CHEST PAIN

*SYSTEMATIC
DIFFERENTIATION
AND TREATMENT*

NATHANIEL E. REICH, M.D., F.A.C.P., F.C.C.P.

Clinical Assistant Professor of Medicine, State University of New York Downstate Medical Center, Brooklyn; Attending Cardiologist, Jewish Chronic Disease Hospital; Attending Physician, Unity Hospital; Consultant, St. Joseph's Hospital, Long Beach Memorial Hospital, Kings Highway Hospital, Linden General Hospital, and Interboro General Hospital

RUDOLPH E. FREMONT, M.D., F.A.C.P., F.C.C.P.

Clinical Assistant Professor of Medicine, State University of New York Downstate Medical Center, Brooklyn; Chief, Cardiovascular Service, Veterans Administration Hospital, Brooklyn; Associate Attending Physician, Jewish Chronic Disease Hospital and Maimonides Hospital

THE MACMILLAN COMPANY - NEW YORK

First printing, February, 1961

Library of Congress catalog card number: 61-5507

The Macmillan Company, New York
Brett-Macmillan Ltd., Galt, Ontario

Printed in the United States of America

To William Dock, M.D., F.A.C.P. *Provocative thinker, inspiring educator, astute clinician*

PREFACE

The anatomic approach to the differential diagnosis of chest pain is not only practical but also logical. The thorax and its contents are more easily visualized moving from the outermost anatomic layers to the innermost structures. This unique and encompassing approach to the systematic diagnosis of chest pain should prove most valuable to the general practitioner, internist, and cardiologist. However, it may also be helpful to many other specialists, such as the chest physician, thoracic surgeon, orthopedist, dermatologist, neurologist, and even the gastroenterologist, all of whom become involved in diagnostic problems in this large area at one time or another.

The planning of this comprehensive project demanded a sense of selectivity and balance. More common disease processes have, of necessity, required more detailed discussion. A brief, but complete, consideration of current therapy completes each discussion. Theoretical aspects have been omitted generally or have been dealt with briefly, when necessary. Pathophysiology and the mechanisms of specific pains have been given due consideration in order to lay the groundwork for a better understanding of each disease process.

Several physicians have critically reviewed those chapters most concerned with their respective specialties and have contributed comments and criticisms in a most constructive manner. We are especially indebted to the following persons for their interest in our work: Dr. W. Dock, who reviewed the entire manuscript and made valuable suggestions; Drs. S. Chessid, M. E. Margulies, and K. Steiner; Dr. J. Dubowy, who helped select many of the x-ray illustrations; Mrs. R. Davison and Mrs. F. Willner, who gave faithful performance in secretarial duties; Mr. P. Glass, who contributed information on cardiopulmonary evaluation; and Mr.

F. Hertling, who helped prepare the illustrations. Please note that a few of the electrocardiograms and other tracings have been touched up slightly to ensure clarity. The publisher has been most helpful in many directions.

THE AUTHORS

Spring, 1961

CONTENTS

CHAPTER 1 *A SUGGESTED APPROACH TO THE DIAGNOSIS OF CHEST PAIN*

No greater opportunity or obligation can befall the physician than to become as proficient as possible in his chosen field. It soon becomes evident to the novitiate that the intelligent care of the suffering demands diagnostic acumen as well as a knowledge of basic science and technical skills. This is essential in order to attain therapeutic objectives. However, although medicine is rapidly advancing as a science, basically it continues to retain many aspects of an art. This is especially true in the interpretation and understanding of the patient's reactions.

The same symptoms are rarely described in the same way by different individuals. Hence, the approach to each patient must be varied in order to conform to the age, sex, intelligence, environmental, psychogenic, economic, and other factors which are the integral ingredients in each case. Experience is the obvious key to this phase of the practice of medicine. The proper attack upon every problem begins with the determination of the urgent and immediate issues. Each statement by the patient must be weighed and scrutinized carefully before it is accepted. The mind of the physician must be alert to all the possibilities of questioning which may lead him toward the crux of the problem. He must quickly learn to recognize and to avoid labyrinths and blind alleys. The subjective manifestations may be colored or camouflaged by language difficulty, fears, confusion, mental deficiency, misconceptions, and other distractions. Thus, the recognition of their true nature requires skill, tact, understanding, and—above all—patience. A sympathetic interview also establishes the foundation for a good patient-physician rela-

1

tionship. There, careful history-taking constitutes the most important part of the examination in almost all instances.

Each symptom must be carefully explored. Eventually, a pattern may emerge which will permit a tentative conclusion. In some instances, the initial impression derived from the history may prove to be the most important part of the entire examination, since it can save valuable time and prevent unnecessary expense. This is especially true when the classic symptom complex of a disease process (such as angina pectoris or peptic ulcer) is elicited. Unfortunately, most diseases do not permit the formulation of a clear or definitive word picture; physical findings or appropriate laboratory examinations may then supply the necessary clues. The final diagnosis involves correlation and integration of all the facts obtained from the carefully taken history, meticulous physical examination, and appropriately chosen laboratory studies.

The subjective complaint that most frequently calls the attention of the patient to his departure from good health is *pain*. The reaction of each individual to pain depends in part on the meaning of the sensation interpreted in the light of his past experiences and in part on his own sensitivity or threshold of pain. It may be well localized in many instances. Unfortunately, pain may also arise from contiguous structures or may be referred to distant structures. The occurrence of referred pain may either blur or, by producing a characteristic picture, sharpen the focus. Perception and reactions to pain, nerve pathways, pain references, pain-sensitive structures, and the qualities of pain will be discussed in detail in the following chapter.

The recognition and differentiation of the various causes of chest pain are most important from the standpoint of their frequency, potential gravity, and apprehension which is apt to accompany the complaint in this vital area of the body. As previously stated, the proper interpretation of the cause of an obscure thoracic pain depends upon its capacity to arouse a suspicion of the true cause and upon the confirmation of its presence by physical findings or laboratory procedures. The areas of location and referral are important to define. The duration of pain is also significant. Brief pains tend to produce less confusion than do longer-lasting pains. The severity and character of each pain are also important. A preceding history of the effects of exertion and body movements or accompanying symptoms can be most helpful. The ability to reproduce the pain may be pathognomonic. Thus, an exercise test may reproduce the characteristics of an anginal syndrome.

The complicated origins due to combinations of thoracic pain (see Figs. 1-1 and 1-2) are numerous and require careful analysis of the exact nature and timing of sequences of pain in each instance. For example, consider

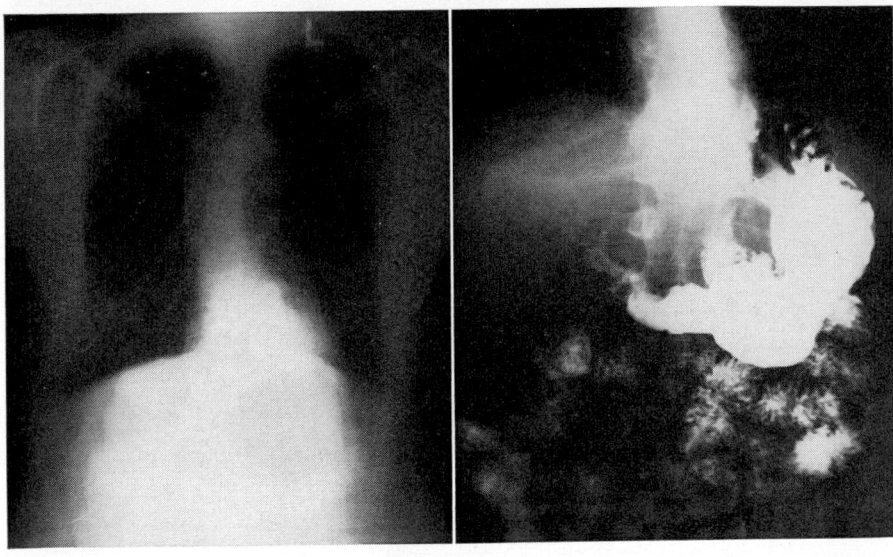

A   B

Fig. 1-1. Three concurrent sources of chest pain. Forty-eight-year-old male hospital-ized for an *acute coronary occlusion*, confirmed by an electrocardiogram which revealed posterior wall myocardial infarction with ischemia of anterior wall. On the third day (*A*), the patient developed radiating pain in the left hemithorax, which was due to *nerve root compression* caused by twenty-year-old fractures of five thoracic vertebrae, with resultant marked scoliosis, and precipitated by jackknifed position in bed. Four days later (*B*), the patient developed acute epigastric pain due to *acute duodenal ulcer* (stress reaction?).

some of the possible causes of chest pain following a coronary occlusion. A shoulder-hand syndrome or postinfarction syndrome may complicate the myocardial infarction as well as the more immediate complication of an extension of the thrombus to a proximal branch with recurrence of coronary thrombosis. Embolization from a mural thrombus (usually during the sec-ond week) results in pain of pleuropulmonary origin. Anginal distress may also be due to the appearance of an intractable arrhythmia which diminishes coronary blood flow. Aortic valve stenosis due to concomitant degenerative changes in this valve may contribute to the degree of coronary insufficiency. The presence of an unrelated severe anemia or thyrotoxicosis may add to the diminished oxygen-carrying capacity of the blood or to the increased work of the heart, respectively. Recurrent pain is then the result of a state of chronic coronary insufficiency. A superimposed anxiety neurosis is common and always magnifies or complicates the distress. Pain of coronary origin may be further complicated by nerve root pain caused by the acute flexion of an osteoarthritic spine owing to the jackknifed body position which is

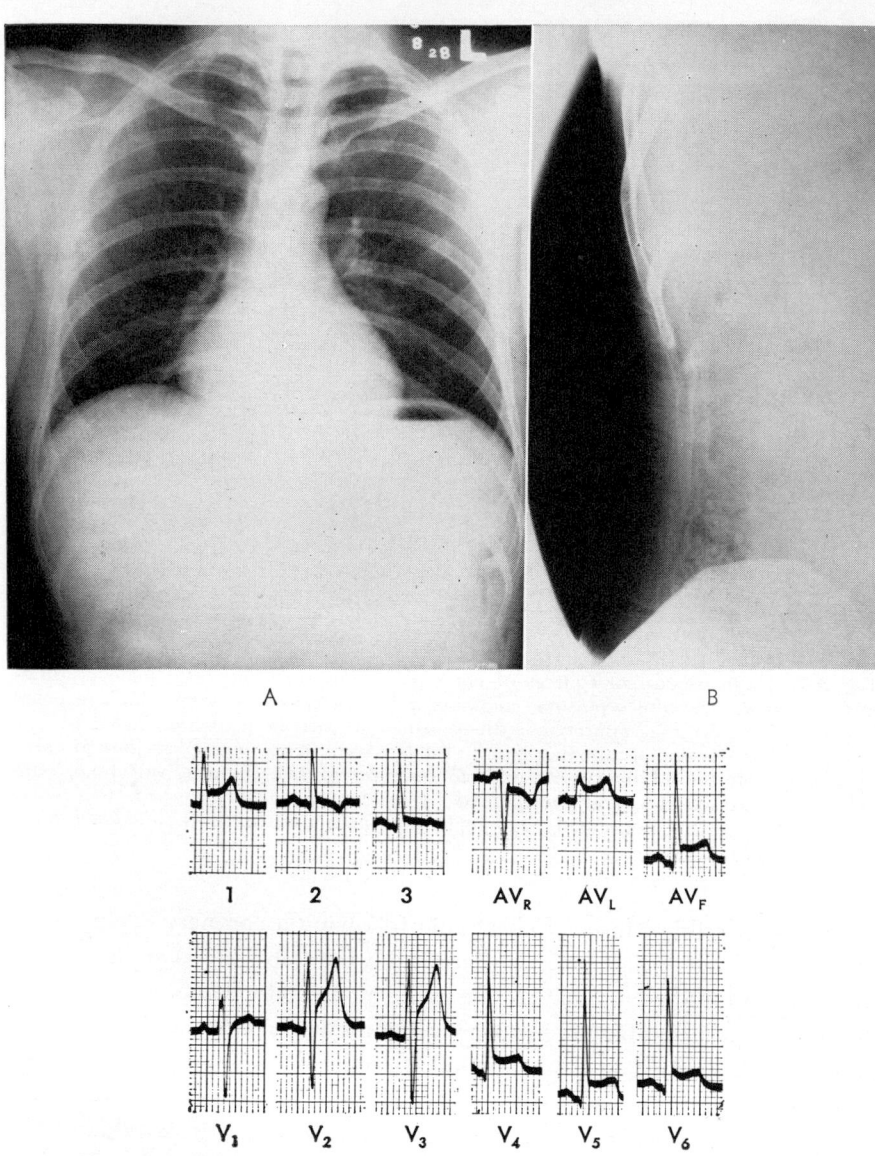

Fig. 1-2. Dual source of lower left chest pain. Twenty-five-year-old male admitted in shock with stab wounds of upper left abdomen and precordium at left fourth interspace. Posteroanterior chest film (*A*) shows early *hemopericardium*, as evidenced by configuration of right heart border and acute cardiohepatic angle. Flat abdominal plate (*B*) reveals *subcutaneous emphysema* (evisceration occurred). Electrocardiogram (*C*) demonstrates elevations of ST segments characteristic of acute pericarditis. (Courtesy of Dr. Benjamin Shafiroff.)

4

maintained in bed for many weeks; hypoxia due to various pleural and pneumonic complications may add a burden—and so on.

While our basic object is to propound a systematic program for the investigation of *all* causes of thoracic pain, it is the first duty of the physician to think of the heart as the source of trouble in most instances of chest pain because of its great frequency and serious nature. If careful study absolves the heart with reasonable assurance, other intrathoracic lesions must then be investigated as the cause of the distress. After chest wall, pleuropulmonary, and mediastinal structures have been considered carefully, attention must then be directed to the digestive tract and diaphragm as the possible cause of pain. The thoracic wall and upper extremities, which are available for more direct examination, may supply either an obvious or an occult cause for the pain.

Rare or unusual conditions may require confirmation by an appropriate competent consultant before the exact cause of the pain is finally established. Thus, the opinion of a neurologist may become necessary in an occasional condition, such as chest pain due to preherpetic lesions or nerve root lesions. The dermatologist may be called upon when the rash appears. The x-ray therapist may become involved when intractable pain results. Expert consultation may become essential in the performance of unusual procedures, such as esophagoscopy or bronchoscopy. Practically any medical specialty may become involved in some special diagnostic or therapeutic situation, as the reader will discover repeatedly. However, with an average degree of common sense, the cause of the thoracic pain can be established by the general practitioner alone in the majority of instances. In other words, comprehension of the clinical features of most of these disorders will minimize difficulties in differential diagnosis which arise within the thorax. It is for this reason that the pertinent clinical features of each condition are presented.

The number of causes of chest pain seems to be increasing. Doubtless, a new cause will appear from time to time, or an ancient condition may be rediscovered under a new name. Such synonyms already form a ponderous phase of medical literature and result in a great deal of semantic confusion. However, the authors hope that most of the future discoveries will be made in the fields of etiology and therapy of established disorders. The patient as well as the physician will profit immeasurably from such advances.

At the risk of tiresome repetition, it is reiterated that the cause of chest pain in any given patient will rarely be identified unless it is first suspected. The index of suspicion can be raised only by a knowledge of the special characteristics of that pain as well as other diagnostic features and confirmatory tests. (See Table 1-1.)

Table 1-1

**Diagnoses Made in 86 Cases
of Proven Dissecting Aneurysm * †**

Primary		Secondary	
Dissecting aneurysm	27	Dissecting aneurysm	7
Hypertensive heart disease	17	Hypertensive heart disease	4
Cerebral accident	13		
Acute myocardial infarction	9	Coronary occlusion	6
Cardiac failure	5		
Arteriosclerotic heart disease	2	Arteriosclerosis	5
Embolism to femoral artery	2		
Uremia	2	Uremia	2
Bleeding ulcer	1	Bleeding ulcer	1
Pneumonia	1	Pneumonia	3
Carcinoma of esophagus	1		
Echinococcus cyst of liver	1	Renal calculus	2
Renal calculus	1	Aortic aneurysm	1
Carcinoma of lung	1	Lymphoma	1
Volvulus, ileitis	1		
Gastrointestinal obstruction	1		
Subarachnoid hemorrhage	1		

* Clinical diagnosis was correctly made in less than one third of all cases.
† From Baer, S.: Varied manifestations of dissecting aneurysm of the aorta. *J.A.M.A.,* **161:**689, 1956.

Since the immediate launching of multiphasic studies may prove time-consuming and expensive, attention should be first directed to a specific structure or area during the course of obtaining a detailed history. When inconclusive symptoms or findings suggest several possibilities, the following basic workup is advisable, since it may lead more quickly to the diagnosis of the majority of conditions capable of causing the chest pain. This is especially true since the heart is most commonly at fault and usually contributes to the most serious of all thoracic conditions.

1. Fluoroscopy or x-ray of the chest.

2. Electrocardiogram. If negative or inconclusive and coronary disease is still suspected, an exercise electrocardiogram (two-step test) should be recorded. If the suspicion persists because of equivocal findings, a double two-step test may then be performed.

3. Routine blood count and urinalysis.

In addition to the discovery of suggestive but inconclusive findings of coronary origin, this basic workup may uncover, through serendipity, gross evidence of other disease processes. Thus, a thorough history may suggest the presence of a strong psychogenic overlay, or the existence of two or more common conditions capable of producing thoracic pain at the same time (e.g., coronary artery disease, marked arthritis of the spine, and severe anemia). The chest x-ray may reveal the presence of many pulmonary, pleural, bony, and mediastinal lesions as well as the size and configuration of the cardiovascular structures.

As previously stated, careful and thorough physical examination is most important after history has been elicited. For example, the finding of enlarged lymph nodes with marked pallor may suggest the presence of mediastinal involvement due to lymphoblastomata; this may then be confirmed by the blood count and sternal marrow studies or biopsy.

Routine urinalysis may be quite revealing when glycosuria, albuminuria, casts, and cellular elements are found. It can be supplemented by appropriate blood chemistry studies at a reliable laboratory. Thus, the presence of glycosuria demands a determination of the blood glucose level and even a glucose tolerance test when necessary for additional confirmation. The presence of acetone and diacetic acid may readily account for the marked weakness, while the radiating burning pains around the thorax and along the extremities may account for the presence of diabetic polyneuritis.

When the symptoms are suggestive of a lesion of the digestive system, the following preliminary x-ray studies may be performed as needed:

1. Upper gastrointestinal series (to exclude diverticulum, esophagitis, peptic ulcer, or gastric malignancy). The Trendelenberg position should be added to demonstrate the presence of an elusive hiatus hernia. Calculi on a flat abdominal film may suggest a renal, cholecystitic, or pancreatic origin of pain.

2. Gallbladder series.

Colonic gas syndromes may be delineated on an ordinary chest film, which usually includes the uppermost abdomen. Serum amylase determination is important during the early phase of acute pancreatitis. Other chemical studies may be limited to investigation of a particular structure. Thus, a complete liver profile may be helpful in the diagnosis of many hepatic lesions. A barium enema may be necessary to exclude a suggestive lesion of the transverse colon as the cause of upper abdominal or lower thoracic pain.

The skeletal system may require special roentgenographic investigation when a lesion appears to originate in the cervical or thoracic segments of the spine, shoulder joints, or ribs. A shoulder-hand syndrome, the radiation to the left shoulder of an anginal seizure, or bony metastases may be excluded at once when a shoulder joint shows evidence only of osteoarthritic changes or subdeltoid calcification. Examination of the ribs may reveal Tietze's syndrome, multiple myeloma, metastases, eosinophilic granuloma, notching due to coarctation, or an obscure fissure fracture as the cause of localized pain. Detailed studies pertaining to the diagnosis of all the specific disease processes which can cause thoracic pain will be elaborated upon in this text.

When all organic possibilities of a particular thoracic pain have been thoroughly exhausted, a psychologic evaluation of the patient (by psycho-dynamically oriented interviews when necessary) may confirm the initial suspicion of the existence of a nonorganic distress. Distinct phobic, hyster-ical, and hypochondriacal tendencies may be observed after several inter-views. These may also be necessary to evaluate the presence and degree of a psychogenic overlay, which may be in greater need of correction than the actual organic lesion that may be present.

Finally, the criteria for the diagnosis of any given condition must be thoughtfully evaluated after all the medical evidence has been gathered. Indeed, this may be necessary on several occasions during the course of the disease so that the clinical course, the presence of concomitant diseases or complications, the degree of psychogenic overlay, and the therapeutic re-sponse may be properly evaluated. It is the modest hope of the authors that the systematic plan of this text will guide the physician through the maze of conditions capable of producing chest pain. With this objective in mind, we can now turn our attention to an understanding of the nature and distribution of the pain itself.

CHAPTER 2 **THE ANATOMY OF CHEST PAIN**[*]

Pain is the most common of all symptoms. It is a warning signal against potential or actual damage to tissue cells. The thorax, especially the precordium, is one of the most frequent and confusing sites of this prime complaint.

[*] This chapter is based on an article originally published in the *American Journal of Cardiology* (Reich, N. E.: "The Anatomy of Chest Pain," *Am. J. Cardiol.*, **2**:95, 1958); reprinted by permission.

The increased frequency of precordial pain due to lengthening of the life span and the importance of differentiating cardiac from noncardiac pain cannot be overemphasized. It is the seasoned opinion of most competent observers that a good understanding of the origin and nature of this important symptom usually aids diagnosis more than any other single element.

Major dependence on some laboratory tests frequently proves misleading. In some instances, the pain characteristics associated with some disorders are so diagnostic as to make a lengthy clinical appraisal unnecessary. For example, this is typical of the severe tearing pain which occurs with most dissections along the aorta. However, precordial pains of various origins frequently bear a confusing resemblance to one another, especially at the onset. To complicate matters, it is not unusual for several factors capable of causing precordial pain to occur in combinations. Thus, the aged patient with advanced osteoarthritis of the spine, who is bedridden in a jackknifed position because of coronary occlusion, may develop an aggravation of chest pain due to nerve root compression. Occasionally, two "stress" conditions may occur simultaneously—e.g., squeezing upper substernal pain of angina pectoris, which is relieved by nitroglycerin, and postprandial burning pain at the lower end of the sternum caused by peptic ulcer and relieved by antacids. Then there is the patient with chronic coronary insufficiency who suddenly develops marked aggravation of pain which arises in the center of the back, and which is suggestive of a posterior wall myocardial infarction. Four days later, characteristic herpetic lesions become discernible over the left side of the back.

A knowledge of the precise anatomy of the nervous innervation of the precordium and areas of referred pain is an invaluable aid in the differential diagnosis of precordial pain (see Fig. 2-1). Unfortunately, investigation of the nervous system by anatomic methods has failed to give the complete answer to the intricate mechanisms by which cutaneous or visceral pain reaches the sensorium. Physiologic studies have carried the frontier of knowledge much further. The ideal experimental subject is not the laboratory animal, because of species differences, but man himself.

Furthermore, different portions of the body vary widely in their sensitivity to pain and the stimuli whereby it is produced. Certain structures, such as the cornea, gastrointestinal tube, and arteries, have little capacity for registering anything but painful stimulation. Other structures, such as the heart and lungs, usually present pain as the most important symptom. Pain may range from slight uneasiness to extreme distress. The threshold for its perception is defined as the lowest intensity of stimulus which is recognized as pain. A stimulus which causes pain in the skin may not produce pain in

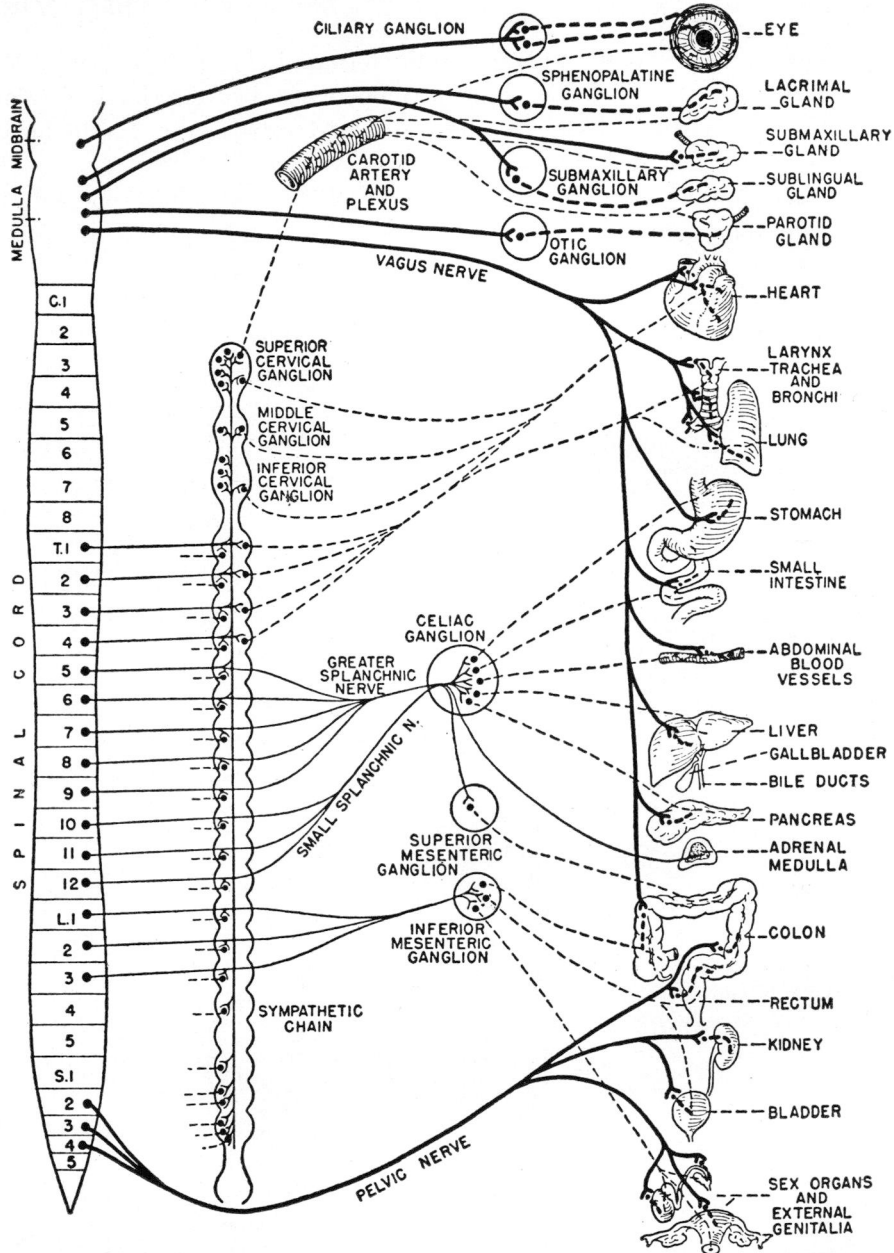

Fig. 2-1. Diagram of distribution of the autonomic nervous system. Heavy lines, the parasympathetic division; fine lines, the sympathetic division; continuous lines, preganglionic fibers; broken lines, postganglionic fibers. (From Youmans, W. B.: *Basic Medical Physiology.* Year Book Publishers, Inc., Chicago, 1952.)

11

the heart. A pin-prick causes distress in the former, ischemia in the latter. It may have both emotional and physical components. The threshold of pain depends upon emotional stability, age, sex, past experiences, conditioned reflexes, and other intangible factors.

Pricking painful sensations are conveyed by thick and rapidly conducting myelinated fibers. Burning pain is transmitted by small, slowly conducting fibers. Visceral pain is carried by myelinated and nonmyelinated fibers which pass through the sympathetic chain. The afferent sensory fibers of the heart pass through this chain and enter the cord in the upper four or five thoracic posterior roots; they then pass into the spinothalamic tracts. Other thoracic structures, such as the aorta, esophagus, mediastinum, and portions of the chest wall, possess sensory nerves with the same general afferent course. (See Figs. 2-2 and 2-3.) The parietal pleura and diaphragmatic sur-

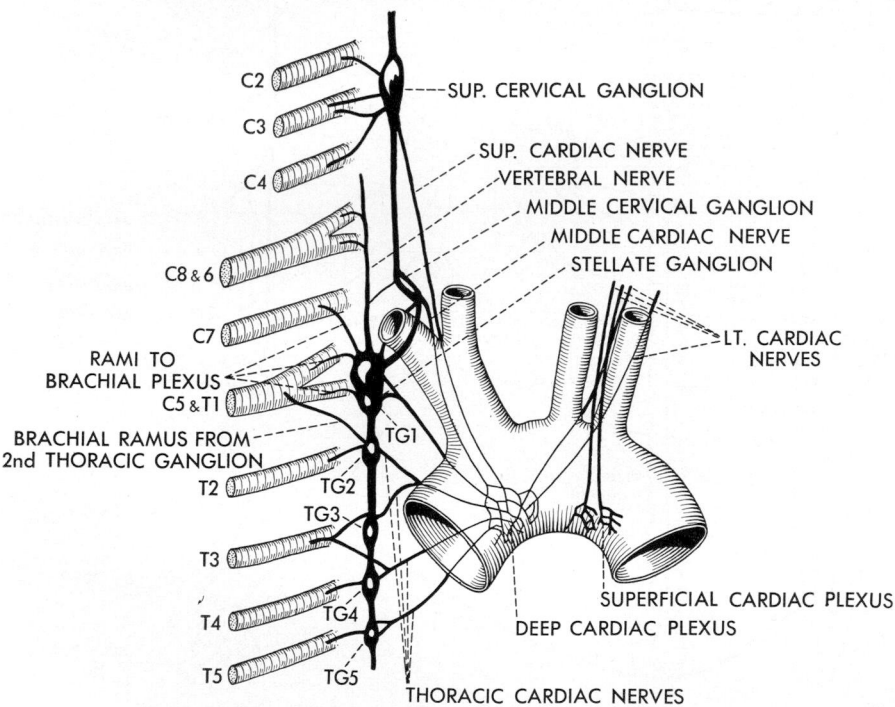

Fig. 2-2. Segmental innervations. (From Reich, N. E.: *Diseases of the Aorta.* The Macmillan Co., New York, 1949.)

face of the parietal pericardium are also pain sensitive but are supplied by the intercostal and phrenic nerves. The intercostal nerves also contain the pain fibers for the parietal peritoneum.

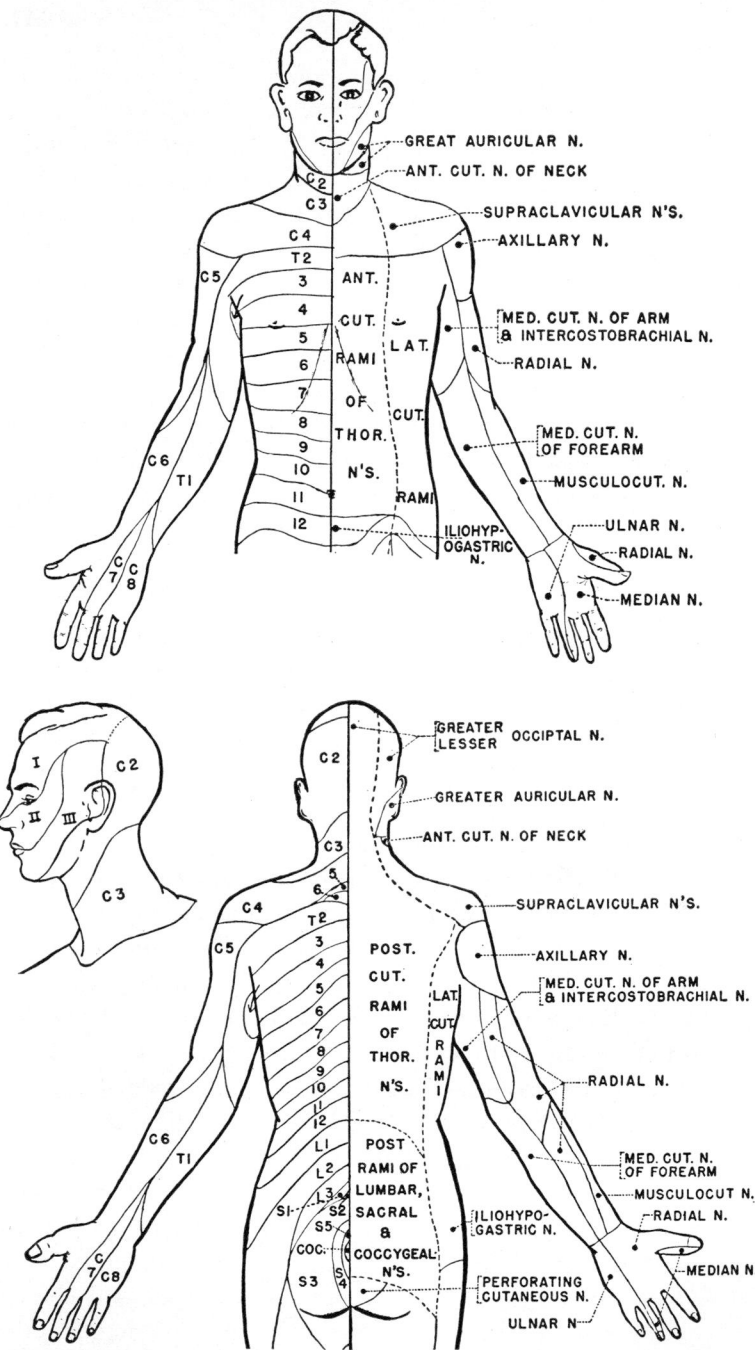

Fig. 2-3. Segmental innervation of dermatomes. (Adapted from Wolff, H. G., and Wolf, S.: *Pain*. Charles C Thomas, Publisher, Springfield, Ill., 1948.)

Pain from the skin can be sharply localized. Direct stimulation of the cutaneous nerves produces the same type of pain that arises from the skin. The intensity may vary, but the quality is the same regardless of the stimulus (e.g., pinch, prick, burn, etc.). The quality of pain from deeper structures, such as the heart, differs from that of skin pain. It is longer-lasting, more diffuse, and frequently radiates to a remote region. This is true of deep somatic structures as well as visceral organs. The distribution is segmental in part but may fill only a portion of a segment, or overflow into adjacent segments. Hence, anginal pain may radiate down the inner surface of the left arm in the area which is innervated by C_8 and T_1 spinal segments. Some of the sensory nerves from the heart travel in the sympathetic chain and establish central connections at these cord levels. In some instances, referred pain is accompanied by superficial or deep hyperalgesia. It may be decreased by the injection of procaine or the spraying of ethyl chloride over this hypersensitive area.

Since the heart is a midline organ, pain is often referred to the retrosternal area and to one or both arms, although the reference is primarily to the left. Recent embryologic and clinical evidence suggests that the left chambers of the heart, pulmonary veins, and interatrial septum develop and receive their nerve supply from the left side. As the right atrium and right ventricle develop on the opposite side, disease involving these structures is likely to be referred primarily to the right. Thus, in dextrocardia with accompanying angina pectoris, the pain is predominantly right-sided. Painful impulses from the heart travel along the sympathetic nerves, entering the sympathetic chains anywhere from the middle cervical to the fifth thoracic ganglion. Here the fibers may travel up or down in the chain but enter the cord in the upper five thoracic roots. Characteristically, pain from the heart is felt beneath the sternum. Referred pain to the surface is localized mainly in the anterior portion of the third to the sixth thoracic segments, with hyperesthesia involving the precordial area, and along the medial aspect of the left shoulder and arm in the distribution of T_1 and T_2. The area of reference of cardiac pain may, however, extend more widely from C_3 to T_{10}. Thus, it may be confused with pain arising from stimulation of other structures innervated by the same segment, notably the biliary passages, diaphragm, mediastinum, esophagus, apex of the lung, spinal cord, nerve roots, and skeletal and muscular structures about the left shoulder and chest. When atypical cardiac pain reaches to the lower jaw, it may suggest disease of the apices of the lower teeth. Roberts has shown that pain referred from the heart is due to ischemia of the somatic nerves caused by spasm of the vasa nervorum. This mechanism could account for the occasional relief of angina by local anesthesia, the occasional occurrence of silent infarction, the shoulder-hand syndrome or Dupuytren's contracture sometimes observed following myocardial infarction, and, finally, the influence of psychic or stress situations on the precipitation of angina. Cardiac muscle hypertrophy results in a relatively decreased blood supply to the myocardium but does not cause pain in the absence of other factors.

PLEUROPERICARDIAL PAIN

The visceral pleura does not originate pain impulses and thus is not pain sensitive. From the parietal pleura, pain sensation reaches the cord via the intercostal nerves. Hence, pains are felt in the area of the cutaneous segment immediately overlying the site of stimulation. This is true also of the area of the parietal pleura reflected over the peripheral border of the diaphragm. Posteriorly where a considerable portion of the diaphragm lies against the chest wall, pain from the pleural surface may be felt in parts of the seventh to the twelfth thoracic segments, including the lower thorax, lumbar region, epigastrium, and even further down in the abdomen. For example, the occurrence of pain has been described in the right lower quadrant of the abdomen with localized tenderness, cutaneous hyperesthesia in the region of McBurney's point, and spasm of the underlying muscles in certain instances of diaphragmatic pleurisy.

Stimulation of the central portion of the diaphragmatic pleura which is supplied by branches of the phrenic nerve gives rise to pain in the region of the trapezius muscle in the neck and shoulder (cutaneous distribution of the third and fourth cervical segments of the cord).

Phrenic nerve endings also supply the lower portion of the parietal pericardium, and its stimulation also causes pain in the trapezius region. Noxious stimuli applied to the parietal pericardium at a distance from the diaphragm, however, do not induce pain. The frequent association of chest pain in acute pericarditis has been ascribed to stimuli reaching the pleural surfaces adjacent to the pericardium.

PULMONARY AND DIAPHRAGMATIC PAIN

The lungs and bronchi originate embryologically as outpouchings from the primitive gut tube in the neck region. Fibers from the third and fourth cervical segments are carried in the vagal rami to the cord in order to innervate it. Sensations arising from these structures are not necessarily referred to the cervical region, however, and are often correctly localized.

Thus, in tracheitis the pain is felt beneath the sternum, and in centrally located bronchiogenic carcinoma pain may be felt in the chest immediately overlying the lesion.

Noxious impulses from the diaphragm travel mainly in the phrenic nerve, entering the cord in the third, fourth, and fifth cervical roots. The peripheral portion of the diaphragm receives fibers from intercostal nerves, and thus, as in the case of its pleural surface, painful stimulation of the muscle near its insertion will give rise to pain felt in the thoracic segments. Areas of reference for pain in the diaphragm may extend as far down over the abdomen and lumbar region as T_{12}. For this reason, the pain of coronary occlusion has been closely simulated by diaphragmatic spasm.

GASTROINTESTINAL PAIN

Diseases of the digestive tract are capable of producing pain in the lower chest or upper abdomen which may be confused with disease of many thoracic structures. In the gastrointestinal tract, noxious impulses arise principally as a result of (1) local stimulation of an engorged or inflamed mucosa, (2) distention or spasm of muscular elements of the tube, and (3) traction upon mesenteric attachments.

From the esophagus, impulses travel in fibers carried by the sympathetic nerves to the chains of sympathetic ganglia. From here they may enter the cord anywhere from the lowest cervical through the entire thoracic distribution. Whether or not the vagus participates in carrying afferent fibers which relay painful stimuli is still undetermined. The most common pain from the esophagus is "heartburn," a burning pain felt substernally and fairly well localized over the site of stimulation. This pain is caused by cardiospasm. The most common cause of heartburn in man results from the regurgitation of highly acid gastric juice into the esophagus which has already had its pain threshold lowered by the presence of engorgement or inflammation (esophagitis).

The pain of peptic ulcer which arises from the stomach or duodenum is frequently described as burning. It is of special interest that burning pain, ordinarily associated with noxious stimulation of the skin, can be elicited from the upper gastrointestinal tract. Hyperperistalsis, pylorospasm, antral distention, hyperacidity, and inflammation augment the pain of ulcer.

Impulses from the pancreas, liver, and biliary tracts appear to travel in the same pathways as do those from the stomach. This fact indicates the difficulties encountered in the differential diagnosis of epigastric pain. It may arise not only from the above structures, but also from retroperitoneal tissues, skeletal muscles, or lesions of the nervous system (such as herpes zoster or cord tumors) which involve dorsal roots. Epigastric pain may even be referred from the heart or other thoracic structures or from impulses arising in the lower bowel, including the transverse colon and appendix. The hepatic parenchyma has been shown to be pain insensitive, but rapid distention of its capsule does give rise to pain. The same generalizations apply to other solid organs, including the spleen and possibly the kidneys. Pain from distention of bile ducts and the gallbladder has been found to be commonly localized in the distribution of T_9, either anteriorly beneath the right costal margin or posteriorly at the angle of the right scapula. Noxious impulses from the small intestine also travel in splanchnic pathways but enter the cord slightly lower than T_9 to T_{11}. The afferent innervation of the colon above the sigmoid is also carried in the sympathetic trunks.

CLINICAL APPLICATION

An understanding of the distribution and characteristics of the pain is vital in the differential diagnosis of the numerous conditions which may cause chest pain. The history should be elicited directly from the patient at the time of the attack, if possible, without presenting leading questions. Since many patients are distraught at such times, they may agree to almost any questions or may exaggerate its significance.

Characteristics of Pain

The following characteristics of the pain should be elicited in each instance.

1. **Location.** The exact area of pain should be delineated, if possible. This may not be possible at all times, especially when radiation is prominent. In some instances (cardiac neurosis), the distribution of pain may be quite bizarre.

2. **Depth and intensity.** The depth and intensity of pain should be determined. Is the pain deep or superficial? Is it severe, moderate, or mild? The physician learns to evaluate the organic and superimposed nonorganic components from experience.

3. **Quality.** The patient should describe the quality of pain in his own words. Is it heavy, boring, burning, pins-and-needles, wave-like, intermittent or continuous, pressing, sharp or dull, sticking, spreading, squeezing, etc.? Pricking, itching, or burning pains arise from the skin. Burning pains arise also from the esophagus and stomach. Dull aching pains are more characteristic for deeper structures.

4. Duration and frequency. How long has this attack lasted? Is this attack abating or increasing? How often have such attacks occurred? Have they been getting worse lately? Is there any regularity of recurrence? The recurring postprandial pain of peptic ulcer has a regularity and seasonal incidence not recognizable in other diseases, while an anginal seizure lasts but several minutes.

5. Radiation. Are any secondary areas involved, or did the pain seem to move elsewhere? These areas should be mapped as carefully as possible, since the major area of confusion lies in the evaluation of referred pains. An anginal seizure tends to radiate down the ulnar side of the left arm. It may also be referred to either shoulder, neck, jaw, lower teeth, and back.

6. Factors that influence pain. Most pains may be noted to begin, become aggravated, or improve under certain specific circumstances. Careful questioning frequently proves highly rewarding in establishing the diagnosis. Walking uphill against a cold wind is a common description of a precipitating factor in angina pectoris; the fact that it is quickly relieved by nitroglycerin or rest is equally characteristic. Pleuritic pain is influenced by coughing or breathing. Spinal root lesions are aggravated by coughing, straining, or sneezing. Since analgesics reduce the intensity of most pains when taken in sufficient dosage, this does not aid much in differential diagnosis unless one takes into account the potency of the drug and its dosage. A tablet of aspirin may relieve intercostal neuralgia, whereas dissecting aneurysm may remain unrelieved following huge doses of opiates.

7. Associated symptoms and findings. The appearance of other symptoms and findings may prove diagnostic. For example, coexisting cyanosis, dyspnea, and feeble heart sounds would be expected to occur in coronary occlusion rather than in intercostal neuritis. However, the subsequent appearance of a pericardial friction rub may make it difficult to differentiate between acute pericarditis and coronary occlusion without the benefit of other findings and studies. Considerable time and effort may be saved in office practice by having the patient fill out a prepared questionnaire (Fig. 2-4) prior to examination.

In summary, it may be stated that the pitfalls in the differential diagnosis of chest pain are numerous. Meticulous attention to the anatomy and mechanism of various pains as well as proper history-taking in clinical application will minimize the possibility of error in clinical diagnosis.

CHEST PAIN QUESTIONNAIRE

Name..Date..History No............

Sex............................Age..Occupation..

COMPLETED BY.......................................(patient) or...M.D.

INSTRUCTIONS: Please FILL IN EVERY SPACE ON THIS FORM, using check mark (V) for "yes" and zero (0) for "no." LEAVE BLANK ONLY IF UNKNOWN.

DURATION of chest pain or pressure.......................years.......................months.

TYPE:

Squeezing..................	Sticking....................
Constricting..............	Gnawing....................
Strangling..................	Aching....................
Compressing.............	Vise-like....................
Burning..................	Choking....................
Heaviness..................	Tightness..................
Pressure....................	Knife-like..............
Boring........................	Discomfort............
Dull..................	Others....................

LOCATION OF PAIN OR PRESSURE:

Substernal (under breast bone).....................
Precordial (over heart in left lower chest)....
....
Pit of Stomach..
Back..
Chest—entire............left............right............
Other ....

DURATION OF PAIN OR PRESSURE:
each attack.

Up to 1 minute....................................
1 to 2 minutes....................................
2 to 5 minutes....................................
5 to 10 minutes....................................
10 minutes to 1 hour............................
Over 1 hour....................................
Continuous....................................

FREQUENCY OF ATTACKS:

More than once a day..............................
Once a day..
Few times a week..................................
Few times a month................................
Rare—Under once a month.......................

RADIATION OF PAIN OR PRESSURE:

None..
Back..
Shoulder—both............left............right............
Arm   —both............left............right............
Hand   —both............left............right............
Jaw..
Neck..
Other..

ONSET:

Effort..
Walking..
Climbing..
Emotion..
Meals..
Walking after meals................................
Cold..
Walking in the cold..................................
Walking against the wind........................
Spontaneous (no apparent cause)...............
Smoking..
Intercourse..
Fatigue..
Lying down..
Other..

RELIEF OF PAIN OR PRESSURE:

	Relieves?		
	Yes How many minutes?	*No*	*Not* *used*
Nitroglycerin			
Whiskey			
Rest			
Belching			
Spontaneous			
Other			

TOBACCO: Cigarettes..............daily.
                         Cigars

E.C.G..
"2-step"..
"2-step"..

B.C.G.—Normal............Abnormal............

REMARKS:

Fig. 2-4. Chest pain questionnaire. (From Master, A. M.; Jaffe, H. L.; and Pordy, L.: Cardiac and non-cardiac chest pain: a statistical study of "diagnostic" criteria. *Ann. Int. Med.*, **41**:315, 1954.)

CHAPTER 3 *ORIGINS OF CHEST WALL PAIN*

CHAPTER OUTLINE

CUTANEOUS LESIONS
    Hyperemia and inflammations
        Erythema nodosum
        Neurotic excoriations
        Herpes zoster
        Impetigo herpetiformis
        Cellulitis, or deep abscess
        Relapsing, febrile, nodular, nonsuppurative panniculitis
        Phlebitis
    Collagen diseases
        Polyarteritis nodosa
        Scleroderma
        Dermatomyositis
        Disseminated lupus erythematosus
    Degenerations
        Xanthomatosis
        Amyloidosis
    Tumors
        Neurofibromatosis
        Lipoma
        Glomus tumor
        Malignant neoplastic lesions

DISEASES OF THE BREAST
        Cystic disease
        Fibrous disease
        Mammary duct ectasia

Fat necrosis
Adenofibroma
Carcinoma
Mondor's disease

SKELETAL DISEASES
Diseases of costosternal structures
Trauma
Costochondral syndrome (Tietze)
Xiphoidalgia
Tumors
Primary rib tumors
Eosinophilic granuloma
Other malignant tumors
Infections
Lesions of the cervicodorsal spine
Rheumatism
Rheumatoid arthritis (spondylitis, Marie-Strumpell disease)
Osteoarthritis (degenerative joint disease)
Spondylitis due to infections
Tuberculosis
Syphilitic spondylitis
Brucellosis of the spine
Typhoid spondylitis
Suppurative spondylitis
Coccidioidomycosis
Histoplasmosis
Blastomycosis
Actinomycosis
Trauma
Miscellaneous conditions of the spine
Congenital disorders
Vertebral epiphysitis
Neoplastic involvement
Metastatic lesions
Multiple myeloma
Osteoporosis
"Straight back" syndrome

MUSCULAR DISORDERS OF THORAX AND SHOULDER
Conditions involving musculature of the chest wall
Trauma
Myofascial pain syndromes
Inflammatory diseases involving the chest muscles
Myositis due to infectious agents
Acute suppurative myositis
Myositis due to clostridial infection

Tuberculous myositis
Actinomycosis
Trichinosis
Epidemic myositis
Myositis due to poliomyelitis
Myositis of unknown etiology
Polymyositis
Dermatomyositis
Neuromyositis
Interstitial (nodular) polymyositis
Myositis associated with sarcoidosis
Polyarteritis nodosa
Miscellaneous conditions involving the chest muscles
Fibromyositis
Idiopathic myohemoglobinuria (rhabdomolysis)
Myositis ossificans
Psychogenic rheumatism
Conditions involving musculature of the shoulder
Bursitis
Tendinitis
Scalenus anticus syndrome

DISEASES OF THE SHOULDER JOINT
Arthritis of the shoulder joint (glenohumeral joint)
Osteoarthritis
Acute rheumatic fever
Tuberculous arthritis
Infectious arthritis
Reiter's syndrome
Rheumatoid arthritis
Allergic arthritis
Gouty arthritis
Periarthritis of the shoulder
Traumatic joint disease
Psychogenic rheumatism
Palindromic rheumatism
Blood dyscrasias
Paget's disease

CUTANEOUS LESIONS

The skin represents a vast area of sensitive nerve terminals. Pain and other noxious sensations are frequently limited to the skin of the chest. The cutaneous disorders may arise primarily within the integument and remain limited to this area, or the skin may become involved as part of a systemic disease process. Thus, it may exhibit primary or secondary manifestations of a disseminated disorder.

There are several conditions involving the integument of the chest which may cause pain or other discomforting sensations, such as tightness, itching, burning, smarting, prickling, tingling or other paresthesias, and hyperesthesia. These symptoms are usually due to irritation of the skin nerve endings by morphologic changes, which include edema, exudates, nodules or diffuse thickening, vesiculation, excoriation, or ulceration of the cutaneous layers. These conditions are listed according to the structural involvement of the skin. Since some of the disorders listed can be diagnosed with ease or are of limited significance, they do not merit elaboration. Others deserve special emphasis because they represent the earliest manifestations of serious systemic diseases or because they are associated with diseases causing chest pain by systemic involvement. In many instances, the lesion may lie deeply within the subcutaneous area. Ensuing pain may not be identified with a skin lesion in such cases, but may be falsely interpreted as due to disease of deeper structures such as the coronary arteries or other intrathoracic structures.

Hyperemia and Inflammations

Erythema nodosum is characterized by nodules in the subcutaneous layers which are most commonly localized bilaterally on the extensor surfaces of the extremities (usually legs), although the trunk may also become involved. The importance of this condition lies in its allergic character and association with other diseases, such as acute rheumatic fever and tuberculosis. These nodules are painful and very tender to pressure. The color of these lesions is variegated and frequently resembles the appearance of a contusion. Nodules associated with sarcoidosis tend to be painless.

Neurotic excoriations are usually seen in areas accessible to the hands and are, perhaps, precipitated by a pruritus of psychogenic origin. These surface lesions are mentioned only because they may supply a helpful clue to the recognition of a severely neurotic personality with complaints about chest pain which are produced by a variety of psychosomatic mechanisms (see pp. 91–94) and are often misinterpreted as angina.

Herpes zoster is an acute viral disease related to chickenpox in certain clinical and immunobiologic respects. The infection tends to be more severe and prolonged in older patients. The cutaneous lesions show a strong predilection for the thoracic and lumbar areas, but in later life other areas of the body are also involved. The lesions show the characteristic evolution from erythematous papules to umbilicated unilocular vesicles and pustules which usually affect one or more dermatomes, appearing first over the proximal portion of the involved nerve root and then spreading distally. Thus, the vesicles rarely cross the midline of the body.

Pain of varying intensity may precede, accompany, and follow the appearance of the skin lesions. The discomfort is described as pruritic, stabbing, burning, or aching. It may be constant or intermittent. Hyperesthesia is always present. Systemic symptoms may include fever, headache, malaise, nausea, stiff neck (with concomitant meningo-encephalitis), and regional lymphadenopathy.

Preherpetic pain is described as a superficial, severe, burning, or stabbing sensation which may affect the precordial area. Until the characteristic skin lesions appear, the exact diagnosis may be elusive. It is at the preherpetic stage (especially in older patients) that angina pectoris may be wrongly suspected. However, the segmental distribution and the cutaneous hyperesthesia are helpful clues in immediate differentiation, even before the electrocardiogram and other laboratory tests are obtained.

Generally, herpes zoster resolves itself without complications. In some patients, it produces sequelae that may incapacitate the patient. The most important among these is postherpetic neuralgia. The exact cause of the pain following herpes zoster is unknown. Secondary changes in the posterior root ganglion and the peripheral nerves have been demonstrated. An alteration in the physiology along the principal thalamic tracts in the afferent pathway of the involved nerves has been suggested.

The common occurrence in the older age groups and the frequent localization in the precordial region may cause diagnostic difficulties, since angina pectoris, intercostal neuritis or neuralgia, and nerve root compression by cervicodorsal lesions of the spine may give rise to similar symptoms. In some instances, localized visceral lesions may be seen with the skin lesions causing tachycardia, pleuritic pain, pleural effusion, and a friction rub.

The pain due to herpes zoster may be severe and persistent despite all therapeutic endeavors. This is exemplified by the large variety of measures that have been employed. They include salicylates; protamide (a proteolytic enzyme extract); immune globulins; vitamins B_1 and B_2; infiltration with procaine hydrochloride; corticosteroids; chlorpromazine; x-ray therapy to the affected ganglia; and, finally, rhizotomy and electroshock therapy in the most severe forms.

Impetigo herpetiformis is a very rare cutaneous disorder which usually affects women during pregnancy or the puerperium. It is characterized by the appearance of pustular lesions in groups over the breasts, axillary regions, groin, inner surfaces of the thighs, and umbilical region, and by their association with marked constitutional symptoms.

Cellulitis, or deep abscess, of the chest wall is an uncommon cause of chest pain. It may not be apparent on the surface of the chest at the onset but may cause a constant diffuse pain. Obviously, the presence of tenderness to pressure will exclude pain of intrathoracic origin. It is usually associated with diabetes or debilitating states. Antibiotics and adequate drainage are indicated.

Relapsing, febrile, nodular, nonsuppurative panniculitis (Pfeifer-Weber-Christian disease) is a syndrome of unknown etiology usually found in middle-aged women. As the name implies, it manifests itself by recurrent, nodular, plaque-like inflammatory changes of the subcutaneous fat, which involve not only the legs, thighs, and abdomen but also the breasts and other adipose tissues. The lesions appear as hard sclerotic masses which usually undergo fibrosis or resolution with subsequent atrophy. Subjective sensations include tenderness in the region of the nodules as well as fever and generalized aching. Although some allergic factors have been invoked as the cause, the treatment is usually symptomatic. A trial with corticosteroids may prove beneficial.

Phlebitis. Inflammation of deep veins beneath the skin may provide a rare cause for chest pain, the exact nature of which may not be readily discernible. This is usually secondary to infections, blood dyscrasias, migrating phlebitis, and malignancy of the pancreas or digestive tract. It produces a boring, constant, aching pain; deep palpation may reveal a linear distribution of the tenderness. An unusual type of phlebitis is Mondor's disease, which produces breast pain (see p. 31).

Collagen Diseases

Polyarteritis nodosa is a widely disseminated disease of the small arteries and veins. It is one of the so-called "diffuse collagen diseases" that produce vascular involvement. Most patients present various types of cutaneous or subcutaneous lesions at some time during the course of the illness. Resulting pathologic changes are characterized by necrosis, infarction, hemorrhage, and fatty changes. These may be the earliest manifest lesions. Since the disease also affects arteries of the viscera, chest pain may also occur because of coronary or other arterial involvement.

Nodules, petechial hemorrhages, purpura, localized areas of skin necrosis, urticaria, and erythema-multiforme-like rashes have been described in polyarteritis nodosa. Crops of painful nodules or papules are seen mainly on the extremities and trunk and usually follow the course of a superficial artery. Remissions and exacerbations are common. The cardiac picture may predominate when the coronary arteries are involved. Tachycardia, heart failure, and serial electrocardiographic changes are most common. Thus, acute coronary insufficiency or actual occlusion may result from thrombotic or aneurysmal changes in these arteries. The painful cutaneous lesions respond best to corticosteroid treatment. At times, anticoagulant and vasodilator drugs may be beneficial.

Scleroderma (generalized or diffuse) is a chronic progressive disease with gradual deterioration. The cause is unknown. It is also considered to be a "diffuse collagen disease." As a rule, no subjective sensations precede the cutaneous manifestations except in the case of involvement of the extremities, when neuralgic, arthritic, or vascular pain may be the first symptom. Thus, pain in the arms may be confused with anginal radiation or with the shoulder-hand syndrome. However, the cutaneous lesions are usually rather characteristic. The skin has a hard or leathery, waxy, irregularly pigmented or depigmented, and smooth glossy appearance. Eventually, the skin becomes firmly bound to the underlying structures.

The earliest subjective sensation is usually that of diffuse stiffness or tightness of the skin. When this affects the integument of the chest, a sense of oppression may ensue. Visceral lesions usually appear following the cutaneous lesions, and may involve the lungs, esophagus, gastrointestinal tract, heart, kidneys, and joints. They may produce dysphagia, pleural or pericardial effusion, digestive disturbances, dyspnea, palpitations, and anasarca. Pericarditis and pleuritis may also be the cause of chest pain. Fixity of the thoracic cage may produce further cardiopulmonary embarrassment. (This condition is also considered among the neurologic causes of thoracic pain.)

Treatment is generally unsatisfactory, and of the many recommended therapeutic measures only corticosteroid therapy has provided some improvement in mild cases. This affects only the cutaneous lesions. Unfortunately, continued corticosteroid treatment may lead to relentlessly progressive hypertension in patients with scleroderma, perhaps because of associated renal lesions of the glomeruli and small blood vessels.

Dermatomyositis is a rare nonsuppurative disease of unknown cause. Most investigators tend to incriminate several bacteria with either direct invasion or toxic damage of the tissues by bacterial products. It is characterized by a variety of cutaneous changes, inflammatory and degenerative involvement of the striated musculature, and also the presence of vasomotor disturbances, all of which are capable of producing pain in the thorax and elsewhere. The cutaneous lesions vary from simple erythema to more serious forms of dermatitis, sclerosis, pigmentation, and even lupus-erythematosus-like lesions. Since cardiac muscle is probably not involved, electrocardiographic changes are due to peripheral cutaneous changes which affect electrical conduction. Of the various therapeutic measures, only corticosteroids bring significant, though temporary, improvement. Unfortunately, the disease eventually proves fatal in about half the cases.

Disseminated lupus erythematosus was originally considered a dermatologic disease but is now regarded as another diffuse vascular disease of the "collagen disease" order. It is responsible not only for a fairly characteristic skin lesion (facial "butterfly") but also for severe blood, joint, cardiovascular, and renal involvement. The cutaneous manifestations may at times also involve the chest. They usually cause no pain, but when the erythematous lesions change to vesicles or bullae, itching and burning of variable degree may be experienced. Lesions of the endocardium, myocardium, and pericardium are considered elsewhere. The treatment with corticosteroids has provided considerable palliation in most cases.

Degenerations

Xanthomatosis is a disease which may involve the skin of the chest in addition to the extremities and the eyelids. It is included here not only because the nodular or plaque-like lesions produce pain and are slightly tender to pressure, but also because of the high incidence of coronary artery disease (40 per cent) found in this metabolic disorder, especially in the type associated with hypercholesteremia. This is especially true in primary familial hypercholesteremia. Blood lipids are markedly elevated. Cardiac symptoms develop before the age of 50 due to the marked atherosclerotic involvement of the coronary arteries.

Amyloidosis is a degenerative disorder which may be primary or secondary to chronic infectious diseases, such as tuberculosis or chronic infections. Amyloid is a foreign material (glycoprotein) which is produced and deposited in various body tissues. Nodules may involve the skin of the chest, although they occur most commonly about the lips and eyelids. The yellowish, often glistening lesions may resemble lichen planus but their histologic features are quite diagnostic. They are usually not painful but may cause itching. Their instant significance lies in the fact that they may provide the first clue to the presence of disseminated visceral involvement. Thus, amyloid heart disease may produce symptoms and signs of cardiac failure or coronary insufficiency. Involvement of the lungs may give rise to chronic cor pulmonale.

Electrocardiographic changes are found in more than half the cases. The Congo red test is positive, and skin biopsy reveals the pathognomonic changes. They may also be associated with multiple myeloma and rheumatoid arthritis. The latter two conditions may also be primary sources of chest pain and are considered elsewhere. The present treatment of these conditions is ineffectual, although improvement may be expected by the removal of primary disorders.

Tumors

Neurofibromatosis (Recklinghausen's disease) consists of melanotic pigmentation of the skin associated with multiple fibromata along the peripheral nerves. The neurologic manifestations usually do not appear until later life. Neurofibromatous involvement of intercostal nerves or the spinal cord itself may cause continuous or intermittent pain over the chest wall. It is interesting to note that this condition occurs in 5 per cent of patients with pheochromocytoma, which may also cause paroxysms of chest pain (see p. 212). Treatment consists of extirpation of the local tumor masses.

Lipoma. This benign tumor may be single or multiple and is nodular, circumscribed, and encapsulated. It is more common in women and as a rule causes no subjective sensation, although pressure on nerves may lead to pain. Removal of the tumor is curative. The condition called *adipositas dolorosa* (Dercum's disease) is usually considered a rare variety of fat deposit encountered in women at the menopause and is characterized by the deposition of irregular cutaneous fatty deposits with symmetrical distribution. They are either preceded by or associated with neuralgic symptoms. The treatment is similar to that of simple obesity. Occasionally, surgical removal of the fat masses may become necessary.

Glomus tumor. The glomic structure is an end-organ apparatus consisting of a direct arteriovenous anastomosis, usually of tortuous nature and rich in glomal cells and nonmyelinated nerve fibers. It is under autonomic nerve control. These structures are found in the stratum reticulare of the skin and distributed widely over the body. The tumors arising from the glomic apparatus may involve not only the extremities, particularly the fingers and toes, but also the thoracic integument. Thus, severe pain in the left arm may falsely suggest the presence of an anginal syndrome. The lesions are minute and frequently invisible. The presence of severe persistent pain in a sharply localized area may lead to a correct diagnosis. This is confirmed by excision and microscopic examination. The slightest pressure on these lesions or change in temperature may cause severe lancinating or radiating pain, which may persist for months after operative removal.

Malignant neoplastic lesions of the skin, whether primary or secondary, are usually not painful except when associated with severe inflammatory reactions. Because of the differential diagnostic problems encountered and because they may represent the initial manifestations of diffuse visceral involvement, the cutaneous lesions of lymphoblastomata and mycosis fungoides should be briefly mentioned. Intensely itching lesions often associated with an erythroderma-like appearance of the skin or a picture of exfoliative dermatitis are not rare in these conditions. Many neoplastic lesions may metastasize to structures of the chest wall (e.g., bones) or the intrathoracic contents (e.g., heart and lungs).

DISEASES OF THE BREAST

A number of painful conditions of the breast may affect males as well as females. The mobility of the female breast is one of its outstanding characteristics. Normally, it occupies the space between the third and seventh ribs. The growth of the breast during the period of sexual development may, at times, become excessive. This so-called "adolescent hypertrophy" of the female breast may cause a "dragging" discomfort and may be also associated with vague localized aching. It is aggravated during the premenstrual period due to engorgement. Hypertrophy of the male breast may be produced by disorders of gonadal function, administration of estrogens and androgens, or digitalis. Acute swelling and pain may occur in the male breast following puberty; this may affect one or both breasts. A similar state is possible in older males following the use of estrogens for prostatic malignancy or the experimental treatment of atheromatous degeneration. Reduction of the elastic tissue occurs with advancing years, and female breasts become very pendulous. This causes a constant pulling or drawing painful sensation which may be unilateral. When it affects only the left side at this age level, anginal distress may be suspected. In the elderly patient, gynecomastia may develop which may also cause a mild ache. A well-fitting breast support rapidly improves the distress.

Nonspecific breast pain has been described following hysterectomy or during the premenstrual period. Either or both breasts may be affected. They are painful to touch or on movements of the arms due to contraction of the underlying pectoral muscle. Small doses of testosterone or x-ray treatment usually give relief in the first instance. Measures reducing the vascular engorgement and sodium retention responsible for the premenstrual mammary discomfort, such as chlorothiazide, ammonium chloride, or progesterone, may afford relief.

Cystic disease of the breast, whether gross or microscopic, is associated with symptoms of pain and tenderness on palpation. Pain may be more common or severe in cystic disease than in benign tumors (adenofibroma) or even carcinoma of the breast. Symptoms may be present continuously or may be limited to the premenstrual period. Pain increases when cysts enlarge rapidly. Aspiration of the cystic contents often produces relief of the pain. The differential diagnosis of cystic disease and of malignancy of the breast is often difficult, especially since both conditions occur in the same age group.

Fibrous disease of the breast is a benign tumorous involvement of the stroma of the breast which is usually painless. Patients complaining of pain and tenderness in the region of the tumor usually develop these symptoms after discovery of the lesion. This tumor occurs during the period of highest ovarian activity; it grows very slowly and tends to develop in large pendulous breasts. Biopsy is usually necessary for differentiation from carcinoma.

Mammary duct ectasia is a benign condition affecting the aging breast and consists of dilatation of the collecting ducts in the subareolar region with surrounding fibrosis and inflammation. The earliest and most significant manifestation of this disease may be a yellow or blood-tinged discharge from the nipple. However, early complaints of pain and tenderness in the breast are also encountered. The pain may be limited to the nipple region or may involve larger areas when rapid enlargement takes place. Differentiation from carcinoma is important, since this lesion does not necessitate radical surgery. Examination of a frozen section is most helpful and permits the local excision of this benign lesion.

Fat necrosis. The vulnerable position of the breasts makes them especially prone to direct trauma. Necrosis of the fat tissue may result. The significance of this lesion lies in the fact that it simulates carcinoma. A traumatic origin is supported by the history of injury and the presence of gross or microscopic hemorrhage. Pain or tenderness occurs in at least one-third of all cases. The lesion is usually quite superficial but may involve large areas of breast tissue. New growths, fibrosis with resultant retraction, and suppurative lesions may cause differential diagnostic difficulties. Transillumination, biopsy, and frozen sections aid in the diagnosis. The treatment consists of local excision if resorption does not take place within a reasonable period of time.

Adenofibroma, a benign fibroepithelial tumor, rarely causes pain and tenderness. This is also true for *cystosarcoma, intraductal papilloma,* and other benign nonepithelial tumors of the breast.

Carcinoma. As regards carcinoma of the breast and other malignant neoplasms of the breast, they are far too often unattended by any painful sensation. However, chest pain may occur even in so-called *occult carcinoma* of the breast. This term implies histologically proved carcinoma of the breast with axillary nodal involvement in the absence of symptoms or signs of any abnormality of the breast. The pain is limited to the axilla in such instances. The prognosis is not hopeless if surgery is performed when the axillary nodes are detected early in the disease. Similar occult malignancies are known to arise in the male breast and may cause pain. Women suffering from pain of the anterior chest wall due to a variety of causes may show great anxiety about breast malignancy. As a matter of fact, this form of cancerophobia is fairly common.

Mondor's disease. Another condition which may produce chest pain is thrombophlebitis of the superficial veins of the breast and the anterior chest wall. Minor trauma or breast surgery is the usual cause of this condition. Treatment is rarely required, since the condition subsides spontaneously and without recurrence or complications. Women with large pendulous breasts are especially prone to this disease. The sudden onset of localized pain and tenderness is accentuated by any maneuver that stretches the breast tissues, such as raising the arm. This localized condition is not to be confused with the distention of the veins of the chest wall and breasts due to superior vena caval obstruction or thrombosis of the subclavian veins.

SKELETAL DISEASES

Diseases of the skeletal framework of the thorax are among the common causes of chest pain. Those involving the ribs and costal cartilages usually cause pain anteriorly and laterally. Those involving the spine cause pain which is usually most severe posteriorly but frequently radiates around the entire chest. On rare occasions, it may be experienced anteriorly only. Thus, the differential diagnosis of chest pain includes a consideration of both the costosternal structures and the spine and its associated structures such as the intervertebral discs and joints. The clavicles and scapulae, which form an integral part of the thorax, complete the bony cage.

Diseases of Costosternal Structures

Trauma. The obvious purpose of the rib cage is to protect the vital intrathoracic structures from external injury. Trauma to the ribs is one of the most common of all chest injuries. Rib fracture may also occur as a result of an unrecognized minor injury (as in the case of pathologic fractures at the site of a metastatic tumor) or in patients with high pain threshold levels. The appearance of pain over the left chest may lead to a suspicion that heart disease exists. Rib fractures may also be associated with more serious injury to the thoracic viscera. It has been estimated that from 10 to 20 per cent of patients with associated pleural or lung complications die because these have been recognized too late or not at all.

Rib fractures may occur following severe anteroposterior compression of the chest, as in steering-wheel accidents or other direct violence to the chest. The more exposed fourth to eighth ribs are usually involved and may injure the pleura, lungs, heart, and intercostal vessels, leading to pneumothorax, hemothorax, subcutaneous emphysema, and even pericardial tamponade. Such fractures are prone to occur in adult life because of the loss of elasticity of the rib cage incident to increasing calcification of the costal cartilages as well as decalcification of the bony structures themselves. Although displacement of the fragments is usually slight, a severe blow may lead to serious complications affecting pleural, pulmonary, mediastinal, or abdominal structures. Slipped costal cartilage may occur at the osseous or sternal attachment and is most difficult to visualize on x-rays.

Chest pain due to rib fracture is aggravated by breathing, coughing, sneezing, or bending. Tenderness and swelling at the site of the fracture may be diagnostic. Crepitus may be palpated over the fracture site or may be heard occasionally with a stethoscope. In the presence of accompanying subcutaneous emphysema, crepitus due to air in the tissues can be easily palpated. Gentle anteroposterior compression of the bony cage may produce localized pain at the site of the fracture. X-rays may be unable to reveal fine fissure fractures or breaks in the continuity of cartilaginous tissues. Such lesions may not be demonstrable until appreciable callus formation occurs.

Occasionally, an *isolated fracture of the first rib* may be sustained without concurrent fracture of the overlying clavicle. Usually there is no displacement of the fragments. It is apt to be missed due to the deep location of the first rib in the base of the neck, where it is protected from trauma by the shoulder girdle. This fracture may result in rupture of the apex of the lung, abscess formation, pleurisy with effusion, hemorrhage, nerve pressure, and Horner's syndrome. The pain is usually sudden and excruciating, localized in the upper portion of the chest, and associated with breathlessness and faintness. The pain may also radiate into neck, shoulder, and arms, suggesting coronary disease. Fracture with displacement of the first rib, either anterior or posterior to the insertion of the scalenus anticus, may cause laceration, distortion, or compression of the subclavian artery and vein, phrenic nerve, or pleura.

It should also be noted that partial immobilization following rib fracture may cause decreased aeration. In the presence of underlying coronary disease, especially in the older age group, this may in turn result in super-imposed pain caused by coronary insufficiency. Crushing injury of the chest may also result in acute pulmonary edema.

The symptomatic treatment of uncomplicated rib fractures consists of ordinary adhesive strapping of the chest wall in order to limit respiratory movements. An intercostal nerve block or local infiltration may be employed in order to control the pain. It is advisable to block at least two nerves above and below the injured rib because of the overlapping distribution of inter-costal nerves. This gives immediate relief of pain and permits normal re-spiratory excursions. This approach is especially indicated among older pa-tients. This group may also benefit from the prophylactic administration of an antibiotic, since impairment of respiration may lead to the accumulation of secretions and pneumonitis, especially in the presence of chronic bronchitis or bronchiectasis. Complicated rib fractures occasionally require additional measures, including tracheostomy, drainage of the chest, and cautious maintenance of proper fluid and electrolyte balance.

Costochondral syndrome (Tietze). The cartilaginous origin of chest pain has been re-emphasized recently. This condition was described originally by Tietze in 1921 and subsequently reported in the foreign literature with in-creasing frequency. In the United States, an increasing number of in-vestigators have recently reconfirmed its occurrence.

The exact cause of this disorder is unknown, since there is seldom any definitive proof of any of the causative factors which have been found to be associated with this condition. These include infection, malnutrition, re-peated trauma from jarring of the trunk or coughing, respiratory diseases, and sudden movements.

Although there are variations in etiology, pathology, and therapy, the following characteristic features are usually present: (1) pain in the chest; (2) tenderness with or without swelling of one or more of the costochondral junctions, often associated with tenderness over the corresponding costo-thoracic joints; (3) history of injury or of unusual stress to the chest wall; (4) high incidence of anxiety induced by pain in the chest; and (5) im-provement after anxiety has been alleviated and when the chest is protected from further injury or stress. The pain itself is ill-defined, recurrent, and localized at the tender nodular swelling. It may resemble a heavy pressure in the chest, or a vague soreness or tightness, or may radiate into the shoulder, arm, or neck. The upper ribs are more commonly involved than the lower ribs. The second to the fourth costochondral junctions are actually affected in most instances. Hence, the confusion with other origins of precordial distress. Characteristic findings are limited to the surroundings of the involved costochondral or sternoclavicular junction. The tender bulbous or fusiform swelling (when present) involves the soft tissue, cartilage, and bone. The skin itself shows no alteration and moves freely over the underlying mass.

Of special interest is the fact that this benign disorder can mimic the pain of various visceral origins, including pleuropulmonary, abdominal, and, most significantly, coronary disease. Anxiety about the possible presence of heart disease is obviously the most common finding in patients complaining of this condition.

Occasionally, the swelling is large enough for the patient to seek advice from a surgeon, and differential diagnostic consideration of various neoplastic diseases involving the ribs and chest wall becomes necessary. Although it tends to subside eventually, recurrences of this benign condition are not infrequent and may give rise to considerable difficulty in management.

Treatment consists essentially of firm reassurance of the patient regarding the benign character of the disease in order to allay his fears, as well as symptomatic measures to relieve pain. These include the local application of heat, analgesics, ethyl chloride spray, and in some instances local infiltration with procaine or corticosteroids. The oral use of corticosteroids has recently found enthusiastic advocates and may be effective in preventing relapses. Surgical exploration and excision of the swelling has been employed in an occasional case for positive identification of the mass, and has resulted in permanent relief.

Xiphoidalgia. A painful disorder which resembles Tietze's syndrome is the so-called "hypersensitive xiphoid syndrome," xiphoidalgia, or xiphidynia. This syndrome is occasionally found in association with various diseases of the chest and abdomen, such as various heart disorders, cholecystitis, peptic ulcer, and bronchial asthma. There is usually no correlation between the frequency and severity of asthma and the degree of tenderness and pain in the xiphoid. Organic disease directly responsible for this condition is usually not detected.

The diagnosis of xiphoidalgia is readily established when lower chest or upper abdominal pain can be reproduced by direct pressure upon the xiphoid. The pain is usually felt as a deep, slightly nauseating ache located in the lower chest behind the sternum, and it may radiate to the epigastrium, the back, both shoulders, the arms, or over the entire precordium.

The innervation of the xiphoid explains the reference of pain and tenderness when disease exists in adjoining structures, and vice versa. Pain is referred from the gastrointestinal tract through the fourth to sixth thoracic nerves. Overlapping of the cardiac afferent and xiphoid nerves exists, since pain from the heart is transmitted through the first to sixth thoracic nerves. Reference of this xiphoid pain to the shoulder is usually mediated via ramification of the phrenic nerves.

Treatment with procaine infiltration appears to give somewhat better relief than ethyl chloride spray. Adequate reassurance is of considerable importance. Treatment of any underlying condition is imperative. Surgical removal of the hypersensitive xiphoid is rarely necessary.

Tumors. Tumors of the rib cage frequently give rise to chest pain. Malignant costal and sternal tumors are rarely asymptomatic, but approximately one-third of benign neoplasms escape detection because they are symptomless. Occasionally, pain may occur as the result of a pathologic fracture. Many rib tumors are not metastatic, and primary malignant tumors are not more common than benign tumors.

Primary rib tumors. Pain and/or tumefaction are the symptoms most frequently encountered in patients with primary tumors of the rib, regardless of whether they are benign or malignant. No conclusions can be drawn as to the nature of the tumor from the duration of symptoms alone. However, the patient with a malignant tumor tends to seek medical care earlier than one who has a benign tumor because of the more rapid expansion and more persistent severe pain.

Histologically, a large variety of tumors may involve the ribs and the sternum (see Table 3-1), since the ribs are mesodermal in origin. The most common benign neoplasms are fibrous dysplasia, chondromas, and osteochondromas. Fibrous dysplasia produces a mass which may include one or more ribs. Symptoms are strikingly few, and the lesion is frequently mistaken for a cartilaginous tumor. Although this is usually a benign lesion, malignant changes have occurred on occasion. This potential malignancy is obviously shared by any primary tumors.

Eosinophilic granuloma. An interesting condition which must be differentiated from primary rib tumor is eosinophilic granuloma. This lesion is actually inflammatory rather than neoplastic. Although the lesion is a disorder of the lipoid metabolism related to Letterer-Siwe's disease and lipid histiocytosis of the cholesterol type (Hand-Schiller-Christian disease), it is advisable to excise the affected segment of rib in doubtful cases. Since it may cause a painful swelling localized to a rib, it is also confused with Tietze's syndrome or multiple myeloma.

Other malignant tumors. Chondrosarcoma, endothelioma, and fibrosarcoma are the types most frequently encountered. Malignant tumors of the

Table 3-1

**Pathology of 212 Collected Cases
of Primary Tumor of the Rib** *

		Per Cent of Benign Tumors	*Per Cent of All Tumors*
Benign Tumors	111 Cases		52.36
Chondroma		22.5	11.8
Osteochondroma		13.5	7.1
Myxochondroma		1.8	0.9
Osteoma		3.6	1.9
Osteoid osteoma		1.8	0.9
Osteofibroma		1.8	0.9
Fibrous dysplasia		31.5	16.5
Hemangioma		7.2	3.8
Xanthomatous giant cell		9.0	4.7
Miscellaneous—myxoma, solitary myeloma, xanthoma, lipoma, fibroma, chondromyxoid fibroma		7.2	3.8

		Per Cent of Malignant Tumors	
Malignant Tumors	101 Cases		47.64
Chondrosarcoma		35.6	17.0
Osteogenic sarcoma		5.9	2.8
Fibrosarcoma		11.9	5.6
Mixed sarcomas		7.9	3.8
Endothelioma (Ewing's tumor)		24.8	11.8
Giant cell		1.0	0.5
Miscellaneous—myeloma, lymphosarcoma, reticulum cell, hemangioendothelioblastoma, hemangiosarcoma, liposarcoma		12.9	6.1

* Modified from Hochberg, L. A., and Crastnopol, P.: Tumors of the ribs. *Dis. Chest,* **28**:406, 1955.

ribs most frequently occur near the costochondral junction of the upper five ribs. *Multiple myeloma* frequently involves the ribs as well as other bones (see Fig. 3-1). It causes pathologic fractures with resultant stabbing pain as well as a persistent boring type of pain usually related to expanding lesions in the marrow. The bone pain occurs in 95 per cent of the cases and especially affects the lumbar and costal areas. Hyperglobulinemia and Bence-Jones proteinuria are usually present, and x-rays present a more or less characteristic picture in 90 per cent of all cases. Bone marrow biopsy shows an increase in the plasma cell series in 85 per cent of all cases. Electrophoretic patterns are demonstrable.

In view of the great difficulty in recognizing the exact nature of many of these tumors by gross inspection, by x-ray examination, or even by micro-

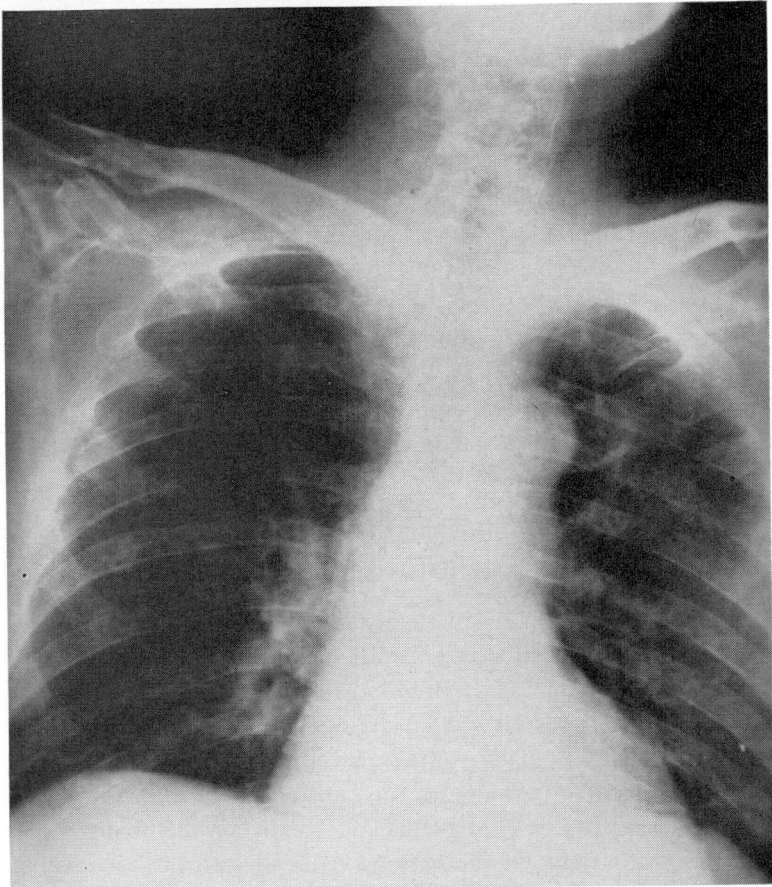

Fig. 3-1. Multiple myeloma of ribs. Note the multiple discrete and confluent osteolytic lesions in the shoulder girdle and ribs without any perifocal bone reaction.

scopic study of the biopsied tissue, most authorities are in agreement as to the need for surgical removal in such instances.

Infections. Staphylococcal infections, tuberculosis, and typhoid fever may cause osteitis of the ribs. Syphilis may cause periostitis. Involvement at these atypical sites may follow mild but repeated trauma to which the ribs are exposed because of their subcutaneous position. Following rib resection for empyema, pericardial infection, or thoracotomy, osteitis of the open rib ends may occur; the infection may then travel along the intercostal muscle planes. Since the infection may not be visible at the surface, the exact nature of the pain and temperature may be difficult to explain initially. X-rays and aspiration may be helpful diagnostic procedures.

Brock considers the location of the osteomyelitic involvement of considerable importance, since it may affect not only the clinical picture but also the prognosis of the disease. Thus, involvement of the anterior ribs, usually near the costochondral junction, is almost exclusively encountered in children and may resemble acute serofibrinous pleurisy or frank empyema. Spread into pleural space and lungs tends to be limited by the endothoracic fascia. Involvement of the lower ribs is evident much earlier than that of the upper ribs, where the heavy pectoral musculature may obscure an enlarging abscess. Involvement of the posterior ribs, usually near the angle, leads often to spread into the lung and pleural cavity. It is associated with severe manifestation of pulmonary or pleural disease.

The treatment of rib infections follows the same principles as that of infections in general. The local injection and oral administration of antibiotics are imperative. Incision and drainage are indicated for localized areas of suppuration.

Lesions of the Cervicodorsal Spine

Rheumatism. Of 10 million Americans afflicted with some form of rheumatism, it has been estimated that 4.5 million actually have arthritis and that 1 million are partially or totally disabled because of this affliction. For our purposes, the heading of this section denotes a broad group of disorders of the joints, manifested by pain, stiffness, swelling, and other musculoskeletal reactions. Inadequate knowledge of the cause and nature of many common rheumatic diseases has created points of controversy involving almost any phase of these disorders. Of the various types of arthritis (see Table 3-2), rheumatoid arthritis and chronic hypertrophic osteoarthritis are the two types which most frequently affect the spine. Infectious lesions of the spine include tuberculosis, brucellosis, syphilis, typhoid, and actinomycosis. Since the introduction of effective antibiotic therapy, the major problem in infectious arthritis has become one of prompt recognition for purposes of early and adequate therapy.

Rheumatoid arthritis (spondylitis, Marie-Strumpell disease). It has been estimated that between 2 and 3 million persons in the United States alone have rheumatoid arthritis.

More than one-quarter of all patients with "rheumatic" complaints have rheumatoid arthritis. This disease has an incidence of 1 in 2000 of the general population and has a predilection for young male adults, although no age is spared. Unfortunately, the problem of etiology has not been resolved. Variants of the disease have added confusion. Heredity, trauma, hypersensitivity, altered metabolism, endocrine and autonomic imbalances,

Table 3-2

Differential Diagnosis of the Arthritides

Arthritis	Pattern	Sex	Age	Fever	Signs of Inflammation	Leuko-cytosis	Anemia	Sedimentation Rate
Rheumatoid (atrophic)	Small joints, symmetric	Male and female	Youth	Occasional	Frequent	Slight	Microcytic hypochromic	Elevated
Degenerative (osteoarthritic) (hypertrophic)	Weight-bearing joints, asymmetric	Male and female	Elderly	0	0	0	0	Unaffected
Lupus erythematosus disseminatus	Rheumatoid pattern	Female	18–40	Present	Present	Leuko-penia	Present	Elevated
Tuberculosis	Weight-bearing joints, mono-articular	Male and female	Child-hood	Present	Variable	0	Present	Elevated
Traumatic	Asymmetric, monoarticular	Male pre-dominate	Any age	0	Present	0	0	Unaffected

and psychogenic disturbances are among the important factors. Although both types have a number of features in common, the ineffectiveness of chrysotherapy, the better response to x-ray therapy, and the general negativity of serologic tests have led many authorities to consider spondylitis as a condition which differs from rheumatoid involvement of the peripheral joints.

The clinical importance of rheumatoid spondylitis resides in the fact that it frequently causes pain which may be mistaken for angina pectoris. This is due to the cervicodorsal involvement in 10 per cent of patients with rheumatoid spondylitis. Impingement of the nerve roots produces pain which is usually of a sharp or "catching" character and may be intercostal, substernal, or precordial in location. A feeling of tightness or stiffness of the chest, often with markedly decreased or even absent chest expansion, may be associated with or occasionally precede the onset of pain. This is due to involvement and fixation of the costospinal articulations, which interfere with the vital capacity. Atelectasis or recurrent pneumonitis may be troublesome complications. In some cases, tenderness and swelling of the sternoclavicular and manubriosternal joints are present, and similar changes may also affect the costochondral cartilage. In the latter instance, a pleuritic type of pain may mimic pulmonary or cardiac disease. Involvement of the shoulder or hip joints suggests a poor prognosis.

These symptoms may occur intermittently over a long period of time in many patients. However, the pain tends to be quite severe, the fixation of the chest increases rapidly, and progressive deformity of the spine with ankylosis may occur over a very short period of time. Resultant kyphoscoliotic deformities may become severe enough to interfere with normal cardiopulmonary function. Eventually, the picture of chronic cor pulmonale (kyphoscoliotic heart disease) may emerge.

Occasionally, symptoms and physical findings characteristic of rheumatoid spondylitis may be evident without detectable x-ray abnormalities. The diagnosis of this condition is not particularly helped by the acute phase reactants but is best confirmed by roentgenograms. The earliest changes detectable by x-rays are first seen in the sacroiliac joints and pelvic bones. The x-ray lesions tend to progress from narrowed joint spaces, with blurring of the subchondral bone; to sclerosis of the adjacent bone, with spotty demineralization; and to ultimate obliteration of the joint spaces. (See Fig. 3-2.) During the final phases, calcification of paraspinal ligaments appears, giving the spine a "bamboo" appearance. Serologic diagnosis includes many variants of hemagglutination tests. Relatively specific serum elements occur with rheumatoid arthritis, and the rheumatoid factor is a macroglobulin

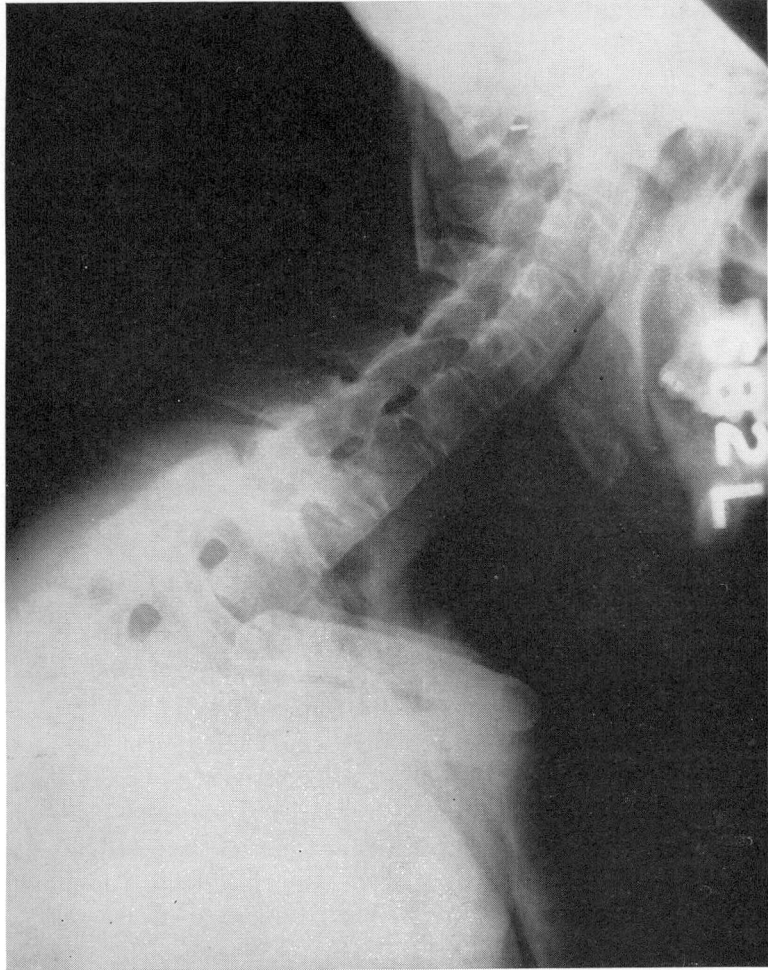

Fig. 3-2. Rheumatoid arthritis of cervical spine. Note decalcification of vertebrae, calcification of the anterior interspinal ligament and indistinctness and narrowing of the zygo-apophyseal joints.

with a protein complex of high molecular weight. The development of a reliable and sensitive serologic test has been most fruitful; there are now agglutination tests available employing bentonite and styrene latex as well as red cells from sheep, humans, and alligators. (By most technics, 70 per cent of rheumatoid patients and 5 per cent of those without the disease give positive results.)

The differential diagnosis of chest pain due to spondylitis is made difficult by the not infrequent association of valvular heart disease (usually aortic insufficiency), endocarditis, pericarditis, or pleuritis with rheumatoid spondylitis. An aortitis resulting in aortic regurgitation and occurring almost exclusively in males with rheumatoid spondylitis is being described more frequently, with more than fifty cases now on record. The lesion is limited to the root of the aorta and shows intimal thickening and deformity of the valve cusps. Rheumatoid nodules have been observed in the myocardium and the pericardium. Necrotizing vascular disease in arteries of the small muscular type has also occurred but has been attributed to the use of steroid therapy. Although the evidence is not yet definitive that any form of heart disease is more frequent in spondylitis than in the general population, it is possible that if cardiac involvement is sought for more carefully, a greater incidence will be found in arthritic patients.

In addition, coronary artery disease has to be considered, and the whole gamut of procedures, including exercise electrocardiography, may have to be used to elucidate the nature of complaints. Not rarely, both rheumatoid spondylitis and coronary artery disease may be present in the same patient. In addition to visceral disease (especially the heart and lungs), differential diagnosis also includes rheumatic fever, Reiter's disease, psoriatic arthritis, and, less frequently, osteoarthritis, senile ankylosing hyperostosis, disc lesions, or a rare heredofamilial spondylitis.

Treatment is essentially the same as for rheumatoid arthritis of the peripheral joints. Countless therapeutic approaches to the problem of rheumatoid arthritis have not yet produced any modality which can be considered specific. Diet, chrysotherapy, vitamins, removal of infected foci, vaccines, antibiotics, physiotherapy, estrogens, and even the much vaunted corticosteroids offer ameliorating benefits rather than the possibility of cure. Since rheumatoid arthritis is a chronic disease and usually a lifetime problem, emphasis should be placed on long-term treatment. In view of the frequency of unfavorable physiologic effects associated with long-term corticosteroid therapy, together with the high failure rate experienced, careful selection of patients is required. Corticosteroid therapy for palliative effects is best indicated in early active rheumatoid arthritis. Phenylbutazone and salicylates are presently the preferred drugs in rheumatoid spondylitis. X-ray therapy to the spine is most helpful in many cases. In the final analysis, a basic program of treatment based on at least the following eight items is essential: (1) psychologic adjustment, (2) a balance between rest and activity, (3) management of food intake and bowel function, (4) correction of anemia, (5) removal of frank foci of infection, (6) relief of pain, (7) corrective and postural exercises, and (8) prevention and correction of deformity.

Osteoarthritis (degenerative joint disease). Osteoarthritis is still regarded as the most common of the rheumatic diseases and a major cause of disability among the aged. Everyone beyond middle age has acquired some degree of osteoarthritis. Since Neolithic man, this condition has been a frequent cause of pain in the thoracic, cervical, and shoulder regions.

The prevalent concept regarding the pathogenesis of osteoarthritis is that of a degenerative disorder of the superficial layers of the cartilages with secondary reactive changes of the subchondral bone consisting of condensation, marginal overgrowth of both cartilage and bone lesions of discs, and ultimate disorganization of the joints. No single etiologic factor has yet been detected. Although "wear and tear" is generally considered as the most common factor, the exact mechanism remains unknown.

The uncomplicated development of degenerative articular disease as a result of ordinary use is known as primary osteoarthritis. Secondary osteoarthritis may occur when joints are injured by either acute trauma or chronic microtrauma such as may result from obesity, postural abnormalities, scoliosis, etc. It may also occur following misuse of joints damaged by other types of arthritis, such as rheumatoid arthritis, articular infection, or gouty arthritis, or when cartilage is weakened or altered by such conditions as ochronosis or certain hereditary factors.

Pain associated with osteoarthritis may result from the articular lesion, nerve root compression, chronic ligament strain, or associated muscle spasm. Involvement of the cervical spine may cause a radicular type of pain involving the arms, head, and shoulder girdle.

These changes are found most often in the lower cervical vertebrae, from which emerge the sixth, seventh, and eighth cervical nerves. These segments contain fibers which supply the pectoralis major and minor, the subscapularis, and the deeper portion of the latissimus dorsi muscles.

When the foramina from which these nerves emerge are narrowed, pain occurs over the pectoral regions, shoulders, or arms. Occasionally, a patient with osteoarthritis of the cervical portion of the spinal column will complain of a dull ache largely confined to the region of a shoulder and arm. He may not experience cervical pain, but certain movements of the neck, such as hyperextension, will produce this pain. Occasionally dizziness may be associated with the pain, but this may be traceable to concomitant hypotension.

This pain distribution may resemble that of coronary artery disease. At times, considerable cardiac anxiety persists even after coronary disease has been excluded and in spite of complete reassurance of the patient. This is frequently due to the chronicity of the osteoarthritic condition and the lack of effective therapy. In milder cases, the response of pain to salicylates and local heat should provide further reassurance. The fairly common finding of muscular weakness may be of further diagnostic help. Involvement of the thoracic spine is more frequent in the lowermost region but may also involve the first two to four vertebral regions. In the first instance, pain is referred to the shoulder or precordial region; in the second instance, a burning or causalgic type of pain is experienced, or a cutaneous hyperesthesia may exist in the corresponding dermatome segment.

Clinical symptoms develop insidiously because of the slow progression of the pathologic process. The first symptom may be increased soreness and stiffness after physical exertion, which is relieved by rest. Since joint pain is closely related to activity, joint discomfort usually increases with the progress of the day. Though there may be considerable stiffness on awaking, this may be a relatively comfortable time of the day. This picture is in sharp contrast to the pain of rheumatoid arthritis. Roentgen studies reveal the characteristic osteophytes in most instances (see Fig. 3-3).

The treatment of osteoarthritis of the spine is not curative, but a carefully planned program can be of considerable benefit to the patient. This should include the use of analgesics and local heat, as well as the avoidance of undue stress leading to further injury of the structures involved. The use of oral corticosteroid therapy is seldom indicated, although it may be injected into the joint for subjective relief. The emotional attitude of the patient toward the disease is of considerable importance, as has been well demonstrated in studies employing placebo medication, given orally or by injection.

In more severe cases of cervicodorsal osteoarthritis, traction and manipulation have proved greatly beneficial. It is seldom necessary or advisable to resort to surgical removal of spurs or arthrodesis, even when there is evidence of significant nerve root compression.

Spondylitis due to infections. The introduction of effective antibiotics has made the problem of infectious arthritis one of prompt recognition and adequate treatment. With the progressive decline in infectious diseases, complicating forms of arthritis are becoming clinical curiosities.

Tuberculosis. Although there has been a tremendous decrease in the incidence of pulmonary bone and joint tuberculosis during the past twenty years, tuberculous spondylitis has remained the most common form of tuberculous arthritis. It occurs in half of all cases of bone tuberculosis. In countries such as Brazil, where tuberculosis is epidemic, dissemination frequently involves the skeleton even without appreciable pulmonary involvement. This disease favors the upper thoracic vertebrae in children and the lower ones in adults. Various portions of the vertebrae may be attacked as well as the adjacent soft tissue. This leads to caseation of bone

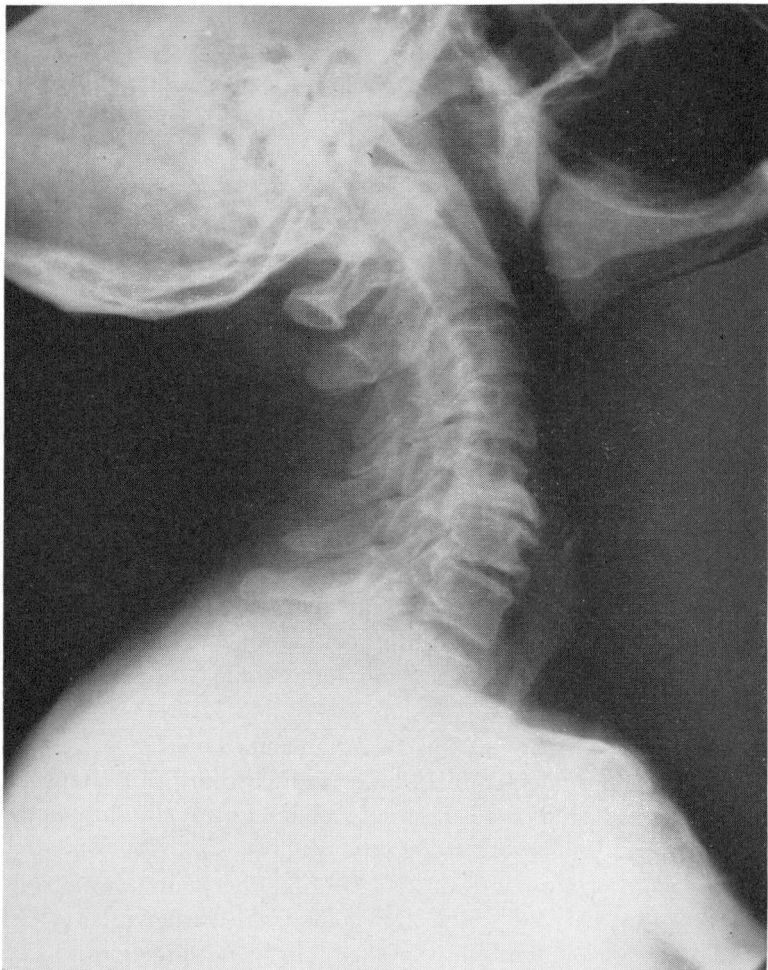

Fig. 3-3. Hypertrophic arthritis of cervical spine. Note narrowed inter-spaces, particularly between C₅ and C₆, C₆ and C₇ with juxta-articular sclero-sis, and osteophyte formation anteriorly and posteriorly.

and the formation of cold abscesses in the paravertebral gutter. About one-third of these patients die.

Chest pain may be located in the region of the spine itself, where it is frequently intensified by movement or even ordinary weight bearing, or it may be present in the anterior or lateral aspects of the chest. The pain may be due to radicular involvement, or to mediastinal, pleural, or pulmonary involvement following the rupture of a paravertebral abscess into these structures. The pain then becomes boring and persistent and is frequently aggravated by respiration or by body movements in the case of mediastinal involvement; or it becomes sharp on respiratory excursions of the thorax in the presence of pleuropulmonary spread. The presence of a paravertebral abscess may produce intrathoracic pain. Intense pain and even paraplegia may occur following vertebral collapse (Pott's disease). Constant pain is due to compression of the intervertebral foramina. Following therapeutic arrest of the process, the resulting kyphosis may give rise to chronic cor pulmonale.

The diagnosis of tuberculous spondylitis is greatly aided by roentgenography (see Fig. 3-4). This may reveal early narrowing of the intervertebral joint space, vertebral caries in the anterior portion, a fusiform paravertebral shadow, and extensive destruction of the disc with resultant complete disappearance of the latter. Extensive vertebral caries and vertebral collapse are easily recognized findings in more advanced cases.

While these signs may help to differentiate tuberculous from pyogenic osteomyelitis of the spine (see Fig. 3-5), the demonstration of the tubercle bacilli provides absolute confirmation.

The treatment of tuberculous spondylitis has been more effective since the introduction of specific antituberculous chemotherapy—e.g., para-aminosalicylic acid (PAS), streptomycin compounds, and isoniazid (INH). Surgery is still indicated in appropriate cases, and arthrodesis of the spine retains a useful place in the therapeutic armamentarium.

Syphilitic spondylitis is a rare form of syphilitic arthritis. It usually involves the cervical spine and responds characteristically to appropriate antiluetic therapy. Primary or secondary syphilis is capable of mimicking any type of acute or chronic arthritis. Neuropathic joints may result from lues of the central nervous system. Of course, the cardiovascular or other systems may be concomitantly involved in late luetic infections.

Brucellosis of the spine constitutes the most common articular or osseous complication of brucellosis. The diagnosis is first suggested by joint and muscle aches and pains with fever, but the precise diagnosis is dependent upon serologic and cultural evidence. The disease itself has decreased, largely as a result of an intensive program designed to eliminate the disease in cattle. The organism tends to attack the thoracic and lumbar vertebrae. The lesions consist of granulomata with a tendency to osteomyelitis and sclerosis, in contrast to the destructive changes found in tuberculosis. The symptoms produced by the osteomyelitic lesions resemble those of a herniated disc as well as other types of spondylitis. However, the clinical picture is usually more acute but more benign than that of tuberculous spondylitis. Paravertebral and epidural abscesses may occur, but there is

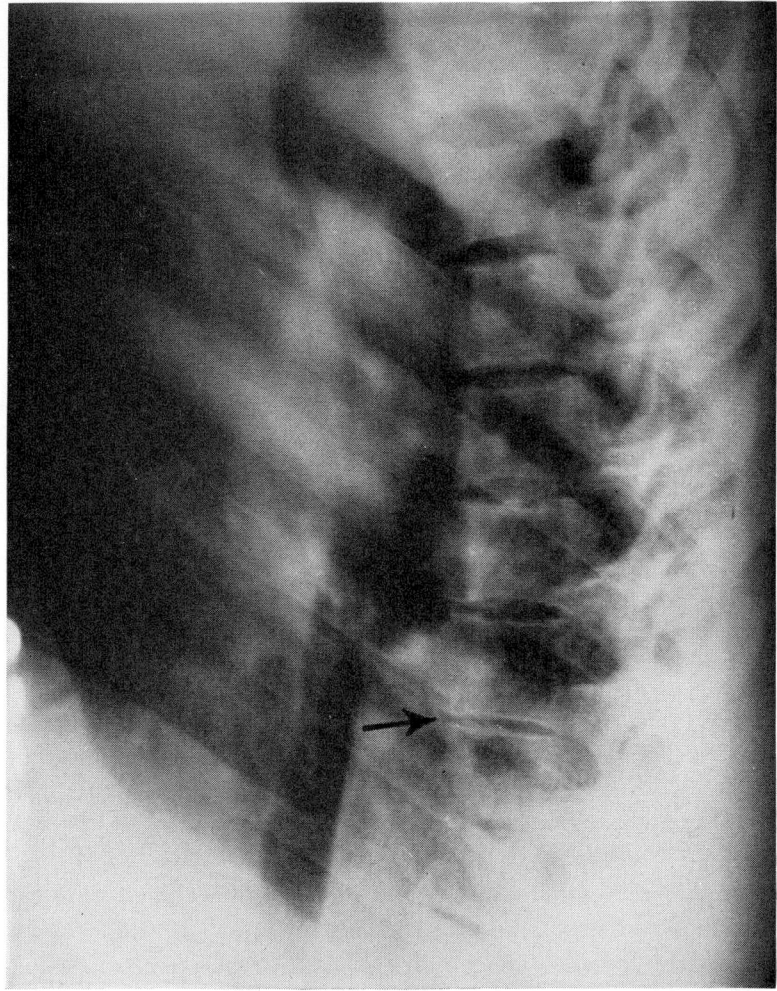

Fig. 3-4. Tuberculosis of spine. Lateral projection of dorsal spine shows narrowing of interspace between D_4 and D_5 with irregular destruction of the contiguous vertebral borders.

usually little disability. A peculiar form closely resembling rheumatoid (ankylosing) spondylitis of the Marie-Strumpell type has also been described.

The diagnosis of brucellosis is confirmed by culture of the organism from blood or tissue fluids on special culture media. Skin tests and complement-fixation tests offer secondary help, but there is considerable controversy as to their diagnostic reliability. Careful re-evaluation of occasional cases previously labeled as neurocirculatory asthenia, depression state, or postin-

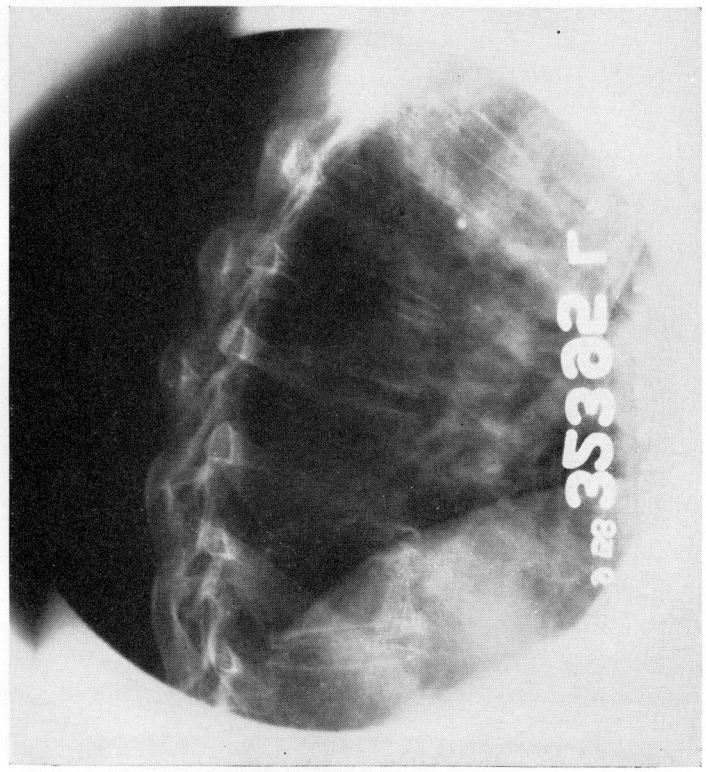

Fig. 3-5. Osteomyelitis of spine due to *Staphylococcus aureus*. Note destruction of the interspace between D_7 and D_8 and paraspinal abscess.

fectious asthenia eventually reveals the presence of chronic brucellosis. It is of interest to note that cardiovascular complications of this infection are quite common. Subacute bacterial endocarditis and electrocardiographic changes consistent with myocarditis have been observed. Thus, the chest pain may have multiple origins.

The treatment has greatly improved due to the availability of antibiotic agents. Of these, the combination of sulfadiazine or chlortetracycline (Aureomycin) and streptomycin appears most effective. Unfortunately, relapses frequently occur.

Typhoid spondylitis is found occasionally where typhoid fever is endemic. It usually involves the periosteum of the lower thoracic and lumbar vertebrae. Tenderness, localized or referred, and muscle spasm are the earliest clinical manifestations. Usually two contiguous vertebrae are affected by the inflammatory process, which leads to irregular sclerotic changes of the vertebral bodies, narrowing of the disc, and frequently associated paraspinal ligamentous ossification. Rarely does suppuration occur, with its possible rupture into intrathoracic structures. Positive culture and agglutination tests are diagnostic. It is interesting to note that as many as 70 per cent of the cases studied also reveal a number of nonspecific electrocardiographic changes characteristic of acute nonspecific infectious myocarditis, which may persist up to three weeks and respond to niacin. Treatment includes chloramphenicol (Chloromycetin), in addition to rest and immobilization. Surgical procedures are rarely indicated unless an abscess becomes apparent.

Suppurative spondylitis usually results from adjacent bone disease, penetrating injury, or hematogenous spread. Staphylococci are more frequently responsible than streptococci. The process resembles osteomyelitis. Antibiotics are effective, with oleandomycin and novobiocin (Albamycin) the drugs of choice for resistant staphylococcal infections. Neurosurgical intervention is effective with epidural granulomas of the mid-dorsal spine. These lesions are due mainly to staphylococci and produce a definite clinical syndrome consisting of boring back pain, radiculitis, and spinal cord damage.

Coccidioidomycosis, a mycotic infection, occurs endemically in the Southwest but is found sporadically in other states. It may involve the vertebrae as well as the short bones of the extremities, ribs, scapulae, and clavicles. The clinical, pathologic, and x-ray pictures closely resemble those of tuberculosis. Chest pain may occur as the result of associated involvement of the spine, ribs, or sternoclavicular articulation. The osteolytic skeletal lesions are relatively benign and rarely give rise to severe disability or complications. The myocardium may be directly affected by any of the fungal disorders. No specific therapy is known, but many drugs have been used, the most effective of which appears to be amphotericin B.

Histoplasmosis (reticuloendothelial cytomycosis) is another fungal disease which usually affects the lungs, oropharynx, liver, spleen, lymph nodes, and adrenals but which may occasionally cause osteolytic lesions of the spine. A recently developed skin test may prove diagnostic when the parasites are not recoverable.

Blastomycosis of the spine occurs not uncommonly as part of the systemic type of involvement by this fungal disease. The clinical, x-ray, and pathologic pictures also resemble tuberculosis. The diagnosis may be suspected when pulmonary, osseous, and cutaneous lesions coexist. Skin and complement-fixation tests are available, but diagnosis can be established definitely only following the identification of the causative organism in the sputum or in direct smears of purulent exudate. The systemic involvement and bone lesions may respond to stilbamidine treatment.

Actinomycosis is a fungal disease which rarely involves the spine. Suppuration is a feature of active infection. It usually occurs secondarily to contiguous infection, but there may also be primary involvement. The lesions are usually limited to the vertebrae and tend to spare the intervertebral discs. The presence of small abscess cavities and areas of dense sclerosis give the vertebrae a peculiar honeycomb or "soap-bubble" appearance on x-ray. Bacteriologic and sensitivity tests are now available to confirm early diagnosis. The presence of sulfur granules and positive smear and culture are diagnostic. The treatment with large doses of penicillin or chlortetracycline yields good results. However, surgical drainage is indicated when purulent secretions accumulate.

Trauma. Trauma to the spine can produce a variety of lesions, from simple "strain" to more severe injuries such as sprains, dislocation, fractures, and traumatic arthritis.

Trauma may affect any part of the vertebral bodies, including the neural arches, transverse and spinous processes, and the intervertebral discs. Fractures of the dorsal spine are usually of the compression type and most frequently involve the body of one or more of the lower thoracic vertebrae; less frequently involved are the upper thoracic vertebrae. Fracture of the transverse process of the first thoracic vertebrae probably represents the most painful fracture. Upper dorsal vertebral fractures are particularly common following electroshock therapy. Since there seldom is disc involvement, pain is due to injury of the articulating facets.

The most common lesions of the spine usually involve the vulnerable intervertebral discs. The discs most frequently injured are those in the lumbar region, but injuries to the third to the sixth thoracic and seventh to eleventh cervical intervertebral discs are not uncommon. The latter are especially prone to "whiplash" injuries, usually sustained in automobile collisions. Degeneration or protrusion of discs may occur also during the course of the aging process, which results in increasing fibrosis of the disc with resultant loss of resiliency and flexibility. It is probably for this reason that disc lesions are much more common during middle age.

Although protrusions occur at every thoracic level, the lower thoracic vertebrae are most frequently involved. Thoracic intervertebral discs may be displaced posteriorly with compression of the anterior tracts of the spinal cord or laterally with compression of the nerve roots.

The pain is not necessarily limited to the mid-dorsal region but may appear in the anterior or sternal region. Pain may be differentiated from cardiac pain, since it tends to be aggravated by movements of the trunk and deep inspiration. Both dorsal and anterior referred pain may be present following thoracic disc lesions. Obviously, until they are properly identified, the symptoms may be confused with those due to angina pectoris, epidemic pleurodynia, intercostal neuralgia, fibrositis, or occasionally abdominal disease.

The typical acute disc syndrome consists of a sudden pain usually precipitated by forceful hyperextension. After a few days, the pain subsides, but it tends to recur for months or years. Pressure on a nerve root gives rise to a radiating type of pain. In chronic cases, there may be no definite history of an acute onset and radiation may be absent. Characteristically, the pain is usually increased by extension and reduced by flexion of the spine, although this depends upon the location of the herniation. Lateral flexion toward the affected side causes pain which is relieved by lateral flexion to the contralateral side. Bending, lifting, rising from a sitting position, coughing, sneezing, or straining also increases the pain.

Cervical disc lesions frequently occur in the fifth and sixth decades of life but often affect younger age groups. As a rule, there is lateral protrusion which most commonly involves the sixth cervical interspace. Trauma is most commonly associated with an unguarded rotation movement of the head. A common type of injury encountered is the "whiplash" injury (see Fig. 3-6). Damage is sustained by the cervical ligamentous structures when the body, in propulsion, comes to a sudden stop or when it is suddenly propelled forward and the head thrust suddenly and forcibly forward, and/or backward, and/or to either side. During automobile collisions, abnormal forces may be transmitted to the neck, with damage to the cervical vertebrae, intervertebral discs, or, rarely, the odontoid process.

The onset of the cervical disc syndrome may be insidious, with aching neck pain. Later, there is referred or radicular pain into the scapular area, shoulder, arm, the pectoral region, and, finally the hand and fingers. This may be confused with the pain of the anginal syndrome or even of the shoulder-hand syndrome.

The diagnosis of intervertebral disc damage can usually be established following a careful history and neurologic examination and may be confirmed by roentgenologic and myelographic examinations. The early enthusiasm for the latter study has waned considerably, and there are now opposing opinions regarding its reliability. Recording the electrical impulses in the muscles of the arms (electromyography) is a practical diagnostic test for herniated intervertebral disc. The procedure can be performed quickly with practically no trauma and is more sensitive than myelographic studies. About 97 per cent of the lesions are detected when both electromyograms and myelograms are used, but either procedure alone reveals less than 85 per cent of the cases. However, myelographic examination may be obviated when the electric recording does not reveal evidence of root irritation.

The treatment is usually surgical when nerve root compression is un-

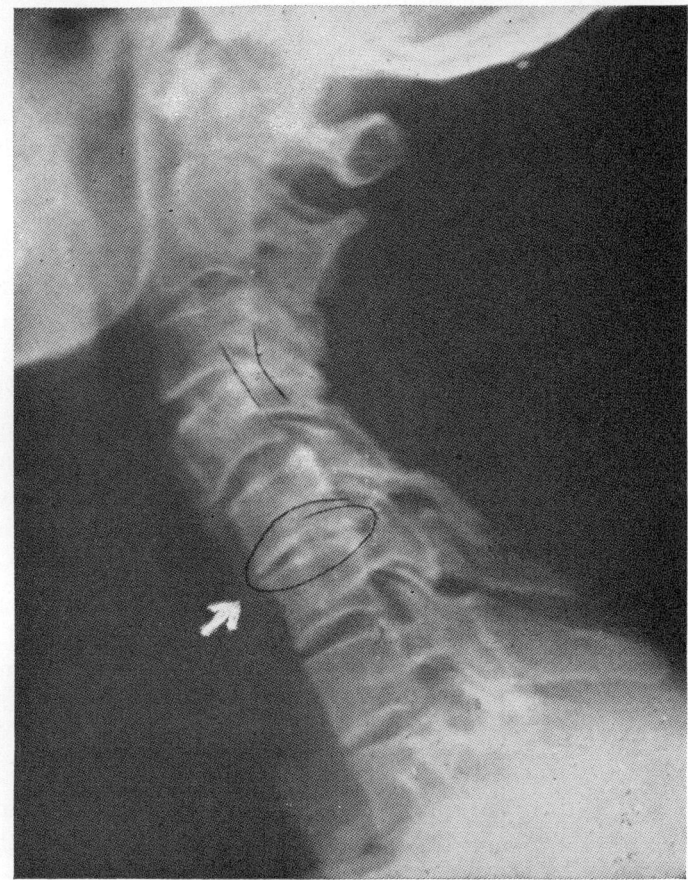

Fig. 3-6. Lateral roentgenogram of the cervical spine of a fifty-three-year-old man, who had received a *whiplash injury* of the neck, reveals marked narrowing of the intervertebral space between C₅ and C₆, accompanied by localized hypertrophic changes and segmental loss of the lower portion of the lordotic curve. In addition, there is a pronounced forward displacement of the fourth cervical vertebra, producing a marked subluxation at the level of C₃ and C₄. Rupture of the intervertebral disk between C₅ and C₆ was found at surgery. (From Braaf, M. M., and Rosner, S.: Whiplash injury of the neck: symptoms, diagnosis, treatment, and prognosis. *New York J. Med.*, **58**:1504, 1958.)

relieved by conservative treatment such as stretching procedures or a fitted brace.

Miscellaneous Conditions of the Spine

Congenital disorders. Of the congenital lesions of the spine which may give rise to chest pain, the only one of pertinent interest is *spondylolisthesis*.

Although this commonly affects the lumbosacral junction, it occasionally involves the cervical spine. The same is true of spina bifida occulta. Spondylolisthesis is characterized by a break in the bony continuity of the pars interarticularis or isthmus, although other anomalies, including fractures and destructive lesions (inflammatory or malignant) of the isthmus or articular processes, may be the cause.

This may bring about a recurrent dull, aching pain with periods of variable severity and frequently precipitated by a strain. There is often localized tenderness over the involved spinous area. When displacement of the vertebral body occurs with resultant changes in the intervertebral disc, findings, both subjective and objective, of a collapsed intervertebral disc may be obtained. Obviously, the nerves are compressed by the narrowed foramina, with the production of pain. Spondylolysis consists of the same defect without displacement. Pseudospondylolisthesis is displacement without defects in the neural arch.

The diagnosis can be ascertained by focal x-ray studies. The treatment is supportive in the uncomplicated case. It consists of heat, massage, analgesics, and a brace. However, correction by spinal fusion may eventually become necessary.

Vertebral epiphysitis is probably a disorder of developmental origin. However, nutritional disturbances, hormonal deficiencies, and trauma have also been held responsible for this condition. It usually occurs in adolescence and most commonly involves the dorsal spine as well as the upper lumbar region.

Symptoms consist of a dull ache in the dorsal region with not infrequent radiation around the chest aggravated by exertion and fatigue. Associated with the pain is an inability to stand or sit erect. The physical findings consist of marked dorsal kyphosis. Jarring may elicit severe pain over the involved spinal segment. X-ray examination reveals the diagnostic findings of fragmented epiphyseal ends, anterior wedging of the vertebral bodies, irregularity of the vertebral surfaces, narrowing of the intervertebral spaces, and osteoporosis of the vertebral bodies.

Neoplastic involvement. This may be primary or secondary and may cause pain similar to some infectious disorders of the spine. The pain is severe, constant, and boring with aggravation following movement of the spine. Pain frequently follows slight jarring due to direct trauma or cervical compression. The latter can usually be reproduced by jarring the spinous region of the spine with the fist or rising on the toes and dropping to the heels. The nature of the neoplastic involvement of the dorsal spine is essentially the same as of the ribs.

Of particular interest are those neoplasms which tend to afflict older patients in the coronary age group. They usually are of the malignant type, and they represent either the osseous counterpart of a generalized involvement, such as occurs with multiple myeloma, or a metastatic lesion.

Metastatic lesions represent the most frequent type of neoplastic involvement. Not infrequently, a clue is obtained from the history of a neoplasm of the prostate, breast, uterus, or gastrointestinal tract. Appropriate studies, such as x-rays (see Figs. 3-7 and 3-8) and blood acid phosphatase, are indicated. At times, chest pain due to metastases of the spine may be the first symptom of an occult neoplasm. Extensive roentgenologic search for

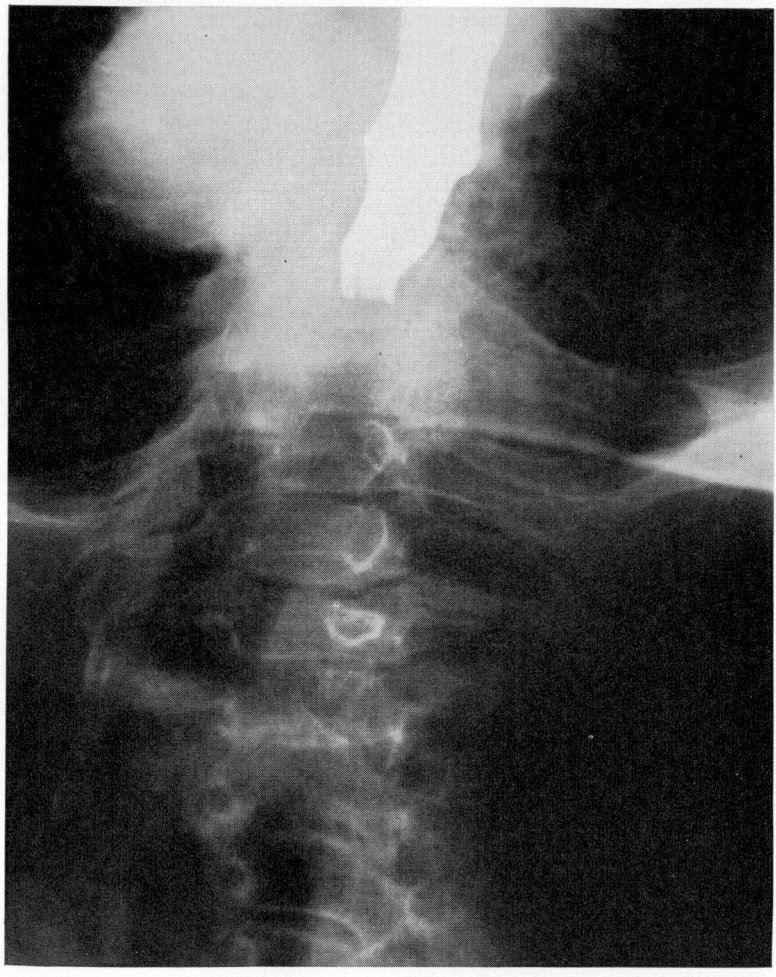

Fig. 3-7. Complete block of myelogram caused by metastasis to spine from carcinoma of lung.

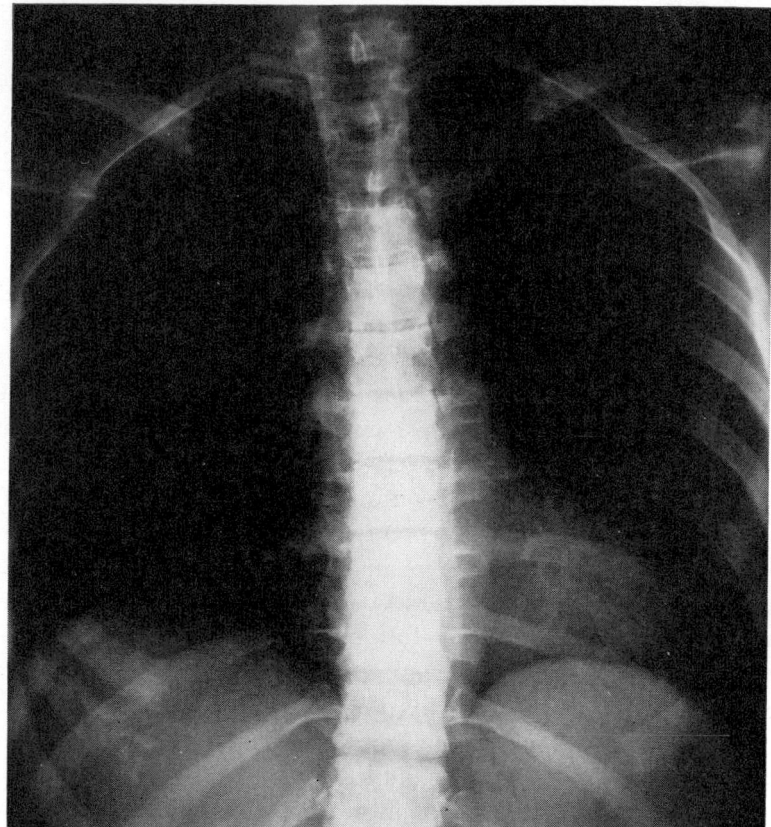

Fig. 3-8. Osteoblastic vertebral metastases from carcinoma of the breast. Note the rather uniform increase in density of the bodies of D_7, D_8, D_9, and D_{10}.

skeletal metastases is then indicated. Tumors of the spinal cord are discussed in the section on nerve disorders (pp. 86–87).

Multiple myeloma occurs with increased frequency around the age of sixty years. The chief pathologic feature is the marked proliferation of a cell resembling a plasma cell found in the marrow. Spinal cord compression occurs mostly in the region of the lower thoracic or lumbar vertebrae, usually with compression of the nerve roots. However, a protracted course without pain is present in some patients. Pain is of the boring type due to involvement of the marrow cavity, aching and radiating type due to nerve root compression, or stabbing type due to occurrence of pathologic fractures. Susceptibility to pulmonary and other types of infections is remarkable and may be the earliest manifestation of the disease. Chest infections and renal failure, or both, cause death in at least 50 per cent of the patients.

Renal involvement frequently occurs secondarily to tubular degeneration arising from plugs or casts of abnormal globulin in the kidney tubules and from droplets of these proteins in the renal epithelial cells. It may present as proteinuria and may progress to uremia. Occasionally, hypertension may be encountered and may give rise to difficulties in differential diagnosis. The associated chest pain resembling atypical anginal seizures may further complicate the clinical picture.

The presence of the characteristic Bence Jones proteinuria, and characteristic bone marrow changes are the most important diagnostic criteria. Elevation of serum proteins and serum globulin provides a valuable diagnostic clue. Roentgenologic changes consist of multiple, punched-out osteolytic lesions, without evidence of osteoblastic reaction. Associated with these findings may be a diffuse type of osteoporosis, and deformity of the intervertebral discs and fractures of the vertebrae.

Excellent clinical results have been obtained by use of a combination of corticotropin (ACTH) or the corticosteroids and urethan. The following effects are noted: (1) decreased myeloma cells in the marrow, (2) decreased abnormal proteins in the blood, and (3) arrest of lytic bone lesions. Urethan seems to act chiefly on the more mature plasmocyte, while corticotropin and the corticosteroids are apparently more effective against the less mature cells. Unfortunately, urethan usually produces only a temporary effect, but bone pain is alleviated and anemia improves. It is administered as long as the patient shows improvement or until toxic effects, such as leukopenia or liver damage, preclude further administration. Corticosteroid therapy has not been found helpful by other observers. The growth process of multiple myeloma may be also inhibited by the administration of chlorambucil, an aromatic nitrogen mustard. Pain is also relieved and renal function improved. However, no alterations in bone marrow or metabolic changes are noted with this treatment. X-ray therapy may relieve pain but seldom affects bone lesions.

Osteoporosis of the postmenopausal or senile type is a frequent cause of chest pain. Many other causes of osteoporosis, such as parathyroid dysfunction, may also be at fault. Bone decalcification is the most common of all osteopathies.

It is attributed mainly to a loss of estrogenic hormone with a resultant decrease of osteoblastic activity and inadequate bone formation. The degree of osteoporosis is directly related to the period of estrogen deprivation and is more severe following artificial menopause. The inadequate bone formation frequently leads to spontaneous fractures of the vertebrae.

X-ray changes reveal decalcification primarily of the lower dorsal and upper lumbar vertebrae bodies. As the disorder progresses, the nucleus pulposus shows increasing indentations, anterior wedging of vertebrae, and finally complete compression with collapse of the vertebrae. Pain is deep-rooted and may occur even in the absence of spontaneous fractures. Progressive compression of the foramina obviously causes increasing nerve root pain. The development of marked kyphoscoliosis eventually gives rise to chronic cor pulmonale in many instances. Thus, pain occurs either along the thoracic spine or may radiate around the chest wall. Occasionally, this pain may become exacerbated and localized following minimal trauma of direct or indirect nature. The pain is ordinarily increased by physical exertion such as stair climbing. Acute attacks of pain usually denote collapse or spontaneous fracture of vertebrae.

Other conditions causing demineralization of the spine and resembling osteoporosis are osteomalacia, osteitis fibrosa generalisata, and parathyroid dysfunction. In contrast to these disorders, osteoporosis is not associated with abnormal values of serum calcium, inorganic phosphorus, or alkaline phosphatase. Conditions such as multiple myeloma, malignancies, and sarcoid usually present either abnormal blood chemistry or characteristic x-ray changes.

The treatment of senile osteoporosis consists of the combined administration of estrogenic and androgenic hormones; this has been demonstrated to enhance both nitrogen and calcium retention. Hormonal therapy may relieve the pain within several weeks to months. In addition, a high-protein diet, relatively low in calcium and vitamin D, and a liberal fluid intake appear useful. Continued activity is important, since disuse may cause further demineralization, systemic infection, and muscular atrophy. A supportive brace and general physical measures designed to improve muscle tone and prevent muscle spasm are helpful.

"Straight back" syndrome. In this new chest syndrome, the normal curve of the upper dorsal spine becomes straightened so that the examiner's flattened palm may be made to rest upon this area without deviation of the extended fingers.

This "straight back" syndrome may produce pseudo heart disease in two ways. First, as in funneling of the sternum, there is a decrease in the anteroposterior diameter of the chest, which may compress the mediastinal structures and cause false heart enlargement in the frontal view, particularly in the great vessel area. This is due to a relative inward displacement of the straightened dorsal spine. The condition is easily recognized when lateral views are taken. Secondly, in cases of less severe mediastinal compression, the defect may be associated with the production of mechanical murmurs.

These murmurs are systolic in timing, usually basal in location, and would seem related to impingement or distortion of the great vessels. Rarely is the defect found without either false heart enlargement or mechanical murmurs.

MUSCULAR DISORDERS OF THORAX AND SHOULDER

It is most practical to discuss musculofascial origins of chest pain according to the two general regions which may become involved: (1) the chest wall and (2) the shoulder region. The latter presents special aspects because of its multiplicity of anatomic structures and integrated function, and because of certain characteristics of the pain patterns. Confusion may arise from the fact that it may also be the sole source of pain referred from coronary disease.

Before discussing the various causes of pain involving the myofascial structures of the chest wall, it must be emphasized that muscular pain is not necessarily due to an intrinsic disease process but may have a distant origin. For example, it may at times be caused by ventral nerve radiculitis or by anterior horn cell disease (poliomyelitis). These aspects are considered in detail in the section on nerve disorders (see pp. 85–90). Fascial and tendinous structures are included in the following discussion, because they are obviously an integral part of the muscular system.

Conditions Involving Musculature of the Chest Wall

A classification of the conditions involving the musculature of the chest wall on an etiologic basis is difficult, because the causes are obscure in many instances. It is similarly difficult to employ morbid anatomy as a foundation, because many conditions of different origins may result in somewhat similar morphologic changes of the affected muscles. Therefore, it appears most useful to discuss this subject under the following headings: (1) trauma, (2) inflammations, and (3) miscellaneous.

A brief anatomic discussion of the muscles of the chest wall is in order for a better understanding of the effects of all lesions of muscular origin. These muscles consist of the external and intrinsic groups. The first category includes the pectoralis major and minor and the serratus anterior (magnus) muscles. They constitute a portion of the anterior and lateral wall of the chest. The wide, fan-shaped pectoralis major muscle has clavicular, sternocostal, and abdominal origins which converge and insert near the head of the humerus. The pectoralis minor is a thin triangular muscle with origins from the third to the fifth ribs and an insertion onto the scapula; it lies under the pectoralis major. The serratus anterior occupies the lateral aspect of the chest wall. The large trapezius muscle is found in the cephalad part of the back. The broad latissimus dorsi and the rhomboid muscles are the other important muscle groups of the back.

Trauma. The powerful muscles of the chest are frequently subjected to strains, sprains, direct injuries, and even rupture on rare occasions during the course of work or play. The resulting painful muscle spasm is not uncommonly confused with coronary disease because of its location. This error is the source of much confusion, especially in liability or compensation matters. It occurs even more frequently in the presence of varying degrees of heart disease, especially when a definite history of trauma is not elicited. However, muscular pain and tenderness are limited to the distribution of the affected muscle tissues, and they are aggravated by movements of these specific muscular structures. Muscle spasm may be exceedingly painful even at rest soon after trauma. The absence of shock and of abnormal serial electrocardiograms and other laboratory tests help to exclude coronary disease. In this connection, it should be emphasized that the serum glutamic oxalacetic transaminase (SGO-T) test may prove misleading, since this enzyme is released following an injury to either skeletal or cardiac muscle. However, it must be stressed that in the case of some steering-wheel injuries or other serious traumata, both structures may be affected. Differentiation rests mainly on serial electrocardiograms as well as the superficial pain and tenderness of skeletal muscle involvement.

Myofascial pain syndromes. Trauma involving these muscles may lead to several so-called "myofascial pain syndromes." They are encountered most frequently in the shoulder girdle region and are discussed in detail in the following section dealing with the shoulder (see pp. 67–68). Suffice it to state here that the myofascial pain syndromes constitute a group of disorders which are characterized by the presence of a hypersensitive region or trigger zone in one of the muscles or in the connective tissue. In addition, there are muscle spasm, tenderness, stiffness, limitation of motion, weakness, and an occasional autonomic dysfunction in an area of reference, usually at some distance from the trigger point. Painful syndromes involving the pectoralis and serratus anterior musculature are especially pertinent.

A myalgia of isolated form has been reported to occur secondary to excessive use of the serratus magnus. This results in sharply localized pain and tenderness at the lower angle of the scapula which may be confused with acute posterior wall myocardial infarction.

The deep-lying internal and external intercostal muscles represent the intrinsic musculature of the chest wall. These muscles may also be injured by direct trauma to the chest wall, exercise, coughing, and sneezing spells.

However, they are most commonly affected by rib fractures or diseases of the ribs. They provide essentially the same diagnostic problems as lesions of the extrinsic muscles. The history of trauma is obviously the most important element in establishing the correct diagnosis.

The management of these painful conditions usually consists of immobilization, heat, and local anesthesia when necessary. The latter approach is particularly helpful when trigger zones are present. More recently, muscle relaxants have found a useful niche in therapy. The local injection of corticosteroids has been advocated in intractable cases.

Inflammatory diseases involving the chest muscles. Myositis denotes an inflammatory process in skeletal muscle usually related to infectious, allergic, or unknown factors. A true myositis is characterized by exudation of plasma, infiltration of the supporting tissues by neutrophilic leukocytes or other inflammatory cells, and damage to the parenchymal and interstitial elements of muscle. Activation of histiocytes, hyperplasia of surviving sarcolemmal nuclei of the type regularly promoted by destruction of muscle fibers, and proliferation of fibroblastic connective tissue constitute the usual reaction to injury. The implication of infection derives from the presence of inflammatory cells even though a bacterial, viral, or parasitic agent cannot be isolated. The agent responsible for the myositis is frequently elusive and makes a precise classification impossible. One can generally distinguish between the cases of myositis caused by a known bacterial, viral, or parasitic agent and those revealing an inflammatory histopathologic picture without an established cause. The latter group comprises polymyositis, dermatomyositis, neuromyositis, and interstitial (nodular) polymyositis associated with rheumatoid arthritis, rheumatic fever, scleroderma, lupus erythematosus disseminatus, and polyarteritis nodosa.

Myositis due to infectious agents. Acute suppurative myositis usually appears secondary to septicemia, infectious pleuritis, or direct trauma followed by infection. Constant boring or sharp pain may be present. Actual abscesses or phlegmon within the muscle are rarely encountered because of the availability and use of effective antibacterial agents.

Myositis due to clostridial infection is rare but may be found in association with the severe direct trauma produced by punctures or lacerations of the chest wall. The crepitation felt over the swollen area due to anaerobic gas production and the acid odor of the wound infection are clinically diagnostic.

Tuberculous myositis is usually secondary to tuberculous infection of an adjacent bone or joint or cold abscess. It may give rise to a diffuse type of polymyositis or to a localized abscess, or it may lead to local involvement by direct extension. Thus, the intercostal and other thoracic muscles may become affected in the presence of a tuberculous empyema. Pain arising from such a deep source may not be evident on the skin surface.

Actinomycosis causes myositis of the chest wall muscles by direct extension from the pleural infection.

Trichinosis is the most common parasitic type of infestation involving the muscles. The diaphragm is commonly affected and may cause lower chest or upper abdominal pain. Since the muscle tissues invaded by the parasites are of the striated and cardiac types, chest pain may also be caused by a concomitant severe invasion of the myocardium. Cardiac signs of myocarditis include dilatation, hypotension, tachycardia, apical systolic murmur, arrhythmias, and, finally, myocardial insufficiency. Electrocardiographic changes of myocardial damage are caused by the direct migration of larvae to the heart and not by any toxic substance. The most common abnormality found is flattened T waves. A history of ingestion of pork products (especially raw) is significant. Eosinophilia and skeletal muscle biopsy confirm the diagnosis. A skin test is also available.

Epidemic myositis ("devil's grip," epidemic pleurodynia, Bornholm disease). This disease represents the only known form of epidemic myalgia. The Coxsackie virus has been found to be present in many cases. The clinical features of this disease may vary somewhat in different epidemics. It is mentioned here as well as under pleuropulmonary disease (see pp. 105–6), because painful involvement of the diaphragm, chest, and shoulder muscles, and/or the muscles of the abdominal wall is common. The myalgia may also involve the costal, trapezius, or deltoid muscles. However, constant cramping pains are usually limited to the site of insertion of the diaphragmatic musculature. The degree of fever and prostration, the frequency of pharyngitis, orchitis, and pleural and central nervous system involvement, and the duration of this bizarre illness are variable. This condition may mimic acute diseases of the lungs and pleura, the digestive tract, and coronary arteries. However, lung findings are usually absent, and the electrocardiogram is negative. The absence of objective findings characteristic of any of these diseases, the epidemic occurrence, and the usually short benign course of epidemic myositis are helpful clues in the differential diagnosis.

Myositis due to poliomyelitis. The so-called "nonparalytic" form of poliomyelitis constitutes an important aspect of this viral infection. Its incidence is reportedly as high as 26 per cent of all the cases.

Inflammation of the anterior horn cells affects adults more frequently than is generally supposed. It is for this reason, that a national campaign has been under way to inoculate all adults under forty years of age with Salk vaccine. Painful involvement of muscles is a frequent finding and may occur before paralysis becomes evident. In the paralytic forms, painful spasm of the involved muscles may be the outstanding characteristic. Indeed, the hot-pack treatment employed at this stage is directed to the control of spasm due to myositis.

Diagnosis becomes more certain as flaccid muscular paralysis ensues. The spinal fluid shows pleocytosis, an elevated protein level but a normal glucose level, and an initial predominance of polymorphonuclear leukocytes followed by an increase of lymphocytes. In recent years, it has been repeatedly demonstrated that this infection may secondarily affect the myocardium in a large number of cases. Findings of an acute nonspecific myocarditis may appear at any stage of the disease. They include the sudden onset of tachycardia or other arrhythmias, dyspnea, palpitation, and chest pain. Serial electrocardiographic changes confirm the occurrence of this serious complication. Pathologic changes in the myocardium are demonstrable in almost all fatalities.

Myositis of unknown etiology. Polymyositis. Muscular weakness and wasting due to widespread local inflammatory changes of unknown etiology are the cardinal features of polymyositis. The disorder is probably related to collagen and vascular diseases, since it frequently occurs in association with scleroderma, disseminated lupus erythematosus, or polyarteritis nodosa. The possibility of an unrecognized viral etiology cannot be entirely discarded, since a similar clinical picture has been observed following proven Coxsackie viral infection.

The acute and subacute forms alone are pertinent, since the chronic progressive form usually remains limited to the muscles of the extremities. Obviously, the differentiation between polymyositis and dermatomyositis depends mainly upon the presence or absence of skin involvement. However, the occurrence of acute polymyositis without associated skin lesions is rare.

The nature of the muscular disorder both in regard to the clinical and histopathologic findings is essentially the same in both conditions. Weakness, tenderness, pain, and induration of the muscles (with occasional progression to fibrous contractures) are the usual clinical manifestations. The shoulder girdle muscles are affected most frequently. Degenerative changes manifested by vacuolation, granulation, and fragmentation with frequent displacement by fibrous tissue stroma comprise the microscopic picture, along with variable degrees of perivascular and diffuse infiltration of lymphocytes, plasma cells, and histiocytes. Occasionally, hemorrhagic changes may be found. Although rare, the occurrence of myocardial changes has been noted.

The differential diagnosis can be difficult, particularly in the absence of cutaneous changes. The conditions commonly giving rise to confusion are trichinosis, epidemic pleurodynia, myasthenia gravis, and scleroderma. The symmetrical involvement of large muscle groups in polymyositis is the most significant differentiating feature. Electromyograms may also be helpful aids.

Dermatomyositis. This collagen disorder is frequently unrecognized because of its variable clinical manifestations and its rarity. It presents with considerable cutaneous involvement, in addition to the muscular disorder which is caused by nonsuppurative inflammation and degeneration of striated muscle. The cutaneous lesions are quite prevalent and range from simple erythema and edema to sclerosis, atrophy, lupus-erythematosus-like efflorescences, and poikiloderma, and hypertrichosis or alopecia.

Dermatomyositis is fatal in half the cases, but remissions and even recovery have been observed. Muscular involvement may produce pain, tenderness, stiffness, and fatigue. Symmetrical atrophy and secondary contractures may result. A fatal outcome is inevitable when the muscles of respiration or deglutition are affected. Urinary creatine and creatinine are elevated, eosinophilia may be present, 17-ketosteroids are very low, and biopsy shows the characteristic microscopic findings.

Differential diagnosis from scleroderma may be very difficult, particularly in the later phases. The characteristic visceral involvement seen in scleroderma may be helpful. Glomerulonephritis, lupus erythematosus disseminatus, myasthenia gravis, pellagra, and trichinosis must be excluded. The cardiac muscle is probably not involved, and any changes on the electrocardiogram are produced by peripheral cutaneous changes which affect conduction. ACTH and corticosteroids offer the best therapeutic hope, but the effects are usually temporary.

Neuromyositis is characterized by the association of acute polymyositis (as described above) with acute polyneuritis. Thus, pain may have a dual origin in the affected sites.

Interstitial (nodular) polymyositis has been noted to occur in rheumatoid arthritis, rheumatic fever, scleroderma, and lupus erythematosus disseminatus. Indeed, its presence in all these conditions is a striking feature. The lesions consist of very small nodules of perivascular infiltrations of inflammatory cells associated with variable degrees of degeneration of muscle fibers. Although this form is seldom associated with marked tenderness, pain may be quite severe occasionally.

An allergic factor is presently considered as the most likely etiologic mechanism. Myositis occurring in these diseases is nonspecific and cannot be used to differentiate them, although the extent of secondary degenerative changes may be strikingly different. Thus, while the muscular lesions in rheumatic fever are rarely marked, those in rheumatoid arthritis not infrequently lead to atrophy and those in scleroderma lead to atrophy and contractures. The lesions in lupus erythematosus disseminatus closely resemble dermatomyositis. The treatment of this type of myositis is that of the primary disorder.

Myositis associated with sarcoidosis. Sarcoidosis is usually a relatively benign disease free from constitutional symptoms. However, almost half the cases die if caseous tuberculosis can be considered as a terminal stage of this disease. This form of muscular disorder rarely involves the chest wall muscles. Multiple disseminated nodules with the histologic features of Boeck's sarcoid (chronic benign granulomatosis) may be found in striated muscles in addition to the lymphatic, cutaneous, and visceral lesions. The nodular infiltrations may cause localized weakness and pain and even lead to muscular atrophy. The latter may have to be distinguished from the atrophy secondary to nerve involvement, which may also be caused by this disease. It is important to note that a variety of clinical syndromes may occur, since any tissue in the body may become involved. Thus, generalized aches and pains are also common. Adenopathy, skin, uveoparotid lesions, and pulmonary involvement usually dominate the picture.

The heart muscle itself may be affected by a focal or diffuse granulomatous myocarditis associated with cardiac hypertrophy. Cardiac failure may ensue from this cause or from chronic cor pulmonale secondary to marked pulmonary sarcoidosis. The electrocardiogram may show T wave changes suggestive of myocardial damage or various arrhythmias. A negative tuberculin test, hyperglobulinemia, hypercalcemia, characteristic bony reticulation and rarefaction, and biopsy help establish the diagnosis of this type of muscular involvement.

Polyarteritis nodosa. This is a relatively rare but generally fatal inflammatory disease of the medium and small arteries and arterioles. It is characterized by medial necrosis and fibrinous exudation. It usually occurs in males during the second and third decades. Muscular involvement may occur in about 30 per cent of the patients. It rarely gives rise to tenderness in the muscles involved. The pain and paresthesia present are more closely related to the neural involvement. The muscles frequently tend to show weakness or paralysis and striking atrophy where the nerves supplying the muscle are involved.

The primary arterial lesions which may lead to disturbances of the muscle (and all other tissues) usually cause ischemic necrosis and hemorrhage of the muscle fibers with ultimate fibrous displacement. Infiltrative cells consist of neutrophils, eosinophils, and lymphocytes. Occasionally, the lesion may resemble a nonspecific myositis. Small aneurysms and vascular throm-boses may ensue. Since the disease process may involve any tissue or may become widely disseminated, almost any symptom complex may occur. However, the general picture is that of an infectious disorder. The cardiac aspect may predominate when the coronary arterial branches are heavily involved. The electrocardiogram is often bizarre and rapidly changing be-cause of the progressive coronary involvement. Eosinophilia, urinary find-ings, cardiac enlargement, and biopsy are helpful diagnostic features. Corticosteroid therapy is the most helpful approach but rarely effects a permanent cure.

Miscellaneous conditions involving the chest muscles. *Fibromyositis* (myositis fibrosa, muscular rheumatism, nonarticular rheumatism, fibrositis) remains one of the most controversial and nebulous conditions in the "realm of rheumatism." It is characterized by inflammation of the connective tissue of the muscle sheaths, fasciae, and aponeuroses. Several varieties are dis-tinguishable, depending upon whether the condition is localized or gen-eralized, and whether muscle, tendon, fascia, or periarticular structures are affected.

The exact cause of this syndrome remains unestablished. It may be pro-voked by a number of factors such as dampness, cold, trauma, and excessive fatigue. Vascular, metabolic, postural, occupational, and psychogenic fac-tors have also been held responsible. The pathologic picture of the nodules offers considerable disagreement as to whether there is any characteristic tissue alteration. The reported prevalence of this syndrome in some geo-graphic areas, such as Great Britain, is subject to considerable controversy. It is usually characterized by pain and stiffness of muscles or muscle groups in any part of the body, and frequently involves the upper back, shoulders, and interscapular region. The presence of firm, tender nodules in the affected regions is a most helpful diagnostic finding. According to some ob-servers, the pain may be due to involuntary muscle spasm arising reflexly from other lesions and the nodule may represent small groups of muscle fibers in spasm due to irritation of the corresponding nerve roots. The pain is characteristically aggravated by both active and passive movements of the affected parts. Stiffness tends to be most marked after prolonged rest of the part. Generalized fatigue is also frequently encountered as a systemic manifestation. The tenderness in localized forms may be manifested at trigger points or zones.

This condition assumes increased significance for us when muscle groups of the anterior chest area are involved. The differentiation from atypical anginal syndrome and from the shoulder-hand syndrome occurring in association with coronary disease is particularly important. The diagnosis of fibrositis should be made only after coronary disease has been excluded on the basis of a careful evaluation of the history, physical findings, and laboratory studies. However, fibrositis may be found in patients with coronary disease, since it commonly affects the same age group. The characteristic relation of pain of fibrositic origin to cold and dampness, its aggravation by movement of the affected parts, the relief afforded by rest and warmth applied to this area, and the response to salicylates are further considerations.

The varied treatment reflects the manifold concepts of etiology. For example, it is not surprising that the occasional effectiveness of placebo (saline) injections tends to support the presence of a psychogenic factor. Supportive and symptomatic measures are essentially the mainstay of therapy. Thus, physical therapy includes stretching and active exercises, heat, and massage. Even vitamin E therapy still retains a few proponents. However, corticosteroids are the most effective therapeutic agents during the active stages of the disease.

Idiopathic myohemoglobinuria (rhabdomyolysis). This is a rare disorder with a familial tendency but of unknown etiology. The attacks or paroxysms are heralded by muscular pain and weakness followed by passage of dark red urine. Muscle fibers lose striation and become swollen and fragmented. No inflammatory reaction appears. Atrophy and weakness may persist after paroxysms. The pectoralis major and the intercostal muscles are frequently involved and may, on occasion, give rise to diagnostic difficulty. The disease may be fatal because of the development of either uremia or respiratory paralysis. Spectroscopic examination of the characteristic urine reveals the presence of myohemoglobin.

Myositis ossificans. Myositis ossificans is characterized by progressive and widespread ossification of soft tissue (primarily muscle and tendon), which leads to crippling immobility. The ossifications occur in the connective tissue surrounding the muscles rather than in the muscles themselves. The disease probably represents an inborn error of metabolism or a primitive mesenchymal defect. Actual bone formation distinguishes this disease from myositis fibrosa, dermatomyositis, polymyositis hemorrhagica, multiple exostoses, and calcinosis interstitialis ossificans. Almost any of the striated muscles may be involved, including the heart and diaphragm and the muscles of the shoulder, back, and ribs.

The sequence of events is usually initiated by the appearance of firm swellings of varying size. They increase in size initially but then regress, leaving stony, hard areas in the muscle; this process recurs until the muscle is ossified and immobilization is completed. The masses are usually painless, although mild discomfort may be present. The patient usually succumbs to pulmonary infection when involvement of the intercostal muscles leads to severe respiratory embarrassment. Corticosteroid treatment may afford marked relief, especially in the early phases.

Psychogenic rheumatism. Psychogenic rheumatism implies the occurrence of musculoskeletal symptoms on a purely functional or psychoneurotic basis. The primary form is characterized by a complete absence of any organic rheumatic disease and by a distinct relationship to psychic stress. The secondary form implies that psychic stress may be superimposed upon active or quiescent organic rheumatic involvement. The most striking example of the primary type of this musculoskeletal disorder is the ubiquitous "aching back," although similar pains in the shoulder region and left precordial portions of the chest are also quite common. These pains require careful evaluation, especially in the coronary age group or when apprehension becomes marked following an erroneous diagnosis of cardiac disease or when a cardiac neurosis already exists. Thus, careful evaluation of the organic and psychogenic components of the chest pain is paramount.

Since anxiety plays a predominant role in the personality of these patients, the term "rheumatism" often causes further apprehension regarding the possible development of a crippling arthritis. "Muscle spasm due to tension" might serve as a better label for the disorder. A good example of this condition is the tightness and pain of the posterior cervical muscles which are an integral part of the tension state. In this connection, it is of interest to note that psychosis and rheumatoid arthritis appear to be mutually exclusive.

Treatment should be directed toward relief of the emotional conflict, rationalization of the problems, and correction of the psychoneurosis.

Conditions Involving Musculature of the Shoulder

Pain in the shoulder region is one of the most common complaints. It is probably exceeded in frequency only by headache and backache. Visceral lesions of the upper abdomen (gallbladder, stomach, pancreas) and of the thorax (especially heart) frequently give rise to referred pain in the shoulder region. Such pain must be distinguished carefully from local causes of shoulder pain. On the other hand, a primary shoulder pain may be referred to the thorax.

As previously indicated, the shoulder region is composed of anatomic structures which perform a highly integrated function. Any of its individual units (bones, joints, bursae, tendons, or muscles) may be subjected to a painful disorder. However, because of the interdependence of all the structures, disturbed function of the shoulder as a whole results. The pain itself is frequently not sharply localized. The present discussion is concerned only with the muscular involvement of the shoulder area, but involvements of the tendons and bursae have been included for the sake of convenience. Bony and articular lesions are considered separately with the analogous structures of the thorax.

It is often impossible to detect the exact cause and pathogenetic mechanism of some painful shoulder disorders. This has led to a loosely applied terminology, such as "painful shoulder" and "fibrositis." The inability to relate a shoulder pain specifically to the basically involved structure has also caused some observers to continue the use of ambiguous terms such as "pain patterns" and "pain syndromes." (See Fig. 3-9.)

Tarsy has attempted to classify these painful shoulder conditions on the basis of pain patterns observed. They are divided into supraspinatus, infraspinatus, teres, serratus magnus, and bicipital syndromes. These pain patterns are based upon the findings of localized trigger points and corresponding trigger zones. Travell has shown that these trigger points can be readily recognized. The pain elicited by pressure upon these points which involve the corresponding segment (the so-called "trigger zone") is usually abolished promptly by local infiltration with procaine. (See Figs. 3-10 and 3-11.)

1. The pain of the *supraspinatus syndrome* involves the entire supraspinatus area in the superior or muscular form and the deltoid area in the anterior or tendinous form. Only the muscular form actually causes dull, aching pain in the shoulder with occasional limitation of motion.

2. The *infraspinatus syndrome* is characterized by pain referred into the shoulder and arm with some limitation of the shoulder and occasional extension of pain down the arm over a variable distance.

3. In the *teres syndrome,* the referred pain also involves the shoulder and arm according to the location of the muscle and its tendinous insertion.

4. In the *serratus syndrome,* the trigger point lies in the interscapular region with the pain felt in the lower portion or part of the chest.

Musculofascial disorders of the shoulder do not differ, in regard to the responsible etiologic factors, from the lesions of the chest wall muscles which were previously discussed. Thus, trauma or various inflammatory and miscellaneous types of myositis and fibrositis, including psychogenic and psychosomatic factors, may cause pain in the shoulder and impaired mobility by affecting the muscles and fascia of the shoulder region. These conditions may all give rise to myalgias, which may in turn present one of the four pain syndromes.

Bursitis. It is now generally accepted that the subdeltoid and subacromial bursae are actually the same structure. With abduction of the arm, the posi-

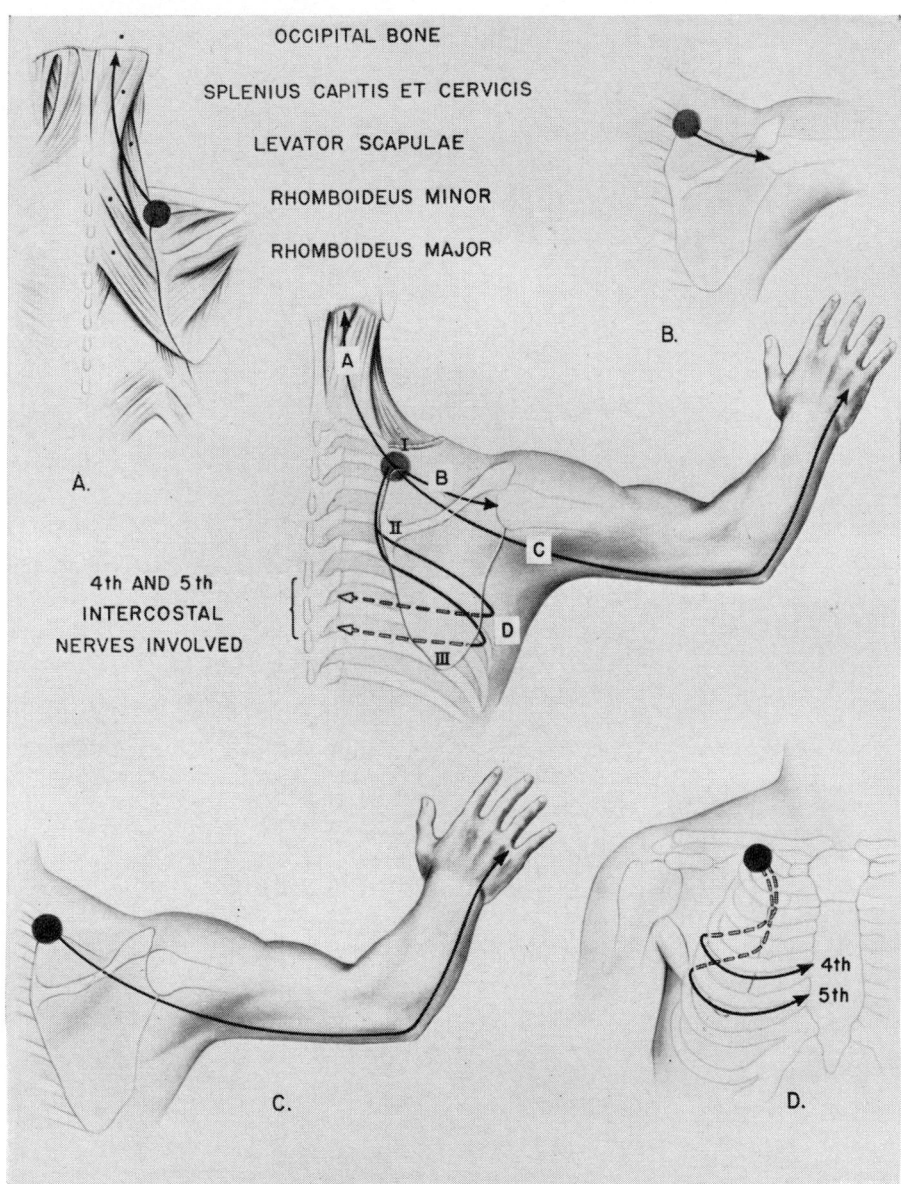

OCCIPITAL BONE

SPLENIUS CAPITIS ET CERVICIS

LEVATOR SCAPULAE

RHOMBOIDEUS MINOR

RHOMBOIDEUS MAJOR

4th AND 5th
INTERCOSTAL
NERVES INVOLVED

A.

B.

C.

D.

Fig. 3-9. Pain pattern distribution at A, B, C, and D. Point of irritative phenomenon at (*I*) the superior medial angle of the scapula in conjunction with the posterior thoracic cage, (*II*) spine of scapula at the vertebral border of the scapula, (*III*) inferior spine of the scapula. (From Michele, A. A.; Davies, J. J.; Krueger, F. J.; and Lichter, J. M.: Scapulocostal syndrome [fatigue-postural paradox]. *New York J. Med.*, **50**:1353, 1950.)

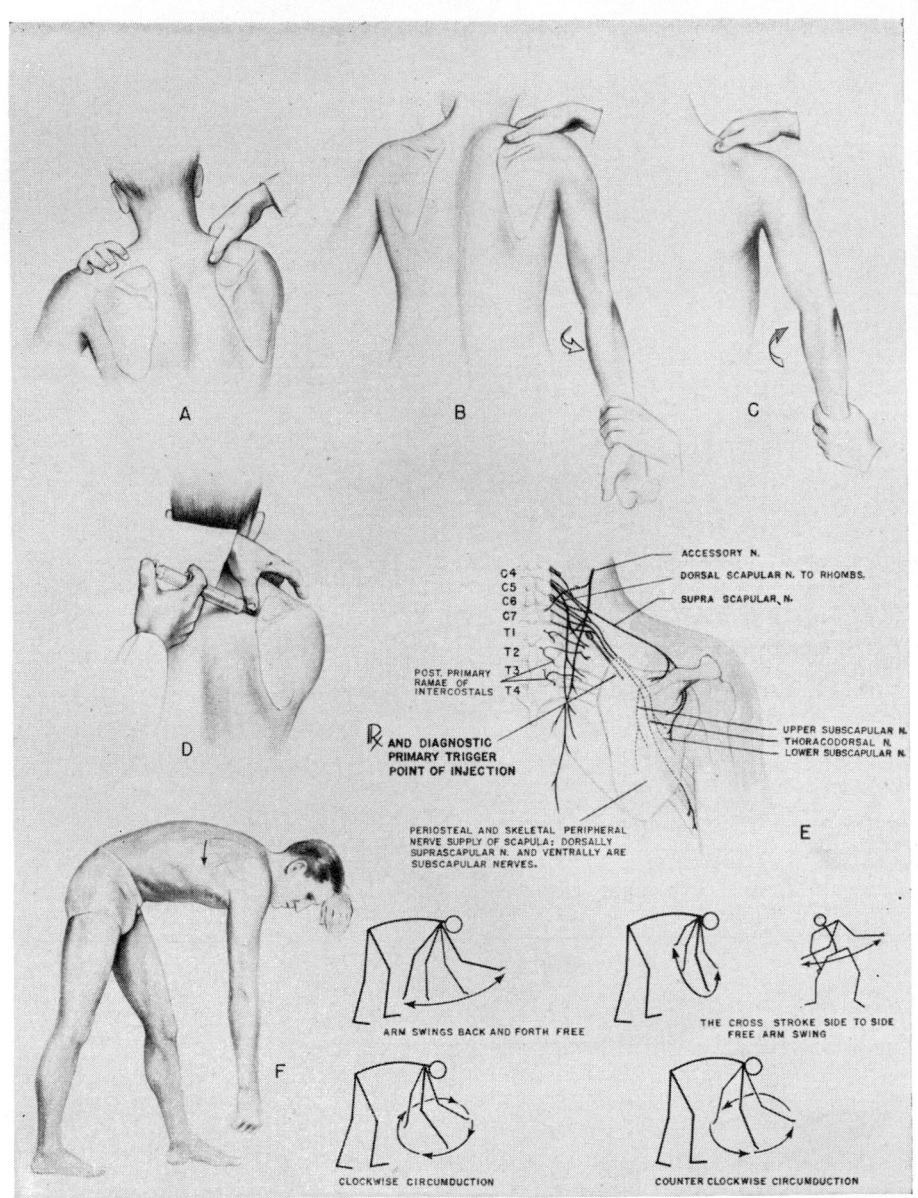

Fig. 3-10. *A, B, C,* Clinical tests for scapulocostal involvement; *D,* site of procaine infiltration; *E,* nerve supply in the vicinity of the scapulocostal region; *F,* Codman or pendulum exercises. (From Michele, A. A.; Davies, J. J.; Krueger, F. J.; and Lichter, J. M.: Scapulocostal syndrome [fatigue-postural paradox]. *New York J. Med.,* **50:**1353, 1950.)

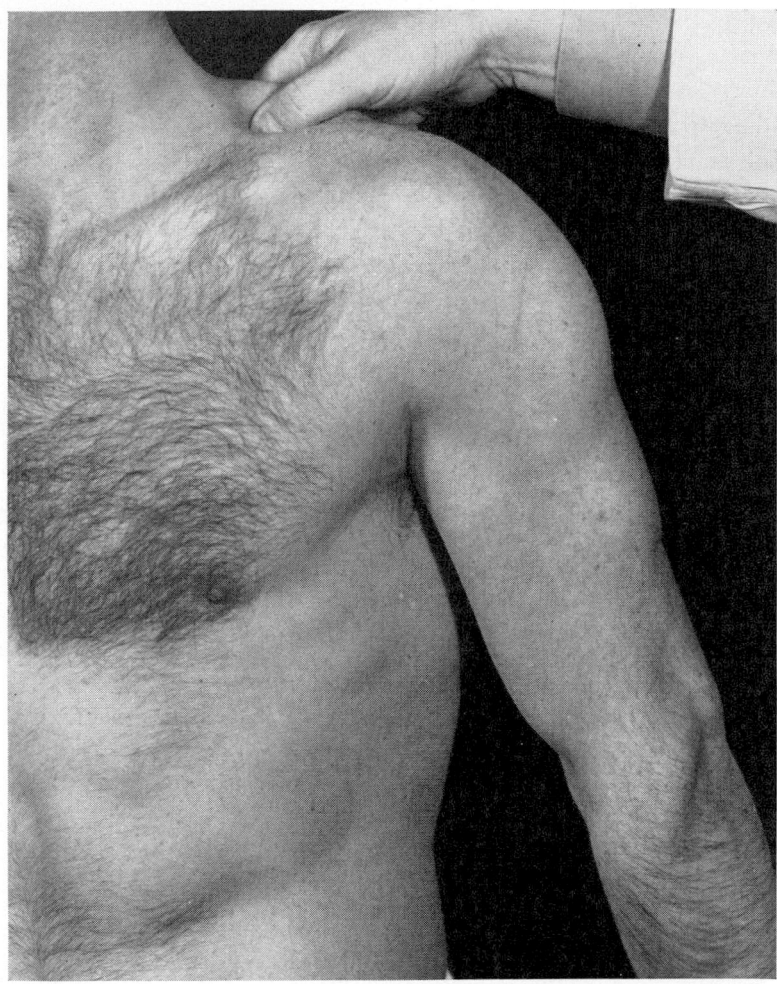

Fig. 3-11. Trigger-point scapulocostal syndrome. (From Michele, A. A.; Davies, J. J.; Krueger, F. J.; and Lichter, J. M.: Scapulocostal syndrome [fatigue-postural paradox]. *New York J. Med.*, **50**:1353, 1950.)

tion of the entire bursa is subacromial; but with its adduction, much of the bursa becomes subdeltoid. Most authorities agree that subdeltoid bursitis is always secondary to an adjacent lesion, which is most commonly a tendinitis with or without calcification of the supraspinatus tendon. However, there is considerable disagreement as to whether or not bursitis (subacromial or subdeltoid) can be differentiated by clinical means from the tendinitis of the rotator cuff of the shoulder joint. This is especially significant for those lesions not yielding precise roentgenologic evidence of calcific deposits as well as those of a chronic nature. However, acute and chronic bursitis are closely related to tendinitis, which frequently represents an involvement of the bursa secondary to calcific lesions of the short rotator tendons of the shoulder.

Another pain syndrome which has recently evoked considerable interest is "the scapulocostal syndrome." This attempts to account for otherwise unexplained shoulder involvement associated with various pain patterns. This syndrome resembles a great number of painful conditions of the shoulder girdle and neck, including the cervical rib, scalenus anticus, pectoralis major, and supraspinatus syndromes. This has been considered to be due to a common factor—namely, a derangement of the deep cervicobrachial fascia, secondary to anterior drooping of the shoulder and undue pronation of the upper extremity. Abnormal postural pull or strain of this fascial carpet may be due to reflex fatigue, reflex imbalance, and degeneration in the somesthetic system and spinal effector mechanism. Trigger points may be found at the stretch sites of the points of fixation of this fascia to bone or muscle, usually beneath the upper medial angles of the scapula in conjunction with the posterior chest wall.

The treatment of this syndrome rests mainly on the correction of the faulty postures responsible for its causation, in addition to the measures generally in use for the treatment of fibrositis and related conditions.

The acute form of bursitis usually presents a characteristic picture of sudden pain which increases quickly in intensity and which leads to complete restriction of all movement of the affected shoulder and arm. Usually, this condition is brought on by slight trauma or strain (of the region), which activates a dormant lesion previously limited to the tendinous structures of the shoulder.

In the subacute and chronic forms, the symptoms include tenderness over the greater tuberosity and a "catching" pain upon elevation or abduction of the arm. The chronic form is often further complicated by adhesions of the chronically inflamed bursa, and symptoms usually resemble those of periarthritis.

Tendinitis. According to many observers, tendinous involvement is a common cause of shoulder pain. Bosworth found this lesion present in forty-three out of fifty-eight shoulders which he explored. The tendinous lesions of the shoulder occur most commonly in the short rotator tendons, which consist of the supraspinatus, infraspinatus, teres minor, and subscapularis tendons. They may also occur in the biceps tendon.

The supraspinatus tendon is most frequently involved, probably because of its adherence to the capsule of the shoulder joint and the frequent pressure placed upon it both by the acromion and the greater tuberosity following arm movements. Thus, stiffness or soreness in the region of the greater tuberosity upon elevation of the arm is a frequent complaint.

The most common factors are chronic trauma, frequently occupational, and degeneration incidental to the aging process. The latter cause is supported by the high incidence of this lesion in persons over fifty years of age.

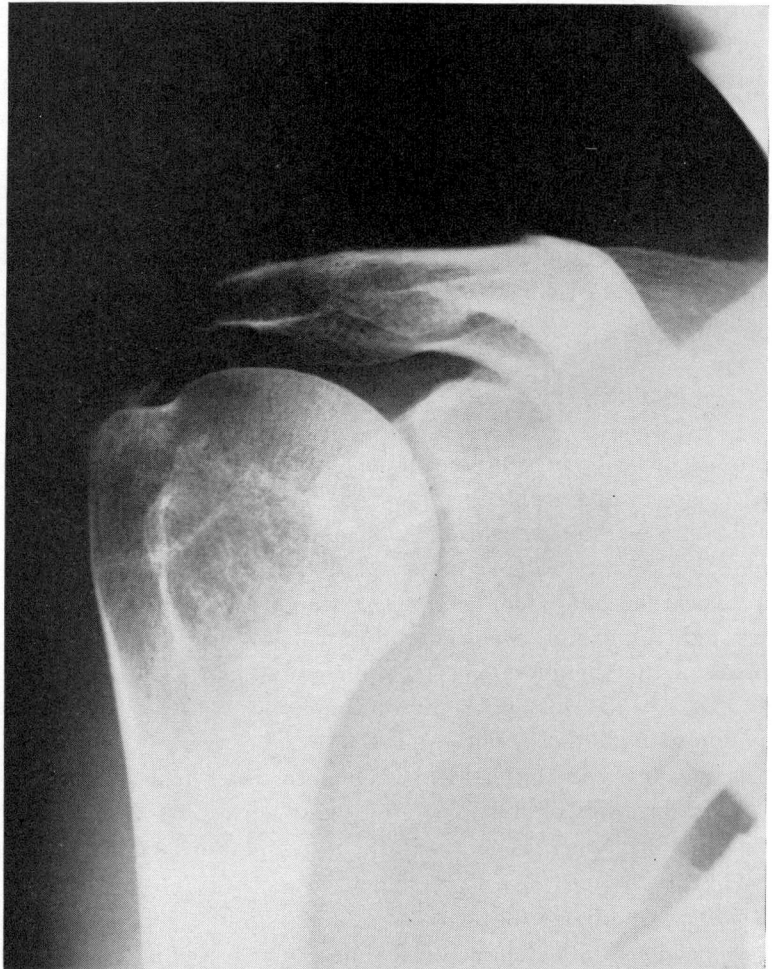

Fig. 3-12. Calcific tendinitis of shoulder. Note the dense calcific plaque adjacent to the greater tuberosity of the humerus, at the insertion of the rotator cuff tendons.

Calcification occurs frequently as the end stage of the degenerative and ischemic lesions. (See Fig. 3-12.) In turn, it becomes the most common cause of acute flareups of bursitis, with further calcification and adhesions and with fibrositis of the muscles of the shoulder girdle. The lesions may cause a variable degree of pain and dysfunction of the shoulder, depending upon the amount of irritation provoked in the involved tissues. The pain may vary from a mild, nagging ache and slight stiffness to a sharp lancinating pain.

Although these lesions are seen in young adults, they are particularly common in the older age groups. Their association or confusion with coronary artery disease has been stressed by many observers.

Scalenus anticus syndrome is the result of pressure of the anterior scalenus muscle on the branches of the brachial plexus. This pain is commonly felt in the shoulder or arm, and less frequently in the upper pectoral region. It may be sharp or constrictive but is increased on weight lifting and disappears when this activity ceases. Thus, it may be confused readily with angina pectoris. Dramatic but temporary relief is experienced following injection of procaine into the muscle. Occasionally, a cervical rib is found and produces circulatory changes in the arm due to pressure on the subclavian vessels.

DISEASES OF THE SHOULDER JOINT

A number of acute and chronic diseases may affect the shoulder joint itself. Although located at the periphery of the chest, this area is not uncommonly the site of referred pain or, at times, of the most pronounced pain due to angina pectoris. The shoulder-hand syndrome, which is a complication of myocardial infarction, hemiplegia, trauma, diffuse vasculitis, cervical arthritis, and panniculitis, is considered in Chapter 4.

Arthritis of the shoulder joint (glenohumeral joint). Special consideration must be given to this important joint, not only because it is in close approximation with the thorax but also because a variety of diseased structures (such as the heart or gallbladder) frequently refer pain to this site. Of course, local disorders of this joint are almost always associated with pain and limitation of motion. Tenderness, fever, crepitation, redness, and swelling may also be found. (See Table 3-2, p. 39.)

The entire shoulder girdle actually consists of four independent joints: the sternoclavicular, the acromioclavicular, the scapulothoracic, and the glenohumeral. The glenohumeral joint is responsible for only 50 per cent of all shoulder motion. While it is subject to all types of acute and chronic arthritis, it appears less prone to sustain severe damage than many other joints. Several reasons for this have been suggested. First, this articulation is characterized by certain anatomic and functional differences from other joints. It is not constantly or statically weight-bearing. The articulating surfaces are relatively small, and the range of motion is relatively free except for extreme movements. However, dislocations are common because of the small articulating surfaces.

Osteoarthritis causes only slight articular changes with crepitation but very seldom results in ankylosis of this joint. Osteoarthritis of the gleno-humeral joint is noted mostly after the fifth decade. The cartilaginous surfaces of the joint show evidence of fibrillation and thinning. Osteophytic changes may exist about the articular rim. Clinical findings in the early stages are stiffness and pain after moderate use of the shoulder and ready fatigue. As the disease progresses with changes within the articular cartilage, the range of shoulder movement becomes gradually smaller. X-rays show marginal lipping with spur formation and secondary narrowing of the glenohumeral articulation.

Acute rheumatic fever occasionally involves the shoulder joint tempo-rarily, as it does other joints of the body, but never leaves residual damage as a result of the polyarticular "flitting pains." This involvement is, of course, only one phase of a systemic disease which involves the collagen tissues throughout the body. These tissues may also be affected by other diseases in this category, such as rheumatoid arthritis, lupus erythematosus dis-seminatus, dermatomyositis, and scleroderma.

Tuberculous arthritis may also involve the shoulder joint. Though it is usually associated with pulmonary lesions, the initial symptoms may be mild enough to be misleading, particularly since the distress resembles pain syndromes observed in "myalgia" or periarthritis.

Infectious arthritis may attack the shoulder joint on rare occasions. It has been found in gonorrhea, pneumonia, typhoid fever, brucellosis, septicemias, and bacillary dysentery.

Reiter's syndrome consists of a characteristic triad of arthritis, urethritis, and conjunctivitis which may create prolonged morbidity. The shoulder joint alone is seldom involved.

Rheumatoid arthritis is one of the most common and crippling forms of arthritis that may involve the shoulder joint. This is a chronic systemic dis-ease belonging to the collagen disorders which has been previously dis-cussed (see pp. 38–42). One or both shoulder joints may be involved as well as other joints. It may present various clinical forms, such as Felty's syn-drome, Still's disease, the psoriatic type, and Marie-Strumpell disease. The last of these may eventually cause ankylosis of the shoulders as well as of the spine and hips. However, in all types of rheumatoid arthritis, it appears likely that the pain and stiffness in the shoulder region are not particularly due to the articular or synovial involvement, but mainly to involvement of the brachial plexus by perineuritic nodules and to the nodular polymyositis, both of which are frequently associated with this disease.

The onset may be acute with polyarthritis, fever, and prostration. It begins most often in the fourth decade, and males and females are equally vulnerable. The shoulder region is involved in half of the cases of any geriatric series, since rheumatoid and osteoarthritis of the shoulder may exist together (mixed arthritis). Pain and stiffness are usually present on awakening in the morning but tend to subside following motion. Joint changes become apparent with progress of the disease. The joint space is reduced due to destruction of the cartilage by pannus formation. With continuing pain and disability of the shoulder area, the muscles are spastic and fixed and later become atrophied. X-rays show punched-out areas in the bone close to the joint and general decalcification. Corticosteroids usually produce quick remission.

Allergic arthritis may sometimes involve the shoulder joint, although the small joints, knees, elbows, and wrists are most commonly affected. The nature of this type of arthritis is usually evident from the associated manifestations of cutaneous allergy and the transitory edema about the joint involvement. The causative allergen is not easily detected even when penicillin and other obvious allergic agents are excluded.

Gouty arthritis. Of the metabolic disturbances causing arthritis, gout has been found to involve the shoulder joint. Tophi and hyperuricemia aid in diagnosis as well as the therapeutic response to colchicine. Punched-out areas in the bone near the joint provide a diagnostic x-ray feature (see Fig. 3-13). Attacks tend to occur following surgery or other stress situations, as well as dietary indiscretions.

Periarthritis of the shoulder is a term used synonymously with painful shoulder, "frozen shoulder," Duplay's disease, fibrositis, bursitis, and adhesive capsulitis of the shoulder. The semantic confusion arises from the fact that some authors define it merely as a state of "pain" and "stiffness in the shoulder," while others consider it due to "periarticular fibrosis" without indicating the particular anatomic structure involved. Some consider it as a fibrositis of the glenohumeral joint with involvement of the muscular structures. Others distinguish a primary idiopathic and secondary post-traumatic form.

Thorough pathologic studies have demonstrated degenerative changes in the articular cartilage of the glenoid cavity and the glenoidal labrum already present from the second decade, and a degenerative change involving the rotator cuff from the fifth decade on. However, these degenerative processes

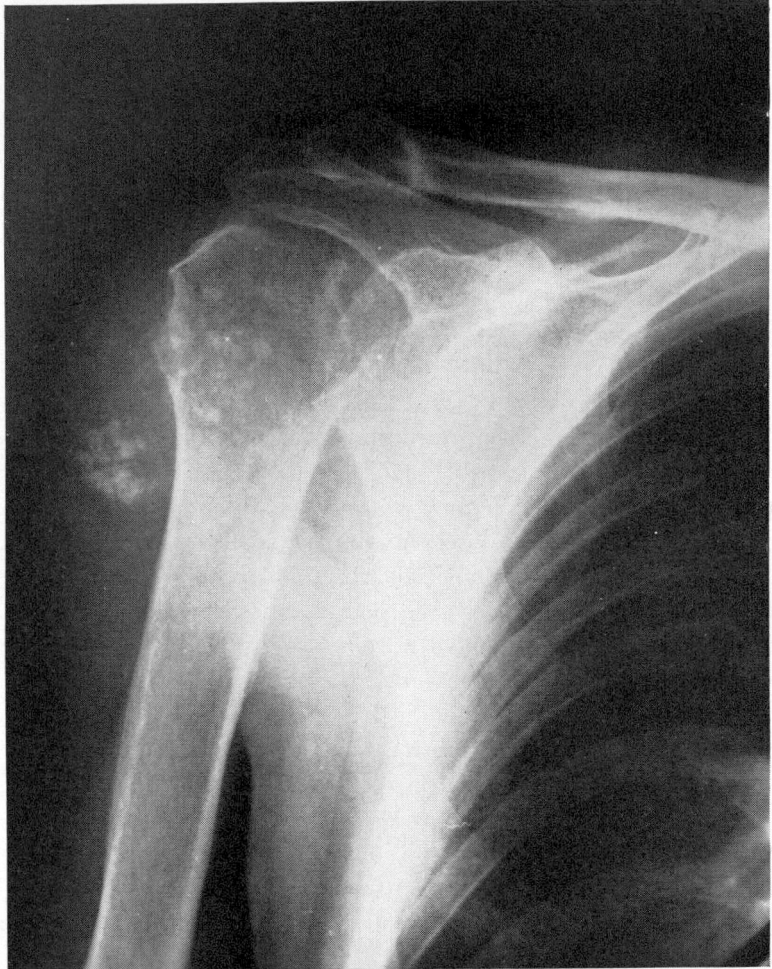

Fig. 3-13. Gout of the shoulder. Note the well-defined destructive bone lesions at the acromioclavicular joint and in the head of the humerus as well as the large calcified tophus laterally.

need not be associated with abnormal function, nor is there any unequivocal relation to the presence of shoulder pain.

There is agreement among most observers that the association of gleno-humeral periarthritis and coronary disease is not accidental. The incidence of myocardial impairment due to coronary disease is definitely greater among persons with periarthritis than among healthy persons of the same age group. In some instances, the association of the two syndromes is particularly evident because they occur concurrently or successively.

However, even an isolated periarthritis should suggest the possible presence of coronary disease.

The pathogenesis is not understood. Most observers agree on the significant role played by disuse of the shoulder. This does not, however, explain the not infrequent occurrence of this condition prior to the clinical manifestation of coronary disease. An emotional pattern termed the "periarthritic personality" may provide an additional basis for the development of this condition. This personality is defined as exhibiting passive and apathetic attitudes. The patients are frequently tense and fatigued and possess a low pain threshold. They are hyperemotional, exhibit hyperactive vasomotor responses, lack drive, and are dependent on others for initiative and decisions.

A similar psychosomatic concept described by Lorenz and Musser is not generally accepted. The possible neurogenic and circulatory factors involved in periarthritis which may initiate the fully developed shoulder-hand syndrome are also discussed in the section dealing with neurogenic causes of painful chest conditions (see pp. 95–96). The early recognition of this disorder is important before the periarthritis becomes full-blown as a frozen shoulder or shoulder-hand syndrome.

Treatment consists of early measures to mobilize the shoulder and to relieve pain. Corticosteroid therapy by local injection or systemic form expedites the relief of pain and the recovery of shoulder motion. However, there is great individual variation in response to treatment, and manipulation may become necessary. Therapy is discussed further in connection with the shoulder-hand syndrome (see pp. 95–96).

Traumatic joint disease. Fracture, dislocation, or sprain plays a significant role in the causation or perpetuation of shoulder-joint disease. A history of trauma is always evident.

Psychogenic rheumatism. Emotional factors influence the course of most cases of chronic joint disease to some degree. Occasionally, they appear to play a major role in the aggravation of the underlying organic disease. In cases of pure psychogenic rheumatism, a previous history of psychoneurotic complaints or a family history of arthritis can often be elicited. Such patients are apt to complain of a tightness or tenseness of the muscles about the joint area. Laboratory tests are entirely negative.

Palindromic rheumatism is an unusual syndrome manifested by very transient "white" articular or periarticular swellings with frequent recurrences. The cause is unknown. Some authorities consider it a variant of rheumatoid arthritis, while others consider it an allergic or psychogenic response.

Blood dyscrasias may cause bleeding into or around the shoulder joint with pain. This may occur in hemophilia, leukemia, sickle-cell anemia, and Henoch-Schönlein purpura.

Paget's disease. This frequently generalized disorder of bone metabolism may also involve the bony structures of the shoulder and give rise to vague pain in this region and characteristic x-ray findings (see Fig. 3-14).

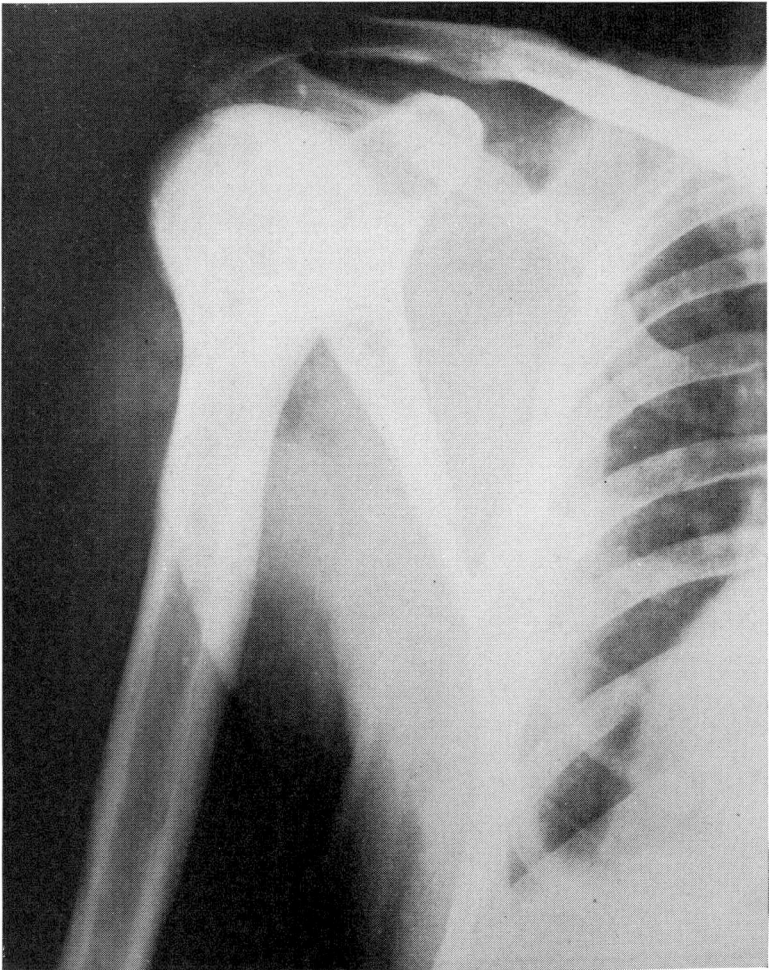

Fig. 3-14. Paget's disease of shoulder. Note increased density in head and neck of humerus with interspersed radiolucent mottling, coarsened trabeculations, and cortical thickening.

REFERENCES

Adams, R. A.; Denny-Brown, D.; and Pearson, C. M.: *Diseases of Muscle: A Study in Pathology.* Paul B. Hoeber, Inc., New York, 1953.

Baylin, G. J., and Wear, J. M.: Blastomycosis and actinomycosis of the spine. *Am. J. Roentgenol.*, **69:**395, 1953.

Benninghoven, C. D., and Miller, E. R.: Coccidioidal infection in bone. *Radiology,* **38:**663, 1942.

Benson, E., and Zavala, J. C.: Importance of the costochondral syndrome in evaluation of chest pain. *J.A.M.A.*, **156:**1244, 1954.

Bickel, W. H.: Tuberculosis of bones and joints. *Proc. Staff Meet., Mayo Clin.*, **28:**370, 1953.

Blatner, R. J.: Recent advances in clinical aspects of poliomyelitis. *J.A.M.A.*, **156:**9, 1954.

Blockey, N. J.; Wright, J. K.; and Kellgren, J. H.: Periarthritis of the shoulder. *Brit. M.J.*, **1:**1455, 1954.

Boland, E. W., and Present, A. J.: Rheumatoid spondylitis; a study of one hundred cases, with special reference to diagnostic criteria. *J.A.M.A.*, **129:**843, 1945.

Bonica, J. J.: Management of myofascial pain syndromes in general practice. *J.A.M.A.*, **164:**732, 1957.

Bosworth, D. M.; Wright, H. A.; Fielding, J. W.; and Wilson, H. J.: The use of iproniazid in the treatment of bone and joint tuberculosis. *J. Bone & Joint Surg.*, **35A:**577, 1953.

Brett, M. S.: Advanced actinomycosis of the spine treated with penicillin and streptomycin; report of a case. *J Bone & Joint Surg.*, **33B:**215, 1951.

Brock, R.: Osteomyelitis of the ribs. *Guy's Hosp. Rep.*, **106:**156, 1957.

Campbell, E. H., Jr., and Whitfield, R. D.: Tumors of the spine and spinal cord with a discussion of the diagnostic significance of back pain. *J. Kansas M. Soc.* (Supp.), **52:**40A, 1951.

(Clinical Conference): Histoplasmosis. *J. Pediat.*, **31:**98, 1947.

Cope, V. Z.: Actinomycosis of bone with special reference to infection of the vertebral column. *J. Bone & Joint Surg.*, **33B:**205, 1951.

Cyriax, J.: Thoracic disc lesions. *St. Thomas Rep. (London)*, **6:**171, 1950.

Davis, A. G.: Injuries of cervical spine. *J.A.M.A.*, **127:**149, 1945.

DePalma, A. F.: Accurate diagnosis in lesions of the shoulder and knee joint. *S. Clin. North America*, **32:**1761, 1952.

DePalma, A. F.; Callony, G.; and Bennett, G. A.: Variational anatomy and degenerative lesions of the shoulder joint. *Am. Acad. Orthoped. Surgeons, Instructional Course Lectures*, **VI**, 1949.

Epstein, B. S.: *The Spine. A Radiological Text and Atlas*. Lea & Febiger, Philadelphia, 1955.

Epstein, J. A., and Davidoff, L. M.: Recognition and management of spinal cord and nerve root compression caused by osteophytes. *Bull. Rheumat. Dis.*, **3**:29, 1953.

Farrow, F. H.: Thrombophlebitis of the superficial veins of the breast and anterior chest wall (Mondor's disease). *Surg., Gynec. & Obst.*, **101**:63, 1955.

Gershon-Cohen, J.; Rechtman, A. M.; Schraer, H.; and Blumberg, N.: Asymptomatic fractures in osteoporotic spines of the aged. *J.A.M.A.*, **153**:625, 1953.

Goldfain, E.: Chronic brucellosal type of ankylosing spondylitis. *J. Lab. & Clin. Med.*, **28**:1226, 1943.

Gordon, A.: Myalgia of an isolated portion of a muscle; the therapeutic value of its recognition. *Am. Pract. & Digest Treat.*, **3**:804, 1952.

Griffin, E. H., and Minnis, F. J.: Traumatic fracture displacement of the first rib. *N.Y. J. Med.*, **57**:2407, 1957.

Guest, C. M., and Jacobson, H. G.: Pelvic and extra-pelvic osteopathy in rheumatoid spondylitis; clinical and roentgenographic study of 90 cases. *Am. J. Roentgenol.*, **65**:760, 1951.

Haagenson, C. D.: *Diseases of the Breast*. W. B. Saunders Co., Philadelphia, 1956.

Hart, G. M.: Post-menopausal osteoporosis of the spine. *Geriatrics*, **5**:321, 1951.

Hendrick, J. W.: Intraductal papilloma of the breast. *Surg., Gynec. & Obst.* **105**:215, 1957.

Herrell, W. E., and Barber, T. E.: Treatment of brucellosis with Aureomycin or Terramycin combined with dihydrostreptomycin. *Postgrad. Med.*, **11**:477, 1952.

Hochberg, L. A., and Crastnopol, R.: Tumors of the ribs. *Dis. Chest*, **28**:406, 1955.

Holbrook, W. P.; Hill, D. F.; and Stephens, C. A. L. Z.: 7B. Current status of the treatment of rheumatoid arthritis. *J.A.M.A.*, **164**:1471, 1957.

Horwitz, M.: Syphilitic spondylitis with a report of 2 cases. *Ann. Rheumat. Dis.*, **7**:200, 1948.

Johnson, E. K., and James, A.: Suppurative typhoid spine perforating into the bronchus; case report. *Am. J. Surg.*, **68**:103, 1945.

Kayser, H. L.: Tietze's syndrome. A review of the literature. *Am. J. Med.*, **21**:982, 1956.

Kenny, J. J., and Maloney, W. C.: Multiple myeloma: diagnosis and management in a series of 57 cases. *Ann. Int. Med.*, **46**:1079, 1957.

King-Brown, R., and Recht, W.: Brucella spondylitis; review of the literature and report on two cases. *Postgrad. M. J.*, **28**:251, 1952.

Kunkel, M. G.; Dahlin, D. C.; and Young, H. H.: Benign chondroblastoma. *J. Bone & Joint Surg.*, **38**:817, 1956.

Lipkin, M.; Fulton, L. A.; and Wolfson, E. A.: The syndrome of the hypersensitive xiphoid. *New England J. Med.*, **253**:591, 1955.

Lorenz, T. H., and Musser, M. J.: Life stress, emotions and stiff shoulder. *Ann. Int. Med.*, **37**:1232, 1952.

Loutzenheiser, J.: Surgery of osteoarthritis. *J.A.M.A.*, **157**:491, 1955.

Malloy, C. J.: Xiphodynia as a concomitant of asthma. *Canad. M.A.J.*, **77**:585, 1957.

McVay, L. V., Jr.; Guthrie, F.; and Sprunt, D. H.: Aureomycin in the treatment of actinomycosis. *New England J. Med.*, **245**:91, 1951.

Michele, A. A.: The conservative management of the painful shoulder. *N.Y. J. Med.*, **56**:49, 1956.

Michele, A. A.; Davies, J. J.; Krueger, F. J.; and Lichtor, J. M.: Scapulocostal syndrome (fatigue-postural paradox). *N.Y. J. Med.*, **50**:1353, 1950.

Myers, A.: Degeneration of cervical intervertebral discs following whip-lash injury. *Bull. Hosp. Joint Dis.*, **14**:74, 1953.

Niehaus, F. W.: Pain in the spine, thorax, shoulders and arms simulating an anginal syndrome. *Nebraska Med.*, **28**:72, 1943.

Nix, J. T., and Albert, M. A.: The surgical management of Tietze's syndrome. *J. Louisiana M. Soc.*, **107**:452, 1955.

Odom, G. L., and Woodhall, B.: Cervical disc lesions. *J.A.M.A.*, **166**:23, 1958.

O'Leary, P. A., and Waisman, M.: Dermatomyositis. A study of 40 cases. *Arch. Dermat. & Syph.*, **41**:1001, 1940.

Olsson, O.: Degenerative changes of the shoulder joint and their connection with shoulder pain. *Acta chir. scandinav.* (Suppl.), **181**:1, 1953.

Pascuzzi, C. A.; Dahlin, D. C.; and Clagett, O. T.: Primary tumors of ribs and sternum. *Surg., Gynec. & Obst.*, **104**:390, 1957.

Phalen, G. S.; Prickman, L. E.; and Drusen, F. J.: Brucellosis spondylitis; treatment by physically induced hyperpyrexia. *J.A.M.A.*, **118**:859, 1942.

Polley, H. F., and Slocumb, C. H.: Medical treatment of osteoarthritis. *J.A.M.A.*, **157**:489, 1955.

Primer on the rheumatic diseases, prepared by Committee of American Rheumatism Association. *J.A.M.A.*, **139**:1068, 1949.

Rapport, R. L.; Allen, R. B.; and Curry, G. J.: Complications of rib fractures. *A.M.A. Arch. Surg.*, **71**:7, 1955.

Reich, N. E.: Acute rheumatic fever in uncommon sites. *Am. Pract. & Digest Treat.*, **2**:328, 1951.

Reich, N. E.: Protean manifestations of acute rheumatic fever. *Am. Pract. & Digest Treat.*, **1**:645, 1947.

Reich, N. E.: Use of large doses of progesterone in rheumatoid arthritis. *Am. Pract. & Digest Treat.*, **4**:1, 1949.

Reich, N. E., and Reinhart, J. B.: Dermatomyositis associated with hypertrichosis. *Arch. Dermat. & Syph.*, **57**:725, 1948.

Reifenstein, E. C., Jr., and Albright, F.: The metabolic effects of steroid hormones in osteoporosis. *J. Clin. Invest.*, **26**:24, 1947.

Riley, H. D., Jr., and Christie, A.: Myositis ossificans progressiva. *Pediatrics*, **8**:753, 1951.

Schlesinger, E. B., and Traveras, J. M.: Syndromes of cervical root compression: neurologic and roentgenologic aspects. *M. Clin. North America*, **37**:451, 1953.

Schwarz, J., and Muth, J.: Coccidiomycosis; a review. *Am. J. M. Sc.*, **221**:89, 1951.

Tarsy, J. M.: *Pain Syndromes and Their Treatment.* Charles C Thomas, Publisher, Springfield, Ill., 1953.

Tietze, A.: Ueber eine eigenartige Häufung von Fällen mit Dystrophie der Rippenknorpel. *Klin. Wchnschr.*, **58**:829, 1921.

Traut, E. F., and Passardli, E. W.: Annual meeting of the American Rheumatism Association, abstracted. *Am. Rheum. Dis.*, **6**:91, 1955.

Travell, J., and Ringler, S. H.: Pain syndromes of the chest muscles. Resemblance to effort angina and myocardial infarction and relief by local block. *Canad. M.A.J.*, **59**:333, 1948.

Valentine, M.: Aetiology of fibrositis, a review. *Am. Rheum. Dis.*, **6**:241, 1947.

West, H. F.: Aetiology of ankylosing spondylitis. *Ann. Rheumat. Dis.*, **8**:143, 1949.

Wise, C. S., and Ardizzone, J.: Electromyography in intervertebral disc protrusions. *Arch. Phys. Med.*, **35**:442, 1954.

Yoss, E.; Corbin, B.; McCarty, S.; and Love, J.: Significance of symptoms and signs in localization of involved root in cervical disc protrusion. *Neurology*, **7**:673, 1957.

Young, H. H.: Non-neurological lesions simulating protruded invertebral disk. *J.A.M.A.*, **148**:1101, 1952.

CHAPTER 4 *NEUROLOGIC AND FUNCTIONAL CAUSES OF CHEST PAIN*

CHAPTER OUTLINE

84

Neurogenic pain may be either organic or functional in origin. When such pains originate in the chest or are referred there from a distant primary focus, they may cause considerable difficulty in diagnosis. The organic type of pain is characterized by radiation along the course of specific nerves. Functional neurogenic disorders encompass the more common types of chest discomfort encountered in practice. Organic causes may be overlooked occasionally when the psychogenic overlay predominates the clinical picture. Thus, a thorough search for underlying organic causes is essential.

The organic causes of neurogenic chest pain may be grouped according to their primary site: (1) lesions of the cervicodorsal spinal cord itself, (2) lesions of the spine resulting in irritation and compression of nerve roots, (3) disorders involving the peripheral nerves, and (4) miscellaneous disorders.

LESIONS OF THE CERVICODORSAL SPINAL CORD AND NERVE ROOTS

Vascular Lesions

Spinal meningeal hemorrhage may begin with pain in the back and with secondary radiation to the chest. It is usually secondary to trauma but may also occur as a result of aneurysmal rupture or of various contiguous vertebral diseases. Initially, such lesions may provoke pain by compression or by irritation of dorsal nerve roots. This pain may be described as lancinating, burning, soreness, or tingling and tenderness. Motor or sensory paralysis may supervene. In cases of traumatic lesions, prompt surgical exploration and laminectomy may be lifesaving. In nontraumatic spinal hemorrhage, the treatment is essentially that of hemorrhage anywhere along the cerebrospinal system tract. This includes absolute bed rest, analgesics, special positioning, removal of excess spinal fluid, and laminectomy in the most serious instances.

Spinal intramedullary hemorrhage is relatively rare but may also produce initial pain in the back and occasional girdle sensations. Root pain appears very rarely. This usually leads to the rapid onset of paraplegia and associated findings, depending on the level of involvement.

Spinal thrombosis and embolism. Vascular lesions (which are mainly atherosclerotic) may lead to complete or partial obstruction to the cerebral blood flow. When factors appear which cause sudden changes in blood composition (such as dehydration or hematologic disorders), thrombosis may occur without total occlusion and produce severe ischemia. Embolism is quite rare and is usually secondary to acute or subacute bacterial endocarditis. The clinical picture is frequently ushered in abruptly by subjective sensations of tingling and numbness. Involvement of the anterior spinal artery is often manifested by initial pain and weakness in the shoulder, neck, and arms, followed by quadriplegia. Involvement of the lower thoracic segments may also be accompanied by painful sensations around the chest wall.

Neoplastic Lesions

Although tumors involving the spinal cord are relatively rare, they exhibit a variety of syndromes, depending upon their state of benignity or malignancy as well as the site of occurrence. They usually manifest local symptoms, depending upon the level of involvement, and characteristic disturbances of spinal cord function below this level either concurrently or soon afterward. In view of the topography of the spinal cord and the small size of the tumor, a differentiation of these neoplastic lesions on the basis of clinical findings alone is frequently difficult. Spinal taps with cell stains and contrast-dye studies are usually helpful prior to exploration.

The pain, which is usually due to sensory root involvement, shows radicular distribution. It is frequently unilateral and may be described as lancinating, burning, boring, stabbing, pricking, or tingling. It may be paroxysmal, waxing and waning, and aggravated by coughing, sneezing, or bending and other movements of the spine, and may occur at particular times. Findings may be limited to hyperesthesia and hyperalgesia during this phase. Subsequently, more striking sensory root and cord as well as motor disturbances may ensue. The most misleading symptom in the region of the thorax is a constant dull ache, at times associated with intermittent dart-like attacks of fleeting pain.

Tumors involving the *cervical* segments of the spinal cord may be responsible for pain and paresthesias in the region of the neck and throat and, rarely, in the region of the thoracic outlet. Of greater interest are lesions involving the *thoracic* segments. Distribution of pain, paresthesia, and motor disturbances are, of course, related to the specific segments involved. Sensory disturbances above the nipple line are usually caused by lesions above the fourth segment. Disturbances below the nipple line suggest the fifth thoracic segment as the upper limit.

A detailed differential diagnosis of the various primary and secondary tumors which affect the spinal cord is beyond the scope of this text. Suffice it to call attention to the possible occurrence of such lesions when chest pain of a neuralgic type exists which cannot be explained on the basis of more common and readily detectable disease. Awareness of such lesions before irreversible motor and sensory disturbances make their appearance may permit early exploration and curative surgery.

Neoplastic lesions may also arise from neural tissue in the thoracic region outside of the spinal cord. A tumor which may produce chest pain and dyspnea is the *neuroblastoma* of the retropleural space. It is a highly malignant tumor which is usually found in childhood. It frequently arises within the adrenal medulla and the sympathetic nervous system. The clinical picture is often misleading, since it is suggestive of leukemia or bone disease. Early recognition and removal of this tumor may be curative. Radiation therapy, used after surgery or when surgery is contraindicated, is a valuable adjunct, since it may alleviate the symptoms caused by this radiosensitive tumor.

Miscellaneous Lesions

Tabes dorsalis. Pains and paresthesias are the common symptoms of tabes and are thought to be due to irritation of the dorsal spinal roots. These pains are lancinating, severe, agonizing, and shooting ("lightning") and may last up to several days. They may involve the legs, girdle, abdomen ("gastric crisis"), and thorax. Precordial or substernal pain may occur early and may persist as the most prominent feature of dorsal column involvement. It appears suddenly with a severe burning abdominal or chest ("lightning") pain, with radiation to the back. Paresthesias, ataxia, urinary difficulties, and optic phenomena are associated findings. Postural hypotension may occur due to involvement of the autonomic nervous system.

It is important to stress the fact that patients with tabes may also have associated luetic cardiovascular involvement, such as aortic insufficiency and aortitis. True anginal seizures may occur because of active inflammatory disease of the aortic wall with involvement of the coronary ostia. (Aortic insufficiency produces a sucking effect on the coronary blood content during diastole.) Such seizures are often associated with sudden rises in blood pressure and tachycardia. These so-called "hypertensive crises" (paroxysmal hypertension) are described in greater detail in Chapter 8.

Spinal fluid studies and blood serology are important diagnostic laboratory procedures. A diagnosis of meningovascular lues should not be made if these tests are normal.

Spinal cord injuries. The incidence of spinal cord injuries is increasing because of the frequency of automobile accidents. Compression fractures (see Figs. 4-1 and 4-2) and "whiplash" effects (see Fig. 3-6, p. 52) frequently involve the cervicodorsal spine and may injure the spinal cord and

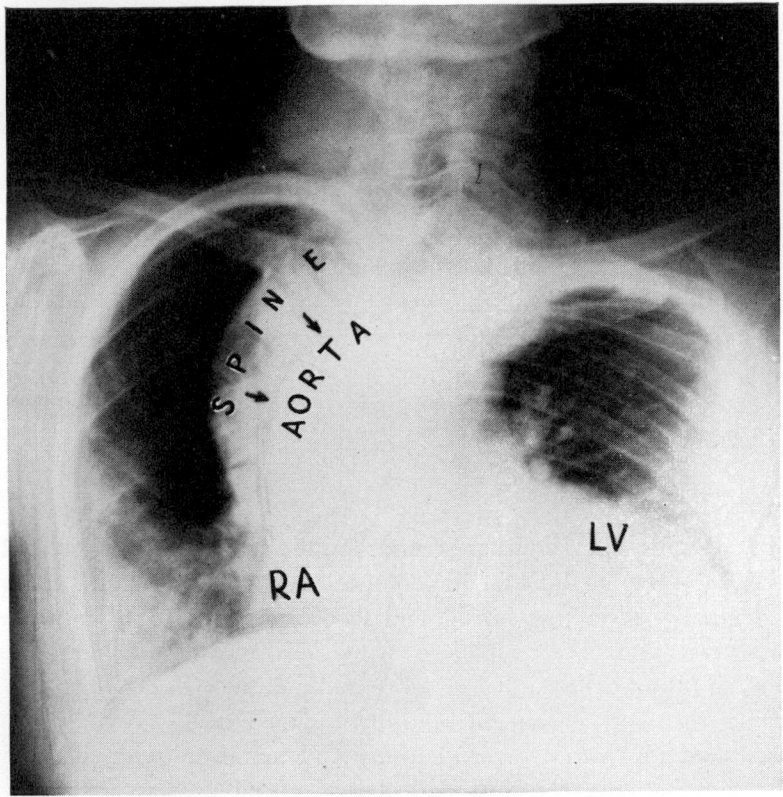

Fig. 4-1. Marked kyphoscoliosis with nerve root compression of intercostal nerves of left side with radiation to precordial area. (From Reich N. E.: *The Uncommon Heart Diseases.* Charles C Thomas, Publisher, Springfield, Ill., 1954.)

nerve roots. Although paralyses and loss of sensory perception are the usual manifestations of cord injuries, direct contusion may cause early pain owing to the rupture of blood vessels with hemorrhage into the cord, nerve roots, and epidural space. In the localization of lesions in the thoracic region, it is helpful to remember that the sensory segments of the skin correspond to cord segments found one or two vertebrae higher than the dermatomes involved. Spinal fluid may be bloody and under increased pressure in more serious injuries. They may cause paraplegia or quadriplegia.

Successful management depends upon the manner in which the patient is treated initially. He must be kept flat on his back or abdomen, and the spine should be neither flexed nor hyperextended. If there is considerable deviation, the head and neck should be straightened only in the long axis of the body. Considerable controversy exists at present as to the advisability of

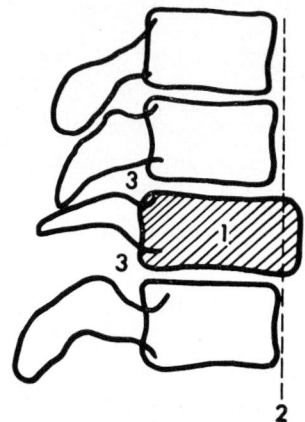 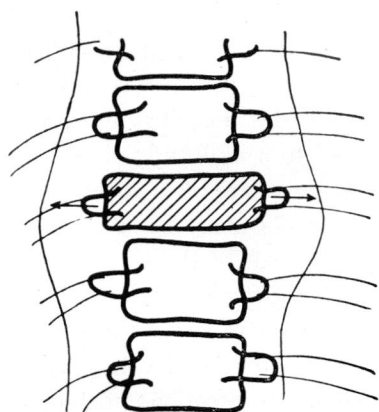

Fig. 4-2. *A*, Compression fracture of a cervical body, lateral view. The vertebral body is decreased in height and flattened horizontally (*1*). The physiologic cervical curve is lost (*2*). The intervertebral foramina are changed (*3*).

B, Compression fracture of a dorsal vertebral body, anteroposterior view. The height of the vertebral body is decreased, its width increased. The posteromedial pleural line is pushed laterally owing to the increased transverse diameter of the vertebral body and to the associated hematoma (→). (From Markovits, E.: *Bone and Joint Radiology.* The Macmillan Company, New York, 1949.)

laminectomy, particularly in the absence of a demonstrable spinal block.

Poliomyelitis. Pain due to acute involvement of the anterior horn cells has already been discussed in the section on chest pain of muscular origin (pp. 61–62).

Herpes zoster. This significant skin lesion, presumably caused by a viral infection of the dorsal nerve ganglia, has been discussed in greater detail in the section on skin diseases (pp. 23–24). Mild symptoms of a systemic infection may precede the vesicular eruption. Preherpetic pain is a severe burning or stabbing pain which may affect spinal nerves innervating the thorax, and thus affect the precordial area. Until the characteristic skin lesions appear, the exact diagnosis may be elusive. Clusters of vesicles eventually appear and closely follow the course of the affected intercostal nerves. Since it frequently occurs in the older age group, coronary disease may be suspected during the preherpetic stage. When the herpetic lesions appear eventually, they never cross the midline, since they follow the course of the nerve rather closely. The postherpetic pain may be more severe and persistent. In some instances, treatment with ACTH or corticosteroids may be helpful. X-ray therapy over the involved cord segment, injections of protamine or B complex, and many other modalities of treatment have been employed with varying degrees of success.

MISCELLANEOUS DISORDERS

Intercostal neuritis and neuralgia. These expressions are commonly applied to a multitude of chest pains of different origins. Intercostal nerve involvement causes a superficial tenderness or ache along the nerve at the three points near the sternum, axilla, and spine, which correspond to the points of exit of the three cutaneous branches. The pain is aggravated by specific movements which affect the nerves and has the quality of pain which arises in the chest wall itself. The causes are manifold and include vitamin B deficiencies, trauma, diabetes mellitus, viral infections, and toxic reactions to infections, metals, and drugs. Phlegmon of the chest wall or disease of an adjacent rib may be at fault. Thoracic surgery may be followed by traumatic neuritis. The pain may be sharp, darting, stinging, or burning and tends to follow the course of the affected nerve. Treatment is that of the underlying condition. Large doses of vitamin B complex may be given empirically.

Visceral epilepsy. This nebulous condition may appear during the aura of an epileptic attack or as an epileptic equivalent. There may be brief paroxysmal attacks consisting of gastrointestinal, genitourinary, or cardio-respiratory manifestations. In the latter instance, vague chest distress, palpitation, hyperventilation, sweating, and other vasomotor changes may appear; thus, a careful investigation must be made in order to exclude organic cardiac disease. The proper recognition of visceral epilepsy is aided by the bizarre and atypical character of the symptoms and the prevalence of associated motor or psychopathologic disturbances which may have their origin in cerebral lesions. Electroencephalography and other studies detect foci of disease in 80 per cent of all cases. The management obviously depends upon the nature of the underlying lesion.

Precordial migraine. Migraine is usually characterized by a severe throbbing, unilateral headache frequently associated with nausea or vomiting, visual disturbances, and other symptoms. Precordial migraine represents an unusual variant of this condition. The occurrence of precordial pain as a migraine equivalent has been rediscovered recently. The condition is often incorrectly interpreted as organic heart disease. Migraine equivalents may also involve the psyche, abdomen, pelvis, or extremities. In a recent review of 3800 consecutive patients, 684 individuals were found to be suffering from migraine; of these, 34 had precordial pain and/or tachycardia as a component of the migraine seizure. Laboratory studies, including electro-encephalogram, do not show any constant deviations from the normal.

The vascular changes and the basic personality structure and family history encountered in these equivalents are presumed to be the same as in the typical migraine case. Relief usually occurs after the administration of ergotamine compounds, preferably given parenterally early in the course of an attack. This also serves as a therapeutic test.

FUNCTIONAL CAUSES OF CHEST PAIN

The most important types of functional chest pain are cardiac neuroses of various types (including neurocirculatory asthenia) and the causalgic syndromes (including the classic type, the shoulder-hand syndrome, and the anterior chest wall syndrome). These indefinite or nebulous syndromes frequently give rise to considerable confusion in diagnosis and treatment. They may occur as a primary condition or as an overlay or a late complication. The proper recognition and evaluation of the different components of the thoracic distress is most important.

Cardiac Neuroses

Cardiac neurosis is more accurately described as an anxiety neurosis with cardiovascular manifestations or fixation. However, the commonly used heading has the advantage of brevity. The anxiety may eventually become focused on the cardiac region or apparatus. It is one of the most common and frequently disabling disorders of mankind. It will be discussed at length, since half the patients who consult a cardiologist are suffering from an anxiety about their hearts and because pain and tenderness of the anterior chest wall are major manifestations. It may occur even in a well-adjusted individual who is suddenly exposed to overwhelming stress or a psychic shock, such as the loss of a close relative or friend, especially following a heart attack. The subconscious identification with the deceased leads to a reproduction of similar cardiac symptoms. A thorough examination and full explanation with firm reassurance are usually sufficient to abolish the anxiety. If the examining physician equivocates, a superimposed *iatrogenic* factor may exacerbate or prolong the anxiety about the state of the heart. Unfortunately, this arises far too frequently in medicolegal cases, often because of improper interpretation of symptoms and findings such as normal electrocardiographic variations.

Much more commonly, cardiac manifestations form only part of a generalized anxiety state. They form a syndrome which has fascinated the medical profession since its original description by DaCosta in 1871. It is generally known as neurocirculatory asthenia (NCA), irritable heart, effort syndrome, or soldier's heart.

The chief symptoms are breathlessness, palpitation, nervousness, irritability, chest discomfort, fatigability, headache, spells of dizziness, faintness, and "anxiety attacks." While the cause is not known, the similarity of the symptoms to those associated with stimulation or inhibition of the sympathetic and parasympathetic nervous systems suggests that it is a disorder of the autonomic nervous system. Its incidence is reported to be as high as 13.7 per cent in a series of 5000 private patients with cardiac symptoms or signs. An excellent study (dealing with 576 such patients) classified the cases into three categories:

1. Those with stigmata of constitutional inadequacy.
2. Those with poor physical endowment plus anxiety.
3. Those with primary neurotic manifestations.

The majority (69 per cent) of these patients belonged to group 2, while the remainder were divided almost equally between the other two groups. The majority of these patients (77 per cent) were asthenic and underweight. They also showed a tendency to cold, moist extremities which were susceptible to frostbite and trench foot. Numerous physical and psychologic factors predisposed the onset of clinical manifestations. Coarse tremors, hyperreflexia, and diminished ocular and gag reflexes were also found.

Although this syndrome has been considered to represent a hypothalamic dysfunction, with resultant excitation of the sympathetic nervous system, it has been shown more recently that the cerebral cortex occupies a higher level and is intimately associated with autonomic function. Areas of the orbital cortex, paraolfactory area, and the island of Reil, the cortical representations of the autonomic system, probably can influence the lower discharge centers both directly and through the hypothalamus. It is postulated that these cerebral mechanisms eventually may even turn initial functional cardiovascular changes into organic disease. The mechanism by which this pain is produced is not fully understood. It probably stems from a physiologic peripheral disturbance, and in part from a cramp of the muscles of the diaphragm. The circumscribed location suggests that some of the sensations originate in the muscles of the chest wall near the cardiac apex. At any rate, it occurs predominantly in highstrung and nervous individuals. The excessive use of coffee and tobacco, and emotional upset or fatigue are important factors. It tends to occur at an earlier age level than does coronary disease but may become engrafted on the latter.

Left chest pain may be vague, linear, or generalized, but it is usually localized at the nipple, along the left cardiac border, or in the left axilla. The periapical type is most frequently encountered, because this region receives the shock of the heart beat. Precordial pain presents itself as an ache, as a momentary, sharp stabbing or sticking pain, or as a "twinge." Radiation is either absent or bizarre, covering the widest or unrelated areas.

The pain may last for seconds to days and may be accompanied by tenderness over the affected area. There is usually no relationship to exertion, and distress may actually cccur more frequently at rest.

Because of the vagaries of this condition, objective tests have been devised to document the inability of these patients to adapt their circulation to increased demands such as physical exercise. The ordinary basal measurements are normal at rest. The electrocardiogram may show ST segment elevations and nonspecific T changes, especially in leads 2, 3, and aVF, which may be confused with myocardial damage and even with posterior wall myocardial infarction. These changes are due to rotation of the heart in vertical and clockwise direction (especially since many of these patients are hyposthenic), to disturbances in neurogenic tone, and/or to hyperventilation which commonly occurs in anxiety states. The myocardium may also be especially sensitive to epinephrine and related substances. Although these may not cause the electrocardiographic changes by affecting coronary blood flow, they may act directly upon the myocardium and may affect the potassium balance of the myocardial cell. An exercise test is often employed to remove any doubt as to the innocuous nature of these variations. However, electrocardiographic interpretation may be difficult, and errors are, at times, responsible for the induction or aggravation of the cardiac anxiety.

Other stress tests, such as the Schneider index and Friedman's ventilation test, are strikingly abnormal. The latter demonstrates that even after a period of hyperventilation these patients cannot remain apneic for more than a brief period, whereas more normal individuals can hold their breath for a much longer period after hyperventilation than before. Testing is performed as follows: the patient is instructed to hold his breath as long as he can, both before and after a 45-second period of hyperventilation. The test is considered negative if the patient can hold his breath 1.3 times as long after hyperventilation as before. In this connection, it should be added that when dyspnea is the main complaint, careful observation will reveal a characteristic sighing type of respiration. This may eventually assume the aspects of a hyperventilation syndrome which is linked with acute or chronic anxiety. The most common manifestations of this are hyperpnea, dizziness, tachycardia, precordial pain, and transitory changes in the ST and T waves.

The treatment of this condition may be quite difficult unless it is recognized early. Sedation, tranquilizers, and firm assurance and encouragement are most important modalities. Combinations of drugs that dampen both the increased sympathetic and vagal tone, such as Bellergal, may be helpful. In severe instances, psychotherapy may be required to abolish the source of symptoms.

In the final analysis, the proper recognition and management require not only the elimination of any possible organic findings by thorough examination, but also a search for the responsible psychologic factor. This is not always easy. It must be realized that changes in emotional states and cardiovascular alterations are both parts of man's adaptive reactions to his life situation. Moreover, changes in cardiovascular function can take place in response to threatening life situations in persons who are either unaware or who show no overt evidence of an emotional disturbance. Hence, the management of patients with cardiac anxiety must include an explanation of the mechanism of these "psychosomatic" or neurogenic factors as well as the discovery of the responsible psychologic factor.

The term *iatrogenic heart disease* has recently come into common usage. It applies to cardiac symptoms of the type described above but which stem from or have become aggravated by the physician himself. Usually they occur when findings of questionable or borderline significance are discovered and are mentioned or inferred to the patient without an adequate explanation of the exact nature and benignity of these findings. These include innocent murmurs, minor electrocardiographic changes, insignificant blood pressure variations, and benign arrhythmias. The induction of such anxiety in the patient can be effectively prevented by the physician who is constantly on guard against misinterpretation of either an innocuous statement or an ill-considered remark or act, and who strives to avoid errors in his interpretation of symptoms and findings.

Causalgic Syndromes

Pain in the chest or an extremity may have a causalgic origin. The three syndromes to be discussed under this heading have one common basis—a local injury produces a reaction which appears to be the result of sensory stimuli arising from the injured part. Thus, the origin of this focus may vary from a nerve injury to coronary occlusion. It is characteristic that disturbances which develop in the nervous system permit the process to continue long after the initiating factor has disappeared.

Classic causalgia. Causalgia may resemble cardiac pain referred to the left upper extremity. A severe or trivial injury to any nerve may provoke a throbbing or burning pain after a few days or weeks. It may result from the activation of sensory fibers by sympathetic impulses. Light, heat, and friction may precipitate subsequent attacks. The skin soon becomes smooth, shiny, red, and moist. Muscles supplying the part enter a state of increased tone. The pain is almost invariably confined to the area of injury at the outset, but subsequently the periarticular edema spreads to surrounding parts. Pain is superficial rather than deep. Distress may be described as throbbing, aching, or constricting and is intermittent initially but becomes constant subsequently. The affected limb becomes cold and cyanotic, and joints stiffen followed by muscle atrophy. Muscle spasm and vasomotor changes induced by this mechanism become foci for other reflexes that may augment the pain. The distress may eventually become continuous and more diffuse.

Pain may subside if the trigger point is eradicated early. Local infiltration with procaine or corticosteroids, paravertebral block, or sympathectomy may be employed. Tolazoline (Priscoline) or Hydergine, injected intra-arterially, may be of benefit. When painful impulses spread over larger areas or when the thalamus is involved, pain may persist long after the original cause is removed despite therapy. Chordotomy may then become necessary in an occasional intractable case.

The shoulder-hand syndrome. The painful disability of the shoulder and hand may persist following an injury to the arm. Hemiplegia, herpes zoster, cervical osteoarthritis, diffuse vasculitis, panniculitis, and coronary artery disease are other causative factors. In fact, the incidence is great enough to make it evident that visceral changes can give rise to somatic alterations of the adjacent musculoskeletal structures. This interesting viscerosomatic interrelationship has been attributed to disuse of the extremity, reflex vasomotor changes, hypoxia secondary to heart failure, trophic alterations, and poor circulation.

No relationship has been found to exist between the transmission of the cardiac pain in acute myocardial infarction to the shoulder area and the development or location of pain of the shoulder-hand syndrome. Nor is the severity of the latter in any way related to the severity, extent, or location of the myocardial injury. The secondary trophic and inflammatory changes are best explained on the basis of the proximity of the corresponding centers in the spinal cord. The trophic and sympathetic centers of the upper extremities are thus constantly bombarded, giving rise to the reflex neurovascular dystrophy. Trophic and vasomotor changes in the hands are often conspicuous in this disorder. The skin in the early stage is pink or red; later, cyanotic or pale. As the condition progresses, the involved hand appears smooth, cold, and glossy. Disturbances in the sweat mechanism may ensue. In the advanced stage, there is atrophy of bone, subcutaneous tissue, and musculature. Contracture of the flexor tendons of the hand is a late development. Involvement of the palmar and digital fascia leads to characteristic deformity resembling the so-called Dupuytren's contraction.

Occasionally, bizarre but persistent painful sensations associated with weakness and discomfort and trophic alterations in the upper extremities may be encountered. They probably represent abortive forms or equivalents of the shoulder-hand syndrome. Significantly, this syndrome may occasionally precede the onset of myocardial infarction. Early recognition is important, since results are poor if treatment is long delayed. No form of therapy is entirely satisfactory, but the use of corticosteroids in addition to judicious rest with early passive and then increased active movements appear to give the best results. When they prove effective, corticosteroids exhibit a dramatic effect, with complete relief of pain and improvement of associated vasomotor disturbances within twenty-four to forty-eight hours. Steinbrocker prefers treatment by stellate ganglion block.

Anterior chest wall syndrome. The anterior chest wall syndrome has certain similarities to the shoulder-hand syndrome but can be readily confused with coronary artery disease. The symptom complex consists of a painful involvement of the somatic structures of the anterior chest wall associated with exquisite tenderness on finger-tip pressure. It occurs following a coronary occlusion but may also develop in healthy persons. Histologic changes in the soft tissues of the anterior chest are inconstant. When present, they consist of lymphocytic infiltration in the connective tissue, muscular degeneration, and increase in collagen fibrils.

The condition is commonly encountered between the ages of thirty and seventy-five years, with the greatest incidence about forty-five years of age. It occurs very commonly from four to six weeks, and occasionally several months, after a coronary occlusion. In a smaller proportion of the cases, the pain begins soon after coronary occlusion. When unrelated to coronary artery disease, the history is usually negative. In postinfarction cases, the pain is usually continuous and spreads throughout the anterior chest wall but is usually most severe over the precordium. Patients are often aware of the different character and superficial localization of the pain. The pain is subject to spontaneous exacerbations. Unlike those of angina pectoris, however, they are not accompanied by radiation of pain to the neck, jaw, shoulders, arms, and fingers; they are not brought on by physical exertion; and they are not associated with vasomotor changes, such as salivation and perspiration. The onset of exacerbations may be sudden and is often occasioned by a quick movement of the body. The duration of pain is generally several hours, and the termination is usually gradual. Patients are seldom free of pain between the attacks. Certain positions of the body and movement of the chest and arms may provoke an acute exacerbation of pain. There is no relationship to food, but emotional stress seems to have an aggravating effect. The pain is present and of the same intensity during hours of activity. Nocturnal attacks of pain are uncommon but may awaken the patient only to disappear with change of body position. Laboratory tests are entirely negative. Glyceryl trinitrate (nitroglycerin) is without effect.

Without therapy, the pain may persist for months and even years. It is often severe and incapacitating. The acute exacerbations may be so excruciating that repeated doses of narcotics are eventually required for relief. The response of the symptom complex to proper therapy is usually gratifying. Several days of therapy with corticotropin or corticosteroids is often sufficient to bring about relief and even cure of pain. If protracted treatment with corticosteroids is undesirable, roentgen radiation may be attempted.

REFERENCES

Bartlett, W. M.: Neurocirculatory asthenia. *Ann. Int. Med.*, **30**:966, 1949.

Basen, P. S., and Graham, W.: The shoulder-hand syndrome. Historical review with observations on 73 patients. *Canad. M.A.J.*, **77**:86, 1957.

Boshes, B.: Emotions, hypothalamus, and cardiovascular system. *Am. J. Cardiol.*, **1**:212, 1958.

Briggs, J. F.: Precordial migraine. Presented at the 24th Annual Session, Am. Heart Assoc., Atlantic City, N. J., June 8, 1951.

Edeiken, J.: Shoulder-hand syndrome following myocardial infarction with special reference to prognosis. *Circulation*, **16**:14, 1957.

Editorial. *J.A.M.A.*, May 30, 1953.

Edwards, W. L. J.: Musculoskeletal chest pain following myocardial infarction. *Am. Heart J.*, **49**:713, 1955.

Friedman, M.: Functional cardiovascular disease. Williams & Wilkins Co., Baltimore, 1947.

Gammon, G. D.; Burge, F. W.; and King, G.: Neural toxicity in tuberculous patients treated with isoniazid. *A.M.A. Arch. Neurol. & Psychiat.*, **70**:64, 1953.

Goldwater, L. J.; Bronstein, L. H.; and Kresby, B.: Study of one hundred seventy-five "cardiacs" without heart disease. *J.A.M.A.*, **148**:89, 1952.

Hart, A. D.: Iatrogenic and cardiac neurosis—a critique. *J.A.M.A.*, **156**:1133, 1954.

Ischlondsky, N. D.: Brain dynamics and heart disease. Presented at 24th Annual Session, Am. Heart Assoc., Atlantic City, N. J., June 8, 1951.

Mitchell, J. H., and Shapiro, A. P.: The relationship of Adrenalin and T wave changes in the anxiety state. *Am. Heart J.*, **48**:323, 1954.

Mulder, D. W.; Daly, D.; and Bailey, A. A.: Visceral epilepsy. *A.M.A. Arch. Int. Med.*, **93**:481, 1954.

Perret, G.: The emergency of spinal cord injuries. *J. Iowa M. Soc.*, **47**:252, 1957.

Prinzmetal, M., and Massumi, R. A.: The anterior chest wall syndrome. *J.A.M.A.*, **159**:177, 1955.

Raab, W.: *Hormonal and Neurogenic Cardiovascular Disorders; Endocrine and Neuro-endocrine Factors in Pathogenesis and Treatment.* Williams and Wilkins Co., Baltimore, 1953.

Reich, N. E.: The anatomy of chest pain. *Am. J. Cardiol.*, **2**:95, 1958.

Reich, N. E.: Neurocirculatory asthenia. *Am. Pract. & Digest Treat.*, **2**:120, 1951.

Reich, N. E.: *The Uncommon Heart Diseases.* Charles C Thomas, Publisher, Springfield, Ill., 1954.

Rowbotham, G. F.: Early diagnosis of compression of the spinal cord by neoplasms. *Lancet,* **2**:1220, 1955.

Russek, H. I.; Russek, A. S.; Dormer, A. A.; and Zohman, B. L.: Cortisone in the treatment of the shoulder-hand syndrome following acute myocardial infarction. *A.M.A. Arch. Int. Med.,* **91**:487, 1953.

Sauer, G. C.: Herpes zoster; treatment of postherpetic neuralgia with cortisone, corticotropin and placebos. *A.M.A. Arch. Dermat.,* **71**:488, 1955.

Sheeley, R. F.; Johnson, C. H.; Baker, J. J.; and Harbough, R.: Effect of cortisone and hydrocortisone in hemiplegia after cerebral infarction. *J.A.M.A.,* **158**:803, 1955.

Steinbrocker, O.: Painful homolateral disability of shoulder and hand with swelling and atrophy of hand. *Ann. Rheumat. Dis.,* **6**:80, 1947.

Weiss, E.: *Emotional Factors in Cardiovascular Disease.* Publication 97, American Lecture Series, Monograph in American Lectures in Circulation, Charles C Thomas, Publisher, Springfield, Ill., 1951.

White, P. D.: *Heart Disease,* 4th ed. The Macmillan Co., New York, 1951.

CHAPTER 5 *PLEUROPULMONARY CAUSES OF CHEST PAIN*

CHAPTER OUTLINE

DISEASES OF THE PLEURA
Pneumothorax
Pleuritis (pleurisy)
Epidemic pleurodynia (Bornholm disease)
Hydrothorax
Chylothorax
Tumors of the pleura

DISEASES OF THE LUNGS
Pulmonary infarction and embolism
Pulmonary artery thrombosis
Infectious diseases of the lungs
Middle lobe syndrome
Hamman-Rich syndrome
Polyarteritis nodosa
Primary pulmonary hypertension
Tumors of the lung
"Smoker's lung"
Cystic disease of the lung
Trauma of pleura and lungs

The prime complaint in most pleuropulmonary disorders is chest pain. Although pain of pleural origin is usually characterized by the aggravating effect of respiration, this is not always the case. For example, pulmonary infarctions associated with marked pulmonary hypertension or deep-seated pulmonary parenchymal lesions may cause chest pain which is not exacerbated by respiration. On the other hand, pain due to chest wall, diaphragmatic, or pericardial lesions may, on occasion, become aggravated by respiration. Therefore, it is not surprising that some cardiac and pleuropulmonary disorders are sometimes mistaken for each other. Since concomitant or complicating cardiac and pulmonary disorders often occur because of their close anatomic relationship, a differentiation of the pain caused by the diseases of both organs becomes important for accurate diagnosis and treatment.

DISEASES OF THE PLEURA

The pleura may be defined as a reflection of serous membrane which not only invests the lung (visceral layer) but also lines the chest wall and diaphragm (parietal layer). This membrane consists of a thin layer of mesothelium on a connective tissue base, both of which are extremely rich in lymphatics, nerve endings, and blood supply. In health, the parietal and visceral membranes lie in close contact and are separated only by a thin lubricating film. In disease, this potential cavity can be expanded with air, fluid, or foreign material.

The rich lymphatic and vascular networks account for the rapid accumulations of marked pleural exudates and pleural effusions as well as the susceptibility to the spread of infection or neoplasm from either the lung, the chest wall, or the blood stream.

Pneumothorax. Pneumothorax is caused by the sudden accession of air into the pleural space through an adventitious communication with the parenchyma of the lung or the chest wall. Spontaneous pneumothorax is usually due to congenital or acquired defects in the lungs which produce emphysematous blebs, bullae, or air vesicles, and which tend to rupture in one or more sites. Torn adhesions between the parietal and visceral pleurae may also result in leaks following therapeutic pneumothorax. Bronchopleural fistula is also capable of producing this condition, and bronchial and bronchiolar obstructions following infection or spasm and leading to emphysema have become an increasingly significant factor. Obstructions commonly occur in necrotizing pneumonias of the newborn and young children; this leads to overdistention and rupture of the alveoli.

The extent of pathophysiologic derangement that attends a pneumothorax depends to a great extent upon the amount of air which invades the pleural space. In mild cases, there may be slight or partial collapse of the lung without any gross physiologic disturbance. In more severe cases, the lung may collapse completely with considerable respiratory distress. Severe circulatory embarrassment may also ensue when the mediastinal structures are displaced appreciably. Finally, air may continue to accumulate in the pleural space with the production of a tension pneumothorax which may lead to circulatory collapse. The tension is caused by the valve-like action of the torn pleura; air is admitted with each inspiration but cannot escape until the pneumothorax is under greater pressure than the atmosphere. Pneumothorax occurs more frequently on the left side but also occurs bilaterally and has a tendency for recurrences. Pneumothorax is sometimes complicated by the escape of air into the mediastinum (mediastinal emphysema). Symptoms are severe and resemble those of spontaneous pneumothorax, but crepitus may appear in the subcutaneous tissues of the neck and chest.

The *diagnosis* of spontaneous pneumothorax is readily established on the basis of the symptoms, signs, and roentgenologic findings (see Fig. 5-1). Characteristically, the patient abruptly develops severe, sharp, and continuous chest pain, with radiation to the ipsilateral shoulder, back, or upper abdomen. Invariably there is a feeling of weakness, occasionally terminating in syncope or shock. This may develop some time after the onset of pain and is related to the degree of intrathoracic hemorrhage and hypoxia. The pain itself may be of sufficient severity to precipitate shock. It is aggravated by deep inspiration, and there are varying degrees of dyspnea and orthopnea. Chest pain may persist for an hour up to several days. There is no correlation between the duration of symptoms and the extent of pneumothorax. Hyperresonance, distant to absent breath sounds, fremitus and egophony, and decreased pulmonary excursion over the affected side with dullness are the most common signs.

Bleeding into the pleural space (hemopneumothorax) may also occur as a complication due to the tearing of pleural adhesions or wound of the chest wall. Many of these cases exhibit varying degrees of shock. The determination of the hematocrit at the time of each thoracentesis is helpful in determining whether bleeding persists, recurs, or ceases.

The degree of collapse cannot be measured directly on x-rays. However, the evaluation of the areas of the collapsed lung and the size of the affected hemithorax offers a fair estimate of the size of the pneumothorax comparable to the actual volume per cent of pneumothorax. The area of the collapsed lung is subtracted from the area of the hemithorax. This difference divided

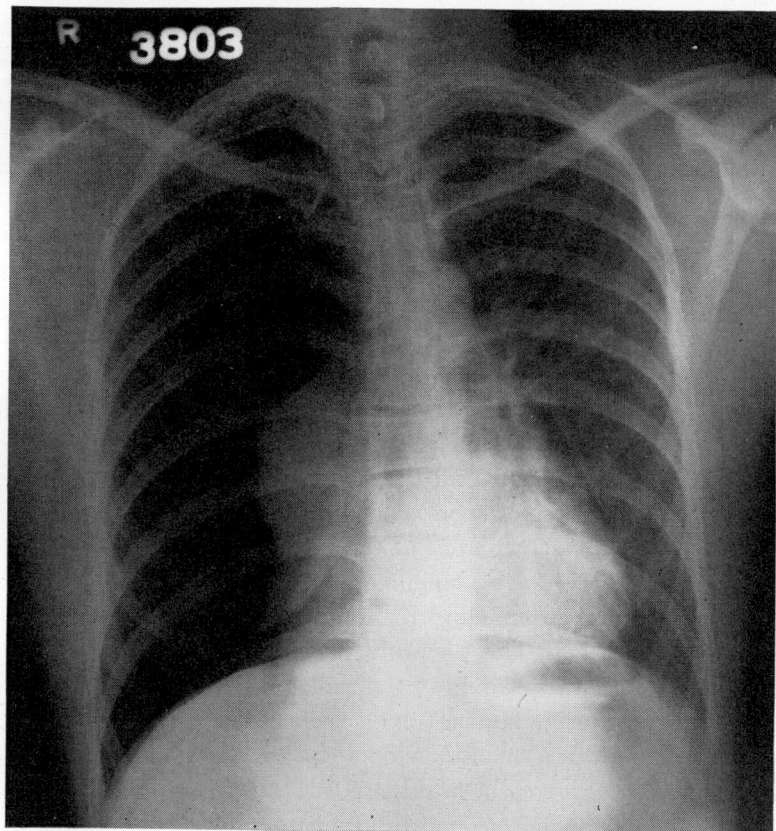

Fig. 5-1. Spontaneous pneumothorax on right with total collapse of lung.

by the area of hemithorax gives an estimate of the percentage of the pneumo-thorax. When air is not visible in the pleural cavity, the precordium should be carefully auscultated, and a careful search for roentgenographic evidence of mediastinal emphysema should be performed.

Differential diagnosis includes coronary occlusion, dissecting aneurysm, intercostal neuralgia, perforated peptic ulcer, acute pleuritis, acute pan-creatitis, and acute pericarditis.

The primary aim is to restore cardiorespiratory physiology as quickly and safely as possible and to return the patient to productive activity with a minimum loss of time. Thus, active treatment of spontaneous pneumothorax in the antibiotic era has been found to be preferable to a program of watch-ful waiting in the average case. When the lung re-expands quickly, symp-toms are promptly relieved, complications are avoided, and the period of hospitalization is shortened.

Underwater sealed drainage may be employed in initial and minimal degrees of pneumothorax. It is employed as an emergency measure in tension or bilateral pneumothorax. Needle aspiration and expectant management seldom result in prompt and complete re-expansion of the lung, and the rate of recurrence remains high with this type of treatment. The main indications for surgical intervention are recurrent tension pneumothorax (intrapleural pressure greater than atmospheric pressure), chronically unexpanded lung, recurrent attacks of pneumothorax, and drainage of blood, excessive hydrothorax, hemothorax, or secondary infection. Surgical or x-ray visualization of subpleural blebs as the cause for the spontaneous pneumothorax constitutes an indication for their excision.

In cases of increasing hemopneumothorax, thoracotomy is indicated in order to ligate or electrocoagulate the bleeding site as a lifesaving procedure. Although it decreases the intrapleural pressure, immediate and repeated aspiration ordinarily does not aggravate bleeding and will prevent the restrictive effects of fibrothorax. The formation of a "peel" on the contracted lung surface after hemothorax can now be prevented by the intrapleural instillation of fibrinolytic enzymes. A combination of streptokinase and streptodornase (Varidase) is usually employed, but more recently trypsin has been used with equal success. Thoracotomy with pulmonary decortication is employed when there is a poor response to this therapy.

The use of extensive pleurectomy has been employed successfully. Pleurectomy effects two significant changes: (1) obliteration of the pleural space and prevention of recurrences and (2) revascularization of the peripheral portion of the lung in which pathologic changes are usually most marked. This operation is seldom followed by a recurrence of spontaneous pneumothorax.

Pleuritis (pleurisy). Inflammatory involvement of the pleura is rarely due to primary disease but results usually from the extension of disease of neighboring structures, such as lung, pericardium, and diaphragm. Pleuritis is encountered following various infections of the lung, pulmonary infarction, and neoplasms. It also occurs following abdominal disorders, such as bacterial or amebic abscess of the liver, and subphrenic abscess. Pleuritis may occur as an integral phase of many systemic diseases, such as lupus erythematosus disseminatus and periarteritis nodosa. The exudate of acute pleuritis tends to be fibrinous initially, but in most instances an effusion develops rapidly. The fluid collection may be serous, serofibrinous, hemorrhagic, or purulent, depending on the nature of the underlying disease process. (See Table 5-1.)

Chest pain and dyspnea synchronous with respiratory movement are the

Table 5-1

Etiology of Serous Pleural Effusion in 193 Cases *

Etiology	Per Cent
Carcinoma	42
Congestive failure	18
Pneumonia	12
Lymphoblastoma	9
Tuberculosis	8
Chronic nephritis with nephrosis	4
Cirrhosis	3
Miscellaneous	4

Etiology of Hemorrhagic Pleural Effusion in 81 Cases

Etiology	Per Cent
Carcinoma	73
Lymphoblastoma	12
Congestive failure	10
Cirrhosis of the liver	2
Pneumonia	1
Tuberculosis	1

* Modified from Tinney, W. S., and Olsen, A. M.: The significance of fluid in the pleural space. *J. Thoracic Surg.*, 14:248, 1945, The C. V. Mosby Co., St. Louis.

most important symptoms of acute pleural disease. Chest pain may be severe enough to require narcotics. Although it is frequently localized to the lower half of the thorax, it may be referred to the abdomen or to the neck. Neck and shoulder pain are usually referred from diaphragmatic pleurisy. The pain is usually more severe in acute fibrinous pleuritis but diminishes or subsides with the development of effusion which separates the diseased pleural. Physical signs of fluid include dependent dullness to flatness on percussion with a pathognomonic shift on changing position of the thorax from right to left, distant or absent breath sounds and fremitus, and diminished excursion on the affected side. Tietze's syndrome or rib fracture may follow a severe coughing spell and must be considered in the differential diagnosis. Fractures are aggravated by sudden anteroposterior chest wall compression, which produces a sharply localized pain in the area of the fractured rib or inflamed costochondral junction.

Examinations (smear, culture, cell block, and guinea pig inoculation) of the pleural fluid are frequently diagnostic. Hemorrhagic fluid occurring in late adulthood may be due to pulmonary or pleural malignancy, tuberculosis, leukemia, or pulmonary infarction. The fluid consists of frank blood in ruptured dissecting aneurysm and is usually found in the left chest. The finding of malignant cells in aspirated fluid is of diagnostic help. Purulent fluid with a high lymphocyte count suggests tuberculosis, while a high poly-morphonuclear count is usually found following bacterial pneumonias. Not infrequently, pleurisy with effusion appears without obvious or detectable etiology. This so-called "idiopathic" pleural effusion, manifested by a pleuritic type of chest pain, dyspnea, and fever when occurring in young adulthood, is strongly suggestive of a tuberculous origin. Although the tubercle bacillus may not be isolated, numerous studies have demonstrated that such patients usually develop active pulmonary tuberculosis within a few years. The estimated percentage varies from 23 to 65 per cent. Since recent studies (pleural biopsy by either thoracotomy or aspiration) have further confirmed this view, it has been recommended that in the absence of positive sputa, pleural biopsy should be employed before long-term treat-ment with antituberculous drugs is initiated.

The specific gravity of pleural fluid previously used to differentiate be-tween transudates (congestive heart failure) and exudates (inflammatory or neoplastic) has recently been found to be modified by extraneous factors which limit the usefulness of this test. X-rays are important for diagnosis and for following the clinical course. They may also reveal serious displace-ment of mediastinal structures toward the opposite side by sudden rapid accumulations.

The treatment of pleural effusion consists of removal of the fluid in order to permit re-expansion of the lung and to alleviate dyspnea. In addition, treatment is directed at the underlying disease and may include various antibiotic and antituberculous drugs. Chronic or recurrent pleural effusions have responded to the use of corticosteroids orally or by pleural instillation even in many cases of tuberculous nature. Empyema of the pleura, whether of tuberculous or other bacterial origin, may require surgical measures in-cluding drainage, decortication, thoracoplasty, or resection.

Epidemic pleurodynia (Bornholm disease). This condition is also known as epidemic muscular rheumatism, acute benign dry pleurisy, epidemic pleuritic pain, Bamle disease, and "devil's grip." It has been discussed previously under chest pain of muscular origin (see p. 61), since the muscles of the chest and shoulder girdle may also be involved. It tends to occur in epidemic form. The Coxsackie virus has been recovered in most epidemics. The clinical picture is characterized by the abrupt onset of severe pleuritic pain along the costal margins at the diaphragmatic insertions or muscular pains arising in the abdomen or the shoulder girdles. The pain has been de-scribed variously as "smothering," "stabbing," "knife-like," and "like a vise around the lower ribs." It is aggravated by deep breathing, yawning, cough-ing, and body movements. The lungs occasionally present basal rales and dullness. Pleuritic friction rub, cutaneous hyperesthesia, abdominal tenderness, and rigidity are less frequently observed. The duration of the pain varies from two to seven days. Although the distress is great, the condition tends to run a short, benign course.

The acute onset and severity of the pain may be highly suggestive of a coronary occlusion or acute pancreatitis. These may be excluded by various enzymatic tests (serum transaminase or amylase) and electrocardiograms. Acute pleuritis, spontaneous pneumothorax, and perforation of the gallbladder or a peptic ulcer must also be excluded.

This condition may be complicated by meningo-encephalitis, orchitis, and acute nonspecific infectious myocarditis or pericarditis. The blood picture presents an early leukocytosis followed by leukopenia. X-ray of the chest is usually negative. The treatment is symptomatic and includes bed rest and analgesics.

Hydrothorax. The pleural effusion of heart failure is rarely associated with the pleuritic type of chest pain. Unilateral effusions almost always begin on the right side due to the azygos vein distribution. Pleural effusion due to congestive heart failure eventually involves both sides. An occasional patient with pneumonia in one lung may develop effusion on the controlateral side. It may also become loculated or interlobar. Changes suggestive of subphrenic effusion (see Fig. 5-2) are elevation of the diaphragm; separation of the gastric bubble from the diaphragm; and flattening of the midsection of the diaphragm, with the highest part of the dome being located in the lateral third of the chest cavity. Pneumoperitoneum or distention of the fundus of the stomach with carbonated beverages shows separation of the inferior surface of the diaphragm from the lung. Breath holding may cause the effusion to assume a more typical configuration. Treatment consists of aspiration when the effusion is massive and not adequately controlled by therapy directed at the underlying disease process.

Chylothorax. When the thoracic duct is interrupted, the pleural effusion consists of a milky fluid which is found, microscopically, to contain large fat droplets. The incidence of chylothorax (and also chylous ascites) has been rising of late with the increasing use of surgical procedures such as aortic grafts, cardiovascular surgery, lung resection, and hepatic and pancreatic resections. It is frequently associated with external trauma or malignant invasion. The diagnosis of chylothorax is rarely established prior to thoracentesis. The surprisingly large volume of thoracic duct flow explains the rapid accumulation of chylothorax. The clinical signs and symptoms result from a combination of mechanical compression and chylous fluid loss. If chest pain is present, it is usually a dull ache and is frequently associated

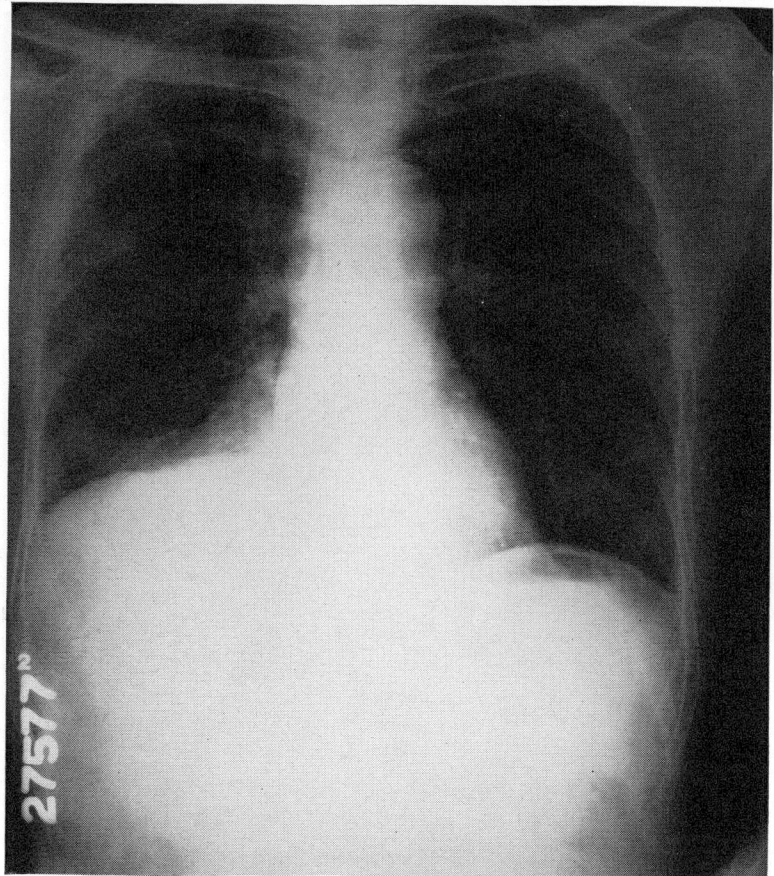

Fig. 5-2. Infrapulmonary pleural effusion on right. Note similarity to an elevated diaphragm.

with dyspnea. Repair of the duct should be attempted in nonmalignant cases.

Tumors of the pleura. Primary pleural tumors are rare occurrences, and the most common type found is mesothelioma. This is usually malignant in nature and may occur as a localized or diffuse lesion. Chest pain, cough, and dyspnea are common. At times these tumors are discovered following routine x-ray examination (see Fig. 5-3). Better visualization is possible following the introduction of air into the pleural space. In some instances, atypical arthritic involvement is present with clubbing of the fingers. The tumor may invade the underlying lung, or it may compress the lung and produce atelectasis. Occasionally, a pleural effusion ensues, and malignant cells may be found in smears and cell blocks. Thoracotomy and operative removal have proved successful in several instances. Secondary metastases

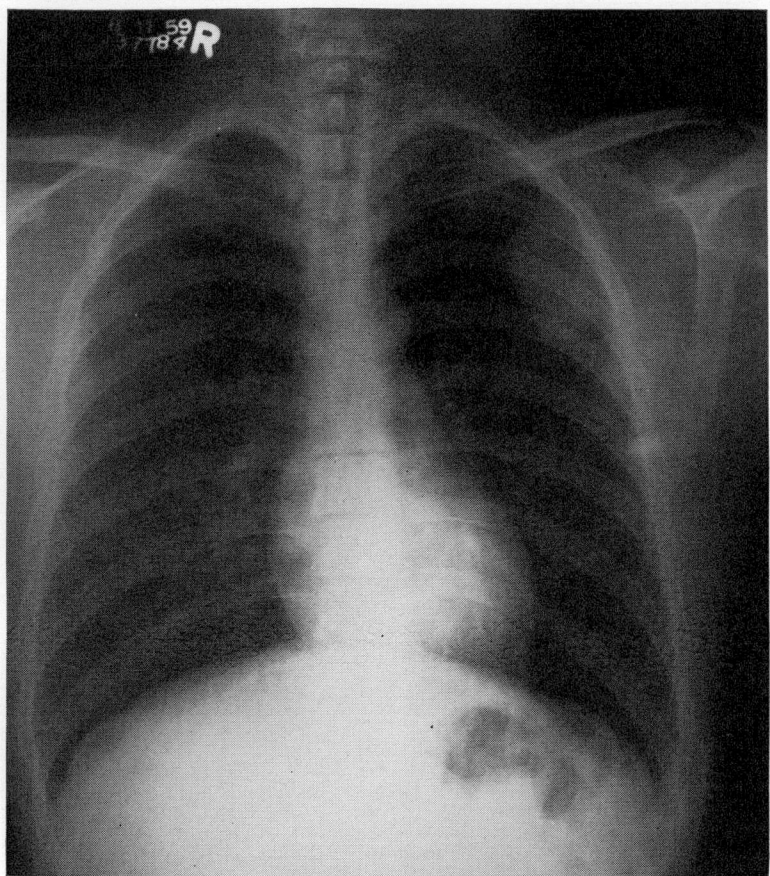

Fig. 5-3. Pleural tumor: sharply marginated, dense, homogenous soft tissue mass attached to left lateral chest wall at level of second and third ribs. Histopathology: neurofibrosarcoma.

which affect the pleura may produce huge serohemorrhagic accumulations but seldom cause chest pain. They may also metastasize to the opposite hemithorax, pericardium, or peritoneum.

DISEASES OF THE LUNGS

Pulmonary infarction and embolism. In spite of increasing alertness and improved diagnostic measures, the autopsy incidence of pulmonary embolism remains much higher than the number of cases that are suspected or diagnosed by all clinical means. Pulmonary embolism is found more commonly with medical conditions rather than following surgical procedures. Fatal pulmonary embolism tends to occur with these predisposing factors:

advanced age, limitation of activity, obesity, infections, hypoproteinemia, hemoconcentration, anemia, varicosities, dehydration, and the presence of cancer. Malignancies of the pancreas, stomach, and lungs are prone to result in multiple venous thromboses, supposedly due to the intravascular liberation of various enzymes which increase coagulability of the blood. Certain blood dyscrasias such as polycythemia vera and essential thrombophilia are also prone to result in thrombosis and embolism.

With regard to the pathologic aspects, two types of pulmonary embolism exist: (1) massive, rapidly fatal pulmonary embolism without pulmonary infarction and (2) pulmonary embolism with pulmonary infarction. In fatal pulmonary embolism without pulmonary infarction, the main pulmonary artery or its major branches are blocked by a clot. Because death is usually sudden, there is inadequate time for pulmonary infarction and secondary pathologic changes to develop. The lungs are only slightly edematous and hyperemic. In infarction of the lung secondary to pulmonary embolism, the infarction is usually pyramidal or wedge-shaped, with its base directed pleurally and its apex at the site of vascular occlusion. The secondary pleuritis accounts for pain on respiration. Very fresh infarctions are not so sharply defined.

According to several large autopsy series, the incidence of pulmonary infarction averages 14 per cent. It is responsible for the majority of deaths in congestive heart failure. The most common sources of emboli are the peripheral and pelvic veins, but clots may arise from the right heart or pulmonary arteries and veins per se. Careful dissection will reveal the presence of thrombophlebitis or phlebothrombosis in most cases. The clot is only loosely adherent in phlebothrombosis and is very prone to break loose as compared to the adherent clot associated with thrombophlebitis. The vessels most commonly involved are the deep calf, femoral, saphenous, and plantar veins. Local tenderness and linear swelling or reddish discoloration and positive Homan's sign may reveal the local site of thrombosis. The application of a tourniquet or blood pressure cuff sufficiently to distend the affected vein segment will quickly produce severe pain. The prostatic and uterine venous plexi may also be the seat of thrombosis; they account for many of the small calcific shadows following healing, which are found accidentally on flat plates of the pelvis and abdomen.

The most frequent site of pulmonary embolization is found in the lower lobes. The right lower lobe is most commonly affected, probably because the artery to the right lower lobe lies in a more direct line with the blood flow from the main pulmonary artery than do the slightly angulated branches to the other lobes.

The sudden appearance of marked apprehension and anxiety may herald the attack of pulmonary embolism. The clinical patterns of thromboembolism of the lung have been found to correlate well with the caliber of the pulmonary arteries and the size of the infarcted area. The diagnosis of pulmonary infarction following an embolus to the pulmonary artery or one of its branches is not difficult when the syndrome is dramatically ushered in by symptoms which include sudden chest pain, dyspnea, cough with hemoptysis, fever, signs of consolidation, and an evident focus of peripheral venous thrombosis. Pain is aggravated by breathing in many instances. Unfortunately, this typical picture is present in only a minority of cases (20 per cent). Hemoptysis is not a common finding. Eventually, pulmonary

Table 5-2

**Frequency of Various Syndromes in
90 Cases of Pulmonary Embolism** *

Syndromes	Number of Patients
Manifestations suggestive of	
Pneumonia	18
Dry pleurisy	10
Pleurisy with effusion	7
Lung abscess	2
Tuberculosis	1
Lung cancer	1
Pulmonary syndromes	39 (43.3%)
Myocardial infarction	22
Coronary insufficiency	4
Postinfarction syndrome	3
Congestive failure	3
Cor pulmonale	1
Cardiac syndromes	33 (36.7%)
Acute surgical abdomen	2
Subdiaphragmatic abscess	2
Primary hepatic disease	2
Abdominal syndromes	6 (6.7%)
Syncope	2
Convulsions	1
Hemiplegia	1
Neurologic syndromes	4 (4.4%)
Other manifestations	8 (8.9%)

* Modified from Israel, H. S., and Goldstein, F.: The varied clinical manifestations of pulmonary embolism. *Ann. Int. Med.*, **47**:202, 1957.

hypertension may occur following repeated infarctions. More often, pulmonary embolism mimics other diseases (see Table 5-2) and thus may present major diagnostic difficulties. Viral pneumonia, postoperative atelectasis, localized empyema or effusion, infectious pleuritis, bronchogenic carcinoma with atelectasis, and chronic bronchiectasis with acute pneumonitis are often incorrectly diagnosed. When massive embolism occurs, the overwhelming clinical picture may resemble that of an acute myocardial infarction.

Pain is often the first and most prominent symptom. This distress may be caused by the pleuritic reaction of the periphery of the infarction. When an embolus occludes one of the larger pulmonary arteries, the severe chest pain is often indistinguishable from that of myocardial origin, especially when the mediastinal or precordial surface of the pleura is affected. Some authorities believe that this pain is the result of an actual diminution in the coronary flow secondary to vasospasm and profound disturbances in the local hemodynamics. Other investigators are of the opinion that the pain originates in the pulmonary artery itself.

Symptoms and signs suggestive of cardiac disease are the dominant manifestations in about one-third of all patients. (See Table 5-3.) This is

Table 5-3

Frequency of Signs in 90 Cases
of Pulmonary Embolism *

Sign	Per Cent
Fever	78.9
Rales	63.3
Tachycardia	58.9
Tachypnea	44.4
Hemoptysis	28.9
Hypotension	25.6
Congestive failure	25.6
Friction rub	24.4
Rib tenderness	17.8
Cyanosis	7.8
Jaundice	2.2

* Modified from Israel, H. S., and Goldstein, F.: The varied clinical manifestations of pulmonary embolism. *Ann. Int. Med.*, **47**:202, 1957.

especially true when the first physical or roentgenologic sign of embolism is pleural effusion on the right side. Thoracentesis may even reveal blood. Thus, tuberculosis and malignancy must be excluded, as well as congestive heart failure. Pulmonary embolism must be suspected when congestive failure is suddenly aggravated during the course of heart disease. This occurs in conjunction with chest pain, low-grade fever, mild icterus and tachycardia, and loss of response to diuretics. Sometimes other subjective thoracic sensations may be present, such as a "catch," a tight feeling, a fullness, or an inability to take a deep breath. Localized chest tenderness may also be found and is apparently produced by spasm of intercostal muscles secondary to contiguous pleural inflammation.

Not only may pulmonary and myocardial infarction (especially of the posterior wall) resemble each other, but pulmonary embolism may occur as a sequel to acute myocardial infarction with mural thrombus. Electrocardiograms are somewhat similar and confusing when a pattern of posterior wall infarction emerges before or after a proven pulmonary infarction. The electrocardiogram in pulmonary infarction usually consists of a deep S in lead 1, an abnormal Q in lead 3, and negative T waves in leads 2 and 3 and in the right precordial leads. The latter also present a delayed "intrinsicoid" deflection. Complete or incomplete right bundle-branch block may be found, or a previously incomplete right bundle-branch block may evolve into a complete block. ST segment depressions may appear in the precordial leads derived from either the left or right ventricular surface leads or both. Arrhythmias may appear and may be attributed incorrectly to digitalis toxicity. Prominent P waves may also appear. (See Figs. 5-4A and 5-4B.)

Determination of SGO transaminase levels is especially useful in these circumstances. A normal value found twenty-four to forty-eight hours after the onset of pain excludes myocardial infarction. The icterus index may be slightly elevated in pulmonary infarction due to the changes in the red blood cells of the infarcted area.

Occasionally, chest roentgenograms (see Fig. 5-5) are suggestive or diagnostic of pulmonary infarction when the infarction presents a triangular, oval, or round shadow, although irregular shapes are also common. However, the evanescent nature of pulmonary infarction and its tendency for multiple and bilateral occurrences are suggestive clues in the differential diagnosis. The high position of the diaphragm, obscurity near the bases, and a shortened interlobar-diaphragmatic distance are important roentgenologic signs.

Effective prophylaxis and treatment of this condition are now possible in most instances. Pulmonary emboli may be prevented if care is given, in both medical and surgical patients, to the predisposing factors previously mentioned. Anticoagulant therapy has been the most potent factor in the significant reduction of the incidence of pulmonary embolization following congestive failure, atrial fibrillation, and acute or recurrent myocardial infarction. Femoral, saphenous, or even inferior vena caval ligation can prevent

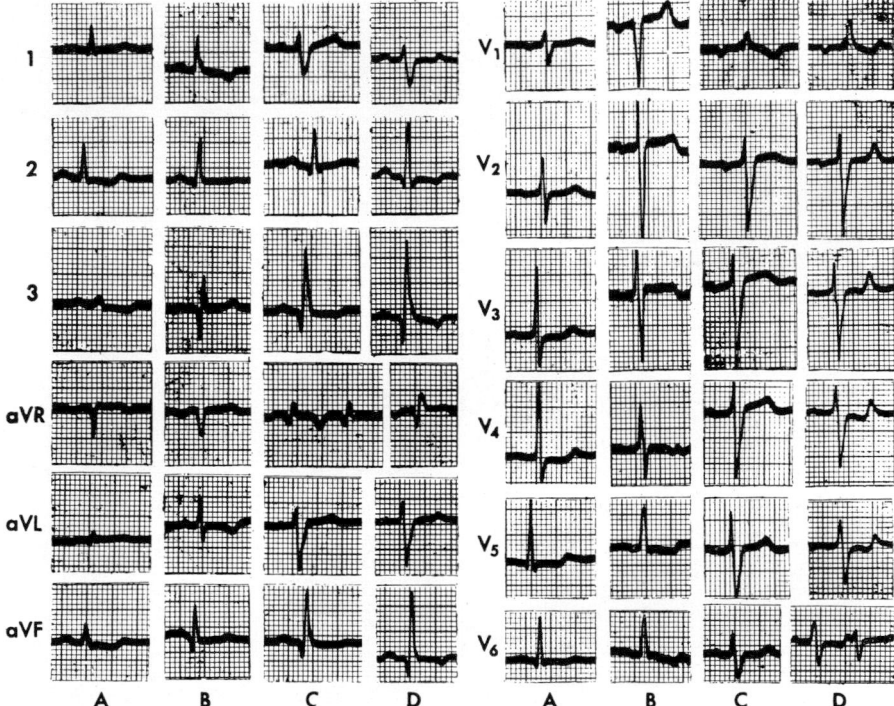

Fig. 5-4A. Electrocardiographic changes after acute pulmonary infarction. Note appearance of S_1Q_3 pattern associated with increasing clockwise rotation and pattern of incomplete right bundle-branch block in the tracings after pulmonary infarction. (*B, C,* and *D* obtained 1, 3, and 19 days after acute episode, respectively.) Note also close resemblance to a posterior wall myocardial infarction.

recurrent pulmonary embolization in thrombophlebitis or phlebothrombosis of the pelvis or lower extremities. Elimination of predisposing factors prior to major surgery and/or institution of anticoagulant treatment immediately after operation is of considerable prophylactic importance. Weight reduction, treatment of varicosities, and eradication of foci of infection are of great value. Once pulmonary embolization and/or infarction has occurred, treatment is directed at (1) the control of the circulatory reaction to embolism, (2) relief of symptoms resulting from infarction, and (3) prevention of recurrent embolism. Control of the circulatory reaction may be very difficult. The use of atropine in large doses has produced equivocal results. Attempts at the reduction of the sudden elevation of pulmonary artery pressure often fail, since nearly all the drugs available for this purpose also reduce the peripheral arterial pressure. Thus, various ganglionic blocking agents, including such drugs as tetraethylammonium (Etamon) and hexamethonium, have been more or less abandoned. Intravenous papaverine and amino-

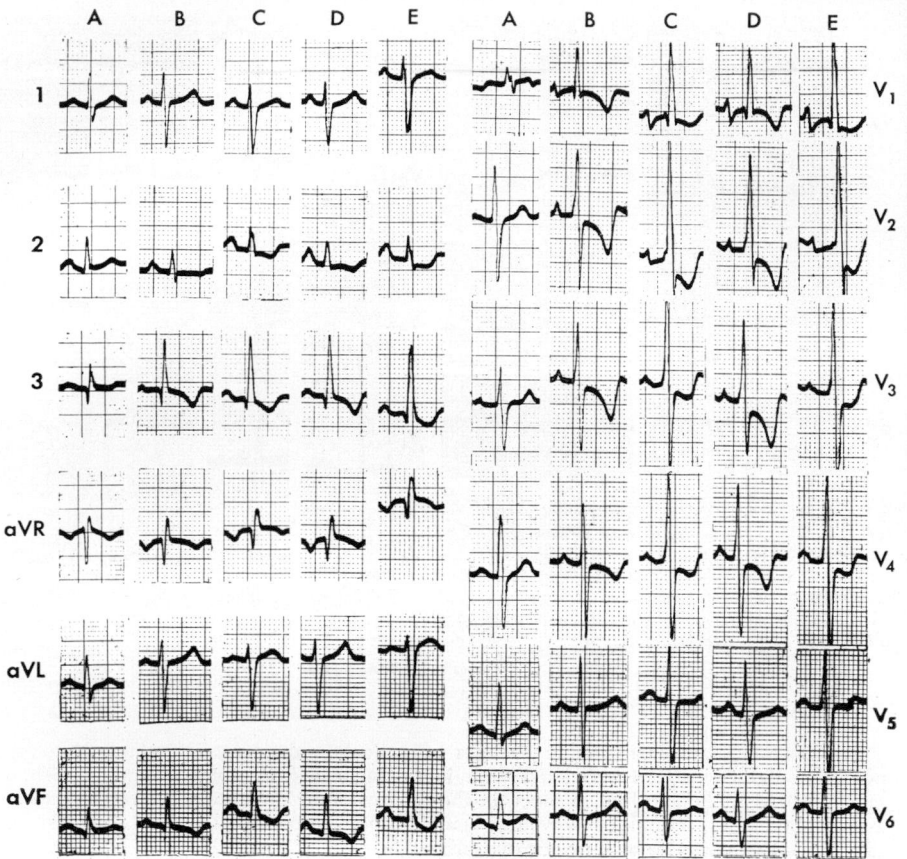

Fig. 5-4B. Recurrent pulmonary infarctions. Note appearance of right ventricular strain pattern following initial episode (*B*) and exacerbation following each recurrent episode (*D* and *E*).

phylline may be useful. Symptomatic relief of pleuritic pain and cough is afforded by narcotics. Circumscribed pain may be treated by local intercostal infiltration with procaine. Antibiotics are administered in order to prevent secondary infection of the infarcted area.

Further embolization is prevented by the initial use of heparin and concomitant and continued oral anticoagulant therapy. This should be continued for a period of at least four to six weeks following the onset of embolization. Heparin may also be administered by continuous infusion or by intermittent intravenous or subcutaneous injections. Its great expense and the necessity for frequent injections have not popularized this form of treatment. Thrombolysin is now most effective in dissolving a fresh clot when administered early and intravenously.

Pulmonary artery thrombosis. Thrombotic occlusion of the pulmonary

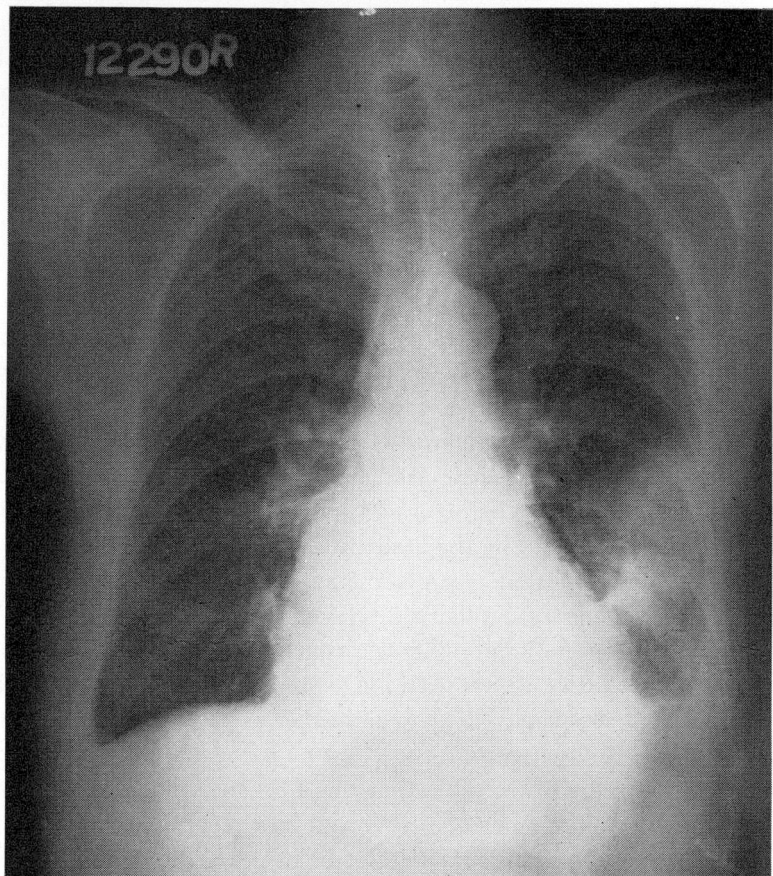

Fig. 5-5. Pulmonary infarction. Note consolidation and secondary pleural effusion at left base.

arteries may occur with or without associated diseases of the lungs, heart, and occasionally the gastrointestinal tract (especially the pancreas and stomach). Increased coagulability of the blood due to many blood dyscrasias and pulmonary hypertension are also factors. Syncope, dyspnea, or chest pain may be insidious. Eventually, pain and dyspnea may be out of proportion to the underlying disease. Frequently, there is early onset of progressive right ventricular failure. The clinical picture may resemble closely that of primary pulmonary hypertension (see p. 118). In many instances, the underlying chronic pulmonary disease may overshadow the symptoms and signs arising from the pulmonary artery thrombosis. Pulmonary abscess may occasionally develop in the area of infarction.

The roentgen film may reveal an abnormal hilar shadow due to enlargement of the pulmonary artery. Because of the vascular obstruction, the lung fields appear abnormally clear as a result of the marked decrease of vascular markings. On fluoroscopy or kymography, there may be diminished or absent hilar pulsation in the affected hilum. Angiocardiography can confirm the presence of pulmonary obstruction when massive thrombosis is suspected. Treatment should include antibiotics to prevent secondary pulmonary infection and anticoagulants to prevent extension of the thrombosis or embolization. With the patient in fair condition, surgical removal of the thrombus in a major branch may be attempted. However, the recent introduction of fibrinolytic enzyme therapy may permit solution of thrombi.

Infectious diseases of the lungs. Chest pain occurs in a large number of specific infections of the lungs (see Table 5-4). The pain does not originate in the lungs, which do not possess pain fibers, but is derived from nerve fibers of the bronchi or the pleura. Thus, pulmonary infections which involve the bronchial tract to an appreciable degree may be associated with chest pain. This is usually characterized by mild substernal soreness, burning, or "rawness," at times aggravated by respiration or by the occasional occurrence of slight substernal pressure. Since some pulmonary infections tend to involve the pleura, a pleuritic type of pain is quite common. When secondary bronchospasm is prominent, a constrictive or choking discomfort may be experienced. In patients with long-standing asthma, any acute bronchopulmonary infection may lead to a further increase of the pulmonary hypertension due to the hypoxia. The chest pain encountered in pulmonary hypertension may closely resemble that due to myocardial ischemia. When the diaphragmatic surface becomes involved in a pleuropulmonary process, pain may be experienced in the shoulder or neck on the affected side and is usually quite sharp.

In pleuropulmonary amebiasis, three major syndromes may be encountered: (1) diffuse pleuropulmonary involvement of the base of the right lung; (2) parenchymatous foci, either pneumonic or in the form of disseminated infiltrates; and (3) serofibrinous pleural effusions. Amebic hepatitis is invariably found in these patients. Chest and shoulder pain may also occur as a result of diaphragmatic involvement.

Middle lobe syndrome. This syndrome is prone to develop after any inflammatory or other process in the chest that gives rise to enlarged hilar nodes on the right side. Although enlarged hilar nodes encroach upon the contiguous bronchi, the right middle lobe bronchus is peculiarly susceptible, since it originates at a very acute angle and is almost entirely surrounded by lymph nodes. Tuberculous hilar adenopathy is the most common etiologic factor, but it has been also described in other pulmonary infections as well

Table 5-4

Classification of Pneumonias °

I. Bacterial
   a. Pneumococci
   b. Streptococci
   c. Staphylococci
   d. Klebsiella pneumoniae
   e. Hemophilus infections
      1. Pertussis
      2. H. influenzae
   f. Pasteurella infections
      1. Pasteurella pestis
      2. Pasteurella tularensis
   g. Coliform, proteus, and pseudomonas (gram-negative bacilli present in the intestinal tract)
   h. Salmonella group
      1. Typhoid
      2. Paratyphoid A, B, and C.
   i. Brucella
   j. Anthrax
   k. Glanders

II. Viral (known and probable)
   a. Psittacosis
   b. Influenza A & B
   c. Variola
   d. Varicella
   e. Rubella
   f. Lymphocytic choriomeningitis
   g. Primary pneumonitis of infants
   h. Infectious mononucleosis
   i. Erythema exudativum multiforme
   j. Primary atypical pneumonia

III. Rickettsial
   a. Typhus
   b. Rocky Mountain spotted fever
   c. Q fever

IV. Mycoses (producing a pneumonia-like picture)
   a. Actinomycosis
   b. Nocardiosis
   c. Blastomycosis
   d. Coccidioidomycosis
   e. Histoplasmosis
   f. Moniliasis
   g. Cryptococcosis
   h. Aspergillosis
   i. Geotrichosis
   j. Penicilliosis
   k. Sporotrichosis

° Committee on Chemotherapy and Antibiotics: Chemotherapy of specific infectious diseases of the lower respiratory tract: report of the Committee. *Dis. Chest,* **33**:203, 1947.

as in lymphoblastomata or direct invasion or stricture of this bronchus. The symptoms consist of chronic cough, hemoptysis, and chest distress of the type encountered in asthma or pneumonitis. The x-ray films reveal an atelectatic right middle lobe in the posteroanterior or oblique views. Bronchoscopy may become necessary to exclude an endobronchial lesion. The treatment consists of removal of the affected lobe, since it rarely regains its normal function but almost always degenerates despite seemingly adequate medical therapy.

Hamman-Rich syndrome. This condition is characterized by a fulminating diffuse interstitial fibrosis of the lungs of unknown cause. The symptoms at the onset often resemble those of chronic bronchitis. After a period of months to years, progressively increasing dyspnea, orthopnea, and cyanosis make their appearance. Pain in the chest, bloody expectoration, and a nonproductive, paroxysmal cough are common. There is no fever, leukocytosis, or increased sedimentation rate, unless intercurrent infection occurs. The dyspnea is not due to ventilatory insufficiency, such as occurs in emphysema; it is a result of interference with gas exchange by the presence of interstitial fibrosis and the resultant "alveolar capillary block." (See Table 5-5.) Evidences of chronic cor pulmonale with clubbing of the fingers and secondary polycythemia may develop. Roentgen study shows bilateral reticulations of the lung fields with increased hilar and vascular markings. The antiinflammatory effect of corticosteroids appears to inhibit the deposition of fibrotic tissue, thus increasing the duration of life. Death usually results from intercurrent pulmonary infection or right heart failure due to resulting chronic cor pulmonale.

Polyarteritis nodosa is a systemic disease involving the small and medium-sized arteries which may affect the lung in a considerable percentage of cases (33 per cent). The respiratory illness generally precedes evidence of periarteritis in other organs and is suggestive of pneumonia, bronchitis, or asthma. Radiologically, the appearance of the lesions is variable, and no specific patterns can be recognized. A diagnosis of polyarteritis nodosa should be considered whenever an atypical pulmonary disease coexists with unexplained lesions in other organs, and especially in the presence of eosinophilia or asthma. Its early recognition is vital, since the introduction of corticosteroids and corticotropin has occasionally controlled the progress of the disorder.

Primary pulmonary hypertension. This condition of unknown cause resembles essential hypertension of the systemic circulation in that it is associated with an abnormal increase of the arteriolar resistance of the lesser circulation. Vascular changes of the lungs induced by hypertension include marked intimal thickening in the small arteries and arterioles, atheromatous

Table 5-5

Pulmonary Function Evaluation in Chronic Obstructive Pulmonary Disease

	Predicted	Determined	% of Predicted	Normal Values
Lung Volumes (BTPS)				
Inspiratory capacity		1649 ml		3600 ml
Expiratory reserve volume		780 ml		1200 ml
Vital capacity	3284 ml	2429 ml	74	>80%
Residual volume (RV)	1461 ml	2635 ml	180	<140%
Functional residual capacity		3415 ml		2400 ml
Total lung capacity (TLC)	4745 ml	5064 ml	107	
RV/TLC × 100		52%		20%
Ventilation (BTPS)				
Tidal volume		374 ml		400–800 ml
Frequency		20/min		12/min
Minute volume		7.48 l/min		6–8 l/min
Respiratory dead space		221 ml		150 ml
Alveolar ventilation		3.06 l/min		4–6 l/min
Distribution of Inspired Gas				
Pulmonary nitrogen empty-				
ing rate (7-min test)		7.34%		<2.5%
Alveolar Ventilation/Pulmonary				
Capillary Blood Flow				
Dead space/tidal volume				
ratio		59%		<30%
Venous admixture		25%		<10%
Alveolar Gas				
Oxygen partial pressure		92 mm Hg		100–110 mm Hg
Carbon dioxide partial pres-				
sure		52 mm Hg		38–43 mm Hg
Gas Exchange				
O_2 consumed		132 ml/min		200–250 ml/min
CO_2 output		114 ml/min		200–250 ml/min
Respiratory exchange ratio				
(CO_2 output/O_2 consumed)		0.867		0.800
Arterial Blood				
O_2 saturation (% saturation				
of Hb with O_2)		92%		94–98%
O_2 tension		65 mm Hg		80–95 mm Hg
CO_2 tension		52 mm Hg		38–43 mm Hg
Alveolar-arterial PO_2 dif-				
ference		27 mm Hg		<10 mm Hg
pH		7.33		7.38–7.43
Mechanics of Breathing				
Maximum breathing capacity				
(BTPS)		16.7 l/min		
Predicted M.B.C.		87.0 l/min		
% of predicted M.B.C.		19%		>80%
Timed vital capacity				
1 second		39%		>75%
3 seconds		61%		>95%

(Courtesy of P. Glass, biochemist, Brooklyn Veterans Administration Hospital, Brooklyn, N.Y.)

plaques, and hypertrophy of the media. Occasionally, degeneration of the media and the elastica may be noted in the arterioles. The definitive diagnosis can be established by cardiac catheterization. The most significant findings are elevation of pulmonary artery pressures and increased vascular resistance. Pulmonary capillary pressure is at the lower limits of normal. Arterial oxygen saturation is somewhat decreased, and cardiac minute output is reduced.

Chest pain, exertional dyspnea, cyanosis, fatigue, and syncope are early symptoms of primary pulmonary hypertension. Precordial aching pain which is indistinguishable from angina pectoris may occur during exertion. However, syncopal attacks are not related to exertion and are unaccompanied by chest pain or palpitation. Dizzy spells may occur without syncope.

The electrocardiogram presents a characteristic picture of right ventricular strain pattern, and the roentgenogram reveals prominence of the main pulmonary artery, pulmonary conus, and right ventricular hypertrophy. Though definitive diagnosis is made only by biopsy or post-mortal examination, a presumptive diagnosis may be reached by exclusion of conditions known to cause secondary pulmonary hypertension. The clinical course terminates with right-sided failure and death.

Tumors of the lung. Chest pain is frequently present in patients with neoplasms of the lung. It was reported in 50 to 62 per cent of a large series of cases of primary cancer of the lung. It has also been described in eosinophilic granuloma of the lung.

Symptoms produced by carcinoma of the lung depend mainly on the location of the tumor (see Fig. 5-6). This may be (1) in the main bronchus, (2) in the lobar bronchus, (3) in the midlung, and (4) below the pleura.

The early symptoms of bronchial malignancies are those of bronchial irritation and eventually of obstruction to the air passage. They include cough (dry initially and productive later), hemoptysis, and localized wheezing. Chest discomfort is rarely present in the early stages and is then usually of vague character. In this group of cases, bronchoscopy is extremely valuable for the early detection of cancer, since the x-ray usually reveals secondary effects of the tumor.

In the second category, the symptoms are similar but most commonly associated with symptoms and signs of an acute bronchopulmonary infection which occurs distally to the obstructive lesion. The infectious element frequently masks the underlying malignancy. Therefore, any persistent respiratory infection severe enough to warrant antibiotic therapy should have serial chest roentgenograms. The persistence of an x-ray shadow following

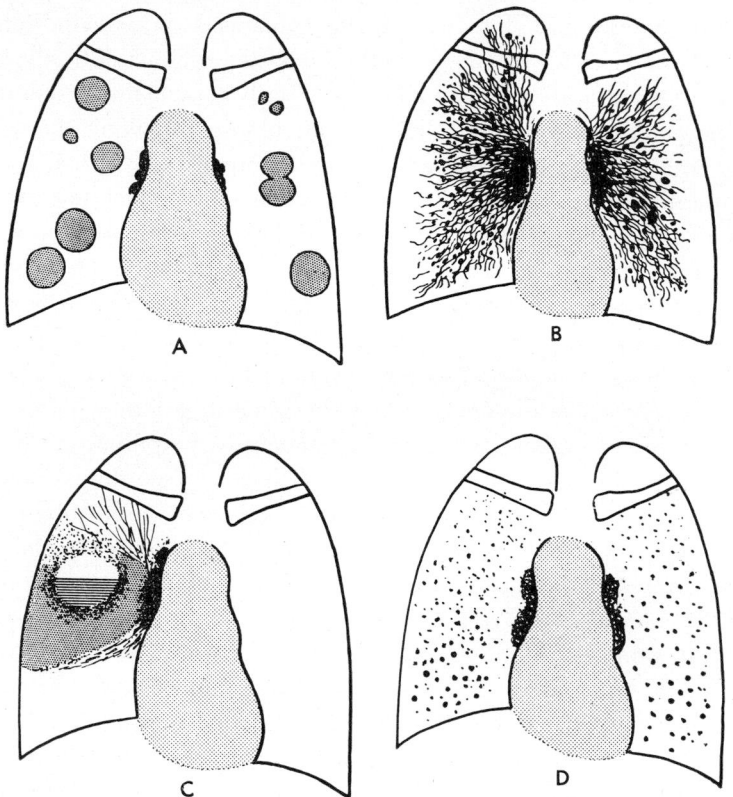

Fig. 5-6. *A*, Secondary pulmonary tumor, nodular type. *B*, Secondary pulmonary tumor, lymphangitic type with nodular infiltrations. *C*, Secondary pulmonary tumor, pneumonic type with cavitation. *D*, Secondary pulmonary tumor, miliary carcinomatosis. (From Markovits, E.: *Visceral Radiology.* The Macmillan Co., New York, 1951.)

the subsidence of an acute infection should lead to further investigation for a possible presence of carcinoma.

The third type, the midlung cancer, rarely causes chest discomfort. A mild pneumonitis is the most prominent finding in this type of lesion. It is frequently asymptomatic, and the differential diagnosis commonly involves the so-called "solitary," or "coin" lesion.

Finally, the occasional subpleural lesion is commonly associated with pleural pain which is due to an acute pleurisy and which may persist. The circumthoracic radiation of intercostal pain is indicative of the involvement of the intercostal nerves. Cough is a late symptom, and hemoptysis occurs rarely, since the lesion is far removed from the larger bronchi.

Thus, chest pain may occur in all types of pulmonary cancer with involvement of the pleura and chest wall during advanced stages. The diagnostic means for the detection of cancer of the lung may include not only conventional roentgenography and bronchography with Papanicolaou staining, but also tomography, scalene node biopsy, and biopsy following thoracotomy.

Other lesions to be differentiated include sarcoma, bronchial adenoma, metastatic tumors, tuberculoma, histoplasmoma, coccidioidal granuloma, hamartoma, bronchogenic cyst, mesothelioma, lipoid granuloma, pulmonary arteriovenous aneurysm, and hemangioma. As regards the indications for surgical or radiation treatment and chemotherapy, the reader is referred to any standard text on pulmonary diseases.

"Smoker's lung." The possible relationship of tobacco smoking and cancer of the lung has led to numerous and varied investigations which have not proved conclusive to date. However, precancerous symptoms and lesions in smokers have been described on many occasions. According to some investigators, a "smoker's respiratory syndrome" can also be distinguished. It is characterized by a clear-cut triad consisting of (1) chronic pharyngitis, (2) wheezing and dyspnea, and (3) a tendency to respiratory infections. Eventually, chronic bronchitis ("smoker's cough") may dominate the picture. Chest pains and tightness also occur in tobacco-sensitive individuals. These are rhythmic, darting, and anginoid in character. They occur in practically any part of the thorax but are most frequent around the heart and hypogastrium and may radiate into the neck and arms. They are also associated with a sensation of precordial constriction and premature contractions. These symptoms tend to disappear following the cessation of the smoking habit.

Cystic disease of the lung. This is usually a congenital abnormality, probably caused by the early isolation of a small lung bud in the parenchyma or in the mediastinum. It is usually solitary but occasionally may be multiplied and scattered throughout both lungs. Congenital cysts of the lung are compatible with a long life and may never come to light unless infection supervenes or unless they are discovered in a routine film of the chest. Chest pain may be secondary to bronchopulmonary infection, or it may be due to pneumothorax as a result of the rupture of a subpleural cyst. The development of a high intrathoracic pressure and mediastinal shift produces marked respiratory difficulty. Cysts are a frequent cause of lung disease and not uncommonly masquerade as malignancy, bronchiectasis, and, occasionally, tuberculosis. The differentiation of emphysematous bulla, diaphragmatic hernia, or pneumothorax depends mainly on the x-ray film as well as tomograms and bronchograms. Treatment is surgical and consists of careful excision of the involved pulmonary segment.

Trauma of pleura and lungs. Most features of pneumothorax due to trauma and other causes have been considered previously. Generally, trauma to the thorax may result in hemorrhage into the lung tissue as a result of tears in the pulmonary arterial or venous systems. Since the pressures in the pulmonary system are low (about 20 mm Hg), fatal hemorrhage is uncommon except in extensive wounds directly involving major pulmonary vessels. Blast injuries are capable of producing multiple small hemorrhages in lung tissue due to rupture of tiny vessels caused by transmission of the blast waves.

Small *lacerations* in lung parenchyma caused by fractured ribs or sharp objects will often seal themselves, and a tension pneumothorax will not develop. The seriousness and extent of the pneumothorax will depend, therefore, upon the size of the bronchi injured. If a ball-valve action is produced at the site of the injury and air constantly enters the pleural space and cannot escape, the resulting tension pneumothorax may be fatal.

The possibility of a *fracture* of a bronchus or even the trachea should be considered in all cases of severe pneumothorax associated with emphysema. The following findings suggest the possibility of a fracture of a major bronchus: a tension pneumothorax with associated subcutaneous and mediastinal emphysema, and atelectasis of the lobe or lung in connection with the tension pneumothorax. There is often little or no evidence of associated fractures of ribs with minimal hemothorax considering the gravity of the wound.

Subcutaneous emphysema may result from penetration of the lung by fractured ribs or, in patients with tension pneumothorax and injury to the chest wall, from allowing the air to take the line of least resistance into the tissues of the chest wall, particularly the subcutaneous tissues. Dissection of air (crepitus) may progress into the neck, face, and sometimes over the entire body surface. The type of chest distress is often modified by the additional presence of thoracic pain due to the injury to the chest wall and its structures, such as the ribs, sternum, and muscles. Other features of pneumothorax have been discussed elsewhere (see pp. 100–103).

REFERENCES

Anderson, M. C., and Shields, T. W.: Significance of fatal pulmonary embolism in immediate postoperative period. *J.A.M.A.*, **161**:422, 1958.

Ball, K. P.; Goodwin, J. F.; and Harrison, C. V.: Massive thrombotic occlusion of the large pulmonary arteries. *Circulation*, **14**:766, 1956.

Barry, F., Jr.: Infrapulmonary pleural effusion. *North Carolina M.J.*, **18**:148, 1957.

Bauer, G.: Heparin therapy in acute deep venous thrombosis. *J.A.M.A.*, **131**:196, 1946.

Bean, C. N.: Bronchiectasis: Concepts of therapy. *Dis. Chest*, **30**:202, 1956.

Benoit, H. W., Jr., and Ackerman, L. V.: Solitary pleural mesotheliomas. *J. Thoracic Surg.*, **25**:346, 1953.

Blades, B.: Management of injuries to the thorax. *J.A.M.A.*, **159**:419, 1955.

Breckler, I. A.; Hensler, N. M.; Hill, H. E.; Hoffman, M.; and Hukill, P. B.: Biopsy technics in the diagnosis of intrathoracic disease. *Ann. Int. Med.*, **46**:706, 1947.

Brewer, L. A.; Bai, A. F.; Little, J. N.; and Rabagoy, P. G.: Carcinoma of the lung. *J.A.M.A.*, **166**:1149, 1958.

Calvert, R. J., and Smith, E.: Analytical review of spontaneous hemopneumothorax. *Thorax*, **10**:64, 1955.

Campbell, G. S., and Varco, R. L.: Management of spontaneous pneumothorax. *Lancet*, **77**:443, 1957.

Coirault, R.; Coudreau, H.; and Girard, J.: Nonsuppurative intrathoracic complications of amebiasis. *Semaine hôp. Paris*, **31**:1591, 1955.

Coutinho, A.: Tropical eosinophilia. *Ann. Int. Med.*, **44**:88, 1956.

Daniels, A. C., and Childress, A. E.: Pleuropulmonary amebiasis. *California Med.*, **85**:369, 1956.

DeLaughter, G. D., Jr., and Anlyan, W. G.: A clinical study of pulmonary embolism. *Surg., Gyec. & Obst.*, **103**:695, 1956.

Dittler, E. L.: Unorthodox clinical and roentgenological features of pulmonary embolism. *Dis. Chest*, **29**:215, 1956.

Ehrenhaft, J. L.; Taber, R. E.; and Lawrence, M. S.: Spontaneous pneumothorax, a review with the results of pulmonary resection in nineteen patients. *Am. Rev. Tuberc.*, **72**:801, 1955.

Finn, J. J.; Weller, T. H.; and Morgan, H. R.: Epidemic pleurodynia: clinical and etiologic studies based on one hundred and fourteen cases. *Arch. Int. Med.*, **83**:305, 1949.

Heaney, J. P.; Overton, R. C.; and DeBakey, M. E.: Benign localized pleural mesothelioma: report of two cases. *J. Thoracic Surg.*, **34**:553, 1957.

Horwitz, M., and Findlay, W.: Supraclavicular lymph node biopsy in the diagnosis of intrathoracic lesions. *New York J. Med.*, **57**:2065, 1957.

Hussey, H., and Katz, S.: Pulmonary embolism. *GP*, **12**:59, 1955.

Israel, H. L., and Goldstein, F.: Clinical manifestations of pulmonary embolism. *Ann. Int. Med.*, **47**:202, 1957.

Kircher, L. T., Jr., and Swartzel, R. L.: Spontaneous pneumothorax and its treatment. *J.A.M.A.*, **155**:24, 1954.

Krause, S., and Silverblatt, M.: Pulmonary embolism: a review with emphasis on clinical and electrocardiographic diagnosis. *A.M.A. Arch. Int. Med.*, **96**:19, 1955.

Kuida, H.; Dammin, J.; Haynes, F. W.; Rapaport, E.; and Dexter, L.: Primary pulmonary hypertension. *Am. J. Med.*, **23**:166, 1957.

Lindskog, G. E.: Present-day management of pleural empyema in infants and adults. *New England J. Med.*, **255**:320, 1956.

Mazzitello, W. F.: Eosinophilic granuloma of the lung. *New England J. Med.*, **250**:804, 1954.

Moore, S. W., and Cole, D. R.: Primary malignant neoplasms of the lung. *Ann. Surg.*, **141**:457, 1955.

Myers, J. A.: Simple spontaneous pneumothorax. *Dis. Chest*, **26**:420, 1954.

Myers, J. A.: Tuberculous pleurisy with effusion. *A.M.A. Arch. Int. Med.*, **96**:191, 1955.

Nix, J. T.; Albert, M.; Dugas, J. E.; and Wendt, D. L.: Chylothorax and chylous ascites: a study of 302 selected cases. *Am. J. Gastroenterol.*, **28**:40, 1957.

Race, G. A.; Scheifley, C. H.; and Edwards, J. E.: Hydrothorax in congestive heart failure. *Am. J. Med.*, **22**:83, 1957.

Reich, N. E.: Protean manifestations of acute rheumatic fever. *Am. Pract. & Digest Treat.*, **12**:645, 1947.

Reich, N. E.: Pulmonary complications of heart disease. *Dis. Chest*, **25**:649, 1954.

Reich, N. E.: Pulmonary diseases secondary to heart diseases. *Am. J. Surg.*, **89**:252, 1955.

Reich, N. E., et al.: Primary atypical pneumonia: the diagnosis and treatment of 440 consecutive cases without a fatality. *Am. Pract. & Digest Treat.*, **2**:85, 1947.

Ring, A., and Bakke, J. R.: Chronic massive pulmonary artery thrombosis. *Ann. Int. Med.*, **43**:781, 1955.

Rose, G. A.: Clinical features of polyarteritis nodosa with lung involvement. *Brit. J. Tuberc.*, **51**:113, 1957.

Rubin, E. H., and Lubliner, R.: The Hamman-Rich syndrome: review of the literature and analysis of 15 cases. *Medicine*, **36**:397, 1957.

Sada, E., and Ravetta, A.: Use of cortisone and hydrocortisone in treatment of pleural effusion. *Minerva med.*, **47**:1896, 1956.

Scott, S. M.: A critical review of one hundred and sixty consecutive scalene node biopsies. *Am. Rev. Tuberc.*, **76**:1002, 1957.

Small, M. J., and Landman, M. E.: Etiological diagnosis of pleural effusion by pleural biopsy. *J.A.M.A.*, **158**:11, 1955.

Thomas, P. A., and Gebauer, P. W.: Pleurectomy for recurrent spontaneous pneumothorax. *J. Thoracic Surg.*, **35**:111, 1958.

Tinney, W. S., and Olsen, A. M.: The significance of fluid in the pleural space. *J. Thoracic Surg.*, **14**:248, 1945.

Towbin, A.: Pulmonary embolism. Incidence and significance. *J.A.M.A.*, **156**:209, 1954.

Tramujas, A., and Artigas, G. V.: Malignant mesothelioma of the pleura. *Dis. Chest*, **32**:340, 1957.

Waldbott, G. L.: Further observation on smoker's respiratory syndrome. *Ann. Int. Med.*, **39**:1026, 1953.

White, F. C.: Chronic pulmonary disease in histoplasmin reactors: a review of 229 cases discovered through chest clinic examinations. *Am. Rev. Tuberc.*, **72**:274, 1955.

CHAPTER 6 *MEDIASTINAL ORIGINS OF CHEST PAIN*

The mediastinum is that part of the thoracic cavity contained between the right and left pleural sacs. A line from the manubriosternal angle to the fourth thoracic vertebra divides the mediastinum into superior and inferior compartments, while the heart itself separates the inferior part into anterior, middle, and posterior portions. Many vital structures are crowded into the relatively small space of the mediastinum (see Fig. 6-1). These include the heart and its great vessels, thymus, trachea, bronchi, esophagus, thoracic duct, lymph nodes, and important nerve plexi, especially the phrenic, vagus, and recurrent laryngeal nerves.

127

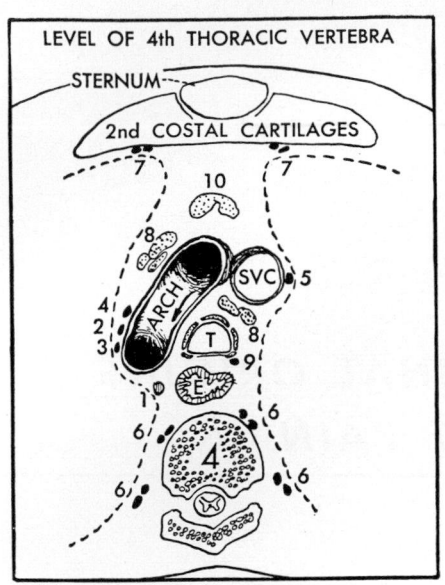

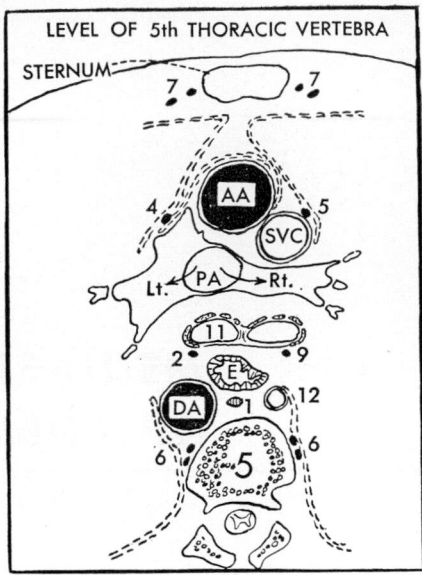

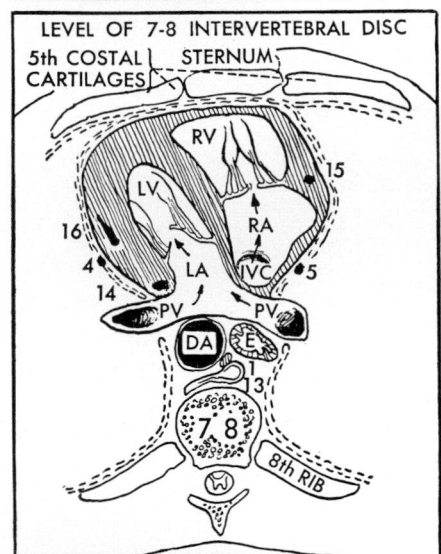

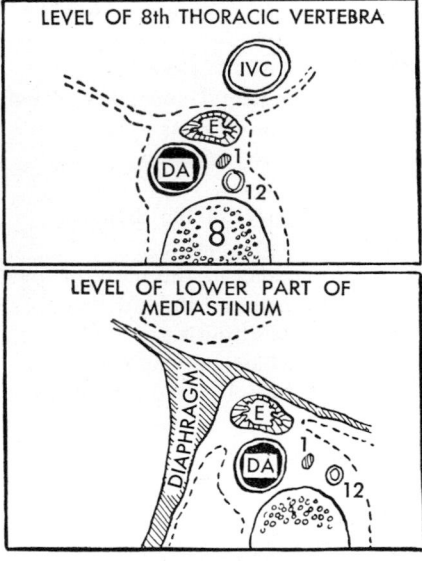

Fig. 6-1. Relation of mediastinal structures by means of transverse sections.

T	Trachea	1	Thoracic duct	8	Lymph glands
E	Esophagus	2	Left vagus nerve	9	Right vagus nerve
SVC	Superior vena cava	3	Left recurrent	10	Remains of thymus gland
IVC	Inferior vena cava		laryngeal nerve	11	Carina of trachea
PA	Pulmonary artery	4	Left phrenic nerve	12	Azygos vein
PV	Pulmonary vein	5	Right phrenic nerve	13	Superior hemiazygos
AA	Ascending aorta	6	Intercostal vessels	14	Coronary sinus
DA	Descending aorta	7	Internal mammary	15	Right coronary artery
			vessels	16	Left coronary artery

Dotted lines: serosal surfaces

(From Reich, N. E.: *Diseases of the Aorta.* The Macmillan Co., New York, 1949.)

Pressure, inflammation, or invasion of the mediastinal contents may cause pain which may vary from a vague intrathoracic discomfort to severe pain which is referred to many areas. Symptoms and signs of more or less specific or localizing character may appear. For example, compression of the aortic branches may lead to a marked difference in the blood pressure readings in both arms. Obstruction or pressure on the superior vena cava produces a syndrome characterized by edema and congestion of the head, neck, and upper extremities; cyanosis; exophthalmos; and dilatation of veins over the neck, chest, and arms. An inferior vena caval syndrome may similarly affect the lower half of the body.

Interference with the cardiac output or with the venous return by large tumors, scar tissue, or effusion may cause tamponade or congestive heart failure. Dyspnea, stridor, and dry cough suggest compression of the trachea or bronchi; dysphagia and regurgitation may indicate involvement of the esophagus. Chylothorax or chylous ascites (discussed on p. 106) can follow obstruction or rupture of the thoracic duct. Pressure or invasion of several important nerves will produce characteristic clinical pictures: recurrent laryngeal nerve, hoarseness; roots of the cervical sympathetics, Horner's syndrome; phrenic nerve, hiccup or diaphragmatic paralysis; vagus, brady-cardia; and intercostal nerves, neuralgia. Even after the location of a tumor mass has been ascertained following various diagnostic procedures, uncertainty may remain as to the exact nature of the lesion, and exploratory thoracotomy may be indicated. A large number of mediastinal masses of varied etiology will first be considered. Subsequently, in Chapters 7 and 8, significant disorders of two major mediastinal structures (esophagus and aorta) will be discussed. This sequence seems especially appropriate because they lie in close proximity in the posterior mediastinum.

MEDIASTINAL MASSES

Tumors of the *anterior* mediastinum are commonly cystic or solid tera-tomas, lipomas, thymomas, or pericardial celomic cysts. Tumors of the *posterior* mediastinum and the posterior aspect of the superior mediastinum are generally of neurogenic origin (neurilemmoma, neurofibroma, gangli-oneuroma, and sympathicoblastoma). (See Fig. 6-2.) Not infrequently, mediastinal tumors are asymptomatic and discovered on routine x-ray. A mediastinoscope can now be introduced through an incision in the supra-sternal notch. Exploratory thoracotomy can often be avoided if the extent of a bronchial carcinoma or the presence of a questionable lesion is first as-sessed by mediastinoscopy; this permits inspection and biopsy of any sus-

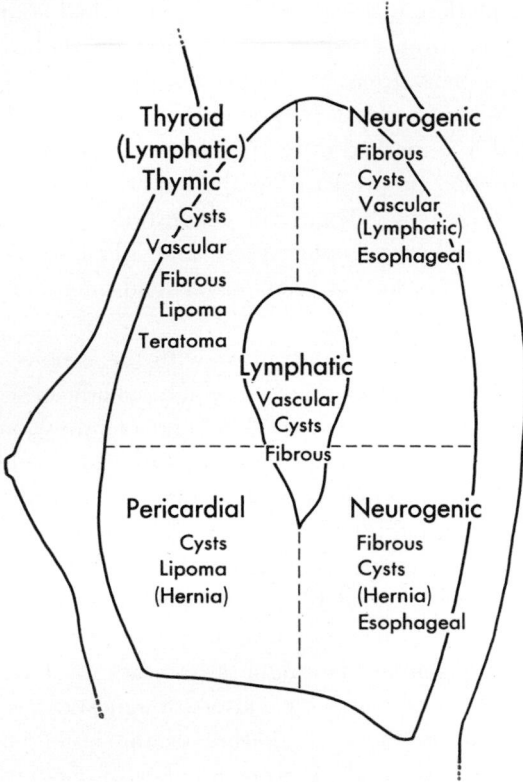

Thyroid
(Lymphatic)
Thymic
Cysts
Vascular
Fibrous
Lipoma
Teratoma

Neurogenic
Fibrous
Cysts
Vascular
(Lymphatic)
Esophageal

Lymphatic
Vascular
Cysts
Fibrous

Pericardial
Cysts
Lipoma
(Hernia)

Neurogenic
Fibrous
Cysts
(Hernia)
Esophageal

Fig. 6-2. Most common location of mediastinal tumors. Hernias are also shown, since they present tumor-like shadows. (From Overholt, R. H., and Neptune, N. B.: Hazards to the host of benign intrathoracic tumors. *J.A.M.A.*, **170**:664, 1959.)

picious area. Occasionally, mediastinal tumors may cause dyspnea, cyanosis, and even syncope without chest pain, particularly in infancy and childhood. Several of the more significant masses capable of producing thoracic pain are now considered.

Chest pain is especially frequent with *teratomata* and may occur as an isolated symptom or may be associated with cough or dyspnea. The character of the pain is ill defined. These tumors are usually found in the anterior mediastinum and present the roentgenographic appearance of a fairly dense mass which occasionally contains scattered amorphous deposits of calcium. The margins of the mass tend to be well defined.

Congenital anomalies of enterogenous origin may occur as cysts lined with bronchial, esophageal, or gastric epithelium. The cysts tend to lie in the midmediastinum in the region of the bifurcation of the trachea. They may produce severe symptoms of respiratory impairment, at times associated with chest discomfort and pain.

Dermoid cysts are relatively uncommon but usually occur in the anterior mediastinum and may give rise to chest pain. They may be associated with various complications such as infection, perforation, and malignant degeneration. These developments may intensify and modify the chest pain.

Cystic hygromas are comparatively rare but occur more commonly in infants and children. The lesions are made up of masses of dilated lymphatic channels lined with flat endothelium and containing watery, clear fluid. Dyspnea, deep chest pain, and dysphagia may be associated symptoms. The tumor has the roentgenographic appearance of a rather large, unilateral or bilateral mass in the superior mediastinum which usually extends toward the neck and has a well-defined margin.

Lipomas are rarely encountered in the thorax but may be found in the anterior mediastinum. The largest lipomas may exceed the bounds of the mediastinal compartment. Although they are frequently asymptomatic, dyspnea and/or vague, dull chest discomfort may be experienced, especially on stooping over. These tumors are of differential diagnostic significance, since their close proximity and blending with the cardiac silhouette may give the misleading appearance of cardiac enlargement. They also are frequently related to the thymus (lipothymomas) and are found in children between ten to fifteen years of age. Some of them may originate in the thymus itself, as a result of the infiltration of the organ with fat during its involution. Thus, when this tumor is discovered early in life, both thymus and fatty elements may be found. Following normal thymic involution, fatty tissue predominates.

Tumors of the thymus are probably the most common of the anterior mediastinal neoplasms. They are frequently associated with myasthenia gravis, especially when they are benign. Tumors of thymic origin vary widely in gross and microscopic appearance and may be confused with other growths which occur in the anterior mediastinal area, such as undifferentiated bronchogenic carcinomas, lymphosarcomas, or dermoid cysts. The thymus tumors may be solid or cystic, sharply circumscribed or extremely invasive, soft or calcific. *Thymic cysts* may be congenital, inflammatory, or neoplastic. The non-neoplastic, noninflammatory cysts of the thymus are probably congenital in origin. Cysts resulting from infection are mainly due to syphilis and are quite rare. Cysts occurring in thymic neoplasms can probably be attributed to degeneration and necrosis of the tumor. They are potentially malignant. Malignant thymomas may be either lymphomatous or carcinomatous. The differentiation between benign and malignant thymus tumors is at times difficult.

The clinical symptoms are not characteristic. Signs of displacement usually predominate and are similar to those of any mediastinal tumors. An irritating cough and the feeling of pressure behind the sternum are frequent complaints. Pressure of the thymus upon the trachea may cause mechanical interference with respiration. The obstruction produces a picture that resembles a circumscribed bronchial asthma. Clinical symptoms generally do not permit a definite diagnosis, but roentgenologic examination may prove valuable. (See Fig. 6-3.) The lateral view is especially helpful in the visualization of the retrosternal mass which appears sharply delineated. Percussion may reveal an area of parasternal dullness. Muscular weakness,

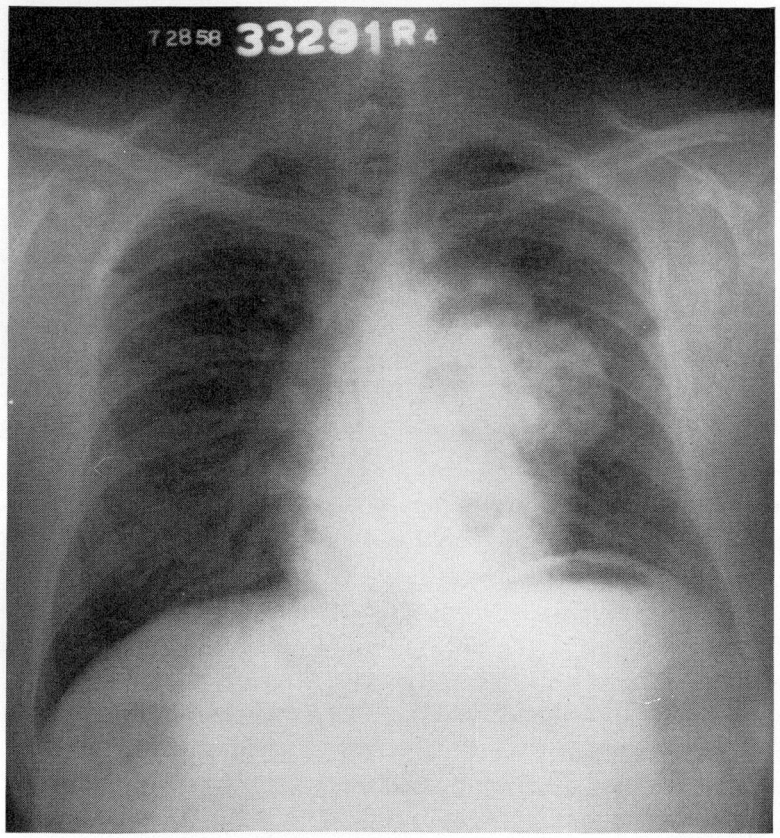

Fig. 6-3. Mediastinal tumor. Large, lobulated soft tissue mass in superior mediastinum. Left diaphragm elevated. Histopathology: malignant tumor, probably of thymic origin.

especially of the muscles of the head and orbicularis oculi, is strongly suggestive of myasthenia gravis. The diagnosis can be readily confirmed by the
rapid response to neostigmine.

Lymphomas are generally of systemic nature, but are frequently discovered initially in the mediastinum on routine chest film and must, therefore, always be included in a differential diagnosis of mediastinal tumors.
Lymph node enlargement gives rise to chest discomfort by compression of
vital structures. The diagnosis is facilitated by appropriate blood studies,
biopsy, and therapeutic response to x-ray therapy and chemotherapeutic
agents.

Tumors of the posterior mediastinum are usually of neurogenic origin.
They may also cause chest discomfort and pain. Their proximity to the
cardiac shadow may be confused with cardiac enlargement, while encroachment upon the lungs may give rise to respiratory symptoms and findings.
They may become massive, especially ganglioneuroma. An accurate differentiation of the various tumors involving the anterior and posterior medias-
tinums and the degree of malignancy almost always demands biopsy or
surgical excision and histologic study.

Substernal thyroid. Enlargements of the thyroid gland which grow downward may be substernal or entirely intrathoracic. The substernal type is
more common. Substernal extension of a goiter can be easily detected as a
pyramidal shadow, with the narrow end extending distally into the superior
mediastinum. The mediastinal portion is continuous with the thyroid enlargement of the neck and may compress the trachea laterally. With true
intrathoracic goiter, no thyroid tissue is palpable in the neck. Intrathoracic
goiters may undergo toxic or malignant changes, but the incidence of such
changes is not unusually high. "Plunging goiter" results when respiration,
swallowing, neck flexion, or gravity displaces the enlarged gland into the
chest. Prolonged coughing or straining may push the mass back into the
neck. This can be confirmed by employing the Valsalva maneuver.

When the growth does not compress any important structures, no signs or
symptoms are noted. The chest discomfort produced by the goiter is usually
due to dysphagia caused by compression of the esophagus. Pressure on the
trachea may cause dyspnea, cough, and inspiratory stridor, particularly
among elderly patients with emphysema. Sudden flexion or extension of the
head or lateral movement can cause tracheal compression with coughing or
choking. There may also be involvement of the recurrent laryngeal nerve
with resultant aphonia. Intrathoracic goiter must be differentiated from
bronchogenic cyst, thymoma, enlarged lymph nodes, and aneurysm of the

arch. Upward movement of the thyroid mass during the act of swallowing is diagnostic upon fluoroscopy because of its attachment to the tracheal region by the long pedicle.

Roentgenologic findings (see Fig. 6-4) may reveal downward displace-

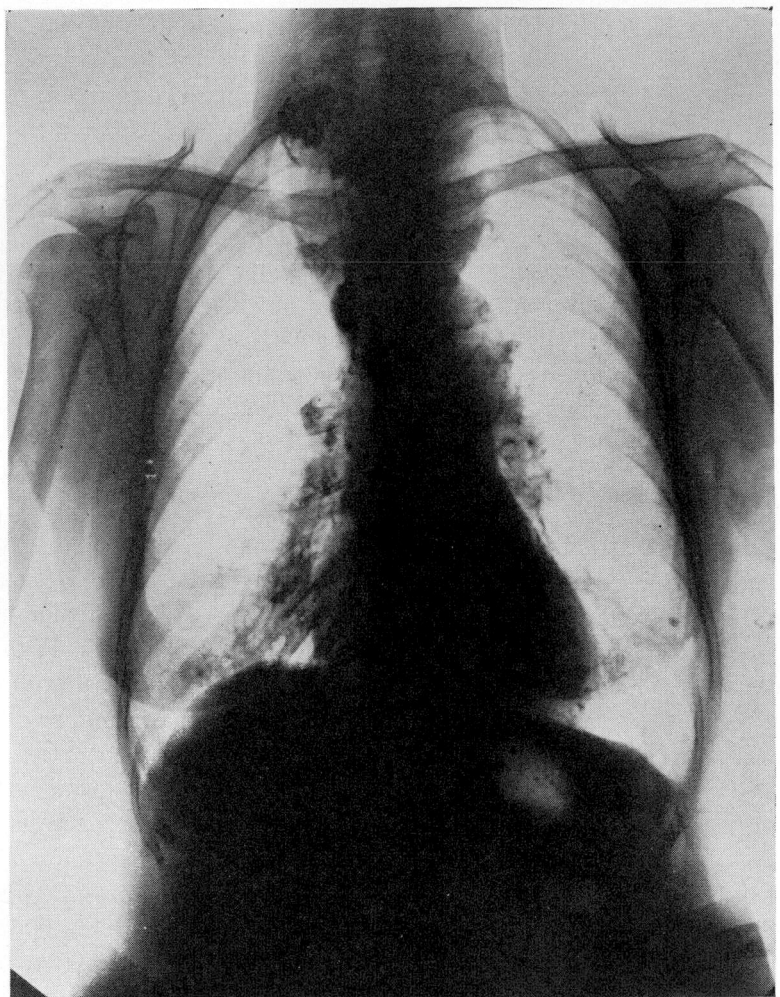

Fig. 6-4. Substernal thyroid in seventy-four-year-old female. Note calcified cysts, calcified costal cartilage, and calcification due to old healed tuberculosis.

ment of the aorta with increasing prominence of the arch. In some cases, the mediastinal shadow appears widened due to displacement of the innominate and subclavian arteries. The trachea and esophagus are often displaced anteriorly. Since they contain little if any functioning thyroid tissue, I[131] uptake studies are usually inadequate for the differential diagnosis. The treatment generally recommended is surgical removal unless the patient's general condition precludes operation. Operation becomes imperative if manifestations of toxicity occur or if compression on mediastinal structure is severe.

Mediastinitis. Inflammatory disorders of the mediastinum (acute mediastinitis) are due to (1) trauma (gunshot or stab wounds), and perforation of the esophagus or trachea by foreign bodies or instruments; (2) secondary infections from contiguous mediastinal structures; or (3) infections from the respiratory tract (empyema and lung abscess) or the neck. The chest pain due to mediastinitis of nonsuppurative character tends to be mild and nebulous. On the other hand, suppurative mediastinitis is accompanied by high fever, chills, sepsis, and prostration. The substernal and interscapular pain is intense. Pain occurs on swallowing and breathing. Mortality and morbidity rates have been markedly improved following intensive antibiotic therapy. When the presence of an abscess becomes evident, surgical exploration and drainage are mandatory. Occasionally, chronic mediastinitis may develop with recurrent symptoms of thoracic discomfort. This depends upon the intrathoracic structure which becomes involved in the ensuing sclerosing process. For example, superior or inferior vena caval syndrome may ensue with the production of characteristic symptoms and findings.

Mediastinal emphysema. Mediastinal emphysema (pneumomediastinum) is an uncommon condition occurring either spontaneously or following direct trauma to the chest or neck or perforation of the air-containing esophagus or trachea. It may also occur following pneumoperitoneum therapy and respiratory diseases such as asthma, influenza, or pneumonia. Spontaneous onset has been attributed to the intrapulmonary dissection of air along the interstitial tissues and bronchial vessels to the hilum and thence into the mediastinum. Its association with pneumothorax has been discussed elsewhere (see pp. 100–103). Air may penetrate to the neck tissues, producing subcutaneous emphysema; to the pleural space, producing pneumothorax; and to the lung tissue, producing interstitial emphysema. (See Fig. 6-5.)

The onset is usually sudden. The accompanying substernal pain is severe, with radiation into the neck and arms. Dyspnea and cyanosis may be present. The acute onset and symptomatic pattern may suggest acute myocardial infarction, pericarditis, or pulmonary embolism. The pain may be intense enough to cause shock. It tends to be worsened by inspiration, movement of the neck, and lying down. When associated with pneumothorax, the condition causes the chest pain to radiate toward the side of the pneumothorax.

Other important symptoms include throat pain, dysphagia, hoarseness or

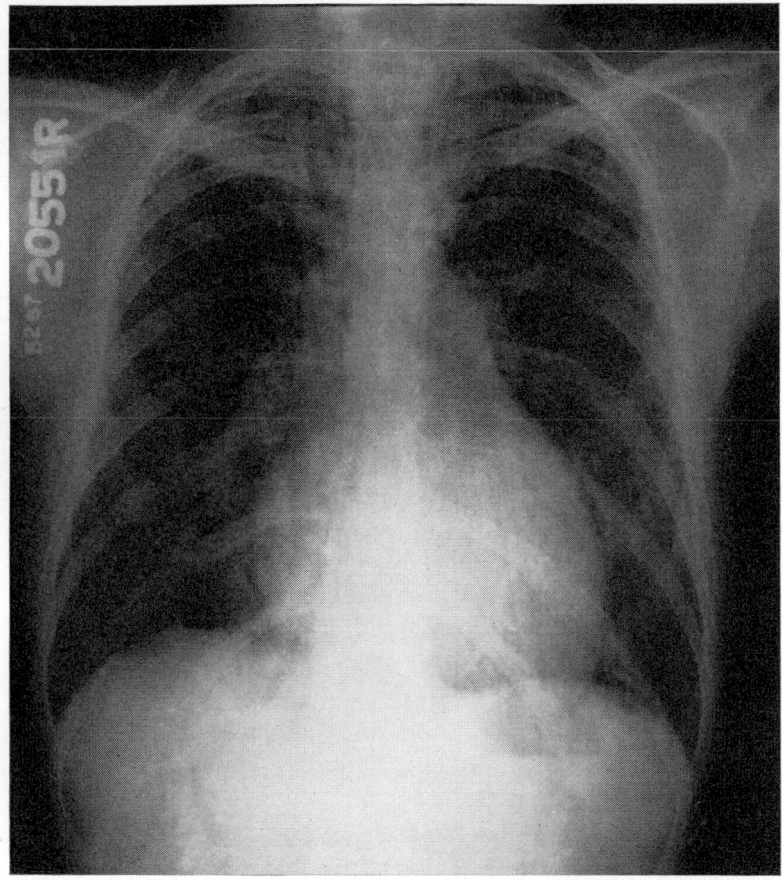

Fig. 6-5. Mediastinal emphysema. Note radiolucent halo around cardiovascular shadow, extending craniad along the superior mediastinum.

aphonia, and a variable degree of dyspnea. Heart sounds become distant
due to the overlying gaseous invasion of tissues. Crepitation, crackling, or
crunching noises may be heard on auscultation or may even be audible at a
considerable distance from the chest. Occasionally, these sounds are heard
when only a small pneumothorax is present without mediastinal emphysema.

No specific treatment is available. The condition is benign and usually
clears up spontaneously. The only complications requiring vigorous and
definitive therapy are tension pneumothorax and secondary infection.

Traumatic mediastinal hematoma. Because of the frequency of accidents,
injury to the mediastinal structure is not unusual. Hematoma may occasionally be found in association with these injuries. Sometimes, there may
be no demonstrable injury to adjacent structures, and hematoma may then

become difficult to diagnose; such a slowly growing mass may arise from venous or arterial bleeding. If the hemorrhage is large, the patient may suffer from esophageal, tracheal, or superior vena caval compression. Pain may be associated with dysphagia, dyspnea, or even shock.

A hematoma that soon decreases in size offers no problem, but one that remains the same size or enlarges slowly must be differentiated from tumors and aneurysms. X-rays show a bilateral widening of the mediastinum with straight, sharp margins; and maximal widening occurs within hours to days. Angiocardiography is helpful in the exclusion of aneurysm or other vascular abnormality. Surgical exploration is indicated if a preoperative diagnosis is not possible or if the enlarging mass causes serious compression.

REFERENCES

Alden, J. F.; Bjornson, R. B. G.; Sterner, E. R.; and Sprafka, J. L.: Mediastinal lipoma. *Dis. Chest,* **32**:580, 1957.

Berger, M.: Mediastinal emphysema as a complication of pneumoperitoneum therapy. *Dis. Chest,* **26**:354, 1954.

Betts, R. H.: The treatment of intrathoracic hydatid disease. *Dis. Chest,* **26**:584, 1954.

Blades, B., and Adkins, F. C.: The management of substernal and intrathoracic goiters. *South. M.J.,* **50**:1123, 1957.

Carlens, E.: Mediastinoscopy: a method for inspection and biopsy in the superior mediastinum. *Dis. Chest,* **36**:343, 1959.

Effler, D. B., and McCormack, L. J.: Thymic neoplasms. *J. Thoracic Surg.,* **31**:60, 1956.

Ellis, F. H., Jr., and Dushane, J. W.: Primary mediastinal cysts and neoplasms in infants and children. *Am. Rev. Tuberc.,* **74**:940, 1956.

Inada, K.: Dermoid cysts of the mediastinum communicating with a bronchus. *Dis. Chest,* **31**:710, 1957.

Jackson, A. S.: Intrathoracic goiter. *Jackson Clin. Bull.,* **16**:48, 1954.

Kastrup, H.; Kny, W.; and Wilhelm, W.: Clinical, pathological, and therapeutic aspects of tumors on the thymus. *Thoraxchirurgie,* **2**:163, 1954.

Keeley, J. L., and Vana, A. J.: Lipomas of the mediastinum. 1940–1945. *Internat. Abst. Surg.,* **103**:313, 1956.

Krech, W. G.; Storey, C. F.; and Umiker, W. C.: Thymic cysts: review of the literature and report of two cases. *J. Thoracic Surg.,* **27**:477, 1954.

Lasley, C. H.: Excision of massive ganglioneuroma of mediastinum. *Dis. Chest,* **31**:709, 1957.

Levinson, B.; Walter, B. A.; Wintrobe, M. M.; and Cartwright, G. E.: A clinical study in Hodgkin's disease. *A.M.A. Arch. Int. Med.,* **99**:519, 1957.

Reich, N. E.: *The Uncommon Heart Diseases.* Charles C Thomas, Publisher, Springfield, Ill., 1954.

Rubin, M., and Mishkin, S.: Relationship between mediastinal lipomas and the thymus. *J. Thoracic Surg.,* **27**:494, 1954.

Sarinana, C.; Torres de Anda, A.; Figueroa, M.; and Sales, M.: Teratoma of anterior mediastinum in infant two months old. *M. Bol. med. Hosp. Inf.,* **11**:279, 1954.

Small, M. J., and Fremont, R. E.: Mediastinal emphysema complicating induction of pneumoperitoneum. *Am. Rev. Tuberc.,* **63**:591, 1951.

Williams, W.: Traumatic mediastinal hematoma. *U.S. Armed Forces M.J.,* **10**:1405, 1959.

CHAPTER 7 *DISEASES OF THE ESOPHAGUS*

CHAPTER OUTLINE

Cardiospasm (esophageal achalasia)
Diffuse spasm
Scleroderma
Dysphagia due to vascular ring anomalies
    Right aortic arch
    Double (bifid) aortic arch
    Anomalous right subclavian artery
Dysphagia due to arteriosclerosis of the aorta
Esophagitis
Peptic ulcer of the esophagus
Esophageal hiatus hernia
Diverticula of the esophagus
Tumors of the esophagus
Spontaneous rupture of the esophagus

Recognition of primary disorders of the esophagus in patients complaining of chest pain is important, since such disorders may cause pain which frequently simulates, or is even indistinguishable from, cardiac pain. The mechanism of production of esophageal pain is similar to that encountered in disorders of the gastrointestinal tract and has been discussed previously (see pp. 16–17).

The pathophysiology may be summarized as follows: Because of the nature of the nerve supply of the esophagus, pain originating in the esophagus may have a bizarre distribution. The esophagus receives its nerve supply primarily from the vagus nerve and the sympathetic trunks. Visceral afferent impulses are carried to the central nervous system by way of the visceral rami of the sympathetic trunk. Sensation may be referred to the same or other somatic segment. Visceral afferent pain impulses may also be transmitted by way of the vagus nerve. Whether or not the phrenic nerve supplies the lower end of the esophagus has not been definitely established. It does, however, supply the central portion of the diaphragm through which the esophageal hiatus passes. Thus, any disorder involving the esophageal hiatus will irritate afferent visceral pain endings of the phrenic nerve. The phrenic nerve, arising from the third to the fifth cervical roots, allows pain to be referred to the peripheral distribution of these roots, which also supply the outer aspect of the shoulder and arm. Thus, pain due to esophageal disturbances or disease may be referred to a considerable part of the chest and neighboring structures (see Fig. 7-1).

Intraesophageal balloon studies in cardiac patients with normal and diseased esophagi and with angina pectoris revealed that half of those suffering from angina pectoris could not distinguish esophageal pain from anginal pain. Electrocardiograms obtained during this procedure in patients with angina pectoris failed to reveal ischemic changes in contrast to the tracings obtained after the exercise test.

The most common manifestation of esophageal disease is pain on swallowing (dysphagia). Dysphagia may be due to any interference with transport of food, or even saliva, through the esophagus. The intrinsic process may be inflammatory, as in esophagitis; obstructive, as in carcinoma or benign

Table 7-1

Esophageal Causes of Chronic Dysphagia
According to Their Approximate Incidence
in Two Age Groups *

Over 45 Years	*Under 45 Years*
Cancer	Peptic esophagitis
Peptic esophagitis	Cardiospasm
Lower-esophageal ring	Benign tumor
Cardiospasm	Extrinsic masses
Diffuse spasm	(vascular anomalies, mediastinal tumors)
Extrinsic masses	Scleroderma
(aneurysm, mediastinal tumors)	Cancer
Zenker's diverticulum	Lower-esophageal ring
Paraesophageal diaphragmatic hernia	Paraesophageal diaphragmatic hernia
Benign tumor	Zenker's diverticulum
Scleroderma	Diffuse spasm

* From Ingelfinger, F. J.: Swallowing disorders in clinical practice. *Med. Science,* Apr. 10, 1960, p. 456.

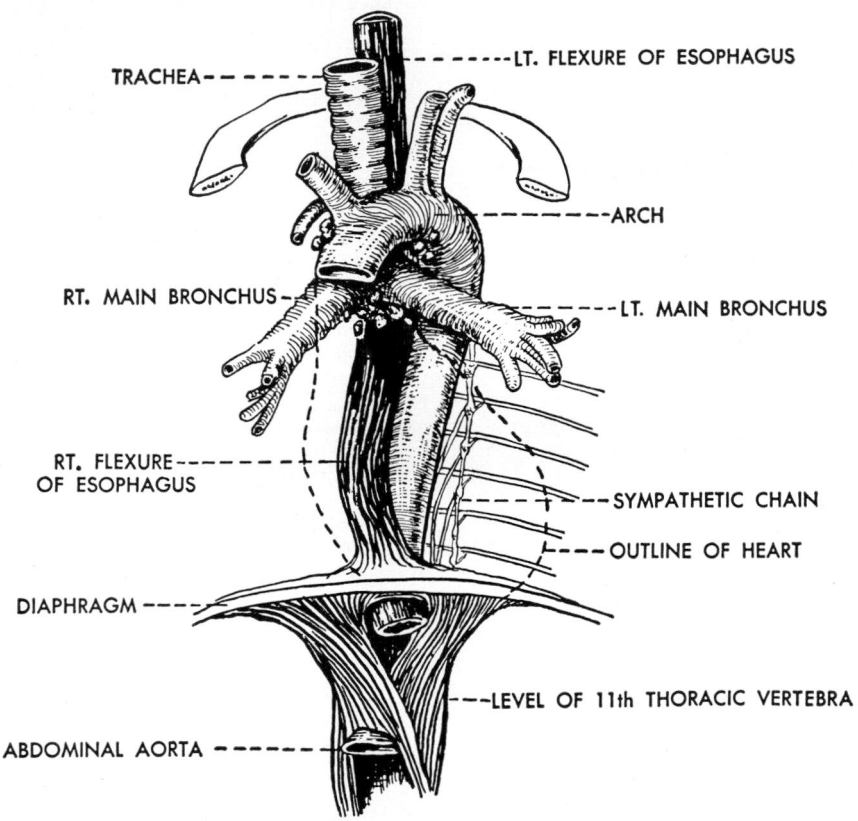

Fig. 7-1. Relation of esophagus to trachea, aorta, and heart. (From Reich, N. E.: *Diseases of the Aorta*. The Macmillan Co., New York, 1949.)

stricture; neurogenic, as in cardiospasm or possibly diffuse spasm; or due to a systemic disease such as generalized scleroderma. (See Tables 7-1 and 7-2.) In general, most conditions causing mechanical obstruction of the esophagus produce similar disturbances in motility along its course.

Cardiospasm (esophageal achalasia). This spastic disorder is often recognized during the fourth decade when an obstruction appears at the esophocardiac junction with proximal dilatation of the esophagus. The most commonly accepted etiologic factor is a degeneration of the myenteric plexus of Auerbach.

Recent studies of this functional disorder indicate the presence of an exaggeration of the normal sphincter-like action of the terminal segment (vestibule) with the generation of abnormally high intraesophageal pressures after swallowing. Methacholine (Mecholyl) has been demonstrated to have a relaxing effect on the vestibule, a reaction opposite to that of the body of the esophagus. Amyl nitrite also induces a temporary relaxation of the

Table 7-2

Helpful Features in the Evaluation of
Esophageal Dysphagia *

	Predominant Sex Incidence	Salient Historical and Related Characteristics
Cancer	M	Duration of symptoms less than 2 years
Peptic esophagitis	M	Heartburn for years, often preceding other symptoms
Cardiospasm		Liquids, especially cold drinks, may cause dysphagia early
Lower-esophageal ring	M	Brief, intermittent attacks of dysphagia with no interval symptoms
Diffuse spasm	M	Elderly person
Zenker's diverticulum	M	Sticking feeling in neck, gurgling sounds on swallowing; occasional regurgitation of decayed food
Scleroderma	F	Skin changes; Raynaud's phenomena
Paraesophageal diaphragmatic hernia	F	Attacks of substernal pressure and belching occurring during meals
Extrinsic masses		Symptoms of primary disorder
Acute disorders		Sudden onset, sometimes following vomiting and accompanied by phenomena such as shock, severe pain, fever, cough, or mediastinal emphysema

* From Ingelfinger, F. J.: Swallowing disorders in clinical practice. *Med. Science,* Apr. 10, 1960, p. 457.

vestibule. It is now generally believed that cardiospasm is not a localized process that produces spasm of the cardiac end of the esophagus alone, but one in which almost the entire esophagus is involved.

The initial symptoms are a sense of oppression or heaviness in the chest. Constriction may be induced during stress situations. Food causes only slight discomfort at first, but the disease usually progresses until dysphagia and substernal distress are practically constant. Eventually, liquids are regurgitated, and only solid foods can force their way through the area of constriction. Fluoroscopically, spasmodic contractions of the entire esophagus are visible early. As the disease progresses, this gives way to a smoothly outlined dilatation, which may assume massive distention (see Fig. 7-2). Since cardiospasm may also occur secondarily to carcinoma of the proximal portion of the stomach, the gastric cardia must be x-rayed carefully in order to exclude this elusive cause of obstruction. Achalasia of the esophagus will respond to an intramuscular injection of 10 mg of methacholine with tetanic contraction of the entire esophagus. This results in very severe retrosternal pain, simulating angina pectoris. Indeed, the pain may be so severe as to require the administration of nitroglycerin for relief. Esophagitis and pulsion diverticula are not uncommon complications. Medical

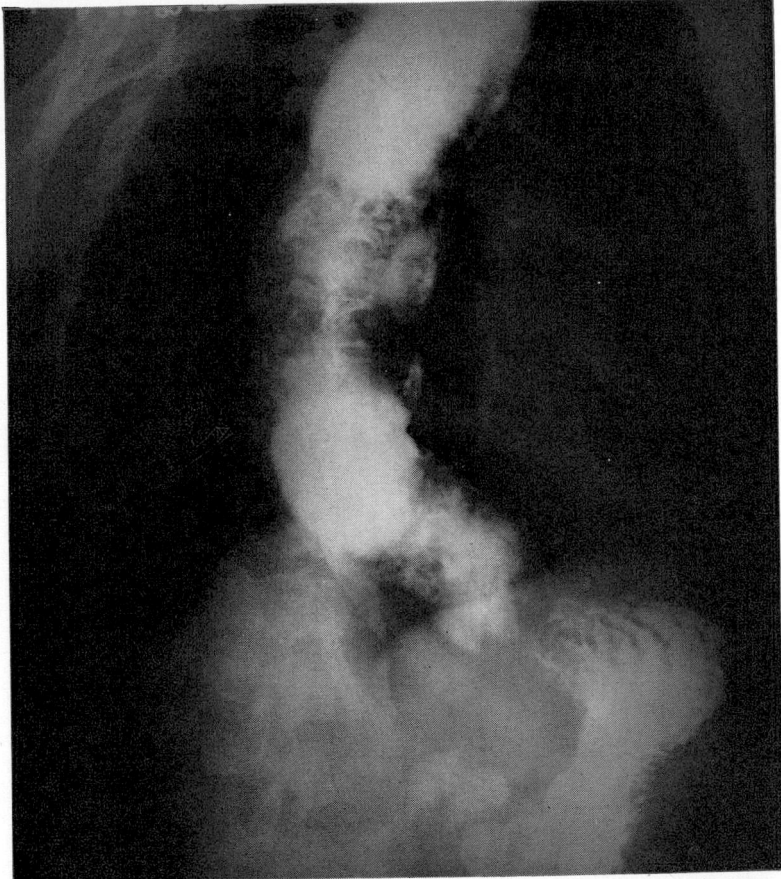

Fig. 7-2. Achalasia of esophagus. Note markedly dilated esophagus secondary to characteristic narrowing below diaphragm.

treatment is usually effective and consists of antispasmodics and sedatives. However, bougie dilatation of the spastic area and even surgery may become necessary in intractable cases.

Diffuse spasm. Dysphagia may occur following diffuse spasm which involves the lower half or third of the esophagus. It is due to a reflex disturbance secondary to gastrointestinal disease. There is no dilatation present above the area of spasm, and methacholine produces no contraction response. The pain produced by this lesion is intermittent and resembles that of cardiospasm. The pain may occur both with and without the ingestion of liquids or foods. When dysphagia is present, the patient may complain that food obstructs or "seems to stick" at a higher level in the esophagus than would occur in achalasia.

Scleroderma. Scleroderma remains somewhat enigmatic, since its etiology is not known and its pathogenesis is poorly understood. A diffuse sclerotic process affects tissues of mesenchymal origin. These profound alterations begin in the skin (induration and atrophy) and also affect muscle tissue, blood vessels, esophagus and gastrointestinal tract, lungs, heart, and kidneys. These profound structural alterations inevitably give rise to disturbances of the function of the involved organs. The clinical course is obviously variable and unpredictable.

A serious neuromuscular disturbance of esophageal function occurs in progressive scleroderma, due to interference with the intrinsic nerve supply caused by the progressive thickening of the submucosa and to muscle atrophy. The esophagus eventually becomes dilated (see Fig. 7-3) and

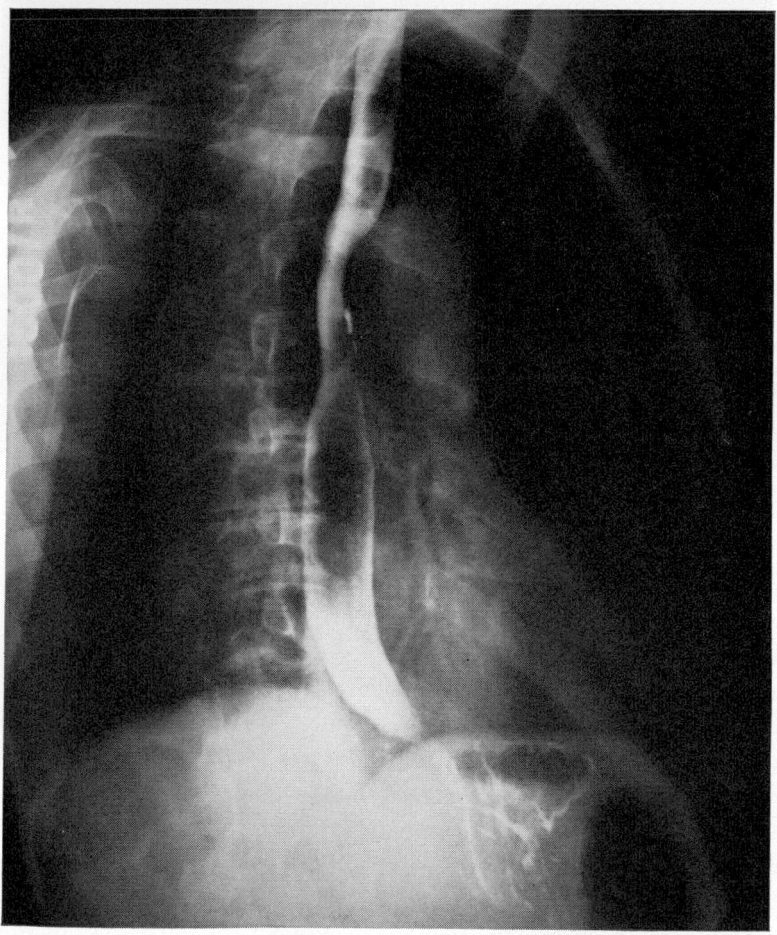

Fig. 7-3. Scleroderma of esophagus. Esophagus is smooth, hypotonic, and slightly dilated.

loses its normal peristaltic activity. There may be ulceration and inflammation associated with mucosal thickening. Dysphagia due to a derangement of the esophageal transport mechanism occurs almost always in individuals who already have other manifestations of the disease. However, in rare instances, esophageal involvement may first cause the patient to seek medical attention. Treatment consists of (1) systemic antifibrosis therapy with para-aminobenzoic acid or its potassium salt and (2) methacholine for the alleviation of dysphagia.

Dysphagia due to vascular ring anomalies. Although these vascular anomalies are quite rare, symptoms of esophageal or tracheal compression or both are common to all.

1. *Right aortic arch* is formed by the abnormal persistence of the right fourth branchial artery, while its left counterpart disappears. The aorta ascends well to the right of the midline, proceeds toward the left behind the esophagus, and usually continues downward slightly to the right of its normal position. Occasionally, there may be a right aortic arch with a left descending aorta; a diverticulum of the aorta may be present into which the ductus is attached. The diverticulum represents the posterior remnant of the left arch. The main branches arising from the arch are mirror images of normal. The right aortic arch may sometimes form a vascular ring by its connection to the right pulmonary artery through the ductus arteriosus. It deserves special consideration because it may produce symptoms (a) by resting upon the right upper lobe bronchus with the production of atelectasis, obstructive emphysema, or recurrent infection, or (b) by compression of the anterior surface of the trachea by the pulmonary artery. Traction is produced on this vessel by the pull of the ligamentum arteriosum because of the posterior displacement of the arch to which it is also attached. Although a right aortic arch usually produces no symptoms, on occasion it may result in dysphagia, dyspnea, cyanosis, cough, hoarseness, stridor, and chest pain.

2. *Double (bifid) aortic arch* occurs when both fourth branchial arteries persist. The left (anterior) arch, which is almost always smaller than the right (posterior), may undergo varying degrees of atresia. More rarely, there is a suppression of the posterior arch. When the vascular ring is small, there will be encroachment upon the esophagus and trachea, especially the latter. Symptoms are similar to those listed above.

3. *Anomalous right subclavian artery* has its peculiar origin from the left side of the arch or from the left subclavian artery. In order to supply the right arm, the aberrant vessel must cross the midline, usually at the level of the third dorsal vertebra. It almost always runs behind the esophagus but may be found between the esophagus and trachea or in front of the trachea.

Although it does not give rise to important symptoms, it may produce pressure on the esophagus of the newborn, resulting in hesitancy in swallowing (dysphagia lusoria). However, symptoms may first appear in later life owing to arteriosclerosis or dilatation of the vessel, which contributes to the compression. Diagnosis is established as follows:

a. Dysphagia, with esophageal dilatation and ulceration above the point of compression.

b. Dyspnea and cyanosis due to tracheal compression. Head retraction and stridor may occur in infants.

c. Recurring tracheobronchitis and pulmonary infections with chronic cough.

d. X-ray studies of the barium-filled esophagus reveal the compression from the right and behind in right aortic arch and bilaterally in double arch. The former causes the esophagus to be displaced to the left and anteriorly at the level of the third or fourth thoracic vertebra. Erosion of the anterior aspect of the thoracic vertebrae is possible in advanced cases. An aberrant right subclavian artery may be visualized by its compression of the barium column in an oblique direction at the level of the third thoracic vertebra.

e. Lipiodol studies, in the lateral position, reveal the direction of tracheal compression occurring anteriorly just above the carina or at the level of the aortic arch.

f. Angiocardiography may clearly outline the characteristic position of right aortic arch or delineate double aortic arches in the seven-second film. In the former, the prominence of the aortic knob to the right compresses the superior vena cava, which may appear as a ribbon-like density. Anomalous right subclavian artery may be delineated with angiocardiographic studies as arising from the left side of the arch.

When the obstruction is of marked degree and is caused by the presence of a right aortic arch, it is possible to relieve the condition by cutting the ligamentum arteriosum, thus allowing the pulmonary artery to fall forward. Removal of the left (anterior) portion of a double arch also gives relief. An anomalous subclavian artery which produces symptoms of compression should be doubly ligated with removal of the offending segment.

Dysphagia due to arteriosclerosis of the aorta. Dysphagia due to compression of the esophagus by an enlarged, widened, and uncoiled arteriosclerotic aorta may be seen occasionally in elderly people. Most of them complain of dyspnea or angina, symptoms that seem to have been aggravated since the onset of dysphagia. Difficulty in swallowing is noticed, particularly with solid food, which seems to "stick in the throat," and the severity of the dysphagia varies from time to time. A distinct delay of barium flow is visible at the level at which the esophagus is compressed by the aorta. The deviation of the sclerosed aorta from its normal course through the relatively restricted space of the mediastinum accounts for the x-ray impression on the compressible esophagus.

Esophagitis. Peptic esophagitis (subacute erosive esophagitis) is probably the most common disease of the esophagus. It is usually encountered in older people in association with or secondary to hiatus hernia with esophageal ulceration, frequent vomiting during early pregnancy, pyloric obstruction, duodenal ulcer, chronic gastritis, instrumental dilatation of the esophagus, and diverticula.

The erosions extend deeply through the epithelial layers. Acidic-peptic corrosion, secondary to transcardial reflux, is probably the direct cause of the disease. The frequency with which esophagitis occurs with hiatus hernia, pregnancy, and prolonged vomiting also suggests an association with cardial incompetence. In healthy persons, backflow of gastric contents is prevented by an esophagogastric valve, with the upper lip of the cardiac orifice acting as a flap-valve mechanism. Competence of the valve apparently depends upon the normal anatomic relationships of the adjacent viscera, maintained by the integrity of the hiatus and, particularly, by the phrenoesophageal ligament which anchors the lower end of the esophagus below the diaphragm.

Hyperchlorhydria is common. This juice digests living tissue much faster than normal juice, and highly acid vomit or reflux is more likely to cause esophagitis. Death may follow perforation into the mediastinum, pleura, or pericardium at any stage of the disease. If the leak is below the hiatal elastic ligament and into the upper abdomen, chemical peritonitis may ensue. There is a tendency to aspiration bronchopneumonia. Anemia may result from chronic or intermittent oozing from the raw surface, as well as from the pain which interferes with food ingestion.

Low retrosternal pain and "heartburn" are the most common symptoms. Pain may radiate to the neck, back, or down both arms and is felt most commonly after meals. It is aggravated by stooping or lying down. "Heartburn" may be accompanied by flushing of the face and acid regurgitation into the oropharynx.

Dysphagia may develop initially following spasm of the lower end of the esophagus, but a true stenosis may develop later. Some patients are labeled neurotic because a persistent complaint of indigestion is coupled with negative x-rays of stomach and duodenum. The medical treatment of esophagitis and its complications should include:

1. Ulcer diet.
2. Prevention of regurgitation by:
   a. elevation of head of bed,
   b. reduction of pressure within the abdomen by weight reduction and avoidance of tight garments.
3. Neutralization of gastric acids by regular use of antacids and anticholinergic drugs.
4. Dilatation of esophageal strictures by mechanical means. When esophagitis is associated with hiatal hernia or when medical treatment is unsuccessful, surgery may provide relief.

Peptic ulcer of the esophagus. Peptic ulcer of the esophagus (Barrett ulcer) is characterized by the presence of an ulceration in a "gastric-lined esophagus." This is in contrast to the diffuse inflammatory process with or without ulceration seen in peptic esophagitis. Thus, peptic ulcer of the esophagus is based on a developmental anomaly, since the lower esophagus is lined by an atypical cardiac type of columnar epithelium. This epithelial lining may show poorly developed rugae or may be completely flat and indistinguishable grossly from squamous epithelium. A peptic ulcer in a gastric-lined segment of esophagus resembles a gastric ulcer and is usually associated with an acquired sliding hiatus hernia of the (true) stomach as well as with regurgitation.

Dysphagia is the most frequent symptom and may be a result of spasm or stricture. When due to spasm, dysphagia is intermittent and is equally severe when ingesting liquids or solids. When due to stricture, difficulty in swallowing is more severe and more constant following solid foods. Burning in the upper epigastrium and the retrosternal area is frequent and is aggravated by reclining. Patients may be forced to sleep in a sitting position. Pain often extends to the back between the tenth and twelfth thoracic vertebrae or radiates into the neck and arms. This discomfort must be differentiated from coronary disease, especially that affecting the posterior wall of the myocardium. Associated symptoms of duodenal ulcer are common.

Aerophagia, upper abdominal distention, and a sensation of fullness over the left anterior chest relieved by belching are frequent accompanying symptoms. Hemorrhage and perforation are serious complications. On roentgenologic examination, a discrete crater or niche may be demonstrated within the tubular structure, with absent or atypical rugae distal to the crater.

Causes of vomiting should be eliminated. In most instances, cardiospasm and benign stricture are treated satisfactorily by dilatation. Although no treatment is entirely satisfactory after the ulcer niche has formed, the usual ulcer regimen and sleeping with the head of the bed elevated about 6 inches are often helpful. Radical surgery may eventually become necessary in some instances. With a careful choice of operative procedure, a satisfactory clinical result may be obtained in at least 90 per cent of all cases.

Esophageal hiatus hernia. Primary disturbances of esophageal anatomy and physiology may also lead to a hiatal hernia (see Fig. 7-4). The most com-

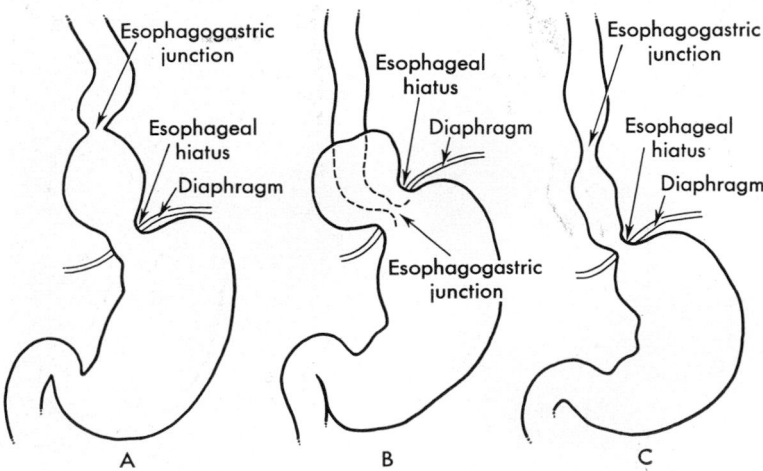

Fig. 7-4. Esophageal hiatus hernia (*A*) without shortening of the esophagus but with upward displacement of esophagogastric junction (sliding type), (*B*) without shortening of the esophagus or displacement of esophagogastric junction (paraesophageal type), and (*C*) with acquired shortening of esophagus and associated stenosis. (From Mobley, J. E., and Christensen, N. A.: Esophageal hiatal hernia: prevalence, diagnosis, and treatment in an American city of 30,000. *Gastroenterology,* 30:1, 1956.)

mon type encountered is due to a congenital shortening of the esophagus with variable amounts of the stomach in the thorax (see Fig. 7-5). The esophagogastric type of hiatus hernia is characterized by the protrusion of the lower end of the esophagus and the adjoining stomach through the hiatus. These two types cause clinical manifestations similar to paraesophageal hiatus hernia, which is discussed in greater detail on pages 320–24.

Pneumoperitoneum may be used as a diagnostic and therapeutic procedure in patients with esophageal hiatus hernia. The pneumoperitoneum may help to differentiate between the pain of coronary insufficiency and hiatus hernia.

Two types are recognizable: (1) sliding hernia, in which the esophagus and stomach slip through the hiatus as a whole in an axial fashion (axial or concentric hernia) or because of the incomplete peritoneal investment; and

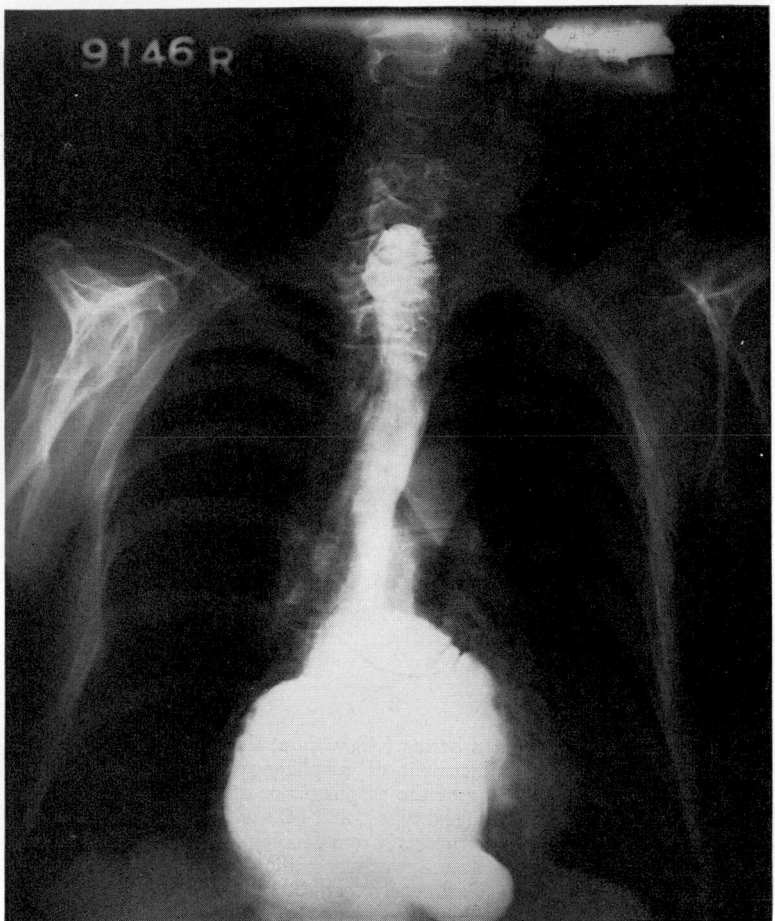

Fig. 7-5. Esophageal hiatus hernia. Major portion of barium-filled stomach is in the thorax.

(2) rolling hernia (paraesophageal), in which the fundus of the stomach slips upward along the esophagus. Sliding hernia implies that the herniated viscus is invested by peritoneum for a portion of its circumference. While this feature is important to recognize prior to surgery, it cannot be predicated. Mamory and Weiss observed longitudinal mucosal lacerations in the cardiac portion of the stomach at autopsy in patients with fatal hemorrhage and incriminated the preceding retching and vomiting as the main causative factor. These lacerations may be considered as an incomplete rupture of the esophageal wall which extends through the mucosa and submucosa and may lead to ulceration and hermorrhage, or may heal spontaneously. As a

general rule, the smaller the hiatus hernia, the more severe are the subjective manifestations.

Diverticula of the esophagus. Traction diverticula of the esophagus are usually located in the middle third of the esophagus behind the heart and are prone to give rise to substernal distress which may resemble coronary disease.

The diverticulum is usually caused by the contraction of fibrous tissue following mediastinal infections, especially tuberculous hilar lymphadenitis. Since the orifice usually lies below the fundus of the sac, it remains empty and small. Although this diverticulum is usually asymptomatic, dysphagia, substernal distress (usually related to food intake and associated with dysphagia and regurgitation), and hemorrhage may occur. Perforation into the mediastinum may result in rare instances.

Epiphrenic diverticulum occurs very infrequently. However, it may also give rise to dysphagia and substernal distress. It is located in the distal part of the esophagus and is frequently associated with considerable cardiospasm. This type usually requires surgical excision, particularly when the associated cardiospasm has become refractory to medical treatment.

Pulsion diverticula are located in the posterior and upper third of the esophagus and are associated with the vomiting of undigested food. Diverticula are readily identified following fluoroscopic examination with barium. Surgery may become necessary when symptoms are intense or persistent.

Tumors of the esophagus. The esophagus is rarely the site of benign tumors. Carcinoma is the most common type of malignancy. Sarcoma rarely occurs but resembles carcinoma in its clinical manifestations. Adenocarcinomas may originate in the esophagus or at the esophagogastric junction. Portions of the esophageal mucosa, usually found in the lower third of the esophagus, may fail to undergo squamous transformation before birth and remain columnar-celled. Esophageal adenocarcinomas probably originate in such areas. Hence, they are commonly found in the lower third of the esophagus. However, squamous-cell tumors occur with equal frequency throughout the entire length of the esophagus.

Dysphagia is the most common symptom and is present in 90 per cent of the cases. It is observed when the neoplasm involves the gastroesophageal area and in 90 per cent of thoracic segment involvement. It is one of the earliest symptoms (in 43 per cent of a large series). Retrosternal pain is found in half of the patients and is often associated with salivation and regurgitation.

Prompt recognition of early symptoms is most important for effective management and improved prognosis. Persistent dysphagia due to carcinoma is confirmed by roentgenography and esophagoscopy. X-ray examination of the esophagus and stomach usually demonstrates the irregular or fixed defect. Esophagoscopy can also help to differentiate between benign cardiospasm and infiltrating cancer of the cardia. Papanicolaou staining may reveal characteristic cells.

Improved surgical technics now permit the radical removal of malignant tumors of the esophagus and cardiac end of the stomach, with restitution of the normal act of swallowing and with a general operative mortality under 15 per cent.

Spontaneous rupture of the esophagus. Spontaneous rupture of the normal esophagus may follow excessive intraluminal pressure (generally induced by severe vomiting and occurring about an inch above the diaphragm), perforation by instrumentation, and ingested foreign bodies. It may also occur in malignant diseases of the esophagus. Unfortunately, diagnostic and therapeutic endoscopic procedures are the most common causes of rupture.

This catastrophe is most frequently confused with perforated peptic ulcer of the stomach or duodenum, dissecting aotric aneurysm, acute hemorrhagic pancreatitis, coronary occlusion, and spontaneous pneumothorax. Esophageal rupture following violent emesis produces extreme upper abdominal and chest pain. The latter is most often noted on the left side, and may extend into the left shoulder and interscapular region. A sensation of something "bursting in the chest" is frequently described. Clammy cold skin, rapid respirations, and other evidences of shock may ensue. Crepitation due to escape of the air into the cervical tissues is readily recognized and may extend anteriorly to the upper chest, although obliteration of mediastinal planes by inflammation may prevent seepage. Pain is unrelieved by the usual doses of narcotics.

The triad of vomiting, severe low chest pain, and emphysema of the neck is diagnostic of this condition. However, because of its rarity, the diagnosis may be overlooked. A simple chest film may reveal air in the mediastinum or subcutaneous tissues of the neck or mediastinum. When in doubt, spontaneous esophageal rupture may be confirmed by the oral administration of a small amount of Lipiodol followed by a roentgenogram of the chest. If the esophagus is perforated, the dye will appear in the mediastinum or in the pleural cavity. Methylene blue in dilute solution may be administered by mouth and recovered by thoracentesis if signs of fluid are present in the chest. The pleural fluid will react acidly to litmus paper due to the hydrochloric acid content of the escaped gastric juice. Dyspnea and peripheral vascular collapse ensue and, with the added burden of biochemical derangements, usually cause death within forty-eight hours. Occasionally, localized mediastinal or pleural suppuration develops when treatment is delayed, and the patient survives for several weeks or more. Appropriate drainage or reparative procedure can be curative.

REFERENCES

Arata, J. A.; McEachern, C. G.; and Zwick, W.: Spontaneous rupture of the esophagus. *Dis. Chest*, **27**:685, 1955.

Ballem, C. M.; Fletcher, H. H.; and McKenna, R. D.: The diagnosis of esophagitis. *Am. J. Digest. Dis.*, **5**:88, 1960.

Beaconsfield, P.: Reflux esophagitis; its diagnosis and treatment. *Gastroenterology*, **24**:369, 1953.

Christoforidis, A., and Nelson, S. W.: Spontaneous rupture of esophagus with emphasis on the roentgenologic diagnosis. *Am. J. Roentgenol.*, **78**:574, 1957.

Friesen, S. R., and Miller, D. R.: Competence of the esophagogastric sphincter in hiatal hernia; some experimental observations. *Am. Surgeon*, **22**:42, 1956.

Garlock, J. H.: Cancer of the esophagus. *New York J. Med.*, **58**:1741, 1958.

Harrison, T. R., et al.: *Principles of Internal Medicine*, 3rd ed. McGraw-Hill Book Co., Inc., New York, 1958.

Hightower, N. C., Jr.: Esophageal motility in health and disease. *Dis. Chest*, **27**:150, 1955.

Hightower, N. C., Jr.; Olsen, A. M.; and Moersch, H. J.: A comparison of the effects of acetyl-beta-methylcholine chloride (Mecholyl) on esophageal intraluminal pressure in normal persons and patients with cardiospasm. *Gastroenterology*, **26**:592, 1954.

Johnstone, A. S.: Oesophagitis and peptic ulcer of oesophagus: the Mackenzie Davidson memorial lecture. *Brit. J. Radiol.*, **28**:229, 1955.

Jones, C. M.: Hiatus esophageal hernia; with special reference to a comparison of its symptoms with those of angina pectoris. *New England J. Med.*, **225**:963, 1941.

Kramer, P., and Ingelfinger, F. J.: Esophageal sensitivity to Mecholyl in cardiospasm. *Gastroenterology*, **19**:242, 1951.

Lindskog, G. E., and Kline, J. L.: The problems of hiatus hernia complicated by peptic esophagitis. *New England J. Med.*, **257**:110, 1957.

Lindskog, G. E., and Stern, H.: Diverticulum of the esophagus. *Yale J. Biol. & Med.*, **26**:285, 1954.

Maisel, B.; Cooper, W; and Glenn, F.: Pneumoperitoneum in the management of esophageal hiatus: a new diagnostic and therapeutic procedure. *J. Am. M. Women's A.*, **11**:299, 1956.

Mayer, H. C.: Rupture of the esophagus by emesis. *New York J. Med.*, **55**:1625, 1955.

Mazzoni, G.: Clinical symptoms of cancer of esophagus with particular reference to the initial symptoms. *Policlinico*, **61**:1492, 1954.

Moersch, H. J., and Donoghue, F. E.: Esophageal disease as a cause of anterior thoracic pain. *Dis. Chest*, **34**:1, 1958.

Mustard, R. A.: Reflux esophagitis. *Canad. M.A.J.*, **76**:811, 1957.

Palmer, E. D.: Dysphagia lusoria: clinical aspects in the adult. *Ann. Int. Med.*, **42**:1173, 1955.

Palmer, E. D.: Esophageal ulcer in the adult: clinical aspects and experiences with conservative treatment. *A.M.A. Arch. Int. Med.*, **99**:695, 1957.

Palmer, E. D.: Serious heart disease simulated by hiatus hernia. *U.S. Armed Forces M.J.*, **8**:477, 1957.

Palmer, E. D.: Subacute erosive (peptic) esophagitis; clinical study of 100 cases. *A.M.A. Arch. Int. Med.*, **94**:364, 1954.

Plotz, M., and Reich, N. E.: Esophageal varices in portal hypertension. *Am. J. Digest. Dis.*, **5**:357, 1938.

Reich, N. E.: *Diseases of the Aorta.* The Macmillan Co., New York, 1949.

Reich, N. E., and Ehrlich, D. E.: Displacements of the barium-filled esophagus by cardiovascular lesions. *Dis. Chest*, **29**:376, 1956.

Smithers, D. W.: Adenocarcinoma of the oesophagus. *Thorax*, **11**:257, 1956.

Symposium on diseases of the esophagus. *J. Mt. Sinai Hosp.*, **23**:14, 1956.

Templeton, F. E.: Movements of the esophagus in the presence of cardiospasm and other esophageal diseases. A roentgenologic study of muscular action. *Gastroenterology*, **10**:96, 1948.

Winkelstein, A.; Wolf, B. S.; Som, M. L.; and Marshak, R. H.: Peptic esophagitis with duodenal or gastric ulcer. *J.A.M.A.*, **154**:885, 1954.

CHAPTER 8 *DISEASES OF THE AORTA*

CHAPTER OUTLINE

Congenital lesions of the aorta
Congenital aneurysm of the right aortic sinus
Coarctation of the aorta
Acquired aneurysms of the aorta
Dissecting aneurysm
Aortitis
    Uncomplicated leutic aortitis
    Aortitis with aortic insufficiency
    Aortitis with aneurysm
    Aortitis with coronary ostia involvement
    Aortitis due to rheumatic fever
    Aortitis due to rheumatoid arthritis
Pulseless disease (Takayasu's disease, aortic arch syndrome)
Trauma to the aorta

Aortic lesions that give rise to chest pain are usually due to inflammatory involvement, dilatation, dissection, or rupture. (See Fig. 8–1.) The pain was originally considered to be of aortic origin and to be produced by a rise in aortic pressure with resultant distention of the root of the aorta. Most instances of pain were later shown to be due to secondary coronary insufficiency with myocardial ischemia. Pain sensibility of aortic origin has its source mainly in the sympathetic nervous system. Pain sensation is con-

155

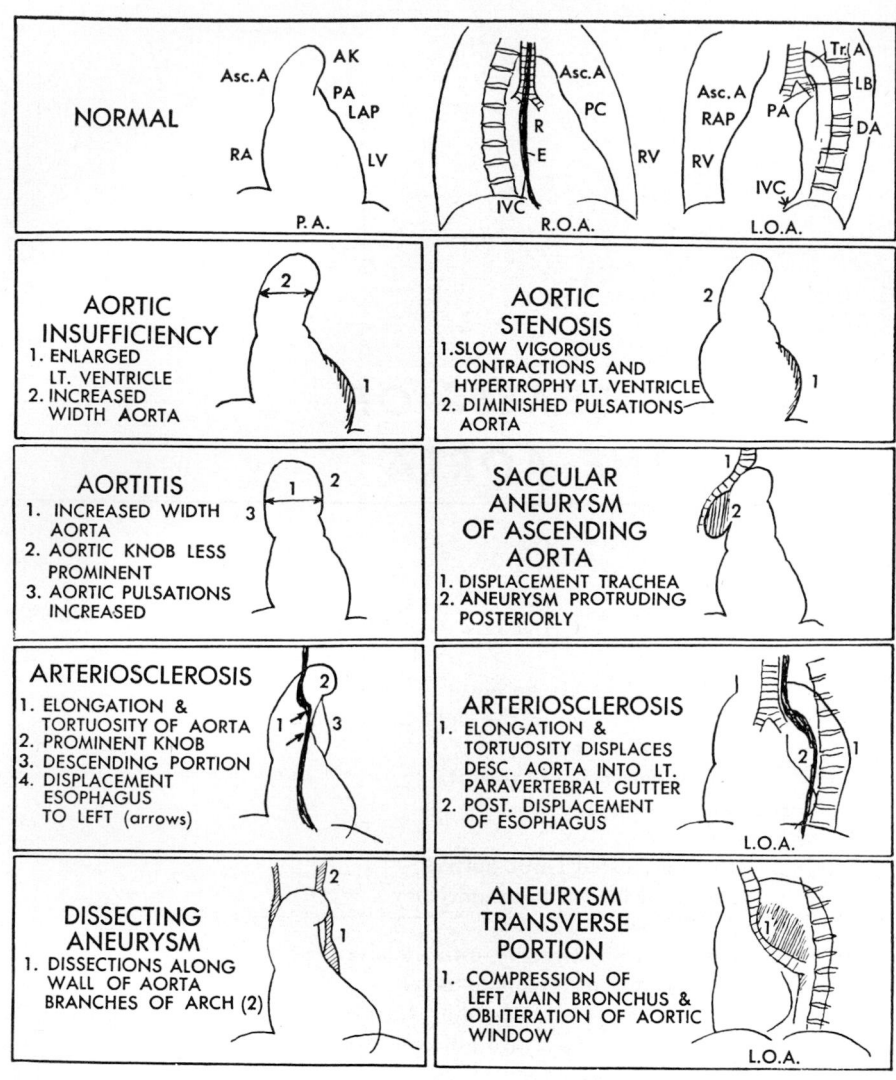

Fig. 8-1. Various lesions and configurations of the aorta.

L.O.A. Left anterior oblique position   LA Left atrium
R.O.A. Right anterior oblique position   LAP Left auricular appendage
  P.A. Posteroanterior position   RAP Right auricular appendage
Asc. A Ascending aorta   IVC Inferior vena cava
   AK Aortic knob   PC Pulmonary conus
 Tr. A Transverse aorta   IVG Interventricular groove
   DA Descending aorta   PA Pulmonary artery
   RV Right ventricle   R Retrocardiac space
   RA Right atrium   E Barium-filled esophagus
   LV Left ventricle   LB Left main bronchus

(From Reich, N. E.: *Diseases of the Aorta.* The Macmillan Co., New York, 1949.)

ducted by nerve fibers and by ganglia of this system, which include the left
stellate ganglion and the upper four thoracic ganglia. Blocking or resection
of these ganglia abolishes all pain sensation.

The recognition of many aortic lesions has been made possible by the
development of newer diagnostic technics, such as angiocardiography and
catheterization. Recently developed surgical technics have made possible
the correction of many of these lesions.

Congenital lesions of the aorta. Congenital anomalies involving the aortic
arch usually cause pain in the upper part of the chest due to encroachment
upon the esophagus and/or trachea. These include various types of developmental anomalies, such as right-sided aortic arch (with ligamentum arteriosum), double aortic arch, and aberrant right subclavian artery. (See Fig.
8-2.) So-called "dysphagia lusoria," which is produced by the encircling or

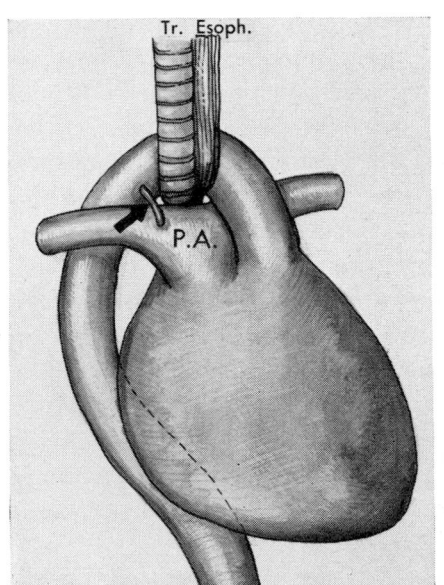
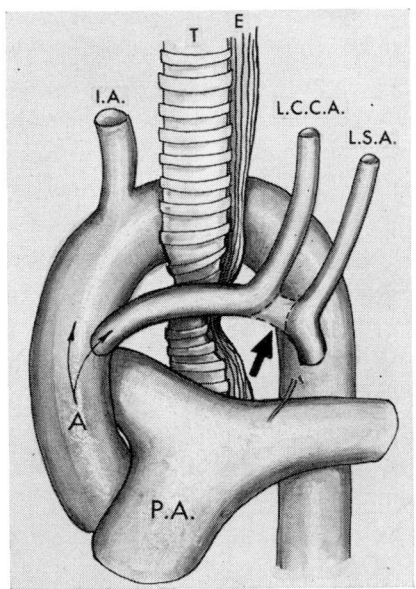

Fig. 8-2. Vascular ring anomalies. A, Right aortic arch; B, double aortic arch. Arrows
point to areas of surgical division. (From Reich, N. E.: *The Uncommon Heart Diseases.*
Charles C Thomas, Publisher, Springfield, Ill., 1954.)

compressing effects of these congenital lesions, has been discussed in detail
and more appropriately in the preceding chapter (see pp. 145–46). Chest
pains may also result from bronchitis and pneumonitis secondary to tracheal
compression by the same lesions. Congenital elongation of the arch with
buckling due to a taut ligamentum arteriosus has been described recently.
This produces an x-ray configuration which consists of two bulges along the

left aortic margin which resembles coarctation with poststenotic dilatation.

Congenital aneurysm of the right aortic sinus is due to a failure of complete development of the right aortic septum. There is usually no pain or other symptoms before rupture, although mild pain may occur due to progressive dilatation caused by the defect in the elastic tissue of the media. Overwhelming precordial pain occurs after rupture of the aneurysm, and is associated with severe dyspnea. Cyanosis is absent, since the flow of blood is from the arterial to the venous side ("intracardiac aneurysm"). Signs accompanying a wide pulse pressure may be produced as a result of the false communication (with the right ventricle or atrium or pulmonary artery).

Paroxysmal tachycardia and a continuous "machinery" murmur with accentuation of the second sound are other concomitant findings. The diastolic murmur may be heard in the region of the valve due to the dilatation. Percussion may reveal increased aortic dullness to the right of the sternum, and this may be confirmed by x-ray. Angiocardiography may reveal a bulge at the right aortic sinus or the actual site of rupture by flow of the dye from the aorta to the right heart. Since the aneurysm may encroach on the neighboring conduction system, the electrocardiogram frequently shows an intraventricular block. The importance of recognizing such lesions is enhanced by the opportunity for repair of the defect following open-heart surgery. Cardiopulmonary bypass, utilizing an extracorporeal circulation, now makes it possible to treat this unusual condition by resection of the aneurysm. The wrapping of the aneurysmal dilatation with reactive cellophane to give support by a fibrosing reaction may be feasible prior to rupture. This treatment is also advisable in congenital aneurysmal dilatation of the ascending aorta which occurs as the result of a defect in the development of the elastic tissue of the media. New plastic and woven aortic valves are now being employed to replace the diseased leaflets, as well as the proximal ascending aorta and even diseased coronary ostia.

Coarctation of the aorta. This correctible congenital anomaly rarely manifests chest pain. Pain usually occurs only at the time of rupture or dissection (17 per cent). This may happen quite early in life, although most tears usually appear during the third decade. The nature of the pain resembles that of dissecting aneurysm of the acquired type. Precordial pain may also be due to the associated congenital lesions involving the aortic valve or coronary ostia. Thus, coronary insufficiency is found in one-fourth of the cases and is usually caused by congenital aplasia or absence of a coronary artery, by arteriosclerotic changes of a concomitant bicuspid valve, or by an associated congenital aortic stenosis. This type of pain is discussed in detail in the chapter dealing with aortic valve lesions (see pp. 181–86). The clinical picture depends upon the degree of obstruction in the thoracic aorta and the development of a compensatory collateral circulation. Important signs include lower blood pressure and diminished to absent pulsations from the femoral arteries down. Thus, a weak or late femoral pulse is characteristic. Intra-arterial pressure measurements and even ordinary blood pressure recordings are confirmatory of the differences in upper and lower extremities. (See Fig. 8-3.) Signs of collateral circulation

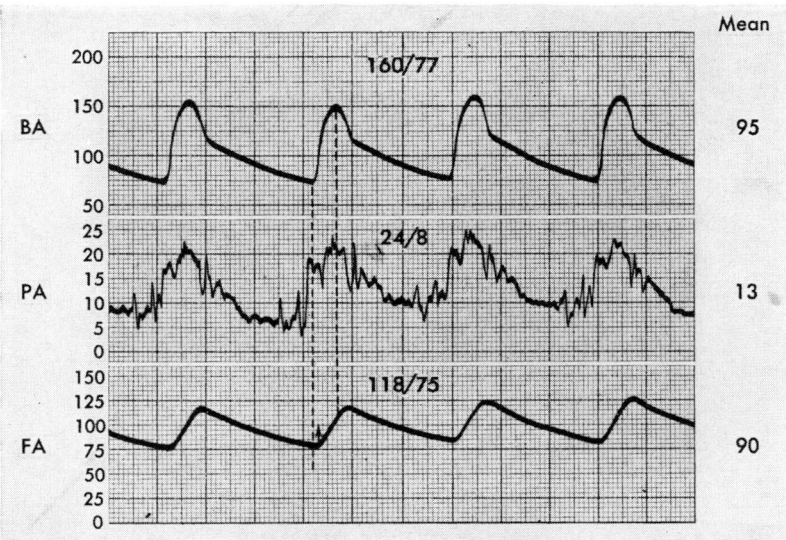

Fig. 8-3. Direct pressure tracings of brachial artery (*BA*), pulmonary artery (*PA*), and femoral artery (*FA*) in *coarctation of aorta*. Note onset of femoral pressure curve occurs later than that of brachial one in contrast to normal. Note also lower systolic pressure in femoral artery.

involve the intercostal, scapular, internal mammary, and deep epigastric arteries. The aneurysmal dilatations of the intercostal arteries actually produce pathognomonic scalloping of the lower rib margins in many instances (see Fig. 8-4). Angiocardiography may reveal a poststenotic dilatation of the aorta as well as the narrowed segment.

Occasionally, hypertension secondary to coarctation may lead to the same sequelae as with essential hypertension and may become complicated in like manner by coronary artery disease. Chest pain may then occur as a result of the latter. The most effective treatment is resection of the aortic constriction and, if necessary, replacement with a homograft or synthetic prosthesis.

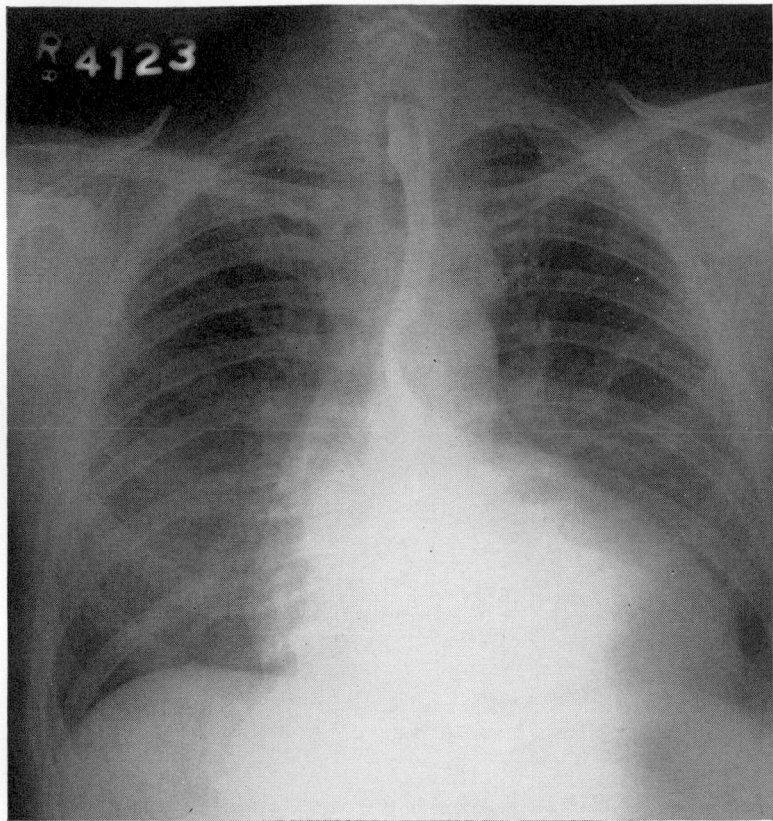

Fig. 8-4. Coarctation of aorta (verified at surgery). Note double contour of aortic arch, large left ventricle, and characteristic rib notching.

Acquired aneurysms of the aorta. At the present time aneurysms of the thoracic aorta more commonly result from arteriosclerosis than from syphilis.

The pain may be due to several mechanisms. Involvement of the aortic wall itself or the coronary ostia may cause pain. The expanding aneurysm (particularly when aggravated by hypertension) tends to exert a continuous expansile effect upon neighboring structures. Thus, pain may occur as a result of erosion of the sternum or vertebrae, more rarely by compression of structures such as the esophagus or nerves. Occasionally, vague epigastric pain may be experienced with radiation to the back. At times, the pain is sharp and localized to the left scapular area. The pain may become overwhelming at the moment of rupture of the aneurysm into the esophagus, trachea, or pleural cavity. Rupture into the pericardial sac results in the triad of falling blood pressure, rising venous pressure with prominence of all veins, and distant heart sounds with increased cardiac dullness (cardiac tamponade). Less frequently, the rupture involves the left hemithorax or retroperitoneal tissue.

The diagnosis of arteriosclerotic aneurysm of the aorta depends upon a detailed history and negative serologic tests for syphilis in the older age groups. The second aortic sound has a ringing quality, and a harsh systolic murmur may be heard over the aortic area. Lesser grades of dilatation and a regular, smooth ascending aorta also favor the diagnosis of arteriosclerosis. Tortuosity and elongation of the thoracic aorta with accentuation of the aortic knob are well visualized. Semilunar plaques may be identified in the wall. The barium-filled esophagus is pulled to the left and posteriorly, and the trachea is pushed to the right.

Luetic involvement of the aorta has recently been reported to be on the ascendency again. The correct diagnosis is important, since effective medical and surgical therapy can be instituted. The presence of linear calcific deposits (in half the cases) in the wall of the ascending aorta with strongly positive serologic tests (in about 85 per cent of all cases) is good evidence of syphilitic aortitis. The conventional roentgenogram (left anterior oblique view) may also reveal calcification in the intracardiac portion of the ascending aorta and often clearly outlines the dilated aortic sinuses. Unlike congenital aneurysm of the sinus of Valsalva, syphilitic aneurysm may become huge. (See Fig. 8-5.) Perforation and massive hemorrhage generally cause death within two years after the diagnosis of an aneurysm has been made. Therefore, prompt surgical intervention is advisable following an established diagnosis. Advances in surgery, including utilization of complete cardiac or cardiopulmonary bypasses and the employment of synthetic replacements or homografts, have greatly enhanced chances for longer survival (see Fig. 8-6). Other types of luetic involvement of the aorta are considered in detail elsewhere in this chapter (see pp. 167–69).

Dissecting aneurysm. Proper recognition of this condition has become more important than ever, since it is now possible to prevent the disastrous course of this disease following surgical intervention. With the increase of the life span and with improved means of diagnosis, its incidence has increased in recent years. Nevertheless, the diagnosis remains difficult in many cases because of the absence of a characteristic syndrome. Dissecting aneurysm of the aorta is twice as common in men as in women. The great majority of cases occur in the fifth and sixth decades of life. However, the occurrence in younger people is not as rare as was once believed, and many patients under forty years of age are now on record. It is also found in

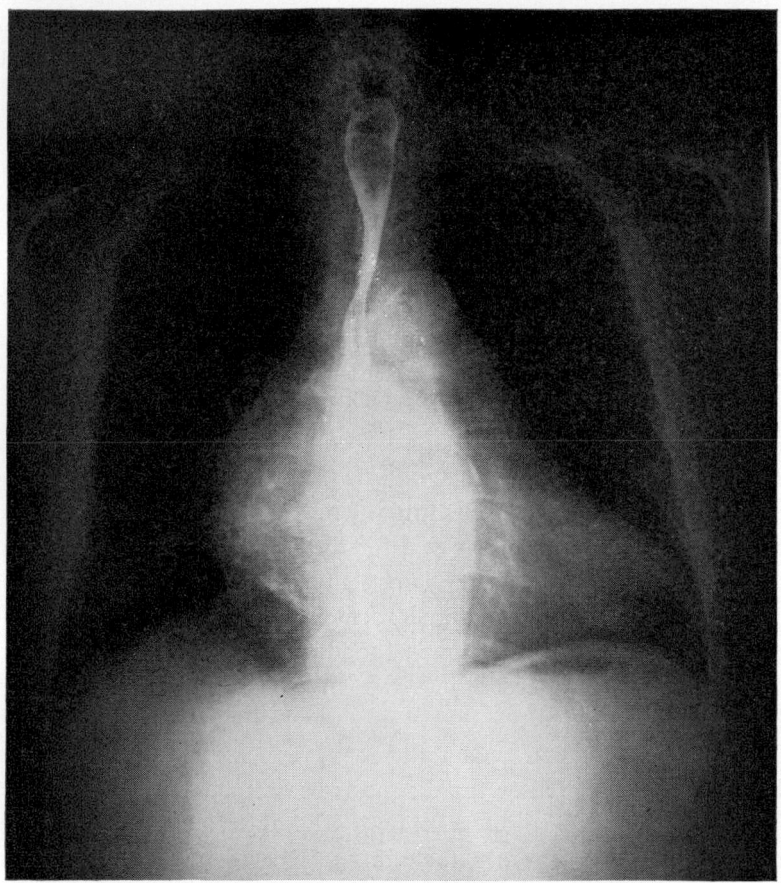

Fig. 8-5. Aneurysm of sinus of Valsalva. Note large circular calcification superimposed over right side of heart shadow, spreading the carina of the trachea.

association with pregnancy, coarctation of the aorta, and hypertension. It is a not infrequent complication of Marfan's syndrome, which is an inherited mesodermal disorder.

There is a distinct absence of unanimity concerning the etiologic and pathologic nature of the disease. Efforts at limiting the pathology to a single factor have been generally unsuccessful. Medionecrosis aortae idiopathica cystica, described by Erdheim, is probably the most important factor. However, the frequent finding of atheromatous degeneration cannot be lightly dismissed. Although degeneration of the media is the most acceptable concept today, controversy still rages as to the tissue primarily involved. Smooth muscle necrosis has vied with mucoid degeneration of the elastic laminae or a ground substance disorder of the basic underlying process.

In most cases, actual dissection originates with rupture and bleeding of vasa vasorum in the media, beginning as a horizontal tear usually around 3 cm above the aortic cusps. The intimal tear then allows the entrance of aortic blood under much higher pressures, which results in dissection of varying degrees.

In the vast majority (two-thirds) of cases, the rupture is initiated in the ascending aorta; in a small number of cases, it occurs in the transverse and remaining portion of the aorta. The length of the dissection may be only a few centimeters or may extend down the entire length to the popliteal arteries. The points of rupture are most commonly the pericardial, the left pleural, and retroperitoneal space; less commonly the mediastinum, peritoneal, and subcutaneous space (see Fig. 8-7).

While the extent and course of dissection vary, three patterns of the disease may be recognized. In the most acute and severe form, there is rapid dissection with terminal perforation through the adventitia, with death in a few hours or days. In the subacute type, the process may begin abruptly but then progresses gradually over a period of days or weeks with eventual rupture and death. In the chronic form, re-entry of the dissected passage into the lumen of the aorta usually takes place, thus forming a double-barreled aorta; or it may tear for a few centimeters and then heal completely with scar tissue.

The event itself is usually most dramatic in the acute and subacute types. Characteristically, there is an abrupt onset of severe chest pain without the gradual build-up which occurs so frequently in myocardial infarction. This may be described by the patient as a sudden, severe, tearing, crushing, excruciating, or ripping pain in the chest. Most often the pain originates substernally and progresses to the neck, head, shoulders, arms, back, abdomen, groin, and lower extremities; this sequence is diagnostic, since it obviously traces the involvement of specific arteries as the dissection progresses along the course of the aorta. Occasionally, there is dysphagia due to pressure of the aorta on the esophagus. As the pain becomes more severe, it responds only slightly to massive doses of narcotics. Chest pain may also be due to involvement of the ostia of the coronary or intercostal arteries. The neurologic changes produced by the aortic dissection are due to interference with the spinal cord circulation. Paresthesia and weakness of extremities are not uncommon.

An unusual diagnostic sign of dissecting aneurysm of the aorta is ecchymosis of the neck, chest, abdomen, and lumbar areas. The combination of sudden unexplained back pain, hematuria, and lumbar ecchymosis is pathognomonic of retroperitoneal hemorrhage following dissection and

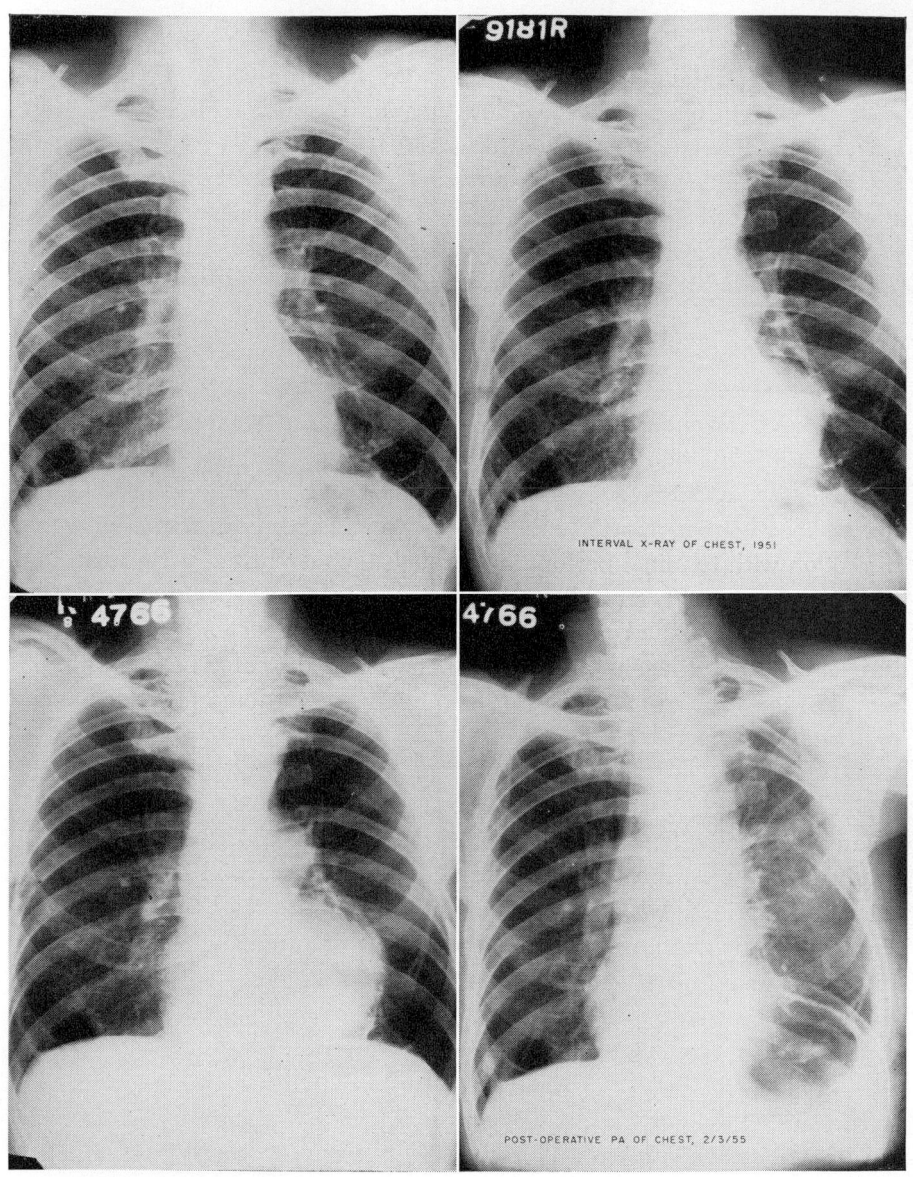

Fig. 8-6A. Serial x-rays and tomograms of chest demonstrating development of multiple aneurysms of descending aorta and removal by complete resection of thoracic aorta and replacement by homograft.

Top, left and right, and bottom left: Preoperative series of posteroanterior chest films (1949, 1951, and 1955, respectively).

Bottom right: Postoperative posteroanterior chest film.

164

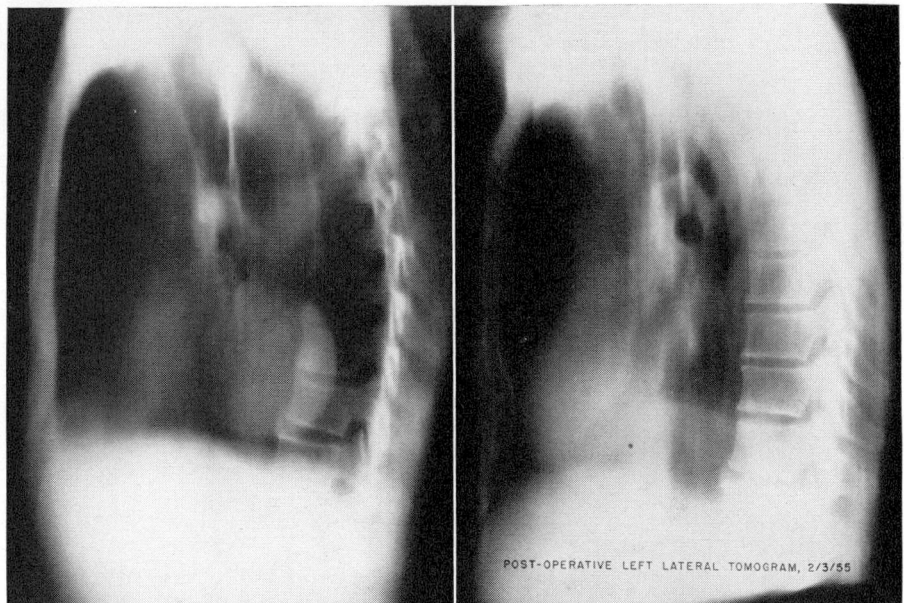

POST-OPERATIVE LEFT LATERAL TOMOGRAM, 2/3/55

Fig. 8-6B. *Left:* Preoperative left lateral tomogram.
Right: Postoperative left lateral tomogram.

rupture of the abdominal aorta. The superior vena caval syndrome may also be a striking manifestation of dissecting aneurysm. It is characterized by cyanosis and edema of the face, neck, and upper extremities, and is accompanied by distended veins in these locations. Other rare symptoms and signs include hissing and rumbling murmurs along the aorta, dysphagia (esophageal compression), severe hemoptysis (intrabronchial rupture), cough, palpable mass over the abdominal aorta, and massive hematemesis (rupture into esophagus).

Dissection may cause instant fatal shock with death within the first few minutes of rupture (65 per cent); 10 to 15 per cent die within a few days; and the remainder may linger for months or heal entirely (symptomless or incomplete tears). Recurrence and multiple dissections are fairly common, as proved by autopsy studies.

Hypertensive and arteriosclerotic cardiovascular disease are most important considerations in the differential diagnosis. The differentiation is vital because of the common use of anticoagulant therapy in acute myocardial infarction and its contraindication in dissecting aneurysm. The differentiation of an aortic dissection from a myocardial infarction may be further complicated by the fact that the former may extend to the orifices

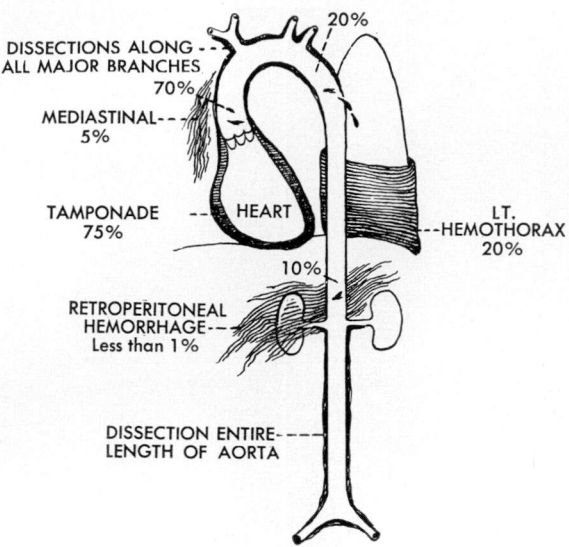

Fig. 8-7. Diagrammatic representation of aortic tears and dissections. (From Reich, N. E.: *Diseases of the Aorta.* The Macmillan Co., New York, 1949.)

of the coronary arteries, causing myocardial ischemia or infarction. While electrocardiographic tracings characteristic of secondary myocardial involvement may be obtained, rarely do these changes follow any characteristic pattern.

Aortic dissection is to be suspected in the presence of hypertensive and coronary disease when the intensity and persistence of chest pain appear out of proportion to the electrocardiographic changes, particularly as observed in early serial tracings. Embolism of a large blood vessel is not fatal as a rule and is usually associated with previous disease of the heart or veins. Syphilitic aneurysm develops gradually and presents a history of earlier lesions and positive serologic tests. Other rare conditions which may be confused with dissecting aneurysm include mediastinal, pleural, retroperitoneal, pancreatic, or renal tumors; perinephric abscess; hydronephrosis; pleurisy; adrenal disease; and acute abdominal conditions (see Table 1-1, p. 6). Aspiration of bloody fluid from the left pleural cavity is highly significant for dissection, but pleuropulmonary malignancy may reveal characteristic metaplastic cells in addition, while tuberculosis presents the organism on smear or culture.

Medical treatment is entirely ineffective. A new surgical procedure permits re-entry of the blood flow in the dissected passage at a distal approachable site in the aorta. In cases in which the dissection begins in the ascending or descending portion of the aortic arch, the creation of a re-entry passage into the aortic lumen above, with obliteration of the false passage below, is achieved by cross-clamping the descending thoracic aorta, dividing it completely between the clamps, obliterating the false passage below by approximating the outer and inner layers, excising a small segment from the inner intimal and medial layer above to produce re-entry of the outer lumen, and then completing the procedure by end-to-end anastomosis. When the lesion is fairly well localized or arises at or below the level of the left sub-clavian artery, this procedure may be combined with excision of the segment involved at the origin of the dissection and completed with end-to-end anastomosis or insertion of an aortic homograft. Cellophane wrapping of the involved segment of the aorta is a simpler method which has had occasional success. Gelatin sponge packs and sutures may be employed to control the source of bleeding at actual rupture sites.

Aortitis. Inflammatory disease of the aorta commonly gives rise to chest pain. Although no definitive proof exists that inflammation of the aortic wall can cause pain unless the coronary ostia are also involved, such in-stances are actually encountered clinically. Very rare causes of aortitis are tuberculosis, acute and subacute bacterial infections, rheumatoid arthritis, rheumatic fever, and other collagen disorders. However, the most common cause of aortitis is syphilis. This infection may cause various types of aortic involvement. It may cause uncomplicated aortitis (27 per cent); aortitis with involvement of the aortic valve, resulting in regurgitation (50 per cent); aortitis with aortic aneurysm (14 per cent); and, finally, aortitis with involvement of the coronary ostia (30 per cent). The diagnosis of cardio-vascular syphilis has been facilitated by the recent introduction of new tests such as the treponema immobilization (TPI) and the treponema immune adherence tests (TPIA).

Uncomplicated luetic aortitis. The clinical recognition of this lesion is of great importance, since the institution of specific antisyphilitic therapy at this stage will prevent progression of the disease and its complications. Unfortunately, many cases of this type are entirely asymptomatic and escape detection.

Pain is localized to the substernal region and is dull, aching, and relatively constant, though of short duration. It is not dependent upon exertion, nor does it radiate down the arms, as is frequently the case in coronary disease. A continuous burning sensation may also occur behind the sternum, lasting for months and slightly increased by effort. If this pain is associated with the findings of a tambour-like second aortic sound, an increased area of dullness over the aorta toward the right side, and/or x-ray evidence of dilatation or calcification of the ascending aorta, a diagnosis of aortitis is nearly certain even in the absence of a positive serologic reaction for syphilis. Serology is positive in 85 per cent of untreated cases.

Occasionally, shortness of breath or an oppressive sensation in the chest, which is paroxysmal and nocturnal, may occur as a pain equivalent. In the absence of other detectable cardiac disease, aortitis should be suspected, particularly if both pain and paroxysmal nocturnal dyspnea coexist. Sudden paroxysms of pain may also occur in this form of aortitis and may be associated with a transitory rise of the blood pressure. These crises are discussed in connection with aortic insufficiency, where they occur more frequently.

Aortitis with aortic insufficiency. The aortic valve is very rarely affected by a primary syphilitic valvulitis. It almost always becomes incompetent secondary to the dilatation of the diseased aortic wall and the loss of elastic tissue. This complication is found in 50 per cent of cases of cardiovascular syphilis. The pain is attributed either to the associated aortitis or to the coronary insufficiency caused by the reduced coronary inflow. Since coronary blood flow depends considerably upon an adequate mean and diastolic pressure, there will be marked reduction when the latter decreases with advancing incompetence of the aortic valve. The type of pain produced by this dynamic disturbance is similar to that seen in aortic insufficiency, aortic stenosis, or tight mitral stenosis due to rheumatic fever. It usually occurs after exertion and is relieved by rest and nitroglycerin. In more advanced cases, it may also be present at rest (angina decubitus).

In some instances, the pain is actually due to an associated luetic coronary osteal stenosis. At times, the clinical picture of a "hypertensive crisis" occurs in luetic aortic insufficiency. These paroxysms of pain and hypertension resemble the attacks that are associated with pheochromocytoma. Sudden palpitation with substernal or precordial oppression of increasing intensity and radiation resembles angina pectoris. There is usually initial pallor followed by a pronounced facial flush and drenching perspiration. The systolic blood pressure may rise to 300 mm Hg and over, while the diastolic rises to a lesser extent. These attacks may appear without any obvious precipitating factor but may follow mental or physical strain. They are of variable duration, lasting a few minutes to several hours. They may disappear spontaneously and permanently. The blood pressure rise is the primary event which initiates the severe anginal pain when the former reaches a critical level. These attacks are obviously a manifestation of sympathetic overactivity; however, the exact mechanism is unknown. Although the attacks are accompanied by an increase in circulating epinephrine, this is far below the level seen in pheochromocytoma. Such attacks have actually been halted by benzodioxane, which neutralizes epinephrine and norepinephrine in pheochromocytoma.

The drug of choice for severe episodes is protoveratrine, since it not only reduces the blood pressure but also slows the tachycardia. Phentolamine (Regitine) is also useful, since it lacks the centrally stimulating effect of benzodioxane.

Aortitis with aneurysm. As dilatation of the diseased wall progresses, a fusiform or saccular dilatation ensues at the weakest point. Aneurysms of syphilitic origin have been discussed previously under acquired aneurysms of the aorta (pp. 160–61). The pain is frequently due to pressure upon neighboring structures (spine and intercostal nerves) as well as to the underlying aortitis. The special characteristics of aneurysms of the ascending ("aneurysm of signs"), arch ("aneurysm of symptoms"), and descending portions of the aorta are well known and require no detailed explanation.

Aortitis with coronary ostia involvement. Coronary osteal stenosis is a frequent complication of luetic aortitis, occurring in about 30 per cent of autopsied cases of cardiovascular syphilis. Both orifices are frequently involved (22 per cent) by concentric or eccentric narrowing. Although anginal pain may be minimal or absent (65 per cent), myocardial infarction rarely ensues because of the very gradual stenosis of the ostia which permits the development of an adequate collateral circulation. However, a diffuse myocardial fibrosis is commonly encountered and eventually results in myocardial insufficiency. The clinical diagnosis may be difficult. However, when severe angina develops in a patient with other findings of cardiovascular syphilis or neurosyphilis, this diagnosis must be seriously considered. The angina of coronary osteal stenosis greatly resembles that of arteriosclerotic coronary disease and may be located in the substernal area, between the shoulders, or in the epigastrium. It is not only present after exertion or excitement, but may occur even at rest. Not infrequently such patients exhibit great anxiety and an inexplicable restlessness. The electrocardiogram may reveal changes usually associated with transient coronary insufficiency. ST segment depression and T wave inversion occur, although the ST may be elevated as in acute myocardial infarction. Even Q waves may appear transiently. The exercise electrocardiogram may be of help in detecting asymptomatic coronary osteal stenosis in aortitis or luetic aortic aneurysm. On the other hand, negative exercise electrocardiographic tests have been reported in patients with complete occlusion of one coronary orifice. Sudden death is not uncommon with this complication of cardio-vascular syphilis, but progressive congestive heart failure is the usual terminal event due to extensive myocardial fibrosis.

The medical treatment of luetic aortitis gives greatest promise of arresting the disease when administered before signs of cardiovascular syphilis have developed. Nevertheless, it can retard or halt aneurysmal formation, aortic valvular insufficiency, and coronary osteal stenosis. Congestive heart failure and severe coronary insufficiency must be treated adequately. Saccular aneurysm may now be treated surgically with homograft or synthetic re-placements. Diffuse fusiform dilatations may be retarded by the fibrosing action of cellophane wrapping.

Aortitis due to rheumatic fever. In severe cases of rheumatic fever, the aorta may be affected in a manner similar to that found in the cardio-vascular system and other sites containing collagen tissue. It is not generally appreciated that rheumatic involvement of the aorta itself may give rise to chest pain by encroaching upon the coronary ostia.

The precordial pain, when present, is the result of coronary insufficiency which resembles that of arteriosclerotic or luetic coronary disease. Of added diagnostic aid is the appearance of systolic and diastolic murmurs, which may not be of valvular origin but may be due to turbulence and eddy cur-rents of blood about the roughened aortic wall and to the stretching of the aortic orifice, respectively. Serum mucoprotein and antistreptolysin titer elevations, positive C-reactive protein test, and electrocardiographic evi-dence of PR or QT prolongation or the occurrence of arrhythmias are help-ful. This acute complication of rheumatic fever responds to corticosteroid therapy.

Aortitis due to rheumatoid arthritis. Rheumatoid disease may cause aortic lesions with scarring and retraction of the aortic cusps, rolling of the free edges, focal calcification, and destruction of elastic tissue in the aortic ring. This may result in aortic insufficiency. Microscopy reveals a thickened intima with foci of inflammation, loss of elastic tissue, replacement fibrosis in the media, and endarteritis obliterans of the vasa vasorum of the externa. However, rheumatoid lesions, unlike those of syphilitic heart disease, usually remain localized to the region of the aortic valve and rarely involve the aorta distal to the ascending portion. Pain closely resembles the anginal syndrome. At times, this may be due to coronary insufficiency caused by the "sucking effect" of the regurgitation. Aortic dilatation is usually not apparent in the roentgen films. On the other hand, the electrocardiogram may reveal conduction disturbances and nonspecific ST and T wave changes. Bentonite and latex fixation tests may prove helpful in diagnosing about 70 per cent of these cases.

Pulseless disease (Takayasu's disease, aortic arch syndrome). This condition is a chronic disorder of the great arteries which arise from the aortic arch or of their ostia. It results in diminished caliber or total obstruction of the lumina of these vessels, which causes diminished or absent pulsations in the arteries supplying the head, neck, and upper extremities.

The term "reversed coarctation" has also been applied to this interesting condition because of the development of a collateral circulation similar to that in coarctation. The exact etiology is not well established, since it has been found in cardiovascular syphilis, healed dissecting aneurysm, and congenital anomalies. In young women, it may be due to an obscure form of arteritis which affects the aortic arch and/or its main branches.

Patients with this disorder may occasionally have chest pain resembling that of coronary artery disease. Pain in the upper extremities may be mistaken for referred anginal pain or anginal equivalents when it is actually due to arterial insufficiency of the subclavian arteries. Similarly, vertigo and syncope following exercise may be mistaken as cardiac symptoms when they actually are due to common carotid artery insufficiency. The latter must also be differentiated from carotid artery thrombosis and carotid sinus syndrome.

The diagnosis can be ascertained by means of angiocardiography or aortography, which reveals the marked narrowing or complete obstruction of the arterial branches arising from the aorta. Luetic involvement or congenital hypoplasia of the aortic arch is excluded by the aortic widening or narrowing, respectively. Treatment is unsatisfactory in the absence of an established cause. In proven cases of arteritis, corticosteroid therapy can be tried. Antisyphilitic therapy should be used in appropriate cases. In other instances, the treatment is merely symptomatic. Surgical resection with replacement of the affected segment has been performed successfully and is curative in selected cases.

Trauma to the aorta. Since the aorta is a highly resistant elastic structure protected by the spine and internal organs, trauma seldom affects this structure unless it was previously diseased. Traumatic injury of the aorta is most commonly encountered in those who have experienced severe compression during automobile collisions or in those caught beneath wreckage during a war or other catastrophe. The isthmus of the aorta is involved most frequently, since it is at the junction of the relatively fixed and mobile segments of the aorta and thus is subject to the greatest strain during nonpenetrating trauma which may cause a tear or may shear off at this point.

There is obvious external evidence of chest wall injury in practically all such instances. Since some patients with incomplete tears survive for a variable period, from a few hours to many months, surgical repair can prove lifesaving.

Occasionally, the aorta may simply buckle at its fixed point near the arch. The tearing of vasa vasorum at this site may result in local degenerative changes which may cause the slow evolution of an aneurysmal dilatation over a period of several months or years. This can have medicolegal significance. These delayed effects can be demonstrated by aortography.

Wars, civil violence, and bizarre accidents account for the great majority of penetrating wounds of the aorta. They are caused by bullets, knives, shrapnel, ice-picks, and other pointed instruments. Early recognition of the serious nature of such wounds can lead to immediate surgical intervention and lifesaving arteriorrhaphy.

Arteriovenous aneurysm ("fistulae") may occur when the aorta ruptures into the atria, pulmonary artery, venae cavae, or other vessels. This may be due to trauma caused by shell fragments, bayonets, and bullets. Arteriosclerosis, syphilis, ulcerating bacterial endaortitis, and congenital defects are also factors. Death results from the sudden overloading of the pulmonary circulation when the aorta ruptures into the right atrium or pulmonary artery. A continuous loud bruit with thrill and high pulse pressure are important diagnostic signs. Cardiac catheterization and angiocardiography are essential to establish the presence of the fistula. Restorative surgical procedures are now available.

REFERENCES

Baer, S.: Varied manifestations of dissecting aneurysm of the aorta. *J.A.M.A.*, **161**:689, 1956.

Baer, S., and Goldburgh, H. L.: The varied clinical syndromes produced by dissecting aneurysm. *Am. Heart J.*, **35**:198, 1948.

Bean, W. B., and Ponseti, I. V.: Dissecting aneurysm produced by diet. *Circulation*, **12**:185, 1955.

Brindley, P., and Stembridge, V. A.: Aneurysms of the aorta: a clinicopathologic study of 369 necropsy cases. *Am. J. Path.*, **32**:67, 1956.

Burchell, H. B.: Aortic dissection (dissecting hematoma; dissecting aneurysm of the aorta). *Circulation*, **12**:1068, 1955.

Campbell, C., and Baylis, J. H.: The course and prognosis of coarctation of the aorta. *Brit. Heart J.*, **18**:475, 1956.

Clark, W. S.; Kulka, J. P.; and Bauer, W.: Rheumatoid arteritis with aortic regurgitation. *Am. J. Med.,* **22**:580, 1957.

DeBakey, M. E.; Cooley, A.; and Creech, O., Jr.: Aneurysm of the aorta treated by resection. *J.A.M.A.,* **163**:1439, 1957.

DeBakey, M. E.; Cooley, D. A.; and Creech, O., Jr.: Surgical considerations of dissecting aneurysm of the aorta. *Ann. Surg.,* **142**:586, 1955.

DeBakey, M. E., and Crawford, E. S.: Resection and hemograft replacement of innominate and carotid arteries with use of shunt to maintain circulation. *Surg., Gynec. & Obst.,* **105**:129, 1957.

Erb, B. D., and Tullis, I. F.: Dissecting aneurysm of the aorta. The clinical features of 30 autopsied cases. *Circulation,* **22**:315, 1960.

Fremont, R. E.: Hypertensive crisis and severe myocardial ischemia induced by piperoxan with comments on the differential diagnosis and treatment of hypertensive crises. *Angiology,* **5**:381, 1954.

Friedberg, C. K.: *Diseases of the Heart,* 2nd ed. W. B. Saunders Co., Philadelphia, 1959.

Lillehei, C. W.; Stanley, P.; and Varco, R. L.: Surgical treatment of ruptured aneurysms of the sinus of Valsalva. *Ann. Surg.,* **146**: 459, 1957.

Merten, C. W.; Finby, N.; and Steinberg, I.: The antemortem diagnosis of syphilitic aneurysm of the aortic sinuses: report of nine cases. *Am. J. Med.,* **20**:345, 1956.

Parmley, F., Jr.; Mattingly, W.; Manion, C.; and Jahnke, J., Jr.: Non-penetrating traumatic injury to the aorta. Presented at 29th Annual Session, Am. Heart Assoc., 1956.

Prior, J. T.; Buran, R. T.; and Perl, T.: Chronic (healed) dissecting aneurysms. *J. Thoracic Surg.,* **33**:213, 1957.

Reich, N. E.: *Diseases of the Aorta.* The Macmillan Co., New York, 1949.

Reich, N. E.: Dissecting aneurysms of the aorta: a clinicopathologic correlation of 19 cases. *Clinics,* **3**:346, 1944.

Reich, N. E.: Nonatheromatous lesions of the coronary ostia. *New York J. Med.,* **52**:2365, 1952.

Reich, N. E.: Occlusions of the abdominal aorta. *Ann. Int. Med.,* **19**:36, 1943.

Reich, N. E.: Roentgenology of the aorta (chapter in *Roentgenology of the Chest*). Charles C Thomas, Publisher, Springfield, Ill. (in press).

Reich, N. E.: Unusual conditions involving the aorta. *Am. Heart J.,* **28**:742, 1944.

Reich, N. E., and Ehrlich, D. E.: Displacements of the barium-filled esophagus by cardiovascular lesions. *Dis. Chest,* **29**:376, 1956.

Rimsa, A.; and Griffith, G. C.: Trends in cardiovascular syphilis. *Ann. Int. Med.*, **46**:915, 1957.

Ross, R. S., and McKusick, V. A.: Aortic arch syndromes. *A.M.A. Arch. Int. Med.*, **92**:701, 1953.

Scherf, D., and Boyd, L. J.: *Cardiovascular Disease*. J. B. Lippincott Co., Philadelphia, 1958.

Steinberg, I.: Diagnosis of arteriosclerotic aneurysms of the thoracic aorta. *Ann. Int. Med.*, **46**:218, 1957.

Steinberg, I., and Geller, W.: Aneurysmal dilatation of aortic sinuses in arachnodactyly. Diagnosis during life in three cases. *Ann. Int. Med.*, **43**:120, 1955.

Warren, R., and Triedman, L. J.: Pulseless disease and carotid artery thrombosis: surgical considerations. *New England J. Med.*, **257**:685, 1957.

Weir, A. B., Jr., and Kyle, J. W.: Reversed coarctation: review of pulseless disease and report of a case. *Ann. Int. Med.*, **45**:681, 1956.

CHAPTER 9 *DISEASES OF THE ENDOCARDIUM*

ENDOCARDIAL DISEASES

The endocardium does not contain any pain-sensitive nerve fibers. Hence, endocardial diseases do not produce chest pain as a direct result of disease or injury of the endocardium per se, but because of secondary or associated pericardial or coronary involvement. The characteristics of chest pain encountered in certain endocardial diseases will now be discussed.

175

Acute rheumatic endocarditis. The endocarditic manifestations of acute rheumatic fever appear as a very early feature in many instances. However, an isolated endocarditis (without an appreciable degree of pericarditis or pancarditis) does not give rise to any subjective symptoms, such as chest pain. It is usually discovered by the appearance of new murmurs or alteration of pre-existent ones, and by abnormal changes of heart sounds. Since the chest pain encountered in acute rheumatic endocarditis is due to pericarditis or coronary artery involvement, it is discussed in the chapters dealing with these entities (see Chaps. 11 and 12). Thoracic pain appearing during acute rheumatic fever may also be due to transitory involvement of the sternoclavicular and shoulder joints as well as to pleural involvement. The special characteristics of the pain in these conditions have already been discussed (see pp. 75, 103).

Postcommissurotomy syndrome (postcardiotomy). This syndrome, consisting of chest pain, fever, atrial fibrillation, cardiac failure, and pericardial, myocardial, and pleural involvement, has been observed following cardiac surgery and especially mitral commissurotomy. Because of a close similarity, a more detailed discussion of this interesting disorder is presented in the chapter on pericarditis (see p. 230). As in acute rheumatic endocarditis, the chest pain is not caused by the endocardial involvement but by the pericardial involvement. Chest pain following cardiotomy may also be caused by secondary involvement of the pleura, or by the interrupted intercostal nerves and ribs produced by the extensive incision.

Acute and subacute bacterial endocarditis. Chest pain is seldom encountered in endocarditis of bacterial origin and is not caused by endocardial involvement per se. The verrucae of the acute and subacute forms are the potential sources of embolism and pain in various structures. It may be pleuritic in character when the pulmonary arteries are affected and is usually located in the lower left chest. The left upper abdomen becomes acutely painful following splenic infarction. It closely resembles anginal pain when produced by coronary embolism or when coronary insufficiency is secondary to aortic stenosis, aortic insufficiency, tight mitral stenosis, or large obstructing verrucae on the aortic valve. Thus, involvement of the aortic valve by extensive thrombotic vegetations may encroach upon the adjacent coronary ostia, or the emboli may enter the coronary arteries. When actual myocardial infarction occurs secondary to embolization, the pain may be indistinguishable from that which occurs in primary coronary disease, with resultant myocardial infarction. The diagnosis of acute or subacute bacterial endocarditis is usually well established or is highly suspected when the chest pain occurs. However, the pain may antedate the valvular infection in cases of pre-existent healed valvular lesions. The anginal pains which are associated with valvular lesions are discussed later in this section (pp. 180, 182–83).

The diagnostic criteria of acute or subacute bacterial endocarditis need not be discussed here in any great detail. The former causes death when untreated in less than six weeks. The classic manifestations are mainly embolic but include chills, fever, diaphoresis, emaciation, various cardiac symptoms, splenomegaly, changing murmurs, renal disturbances, tender cutaneous lesions, petechiae, Osler nodes, purpura, pulmonary symptoms and findings, sternal tenderness, *café-au-lait* color, joint and ocular changes, other embolic phenomena, and, finally, intractable congestive heart failure.

Since subacute bacterial endocarditis may be superimposed upon valvular lesions of variable etiology, the angina-like chest pain may be related to the underlying congenital, luetic, or rheumatic involvement of the heart and aorta, including involvement of the coronary ostia. Chest pain may be also caused by an associated pneumonia which is bronchitic or pleuritic in character.

Pain may result from pulmonary embolization secondary to subacute bacterial endocarditis, involvement of the tricuspid valve, interventricular septal defect, and patent ductus arteriosus as well as from peripheral venous thrombosis or a fibrillating right atrium. Pericarditis as a cause of chest pain is rarely seen in subacute bacterial endocarditis but may occur with staphylococcal infections which reach the pericardial sac through the blood stream or by contiguous spread.

Atypical verrucous endocarditis, Libman-Sacks disease (L.E.D.). This type of endocarditis is part of a systemic disorder which involves the connective tissue of the smaller arteries and arterioles of the skin, serous membranes, myocardium, endocardium, and kidneys. The "wire-loop" glomeruli and atypical verrucous endocarditis appear to be specific manifestations of L.E.D. It is further differentiated from the other collagen disorders by the hematoxylin-staining bodies found in the tissues and the Hargraves bodies found in the leukocytes of the bone marrow and peripheral blood.

This disease has long been considered a collagen disorder, based on certain features which bear superficial resemblance to those found in other so-called "collagen diseases." The endocardial lesion is larger than that usually seen in rheumatic endocarditis and tends to involve the mural endocardium and that of the valve pockets. Since it frequently affects the right side of the heart, tricuspid and pulmonic valves are damaged more frequently than mitral and aortic ones. A superimposed acute bacterial endocarditis may occur terminally.

Chest pain is frequently encountered in this condition. Again, it is not related to the endocardial lesion but to the pleural or pericardial involvement. Adhesive and even serofibrinous pericarditis are not uncommon features of disseminated lupus erythematosus. Pleuritis with and without effusion is seen occasionally as the first or dominant manifestation. Therefore, chest pain occurring in atypical verrucous endocarditis may be of the pleuropericardial type. Concomitant myocardial involvement does not produce chest pain but tends to result in electrocardiographic abnormalities and cardiac failure. The diagnosis is established by the demonstration of lupus erythematosus cells. At least three technics are now recommended to detect these characteristic cells. The sieved two-hour clot test, the Zinkhan-Conley method of rotating heparinized blood with glass beads, and the Snapper ring technic appear to give the highest percentage of positive results.

Treatment consists of the administration of corticosteroid drugs in more severe cases. Antimalarial drugs are useful when the disease is mild. The effect of quinacrine (Atabrine), amodiaquin (Camoquin), or chloroquine (Aralen) on the cutaneous lesions is almost specific, and even the arthritic manifestations often abate. Concurrent use of antimalarials and corticosteroids may permit lowering of the corticosteroid dosage or discontinuance of the hormones entirely.

Specific endocarditis. Endocarditis of syphilitic and tuberculous origins is extremely rare. The reader is referred to a previous text by the senior author (*The Uncommon Heart Diseases,* 1954), which includes a detailed discussion of such cardiac rarities. When chest pain occurs, it is due to coronary or pericardial involvement, or to involvement of the lungs, aorta, and other intrathoracic structures.

Endocardial fibroelastosis. The term "endocardial fibroelastosis" is synonymous with "endomyocardial fibrosis," "endomyocardial sclerosis," and "endocardial sclerosis." It has received increasing recognition in recent years despite an obscure etiology and pathogenesis. A white, opaque, fibroelastic thickening of the endocardium occurs and frequently involves the cardiac valves and myocardium. Primary and secondary types of endocardial thickening may be recognized. The secondary (acquired) type is actually a reparative fibrosis and may be found in myocardial infarction, rheumatic fever, diphtheria, subacute bacterial endocarditis, malignant nephrosclerosis, polyarteritis nodosa, disseminated lupus erythematosus, and beriberi. A history of chronic alcoholism is obtainable in most adult cases. The primary (congenital) type may be found at any age but is especially common in infants and children. It is best explained as a developmental anomaly, perhaps as an overgrowth of the endocardium of the left bulbus cordis due to a genetically determined metabolic disorder. Gargoylism may also be encountered. It may also be secondary to valvular or other cardiac defects leading to hypoxia of the endocardium.

Symptomatology is related to the altered pathologic physiology of the left ventricle, which is most commonly involved. Wean has demonstrated the intramyocardial circulation and considers the changes in the left ventricle secondary to interference with this circulation. The changes in the endocardium may interfere with the emptying of the arterioluminal vessels into the left ventricle because of their constriction by the firm elastic tissue. The inner myocardium becomes ischemic and fibrotic with early dilatation and ultimate failure of the left ventricle. In children, there is frequent association with congenital lesions such as coarctation of the aorta, interatrial septal defect, hypoplasia of the left atrium or ventricle, and valvular defects, most commonly involving the tricuspid valve.

As regards the clinical course, three major types may be recognized. Patients in the first group die either before any cardiac abnormality is suspected or after a brief and progressive downward course. Irritability, anorexia, restlessness, and a terminal shock-like condition in conjunction with neck and limb stiffness, cyanosis, and respiratory distress are symptomatic. The second group responds to good medical management over a period of months or years after an initial attack of congestive failure in infancy, and may become amenable to surgical therapy of an underlying lesion. The third group lives long beyond infancy, and an occasional patient may live a full, asymptomatic existence.

The adult cases show fibroelastic endocardial thickening which is qualitatively identical with that found during childhood, in some as severe and in others less severe but more patchy in extent. When the clinical picture in the adults is contrasted with that in children, it is found that the average duration of symptoms in the former is much longer, congestive failure is more prominent, mural thrombi are present in three-quarters of the patients, and embolization is very frequent.

Chest pain of anginal character is seen in adult patients but is not a very pronounced feature of the disease, although it may occur in the presence of normal coronary arteries. A similar clinical picture has been encountered in East African endomyocardial necrosis and in South African cardiovascular collagenosis with parietal endocardial thrombosis. The extent and distribution of the endocardial thickening vary in these cases, but the etiology is equally obscure.

Not infrequently, the cardiodynamic disturbance closely resembles that of constrictive pericarditis, with the thickening of the endocardium markedly restricting diastolic expansion of the ventricles. This is readily recognizable on kymography, fluoroscopy, and angiocardiography. The treatment of congestive failure is palliative. Underlying congenital cardiovascular lesions may be attacked surgically. More recently, poudrage has been employed in an effort to stimulate collateral circulation.

VALVULAR DISEASES

Chest pain occurs frequently in patients with valvular heart disease. Pain may have a cardiac or noncardiac origin, regardless of the type of valve lesion present. Since the latter may, however, determine the mechanism as well as the frequency of chest pain, it is best to discuss this subject in accordance with the type of valvular lesion present.

Mitral stenosis. This valvular defect is almost always due to rheumatic involvement and leads to a variety of mechanisms of chest pain. Chest pain may be anginoid in character and has been encountered in as many as 85 of a series of 100 patients with mitral stenosis; most of these patients were under thirty-seven years of age and showed very little coronary artery disease. Angina appears to be related to the severity of the stenosis. Low cardiac output is suggested by the small pulse volume, low systemic blood pressure, and cold vasoconstricted extremities. Inadequate coronary blood flow due to the lack of improved cardiac output following exercise causes angina. Electrocardiographic changes are caused by the myocardial ischemia and may be more prominent in left ventricular surface leads, even though a predominantly right ventricular hypertrophy exists.

Pain in mitral stenosis has been variously attributed to relative coronary insufficiency, to compression of the left coronary artery between the enlarged left atrium and a prominent pulmonary conus, and to traction on the coronary orifice due to contraction of a scarred mitral valve with shortened chordae. Angina due to primary coronary artery disease is actually rare in mitral stenosis unless there is concomitant rheumatic coronary arteritis. A recent series of nearly 3000 cases of angina or myocardial infarction revealed the presence of mitral stenosis in only 0.6 per cent.

The noncardiac type of chest pain in mitral stenosis may be caused by several conditions. Cardiac neurosis is frequently responsible for a vague, sticking, or aching precordial sensation occurring even at rest. The apical or nipple region is similarly affected. A deep morbid anxiety regarding the cardiac condition or contemplated cardiac surgery is the usual precipitating cause. This functional factor has been discussed in detail in Chapter 4.

Active rheumatic carditis may also cause chest pain which may closely resemble angina pectoris but which does not respond well to nitroglycerin. Pain may also possess the characteristics of dysphagia caused by compression of the esophagus by an enlarged left atrium. This enlargement is more common with combined mitral stenosis and regurgitation or pure or predominantly mitral regurgitation. Massive dilatation of the left atrium (especially due to pure mitral insufficiency) may on rare occasions even cause spinal erosion with a deep boring pain in the back. An aching or stabbing type of chest pain, usually in the right side of the chest with radiation to the right scapula or shoulder, occurs in some instances of mitral stenosis. Occasionally, the pain may be limited to the left chest. In general, the cause of the pain is obscure, although it has been postulated that it may be due to a disproportion between the available blood supply and the metabolic demands of the expanded atrial wall, since the pain frequently occurs following exertion. It is also related to pulmonary hypertension and has been termed hypercyanotic angina. Pain may also occur in paroxysms and is associated with dyspnea, orthopnea, and severe cyanosis. It responds poorly to nitroglycerin but may improve when cardiac failure is treated intensively with oxygen and digitalis. This chest pain as well as the other clinical features respond promptly to corticosteroid therapy, although salicylates are preferred in mild cases.

Phonocardiography (see Fig. 9-1) constitutes one of the most helpful aids in evaluation of the degree of stenosis present. Roentgenography or electro-kymography also help in the differentiation of various valvular lesions (e.g., between mitral stenosis and insufficiency). (See Fig. 9-2.) Mitral commissurotomy is generally indicated when the stenotic lesion begins to show evidences of cardiac embarrassment. The mortality rate due to operative intervention is currently 4 per cent.

A not uncommon cause of postoperative chest pain is *intercostal neuritis,* which may become very troublesome. Originally, local alcohol blocks were used to prevent this severe incisional type of pain, but this has been abandoned since it does not prevent the pain reliably. Occasionally postoperative pain may be due to myocardial ischemia caused by prolonged hypoxia during surgery. *Myocardial infarction* has also occurred due to the inadvertent ligation of the left circumflex artery during manipulation and suture of the left atrial appendage. *Postcommissurotomy syndrome* as a cause of chest pain has been previously discussed (see p. 176).

Aortic stenosis. This obstructive lesion of the aortic valve is commonly due to rheumatic fever, but arteriosclerosis, healed or active subacute bacterial endocarditis, and congenital defects (supernumerary cusps, bicuspid valve,

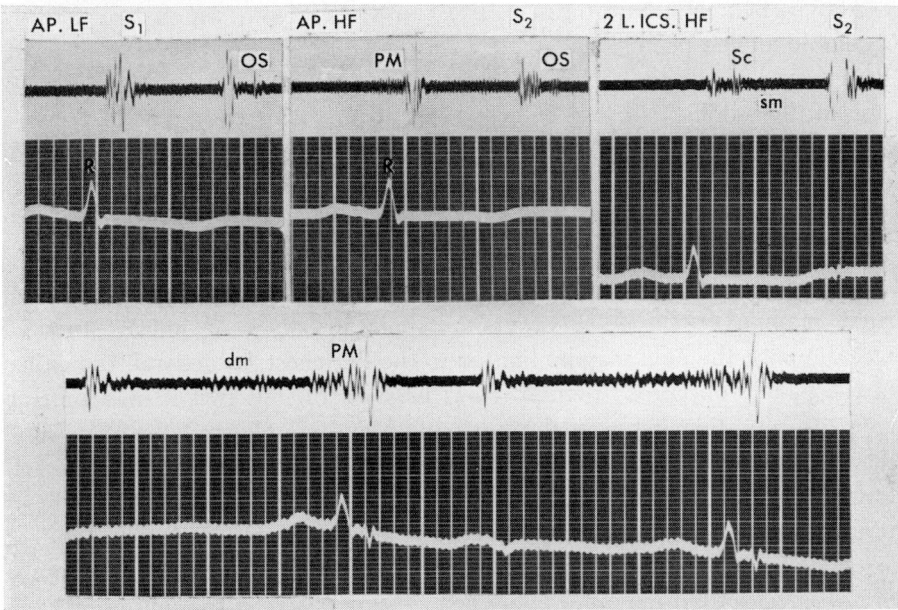

Fig. 9-1. Phonocardiogram in mitral stenosis. Note first sound (S_1) of high frequency and amplitude and of delayed onset (R-S_1 interval exceeds 0.04 sec.), prolonged diastolic rumble (*dm*) with presystolic accentuation (*PM*) and presence of opening snap (*OS*) with short S_2-*OS* interval (0.06 sec.). These findings indicate dynamically significant and fairly tight mitral stenosis. Note also: in the pulmonic area the early systolic click (*SC*), slight systolic murmur (*sm*), and markedly accentuated second sound (P_2)—all related to pulmonary hypertension. *LF*, Low frequency record; *HF*, high frequency record; *AP*, apex; 2 L. *ICS.*, second left intercostal space.

congenital aortic atresia) may also be at fault. Of all the valvular lesions, aortic stenosis is most frequently responsible for cardiac pain, since it occurs in 10 to 20 per cent of proven cases. In severe aortic stenosis, angina pectoris is the most common symptom after fatigue and exertional dyspnea.

Comparison of the natural history of aortic stenosis with that of mitral stenosis shows that the former has a longer symptomless period. When fatal left ventricular failure ensues, it is of brief duration. By contrast, mitral stenosis presents a comparatively long period of severe symptoms, and the downhill progress is marked by exacerbations that are often associated with pain due to bronchitis or pulmonary infarction.

Although aortic stenosis ordinarily takes much longer to develop, angina pectoris may be an early symptom. It is aggravated by physical effort, and the pain resembles that encountered in acute coronary insufficiency. Several explanations have been advanced for the pathogenesis of cardiac pain. Concomitant coronary atherosclerosis is frequently found in cases of aortic stenosis exhibiting symptoms of angina pectoris. Primary aortic valve

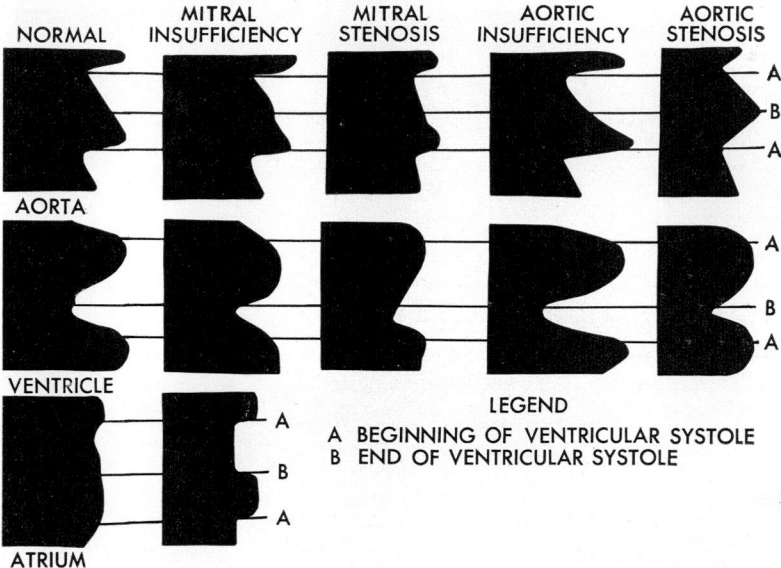

Fig. 9-2. Aortic, ventricular, and atrial kymographic patterns of valvular lesions. Note variation of slope contour during systole and diastole. (From Reich, N. E.: *Diseases of the Aorta.* The Macmillan Co., New York, 1949.)

stenosis may very well be of arteriosclerotic origin in many of these cases. However, anginal seizures frequently occur in the presence of normal coronary arteries and may even present findings of various degrees of myocardial necrosis. This pathogenetic mechanism derives from the diminished blood flow past the stenosed valve with a functional or relative coronary insufficiency of varying severity. This results in varying degrees of myocardial ischemia, from slight transient and reversible states to prolonged hypoxia leading to myocardial necrosis. It has also been suggested that the manner in which blood is ejected through the narrowed aortic opening exerts suction on the coronary ostia during systole, thus producing a significant drop in coronary blood flow. The work of the left ventricle is also increased as a result of the obstruction and produces a relative ischemia of the cardiac musculature. Diminution of the coronary blood flow is enhanced by an increased peripheral resistance in the coronary vessels, which has been attributed to the marked increase in intraventricular pressure necessary to maintain a near-normal aortic pressure in spite of severe narrowing of the aortic orifice.

Pain obviously appears more frequently and is more severe in the calcified type of aortic stenosis (see Fig. 9-3). This is due not only to the more severe degree of aortic stenosis encountered, but also to the higher incidence of

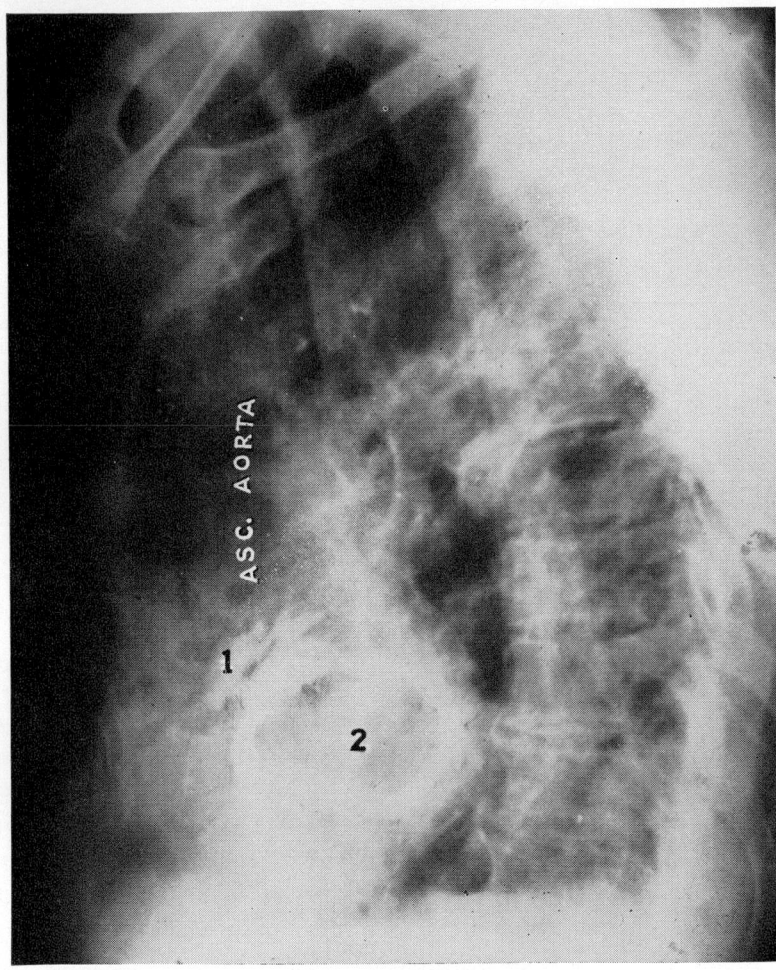

Fig. 9-3. Calcification of valves. Left anterior oblique view shows marked
calcium deposits in aortic valve (*1*) and annulus fibrosis of mitral ring (*2*).
Calcification extends into adjacent myocardium. (From Reich, N. E.: *Diseases of the Aorta.* The Macmillan Co., New York, 1949.)

associated coronary atherosclerosis, since primary calcific aortic stenosis
frequently represents another manifestation and localization of atherosclerosis resulting from a disturbed lipid metabolism. On the other hand, previous
damage by rheumatic infection probably represents a predisposing factor
for the development of these sclerotic changes, since this may be the end
stage of the healing process. In a group of patients with aortic stenosis, the
average total serum cholesterol was 282 mg per 100 ml; it was over 279 mg
per 100 ml in more than half the cases. In contrast, hypercholesteremia in

aortic stenosis closely paralleled levels found in patients with coronary atherosclerosis. Xanthomas are occasionally found as another manifestation of the disturbed lipid metabolism.

Sudden death occurs fairly frequently in aortic stenosis. It may be caused by cerebral ischemia or by severe acute coronary insufficiency with terminal cardiac standstill or ventricular fibrillation, or by obstructing thrombi on the stenosed aortic valve which interfere with coronary flow. Angina-like pain in aortic stenosis, which may be due to "hypertensive crises," has been discussed previously (see p. 168). These episodes occur even in young individuals and are of the same character as those encountered in patients with aortic insufficiency, aortitis, coronary sclerosis, and essential hypertension.

Surgical treatment for aortic stenosis is performed by closed or open technics. When the blind method is employed in the treatment of calcified aortic stenosis, the transventricular route is preferred. For noncalcified disease, open direct-vision aortic valvulotomy with bypass or hypothermia is recommended. Many cases cannot be satisfactorily fractured by finger alone and require additional instrumentation. In the presence of marked calcific distortion, an attempt may be made to "tease" out the deposits. Surgical mortality usually ranges between 15 to 20 per cent. Advisability of surgical correction is determined by the functional capacity of the left ventricle.

Attacks of angina pectoris or cerebral ischemia also represent important indications for operation, since they are not likely to improve with medical treatment and may terminate in sudden death. Accurate assessment of the degree of valvular stenosis can be determined by left-heart catheterization through the left atrium or by direct percutaneous left ventricular puncture. The aortic pressure is also determined. This provides the most reliable means of determining the pressure gradient across the aortic valve. The gradient may be deceivingly high when significant regurgitation coexists. Pressure in the left ventricle and brachial artery should be measured before, during, and after surgery. Where cardiac catheterization is not possible, a determination of the carotid and brachial pulse contour may be of considerable diagnostic value (see Fig. 9-4). The results of aortic stenosis surgery have been difficult to assess at this stage. Patients with moderate to severe lesions fail to benefit frequently when the severely calcified and distorted valve defies surgical repair.

Subaortic stenosis is a curious congenital annular thickening of the endocardium a few millimeters below the aortic valve. Unless it is of marked degree, it does not usually produce cardiac pain, since the valves themselves are not involved and do not interfere with the normal egress of blood.

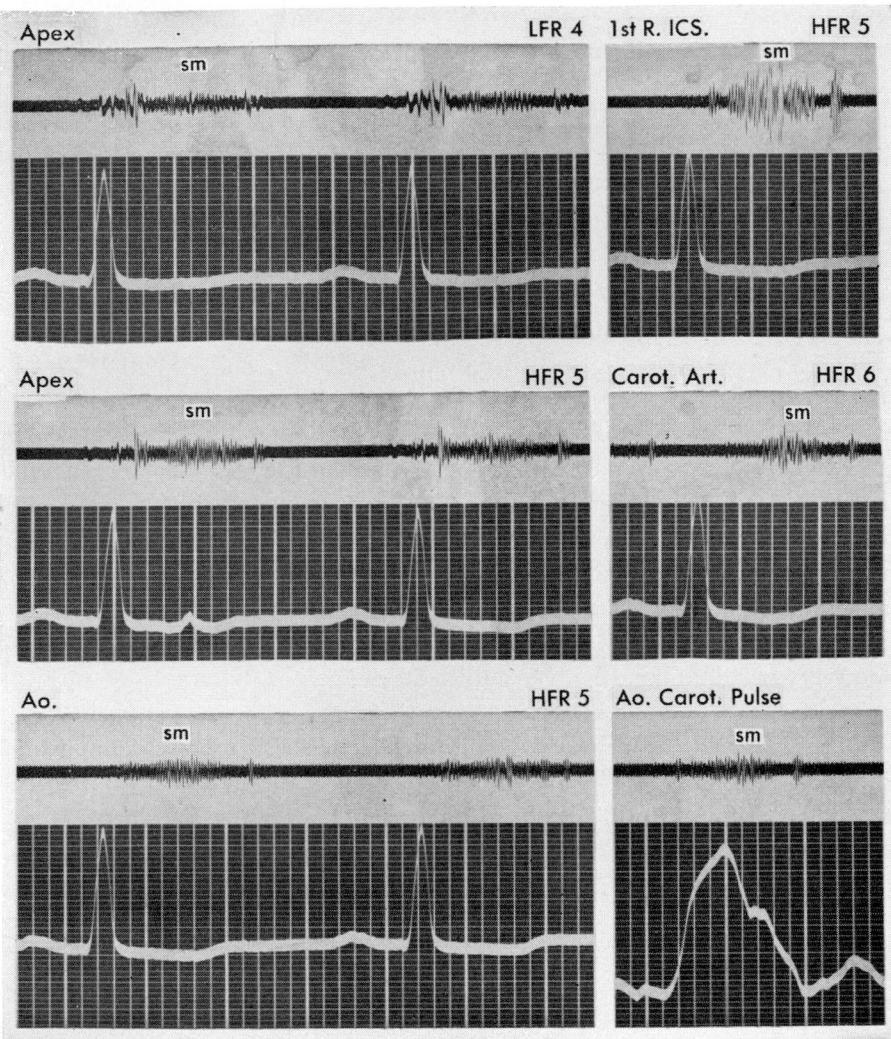

Fig. 9-4. Phonocardiogram and carotid pulse tracing in aortic stenosis. Note characteristic diamond-shaped configuration of systolic murmur (*sm*) of high frequency and wide transmission. Note also characteristic contour of pulse wave with anacrotic break and delayed peak. *LFR,* Low-frequency record; *HFR,* high-frequency record; 1st R. *ICS,* first right intercostal space.

Congenital aortic stenosis presents the usual findings of aortic stenosis as observed in adults. Bicuspid or supernumerary cusps may adhere to each other as a result of fetal endocarditis, or atresia or marked hypoplasia of the ascending aorta may be at fault. Cardiac pain is rare. Fatigue, shortness of breath, and profuse perspiration are the most common symptoms.

Aortic insufficiency. The same etiologic factors are found as those that occur with the stenotic lesion, except that syphilis and rheumatoid arthritis may also be implicated due to involvement and stretching of the aortic wall.

This lesion may show marked variation in the degree of valvular incompetence. Mild involvement in many patients may permit survival for twenty years or more, and the patients are able to lead almost normal lives. However, the mortality rate is markedly elevated in the presence of extensive aortic regurgitation. After the onset of angina pectoris, few patients survive more than a year or two, and some die within a few months. The diminished diastolic blood pressure results in an impoverished coronary circulation, which may be induced by the "sucking" effect of regurgitation. This effect is in addition to any organic disease involving the coronary ostia, such as arteriosclerosis or syphilis, or associated disease of the coronary arteries per se.

The subjective and objective features of the anginal syndrome are quite consistent and probably represent a special type of angina pectoris. Sinus tachycardia, palpitation, generalized flushing of the skin, profuse sweating, and difficult respiration usually precede pain but occasionally occur without pain. Hypertension may be found at the onset and suggests "hypertensive crisis" as the primary cause for a myocardial rather than a coronary insufficiency. Severe precordial pain spreads transversely to both sides of the sternum and to the left side of the neck.

Since the outcome is nearly always unfavorable after onset of intractable congestive heart failure and, especially, of nocturnal angina pectoris, surgical intervention is justified. Insertion of a plastic Hufnagel valve in the descending thoracic aorta has been employed to relieve the reflux load on the heart. At present, attempts are being made to replace the diseased valve with synthetic valves employing bypass or hypothermia. A polyvinyl sponge prosthesis or woven tetraflorethylene (Teflon) replacement has been employed. At times, it may be important to ascertain the correlation of anginal episodes with the degree of valvular incompetence with utmost accuracy. Left heart catheterization appears the most suitable tool for this purpose, but unfortunately it fails to correlate well with findings obtained at the time of operation.

In patients with syphilitic aortic insufficiency, (Fig. 9-5) cardiac pain of anginal character is usually due mainly to coronary osteal stenosis caused by the luetic aortitis. Because of the extensive myocardial ischemia provoked, electrocardiograms obtained during transient episodes of angina may show the pattern of acute myocardial infarction even with pathologic Q waves. Active luetic infection must first be controlled by intensive antibiotic therapy before considering the necessity for surgical therapy.

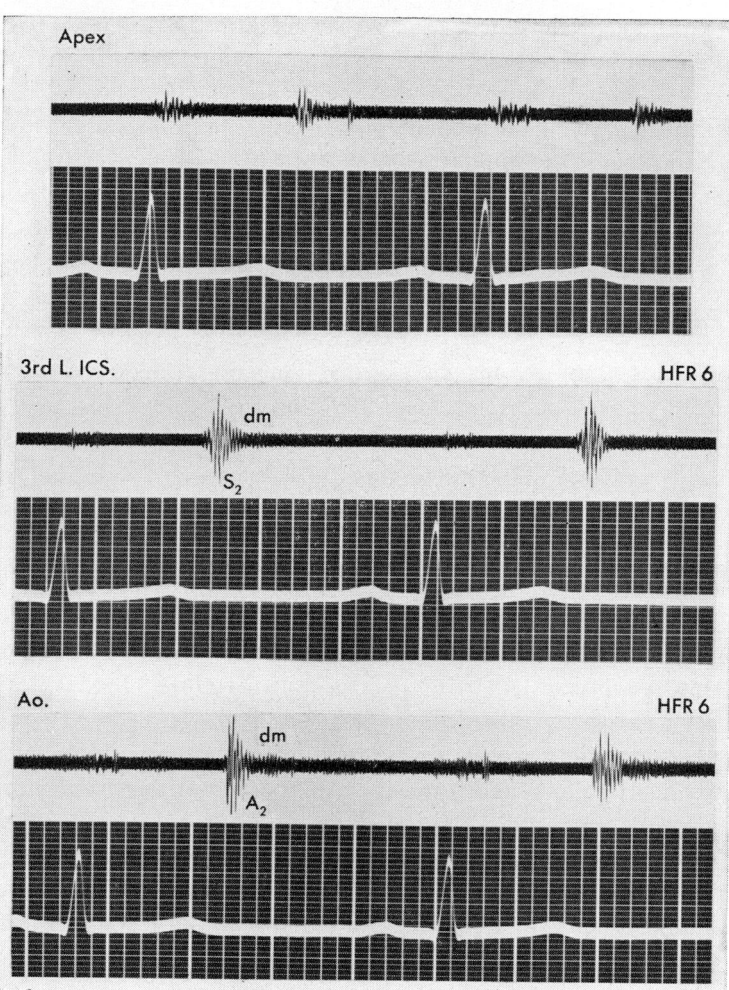

Fig. 9-5. Phonocardiographic changes in syphilitic aortitis with aortic insufficiency. Note musical or tambour characteristics of second aortic sound (A_2) and high-pitched early diastolic murmur (dm) of characteristic decrescendo configuration.

REFERENCES

Abelmann, W. H., and Ellis, L. B.: Severe aortic stenosis in adults: evaluation by clinical and physiological criteria and results of surgical treatment. *Ann. Int. Med.,* **51**:449, 1959.

Ashworth, H., and Jones, A. M.: Aneurysmal dilatation of the left auricle with erosion of the spine. *Brit. Heart J.,* **8**:207, 1946.

Ball, J. D.; Williams, A. W.; and Davies, J. N. P.: Endomyocardial fibrosis. *Lancet,* **1**:1049, 1954.

Becker, B. J. P.; Chatgidakis, C. B.; and Lingen Van, B.: Cardiovascular collagenosis with parietal endocardial thrombosis. A clinicopathologic study of forty cases. *Circulation,* **7**:345, 1953.

Bedell, G. N.; Culbertson, J. W.; and Ehrenhaft, J. L.: Management of patients with mitral stenosis before, during, and after mitral valvuloplasty. *A.M.A. Arch. Int. Med.,* **94**:718, 1954.

Bergeron, H.: Aortic stenosis—clinical manifestations and course of disease; review of 100 proved cases. *A.M.A. Arch. Int. Med.,* **94**:911, 1954.

Bland, E. F., and Wheeler, E. O.: Severe aortic regurgitation in young people. *New England J. Med.,* **256**:667, 1957.

Brock, R. M. S.: Surgical treatment of aortic stenosis. *Brit. M.J.,* **5026**:1019, 1957.

Brunsting, L. A.; Stickney, J. M.; Pease, G.; and Reed, W. B.: The clinical significance of the L.E. clot test. *A.M.A. Arch. Dermat.,* **73**:307, 1956.

Burgess, C. M., and Ellis, L. B.: Chest pain in patients with mitral stenosis, with particular references to so-called "hypercyanotic angina." *New England J. Med.,* **226**:937, 1942.

Christiansen, J. V.: Treatment of lupus erythematosus with chloroquine. *Brit. J. Dermat.* **69**:157, 1957.

Denton, C.; Pappas, E. G.; Uricchio, J. F.; Goldberg. H; and Likoff, W.: Endocarditis after cardiac surgery. *Circulation,* **15**:525, 1957.

Downing, D. F.: Congenital aortic stenosis. *Circulation,* **14**:188, 1956.

Dubois, E. L.: Prednisone and prednisolone in treatment of systemic lupus erythematosus. *J.A.M.A.,* **161**:427, 1956.

Dubois, E. L.: Systemic lupus erythematosus: recent advances in its diagnosis and treatment. *Ann. Int. Med.,* **45**:163, 1956.

Ellis, L. E.; Harken, D. E.; and Black, H.: A clinical study of 1,000 consecutive cases of mitral stenosis two to nine years after mitral valvuloplasty. *Circulation,* **19**:803, 1959.

Friedberg, C. K.: Acute myocardial infarction not due to coronary artery occlusion. *J.A.M.A.,* **112**:1675, 1939.

Friedberg, C. K.: *Diseases of the Heart,* 2nd ed. W. B. Saunders Co., Philadelphia, 1956.

Friedberg, C. K., and Sohval, A.: Non-rheumatic calcific aortic stenosis. *Am. Heart J.,* **17**:452, 1939.

Halliday, W. R.: Endomyocardial fibroelastosis: a study of 30 cases. *Dis. Chest,* **26**:27, 1954.

Landtman, B., and Wallgren, E. I.: Congenital aortic stenosis in children. *Ann. paediat. Fenniae,* **2**:259, 1956.

Likoff, W., and Berkowitz, D.: Transventricular commissurotomy in aortic stenosis; clinical evaluation. *J.A.M.A.*, **157**:1367, 1955.

Lisaw, P.; Reale, A.; and Likoff, W.: The postmitral commissurotomy syndrome, a 4 year clinical, pathological, and serological study, and its relation to restenosis. *Ann. Int. Med.*, **50**:1352, 1959.

Luisada, A. A.: Recent advances in the diagnosis of rheumatic heart disease. *Am. J. Med.*, **17**:781, 1954.

McEwen, C.: The treatment of rheumatic fever. *Am. J. Med.*, **17**:794, 1954.

Matthews, M. B.; Medd, W. E.; and Gorlin, R.: Aortic stenosis: a clinical study. *Brit. M.J.*, **2**:759, 1955.

Mitchell, A. M.; Sackett, C. H.; Hunzicker, W. J.; and Levine, S. A.: The clinical features of aortic stenosis. *Am. Heart J.*, **48**:684, 1954.

Morris, H., and Friedman, W. C.: Endocardial fibroelastosis. *New York J. Med.*, **54**:1378, 1954.

Papp, C., and Zion, M. M.: Postcommissurotomy syndrome. *Brit. Heart J.*, **18**:153, 1956.

Reich, N. E.: Calcific aortic stenosis: a clinicopathological correlation of 22 cases. *Ann. Int. Med.*, **22**:234, 1945.

Reich, N. E.: The earlier recognition of minimal aortic valve insufficiency. *Am. Pract. & Digest Treat.*, **1**:475, 1947.

Semans, J. H., and Taussig, H. B.: Congenital "aneurysmal" dilatation of the left auricle. *Bull. Johns Hopkins Hosp.*, **63**:404, 1938.

Sloan, S.; Pollock, R. C.; Kirshbaum, J.; and Freedman, T.: Massive dilatation of the left auricle: report of 3 cases. *Ann. Int. Med.*, **40**:75, 1954.

Soloff, L. A.; Zatuchni, J.; Janton, O. H.; O'Neill, T. J. E.; and Glover, R. P.: Reactivation of rheumatic fever following mitral commissurotomy. *Circulation*, **8**:481, 1953.

Stuckey, D.: Cardiac pain in association with mitral stenosis and congenital heart disease. *Brit. Heart J.*, **17**:397, 1955.

Thomas, W. A.; Randall, R. V.; Bland, E. F.; and Castleman, B.: Endocardial fibroelastosis: a factor in heart disease of obscure etiology. A study of 20 autopsied cases in children and adults. *New England J. Med.*, **251**:327, 1954.

White, P. D., and Fennell, R. H., Jr.: Endocardial fibroelastosis with marked cardiac enlargement and failure in a man who died at the age of 71 after 15 years of angina pectoris and two years of congestive heart failure. *Ann. Int. Med.*, **41**:333, 1954.

DISEASES OF
THE MYOCARDIUM

CHAPTER OUTLINE

Pheochromocytoma
Addison's disease
Waterhouse-Friderichsen syndrome
Gout

BLOOD DYSCRASIAS

DEGENERATIVE MYOPATHIES

TUMORS OF THE MYOCARDIUM

TRAUMATIC LESIONS OF THE MYOCARDIUM

Diseases of the myocardium probably do not produce pain by direct involvement of the heart muscle, since the myocardium is not innervated by pain-sensitive nerve fibers. However, chest pain of both cardiac and noncardiac origin can occur. The former is usually related to an associated pericardial or coronary artery involvement. The following pertinent types of myocardial diseases may be encountered.

INFLAMMATORY LESIONS OF THE MYOCARDIUM

A correct diagnosis of "myocarditis" as a specific entity was proffered at one time with remarkable rarity. These inflammatory lesions are being clinically recognized more often today. However, many patients are still dying from undiagnosed types of myocarditis of both specific and nonspecific types. This is most unfortunate, since they may even be reversible with appropriate therapy.

Acute Specific Myocarditides

Specific inflammatory lesions of the myocardium imply a distinct etiologic factor which can be identified in the lesion or by peculiarly distinctive pathologic changes caused by these infectious processes.

Luetic myocarditis. Although luetic aortitis is by far the most commonly described manifestation of cardiovascular syphilis, the possibility of involvement of the myocardium has been generally neglected. Despite mass-screening procedures and a free supply of drugs, syphilis is not only quite prevalent but has actually been increasing in frequency in recent years. Indeed, the more frequent recognition of cardiovascular syphilis at the autopsy table indicates that the incidence is much greater than that found by clinical study.

Sufficient evidence has now accumulated to indicate that cardiovascular involvement may occur even in *early syphilis*. Exactly half such cases show definite electrocardiographic abnormalities consisting of T wave and ST segment changes.

Although *luetic aortitis* is not under detailed consideration in this section, it must be stressed that it may indirectly affect the myocardium by the production of two lesions:

1. *Aortic regurgitation.* This results in anginal attacks because of coronary insufficiency caused by a sucking effect, and also produces progressive myocardial hypertrophy which eventuates in heart failure.

2. *Coronary ostial stenosis.* This causes around 1.6 per cent of all cases of myocardial infarction, and such patients are likely to die suddenly. However, a slowly progressive closure of an ostium usually results in a diffuse myocardial fibrosis. Since an associated aortic insufficiency is usually present in about three-fourths of such cases, intractable myocardial failure ensues in most instances. The typical history of angina pectoris, physical signs, and serologic tests aid in establishing the correct diagnosis. Exertional dypsnea and nocturnal dyspnea are also common. Around 85 per cent of all cases have atypical angina. When pain persists for more than fifteen minutes, significant organic coronary changes must be suspected. Electrocardiographic changes are mainly concerned with T wave alterations due to coronary insufficiency, although the findings may also become characteristic of an acute myocardial infarction. The association of coronary sclerosis in the older age groups must be correctly evaluated, since almost 95 per cent of all coronary artery diseases is statistically attributed to atherosclerotic changes. Calcification of the wall of the ascending aorta is far more characteristic of luetic aortitis than of an arteriosclerotic aorta. The response to treatment (specific and supportive) is usually poor.

Gumma of the myocardium is rare, but there are two distinct types of luetic myocarditis: (1) diffuse gummatous myocarditis and (2) large localized gummatous lesions. Since the upper part of the ventricular septum is frequently affected, conduction disturbances and septal rupture with severe pain and early death may ensue. Strongly positive serology and electrocardiographic changes in the presence of gummata elsewhere in the body should strongly suggest similar involvement of the myocardium.

Tuberculous myocarditis. Although tuberculosis usually avoids the heart, a sufficient number of cases have been reported which establish the fact that the three heart layers and the coronary arteries may also be involved.

Tuberculous pericarditis is discussed in Chapter 11 (see p. 232); tuberculous endocarditis is rare and almost always secondary to myocardial involvement.

Three pathologic types of myocardial involvement are recognized: (1) caseous nodular necrosis, (2) diffuse tuberculous myocarditis, and (3) miliary tuberculosis (usually during childhood).

Tuberculosis of the heart may be suspected when electrocardiographic evidence of myocardial damage, ectopic rhythms, or pericarditis appears in a person known to have active and far advanced tuberculosis of the lungs, hilar nodes, or blood stream (miliary). Rare complications are spontaneous rupture or aneurysmal formation of the left ventricle and congestive heart failure.

Mycotic infections. A number of mycotic infections of exogenous or endogenous source are capable of systemic spread with myocardial involvement. The three fungal diseases most frequently affecting the myocardium are actinomycosis, blastomycosis, and moniliasis, but sporotrichosis and histoplasmosis are also encountered. Most other mycotic infections fail to affect the heart. Cardiac pain is obviously a rare feature unless a concomitant pericarditis exists.

Parasitic inflammations. Following World War II, many tropical diseases were no longer considered as medical curiosities. The most important of these are amebiasis, schistosomiasis, malaria, leishmaniasis, filariasis, and hookworm disease. Parasitism of the myocardial fibers is not always associated with an inflammatory reaction (e.g., toxoplasmosis). The cardiovascular manifestations of malaria include syncope, angina pectoris, and peripheral circulatory collapse. Secondary anemia not only adds to coronary insufficiency but may contribute to the fatty degeneration of the myocardium. Thrombosis in the capillaries is enhanced. Vague precordial pain (which may also be referred to the abdomen), dyspnea, and palpitation may be clinical features of Chagas' disease (American trypanosomiasis). Various types of heart block and serial changes in the ST and T segments are found in the chronic form of this heart disease. Helminthic infections (strongyloidiasis, schistosomiasis, filariasis, trichinosis, and others) also affect the myocardium directly. Thrombosis of the small coronary arteries has been well established as a finding in trichinosis and heterophyiasis. Cardiac cysts may be formed following the entrance of the echinococcus larvae into the coronary system.

Other specific infections of the myocardium may accompany various septic states due to pyogenic bacteria and subacute bacterial endocarditis. The latter organisms not only invade the heart muscle directly from contiguous valvular involvement but also embolize to the coronary arteries. Multiple abscesses of the myocardium are usually due to bacterial invasion of the terminal coronary branches following pyemia or septicemia.

Acute Nonspecific Myocarditis

Inflammations of the myocardium due to many bacterial, rickettsial, or viral infections are a commonly neglected aspect of heart disease. Many of the responsible specific infections have been identified by means of the electronic microscope and serologic tests. In other instances, the lack of recognition of the primary disease process (usually of viral origin) has given rise to a number of vague diagnostic labels (idiopathic, Fiedler's primary, interstitial, isolated, and fibrous myocarditis). Bacterial or rickettsial infections usually produce more recognizable symptoms and signs. Infectious myocarditis, which is an inflammatory alteration, is not to be confused with toxic myocarditis, which is in reality a degenerative lesion. The myocardium is usually soft, pale, and flabby but may appear hemorrhagic or edematous.

Angina pectoris or precordial discomfort is a common symptom. It may be associated with asthenia, dypsnea, palpitation, fever, gallop rhythm, arrhythmias, poor heart sounds, changing murmurs, embolization, cardiomegaly, and, finally, myocardial failure.

Laboratory tests show leukocytosis and elevated sedimentation rate, diffuse heart enlargement, and serially changing electrocardiographic abnormalities which affect any of the complexes and may show conduction disturbances and arrhythmias. The ballistocardiogram is also frequently altered (see Fig. 10-1). Blood cultures, agglutination tests, and other specific procedures are important in the diagnosis and treatment of underlying specific etiologic factors. Bacterial and viral pneumonias, glomerulonephritis, diphtheria, typhoid fever, brucellosis, scarlet fever, typhus infections, influenza, poliomyelitis, and acute infectious mononucleosis are among the more common primary diseases which have been proved to foster secondary myocardial inflammation. Thus, extensive treatment is directed at the primary infectious process. Adequate symptomatic treatment (fluids, diet, etc.) and adequate bed rest are imperative. Cardiac drugs are not indicated unless evidences of incipient myocardial failure appear.

Diffuse Collagen Diseases

Acute rheumatic fever. The most common inflammatory lesion of the myocardium is caused by acute rheumatic fever, which is a specific inflammation identifiable by the presence of Aschoff bodies. The younger age

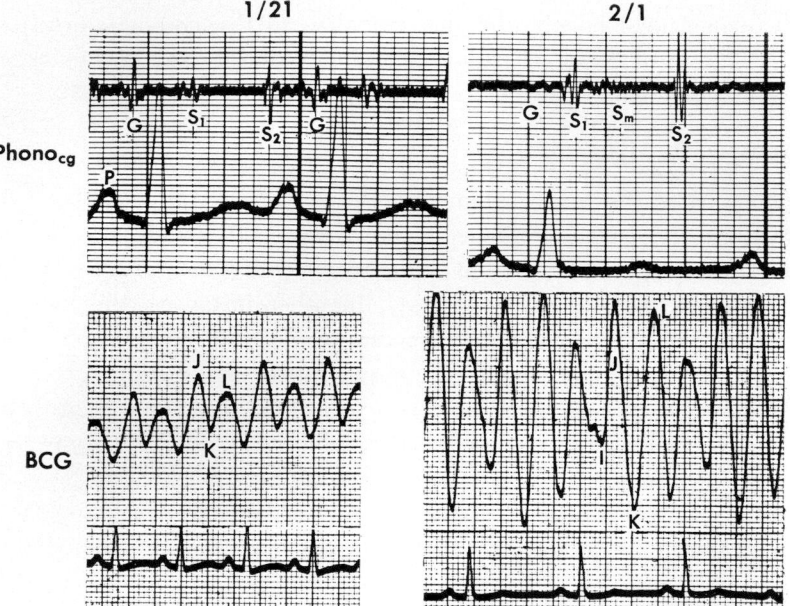

Fig. 10-1. Twenty-four-year-old patient with acute "nonspecific" myocarditis manifested by anginoid chest pain and cardiac failure. First attack treated successfully with corticosteroids and digitalis. Note diminished and delayed first sound (S_1) and presystolic gallop (G) in phonocardiogram shortly after admission 1/21, with marked improvement twelve days later. Note also concurrent abnormality in ballistocardiogram (1/21), with similar marked improvement seen 2/1. Recurrence six months later resulted in death. (Autopsy revealed acute rheumatic myocarditis and endocarditis.)

group is usually affected. Although myocarditis may occur in isolated form or may predominate the clinical picture, it usually occurs as a feature of pancarditis. Chest pain occurring in proven rheumatic myocarditis is attributed to an associated coronary arteritis or pericarditis. The sudden intensification of precordial pain during a bout of acute rheumatic fever, unrelieved by massive doses of salicylates or corticosteroids, and accompanied by characteristic electrocardiographic changes, should raise the suspicion of severe rheumatic coronary arteritis, complicated by a superimposed intraarterial thrombus with resultant myocardial infarction. History of a preceding infection with group A beta-hemolytic streptococci, articular and other clinical manifestations, and high antistreptolysin-O and fibrinolysin titers in a patient under thirty years of age who suffers a myocardial infarction strongly suggests a rheumatic origin. Both C-reactive protein and serum glutamic oxalacetic transaminase (SGO-T) tests tend to be positive. Serial electrocardiographic studies are confirmatory. However, it is well to remember that myocardial infarction on an atheromatous basis may also follow certain acute illnesses which produce hypercoagulability of the blood.

Since the rheumatic vascular lesions predominantly affect the small arteries, collateral circulation in the rheumatic group quickly compensates for ischemia produced by the inflammatory narrowing of the affected vessels. Pain due to coronary arteritis is anginoid in character, whereas pain due to pericarditis is usually aggravated by deep inspiration and is more constant. Its severity is variable, and it may be atypical in its location and other characteristics. A friction rub is common in early pericarditis but may disappear following effusion. The initial appearance of rheumatic arthritis in the left wrist, elbow, or shoulder may incorrectly suggest anginal radiation, but the transitory and migratory character of the polyarthritis, with redness, swelling, and heat, soon clarifies this impression. However, because of the occasional protean nature of acute rheumatic fever, atypical involvement of single joints may prove confusing at times.

Chest pain in acute rheumatic fever may also be due to rheumatic *pneumonitis*. The chest pain is then pleural in character, as it is in other forms of pneumonitis. However, the transitory nature of the patchy hemorrhagic exudates is pathognomonic, since the rapid clearing and reappearance of the lesion elsewhere in the pulmonary parenchyma within a matter of days are striking features on serial roentgenograms. It occurs most commonly following severe attacks of acute rheumatic fever. Upper or lower abdominal pain may be due to similar rheumatic involvement of the abdominal peritoneum.

Other clinical evidence of myocardial involvement is suggested by progressive cardiac enlargement (not due to pericardial effusions), which may recede quickly with improvement following therapy. Poor quality of the heart sounds and changing murmurs are also significant. Death due to rapid congestive heart failure in a patient under twenty-five years of age is an important feature when no other cause is discernible.

The presence of isolated inflammatory involvement of the myocardium is strongly suggested by serial electrocardiographic changes (various degrees of atrioventricular or intraventricular block, T wave changes, low slurred QRS complexes, QT prolongation, and arrhythmias). Diminution of the first heart sound, the appearance of gallop rhythm, and abnormal diastolic deflections in the ballistocardiogram are other important findings.

Since no specific test is available as yet, the modified Jones criteria remain our most important guide in the diagnosis of rheumatic fever. However, certain laboratory tests may prove useful (see Fig. 10-2). The time-honored test for rheumatic activity is the *erythrocyte sedimentation rate*. Because of

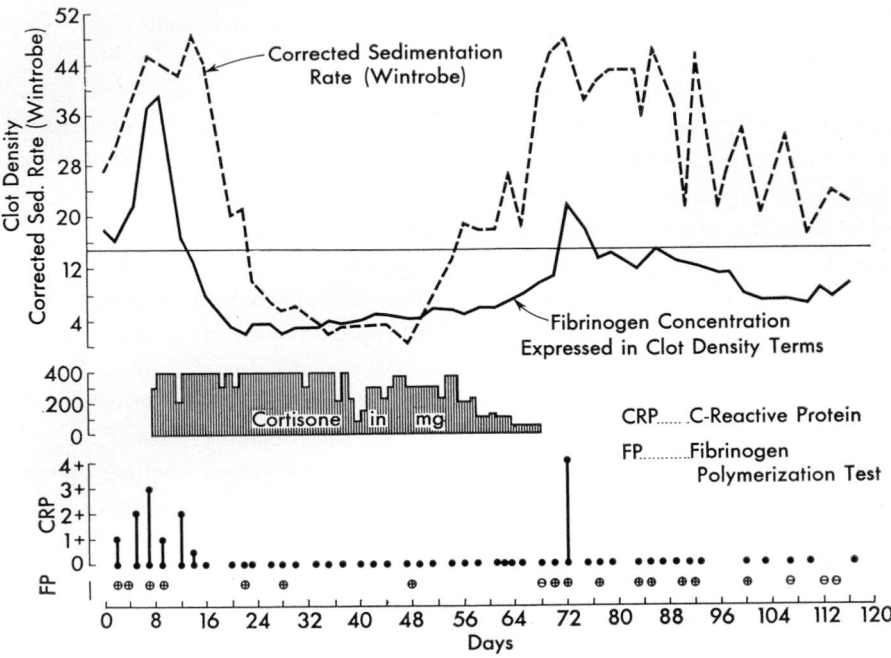

Fig. 10-2. Comparative course of fibrinogen polymerization test (*FP*), clot density (*CD*), C-reactive protein, and corrected sedimentation rate in a sixteen-year-old girl with acute rheumatic fever treated with cortisone.

Fibrinogen in milligrams per 100 cc is obtained from the clot density utilizing the formula F (fibrinogen) = 18 d (clot density) + 120. (From Losner, S., and Volk, B. W.: The fibrinogen polymerization test in active rheumatic disease. *Am. J. M. Sc.,* **229**:371, 1955.)

its simplicity, it will probably continue to be the most widely used single test for the determination of rheumatic activity. Unfortunately, it is limited in value because of its nonspecificity and poorly defined range of normal. The *white blood count* may be in the vicinity of 12,000 per cubic millimeter, and anemia is usually present. Of the newer nonspecific tests, the *C-reactive protein* is far more diagnostic for acute rheumatic fever. It appears more useful than another acute phase test known as the mucoprotein tyrosine test. Serial determinations of the *plasma fibrinogen concentration,* although non-specific in nature, have also proved to be valuable in the estimation of rheumatic activity. Another sensitive test is based on the *cationic detergent* technic for *serum protein fractionation.* This test appears to be as reliable as electrophoretic studies. It demonstrates that the alpha globulin and fibrinogen concentrations are increased while the albumin concentration is decreased during the acute phase of the illness. The degree of protein altera-tions and the duration of the abnormal pattern parallel the severity of the rheumatic inflammation. *Serum antistreptolysin and fibrinolysin* titers are generally employed to determine the degree of activity in children.

The most valuable test may eventually prove to be the *fibrinogen polymerization test* (see Fig. 10-2). Detectable amounts of fibrinogen following gross coagulation of a slightly heparinized venous blood sample indicate normal fibrinogen polymerization or a "negative" test. The fibrinogen polymerization test is "positive" when such a specimen of serum no longer contains any clottable fibrinogen. Since it is independent of the effects of salicylates, corticosteroids, or ACTH, this test indicates more specifically the presence of activity.

Another new test is the *longchain test* (chains containing 100 or more organisms). It is simple and rapid and detects the specific antibodies that produce immunity to group A streptococci within two or three weeks of infection and as long as six months or more thereafter. Health departments in nearly thirty states now have the necessary equipment and trained personnel to conduct fluorescent antibody test for rapid identification of group A beta-hemolytic streptococci as a forerunner of rheumatic fever.

The treatment of the various types of chest pain encountered in acute rheumatic myocarditis obviously depends upon their mechanism. Anginoid pain may respond to nitroglycerin. Since this effect is inconstant, analgesics and even meperidine (Demerol) may be required. The response to corticosteroids is usually excellent. Anticoagulants are contraindicated in occlusive coronary arteritis, since the presence of an associated pericarditis may give rise to bleeding and tamponade. Pain due to pericarditis responds best to salicylates in the milder cases, but corticosteroids are preferable in the more severe cases, especially in the presence of pancarditis. The pleuritic type of pain that is associated with rheumatic pneumonitis may respond to massive salicylate administration. However, the beneficial effect is somewhat difficult to evaluate as a therapeutic test, since this clinical manifestation is quite evanescent.

Rheumatoid arthritis. The confusion in differentiating the myocardial and other cardiac lesions in both rheumatic fever and rheumatoid arthritis has led to a number of etiologic and pathologic studies. Unfortunately, the pathologic evidence is not always consistent, and the etiologic investigations remain incomplete at present. Further confusion may occur, since more than a third of patients with rheumatoid arthritis show clinical evidence of rheumatic heart disease. The lesions are surprisingly similar in many instances, although less severe in rheumatic fever. In addition to pericarditis and gross valvular deformities, myocardial lesions in rheumatoid arthritis are predominantly those of active chronic inflammatory interstitial myocarditis. Cardiomegaly, murmurs, and nonspecific electrocardiographic changes are diagnostic features of cardiac involvement in the presence of evidence of joint involvement. It is interesting to note that spinal involvement (Marie-Strumpell) may also produce chest pain due to nerve root compression. Synovial involvement of the left shoulder, elbow, or wrist may be confused with the radiation of coronary origins of pain. Aortic inflammation with secondary aortic valvular insufficiency is being described with increasing frequency. The sucking effect of regurgitation on the coronary circulation may also produce pain due to relative coronary insufficiency. Other diagnostic features and treatment of rheumatoid arthritis are described elsewhere (see pp. 38, 75–76).

Lupus erythematosus disseminatus may lead to myocardial involvement manifested by fine scars resembling small infarctions, increased density of collagen along the intermuscular septa, and thickening of the small arteries. These lesions are usually found beneath the mural vegetations or adjacent to arteries with partial or complete occlusion. Fresh fibrinoid necrosis of collagen is a frequent finding in more severe cases. There is no characteristic pain, although cardiac distress may manifest itself as vague precordial discomfort. True chest pain is usually produced by associated pleuritic or pericardial involvement. Pericardial effusion may occur at any time during the disease and is usually preceded by typical precordial pain and friction rub. Signs of impending heart failure due to extensive myocardial involvement may appear terminally. Diagnostic aspects and treatment are discussed elsewhere (see pp. 27, 233).

Polyarteritis nodosa. The typical lesions found in the myocardium are of the same character as in other tissues in which the small and medium-sized vessels are affected by medial necrosis and fibrinous exudation. Chest pain occurs only when there is aneurysmal or thrombotic involvement of the coronary arteries. In such instances, pain of anginal character is present, and the picture may be undistinguishable from that of acute (transient or protracted) coronary insufficiency or of coronary occlusion produced by coronary atherosclerosis.

Electrocardiographic changes are also similar to those which occur in coronary atherosclerosis, although they tend to be atypical, changing, and bizarre because of the widespread and progressive involvement. Polyarteritis nodosa is divisible clinically into two groups, primary and secondary periarteritis nodosa. The only differences in the morphology of the lesions are those attributed to variations in the duration and extent of the pathologic process. Myocardial involvement appears more frequently in hypersensitivity angiitis, which may be considered as a secondary form manifested by fever, skin rash, nephritis, myocarditis, and a frequent history suggesting recent exposure to some antigenic substance. It usually runs a fulminating course. Treatment is generally unsatisfactory, and even corticosteroid therapy gives only temporary relief. Details of therapy and other diagnostic features are discussed on pages 38–42, 75.

Diffuse scleroderma. This disease tends to involve the fibrous tissue of the skin, myocardium, lungs, esophagus, skeletal muscle, and other organs. Symptoms and signs of cardiac involvement are the result of the peculiar myocardial scarring caused by this disease. However, chest pain is rarely present and is not due to myocardial involvement. The chest pain is caused by pericarditis or pleuritis following collagenous degeneration of the subendothelial connective tissue. Distress in the thorax may also originate in esophageal involvement (dysphagia). The myocardial changes may result in cardiac failure. As in lupus erythematosus disseminatus, the most common electrocardiographic findings are various types of bundle-branch block. Ballistocardiographic abnormalities are also found with considerable frequency. The most effective treatment consists of corticosteroid administration. Serial ballistocardiograms have been shown to be valuable objective guides to the efficacy of the treatment.

Dermatomyositis. Cardiac involvement is present in 25 per cent of cases, with diffuse and focal changes in the myocardium and signs of cardiac enlargement, systolic murmurs, tachycardia, and pericardial friction rub. Abnormalities of the electrocardiogram include atrial fibrillation, low voltage, nonspecific T wave changes, and evidence of ventricular strain patterns. Hypertension may also ensue. Although the lesions of the myocardium are not extensive, they may cause death by producing rapidly progressive cardiac failure. Chest pain of cardiac origin is usually not present. However, chest pain may be of musculoskeletal origin due to involvement of the intercostal muscles, as has been discussed previously (p. 63). The lesions of the small arteries and arterioles which produce thickening with concomitant narrowing of the lumina are rarely extensive enough to produce myocardial ischemia or hypoxia.

CARDIAC HYPERTROPHIES

Hypertrophy of the myocardium most frequently occurs in response to persistent or increasing systemic or pulmonary hypertension due to a large number of causes. This can lead to hypertrophy of the heart in less than eighty days (as has been shown in experimentally produced stenosis of the ascending aorta). The only reliable criterion of cardiac hypertrophy is the increase in muscle mass as demonstrated by an increase in general heart weight.

According to Wiggers, heart muscle hypertrophies in response to constant stretching of the muscle fibers, as in heart failure, and also when the heart is required to work near the limit of its reserve. The latter occurs when more work is performed without a corresponding increase in oxygen supply. Intimately associated with the appearance of cardiac pain in cardiac enlargement is the well-documented observation that the heart muscle suffers a relative reduction in its blood supply as the vascularization ratio per unit of myocardial weight diminishes. This eventuates in hypoxia of the myocardium.

Although cardiac hypertrophy is the result of numerous common disorders, such as essential hypertension and chronic bronchopulmonary, rheumatic valvular, and coronary artery diseases, it has been noted frequently in the absence of any recognizable or proven cause. However, a number of clear-cut entities, such as acute nonspecific infectious myocarditis and endocardial fibroelastosis, are beginning to emerge out of the nondescript title of "idiopathic cardiac hypertrophy." Other causes are thyroid diseases, acromegaly, and blood dyscrasias. In children, developmental anomalies, such as Von Gierke's disease and a single coronary artery, may produce a similar clinical picture. Perhaps other specific entities will become identifiable eventually.

The chest pain in *left* ventricular hypertrophy due to essential hypertension (see Fig. 10-3) may be of various origins. If anginal in character, it may be due to relative coronary insufficiency, or it may be due to an associated atheromatous degeneration of the coronary arteries which is frequently accelerated by the hypertensive state. Vague transitory precordial pains which fail to respond to nitroglycerin frequently occur in hypertensive states. Their origin is not clear, although it has been postulated that they are caused by the relative disparity between the increased muscle mass and the blood supply.

Similarly, in instances of severe *right* ventricular hypertrophy secondary to bronchopulmonary or valvular disease, cardiac pain of anginal character may occur. (See Fig. 10-4.) It is probably caused by ischemia of the right ventricular muscle in the absence of significant coronary artery disease. It may also occur in children and adolescents with congenital or acquired heart diseases. The relation of chest pain to pulmonary hypertension has been discussed previously (p. 111). Precordial pain encountered in cor pulmonale may also be due to compression of the origin of the left coronary artery, since this vessel passes between the aorta and the pulmonary artery for the

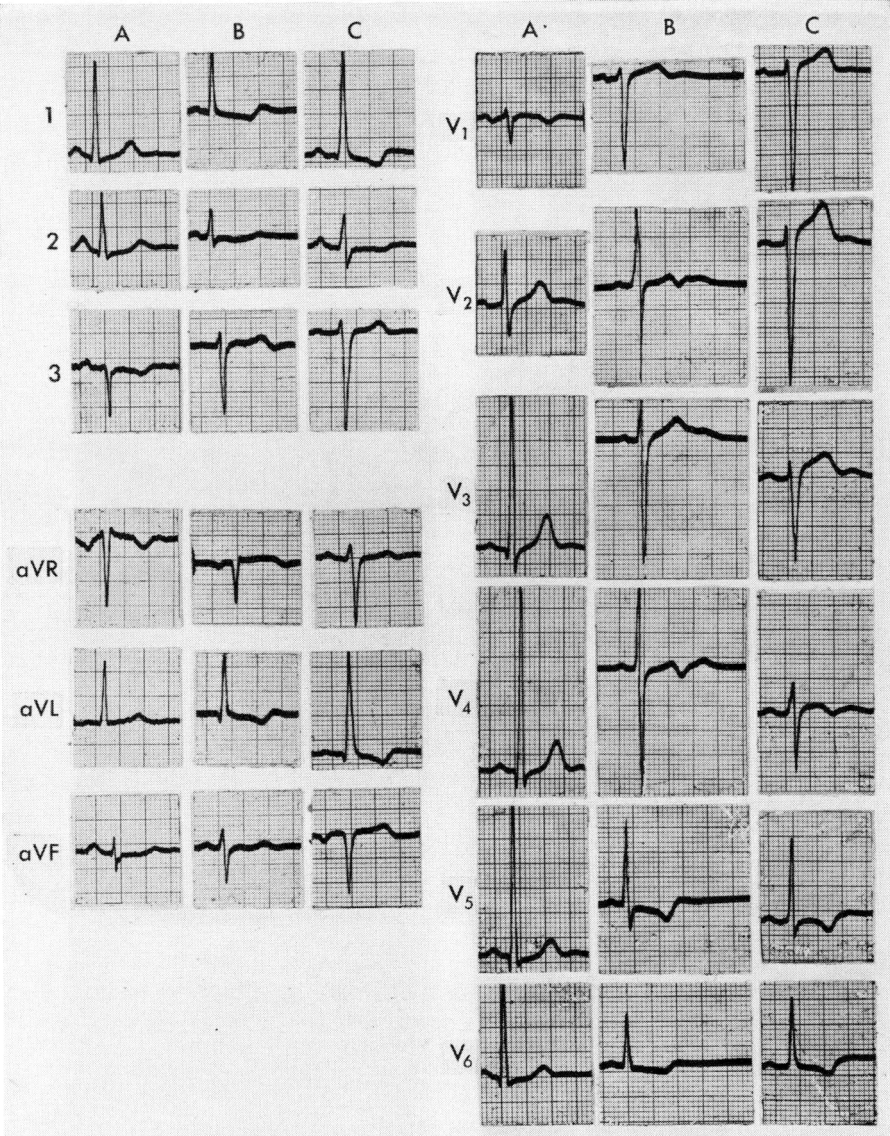

Fig. 10-3. Various degrees of left ventricular enlargement. *A,* Early left ventricular hypertrophy with only abnormally high voltage of QRS present in standard limb and chest leads. *B* and *C,* More advanced degrees of left ventricular enlargement with ST and T changes present in addition to high voltage of QRS and more marked deviation of QRS vector in frontal plane.

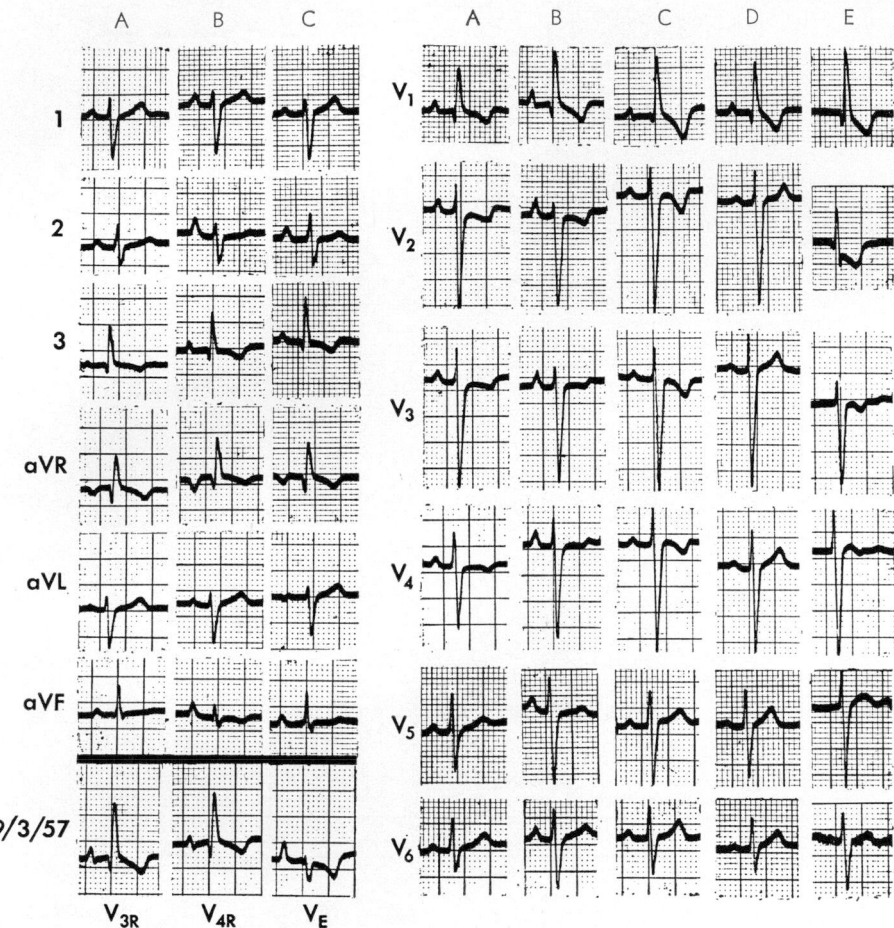

Fig. 10-4. Serial electrocardiograms of progressive right ventricular enlargement (A-E) secondary to idiopathic pulmonary fibrosis, changing from right bundle-branch block to diagnostic pattern of Q in V₁ (*B* through *E*) and more clearly seen in V₃ᵣ, V₄ᵣ, and Vₑ (*C*). Note also temporary increase of T wave abnormality in V₂₋₄ due to superimposed episodes of acute right ventricular strain (*C* and *E*). *A*, 1/17/1956; *B*, 4/12/1957; *C*, 9/3/1957; *D*, 10/30/1957; *E*, 1/30/1958.

first centimeter of its length. At this point, the aorta and the pulmonary artery are tightly bound together by a pericardial reflection so that expansion of either is restrained by the pericardial sheath. Thus, any severe changes in the pulmonary artery pressure may cause compression of the left coronary artery at its origin.

In *idiopathic* cardiac hypertrophy, cardiac pain of anginal character is infrequent, and the most common clinical manifestation is progressive cardiac failure. However, chest pain of noncardiac origin is frequent, is usually pleuritic in origin, and is caused by embolization with pulmonary infarction, which is a frequent complication of this obscure disease.

AMYLOIDOSIS OF THE HEART

This degenerative disorder can result in intrinsic cardiac involvement which may lead to heart failure. Two forms of this somewhat infrequent myocardial condition are distinguishable. The primary type is a progressive, insidious, and irreversible entity which usually terminates in congestive failure, while the secondary disease is more rapid in progress, and potentially reversible, but generally ends in renal failure. Primary amyloidosis is essentially a disease of older persons; secondary amyloidosis may develop at any age, depending on the nature of the underlying disease (tuberculosis, chronic suppuration, malignancy, etc.).

Primary amyloidosis affects mesenchymal tissues such as the heart, blood vessels, skeletal muscle (including the tongue), and the digestive tract. Secondary amyloidosis mainly involves parenchymatous organs, such as the liver, spleen, kidney, and adrenal cortex. About 25 per cent of cases of the primary form also involve parenchymatous organs. Amyloidosis associated with multiple myeloma resembles the primary variety in its distribution and staining characteristics.

Although the etiology of amyloidosis is unknown, it has been suggested that (1) amyloidosis represents a general or localized disturbance of protein metabolism, with precipitation of abnormal intermediary protein products in the tissue; (2) the disease is an allergic disorder involving the immune mechanism, and amyloid is a result of an *in vivo* antigen-antibody reaction; (3) amyloidosis represents some abnormality or disturbance in the reticuloendothelial system; and (4) amyloidosis is a consequence of hyperglobulinemia.

Amyloid is deposited between (not within) the cells. It injures the myocardium by compressing the cells which it surrounds, producing atrophy and necrosis, and eventually leaves a rigid amyloid "skeleton." Amyloid in the walls of coronary vessels narrows the lumina and produces fatty and hyaline droplet degeneration of the parenchymal cells as a result of impaired nutrition.

The following types of cardiovascular involvement may occur:

1. Chronic cor pulmonale (right ventricular hypertrophy and failure) due to marked infiltration of the pulmonary vascular system.

2. Deposition of amyloid in the coronary arteries.

3. Diffuse or localized nodular interstitial deposition of amyloid in the myocardium with or without secondary degeneration of the myocardial fibers.

4. Pericardial or endocardial deposition of amyloid.

5. Valvular deposition of amyloid resulting in stenosis or insufficiency. Thus, the clinical picture is frequently aggravated by involvement of the various cardiac structures, each of which contributes its individual burden.

The heart is most commonly involved in the primary form. The greatest concentration of amyloid is distributed throughout the myocardium. As a result, cardiac enlargement and congestive failure are the usual features. In fact, congestive failure occurs in half of all cases. Chest pain is caused by variable degrees of perivascular involvement of the coronary vessels which give rise to coronary insufficiency. Hypertension occurs in 20 per cent of cases of primary amyloidosis. The electrocardiogram usually shows non-specific changes of diffuse myocardial damage with low voltage, flattening or inversion of T waves, prolongation of the P-R interval, bundle-branch block, and atrial fibrillation. Fluoroscopy reveals decreased amplitude of pulsations and marked cardiomegaly. A positive Congo red test and biopsy of the skin or tongue may be diagnostic. The electrophoretic pattern of blood proteins shows hyperglobulinemia. Treatment is symptomatic, and the average life span is four years. The outlook is somewhat better for the secondary type if the underlying disease is halted.

SARCOIDOSIS OF THE HEART

Sarcoidosis is a systemic disease that may involve any organ. It is usually a benign granulomatous process. Gross lesions, when present in the skin, appear as brown nodular thickenings of various sizes; those encountered in other tissues appear as pale gray nodules. Microscopically, the picture resembles tubercle formation but without caseation.

Although myocardial involvement is not rare and may occur either as a primary or more commonly as a secondary sarcoidosis, cardiac pain is unusual. However, chest pain of noncardiac origin is not uncommon. It is usually of vague character and similar to the generalized aches and pains encountered in this disorder.

Involvement of the myocardium may be due to a focal or diffuse granulomatous myocarditis associated with cardiac hypertrophy. Electrocardiographic changes which have been noted include inverted T waves suggestive of myocardial damage, premature contractions, conduction disturbances, and paroxysmal ventricular tachycardia. Findings have been present which also suggest pericardial involvement. Chronic cor pulmonale secondary to marked pulmonary sarcoidosis may result in signs of right heart failure and death. Direct involvement of the myocardium may produce fatal heart block or other serious arrhythmias.

Diagnosis may be quite difficult, particularly in cases of primary myocardial sarcoidosis. It should be suspected in cases of systemic sarcoidosis when there is persistent tachycardia in the absence of fever. The tuberculin test is usually negative due to an anergy. The Nickerson-Kveim test may be helpful but is difficult to perform. Biopsy may reveal the characteristic tubercle formations without caseation. X-rays of bones show rarefaction and reticulation. The lungs reveal an extension of the lesion from the hilum to the periphery. Cardiac hypertrophy is also evident.

Treatment of primary sarcoidosis includes the cautious use of corticosteroids; it is advisable to limit their use in the severe exudative forms. Spontaneous healing occurs in most instances but may take long periods of time. X-ray irradiation has been successful with mediastinal and pulmonary involvement.

METABOLIC AND HORMONAL CAUSES
OF MYOCARDIAL DISEASE

Thyrotoxic heart disease. The occurrence of myocardial involvement in hyperthyroidism is well recognized. Persistent overactivity results in variable degrees of hypertrophy of the heart muscle and dilatation. Eventually, the cardiac reserve becomes completely exhausted, and congestive heart failure ensues. Thus, the increased work of the heart plays an important role in the production of heart failure. The toxic effect of thyroxin on the heart muscle and the arteriovenous shunt-like effect of the dilated thyroid vessels may be other factors which create a strain on the myocardium. Disturbance of the carbohydrate metabolism due to excessive utilization and requirements of vitamins with resultant accumulation of acid metabolites, such as lactic acid and pyruvic acid, may also play an important role in the breakdown of myocardial function.

Vague precordial or apical pains of paroxysmal nature are common. True angina does not occur as a rule except in the presence of coronary artery disease, when the degree of coronary insufficiency is usually increased by the hypermetabolic demands. Forceful pulsations with heart consciousness, palpitation, and dyspnea are also disturbing characteristics. Cardiac enlargement does not occur until thyrotoxicosis has been present for many years.

The diagnosis is reliably confirmed by determination of the uptake of radioactive iodine and the protein-bound iodine test. Some cases are not

[*Text continued on page 210.*]

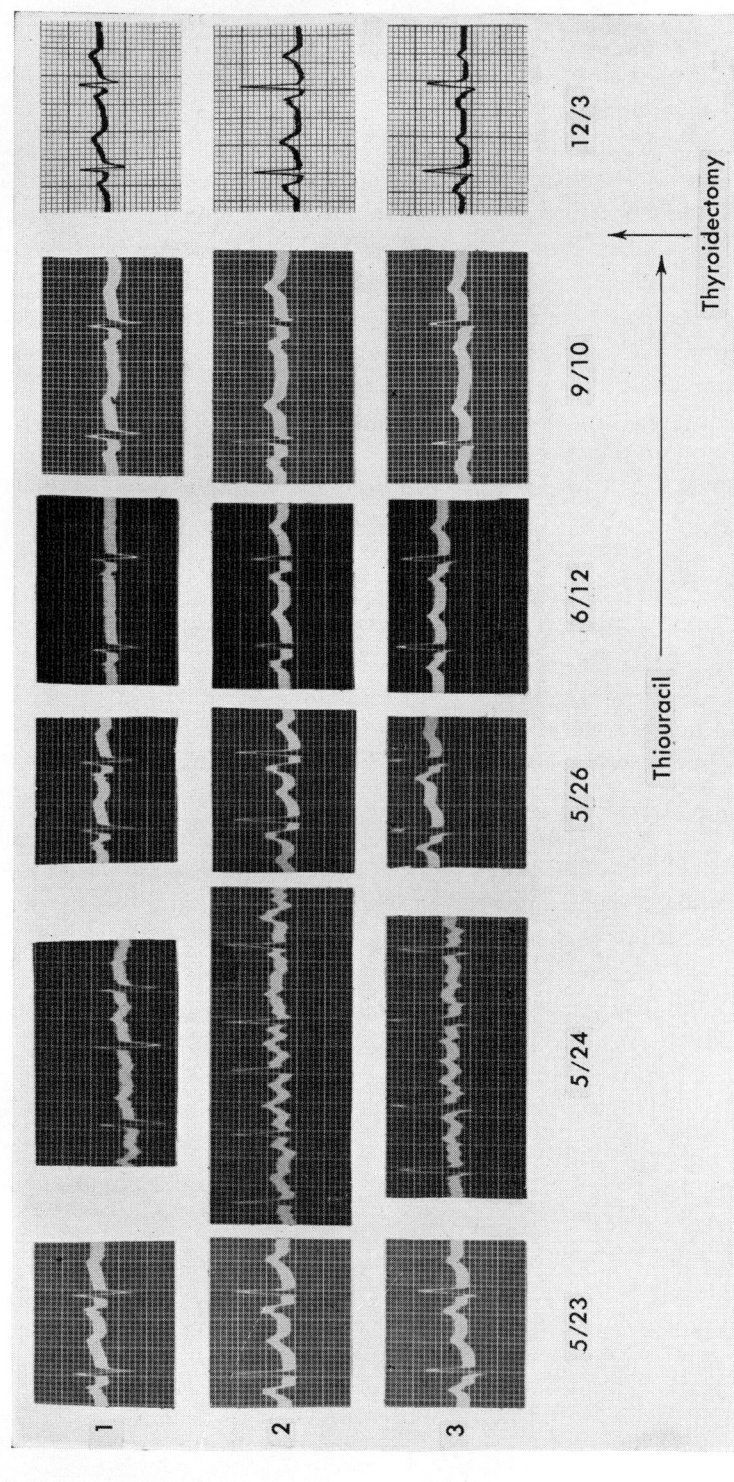

Fig. 10-5. Electrocardiographic changes in thirty-three-year-old man with thyrotoxicosis. Note tall P waves, sharply inverted T waves, and a transient episode of atrial fibrillation during thyrotoxic state, partial return to normal while on thiouracil, and complete return to normal following thyroidectomy. Precordial leads appear on opposite page.

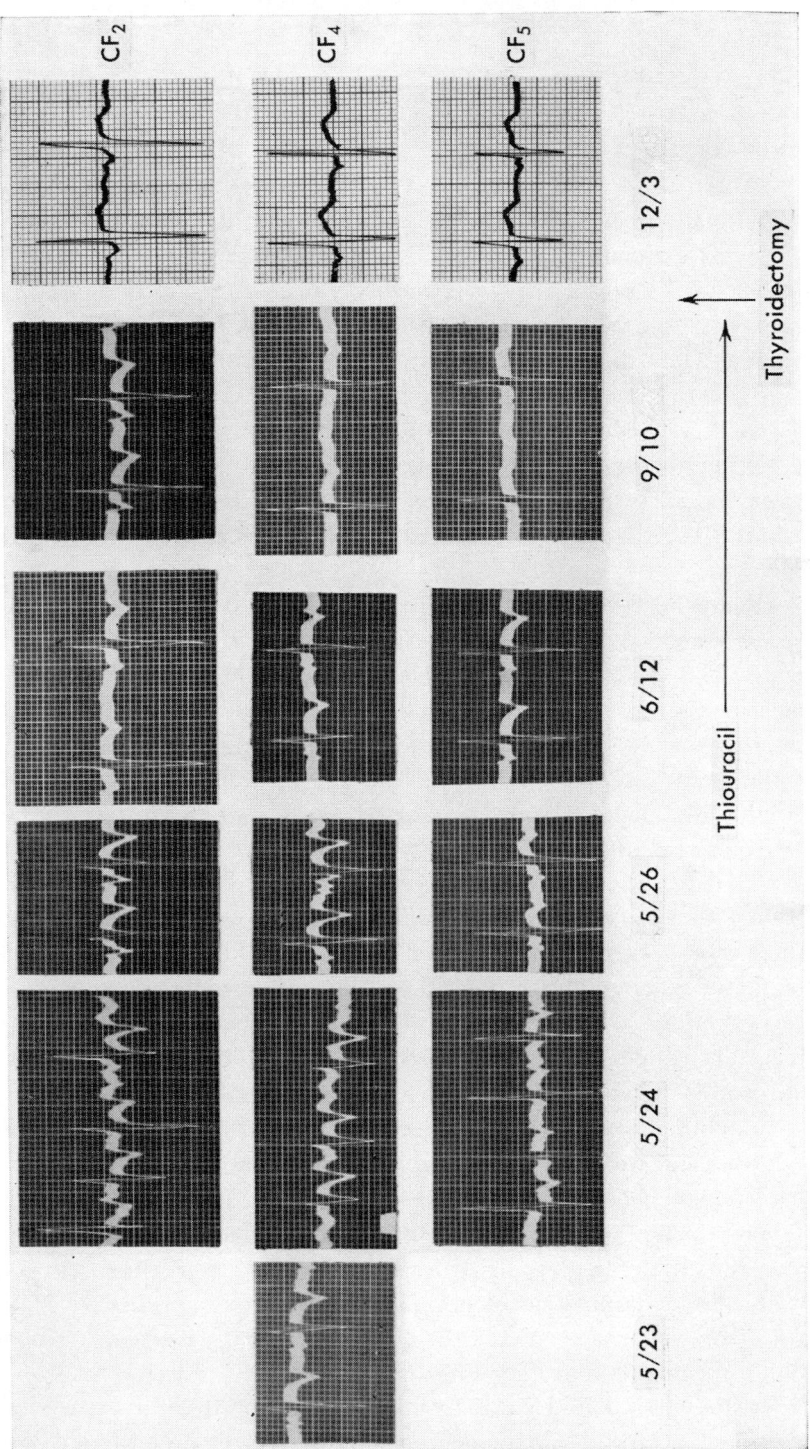

readily recognized because of the presence of masked thyrotoxicosis, usually found in older patients. The clinical picture may be merely that of paroxysmal atrial fibrillation and progressive cardiac failure. However, a persistently rapid ventricular rate or intractable heart failure despite adequate digitalization should cast suspicion on the possible presence of thyrocardiac disease. Warm, moist extremities in aged individuals with cardiac failure may also provide a clue. Fluoroscopy reveals markedly increased amplitude of cardiac contractions and progressive enlargement of the left ventricle. The electrocardiogram is not diagnostic and may show left ventricular strain, arrhythmias, and nonspecific T wave changes. (See Fig. 10-5.)

The treatment consists of the prolonged administration of antithyroid drugs—propylthiouracil or methimazole (Tapazole)—or of one or two doses of radioactive iodine. Surgical extirpation is preferable for toxic adenoma of the thyroid, since this lesion also exhibits a tendency toward malignancy.

Myxedema heart disease. Underactivity of the thyroid gland leads to cardiac dysfunction as a result of myxedematous changes. However, the hypometabolic state frequently prevents many of the cardiac symptoms from becoming evident until the process is long-standing or well advanced. In fact, they may not make an appearance unless sudden demands are made upon the decreased cardiac reserve. Cardiac enlargement encountered in hypothyroidism may be due to myocardial changes with resultant dilatation and pericardial effusion.

Precordial pain occurs frequently when hypothyroidism is found in association with coronary artery sclerosis. It occurs as a result of the decreased cardiac output in the presence of a deficient coronary circulation. It may also follow thyroid therapy, since the sudden increase in metabolism may result in relative coronary insufficiency. Sudden deaths due to severe acute coronary insufficiency have been reported. It is also interesting to note that the hypothyroid state tends to accelerate atheromatous degeneration of the coronary and other arteries due to lipid disturbances. Tiredness, dyspnea, bradycardia, and weakness of heart sounds are also evident.

Characteristic electrocardiographic changes (see Fig. 10-6) consist of sinus bradycardia, low voltage of QRS complexes, and flat or inverted T waves, with varying degrees of atrioventricular block. The diagnosis is confirmed by the determination of protein-bound iodine or radioactive iodine uptake. X-rays show a generalized increase in heart size which responds rapidly to specific therapy (see Fig. 10-7).

The treatment is based on the administration of thyroid extract or its active principle (tri-iodothyronine). It is important to give thyroid extract

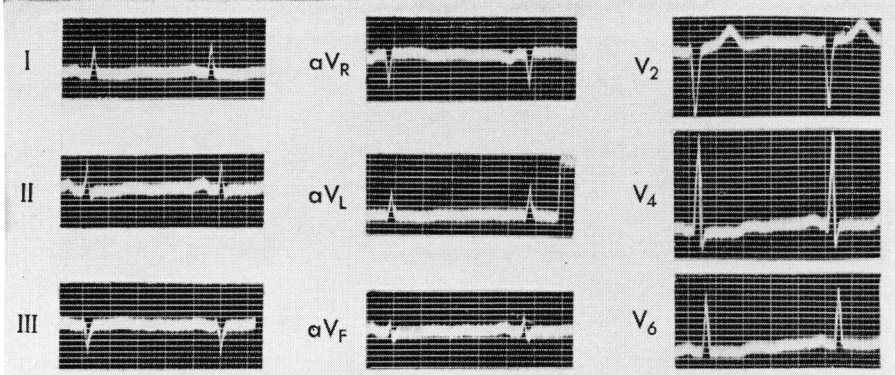

Fig. 10-6. Electrocardiogram in myxedema heart disease. Note low voltage of QRS in limb leads and also low and diphasic T waves. (From Reich, N. E.: *The Uncommon Heart Diseases.* Charles C Thomas, Publisher, Springfield, Ill., 1954.)

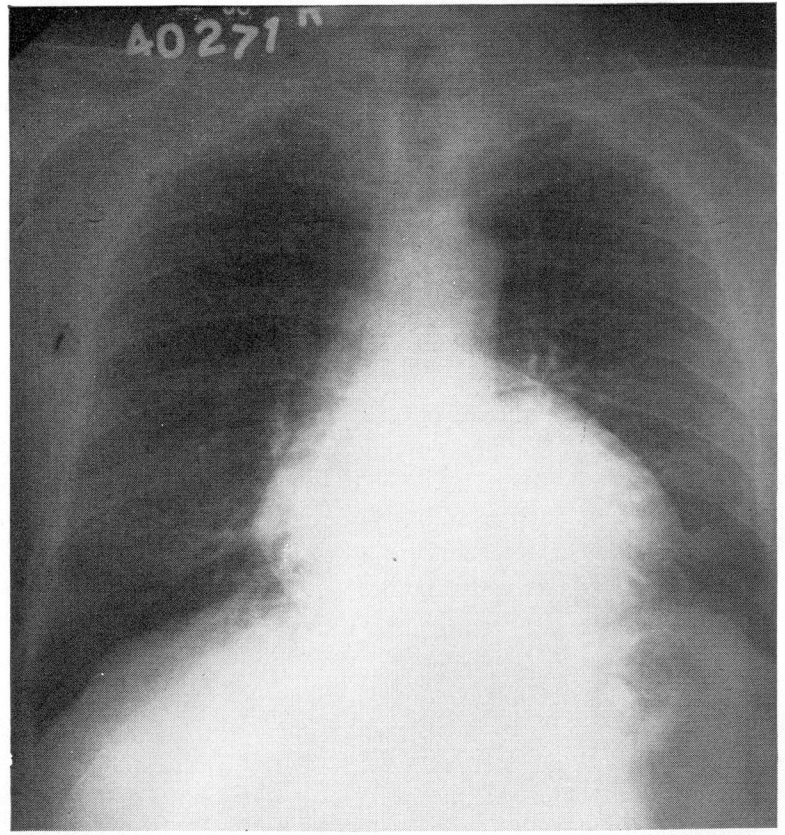

Fig. 10-7. Heart in myxedema. Note generalized enlargement and globular shape of heart. Size and configuration promptly returned to normal following the administration of thyroid extract.

cautiously in order to avoid sudden increased demands on a heart afflicted with coronary artery disease.

Diabetes mellitus. The acceleration of coronary atherosclerosis by diabetes has long been an established fact. Since it appears earlier and to a more marked degree in diabetic persons, coronary artery disease is the most important single cause of death in diabetic persons. The pain related to this complication is described in Chapter 12 (see pp. 249–50).

Hypoglycemia. Whether spontaneous or insulin-induced, hypoglycemia is accompanied by increased cardiac work which may have serious effects on a previously damaged heart. Electrolyte disturbances involving potassium may play a contributory or even basic role. Angina pectoris associated with electrocardiographic changes may be noted. Diminished nutrition of the myocardium may be another factor in the causation of chest distress.

Hyperfunction of the adrenal glands. Of the various clinical syndromes produced by overactivity of the adrenal cortex, only *Cushing's syndrome* falls within the scope of this text. Hypertension with secondary myocardial hypertrophy may lead to the appearance of chest pain of cardiac origin similar to that of essential hypertension. However, this is less common, since the disease rarely lasts long enough for the development of severe coronary insufficiency. Cardiac failure ensues early in the course of this type of hypertension because of the disturbance of salt and water metabolism related to the primary endocrine disorder.

Pheochromocytoma (paraganglioma) is a chromaffin tumor arising either in the adrenal medulla or in chromaffin tissue located elsewhere in the body. The characteristic clinical picture develops as a result of the irregular release of significant amounts of epinephrine and norepinephrine. This precipitates paroxysmal attacks of hypertension (which may last from seconds to hours), palpitation, precordial distress, and tachycardia. In some cases, hypertension may be of the same character and origin as in essential hypertension. The nature of chest pain directly attributable to chromaffin tumor has been discussed on page 28.

Addison's disease results in marked hypotension and myocardial weakness. The electrocardiogram reveals low voltage of QRS complexes and T waves. Electrolyte studies reveal characteristic disturbances in the sodium values.

Waterhouse-Friderichsen syndrome. The marked fall in blood pressure and collapse may also induce coronary thrombosis in previously diseased arteries. Massive adrenal hemorrhage may also give rise to the acute upper abdominal pain and is usually fatal.

Gout. This disturbance in purine metabolism is associated with an increased incidence of arteriosclerosis and hypertension, and advanced coronary disease frequently results in anginal seizure. Bursal and arthritic involvement of the upper extremities may be confused with true anginal radiation (see p. 76).

BLOOD DYSCRASIAS

Although precordial pain is frequently an outstanding symptom in severe anemias, it is not related to the fatty degenerative changes in the myocardium but to relative or functional coronary insufficiency. It is discussed in the section on coronary causes of chest pain (see pp. 249, 250, 272).

DEGENERATIVE MYOPATHIES

Friedreich's ataxia, progressive muscular dystrophy, and myotonia atrophica are degenerative myopathies which may affect the myocardium. There may be severe anatomic changes, consisting of degeneration and replacement fibrosis. Marked electrocardiographic abnormalities consist of deep Q waves, T wave inversions, arrhythmias of paroxysmal and permanent types, and conduction disturbances. The clinical manifestations, however, do not ordinarily include precordial pains, but they may occur during rapid paroxysmal arrhythmias found especially in many instances of progressive muscular dystrophy.

TUMORS OF THE MYOCARDIUM

The myocardium may be the site of either primary or secondary tumors. *Primary* tumors, which occur less frequently than secondary ones, may be intracavitary and are usually situated in the atria. They are myxomas, myomas, or sarcomas. The growing tumor (especially when pedunculated) interferes with valvular function or mechanically obstructs the orifice of the valves. Paroxysms accompanied by cyanosis and dyspnea are prone to occur with changes in position which cause the growth to block the opening. Thus, primary tumors of the atria may mimic rheumatic valvular stenosis or ball-valve thrombus and usually escape clinical detection unless angiocardiography is used routinely in the evaluation of all patients being considered for valvulotomy. Exertional dyspnea is common, and when cardiac failure develops, it is usually intractable because of the mechanical interference with atrial or ventricular filling. Anginal pain may result owing to the reduced cardiac output and consequently inadequate coronary blood flow.

The ante-mortem diagnosis of primary cardiac tumors (see Fig. 10-8) is

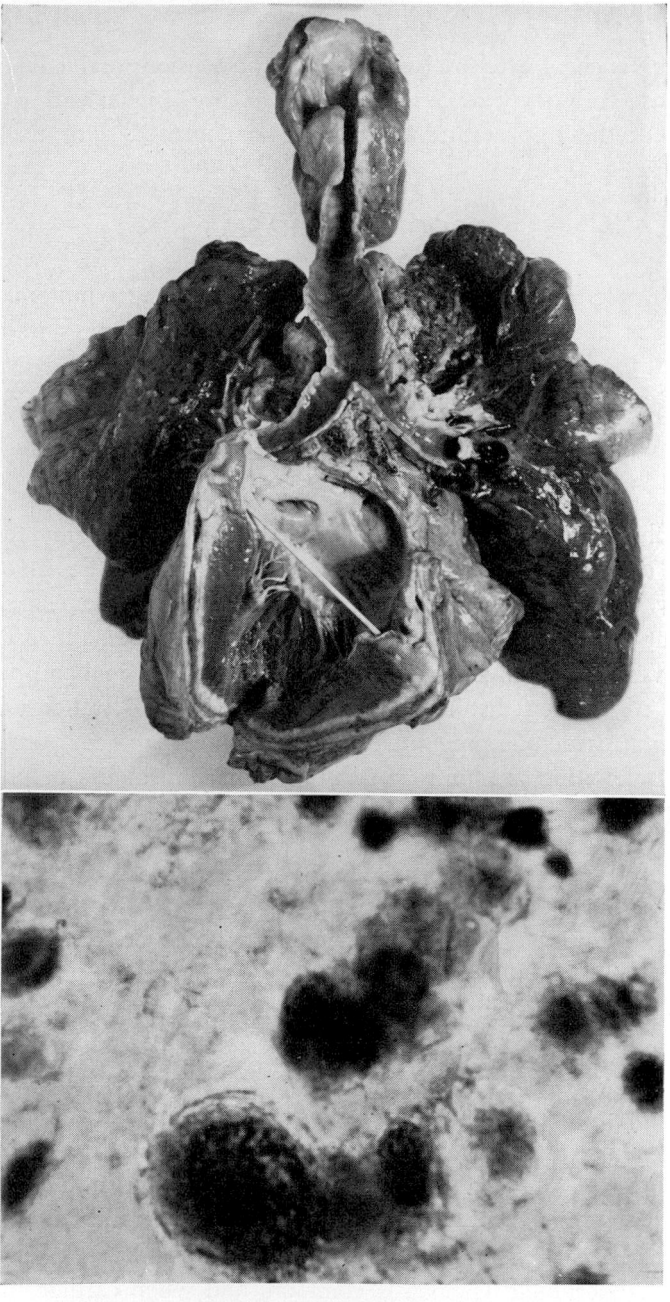

Fig. 10-8. (*Top*) Primary sarcoma of the heart with metastases to the lungs and atelectatic compression of lung tissue by massive pericardial effusion. (*Bottom*) Tumor cells found in pericardial and pleural taps. (From Reich, N. E.: *The Uncommon Heart Diseases.* Charles C Thomas, Publisher, Springfield, Ill., 1954.)

now being reported with increasing frequency. These lesions are receiving more attention, because some tumors of the heart (especially myxoma) are now resectable with improved technics which employ open-heart surgery. The positive diagnosis of certain primary neoplasms of the heart is now possible by means of angiocardiography, cytologic examination of pericardial effusions, intractable cardiac failure despite effective therapeutic regime, and electrocardiographic changes.

Secondary neoplastic invasion of the myocardium is not infrequent, the reported autopsy incidence varying from 0.24 to 6.45 per cent. Although cardiac metastases may arise from a malignant lesion of almost any organ, carcinoma of the breast, bronchogenic carcinoma, malignant melanoma, and malignant lymphomas constitute the most frequent sources. Most of these tumors reach the heart or pericardium by direct extension from neighboring intrathoracic organs. Another pathway is possible by invasion of the pulmonary veins and implantation within the myocardium via coronary artery embolization. Less commonly, hematogenous dissemination from more distant sites and retrograde lymphatic extension may occur.

Cardiac involvement may consist of (1) neoplastic lymphangitis; (2) miliary infarctions, due to tumor emboli in the coronary vessels but without gross metastases; (3) single or multiple nodules, presumably due to hematogenous dissemination; or (4) diffuse infiltration. In some instances of the latter, the tumor may encroach upon and fill the cardiac chambers, or markedly thicken the myocardial or pericardial walls, or even obliterate the pericardial cavity with the production of chronic constrictive pericarditis.

Tumors of the heart are often clinically silent, and, even when they produce symptoms or signs, these are usually overshadowed by the effects of the primary tumor or metastasis to another organ. When cardiac pain occurs in the presence of secondary cardiac tumors, it is due to coronary or pericardial involvement. Thus, if a coronary artery is compressed or invaded, angina usually ensues. Myocardial infarction may eventually occur with evidence of typical electrocardiographic changes. However, unexplained heart failure (often of sudden onset and intractable nature) is the most common clinical manifestation of myocardial metastasis. Cardiac decompensation may also occur as a result of pericardial or endocardial involvement. Unexplained sinus tachycardia, premature atrial or ventricular contractions, atrial flutter or fibrillation, bundle-branch block, or complete heart block with Stokes-Adams syndrome probably constitute other frequent manifestations of myocardial involvement. These disturbances of rhythm or conduction are usually encountered in cases with metastatic invasion of the atria, particularly the right atrium.

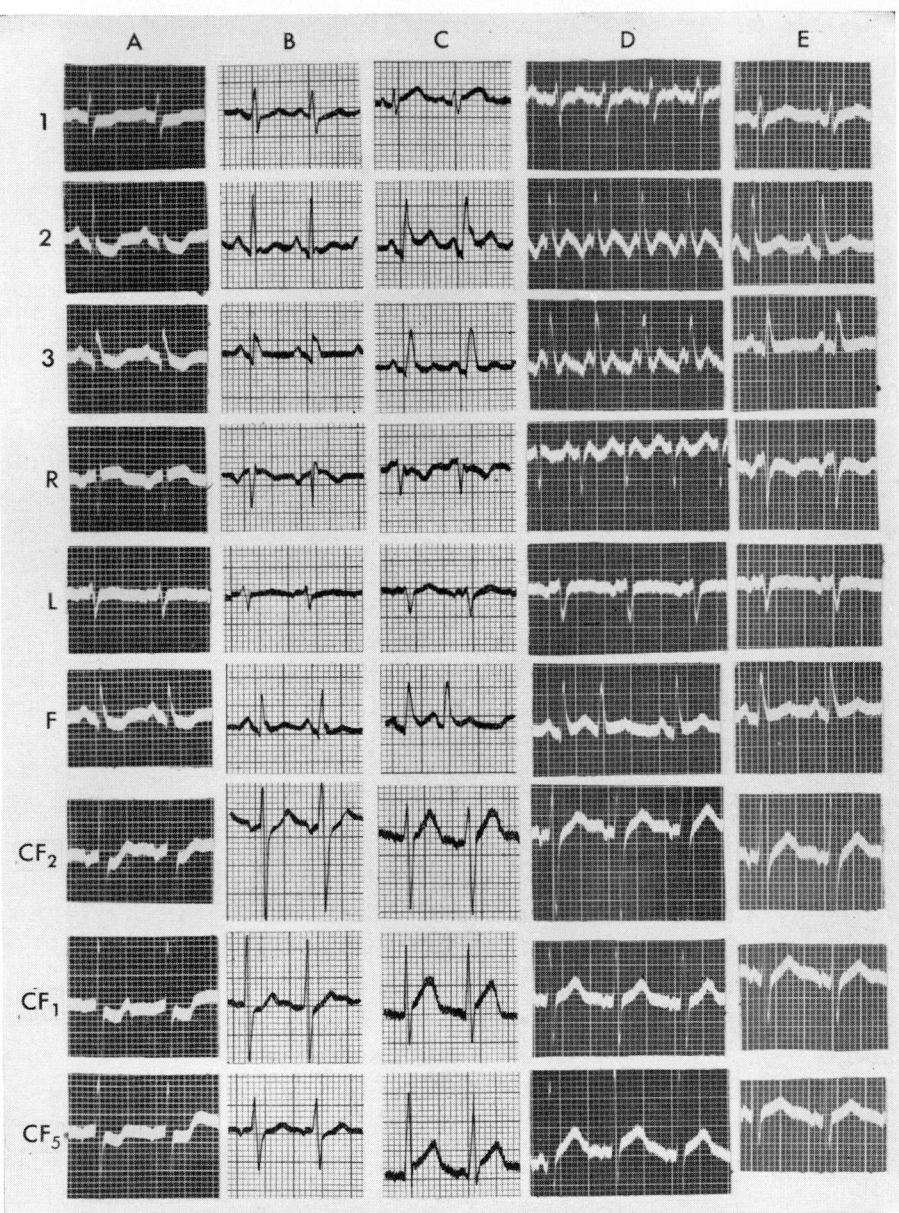

Fig. 10-9. Serial electrocardiographic changes caused by myocardial and pericardial metastases from bronchogenic carcinoma (proven by autopsy). Note nonspecific ST and T changes, atrial premature beats (C, D) followed by transient episode of atrial flutter (D). (A, 7/13; B, 8/7; C, 10/18; D, 10/26; E, 10/29.)

Rhythm and murmurs usually change rapidly from one examination to another. Pericardiocentesis of a bloody fluid which contains tumor cells confirms the diagnosis with certainty. X-rays may reveal bulges of the heart and irregularities or shagginess of its contour. After air is introduced into the pericardial sac, x-rays may delineate localized enlargements of the heart or a shaggy contour. Angiocardiographic studies may reveal an irregular outline of a cardiac chamber. Electrocardiographic findings, especially rapidly changing complexes, arrhythmias, or a pericarditis pattern are suggestive of cardiac malignancy (see Fig. 10-9).

The use of anticarcinogenic agents is far from satisfactory at present. However, radioactive gold may control effusions, and x-ray irradiation may temporarily influence certain lymphomas. Certain localized or pedunculated tumors have been removed successfully, especially since the perfection of heart-lung devices.

TRAUMATIC LESIONS OF THE MYOCARDIUM

Trauma may be nonpenetrating or penetrating. The first type is usually produced by serious steering-wheel accidents which compress the chest (see Fig. 10-10); direct blows by fist, baseball, or a heavy blunt object; or falls from great heights. This may result in small hemorrhages into the myocardium (contusio cordis). Softening and fibrosis of an extensively and severely contused area may eventually lead to the formation of an aneurysm.

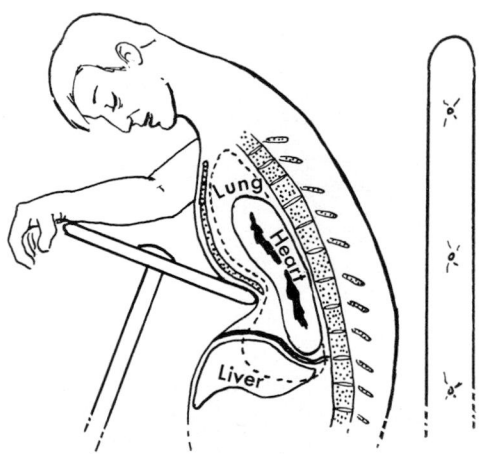

Fig. 10-10. Effect of steering wheel compression on the heart (after Beck). (From Reich, N. E.: *The Uncommon Heart Diseases*. Charles C Thomas, Publisher, Springfield, Ill., 1954.)

Rupture of a papillary muscle may also take place, although an underlying disease process is usually found to be at fault. It is characterized by a sudden onset of severe pain and progressive failure. Chest pains of cardiac origin very rarely result from indirect injuries to the anterior coronary arteries because of their linear nature and fat envelopes. They may be affected following direct, penetrating trauma. Dyspnea may also appear following severe contusion of the myocardium, as in steering-wheel accidents. Cardiac pain may be of sharp character when myocardial lesions are associated with pericardial lesions.

REFERENCES

Biegelman, P. M.; Golner, F., Jr.; and Bayles, T. B.: Progressive systemic sclerosis. *New England J. Med.*, **249**:45, 1953.

Blankenhorn, M. A., and Knowles, H. C., Jr.: Periarteritis nodosa. Recognition of clinical symptoms. *Ann. Int. Med.*, **41**:887, 1954.

Cohen, G. U.; Peery, T. M.; and Evans, J. M.: Neoplastic invasion of the heart and pericardium. *Ann. Int. Med.*, **42**:1238, 1955.

Davis, T. W., and Andrus, E. C.: Mitral stenosis in facsimile. *New England J. Med.*, **251**:297, 1954.

Goldberg, H. P., and Steinberg, I.: Primary tumors of the heart. *Circulation*, **11**:963, 1955.

Goudie, R. B.: Secondary tumours of the heart and pericardium. *Brit. Heart J.*, **17**:183, 1955.

Harrison, J. W.; McCormack, L. J.; and Ernstene, A. C.: Myxoma of the left atrium simulating mitral stenosis. *Circulation*, **10**:766, 1954.

Likoff, W.; Geckeler, G. D.; and Gregory, J. E.: Functional mitral stenosis produced by an intraatrial tumor. *Am. Heart J.*, **47**:619, 1954.

Losner, S., and Volk, B.: Newer laboratory procedures indicating rheumatic activity. *New York J. Med.*, **59**:2665, 1959.

Mandelbaum, R. A.: The ballistocardiogram in the diagnosis of myocarditis of non-rheumatic origin. *Am. J. Cardiol.*, **3**:537, 1959.

Morlon, E. V. B.: Benign polypoid tumors of the left auricle. *Edinburgh M.J.*, **41**:227, 1954.

Peacock, R. A.; Lippschutz, E. J.; and Lukas, A.: Myocardial sarcoidosis. *Circulation*, **16**:67, 1957.

Reich, N. E.: Non-diagnostic electrocardiographic patterns. *Dis. Chest*, **25**:516, 1954.

Reich, N. E.: Protean manifestations of acute rheumatic fever. *Am. Pract. & Digest Treat.*, **1**:645, 1947.

Reich, N. E.: *The Uncommon Heart Diseases.* Charles C Thomas, Publisher, Springfield, Ill., 1954.

Stollerman, G. H.; Glick, S.; Patel, D. J.; Hirschfield, I.; and Rusoff, J. H.: Determination of C-reactive protein in serum as a guide to the treatment and management of rheumatic fever. *Am. J. Med.,* **15:**645, 1953.

Wood, H. F., and McCarty, M.: Laboratory aids in the diagnosis of rheumatic fever and in evaluation of disease activity. *Am. J. Med.,* **17:**768, 1954.

CHAPTER 11 *DISEASES OF THE PERICARDIUM*

Chest pain produced by involvement of the pericardium is one of the most commonly encountered and severe types of cardiac pain. Its proper recognition is of practical importance, since it closely resembles that of acute myocardial infarction, which has an entirely different prognosis and treatment. The various types of pericardial disease producing chest pain will be discussed in accordance with the classification indicated in Table 11-1.

Table 11-1

A Complete Etiologic Classification of Pericardial Diseases °

I. Acute (and Subacute) Disorders

   A. Acute nonspecific (benign, idiopathic) pericarditis
   B. Pericarditis due to living agents
      1. Tuberculous
      2. Purulent (pyogenic)
         a) Pneumococcal
         b) Streptococcal
         c) Staphylococcal
         d) Neisserian
         e) Friedlander's
         f) Tularemic
         g) Meningococcal
         h) Secondary to hepatic or subphrenic abscess
         i) *Hemophilus influenzae*
      3. Protozoal
         a) Echinococcal
         b) Amebic
         c) *Necator americanus*
      4. Mycotic
         a) Actinomycosis
         b) Coccidioidomycosis
      5. Viral, e.g., mumps(?), lymphopathia venereum, infectious mononucleosis
   C. Connective tissue disorders and allergic diseases
      1. Rheumatic fever
      2. Systemic lupus erythematosus
      3. Allergic granulomatosis
      4. Rheumatoid arthritis
      5. Serum sickness
   D. Chemical or metabolic
      1. Uremia
      2. Diabetic acidosis
      3. Addison's disease
      4. Myxedema
   E. Neoplastic
      1. Primary
      2. Metastatic
      3. Lymphomatous (Hodgkin's disease, lymphosarcoma, leukemia)
   F. Pericarditis secondary to abnormalities of heart and great vessels
      1. With myocardial infarction
      2. With coronary embolism
      3. With dissecting aneurysm of the great vessels
      4. With bacterial endocarditis

Table 11-1 (continued) °

_____

   G. Pericarditis with a physical basis
     1. Trauma
     2. X-ray

II. Chronic Disorders

   A. Chronic constrictive pericarditis
   B. Chronic mediastinopericarditis
   C. Chronic pericardial effusion
     1. Myxedema
     2. Cholesterol pericarditis
     3. Chylopericardium
     4. Cholopericardium
     5. Anemia
     6. Trauma
     7. Chronic idiopathic pericardial effusion
   D. Pericardial cyst and diverticulum
   E. Congenital absence of pericardium

_____

° From McKusick, V. A., and Harvey, A. M.: Diseases of the pericardium. *Advances in Internal Medicine,* Vol. 7, Year Book Publishers, Chicago, 1955.

THE ACUTE PERICARDITIDES

A number of etiologic agents are responsible for attacks of acute pericarditis. They will be discussed individually. The pathologic changes of almost any type of acute pericarditis consist of grossly visible roughening of the membranes due to the deposition of fibrin. In more severe cases, the latter may accumulate in the form of large tufts and gives the pericardium a so-called "bread and butter" appearance. A small amount of fluid usually accumulates. The normal amount of 25 ml may increase to 250 ml before a significant rise in intrapericardial pressure occurs. Amounts up to 4000 ml may collect very slowly. Healing results in complete absorption of the small exudate, the formation of whitish flat scars ("milk spots"), or the production of adhesions between the two pericardial membranes or between the parietal membrane and adjacent structures. The serofibrinous form of pericarditis is characterized by the presence of variable amounts of fluid in the pericardial sac in addition to the fibrinous changes of the membranes. The fluid may be serous, serosanguinous, purely hemorrhagic, or frankly purulent.

The type of pain produced by various inflammatory disorders of the pericardium is essentially the same. The pain experienced in acute pericarditis is often attributed to involvement of the epicardium. However, the visceral membrane carries no pain fibers and is, therefore, insensitive to pain. This also holds true for the parietal membrane except for its lower part, which contains fibers deriving from the phrenic nerve. This explains the absence of pain in some types of acute pericarditis, such as uremia. When pain is present in acute pericarditis, it is usually caused by involvement of adjacent structures, such as the pleura, diaphragm, and mediastinum. This is consistent with the exacerbation or provocation of the pain by deep respiration and coughing, its frequently sharp character, and its radiation to the neck, shoulder, or back. A wide variation in the nature of the pain is noted. It may be described by the patient as a sharp, aching, heavy, oppressive, cutting, squeezing, twisting, or burning sensation. The nature of the pain may change during the course of the illness. Sharp or cutting pain often tends to become persistent and produces an aching sensation at a later stage. The pain is usually aggravated by taking a deep breath, torsion of the thorax, and swallowing or coughing, but not by exercise.

Systemic symptoms of fever, chills, sweating, fatigue, etc., depend to a great extent on the etiologic factors responsible for acute pericarditis. The symptoms of acute pericarditis associated with effusion depend mainly on the amount and rate of accumulation of the pericardial effusion present. Large pericardial effusions may eventually compress the esophagus with resultant dysphagia. In addition to the sharper types of pain noted in dry fibrinous pericarditis, a dull oppressive pain may also appear. It is presumably related to the acute distention of the pericardial sac itself. The pericardial sac can tolerate the accumulation of large amounts of fluid (3500 to 4000 ml) if this occurs slowly. This leads to considerable disturbances of cardiovascular dynamics.

The following *signs* may be encountered in acute pericarditis regardless of the etiologic factor:

A *rub* is frequently produced by the friction of the fibrinous surfaces of the two pericardial membranes. Its variability is related to the location and extent of the morphologic changes of the pericardium. A pericardial friction rub may continue occasionally after pericardial fluid appears. The incidence and loudness of the rub vary greatly, as does its extent over the precordial area.

The following features help to differentiate the rub from a cardiac murmur: It varies with the phase of respiration and the position of the patient as well as in duration and intensity. It is rougher and more "scratchy" and has a "to and fro" quality. It is heard best with the patient in the upright position. Its audibility can be further increased by pressing the chest piece of the stethoscope against the precordium—rubs increase in intensity, while murmurs tend to disappear.

The objective signs encountered in a pericardial *effusion* depend upon the hemodynamic disturbances and the compression of adjacent structures caused by the pericardial effusion. Rapid accumulation of even small amounts of fluid may lead to severe disturbances which cause alarming symptoms and signs. The progressive increase in intrapericardial pressure tends to interfere with the filling of the right atrium and ventricle; inflow stasis ensues with the increasing pressure in the right atrium and large veins. There is also an increase of the right ventricular diastolic pressure. The increased intrapericardial pressure may directly compress the superior vena cava or the right atrium; this in turn is responsible for the engorgement of the jugular veins and their failure to collapse normally during the inspiratory phase. Compression of the hepatic vein results in hepatomegaly and ascites. Large effusion may also interfere with the emptying of the cerebral veins, resulting in cerebral symptoms of dizziness or fainting.

The presence of a large pericardial effusion is often associated with orthopnea and dyspnea. This is probably due to compression of the lung, with resultant atelectasis and decreased vital capacity. Pressure on the recurrent laryngeal nerve may cause voice changes. The finding of an increased area of cardiac dullness with flat percussion note is a significant physical finding. The area of dullness below the angle of the left scapula, which may extend considerably over the left lower chest posteriorly (Ewart's sign), is related to the compression of the lung with resultant atelectasis. A dull percussion note is found frequently in the fifth right intercostal space parasternally (Roche's sign). The apex beat may be diminished or absent, but at times it persists even in the presence of massive effusions. It is often felt inside the left border of cardiac dullness.

With marked and rapid increase of the intrapericardial pressure exceeding 100 mm of saline, cardiac tamponade may evolve, characterized by a diminished venous return with resultant reduction of the stroke volume and a reduced pulse pressure. The triad consists of distant heart sounds, rising venous pressure, and falling systolic pressure. Another phenomenon observed with large pericardial effusions is pulsus paradoxus, which is a marked reduction of the pulse amplitude during inspiration.

The following *laboratory findings* aid in the diagnosis of the many etiologic forms of acute pericarditis:

The *electrocardiogram* shows characteristic changes (see Fig. 11-1) which involve the ST segments and the T waves. In rare instances, an electrical alternans occurs even in the absence of any other demonstrable myocardial involvement.

Pathognomonic ST segment changes occur early and tend to disappear before the T wave changes appear. The elevated ST segment exhibits either

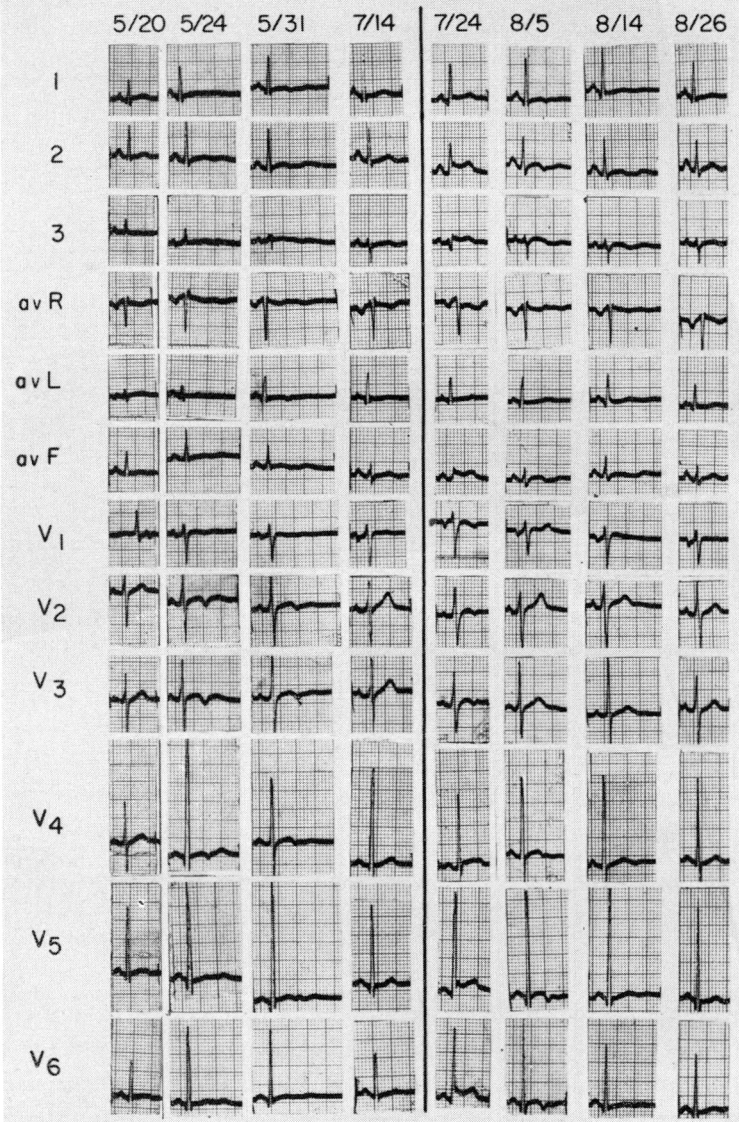

Fig. 11-1A. Serial electrocardiograms in acute nonspecific pericarditis obtained during initial (5/20) and recurrent episode (7/24). Note presence of ST and T wave changes and absence of abnormal Q waves.

a straight oblique course upward to the peak of the T wave or retains the upward concavity of a normal ST segment, as differentiated from the upward convexity (coving) which is seen in acute myocardial infarction and usually occurs at the time the T wave becomes inverted. The ST elevation

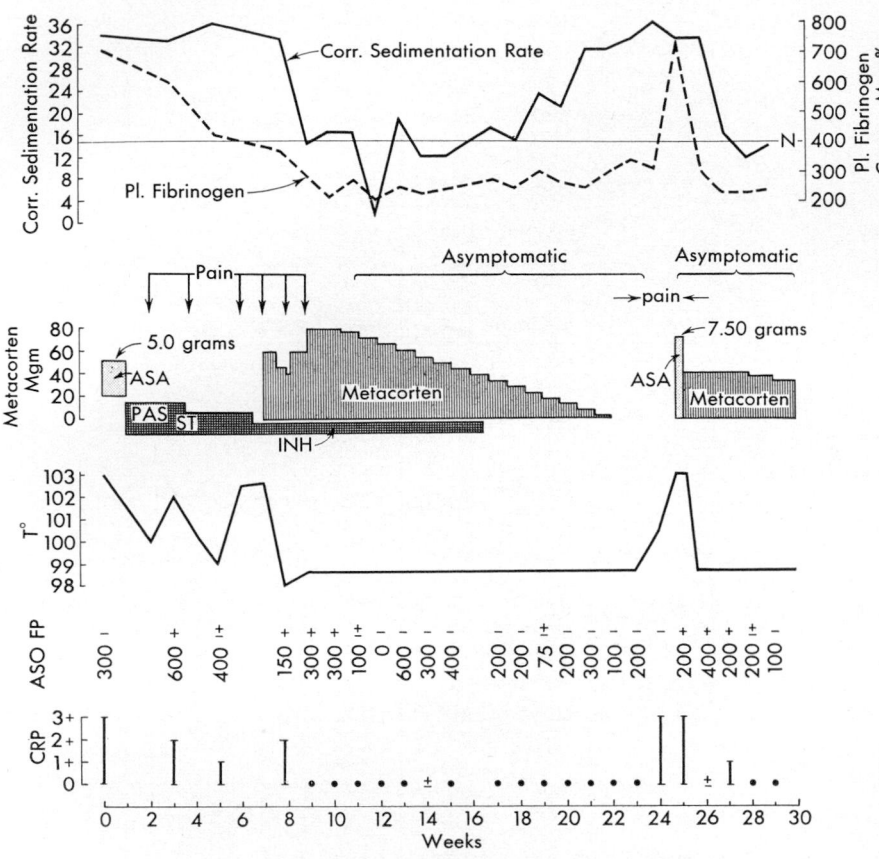

Fig. 11-1B. Graph demonstrating the correlation of the FP test, the acute phase re-actants, and the ASO titer with the temperature, chest pain, and the therapy used in a patient with recurrent idiopathic pericarditis. (From Fremont, R. E.; Losner, S.; and Volk, B. W.: Newer laboratory aids in the differential diagnosis of acute pericarditis. *Am. J. Cardiology*, 1:480, 1958.)

lasts a variable period of time (usually about one week). It may be found in all limb and precordial leads, or it may be present in only two of the standard limb leads and in a variable number of the precordial leads. This depends upon the extent of the pericardial involvement and the spatial rela-tionship of the electrodes to the involved area. Therefore, the findings of a reciprocal depression of the ST segment in some leads should not be relied upon for the differentiation of acute pericarditis and acute myocardial in-farction. Only the presence of abnormal Q waves offers conclusive evidence for the presence of the latter condition. The T waves undergo usually a gradual change from low amplitude and notching to isoelectricity and ulti-mate inversion. The inverted T wave phase lasts longer than that of the ST changes. It may persist for several months after complete clinical recovery has occurred. These late T wave changes are often characterized by deep inversion and peaking. In pericardial effusion, the electrocardiogram often shows a diminution of the voltage of the QRS and T elements, in addition to the ST segment and T wave changes which occur in fibrinous pericarditis. This is probably due to a short-circuiting of the current by the large fluid mass.

Acute nonspecific phase reactants are also of considerable importance. Of the nonspecific tests, the *erythrocyte sedimentation rate* and *white blood cell* count tend to be abnormally elevated in most cases—the sedimentation rate more frequently so than the white blood count. In fact, the latter may be abnormally low in some instances as a response to a viral infection. Of the newer nonspecific acute phase reactants, the *C-reactive protein* (CRP) and the *plasma fibrinogen concentration* commonly yield abnormal findings in acute rheumatic, acute nonspecific, and tuberculous pericarditides, usually in the most severe forms. In general, however, they behave erratically. The *antistreptolysin-O titer* (ASO titer) is of limited value. It is frequently elevated in acute rheumatic pericarditis, particularly in childhood and adolescence, but is usually normal in adulthood. It is rarely elevated in acute nonspecific pericarditis.

The *fibrinogen polymerization test* is positive in acute rheumatic and nonspecific pericarditides. The fibrinogen polymerization test offers the particular advantage of not being suppressed promptly by salicylates or corticosteroids in contrast to the nonspecific acute phase reactants. It appears to reflect faithfully the duration of activity of the disease process. Since the fibrinogen polymerization test is negative in myocardial infarction, it is of value in the differential diagnosis between acute or subacute pericarditis and acute myocardial infarction, particularly when used in combination with the determination of serum enzyme levels (serum glutamic oxalacetic transaminase or aldolase).

Roentgenologic features are usually revealing (see Figs. 11-2 and 11-3). The normally sharp outline of the cardiac segments is usually obliterated. This is best noted in the region of the pulmonary artery segment. It leads to a pear-shaped or water-bottle appearance of the cardiac silhouette. There is also a widening of the supracardiac vascular area, and a bulge may appear in the posterior and inferior area of the cardiac silhouette in the right anterior oblique view. Vertical and horizontal roentgenograms show variations in configuration as the fluid shifts. An acute right cardiohepatic angle is visible in overexposed films, because the pericardium is anchored at this site. *Fluoroscopy* frequently reveals a marked reduction or complete absence of

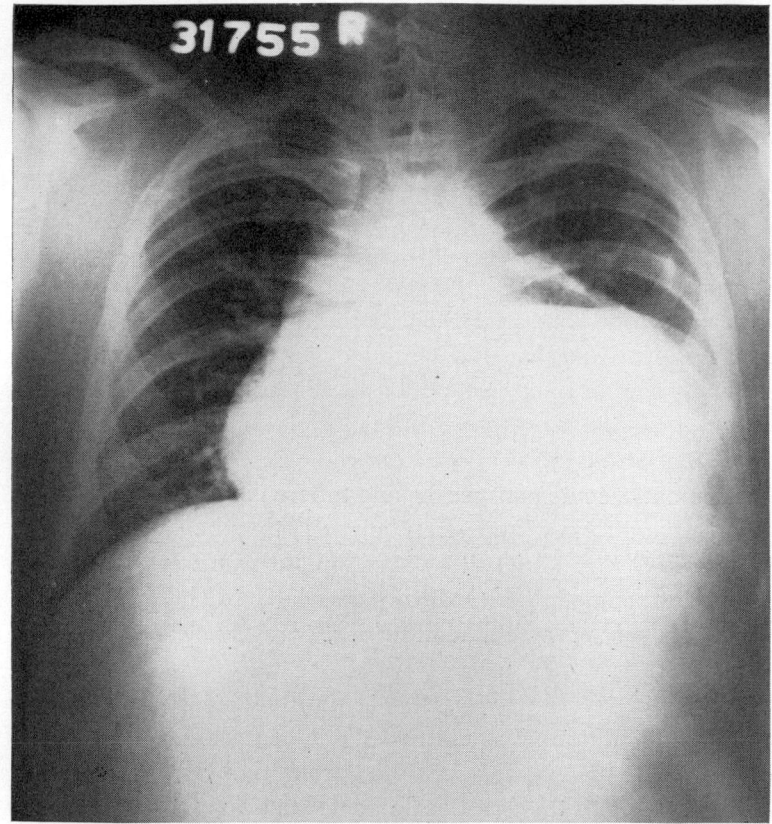

Fig. 11-2. Pericarditis with effusion. Markedly enlarged cardiac shadow. Note the air fluid level within the pericardial cavity following needle tap.

cardiac pulsations ("quiet heart"), which can be confirmed by kymography. *Angiocardiographic studies* reveal normal-sized heart chambers heavily opacified by the contrast medium well within the pericardial effusion. Carbon dioxide has been employed recently, without any detrimental effects, to fill the right-sided chambers while the patient is lying on the left side. The fluid density in the pericardium is noted just above the atrial gas. In the lateral projection, the fluid is in the anterior, retrosternal, and infracardiac area, displacing the heart posteriorly. Small amounts of fluid appear to accumulate below the heart initially. With massive accumulation of fluid, the lateral processes of the pericardial sac fill.

Pericardiocentesis is a diagnostic (and therapeutic) procedure which may be employed for the detection of small effusions or for the differential diagnosis of an enlargement of the cardiac silhouette consistent with either cardiac dilatation or pericardial effusion. Since angiocardiography has dem-

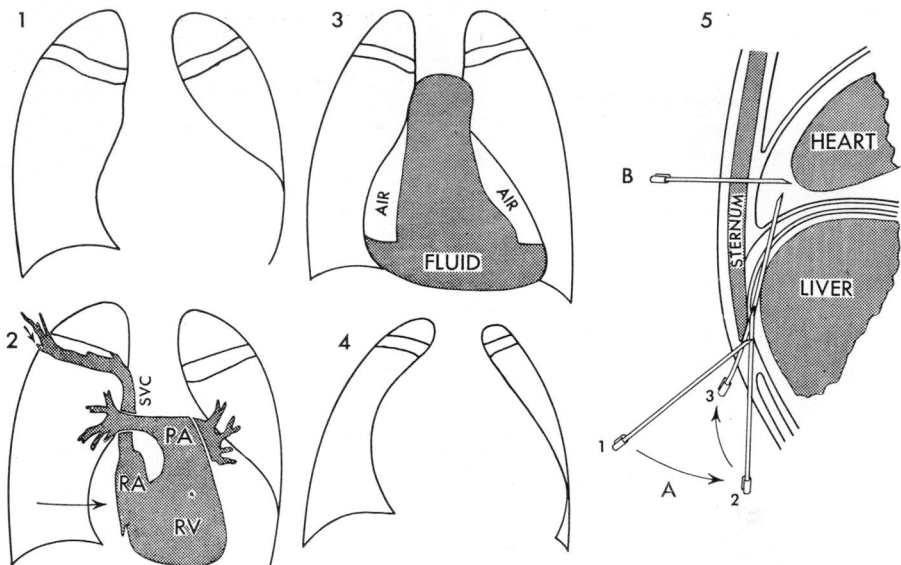

Fig. 11-3. Pericardial fluid. *1*, Marked globular enlargement of cardiac silhouette due to massive effusion. *2*, Frontal angiocardiogram (3 sec.) shows characteristic wide interval (*arrow*) between right atrium and right heart border, thus excluding cardiac hypertrophy. *3*, Hydropneumopericardium. *4*, Appearance of massive pericardial effusion or suppuration in an infant. *5*, Two satisfactory methods of pericardiocentesis: *A*, subxiphoid approach; *B*, intercostal approach in fourth or fifth interspace in left parasternal line. (From Reich, N. E.: *The Uncommon Heart Diseases*. Charles C. Thomas, Publisher, Springfield, Ill., 1954.)

onstrated the localization of small amounts of pericardial effusion below the heart, the subxiphoid approach is safest and most likely to yield fluid. Smear, culture, cell block, and guinea pig inoculation are employed to ascertain the etiologic factor. Pericardial tapping may also be utilized for the determination of the intrapericardial pressure (see Fig. 11-4). It is markedly elevated in cardiac tamponade. The diagnostic value of the pericardial tap can be enhanced significantly by the instillation of air following withdrawal of fluid. This permits evaluation of the heart size, of the thickness of the parietal pericardium, and of the presence of adhesions and epicardial or pericardial shagginess or irregularity. Furthermore, induction of a pneumopericardium may have therapeutic value and may prevent the development of constrictive pericarditis. Differentiation of cardiac dilatation and pericardial effusion is also possible during cardiac catheterization. Contact of the catheter with the right atrial wall and the relation of this point to the right lung field may prove the presence or absence of pericardial effusion.

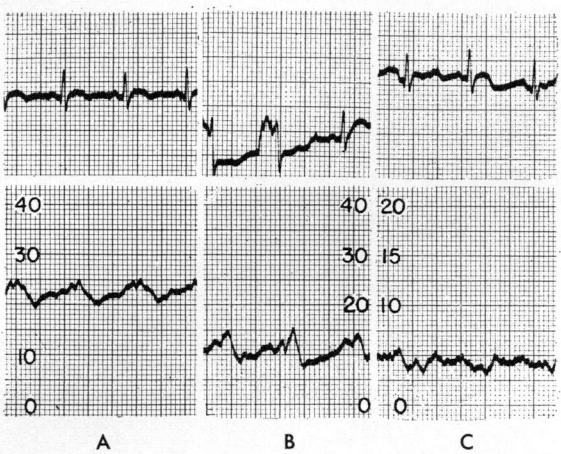

A   B   C

Fig. 11-4. Lower graphs show intrapericardial pressures obtained in massive pericardial effusion before (*A*) and after repeated withdrawal (*B* and *C*) of pericardial fluid. The pressure dropped from an initial average 23 mm Hg to a final average of 3.5 mm Hg. This coincided with marked subjective relief of the patient and markedly reduced engorgement of the neck veins. (From Fremont, R. E.: Pathophysiology of acute and chronic pericarditis. In Gordon, B. L. [ed.]: *Clinical Cardiopulmonary Physiology,* 2nd ed. Grune and Stratton, New York, 1960.)

Special Types of Pericarditis

There are infectious and noninfectious types of pericarditis, many of which have an uncertain etiology. Certain types of infectious pericarditis are curable. The tuberculous and pyogenic groups are especially serious and tend to produce constrictive lesions. Rheumatic pericarditis may be the overwhelming feature of a pancarditis. Noninfectious types of pericarditis may be due to uremia, neoplasms, or collagen disorders.

Acute nonspecific (idiopathic) pericarditis is probably the most common type of pericarditis encountered in adulthood, but it also occurs in adolescence and childhood. This benign lesion frequently follows in the wake of an upper respiratory infection, shows a marked tendency to relapse, and is often accompanied by pneumonitis and pleuritis. A past or family history of allergic manifestations is not uncommonly obtained, but the exact etiology has not been identified. It has been postulated that it may follow an upper respiratory infection which spreads to the mediastinal lymph nodes and pericardium. The clinical course closely resembles that of rheumatic and tuberculous pericarditis as well as pericarditis following cardiac surgery (postcardiotomy syndrome). A similar type of pericarditis (postinfarction

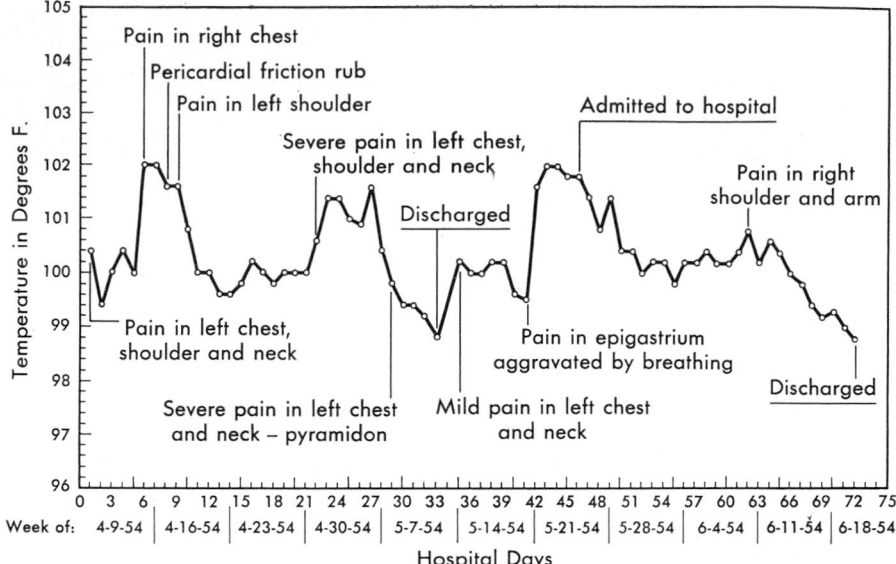

Fig. 11-5. Following acute myocardial infarction, six bouts of fever occurred during a period of ten weeks, each associated with a flare-up of pain in the chest, shoulders, arms, neck, and epigastrium. (From Dressler, W.: Post-myocardial infarction. *J.A.M.A.*, **160:**1379, 1956.)

syndrome) has been described recently following acute myocardial infarction (see Fig. 11-5). This has led to the assumption that nonspecific pericarditis may be of rheumatic nature or, like the latter, may also represent a hypersensitivity reaction of the pericardium in a patient with a rheumatic or allergic diathesis.

This condition is frequently associated with variable amounts of pericardial effusion but rarely leads to cardiac tamponade. However, death may occur as a result of pericardial hemorrhage when the chest pain is erroneously attributed to acute myocardial infarction and treated with anticoagulants. The early appearance of the pain, fever, pericardial friction rub, and confirmatory electrocardiographic changes establishes the diagnosis of acute benign pericarditis.

The amount of pericardial effusion rarely requires a pericardial tap or pericardiectomy for therapeutic relief. The fluid is frequently serosanguinous, but microscopic examination usually fails to yield any etiologic clue.

The most effective treatment consists of the administration of salicylates in mild cases and of corticosteroids in more severe cases. Whether the corticosteroids actually affect the duration of the disease is uncertain, but prompt reabsorption of the pericardial effusion follows, and there is usually rapid improvement of the pain with disappearance of the systemic symptoms, such as fever, malaise, and sweating. Relapses may occur even when the corticosteroids are used in large doses over a long period of time. Since the disease has a tendency to recur, especially when the patient attempts to resume activity, prophylactic surgery (pericardiectomy) has been advocated in pericarditis that has not yet advanced to the constrictive phase. It also has the advantage of preventing attendant cardiac failure and liver damage.

Acute rheumatic fever presents microscopic evidence of pericardial involvement in nearly all fatal cases. The pericarditis is usually overshadowed by the associated acute myocardial and endocardial involvement and is frequently of very serious nature. It may lead to formation of adhesions between the visceral and parietal membranes or between the latter and mediastinal structures (adhesive mediastino- or pleuropericarditis). Constrictive pericarditis is a rare complication.

Serofibrinous pericarditis with variable amounts of effusion also occurs in acute rheumatic fever. It is most common in childhood and adolescence and is usually associated with other manifestations of cardiac involvement. When it represents the only cardiac findings, it may resemble acute idiopathic pericarditis. A history of previous joint involvement, unexplained fever, or other manifestations of rheumatic disease may be elicited and confirmed by the laboratory tests previously described. Pericarditis is frequently associated with rheumatic valvular disease, high fever, pneumonia, pleuritis, or heart failure. Subcutaneous nodules are more common in the presence of rheumatic pericarditis.

Tuberculosis may cause fibrinous pericarditis with a small amount of effusion but large amounts of fibrin. The rapid development of partial or complete obliteration of the pericardial space frequently leads to chronic constrictive pericarditis. Adhesions with the adjacent mediastinum or pleura frequently produce adhesive mediastino- or pleuropericarditis.

A serofibrinous exudate represents the most frequent type of tuberculous pericardial disease. The fluid is usually hemorrhagic, and massive amounts may accumulate. Thus, marked hemodynamic disturbances caused by large pericardial effusion or by cardiac tamponade are commonly encountered. Large masses of fibrin are deposited, and constrictive pericarditis may also occur early while the tuberculous infection of the pericardium is still in the active stage. Fortunately, the use of streptomycin, aminosalicylic acid (PAS), and isoniazid therapy has not only greatly reduced the incidence of tuberculous pericarditis but has permitted the institution of early surgical drainage, and of pericardiectomy in the presence of constrictive pericarditis.

Pyogenic infections of the pericardium may also lead to large pericardial effusion and eventually to constrictive pericarditis. They usually originate from suppurative infections, which most commonly affect contiguous structures such as the lungs and pleura. The pericardial involvement is often overshadowed by the systemic manifestations of a severe pyogenic infection. Aspiration of the thick fluid has been made possible by the introduction of enzymatic substances (e.g., streptokinase). Antibiotics have reduced effectively the incidence and increased the recovery rate of this type of pericarditis. When used in connection with pericardiectomy, antibiotics facilitate the recovery from the acute infection and combat the development of constrictive pericarditis.

Disseminated lupus erythematosus frequently causes pericardial involvement. It appears in about half the cases and may even be the first clinical manifestation. It is occasionally associated with a large effusion, but most commonly is of the dry fibrinous type. Recurrences are frequent, and associated myocardial involvement may occur. It may be difficult to distinguish between myocardial and pericardial involvement, but the presence of chest pain and electrocardiographic changes usually suggest pericardial involvement. Typical lupus erythematosus cells are occasionally found in the pericardial fluid. Evidence of endocarditis may also be in evidence (Libman-Sacks disease).

Uremic pericarditis frequently tends to be of the dry fibrinous type, but large effusions may occur occasionally. It is usually associated with the terminal phase of various renal lesions. The appearance of a "to and fro" rub is an ominous sign. However, recurrences of pericarditis and even complete healing with the formation of adhesions have been observed. The exact pathogenesis of this pericarditis is unknown, but metabolic and chemical alterations have been incriminated. Pain is rare in this type of pericarditis. The history, urinary findings, and blood chemistry are usually revealing. The use of the artificial kidney apparatus has been helpful in an occasional patient.

Pericarditis and Addison's disease. Pericarditis has been encountered in Addison's disease. The clinical picture closely resembles that of acute benign idiopathic pericarditis except for an extremely rapid demise, which may be attributed to the adrenocortical insufficiency.

Pericarditis and diabetic acidosis. Pericarditis has also been reported in several instances of diabetic acidosis. It is quite conceivable that a basic mechanism of hypersensitivity reaction is common to many disorders of inflammatory, infectious, metabolic, and other types which may precipitate an acute pericarditis of the so-called "idiopathic" or nonspecific variety. All of them appear to respond to corticosteroid administration.

Neoplastic involvement of the pericardium. The pericardium may be involved by primary or secondary neoplasms. These have been discussed elsewhere in greater detail (see pp. 213–17). However, a brief discussion of their effects on the pericardium is in order. Of the primary malignancies, sarcoma is the most noteworthy type. It may cause extensive pericardial involvement with large effusions or complete obliteration of the pericardial space. Involvement of the pericardium by secondary tumors is even more common than that of the myocardium. Teratomas of the mediastinum may involve the pericardium and even cause purulent pericarditis when superimposed infection occurs. Other types of neoplasm affecting the pericardium by contiguous or metastatic invasion are essentially the same as in the case of myocardial invasion, which has been discussed in Chapter 10.

These lesions are rarely the cause of chest pain. If pain is present, it is of vague, dull, oppressive type and is often due to the accumulation of a large effusion in the pericardial sac. Such effusions are serous or sanguinous and may lead to cardiac tamponade; they tend to reaccumulate rapidly following aspiration. However, neoplastic lesions of the pericardium may produce a dry fibrinous type of pericarditis with typical pain and a friction rub which may persist for several weeks or months. In some instances, the clinical picture of chronic constricture pericarditis may be produced.

Systemic neoplastic disease may also involve the pericardium. This occurs most commonly in Hodgkin's disease, lymphosarcoma, reticulum-cell sarcoma, and malignant lymphoma. While the clinical picture is usually that of asymptomatic pericardial effusion (frequently hemorrhagic), chest pain resembling that of acute pericarditis may also be encountered. Radioactive gold may be instilled into the pericardial sac in order to reduce the accumulation of fluid.

Pericardial involvement due to abnormalities of heart and great vessels. Since these lesions have been described in great detail in appropriate sections, they will be mentioned only briefly at this point. *Dissecting aortic aneurysm* may rupture into the pericardium and produce the clinical picture of acute pericarditis. Occasionally, the latter may completely obscure the underlying primary disorder. However, the pain is usually very severe and sudden in onset. Aspiration reveals frank blood in the pericardium. Pericarditis occurs frequently in association with *acute myocardial infarction* or *coronary embolism*. However, chest pain of pericardial origin is rare, and the friction rub is of brief duration. During the course of these diseases, the onset of typical pain of acute pericarditis associated with a persistent friction rub, but without electrocardiographic changes of infarction, strongly suggests a *postmyocardial infarction syndrome*.

Traumatic involvement of pericardium. The pericardium is most frequently injured by blunt or direct trauma to the chest. This may result in typical chest pain due to fibrinous pericarditis or to an acute effusion of serous or sanguinous nature which rapidly distends the pericardial sac. This may also lead rapidly to cardiac tamponade. However, chest pain due to trauma of the pericardium may be overlooked owing to the presence of more obvious injuries of the bony cage or pulmonary system. Acute pericarditis may not develop directly following penetrating wounds of the heart or pericardium, but may arise following surgical intervention for the myocardial or pericardial injuries. Acute pericarditis resulting from penetrating or nonpenetrating injuries produces electrocardiographic changes similar to other etiologic forms of acute pericarditis.

The treatment includes analgesics, supportive measures in cases of severe associated hemorrhage or shock, pericardiocentesis in impending cardiac tamponade, and measures directed at any cardiopulmonary abnormalities. Surgical intervention is indicated if myocardial rupture or laceration of a coronary artery is suspected or following rapid reaccumulation of blood in the pericardial sac.

Pericardial lesions produced by physical agents. Pericardial reaction of severe degree may be produced by roentgen therapy administered for neoplastic lesions involving the thorax and its contents, such as lymphoma or cancer of the breast, thyroid, or lungs. Chest pain may occur as a result of the pericardial reaction. Massive pericardial effusion may be encountered occasionally.

CHRONIC LESIONS OF THE PERICARDIUM

Chronic Constrictive Pericarditis

Long-standing disorders are fairly quiescent and are rarely associated with symptoms of pain. The most important chronic lesion is chronic constrictive pericarditis. This disorder is most frequently attributed to tuberculous pericarditis. Pain may occur in this type of chronic pericarditis, since the constrictive process may originate very early in the course of the tuberculous infection. However, the tuberculous type is usually painless and is characterized by asymptomatic hemorrhagic pericardial effusion. Chest pain may also be due to an associated tuberculous pleuritis. Low thoracic or epigastric distress may also be present due to hepatomegaly. As mentioned elsewhere (pp. 229, 232), chronic constrictive pericarditis may be secondary to other types of acute or recurrent pericarditis, such as pyogenic infections and benign idiopathic and acute rheumatic pericarditis. Neoplastic and traumatic lesions rarely lead to constrictive pericarditis. Concretio cordis and chronic adhesive pericarditis are not associated with pain of pericardial

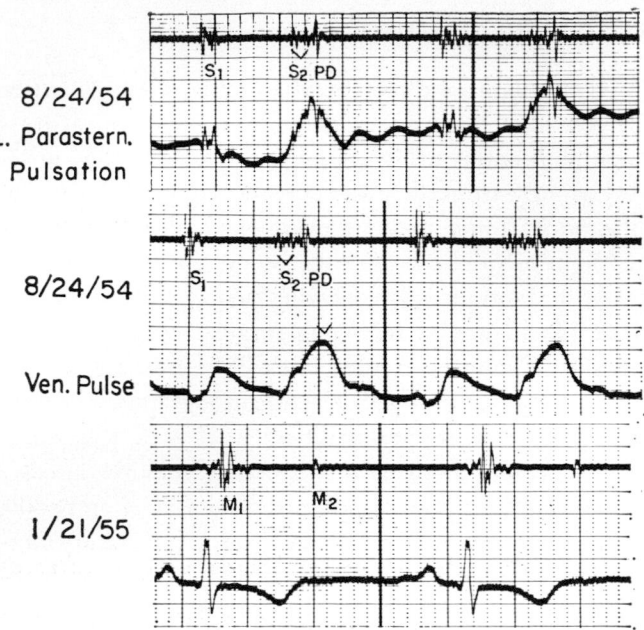

Fig. 11-6. Phonocardiographic and pulsatory findings in constrictive pericarditis. Note early protodiastolic sound (*PD*) coinciding with outward movement of left parasternal region of chest wall but preceding peak of V wave of venous pulse (in contrast to protodiastolic gallop due to myocardial disease). Phonocardiogram obtained after successful cardiolysis (1/21/55) reveals disappearance of adventitious sound. (From Fremont, R. E.: Pathophysiology of acute and chronic pericarditis. In Gordon, B. L. [ed.]: *Clinical Cardiopulmonary Physiology,* 2nd ed. Grune and Stratton, New York, 1960.)

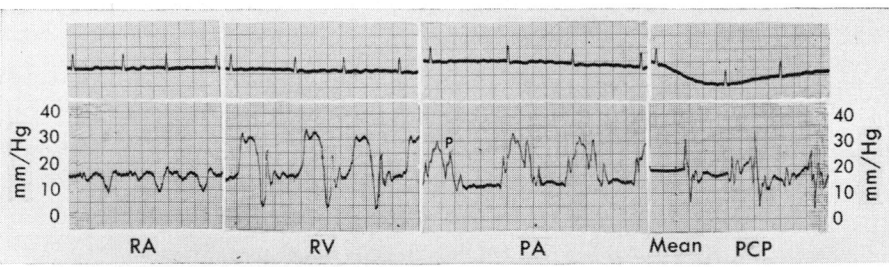

Fig. 11-7. Cardiodynamics in constrictive pericarditis (lower graphs). Note elevated and nearly identical levels of mean pressure of right atrium (*RA*), end-diastolic pressure of right ventricle (*RV*), diastolic pressure of pulmonary artery (*PA*), and mean pulmonary capillary pressure (*PCP*). Note also early diastolic dip of right ventricular pressure, low voltage of QRS complex, and presence of atrial fibrillation. (From Fremont, R. E.: Pathophysiology of acute and chronic pericarditis. In Gordon, B. L. [ed.]: *Clinical Cardiopulmonary Physiology,* 2nd ed. Grune and Stratton, New York, 1960.)

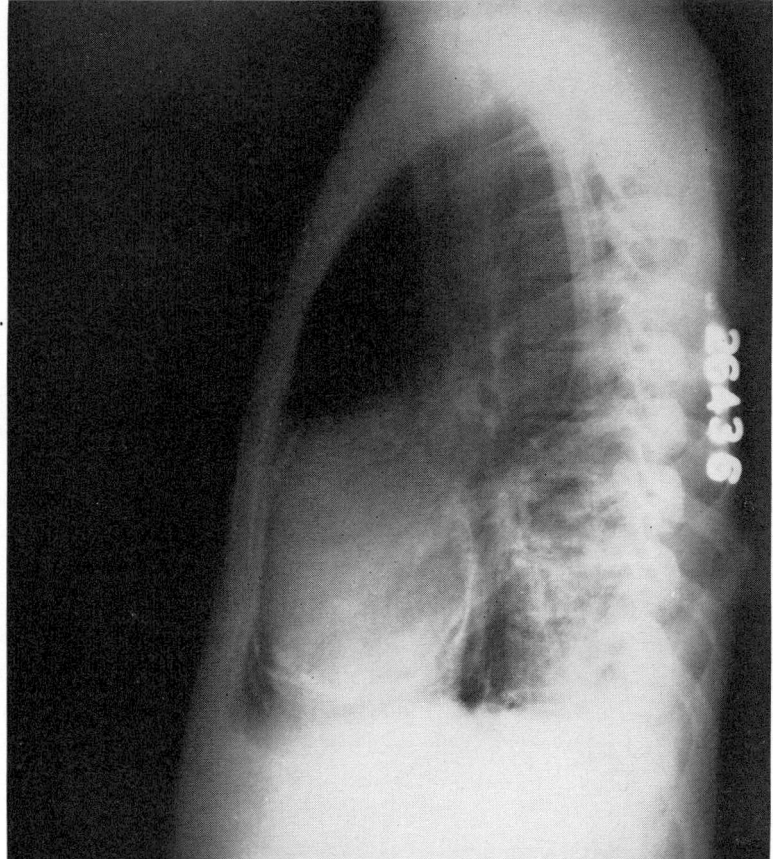

Fig. 11-8. Extensive pericardial calcification encircling the cardiac shadow on lateral projection.

origin. A detailed discussion of the hemodynamic disturbances which result from pericardial constriction regardless of the etiologic factor is not within the scope of this text. (See Figs. 11-6, 11-7, and 11-8.)

Miscellaneous Pericardial Disorders

A number of unusual conditions which are characterized by large recurrent pericardial effusions do not cause chest pain of the type ordinarily encountered in acute pericarditis. Chest pain of a vague, dull, oppressive nature ("crowding in the chest") is usually present in these cases. The etiologic and pathogenetic factors are seldom clarified. In rare instances, a so-called *cholesterol pericarditis* may be found as the cause. It may lead to massive accumulation of fluid and even to cardiac tamponade. Myxedema, pericardial effusion, and cholesterol pericarditis are often associated. A crystalline suspension of cholesterol injected into the pericardial sac has been shown to lead to pericardial effusion, pericardial granulation tissue, and pericardial and epicardial thickening. In other instances, tuberculosis, trauma, lupus erythematosus, chylopericardium, and myxedema may be found to produce chronic pericardial effusion. Occasionally, no cause whatsoever can be detected. The treatment consists of pericardiectomy when constrictive lesions ensue.

Chylopericardium and pseudochylous fluids may also be found on aspiration of the pericardial sac. Indirect or direct trauma to the thoracic duct is usually the cause, although this has also been noted following neoplastic or tuberculous invasion of the duct. There is an initial period of shock and then recovery, which may be followed in two to six days by a third stage of profound collapse and the usual signs of pericardial fluid. The rapid development of an adequate collateral lymphatic circulation results in quicker recovery. Aspiration of a cloudy or milky fluid is characteristic. The appearance of pseudochylous fluid is not due to fat but to the presence of fine albuminous particles which are not soluble in ordinary fat solvents.

Cholopericardium is exceedingly rare but may follow gallbladder or liver injury or disease with the development of a fistulous tract which communicates with the pericardium. Bile is very irritating to any serous surface. It is very painful and may precipitate enormous effusions. The primary condition is usually so evident and dramatic as to overshadow the picture of cholopericardium.

Pneumopericardium signifies the presence of gas within the pericardial sac due to a variety of causes. The gas may be irritating and gives rise to fluid. In the case of trauma, the fluid is bloody. The history of a primary disease process is significant. Perforating lesions of the esophagus are especially important. Precordial tympany and splashing churning sounds (bruit de moulin) may be heard as the heart beats within the mixture of air and fluid. X-rays are characteristic and show a distinctive pericardial fluid level.

Congenital lesions of the pericardium include a deficiency or total *absence* of the pericardium and *pericardial celomic cyst.* "Pleurodiaphragmatic cysts," "springwater cysts," and "serosal cysts" are other synonymous terms for the latter, which refers to a congenital thin-walled cyst of the pericardium that usually lies on or near the diaphragm in the right cardiophrenic space (see Fig. 11-9). The majority of pericardial cysts are asymptomatic. When symptoms do occur, they are usually the result of increased pressure within the thoracic cavity with resulting compression of the heart, lungs, or mediastinal structures. The treatment of these cysts consists of surgical removal.

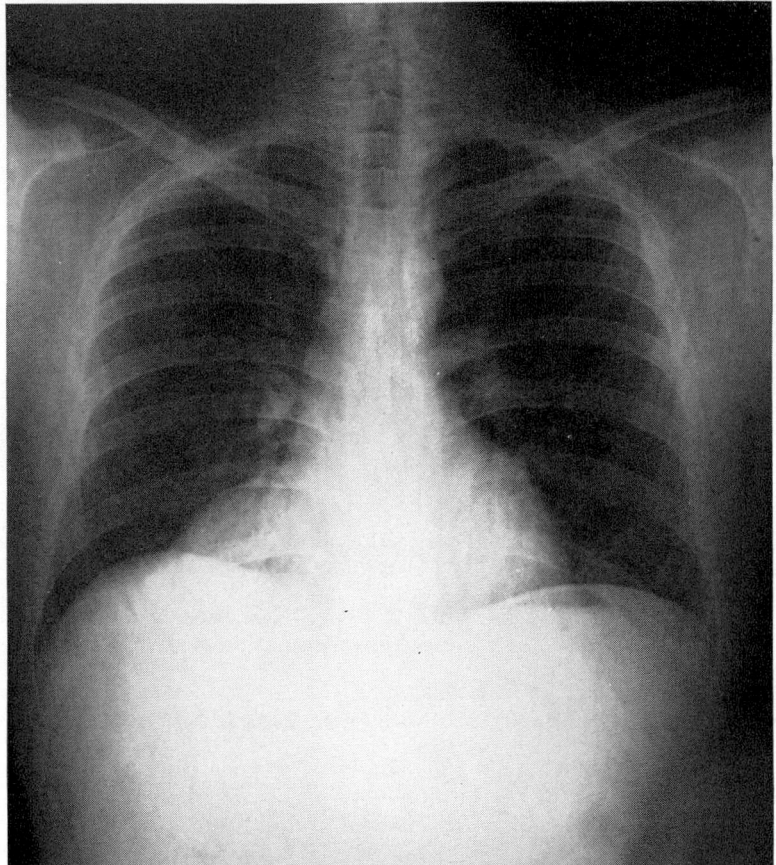

Fig. 11-9. Pericardial celomic cyst. Note smooth, homogenous soft tissue density in the right cardiophrenic angle (surgically proven).

REFERENCES

Andrews, G. W. S.; Pickering, G. W.; and Holmes, S. T.: The aetiology of constrictive pericarditis with special reference to tuberculous pericarditis together with a note on polyserositis. *Quart. J. Med.,* **17:**291, 1948.

Barker, P. S., and Johnston, F. D.: Chronic pericarditis with effusion. *Circulation,* **2:**134, 1950.

Burwell, C. S., and Ayer, G. D.: Constrictive pleuritis and pericarditis. *Am. Heart J.,* **22:**267, 1941.

Chamblis, J. R., et al.: Chronic cardiac compression (chronic constrictive pericarditis): critical study of 61 cases with follow-up. *Circulation,* **4:**816, 1951.

Clark, G. M.: Endocardial fibrosis. M.S. thesis, Department of Medicine, University of Colorado, 1952.

Couter, W. T., and Reichert, R. E., Jr.: Primary systemic amyloidosis mimicking chronic constrictive pericardial disease. *Circulation*, 2:441, 1950.

Crastnopol, P.; Kroop, I. G.; and Levy, G.: Management of pericardial effusions by pericardiectomy. *New York J. Med.*, 58:2367, 1958.

Dressler, W.: *Clinical Cardiology*. Paul B. Hoeber, Inc., New York, 1942.

Dressler, W.: Idiopathic recurrent pericarditis: comparison with the postcommissurotomy syndrome; considerations of etiology and treatment. *Am. J. Med.*, 18:591, 1955.

Dressler, W.: A post-myocardial infarction syndrome. *J.A.M.A.*, 160:1379, 1956.

Findley, J. W., Jr., and Adams, W.: Primary systemic amyloidosis simulating constrictive pericarditis with steatorrhea and hyperesthesia. *Arch. Int. Med.*, 81:342, 1948.

Freilich, J. K.: Acute nonspecific pericarditis complicated by the development of a fibrous pericardium. *Ann. Int. Med.*, 37:388, 1952.

Fremont, R. E.; Losner, S.; and Volk, B. W.: The fibrinogen polymerization test in nonspecific myocarditis and pericarditis (abstr.). *Circulation*, 14:938, 1956.

Fremont, R. E.; Losner, S.; and Volk, B. W.: The fibrinogen polymerization test in nonspecific myocarditis and pericarditis. *A.M.A. Arch. Int. Med.*, 102:41, 1958.

Fremont, R. E.; Losner, S.; and Volk, B. W.: Newer laboratory aids in the differential diagnosis of acute pericarditis, with particular emphasis upon the value of the fibrinogen polymerization test. *Am. J. Cardiol.*, 1:480, 1958.

Fremont, R. E.; Volk, B. W.: Newer aspects of diagnostic and therapeutic management of acute idiopathic pericarditis. *Dis. Chest*, 36:319, 1959.

Fremont, R. E.: Pathophysiology of acute and chronic pericarditis. In Gordon, B. L. (ed.): *Clinical Cardiopulmonary Physiology*, 2nd ed. Grune and Stratton, New York, 1960.

Friedman, S.; Ash, R.; Harris, T. N.; and Lee, H. F.: Acute benign pericarditis in childhood: comparison with rheumatic pericarditis and therapeutic effects of ACTH and cortisone. *Pediatrics*, 9:551, 1952.

Gibb, W. E.: Pulsus paradoxus and pleurisy. *Brit. J. Tuberc.*, 43:1, 1949.

Hansen, A. T.; Eskildsen, P.; and Gotzsche, H.: Pressure curves from right auricle and right ventricle in chronic constrictive pericarditis. *Circulation*, 3:881, 1951.

Harrison, T. R., et al.: *Principles of Internal Medicine*, 3rd ed. McGraw-Hill Book Co., Inc., New York, 1958.

Holman, E., and Willett, F.: Treatment of active tuberculous pericarditis by pericardiectomy. *J.A.M.A.*, 146:1, 1951.

Kaltman, A. J.; Schwedel, J. B.; and Strauss, B.: Chronic constrictive pericarditis and rheumatic heart disease. *Am. Heart J.*, **45**:201, 1953.

Loeffler, W.: Endocarditis parietalis fibroplastica mit Bluteosinophilie. *Schweiz. med. Wchnschr.* **66**:817, 1936.

McKusick, V. A.: Chronic constrictive pericarditis. II. Electrokymographic studies and correlations with roentgenkymography, phonocardiography and right ventricular pressure curves. *Bull. Johns Hopkins Hosp.*, **90**:27, 1952.

McKusick, V. A., and Harvey, A. M.: Diseases of the pericardium. *Advances in Internal Medicine,* Vol. 7. Year Book Publishers, Chicago, 1955.

Meyers, T. M., and Hamburger, M.: Tuberculous pericarditis. Its treatment with streptomycin and some observations on the natural history of the disease. *Am. J. Med.*, **12**:302, 1952.

Murphy, T. R.; Meyer, J. M.; and Chase, J.: Constrictive pericarditis; serial hemodynamic studies with an explanation for reversible congestive phenomena. *Circulation*, **18**:526, 1958.

Overholt, R. H., et al.: Constrictive pericarditis and constrictive pleuritis treated by pericardiectomy and pulmonary decortication. *J. Thoracic Surg.*, **23**:1, 1952.

Reich, N. E.: Restrictive heart diseases: diagnosis and treatment. *Angiology*, **2**:387, 1960.

Reich, N. E.: *The Uncommon Heart Diseases,* Charles C Thomas, Publisher, Springfield, Ill., 1954.

Reich, N. E.: Less common causes of cardiovascular disease. In *Cardiology*, Vol. 4, Blakiston Div., McGraw-Hill Book Co., 1959.

Shapiro, J. B.: Tuberculous pericarditis with effusion: the impact of antimicrobial therapy. *Am. J. M. Sc.*, **225**:229, 1953.

Soloff, L. A., and Zatuchni, J.: The definitive diagnosis of effusive or constrictive pericarditis. *Am. J. M. Sc.*, **234**:687, 1957.

Steinberg, I.; VonGal, H. V.; and Finby N.: Roentgen diagnosis of pericardial effusion: new angiocardiographic observations. *Am. J. Roentgenol.*, **79**:321, 1958.

Williams, R. G., and Steinberg, I.: The value of angiocardiography in establishing the diagnosis of pericarditis with effusion. *Am. J. Roentgenol.*, **61**:41, 1949.

Wood, P.: Diagnosis of pericardial effusion by means of cardiac catheterization. *Brit. Heart J.*, **13**:574, 1951.

Yu, P. N. G., et al.: Right auricular and ventricular pressure patterns in constrictive pericarditis. *Circulation*, **7**:102, 1953.

CHAPTER 12 *DISEASES OF THE CORONARY ARTERIES*

242

Electrocardiography
Vectorcardiography
Ballistocardiography
Phonocardiography
Roentgen procedures
    Fluoroscopy
    Electrokymography
    Roentgencinematography
    Roentgenkymography
    Tomography
    Angiocardiography
General laboratory tests
    Acute phase reactants
        erythrocyte sedimentation rate
        C-reactive protein test
        plasma fibrinogen concentration
    Fibrinogen polymerization test
    Leukocyte count
    Enzyme tests
        serum glutamic oxalacetic transaminase
        lactic acid dehydrogenase
        aldolase
    Lipid determinations
        plasma-cholesterol-phospholipid ratio
        blood triglyceride level
        beta-lipoproteins
        fat tolerance tests
    Determination of radioiodine uptake
    Trace metal determinations

TREATMENT

Medical treatment
    Angina pectoris and coronary insufficiency
    Coronary occlusion
        Other forms of treatment
            the use of anticoagulants
            fibrinolytic agents (for dissolution of fresh thrombi)
            anticholesterol regimen (to reduce progress of atheromatous
            degeneration)
        Treatment of complications
            shock
            cardiac failure
            cardiac arrhythmias
Surgical treatment
    The neurosurgical approach
    Surgical revascularization

By far the most common and thus the most important cause of chest pain is that associated with disease of the coronary arteries. It also has a more serious import and prognosis than most of the conditions which are capable of producing thoracic pain. Hence, its many phases are considered in far

Table 12-1

Differentiation of Angina Pectoris, Coronary Insufficiency, Coronary Occlusion, Cardiac Contusion

	Angina Pectoris	*Coronary Insufficiency*	*Coronary Occlusion*	*Cardiac Contusion*
Physiology	Transitory ischemia Diminished coronary flow due to increased heart work or coronary spasm	Prolonged ischemia Diminished coronary flow, increased heart work	Complete block of coronary flow	Direct or indirect trauma
Pathology	No acute changes	Infarction: focal or disseminated, subendocardial (often microscopic)	Transmural infarction Pericarditis Mural thrombosis with embolism	Myomalacia Contusio cordis Pericarditis, depending on severity of trauma
Predisposing Factors	Coronary sclerosis Hypertension	Diseases of aorta and coronary ostia Coronary sclerosis Cardiomegaly Hypertension Aortic stenosis and insufficiency	Coronary sclerosis Hypertension	None
Exciting Cause	Exertion Excitement Heavy meals Cold and windy weather Tobacco Hypoglycemia	Exertion Severe excitement Tachycardias Shock Hemorrhage Heart failure Operations Infection Trauma Endocrinopathy	Factors which increase blood coagulability, or rare subintimal hemorrhage	Trauma
Duration of Pain	Up to 15 min	Variable	Prolonged	Variable, dependent on other structures
Effect of Nitroglycerin	Relieved	Usually unrelieved	Ineffective or intensifies pain	Ineffective

Table 12-1 (continued)

	Angina Pectoris	Coronary Insufficiency	Coronary Occlusion	Cardiac Contusion
Shock	Absent	Absent	Present	Variable
Nausea and Vomiting	Absent	Uncommon	Common	Occasional
Heart signs:				
Sounds	Unchanged	Decreased	Poor, gallop	Usually decreased
Failure	Absent	Absent	Present	Variable
Arrhythmia	Absent	Occasional	Common	Common
Blood Pressure	Same or rises	Falls slightly	Falls greatly	May fall
Lungs	Unchanged	Unchanged	Congestion from heart failure or embolization	Trauma to pleura and lungs
Electrocardiogram	Unchanged or transitory ST depressions Stress tests	ST depressions with or without T wave changes Stress tests	Coved negative T waves Early ST elevations, late depressions Q waves	ST depressions with or without T wave changes (ST elevations in pericarditis are transitory)
Laboratory Findings	Normal	Variable, usually depending on severity of attack	Elevated serum enzyme levels Fever Leukocytosis Sedimentation rate rapid Glycosuria initially	Leukocytosis Fever SGO-T elevation from cardiac and chest wall muscle injury
Complications	None	None	Thromboembolism Congestive failure Shock Arrhythmias Shoulder-hand syndrome Ventricular aneurysm S.B.E. Postinfarction syndrome Rupture	Ventricular aneurysm or rupture

greater detail than other areas of this text. Atherosclerosis accounts for nearly 95 per cent of all causes of coronary artery disease, but there is a large number of lesser conditions that may affect the coronary arteries.

Pain of coronary origin may be produced by intrinsic disease of the coronary arteries, by functional interference with the blood flow through the coronary arteries, or by decrease of myocardial oxygenation. The three main types of coronary disease are classified as follows: angina pectoris, coronary insufficiency, and coronary occlusion (see Table 12-1). This classification is most convenient, although it is by no means a universally accepted one. "Coronary insufficiency," "intermediate coronary syndrome," "coronary failure," "acute coronary insufficiency," and "acute atypical coronary insufficiency" are terms which are used interchangeably. Semantics of this type have produced confusion on many occasions.

Angina pectoris implies a brief attack of chest pain due to myocardial hypoxia (usually up to fifteen minutes). It occurs most commonly on the basis of underlying coronary artery disease with the superimposed stress of exertion or excitement. *Acute coronary occlusion* connotes a prolonged bout of chest pain associated with variable degrees of myocardial necrosis associated with characteristic laboratory findings. However, the term *"acute coronary insufficiency"* has led to some confusion, since it has come to mean more than the physiologic disturbance of angina pectoris. It is a relative inadequacy of coronary blood flow for the myocardial needs following effort or even at rest in more severe instances. It may be associated with many other conditions (severe anemia, hyperthyroidism, fever, etc.) and usually results in subendocardial ischemia or necrosis if the condition is severe or prolonged. It is characterized by a prolonged bout of chest pain of angina-like character, usually lasting at least twenty minutes but less than one hour and associated with electrocardiographic ST and T wave changes. It has been termed "chronic" when pain recurs at frequent intervals.

Unfortunately, the basis for the disease entity of "acute coronary insufficiency" as originally defined by Master is not thoroughly descriptive. The ST segment depressions and T wave inversions which form the electrocardiographic basis for this diagnosis do not always disclose whether there is impending or early coronary occlusion or not, nor do they distinguish between myocardial ischemia without necrosis and myocardial ischemia with necrosis. Ordinarily, when the hypoxic state is severe or prolonged, ischemia may proceed to irreversible necrosis. The term "coronary insufficiency" is best employed in its original and broadest sense and should indicate the underlying pathology as well as the precipitating mechanism responsible for the attack of coronary pain—e.g., acute coronary insufficiency secondary to gastrointestinal hemorrhage. All coronary diseases, regardless of the underlying cause, have one cardinal manifestation in common—pain.

CLASSIFICATION

Angina Pectoris

Heberden's original description of angina pectoris in 1768 as a sudden substernal pain associated with a feeling of constriction around the chest, with radiation down the left arm and with a sense of impending death, is still accurate and tenable. Although the original characteristics of the pain were stated to be its reproducibility, repetition, and constancy of pattern, the incidence of atypical symptoms of coronary artery disease is almost as frequent and more difficult to evaluate. Instead of arising in the upper substernal area, the pain of angina pectoris may be experienced in many less typical locations, such as the precordium, lower left axilla, right or left infraclavicular region, mid-dorsal or left scapular area, various parts of one or both upper extremities (occasionally the wrist only), and the throat, jaws, teeth, or epigastrium. Many describe their discomfort not as actual pain, but rather as a sense of constriction, tightness, sticking, choking, burning, pressure, aching, heaviness, oppression, or fullness. In rare cases, dysphagia, dyspnea, or palpitation may be the only subjective equivalent of angina. Its intermittent occurrence may be due to variations in parasympathetic tone.

The anginal episode may be accompanied by a desire to belch. This is due to air swallowing which occurs as a manifestation of anxiety. The substernal discomfort is a severe type of pain which the patient feels he would be unable to tolerate for a long period of time. Fortunately, the pain seldom lasts more than about fifteen minutes and recedes quickly and spontaneously; it may persist for as little as a half-minute but usually averages two to three minutes. It is associated with a transitory rise in blood pressure and increased pulse rate. Dizziness, syncope, and palpitation also may be experienced.

Although typical angina is considered to be related to the stress of effort or excitement, it may occur spontaneously in many patients. The pain may be induced by a large meal, by sudden exposure to cold or wind, or by walking rapidly or proceeding up an incline. It may occur in more advanced cases even during sleep and has been ascribed to nightmares, fall in blood pressure, pooling of blood in splanchnic areas, or pressure on the diaphragm by abdominal contents. The exact mechanism has not been adequately explained as yet, although the pain is almost certainly due to an insufficiency of the coronary circulation. When angina occurs following effort, it is relieved by rest or by nitroglycerin. The response to nitroglycerin is a helpful finding but has been noted in only 80 per cent of patients with proven coronary disease. Some patients may actually exhibit a seemingly paradoxical response to nitroglycerin which intensifies or prolongs pain instead of alleviating it. This may be due to a marked drop in peripheral resistance and a resultant reduction of venous return, cardiac output, and coronary blood flow. When nitroglycerin causes a severe flush, dizziness, or marked headache, the dose should be reduced. In many instances, nitroglycerin may be employed prior to an anticipated but necessary increase in effort. It is interesting to note that this drug may also relieve sphincteric spasm. Hence, it does not aid in the differentiation of pain due to spasm of the spincter of Oddi in gallbladder disease.

Various somatic effects may be produced by decreased coronary flow of even short duration. The following atypical features may result: Spasm of the intercostal musculature may cause severe knife-like, constricting pain around the chest. A vascular phenomenon may occur, causing the fingers to appear blanched, resembling Raynaud's phenomenon. Other individuals may develop severe sweating, which may be sharply localized to the region of the left shoulder, chest, and arm, or they may develop excessive salivation. In still other patients, the lumbar sympathetic nerves may be stimulated, and a desire to defecate or void may occur. Some patients, particularly in the older age group, may suffer attacks of paroxysmal nocturnal dyspnea.

A basic consideration in evaluating cardiac pain is the sensitivity of the patient and his ability to perceive pain. It is well known that the incidence of atypical or even painless angina (as well as coronary insufficiency and acute myocardial infarction) is high among patients who are hyposensitive or entirely insensitive. The degree can sometimes be gauged by the reaction of the patient to strong pressure applied to the styloid process of the mastoid bone. Often the physical attitude of the patient while he presents his complaints, his manner of presentation, and general characteristics of his personality will aid in the differentiation of atypical symptoms of angina pectoris. For example, P. D. White has described the peculiar curling or clutching of the fingers to the chest during an attack as characteristic of true angina. Recently, other bizarre connotations of angina have been described. "Alcohol angina" may result when the patient gets overly enthusiastic about the sedative effects of alcohol. Thus, he may become involved in emotional events that he would have the sense to avoid when sober. "Food angina" occurs when postprandial distress causes the development of a conditioned reflex so that eventually the mere sight of food produces an attack; inanition and vitamin deficiencies may result. This can be avoided by smaller and more frequent feedings. "TV angina" (a new diagnosis suggested by Briggs) induces attacks following the excitement of watching events such as ball games or prize fights. Iatrogenic and "compensation angina" are considered under anxiety states (see pp. 91–94). Paradoxically, angina sine dolore is angina without pain. Such patients are generally more vaguely distressed and perspire or have dyspnea as anginal equivalents. Attacks have been precipitated by lying or sleeping on the right (left-side pain usually signifies neurocirculatory asthenia) or by flexing the trunk forward. Angina pectoris inversa has been described as a pain which occurs at rest and which presents electrocardiographic evidence of transitory ST segment elevations rather than depressions, due to chemical changes in the myocardium.

Nearly one-fourth of all cases of angina pectoris show an apparently normal heart by all available methods of examination, including blood pressure, physical signs, x-ray, and even electrocardiography. The remainder show cardiac enlargement, murmurs or gallop rhythm, or hypertension or abnormal electrocardiograms.

Coronary Insufficiency
(Intermediate Coronary Syndrome, Coronary Failure, Acute Coronary Insufficiency, Acute Atypical Coronary Insufficiency)

The pain caused by this disorder of the coronary circulation generally resembles angina pectoris except for the duration, which usually extends beyond twenty minutes. This condition also occurs both in typical and atypical forms. Thus, it may resemble the classic anginal syndrome or may exhibit the whole gamut of atypical features described under angina pectoris.

The recognition of the nature of this type of coronary pain is facilitated (or sometimes overlooked) by the presence of a serious precipitating factor, such as shock, acute hemorrhage, pulmonary embolism, arrhythmias, etc. These conditions (Table 12-2) may frequently overshadow the discomfort produced by coronary insufficiency itself and may explain many of the atypical or painless variants. Thus, acute coronary insufficiency may be precipitated by the development of a severe anemia. This pain is usually not completely relieved by nitroglycerin, whereas transfusion or hematinics may afford relief.

In addition to *acute* coronary insufficiency, a *chronic* variety due to intrinsic coronary disease (usually atherosclerotic) is recognizable. Frequent bouts of pain may occur without the detectable presence of any of the

Table 12-2

Causes of Acute Coronary Insufficiency *

Increased Cardiac Work	Reduced Coronary Flow	Altered Blood
Effort	Paroxysmal tachycardia	Acute anemia
Emotion	Shock	Carbon monoxide poisoning
Overeating	Acute hemorrhage	Asphyxia
Hypertensive crisis	Hypotensive crisis	High altitude
Fever and infections	Aortic stenosis	Pulmonary insufficiency
Hyperthyroidism	Pulmonary embolism	
Paroxysmal tachycardia	Insulin shock	
	Congestive failure	
	Acute abdominal conditions	
	Exposure to heat and cold	
	Excessive smoking	

* From Master, A. M., et al.: Acute coronary insufficiency, its differential diagnosis and treatment. *Ann. Int. Med.,* **45**:561, 1956.

precipitating factors. The pain usually occurs at rest, although not necessarily in the form of *decubital angina.* There may be frequent recurrences of distress characteristic of *status anginosus.* In some patients, psychodynamic disturbances may be found responsible for the perpetuation and prolongation of the anginal episodes, since severe cardiac anxiety superimposed upon the organic disease is very common. A hyperventilation syndrome may precipitate prolonged and atypical attacks of precordial pain. In most instances, this prolonged type of coronary insufficiency heralds the onset of a true coronary occlusive process. The findings may be similar to those in angina pectoris. However, the resulting subendocardial ischemia takes about two or three weeks to heal. It is usually represented by ST segment depressions over the affected areas. The serum glutamic oxalacetic transaminase (SGO-T) test is elevated slightly in a small proportion of the cases. Treatment consists of complete bed rest for about two weeks. Anticoagulants may be employed prophylactically, and coronary vasodilators with or without a tranquilizer are beneficial. The primary cause (Table 12-2) must be remedied if possible.

Coronary Occlusion

Although the term "acute myocardial infarction" is preferred by many to "coronary occlusion" because it differentiates myocardial necrosis with and without complete coronary occlusion, the term "acute coronary occlusion" is generally employed. Pain may occur following an incomplete occlusion even though no infarction may be demonstrable anatomically.

This is usually found when death occurs as a result of shock or cardiac arrest or ventricular fibrillation due to electrical instability of the heart which occurs soon after the onset of the occlusion but before a true myocardial infarction can become evident. Most instances are due to an underlying progressive atheromatous degeneration of the coronary arteries upon which a more recent thrombotic process becomes engrafted. In a smaller number of cases, the degenerative process itself proceeds to complete closure. Nonatheromatous lesions are discussed later in this chapter (pp. 258–62).

There may be a great variation of complaints. Typical constricting chest pain occurs in the majority of cases. It may be slight to overwhelming and may mount from a slight discomfort to squeezing, crushing, pressing, burning, aching, boring, tightening, or constricting pain. Radiation is possible to all the sites mentioned under angina pectoris (see p. 247). However, atypical distress is found in about 8 per cent and absence of any pain in about 5 per cent of cases. Very mild or insignificant pain occurs in about 3 per cent. Thus, the nature of the distress is of small help in the diagnosis of about 16 per cent of cases.

An occasional feature of the pain in acute coronary occlusion is a tendency of the patient to seek relief from the pain by walking around. This is in marked contrast to the pain of angina pectoris which occurs during physical exertion such as walking, "freezes" the patient, and is promptly relieved by rest. Acute coronary occlusion may also present pain of many varieties of atypical location and character. However, this occurs less frequently than with the anginal syndrome or acute coronary insufficiency.

When pain is absent or minimal, it is important to search for other diagnostic clues known as pain equivalents. A common pain equivalent is shortness of breath. This appears as dyspnea on slight effort, orthopnea, paroxysmal nocturnal dyspnea, Cheyne-Stokes respiration, or even as a fulminating pulmonary edema, which may initiate the entire clinical picture. A complicating arrhythmia such as paroxysmal tachycardia or complete atrioventricular block with syncope, precipitated by acute coronary occlusion, may also modify, replace, or completely mask the initial presence of any pain. The resulting palpitation is variously described as a "bounding, thumping, or beating of the heart." The pain is frequently associated with other symptoms, such as excessive sweating (63 per cent), weakness (18 per cent), and other constitutional disturbances, such as chills, heat sensation, flushing, and shivering. Pain may be absent or minimized in patients overwhelmed by malignancy, biliary tract disease, uremia, pneumonia, or mental disease. The episode may be ushered in by dizziness, unsteady gait, syncope, and occasionally tonoclonic movements. Such neurogenic symptoms may occur in about 21 per cent of cases. Gastrointestinal symptoms, such as nausea, vomiting, diarrhea, hiccup, and abdominal pain and tenderness, may be present in about 15 per cent of the cases and account for the ancient impression of "acute indigestion" as the cause of death. It may suggest an acute surgical abdomen, just as many acute upper abdominal disorders may first simulate coronary disease. It has been shown, on the other hand, that coronary occlusion may be associated with an increased gastric secretory response and activation or appearance of peptic ulcer. This complication should obviously be suspected following myocardial infarction and suggests a relation between increased adrenocortical activity and ulcer formation.

The onset of shock may prevent the appearance of pain. Shock due to other causes may precipitate a coronary thrombosis. Fever and friction rub tend to occur on the second or third day and may be suggestive features.

The most important factor in the failure to recognize healed or acute infarctions is the absence of angina or a history of prolonged chest pain. A history of characteristic chest pain is often absent when acute coronary occlusion results in shock or occurs in the immediate postoperative period, or when the state of consciousness is altered by other systemic diseases (uremia and other comas). Concomitant strokes or the sudden occlusion of other major arteries may also obscure the cardiac status. In some instances, the pain is neither severe nor prolonged and may be overlooked or forgotten by the patient. Other causes for atypical or silent infarctions are alcoholism, memory defects, and even language difficulty. In such cases, pain may be experienced but is not related well by the patient. Atypical episodes of acute coronary occlusion frequently occur in psychotic patients, who do not verbalize since their withdrawal prevents the pain from penetrating to their consciousness. A sudden change in their behavior may be the only indication of an acute episode of coronary occlusion. Such patients may suffer other catastrophic episodes, such as perforated peptic ulcer, without complaints.

Sometimes the pain accompanying acute coronary occlusion is not of the characteristically long duration or marked severity but resembles a brief anginal seizure. In such cases, there is usually a marked and seemingly inexplicable increase in frequency of the anginal attacks, each of which yields to rest or nitroglycerin. The first evidence of the existence of a heart attack may be heralded by thromboembolic episodes or rupture of the infarction.

The sequence of the painful episodes due to acute coronary occlusion may be divided into three stages. Careful questioning will reveal the presence of prodromal symptoms in a large number (10 to 50 per cent). These symptoms may be increasing frequency or severity of episodes of angina pectoris or any of its equivalents and may precede the acute episode by several days or weeks. The main stage is usually ushered in by severe pain of prolonged duration or its equivalents of atypical nature, as discussed above. This pain may occur at work, at rest, at play, or during sleep with equal frequency, although the greatest incidence appears to occur in the early-morning hours between 3 and 7 A.M. If the attack is initiated during physical activity, it fails to subside with immediate rest, in contrast to the brevity of anginal seizures. The pain may last for many hours and even days unless it is abolished by the administration of a narcotic. When of longer duration, it may be constant or intermittent.

Chest pain may occur in the early phase following acute occlusion. If it recurs early, it may be due to marked coronary insufficiency or myocardial ischemia or thrombotic extension to a neighboring arterial branch. It is usually encountered following an extensive infarction and/or inadequate collateral circulation. Continuation of the pain after several days may be due to a superimposed anxiety. This does not respond to nitroglycerin but improves following firm reassurance and mild sedative.

After the patient resumes ambulation, pain may reappear. This is either typical angina of effort or pain of psychogenic origin, caused by the apprehension of resuming normal activities. In sharp contrast, many patients who have suffered frequent and severe anginal episodes prior to a complete coronary occlusion subsequently remain free of angina if the other coronary arteries are sufficiently patent.

The pain of acute coronary occlusion is not affected by nitroglycerin in most instances. Indeed, this may be dangerous, since it may cause a further fall in blood pressure below critical levels.

Other features of angina pectoris, coronary insufficiency, and coronary occlusion will now be discussed in connection with the etiology and pathology of the lesions responsible for the production of chest pain.

PATHOGENESIS

Atherosclerotic Lesions

Etiology. This group constitutes the vast majority of all coronary arterial disorders. Many investigators are seeking to unravel the complex relationship of heredity, body type, sex, race, stress, exercise, diet, obesity, hypertension, blood lipids, enzyme disturbances, and hypercoagulability of blood.

They will be discussed briefly for a better understanding and evaluation of the nature of chest pain.

Atherosclerosis is generally defined as a degenerative process which affects large and medium-sized arteries in a patchy pattern and is characterized by plaque-like subintimal deposits which contain neutral fats, cholesterol, and lipophages and by destruction of elastic tissue. The lesions enlarge insidiously, fibrose, calcify, and gradually encroach upon the lumen. The intimal surface degenerates and acts as a nidus for more acute thrombotic occlusions.

The etiology of human coronary atherosclerosis has thus far eluded myriad and diverse painstaking clinical, anatomic, and experimental investigations. Many theories have been advanced to explain the genesis of atherosclerosis. One theory considers the degenerative process as an irreversible change related to the aging of man. However, sufficient data have been accumulated to indicate that this process may be extensive and lethal even in young adulthood and, contrariwise, that it may be minimal and without consequence in numerous elderly individuals. It was quite surprising to discover that the coronary arteries of 300 "healthy" American soldiers (average age, 22.1 years) killed in the Korean action showed 77.3 per cent gross evidence of disease ranging from fibrous thickening to complete occlusion in one or more branches.

Another theory assumes a primary metabolic disturbance of the lipids. It is supported by the presence of cholesterol in atherosclerotic lesions, by the favorable influence of unsaturated fatty acids, by the production of hypercholesteremia and atherosclerotic lesions in experimental animals fed cholesterol, by the frequent association of hypercholesteremia in human patients with premature coronary disease, and by the relatively low incidence of atherosclerosis in populations subsisting on a diet containing little or no animal fat. However, it has not been possible to prove a causal relationship between a primary disturbance of the lipid metabolism (manifested by elevated serum cholesterol, elevated beta-lipoproteins, and a decreased phospholipid-cholesterol ratio) and the atherosclerotic lesions. This is mainly due to the inability to detect atherosclerosis in man before the appearance of clinical abnormalities produced by the more severe forms of the pathologic changes.

It has been shown that the cholesterol deposit in the arterial wall may be secondary to repeated intra-arterial thromboses ineffectively neutralized by normal fibrinolytic processes. The fibrin strands may be overgrown by endothelium and so form a thickened cushion which obstructs filtration, ultimately leading to deposition of lipid. It has also been suggested that the metabolic changes within the vessel wall itself are more important than those within the blood stream, since it has been shown that both cholesterol and phospholipid can be synthesized by the vessel wall itself.

In addition to these theories, many other predisposing factors have been offered, leading to the generally held concept that atherosclerosis may be a polyetiologic disease. These predisposing factors are helpful in the evaluation of each patient. While suggesting a tendency to atherogenesis, the quantitative determination of the various lipid fractions, total cholesterol, beta-lipoproteins, triglycerides, and others is of limited diagnostic or prognostic value in a particular individual. This is partly due to considerable overlapping of values in so-called "normals," or at least in individuals without clinically detectable coronary disease and those with clear-cut evidence of the latter. Predisposing factors worthy of mention are heredity, diabetes mellitus, sex, and familial hypercholesteremia. Their influence is well established, although their exact mode of action is unknown. A family history of premature coronary disease, diabetes mellitus, or hypercholesteremia is considered an unfavorable factor. Since females infrequently suffer from the effects of coronary sclerosis before the menopause (in the absence of hypertension or diabetes), the favorable influence of estrogenic hormones has also been studied.

Hypertension may represent an aggravating factor, but it is usually the sclerotic process which unfavorably influences the natural course of hypertensive vascular disease.

Obesity has long been considered a factor which decreases the life span and is associated with an increased incidence of diabetes mellitus, hypertension, and coronary disease. However, recent data have cast considerable doubt as to a causal relationship of obesity to coronary atherosclerosis, since an equally high incidence of overweight was found in males under forty years without appreciable lesions. The incidence of obesity was about the same among a group of young American soldiers who died suddenly during World War II from acute coronary disease, as compared to healthy soldiers who had been killed in action or by accident. As has been previously mentioned, a surprisingly high incidence of atherosclerosis, regardless of weight, was found also during the Korean conflict in "healthy" young American soldiers killed in action, while a comparable group of Korean soldiers showed far less evidence of degenerative vascular disease. While the total caloric consumption seems to have no definite relationship, the relative quantity and quality of the fat content appear to be much more significant.

As regards *hormonal* influence, it has been shown that the administration of estrogens lowers serum cholesterol, beta-lipoproteins, and the cholesterol-phospholipid ratio and prevents and even reverses the development of experimentally induced atherosclerosis. It may also be responsible for the protection of women from coronary atherosclerosis prior to the menopause. When estrogens are deficient following bilateral oophorectomy, women are subject to as great an incidence of coronary disease as men in the same age group.

The role of *thyroid* function is less clear-cut, although the thyroid hormone is known to influence the level of serum cholesterol and the experimental development of atherosclerosis. The role of the adrenal cortex in the development of human atherosclerosis is obscure, although its influence upon serum cholesterol and other lipids is evident.

An analysis of the influence of *body constitution* revealed the prevalence of premature coronary disease among endomorphic mesomorphs (stocky, muscular individuals).

Emotional stress and its possible role in predisposing to coronary sclerosis have been investigated. While no definitive proof has been elicited as to its effects, a causal relationship to prolonged stress has been suggested by some investigators. These data include the cholesterol-raising effect of periods of increased mental and emotional stress (Sisyphus complex) and the possible mediating role of neurohormonal and hormonal mechanisms. It has been suggested that emotional stress acting through the cerebral cortex and hypothalamus may be responsible for (1) an increase in the lipid receptiveness of the vascular walls, (2) an elevation of blood cholesterol, and (3) an acceleration of blood clotting time.

Pathology. The pathologic changes common to the three clinical forms of coronary artery disease (angina pectoris, coronary insufficiency, and coronary occlusion) almost always (95 per cent) consist of basic atheromatous alterations in the coronary arteries. The lesions are essentially intimal plaques which are formed by fibrous tissue deposits with subsequent hyalinization and later deposition of lipids. However, the very earliest lesion may begin as reversible fatty streaks soon after birth. The intimal thickenings are accompanied by degenerative changes in the adjacent elastic tissue that possibly are related to the stress of intravascular pressure acting over a period of time. The disorganization of elastic lamellae involves fragmentation, spreading, wandering, or disappearance of elastic tags, a granular microscopic appearance, and eventually an increased affinity for calcium. While the endothelium in normal young individuals shows few vasa vasorum, thickening of the intima eventually leads to vascularization from the adventitia by way of the media or from organizing mural thrombi. Presumably, the normal intimal elastica prevents the passage of the blood lipoproteins through the arterial wall. When this elastica breaks down, lipids enter the media. Many factors facilitate the passage of lipids into the arterial wall, such as the hydrostatic pressure of the blood and changes in osmolarity and enzymatic activity, in addition to the physicochemical make-up of the lipids themselves. The lifting effect of the hydrostatic forces on the vascular structures has recently been introduced as another factor.

It has also been suggested that the atherosclerotic lesions evolve by the primary formation of arterial thrombi and not by fatty degeneration of the intima. The arterial thrombus then undergoes organization as follows: When the thrombus first forms in the artery, it may first occlude the lumen but later retracts to form a channel through which the circulation is partly restored. This channel becomes lined with endothelium, and the thrombus beneath it is organized into fibrous tissue. Complete organization of the mass may be brought about in this way, but more often fatty degeneration and softening occur at the center. Most arterial thrombi merely form fibrous deposits on the intimal surface. These become covered with a layer of endothelium, and while the subendothelial layers undergo direct transformation into fibrous tissue, the deeper ones may vascularize. In large deposits, fatty degeneration may occur; softening and even calcification may also take place with relatively limited organization. In such instances, rupture of the surface may occur with the formation of atheromatous ulcers. The thickening which appears in the arteries of old people is often the cumulative effect of recurring mural thrombi. Since most mural thrombi show some fatty change, they give rise to that combination of fatty change and fibrosis that is characteristic of atherosclerosis. There is experimental confirmation that thrombi can be converted into fibrous tissue. Although there are considerable correlative clinical and pathologic as well as experimental data available regarding the association of abnormal lipid content and the presence of atheromatous lesions, a relationship has also been demonstrated between excessive lipid content and the occurrence of intravascular clotting abnormalities. Thus, the hypothesis that primary arterial thrombi are the basis of the atherosclerotic process is undergoing intensive investigation.

Angina pectoris and coronary insufficiency. In coronary disease, an atheromatous narrowing of the coronary lumen impedes coronary blood flow temporarily when an increase of the latter is required to fulfill extra myocardial oxygen demands. This may be brought about by such factors as exertion or excitement. Unfortunately, far greater emphasis has been placed on the larger vessels of the coronary circulation than on the smaller vessels. Recent studies on canine and human hearts indicate that there is an anatomic muscle–sphincter-nerve unit which functions to regulate the caliber of smaller vessels of the myocardium and that this muscle-nerve unit in the capillary circulation is very responsive to various stimuli. Coronary spasm of this type may even influence the pathogenesis of coronary disease.

In prolonged coronary insufficiency, more severe damage may result in a so-called "acute" type or the intermediary syndrome with subendocardial ischemia or necrosis, which produces a characteristic clinical and electro-cardiographic picture. Patients who suffer from prolonged coronary insufficiency precipitated by various extracardiac factors may show more extensive pathologic changes.

Coronary occlusion. Acute infarction of the myocardium is usually the result of occlusion of a coronary artery. Occlusion usually occurs following thrombus formation on an atheromatous plaque or ulcer, but may also follow progressive and severe narrowing of the lumen by atheromatous degeneration. Emboli, subintimal hemorrhage, and rare causes of coronary artery disease account for a very small number of coronary occlusions.

Myocardial infarction is the usual recognizable consequence of acute coronary occlusion, except in those instances when death occurs within the first few hours. The extent of the infarcted area depends on a number of factors. These include the size and location of the occluded vessel, the concomitant state of the other vessels, the availability of an adequate collateral circulation, and the presence of hypertension or other cardiac disease. A good collateral circulation plays an important role in preventing the extension of infarction by revascularizing adjacent ischemic area of myocardium.

Myocardial infarction usually extends to the pericardial surface and may cause a localized or diffuse type of acute pericarditis. The latter may give rise to the type of chest pain and associated symptoms and signs resembling those seen in acute benign idiopathic pericarditis.

The occurrence of *mural thrombi* following acute myocardial infarction in the right heart is of pertinent interest, since this may lead to pulmonary embolism and infarction, which also cause chest pain. Mural thrombi are found in almost half of all cases of acute myocardial infarction, and are commonly situated in the left ventricle, usually near the apex. Extensive infarction involving the septum can obviously cause thrombus formation on either side of this structure. However, most pulmonary emboli actually originate from the thrombotic involvement of deep pelvic veins or the veins of the legs rather than those of the heart.

Nonatherosclerotic Lesions

Although this group of lesions accounts for a very small proportion of coronary disorders, the most important conditions which may involve the coronary arteries are syphilis, rheumatic fever, other infections, polyarteritis nodosa, embolism, aneurysms, trauma, congenital anomalies, thromboangiitis obliterans, and neoplasms.

Syphilis. This specific infection impairs coronary blood flow by concentric or eccentric narrowing of the coronary ostia due to the effects of an ascending luetic aortitis (see Fig. 12-1). This begins as an involvement of the

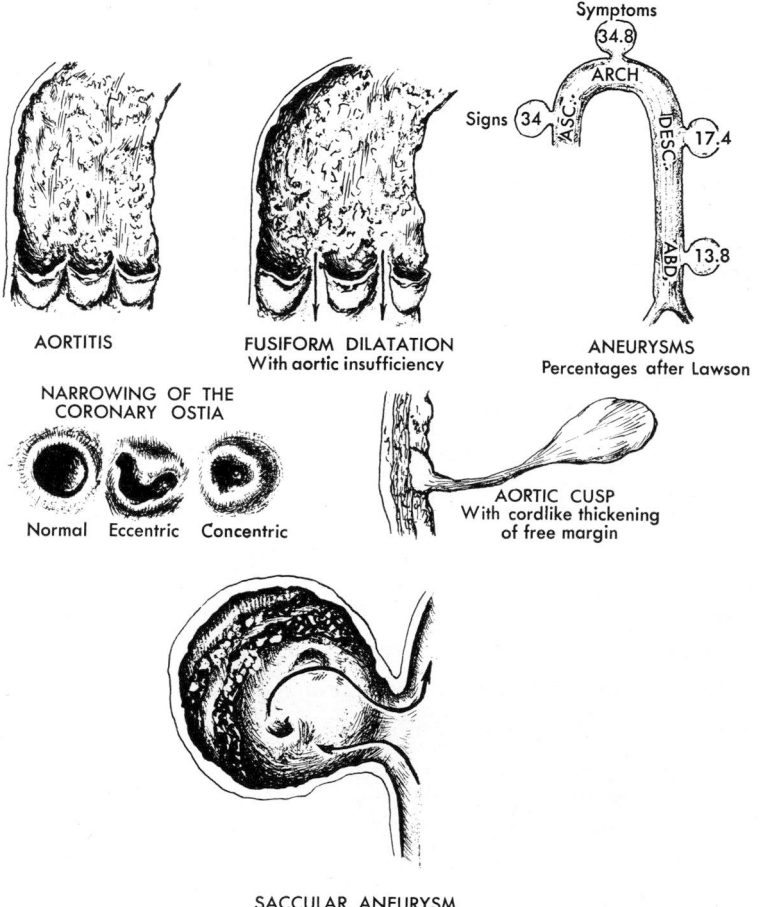

Fig. 12-1. Effects of syphilis on the coronary ostia and aortic structures. (From Reich, N. E.: *Diseases of the Aorta*. The Macmillan Co., New York, 1949.)

lymphatics which accompany the small nutrient vasa vasorum into the adventitia and media. Since the ascending aorta is especially rich in these lymphatics, the most common point of attack is around 2 to 5 cm above the aortic valve. Destruction of the connective and elastic tissues of the media and central areas of necrosis are found. Collagen replacement eventually results in diffuse scarring, distortion, and aneurysmal formation, which may directly affect the coronary ostia. Complete occlusion with diffuse myocardial fibrosis is not rare, and even aneurysms of the proximal portion of the coronary arteries have been reported. Syphilitic coronary ostial stenosis rarely leads to myocardial infarction. It causes a diffuse myocardial fibrosis which eventually leads to myocardial failure.

Rheumatic fever. Acute rheumatic fever may affect the coronary vessels but tends to involve the small arteries and rarely impedes the coronary blood flow to a major degree. Rheumatic lesions also may involve the aorta and encroach upon the coronary ostia. The histologic character of these lesions is essentially as elsewhere in the heart (Aschoff nodules). A similar type of involvement is occasionally found in rheumatoid arthritis and tends to produce aortic insufficiency.

Valvular lesions caused by rheumatic fever may interfere seriously with coronary blood flow and cause coronary insufficiency and even acute myocardial infarction. These lesions (aortic stenosis, aortic insufficiency, and mitral stenosis) have been discussed in the section dealing with endocardial causes of chest pain (pp. 180–87).

Other infections. A variety of acute infections, including diphtheria, influenza, scarlet fever, typhoid, and pneumonia, may produce inflammatory changes of the coronary arteries, just as they may produce acute nonspecific infectious myocarditis. They rarely encroach upon the lumen of the involved vessels. *Bacterial endocarditis* may give rise to a clinically recognizable syndrome of acute myocardial infarction. It is usually the result of emboli originating from the bacterial thrombotic vegetation (see below under embolism) or from direct obstruction of the lumen by extensive involvement of the aortic valve or ascending aorta. Mycotic aneurysms of coronary arteries due to embolization may complicate bacterial endocarditis.

Polyarteritis nodosa. The coronary arteries are involved in 60 to 70 per cent of patients with this serious malady. The gross and histologic lesions are characteristic. Since the intima becomes involved frequently, thrombosis may result in the clinical picture of acute myocardial infarction. Most commonly, however, only the small vessels are affected or the arteritis produces very gradual narrowing, allowing for the development of an adequate collateral circulation. In these cases, coronary insufficiency may be absent or minimal. Rarely, a necrotizing coronary arteritis may lead to aneurysmal rupture with consequent hemopericardium and fatal tamponade.

Coronary embolism. The most common source of coronary embolization are the vegetations caused by bacterial endocarditis of the aortic valve.

Emboli may occur in two forms. In the first, multiple minute emboli enter the coronary bed and cause small infarcts, abscesses, and aneurysms; these are usually not productive of coronary pain because of their small size. The other form consists of larger emboli, which may occlude a large coronary artery and produce acute myocardial infarction that is indistinguishable clinically from that due to coronary atherosclerosis, or the infarction may cause sudden death. Coronary emboli may also arise from a mural thrombus secondary to acute myocardial infarction or from a thrombus resting on a neighboring arteriosclerotic plaque in the aorta.

Coronary aneurysms. Aneurysms of the coronary arteries are rare and seldom cause pain prior to rupture. They are most commonly caused by polyarteritis nodosa, embolization from bacterial endocarditis (mycotic aneurysm), and congenital defects. A not uncommon complication is rupture of the aneurysm into the pericardial sac with hemopericardium and acute tamponade. Congenital coronary arteriovenous aneurysms have also been described. Cases of arteriovenous fistula formed by communication between a coronary artery and the right atrium are on record. Proximal extension of a dissecting aneurysm of the aorta may involve the coronary circulation by direct compression of the coronary ostia by the advancing hemorrhage. This may cause acute myocardial infarction with characteristic clinical manifestations when the patient survives the dissection.

Traumatic lesions. Blunt and penetrating injuries of the chest wall may involve the coronary arteries. Blunt injuries resulting in coronary thrombosis and myocardial infarction have been reported, but the evidence is usually inconclusive. The usual lesion found is a myocardial or epicardial contusion of varying degrees. When a fall with subsequent injury to the chest occurs, the ensuing manifestations of myocardial infarction may not be the sequelae but the cause of the fall itself.

Bullets, sharp instruments, and broken ribs are common causes of such injuries. Penetrating injuries of the chest usually affect the myocardium, but the coronary circulation may also be involved. Direct damage to a coronary artery may lead to thrombosis. Laceration of a coronary vessel may eventuate in hemopericardium (tamponade). However, penetrating knife wounds of the myocardium may not lead to excessive bleeding because of the spiral arrangement of the thick musculature. The coronary arteries may be damaged during cardiac surgery—e.g., during commissurotomy when ligatures are inadvertently placed around a coronary vessel; and this will lead to acute myocardial infarction.

Congenital anomalies. These may cause disturbance of the coronary circulation by involving the coronary arteries directly. The most common type is an anomaly consisting of the origin of the left coronary artery from the pulmonary artery. Since the left side of the heart fails to receive an adequate supply of oxygenated blood, fibrosis, weakness, and dilatation of the left ventricle develop. Symptoms resembling angina pectoris occur in patients suffering from this malady.

Eisenmenger's complex is usually associated with deformity of the aortic cusp, with resultant aortic insufficiency, and also with displacement of the coronary ostia. These lesions may deplete the coronary circulation.

Aneurysm of the right sinus of Valsalva may occur on a congenital basis and encroach upon the coronary ostia, with disturbance of the coronary blood flow. Hypoplastic or absent coronary arteries may be responsible for coronary insufficiency very early in life. Other anomalies identified with aortic atresia, truncus arteriosus, or accessory coronary arteries usually have no clinical significance per se.

Thromboangiitis obliterans. The presence of coronary disease in patients (usually under forty years of age) with peripheral manifestations of thromboangiitis obliterans is uncommon. Careful investigation should be made, since the peripheral lesions in patients with coronary disease may not be due to thromboangiitis obliterans, but rather to premature arteriosclerosis obliterans (especially in juvenile or brittle diabetics). The pathologic differentiation may also be difficult, since thromboangiitis obliterans is often associated with atherosclerotic lesions. Furthermore, a histologic and gross differentiation between these two conditions is possible only during the inflammatory phase of thromboangiitis obliterans. The acute phase of thromboangiitis obliterans shows inflammatory changes involving segments of the peripheral veins in almost half the cases.

Neoplastic lesions. The coronary circulation may become affected by the contiguous or metastatic spread of some malignancies, especially bronchogenic carcinoma. These lesions may compress or invade the coronary arteries, producing either coronary insufficiency or acute myocardial infarction. The presence of pericardial effusion containing blood and malignant cells is helpful. It is also of interest to note that certain malignancies of the pancreas, gastrointestinal tract, and lungs are associated with a tendency to increase intravascular clotting.

CLINICAL DIAGNOSIS

The diagnostic features of both the predominantly atherosclerotic and the infrequent nonatherosclerotic forms of coronary artery disease will be discussed under the same heading, since they share many common clinical features.

Evaluation of Symptoms

The need for a painstaking evaluation of the patient's complaints has been stressed repeatedly and cannot be overemphasized. The frequency of atypical chest pains and of the admixture of symptoms produced by cardiac anxiety or concomitant disease often make the differential diagnosis extremely difficult. On the other hand, there may be minimal or even absent pain, or it may be very short in duration and easily missed. At times, anginal equivalents, such as dyspnea or tachycardia, may be misinterpreted. In the middle-aged and particularly the elderly patient chest pain due to noncardiac disease is not infrequently present in addition to an underlying coronary disease and reveals its true character only after intensive inquiry and examination. Cervicodorsal arthritis and hiatus hernia are the two most common conditions to be considered in this connection. An elaboration of the differential points of the symptomatology would be repetitious, since the characteristics of chest pain produced by various conditions has been described in detail in preceding sections.

The most important reason for the failure to recognize healed or even acute infarctions is the absence of angina pectoris or of a history of prolonged chest pain. Such a history is obtained almost twice as frequently in patients with healed infarctions who are seen repeatedly as in patients who are seen only for their terminal illness.

Narcotics given for postoperative pain may mask secondary cardiac pain. Fatal myocardial infarction may also occur during the course of uremia, diabetic coma, psychosis, or serious metabolic disturbances that impair cerebration. It is also likely to occur because of impaired cerebral circulation following a cerebral vascular accident, extensive hemorrhage, surgery, or spinal anesthesia. The average age of patients with unrecognized acute infarction has been demonstrated to be about four years greater than that of patients with correctly diagnosed infarction. The presence of congestive heart failure favors recognition of pain due to infarction, although this condition is frequently associated with thromboembolic episodes.

In addition to the careful evaluation of symptoms, observations as to the therapeutic response are often helpful. The response to nitroglycerin, in particular, should be noted. Its diagnostic value has been known for a long time and may often prove superior to exercise electrocardiography. In typical instances of angina pectoris, nitroglycerin gives prompt relief. Even in the more severe protracted form of coronary insufficiency, relief may be prompt, although it tends to be partial or transitory. The chest pain of acute coronary occlusion is usually not relieved by nitroglycerin, or only to a minimal degree and for a very brief period. Therefore, lack of relief by nitroglycerin in a patient with brief attacks of anginoid pain suggests a noncardiac cause or perhaps that the dose has been insufficient to produce a definite and recognizable pharmacologic effect (pounding headache or flushing of the face). On the other hand, a good response to nitroglycerin does not always imply the presence of coronary disease, since chest or upper abdominal pain produced by esophageal spasm, peptic esophagitis, or gallbladder dyskinesia also responds favorably to this medication. A partially favorable response to nitroglycerin may also occur in patients suffering from pulmonary hypertension ("cyanotic angina"). Finally, relief must be almost immediate and complete and not duplicated by the sublingual administration of placebos.

It should be stressed that a poor response to nitroglycerin may occasionally by due to deterioration of the tablets, since they fail to dissolve promptly. Questioning of the patient in this regard is important, especially in those cases of recurrent angina that eventually fail to respond to nitroglycerin.

The diagnostic value of therapeutic response also extends to the use of salicylates. For example, cervicodorsal arthritis may produce chest pain which simulates angina pectoris but is relieved by adequate doses of salicylates. Anginal symptoms that fail to respond to nitroglycerin are not infrequently due to cardiac neurosis. It is obviously important to exclude all organic factors, but it is equally vital to determine the psychodynamic disturbance leading to chest pain. Frequently, the sudden cardiac death of a close friend or relative to whom the patient has had a close emotional attachment precipitates chest pain of anginoid character.

Cervicodorsal arthritis and hiatus hernia must be considered as possible causes of the chest pain, particularly in cases of angina decubitus or status anginosus. The jackknifed position of the spine in bed aggravates arthritis of the spine, while the horizontal position may induce an acute exacerbation of hiatus hernia. The differential diagnosis is made difficult by the frequent lack of response to nitroglycerin even in proven cases of decubital angina.

In the differentiation of pain produced by coronary artery disease, additional clues are provided by (1) family history, (2) relationship of pain to time of day, (3) relationship of pain to stress or effort, and (4) presence of other precipitating factors (e.g., tachycardias and hypertension). The family history may reveal premature deaths of ancestors due to the occurrence of premature coronary disease, hypertension, diabetes, or gout. The greater the incidence of such a history, the greater is the likelihood of transmission of these characteristics to the patient. Cholesterol determinations of family members may establish primary familial hypercholesteremia as the cause of premature coronary deaths or coronary disease in females.

It has been observed that angina may occur more frequently at the beginning of the day, when the patient gets out of bed, engages in the effort of the morning toilet, and then walks briskly to his job after eating a large breakfast. Angina may be common at the onset of prolonged though moderate exercise such as golf or swimming. Consideration should be given to the precipitating factors, which not only include exposure to cold, meals, physical exertion, and emotional tension, but may also include paroxysmal increase of the cardiac rate or of the blood pressure. Reproduction of the pain is often the most valuable and sometimes the only means of diagnosis.

Arrhythmias such as atrial tachycardia, flutter, or fibrillation and ventricular tachycardia are not always manifested by palpitation. Angina may be the only symptom due to progressive coronary insufficiency and myocardial ischemia resulting from the rapid heart rate. Compensatory cardiac and extracardiac mechanisms tend to maintain the coronary circulation during tachycardias and where hypotension supervenes. Thus, antiarrhythmic agents are indicated in order to maintain coronary flow. Occasionally, the patient may relate a vague or peculiar sensation in the thorax prior to the onset of chest pain. Paroxysmal rise of blood pressure may be noted in some patients. It produces angina only when accompanied by a marked increase in heart rate. This occurs in hypertensive crises or pheochromocytoma. The first is found more frequently than the second but is often unrecognized. It has been encountered in patients with aortic and aortic valvular disease and arteriosclerotic heart disease as well as in those with hypertensive vascular disease. Since an elevation of the blood pressure occurs frequently during the course of the anginal syndrome, symptoms preceding or accompanying the anginal attack are important clues. A throbbing headache or a flushed face may be significant. Palpitations are also felt by some of the patients during this phase of the acute attack. This condition occurs often in elderly patients with hypertensive and arteriosclerotic heart disease and may lead to concomitant symptoms of cerebral ischemia, such as giddiness, dizziness, and even fainting. The systolic blood pressure is usually elevated above 200 mm Hg. The relation of pain to rapid heart rates is further confirmed by simple carotid sinus pressure, which slows the rate and tends to abolish an anginal attack.

Crises due to pheochromocytoma may involve similar symptoms except for marked pallor of the face and profuse sweating. "Angina pectoris inversa" has recently been described as a new anginal syndrome with characteristics opposite to those of classic angina. Attacks occur at rest, with more severe pain lasting only one or two minutes. Although an individual attack may be terminated with nitroglycerin, another attack may occur within minutes. The electrocardiogram shows marked ST elevation with reciprocal depression, which disappear after the attack. The precise or objective method of differential diagnosis is discussed in the section on diagnostic procedures (see pp. 267–95).

Finally, an impending myocardial infarction may be anticipated by three features: (1) onset of ischemic cardiac pain for the first time, particularly when occurring during rest; (2) progressive intensification of previous anginal seizures; and (3) recurrence of pain at rest or on slight provocation following a previous myocardial infarction which has healed. Early anticipation of an impending coronary occlusion permits early confirmation by serial changes in laboratory studies and prompt institution of anticoagulant therapy and adequate rest. Whether prophylactic use of anticoagulants in impending infarction is beneficial remains undecided.

Evaluation by Physical Examination

Signs elicited by physical examination are generally less important clues than symptoms in the diagnosis of coronary pain. Obvious external signs pointing to premature atherosclerosis are early grayness and baldness and arcus senilis. The latter is due to the deposition of cholesterol in the outer cornea. However, there are so many exceptions that the presence of these signs is at best suggestive, while their absence may be of no significance at all.

Xanthelasmas are small, slightly elevated yellow deposits of cholesterol in the skin around the eyelids, and xanthelomata are deposits of cholesterol in the tendon sheaths. Both are strongly suggestive of the presence of atherosclerosis. Arcus senilis has a similar significance. The presence of peripheral arteriosclerosis or thickened tortuous temporal and brachial arteries is also significant.

Any abnormalities found on physical examination of the cardiovascular system make it mandatory to exclude an asymptomatic but organic origin of cardiac pain before dismissing the latter as a symptom of an anxiety neurosis or other noncardiac condition. This is also true in the case of atypical angina and the presence of readily detected concomitant noncardiac conditions. Considerable significance may be given to the simple observation of clutching or curling of the patient's fingers to the precordium during an anginal seizure. Carotid sinus pressure may prove useful in the alleviation of an anginal attack when the physician is fortunate enough to be present during one of these transitory episodes.

Coronary artery disease produces very few abnormal physical findings and none that are truly specific. However, the presence, in an adult or elderly patient who complains of angina, of an audible third sound or protodiastolic gallop not associated with a rapid rate strongly suggests an old or recent myocardial infarction; this suspicion is intensified by the associated presence of a diminished first sound. At times, a diastolic pulsation of the precordium may be felt during an attack of angina pectoris.

Many signs may appear following acute myocardial infarction. Most of these are related to the effects of the myocardial infarction upon myocardial function. They include the reduction of intensity and pitch of the first sound, the appearance of gallop sounds of either the presystolic or the protodiastolic type, and the increased intensity of the second pulmonic sound. In addition, a transitory pericardial friction rub may appear between the second to fourth day in a small number of cases. A greater incidence depends on more frequent observations. When it persists and is accompanied by prolonged fever and recurrence of pain of pleuropericardial type, a postmyocardial infarction syndrome should be suspected. This can be confirmed by the acute changes in elevation of the ST segments and therapeutic response to corticosteroids. Cardiac murmurs may also appear, usually in the early systolic phase of the cardiac cycle. In addition, blood pressure levels may become abnormally low. Signs of shock, such as cold, clammy skin, are usually evident when a marked fall or complete disappearance of the blood pressure occurs. Irregularities of the pulse and marked increase or reduction of the pulse and cardiac rate occur as various arrhythmias or atrioventricular conduction disturbances complicate the clinical picture. Cyanosis or ashen-gray pallor is noted in more severe cases which are complicated by congestive failure or shock, respectively. Increasing pulmonary congestion appears in both conditions.

Diagnostic Laboratory Procedures

The laboratory diagnosis of early coronary artery disease has come to rest mainly upon the electrocardiographic changes which are noted at rest or, when necessary, after a stress test. In recent years, ballistocardiography, electrokymography, and vectorcardiography have appeared, but they present certain limitations which will be discussed subsequently. In addition, the blood lipid pattern in coronary sclerosis has been explored and may be evaluated, albeit only as supportive information. The discovery of increased amounts of certain enzymes in serum following their release by severely injured or necrotic myocardial tissue has led to the application of several enzyme tests to the diagnosis of acute myocardial infarction. A number of miscellaneous laboratory tests of varying values are also available.

Electrocardiography. The electrocardiograms of patients suffering from an anginal syndrome are frequently normal at rest. In the early phases of coronary sclerosis (prior to the occurrence of myocardial infarction), electrocardiographic evidence of the disease may be lacking in 40 to 60 per cent of the cases. Negative electrocardiograms may be obtained in spite of the presence of anatomically demonstrable infarctions. They are most often associated with infarctions limited to the apex, high lateral infarctions, and infarctions during rheumatic carditis. Thus, it became necessary to develop an objective test to demonstrate the diminished coronary reserve. This is especially significant since a diagnosis based on the subjective description of pain and its interpretation may sometimes be inadequate.

If an electrocardiogram is obtainable during an anginal episode, characteristic but transitory changes may be present. The ST segment is commonly depressed, and the T waves may be inverted. This is considered a manifestation of transitory ischemia of the subendocardial layers of the heart muscle. Arrhythmias may also appear, such as ventricular premature beats (even in coupled form) and atrial fibrillation or conduction disturbances such as atrioventricular and bundle-branch block. Not infrequently, abnormally large or inverted U waves may appear. The ST and T wave changes are rarely of the type encountered in acute myocardial infarction, and there are no significant Q waves. Transient but severe coronary insufficiency may in rare cases produce temporary elevation of the ST segment and reversible changes of the QRS complex, such as usually accompany transmural myocardial infarction. It must be remembered that ST segment elevations are not necessarily due to severe diffuse myocardial ischemia or to acute myocardial infarction but may on occasion persist following an old healed myocardial infarction or may suggest a postinfarction syndrome. ST elevation may also be produced by acute transient ischemia occurring in cases of healed infarction; it usually appears in the leads exhibiting abnormal Q waves, which may be the only residual evidence of an old healed infarction.

Since it is rare to record an electrocardiogram during the spontaneous and brief interval of an anginal episode, various tests have been employed to produce a relative state of coronary insufficiency sufficient to promote electrocardiographic changes which duplicate those seen in spontaneous angina pectoris. These tests utilize generalized hypoxemia or exercise as the precipitating factor.

The *hypoxemia test* of Levy consists of the inhalation of a mixture of 10 per cent oxygen and 90 per cent nitrogen for a period of twenty minutes or until cardiac pain is experienced. ST depression and T wave changes appear

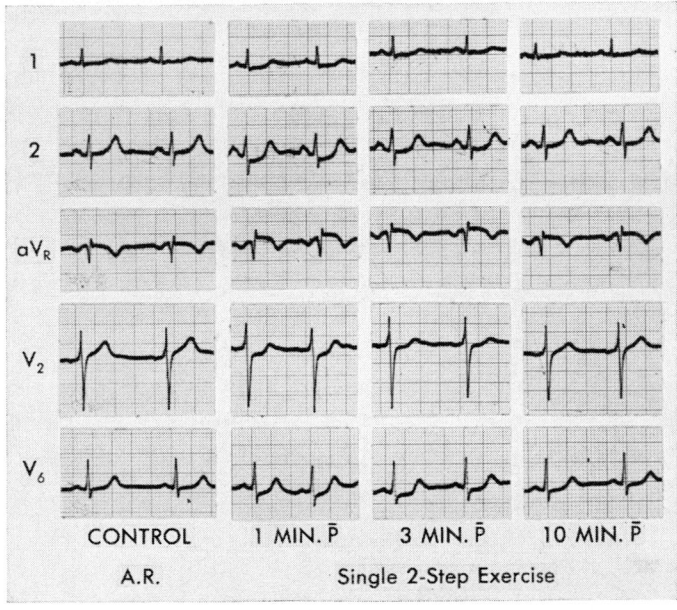

CONTROL   1 MIN. P̄   3 MIN. P̄   10 MIN. P̄

A.R.   Single 2-Step Exercise

A

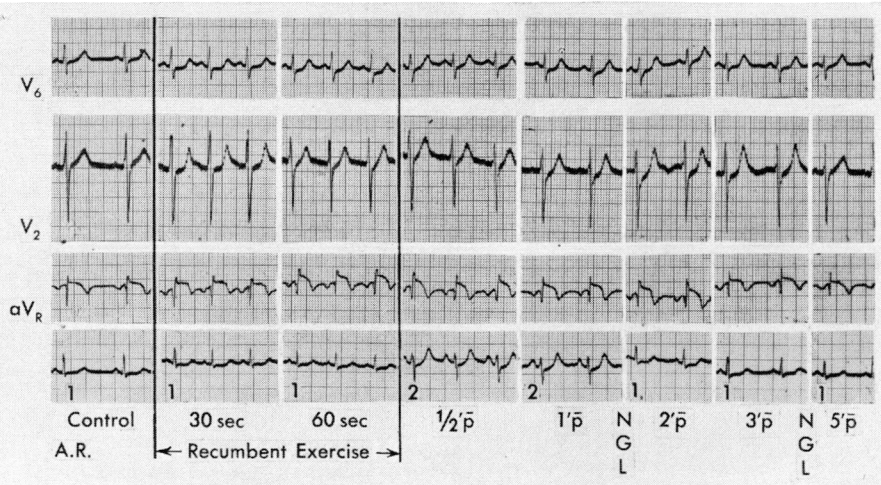

Control   30 sec   60 sec   ½'p̄   1'p̄   N   2'p̄   3'p̄   N   5'p̄

A.R. |←— Recumbent Exercise —→| G   G
                                             L   L

B

Fig. 12-2. A, *Two-step exercise* test in patient with severe anginal syndrome. Note characteristic configuration and depression of ST segment in leads 1, 2, V₂ and V₆ with reciprocal elevation of ST in aVR.

B, A *recumbent exercise test* in same patient involving approximately same amount of effort yields quite similar changes of ST segment. Even though exercise was terminated before onset of pain in view of ST changes, severe pain set in shortly afterward, requiring two tablets of nitroglycerin in short succession.

269

in about 30 to 50 per cent of patients suffering from probable or definite coronary disease and in 15 to 20 per cent of suspected cases. However, the limitations of the test because of technical equipment and the need for careful choice of patients have hindered its widespread acceptance.

On the other hand, standardized exercise tests are now widely employed to obtain objective evidence relative to the patency of the coronary circulation. The most popular stress test is the Master standard two-step exercise test (see Fig. 12-2). While the test is simple and easy to perform in most instances, the results are often difficult to interpret, especially since factors other than acute coronary insufficiency are known to affect the electrocardiogram. Following is a partial list of the extracardiac factors which influence the electrocardiogram: body position, cold drinks, digitalis, quinidine, quinine, quinacrine (Atabrine), pamaquine (Plasmochin), epinephrine,

Table 12-3

Abnormal ST and T Wave Changes Caused by Nonatheromatous Disease

1. Drugs
   a. Digitalis
   b. Quinidine
   c. Tobacco
   d. Emetine

2. Myocardial Infection
   a. Rheumatism
   b. Diphtheria
   c. Trichinosis

3. Other General Infections
   a. Pneumonia
   b. Infectious mononucleosis

4. Pericarditis

5. Toxemia and Metabolic Disorders
   a. Uremia
   b. Diabetic acidosis
   c. Hypocalcemia
   d. Hypokalemia
   e. Hyperkalemia
   f. Hyperthyroidism
   g. Hypothyroidism
   h. Insulin shock
   i. Addison's disease
   j. Anemia
   k. Avitaminosis, especially beriberi
   l. Acidosis
   m. Alkalosis
   n. Anoxemia
   o. Shock

6. Changes in Posture of the Patient

7. Axis Deviation

8. Abnormal Heart Rhythms
   a. Paroxysmal tachycardia and atrial fibrillation
   b. Sinus tachycardia

9. Alterations in Vagosympathetic Tone
   a. Pain
   b. Fear
   c. Anesthesia

10. Pulmonary Embolism

11. Miscellaneous
    a. Periarteritis nodosa
    b. Trauma
    c. Malignancy of myocardium
    d. Dissecting aneurysm of coronary artery
    e. Dissecting aneurysm of aorta
    f. Syphilis of aorta
    g. Gallbladder disease
    h. Scleroderma
    i. General anasarca
    j. Cooling the heart through ingestion of ice water
    k. Terminal states of all kinds
    l. Unexplained

atropine, methacholine (Mecholyl), emetine, tobacco, exercise, infections, pericarditis, metabolic disorders, renal disease, visceral disease, pancreatitis, gallbladder disease, peptic ulcer, and autonomic nervous system imbalance. (See Table 12-3.)

Careful consideration must be given to the effect of increased rate upon the ST segment. A sagging of the PR segment followed by a false depression of ST segment due to an enlarged atrial T wave produced by tachycardia is the most common cause for the falsely positive exercise test. A horizontal configuration of the depressed ST segment greatly increases the significance of the depression. The recently introduced QX/QT ratio may prove a most valuable additional criterion of ST and T wave abnormality.

Long-term evaluation of the exercise test indicates that an abnormal double two-step exercise test is fairly reliable evidence of coronary insufficiency and that ST depression after exercise is more significant than T wave inversion.

In addition to hypoxemia and exercise, objective tests have also employed drugs which are known to cause coronary artery constriction; these include vasopressin (Pitressin) and ergonovine (see Fig. 12-3). However, these tests have not been popular because of the hazard of drug-induced coronary insufficiency.

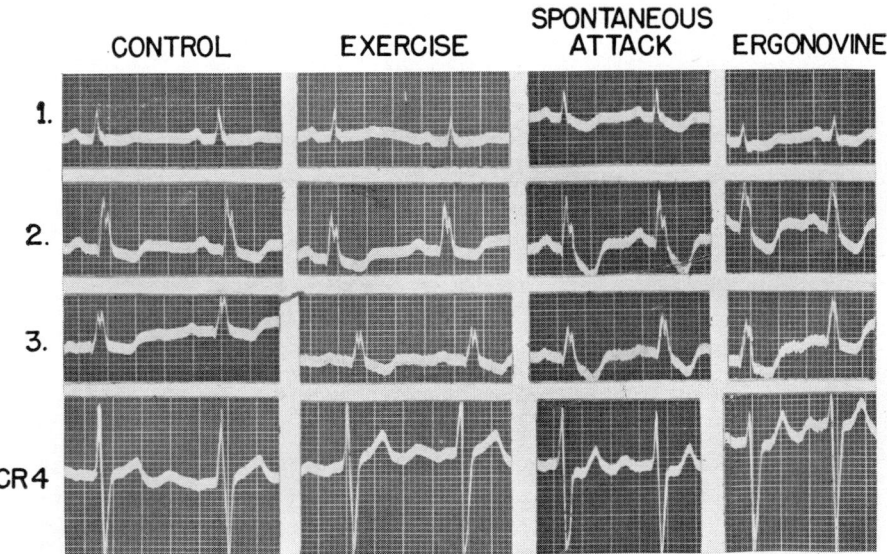

Fig. 12-3. Effects of exercise, spontaneous attack of angina, and ergonovine (0.4 mg intravenously). Note absence of electrocardiographic response to exercise but similarity of a spontaneous attack of angina and the ergonovine test for coronary insufficiency. (Courtesy of Dr. I. Stein.)

The details of the electrocardiographic diagnosis of acute myocardial infarction are included in many standard texts on the subject. Generally, transient coronary insufficiency reveals ST depressions and T wave changes as a result of subendocardial ischemia. Severe or persistent coronary insufficiency may lead to myocardial infarction, located intramurally or subendocardially (see Fig. 12-4). Acute myocardial infarction (see Fig. 12-5) usually presents abnormal Q waves and RST elevations over the affected areas if it is of transmural type; persistent ST depression with or without abnormal Q waves if it is subendocardial; and only T wave inversion if it is of patchy intramural type. Tall peaked T waves may be observed in the very early phase of acute myocardial infarction, indicative of ischemia preceding injury and necrosis. In most instances, the electrocardiographic pattern is not only pathognomonic but also permits accurate localization of the infarcted area. Unfortunately, a large percentage of cases produce atypical changes in the electrocardiogram, depending upon the stage of the attack and the location and extent of the myocardial changes. Following acute occlusion of a coronary artery, the area of the myocardium deprived

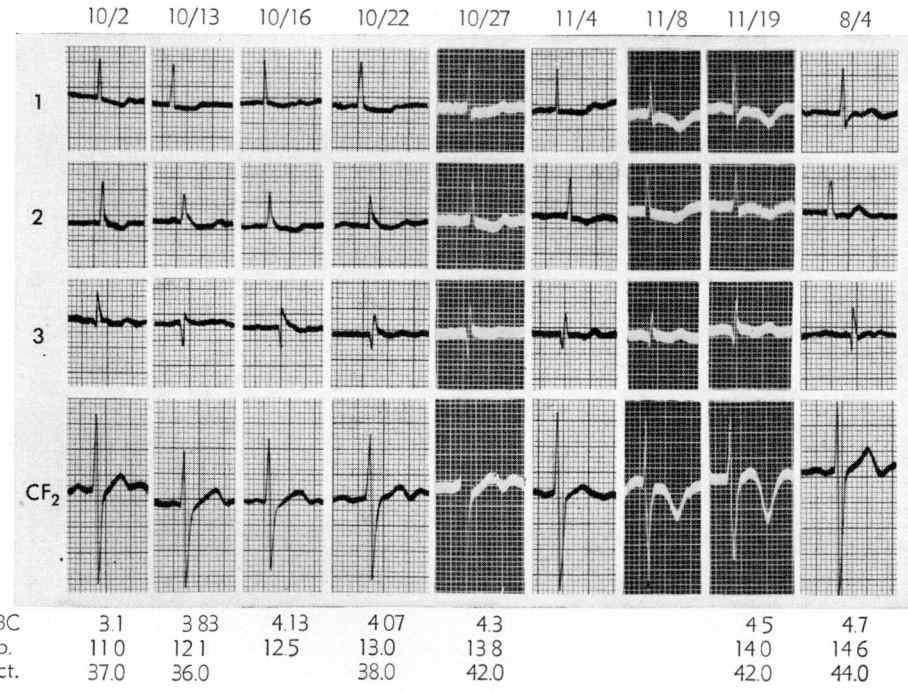

Fig. 12-4. Serial electrocardiogram changes in fifty-four-year-old patient with coronary disease following acute gastrointestinal hemorrhage. Note progressive T wave changes demonstrating intramural or subendocardial infarction due to coronary insufficiency precipitated by gastrointestinal hemorrhage. Note delayed onset of electrocardiographic changes.

of blood supply undergoes progressive changes; ischemia, injury, necrosis, and, finally, healing. Each stage of the process causes specific alterations in the electrical activity of the heart which can be detected in the serial electrocardiograms.

Characteristics of an acute myocardial infarction may be masked by bundle-branch block, paroxysmal arrhythmias with rapid rate, superimposed acute pericarditis, or drug effects such as those caused by digitalis and quinidine. In some instances, the electrocardiogram fails to show any abnormalities for an appreciable period after the onset of the acute episode. This usually occurs when the infarction has a patchy distribution, when it is located intramurally, or when it is in an unusual area. Thus, the inversion of T waves which is characteristic of this lesion may be delayed for many days following the attack because of the initial appearance of the infarction in the deeper layers. Changes do not become manifest until the lesion involves more superficial areas.

Occasionally, the tracing remains normal in spite of clinical evidence of acute myocardial infarction because of the position of the heart and the location of the infarcted area. In the first instance, the heart is most commonly in a markedly horizontal position, and the conventional twelve leads do not face the infarcted zone, which may lie high on the anterolateral or posterolateral wall of the left ventricle. In order to circumvent this drawback, additional precordial leads are employed one or two interspaces above the usual levels, or V_7 to V_9 leads are obtained over the back of the chest. In the second instance, the infarction may be situated in a silent zone of the myocardium, such as the septum. In rare instances, the electrocardiogram may show temporary improvement between the fourth and tenth days so that it may approach normalcy for several days. This effect may be due to an incomplete or slowly progressive occlusion, to the temporary effectiveness of the collateral circulation, or to an associated pericarditis.

Atypical electrocardiographic changes may also be encountered in the following conditions: (1) small and intramural infarction surrounded by healthy heart muscle; and (2) combined anterior and posterior infarctions in which the altered electrical forces are neutralized by each other. Other difficulties and errors in electrocardiographic diagnosis lie in commission rather than omission. The most common patterns misinterpreted as due to myocardial infarction may be detailed as follows:

A. Leads from the right precordium: (1) abnormal QR patterns attributable at autopsy to right ventricular hypertrophy, or abnormal QS patterns referable to right ventricular dilatation rather than anteroseptal infarction; (2) abnormal RST elevation attributable to left ventricular hypertrophy, digitalization, or pericarditis; (3) fixed or rapidly evoluting cove plane inversion of the T waves

[*Text continued on page 276.*]

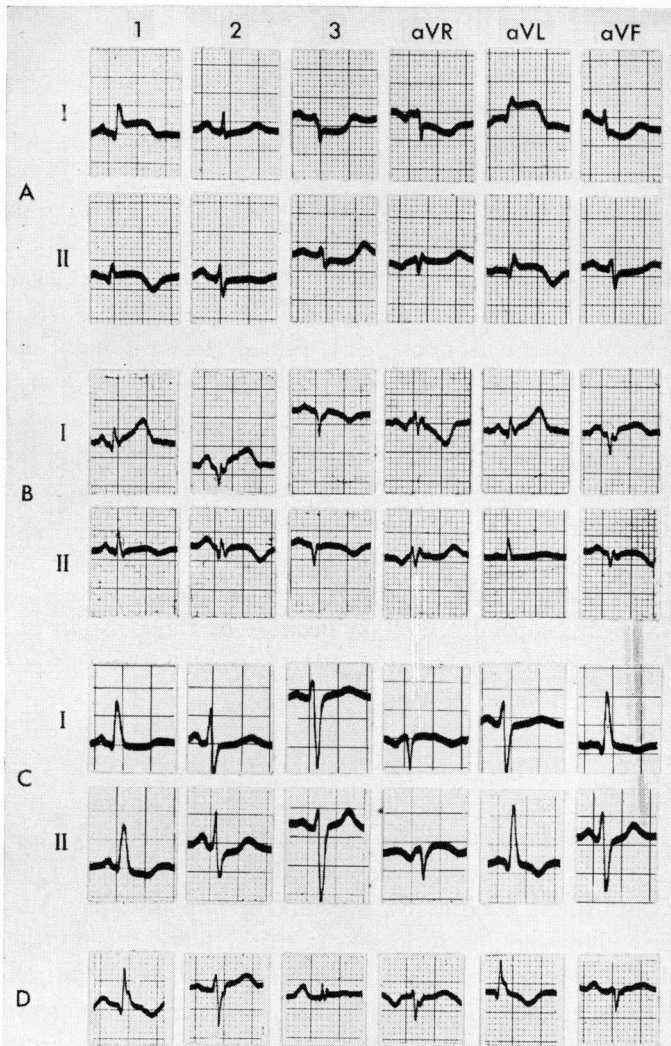

Fig. 12-5. Typical patterns of acute myocardial infarction.

A (*I* and *II*): Acute extensive anterior infarction (transmural). Note abnormal Q waves in V_{2-5} and progressive ST and T changes in 1, 2, V_{2-5} with reciprocal changes in 3, aVR, and aVF.

B (*I* and *II*): Acute posterolateral infarction (transmural). Note abnormal Q waves in 2, 3, aVF, and V_2 and V_6. Note very high and peaked T waves in V_{2-4} of earlier top tracing and relatively prominent R in V_1 in bottom tracing.

C (*I* and *II*): Acute subendocardial infarction of anterior wall. Note persistent and increasing ST depression in V_{2-6}.

274

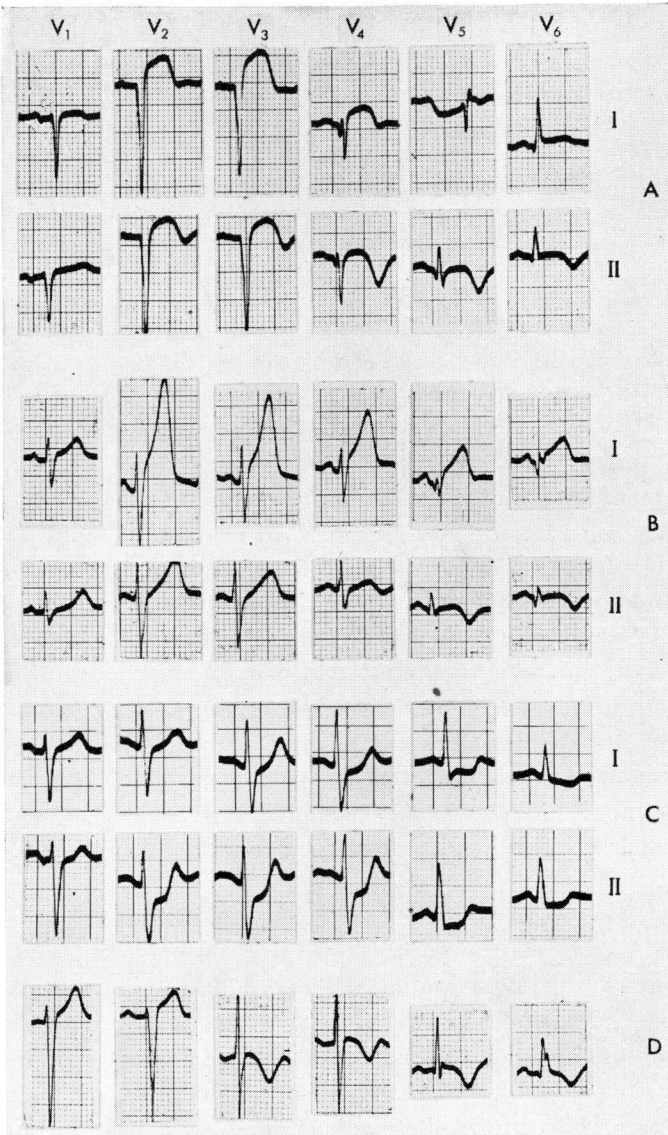

D: Acute intramural infarction of anterior wall. Note changes limited to moderately deep inversion of T waves in 1, 2, and V_{3-6}. The Q in 1, aVL, and V_6 is consistent with the transmural involvement of anterolateral wall which occurred three years before present infarction.

that could be correlated with right ventricular hypertrophy or dilatation at autopsy.

B. Leads from the transitional zone: (1) reduction in the amplitude of the initial R wave, or replacement by a QS deflection as the electrode is moved leftward from the V_1 or V_2 position, referable to transitional zonal effects in the presence of right ventricular dilatation, rather than to anteroseptal infarction; (2) abnormal elevation of the RST junction, followed by cove plane inversion of the T wave found localized to leads at the transitional zone in the absence of infarction.

C. Leads from the left axilla: (1) deep Q and tall succeeding R waves, that could be correlated with uncomplicated left ventricular hypertrophy; (2) abnormal RST depression referable to left ventricular hypertrophy and/or digitalization or abnormal T wave inversion secondary to left ventricular hypertrophy or subendocardial myocarditis; (3) abnormal QRS or notched QS deflections referable to right ventricular hypertrophy and dilation.*

Although ST segments and T waves show improvement, Q wave changes which appear during the acute or massive phase of transmural infarction rarely disappear completely. A return to normal is far more common in intramural or subendocardial infarctions which are manifested initially by ST and T changes. A completely normal twelve-lead electrocardiogram one year following an acute infarction is strong evidence against the previous existence of an acute myocardial infarction of the classic anterior or posterior wall type. Conglomerate and transmural acute or healed infarcts are more frequently recognized ante mortem than are patchy and subendocardial lesions. Of the transmural infarctions, those located laterally are the ones most difficult to diagnose. Lateral and posterior subendocardial infarcts are most often missed.

Vectorcardiography is actually fundamental electrocardiography studied in three dimensions. A vector has three characteristics: (1) magnitude, represented by arrow length; (2) direction of inclination, illustrated by deviation of the line from the horizontal or vertical; and (3) "sense," with the arrow lead indicating the direction of the force. Direct or indirect methods of recording are employed. The indirect methods require detailed measurements and calculations which utilize the electrocardiogram as the starting point. Direct spatial vectorcardiography permits the visualization of the termini of the instantaneous vectors of ventricular activation by means of the cathode-ray oscilloscope which is used to record the loop in several planes.

The vectorcardiogram is especially useful in the localization of a myocardial infarction, since the conduction of electrical impulse is a property of living cells. Therefore, an area of dead muscle without electrical potential

---

* From Myers, G. B.: QRS-T patterns in multiple precordial leads that may be mistaken for myocardial infarction. *Circulation*, 2:60, 1950.

causes a change in the instantaneous vectors at the moment that the area normally would have shown activity. It is manifested by changes in the initial inscription of the vectors and/or by a "shunning" of the involved area (see Fig. 12-6).

The vectorcardiogram appears to be superior to the electrocardiogram in the diagnosis of certain types of myocardial infarctions—e.g., combined infarctions of the anterior and posterior wall of the left ventricle and high posterior myocardial infarction. However, it has not been sufficiently appreciated that all vectorcardiograms and vector methods of presentation depend on data obtained from more or less commonly used surface leads.

In brief summary, vector methods of all kinds are simply different schemes for the display of information frequently already available in more conventional electrocardiograms. Disorders of rate and rhythm can be analyzed better with the conventional electrocardiogram. Small areas of necrosis can also escape detection by the vectorcardiographic method. Thus far, correlation of pathologic and vectorcardiographic findings in myocardial infarction is based on a much smaller number of cases compared with conventional electrocardiography. For these reasons, as well as the necessity for expensive instrumentation or apparatus which may be crude or inexact, vectorcardiography appears to have limited clinical value at present.

Ballistocardiography. A ballistocardiogram is a graphic representation of the motions imparted to the body in response to physical movements of the heart and the passage of the blood through the vascular system. Although the exact mechanisms responsible for the ballistocardiographic changes have not as yet been fully explained, empirical correlations with clinical and autopsy findings have demonstrated the value of ballistocardiography in the diagnostic evaluation of coronary artery disease. Three methods are generally employed: (1) Starr's high-frequency, undamped bed, (2) Nickerson's low-frequency, critically damped bed, and (3) Dock's direct body pickup. The last method is inexpensive, simple, and effective. Many ballistocardiographic studies of normal individuals in various age groups have led to the generally accepted conclusion that an abnormal tracing under the age of forty-five to fifty years and a normal tracing over the age of sixty years are significant. The high incidence of abnormal tracings in older normal individuals probably is a manifestation of latent coronary disease, which may be demonstrable before clinical or electrocardiographic evidence appears. However, in some older subjects, an abnormal ballistocardiogram is obtained in the head-foot axis, while normal tracings are obtained in lateral direction. This is probably related to the tortuosity of the aorta and the transmission of the ventricular ejection force into a more lateral direction.

[*Text continued on page 280.*]

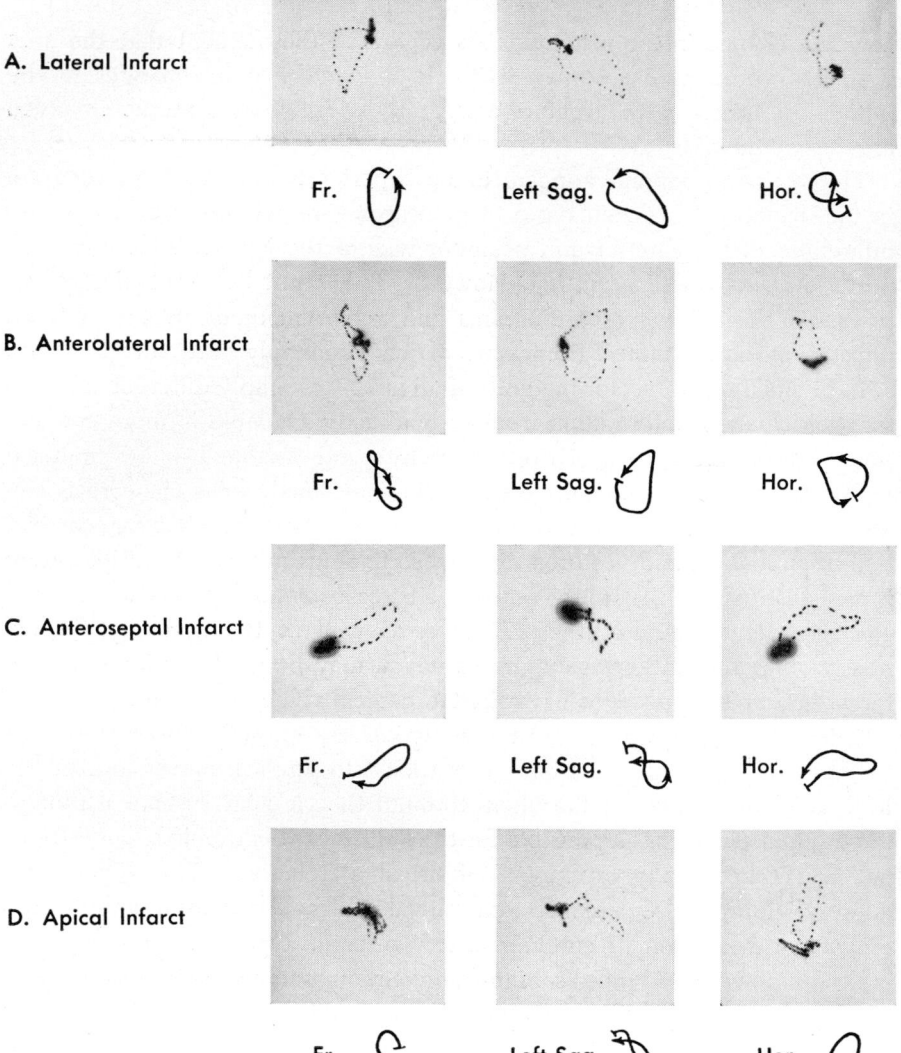

A. Lateral Infarct

Fr.   Left Sag.   Hor.

B. Anterolateral Infarct

Fr.   Left Sag.   Hor.

C. Anteroseptal Infarct

Fr.   Left Sag.   Hor.

D. Apical Infarct

Fr.   Left Sag.   Hor.

278

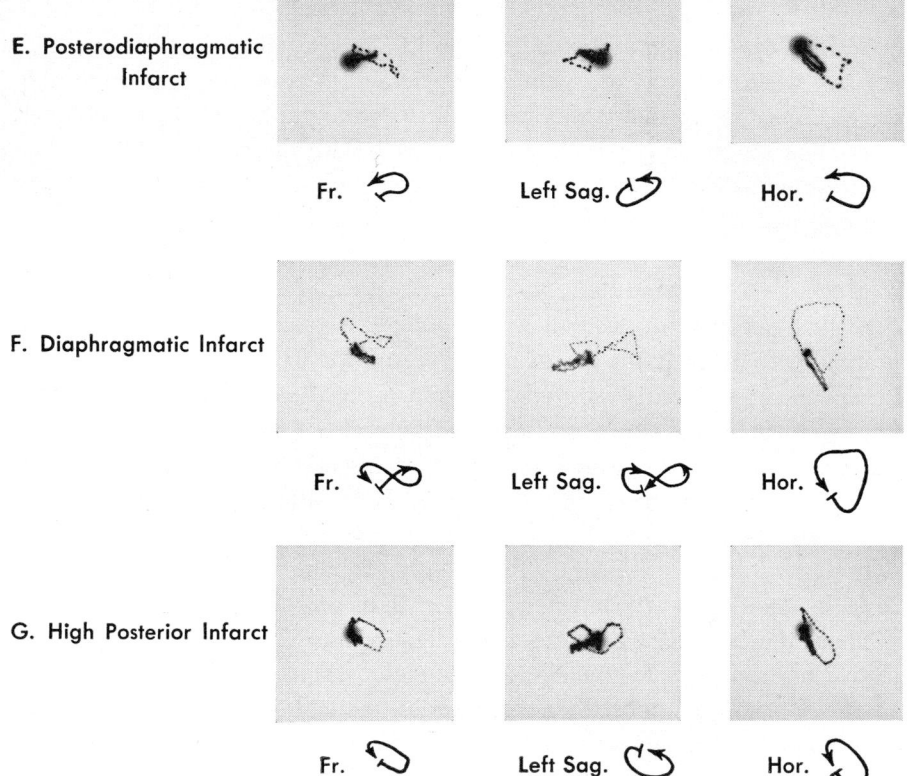

E. Posterodiaphragmatic
Infarct

Fr.   Left Sag.   Hor.

F. Diaphragmatic Infarct

Fr.   Left Sag.   Hor.

G. High Posterior Infarct

Fr.   Left Sag.   Hor.

Fig. 12-6. Vectorcardiograms of the most common types of myocardial infarction. (*Fr.*, frontal plane; *Sag.*, sagittal plane; *Hor.*, horizontal plane.) (Courtesy of D. H. Pipberger, Mount Alto Veterans Administration Hospital, Washington, D.C.)

The ballistocardiogram has been found to be six and one-half times more accurate than the electrocardiographic exercise tolerance test in confirming the presence of coronary disease. Ballistocardiographic changes obtained after cigarette smoking correlate more closely with the coronary status than the resting ballistocardiogram or the tracing obtained after exercise. An exercise ballistocardiographic test may also be helpful. Ballistocardiograms may also demonstrate abnormalities after the consumption of a heavy meal in patients with coronary artery disease. (See Fig. 12-7.)

Angina pectoris produces a marked deterioration of the ballistocardiographic pattern; after the use of nitroglycerin, the ballistocardiogram shows improvement as pain is relieved. (Angina pectoris sine angina often shows improvement in ballistic form after nitroglycerin.) In some older persons without clinical evidence of coronary heart disease but with abnormal ballistocardiograms, marked improvement is shown after nitroglycerin; but in apparently similar cases, the ballistic form may remain unchanged or may deteriorate following this drug. It is highly probable that this improvement in the ballistic form after nitrites is evidence of coronary heart disease.

Thus, the ballistocardiogram may demonstrate the only abnormal objective finding prior to the development of overt coronary artery disease. In Starr's original supposedly normal series, the eight- to ten-year follow-up showed that among those over the age of forty with normal tracings, none developed coronary artery disease. The incidence of lesions was considerable among those with abnormal ballistocardiograms. Yet it should be noted that normal ballistocardiograms may be present in those with severe coronary artery disease, even during the acute phase of myocardial infarction. In most cases of *acute* myocardial infarction, the ballistocardiogram has limited value and constitutes only a confirmatory objective test. However, following the immediate recovery from the acute attack, serial ballistocardiographic tracings permit an objective assessment of the recovery of cardiac function and of the ability of the patient to resume regular activity, since the ballistocardiogram is a record of the ejection force of the ventricles and thus reflects the mechanical efficiency of the heart. The correlation between clinical course and serial ballistocardiographic findings is usually excellent. Furthermore, the objective documentation of the degree of cardiac efficiency following acute myocardial infarction is helpful in the differential diagnosis of chest pain which persists after an infarction.

Vectorballistocardiography employs multidirectional tracings (head-foot, lateral, and dorsoventral) using vector principles. Other developments along this line include a torsion ballistocardiogram and a tilting ballistocardiogram. The ultra-low-frequency method utilizing a mercury bed or an extremely

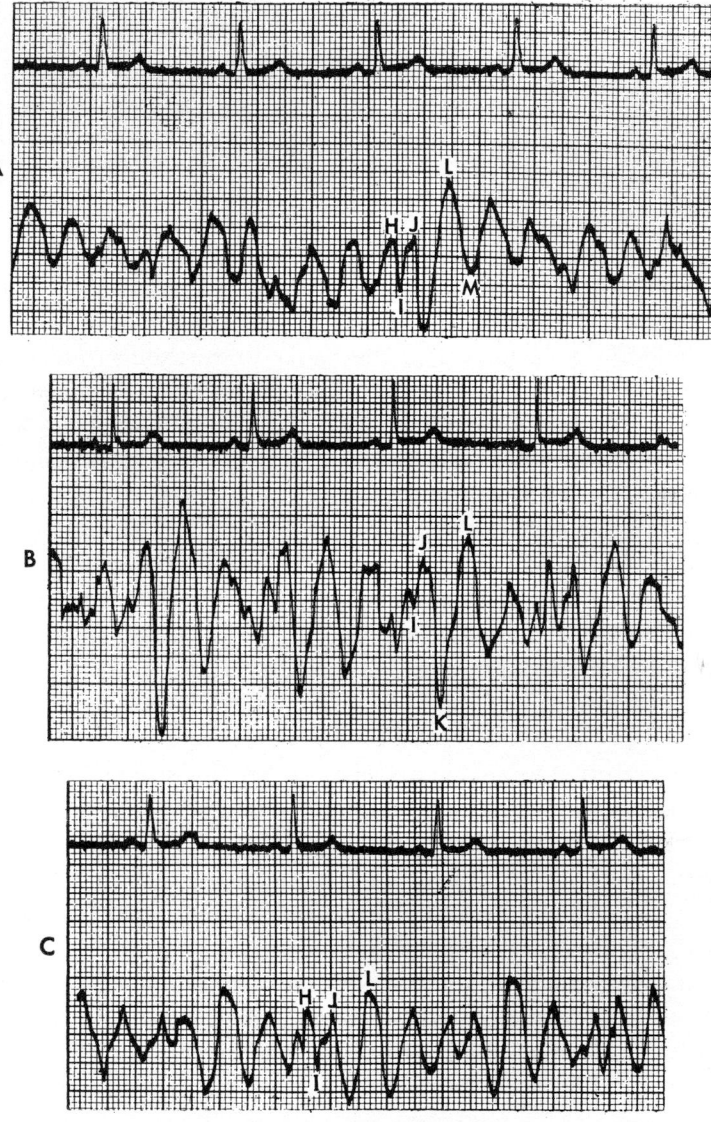

Fig. 12-7. Ballistocardiographic changes two months after acute myocardial infarction. Note marked respiratory variations of the amplitude, abnormally notched J wave, and abnormally prominent L wave. (*A*, Normal respiration; *B*, inspiratory phase; *C*, expiratory phase.)

light suspended bed permits the most accurate recording of ballistic deflections. Further investigation is necessary to prove the accuracy and clinical usefulness of these promising methods.

Phonocardiography. Phonocardiography represents a graphic recording of auscultatory findings. It has the additional advantage of amplifying and recording heart sounds and murmurs of frequencies which exist beyond human audibility. Thus, faint diastolic gallop sounds which may be encountered following myocardial infarction and which consist of frequencies below 30 cycles per second are clearly demonstrable with the phonocardiograph.

In myocardial infarction, the phonocardiogram may reveal or document abnormalities of the first and second sound, the presence of adventitious sounds such as presystolic gallop, protodiastolic gallop, and third sound, and also the presence of systolic murmurs. (See Fig. 12-8.) As regards the first sound, studies have demonstrated the marked reduction in amplitude and frequency of the second component of the first sound. This change is responsible for the dull, muffled, or low-pitched character of the first heart sound frequently noted in acute myocardial infarction. This component is related in time to the isometric contraction phase, and its diminution may be the result of impaired contractile power of the heart muscle and/or impaired atrioventricular valve closure. The second sound is frequently higher in amplitude and frequency both relative to the first sound and also in the absolute sense. The latter may be related to the increased pulmonary artery pressure due to left ventricular failure. The appearance of a third sound (related to the rapid ventricular filling phase) in a phonocardiogram of a person over forty years should be considered abnormal. It is a frequent finding in myocardial infarction and may be present several years after the acute episode, even in the absence of cardiac failure. When the third sound shows markedly increased amplitude, it constitutes a protodiastolic gallop sound. This is a not infrequent finding in acute myocardial infarction. Presystolic gallop sounds which represent atrial (or fourth) sounds of accentuated amplitude are frequently associated with cardiac failure. Both gallop sounds are usually associated with rapid heart rates and can be made to disappear by slowing the cardiac rate by means of carotid sinus pressure. However, the abnormal "third" sound may be present in coronary disease even if the heart rate is quite slow. In some patients, this finding may be the only cardiac abnormality detectable aside from the abnormal electrocardiogram. Phonocardiograms may also document the appearance of systolic murmurs after acute myocardial infarction, although this is rarely necessary. The murmur usually possesses the characteristics of mitral regurgitation. It is well fused with the first sound, and is of relatively high frequency and slight to moderate amplitude, with the latter showing decrescendo configuration. It may persist throughout systole and is usually loudest at the apex. This murmur is found mainly in posterior wall infarction. Systolic

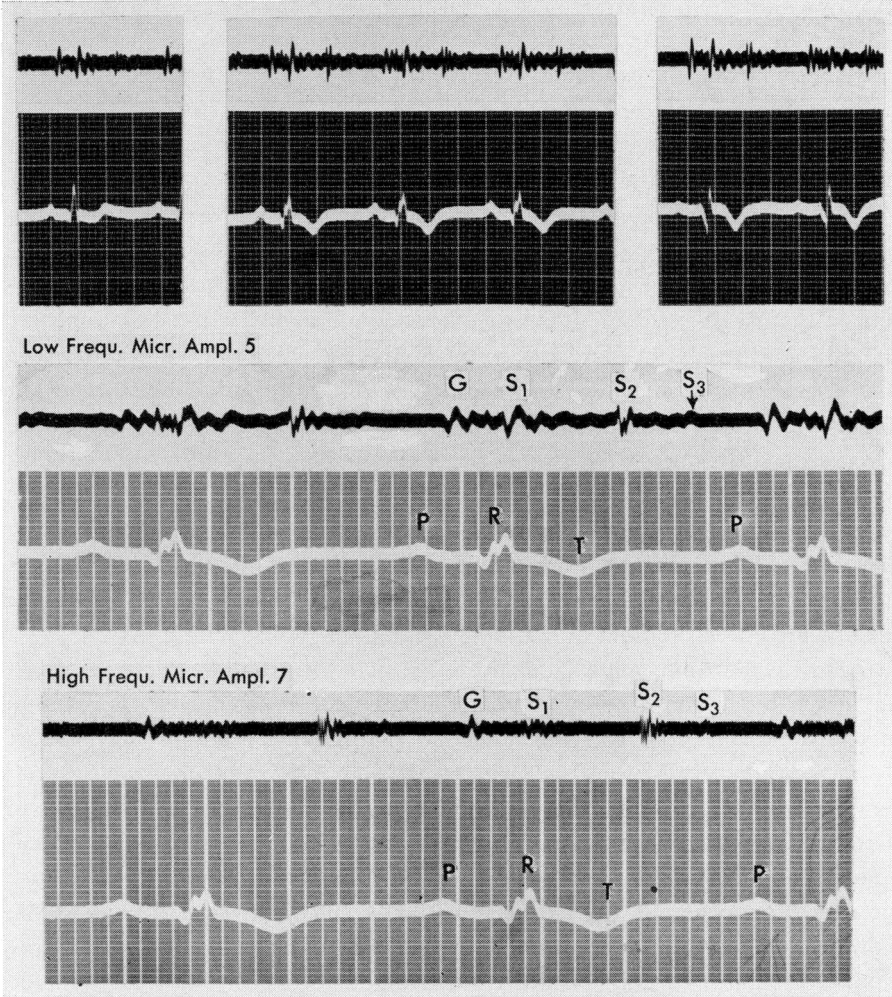

Fig. 12-8. Phonocardiographic changes in acute myocardial infarction. Note relatively low-pitched first sound (S₁), accentuated atrial sounds (A), and third sounds (S₃) representing presystolic and protodiastolic gallops.

murmurs of different characteristics may appear following rupture of papillary muscles, chordae tendineae, or septum. These murmurs tend to be of greater intensity and usually show an amplitude of gradually increasing degree corresponding to the dynamic disturbance produced by these lesions.

Occasionally, abnormal heart sounds in coronary artery disease may simulate mitral stenosis. Phonocardiograms reveal, in these cases, the presence of a diminished, reduplicated, and prolonged first sound often preceded by a presystolic gallop. This may give the auscultatory impression of a late rumbling diastolic murmur. The reduplication is due to asynchronic valve closure and is related to the presence of bundle-branch block.

Roentgen procedures. Roentgen procedures are especially useful in determining the size and configuration of the heart in coronary disease, the possible presence of a ventricular aneurysm, abnormal cardiovascular pulsations, and lesions of the aorta and coronary arteries.

Each of the procedures finds its proper niche in the evaluation of coronary disease. Initial and serial determination of the heart size is of value in assessing the damage caused by acute myocardial infarction and by coronary disease in general. Cardiac enlargement involves the left ventricle initially and results in the lengthening of the left lower cardiac border and the appearance of an undue prominence of the posterior border in the left anterior oblique view. Later, left atrial enlargement ensues. With progressive myocardial weakness, the right ventricle and atrium also dilate. This eventually causes a generalized enlargement of the cardiac silhouette which must be differentiated from pericardial effusion, particularly when the congestive failure is predominantly right-sided. A circumscribed area of calcification of the myocardium always suggests the presence of an old healed area of infarction.

An x-ray film may reveal the presence of a ventricular aneurysm characterized by an eccentric bulge near the left ventricular border. This bulge may extend abruptly from the adjacent ventricular border or may depart from it gradually. At times, a large ventricular aneurysm may cause only marked rounding of the left ventricular border, such as is also found in hypertension or aortic valvular disease. The ascending aorta may reveal calcification or dilatation due to old luetic disease, and this may be the cause of encroachment upon the coronary ostia. Calcification of the walls of the coronary branches may be directly visible on roentgenograms employing special technics (Fig. 12-9), but this does not necessarily indicate that the lumina are not patent. Calcification of the coronary arteries may also be discernible on ordinary roentgenograms.

The arteriosclerotic process must be advanced and rather dense to become visualized. Other considerations which play a definite role in the roentgenographic recognition of coronary sclerosis are (1) awareness of the common sites and characteristics of such densities; (2) good technical quality of roentgenograms with multiple projections including posteroanterior, both oblique, and lateral views; and (3) differentiation from other intra- and extracardiac densities, such as calcification of the pericardium, valves, annulus fibrosus, costal cartilages, hilar lymph nodes, and pulmonary vessels projected through the cardiac borders. Characteristically, these

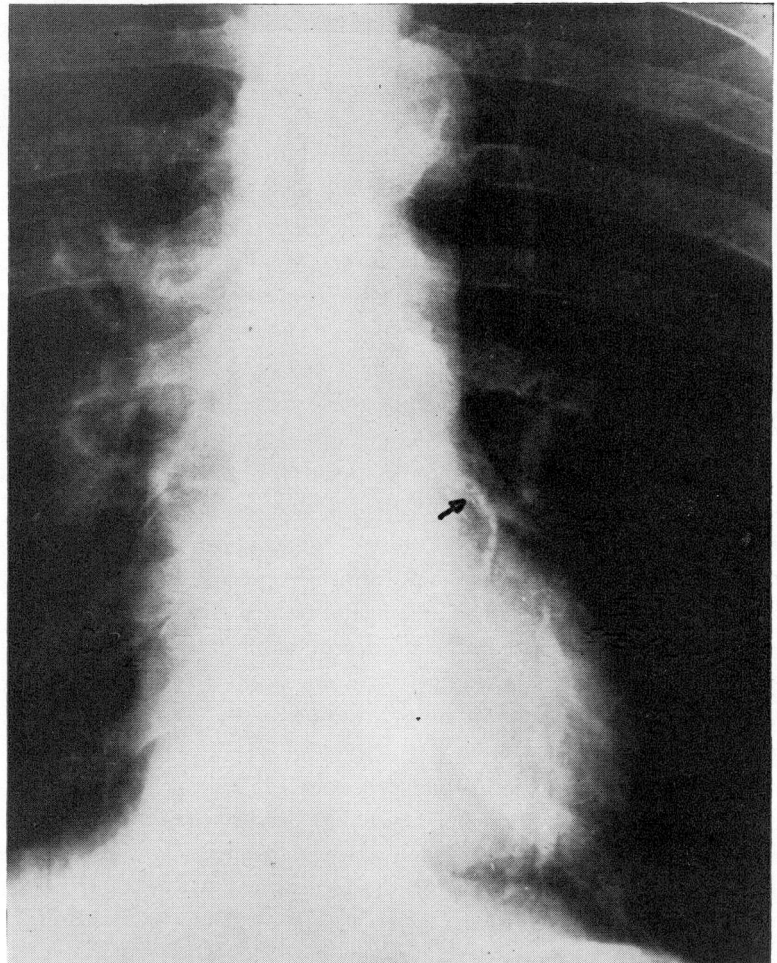

Fig. 12-9. Calcification of a coronary artery visible on routine x-ray.

calcifications have the appearance of linear streaks and interrupted plaques arranged in parallel segments.

Contrast visualization of coronary arteries has recently been introduced to demonstrate the patency of the coronary arteries. Minute quantities of contrast medium are rapidly injected (one and one-half seconds) into the aorta by retrograde catheterization under pressure, while carotid arteries are compressed briefly. More recently, Dotter has added a balloon type of catheter which can occlude the ascending aorta while the dye is injected at the level of the coronary ostia.

Acetylcholine has also been injected to produce brief cardiac arrest preliminary to the coronary filling. Lehman and Sones, working independently, have recently introduced the catheter through the brachial artery to a point just above the aortic valves and have injected radiopaque dye (during diastole preferably) with excellent visualization of the coronary arteries in a large percentage of the cases; selective filling of either coronary artery is possible by careful positioning of the catheter tip. This has been supplemented by cineangiocardiography. Thus far, contrast visualization has been a fairly safe procedure in man. Excellent demonstration of narrowing and occlusion of vessels can be obtained, which may eventually prove practical in the evaluation of patients with suspected or proven coronary artery disease prior to direct surgical attack on the narrowed segments.

In addition to opaque media, it is possible to use intravenous injection of gas (50 to 100 cc of carbon dioxide) (patient lying on the left side) in order to outline the right heart. This aids in the differentiation of pericardial effusion, constrictive pericarditis, and intracardiac lesions.

Fluoroscopy may be of considerable value in coronary artery disease by detecting abnormal cardiovascular pulsations, especially of the left ventricle and aorta. The left ventricular border normally moves inwardly during systole, while the pulmonary artery and aortic segments immediately above show an opposite movement. Following myocardial infarction, the infarcted or aneurysmal area of heart muscle is often passively distended and exhibits an outward movement or bulge during systole. This phenomenon is called "paradoxical pulsation." Diminished pulsations of the apical region are not indicative of myocardial infarction, since they are frequently found in cardiac enlargement due to various causes. They represent an accentuation of the normally present gradient of pulsations between the upper left ventricular border and the apex.

Electrokymography employs a photoelectric device and fluoroscopy with screen and slit to trace the movements of the cardiac chambers and large vessels as well as the hilar shadows, small pulmonary vessels, and venae cavae. Dissociation between various heart chambers may also be studied. Variations of density due to motion of the cardiac border appear in the slot of a photosensitive tube overlying the area to be explored. This causes changes in the electric current emitted, which are transformed into graphic deflections.

Electrokymograms are usually taken together with the electrocardiogram or carotid pulse tracings for time reference. The method is somewhat cumbersome, requires special equipment, and results easily in excessive exposure to radiation.

Roentgenkymography (slit-kymography) employs a single- or multiple-slit method. The inthrust and outthrust of each point of the cardiovascular silhouette are visualized and may be graphically recorded. Analysis of the wave-like motion of these points can be made in respect to amplitude, form, duration, and time. Thus, the cardiac areas and those of the aorta and pulmonary artery can be measured in systole and diastole. Myocardial infarctions or cardiac aneurysms may be recognized by the paradoxical pulsations. The electrokymogram is superior to the roentgenkymogram for recognizing old infarctions.

Tomography is sectional roentgenography. Serial planes of the thorax appear well delineated, with a blurring of overlying and underlying structures. This method is especially valuable in the study and localization of intrapulmonary or mediastinal lesions and aneurysms.

Roentgencinematography is the use of motion-picture technics in recording the images on a fluoroscopic intensifying screen adopted for direct photography. Although it is not a popular method because of expense and dangers of x-ray overexposure, this procedure may contribute valuable information on a permanent record which indicates all phases of the part to be studied. Sones has recently employed this method successfully to record coronary angiograms by means of retrograde aortography.

Angiocardiography is a technic which employs contrast media for visualization of size, shape, and position of the cardiac chambers and intrathoracic blood vessels. Shunts are readily demonstrable. It is of special value in determining the nature of aortic lesions and in the exclusion of mediastinal tumors, pericardial effusion, and diaphragmatic hernia. Translumbar or retrograde aortography are especially valuable for the arteriographic study of the aorta and its branches. Even the coronary arteries may be visualized with this method, by placing the tip of the catheter at the coronary ostia. Direct intracardiac and great-vessel opacification studies are possible by percutaneous introduction of the needle directly into the right or left ventricle, or even into the aorta through the suprasternal notch.

General laboratory tests. A battery of the following laboratory tests is usually required to ascertain the exact nature of atypical chest pain or of limited areas of infarction (see Table 12-4 and Fig. 12-10).

Acute phase reactants. The inflammation and necrosis associated with acute myocardial infarction cause abnormalities of a number of so-called "acute phase reactants." These include the erythrocyte sedimentation rate (ESR), the C-reactive protein (CRP) test, and the plasma fibrinogen concentration. They are all of nonspecific character and merely indicate the

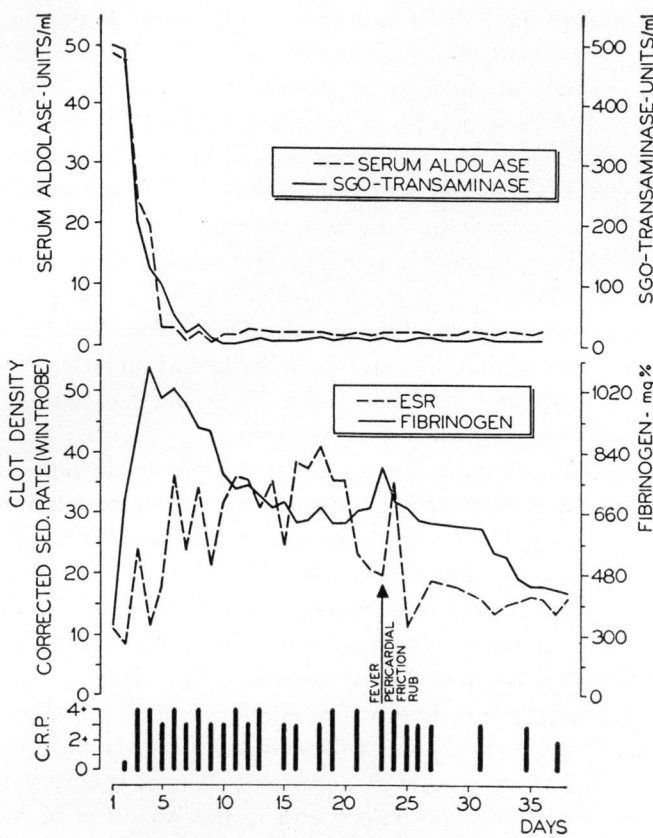

Fig. 12-10. Serial determinations of fibrinogen concentration, SGO-T, serum aldolase, ESR, and CRP in a forty-four-year-old man with massive posterior wall myocardial infarction. (From Losner, S.; Volk, B. W.; and Aronson, S. M.: Diagnostic aids in acute myocardial infarction: clinical and experimental. *Am. Heart J.*, **54**:225, 1957, The C. V. Mosby Co., St. Louis.)

presence of inflammation, infection, or necrosis anywhere within the body. Therefore, the chief objection to these tests is that they may prove confusing in the presence of concomitant disease.

Erythrocyte sedimentation rate (normally: male, 2 to 8 mm; female, 2 to 10 mm) is the least specific of the tests but is commonly employed as a laboratory guide for the clinical evaluation of patients with acute coronary occlusion. In most instances of major infarction, the rate is rapid early in the course of the infarction but seldom rises before the first day; therefore, results are erratic or misleading in many instances. The sedimentation rate may fail to rise at all during the first two weeks of illness, due to the retarding effect of an increased hematocrit reading. This is frequently encountered in patients who display hemoconcentration and shock during the early stages of the disease. When the hematocrit returns to normal levels, the sedimentation rate increases in accordance with the pathologic condition present. Elevated levels may persist for four to thirty-six days, although the range varies widely. Rates above 100 mm per hour are very rarely reported. Persistent elevation of the sedimentation rate signifies the existence of an active or unhealed infection anywhere in the body (e.g., common cold) or the presence of congestive heart failure, or even of severe anemia. If healing is retarded because of extensive coronary sclerosis of the other coronary vessels, the rate may remain elevated for a long time after myocardial infarction. The rate may also be slow to recede when the infarction is massive or has extended elsewhere, or if completion of revascularization is delayed.

The C-reactive protein test (normally negative) is nonspecific and is based on the appearance of alpha-globulin in the serum when inflammation is present anywhere in the body. Since it forms a precipitate with the somatic-C polysaccharides of the pneumococcus, it has been called C-reactive protein. It has also been demonstrated in the blood of patients with congestive failure. However, in the absence of carcinoma, trauma, and inflammatory conditions (such as rheumatic fever), it can be used to advantage in the diagnosis of acute myocardial infarction. It is positive initially (one to six) but becomes negative again in most cases one to two weeks after myocardial infarction. It correlates with other laboratory indices of infarction, such as leukocytosis and elevated erythrocyte sedimentation rate, and with the presence of fever. It is highly positive in patients with acute myocardial infarction. Qualitative changes in C-reactive protein lag behind clinical and electrocardiographic improvement but appear more reliable than the erythrocyte sedimentation rate in following the natural evolution of myocardial infarction. Serial determinations may help to establish the complete subsidence of myocardial necrosis and inflammation. It may also be used to differentiate between acute myocardial infarction and protracted coronary insufficiency without infarction. It is negative in coronary insufficiency, in the premonitory phase of infarction, and in healed infarction. The persistence of a positive C-reactive protein test may be indicative of progressive infarction, phlebothrombosis, or some other embolic phenomenon.

Plasma fibrinogen concentration (normally less than 390 mg per 100 ml) may rise whenever an inflammatory or necrotizing process takes place in the body. A significant elevation of the fibrinogen level occurs in acute myocardial infarction. The maximum fibrinogen concentration (up to 800 mg per 100 ml), which is reached during the first few days of illness, usually correlates closely with the severity of the clinical picture. This occurs frequently while the erythrocyte sedimentation rate is still normal. Levels usually return to normal by the third week. During convalescence, the sedimentation rate often remains elevated long after the fibrinogen concentration has returned to normal. The plasma fibrinogen concentration can be determined by the clot density method, which is based on the increasing optical density of coagulating plasma. It yields results within a few minutes after withdrawal of venous blood. The normal values range from 5 to 15, corresponding to a fibrinogen concentration of 210 to 390 mg per 100 ml. Plasma fibrinogen elevation is suggestive of, but not specific for, myocardial necrosis. Necrosis due to injured tissue or inflammatory disease must be excluded. Fibrinogen concentration is not elevated when hepatic disease coexists, since the liver is the principal source of fibrinogen production.

The fibrinogen polymerization test offers diagnostic aid in differentiating myocardial infarction from pericarditis (Table 12-4). It is negative in myocardial infarction but positive in acute and subacute pericarditis. It may be particularly helpful in cases of atypical chest pain and instances where the

Table 12-4

The Differential Diagnosis of Various Laboratory Findings in
Myocardial Infarction and Pericarditis *

Laboratory Data	Acute Myocardial Infarction		Pericarditis	
	Transmural	Atypical	Acute	Subacute
E.S.R.	frequently elevated	frequently normal	elevated	frequently elevated
C.R.P.	usually elevated	frequently normal	frequently elevated	frequently normal
Fibr. Conc.	usually elevated	frequently normal	frequently elevated	frequently normal
F.P.	negative	negative	positive	positive
S. Enz.	elevated	frequently normal	normal	normal
Ekg. Q	abnormal	usually normal	normal	normal
ST	frequently elevated	normal, depressed, or elevated	frequently elevated	normal
T	progressively inverted	frequently inverted	may be inverted	may be inverted

F.P.—Fibrinogen polymerization
Fibr. Conc.—Plasma fibrinogen concentration
S. Enz.—Serum enzyme level (SGO—T or serum aldolase)

* Modified from Fremont, R. E., and Volk, B. W.: Newer aspects of diagnostic and therapeutic management of acute idiopathic pericarditis. *Dis. Chest*, **36**:319, 1959.

electrocardiogram reveals changes consistent with intramural infarction manifested only by T wave changes.

Leukocyte count. Leukocytosis occurs in more than 90 per cent of patients within the first day and reaches a peak by the third day. The leukocyte count then returns to normal levels (up to 10,000 per cubic millimeter) by the eighth day. The white-count elevation is usually below 15,000 but may rise as high as 85,000. The higher the count, the worse the prognosis. The polymorphonuclear leukocytes reach a peak at about the same time as the leukocytosis. An eosinopenia is usually found.

Enzyme tests. Serum glutamic oxalacetic transaminase. The serum contains numerous enzymes that cause transamination, a reversible metabolic reaction. All natural amino acids participate in transamination, a reaction believed to play an important but not well-understood role in amino acid metabolism. This enzyme has its greatest concentration in heart muscle, skeletal muscle, and brain, liver, and kidney tissue but is low in lung tissue. This observation was made in 1941 by Cohen and Hekhnis, who found that transaminase occurs in high concentration in cardiac and skeletal musculature. LaDue, Wroblewski, and associates described its existence in the other tissues in 1954.

Thus, serum glutamic oxalacetic transaminase (SGO-T) activity was found to be a valuable aid in the diagnosis of acute myocardial infarction,

Table 12-5

Clinical Applications of SGO-T Test

1. SGO-T activity is within normal limits in infectious, degenerative, neoplastic, toxic, allergic, reactive, and metabolic diseases when heart and skeletal muscle and liver are undamaged.
2. SGO-T activity rises within twelve hours and persists as long as six days after acute transmural myocardial infarction.
3. The height and duration of elevation of SGO-T are roughly proportional to the size of infarction.
4. Angina pectoris or coronary insufficiency does not increase SGO-T activity if heart muscle cells are undamaged.
5. Rheumatic fever with active carditis is frequently associated with concomitant increases in SGO-T activity.
6. Elevation of SGO-T in toxic, infectious, and homologous serum hepatitis is so great in the early stages of liver cell injury as to be almost diagnostic.
7. SGO-T is moderately elevated in obstructive jaundice but falls promptly after surgery.
8. SGO-T activity is variable in cirrhosis of the liver.
9. An increase in SGO-T activity appears to be a relatively sensitive index of liver metastasis.
10. The level of SGO-T activity in liver disease does not parallel the tests of liver function now in use. An increase in activity appears to indicate active liver cell destruction.

since it rises from two to twenty times the normal value (up to 40 units) (see Table 12-5). Other enzyme levels are also elevated following acute myocardial infarction (see Fig. 12-11). These include serum adolase, lactic

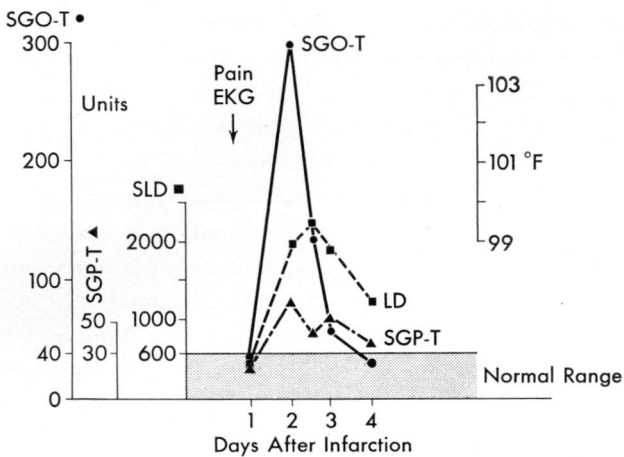

Fig. 12-11. Average changes in SGO-T, SLD, and SGP-T activity following acute transmural myocardial infarction in a patient. (From LaDue, J. S.: Laboratory aids in diagnosis of myocardial infarction. *J.A.M.A.*, **165**:1776, 1957.)

acid dehydrogenase (LAD), malic dehydrogenase, and serum glutamic pyruvate transaminase (SGP-T). They are not as valuable as SGO-T in the diagnosis and prognosis of acute myocardial infarction, although the LAD is the preferred test in the Boston area. The height of the enzymatic activity is roughly proportional to the size of the infarction and frequently provides a rough estimate as to prognosis. However, levels up to 1800 units have been reported with recovery. Elevated enzyme activity is apparently produced by enzyme leakage through the severely damaged cell membrane. A rise generally occurs six hours after the onset of acute infarction, and values often return to normal between the third and the sixth day. Therefore, the test may have no value and may even prove confusing when determinations are made too early or too late. The test is especially useful before electrocardiographic changes appear or when the electrocardiographic pattern of infarction is obscured by the presence of rapid paroxysmal arrhythmias or a bundle-branch block. Secondary peak elevations occur when recurrent chest pain is caused by an extension of the original infarction or following the occurrence of a new infarction. A rise above 250 units indicates a poor prognosis. It is not elevated by angina pectoris, mild or chronic coronary insufficiency, heart failure, or digitalis in the absence of active heart cell damage. However, if subendocardial ischemia is marked, it may result in a slight elevation of the levels.

Patients suffering skeletal trauma may exhibit serial SGO-T levels simulating those of an acute myocardial infarction. When such patients undergo simultaneous cardiac injury (as in steering-wheel injuries to the chest), the SGO-T test may prove confusing as a differential diagnostic test. False positive elevations are also found in certain other types of tissue necrosis, such as liver disease, jaundice, acute pancreatitis, and pulmonary embolism.

In summary, the SGO-T test may be of considerable aid in the following ways: (1) it is usually elevated before diagnostic electrocardiographic changes appear; (2) it is helpful in differentiating pulmonary and myocardial infarctions; (3) it may confirm the presence of an acute myocardial infarction which is masked by the presence of certain cardiac arrhythmias or left bundle-branch block, or by marked digitalis effect; (4) it can differentiate a recent myocardial infarction from acute pericarditis; and (5) it may confirm the diagnosis of a second acute myocardial infarction superimposed upon a healing infarction.

The lactic acid dehydrogenase (LAD) values (normally 200 to 680 units) run parallel to the SGO-T values and offer little additional aid in establishing the diagnosis of myocardial infarction. LAD remains elevated longer than SGO-T in less than 50 per cent of the cases. Abnormal serum glutamic pyruvate transaminase (SGP-T) activity is also noted in 50 per cent of the cases, but no consistent relationship of SGP-T to SGO-T has been noted. When clinical shock complicates a myocardial infarction (regardless of its size), elevations of the SGP-T level invariably occur. Occasionally, the LAD elevation appears earlier than SGO-T and persists longer. SGP-T is low in relation to SGO-T when no hepatic dysfunction is present and relatively high when the reverse occurs. More recently, Wroblewski has found that of the five fractions of LAD, rises in LAD_4 and, especially, LAD_5 are almost specific for myocardial infarction.

Determinations of SGO-T, LAD, and SGP-T aid in diagnosis of minimal myocardial infarcts or those complicated by hepatic dysfunction. Enzyme levels do not correlate well with white-cell count, temperature, or erythrocyte sedimentation rate. Angina pectoris, severe coronary insufficiency, or myocardial ischemia do not affect dehydrogenase activity of the serum. Elevation of all enzyme levels is roughly proportional to the extent of necrosis.

Aldolase. Another enzyme that becomes elevated in the serum following acute myocardial infarction is aldolase. Aldolase levels rise to a peak twenty-four hours after infarction and return to normal during the next four days. Serum aldolase levels are normal in patients with coronary insufficiency without myocardial infarction.

Lipid determinations. The tests which explore abnormal lipid patterns in coronary artery disease fall into two categories: (1) lipid tests obtained in the fasting state, and (2) lipid tolerance tests. Unfortunately, there is still much controversy regarding the value of these tests for the prediction or diagnosis of coronary artery disease. According to a recent large-scale study reported by the Committee on Lipoproteins and Atherosclerosis of the National Advisory Heart Council, the value of the lipoprotein and cholesterol measurements as effective predictors of coronary artery disease is not yet established. Total blood cholesterol remains the simplest and cheapest blood test. Even the concept of normal cholesterol levels remains controversial and varies in different areas; in this country, it varies between 150 to 275 mg per 100 ml, depending in part upon the method employed. Serial determinations of the cholesterol are important, since its level is usually constant in normal individuals but inconstant and widely fluctuating in patients with coronary artery sclerosis.

Wherever possible, the determination of the *plasma-cholesterol-phospholipid ratio* appears advisable, since careful investigations have revealed that this ratio has greater significance than the determination of the total cholesterol level alone. The ratio has been found to be significantly higher in patients with coronary artery sclerosis and myocardial infarction than in normal individuals.

The determination of the *blood triglyceride level* shows a closer correlation with the presence of coronary artery sclerosis than does the total cholesterol.

A determination of *beta-lipoproteins* appears to be particularly valuable in ascertaining the presence of coronary atherosclerosis. These proteins carry the lipids of presumably atherogenic nature. Increased amounts of lipoproteins in patients with coronary artery disease can be determined by the ultracentrifuge method. The significant atherogenetic fraction occurs mainly in the range of Sf 12 to 200. Although claims have been made that the elevation of these lipoproteins may provide a clue to the genesis and presence of coronary artery sclerosis, they have not been generally confirmed. A simpler method of lipoprotein determination employing paper electrophoresis is available but does not offer complete reliability.

Fat tolerance tests have been employed recently to determine any possible deviation in handling regested fat in patients with coronary artery sclerosis.

From a practical viewpoint, when hyperlipemia is induced in patients with the anginal syndrome, some will develop typical attacks of angina. These episodes occur near the peak of the postprandial lipemic curve, usually several hours after the test meal. Definite but transient changes in the electrocardiograms and marked ballistocardiographic changes tend to appear in these patients. This has provided the basis for the repeated use of sublingual heparin as a fat-clearing substance. Unfortunately, consistently good results have not been obtainable.

Determination of radioiodine uptake by an area of infarcted myocardium has shown concentrations of I^{131} about 50 per cent higher than in the intact myocardium after the precordium was explored at half-hour intervals with a scintillation counter.

Trace metal determinations have recently been found to give a fairly accurate measure of the extent of damage to the myocardium following an infarction, and may prove to be less likely to yield false positive results since the measure is fairly specific for myocardial damage. Thus, *serum manganese* (normally up to 19 mcg) may be found elevated up to 35 mcg per milliliter. Following pulmonary infarction, *serum aluminum* values rise. Thus, a differentiation, which is sometimes difficult, may be resolved by trace metal determinations.

TREATMENT

Medical Treatment

Angina pectoris and coronary insufficiency. Chest pain due to angina pectoris or coronary insufficiency must be treated with due consideration for all somatic and psychic factors. Because of the great variability in the natural course of coronary artery disease and the overlapping of multiple psychosomatic factors, treatment must be tailored to fit the individual needs of each patient. Promising claims are constantly made for many new drugs and various combinations of drugs. These appear almost daily and plague the physician as well as the patient. Unfortunately, there are very few effective drugs other than the nitrites.

The therapeutic effect of almost any antianginal agent is proportional to that of the personality of the physician and the suggestibility of the patient. Thus, physician-patient rapport is the most ancient yet the most potent factor in the management of such patients at our present state of knowledge. In evaluating any new antianginal agent, proper assay must include a study of its effectiveness during the postrapport period, preferably by means of double-blind studies or objective data.

Therapy for the relief of an acute anginal seizure is predicated upon the use of promptly acting coronary dilators to relieve the myocardial ischemia. *Nitroglycerin* (hypodermic tablets) taken sublingually remains the most effective and dependable drug, acting directly on the musculature of the vessels irrespective of their autonomic innervation. Sublingual administration bypasses the portal circulation and affords rapid action. Nitroglycerin relieves the chest pain promptly, particularly when produced by exertion. Most decubital or nocturnal attacks also respond to this drug. At times, the dosage requires adjustment. When a severe throbbing headache ensues, dosage may have to be reduced. Failure to respond to nitroglycerin suggests that the tablet may be deteriorated and has not dissolved promptly. Unless compensated for by reflex mechanisms, nitroglycerin induces a number of changes which counteract or outweigh the beneficial effects derived from direct coronary vasodilatation. Thus, venous pooling in the lower extremities with diminished venous return to the heart, tachycardia, and fall in blood pressure are other actions of the drug which would exclude its use in acute myocardial infarction. It may also be responsible for the occasional aggravation of angina encountered after the use of nitroglycerin. Nitroglycerin is also useful for the immediate prevention of anginal attacks and may be employed prior to physical or emotion stress (such as during sexual intercourse) that is prone to produce an anginal attack. The liberal use of nitroglycerin as a prophylactic medication may be extremely helpful in patients with severe angina.

Ever since the efficacy of nitroglycerin was first recognized, much research has centered about the discovery of a similar preparation with more prolonged action. This has led to the use (generally followed by discard) of various nitrate compounds.

Of the older vasodilators, *octyl nitrite* is a drug administered by inhalation and is more agreeable than *amyl nitrite*. Of the newer types, *pentaerythritol tetranitrate* (Peritrate) and *triethanolamine trinitrate* (Metamine) have found considerable acceptance. Many of these drugs have been coated to permit slow and uniform disintegration during the day. Others have been combined with tranquilizers and sedatives in order to control psychogenic overlay. Two promising nitrate compounds are Cardilate and Isordil. The first is a sublingual preparation of *erythrol tetranitrate,* which has been shown to cause considerable improvement of angina pectoris. The second is an *isosorbide dinitrate* preparation and appears equally effective in oral and sublingual form.

Although *theophylline* preparations have vasodilating effects, their popularity has declined, mainly because of the necessity for large doses, gastrointestinal intolerance, and unreliability or variability of response. *Papaverine* in large doses (3 to 8 grains) relieves angina and improves exercise tolerance, as judged by exercise electrocardiographic tests. Other drugs reputedly effective in some cases of angina pectoris are the monoamine oxidase inhibitors (e.g., *iproniazid* [Marsilid], *isocarboxazid* [Marplan], and *pivalylbenzhydrazine* [Tersavid].) These "psychic energizers" frequently do not affect the anginal syndrome except by mood change. Their antianginal efficacy appears to run parallel to their toxic properties, which may include dryness of mouth, flatulence, constipation, difficulty in starting micturition in males, and psychic stimulation to the point of mania. The constant search for a drug with reliable and predictable effect upon angina has led to several unique approaches. Thus, *ethylenediamine tetraacetic acid* (EDTA) has been injected to chelate-bound calcium in order to permit disintegration of the atheromatous matrix. *Tetrahydroxethyl ethylenediamine tetranitrate* (THEN) seems to have been successful in experimental trials.

The failure of *ethyl alcohol* to influence the electrocardiographic response to exercise suggests that this "popular agent" is without effective coronary vasodilation but may relieve anginal pain through its sedative effect. Other vasodilating drugs, such as *nicotinyl alcohol* (Roniacol), *tolazoline* (Priscoline), *khellin,* and *dioxyline phosphate* (Paveril), have been found to be relatively ineffectual or to demonstrate undesirable side effects.

A recent method employed for intractable anginal seizures consists of inserting a needle 15 to 18 cm long into the jugular fossa downward behind the sternum until aortic pulsations are felt. From 60 to 80 ml of 0.5 per cent *procaine* are then injected into the anterior mediastinum. Presumably, the anesthesia of the para-aortic and cardiac plexuses paralyzes pain-conducting fibers and has a dilating effect upon the coronary arteries. *Reserpine* may be useful in patients with angina pectoris who are apprehensive and have a labile hypertension or exhibit a tendency to tachycardias. Sedatives (e.g., *barbiturates*) and tranquilizers (e.g., *meprobamate*) may be effective in those who exhibit a strong psychogenic overlay.

Nocturnal angina may respond to the parenteral injection of a mercurial diuretic or the administration of the oral diuretics (e.g., *acetazoleamide, chlorothiazide, hydrochlorothiazide,* and related compounds). Simple elevation of the bed may alone prevent a distressing attack. *Aminophylline,* administered by slow intravenous injection in the late afternoon or by suppository or rectal instillation, has been helpful occasionally. Nightmares which may precipitate nocturnal attacks require firm reassurance and sedation.

The treatment of the status anginosus or refractory angina is extremely difficult. Severe anxiety due to a fear of death is the underlying mechanism in most instances. Adequate explanation as to healing processes and encouragement regarding the generally favorable outlook of this disease may be more helpful in reducing the frequency and severity of chest pain than many medications. The individual must be taught to avoid or minimize nervous tension and emotional fatigue. The physician must be careful in action and speech to avoid creating disability and fears in the victim of coronary heart disease (iatrogenic heart disease). At times, individual or group psychotherapy may become necessary.

In intractable instances (probably not more than 5 per cent of cases), the induction of a hypometabolic state by *antithyroid drugs* or *radioactive iodine* is indicated. This approach has largely supplanted the risks of surgical thyroidectomy introduced in 1933 for the alleviation of intractable angina or congestive heart failure. It reduces systemic circulatory requirements and exerts a palliative effect. The greatest benefits following treatment with I^{131} occur when the disease has been relatively stationary or only slightly progressive over a period of one year or more.

The indications may be summarized as follows:

1. Severe intractable angina.

2. Angina which fails to respond to conventional medical therapy such as weight reduction, limitation of activity, vasodilators, sedation, etc.

3. Symptoms which have persisted and which indicate that significant spontaneous remission is unlikely.

4. Symptoms which are relatively stable or very slowly progressive, but cause considerable disability.

5. Patients who are expected to live long enough to develop the necessary state of hypothyroidism.

Unfortunately, the basic atherosclerotic process in the coronary arteries progresses until the coronary flow again becomes inadequate.

Patients with radioactive iodine uptakes of about 30 per cent should receive an initial dose no larger than 20 mc. Higher dosage is used in patients with greater uptakes or with angina decubitus. Three doses are given at weekly intervals. Patients with angina pectoris decubitus must restrict activities for the first three weeks, since temporary hypermetabolism may be noted in the second or third week of therapy. Generally, improvement is noted two to six months after initiation of therapy. Myxedema heart disease, which occurs with spontaneous myxedema and which may precipitate congestive failure or angina, does not occur in hypothyroidism induced by radioactive iodine. Disturbing symptoms due to the ensuing hypothyroidism may be treated with small doses of desiccated thyroid.

Other long-term measures to reduce the frequency of anginal episodes include regimens which attempt to influence the cholesterol metabolism and the clotting mechanism (long-term prophylactic anticoagulant drug therapy). These are discussed in detail on pages 300–302.

A large study based on 275 patients treated with anticoagulants for about two and one-half years showed that the mortality rate was about 5 per cent during the first year, 6.8 per cent during the second year, and 5.4 per cent during the third year. In contrast, mortality among patients not treated with anticoagulants was about 15 per cent during the first year, and 8 or 9 per cent thereafter. During the same period, effort tolerance had improved in 37 per cent of patients, and lesser improvement was noted in 12.5 per cent. Difficulties which attend anticoagulant treatment in the ambulatory patient make the routine employment of such a regimen in simple angina pectoris inadvisable at this time. It has found more universal acceptance following attacks of acute protracted coronary insufficiency or coronary thrombosis.

Coronary occlusion. Basically this involves the control of chest pain, accompanying symptoms, and the treatment of complications. Since pain and apprehension may be severe enough to precipitate shock, they must be relieved as soon as possible. However, because of differences in pain tolerance, the intensity of the pain which ushers in the attack is not an accurate gauge of the actual severity of the attack. Not infrequently, coronary occlusion heralded by very severe pain may run a remarkably smooth course after the pain has eased. Reduction of the anxiety factor and fear of death is also of prime importance. *Morphine* is the preferred agent for these purposes, because of its ability to induce euphoria. The initial dose can be given intravenously when a prompt effect is desirable. Administration should be slow and is discontinued as soon as the pain is relieved. The dosage required ordinarily is about 30 mg (½ grain), but as much as 60 mg (1 grain) may be required. *Meperidine* (Demerol) is of value only in the milder pain episodes, generally after the first or second day; the anticholinergic effects of the drug may lead to suppression of the bladder reflex in older patients, and it is poorly tolerated by the central nervous system. Occasionally, *methadone* causes less nausea and vomiting than morphine. *Atropine* may be combined with morphine in order to overcome side effects; in the dosage used for this purpose, it rarely increases the heart rate. Persisting pain may be entirely relieved or reduced by *oxygen* therapy. Psychologic support is highly beneficial in the form of firm reassurance and constant encouragement.

Nitroglycerin (which is the most useful agent for angina pectoris) is distinctly contraindicated, because the additional induced fall in blood pressure is obviously detrimental. The intravenous use of 0.2 per cent *procaine hydrochloride* by slow infusion has been employed as an analgesic and anti-arrhythmic agent, but the occasional hypotension encountered makes its use somewhat hazardous. New approaches are constantly being investigated. Massive doses of *hyaluronidase* (100,000 units intravenously every four to six hours for three days) appear to improve the prognosis in acute myocardial infarction by decreasing the intramyocardial edema which tends to produce mechanical compression of the myocardial cells and the small collateral channels.

As regards other modalities of treatment, bed rest and diet, while not directly concerned with the relief of pain, are of importance in helping to reduce cardiac work and thereby lessening demands upon the coronary blood flow. It has also been shown more recently that patients with acute coronary thrombosis in the absence of shock often get along better when they are allowed to sit up in a chair after the first day than when they are kept in bed. However, while cardiac work and dyspnea are less in the sitting position than in the recumbent position, dependency of legs may favor venous thrombosis, cerebral ischemia may occur following marked hypotension, and movement between chair and bed may produce an added strain.

Nausea and vomiting may be closely associated with severe pain during the acute phase of myocardial infarction. Occasionally, small oral doses of *chlorpromazine* (Thorazine) or a gastric sedative may be necessary. However, the parenteral use of chlorpromazine is hazardous because of the possibility of orthostatic hypotension or possible hepatitis. Bowel movements may be facilitated with bulk and softening agents. The diet should be bland and salt poor, with decreased caloric intake for the obese patient.

The clinical picture of dynamic ileus may appear on rare occasions. This is probably of reflex origin but may require specific measures, since it may persist even after disappearance of the chest pain. It may be present without any other complications or sequelae of myocardial infarction. Mesenteric embolism must also be considered as a cause of ileus, especially during the second week, when mural thrombi are most apt to embolize.

Other forms of treatment. 1. The use of anticoagulants. Although anticoagulant therapy represents an important advance in the treatment of acute myocardial infarction, considerable disagreement has arisen as to whether the risk of thromboembolism in patients with an uncomplicated first attack is sufficiently great to justify the hazards inherent in the use of anticoagulant drugs. However, anticoagulants may be employed in the presence of the following signs of unfavorable prognostic import: previous infarction or embolism, congestive failure, intractable pain, severe shock, gallop rhythm, significant cardiac enlargement, arrhythmias, and various other conditions predisposing to thromboembolism. To these may be added some secondary considerations such as age, obesity, varicosities, and venous thrombosis and concomitant diseases. Since it is usually difficult to determine with certainty the prognosis of an acute myocardial infarction during the first twenty-four or forty-eight hours ("good risk" vs. "bad risk"), the above may serve as the general indications for its use. *Heparin* is usually given parenterally during the first thirty-six to forty-eight hours, while the slower-acting coumarin derivatives are reaching therapeutic levels. Prothrombin time determinations are necessary to maintain effective therapeutic levels (two and one-half times the control value, or usually around thirty seconds). Heparin may be given by continuous or intermittent venous administration, but a simpler method is to give the average patient 200 mg of the repository intramuscular form (Depo-heparin) every twelve hours for three or four doses. Recently, H. Engelberg has advised the constant intravenous or intermittent subcutaneous use of heparin as the sole anticoagulant for three weeks. The cost and inconvenience of administration are great objections.

The starting dose of *bishydroxycoumarin* (Dicumarol) is usually 300 mg, and 200 mg are given the second day. Subsequent doses depend upon the daily prothrombin times. Serious difficulties are seldom encountered with these conservative doses. In recent years, *warfarin sodium* (Coumadin) has tended to replace bishydroxycoumarin because of greater predictability of response. The initial dose is usually 50 to 75 mg. It has been found best to skip the drug the second day and to then alter the dose only at three-day intervals and in small degrees.

Other drugs employed in the prevention of clotting include *ethyl biscoumacetate* (Tromexan), *phenindione* (Danilone, Hedulin), *acenocoumarol* (Sintrom), *diphenadione* (Dipaxin), and *Marcoumar*. Various claims are laid to potency of their hypoprothrombinemic effects, decreased toxicity, speed of action, decreased dosage, and freedom from fluctuation of prothrombin levels.

Overdosage (dangerous elevation of prothrombin times and gross or microscopic evidences of bleeding) is treated by judicious reduction or discontinuation of the drug. Bleeding of gingiva or nasal mucosa is rarely serious, but hemorrhagic complications of the kidney, gastrointestinal tract, pericardium, and brain are of increasing danger in the order mentioned. Tamponade should always be suspected in the presence of falling blood pressure, distended cervical veins due to rising venous pressure, distant heart tones, and rapidly increasing anemia. *Vitamin K_1 oxide* (Mephyton) is a most effective antidote when given slowly and intravenously in a dose of 50 to 150 mg. Vitamin K_1 is also employed orally in doses of 1 to 20 mg.

Transfusion of fresh whole blood for anticoagulant effect alone is seldom necessary. Antiheparin measures include the injection of *protamine sulfate, toluidine blue,* or *fresh whole blood.* However, these are seldom necessary, since the transitory heparin action recedes promptly following its withdrawal.

Treatment with anticoagulants is usually continued for at least four weeks. Thereafter, a decision must be made as to the advisability of long-term treatment with anticoagulants. Experiences with the long-term administration in ambulatory patients has been favorably reported by many investigators. However, most reports suffer from certain inadequacies inherent in patient selection and matching of control groups. Although most coronary occlusions are caused by thrombus formation, it has been estimated that anywhere from 15 per cent to as many as 60 per cent of the cases occlude because of progressive sclerotic narrowing alone or because of other coronary disease processes. Subintimal hemorrhages also play a variable role. Furthermore, considerable basic data are accumulating to show that the coumarin derivatives usually employed are not true antithrombotic agents as compared with heparin. Hence, the problem of routine long-term anticoagulant therapy in the prevention of recurrent coronary thrombosis remains unresolved at this time. However, while data regarding long-term therapy are difficult to evaluate because of many variables, much evidence is accumulating that suggests that patients who remain on long-term anticoagulant therapy after their first or subsequent myocardial infarctions have a better prognosis in terms of future coronary occlusions or thromboembolic complications. Recent well-carried-out studies suggest, however, that this favorable effect is present only during the first three to six months after acute infarction.

Among the contraindications for the use of the anticoagulants are hemorrhagic diseases, bleeding peptic ulcer or other bleeding lesions, severe liver disease, jaundice, cancer, vitamin C or K deficiency, renal insufficiency, immediate postoperative conditions in which there are wide areas of open tissues (such as prostatectomy and neurosurgery), and complicating pericarditis of the so-called "postinfarction syndrome." Recent reports concerning adaptive enzyme mechanisms have led to renewed interest in the influence of some drugs on others. Weiner and Dayton have shown that barbiturates markedly inhibit the prothrombin response to coumarin medication.

2. *Fibrinolytic agents (for dissolution of fresh thrombi).* An entirely new approach to the problem of vascular thrombosis is based upon the use of several unrelated substances which are now emerging from the experi-

mental stage. These compounds have the ability to promote the dissolution of the fibrin framework which is necessary for the support of a thrombus. They must be employed as early as possible (up to six hours) and before the thrombus becomes "fixed" and resists lytic action. Future developments in this area may resolve the problem of thromboembolism, while the basic underlying problem of the atheromatous process continues to await solution. Enzymatic agents, such as *streptokinase* (SK), have proven unsuitable for therapy thus far, because allergic and inhibitory phenomena are likely to be enhanced by their administration. Streptokinase has also been used in combination with *streptodornase* (Varidase). As regards *trypsin* (Tryptar, Enzar), this thrombolytic agent can lyse fibrin directly and also acts as an activator of profibrinolysin. It has been employed previously as an anti-inflammatory agent in the treatment of thrombophlebitis. Unfortunately, it has a potent action against other protein components of plasma besides those necessary for blood coagulation and produces marked febrile responses. More recently, experimental studies have failed to demonstrate proteolytic dissolution of preformed coronary artery thrombi regardless of the amount injected.

Fibrinolysin (Actase, Plasmin) has been investigated as to its clinical applicability as a thrombolytic agent, since it has become possible to obtain it directly from both human and bovine plasma. Unlike trypsin, intravenous fibrinolysin does not seriously affect other plasma proteins but chooses fibrin as its major target of enzymatic activity. Both substances also exert an anti-inflammatory effect. Minor toxic reactions may appear due to the release of protein fractions when fibrinolysin acts upon fibrin. Whatever its exact nature, the danger of pyrogenicity presently limits its clinical application. Chills, hypotension, digestive disturbances, and skin rash may also occur. However, purification has now reduced such reactions to a minimum. It must be employed within the first few hours for maximum efficiency except in the case of thrombophlebitis where it has proven effective even following the first week or two. Fibrinolysin has similarly been employed with streptokinase. Its practical use at present is limited to acute thrombophlebitis, acute pulmonary embolism, and acute peripheral arterial thrombosis. Equivocal results in coronary thrombosis have been reported thus far. A more direct approach has recently proved more successful. This consists of introducing the tip of a catheter at the ostium of the affected coronary artery while the heart itself monitors the delivery of the drug during the diastolic phase. It has also been used in conjunction with the anticoagulants, especially heparin, during the early phase of the thrombotic obstruction.

Even a mold has been suspected of harboring an effective thrombolytic substance. Purified bacterial pyrogens (lipopolysaccharides) have recently been shown to produce some favorable results. The direct attack on the thrombotic element in coronary occlusion has stimulated a fresh and encouraging approach to a major problem in therapeutics. It is hoped that an effective and inexpensive agent will soon be forthcoming, and one which will also be beneficial in coronary, cerebral, or pulmonary thrombosis in addition to peripheral vascular thrombosis.

3. *Anticholesterol regimen* (*to reduce progress of atheromatous degeneration*). While the exact relationship between hypercholesteremia, atherosclerosis, and coronary heart disease still remains to be determined, evidence is steadily accumulating on the desirability of reducing cholesterol levels in those patients where they are elevated. This has added significance in the presence of diabetes mellitus, hypothyroidism, gout, nephrosis, hypertension, and primary familial hypercholesteremia. Interest has been focused principally upon cholesterol and the fatty acids. Recent investigations have demonstrated that the blood cholesterol value as a predictor of atherosclerotic events in diabetic patients is at least as good as lipoprotein fractionation, especially since the complexity and expense of the ultracentrifuge apparatus make it impractical for ordinary clinical use. Although there has been criticism regarding the value of numerous indirect correlative studies of lipid abnormalities and coronary artery disease, there has been increasing interest in the clinical application of various methods of reducing the elevated blood cholesterol and other lipids. These methods generally consist of dietary regimen (low fat, low cholesterol) alone or in combination with administration of several types of anticholesterol agents. Although plant sterols (sitosterol) prevent the intestinal absorption of ingested cholesterol, their administration has fallen into disrepute for a number of reasons. Triparanol is an efficient inhibitor of cholesterol biosynthesis in doses of 250 mg per day. The average reduction in blood cholesterol is 43 mg per 100 ml. It has been shown to reduce the miscible cholesterol pool as well as the number of anginal seizures. *Benzmalecene* (750 mg daily) has also been shown to exhibit interference with the conversion of acetate and mevalonic acid cholesterol. Unfortunately, it produces marked gastrointestinal complaints.

Highly unsaturated fatty acids, such as *linoleic acid, safflower oil, corn oil,* and other vegetable and fish oils, have been found to reduce the blood cholesterol and triglyceride levels significantly. The active principle appears to be beta-sitosterol, since its administration results in highly significant reductions in serum cholesterol and beta-lipoprotein lipid levels, with a lesser reduction in total lipid and a slight rise in beta-lipoprotein lipid. Unfortunately, the results with this group of anticholesterol agents have been variable and limited by disagreeable side effects in addition to the high caloric value of these substances. The most useful regimen is one consisting of adequate polyunsaturated fatty acids, low-saturated fatty acids, and a total caloric value able to achieve reduction to or maintenance of ideal weight.

It has also been demonstrated that the serum cholesterol can be reduced experimentally and clinically in normal and hypercholesteremic subjects following the ingestion of *nicotinic acid*, although the mechanism is not clearly understood. Three to 10 gm are employed daily. The ratio of fractions of beta-lipoprotein cholesterol to alpha-1-lipoprotein cholesterol is also reduced by therapy with nicotinic acid. Phospholipids remain essentially unchanged, resulting in lowering of the cholesterol-phospholipid ratio. Unfortunately, the nicotinic acid effect does not occur with regularity. Side effects consist mainly of disturbed glucose tolerance, marked unpleasant flushing of head and neck, which may disappear as the dosage is further increased, and increased serum uric acid levels.

A third approach to the treatment of hypercholesteremia is based upon the experimental observation that the turbidity of plasma caused by alimentary lipemia disappears completely after injection of *heparin* and is independent of any anticoagulant effect. This lipid-clearing phenomenon appears to be mediated through an alteration in the physical state of the blood lipids (chylomicrons) rather than by any significant change in total lipid concentration. Thus, plasma ultracentrifuge studies have shown that there is a marked shift in the distribution of lipoproteins in human plasma with a rapid conversion of lipoproteins of low density to those of higher density. The lipoproteins most affected by heparin are also those most likely to be found in high concentration in atherosclerosis, since these low-density lipoproteins are believed to contain abnormally large proportions of cholesterol. Since heparin activity is destroyed in the stomach, it has been employed buccally (with poor absorption) and intramuscularly. However, valid evidence is presently lacking to support the view that even parenteral heparin exerts a significant effect in preventing, reducing, or delaying atherosclerotic changes or in reducing the incidence of anginal seizures.

Thyroid analogs and *estrogens* have also been employed to lower hypercholesteremic levels. However, the former probably increase myocardial metabolism even in the absence of any effect on basal metabolic rate; the latter induce feminization. More recently, *androsterone* (a normal hormonal constituent in both sexes) has been shown to play a key role in lowering blood cholesterol and appears to act in conjunction with thyroid secretion. Although thyroidectomy has been abandoned in cases of intractable anginal pain, hypothyroidism may now be induced in appropriate cases of intractable angina as well as intractable congestive failure by the use of radioiodine or thiouracil compounds. Newer methods include the experimental use of chelating agents (such as EDTA) intravenously in an effort to remove calcium ions in the coronary atheroma.

In summary, it is fair to state that the present knowledge of the relationship between cardiovascular disease and dietary fat is far from conclusive. Experimental arteriosclerosis is not the counterpart of human arteriosclerosis—in fact, myocardial infarction is rare in experimental animals; population studies suggesting a correlation between high plasma cholesterol and arteriosclerosis do not apply to individuals; a diet rich in saturated fatty acids has been linked with cardiovascular disease—yet it has been shown that dietary cholesterol has only minor influence on human plasma cholesterol, and that alimentary lipemia has no clear-cut influence on blood clotting and thrombus formation. A satisfactory solution to the multifaceted and universal problem of cardiovascular disease awaits further elucidation before any specific or truly effective therapy will be forthcoming.

Treatment of complications. In addition to the relief of pain, the therapy of myocardial infarction actually consists of the treatment of its complications. Three major complications are shock, cardiac failure, and cardiac arrhythmias. They must be recognized promptly and treated intensively. Other early complications of significance are myocardial rupture with tamponade, postinfarction syndrome, localized pulmonary edema, and, rarely, pneumonia. Among the later complications are ventricular aneurysm, shoulder-hand syndrome, psychoneurosis, and, rarely, subacute bacterial infections.

1. Shock. This is the most serious complication following myocardial infarction, since the mortality rate ranges between 75 to 90 per cent. Therefore, combating this dire complication assumes prime importance. Plasma, whole blood, and plasma extenders were formerly the most effective measures used. Intra-arterial transfusions have also fallen into disrepute. The most effective agents are the pressor drugs, which have reduced the mortality rate by about 50 per cent.

The commonly employed pressor agents are *hydroxyamphetamine hydrobromide* (Paredrine), *phenylpropanolamine hydrochloride* (Propadrine), *phenylephrine hydrochloride* (Neo-Synephrine), and *mephentermine sulfate* (Wyamine). In addition to their vasopressor effect, the latter two drugs have an inotropic myocardial action (affecting the force of muscular contractions). They are administered by intramuscular or intravenous injection in doses of 5 to 25 mg, although mephentermine has been safely used in doses up to 50 mg. The duration of the pressor response to these drugs rarely exceeds a half-hour, and they must be given repeatedly as indicated.

Metaraminol (Pressonex, Aramine) possesses the great advantage of raising the blood pressure by inotropic effect on both heart muscle and increase of peripheral vascular resistance. It may be administered intravenously as a drip infusion in a dose of 300 to 1000 mg per liter of 5 per cent glucose or by the parenteral (subcutaneous or intramuscular) injection of 5 to 25 mg. Excessive rises which are often observed following the use of other pressor agents are not observed with this drug. Metaraminol generally retains its pressor effect for thirty to 120 minutes. This maintenance effect is quite stable. Since blood pressure drops gradually over a ten- to fifteen-minute period when metaraminol is stopped, accidental interruption of therapy does not precipitate severe hypotension. When treatment is discontinued, blood pressure readjusts within several hours after the initial fall. Thrombophlebitis and tissue slough are not observed.

L-norepinephrine or *levarterenol* (Levophed) has proved to be the most potent, prompt, and effective vasopressor for the treatment of severe hypotensive states and shock following acute myocardial infarction. Intravenous infusion may also be introduced into the inferior vena cava via the femoral vein when long periods of infusion are indicated. The drug is given in a concentration of 4 mg per liter of 5 per cent glucose solution but is inactivated if given in blood or plasma. If this concentration is ineffective, the amount may be increased to 8 mg or more. This may also be required when the presence of cardiac failure necessitates fluid restriction.

During therapy, the patient must be constantly monitored, and quarter- to half-hourly records of flow rate, drug concentration, blood pressure, pulse, and respiration must be maintained. The cessation of the infusion is attempted only after gradual decrease of dosage; and a glucose solution drip is maintained for at least one hour after the drug is stopped, since the reappearance of severe hypotension may quickly result in intractable shock if the flow cannot be rapidly started. Levarterenol has several undesirable effects: (1) It may cause slough of skin and deeper tissue following accidental extravasation of fluid; this may be counteracted by prompt multiple subcutaneous injections of 10 to 20 mg of *tolazoline hydrochloride* (Priscoline) or of *phentolamine hydrochloride* (Regitine), in 20 ml of saline solution. (2) The transitory action of levarterenol may result in prompt hypotension if the infusion flow ceases abruptly.

The not infrequent coexistence of myocardial failure and shock requires the administration of digitalis glycosides in addition to a vasopressor drug for the successful abolition of shock.

2. Cardiac failure. The use of *digitalis* is indicated for heart failure, but dosage must be carefully adjusted, since the myocardium tends to be hypersensitive during the acute phase of myocardial infarction. At times, the constrictive sensation in the chest represents an equivalent of dyspnea and orthopnea due to left ventricular failure, and treatment of the latter with mercurials and digitalis may promptly alleviate this discomfort. Since left ventricular failure is often partly responsible for severe hypotension or shock, the treatment with digitalis may suffice to combat shock or may prove an effective addition to vasopressor therapy. The frequent association of thromboembolic episodes with congestive heart failure is another indication for the use of anticoagulants.

Not uncommonly, coronary occlusion may have a dramatic onset as an attack of acute pulmonary edema. The treatment of this condition is the same regardless of the etiologic factor involved. *Morphine* given intravenously or intramuscularly is usually efficacious, but intravenous *aminophylline* or a parenteral digitalis preparation (strophanthin, cedilanid, or digoxin) may be added. Aminophylline must be diluted to 10 ml and administered very slowly in a dosage of 0.5 gm. The initial dose of strophanthin K is 0.25 mg. Injection of 0.1 mg may be repeated every hour until 1 mg has been given in twenty-four hours. Digitalis maintenance should be carefully observed. Oxygen under positive pressure, rotating tourniquets or phlebotomy of 500 ml (in the absence of shock), and an intravenous mercurial diuretic may be helpful. The inhalation of 70 per cent alcohol or 2-ethyl hexanol vapor, with or without intermittent positive pressure breathing, has been found to be effective, since it lowers the surface tension of the frothy transudate. The lungs can actually withstand the presence of a relatively large amount of fluid providing it does not froth because of labored and rapid respirations.

3. Cardiac arrhythmias. Atrial, nodal, and ventricular tachycardias are of serious import, since rapid rates are frequently responsible for the aggravation of myocardial ischemia and persistent chest pain because of the fact that they result in a fall in blood pressure with decreased cardiac output and deficient coronary blood flow. Compensatory cardiac and extracardiac mechanisms which tend to maintain the coronary circulation during tachycardias may fail eventually in extremely rapid tachycardias and where hypotension supervenes. Persistent sinus tachycardia following an acute infarction may also be deleterious.

Prevention of paroxysmal arrhythmias by the routine use of *quinidine* or *procainamide* (Pronestyl) is suggested when premature beats appear, but its practice varies widely, since many clinicians consider the arrhythmias to be of transient nature in most instances of acute myocardial infarction. If they persist or if an element of shock or heart failure is present, such treatment is indicated. Atrial or nodal tachycardias often respond to simple pressure on the carotid sinus or eyeball; if this does not help, 0.5 mg of *phenylephrine* (Neo-Synephrine), 5 to 10 mg of *metaraminol* (Aramine), or 2.5 to 5 mg of *methoxamine* (Vasoxyl) may be administered intravenously, particularly if the blood pressure is low. If this is not effective, digitalis is given parenterally or orally. If necessary, quinidine or procainamide may be given orally or intramuscularly.

Ventricular tachycardia should be treated promptly with either quinidine or procainamide. If these drugs are ineffective by the oral or intramuscular routes, procainamide should be given intravenously, well diluted and slowly. Since intravenous procainamide is apt to cause a considerable drop in blood pressure, *levarterenol* (Levophed) may be administered simultaneously in order to maintain the blood pressure. Of all the conduction disturbances, the most important is complete atrioventricular block. The danger of complete block lies in the development of Adams-Stokes seizures which may eventuate in asystole or ventricular fibrillation, or both. Loss of consciousness at the onset of myocardial infarction which produces the heart block may be responsible for the lack of precordial pain. Treatment includes *isoproterenol* (Isuprel) given by various routes, *epinephrine*, and application of an electrical cardiac pacemaker. Cardiac massage may have to be employed in the presence of cardiac arrest or ventricular fibrillation. The former can be controlled with a substitute pacemaker; the latter demands immediate application of an electrical defibrillator to the precordium or directly to the heart surface.

Surgical Treatment

In the search for a more direct method to treat severe coronary disease, various surgical procedures have been devised. Two general approaches are employed for its relief. The first method utilizes neurosurgery, which relieves intractable angina but has no direct effect upon the myocardial ischemia or upon the course of the disease. The second approach is by revascularization procedures, which may improve myocardial ischemia by furnishing additional blood supply.

The neurosurgical approach is made upon the vasomotor nerves in an effort to prevent spasm of the coronary arteries; this method is of dubious value. Another point of attack has been made upon the motor accelerator nerves in order to slow the heart and to improve its limited capacity for work; unfortunately, this results in a slowing of the heart rate only during rest. The third and most logical point of attack is by interruption of the pain pathways. This is accomplished by blocking the upper four or five thoracic sympathetic ganglia with alcohol injections, by surgical removal of these same ganglia, or by posterior rhizotomy. Thoracic ganglionectomy carries a mortality of 14 per cent. It gives partial relief of pain in 50 per cent and complete relief of pain in only 30 per cent. Seventeen per cent of the patients are unimproved, and there is a late recurrence of pain in 25 per cent. Unfortunately, anginal seizures may subsequently originate in other areas, and myocardial infarction tends to occur rather frequently after the procedure. Other complications include traumatic neuritis, Horner's syndrome, nasal congestion, and changes in peripheral vascular tone. Posterior rhizotomy enables a bilateral denervation to be done in one stage, but it is a formidable procedure. This operation gives excellent relief of chest and arm pains but minimal relief of neck and jaw pains. Paravertebral alcohol injections require an accurate knowledge of neuroanatomy and technical skill in order to avoid tissue destruction or serious complications. It gives partial and complete relief in 64 per cent, with enduring good results in only 23 per cent. Recurrence of the pain within three to six months occurs in 35 per cent, and 28 per cent of the cases are entirely unrelieved.

The neurosurgical procedures are most useful when the more formidable revascularization procedures cannot be tolerated. The choice of the proper surgical procedure depends on the relative competence of the heart. Those patients with a fair degree of cardiac reserve may undergo laminectomy or root section with reasonable safety. Thoracic ganglionectomy is preferable for questionable risks, especially if anginal pain is unilateral. For the poorest-risk cases (those who have had repeated or recent attacks of myocardial infarction with large hearts and great reduction in cardiac reserve), interruption of the nerves by paravertebral alcohol block may be the only possible surgical measure.

Surgical revascularization of the myocardium depends upon three major approaches: (1) the use of extracardiac tissues (omentum, pectoral muscle, lung, etc.) or vascular anastomoses (grafts), (2) the stimulation and development of the residual myocardial circulation, and (3) endarterectomy. The extracardiac tissues must have or be capable of producing a satisfactory collateral blood supply, while the vascular grafts bring blood directly to the coronary system. A certain degree of stimulation of the myocardial circulation occurs in all of the operations upon the heart as a result of the irritation produced by surgical trauma. In many instances, the major effect is of psychogenic nature.

Cardiopericardiopexy is the fixation or grafting of the pericardium to the surface of the myocardium, which is a fairly good source of extracardiac collateral circulation. A number of irritants (talc, asbestos, bone dust, and even large penicillin crystals) have been applied directly to the pericardium in an effort to stimulate granulomatous tissue. Powdered magnesium silicate (talc) is the current favorite; it produces a marked inflammatory reaction which spreads from the pericardium and myocardium to the mediastinal structures and is attended by a severe hyperemia. The epicardial "barrier" may first be destroyed by mechanical abrasion or by the application of phenol. Anatomic studies reveal that the coronary system anastomoses in variable degrees through the vascularized granulomatous area of induced pericarditis with vessels in the mediastinum, parietal pericardium, diaphragm, and hila of the lungs, vasa vasorum of the ascending aorta, and pericardial branches of the internal mammary arteries. The extracardiac anastomoses constitute a significant reserve for cardiac circulation, augmented by the presence of vascularized pericardial adhesions. Unfortunately, there is no unanimity of opinion as to its efficacy.

Inplantation of the internal mammary artery directly into the ventricular myocardium, with the end of the artery left open to allow free bleeding, has been employed. Anastomoses between the transplanted artery and the left coronary arterioles begin within five days and are fully developed in about two months. Lung, left pectoralis major muscle, omentum, and diaphragmatic muscle have been grafted to the myocardium. Various combinations have also been employed by a number of investigators.

The *Beck No. 1 operation* consists of abrasion of the epicardium and pericardium, partial ligation of the coronary sinus, application of 0.2 gm of powdered asbestos, and grafting of the abraded pericardium to the cardiac surface. Most intercoronary communications thus produced are located on the surface. The *Beck No. 2 operation* consists of first shunting arterial blood into the coronary sinus by a free vein graft between the aorta and the coronary sinus or by direct anastomosis between these structures. Two or three weeks later, the coronary sinus is partially occluded where it enters the right atrium in order to raise the blood pressure in the sinus and produce a retrograde flow. This procedure has been largely abandoned because of the spontaneous eventual closure of the graft. Unfortunately, the procedures which are directed at the production of vascular adhesions usually fail to produce enough channels of sufficient size to carry either water-soluble dyes or the lead acetate-agar injection mass of Schlesinger, which enters vessels 40 μ or larger in diameter, unless preliminary phenolization is employed.

Coronary endarterectomy has been employed as a most direct surgical approach. This is significant since animal experimentation indicates that a

40 per cent reduction in blood flow to the heart represents a critical point. It may eventually prove useful for localized atherosclerotic disease, since procedures (coronary arteriography) that demonstrate occlusive segments are now being developed. Selective coronary arteriography by means of cineangiocardiography is a recent refinement of this diagnostic method and has obviated the necessity for the use of acetylcholine or balloon obstruction of the ascending aorta in order to obtain a better concentration of dye in the coronary arteries.

Bilateral ligation of the internal mammary arteries in the second intercostal spaces has been advocated as a simple, safe, and effective surgical procedure. There is little reason to expect benefits on physiologic and experimental grounds from this procedure. Although small arterial communications between the internal mammary branches and the perivascular arteries along the great vessels entering the heart can be demonstrated by injection technics, the volume of blood is quite small and the procedure does not protect against experimental coronary occlusion. The simplicity and safety of this operation, however, have led to widespread clinical trials. Further observations utilizing adequate controls, including a double-blind technic, and objective data failed to show any appreciable benefit from this operation except that attributable to its psychologic effect.

Other novel approaches are certain to be forthcoming in the immediate future. For example, the experimental irradiation of dogs' hearts has been shown to increase collateral circulation. Present reports of salutary effects of this therapy on dogs may be due to a nonspecific response or may represent a transitory beneficial effect which can be harmful in the long run by damaging blood vessels. Recently procaine has been applied to the pericardium in order to increase coronary flow by dilatation of the coronary vessels secondary to the arterial hypotony. Ventricular aneurysms have been excised with success. This has removed a source of myocardial failure and systemic embolization.

The clinical results of the various revascularization approaches and technics have been similar in some respects. Since their effect upon coronary backflow appears to be relatively minute and since there is relief of symptoms in many instances, a mechanism other than increased blood flow may be likely. A common factor appears to be effective denervation of the heart or diminished response to epinephrine or sympathetic nervous stimulation, with secondary relief of anginal anxiety. The latter may be a nonspecific psychologic effect of a major therapeutic measure or a product of the relief of pain. Whatever the mechanism, the total effect may result in the return of many patients to normal activities.

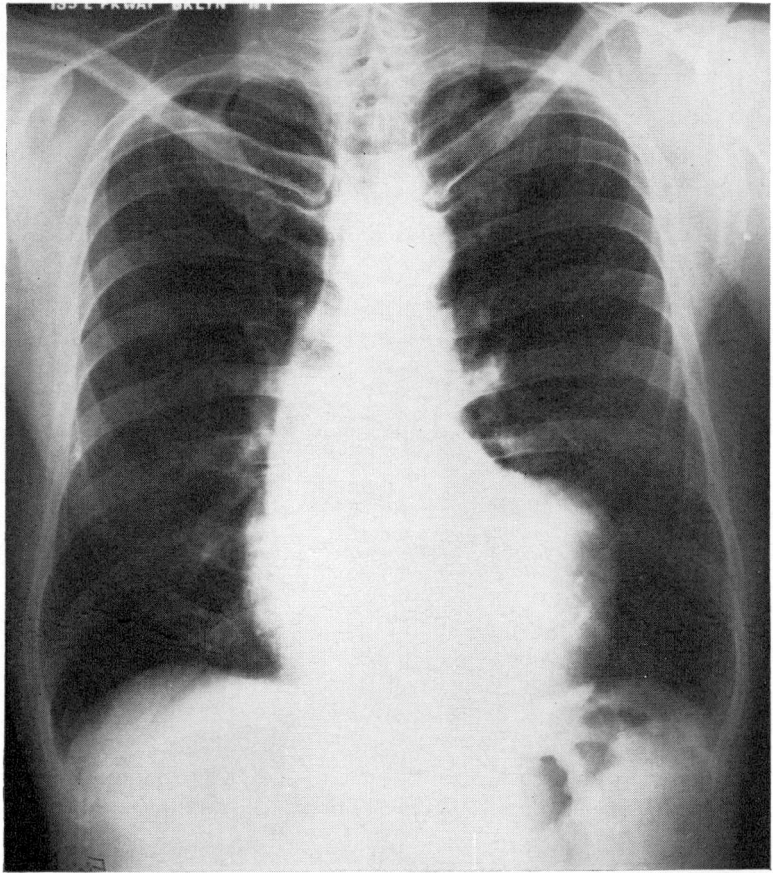

Fig. 12-12. Ventricular aneurysm. Patient, aged sixty years, developed prodromal anginal attacks for one month prior to an acute anterior wall myocardial infarction. Aneurysm first noted about eight months later while still on anticoagulants. Note eccentric bulge of left ventricular border.

Ventricular aneurysmectomy. Aneurysm of the left ventricle is one of the most common complications of myocardial infarction, with an incidence of 10 to 38 per cent. It may prove serious if it increases the work load of the heart, harbors mural thrombi, or ruptures. These complications may develop within days or years of an infarction; however, the usual end is congestive heart failure. The clot or the thinned wall may become calcified, which is easily recognizable on x-ray. When of sufficient size, characteristic paradoxical movements of the affected area may be visible with fluoroscopy or kymography and proper positioning. The electrocardiographic picture may also be characteristic. Such aneurysms have already been removed successfully in a number of recorded instances.

REFERENCES

Albright, E. C.; Soder, D.; and Crumpton, C.: I^{131}-induced hypothyroidism in intractable angina pectoris. *Ann. Int. Med.*, **49**:271, 1958.

Beck, C. S., and Brofman, B. L.: The surgical management of coronary artery disease: background, rationale, clinical experiences. *Ann. Int. Med.*, **45**:975, 1956.

Belle, M., and Halpern, M. M.: Oral nicotinic acid for hyperlipemia. *Am. J. Cardiol.*, **2**:449, 1958.

Blumgart, H. L.; Freedberg, A. S.; and Kurland, G. S.: Hypothyroidism produced by radioactive iodine (I^{131}) in treatment of authyroid patients with angina pectoris and congestive heart failure: early results in various types of cardiovascular diseases and associated pathologic states. *Circulation*, **1**:1105, 1950.

Brown, H.; Rinzler, S. H.; and Benton, J. C.: Correlation of the ballistocardiogram with work performance and energy cost for guidance in rehabilitation of cardiac patients. *Circulation*, **7**:740, 1953.

Cole, S. L., and Griffith, G. C.: Assay of antianginal agents—the rapport period. *J.A.M.A.*, **168**:275, 1958.

Davis, F. W., Jr.; Scarborough, W. R.; Mason, R. E.; Singewald, M. L.; and Baker, B. J. J.: The effects of exercise and smoking on the electrocardiograms and ballistocardiograms of normal subjects and patients with coronary artery disease. *Am. Heart J.*, **46**:529, 1953.

Dock, W.: Evil sequelae of complete bed rest. *J.A.M.A.*, **125**:1083, 1944.

Dock, W.; Mandelbaum, H.; and Mandelbaum, R. A.: *Ballistocardiography*. C. V. Mosby Co., St. Louis, 1953.

DuGuid, J. B.: Thrombosis as a factor in the pathogenesis of coronary atherosclerosis. *J. Path. & Bact.*, **58**:207, 1946.

Enos, W. F.; Holmes, R. H.; and Beyer, J.: Coronary disease among United States soldiers killed in action in Korea. *J.A.M.A.*, **158**:912, 1955.

Fremont, R. E.: Newer methods of medical treatment of coronary insufficiency (use of monamine oxidase inhibitors). Handbook of 6th International Cong. Int. Med., Basel, Switzerland, 1960.

Fremont, R. E.: The medical treatment of coronary insufficiency; new drugs and new methods (Abstract). 5th International Cong. of Gerontology, San Francisco, 1960.

Fremont, R. E., and Jagendorf, B.: Clinical observations on use of warfarin (Coumadin) sodium, a new anticoagulant. *J.A.M.A.*, **165**:1381, 1957.

Fremont, R. E.; Klopstock, R.; and Glass, P.: Controlled studies on the efficacy of bilateral internal mammary artery ligation in patients with angina pectoris. *Angiology*, **10**:20, 1959.

Fuller, H. L., and Kassel, L. E.: Metamine (triethanolamine trinitrate biphosphate) in angina pectoris. *J.A.M.A.*, **159**:1708, 1955.

Gertler, M. M., and White, P. D.: *Coronary Heart Disease in Young Adults: A Multidisciplinary Study.* Harvard University Press, Cambridge, Mass., 1954.

Glover, R. P.; Kitchell, J. R.; Kyle, R. H.; et al.: Experience with myocardial revascularization by division of the internal mammary arteries. *Dis. Chest*, **33**:637, 1958.

Goldner, M. G.: Obesity and its relation to disease. *New York J. Med.*, **56**:2063, 1956.

Gorelik, A. N.: Critical analysis of cardiopericardiomyopexy with eight year follow-up. *J. Internat. Coll. Surgeons*, **28**:401, 1957.

Harken, D. E.; Black, H.; Dickson, J. F., III; and Wilson, H. E., III: De-epicardialization: a simple effective surgical treatment for angina pectoris. *Circulation*, **12**:955, 1955.

Hellerstein, H. K.: Evaluation of surgical methods in the treatment of coronary artery disease. *Mod. Concepts Cardiovas. Dis.*, **26**:411, 1957.

Kelly, J. J., Jr.; Caccese, A.; Ortiz-Marquez, J.; and Taubman, F.: Effects of cigarette smoking on ballistocardiograms of high school youths. *Am. Heart J.*, **47**:30, 1954.

Keyes, J. W.; Drake, E. H.; and Smith, F. J.: Survival rates after acute myocardial infarction with long term anticoagulant therapy. *Circulation*, **14**:254, 1956.

Krantz, J. C., Jr., and Ling, J. S. L.: The pharmacological approach to coronary insufficiency. *Am. J. Cardiol.*, **2**:479, 1958.

Lee, R. E., and Schneider, R. F.: Hypertension and arteriosclerosis in executive and non-executive personnel. *J.A.M.A.*, **167**:1447, 1958.

Lepeschkin, E., and Surawicz, B.: New criteria for the recognition of "false positive" electrocardiographic exercise tests. Characteristics of true-positive and false-positive results of electrocardiographic Master two-step exercise tests. *New England J. Med.*, **258**:511, 1958.

Levine, A. A.: The myth of strict bed rest in the treatment of heart disease. *Am. Heart J.*, **42**:406, 1951.

Levy, R. L.; Williams, N. E.; Bruenn, H. G.; and Carr, H. A.: The "anoxemia test" in the diagnosis of coronary insufficiency. *Am. Heart J.*, **21**:634, 1941.

Lewis, B. I.; Lubin, R. I.; January, L. E.; and Wild, J. B.: Rauwolfia serpentina in the treatment of angina pectoris. *Circulation*, **14**:227, 1956.

Littman, D., and Barr, J. H., Jr.: Acute atypical coronary artery insufficiency. *Circulation*, **5**:189, 1952.

Mandelbaum, H., and Mandelbaum, R.: Studies utilizing the portable electromagnetic ballistocardiogram: IV. The clinical significance of serial ballistocardiography following acute myocardial infarction. *Circulation,* 4:920, 1953.

Master, A. M.; Friedman, R.; and Dack, S.: The electrocardiogram after standard exercise as a functional test of the heart. *Am. Heart J.,* 24:777, 1942.

Master, A. M.; Pordy, L.; and Chesky, K.: Two-step exercise electrocardiogram: follow-up investigation in patients with chest pain and normal resting electrocardiogram. *J.A.M.A.,* 151:458, 1953.

Montgomery, G. E., Jr.; Dry, T. J.; and Gage, R. P.: Further observations on the prognosis in angina pectoris due to coronary sclerosis. A study of 405 patients who survived ten or more years. *Minnesota Med.,* 30:162, 1947.

Moser, K. M.: Thrombolysis with fibrinolysin (Plasmin)—new therapeutic approach to thromboembolism. *J.A.M.A.,* 167:1695, 1958.

Myers, G. B.: QRS-T patterns in multiple precordial leads that may be mistaken for myocardial infarction. *Circulation,* 2:60, 1950.

Nisnewitz, S.; Stein, I.; Silverstone, F.; and Slater, S. R.: The inverted "U" wave in coronary artery disease. *New York J. Med.,* 54:2078, 1954.

Ostapiuk, F. E.: Retrosternal novocaine anesthesia therapy of coronary insufficiency. *Terapeyticheskiy Arkhiv.,* 29:58, 1957.

Owren, P. A.: Permanent anticoagulation therapy in cardiovascular disease. *Northwest Med.,* 56:298, 1957.

Pollock, B. E.: The early management of myocardial infarction. *J.A.M.A.,* 161:404, 1956.

Raab, W.: Loafers' heart. *A.M.A. Arch. Int. Med.,* 101:194, 1958.

Raab, W.: Neurohormonal atherogenesis. *Am. J. Cardiol.,* 1:113, 1958.

Reich, N. E.: Coronary deaths in "healthy" young soldiers: a clinicopathologic study. *Am. Pract. & Digest Treat.,* 2:731, 1948.

Reich, N. E.: Non-atheromatous lesions of the coronary ostia. *New York J. Med.,* 52:2365, 1952.

Reich, N. E.: Non-diagnostic electrocardiographic patterns. *Dis. Chest,* 25:516, 1954.

Reich, N. E.: *The Uncommon Heart Diseases.* Charles C Thomas, Publisher, Springfield, Ill., 1954.

Reich, N. E.: The versatility of the carotid sinus in diagnosis and treatment. *Angiology,* 8:328, 1957.

Reich, N. E.: Less common causes of cardiovascular disease. In *Cardiology,* Vol. 4, Blakiston Div., McGraw-Hill Book Co., New York, 1959.

Reich, N. E.; Rosenberg, B. A.; and Metz, M.: The use of 2-ethylhexanol in acute pulmonary edema. *Dis. Chest,* **23**:43, 1953. A new therapy for acute pulmonary edema. *New York J. Med.,* **52**:2647, 1952. The combined use of intermittent positive pressure oxygen and 2-ethylhexanol in acute pulmonary edema. *Am. Pract. & Digest Treat.,* **4**:616, 1953.

Reich, N. E., and Witten, M.: Roentgenographic visualization of the coronary arteries. *Am. J. Roentgenol.,* **77**:274, 1957.

Rinzler, S. H., and Travell, J.: Therapy directed at the somatic component of cardiac pain. *Am. Heart J.,* **351**:248, 1948.

Robb, G. P.; Marks, H. H.; and Mattingly, T. W.: The value of the double standard two-step exercise in the detection of coronary disease. *Trans. A. Life Insur. M. Dir.,* **40**:52, 1957.

Roesler, H., and Dressler, W.: Transient electrocardiographic changes identical with those of acute myocardial infarction accompanying attacks of angina pectoris. *Am. Heart J.,* **47**:520, 1954.

Rosenman, M. D.: Painless myocardial infarction: a review of the literature and analysis of 220 cases. *Ann. Int. Med.,* **41**:1, 1954.

Rosenman, R. H., and Friedman, M.: Emotional stress and blood changes. Presented at Annual Meeting, Am. Heart Assoc., Chicago, Ill., October, 1957.

Russek, H. I.: Emotional stress and the etiology of coronary artery disease. *Am. J. Cardiol.,* **2**:129, 1958.

Russek, H. I.: Hazards in the treatment of acute myocardial infarction. *Am. J. M. Sc.,* **232**:403, 1956.

Russek, H. I., and Zohman, B. L.: Relative significance of heredity, diet and occupational stress in coronary heart disease of young adults. *Am. J. M. Sc.,* **235**:266, 1958.

Russek, H. I., and Zohman, B. L.: Selection of patients for anticoagulant therapy in acute myocardial infarction. *Am. J. M. Sc.,* **228**:133, 1954.

Sabiston, D. C., Jr., and Blalock, A.: Experimental ligation of the internal mammary artery and its effect on coronary occlusion. *Surgery,* **43**:906, 1958.

Sampson, J. J., and Zipser, A.: Norepinephrine in shock following myocardial infarction: influence upon survival rate and renal function. *Circulation,* **9**:38, 1954.

Scarborough, W. R.; Mason, R. E.; Davis, F. W., Jr.; Singewald, M. L.; Baker, B. M., Jr.; and Lore, S. A.: A ballistocardiographic and electrocardiographic study of 328 patients with coronary artery disease; comparison with results from a similar study of apparently normal persons. *Am. Heart J.,* **44**:645, 1952.

Scherf, D., and Boyd, L. J.: *Clinical Electrocardiography,* 2nd ed. J. B. Lippincott Co., Philadelphia, 1946, p. 110.

Scherf, D., and Schaffer, A. I.: The electrocardiographic exercise test. *Am. Heart J.*, **43**:927, 1952.

Schlachman, M.: Dysphagia as a symptom of coronary artery disease. *New York J. Med.*, **56**:79, 1956.

Schnur, S.: The current dispute concerning anticoagulants in acute myocardial infarction. *J.A.M.A.*, **156**:1127, 1954.

Sensenbach, W.: Some common conditions, not due to primary heart disease that may be associated with changes in the electrocardiogram. *Ann. Int. Med.*, **25**:632, 1946.

Sigler, L. H.: Suggestive manifestations of acute coronary occlusion or insufficiency. *A.M.A. Arch. Int. Med.*, **94**:341, 1954.

Spain, D. M.; Bradess, V. A.; and Huss, G.: Observations on atherosclerosis of coronary arteries in males under age of 46: necropsy study with special reference to somatotypes. *Ann. Int. Med.*, **38**:254, 1953.

Stechel, G. H.; Fishman, S. I.; Schwartz, G.; Turkowitz, H.; Madonia, P. F.; Fankhauser, A.: The use of Aramine in clinical shock. *Circulation*, **13**:834, 1956.

Suzman, M. M.; Ruskin, H. D.; and Goldberg, B.: An evaluation of the effect of continuous long-term anticoagulant therapy on the prognosis of myocardial infarction. *Circulation*, **12**:338, 1955.

Thompson, S. A., and Plachta, A.: Fourteen years' experience with cardiopexy in the treatment of coronary artery disease. *J. Thoracic Surg.*, **27**:64, 1954.

Vineberg, A.: Internal mammary artery implant in the treatment of angina pectoris; a three year follow up. *Canad. M.A.J.*, **70**:367, 1954.

Waaler, B. A.: The effect of permanent anticoagulant therapy on symptoms and mortality in angina pectoris. *Acta med. scandinav.*, **157**:289, 1957.

Weil, M. H.: Current concepts on management of shock. *Circulation*, **16**:1097, 1957.

Wertlake, P. T.; Wilcox, A. A.; Haley, M. L.; and Peterson, J. E.: Serum cholesterol values during mental and emotional stress. *Proc. Soc. Exper. Biol. & Med.*, **97**:163, 1958.

Winsor, T., and Humphreys, P.: Peritrate in angina pectoris. *Angiology*, **3**:1, 1952.

Yater, W. M.; Traum, A. H.; Brown, W. G.; Fitzgerald, R. P.; Geisler, M. A.; and Wilson, G.: Coronary artery disease in men 18 to 39 years of age: a report of 866 cases, 450 with necropsy examination. *Am. Heart J.*, **36**:334, 1948.

CHAPTER 13 *DISEASES OF THE DIAPHRAGM*

The diaphragm is a dome-shaped musculomembranous structure which separates the thoracic and abdominal cavities and acts as the most important muscle of respiration. Because of its divisive position as the anatomic border between the chest and the abdomen, abnormalities involving the diaphragm may cause secondary involvement of either thoracic or abdominal organs; this may lead to chest pain. Since the distress very frequently suggests cardiac disease, a careful differential diagnosis of the pain must always include the possibility of diaphragmatic involvement.

DIAPHRAGMATIC HERNIAE

Anatomic weaknesses are often inherent in the diaphragmatic openings. Of all the orifices, the esophageal hiatus presents the greatest weakness.

319

The aortic and vena caval hiatuses and the peripheral attachments present other potential congenital or acquired weaknesses.

Although portions of thoracic organs, such as the lungs, may protrude through the defect, diaphragmatic hernia is usually defined as a protrusion of abdominal viscera through a diaphragmatic hiatus into the thoracic cavity. Compound diaphragmatic hernia implies that several abdominal organs protrude through the involved foramen. Certain phases of diaphragmatic hernia have already been discussed in conjunction with diseases of the esophagus (see pp. 149–51).

Etiologic factors include congenital weakness of the diaphragm, trauma to the trunk, and any condition causing increased intra-abdominal pressure, such as pregnancy, ascites, obesity, and chronic constipation. Protrusion of part of the stomach through the widened esophageal opening is the most common type of diaphragmatic hernia. Except for the rare occurrence of a true congenitally short esophagus, hiatus hernia occurs mainly in the hypersthenic, obese, middle-aged person and is slightly more common in women than in men. Fixation of the diaphragm to the lower end of the esophagus and to the cardia of the stomach normally exists, by a condensation of fibroelastic tissue, the esophagophrenic membrane. Laxity of this membrane is generally accepted as being the initial lesion in the development of the sliding hiatus hernia. Three types of hiatus hernia may occur: (1) esophagogastric hernia, (2) paraesophageal hernia, and (3) short esophagus hernia. (See Fig. 13-1.)

In rare instances, the diaphragmatic hernia may be of the parasternal or subcostosternal type. The abdominal organs, usually the stomach and occasionally the colon, may protrude through the Morgagni foramen (Larrey's space). This is a triangular space between insertion of the muscular fibers of the diaphragm at the posterior surface of the xiphoid process, and at the cartilage of the seventh rib. Although this is a relatively rare type of hernia, it almost invariably produces substernal and left shoulder pain.

The manifestations of herniation through the esophageal opening in the diaphragm are often vague and confusing, since the symptoms commonly simulate those of gallbladder disease, stomach disease, angina pectoris, and even coronary occlusion. Indeed, coronary occlusion is commonly suspected because of the severity and location of pain. However, the most frequent symptoms are dysphagia, "heartburn," and pain. Regurgitation and belching may also be encountered. Recent studies of the intraluminal pressures within the esophagus with multiple-opened catheters have demonstrated the exact nature of the disturbances in dysphagia. Normally, the peristaltic wave traverses the esophagus in about eight seconds and devel-

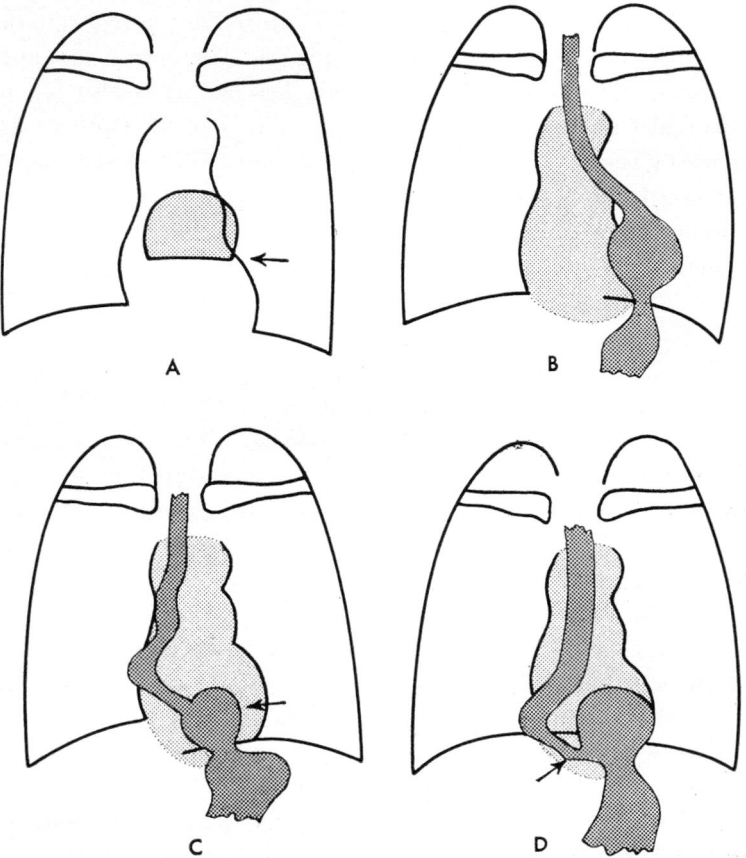

Fig. 13-1. *A,* Diaphragmatic herniation. Gas-filled stomach with horizontal fluid level (←) within the cardiac shadow on routine chest exposure.

B, Congenitally short esophagus, esophageal hiatal hernia with the larger
part of the stomach in the thorax (congenital thoracic stomach). Posteroanterior view.

C, Diaphragmatic hernia with upward displacement of the unshortened
esophagus. The esophagus is tortuous and does not enter the abdomen.
(Herniated portion of the stomach: ←.)

D, Paraesophageal hiatus hernia. The esophagus is dilated and displaced
to the right, the esophagogastric junction is intra-abdominal (→). (From
Markovits, E.: *Visceral Radiology.* The Macmillan Co., New York, 1951.)

ops pressures up to 100 mm Hg. The most distal portion of the esophagus
(the vestibule) presents lower pressures and delayed or absent propagation
of the peristaltic wave. Observations on patients with hiatus hernia have
demonstrated decreased deglutition pressures at the esophagogastric junction and the herniated stomach, with normal pressures in the more proximal
esophagus. An increased duration of the peristaltic wave also resembles
cardiospasm.

The sensation of "heartburn" is probably caused by a regurgitation of irritating gastric contents into the lower esophagus. The most common symptom is epigastric or substernal pain or both. Discomfort is also felt in the upper abdominal quadrants and in the left or right chest. Gaseous eructations commonly relieve the pain. The pain of hiatus hernia is ordinarily induced by exertion or heavy meals and occasionally awakens the patient during the night. Sitting up, drinking water, or antacids may provide temporary relief. Acute precordial distress which radiates to the neck and left arm may appear, particularly after eating, accompanied by a sense of fullness in the left thorax. The pain is usually sharp, stabbing, or knife-like. These symptoms depend on the patient's posture; recumbent position or raising the intra-abdominal pressure bring on the symptoms, whereas an upright position alleviates the condition. Esophagitis may be a concomitant factor and may cause a burning sensation in the chest which may radiate to the back, neck, jaw, ear, palate, shoulders, or arms. Patients may have an awareness of food passing down the entire gullet, and this may be associated with actual pain. Increasing difficulty in swallowing may ultimately ensue.

Massive diaphragmatic hernia causes severe embarrassment of the cardiorespiratory system by direct compression of lung tissue. Even the colon and small intestines may herniate through the increased opening, especially if it is of congenital origin with a large developmental defect.

Pain following incarceration of a diaphragmatic hernia may be especially severe and at times simulates the pain of angina pectoris or even coronary occlusion. The onset is marked by vomiting and pain in the epigastrium radiating to the chest and left shoulder. Hiccup and sudden shortness of breath may occur, due to phrenic nerve or diaphragmatic irritation. In general, the picture is frequently more suggestive of a chest condition than of an abdominal situation. The relieved herniation may progress to rupture of the esophagus, and the picture of an acute mediastinitis rapidly emerges. The mediastinum is often displaced by the escaped air, which causes increasing respiratory difficulties. A flat plate will reveal gas above and below the diaphragm. Crepitus may appear about the neck and upper chest.

The differential diagnosis of the pain includes peptic ulcer and coronary disease, and in some instances gallbladder disturbances also. The pain due to ulcer is usually characterized by its periodicity and food relationships. Occasionally, an accompanying hiatus hernia is discovered accidentally during the search for an acute peptic ulcer when Trendelenburg views are taken. Coronary disease is differentiated by electrocardiographic studies. Secondary anemia may occur as the result of ulceration with hemorrhage either in the lower esophagus or, more commonly, in the portion of the stomach lying above the diaphragm. In such instances, positive electro-cardiographic findings may be obtained that are not primarily due to coronary artery disease but rather to the severe anemia with resultant myocardial ischemia. Not infrequently, both hiatus hernia and coronary artery disease may occur concomitantly, requiring the most careful evaluation. Therapeutic tests with nitrites and antacids may be of diagnostic help.

It must be emphasized, however, that occasionally angina pectoris may falsely appear to respond to antacids because of its transitory nature. Furthermore, the relief of pain following the use of nitroglycerin does not exclude hiatus hernia with esophageal spasm or esophagitis, since the latter conditions may also respond favorably to nitroglycerin. ST and T changes in the electrocardiogram can also be produced by balloon distention of the esophagus. These changes may resemble superficially those seen after exercise tests. Finally, pain due to hiatus hernia or esophageal disease may reflexly "trigger" an attack of angina pectoris or acute coronary insufficiency in the presence of underlying coronary disease.

Roentgenologic studies should be performed in the Trendelenburg position, employing an abdominal binder or the Valsalva maneuver.

Preliminary medical treatment of hiatus hernia should be undertaken first because incisional pain after transthoracic repair may be quite severe, because the defect may recur, and because not all patients are completely relieved by hernial reduction. Small meals, exclusion of gas-producing foods, and an upright position for at least an hour after eating are helpful. Bland foods may lessen epigastric distress. Antispasmodics before eating, antacids after meals, and sedatives may be of value. Tight belts, abdominal binders, girdles, or corsets should be avoided. A weight-reduction program is advisable for the obese patient. Sleeping in a more erect position is occasionally helpful. Treatment in cases with esophagitis is directed mainly against the hyperacidity.

Surgery is performed when the condition does not improve or when complications occur, such as severe vomiting due to obstruction, serious hemorrhage, or marked strictures of the esophagus. Unfortunately, there is a tendency to recurrences.

Attempts have been made to predetermine the likelihood of good surgical results. Thus, it was found that the response to a preoperative pneumoperitoneum produced by the injection of 300 cc of air correlated closely with the degree of postoperative improvement. Surgical intervention is indicated in cases of compound diaphragmatic hernias before respiratory function becomes impaired, and operation makes surgical intervention hazardous. Medical treatment for compound hernia is usually ineffective.

Subcostosternal hernia may interfere with the heart action as well as the intrathoracic circulation, producing substernal pain or pain in the shoulder region, palpitation, a sense of suffocation, cyanosis, and weakness. These chest symptoms are prone to occur after physical exertion or voluminous intake of food or liquids. Most cases respond to medical management. Indication for surgical interference is the same as in hiatus hernia.

OTHER DISORDERS OF THE DIAPHRAGM

Eventration. Another disorder which may be the cause of pain in the chest and minor cardiovascular disturbances is eventration of the diaphragm (see Fig. 13-2). An entire hemidiaphragm or a segment lies at an abnormally

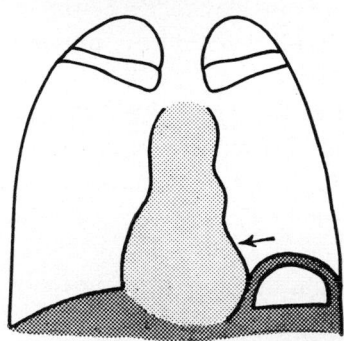

Fig. 13-2. Diaphragmatic eventration on the left side with displacement of the heart to the right. Paralysis of the left phrenic nerve. (From Markovits, E.: *Visceral Radiology.* The Macmillan Co., New York, 1951.)

high level in the thorax. This is also known as "elevation" or "relaxation" of the diaphragm. It may be total or partial. Partial eventration or relaxation usually involves the right hemidiaphragm.

Eventration is probably due to a congenital developmental anomaly. However, injury or involvement of the phrenic nerve by an inflammatory or a malignant process occasionally may be responsible.

Symptoms caused by displacements are of three types: (1) dyspeptic—abdominal pain, nausea, vomiting, and belching; (2) respiratory—chest pain, cough, and cyanosis; and (3) cardiac—palpitation, tachycardia, and extrasystoles.

Total eventration of the diaphragm is occasionally found in children. It is treated surgically, particularly when there is significant respiratory embarrassment, resulting in dyspnea and cyanosis. Older children or adults with mild symptoms may be treated medically. This requires the restriction of physical activity, avoidance of heavy lifting, reduction of excess weight, avoidance of heavy meals, and the use of antispasmodics. Surgical treatment of eventration is directed toward strengthening the thin, overstretched hemidiaphragm and lowering it to an approximately normal position. The procedure most often used to attain this objective consists of imbrication or plication of the diaphragm by suture in as many layers as necessary.

Diaphragmatic tic and flutter. These unusual rapid rhythmic motions of the diaphragm produce severe pain which may be confused with angina or coronary insufficiency. Pain occurs along the costal margins or lower chest and is frequently accompanied by marked dyspnea.

Tic is characterized by diaphragmatic movements of up to 100 or more per minute and affects the entire diaphragm. Flutter presents movements at about 300 per minute and usually affects only one-half of the diaphragm. The cause is usually unknown, but both conditions have occurred in hysteria, in hypocalcemia, and after encephalitis, or as a result of phrenic nerve or muscular irritation. The condition may develop and terminate suddenly. Fluoroscopy reveals characteristic fluttering of the diaphragm.

Treatment may be effective only by blocking the phrenic nerve by injection, freezing (ethyl chloride spray), or crushing.

Diaphragmatic rupture. Tearing of the diaphragm may be caused by (1) direct injury as a result of thoracoabdominal wounds (e.g., from stabbing or bullets), (2) indirect injury as a result of crushing accident (e.g., automobile accident) or heavy blows to the chest (e.g., as in boxing), and (3) inflammatory necrosis of the diaphragm following subphrenic abscess, empyema, or malignancy. The left leaf of the diaphragm is usually affected more often than the right.

The diagnosis depends upon the history of a missile, blow, or infection; low chest pain and dyspnea; and physical and roentgenologic findings. X-rays may reveal pneumoperitoneum or pneumothorax with or without atelectasis, intermittent tic or flutter of the diaphragm on fluoroscopy, or indistinct diaphragmatic structure due to contracted muscle or blood clots.

Treatment consists in combating shock and hemorrhage before suture of the diaphragm is considered.

Infections of the diaphragm. Although trichinosis is a generalized infection due to *Trichinella spiralis*, the diaphragm is commonly invaded. In addition to generalized symptoms—a history of raw pork ingestion, hiccup, and diaphragmatic pain—the diagnosis can be confirmed by a biopsy of voluntary muscle, periorbital edema, and skin tests.

Localized infections of the diaphragm are rarely recognized as such. The muscular membrane participates in infections above or below the diaphragm, such as subphrenic abscess, peritonitis, or empyema. Amebic infection of the liver frequently traverses the diaphragm by way of the lymphatic system to enter the pleural space and lungs, although it may produce actual rupture into the pleural space with sudden onset of severe pain in the chest and right shoulder.

Diaphragmatic pleurisy (epidemic pleurodynia). The diagnosis and treatment of this condition have been described in detail in the chapter concerned with pleuropulmonary causes of chest pain (Chap. 5).

REFERENCES

Brown, C. H.; Moberg, C. H.; and Effler, D. B.: Compound diaphragmatic hernia. *Ann. Int. Med.,* **44**:534, 1956.

Christensen, P.: Eventration of the diaphragm. *Thorax,* **14**:311, 1959.

Des Forges, G., and Lynch, J. P.: Traumatic rupture of diaphragm. *J. Thoracic Surg.,* **34**:779, 1957.

Donald, C. J., and Clayton, O. W.: Diaphragmatic hernia, report of 83 cases. *Am. Surgeon,* **21**:45, 1955.

Edmunds, V.: Hiatus hernia; a clinical study of 200 cases. *Quart. J. Med.,* **26**:445, 1957.

Hoffman, K. F., and Chilko, A. J.: Subcostosternal diaphragmatic hernia. *Ann. Int. Med.,* **41**:616, 1954.

Izzedine, A.: Anginal symptoms in diaphragmatic hernias. *J. Med. Liban.,* **12**:482, 1959.

Kohli, J., and Pearson, C. C.: Study of hiatus hernia. *Gastroenterology,* **23**:294, 1953.

Master, A. M.; Dack, S.; Stone, J.; and Grishman, A.: Differential diagnosis of hiatus hernia and coronary artery disease. *Arch. Surg.,* **58**:428, 1949.

Newman, H. W.; Ellis, F. H.; and Andersen, H. A.: Eventration of the diaphragm. *Proc. Staff Meet. Mayo Clin.,* **30**:310, 1955.

Texter, E. C., Jr.; Smith, H. W.; Sippy, H. I.: Hiatal hernia and related disorders of the esophagogastric junction. *J.A.M.A.,* **160**:830, 1956.

Vogl, A., and Small, A.: Partial eventration of the right diaphragm (congenital diaphragmatic herniation of the liver). *Ann. Int. Med.,* **43**:61, 1955.

CHAPTER 14 *ABDOMINAL CONDITIONS CAUSING CHEST PAIN*

327

DISORDERS OF THE ADRENAL GLANDS
Pheochromocytoma
Waterhouse-Friderichsen syndrome

A number of subdiaphragmatic conditions may refer a significant degree of pain to the precordium, xiphoid, shoulders, or back. However, gastric, duodenal, and gastrojejunal ulcers, cholecystic and pancreatic disease, diaphragmatic hernia, and certain of their complications generally present characteristic patterns of pain. With a careful history relative to the site and type of pain and its time sequence, the pain pattern can be determined, and the causative lesion may thus be suggested. The integration of this information with other symptoms and findings will usually establish the clinical diagnosis with a fair degree of certainty, and appropriate tests may then be employed for final confirmation.

The pain patterns produced by the above-mentioned abdominal conditions and the locations of pain referable to body segments are listed in Table 14-1 and illustrated in Figure 14-1. The mechanisms by which the patterns of pain are generated involve the splanchnic pathways through the stimulation of the plexuses of Meissner and Auerbach. The nerve impulses are transmitted through the splanchnic fibers, which pass, uninterrupted, through the celiac ganglia, the sympathetic trunk, and the rami communicantes to the splanchnic cell bodies in the dorsal root ganglia, and terminate centrally in the lateral portion of the spinal cord. The cerebrospinal nerve endings are thought to be in the parietal peritoneum, the mesentery, and the lesser omentum, within 1 or 2 cm of the free border of the viscus. Adequate stimulation of these nerve endings sends impulses by way of the segmental cerebrospinal nerves to the ordinary sensory ganglia in the dorsal root and from there centrally to the lateral portion of the spinal cord.

Many intra-abdominal conditions frequently manifest themselves as "acute indigestion." This vague, uncomfortable infradiaphragmatic sensation may also be initially experienced in many instances of acute involvement of the coronary circulation, including acute myocardial infarction. Improved methods of diagnosis of the latter condition in recent years, especially serial electrocardiography, have led to an overemphasis of the frequency of coronary disease as a basis of "acute indigestion." Thus, both the layman and the press have come to confuse this term with coronary artery disease. Unless the physician is unaware of the fact that electrocardiographic changes may also occur in certain digestive disorders of functional or organic nature,

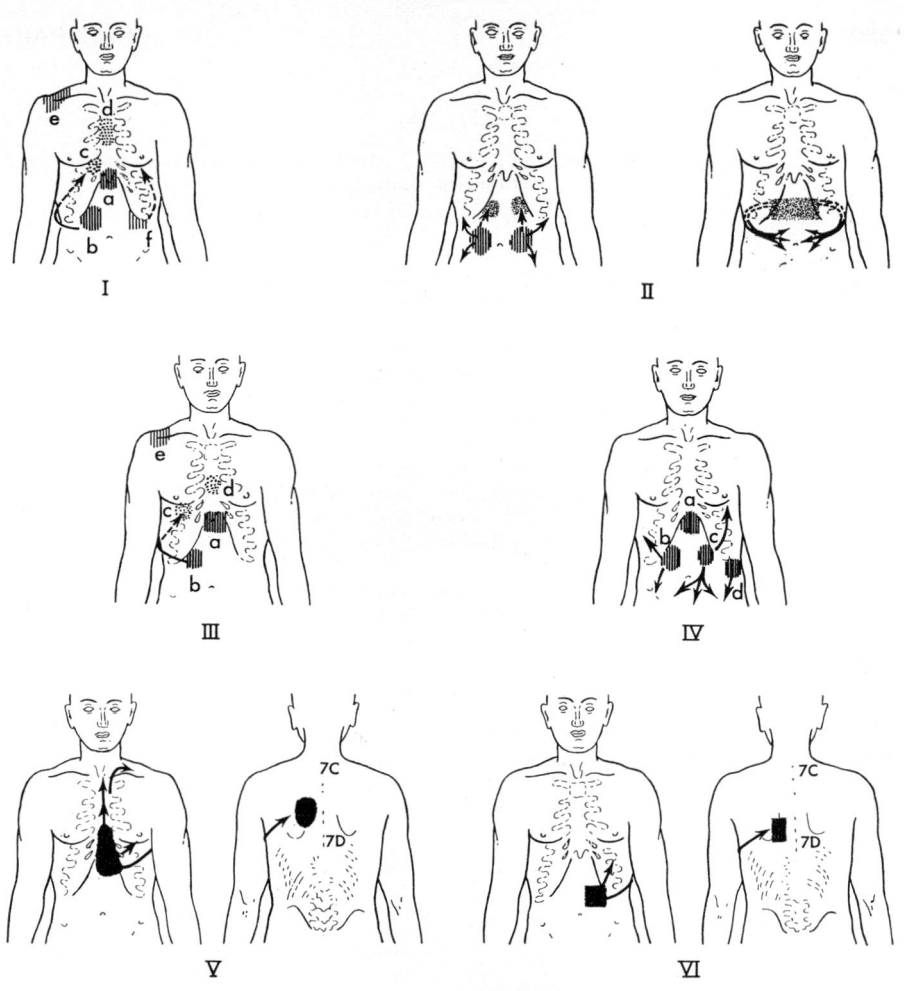

Fig. 14-1. Pain patterns in abdominal disease.

I, Sites of pain that may occur in a case of cholecystitis with stones. *a,* Visceral pain alone; *b,* summation pain; *c,* subscapular pain of summation or of mixed visceral and somatic origin; *d,* interscapular somatic pain alone; *e,* special right phrenic referral of pain; *f,* uncommon left-sided pain.

II, Left, site of pain of pancreatitis; right, back pain and engirdling pain of pancreatitis.

III, Common sites of pain in cases of duodenal ulcer. *a,* Original visceral pain; *b,* summation pain; *c,* extension to subscapula in summation pain or pain of mixed visceral and somatic origin; *d,* interscapular somatic pain in involvement of lesser omental tissues; *e,* rare, special phrenic pain with referral to the right.

IV, Sites of pain in anastomotic ulcer. *a,* Visceral pain of uncomplicated duodenal ulcer; *b,* right shift of pain during perforation of duodenal ulcer; *c,* left and downward shift of pain of gastrojejunal ulcer involving stomach and mesocolon; *d,* downward shift of pain of perisplenic involvement.

V, Site of pain in a case of gastric ulcer associated with diaphragmatic hernia.

VI, Site of pain in a case of ulcer of the lesser curvature of the stomach.

(From Smith, L. A.: The pattern of pain in the diagnosis of upper abdominal disorders. *J.A.M.A.* **156:**1566, 1954. Figs. 4, 5, 9, 10.)

Table 14-1

Diagnoses Suggested by Certain Pain Patterns and Certain Locations of Pain Referable to Body Segments *

Location of Pain or Radiation	Body Segment	Diagnosis
Upward radiation	T_5–T_6	Diaphragmatic hernia; gastric ulcer; esophageal ulcer
Epigastrium	T_6–T_{10}	Diaphragmatic hernia; gastric ulcer; duodenal ulcer; gallbladder disease; pancreatic lesions; esophageal lesions; angina; carcinoma of cecum
Interscapular region	T_6	Lesser omental involvement by gastric ulcer; cystic duct stone; perforating duodenal ulcer; esophagitis
Left radiation	T_6–T_8	Gastric ulcer; lesion in tail or pancreas; pyloric obstruction from duodenal ulcer or carcinoma; gallbladder disease (rare)
Right radiation	T_8	Duodenal ulcer; gallbladder disease; pancreatic involvement; prepyloric gastric ulcer (rare)
Subscapular region	Right or left	Right: duodenal ulcer; gallbladder disease; involvement of head of pancreas
	T_8	Left: gastric ulcer; lesion of tail of pancreas; perforating carcinoma of colon; gallbladder disease (rare)
Pancreatic region	T_{10}–L_2	Pancreatic lesions
Downward radiation; mesocolon, renal, or splenic involvement	T_{10}–L_1	Shift to right lower quadrant, testis, or thigh; duodenal ulcer
		Shift to lower part of abdomen: gastric ulcer; splenic lesion; gastrojejunal ulcer; jejunal ulcer
Supraclavicular region	Right or left	Right: gallbladder disease; subdiaphragmatic abscess; duodenal ulcer (rare); amebic liver abscess
		Left: involvement of dome of left hemidiaphragm by diaphragmatic hernia or by perforating gastric ulcer; left subdiaphragmatic abscess; high anastomotic ulcer

* Modified from Smith, L. A.: The pattern of pain in the diagnosis of upper abdominal disorders. *J.A.M.A.*, **156**:1566, 1954.

even he may be misled into attributing the origin of the pain to the heart rather than to the abdomen. Electrocardiographic changes have been described in many functional or organic abdominal disorders, such as spasm and distention or hiatus hernia of the digestive tract, and they have also been reproduced experimentally. These disorders may produce "cardiac discomfort" as well as serious arrhythmias. Electrocardiographic changes may be due to reflex changes in coronary blood flow initiated by mechanical irritation of vagal fibers. In severe disorders, electrolyte disturbances, rotation of the heart, and torsion of the great vessels due to marked elevation of the diaphragm, acute gastrointestinal loss with secondary coronary insufficiency and shock may be responsible for cardiac and electrocardiographic manifestations. Their secondary character becomes evident when they disappear following the proper recognition and adequate treatment of the primary abdominal disturbance. Finally, pain due to gallbladder dysfunction or disease is commonly radiated to the shoulder region, back, or chest, and this is occasionally confused with coronary pain.

DISORDERS OF THE BILIARY TRACT

The main function of the gallbladder is the concentration and storage of bile. It is generally agreed that gallbladder disorders constitute one of the most common causes of "indigestion," especially in women. The diseased gallbladder is the most common cause of operation in the aged and the second most common reason for surgery in all age groups. Marshall states that 15,000 people die yearly in the United States because of gallstones or their complications.

There has been a good deal of speculation in the past about the relation of gallbladder disease to disturbances of the heart and disorders of the digestive tract. While attacks of cholecystitis are occasionally mistaken for heart attacks, anginal seizures seem to be relieved by removal of the diseased gallbladder which "triggers" such attacks. Thus, painful impulses arising in the biliary tract and other abdominal viscera may act as provocative mechanisms in the production of various cardiac arrhythmias or angina pectoris. The differential diagnosis between the two conditions is often difficult because of the fact that the pain impulses may be transmitted to the same or overlapping areas in the spinal cord.

Gallbladder disorders are generally classified into two major groups—functional and organic. The *functional* type of disorder, commonly termed "biliary dyskinesia," frequently represents the initial stage of gallbladder disease. The hypotonic (distended) type is usually found in obese and sedentary individuals and causes dyspepsia, flatulence, and constipation without colic. The hypertonic (spastic) type, usually found in nervous, tense, and ambitious individuals, tends to cause pain or colic. Autonomic imbalance leads to excessive and persistent spasm of the common duct sphincter. The resulting increased intraductal pressure causes overdistention of the common duct in this form of dyskinesia. An irritable and spastic state of the common duct sphincter may be aggravated by a focus outside the biliary tract, sometimes known as a "trigger mechanism." The source of the extrabiliary stimulation may be of cerebral origin following mental anxiety, unfavorable environmental conditions, or other unrelated condi-

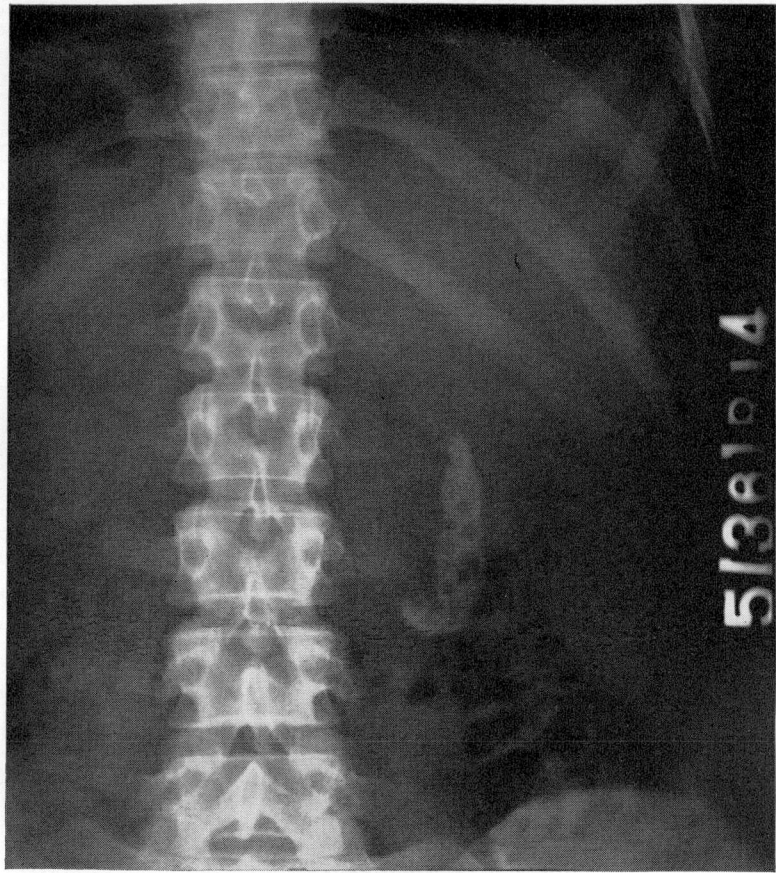

Fig. 14-2. Cholelithiasis. Multiple radiolucent biliary calculi in opacified gallbladder.

tions. Interestingly enough, this pain may not disappear completely following average doses of morphine, but may be relieved by nitroglycerin.

Organic disease of the gallbladder may be chemical, bacterial, metabolic, or mechanical in origin. The sequence of events—whether beginning as acute or latent infectious cholecystitis with subsequent stone formation (see Fig. 14-2); as initial stone (cholesterol) formation; as kinking; or as a stricture with resultant trauma and inflammation of the gallbladder and further complications—is not within the scope of this text. Whatever the exact etiology, it is a recurrent progressive disease of middle and old age, and of the obese.

From the viewpoint of differential diagnosis, the situation is complicated by the fact that the symptoms of biliary functional disorders are often identical with those of organic disease. Some symptoms are common to both functional disorders and organic disease, while other symptoms occur only with organic disease. The symptoms usually limited to the latter include recurrent attacks of pain with nausea, vomiting, chills, or fever. The symptoms common to all biliary tract disorders are a vague sensation of "dyspepsia" or discomfort after meals, belching, distention, bloating, and flatus. Intolerance to certain foods, such as fats, fried foods, and eggs as well as "heartburn," acid eructation, and chronic constipation may occur as associated symptoms.

Pain is the predominant symptom in almost all patients with biliary tract disorders. This pain is apt to be precipitated by overindulgence in spicy and fried foods, fats, or alcohol. Its character ranges from a mild nagging discomfort to the most severe colic. A constant severe pain in the abdomen usually marks the onset of acute cholecystitis. It may wax and wane but seldom ceases. In about 50 per cent of proved gallbladder cases, pain is found to be localized in the epigastric region. It may extend to the lower abdomen or lower substernal regions. The colic caused by a common duct stone is frequently associated with nausea and vomiting and may be followed by jaundice. After the severe pain subsides, a constant ache in the right hypochondrium may be experienced. Early epigastric pain is aggravated by motion, but not particularly so in the later stages. Naturally, the possible radiation of pain to the lower substernal or precordial region may be confused with a cardiac source of pain. Differentiation between the two conditions is extremely important, because a patient with acute coronary disease may be subjected to unnecessary surgery, or a cholecystectomy needed to remove gallstones may not be performed because the symptoms simulate those of coronary disease. Nausea, vomiting, anorexia, abdominal distention, or fever usually accompany gallbladder pain. Localized tenderness, palpable gallbladder, and spasm of the overlying abdominal muscles are important findings. Punch tenderness may be elicited in mild or subsiding instances. Right-sided inspiratory distress may resemble pleurisy. Indeed, inconstant rales may be found at the right base due to splinting and localized atelectasis. The appearance of obvious jaundice simplifies the differentiation.

The tendency of gallstones and heart disease to coexist increases after the age of fifty years. Nervous stimuli originating in the gallbladder or the common duct may reflexly alter the degree of coronary blood flow. A primary disturbance of lipid-cholesterol metabolism may also be implicated, since this is frequently concerned in stone formation due to overconcentration and precipitation in the gallbladder or due to absorption from the digestive tract. Cardiac pain is usually referred along the fifth cervical through the fourth thoracic nerves. Biliary tract pain occurs along the seventh and eighth thoracic spinal segments and may radiate to the shoulders and down the arms. Pain regarded as anginal in patients with gallstone disease is often unrelated to effort and most frequently occurs at night while the patient is in bed. It frequently follows the ingestion of food which is known to be poorly tolerated. Cholecystography confirms the presence of organic biliary tract disease in 90 per cent of cases. Perhaps many patients with symptoms of heart disease should have a cholecystogram, and most patients with symptoms of gallbladder disease should have an electrocardiogram when warranted because of referred pains. Duodenal drainage revealing the absence of concentrated gallbladder bile provides diagnostic import in those instances which fail to reveal gallbladder filling.

The electrocardiogram may be very helpful in elucidating the nature of the pain. It must be reiterated that any changes may be due to primary disorders of the biliary tract, although some doubt has recently been cast upon this clinical observation by experimental work. The effect of gallbladder distention on the electrocardiogram was determined before and after the experimental production of myocardial infarction. The electrocardiograms taken before, during, and after distention showed occasional vagal effects during periods of dilatation but no ectopic beats. Following the production of myocardial infarction by coronary artery ligation, gastric and gallbladder distention resulted in the production of multifocal extrasystoles, and when maintained for several minutes, a paroxysmal tachycardia ensued. Sinus rhythm returned in about five minutes after the distention was released. These changes could be repeatedly produced up to the fifth day following the production of the myocardial infarction. These studies suggest that gastric and gallbladder distention may produce serious abnormalities in rhythm in the damaged heart but fail to do so in the normal heart.

This confirms the clinical observations that when gallbladder and coronary disease coexist, considerable improvement may be achieved by the removal of gallstones or an otherwise diseased gallbladder. Not only pain, but severe arrhythmias and conduction disturbances such as complete heart block associated with Adams-Stokes attacks may respond favorably. Therefore, the possibility of gallstones should be diligently explored in all cases of Adams-Stokes syndrome. If stones or an abnormal gallbladder are found, cholecystectomy may not only relieve the patient of biliary symptoms but may improve his cardiac status by decreasing the frequency of recurrent arrhythmias and anginal or syncopal attacks. It is now deemed advisable to remove asymptomatic stones in most instances in view of potential complications such as neoplasm, secondary hepatic or pancreatic involvement, and obstructions, provided no contraindications to elective surgery exist.

Interestingly enough, the risk of cholecystectomy among patients with symptomatic coronary heart disease is relatively low (10 to 15 per cent). Anesthesia, hypotension, and other postoperative factors which increase coagulability of the blood may enhance the possibility of coronary thrombosis. Of course, surgery is preferred during the quiescent phases of gallbladder disease, because postoperative complications of chronic biliary disease are more severe than usual when coronary heart disease coexists.

In regard to medical treatment of biliary tract disease in general, a recent survey covering 381 patients reveals that 15 per cent of all patients with acute cholecystitis failed to respond to medical treatment. When medical treatment succeeded in producing clinical remission, the mortality, complication, and cholecystostomy rates were the lowest in the series. Patients who failed to respond to medical treatment had much higher rates. Thus, early operation should be reserved for the older age group with advanced acute cholecystitis. The patient with less severe forms of acute cholecystitis can best be served by medical treatment and delayed surgery.

In regard to chronic cholecystitis, there is general agreement that cholecystectomy is indicated, preferably during a period when the patient is free from acute symptoms. Recurrent pain is the most urgent indication for operation, particularly when associated with attacks of jaundice. There is also general agreement that cholecystectomy is indicated for cholelithiasis in patients under forty years of age, regardless of the presence of symptoms. For those over sixty years of age with no symptoms, elective surgery is inadvisable because of the higher operative mortality. At times, pain may persist after cholecystectomy. This is particularly common (50 per cent) in noncalculous biliary disease. The major conditions responsible for the so-called "postcholecystectomy distress" may be secondary hepatitis or pancreatitis, duodenal diverticulum, peptic ulcer, diaphragmatic hernia, bronchiectasis, diabetes, or overlooked coronary artery disease.

Two other conditions worthy of brief mention are tumors of the gallbladder and rupture of the gallbladder into the pericardial sac. Cholopericardium has already been considered on page 238. Tumors (adenocarcinoma) resemble chronic cholecystitis with cholelithiasis. The pain is dull, boring, and spasmodic or progressive. It is associated with nausea, vomiting, anorexia, and jaundice. The prognosis is usually very grave. The prevention of adenocarcinoma demands the early removal of stones, with which it is so frequently found in association. Benign tumors may also be found, but they are rather rare.

DISORDERS OF THE PANCREAS

The diagnosis of pancreatic disease is still being missed in too many instances because of the deep position of the organ, the type of symptomatology, and the lack of consistent or specific tests. However, the diagnostic procedures listed in Table 14-2 may be of considerable help.

Table 14-2

Diagnostic Aids in Pancreatitis

Test	Acute Pancreatitis	Chronic Pancreatitis
Serum amylase	Elevated	Normal or low
Serum lipase	Elevated	Normal or low
Blood sugar	Frequently elevated	Elevated fasting level
Serum calcium	Low	Normal or low
Serum bilirubin	May be elevated	May be elevated
Urinary amylase	Elevated	Normal or low
Glucose tolerance curve	Abnormal	Abnormal
Stool examination	Usually not indicated	Increased content of total and neutral fats
Peritoneal aspiration	Turbid or hemorrhagic aspirate	Usually not indicated
Secretin test	Usually not indicated	Low bicarbonate and enzyme content of duodenal aspirate
Radiologic signs	Loss of psoas shadow; paralytic ileus; elevated diaphragm on the left; basal pneumonitis or pleuritis	Calcific deposits within pancreatic shadow; widened duodenal loop; pressure defects in walls of stomach and duodenum
Absorption studies	Usually not indicated	Impaired absorption of triolein labeled with 1^{131}

Acute pancreatitis is frequently confused with acute myocardial infarction, since both conditions begin with severe upper abdominal or high epigastric pain and both may be associated with shock. The differential diagnosis is further complicated by the early occurrence of electrocardiographic changes in both conditions.

In general, pain sensations caused by pancreatic involvement are transmitted bilaterally along visceral afferent fibers accompanying the splanchnic nerves on both sides. Pain is also conducted along somatic afferent pathways, because most of the anterior surface of the pancreas is covered by parietal peritoneum. The distribution of pain arising from the pancreas depends largely on the portion of the gland affected. Studies have demonstrated that when the head of the pancreas is electrically stimulated, pain is distributed over the right epigastrium; that stimulation of the body of the pancreas produces pain in the midepigastrium; and that stimulation of the tail gives rise to pain in the left lower epigastric region, and sometimes in the left lower quadrant. When all parts of the gland are stimulated simultaneously, a band-like pain is felt across the epigastrium, with radiation to the back.

The intensity of pain varies with the extent and degree of pancreatic involvement. In chronic pancreatitis and in cancer of the pancreas, pain tends to be mild to moderate with severe exacerbations. The greatest intensity of pain occurs in acute pancreatic necrosis. Pancreatic pain is usually constant and often boring, although it may be paroxysmal and colicky or even intermittent. Posterior radiation and exacerbation during the night or while in the supine position are highly characteristic. Relief is often experienced by sitting up or bending forward (as in many cases of pericarditis) or by walking around (as in some cases of acute myocardial infarction), except that there is a marked tendency to keep the trunk flexed with pressure exerted upon the epigastrium with pancreatic disease. Radiation may also extend to the sternum, lower abdominal quadrants, flanks, and either scapula.

The differentiation of pain is also complicated by the frequent association of pancreatic and biliary tract disease, which may be as high as 37 per cent. The patient with acute pancreatitis is always very ill. Abdominal distention, deep tenderness, and rigidity are present. Shock develops in severe cases, and jaundice may appear. Laboratory findings depend upon the severity of the disease. Thus, serum amylase and lipase are frequently elevated. The former also appears in the urine and tends to be increased only during the first two or three days. Hyperglycemia, glycosuria, bilirubinemia, bilirubinuria, low prothrombin time, hypocalcemia, and positive liver function tests may also be found.

The close clinical relationship of acute pancreatic disease to the heart has been re-emphasized recently by some authors. Attention has been directed not only to the marked alterations of the blood pressure which occur as an integral manifestation in severe forms of acute pancreatitis but also to the pronounced electrocardiographic changes. The latter have been attributed to four mechanisms: (1) the state of shock with marked hypotension results in coronary insufficiency which is related to a diminished coronary circulation; (2) a reflex originating in the diseased pancreas causes spasm of the coronary arteries; (3) the altered electrolyte equilibrium, often present in acute pancreatitis, causes changes in the QT segment and the T waves; and (4) the pancreatic enzymes exert a direct action on the cardiac structures. Experimental work utilizing direct intravenous injection of sterile pancreatic juice or crystalline trypsin has produced upright spiking of the

T waves. Pancreatic serum enzyme determinations are most important for the diagnosis of pancreatic disease. The serum amylase test is the most widely used procedure in diagnosing and following the course of acute pancreatitis as well as the acute episodes in chronic relapsing pancreatitis. This enzyme attains its greatest value within twenty-four hours of onset of the acute attack and retains it for a variable period, depending upon the severity of the disturbance. It usually returns to normal within two to three days. The serum lipase rises later than the amylase but remains elevated for a longer period of time. The behavior of the amylase enzyme is not infrequently irregular and is also affected by the administration of opiates as well as by conditions simulating the clinical picture of pancreatitis, such as anterior perforation of a duodenal ulcer (about 15 per cent have high serum amylase values), intestinal obstruction, peritonitis, and even hepatic disease. Therefore, determinations of both enzymes increase their diagnostic and prognostic value.

Certain limiting factors must be also considered in interpreting the significance of the serum pancreatic enzyme levels. Chief among these factors are (1) the degree of obstruction of the larger pancreatic ducts, (2) the extent of destruction of acinar tissue, and (3) the stage of the disease at the time the determinations are made. Values of serum amylase in excess of five times the normal value almost always indicate the presence of primary pancreatitis. Analysis of peritoneal fluid for amylase content provides another approach to the identification of acute pancreatitis. Values in excess of 300 Somogyi units strongly suggest the presence of acute pancreatitis but should not be considered pathognomonic of this disease. The antithrombin test represents another method for the diagnosis of pancreatic disease, based on alterations in the factors responsible for coagulation of blood. This test measures the antithrombin titer of the blood by determining the clotting time of defibrinated plasma to which standardized thrombin and fibrinogen aliquots are added. Increased plasma antithrombin titers have been observed in the following conditions: acute pancreatitis, acute exacerbations of chronic relapsing pancreatitis, cancer of the pancreas with jaundice of less than four weeks' duration, and pancreatic cyst. Since the plasma antithrombin titer remains elevated throughout the acute phase of pancreatitis, diagnostic plasma antithrombin values may be obtained at stages of acute pancreatitis when serum pancreatic enzyme levels are no longer increased.

In the diagnosis of chronic pancreatitis (with or without calcification), the determination of the concentration of enzymes in aspirated duodenal juice before and after the administration of a suitable stimulant, the microscopic examination of stools for undigested fat and meat fibers, the chemical analysis of feces for total and split fat and nitrogen, and the oral glucose tolerance test are the most useful procedures.

In addition, x-ray studies of the chest and abdomen are advisable, since acute pancreatic disease may not only produce changes in adjacent segments of the gastrointestinal tract through peripancreatic inflammation, scar formation, pressure or invasion, but supradiaphragmatic changes may also appear in the form of basal pneumonitis, pleurisy, or even pleural effusion, which usually occurs on the left side. Radiopaque gallstones and calcification (see Fig. 14-3) in the region of the pancreas are, of course, distinctive clues.

Chronic pancreatitis may result from recurrent attacks of acute pan-

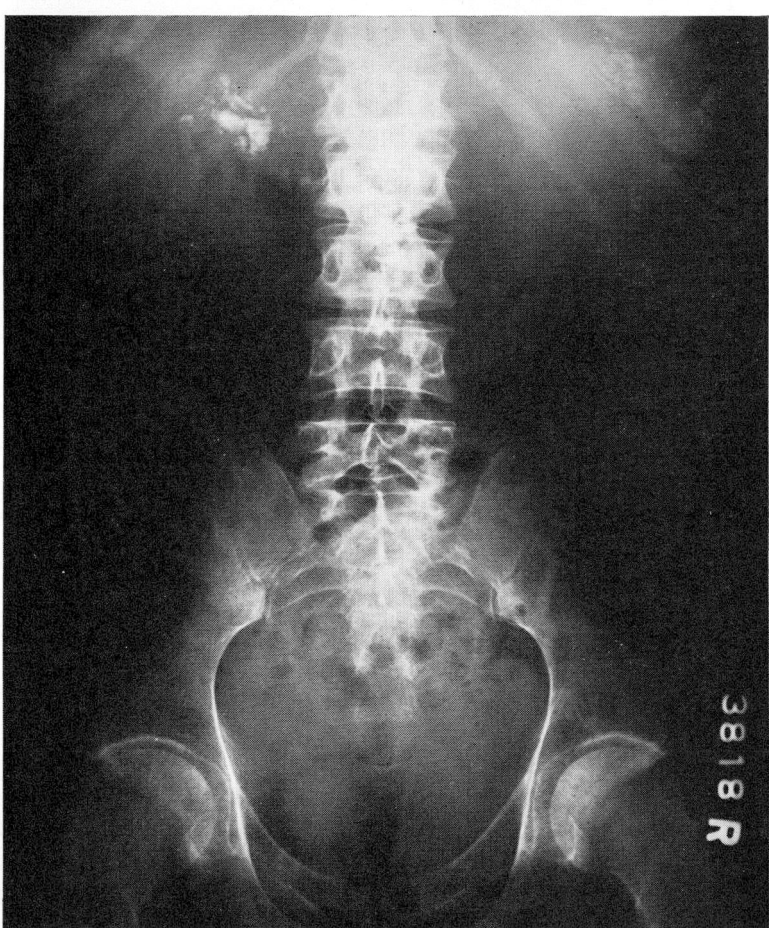

Fig. 14-3. Chronic pancreatitis. Note calcifications outlining anatomic position of pancreas.

creatitis or inflammatory disease of the gallbladder, stomach, or duodenum; penetrating ulcers; tuberculosis; syphilis; or arteriosclerosis. There is a deposition of fibrous tissue which produces a firmness and enlargement of the pancreas. Diabetes may occur due to involvement of the islet tissue. Interference with digestive juice production results in bulky, light, and foul stool. This condition gives rise to weight loss, diarrhea, anemia, edema, ascites, arthritis, achlorhydria, and cutaneous pigmentation. X-rays may reveal distortion or compression of the duodenal loop and pancreatic lithiasis. When jaundice occurs due to compression of the common bile duct, surgery may be indicated to sidetrack the flow of bile.

The medical management of acute pancreatitis is directed toward early and complete control of its physiologic and anatomic sequelae. Alleviation of pain, treatment of shock, replacement of lost fluids and electrolytes, dietary measures which inhibit pancreatic function, neutralization of extravasated pancreatic enzyme activity, relief of ileus, combating of infection, and prevention of recurrences are major lines of attack. Upper abdominal pain may not only be excruciating and highly resistant to opiates in the acute phases of pancreatic disease, but may become intractable in advanced phases of chronic pancreatic disease. The frequent severe emotional disturbances leading to behavior and personality changes encountered in these instances may make the medical management extremely difficult and may necessitate surgical measures for relief of pain, such as splanchnic denervation and even rhizotomy.

Carcinoma of the pancreas may originate in the parenchyma or ducts. The head of the gland is involved in the majority of instances and usually compresses the common bile duct and duodenum. Metastases occur early and especially invade the liver. Indefinite symptoms such as vague epigastric discomfort occur, but pain may be dull, boring, and penetrating. It is usually increased in the supine position and is relieved by curving the spine forward. Pain is worse at night and may be accompanied by rapid weight loss, nausea, vomiting, and abdominal fullness. Jaundice appears eventually, due to involvement of the liver by metastases of compression and invasion of the biliary tract, but may be absent when the tumor affects the body or the tail.

Hepatomegaly occurs as a result of common duct obstruction or metastases. A large gallbladder may be palpated if a fair degree of relaxation of the abdominal wall is possible. It is of special interest that pancreatic tumors are commonly associated with multiple venous thrombosis. Hypercoagulability may extend to the arterial system and may even give rise to coronary thrombosis. Serum lipase may be elevated in the early stages but falls as the acinar tissue is destroyed. Serum trypsin may also become elevated (normally up to 100 units) due to obstruction of the ductal or acinar system. Serum bilirubin is elevated due to the obstructive lesion, and increasingly light stools and darker urines appear. Diabetic findings may appear due to destruction of islet tissue. X-rays may reveal compression of the duodenal loop or common bile duct (see Fig. 14-4). Treatment consists mainly of the

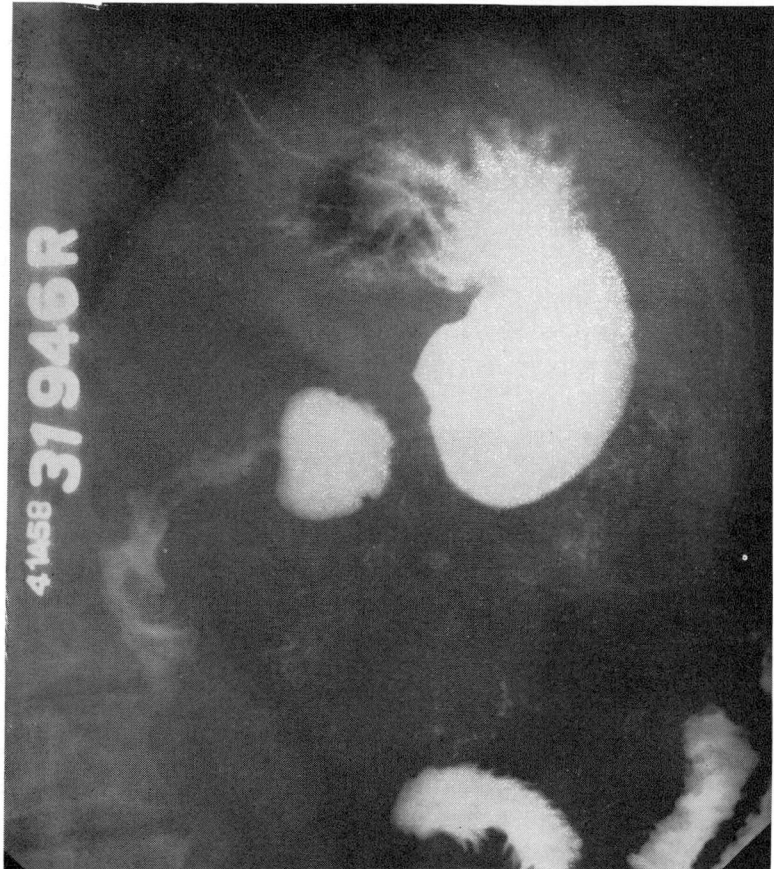

Fig. 14-4. Carcinoma of pancreas. Stomach and duodenum visualized with barium. Duodenal loop not enlarged, but shows thickening and irregularity of the mucosa as well as extrinsic pressure defects along its internal contour.

alleviation of the jaundice by surgical procedures. It is possible to extirpate an early lesion of the pancreas, especially one involving the body or the tail. Even total pancreatectomy has been performed on a number of occasions.

Cysts of the pancreas. Although rare, pancreatic cysts may vary tremendously in size. Pain of variable character and severity is most common. It is located in the epigastrium or left hypochrondrium and may radiate to the back. As the cyst increases in size, it may compress the duodenum, stomach, gallbladder, common duct, or inferior vena cava. A large fluctuant mass may occasionally be palpated. X-rays reveal a smooth compression on the above structures rather than the irregularity produced by pancreatic malignancy. Treatment is marsupialization or complete removal of the cyst.

DISORDERS OF THE UPPER GASTROINTESTINAL TRACT

Noxious impulses may arise within the upper gastrointestinal tract and may produce chest distress, especially in the substernal or epigastric region. Thus, these upper digestive disorders require careful differentiation from pain of cardiac origin. Such noxious impulses may be caused by local stimulation of an inflamed or engorged gastric mucosa or by distention or spasm of the gastric musculature. The former mechanism is usually present in the various types of nonspecific and specific gastritis. The latter mechanism is responsible for the pain experienced in *aerophagia, cardiospasm*, and *pylorospasm*. Not infrequently, both mechanisms operate simultaneously. The pain sensation may vary from a feeling of vague "indigestion," as occurs in gastritis, to severe pain, such as is encountered in peptic ulcer. Of less diagnostic value are symptoms of epigastric fullness, anorexia, nausea, and vomiting.

Various types of *acute gastritis* include the acute simple exogenous (alcohol and spices), corrosive (lye), infectious, and suppurative types. The chronic forms encompass the atrophic, hypertrophic, and superficial types. A precise history of the factors attending the appearance and the relief of the "indigestion" or pain is most helpful in cases of acute gastritis. X-ray studies and gastroscopy are important diagnostic aids in chronic gastritis and are often indispensable, since the pain may resemble that of gastric neoplasm or peptic ulcer. Psychogenic causes may also be responsible for symptoms of both acute and chronic "indigestion" or actual pain, or they may become superimposed upon organic disorders of the stomach.

The management of these causes of indigestion obviously depends upon the underlying factors involved. In general, it consists of a bland diet, avoidance of irritating foods and condiments, interval feedings, antacids for hyperacidity, and antispasmodics. Occasionally, psychotherapy and antibiotic therapy are also indicated. Gastritis due to syphilis or tuberculosis requires specific therapy.

Of all the stomach disorders causing pain by distention, the most prevalent is *aerophagia. Cardiospasm* is discussed in the chapter on esophageal disorders (see pp. 141–43), since it is usually due to or associated with disease of the lower esophagus. *Pylorospasm* is frequently secondary to a prepyloric peptic ulcer or malignancy and is included in the appropriate section.

Aerophagia is the leading cause of functional digestive symptoms. Although excessive air swallowing may be initiated by any disorder causing nausea or hyperventilation, the most common cause for this subconscious act is an emotional disturbance, such as tension or anxiety. Symptoms of aerophagia may be erroneously attributed to either cardiac or biliary disease. Conversely, gaseous pressure may mask symptoms of underlying heart disease, cholecystitis, peptic ulcer, or emphysema. Belching may be habitually induced to relieve discomfort from anginal seizures. Aerophagia is mainly responsible for the so-called "magenblase" and the hepatic and splenic flexure colon syndromes. "Magenblase" is produced by a large gastric air bubble which appears during or shortly after meals. Pseudo-angina results when the "magenblase" causes stabbing pain along the left rib margin or in the pectoral area. Pressure on the diaphragm may also cause secondary radiation to the left shoulder, which may prove confusing. The hepatic and splenic flexure colon syndromes are discussed on pages 347–49.

The diagnosis of aerophagia is not difficult. Tension and frequent air swallowing may be noted even during the interview. Characteristically, the distress increases as more and more air is swallowed. This becomes aggravated as the body temperature causes further expansion of the gas. Eventually, the increasing pressure overcomes the cardiosphincteric control, and complete relief is obtained after belching occurs; unfortunately, the cycle is repeated again and again. Examination may disclose tympany, distention, and borborygmi. Aerophagia may also be evident beneath the left diaphragm during fluoroscopic and x-ray examinations, where it appears as a large air bubble in the fundus.

For effective treatment, one must uncover the underlying causes of aerophagia and attempt to remove them. A dietary regimen based on the avoidance of gas-producing varieties of vegetables and of raw fruits and vegetables is helpful, as are walking, abdominal massage, and heat. Reassurance is important, since patients are tense and frequently concerned because of the precordial location of pain. A tranquilizer may control an underlying anxiety or tension state. Psychotherapy may be indicated in more severe instances of psychoneuroses.

Peptic ulcer. Ulceration of the stomach, especially of the prepyloric portion, gives rise to pain which is commonly experienced in the upper abdomen and less frequently in the chest, and which may be referred to either anterolateral or dorsal regions. At times, the pain may be felt in the lower anterior chest alone. An understanding of the pathways responsible for the typical and atypical pain patterns is essential for the proper differential diagnosis (see Chap. 2). All nervous impulses arising in the upper abdomen are transmitted over three general pathways: parasympathetic (vagus), sympathetic (splanchnic), and somatic (intercostal). All painful stimuli from the upper abdomen are transmitted over the splanchnic and intercostal nerves. The vagal fibers conduct motor impulses which stimulate gastrointestinal motility and secretion. The afferent impulse of visceral pain is transmitted through the celiac ganglion, over the great splanchnic nerve, through the sympathetic chain, and then to the spinal core and through the spinothalamic tract to the brain. The afferent impulse of somatic pain is transmitted through the intercostal nerves to the spinal cord and then proceeds to the brain along the same pathway as the visceral afferent impulse. The close anatomic relationship of visceral and somatic fibers in the posterior horn probably explains referred pain by the so-called "overflow mechanism." Visceral pain is ill defined and arises from distention or spasm of the viscus or from traction on the mesentery. Chemical and physical stimuli of various types cause visceral pain only if the mucosa is inflamed or engorged. Somatic pain is more sharply defined and localized and results from a variety of chemical and physical stimuli. The parietal peritoneum, body wall, diaphragm, mesentery, and lesser omentum have a rich supply of pain fibers from the intercostal nerves.

The pain of peptic ulceration has been ascribed to a large number of mechanisms. Of these, hyperacidity, disturbed motility, and local inflammatory reaction of the ulcer lesions are the most commonly invoked theoretic explanations. According to studies utilizing a balloon-kymographic technic on patients with symptomatic ulcers, no constant relationship was found either between acidity and pain or motility and pain. The instillation of a 0.5 per cent solution of hydrochloric acid produced pain with regularity, and that of sodium bicarbonate led to relief in all cases. This study supports local inflammatory reaction as the basic mechanism for the production of pain. Regardless of the actual mechanism, peptic ulcer may be considered as the product of an abnormal physiologic state characterized by inability of localized areas of the stomach and duodenum to withstand the digestive action of acid gastric juice. In gastric ulcer, the output of hydrochloric acid is normal or low, but its corrosive effect presumably surpasses the diminished resistance of the gastric mucosa. In duodenal ulcer, the secretion of hydrochloric acid is excessive, and its digestive capacity exceeds the normal resistance of the duodenal mucosa. However, localized areas of vulnerability also may exist in the duodenum. Present evidence tends to emphasize the role of vagal hyperactivity, effecting a more responsive gastric secretory mechanism. However, other factors, chemical and humoral, undoubtedly are involved.

The relationships of gastric or duodenal ulcer to cardiac disease are manifold. The pain due to ulcer may be referred or limited to the thoracic region. For example, chest pain occurring in the dorsal and right anterior chest region may actually constitute the only symptom of gastric ulcer. Atypical location or superimposed digestive lesions must also be investigated, since an ulcer may also occur high on the lesser curvature or along the greater curvature. The differentiation from pain produced by intrathoracic structures, such as the heart, lungs, pleura, and skeletal structures, may be facilitated by noting its relation to eating and the frequent association of dysphagia.

Pain may be confined to the interscapular area or may extend to the lateral chest wall or abdomen, simulating intercostal neuralgia. Discomfort is often severe and may awaken the patient from the deepest sleep. Frequently, interscapular tenderness is not associated with visceral symptoms and is not influenced by food intake. The pain may be constant and not modified by movement or change of position. Anesthetizing the skin over the spinous processes of D_6 and D_7 has been found to abolish this pain. Interscapular symptoms often persist until after complete healing of the ulcer. In differentiating this type of pain, herniated cervical disc, cervical rib and scalenus anticus syndromes, intercostal neuralgia, and esophageal or coronary disease must be excluded.

The differentiation of peptic ulceration from cardiac disease may be complicated by their not infrequent association. After all, stress may play an important role in both conditions. The difficulty in differential diagnosis extends also to the therapy, since the appropriate dietary regimen must be applied. Present coronary diets demand less cholesterol and fats, whereas they are usually considered an integral dietary feature in ulcer management.

An interrelationship with heart disease may be encountered in gastrointestinal hemorrhage. Peptic ulceration with hemorrhage is known to occur following surgery for congenital or acquired heart disease and may be fatal unless suspected. It has also been reported following acute coronary occlusion, suggesting an acute stress reaction. On the other hand, myocardial infarction or acute coronary insufficiency may follow perforation with shock or a severe hemorrhage from a peptic ulcer, due to the ensuing fall in blood pressure and decreased coronary blood flow in the presence of coronary disease. Since hemorrhage may not be preceded by pain, rapid blood loss may reach critical levels because of the lack of any obvious warning. Such cases, especially among the aged, require prompt and adequate replacement of blood in order to prevent shock and to avoid coronary insufficiency or thrombosis. If bleeding continues or recurs, early operation is imperative. A hematocrit and serial blood urea nitrogen determinations, in addition to the usual roentgenographic and gastric content studies, may be of considerable help in evaluating the status. Two major problems in diagnosis and management are dependent on the differentiation of benign ulcer from malignant ulcer and the possible malignant transformation of benign gastric ulcer. The first is usually possible with the help of extensive diagnostic procedures. The latter is actually quite rare but nevertheless requires careful observation of the rapidity of the healing process. Size of the ulceration is no longer considered very significant. A gastric ulcer should show complete healing within two to three months; otherwise, additional investigations, such as gastroscopy, are indicated.

Carcinoma of the stomach. This common neoplastic lesion usually involves the antral and pyloric regions and less commonly affects both curvatures and the remaining regions of the stomach. Pain is usually epigastric in location and not infrequently vague and variable in character. Of particular interest is carcinoma of the proximal third of the stomach, since it is not only in closer proximity to the thorax but is more difficult to diagnose. In contrast to lesions occurring in other regions of this viscus, it is characterized by the greater frequency of dysphagia as an initial symptom and by the presence of a gnawing pain which is usually localized to the epigastrium, although it may be referred to other regions of the upper abdomen or the chest. Radiation to the back or chest is infrequent. The intensity of pain varies, and it may occur continuously or intermittently. The recognition of a lesion of the proximal third of the stomach is not only complicated by the somewhat atypical character of the pain but is made more difficult by the infrequency of a palpable abdominal mass. Unfortunately, even radiographic studies have distinct limitations in uncovering lesions in this area. However, gastroscopic examination and stained specimens may be of considerable aid in the diagnosis of malignancy. Certain complications of gastric neoplasms may produce confusing symptomatology because of referred pain. For example, they may require careful differentiation from acute pancreatitis and acute coronary disease when they perforate into the upper abdomen or penetrate into the neighboring pancreas. Acute pancreatitis tends to produce a pain which is boring and which is worse on lying down. Other differentiating features have been described previously in this chapter.

Gastric diverticula. While the majority of gastric diverticula are asymptomatic, some may give rise to upper abdominal pain of varying severity.

Congenital and acquired types are recognizable. The congenital variety tends to occur near the fundus. Pain occurs more frequently in the acquired type, which is usually caused by traction of inflammatory lesions of adjacent structures and is usually localized near the pylorus. The pain may resemble "acute indigestion" or acute gastritis. It may be located in the epigastrium, the xiphoid region, or under the left costal margin toward the midline. It tends to be relieved by belching or vomiting.

Since acquired diverticula occur in the coronary age group, the pain requires differentiation from atypical anginal seizures with localization at the xiphoid area. Diaphragmatic hernia, low esophageal diverticulum, or penetrating gastric ulcer must also be excluded. A pathognomonic roentgenographic picture usually shows the round, well-delineated pouch along the upper border of the lesser curvature. Mucosal studies exclude the erosive penetration of a gastric ulcer.

Colon flexure syndromes. The mere presence of gas collections in one or both colonic flexures does not necessarily indicate disease. These syndromes involve either the hepatic or the splenic flexure of the colon. Both syndromes are due to large collections of gas which are trapped in the respective segments of the large bowel by colonic spasm or by angulation caused by adhesions or bowel redundancy. Chronic fatigue, constipation, overeating, or consumption of gas-producing foods may also initiate an attack. Pains are usually paroxysmal and begin rather suddenly. They last from a minute to several hours and subside fairly rapidly, sometimes leaving a persistent discomfort. Although the pathophysiology is similar, symptoms are greatly different because of their locations. The *hepatic flexure syndrome* simulates gallbladder disease; the *splenic flexure syndrome* may produce symptoms suggestive of coronary artery disease.

In the hepatic flexure syndrome, periodic right upper quadrant pressure of varying severity frequently occurs. This discomfort may radiate into the epigastrium and may even be transmitted to the right shoulder. This pain requires differentiation from that due to a biliary dyskinesia, chronic cholecystitis without stones, postcholecystectomy syndrome, or chronic liver disease. The abnormal accumulation of gas in the hepatic flexure is readily percussed and is easily demonstrated on a flat plate of the abdomen or by fluoroscopic examination.

In the splenic flexure syndrome, a sensation of fullness or aching in the region of the precordium or left chest is a common symptom. Later, pain occurs in the subscapular or supraclavicular regions and extends to the left shoulder and upper arm but rarely radiates to the wrist. Deep breathing or manual compression of the left upper quadrant will usually aggravate the symptoms. Abdominal symptoms include a sense of fullness, distention, and discomfort in the left upper quadrant. The trapped gas can be easily demonstrated by percussion, which reveals an abnormal area of hyperresonance in the left lower chest and left upper abdomen. This finding is readily confirmed by x-ray (see Fig. 14-5) or fluoroscopy. The splenic flexure syndrome

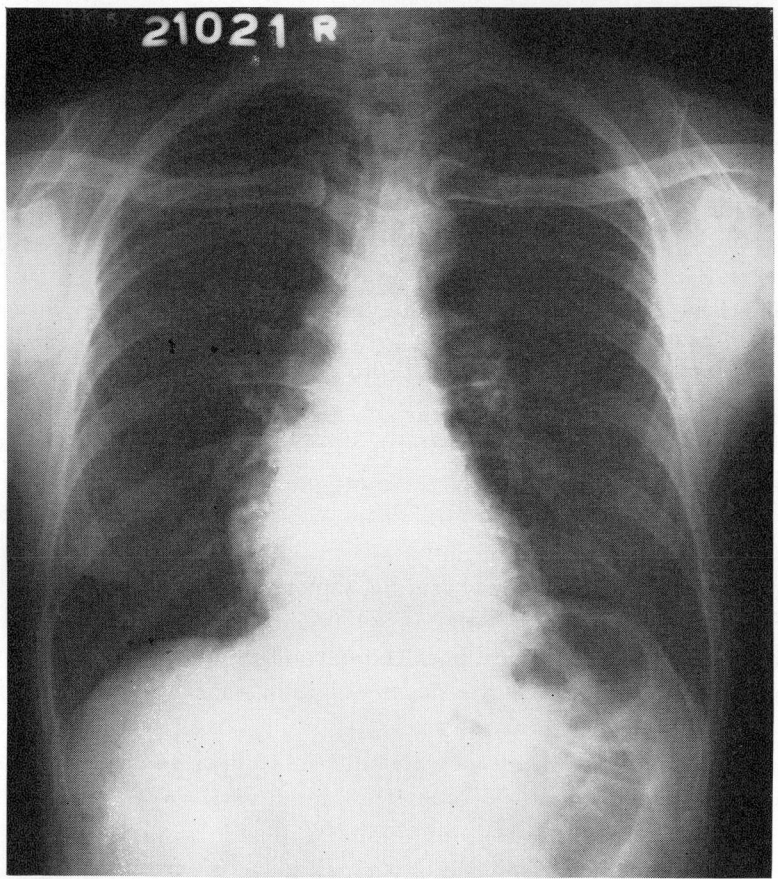

Fig. 14-5. Splenic flexure syndrome. Note splenic flexure, distended with gas, immediately beneath elevated left dome of diaphragm.

must be distinguished from acute myocardial infarction or coronary insufficiency, gastric ulcer, hiatus hernia, left renal disease, gastric cancer, and pancreatic tumor. Obviously, patients with gas accumulations do not present the general appearance of a serious illness. The development of a cardiac neurosis and the subsequent necessity for excluding organic heart disease usually require electrocardiograms and other laboratory studies (transaminase and blood counts). "Laubry-Soulle syndrome" is a term which has been employed to describe the appearance of a new chest pain about three or four days after a myocardial infarction. It is caused by the colonic gas and subsides spontaneously in about two weeks.

Management is made difficult by the neurotic personality of the patient, who may also suffer from related conditions, such as spastic colon or cardiac anxiety. To prevent recurrences, psychologic readjustment is necessary. Encouragement and reassurance are essential, and antispasmodic drugs as well as sedatives or tranquilizers are most helpful. Enemas may be necessary to initiate the expulsion of gas; a buttermilk diet has been found to be effective in some instances.

The "dumping" syndrome. This condition is not infrequently encountered following a short circuiting procedure such as gastroenterostomy or subtotal gastric resection. A relationship to the cardiovascular system exists on clinical and physiologic grounds. Palpitation and pain may be referred to the precordial region, as may other manifestations due to acute alterations in blood volume. Clinical and electrocardiographic changes are triggered by rapid enzymatic hydrolysis of foodstuffs within the jejunal lumen, and a subsequent breakdown of larger molecular particles into their smaller molecular components with a corresponding increase in osmolarity. As a result of the increased osmolarity, extracellular fluid is shifted into the jejunal lumen in an attempt to maintain isotonicity of the jejunal contents with the plasma. This is associated with an acute decrease in circulating blood volume and extracellular fluid, a fall in blood pressure, and electrocardiographic changes resembling myocardial ischemia. The electrocardiographic variations include low, flattened, or inverted T waves, abnormally large U waves, sagging ST segments, and increased voltage of P waves. Since similar changes can be produced by subcutaneous or intravenous injection of epinephrine, it has been suggested that adrenal stimulation plays a part in this syndrome. However, the mechanism responsible for at least the electrocardiographic changes is probably a shift in potassium which may be related to the rapid absorption of carbohydrates.

The diagnosis depends upon the history or the roentgenographic evidence of gastric surgery. Symptoms consist of a feeling of warmth, weakness, sweating, epigastric or low substernal tightness or pain, vertigo, nausea, palpitation, and collapse. These symptoms occur with variable severity and usually appear soon after meals. The treatment varies with the etiologic concept. Some authorities advocate atropine or tetraethylammonium (Etamon) before meals, and the omission of fluids from meals. Others employ a high-protein, low-carbohydrate diet.

Carcinoid tumor. This unique tumor of the digestive system is found in the stomach, gallbladder, duodenum, small intestine, Meckel's diverticulum, appendix, ileocecal valve, cecum, colon and rectum, and in the gastrointestinal components of teratomas of the ovary. They are most frequently found in the appendix. It is generally agreed that all carcinoids have malignant potentialities, especially those of the small intestine (25 to 50 per cent).

The malignant carcinoid also acts as an endocrine tumor, producing high concentrations of serotonin. The manifestations of functioning carcinoids may be gastrointestinal, vascular-cutaneous, cardiovascular, or metabolic. Carcinoid may be responsible for chest pain or discomfort by referring pain from its primary site in the gastrointestinal tract, or by causing a bronchospastic condition with resultant discomfort resembling other conditions. Recognition of such tumors may be difficult, since the earliest manifestations may not produce intestinal symptoms but may be of respiratory origin with paroxysmal dyspnea, wheezing, and cyanosis. This may lead to its confusion with a primary bronchopulmonary disorder, while the findings of an associated valvular lesion may be mistaken as evidence for a primary cardiac disorder. Flushes and occasional palpitation in women may be mistaken for a menopausal syndrome.

Because of its protean clinical manifestations, the "carcinoid syndrome" may mimic a number of diseases. Paroxysmal flushing of the skin is one of the most frequent extraintestinal findings. Latent cardiac involvement, with endocardial lesions affecting the pulmonic and tricuspid valves and producing right-sided heart failure, is another outstanding lesion. The metabolic disorder consists of altered tryptophan metabolism with loss of weight and the development of a protein deficiency and a related niacin deficiency.

These phenomena can best be explained by the chemical abnormalities caused by serotonin. Direct chemical irritation may damage the endocardium following the liberation of serotonin directly into the blood stream. Predominance of right-sided heart lesions has also been attributed to destruction of free serotonin in the lungs. In 1953 Lembeck isolated a substance from a carcinoid tumor that was identified chemically as 5-hydroxytryptamine and which is identical with vasoactive material called enteramine or serotonin. This substance is found in enterochromaffin tissue. It is pharmacologically active on smooth muscle, producing intestinal peristalsis, bronchoconstriction, and varying effects on blood vessels. Thus, the concept gradually evolved that many carcinoid tumors are "truly functioning tumors." The finding of elevated urinary 5HIAA (hydroxyindoleacetic acid), a metabolite of serotonin, is diagnostic of malignant carcinoid (values usually exceed 30 mg daily in a twenty-four–hour specimen). Hydergine is an antimetabolite substance which can neutralize the action of serotonin and thus relieve or abolish the resultant symptoms. Chlorpromazine has been found helpful in combating nausea and flushing. Complete extirpation of the tumor is essential. Small tumors up to about 1 cm, if noninvasive and not fixed in position, may be safely treated with wide local excision.

MISCELLANEOUS ABDOMINAL DISORDERS

"Abdominal angina." The occasional and unwarranted use of this vague diagnostic label is confusing and one which requires further clarification. Both the etiology and pathophysiology are nebulous. The abdominal distress frequently proves to have a coronary origin in such cases, since the pain of anginal syndrome or acute coronary insufficiency may be referred atypically to the epigastric region. On the other hand, epigastric pain or pain referred to or localized in the substernal or precordial region may also occur in biliary disease.

It has also been suggested that kinking, torsion, or angulation of the mesenteric artery, caused by peristaltic movements or the weight of excess fatty omental deposits, may also produce "abdominal angina." It is obviously very difficult to establish such etiologic factors because of their transitory character.

"Abdominal migraine." "Migraine" is a term employed to describe nebulous pain in the head, chest wall, or abdomen. However, careful study can frequently uncover the exact nature of the pathologic changes and the mechanism for the production of typical "migraine" symptoms or their equivalents. "Thoracic migraine" is discussed on page 90.

"Abdominal migraine" is an equivalent which describes epigastric or abdominal distress of variable severity. There is a familial tendency, and the attack may last an hour or longer. Chronic pancreatitis, cysts of the pancreas, disturbances of the biliary tract (biliary dyskinesia, cholelithiasis, cholecystitis), disturbances of the stomach (chronic hypertrophic gastritis), spastic colon, and food allergy must be carefully investigated as possible causes of "abdominal migraine." The label may be employed only as an exclusion diagnosis. The term "abdominal migraine" appears justified only when typical cranial migraine attacks develop with associated symptoms of abdominal pain, nausea, vomiting, and diarrhea and are confirmed by the therapeutic response to the administration of ergotamine tartrate (Gynergen) or ergotamine and caffeine (Cafergot). Chlorpromazine (Thorazine) and its newer derivatives are helpful adjuncts because of their antiemetic and tranquilizing properties.

Mesenteric artery disease. A disorder of the abdominal circulation, specifically of the mesenteric arteries, may be responsible for anginoid pain which occurs more commonly in the epigastric or midabdominal region and is occasionally referred to the chest, back, or shoulder. The disturbance is due to incomplete vascular obstruction caused by atheromatous changes of the mesenteric arteries. Such a condition may be termed "intermittent mesenteric ischemia." Since it has a counterpart in coronary insufficiency, the label "mesenteric insufficiency" may be simpler and more accurate terminology. Complete occlusion of mesenteric arteries presents the clinical picture of an acute abdominal catastrophe with severe pain, usually involving the midabdominal region. Ileus or bloody stool may occur. It is usually caused by thromboarteriosclerosis or embolism and is a surgical emergency. The diagnosis of mesenteric ischemia is more difficult to evaluate. Aortography with the catheter or needle at the level of the celiac axis or mesenteric arteries may show narrowing of a mesenteric arterial segment. The pain is usually both postprandial and greatly dependent upon position. Relief is usually obtained in the prone position and by leaning forward.

Ruptured ectopic pregnancy. The outstanding symptom following rupture of an ectopic pregnancy is abdominal or pelvic pain of a tearing, stabbing character. The pain may be generalized or localized but is often referred to the shoulder, where it may also be the presenting symptom. This may not always occur on the same side as the rupture. Abdominal distention, nausea and vomiting, constipation, and urinary disturbances are commonly associated symptoms. The history and clinical picture may deviate from the classic syndrome to such an extent that a correct diagnosis may be impossible prior to surgical exploration. Because it occurs in women during the childbearing age, it is seldom confused with a coronary type of radiation unless there is a coexisting hypertensive disorder or other condition commonly associated with coronary disease. Therefore, the history of a missed menstrual period and the age of patient strongly militate against coronary disease but not against pulmonary embolism, diaphragmatic pleurisy, or gallbladder disease. The Trendelenburg position may facilitate irritation of the diaphragm with the production of shoulder pain by the presence of intraperitoneal blood. Gynecologic examination may establish the presence of a pelvic mass and tenderness.

DISORDERS OF THE SPLEEN

The two most common diseases of the spleen which are capable of causing left chest as well as abdominal pain are rupture and infarction.

Rupture of the spleen. The spleen is the organ which is most commonly ruptured in nonpenetrating abdominal injuries. The frequency of splenic rupture is due to its friable nature, to its mobility and free suspension by the lienorenal and gastrosplenic ligaments, and to its close proximity to the chest wall. Obviously, a malarial spleen or other splenic disorder predisposes to rupture. The injury which causes rupture of the spleen most frequently is an automobile or motorcycle accident. When the violence is severe and more apparent, there may be associated pathology such as fractures of the left lower ribs or damage to the left kidney. However, the injury may be surprisingly slight, particularly when it occurs in children while sledding or cycling.

A ruptured spleen may produce a great variety of clinical symptoms and signs, the most serious of which is evidence of progressive intraperitoneal hemorrhage. Pain is invariably present and may vary from a dull ache to a most excruciating agony. Kehr's sign (pain at the tip of the left shoulder) is referred from irritation of the central part of the diaphragm. It is present in about 24 per cent of the cases. If the sign is absent, it may often be produced by maintaining the Trendelenburg position for a few minutes. Pain in the shoulder or neck often may occur only in the supine position. Frequently, deep breathing will precipitate or enhance the pain.

Peritoneal tenderness on rectal examination, pallor, abdominal tenderness and distention, and increased dullness in the splenic area and left flank are frequent signs. Roentgenologic signs consist of increased density in the left hypochondrium, elevation of the left leaf of the diaphragm, displacement of the stomach to the right, and the presence of free fluid between loops of intestine. Depression of the splenic flexure of the colon by a perisplenic hematoma may be of assistance in doubtful cases. Careful needling in the lower abdominal segment may reveal frank blood. Ruptured spleen may escape detection when symptoms are attributed to fractured ribs or bruised muscles, ruptured intestine, ruptured liver, lacerated kidney, perforated ulcer, or ruptured ectopic gestation. Immediate splenectomy and blood replacement are indicated.

Infarction of the spleen. Infarction of the spleen with secondary perisplenitis may be responsible for severe pain, which is not always experienced in the left upper abdominal quadrant alone but may be referred to the left lower chest and even to the left shoulder.

Infarction of the spleen may be secondary to emboli originating in the left heart from a mural thrombus following myocardial infarction or atrial fibrillation or subacute bacterial endocarditis, or it may be due to thrombosis of splenic vessels. Sickle-cell hemoglobin C disease may lead to painful splenomegaly with fibrinous perisplenitis. The degree of sickling of the erythrocytes of individuals with sicklemia is related to the oxygen tension to which the blood is exposed. Victims of sicklemia may be adversely affected by exposure to reduced oxygen tension, such as occurs during high-altitude flight. Splenic infarcts may also develop during flight even in individuals who have only the sickle-cell trait. Polycythemia, thrombocytopenic purpura, and leukemias may also cause splenic phlebothrombosis and infarction. It may also occur in the presence of enzyme-secreting tumors of the pancreas, stomach, and lungs, as well as in postoperative states, due to hemoconcentration and transitory rise in platelets.

Splenic vein thrombosis, torsion of the pedicle of the spleen, and pressure on the splenic artery by an adjacent neoplasm are other less frequent causes of pain due to splenic involvement which are not infrequently referred to the thoracic region. In the presence of cardiac disease, pulmonary and renal embolization with secondary infarction have to be differentiated from splenic infarction. In mild cases, it may be impossible to arrive at a definite diagnosis, since no significant localizing signs or laboratory evidence of any significance may appear. A friction rub may be palpated or heard over the splenic area. In more severe cases, the presence of hemorrhagic pleural effusion, pleural friction rub, hemoptysis, and electrocardiographic changes may favor the diagnosis of pulmonary infarction. Hematuria (and occasional evidence of renal dysfunction) strongly suggests renal infarction. Treatment is that of the primary disease process. Anticoagulants are indicated in appropriate cases.

DISORDERS OF THE ADRENAL GLANDS

Pheochromocytoma. This is the most important lesion of the adrenal glands responsible for the appearance of chest pain. This tumor usually arises in the adrenal medulla, slightly more often on the right side than on the left. It may also originate in extra-adrenal sites of chromaffin tissue, which are usually found along the sympathetic chain of the aorta. These tumors may be bilateral or multiple. There is a familial tendency. They are not infrequently associated with neurofibromatosis and may be malignant, metastasize, or undergo hemorrhage, necrosis, or secondary infection with abscess formation. The tumor consists of functioning cells which are capable of releasing epinephrine and norepinephrine directly into the blood stream. The intermittent secretion of these substances is responsible for the characteristic crisis, which occurs in less than half the cases.

Chest pains, or more specifically anginal episodes, are frequently present during the crises, which are also manifested by palpitation, drenching perspiration, hypertension, headache, diarrhea, pallor, and psychic disturbances. Myocardial infarction has been known to occur following an episode; it appears spontaneously or can be precipitated by simple palpation or massage of the tumor or by changes in body position, such as flexing the trunk.

A number of pharmacologic tests which precipitate such crises are available for diagnostic purposes. The histamine test produces a paradoxic elevation of blood pressure and may not be entirely safe. Tetraethylammonium (Etamon) and methacholine (Mecholyl) have also been employed. During a crisis with the associated hypertension, the administration of piperoxan (Benodaine) or, preferably, phentolamine hydrochloride (Regitine) is also of diagnostic help, since it terminates the crisis by blocking or neutralizing both medullary hormones.

The chemical determination of epinephrine and norepinephrine content of urine and plasma shows a significant elevation not only during the intermittent crises of pheochromocytoma but even during the normotensive interval. The hormones are also found to be elevated in the form that resembles sustained essential hypertension of either benign or malignant type. However, these chemical tests have their limitations. For instance, the fluorescence which is used to determine the presence of epinephrine and norepinephrine may be due to the presence of therapeutic substances, such as tetracycline and other antibiotics. Careful and repeated observations of the blood pressure during the course of surgical intervention for pheochromocytoma are essential, and appropriate depressor and pressor drugs should be available for prompt administration during operation. Hypotension commonly follows removal of a pheochromocytoma and requires treatment with pressor agents and corticosteroids. Hypertension may occur from the handling of the tumor during surgery.

Since pheochromocytoma produces a curable form of both hypertension and angina, it should always be considered in the differential diagnosis of angina pectoris. The rise in blood pressure due to a pheochromocytoma tends to be much greater than that usually observed during an anginal seizure. Other evidences of hyperadrenalism, such as hyperglycemia and increased basal metabolic rate, may be helpful differentiating features.

Waterhouse-Friderichsen syndrome occurs in a small percentage of cases of acute septicemia and severe hemorrhagic disorders which are complicated by extensive hemorrhages into the adrenal glands. Acute meningococcemia is the most common type of infection. Massive adrenal bleeding may also occur in the newborn. Abdominal pain may be referred to the thorax. Malaise, petechiae, cyanosis, marked fall in blood pressure, and fatal collapse occur within twenty-four hours. Treatment is directed at the under-lying infection or blood dyscrasia. Corticosteroids and the medullary hor-mones are employed in large doses.

REFERENCES

Bauer, J., and Fisher, L. J.: Sickle cell disease. *Arch. Surg.*, **47**:533, 1943.

Berman, L. G., and Russo, F. R.: Abdominal angina. *New England J. Med.*, **242**:611, 1950.

Cahill, G. F.: Pheochromocytomas. *J.A.M.A.*, **138**:180, 1948.

Caini, B., and Modigliani, V.: Cardiovascular syndrome of acute pancreatitis. *Settimana med. sper.*, **44**:349, 1956.

Colcock, B. P., and McManus, J. E.: Cholecystectomy for cholelithiasis: a review of 1,356 cases. *S. Clin. North America*, **35**:765, 1955.

Connell, J. L.: Rupture of the spleen. *M. J. Australia*, **1**:676, 1955.

Craver, W. L., and Glenn, F.: Massive hemorrhage from peptic ulcer: a cause of myocardial infarction in the aged. *J. Am. Geriat. Soc.*, **5**:969, 1957.

Eisenbud, M., and Finby, N.: Carcinoma of the proximal third of the stomach: a critical study of clinical observation in 74 cases. *Ann. Int. Med.*, **46**:43, 1957.

Emlet, J. R.; Grimson, K. S.; Bell, D. M.; and Orgain, E. S.: *J.A.M.A.*, **146**:1383, 1951.

Field, L. E.; Pordy, L.; and Master, A. M.: Acute coronary occlusion simulating acute abdominal disease. *New York J. Med.*, **49**:1419, 1949.

Fremont, R. E.: Hypertensive crisis and severe myocardial ischemia induced by piperoxan with comments on the differential diagnosis and treatment of hyper-tensive crises. *Angiology*, **5**:381, 1954.

Garrett, R. M.: Cholelithiasis and cardiac disease. *Am. J. Surg.*, **19**:503, 1953.

Gilbertsen, V. A.: Use of Trendelenburg position in diagnosis of intraperitoneal hemorrhage: a maneuver to facilitate production of shoulder pain. *J.A.M.A.*, **158**:650, 1955.

Goldenberg, M.; Snyder, C. H.; and Aranow, H., Jr.: New test for hypertension due to circulating epinephrine. *J.A.M.A.*, **135**:971, 1947.

Hayes, A. M.: Biliary tract surgery in patients past 60 years of age. *J. Am. Geriat. Soc.*, **3**:146, 1955.

Hinshaw, D. B. et al.: Peripheral blood flow and blood volume studies in the dumping syndrome. *A.M.A. Arch. Surg.*, **74**:686, 1957.

Iseri, L. T.; Henderson, H. W.; and Derr, J. W.: *Am. Heart J.*, **42**:129, 1951.

Judovich, B., and Pincus, I. J.: Interscapular pain. *Lancet*, **16**:204, 1956.

Kalser, M. M.; Bockus, H. L.; Roth, J. L. A.; Bogoch, A.; and Stein, G. N.: Clinical features of acute inflammation of the pancreas: analysis of 80 cases. *Arch. Int. Med.*, **96**:308, 1955.

Keys, J. R.; Dry, T. J.; Walters, W.; and Gage, R. P.: Cholecystectomy in patients with coronary heart disease. *Proc. Staff Meet. Mayo Clin.*, **30**:587, 1955.

Kirsner, J. B.: Current status of therapy in peptic ulcer. *J.A.M.A.*, **166**:1727, 1958.

Kvale, W. F.; Priestley, J. T.; and Roth, G. M.: Pheochromocytoma: clinical aspects and surgical results. *A.M.A. Arch. Surg.*, **68**:769, 1954.

McLemore, G. A., Jr., and Levine, S. A.: The possible therapeutic value of cholecystectomy in patients with coronary heart disease. *Proc. Staff Meet. Mayo Clin.*, **30**:587, 1955.

Marshall, J. M.: The silent gallstone. *Am. J. Surg.*, **88**:365, 1954.

Mattingly, T. W.: The functioning carcinoid tumor—a new clinical entity: review of the clinical features of the nonfunctioning and functioning carcinoid, including a review of thirty-eight cases from the literature (parts I and II). *M. Ann. District of Columbia*, **25**:239, 304, 1956.

Mikkelsen, W. P., and Zars, J. A., Jr.: Intestinal angina: report of a case with preoperative diagnosis and surgical relief. *New England J. Med.*, **260**:912, 1959.

Minno, M.; Bennett, A.; and Kvale, W. F.: Pheochromocytoma: a study of 15 cases diagnosed at necropsy. *New England J. Med.*, **251**:959, 1954.

O'Brien, G. F., and Schweitzer, I. L.: Biliary tract syndromes and their treatment. *M. Clin. North America*, **37**:155, 1953.

Palmer, E. D.; Deutsch, D. L.; and Scott, N. M.: Clinical experience with the splenic flexure syndrome and the hepatic flexure syndrome. *Am. J. Digest. Dis.*, **22**:193, 1955.

Patterson, H. A.: The association of gall stones and heart disease. *Ann. Surg.*, **139**:683, 1954.

Perchuk, E., and Liveson, A.: Unusual complications of acute coronary occlusion: gastrointestinal hemorrhage and hiccup. *New York J. Med.*, **55**:1175, 1955.

Pollock, A. V., and Bertrand, C. A.: Electrocardiograph changes in acute pancreatitis. *Surgery*, **40**:951, 1956.

Pulvertaft, C. N.: Electrocardiographic changes in the dumping syndrome. *Lancet*, **6806**:337, 1954.

Ravdin, I. S.; Fitz-Hugh, T., Jr.; Wolferth, C. C.; et al.: Relation of gallstone disease to angina pectoris. *A.M.A. Arch. Surg.*, **70**:333, 1955.

Reich, N. E.: Bleeding peptic ulcers. *J.A.M.A.*, **118**:9, 1942.

Reich, N. E.: Gastric diverticula. *Am. J. Digest Dis.*, **8**:70, 1941.

Reich, N. E.: Protean manifestations of acute rheumatic fever. *Am. Pract. & Digest Treat.*, 1:645, 1947.

Reich, N. E.: A review of recent advances in the hepatorenal syndrome. *New Internat. Clin.*, 4:135, 1941.

Reich, N. E.: Spontaneous rupture of a normal hepatic duct. *Ann. Surg.*, 116:137, 1942.

Roberts, K. E.; Randall, H. T.; Bane, H. N.; et al.: Studies of the physiology of the dumping syndrome. *New York J. Med.*, 55:2897, 1955.

Roth, J. L. A., and Bockus, H. L.: Aerophagia: its etiology, syndromes, and management. *M. Clin. North America*, 41:1673, 1957.

Roth, G. M., and Kvale, W. F.: Pharmacologic tests as an aid in diagnosis of pheochromocytoma. *Mod. Concepts Cardiovasc. Disease*, 18:41, 1949.

Sedlacek, A., and Bean, B.: Abdominal "angina": the syndrome of intermittent ischemia of mesenteric arteries. *Ann. Int. Med.*, 46:148, 1957.

Shedrow, A.: Chest pain as the only symptom of gastric ulcer. *South African M. J.*, 31:802, 1957.

Sjoerdsma, A.; Weissbach, H. D.; Terry, L. L.; and Udenfriend, S.: Further observations on patients with malignant carcinoid. *Am. J. Med.*, 23:5, 1957.

Smith, A. W. M.: The pain of peptic ulceration. *Quart. J. Med.*, 24:393, 1955.

Smith, E. W., and Conley, C. L.: Sicklemia and infarction of spleen during aerial flight: electrophoresis of the hemoglobin in 15 cases. *Bull. Johns Hopkins Hosp.*, 96:35, 1955.

Smith, L. A.: The pattern of pain in the diagnosis of upper abdominal disorders. *J.A.M.A.*, 156:1566, 1954.

Sohmer, M. F., Jr.; Johnston, D. H ; and Ruffin, J. M.: Pain patterns in peptic ulcer: clinical application. *South M. J.*, 49:393, 1956.

Spear, H. C., and Griswold, D.: The use of Dibenamine in pheochromocytoma. *New England J. Med.*, 259:736, 1948.

Tagart, R. E. B.: Ruptured spleen. *Brit. J. Surg.*, 43:283, 1955.

Thorson, A. H.: Hemodynamic changes during "flush" in carcinoidosis (the carcinoid syndrome). *Am. Heart J.*, 52:444, 1956.

Thorson, A. H.; Biorck, G.; Bjorkman, G.; and Waldenstrom, J.: Malignant carcinoid of the small intestine with metastases to the liver, valvular disease of the right side of the heart (pulmonary stenosis and tricuspid regurgitation without septal defects), peripheral vasomotor symptoms, bronchoconstriction, and an unusual type of cyanosis: A clinical and pathologic syndrome. *Am. Heart J.*, 47:795, 1954.

Zollinger, R. M.; Boles, E. T.; and Crawford, G. B.: The diagnosis and management of biliary tract disease. *New England J. Med.*, 252:203, 1955.

INDEX

Colonial America

Volume One

Colonial America

An Encyclopedia of Social, Political, Cultural, and Economic History

Volume One

Edited by James Ciment

With an Introduction by
Michael Zuckerman, University of Pennsylvania

SHARPE REFERENCE
an imprint of M.E. Sharpe, Inc.

SHARPE REFERENCE

Sharpe Reference is an imprint of M.E. Sharpe, Inc.

M.E. Sharpe, Inc.
80 Business Park Drive
Armonk, NY 10504

Cover Photo: Tontine Coffee House, c. 1797 (oil on linen), Francis Guy (1760–1820) / © New York Historical Society, New York, United States; www.bridgeman.co.uk.

Maps: Adapted by Carto-Graphics from the following sources:

Kwame Anthony Appiah and Henry Louis Gates, Jr., eds., *Africana: The Encyclopedia of the African and African American Experience* (New York: Basic Books, 1999). See map: Volume 3, page 788.

Geoffrey Barraclough, ed., *The Times Atlas of World History,* 6th edition (Maplewood, NJ: Hammond, 1982). See maps: Volume 1, pages xlii, xliii, 15, 214; Volume 2, pages xx, xxi; Volume 3, pages xx, xxi; Volume 4, pages xx, xxi, 850; Volume 5, pages xx, xxi.

James Ciment, ed. *Encyclopedia of American Immigration* (Armonk, NY: M.E. Sharpe, 2001). See map: Volume 1, page 55.

James Henretta, et al. *America's History.* 2nd edition (New York: Worth Publishers, 1993). See maps: Volume 1, pages xli, xlii, xliii, 59; Volume 2, pages xix, xx, xxi, 327, 362; Volume 3, pages xix, xx, xxi, 581, 738, 788; Volume 4, pages xix, xx, xxi; Volume 5, pages xix, xx, xxi.

Mary Beth Norton, et al. *A People and a Nation.* 6th edition (Boston: Houghton Mifflin, 2001). See maps: Volume 1, pages xliv, xlv; Volume 2, pages xxii, xxiii, 324; Volume 3, pages xxii, xxiii, 812; Volume 4, pages xxii, xxiii.

Library of Congress Cataloging-in-Publication Data

Colonial America: An encyclopedia of social, political, cultural, and economic history/James Ciment, editor.
    p. cm.
  Includes bibliographical references and index.
  ISBN 0-7656-8065-3 (Set: alk. paper)
    1. United States—Civilization—To 1783—Encyclopedias. I. Ciment, James.

E162.C68 2005
973.2'03—dc22
                                        2003023235

Printed and bound in the United States of America

Publisher: Myron E. Sharpe
Vice President and Editorial Director: Patricia Kolb
Vice President and Production Director: Carmen Chetti
Executive Editor and Manager of Reference: Todd Hallman
Senior Development Editor: Jeff Hacker
Project Editor: Laura Brengelman
Program Coordinator: Cathleen J. Prisco
Text Design: Carmen Chetti and Jesse Sanchez
Cover Design: Jesse Sanchez

Contents

Volume 2

Volume 3

VOLUME 4

Chronologies

Thematic

Geographic

VOLUME 5

Documents

List of Maps

Topic Finder

Jay, John
Jefferson, Thomas
Johnson, Sir William
Jolliet, Louis
La Salle, René Robert Cavelier, Sieur de
Las Casas, Bartolomé de
Lee, Richard Henry
Leisler, Jacob
Locke, John
Louis XIV
Marquette, Jacques
Mary I
Massasoit
Mather, Cotton
Mather, Increase
Menéndez de Avilés, Pedro
Montcalm, Louis-Joseph
Montezuma II
Murray, Judith Sargent
North, Lord
Oglethorpe, James
Oliver, Andrew
Oñate, Juan de
Opechancanough
Otis, James
Paine, Thomas
Penn, William
Philip, King (Metacom)
Philip II
Pitt, William
Pocahontas
Ponce de León, Juan
Pontiac
Powhatan
Quincy, Josiah, Jr.
Raleigh, Sir Walter
Revere, Paul
Rolfe, John
Rowlandson, Mary
Rush, Benjamin
Serra, Fray Junípero
Smith, John
Squanto
Stuyvesant, Peter
Taylor, Edward
Townshend, Charles
Verrazano, Giovanni da
Vespucci, Amerigo
Warren, Mercy Otis
Washington, George
West, Benjamin

Wheatley, Phillis
Whitefield, George
Wilkes, John
William III of Orange and Mary II
Williams, Roger
Winslow, Josiah
Winthrop, John
Wolfe, James
Wright, Susanna
Zenger, John Peter

British Colonies
Acadia, Nova Scotia
Antigua
Army, British
Barbados
Bermuda
Canada
Connecticut
Connecticut (Chronology)
Delaware
Delaware (Chronology)
Florida
Georgia
Georgia (Chronology)
Jamaica
Kentucky
Maine
Maryland
Maryland (Chronology)
Massachusetts
Massachusetts (Chronology)
Massachusetts Bay Colony
Native American–European Conflict
Native American–European Relations
New England, Dominion of
New Hampshire
New Hampshire (Chronology)
New Haven
New Jersey
New Jersey (Chronology)
New York
New York and New Netherland (Chronology)
Newfoundland
North Carolina
North Carolina (Chronology)
Pennsylvania
Pennsylvania (Chronology)
Rhode Island
Rhode Island (Chronology)
Roanoke Colony

Patriots
Paxton Boys
Piracy
Pontiac
Queen Anne's War
Regulators
Revolutionary War
Riots
Ship's Stores
Slave Rebellions
St. Augustine
Tordesillas, Treaty of (1494)
Transportation, Land
Transportation, Water
Tuscarora War
War
War of Jenkins' Ear
Washington, George
Weaponry
Wolfe, James

Native Americans

Abenaki
Albany Congress (1754)
Arawak
Aztec
Bacon's Rebellion
Beaver Wars
Brant, Joseph
Brant, Mary "Molly"
Captivity (by Native Americans)
Carib
Cayuga
Cherokee
Chickasaw
Choctaw
Creek
Erie
Family
Food and Diet
French and Indian War
Furs
Hopi
Huron
Iroquois Confederacy
King Philip's War
Las Casas, Bartolomé de
Lenni Lenape (Delaware)
Massasoit
Maya
Missions

Mohawk
Mohegan
Montezuma II
Natchez
Native American–African American Relations
Native American–European Conflict
Native American–European Relations
Native Americans
Native Americans and Slavery
Navajo
Oneida
Onondaga
Opechancanough
Ottawa
Paxton Boys
Pequot
Philip, King (Metacom)
Pocahontas
Pontiac
Powhatan
Powhatan Confederacy
Praying Towns
Pueblo
Race and Ethnicity (Chronology)
Race and Ethnicity (Essay)
Religions, Native American
Seminole
Seneca
Slavery, African American
Smallpox
Squanto
Taino
Tuscarora
Tuscarora War
War
Yamasee
Yamasee War
Zuni

Politics, Law, and Government

Adams, John
Adams, Samuel
Albany Congress (1754)
Anne, Queen
Assemblies, Colonial
Berkeley, Sir William
Bradford, William
Brant, Joseph
Calvert, Cecilius
Calvert, George (First Lord Baltimore)
Carteret, Sir George

Religion

Bible
Bradford, William
Calvinism
Catholic Church
Christ and Christianity
Covenants
Cromwell, Oliver
Deism
Dominicans
Edict of Nantes, Revocation of
Education
Education, Higher
Edwards, Jonathan
English Civil War
Franciscans
God
Great Awakening
Huguenots
Hutchinson, Anne
Jesuits
Jews
Las Casas, Bartolomé de
Marquette, Jacques
Mather, Cotton
Mather, Increase
Methodist Church
Ministers and the Ministry
Missions
Of Plymouth Plantation
Pietism
Pilgrims
Praying Towns
Presbyterianism
Puritanism
Quakers
Reformation
Religion (Chronology)
Religion (Essay)
Religions, African
Religions, Native American
Sermons
Serra, Fray Junípero
Shakers
Slave Communities and Culture
Whitefield, George
Williams, Roger
Witchcraft and Witch Trials

Spanish Colonies

Acapulco
Armada, Spanish

Borderlands, Spanish
Cabrillo, Juan Rodríguez
California
Canary Islands
Caribbean (Chronology)
Caribbean Sea
Catholic Church
Charles V
Columbian Exchange
Columbus, Christopher
Coronado, Francisco Vázquez de
Cortéz, Hernando
Cuba
De Soto, Hernando
Dominicans
Ferdinand and Isabella
Florida
Franciscans
Government, Spanish Colonial
Hispaniola
Jamaica
Jesuits
King George's War
Las Casas, Bartolomé de
Menéndez de Avilés, Pedro
Mexico City
Missions
Mississippi River
Native American–European Conflict
Native American–European Relations
New Mexico
New Orleans
New Spain
Philip II
Piracy
Ponce de León, Juan
Precious Metals
Puerto Rico
Queen Anne's War
Santa Fe
Serra, Fray Junípero
Slavery, Caribbean
St. Augustine
Texas
Tordesillas, Treaty of (1494)
Vespucci, Amerigo

Women and Gender Issues

Adams, Abigail
Alexander, Mary Spratt Provoost
Anne, Queen

General Editor
James Ciment

Advisory Board

Angelo Angelis
Hunter College

Wayne Bodie
Indiana University of Pennsylvania

Charles L. Cohen
University of Wisconsin

Matthew Dennis
University of Oregon

Leslie Horowitz
Hobart and William Smith Colleges

Russell Menard
University of Minnesota

Contributors

Cameron Addis
Texas A & M University

Donna L. Akers
Purdue University

Rolando Avila
University of Texas, Pan-American

David Ballew
Chowan College

John H. Barnhill
Independent Scholar

Karen B. Bell
National Archives and Records Administration

Richard Bell
Harvard University

James R. Belpedio
Becker College

Christophe J. M. Boucher
College of Charleston

Peter Bratt
Ohio State University

David Broadnax, Sr.
Northwestern University

R. Blake Brown
Dalhousie University, Canada

Judkin Browning
University of Georgia

William E. Burns
Independent Scholar

Edward F. Butler, Sr.
Independent Scholar

Abigail B. Chandler
University of Massachusetts

Arthur E. Chapman
Georgia Perimeter College

Jorge L. Chinea
Wayne State University

Aaron F. Christensen
Oklahoma State University

Charles L. Cohen
University of Wisconsin

Aaron N. Coleman
University of Kentucky

Tonia M. Compton
Independent Scholar

James A. Denton
University of Colorado

Michael F. Dove
University of Western Ontario, Canada

Carole Emberton
Northwestern University

Alexander Engel
Göttingen University, Germany

David M. Fitzsimons
University of Rhode Island

Kevin M. Gannon
Grandview College

Anna Gersh
Washtenaw Community College

Larry Gragg
University of Missouri, Rolla

John Grenier
United States Air Force Academy

Lisa Guinn
Oklahoma State University

Lynne Guitar
Council on International Educational Exchange

Joan R. Gundersen
Independent Scholar

John Craig Hammond
University of Kentucky

Tamara Harvey
George Mason University

David Head
State University of New York, Buffalo

Jeffrey Heeren
University of California, Irvine

Marjorie L. Hilton
Georgia State University

Arthur Holst
Independent Scholar

Jay R. Hopler
Purdue University

Leslie Horowitz
Hobart and William Smith Colleges

Charles A. Israel
University of the South

Gail L. Jenner
Etna (California) High School

Matthew Jennings
University of Illinois

Thomas F. Jorsch
Oklahoma State University

Neil Kennedy
Brock University, Canada

James E. Klein
Oklahoma State University

Andrew C. Lannen
Louisiana State University

Todd E. A. Larson
University of Illinois

Robert Leach
Indiana Wesleyan University

Todd Leahy
Oklahoma State University

Katherine A. Libby
East Tennessee State University

Daniel R. Mandell
Truman State University

Douglas Mann
University of Georgia

Kevin P. McDonald
University of California, Santa Cruz

Mitchell McNaylor
Our Lady of the Lake College

Florene S. Memegalos
Hunter College

Charlene Merithew
Assumption College

Amy Meschke
Southern Methodist University

Craig Miller
*State University of New York,
Buffalo*

Janet Butler Munch
Lehman College

Dan Murphree
University of Texas, Tyler

Aubrey L. Muscaro
University of Florida

Thomas Nester
Texas A & M University

Caryn E. Neumann
Ohio State University

Karen O'Brien
Ramapo College

Keith Pacholl
*California State University,
Fullerton*

Thomas L. Purvis
Independent Scholar

Lisa Y. Ramos
Columbia University

Ty M. Reese
University of North Dakota

Michael A. Rembis
University of Arizona

Joann M. Ross
University of Nebraska

Ryan L. Ruckel
Louisiana State University

Margaret Sankey
*Minnesota State University,
Moorhead*

Kenneth A. Shelton
Boston College

Frank Shuffelton
University of Rochester

Phillip L. Sinitiere
University of Houston

Michael Sletcher
Yale University

Solomon K. Smith
University of Georgia

Penny M. Sonnenburg
Independent Scholar

Mary Stockwell
Lourdes College, Ohio

Barbara Schwarz Wachal
Saint Louis University

Jeffrey B. Webb
Huntington College

Leigh Whaley
Arcadia University

Elizabeth McKee Williams
University of Michigan

Charles H. Wilson, III
Gainesville College

Ronald Young
Georgia Southern University

Michael Zuckerman
University of Pennsylvania

Documents

Compiled by Janet Butler Munch
of Lehmann College

Glossary

Compiled and written by Katherine A. Libby
of East Tennessee State University

Bibliography (Primary Sources)

Compiled by Arthur Chapman
of Georgia Perimeter College

Bibliography (Secondary Sources)

Compiled by Dan Murphree
of University of Texas, Tyler

Acknowledgments

In the course of editing this seemingly endless project on the history of colonial North America through to completion, I was sometimes reminded of Columbus's first trans-Atlantic crossing, with one big difference. Where the determined captain of that voyage suffered a despairing crew, I was ever reassured by a team of very dedicated and able people.

First, I want to thank Executive Editor Todd Hallman for launching the project and navigating it through the myriad shoals of publishing bureaucracy. M. E. Sharpe Project Editor Laura Brengelman, Senior Development Editor Jeff Hacker, and a talented team of copyeditors and proofreaders dotted the "i"s, crossed the "t"s, and did a whole lot more in whipping the manuscript into shape.

M. E. Sharpe Program Coordinator Cathy Prisco did her usual remarkable job tracking the book's vast cargo of articles, pictures, maps, chronologies, and appendices. Cartographer Alice Thiede provided a fine set of informative maps, while our photo researcher Anne Burns uncovered a wealth of captivating and worth-a-thousand-word images.

Special appreciation goes to my editorial assistant. Every large reference book sails upon a sea of details; Rebecca Black made sure they never swamped us.

I also want to thank the advisory board for their encouragement and assistance.

Last, and, of course, not least, I must extend my heartiest appreciation to the dozens of scholars who gave generously of their time and their expertise. Without their enormous contribution, this ship would have never reached its destination.

James Ciment

Preface

All things American begin with the colonial era. Our democracy and free enterprise system, our tortured race relations, our ability to absorb a diversity of immigrants, our relationship to the environment, even our social mores—all have their roots firmly planted in the nearly two centuries between the founding of the first permanent English settlement at Jamestown in 1607 and the 1783 Paris Peace Treaty recognizing American independence.

There was, of course, a North American history before 1607, just as there were people living in the territory that is now the United States long before the first colonists arrived in Virginia—lots of them, in fact. Although figures vary widely, the general consensus within the historical and archaeological communities is that, in 1492, about 10 million persons lived between the Rio Grande and what is now the Canadian border. While some of these native peoples have origin legends that situate them in North America since the beginning of time, most archaeologists believe that their ancestors migrated to the continent over the Bering Strait from Siberia at some point in the past 12,000 to 50,000 years.

Other Europeans, and a few Africans, were also here in 1607, most notably in the Spanish colonies planted in Florida and the Southwest in the mid- to late sixteenth century. The French and Dutch also would settle their first North American colonies around the same time as Jamestown. That said, the arrival of English colonists in the Chesapeake Bay region in the early seventeenth century would set in motion forces that would forever change the lives of the Native Americans, as well as the lives of the other European colonists who inhabited the continent at the beginning of the English colonial era.

The first English colonies were founded for two quintessentially American reasons—freedom and money. The settlers at Jamestown hoped to get rich, like the Spanish before them, mining precious metals or, more precisely, getting the native peoples to do the work for them. When no precious metals were to be found, the colonists turned to the lucrative plantation agriculture system first established in the Caribbean. Instead of sugar, the commodity was another addictive substance, tobacco. When the English found that the Native Americans refused to work for them and that exploiting their own proved too socially contentious—white indentured servants and small farmers rose up against the planter elite in the rebellion of 1676—they turned to imported African slaves.

Hundreds of miles to the north, the first settlers in New England had anything but money on their minds. Dissenting Puritans—called such by their opponents for their zealous desire to purify the Anglican church of ritual and hierarchy—created a theocracy of sorts in Massachusetts, with the clergy acting as both spiritual and secular rulers. Ironically, the Puritans proved as intolerant as their own Anglican tormentors back in England, exiling dissenters to the neighboring colony of Rhode Island. While the theocratic model of government never took hold in America, the Puritan ideal that all worldly activities should be infused with a duty to God did, albeit corrupted with the notion that one's worldly success was a sign of God's favor.

North America also was seen by the English and other colonizers as virgin territory, as a place to exploit and to transplant European social models. The Dutch attempted to create a feudal order of landlords and tenants in their colony of New Netherland, which was later adopted by the English after they seized it and renamed it New York. But land was too plentiful for a feudal order, and tenants resisted the dominance of the patroons, as the great landholders were called, and instead chose to strike out on their own.

William Penn's Quaker colony of Pennsylvania, although somewhat more egalitarian and certainly more considerate of American Indian sensibilities, also saw its original paternalistic order transformed by the realities of North America. As non-Quakers flooded into the colony, it became more commercially oriented, more socially stratified, and less willing to respect the native peoples' prior claims to the land.

In the Carolinas, political philosopher John Locke's model for an idealized feudal order of aristocratic landholders, free farmers, and serfs similarly failed to take root. Poor whites proved unwilling to accept the paternalism inherent in such a system, and landholders, more eager to make money than to realize a philosopher's dream, began importing African slaves by the thousands to work their rice and indigo plantations.

Paradoxically, slavery offered a foundation for a new kind of democracy. As the eminent historian Edmund Morgan has argued for the Chesapeake, American slavery and American freedom were intricately bound up with one another. By equating blackness with servitude, the slave system gave every white man—poor, as well as rich—a stake in the system, a form of property in their white skin. This allowed for a social cohesion that would eventually make it possible to extend representation down through the social ranks of white men, although this process would not be fully completed until half a century or so after the American War for Independence.

The Native Americans or—more accurately put—the removal of the Native Americans also helped make possible a more republican order in the North, where slavery was far more marginal to the well-being of the economy. With land widely available, the American colonies became, in the words of one contemporary essayist, the best poor man's land on Earth. That is to say, the colonies allowed for unprecedented opportunity, and this sense of possibility drew tens of thousands of European immigrants across the Atlantic. Not just from the British Isles, but from Germany, France, and elsewhere, they created the multi-ethnic, multi-denomination population that became a hallmark of the American way of life. Opportunity also alleviated social tensions, making, if possible, room for a more inclusive form of political order to emerge. In short, the roots of American republicanism were established in the colonial era.

Before that could emerge, however, the old order had to be overturned. For all the egalitarianism of the colonies—at least, for white males—old English and European ideas about deference to the will and leadership of social elite still held sway. Despite the fact that opportunity was more widely available here than in almost any place else in the world, the British government still tried to maintain a mercantilist economic system that restricted trade and commerce in a way that benefited the mother country. Finally, the old English system of virtual representation—in which Parliament as a whole upheld the interests of all the empire's subjects—just would not do in this faraway land, where local interests demanded their own direct representation.

It started with taxes but went a whole lot further. Having financially exhausted itself ousting the French from North America, the British government insisted the colonists pay their fair share of the military burden. But his majesty's American subjects had a different idea. They demanded a say in their own political affairs and the right to control their own economic destiny, including, as it turned out, the right to own human beings of one race and seize the lands of another.

When the British military band at Yorktown, the final imperial defeat in the American Revolution, played "The World Turned Upside Down," the musicians may not have been aware of how appropriate their choice of song was. The American Revolution did not merely replace a government on one side of the Atlantic with one on the other. It set in place a whole new political, social, and economic system in which merit, talent, and hard work counted for more than parentage and class.

While the Revolution paved the way for the future, it also was the culmination of the past. The revolution and the republic it founded were shaped by nearly two centuries of colonial history.

James Ciment

How to Use This Encyclopedia

Colonial America: An Encyclopedia of Social, Political, Cultural, and Economic History is divided into four major parts, plus ancillary materials at the beginning and end of the encyclopedia. A topic guide—by general subject area—is provided to help guide the reader. The topic guide, which appears at the front of the book, covers essays, topical entries, and chronologies, but it does not include documents.

The first section consists of seven thematic essays on arts, culture, and intellectual life; economy, business, and labor; gender issues; military and diplomatic affairs; politics and government; race and ethnicity; and religion. These essays provide an overview and analysis of these major issues in colonial American life.

The second section contains the bulk of the encyclopedia—A to Z entries on individuals, places, events, institutions, ideas, peoples, commodities, and a host of other topics.

The third section consists of various chronologies, seven of which correspond to the themes explored in the encyclopedia's opening essays. In addition, there is a chronology encompassing scientific and technological developments. Finally, there are sixteen chronologies corresponding to the thirteen British North American mainland colonies, and one each on French colonies in North America, Spanish colonies in North America, and the Caribbean.

The final section includes nearly sixty primary documents, covering the history of the colonial era. Listed in chronological order, each includes a brief introduction that describes the contents of the document and its historical context.

The ancillary materials at the back of the book include a glossary of terms used throughout the encyclopedia and two bibliographies. The first is a bibliography of primary sources (sources written in colonial times); the second covers secondary sources (written since the end of the colonial era). Finally, there are three indexes: general, biographical, and geographical.

Also, readers should note that most of the A to Z entries are cross-referenced to related essays, other entries, chronologies, and primary documents. In addition, all essays and entries include bibliographies of books and articles for further research.

James Ciment

Introduction: Studying the Colonial Era

The day that they declared their independence, there were fewer people in all the thirteen rebellious colonies than there are in the St. Louis metropolitan area today. Sometimes it seems that there are more twenty-first-century students of early Puritanism than there were Puritans in the seventeenth century. In fact, there are more scholars of early America in our own time than there ever were Anglo-Virginians in the time of Captain John Smith and the Virginia Company.

In 1650, there were just 50,000 Europeans in the British Mainland colonies, not nearly enough to fill the stadium of a first-rate college football power on a Saturday afternoon in October. In 1700, almost a century after the founding of that first enduring English settlement in the New World in Virginia, there were still only 250,000 colonists. And the best estimates of colonial populations put them at little more than a million—almost a fifth of them African American slaves—in the middle of the eighteenth century. Taken together, all the men, women, and children who ever lived in any of the provinces that proclaimed the Revolution in 1776 amounted to less than one-tenth of one percent of all the people whose history we now call "American."

Nonetheless, the history of colonial America engages the interest of academics and their audiences out of all proportion to the paltry number of colonists in whom they are interested. Books about the period proliferate beyond any possibility of keeping up with them, and the best of them claim a lion's share of the most prestigious prizes conferred on historical writing. The *William and Mary Quarterly,* the scholarly journal of the field, turns up on every survey of the subject as one of the five most distinguished historical periodicals in the English language. It is not for nothing that Bernard Bailyn wrote recently of a "creative ferment" in early American studies, unparalleled in any other realm of American historical scholarship and "perhaps unique in western historiography."

Remarkable as this extravagant disproportion between subject and scholarship is, it may be even more remarkable that there is nothing novel in it. For much of the nineteenth and early twentieth centuries, colonial and Revolutionary American history actually commanded more attention than it has in the past three or four decades.

In the nineteenth century, newly established historical and genealogical societies devoted their best efforts to the colonial era, and local historians scarcely studied anything else. The greatest of the midcentury romantic historians, Francis Parkman and George Bancroft, did much of their best work on the years before the Revolution, and Bancroft barely went beyond them. Although he originally intended to carry his ten-volume history of the United States to his own time—he died in 1891—he never got past the eighteenth century. The colonial era was sufficient to his purpose. "The maturity of the nation," he concluded, "is but a continuation of its youth." The seventeenth century made manifest "the germ of our institutions."

Canvassing the nation's leading historical magazines near the end of the nineteenth century, J. Franklin Jameson noted derisively their preoccupation with "voyages and discoveries," the Revolution, the "Fathers," and "the local and antiquarian details of the colonial period." These, he observed, "were regarded as the main matters of American history," and he intended to do differently. The first editor of the first journal of the first professional historical association in America, he declared his determination to pursue a much less parochial path.

Yet when Jameson's first issue of the *American Historical Review* appeared in 1895, three of its five articles took early America for their topic. Over the *Review*'s first year, more than half of its articles pertained to America in the era of the colonies, the Revolution, and the early republic. Over its first five years, 40 of its 108 articles did the same, despite the explicit dedication of the journal to a vastly more encompassing coverage of Europe and the wider world, as well as of the United States.

There were several sources of this extraordinary obsession with the history of early America. Some were internal to the politics and problematics of the historical profession as it emerged in the late nineteenth century. Others were rooted in the demands that society made on historians and those that historians made on themselves.

History as a discipline both presupposed and promoted the nation. It took nations as its units of analysis, and it celebrated nations as its assumptive centers of allegiance and identity.

History as a discipline in America took for granted that the United States was the nation of nations, divinely appointed to light the world's way. Though they prided themselves on their "scientific" skepticism, American historians rarely doubted their country's manifest destiny. Their task was, rather, to explain it. How had their exemplary nation grown from a few straggling settlements on the Atlantic seaboard? What were the origins of its distinctive democracy and its freedom of religion and enterprise? Many of them were convinced that the answers to such questions would be evident in the country's colonial past.

But colonial history was more than merely a field in which academics sought to find solutions to pressing professional problems. Colonial historians were citizens, as well as scholars. They knew more self-consciously than most of their fellow citizens that American nationality could not be entrusted to shared language or religion or to an ancient ethnicity. They were acutely aware that American identity could only come of embracing American foundation myths and its founding texts. As custodians, and indeed as creators, of that cultural inheritance, they understood that the colonial and Revolutionary record represented the vital heart of the tradition they conserved, and indeed invented, so that their countrymen might know themselves.

Of course, the identity that colonial historians proffered was always a partisan identity. Through the first half of the twentieth century and beyond, colonial history provided a refuge for old-stock Americans. It was studied and supported as an Anglophilic foil for a pluralism that seemed suddenly all too prevalent. In a nation increasingly contaminated (as the descendants of the earlier invaders believed) by invasion from the wrong parts of Europe, colonial history enabled the children of the earlier immigrants to claim one part— one crucial part—of the country's history as uniquely their own. The story of American settlement was an Anglo-Saxon story. (Indeed, the colonists were called settlers, so they could not be confused with the later comers, who were called immigrants.) The values of the founding defined the authentic ideals of the nation. And since those ideals affirmed national unity, differentiation had no real place in the story.

In a concerted effort to reconcile recently warring regions and to resist recently arriving newcomers, New England and Virginia were set at the center of the colonial narrative. New England, the one corner of the colonies that was in fact as English as the Yankee gentry fancied, was celebrated as the purest distillation of genuine Americanism, especially in its Boston hearth, where the Brahmins clung rabidly to their anti-Irish and anti-Catholic prejudices. Residents of polyglot Pennsylvania and New York were excluded almost totally from the tale, and so were the other colonists who did not fit the New England model.

After the 1960s, however, new idealizations of America arose. Nostalgic norms of a racially and ethnically homogeneous America ceased to prevail unproblematically. As the elites who craved an English imprimatur were increasingly challenged by others who cast about for more pluralistic ways of understanding our origins as a people, we reached for reconceptualizations of our colonial heritage that could accommodate deeper diversity and more inclusive ideals.

Carl Bridenbaugh's cranky manifesto of the early 1960s marked the transition. In his presidential address to the American Historical Association, Bridenbaugh resented the new generation of early Americanists. They were "urban-bred" men of "lower middle-class or foreign origins," and they were the worse for that "environmental deficiency." They could not comprehend the first centuries of American life. They did not share the common culture "vouchsafed to historians who were raised in the countryside or in the small town."

Bridenbaugh's address was widely understood as a diatribe against the increasing presence of Jews in the historical profession, but it was perhaps more prescient than that. Soon enough, Jews would be far from the most militant disturbers of the old order. Within a decade of his rant, Bridenbaugh saw early American studies aflame with brilliant and influential work by women, African Americans, gays and lesbians, pacifists, and Marxists.

America changed in the 1960s and so did the

study of its history. Historians gave up the preoccupation with elite politics that had defined their profession from the time of its late-nineteenth-century formation. They evolved an increasingly inclusive interest in the everyday affairs of common people. As they did, they found that the discovery of America lay before them.

Before the '60s, historians had been wary, or dismissive, of the universalizing endeavors of the social sciences. Their discipline was predicated upon particularity and suspicious of sweeping generalities. It scorned broad propositions about social life and gloried in intricately specified accounts of great men and great events that bore on state building.

Without any resonant ideas of society or coherent concepts of culture, historians were bound to disdain social history. They could only comprehend it as an antiquarian pursuit, "pots and pans" history as they colloquially called it, history "with the politics left out" as Trevelyan said.

But sociology's idea of society was out there, in the air, and so was anthropology's concept of culture. Slowly, those more systemic, holistic notions seeped into the study of the past. Grudgingly, almost despite themselves, historians absorbed these notions, and, as they did, they changed. Some changed modestly, like Keats's "watcher of the skies / When a new planet swims into his ken." Others changed mightily, like Keats's Cortez, staring for the first time at the Pacific, "silent, upon a peak in Darien."

Once they understood society and culture as the subject of their study, historians could contemplate a radical redirection of their interests and reorientation of their work. And no American historians could do so more completely or congenially than colonial historians. The turn to the "new social history" occurred most visibly and sustained itself most vigorously among students of early America. Just as there were both internal and external sources for the preceding century of obsession with colonial history, so there were both internal and external sources for the transformation of the field.

Perhaps the most powerful facilitating factor within early American studies was also the most obvious. Colonial historians had never had to deal with national politics. They had never operated on the premise prevalent in the study of all subsequent periods, that the proper business of history was the politics of nation building. They could let go of politics, or subsume politics in a more encompassing frame of interpretation, without abandoning the paradigm in which they practiced or any immense body of hard-won knowledge.

They simply had less to lose than other American historians.

They also had more to gain. Social science after 1945 was, inevitably, embroiled in the Cold War contest between Marxists and liberals. As that contest touched history, it did so in an illuminating dispute over the economic development of the West.

Some time, somehow, between, say, 1400 and 1900, Europe became modern. An insular civilization that had previously lagged at least half a dozen others on three or four continents in population, production, and knowledge became, in that half-millennium, the preeminent power on the planet, with the most sophisticated science, innovative technology, and dynamic economy.

Marxists attempted to explain the change as a convulsive evolution from feudalism to capitalism. Liberals looked to more incremental evolutionary explanations. But on both accounts, the decisive developments occurred in the seventeenth and eighteenth centuries, and these developments concerned Europe's overseas expansion.

Suddenly, colonial American history was more than a provincial prologue to a provincial revolution. Now, it commanded the crossroads of the most momentous transformation in human history and the most importunate intellectual issues of the modern world.

Most of the vibrant controversies in early American history since the '60s have been controversies that came out of that larger inquest into the vicissitudes of modernity. Students of the colonies had no qualms appropriating *gemeinschaft* (community) and *gesellschaft* (corporate) models for their community studies, premarket and market models for their contretemps over the coming of capitalism, and patriarchal models for their inquiries into gender and family relations.

These topics and these models had, of course, a special salience—a special theoretical load, often a special polemic implication—for scholars of the early modern era. They also had a special accessibility. All of them took (and shifted) shape over long periods of time. Patriarchy persisted (and mutated) for millennia. Witch beliefs flowed (and ebbed) for centuries. Racism rose (and was augmented) as witchcraft fell, and it is with us still. Lived religions and ideologies crystallized (and fractured) across generations.

Other American historians do not specialize in such spans. Students of the Jacksonian era, the Civil War, Reconstruction, the Gilded Age, the Progressive Era, and the New Deal confine themselves to a couple of decades, or less. Only colonialists work on a temporal scale commensurate with the larger issues that social history raises. Colonialists produced the first and the most provocative demographies, family histories, and community studies.

But early Americanists did not desert the historical ideas they had argued for a century simply because social history made them a better offer. Bridenbaugh's anti-Semitic screed had an element of truth in it. The profession *was* changing, even before the upheavals of the '60s. And those upheavals amplified a gathering alienation from what had come to be called "the establishment," releasing forces that we cannot count or contain to this day. The call to write history from the bottom up came first and most famously from Jesse Lemisch, an early Americanist. So did the plea to listen to the inarticulate, those who had left few written records.

Others heeded those appeals. In no time, the journals were teeming with studies of artisans and indentured servants, of transient laborers and slaves, of soldiers and camp followers, of wives and widows, of parents and children, of Mennonites and Moravians. Books followed close behind the journal articles, on fishermen and frontier farmers, on free blacks and founding mothers, on debtors and creditors, on criminals and righteous rioters, on pirates and child abusers. More, perhaps, than historians of any other period, historians of the seventeenth and eighteenth centuries set out to recover the rhythms, rhymes, and reasons of everyday experience, among the lowly as much as among the lofty.

The study of early America had long been a study of politics, institutions, and wars. After the '60s, it was impossible to presume the primacy of such subjects and difficult even to assert their importance. Domestic violence came to seem more interesting than the martial kind, and gender politics more significant than the electoral sort.

The study of early America had long been a study centered on New England. After the '60s, it was impossible to treat New England as a template for America, and there was a genuine danger that New England histories would be dismissed as deviant. The Chesapeake became the vital center of early American history, and then perhaps the Middle Atlantic and the West Indies. By the beginning of the twenty-first century, colonialists were working on Africa and Arkansas, the backcountry and the low country, New Orleans and New Netherland. As Daniel Vickers observed, colonial history ran "from Bordeaux and Bristol to Barbados and the Bight of Benin."

The study of early America had long been a study almost entirely of men. After the '60s, it was impossible to think solely of men, even in male milieus such as militia companies and taverns. There were gendered meanings in everything.

The study of early America also had long been a study overwhelmingly of whites. After the '60s, it was impossible to think solely of whites, even in colonies largely populated by them. The New World swarmed with blacks, browns, tawnies, and reds, and the very names by which whites knew them held crucial clues to the unriddling of the origins and extent of American racism.

The story of early America had long been the story of the expansion of English liberties in the favorable settings of America. After the '60s, it was impossible to perpetuate that saga of the superiority of the Anglo-Americans who told the story. The paradigmatic tales of the new social history were tales of the encounters—and, often, the collisions—of the disparate cultures that laid the foundation for the nation's diversity.

Few colonialists who participated in these transitions saw much to lament in the passing of what was once, in Ian Steele's words, "the tidy domain of colonial American history." Indeed, a great many saw much to celebrate. Engaged in what seemed at the time a concerted campaign to recover the richness and complexity of provincial life in its totality, early Americanists researched and wrote with an unrivaled verve and sense of communal purpose. When Jack Greene and J. R. Pole canvassed the state of the art in the mid-1980s, they sensed that the study of the colonies had achieved an integrity over the preceding quarter-century it had never had before.

Yet that integrity was not evident in the separate surveys they had commissioned. As they admitted, those surveys suggested a "paradoxical result" of the remarkable "reinvigoration" of early American history in the years since the 1960s. Impressive advances had led to "a severe case of intellectual indigestion." The new work left the traditional themes of colonial history "obsolete," but put nothing in their place. Even in 1984, a "signal loss of overall coherence" was apparent, noted Greene and Pole. Colonialists were "less clear than ever before about precisely what the central themes and the larger questions are in the field as a whole."

Worse, Greene and Pole detected no inclination to come to clarity. Worried that the study of early America both flourished and floundered, they had urged their fourteen contributors, senior scholars every one, to write about the *general* themes that "might help to structure studies [of] the field." Not one of the fourteen did. None of those leading academic authorities were able to generalize across the colonies, even when they were explicitly instructed—or begged—to do so.

In the two decades since Greene and Pole noted that the propulsive vitality of colonial studies resisted efforts to articulate any larger logic of the field, a succession of scholars have written ruefully of the same conundrum. So far from seeing the unprecedented "integrity" that Greene and Pole did, they have seen only "disintegration." As ever more expansive and ingenious books and articles appeared, colonial history itself seemed ever more "confused and incoherent."

The very profusion of publication compounded the confusion. And the very expansiveness and ingenuity of the new work left the boundaries of the field more distended than ever—in time, as well as in space. The era of significance to early America increasingly ran backward into the sixteenth century, or even the late Middle Ages, and forward into the mid-nineteenth century. It extended eastward to Europe and Africa and westward to American Indian territory and the Spanish borderlands. It reached outward to phenomena such as riot, ritual, and occult religion, which it had once disdained as realms of the irrational. It reached inward to subjects such as death, desire, and marital discord, which it had once put off limits as spheres of the intimate that were inaccessible to historical investigation.

Even aspects of the colonial scene that seemed neglected in 1984 have, on the whole, been addressed extensively since. Greene and Pole thought that the Caribbean colonies, the Atlantic islands, Nova Scotia, women, children, Native Americans, lower-class whites, and the Lower South were all understudied. Newfoundland, Bermuda, and Nova Scotia may still be. But studies of the West Indies and the Lower South are burgeoning. Children and lower-class whites are markedly better understood. Women and gender are now required considerations in colonial studies. And all of that pales beside the explosive growth of Native American studies.

American Indians are today, as they never were at any time until now, indispensable to the interpretation of early America. A century ago, when he set the agenda for American historians of his generation and the next, Frederick Jackson Turner consigned the natives of the New World to inconsequence. The conquest of the continent was, he assured his avid readers, an appropriation of "virgin soil." The colonists and their westward

spreading descendants came to "an unexploited wilderness." It was "the fact of unoccupied territory in America that [set] the evolution of American and European institutions in contrast."

Even when Turner acknowledged that the native peoples were there, he accorded them no role of their own design in the American saga. At the outside, they constituted "a common danger" that called forth "intercolonial conferences" and other "common measures of defense." They were, inadvertently, "the military training school" that taught the "rugged qualities of the frontiersman." They were, unwittingly, "a consolidating agent in our history." Their menace motivated the "unifying tendencies" that helped prepare America for nationhood. In colonies with no Native American frontier, where there was no specter of native attack, "particularism was strongest." As Turner saw it, the native peoples had no significance in the history of the United States beyond being a necessary condition of any explanation of American emergence as "one nation, rather than a collection of isolated states."

When Greene and Pole took the temperature of colonial study, ninety years after Turner pronounced the significance of the frontier in American history, there was no prospect of a remedy for the repression of native peoples in American memory. Scarcely a single major center of graduate training in colonial history had a specialist in Native Americans. Today, just twenty years later, there is scarcely one without such a specialist.

This massive advent of Native American history represents more than a mere correction of the "underemphases" that Greene and Pole regretted. It means more than the addition of a few more tiles to the totalizing mosaic of early American history that Greene and Pole urged. It indicates a radical re-visioning of that history. It ends the occlusion of the American Indians that Turner inherited and amplified. It ends four centuries of seeing the colonies solely from a European perspective, and it introduces the profoundest fracture of colonial history that we have ever had. As Daniel Richter suggests, we must now attempt to understand that history dialogically, not only looking west across the continent but also "facing east from Indian country."

As if such postmodern pluralization of perspectives were not enough, another major viewpoint in the scholarship of the past two decades looks implicitly to reinstate the angle of the omniscient narrator. The recent rage for Atlantic history situates colonialists neither in Europe looking west nor in America facing east. It puts them metaphorically in the middle of the

Atlantic Ocean, observing the passage of people and goods all around. The new Native American history de-centers, demanding self-awareness of our inescapably, irreconcilably partisan postures. The new Atlantic history re-centers, inviting revival of the myth of objectivity, as Bernard Bailyn made plain when he fantasized monitoring Atlantic passages from high above the earth and the water, by means of "a satellite . . . with a camera of perfect accuracy."

Much of the most enlivening recent work on the colonies—on empire, capitalism, consumption, and migration—presupposes an Atlantic perspective. But much of it—on Native Americans, the backcountry, and the environment—carries us farther into the interior of the continent. One approach situates the colonies in the wider world. The other reinforces American exceptionalism. Still other innovative initiatives and persisting concerns—slavery, the encounter of cultures, gender, staple economies, war, religion, and family—look simultaneously to what was embedded in worlds beyond America and what was unique to America.

We go back and forth, from an oceanic to a continental outlook, without ever achieving coherence or even a common point of view. Despite our misgivings, we compound what Ian Steele calls the "cacophony of recent approaches to the study of early modern North America."

Twenty years ago, Darrett Rutman wrote that colonial life was "essentially disorganized." Whether or not he was right about colonial life itself, he was certainly right about writing about colonial life, then and now. So it may well be that the encyclopedia is the genre that best represents our current understanding of colonial history.

The encyclopedia does not depend on grand interpretations or general themes. It does not even seek to synthesize the vast outpouring of scholarship in the field. It simply attempts to encompass the sweep of contemporary research and writing. It feasts on the multitudinous fruits of the many orchards that colonial historians cultivate.

Consider the first entries in this encyclopedia. Abenaki, Acadia, Acadians, Acapulco, and African Americans flank the Adamses. None of these first eight

subjects but John and Samuel Adams—not even Abigail Adams—would have been in an encyclopedia of early America half a century ago.

Also consider the entries under C. Among the first listings are John Cabot and the Calverts, stalwarts of the old narratives of exploration and founding, and, equally, Juan Rodriguez Cabrillo and California, elements until just yesterday of a history 3,000 miles removed. Later listings include not only the Coercive Acts, *Common Sense*, and the Continental Congresses, staples of the old political ordering, but also Child Rearing, Clocks and Timekeeping, Clothing, and Corn, vital expressions of the new social view.

Under P, entries such as Thomas Paine, William Penn, and the Pilgrims jostle with Pietism, Poverty, Prostitution, and Pueblos. Under S, the Sons of Liberty and the Stamp Act mingle with Servants, Domestic, Slave Rebellions, Sugar, and Syphilis. Under W, George Washington appears with Phillis Wheatley, Roger Williams, Widows and Widowers, and Witchcraft and Witch Trials. And so it goes. This is not your father's encyclopedia.

The syntheses that shaped colonial history in the past set forth unifying myths that served to consolidate American identity and attachment. But the cosmopolitan classes today do not identify as ardently with the nation as their forebears did. Though some remain so moored, others find their most meaningful anchorages in larger or smaller affiliations. They worry about the fate of the planet or seek to be citizens of the world. They prefer regional loyalties to global ones. They pursue identity politics, or they think of themselves primarily in terms of their profession or their work.

The encyclopedia may be the one form that can consolidate knowledge that suits these disparate sensibilities. And if it is, we have come an exquisite rounding of the circle. The dream and the dawn of a distinctly modern learning were embodied in the great compendia of the Enlightenment: Diderot's and D'Alembert's *Encyclopedie,* Johnson's *Dictionary,* and *The Encyclopaedia Britannica.* There is a delicious irony if, a quarter of a millennium later, we are back where we began.

Michael Zuckerman

Maps

North America, 1600. The above map shows the multiplicity of native peoples on the North American continent in 1600, as well as the extensive Spanish presence in Mexico, Central America, the Caribbean, and southwestern portions of what is now the United States. Note that the English colony of Roanoke mysteriously disappeared shortly after its establishment in 1587. *(Carto-Graphics)*

North America, 1700. The above map shows the presence of European colonial powers on the North American continent circa 1700. Note that the presence of Europeans varied: British holdings in the Hudson Bay region were little more than claims on maps, while settlements along the Atlantic seaboard of what is now the United States included tens of thousands of European settlers and African slaves, as well as the remaining native peoples. *(Carto-Graphics)*

North America, 1775. The above map shows the presence of European colonial powers on the North American continent on the eve of the American Revolution. Note that some regions—particularly in the heart of Mexico and along the Atlantic seaboard of what is now the United States—were more heavily populated by colonists than other areas. *(Carto-Graphics)*

European Settlement Areas, Eastern North America, 1650. The above map shows the thin line of European settlements along the Atlantic seaboard and the St. Lawrence River Valley. At the time, the total European and African populations in the British colonies stood at about 50,000, with a few thousand more in the Dutch, French, and Spanish colonies. *(Carto-Graphics)*

British Colonies, Mainland North America, 1765. By 1750, British settlements on mainland North America had pushed westward to the eastern edge of the Appalachian Mountains. The population of the thirteen colonies in 1750 was roughly 1.2 million, including about a quarter of a million slaves. *(Carto-Graphics)*

Thematic Essays

Arts, Culture, and Intellectual Life

When the first permanent colonies were established in British North America, the colonists brought with them aspects of the culture they had left behind in England, but the colonial experience demanded extraordinary efforts to maintain an approximation of the cultural values of their old home. Two examples suggest the directions these efforts might take.

George Sandys, the youngest son of the archbishop of York, came to Virginia in 1621 as the colony's treasurer, and while there, he completed his important translation into heroic couplets of Ovid's *Metamorphoses.* This was published in London in 1626, a year after his return from Virginia, manuscript in hand, and it influenced English poets for generations to come. Sandys stands at the head of a long classical tradition in American verse and prose that reaffirmed the values of European civilization in the New World.

Sandys's work also initiated a long tradition of poets, diarists, letter writers, and other men and women of letters, who worked in relative isolation on literary projects. Unlike Sandys's Ovid, however, much of this work remained unpublished until the nineteenth or twentieth century. If Sandys had enjoyed less powerful connections and had stayed in Virginia, his translation might have become a part of this extensive manuscript culture that included some of the best literature produced in colonial America. William Byrd's writing remained mostly in manuscript until the nineteenth century, Edward Taylor's poetry was not published until the mid-twentieth century, and Dr. Alexander Hamilton's comic masterpiece, *The History of the Ancient and Honorable Tuesday Club,* appeared only in 1990.

In colonial America, however, manuscript writings often circulated among friends and relatives as a central part of a thriving literary culture. When print culture emerged in later years, it operated in parallel with this manuscript culture, feeding from it and offering a public alternative to its private expression, but at the same time reflecting its preferences for anonymity and for personal experience and address.

The First Printing Presses

A dozen years after the appearance of Sandys's Ovid, the Reverend Jose Glover emigrated to New England. Glover died en route in the summer of 1638, but the printing press he was bringing with him arrived safely. The president of Harvard College, Henry Dunster, married Glover's widow and set up the first press in British North America at Harvard, which itself had been in existence for only two years. Stephen Daye, the first printer in Cambridge, brought out the press's first big project, *The Whole Booke of Psalmes Faithfully Translated into English Metre*, in 1640. *The Bay Psalm Book*, as it is known, went through several editions and set the tone for much of the publishing in the earliest years of the North American colonies, which predominantly included religious titles: sermons, treatises, and John Eliot's translation of the Bible into the Massachusetts Native American language (1661–1663), as well as other religious publications in the Native American language, and even religious verse.

After a second press set up operation in Boston, however, publications with a more secular orientation began to appear, although not always with the authorities' approval. Marmaduke Johnson was fined in the 1660s for printing a romance titled *The Isle of Pines.* Even so, when Mary Rowlandson's captivity narrative first appeared from the Boston and Cambridge presses, it was titled *The Soveraignty and Goodness of God, Together with the Faithfulness of His Promises Displayed; Being a Narrative of the Captivity and Restauration of Mrs. Mary Rowlandson* (1682), whereas the London reprinting was more simply *A True History of the Captivity and Restoration of Mrs. Mary Rowlandson* (1682). The New England edition emphasizes the divine framework, while the English edition emphasizes the human drama. Daye was soon succeeded as printer by Samuel Green, who became the patriarch of a veritable dynasty of New England printers, with shops opening in Cambridge, Boston, New London, and New Haven, and even an office in Annapolis, Maryland, during the course of the next century.

If religious texts were a mainstay of the printer's business, government publications were another important, reliable source of income, and printers eventually vied for the right to publish the laws and official proceedings and announcements of colonial governments. Green's publication of the laws of Massachusetts in 1660 was a major accomplishment and implicitly signaled, perhaps, the connection in early Massachusetts between the ministerial and political orders.

The intellectual center of the community was thus bounded by the General Court in Boston, Harvard College, and its press. The culture bearers of the early generations there and throughout New England were, for the most part, the ministers, men like John Cotton, Thomas Hooker, Thomas Shepard, and a host of others who were memorialized in Cotton Mather's *Magnalia Christi Americana* (1702). Their most ambitious productions were typically published in London, both because of the limited abilities of the New England press and because of the desire to speak to the larger British evangelical audience.

The first generation of preachers was concerned with defending and defining the New England ecclesiastical order and its covenant theology with books such as John Cotton's *Keys of the Kingdom of Heaven* (1644) and *The Way of the Congregational Churches Cleared* (1648), Thomas Hooker's *A Survey of the Summe of Church Discipline* (1648), and Peter Bulkeley's *The Gospel Covenant* (1646). Samuel Willard, a third-generation minister, culminated the defense of the covenant theology of the New England Way, or clergy-led society, with his posthumously published *A Compleat Body of Divinity* (1726). At the time, it was the longest book published on an American press, and it remained an influential statement of Puritan religious orthodoxy for a century to come. Cotton's controversy with Roger Williams went beyond arguments about church government and became a major debate about the freedom of conscience. Williams's *Bloudy Tenent of Persecution* (1644) was answered by Cotton's *The Bloudy Tenent Washed and Made White in the Bloud of the Lambe* (1647), to which Williams fired back *The Bloudy Tenent Yet More Bloudy* (1652), restating his landmark defense of religious freedom.

Although defenses of the congregational form of church order and the New England Way were, in the first generation, largely arguments with critics in England and Europe, the more immediate concerns of ministers were with the spiritual welfare of their congregants. In elaborating the process of salvation and

the difficulties troubled souls could meet, many of them published sermon collections that revealed a shrewd understanding of religious psychology. Eminent examples are Thomas Hooker's final series of sermons published as *The Application of Redemption . . . the First Eight Books* (1656) and *The Application of Redemption . . . the Ninth and Tenth Books* (1659), and Thomas Shepard's considerations of the grounds of true faith in *The Sincere Convert* (1641) and *The Sound Believer* (1645). Shepard also wrote about the beginnings of the attempts to convert Native Americans in New England to Christianity in *The Clear Sunshine of the Gospel Breaking Forth upon the Indians of New England* (1648), a project later discussed by its chief missionary, John Eliot, in a series of reports that appeared between the 1650s and 1680s. Sermons that warned of divine judgments and the necessity to preserve the piety of the founding generation were a staple of the clergy, and these jeremiads appeared particularly at times of religious or political crisis. Nathaniel Ward's *The Simple Cobbler of Aggawam in America* (1647) assailed the vices of the day with energetic comic satire, a reminder that for Puritans, being morally serious did not necessarily mean being humorless.

Seventeenth-Century Secular Writing

If the New England ministers were the chief intellectual class of the early British colonies in North America, they were by no means the only writers, nor were religious topics the only matters of discussion. From the very beginning, there was promotional literature of various sorts that attempted to persuade Englishmen or other Europeans to emigrate to America or to invest in various colonial enterprises there. Captain John Smith was both a leader of the Virginia settlers and an indefatigable promoter of North American British colonization. His *A True Relation of . . . Virginia* (1608) was followed by *A Map of Virginia* (1612), *The Proceeding of the English Colony in Virginia* (1612), and *A Description of New England* (1616), the latter based on his voyages along the New England coast in 1614. Smith's most famous work, however, was his 1624 *Generall Historie of Virginia, New-England and the Summer Isles,* which incorporated earlier materials he had written, though often revised and "improved" for this edition, along with maps, a portrait of Pocahontas, and congratulatory poems, including one by John Donne.

Other early promoters of Virginia and the Chesapeake include Alexander Whitaker, an Anglican minister and missionary who instructed and baptized Pocahontas and whose *Good News from Virginia* (1612) urged Englishmen to have compassion on the native people, "these naked slaves of the devil." William Strachey, first recorder and secretary of the Virginia colony from 1610 to 1611, reported in 1609 on his shipwreck with Sir Thomas Gates in a narrative that is credited with inspiring Shakespeare's *The Tempest.* Strachey's subsequent *History of Travel into Virginia Brittania* (1612) included his thoughtful observations of Native Americans, their language, and beliefs.

After its beginnings in the early 1630s, the colony of Maryland had its own promoters, among them two with some real literary distinction. John Hammond's *Leah and Rachel; Or, The Two Fruitfull Sisters, Virginia and Maryland* (1656) urged the English poor to seek a better life in Maryland where opportunity beckoned, and he systematically tried to rebut the "calumnies" about the Chesapeake colonies that were then circulating in England. Ten years later George Alsop's *A Character of the Province of Maryland* (1666) both painted the charms of the colony's natural scene and viewed its social and political life as a comic spectacle, praising "Nature's extravagancy," but also giving preposterous accounts of Native American life. In New England, the wonders of nature were celebrated by William Wood's *New England's Prospect* (1634) and John Josselyn's *New-England's Rarities Discovered* (1672) and *An Account of Two Voyages to New England* (1674).

Alsop's *Character* included poetry and letters interspersed with the expository and persuasive prose that was more typical of the promotional literature, and, in effect, he transcended the form. In fact, the most ambitious defenses of colonial life went beyond the promotional tract or narrow argument directed toward the English authorities and offered expansive histories of Virginia and New England. Smith's *Generall Historie* summed up the first quarter century of English colonization in America and was the only attempt at a comprehensive history of Virginia until Robert Beverley's *The History and Present State of Virginia* (1705; 1722). Virginia, like the other colonies outside of New England, did not have a well-established press until the eighteenth century—Governor William Berkeley told English commissioners in 1670, "I thank God there are no free schools, nor printing; and I hope we shall not have these for a hundred years; for learning has brought disobedience and heresy and sects into the world, and printing has divulged them, and libels against the best government."

The accounts of an event as important as Bacon's Rebellion remained in manuscript form until the nineteenth century, although they were circulated among interested contemporaries and preserved by families like the Burwells of the Northern Neck. John Cotton of Queen's Creek, who wrote *The History of Bacon's and Ingram's Rebellion,* was both sympathetic and critical of Bacon, playing his wit and satiric thrusts against both sides in the conflict. Beverley's *History* inaugurated a new era of historical writing in Virginia, even as it preserved signs of its origins in promotional literature. Divided into four books, it offered a narrative of the first settlement to the present time, followed with an account of the natural productions and a longer account of Native Americans, and concluded with a description of the present state of the country and its prospects.

Having a press available did not always guarantee publication, however; the greatest of the seventeenth-century histories, William Bradford's *Of Plymouth Plantation,* circulated in manuscript and was eventually acquired by the Boston antiquarian Thomas Prince. It disappeared at the time of the Revolution and was only rediscovered in 1855 and published in 1856. In the meantime, Bradford's history was an important resource for Nathaniel Morton's *New England's Memorial* (1666) and for the parts of Cotton Mather's *Magnalia Christi Americana* that dealt with the Plymouth colony. Bradford narrated the story of the Pilgrim community from its origins in late sixteenth-century England, through its years in exile in the Netherlands, its emigration to New England, and the difficult first years at Plymouth. He hoped to write a providential history of a chosen people, but when he broke off in 1646, it was clear that he would not live to see the hoped-for millennial promise. Nevertheless, his expansive plan, his fullness of detail, and his inclusion of documentary evidence make his history a landmark of early American writing. As longtime governor of Plymouth, he was in a unique position to gather information, but he also drew upon the knowledge and writings of other members of the colony, notably Edward Winslow's *A Relation or Journal of the . . . English Plantation Settled at Plymouth in New England,* commonly known as *Mourt's Relation* (1602, printed in London in 1622).

In the Massachusetts Bay Colony, John Winthrop kept an extensive diary, which he quite possibly intended to turn into a full-fledged history. But the first published major historian of that colony was Edward Johnson with his work best known as *The Wonder-Working Providence of Sion's Savior in New England* (1653). Johnson memorialized the settlement of Massachusetts, town by town, as God worked through chosen religious and secular leaders whom the historian eulogized with heartfelt but clumsy poems. William Hubbard's *A General History of New England* was written around 1682, but apparently did not find support from his fellow clergy members, particularly the Mathers, and remained unpublished until 1815. Cotton Mather's *Magnalia* was the last great work of Puritan historiography, with its compendium of narratives, biographies, miraculous providences, and providential rescues from Native Americans, shipwrecks, lightning, and other natural catastrophes.

New England writers also responded to specific historic crises with a variety of narratives, to say nothing of the inevitable sermons and jeremiads from the pulpit. The Pequot War of 1637–1638 was described by participants Lion Gardiner, John Mason, and John Underhill, as well as by Phillip Vincent. Underhill's *News from America* (1638) defended the colonists' behavior, including the massacre at the Pequot fort, but Vincent, a visitor from Virginia at the time, gave a more even-handed account in his *A True Relation of the Late Battle Fought in New England* (1638).

Interest in Native Americans, their culture, and their relationships with the English settlers ran high both in New England and in the home country, and New England writers spoke to it in various ways. Reports on the missionary efforts by John Eliot and Thomas Mayhew have been mentioned above, and William Wood's and John Josselyn's narratives contained lengthy accounts of Native Americans. The most interesting and sympathetic early account of native people in New England, however, may well be Roger Williams's *A Key into the Language of America* (1643), a pioneering work of ethnography that linked lessons in Narragansett vocabulary with descriptions of their culture and beliefs.

War, with all its sufferings and terrors, seemingly prompted a large part of the writings about Native Americans. King Philip's War in 1675–1676, the most disruptive event in seventeenth-century New England, brought forth Nathaniel Saltonstall's news-bulletin-like accounts of 1676, Increase Mather's *A Brief History of the War with the Indians in New-England* (1676), William Hubbard's *A Narrative of the Troubles with the Indians* (1677), Mary Rowlandson's narrative of her captivity, and the Indian fighter Benjamin Church's *Entertaining Passages Relating to Philip's War* (1716). Daniel Gookin, superintendent of the "praying Indians" converted by Eliot, wrote *Historical Collections of the Indians in New England* in 1674, before the war broke

out, but his sympathetic and knowledgeable account was not published for more than a century, as was his subsequent *An Historical Account of the Doings and Sufferings of the Christian Indians in New England in the Years 1675, 1676, 1677*. Of all these accounts, Mrs. Rowlandson's was the most frequently reprinted in the course of the next century of Native American warfare in New England, and it set a model for the scores of captivity narratives that came out during that same period.

Not all of the writing stimulated by the experience of the war dealt directly with military action or was prose narrative. Benjamin Tompson's *New England's Crisis* (1676), a mock-heroic poem that lamented the destruction of New England towns and jeered at Native American "savagery," was an important addition to an emerging body of New England poetry. The New England Way faced challenges in the 1670s and after, from both Native American rebels and the English authorities who sought to recall the Massachusetts charter, and the subsequent anxieties fed into events like the Salem witch trials. Increase and Cotton Mather were at the center of efforts to preserve and reassert the traditional order and the sense of a divinely guided community. In *An Essay for the Recording of Illustrious Providences* (1684) and related publications, Increase Mather attempted to use natural phenomena and science to authenticate Puritan theology. His son Cotton continued his interest in collecting providential anecdotes, which he published in his *Magnalia,* in his 1689 *Memorable Providences Relating to Witchcrafts and Possessions,* and in his 1693 *Wonders of the Invisible World* about the Salem witchcraft cases. Cotton Mather's interest in science—he was elected to the Royal Society of London—figured in his *The Christian Philosopher* (1721) with its attempt to link God's providential care for the world with scientific explanations of natural phenomena.

Benjamin Tompson's poems on King Philip's War were by no means the first such writings, for Puritans of both sexes had been composing poetry from the earliest days of settlement. A decade after the Antinomian Controversy initiated by Anne Hutchinson, leading Puritans encouraged the London publication of Anne Bradstreet's poems, perhaps both as an exemplary female voice and as a demonstration to the home country of the cultural achievements of the colony. Published in London in 1650 under the title *The Tenth Muse Lately Sprung Up in America,* the collection was reprinted in Boston in expanded form in 1678. In a society in which grace was the measure of all things, grace came equally to men and women, and Bradstreet's poetry quietly exemplified the implicit equality of the sexes on the scale of grace.

Bradstreet's poems are often moving and accomplished, but the most locally popular poet of the era was Michael Wigglesworth, whose *Day of Doom; or, A Poetical Description of the Great and Last Judgment* (1662), with its nearly 1,800 lines of relentless rhyme, went through numerous editions. The *Daily Meditations* (1666) on death and salvation by the otherwise unknown Philip Pain is a collection of more skillful poems, and poetry by John Saffin, Richard Steere, Urian Oakes, and Benjamin Colman, to single out only a few, can still be read with pleasure.

The major poet of the period, however, and perhaps America's first major poet, was Edward Taylor, the minister of Westfield, Massachusetts, who wrote meditative poems in connection with officiating at the Lord's Supper with his congregation. Taylor's poems reflect the taste for metaphysical wit that was popular a generation or two before he wrote, at the end of the seventeenth century and the beginning of the eighteenth. His work was appreciated only in the twentieth century, when literary taste in the wake of T. S. Eliot and others reevaluated the metaphysical poets. Taylor has a voice all his own, and his poems are dense, witty, and surprising plays of language and feeling.

While there is relatively less poetry surviving from the Southern colonies in this period, the two poems on Nathaniel Bacon by John Cotton of Queen's Creek are worth notice. In Pennsylvania, the Reverend Francis Daniel Pastorius filled a manuscript with poems and other writings in English, German, French, Latin, and Greek. Most of these still await publication, although some charming examples have appeared in various anthologies.

New England produced more literature and had a richer intellectual community than other colonies in the seventeenth century for several reasons. The Puritans believed in the importance of an educated ministry and set up Harvard College to produce young men knowledgeable in the classics, the languages of the Bible, science, philosophy, and rhetoric. Massachusetts had presses, which increasingly were able to turn out literature for local consumption. Boston was, from the beginning, an urban focus for the intellectual, religious, and political life of the colony. New Englanders settled in towns because of the organization of their communities around the churches, while settlement in Virginia, Maryland, and the Carolinas tended to be dispersed onto individual plantations. Although New

Amsterdam (later New York) had a number of writers in Dutch, such as Henricus Selyns and Adriaen Van der Donck, it went through various political upheavals after the English acquired control of the colony. Pennsylvania was settled later, and its emergence as a cultural center is a phenomenon of the eighteenth century.

Eighteenth-Century Enlightenment and Expansion

After the Glorious Revolution of 1689 brought William III and Mary II to the English throne, the colonial system was reorganized and energized by an emerging commercial empire. The American colonies developed a more complex and lively cultural and intellectual life than before, although the continuing wars with France meant that crises did not disappear.

New England had developed a lively literary culture in the seventeenth century, albeit a culture predominantly organized around religious concerns. New Englanders had acquired wealth enough, however, to enjoy other pleasures of life, as evidenced by the oil portraits of John and Mary Freake and of Captain Thomas Smith of Boston that are now in the Worcester Art Museum. Samuel Sewall's diary records the day-to-day details of a sophisticated layman, including his observation of the polite rituals of courtship in the Boston of his day as he looked for a third wife. But other colonies saw an ever more complex and polished cultural and intellectual life as well. In addition, wealthier colonists increasingly tried to emulate English fashions. As the century went on, the system of royal government also brought increasing friction between royally appointed governors and locally elected legislatures, leading to diverse expressions of political opinion.

Literature in the Middle Colonies

The printer William Bradford set up the first active press in Philadelphia. When the Quaker authorities tried to censor some of his publications, he transferred his business to New York, inaugurating the first press there. Printers set up shop in Maryland and Virginia, and Annapolis and Williamsburg became centers of cultural and social life, as well as of political and economic activity.

The first newspaper, the *Boston News-Letter,* appeared in Boston in 1704, but more significant was James Franklin's *New England Courant* of 1721 because it presented local news, offered local writing, and challenged the governing authorities. When James was censured for the contents of the paper, his younger brother, Benjamin, took nominal control of the paper, even though he was still an apprentice.

When Benjamin Franklin moved to Philadelphia in the 1720s, he was involved in efforts to establish another printing office that would give a venue to opposing political opinions. When he took over the press in 1729 from Samuel Keimer, its first owner, he built a thriving business by capturing government printing commissions. A shrewd competitor, he also published a wide variety of material to suit every range of interest and opinion. His *Pennsylvania Gazette* became an important newspaper, and its appearance, along with that of numerous presses and papers in other colonies, signaled the arrival of the phenomenon Jürgen Habermas has called the bourgeois public sphere. It gave individuals a place to reason in public about religion, government, science, and the arts.

Growth of a print culture in the colonies in the early eighteenth century accompanied an increased attention to the values of learning, politeness, and sociability, which had been promoted in England in Lord Shaftesbury's *Characteristics* and Addison and Steele's *Spectator*. Franklin invigorated not only the Philadelphia press but also the intellectual scene by organizing his Junto, a group of young tradesmen like himself who wished to improve themselves and stay abreast of the latest accomplishments of the Enlightenment. Franklin printed George Webb's poem "Bachelor's Hall" (1736), a defense of a Philadelphia club rumored to be licentious and dissolute, and his friend Joseph Breintnall assisted him in writing his essay series "The Busy Body," which appeared in the *Gazette.* The glazier and Junto member Thomas Godfrey (father of the poet and playwright of the same name) independently invented the sextant, among his other scientific interests. Clubs and other informal literary circles in Philadelphia and elsewhere created the scene for the production of a variety of writing—poetry, essays, satires, scientific papers—which continued the manuscript culture of the previous century, but added a sense of intimacy and sentiment different from the political and public world of the printed text.

Philadelphia, scarcely forty years old when Franklin arrived, was no intellectual wasteland. William Penn, the colony's founder, wrote extensively about religion and his vision of an egalitarian society. He encouraged young men of learning and promise such as Gabriel Thomas, Thomas Frame, and John Holme to emigrate to Pennsylvania; they repaid his confidence by writing favorably about the opportunities there.

Penn's greatest protégé was James Logan, who came to Pennsylvania in 1699 and was at the center of political and intellectual life there until his death in 1751. Logan was a polymath, interested in politics, philosophy, science—he first described the sexual fertilization of corn in a paper published in the *Transactions of the Royal Society*—and the classics. (Franklin published his translation of M. T. Cicero's *Cato Major* in 1744.) He encouraged the scientific interests of Franklin and John Bartram, the naturalist, and amassed one of the best libraries in colonial America. At the time of Logan's death, Philadelphia was in the process of becoming the intellectual center of colonial America. The Philadelphia Library Company had begun in 1731, the first steps had been taken to found the American Philosophical Society on the model of the Royal Society, and discussions were under way to establish a college. The Reverend William Smith arrived in 1754, after Franklin invited him to become the provost of the new academy at Philadelphia. Smith encouraged literary and dramatic performances in the college and wrote competent poetry.

The Society of Friends, frequently known as Quakers, had a powerful impact on the culture of eighteenth-century Pennsylvania. Quakers disdained theological treatises of the sort popular with other Protestant divines, such as those in New England, and instead encouraged narratives that testified to personal spiritual experience. Furthermore, because of their belief in the central importance of an inner light, they authorized women speakers in their community and initiated a line of outspoken women reformers from Mary Dyer in early New England to Lucretia Mott in nineteenth-century America. Narratives by women such as the eccentric Bathsheba Bowers's *An Alarm Sounded* (1709) and Elizabeth Ashbridge's *Some Account of the Fore-Part of the Life of Elizabeth Ashbridge* (1774) stood with John Woolman's *Journal* (1774) and John Churchman's *An Account of the Gospel Labours and Christian Experiences of Christ* (1779).

Slavery had been condemned as early as Samuel Sewall's *Selling of Joseph,* published in Boston in 1700, but the Quakers' eagerness to reform the world made them particularly effective critics of slavery. John Woolman made it his life's work to convince his coreligionists of the sin of slave owning by traveling up and down the Atlantic seaboard, visiting Quakers in their meetings and as individuals. Woolman published the first part of his long essay, *Some Considerations on the Keeping of Negroes* in 1754, with a second part in 1762. Anthony Benezet took the campaign to a larger audience, writing and speaking against slavery and racial injustice from his first tract, *An Epistle of Caution and Advice* (1754), to his last publication, *Some Observations on the . . . Indian Natives* (1784).

Quaker tolerance, both for other varieties of opinion and for women's participation in public discourse, underwrote the diverse intellectual and cultural life in early Philadelphia. It was here that in the years before the Revolution, Elizabeth Graeme Fergusson became the center of a group of fellow poets. She encouraged Nathaniel Evans and Francis Hopkinson, who published their poetry, as well as many women poets who published only occasionally or shared their writing in manuscript. Much of this group's work has been recently brought to light with the publication of *Milcah Martha Moore's Book* (1997), a collection of writings by Fergusson, Susanna Wright, and Hannah Griffits.

The urban centers of other colonies were also developing centers of intellectual and polite life. New York recovered from its political upheavals in the late seventeenth century, and when Cadwallader Colden, a Scots physician, arrived in 1718 in response to an invitation from Governor Robert Hunter, he became an energetic agent of enlightenment. Appointed surveyor general by Hunter, Colden played an active role in New York politics, serving as lieutenant governor from 1761 until his death in 1776. He took part in treaty-making sessions with the Iroquois and published his *History of the Five Indian Nations Depending on the Province of New York* in 1727, with a revised edition in 1744. He wrote widely on scientific subjects and corresponded with an international circle of scientists that included Linnaeus, who applauded his account of the flora of New York. Colden's medical writings were fairly well received, but his misguided attempt to revise Newton's theory of gravity, *An Explication of the First Causes of Action in Matter* (1747), was rejected by the scientific community. In correspondence with Franklin and John Bartram, he made the initial proposal that led to the formation of the American Philosophical Society. Colden also encouraged the botanic interests of his daughter Jane and exchanged letters on botanic matters with Bartram and Alexander Garden of Charles Town, South Carolina.

New York intellectual circles at midcentury focused more on medical or legal interests than on bel-letristic culture, but a number of young lawyers who opposed the Anglican foundation for a proposed college wrote poetry, history, and essays, in addition to their legal activities. William Livingston, William Smith, Jr., and John Morin Scott published *The Independent Reflector* (1752–1753) as a "Reformer of Public Abuses," but the main target was the attempt to make the proposed King's College (eventually Columbia) an Anglican institution. Their essays demonstrated familiarity with John Trenchard and Thomas Gordon's *Independent Whig,* a staple of British Whig discourse, and covered a range of topics from extravagant funerals to passive obedience and nonresistance. Livingston earlier published a popular poem in the Epicurean manner of John Pomfret; *Philosophic Solitude* (1747) praised the choice of a rural life and went into its thirteenth edition in 1790. Livingston became a patriot leader in the Revolution, serving as member of Congress and governor of New Jersey while he continued to attack Tories and encourage "the cause of liberty and virtue." Smith collaborated with Livingston on *The Art of Pleading in Imitation of Part of Horace's Art of Poetry* (1751) and contributed frequently to New York newspapers. But he was best known for his *History of the Province of New York* (1757); a continuation not published until 1829 brought the history up to 1762, and it remains one of the best historiographic performances of the colonial era.

Literature in the Southern Colonies

In Annapolis, Southern writers carried on a tradition of genial satire. Ebenezer Cooke's *The Sot-weed Factor* (1708, 1731), a masterpiece of colonial humor, details the misadventures of a naive newcomer to what is basically a frontier society. Cooke also wrote elegies on Maryland worthies, as well as a satiric poem on Bacon's Rebellion printed in *The Maryland Muse* (1731).

Richard Lewis's 1728 translation of *Muscipula,* Edward Holdsworth's mock heroic satire of the Welsh, was the first poem printed at William Parks's new press in Annapolis and appeared with Lewis's critical introduction, which discussed poetic genres, literary theory, and polite literature. His poem "A Journey from Patapsco in Maryland to Annapolis, April 4th, 1730," which appeared in several colonial newspapers and in the *Gentleman's Magazine* in London, is perhaps the earliest nature poem in America. He wrote other occasional verse and sent letters on the aurora borealis, an earthquake, and insects to the Royal Society.

In 1745, the Tuesday Club, organized by Dr. Alexander Hamilton, began meeting. Sociability was its purpose, and one of its earliest bylaws proposed that if any person raised a topic of local politics, or for that matter any topic disagreeable to other members, it would be the duty of the club to laugh at the offending member in order to divert the discourse. Until his death in 1756, Dr. Hamilton kept a witty record of the club's minutes and converted them into *The History of the Ancient and Honorable Tuesday Club*, a three-volume manuscript not published until 1990. Hamilton's witty *History* is the most ambitious and successful piece of literary satire from colonial America. At the same time, it reveals the rich variety and possibility of "clubbical life" in the period better than any other document we have.

The same William Parks who had printed Lewis's *Muscipula* also established the first successful press in Williamsburg, an event that was celebrated in John Markland's *Typographia: An Ode on Printing* (1730), with its flattery of Governor William Gooch, who had promoted a press. Virginia planters, widely separated on their individual plantations, had already developed a rich manuscript culture that is perhaps best exemplified by William Byrd II. Educated in England, Byrd spent considerable stretches of his early life there. At his home in Virginia, he amassed one of the most important private libraries in colonial America—the others were Cotton Mather's and James Logan's—and kept a diary that recorded the daily life of a tidewater grandee. When appointed in 1728 as one of the leaders of the commission to survey the boundary between Virginia and North Carolina, he produced two versions of the expedition, one known as "The History of the Dividing Line Betwixt Virginia and North Carolina" and the other as "The Secret History of the Line." In the latter, Byrd portrayed himself as "Steddy," who stood for good sense, courage, and leadership, as opposed to his rival, "Firebrand," or the North Carolinians "Shoebrush" and "Puzzlecause." Byrd's combination of satire and close observation has made his narratives literary classics.

Other Virginians such as William Dawson and Charles Hansford circulated their poetry in manuscript, as did the satires directed against Governor Dinwiddie, first published by Richard Beale Davis in 1967 as *The Colonial Virginia Satirist*. Hugh Jones surveyed *The Present State of Virginia* (1724), and William Stith improved upon Beverley's history with his *History of the First Discovery and Settlement of Virginia* (1747).

Colonial elites such as Byrd and Stith met in urban centers like Williamsburg to take care of government or business matters, to meet with their friends, and to participate in a culture of virtue and social politeness. As towns like Williamsburg and Charles Town acquired presses and newspapers, writers contributed essays like those in the *South Carolina Gazette*'s "Meddlers Club Papers" (1735) or the *Virginia Gazette*'s "Monitor" essays (1736).

Theater

In the same period, theatrical performances began in a number of colonial towns, first by amateurs and later by traveling companies of professional actors. Although Governor Robert Hunter of New York had written a satiric play, *Androboros,* in 1714, most plays were British, and Addison's *Cato* and Farquhar's *The Recruiting Officer* and *The Beaux' Stratagem* were favorites in New York, Williamsburg, Annapolis, and Charles Town in the 1730s. In 1735, a company advertised in Charles Town for the performance of the first opera in America, *Flora, or Hob in the Well.* When the Lewis Hallam company of actors came from Britain in 1752 to perform regular seasons in buildings erected specifically as theaters, plays were a frequent entertainment in colonial cities.

Authorities had moral reservations about theater in some areas, especially Boston and Providence, but also Philadelphia to some extent, and the players sometimes had to use stratagems to perform. When David Douglass took his company to Newport, Rhode Island, in 1761, he advertised a "Moral Dialogue" on the dangers of envy that was, in fact, a performance of *Othello.* In 1767, *The Prince of Parthia*, by Thomas Godfrey, Jr., became the first play by an American playwright to be performed by a professional company, and the same Philadelphia company almost performed in the same year Thomas Forrest's *The Disappointment,* a ballad opera whose satire was finally deemed too pointed toward local persons.

Music and Fine Arts

As colonists accumulated more wealth, the desire for more genteel, that is, more English, lifestyles led to the encouragement of other arts as well. In addition to theater, musical performances by professionals and amateurs became more widespread.

Cabinetmakers like the Goddards of Newport supplied fine pieces of furniture in the latest fashion for the homes of wealthy merchants and professional men. Artists from Europe arrived to paint the portraits of the colonial elite. Gustavus Hesselius came from Sweden to Delaware in 1711 and began to do portraits there, in Philadelphia, and in the Chesapeake region. He later turned to organ building, while his son John followed in his footsteps as a portraitist. Peter Pelham, a mezzotint engraver, began working in Boston in 1726, and three years later, John Smibert arrived in the company of Bishop Berkeley. Jeremiah Theüs, a Swiss painter, came to Charles Town in 1739, and in 1750 John Valentin Haidt came to the Moravian community in Bethlehem, Pennsylvania.

A number of American-born painters emerged in the same era, notably Nathaniel Emmons, Joseph Badger, and John Greenwood in Boston, Robert Feke in Newport, and James Claypoole in Philadelphia. John Wollaston and Joseph Blackburn emigrated from England at midcentury, bringing with them new fashions in portraiture. This later generation of American painters, active in the two decades before the Revolution, included John Singleton Copley, Benjamin West, and Charles Willson Peale, three of the best artists of the period. Copley was the stepson of Peter Pelham, and

Charles Willson Peale, one of the great American painters of the Revolutionary period, was the father of a distinguished family of artists in the eighteenth and nineteenth centuries. This portrait is by Benjamin West, Peale's teacher and the first American painter to gain an international reputation. *(New York Historical Society, New York/Bridgeman Art Library)*

his portraits done in Boston and New York are notable for their masterly capturing of individuality, their luminousness, and their exquisite representation of textures and surfaces. Copley went to England during the Revolution, partly for political reasons but mostly in search of more lucrative commissions. Benjamin West, however, left Philadelphia to develop his skills as a painter in England and on the Continent. His historical painting *The Death of General Wolfe* (1770) attracted favorable attention in England, including the interest of King George III, who appointed West as keeper of the royal pictures; West eventually succeeded Joshua Reynolds as president of the Royal Academy. West encouraged young American painters both in Philadelphia and London, and one of his students, Charles Willson Peale, became the great painter of the Revolutionary generation and the father of a family of talented artists.

Culture in the Great Awakening

Religious questions remained central to the lives of most European Americans, however, and the central religious event of the eighteenth century, the Great Awakening, prompted new directions in theological writing and practice. Revivals of religious spirit had been promoted in individual churches, particularly by Solomon Stoddard and his grandson Jonathan Edwards in their church in Northampton, Massachusetts. William Tennent and Theodore Frelinghuysen also spread this spirit in the Middle colonies.

The Great Awakening took off when the famous English evangelist George Whitefield arrived in 1738, to begin a two-year tour of the colonies from Georgia to New England. Huge crowds turned out to hear him wherever he went, preaching the need of individuals to come to terms with their sinfulness and their need for redemption. The clergy generally welcomed him and built upon the enthusiasm he invoked, and newspapers reported on his arrival and preaching successes as celebrity events. Notable supporters of the Awakening included Jonathan Edwards, William Tennent's son Gilbert, and Samuel Davies in Virginia, and many others, including so-called itinerants, who spoke to public assemblies outside of their own towns. Such itinerants as James Davenport of Connecticut promoted an enthusiastic experience at the expense of religious and civil order—or so Davenport's critics charged. Edwards, perhaps the deepest philosophical mind of the colonial era, wrote *The Distinguishing Marks of a Work of the Spirit of God* (1741) and *A Treatise Concerning*

Religious Affections (1746) in order to analyze and describe the changes in mind and behavior that accompanied a genuine spiritual rebirth. Thomas Prince, minister of the Old South Church in Boston, who had earlier written the first volume of *A Chronological History of New England* (1736; second volume in 1755), edited a magazine reporting on the spread of the Awakening. Charles Chauncy of Boston published some of the most effective critiques of the awakeners in his *Enthusiasm Described and Cautioned Against* (1742) and *Seasonable Thoughts on the State of Religion in New England* (1743).

The Awakening's emphasis on the necessity of individuals' taking responsibility for their own lives, although restating the basically Calvinist belief that saving grace was in God's hands alone, strengthened individualist sensibility in the colonies. The movement's evangelizing energies supported the careers of the American Indian missionary Samson Occom and Eleazar Wheelock's efforts to educate Native Americans at his school. Edwards's powerful theology was recognized when he was appointed as president of the College of New Jersey (later Princeton University). Although he died shortly thereafter, his renewal of Calvinism echoed for generations in followers such as Joseph Bellamy and Nathaniel Emmons.

Political and Military Issues

Newspaper coverage of Whitefield's evangelical tour and of other moments of the Awakening signaled it as one of the first events that was a shared experience across the Eastern seaboard colonies. Intercolonial trade strengthened connections during the eighteenth century, but in the early years, at least, travel between colonies was difficult and a bit unusual, as is revealed in Sarah Kemble Knight's 1704 *Journal* of her trip from Boston to New York (published in 1825). Dr. Alexander Hamilton's 1744 *Itinerarium* (published 1907) revealed that during his pleasure tour from Annapolis to New England and back, his presence was regarded as a considerable curiosity in rural communities, although he found comfortably polite society in Philadelphia, New York, and Boston.

Military and political events originating outside the colonies in the 1750s and 1760s furthered the sense of intercolonial connection begun by the Awakening. The Seven Years' War of 1756 to 1763, known as the French and Indian War in North America, involved all of the colonies in the struggle against France and the French-led Native American forces, as well as shared expansionist ambitions. The subsequent efforts of the

British government to make the colonies pay a greater share of the costs of empire, beginning with the Stamp Act of 1765, brought the colonies together in a spirit of resistance. The cultural and intellectual life of the colonies became increasingly overshadowed by the political struggles over who was to govern them, or so it seems to historians who have written from a post-Revolutionary viewpoint.

The culture of politeness continued to thrive in all of the colonies. Boston's Reverend Mather Byles emerged as one of the best neoclassical poets of the age in his *A Collection of Poems by Several Hands* (1744) and in later works. He advised the young African poet Phillis Wheatley as she wrote the poems that appeared in her 1773 *Poems on Various Subjects, Religious and Moral*. But Boston seemed more consumed by the conflicts between the royal governors and the legislature that produced influential tracts like James Otis, Jr.'s *The Rights of the British Colonies Asserted and Proved* (1764). When the poet and historian Mercy Otis Warren published her first work, it was *The Adulateur* (1772), a satiric play targeting Governor Hutchinson and his

Brought to America and sold into slavery as a child in 1761, Phillis Wheatley created a sensation a decade later with her poems on classical and Christian themes, most notably in the book *Poems on Various Subjects, Religious and Moral* (1773). *(Private Collection/Bridgeman Art Library)*

circle. The Stamp Act also met with widespread criticism.

John Dickinson's *Letters from a Farmer in Pennsylvania* first appeared in the *Pennsylvania Chronicle* in 1767, and it was subsequently widely reprinted in other newspapers and in pamphlets. Dickinson, a lawyer and member of the Pennsylvania and Delaware elite, managed to make the "Farmer" a powerful image of American self-identity. In subsequent controversies after the Revolution, the "Westchester Farmer" and the "Federal Farmer" delivered their opinions, and Guillaume Crevecoeur's *Letters from an American Farmer* (1782) identified the literate farmer, skilled at agriculture and epistolary art, as the quintessential American.

The pamphlet war intensified in the 1770s as American rights and American identity increasingly became issues of concern. James Wilson's *Considerations on the . . . Legislative Authority of the British Parliament* (1774) and Thomas Jefferson's *Summary View of the Rights of British America* (1774) were powerful, literate arguments before the fact for American self-rule. The political culture that led to the First and Second Continental Congresses culminated in the Declaration of Independence, the last piece of literature from the American colonies and, at the same time, the first from the United States.

The larger cultural developments of colonial America presaged independence, a fact realized in the 1771 commencement piece at Reverend William Smith's College of Philadelphia. The young poets Hugh Henry Brackenridge and Philip Freneau titled their work *A Poem on the Rising Glory of America*. It avoided politics, but its assertion of an imagined "America" was more than merely colonial.

Frank Shuffelton

Bibliography

Amory, Hugh, and David D. Hall, eds. *The Colonial Book in the Atlantic World,* Vol. 1 of *A History of the Book in America.* Cambridge, UK: Cambridge University Press, 2000.

Bercovitch, Sacvan, ed. *The Cambridge History of American Literature.* Vol. 1, 1590–1820. New York: Cambridge University Press, 1994.

Blecki, Catherine LaCourreye, and Karin A. Wulf. *Milcah Martha Moore's Book: A Commonplace Book From Revolutionary America.* University Park: Pennsylvania State University Press, 1997.

Crawford, Richard. *America's Musical Life: A History.* New York: W. W. Norton, 2001.

Davis, Richard Beale, ed. *The Colonial Virginia Satirist: Mid-Eighteenth-Century Commentaries on Politics, Religion, and Society. Transactions of the American Philosophical Society* 57:1 (1957).

Hall, Clayton Colman, ed. *Narratives of Early Maryland.* New York: Scribner's, 1910.

Jehlen, Myra, and Michael Warner. *The English Literatures of America, 1500–1800.* New York: Routledge, 1997.

Jones, Howard Mumford. *The Literature of Virginia in the Seventeenth Century.* Charlottesville: University Press of Virginia, 1968.

Larkin, Oliver W. *Art and Life in America.* New York: Holt, Rinehart and Winston, 1960.

Lemay, J. A. Leo. *Men of Letters in Colonial Maryland.* Knoxville: University of Tennessee Press, 1972.

Levernier, James A., and Douglas R. Wilmes, eds. *American Writers Before 1800: A Biographical and Critical Dictionary.* 3 vols. Westport, CT: Greenwood Press, 1983.

Meserole, Harrison T., ed. *Seventeenth-Century American Poetry.* New York: New York University Press, 1968.

Meserve, Walter J. *An Emerging Entertainment: The Drama of the American People to 1828.* Bloomington: Indiana University Press, 1982.

Miller, Perry. *The New England Mind: From Colony to Province.* Cambridge, MA: Harvard University Press, 1953.

———. *The New England Mind: The Seventeenth Century.* Cambridge, MA: Harvard University Press, 1954.

Miller, Perry, and Alan Heimert, eds. *The Great Awakening: Documents Illustrating the Crisis and Its Consequences.* Indianapolis, IN: Bobbs-Merrill, 1967.

Morison, Samuel Eliot. *The Founding of Harvard College.* Cambridge, MA: Harvard University Press, 1935.

Mulford, Carla, Angela Vietto, and Amy E. Winans. *Early American Writings.* New York: Oxford University Press, 2002.

Quinn, Arthur Hobson. *A History of the American Drama From the Beginning to the Civil War.* New York: Appleton-Century, 1943.

Richardson, E. P. *Painting in America From 1502 to the Present.* New York: Crowell, 1956.

Shields, David S. *Civil Tongues & Polite Letters in British America.* Chapel Hill: University of North Carolina Press, 1997.

Silverman, Kenneth, ed. *Colonial American Poetry.* New York: Hafner, 1968.

———. *A Cultural History of the American Revolution: Painting, Music, Literature, and the Theater in the Colonies and the United States from the Treaty of Paris to the Inauguration of George Washington, 1763–1789.* New York: Crowell, 1976.

Sonneck, O. G. *Early Concert Life in America.* Leipzig, Germany: Breitkopf and Härtel, 1907.

Stearns, Raymond Phineas. *Science in the British Colonies of America.* Urbana: University of Illinois Press, 1970.

Wright, Thomas Goddard. *Literary Culture in Early New England, 1620–1730.* New Haven, CT: Yale University Press, 1920.

Economy, Business, and Labor

From the settlement of Jamestown to the American Revolution, colonial economic expansion played an important role in imperial and colonial development. The increasingly strong colonial economy laid the foundations for America's continued economic growth.

The traditional framework for understanding the colonial economy comes from the so-called staples thesis, which views economic activity through the role of exported such staples as corn and tobacco. While the staples thesis explains much of the colonial role within Great Britain's imperial system, it fails in other important aspects.

One overlooked area concerns importation to the colonies. Over the course of the eighteenth century, the growing colonial population consumed more and more commodities and goods, making the colonies an important English market. A growing population also contributed to economic diversification. Meanwhile, increasing discrepancies in levels of individuals' prosperity began to occur.

Finally, the staples thesis generally maintains the traditional idea of the hardy yeoman farmer toiling within a subsistence economy, but it often ignores regional variations. Examining the colonies within a market economy context expands our understanding of the complexity of their economy. Thus, while earlier studies of the colonial economy stressed issues of exportation and the colonies' role within an imperial economy, more recent research has focused on importation and consumption.

Historians often examine the colonial economy within a local or regional context, and specialized studies of merchants, farmers, and laborers have all extended our knowledge of the subject. Other studies have included the nature of colonial agriculture and the agrarian origins of American capitalism. Recently, scholars have clearly shown how economic development affected various colonial groups and the expansion, by the mid-eighteenth century, of growing divisions between rich and poor.

Foundations

In the fifteenth century, the Portuguese began the European exploration of the New World that culminated in Christopher Columbus's discovery of the Americas. These early adventurers were followed by explorers from other European nations, particularly Spain. Britain's earliest attempts at colonization, first at Roanoke and then in Jamestown, New England, and the West Indies, continued the process of European expansion into the Atlantic.

During this expansion, the slave-labor-based plantation complex, centered on sugar production, developed. The West Indies and coastal Brazil possessed the perfect environment for sugar cultivation, and Portuguese trade enclaves in West Africa provided slave laborers. Britain's establishment of colonies occurred within an already established and defined system of expansion in which colonization played a role in the development of European state structure. That is, the need to govern colonies reinforced the bureaucracy of the centralized government back in the home country.

Early English colonization efforts were primarily private ventures through joint-stock companies. The private financing of these efforts meant that the colonies were intended as profit-making ventures, providing the foundation for colonial economic development.

English colonization began with the Virginia Company's settlement at Jamestown, where settlers suffered through a decade of starvation, brutal discipline, and strife until the first successful tobacco harvest in the late 1610s. The subsequent tobacco boom led to the development of a plantation-based economy on mainland North America, which reinforced the profitability of colonization. Virginia's tobacco production supports the staples thesis focus on exports and helps explain the rise of African slavery. Virginians discovered that an abundance of land, once appropriated from its original inhabitants, necessitated affordable labor to work it. While Virginia experimented with several

North American Economy, 1750. The North American economy in colonial times was largely geared toward the output of raw materials from forests, mines, and farms. *(Carto-Graphics)*

labor systems, including indentured servants, African slavery proved the most effective solution.

A counter to the staples thesis occurred twenty years later with the founding of the Massachusetts Bay Colony. There, the Puritan founders came not to create dividends for their investors but to obtain religious freedom. To accomplish this goal, they needed to find ways to survive and thrive in the New World. The region they settled in was ill suited for plantation agriculture, and so small, family farms developed in-

stead. New England was mainly settled by these farmers; however, a more diversified economic system of agricultural production, manufacturing, and trade developed over time.

As these first colonial ventures were established, the English Civil War (1638–1660), which was caused by political, religious, constitutional, social, and economic factors, interrupted the focus on colonization for over a decade. The most important colonial result of this conflict involved a second wave of settlements, governed by a newly created mercantile system. The foundations of this system came during the Puritan Commonwealth period, when Parliament defined the economic relationship between England and its colonies.

Mercantilism, as an economic philosophy, was not yet a cohesive body of thought in the seventeenth century. Adam Smith first used the term in his 1776 *Wealth of Nations*, but it can best be defined as a system designed to generate revenue and wealth for the state. Some basic tenets of mercantilism, a mixture of feudal and capitalist economic beliefs, had previously existed, such as the concept that wealth was finite and the desire to create a favorable balance of trade was a key to prosperity.

Early English mercantilists, such as Thomas Munn, argued that foreign trade constituted the best way for England to increase its treasury, and the Navigation Acts embodied these ideas. The Navigation Act of 1651, in an attempt to reduce the Dutch role in the carrying trade, stipulated that all goods imported into England and its colonies must arrive on English ships, with predominantly English crews. (The act excluded goods coming from Europe to England.) In 1660, another parliamentary act set the nationality of crews at least at three-quarters Englishmen and defined a set of enumerated goods, including tobacco, cotton, sugar, and indigo, which could go only from the colonies directly to England. The 1663 Staple Act required that all goods shipped from Europe to the colonies first go through England. Through this re-export trade, the British government controlled the flow of goods from the colonies to Europe and vice versa.

In 1673, the final Navigation Act regulated trade between colonies by requiring every ship carrying enumerated goods either to give a bond if sailing to England or to pay the duty up front if sailing to another British colony. While the Navigation Acts successfully increased England's wealth, a major problem was the difficulty of enforcement. The strengths and weaknesses of the Navigation Acts benefited both England and the colonies. While they restricted colonists' trade with other countries, they also limited other nations' intrusion into colonial trade.

Meanwhile, the second wave of colonization started with the eight lord proprietors of the Carolinas and ended with the founding of Georgia. The major difference between the first and second wave of settlement was that the latter occurred through the Crown distributing proprietary grants. The proprietary system involved granting large tracts of land to individuals or groups. Following the 1664 conquest by the English of New Netherland, which was renamed New York, this colony was divided into two, when the Duke of York presented proprietary grants to Sir George Carteret and Lord John Berkeley to form New Jersey. The next proprietary grant was to William Penn, who hoped to create a Quaker commonwealth in Pennsylvania. The final colony, granted to twenty-one trustees, was Georgia.

All of the grants focused on land and the desire to make it productive, while ensuring state revenue. What quickly happened was that the complex and hard-to-enforce proprietary systems, often modeled upon feudal practices, broke down, and land ownership was dispersed. Whether within the proprietary tenant system or the developing system of private ownership, the new colonies, like those before them, centered their early economic development on agricultural production.

Over time, diversification and specialization occurred in three colonial regions. From north to south, these regions were the New England colonies, the Mid-Atlantic colonies, and the Southern colonies. Within these regions, environmental and geographic variations further defined each colony's economic opportunities.

In New England, the often sandy, rocky soil did not prohibit farming, but it did limit production. Most New England farms were small and family run, and they produced mainly for a local market. For this reason, New England developed a diversified economy.

The Mid-Atlantic colonies contained productive farmland, more suited to the production of wheat and corn than of cash crops. These crops required control of both land and labor, although these staples were not as labor-intensive as the cash crops grown farther south. The food surplus in the Mid-Atlantic region provided an export commodity, but these colonies also developed a diversified economy for local consumption.

Of the three regions, the Southern colonies were the least diversified because of the plantation system, within which landowners utilized almost all available land and labor in the production of one or two crops such as tobacco in Virginia and rice and indigo in South Carolina. The Southern plantation system created a slave society where the economic, social, and political system evolved from the control of land and labor. During the course of the eighteenth century, the Southern economy did become more diversified.

It is worth noting that while such economic differences defined each region, their economic interaction and consumption of similar commodities muted many of these differences.

Agriculture

Since most settlers and slaves toiled to make the land productive, agricultural production dominated the colonial economy. Environmental factors dictated each colony's agricultural production, but similarities existed.

The first involved the abundance of cheap land and the competition to possess it. The result was the accumulation of land by wealthy landowners and speculators, thereby pushing settlement westward as poor settlers sought less expensive land. Another important similarity was the fact that most people in the British colonies labored within a larger imperial economy and operated within a market economy.

Colonial agriculture produced an assortment of crops. Cash crops, such as tobacco, were often seen as the most important because of their profits and their place within the imperial system. The early Virginia tobacco boom illustrated the profitability of colonization while making it clear that profits resulted from exploiting different classes of agricultural laborers. By the eighteenth century, most farmers, especially in the Mid-Atlantic colonies, produced food for a market that included slave plantations, urban areas, and the West Indies.

As European colonists arrived and settled, they brought with them a deferential and hierarchical social system that defined most people, European and non-European, by their relationship to the land. Because the social system of Native Americans was not agriculturally based and sedentary, Europeans defined natives as less civilized, thereby justifying appropriation of their land.

Colonial society consisted of slaves, indentured servants, tenants, yeomen, artisans, husbandmen, planters, gentry, and proprietors, depending upon their ownership of land and the amount possessed. What united the settlers was that most were unprepared to survive in the American wilderness since they lacked the skills to clear the land and begin their life anew. Ironically, it was the knowledge and skills, including hunting, fishing, gathering, and farming, provided by local Native Americans that ensured many of the early European settlers' survival.

While most farmers focused on crop production, they diversified their income through other pursuits. As they cleared their land, they acquired timber to sell in local and regional markets. Keeping and raising cattle, swine, chickens, horses, and other domesticated animals supplemented their diets and their income. Cattle were important not only as a food source but also for their hides, and dairy cows provided milk, butter, and cheese. Swine were popular in that they required little upkeep and were an important foodstuff. Horses served as beasts of burden, and provided transportation, while other animals served additional roles.

In coastal areas, farmers could become fishermen during the winter months, and fishing provided another important food source and trade item for the colonies. Farmers also developed other skills and practiced various crafts in the off season. The ability of farmers to diversify ensured their survival and bolstered the developing economy.

Trade

Mercantilism, coupled with agricultural production, made trade an important part of colonial economic development. Colonists participated in the market economy when they sold excess crops and, increasingly in the eighteenth century, when they consumed British and global commodities. Mercantilism allowed American wealth and products to flow to England, and it made the colonies a profitable market. Thus colonists, Native Americans, and Africans throughout British North America contributed to this development.

The expansion of trade depended on the rise of a merchant class that exported colonial products and imported manufactured goods. The largest merchants engaged in overseas trade; while some specialized in specific commodities, most dealt with a variety of goods. Next in size were regional merchants who purchased products from large merchants and then sold or traded the products in the hinterland. There, local merchants bought local products and sold various goods.

All these merchants depended upon credit, and bookkeeping advances, along with increasing amounts of capital, allowed merchants to negotiate numerous long-term exchanges. Especially in the seventeenth century, however, there were traditional economic and social constraints that regulated them. An example was the New England "just price," which limited profits by setting a fair value. The just price was especially important during famines when, if food prices remained at market value, the poor would starve. Thus, the just price placed the common good ahead of individual profits. During the eighteenth century, these domestic restraints broke down.

Internationally, the triangle trade created three lines of commodity movement: from Europe to West Africa, from West Africa to the Americas, and from the Americas to Europe. Within this triangle, goods, including firearms, alcohol, and textiles, flowed to West Africa to be exchanged for slaves who, after they were transported to the Americas, became a permanent unfree labor force.

American products, including crops, naval stores, furs, and raw materials, then traveled to Europe, where the process began again. The triangle trade explains the general flow of goods in the Atlantic, but it creates a simplistic understanding of a complex and interconnected trading network. The goods being carried to West Africa came from not only Europe and the Americas but also the Far East, and it was not just European-based merchants who became involved in the slave trade.

The flow of goods within the colonial economy also occurred on multiple levels. The first for most settlers involved their local economic network. As most colonists engaged in agriculture, they purchased goods that they could not produce at home. Often, this involved bartering with their neighbors or creating a reciprocal relationship, but it usually involved selling a surplus crop. A Pennsylvania farmer who sold his surplus corn contributed to Philadelphia's development when a Philadelphia merchant purchased this corn to sell to urban consumers. The same corn might be placed in a ship and sent to the Southern colonies or the West Indies to feed slaves. The development of, and connections between, these economic networks created profit through surplus production, thereby providing access to a growing variety of consumable goods.

As colonial trade developed, so did the carrying trade, sometimes referred to as merchant capital. This involved the movement of goods from the producer to market by someone other than the producer. The success of the Navigation Acts in displacing the Dutch from this trade allowed the colonists to become more involved.

An early example of the carrying trade occurred between Virginia and New England. Virginian tobacco production created a profitable commodity, but the planters' focus on land and labor made them reliant upon New Englanders' sailing vessels and crews to carry their goods to the European market. The profit in the carrying trade came from the difference between the purchase and selling price, minus transportation and other costs. While the carrying trade provided an effective way for producers to sell their commodities, they lost a percentage of their profit to middlemen. By the eighteenth century, a complex carrying trade operated within the Atlantic world.

As the carrying trade integrated regions, an important local and regional exchange system also occurred between settlers and Native Americans. For the Europeans, this commerce, especially in the fur trade, was particularly lucrative. A profitable market for furs, especially beaver pelts, existed in Europe, and there also were local and regional markets for clothing created from animal skins and furs. In some cases, European fur traders, such as the French coureurs de bois, trapped the furs themselves.

Although the fur trade was profitable for the colonists, it had a negative impact on the Native Americans who engaged in it. As native peoples focused on trapping, they quickly depleted resources within their tribal lands, and their search for new furs caused intertribal conflict. Many historians also believe that the fur trade was primarily responsible for creating Native American dependency upon European goods.

Another important trade item for the colonies was rum. New England merchants carried foodstuffs and other goods into the West Indies and, in return, received sugar, molasses, or rum. The popularity and value of West Indian rum caused New England merchants to distill their own. While of a lesser quality than West Indian rum, New England rum quickly became popular because of its low cost. Rum provided New England merchants with a durable and valuable commodity in demand throughout the Atlantic.

Rum's profitability, coupled with its declining production in the British West Indies and rising production in the French West Indies, caused Parliament in 1733 to pass the Molasses Act, which placed a tax of 6 pence per gallon on all imported molasses. The Americans frequently avoided the tax by smuggling in cheaper illegal molasses. By the 1760s, New England imported 6 million gallons of molasses per year, which they distilled into 5 million gallons of rum. Thus, the production of rum, like numerous other areas of trade, allowed both the colonies and England to profit.

Yet another area of commerce, with direct connections to the triangle trade, was the slave trade. As slavery grew in importance to colonial development, so did the demand for more slaves. In 1672, Parliament created the monopolistic Royal African Company to carry slaves to the Americas. The company supplied about 5,000 slaves to Britain's colonies in the Western Hemisphere, but its monopoly powers were resented by other merchants; they were able to get its monopoly status overturned in 1698.

Parliament then opened the slave trade to the so-called ten percenters, who were required to pay a 10 percent duty, thus allowing England to become the dominant slave carrier. The success of the ten percenters and free trade ensured a continuous supply of slave laborers and a growing West African market for colonial goods. Most colonies relied upon English slavers; in fact, Rhode Island was the only colony extensively involved in the slave trade.

While Britain's mercantile system proved beneficial to the motherland, the colonists often found it overly restrictive or unprofitable. As a result, smuggling became an important and hard-to-curtail practice. Parliament had designed the 1733 Molasses Act to raise revenue through the colonial production of rum, but that legislation brought in little revenue since legal molasses, because of the tariff, cost more then illegal smuggled molasses. The continued and growing production of rum, coupled with the lack of revenue created by the Molasses Act, clearly demonstrated colonial involvement in clandestine trade.

In addition, the colonists developed other ways to manipulate the system. The colonial customs structure was limited; customs agents could not cover every port and inspect every ship, and many officials were corruptible. In a number of instances, however, smuggling proved more beneficial than harmful to the larger imperial economy, as it allowed the colonies to obtain currency they could use to pay their debts to England.

Another problem with the mercantile system involved its success in causing specie, gold and silver coins, to flow from the colonies to England. This meant that the colonies encountered a dearth in a common medium of exchange. To counteract this problem, the colonists utilized bills of exchange. Bills of exchange began as a system of credit when producers, such as farmers, took their product to a local merchant for sale. The merchant might not possess enough gold or silver to pay the farmer, and the farmer might not be ready to utilize all of his credit. To solve this problem, the merchant provided the farmer with a bill of exchange with a specified amount to be paid by the merchant at a later date. These bills were soon being exchanged as a form of currency, becoming a limited but usable form of paper money, and setting the basis for the individual colonies to print their own currency.

The development of paper money solved one in-ternal problem, but the same issues of debt existed between the colonies and England. The majority of colonial exports were agricultural products and raw materials, and most imports were finished goods produced in or re-exported through England. This created debt on the colonists' side, since export profits were generally less than import costs. While many factors alleviated this problem, the development of the colonial economy, especially as a market for English goods, depended upon the willingness of British merchants to extend credit to colonial merchants and consumers.

During the eighteenth century, credit, coupled with the growing colonial population, allowed the colonial market to grow. Large British merchants extended credit to large American merchants, who then extended credit to regional merchants, who extended it to local merchants, who extended it to consumers. During the so-called American crisis (1763–1776), as tensions between colonists and Britain grew over the issue of imperial economic control, this credit/debt situation became an important element in colonial resistance to Britain's changing imperial policies and increasing taxation.

Manufacturing

While farming and trade were the two most important aspects of the colonial economy, other factors contributed to its development. Most colonial export involved the production of agricultural products, whereas most production of finished goods filled local demand only.

One reason for this was that Britain's mercantile approach meant that colonies should not compete with the motherland when it came to manufactured goods. Almost anything produced in England could not be produced in the colonies; while this stricture limited colonial manufacturing, it did not prevent it.

Important colonial manufacturing efforts that were encouraged by Britain were naval stores and ship-building. As they were part of an economic system dependent upon oceanic trade, both Britain and the colonies required large and small vessels to move commodities. Shipbuilding required the right materials, skilled and unskilled labor, and proper construction facilities, making it an important part of the urban port economy.

As the colonies grew, the demand for other manufactured goods expanded as well. One important specialty was the production of metal goods, since settlement required a wide variety of tools and other metalware. Over time, growing colonial refinement also

Shipbuilding, as portrayed in this period woodcut, was a mainstay of the colonial economy and vital to a commercial system dependent on oceanic trade. *(Brown Brothers, Sterling, Pennsylvania)*

created a demand for fine metalware produced by jewelers, goldsmiths, and silversmiths. Blacksmiths were important, as were gunsmiths, clockmakers, and printers.

Other areas of production included making pottery and glass, shoemaking, and hat making, as well as the development of a local woolen goods industry, mainly in the form of homespun produced by women. The development of production coincided with the development of a more advanced and permanent colonial infrastructure and the growth of a skilled workforce.

Labor

To be successful, all segments of the colonial economy depended upon the effective utilization of a variety of labor systems. The staples thesis clearly explains the importance of labor to the colonial economy. While some labor systems proved more effective for specific regions and within specific types of production, all forms of labor existed throughout British North America and involved a change over time of the types of labor needed.

Virginia was the first colony to encounter a major labor shortage and the first to experiment with a variety of labor sources. The introduction of West Indian tobacco in Virginia, coupled with Edwin Sandys's reorganization of the Virginia colony, created the proper elements for a tobacco boom. Tobacco was a labor-intensive crop, and the colony lacked labor. Sandys's "headright" system solved this problem by providing the incentive, in the form of land, to bring laborers to Virginia. Under the system, planters paid for the passage of indentured servants in exchange for land grants.

From this developed the indentured servant system, which stemmed from traditional English contractual systems of labor. Agricultural, demographic, and social changes within England created a growing population of displaced men and women searching for work but lacking the means to travel to the Americas. The indentured servant system provided a way to transfer these laborers from Europe to the colonies.

Servants entered into a contract, whereby the passage from England to North America was paid for by their master. In exchange, the servant agreed to labor for a set number of years; upon serving this term, he or she became free. The contracts stipulated length of service, servant behavior, and master responsibilities. Some contracts also included freedom dues (in the form of money, goods, or land) payable to the servant upon the termination of his or her contract.

Early in Virginia's settlement, landowners generally utilized indentured servants only as tobacco producers. As indentured servants could only be held for a limited number of years, and as tobacco was extraordinarily profitable, the system led to brutal exploitation of these servants. The indentured servitude system existed in all colonies, however, and, while it mainly fulfilled agricultural laboring needs, such servants could be found laboring in urban areas in a variety of occupations. Over time, indentured servants were used less for farming and more for skilled and unskilled labor.

Eventually, the system brought people from throughout the British Isles and continental Europe, consequently diversifying the colonial population. As German immigration into North America increased in the eighteenth century, the so-called redemptioner system developed. This system was similar to indentured servitude, except that many Germans could afford to pay some of their passage, leading to shorter periods of indenture or better compensation. Generally, on arrival, they would contract for a term of indenture to pay for the rest of the amount owed; if no contract was obtained, their services would be sold to the highest bidder. This developed as a way to bring new immigrants, again under a defined obligation, from the German territories into North America.

As the indentured servant system grew and developed, so did an alternative. Early European forays into the Atlantic discovered that West Africa possessed not only gold but also human commodities in the form of slaves. These fifteenth- and sixteenth-century voyages set the foundations of the trans-Atlantic slave trade, but it was not until the seventeenth and eighteenth centuries that the slave trade flourished in the Americas. Of all the labor systems available for use, African slavery provided the cheapest and most permanent form of labor.

While American slavery is most often associated with the plantation complex, slavery existed in all thirteen colonies, and masters utilized their slaves in a variety of occupations. The majority supported agricultural production on small and large plantations and farms, but slaves contributed to colonial economic development in all segments. Some slaves became skilled laborers, others engaged in physical labor in the developing colonial ports, others went to sea as sailors, and some served as domestic servants.

Slavery was important to economic development because of the profits it created. In addition, the use of slaves created economic demands that other regions filled. The Southern plantations purchased food and goods for plantation consumption, creating a market for food from the Mid-Atlantic colonies and the carrying trade for New England.

A final form of unfree or contractual labor developed early in the eighteenth century because of rising crime, stemming from social and economic changes, in England. As Parliament created more laws to protect private property, and the situation of the laboring poor worsened, increasing numbers of people faced trial for crimes against property. The majority of these laws carried the death penalty, but judges and juries found it difficult to execute someone for stealing to survive. Because of this, Parliament created the alternative punishment of deportation and enforced labor: those found guilty could be transported to the colonies to serve their sentences as laborers. Georgia was created not only as a buffer colony between British colonies to the north and Spanish Florida to the south, but also as a penal colony. While the convicts served as a cheap source of labor, they were not a labor supply looked upon favorably by the colonists.

The final form of labor, which developed over the course of the eighteenth century, was wage labor. It was the situation of these wage laborers that created the idea of America as the "best poor man's land."

As the colonial population grew, so did colonial refinement and consumption. Growing prosperity, especially in cities and towns, but also in rural areas, called for the construction of brick houses, fine furniture, and various other displays of wealth and status. This growing demand required skilled labor, which, over time, was largely filled by wage laborers. Many indentured servants, once freed, became wage laborers until they accumulated enough money to purchase land and become farmers.

Early Virginia tobacco harvests demonstrated the profit potential of North American colonization, laid the foundation for the plantation system, and drove demand for African slave labor. This lithograph depicts slaves preparing Virginia tobacco in the late 1700s. *(The Stapleton Collection/Bridgeman Art Library)*

Land of Opportunities

The development of the colonial economy depended upon a variety of factors, including the relationship between land and labor, the development of export agriculture, colonial consumption, credit and available currency, and a growing and diverse population.

Economic expansion fulfilled the colonial role within England's imperial system while providing the colonists with not only a means of survival but, in time, prosperity. This economic growth depended upon the colonists' ability to utilize effectively, or exploit, a variety of labor systems, but the benefits were not equally shared.

The American Revolution did not dramatically alter economic relations in the new nation, in the way that later revolutions in France and Russia did. Other than loyalists, the elite in the former colonies did not see their land or property taken from them. Still, the Revolution did expand economic opportunities, by lifting imperial restrictions on manufacturing and westward expansion.

Ty M. Reese

Bibliography

Bailyn, Bernard. *The New England Merchants in the Seventeenth Centuries.* Cambridge, MA: Harvard University Press, 1955.

Berlin, Ira. *Many Thousands Gone: The First Two Centuries of Slavery in North America.* Cambridge, MA: Harvard University Press, 1998.

Brewer, John. *The Sinews of Power: War, Money and the English State, 1688–1783.* New York: Random House, 1989.

Clemens, Paul G. E. *The Atlantic Economy and Colonial Maryland's Eastern Shore: From Tobacco to Grain.* Ithaca, NY: Cornell University Press, 1980.

Curtin, Philip D. *The Rise and Fall of the Plantation Complex: Essays in Atlantic History.* Cambridge, UK: Cambridge University Press, 1990.

Davis, Ralph. *The Rise of the Atlantic Economies.* Ithaca, NY: Cornell University Press, 1973.

Dickerson, Oliver. *The Navigation Acts and the American Revolution.* Philadelphia: University of Pennsylvania Press, 1951.

Doerflinger, Thomas. *A Vigorous Spirit of Enterprise: Merchants and Economic Development in Revolutionary Philadelphia.* Chapel Hill: University of North Carolina Press, 1986.

Dunn, Richard. *Sugar and Slaves: The Rise of the Planter Class in the English West Indies, 1624–1713.* Chapel Hill: University of North Carolina Press, 1972.

Galenson, David W. *Traders, Planters, and Slaves: Market Behavior in Early English America.* Cambridge, UK: Cambridge University Press, 1986.

Hancock, David. *Citizens of the World: London Merchants and the Integration of the British Atlantic Community, 1735–1785.* Cambridge, UK: Cambridge University Press, 1995.

Innes, Stephen. *Creating the Commonwealth: The Economic Culture of Puritan New England.* New York: W. W. Norton, 1995.

———, ed. *Work and Labor in Early America.* Chapel Hill: University of North Carolina Press, 1988.

Kulikoff, Allan. *From British Peasants to Colonial American Farmers.* Chapel Hill: University of North Carolina Press, 2000.

Liss, Peggy K. *Atlantic Empires: The Network of Trade and Revolution, 1713–1826.* Baltimore: Johns Hopkins University Press, 1983.

McCusker, John J., and Russell Menard. *The Economy of British America, 1607–1789.* Chapel Hill: University of North Carolina Press, 1985.

Merrell, James H. *The Indian's New World: Catawbas and Their Neighbors From European Contact Through the Era of Removal.* Chapel Hill: University of North Carolina Press, 1989.

Morgan, Edmund. *American Slavery American Freedom: The Ordeal of Colonial Virginia.* New York: W. W. Norton, 1975.

Morris, Richard B. *Government and Labor in Early America.* New York: Columbia University Press, 1946.

Vickers, Daniel. *Farmers and Fishermen: Two Centuries of Work in Essex County, Massachusetts, 1630–1850.* Chapel Hill: University of North Carolina Press, 1994.

Wallerstein, Immanuel. *The Modern World System: Mercantilism and the Consolidation of the European World Economy, 1600–1750.* New York: Academic Press, 1980.

Williams, Eric. *Capitalism and Slavery.* Chapel Hill: University of North Carolina Press, 1944.

Gender Issues

The first immigrants to mainland North America encountered an environment vastly different from the one they had left behind. In this new setting, women's relationships and experiences were influenced by their race, ethnicity, and status, as well as by the region in which they settled. Throughout the colonies, however, English, Native American, and African women all would help to create their new societies.

In the seventeenth century, English emigrants settled mainly in two regions: the Chesapeake Bay area and New England. Life for these early women settlers proved difficult. But the difficulties faced by English women in New England would be much different than their counterparts' experiences in the South.

Chesapeake

The conditions women encountered in the Chesapeake were particularly harsh. Early immigrants experienced disease, warfare, and starvation. They found the weather in North America much more extreme than in England, and more dangerous. Here the summer heat provided a breeding ground for germs. Malaria was especially prevalent and claimed the lives of many. During the winter, food was scarce, and the chance of dying of hunger was all too possible. Only if colonists lived through what they called the "seasoning" did their chances of survival increase.

Many of the immigrants came to the Chesapeake as indentured servants. In this capacity, they agreed to work for their sponsor for a period of four to seven years. In return, they would receive passage, room and board, and, in the early years of settlement, a parcel of land to settle on after their contract was up. From 1630 until 1680, approximately one-half to three-quarters of the indentured servants were male. Thus, in the earliest decades, men outnumbered women by a ratio of six to one. By as late as the 1680s, the ratio was three to one. Thus, women had their choice of husbands.

At the same time, marriages in the Chesapeake tended to occur later in life than in England or New England. The demographic figures are startling. Approximately one-quarter of all babies who survived birth would die before their first birthday and 55 percent of all white children died before they reached their twentieth birthday. The combination of this high mortality rate and late marriages meant that the Chesapeake population could not reproduce as quickly as did settlers in other regions.

Although the family remained, as in England, the fundamental unit of Chesapeake society, it was constantly undergoing transformations because brutal conditions in the area disrupted family life. Adult life expectancy in the Chesapeake was also lower than in England or New England. Men generally survived into their mid-40s, and women until they were approximately 39 years of age. This mortality rate led to a series of complex familial relationships. Most marriages ended by the death of a spouse, and remarriage was common. Families often contained stepparents and stepsiblings. Chesapeake society had to develop ways of dealing with early death, and orphan courts were created to care for the large number of parentless children.

Despite these dramatic statistics, Chesapeake families may not have been so different from the English family across the Atlantic. There, too, fathers often did not live long enough to supervise their children's later lives, and other similarities existed. The Chesapeake family, in its ideal, resembled the patriarchal English family. Men were responsible for their wives and children and were expected to represent them in religious and legal affairs. For their part, wives and children were expected to remain deferential to their husbands and fathers.

The legal system was critical to the maintenance of Chesapeake society because of the fluidity in family relationships. English common law applied to the colonists. Women of adult age fell into two categories. The first was an unmarried woman, or *femme sole* (woman alone). Theoretically, a *femme sole* had all the same legal rights as a man. She could sue, be sued, make contracts,

From New England to the Chesapeake, women in the seventeenth-century colonies were expected to perform traditional household tasks—such as spinning wool, keeping a kitchen garden, and running the household—and to labor in the fields alongside their husbands as needed. *(Brown Brothers, Sterling, Pennsylvania)*

earn and pay wages, own and sell property, and leave a will designating her heirs. The second category was the married woman, or *femme covert* (literally, "covered woman," as in legally covered by her husband). Legally, a *femme covert* had few independent rights. She had no standing in court. She could not own property. She had no right to her children. In other words, a married woman was totally dependent upon her husband. When a woman married, whatever property she had became her husband's. English common law did allow for a premarital contract, but few women knew about this or took advantage of it.

This was a society whose family relationships were constantly being negotiated and redefined. Because marriages often ended in the death of a husband, it was imperative that colonists follow English law when it came to a widow's dower rights. Husbands were expected to provide for their widows even after death, since the last thing a developing colony wanted was to be responsible for indigent widows. Under dower law, women were entitled to a life interest in their husband's

real property. In other words, a widow was entitled to the profits from his land. However, she could neither sell this property nor leave it in her will, and when a woman died, the property passed into the hands of her husband's designated heirs. Because of the likelihood of remarriage, men did not want their property transferring over to a wife's new husband, so husbands were careful to ensure a wife's dower rights were firmly established.

Seventeenth-century Chesapeake colonists believed in maintaining a gender division of work whenever possible. Men were expected to do the fieldwork, while women maintained the garden, dairy, and household. A wife's homemaking skills were necessary to the family's survival, for it was the wife who transformed raw materials into usable products through butchering, food preservation and preparation, spinning, and manufacturing other domestic supplies. This traditional gendered division of work was difficult to maintain in seventeenth-century Maryland and Virginia, however, since all hands were needed in the field to cultivate tobacco. Therefore, men and women, both free and not free, often worked side by side in the tobacco fields.

New England

Immigrants arriving in New England came primarily as families, although there also were single people who traveled to the New World. About one-third of the immigrants to New England were adult males. From 1621 to 1651, historians estimate that there were four single men for every single woman.

The earliest New England settlers tended to establish communities like the ones they left behind in England, although their religious loyalties were radically different from the Anglican population that remained behind. New England was primarily settled by dissenters from the Anglican Church: the Pilgrims, who settled in the Plymouth Colony, and the Puritans, who established the Massachusetts Bay Colony. The Puritans wanted to create the perfect religious community. To achieve their aims, the first generation of colonists established small, close-knit, farming communities, defined by long marriages, multigenerational households, and strong religious institutions.

This first generation of New Englanders also tended to marry later than their counterparts back in England. The average age for single brides was 23 years, 4 months. Female servants, however, were often married by the time they turned 20. By the 1650s, the marriage age for servants had dropped to 17. Most women born in New England before 1650 had their last children by the time they were 37 years old. They averaged seven children, just like their Southern counterparts. Here, as in England and in the Chesapeake, childbirth proved dangerous for colonial women. Somewhere between 3 percent and 10 percent of women who became pregnant between 1630 and 1670 died following childbirth. The greatest danger of dying after childbirth was after the birth of a woman's fourth, fifth, or sixth child.

Before 1650, two-thirds of the immigrants were between the ages of 10 and 40, with 8,000 babies having been born. Life expectancy in New England was high, although infants, children, and young adults were more likely to succumb to disease. Colonists who survived into adulthood also had a longer life span than their counterparts in the Chesapeake. In fact, once acclimated to their surroundings, New Englanders tended to be healthier than the population in both England and the Chesapeake. The healthier environment of New England created a generation of parents who lived to become grandparents.

The patriarchal family and the Congregational Church influenced and shaped New Englanders' lives. Both religious and legal notions reinforced the father's role as the head of the family. Wives stood below their husbands and above their children and servants on the social ladder. The law supported by the Fifth Commandment—"Honor thy parents"—ensured that parents had ultimate control over their children. In colonial New England, the family was considered a "little commonwealth." If society were to maintain order, then each family must be stable. To that end, the legal system reinforced the orderly workings of the family by dictating inheritance laws and a criminal code that preserved male authority. Eldest sons inherited land over their mothers, and sexual indiscretion was punished more severely in women than in men.

Wives' productive duties were considered vital to the proper functioning of the household. New England women labored at their husbands' sides in the fields. A good wife was considered a "helpmeet" to her husband. Those women who succeeded in their wifely duties were honored with the title "notable housewife." Colonial New England wives were expected to spin cloth, maintain the garden, and process raw materials into usable goods. To this end, they had to know how to manage their time and resources.

Women in New England towns could trade for the things they needed, such as flour, grain, and, possibly, bread and meat. These women learned how to haggle for a good price—another way of proving their "goodwife" status. In addition to their other chores, women who lived close to or in town added cleaning and neatness to their list of concerns, although women who lived in rural or frontier communities found far less time for these luxuries. Without a nearby town where they could acquire goods, these women spent more time on the land and with the livestock, striving to produce their family's necessities.

New Englanders lived near each other and learned to depend on each other. Women borrowed and lent each other goods. They also kept each other company during childbirth, which was surrounded by ritual and ceremony, as women assisted and witnessed their neighbor's deliveries. After childbirth, women spent about ten months in confinement, working inside the house only and tending to their babies. When this period of confinement ended, women often weaned their children by leaving home for a short period of time.

Our modern notion of childhood did not exist in seventeenth-century New England. As potential heirs to property, children were also the concern of their fathers. Both parents provided vocational training for their children, with fathers training their sons in agriculture and the family trade and mothers teaching their daughters the art of housewifery. Thus, gender divisions within the family were created at an early age.

In addition to the family, Puritanism was central to women's lives, although they were excluded from positions of power, both in the religious and secular realm. Indeed, the Puritan Church maintained a strict gender division. Men and women entered the church by separate doors. Wives sat apart from their husbands. Women were not accorded a formal voice in the church, even though they could enter into full membership. As their numbers began to increase, their influence in church affairs did as well. But the power that they began to exercise was more informal than formal. For instance, women would lobby for the church to be located in close proximity to their homes, because they had children to carry. For a minister to have any success, he would need the approval of his female congregants. Church membership did not ensure political rights for women as it did for men.

Throughout the seventeenth century, the Puritan church in New England maintained a relatively tight control over the population, but that control would eventually be challenged. By 1690, the population in the colonies had doubled. Huguenots, Quakers, Anglicans, and Anabaptists began to challenge the Puritans for political and social power. In addition, seventeenth-century New Englanders experienced repeated hostilities with Native Americans. The social tensions created by an increase in population and wartime dislocation undermined already fragile community and political relationships.

In 1692, New England suffered a dramatic outbreak of witchcraft accusations that came to be known as the Salem witch trials. Accusations of witchcraft were not unknown in New England, but the number of such incidents made this an exceptional crisis. Prior to the Salem outbreak, only 107 accusations of witchcraft had been made in the entire New England area, but in 1692, 178 people were accused of witchcraft, 141 were arrested, and more than half of this number confessed. More than two dozen people were tried and convicted; the majority of those convicted were women. In the end, thirteen women were hanged, and one man was pressed to death by stones. The number of women accused and prosecuted is striking. One factor may have been the fact that the proportion of women persecuted for crime had been on the rise, especially for sexual offenses, and cases of infanticide had peaked in the 1690s.

The Salem witchcraft crisis began in the winter of 1692, when a group of girls, including the daughter of the Reverend Samuel Parris, became involved in fortune telling with a slave named Tituba. When the girls reported experiencing fits, accusations began. Tituba was the first of those to be accused. Many of the accused women were old and had reputations for being aggressive or inclined to assertive behavior; some were known to have had trouble with their neighbors or family members. Several of the women accused were at the age of menopause, a period in the life cycle when they carried heavy responsibilities and enjoyed a modicum of power. One-sixth of these women were childless, and others had only one or two children. Some had medical knowledge, which gave them suspicious power in the community. The earliest accusations were made against poor women, but as the accusations continued, wealthy women also were named. These accusations against elite women made judges skeptical, and soon the trials were ended.

New England never again experienced a witch hunt such as the one that began in Salem. And as the new century began, interest in taking legal action to regulate women's sexual or moral behavior diminished. By the early 1720s, the number of women brought up on charges of fornication or infanticide dropped dramatically.

Native Americans

Native American women experienced English colonization differently from the settlers in either the Chesapeake or New England. Unfortunately, Native American women of the seventeenth century have left no written documents for historians. Much of what we know about their experiences, therefore, comes from the biased observations of European men. We do know, however, that there was no uniform Native American social custom.

At least four distinct language groups have been identified—Algonquian, Iroquoian, Caddoan, and Siouan—and political and familial organization within and among these groups varied considerably. Where agriculture was part of the primary economic foundation, a sexual division of labor existed. Men hunted, and women tilled the land. If hunting was the key to a community's subsistence, men had more responsibility and power in the society; if cultivation was the primary mode of subsistence, women wielded more power and had greater control over resources. In both cases, men, as hunters and warriors, had more geographic mobility. Women remained closer to home, tilling crops and rearing children.

Family organization varied from tribe to tribe. In the Mid-Atlantic and southeastern regions, for example, family connections were defined through the mother's lineage. When men married, they moved in with the wife's family. Europeans had great difficulty understanding this, as their families were defined through the father's lineage, and differences such as these led to considerable cultural misunderstanding on the part of European and English observers. For example, Europeans tended to visit Native American communities during the summer, when men did not hunt but remained close to home, keeping fit by playing games. Europeans, unaware that fall and winter were "work" periods for these hunters, assumed the men were lazy. At the same time, Europeans saw women busy at work in the fields. Europeans did not view hunting as serious work, since in their society hunting was a sport. Their conclusion was that lazy Native American men exploited women as drudges.

Europeans assumed that Native American men enjoyed a monopoly on power in their societies. In fact, it was the women who were responsible for some of the most important community decisions. In the Iroquois tribe, matrons nominated male chiefs and had the power to remove them as well. Because Iroquois women controlled the food supply, they also had the power to decide if and when the tribe went to war. Warriors could not wage war without access to a food supply.

In Iroquois society, both a man and a woman could initiate a divorce, but the children of the marriage stayed with the mother. When the marriage was dissolved, the husband returned to his mother's house, and property stayed with the wife. Land was held in common by women of the clan or village and was passed down through the maternal line. The fact that Native American men did not own the land was especially confusing to European men, who, nevertheless, tried to negotiate land sales with their Native American male counterparts. In the end, contracts were void if the women did not agree to the sale.

While the Iroquois women enjoyed decision-making powers, women of tribes on the Western Plains did not. Among the Blackfeet, for example, both sexes were involved in producing the food supply. And, until contact was made with Europeans, there was little difference in their status. Once Plains Indians such as the Blackfoot acquired horses from the Europeans, this equality changed. Because they had horses, Blackfoot men could travel longer distances in their hunt for buffalo; as a result, women's work of gathering seeds and berries became less important. Hunting became the primary mode of subsistence, and thus the ownership of horses made Native American men dominant.

The Plains Indians were organized around the male household. Men had multiple wives, who were often sisters. The more wives a man had, the more status he maintained in the community. Divorce was fairly easy, but it usually was initiated by men. Often, a divorced woman would kill herself. If a woman was a widow, she was expected to marry her dead husband's brother.

In many Native American societies, whether patrilocal (where the woman went to live with her husband's family) or matrilocal (where a husband went to live with his wife's family), young girls spent time with older women, who taught them how to farm and guided them into gender-appropriate activities. Among the East Coast tribes, young girls also would be isolated as they reached puberty. And among some tribes, girls and women would isolate themselves each month during menstruation.

Marriage tended to be a significant rite of passage for both men and women, although premarital sex was normally permitted. Usually, couples married by choice, although the right to marry was generally granted by the clan leaders. Marriages were celebrated with a feast, which, in a number of tribes, excluded all women, except the bride and groom's mothers.

Women often gave birth in isolation, and children often spent their first few months swaddled and carried on a board. In many tribes, parents believed in letting children have their freedom, a child-rearing pattern quite unlike the more restrictive European policy.

In the seventeenth century, some New England women, captured from their towns during Native American raids, chose to stay with their "adoptive" families. Some made this choice in the belief that they would enjoy a life less circumscribed by gender ideals.

Eighteenth Century

At the turn of the century, life in the colonies began to change drastically as the population increased dramatically. In 1700, there were approximately 250,000 Europeans and Africans living in the North American colonies. By 1730, the population more than doubled, and by the eve of the Revolution, America boasted a population of nearly 2.5 million people. This growth resulted from both non-English migration and a natural population explosion.

The natural increase can be accounted for by the colonists' acclimation to their new climate. The difficulties of the early years had passed. White women were marrying in their 20s, and African American women were marrying in their teens. Thus, women were beginning to reproduce at earlier ages, extending their childbearing years and producing more children. Many more people lived to their maturity and started their own families. As a result, about half the American population, both black and white, was under the age of 16 in 1775.

The increase in the population would lead to drastic changes for women's lives and experiences. Many of the same English laws would remain, and gender ideals remained firmly embedded in the colonial psyche. Women's everyday experiences changed, however, largely because of the growth of an urban population. By today's standards, colonial cities were not large: In 1750, Boston had a population of 17,000 and Philadelphia, 13,000. But the differences between city and country life were great.

In the urban areas, life was governed by clocks. People could purchase foodstuffs year round and see each other whenever they wished. City people also had greater access to information. By 1750, every major city had a newspaper, and while many women could not read, they could often find someone to read to them. Cities attracted people looking for work. Widows, for example, often moved to a city, where they hoped to find work as cooks, nurses, and servants.

African Americans

Population increase also changed the lives of African American women. When the English economy began to recover between 1660 and 1690, fewer indentured servants migrated to North America. Facing a labor shortage, the British colonists turned to African slaves. By the eighteenth century, 95 percent of colonial blacks were slaves whose lives fell under the authority of white males. Blacks made up a high proportion of the population in plantation colonies. In many Southern areas, blacks outnumbered whites.

Just as the relationship between the English settlers and the Native Americans was defined by cultural misconceptions, so, too, was the relationship between the white settlers and the Africans brought to North America. Like women in many of the Native American communities, West African women were primarily responsible for cultivation. And as in European society, agriculture was the predominant mode of production in Africa. The early slave traders, however, assuming African men were the agriculturists, preferred male slaves to females.

Many African practices would survive in the harsh realities of the New World. In their new homeland, family was organized around clan groups, many of which practiced polygamy. The family compound often consisted of several buildings housing wives and children. In many African cultures, both men and women could initiate divorce. Normally, children would stay with their mothers. As a rule, men governed the behavior of men, and women governed women. Women could be property owners and were frequently traders within their communities.

The sexual division of labor persisted into the eighteenth century. Men were blacksmiths, carpenters, and shoemakers while the women worked as cooks, seamstresses, and midwives. Because of the need for labor, both sexes often worked in the field.

Slaves had no legal rights and were often at the whim of the master. Life in such a circumscribed society made familial relationships critical to the slave's survival. The extended family proved pivotal, since nuclear families could be broken up at any moment through the sale of a father or mother. Parents thus relied on extended kin to look after their children. Kin provided support, assistance, and comfort. Historians have discovered that children were named for relatives in such a way as to cement these extended family ties.

Religious upheavals influenced both black and white women's lives in the eighteenth century. Between 1730 and 1760, the North American colonies were introduced to new religious ideas. These ideas were spread through large gatherings called religious revivals. Preachers began to emphasize emotion over intellect, making even those who could not read equal participants in religious practices. The focus of revivalist preachers such as George Whitefield was the individual. This meant that women could participate without a male intermediary. Women flocked to the religious revivals. They began to rethink their own capabilities and their place in the world.

Although revivalism seemed to have its greatest impact in the North, the South was not immune. Virginia experienced the greatest religious fervor in the South, but here the impact of the revivals was complicated by race. Many of the new religious sects, especially Baptists, referred to members as brothers and sisters. But "brother and sister" implied a sense of equality impossible in a society built on the institution of slavery. Some of the more radical sects were forbidden to preach in the South unless they avoided the condemnation of slavery.

Perhaps the most important episode in the eighteenth century was the Revolutionary War. Nobody was immune to the changes that this cataclysmic event wrought. For African American women, the notions of equality led in some cases to freedom. Some slave owners in the South, understanding the implication of revolutionary rhetoric, freed their slaves. Other slaves took advantage of wartime disruption and fled their plantations. In the North, many of the newly formed states began to outlaw slavery.

For Native American women, however, the colonists' victory was detrimental to their communities. With the British loss, Native Americans were left with no buffer between their lands and the colonists. Removal of the native peoples and the disruption of their lives would become the norm.

Impact of the American Revolution

Wartime events also provided women, of all heritages, with new opportunities. With their husbands away

A British cartoon of 1775 satirizes the "patriotic ladies" of Edenton, North Carolina, who pledged to boycott English tea. Colonial women played a key role in the revolutionary cause. *(Library of Congress, LC-USZC4-4617)*

fighting, a number of women took over businesses, ran the farm or plantation, and supervised the household. At first, these changes proved daunting. But as time passed, women rose to the challenge. Women also performed crucial services for the army. They were nurses and cooks, and some even fought in battle.

As a result of wartime activities, several women began to agitate for reforms. Although there were no significant changes in the legal status of women, there were significant changes in education. Beginning in the 1780s, tax money was used to finance public education. Massachusetts became the first state to require towns to offer free elementary education to its citizens, including women.

To advance the cause of women's education, advocates like Judith Sargent Murray, a famous author, began to construct arguments emphasizing women's critical role to the new republic. Sargent and others argued that women were the foundation of the new republic, because it was their duty to raise virtuous citizens. In order to guide the rising generation, women had to be educated themselves. In the nineteenth cen-

tury, reformers relied on this notion of "republican motherhood" to fight for further advances in women's lives.

Leslie Horowitz

Bibliography

Berkin, Carol. *First Generations: Women in Colonial America.* New York: Hill and Wang, 1996.

Berlin, Ira, and Ronald Hoffman, eds. *Slavery and Freedom in the Age of the American Revolution.* Evanston: University of Illinois Press, 1983.

Carr, Lois G., Phillip Morgan, and Jean B. Russo, eds. *Colonial Chesapeake Society.* Chapel Hill: University of North Carolina Press, 1988.

Colloway, Colin G. *The American Revolution in Indian Country: Crisis and Diversity in Native American Communities.* Cambridge, UK: Cambridge University Press, 1995.

Isaac, Rhys. "Evangelical Revolt: The Nature of the Baptists Challenge to the Traditional Order in Virginia, 1765–1775." *William and Mary Quarterly* 31 (1974): 345–68.

Kerber, Linda. *Women of the Republic: Intellect and Ideology in Revolutionary America.* Chapel Hill: University of North Carolina Press, 1980.

Kulikoff, Allan. *Tobacco and Slaves: The Development of Southern Cultures in the Chesapeake, 1680–1800.* Chapel Hill: University of North Carolina Press, 1986.

Merrell, James H. *The Indians New World: Cataubas and Their Neighbors from European Contact through the Era of Removal.* Chapel Hill: University of North Carolina Press, 1989.

Norton, Mary Beth. *Founding Mothers and Fathers: Gendered Power and the Forming of American Society.* New York: Alfred A. Knopf, 1996.

———. *In the Devil's Snare: The Salem Witchcraft Crisis of 1692.* New York: Alfred A. Knopf, 2002

———. *Liberty's Daughters: The Revolutionary Experience of American Women, 1750–1800.* Ithaca, NY: Cornell University Press, 1996.

Richter, Daniel K. *The Ordeal of the Longhouse: The Peoples of the Iroquois League in the Era of European Colonization.* Chapel Hill: University of North Carolina Press, 1992.

Sobel, Mechal. *The World They Made Together: Black and White Values in Eighteenth-Century Virginia.* Princeton, NJ: Princeton University Press, 1987.

Tate, Thad, and David Ammerman, eds. *The Chesapeake in the 17th Century: Essays in Anglo-American Society.* Chapel Hill: University of North Carolina Press, 1979.

Ulrich, Laurel Thatcher. *Good Wives: Image and Reality in the Lives of Women in Northern New England, 1650–1750.* New York: Random House, 1980.

Westerkamp, Marilyn J. *Women and Religion in Early America, 1600–1850: The Puritan and Evangelical Traditions.* New York: Routledge, 1999.

Military and Diplomatic Affairs

Warfare and diplomacy profoundly shaped the colonial era as Native Americans, European colonists, and dynastic European states struggled for control of North America. Internecine conflicts among native peoples, confrontations between them and white settlers, and imperial wars and diplomacy shaped the lives of nearly everyone in early America. In the end, warfare and diplomacy allowed European Americans to dominate the eastern quarter of North America.

Precontact Native American Warfare and Diplomacy

Precontact Native American warfare and diplomacy was generally limited in its scale and scope of violence. Among the Eastern Woodland peoples, "mourning war" reigned supreme. Mourning war was a highly ritualized form of warfare and diplomacy, in which vanquished foes and captives often served to "replace" those lost due to disease, war, or migration in native communities.

Raiding parties would venture forth, take captives, and return to the war party's home village with those captives in order to apportion them among grieving clans. At that point, the elder women of the clan determined the fate of the captive. Males usually suffered death by excruciating torture; the women and children were most often incorporated into the clan via adoption. Mourning war also offered young men the prestige that came with leading war parties and taking captives.

Europeans would speak of the "savagery" of native warfare—"proof" being the brutal torture of prisoners. Mourning wars, however, included relatively limited violence, especially when compared to the gross slaughter that Europeans subjected each other to in the so-called Wars of Religion in the sixteenth and early seventeenth centuries. At its basic level, war among precontact native peoples was primarily a personal affair

and rarely required the full resources of a native community.

A key to the limited nature of Native American warfare was the dichotomous relationship between cultural exchange and warfare within native communities. Most indigenous peoples understood diplomacy, and thus issues of war and peace, as hinging on reciprocal relations. As long as a "tributary" person, group, or village submitted to a putative dominant group, affairs—meaning trade and cultural exchange—could proceed normally. The breakdown of reciprocity, caused by migration, poor harvests, changes in leadership, or pandemics, often led to war.

Indeed, most native peoples sought to end war quickly and with as little dislocation to their group as possible. Some civilizations, such as the precontact Mississippian peoples at Cahokia, could not survive in a world in which war, rather than reciprocity, ruled. Others, like the tribes who fled the Iroquois to the area the French called the *pays d'en haut* (the Upper Ohio Valley), built peaceful communities on a middle ground that rested on a foundation of trade and cultural exchange.

Native American confederacies played an important role in arbitrating issues of war and peace. The English placed their first permanent settlement in North America in the territory of the most powerful native confederacy on the eastern seaboard, the Powhatan League. The Powhatan naturally saw the English settlers as interlopers but, because of the latter's weak state, they assumed the Europeans would become another tributary people. The military and diplomatic history of the early Chesapeake is one of tentative attempts by Native Americans and Englishmen to build a reciprocal relationship, based on trade and exchange, which fell apart in periods of violence and destruction.

Ironically, the Powhatan's success as masters of the precontact Tidewater contributed to their downfall. English settlers capitalized on discontent among the Powhatan's tributary nations and encouraged them to break free of Powhatan dominance. By the mid-

In 1609, the French explorer Samuel de Champlain encountered and subdued Huron Indians in southern Ontario. Unlike other native peoples, who faced annihilation at the hands of Anglo-Americans, the Huron formed a fur trade alliance with the French that enabled both groups to dominate the region. *(Brown Brothers, Sterling, Pennsylvania)*

seventeenth century, English colonists, their native allies, and, most significantly, diseases had destroyed the Powhatan confederacy and made the colonists the new masters of the Chesapeake.

Not all Native American confederacies fell as quickly as the Powhatan. The Iroquois League, founded in the sixteenth century among the five Iroquois nations of present-day upstate New York (the Mohawk, Oneida, Onondaga, Cayuga, and Seneca), was the linchpin on which inter-native and European-native affairs in the Northeast hinged throughout the colonial period. English colonists and imperial administrators focused their diplomacy and distribution of annual "presents" of European trade goods, weapons, and alcohol on the League, in hopes of making the Iroquois proxies in the settler-native and imperial wars. Only in 1701, after the League staked out a neutral position between the English and French in the "Grand Settlement" at Montreal, did the Iroquois break free from their descent into European wars.

The eighteenth century witnessed a diplomatic dance among the Iroquois League, the British, and the French. Anglo-Americans sought to turn the Iroquois into their janissaries, while officials in Montreal and Quebec tried to win Iroquois support as a foil against British imperial ambitions. Complicating matters were the pro-French Kahnawake Iroquois, who had moved from New York to near Montreal. Neutralists within the League struggled to remain aloof from European wars and to prevent civil war between pro-English and pro-French native factions.

The Creek Confederacy in the Southeast shared much in common with the Iroquois League. Comprised of Muskogee peoples, who migrated from the west in the precontact period, the Creek Confederacy proved to be one of the most permanent and robust native groupings throughout the colonial period. Much like the Iroquois, the Creek played European powers against one another. The Creek juggled relations with the English settlers of Georgia and the Carolinas, the Spanish in Florida, and the French in the Lower Mississippi Valley. Unlike the other native peoples of the Southeast—the factious Cherokee, for example—the Creek offered a unified front against the European powers. In the end, the Confederacy's demise came only in the early nineteenth century, after Americans had driven the other colonial powers from the Southeast and the Creek had lost their bargaining leverage.

Impact of European Arrival

The settlement by Europeans in the seventeenth century dramatically altered the military and diplomatic landscape of early America. Within one generation, settler-native wars and diplomatic relations had replaced precontact ways of war and diplomacy.

European–Native American wars dominated war making and statecraft in North America for a century. The settler-native wars were primarily local affairs fought without the support of the European states. Especially between the English and native peoples, military strategies became increasingly less formal as Europeans struggled to adapt to native ways of war.

Perhaps no factor shaped the seventeenth-century settler-native wars more than the European experience of war. The first European settlers, particularly the English mercenaries who arrived in Virginia and New England, were products of the Wars of Religion. As such, they knew war as all encompassing. For them, there were no distinctions between combatants and noncombatants. Everything, from villages and fields to women and children, was considered a target for military action.

While the devastation wrought during the Wars of Religion appalled Europeans and inspired them to moderate and limit war, Europeans in North America made no such transition. While Europe progressed toward the eighteenth century's "age of limited warfare," Anglo-American colonists normally looked to exterminate their enemies or, at least, drive them out of the area.

Affairs of war and diplomacy between settlers and Native Americans varied. The relative strength of the settler community vis-à-vis the neighboring native peoples, as well as the colonists' motivation for coming to North America, influenced the nature of relations.

The settlers, priests, and traders of New France and New Spain, because of their small numbers and interest in trade and proselytizing, found themselves largely unwilling to confront Native Americans, other than in cases where they needed to assert their authority. As a result, they generally had positive, or at the least ambivalent, relations with indigenous peoples.

The English, with their rapidly increasing population that voraciously sought to claim native lands and the resources that could be extracted from those lands, had much more contentious and hostile relations

with native peoples. Indeed, the uses and need for land were the key factors that governed English-Native American relations. Within the mix of population, interests, ambitions, and attitudes, two series of conflicts—wars to establish a settler foothold and wars to expand English settlement beyond the "first frontier"—shaped their wars and diplomacy.

The major wars fought to establish a European foothold include the wars in Virginia (the Indian War of 1607–1608, the misnamed First Indian War of 1622–1632, the Tidewater War of 1644–1646, and the Susquehannock War of 1675–1676) and New England's seventeenth-century wars (the Pequot War of 1637–1638 and King Philip's War of 1675–1676). In these wars, settlers enlisted Native Americans to kill other native peoples. For example, in the Pequot War, the English turned to the Narragansett to help them extirpate the Pequot. While the unrestrained slaughter that the English perpetrated on the Pequot at the Mystic River Fort supposedly shocked the Narragansett, these English allies didn't hesitate to enslave the Pequot and expropriate their lands.

Throughout the seventeenth century, there was a rush to secure native allies and proxies. As noted, the English focused their diplomatic energies on the Iroquois, while the French in Canada wooed the Iroquois' traditional enemies, the Huron, Mi'kmaq, Malisett, Abenaki, Shawnee, Delaware, Miami, Ottawa, Pottawatami, and others.

During King Philip's War, the English had forged a diplomatic alliance with the Iroquois known as the Covenant Chain; this alliance proved decisive in both King Philip's and the Susquehannock wars. Of course, Mohawk warriors were also motivated by economic rewards, such as the bounties that settlers had placed on their enemies' scalps.

Meanwhile, the governor of New France became "Onontio," or "father," to the native peoples of the Maritimes and the St. Lawrence River area, the Ohio *pays d'en haut*, and the Choctaw of the Lower Mississippi Valley. In the 1680s and 1690s, Onontio unleashed his native "children" on the Iroquois of the Covenant Chain. The result was a major diplomatic coup for New France in the Grand Settlement of 1701 that, in effect, left the English without reliable native allies in the Northeast.

Of course, neither the English nor the French depended solely on Native Americans to fight their wars. After decades of fighting alongside and against Native Americans, the Europeans, starting with the French, also began to incorporate native forms of warfare in their style of fighting. By the late seventeenth century, France's regular troops stationed in North America (called the *Troupes de la Marine*) and the Canadian militia had adopted native-style warfare: small-unit operations, skirmishing, and what today we call guerrilla warfare.

The English made similar attempts to learn from both their Native American enemies and allies. In King Philip's War, some English settlers recognized the difficulties of protecting a porous frontier, as well as the potential impact that destroying the Native American base of supply would have in stopping the guerilla attacks. Captain Benjamin Church of Plymouth therefore formed a company-sized unit of around thirty settlers, supported by native guides. Church's aim was to take the field and best the native raiders that were then infesting the New England frontier. By the 1720s, British "rangers" could be found wherever and whenever the English and Native Americans came into conflict.

In time, the rangers took advantage of the generous bounties on scalps that the British assemblies first had offered to their Native American allies. When combined with their forefathers' legacy of extirpative war, they created Americans' first way of war. Built on wide-ranging forays, scalping, and violence directed against enemy noncombatants, this first way of war became the centerpiece of American military culture well into the nineteenth century.

Wars of Expansion

In the wars to expand British settlement beyond the first frontiers of southern New England and the Virginia Tidewater, British Americans embraced both the first way of war and Native American allies. During the Tuscarora War (1711–1715) in North Carolina, British rangers and tributary Catawba waged a war of extermination and enslavement on the Iroquoian Tuscarora. The English thoroughly pummeled the Tuscarora and drove them to seek protection from their cousins in New York, where they became the sixth member of the Iroquois League.

A similar chain of events transpired in South Carolina during the Yamasee War (1715–1717). Ironically, the Yamasee had helped the English defeat the Tuscarora. The English, now aided by Covenant Chain Iroquois, crushed the Yamasee and thereby opened much of South Carolina to slave-based plantation agriculture.

In New England, in Dummer's War (1724–1725)—also known as Father Râle's War, Lovewell's War, and Gray Lock's War—British-American rangers roamed the Maine frontier, seeking Abenaki men, women, and children to scalp. The events of the war included the English destruction of the Abenaki village at Norridgewock and the death of Captain John Lovewell, a British ranger who had made a small fortune cashing in on scalp bounties.

The wars to expand British settlement saw both the creation of "new" and the strengthening of "old" European-Native American alliances. The English, in the Catawba and Savannah, found trusted allies, who would help protect the southern frontier from the encroachments of other native peoples (Cherokee and Creek) and Europeans (Spaniards and Frenchmen), as well as become partners in expanding the native slave trade. The Catawba became the most trusted of the southern tribes and prospered in a "New World" of British domination. The Yamasee, driven from Carolina, fled to Florida, where they allied themselves with the Spanish. In return for Spanish protection, the Yamasee served as a buffer against British advances southward from Charles Town.

In the North, the French redoubled their commitment to their allies. They understood that the protection of Canada depended on maintenance of the good relations with native peoples, and, in the 1720s and 1730s, they built more Jesuit missions among Native Americans. By the 1740s, a well-developed system of alliances and pacts had been created in North America.

Imperial Warfare

Imperial warfare came to North America at various times during the second Hundred Years' War (1689–1763). The imperial wars among Great Britain, France, and Spain consisted of four conflicts that ran concurrently with European wars: King William's War, Queen Anne's War, the Wars of King George II, and the French and Indian War. The European monarchies saw North America as a theater of secondary importance, after their struggles for dynastic control of Europe. As a result, they generally sought to wage war in America "on the cheap."

France fought in North America for the preservation of the status quo, England, originally, for commercial advantage, and Spain, for the survival of its colonial outposts on mainland North America. Colonists fought for expansion of dominion and empire in

North America, while Native Americans increasingly found themselves mired in wars of anticolonialism.

King William's War (1689–1697), known in Europe as the War of the League of Augsburg, set the pattern for the rest of the imperial wars: French and Native American offensives against the frontier, followed by unsuccessful British invasions of Canada. Indigenous forces (British American provincials and rangers, Native Americans, and English-speaking Canadian forces) conducted virtually all the fighting. The French and their allies struck first, when Louis de Baude de Frontenac turned his *Troupes de la Marine* and native warriors loose on the New England frontier. In the summer of 1689, they destroyed several towns in present-day New Hampshire and Maine; in February 1690, they sacked Schenectady, New York.

British Americans responded with grandiose plans for a two-pronged invasion of Canada. A land force was to march up the Hudson River Valley and cross Lake Champlain to take Montreal from the west, while a seaborne expedition under William Phips would approach New France from the east. The land force never materialized, as New Yorkers feuded with one another over who would command the army. Phips, at least in the beginning, proved more successful. His fleet and army of British American provincials—colonials in the service of the British army—took poorly defended Port Royal in Acadia before setting out for Quebec. In the face of the guns and defenses of New France's most heavily defended town, however, Phips beat a hasty retreat to Boston.

After 1690, the French and Native Americans operated freely on the northern frontier. The New England colonial assemblies responded by issuing bounties on native scalps and calls to their native allies for assistance. Major Benjamin Church led his rangers on the "Eastward Expeditions" to Maine to kill the Abenaki. By 1697, when the Treaty of Ryswick ended the war in Europe, New Englanders were relieved to be able to put what Reverend Cotton Mather had termed their *Decennium Luctuosum*, or Mournful Decade, behind them.

Queen Anne's War (1702–1713), or Europe's War of the Spanish Succession, saw the Native American, settler-native, and imperial wars coalesce. For European Americans, success in the war depended on their relations with Native Americans. New France's governor initiated the conflict when, after having secured Iroquois neutrality at Montreal in 1701, he sent his native allies against New England's settlements to keep the English on the defensive. New England, with New York bowing out of the war for fear of alienating the Iroquois and driving them into the French camp, stood alone against New France.

The New Englanders responded by fortifying their frontier and offering bounties on Native American scalps. Despite the rangers' scalp-hunting efforts, French and Native American raiders operated with near impunity, and in 1704, they destroyed Deerfield, Massachusetts, in the Connecticut River Valley.

New Englanders hoped to drive New France from the war in 1707, but without the assistance of the Iroquois or New York, they could not advance up the Hudson River and Lake Champlain. British American spirits soared when the Crown promised them regulars for an attack on Canada. The 1709 campaign, in which colonial militia planned to advance up the Hudson River while British regulars attacked down the St. Lawrence River, was stillborn, however, when the Crown diverted the regulars promised for North America to Portugal.

The following year, a provincial army under Francis Nicholson took Port Royal, Acadia. In 1711, a storm at sea took the lives of 800 British troops en route to Canada and led to the abandonment of major offensive operations against the center of French power on the North American continent.

On the southern frontier, the colonists focused on the Spanish and their native allies. In 1702, Governor James Moore of Carolina unsuccessfully besieged Spain's main outpost in St. Augustine, Florida. The next year, Moore devastated the Spanish missions in the Florida Panhandle and captured nearly 300 Native Americans, whom he enslaved.

After 1703, British rangers focused on securing their frontier and enslaving indigenous peoples. In the Caribbean, offensive operations remained important as the English and French forces raided each other's colonies to destroy sugar plantations and seize black slaves.

The 1713 Treaty of Utrecht signaled a British victory. Great Britain, based on the provincials' success at Port Royal, took possession of Acadia (which it renamed Nova Scotia), won recognition of the Iroquois as British subjects, and garnered the right to a limited but annual trade (the *asiento*) in the Spanish Caribbean.

France took consolation in the fact that Canada remained firmly in its hands and seemed impenetrable to British attacks. With the loss of Port Royal, now called Annapolis Royal in honor of Queen Anne, the French began construction of the fortress at Louisbourg, on Cape Breton Island. A naval base at Louisbourg would protect the mouth of the Saint Lawrence River and the French merchant and fishing fleets in the North Atlantic, as well as provide a base for France's Native American allies to harass the British in the Maritimes.

Spain lost the most. Large parts of the Florida frontier became a no-man's land, as Spain directed a strategic withdrawal from the Florida Panhandle and abandoned its missions.

Following Queen Anne's War, the imperial struggle for North America entered the period of the "Long Peace." The European monarchs interfered little in the colonists' dealings with Native Americans. While peace ruled in Europe, the English settlers in North America fought the Tuscarora, Yamasee, and Dummer's wars. Great Britain's primary interest in North America remained in using the colonies to benefit the mercantilist system. When British merchants sought to extract more wealth from the *asiento* concession formalized following Queen Anne's War, war erupted on the southern and Caribbean frontiers.

The first of the Wars of King George II, the War of Jenkins' Ear (1739–1743), or the Anglo-Spanish War, originated from Great Britain's desire for a larger piece of Spain's trade with its North American colonies. Jingoists used Captain Robert Jenkins's confrontation with Spanish customs officers to justify a war.

British forces struck first in November 1739. Admiral Edward Vernon's British fleet sacked Porto Bello on the Isthmus of Panama. Both British and Spanish privateers, merchant ships commissioned by their respective governments to wage war, took to the seas and wreaked havoc on the other side's shipping.

In 1740, Brigadier General James Oglethorpe, operating out of Georgia, which the British had established in 1733 as a buffer between Spanish Florida and Carolina, invaded Florida. He hoped to destroy St. Augustine as a base for privateers and a haven for runaway slaves from the British colonies. While he could not penetrate the walls of the Castillo de San Marcos there, his rangers and Native American allies devastated the Spanish frontier.

The next year, a combined British-American force floundered outside Cartagena (in what is now the South American nation of Colombia) and failed to capture the city. Spanish forces seized the initiative in 1742 and invaded Georgia, but Oglethorpe easily drove them back to Florida.

In the war's last major action, in March 1743, Oglethorpe raided Florida, and his troops ravaged Spanish and native settlements. Nonetheless, the British did not see the war as a success. Despite a significant investment in lives and money, British traders remained excluded from Spain's North American colonies, although some privateers profited handsomely.

By the close of the War of Jenkins' Ear, it had merged into Europe's War of the Austrian Succession, which the colonists knew as King George's War (1744–1748). This was a limited affair for the European powers, but for the American colonists and Native Americans, it was alternately a war for dominion and anticolonialism. In Europe, Great Britain faced the combined armies of France and Prussia, as well as the threat of Jacobitism in Scotland. As a result, both France and Britain left their colonists and Native American allies to carry the burden of the fighting in North America.

British Americans welcomed the declaration of war as an opportunity to improve their economic and territorial standing at New France's expense. Once again, however, the French struck first and flooded the New England, New York, and Nova Scotia frontiers with raiders.

The American colonists, meanwhile, eyed Louisbourg. In 1745, Massachusetts Governor William Shirley raised nearly 4,300 colonial troops for an expedition against the French fortress. After a forty-seven-day siege, the New England forces, under the combined command of William Pepperrell and Commodore Peter Warren of the Royal Navy, victoriously entered Louisbourg. Jubilation swept the British colonies. Storms at sea wracked the French armada sent to retake Louisbourg and compelled it to limp back to Europe in 1746 without relieving the fortress.

Still, all was not lost for the French. They countered the fall of Louisbourg by increasing their efforts on the frontier. In February 1746, *Troupes de la Marine* and native warriors wiped out the British American garrison at Grand Pré, Nova Scotia. Other Canadians laid siege to Fort Massachusetts in the Berkshire Mountains of western Massachusetts and attacked Saratoga, New York. William Shirley's plan to take Canada then unraveled in the fall of 1746 in the face of poor planning and because the British regulars—troops the British government again had promised the provincials to support an invasion up the St. Lawrence—failed to arrive at Louisbourg.

The only tangible British American success in this war on the frontier occurred when Captain John Gorham and his rangers, in concert with their native allies from Maine, pacified the hinterlands of Nova Scotia. Gorham waged a ghastly guerrilla war against the Acadians and Mi'kmaq. His operation poisoned relations between British Americans and the Acadians, and it contributed to the British decision to deport the French population of Nova Scotia in 1755.

By 1747–1748, both sides had tired of the inconclusive war and awaited developments in Europe. The 1748 Treaty of Aix-la-Chapelle returned combatants to the *status quo ante bellum* (status quo before the war). To the great consternation and disappointment of New England, the British returned Louisbourg to France in exchange for Madras, India.

One positive wartime development for the British, however, was the improvement of their relations, driven by increased gift giving, with the Native Americans of the Ohio Valley. The Iroquois, particularly the Mohawk, feared that the British might supplant them with other native peoples as the primary benefactors of British largesse. William Johnson deftly capitalized on Iroquois insecurity, and, as a result, Iroquois commitment to neutrality started to waiver. France, for so long dependent on native allies, decided to act.

French and Indian War

France's decision to reassert its authority in the Ohio Valley precipitated the French and Indian War (1754–1763), also known as the Seven Years' War (1756–1763) in Europe. The French and Indian War is perhaps the best known of all the colonial wars, and it is certainly the most significant. Great Britain's eventual victory in the conflict radically altered the balance of power among British Americans, Frenchmen, Englishmen, and Native Americans in North America. At the time of the war, however, the British could not foresee the tremendous consequences their victory would have.

The French and Indian War began with the 1754 mission of George Washington to deliver Virginia's message to the French that they must evacuate their forts in the Ohio Country. Washington's skirmish at Jumonville's Glen sparked a worldwide conflagration.

In 1755, Britain sent Major General Edward Braddock and his army to remove the French from Fort Duquesne at present-day Pittsburgh. Braddock met with disaster on the Monongahela River, and another combined British American–Native American force under William Johnson stalled after fighting the French and their allies under Jean-Armand, Baron de Dieskau, to a draw on Lake George.

The one success of the British plan for 1755, which was supposed to win the war in one season, was the capture of Fort Beauséjour in Acadia, followed by the deportation of the French-speaking and Catholic

Acadians. British failures on the frontier led to a repeat of the earlier imperial wars, as British Americans fled the backcountry in waves.

In 1756, the French complicated British efforts when they and their Native American allies took Fort Oswego in western New York. French officers, in an effort not to antagonize their allies, turned a blind eye as native warriors looted the fort and killed their prisoners. In 1757, the new British commander, John Campbell, fourth earl of Loudoun, sailed to take Louisbourg. The French, under Louis-Joseph, marquis de Montcalm, counterattacked on Lake George and laid siege to Fort William Henry. The infamous "Massacre" ensued when French officers again watched their Native American allies seize the spoils of war.

Campbell returned to New York to find that the Crown had replaced him as commander-in-chief with Major General James Abercromby. In July 1758, Abercromby snatched defeat from the jaws of victory at Fort Ticonderoga. The year 1758 also offered the British promise of what was to come. Lieutenant Colonel John Bradstreet led a force primarily composed of British Americans and captured Fort Frontenac on Lake Ontario, Brigadier General John Forbes and Colonel Henry Bouquet captured Fort Duquesne, and Major General Jeffery Amherst and Brigadier General James Wolfe took Louisbourg.

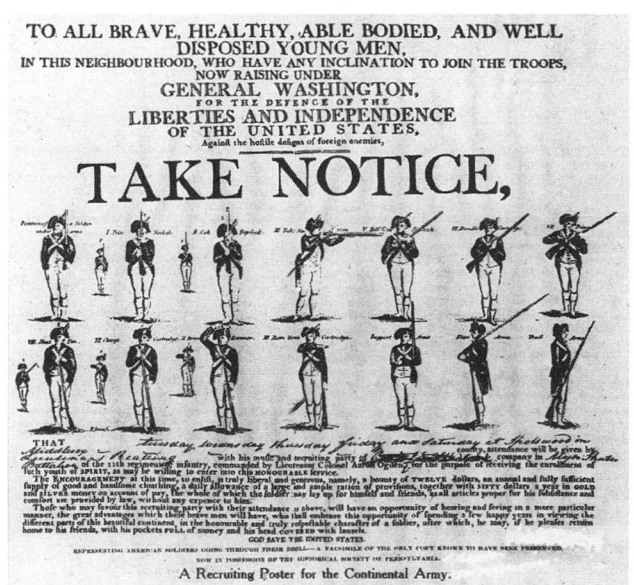

A recruiting poster for the Continental Army offers enlistees "a bounty of twelve dollars," "sixty dollars a year in gold and silver money," and other benefits. By the end of the colonial period, Americans had a tradition of war making and diplomacy that stretched back nearly 170 years. *(Brown Brothers, Sterling, Pennsylvania)*

Amherst took command of the British armies, and, for the 1759 campaign, he moved northward along the Hudson River–Lake Champlain front toward Montreal, while Wolfe approached Quebec along the Saint Lawrence. Wolfe won a place for himself in Britain's pantheon of heroes when he lost his life in his army's victory at the Plains of Abraham.

French forces attempted to retake Quebec at the Battle of Sainte-Foy in April 1760, but they failed. Amherst used his larger and better-equipped army to methodically reduce the French positions and, in September 1760, entered Montreal. Following the 1763 Treaty of Paris, France abandoned its claims to Canada, and Britons and British Americans toasted each other as members of the world's greatest empire.

Beyond witnessing the British Army's tremendous military and diplomatic victory, the French and Indian War saw a clash between American and British military cultures. The war was seen to continue colonial-British arguments over the proper role and place of British professional soldiers, colonial provincial troops, and British American rangers. Great Britain entered the war, assuming that it would be a limited conflict. American colonists, on the other hand, fought their part of the Seven Years' War to conquer their French and Native American enemies.

In time, Prime Minister William Pitt embraced the colonists' goals and promised to repay them for their costs in fighting the war. British field commanders, most notably Amherst and Wolfe, grudgingly came to value the colonial troops. Both Amherst and Wolfe had increasingly used American-born rangers, most notably the companies under Major Robert Rogers and Captain Joseph Gorham, to wage war directly against Native Americans and terrorize Canadian civilians.

The eviction of France from North America meant that Native Americans could no longer play Great Britain and France against one another. Their insecurity manifested itself in Pontiac's Rebellion, as the native peoples of the *pays d'en haut* sought to define the parameters of reciprocity in a new British-Native American relationship. British imperial administrators, having to contend with both Native Americans and American colonists who hoped to expand into the lands taken from France, faced a daunting task. The Proclamation of 1763 proved only a temporary salve to the concerns of Native Americans that colonial Americans would overwhelm them.

The colonial wars began to merge into Americas' expansionist wars at the end of the French and Indian War. Colonial Americans reacted negatively to ambiguous British policies, like the Proclamation of 1763

that would have limited their expansion west of the Appalachian Mountains. Beginning at the end of the colonial period, and stretching through the War of 1812, colonists fought a series of wars of conquest against the native peoples of the Transappalachian West. In each of those wars, all of them Native American wars against colonialism, colonial fighters turned to the first way of war.

Following the deportation of the Acadians in 1755, Americans focused their military energies on completely subjugating the Mi'kmaq of the Maritimes. In 1760 and 1761, combined British and colonial armies laid waste to huge tracts of the Cherokee homelands in a war to spread colonial settlement into present-day western North Carolina and eastern Tennessee. The "winning of the West" and Kentucky began in 1774 with the outbreak of Lord Dunmore's War in western Virginia. During the American War for Independence, the colonists would continue to fight Native Americans on the southern, western, and New York frontiers.

At the end of the colonial period, America had a tradition of war making and diplomacy that stretched back nearly 170 years. Although wars in colonial America paled in terms of the number of forces engaged as compared to contemporary European conflicts, they were no less important. Warfare and diplomacy were the colonists' tools to "clear" North America for settlement.

The colonists' wars were unlike most contemporary European wars in that they were unlimited wars for the conquest of enemy lands, and, therefore, were wars of extermination and removal. Native Americans, in that sense, fought all the colonial era's wars as wars of anticolonialism. Their goals centered on maintaining their independence, whether that independence revolved around maintaining the proper boundaries of reciprocity with Onontio or preserving their lands from colonial encroachments.

Ultimately, the Native Americans failed. The product of the colonial wars and diplomacy was the eventual European American conquest and settlement of the lands between the Atlantic seaboard and the eastern range of the Appalachian Mountains.

John Grenier

Bibliography

Anderson, Fred. *Crucible of War: The Seven Years' War and the Fate of Empire in British North America, 1754–1766.* New York: Alfred A. Knopf, 2000.

Grenier, John. *The First Way of War: American Warmaking on the Frontier, 1607–1814.* New York: Cambridge University Press, 2005.

Holland-Braund, Kathryn. *Deerskins and Duffels: Creek Indian Trades with Anglo-America, 1685–1815.* Lincoln: University of Nebraska Press, 1993.

Merrell, James. *The Indians' New World: Catawbas and Their Neighbors from European Contact through the Era of Removal.* New York: W. W. Norton, 1989.

Richter, Daniel. *Ordeal of the Longhouse: The Peoples of the Iroquois League in the Era of European Colonization.* Chapel Hill: University of North Carolina Press, 1992.

Steel, Ian. *Warpaths: Invasions of North America.* New York: Oxford University Press, 1994.

White, Richard. *The Middle Ground: Indians, Empires, and Republics in the Great Lakes Region, 1650–1815.* New York: Cambridge University Press, 1991.

Politics and Government

Five European nations founded enduring societies north of the Gulf of Mexico. Only one of them left any lasting legacy upon the political history of postindependence North America: Great Britain.

Royal authority in New France and New Spain operated through appointive officials, who owed their posts to court patronage and whose duty it was to maintain order and dispense justice on behalf of absolute monarchs. Under such circumstances, no opportunity arose for settlers to gain experience in lawmaking or to master crucial aspects of civil administration.

New Netherland and New Sweden functioned as corporate enclaves staffed by managers, employees, and various independent contractors—not as political societies based upon the rights and duties of citizenship. Their formative period left no tradition of self-government, much less any ethos of public service. Only colonists from England established institutions that would influence the future course of both constitutional history and political thought during later centuries.

Imperial Institutions

No factor shaped the founding of English-speaking North America more fundamentally than a strong disinclination by both Crown and Parliament to bear the heavy, initial costs entailed in acquiring overseas dominions before the 1660s. English monarchs and statesmen were also long distracted from colonization ventures by the events preceding the civil wars of the 1640s and then by the Interregnum (1649–1660) that followed the beheading of Charles I. During the first half century of trans-Atlantic expansion, the burden of empire instead fell upon such corporations as the Virginia and Massachusetts Bay Companies, such proprietors as the first two generations of Maryland's Baltimore dynasty, and such privately organized, self-financing groups of emigrants as the religious exiles who founded Plymouth, Rhode Island, and New Haven.

English settlers consequently found themselves thrown upon their own devices for keeping order and resolving controversies by the general inattention of officials in London toward colonial affairs. In order to enlist cooperation from their resident populations, leaders in the early colonies eventually granted the right of making laws to democratic assemblies by entitling a large portion of free, adult males to vote and hold office (subject to qualifications based on property ownership and, sometimes, religion). The rise of representative government was crucially important for Anglo-American political history, not only as the root of all subsequent constitutional development but also as the basis for later claims that long-standing custom had endowed the colonial assemblies with near-autonomous rights of self-governance.

For almost three decades after Charles II's coronation in 1660, however, the restored Stuart dynasty pursued ambitions of turning Great Britain into an absolutist state modeled after the example of Louis XIV in France. The Stuarts sought to tighten control over their overseas possessions through royal bureaucrats, much as the Bourbons did in New France. Beginning in late 1660, the monarchy started supervising overseas affairs through a special committee of the Privy Council. By 1675, when it was reconstituted as the Committee on Trade and Plantations (or Lords of Trade), this committee had emerged as the first effective agency for monitoring colonial developments and enforcing Crown policies in America. The Stuarts eventually moved to increase the number of dominions under their direct control (known as royal colonies, as opposed to those created by charters to corporate entities or grants to proprietors). Before 1660, the only royal government on the North American mainland had been in Virginia, but during the early 1680s, New Hampshire, New York, and Massachusetts came under the monarchy's immediate rule. By 1732, eight of the thirteen original colonies had Crown status. (Connecticut and Rhode Island retained charter privileges, while Maryland, Pennsylvania, and Delaware continued as proprietaries.)

James II showed exceptional animosity toward parliamentary institutions during his brief reign (1685–1688). Striving to curb legislative rights and privileges both at home and abroad, he moved first to dispense with representative government in North America. The king consolidated every colony from West Jersey through New Hampshire into the Dominion of New England. The dominion was a prototype for reorganizing the empire along the model of Spanish America, where viceroyalties were administered by governors-general, appointed by the court at Madrid with power to promulgate ordinances and impose revenues within their jurisdictions. No provision was made for elective assemblies to pass laws or enact taxes. Before James II could abridge legislative self-government in his other American dependencies, however, he was driven from power by the Revolution of 1688, which established constitutional protections for Parliament's traditional rights.

William III and Mary II, who succeeded James II, countermanded his autocratic measures and reinstated the legislatures annulled by him. The British government thereafter treated Anglo-American assemblies as an integral part of colonial administration. Representative government functioned as a highly effective and practical vehicle for mobilizing support from American elites and taxpayers, whose financial resources not only paid the salaries of each colony's executive officers and judges, but often provided sub-

The Declaration of Rights, presented to William and Mary in 1689, defined the conditions under which they would be recognized as king and queen of England, opening the way to constitutional monarchy. William and Mary reinstated representative assemblies as an integral part of colonial administration. *(British Museum, London, United Kingdom/Bridgeman Art Library)*

stantial military assistance during wartime. British ministries consequently enjoyed the luxury of reaping a significant influx of customs duties from American commerce, while the cost of governing those overseas possessions amounted to a pittance of the Treasury's annual budget.

In 1696, the Privy Council formed a new committee, the Lords Commissioners of Trade and Plantations (or Board of Trade), to monitor commerce and fisheries, evaluate candidates for royal governorships and other positions, formulate policy concerning events in America, and identify any acts passed by colonial legislatures that should be disallowed by royal veto. Interest in colonial affairs steadily waned among members of Parliament and the royal bureaucracy after 1725, however, and, over the next two decades, the Board of Trade reflected this general apathy by pursuing its duties indifferently, if not lethargically. Aside from a brief resurgence of activity and influence at the Privy Council under the Earl of Halifax for nearly a decade after 1748, the Board had minimal impact upon politics

in the British colonies. Its most important activity was reviewing legislative acts for the royal signature, and in this task the Board proved quite accommodating to colonial wishes by approving all but 469 (5 percent) of the 8,563 statutes submitted through 1776. British policy and attitudes toward America evolved in an atmosphere of reasonably well intentioned—if poorly informed—neglect, so that imperial oversight from London was rarely intrusive or heavy-handed.

By the 1750s, the British Empire, which then included about 1.5 million inhabitants throughout the Western Hemisphere, had matured into a conglomeration of self-governing political units whose constitutional relationship to the British monarchy and Parliament lacked any formal definition or even mutual understanding. Parliament saw itself as having virtually unlimited lawmaking authority within all the monarchy's possessions except Ireland, which had its own parliament, endowed with essentially sovereign powers over taxation, and its own internal governance.

Colonial legislative leaders conceded that, as a

In March 1765, the Stamp Act challenged colonial notions of local autonomy and awakened a dormant dispute over the degree of American exemption from parliamentary laws. Angry protests led to repeal of the tax—as depicted in this British cartoon funeral—in March 1766. *(New York Public Library, New York)*

matter of practical necessity, deference should be accorded to Parliament for standardizing legal institutions critical to ensuring justice and promoting prosperity equally throughout the empire. These measures included amending the common law, bringing efficiency to judicial proceedings, and making uniform regulations for contracts, currency, or commerce. Otherwise, however, Anglo-Americans assumed that their assemblies occupied a status similar to Ireland's parliament: subordinate in authority and prestige to Parliament, but still endowed with exclusive rights of levying taxes within their own boundaries and of regulating their own internal affairs by statutes enacted under the royal signature. A latent conflict thus existed over the degree to which Americans could claim exemption from parliamentary laws. This issue remained dormant until the 1765 Stamp Act challenged American notions of local autonomy by imposing taxes upon a wide range of legal and business transactions in the colonies.

Representative Government

The first colonial assembly convened at Jamestown, Virginia, in 1619, twelve years after the colony's founding. The Virginia Company permitted any parish or other community to elect two deputies who could attend sessions with the governor and his appointed council, provided that the constituency paid its delegates' expenses. While at the assembly, the representatives' primary duties were to endorse decisions made by the company shareholders in London and enact necessary ordinances. The assembly's actions lacked legal force without later approval from company headquarters, however, and it had no right to meet on a recurring basis.

When Virginia became a royal colony in 1624, the Crown clearly hoped to govern the colony with officials independent of popular influence, since its governors dispensed with calling the legislature into session. The king's need for local sanction of his plan to inaugurate a tax on exported tobacco finally led to calling an elected assembly in 1628 to enact the levy. Annual sessions only began to be held on a regular basis after 1630. The members organized themselves on the model of the House of Commons in 1634 by setting counties as the basic constituency (along with a few boroughs) and allocating two seats for each, regardless of population.

Representative institutions next developed under the Massachusetts Bay Company, whose charter established a governmental structure appropriate for a busi-

ness corporation. The charter stipulated that the investors (or "freemen") would elect a board of trustees (or "assistants," chaired by a "governor") at shareholders' meetings (or "General Court") where all major decisions and regulations would be debated and adopted. The company moved its headquarters to the colony by instructing the first governor to carry the charter to New England in 1630. When the General Court first convened soon after, fewer than a dozen shareholders had apparently emigrated, and just eight attended the meeting in their role as freemen. They transferred the power of choosing executive officials, making laws, and laying taxes from the freemen in general to the assistants and governor, who—of necessity—consisted of the same eight individuals. The assistants broadened the definition of a freeman in 1631 to include all adult men who were full church members, by which citizenship came within the reach of every male settler, although their political duties by then extended no further than voting for a legislative council.

In response to objections made in 1632 that the assistants had exceeded their authority by levying the colony's first tax, the General Court decreed that prior notice would be given when future revenues were needed and that no tax would be imposed without majority approval from a deputation comprised of two freemen sent from each of the towns specifically to vote on that subject. Two years later, other protests arose that the freemen had been denied their right under the charter to participate in the making of laws as well. This grievance defied any solution based on a literal reading of the charter, since, even at that early date, it was impractical for the several hundred men admitted as citizens to function efficiently as a legislature, and within a few years, the number of freemen would certainly exceed 1,000. The colony's leaders therefore directed each town to elect two delegates to join with the assistants and governor in enacting ordinances. The transmutation of a commercial bureaucracy into a civil republic was then essentially accomplished.

Representative government did not mature in Virginia and Massachusetts until after each was first settled. Legislative bodies emerged in both colonies out of the administrative apparatus of a business enterprise, but each proved sufficiently durable to continue functioning after the chartered company from which it sprang had expired. In neither colony was the government consciously fashioned after England's parliamentary system of a popularly chosen House of Commons, a hereditary House of Lords, and the reigning monarch. Elected representatives in both Virginia and Massachusetts did not at first organize themselves into a separate chamber interacting with the other branches of government, but rather sat together with the governor and his appointive council, to whose agenda and judgment they generally deferred. Virginia's legislature almost certainly continued to hold unicameral sessions until 1642, while the Massachusetts General Court became bicameral in 1644.

Democratically chosen assemblies emerged elsewhere in Anglo-America in a manner similar to developments in Virginia and Massachusetts. Rarely did the first sitting of any colony's legislature occur until two years after its earliest settlers had arrived, while in Virginia, Plymouth, Rhode Island, New York, and Georgia, the opening sessions of their assemblies were not held until a decade or more after their founding. Most assemblies either evolved from corporate structures or were designed by proprietors given royal land grants to encourage overseas expansion, and many bore absolutely no resemblance to the British Parliament's structure or manner of lawmaking. For example, the Fundamental Constitutions of Carolina (1669) envisioned a single-chamber parliament wherein the proprietors, commoners, and indigenous nobility—a fanciful mix of landgraves, caciques, and manor lords—sat together. Bills could only be drafted by the proprietors, however, and the role of commoners and nobles was limited to accepting or rejecting what was placed before them.

Most colonies required about two decades for legislative government to establish continuity and mature into bicameral institutions. As in Virginia and Massachusetts, elected representatives initially met in joint sessions with the governor and his council, and they routinely acted in a judicial capacity on an *ad hoc* basis. No assembly attempted to base representation upon districts of equal populations (along lines of the modern concept of "one man, one vote"); instead, members were apportioned among various units of local government at a fixed ratio (usually two for each county, town, or parish).

Colonial assemblies developed in most respects along parallel lines after 1690. Despite their varied origins, Anglo-American governments ultimately came to resemble Great Britain's bicameral legislative system, in which bills required approval by both a popularly chosen assembly and an appointive governor's council, save for a few exceptions: Pennsylvania's legislature was unicameral since its council could not reject acts passed by the lower house, while in the de facto republics of Rhode Island and Connecticut, both houses

of the legislature were elected by voters. In the royal colonies, especially where the chief executive was a Crown official, it was natural for Americans to see their governments as "little Parliaments" and to idealize them as having inherited the full panoply of constitutional rights and liberties won during the long struggle since Magna Carta to secure the "rights of Englishmen."

Local Government

Anglo-Americans patterned their own local governments after institutions long established in their homeland. England's basic unit of local jurisdiction was the county (or shire), and its chief officials—the sheriff, justices of the peace, clerk of registration, coroner, and constables—were all appointed directly or indirectly by the Crown and not elected. It was common for members of the town councils in larger cities to be appointed to office for life by the incumbents, independently of any elections. Even when self-governing boroughs chose their administrative councils by popular vote, rarely did the franchise include more than a quarter of adult men.

Many of England's unincorporated, agrarian villages, nevertheless, had inherited customary practices of self-government from medieval times. Heads of households within an isolated parish or tenants on a large manor frequently would meet each year to address neighborhood problems, allocate access to shared resources like common lands, review maintenance of pathways or boundary fences, pass village bylaws, and elect officials to oversee local affairs. The first generation of New Englanders adapted this precedent to their own settlements through town meetings convened at least once every year, so all heads of families could vote for selectmen, who would supervise the next year's communal business. Town government quickly spawned many lesser officers with specialized responsibilities, such as a moderator of meetings, clerk, treasurer, tithing-man, tax assessor and collector, surveyor of highways, fence viewer (person hired to make sure fences were in good order), livestock brander, keeper of the animal pound, and weight or measure sealer (official who verified the accuracy of weights and measures). By 1750, the average Connecticut town was appointing over sixty adults to oversee various responsibilities for the local government.

Outside of New England, eastern Long Island, and parts of northeastern New Jersey, few colonists lived in towns. The largest cities usually had municipal councils elected by property-owning citizens—but not always. Philadelphia's charter of 1691 vested its government in aldermen who were appointed with lifetime tenure; the aldermen nominated and approved their own successors and, for good measure, also chose the mayor. Charles Town, South Carolina, survived the entire colonial era without any municipal government; law and order in the city rested on justices of the peace and a sheriff, whom the governor appointed, while Anglican parish vestries dispensed poor relief and performed other social services.

Counties were the basic unit of local government in the Southern and mid-Atlantic colonies (except South Carolina, which was divided into parishes). Even in New England, with its strong tradition of direct democracy through town meetings, counties served as the chief jurisdiction for civil administration and the primary venue for legal proceedings. As in Great Britain, the key personnel of county government were the justices of the peace (or magistrates), who formed a collective tribunal empowered to try misdemeanors, settle disputes over debts and contracts, and enforce the slave codes with rigor. Magistrates could dispense decisions individually in petit sessions, without a jury, on minor matters or collectively at quarter sessions, with a jury, in major cases. The county court also functioned in an executive capacity as an omnicompetent institution that could initiate almost any action necessary for the public welfare and had authority to levy small taxes for essential community expenses. The magistrates, furthermore, appointed lesser officials responsible for various public services, such as overseers of the highways, overseers of the poor, the slave patrons officers, and constables, and they could rebuke or remove these subordinates for nonperformance of their duties. The sheriff publicized and enforced the county court's orders; he also maintained the tax rolls and conducted elections. The clerk acted as secretary when the justices conducted business, and he kept the courthouse open on a daily basis in the course of serving as a general registrar.

Magistrates, sheriffs, and clerks all obtained their posts through the governor's patronage and held office until either their commission was rescinded or, as under British law, the current monarch's death obliged them to resign. Vacancies within county government were usually filled out of recommendations to the governor from the sitting justices, who invariably nominated relatives, friends, and other associates drawn from the ranks of the wealthiest tenth of landowners, usually termed the gentry. Wherever communities had been settled for two or three generations, county government

assumed an oligarchic and quasi-hereditary character, until the interconnections between its justices, sheriffs, and clerks formed a tangled cousinry of the area's leading families.

The county court system ensured that local affairs would be administered by local residents, who could make knowledgeable decisions for their neighbors based on the familiarity that comes with long residence. It was also a fundamentally elitist arrangement for sharing power that excluded men of average means and middling families from any influence or participation.

Voters, Candidates, and Elections

In every colony but Rhode Island and Connecticut, the choice of a representative to the assembly was the only occasion when voters participated in a colonial-level contest. Massachusetts, Rhode Island, Connecticut, Pennsylvania, and Delaware elected a new lower house each year. In the other eight colonies, governors had complete discretion of calling for a new assembly as they saw fit, as long as no house sat for more than seven years, and they usually scheduled elections about every three or four years.

By the 1750s, legal qualifications for voters were fundamentally similar in all the mainland colonies. Every colony restricted political participation to white, adult, male property owners, but relatively few possessions were needed to qualify as an elector. The usual stipulation was that a man either had to have negotiated a mortgage on at least 50 acres or have accumulated other property worth 40 to 50 pounds. Most married men would have owned tools, household furnishings, or livestock valued at 50 pounds by age 30, if not before then, and the majority of farmers probably had saved the down payment for 50 acres by age 35 or shortly thereafter. Property qualifications primarily excluded young men from the polls, but over the course of their lifetime, likely nine-tenths of adult, white males acquired enough wealth to vote by age 40. The main effect of property qualifications was to keep most men from becoming enfranchised for a decade or more after they turned 21, but not to block them from exercising the suffrage permanently.

Only four colonies set property qualifications for sitting in the legislature that were beyond the means of most persons with middle-class status (500 acres in South Carolina and Georgia, 1,000 acres in New Jersey, and real estate worth 300 pounds in New Hampshire; total net worth of 500 pounds also qualified a person in all the preceding except Georgia). In eight colonies, including all six with the largest populations, anyone who could vote was eligible to serve as a representative. It was nevertheless not practical for ordinary citizens to perform assembly duty, because the position placed a heavy burden on an individual's time and resources. Legislators received no salary for their services and only a modest living allowance, which was set at minimum level and did not always cover full costs, while at assemblies. Assembly sessions rarely lasted less than one month, often two, and sometimes three, and, during this time, members could not pursue their usual employment. Few middle-class persons would have been able to afford the sacrifice of time and money, particularly if the governor summoned the legislature for business at planting or harvest seasons, when even wealthy planters with overseers tried to personally supervise the work on their estates.

As a consequence, it was virtually foreordained that colonial legislatures would be overwhelmingly comprised of the economic and social elite. By the end of the colonial period, the typical member of Virginia's lower house owned 1,800 acres and 40 slaves. Two-thirds of all South Carolina assemblymen after 1750 were planters who worked their estates with eighty or more slaves. Nearly three-quarters of all New Jersey representatives held 600 acres or more and ranked among the wealthiest 5 percent of that colony during the quarter century prior to the Revolution.

The assemblies also began to spawn dynastic groups like the First Families of Virginia, which were notable for sending successive generations of kinsmen into the legislature. In South Carolina's lower house, for example, about half the members were related to other representatives as sons, fathers, or brothers in the half century before 1775. Similarly, John Adams once remarked that in most Massachusetts towns, the office of assemblyman usually rotated among a circle of extended relatives descended from or connected by marriage to just three or four distinct family groups.

The manner of conducting elections acted as a deterrent to high turnout among voters. Eight of the colonies had no regular schedule for balloting. Governors could issue the writs at any time, and the law directed that sheriffs need give only a few weeks' notice by posting announcements at commonly frequented sites, such as taverns. In rural areas, where few—or no—newspapers circulated, many electors were not likely to learn that a new assembly was to be chosen until after the fact. The county courthouse generally served as the only polling place, so that outlying voters had to travel long distances over unpaved, narrow roads, and some would have to bear the expense of overnight lodging. These circumstances made it inevitable that numerous freeholders would be left uninformed of elections and many others would find it personally inconvenient, time consuming, and even expensive to get to polls.

Turnout at elections consequently remained low during colonial times. It was unusual for a majority of adult white males to cast ballots, although participation rates sometimes ranged from 67 percent to 80 percent on rare occasions when hotly contested issues were at stake. The usual level of turnout ranged from 25 percent to 40 percent of adult white males. Assuming that 25 percent to 40 percent of free males over 21 were likely without sufficient property to exercise suffrage at any given moment, such a rate of turnout would suggest that slightly less than half of qualified voters went to the polls on average.

Colonial elections usually resulted in a high percentage of new members being freshly chosen. Turnover among assemblymen was lowest in Delaware, at about 20 percent, and highest in Rhode Island, at over 60 percent. Elections in the colonies produced significantly more change than in Great Britain. Turnover in the House of Commons alternated between 27 percent and 35 percent, while most colonial assemblies had approximately 35 percent to 50 percent of their membership change during most of the period after 1760.

As the eighteenth century progressed, however, elections in America became less volatile. Turnover in many colonies began to approximate that of Britain's House of Commons. As the colonial period came to an end, only in Rhode Island did elections routinely send a majority of newcomers to the legislature.

The explanation for early America's high rate of legislative turnover does not seem to have been a high level of partisan rivalry (unlike Great Britain, no organized parties existed in the colonies), but rather a tendency for most representatives to retire voluntarily after two or three terms. In large part, legislators seem to have left public office after relatively short tenures because of the inconvenience to their private lives and the interruption of their financial affairs caused by attending lengthy sessions at the capital. Politicians consequently found themselves shouldering a public burden that offered little monetary or personal award—save recognition of one's abilities in a society that offered few other chances to win esteem from the community at large—and, not surprisingly, most of them tired of its demands after a few years.

Rise of the Assemblies

The upper class of the British mainland colonies increasingly identified their own collective interest with the colonial government's representative element after 1690. Accordingly, they strove to buttress the standing of their local assemblies with the same powerful privileges that had been confirmed as belonging to the British House of Commons following the Revolution of 1688. This development reversed the balance of legislative power established in the early seventeenth century, when the legislatures' lower houses did little more than ratify measures initiated by the governors or their councilors. Continued deference to the chief executive and his appointed advisors ultimately proved incompatible with defending local interests against outside interference, since the Crown (or an absolute proprietor) named the governor, who then appointed his own advisers to the upper house everywhere but in Connecticut and Rhode Island (where they were popularly elected). The lower houses of assembly increasingly asserted their own authority during the eighteenth century as a means of checking the potential threat to local autonomy posed by royal and proprietary officials.

The assemblies simultaneously began shedding the amateurishness and inefficiency that had characterized their deliberations for much of the 1600s. The lower houses steadily became more proficient in such areas as keeping accurate and detailed records of official activities, gaining greater mastery over parliamentary procedure and rules of order, and making their internal organization more efficient and flexible through greater reliance upon standing committees to conduct recurring business and by taking greater care in naming competent individuals to key leadership positions. The assemblies became more professional and hard working, in large part through the emergence of a new generation of speakers of the house, who were more politically sophisticated, strong-willed, and determined to elevate their assembly's standing to a level commensurate with the status of Britain's House of Commons. These speakers frequently held long tenures, and they led the members in an often spirited offensive to expand their assembly's institutional rights and privileges.

The lower houses eventually shifted the locus of constitutional power away from the governor and councilors by refusing to permit any external meddling in their own internal proceedings, by gaining firm control over taxes and the budget, and by refusing to appro-priate permanent, independent salaries or other incomes to executive officers. By keeping governors dependent upon the passage of an annual bill for their compensation, the lower houses used the power of the purse to ensure that governors could not allow long periods to pass without calling the legislature into session. They also generally withheld final approval of the government's budget until the governor had agreed to sign the major acts sought for passage by the speaker. Despite a considerable range of gubernatorial powers (including the rights of vetoing any measure, of summoning or dismissing a legislative session at will, of calling elections with little advance notice, and of packing the upper house with his own supporters), a determined lower house had the advantage because the governor was dependent upon local revenues to carry out his duties—not to mention receive his pay.

Because of the general inattention to colonial affairs by the Privy Council and even the Board of Trade's members, governors rarely obtained any effective backing from the British government that would enable them to coerce assemblies into compromising on most disputes, much less to press a lower house into backing down on matters of constitutional principle or measures strongly demanded by the voters. Under such conditions, the lower house succeeded in gaining the initiative in legislative proceedings, establishing itself as the dominant force in colonial government, and maintaining that position throughout the eighteenth century.

Well before the colonial period ended, representative government had displaced imperial or proprietary institutions as the center of political power in Anglo-America. The lower houses of assembly no longer acquiesced to the constitutional primacy of the governor and his council as they had during the seventeenth century. They saw themselves as entitled to the same legislative privileges accorded by the British Crown to the House of Commons, and they exercised de facto local autonomy in nearly all matters of lawmaking, except regulation of oceanic trade, issuing currency, and amending the common law.

Thomas L. Purvis

Bibliography

Bailyn, Bernard. *The Origins of American Politics.* New York: Alfred A. Knopf, 1968.

Clarke, Mary P. *Parliamentary Privilege in the American Colonies.* New Haven, CT: Yale University Press, 1943.

Dinkin, Robert J. *Voting in Provincial America: A Study of*

Elections in the Thirteen Colonies, 1680–1776. Westport, CT: Greenwood, 1977.

Greene, Jack P. *Peripheries and Center: Constitutional Development in the Extended Polities of the British Empire and the United States, 1607–1788.* Athens: University of Georgia Press, 1986.

———. *The Quest for Power: The Lower Houses of Assembly in the Southern Royal Colonies, 1689–1776.* Chapel Hill: University of North Carolina Press, 1973.

Hofer, Peter C., and N.E.H. Hull. *Impeachment in America, 1635–1805.* New Haven, CT: Yale University Press, 1984.

Johnson, Richard R. *Adjustment to Empire: The New England Colonies, 1675–1715.* New Brunswick, NJ: Rutgers University Press, 1981.

Kammen, Michael. *Deputyes & Liberves: The Origins of Representative Government in Colonial America.* New York: Free Press, 1969.

Kettner, James H. *The Development of American Citizenship, 1608–1870.* Chapel Hill: University of North Carolina Press, 1978.

Labaree, Leonard W. *Royal Government in America.* New Haven, CT: Yale University Press, 1930.

Leder, Lawrence H. *Liberty and Authority: Early American Political Ideology, 1689–1763.* Chicago: Quadrangle, 1968.

Lutz, Donald S. *Colonial Origins of the American Constitution.* Indianapolis, IN: Liberty Fund, 1998.

———. *The Origins of American Constitutionalism.* Baton Rouge: Louisiana State University Press, 1988.

McLaughlin, Andrew C. *The Foundations of American Constitutionalism.* New York: New York University Press, 1932.

Murrin, John M. "Political Development." In *Colonial British America: Essays in the New History of the Early Modern Era,* edited by Jack P. Greene and J. R. Pole. Baltimore: Johns Hopkins University Press, 1984.

Pole, Jack R. *The Gift of Government: Political Responsibility from the English Restoration to American Independence.* Athens: University of Georgia Press, 1983.

———. *Political Representation in England and the Origins of the American Republic.* London: Macmillan, 1966.

Steele, Ian K. *Politics of Colonial Policy: The Board of Trade in Colonial Administration, 1696–1720.* New York: Oxford University Press, 1968.

Tully, Alan. *Forming American Politics: Ideals, Interests, and Institutions in Colonial New York and Pennsylvania.* Baltimore: Johns Hopkins University Press, 1994.

Race and Ethnicity

At the beginning of the twenty-first century, Americans tend to differentiate between race and ethnicity, seeing the former as inherited physical differences and the latter as a distinctive sense of common ancestry and culture. But between 1500 and 1700, as Europeans, Africans, and Native Americans met, traded, fought, and talked about each other, concepts of race and ethnicity (and nation) blended together in an ambiguous, often inconsistent, fashion, similar to modern notions of ethnicity. Appearance, clothing, religion, politics, manners, and even food preference and preparation—all were investigated as aspects of a distinct lineage, group, or nation. Sometimes these aspects were viewed as permanent and inherited, and sometimes they were viewed as shaped (and potentially reshaped) by environment.

After 1700, more rigid perceptions of race and ethnicity emerged with a clear hierarchy, as skin color increasingly demarcated legal status, social rank, occupation, and other differences in lifestyle and social relations. On the "colored" side of this dividing line, Native Americans and Negroes were viewed as inferior to whites, with their skin colors (red and black) and "racial" characteristics subsuming ethnic variations. On the white side of the line, colonists perceived substantial variations among different ethnic groups—English, Germans, Scots-Irish, French Huguenots—even though their Christian religion and European heritage provided a fundamental connection.

The history of group identity in colonial North American has three distinctive themes, all of which became more prominent in the eighteenth century. First, there was an emphasis on skin color as the key indicator of group distinctiveness, denoting a cluster of physical, behavioral, psychological, and cultural attributes; this applied not only to Africans and Native Americans but also to Europeans. Second, resulting perhaps from the need to justify the legal and social distinctions of black slavery and the dispossession of Native Americans, Europeans, particularly colonists, increasingly perceived a rigid hierarchy of races, with whites at the top, Native Americans in the middle, and blacks at the bottom. And third, the British colonies in North America, especially New York and Pennsylvania (and, after 1720, the western border areas along the Appalachian Mountains), became more diverse as they attracted a growing mélange of peoples from many areas of Europe, as well as more Africans being brought into slavery.

These three developments encouraged distinctions of race in colonial British America that supplanted traditional English demarcations of class and even gender. Ironically, these distinctions became even more rigid and comprehensive after 1750 among some of the Anglo-American intellectuals who embraced the new Enlightenment notions of objectivity and scientific truth.

First Impressions

In the fifteenth century, as Europeans began to explore and trade on other continents, they brought with them various preconceptions that would shape how they perceived the many peoples they would meet. The biblical book of Genesis taught them that all humans came from a single ancestor, created by the same God. All of those descendants (and other creatures on earth) were assigned a permanent place in life in the Great Chain of Being, which connected all existence, from the lowest insects to the heavenly hosts—a concept with roots in ancient Greece but which served Europe's relatively rigid social hierarchy. Those descendants were divided into two clearly delineated groups, Christians and unbelievers. All Christians were to be brethren, responsible to each other and the Church; slavery was barred among Christians, although not servitude.

While Europeans were attentive to how different peoples looked, dressed, and acted, their intellectual framework was founded on Aristotelian philosophy and physics, which reinforced biblical concepts that the environment shaped human variation. English writers, like other Europeans, focused on the body as a reflection of the universe, with the body's four humors (black bile, blood, yellow bile, and phlegm) corresponding to the universe's elements (earth, air, fire, and water). The balance between those humors shaped a person's (and a people's) nature. That balance was influenced by the local climate, as well as by inheritance and various aspects of culture such as food.

European notions of exotic peoples and cultures evolved rapidly in the sixteenth century. The expansion of direct trade with Africa and the discovery of the Americas, which came as the printing press and literacy became more widespread, spawned a growing literature of travel stories and other writings, which focused on those strange places and peoples. These accounts focused on religion, clothing, physiognomy (including skin color), and temperament, and often speculated about how those characteristics were shaped by the group's climate and environment.

Europeans generally agreed that Africans' skins had been burned black by the equatorial sun, and, given their biblical ideas about creation and monogenesis, they rejected the idea that Africans were not fully human or somehow created differently. But intellectuals used to arguing over whether the English or French climate was more conducive to high civilization were easily able to agree that the equatorial heat of Africa fostered durable, insensitive bodies, inherently fitted for heavy labor and low social status.

Some writers, drawing on older Catholic literature, connected the Africans' skin color with God's curse on Ham or his son Canaan as described in Genesis 9–10. That tradition included the notion that Ham and his male offspring were particularly libidinous, and Europeans tended to view West Africans (who wore relatively few clothes) as innately sensual and driven by lust. Some Europeans even tried to connect African humans to African apes, describing similarities between the beast-like man and the man-like beast, and theorizing that apes had attacked and copulated with African women. While writers continued older traditions

Early European commentators often described Native Americans either as simple, noble, and Edenic—as in this depiction of Florida Indians by the Flemish-German engraver Theodore de Bry—or as cannibalistic savages. *(New York Public Library, New York)*

of viewing Africans' animist and Moslem religions as a crucial division between savage cultures and Europe's civilized ways, the intellectual foundations for racism and for plantation slavery in the Americas were set during the early stages of exploration and trade with Africa.

Also important was how the Europeans' notion of race shifted noticeably after they began exploiting the Americas. Initially, Native Americans were not described in terms of color, or, if they were, they were considered white like Europeans, although somewhat tanned by paint or dye or "smoked" by the fires in their wigwams. Since many Native Americans lived along the same latitude as darker-skinned Africans, Europeans began to reject the concept that skin color was determined by one's distance from the equator, and by extension began questioning older notions that the environment generally determined human characteristics.

Native Americans became a cultural mirror: Europeans tended to describe them as simple, noble, and Edenic (in order to criticize unwanted developments in their own countries, such as crowded cities and capitalism) or as hideous cannibalistic savages (in order to excuse their hostility and aggression toward the native peoples). While this bifurcated view persisted past the colonial period, most European intellectuals depicted Native Americans as nearly at the level of animals, because the men were relatively hairless and were seen as exerting little control over their environment, and the women wore few clothes and were supposedly insubordinate, with high sexual appetites.

Again, Christianity was often depicted as the most significant distinction between Europeans and others. At best, Native Americans were seen as having no religion and, at worst, as devil worshipers. While many writers thought that culture and environment alone made Native Americans different—that even their skin color was a result of culture (unlike those in Africa)—descriptions of Native American savagery supported ideas of innate European superiority.

Race and Slavery in the Americas

When sparsely settled or easily conquered subtropical lands were found to the west, Europeans established plantations and saw Africans as ideally suited to forced labor in those environments. In the 1340s, the Portuguese found the Azores, Madeira, and Canary Islands off the west coast of Africa; they established sugar plantations worked first by natives and then by imported African slaves who were worked to death. In the 1500s, the Spanish and Portuguese imported this barbaric but profitable system to the West Indies and Brazil; the Dutch, French, and English would copy the model in areas suitable for growing sugar, tobacco, rice, and other plantation crops.

Such treatment was justified in part by the ideology of the Crusades, which allowed unlimited war against (and exploitation of) non-Christians. European laws generally distinguished between slavery and servitude, with the former permanent and the latter temporary, and limited slavery to war captives or condemned criminals. During the long *Reconquista*, the reconquest of the Iberian Peninsula, however, the Spanish and Portuguese became used to taking Muslim captives (some from North Africa) as slaves. By the thirteenth century, Iberian legal codes allowed for Muslim slaves and distinguished between a range of ethnic and religious categories based on ancestry and religion. Europeans also had been hardened to abuse and death by the system of feudalism and by wave after wave of epidemics, particularly the bubonic plague of the mid-fourteenth century. Most important to the development of slavery was the gradual evolution of the concept of race, which transformed Africans into a different type of human, somewhere on the Great Chain of Being between Europeans and animals.

The Spanish and Portuguese initially tried to make Native Americans labor in their mines and plantations but quickly discovered problems with that system. Native Americans resisted compulsory labor (often killing themselves), and they were extremely susceptible to epidemics. Their enslavement was hotly debated and finally outlawed by Spain (in the 1520s) and Portugal (in the 1570s), although those laws were frequently violated. The colonists therefore had a strong motivation and the legal tradition to import large numbers of Africans as slaves on sugar plantations in the Indies and Brazil. By 1550, the slave trade was firmly established in Latin America.

Spanish and Portuguese colonial laws distinguished between whites, Native Americans, and slaves; thus slavery and racism were joined from the beginning and became a mutually reinforcing system. But the Iberian tradition of slavery and relative willingness to intermarry with others, based on the notion that European "blood" was strongest and would therefore gradually "whiten" others, created a more complex racial structure in Latin American society and culture. Many African slaves and their (often mixed) descendants gained freedom in various ways; in addition, a growing number of Native Americans and their mixed descendants moved to the towns, away from their indigenous communities. The result in Latin America was a hierarchical continuum of racial categories based on the degree of European, Native American, or African ancestry, each defined and regulated by an increasingly complex social code but not necessarily (as in British North America) distinguished and restricted by legal codes.

England began its efforts to understand and exploit the Americas with a deep sense of rivalry with Catholic Europe, and English writers frequently criticized how the Spanish and Portuguese abused Native Americans. Promoters of colonization such as the Hakluyts frequently trumpeted that English traditions of liberty and Protestant values would result in fair and just treatment of Native Americans. The reality, however, proved very different.

English leaders and colonists were fearful and contemptuous of the indigenous peoples and preferred to keep their communities separate while attempting to subject the natives to the colony's sovereignty and rule. When the English began establishing colonies in the West Indies, they copied the Spanish and obtained African slaves from Dutch merchants to work their sugar plantations.

The English also adopted the harsh Spanish and Portuguese laws regulating slaves, as well as the terms "Negro" and "mulatto" for Africans and their mixed descendents. In the long run, the Spanish tended to be much more precise about how they categorized race, but they also were more open to intermarriage between Europeans and native peoples, and they made racial variations an important shaper of class. For the English, notions of race, as they developed, proved more important than class or even the condition of servitude.

In the English colonies, racism developed as part of the institution of slavery. The first Africans to arrive were sold by Dutch merchants to Virginians in 1619, only twelve years after the colony was founded and just as those colonists were embracing tobacco—a very profitable crop if one had rich soil and sufficient laborers. But most of the unfree laborers obtained by planters in the Chesapeake region over the following half century were young Englishmen indentured for four to seven years of servitude. More Africans also were acquired, primarily from the West Indies; while the records are sparse and incomplete, initially some were apparently treated as bound servants and even gained their freedom, even though they were held longer than whites, while others were held as slaves without redemption.

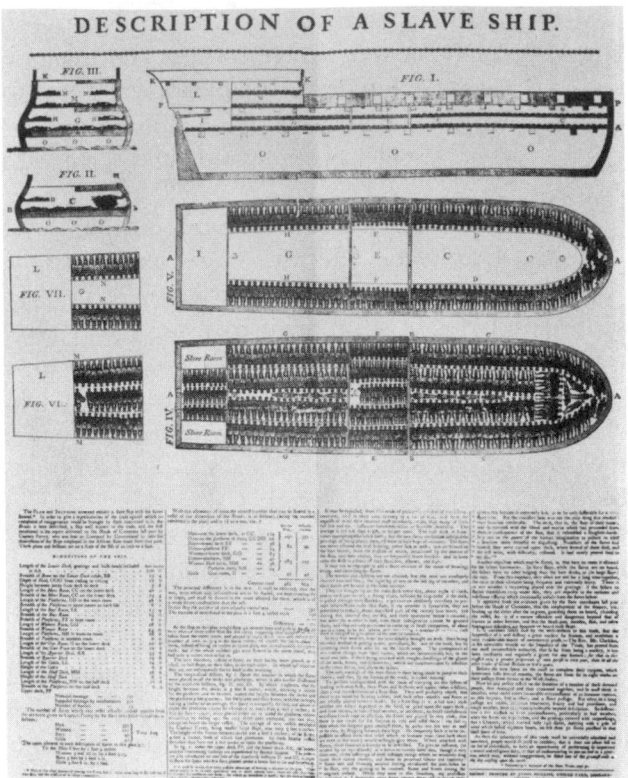

The Middle Passage—marked by overcrowding, a lack of proper nourishment and sanitation, and outbreaks of disease—was only the beginning of a long nightmare for African slaves and their descendants in the New World. *(Wilberforce House, Hull City Museums and Art Galleries, United Kingdom/Bridgeman Art Library)*

Whether free or slave, Africans and their descendants were set apart by the label "Negro," and that difference widened over time. After 1640, some were put into slavery for life by courts, which never happened to whites. Probate records and other documents show that Africans and their descendants were worth more than whites, which pointed to longer or unlimited servitude; the higher prices of black women pointed to inherited servitude for their children, a practice that did not apply to the children of English indentured servants.

The emergence of new concepts of race appeared in the changing terminology used by English colonists. They increasingly tended to refer to themselves as "English," free," and "white" rather than "Christians," and described Africans and their descendants as "Negroes" and "blacks" rather than "heathens" or "pagans."

Fashioning Racial Barriers

Anglo-American concepts of racial differences were not initially set in law, but that began to change by the end of the seventeenth century. Not surprisingly, the plantation colonies of Virginia and Maryland were the first to create laws that discriminated against Africans whether slave or free. In 1640, Virginia barred blacks from carrying arms in militia service. Other English colonies showed the same tendencies: Massachusetts passed a similar statute in 1656, and Connecticut followed four years later.

After 1660, the plantation colonies began to create laws that explicitly connected slavery and subordination to Africans and their descendents. The first comprehensive set of racial laws was created by Barbados in 1661; this primarily regulated slaves, but its criminal provisions were also explicitly directed at free blacks. This code was reflected in many of the Virginia and Maryland laws passed after 1660, and it was adopted wholesale by the infant colony of Carolina in 1692. Southern colonies increasingly treated descendants of Africans as property rather than people—for example, taxing slaves as chattel rather than as servants—and that line also crept into Northern colonies, where slavery was relatively less significant.

These laws continued to equate slavery (and Africans) with heathenism, although they also clearly exempted white heathens from slavery and made sure that an African's conversion to Christianity would not result in freedom. The result was a system that connected slavery with a particular people and connected that people with slavery. Native American slavery, on the other hand, declined in the English colonies as natives were increasingly viewed as innately disorderly and impossible to control in permanent servitude.

The growing emphasis among Anglo-American colonists on skin color and "pure blood" as the source of identity, social status, and legal privileges (or handicaps) can be viewed in the growing body of laws that sought to shore up the expanding institution of slavery by isolating and dominating *all* blacks. Anglo-Americans were particularly concerned about preventing interracial sex, which highlights the emerging sense of race as a fundamental, biological distinction between superiors and inferiors. In 1691, Virginia made marriages between blacks and whites (free or not) punishable by banishment, and a white woman who bore a mulatto child out of wedlock would be fined or sold into service and the child bound for thirty years of servitude. Similar bans on intermarriage were quickly passed by nearly every colony; even Massachusetts enacted such a law in 1706. Such laws were inspired by the desire to avoid weakening the physical boundaries between slaves and free whites, a perception of inter-

racial sex as polluting white purity. There also was a continued belief in the mythology that African men were extremely aggressive sexually—and perhaps more desirable to white women. Colonial laws and practices also lumped "mulattos" together with "Negroes," thereby reinforcing racial boundaries and spurning the Spanish pattern of creating different terminology and rules for varying percentages of African ancestry.

Colonies also limited the civil rights of free blacks. A 1705 Virginia law denied free blacks the right to hold office or testify as a witness in court, and deemed it a crime if they struck any white person, even in self-defense. In 1723, the colony barred free blacks from voting. Such laws point to how America slavery and racism absorbed the fear and contempt felt in England by the upper and middling classes for the inarticulate lower class, allowing an ideology of equality to emerge after 1700.

Other colonies with sizable black populations passed similar measures, although the South was far more obsessed with barring free blacks from civil and political privileges. The New England colonies, for example, required blacks, Native Americans, and mulattos, free or slave, to have permission from their employers or owners to travel or visit taverns at night, but they encouraged literacy and allowed slaves to testify against whites.

Regardless of such differences, a growing body of colonial laws created a reinforcing connection between skin color and subordinate status. This further linked black people and slavery, although the continued ambiguity of racial concepts and persistent legal differences between free and slave status continued to provide a niche for free black households even in the Southern slave societies. Race, as indicated by skin color, thus became one of the most significant Anglo-American paradigms, as the colonists separated their world into discrete segments of whites, blacks, and "tawny" Native Americans.

The growing racial boundaries still did not create a sealed system. Many white slave owners used the black women they owned as sexual partners. While such relationships were often on the level of rape, some may have been affectionate—apparently including the probable relationship between Thomas Jefferson and Sally Hemings—and occasionally their offspring were given special status or privileges. Such illicit liaisons were generally condemned and concealed in the upper South but openly conducted in the lower South and in French Louisiana. Lawmakers and ministers complained that whites of the "lower sort" socialized with blacks in taverns and during the occasional "African election festivals." They also occasionally noted intimate relationships between black men and white (especially Irish) serving girls, indicating that class continued to trump race among some colonists. Some slaves also managed to escape, occasionally with the assistance and companionship of a white servant. Some black freedmen became semi-respected members of their local community, in both the North and the South. Free mariners of color from the Americas, Africa, and Europe traveled within the Atlantic world of seaports and coastal settlements.

All of this posed a symbolic and potentially real threat to the system of race-based slavery and domination. Anglo-Americans increasingly came to fear uprisings in which free blacks would join slaves in a threat not just to slavery but also to the lives and property of all whites. Conspiracies emerged or real uprisings actually took place in New York City in 1712 and 1741, in Charles Town, South Carolina, in 1739, and in Maryland in the late 1730s.

Evolving Racial Identity

Ironically, non-Europeans in the Americas were compelled or influenced by their relationships with the colonists to adopt similar paradigms. Soon after colonization began, native peoples were referring to themselves as "Indians," even as tribal, village, and clan identities remained preeminent. This was in part because Europeans used this term and in part because Native Americans felt the need for a collective term to distinguish themselves from the newcomers.

After more than a century of seeing how Europeans saw themselves as "white" and more alike than different, Native Americans began to see themselves as *red* American Indians, with the same ancestry and essential characteristics. Southeastern tribes also had traditions of symbolic meanings for colors, including red and white, which made those terms metaphors for a host of cultural meanings that paralleled modern notions of race. At about the same time, a radical and powerful pan–Native American movement developed among Eastern Woodland tribes, whose prophets often described separate creation stories for native peoples, whites, and blacks, and sought to unite all tribes into a single community to resist the colonial invasion.

Africans and their descendants in North American were similarly compelled by the circumstances of slavery to subsume tribal, religious, and national divisions, although some distinctions persisted. Initially,

most bound Africans were brought from the West Indies or South America, and some were born in European colonies. As British American slave societies developed after 1680, the balance of new slaves shifted to those brought from West and Central Africa. Between 1690 and 1740, the sudden and heavy importation of Africans into the Chesapeake created social conflicts between native-born slaves and new arrivals, particularly since Creole women often refused to marry African men.

After 1740, the importation of slaves rapidly declined, plantation sizes increased, and communities developed as slave demographics became more balanced. Slaves and their descendants forged a new and unique African American identity, encompassing shared or particularly appropriate aspects of tribal cultures, even as distinct experiences of enslavement and subordination created two distinct black communities (and cultures) in the Chesapeake and coastal Carolina.

Anglo-American preferences for lighter skin also may have been partially accepted by African descendants. Scattered evidence indicates that some mulattos considered themselves superior to those with darker skins, a propensity that became clearer in the nineteenth century.

Diversity in the Mid-Eighteenth Century

After 1700, colonial British America became increasingly diverse: as growing numbers of Africans were imported into the coastal South, large numbers of Germans and Scots-Irish immigrated to New York and Pennsylvania. By the middle of the century, Africans were about a third of the population in the South (and a majority in some coastal counties), and more Irish and Germans than English were coming to the mainland colonies. Most of the Irish were Scottish Presbyterians, but about a quarter were Catholic. The Germans were primarily members of pietistic Protestant movements such as the Moravians, who tended to form insular settlements and sought to maintain their distinctive language and culture.

Some Anglo-Americans reacted to the growing diversity in racial terms. For example, Benjamin Franklin, who noted in *Observations Concerning the Increase of Mankind* (1751) that "the Number of purely white People in the World is proportionably very small," called the German immigrants (and most Europeans) an alien "swarthy" race, and advocated keeping out

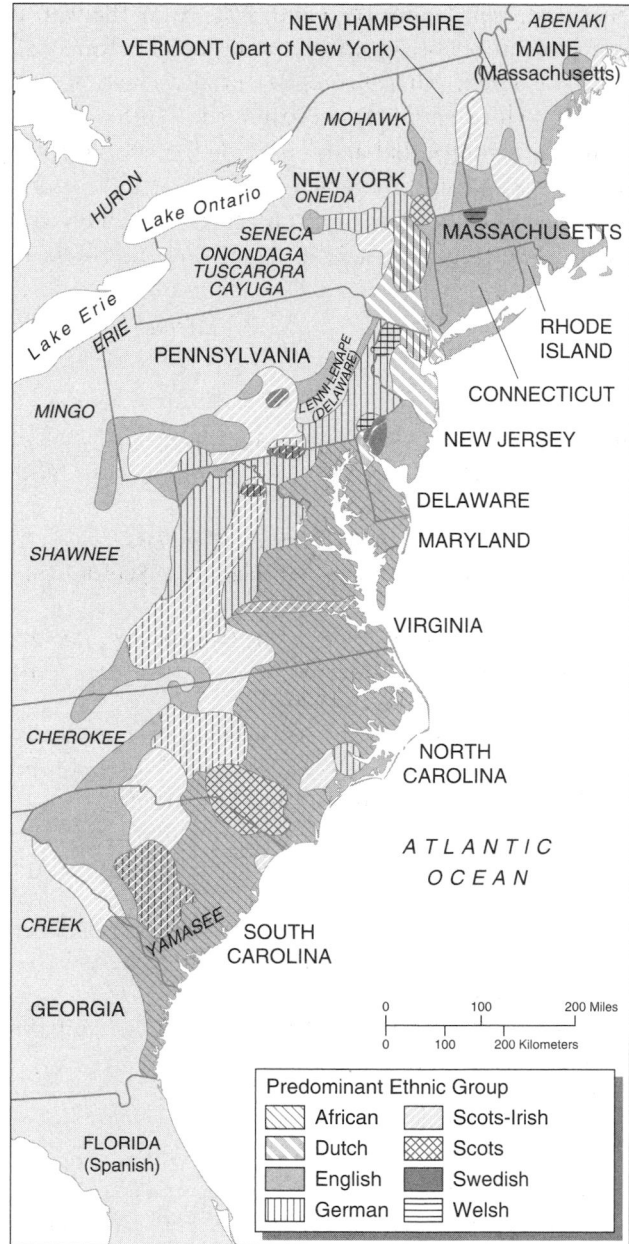

European and African Ethnic Groups, North America, 1775. While administered by the British government, on the eve of the American Revolution, the thirteen colonies were made up of a complex mix of European and African ethnic groups. *(Carto-Graphics)*

"Blacks and Tawneys" in order to ensure that "the lovely White and Red" remained "the Complexion of my country."

Franklin's outburst not only showed the ambiguous nature of Anglo-American racial concepts and how some white men continued to see an essential brotherhood between themselves and Native Americans, but it also pointed to how even the few colonists who, like Franklin, objected to the practice of slavery

still accepted racist beliefs. In fact, the first American antislavery tract, Samuel Sewall's *Selling of Joseph* (1700), while positing the essential unity of mankind beginning with a single creation, called for an end to importing African slaves because "there is such a disparity in their Conditions, Color & Hair, that they can never embody with us . . . but still remain in our Body Politic as a kind of extravasat[e] the Blood"—that is, outside the community.

By the middle of the eighteenth century, Anglo-American concepts of race were a confusing mélange of concepts, prejudices, fears, norms, and laws—all of which coalesced into two seemingly contradictory yet reinforcing tendencies. The first was a bichrome, hierarchical demarcation of "white" versus "colored," which was driven by the race-based slave system, generations of laws that painted blacks as inferior, and insecurities about black revolts. In this sense, differences among Europeans were perceived as ethnic rather than racial; the former could be readily altered or reshaped over time, while the latter was innate and unchangeable and marked the boundary between superior and inferior peoples.

One element shaping this shift in perception was the increasing intermarriage between Native American survivors and blacks within areas of English domination. Anglo-Americans came to view the remaining coastal Native Americans as part of an undifferentiated "people of color," and legislatures began to link Native Americans and blacks in restrictive racial laws. This bichrome view of race expressed the most fundamental characteristic of power and domination in colonial British America by the mid-eighteenth century. It would be embedded in the first federal census of 1790, with categories of "slave," "white," and "all other free persons."

The second tendency was to emphasize human complexity and diversity, which was expressed primarily by the Enlightenment effort to catalogue and order the natural world by detailing innate and unvarying differences between species, including humans. This was driven in part by the continuing discovery of new and strange animals in the Americas, Africa, and Asia; it also was based on a growing understanding of reproduction, which emphasized the continuity of physical traits.

In 1684, François Bernier differentiated mankind into four to six groups and, not surprisingly, picked skin color as the best characteristic to distinguish each race. A half century later, Charles Linnaeus in *Systema Naturae* tried to catalogue all living things, including humans, and nearly every subsequent scientific study began with that paradigm. This new system was vague and malleable, and, while it was not innately judgmental, it could be used to prove or disprove a hierarchy of races.

Many Anglo-American intellectuals, including Benjamin Rush, proclaimed that whites and blacks were equal, and that all differences were environmental—much as John Locke described the human mind, regardless of race, as a tabula rasa, or blank slate. Others, particularly Southerners deeply rooted in their slave societies, utilized Enlightenment ideas to solidify older, amorphous notions of race. Thomas Jefferson's *Notes on the State of Virginia*, which he wrote between 1782 and 1783, used his observations of slave behavior to detail how they lacked "reflective" and "imaginative" abilities; he strongly suggested ("a suspicion only") that blacks "are inferior to the whites in the endowments both of body and mind." Ironically, he also countered French scientist Georges Buffon's contention that the North American environment "degenerated" animals (including humans), vigorously defending the essential equality between Europeans and Native Americans and pointing to cultural factors as the sole causes of Native American barbarity.

By the outbreak of the Revolutionary War, scientific ideas of innate racial differences had joined with less reasoned prejudices to form the dominant concept of race. Despite an upsurge of Enlightenment egalitarianism among some American intellectuals in the wake of the Revolution, most considered race to be considered innate and hierarchical: it was connected to skin color, denoted an individual's intellectual and moral condition, and served as the key indicator of one's social and legal status. Any recognizable amount of African ancestry would condemn an individual to the lowest rank.

By the early nineteenth century, European and American intellectuals had rejected Enlightenment notions of environmentalism and, extending Jefferson's ideas, constructed an increasingly elaborate system that ranked human races in terms of innate intelligence and morals, with Africans (or one particular group of Africans, which Europeans called the Hottentots) at the bottom. This marked the genesis of modern racism, because the notion of black inferiority was justified by supposedly dispassionate, provable scientific data, and also because such distinctions were unchangeable, and any modifications violated natural law.

In this form, racism became deeply rooted in American culture and institutions, Northern as well as Southern, well before the Civil War. After the war, it continued to shape American thought and culture well into the twentieth century, essentially creating two worlds, white and black, within the United States. While the intellectual and legal tide has since turned, and race is increasingly depicted as a social and cultural construct akin to ethnicity, contests for economic and political power continue to divide whites and blacks in America.

Daniel R. Mandell

Bibliography

Berkhofer, Jr., Robert F. *The White Man's Indian: Images of the American Indian from Columbus to the Present*. New York: Alfred A. Knopf, 1978.

Berlin, Ira. *Many Thousands Gone: The First Two Centuries of Slavery in North America*. Cambridge, MA: Harvard University Press, 1998.

Breen, T. H., and Stephen Innes. *"My Own Ground": Race and Freedom in Virginia's Eastern Shore, 1640–1676*. New York: Oxford University Press, 1980.

Brown, Kathleen. *Good Wives, Nasty Wenches, and Ancient Patriarchs: Gender, Race, and Power in Colonial Virginia*. Chapel Hill: University of North Carolina Press, 1986.

Chapin, Joyce. *Subject Matter: Technology, the Body, and Science in the Anglo-American Frontier, 1500–1676*. Cambridge, MA: Harvard University Press, 2001.

Dowd, Gregory. *A Spirited Resistance: The North American Struggle for Unity, 1745–1815*. Baltimore: Johns Hopkins University Press, 1992.

Godbeer, Richard. *Sexual Revolution in Early America*. Baltimore: Johns Hopkins University Press, 2002.

Handlin, Oscar, and Mary Handlin. "Origins of the Southern Labor System," *William and Mary Quarterly*, 3rd ser., 7 (1950): 199–222.

Jordan, Winthrop D. *White Over Black: American Attitudes Toward the Negro, 1550–1812*. Chapel Hill: University of North Carolina Press, 1968.

Kulikoff, Allan. *Tobacco and Slaves: The Development of Southern Cultures in the Chesapeake, 1680–1800*. Chapel Hill: University of North Carolina Press, 1986.

Mandell, Daniel R. "The Saga of Sara Muckamugg: Indian and African American Intermarriage in Colonial New England." In *Sex, Love, Race: Crossing Boundaries in North American History*, edited by Martha Hodes. New York: New York University Press, 1998.

McGiffert, Michael, ed. "Constructing Race: Differentiating Peoples in the Early Modern World," *William and Mary Quarterly*, 3rd ser., 54 (January 1997): 1–252.

Morgan, Edmund. *American Slavery, American Freedom: The Ordeal of Colonial Virginia*. New York: W. W. Norton, 1975.

Morgan, Philip. *Slave Counterpoint: Black Culture in the Eighteenth-Century Chesapeake and Lowcountry.* Chapel Hill: University of North Carolina Press, 1998.

Shoemaker, Nancy. "How Indians Got to Be Red." *American Historical Review* 102 (1997): 625–44.

Sweet, John W. *Bodies Politic: Negotiating Race in the American North, 1730–1830.* Baltimore: Johns Hopkins University Press, 2003.

Vaughan, Alden. *Roots of American Racism: Essays on the Colonial Experience.* New York: Oxford University Press, 1995.

Wade, Peter. *Race and Ethnicity in Latin America.* London: Pluto Press, 1997.

Religion

Religion, which is to say, essentially, Christianity, figured mightily in the European settlement of North America. Personal commitments to build a godly society, escape persecution, or proselytize the "heathen" impelled individuals by the tens of thousands to cross the Atlantic, while national religious identifications helped fuel monarchs' determination to quash the imperial ambitions of their "heretical" or "papist" rivals. Nevertheless, in none of the territories claimed by the major European combatants did organized churches resembling those of the homeland appear quickly, if at all, although the Catholic powers—Spain and France—erected systems of missions and *reserves* for converted natives.

In seventeenth-century Anglo-America, the spawn of Protestant England, only New Englanders erected a stable church order; in the South, most settlers lived outside any congregation. That situation changed significantly during the eighteenth century. The migration of non-English Europeans increased the colonies' ethnic diversity and, concurrently, their religious pluralism; scattered churches consolidated themselves into permanent denominations; a major mechanism for recruiting the mass of unchurched settlers—the evangelical revival—took root; church membership grew apace; and an increasing percentage of European Americans styled themselves true Christians.

Pluralism and Christian identity had their limits, however; colonists dismissed the faiths of Native Americans and of African slaves. For their part, most native peoples rejected the cross and militantly defended their own faiths. African Americans, struggling to salvage what shards of their traditions the Middle Passage had spared, remained almost entirely outside Christian orbits until the nineteenth century.

Religion also played a role in the American Revolution. Many churchgoers understood rebellion as the godly duty to defend themselves from British corruption and perceived the republic as the political embodiment of Protestant values. At the same time, the framers of the Federal Constitution and Bill of Rights took pains to recognize the rights of religious minorities. The colonial and revolutionary experience deeded to future Americans the dual and potentially discordant images of the United States as both a nation "under God" and a haven for religious freedom.

European Background and Non-English Settlement

European colonization began against the backdrop of medieval Christendom's fragmentation. Inaugurated by Martin Luther's promulgation of his Ninety-five Theses in 1517, the Protestant Reformation challenged Roman Catholic theology, liturgy, piety, and ecclesiology across a wide front. From Protestants' fundamental principles of *solafideism* (sinners are judged by their faith alone, not for any merit accruing to their deeds) and *sola scriptura* (the Bible is the only authority for salvation) derived two important corollaries: The priesthood is neither a superior order nor a requisite means for salvation, since individuals guided by Scripture have access to God without clerical mediation, and most Catholic ceremonial practice is false, because it lacks biblical sanction.

Protestants themselves were divided on many issues, such as how much power to accord the laity in running the church and the state in overseeing it. Those known as Reformed Protestants (or Calvinists, after the leading theologian John Calvin) were more willing than were Lutherans to grant the male laity substantial authority in exercising discipline over their congregations and to assert the church's independence from state control in all matters pertaining to theology and worship. Calvinists also declared that magistrates wield power by God's authority and have an obligation to protect the true church, for which duties the people owe them full obedience—except when they transgress divine law, in which case God ordains their overthrow.

The Protestant Reformation galvanized the Roman Catholic Church to address the conditions that

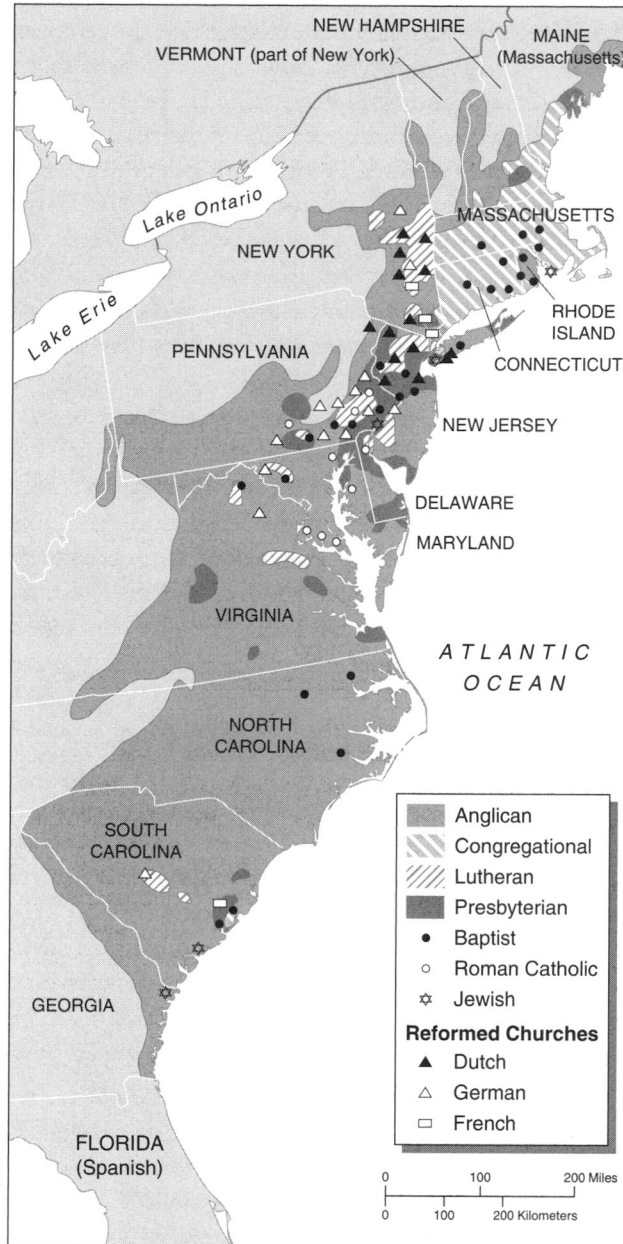

European Religions, North America, 1750. The above map shows the various Christian (and Jewish) sects in the thirteen colonies in 1750. This diversity reveals one of the primary reasons the founders of the American republic decided against the establishment of a state religion. *(Carto-Graphics)*

had precipitated schism. Although affirming traditional dogmas, the Catholic Church sought to improve the clergy's education and heighten the importance of individual (as opposed to collective) devotions; it also launched a number of new clerical orders, most notably the Jesuits, dedicated to rolling back Protestantism.

By 1600—the eve of Europe's permanent settlement of North America—the Catholic Church had

stabilized its control over much of the Continent, while Protestants appeared more frequently the farther north and northwest one went. This latitudinal religious topography combined with a longitudinal economic and racial one—colonizing was a western European activity—and with a general theory concerning the relationship between religion and the state to shape the contest for the "New World."

Since the Roman Empire had adopted Christianity as its official faith in the fourth century, convention held that a state should prescribe religious uniformity, for to countenance multiple beliefs invited political and social discord. Spain's national church was Catholic, as was France's (although a Protestant minority, the Huguenots, fortified towns along the Atlantic Coast), while the United Provinces (the Netherlands) embraced Reformed Protestantism, and England developed a Protestant Episcopal church. Where these powers were successful in establishing settlements would profoundly influence North America's religious geography.

Attempting to protect the wealth of Mexico and Central America, the Spanish flung outposts across the northern extremities of their American empire in an arc running through modern Florida, Texas, New Mexico, Arizona, and California. The church participated integrally in the Spanish scheme to conquer and convert the native peoples. Hence, in the Borderlands, where remote, impoverished garrisons attracted few colonials, it characteristically took the form of missions staffed by members of the Franciscan order who ministered to native peoples, rather than parishes occupied by "secular" priests who served European Americans. Mission compounds (*doctrinas*) centered about a sanctuary, surrounded by outbuildings, fortifications, and natives' fields. Spanish colonization expropriated native labor whenever possible. While the church often succeeded in mitigating the worst exploitation, the missions themselves depended on it.

The Spanish launched three major campaigns in the Borderlands. In northern New Mexico, as early as 1630, twenty-five missions included 25,000–30,000 Pueblo peoples. In Florida, two lines of *doctrinas*—one running north along the Atlantic coast, the second reaching west toward the Panhandle—reached perhaps 60,000 people by 1634. And in California, as a result of a campaign initiated in 1769, total conversions reached perhaps 100,000.

In the long run, however, the devastation of native populations by epidemic disease, aggression by European and indigenous foes, and resistance by the mission Native Americans themselves diminished Catholicism's presence in the region. The Timucuan Revolt of 1656 weakened the central Florida missions; fifty years later, the English, with their Creek allies, collapsed the entire system. The California missions disappeared when Americans swarmed into the territory in the mid-nineteenth century. Only in New Mexico—and only after the Spanish had suppressed the Pueblo Revolt, which expelled them from the region between 1680 and 1692—did the missions establish a lasting group of Catholic indigenes. With the exception of Maryland, Catholicism came of age in the United States only in the nineteenth century, long after Protestantism had established the cultural ground rules.

In New France, parishes of European American Catholics arose alongside—but ecclesiastically, politically, and culturally segregated from—Native American churches. Proselytizing the native peoples was a major goal in New France, especially after Cardinal Richelieu, head of the Royal Council of State, reorganized the faltering colony in 1627. But because neither the Crown nor the mercantile companies that promoted French colonization could afford to send clerics, responsibility devolved upon the religious orders themselves.

The most effective missionaries during the seventeenth century were the Jesuits, who paddled hundreds of miles to preach the Gospel in Huron and Algonquin villages. As warfare with the Five Nations of the Iroquois forced tribes from ancestral homes, the French established *reserves* for Christianized Native Americans, who obtained educational and medical services from nuns like the Ursulines, the Hospitallers, and the Sisters of Charity—a female religious presence unique in colonial North American history.

The Jesuits claimed to have baptized 16,000 souls from 1632 to 1672, only a minority of the native population, but the ministrations of the Catholic orders, male and female, played a critical role in New France's survival. The good relations they fostered with native peoples facilitated the trade in furs, New France's signal export commodity, and military alliances, on which the colony's existence depended.

The parochial church took longer to organize. Not until 1674 did the pope appoint a bishop, and only in the eighteenth century were the majority of priests themselves colonial-born Creoles. Operating in different intellectual and social contexts, the Canadian church departed in some ways from French norms. Less defensive about Protestant polemics and relatively untouched by Enlightenment skepticism, the clergy preached—and, far more than their European peers, practiced—the moral rigor characteristic of the French

Catholic Reformation. They also presided over congregations of independent landowners, who paid lower tithes than did French peasants. The landowners' sense of autonomy led to practices—such as a casual view of when it was necessary to baptize one's child—that prompted chronic clerical scolding. Nevertheless, the laity heeded their priests (conceptions plummeted during Lent, for instance) and gave the church their full loyalty. Catholicism became a major marker of French Canadian identity after Britain took over New France in 1763.

Leery of settling too close to the Spanish, who had massacred one settlement in 1565, the French left a thousand-mile gap between themselves and their Catholic rivals, a territory that was open to Protestant occupation. The Dutch seized the opportunity to sprawl New Netherland across the Hudson and Delaware Rivers. Commerce, not religion, drove Dutch colonization, reflecting a sentiment common in civic and mercantile circles that toleration preserved comity and commerce more readily than did religious exclusivity.

By 1600, most of the Dutch Republic's seven provinces in Europe had recognized the supremacy of the Reformed Church. Although the *predikanten* (preachers) of the Dutch Reformed Church urged the state to impose uniformity, the magistrates' unwillingness to cede power to the clergy, coupled with merchants' fears that enforcing doctrinal orthodoxy would hurt trade, frustrated the ministers' hopes. Known for its toleration, the Netherlands attracted Jews and Protestant dissenters from across Europe.

These attitudes carried over into New Netherland, where the Dutch Reformed Church had little influence. The ruling West India Company preferred making profits to saving souls. It sought to dampen religious controversy in order to maintain political stability and welcomed anyone who would settle, regardless of their faith. As late as 1650, only two Reformed congregations, 150 miles apart, served the colony.

Peter Stuyvesant, New Netherland's longest-serving and most competent director-general, did try to implement a policy of religious uniformity in the 1650s, but the company overrode his plans to expel Lutherans, Jews, and Quakers. The Dutch Reformed Church gained greater cultural authority among ethnic Dutch settlers only after England conquered the colony in 1664, by which time the newly named province of New York had gained a reputation for religious heterogeneity.

Seventeenth Century

The notion that religion in Anglo-America enjoyed a "golden age" in the seventeenth century comes from two perspectives, both of which focus overmuch on New England. The scholarly version comprehends Puritanism as a tightly argued intellectual construction that declined in the century following the founding of Massachusetts under the pressure of internal contradictions, social change, and secularization. The popular variant focuses on the intensity of Puritan spirituality, declares America to have been founded on Christian principles, and laments the present's alleged falling away from the faith of our fathers.

Both stances are flawed. The first essentializes Puritanism and fails to track how it adapted to America. The second perspective imputes the prevailing minority's piety to the entire population and misses how ecclesiastically unique seventeenth-century New England was. More accurately, religious authority outside New England struggled to assert itself. Churchmen did not exercise their accustomed power, the majority of colonists attended services sporadically, if at all, and unorthodox beliefs infiltrated popular practice.

At the same time, the outlines of a distinctive American religious culture began to take shape. This was based on more extensive lay governance than existed in Europe, a greater variety of churches from which to choose, religious affiliation increasingly dependent on individuals' voluntary choices rather than on custom, decree, or family habit, and, in many places, the state's inability (even unwillingness) to enforce religious uniformity.

Although their theological commitments varied, English monarchs from Henry VIII (r. 1509–1547) to Charles I (r. 1625–1649) dreamed of erecting a national church to which all subjects belonged. None of them achieved that goal, however, and the Church of England's failure to include all the king's men (and women) dogged efforts to realize it in the colonies. The church that emerged adopted a Protestantized worship that nevertheless retained Catholic practices (such as allowing priests to wear ornate clerical garb); it also inscribed Reformed theology into its creeds without encouraging Calvinism's disciplinary apparatus or its scripturalism.

This "middle way" angered both loyal Catholics (recusants), who detested any departure from the "good old religion," and the "hotter sort of Protestants." The latter were derided as Puritans, although they denominated themselves the "godly"; they maintained that the Church of England had neither sufficiently purged itself of "Romish" practices nor effectively instituted a Reformed ecclesiology. In the interest of achieving uniformity, the government suppressed the Catholics, sometimes lethally, and periodically harassed the Puritans.

Unlike the Catholic Church in Spanish and French dominions, the Church of England did not deeply involve itself in seventeenth-century English colonizing efforts, which were undertaken by private parties—mercantile companies or aristocratic proprietors—not the Crown. Nor did it work actively on its own behalf. Internal conflicts over its constitution, theology, and liturgy, culminating during the 1640s and 1650s in the attempt to institute a presbyterian form of government, distracted it from organizing its American dominions. Meanwhile, Puritans, Catholics, and Quakers, fleeing religious turmoil, set up their own churches. In places like New England, these dissenters vastly outnumbered the established church's own adherents.

Virginia, the first permanent English colony, formally established the Church of England as early as 1619. Governor William Berkeley expelled Puritan dissenters in the 1640s, but no one in England took permanent responsibility for managing the church until the Bishop of London did so in 1677. By this point, the Old Dominion's laity had arrogated substantial power to themselves.

In the absence of a presiding bishop, the House of Burgesses watched over the clergy's behavior and created lay vestries that took care of the congregation's property, levied ecclesiastical taxes, and chose the clergyman they wanted the governor to install, a liberty unimaginable in England. As the Crown rationalized English imperial administration late in the century, the Bishop of London in 1693 installed a commissary, his personal representative, to try clergy for malfeasance, oversee their parishes, and convene them to discuss church business. The lay vestries, however, retained their authority, and the church never seated an American bishop.

Elsewhere, the Anglican Church lay thin on the ground. One minister complained in 1676 that Maryland's three "conformable" clergy could not possibly take charge of an estimated 20,000 souls. Hence, the colony had become "A Sodom of uncleanness." In New England, the state church played the unaccustomed role of minority dissenter to the most powerful eccle-

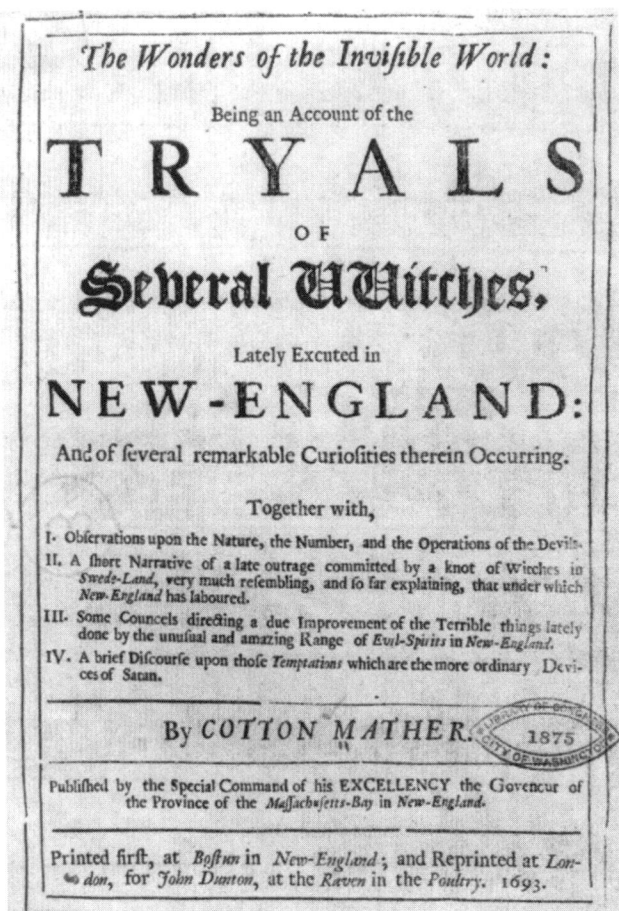

The Wonders of the Invisible World:

Being an Account of the

TRYALS

OF

Several Witches,

Lately Excuted in

NEW-ENGLAND:

And of several remarkable Curiosities therein Occurring.

Together with,

I. Obfervations upon the Nature, the Number, and the Operations of the Devils.

II. A fhort Narrative of a late outrage committed by a knot of Witches in *Swede-Land*, very much refembling, and fo far explaining, that under which *New-England* has laboured.

III. Some Councels directing a due Improvement of the Terrible things lately done by the unufual and amazing Range of *Evil-Spirits* in *New-England*.

IV. A brief Difcourfe upon thofe *Temptations* which are the more ordinary Devices of Satan.

By COTTON MATHER.

Publifhed by the Special Command of his EXCELLENCY the Governour of the Province of the *Maffachufetts-Bay* in *New-England*.

Printed firft, at *Bofton* in *New-England*; and Reprinted at *London*, for *John Dunton*, at the *Raven* in the *Poultry*. 1693.

In his pamphlet *The Wonders of the Invisible World* (1693), the influential Puritan clergyman Cotton Mather offered an account and defense of the Salem witch trials. Mather's teachings epitomized the strict Puritan orthodoxy of seventeenth-century New England. *(Library of Congress, LC-USZ62-75554)*

siastical organization in colonial Anglo-America, Puritan Congregationalism.

Puritanism is best understood not as a theological system but as a religious temperament centered around the experience of conversion (the New Birth in which the Holy Spirit regenerates the soul by grace). As such, it is fashioned within Reformed Protestant theology and dedicated to morally reforming society through the collaboration of ministers, magistrates, and laity. Puritanism took root in, as one historian has remarked, a "mood of sour discontent" with the Church of England's incomplete reformation. For some six decades thereafter, the Puritans remained (with the exception of a few hundred Separatists) within the church, while setting themselves apart from their less godly neighbors in closely knit groups committed to prayer, study, and moral improvement.

The ascendancy during the 1620s of an Arminian clerical clique, who subscribed to a nonorthodox theology of grace and a sumptuous liturgical style hugely at odds with the Puritans' preferences for plainness, helped precipitate the "Great Migration" to New England. The Puritans emigrated to this New World to form what Massachusetts Governor John Winthrop christened the "City upon a Hill," a society that, like ancient Israel, had collectively entered into a national covenant with God. Its members would perform all of God's commandments and, for their obedience, he would bless their enterprise.

In what might be called the "First Puritan Reformation," the founding generation of settlers constructed what they considered a biblically sanctioned church order. Far from implementing a theocracy (a state governed by religious authority), it delegated responsibilities for its maintenance to its three sociological constituents: The clergy would define doctrine, rulers would enforce religious uniformity, and families would patrol their neighborhoods to enforce moral standards.

Under this system, encoded in the Cambridge Platform of 1648, the male laity, not an ecclesiastical hierarchy, held the power to create new churches. They did this by voluntarily gathering regenerate "Saints" (those who had experienced conversion), calling for the minister, and, with their pastor, judging who should be admitted or expelled.

The survival of the City upon a Hill was predicated, Puritans believed, on the continued existence of a godly majority, committed to suppressing dissent and upholding moral norms. From a historical perspective, we can determine that it also depended on a population characterized by relatively little occupational differentiation or inequalities of wealth, a group bound together both by strong social networks and by high levels of ideological commitment.

By the later seventeenth century, changing conditions were undermining these prerequisites. Families seeking land broke away from town centers, religious dissenters (Quakers, Baptists, and Anglicans) claimed the right to form churches, piety among the second and third generations flagged, economic change precipitated the appearance of a "counterculture" of festivity contemptuous of the Saints' highhanded righteousness, and imperial authorities increasingly intruded into colonial affairs. In the face of these challenges, ministers launched the "Second Puritan Reformation," an effort to recover the presumed godliness of the first generation in circumstances (such as the loss of the Massachusetts charter in 1684) that made the old moral alliance of ministers, magistrates, and laity increasingly difficult to sustain.

The ministers' program took various forms. They applied a rhetorical style, called the "Jeremiad," urging magistrates to continue supporting the church and the laity to tighten family government. They proposed innovations to the sacramental system that allowed a greater number of people to undergo baptism or take the Lord's Supper. A concerted effort was made to suppress, or at least rein in, the counterculture. They also experimented with various devices—covenant renewal ceremonies, a more emotional homiletic style—to revivify piety and excite large numbers of people to experience the New Birth concurrently. The Saints never recaptured their majority status, and the British government ultimately forced them to tolerate other churches, but the Congregationalists continued to dominate New England's cultural and religious life throughout the eighteenth century.

While Virginia, Massachusetts, and Connecticut strove (with varying degrees of success) to impose religious uniformity, three colonies took the step—radical for the seventeenth century—of promoting religious liberty. The Calvert family founded Maryland in 1632 as both a refuge for English Catholics and a proprietary domain from which they hoped to profit. Since Protestants comprised the vast bulk of English people, the Calverts encouraged them to settle, promising that they might worship as they pleased. In 1649, the Maryland assembly codified such an arrangement in an Act Concerning Religion, which assured that authorities would trouble no one professing any form of Trinitarian Christianity.

Roger Williams developed a more liberal policy for Rhode Island, which he founded in 1636 after Massachusetts had banished him. Williams believed that papal corruption had broken the apostolic succession and so made constituting any pure church impossible until Christ's return. Consequently, the state had no business either supporting any church (since none warranted its aid) or punishing dissent (since none could claim to hold the truth). Rhode Island soon attracted dissenters unwelcome in either Old or New England.

Similarly disposed to Williams, Pennsylvania's proprietor, William Penn, based his apology for religious liberty on Whig theories of personal liberty and Quaker doctrines of the "inner Light," that is, the divine spark that all human beings possess and that no government has the right to coerce. Forced worship both "stinks in God's nostrils," Penn declared, and works

contrary to its political intentions by alienating subjects from rather than bonding them to their prince. These attitudes grounded Pennsylvania's policy of permitting all theists to worship as they wished, although laws forbade Catholics from holding office.

Few colonists heeded the experiments in Rhode Island or Maryland. Rhode Island's reputation as a sectarian sinkhole and, during the Revolution, a political pariah isolated it; while in Maryland, Protestants stripped Catholics of their political rights in the eighteenth century. Pennsylvania's growing wealth, however—it quickly earned the sobriquet "the best poor man's country"—provided a widely noted counterexample to the ancient notion that only religious uniformity could underwrite prosperity.

Eighteenth Century

Christian institutions and beliefs solidified their presence in Anglo-America during the century following 1680. The number of Protestant churches multiplied and consolidated themselves into recognizable denominations. Presbyterians organized their first presbytery (a court composed of local ministers and lay elders) in 1706 and their first synod (a council of representatives from presbyteries) a decade later. Quakers erected a hierarchy of meetings—weekly, monthly, quarterly, and yearly—and corresponded with similar bodies in Britain. Particular (Calvinistic) Baptists put together the Philadelphia Association in 1707. And the German Reformed churches adopted a *coetus* (an administrative gathering of ministers and elders) in 1747.

Nevertheless, large numbers of people—especially Eastern Woodlands natives and African slaves—remained virtually unincorporated. To recruit unchurched European Americans (and, to a far lesser extent, people of color), ministers in several denominations fastened upon the revival. These mass meetings, in which preachers, using highly emotional language, exhorted audiences to accept Christ immediately, served as a mechanism that might catalyze hundreds of conversions at once.

These developments elaborated on but did not substantially alter patterns previously laid down. Many colonies granted certain churches taxation privileges, but nowhere—neither in the South, where provincial legislatures from Maryland to Georgia formally established the Church of England, nor in much of New England, where the Congregational churches predominated—did a single church holding monopoly privileges over taxation and attendance prevail. Rhode

Island, Pennsylvania, Delaware, and New Jersey erected no such establishments at all, although most colonies did restrict office holding to certain groups.

The ideas of Roger Williams and William Penn notwithstanding, most colonists did not regard religious freedom as a positive value. In some instances, religious majorities sought to curtail the activities of minorities. Examples include Anglican persecution of evangelicals in the Southern interior and Congregational harassment of Anglicans, Baptists, and Quakers in New England.

Nevertheless, in most places, a "grudging toleration" prevailed. Moreover, even though the churches bickered with, competed for converts against, and occasionally tried politically to hamper each other, colonists constructing their religious identities in opposition to Britain's enemies considered themselves as resolutely Protestant. To their minds, Catholicism nurtured not only doctrinal error but also subservience to the papacy, political authoritarianism, and tyranny, evils that would befall them should the world's freest empire—in the sense of allowing its subjects basic freedoms and limited self-rule—falter.

Religious diversity emerged in part from divisions over theology, liturgy, and devotional styles, such as the Baptist schism from New England Congregationalism, or from the appearance of such new European traditions as Methodism. The major factor, however, was immigration. Most eighteenth-century migrants traveled from parts of the British Isles other than England, and from northwest Europe, Africa, or the West Indies; ethnicity and national origin frequently correlated strongly with religious affiliation.

The preferred church government of perhaps half a dozen seventeenth-century congregations, Presbyterianism, grew rapidly in the Mid-Atlantic colonies with the arrival of Highland, Lowland, and Ulster Scots. A few thousand Huguenots expelled from France by the revocation of the Edict of Nantes in 1685 ultimately found their way to Massachusetts, New York, and South Carolina, although by mid-eighteenth century, they had merged with the Anglicans. The largest European American exodus issued from southwest German states, strewing Lutherans, German Reformed, and various sectarians—Mennonites, Schwenkfelders, Moravians—across the Mid-Atlantic provinces (especially Pennsylvania) and the Southern interior.

The rising number of non-English European Americans and of African Americans fostered pluralism, albeit of a decidedly Protestant cast. Britain's Protestant identity and the colonists' virulent anti-Catholicism kept the number of Catholics to a bare minimum. Although Parliament allowed the colonies (but not the home country) to naturalize Jews, only a few thousand resided there.

Pluralism had other limits as well. Despite sporadic missionary efforts, Native Americans, for the most part, remained outside colonial churches. Eastern Woodland religious beliefs traversed an axis radically different from that of Christianity, which construes the central relationship between people and God in terms of sin and redemption: Human sinfulness, both innate (original sin) and volitional (specific transgressions), indicts every individual and requires Christ's intercession for eternal life. Native Americans, on the contrary, did not conceive a radical split between "natural" and "supernatural" realms. Instead, they interacted constantly with myriad spirits that conferred or withheld "power" (the Algonquin word is *manitou*), the ability to grow or catch food or kill enemies. A life well lived consisted in navigating the natural world in such a way as to maintain cordial relationships with all of the power-giving spirits, thereby maintaining one's health and strength.

Notions of proselytizing the natives appeared at the outset of English colonization. The seal of the Massachusetts Bay Company even featured a Native American saying, "Come over and help us." Despite some major efforts, such as John Eliot's project of founding English-style towns and churches among the Massachusetts Algonquin and the Mayhew family's longstanding mission to the Martha's Vineyard Wampanoag, New Englanders generally were not interested in such conversion efforts.

The greatest success in Anglo-America came not from the English but from the German Moravians, who, in the eighteenth century, converted hundreds of Native Americans in Pennsylvania and the Ohio territory. Compared to Spanish and French efforts, however, Anglo-American proselytizing did not amount to much, thwarted as it was by the absence of royal involvement (the British monarchy never sponsored missions), the lack of means (exacerbated by the dearth of clerics who could free themselves from serving their own congregations), and, most importantly, the Native Americans' resistance, both passive and active.

Most native peoples spurned the Gospel message, because it required them to renounce their own deities or because they did not witness European American Christians practicing what they preached. Quiet dismissal turned to violent rejection as the Anglo-American population doubled each quarter-century, pressuring Native American lands and catalyzing native "revitalization movements." Native "prophets" diagnosed their peoples' debilitation as the result of embracing European American goods and their god; utter renunciation of these influences was prescribed as the only means of reacquiring spiritual power and tribal strength. One such movement, "Pontiac's Rebellion," ravaged the western frontier in 1763, and others dogged American expansion throughout the nineteenth century.

Africans lay equally outside Anglo-American Protestantism. Slavery's solution to the colonies' habitual labor shortage and its consequent pervasiveness, particularly in the South, spurred imports. By 1775, half a million African Americans, virtually all of them slaves, inhabited the colonies. The West African peoples who "provided" most of these slaves practiced a number of religions. Some had converted to Islam, but most believed in a High God, who remained distant from human affairs, and a multitude of lesser divinities, including one's ancestors, who involved themselves deeply in human affairs and had to be ritually appeased.

The Middle Passage ripped slaves from ceremonial observances and their sustaining kinship networks, prohibiting their replication in America. Recent captives might reinvigorate memories of specific African traditions. As the mainland slave population began to sustain itself by the later eighteenth century and importations directly from Africa declined, however, African Americans lost direct knowledge of their homeland. "The gods of Africa died," as one historian put it, but the broader African religious background did not. Spirit possession, accompanied by spiritually passionate singing and dancing, would eventually resurface in African American Christianity and infuse evangelical Protestantism.

Nevertheless, colonial missionaries reached fewer slaves than they did Native Americans. Strongest in the South, where most slaves lived, the Church of England initiated the most substantial effort, but it faced numerous obstacles. Imbued with a sense of their racial and cultural superiority, missionaries did not warm to their task and had trouble communicating with people who knew little or no English. Also, planters, many indifferent to Christianity, did not like losing their laborers' time and feared that the spiritual equality with masters implied by baptism would instigate slaves' indolence, sauciness, and rebellion.

It would be evangelical Protestants, particularly Methodists and Baptists, who took the conversion of African Americans seriously. Their activity began during the Revolutionary era, when blacks made up perhaps a quarter of their adherents in the South, but the full-fledged "plantation mission" took place only in the nineteenth century. Before then, the majority of slaves remained outside Christianity.

The presence of evangelical Protestants in the late-eighteenth-century South was largely due to the invention of revivalism. During the Second Puritan Reformation, ministers searched for ways to quicken the rates of conversion and recruit church members en masse, rather than waiting for the Spirit to work on individuals ad hoc. Solomon Stoddard of Northampton, Massachusetts, discovered the solution: a "season of refreshing," during which hortatory sermons, including invocations of hell (extremely rare among earlier Puritans), drew dozens into the church and improved the town's moral comportment (if only for a time).

A similar predilection for highly wrought preaching to stimulate the New Birth occurred in other Reformed Churches. Influenced by Pietism, a movement within German Lutheranism emphasizing the importance of personal feeling for spiritual living over assent to creedal formularies or the observance of ritual niceties, Theodore Jacob Frelinghuysen excited congregations in New Jersey's Raritan Valley during the 1720s. Based on precedents from a century earlier—when Presbyterians in Scotland and Ulster had celebrated the Lord's Supper at outdoor gatherings that occasionally sparked dozens of conversions—a group of ministers, gathered around William Tennent, lobbied the Philadelphia Synod in the 1730s to endorse "heart–religion" over doctrinal exactitude as the hallmark of Presbyterianism.

These local developments were subsumed in 1739–1741 by the "Great Awakening," which was catalyzed by George Whitefield. An ordained Anglican who, with John Wesley (Methodism's founder), pioneered the technique of "field preaching," Whitefield traveled throughout the colonies preaching the New Birth and eliciting enthusiastic crowds. The Awakening's manifest success in stimulating religious feeling led to the creation of two forms of revivalism. The first, theorized and practiced by Stoddard's grandson, Jonathan Edwards, took place in settled churches under the direction of their own pastors; the second followed Whitefield's model of an itinerant preacher converting the unchurched, who, in time, gathered new congregations. The Edwardsean type operated in New England, the region long accustomed to town settlements centered around church greens, but the Whitefieldian strain was far better suited to the dispersed and less

The English evangelist George Whitefield preached the "New Birth" to enthusiastic crowds throughout the colonies, helping to launch the religious revival known as the Great Awakening in the 1720s. *(Private Collection/Bridgeman Art Library)*

ecclesiastically organized populations more typical everywhere else, and, for this reason, it became the American Protestant norm.

Revolutionary Era

American religious culture played a subsidiary role in instigating the Revolution, but a major one in constituting the new nation. One scholar has deemed the Revolution a "religious war," fought between the Anglican British state and colonial dissenting Protestants concerned more about losing their religious freedom than their liberty and property. This interpretation rightly recognizes that non-Anglicans formed a majority in the colonies as a whole (Anglicans predominated in the South), that they perceived any attempt to strengthen the colonial Church of England as necessarily endangering their own churches' autonomy, and

that most of the Dissenters came out of Reformed Protestantism, which allowed the public to unseat transgressive rulers. Nevertheless, this argument wrongly assumes that eighteenth-century colonists identified themselves primarily as church members rather than as subjects heir to British liberty, fails adequately to explain why the majority of the Anglican laity (including George Washington, Thomas Jefferson, James Madison, and Patrick Henry) lined up with the patriots while some Dissenters joined the loyalists, and undervalues the political and constitutional issues that most agitated patriots. First and foremost, Americans fought for liberty and property.

Religion did, nevertheless, affect how colonists mobilized to rebel. For one thing, Reformed Protestantism formed an important element of the ideology of resistance; its standard themes about human sinfulness, the necessity of regeneration, the Christian duty to create a moral society, and God's never-ceasing governance of the universe intersected with "secular" ideologies depicting history as the incessant struggle to secure liberty against despots' drive to aggrandize power. The ingrained Protestant identity that had caused colonists previously to regard Britain as the bulwark of liberty against Catholic slavery now depicted the empire itself as equally tyrannical. Protestant ideology helped some colonists define the massive program of imperial reorganization that Parliament launched after 1763 as not simply a misguided attack on American rights but, more essentially, a manifestation of an eternally occurring type of corruption from which only independence could inoculate them.

Certain imperial actions disturbed colonists on grounds of interest as well as ideology. During the 1760s, some Anglicans, especially in the North (where the Church of England was weakest), lamented the absurdity of an episcopal church lacking a bishop and petitioned for an American see. Dissenters and Southern lay Anglicans protested. The former protested because they feared a bishopric as the first step to losing their religious freedom, the latter because they did not wish to cede their hold on church administration, and both protested because they regarded the plan as part of a larger conspiracy to deprive them of liberty. As the crisis over the Boston Tea Party spun toward war, Parliament recognized the Catholic Church in Quebec (whose European American population was almost entirely Catholic) without granting the French Canadians a legislature (which they did not want), firing Anglo-Americans' endemic anti-Catholicism and suggesting that Britain endorsed both authoritarian government and papism. Some people dreamed that the United States would create an utterly new society (a hope stamped into the Great Seal of the United States in the motto *novus ordo seclorum*—"a new order of the ages"). At some point, such thoughts helped convince colonists to revolt.

The settlement of religion—the formal acts and popular attitudes that realigned the relationship between church and state following independence—comprised one of the American Revolution's most radical consequences. The settlement exploded the notion that political stability and prosperity require religious uniformity, yet it did not completely wall off church from state. The American republic's system of dual federalism, which accorded the individual states substantial sovereignty over the national government, and Americans' identification of the United States as a "Christian"

(by which they meant "Protestant") nation, mitigated against such absolute segregation.

Building upon the colonies' de facto toleration, the revolutionary rhetoric about the individual's "unalienable" rights, and the participation of every religious group on the patriot side, all of the state constitutions provided for religious liberty. At the same time, most states did not consider freedom of conscience to be incompatible with either publicly financing religion in general or imposing religious qualifications for office holding. Three New England states (which had a long-standing history of state support for churches) and five states in all made some provision for fiscally supporting religion.

In Virginia, however, a concerted campaign orchestrated by Madison among evangelical Protestants influenced the legislature to vote down a controversial general assessment bill that would have allowed each person to designate to which church (or, as an option, school) his tax proceeds should go "to encourage public order." This bill was rejected in favor of Jefferson's Act Establishing Religious Freedom, which prohibited any such arrangement, because it violated the individual's right to worship according to one's conscience.

Eleven states passed test acts limiting one group or another (most often Roman Catholics, sometimes non-Trinitarians, more generally) from office. Although such disqualifications are antagonistic to modern notions of religious liberty, they did not appear so at the time, because virtually all Americans held republican and Protestant values to be indistinguishable. So axiomatic did this equation appear that even Virginia, the only state besides Rhode Island to hold that any government action concerning religion infringed on religious freedom, passed a law in 1792 discouraging anyone's celebrating the Sabbath on a day other than Sunday; this was done without any apparent sense of inconsistency.

Defining their task as deriving a republican solution for the problems of a republican polity, the framers of the federal Constitution of 1787 shied away from any discussion promoting religion. Drawn from diverse Protestant backgrounds (although as a group they tended overwhelmingly toward rationalism, and only one might be considered an evangelical) and disinclined to promote the interests of any specific creed or denomination, they sought to create a national governing structure that would avert the sectarian discord they feared would corrode republican institutions.

Unlike the Declaration of Independence, which postulates rights as "endowed" in human beings "by their Creator," the Constitution locates the source of federal power in "We, the People," and does not mention any divinity—about which failure some contemporary Christians complained. The document takes up religion in only two places: It allows federal and state officers to affirm, rather than swear, their loyalty to the Constitution (a concession to Quakers, who objected to oath taking because they claimed that forcing them to swear implied that they never told the truth except under pledge), and it forbids any religious test for national office—a provision contrary to what most state constitutions provided.

Because opponents of ratifying the Constitution argued that it did not properly protect individual rights, the first federal Congress drafted ten amendments that eventually became the Bill of Rights. The First Amendment secured the "free exercise" of religion, as had the states, but it also dictated, "Congress shall make no law respecting an establishment of religion." Many colonial and state governments had legislated financial support for churches or passed test acts, but contemporaries generally concurred that the term "establishment" referred not to these sorts of arrangements but only to "an exclusive government preference for one religion." Working from this definition, the Bill of Rights, in concert with the Constitution, seemed to suggest that the national government possessed no authority in religious matters. In practice, however, interpretations varied.

Some Americans regarded presidential proclamations for Americans to hold fast or thanksgiving days as representing an unwarranted governmental intrusion into religion. (As president, Jefferson refused to issue them.) While to most contemporaries, such actions appeared so consonant with Protestant (i.e., Christian), hence republican, values that they seemed merely commonplace moral expressions, not partisan pieties.

Toward Nineteenth-Century Evangelism

Developments during the colonial and revolutionary eras grounded the nineteenth-century religious order. This was characterized by the removal of all constitutional impediments to full religious freedom, such as test acts; widespread Protestant acceptance that no denomination can call itself the one true church; acceptance of the voluntary principle that private contributions, not state funding, should support religion; the tendency, albeit not absolute, to keep government from intruding into religious matters; and the assertion that the United States was a Christian Protestant nation, a device that extended the Puritans' national covenant to the entire nation.

These patterns underlay the "evangelical surge" that transformed American religious life in the first half of the nineteenth century, resulting in rates of church membership higher than anything attained in the seventeenth and eighteenth centuries. They also created two discrepant visions of the United States: a Christian nation specially privileged by God, and a haven of religious freedom. The first view is exclusivist, the second more liberal. Modern advocates of each position argue that early American history credits their view alone. In fact, it endorses both.

Charles L. Cohen

Bibliography

Andrews, Dee E. *The Methodists and Revolutionary America, 1760–1800: The Shaping of an Evangelical Culture.* Princeton, NJ: Princeton University Press, 2000.

Axtell, James. *The Invasion Within: The Contest of Cultures in Colonial North America.* New York: Oxford University Press, 1985.

Bonomi, Patricia U. *Under the Cope of Heaven: Religion, Society, and Politics in Early America.* New York: Oxford University Press, 1986; 2nd ed., 2003.

Butler, Jon. *Awash in a Sea of Faith: Christianizing the American People.* Cambridge, MA: Harvard University Press, 1990.

———. "Religion in Colonial America." In *Religion in American Life: A Short History,* edited by Jon Butler, Grant Wacker, and Randall Balmer. New York: Oxford University Press, 2003.

Cohen, Charles L. "The Colonization of North America as an Episode in the History of Christianity." *Church History,* 72 (September, 2003): 553–68.

———. "The Post-Puritan Paradigm in Early American Religious History." *William and Mary Quarterly,* 3d ser., 54 (1997): 695–722.

Crawford, Michael J. *Seasons of Grace: Colonial New England's Revival Tradition in Its British Context.* New York: Oxford University Press, 1991.

Curry, Thomas. *The First Freedoms: Church and State in America to the Passage of the First Amendment.* New York: Oxford University Press, 1986.

Dowd, Gregory Evans. *A Spirited Resistance: The North American Indian Struggle for Unity, 1745–1815.* Baltimore: Johns Hopkins University Press, 1992.

Foster, Stephen. *The Long Argument: English Puritanism and the Shaping of New England Culture, 1570–1700.* Published for the Institute of Early American History and Culture in Williamsburg, Virginia. Chapel Hill: University of North Carolina Press, 1991.

Frey, Sylvia R., and Betty Wood. *Come Shouting to Zion: African American Protestantism in the American South and British Caribbean to 1830.* Chapel Hill: University of North Carolina Press, 1998.

Gutiérrez, Ramón A. *When Jesus Came, the Corn Mothers Went Away: Marriage, Sexuality, and Power in New Mexico, 1500–1846.* Stanford, CA: Stanford University Press, 1991.

Hall, David D. *Worlds of Wonder, Days of Judgment: Popular Religious Belief in Early New England.* New York: Alfred A. Knopf, 1989.

Heyrman, Christine Leigh. *Southern Cross: The Beginnings of the Bible Belt.* New York: Alfred A. Knopf, 1997.

Lambert, Frank. *The Founding Fathers and the Place of Religion in America.* Princeton, NJ: Princeton University Press, 2003.

———. *Inventing the "Great Awakening."* Princeton, NJ: Princeton University Press, 1999.

Levy, Barry. *Quakers and the American Family: British Settlement in the Delaware Valley.* New York: Oxford University Press, 1988.

Longenecker, Stephen L. *Piety and Tolerance: Pennsylvania German Religion, 1700–1850.* Metuchen, NJ: Scarecrow Press, 1994.

May, Henry. *The Enlightenment in America.* New York: Oxford University Press, 1976.

Noll, Mark. *America's God: From Jonathan Edwards to Abraham Lincoln.* New York: Oxford University Press, 2002.

Schmidt, Leigh Eric. *Holy Fairs: Scottish Communions and American Revivals in the Early Modern Period.* Princeton, NJ: Princeton University Press, 1989.

Westerkamp, Marilyn. J. *Triumph of the Laity: Scots-Irish Piety and the Great Awakening, 1625–1760.* New York: Oxford University Press, 1988.

Woolverton, John Frederick. *Colonial Anglicanism in North America.* Detroit, MI: Wayne State University Press, 1984.

A-Z Entries

Abenaki

"Abenaki" (or Wabanaki) is a broad term that refers to a number of loosely related Algonquian-speaking peoples of northern New England. In the colonial period, Abenaki territory included pieces of Canada, Massachusetts, and New York, though the group is most closely associated with Vermont and Maine (the respective heartlands of the Western and Eastern Abenaki).

When Europeans first arrived in northern New England, they encountered peoples who relied on hunting and gathering, and supplemented these activities with corn agriculture and freshwater fishing. Abenakis living on the Atlantic coast also took advantage of the resources offered by the ocean. As far as Abenaki social and political organization was concerned, the family band was the main unit, and village life and the process of making major decisions was overseen by a council of elders. This type of organization allowed for a fluid political situation.

As with other Native American communities, the arrival of Europeans brought disease epidemics to the Abenaki. Thousands of Abenakis died in 1616–1617 from an undiagnosed "plague," and thousands more died in a smallpox outbreak in 1633–1634. Additional epidemics swept through northern New England in 1669, in 1684, and throughout the 1690s.

In addition to disease, Europeans brought new religions and technologies to Abenaki country. The fur trade flourished, with Abenakis bringing in beaver pelts for manufactured cloth, glass bottles and mirrors, metal goods, and wampum (a seventeenth-century currency made from drilled shell beads, which took on spiritual significance for some Native Americans). Although the fur trade's effects were not as immediate as those of the diseases Europeans introduced, the Abenaki did trade at a disadvantage and eventually became dependent on European goods. Trade also had profound effects on Abenaki social organization. Before the development of extensive European trade, band chiefs wielded symbolic power but had little authority. As trade increased, chiefs redistributed goods. Europeans enforced this centralizing tendency by preferring to deal with a single major chief.

The arrival of the English and the rapid expansion of New England brought a new threat to the Abenaki. The French inhabitants of Abenaki country made relatively few demands. They forced the Abenaki to convert to Catholicism, at least minimally, and carried on a brisk trade in beaver pelts. Many Abenakis converted to Catholicism, as Jesuit priests made easy converts in disease-devastated communities. The English wanted land, and, moreover, they wanted the Abenaki to give up their long-standing cultural institutions and lifeways. Relations with the Iroquois were never that strong, and, in the second half of the seventeenth century, the Abenaki found themselves wedged between three empires: Iroquois, French, and English.

The result of this tension was a series of devastating wars, first with the Iroquois (1664–1669) and later with the English (1675–1676, 1689–1697, and 1702–1713). The Abenaki remained allied with the French through the French and Indian War (1754–1763). In the aftermath of the French defeat, the Abenaki faced a colonial situation similar to that of other Native American groups.

English settlers poured into Abenaki country, cutting down forests and replacing them with farms, mills, roads, and bridges. This new wave of settlement, together with a British decision to deal mainly with the Abenaki at St. Francis (Odanak, a mission community on the St. Lawrence River), persuaded many Abenakis to withdraw farther into their traditional territory.

The onset of the American Revolution was a time of great turmoil in many native communities. Although

A 1768 woodcut depicts a sachem of the Abenaki nation saving an English officer from attack by two tribesmen. The influx of British settlers and clearing of forests forced these native peoples deep into traditional lands in northern New England. The Abenaki fought on both sides in the Revolutionary War. *(Library of Congress, LC-USZ62-45552)*

the Abenaki likely would have opted for neutrality had they been given a choice, they fought on both sides of the War for Independence, usually serving as rangers or scouts. As the American government took control of the region, it did not distinguish between loyalist and rebel communities; it simply saw all native peoples as potential enemies. The Abenaki survived in the face of overwhelming odds.

Many Abenaki hid their identity through the nineteenth and twentieth centuries; some "passed" as French Canadians. In fact, the 1900 U. S. census listed only five Native Americans in Vermont. Today, the situation is more hopeful. The Abenaki people have recovered remarkably from the devastation of colonialism, both numerically and in terms of cultural and political autonomy, in both the United States and Canada.

Matthew Jennings

See also: Native American–European Relations; Native Americans.

Bibliography

Calloway, Colin G. "Abenaki." In *Encyclopedia of North American Indians,* edited by Frederick E. Hoxie. New York: Houghton Mifflin, 1996.

———. *The Western Abenakis of Vermont: War, Migration, and the Survival of an Indian People.* Norman: University of Oklahoma Press, 1990.

Haviland, William A., and Marjory W. Power. *The Original Vermonters: Native Inhabitants, Past and Present.* Hanover, NH: University Press of New England for the University of Vermont, 1981.

Acadia, Nova Scotia

Acadia was the French colony in what became the Canadian provinces of Nova Scotia, New Brunswick, and Prince Edward Island. It was distinct from the French colony around the St. Lawrence River, known as "Canada." Despite their mutual French roots, Acadians and Canadians had little contact with one another, and the Acadians developed a unique culture prior to their tragic expulsion by the British, which began in 1755.

The colony of Acadia succeeded only after several failed attempts. In 1604, a group of French settlers wintered on an island in the St. Croix River, and, in 1605, the French began a settlement at Port Royal, on the Nova Scotia mainland. After the establishment of Quebec in 1607, Canada became a more important colony to France. The settlement of Acadia ended temporarily when British forces under Virginian Samuel Argall destroyed Port Royal in 1613. In 1632, however, Isaac de Razilly arrived in Acadia and finally began a permanent French settlement.

Unlike many European settlers in North America, the Acadians did not clear large sections of forests for their farms. Instead, most Acadians settled around the shorelines of the Bay of Fundy, becoming skilled at constructing dikes to reclaim fertile land. This less intrusive form of development encouraged good relations with the indigenous peoples of Nova Scotia and New Brunswick, the Mi'kmaq and Maliseet. Acadian and aboriginal intermarriage was relatively common, and the French and native peoples became allies against the British.

The Catholic Church and the family were more important in Acadia than the seigniorial system then dominant in France. The population of Acadia increased rapidly through natural reproduction. There were more than 800 Acadians by 1686, about 2,300 by 1714, and approximately 13,000 in 1754.

Both economic cooperation and military conflict marked the relationship between Acadia and the British colonies of North America. Acadia carried on an extensive trade with the Massachusetts Bay Colony, but whenever war broke out between England and France, New Englanders almost invariably attacked Acadia. For example, after King William's War broke out in 1689, 700 New England troops under William Phips captured Acadia, holding it until 1697. During the War of the Spanish Succession, known as Queen Anne's War in North America, which broke out in 1702, New Englanders conquered Acadia again in 1710. The 1713 Treaty of Utrecht, ending the war, permanently made the peninsula of Nova Scotia a British colony, although the French retained Cape Breton Island (Ile Royale), New Brunswick, and Prince Edward Island (Ile Saint-Jean).

Despite living under British control, the first half of the eighteenth century was a "golden age" for Acadians. Their population increased, and their economy remained healthy. Given the large number of Acadians and their close ties to the native peoples, the British were generally reluctant to enforce their authority. To prevent the Acadians from taking up arms against Britain, the British tried to force them to swear an oath of allegiance. The Acadians, however, refused and insisted that they were neutral, thus becoming known as the "neutral French."

Their neutrality became increasingly contentious. The French established a strong military presence with their fortress of Louisbourg on Cape Breton. Britain responded by establishing Halifax in 1749 and bringing in Protestant settlers. This increased English presence brought greater conflict with the Mi'kmaq. In 1749, the Acadians again refused to take an oath of allegiance. In 1753, the British appointed a new governor, Charles Lawrence, who worried about the Mi'kmaq threat and doubted the sincerity of the Acadian's neutrality.

In July 1755, the British decided to forcibly expel the Acadians from the region. The expulsion was poorly planned and brutal. Despite Acadian resistance, much of their society was destroyed. The British separated family members as they loaded transport ships with Acadians, who were allowed to bring only what they could carry. Many died at sea; others perished while interned, often of disease.

The British were reluctant to send the Acadians to other French colonies for fear that this would strengthen French defenses. They therefore attempted to disperse the Acadians throughout the thirteen colonies. The expulsion lasted until 1762, by which time the British had deported approximately 11,000 Acadians.

Some Acadians fled to Prince Edward Island and Cape Breton Island, although the British eventually rounded up many of these exiles and deported them as well. Other Acadians went to France, but they had difficulty adjusting to the social strictures of eighteenth-century European society, and many returned to North America.

The largest number of Acadians, about 2,500, migrated to Louisiana, a Spanish colony, where they could apply their expertise in reclaiming marshland and practice Roman Catholicism. In time, they became known as "Cajuns."

In 1764, Britain permitted the Acadians to return to Nova Scotia. About 3,000 did so, but they were not welcomed by the new British settlers, many of whom had established themselves on the old Acadian lands. By the end of the eighteenth century, the Acadian population of Nova Scotia had risen to about 8,000, but their society was significantly less cohesive and less affluent than it had been before their expulsion.

R. Blake Brown

See also: Canada; French; French and Indian War; French Colonies on Mainland North America (Chronology). *Document:* Evangeline, A Tale of Acadie (in 1755; pub. 1847).

Bibliography

Brebner, J. B. *New England's Outpost; Acadia Before the Conquest of Canada.* New York: Columbia University Press, 1927.

Griffiths, Naomi. *The Acadians: Creation of a People.* Toronto: McGraw Hill-Ryerson, 1973.

———. *The Contexts of Acadian History, 1686–1784.* Montreal: McGill-Queen's University Press, 1992.

Rawlyk, George A. *Nova Scotia's Massachusetts: A Study of Massachusetts-Nova Scotia Relations, 1630–1784.* Montreal: McGill-Queen's University Press, 1973.

Acadians

L'Acadie, or the original land of the Acadians, was settled by the French beginning in 1632. Encompassing the area located between the St. Lawrence River and the Atlantic Ocean, and including what is now called Nova Scotia, New Brunswick, and the eastern part of Maine, it became the site of intense colonial conflict between the French and the English.

Rivalry between England and France revolved around control over the northeastern section of North America. Starting roughly with the beginning of King William's War in 1689, and ending with the Treaty of Paris in 1763, the fight over who would dominate the region continued for about seventy-five years. Periods of peace were relatively short-lived, as each country attempted to widen its colonial borders. Throughout this period, the French aligned themselves with Native American tribes from Canada and Maine, while the British aligned themselves with the Iroquois nation.

For the Acadians, serious trouble began after the British defeated the French in 1713. With the signing of the Treaty of Utrecht, Britain took over Hudson Bay, as well as the areas of Newfoundland and Nova Scotia. France, on the other hand, was allowed to keep only Cape Breton Island. France's regional dominance was severely shaken.

This important treaty—signed by Britain,

In 1755, British authorities began the forcible expulsion of 6,000 French-speaking residents from Acadia (Nova Scotia). The banishment was later recounted in Henry Wadsworth Longfellow's narrative poem, "Evangeline," published in 1847. (*Musée Acadien de l'Université de Moncton, Canada/Archives Charmet/Bridgeman Art Library*)

France, Holland, Spain, Portugal, Savoy, and Prussia—established Protestantism as the official religion of English monarchs. The treaty also separated the Crowns of France and Spain and the kingship of Prussia. In addition, it gave Britain control of Gibraltar and Minorca and control over the African slave trade in Spanish America.

At first the British tolerated the Acadians, who numbered 6,000 to 8,000. Acadians were allowed to keep their language, their religion, and even their government. As hostility increased between the French and the British, however, French Acadians were seen as a potential threat to British rule, despite the Acadians claim of neutrality.

When 1,400 British subjects, led by Edward Cornwallis, arrived from England to settle in Nova Scotia in 1749, tension multiplied. The Acadians feared the establishment of permanent English settlements. In 1755, in order to safeguard the settlers and maintain control over the area, Governor Shirley, supported by British authorities, decided to expel all French people living there. This exodus and resettlement of the Acadian people would eventually be recaptured almost 100 years later in Henry Wadsworth Longfellow's classic poem "Evangeline."

The British confiscated Acadian farms and businesses, split up families and neighbors, then deported approximately 6,000 people to various places around the globe. Many Acadians were quartered in towns or settlements in other British colonies, while some were returned to France. Others escaped by sea or through dense forests to Canada. In time, many of these refugees returned to Nova Scotia, though the returning Acadians were never given back their lands.

Today, we think of Acadians as living in Louisiana and other parts of the South, but none of the refugees was sent there by the British during the deportation. Instead, a number of Acadian refugees managed to reach the southern portion of the United States as early as 1756.

The largest migration of Acadians occurred under Spanish rule. Louisiana, under French rule until 1762, then belonged to Spain until 1800. The Spanish authorities welcomed the industrious Acadian farmers. Many even offered the new immigrants parcels of land and seed in return for settling the land. To this day, many Acadians (now known as Cajuns) are still farmers.

During the latter part of the eighteenth century, thousands of Acadians settled in the southern portion of Louisiana. Some came from the West Indies, some from other British colonies, and some from France. In the 1810 census, more than 6,000 Acadian residents, along with 2,500 slaves, were listed as living in two parishes.

Most Acadians moved into what is known as bayou country. Isolated geographically, they staunchly maintained and protected their distinct culture, including their language (now known as Cajun French) and their Roman Catholic roots. Nevertheless, the population of the region continued to grow, from 35,000 in 1815 to more than 270,000 in 1880.

Over time, intermarriage with people of other ethnic backgrounds became acceptable, and, these days, it is common for Cajun-speaking families to carry such names as Smith, Schneider, or Hernandez. Most importantly, the descendants of the French Acadians who settled the area take pride in their long and complex history, a history that sets them apart from any other ethnic group in the United States.

Gail L. Jenner

See also: Canada; French; French and Indian War; French Colonies on Mainland North America (Chronology); Louisiana; New Orleans; Race and Ethnicity (Essay). *Document*: Evangeline, A Tale of Acadie (in 1755; pub. 1847).

Bibliography

Athearn, Robert G. *American Heritage Illustrated History of the United States.* Vol. 2, *The New World.* New York: Choice, 1988.

Daniels, Roger. *Coming to America: A History of Immigration and Ethnicity in American Life.* New York: HarperCollins, 1990.

Morison, Samuel Eliot. *The Oxford History of the American People.* New York: Oxford University Press, 1965.

Acapulco

Acapulco is a major seaport located on a deep bay that provides easy access and secure anchorage, making it the best harbor on Mexico's Pacific coast. The name of the city means "place of dense reeds" in the native Nahuatl language, and it is built on a narrow strip of low land between the shoreline and the mountains that encircle the bay. These rugged mountains have historically made access from the interior difficult.

Acapulco has been a crossroads for the people of Mexico for at least a millennium. The earliest remains found in the area date from the third millennium. Archaeologists have also discovered artifacts that are similar to those found in highland Mexico and show influence by Tarascan, Mixtec, Zapotec, and Aztec civilizations; however, Acapulco never came under direct control of these groups. Instead, it remained subject to local leaders until the Spanish conquest in the sixteenth century.

Soon after the conquest of the Aztec empire in central Mexico in 1521, the Spanish arrived in present-day Acapulco. A royal decree in 1528 brought the site under the control of the Spanish Crown. Spaniards continued to settle Acapulco in the 1530s, using it as a site to build ships to explore the Pacific coast. From Acapulco, the Spanish traveled both south to Peru and north to explore the Colorado River.

Then, during the 1560s, the Spanish established a regular trading link between Acapulco and Manila in the Philippines. Even before the arrival of the Spanish, Manila had served as a center of Asian trade, and Spain took advantage of this position. Colonists in Spanish America increasingly looked to Asia for luxury goods such as silk, porcelain, jade, ivory, and perfumes. Thus, for more than 200 years, a special yearly trading ship, known as the "Manila Galleon," sailed between Acapulco and Manila.

The trip across the Pacific Ocean was not an easy one. The westward journey from Acapulco to Manila was relatively safe and took about three months. However, the eastward trip was long and difficult, lasting from six to eight months.

When the Asian goods reached Acapulco, some merchants crossed Mexico overland in order to ship them to Spain. But many of these products remained in the Americas, sometimes influencing New World artists. For example, Mexican ceramics demonstrate the impact of the Galleon trade, and Chinese silk designs may have inspired some of the patterned garments of Guatemalan sculptures.

From Acapulco, merchants sent small amounts of chocolate, a dye known as cochineal, oils, and Spanish wines, but the most important product that filled the Manila-bound ships leaving from Acapulco was silver. Large quantities of silver from the great mines of Zacatecas, Guanajuato, and San Luis Potosí flowed through Acapulco, and there was a great demand for this precious metal, especially in China. This demand led to a large-scale diversion of silver that would have gone to Spain but instead was sent to Asia. There was some attempt to regulate this trade, such as limiting it to one Manila Galleon each year. These attempts were largely ineffective and often resulted in contraband trade.

Acapulco's yearly treasure attracted Spain's European rivals. In 1579, Francis Drake attacked but failed to capture the Galleon. In 1587, off Cabo San Lucas, Thomas Cavendish seized the ship *Santa Anna.* By 1615, the Dutch had appeared along the Pacific coast of Spain's American empire. This Dutch presence led the Spanish to construct fortifications at Acapulco to protect their interests. Spanish authorities did benefit from taxes on the Acapulco trade. Initially, "China goods" paid 10 percent tariff. By the eighteenth century, that figure had risen as high as 33 percent.

Due to its hot and unhealthy climate, the population of Acapulco remained small, despite its importance as a port city. By 1800, there were only about 4,000 inhabitants, including many blacks and mulattos. The population increased dramatically, however, when the Galleon arrived. Its return started an annual merchant fair in Acapulco, where traders bargained for the Galleon's cargo of luxury goods. During the two-week fair, there could be as many as 12,000 people in Acapulco.

In the 1820s, Mexico's War of Independence permanently ended the Manila Galleon. Acapulco declined in importance until the early twentieth century, when tourism revived the city's fortunes.

Ronald Young

See also: Mexico City; New Spain; Spanish Colonies on Mainland North America (Chronology); Trade.

Bibliography

Bethell, Leslie, ed. *The Cambridge History of Latin America.* Vol. 1. Cambridge, UK: Cambridge University Press, 1984.

Parry, J. H. *The Spanish Seaborne Empire.* New York: Alfred A. Knopf, 1966.

Schell Hoberman, Louisa. *Mexico's Merchant Elite, 1590–1660.* Durham, NC: Duke University Press, 1991.

Schurz, William. *The Manila Galleon.* New York: E. P. Dutton, 1939.

Williams, Martha N., and John Hoyt Williams. "The Route To Riches." *Américas* 36:6 (November–December 1984): 24–29.

Adams, Abigail (1744–1818)

Abigail Smith Adams was the wife of John Adams, founding father and second president of the United

Abigail Adams, the wife and confidante of John Adams, is best remembered for her advocacy of women in a letter to him in March 1776 at the Second Continental Congress. "I desire you would Remember the Ladies," she wrote, "and be more generous and favourable to them than your ancestors." *(Brown Brothers, Sterling, Pennsylvania)*

States. In addition, she was the mother of John Quincy Adams, the sixth president of the United States.

Abigail was born on November 22, 1744, in Weymouth, Massachusetts, to Elizabeth Quincy Smith and the Reverend William Smith. Her father was the minister of the First Congregational Church of Weymouth. Elizabeth Quincy Smith came from a family of Puritan ministers, and her father, John Quincy, was a substantial landowner and politician. Abigail was one of four children; she had two sisters, Mary and Elizabeth, and a brother, William.

Abigail lacked a formal education, but an innate curiosity stimulated her keen intelligence. She avidly read books at home, mainly literature, including Shakespeare, Pope, and Cowper. She also learned some French and the important practical skills of basic mathematics and keeping accounts. Thus her education was geared toward her role in life, the only role open to women at the time: that of wife, mother, and household manager. Education, however, would remain a lifelong passion,

one she continued to pursue after marrying. In her husband's well-stocked library, she read history and political theory in addition to many scientific and medical works. One of her pivotal concerns was the improvement of female education. She wrote, "Female education in the best of families went no further than writing and arithmetic; in some few instances, music and dancing."

A love of literature created a bond between Abigail and John Adams, a Harvard law graduate with a promising future. They were married in 1764, when she was only 19; he was ten years her senior. Upon her marriage, Abigail moved from Weymouth to Braintree (now Quincy), where she not only managed the Adams' family farm and its workers but also conducted extensive financial enterprises unusual for women at the time. She purchased and speculated in land, and she also sold goods that John brought back from England.

Within ten years, she bore three sons and two daughters. She looked after family and home when her husband went traveling as circuit judge, delegate to the Continental Congress, envoy abroad, and elected officer under the Constitution.

Abigail Adams courageously expressed her opinions in private and in public. She wrote hundreds of letters that recorded the history of colonial America and the many perils it faced on the road to independence. Her humorous and lively correspondence details her life at the time of the Revolution. They tell the story of a woman who stayed at home to struggle with wartime shortages and inflation, to run the farm with a minimum of help, and to teach her children when their schooling was interrupted.

Historians have long disputed the nature of her feminism or lack of it, however, it is clear that many of her ideas were ahead of their time. These views are revealed in the letters she wrote to her husband while he was attending the Second Continental Congress in Philadelphia:

"I long to hear that you have declared an independency—and by the way the new Code of Laws which I supposed it will be necessary for you to make. I desire you would Remember the Ladies, and be more generous and favourable to them than your ancestors. Do not put such unlimited power into the hands of the Husbands. . . . If perticuliar care and attention is not paid to the Ladies, we are determined to foment a Rebelion, and will not hold ourselves bound by any Laws in which we have no voice, or Representation."

The fact that John did not take his wife's views seriously is demonstrated by his reply: "As to your extraordinary Code of Laws, I cannot but laugh. . . . We know better than to repeal our Masculine systems."

After the American Revolution, Abigail and John lived in Paris, London, and The Hague, where he represented the new republic in a number of diplomatic positions. During this period and while he was president, Abigail continued to write numerous letters to friends and family. Her collected letters provide an excellent portrayal of life in late-eighteenth-century America. Abigail Adams died from typhoid fever in 1818 at the age of 74.

Leigh Whaley

See also: Adams, John; Massachusetts; Revolutionary War. *Document*: Letters between Abigail Adams and John Adams (1776).

Bibliography

Akers, Charles W. *Abigail Adams: An American Woman.* Boston: Little, Brown, 1980.

Gelles, Edith Belle. *First Thoughts: Life and Letters of Abigail Adams.* New York: Twayne, 1998.

————. *Portia: The World of Abigail Adams.* Bloomington: Indiana University Press, 1992.

Keller, Rosemary Skinner. *Patriotism and the Female Sex: Abigail Adams and the American Revolution.* Brooklyn, NY: Carlson, 1994.

Adams, John (1735–1826)

John Adams, lawyer, statesman, vice president, and president of the United States, was born in Braintree (now Quincy), Massachusetts, on October 19, 1735. He was the third son of Susanna Boylston Adams and John Adams, a farmer, shoemaker, selectman, and deacon of the local congregational church.

Although Adams had decided at an early age that he wanted to be a farmer, his father convinced him to enter Harvard College and become a minister. By the time he graduated in 1755, however, Adams had given up the idea of entering the ministry and instead took a position teaching at a grammar school in Worcester, Massachusetts. Resolving to enter the legal profession, he taught during the day and read law at night with James Putnam. After completing his studies, he re-

turned to Braintree in 1758 and, with the assistance of Jeremiah Gridley and Oxenbridge Thacher, was admitted to the Boston bar in November.

Adams lost his first case, involving two feuding neighbors, on a technicality and resolved to become a better lawyer. His diary reveals numerous occasions of self-doubt and despair during this period of his life, but with each successive case he gained more confidence. He soon revealed to Jonathan Sewall that he had a newfound admiration for his profession.

While practicing law, Adams met and married Abigail Smith, a minister's daughter from Weymouth, Massachusetts, who had schooled herself well in the art of politics and literature. Their partnership was both an intimate and intellectual one, as their many surviving letters attest, and Abigail soon became Adams's most trusted political advisor and confidante. They had five children together, four of whom survived into adulthood. Abigail, otherwise known as Nabby by the family, was the eldest, followed by John Quincy, who became the sixth president of the United States, Charles, and Thomas Boylston.

As a leader of the revolutionary cause, European diplomat, first vice president, and second president of the fledgling nation, John Adams was acclaimed by his friend and rival Thomas Jefferson as the "Colossus of Independence." *(Private Collection/Christie's Images/Bridgeman Art Library)*

Resistance to the British Government

Shortly after marrying Abigail, Adams became a key player in the resistance to Parliament's right to tax the American colonists. In response to the Stamp Act, he wrote a series of essays for the *Boston Gazette* in 1765 (published three years later as *A Dissertation on the Canon and Feudal Law*), in which he denounced Parliament's recent interference in the colonies. In it he praised the Puritan founders as reformers and opponents of tyranny, acknowledged a providential plan for enlightenment and liberty in the colonies, and claimed that the British government had become characteristically coercive and corrupt, denying the English colonists their two basic rights under the Magna Carta: the right to be taxed only by consent and the right to be judged only by a jury of one's peers.

Although the Stamp Act was repealed in 1766, Adams knew that Parliament would impose another tax on the colonies, and so he continued to oppose its right to do so. In 1769, two years after the Townshend Acts had been passed, he defended John Hancock, a wealthy Boston merchant who had been charged with smuggling wine. Acknowledging Hancock's obvious guilt, he argued the case on the merits that the colonists were not represented in Parliament, which had passed the trade acts, and that they were subsequently tried without juries after being accused of violating the acts. The Crown, recognizing the dangers of pursuing the case, dropped the charges.

Adams continued to oppose Parliament's right to tax the colonies, but he was also opposed to mob rule. This probably contributed to his decision in 1770 to team up with Josiah Quincy and defend eight British soldiers and an officer who had been accused of firing on a Boston crowd, killing five people and wounding others, in an incident that quickly became known as the Boston Massacre.

During the first trial, Quincy and Adams successfully defended Captain Thomas Preston; in the second trial, six of the British soldiers were acquitted, while the remaining two were found guilty of manslaughter. After pleading benefit of clergy (a clause in English law under which anyone who was able to read— formerly the province only of clergy members—could be exempted from the jurisdiction of the secular courts), the two convicted soldiers were branded on the thumb and released. Adams's defense of the British soldiers made him temporarily unpopular in the colonies. But it also earned him a reputation for fairness and honesty, a reputation he upheld throughout his political career.

Continental Congresses

The same year as the Boston Massacre, Adams was elected to the Massachusetts General Court and served as clerk of the Suffolk County Bar Association. He continued to practice law but became increasingly involved in intercolonial politics as tensions between the mother country and colonies escalated. After taking a brief break from politics for much of 1771 and 1772, he was reelected to the General Court in 1773, and, in June 1774, he was appointed to represent the Commonwealth of Massachusetts at the First Continental Congress. He and his cousin, Samuel Adams, became leaders of the radical faction at the Philadelphia convention, and both were disappointed by Congress's reluctance to go beyond written protest to Parliament as a means to repeal the Coercive Acts (1774). Already committed to independence, Adams returned to Boston later that year and wrote a series of essays against the loyalist Daniel Leonard using the pseudonym "Novanglus," in which he questioned not only Parliament's right to tax the colonies but its declared authority in North America.

At the Second Continental Congress, following the battles of Lexington and Concord, Adams once again took a leading role. He was involved in as many as ninety committees, chairing twenty-five of them, and worked diligently on the Board of War to equip the Continental army and build an American navy. One of his first acts was to nominate George Washington to take command of the Continental army, and, as early as 1775, he proposed independence from Britain. In a move to secure Virginia's allegiance to the independence movement, in 1776, he asked Congress to appoint Thomas Jefferson to draft the Declaration of Independence, a document that both he and Benjamin Franklin helped to edit and which he signed after it had passed through Congress. Working tirelessly, that year Adams also helped to draft "The Plan of Treaties," a foreign policy manual that influenced American politics for years to come, and wrote *Thoughts on Government*, a political treatise on the superior merits of balanced governments, intended to assist North Carolinians in framing a new constitution.

After Independence

After the signing of the Declaration of Independence, Congress sent Adams to France to negotiate a treaty of alliance. He returned home in 1779 and drafted the Massachusetts Constitution (1780), then went back to France to negotiate a peace and commercial treaty with England. He was unpopular as a diplomat in Europe but managed to obtain Dutch recognition of U.S. independence and a $400,000 loan, and he played an important role in the ratification of the peace treaty in 1783. He was then appointed ambassador to England, where he wrote *Defence of the Constitutions of Government of the United States of America* (1787), a three-volume political treatise defending mixed forms of government.

When Adams returned to the United States in 1788, he was very popular and soon found himself on the 1789 presidential election ballot. He was easily defeated by George Washington, but, according to the electoral rules of the day, he was elected to the office of the vice presidency. In that office, to which he was reelected in 1792, he supported the major policies of the Washington administration, including Alexander Hamilton's financial program, the Neutrality Proclamation (1793), the suppression of the Whiskey Rebellion (1794), and Jay's Treaty (1794). In the third presidential election (1796), Adams, who represented the Federalist interest, defeated Thomas Jefferson by a narrow margin and became the second president of the United States.

Most of Adams's presidency was consumed by avoiding a costly war with France. In working so hard to avoid the war, he alienated both Federalist and Republican support. That, combined with the unpopularity of the Alien and Sedition Acts (1798), led to his defeat in the next presidential election.

After losing the election of 1800 to Thomas Jefferson, Adams retired from politics and spent the remaining twenty-six years of his life on the family farm in Quincy, writing letters, commentaries, and his autobiography. While he did not refrain from offering his political views to friends and correspondents, as when he supported Jefferson's embargo and opposed the Federalists during the War of 1812, he stayed out of political life and lived long enough to see his eldest son, John Quincy, elected the sixth president of the United States.

In 1812, thanks to the intervention of Benjamin Rush, Adams reconciled with his old friend and political rival Thomas Jefferson. On July 4, 1826, the fifty-year anniversary of independence, their friendship came to a sudden end. Adams, not knowing that his friend in Monticello had died earlier that day, breathed his last words: "Thomas Jefferson survives."

Michael Sletcher

See also: Adams, Abigail; Boston Massacre; Massachusetts; Politics and Government (Essay); Revolutionary War. *Document:* Letters between Abigail Adams and John Adams (1776).

Bibliography

Ellis, Joseph J. *Passionate Sage: The Character and Legacy of John Adams.* New York: W. W. Norton, 1993.

Ferling, John. *John Adams: A Life.* Knoxville: University of Tennessee Press, 1992.

McCullough, David G. *John Adams.* New York: Simon & Schuster, 2001.

Shaw, Peter. *The Character of John Adams.* Chapel Hill: University of North Carolina Press, 1976.

Smith, Page. *John Adams.* 2 vols. New York: Doubleday, 1962–1963.

Adams, Samuel (1722–1803)

Writer, organizer, and agitator, Samuel Adams led the revolutionary movement in Massachusetts against English rule. Born in Boston on September 27, 1722, Adams was one of a dozen children born to Samuel and Mary Fifield Adams. His merchant father was a leading figure in town politics, serving both as town selectman and as representative to the provincial assembly.

After attending the Boston Latin School, Adams entered Harvard College at the age of 14, receiving a bachelor's degree in 1740 and a master's degree in 1743. Although his parents hoped he would become a minister or a lawyer, Adams rejected both careers. He demonstrated little promise as a businessman, quitting a job at a counting house and failing in his own business despite a substantial loan from his father. Adams did work in the family malt house, and he assumed control of the family's business interests, including several commercial investment properties, when his father died in 1748, but he never enjoyed commercial success. He was married twice, in 1749 to Elizabeth Checkley, who died in 1757, and then in 1764 to Elizabeth Wells. Only two of his children survived to adulthood.

As he took over his father's business interests and began a family, Adams also entered upon a career of public service, with appointments to minor municipal posts. In 1756, he began nearly a decade of service as one of Boston's tax collectors. It was a task for which he demonstrated little diligence, and he ended up 8,000 pounds in arrears to the town. Nonetheless, town leaders found Adams useful and drew upon his talents as a writer. He drafted the town meeting's instructions to Boston's representatives in the provincial legislature. Thereafter, Adams rapidly became a leader in town politics. Because he belonged to several political clubs, both those of merchants and those of artisans, he became a key figure in the town caucus, an informal organization of merchants and artisans that essentially ran the town meetings. Adams particularly enjoyed the company of Boston's artisans, often dropping by their clubs and taverns. He even came to see himself as a defender of the interests of the artisan class.

As Adams's star rose in town politics, the attention of many shifted to changes in imperial policies. After its victory over France in the French and Indian War in 1763, the English government sought new ways

Writer, orator, and publicist, Samuel Adams was a leading light of the American Revolution in colonial Massachusetts. The royal governor complained that Adams "obtained such ascendancy as to direct Boston . . . just as he pleases." *(The Stapleton Collection/Bridgeman Art Library)*

to pay for the increasing costs of its expanding empire. Because of growing opposition to taxes at home, British leaders turned to the colonies as a source of revenue. Beginning with the Sugar Act in 1764, Parliament passed a series of revenue measures, including the 1765 Stamp Act and the 1767 Townshend duties, all of which Adams opposed.

Adams drew upon several sources in condemning these British impositions. At Harvard, he had become an advocate of John Locke's political theory. He embraced the notion that a covenant existed between government and the people. Citizens owed their compliance to government only as long as it preserved their life, liberty, and property, the natural rights of all men. When it failed to do so, citizens had an obligation to resist.

From his father's experiences, Adams had also learned that it was dangerous to entrust the liberties of citizens to a distant government. In 1739, his father had helped create a land bank in Massachusetts that issued paper money to borrowers who secured loans with their real estate. Two years later, Parliament, influenced by Boston merchants who wanted a sole currency backed by gold or silver, dissolved the bank, leaving the directors, including Samuel Adams, Sr., liable for the bank's debts. Although his father died in 1748, Adams was still struggling to protect the estate from legal challenges ten years later.

Most important in framing Adams's opposition politics was his faith. A pious man, Adams shared with the seventeenth-century Puritans a profound belief that America had a mission to create a virtuous society of frugal, temperate, and hardworking people who would subordinate self-interest to the needs of the community. The biggest threat to this mission lay in liberty's vulnerability to power. If government was not in the hands of virtuous men, the only check to this threat lay with a vigilant citizenry, ever ready to respond to the challenges to their rights.

Revolutionary Activity

Committed to these fundamental principles, the politically connected Adams was prepared to play a key role in American resistance to changes in British policies. As clerk of the Boston town meeting and as clerk of the House of Representatives, after his selection to that body in 1765, Adams was able to agitate against British policies on both the local and provincial levels. He drafted petitions, resolutions, and letters condemning all the revenue acts as unconstitutional violations of the liberties of English colonists. Drawing upon John Locke's theories, he argued that the imperial government could not take the colonists' property in the form of taxes without their consent, and since the colonists were not represented in Parliament, they could never consent. Adams mobilized popular opposition against the legislation in dozens of newspaper articles, in town meeting debates, in his frequent visits to clubs and taverns, and in casual conversations in the streets and along the town docks. He called upon his fellow citizens to boycott English imports, and he supported the public demonstrations organized to intimidate stamp distributor Andrew Oliver into resigning his post. Yet when a mob destroyed Lieutenant Governor Thomas Hutchinson's home, Adams condemned the action. He was always reluctant to sanction violence in seeking redress of grievances, although in this case it contributed to the repeal of the Stamp Act.

In 1768, Adams learned of the English dispatch of two regiments to Boston, which had become the focal point of the opposition to imperial politics. Eighteenth-century political opposition writers in England had persuaded Adams that a standing army was the most ominous threat to liberty. In newspaper articles he condemned the decision as unmistakable evidence of the arbitrary power wielded by imperial officials, and his worst fears were realized when British soldiers fired into a threatening crowd, killing five, on March 5, 1770. Adams headed a delegation that persuaded the governor to remove the troops from Boston, and then spent weeks spreading the word in the colonies and overseas of the "massacre." Yet Adams supported a fair trial for the soldiers, to demonstrate the virtue of Bostonians.

In his almost constant agitation, Adams worked to broaden opposition to British policies. In 1768, as House clerk, he drafted a letter to the other colonial legislatures, seeking their support in opposing the Townshend duties. In 1772, he helped create a committee of correspondence to unite the towns of the province in defying the British, and the following year he contributed to the development of a network of intercolonial committees of correspondence.

In 1773, Adams came into possession of what he considered proof of a conspiracy involving imperial officials and their royal governors to destroy liberty in the colonies. Benjamin Franklin sent Adams letters written by Massachusetts governor Thomas Hutchinson that recommended limitations on colonists' liberties. After securing publication of the letters and calling upon the king to recall Hutchinson, Adams turned his attention to the Tea Act. This legislation represented yet another attempt by Parliament to raise revenue in the colonies. By allowing the East India Company to ship tea directly to the colonies, the company would not have to pay the import tax normally levied in England and could sell its tea through the merchants, or consignees, it selected rather than through public auctions. As a result, the cost of tea to colonial consumers would be much lower. Adams and other revolutionaries saw the Tea Act as a ploy to get colonists to accept Parliament's taxing power through their purchase of cheap tea. Intimidated by mass meetings, tea consignees in Philadelphia, New York, and Charles Town all resigned. On December 16 in Boston, Governor Hutchinson refused to grant the captains of tea ships a clearance to return to London with their tea cargoes. When he received the news, Adams announced to a packed town meeting that nothing more could be done to save the country. His statement was apparently a signal for action, because that night several dozen men dressed as Native Americans boarded the tea ships and tossed their cargoes overboard.

The English response to what became known as the Boston Tea Party triggered a chain of events that ultimately led to revolution. Parliament passed a series of acts (which the colonists called "Intolerable Acts") that, among other things, closed the port of Boston and limited town meetings to one session per year. To Adams, these punitive measures directed at Massachusetts were a warning to all colonists of the vulnerability of liberty, and he joined delegates from twelve colonies in September 1774 at the First Continental Congress in Philadelphia to unite in opposition. Adams not only supported a complete boycott of English trade but also helped draft the Declaration of Rights. After the Continental Congress adjourned, Adams returned to Massachusetts, where he won election in February 1775 to an extralegal provincial congress that met first in Cambridge and then in Concord. On the morning of April 19, Adams was staying at nearby Lexington with John Hancock, when Paul Revere gave them sufficient warning to escape from approaching British troops, who had come to capture them and seize military supplies in Concord.

The following month, Adams was back in Philadelphia to attend the Second Continental Congress, where he served for six years. He also helped write the Massachusetts state constitution, one based firmly on the principle that all power came from the people. Throughout the revolutionary struggle, Adams remained persuaded that power always threatened liberty, and that concentrated power in a distant government should be avoided. Consequently, as a delegate to the Massachusetts ratifying convention, he endorsed the 1787 Constitution only after obtaining assurances that it would be amended to protect basic liberties. The ultimate safeguard for liberty, however, was his faith that the people, though they might often stray from the virtuous life, shared an essential commitment to a republican form of government.

Adams held a number of political posts after the American Revolution. Besides serving as a delegate to the Massachusetts ratification convention, he served as a state senator, lieutenant governor, and governor. He retired in 1797 and died in Boston on October 2, 1803.

Larry Gragg

See also: Boston Tea Party; Revolutionary War; Townshend Acts (1767). *Document*: Townshend Revenue Act (1767).

Bibliography

Alexander, John K. *Samuel Adams: America's Revolutionary Politician.* Lanham, MD: Rowman & Littlefield, 2002.

Brown, Richard D. *Revolutionary Politics in Massachusetts: The Boston Committee of Correspondence and the Towns, 1772–1774.* Cambridge, MA: Harvard University Press, 1970.

Canfield, Cass. *Samuel Adams's Revolution, 1775–1776.* New York: Harper and Row, 1976.

Fowler, William M. *Samuel Adams: Radical Puritan.* New York: Longman, 1997.

Maier, Pauline. *From Resistance to Revolution: Colonial Radicals and the Development of American Opposition to Britain, 1765–1776.* New York: Alfred A. Knopf, 1972.

———. *The Old Revolutionaries: Political Lives in the Age of Samuel Adams.* New York: Alfred A. Knopf, 1980.

African Americans

The history of Africans in the Americas began long before the famous sale of "twenty Negars" to Virginia's John Rolfe in 1619. African slaves participated in Spanish expeditions throughout the sixteenth century and were present in large numbers in Spanish, Portuguese, and other European colonies throughout the Atlantic world.

By the time of the American War for Independence, African American men and women were present in every British colony in North America, although their numbers were largest in the plantation societies of the Southern colonies. Both enslaved and free, they worked in a striking variety of rural and urban jobs.

Through the horrors of the Middle Passage and nearly two centuries of colonial enslavement, Africans in America forged a new cultural identity, blending remembered traditions from all over Africa with borrowed European American practices. It is impossible to imagine how colonial America would have grown, especially economically, without the institution of black slavery and the contributions of African men and women.

Atlantic Slave Trade and Early Generations

Four centuries of contentious race relations in North America have made it difficult to reconstruct the first

The first African Americans in the British colonies date to 1619, when John Rolfe had "twenty Negars" transported from Africa to the Jamestown colony. Black slaves also are believed to have been part of earlier Spanish and Portuguese explorations. *(Brown Brothers, Sterling, Pennsylvania)*

meetings of diverse groups of Africans and Europeans without imagining the people concerned as "white" and "black." Distinctions like "European" and "African" also fail to represent the situation accurately, since, in the fifteenth and sixteenth centuries, few people identified themselves with their continent of origin; instead, they thought in terms of nation, tribe, or clan.

Europeans in the fifteenth century were unable to penetrate the African interior and raid for slaves. Rather, they entered into commercial relationships with traders on the coast of Africa. European and African traders, merchants, and monarchs all benefited.

Slavery was a fact of life in West and West Central Africa—the regions from which most African Americans were imported—but there were several key differences between African slavery and its American cousin. First, slavery in Africa was rarely hereditary. Indeed, slaves were often adopted or married into the master's family, clan, and tribe. Most importantly, slaves in Africa were physically identical to their masters. Thus, no permanent stigma of slavery was attached to them. (None of this applies, however, to the slave trade with the Arab world, where slaves were often reduced to nothing more than property, much as they were in the Americas.)

The barracoon (slave compound) and the infamous Middle Passage were crucial first steps in the creation of African Americans from the myriad ethnicities of Africa. Disoriented and surrounded by disease and death, Africans forged bonds that transcended ethnicity and religion and began to approach race consciousness. Approximately 10 million slaves arrived alive in the Americas over the four centuries of the trade, out of an estimated 20 to 30 million captured in Africa, the rest dying somewhere en route. Of those who lived, about 400,000 ended up in British North America before the trade stopped in 1808. The Caribbean and Brazil received far more slaves than North America.

The legal status of the first group of Africans in English North America is not precisely clear. In the earliest years of the English colonies on Chesapeake Bay, Africans—mainly men—worked alongside English and Irish servants in various states of semi-freedom. Some Africans were able to gain their freedom and operate tobacco farms, complete with their own servants and slaves. Even when they could not reach such heights, Africans created their own vibrant, independent economy of small farmers, laborers, and artisans. Many of the legal obstacles that faced later generations of African Americans were not yet in place. For instance, Africans could sue and testify in court. Some of the

earliest laws regarding race were an effort to stop sexual relations between black and white people, indicating Africans' presence in the community.

In South Carolina, where slavery was the norm from the outset, frontier conditions allowed for a rough equality as both masters and slaves worked together to create plantations in a subtropical climate. Maroon, or run-away, communities, though never as numerous or populous as those in the Caribbean, existed in the Southern backcountry during these early years. In sparsely settled Spanish Florida, Africans maintained a greater level of autonomy than in the English colonies; this balance continued until the British took control of the area in the late eighteenth century.

In urban areas of the Northern colonies in the seventeenth century, such as Dutch New Amsterdam, New York (after 1670), Boston, and Newport, Africans plied a variety of trades and experienced freedom of movement that would be unheard of on the established plantations farther south later. African Americans in the Northern colonies were primarily agricultural laborers, like most of their European neighbors. A minority laborer might work in mines, tanneries, and iron furnaces. Because of their experiences around the Atlantic world, Africans also participated in shipping and associated jobs in northern port cities.

The earliest generations of Africans in America lived at a crossroads of sorts. They were African-born, but had close ties to European colonists. Because of their small numbers and their relationships with Europeans, they picked up a variety of trades and a deep understanding of European culture, including Christianity.

Slave Culture in Mature Colonial Societies

In the late seventeenth and early eighteenth centuries, drastic changes took place in the African American population. While the first generations of Africans in America were generally not directly from Africa, but had spent time in other European colonies, increasing numbers of people came directly from West and West Central Africa.

The first generations had experienced some level of autonomy and equality, but the spread of the plantation worsened the conditions of African American life. African Americans struggled to maintain family ties and were isolated on large plantations. Because of the strenuousness of plantation life, they also died younger. Race took on new importance, and racist laws and policies began to emerge, curtailing Africans' activity in several arenas. As they confronted the harsh realities of plantation life, Africans created new institutions and worldviews that allowed them to survive slavery. In the process, a distinctly African American culture emerged.

The shift to plantation agriculture affected African American communities differently, depending on the region. In the Chesapeake, plantation agriculture developed slowly over several decades in the late seventeenth century. As a result of planter demand and improved conditions in the British Isles, African slaves, bound for life, gradually replaced white indentured servants. Slaves came increasingly from the interior of Africa, from provincial areas rather than from the coast and other areas around the Atlantic world. Men outnumbered women even more than they had decades earlier.

As a result, the large plantations of the Chesapeake began to resemble parts of Africa in speech patterns—many Virginian slaves spoke variants of Igbo, for instance—music, food, and religion, both polytheistic and Islamic. Movement between plantations came under tighter control, and African Americans fell victim to increasingly harsh punishments as planters strove to legitimatize their power. Plantation life also became increasingly regimented as planters devised new ways to maximize their profits.

Slaves resented the rising power of planters and resisted them at every turn. Although large-scale uprisings were rare, slaves could, and did, withhold labor, slow down, and feign ignorance to negotiate the terms of their bondage. While earlier generations could hold out hope for freedom, property ownership, and some legal rights, plantation slaves could not.

In the second half of the eighteenth century, the Chesapeake's African American population underwent another dramatic transformation. Africans born in Africa became a minority and a new generation of African Americans rose to prominence in the slave quarters. Slave health improved, and American-born slaves lived longer and had more children than their African parents. Slave families, though under constant threat, did achieve some measure of stability.

The new generation of African Americans also picked up the precepts of evangelical Christianity. They generally shunned white instruction, taking control of their own religion and shaping it to their particular needs, combining remembered African concepts with a redemptive, egalitarian vision of Christianity. Skilled black preachers became powerful within African American communities.

In South Carolina, similar change occurred, but more rapidly and to a greater extent. South Carolina's planters crafted a society based upon the holding of large numbers of slaves. In the first decade of the eighteenth century, the black population surpassed the white population. In several crucial ways, South Carolina was, in the words of one Swiss settler, "more like a negro country than one settled by white people."

Rice production lent itself particularly well to the "task," as opposed to the "gang," system of labor, whereby individual slaves were given a set of tasks to accomplish. Once the tasks were accomplished, slaves had the remainder of their time to themselves. Interestingly, low country planters learned from their African slaves how to grow rice. While most South Carolina slaves were from Angola, skilled slaves from the rice-producing area between the Senegal and Gambia rivers were particularly sought after.

Most white planters found plantation life distasteful, and they moved to Savannah, Charles Town, and Beaufort, leaving their plantations in the hands of managers, overseers, drivers, and slaves. A class of free, light-skinned African Americans and urban slaves grew up in Charles Town, but the vast majority of black men and women in the low country were plantation slaves.

South Carolina's plantation slave population was large, restive—in 1739, they launched a frontal assault on slavery at Stono—and overwhelmingly African. Planters laid out the designs of their plantations, but slaves altered these plans, constructing African-style dwellings and filling them with objects representing a mix of European, African, and Native American cultures. Slaves in South Carolina spoke a variety of African languages, and their influence can still be heard in the distinctive Gullah and Geechee languages of the Sea Islands. Carolina slaves also braided their hair in traditional ways and continued to file their teeth, mark their faces and bodies, and name their children in accordance with older cultural mandates, rejecting the names given to them by their generally absentee masters.

Christianity made slight inroads among low-country slaves in the first half of the eighteenth century, as African traditions remained powerful. When Africans accepted Christianity, they did so on their own terms, often adapting the new beliefs to older forms, such as the ring shout.

At the same time as the plantation model gained strength in Carolina and the Chesapeake, it was undermined in the sugar-producing areas of the lower Mississippi Valley. French planters had established large-scale plantations there, but, in 1729, the Natchez chiefdom allied with some 200 slaves, mainly Bambaras, to kill slightly more than 10 percent of the French population. The revolt did not end slavery in the region, but it altered its tenor considerably, and planters gradually ceased their importation of new slaves. Some Africans were employed by the government to retaliate against the Natchez.

There were significant numbers of free African Americans, who in their employment as slave catchers and soldiers grew close to European American society. Some free people of color were even able to make modest moves up the social ladder. This happened in Louisiana to a greater extent than anywhere in British North America, although the process was not unheard of elsewhere. In Louisiana, African Americans, both slave and free, participated in a flourishing economy independent of the planters, and Louisiana's slaves had a greater chance of attaining their freedom than their counterparts in British North America.

Slavery in the Northern Colonies

Britain's Northern colonies did not experience what Ira Berlin, one of the preeminent scholars of the African American experience in the colonial era, has termed the "plantation revolution." Still, it would be a mistake to assume that slavery was not important to the Northern colonies or that the life of African Americans in those colonies changed little over time.

As in other colonies, direct importation of slaves from Africa altered the makeup of black communities. In areas where black men and women worked and lived in close proximity to white people, they began to forge an identity that was neither African nor European but rather a hybrid African American one.

Northern cities, particularly Philadelphia and New York, boasted large black populations. There, slaves and free people of color united in ways they could not in the plantation colonies in the South. Urban slavery, though still degrading, took on a different character than plantation labor. African Americans in the Northern colonies could move around more freely, occasionally hiring out their own time. They also came under the cosmopolitan influences of the wider Atlantic world, and many took up skilled and semi-skilled jobs.

As race prejudice hardened throughout the colonies during the eighteenth century, northern people of African descent built their own African American communities. These communities demonstrated a vibrant mix of African and African American traditions: Negro Election Day in New England is one example; Pinkster Day in New York is another. On one day of the year, slaves and free people paraded through the streets, playing music and singing. In a ritual reversal of the social order, the revelers elected black kings, governors, and magistrates. Though white observers wrote off the proceedings as silly, the officials elected by blacks on these holidays held sway over the emerging black community.

Revolution

The American Revolution would profoundly alter African American life and the role of African Americans in the society of the new American republic. Many slaves were freed to fight in the war. Of these, the vast majority fought for the British and were largely removed to Canada after Britain's defeat in 1781. Those freed because of their service in the patriot army were soon joined by thousands of others freed by emancipation laws in the North or by acts of manumission in the South, many by planters influenced by the egalitarian rhetoric of the revolution.

As the free black community grew, it began to develop institutions of its own, most notably churches, particularly in urban areas where a critical demographic mass developed. These institutions, along with continuing white racism, led to the development of a distinct African American culture, again, separate from European American culture, but heavily influenced by it.

Developments in the history of the early republic, however, also condemned future generations to the rigors of plantation slavery. The invention of the cotton gin led to the vast expansion of the slave empire, throughout the existing South and into new territories farther west. Ultimately, it would take a second and even third revolution, the Civil War of the nineteenth century and the Civil Rights movement of the twentieth, to win blacks an equal share in the society partially founded on their labor centuries earlier.

Matthew Jennings

See also: Agriculture; Cotton; Equiano, Olaudah; Free Blacks; Indentured Servitude; Laborers, Rural; Laborers, Urban; Native American–African American Relations; Native Americans and Slavery; Race and Ethnicity (Chronology); Race and Ethnicity (Essay); Religions, African; Rice; Royal African Company; Slave Communities and Culture; Slave Rebellions; Slave Trade; Slavery, African American; Slavery, Caribbean; Sugar; Wheatley, Phillis. *Documents:* Virginia Slave Laws (1660s); The Demand for Slavery in Georgia (1743); On Being Brought from Africa to America (early 1770s); Slave Petition to the Governor, Council, and House of Representatives of the Province of Massachusetts (1774).

Bibliography

Berlin, Ira. *Many Thousands Gone: The First Two Centuries of American Slavery.* Cambridge, MA: Belknap Press, 1998.

Franklin, John Hope, and Alfred A. Moss. *From Slavery to Freedom: A History of African Americans.* 7th ed. New York: McGraw-Hill, 1994.

Gomez, Michael A. *Exchanging Our Country Marks: The Transformation of African Identities in the Colonial and Antebellum South.* Chapel Hill: University of North Carolina Press, 1998.

Morgan, Philip D. *Black Culture in the Eighteenth-Century Chesapeake and Lowcountry.* Chapel Hill: University of North Carolina Press, 1998.

Thornton, John. *Africa and Africans in the Making of the Atlantic World, 1400–1800.* 2nd ed. Cambridge, UK: Cambridge University Press, 1998.

Wood, Peter H. *Black Majority: Negroes in Colonial South Carolina from 1670 through the Stono Rebellion.* New York: Alfred A. Knopf, 1974.

Agriculture

American agriculture has gone through many dramatic, even traumatic, changes in its more than 350-year history. To begin with, according to Thomas Wessel, author of "Agriculture, Indians, and American History," the early colonists' survival was inextricably linked to the way Native Americans farmed and cultivated the land.

Native American Agriculture

Most of the tribes living in the East practiced some form of agriculture. Tribes like the Iroquois planted corn and other vegetables. Others, like the Ottawa, depended more on hunting or fishing, farming only a little.

Unfortunately, as these tribes established contact with the colonists, they exchanged many of their old traditions for new ones. The Huron, for example, began transporting maize and tobacco to trade for furs (to sell to the colonists). "The Hurons found the fur trade so profitable and the Petun and Neutral Nations agricul-

ture so reliable that they abandoned their own agricultural labors," writes Wessel. Rivalry in the growing fur trade led to increased hostilities between otherwise peaceful tribes. In fact, Wessel adds, after one midwinter attack by the Iroquois, "the Hurons starved and became nearly extinct."

In the Southeast, Native American tribes were heavily dependent on agriculture. Many lived in sedentary villages, and with increased European contact, some, like the Choctaw, even began herding livestock.

In spite of the conflicts that existed, Native American tribes provided the colonists with the knowledge and skills they needed in order to survive. The Pilgrims learned to plant corn from their Native American neighbors, a crop that yielded well and could ripen on the stalk. They planted it in Native American-style: piles of earth were mounded up with a hoe, and corn, bean, and squash seeds were planted together. As the corn grew out of the top, the bean plants used the corn as a trellis, and the squash plants kept weeds to a minimum. A dead fish, placed in the mound, provided fertilizer. According to Wessel,

> Native American agriculture fed the first colonists at Jamestown and Plymouth and largely accounted for their survival. Native American crops and farming techniques sustained the early settlements and provided the United States and a good portion of the world with its most prolific feed grain. Agriculture was a vital ingredient in the fur trade. More often than not, frontiersmen carried Native American agriculture into the woodland farms of the Ohio and beyond. . . . Throughout American history, in sometimes benign and sometimes tragic circumstances, agriculture forged a bond between Native Americans and whites in North America.

Turkeys, oysters, and many kinds of fish were introduced to the colonists. Other important crops adopted from Native American tribes included tomatoes, sweet potatoes, squash, pumpkins, beans, watermelons, berries, nuts (pecans, black walnuts, peanuts), maple sugar, tobacco, and cotton. A few plants were initially rejected by the settlers, who considered them poisonous or inedible, and some were rejected by Europeans when they were exported later on, but most were gratefully adopted.

From the beginning, the colonists derived their living from farming. Even on the eve of the American

Revolution, more than 75 percent of the colonists still practiced agriculture. Many immigrants were displaced tenant farmers seeking opportunities to settle their own farms. Some worked as tenant farmers in the colonies, while others arrived as indentured servants. (In fact, by 1750, more than half the immigrants arriving south of New England came as indentured servants.) For members of both groups, there was still the promise that some day they would own their own land.

Small family farms were most common in the colonies, except in the South where plantations began to evolve. Houses were often crudely made and small, and most farm families manufactured their own tools and products, relying little on the outside world. Even if the farmers' role in government and policy making would not be established for many years, it wasn't long before the ownership of land became the standard for wealth and status in all of the colonies.

Agricultural Technology

In the beginning, technology was limited. The colonists possessed few implements and little technological knowledge. Axes were used to clear the land or fell trees. Simple mauls were made from scraps of timber, and splitting wedges were cut from wood. Shovels and spades were made with wooden blades, plated with iron shoes. Hay forks or pitchforks were made out of split saplings. Sowing and cultivating was accomplished by hand, and in the beginning, there were few plows.

By 1700, some changes had occurred: A-frame harrows were used to break up the soil, and sickles or cradles were used to cut hay and grain. Crudely designed wooden hand plows, enhanced with iron plates,

made it possible for two men to plow 1 to 2 acres a day. By 1750, many farmers in the North were using the cradle scythe. This 10- to 12-pound tool allowed reapers to cut 3 acres a day. Cradles allowed grain to fall into piles, the piles were raked into bundles, and the bundles were bound into sheaves. In the South, farmers preferred the sickle. The sickle didn't "shatter" the grain as much as the cradle, and it also left more straw behind in the field.

Oxen provided the major means of transportation and assisted minimally in other kinds of farm work. It would be many years before horses were used to power more sophisticated farm machinery.

All domestic livestock, except for turkeys, had to be or had been imported. Meat was very important to the colonists' survival and provided the basis of their diet. Mutton, a popular meat in the sixteenth century, became less common after a time because of the number of wild predators that preyed on sheep. Cattle and pigs, which were less susceptible to attack by panthers or wolves, became increasingly popular. Goats were also kept, especially in the early years, for they provided both meat and milk, and they proved hardier than other kinds of livestock.

Livestock was frequently turned loose and only herded when necessary. In the Northern colonies, fences were usually made of stone, while in the South split rail fences were common. These enclosures were used primarily to fence animals out of planted fields or gardens. Along the coast, islands also were used to isolate livestock.

Unfortunately, mice and rats were a frequent problem, so farmers kept cats and dogs, or relied on snakes and other natural predators. Sometimes, farmers built granaries off the ground to discourage infestation.

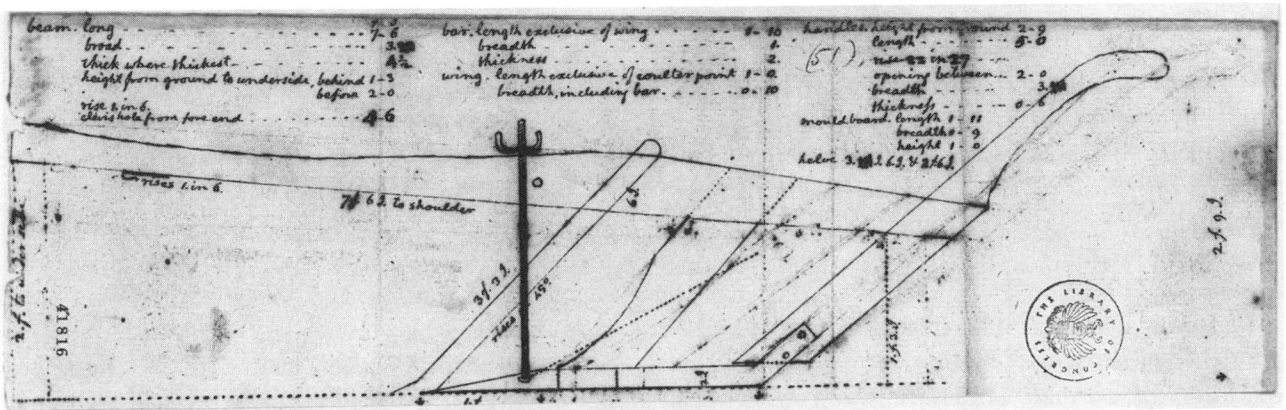

Thomas Jefferson, one of Virginia's most notable planters, regarded agriculture as "a science of the very first order." Among his many innovations was a plow that would delve deeper than the standard wooden plows of the time and help limit soil erosion. *(Library of Congress, LC-MSS-27748-64)*

Birds were also a problem as they devoured grain while it was still in the fields. As a result, they were hunted and added to the farmers' stew pots. Deer were hunted heavily, since they could destroy a cornfield in a very short time.

In the New England colonies, farmers initially worked smaller plots of land and settled in villages. These farming communities were tightly knit and shared similar cultural and religious traditions. Because of the cooler climate and rocky soil, however, much of the region was better suited for cattle and dairy production, and these proved the most profitable endeavors. In fact, by 1650, Boston and the Massachusetts Bay region became major livestock-producing areas.

By the mid-1640s, farmers in Connecticut and Rhode Island were raising crops, including vegetables and fruits, in addition to livestock. Rhode Island was labeled the "garden of New England." Farmers nearest the waterways and along the Atlantic coast grew cash crops, including wheat and corn, which were sent to market. Farmers more inland could not count on this exchange, and they were more likely to be subsistence farmers.

Plantation Agriculture

In the Southern coastal areas, large plantations grew up around the increasingly important and successful tobacco crop. Prior to its introduction in Virginia, all tobacco for English or European markets came from the Caribbean. In 1612, John Rolfe learned how to farm and cure tobacco, and it wasn't long before it was available for trade with England and Europe. In fact, by 1619, most of the nearly 1,000 colonists of Virginia were making their living producing, manufacturing, or transporting tobacco. Jamestown, catching the "tobacco fever," even grew it in the streets.

In order to control quantity and quality, however, regulations were imposed. Poorer quality tobacco, called "mean tobacco" was burned to keep it off the market, while individuals were limited to the amount they could grow. In 1621, Governor Wyatt limited each family to 1,000 plants per person. In 1730, Virginia passed an Inspection Act that further regulated the grading, packing, and marketing of tobacco.

The quantity of tobacco being grown for export increased dramatically after its introduction in the colonies. In 1628, Virginia exported approximately 550,000 pounds of tobacco to England; in 1688, 18 million pounds were exported. This growth spurred the need for more labor, and this in turn spurred the spread of slavery into North America.

The widespread use of African labor during the sixteenth and seventeenth centuries on sugar plantations in the Caribbean soon provided a model for European colonists in North America. The Spanish had already brought more than 100,000 slaves into Mexico during the sixteenth century. The English, slower than the Spanish to turn to slavery as a means of solving their labor problem, began to import Africans in 1619—first as free and bonded servants. But by 1663, the Royal African Company was established, and the slave trade was underway.

With the introduction of slaves, the tobacco industry grew rapidly. Slaves provided a cheap and enormous labor pool. Interestingly, Thomas Jefferson opposed the planters' emphasis on tobacco and tried to encourage greater crop diversification and cultivation, believing it was the key to a more sustainable agricultural foundation.

In addition, a "headright" system granted planters the right to claim more land for each laborer they brought into the country, whether free or slave. The first slaves, many imported from the West Indies in exchange for hogs or cattle, also knew about the cultivation of rice. Rice had been a common staple in West Africa but was unfamiliar to Europeans. With its introduction, however, plantation agriculture expanded from the coastal areas into more inland regions.

Rice soon became the most important agricultural crop in South Carolina and Georgia. By 1726, planters exported 10 million pounds of rice per year. Its production "peaked" in 1770, when 84 million pounds were exported. Because rice plantations were large, the enslavement of 50 to 100 Africans was common. In addition, Africans proved to have a greater resistance to malaria and yellow fever than Europeans, although they were not totally immune.

A new crop, indigo—first introduced by Eliza Lucas in 1739—became a new production crop in many areas of the South. Though it depended on slave labor, it did not require as many slaves, and thus, it offered planters an economical alternative to rice.

In contrast to other parts of the South, Florida remained a Spanish colony. Historical records indicate that oranges and wheat were cultivated and became important exports to the British colonies. Olive oil and wine were also exchanged for commodities the Spanish needed. This agricultural development contributed to the economic and cultural independence of Spanish Florida.

Middle Colonies and Food Crops

It was in the middle colonies (New Jersey, New York, and Pennsylvania), however, that farmers first cultivated a substantial surplus in food crops. Whereas farmers in the North had to clear land before being able to cultivate it and could only afford to take on a few more acres each year, farmers in the middle colonies were able to settle across the rolling hills and wider spaces of the region.

Wheat farming flourished, and it was not long before the middle colonies earned the title as the "breadbasket" of the New World. Yield often reached 40 bushels per acre on newly plowed lands. But because they did not understand the importance of rotating crops, farmers quickly depleted the land. Production often dropped to ten bushels per acre. Not until 1780 did crop rotation become a common practice.

It was also in the middle colonies that farmers began using horses, particularly draft horses, for power because of their speed. This led to increased oat and pasture cultivation where land was farmed as intensively as possible with little thought to conservation. Horses were also used to tread grain; horses could tread thirty bushels a day, but more grain was wasted in this process.

A rising anti-British sentiment took root in the colonies in the eighteenth century. Much of this dissatisfaction was due to the Crown's cynical attitude toward farmers, as well as its inability to deal with agricultural issues. Though farmers typically suffered through periodic low prices, high taxes, crop failures, or debt, their political and social dissatisfaction grew as England demanded more and gave less to its subjects. In several colonies, agriculturalists staged protests and "insurrections" in the decades before the American Revolution. Clearly, controls on agricultural exports, land title restrictions, and bans and restrictions on western settlement by the British ultimately became one of the reasons the colonies rose up against the king.

Agriculture in Spanish Colonies

In contrast to the eastern colonies settled by the English and Northern Europeans, agriculture in the Spanish colonies in the Southwest and California was organized around Native American labor. And, though livestock and horses were brought to North America by the Spanish as early as the sixteenth century—dramatically affecting the lifestyle of Native Americans throughout the West—the Spanish were not engaged in farming for export. Farming, for the most part, was subsistence farming. Spanish colonization was conducted principally by the military and by church missionaries, and the Crown was less concerned with establishing permanent settlements in the New World than in locating treasure to take back to Spain.

At the same time, Spanish settlers, many of whom married Native American women, established ranches all over the Southwest. Spanish land grants were vast, and the system of awarding land to selected individuals guaranteed loyalty to Spain. Some of these holdings in the Southwest and California ranged from 1 to 11 square leagues (1 league = 4,438 acres), and it has been estimated that 750 of these land grants encumbered around 13 or 14 million acres. Spain continued this practice until the Mexican Revolution in 1821.

As a result, the cattle industry grew from its simple roots into an enormous industry. Some of the byproducts, including soap, tallow for candles, and hides, were used for trade. Most importantly, the region remained a livestock-producing area and gave rise to the cowboy and large cattle "spreads" that still exist today.

The American Revolution had a significant impact on agriculture. First, it became a formidable task to feed the army, as well as sustain the newly emerging markets that were developing abroad, including those for flour, wheat, tobacco, indigo, cattle, and barreled pork. In order to keep production going, the wives and daughters of patriots worked the fields, replacing men as farmers.

Livestock production increased during the war years because of the army's growing demand for meat products. Sheep were important for their wool. Although to meet the increased demand for the commodity, wool was often blended with flax, resulting in a fabric known as "linsey-woolsey."

The Revolution affected Southern tobacco planters substantially, not only because of the number of slaves who fled the region, but because the soil on many plantations was worn out. There were surpluses of crops, such as tobacco, rice, and indigo, and prices for many crops dropped. To counter this, some Maryland and Virginia farmers began cultivating wheat. In fact, by 1812, Shenandoah Valley farmers had become the leading wheat producers in Virginia, and their production reached 15 million pounds. Moreover, only a few farmers in North Carolina and Virginia continued to profit from tobacco. It would be a number of years before others recovered.

Cotton farming also expanded into the Gulf Coast regions of Alabama, Mississippi, and Louisiana, and New Orleans soon became the cotton export center for international trade. As cotton was most effectively cultivated by the gang-labor system, slavery did not diminish. In fact, the slave trade took on new importance in the years following the American Revolution.

Gail L. Jenner

See also: Alcohol; Coffee; Corn; Cotton; Economy, Business, and Labor (Chronology); Economy, Business, and Labor (Essay); Food and Diet; Grain; Horses; Indentured Servitude; Indigo; Laborers, Rural; Livestock; Rice; Slavery, African American; Slavery, Caribbean; Sugar; Tea; Tobacco; Trade. *Document*: Tobacco Growing (1775).

Bibliography

McCuskler, John J., and Russell Menard. *The Economy of British North America*. Chapel Hill: University of North Carolina Press, 1985.

Washburn, Wilcomb. *The Indian in America*. New York: Harper and Row, 1975.

Wessel, Thomas. "Agriculture, Indians, and American History." *Agricultural History*, 50: 1 (January 1976).

Albany Congress (1754)

Originally, the Albany Congress was convened at the behest of the English Board of Trade in 1754 to address the fraying relationship of the colonial governments with the Mohawk, and by extension, the entire Iroquois Confederacy. In the process of gathering seven of the thirteen continental American colonies together, the imperial government and the colonies considered a plan for colonial union, although each for different reasons.

The immediate reason for holding the conference was to meet the demands of the Mohawk tribe, which had been hurt by changes in the fur trade and the increasing migration of colonists westward from Albany. In the face of French expansion and aggression, keeping the "Covenant Chain" with the Six Nations of the Iroquois was crucial to colonial defense and imperial policy. Native Americans expected a forum in which they could renegotiate their relationship as subjects and allies of Britain, gain substantial gifts, and obtain such concessions as a ban on liquor sales and the removal of obnoxious Indian commissioners, as in the Dutch-dominated commission of New York.

The colonial governors saw this as an opportunity as well. Governors William Shirley of Massachusetts and Robert Dinwiddie of Virginia wanted to establish a common defense fund, given the increasing likelihood of another war with the French. Connecticut and Pennsylvania saw the conference as an ideal time to carry out negotiations to purchase a large tract of Native American-held land coveted by powerful speculators.

Benjamin Franklin, one of the delegates from Pennsylvania, however, had the most intriguing purpose of all—a plan for colonial union and an "American" government. This was not entirely antithetical to royal authority, since the king, George II, and his ministers were in favor of altering colonial charters to streamline authority and smooth over the various policies and governmental structures. Thus, the plan of union had interested royal support, as long as royal prerogative was preserved.

The conference convened on June 19, 1754 in Albany, on the frontier of British authority in North America, within the crumbling fort whose defenses so concerned Dinwiddie and Shirley. Seven colonies sent delegations: Massachusetts, New Hampshire, Connecticut, Rhode Island, Pennsylvania, Maryland, and New York. Virginia held a separate, lower-profile conference that same summer to deal with frontier issues. While much of the public time centered on restoring the Covenant Chain, including the dramatic late arrival of the Mohawk, who demanded that the king name William Johnson as their representative, the delegates increasingly met privately to debate Franklin's plan for union.

Left deliberately vague in outline, a committee quickly altered Franklin's original plan, suggesting a "Grand Council" with two to seven representatives from each colony, depending on that colony's contribution to an excise on liquor that would support the workings of the council. With royal prerogative preserved by an appointed President-General or Viceroy, the council would have the power to declare war on or make peace with Native Americans and to control how men and supplies were to be impressed by the Crown. The revised plan also gave more control over western frontier land to the colonies. The committee even suggested imposing a Stamp Tax to fund greater bureaucratic efficiency and coordination.

The revised proposal went to the main body of delegates on June 28. It was debated until July 10, with additional features such as the requirement of an Act of Parliament to legalize the union and the reapportionment every three years of the number of delegates.

Although the motion passed unanimously at Albany, it was received poorly by the assemblies and councils of the colonies themselves, who were startled by the surrender of Virginia militia to the French in the Ohio Valley and distracted by the impending Revolutionary War. The issue became lost in the shuffle.

Franklin's widely reprinted "Unite or Die" cartoons attempted to keep the idea going. The royal government did agree with the Mohawks and named two royal Indian Agents—Johnson in the north, John Bruce in the south. But a plan for union did not appear again until 1774, when Joseph Galloway suggested a plan nearly identical to the Albany proposal as a peacemaking measure between the Iroquois and the English colonists.

Historiographically, the Albany Congress was used in the early national period by Franklin and John Adams to indicate the maturity and inevitable independence of the colonies from Britain. Later, it served to emphasize the degree to which the colonies might or might not have been inspired by the Iroquois Confederacy to unite themselves.

Margaret Sankey

See also: Iroquois Confederacy; Johnson, Sir William; Military and Diplomatic Affairs (Chronology); Military and Diplomatic Affairs (Essay); Native American–European Relations.

Bibliography

Fenton, William. *The Great Law and the Longhouse.* Norman: University of Oklahoma Press, 1998.

Newbold, Robert. *The Albany Congress and Plan of Union of 1754.* New York: Vantage, 1955.

Shannon, Timothy. *Indians and Colonists at the Crossroads of Empire: The Albany Congress of 1754.* Ithaca, NY: Cornell University Press, 2000.

Ward, Harry M. *"Unite or Die": Intercolonial Relations 1690–1763.* Port Washington, NY: Kennikat, 1971.

Alcohol

Alcohol was a vital part of colonial life from the earliest establishment of the Dutch and English colonies. One observer to the region commented, "They all drink here, from the moment they are able to lick a spoon," and the remark was apt.

In the seventeenth century especially, alcohol was considered safer than water, and it was often thought to aid in digestion, ward off fever and chills, and mend broken bones. This tradition was carried over from the Old World to the New, but the American colonists adapted and developed new drinking traditions and novel ingredients of their own. From the beginning, alcohol was fundamentally integrated into the colonial experience.

Beer, Cider, and Wine

When the Dutch founded the settlement at New Amsterdam in 1625, one of the first buildings erected was a brewery. The English settlers who followed likewise had a fondness for beer, and local brewing began as soon as the colonists were ashore. The most popular brew was a dark malt made of barley and flavored with hops, and containing about 6 percent alcohol (eventually this evolved into the modern porter and stout). In addition to the licensed breweries, colonial wives incorporated brewing into their household routines, and beer became a dietary staple. For those who could afford it, imported beer from the Old World was also available.

Although brewers used traditional ingredients when they could, hops and malt from Europe were not always available, especially in the settlements away from the coast. Accordingly, the provincials used whatever local substitutes were handy, including corn, pumpkins, parsnips, and walnuts. Local governments attempted to regulate quality but could do little with regard to the home brews. Still, some entrepreneurs, such as Connecticut governor John Winthrop, Jr., were successful enough to receive international recognition. After creating a highly palatable beer from Indian corn, Winthrop was elected to the esteemed Royal Society of London in 1662, one of the highest scientific honors available. In the following century, such famous personages as Benjamin Franklin, George Washington, and Thomas Jefferson all dabbled in brewing and/or distilling.

Hard cider, brewed from apples, also became popular, especially in the Northern colonies, where orchards planted from European seeds flourished in the hospitable climate. Naturally fermented to about 7 percent alcohol, cider ultimately rivaled beer in popularity. By the early 1700s, and likely much earlier, Anglo-Americans were distilling their cider into potent applejack, with a particularly loyal following in the Mid-Atlantic colonies. "Jersey lightning" was fit for serious drinkers only, however, and too much imbibing could bring on a condition known as "apple palsy."

Though popular in the Old World, wine was available in the English colonies only to upper-class citizens who could afford to import it. Unlike the Spanish and French, who planted vines in their New World possessions, the English had no early viticulture to speak of. In Virginia, a promising attempt by French Huguenots to establish vineyards ended when the growers switched to tobacco and tore out the vines.

Thus, the wines served in the English colonies were generally imported at considerable expense from Europe and the Madeira islands, and among the masses, wine never became as popular a beverage as beer or cider.

Hard Liquor

Hard liquor, on the other hand, was another matter. Generically termed "aqua vitae" or "hot water," distilled beverages came in the form of brandy, whiskey, gin, and rum. These contained on average 45 percent alcohol (in distiller's terms, 90 proof), though the rums were often stronger. Colonists valued liquor for this high alcohol content, which enabled it to keep better than

beer. The high alcohol content was also at times responsible for excessive drunkenness, and, from the beginning, distilled spirits were potent enough to raise concerns over misuse.

Colonists nonetheless placed such a premium on distilled liquor that in the early years it was often used as wages. When the Boston town council threatened to halt this practice in the 1640s, one group of laborers responded with what may have been America's first strike, and the authorities backed down and restored the workers' drink.

Around the turn of the eighteenth century, a shift occurred in popular drinking patterns, and distilled spirits replaced beer as the alcoholic beverages of choice. As supply increased and prices dropped, especially in the case of rum (produced from sugar molasses), colonists took to imbibing hard liquor more often, and because of the high alcohol content, they achieved the desired state of inebriation more rapidly. Rum, which was served straight up or mixed in grogs and toddies, grew especially prevalent as sugar cane production in-

Barrels of rum are loaded for shipping in Antigua. In the 1720s, the colonies imported more than 2.1 million gallons of rum from the Caribbean "sugar islands." The colonists drank abundantly, and sailors and other workers received regular rations of alcoholic beverages. *(British Library, London, United Kingdom/Bridgeman Art Library)*

creased in the Caribbean "sugar islands." Colonial officials began to express their concerns about alcohol abuse, drunkenness, disorder, and the lack of control in regulating drinking habits.

Gin, in particular, developed a dubious reputation in both the Old World and the New. Distilled from the juniper berry, gin was produced cheaply and easily and became highly popular among the urban poor. In the view of many Englishmen, the "gin epidemic" had grown out of control by the 1730s, and it was immortalized in the public imagination in Hogarth's famous "Gin Lane" prints, which depicted the ravages of gin on English society. The urban population in the colonies, however, remained small enough so that gin never took on the same social significance as it did in the metropole. Nonetheless, colonial officials attempted to regulate alcohol consumption more closely as the eighteenth century progressed.

Use and Abuse

Two of the main characteristics of alcohol consumption in colonial America were frequency and quantity. Stated simply, most settlers drank often and abundantly. Alcohol consumption was a normal part of personal and communal habits, and in colonial homes beer and cider were the usual beverages at mealtime, including for children. Communal projects such as clearing the fields or raising buildings were usually accompanied by a public cask to fortify the laboring citizens, and farmers usually took a generous ration into the fields. Though this policy may seem foolhardy by modern standards, the rationale in colonial times was that the backbreaking labor required in these pursuits was somewhat allayed by the effects of alcohol.

Drinking became institutionalized in other spheres as well. Both the Anglican and Puritan churches, for example, used communion wine. New England towns held "ordinaries," or weekly community gatherings where the citizens prayed, ate, drank, and gossiped. In the South, alcohol mixed with politics in the practice known as "treating," where candidates for local office provided the electorate with plentiful libations, presumably in return for their vote. In addition to political events, weddings, baptisms, funerals, holidays, ministerial ordinations, and militia musters were normally wet occasions. Most drinking, however, occurred in inns and taverns, which were often among the first structures constructed in colonial towns, and they remained prevalent and popular throughout the colonial period.

Despite the heavy drinking, there was little public outcry against alcoholism, and certainly no prerevolutionary equivalent of the temperance or prohibition movement. Extreme intemperance was held largely in check by traditional cultural and societal norms that stressed common loyalty and standards of individual conduct. If individual willpower wavered, families, friends, ministers, and magistrates served to guard against deviant behavior. The church, especially, played a central role in defending community values, as Increase Mather, the Puritan preacher from Boston, made clear in his sermon "Woe to Drunkards" (1673), which warned against the sin of drunkenness. Civil officials addressed more temporal concerns when alcohol consumption led to crime, and each colony developed extensive legal codes to combat all aspects of liquor violations. Colonial magistrates, however, rarely let concerns over excesses in drinking spill over into general attacks on the consumption of alcohol, which was recognized as a fundamentally necessary product.

Two important exceptions to this rule involved Native Americans and African Americans. Strict regulations were enacted to limit alcohol consumption by members of these two groups, who differed both ethnically and culturally from the European settlers. Native inhabitants of North America had no prior experience with alcoholic beverages before the Europeans arrived, but they quickly learned of its debilitating powers, especially from European fur traders on the frontier. Colonists became convinced that the native people could not hold their liquor, and a long-standing stereotype was born concerning their propensity to alcoholism (some modern anthropologists have termed this the "firewater myth"). Evidence suggests that reactions to alcohol and drinking behavior varied widely from tribe to tribe, but the stereotype held firm, and regulations were enacted in most colonies that strictly limited the sale of liquor to Native Americans, though enforcement was sometimes lax.

Like Native Americans, blacks were often perceived as inferior heathens, and alcohol consumption among African American slaves was generally limited by what the masters would allow. Notwithstanding this general rule, on holidays, Sundays, and special occasions, some masters rewarded their slaves with liquor rations. Overall, however, the discipline and demands placed upon the slaves, as well as white fears of intoxicated blacks, severely limited the amount of alcohol consumed for other than "medicinal purposes." In the New England and Mid-Atlantic colonies, slaves who were caught in taverns without their masters' permission were often flogged, and fines were assessed upon the tavern proprietors who served them. After the New York slave revolt of 1741, anyone caught selling liquor to a free African American was severely fined.

Thus, from the earliest settlements to the American Revolution, alcohol was firmly integrated into colonial life. Though beverage choices and consumption patterns were initially carried over from the Old World, American colonists soon developed beverages and drinking habits different from those of the European world they had left behind.

Kevin P. McDonald

See also: Agriculture; Corn; Grain; Inns and Taverns (Public Houses); Sugar; Triangle Trade. *Document*: Connecticut Blue Laws (1650).

Bibliography

Bridenbaugh, Carl. *Cities in the Wilderness: The First Century of Urban Life in America, 1625–1742.* London: Oxford University Press, 1971.

Conroy, David W. *In Public Houses: Drink and the Revolution of Authority in Colonial Massachusetts.* Chapel Hill: University of North Carolina Press, 1995.

Lender, Mark E., and James K. Martin. *Drinking in America: A History.* New York: Free Press, 1987.

Salinger, Sharon V. *Taverns and Drinking in Early America.* Baltimore: Johns Hopkins University Press, 2002.

Alexander, Mary Spratt Provoost (1693–1760)

Mary Spratt Provoost Alexander entered life as the daughter of an immigrant and became a leading merchant, prominent citizen, and one of the most influential women of the colonial period. As she grew up in New York City, one of the main centers of colonial commerce, it was natural that, later in life, she herself would become a merchant. Dutch women colonists had a tradition of merchandising and trade, even though women in Europe and the other North American colonies generally were not involved in business; in some cases, they were not even allowed to own property.

Born on April 17, 1693, Mary was the daughter of John Spratt, a Scottish immigrant merchant who rose to become an alderman for the City of New York, and Maria DePeyster, an heiress of a prominent Dutch family of goldsmiths, merchants, and politicians. When Spratt died in 1697, his widow remarried, this time to David Provoost, who had an established reputation as both a merchant and a smuggler.

After the death of her mother in 1700, Mary and her siblings acquired a sizable inheritance. In 1711, she married Samuel Provoost, her stepfather's younger brother who also was an importer, and they had three children together. Mary invested much of her inheritance in her husband's enterprises and acted as his business partner. What she accomplished was to build a trading empire of stores throughout New York City for which it was said she imported so many goods that most ships arriving in New York port had a consignment for her.

Sometime in 1719, or perhaps early 1720, Samuel Provoost died. Mary immediately assumed full control of all of his business affairs. With her increased fortune and reputation as a successful merchant, she married again in 1721. Her new husband, James Alexander, was a direct descendant of the Scottish Earls of Stirling, as well as one of New York's leading attorneys and politicians.

With her second husband, Mary Alexander had seven more children, of whom five lived to adulthood. Perhaps the most prominent of her children was her son William Alexander, who later assumed the title Lord Stirling. He served as an aide and secretary to General William Shirley during the French and Indian War and later served as a successful general under George Washington during the American Revolution.

For the rest of her life, Mary continued to raise her family, assist them with their business affairs, and directly manage the Provoost mercantile business. She sold goods in her own store, which she had built, along with a row of counting house offices, in front of her mansion on Broad Street. Her imported inventory was frequently augmented by goods that her husband received as payment for his legal services.

The Alexander's store and home quickly became a meeting spot and salon for many of New York's elite politicians and businessmen, and Mary was reputed to be an informal adviser to many of them, including Andrew Hamilton, the attorney for John Peter Zenger. The stock of goods within the Provoost system of stores was so extensive that during the French and Indian War, they supplied General William Shirley's Fort Niagara expedition with provisions.

Mary Alexander died on April 18, 1760, in New York City. Both she and her husband James are buried in the Trinity Church cemetery in lower Manhattan.

Arthur E. Chapman

See also: Merchants; Trade; Widows and Widowers.

Bibliography

James, Edward T., ed. *Notable American Women, 1607–1950; a Biographical Dictionary.* Cambridge, MA: Harvard University Press, 1971.

Van Rensselaer, John King. *The Goede Vrouw of Mana-ha-ta at Home and in Society, 1609–1760.* New York: Charles Scribner's Sons, 1898.

American Philosophical Society

The first enduring American scientific society was formed as part of a wave of organization that swept the European and American intellectual world in the mid-eighteenth century. The first American Philosophical Society was a short-lived Philadelphia group that met from 1743 to 1746. Leading members included Benjamin Franklin, the group's leading promoter; the inventor of the octant, Thomas Godfrey, Sr.; and plant collector John Bartram.

The group revived in 1767. The new American Philosophical Society was dominated by members of the Church of England and supporters of the Proprietary Party in Pennsylvania politics.

On December 20, 1768, this American Philosophical Society merged with a similar Philadelphia-based group, the American Society for Promoting and Propagating Useful Knowledge. The American Society, which had been meeting since 1750 but had only taken this name in 1766, was dominated by Quakers, traders, and opponents of the Proprietary Party. (At the time of the merger, it had just absorbed yet another group, the Philadelphia Medical Society, a physicians' group founded in 1766 by John Morgan.) The new society's official name was a compromise: American Philosophical Society for the Promotion of Useful Knowledge. The new society's organization was modeled on Britain's Royal Society, with a large, unpaid, and theoretically equal membership and a small body of elected officers.

The officers were originally balanced between the members of the two former societies, but as time went on members of the Philosophical Society group clearly dominated. Franklin was more closely aligned with the original American Society group, but his stature as America's leading scientist made him the obvious choice to be elected president at the new society's first meeting on January 2, 1769. Since he was in England at the time, he was elected president in absentia. He held the office until his death, and dominated the society's image outside America—to Europeans it was "Franklin's Society."

The society made a determined effort to recruit scientists from elsewhere in the colonies as corresponding members, focusing on the Middle and Southern colonies rather than New England. It also had corresponding members in Europe. The new society was supposed to be supported by admission fees and annual dues, both of 10 shillings, but these often went unpaid, particularly as attendance and interest in the society waned after the excitement of its founding. In addition to Franklin, leading colonial scientists among the society's members included Bartram, who was inactive, and the young astronomer David Rittenhouse. Its unofficial leader, from the Philosophical Society group, was Thomas Bond.

The society's first major project was the collection

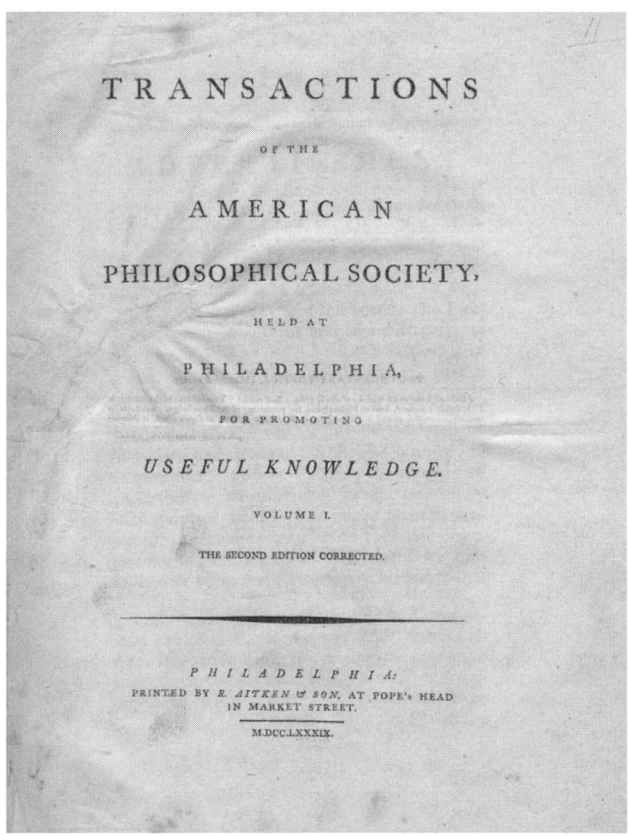

The American Philosophical Society, dating to the 1740s, was the first enduring scientific society in America. Its official organ, *Transactions,* remains the oldest scholarly publication in the country. The first edition appeared in 1771; this issue is dated 1789. *(University of Chicago Library, Special Collections)*

of astronomical observations of the transit of Venus in June. The transit is a time when Venus, as viewed from earth, crosses the disk of the sun. Getting exact measurements of the time Venus first appeared to touch the solar disk and the time it took to cross the sun's face from as many places as possible was extremely important to astronomers. There would be no second chance for anyone alive at the time: there had been a transit in 1761, but after 1769 the phenomenon would not recur for over a century. This called forth a massive coordinated effort from Europe's scientific societies, and provided an ideal opportunity for the new American society to prove its worth. The society applied for and received a grant from the Pennsylvania legislature for this purpose, and coordinated and collected over twenty observations by astronomers throughout the British colonies in North America. The data gathered occupied a major part of the first volume of the society's *Transactions,* published in 1771. (Unofficial transactions had been published in *The American Magazine,* a short-lived publication belonging to society member Lewis Nicola.) Copies were sent to several European scientific societies, and distributed in Europe by Franklin. The observations favorably impressed many European astronomers. The next volume of *Transactions* did not appear until after the Revolution.

Much of the society's activity was devoted to economic development. It received a grant from the colonial assembly of 1,000 pounds, matched by another 1,000 pounds raised by subscription, to start a silkworm industry in Pennsylvania. The society also received 200 pounds from local merchants to examine possible routes for a canal from the Delaware to the Chesapeake.

Meetings of the American Philosophical Society were suspended from 1776 to 1779 by the American Revolution, and a rival, the Boston-based American Academy of Arts and Sciences, was founded in 1780. Although it shared in the general decline of American science after the Revolution, the American Philosophical Society survived to become the leading scientific organization in the new United States.

William E. Burns

See also: Arts, Culture, and Intellectual Life (Essay); Franklin, Benjamin; Philadelphia; Quakers; Science; Science and Technology (Chronology).

Bibliography

Bell, Whitfield J. *Patriot-Improvers: Biographical Sketches of Members of the American Philosophical Society.* 2 vols. Philadelphia: American Philosophical Society, 1997–1999.

McClellan, James E., III. *Science Reorganized: Scientific Societies in the Eighteenth Century.* New York: Columbia University Press, 1985.

Stearns, Raymond Phineas. *Science in the British Colonies of America.* Urbana: University of Illinois Press, 1970.

Anabaptists

Anabaptists were part of a religious movement known as the Radical Reformation, which arose in German-speaking areas of Europe, primarily the Rhine Valley and the Low Countries, during the sixteenth century. The reaction among the established churches of Europe to the Radical Reformation was swift and severe, forcing many Anabaptists to migrate to the New World.

Many Anabaptists who fled to the New World migrated to the religiously tolerant colony of Pennsylvania. In 1683, Anabaptists established their first permanent settlement in colonial North America in Germantown, Pennsylvania. A group of thirteen German families of Dutch ancestry arrived in Philadelphia aboard the *Concord* in October 1683 and immediately laid out their small village just north of the city. They had purchased the land from Jacob Telner, a Mennonite merchant from Amsterdam, and from the Frankfort Land Company, which was led by Francis Daniel Pastorius. Initially, Anabaptists met with their Quaker neighbors in common worship, but, as more Anabaptists arrived in the colony, the two groups began to meet separately. By 1690, Anabaptists were meeting privately in members' homes for religious instruction, which usually consisted of a set of readings from a book of sermons. They had also elected a papermaker, William Rittenhouse, who had arrived in the colony in 1688, to serve as their first minister. In 1708, Anabaptists constructed their first permanent, separate meetinghouse.

Anabaptists held several fundamental beliefs that made them appear radical to many of their contemporaries. They believed in a literal interpretation of the Bible and attempted to carry out a literal following of the teachings of Christ. Among other things, this meant that they rejected anything that might be considered "worldly" and chose to worship in barns, houses, and other secular buildings. Believing in the importance of personal faith in God, they shunned the rituals of established churches, did not conduct Mass, and instead engaged in a memorial Last Supper. They also believed in the baptism of faithful adults rather than infants and considered infant baptism invalid. Their baptismal process, which they conducted by immersing the person in a stream of running water, came to be known as "rebaptism," or "anabaptism," by its detractors. Finally, unlike Catholics and most Protestants, Anabaptists believed in a complete separation of church and state. These pacifists refused to pay taxes, swear oaths, serve in the military, or cooperate in any way with a civil government whose authority rested upon the use of force. Needless to say, Anabaptists became extremely unpopular in many parts of Europe and the New World.

The term "Anabaptist" is actually a misnomer and was used as an epithet by those individuals who opposed the Radical Reformation. Most Anabaptists would not have referred to themselves as such, but would have instead used the term "Brethren," "Hutterite," "Mennonite," or "Amish." Most Anabaptists traced their spiritual beliefs to the teachings of Menno Simons, a Dutch Catholic priest who renounced Ca-

tholicism in 1536, and they referred to themselves as Mennonites.

The first settlers at Germantown were Mennonites. The largest Mennonite settlement during the colonial period was not at Germantown, however. It was actually in Lancaster County, Pennsylvania, along the banks of the Conestoga River.

The other major Anabaptist sect, the Amish, took their name from Jacob Amman, a Swiss Mennonite leader who came into conflict with other Mennonites over the practices of banning and shunning. Amman believed in the maintenance of a strict system of banning and shunning for followers who broke the rules, as well as a strict repudiation of all forms of worldliness. The first Amish settlers arrived in Philadelphia aboard the *Adventure* on October 2, 1727. Initially, the Amish were reluctant to leave their Swiss homeland but many did eventually emigrate. Throughout the remainder of the colonial period, Amish immigrants formed com-

Members of a sixteenth-century Christian movement in Europe, the Anabaptists later settled in Pennsylvania. They rejected baptism for children but believed in it for faithful adults. Detractors called the latter practice "rebaptism" or "anabaptism." *(Library of Congress, LC-USZC4-3265)*

munities in Berks, Chester, and Lancaster counties, Pennsylvania.

The third group of Anabaptists, the Hutterites, took their name from Jacob Hutter, whom they chose as their leader in 1533. For refusing to renounce his faith, he was burned at the stake in 1536 on orders of the government of the Austrian Emperor Ferdinand I, but Hutter's church survived.

Mennonites, Amish, and Hutterites brought the Anabaptist tradition to the New World, primarily to Pennsylvania, but also to the Midwest and the Canadian prairie. Today, there are at least nineteen distinct Mennonite and Amish communities, consisting of approximately 200,000 members. A much smaller group of Hutterite Brethren, who migrated from Russia and Europe, live in communal colonies primarily in the northwestern United States and Canada.

Michael A. Rembis

See also: Bible; Christ and Christianity; Germans; Religion (Chronology); Religion (Essay).

Bibliography

Bender, Harold S., and C. Henry Smith. *Mennonites and Their Heritage: A Handbook of Mennonite History and Beliefs.* Rev. ed. Scottdale, PA: Herald, 1964.

Bennett, John W. *Hutterian Brethren: The Agricultural Economy and Social Organization of a Communal People.* Stanford, CA: Stanford University Press, 1967.

Hostetler, John A., ed. *Amish Roots: A Treasury of History, Wisdom, and Lore.* Baltimore: Johns Hopkins University Press, 1989.

Rich, Elaine Sommers. *Mennonite Women: A Story of God's Faithfulness, 1683–1983.* Scottdale, PA: Herald, 1983.

Smith, C. Henry. *The Story of the Mennonites.* 4th ed., revised and enlarged by Cornelius Krahn. Newton, KS: Mennonite Publication Office, 1957.

Williams, Peter W. *America's Religions: From Their Origins to the Twenty-first Century.* Urbana: University of Illinois Press, 2002.

Andros, Sir Edmund (1637–1714)

Descendent of a distinguished family from the English Channel island of Guernsey, Sir Edmund Andros was born in December 1637. He served under four English monarchs before his retirement from public service in 1706. From 1674 through 1698, Andros served as governor of New York, then of the short-lived Dominion of New England, and finally of Virginia.

Andros was an able and experienced administrator who sought to impose greater Crown control over the colonies and the burgeoning English empire. He constantly found himself at odds with colonists who viewed his measures as arbitrary and hostile to colonial interests. On four separate occasions, colonists from New York (1680 and 1689), Massachusetts (1689), and Virginia (1698) rebelled against Andros's heavy-handed governance.

Prior to 1675, Andros gained administrative experience by holding offices on Guernsey and military experience as an officer in various colonial regiments. In 1675, James Stuart, duke of York, appointed Andros governor of New York, formerly the Dutch colony of New Netherland. Andros's military and administrative experience made him an ideal candidate to govern a colony only recently seized from the Dutch and still exposed to threats from the French and their native allies. As governor, Andros helped forge an alliance, called the Covenant Chain, between the English and the powerful Iroquois of upstate New York. Andros governed New York's European population by creating an oligarchic council dependent on economic privileges conferred by him. When excluded Dutch and English leaders protested, Andros had them arrested and confiscated their property. Andros's actions, though approved by the duke of York, smacked of arbitrary and despotic government.

When the duke of York became King James II in 1685, he moved to consolidate the Crown's control over the colonies, increase its colonial revenues, and better provide for colonial defense against France and Native American nations by creating the Dominion of New England. James II appointed Andros governor-general of this new colony, stretching from Maine to the Delaware River. The Dominion of New England, which incorporated the New England colonies, New York, and New Jersey into a single government, stripped the Northern colonies of their charters and their elected assemblies. The dominion also placed all power in the hands of Andros, his lieutenant governor, and appointed councils. Andros's actions immediately produced protests from the colonists he governed.

Andros's strict enforcement of the Navigation Acts upset New England merchants. Andros then outraged other New Englanders when he began to challenge the legitimacy of land titles issued by New England towns under the old colonial charters. To further weaken Puritan dominance of the local and colonial governments, Andros and James II replaced

Puritan officials such as judges and sheriffs with non-Puritans loyal to him. He also limited town meetings to one session per year, prohibited towns from using tax money to pay ministers' salaries, and forced Boston to give up one of its Puritan churches to the Anglican Church. To pay for his excessive salary of 1,200 pounds, along with his officials' salaries, Andros levied heavy taxes, which a majority of his own council opposed. In 1687, when leading men from the town of Ipswich, Massachusetts, protested Andros's arbitrary rule, he promptly arrested the men, had them tried before an unsympathetic jury (picked by an Andros-appointed sheriff), and then jailed them. In New York, the heavy-handed administration of Andros and his deputy governor, Francis Nicholson, outraged New Yorkers, too.

By the spring of 1689, rumors that William of Orange and his wife, Mary, had claimed the throne abdicated by James II began to reach New York and Boston. Andros and Nicholson responded by imprisoning men who brought news of the "Glorious Revolution" to the colonies. In April, Andros was in Boston, but his main body of troops was in Maine waging war against the Abenakis. On April 18, 1689, Boston and its surrounding towns rose in rebellion against Andros. Within hours, 2,000 or so militia members streamed into Boston in a carefully coordinated uprising led by Puritans. The rebellion leaders promptly arrested and jailed Andros along with twenty-five of his officials. Andros spent nine months in a Boston jail before colonial officials shipped him to England to face charges that he had abused his authority.

In April 1690, a privy council exonerated Andros of the charges the Massachusetts government had brought against him. In 1692, King William III appointed Andros captain general and governor-in-chief of Virginia. Almost immediately, Andros clashed with powerful men in Virginia. In 1697, leading Virginians traveled to London and charged Andros with abusing his power. Facing recall, Andros resigned and returned to London.

After serving as lieutenant governor of Guernsey, Andros retired from public life in 1706. He spent the remainder of his life in London until he passed away in February 1714.

John Craig Hammond

See also: Boston; New England, Dominion of; Politics and Government (Chronology); Politics and Government (Essay). *Document*: Commission of Sir Edmund Andros for the Dominion of New England (1688).

Bibliography

Johnson, Richard R. "The Revolution of 1688–9 in the American Colonies." In *The Anglo-Dutch Moment: Essays on the Glorious Revolution and Its World Impact*, edited by Jonathan I. Israel. New York: Cambridge University Press, 1991.
Lovejoy, David S. *The Glorious Revolution in America.* New York: Harper and Row, 1972.
Webb, Stephen Saunders. "The Trials of Edmund Andros." In *The Human Dimensions of Nation Making: Essays on Colonial and Revolutionary America*, edited by James Kirby Martin. Madison: State Historical Society of Wisconsin, 1976.

Anglican Church

The term "Anglican Church" refers to the reformed Church of England and its dependent churches abroad, such as those in colonial America. The Anglicans were the predominant sect in Virginia and other parts of the South during the colonial era.

English Reformation of the Sixteenth Century

The path to a reformed English church was anything but straightforward under the Tudor monarchs in the sixteenth century. Initially, Henry VIII, as a committed Roman Catholic, wrote a defense of the seven sacraments against the reformed writings of Martin Luther. The king received the title Defender of the Faith from an appreciative Pope Leo X in 1521. But the papacy was not as obliging in 1527, when Henry VIII asked that his marriage to Catherine of Aragon, his wife of eighteen years, be declared invalid. Henry VIII had only one daughter, Mary, who was born in 1516, and he wished to marry again in the hopes of having a male heir. After failing to gain Rome's concurrence, beginning in 1533 Henry VIII and Parliament passed legislation denying papal jurisdiction and making the king supreme head of the Church of England. The king's newly appointed archbishop of Canterbury, Thomas Cranmer, the senior churchman in England, declared the king's marriage to Catherine dissolved. Henry VIII could then marry Anne Boleyn in 1533, the same year their only child, Elizabeth, was born.

In 1536, Henry VIII began the dissolution of the English monasteries and sold off the monastic lands to the gentry. In 1536, Catherine of Aragon died, and Anne Boleyn was executed on purported charges of adultery and treason. Henry VIII's third wife, Jane

Seymour, died in 1537 after giving birth to his long-awaited son, Edward. Henry VIII married three more times but had no more children. By the Act of Six Articles of 1539 the king further defined the church he had created, which remained Catholic in doctrine. Most importantly, the English church still believed in transubstantiation, the real presence of Christ in the communion wine and bread. Henry VIII had created an Anglo-Catholic church.

The Protestant reformation of the Church of England first occurred during the reign of Henry's son, Edward VI. The Act of Uniformity of 1549 abolished the Latin mass and substituted as the official form of worship the new English Prayer Book, written by Archbishop Cranmer and other divines. In 1552, Cranmer, further influenced by Continental reformers, produced a revised *Book of Common Prayer* in which holy communion became a memorial of Christ's last supper, thus denying the Catholic doctrine of transubstantiation.

Before the English people had time to absorb these fundamental changes, Edward VI died and was succeeded by his half sister Mary I, who declared herself Roman Catholic. The English church was to undergo yet another transformation, as Parliament repealed all Protestant legislation, to include the 1552 Prayer Book, and the doctrine of transubstantiation was reinstated. Parliament, however, repealed the legislation against papal authority in England only after the papacy gave assurances that the confiscated church properties would not have to be restored. Mary I also reactivated the laws against heresy by which 300 Protestants were burned at the stake, among them Thomas Cranmer.

When Mary I died childless in 1558, her half sister Elizabeth I ascended the throne. To Catholics, Elizabeth I was illegitimate, having been born to Anne Boleyn while her father was legally married to Catherine of Aragon by the laws of their church. For that reason, as well as her personal preference, Elizabeth I re-created a Protestant Church of England. The pope's authority was once again denied by the Act of Supremacy of 1559, which made the queen the supreme governor of the English church. The Act of Uniformity revived the Prayer Book of 1552, and in 1563 the convocation, or governing body of church clergy, passed the Thirty-Nine Articles of Religion, which were clearly Protestant in content. Nevertheless, in the hopes of creating an all-embracing church, Elizabeth I maintained bishops and left certain matters of ritual and vestments unchanged. During her reign, those who wanted to further "purify" the church and remove all vestiges of Cathol-

icism found that the queen would condone no more innovations.

Religious Conflict in the Seventeenth Century

Elizabeth I's death, in 1603, brought her cousin James VI Stuart of Scotland to the throne of England as James I. He and the succeeding Stuart monarchs of the seventeenth century would have to face the ongoing, oftentimes rancorous, debate about the structure and practices of the Church of England.

At the very start of his reign, James I was presented with the Millenary Petition, signed by over 1,000 ministers, asking for a church conference. This Puritan faction hoped that James I, raised in the Calvinist Presbyterian Kirk of Scotland, would be open to their call for a further "godly reformation." The resultant Hampton Court Conference of 1604, however, failed to produce any changes in the *Book of Common Prayer* or in the episcopate, for James I supported the Elizabethan settlement. The king did authorize a new translation of the Bible. The King James Bible, published in 1611, not only served as a standard text for the church but also became one of the great literary masterpieces of the English language.

It was also under James I that the first successful English colonies in North America were founded. In 1607, Jamestown was established by the Virginia Company, and it was here that the Church of England took strongest root in British North America. The Anglican clergy in the colonies eventually came under the jurisdiction of the bishop of London. This posed a contradiction for the Anglican Church in America, since it was an episcopal church without any resident bishops or local ecclesiastic courts, so that the colonial laity came to assume greater control of church affairs. Nor was the Church of England ever accorded exclusivity within the colonies. Instead, British North America became a haven for nonconformists, those seeking to practice their faith differently than prescribed by the established church. Beginning in 1620, when the *Mayflower* reached Plymouth, the settlements in New England became a refuge for Puritans and their form of worship, called Congregationalism.

James I's son, Charles I, was raised in the Anglican faith. He strongly believed in maintaining the episcopal structure, the ritual, and the sacraments, as did William Laud, his archbishop of Canterbury. The Puritans, who preferred a good sermon expounding on Holy Scripture over ritual, increasingly sought refuge in the colonies at a time when Laud was seeking closer conformity within the English communities abroad. To that end, in 1637, the king issued two decrees that attempted to enforce the conformity of all those emigrating to New England, including the ministers themselves. Laud planned to appoint a bishop to the British North American colonies, but developments within the British Isles soon diverted attention from the colonial church.

Charles I's attempt to impose an Anglican-style prayer book on the Scottish kirk led to the Bishops' Wars of 1639–1640 with Scotland. The English Parliament, back in session in 1640 after an eleven-year hiatus, attempted to limit the king's sovereignty and to reform the Church of England, "root and branch." King and Parliament went to war in 1642, and the English Civil War ended in 1646 with the king's defeat. Both Laud, executed in 1645, and the Church of England were casualties of the war, but the victorious Parliamentarians were themselves divided over the form of a new religious settlement. While a majority wanted a presbyterian-style church government, a powerful minority of Independents, who dominated Parliament's victorious New Model Army, wanted independent congregations. Oliver Cromwell, the cavalry commander of the New Model and a leading Independent, was among those who condemned Charles I to death in January 1649 and abolished the English monarchy.

Under the ensuing Commonwealth (1649–1653) and Cromwell's Protectorate (1653–1658), a certain amount of religious toleration was granted to Protestants, although congregations were prohibited from using the prayer book or rituals of the Anglican Church. After Cromwell's death, in 1658, a restoration of the Stuart monarchy and the Church of England took place in 1660. Soon thereafter, episcopal control from England was again exercised over the colonial established church.

Reestablishment of the Church of England

Under Charles II, a series of acts known as the Clarendon Code defined the religious settlement. The king became supreme governor of the Church of England, and the Act of Uniformity of 1662 authorized a slightly revised *Book of Common Prayer*. The Test Act of 1673, aimed at both dissenting Protestants and Roman Catholics, allowed only those who passed the "test" of taking communion in the Church of England to hold public and ecclesiastic office or military commissions.

A crisis developed during the reign of James II, Charles II's Catholic brother. Wanting toleration for both Dissenters and Catholics, James II issued a Declaration of Indulgence, which the Anglican bishops openly opposed. Then in June 1688, James II's second wife gave birth to a son. This male heir, to be raised Catholic, took precedence over James II's two older daughters, Mary and Anne, who had been raised Anglican. The political elite of England wanted neither a king seeking to suspend parliamentary law nor a Catholic succession. So in a bloodless coup, they invited James II's eldest daughter, Mary, and her Dutch husband, William, Prince of Orange, to England, and James II and his new family fled.

By the Glorious Revolution, William III and Mary II became joint sovereigns of England. The Church of England remained the established church, but the Toleration Act of 1689 did permit Dissenters to have their own chapels. In 1693, the monarchs granted a charter for the Virginia college bearing their names, the first Anglican-affiliated institution of higher learning in the colonies. Since William and Mary had no children, nor did Anne despite many pregnancies, Parliament passed the Act of Settlement in 1701; henceforth, only Protestants who conformed to the Church of England would be permitted to succeed to the English throne. Anne, the last Stuart monarch, was a staunch Anglican and personally provided for the poorer clergy in what became known as Queen Anne's Bounty. Upon her death, she was succeeded by her closest Protestant relation, George, elector of Hanover.

With the firm establishment of the Anglican Church in England, efforts were made to strengthen the church in the colonies by such organizations as the Society for Promoting Christian Knowledge, founded in 1698 to distribute Anglican literature abroad, and the Society for the Propagation of the Gospel in Foreign Parts, a missionary body. Nevertheless, a pattern of religious diversity continued in the American colonies. Although the Anglican church expanded in the eighteenth century, it did not keep pace with other Protestant denominations, and, by the time of the revolution, it had fallen to fourth place, after Congregationalists, Presbyterians, and Baptists.

The Church of England obviously could not survive the American Revolution as such, since its clergy had to pledge allegiance to the English monarch. While many colonial Anglican clergymen were loyalists, some did side with the American patriots. After independence, those who still believed in the Anglican doctrines founded the American Episcopal Church.

Florene S. Memegalos

See also: Bible; Christ and Christianity; Religion (Chronology); Religion (Essay).

Bibliography

Cross, Arthur Lyon. *The Anglican Episcopate and the American Colonies.* Reprint of Harvard Historical Studies 9, 1902. Hamden, CT: Archon, 1964.

Elton, G. R. *Reform and Reformation: England, 1509–1558.* Cambridge, MA: Harvard University Press, 1977.

Prall, Stuart E. *Church and State in Tudor and Stuart England.* Arlington Heights, IL: Harlan Davidson, 1993.

Rhoden, Nancy L. *Revolutionary Anglicanism: The Colonial Church of England Clergy During the American Revolution.* New York: New York University Press, 1999.

Scarisbrick, J. J. *Reformation and the English People.* Oxford, UK: Blackwell, 1984.

Woolverton, John Frederick. *Colonial Anglicanism in North America.* Detroit, MI: Wayne State University Press, 1984.

Anne, Queen (1665–1714)

Born at St. James's Palace on February 6, 1665, Anne was the second surviving child and younger daughter of James, duke of York (James II), and his first wife, Anne Hyde. Raised at the instruction of Charles II as a Protestant, Anne was a pious and conventional noblewoman, kept deliberately from learning the exercise of political power in favor of needlework and housekeeping. Anne deeply resented both her mother's conversion to Roman Catholicism and James II's second marriage to an Italian princess. Anne's own marriage in 1683, to Prince George of Denmark, was a happy one, although of seventeen pregnancies, only one child, William of Gloucester, lived to age 11, dying in 1700.

Anne, living in London when James II became king, was a natural focus for an opposition party. She was at the center of accusations that James II's son, born in 1688, was the "warming-pan" baby rather than a true heir. (As a warming pan kept a bed heated in preparation for someone going to bed, so the son would serve as a substitute until a real heir came along.)

Subsequently, she and her household officials, including John and Sarah Churchill, aided the Revolution of 1688 by abandoning James II and persuading key figures in the military and church to follow them. Anne continued to be the focus of discontented politicians and nobles during the reign of William and Mary, with whom Anne had a strained relationship, although she was treated as heir to the throne by the childless king and queen. She became queen on March 8, 1702, when William III died.

Anne's reign began with England involved in the War of the Spanish Succession, which she popularized by giving overall command of English forces to Churchill, who would be made duke of Marlborough for his victory at Blenheim. In North America, this war was called Queen Anne's War, and it included a major Native American conflict, the Tuscarora War (1711–1715), and a French-provoked Native American raid into Deerfield, Massachusetts. Despite her natural leanings toward the ideology of the Tory party, Anne chose moderate ministers, preferring Churchill and his sons-in-law and largely ignoring the Whigs.

One of the most significant moves of her reign

Queen Anne (r. 1702–1714) came to the British throne amid the War of the Spanish Succession, which played out in the American theater as a prolonged territorial struggle with France that became known as Queen Anne's War. *(Philip Mould, Historical Portraits Ltd., London, United Kingdom/ Bridgeman Art Library)*

was arranging the Union of Scotland and England in 1707; the treaty required the queen to expend huge sums in bribes, special favors, and personal requests in order to achieve a permanent joining of the island as Great Britain. This union, however, allowed Scots legal access to the English colonies, where they were establishing powerful tobacco and banking presence. A Jacobite plot on behalf of James II's Catholic son was launched in 1708, partially in protest against the union, but it was crushed by good intelligence and selective arrests of the Scottish and English ringleaders.

The end of Queen Anne's reign saw significant changes in policy, as a series of crises pushed her from largely passive ruler into active decision maker. Britain's candidate to be king of Spain, Archduke Charles, also inherited the Habsburg Austrian Empire, while fighting bogged down and costs mounted. A personal falling-out with the Churchills led to their removal from court power and replacement by Robert Harley, and the election of a Tory majority in the House of Commons ensured an end to the War through the Treaty of Utrecht. This treaty gave the British the *asiento*, a coveted privilege allowing them to sell a quota of African slaves to Spanish America every year, which created the South Sea Company and encouraged seaborne trade in the Caribbean. Additionally, the treaty was an acknowledgment by other European powers that Britain was a significant and very desirable power with which to ally.

Anne, a chronic invalid with gout and arthritis, suffered a series of strokes in the summer of 1714, provoking a scramble by her ministers to either ensure their places under the legal, Protestant successor, George of Hanover, or launch a Jacobite restoration under Anne's half brother, James Edward Stuart. By the time of Anne's death at Westminster on August 1, 1714, the Jacobite conspirators had failed to organize. George I acceded peacefully to the throne of a united Great Britain, rising on the European scene as a great and colonial power.

Margaret Sankey

See also: James II; Queen Anne's War.

Bibliography

Cowles, Virginia. *The Great Marlborough and His Duchess.* New York: Macmillan, 1983.

Gregg, Edward. *Queen Anne.* New Haven, CT: Yale University Press, 2001.

Waller, Maureen. *Ungrateful Daughters.* New York: St. Martin's, 2003.

Antigua

Antigua, the largest of the Leeward Islands, belonging to the Lesser Antillean chain in the Caribbean Sea, had a difficult existence in the early colonial period but developed into an important English "sugar island" by 1708. The indigenous Carib and Arawak peoples of the circum-Caribbean region shunned the island because of its lack of natural springs and rivers and its limited annual rainfall. And when Columbus set anchor in 1493 and christened the island after the Church of Santa Maria de la Antigua in Seville, neither he nor future Spanish colonists made any efforts at settlement.

Despite considerable acreage and excellent harbors, the fresh-water problem and distance from the mainland led to Antigua being unsettled until 1632. At that time, English colonists ventured over from nearby St. Christopher's (St. Kitts), which had been settled eight years earlier by a rare English and French combined colonizing effort to counter attacks from the Spanish and Carib.

The Antiguan population, which consisted mostly of peasant tobacco farmers and numbered less than 750 before 1646, grew to 1,200 in nine years, but conditions were harsh enough that the settlers, a quarter of whom were Irish, threatened to abandon the struggling colony. Hostilities with the French on the neighboring islands of St. Kitts and Guadeloupe and with the Dutch on St. Maarten exacerbated the difficulties, and, during King William's War, the French marauded and sacked the island. The threat from foreigners persisted and was repeated again in 1712 during Queen Anne's War, though English colonists resettled the island after both incidents. Under the Treaty of Utrecht in 1713, the French ceded their portion of St. Kitts to the English, and Anglo-French friction was moderated for a time.

The increasing economic importance of the sugar plantations in the eighteenth century still led to increased military expenditures on the island. Cannon mounts and army barracks were eventually constructed atop Shirley Heights, and the English fleet was headquartered at the Dockyard in English Harbour. The senior officer of the Dockyard station from 1784 to 1787 was Lord Nelson.

In addition to external threats, Antiguans faced internal difficulties during the early period from corrupt imperial officials and political disruption from the Glorious Revolution. In 1686, Sir Nathaniel Johnson

With a shift from tobacco to sugar cane as the leading crop in the late seventeenth century, Antigua became the most important of the English Leeward sugar islands. Thousands of African slaves were imported to tend the labor-intensive crop. *(British Library, London, United Kingdom/Bridgeman Art Library)*

was appointed governor of the Leeward Islands and moved the seat of power from Nevis to Antigua, but his decision to increase taxes and his pro-French and pro-Catholic policies demoralized the growing number of English gentry planters while stirring up near mutinies by the Irish settlers. The wealthy planter-politician Christopher Codrington replaced Johnson and was commander in chief of the Leeward Islands from 1689 to 1698 (during open hostilities against the French); his son, Christopher Codrington the younger, succeeded him from 1699 to 1704. Internal problems reached a peak under their successor, the domineering and corrupt Daniel Parke, who was gruesomely murdered by planters in 1710 after he threatened the local assembly at bayonet point. Parke was the only English colonial governor in British America to suffer such a fate.

In a move that was more significant for Antigua than his political policies, Codrington the elder established the first major sugar plantation in 1674. In the succeeding decades, Antigua grew to become the most

important of the Leeward English "sugar islands." With the shift from tobacco to cane came a dramatic change in population demographics, as thousands of African slaves began to be imported to tend the labor-intensive sugar crop. In 1678, the ratio of whites to blacks on Antigua was almost exactly 1 to 1 (approximately 2,000 each). By 1708, Africans outnumbered Europeans by more than 4 to 1 (13,000 to 3,000), and Antigua accounted for 50 percent of the Leeward slave population and sugar output. As with all the other Caribbean sugar plantations, the African laborers were forcibly transported from their homeland across the Atlantic in the difficult Middle Passage after being sold at the European slave factories that dotted the West African coast.

As sugar production intensified and became more profitable, absentee ownership increased. Furthermore, there was a high turnover in the Antiguan gentry class population, as only six of the top twenty-nine Antiguans in 1678 left descendants among the mid-eighteenth-century plantocracy. By 1767, in the parish of St. Mary's in the southwest corner of the island, all sixty-five taxpayers were slave owners, a third of whom had very large plantations and held an average of eighty-six slaves each, or roughly one slave for every two acres.

Because of the sugar monoculture that had been firmly established by the time of the American Revolution, Antigua and many of the other English Caribbean islands that sided with the British faced a severe subsistence crisis when open hostilities broke out, which was further exacerbated by inflation and a severe drought. As a result, a fifth of Antigua's 38,000 slaves died between 1778 and 1781. Slavery was finally abolished in 1833, but fundamental political and economic inequalities remained prevalent in the African-Antiguan community long past the colonial era.

Kevin P. McDonald

See also: Caribbean (Chronology); Slavery, Caribbean; Sugar.

Bibliography

Dunn, Richard. *Sugar and Slaves: The Rise of the Planter Class in the English West Indies, 1624–1713.* New York: W. W. Norton, 1972.

O'Shaughnessy, Andrew J. *An Empire Divided: The American Revolution and the British Caribbean.* Philadelphia: University of Pennsylvania Press, 2000.

Appalachia

Often referred to as America's first frontier, Appalachia played a crucial role in the colonies' development. As historian John Alexander Williams relates, the region was first explored by Hernando de Soto and his expedition in the mid-1500s, as the mountains that lay in the distance north of Florida held promises of gold and other extractable resources. The Apalachee, wishing de Soto and his band to move on, encouraged the explorers to continue on their way. Of course, little, if any, gold was found, but the Spanish encounters with the region's Native American populations set the stage for the next 300 years of colonial contact.

Reflecting what historian Richard White terms a "middle ground," Appalachia witnessed the collision of a multiplicity of societies and cultures. Not only did the Spanish, French, and English encounter a variety of Native American communities, but the European incursions into the colonial backcountry also forced disparate native peoples into contact, cooperation, and conflict with each other.

Extending from northern Georgia upward through Pennsylvania, Appalachia covers some 200,000 square miles that stretches from southern New York to northern Mississippi. Within the region are several mountain chains (the Alleghenies, Cumberlands, Blue Ridge, and Great Smokey Mountains), as well agriculturally important valleys (the Great Valley in Pennsylvania and the Shenandoah and Tennessee valleys). But the name "Appalachia" signifies a cultural, as well as geographical distinction.

This cultural identity began to take shape in the early decades of contact and exploration. Insecurity characterized life in Appalachia during the sixteenth and seventeenth centuries as traders and other imperial emissaries forged connections with the native populations. Well into the eighteenth, diversity characterized the region as cultural contact increased and intensified. Most of Appalachia's colonial period found the region's vast landscape the focus of traders and trappers intent on finding pathways that would link the eastern ports with the nation's hinterland and its abundance of commercial resources. This establishment of the transportation corridors to move both goods and people continued well into the antebellum era.

But it was not until the eighteenth century, when migrants from the East began to push south and west in search of land, that the Appalachian character began to take shape. Migration peaked from 1700–1775, and the increase in settlement resulted in what one historian of Appalachia has called "one of the great folk movements in American history."

Traveling south from Pennsylvania, beyond the nearly impassable Alleghenies, following the naturally southward-sloping Great Valley into the Carolinas, where gaps in the Blue Ridge Mountains promised entrance into vast and fertile lands, migrants gradually pushed outward from the crowded eastern seaboard. Men like Squire Boone, accompanied by his young son Daniel, set out in 1750 for "Virginia, Carolina, or elsewhere," a journey that forever changed the face of American geography and culture.

The "Pennsylvania Dutch," who actually were German, accounted for one of the two primary groups making the Appalachian journey. Among them were Moravians seeking in 1753 to establish a North Carolina colony, where they would proselytize to the native peoples and enslaved Africans beginning to crowd the Carolina backcountry, to the irritation of the neighboring slaveholders. Irish Protestants outnumbered Germans in Appalachia and arguably became the region's most influential ethnic group.

The eighteenth century witnessed an increase in Appalachia's population of "involuntary migrants" as well. White masters brought Africans, many of whom had already filtered through the Caribbean before reaching the Southern colonies, to the region as slaves. Many slaves also fled to the mountains as runaways, hoping to escape the abuses of plantations in the East.

While the Southern backcountry eventually would prove to be a weak link in the chain of antebellum slave power, slavery contributed to the settlement and development of the southern Appalachians as it had in the East. Slave labor cleared trails, built mills, and constructed Appalachian stations, or fortified encampments guarded by local militias, which were the region's first European communities. Although there were no plantations comparable to those in the East, enslaved Africans' knowledge of agriculture and their value as farm laborers remained important, as Appalachian migrants sought to develop what Williams identifies as a "farm-and-forest economy."

Appalachia, in the minds of colonial Americans, constituted an imagined frontier that held much promise and danger. By the time of the American Revolution, Appalachia signified the new nation's hope for victory (by denying the British the possibility of native allies), renewal, and, most importantly, expansion. The drama of the Appalachian frontier would be played out again, several times, over the course of American history, as long as the desire for land, wealth, and independence remained.

Carole Emberton

See also: Agriculture; Exploration; Furs; Native American–European Relations.

Bibliography

Rohrbough, Malcolm J. *The Trans-Appalachian Frontier: People, Societies, and Institutions, 1775–1850.* New York: Oxford University Press, 1978.

Sensbach, John. *A Separate Canaan: The Making of an Afro-Moravian World in North Carolina, 1763–1840.* Chapel Hill, NC: Omohundro Institute of Early American History and Culture, 1998.

White, Richard. *The Middle Ground: Indians, Empires, and Republics in the Great Lakes Region, 1650–1815.* New York: Cambridge University Press, 1991.

Williams, John Alexander. *Appalachia: A History.* Chapel Hill: University of North Carolina Press, 2002.

Arawak

The term "Arawak" describes a group of languages spoken by many indigenous peoples in the Greater Antilles and beyond. It also has been applied to the people themselves.

At times, Arawak and Taino have been used interchangeably to describe the original inhabitants of the Greater Antilles, most notably Hispaniola (Española), but this overlooks some major distinctions. The Taino is a common ethnic group. The Arawak is a group of tribes speaking related languages, although, because of the geography of the region, many of the Arawakan languages were mutually unintelligible.

A separate group from the Taino islanders, the Arawak people, who call themselves "Lokono," meaning "the people," are more properly considered the mainland branch of a culture that extended throughout the Caribbean. Most Tainos lived in Cuba, Hispaniola (Haiti and Dominican Republic), Puerto Rico, and southern Florida in pre-Columbian times.

The Arawakan speakers were not the only ethnic group in the area in the years before European colonization; people called the Guanahatabey lived in western Cuba, and the Carib lived in the southern part of the Lesser Antilles. In fact, when Columbus arrived in the area, it was a densely populated patchwork of numerous small polities, ranging from villages to chiefdoms with highly articulated social structures, and the Carib were in the process of conquering other islanders.

At the end of the fifteenth and beginning of the sixteenth century, Arawakan speakers numbered in the millions and inhabited coastal areas of Venezuela, Colombia, and the Guianas and had migrated into the Greater Antilles and even the Florida Keys. The Arawak in the Caribbean bore the brunt of early Spanish colonization in the region. As a result, their population dropped drastically. For Hispaniola, the precontact population figures vary widely, but the island could have maintained upwards of 5 million people. By 1520, only 30,000 or so remained. The Arawak and others perished in droves as a result of European disease, along with the effects of dislocation, enslavement, and conflict with the invading Spanish.

When Columbus reached Hispaniola and Puerto Rico in the last decade of the fifteenth century, he saw large, permanent Arawak settlements. Each individual village was home to 1,000 to 2,000 people, who lived under the governance of a single chief, or cacique. These small chiefdoms were organized into district chiefdoms, which, in turn, were aligned with regional chiefdoms. Commoners lived in multiple-family dwellings of wood and thatch, while elites lived in slightly more elaborate houses.

The Arawak in the Caribbean developed sophisticated agricultural techniques, growing cassavas and sweet potatoes in mounds that slowed erosion and aided drainage. The Arawak mined nuggets of gold (of great interest to Columbus) and fashioned them into ornaments for their elites. Arawak craftspeople also worked in shell, wood, ceramics, bone, and cotton, and they participated in trade with other tribes. When the Spanish arrived, they exploited this indigenous trade network.

Columbus never encountered the Arawak of mainland South America; their experience with European colonization was different than that of the Taino. The Arawak and Spanish met on Trinidad during the 1510s. Since the groups were at peace, it was illegal to enslave the Arawak, but depopulation on other islands led to Spanish slave raids in Arawak territory. The Arawak also served the Spanish as interpreters, river pilots, and in other capacities.

Spanish missionary activity in northern South America made little headway among the Arawak. Beginning in the 1570s, the Arawak of Guiana began to assist in Spanish slave raids and military expeditions against other tribes in the area. As the Spanish began to found permanent settlements, relations with the Arawak deteriorated; some Arawaks left the islands for the mainland, and mainland Arawaks moved to escape the Spanish encroachment. Many allied themselves with Dutch and English parties active in the region.

The history of the Taino and other Arawak was disrupted tremendously by the arrival of Europeans at the end of the fifteenth and the beginning of the sixteenth century. The Arawak outside the Spanish sphere of influence quickly recognized the value of iron tools and weapons and grew dependent on items of European manufacture.

Despite being devastated by disease, dislocation, and slavery, the Arawak people were not entirely destroyed by the colonial onslaught. Their descendants, many of whom continue to identify themselves as Lokono, are scattered throughout the northern regions of South America.

Matthew Jennings

See also: Caribbean (Chronology); Columbus, Christopher; Cuba; Hispaniola; Native American–European Relations; Native Americans.

Bibliography

Boomert, Arie. "The Arawak Indians of Trinidad and Coastal Guiana, ca. 1500–1650." *Journal of Caribbean History* 19:2 (November 1984): 123–88.

Rouse, Irving. *The Tainos: Rise and Decline of the People Who Greeted Columbus.* New Haven, CT: Yale University Press, 1992.

Wilson, Samuel M., ed. *The Indigenous People of the Caribbean.* Gainesville: University Press of Florida, 1997.

Armada, Spanish

The defeat of the Spanish Armada in the summer of 1588 was one of the seminal events in the history of Britain, Spain, and the creation of the New World. The culmination of decades of Anglo-Spanish hostility, it not only forever ended the Spanish invasion menace but also settled the question of which country would dominate the American colonies. The victory helped knock Spain from its position as preeminent world power and elevated Britain in its place. Beyond this, the armada's defeat became part of Britain's national mythology, symbolizing the victory of freedom over tyranny, of the New World order over the Old, and of Protestantism over Catholicism.

The origins of the conflict lay in the aftermath of the Reformation, when Henry VIII abolished Catholic authority in Britain in 1529. The Counter-Reformation that followed, intending to recapture Protestant lands for the Catholic Church, culminated during the reign of Philip II of Spain (1556–1598); he felt that God had granted his nation the divine mission of saving Catholicism in the Old World and firmly establishing it in North America. All that stood in the way of Philip II's plan was Queen Elizabeth I, the British monarch.

Starting in 1554, Philip II had been king of England through his marriage to Queen Mary I, but he lost his influence in Britain following the death of his wife and the ascension of Elizabeth I, her half sister and a Protestant, in 1558. From that point forward, Philip II sought to regain his authority. He supported Elizabeth I's heir, Mary Stuart, the Catholic queen of Scotland and former queen of France; however, an assassination plot against Elizabeth I was uncovered that

Britain's defeat of the "invincible" Spanish Armada in 1588 culminated decades of hostility between the two nations, shifted the balance of power in Europe for centuries, and settled the issue of which country would dominate the North American colonies. *(Society of Apothecaries, London, United Kingdom/Bridgeman Art Library)*

led back to Mary, and she was executed in 1587. Using this as a pretext, Philip II declared himself a claimant to England's throne and began plotting to invade Britain and reclaim it for the Catholic Church.

Philip II immediately began to assemble an "invincible armada," but his plans were delayed due to the actions of Sir Francis Drake, who attacked a portion of the armada at Cadiz in 1587 and destroyed 37 ships. Elizabeth I, still hoping for a peaceful solution, recalled Drake. But Philip II would not be placated. In 1588, he launched a fleet of 130 large ships carrying 19,000 troops and 8,000 sailors bound for England's shores, intending to establish a foothold on the island and to pave the way for another invasion fleet carrying 30,000 troops from the Netherlands, which had rebelled against Spanish authority. With a blessing from the Pope, the armada sailed for Britain in May 1588.

To answer this deadly peril, the British mustered 197 smaller ships, of which only 34 were Royal Navy vessels. The small British ships were more maneuverable than the large Spanish galleons, and in addition to Drake the British were led by the able Lord Howard of Effingham and Sir John Hawkins. The Spanish swept into the English Channel in July as the English fleet waited for the winds to change so that they could counter the armada. Queen Elizabeth I addressed her waiting troops, declaring confidently, "We shall shortly have a famous victory over those enemies of my God, of my kingdom, and of my people."

The queen spoke prophetically. Once out of har-bor, the British fleet hammered the cumbersome Spanish ships, deploying daring hit-and-run tactics, and in a running fight that lasted six days, killed 4,000 Spaniards, and sank six ships. The Spanish Armada took refuge in the French port of Calais, but the British attacked at night with fire ships, and in a panic, the Spaniards cut their anchor cables and ran into a heavy wind. Routed in the ensuing battle of Gravelines, they eventually escaped the British, only to meet their doom on the long voyage home when, damaged and without anchors, they met a powerful Atlantic storm and foundered up and down the Scottish and Irish coast. Only about fifty ships returned to Spain, carrying just 10,000 men. The legend of the "Protestant wind" that saved England was born, but it was only a myth. Britain was saved by able seamanship and Spanish blunders.

Although the defeat of the armada did not end the war, which lasted until 1604, it brought a decisive end to the threat of invasion, solidified once and for all the Protestant Reformation, secured the independence of Holland, and hastened the Spanish decline around the globe. In the end, the most important legacy of the defeat of the Spanish Armada was that after 1588, England's mastery of the seas went unquestioned for the next 300 years. With its powerful navy finally able to ensure the protection of overseas colonies, Britain turned its eyes across the Atlantic, where the untold wealth of New World colonies beckoned, and Spain was no longer able to check her advance. The rest was British—and American—history.

Todd E. A. Larson

See also: Military and Diplomatic Affairs (Chronology); Military and Diplomatic Affairs (Essay); Navy, British; War.

Bibliography

Martin, Colin, and Geoffrey Parker. *The Spanish Armada.* 2nd rev. edition. New York: St. Martin's, 1999.

Mattingly, Garrett. *The Armada.* Boston: Houghton Mifflin, 1959.

Whiting, John Roger Scott. *The Enterprise of England: The Spanish Armada.* New York: St. Martin's, 1988.

Army, British

From 1600 to 1783, the British army was characterized by the growth of a professional force and an increased ability to cooperate with the Royal Navy in order to project power around the globe. In 1600, Britain relied on a militia system for defense. By the end of the American War for Independence, Britain possessed an

The British Army, shown marching into Philadelphia in 1777, was a formidable fighting force—experienced, well equipped, and well trained. Its defeat in the American Revolution is attributed to failures in leadership and repeated underestimations of colonial fighting abilities. *(Brown Brothers, Sterling, Pennsylvania)*

extremely capable professional army, albeit one unable to defeat the American's Continental army.

The 1620s saw the abject failure of the English militia system. In that decade, the English attempted to stage expeditions against Cadiz and New Rochelle. Both were appallingly ad hoc, and both failed completely. Only with the outbreak of the English Civil War would a professional army begin to develop. The parliamentary forces proved far more adept at warfare and incorporated new military developments such as a slower cavalry charge (which was easier to control) and new infantry tactics. Inspired leadership and effective tactics allowed the Roundheads to win against royalist troops in Ireland, and in Scotland as well.

In the 1680s, King James II's relatively large, standing army outraged many in England, especially in light of his tendency toward Roman Catholicism. The Glorious Revolution of 1688 saw James II overthrown and replaced with King William of Orange and Queen Mary. During William's reign, the English army fought on the Continent during the Nine Years' War and in Ireland as well. English forces also fought extensively in Europe during the reign of William's successor, Queen Anne. The War of the Spanish Succession saw British troops in some of the most famous battles of the eighteenth century, under the command of one of Britain's most famous generals, John Churchill, First Duke of Marlborough.

In the late seventeenth and early eighteenth centuries, a debate raged in Britain over the size and character of a standing army in Britain. Many suspected that a permanent standing army would only lead to tyranny, either in the form of a military coup or as the muscle for a tyrannical regime. This debate would be settled in Britain with the acceptance of a relatively small permanent army. The true importance of the debate took place across the Atlantic, as colonists in America studied the arguments used against a standing army and increasingly during the eighteenth century saw the British army in North America as an instrument of tyranny. In the aftermath of the Seven Years' War (known as the French and Indian War in North America), as British troops were stationed throughout the American colonies, many colonists began to fear that those troops would destroy American liberties.

Even today, the British army possesses a unique structure that evolved during the seventeenth and eighteenth centuries. Regiments are the principal units of the British army; many have long lineages and their own distinctive characters. Regiments were commanded by a colonel and a colonel proprietary. The former actually led the regiment and attended to the daily administration; the latter "owned" the regiment. Officers' commissions were secured by purchase, not by merit. This practice helped to reinforce the social structure of Britain and to ensure that only aristocrats or those from prosperous backgrounds could afford to purchase a commission. Regiments were composed of smaller units known as companies, each normally commanded by a captain. In battle, these units would be drawn up in a line two deep that could deliver volleys against an enemy. Contrary to popular images of the British fighting in lines while their opponents sniped at them from cover, the British did develop light infantry tactics of their own and could, in most cases, hold their own in wilderness fighting.

Structure and Operations

During the eighteenth century, the British army developed a rare talent for close and effective cooperation between the army and navy, which allowed the British to project power around the globe. In 1711, the British staged an expedition against Quebec and failed. Thirty-one years later, the British attacked the Spanish fortress city of Cartagena and failed, largely due to the devastation of the expeditionary force by an outbreak of yellow fever. During the Seven Years' War, British conjunct operations came into their own with a long string of successes: Louisbourg (1758), Quebec (1759), Havana (1762), and Manila (1762). Conjunct operations played a major role in the American War for Independence as well.

One of Britain's greatest triumphs, the campaign to take New York City in 1776, came as a result of British dominance of the waterways in the area of operations. The rare occasions when such operations did not succeed led to disastrous results for the British. The American victory at Yorktown in 1781 came about because of the Continental army's ability to corner the British army on the York-James peninsula, and because the French fleet prevented the Royal Navy from rescuing the besieged British troops.

Operations in the coastal areas of North America and in the islands of the Caribbean did expose British soldiers to killer diseases, often far more lethal than their military opponents. Mosquito-borne illnesses such as yellow fever could exact a fearful toll on their victims: yellow fever leads to fever, vomiting, and severe diarrhea, and in extreme cases death. The Cartagena expedition of 1742 largely failed due to the heavy toll taken by yellow fever. In addition, the unhealthy water

and extreme heat of parts of America and the Caribbean devastated soldiers born in Britain's cool climate.

Although the British army performed well in most conflicts of the eighteenth century, it eventually was defeated in the American War for Independence. While the rank and file fought bravely, poor and lethargic leadership failed to destroy the Continental army. At the battle of Bunker Hill in June 1775, British troops charged into the teeth of the colonists' entrenchments, believing that militia would never stand against superbly trained regulars.

During the 1777 campaign, the British high command attempted to attack on three fronts: north from New York City, south from Canada, and against Philadelphia, but a lack of coordination and worse generalship doomed the enterprise. The army of General John Burgoyne, moving south from Canada, suffered a series of defeats near Saratoga, New York, and eventually surrendered to its American opponent on October 17, 1777.

In addition, British prejudices about the colonists' fighting abilities led them astray. In some instances, such as the battle of Cowpens and, later, the 1781 siege of Yorktown, the Americans both outgeneraled and outfought their opponents.

Mitchell McNaylor

See also: Braddock, Edward; Bunker Hill, Battle of; Fortifications; French and Indian War; King George's War; Lexington and Concord, Battles of; Military and Diplomatic Affairs (Chronology); Military and Diplomatic Affairs (Essay); Native American–European Conflict; Navy, British; Queen Anne's War; Revolutionary War; War of Jenkins' Ear.

Bibliography

Anderson, Fred. *Crucible of War: The Seven Years' War and the Fate of Empire in British North America, 1754–1766.* New York: Alfred A. Knopf, 2000.

Beckett, Ian, and David G. Chandler, eds. *The Oxford Illustrated History of the British Army.* Oxford, UK: Oxford University Press, 1994.

Brumwell, Stephen. *Redcoats: The British Soldier and War in the Americas, 1755–1763.* Cambridge, UK: Cambridge University Press, 2001.

Chandler, David G. *The Art of Warfare in the Age of Marlborough.* London: B. T. Batsford Limited, 1976.

Clinton, Sir Henry. *The American Rebellion: Sir Henry Clinton's Narrative of His Campaigns, 1775–1782, with an Appendix of Original Documents.* New Haven, CT: Yale University Press, 1954.

Fortescue, Sir John William. *A History of the British Army.* 13 vols. London and New York: Macmillan, 1899–1930.

Frey, Sylvia R. *The British Soldier in America: A Social History of Military Life During the Revolutionary Period.* Austin: University of Texas Press, 1981.

Gruber, Ira D. *John Peebles' American War: The Diary of a Scottish Grenadier, 1776–1782.* Mechanicsburg, PA: Stackpole, 1998.

Holmes, Richard. *Redcoat: The British Soldier in the Age of Horse and Musket.* New York: W. W. Norton, 2001.

Houlding, J. A. *Fit For Service: The Training of the British Army, 1715–1795.* Oxford, UK: Oxford University Press, 1981.

Mackesy, Piers. *The War for America, 1775–1783.* Cambridge, MA: Harvard University Press, 1964.

Reid, John Philip. *In Defiance of the Law: The Standing Army Controversy, the Two Constitutions, and the Coming of the American Revolution.* Chapel Hill: University of North Carolina Press, 1981.

Schwoerer, Lois G. *"No Standing Armies!" The Antiarmy Ideology in Seventeenth-Century England.* Baltimore: Johns Hopkins University Press, 1974.

Stacey, C. P. *Quebec, 1759: The Siege and the Battle.* Toronto: Macmillan, 1959.

Steele, Ian Kenneth. *Betrayals: Fort William Henry and the Massacre.* New York: Oxford University Press, 1990.

Tarleton, Lieutenant Colonel Banastre. *A History of the Campaigns of 1780 and 1781 in the Southern Provinces of North America.* London: Printed for T. Cadell, 1787.

Art, Cartoons, and Broadsides

The seventeenth and eighteenth centuries saw numerous changes in religion, culture, and politics on both sides of the Atlantic. People were encouraged to profess new religions, new leaders, and new countries. Due to low literacy rates, the best way to convey these messages was through drawings, usually printed from a carved woodblock or engraved copper plate.

As paper was expensive, these drawings were often printed on broadsides, sheets of cheap paper printed on a single side. Broadsides were sold in the street, at fairs, or in small stalls and served as a means of reaching as many people as possible. While wealthy members of society typically looked down on broadsides, their presence was impossible to ignore.

The first broadsides connected with North America were produced in the late fifteenth century to encourage colonists to move to the New World. John White made numerous drawings during his explorations of Virginia and North Carolina in the 1580s. The Flemish engraver Theodore de Bry published White's drawings in 1590, after alterations were made to the images to demonstrate the prosperity settlers would find in the New World. In 1607, de Bry's engravings were used to encourage the foundation of the Jamestown Colony in Virginia. Other artists produced similar maps and drawings, including Simon van de Passe's 1618 engraving *Pocahontas* and Robert Vaughan's *Ould Virginia* in 1624.

By the late seventeenth century, the North American colonists were creating religious and political art of their own. The first known original woodblock in the colonies was made by Boston printmaker John Foster in 1670. Appropriate for a Puritan colony, Foster's print showed the religious leader Richard Mather holding an open Bible.

The captivity narratives composed by Puritans captured by native peoples during the colonial wars also supplied a popular subject for engravings. These drawings served as a demonstration of the Puritan faith surmounting religious and physical attack; they were used as advertisements to sell the narratives, the first bestsellers in North America.

Political cartoons and caricatures became increasingly popular in Europe in the eighteenth century. While these were as much propaganda as the earlier broadsides encouraging North American settlement had been, they allowed artists to make political comments of their own. The earliest known political cartoon in the colonies was drawn by Benjamin Franklin in 1747 to accompany his pamphlet *Plain Truth.* It showed a wagon stuck in the mud, while its owner prayed for heavenly intervention. The caption below it read *"Non Votis,"* "God helps those who help themselves" in Latin.

Franklin continued his career as a political cartoonist in 1754 with a drawing of a snake divided in eight parts. Each part was labeled with the initials of a colony or region. The caption below read "Join, or Die." Franklin's snake continued to resurface throughout the American Revolution. At the end of the war, British engraver James Gilray drew a cartoon of the defeated British army surrounded by a large, joined snake.

In 1770, John Singleton Copley's half brother Henry Pelham designed an engraving showing the Boston Massacre. Shortly afterwards, Paul Revere produced an engraving of the Boston Massacre that copied Pelham's etching. Pelham accused Revere of stealing his drawing, stating that Revere was a silversmith with no artistic talent. It is unknown whether Revere ever responded to the charge.

The primary distinctions between Pelham's and

In this 1774 engraving by Paul Revere, "The Able Doctor, or America Swallowing the Bitter Draught," Britannia weeps as Lord North pours tea into the mouth of America. Political cartoons, broadsides, and other print media were vital in promoting colonial interests both at home and in London. *(Library of Congress/Bridgeman Art Library)*

Revere's drawings demonstrate their differing political beliefs. Both Pelham and Copley attempted to remain neutral throughout the war. Revere, an ardent patriot, added a sign reading "Butcher's Hall" above the British Custom House. Hundreds of copies of Revere's engraving were sold for a few pennies a copy, and the image was actively used as propaganda by the Sons of Liberty in Boston. Later on, Revere produced engravings of the coffins of those killed in the attack.

Other political engravings supporting the American cause include a 1776 series produced by Franz Xaver Habermann in New York to demonstrate the destruction caused by British occupation. American wax sculptor and spy Patience Wright was a popular subject for cartoonists throughout the war. In 1780, John Williams drew a cartoon titled *The "Right" Situation.* It showed the heads of three British officials on stakes while Wright commented, "This is a sight I have long wished to see."

Following the end of the Revolution and the foundation of the United States, political cartoonists continued to thrive. As literacy rates rose and the price of paper dropped, they became a regular part of newspapers, aiming to appeal to an increasingly sophisticated audience.

Abigail B. Chandler

See also: Art, Folk; Franklin, Benjamin; Newspapers and Journals; Revere, Paul.

Bibliography

Bjelajac, David. *American Art, A Cultural History.* New York: Harry N. Abrams, 2001.

Hess, Stephen, and Milton Kaplan. *The Ungentlemanly Art.* New York: Macmillan, 1975.

Preston, Cathy Lynn, and Michael J. Preston, eds. *The Other Print Tradition: Essays on Chapbooks, Broadsides, and Related Ephemera.* New York: Garland, 1995.

Art, Fine

While decorative art, crafts, and folk art flourished in colonial America, and artists and craftspeople worked in styles distinct from those in Europe, fine art devel-

William Penn's Treaty with the Indians (1772) is one of the iconic, large-scale historical works that made Benjamin West so influential in early American painting. Fine art played a major role in the creation of national myth and symbology. *(Brown Brothers, Sterling, Pennsylvania)*

oped much more slowly, and along strikingly English lines. The reasons for this are fairly obvious. Fine art requires patrons with enough money to spend on its production and enough leisure time to appreciate it. In seventeenth-century America, neither of these conditions existed.

As the eighteenth century progressed, the elite men and women of substantial towns such as Boston, New York, Philadelphia, and Charles Town began to patronize the arts. By the era of the War for Independence, the colonies had produced several painters and silversmiths who could match European artists in terms of quality, in spite of their relatively small number.

As the culture of refinement spread throughout the colonies in the second half of the eighteenth century, elites looked to England, and to a lesser extent France, for examples of desirable high culture. Particularly in the Chesapeake Bay area and South Carolina, wealthy families would import goods directly from Europe

rather than accept what they considered to be inferior American products. Fine art began as a European phenomenon transplanted to colonial America, and it remained tied to Europe even as the political relationship between the two continents soured.

Portraiture and Painting

Portraiture was by far the most popular form of fine art in the colonies. In the seventeenth century, portraits were somewhat crude compared to their later counterparts. Limners, or portrait painters, were occasionally trained in England or the Netherlands but often learned by copying prints of European paintings. Since the colonial upper class was relatively small, limners often had to supplement their income by painting signs for businesses or even by painting houses. House painters would also try their hand at painting portraits. Often, limners would travel from town to town with pre-painted bodies and simply fill in the head of anybody who was willing to pay to have his or her portrait made. By the turn of the eighteenth century, wealth and taste had reached a critical mass—at least in prosperous towns—that could support a class of professional artists, most of whom were from Europe.

Henrietta Dering Johnston, an Englishwoman working in Charles Town, South Carolina, was very popular among that city's planter elite for her skill in rendering small pastel portraits. Jeremiah Theüs, a Swiss artist, was active in Charles Town in the middle of the eighteenth century.

Since Virginia, a fairly wealthy colony in its own regard, had no prosperous port city in which to sell completed paintings, painters would be commissioned by individual planters for specific projects. In 1735, for instance, William Byrd II commissioned Charles Bridges to paint portraits of his daughters.

Other European painters were active in Annapolis, New York, Boston, and Philadelphia. Gustavus Hesselius, a Swedish painter, achieved some renown for his paintings of Lenni Lenape leaders and scenes from the Bible and Greek mythology.

Robert Feke also rose to prominence from rather shadowy roots in the middle of the eighteenth century. Unlike most other professional painters, he was born in America, on Long Island. He spent his early life at sea—some have speculated that he was abroad learning to paint—and produced some striking portraits of the Boston and Philadelphia upper classes. His career ended as mysteriously as it began, and one 1767 document simply described him as "mariner, deceased."

John Smibert, an English immigrant, based his work on English court portraits and owned a small copied collection of the works of Titian, Raphael, and other European masters. The collection caused quite a stir in the fledgling Boston art world, and several young painters, including Charles Willson Peale, John Singleton Copley, and John Trumbull, spent time in Smibert's small gallery copying paintings and learning to draw.

This second generation of American painters went a long way toward proving that American artists could hold their own against their European counterparts and even be recognized for their skills in Europe. Foremost in this regard was Benjamin West, who was born in Philadelphia in 1738. West eventually emigrated to Rome and London, where he became president of the Royal Academy in the 1760s. He was particularly adept at depicting momentous occasions in American history that echoed classical forms. *William Penn's Treaty with the Indians* (1772) and *The Death of General Wolfe at Quebec* (1771) are two examples of his large-scale historical paintings. West encouraged the careers of such painters as Gilbert Stuart and the aforementioned Trumbull and Peale. During the Revolution, West remained in England, whereas Stuart, Peale, and Trumbull returned to the United States. All three gained fame through painting the heroes of the Revolution in classical poses. In this way, fine art played a large role in the creation of America's national myths and symbology. Peale's *Washington After Trenton* is a prime example, as are Trumbull's *The Surrender of Cornwallis at Yorktown, Washington Resigning His Commission*, and *The Declaration of Independence*, large versions of which decorate the Rotunda of the Capitol. Simple portrait painting did not decline as more-refined forms took center stage, though. Even as the War for Independence raged, itinerant portrait painters traveled New England, painting in long-established, orderly patterns, even though their palettes had become slightly bolder.

Three main trends are visible in colonial painting. First, the impact of Europe, particularly England, was immense. Colonial painters began by copying European prints and forms of portraiture, moved to emulating English painters living in the colonies, and finally graduated to hold high positions in the Royal Academy in London. Second, the earliest seeds of a distinctly American style of painting are evident when one considers the practical, down-to-earth nature of American portraiture (see Copley's portrait of Paul Revere, for instance). American painters exhibited a fondness for painting the events of contemporary American history, and this choice, combined with the way they executed their historical paintings, laid the groundwork for a more independent American way of painting. Finally, American painters modified what they copied from England, often transforming the end product into something slightly more spare and rejecting the overt sensuality often associated with European high art of the same period.

Decorative Arts and Other Forms of High Culture

Decorative arts and things for the home are not usually considered fine art, but the fact that Americans in the eighteenth century produced some of the finest furniture and silver pieces in the world justifies their inclusion in the category. From humble beginnings in the seventeenth century, colonial artisans working mainly in Boston, New York, Newport, and Philadelphia produced strikingly elegant chests, chairs, desks, and tables for their increasingly wealthy and refined customers. Chairs in the Queen Anne (with a cabriole leg) and Chippendale (like Queen Anne, but replete with rich and varied ornament) styles grace the collections of many art museums. Astute collectors can distinguish between the New York, Philadelphia, and Boston variations of furniture.

Like furniture, American silver production began rather crudely in the seventeenth century but reached the heights of refinement and sophistication by the end of the eighteenth. Most of the early silversmiths (they referred to themselves as goldsmiths, though they rarely worked in that metal) working in America were English immigrants. As in painting, the development of a uniquely American style of silver seems to stem from colonists' unwillingness to "overdecorate" their pieces. The turn of the eighteenth century brought about several important shifts in the production of American silver. Philadelphia joined Boston and New York as a serious center of silver making, tea usage—and its accompanying silver pieces—began to spread in the colonies, and silversmiths began to employ a technique known as gadrooning (parallel vertical convex ornamentation). As the eighteenth century progressed, American silversmiths followed the trends from London at the same time as they modified them slightly. Paul Revere, one of the most famous colonial silversmiths, produced several important tea sets that were variations on English themes.

Other forms of cultural production now considered fine art were hardly present in the colonies before 1776. Classical music was nearly nonexistent, as was the theater. Some concerts took place in large seaport towns, but the performers were invariably talented amateurs and not paid professionals. Sculpture, too, was not prized highly among colonial patrons. Woodcarvers did produce elaborate figureheads for ships, but there were hardly any freestanding sculptures in colonial cities. Colonial grave markers provided another creative outlet, and decorations varied by region and denomination.

The fine arts in colonial America began the eighteenth century as somewhat primitive imitators of European styles and trends. They ended the eighteenth century in much the same fashion, except that the beginnings of a uniquely American style were starting to appear. While colonial artists looked to Europe for examples, their descendants would labor to distinguish themselves from the Old World.

Matthew Jennings

See also: Art, Folk; Arts, Culture, and Intellectual Life (Chronology); Arts, Culture, and Intellectual Life (Essay); Copley, John Singleton; West, Benjamin.

Bibliography

Kolter, Jane Bentley, ed. *Early American Silver and Its Makers.* New York: Main Street, 1979.

Middleton, Richard. *Colonial America.* 2nd edition. Oxford, UK: Blackwell, 1996.

Reich, Jerome R. *Colonial America.* 4th edition. Upper Saddle River, NJ: Prentice Hall, 1998.

Wright, Louis B., et al. *The Arts in America: The Colonial Period.* New York: Charles Scribner's Sons, 1966.

Art, Folk

American folk art is an umbrella term for various types of artistic expressions created by amateurs and craftspeople unschooled in the stylistic trends of academic art. Once referred to as primitive, rustic, or naive, folk art is now more commonly considered nonacademic, self-taught, popular, or vernacular.

Samplers—framed needlework pictures used as references for common stitches and motifs—are prized among collectors of colonial folk art. Letters, numbers, biblical passages, flora, fauna, and local scenery were favorite subjects. *(Victoria & Albert Museum, London, United Kingdom/ Bridgeman Art Library)*

Basic categories of folk art include portraits and pictures in oil, watercolor, and ink; various kinds of needlework; *fraktur* (a form of illustrated lettering); three-dimensional carvings and sculptures from wood and metal such as weathervanes, ship carvings, shop signs, and toys; painted furniture and other household items; and architectural decorations such as fireboards and cornices. Created by and for common people, folk art reflects the social, political, cultural, and economic life of ordinary Americans.

Painting and Portraiture

When European colonists arrived in North America, they brought with them the cultural and artistic traditions of their homelands. These traditions provided the basis for American folk art, which flourished all along the eastern seaboard from the seventeenth until the late-nineteenth century. The early colonists continued the stylistic traditions of their native lands, but they also embraced other traditions, adapted forms, colors, and materials, and introduced new designs, all of which contributed to a distinctive brand of folk art.

Portraiture, the first and most important type of folk art, emerged in the seventeenth century in New England colonial towns. Many portrait artists, known as limners, adopted an itinerant lifestyle, traveling from city to city, painting portraits for a prosperous, middle-class clientele. The work of these painters exhibited familiarity with European artistic traditions, but they also set new standards.

Two of the finest examples of early portraiture were commissioned in 1671–1674 by John Freake, a Boston attorney and merchant, and created by an artist whose name remains unknown. One of the portraits is of Freake himself, and the other is of his wife, Elizabeth, and their baby daughter, Mary. The portrait of Elizabeth and Mary reveals the influence of European Mannerism, an idealized mode of painting that emphasized ornamentation and exaggerated the proportions of the human figure. The painting also suggests the status of the client: success and material wealth are represented by Elizabeth's clothing and jewelry.

A painting of Pau de Wandelaer from 1730 by Pieter Vanderlyn shows another style of portraiture common in the eighteenth century. Vanderlyn's attempt to accurately depict spatial relationships in the portrait, which gave it a three-dimensional quality, was a legacy of the High Renaissance. The artist also attempted to create a realistic likeness of the subject and to convey something of de Wandelaer's personality through references to his life and home in the form of the Hudson River and a sloop, both of which appear in the background. The inclusion of personal references became a characteristic common to American portraiture. By the late eighteenth century, artists had begun to blend the two styles found in the Freake and de Wandelaer paintings and to reshape artistic traditions.

Folk artists also depicted the land, cities, and their farms and houses in their work. Many early paintings were intended to serve as a decorative overmantel, a painted section of wall above a parlor fireplace. One of the first American landscapes—and overmantels—dating to the 1730s, depicted the Van Bergen homestead in Leeds, Greene County, New York. Besides its visual appeal, the painting details eighteenth-century farm life in the Hudson River Valley. A red-roofed farmhouse and lavishly dressed Mr. and Mrs. Marten Van Bergen stand at the center of the painting. On either side, four black slaves, two white servants, Native Americans, livestock, and pets engage in various activities amid the land, mill, hay barracks, and Catskill Mountains. Depictions of the sea and harbors full of boats were also popular subjects for folk paintings, reflecting the importance of shipping and commerce to the Atlantic economy.

Women

Women occupied a place within the folk-art tradition, both in painting and needlework. Because of their household and childrearing duties, they were less likely to pursue careers as painters, although some women painted portraits of their family members and friends or painted to supplement the household income.

Needlework, however, was an integral part of every woman's daily routine. Whether wealthy or poor, every young girl learned to sew and knit in order to make and care for the family's clothing, linens, and towels. Women of prosperous families were sent to schools, where they learned the more complicated skills of ornamental needlework and stitching, skills which indicated social grace and education. Learning to use a needle was important to the management of a household and to some women's status, but it also provided talented women an artistic outlet.

The first piece of needlework that most women created was the sampler. Samplers were usually long, narrow stitched pictures, which were intended to be framed or used as a reference for commonly used stitches and motifs. Favorite subjects for samplers included

Adam and Eve, flora, fauna, the alphabet, numbers, poems, biblical quotations, landscapes, and farm scenes.

Needlework tapestries were normally produced by educated young women. These pictures often incorporated more elaborate materials, such as appliqués, silver and gold spangles, beads, and silk ribbons, and they featured more complex subjects such as allegories or biblical, literary, or historical themes. Intended to exhibit a girl's skills and to enhance a room, tapestries were often framed and hung.

Women also created quilts, blankets, bed rugs, and other kinds of bed coverings, all of which demonstrated artistic talent. Most of these pieces were intended for warmth, but since beds were frequently the focal point of a room, women strived to create items that were also beautiful.

Quilts are the best-known form of American textile folk art. A quilt is made by joining three layers of cloth—the top, interlining, and backing—with stitches. The earliest-known surviving American quilt, made from pieced, triangle-shaped remnants, is believed to have been made by Sarah Sedgewick Leverett, the wife of the governor of Massachusetts Bay Colony, and her daughter, in 1704.

Different regions developed distinct quilting designs and techniques, although most eventually spread throughout the colonies. In New England, quilts were fairly simple and usually created from strips of fabric or geometric pieces. In the South, quilters created more intricate designs using *Broderie Perse*, a technique in which flowers, animals, and foliage were cut from printed cotton and chintz and sewn onto a plain ground fabric to make a larger design. Popular motifs in the colonial period included the Tree of Life, sunburst, floral and fauna, and cityscapes, executed in bright colors with detailed borders.

Other Forms of Folk Art

Another form of folk art was *fraktur*, a style of ornate illustration and lettering derived from European illuminated manuscripts. Ministers, schoolmasters, and itinerant penmen in Pennsylvanian German communities produced *fraktur* work for prayer and hymnbooks and primers for schoolchildren. Individuals also commissioned them to create ornamental family registers, certificates of birth, baptism, confirmation, marriage, and death, valentines, and bookplates. As developed in America, *fraktur* art was rendered in bold designs and bright colors and incorporated various motifs, including tulips, symbolic of the Trinity, unicorns, representa-

tative of virginity, hearts for love and marriage, and such traditional heraldic symbols as lions and crowns.

Gravestones are considered an early form of American folk sculpture. While the idea was not to portray eternal damnation, but the release of the spirit to eternal peace, the symbols most commonly carved onto gravestones included winged skulls, hourglasses with the sands of time running out, and fire- and scythe-bearing skeletons. Other common gravestone images included winged cherubs' heads or angels.

Weathervanes were popularly produced due to farmers' and shippers' need to keep an eye on the weather. Designs for weathervanes often represented local surroundings: horses, pigs, and cows in rural areas; whales, fish, mermaids, and ships in coastal towns. Several excellent examples of weathervanes, created by the Deacon Shem Drowne, a famous Massachusetts weathervane maker, still survive in Boston. They include a metal rooster, the "Blew Ball and Banner," the copper grasshopper vane atop Faneuil Hall, and a vane depicting a Native American.

Prosperous colonists also decorated their homes with carved and painted furniture. By the eighteenth century, almost all American furniture produced in the countryside was painted, either to hide the fact that it was constructed from inexpensive or several different types of wood or to simulate carving. Craftsmen painted pieces in one or several colors and then ornamented them with painted designs, stenciling, gold leaf, or bronze paint. Similar techniques also were applied to other items, including furniture and toys made for children, decorative carvings, and various kinds of signage.

Painted chests were particularly popular. Guilford chests, produced in and around Guilford, Connecticut, were constructed from tulipwood and had a decorated front panel over one decorated drawer and decorated side panels. The Pennsylvania Germans were renowned for the dower chest, a carved, painted wooden chest given to a girl when she reached marriageable age or at the time of her engagement. The front of the chest displayed the girl's name and the date the chest was presented, along with brightly colored unicorns, hearts, a tree-of-life, or the bride and groom in wedding clothing.

Tables, wardrobes, cupboards, and other pieces of furniture adorned with tulips, birds, doves, hearts, and trees also were painted in vivid red, green, blue, and black. These brilliant pieces surely livened up colonial farmhouses and in-town homes.

Marjorie L. Hilton

See also: Art, Cartoons, and Broadsides; Artisans.

Bibliography

Bishop, Robert, and Jacqueline Marx Atkins. *Folk Art in American Life*. New York: Viking Studio, 1995.

Folk Art in America: A Living Tradition. Atlanta, GA: High Museum of Art, 1974.

Lipman, Jean. *American Folk Decoration*. New York: Oxford University Press, 1951.

Lipman, Jean, Robert Bishop, Elizabeth V. Warren, and Sharon L. Eisenstat. *Five Star Folk Art: One Hundred American Masterpieces*. New York: Harry N. Abrams, 1990.

Lipman, Jean, and Alice Winchester. *The Flowering of American Folk Art, 1776–1876*. Philadelphia: Courage, 1997.

Ward, Gerald W. R., Abaigeal Duda, Pamela A. Parmal, Sue Welsh Reed, Gilian Ford Shallcross, and Carol Troye. *American Folk*. Boston: MFA Publications, 2001.

Artisans

Artisans, skilled craftspeople, were found in many communities and social classes in colonial America, from slaves and the urban poor to leading businesspeople. Artisans were among the first American settlers, although they always lagged far behind farmers and agricultural laborers in numbers.

Artisanal skills were vital even to small communities, and skilled carpenters or blacksmiths were found throughout rural America. (Relatively few, however, were adult indentured servants.) These artisans often could not support themselves by their craft alone and commonly divided their time between agricultural and artisan work. A rural blacksmith, for example, might abandon his forge during harvest season. Farmers also acquired artisanal skills, either to support their farming—a farmer's son might learn carpentry to build and maintain farm buildings—or as a form of supplemental income.

The artisanal economy was stronger in the cities, with their developed markets, than in rural areas. It was also stronger in the Northern and Middle colonies than in the South. The less urbanized South had smaller markets, and many of the Southern elite preferred to order the goods they wanted from London or the North. Even in the villages, white artisans in the South, particularly in the Carolina low country, complained about the difficulty of competing with slaves.

Artisans entered their trades through many paths. Often, the eldest son of an artisan's family entered his father's trade and took over the business. This pattern was more common in capital-intensive trades like blacksmithing, where the initial investment for a forge, furnace, and tools daunted the newcomer. Artisans learned their trade by doing, and their children worked in the shops, starting as young as 6 years old and at first doing light tasks like sweeping.

Some trade schools existed. (The Moravians of Nazareth, Pennsylvania, opened a school to train craftsmen in 1757, and "spinning schools" trained poor girls to become spinners.) For those not born into a trade, such as the younger sons of farmers, however, the normal way to enter it was still apprenticeship. Boys, and sometimes girls, were usually apprenticed around the age of 12.

The demand for artisans, however, made it impossible to maintain in the colonies the requirement of the Elizabethan Statute of Artificers, which held that apprentices must serve a full seven years before being released; apprentices often left that status after only three or four years. The overall trend in the colonial period was for artisanal workshops to move from a household model, where apprentices and journeymen were treated as members of the master's family, to one based on contractual relations of work done for wages.

Artisanal work was strongly gendered. Most well-paying occupations were limited to males, either by the need for physical strength, or more often, by custom, although women were occasionally found even in the metalworking trades. Among the few artisanal trades open to women in numbers were hat making, dressmaking, embroidery, and making artificial flowers. However, the male artisan's wife could be an important participant in the business, keeping the books and managing the shop, while not actually practicing the craft.

Slave Artisans

Although the majority of slaves during and after the colonial period were agricultural laborers, some slaves practiced crafts. Like other specialized slave workers, slave artisans were more likely to be found on large plantations than small plantations or farms. Many large plantation owners prided themselves on being able to produce everything they needed on their own property, with their own workers.

Until the mid-eighteenth century, the vast majority of slave artisans were workers in wood. Slaves cut lumber into boards and built houses and plantation buildings. Another major Southern artisanal profession

The work of silversmith Apollus De Revoire and his son, Paul Revere, was among the most prized in colonial Boston. The expanding economy and rise of an economic elite in the eighteenth century created a strong demand for quality craftwork. *(Brown Brothers, Sterling, Pennsylvania)*

employing slaves, as well as indentured servants and free people, was coopering. Also found in the North, barrel makers and the containers they made were indispensable for the export of rice, tobacco, wheat, meat, tar, and other Southern products.

In the second half of the eighteenth century, there was a broadening of the work done by slaves, with slaves specializing in brick making, bricklaying, blacksmithing, and many other trades. In both the North and South, slave craftspeople also worked off the farm or plantation in industrial enterprises, as carpenters in shipyards, or as blacksmiths or carpenters in ironworks.

Artisanal work was sometimes a life-cycle occupation for slaves, as a slave too debilitated by age or disease to be a productive agricultural worker would be reassigned to a craft by the master or overseer. Other slaves learned their crafts when young, either by being apprenticed to white artisans, or, in areas like the Chesapeake, by being hired out to artisans by their owners.

Particularly in the Carolina low country, there was a transition after the mid-eighteenth century, and

slaves more often learned their crafts from other slaves. American-born slaves also were more likely to be put into artisanal occupations by their masters than African-born slaves, even though some African-born slaves had been craftspeople in their own country. Most artisanal occupations also were reserved for male slaves; female slave artisans were usually restricted to textile trades. Slaves, lacking control over their own careers, also might be shifted from one craft to another, according to the need or whim of their masters.

Artisans in the Eighteenth Century

Artisans were much in demand in eighteenth-century British colonies. The expanding economy needed craftspeople, and the growth of the colonial economic elite enabled high-end craftspeople like coach makers, plasterers, and makers of scientific equipment to support themselves in the larger cities. Some cities became centers of specialization in a particular kind of product, exporting it all over the colonies. Germantown, Pennsylvania, for instance, was known for its "Germantown stockings." Lynn, Massachusetts, became the center of American shoemaking after the Welsh shoemaker John Adam Dagyr introduced more advanced techniques in the 1750s.

The relatively high wages paid in America attracted craftspeople from many parts of the British Isles and Continental Europe. Many of them boasted of their European origins, selling their products by appealing to early American prejudice against native-born workers. Europeans brought new skills that were adapted to the American environment. Irish weavers brought expertise in linens. French Huguenots, like Paul Revere's father, Apollus De Revoire, established many silversmith businesses. The American or "Pennsylvania," rifle was adapted from German rifles by German gunsmiths who had immigrated to Pennsylvania.

Not all immigrant artisans stayed artisans. The cheapness of land in America meant that, for many, practicing their craft was principally a means to get the money together to purchase their own land and work as a farmer. Still, some who purchased land continued to practice their craft during seasonal downtimes and to supplement their income.

Even in less lucrative and prestigious crafts, the gap between the master artisan and business owner and the journeymen who worked for wages was growing in the eighteenth century. Rich artisans were leaving the artisan ranks and becoming merchants and investors. This pattern was particularly common among goldsmiths and silversmiths, whose work with precious metals led easily into banking and trade. Rich and ambitious artisans were able to enter the upper classes of Boston and Philadelphia, a few even styling themselves "gentlemen," although the planter aristocracy of the South proved a much tougher challenge to enter.

Artisans at lower levels of their trades also sometimes used their earnings as capital to enter commerce, which was seen as a more financially rewarding field. Artisans often exchanged their wares for other merchandise, which they then sold. Successful artisans who became merchants or shopkeepers might personally stop practicing their craft, while still maintaining an artisan's shop staffed by journeymen.

For those at the bottom of the artisan hierarchy, the shift from household organization to wage work offered freedom and flexibility at the expense of security. Sickness or economic depression could destroy the worker's wages, forcing him and his family to subsist on charity or find other means of support.

Artisanal Societies and Sociability

Artisans operated in a freer market in the American colonies than in Europe, as many European trades had established, conservative guild organizations, whose origins dated back to the Middle Ages. These organizations regulated the prices charged and the wages paid to workers. There were many efforts, more or less successful, to organize American trades on the European model, usually to the benefit of the master artisans.

For example, the Carpenters' Company of Philadelphia, founded in 1724, was an organization of master builders devoted to minimizing competition by establishing uniform rates for their work. They also established a library in 1734, with works of building design, mostly from England. The company split in 1769 over entrance fees and other issues. In 1771, Philadelphia's master tailors organized a similar group to fix prices and limit journeymen's wages.

Although there were many solitary craftspeople, the artisan workshop could be a place of lively conversation. Urban artisans also socialized outside their individual trades, in churches, militia companies, Masonic lodges, and informal clubs. One organization bringing artisans together across trades was the Ancient and Honorable Mechanical Company of Baltimore, founded in 1763. Like many artisans, members of the Mechanical Company supported the patriot movement, lending their headquarters to the first meeting of the Baltimore Sons of Liberty in 1766.

William E. Burns

See also: Art, Folk; Economy, Business, and Labor (Chronology); Economy, Business, and Labor (Essay); Laborers, Urban. *Document*: Advice to a Young Tradesman (1748).

Bibliography

Bridenbaugh, Carl. *The Colonial Craftsman*. Reprint. Chicago: University of Chicago Press, 1961.

Daniels, Christine. " 'WANTED: A Blacksmith who Understands Plantation Work:' Artisans in Maryland 1700–1810." *William and Mary Quarterly* 3:50 (1993): 743–67.

Morgan, Philip D. *Slave Counterpoint: Black Culture in the Eighteenth-Century Chesapeake and Low Country*. Chapel Hill: Published for the Omohundro Institute of Early American History and Culture by the University of North Carolina Press, 1998.

Ward, Barbara McLean. "Boston Artisan Entrepeneurs of the Goldsmithing Trade in the Decades before the Revolution." In *Entrepreneurs: The Boston Business Community, 1700–1850,* edited by Conrad Edick Wright and Katheryn P. Viens. Boston: Massachusetts Historical Society, 1997.

Wolfe, Stephanie Grauman. *As Various as Their Land: The Everyday Lives of Eighteenth-Century Americans.* New York: HarperCollins, 1993.

Assemblies, Colonial

In the realm of politics, there was no more significant trend in British colonial America than the ascendance of representative assemblies to positions of power. Originally intended to automatically approve the mandates of royally appointed governors, they had, in almost every colony, taken on roles far beyond that by the time of the American Revolution. New England, which boasted far less royal control than other areas and a powerful legislature from an early date, was an exception to this rule.

Since there was almost no political contact between colonies, and relatively little royal oversight, the story of how colonial assemblies formed and gained power is the story of political development in colonial America. Several excellent accounts treat the ascendance of the assemblies in the eighteenth century, but the story of each body's origins is not as well known.

Seventeenth Century Beginnings

The first colonial assembly in British North America met in the church at Jamestown in 1619. Part of a larger Virginia Company effort to improve morale and draw colonists after the colony's brutal first years, the "House of Burgesses," as it was known, was to meet once a year and have power to enact any measures it felt would aid in the good government of the colony. The assembly consisted of the governor, his council, and two burgesses from each parish. Any acts could be vetoed by the governor or the company's leadership in London and could not run contrary to English law. The earliest laws were carry-overs from company policies, based on military discipline, that forbade drunkenness, idleness, and other forms of bad behavior. They also regulated trade with neighboring tribes and required regular church attendance.

In the aftermath of the 1622 attack led by Opechancanough, the Virginia Company lost its charter, and Virginia became a royal colony. The status of the legislature was uncertain for a time, largely because nobody in England cared. In 1639, Charles I decided that the burgesses could be called yearly to pass acts concerning the governance of the colony.

If Virginia's early years were marked by a surplus of authority on the part of the London Company, the opposite statement could be made for the island colony of Bermuda. On Bermuda, a divided group of planters viciously fought among themselves in the absence of any real government during the 1610s. In 1620, in an effort to ease factional tension and levy taxes to fund public projects, an assembly was called. Later in the seventeenth century, other English possessions in the Caribbean would undergo similar processes.

Virginia and Bermuda had legislatures granted to them, but in Massachusetts Bay, Plymouth, Maryland, Connecticut, and New Haven—colonies whose legislatures trace their roots to the 1630s—the impulse to form assemblies came from within. By the 1630s, colonists had come to expect assemblies. Even in Maryland, a proprietary colony granted to Lord Baltimore, the charter required that he make laws with the consent of the colonists.

In New England, particularly among the Puritans, the institution of town government was very strong, and some of this strength carried over to colonial assemblies. In the Massachusetts Bay Colony, each town elected deputies to the General Court, which could grant land, charter new towns, and levy taxes. Connecticut and Rhode Island, each essentially an offshoot of the older colony, had similarly powerful assemblies.

The colonies founded after the Restoration exhibited a change in the way representative assemblies were perceived. From the 1660s, assemblies were no longer seen as a response to colonization, but rather as reason for people to settle in a given colony.

With a weaker tradition of local government to draw upon, the South Carolina Commons House of Assembly faced an uphill battle against the will of the lords proprietors. South Carolina's Commons gradually usurped the governor and the council (which became the upper house), claimed for itself wide-ranging powers, and eventually faced little resistance, either from the proprietors, or, after the "Revolution of 1719," the royal governors.

The Dutch ran New Amsterdam as a military and commercial enterprise, especially under the leadership of Peter Stuyvesant in the late 1640s, even though Dutch and English residents complained about the arbitrary nature of Stuyvesant's rule and the lack of local government. Even after the English took over the colony, little effort was made to convene an assembly.

Although most colonies had some representative legislative body, they generally remained politically weak until the end of the seventeenth century. William Penn's "holy experiment" of Pennsylvania featured a legislature that was rather liberal-minded on paper, less so in practice. Free men who owned 50 acres of property or paid taxes were eligible to vote for members of the assembly, which would work with the governor, basically by accepting or rejecting, or amending, the governor and council's proposed legislation.

Impact of the Glorious Revolution

The end of the seventeenth century was the beginning point of a marked rise in the power of several colonial assemblies. The change was halting and uneven, and some legislatures remained comparatively weak into the era of the French and Indian War (known as the Seven Years' War in Europe); governors and their councils were the prime political movers.

One of the main models for the rise of the colonial assemblies was the rise of England's own House of Commons in the wake of the Glorious Revolution. In the decades that followed William and Mary's reign, Parliament became a dominant force in the government of England. Not only that, but local authorities, in England, Ireland, and North America, continued to expand their control.

The rise of the assemblies, particularly in the Southern royal colonies, was closely tied to the development of a class of colonial lawyers, merchants, and planters. These men of property, already masters of their professional offices, trading houses, and plantations, made legislative choices that would make them masters of the colonial political landscape.

Jack P. Greene, the preeminent scholar on the topic, has divided this rise to power into three phases of development. The first stage, chronicled above, saw assemblies in a subordinate position to councils and governors. By the early decades of the eighteenth century, most assemblies were on equal political footing with their respective governors and could even take on London authorities from time to time. In the third and final phase, governors and councils gave way to forceful lower houses.

In Pennsylvania during the 1730s and 1740s, for instance, the lower house surpassed the governor and his council, claiming the power of the purse and denying the right of the council to initiate legislation. At about the same time, the Massachusetts house, which was already powerful, reached new heights of financial and legislative control.

Occasionally, lower houses gained power as a result of administrative mismanagement, often in the form of a corrupt governor, or one who tried to limit the rights of the legislature. This happened in several colonies, including Virginia, Maryland, Massachusetts, North Carolina, and New York. Most royal governors, however, learned quickly that reaching a consensus with the gentry in their respective domains made their lives much easier. Such a position eventually became necessary in plantation colonies like South Carolina and Virginia, where a handful of super-wealthy planters ruled society and politics. Later colonies, such as Nova Scotia and Georgia, built upon the successes of the legislatures long established in places like South Carolina and Massachusetts.

Having risen to dominate the provincial political scene, the lower houses took aim at a much more formidable enemy, the British Empire itself. The organization of the Empire, which had grown tremendously in size with little in the way of overarching vision, promoted colonial legislative resistance. In the aftermath of the Seven Years' War, Great Britain had effectively removed France from North America, but faced crippling debt, a postwar depression, and the trouble of defending a huge empire on a distant continent. As a result, Britain sought a massive reorganization of its empire.

As with previous attempts to reign in the colonies, such as the Dominion of New England, the reorganization effort provoked loud protests from colonial legislatures. The responses to new British policies, including planned boycotts and letters circulated between various colonial legislatures, indicated that the stakes of the game had risen considerably in the years after 1763.

By the time of the American War for Independence, the colonial assemblies were the main political force in the colonies. Their ascendancy during the eighteenth century determined, to a great extent, the form of the war and the Articles of Confederation government of the 1780s.

Matthew Jennings

See also: House of Burgesses; Politics and Government (Chronology); Politics and Government (Essay). *Documents:* Rights of the British Colonies Asserted and Proved (1764); The Declaration of Independence (1776).

Bibliography

Greene, Jack P. *Negotiated Authorities: Essays in Colonial Political and Constitutional History.* Charlottesville: University Press of Virginia, 1994.

———. *The Quest for Power: The Lower Houses of Assembly in the Southern Royal Colonies, 1689–1776.* Chapel Hill: University of North Carolina Press, 1963.

Kammen, Michael. *Deputyes and Libertyes: The Origins of Representative Government in Colonial America.* New York: Alfred A. Knopf, 1969.

Atlantic Ocean

The Atlantic Ocean played a critical role in the colonization of America as the conduit for people, goods, microbes, and ideas from the Old World to the New. The Atlantic was never completely controlled by any single national group, though by the time of the American Revolution, the North Atlantic had come to be dominated by the English.

Prior to the eighteenth century, first Viking Norsemen, then in successive waves the Portuguese, Spanish, Dutch, French, and English adventurers, embarked from the European continent to make contact with and then colonize the Americas. These European emigrants would be joined by millions of Africans, forcibly transported across the Atlantic in the Middle Passage. Throughout the colonial era and beyond, the Atlantic would play a crucial role in the formation of America, composing a transnational region and subregions involving similar economic structures, state formations, political discourses, and institutions, as well as complex relations, identities, and practices involving class, race, and gender.

Celtic and Viking explorers were the first Europeans to venture out into the Atlantic, the Norse reaching as far as Newfoundland around the year 1000, but they created no lasting colonial settlements. Beginning in the fourteenth century, the Atlantic islands of Madeira and the Azores were colonized by the Portuguese, and the Spanish followed suit by conquering the Canary Islands in the 1490s, exterminating the indigenous Guanche population in the process, a precursor to the epidemiological disasters that would occur with all of the indigenous American populations. In 1492, Columbus sailed west across the Atlantic in the name of the Castilian Crown, thinking he would find an alternate route to the spices of the East, thereby circumventing the Portuguese who were monopolizing the Cape route around Africa. Instead, he stumbled into the New World and began the centuries-long process of European colonization of the Americas. The English explorers came next, induced by the rich North Atlantic cod-fishing grounds of the Grand Banks, off the coast of Newfoundland, that provided a staple food product for the maritime European populations. The Dutch and French soon followed suit, establishing North American, South American, and Caribbean trading outposts that would eventually develop into settler colonies.

Once these European colonies were firmly established in the seventeenth century, the transmission of human experience "across the pond" continued apace. Royal officials, merchants, planters, and manufacturers organized workers from four continents and created a new transatlantic economy. The currents of the North Atlantic are circular, so ships sailing from Europe pass by Africa across to the Caribbean and then to North America, where the Gulf Stream moves north to connect with the Labrador and Arctic currents, taking vessels eastward toward Europe. This natural circulation was conducive to the so-called "triangle trade," where, in theory ships from Europe packed with manufactured goods would sail to Africa to trade for slaves, then continue to the Americas to unload manufactured goods and slaves in return for sugar, tobacco, and timber.

In addition to the purposeful movement of people, goods, and ideas and the unwitting transmission of Old World microbes, the Atlantic was itself a site of significant geopolitical and strategic importance throughout the colonial period. Before the establishment of professional navies in the eighteenth century, privateers and pirates plied the seas, plundering ships while practicing a rough form of democracy: electing captains, distributing wealth equally, even establishing a form of insurance for members who became injured or otherwise incapacitated. Once the navies were established, they utilized the North Atlantic seaboard as a blockading ground, the English doing so first with great success against the French in the Seven Years' War (known as the French and Indian War in North America). The favor was returned when the French blockaded the English during the American Revolution.

Thus, the Atlantic Ocean played a crucial role in colonial America. This role encompassed critical areas of historical inquiry, ranging from migration and diasporas to commerce and finance; scientific, military, and technological diffusion; artistic production and tastes; transmission of disease; conquest, colonization, and imperialism; and race relations.

Kevin P. McDonald

See also: Armada, Spanish; Navy, British; Slave Trade; Trade; Transportation, Water; Triangle Trade.

Bibliography

Linebaugh, Peter, and Marcus Rediker. *The Many-Headed Hydra: Sailors, Slaves, Commoners and the Hidden History of the Revolutionary Atlantic.* Boston: Beacon, 2000.

Meinig, Donald. *The Shaping of America: A Geographical Perspective of 500 Years of History.* Vol. 1, *Atlantic America, 1492–1800.* New Haven, CT: Yale University Press, 1986.

Richardson, David. "Shipboard Revolts, African Authority, and the Atlantic Slave Trade." *William and Mary Quarterly* 58:1 (2001).

Avilés, Pedro Menéndez de

See Menéndez de Avilés, Pedro

Azores and Madeira

The Azores and Madeira are two groups of islands in the Atlantic Ocean. The Azores, an archipelago of nine islands stretching over 360 miles of sea, are about 900 miles west of Lisbon, Portugal. Madeira, a group of four islands, is slightly less than 600 miles southwest of Lisbon. Though collectively smaller than the state of Connecticut, these strategically located islands played a crucial role in the colonization of the Americas by Europeans.

The role of the Azores and Madeira in European colonization began in the early years of the fifteenth century, when Portugal's Prince Henry (often referred to as "the Navigator") commissioned a number of voyages to explore the coast of Africa. On one of these voyages, perhaps in 1418, returning mariners were blown far off course and discovered Madeira. In the 1420s or 1430s, Portuguese sailors ventured even farther west before turning east toward home, and this voyage hit the eastern edge of the Azores chain. At the time of their discovery, neither island group was inhabited.

The Portuguese, sensing Madeira's strategic importance, began to colonize the islands in 1425. Madeira quickly became a profitable sugar colony, with the earliest African slaves arriving to cultivate this crop in 1443. The quality and quantity of sugar produced in Madeira wreaked havoc on the European sugar market, and, as early as 1498, Portugal's Manuel I was forced to limit the amount of sugar that could be exported.

These two groups of islands were remarkable fertile, and the Portuguese also were able to grow and export wheat and wine. In fact, Madeira wine grew famous throughout the Atlantic world within a few years of the island's settlement. Much later, the rise of the great Brazilian and Caribbean sugar-producing colonies dwarfed Madeira's relative modest production, and, in the seventeenth century, wine became Madeira's major export. The wine that made up most of Madeira's exports was akin to today's red table wines. The highest class of Madeira wine was a sweet, fortified dessert wine, and its chemical makeup rendered it impervious to the perils of sea travel, temperature change, and even extreme age.

The colonization of the Azores took on a different character. The Portuguese introduced sheep to the islands in the 1430s, hoping that they would provide food to later Atlantic voyagers. Settlement began in the 1440s, but the number of settlers remained small for several decades. Sheep, cattle, goats, and wheat became the main products of the Azores. By the sixteenth century, the Azores had become an integral part of Portugal's Atlantic empire, and Azoreans served in Portugal's army and navy.

The Azores' location might at first glance appear to make them an ideal stopping-off point on long transAtlantic voyages. But prevailing winds made that a treacherous choice for early sailors, and the Azores were initially better known in the context of the exploration of the coast of Africa. The colonization of the Cape Verde Islands after the 1450s gave European mariners a better departure point for crossing the Atlantic; advances in shipbuilding would lead to the Azores playing a similar role in trans-Atlantic commerce.

As English, French, Portuguese, and Spanish traffic to the Americas increased in the seventeenth and eighteenth centuries, the Azores rose to prominence as a way station. Azorean ports experienced growth in population and prosperity. With the emergence of Boston and New York as serious Atlantic ports in the late seventeenth and early eighteenth centuries, trade with the Azores continued to grow. American elites grew particularly fond of wines produced in Madeira, and, to a lesser extent, in the Azores. American and English ships did not always unload their cargoes in the Azores, but trading vessels did stop there for fresh water, food, and repairs. French and Dutch merchants also set up shop on the islands.

Portugal's 1974 revolution resulted in decolonization for much of the nation's empire. While the Azores and Madeira each has its own parliament, both remain part of the Republic of Portugal.

Matthew Jennings

See also: Alcohol; Atlantic Ocean; Exploration; Trade.

Bibliography

Duncan, T. Bentley. *Atlantic Islands: Madeira, the Azores, and the Cape Verdes in Seventeenth-Century Commerce and Navigation.* Chicago: University of Chicago Press, 1972.

Parry, J. H. *The Age of Reconnaissance.* London: Weidenfeld and Nicolson, 1963.

Rogers, Francis M. *Atlantic Islanders of the Azores and Madeiras.* North Quincy, MA: Christopher Publishing House, 1979.

Aztec

The Aztec were descendants of a people who traced their roots to Aztlán and who had migrated to central Mexico in 1175 after the fall of the Toltec empire. Tenochtitlán, the largest city to flourish in the pre-Hispanic New World, was founded in 1325, and the Aztec empire was well established by 1482. In 1519, the Spaniards approached Tenochtitlán, and, by 1521, they had completed the conquest of the Aztec. Elements of continuity and change during the melding of indigenous and Spanish cultures and people characterize the process of colonization that began under Spanish rule.

A civilized society of several million people of distinct indigenous ethnic groups that spoke Nahuatl, the Aztec had an orderly political and social system of city-states and empire across the region of Tenochtitlán and the Valley of Mexico. Agriculture and farming provided a means of subsistence for the Aztec and formed part of their tribute and bartering systems. Commoners gave food in tribute to their nobility, and the city-states paid tribute to the empire. Not only did the Aztec trade food, crafts, and cotton textiles in their large and elaborate marketplaces, but they also used food as offerings to please their multiple gods.

Other religious offerings took place on the many large pyramids the Aztec constructed as temples; they often included human sacrifices to gods of war, death, and blood. The Aztec were astronomers and astrologers. They had a 260-day ritual calendar used for divination, astrology, and religion, as well as a 365-day solar calendar. Together, these calendars formed a major cycle of fifty-two years. When the gods or calendar called for human sacrifices, the Aztec often waged ritualized war on other city-states in order to capture soldiers for this purpose. The wars were also a way to force other city-states to pay tribute. Military service was required of all males, and warfare and the priesthood were ways they could raise their status in society. While Aztec society expected men to aspire to become great warriors, it expected women to accept their fate of marriage.

The Aztec population declined in number with the arrival of the Europeans. Many Aztecs were killed in battle against the Spanish conquerors, led by Hernando Cortéz. Also the Aztec's herbal remedies were not effective against the diseases introduced by the Europeans, and epidemics decimated the native people. Economic and religious objectives governed the Spanish conquest. And with the defeat of the Aztec in 1521, the Spanish conquerors renamed the empire New Spain and founded its capital on the site of Tenochtitlán, renaming it Mexico City. The last Aztec emperor, Cuauhtémoc, died in 1523.

The conquerors founded new cities and towns

The Aztec Calendar, or Sun Stone, is a basalt monolith that measures nearly 12 feet in diameter and 3 feet thick. Carved in the fifteenth century and dedicated to the sun god, this complex astronomical and mythological symbol reflects the sophistication of the Aztec civilization. *(Museo Nacional de Antropologia, Mexico City, Mexico/Sean Sprague/Mexicolore/Bridgeman Art Library)*

located at the previous Aztec cities and towns. The king of Spain distributed land parcels to Spaniards living in New Spain. These parcels were usually divided based on the previously existing Aztec city-state divisions. The distribution of Aztec land and people to the Spanish conquerors formed part of the *encomienda* system, where the indigenous people were obligated to render goods and services as tribute to their Spanish masters, who, in return, protected them and indoctrinated them in Christianity. This system mirrored the previous Aztec system of tribute, except instead of producing goods for their own families and for city-state tribute to the Aztec Empire, the indigenes were now producing goods for their own families, for their Spanish masters, and for the Spanish Crown. This system lasted until 1542, when the New Laws emancipated all native slaves.

Although the Aztec still lived on the same land, the landscape was rapidly and drastically changing. Not only were the Spaniards renaming towns and cities, but in their colonization they were also destroying many fundamental Aztec constructions. They tore down Aztec pyramids in order to build Catholic churches on the site of the rubble. The Aztec were to be converted to Christianity, and human sacrifice was abolished. But many of the natives still followed traditional Aztec religion or adopted characteristics from both religions, and hence syncretism was widespread. The Nahuatl language continued to exist after the conquest, as the native people were able to write in their own language using the Spanish alphabet.

During the conquest and continuing through the colonial period and beyond, the intermarriage of Aztecs and Spaniards produced what would become the mestizo race, children born in Mexico of one indigenous parent and one European parent. This race would become the foundation of the Mexican nation.

Charlene Merithew

See also: Cortéz, Hernando; Mexico City; Montezuma II; Native American–European Conflict; Native Americans; New Spain; Spanish Colonies on Mainland North America (Chronology).

Bibliography

Clendinnen, Inga. *Aztecs.* New York: Cambridge University Press, 1991.

Davies, Nigel. *The Aztecs.* Norman: University of Oklahoma Press, 1980.

Smith, Michael E. *The Aztecs.* Malden, MA: Blackwell, 1996.

B

Bacon, Nathaniel (1647–1676)

Nathaniel Bacon is remembered largely because of his leadership in the event that became known as Bacon's Rebellion, a 1676 attack on Native Americans and the colonial government in Jamestown, Virginia.

Bacon was born in Suffolk in 1647. His father, Thomas Bacon, was a well-heeled aristocrat. Nathaniel was named for an older cousin who was a country theorist, a philosopher opposed to the reign of Charles I, and who served as Oliver Cromwell's master of requests.

Bacon was raised on his father's large estate at Freestone (Friston) Hall. He studied at Cambridge for two-and-a-half years, but his father withdrew him as punishment for extravagant behavior. Subsequently, he was tutored by the scientist John Ray, who praised Bacon's intellect but remarked that the young man lacked the patience for long periods of study. In 1663, Ray took Bacon, two older students, and their servants on a grand tour of Europe. For three years, the group traveled through the Netherlands, present-day Germany, Austria, and the cities of northern Italy. In 1666, while visiting Bologna, Bacon contracted smallpox. Upon his recovery, he returned to England, reenrolled at Cambridge, and took a master's degree there in 1668. Next Bacon took up law, receiving the title of esquire in 1669 or 1670.

Bacon married Elizabeth Duke in May 1670. Elizabeth's father, Sir Edward Duke, so disapproved of Bacon, who had a reputation for being arrogant and brash, that he disowned his daughter. In the early 1670s, Bacon, who also was ambitious and well-spoken, became involved in a scheme to defraud another young man of his inheritance. When this was discovered, Bacon was forced into exile in America.

As Bacon's father had given him 1,800 pounds, upon his arrival in Virginia in 1674, Bacon was already among the colony's wealthiest men. With the help of Governor Berkeley, a cousin by marriage and Bacon's future adversary, and his older cousin and namesake Nathaniel Bacon, Bacon acquired about 1,230 acres of land. Bacon's holdings stretched from his main plantation, Curles Neck, which was 40 miles up the James River from Jamestown, to the Falls of the James, the farthest reach of English settlement and the site of the present-day city of Richmond.

Despite Bacon's youth, Berkeley recognized his high social standing and appointed him to the Governor's Council, the ruling body of the colony. Bacon's attendance record indicates that he was uninterested in government. In June 1675, he missed the entire session; in September, he sat for a day; and in March 1676, he sat for a day and a half.

The 1670s were a tense time in Virginia. Governor Berkeley had been serving intermittently for over thirty years, Native Americans had become worried over increasing English encroachment, and some planters felt that Berkeley was not offering adequate protection in the event of attack. In 1676, these tensions erupted into open warfare. A group of dispossessed Doeg Indians, upset by what they considered crooked trade, raided English settlements, including Bacon's plantation, killing his overseer and three servants. A group of angry planters responded by killing not only Doegs but also Susquehannocks, who had been allied with the English for nearly three decades. The Susquehannock responded in kind, and the planters upriver from Jamestown asked Berkeley to send in the colonial militia.

Berkeley replied by claiming that Bacon and others had indiscriminately murdered both friendly and hostile Native Americans and had generally disregarded the authority of law and government. Instead of sup-

Nathaniel Bacon, a wealthy Virginia landholder, is remembered for a short-lived rebellion—which took his name—against the royal governor, Sir William Berkeley, and Native American tribes in 1676. *(Brown Brothers, Sterling, Pennsylvania)*

porting the planters, Berkeley sent 300 militiamen to capture Bacon.

Bacon, who had raised an army of his own to engage in warfare against the natives, now turned on Jamestown itself, finally burning it to the ground on September 19, 1676. He briefly gained control of the colonial government and enacted a series of statutes known as "Bacon's Laws." Bacon, however, died of dysentery on October 26, 1676, at the age of 29. In January 1677, Berkeley returned from exile on the Eastern shore of Maryland with royal troops and resumed control of the colony.

Matthew Jennings

See also: Bacon's Rebellion; Berkeley, Sir William; Chesapeake; House of Burgesses; Riots; Tobacco. *Document*: Governor William Berkeley on Bacon's Rebellion (1676).

Bibliography

Nash, Gary B. *Red, White and Black: The Peoples of Early North America.* Upper Saddle River, NJ: Prentice Hall, 2000.
Washburn, Wilcomb E. *The Governor and the Rebel: A History of Bacon's Rebellion in Virginia.* Chapel Hill: University of North Carolina Press, 1957.
Webb, Stephen Saunders. *1676: The End of American Independence.* Cambridge, MA: Harvard University Press, 1985.

Bacon's Rebellion

Historians have interpreted Bacon's Rebellion variously as a race war, a class war, a battle over patronage, and the "[temporary] end of American independence." Each of these interpretations is valid to a certain extent. Bacon's Rebellion, which shook the colony of Virginia to its very foundations in 1676, arose from complex origins and achieved complicated results.

Virginia in 1676 had enjoyed several decades of peace, thanks to a treaty signed by the Powhatan in 1644. Virginia had also enjoyed half a century of prosperity from the export of tobacco. However, rifts had developed between those who benefited from patronage and those who were not so favored, between Native Americans and English colonists, and between the eastern and western parts of the colony. These tensions would erupt into violence in 1676.

William Berkeley and Nathaniel Bacon

The two central figures in the saga of Bacon's Rebellion are William Berkeley, the longtime governor of Virginia, and Nathaniel Bacon, one of the colony's wealthiest residents. The two were related by marriage; Berkeley's second wife was Bacon's cousin.

William Berkeley was appointed governor in 1641 and brought an unabashedly elitist view to the post. He believed fervently that the upper classes should rule over the lower classes. He also praised the fact that in 1671, Virginia had no free public schooling or printing presses, reasoning that both developments led to disobedience and heresy. Berkeley's government focused on making the colony's wealthiest men even wealthier. Through an oppressive system of taxation and stuffing the pockets of legislators with the taxes of common planters and the profits from the Crown's lucrative monopoly on the deerskin trade, Berkeley managed to offend large numbers of people. If Bacon's Rebellion was a class war, Berkeley was clearly among the elite.

Nathaniel Bacon, the leader of the revolt against Berkeley, was a recent arrival in Virginia, having moved to the colony in 1674. When he reached America, he was already one of Virginia's wealthiest individuals, as his father had given him 1,800 pounds to start him off in a world where small-time planters could hope to clear 3 pounds a year after expenses. Bacon was a charismatic man in his mid-20s, whose exposure as a confidence man had forced his exile to Virginia. He took up residence along the James River on a previously established plantation and began to purchase lands as far north as the Falls of the James, site of the present-day city of Richmond. Though Berkeley offered the young man a post in the prestigious Governor's Council in recognition of his high social standing, Bacon initially took little interest in politics. But when his personal property came under threat from attack by natives, he became overtly critical of the Berkeley regime.

Anglo-Indian Conflict

As mentioned, Virginia had been at peace with most of its native neighbors for three decades. A brisk trade in deerskins had allowed Native Americans access to the trade goods they desired, and the colonial legislature, mainly friends of Berkeley, reaped the profits. In 1675, however, the peace began to unravel. A group of Doeg Indians, who had been swindled by an English planter, began to conduct raids on frontier plantations. The Virginia settlers, who had been able to disguise their hatred of Native Americans during a time of peace, retaliated. Unfortunately, they attacked the Susquehannock, another Iroquoian-speaking people who, while not particularly numerous, were adept at hit-and-run tactics and could strike plantations quickly with minimal risk of casualties on their part. The English settlers' inability or unwillingness to distinguish between groups of Native Americans sparked further conflict. The situation worsened when the English murdered a group of Susquehannock headmen, who were attempting to negotiate terms of peace.

Frontier planters, already disgruntled with the power and arrogance of the colonial establishment and hungry for new lands to put under the plow, seized the opportunity. They proposed an all-out race war between Native Americans and whites, regardless of whether Virginia had established friendly relations with specific native communities. Governor Berkeley balked at the idea, which would remove one of the forces that had increased his and his friends' fortune. He also resisted the proposal because rapid settlement in the western part of the colony would siphon off valuable labor and

rents from the eastern part. Berkeley instead proposed a system of defensive forts, which planters to the west viewed as wasteful and expensive.

The dispute led to a civil war pitting Berkeley and his followers (and to a lesser extent the Crown) against Bacon and a coalition of westerners, those who had not benefited from patronage, small planters, and indentured servants. Bacon promised immediate freedom to servants who aided his destruction of Berkeley's government.

Bacon's first action as a rebel leader was to carry out indiscriminate attacks on the region's Native Americans, including Algonquian speakers, who had long been friendly toward Virginia. While this increased his popularity among his neighbors, it angered Berkeley to the point that he declared Bacon guilty of treason, and the governor raised an army to deal with Bacon's threat. For his part, Bacon, having subdued or sufficiently terrorized Native Americans to force them into exile, turned his army toward Jamestown in early 1676 with the intention of unseating Berkeley.

While it may be appealing to view Bacon as a champion of the common white man, it is equally likely that he and his followers simply wanted a larger piece of the tax revenue pie. Still, Bacon was shrewd enough to recognize his need for allies wherever he could find them. In addition to freeing indentured servants, he also encouraged his followers to sack the plantations of those who remained loyal to Governor Berkeley.

Bacon's Rebellion succeeded in the short term. In the summer of 1676, Bacon's army pushed Berkeley's forces out of Jamestown. The governor and his supporters took refuge on the Eastern shore of Chesapeake Bay. In September, to dissuade them from returning, Bacon took the symbolic step of burning the colonial capital. During the rebellion, Bacon and his supporters enacted a series of laws that came to be known as Bacon's Laws.

The success of Bacon's Rebellion was short-lived, and so was Nathaniel Bacon. Just over a month after the burning of Jamestown, Bacon died from dysentery. Without its charismatic leader, the rebellion that bore his name crumbled quickly, and Berkeley's retribution was fast and harsh. Twenty-three of the rebels were hanged, and Berkeley turned his forces loose on the plantations of Bacon's followers.

The government of Charles II took an interesting stand on the issue. The king could not stand for open rebellion against authority, but his advisers also recognized that Berkeley's policies had incited the conflict. Though Virginia had become a Crown colony in the wake of Native American attacks in the 1620s, the Crown developed a greater interest in Virginia's affairs after Bacon's Rebellion. Charles II dismissed Berkeley, calling him a fool, and sent an army to Virginia to restore order.

The long-term effects of Bacon's Rebellion are as complex as its origins. Though the Crown takeover weakened when the newly appointed governor and many of the royal troops died of disease, former supporters of Berkeley did not use the opportunity to retaliate against the remaining Baconites. Instead, they extended an olive branch to western planters. And the House of Burgesses reduced the poll tax, seeking a broader-based coalition of planters.

Interestingly, one effect of the rebellion was racial. One of the last parties of Bacon's supporters contained African Americans, and as such raised the specter of class warfare against the great planters. The great planters, in turn, reached out to other white Virginians and began to divide Virginia even more sharply along lines of black and white. Similarly, colonial leaders recognized that Bacon's harsh Native American policy was exceedingly popular, particularly in western areas, and began to lead incursions against Native Americans, dividing peoples that had coexisted between 1644 and 1676. Virginia society was transformed in the wake of Bacon's Rebellion, and the main result was a united front of great planters and common planters against the colony's nonwhite population. Categories of race that had previously been fluid hardened into a caste-like system.

Bacon's Rebellion should not be held responsible for all of the changes in Virginia at the time. (For instance, an increase in tobacco prices helped large and small planters recognize their similarities.) It did, however, highlight the tensions of colonial society. Virginia emerged from the conflict a more prosperous, yet increasingly racialized, colony.

Matthew Jennings

See also: Bacon, Nathaniel; Berkeley, Sir William; Chesapeake; House of Burgesses; Riots; Tobacco; Virginia; Virginia (Chronology). *Document*: Governor William Berkeley on Bacon's Rebellion (1676).

Bibliography

Middlekauff, Robert, ed. *Bacon's Rebellion.* New York: Rand McNally, 1964.

Taylor, Alan. *American Colonies.* New York: Viking, 2001.

Washburn, Wilcomb E. *The Governor and the Rebel: A History of Bacon's Rebellion in Virginia.* Chapel Hill: University of North Carolina Press, 1957.

Webb, Stephen Saunders. *1676: The End of American Independence.* Cambridge, MA: Harvard University Press, 1985.

Baltimore

In 1729, Maryland's colonial assembly appointed seven commissioners to purchase 60 acres of land on the north bank of the Patapsco River and establish a city named Baltimore. Although a latecomer among East Coast cities, Baltimore experienced phenomenal growth, and it quickly became an important part of the social, political, cultural, and economic landscape of colonial North America.

Initially, the site upon which Baltimore was founded consisted of three small settlements, Jonas Town (Jones Town), Fell's Point, and Baltimore Town. The commissioners who purchased the land for Baltimore Town divided it into sixty 1-acre lots, which they then sold for 40 shillings each. Each new settler was allowed the purchase of a single lot and was required to build a house on the land within eighteen months of the date of purchase or forfeit the title.

For almost thirty years, the area did not experience much growth. The settlement at Baltimore Town consisted of twenty-five houses, a church, a brewery, a tobacco inspection house, a tavern, and a barbershop. By the 1760s, however, Baltimore became increasingly attractive to sailors and merchants, who recognized its value as a port that could easily accommodate local, as well as overseas, trade. Baltimore annexed both Jonas Town and Fell's Point by the 1770s and, by 1776, had a population of 6,755, a much larger number than Maryland's capital, Annapolis.

Like most other colonial cities, especially those located on or near the coast, Baltimore owed its existence to trade. In the years preceding the Revolution, Baltimore became the center of trade in Maryland, and a variety of goods passed through the burgeoning port on a daily basis. After 1760, large amounts of wheat, corn, and flour from Maryland's upper Eastern shore, as well as tobacco and flax, passed through Baltimore on its way to ports as far off as the West Indies and Europe. By 1760, Baltimore had also become a critical link in a network of local trade that extended to all parts of Chesapeake Bay.

The coming of the Revolution only served to further enhance Baltimore's status as a social, political,

Founded in 1729, Baltimore was a relative latecomer among East Coast cities, but it soon became one of the busiest ports in the Chesapeake and a center of shipbuilding, maritime trade, finance, crafts, education, and medicine. *(Private Collection/ Bridgeman Art Library)*

and economic leader within the colonies. It became the county seat in 1768. Baltimore residents also formed their own Sons of Liberty political club and swore resistance to the Stamp Act. Following the Boston Tea Party, Baltimore residents decided to send much-needed food to Boston to help those individuals who could not work because of the British blockade of Boston Harbor. Baltimore also became the temporary site (from December 1776 to February 1777) of "the United States in Congress Assembled," when British capture of Philadelphia seemed inevitable. Countless Baltimore residents fought in the Revolution, and more than 240 privateers left the port of Baltimore to attack British commercial vessels. The first cruisers of the Continental Navy, the *Hornet* and the *Wasp,* were at least partially constructed in Baltimore shipyards.

Baltimore experienced a growth spurt during the Revolution and by 1790 had a population of 13,503 inhabitants. By the 1790s, Baltimore's average annual exports included approximately 260,000 barrels of flour, 20,000 barrels of beef and pork, 20,000 barrels of fish, 8,000 casks of butter and lard, 8 million board feet of lumber, and 5 million shingles, with a total value of approximately $3.6 million. In addition, Baltimore was exporting "foreign articles" worth approximately $9 million, mostly West Indian sugar that was sent to Europe aboard American ships. Trading was often conducted in one of Baltimore's many public markets, the first of which, located on the northwest corner of Baltimore and Gay streets, was in operation by 1765.

A few wealthy merchants dominated trade in Baltimore and in most cases also assumed the role of civic and social leader. In addition to overseeing the activities at their warehouses and wharves, located along the waterfront, and their counting houses, located in the center of Baltimore's financial district, wealthy merchants served as town commissioners and were the majority of stockholders in the Bank of Maryland as well as the local branch of the Bank of the United States.

By 1790, Baltimore had become the fifth-largest city in the United States and one of the busiest ports on the Chesapeake. It was a center for shipbuilding and the related crafts of rope making, sail making, and rigging manufacture, as well as the home of many skilled artisans and craftsmen, including carpenters, masons, tanners, saddlers, butchers, bakers, and cabinetmakers. In the early nineteenth century, Baltimore would become a center of education and medicine as well.

Michael A. Rembis

See also: Calvert, George (First Lord Baltimore); Maryland; Maryland (Chronology).

Bibliography

Land, Aubrey C. *Colonial Maryland: A History.* Millwood, NY: KTO, 1981.

Maryland Historical Society. *Maryland Heritage: Five Baltimore Institutions Celebrate the American Bicentennial.* Baltimore: Maryland Historical Society, 1976.

Middleton, Arthur Pierce. *Tobacco Coast: A Maritime History of Chesapeake Bay in the Colonial Era.* Baltimore: Johns Hopkins University Press, 1984.

Reps, John W. *Tidewater Towns: City Planning in Colonial Virginia and Maryland.* Williamsburg, VA: Colonial Williamsburg Foundation, 1972.

Baltimore, First Lord

See Calvert, George

Banks and Banking

The concept of banking dates centuries back to the days of biblical moneychangers. In every transaction, moneychangers took a percentage. They collected a profit, which is what every bank does in order to extend credit or loan money.

The first country to impose mercantilism and profiteering on its American colonies was Spain. The Spanish American colonies were not allowed independent access to markets in Europe or abroad. All trade had to be filtered through Spain first, and heavy tariffs were imposed on all imports. The rationale, of course, was that the colonies only existed to support the mother country; and all profits were to return to her.

Profit seeking also influenced the settlement of the British colonies. For example, Jamestown was funded by the English shareholders of a joint-stock company. And though the colony faced major setbacks at the outset, when it began raising and selling tobacco the company's shareholders began receiving substantial profits.

First Colonial Bankers

The first "bankers" in the colonies were most likely goldsmiths, and the first paper money, merely receipts for gold deposits. These receipts were easy to handle and carry; nevertheless, they represented real backing (gold, bullion, or coin). As people neglected to collect the real gold, using the receipts instead as a form of tender, some goldsmiths merely extended credit on the basis of the gold deposits.

British colonists derived their concept of banking from the English system. In the seventeenth century, after a series of international wars, England turned to a "government-sanctioned" but privately owned Central Bank, erroneously named the Bank of England. Operated by foreign banks, it loaned money that was supposed to be secured "by the direct taxation of the people." For a time, England appeared to prosper as a result of these loans, but in reality, the national debt rose by 1,280 percent from 1694 to 1698.

It has been suggested by Andrew McFarland Davis in his two-volume history on colonial currency, first published in 1900, that

> it may be doubted whether the founders of the Bank of England, in 1694, had before them any other well-defined precedents upon which to base an opinion as to the probable success of paper money, than were to be found in the ordinary mercantile bills of exchange, the goldsmiths' notes, and the bills of public credit of the Colony of the Massachusetts Bay.

Thus, the Bank of England, in spite of its poor beginnings, was stepping into a new era and offering a new definition of banking. Other banks that might have influenced the Bank of England's design included the Bank of Amsterdam, the Bank of Venice, and the Bank of Genoa. Also, the move by the Colony of Massachusetts Bay several years earlier to extend public credit was apparently an important catalyst in the emerging history of banking.

As Davis writes, "When the Assembly of the Colony of the Massachusetts Bay first authorized the emission of bills of public credit, they were securing for themselves the right to claim that they were practically the pioneers in a great economic experiment."

Indeed, in an act proposed by the magistrates of

the Massachusetts Bay Colony as early as May 1654, they wrote:

> [W]hatever person or persons be they stranngers or Inhabitants that shall directly or Indirectly export out of this Jurisdiccon any of the coine of this countrie after the publication hereof shall forfeite his or their whole estate one halfe to the countrie and the other halfe to such pson or psons as shall sue for the same.

They also proposed that "there should be a Water Bayly or searcher appointed in every port-towne who would search any suspistious persons or vessells, chests, truncks or any other things." The discovered coin would then be divided, half to the officer who discovered the theft and half to the "countrie."

By the mid-1700s, however, with British debt skyrocketing, the Crown looked to its American colonies for revenue. At this time, the colonies issued their own paper currency. According to Benjamin Franklin, when asked to explain the colonies' economic prosperity, "We issue it [colonial scrip] in proper proportion to make the goods pass easily from the producers to the consumers. In this manner, creating ourselves our own paper money, we control its purchasing power and we have no interest to pay to any one."

On the heels of this, Britain moved to forbid the minting or regulation of colonial currency within the colonies, forcing the colonists to rely on British or European money. This led to incredible hardships, because coin had always been scarce and its value was never standardized. What foreign specie came into the colonies was always quickly spent on imports and foreign goods.

From Spanish pieces of eight to British sterling, there was no consistency in money's exchange rate. Not until 1672 was there a legal rating of Spanish pieces of eight in New England, and "it seems probable that this legislation was the result of two circumstances: first, that the piece of eight having a recognized rate in shillings at which it would pass, people could and did avail themselves of it as a medium of trade . . . ; and second that the General Court was desirous of protecting the public against the light weight pieces if possible."

Creation of Colonial Money

In spite of Britain's ban on issuing money, however, and without banks to offer credit or loans, several colonies went ahead and devised their own money.

Unfortunately, it was rarely accepted or redeemable in other colonies. As Franklin later wrote in his autobiography,

> The colonies would gladly have borne the little tax on tea and other matters, had it not been that England took away from the colonies their money, which created unemployment and dissatisfaction. The inability of the colonists to get power to issue their own money permanently out of the hands of George III and the International Bankers was the Prime reason for the Revolutionary War.

Clearly, not only was there a great need for a form of standardized and universal currency within the colonies, there was also a growing need for banks that could provide venture capital and secure loans to individuals. However, even as late as 1775, the few lending institutions that did exist were not the kind that we know today. Most were land banks, which required land as collateral. Moreover, the Bank of England, now a century old, was not a place where colonists went for investment purposes. Their distrust of all things British was most evident in their disdain for its institutions.

These early banks, many of them private institutions, did offer a place to store money. Many also made loans, but there was no uniform code of standards, no rules by which they were held accountable. There was also no consistency in the type or management of loans. Bills of credit were often signed over to the next merchant or manufacturer and could be passed on and on, down the line, almost as a form of specie. Debt followed the bills until, perhaps, the last bearer turned and sued for payment, unleashing "a flurry of letters and sometimes a chain of lawsuits until all debts, once thought canceled, were again made good." Sometimes payment never found its way to the last "payee."

As a result, most individuals looking for credit or loans sought the assistance of private lenders such as merchants. In this way, merchant capitalists became the primary source of money or credit throughout the colonies for a span of time. Many of these wealthy merchants, along with a number of Southern landowners, eventually emerged as leaders in the rebellion against the British.

One such patriot merchant was Robert Morris, of Philadelphia. Having signed the Non-Importation Agreement in 1765, an act that attempted to force the repeal of the Stamp Act and other taxes, Morris quickly joined the growing throng of revolutionaries who opposed Britain's control over every aspect of colonial life. He served as a delegate to the Second Continental

Philadelphia merchant Robert Morris was known as "the financier of the American Revolution" for his role in securing materiel and financial assistance. Congress named him superintendent of finance, in which capacity he helped found the Bank of North America. *(Library of Congress, LC-USZ62-3596)*

Congress, where he contracted for equipment needed by the Continental army, from which his firm, Willing, Morris & Company, benefited by the contracts drawn up with the emerging American government. Later appointed superintendent of finance in 1781, he helped create the Bank of North America. Stephen Gerard, another private banker, was also America's wealthiest shipping merchant.

The banking activity these colonial merchants engaged in became a lucrative enterprise, but it still left many prospective borrowers without a way to obtain credit or loans. Even the Continental Congress, when it chose to finance Washington's Army, turned to issuing notes or bills of credit in increasing quantities, because the contributions made by the individual states were not enough to finance a war. One of the first orders of business for the newly formed United States under the Constitution was the appointment of Alex-ander Hamilton as the first secretary of the treasury and the formulation of a sound economic policy.

Gail L. Jenner

See also: Currency; Economy, Business, and Labor (Chronology); Economy, Business, and Labor (Essay). *Document*: A Modest Enquiry into the Nature and Necessity of a Paper Currency (1729).

Bibliography

Davis, Andrew McFarland. "Currency and Banking in the Province of the Massachusetts Bay Colony." http://etext.lib.virginia.edu/users/brock/davisch1.html.

Todd, Lewis Paul, and Merle Curti. *Rise of the American Nation.* New York: Harcourt Brace Jovanovich, 1982.

Wright, Robert E. "Commercial Banking in Colonial America." http://earlyamerica.com/review/summer97/banking.html.

Baptists

Despite the similarity in their names, American Baptists are not the spiritual descendants of the Anabaptists of Switzerland, Germany, and the Netherlands. Rather, Baptists in America can trace their heritage to left-wing Puritans of the English Reformation. Today's largest American Protestant denomination owes much to these founders and to the growth achieved by its forbears during and after the Great Awakening.

English Beginnings of the Baptist Faith

Baptists in England had strong roots in the Westminster Confession of Faith dating to 1640. These dissenting Englishmen were decidedly liberal, however, and parted ways with traditional Puritan beliefs. Some early Baptists were Calvinist in their beliefs, especially concerning the issues of limited atonement and special or "particular" election of God's chosen saints; accordingly, this group came to be known as Particular Baptists. Other, more radical, Baptists were decidedly Arminian in their beliefs concerning the exercise of the individual's free will and in their belief in the unlimited atonement for sinners provided by Christ's redeeming death. This group became known as General Baptists. Both Particular and General Baptists, however, agreed on the necessity of the individual's conversion experience as a manifestation of his or her right relationship with God. Accordingly, Baptists parted from the usual Puritan practice of infant baptism, arguing that without this personal conversion, a believer was in fact unfit to receive the Holy Spirit via the ritual of baptism. Further, Baptists posited that only baptism by immersion was acceptable, as it was necessary to wash away one's sins to begin a new spiritual life—a task that simple sprinkling could not accomplish. The particulars of how each group of English Baptists approached their mission of correcting the errors they perceived in Puritanism are significant, and both groups' activities have a bearing on the spread of the Baptist church to America.

Particular Baptists shared many of their Anglican brethren's beliefs, especially the Calvinist tenet of God's special election of the saints. While they disagreed with the Church of England's practice of infant baptism, this group felt it was possible to correct the church's errors from within. Accordingly, Henry Jacob founded a Baptist congregation in Southwark near London in 1616. By 1622, however, Jacob decided to relocate to Jamestown in the new Virginia colony, and he was replaced at Southwark by John Lathrop. As time went on, Lathrop's group came under increasing persecution for their beliefs; in 1634, the minister led thirty of his parishioners to the New World in search of religious tolerance. The group went first to Scituate, in Plymouth Colony, and then relocated to the Barnstable area of Cape Cod.

Jacob's Southwark congregation remained a vital and dynamic group after his departure. Part of the group split off in 1633, troubled by the reluctance of the entire group to separate from the Church of England; by 1638, more congregants joined them, and this group declared publicly that infant baptism was wrong, refining this belief in 1640 to state that only baptism by immersion (rather than sprinkling) was sufficient to seal the relationship between man and the Holy Spirit. Other Particular Baptists in London remained more closely Calvinist and thus were more in agreement with Congregationalists and Anglicans. Through the mid-seventeenth century, Particular Baptists remained a strong presence in and around London and even spread to Wales. As the century progressed, Particular Baptists from Wales created a strong presence in the middle colonies and in the Philadelphia Association, which was formed in 1707.

Early General Baptists were led by John Smyth, a Cambridge-educated minister. Smyth came to believe that a personal profession of faith was necessary for the individual to have a personal relationship with God. As

a result, he saw the tenets of the Church of England as being in error; consequently, because the Anglican views on man's ability to be in direct communion with God were wrong, Smyth concluded that the Anglican baptism must also be in error. As a result, the General Baptists under Smyth felt it necessary to separate themselves from the Anglican faith, believing that it was impossible to reform the church from within.

By 1608, the Separatist congregation established by Smyth at Gainesboro had fled to Amsterdam to escape English persecution for its heresy. In 1609 Smyth declared the need for a new start for himself and his congregation, and he baptized himself and his followers anew. Soon Smyth became increasingly interested in merging with local Dutch Mennonites. A number of parishioners, led by Thomas Helwys, became convinced that they had erred in leaving England. In 1612, this group returned and formed the first Baptist congregation in England in Spitafields, near London. General Baptists enjoyed a period of quick yet sustained growth under the rule of Cromwell that even continued under the Stuart Restoration after 1660. General Baptists eventually spread to western counties of England, with many of these believers eventually migrating to the American colonies of Rhode Island, Virginia, and North Carolina.

Baptists in Colonial America

Roger Williams played a key role in the establishment of the colony of Rhode Island as a haven of religious toleration. He and his followers established the first native Baptist church in America at Providence in 1639. However, it is important to mention that over time Williams's views changed; eventually, he came to deny the legitimacy of all organized churches and to believe that only God's interposition could restore the church on earth to fullness. After Williams's withdrawal from the Providence Baptist fellowship, Thomas Olney, a strong Calvinist, took charge of the congregation. Eventually, the group's views evolved to include a strong belief in the necessity of the laying on of hands as a requisite for the visitation of the Holy Spirit. Because this belief was one of the six tenets listed in Hebrews 6:1–2, the local church became known as "Six Principle Baptists." By 1652, the Providence church was divided over these six principles; overall, this and other Six Principle churches had little influence on American Christianity. And despite these changes within the Baptist community, Rhode Island remained a safe haven for a variety of religious groups.

The Baptist message was attractive in other colonies as well. Henry Dunster, president of Harvard College, was forced to resign his position in 1654, a year after he refused infant baptism for his fourth child. Thomas Gould led the Boston Baptist membership after the church was formed there in 1665. From that year through 1680, Baptist churches experienced steady growth but increasing persecution, particularly along the border region where Massachusetts met Rhode Island.

Connecticut Baptists also were influenced by their colleagues in Rhode Island. In 1705 the church at Groton was founded and led by Valentine Wightman. Following his death in 1741, his son and grandson took up Wightman's mantle and led the congregation for the following 100 years. Nearly all New England Baptist churches were associated via the Rhode Island Yearly Meeting of General Baptists, which had been established at the beginning of the eighteenth century.

Interestingly, the early years of colonial settlement were not a prosperous time for Baptists in the Southern Colonies. Banned from organizing in Virginia by a 1661 law, there were Baptists in North and South Carolina in the seventeenth century, but none were especially effective. The following century, however, was a far different story.

Perhaps the most far-reaching event for Southern churches, especially for Baptists and Methodists, was the advent of the Great Awakening in the early 1700s. Baptists particularly benefited from the basic premises of this evangelistic movement: the revivalists' emphasis on the necessity of "being saved," the view that infant baptism was an anomaly at best and sinful at worst, and the belief that the sacraments of baptism and communion—while important rituals—were insufficient as the means of grace. All resounded with the core beliefs of the Baptist faithful. Statistics and anecdotal evidence certainly suggest that the Awakening's zeal lingered longer in Southern Baptist communities of worship than in many other groups and regions. The personally charismatic, energetic, emotional, and sometimes eccentric preaching of early Methodist revivalists, including George Whitefield, was quickly adopted by many Baptist preachers, particularly those in rural and frontier areas of the South. Combined with his methodology, Baptists' simplicity of doctrine and egalitarian ethic strongly appealed to these uneducated and unsophisticated flocks. As a result, Baptist missionary preachers in the South (and, soon, also in the western territories of Kentucky and Tennessee) were joined by the newly converted farmer-preacher, a phenomenon that helped lead to the church's astounding rural growth in the mid- and late-eighteenth century. In the agrarian South, there were only two plausible hindrances to the adoption of the Baptist faith: First, in isolated instances, a local group might be repelled by a given preacher's personal enthusiasm; or, more often, a Methodist preacher might have evangelized and converted a given area before a Baptist could arrive to do the job.

Perhaps the same traits that made Great Awakening evangelism so popular in the South made it equally distasteful to New England Baptists, who largely fancied themselves too sophisticated to be swayed by such emotional displays. Mostly, though, Baptists' general opposition to a paid, settled, college-educated clergy made the denomination a good fit with the mood of colonists as they migrated westward.

In addition to their spiritual legacy to contemporary church members, colonial Baptists established the College of Rhode Island in 1764. Although the American War for Independence disrupted its operations for a time, the school survived and was renamed Brown University in 1804. It remains one of the nation's finest institutions of higher education.

Barbara Schwarz Wachal

See also: Christ and Christianity; Religion (Chronology); Religion (Essay).

Bibliography

Davis, Lawrence B. *Immigrants, Baptists, and the Protestant Mind in America.* Urbana: University of Illinois Press, 1973.

McLoughlin, William G. *New England Dissent, 1630–1833: The Baptists and the Separation of Church and State.* Cambridge, MA: Harvard University Press, 1971.

———. *Soul Liberty: The Baptists' Struggle in New England, 1630–1833.* Hanover, NH: University Press of New England, 1991.

Torbet, Robert G. *A History of the Baptists.* Valley Forge, PA: Judson, 1965.

Barbados

The island of Barbados is the most windward, or easternmost, of the Lesser Antilles, bounded by the Caribbean Sea on its western coast and the Atlantic Ocean on the east. Barbados was originally peopled by Amerindian migrants from the South American mainland. The Spanish explorers of the first quarter of the six-

The most easterly of the Antilles islands, Barbados (viewed here in the late seventeenth century) was settled by English colonists in 1627. Sugar exports made it the wealthiest colony in the British Empire. *(Yale Center for British Art, Paul Mellon Collection, New Haven, Connecticut/Bridgeman Art Library)*

teenth century encountered a number of indigenous settlements, but when the Portuguese arrived in 1536, they found the island to be deserted. They christened it Los Barbados, which means "the bearded ones," after bearded fig trees they found on the island.

English mariners led by Captain John Powell arrived in 1625 and confirmed the uninhabited status of the island, and Barbados was claimed for the English Crown. The first settlement was established two years later at Jamestown (present-day Holetown) on the western coast, and consisted of eighty European settlers and ten African slaves. The European and African populations would continue to grow from emigration, forced or otherwise, over the course of the seventeenth century.

Within a few years of settlement, the colonists had cleared much of the native forest to plant tobacco and cotton, but neither crop performed well. In the 1640s, following the success of sugar growth in Brazil, the settlers began replanting the fields with sugarcane, which was in great demand in Europe and the colonies, both in granulated form and as molasses, which was fermented and distilled to produce rum. Until the introduction of sugar, indentured servants, mainly Irish, performed most of the labor. Some had been kidnapped to the island, inaugurating the colloquialism "to be barbadosed," the seventeenth-century equivalent of the later term "shanghaied." In order to meet the increased labor demands of sugar cultivation, the planters began importing large numbers of African slaves.

Due to its sugar production, Barbados soon became the wealthiest colony of the English empire. The wealth of the sugar plantations, though built on the backs of slave laborers, was nonetheless highly concentrated in the hands of the British-educated elite. This elite planter class dominated all of the important ranks in society, including the English-style administrative positions of council members, assemblymen, militia officers, judges, and justices of the peace. Throughout the course of the seventeenth century, they maintained a black-to-white ratio of 4 to 1, the lowest in the British West Indies. To avoid slave revolts, the planters deliberately avoided the purchase of Coromantees (from West Africa's Gold Coast, present-day Ghana), as this group had played a key role in the rebellions of Jamaica. This factor, in combination with the island's open and level terrain (unlike the mountainous and rugged geography of Jamaica, which is more conducive to hiding) and the maintenance of a strong militia, led to a limited number of slave revolts in Barbados, although uprisings occurred, and were suppressed, in 1675 and 1692. Many Barbadians emigrated to South Carolina in the late seventeenth century, where they established slavery and the plantation system for the cultivation of rice.

The Legislative Assembly was founded in 1639, and in 1652, Barbados signed a charter with London that guaranteed rule by a governor and a freely elected assembly, dominated by the planter elite, who were granted freedom from taxation without local consent. In addition, customs duties placed on sugar were significantly lower than those placed on tobacco grown on the mainland colonies. This measure of political and economic freedom caused the Barbados colonial elites to side with the British Crown a century later during the Stamp Act crisis of 1765–1766 when the governor, Charles Pinfold, and the legislative assembly voted to pay stamp duties.

During the subsequent American War for Independence, Barbados again sided with the Crown. The hardship of the war, however, was exacerbated by years of declining profits, lower productivity, and decreased production due to soil erosion. Furthermore, a severe hurricane wrought havoc upon the island in 1780, causing damage with an estimated cost of 1.3 million pounds.

The major effect of the American Revolution on Barbados was to weaken the political leverage of the elite planters and deteriorate the foundations of slavery upon which the economy was based. The sugar trade continued to be profitable, but demands for a full resumption of trade with the United States, which had accounted for one-fourth of all produce exports in the prewar years, were met by firm opposition in London; the traditional mercantilist principles of colonial policy demanded a balance of trade in favor of Britain.

The war elevated the status of both free blacks and slaves. In addition to military service, they became essential to the economy as peasant farmers, following the virtual loss of imports from North America. Abolition finally came to Barbados in 1834, but it failed to solve the extant inequalities in the distribution of land and wealth.

Kevin P. McDonald

See also: Caribbean (Chronology); Slavery, Caribbean; Sugar.

Bibliography

Beckles, Hilary. *A History of Barbados: From Amerindian Settlement to Nation-State.* Cambridge, UK: Cambridge University Press, 1990.

Dunn, Richard. *Sugar and Slaves: The Rise of the Planter Class in the English West Indies, 1624–1713.* New York: W. W. Norton, 1972.

Handler, Jerome S., and Frederick W. Lange. *Plantation Slavery in Barbados: An Archaeological and Historical Investigation.* Cambridge, MA: Harvard University Press, 1978.

O'Shaughnessy, Andrew J. *An Empire Divided: The American Revolution and the British Caribbean.* Philadelphia: University of Pennsylvania Press, 2000.

Watson, Karl. *The Civilised Island, Barbados: A Social History, 1750–1816.* Ellerton, Barbados: K. Watson, 1979.

Bartram Family

This extended family, centering on the Pennsylvania farmer John Bartram, contributed substantially to the study of botany and natural history in British North America.

Beginning around 1727, when he was about 28 years old, Bartram became interested in botany, a subject in which he was largely self-taught. Through his correspondence with the London Quaker merchant Peter Collinson, one of the most important intermediaries between English and American science, Bartram entered the world of international botanical exchange, sending seeds, bulbs, and cuttings of American plants to Europe; he received European and other foreign specimens in exchange, as well as monetary payment. Bartram's efforts contributed to a marked rise in the number of American plant species cultivated in England in the mid-eighteenth century.

As his skills were recognized in the learned community in Europe and America, Bartram acquired Benjamin Franklin as a patron and the great Swedish botanist Carl Linnaeus as an admirer. He also published several papers on natural history in the journal of Britain's Royal Society, *Philosophical Transactions,* although, curiously, none on botany. Bartram contributed specimens to enable Mark Catesby, who was in London at the time, to finish his *Natural History of Carolina, Florida and the Bahama Islands* (published 1729–1747).

Bartram also corresponded and exchanged plants and seeds with other North American botanists and gardeners, such as Cadwallader Colden of New York and Martha Logan of Charles Town. The botanical garden Bartram started in 1728 at his home outside Philadelphia attracted many distinguished visitors. He participated in the first American Philosophical Society from 1743 to 1746 and was an inactive member of the subsequent Philadelphia organization bearing that name.

Bartram made several journeys in search of new American plants. The height of his career was an expedition to the southeastern British colonies in 1765, when George III appointed Bartram king's botanist. This appointment shocked some American scientists.

Largely self-taught, John Bartram came to be regarded as "the father of American botany." He collected, studied, and exchanged countless plant species and conducted what are believed to be the first experiments in hybridization. *(Library of Congress, LC-USZ62-68176)*

Bartram, for all his undoubted skill in collecting and raising plants, was not a learned botanist—he had little knowledge of Latin and botanical science.

Regardless of his colleagues' skepticism, the trip was a success. Bartram published two accounts of his journeys, *Observations on the Inhabitants, Climate, Soil, Rivers, Productions, Animals, and other matters worthy of notice. Made by Mr. John Bartram, in his travels from Pensilvania to Onondago, Oswego, and the Lake Ontario, in Canada* (1751) and a journal included in William Stork's *An Account of East Florida, with a Journal, Kept by John Bartram of Philadelphia, botanist to his majesty for the Floridas; upon a journey from St. Augustine up the River St. Johns* (1767).

Bartram's success helped attract his cousin Humphrey Marshall to the sciences. Marshall supplemented Bartram's botanical exports by sending small American animals and insects to European collectors. Marshall, with broader scientific interests than Bartram, was also a keen astronomer whose observations of sunspots were

published in *Philosophical Transactions.* In his work as a botanist, Marshall wrote a catalogue of American trees and shrubs, *Arbustrum Americanum* (1785), which attracted considerable interest in Europe, with two reprints.

Two of John Bartram's sons, Isaac and Moses, were apothecaries, active members of the American Philosophical Society, and dabblers in the sciences. Isaac's interests were in chemistry, botany, and agricultural improvement, while Moses was mostly interested in natural history. Both were deeply involved in the American Philosophical Society's project to create a silkworm industry in Pennsylvania.

The most prominent scientist and writer among John Bartram's sons was the youngest, William Bartram. William Bartram's keen interest in botany and natural history was manifest in his youth, causing his father to despair of finding him a remunerative career. William was a gifted illustrator and accompanied John on his trip to the southeastern colonies in 1765. He hoped to start a slave-worked rice plantation in Florida, an effort that came to nothing.

William Bartram is best known for his narrative of a series of his own expeditions in southeastern North America from 1773 to 1776, *Travels through North & South Carolina, East and West Florida, the Cherokee Country, the Extensive Territories of the Muscogulges, or Creek Confederacy, and the Country of the Choctaws, containing an Account of the Soil and Natural Productions of these Regions, together with Observations on the Manners of the Indians* (1791). His scientific interests were broader than his father's. In addition to information on botany, his writings contain much information about animal life and both colonial and Native American society. Bartram was more sympathetic to Native Americans than were most white American writers at the time. *Travels* was far less popular in the United States than in Europe, where its influence was greatest among Romantic poets, rather than natural historians.

William E. Burns

See also: Environment and Nature; Science; Science and Technology (Chronology).

Bibliography

Earnest, Ernest. *John and William Bartram, Botanists and Explorers.* Philadelphia: University of Pennsylvania Press, 1940.

Slaughter, Thomas P. *The Natures of John and William Bartram.* New York: Alfred A. Knopf, 1996.

Stearns, Raymond Phineas. *Science in the British Colonies of America.* Urbana: University of Illinois Press, 1970.

Bathing and Hygiene

The importance placed on bathing and hygiene fluctuated greatly throughout European history. A Roman emphasis on cleanliness led to the creation of public baths in Europe and southern Britain during the Roman Empire. For wealthy families, this attention continued from the fall of the Roman Empire through the medieval period. Most castles were equipped with tubs for bathing, usually with water hauled both in and out by servants.

By the sixteenth and seventeenth centuries, however, bathing was no longer valued. Public baths were viewed as dangerous and promiscuous places, where disease spread easily. The close, cramped quarters endured by most people and their lack of access to water also made bathing difficult. As colonists began moving to North America in the early seventeenth century, these obstacles to bathing, both societal and practical, were compounded by the difficulties of early settlement.

The late eighteenth century saw a renewed focus in bathing and hygiene on both sides of the Atlantic, predominantly for the upper classes. This renewed interest in cleanliness reflected many changes of the period. Increased trade led to often-rapid transformations of fortune, simultaneously threatening the traditional upper class while creating a larger middle class. Wealthy families needed a means of demonstrating their continued superior position in society. In contrast, families suddenly made financially comfortable as a result of exploration and trade needed a means of demonstrating how they were different from those in the lower class. Both groups sought recognition through the same means: the demonstration of gentility through personal refinement. While well-tailored clothing, a large house, and elegant furniture were an instant indication of wealth, they were all things that could be purchased. Good grooming implied custom and background that could be gained only through birth.

The other motivation for greater hygiene reflects the scientific discoveries of the age. In the Renaissance period, some people had believed that bathing was harmful to the skin, removing oils necessary for good health. This belief also may have been reinforced by concerns about the dangers of public baths. By the late eighteenth century, new research suggested that the skin created grease and perspiration, which should be removed with soap and water. A popular source for this information was William Buchan's *Domestic Medicine.*

First published in London in 1769, it had gone through seventeen American editions by 1800.

Bathing and Health

The initial trend toward bathing began in the 1740s, although it had little to do with becoming clean. Certain types of water were thought to provide specific medical benefits. A cold bath would strengthen constitutions prone to ill health and indigestion. A warm bath would soothe nervousness. Other options included baths that contained mineral salts or with some form of added electric shock. Doctors often suggested that their wealthy patients "take the waters," whether at a popular seaside town or in private baths at their own homes. While the organized resorts of Britain never fully materialized in the colonies, the custom was known in North America. The first baths primarily meant for becoming clean did not emerge until the 1780s.

Further evidence that bathing was not initially connected to hygiene is found in the general absence of soap for bathing during the period. For most people, soap was made at home from a combination of fat, usually lard from pigs, and lye, composed of wood ash and water. While curing for a month or more took away some of its harshness, lye soap was always hard on the hands. It was used predominantly for washing clothes, dishes, and homes rather than bodies; cold water and a hard scrub with a rough towel were generally thought sufficient. Wealthy women had access to perfumed soaps from Europe, but the emphasis was on the perfume rather than its ability to wash. Toilet soaps were not commonly manufactured in the United States until the early nineteenth century.

In France, the palace at Versailles was designed to include a bathroom for every suite of rooms. The bathroom customarily held two tubs. The bather removed any dirt, sweat, or grease in the first tub, then rinsed in the second tub.

American colonists were gradually able to obtain bathtubs for their own houses. While these were first made from marble, copper gradually became preferred, as it offered better heat retention as well as lower cost. In time, tubs also were made from tin, bringing the price down even more. While some tubs were large enough for the bather to lie down in, most came to the bather's hips. Other, shallow tubs, designed to catch water dripping from the standing occupant, provided only for a glorified sponge bath.

By the late eighteenth century, furniture also was being built to aid in bathing. One such item was the washstand. Often elaborately carved, it usually featured some form of basin for holding water. It also might include shelves for cosmetics or a rack for towels. The nightstand was often used to conceal a chamber pot, still a necessity. Again, these stands could be carved or painted. Other pieces of furniture connected to hygiene included wig stands, shaving tables, and dressing chests.

At this time, these specialized pieces of furniture were articles used predominantly by the upper classes and were rarely found anywhere else. A study of probate inventories in Chester County, Pennsylvania, shows only one washstand in 694 estates for the years 1780–1789. A similar study in Essex County, Massachusetts, shows no washstands prior to 1763. Washstands did not become common household items until the mid-nineteenth century.

Literature, Bathhouses, and Bathrooms

The attention placed on gentility, and so on cleanliness, is also reflected in books and pamphlets written in the early to late eighteenth century. In 1715, a Boston schoolmaster named Eleazar Moody published *The School of Good Manners.* Likewise, George Washington produced his *Rules of Civility and Decent Behaviour in Company and Conversation* a few years later. While these volumes largely reworked materials from books published in France and England, they demonstrate a colonial interest in good behavior. By 1780, the instructive *Letters of Philip Dormer Stanhope, 4th Earl of Chesterfield,* had been published in North America. Written to his son, they exhorted him to clean his teeth and nails, brush his coats, and maintain his wigs.

The years following the American Revolution and the founding of the new republic showed further interest in bathing and hygiene. Now that they were part of a new nation, wealthy Americans were especially anxious to demonstrate to their European counterparts that they were equally genteel and refined.

Public bathhouses began emerging in Europe and England in the 1790s. While New York saw its first public bathhouse in 1792, it appears to have been more in the tradition of the therapeutic baths of the mid-eighteenth century, with its offering of warm, fresh- or saltwater baths. The first bathhouse in Philadelphia, opened in 1801, had bathtubs, running water, and drains. And the second New York bathhouse, opened

in 1804, advertised hot and cold water, and it also provided a private space for women.

Wealthy families also began creating bathhouses or bathrooms within their own homes. In time, these attentions to bathing and cleanliness became part of daily life for the rest of the population, largely through the work of the domestic economists of the 1840s and 1850s and the continued scientific discoveries resulting from the American Civil War.

Abigail B. Chandler

See also: Disease; Housing.

Bibliography

Busham, Richard L., and Claudia L. Busham. "The Early History of Cleanliness in America." *Journal of American History* 74 (1988): 1213–38.

Hoy, Suellen. *Chasing Dirt.* New York: Oxford University Press, 1995.

Wright, Lawrence. *Clean and Decent.* London: Routledge and Kegan Paul, 1963.

Battle of Bunker Hill

See Bunker Hill, Battle of

Battle of Lexington and Concord

See Lexington and Concord, Battles of

Beaver Wars

As rivalries between the French, Dutch, and English traders increased, the native peoples began to struggle among themselves for an economic advantage. The competition among the Europeans led to conflicts among their native trade partners that became known as the Beaver Wars. In the 1640s, the long struggle between the Huron and the Iroquois illustrated not only the seriousness of these wars for animal pelts—preferably beaver—but also the increasing ferocity of such contests.

The Dutch merchants in the Hudson River Valley, attempting to enter the lucrative fur trade, turned to the Iroquois League as a trading partner, as the French had already done with the Huron. In the beginning, these trade partnerships were on equal ground—trading furs for similar goods accessible to both the French and Dutch. Since the beaver was hunted to extinction in most of Europe, the demand for North American beaver pelts was high.

In their attempt to satisfy this demand, the Huron and Iroquois both hunted beaver at a pace previously unknown to them. At first, the Native Americans sought trading within their own cultural boundaries. They perceived all things, material as well as living, as possessed with some spiritual power—an animistic concept of the world. Therefore, the allure of the shiny objects that both the French and Dutch offered for beaver pelts was irresistible. By the 1630s, the high demand for pelts resulted in the killing of nearly all the beavers on the lands of the Huron and Iroquois. This caused these native peoples to look elsewhere for furs.

The Huron began by clearing new fields to increase their corn harvest, resulting in a surplus that they could trade for furs with tribes north of the Great Lakes, an area where the beaver were still abundant. The Iroquois responded quite differently: They began to raid Huron trading parties and attack Huron villages. The Iroquois were victorious, because the Dutch readily supplied them with guns, and the French were reluctant to supply guns to their own trading partners, the Huron. The end of the first phase of the Beaver Wars came as the Huron were destroyed; thousands were killed or captured, while some fled westward.

This cycle of warfare for pelts did not end with the demise of the Huron. The victorious Iroquois, in an attempt to maintain control over the fur supply, began to challenge other native nations in areas where beavers were still found. A brief renewal of the Beaver Wars occurred in the 1680s as the French began to look for new trading partners to replace the Huron. Once again, this pitted the French against the more powerful Iroquois nation.

Penny M. Sonnenburg

See also: Dutch; French; Furs; Hudson River; Huron; Iroquois Confederacy; Native American–European Conflict.

Bibliography

Axtell, James. *The Invasion Within: The Contest of Cultures in Colonial North America.* New York: Oxford University Press, 1985.

White, Richard. *The Middle Ground: Indians, Empires, and Republics in the Great Lakes Region, 1650–1815.* New York: Cambridge University Press, 1991.

Berkeley, Sir William (c. 1605–1677)

Born about 1605 to Sir Maurice Berkeley and Elizabeth Killigrew Berkeley, favorites of James I, Sir William Berkeley grew up in a family that had invested heavily in the Virginia Company. He studied at St. Edmund Hall and earned a master of arts degree from Merton College, Oxford.

Berkeley won the attention of Charles I through his literary works, including several plays performed at court. Horrified by his experiences in the early stages of the English Civil War, Berkeley parlayed his knighthood, which he was awarded for valor, as well as his personal wealth, into a royal appointment as governor of Virginia in August 1641.

Berkeley quickly became enamored of Virginia. He was popular with the colony's elite planters, whom he emulated by establishing his own plantation, Green Spring, and promoting agricultural improvements, colonial self-sufficiency in products such as flax and rice, and trade with England. Berkeley was applauded for sharing authority with the House of Burgesses and for using his contacts in London to supply weapons when the colony went to war with Native Americans under Opechancanough in the Third Anglo-Indian War (1644–1646). Despite this war, he was strongly in favor of a policy encouraging friendly relations with the neighboring Native American tribes, with whom he and other elite families had a substantial and lucrative trade in furs, and he arranged a generous peace treaty with the Powhatan Confederacy. In 1650, Berkeley married, but the name and family background of his first wife are unknown.

The Great Civil War in England spilled over into Virginia with the 1652 arrival of Cromwellian troops, who accepted Berkeley's surrender in exchange for Virginia retaining most of its self-government and a generally amicable relationship between royalists and supporters of Oliver Cromwell. Berkeley spent the years 1652–1661 in quiet retirement at Green Spring until recalled by the Stuart Restoration of Charles II in 1661. Unfortunately, Berkeley was out of step with both the Stuart continuation of commonwealth policies such the Navigation Acts and the influx of new settlers, many of them former supporters of Cromwell.

Tensions built as the old elite planters, suffering from a downturn in the tobacco market, were challenged by a new generation of settlers, who pushed the frontiers of Virginia and established themselves on lands claimed by Native American tribes with treaty and economic connections to Berkeley and his circle of friends. Under the influence of his second wife, Frances Culpeper (sister of the Virginia governor Thomas Culpeper), whom he married in 1670, Berkeley's governing style became more dictatorial, and he clashed repeatedly with the leader of the new settlers' faction, Nathaniel Bacon.

After an attack by Doeg Indians, Bacon's followers waged a campaign against all neighboring tribes. This campaign also was fueled by the settlers' jealousy of Berkeley's protection of the natives in the interest of his trade investments and by fierce competition for frontier land.

When Bacon assembled a militia in the spring of 1676, Berkeley declared him outlawed. Berkeley eventually pardoned Bacon and sent him home, hoping to deescalate the situation, but Bacon returned from Henrico County with a band of more than 500 men and extorted a general's commission from the House of Burgesses. Again outlawed, Bacon led a terror campaign against the peaceful Pamunkey tribe before coming back, capturing Jamestown, burning most of the capital to the ground, taking hostages, and outlawing Berkeley's supporters in the process. The reign of terror might have continued, but Bacon died a month later.

Berkeley had retired to Green Spring on Virginia's Eastern Shore after sending to London for help. It arrived in the form of regular English soldiers and naval support, months after the rebellion fizzled out with Bacon's death. Displeased by the incident and by Berkeley's hanging of twenty-three rebel leaders, Charles II ordered the commander of the military expedition, Colonel Herbert Jeffreys, to replace Berkeley.

Berkeley returned to England to beg the king to reinstate him. Shortly after landing in England and before reaching the king to plead his case, Berkeley died on June 9, 1677. He is the longest-serving governor in Virginia's history.

Margaret Sankey

See also: Bacon, Nathaniel; Bacon's Rebellion; Chesapeake; House of Burgesses; Virginia; Virginia (Chronology). *Document*: Governor William Berkeley on Bacon's Rebellion (1676).

Bibliography

Middlekauff, Robert. *Bacon's Rebellion*. Chicago: Rand McNally, 1964.

Washburn, Wilcomb E. *The Governor and the Rebel*. Chapel Hill: University of North Carolina Press, 1957.

Webb, Steven Saunders. *1676: The End of American Independence*. New York: Alfred A. Knopf, 1984.

Bermuda

Bermuda is a group of small, isolated islands about 600 miles off the coast of Virginia. The islands are named for a Spanish sea captain, Juan de Bermdez, who probably spotted them in the opening years of the sixteenth century. Various early adventurers tried to land on the islands, but the sharp reefs and rocks that surround Bermuda discouraged them. At the time of European discovery, the islands were uninhabited, though they became a crucial navigational point on trips between Spain and its colonies in the Caribbean and Mexico.

The Portuguese made a halfhearted attempt at settlement in 1527, but it seems as if the first Europeans to actually land on Bermuda were a group of Portuguese whose ship was wrecked there on a trip between Santo Domingo and Portugal. They promptly built a new ship and returned to Santo Domingo. A party of French sailors shipwrecked there between 1560 and 1570, but they, too, built a ship and sailed for Newfoundland.

The English also came to Bermuda as the result of a shipwreck. In 1609, the *Sea Venture,* en route from Plymouth, England, to Virginia, began taking on water and was wrecked off Bermuda. The people on board, including notables such as John Rolfe, the admiral Sir George Somers (with his secretary William Strachey), Sir Thomas Gates (deputy governor of Jamestown), and Christopher Newport (head of the first expedition to Jamestown), stayed for nine months, until they had finished two boats. Then, they made their way to Virginia.

Serious attempts at settlement date from 1612, when the *Plough,* an English ship, landed on purpose, bringing fifty settlers and the colony's first governor, Richard Moore. This was done under the auspices of the Bermuda Company, which, like the Virginia Company in Jamestown, raised money for colonial ventures. In the first half of the sixteenth century, the English desperately wanted profitable colonial holdings, and they considered Bermuda a key to their enterprise.

The history of Bermuda's colonial development is intricately linked with that of Virginia. When relations with the Powhatan Confederacy soured, white Virginians considered planting tobacco in Bermuda. To this end, African slaves were imported beginning in 1616. Since Bermuda's soil was not particularly rich and the supply of fresh water was relatively limited, commercial agriculture, either in tobacco or sugar, never caught on as it did elsewhere, and most Africans were employed as house servants or artisans. White Bermudians and their black slaves continued to grow tobacco, though it played a decreasing role in the colony's economy. In 1834, when slavery was abolished by act of Parliament, about 4,000 of the island's 9,000 people became free.

Though commercial agriculture failed to reap the massive profits it did elsewhere in England's empire, Bermuda's colonial economy should not necessarily be seen as stagnant. Salt from the Turks Islands, in the Bahamas, allowed Bermudians who shipped the salt to trade for food and other supplies with the mainland American colonies. Bermuda's economy was also tied to the sea, and its cedar forests provided timber for shipbuilding. Both black and white Bermudians worked as sailors; in fact, Bermuda ship captains were often able to underbid competing Atlantic carriers because they used skilled slave labor. One of Bermuda's main exports during the seventeenth century was people. Disillusioned settlers from overpopulated areas such as Bermuda and Barbados contributed to the English settlement of Jamaica in particular, but also to places on the American mainland—most notably South Carolina, officially founded in 1670.

By the 1680s, Bermuda, though it retained strategic importance, was overshadowed by the rest of England's Atlantic empire. Recently, England had taken Jamaica, a profitable sugar colony, from the Spanish, and New Amsterdam, a growing center of shipping and trade, from the Dutch. The older colonies in New England and Virginia were prospering and attracting many more immigrants. Bermuda became a British Crown colony in 1684. In 1776, when Britain's mainland colonies chose to fight for independence, Bermuda did not.

During the War of 1812, Bermuda was an important staging ground for the British assault on Washington, D.C., and a joint American–British air base constructed on Bermuda aided Allied efforts during World War II. Bermuda continues to rely on Great Britain in matters of defense, security, and diplomacy, although a 1968 constitution provided for full internal self-government, bringing a peaceful end to colonial rule.

Matthew Jennings

See also: Atlantic Ocean; Trade.

Bibliography

Craven, Wesley Frank. *An Introduction to the History of Bermuda.* New York: New York University Press, 1938.

Zuill, W. S. *The Story of Bermuda and Her People.* London: Macmillan Education, 1973.

Bible

The Bible is a collection of writings that Christians believe to be divinely inspired. The word is derived originally from the Greek *biblia,* meaning "books." Another term for the Bible is "Scriptures," or writings. For Christians, the Bible consists of the Old Testament (the Jewish Bible), written primarily in Hebrew, before the coming of Jesus Christ, and the New Testament, written in Greek, about the life and teachings of Christ. The Bible remains the most published book in history.

Throughout the Middle Ages, the Roman Catholic Church relied upon a Latin translation, the Vulgate Bible, made by St. Jerome in the early fifth century. The Roman Catholic Church, however, placed equal importance on tradition, the writings and pronouncements made by the Church through the ages, and laymen were not encouraged to read and interpret scripture for themselves. The invention of the movable type printing press by Johann Gutenberg in the 1450s did, however, give a new impetus to Bible production, and the first book Gutenberg printed was the Latin Bible. Christian humanists of the Renaissance also stressed biblical scholarship.

The Protestant Reformation of the sixteenth century provided a further major stimulus to Bible study. Martin Luther, in his break with Catholicism, placed the Scriptures above pope or church council as divine authority. He believed every Christian should be able to read the Word of God in the vernacular, and he prepared a new translation of the Bible in his native German. John Calvin, based at Geneva, also stressed the primacy of the Bible, in which, he believed, God had provided a written law for humans to live by.

William Tyndale, inspired by the Continental reformers, translated the Greek New Testament into his native English. Tyndale's work, which would influ-

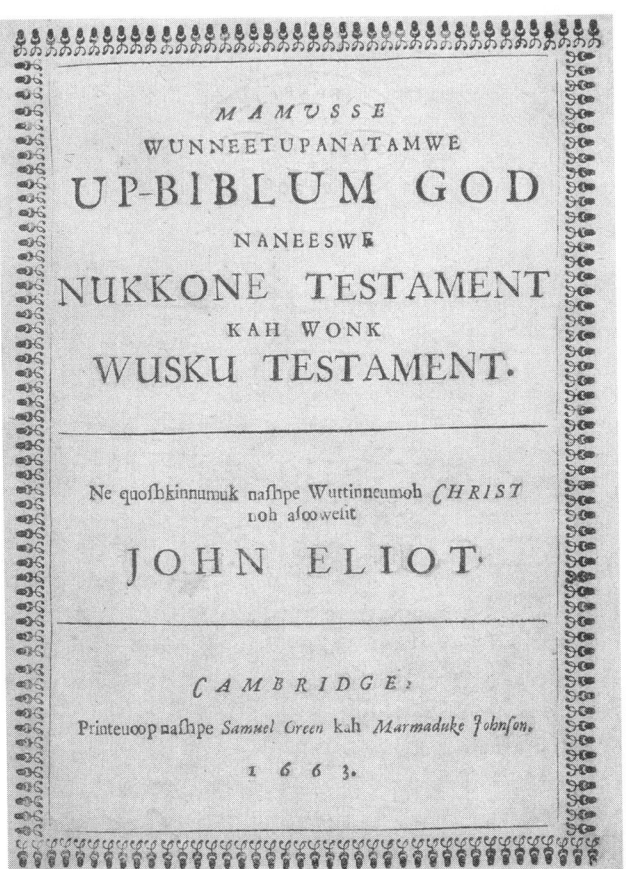

The Eliot Indian Bible, translated into Algonquian by the Puritan minister and missionary to the native peoples John Eliot, was the first complete edition of the Bible to be published in North America, in 1663. *(Massachusetts Historical Society, Boston, Massachusetts/Bridgeman Art Library)*

the Church of England prelates were concerned that the marginal commentaries offered scriptural interpretations over which they had no control. Nevertheless, by the end of Elizabeth's reign, the Geneva Bible had eclipsed the official Bishops' Bible of 1568 in popularity because of its portable size, reasonable price, and annotations.

James I was displeased with the Geneva Bible, for he, too, did not like the commentaries, especially those that contradicted his belief in the divine right of kings. He also was aware that English Catholic exiles on the Continent were producing their own translation, the Douai Bible of 1609–1610. Instead, James approved a new translation, known as the Authorized Version. Published in 1611 and more commonly known as the King James Bible, it became a landmark literary work in the English language.

It was also under James I that the first permanent English settlements were established in North America. The one book that nearly all colonists brought with them was the Bible. It was the divine book by which they would guide their lives, particularly in New England, and it was also the link to their native language. The family Bible became an important source of family history in America, for in it major events such as births and deaths were recorded.

Initially, both the Geneva and King James versions were brought to the colonies. Governor William Bradford used his Geneva Bible—preserved at Pilgrim Hall, Plymouth—for all the scriptural quotes in his *History of Plymouth Plantation* (1646). John Winthrop of the Massachusetts Bay Colony used the King James version, which remained the Bible of choice even after the Boston Puritans separated from the Church of England. The King James version eventually displaced the Geneva Bible, last printed in England in 1644.

The first book published in New England was the *Bay Psalm Book* of 1640. The King James Bible, however, had to be imported from England throughout the colonial period, because it could be printed only under royal license. Ironically, the first two complete Bibles published in colonial British America were not in English. John Eliot translated the Bible into an Algonquian language and published this version at Cambridge, Massachusetts, in 1663, and Christopher Sauer published a German Bible at Germantown, Pennsylvania, in 1743.

In 1777, with the growing rift between the colonies and England, there was a demand for the Bible to be produced in America. While colonial printers did not have the necessary supplies for a work of this

ence subsequent English translations, was published in Germany in 1526 but prohibited in Catholic England. Only after King Henry VIII broke with Rome did he require an officially sanctioned English-language Bible. Miles Coverdale published the first complete English Bible in 1535, and government authorization was subsequently given to the Great Bible of 1539–1540, which combined the work of Tyndale and Coverdale.

Under Edward VI, the English Reformation advanced, but Mary I brought England back to Roman Catholicism. A number of learned Protestants, known as the Marian exiles, fled to Calvin's Geneva; there, they produced a new English Bible in 1560, known as the Geneva Bible. Not only was this version considered the best translation to date, it also contained detailed marginal notes to help readers understand the text.

With the accession of Elizabeth I in 1558, Protestantism was firmly reestablished in England. The returned Marian exiles hoped that their Geneva Bible would be given official sanction. It was not, because

magnitude, several editions of the New Testament were printed during the Revolutionary War. Only in the 1790s, after independence was gained, were the first complete English Bibles produced in the United States by printers such as Isaiah Thomas of Worcester, Massachusetts. The King James version remained the Protestant Bible of choice in the early Republic.

Florene S. Memegalos

See also: Christ and Christianity; Puritanism; Religion (Chronology); Religion (Essay). *Document:* Psalm 23 from *The Bay Psalm Book* (1640).

Bibliography

Daniell, David. *The Bible in English, Its History and Influence.* New Haven, CT: Yale University Press, 2003.

Frerichs, Ernest S., ed. *The Bible and Bibles in America.* Atlanta, GA: Scholars Press, 1988.

McGrath, Alister. *In the Beginning: The Story of the King James Bible and How It Changed a Nation, a Language, and a Culture.* New York: Doubleday, 2001.

Board of Trade

Established by King William III in 1696, the Lords Commissioners for Trade and Plantations (more commonly known as the Board of Trade) were charged with promoting commerce in the British Empire and improving the administration of British colonies. The Board of Trade was separate from, but still subordinate to, the royal Privy Council, which had previously attended to such responsibilities. Members of the fifteen-person board were supposedly appointed because of their economic and political expertise, but positions were often distributed on the basis of political expediency rather than merit.

In theory, the Board of Trade was the center of colonial administration. The panel drafted detailed instructions for newly appointed royal governors to follow and maintained an active correspondence with a large number of royal officials and elected assemblies throughout the British Atlantic world. The board received political petitions and legal appeals from overseas settlements and soon became a lobbying forum for paid agents representing the interests of their individual colonies.

Perhaps the most important and controversial task of the panel was the review of all laws passed by colonial legislatures. The Board of Trade examined such acts to ensure that they contained nothing contrary to English law, harmful to the economic interests of the mother country, or tending to undermine the king's powers over his American subjects. Though this routine legal review rarely ended with the disallowance of laws, colonial assemblies resented the limitation on their legislative powers and privileges.

In reality, the Board of Trade had few formal powers. Its role was mainly advisory rather than executive. The panel held hearings on specific issues, drew up recommendations, and then forwarded those to a higher authority—typically the Privy Council or the secretary of state—for definitive action. The Board of Trade's advice carried weight and was frequently followed, but its recommendations were not binding. Commissioners found that their powers only went as far as their audience's willingness to listen. In particular, the panel lacked the ability to appoint or remove officials on its own authority—a limitation that severely constrained the commissioners' control over colonial officeholders.

The board approached its tasks with enthusiasm for the first two decades of its existence, but after 1714, its activities became increasingly passive and routine. It became little more than a clearinghouse for correspondence to and from the colonies. The driving force behind imperial policy was instead the secretary of state for the southern department.

The Board of Trade's prominence waxed and waned depending on the interest and effectiveness of its members. In the 1720s and 1730s, Martin Bladen unsuccessfully sought to rescue the panel from its reduced position and shake the British Crown out of its policy of "salutary neglect" toward overseas settlements. A trade commissioner for more than thirty years of his life, Bladen believed that the colonies enjoyed far too much independence. He wanted to use the board as an instrument to tighten direct royal control over the British Empire. Among his various proposals, nearly all of which were rejected, was a plan for a union of all the American colonies that would have been placed under the direct governance of the Board of Trade. When Bladen died in 1746, his immediate successors discarded most of his ambitious regulatory schemes.

The next burst of activity came during the presidency of the Earl of Halifax from 1748–1761. Like Bladen, Halifax disliked the home government's lax and inconsistent colonial policies and worked to enforce a greater administrative uniformity among British settlements. Under his aggressive leadership, the board extended its formal powers. The most significant gain was the commissioners' right to appoint a wide range of colonial officials, including governors. Throughout the 1750s, the Board of Trade grew into a reasonable approximation of the centerpiece of colonial oversight originally envisioned in 1696. Halifax's departure in 1761 and the resulting lack of leadership, however, again brought a sharp decline in the board's power.

During the troubles that gripped the British Empire in the aftermath of the Seven Years' War, control over imperial policy slipped away from the board. Correspondence from the colonial governors went directly to the secretary of state for the colonies. By the outbreak of the American Revolution, the Board of Trade had again been reduced to a largely advisory and passive role in American affairs.

Andrew C. Lannen

See also: Mercantilism; Merchants; Trade.

Bibliography

Basye, Arthur Herbert. *The Lords Commissioners of Trade and Plantations, Commonly Known as the Board of Trade, 1748–1782.* New Haven, CT: Yale University Press, 1925.

Steele, Ian K. *Politics of Colonial Policy, The Board of Trade in Colonial Administration, 1696–1720.* Oxford, UK: Clarendon Press, 1968.

Boone, Daniel (1734–1820)

Daniel Boone lived an extraordinary life. In his lifetime, Boone engaged in a variety of notable vocations; however, he gained fame as a legendary hunter, explorer, and Indian fighter. As a frontiersman in the colonial American West, Boone explored the wilderness and worked toward the settlement of Kentucky. As many stories surrounding Boone's adventures have served to catapult him to mythical status, separating myth from fact has become an ongoing labor for historians over the years.

Boone's grandfather, George Boone, was a Quaker, a weaver, and a farmer in Exeter, England. In 1717, George Boone immigrated with his family to the North American colonies. Daniel Boone was born near Reading in Berks County, Pennsylvania, in 1734. His parents, Squire Boone and Sarah Morgan Boone, raised him as a Quaker.

Squire Boone was a blacksmith and a stock raiser,

and he taught his son these trades. Aside from his father's training, Boone received little formal education. From a very early age, however, Boone exhibited a great aptitude and fondness for the wilderness, and when he was 12, his father gave him a rifle, which he used for hunting. In 1753, the Boone family moved to the Yadkin River valley, which placed the Boones in close contact with Native Americans. In fact, Boone befriended some local Native Americans and gleaned many wilderness survival skills from them. Living on the frontier afforded Boone the opportunity to practice his skills, and he soon became an excellent hunter, tracker, and trapper. In 1756, Boone married Rebecca Bryan, the 17-year-old daughter of his neighbor.

During the French and Indian War, Boone served as a teamster and a blacksmith under General Edward Braddock, and he took part in Braddock's campaign against Fort Duquesne, which ended in failure. In 1758, however, Boone served in a successful march against

The exploits of Pennsylvania-born frontiersman and Indian fighter Daniel Boone had attained legendary status even before his death in 1820. Mythologized or not, Boone made important contributions as an explorer, surveyor, and settler. *(Special Collections, University of Chicago Library, Illinois)*

the fort under General John Forbes. During the war, Boone met John Finley, a hunter, who told him about the Kentucky wilderness. The stories piqued his interest, but he set his sights on Pensacola, Florida, instead. When his wife refused to move to Florida, Boone reconsidered Kentucky.

A few years later, John Finley rejoined Boone, and they made plans for a Kentucky expedition. In 1769, Boone and a few other men explored eastern Kentucky by following a trail through the Cumberland Gap. When Judge Richard Henderson, a North Carolina land speculator and owner of the Transylvania Company, heard about Boone's journey, he decided the Kentucky wilderness was a business opportunity too good to pass up. Henderson hired Boone to negotiate a sale of land in Kentucky from the Cherokees. After returning from a successful mission, Boone was ordered by Henderson, who planned to settle Kentucky, to fix a road that settlers could use to reach the newly acquired land. Consequently, in 1775, Boone and a small group of armed men passed through the Cumberland Gap, cleared the way for the Wilderness Road, and built a fort in Boonesborough, by the Kentucky River.

In the years that followed, Boone led settlers, including his own family, to Kentucky and aided them as a hunter and an Indian fighter. Native American raids were a constant threat to the new settlement. In 1776, for example, Shawnees captured three girls, including Boone's 14-year-old daughter, Jemima, and he immediately sprang into action. Boone organized a small party of men, tracked the Shawnees, and freed the captives.

In the years that followed, the new settlement continued to suffer through several Native American raids, and Boone was taken prisoner by the Shawnee tribe in 1778. After four months of captivity, however, he managed to escape and resumed his settlement activities.

During the American Revolution, Boone became a captain in the Virginia militia and defended Kentucky against the British and their Native American allies. After the colonial period, Boone served as sheriff, lieutenant colonel of the Fayette County militia, delegate to the Kentucky legislature, and deputy surveyor. Due in great part to his efforts, Boonesborough continued to prosper and Kentucky was eventually settled. The Transylvania Company awarded Boone a large tract of land in Kentucky as payment for his labors, but he lost it a few years later when the company suffered an economic downturn.

In 1784, Daniel Boone gained world fame and legendary status with the publication of John Filson's *The Discovery, Settlement, and Present State of Kentucke.* The American author James Fenimore Cooper was so impressed by Boone's frontiersman image that he used Boone as inspiration for the character of Natty Bumppo in the novels that make up his "Leatherstocking Tales." Lord Byron paid tribute to Boone posthumously in a poem titled *Don Juan.* In fact, so many works of fiction were inspired by Boone that, by the time of his death in 1820, he had become the most famous American frontier hero.

Rolando Avila

See also: Appalachia; Cumberland Gap; Exploration; Kentucky.

Bibliography

Bakeless, John. *Daniel Boone, Master of the Wilderness.* New York: William Morrow, 1939.
Faragher, John Mack. *Daniel Boone: The Life and Legend of an American Pioneer.* New York: Henry Holt, 1992.
Thwaites, Reuben Gold. *Daniel Boone.* Williamstown, MA: Corner House, 1977.

Borderlands, Spanish

Serious consideration of the Spanish borderlands as a legitimate field of history was inaugurated by Herbert Bolton, who, in 1921, published the landmark study *The Spanish Borderlands: A Chronicle of Old Florida and the Southwest.* Bolton, along with many of his followers, found Frederick Jackson Turner's frontier thesis (that U.S. society was shaped by its frontier experience) interesting, but he pointed out correctly that it did not take into account areas colonized by the Spanish.

Since its inception, the study of the Spanish borderlands has expanded in geography and chronology. These borderlands now are considered to include parts of the Southwest, Texas, the Southeast, and northern Mexico. Chronologically speaking, the history of the borderlands begins with the colonization efforts of the Spanish in these various regions. Although many of the former borderlands have been divided by the border between the United States and Mexico, they continue to exist in cultural terms on both sides of the fence that separates the two modern nations. To define the borderlands rigidly in time and place is difficult; they are the fluid middle ground that exists whenever cultures meet and neither dominates the other.

As they relate to the region and time traditionally

known as colonial America—the present United States prior to 1776—the Spanish borderlands consist of the Spanish colonies in Florida, New Mexico, Texas, and California. It bears mentioning that 1776 is not a particularly significant date in the history of the Spanish borderlands, though it did eventually result in the creation of the United States, a force that would eventually come to dominate much of the region.

Spanish colonial goals and institutions are essential to understanding the borderlands. It is easy, though overly simplistic and inaccurate, to dismiss Spanish motives in the New World solely as having to do with plunder. The old story goes that while the English came to the Americas to settle and the French came to trade, the Spanish sought to extract precious metal. The Spanish actually had a number of reasons, not all of them financial, for colonizing the borderlands, and a closer look at the mission system reveals some of these complexities.

Throughout their history in the New World, the Spanish founded missions, beginning in Florida in the 1570s and New Mexico in 1590s and stretching in a thin line across the American Southwest all the way to California by the 1760s. Although a few of these were Jesuit missions, the overwhelming majority were Franciscan undertakings. The role of the missions helps to explain the ambiguities of the borderlands. On one hand, the missions were instruments of imperial control. Friars could extract labor and other forms of tribute from Native Americans, and their basic goal was to remove traces of indigenous religious belief. However, Native Americans resisted this cultural imperialism and sometimes relied on friars to protect them from exploitation at the hands of Spanish colonists.

Revolts in New Mexico and Florida in the 1680s, the latter undertaken under the auspices of English slave traders, convinced Spanish authorities of the necessity of military outposts, or presidios. These were intended to "pacify" restless Native American populations. As with the missions, the real-world application of the military posts was complicated. Some Native Americans, such as the Apaches, attacked the posts as soon as they were established, seeking to continue slave raids among natives associated with the missions. Other native peoples sought the protection of the Spanish.

The presence of the English in South Carolina and later Georgia and of the French in the Gulf of Mexico signaled a shift in the history of the borderlands. Increasingly, the region's Native Americans found themselves embroiled in international disputes between European powers. At the same time, they struggled to maintain their own cultural and political autonomy, a viable land base, and their diplomatic relations with other Native American communities.

The Spanish borderlands are crucial to a full, accurate understanding of colonial America. The European colonization of America does not begin only at Roanoke, Jamestown, and Plymouth; it also must take into account the interactions between Spanish and Native American peoples all across the continent. Many of these interactions occurred prior to English colonization, and their effects were long lasting, yet they still are not fully understood or incorporated into colonial history. Finally, the careful study of these borderlands can be applied to many different fields and allow for fruitful comparisons that transcend the once-rigid boundaries of American history.

Matthew Jennings

See also: New Mexico; New Spain; Santa Fe; Spanish Colonies on Mainland North America (Chronology).

Bibliography

Adelman, Jeremy, and Stephen Aron. "From Borderlands to Borders: Empires, Nation-States, and the Peoples in Between in North American History." *American Historical Review* 104:3 (June 1999): 814–41.

Jones, Oakah L., Jr., ed. *The Spanish Borderlands: A First Reader.* Los Angeles: Lorrin L. Morrison, 1974.

Weber, David J. *The Spanish Frontier in North America.* New Haven, CT: Yale University Press, 1992.

Boston

In 1629, a group of English Puritans, led by merchants and country gentlemen, obtained a charter from King Charles I for the Massachusetts Bay Company. This was in many respects a typical joint-stock company, except for one critical feature: The charter did not specify the company's location.

Led by John Winthrop, the Puritans used the charter to create the Massachusetts Bay Colony in New England, putting the vast expanse of the Atlantic Ocean between them and the hostile rule of Charles I. In 1630, after leaving Salem and Charlestown, Winthrop and his followers settled on the Shawmut Peninsula, in Boston.

City upon a Hill

While sailing aboard the *Arabella* en route to Massachusetts, Winthrop delivered a sermon entitled "A Modell of Christian Charity," in which he informed his followers that they would be creating a "City upon a Hill." Boston would be a close-knit community. The settlers, most of whom came from England's middle classes and migrated with their families, would have their own homes and gardens, and access to surrounding fields to grow crops and graze cattle. The more wealthy and prominent of Winthrop's followers would have larger enclaves in the surrounding wilderness, but the city would be the center of the community. It would be the seat of the church and of government, and it would be a place where settlers would take refuge from outside attack.

Winthrop declared that Boston would be a "city of God." Settlers would serve God in all ways, and a meetinghouse where God's word could be heard would be the center of life in Boston. Settlers would also serve each other in accordance with God's wishes. Winthrop

recognized the social and economic inequities that existed in society, but he hoped his followers would work to overcome them. He urged his congregation to share supplies and produce and to temper their commerce with mercy. According to Winthrop, the settlers had entered into a covenant with God when they placed themselves under his protection, both on the voyage to Massachusetts and in their new community, and they subsequently agreed to live in a godly fashion. Winthrop considered England a "sinfull lande" and dreamed of creating a better society in Boston where the so-called natural leaders—wealthy gentlemen—would rule in the best interest of the people, and the people would accept the government of their leaders.

Unfortunately for Winthrop, his dream of creating a city upon a hill was not shared by all of his followers. Englishmen arriving in Boston in 1630 and in the years that followed learned quickly of the tremendous opportunity for individual profit available in the New World. Almost immediately, the acquisitive instincts of English settlers overwhelmed Winthrop's

Founded as a "city of God," Boston became the heart of a thriving maritime economy, a center of higher learning, and the crucible of an independent secular nation. Town hall is the subject of this mid-seventeenth-century engraving. *(Bibliotheque Nationale, Paris, France/Lauros/Giraudon/Bridgeman Art Library)*

communal vision, and conflicting ideas fragmented the united society he sought to create.

Port City

Though Winthrop's party initially intended to become farmers, they found the area's rocky soil difficult to cultivate, and some colonists turned to the sea for their livelihood. Settlers used small boats, called shallops, to fish and trade with Native Americans and with English settlers in other coastal villages. Trade increased rapidly, and, before long, Boston became the chief trading port in the area.

More distant coastal trade soon followed. Boston established trade relations with Virginia in 1631, and, in 1633, 10,000 bushels of corn from Virginia arrived in Boston Harbor. In return, Boston shipped many barrels of salted codfish south. Boston had also established trade with Maryland, the Dutch colonies of Manhattan and Long Island, and French colonies in Canada during the 1630s. By the time of Winthrop's death, in 1649, Boston had established a vigorous and profitable commerce with ports throughout the New World.

Boston's early settlers, under Winthrop's guidance, also became skilled shipbuilders. Their first sizable vessel, the *Blessing of the Bay,* was launched on the Mystic River near Winthrop's Medford estate in 1631. Medford and the Mystic quickly became the center of Boston's shipbuilding industry. Within thirty-five years of Boston's founding, there were 300 New England ships, most of them Boston-owned, engaged in coastal and overseas trade. There were also 1,300 smaller ships fishing off the Massachusetts coast.

When immigration to Boston lagged in the 1640s, the city increased its development of maritime commerce. Strife between the Puritans in England and King Charles erupted into a civil war known as the Puritan Revolution in 1640, causing immigration to Boston to dwindle. Decreased immigration brought hard times to many colonists who during the 1630s had counted on new immigrants to stimulate Boston's growing economy. When immigration ceased, Boston's residents sought other economic outlets. New England's rocky soil and short growing season prohibited common cash crops such as tobacco, sugar, and rice. Thus, Boston residents increasingly exported manufactured goods and surplus foodstuffs. Traders began sailing to ports as far away as Europe, Barbados, Jamaica, and even Madagascar and became directly involved in the trade of rum, slaves, and molasses, among other commodities.

Parliament attempted to control Boston traders with the passage of a series of Navigation Acts in the 1660s that required the transport of goods through English ports. While many Boston merchants sailed to England with their goods, most sea captains carried on their trade illegally. Finally, in 1684, the charter of Massachusetts was annulled, and in 1686 the frigate HMS *Rose* was stationed outside Boston Harbor to apprehend smugglers. Sir Edmund Andros was appointed governor of the New England colonies in 1687. Boston's trade was crippled, and a severe depression set in. The Andros government lasted two years and four months and ended in violent revolt by Boston's residents.

Following Andros's deportation, Boston traders were once again free to sail to the West Indies and Europe. New England became a royal province in 1692, but the new royal governors made little effort to enforce the Navigation Acts.

Eighteenth-Century Boston

Though the rate of immigration to Massachusetts lagged behind that of other colonies, its population grew sixfold in the eighteenth century, mainly from natural increase. As the population increased, Puritan communities lost much of their cohesion, and new networks emerged that centered on trade and manufacturing. Many New England residents lived on relatively small family farms, which were connected to the cities through trade. Farmers acquired manufactured goods from cities; in return, they provided urban dwellers with surplus grain and livestock. About one-third of Boston's adult men were skilled tradesmen, but it was the wealthy merchants who dominated Boston's commercial economy. New England's wealthiest and most powerful merchants lived in Boston. They bought and sold imported goods and owned and insured the ships that carried the goods. The commerce generated by wealthy Boston merchants affected the entire New England economy.

Throughout the eighteenth century, a marked polarization of wealth became increasingly apparent in Boston. By the 1760s, the richest Boston merchants built sumptuous mansions along King Street in the fashionable North End; they imported ornate luxury items and used servants and slaves to perform the menial tasks of daily living. By 1770, the richest 5 percent of Boston's residents owned half the city's wealth. In contrast, the share of wealth owned by the city's poorest two-thirds decreased during the eighteenth century from one-sixth to less than one-tenth. During the eighteenth century, approximately 5 to 6 percent of New England's population qualified for poor relief, which was usually distributed directly to local families or through almshouses. To minimize taxes, Boston also built workhouses in the hope that poor residents would earn their keep. Although New England was comparatively better off than other colonies, as well as England, during the eighteenth century, the explosive growth of transatlantic trade caused serious social and economic inequities.

During the eighteenth century, Boston also found itself at the center of a number of social, political, and economic conflicts. The Sugar Act (1764) and the Stamp Act (1765), which were meant to curb smuggling and increase revenue for the British Crown, enraged Boston residents, who destroyed the home and office of Andrew Oliver, the Massachusetts collector, and then hanged him in effigy. The Stamp Act was repealed the following year. The Townshend Acts (Revenue Act of 1767) were met with similar resistance from angry Boston merchants, who organized residents in a boycott of British-made goods. Their actions led, at least in part, to the presence of British troops in Boston and the famous Boston Massacre (1770).

The Townshend Acts were repealed in 1770 with the exception of the tax on tea. To avoid rising tea prices, as well as the tax, Boston merchants smuggled Dutch tea into the city. Parliament decided to provide Boston residents with less expensive tea by allowing the East India Company to import tea directly from India, thus avoiding the tax. Fearing the loss of profits gained from the sale of smuggled tea, Boston merchants turned radical and on November and December 17, 1773, staged the historic Boston Tea Party. England responded with the Boston Port Bill (1774), which severely crippled Boston's economy and imposed a formidable military presence on the bay.

Initially, a number of Boston merchants favored simply paying for the tea that had been cast into the harbor, but England's rapid issuance of a whole series of Coercive Acts in the wake of the Boston Tea Party ultimately changed many colonists' minds. In September 1774, Massachusetts, along with every other British colony in North America except Georgia, sent delegates to the First Continental Congress in Philadelphia.

Michael A. Rembis

See also: Boston Massacre; Boston Port Bill; Boston Tea Party; Bunker Hill, Battle of; Cities; Harvard College; Massachusetts; Massachusetts (Chronology); Massachusetts Bay Colony; Puritanism; Revolutionary War. *Documents:* Newspaper Account of the Boston Massacre (1770); The Boston Port Act (1774).

Bibliography

Boston Looks Seaward: The Story of the Port, 1630–1940. Compiled by the workers of the Writers' Program of the Work Projects Administration in the State of Massachusetts. Boston: Northeastern University Press, 1985.

Kennedy, Lawrence W. *Planning the City upon a Hill: Boston Since 1630.* Amherst: University of Massachusetts Press, 1992.

Levesque, George A. *Black Boston: African American Life and Culture in Urban America, 1750–1860.* New York: Garland, 1994.

Rutman, Darrett B. *Winthrop's Boston: A Portrait of a Puritan Town, 1630–1649.* New York: W. W. Norton, 1972.

Tager, Jack. *Boston Riots: Three Centuries of Social Violence.* Boston: Northeastern University Press, 2001.

Tyler, John W. *Smugglers and Patriots: Boston Merchants and the Advent of the American Revolution.* Boston: Northeastern University Press, 1986.

Vale, Lawrence J. *From the Puritans to the Projects: Public Housing and Public Neighbors.* Cambridge, MA: Harvard University Press, 2000.

Wright, Conrad Edick, and Katheryn P. Viens, eds. *Entrepreneurs: The Boston Business Community, 1700–1850.* Boston: Massachusetts Historical Society, 1997.

Zobel, Hiller B. *The Boston Massacre.* New York: W. W. Norton, 1970.

Boston Massacre

The incident known as the Boston Massacre occurred on the bitterly cold night of March 5, 1770. It was the culmination of eighteen months fraught with tension between British soldiers and angry townspeople.

In September 1768, Lord Hillsborough, secretary of state for the American colonies, ordered the 14th West Yorkshire Fusiliers and the 29th Worcestershire Regiment to Boston to protect the customs collectors from harassment by the townspeople. The soldiers arrived on September 28, 1768, and tumultuous street fights with town boys and rowdies would mark their time in Boston. The colonists, who had been fighting Parliament for the right to tax themselves, viewed the arrival of the soldiers as coercion. The British troops angered the townspeople with their perceived insolence,

As depicted in this engraving by Paul Revere, nervous red-coats, taunted by unruly colonists in front of Boston's Customs House on May 5, 1770, opened fire on the crowd, killing five. Patriots publicized the event as the "Boston Massacre" to stir resentment against British rule. *(Library of Congress, LC-USZ62-35522)*

as well as for their competition for jobs, as the soldiers often worked in town during their off-duty hours to make extra money.

Tensions reached a fever pitch in early March 1770. On March 2, a Bostonian employed at John Gray's ropewalk insulted a soldier looking for work. The soldier left, but he later returned with some friends, and a brawl ensued.

On March 5, although a foot of snow covered the ground, townsmen and soldiers engaged in another fight near the British military barracks. The soldiers wielded cutlasses and injured some townspeople in the fight before officers ordered them back inside the barracks. Angry townspeople followed the soldiers to the barracks' gate, verbally abusing them.

Shortly before nine o'clock that night, David Garrick, a wigmaker's apprentice, goaded a passing British captain for a delinquent payment of a bill. While the officer walked on, ignoring the taunt, a sentry standing guard at the Customs House on the corner of King Street and Royal Exchange Lane came to the officer's defense. He exchanged words with Garrick and then hit him in the head with his musket. A crowd

gathered, still seething from the earlier actions with the soldiers near the barracks. Soon church bells started ringing in the town (normally a signal for fire), which drew even more townspeople out. After harassment by the crowd increased, the nervous sentry loaded his gun and called for the main guard. Captain Thomas Preston led the seven-man main guard out and formed a semicircle defensive perimeter, with bayonets fixed, in front of the Customs House.

Preston put his men through a brief series of drills, concluding with an order to load their weapons. A growing mob of between 300 and 400 people baited and taunted the guards. The mob hurled snowballs, chunks of ice, oyster shells, and lumps of coal at the soldiers, accompanied by many abusive insults, all from very close range. In some cases, there were mere inches between the bayonets and the pressing crowd. Several townspeople wielded clubs or sticks in a threatening manner and belligerently dared the soldiers to fire, believing that they legally could not unless ordered to do so by a civil authority.

Many of the projectiles hit the soldiers and their weapons. One knocked Private Hugh Montgomery down. The beleaguered private got back to his feet and fired his musket into the crowd. In the confusion of shouting and insults, the other anxious and stressed soldiers let out a ragged, disjointed volley into the crowd at point-blank range. The shots killed four, including Crispus Attucks (the first African American to die in the Revolution), mortally wounded one, and slightly wounded six others.

Captain Preston (who had not given the order to fire) immediately ordered his men to cease firing, and the stunned crowd slowly dispersed. Acting governor Thomas Hutchinson rode up and reprimanded Captain Preston and the soldiers for firing on the crowd. He convinced the British officers to have the soldiers withdraw to their barracks.

Nine men, including Captain Preston, were arrested and indicted for murder. The soldiers spent the summer in jail awaiting their trial. With John Adams and Josiah Quincy leading the defense, Preston and six of the soldiers were acquitted, while two privates were found guilty of manslaughter. The two pleaded benefit of clergy, or exemption for a first felony; they were branded on their left thumbs and released.

This incident, dubbed the "Boston Massacre" by radicals, illustrated the dangers of forcing troops on townspeople against their will. The Massacre, which carried much rhetorical power as propaganda, especially in the skillful hands of Samuel Adams and Paul Revere, proved to be a major stepping-stone on the path that led to colonial independence from England.

Judkin Browning

See also: Adams, John; Boston; Politics and Government (Chronology); Politics and Government (Essay); Revolutionary War; Riots. *Document:* Newspaper Account of the Boston Massacre (1770).

Bibliography

Hansen, Harry. *The Boston Massacre: An Episode of Dissent and Violence.* New York: Hastings House, 1970.

Payne, Samuel B. "Was Crispus Attucks the First to Die?" *New England Journal of History* 57:2 (2000): 1–10.

Zobel, Hiller B. *The Boston Massacre.* New York: W. W. Norton, 1970.

Boston Port Bill

The Boston Port Bill was the first in a series of legislative measures known as the Coercive Acts or Intolerable Acts. Passed in 1774 by the British Parliament in response to the 1773 Boston Tea Party, the Boston Port Bill closed the port at Boston, Massachusetts. This bill was specifically designed to punish Boston, as well as the entire colony, by depriving the colonists of their main source of revenue, maritime commerce.

The port of Boston was closed, the bill stated, because of the hostile atmosphere and the consequent inability to safely conduct commerce or collect custom duties. All royal customs officers were required to leave Boston. No commercial ships were allowed entry, and any contract entered into while the act was in force was declared null and void.

Royal and military ships were allowed to dock at the port, as were ships carrying the bare necessities of survival for the colony. Ships in the latter group, however, were required to have the proper paperwork. Any ship that violated the terms of the act was to be confiscated along with its cargo. Furthermore, the Royal Navy was authorized to force ships from the port; any ship that did not leave after sufficient warning also became royal property. In addition, under the provisions of the act, those who assisted violators forfeited a sum equal to what the profits from the goods would have been had they been sold, and all the items used to violate the act would be confiscated.

The Boston Port Bill authorized that upon a warrant from either the lord high treasurer or commissioners of the Royal Treasury, any admiral, chief commander, commissioned officer of the Royal Navy, customs officer, or other specially designated person would be allowed to enforce the act. If those charged with enforcing the act were caught allowing any prohibited ship to enter the port because of bribes or other influences, they would have to pay a fine of 500 pounds per offense and would never again be allowed to serve in any civil or military position. Those who offered the bribe or other influence were to be fined 50 pounds per incident.

The Boston Port Bill was to be in effect until the fulfillment of two conditions. First, it had to appear to King George III and the Privy Council that law and order had been restored to Boston. Second, the East India Company had to be duly compensated for its losses resulting from the Boston Tea Party. Once both conditions had been satisfied, either a proclamation or an order-in-council could declare the entire port or certain parts of it reopened. Until those conditions were met, the port would remain closed.

The Boston Port Bill was passed in March 1774 and was signed by King George III on March 31, 1774. The act was to go into effect on June 1, 1774. News of the act was met with widespread shock and condemnation throughout the colonies. The act prompted Josiah Quincy to write and publish "Observations on the Boston Port Bill with Thoughts on Civil Society and Standing Armies," one of the most famous prerevolutionary tracts.

On June 1, 1774, when the port of Boston was closed, the town of Williamsburg, Virginia, condemned the Boston Port Bill and declared a day of prayer and religious exercises in a display of colonial solidarity. Philadelphia also acted in favor of Boston by condemning the act and closing its houses; its citizens met in public to voice their grievances against Parliament and held religious services. The remaining colonies followed a similar pattern, condemning the act and holding religious services in support of Boston.

The port of Boston remained officially closed until the end of the American War for Independence.

Aaron N. Coleman

See also: Boston; Coercive Acts (1774); Navy, British; Trade. *Document:* The Boston Port Act (1774).

Bibliography

Ammerman, David. *In the Common Cause: American Response to the Coercive Acts of 1774.* Charlottesville: University Press of Virginia, 1974.

Quincy, Josiah, Jr. "Observations on the Act of Parliament Commonly Called the Boston Port Bill: With Thoughts on Civil Society and Standing Armies." In *Memoir of the Life of Josiah Quincy.* New York: Da Capo, 1971.

Reid, John Phillip. *Constitutional History of the American Revolution.* Abridged edition. Madison: University of Wisconsin Press, 1995.

Boston Tea Party

In the 1770s, tea was an immensely popular drink in America. Although supposedly boycotting tea—as a part of the Non-Importation Agreement established in resistance to the Townshend Acts—colonists in Boston actually imported large amounts from the British and smugglers.

Parliament repealed the Townshend Acts and, on May 10, 1773, passed the Tea Act, which placed a tax of threepence on the beverage. Parliament also granted the East India Company a monopoly on the sale of tea in the colonies, which reduced the price of tea considerably. If colonists wanted to buy tea, they would have to buy it from the East India Company (through consignees at each colonial port), and they would have to pay the tax and acknowledge Parliament's right to impose taxes on the colonies.

Unlike the cities of New York and Philadelphia, Boston had been unable to force the colonial governor to back down over the Tea Act. Governor Thomas Hutchinson supported the East India Company agents (two of his sons and a nephew were tea agents), and the Boston consignees refused to resign. The radicals, led by the Sons of Liberty, knew that if the tea was landed, it would make its way into the colonial market and be heartily consumed by the colonists, undermining their opposition to British authority. The radicals, led by Samuel Adams and John Hancock, cast the Tea Act as another parliamentary attempt at colonial oppression, an infringement on their fundamental rights, the forerunner of more destructive laws, and the beginning of the end of the colonial assemblies.

The radicals began organizing mobs and threatening the local consignees with violence if they did not resign. The consignees fled to Castle William in Boston Harbor for safety. In November and December, the Sons of Liberty held several town meetings. On November 28, the *Dartmouth* arrived in the harbor with 114 chests

On December 16, 1773, a band of patriots disguised as Mohawk Indians boarded three ships in Boston Harbor, broke open 342 chests of tea, and dumped the contents overboard to protest the Tea Act. Not until the nineteenth century was the event called the "Boston Tea Party." *(Brown Brothers, Sterling, Pennsylvania)*

of East India tea and anchored at Griffin's Wharf. The radicals prevented the unloading of the tea but were pressed for time: Under British customs law, officers could seize dutiable goods if no payment had been made within twenty days. On December 17, the tea would be seized by the customs agents, who would be supported by royal arms if necessary.

On November 29 and 30, meetings were held that drew about 5,000 people each. The committee agreed to set up a twenty-five-man guard to keep watch at the wharf, ostensibly to protect the ships from the mob, but in reality to make certain the tea was not unloaded. In early December, two other ships arrived with cargoes of tea, heightening the tension.

The radicals tried to persuade the consignees to send the tea back to England. The agents either refused or pleaded their inability to contravene British law. Hutchinson refused to allow the ships to leave without unloading their cargo. The cannon at Castle William and on the ships of the Royal Navy would physically prevent such an illegal exit. On Thursday, December 16, in the freezing rain, over 5,000 people made their way to the Old South Church to support the radical leadership as they tried to force Francis Rotch, owner of the *Dartmouth,* to send the shipment back to England. The merchant pleaded that he could not gain clearance from customs, and therefore the ship could not leave the harbor. The radicals insisted he get a permit from Governor Hutchinson allowing safe passage past Castle William. Hutchinson refused.

The weather had cleared when Rotch returned around six that evening to report the bad news. Samuel Adams gave the signal, and a small group of men crudely disguised as Mohawk Indians appeared and led a procession to Griffin's Wharf. Along the way, more men appeared in disguise, with blackened faces, and carrying hatchets. They boarded the three ships resting at Griffin's Wharf, removed the customs officers, and hoisted the tea chests from the ships' holds, taking care not to damage the ships or any of their other cargo. The tea chests were broken open with hatchets and the contents dumped into the harbor. Over the course of three hours, while thousands watched quietly from the water's edge, the "Mohawks" emptied 342 chests of tea, worth over 10,000 pounds.

Although estimates of the number of participants range from twenty to sixty, their identities have remained a secret, with very few exceptions. Their actions did not become known as the "Boston Tea Party" until nineteenth-century writers created that moniker.

The colonists' act of resistance to parliamentary authority led to Parliament enacting the Boston Port Bill, which closed Boston Harbor. Other Americans rallied to Boston's support, creating a greater sense of unity in the colonies against British oppression than had previously existed.

Judkin Browning

See also: Adams, Samuel; Boston; East India Company; Hancock, John; Politics and Government (Chronology); Politics and Government (Essay); Revolutionary War; Tea; Tea Act (1773).

Bibliography

Labaree, Benjamin Woods. *The Boston Tea Party.* New York: Oxford University Press, 1964.

Thomas, Peter D. G. *Tea Party to Independence: The Third Phase of the American Revolution, 1773–1776.* Oxford, UK: Clarendon, 1991.

Young, Alfred F. *The Shoemaker and the Tea Party: Memory and the American Revolution.* Boston: Beacon, 1999.

Braddock, Edward (1695–1755)

Born in January 1695, the son of an officer in the elite Coldstream Guards, Edward Braddock came of age during Queen Anne's War (1702–1713), hearing of the glories of English arms and especially the duke of Marlborough. Although a commoner, Braddock secured a commission as an ensign in the Coldstream Guards on October 10, 1710.

Braddock, who could be peevish and quick-tempered, developed a mild reputation as a profligate young officer, partaking of the vices of Covent Garden and developing a lifelong addiction to snuff. As he progressed through the ranks, however, first as a lieutenant colonel in the Coldstream Guards and later as a colonel in the 14th Foot, the brown-haired, portly officer was generally regarded as a noted administrator, effective disciplinarian, and dedicated soldier who possessed impressive personal courage and honesty.

Braddock spent nearly all of his unremarkable, but unblemished, forty-four-year career serving in garrison duty in London, Flanders, and Gibraltar. In 1754, he finally earned a chance to achieve military distinction when William Augustus, duke of Cumberland, promoted the politically reliable colonel to major general and appointed him commander of all British forces in North America. Cumberland ordered Braddock to drive the French from Fort Duquesne in the Ohio Valley before reducing the forts at Niagara, Ontario, Champlain, Crown Point, and Nova Scotia.

Braddock sailed for Virginia on December 22, 1754, arriving there on February 20, 1755, three weeks ahead of two regiments of British regulars, the 44th and 48th Foot, who were to serve as the backbone of his expeditionary force. Braddock spent the next several weeks trying to gather supplies and recruit colonial troops to join his force. His inflexibility and lack of imagination hindered his preparations. He refused to deviate from the letter of his orders. He commanded rather than cajoled colonial governors, took a dim view of colonial volunteers, and did not behave very diplomatically to potential Native American allies. The lack of supplies, transportation, and provincial assistance delayed his march.

Finally, on May 30, Braddock's force, nearly 2,300 strong, marched from Fort Cumberland near the Potomac River toward Fort Duquesne. Progress was slow, as 300 axmen had to hack a road ahead of the main body so that Braddock could drag his immensely heavy 8-inch howitzers and 12-pound cannon, as well as an enormous wagon train of supplies and baggage,

General Edward Braddock served as commander of British forces in North America from his arrival in Virginia in February 1755 until his death the following July near Fort Duquesne (present-day Pittsburgh) in an early campaign of the French and Indian War. *(Brown Brothers, Sterling, Pennsylvania)*

through 100 miles of dense wilderness and mountains. Soon, Braddock divided his army into two columns in order to travel faster.

On July 9, 1755, just on the northern side of the Monongahela River, about 8 miles from Fort Duquesne (in present-day Pittsburgh), Braddock's flying column of nearly 1,400 men was ambushed by 108 French colonial regulars, 146 Canadian militiamen, and 637 Native Americans. The French forces initially attacked Braddock's vanguard, led by Lieutenant Thomas Gage (who would later lead British troops to Lexington and Concord in April 1775, beginning the Revolutionary War). Gage's troops recoiled and collided with those behind them. Braddock sent reinforcements forward, only to see them become entangled with Gage's troops. Bunched together, the troops were easy targets for the hidden enemies firing from both flanks.

Though his men suffered terrible casualties, Braddock insisted on keeping them in line of battle. He knew his regulars were not trained for irregular fighting and feared their reaction if he allowed them to seek cover. Riding up and down the line with his hat tied on with a white handkerchief knotted under his chin, Braddock displayed conspicuous bravery in the fight, having four horses shot out from under him while trying to rally his troops and maintain order. Nearly all of his officers were killed or wounded. Finally a bullet penetrated Braddock's right arm and pierced his lungs. After his wounding, his men retreated pell-mell back across the Monongahela and toward the safety of the second column, several days behind them. Two-thirds of Braddock's force had been killed or wounded, while the French suffered only twenty-three killed and sixteen seriously wounded. A number of Canadians and Native Americans also were dead or wounded.

Braddock suffered in agonizing pain for four days before finally succumbing to his wound on July 13, 1755. He was buried in the road, and the army and wagons trudged over his grave to obliterate any trace of it in order to keep enemy natives from desecrating it.

Braddock had failed in his only field command. His training and traditional sense of warfare had left him unprepared for the type of fighting necessary to succeed in the North American wilderness.

Judkin Browning

See also: Army, British; French and Indian War; Military and Diplomatic Affairs (Chronology); Military and Diplomatic Affairs (Essay); Queen Anne's War.

Bibliography

Anderson, Fred. *Crucible of War: The Seven Years' War and the Fate of Empire in British North America, 1754–1766.* New York: Alfred A. Knopf, 2000.

Kopperman, Paul E. *Braddock at the Monongahela.* Pittsburgh: University of Pittsburgh Press, 1977.

McCardell, Lee. *Ill-Starred General: Braddock of the Coldstream Guards.* Revised. Pittsburgh: University of Pittsburgh Press, 1986.

Bradford, William (1590–1657)

William Bradford was arguably the most important and influential individual in the earliest days of America's colonial period. A voracious reader from childhood and largely self-educated, Bradford is remembered as a statesman, a pious Puritan, a devout defender of democratic ideals, and a comprehensive historian of life in the New World. His *Of Plymouth Plantation*, written in a "plain style" and with a "singular regard unto the simple truth," remains one of the best records of life in his time.

Early Life

Bradford was born in Austerfield, England, in 1590 to relatively prosperous parents; however, his father died before William's first birthday. His mother soon remarried, and the young William was shunted off to be raised by male members of his father's family, who readied him for a career as a farmer, training the boy in animal husbandry and agricultural practices. Unlike many farm boys, William had a thirst for theoretical as well as practical knowledge. He read widely in the libraries of family friends and acquaintances and, by the age of 12, was particularly interested in studying the Scriptures.

In his midteens, Bradford was introduced to the rhetoric of the Pilgrims, who believed the Church of England was so corrupt that it was impossible to reform and purify it from within. Bradford was enthralled by the preaching of Richard Clyfton, the leader of a particularly nonconforming congregation. To save their own souls, these "Scrooby Pilgrims," named for the home location of their group, believed it was necessary to completely sever their ties with the Anglican hierarchy. Because it was unlawful for an English citizen to separate himself from the state-established Church, these separatists were persecuted as traitors.

Bradford made the Pilgrims' cause his own, and by 1607, he had joined the group in their quest for religious tolerance in the Netherlands. After living for a time in Amsterdam, Bradford settled in Leyden, where he became somewhat prosperous as a weaver. Continuing his love of reading, Bradford learned Dutch, French, Latin, Greek, and Hebrew, largely teaching himself these new languages.

Life in America

After some ten years in Leyden, the Pilgrims began to fear that they were losing their English identity and "becoming Dutch." Further, they were not prospering, and their numbers were diminishing. In hopes of reversing these trends, the Scrooby Pilgrims decided to strike out for the New World. Bradford, 27 years old and a leader of the congregation in Leyden by this time, was part of the committee that obtained a charter to settle on land owned by the Virginia Company, as well as financing from merchant speculators who hoped to profit from return shipments of fish, furs, and minerals from the colony. The details settled, Bradford and his companions, along with the ship's other passengers, most of whom were not Pilgrims, sailed for America on the *Mayflower*. Bradford was named a leader of the colony even before the new arrivals reached their American home. Shortly before landing, those on board signed the Mayflower Compact, the first document arranging for democratic governance in the New World. Despite arriving at Cape Cod in the Massachusetts (not Virginia) territory in November 1620, the settlers decided to remain in New England without a charter, eventually establishing a home at Plymouth in Massachusetts Bay.

Numerous accounts relate the difficulties faced by the Pilgrim group in the early days of their settlement in Plymouth. Fifty of the 102 Pilgrims who survived the difficult three-month journey died within the first year after their arrival; Bradford's own wife drowned while he was gone from Cape Cod seeking a place to settle the community permanently. Still, like his companions, Bradford was a man of strong faith and convictions, and, like them, he prospered in the New World. After the death of John Carver, Plymouth's first governor, Bradford was elected to replace him; over the ensuing years from 1621 through 1656, he would be elected governor a total of thirty times—a telling indication of the respect and veneration afforded him by his companions.

Bradford carefully recorded his observations and reflections on life in the colony in his masterful *Of Plymouth Plantation*, arguably the most historically useful text that has survived that period. Written from 1630 to 1647, the massive volume tells the settlers' story, beginning with their persecutions in England. Bradford's emphasis throughout the work remains on spiritual, not material, wealth. Like his fellow Pilgrims, Bradford anticipated the Christian millennium as a spiritual, rather than a physical, utopia; however, as the length of time from the original settlement of the colony grew, piety among the group declined. Bradford felt moved to write *Of Plymouth Plantation* to renew the often-repeated sense of mission and calling of the Pilgrims. His text frequently compares the settlers to the Israelites, and his language, style, and rhetoric are all strongly Biblical in nature.

The original manuscript was long presumed to have been destroyed in the Revolutionary War. In the mid-nineteenth century, however, it was found in the library of the Bishop of London, apparently taken there among the spoils of war. The original manuscript was returned, after extended legal haggling, to the Massachusetts State House in 1897. Although portions of the text had been published piecemeal in heavily edited versions over the years by Bradford's nephew, the first faithful edition of *Of Plymouth Plantation* was not published until 1856, over 200 years after Bradford had finished writing it.

Throughout the years since, Bradford's book has remained the premier source of information about life in the early days of colonial settlement. Along with his other accomplishments, William Bradford's creation of this seminal American text makes him a critical component of the early life of the nation.

Barbara Schwarz Wachal

See also: Mayflower Compact; *Of Plymouth Plantation;* Pilgrims; Plymouth. *Document:* The Mayflower Compact (1620).

Bibliography

Anderson, Douglas. *William Bradford's Books: Of Plimmoth Plantation and the Printed Word.* Baltimore: Johns Hopkins University Press, 2003.

Davis, William T. *Bradford's History of Plymouth Plantation, 1606–1646.* New York: Barnes Publishing, 1946.

Smith, Bradford. *Bradford of Plymouth.* Philadelphia: Lippincott, 1951.

Bradstreet, Anne (1612–1672)

Anne Bradstreet was born in 1612 in Northampton, England. Her position as the daughter and wife of two influential figures in the governance of the American colonies would have made her a woman of some note, but her own creativity leads modern scholars to recall her as the first significant poet in American literature.

The daughter of Thomas Dudley, a steward of the estates of the Earl of Lincoln, and Dorothy Yorke, an educated gentlewoman, Anne had the advantage of more education than most girls and women of her day received. From an early age, she received tutoring and read widely in the Scriptures, Puritan texts, and history and literature in Greek, Latin, French, and Hebrew; she was also familiar with the works of Shakespeare, Bacon, and John Foxe. Her family's strong Puritan views exposed her early to lively religious and intellectual debate.

In 1628, 16-year-old Anne Dudley married Simon Bradstreet, a young man, nine years her senior, who had been in her family's care since his mother's death some years earlier. Bradstreet was a graduate of Emmanuel College at Cambridge University, a center of nonconformist thought, and his father was a Puritan minister of some note.

Thomas Dudley and Simon Bradstreet came under increasing suspicion by Charles I for their separatist beliefs. Finally, in 1630, the young married couple and the Dudleys joined John Winthrop and other Puritans on board the *Arabella,* bound for the American colonies in search of freedom from religious persecution.

Life in America

Arriving in the Massachusetts Bay Colony following a difficult three-month voyage, many survivors of the journey quickly died of disease; others decided to return to England. Those who remained elected John Winthrop governor, Thomas Dudley deputy governor, and Simon Bradstreet chief administrator. Both Dudley and Bradstreet would continue their service in colonial government, with Anne's father eventually acting as the governor of the Massachusetts Bay Colony four times and Bradstreet serving as a judge, as the colony's representative to British Crown, and eventually as the colony's governor for some ten years.

Daily life in the colonies was difficult, characterized by scarce provisions, unsafe water, and the continual worry of attack by Native Americans against the European settlers. Anne had suffered from both rheumatic fever and smallpox before leaving England. She remained sickly in her new home and succumbed again to smallpox, lameness, and fainting spells. She presumed she would die as a young woman, presumably in childbirth, but despite her sickly disposition, she bore eight children, who all lived to adulthood. Adding to the difficulties of her life were the Bradstreets' frequent relocations in their early marriage.

From their first home in Salem, the Bradstreets moved to Charlestown, but since the water supply there was bad, in 1631, the couple moved to Newtown (now Cambridge). Shortly thereafter, they settled in Agawam (now Ipswich), where a vigorous intellectual life in the community inspired Anne to begin writing poetry in 1632. By 1645, the family included five of their eventual eight children, and Simon decided to move to a 20-acre homestead in the farming settlement of Andover, where the village's setting near dense woods made wolves a serious and constant threat to its human inhabitants.

Anne's life was further complicated by Simon's frequent absences. His business dealings on behalf the Massachusetts Bay Company demanded extensive travel, as did his lengthy attempt in 1661 to renegotiate the company's charter at Charles II's court in London. Drawing on her strong faith in God, Anne was often left alone to cope with raising children, handling domestic duties, facing the hardships of everyday colonial life, and dealing with her own loneliness. Her poetry reflects all of these facets of life in the American colonies, as well as her personal experience of universal truths.

Her Poetry

Anne Bradstreet's earliest poems were collected and published, with many printing errors and without her consent, by her brother-in-law in England in 1650 as *The Tenth Muse Lately Sprung Up in America.* This work reflects her reading of Raleigh, Spenser, Donne, and Herbert; her derivative style is largely applied to cosmic themes.

Her later poems deal much more extensively with religious themes and with Nature, life in the New World, domestic matters, and the intimacies of married life. In fact, late-twentieth-century feminist scholars have pointed to the latter two categories of Bradstreet's poems as examples of the visionary and enduring value of her work. She revised all of her poetry in 1666 in

anticipation of a new collection of her works, but this edition was not published until after her death in 1672.

Barbara Schwarz Wachal

See also: Arts, Culture, and Intellectual Life (Chronology); Arts, Culture, and Intellectual Life (Essay); Literature; Massachusetts Bay Colony; Women. *Document*: Upon the Burning of Our House (1666).

Bibliography

Bradstreet, Anne. *The Complete Works of Anne Bradstreet.* Edited by Joseph R. McElrath, Jr., and Allan P. Robb. Boston: Twayne, 1981.

Rosenmeier, Rosamond. *Anne Bradstreet Revisited.* Boston: Twayne, 1991.

Stanford, Ann. *Anne Bradstreet, the Worldly Puritan: An Introduction to Her Poetry.* New York: B. Franklin Publishing, 1974.

White, Elizabeth Wade. *Anne Bradstreet: "The Tenth Muse."* New York: Oxford University Press, 1971.

Brant, Joseph (1743–1807)

Joseph Brant (whose Mohawk name was Thayendanegea, "He Places Together Two Bets") flourished in both the Mohawk world and the British colonial world. He led the Mohawks against the Americans during the War for Independence and advocated a pan-tribal identity that would continue to influence the region's native peoples through the era of Tecumseh and the War of 1812.

Brant was born in Ohio in 1743 to Tehonwaghkwangeraghwa of Canajoharie, New York, and his wife, Margaret Aoghyatonghsera. Shortly after his birth, Joseph's father died. The surname Brant came from Joseph's stepfather, an elite Mohawk and contemporary of the highly respected chief King Hendrick. This was one of the avenues through which Brant rose to prominence in Mohawk society. It bears mentioning that Sir William Johnson, the de facto British ambassador to the Iroquois, took a special interest in Brant's education. Johnson intended to create a peaceful trading empire using an army of fluent translators who could maneuver between the British colonial and Mohawk worlds.

Brant's family connections allowed him access to the highest rungs of colonial society. From 1761 to 1763, he studied English at Eleazar Wheelock's famous missionary school in Lebanon, Connecticut. (The school

Mohawk chief Joseph Brant—known as Thayendanegea in his native tongue—fought with the British in the War for Independence, because he believed that an American victory would destroy the Indian nation. *(Brown Brothers, Sterling, Pennsylvania)*

was the alma mater of Samson Occom, a well-known Mohegan preacher, and later it would relocate to New Hampshire and become Dartmouth College.) While under Wheelock's tutelage, Brant learned the skills necessary to be a missionary. Reverend Wheelock described his appearance and demeanor in 1763, noting that Joseph was "a young Mohawk . . . of a Family of Distinction in that Nation . . . of a Sprightly Genius, a manly and genteel Deportment, and of a Modest courteous and benevolent Temper."

Brant returned to Canajoharie in 1763 and, by 1770, was the head of a fairly profitable European-style farm, where he grew wheat for profit and kept livestock. He also continued to raise more traditional Mohawk crops, namely, corn, beans, and squash. During this period, Brant married Margaret, an Oneida woman, who bore his first child, Isaac, at Fort Ontario in 1767, as well as his daughter. Brant remained active in politics as well, translating for Sir William Johnson and John-

son's nephew Guy Johnson, who replaced William as superintendent of Indian affairs. Brant's first wife and his second wife, Susanna, both died; he had seven children by his third wife, Catherine.

Brant's ties to the British in North America ran deep; he owed his success to men such as William Johnson and Eleazar Wheelock. For Brant, however, the years before the American War for Independence made clear the difficulties of maintaining both white and Native American ways, or at least maintaining a semblance of Mohawk autonomy in the face of an expanding American empire. Settlement during this time period pushed farther and farther into Iroquois country, with devastating results for traditional Iroquois hunting grounds. On the eve of war, in 1775 and 1776, Brant visited London. He met King George III and became convinced that the British, and not the Americans, had the best interests of the Iroquois in mind. The British guaranteed their support and protection against American encroachment. Brant returned home confident in his own abilities as a statesman and in the Iroquois's ability to resist American imperialism.

The Iroquois Confederation as a whole tried to remain neutral in the Revolutionary War. This policy actually broke apart the confederation, as the Oneida and Tuscarora chose to support the Americans and the Mohawk, Cayuga, Onondaga, and Seneca fought on the British side. Joseph's leadership against the Americans during the war was truly remarkable. He led an army of loyalist whites and Native Americans into Oriskany, New York, on August 6, 1777, and surprised a sizable force of American militia stationed there. Although not technically a war chief, Brant led an army in New York and Ohio for most of the war.

Despite Brant's accomplishments, the British lost the war; to make matters worse, reneging on their earlier promises, the British did not mention Native American rights in the Treaty of Paris. The end result of these negotiations was that Native Americans who supported the British during the war were now left on their own to face the fledgling American nation. That nation, in turn, began to expand through conquest, treaty, and purchase, with little regard for Native American cultures or peoples.

Brant's leadership against the Americans did not go entirely unrewarded. In exchange for his military service (and the land in New York from which he was forced), Brant and his allies received a vast tract of land in Ontario, on the Grand River. Brant, who viewed military action as a last resort, continued to advocate pan-tribal resistance to American expansion until his death in Burlington, Ontario, on November 24, 1807.

Matthew Jennings

See also: Brant, Mary "Molly"; Iroquois Confederacy; Mohawk; Native American–European Conflict; Native American–European Relations; Revolutionary War.

Bibliography

Kelsay, Isabel Thompson. *Joseph Brant, 1743–1807: Man of Two Worlds.* Syracuse, NY: Syracuse University Press, 1984.

Robinson, Helen Caister. *Joseph Brant: A Man for His People.* Don Mills, Ontario: Longman Canada, 1971.

Sugden, John. "Brant, Joseph." In *Encyclopedia of North American Indians,* edited by Frederick E. Hoxie. New York: Houghton Mifflin, 1996.

Brant, Mary "Molly" (c. 1736–1796)

Probably born in 1736, Mary Brant, sometimes called Konwatsi'tsiaienni ("someone lends her a flower"), was the daughter of Margaret, a Mohawk woman, and her first husband, whose name is unknown. Educated by British missionaries, she was literate in English and held status in Anglicized Mohawk circles, although she does not seem to have held any particular matrilineal importance as a clan mother or hereditary female leader, as is sometimes reported in older texts. She appears in records of a 1754–1755 diplomatic mission of the Mohawk to Philadelphia, among twelve men representing the Iroquois.

Best known by the surname of her stepfather, the Mohawk sachem Nichus Brant, Mary came into contact with the British Indian Agent and land magnate Sir William Johnson through her brother (perhaps halfbrother) Joseph Brant at Johnson Hall, New York. By September 1759, she was living as "housekeeper" with Johnson, his children by his previous German commonlaw wife, and the first of the couple's eight children.

Given tremendous status as the unofficial "Lady Johnson," Brant was able to dispense patronage to the Six Nations of the Iroquois. She also added to Johnson's prestige among the native population, especially as he acknowledged, educated, and provided for their two sons and six daughters in a generous and magnanimous style. Johnson and Brant may have married in a Mohawk ceremony, but they never wed legally under British law or in the Church of England, although the local parish treated her as his wife.

In 1765, Brant fell seriously ill from smallpox and was badly scarred. Johnson died in 1774, leaving her considerable property, slaves, and a substantial financial settlement carefully structured to protect her holdings from her stepchildren.

During the American Revolution, Brant was crucial in holding the Mohawk to their loyalty to the British Crown, using Johnson's prestige to involve them in the contest for the Mohawk Valley. She provided key intelligence, obtained from Mary Aaron, the Mohawk mistress of General Philip Schuyler, and warned General Barry St. Leger that the patriots were sending relief to the besieged Fort Stanwix; this information allowed the British to plan the bloody ambush at Oriskany.

After 1777, subject to increasing harassment, including the sack of Johnson Hall, Brant and her younger children fled to Cayuga and Niagara. There, she worked amongst the Mohawk and loyalist Oneida to refuse a peace offer after the British surrender at Saratoga.

As a refugee in British Canada, Brant was invaluable in keeping order among loyalist British and Native American refugees. Several times, she arranged safe passage for British loyalists through hostile Oneida lands to Canada. She demanded privileged treatment from the British commanders of Fort Carleton (Kingston, Ontario), who provided for her entourage, including slaves, out of the slim resources of the official provisions list and built her a house. In 1783, Brant submitted a claim for 1,206 pounds in damages to her property, which was promptly paid by Guy Carleton, who also granted her a pension of 100 pounds per year, the largest granted to any Native American by the British during the American Revolution. Brant also insisted that all her daughters continue their British education, and she saw four of them married into the loyalist landowners of Ontario.

Mary Brant's contributions to the British cause and her role in loyalist activities were overlooked in nineteenth-century histories of the American Revolution, which characterized her as a virtuous helpmeet of Sir William Johnson rather than an independent actor in the conflict. Recognized as a leader of the local elite in British Upper Canada, she died in April 1796 and was buried from the Kingston Episcopal church.

Margaret Sankey

See also: Brant, Joseph; Mohawk; Native American–European Conflict; Native American–European Relations; Revolutionary War.

Bibliography

Flexner, James Thomas. *Lord of the Mohawks.* Boston: Little, Brown, 1979.

Gundy, Pearson. "Molly Brant: Loyalist." *Ontario Historical Society Papers and Records* 45 (1953): 97–108.

Kelsay, Isabel Thompson. *Joseph Brant: 1743–1807.* Syracuse, NY: Syracuse University Press, 1984.

Potter-Mackinnon, Janice. *While the Women Only Wept: Loyalist Refugee Woman.* Montreal and Quebec: Queens-McGill University Press, 1993.

Brent, Margaret
(c. 1601–c. 1671)

Margaret Brent, landowner and executor of the estate of Maryland governor Leonard Calvert, was the daughter of two prominent Gloucester English Catholics, Richard Brent (Lord Admington and Lark Stoke) and Elizabeth Reed Brent.

Born about 1601, she arrived in the new colony of Maryland with her sister and two brothers in 1638. As kin of the Calverts, they expected a warm welcome, and they bore letters from Lord Baltimore, recommending that they be granted land on the same terms as the original proprietors. The patent for land near St. Mary's City that Margaret and her sister Mary took out in 1639 made them Maryland's first women to own land in their own right. Colonists called the property "Sisters Freehold." In 1642, Margaret added 1,000 acres on Kent Island, transferred to her by her brother to settle a debt.

Margaret Brent actively managed her estate, appearing in court more than 124 times in eight years to pursue debt claims or represent others through power of attorney. It was not necessary to have studied law or to be admitted to the bar to represent one's self or others in Maryland courts. She also was co-guardian, with her brother, of Mary Kitomaquund, daughter of the chief of the Piscataway Indians. When Giles Brent later married Mary Kitomaquund, some feared he was trying to build a source of power separate from the Calverts.

By 1643, England was deep into civil war, and Leonard Calvert was called home. Maryland Protestants, encouraged by William Claiborne and Richard Ingle, rose against the government of the Catholic proprietors while Calvert was gone. When he returned from England in 1645, the Protestants drove Calvert into Virginia, and Ingle sent Giles Brent as a prisoner to England.

In August 1646, Calvert returned to Maryland, leading an army of soldiers recruited in Virginia, and he regained control of the colony. Margaret Brent may have helped gather the troops. On his deathbed in May 1647, Calvert appointed Brent his executor, giving her authority to "take all and pay all." It was not an easy task, for the governor's estate was besieged with claimants for debt. Brent defended against these claims, acting as the estate's attorney.

Calvert's will made Brent, for all practical purposes, the fiscal administrator for the colony. Unfortunately, the colony faced a severe corn shortage. Hungry, unpaid soldiers were a threat to Maryland that she could not ignore; however, Leonard Calvert's estate was not large enough to meet all of these payments. To maintain peace and retain control of the Virginia troops, Margaret Brent imported food from Virginia and sold some cattle from Lord Baltimore's estate (which had been managed by his brother, Leonard Calvert) to pay the soldiers.

Both as executor with power of attorney of Calvert's estate and as a proprietor in her own right, Margaret Brent qualified for a vote in the Assembly. (All other large landowners had a seat by virtue of their property.) On January 21, 1648, she requested two votes. She thus became the first woman in the colonies to request political participation in a legislative assembly. The Assembly denied her request without giving a reason, apparently believing that her request went beyond acceptable roles for a woman, even when acting as representative (executor) for a man. Margaret was surprised and angry, but she continued managing Maryland's finances until the estate was settled. Lord Baltimore was displeased to learn that she had used her power as executor to sell some of his property, but the Assembly defended her actions as necessary to save the colony.

In 1650, no longer in favor with the proprietor, the Brents moved to land in nearby Westmoreland County, Virginia. There, Margaret Brent imported numerous settlers and presided over a manorial court on her estates. Brent managed her Virginia estate, which she named "Peace," until her death in 1670 or 1671. Her will was offered for probate in 1671.

Often incorrectly hailed as the first woman to ask

to vote in the colonies and as the first woman attorney in the British colonies, Brent best illustrates the way an upper-class woman could assume roles of power by acting as an agent of her family. As a single woman, she escaped the limits English law placed on a married woman's control of property. She carved a niche for herself in history as an entrepreneur and competent manager, who provided crucial leadership to Maryland at a critical point in the colony's development.

Joan R. Gundersen

See also: Landlords; Maryland.

Bibliography

Morello, Karen Berger. *The Invisible Bar: The Woman Lawyer in America, 1638 to the Present.* Boston: Beacon Press, 1986.

Norton, Mary Beth. *Founding Mothers and Fathers: Gendered Power and the Forming of American Society.* New York: Alfred A. Knopf, 1996.

Spruill, Julia Cherry. *Women's Life and Work in the Southern Colonies.* Chapel Hill: University of North Carolina Press, 1938.

British East India Company

See East India Company

British Navy

See Navy, British

Broadsides

See Art, Cartoons, and Broadsides

Bunker Hill, Battle of

Soon after the British soldiers returned to Boston from their disastrous venture to Lexington and Concord on April 19, 1775, to participate in the battles that began the American Revolution, colonial troops laid siege to the city. In June, reinforcements arrived from England to strengthen General Thomas Gage's attempts to drive away the rebels menacing his army.

Once they learned that the British were planning an attack against the colonial positions, the colonials decided to surround Bunker Hill near Charlestown in order to strengthen their position. On the night of Friday, June 16, 1775, approximately 1,140 men, under the command of Colonel William Prescott, marched across Charlestown Neck. After a discussion with his fellow officers, Prescott opted to fortify Breed's Hill, which was lower than Bunker Hill but threatened British lines, in the hope of provoking them to attack. At midnight, the troops began digging earnestly to create a substantial redoubt near the crest of the hill. On the left flank, New Hampshire troops of Captain Thomas Knowlton fortified some fence rails with rocks and straw, while shortly before the battle, reinforcements under Colonel John Stark entrenched on the beach of the Mystic River on the far left flank.

At dawn, the British officers spotted the fortifications and crafted a plan to defeat the rebels. Sir Henry Clinton advocated an amphibious landing behind the hill to cut off their retreat, but General Gage overruled his plan in favor of one by Sir William Howe. Howe advocated two separate landings of troops, who would attack simultaneously against the left flank and the center of the position. Howe believed that when confronted with disciplined redcoats with bayonets ready, the colonists would break and run. Shortly after noon, on a perfectly clear but oppressively hot day, Royal Navy barges ferried Howe's 2,800 troops onto the Charlestown peninsula. Unforeseen delays ensued, allowing the colonists time to further strengthen their defenses.

Hungry, thirsty, and exhausted, nearly half of the original colonists slipped to the rear by late morning, while reinforcements passed them on the way to the fortifications. By the time the British began their advance, at around three in the afternoon, Prescott had nearly 900 men in his lines. While thousands of spectators sat on roofs in Boston to watch, Howe advanced. Stark's men decimated the initial British thrust on the colonial left flank, along the banks of the Mystic River. Howe personally led the attack on the rail fence with his grenadiers and the 5th and 52nd Foot Regiments. As the redcoats marched in the searing 95-degree heat under full pack, through knee-high grass, and over numerous fences and low stone walls, they encountered

British regulars under General William Howe and colonial volunteers under Colonel William Prescott met in the first major engagement of the American Revolution on June 17, 1775. The misnamed Battle of Bunker Hill was actually fought on Breed's Hill across the Charles River from Boston. *(Brown Brothers, Sterling, Pennsylvania)*

withering rebel fire. Within fifteen minutes, Howe lost over 50 percent of his forces, including 80 percent casualties in the grenadiers.

On the colonial right flank, British warships set the abandoned town of Charlestown ablaze in an effort to drive off rebel sharpshooters. Three British regiments and a battalion of marines suffered an equally bloody repulse from Prescott's troops.

Howe rejected the advice of some of his officers to retreat and instead called for reinforcements. He pinned the rebel left with artillery fire and concentrated his next thrust on the redoubt atop the hill, where Prescott's 150 men had nearly exhausted their ammunition. Ordering his men to drop their gear, Howe ordered a fast march up the hill, over the bodies of comrades fallen in earlier engagements. Prescott's men staggered them for a short time, but the well-trained redcoats breached the walls and overran the redoubt with bitter hand-to-hand fighting, forcing the

rebels to retreat. Stark conducted a solid fighting withdrawal, preventing a rout.

The British gained the summit of Bunker Hill a few minutes later, shortly after five o'clock, with little opposition. At this point, Howe chose not to press on the attack across Charlestown Neck toward the main rebel army stationed at Cambridge, and the battle thus came to a close.

The British army won the field but paid a steep price, suffering 226 killed and 828 wounded, while 140 Americans were killed and 271 wounded. Although holding a relatively poor military position and fighting with untrained soldiers, the Americans had held out for over two hours against some of the best British soldiers and generals. The Americans learned that they could stand up to the British, and the British learned that the colonial rebels could be a formidable foe when properly motivated.

After the Battle of Bunker Hill, the British never

mounted another local offensive against their besiegers, and they eventually evacuated Boston on March 17, 1776.

Judkin Browning

See also: Army, British; Gage, Thomas; Military and Diplomatic Affairs (Chronology); Military and Diplomatic Affairs (Essay); Revolutionary War; War.

Bibliography

Brooks, Victor. *The Boston Campaign: April 1775–March 1776.* Conshohocken, PA: Combined, 1999.

Fleming, Thomas J. *Now We Are Enemies: The Story of Bunker Hill.* New York: St. Martin's, 1960.

Ketchum, Richard M. *Decisive Day: The Battle for Bunker Hill.* Garden City, NY: Doubleday, 1974.

Cabot, John
(c. 1450–c. 1498)

Born Giovanni Caboto (or Cabato) in one of the Italian states, John Cabot first surfaces in Venetian records in 1476, when he gained citizenship after fifteen years of residence. Married to a Venetian, Mattia, in 1484, Cabot gained a reputation as an expert navigator and ship captain in the service of Venice.

In 1496, perhaps inspired by the rush of proposals following Christopher Columbus's voyages, Cabot approached England's King Henry VII for sponsorship in a voyage across the North Atlantic. Henry VII, reluctant to challenge Spanish claims in the Atlantic because of treaty obligations, agreed to lend his patronage to an exploration of the northern latitudes. In lieu of cash financing, he waived customs duties for profitable products brought back and encouraged nobles to invest in the plan in exchange for 20 percent of any eventual profits.

An abortive 1496 expedition from Bristol was followed by the May 20, 1497, launch of the ship *Matthew*, with the support and investment of Bristol merchants and fishermen. Cabot sailed west to Ireland and then westward across the Atlantic on a route that fell between 51 and 55 degrees north latitude. After thirty-five days at sea, Cabot and his crew of eighteen made landfall on June 24, 1497, not in Japan, as they had hoped, but somewhere on the coast of Canada between Newfoundland's Avalon Peninsula and Cape Breton Island. He described the landfall as "the mainland and some islands" and reported encountering native people who used ochre and supplied him with a needle and snares for small game. Cabot and the crew enacted a formal ceremony claiming the land for England, noted the large number of trees that could provide masts for ships, then collected fresh water and sailed east for fifteen days, arriving off the coast of Brittany.

Henry VII was delighted to receive Cabot back in London in August 1497 and rewarded him with 10 pounds in gold and a pension of 20 pounds per year to be taken from the Bristol customs revenue. The following year, Cabot collected London investors and ships for a six-vessel expedition to the North Atlantic. Again, he hoped to open a lucrative spice trade between England and the East Indies, and departed with trade goods for prospective negotiations. Cabot failed to return from this voyage, although one ship that had turned back made it to England. In 1501, explorer Gaspar Corte-Real discovered a broken Italian sword in Canada, which he proposed must have been Cabot's, but there is no trace or record of his survival.

In 1508, Cabot's son, Sebastian, who probably also had gone on the 1497 voyage, sailed for Labrador in the employ of a consortium of Bristol and Azores merchants. A gifted cartographer, Sebastian later went into the pay of the Spanish monarchy and claimed nothing further for England.

Henry VII and his son Henry VIII were increasingly bound by French and Spanish interests not to interfere in exploration claims, but the timber and cod fishing intrigued English merchants. Through Cabot's expedition, the monarchy did, however, establish a tenuous claim on Canada and the Americas that British rulers called back into play at the time of Queen Elizabeth I in the 1590s.

Cabot himself is the subject of intense national interest in Canada, where numerous towns wish to claim the prestige of his landfall. He also serves as a viable alternative for English-speaking Canadians to the French Catholic explorer Jacques Cartier as the true European founder of the country.

Margaret Sankey

See also: Exploration; Newfoundland. *Document*: John Cabot's Discovery of North America (1497).

The Italian navigator John Cabot and his son, Sebastian, sailing under the flag of England, depart from Bristol on their first voyage of discovery in May 1497, seeking Cathay. They landed somewhere on the Newfoundland coast. *(Brown Brothers, Sterling, Pennsylvania)*

Bibliography

Pope, Peter Edward. *The Many Landfalls of John Cabot.* Toronto: University of Toronto Press, 1997.

Simons, Eric N. *Into Unknown Waters: John and Sebastian Cabot.* London: D. Dobson, 1964.

Williams, Alan F. *John Cabot and Newfoundland.* St. John's, Canada: Newfoundland Historical Society, 1996.

Cabrillo, Juan Rodríguez (c. 1498–c. 1543)

Juan Rodríguez Cabrillo, a Spanish explorer, was one of a trio of explorers active in North America at the beginning of the 1540s, which included Hernando de Soto and Francisco Váquez de Coronado. Cabrillo's voyage up California's Pacific coast gave Spain a claim to the region that no European power could challenge until the eighteenth century.

Not much is known about Cabrillo's early life. He was probably born around 1498, perhaps in Seville. The place of his birth has created something of a controversy. Many scholars believe he was a Spaniard, although a contemporary document describes him as being Portuguese.

Cabrillo came to the Americas as a young boy, perhaps as a page to a Spanish soldier. He was with Pánfilo de Narváez during his expedition to conquer Cuba in the 1510s. During the conquest of Mexico's central valley, Cabrillo was a captain of crossbowmen, first against the renegade Hernando Cortéz and later in his service. It was rumored at the time that Cabrillo used rendered human body fat in the production of pitch.

Cabrillo rose to prominence in the army that conquered Guatemala and Honduras, and, by the 1530s, as a merchant, mine owner, and shipbuilder, he was one of the richest men in Guatemala. His military prowess also garnered him several highly profitable *encomiendas* (grants of land and people). Cabrillo ran into some financial difficulties at the end of the 1530s, and it is possible that money problems prompted him to undertake his famous voyage, sponsored by Viceroy Antonio de Mendoza. Cabrillo's 1541 pamphlet describing an earthquake in Guatemala is generally understood to be the first secular work published in the Americas.

In 1542, Cabrillo set sail to explore the western coast of New Spain and then to travel onward to China. At the same time, another Spanish fleet would attempt to reach the Spice Islands and China by sailing directly across the Pacific. Of course, both of these goals were impossible to achieve.

Cabrillo's group consisted of three ships, whose construction he had overseen himself. In September of 1542, he anchored the ships near Point Loma, near present-day San Diego, and went ashore. Through interpreters, he learned that the native people in the interior recently had been terrorized by Europeans. According to his account, "men like us were traveling about, bearded, clothed and armed . . . killing many native Indians, and . . . for this reason they were afraid." Farther to the north, Cabrillo again heard reports of such atrocities. During the early 1540s, Coronado's expedition on the Colorado River had come within 150 miles of San Diego, and word of the force's brutality had spread rapidly through the region's native communities. Cabrillo, however, seems to have maintained peaceful relations with most of his native hosts—some even went so far as to spend the night on the Spanish ships.

Sometime during the winter of 1542–1543, Cabrillo died, probably from the infection of a broken shinbone, an injury he had sustained earlier in the year when he had slipped on rocks trying to rescue some of his men from an attack by natives. With Cabrillo gone, the voyage continued under the direction of the chief pilot, Bartolomé Ferrer. Ferrer led the ships to the area of the present-day border between California and Oregon. There, the combination of high seas and a shortage of supplies, which apparently drove some of the sailors to the brink of madness, forced Ferrer to abandon the original plan to reach China, and he turned back south.

The Cabrillo expedition did not find a strait to the interior, the alleged home of fabulously wealthy native civilizations. It did succeed in exploring more than 1,000 miles of coastline and went a long way toward proving, once and for all, that Asia and the Americas were separate continents. The expedition also established a Spanish claim to the West Coast, providing a legal basis for the continued exploration and eventual colonization of the region for the Spanish.

Matthew Jennings

See also: California; Exploration; Spanish Colonies on Mainland North America (Chronology).

Bibliography

Kelsey, Harry. *Juan Rodríguez Cabrillo.* San Marino, CA: The Huntington Library, 1986.

Morison, Samuel Eliot. *The European Discovery of America: The Southern Voyages, A.D. 1492–1616.* New York: Oxford University Press, 1974.

Weber, David J. *The Spanish Frontier in North America.* New Haven, CT: Yale University Press, 1992.

California

The earliest settlement of California dates back at least 12,000 years. By 9000 B.C.E., evidence suggests that the indigenous peoples began to transition from a nomadic hunting-gathering culture to a more settled tribal culture. Without the introduction of the horse, which so dramatically altered the lifestyle of the Great Plains tribes, California's various tribes remained more isolated from one another. Warfare was impractical and less common.

California's varied topography also affected culture contact, but ample food supplies, including the acorn, made life reasonably healthy and comfortable. For these reasons, California's native population grew to equal 13 percent of all indigenous peoples in North America, and, by the eighteenth century, they numbered 300,000 with more than 135 distinct dialects.

European exploration of California predates the colonial settlements of the eastern seaboard, including Jamestown. Fueled by the desire to locate a Northwest Passage leading directly to the East Indies and the Far East, as well as legendary cities of gold, European explorers headed west across the Atlantic Ocean, then across Mexico or around Cape Horn. Even the name California was taken from a mythical island believed to be inhabited by Amazons.

The greatest exploration was accomplished by Spain. The earliest Spanish settlements grew up around the Caribbean and in Mexico; however, more than 200 years would pass before Spanish colonies would take hold in California.

In 1542, Juan Cabrillo, a Portuguese explorer sailing for Spain, headed for Upper, or Alta, California. On September 28, 1543, after 103 days at sea, Cabrillo's envoy landed in a harbor he named San Miguel (later renamed San Diego). Although Cabrillo died on San Miguel Island, his crew, led by his pilot Bartolomé Ferrer, would become the first Europeans to explore California and Oregon's coastline. In 1565, Lopez de Legazpi mapped a route from the Philippines to Alta California and down to the coast of Mexico. This exploration led to trans-Pacific trade that would continue for 200 years.

The English privateer Francis Drake—having plundered Spanish ships—sailed up the coast of California in 1579. Not wanting to retrace his steps, he sought a route that would take him through to the North Atlantic. He traveled north as far as the Rogue River, then anchored near present-day San Francisco. He claimed the whole territory for England, and, like Spain, did not acknowledge the Native Americans' right of possession.

Other voyages took Spanish explorers up the California and Oregon coast, but none produced more than a cursory description of the shoreline. Sebastiano Vizcaino's discovery of Monterey Bay, in 1602, was important, but an outpost there would not be established for another 168 years.

The Russians did not reach the Pacific coast until 1639. When they returned home with luxurious furs, they were followed to the Northwest by a stampede of Russian hunters and trappers.

Finally, in 1768, when King Charles III of Spain heard that Russia planned to settle the Pacific North-

San Carlos Borromeo in Monterey, dating to 1770, was the second—and, according to many, the most beautiful—of the original Franciscan missions established in California by Fray Junípero Serra. He was buried there in 1784. *(Mr. Pat Hathaway photo collection, Monterey, California, #89-033-0503)*

west, he called for Spanish occupation of its claimed lands. To accomplish this, the king sent over both soldiers and missionaries. It was the Crown's desire not only to settle the land but to convert and conquer the native peoples living there.

Don Gaspar de Portolá was made the acting military governor of California, and Fray Junípero Serra was chosen to build a series of missions. The first mission was dedicated near San Diego on July 16, 1769. Portolá and sixty of his men set off for Monterey. The journey took nine difficult months, during which Portolá stumbled across another bay far to the north. It was so large that Fray Juan Crespi wrote, "doubtless not only all the navies of our Catholic Monarch, but those of all Europe might lie within the harbor." This bay would later become known as San Francisco.

Meanwhile, the Kumeyaay around San Diego resisted Serra's attempts to convert them. When Portolá returned, he found illness rampant among Serra's men; only twenty of the forty had survived. It was only after a fully provisioned ship, the *San Antonio*, reached them that Portolá decided not to abandon the mission.

In the end, twenty-one missions would be established by Serra, four of which were located around Monterey. These missions adversely affected native life in California. Conversion was rarely voluntary, and diseases devastated the population. After sixty-five years, more than 50 percent of the Native Americans in the region had been eliminated. The mission system would not be abandoned until 1834.

In addition, claims made by Spain, England, and Russia were eventually overturned by American settlement. With the arrival of an American trading vessel, the *Otter*, in 1796, trade with the East Coast began in earnest, and California took a giant step toward Americanization.

Gail L. Jenner

See also: Cabrillo, Juan Rodríguez; Missions; Serra, Fray Junípero; Spanish Colonies on Mainland North America (Chronology).

Bibliography

Gutiérrez, Ramón, and Richard J. Orsi. *California Before the Gold Rush.* Berkeley: University of California Press, 1998.

Kessel, John L. *Spain in the Southwest: A Narrative History of Colonial New Mexico, Arizona, Texas, and California.* Norman: University of Oklahoma Press, 2002.

Calvert, Cecilius (1605–1675)

Cecilius Calvert founded Maryland and served as its first proprietor from 1632 until his death. A convert to Catholicism, he established the first legislation in the English world that guaranteed the right of any Christian to worship freely, without interference from secular authorities.

Calvert was born on August 8, 1605, in Kent County, England, the first son of Sir George Calvert, first Lord Baltimore. He attended Trinity College, Oxford, but left without a degree and converted to Catholicism in 1625. In Britain, Catholicism was outlawed, though followers did not suffer severe persecution. George Calvert, one of the principal secretaries of state and also a Catholic convert, began to establish Catholic colonies in the New World with the permission of the British Crown. While his father traveled to America, Cecilius remained in England to manage the family businesses.

George began the process of obtaining a charter to settle land along Chesapeake Bay, but he died in 1632, just before Charles I granted it. Cecilius then became the second Lord Baltimore and inherited the proprietorship of the province of Maryland. Unlike other settlements, the primary aim of the Maryland patent was to advance the Calvert family fortune through land sales, not to add to the wealth of a group of shareholders.

Although he was the colony's founder, Calvert never visited Maryland. His status as proprietor was under constant threat from political rivals in England who challenged the validity of his charter, and Calvert believed that his time was best spent defending his interests at home. He sent his younger brother, Leonard, in his stead to serve as the colony's first governor. While Calvert had intended Maryland to be a sanctuary for Catholics, his government did not officially support any religious denomination, and religion remained a private matter, not a public one. The charter invested the proprietor with nearly kinglike powers through which he attempted to re-create a little England. Calvert's goal was to give Maryland the economic, social, and political stability that other colonies usually lacked, and thereby ensure its survival and prosperity. His charter enabled him to create a number of manors, self-contained administrative units based on the distribu-

Cecilius Calvert, the second Lord Baltimore, was the official founder and first proprietor of the colony of Maryland. He never set eyes on the colony, however, as he was too busy defending his possession against rivals in England. *(Courtesy of Maryland Department, Enoch Pratt Free Library, Baltimore, Maryland)*

tion of land to parties loyal to him. Despite Calvert's efforts, few settlers of any faith were interested in Maryland. It took him eighteen months to find the first group of 200 immigrants, who left Portsmouth for Maryland in November 1633.

To make matters worse, the English Civil War hampered Calvert's efforts to establish a colony by giving agitators a religious excuse to attack Catholics. Claiming authority from the Protestant Parliament, pirate Richard Ingle plundered Maryland in 1645 and sent the governor fleeing into Virginia. Maryland lay in chaos until December 1646, when Calvert regained control. To prevent this situation from being repeated, Calvert appointed a Protestant governor to replace his now-deceased brother, chose a Protestant Council of

State (which formed the upper house of the Maryland General Assembly), and presented the assembly with a bill for religious tolerance in 1649. Calvert's proposal anticipated the Bill of Rights in its provisions for religious tolerance and constitutes a landmark for its view of the proper purview of religious and political authorities. It prohibited intolerant language, as well as actions. The legislation extended only to Christians, excluding Native American and African religious beliefs. With these measures, Calvert hoped to reduce tensions in the colony, as well as please Protestant authorities in England.

Calvert's success at reducing religious tensions was short-lived. Puritans from Virginia, lured to settle in Maryland by Calvert in 1649, turned against him in a successful armed uprising in 1652. Calvert, a man of formidable political skills, appealed to the government of Oliver Cromwell for assistance. In 1657, he was reinstated as proprietor by Cromwell, in return for which Calvert pardoned his opponents, who then accepted the Act Concerning Religion.

The restoration of Charles II in 1660 brought a more relaxed attitude toward Catholics in England and English America. Calvert's colony finally began to flourish. Blessed by mild weather and good soil, Maryland eventually grew rich with tobacco and slaves. Calvert died on November 30, 1675, near London, England, and left the proprietorship to his eldest son, Charles.

Cecilius Calvert envisioned Maryland as a replica of England, with large manors and a noble class, but additionally with freedom for a religiously pluralistic society. The Maryland that existed upon his death was a province of small tobacco farms dominated by Protestants. Calvert did succeed in establishing a prosperous colony, if not the colony that he had intended to create.

Caryn E. Neumann

See also: Calvert, George (First Lord Baltimore); Catholic Church; Charles I; Maryland; Maryland (Chronology). *Document*: Maryland Toleration Act (1649).

Bibliography

Browne, William Hand. *George Calvert and Cecilius Calvert: Barons Baltimore of Baltimore.* New York: Dodd, Mead, 1890.

Krugler, John D. "Lord Baltimore, Roman Catholics, and Toleration: Religious Policy During the Early Catholic Years, 1632–1649." *Catholic Historical Review* 65 (January 1979): 49–75.

Calvert, George (First Lord Baltimore; c. 1580–1632)

Born about 1580 to a gentry family in Kiplin, Yorkshire, George Calvert was educated at Oxford and sent on a grand tour of Europe to prepare him for a career of service to the British Crown. A friend of Secretary of State Robert Cecil, Calvert became Cecil's personal secretary before being made a clerk of the Privy Council and elected to a seat in the House of Commons in 1609.

Calvert became a trusted friend of James I, valued for his support of the king's pro-Spanish policies and refusal to be drawn into the Thirty Years' War on behalf of the Palatinate, a German principality opposed to the Spanish Crown. James I sent Calvert on several sensitive missions as his representative, including an assignment to negotiate with France and to compile a report on the progress of Protestant settlement in Ireland. Calvert returned to Ireland as a commissioner empowered to hear Irish grievances against the government and English settlers. In recognition for these services, he was knighted in 1617 and given both a 2,000 pound pension from customs revenue in 1620 and a 2,300-acre Irish estate the following year, although Calvert refused the estate unless the king agreed that settlers and tenants could be Roman Catholic, a condition James I conceded.

In 1625, Calvert announced his conversion to Roman Catholicism, a decision that put him on the outside of English power and politics, despite his being raised to the Irish peerage as Baron Baltimore by James I. In order to keep Calvert at court, Charles I offered to waive the obligatory oath of religious allegiance, but Calvert chose to leave and instead pursue his interest in the New World.

An investor in the East India Company and the Virginia Company, Calvert purchased a patent for a colony in Newfoundland for the sum of 25,000 pounds in 1620. The patent gave Calvert distinctly feudal rights to the area, perhaps as a royal rebuke to the self-governing tendencies of Virginia and Massachusetts Bay. To encourage settlement, Calvert and his wife visited the colony, named Avalon, and its port, Fairyland, in 1627. They discovered that the climate and resources were poor and the life of the settlers a subsistence struggle, especially as the French disrupted local cod fishing as an act of war against England.

During his return trip to England, Calvert visited Virginia, where he scouted locations for a better patent, choosing the upper reaches of Chesapeake Bay. Virginians were horrified at the prospect of a Roman Catholic colony as a neighbor and protested vehemently. Charles I, however, granted the patent, naming the new land Terra Maria after his Catholic queen, Henrietta Maria, as well as for the Virgin Mary. The royal patent defined the boundaries of the 6,769,290-acre grant as along the 40th parallel from the Atlantic Ocean to the first fountain of the Potomac River, south to the Chesapeake Bay, then east to the Atlantic Ocean, a vague enough construction to busy lawyers for a generation.

The patent gave Calvert the same palatinate powers he enjoyed in Newfoundland, setting Maryland apart from other colonies and making the Calverts lords proprietor. Calvert never enjoyed this dignity himself, as he died on April 6, 1632, shortly before the patent formally passed the royal seals.

Margaret Sankey

See also: Calvert, Cecilius; Catholic Church; Charles I; Chesapeake; East India Company; James I; Maryland; Maryland (Chronology); Virginia Company. *Document:* Maryland Toleration Act (1649).

Bibliography

Browne, William Hand. *George Calvert and Cecilius Calvert, Barons Baltimore of Baltimore.* New York: Dodd, Mead, 1890.

Codignola, Luca. *The Coldest Harbor of the Land: Simon Stock and Lord Baltimore's Colony in Newfoundland, 1621–1649.* Kingston, Ontario, Canada: McGill-Queen's University Press, 1988.

Foster, James W. *George Calvert: The Early Years.* Baltimore: Maryland Historical Society, 1983.

Calvinism

Calvinism is a set of doctrines and a distinct set of cultural assumptions associated with sixteenth-century Protestant reformer John Calvin. Born in France in 1509, Calvin was educated at the University of Paris, where he studied law and theology and eventually embraced the Protestant faith. Desiring a life of secluded study and contemplation, Calvin was invited to preach in Basel, Switzerland, and eventually settled in Geneva.

Calvin established a theocracy in which God's law was the civil law and the ministry held a decided political, ecclesiastical, and theological influence over the city. Protestant sympathizers from every corner of Europe came to Geneva to study, and the teachings of Calvin spread throughout the Continent during the sixteenth and seventeenth centuries.

Calvin's followers at the Synod of Dort (1618–1619) coined the term "Calvinism." Convened in Holland, this church meeting witnessed intense theological conversation between the followers of Dutch theologian Jacob Arminius, the Arminians (or Remonstrants), and the followers of John Calvin. Arminians believed that human beings were endowed with free will and could respond to or reject God's spiritual overtures. Arminians also maintained that the death of Jesus Christ was sufficient and satisfactory for the salvation of the entire human race. Finally, Arminians held that human beings retain salvation so long as faith and holy practice are sustained. The Calvinists felt that the Arminians overemphasized human effort in matters of salvation and that they therefore placed a premium on God's exhaustive knowledge and ability to instill irrevocable faith. Unlike the Arminians, the Calvinists maintained that human beings were sinful by nature and spiritually unable to respond to God's spiritual prodding. Calvinists believed that God chose a special group for heaven and left the rest to suffer eternal damnation.

The spirit of the Protestant Reformation was born in England with the fourteenth-century reformer John Wycliffe; William Tyndale, who first translated the Bible into English in the sixteenth century; and his contemporary Thomas Cranmer, who authored the Anglican *Book of Common Prayer* and served as archbishop of Canterbury. Calvin's connection to England began with a French-speaking congregation in London and with significant and extended correspondence with the duke of Somerset. This communication was integral to several Calvinists gaining social prominence in England in the sixteenth century, including Martin Bucer, a professor of divinity at Cambridge, and Peter Martyr Vermigli, a professor of divinity at Oxford.

After the reign of Mary I (known as Bloody Mary for her execution of Protestants), Queen Elizabeth's moderate religious position allowed many Calvinists safe return to England. The Geneva Bible became the scripture of choice, and Calvinism was supported at the end of the sixteenth century by another archbishop, John Whitgift. Other major expositors of Calvinism in England were William Perkins and Richard Sibbes, who was instrumental in the conversion of John Cotton, the leading minister in the early days of the colonial Massachusetts settlement. The English Calvinists Thomas Hooker and William Ames also influenced Cotton and other colonial ministers, as did the Westminster Assembly, from which the Calvinistic Westminster Confession of Faith came. These formidable English Calvinistic influences provided the marrow for colonial North American Puritan theology.

Puritans began migrating to North America during the 1620s and 1630s. Led by spiritual leaders such as John Winthrop, the Puritans fashioned a solid Calvinistic foundation for the colonies of New England. Serious in theology and purposeful in morality, the Puritans were noted for spiritual exactitude. The Calvinist outlook of the Puritans placed a premium on God's action in the world and made prodigious use of the intellect in an attempt to understand God's ways. Another key colonial Calvinist was notorious Salem minister Cotton Mather, famous for his role in the witch trials of the 1690s. Notable eighteenth-century Calvinists included Jonathan Edwards and George Whitefield, the major figures of the colonial religious revival known as the Great Awakening. Many of Edwards's sermons, such as "Justification by Faith Alone" (1734–35) and "Sinners in the Hands of an Angry God" (1741), along with his formidable *A Treatise Concerning Religious Affections* (1746), bolstered the Calvinist cause in New England.

Even though Calvinism still claimed notable advocates by the mid-eighteenth century, it had to compete with a plurality of ideas (e.g., Deism) in the growing religious marketplace of colonial America. It eventually succumbed to more voluntarist forms of religious expression.

Phillip L. Sinitiere

See also: Bible; Christ and Christianity; Religion (Chronology); Religion (Essay).

Bibliography

Benedict, Philip. *Christ's Churches Purely Reformed: A Social History of Calvinism.* New Haven, CT: Yale University Press, 2002.

Bouwsam, William J. *John Calvin: A Sixteenth-Century Portrait.* New York: Oxford University Press, 1989.

Calvin, John. *Institutes of the Christian Religion.* Translated by Henry Beveridge. Grand Rapids, MI: Eerdmans, 1997.

Reid, W. Stanford. *John Calvin: His Influence on the Western World.* Grand Rapids, MI: Zondervan, 1982.

Canada

European activity in Canada began in the tenth century, but it was insignificant until the seventeenth century. Vikings from Greenland had probably seen Labrador around 985, but the fragile early-eleventh-century settlements of Leif Ericsson and Thorfinn Karlsefni left no impact, and the Vikings were gone by 1020. The Viking settlements in Greenland and Iceland disappeared, too, and Europe turned away until the voyages of Christopher Columbus brought the New World to its attention.

Following Columbus's voyages to the Caribbean, the Italian-born John Cabot, sailing for England, explored the northern coast in 1497, giving England claim to eastern North America. After that, an occasional European vessel from the fisheries off Nova Scotia and Newfoundland entered the Gulf of St. Lawrence to trade with the natives. European interest was primarily in the south, however, where the Spanish and Portuguese found gold and silver. It was only in 1524 that France formally began exploration, when Giovanni da Verrazano explored the coast from North Carolina to Newfoundland. After Verrazano, France neglected the area for a decade.

Between 1534 and 1541, French explorer Jacques Cartier sailed the St. Lawrence River. Following his final exploration and a failed settlement effort, for the next sixty years, France ignored the colony for all activities but offshore fishing. Then, the beaver hat came into fashion, reviving French interest. The Canadian countryside was rife with beaver, and France established beaver-pelt trading colonies in 1598, 1600, and 1604, but all failed due to disease or native hostility.

Finally, in 1607, Samuel de Champlain, geographer for the last failed colony, relocated the colonists to Quebec, France's first permanent settlement. Champlain's colony struggled while he and his subordinates continued exploring. Étienne Brûlé became the first European to see Lake Superior; Champlain became the first to encounter Lake Champlain. Even as they surveyed the countryside, these explorers were already getting involved in the rivalries of native peoples. While exploring Huronia, Champlain aided the Hurons against the Iroquois, turning the Iroquois against New France.

Government

Champlain became governor of New France in 1633. New France was feudal, with seigneurs, vassals of the king, and habitants, vassals of the seigneur. Agriculture was secondary; colonial wealth was in fur. But New France expanded. New settlements included Trois-Rivières, founded in 1634, and Montreal, established in 1642. A forty-year missionary effort ended in 1648 when the Iroquois dispersed the Huron and killed missionaries serving Huronia. The Iroquois continued to hinder French settlement into the 1690s.

The French government structure divided power between a royal governor and an *intendant*, the latter responsible for finance and justice, but did not clearly delineate the functions of the two positions. The most significant of the *intendants* was Jean Talon, who took office in 1665. He promoted exploration, agriculture, and immigration and took the first census. His census of 1666 showed only 3,215 souls in all of New France, not nearly enough people to match the ten British colonies to the south.

Another important leader in New France was Count Louis de Frontenac, governor from 1672, who established peace with the Iroquois and sponsored the voyages of Louis Jolliet, Father Jacques Marquette, and René-Robert Cavelier, Sieur de La Salle. In 1682, Frontenac and his *intendant* clashed over jurisdiction, leading the king to recall them both. Frontenac returned to the colony in 1689.

In 1674, during Frontenac's governorship, François Xavier de Laval-Montmorency became the first bishop of New France. He established the parish system and Quebec Seminary and encouraged missionary efforts. Meanwhile, the harvesting of furs continued.

Arrival of the English

The English entered the fur trade when they founded the Hudson's Bay Company in 1670. The traders' rivalry matched the two nations' rivalry for the continent. While the English settled from the coast westward, French explorers and trappers used rivers and lakes to penetrate the interior. LaSalle reached the mouth of the Mississippi in 1682, extending New France from the Great Lakes and the Ohio River to the Gulf of Mexico and blocking English expansion.

Competition in Europe and America flared into violence periodically. England and France fought four

Britain's stake in Canada dates to May 2, 1670, when King Charles II granted a charter to the Hudson's Bay Company for "sole trade and commerce" (chiefly in furs) and ownership of "all lands and territories" drained by the waters that flowed into Hudson Bay. *(Hudson's Bay Company, Canada/Bridgeman Art Library)*

wars from 1690 through 1763. After Queen Anne's War, France lost Hudson Bay, Newfoundland, and Acadia but kept Cape Breton Island and the inland areas. In 1713, the French established Fortress Louisbourg on Cape Breton Island to protect the St. Lawrence entry to the empire—and to prey on English shipping. The English took Louisbourg in 1745, but three years later, the Treaty of Aix-la-Chapelle, which ended the War of Austrian Sucession, returned it to France, forcing the English to settle 2,500 colonists at Halifax as a counter. The final war, the French and Indian War (known as the Seven Years' War in Europe), ended the existence of New France, shifting 60,000 Francophones to British rule in 1763.

The British inherited the forts around the Great Lakes. Native Americans, including the Ottawa chief Pontiac, recognized that permanent English settlers were more of a menace than were transient *couriers du bois* (French trappers and explorers). Pontiac's confederation forced the English out of all forts west of Lake Erie except Detroit in 1763. The English finally bested Pontiac's forces in 1764, forcing the native leader to sign a peace treaty with the British in 1766.

Within a few years of taking control of Quebec, England moved to establish administrative control with new acts and laws. In 1774, England's Quebec Act set the colony's boundary at the Ohio River Valley, established British criminal law, and recognized the Roman Catholic Church and French civil law, but it provided no elected assembly.

Within a year, England's rebellious Atlantic colonies, most notably, those of New England and the mid-Atlantic region, attempted to capture Quebec from the British. They took Montreal and then laid siege to the city of Quebec but retreated when a British fleet arrived. At that point, the colonies were engaged in a broader conflict, the American Revolution. Canada remained loyal to England, not achieving its independence until 1867.

John H. Barnhill

See also: Acadia, Nova Scotia; Acadians; Cabot, John; Cartier, Jacques; Champlain, Samuel de; French; French and Indian War; French Colonies on Mainland North America (Chronology); Furs; Great Lakes; Hudson, Henry; Huguenots; Huron; La Salle, René Robert Cavelier, Sieur de; Montreal; Newfoundland; Northwest Passage; Ottawa; Quebec Act (1774); Quebec City; St. Lawrence River. *Documents:* John Cabot's Discovery of North America (1497); The French and the Fur Trade (1724); Evangeline, A Tale of Acadie (in 1755; pub. 1847).

Bibliography

Belton, Robert J. "Important Moments in Canadian History." http://www.arts.ouc.bc.ca/fiar/his_home.html.

Eccles, W. J. *The Canadian Frontier, 1534–1760.* Albuquerque: University of New Mexico Press, 1974.

Hudson's Bay Company. "A Brief History of the Hudson's Bay Company." http://www.gov.mb.ca/chc/archives/hbca/about/the_bay.html.

———. "Historic HBC," http://www.hbc.com/hbc/e_hi/historic_hbc/earlyyears.htm.

Leeck, Beverly. "Oh Canada!" http://www.ualberta.ca/bleeck/
canada/canhist.html.

Morgan, Ted. *Wilderness at Dawn: The Settling of the North
American Continent*. New York: Simon and Schuster, 1994.

Raddall, Thomas Head. *The Path of Destiny: Canada from the
British Conquest to Home Rule, 1763–1850*. New York: Popular Library, 1957.

Canary Islands

Named not after the little yellow birds but after the huge dogs that inhabited the islands ("Canis" in Latin means dog), the Canary Islands, an archipelago of seven volcanic islands, lie off the northwest coast of Africa, approximately 60 miles from Morocco. Like other island groups in the Atlantic, the Canary Islands served as the backdrop for early European attempts at colonization. Unlike the Azores and Madeira, however, the Canaries were inhabited when Europeans rediscovered them in the fourteenth century. The patterns established by Castilians and others in dealing with Canary Islanders would shape colonization in the Caribbean and elsewhere in the Americas.

The Canary Islands were known to the ancient Romans and Phoenicians. The islands also may have been known as the "Fortunate Isles" by later Europeans, although that term also could describe any number of real or imaginary islands. The Canaries were rediscovered by sailors from Genoa, Catalan, and Mallorca in the first half of the 1300s and then explored and colonized by French, Portuguese, and Castilian forces throughout the fifteenth century.

At the time of rediscovery, the islands were already inhabited by people—similar, ethnically, to the Berbers—who had migrated from North Africa, bringing their domesticated goats, sheep, pigs, and dogs, along with the staples of wheat and barley. Over several centuries, the people known as Guanches had developed hierarchical societies with distinct ceramic traditions, religious beliefs, and worldviews. On the largest island, Gran Canaria, Guanche society was particularly complex, and chiefs maintained power by distributing food stored in communal silos.

During the early stages of Europe's expansion—sometimes referred to as the Age of Discovery—Mallorcans and Catalans began to Christianize and trade with inhabitants of the Canary Islands. In 1402, Enrique III of Castile granted Jean de Bétancourt, a Norman lord, permission to conquer the islands. Within a few years, the Norman venture had succeeded in taking control of the smallest, most sparsely populated, and least productive of the Canaries. By the 1430s, Spanish slave raiders and gold seekers also had come into contact with the Guanches.

After Castile and Aragon were joined by the marriage of King Ferdinand and Queen Isabella in 1469, Spain sent better equipped and organized forces to try to take the larger Canary Islands, with the goal of enslaving the Guanches and forcing them to labor on profitable sugar plantations. The Spanish suffered heavy losses during their campaigns against the islanders, but, by 1496, they had succeeded in conquering Tenerife, the last of the Canaries to fall.

The tactics and strategies employed by Guanches and Spaniards shared many characteristics with those used in the conquest and exploration of the Americas. Tribal societies tried to avoid pitched battles and attempted to wear down Spanish forces instead. The Spanish relied on the advantage of swords, crossbows, and horses whenever they could. They also identified the tribal divisions between native communities at an early date and exploited these to their benefit. Many Guanches died as a result of conflict with the Spanish, and those who survived were forced to serve their conquerors as slaves.

After the conquest of the Canary Islands was complete, Genoese and Spanish merchants set up sugar plantations. Sugar was a driving force behind the colonization of many of the Atlantic islands, especially those with a tropical or semitropical climate. As new, more profitable sugar operations popped up in the Caribbean, the Canaries became marginal to Spanish colonization.

One lasting effect of the conquest of the Canaries was that, after attempting a mercantile approach to colonization, the Spanish turned to the "full settlement" model. In the future, they would conquer areas as completely as possible and then send settlers in an effort to recreate Spanish institutions.

The Canary Islands remain a possession of Spain, but they maintain their own parliaments and regional governments. The islands' ideal climate led to their emergence as a popular tourist destination in the twentieth century.

Matthew Jennings

See also: Atlantic Ocean; Columbus, Christopher; Exploration; Slave Trade; Sugar.

Bibliography

Aznar Vallejo, Eduardo. "The Conquests of the Canary Islands." In *Implicit Understandings: Observing, Reporting, and Reflecting on the Encounters Between Europeans and Other Peoples in the Early Modern Era*, edited by Stuart B. Schwartz. Cambridge, UK: Cambridge University Press, 1994.

Fernández-Armesto, Felipe. *Before Columbus: Exploration and Colonization from the Mediterranean to the Atlantic, 1229–1492.* Philadelphia: University of Pennsylvania Press, 1987.

Kicza, John E. "Patterns in Early Spanish Overseas Expansion." *William and Mary Quarterly* 49:2 (April 1992): 229–253.

Cape Cod

Cape Cod is a sandy peninsula in Massachusetts, which hooks into the Atlantic Ocean. Settled originally by the Wampanoag, the cape attracted many European explorers because of its exposed location. The Norse, French, and English visited the region, but only the Pilgrims established a permanent settlement, stepping off the *Mayflower* onto the tip of lower Cape Cod in 1620. The area briefly supported agriculture, but it is best known for its shipbuilding, ship supplying, fishing, and whaling industries.

The colonial history of Cape Cod begins around 1000 C.E., when Norsemen are thought to have sailed to the area in search of good cod fishing. Other fishing peoples may have also visited the cape, but they left no records. In 1524, Giovanni da Verrazano, an Italian commissioned by the French government, sailed up the coast of North America in search of a westward route to China. He discovered the cape, named it Pallavisino after an Italian general, and returned to France. In 1602, Bartholomew Gosnold sailed down the coast of New England in search of a passage to Asia and sassafras, a tree with a bark that was in heavy demand as a suspected cure for syphilis. Gosnold found abundant supplies of sassafras on Pallavisino and then changed the peninsula's name to Cape Cod in honor of the many cod in its waters. A French explorer, Samuel de Champlain, next visited the cape in 1606. Champlain's brief stay on the peninsula is notable only for his fight with the Wampanoag over a kettle that left seven French and an undetermined number of Native Americans dead. After this incident, the French never returned to Cape Cod. Meanwhile, Englishman John Smith had learned of Gosnold's discoveries, and on a 1614 voyage he charted the coastline along Cape Cod. Smith publicized his map, which prompted the Pilgrims to seek a land grant, ostensibly to profit from the cod to be found in the new country but also to escape religious persecution.

The practice of kidnapping Native Americans into slavery led the Wampanoag to be suspicious of European motives and likely prompted them to initially treat the Pilgrims as enemies. Thomas Hunt, one of several captains known to have enslaved Cape Cod natives, had led a 1614 kidnapping in the future area of Plymouth that claimed a number of Wampanoags, including Squanto, a member of the Patuxet group. When Squanto returned to the cape in 1618, the European diseases that decimated the Wampanoag had already wiped out his village. Eight of the Cape Cod villages identified by John Smith had vanished by the time of the arrival of the Pilgrims at Provincetown. Finding the land at Provincetown to be too sandy to support settlements, the Pilgrims moved across the bay to Plymouth. Instead of a wilderness, they found cleared land ready for planting, villages with small homes, and the remains of many Cape Cod Native Americans. The forested areas of the cape, which created a screen for the villages by extending down to the shoreline, were filled with beeches, several types of oaks, hickories, black and yellow birches, red and white cedars, and pitch pines.

Although the waters around Cape Cod swirled with marine life, the English were slow to benefit from these riches. The Pilgrims disliked clams, declined to eat the abundant supplies of mussels, and only devoured lobsters to avoid starvation. Not especially adept at catching cod, they abandoned attempts at commercial fishing by 1626 to concentrate on fur trading and agriculture. Salt hay from the marshes was used to feed cattle and horses, but forest removal and soil depletion eventually caused farm yields to drop dramatically. When the supply of beaver and otter furs became exhausted by 1688, the Cape Codders were forced to turn to the sea.

In an imitation of the Wampanoag whaling approach, the first English whaling efforts were limited to butchering the giants that beached themselves on the cape. By 1700, almost everyone was involved in whaling. Rather than venturing out for long journeys, the English posted lookouts along the beach and rowed out in an attempt to herd passing whales into the surf. By the middle part of the eighteenth century, whaling had evolved to harpooning passing animals and towing them back to shore. The peak year for shore whaling was 1726, when eighty-six whales were killed. When the whales stopped coming so close to Cape Cod, the whalers simply went on longer journeys to find them.

By 1776, life on Cape Cod revolved almost entirely around the sea. This pattern would continue into the twentieth century.

Caryn E. Neumann

See also: Fish and Fisheries; Massachusetts; Massachusetts (Chronology); Massachusetts Bay Colony; Massasoit; Pilgrims; Squanto.

Bibliography

Kittredge, Henry C. *Cape Cod: Its People and Their History.* Boston: Houghton Mifflin, 1968.

Schneider, Paul. *The Enduring Shore: A History of Cape Cod, Martha's Vineyard, and Nantucket.* New York: Henry Holt, 2000.

Captivity (by Native Americans)

Though the risk of being captured by Native Americans was small when one considers the entire North American continent and the whole period before 1776, it weighed heavily on the minds of white people throughout the colonial era. Among the English, captivity narratives became wildly popular. Puritans in particular used the genre to point out the problems in New England society and suggest a course for improvement.

Capture by Native Americans was not specific to colonial New England, however. John Smith was captured by Powhatan's forces outside of Jamestown. Father Isaac Jogues, a Jesuit missionary, was taken by a Mohawk raiding party near Montreal in 1642; after a brief return to France, he traveled with the Mohawks for four years before being accused of sorcery and put to death in 1646. In the 1520s and 1530s, Álvar Núñez Cabeza de Vaca, treasurer of the ill-fated Narváez expedition, traveled overland from Florida to Mexico as a prisoner of various tribes and later on his own.

Historians and anthropologists have mined the Eurocentric accounts left behind for clues about Native American life and race relations in colonial North America. June Namias, a leading authority on the narratives, writes that "scholars have studied captivity from four perspectives: imperial, cultural, ethnohistorical, and gender-based."

Capture was not a new addition to Native American warfare during the colonial period. For centuries, Native Americans in the Northeast and South-west took captives during war. Among the Iroquois in particular, captives were usually forced to endure torture (in the form of the gauntlet) before being adopted into a village. Women, often the motivating force behind the mourning war, or war of revenge, played a crucial role in whether enemy captives were executed, tortured, or adopted.

Adoption and ransom seem to have been the main reasons Native Americans took captives. Among the Aztecs of central Mexico, however, war captives were used as slaves and religious sacrifices. This practice angered tributary peoples to the point that when Hernando Cortéz arrived in the 1510s, he had a steady supply of allies in his conquest of the Aztec empire. North of the Rio Grande, adoption, not slavery or sacrifice, was much more common, and by the close of the colonial period, Native American communities were ethnically diverse, and many contained refugees from colonial conflicts and both Native American and non–Native American adoptees.

Apart from adoption, ransom, and sacrifice, Native Americans employed capture because of the psychological terror that it inflicted on an enemy. The fantastic popularity of captivity narratives throughout the eighteenth and nineteenth centuries, coupled with the increasing fictionalization and sensationalizing of the genre, inflicted precisely that type of terror.

In the colonial period of American history, the experience of being a captive or captor was not limited by race or gender. Early European explorers often took captives back to Europe for display and to train them as interpreters. Millions of captured Africans were forced into labor throughout the Americas. The Spanish, French, and English also took each other captive as they battled for control of the Americas. Of all of these various experiences, the one that had the most profound effect on colonial America was the capture of white men and women by Native Americans.

John Smith's narrative of his capture and adoption into Powhatan culture is the earliest English example of the genre of the captivity narrative, though it differs from most accounts because Smith was not a Puritan and described his ordeal in a strikingly plain way. In December 1607, Smith was taken by a Powhatan raiding party near the Chickahominy River. For nearly a month, Smith was escorted around Powhatan country. He participated in a number of complicated rituals that he did not understand very well. His life was threatened three times, and he was denied food for long stretches, but he was also the guest of honor at a number of feasts.

Generations of people, many in recent years be-

Women were the writers and subjects of a number of captivity narratives, whose purpose was often to arouse anti–Native American sentiment. A few were even fictitious, including this account of the 1814 capture of Mary Smith and her daughters in Florida. *(Library of Congress, LC-DIG-ppmsca-02973)*

cause of the popular Disney film, know that Smith was saved by Pocahontas, the daughter of a chief named Powhatan. The debate over whether this event actually happened and, if so, why it happened has taken on a life of its own. Some suggest that Pocahontas fell in love with Smith and therefore risked her neck to save his; other scholars believe that Smith fictionalized the account as a particularly English manner of claiming authority over Virginia. The most viable interpretation is that Smith and Pocahontas were the leading players in a complex adoption drama. Through the ritual rescue, Powhatan felt that he had adopted Smith and hoped to cement peaceful relations with the Virginia colony. Smith returned to Jamestown in early 1608, walking over 100 miles to make it back.

Colonial New England was far and away the largest producer and consumer of captivity narratives; it also seems to have been the site of the most actual captivities. One estimate places the number of white captives taken between 1675 and 1763 at 1,641. Although there had been white captives in the region before 1675, Mary White Rowlandson's *The Soveraignty and Goodness of God, Together with the Faithfulness of His Promises Displayed*, the first captivity narrative, was not published until 1682. Interestingly, Rowlandson's captivity narrative was also the first North American publication by a living woman.

In 1675, Rowlandson was captured at Lancaster, Massachusetts, during the conflict known as Metacom's (King Philip's) War, a devastating struggle between the Wampanoag, Nipmuc, and Narragansett on one side and the New England colonies and their Native American allies, chiefly Mohawks, on the other. The two sides had coexisted peacefully for decades, but renewed English expansion and Native American grievances sparked violence. Rowlandson, the wife of a Puritan minister, traveled during her thirteen-week captivity. She met King Philip, Quinnapin, and Weetamoo, all three of whom were Wampanoag sachems. Tellingly, Rowlandson did not get along with Weetamoo, the female sachem, perhaps because Weetamoo did not show her the respect she received from Puritan women or because Rowlandson was not accustomed to seeing a woman in a position of political authority. Rowlandson survived her ordeal because she learned to live like a native. Her narrative enlightened readers about the native world of southeastern New England, but it also served an important social function. Rowlandson put a spiritual spin on her captivity. Her capture was Puritan New England's capture; her redemption was Puritan New England's redemption. Divine providence had brought the wrath of the region's native peoples down upon the English, and divine providence had allowed the English to triumph over their native foes.

Most disturbing of all to white Americans were the captives who chose to remain "unredeemed," giving up white society entirely and permanently in favor of Native American lifeways. As Hector de Crèvecoeur put it, "thousands of Europeans are Indians, and we have no examples of even one of those Aborigines having from choice become Europeans." Perhaps the two most famous examples of this type of captivity are Eunice Williams and Mary Jemison. Eunice Williams was the daughter of John Williams, a Puritan minister. John and his five children were taken captive in a 1704 raid by French and Native American warriors at Deerfield, Massachusetts. John Williams was released and wrote his story in a popular narrative titled *The Redeemed Captive Returning to Zion.* Eunice Williams, however, remained "unredeemed." Her family's horror multiplied tenfold when, years later, she chose to become a Catholic and took a Mohawk husband. There were few greater sins in Puritan New England.

Eunice's story is not unique. Women and children were often adopted into their captors' communities. Mary Jemison was captured in 1758 during the French and Indian War in southwestern Pennsylvania. Like Eunice Williams, Jemison remained in Native American society. She married a Seneca man and refused to move back with the English.

Captivity narratives usually cast Native Americans as "savage" aggressors and whites, particularly women, as helpless victims. As such, they held massive appeal for Anglo-Americans who already disliked Native Americans. Not all women were passive victims, though. Hannah Dustin, captured in 1697, escaped by killing ten of her twelve captors with a hatchet, and she was widely celebrated.

The genre of the captivity narrative has had an impact on American culture stretching far beyond the colonial period. Books such as *Last of the Mohicans* and films such as *Dances with Wolves* continue to offer Americans romanticized visions of Native American captivity.

Matthew Jennings

See also: Native American–European Conflict; Native American–European Relations; Rowlandson, Mary. *Document*: Captivity Narrative of Mary Jemison in the 1750s (pub. 1824).

Bibliography

Axtell, James. "The White Indians." In *The Invasion Within: The Contest of Cultures in Colonial North America.* New York: Oxford University Press, 1985.

Demos, John. *The Unredeemed Captive: A Family Story From Early America.* New York: Vintage Books, 1994.

Gleach, Frederic W. *Powhatan's World and Colonial Virginia: A Conflict of Cultures.* Lincoln: University of Nebraska Press, 1997.

Namias, June. *White Captives: Gender and Ethnicity on the American Frontier.* Chapel Hill: University of North Carolina Press, 1993.

Rowlandson, Mary. *The Soveraignty and Goodness of God.* Edited with an introduction by Neal Salisbury. Boston: Bedford, 1997.

Carib

The Carib or Caribe are one of the least understood and most vilified of the Amerindian peoples. Known variously as Kalina, Kalinago, and Galibi in pre-Columbian times, they originated in the Orinoco River delta of northern South America. Scholars estimate that as many as 100,000 Caribs dwelled in this region at the time of European contact.

Their descendants colonized the eastern Caribbean about a century prior to the arrival of the Europeans, gradually displacing or blending with its previous inhabitants. Population counts in the Lesser Antilles during the European encounter range wildly, from a low of 1,000 to a high of 30,000. Accomplished seafarers, the island Carib fashioned what the historian Philip P. Boucher calls a "commuter economy," harvesting widely scattered natural resources by combining fishing, hunting, gathering, farming, and bartering.

Allegations that they practiced ritual cannibalism, though rarely documented, first appeared in the navigational logs of Christopher Columbus. The Taino, native inhabitants of the Greater Antilles, reputedly depicted the people of Canima or Caniba, located just east of Puerto Rico, as flesh-eating, one-eyed men with snout-shaped noses. A Spanish party reconnoitering the area retrieved four or five human bones and rescued several Taino captives from the island of Guadeloupe. Unaware that the native people may have saved the bones of dead relatives, expedition physician Diego Alvarez Chanca took the findings as proof that the Carib were anthropophagi.

Since then, European explorers, missionaries, colonizers, and chroniclers have customarily portrayed the Carib as a belligerent people, infidels, heretics, sodomites, savages, and cannibals. Worse yet, they frequently misidentified as Caribs unrelated Amerindians who fiercely resisted conversion to Christianity and/or European forays into their territories. For instance, Pietro Martire d'Anghiera (Peter Martyr) attributed the death of Juan Díaz de Solís during his 1516 expedition to the River Plate region (an area occupied today by Uruguay, Paraguay, and Argentina) to the "ominous" and anthropophagic Caribs. Early negative reports had already persuaded the Spanish Crown to authorize the enslavement of the Carib "cannibals." In 1515, Juan Ponce de León led a military offensive against their eastern Caribbean strongholds.

Other slaving and punitive campaigns targeted the native peoples in the so-called Wild Coast of South America. As could be expected, the Carib retaliated against these depredations by repeatedly attacking Spanish settlements in the circum-Caribbean area or by entering into military alliances with rival European colonial powers.

Modern-day scholars critical of European imperial motives question the Columbian characterization of the Carib as cannibalistic savages. They point out that these epithets are based overwhelmingly on self-serving European accounts of the European invasion. They hinged on weak circumstantial evidence (the discovery of bones, the "disappearance" of Europeans on Carib territories) rather than on the testimonies of reliable eyewitnesses. Others maintain that early European narratives of the New World contain similar impressionistic, unsubstantiated tales of Amazon women, Patagonian giants, and mermaids.

Although the Spaniards feared and despised the Carib, after about 1600, their attention shifted from the Caribbean to the mainland mineral enclaves of Mexico and Peru. The gradual colonization of the Lesser Antilles and the Guyana-Suriname littoral by Spain's European rivals thereafter altered the course of Carib-European relations. At first, the new European intruders focused their efforts in the profitable business of capturing Spanish treasure ships, plundering the Spanish American colonies, and challenging Spain's commercial monopoly. The transformation of the Lesser Antilles into slave-based plantation economies after about 1650 brought Europeans once again into direct conflict with the Carib. Settlers pushed out from islands that had undergone the sugar revolution, such as Barbados, searching for greener pastures in those occupied or claimed by the Carib. At the same time, growing numbers of Africans brought in chains to toil on the plantations sought shelter on Amerindian soil. By about 1700, marronage or permanent flight from slavery

contributed to the emergence of powerful Black Carib bands, especially on the islands of St. Vincent and Dominica. Both Red and Black Caribs exploited inter-imperial rivalries to their advantage, thwarting repeated invasions by European slave catchers and colonizers.

Eventually, the destruction of their ecological base of survival, warfare, and European and African diseases took a heavy toll on the already weakened Carib peoples. Just over 4,000 Black Carib holdouts in St. Vincent surrendered to the British in 1796 and were deported the following year to the island of Roatan, off the coast of Honduras. Half of them died while interned or en route to Central America, where their descendants are known today as the Garifuna. Likewise, their counterparts in the Venezuela-Guyana Essequibo area had lost considerable power at the hands of the Spaniards, French, and Dutch by the start of the nineteenth century.

Jorge L. Chinea

See also: Caribbean (Chronology); Columbus, Christopher; Native Americans; Taino.

Bibliography

Boucher, Philip P. *Cannibal Encounters: Europeans and Island Caribs, 1492–1763.* Baltimore: Johns Hopkins University Press, 1992.

Hulme, Peter, and Neil L. Whitehead, eds. *Wild Majesty: Encounters with Caribs from Columbus to the Present Day: An Anthology.* Oxford, UK: Clarendon, 1992.

Whitehead, Neil L. *Lords of the Tiger Spirit: A History of the Caribs in Colonial Venezuela and Guyana, 1498–1820.* Dordrecht, Holland: Foris, 1988.

Caribbean Sea

The islands of the Caribbean Sea or Antilles, originally known by Europeans as the West Indies, were the proving and provisioning grounds for the Spaniards' conquest and settlement of the Americas. They were key to the famous "triangle trade" between North America, the Caribbean, and Africa that thrived throughout the American colonial era.

Created millions of years ago by volcanic action and continental plate uplift, the islands of the Caribbean Sea form an arc that sweeps east from the Florida and Yucatán peninsulas to the Virgin Islands and then dips south to the Venezuelan coast. The largest of the islands

The islands of the Caribbean, seen here in a 1650 map, were the proving ground and strategic base of the Spanish colonial empire in the Americas. *(Royal Geographical Society, London, United Kingdom/Bridgeman Art Library)*

is Cuba, followed by Hispaniola, Puerto Rico, and Jamaica—these, together with the Bahamas, Turks, and Caicos, are the Greater Antilles. The Lesser Antilles comprise the Windward Islands (which face the Atlantic) and the Leewards (which face the Caribbean), all of which lie between Puerto Rico and northern South America.

The ancestors of the native peoples whom Christopher Columbus met in the Caribbean in 1492 began to canoe down the island arc from the Yucatán about 7,000 years ago; we call them Ciboney or Guanahatabey. Other indigenous groups canoed up from the Orinoco and Amazon River valleys in various waves. By 950 C.E. they had merged to become the Taino. Later immigrant groups from the same Orinoco and Amazon regions are known as Carib, and they gave the sea and the region their name. The Carib were the most feared of the region's indigenous peoples because it was rumored that they were cannibals; however, archaeological studies reveal that while the Carib may have ritually

consumed parts of their conquered enemies, human meat did not form part of their daily diet.

It was on Hispaniola, the island presently shared by the Dominican Republic and Haiti, that the patterns for Spanish conquest and settlement of the rest of the Americas were formed. The native peoples of the island (Taino) were forced to work in exchange for being taught Christine doctrine and lifestyle, African slaves were brought in to replace the declining indigenous laborers in the mines and plantations (the Native Americans had no immunity to the diseases that Europeans, Africans, and Asians had exchanged for millennia along with commercial goods), and all three groups of people—Native Americans, Africans, and Europeans—began to intermix culturally and biologically.

By 1509, the Spaniards had also colonized Cuba, Jamaica, and Puerto Rico and had begun to seek pearls in the waters of the Lesser Antilles. When they discovered the densely populated lands of the Aztec, Maya, and Inca, rich with deposits of silver and gold, however, the Caribbean islands became the jumping-off points where Spaniards gathered seasoned men and supplies to outfit their mainland expeditions.

Wars among the European nations spilled over into the Caribbean. Protestant nations such as the Netherlands and England, and even Catholic nations such as France, disputed the pope's right to divide the Americas between Spain and Portugal. Corsairs, privateers with backing from Spain's European enemies, began attacking Spanish ships and settlements in the Caribbean as early as the 1520s. Among the most famous were the Frenchman Jean D'Ango's seizure of two Spanish galleons laden with Aztec gold and other valuables that Hernando Cortéz sent to the Spanish Crown in 1523, and the Englishman Francis Drake's sacking of Santo Domingo in 1586.

By the end of the sixteenth century, it was clear that Spain could not hold on to its islands in the Caribbean. One by one, Jamaica and the islands of the Lesser Antilles fell to the English, French, Dutch, and eventually even the Danes, for they were valuable tobacco and sugarcane lands. With the spread of sugar came a dramatic increase in the number of African slaves brought to the Caribbean to work the plantations and mills.

Sugar and slaves connected Britain's Caribbean colonies to its colonies on the North American coast. The North Americans engaged in small manufacturing, shipbuilding, and trade. They traded manufactured goods from England and basic supplies from North America to the sugar planters of the Caribbean, for which they received tropical products and molasses to make rum. The rum was traded into Africa for more slaves. This was the famous "triangle trade" that connected the European, American, and African continents.

The Caribbean was also the birthplace of the abolition of slavery. Enlightenment philosophies of liberty, equality, and brotherhood were first put into practice in what became the United States and France—and then they spilled over into French Saint-Domingue (present-day Haiti). There, in 1804, for the first time, these principles were applied to all people, not just those of European descent.

For a multitude of economic reasons, not just humanistic ones, the British outlawed slavery throughout their Caribbean colonies in 1833, and the law went into effect the following year. Most other nations soon followed suit.

Lynne Guitar

See also: Antigua; Barbados; Caribbean (Chronology); Cuba; Hispaniola; Jamaica; Puerto Rico; Saint-Domingue; St. Kitts; Sint Eustatius; Slavery, Caribbean.

Bibliography

Boucher, Philip P. *Cannibal Encounters: Europeans and Island Caribs, 1492–1763.* Baltimore: Johns Hopkins University Press, 1992.

Claypole, William, and John Robottom. *Caribbean Story.* Vol. 1, *Foundations.* Kingston, Jamaica: Longman Caribbean, 1980–1981.

———. *Caribbean Story.* Vol. 2, *The Inheritors.* Kingston, Jamaica: Longman Caribbean, 1980–1981.

Knight, Franklin W., and Colin A. Palmer. *The Modern Caribbean.* Chapel Hill: University of North Carolina Press, 1989.

Lewis, Gordon K. *Main Currents in Caribbean Thought: The Historical Evolution of Caribbean Society in Its Ideological Aspects, 1492–1900.* Baltimore: Johns Hopkins University Press, 1987.

Carteret, Sir George (d. 1680)

A prominent figure in seventeenth-century English political, naval, commercial, and colonial affairs, Sir George Carteret was a lifelong servant to the Stuart cause and a strong promoter of English imperial aims overseas. Although he was involved in several commercial and colonial ventures, the establishment of Carolina and New Jersey were his primary interests in North America.

Born sometime between 1609 and 1617 in St. Ouen on Jersey, an island in the English Channel, George was the son of a leading landholding family. Joining the navy as a youth, he made lieutenant in 1632 and captain in 1633. In 1639, he was appointed comptroller of the navy. Following the outbreak of the English Civil War in 1642, he established a base at Saint-Malo in France, which supplied arms and munitions to royalist forces in the west of England.

In 1643, George succeeded his deceased uncle, Sir Philip Carteret, as bailiff of Jersey, which had earlier succumbed to parliamentary forces. Later that year, George reconquered the island for the king and was appointed its lieutenant governor. In 1644, he received a royal commission as vice admiral over the region, and from there orchestrated an effective privateering war against English shipping for several years. Under his direction, Jersey's natural resources were fully developed to provide a safe refuge for royalist refugees, including Charles, Prince of Wales (later King Charles II). In recognition of his loyal service to the Crown, Carteret was knighted and made a baronet. Jersey was the last royalist stronghold when Carteret surrendered to British Commonwealth forces in 1651. Exiled to France, he served as vice admiral in the French navy.

Carteret's allegiance to the king was rewarded after the restoration of the Stuarts in 1660. He was appointed a member of several official bodies, including the Privy Council, the Council of Trade, and the Council of Foreign Plantations. In 1661, he was elected a member of Parliament for Portsmouth and was named to the Tangiers committee. Appointed to the post of vice chamberlain of the household later in the decade, Carteret's principal office was as treasurer of the navy from 1661 to 1667. Although credited with protecting the English fleet from the plague raging in the port of London in 1665, Carteret was later accused of gross mismanagement of naval accounts during the Second Dutch War. These charges forced an exchange of offices with Lord Anglesey in 1667, in which Carteret assumed the position of deputy treasurer of Ireland. Despite this setback and his suspension from the House of Commons on a misdemeanor charge in 1669, Carteret was appointed a commissioner of the Admiralty in 1673.

During his tenure in government, Carteret became closely associated with a small, yet considerably influential, group of gentlemen and courtiers dedicated to expanding England's trading and colonial empire. In 1660, he became a member of the Company of Royal Adventurers to Africa, which managed the slave trade to the American plantations. In 1663, he was appointed to a special committee to examine English interests in America, and he recommended that the Dutch be driven out of New Netherland. That same year, he became one of the eight original proprietors of Carolina.

In 1664, James, duke of York, granted Carteret and Lord John Berkeley a tract of land lying between the Hudson and Delaware rivers, likely in return for their assistance in planning the English conquest of New Netherland. Carteret funded the first expedition to establish a settlement of the tract, named New Jersey in honor of his home island, in 1665. The tract was governed by his cousin Captain Philip Carteret. The Quintipartite Deed of 1676 divided the province into East and West New Jersey. The Carteret family governed the former until 1682, when it was sold to a group headed by William Penn.

Carteret was involved in numerous other ventures.

By 1664, he had acquired stock in the Royal Fishing Company of Great Britain and Ireland. The following year, he met with French fur traders intent on developing the fur trade in the north part of America and was instrumental in laying the groundwork for the eventual establishment of the Hudson's Bay Company in 1670. He was also one of the proprietors of the Bahamas grant in 1670 and a leading stockholder of the newly formed Royal African Company in 1672.

Sir George Carteret died in 1680 and was buried at Hawnes (Haynes), Bedfordshire, England. During his lifetime, his capital and connections were vital ingredients in establishing and nurturing various trading companies, as well as the colonies of Carolina and New Jersey, thereby promoting English imperial designs in North America.

Michael F. Dove

See also: Charles II; Fish and Fisheries; Furs.

Bibliography

Ogg, David. *England in the Reign of Charles II*. 2 vols. Oxford, UK: Clarendon, 1955.

Pomfret, J. E. *Colonial New Jersey: A History*. New York: Charles Scribner's Sons, 1973.

Rich, E. E. *The History of the Hudson's Bay Company, 1670–1870*. Vol. 1. London: Hudson's Bay Record Society, 1958.

Cartier, Jacques (1491–1557)

Jacques Cartier was a sixteenth-century French explorer whose name is inextricably linked to the early colonial history of Canada.

Born in 1491, he was the son of Jamet Cartier and Josseline Jansart. He grew up in Saint-Malo, Brittany, France, a seaport that assumed a dominant position in the North Atlantic economy. While little is known about his early life, not even his parents' professions, Cartier's marriage in 1520 to Catherine des Granges, the daughter of the local constable, bears witness to his respectable socioeconomic status at the time.

In 1534, Cartier gained meteoric fame when Francis I, king of France, commissioned him to seek wealth and new territories in the vicinity of Newfoundland. His unofficial goal was to find a passage to Asia. Cartier's experience as a sailor partially explains Francis's

French navigator Jacques Cartier was the first to explore and map the Gulf of St. Lawrence (1534) and the St. Lawrence River (1535), laying the groundwork for a French colonial presence in North America. *(Brown Brothers, Sterling, Pennsylvania)*

choice. Jean Le Veneur de Tellière, an influential ecclesiastic with access to the king, had vouched for Cartier's competence to handle such an enterprise. Indirect documentary evidence suggests that before this voyage, Cartier had sailed to Brazil and Newfoundland.

Cartier left Saint-Malo on April 20, 1534. Barely a month later, he reached the Strait of Belle Isle, between Newfoundland and Labrador, convinced that it led to Asia. Following the corridor, Cartier entered unknowingly into the Gulf of St. Lawrence, which he proceeded to explore. In search of a passage along the shores of present-day New Brunswick and Quebec, Cartier established contacts with Algonquin and Northern Iroquois peoples. Among the latter, he kidnapped two young men, Domagaya and Taignoagny, to assist him in his enterprise.

As Cartier reached the estuary of the St. Lawrence River, deteriorating weather conditions prevented him from exploring the waterway. Fearing that seasonal storms would impede his return to Saint-Malo, Cartier proceeded back to his hometown, which he reached on

September 5, 1534. Even though he had fallen short of his goals, he had claimed the newly explored territories for Francis I and had gathered an impressive array of information about a little-known region.

The following year, Cartier received another royal commission to resume his exploration. He left Saint-Malo on May 19, 1535, accompanied by Domagaya and Taignoagny. With their assistance, he sailed down the St. Lawrence to Stadacona, a Northern Iroquois village near present-day Quebec City. While part of his crew erected a winter camp nearby, Cartier continued upriver to Hochelaga, another Northern Iroquois settlement standing where Montreal is today. Realizing that some rapids blocked the river farther south, Cartier retraced his steps to Stadacona, where he spent the winter.

During this time, the explorer and his crew benefited from the material support of their native hosts, even though, over time, relations between the French and Native Americans began to deteriorate. From the Stadaconans, Cartier learned about the Kingdom of Saguenay and other fabulous lands that abounded with wealth and chimerical creatures. Before sailing back to France on May 6, 1536, Cartier abducted a number of Stadaconans, hoping that they would vouch for the existence of these fabled lands.

Wars in Europe forced Francis I to postpone any ventures overseas, and it was only in 1541 that Cartier was able to return to the St. Lawrence. This time, the king intended to colonize the area, a task he had entrusted to Jean-François de La Rocque de Roberval. On this occasion, Cartier commanded an advance force consisting of 1,500 colonists. Upon arrival in the region, he ordered the building of Charlesbourg-Royal, a settlement located near Stadacona, and explored the area south of Hochelaga.

For unspecified reasons, Cartier returned to France with his contingent of colonists in June 1542, despite Roberval's objections. As a consolation, he had aboard a large cargo of minerals that he wrongly estimated to be gold and diamonds.

This fiasco sealed the fate of Cartier's notoriety with the king. After 1542, the explorer sank into historical obscurity, even though he continued to be an active and noteworthy inhabitant of Saint-Malo. Cartier died on September 1, 1557.

Despite his royal disgrace, Cartier's influence should not be underestimated. While it is unclear whether Cartier was the first European to explore the St. Lawrence River, it is unquestionable that the earliest European maps of this waterway and its gulf rested on his detailed observations of the region. Furthermore, his three voyages set a historic precedent for further French colonial activities in North America. In the early seventeenth century, the St. Lawrence River Valley became the heart of the French colony in North America and the launching pad for French imperial ventures deep in the continent.

Christophe J. M. Boucher

See also: Canada; Exploration; French; French Colonies on Mainland North America (Chronology); St. Lawrence River.

Bibliography

Bideaux, Michel. *Relations*. Montreal: Presses de l'Université de Montréal, 1986.

Biggar, H. P., ed. *A Collection of Documents Relating to Jacques Cartier and the Sieur de Roberval*. Ottawa: Publications of the Public Archives of Canada, 1930.

———, ed. *The Voyages of Jacques Cartier*. Ottawa: Publications of the Public Archives of Canada, 1924.

Braudel, Fernand, ed. *Le monde de Jacques Cartier: L'aventure au XVIe siècle*. Montreal: Libre Expression, 1984.

Cook, Ramsay, ed. *The Voyages of Jacques Cartier*. Toronto: University of Toronto Press, 1995.

Gagnon, François-Marc, and Denise Pétel. *Hommes effarables et bestes sauvaiges: images du Nouveau-Monde d'après les voyages de Jacques Cartier*. Montreal: Boréel, 1986.

Catholic Church

More than any other nation, the history of America has its origins in the establishment of religious freedom. Many faiths had to struggle, however, to achieve equal access to liberty. Roman Catholicism, the established religion of Western Europe during the medieval period, traveled to the New World with the French and Spanish explorers and fur trappers, but it was soon overshadowed by various Protestant settlements and denominations.

The French came to control an area that stretched from New Orleans to Canada, while the Spanish settled St. Augustine, Florida, the first Catholic colony in America. In addition, the Spanish and French sent Jesuit missionaries to convert Native American tribes. These Jesuits were actually more successful than later Protestant missionaries in converting native populations because they allowed tribes to practice their own traditions.

One Jesuit missionary, Father Isaac Jogues, helped establish a mission for Hurons who were suffering from disease. He was then captured by a band of Mohawks (Iroquois), but, after being kept as a slave for a year, he escaped and returned to France briefly. He returned to take up missionary work with the Mohawks, but was later accused of sorcery, tortured, and killed.

Catholic Maryland

Maryland, named for both the Virgin Mary and Queen Henrietta Maria, was established as a Catholic colony by George Calvert, the first Lord Baltimore, in 1632. The decision to allow Maryland to be settled as a Catholic colony was in part achieved because King Charles I had married a Roman Catholic.

Lord Baltimore was a man devoted to his faith, converting to Catholicism despite the fact that in 1625, Parliament had decreed that Catholics could not aspire to positions of authority. This did not dissuade Lord Baltimore from pursuing the establishment of a colony that protected Catholicism. In fact, he secured the charter in the face of substantial opposition.

Hoping to populate the colony with English Catholics, he granted each of sixty feudal manors 3,000 acres. Though Lord Baltimore died before he could set sail, Cecilius Calvert, the second Lord Baltimore, took up his father's dream. In 1633, the first shipload of Catholic "gentlemen-adventurers" departed London for Maryland. On board the *Ark* and the *Dove* were Leonard Calvert, lieutenant governor and brother to the second Lord Baltimore, and George Calvert, youngest brother to Leonard and Cecilius.

Lord Baltimore was deemed "proprietor of the province of Maryland." As such, he received all profits and had the power to appoint officials. Jealous of sharing authority, he decreed that Jesuit missions could not own land. In 1659, he ordered coins to be struck that bore his likeness on one side, his family's arms and motto on the other: "Increase and multiply." This currency became legal tender throughout Maryland.

Lord Baltimore also extended religious protection to non-Catholics. This staunch belief in the separation of faith and politics was clearly written into Maryland's provisional government's charter, where Catholics and Protestants were instructed to "not give offense" to one another in "matters of religion."

Although there is evidence that a Tolerance Act was passed in Maryland as early as 1635, in 1649, at St.

Mary's City, Maryland's General Assembly enacted a formal Act Concerning Religion. It stated

> . . . no person or persons whatsoever within this province . . . professing to believe in Jesus Christ shall from this day forth be in any ways troubled, molested, or discountenanced for or in respect of his or her religion, nor in the free exercise thereof.

The religious tolerance promulgated in Maryland was an early forerunner of the constitutional principles later established by America's founding fathers.

Another factor unique to Maryland was its constitutional provision—the first of its kind—stating that laws within the province had to be "of and with the advise, assent, and approbation of the free-men of the said Province, or the greater part of them, or of their delegates or deputies." The category of freemen encompassed all adult males not bound by slavery or indenture, and this included Mathias de Sousa, a black man—once indentured—who not only voted but also served in the General Assembly.

Rhode Island was another haven for religious nonconformists for many years. Roger Williams's community of Providence, along with the communities of Portsmouth and Newport, was dedicated to religious tolerance. Under Rhode Island's constitution of 1647, church membership was not a requirement for voting, something almost every other colony demanded. The royal charter of 1663 characterized the smallest American colony as a "ship" with a mixed passenger list of Protestants, Catholics, Jews, and Muslims. Another unique principle included the "notions" of "initiative, referendum, and recall" of officers.

Unfortunately, it was not long before this environment of tolerance within the colonies changed. Lord Baltimore's dream of a safe haven for Catholics turned nightmarish in 1654 when the Protestant majority passed a law keeping Catholics from worshiping according to their traditions. An "insurgent band" marched into Maryland's capital city of St. Mary's and took over the assembly, leaving Lord Baltimore only his property rights. The new capital moved to Protestant Anne Arundel—now known as Annapolis.

Persecutions continued throughout 1655 and 1656. Puritans, aided by Virginians, attacked Catholic colonists in Maryland. Three captives were shot; others, including several priests, surrendered and were imprisoned. They were labeled "imposters," and all of their personal property was either confiscated or destroyed.

Reign of William and Mary

In 1689, after the accession of William and Mary to the English throne, hatred continued to mount against Catholics. In Rhode Island, Catholics were disenfranchised in 1729, and Jews were denied the right to naturalization. Newport later came to represent the center of the thriving slave trade rather than a center for tolerance.

Outside Maryland, the largest population of Catholics settled in and around Philadelphia. But because Catholics numbered only 25,000 in 1776, equaling 1 percent of the colonial population, Rome did not appoint an American Roman Catholic bishop until after the Revolutionary War. In contrast, Congregationalists, Anglicans, and Presbyterians constituted approximately 62 percent of the colonial population. Unchurched slaves accounted for another 22.6 percent.

On the heels of the Revolutionary War, a new wave of anti-Catholicism spread throughout America. Protestant loyalists, fearful of a French alliance because France was a Catholic monarchy, began publishing and distributing anti-Catholic literature. One such piece of

The Reverend John Carroll, a Jesuit priest and founder of Georgetown University, was consecrated as the first Roman Catholic bishop in the United States in 1790. He later became archbishop of Baltimore. *(Brown Brothers, Sterling, Pennsylvania)*

literature—a satirical, fictitious diary—prophesied "horrible events" to come. It appeared in Rivington's *Royal Gazette* on March 19, 1779.

It wasn't until August 15, 1790, that John Carroll, a former Jesuit priest, was consecrated the first Roman Catholic bishop in America by Pope Pius VI. Carroll, who also founded Georgetown University in 1789, became the first archbishop of Baltimore in 1808.

Gail L. Jenner

See also: Bible; Charles V; Christ and Christianity; Dominicans; Franciscans; James II; Jesuits; Mary I; Maryland; Maryland (Chronology); Missions; Religion (Chronology); Religion (Essay). *Document*: Maryland Toleration Act (1649).

Bibliography

Amos, Gary, and Richard Gardner. *Never Before in History: America's Inspired Birth.* Dallas, TX: Haughton, 1998. Bailey, Thomas A., and David M. Kennedy, eds. *The American Spirit: United States History as Seen by Contemporaries.* 8th ed. 2 vols. Lexington, MA: D. C. Heath, 1994.

"Two Acts of Toleration: 1649 and 1826." http://www.md archives.state.md.us/msa/speccol/sc2200/sc2221/000025/html/intro.html.

Cayuga

When they met Europeans for the first time, the Cayuga occupied three large villages in present-day New York State. The Cayuga were (and remain) part of the larger Iroquois Confederacy, which also includes the Oneida, Onondaga, Seneca, Mohawk, and Tuscarora nations. While their main settlements were fairly compact, the Cayuga hunted in territory ranging from Lake Ontario in the north to the Susquehanna River in the south.

The primary unit of Cayuga political life was the village, or town, and each of the three Cayuga towns was home to around 2,000 people. The towns of Iroquois country were the most densely settled places in the Native American or European Northeast until the nineteenth century, with an average population of 200 people per acre. Cayugas lived with their families and other clan members in longhouses. In fact, the Iroquois Confederacy was often conceived as a longhouse, where all five member nations dwelled. Most Iroquois families were matrilineal, meaning that descent was traced through the mother, and matrilocal, in that men often moved into the homes of their wives' mothers.

Between the 1640s and the 1680s, the nations of the Iroquois Confederacy, including the Cayuga, fought continually with their neighbors. Wars broke out over access to European trade goods, and the captives from these wars were often adopted into the Iroquois world as a way of recouping population losses brought on by European diseases. The result of these conflicts was that by the turn of the eighteenth century, the Iroquois had established themselves as the main Native American power brokers in the Northeast and had forced the Huron to scatter into the Great Lakes region. Separate treaties, each of which confirmed Iroquois neutrality, were established in 1701 with the English and the French. In the 1720s, the Cayuga, like the other Iroquois nations, increased their diplomatic power by acting as negotiators between Native American and European worlds. At the same time, they grew increasingly dependent on European trade goods and aware of increasing European military power.

During the early decades of the eighteenth century, the Cayuga succeeded at playing the French and the English off one another to the natives' advantage in terms of trade and diplomacy. They also continued to accept members of defeated tribes into their villages, and Tutelos, Saponis, Nanticokes, and Conoys joined the Iroquois Confederacy in 1753 as nonvoting members under the auspices of the Cayuga.

The French and Indian War pitted the British Empire against the French in an all-out struggle for control of North America. The Iroquois officially remained neutral, but the Cayuga often joined the French and other allied Native American peoples in raiding Anglo-American settlements. The Mohawks, on the other hand, sided with the English as it became increasingly clear that the French would lose. The end of the war brought peace to Iroquois country, but it also took away the option of pitting the English against the French. As a result, Cayuga power was reduced drastically.

After the French vacated Iroquois country in 1763, a new flood of Anglo-American settlers swept over the area. Earlier conflict had erupted when white settlers moved too far up the Susquehanna River, and tensions continued to increase in the region throughout the eighteenth century. In response, when war broke out between Great Britain and its North American colonies in 1776, the Cayuga, like many other Native American groups, sided with the English, hoping that an English victory would slow American expansion. This proved disastrous, as American forces burned the Cayuga heartland in 1779, sending Cayugas as refugees to other tribes.

By 1807, the state of New York had acquired most of the Cayugas' land base. Many Cayugas fled to the Six Nations Reserve in Ontario, Canada, while others moved near present-day Buffalo, New York, and eventually to Kansas, Ohio, and Oklahoma. Part of the Cayugas' current land claim is based on the fact that their treaty was negotiated by the state of New York and the United States Congress never formally ratified the treaties.

Matthew Jennings

See also: French and Indian War; Iroquois Confederacy; Native American–European Conflict; Native American–European Relations; Native Americans.

Bibliography

Becker, Mary Druke. "Cayuga." In *Encyclopedia of North American Indians*, edited by Frederick E. Hoxie. Boston: Houghton Mifflin, 1996.

Richter, Daniel K. *The Ordeal of the Longhouse: The People of the Iroquois League in the Era of European Colonization.* Chapel Hill: University of North Carolina Press, 1992.

Richter, Daniel K., and James Merrell, eds. *Beyond the Covenant Chain: The Iroquois and Their Neighbors in Indian North America, 1600–1800.* Syracuse, NY: Syracuse University Press, 1987.

Champlain, Samuel de (c. 1570–1635)

Samuel de Champlain, a French military officer, is best known for his explorations of North America from Nova Scotia through the Bay of Fundy to New Brunswick and down to Cape Cod. Besides creating charts that aided the westward expansion of Europeans, Champlain established the colonies of Acadia and Quebec. He spent the remainder of his life as the royal governor of New France.

Born about 1570 in Brouage, Saintonge, France, into a seafaring family, Champlain learned navigation, draftsmanship, and cartography as a youth. He served in the army of Henry IV against the Catholic League in the French Wars of Religion until 1598 and then joined a voyage to the West Indies and Mexico. Champlain's popular illustrated account of this trip, *Brief Discours* (1601), helped establish his reputation as an explorer. More than a quarter of the book focused on native plants that were potentially profitable.

In 1603, Champlain began his long association with North America by becoming an observer on François Gravé Du Pont's expedition to the St. Lawrence Valley to trade furs with the Montagnais Indians. His *Des Sauvages* (1603) described the customs of the Native Americans and the region from Tadoussac to Montreal, including an area that Champlain named Acadia. On this trip, Champlain first developed the notion that these lands could be colonized, and he probably brought samples of plants, animals, and minerals back to France to show the wealth of the New World. Once in France, he began to champion the exploration of Acadia and theorized that the area held a route to the Great Lakes that would, in turn, lead to a Northwest Passage to Asia.

Champlain's skills as a naturalist and a mapmaker attracted the notice of the lieutenant general of New France, who invited him to explore and chart the Atlantic Coast from La Have, Nova Scotia, to Martha's Vineyard, off Cape Cod. This expedition, led by Pierre de Monts, lasted from 1604 to 1607 and established a colony in Acadia, which had to return to France when de Monts lost his trading privileges.

Champlain's next journey would lead to the establishment in July 1608 of Quebec on the St. Lawrence River at a point where the waters narrowed enough to ensure that cannons could control passage. Quebec began on behalf of a fur trading company, but the colony would be marred by tragedy due to incomplete medical knowledge about the causes of scurvy and inadequate preparations to treat the disease. Although Champlain knew that a native medicinal remedy had helped save another French expedition, he could not locate the ingredients in time, and scurvy decimated the settlement. Only nine of the twenty-five men at Quebec survived the winter.

Despite this setback, Champlain continued his career as an explorer. The Algonquin and Huron allies of the French allowed him to traverse the interior rivers of Ottawa, Richelieu, and Trent, as well as Georgian Bay, in return for aid against their enemies. Beginning in 1612, Champlain cemented these friendly ties with the Native Americans by sending some of his men to winter with the tribes to learn their languages and customs. In that same year, he was chosen by the French king to govern the new settlement.

Champlain's governorship did not enjoy a resounding success. In 1615, the French joined with the Huron to attack an Iroquois fort. The attack failed, and Champlain was badly wounded. On his return to

France, court politics cost him his position. Determined to regain his post, Champlain submitted a plan to the king to colonize Quebec with 400 families protected by 300 soldiers, to establish agriculture, and to search for the Northwest Passage. In 1620, he became the official commander of Quebec.

In 1627, the king's first minister, Cardinal Richelieu, created the Compagnie de la Nouvelle-France (commonly called the Company of One Hundred Associates) to rule New France and named Champlain as acting governor. The few settlers in New France, however, proved no match for English invaders. After the English conquered the territory and took Champlain prisoner in 1629, he again returned to France. In 1633, following the signing of the Treaty of Saint-Germain-en-Laye, he returned to Quebec once again as governor. Weakened by various infirmities, Champlain died there on December 25, 1635.

Champlain's publications did much to stimulate European interest in the New World. His maps greatly aided navigation by incorporating native geographical knowledge, while his descriptions of potentially profitable minerals, plants, and animals helped spark mercantile interest. His constant promotion of French settlement also makes him one of the founding fathers of Canada.

Caryn E. Neumann

See also: Canada; Exploration; French; French Colonies on Mainland North America (Chronology); Quebec City; St. Lawrence River.

Bibliography

Armstrong, Joe C. W. *Champlain.* Toronto: Macmillan of Canada, 1987.

Charles I (1600–1649)

Born November 19, 1600, in Dunfermline, Scotland, Charles I was the second but eldest surviving son of James I of Great Britain and his wife Anne of Denmark. Becoming heir to the throne in 1612 upon the death of his brother Henry, Charles I was deeply embarrassed by failed marriage negotiations with Spain, and he resented his father's pro-Spanish policies.

Acceding to the throne in 1625, he also inherited his father's last male favorite advisor, George Villiers, the Duke of Buckingham, who became a close friend

and helped to arrange Charles I's marriage that year to Henrietta Maria of France, daughter of Henry IV and Maria d'Medici. The king's marriage to a Catholic was very unpopular, and he was shocked and threatened by the assassination of Buckingham.

Like his father, Charles I relied on private income, rather than on a regular source of parliamentary revenue, and he tried to negotiate a more stable source of financing from the state. The result was the 1629 Petition of Right, a list of demands from Parliament that would curtail royal power, a proposal that Charles I, schooled in the theory of divine right monarchy, angrily refused.

For the next ten years, Charles I ruled without calling Parliament, raising money by combing medieval records for a series of lucrative and obscure royal prerogatives, such as distraint, or forced payment for, knighthood, "ship money" paid by coastal towns, and the sale of monopolies of commodities like soap and imported wine. During these years, the intensely private Charles I avoided public events, preferring to stage elaborate court masques and cultivate collections of European paintings and sculpture.

His personal religion, encouraged by William Laud, whom he created archbishop of Canterbury, was an elaborate form of the Church of England, stressing rituals that Puritan critics in England saw as too close to Roman Catholicism. Meanwhile, Charles I signed charters for a Roman Catholic colony, Maryland (named for Henrietta Maria), to be governed by the Catholic Calvert family, and oversaw the settlement of Bermuda and Barbados, as well as the chartering of the Massachusetts Bay Company. Under Thomas Wentworth, created Earl Stafford, Charles I experimented with a rigorous and heavy-handed policy in Ireland known as "thorough" government.

In 1639, efforts by Charles I and Laud to force a new version of the Church of England prayer book on Presbyterian Scotland triggered a violent political protest by the "Covenanters." Unable to deal with the situation on his own, the king was forced to call Parliament, which refused to grant monies unless their decade of complaints was addressed. Stalling on reform, Charles I faced threats against Laud, the Earl of Stafford, his administrator in Ireland, and even his wife, who was suspected of raising the royal children as Catholics. In 1640, Charles I was forced to sacrifice Stafford to a parliamentary charge of treason; he tried to retaliate by marching on the House of Commons to arrest its leaders. This ill-advised invasion of Parliament sparked off civil war: The king went north to raise his standard at

Nottingham, and Parliament organized its own army to respond.

Although Charles I rallied supporters and carried on a four-year war against parliamentary forces and their Scottish Covenanter allies, he could not match their financial resources or the military strength of the New Model Army, which crushed royal supporters at the Battle of Naseby in 1645. Many Puritans returned from Massachusetts to fight against the king in the Great Civil War. Hoping to drive a wedge between his rebellious kingdoms, he surrendered to the Scots, to whom he promised reform, but they handed him over to the increasingly radical and republican House of Commons. In January 1649, Charles I was tried for treason and sentenced to death, an execution carried out on January 30, 1649, in the Banqueting Hall of Whitehall Palace.

Disliked during his lifetime for his sympathy to Catholicism and favors to Catholic courtiers like the Calverts and Arminian Anglicans like Laud, Charles I was finally brought down by the rickety system of royal finance inherited from the Tudors. Considered a Church of England martyr after his death, he also became the arch-foe of republicans, who insisted on their right to remove and even kill a king. The Petition of Right was considered a precious precedent by English constitutionalists and their American successors, especially those New Englanders who considered Charles I a personal enemy.

Margaret Sankey

See also: Cromwell, Oliver; English Civil War; Puritanism.

Bibliography

Hibbert, Christopher. *Charles I.* New York: Harper and Row, 1968.

Russell, Conrad. *Fall of the British Monarchies 1637–1642.* Oxford, UK: Clarendon Press, 1991.

Sharpe, Kevin. *The Personal Rule of Charles I.* New Haven, CT: Yale University Press, 1997.

Charles II (1630–1685)

Born May 29, 1630, at St. James's Palace, Charles II was the eldest surviving son of Charles I and his wife, Henrietta Maria of France. At his father's side throughout the civil war, he escaped to France, but returned in 1650 as de jure king to lead a rebellion of the Scots

against Oliver Cromwell. Defeated at Worcester in 1651, he again returned to Europe as an exile.

In 1660, with Cromwell dead, and Charles II's son Richard an unacceptable head of state, General George Monck negotiated the return of Charles II as king. At Breda, Charles II declared he would not seek revenge against the regicides and offered an Act of Indemnity. The restored Parliament, however, proving far harsher than the king, limited the religious rights of Presbyterians and Independents (dissenting Protestants) and executed several of the regicides.

Charles II's first years after he was restored to the throne saw the disastrous Fire of London in 1665 and an outbreak of plague. This was balanced by his sponsorship of the Royal Society, founded in 1662, and the magnificent rebuilding of London planned by Sir Christopher Wren under the king's direction. As an ally of France, he also engaged Britain in two wars against the Dutch in 1665–1667 and 1672–1674, which allowed him to seize Dutch property in North America but also included a Dutch raid on shipyards on the Thames River.

The reign of Charles II (1660–1685) saw a major expansion of the British Empire. In North America, he seized New Amsterdam (later New York City) and granted charters for Carolina, New Jersey, and Pennsylvania. *(Private Collection/ Philip Mould, Historical Portraits Ltd., London, United Kingdom/Bridgeman Art Library)*

Charles II married Catherine of Braganza, a Portuguese princess, in 1662, but he had no legitimate children. His relationship with Parliament grew stormy over members' attempts to exclude his Roman Catholic younger brother James from the succession. The king skillfully manipulated Parliament to prevent the exclusion, but he was forced to give in to the Test Act, which prohibited those not communicant with the Church of England from holding public office. During his reign, as the power of Parliament increased, Britain's two leading historical political parties, the Whigs and Tories, developed their identities.

Under Charles II, the British Empire expanded hugely. The king's marriage brought Goa, Bombay, and Tangiers into the empire, while the Dutch Wars allowed him to seize New Amsterdam. In North America, he granted new charters, giving Carolina to lords proprietors, including his friend Lord Anthony Ashley Cooper (the Earl of Shaftesbury) in 1663, New Jersey to Lord George Carteret, and Pennsylvania to William Penn as repayment for a loan made to the king by Penn's father, Admiral William Penn. In 1670, he forced Spain to acknowledge British possession of Jamaica and settlements in the Americas in the Treaty of Madrid, the first time Spain admitted that any other nation had legal possessions in the Western Hemisphere.

Charles II extended Cromwell's Navigation Act in 1663 and 1673, limiting the North American colonies to trade with Great Britain and placing customs agents in the colonial ports to enforce the laws, which were increasingly resented by the colonists. To administer the British colonies, Charles II created the Lords Commissioners for Trade and Plantation in 1675. In 1676, he was called upon to intervene in Virginia, where Nathaniel Bacon had seized power from the royal governor.

Charles II was constantly pressed for cash, especially during the periods when he chose to live without Parliament, preferring to raise funds through the sale of Dunkirk to France and signing a secret agreement with Louis XIV, the Treaty of Dover, in 1670. According to this document, he received a generous allowance from France in exchange for his promise to convert to Catholicism, which he did only on his deathbed. Charles II is famous for his luxurious court, resplendent with a bevy of official mistresses (most notably Nell Gwynne and Louise de Kerouelle), his lavish entertainments, and his reaction to the austerities of the British Commonwealth.

Unfortunately, despite his successful manipulation of Parliament, Charles II failed to reform the system of finance in Britain or fully address the problems of religion in the aftermath of the civil war. When he died of a stroke on February 6, 1685, he was succeeded by his Catholic brother, James II.

Margaret Sankey

See also: Cromwell, Oliver; English Civil War.

Bibliography

Ashley, Maurice. *Charles II: Man and Statesman.* New York: Praeger, 1971.
Coote, Stephen. *Royal Survivor.* New York: St. Martin's, 2000.
Haley, Kenneth. *Politics in the Reign of Charles II.* Oxford, UK: Blackwell, 1985.

Charles V (1500–1558)

Holy Roman Emperor Charles V of Hapsburg received a vast inheritance that included Austria, the Netherlands, Franche-Comté, Aragon, Naples, Sicily, and Castile and its growing American empire. This made him the most powerful European ruler in the first half of the sixteenth century.

The ascendancy of the Hapsburgs, hereditary archdukes of Austria, was the result of fortuitous marriage alliances. Charles was born in 1500 in Ghent, the Netherlands, to Philip of Hapsburg (the only son of Holy Roman Emperor Maximilian I and Mary of Burgundy) and to Princess Juana (the third child of Ferdinand of Aragon and Isabella of Castile). From infancy, Charles was destined for the Spanish throne because of the untimely deaths of Ferdinand and Isabella's eldest children and their offspring. Nevertheless, Charles remained in the Netherlands, even after Isabella's death in 1504, his father's sudden demise in 1506, and his mother's subsequent melancholy and permanent confinement. It was Charles's grandfather Ferdinand who ruled the Spanish kingdoms until his death in 1516.

Charles first traveled to Spain in 1517 to gain recognition as King Charles I of Castile and Aragon. While there, he sponsored Ferdinand Magellan's voyage to find a westward sea route to the East Indies, which resulted in the first circumnavigation of the globe (1519–1522). Charles was at Barcelona in 1519 when he learned that his grandfather Maximilian I had died, leaving the imperial throne vacant. The title of Holy Roman Emperor was an elective one, and Charles won the election by paying the largest bribes to the seven German electors.

The Holy Roman Emperor Charles V dominated European politics in the first half of the sixteenth century. As king of Spain as well, he was able to exploit silver and other exports from the New World to finance his European exploits. *(Prado, Madrid, Spain/Bridgeman Art Library)*

In 1520, he prepared to leave Spain to receive his imperial crown, but, in a pattern that would often repeat itself, Castile was asked to shoulder the financial burden of his journey. This additional monetary demand, combined with Spanish resentment toward Charles's Flemish entourage, led to rebellion. Although royal authority was restored, Charles, now crowned Holy Roman Emperor Charles V, did agree to reduce certain taxes and to use native nobles, not his Flemish followers, in the government of Castile.

The rapid expansion of Hapsburg power within Europe and beyond brought with it an equal number of challenges. The French king, Francis I Valois, himself a failed candidate for the imperial title, not only feared the Hapsburgs' encircling power but also fought Charles V for control of Northern Italy. Francis had captured Milan in 1515, but imperial troops retook it in 1521, and at the Battle of Pavia, in 1525, Francis was captured trying to retake the city. While the French king was forced to make major concessions to Charles V by the Treaty of Madrid of 1526, once freed, he repudiated the terms and set off further hostilities. Another major participant in the constantly shifting

alliances was King Henry VIII of England. It was Charles V's powerful intervention that led the papacy to deny Henry VIII's request to annul his marriage to Catherine of Aragon—Charles V's aunt—and helped set in motion Henry's break with the Catholic Church.

At the same time, Charles V had to face the challenge of Martin Luther and the Protestant reformation. Luther, a German monk who had been excommunicated by the Catholic Church for his attacks on doctrine, was summoned by Charles V in 1521 to the Diet of Worms, an assembly of the secular and ecclesiastic authorities of the German empire. When Luther refused to recant, Charles V outlawed him. Luther eluded capture because of his growing support among the German princes, who began to reform their churches, contrary to the emperor's orders. Charles V and his younger brother, Ferdinand, his deputy in Germany, could not take immediate action against the Lutheran princes because of ongoing threats from both France and the Turks.

The Ottoman Turks, an Asiatic people of the Islamic faith, had ended the Byzantine Empire with the capture of Constantinople in 1453. The Turks continued to advance through the Balkans, and in 1526, at the Battle of Mohács, killed King Louis II of Hungary and Bohemia. Louis II had been married to Charles V's sister Mary, while his own sister was married to Ferdinand. The Hungarians and Bohemians then chose Ferdinand as their new king, which further extended Hapsburg power into central Europe. King Ferdinand and King Charles V had to defend the eastern borders of Christendom and the very heart of the Hapsburgs' possessions, Vienna, against Turkish threats in 1529 and 1532, which thus prevented them from settling religious matters within the empire.

Charles V married Isabella of Portugal, his first cousin, with whom he had one son, Philip, and two daughters. That his family was based in Castile showed the importance of this kingdom among his many possessions, for Castile was the source of the treasure from the New World with which he financed his European enterprises. It was under Charles V that Hernan Cortéz set out from Cuba with some 500 men and sixteen horses and overthrew the Aztec empire (1519–1521). With an even smaller expedition, Francisco Pizarro left Panama in 1531 and, within two years, had conquered the Inca empire. In 1545, the Spanish discovered the silver mines of San Luis Potosí, in present-day Bolivia, which would be developed into a major source of income through the rest of the century.

Despite these vast resources, Charles V was ultimately unable to stop the spread of Lutheranism in a series of German wars. Instead, by the Peace of Augsburg of 1555, he granted each ruler in Germany the right to be Lutheran or Catholic. In 1556, worn down by his constant struggles, Charles V abdicated the thrones of Spain, parts of Italy, the Netherlands, and Spanish America in favor of his son, Philip. His brother, Ferdinand, received Austria and the imperial title, as well as Bohemia and Hungary. Charles V spent his last days in a Spanish monastery, where he died in 1558.

Florene S. Memegalos

See also: Catholic Church; New Spain; Spanish Colonies on Mainland North America (Chronology).

Bibliography

Brandi, Karl. *The Emperor Charles V: The Growth and Destiny of a Man and of a World-Empire.* Translated by C. V. Wedgwood. London: Jonathan Cape, 1968.

Fernández Alvarez, Manuel. *Charles V, Elected Emperor and Hereditary Ruler.* Translated by J. A. Lalaguna. London: Thames and Hudson, 1975.

Maltby, William. *The Reign of Charles V.* New York: Palgrave, 2002.

Charleston

Charleston, South Carolina, located at the confluence of the Ashley and Cooper rivers, was one of the most populous cities in America throughout the eighteenth century. English exploration and settlement began with a three-ship expedition financed by the colony's lords proprietors, eight political allies of Charles II. The original colonists, ninety-three in all, represented a cross section of Atlantic society. A few were wealthy planters from Barbados, some were simply free English men, at least one was an African slave, and about two-thirds were indentured servants.

In 1670, the *Carolina*, the other ships having been lost, sailed into Charleston Harbor. The first English settlement was on Albemarle Point (named for one of the lords proprietors). Within a decade, however, the English had moved across the Ashley River to the present site and renamed the settlement Charles Town, in honor of the king.

Charles Town's early settlement was profoundly influenced by Barbados. The Caribbean sugar island had become overcrowded in the middle of the seventeenth century, and great planters, small farmers, merchants, artisans, servants, and slaves moved to Charles Town and its environs. The Barbadians brought their institutions with them: these ranged from slave codes to the Anglican Church and a rowdy, ostentatious lifestyle. The proprietors, most of whom remained in England, exerted relatively little influence over the colony. Anthony Ashley Cooper, the first earl of Shaftesbury, ordered the colonists to settle in towns; by and large they refused, spreading over the countryside in search of fertile land. The lords proprietors also insisted on the adoption of the Fundamental Constitutions, an enlightened plan of government and religious toleration; the colonists never did adopt them entirely, though religious toleration was more prevalent in Carolina than, for instance, in Massachusetts. By the 1680s, there were Anglicans, Dissenters, Presbyterians, and Quakers worshiping in Charles Town.

The lords proprietors did insist upon the orderly layout of Charles Town. They wanted to avoid the narrow, congested streets of Europe, and the colonists largely complied with this request. In 1680, observers estimated that Charles Town had a population of about 1,000, and the proprietors encouraged new immigration. In its early years, Charles Town was the North American center of the trade in Native American slaves; it was also a significant center of piracy. Charles Town's fortunes would shift dramatically with the introduction of rice. Although Charles Town was an economically diverse early modern city, rice was the engine that would drive South Carolina's economy throughout the colonial period.

Rice, Africans, and Native Americans

The origins of rice culture in Carolina are not exactly clear, though it seems likely that West Africans skilled in rice production played a significant role. Rice agriculture required crop-specific skills and massive amounts of labor, and for both of these, English planters began to import large numbers of West African slaves, preferring people from the region between the Senegal and Gambia rivers. Both Native American and African slaves labored in town and in the surrounding plantations.

By 1708, Africans outnumbered English people in the colony, causing one observer to remark that South Carolina was "more like a Negro country." The governor and council reported in 1708 a population of 4,080 white people, 4,100 black slaves, and 1,400 Native

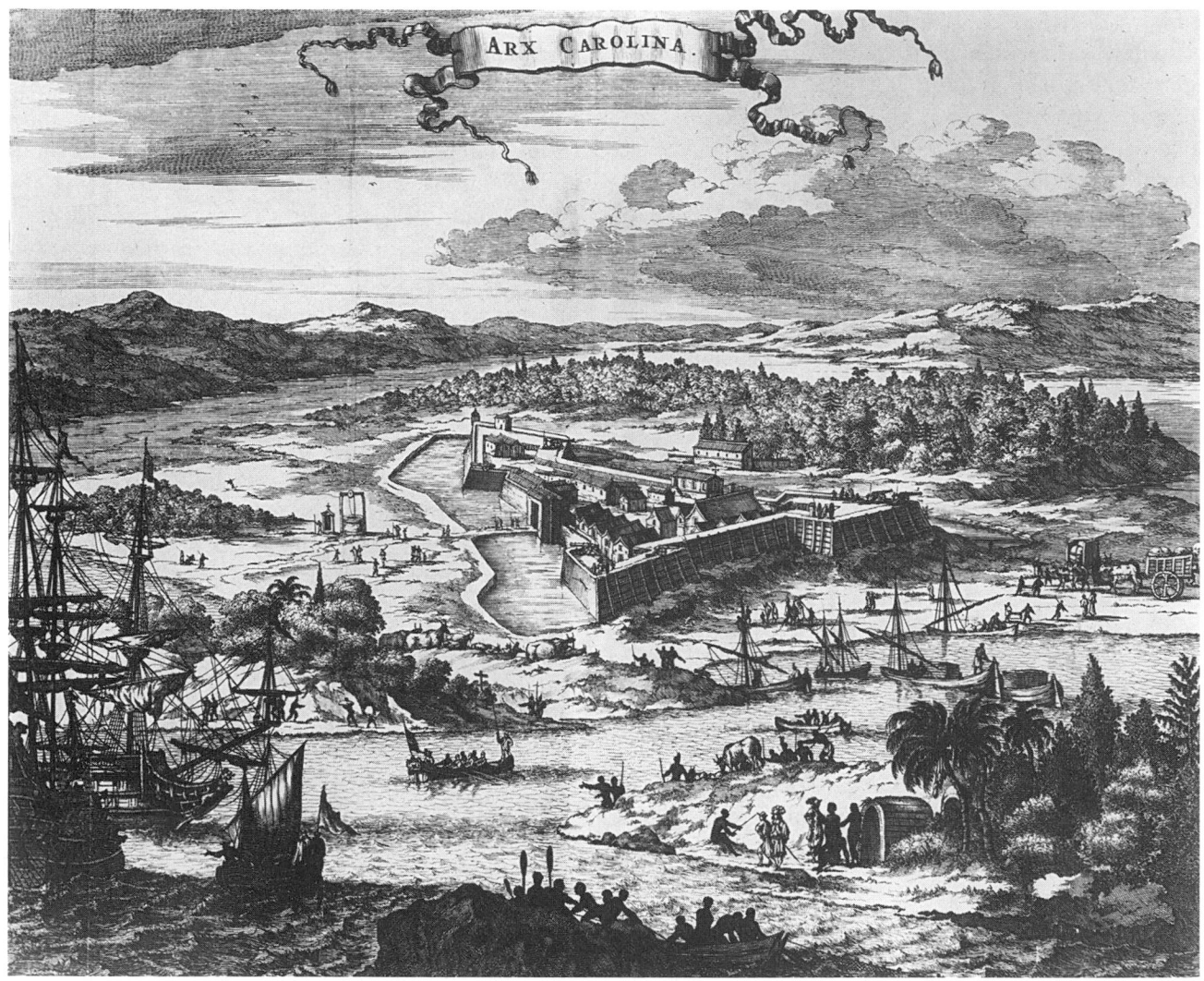

ARX CAROLINA.

Charleston, South Carolina, is viewed in an etching dating to 1673, just three years after its founding. Originally called Albemarle Point, the settlement was moved across the Ashley River a few years later and renamed Charles Town, in honor of King Charles II. *(Brown Brothers, Sterling, Pennsylvania)*

American slaves. By 1720, the situation appeared in even deeper relief: there were 9,000 whites and 12,000 Africans. In 1740, in the aftermath of the Stono Rebellion, slaves outnumbered free whites 39,155 to about 20,000.

At the same time that rice was transforming Charles Town into a major slave trading post and a bustling port city, Native American traders were seeking to establish commercial ties with tribal communities from the nearby Yamasee to groups as far west as the Mississippi River. Although Native Americans mistrusted unscrupulous English trading practices, they came increasingly to depend on Carolina traders for firearms, cloth, and rum. The trade was not, generally speaking, conducted on fair terms, and one by one, the

tribes fell into debt. They also became increasingly suspicious of English encroachment on their lands.

On Good Friday 1715, a combined force of Yamasees and Creeks, together with some smaller tribes, killed all of the traders in their villages, attacked the frontier plantations, and drove the English back to within several miles of Charles Town. Early Native American successes were reversed when the Cherokee joined the war on the English side. By 1720, the English planters at Charles Town were firmly in control of much of present-day South Carolina.

In 1739, Charles Town society was shaken to its very foundation by one of North America's largest slave revolts. In the decades leading up to the Stono Rebellion, Africans had begun to resist slavery in a number of ways, including poisoning, sabotage, arson, and work slowdowns. The white minority grew increasingly anxious about growing unrest among slaves and began to regulate slavery ever more tightly. Slaves were forbidden to carry firearms; they were forced to give up any clothing deemed impractical or flashy. Their diet was restricted. Slaves responded to the increasing regulation by running away in larger numbers. The white minority had entered into a downward spiral of fear and repression.

A group of twenty primarily Angolan slaves gathered near Charles Town under the leadership of a slave named Jemmy. The band broke into a storehouse, where the slaves armed themselves. They marched through the countryside outside Charles Town, gathering support from slaves and killing about twenty white people in the process.

Even though the rebellion was put down in a quick and harsh manner, it left deep scars on the psyche of Carolina's white minority. A new, even more brutal slave code was enacted, and slave patrols were stepped up. The planters at Charles Town also launched a punitive raid on the Spanish at St. Augustine, following the logic that many slaves who escaped from Carolina gained their freedom there. By 1740, the city of Charles Town had subjugated African slaves and Native Americans, and profited wildly from the trade in slaves and rice.

A Mature Colonial City?

Though South Carolina had developed all the characteristics for which it would be known throughout the colonial period, Charles Town itself was undergoing rapid change in the years after the Stono Rebellion. In 1740, a massive fire swept through the city, gutting many of the original buildings. White residents, still in shock from Stono, blamed black arsonists. In 1742, Spain threatened to attack the city, landing a large army about 200 miles to the south, but the attack never came. In 1744, France declared war on England. While the merchants of Charles Town feared a loss of trade, those who were associated with smuggling and shipbuilding actually profited from the conflict.

Interestingly, in the mid-eighteenth century, planters lost political power in the colonial assembly. This was probably because their social status was already secured, and they had become bored with politics. A new class of merchants and lawyers dominated political life during this period.

Charles Town's economy boomed once again after peace with France in 1749, due in large part to the trade in indigo, a plant used for dye in the English textile industry. The year 1756 saw the renewal of hostilities with France. By this time, Charles Town was the most important American commercial center south of Philadelphia, and the British Crown, fearing that the French would recognize this fact, stationed 1,700 royal troops there. South Carolina's role in the French and Indian War was limited in comparison to that of colonies farther to the north. Still, a party from Charles Town attacked Cherokee settlements in the upcountry. The war also had the effect of concentrating even more wealth in the hands of those at the top of Charles Town society.

The end of the French and Indian War brought about a new period of tension between British administrators and their American subjects in Charles Town, as it did in other colonial centers such as New York, Philadelphia, and Boston. The Stamp Act was particularly poorly received, and the South Carolina General Assembly sent several delegates to the Stamp Act Congress. On a more popular level, a local Sons of Liberty group incited eight days of disorder by hanging a stamp distributor in effigy, ransacking the house of another stamp distributor, and leading a mock funeral procession and burying a coffin marked "American Liberty." Charles Town became the center of revolutionary fervor in the South. During the American War for Independence, Charles Town was under British control from May 1780 to 1782.

After the war, the city of Charles Town was chartered as Charleston. Although the state government of South Carolina moved to the city of Columbia in 1786, Charleston's elites loomed large in state politics. In the antebellum period, Charleston remained one of America's wealthiest cities.

Matthew Jennings

See also: Cities; Rice; Slavery, African American; South Carolina; South Carolina (Chronology).

Bibliography

Edgar, Walter. *South Carolina: A History.* Columbia: University of South Carolina Press, 1998.

Fraser, Walter J., Jr. *Charleston! Charleston! The History of a Southern City.* Columbia: University of South Carolina Press, 1989.

Sirmans, M. Eugene. *Colonial South Carolina: A Political History, 1663–1763.* Chapel Hill: University of North Carolina Press, 1966.

Weir, Robert M. *Colonial South Carolina: A History.* Columbia: University of South Carolina Press, 1997.

Wood, Peter H. *Black Majority: Negroes in Colonial South Carolina from 1670 Through the Stono Rebellion.* New York: Alfred A. Knopf, 1974.

Cherokee

When the European colonization of North America began, the Cherokee numbered more than 30,000. Their territory consisted of parts of ten future U.S. states, though most lived in Georgia, Tennessee, and the Carolinas (North and South Carolina were one colony until 1762). The Cherokee were one of the largest Native American groups in colonial America, and, today, the Eastern Band (North Carolina) and the Cherokee Nation (Oklahoma) have more enrolled members than any other tribe.

The pre-Columbian story of the Cherokee is not all that well known, but their language, a distant relative of the Iroquoian languages spoken farther north, indicates an ancient migration southward. By 1000 C.E., Cherokees had settled in the Appalachians' fertile valleys and begun to cultivate corn and build permanent towns. By the time English colonization had any real effect on the Cherokee, they were the most powerful Native American tribe in the Southeast. They controlled trade, hunting, and settlement on more than 40,000 square miles of land.

In the colonial period, Cherokee towns were largely autonomous, though they could band together in times of crisis. Cherokee government was highly decentralized, and life in the towns was governed by relatively strict gender conventions. For Cherokees in the sixteenth, seventeenth, and eighteenth centuries, male and female roles balanced one another. Agriculture was primarily a female pursuit, and the winter hunt and warfare were almost entirely male activities. While occasionally men would work in the fields and women would hunt or go to war, Cherokees tried to adhere to their culturally mandated gender division as much as possible, fearing that a significant alteration could cause crop failure, disease, and other problems.

Though de Soto traveled through Cherokee country during the period 1539–1542, Cherokees did not encounter a serious colonial challenge until the 1700s in South Carolina. Their relative isolation, while it did not protect them entirely from European disease, probably mediated the political and cultural effects of the Europeans' arrival. Relations between the Cherokees and Carolina were fairly complex. Both were major power brokers in the Southeast, and they fought with and against one another throughout the eighteenth century.

The Cherokee first met the English settlers through trade largely administered by Native American middlemen. Deerskins had become a valuable commodity, and the wooded, mountainous homelands of the Cherokee were loaded with deer. The Cherokee shipped thousands of deerskins, baskets, and other commodities to the traders at Charles Town, and received in exchange cloth, firearms, and other items of English manufacture. On occasion, Cherokees themselves became commodities, when they were captured by Carolina's allied Native Americans and sold into slavery. The Native American slave trade affected most of the native peoples living in the Southeast, but for the Cherokee the effects were slight when compared, for example, to the thousands of Native Americans carried off from Florida in the late seventeenth and early eighteenth centuries.

The Cherokee fought alongside the English in the Tuscarora War (1711–1715) and the Yamasee War (1715–1717). They may have recognized the growing power of the English, or they may have recognized a chance to hurt the Tuscarora and Creek, two large neighboring tribes with which the Cherokee skirmished constantly. In both wars, the Cherokee provided the English with a powerful ally, and some credit the Cherokee with saving the Carolina colony from Creek and Yamasee aggression.

The English intended more than simply trade, however, and territorial ambitions eventually brought the Cherokee and English into conflict with each other. The Seven Years' War, a global conflict between the French and English that was known in North America as the French and Indian War, touched the Cherokee and North and South Carolina in a series of skirmishes, sometimes called the Cherokee War. Intending to further the interests of South Carolina, Governor William Henry Littleton incited war with the Cherokee. Official policy was the annihilation of the Cherokee, but local commanders disobeyed their orders and tried to reconcile the differences between the two cultures. The end result was the establishment of a permanent border.

The Cherokee became known in the nineteenth century as one of the "Five Civilized Tribes," large communities of southeastern Native Americans who had adopted Anglo-American practices. This did not protect the Cherokee people from American aggression in the American War for Independence or as they squared off against the early United States government. Most of the Cherokee were forcibly removed to the West during the nineteenth-century expulsion known as the "Trail of Tears."

Matthew Jennings

See also: Native American–European Conflict; Native American–European Relations; Native Americans; Tuscarora War; Yamasee War.

Bibliography

Hatley, Tom. *The Dividing Paths: Cherokees and South Carolinians Through the Revolutionary Era.* New York: Oxford University Press, 1995.

Perdue, Theda. *Cherokee Women: Gender and Culture Change, 1700–1835.* Lincoln: University of Nebraska Press, 1998.

Chesapeake

Encompassing parts of Virginia, Maryland, and Delaware, the Chesapeake region of colonial America was dominated by tobacco culture—the social, political, economic, and racial relationships that developed around the production of tobacco. For over a century, from 1617 through the 1720s, tobacco culture produced disorder and conflict in the Chesapeake. It was only in the 1720s that the planters of Virginia and Maryland secured their authority, and then only after they had permanently enslaved a racially distinct labor force. The colonial Chesapeake came to be characterized by dependence and independence, slavery and freedom.

The Virginia Company of London established the first permanent English colony in North America at Jamestown in 1607. By 1617, only 2,000 of the 10,000 colonists transported to Virginia were still alive, the Virginia Company teetered on the brink of bankruptcy, and it seemed likely that the entire colonial venture might collapse. Then, John Rolfe discovered that Chesapeake tobacco fetched a high price in London. The tobacco boom was on.

By the early 1620s, tobacco production had so taken over the colony that tobacco was a legal form of money and men used it to settle debts, pay fines, and purchase servants and goods. Tobacco saved the Virginia colony and provided an immediate cash crop for Maryland, which was established in the 1630s. It also brought misery to many men and women in the Chesapeake.

Tobacco planters' insatiable appetite for land caused conflicts with earlier settlers, fur traders, and others, especially the Native Americans who lived in the area. Wars and diseases decimated such tribes as the Powhatan, who eventually migrated inland and incorporated themselves into other tribes and nations like the Catawba. Chesapeake natives simply could not withstand the brutality and deceit of the English, the spread of fatal diseases, and the ever-increasing number of settlers.

It was not until the 1680s that Chesapeake planters turned to slave labor. Before then, England's poor fulfilled tobacco culture's demand for labor. Indentured servants, mostly young men, pledged four to seven years of labor in exchange for transportation to the Chesapeake and freedom dues (land, goods, and/or money given to a servant at the end of his or her term). Disease killed many during their first years, and the survivors were worked hard by planters intent on extracting as much labor as possible. Yet, for those who lived through their indenture, life in the early Chesapeake was promising, and many obtained land and began producing their own tobacco.

A great transition in Chesapeake society began around 1660 with the decline of the tobacco economy and the emergence of a more permanent and powerful planter class. The Navigation Acts and overproduction drove down the price of tobacco, while heavy taxes and import duties cut into profits. Well-connected planters moved to consolidate their wealth and power, but they did so at the expense of smaller farmers, landless laborers, and servants.

In 1676, frustration came to a boil when Nathaniel Bacon, a well-bred planter who was excluded from Virginia's ruling circle, led a rebellion against the planter class. Promised freedom, lower taxes, more land, and plunder for all, small farmers, servants, and the few slaves in Virginia flocked to join Bacon's ranks and nearly destroyed the colony.

In the aftermath of Bacon's Rebellion, the Chesapeake's planters instituted a host of reforms and placed more land on the market, placating the white population. At the same time, they began to import ever-growing numbers of African slaves to produce tobacco more profitably.

Prior to the 1670s, the great dividing line in the Chesapeake separated those who controlled land and labor from those who did not. Poor whites and blacks fell indiscriminately on the wrong side of that line. After 1680, poor whites and great planters increasingly

A dispute between Virginia fur trader William Claiborne and the royalist Calvert family over territory in the Chesapeake Bay led to the first naval battles in North America during the mid-1630s. *(New York Public Library, New York)*

united against the common enemy in their midst: African slaves who might rebel at any time.

Between 1680 and 1720, Virginia's enslaved population increased fivefold to more than 25,000 slaves, as planters transformed the Chesapeake from a society with slaves into a slave society, where the economy and the social order rested on the institution of slavery. By 1750, there were more than 150,000 slaves in the Chesapeake, accounting for 40 percent of the region's population.

A new, distinct Chesapeake social order had emerged. At the bottom were slaves, who had produced an African American culture equipped to address the uncertainties of slavery. At the pinnacle stood great planters—the gentry—who ruled over their families, their plantations, their parishes, and their counties. Beneath them were the white landowners, who had perhaps a few servants or slaves, and the landless whites.

When British policies in the 1770s challenged the gentry's control of Chesapeake society, the planters rebelled. The American Revolution brought many changes to this hierarchical society. Planters in Maryland and Delaware lost much of their influence, but Virginia planters maintained their authority. In the early nineteenth century, many Virginians migrated to the cotton belt, bringing the basic institutions of the Chesapeake to Alabama, Georgia, Mississippi, and Texas.

John Craig Hammond

See also: Bacon's Rebellion; Jamestown; Maryland; Maryland (Chronology); Powhatan Confederacy; Slavery, African American; Tobacco; Virginia; Virginia (Chronology). *Document:* The Jamestown Settlement (1607–1609).

Bibliography

Breen, T. H. *Puritans and Adventurers: Change and Persistence in Early America.* New York: Oxford University Press, 1980.

Kulikoff, Allan. *Tobacco and Slaves: The Development of Southern Colonies in the Chesapeake, 1680–1800.* Chapel Hill: University of North Carolina Press, 1986.

Morgan, Edmund. *American Slavery, American Freedom: The Ordeal of Colonial Virginia.* New York: W. W. Norton, 1975.

Chickasaw

According to the Chickasaw, their history began with a migration, perhaps from Mexico. Each day, the people would erect a sacred leaning pole. They moved in the direction the pole indicated until it no longer leaned, and then they settled across a wide swath of what is now the southeastern United States. In colonial times, Chickasaw territory stretched over parts of present-day Alabama, Mississippi, Tennessee, and Kentucky.

The Chickasaw, who numbered perhaps 4,500 at the time of European contact, are ethnically related to the more numerous Choctaw, who numbered 20,000 at about the same time. The Choctaw and Chickasaw languages are very similar and can be considered dialects of a single tongue.

By the end of the seventeenth century, Chickasaws lived in seven towns, mainly along the Tombigbee River; the tribal capital was at Chukafalaya. Chickasaw population and settlement patterns are not that easy to trace. During times of peace with other Native Americans and Europeans, Chickasaws settled widely, ranging far to the east and west. In fact, two Chickasaw villages could be found on the Savannah River between South Carolina and Georgia. When Chickasaws were at war with Europeans or other Native Americans, however, they restricted their movements to the Tombigbee. Further complicating the picture is the fact that Chickasaw often adopted captives and accepted refugees from other tribes. Chickasaw ethnicity seems to have been remarkably fluid in the colonial period.

Chickasaw society was organized along clan lines. The clans were exogamous, meaning that clan members had to marry outside of their particular clan, and Chickasaw society was matrilineal, meaning that descent was traced through the female line. Clans and towns were mainly self-governing, though larger councils could be called in times of crisis. Chickasaws earned the reputation among other Native Americans and Europeans of being particularly aggressive, both in going to war and in individual acts of bravery in battle.

Chickasaws first met Europeans during Hernando de Soto's trek across the Southeast in 1540. De Soto captured several Chickasaws and forced the chiefs to provide his soldiers with shelter and food for the winter. The Chickasaw saw the benefits of an alliance with the Spanish and even planned a joint attack on a neighboring tribe. Relations between the Chickasaw and Spanish soured, however, when de Soto demanded that 200 warriors carry his party's baggage. The Chickasaw viewed this as an insult and attacked the Spanish, burning their camp and killing twelve men and fifty-seven horses.

For the next century and a half, the Chickasaw did not have much contact with Europeans. In 1673, the Jolliet-Marquette party passed through Chickasaw country, as did La Salle's in 1682. In fact, the Chickasaw territory was right in the middle of an area contested by the increasingly aggressive empires of England and France. Although actual European settlement in Chickasaw territory still lay in the future, increasing numbers of traders, missionaries, and soldiers began to filter into Chickasaw lands.

Initially, most Chickasaws sided with the French, mainly because they resented unscrupulous English traders. By 1720, though, most Chickasaw villages had allied themselves with the English because they feared a French-Choctaw alliance. The Chickasaw found themselves a part of the booming colonial trade in skins, cloth, and firearms. They also earned a reputation as fierce slave catchers and ranged far from the Tombigbee to raid tribes for slaves.

Between 1720 and 1763, the Chickasaw fended off assaults by the French and allied tribes (including the Miami, Iroquois, and Illinois). The removal of France from North America, which devastated many tribes, did not affect the Chickasaw; they had proven themselves staunch and valuable allies to the British.

The end of the French and Indian War brought administrative changes to Chickasaw country. They came increasingly under the purview of British colonial policies. White settlers moved into Chickasaw territory, and a fairly large mixed-blood contingent began to make its presence known in tribal affairs. During the American Revolution, the Chickasaw, like most Native American groups, sided with their longtime allies, the British. When Thomas Jefferson, then governor of Virginia, ordered a fort to be constructed south of the Ohio River, the Chickasaw responded by surrounding the fort and burning the settlers' houses.

After the war, the Chickasaw negotiated treaties with Virginia and Spain. Eventually, the United States would force 4,900 Chickasaws and 1,100 African American and mixed African–Native Americans west to Indian Territory along the Trail of Tears.

Matthew Jennings

See also: Native American–European Conflict; Native American–European Relations; Native Americans.

Bibliography

Gibson, Arrell M. *The Chickasaws.* Norman: University of Oklahoma Press, 1971.

Hudson, Charles. *The Southeastern Indians.* Knoxville: University of Tennessee Press, 1976.

White Deer, Gary. "Chickasaw." In *Encyclopedia of North American Indians*, edited by Frederick E. Hoxie. New York: Houghton Mifflin, 1996.

Child Rearing

Child rearing, which may be defined as providing the physical care, education, training, and socialization of children, took place primarily within the nuclear family in colonial America. Parents were largely guided by the values and teachings of Protestant Christianity. Religious and secular institutions reinforced parental authority, but local governments also could place children in other households as servants or apprentices if the parents were judged unfit or too poor. Children also were included in some indenture arrangements, in which case, they might live separately from their parents.

Most seventeenth-century families were patriarchal in structure, with the father seen as wielding ultimate authority, authority that had been given to him by God. Protestant religious traditions supported this view, and ministers often preached sermons emphasizing the parents' duty to train the child properly, as well as the child's duty to obey. This religious influence was strongest in New England, with its many Calvinist ministers, but it existed throughout the American colonies. Over time, parents began to turn from religious traditions to books by such Enlightenment writers as John Locke for advice on how to raise their children.

Infancy and Early Childhood

Infancy and early childhood were considered a dangerous time, both in terms of childrens' physical survival and development. Infants were usually born at home and delivered by a midwife. Pregnancy and childbirth were a leading cause of death for colonial women, which meant that many children were raised by a stepmother. In contrast to much of Europe, most American mothers nursed their own infants, although some Southern slaveholding families had slave women nurse the babies. Parents feared the period of teething and weaning, because many children died at that age. Some early advice manuals blamed early childhood illness and death on teething, rather than on inadequate or unsafe diets, and advised parents to hasten teething by lancing open the baby's gums.

Families were large, and mortality was high, with both disease and accidents claiming many young lives. Infants and toddlers were often cared for by children not much older than themselves, and the home was filled with dangers like open fireplaces and large pots of boiling water. Older children often worked alongside their parents, exposing them to additional dangers. Death was a fact of life for colonial children.

Parents and clergymen used this awareness of death to reinforce religious teachings, particularly the urgency of receiving salvation. Religious training occurred at home and at church, and it was reinforced at school. Children often participated in family prayers at home, typically spent most of Sunday at church, and memorized and were examined on Scripture verses.

Seventeenth-century Puritans believed in original sin, which meant to them that they needed to combat the natural depravity of the child by breaking his or her will. Discipline to eradicate stubbornness and replace it with obedience started in infancy. In the eighteenth century, Jonathan Edwards differed from many earlier clergy by advocating constant discipline without physical force. He sought cheerful obedience from children, believing that obedience to parents would prepare the child for mature obedience to God.

Both religious and medical experts exhorted parents to actively manage their child's physical and social growth. Natural impulses, appetites, and desires were seen as animalistic and to be suppressed. One way parents accomplished this goal was by swaddling their infants—wrapping them tightly in bands of cloth. Parents straightened the baby's arms and legs, molding them to the desired shape and immobilizing them. (The newborn baby's head was also sometimes molded into shape.) Swaddling seems harsh, and infants could be wrapped too tightly for too long, but the practice did keep babies warm and may have helped keep them safe when tended by other children.

Following the advice of physicians, seventeenth-century parents did not want their children to crawl like animals, but to walk upright like humans. Swaddling straightened the infant's legs like an adult's and, at the age of six to nine months, the child was unswaddled and placed in a standing stool. This was a simple device, perhaps made from a hollowed tree trunk, which held the child upright and immobile. The child could not sit, and so could become too tired, but he or she also was kept off the cold, dirty floor. A slightly older child would be placed in a walking stool, a similar device that kept him or her upright, but which had wheels to allow movement from place to place, increasing both autonomy and the risk of accidents.

Seventeenth-century children dressed in clothing that looked like smaller versions of adult clothing. Surviving paintings show small boys in petticoats or long skirts, looking much as their mothers or sisters did. Boys were "breeched" around the age of six or seven, when they gave up skirts and dressed in pants like adult men. Nothing in either boys' or girls' wardrobe was designed specifically for children, a situation that would change during the eighteenth century.

Enlightenment Thinking

By the middle of the eighteenth century, parents were being told they need not try so hard to control and shape their young children. John Locke published *Some Thoughts Concerning Education* in 1693, and his work became increasingly influential in America after about 1750. Locke assured parents that much natural development could be trusted rather than combated. For example, children could be allowed to crawl and would progress to walking without being harmed by having crawled on all fours. Locke disapproved of swaddling and advised simple, nonrestrictive clothing for babies and older children. He introduced the idea of learning through play—the idea of educational play helped make play itself more acceptable—and described educational toys. Memoirists born near the end of the colonial period remembered alphabet blocks, a toy that fostered learning, as did some children's books of this era.

Locke, with other Enlightenment writers like William Buchan, still continued to advise parents to break the child's will. Discipline was to start in infancy. Parents were told to deny requests and to refuse to indulge a child's appetites in order to promote the virtues of self-control and self-denial. This discipline was to be enforced not with physical force but with emotional control, through giving or withholding affection.

In addition, Locke recommended a simple diet, fresh air, cold water baths, and cold feet. He believed this regimen would harden the child, resulting in ro-

bust physical health. Diaries and memoirs show that many parents implemented Locke's advice, occasionally creating lasting resentment in their children.

Both the religious tradition and the Enlightenment authors considered education an important part of child rearing. The religious view emphasized literacy, since believers needed to be able to read the Bible themselves. The Enlightenment celebrated human reason and the reading of the classics. Many children learned to read at home, being taught by a parent or older sibling. Formal schooling, however, became increasingly available to both boys and girls over time.

Of course, children born into slavery had a very different experience. To start with, they could be separated from their parents at any time if either the parent or child was sold or moved to a different location. Even when they lived together, slave parents were denied the authority to make decisions regarding their children's lives. Slave children were almost never taught to read; in fact, teaching a slave to read was later made illegal in many Southern states. Slave children were taught to work, typically starting with lighter versions of the tasks they might spend their adult lives doing. Religious training emphasized obedience over all else, and physical punishments were frequent and sometimes severe.

American Revolution

The American Revolution brought change, creating, perhaps, a more egalitarian family structure. Before the Revolution, families had begun moving away from the patriarchal model; the revolutionary era saw the development of what was called "Republican Motherhood." The mother's role was considered important, because she was the one to educate and train her sons to be virtuous citizens of the republic. In practice, this meant that mothers gained more authority within the home and girls received a more thorough education than in earlier generations, so that they would be able to be good teachers of their sons.

The use of corporal punishment also declined. Parents began to replace the idea of original sin with a view of children as innately good, a view that would underlie many child-rearing ideas and practices in the coming century.

Elizabeth McKee Williams

See also: Children; Education; Family; Reading and Literacy. *Document:* Raising Colonial Children (1699).

Bibliography

Calvert, Karin. *Children in the House: The Material Culture of Early Childhood, 1600–1900.* Boston: Northeastern University Press, 1992.

Greven, Philip J., Jr. *Child-Rearing Concepts, 1628–1861: Historical Sources.* Itasca, IL: F. E. Peacock Publishers, 1973.

Reinier, Jacqueline S. *From Virtue to Character: American Childhood, 1775–1850.* New York: Twayne, 1996.

Children

Prior to the colonial period, children occupied a poorly defined place in society. While it was recognized that they were not adults, their social and moral position was unclear.

They could be married at the age of 3 or 4 with plans to consummate the marriage later. They could be bound out for indentured servitude as a means of providing their own support or support for their families. They also were customarily seen as possessing the same inherited sins and inherent evil as their parents. While these characteristics remained part of childhood for many children, the seventeenth and eighteenth centuries saw a move toward defining children as beings distinct from adults.

Changing Meaning of Childhood

This change is directly reflected in the social and political movements of the early modern period. Religious leaders in Europe and England had advocated religious reform in the sixteenth century, leading to the creation of the Protestant church. By the seventeenth century, their reform interests incorporated politics and society, as well as religion. Among the best-known examples of this movement are the Puritans. Other examples include the smaller, splinter Protestant groups: the Quakers, Moravians, and Anabaptists. In contrast, the eighteenth century saw a different type of reform. Advocates for change became philosophers and scientists, arguing for scientific reason rather than religious justification. Regardless, both religious and scientific thinkers were interested in how children were defined and taught.

The medieval period had also seen drastic change and upheaval with very little thought given as to how children lived. The most likely reasons that reformers were now choosing to address the issue of children were social and economic. Crop rotations that led to greater yields, increased trade and prosperity, and more information about medicine had led to a higher rate of survival for both parents and children. Parents able to contemplate seeing children through to adulthood could more readily contemplate those children as children.

These issues can be traced in the books written about and for children during the colonial period. The rise of the printing press had made printed material more readily available. Books about children could be printed and sold to the middle and upper classes. Broadsheets and small chapbooks for children were available for a penny or less. Many of these were imported to the colonies; some were printed and bound in North America.

While the Puritans hoped that changing church and state would improve society, they also believed that reform had to take place within the family. As a means of advocating these reforms, they wrote numerous how-to manuals on raising children, including Robert Cleaver's *A Godly Form of Household Government* in 1598 and William Gouge's 1622 *Of Domestical Duties*. While these books demonstrate the strictness that the Puritans were known for, they also demonstrate a move toward fairness in raising children. Parents, suggested Gouge, should not beat their children when enraged, and children should be given the opportunity to defend themselves. Direct examples of the application of these beliefs can be found in diaries from the period.

Books written for children by Puritans also took an instructive form. In the 1640s, a Moravian schoolmaster named Jan Amos Comenius moved to London from Czechoslovakia, eager to put his educational theories to work. In 1658, he published a primer to be used in schools, titling it *Orbus Sensualism Pictus*. Each page had a picture showing some aspect of everyday life with captions in both a vernacular language and Latin. Comenius argued that children would be eager to sound out the words as they described their own, familiar world. Following the Restoration of Charles II, Comenius's book and ideas fell into obscurity.

Another example of a book written for children in the seventeenth century is James Janeway's *A Token for Children* in 1671. While its almost saintly boys and girls, none of whom reach adulthood, seem impossible to a modern reader, it was one of the first books to portray children as children, distinct from adults. Janeway even went so far as to suggest that these children served as examples of good behavior to their parents rather than the other way around.

The eighteenth century saw the creation of very

different books about and for children. While the Puritans had advocated reform for children, the belief that all humans, adult or child, were inherently evil was still a tenet of their faith. In contrast, Enlightenment philosophers such as John Locke and Jean-Jacques Rousseau argued that children were born as blank slates, neither good nor bad, and that corruption could come only with experience.

In 1693, Locke published his *Some Thoughts Concerning Education.* In some respects, Locke's work resembled the books published by the Puritans, as it argued for strict, consistent parenting. In contrast, however, he said that children should be encouraged to play more and be "cozen'd" into learning in this context. In 1762, Rousseau's *Emile* was published, suggesting that children be allowed to develop naturally. The ideas put forth by Locke, Rousseau, and others were fully established by the outbreak of the American Revolution. In turn, their philosophies also contributed to some of the rhetoric of the Revolution.

Throughout the medieval period, fairy tales and romances were popular among adults and children alike. By the late seventeenth century, sophisticated writers such as Charles Perrault were retelling traditional stories for the French court. Beautifully illustrated editions of *Beauty and the Beast* and *Cinderella* were highly popular. It is likely they were also read to aristocrats' children. The Enlightenment, in contrast, saw these stories as bad for both adults and children, though for different reasons. Adult attention to fairy tales and magic demonstrated a lack of interest in the sciences. And if fairy tales were written for adults, and children were different from adults, then children needed writing created for children.

The early eighteenth century saw the rise of the nursery rhyme as a genre. Perrault published *Tales of Mother Goose* in 1697 and also attached morals to many of his earlier stories. Isaac Watts, an English dissenter, published *Divine and Moral Songs for Children* in 1715, one of the most popular books of the age. Before 1800, it went through seventy-five different editions in the colonies. Another collection of children's songs, titled *Tommy Thumb's Pretty Songs,* was published in 1744 under the pseudonym of Nurse Lovechild. These works continued to be published well into the nineteenth century.

Regional and Ethnic Differences

While these broader-scale movements were important throughout the colonial period, children arriving in the colonies also had experiences unique to the regions in which they lived. Most of the groups moving from England to the Northern and Middle colonies were Protestant, whether Puritans and Pilgrims who came to New England, or English Quakers who settled in Delaware and Pennsylvania. Other major settlement groups coming from the European continent included the Protestant Lutherans, Moravians, and Amish. Children coming to these colonies had some things in common. Initially, they usually arrived in groups of extended family members. If one or both parents did not survive the first few difficult winters, there were aunts, uncles, cousins, or grandparents to serve in their place.

The Northern colonies, in particular, became established fairly quickly, and family life was able to continue in much the same way it had in England and Europe, with colonists generally lived in towns or on small farms. Most of these Protestant groups argued for strong family structure. They also frequently had justified their move to North America by arguing it was for their children's benefit. Prior to 1620, many Pilgrim families had moved to Leyden, Holland. Concerned about their children becoming too Dutch, the Pilgrims wanted to be able to raise them as English children without the English restrictions on their religion.

The Protestant emphasis placed on literacy meant that most children were likely to learn to read. Their parents, in turn, were apt to have read some of the contemporary writing on raising children. Anne Bradstreet, a New England poet of the mid-seventeenth century, often made reference to her children in her poems, contemplating her love for them and wondering if she would die in childbirth and leave them without a mother.

In contrast, children arriving in the Southern colonies had very different experiences. On arrival, the wealthy planter class of Virginia, Maryland, and the Carolinas were similar to their Northern counterparts. Able to afford the Atlantic passage, they had the option of moving their entire families as a complete group. Upon arrival, however, the warm Southern climate often proved disastrous for initial settlement. Mortality rates were far higher than in the Northern colonies. Only one in three marriages lasted for more than ten years without one or both partners dying. Nearly a quarter of all children died before reaching the age of 1, and 50 percent died before they reached 20. And, unlike the towns and small farms of the Northern and Middle colonies, most Southerners lived on isolated plantations.

Immigrants too poor to afford the cost of passage arrived as indentured servants, trading seven years of service for the journey to North America, a parcel of land, and some tools and clothing. While most servants were single men and, in some cases, women, families occasionally agreed to take their chances with indentures. In these cases, most family members were automatically separated. While women were allowed to keep children under the age of 2 or 3, any other children were taken as servants on separate plantations. Unlike adults, their indentures could last anywhere from seven to twenty years, usually until they were adults. Unable to read or write, separated by the great distances between plantations, family ties were easily broken. By the 1680s, a native-born population was finally able to establish itself in the Southern colonies. While this led to greater stability for wealthy families, poor families were now pushed farther and farther west in the search for more land, further increasing the distance between separated parents and children.

Children of African American descent occupied a still different position. Initially, their parents were brought to the Southern colonies as indentured servants. In time, like their white counterparts, they had the hope of finishing their indenture ships and gaining farms of their own. By the 1670s and 1680s, however, permanent servitude for African Americans had become more common. Race lines were also being established; a child born to an African American woman was automatically a slave, regardless of the father's race. Family members were again frequently separated and isolated on distant plantations.

The late seventeenth century also saw African Americans being brought to the Northern colonies, usually as slaves. While their children were born into slavery, they tended to live and work in close quarters with the families who owned them. Unlike their Southern counterparts, they were more apt to have contact with free African American families, who tended to live in Northern cities. Children of free African American families had few options available to them: working as servants, as day laborers, or in the maritime trades.

Most parents raising children in the colonial period looked to their children's future. Well-off parents could usually guarantee some form of education, if not for their daughters, at least for their sons. Families in the middle and lower classes at least hoped to provide training in some skill for their children, often through apprenticeships. An apprenticeship was a set amount of time, usually five to eight years, during which the apprentice received food, housing, job skills, and, some-times, a small salary in exchange for their labor. Over the course of the apprenticeship an individual passed from apprentice to journeyman and finally to master. Under the best circumstances, apprentices were then able to start businesses of their own. As the system had few regulations, apprentices were often used as a source of menial labor and did not always receive the skills they needed.

While formal apprenticeships were less common for girls, some existed for trades such millinery work, dressmaking, or midwifery. Another means for a young girl to acquire skills was to live with another family for a time, treated either as a servant or an additional daughter, preferably gaining such domestic skills as spinning, weaving, and preserving. Again, like the apprentice system, there was little or no way to govern how beneficial the experience would be.

Poverty

Despite the best hopes of all immigrants, poverty remained an issue for many after the move to North America. High mortality rates meant that children were easily orphaned, parents easily widowed. At the end of the eighteenth century, it was estimated that a quarter of all whites lived in poverty, as did almost all African Americans. Most towns were required to support their own poor. This support took many different forms.

By 1685, Boston had an organized almshouse, and various programs were being established to train its inmates for future work. More commonly, poor members of society were bound out to the lowest bidder in a process similar to indenturing a servant. Young children, unable to provide much in the way of labor or personal defense, were especially vulnerable to abuse. Older children, capable of more skilled work, were often assigned to work off their family's debt. Organized protection for poor children was not established until much later.

The Changing Colonial Family

Like children all over Europe, children in the colonies were shaped by the social and political interests of their families. In addition, their lives were influenced by factors their parents could not have predicted before arrival. The high mortality rates in the Chesapeake for the first three-quarters of the seventeenth century meant that family structure initially lost the importance it held in England and the Northern colonies. All over the colonies, the lure of land farther west further divided families already disjointed by immigration to North America. By the mid-eighteenth century, however, most of these gaps had shrunk. Life in the Eastern colonies was as similar to life in Europe as families wanted it to be.

The outbreak of the American Revolution upset all of these boundaries. Some families were split by political differences. Others were divided by death and long military campaigns. Few families were unaffected by a war fought throughout the colonies. When the war and the turmoil of starting a new country finally ended, family life reestablished itself. New ideas about how children and childhood were defined continued to evolve through the nineteenth century.

Abigail B. Chandler

See also: Child Rearing; Education; Family; Reading and Literacy. *Document*: Raising Colonial Children (1699).

Bibliography

Fischer, David Hackett. *Albion's Seed.* New York: Oxford University Press, 1989.

Greven, Philip J. "Family Structure in Seventeenth-Century Andover, Massachusetts." In *Colonial America: Essays in Politics and Social Development,* edited by Stanley N. Katz, John M. Murrin, and Douglas Greenberg. New York: McGraw-Hill, 1993.

Illick, Joseph E. "Child-Rearing in Seventeenth-Century England and America." In *The History of Childhood: The Untold Story of Child Abuse,* edited by Lloyd deMause. New York: Peter Bedrick, 1988.

Levy, Barry, and James Baker. " 'Tender Plants': Quaker Farmers and Children in the Delaware Valley." In *Colonial America: Essays in Politics and Social Development,* edited by Stanley N. Katz, John M. Murrin, and Douglas Greenberg. New York: McGraw-Hill, 1993.

Pollock, Linda A. *Forgotten Children.* Cambridge, UK: Cambridge University Press, 1983.

Sommerville, C. John. *The Rise and Fall of Childhood.* Beverly Hills, CA: Sage Publications, 1982.

Walzer, John F. "A Period of Ambivalence: Eighteenth-Century American Childhood." In *The History of Childhood: The Untold Story of Child Abuse,* edited by Lloyd deMause. New York: Peter Bedrick, 1988.

Choctaw

The Choctaw are a large nation of Native Americans originally located in the present-day states of Mississippi and Alabama. According to their oral traditions, the Choctaw emerged from the sacred mother mound, Nanih Waiya, thousands of years ago. Another tradition tells about their migration from some unknown place in the West, sometime in the distant past, and how they were given their lands forever by the Great Spirit. Relationships with all other beings and spirits formed the heart of the Choctaw worldview. Everything in their world had a spirit—all plants and animals and even inanimate objects.

According to Western scholars, the Choctaw nation coalesced from the survivors of several groups native to the American Southeast, who had experienced catastrophic population losses from epidemic diseases introduced into America by Europeans in the sixteenth century or earlier. By 1700, however, the Choctaw people viewed themselves as a distinct, unified nation, speaking a dialect of the Muscogee language.

The Choctaw were a sedentary people who lived in semipermanent villages. Their subsistence economy included agriculture, hunting, and gathering. Individuals took their mother's clan identity at birth; thus every Choctaw was integrated into an intricate web of relationships governed by complex social beliefs and traditions.

The first meeting with Europeans occurred in 1540 when Hernando de Soto invaded the Southeast. In the late seventeenth century, Frenchmen entered Choctaw territory in search of furs, allies, and trade. The English also sought alliances with the Choctaw from their colonies on the American seaboard. The Choctaw allied themselves primarily with the French, whom they found to be more compatible, but a strong faction of Choctaws maintained close relations with the English. The English, however, incited the Chickasaw to raid the Choctaw nation to kidnap women and children to be sold into the Caribbean slave trade, which was developing in the British colonies.

In 1748, a terrible civil war erupted between rival factions of Choctaws. The faction favoring the French crushed its opponents in 1750. The Choctaw allied with the French in their epic struggle against the British; with the defeat of France at the end of the French and Indian War, the Choctaw were left to deal with the British. In 1765, the British met with the Choctaw at Mobile and signed a treaty of friendship.

Although nominally allied with the British when the American Revolution erupted, Choctaw warriors instead chose to fight with the Americans. After the defeat of the British, the Americans and the Choctaw entered into a treaty of friendship at Hopewell, South Carolina, in 1786.

Donna L. Akers

See also: Native American–European Conflict; Native American–European Relations; Native Americans.

Bibliography

Akers, Donna L. *Living in the Land of Death: The Choctaw Nation, 1830–1860.* East Lansing: Michigan State University Press, 2003.

Debo, Angie. *The Rise and Fall of the Choctaw Republic.* Norman: University of Oklahoma Press, 1934.

Christ and Christianity

"Christ" refers to the historical figure of Jesus, founder of the Christian religion and believed to be the Son of God by his followers. Jesus was born in 4 B.C.E. and raised in the Galilean village of Nazareth in Jewish Palestine. In his late 20s, Jesus was drawn to John the Baptist's message of repentance, and he began his own ministry in the region of Galilee, preaching the coming of the Kingdom of God.

In about 30 C.E., Jesus and his disciples went to celebrate Passover in Jerusalem, but he was condemned as a political agitator by the Roman governor, Pontius Pilate, and crucified. Three days later, his followers found that his tomb was empty and said that the resurrected Jesus appeared to them for forty days thereafter until he ascended into heaven. Hence, his followers believed that Jesus was the promised Savior of Jewish sacred scripture, the "anointed one," the Messiah (in Hebrew) or Christ (*Christos* in Greek).

The life and teachings of Jesus Christ are chronicled in various first-century sacred writings, known collectively as the New Testament of the Bible (the Old Testament consisting of Jewish sacred writings prior to the coming of Christ). The Gospels of Matthew, Mark, Luke, and John provide the life of Christ; the Acts of the Apostles chronicle the earliest spread of Christianity, as do the Epistles, or letters. The latter two sections refer primarily to the extensive missionary work of Paul, born Saul of Tarsus. Paul believed that Christ's message was for both Jew and non-Jewish Gentile and preached Christianity throughout the Roman Empire until his execution about 63 C.E.

Despite sporadic Roman persecutions, Christianity continued to spread, and, in the early fourth century, Emperor Constantine recognized it as a force that could unite his empire. But there was no consensus among church leaders as to the precise nature of Christ. Constantine, therefore, called a church council at Nicaea (325 C.E.), which produced a statement of faith, the Nicene Creed, which defines God as a Trinity: Father, Son, and Holy Spirit. Jesus Christ is called the Son of God, begotten from the Father.

The Roman Empire was a Christian state by the time of its demise in the late fifth century. Christianity continued to spread throughout Europe, from west to east. However, questions persisted about doctrine, as well as the structure and authority within the church, so that Christianity split in 1054 between the Eastern Greek Orthodox Church and the Western Latin Catholic Church, which was led by the pope in Rome. Western Christendom was further fragmented with the Protestant Reformation of the sixteenth century.

In the age of exploration, the European powers that sponsored voyages did so for economic and political reasons, but also in the hope of spreading the Christian faith. Christopher Columbus, sailing for Spain in 1492, cited conversion of the people of the East as an objective of his voyage. On October 12, on his initial landfall (in the Bahamas) after his transatlantic voyage, Columbus named the island "San Salvador [Holy Savior], in honor of our Blessed Lord." So Christ accompanied Europeans to the New World from the very start.

In the seventeenth century Spain and France, both Roman Catholic countries, were colonizing powers in North America, which meant that the Catholic Church looked after the spiritual well-being of their colonists and fostered the spread of Christianity among the natives. The role of religion in the founding of the Protestant English colonies was somewhat different. Of the thirteen English colonies established along the Eastern seaboard of North America, the settlements in New England had the strongest religious basis. The growing division in the Church of England between the authority of king and bishops and those who believed that the church had not been sufficiently purified of its Catholic past led to the emigration of some of the so-called Puritans. These settlers came to practice their faith as they believed was proper and not as prescribed by the established Anglican Church.

One group of Puritans, aboard the *Mayflower*, landed at Plymouth in 1620. According to the compact they subscribed to on board, their colony was being established "for the glory of God, for the advancement of our Christian faith, and honor of our king and country." Governor William Bradford in his *History of*

Plymouth Plantation (1646) cited "advancing the Gospel of the Kingdom of Christ in those remote parts of the world" as a reason for their settlement.

Yet it was the Old Testament that greatly inspired the Puritans, who believed that, like the biblical Jewish people, they too had a covenant with God. In 1630, the Puritans who founded the Massachusetts Bay Colony were reminded of this in the sermon delivered by Joseph Cotton on their departure from England: "Moreover I will appoint a place for my people Israel, and I will plant them." In this period of increasing religious tensions in England, some who came to America compared their voyage to that of the exodus of the Hebrew people from Egypt.

Jonathan Edwards, a preeminent theologian from Massachusetts, believed in religious experience, while maintaining his strict Calvinist faith in predestination. In 1741, he delivered the sermon "Sinners in the Hands of an Angry God," in which the fearful image of sinners being suspended over hellfire by the hand of God was mitigated by the presence of Christ, who "has thrown the door of mercy wide open."

In the 1740s, colonial America experienced the First Great Awakening, a renewal of religious fervor. It was in the Second Awakening, however, in the early nineteenth century that American Christianity moved away from the stern God of the Old Testament toward the saving grace of Jesus Christ of the New Testament.

Florene S. Memegalos

See also: Anglican Church; Baptists; Bible; Catholic Church; Methodist Church; Pietism; Puritanism. *Documents:* A Modell of Christian Charity (1630); Psalm 23 from *The Bay Psalm Book* (1640); Maryland Toleration Act (1649).

Bibliography

Holifield, E. Brooks. *Theology in America: Christian Thought from the Age of the Puritans to the Civil War.* New Haven, CT: Yale University Press, 2003

Noll, Mark A. *America's God: From Jonathan Edwards to Abraham Lincoln.* New York: Oxford University Press, 2002.

Urban, Linwood. *A Short History of Christian Thought.* Rev. ed. New York: Oxford University Press, 1995.

Cities

Seventeenth-century cities depended upon commercial activity, and cities that possessed distinct trading advantages prospered. Cities with a good natural harbor, readily accessible avenues of trade and communication, and an agriculturally productive hinterland tended to thrive in the seventeenth-century maritime economy.

Five cities that had some or all of these advantages and ultimately proved influential in the social, cultural, political, and economic history of colonial America were Boston, Newport, New Amsterdam (New York), Philadelphia, and Charles Town. In 1760, these also were the only communities in colonial North America with populations exceeding 5,000.

Situated along the Eastern seaboard, each of these cities was ideally suited to benefit from transatlantic trade, and they all quickly became focal points for trade between Europe and the colonies. New Amsterdam, located on the southern tip of Manhattan Island, enjoyed the finest harbor on the North American continent. Founded in 1625 by Cryn Fredricksen, New Amsterdam was the principal New World trading post of the Dutch West India Company. Boston, which was founded by John Winthrop in 1630, was situated on Massachusetts Bay at the mouth of the Charles River and possessed a natural landlocked port that could be kept open most of the year. In 1638, William Coddington and his followers established Newport, Rhode Island, on the best year-round harbor on Narragansett Bay. English settlers set up yet another trading post, which they named Charles Town, on a small piece of land between the Ashley and Cooper rivers in South Carolina in 1680. Though 100 miles from the sea, the Quaker town of Philadelphia, founded in 1682, was situated on the Schuylkill and Delaware rivers, which provided easy access to world markets. Life in the five most populous colonial cities was decidedly commercial.

Economy

Colonial cities set up markets for the exchange of manufactured goods from Europe and produce from rural and frontier settlements in the New World. By 1690, all of the cities had regular markets that they held on a particular day each week at a specific location, both of which were designated by provincial or village authorities. In some of the Northern towns, the custom of yearly fairs had also become well established by 1690.

Boston established the colonies' first market in 1633–1634. Every Thursday, settlers from the surrounding countryside journeyed to Boston to exchange goods and produce with the townsfolk. The market was held outside at the head of King Street until 1658, when funds became available for the construction of a town house. Increased trading at the Boston market ultimately led to the town meeting and the appointment of a market clerk, two of the defining characteristics of politics and trade in Boston for nearly 200 years.

In 1648, a weekly market opened on the Strand in New Amsterdam, where townsfolk and farmers exchanged goods. Every Saturday, meat, pork, butter, cheese, turnips, carrots, cabbage, and other country produce, as well as manufactured goods, were bought and sold. In 1662, both Tuesday and Saturday were designated as market days. When the English seized control of New Amsterdam in 1664, they constructed a building to house the market and, in 1683, they officially introduced English market custom in the form of the Dongan Charter. Newport and Philadelphia established their markets in the 1670s and 1680s, respectively, and Charles Town had its market by the 1690s.

In addition to weekly market days, some seventeenth-century town dwellers instituted annual or semiannual fairs. New Amsterdam held annual cattle and hog fairs. Philadelphia also held an annual fair in which all types of merchandise were exchanged. Philadelphia residents valued their fairs, and each county competed eagerly to host them. By 1688, Philadelphia was holding two fairs a year, on May 20 and August 20. Boston residents had also been granted two fairs per year in 1648, but their experience with fairs proved short-lived. There is no evidence that Newport or Charles Town held fairs in the seventeenth century, but, by the eighteenth century, both towns had a robust economy.

Trade and commerce engaged townsfolk of all classes in the seventeenth century. Most inhabitants worked to support the local shipping industry. Some workers prepared commodities for export. Other residents became the ship's crews. Townspeople also worked as artisans, mechanics, or shopkeepers. Gristmills, sawmills, breweries, bakeries, cooperages, and tanneries all appeared in the towns almost as soon as they were established. As trade grew, these occupations also grew, employing more townsfolk. A corps of artisans and laborers also worked diligently to construct and maintain the many ships passing in and out of the cities' harbors. Controlling and managing all of the economic activity in the growing towns were a few wealthy merchants.

Merchants, artisans, and shopkeepers all acquired their much-needed skilled laborers through a system of apprenticeship similar to the one in place in England. Young boys, and occasionally girls, were given for a set number of years to a master workman, who would train them in a given craft or occupation. The great need for skilled laborers during the seventeenth century meant that apprenticeships usually lasted no more than three or four years. Though slight variations existed, a general system of apprenticeship appeared in all of the towns by the end of the seventeenth century.

Economic activity in colonial cities was governed by the medieval notion that merchants, craftsmen, artisans, and laborers' greatest responsibility was to maintain the welfare of the community. Village authorities sought to maintain a fair and customary price for goods. They also promoted quality standards, supervised the food supply, regulated weights and measures, oversaw payment of debts, and protected trade from outside intruders. The result, at least in part, was that townsfolk often found themselves severely limited in their actions and economic dealings.

Society

Colonial cities grew quite rapidly. Boston had 7,000 residents in 1690 and over 15,000 residents in 1760. Philadelphia had 2,100 residents in 1690, over 9,000 residents in 1740, and over 20,000 residents by 1760. New Amsterdam's population grew from 4,000 in 1690 to over 10,000 in 1740 and to 25,000 by the 1770s. Newport had 2,600 residents in 1690 and over 10,000 residents by the 1770s, and Charles Town grew from 1,100 in 1690 to over 10,000 by the 1770s. Much of the cities' growth, except that of Boston, was fueled by immigration, which led to a diverse population.

Colonial cities were heterogeneous places. The majority of urban dwellers came from England. There were, however, Swedes, Dutch, Scots, Scotch-Irish, Welsh, Swiss, Germans, and Africans living in colonial cities. New Amsterdam, Philadelphia, and Charles Town possessed much more racially and ethnically diverse populations than did Boston and Newport, which remained primarily English throughout the colonial period.

Stark class distinctions also existed in colonial cities. By the end of the seventeenth century, a small, exclusive class of rich English merchants had emerged in each of the towns, assuming all of the characteristics of a commercial aristocracy. Rich Boston merchants, for example, built luxurious mansions made of stone and brick and wore fancy clothes, lace, gold braid, and slashed sleeves. They also prevented lower-class residents from exhibiting "excess" in their apparel. Even the Quakers in Philadelphia, who tended to be more

North American Cities, 1750. North America was a largely rural place in the middle of the eighteenth century. Then, as now, Mexico City was the largest metropolis on the continent with a population of over 100,000. By comparison, cities in the thirteen colonies were tiny. Philadelphia was the largest, with a population of less than 20,000. *(Carto-Graphics)*

modest, wore fine clothes, wigs, and side swords. They also built sturdy brick houses with balconies overlooking the Delaware, ate rich foods, and drank fine wine. Elite merchants in Newport and Charles Town, who had a greater amount of arable land at their disposal, established elaborate country estates. The majority of city dwellers were not wealthy, however. They were common laborers or skilled craftsmen who spent their days working to maintain themselves and their families. Class distinctions affected every facet of life in colonial cities.

Two of the most important institutions in colonial cities were the church and the tavern. Puritans in Boston, Anglicans in Charles Town, and the Society of Friends in Philadelphia dominated the social life and social hierarchy in their respective towns. New Amsterdam and Newport proved more tolerant and more heterogeneous. All of the cities had numerous taverns and inns, which served a number of vital functions during the colonial period. Townsfolk went to the taverns daily to eat, drink, gossip, share important news, and engage in a small amount of trade. They posted notices on tavern walls for all to read. Travelers also lodged at local taverns and inns. Together, the church and the tavern provided the social, economic, political, and religious infrastructure necessary for survival in colonial cities.

Colonial urban dwellers faced many of the same problems that continue to plague American cities in the twenty-first century. Colonists, for example, spent a considerable amount of time and effort constructing and maintaining adequate housing and roadways. With the exception of New Amsterdam, colonial cities looked very English. Initial structures were simple one-story buildings made of stone or wood, covered with thatch, and scattered about the settlement. As the cities grew, the buildings also grew, and residents increasingly took more care in determining their design and location. Initially, colonists created paths to get from one location to another, but as the seventeenth century progressed, paths became roads and roads became highways, all of which required increased maintenance and planning. Charles Town and Philadelphia, which were founded near the end of the seventeenth century, grew much more quickly than the other cities and required more initial planning.

Colonists in all of the cities engaged in land reclamation and the building of bridges, canals, wharves, warehouses, churches, taverns, and other public buildings. Fire was always a major concern, as were maintenance of order and police protection. The relative congestion of colonial towns also forced residents to deal with sanitation and public health issues. Each city also found itself confronted early in its history with the necessity of providing for its poor and dependent residents.

Culture

Much of the city dwellers' time was filled with work. They did, however, enjoy other amusements and entertainment. The majority of townsfolk considered church to be their primary social and cultural outlet. The church dominated life in Boston and Philadelphia, and, in Charles Town, the elite turned church attendance into an elaborate social event filled with cultural meaning and significance.

Townsfolk also pursued other cultural outlets, most of which they brought with them from their homeland. Gaming and card playing as well as dancing, singing, and "fidling" proved quite popular in colonial cities. Young boys also played a kind of football or soccer in city streets. The town's wealthier inhabitants enjoyed country excursions, elaborate dinner parties, and lectures provided by distinguished speakers. In Newport, village men amused themselves by bowling on the green, hunting wildfowl, and fishing. New Amsterdam's (New York) elite engaged in boat racing and a popular form of miniature golf, among other amusements. Townsfolk also passed the time smoking tobacco and drinking alcohol, although these were officially discouraged, if not outright condemned, by most colonial leaders. Virtually all townsfolk celebrated important holidays such as New Year's Day, May Day, and Christmas.

Most town leaders valued education and worked to create both public and private schools in their towns. Boston led the colonial cities in the creation of schools, but it was not the only city with schools. New Amsterdam created the first elementary school in any colonial town in 1638, and, within a year of its founding, Newport's leaders also had made provision for a school. Charles Town, too, established schools, but not until the eighteenth century. Although the Society of Friends in Philadelphia remained somewhat indifferent to higher education, it was noticeably active in creating elementary schools; Philadelphia also had an excellent public library system, founded in large part by Benjamin Franklin, who also created the American Philosophical Society in 1743. Of the four Northern towns, Boston and Philadelphia rapidly became centers of education, attracting students from the city and the surrounding countryside, as well as other English colonies.

Colonial cities also enjoyed a vibrant print culture. In 1638, the first printing press in the North American colonies was set up just outside Boston, in Cambridge. John Foster became the proprietor of the first Boston press in 1674. Printing began in Philadelphia in 1685. Soon, other presses emerged, printing everything from collections of poems and essays to sermons, pamphlets, and almanacs.

Politics

Rapid growth of the cities' population and their respective economies, as well as their distance from England, forced colonial leaders to expand local government. All of the cities except Charles Town gradually assumed self-management of local affairs. They acquired power through either piecemeal grants or charter revisions as the need for more local control increased.

The structure of local government in Philadelphia and New Amsterdam (after 1664, New York) most resembled that of English towns. Both cities were designated as municipal boroughs, incorporated by a royal charter, and governed by a mayor and a city council. Both mayor and council were appointed by a royal governor and tended to be aristocrats. They possessed limited taxing and spending power and were often slow to meet the demands of urban growth.

Local government in Boston and Newport had its roots in the assemblies of rural England and Puritan congregationalism and was centered upon the town meeting and the selectmen. Several times a year, all the male residents (freemen) of each town would gather in a town meeting to conduct business, elect officials, pass laws, levy taxes, and settle disputes. During the time between meetings, the selectmen assumed all of the governmental responsibilities. They made appointments and judicial decisions and oversaw the daily administration of the city. The selectmen tended to be those individuals who held the most power within both the marketplace and the church. In general, local government in Boston and Newport proved much more efficient than that in either Philadelphia or New York.

Colonial Charles Town was governed by a provincial assembly that appointed local commissioners to manage the city. Both assemblymen and commissioners, most of whom were wealthy planters, tended not to live in Charles Town and were often extremely slow in meeting the needs of the city.

Cities and the Coming of the Revolution

Cities played a critical role in the coming of the American Revolution. In most cases, cities bore the brunt of English fiscal policy in both the seventeenth and eighteenth centuries, and, by the 1760s, residents of cities were leading overt resistance to the Crown. By this time, the cities, as well as the colonies, had grown so much that attempts by British authorities to impose restrictions on them resulted in a series of conflicts that forced colonists to reconsider their connection to England.

The cities' meetinghouses, printing shops, taverns, and coffeehouses provided colonists with the means to organize protests and distribute information. The lines of communication that cities had opened to facilitate trade between colonies also helped facilitate

resistance. Wealthy merchants, the growing middle class, and common laborers—all participated in the urban protest that ultimately led to revolt.

Michael A. Rembis

See also: Artisans; Baltimore; Boston; Charleston; Detroit; Halifax; Laborers, Urban; Merchants; Mexico City; Montreal; New Amsterdam; New Bern; New Orleans; New York City; Newport; Ottawa; Philadelphia; Portsmouth, New Hampshire; Providence; Quebec City; St. Augustine; St. Louis; Santa Fe; Savannah; Williamsburg.

Bibliography

Bridenbaugh, Carl. *Cities in Revolt: Urban Life in America, 1743–1776.* New York: Alfred A. Knopf, 1955.

———. *Cities in the Wilderness: The First Century of Urban Life in America, 1625–1742.* New York: Alfred A. Knopf, 1955.

Chudacoff, Howard P. *The Evolution of American Urban Society.* Upper Saddle River, NJ: Prentice Hall, 2000.

Fries, Sylvia Doughty. *The Urban Idea in Colonial America.* Philadelphia: Temple University Press, 1977.

Nash, Gary B. *The Urban Crucible: Social Change, Political Consciousness, and the Origins of the American Revolution.* Cambridge, MA: Harvard University Press, 1979.

Purvis, Thomas L. *Colonial America to 1763.* New York: Facts on File, 1999.

Class

During the colonial period, the role of class varied, depending on time and region. Over time, emerging class divisions marked the development of a new social structure.

As colonists from throughout Europe traveled to British North America, they hoped to re-create their Old World home, while taking advantage of the opportunities in the New World. As they worked to establish traditional social, economic, political, and cultural folkways in North America, they soon learned that many needed to change because of the new environment. Thus, in North America, familiar institutions took on new characteristics, even when they existed side by side with traditional institutions. This created a more open, fluid society, which eventually challenged and destroyed many traditional institutions while creating new ones—with both positive and negative consequences.

In traditional society, for example, deference maintained the hierarchical social system of Europe. Members of the general populace knew their place and responsibilities, and they interacted with their betters in a deferential manner. In North America, the lack of a noble class, coupled with the consequences of open land ownership and economic opportunities, challenged these behavior patterns. An individual's ability played an important role in colonial development, and a self-made citizen earned his or her status rather than inheriting it. Thus, the stabilizing effect of deference gave way to a less stable society based upon individualism, with wide-ranging consequences.

In addition, obligations existed between the various ranks of traditional European society, and, during times of crisis or dearth, the poor could count on the elite for protection and food. Under the more modern social system of colonial America, these mechanisms became strained in many areas.

By the mid-eighteenth century, the partial breakdown of deference, coupled with the abolishment of many traditional customs and increasing economic inequality, further increased instability among workers in towns, who, in turn, slowly developed a class consciousness. "Class" became a modern category that replaced traditional groupings; thus, while old ranks faded away, new ones were established.

Role of Class

The place of class in colonial America has been both denied and celebrated. A traditional perception of the colonial period viewed the New World frontier, which was constantly moving westward, as a great leveler that denied class divisions.

As the colonies developed, the majority of settlers engaged in yeoman agriculture. These farmers were neither tenants nor agricultural laborers; rather, they were landowners who controlled their own means of production. As they constituted the majority, and as many had once been indentured servants or farm laborers, colonial America could either be seen as a classless society or a society with one class. These yeoman farmers, however, were not engaged merely in subsistence agriculture; they also were engaged in market agriculture, and all was not equal between them.

The stress on colonial agriculture downplayed the role of urban development. In fact, it was in urban areas, especially in eighteenth-century port cities, that class became a permanent fixture. Colonial development placed new demands upon the economy and workforce. The wealthy demanded larger and more ornate houses, and an infrastructure needed to be de-veloped and expanded. This, in turn, created an increased demand for both skilled and unskilled labor.

Many people traveled to British North America with the dream of owning land. Over time, however, it became harder to acquire land, as the frontier, where free or cheap land existed, moved farther from the coast. People were willing to travel inland for land, but wealthy speculators had already purchased large tracts and were profiting by reselling it, thereby driving up the costs of even small plots. By the American Revolution, the colonies, and their social structure, were at a very different place than at their founding.

Colonial society was divided into three groups: the "better" sort, the "middling" sort, and the "lower" sort, which, when taken together, created a system of individualism and interdependency. Gradually, relations between the three groups changed. While colonial America lacked an established nobility, an upper class soon emerged.

The best example of this was colonial Virginia where, after the discovery of tobacco as a cash crop, a group of well-connected individuals increasingly used their position to gain more economic, social, and political power over both land and labor. As they grew wealthier, the emerging Tidewater elite worked harder to consolidate and expand their position. In the exploitative plantation system they had developed, clear distinctions existed between the major groups.

The planters dominated all aspects of society. Indentured servants were exploited for their labor and, once free, usually pushed to the frontier. With the development of African slavery, the planters had a new labor source to exploit; they worked to expand and protect their slave labor through the legal system, making slavery an inherited status. The Southern colonies, for the most part, lacked a middle class, but they created a class system based upon control over the means of production.

In the New England and Mid-Atlantic colonies, the better sort did not dominate to the extent of the Southern planters, but, gradually, large landowners and merchants utilized their social and economic power to gain more control over the political system. Parts of New England probably came closest to a classless society because of the large number of small freeholders; yet rank, status, deference, and issues of dependency and independence still created a social, economic, and political hierarchy.

Both the better and middling sort worked to consolidate and expand their social and economic power. The establishment of British political institutions, especially the Forty Shilling Freehold (whereby men with 40 shillings worth of property were given full citizenship and the right to vote), allowed a growing number of colonists, from all classes but especially the middle, to acquire political power.

Better and Middling Sorts

For many, social status came from their relationship to, or control over, the lower sort. A master craftsmen needed laborers for his shop and porters to move his goods. A merchant needed unskilled laborers in the ports along with sailors to man his vessels. A large landowner required tenants, slaves, or agricultural laborers to make his land productive.

It was from among the lower sort, where there existed the greatest diversity of individuals and a vast labor spectrum from free to unfree laborers, that the urban working class would emerge. Especially in urban areas, the status of the lower sort, coupled with issues of race, gender, and ethnicity, was both a divisive and unifying force, with groups sometimes uniting over the economic issues that they all faced and sometimes experiencing conflicts based on racial and ethnic differences.

Members of the lower sort also included Native Americans, who contributed to colonial development through the fur trade, as laborers, and in a variety of other roles. While many tribes were being pushed to the west, Native Americans lived throughout the colonies, and they were readily recognized by their skin color and physical features.

In a similar situation, because of physical appearance, were the close to 1 million African slaves who ended up in British North America. Although slaves are often stereotyped as agricultural laborers, they served many roles during the colonial period, including those of domestic servants, skilled laborers, and sailors.

European laborers were also important to colonial development. The first important group to arrive was the indentured servants of Virginia, who mainly served as contracted agricultural laborers. As slaves replaced indentured servants on the plantations, the role of indentured servants changed. By the eighteenth century, indentured servants served as both skilled and unskilled laborers, with many becoming apprentices in colonial industry.

Another important group of mobile workers were the various Jack Tars (sailors), throughout British North America and the Atlantic world. Jack Tars were important not only on the seas but also on land, as they were a visible force in ports.

The final group of the lower sort was the wage laborers, whose development was seen in eighteenth century urban areas. As they exchanged their labor for wages in a mixed modern and traditional economic and social system, they were the most affected by ongoing changes.

Maintaining and justifying traditional and modern social distinctions, class existed throughout colonial America, but its influence varied over time and place.

Impact of the Revolution

The American Revolution had a critical impact on class or, at least, on the perception of class in American society. Unlike later revolutions—such as those in France and Haiti—the American Revolution did not see a dramatic change in the composition of the ruling class. With the exception of some wealthy loyalists, forced to flee after Britain's defeat, the merchants and landholders who held sway in the colonies composed much of the ruling elite in the new United States.

They were now, however, less likely to command the kind of automatic loyalty, or deference, they once had. Participation in the Revolution led many ordinary farmers and artisans to believe that they had a voice in their own governance. They were no longer willing to except, without question, the rule of their social betters. Of course, this social transformation had been going on during colonial times, but the Revolution accelerated the pace.

By eliminating British imperial restrictions on trade and westward expansion, the Revolution also opened up economic opportunities for poor and middling whites. Along with those opportunities came a more fluid class order.

Ty M. Reese

See also: Artisans; Laborers, Rural; Laborers, Urban; Landlords; Land and Real Estate; Merchants; Property and Property Rights. *Document:* Rules of Civility & Decent Behaviour in Company and Conversation (c. 1744).

Bibliography

Nash, Gary. *Race, Class and Politics: Essays on American Colonial and Revolutionary Societies.* Urbana: University of Illinois Press, 1986.
———. *Red, White and Black: The Peoples of Early America.* Englewood Cliffs, NJ: Prentice Hall, 1974.
———. *The Urban Crucible: Social Change, Political Conscious-*

ness and the Origins of the American Revolution. Cambridge, MA: Harvard University Press, 1979.

Pestana, Carla Gardina, and Sharon V. Salinger, eds. *Inequality in Early America.* Hanover, NH: University Press of New England, 1999.

Schultz, Ronald. *The Republic of Labor: Philadelphia Artisans and the Politics of Class, 1720–1830.* New York: Oxford University Press, 1993.

Clocks and Timekeeping

In the agriculture-based colonial economy, accuracy in the measurement of time proved of little relative importance. The few privately owned clocks, generally brought from Europe, were rarities celebrated as scientific curiosities, treasured for their beauty, and displayed as symbols of prosperity. Clocks for the general public, very large types set in steeples, towers, and public buildings, existed only in the most prosperous and established settlements. Most early Americans judged time in the age-old manner of looking up at the sky and observing the position of the sun or the moon.

Several different types of mechanical timekeepers could be found in colonial America, including lantern, bracket, tall, and tower clocks. At the time, the definition of a clock was a device that strikes, at minimum, on an hourly basis, while a timepiece merely measured the passage of time and did not strike.

European settlers brought the first clocks. These early clocks were probably lanterns, small clocks with a wheel balance that enjoyed great popularity in England and predated the bracket and tall clocks. Bracket clocks, first developed in 1657, were small spring-driven clocks with pendulums.

Tall clocks appeared only after 1659 and, like bracket clocks, were made possible by the commercial application of the pendulum, a much more accurate way of regulating a clock by means of a swinging weight. Five to nine feet in height and standing unsupported on the floor, tall clocks are also known as longcase or grandfather clocks.

Very little is known about tower clocks in America, other than that they constituted a proud achievement for a town that had previously relied either on bells or on a cannon to mark time. The earliest one, probably built to alert townspeople to the start of church services, may be a Massachusetts clock that was in existence in 1650. In the mid-seventeenth century,

The tall clock—also called the longcase or grandfather clock—was 5 to 9 feet high and stood unsupported on the floor. It was made possible by the commercial application of the pendulum in the late 1650s. *(Sturbridge Museum, Sturbridge, Massachusetts/Bridgeman Art Library)*

tower clocks began to employ pendulums and, if kept in good condition, lost only a few seconds a day instead of the minutes lost in the days before pendulums.

American clock makers in the colonial period made clocks in the English style but with slight twists to accommodate American conditions. Tall clocks were English inventions that never became very popular on the Continent but were apparently the only type of clocks made for private use by early American craftsmen. Much of their popularity derives from the fact that they could be made with an absolute minimum of metal parts, since metal was scarce in the colonies. Glass, also hard to obtain, rarely covered a dial. The dial, about 10.5 inches in diameter, consisted of metal, often a strip covering easy-to-acquire wood. Typically, two hands would mark hours and minutes, although some English and Dutch clock makers in 1660 developed a style with only one hand that moved along a dial divided into forty-eight segments for the quarter hours.

The movement, or mechanism of the clock, came in four types: thirty-hour brass, eight-day brass with two weights, thirty-hour wood, and eight-day wood. Wooden movements, generally made of oak, had metal escape wheels to regulate the release of power. Brass movements, cast using sand molds, were made from an alloy of copper, zinc, and occasionally tin in proportions unique to each clock maker.

The cases of American clocks were constructed from native woods such as cherry. In overall design, these clocks owed much to their English cousins and were often indistinguishable from them. Both English and American models were plain with flat-topped hoods.

The clock making industry in America developed very slowly, in part because of the absence of a strong demand for clocks but also because a clock took many months to complete. Clock makers typically worked in other craft jobs, such as blacksmithing or gunsmithing, and only made clocks on occasion at the request of a customer.

Abel Cottey is the earliest known American clock maker. An immigrant from Devon, England, he set up a business in Philadelphia in 1682 and made tall clocks. Perhaps because of Cottey's influence, Philadelphia became the clock making center of the English colonies, although other areas also had established clock makers. By the start of the eighteenth century, tall clocks were being made in numbers in Massachusetts, Connecticut, Rhode Island, New Hampshire, and New York.

By the time of the Revolution, the craft of clock making in America lagged considerably behind that in Europe. Severely hampered by supply difficulties, American clock makers could not match their European counterparts in the beauty or quality of their products, and most Americans saw no need to purchase such items. American clocks would occupy a minor place in history until well into the nineteenth century.

Caryn E. Neumann

See also: Artisans; Science and Technology (Chronology); Technology.

Bibliography

Baillie, G. H., C. Clutton, and C. A. Ilbert. *Britten's Old Clocks and Watches and Their Makers.* New York: Bonanza, 1956.

Palmer, Brooks. *The Book of American Clocks.* New York: Macmillan, 1950.

Clothing

Although separated by 3,000 miles and a long sea voyage, colonists in North America followed clothing customs similar to their European counterparts. Fashion was developed on both sides of the English Channel, usually by members of the royal courts, and it traveled with courtiers and merchants, and in portraits. While the general drape of a gown or jacket could be common across Europe, small regional differences were frequently seen. Once a style became established at court, it gradually trickled down through the middle and working classes.

Fashionable women and men in the colonies were able to follow changing styles through engravings, drawings, letters, and clothing shipped directly from Europe. They were already accustomed to international changes in fashion. The wide sweep of migration to the New World did lead to a broader range of influences on the middle and working classes. A farmer's wife in England would see only what her English neighbors were wearing, but a farmer's wife in one of the colonies could have Dutch or French neighbors. Then, as now, fashion also was a personal choice.

Some aspects of clothing in the colonial period were consistent, despite social class and changes in fashion. Fabric was always expensive and labor relatively cheap. Cloth had to be carefully cut and seamed together if it was not large enough. Most cuts were made on the straight of the goods, rather than on the bias as they are today. Outer fabrics and linings were cut and fit together. While a woman's gown may have resembled one complete piece, it usually consisted of several parts held together with lacings. This required fewer large pieces of fabric, helped with washing, and made it easier to vary gowns, as women could substitute different bodices or petticoats. The upper classes wore garments made from such rich, smooth fabrics as satin, camlet, and russel. Clothing worn by the working classes was made from such fabric as wool, frieze, and tow (a coarse form of linen).

Maintaining cleanliness was a constant challenge before washing machines or dry cleaning. Underneath their clothing, men and women wore a loose garment called a shirt or shift. Throughout the colonial period, linen was the most common fabric for the middle and lower classes. Cotton was prized by the upper classes in the late seventeenth and early eighteenth centuries. Men's shirts were usually made with a collar and could be seen from under a waistcoat or vest. Women's shifts often had a drawstring at the neck to adjust for lower necklines or nursing a child. As the garment was worn next to the body, it soaked up sweat and dirt before it could reach the more expensive outer clothing. Underwear as we know it today was rare. Most people let their shifts or shirts hang loose or tucked them up between their legs.

While working, men and women covered their outer clothing with aprons to protect both wearer and clothing. When they cooked, women wore wool aprons, as wool would smolder rather than burn if a spark touched it. Blacksmiths wore leather aprons for similar reasons.

Pockets as we know them were almost never set into clothing. Men attached small bags or pouches to their belts. Women tied flat, oblong bags, which were called pockets, to their waists. Ordinary pockets were tied under the clothing and reached through a slit in the petticoat. Fancier pockets were heavily embroidered and meant for show on top of a gown.

European clothing in the early seventeenth century resembled the garments of the decades before. Women wore stays—undergarments stiffened with whalebone or metal—about their waists, giving them a square look, and a piece of wood or whalebone, called a busk, fit in a pocket down the front for added stiffening. The farthingale, a flat support holding the skirts out from the waist, was still worn by some women. Heavy ruffs were still worn about the neck by both men and women, and both sexes wore close-fitting bodices or doublets. Lines were either straight or angular, and garment waists were at the natural waistline. Color throughout the seventeenth century was heavy and deep.

In the mid-seventeenth century, the "cavalier" style began to grow popular for the upper classes in England, France, and Holland. Clothing lines were draped and flowing. Women's waistlines rose as their necklines fell. Both men and women's sleeves were often slashed to reveal the fabric beneath; women's skirts were often tucked one on top of the other for the same

reason. Men wore broad, lace-trimmed collars and high boots. Over time, men's breeches grew ever more exaggerated, ending in lace, and were worn with delicate, pointed shoes. Wigs were commonly worn. The overall emphasis was on lavish display.

A counterinfluence on fashion was exerted by the members of the English upper class known today as the Puritans. They sought to reform, or purify, all aspects of English life and chose simply cut garments, though these were usually made from costly, heavy fabrics. Sumptuary laws passed in Massachusetts Bay Colony served primarily to control dress for the lower classes, rather than society as a whole. Portraits from the period show men and women in their best clothing, often dyed with expensive black dyes (black was difficult to obtain with natural dyes), which perhaps led to the image that all Puritans wore black. Other religious groups, including the Quakers and Separatists (or Pilgrims), also instituted similar dress reforms.

Dress lines in the late seventeenth century grew angular once more. The waists of women's garments again fell at the natural waistline and had begun to acquire a pointed front. While women continued to wear layers of skirts, the fullness was usually drawn to the back of the dress (similar to the bustle of the late nineteenth century). Men's clothes also lost some of their fullness. Their breeches were usually covered by heavy, well-cut coats. The same emphasis on brocade and trim remained.

Clothing for both men and women remained angular in the early eighteenth century. Women wore a different form of stays that gave their upper bodies an upside-down-cone look that would remain for most of the century, although the later emphasis on tightly laced stays for a small waist was not as prominent in the colonial period. The deep, bright colors favored during the seventeenth changed to pastels. Trade with the Far East brought patterned, floral printed fabrics into vogue for the very wealthy. Both men and women wore tight-fitting sleeves with large cuffs, trimmed with lace and ribbon.

The most noticeable part of mid-eighteenth-century fashion was the shape of women's gowns. Side hoops, called panniers, held skirts farther and farther out on either side of the woman's waist. In France, the "robe à la française" or sack-back dress, became popular. Cloth flowed down from women's shoulders, held in pleats on the back. The English variation on this fashion was the "robe à l'anglaise," where the draped cloth was tucked smoothly over the back petticoats. Women's

Puritan clothing of the seventeenth century (two figures at left) was characterized by simple cuts and heavy fabrics. The garments of upper-class English settlers in the 1660s (two figures at right) were more elaborate and ornate. *(Brown Brothers, Sterling, Pennsylvania)*

hair was piled higher and higher on their heads. Men's clothing was very well cut, with coordinated waistcoat, jacket, and breeches.

Clothing at the very end of the eighteenth century was a direct reaction to the excesses before it. The American and French revolutions led to an interest in classical design. Women's dresses became loosely draped, often with a broad sash about the waist. Their pockets were worn as small bags, tied about the wrist, as the straight skirts could not accommodate them. Men wore close-fitting breeches and jackets. Fabrics were solid and rarely trimmed.

While clothing for middle- and working-class people roughly followed these changes in elites' clothing, the primary emphasis was on practicality. People needed clothing that was easy to put on and would protect them at work. The average woman dressing in the morning put on a shift, stockings, a pocket, stays, petticoats, a bodice, a kerchief, an apron, and a cap. The average man wore a shirt, breeches, a waistcoat, a jacket, a kerchief, and a cap. Clothing for special occasions was

passed through families and continually altered to keep up with changing fashions. Most rural and working-class colonists continued to maintain this style of dress until the early nineteenth century.

Abigail B. Chandler

See also: Cotton; Furnishings; Indigo. *Document*: Probate Inventory of a Plymouth Colony Estate (1672).

Bibliography

Arnold, Janet. *Patterns of Fashion*. Vol. 1. New York: Drama Book Specialists, 1972.

Baumgarten, Linda, and John Watson. *Costume Close-Up*. Williamsburg, VA: Colonial Williamsburg Foundation, 1999.

Hart, Avril, and Susan North. *Fashion in Detail, from the 17th and 18th Centuries*. London: Victoria and Albert Productions, 1998.

Johnson, Mary Moyars. *Historic Colonial French Dress*. West Lafayette, IN: Ouabache, 1982.

Waugh, Norah. *Corsets and Crinolines*. New York: Routledge/Theatre Arts, 1954.

Coercive Acts (1774)

The Coercive Acts, or Intolerable Acts, were a series of bills passed by Parliament in 1774 as a punitive action against colonial resistance to the Tea Act, particularly the Boston Tea Party. Scholars believe that the Coercive Acts were a critical spur to colonial resistance, which resulted in the organization of the Continental Congress and culminated in the writing of the Declaration of Independence.

The first act, called the Boston Port Bill, took effect on June 1, 1774, under the direction of the new governor, General Thomas Gage. Utilizing a port blockade, the governor prohibited the loading and unloading of ships at Boston until the inhabitants of Massachusetts paid for the damages incurred by the destruction of tea in Boston Harbor (commonly referred to as the Boston Tea Party). The only exceptions were military stores, foodstuffs, and fuel. Before these items were unloaded, they had to clear customs officials in nearby Salem—the location of the new customs house for the colony when Boston was closed. The port closure rallied the other colonies to the cause of Massachusetts; fearing the loss of their own liberties, they called for a Continental Congress in order to develop united measures of resistance to future British persecution.

Next was passed the Massachusetts Government Act, which took effect on August 1, 1774. The act dissolved the colony's charter and changed the structure of the government. The new government consisted of a governor and a council appointed by the king. The governor had the authority to select most office holders in the colony, including judges and sheriffs. The governor also gained control of town meetings. Although this was not the first time Massachusetts had lost its charter, the action, combined with the closure of the port of Boston, became the most threatening aspect of the coercive program for many colonials. They believed that if the Crown could systematically destroy the economic and political viability of Massachusetts, then the future of every colony was jeopardized.

Then came the Administration of Justice Act, which took effect June 1, 1774. It provided protection for royal officials in the colonies by allowing the governor to move court trials outside of the colony. According to the act, any government official accused of a capital crime committed in the execution of government duties could be tried by a court in another colony or in England if the governor believed local opinion made a fair trial impossible. Since the act freed government officials from local bullying, the ministry hoped a more determined supervision of imperial measures within the colonies could occur. The Administration of Justice Act raised suspicions among the colonials, who believed the British government would use it to extend the authority of Parliament over the colonies by limiting their influence over the administration of the colonial government.

Although the Quartering and Quebec Acts were not actually a part of Parliament's program for coercion, the colonists certainly viewed them as such. The Quartering Act went into effect on June 2, 1774. Essentially, the act was an insignificant supplement to a much larger series of bills providing for the supply and quartering of British soldiers throughout the empire, and specifically emerged from the Mutiny Act of 1765. Composed of numerous provisions for military support, the aspect of the act most offensive to the Americans was the stipulation that army officers could house soldiers in private homes when accommodation in government buildings was not feasible.

Not directly related to the thirteen colonies, the Quebec Act took effect with the Quartering Act. It extended the boundaries of Quebec to the Ohio country, permitted the predominantly Roman Catholic citizens of the former French colony of Quebec to practice religious freedom, allowed for the continuation of French law, and set up a government run entirely by individuals appointed by the king without consent of an elected legislature. The expansion of Quebec's borders angered land speculators throughout the colonies, and many Americans feared that Parliament would force them to accept the same type of government. Those fears were never realized, as the American Revolution rendered these acts moot.

Solomon K. Smith

See also: Boston Port Bill; Gage, Thomas; Quebec Act (1774). *Document:* The Boston Port Act (1774).

Bibliography

Ammerman, David. *In Common Cause: American Response to the Coercive Acts of 1774.* New York: W. W. Norton, 1974.

Champagne, Roger. "New York and the Intolerable Acts." *New-York Historical Society Quarterly* 45 (1961): 195–207.

Sosin, Jack M. "The Massachusetts Acts of 1774: Coercive or Preventive." *Huntington Library Quarterly* 26 (1963): 235–52.

Coffee

The use of coffee originated in Ethiopia and expanded to Arabia and elsewhere, beginning in the fifteenth century. Coffee initially became known in Europe as a commodity that was exchanged between the Muslim traders whom European merchants did business with.

Adopted by Europeans in the 1640s, the new drink rapidly grew in popularity. Its advantage over alcoholic beverages of clearing and stimulating the mind made it the symbolic drink of the Enlightenment. Its cost was high at first, but as the price fell, it became popular among the lower classes, not only in imitation of the upper classes but also because its ability to suppress hunger and drowsiness helped people to endure the harsh working conditions common under early industrialization.

To satisfy the growing demand from about 1650 onward, the English and Dutch East India companies began to import an increasing amount of coffee from Yemen, the sole producer. By 1720, the trade reached about 2,000 tons annually, 10 percent of the world's production.

As this trade depended on the goodwill of the Yemeni suppliers, Europeans attempted to establish cultivation of the coffee plant in colonies with the appropriate climate. Permanent cultivation was achieved in the Dutch colony of Java (Indonesia) and the French Île de Bourbon (La Réunion) in the 1710s. The resulting output from the East Indies rendered Europe independent of Arabian production, but it did not exceed 3,500 tons annually.

A massive augmentation of the coffee supply was accomplished only when coffee was introduced to the West Indies. Growing coffee is labor-intensive, as the berries of the coffee plant—from which coffee beans are obtained by peeling and drying—do not mature all at the same time and need to be carefully harvested by hand. Therefore, this tropical crop neatly fitted into the agricultural economies of the Western colonies, already based on plantations using slave labor to grow other labor-intensive tropical crops, such as sugar or indigo. The Dutch initiated coffee production in Suriname in 1724 and, by the 1770s, that colony was producing more than 12,000 tons annually.

The French, the only other colonial power to be a major force in the coffee trade until the end of the eighteenth century, started cultivation on the small islands of Martinique and Guadeloupe in the 1720s and 1730s. By 1765, exports from the French Antilles—still mainly the Lesser Antilles—reached 10,000 tons per year.

The most astounding boost in coffee production, however, was the rapid extension of cultivation on Saint-Domingue in the second half of the eighteenth century, pushing French trading volume to 20,000 tons annually around 1770, to 35,000 tons in the late 1770s, and finally to 45,000 tons by 1790. Coffee had become the second most important commodity in the Atlantic trade after sugar. But slave rebellions in Saint-Domingue and the colony's independence in 1804 reduced its output, and the coffee supply of the Western world dropped. This stimulated coffee cultivation in Brazil and Colombia, which subsequently became the most important coffee producers.

The main part of the coffee produced in the colonies was consumed in central and Western Europe; Spain and Portugal did not develop a taste for the beverage at first, and neither did the American colonies. The British had been a coffee-drinking nation in the seventeenth century, but then the government increased taxes on coffee to protect the British tea trade. Hence, the British started preferring tea, and this habit was adopted by the European inhabitants of the North American mainland. At the end of the eighteenth century, a Continental European on average consumed nearly a pound of coffee annually, but a North American consumed barely an ounce.

In the conflict between the colonists and Britain leading to American independence, however, tea became a symbol of the British rule and was, as such, rejected. The immigration of non-British Europeans was another reason for the rising demand for coffee.

On the supply side, the escape from the Navigation Acts made trade with the near centers of coffee production possible, so that coffee was more readily available than tea. Within 50 years, coffee had ousted tea, and the United States was to become the world's largest market for coffee.

Alexander Engel

See also: Agriculture; Inns and Taverns (Public Houses); Slavery, Caribbean.

Bibliography

Pendergrast, Mark. *Uncommon Grounds: The History of Coffee and How It Transformed Our World.* New York: Basic Books, 1999.

Schivelbusch, Wolfgang. *Tastes of Paradise: A Social History of*

Spices, Stimulants, and Intoxicants. New York: Pantheon, 1992.

Smith, Simon D. "Accounting for Taste. British Coffee Consumption in Historical Perspective." *Journal of Interdisciplinary History* 27:2 (1996): 183–214.

Columbian Exchange

Historian Alfred W. Crosby coined the phrase "Columbian Exchange" in 1972 to describe the significant biological consequences of the meeting of Europe and the Americas in the 1490s and beyond. Since Crosby's landmark study, scholars have expanded the concept to include the cultural and material consequences of this exchange.

The Columbian Exchange is, for many historians, one of the pivotal moments in human history. Its consequences spread far beyond the simple meeting of cultures. The resulting disease epidemics, coupled with the massive mineral and agricultural wealth reaped by Europeans (and their American descendants), affected world history profoundly and touched nearly every part of the globe. Considered together, the effects of the Columbian Exchange are not simply important to understanding the development of European colonies in the Americas; they are one of the key events in human history.

The term "exchange" implies that each side, Europe and the Americas, received and gave something. The first, deadliest, and most significant impact that Europe had on the Americas was disease. Native American history, and likely European history, would have been profoundly different had it not been for the crippling effects of epidemics on native societies. The dramatic decrease in the number of Native Americans after 1492 is startling and tragic, but it tells only part of the story of the effect of diseases such as measles and smallpox. Both of these diseases were unknown in the Americas prior to 1492, but they colored nearly every meeting of Europeans and Americans.

Although the numbers are very much in dispute, and we are unlikely to know for certain how many Native Americans there were before 1492, recent estimates place the Native American population of the area that became the United States between 5 million and 7 million. At its nadir, around the turn of the twentieth century, the native population had dropped to around 250,000. Disease was not the only culprit, but it was a major factor.

The numbers, as horrific as they may be, fail to capture the cultural significance of such a loss of population. In societies where records and cultural traditions are kept orally, the loss of elders exacted a painful cultural price. Diseases that wiped out whole generations of Native Americans made effective resistance against colonial encroachment all but impossible. Since Europeans were, for the most part, immune to these diseases, their populations soared in North America, while native populations plummeted. In some communities, the mortality rate reached 90 percent. The Columbian Exchange, in this regard, was not a fair trade conducted on equal footing.

Disease would appear to have had the most profound impact on Native Americans, but the Columbian Exchange also brought about other changes in native life, not all of which were negative. Columbus's voyages and early Spanish colonization efforts introduced pigs and horses to the Americas. Plains cultures in particular recognized the efficacy of horseback combat and quickly developed skill in riding. Pigs descended from Spanish drifts fed generations of Native Americans, particularly in the Southeast. Among the Navajo of the American Southwest, sheep had been unknown prior to the arrival of flocks from Spanish Mexico, but weaving, particularly among Navajo women, has become one of the defining characteristics of Navajo cultural production. Of course, European-introduced livestock also overran Native American farmland and hunting territory with serious ecological consequences.

The effects of the Columbian Exchange on Europe, while not as devastating, are significant in terms of intellectual, economic, and dietary developments. Prior to 1492, European concepts of the world had changed strikingly little for at least 1,000 years. The world was generally divided into the only three inhabitable parts—Europe, Africa, and Asia. The rest of the world fell under the ominous category of the "Torrid Zone," where the climate was considered too inhospitable to support human life. Columbus, together with Portuguese explorers in Africa, exploded this myth with the revelation that there were people—many of them—inhabiting areas long believed vacant by Europeans.

Europeans in 1491 were familiar with Islam, Christianity, and Judaism, all of which grew from similar monotheistic foundations. After the existence of native peoples in the Americas became known in Europe, European philosophers struggled to fit Native Americans into their medieval categories. Though Columbus had sailed with the intent of crusading for Catholic Spain, the scientific furor ignited by his discoveries promoted skepticism of ancient theories. Knowledge of new plants and animals further challenged European systems. The European pursuits of biology, botany, and anthropology all can be traced to the Columbian Exchange.

From an economic standpoint, the Columbian Exchange encouraged a rise in European wealth, commerce, and productivity that would eventually propel Europe into the dominant position it held during the seventeenth, eighteenth, and nineteenth centuries. The Spanish, for instance, extracted huge amounts of gold and, later, silver from Peru and Mexico. The rise in European wealth prompted countries to pursue trade with the Far East more vigorously than they had previously. This effect is a matter of some disagreement; the new hard currency almost certainly produced great wealth for some and grinding poverty for others. In the wake of Columbus's discoveries, Europe created a world market, with itself at the center.

Not all the wealth extracted from the New World was in the form of precious metals. Furs, skins, sugar, tobacco, and rice became important exports from the Americas, and demand in Europe and elsewhere for these products grew throughout much of the colonial period. As demand grew, planters acquired more and more African slaves to plant and harvest valuable commodities, ensuring that the Columbian Exchange would have a significant impact on the continent of Africa as well. Though estimates vary, about 10 million African slaves arrived in the Americas through the four centuries of the African slave trade. The number is high but becomes even more tragic when it is added to the 5 million or so slaves who left Africa but died before they reached the Americas, not to mention the many millions of people displaced in various West and Central African polities.

In addition to the profits from plants such as tobacco, New World exports such as cassava, potatoes, corn, and turkeys became more common in European and African diets. Cassava grows well enough in harsh environments to support large populations where there had been few people previously. Corn and sweet potatoes, both unknown in Asia prior to their introduction there by Europeans, provide a significant portion of the calories consumed in China. And today the Russian Federation produces about ten times as many potatoes as all of South America, the potato's continent of origin.

One of the more controversial ideas offered, though not by Crosby, concerning the Columbian Exchange is that the relatively egalitarian Native American forms of government influenced leaders, particu-

larly in the United States, to adopt democratic forms of government. Adherents to this view cite Benjamin Franklin's admiration of the Iroquois.

It is likely that the chain of events set in motion by Columbus would have occurred whether he had sailed or not. Nonetheless, the Columbian Exchange provides a useful, broad framework for understanding the effects of the meeting of the New and Old Worlds, an interaction that began in 1492 and has continued through the present day.

Matthew Jennings

See also: Agriculture; Corn; Cotton; Grain; Horses; Indigo; Livestock; Rice; Sugar; Tobacco. *Document:* Tobacco Growing (1775).

Bibliography

Crosby, Alfred W. *The Columbian Exchange: Biological and Cultural Consequences of 1492.* Westport, CT: Greenwood, 1972.

———. *The Columbian Voyages, the Columbian Exchange, and Their Historians.* Washington, DC: American Historical Association, 1987.

Nash, Gary B. *Red, White, and Black: The Peoples of Early North America.* 4th ed. Upper Saddle River, NJ: Prentice Hall, 2000.

Columbus, Christopher (1451–1506)

Few men have been as acclaimed or as maligned as Christopher Columbus, both in his own time and in recent years. Feted by Queen Isabella and King Ferdinand upon returning in 1493 from his famous first voyage as discoverer of a new, fast trade route to the Indies, reports began to filter back to Castile during his second voyage and the conquest of Hispaniola about how badly he was mismanaging royal authority. By August of 1500, the reports were so consistently negative and the rebellions against him so fierce that the queen's investigator, Francisco de Bobadilla, sent Columbus and his brothers home to Spain to be tried by the royal court. The queen forgave him, and Columbus's biographers turned all the denigration around, so his name and deeds became, as Zvi Dor-Ner put it, "the world's most powerful metaphor of discovery."

In the young United States, Columbus came to signify "the essence of qualities we revere—risk taking, entrepreneurship, perseverance." Nearly every state boasts a city named Columbus, and the nation's capital

More than 500 years after his first landfall in North America, Christopher Columbus is both venerated and vilified. His portraits, like his reputation, vary significantly; this etching dates to the 1530s. *(Brown Brothers, Sterling, Pennsylvania)*

is located in the District of Columbia. The 1992 quincentennial of Columbus's first voyage, however, coming hard on the heels of the civil rights movement and the general acknowledgment that Native Americans were given a raw deal in the trade that Columbus began, became less a celebration of his deeds than an occasion to criticize them. Regardless of whether you believe that he was a hero or a villain, it is impossible to deny that what Columbus did changed history.

Columbus was born in 1451, just two years before the Ottoman Turks conquered Constantinople and cut off Europe's trade route to the exotic goods of the East. The young Columbus was attracted to the sea, which dominated the port town of Genoa, Italy, where he grew up. At age 14, he began making short trading voyages, and in his early 20s, he took a position with the Spinola family aboard a ship bound for the eastern Mediterranean island of Chios. Next, he sailed to Northern Europe, but on the return trip the ship was attacked by pirates. Shipwrecked off Portugal, Columbus swam ashore at Lagos, where Prince Henry the Navigator had founded a school for mariners; however, he never attended the school.

Columbus soon moved to Lisbon, where he and his brother Bartholomew worked as mapmakers, but Columbus could not stay away from the sea. He sailed to England, Ireland, and Iceland, among other ports. In Madeira, he married a poor young noblewoman, Felipa Moniz y Perestrello, who gave birth to their son, Diego. In the Atlantic islands, Columbus took note of the winds and ocean currents and listened to sailors' tales of exotic lands and strange things that floated in from the west.

In his 30s, Columbus sailed to the Gold Coast of Africa and entered into correspondence with the renowned Florentine scholar Paolo Toscanelli, whose calculations of the circumference of the earth confirmed that Columbus's theory of sailing west to reach the East Indies was feasible. In 1484, he sought financial support for this great enterprise from King John II of Portugal but was turned down. His wife had died, so he took his young son and went to Spain, while Bartholomew went to England and France, seeking royal backing.

Here's where the story turns so familiar, so legendary, that any schoolchild can recite it: Columbus endured long, frustrating years of disappointment and rejection. But in 1492, the year that Queen Isabella and King Ferdinand completed the Christians' 800-year-long reconquest of Spain from the Moors, Columbus received royal support from the queen. She liked his ideas, for both economic and religious reasons, Columbus having convinced her that proceeds from the enterprise could fund the conversion of millions of Asian pagans to Christianity.

On August 3, 1492, Columbus and his men left the Spanish port of Palos in the *Niña*, *Pinta*, and *Santa María*. They stopped in the Canary Islands to stock up on fresh provisions and to take advantage of the westerly winds, and then they sailed on to keep their rendezvous with history three months later, on October 12.

Columbus made not one but four voyages, claiming most of the Caribbean islands and the American mainland for Spain. Some say he never realized he had not discovered a fast route to the East Indies and had instead stumbled onto lands that the ancients did not know existed. It is more likely, however, that he did know but could not admit it, for admitting it would cancel his contract (known as the Capitulaciones) with the Spanish monarchy, a contract that guaranteed him and his descendents the title of "admiral of the ocean sea, governor and viceroy of the Indies," and a share of all the profits from the new Spanish territories. Instead, another Italian adventurer, Amerigo Vespucci, got credit for recognizing the New World, which today bears his name.

Columbus did not die poor, as the romanticist writer Washington Irving portrayed him, but his fame was short-lived in his lifetime. It was not until his illegitimate son Ferdinand wrote his father's biography that the world at large learned of Columbus's deeds.

Lynne Guitar

See also: Canary Islands; Caribbean (Chronology); Exploration; Ferdinand and Isabella; Hispaniola; Spanish Colonies on Mainland North America (Chronology). *Document*: Columbus's Letter Announcing His Discoveries in the New World (1493).

Bibliography

Colón, Ferdinand. *The Life of the Admiral, by His Son Ferdinand.* Translated by Benjamin Keen. New Brunswick, NJ: Rutgers University Press, 1959.

Columbus, Christopher. *The Diario of Christopher Columbus's First Voyage to America, 1492–1493, Abstracted by Fray Bartolomé de las Casas.* Edited by Oliver Dunn and James E. Kelley, Jr. Norman: University of Oklahoma Press, 1989.

———. *Four Voyages to the New World in His Own Words.* Translated by R. H. Major. New York: Carol, 1992.

Dor-Ner, Zvi. *Columbus and the Age of Discovery.* New York: William Morrow, 1991.

Fernández-Armesto, Felipe. *Columbus.* Oxford, UK: Oxford University Press, 1992.

Morrison, Samuel Eliot. *Admiral of the Ocean Sea: A Life of Christopher Columbus.* Boston: Little, Brown, 1942.

Committees of Correspondence

The American colonists formed the Committees of Correspondence to act as an information network that would essentially maintain correspondence and communication between the thirteen colonies. Members of these committees wrote pamphlets that were distributed throughout the colonies, and called meetings of all colonial committees to deal with problems with the British government.

The intercolonial committees were based on models established in Massachusetts and Virginia, and, by 1774, all the colonies except Pennsylvania had established their own committees. There also were individual committees formed in the different communities within each colony.

The Committees of Correspondence played a central role in the coming of the American Revolution. Because there was no preexisting communication network in the colonies, the committees tied the colonies together and united them in a common cause against England. It was the Committees of Correspondence that distributed the call for a Continental Congress in 1774.

Samuel Adams proposed the establishment of the first Committee of Correspondence at a Boston town meeting in November 1772. The committee began after Adams and his group of patriots learned that the salaries of British officials in the colonies were to be paid from revenue received from the Townshend Duties. Shortly after its establishment, the Boston committee set to work writing a declaration that came to be known as the "Boston Pamphlet." Addressing issues of natural rights and listing specific grievances against the British Parliament, it claimed that the British were out to enslave the American colonists. The grievances included such things as taxation without representation, unlawful force used by the British army in Boston, and Parliament's assertion in the Declaratory Act that it possessed sovereign authority over the colonies. The Boston committee printed hundreds of copies of the pamphlet and distributed it throughout Massachusetts.

By spring 1773, Committees of Correspondence had formed in other colonies. It was these committees that rallied to the support of Boston during the tea crisis that led to the Boston Tea Party. After the passage of the Coercive Acts, several committees, many outside Massachusetts, pledged their support for Boston and denounced the acts.

In March 1773, Thomas Jefferson, Richard Henry Lee, and Patrick Henry submitted a resolution to the Virginia House of Burgesses, which proposed the creation of a standing Committee of Correspondence. Members wanted a permanent committee that could alert the other colonial assemblies to possible threats from the British government. The resolution came in response to the *Gaspee* affair, which began in June 1772, when a British customs vessel, the *Gaspee,* ran aground near Patuxet, Rhode Island. More than 100 raiders boarded the stranded vessel, drove off the crew, and set it afire. The British government sent a commission to the colonies to look into the destruction of the *Gaspee,* and approved the commission's recommendation to expedite the individuals accused of the destruction, along with witnesses and evidence, to England for trial. Although no witnesses stepped forward to name the raiders, the colonists viewed this policy as a violation of their right to trial by a jury of their peers. This was just one of the dangers that Jefferson, Lee, and Henry referred to in their resolution for a permanent Committee of Correspondence.

Anticipating the upcoming War for Independence (in fact, fighting at Lexington and Concord had already occurred), in November 1775 the Continental Congress created a special committee to communicate with foreign powers on behalf of the American colonies. The original members of the committee were Benjamin Franklin, John Dickinson, and Robert Morris from Pennsylvania, Benjamin Harrison and Thomas Jefferson from Virginia, and John Jay from New York. Their goal was to appoint several diplomats to travel to Europe and assess how the European countries viewed the American war. The committee was most interested in the opinion of France, which was England's longtime enemy and which the committee believed would support the American colonists in their bid for independence. Indeed, the delegates convinced the French, and, in 1778, France allied itself with the Americans in the Revolution.

Lisa Guinn

See also: Patriots; Revolutionary War; Sons of Liberty.

Bibliography

Martin, James Kirby. *In the Course of Human Events: An Interpretive Exploration of the American Revolution.* Arlington Heights, IL: Harlan Davidson, 1979.

Middlekauff, Robert. *The Glorious Cause: The American Revolution, 1763–1789.* New York: Oxford University Press, 1982.

Common Sense (1776)

On January 9, 1776, Pennsylvanian James Wilson asked the Continental Congress, meeting in Philadelphia, to issue a statement renouncing any desire for independence. That same day, in the same city, Thomas Paine's pamphlet *Common Sense* first appeared; its message could not have been more different. "Everything that is right or natural pleads for separation," argued Paine.

Promising "to inquire into the pretensions" of monarchy and aristocracy, Paine delivered a scathing critique of hereditary government and an ardent plea for independence. Perhaps the most important political pamphlet produced in Revolutionary America, and certainly the most widely read, *Common Sense* helped

transform the imperial crisis from a colonial struggle for greater autonomy within the British Empire into a revolutionary movement for independence.

The circulation of *Common Sense* was unprecedented in colonial America. Within three months of its first publication, 120,000 copies were in circulation from New Hampshire to Georgia. Most Revolutionary political pamphlets were written by gentlemen for gentlemen and filled with dense, dull prose. Paine instead wrote for a much broader audience, using clear, direct language to argue the cause of independence to all ranks. Paine's appeal to a broader class of the "people" justified popular political action during the crisis of empire leading up to the American Revolution.

Common Sense also helped turn independence into a popular cause. When it first appeared in January 1776, few colonists sought separation from Britain or a revolution within colonial society. Yet, by July 1776,

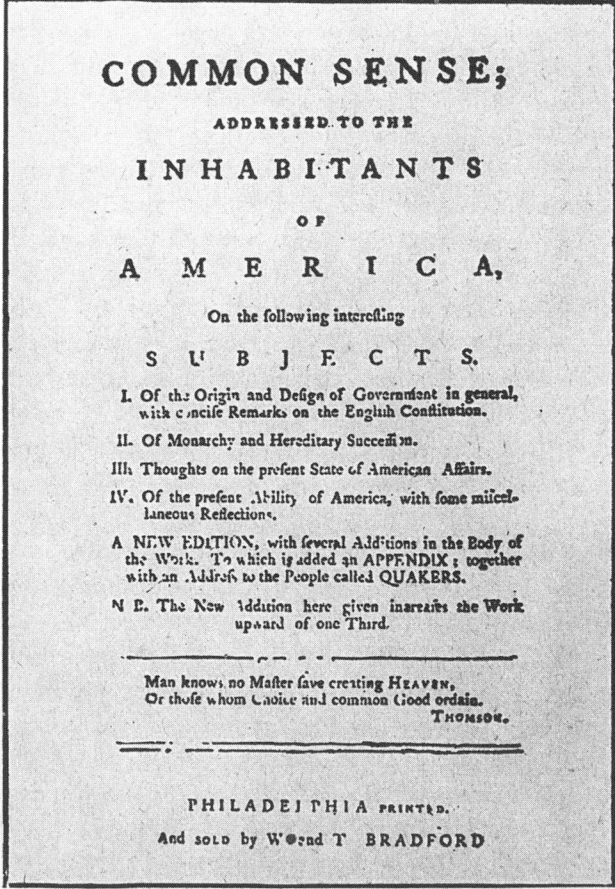

Thomas Paine's call for independence in *Common Sense* had a profound effect on popular thinking. An unprecedented 120,000 copies of the pamphlet were distributed within the first three months of publication in January 1776. *(Brown Brothers, Sterling, Pennsylvania)*

Common Sense had convinced many colonists that independence was not only necessary but desirable.

By so poignantly framing the long train of abuses perpetuated by Britain against the colonies, Paine convincingly established that reconciliation with Britain was no longer a viable option. By so effectively attacking established institutions like the British constitution and the monarchy, Paine made it possible to imagine the colonial rebellion as a revolution. According to Paine, the problems facing the colonies stemmed from monarchy, aristocracy, and the whole British system of hereditary government.

The much-vaunted British constitution, which the colonists had long placed their faith in, was but "the base remains of two ancient tyrannies, compounded with some new republican materials." It could provide the colonists with no protections for their liberties. Because Britain's hereditary government was "independent of the people," it had inevitably become overgrown, excessive, bloated with its own power, and thus tyrannical.

Neither the king nor Parliament would yield to the colonists' demands and recognize their rights. The ongoing British efforts to put down the rebellion in New England demonstrated that reconciliation would be on British terms only. The colonists faced either submission to tyranny or independence and liberty.

After establishing the impossibility of reconciliation, Paine laid out the bright prospects for an independent America. Since "monarchical tyranny in the person of the king" and "aristocratical tyranny in the persons of the peers" contributed "nothing towards freedom," the colonists and freedom would be better served by simple, representative, republican governments in an independent America.

There was not "a single advantage this continent can reap, by being connected with Great-Britain," contended Paine. The colonies had benefited from British mercantilism for sure, but at a cost greater than its worth. The independent colonies would pursue friendship with all of Europe, and, so long as "eating is the custom of Europe," American farmers would find a ready market for their produce.

Paine also challenged his readers to think of themselves as Americans, as members of a new continental union, rather than as British subjects or colonial provincials. Finally, Paine's eloquent defense of rights, independence, and republican government promised a kind of liberty unimaginable in the British Empire. In its most profound and effective parts, *Common Sense* linked the colonial cause to the cause of freedom itself throughout the world, situating the colonists in a near-millennial struggle between freedom and tyranny. Although freedom found itself "hunted round the globe," "We have it in our power to begin the world over again" and "prepare in time an asylum for mankind."

Common Sense did not lead the colonies on a direct path to independence; no single document could generate the consensus needed for such a momentous and difficult decision. It instead further frayed the colonists' ties to the monarchy and the British Empire, sparked public discussion about independence, a topic that had been largely taboo, and provided a framework for understanding the events that eventually pushed the colonies to declare their independence in July 1776.

John Craig Hammond

See also: Paine, Thomas; Politics and Government (Chronology); Politics and Government (Essay); Revolutionary War. *Document*: *Common Sense* (1776).

Bibliography

Foner, Eric. *Tom Paine and Revolutionary America.* New York: Oxford University Press, 1976.

Foner, Philip S. *The Complete Writings of Thomas Paine.* 2 vols. New York: Citadel, 1945.

Maier, Pauline. *American Scripture: Making the Declaration of American Independence.* New York: Alfred A. Knopf, 1997.

Connecticut

Prior to the seventeenth century, Connecticut was home to sixteen Native American tribes, all members of the larger Algonquin confederation. Among these tribes were the Podunk near Hartford, the Niantic along Long Island Sound, the Quinnipiac near Milford, the Pequot in the Southeast, and the Mohegan in the Northeast. While each tribe spoke its own language, there were four distinct language groups: Pequot-Mohegan, Niantic and Narragansett, Nipmuck, and Quinipi.

Thousands of tribal members died as a result of European diseases such as smallpox in 1616 and 1617. By 1630 the total Native American population was about six or seven thousand.

First European Encounter

The first known European exploration of inland Connecticut was a Dutch voyage up the Connecticut River in 1614 by Adriaen Block. In 1633, the Dutch established a fort and trading site at Hartford. The Dutch continued to show interest in Connecticut throughout the seventeenth century but developed no additional settlements in the colony.

In 1632, Edward Winslow, governor of Plymouth Colony, began exploring the lower Connecticut River and established a trading post at Windsor in 1633. By 1634, settlers from the Massachusetts Bay Colony had begun the first permanent towns in Connecticut. Like the original British settlements in Massachusetts and Plymouth, these towns were founded by Puritans, usually individuals and families following dynamic religious leaders. These leaders, seeking their own vision of the Puritan faith, were often controversial. The town of Wethersfield, established in the fall of 1634 by John Oldham, was followed by Hartford, under the leadership of Thomas Hooker, in 1636. While still under the rule of Massachusetts Bay, these settlements sought

recognition in the 1630s as an independent colony from the government in London.

In 1639, leaders from Windsor, Wethersfield, and Hartford agreed on and drafted a system of governing themselves called the "Fundamental Orders," a political document similar to the 1620 Mayflower Compact. Towns established along the coast in the 1640s operated under the same system of government. In contrast, New Haven was founded as an independent colony in 1638 by John Davenport and Theophilus Eaton. Unable to obtain a patent from the British Crown, New Haven remained politically vulnerable to rule by Massachusetts authorities.

Throughout the early 1630s, the English settlers came in constant contact with Native American tribes, especially the Pequot and Mohegan in eastern Connecticut. Both sides were concerned about the control of land and maintaining their separate cultures. Follow-

According to tradition, colonists in 1687 used a white oak tree in Hartford to hide the charter of Connecticut from Sir Edmund Andros; he had been ordered by the British Crown to revoke the charter and establish a dominion comprising all the New England colonies. The great oak, previously revered and used by native peoples as a council tree, became known as the Charter Oak. *(Florence Griswold Museum, Old Lyme, Connecticut/Gift of the Hartford Steam Boiler Inspection & Insurance Company/Bridgeman Art Library)*

ing a series of raids and failed diplomacy between the English colonists and the Pequot, a Pequot village on the Mystic River was attacked by the colonists, Narragansett, and Mohegan in 1637. Other attacks on Pequot villages continued throughout the summer. Surviving tribal members were absorbed into the Mohegan, Narragansett, and Niantic tribes or sold into slavery.

Some Connecticut tribes moved northward, seeking alliances with the powerful Mohawk in New York and Vermont, while others continued to attempt to live alongside the English settlers. The Connecticut River region, with its relatively easy access to Canada, became the most fiercely contested land in New England.

Following the Pequot War, the colonies of Plymouth, Massachusetts Bay, New Haven, and Connecticut joined together as the United Colonies of New England, hoping the alliance would protect them against potential threat from the Dutch, French, and various Native American tribes. While this agreement gave Connecticut local recognition, the colony recognized the need for official recognition from Britain.

In 1662, John Winthrop, Jr., traveled to England to petition Charles II for a charter. The charter was granted, and the colony continued under laws similar to the Fundamental Orders of 1639. Like Massachusetts to the north, colony leaders were elected, although suffrage was limited and based on church membership and property ownership.

Although New Haven fell within the geographical limits of the British charter, it still considered itself an independent colony. Hoping for official acceptance as an independent colony under Dutch protection, New Haven's leaders petitioned the Dutch for a charter in 1663. When this failed, New Haven finally merged with Connecticut in 1665.

King Philip's War began in 1675 between the Wampanoag and their English neighbors in southeastern Massachusetts. Like the Pequot before them, the Wampanoag feared total loss of their lands to the English. Unlike the Pequot War, King Philip's War developed into a region-wide conflict, involving Massachusetts, Rhode Island, Maine, and Connecticut. Although few battles took place in Connecticut, the colony provided troops in western Massachusetts, as well as diplomacy with the Narragansett people. Both efforts created tensions between Connecticut and Massachusetts, as the latter feared Connecticut would seek greater leverage with the Native Americans of western Massachusetts, and eventually led to the end of the United Colonies of New England.

Preoccupied with the English Civil War, the British Crown paid little attention to the political and religious activities of the colonies during the first half of the seventeenth century. Following the restoration of the monarchy in the 1660s, however, Charles II and his successors began exerting greater control over the New England colonies. In 1684, the Massachusetts Bay Colony's charter was revoked. Shortly afterwards, James II created the Dominion of New England. Consisting of Massachusetts Bay, Plymouth, New Hampshire, and Maine, the Dominion was governed by Sir Edmund Andros.

In 1685, Edward Randolph was appointed collector of customs for all New England. Randolph announced that Connecticut was in violation of British laws, citing laws affecting property sales, marriage ceremonies, capital punishment, and freedom of worship, among others. As a result, he argued, Connecticut's charter was in jeopardy and could be legally revoked by the Crown.

Connecticut's leaders were divided on the best way of answering this charge. Some argued that the colony should join with New York, still an independent colony. Others argued that annexation by the Dominion was inevitable and that Connecticut should join Massachusetts Bay.

On October 31, 1687, Connecticut was officially made a member of the Dominion of New England. Unlike the Massachusetts Bay Colony's revoked charter, the actual document of the Connecticut charter was preserved within the colony, giving Connecticut a continued, if symbolic, sense of a separate identity. State legend holds that the charter was hidden in an oak tree, called the Charter Oak.

Following the 1689 Glorious Revolution in England, Massachusetts revolted, and Governor Andros was imprisoned. Shortly afterwards, Connecticut began reasserting its independence, arguing that its charter was still valid, since it had never been officially revoked. In 1690, the colony regained recognition by the British Crown.

Coming of the Revolution

By the time of the American Revolution, Connecticut had changed little in character. Population growth was constant throughout the colonial period, increasing by about 400 people a year in the seventeenth century and about 1,500 a year in the eighteenth century. The estimated total population in 1774 was approximately 200,000.

Initially, most colonists arrived from Massachusetts Bay Colony rather than directly from Europe. Increased emphasis on trade and maritime industries led to a wider range of cultural backgrounds, although minorities such as African Americans remained under 5 percent of the total population. The most common religion was still Congregationalism, in its various interpretations, although there were some Anglicans, Methodists, and Quakers. Similar to the early colonial period, the primary sources of income were fishing and farming, with merchants and artisans clustered in and around the towns.

The earliest signs of the American Revolution in Connecticut were protests in 1765 against the Stamp Act, followed by more protests against the Townshend Duties in 1767. After the Battle of Lexington and Concord in 1775, Connecticut called up a quarter of its militia and began readying its soldiers to march to Boston. Bounties were offered for military supplies, sulfur, and saltpeter. The colony also prepared shore defenses for coastal towns and began forming a navy.

In 1777, William Tryon, the royal governor of New York, led an attack on Danbury to destroy supplies intended for the Continental army. In February 1779, Governor Tryon attacked the salt works in Greenwich. Later that year, he also attacked New Haven, Fairfield, and Norwalk, again seeking to destroy local support for the colonial war effort. The most devastating attack was led by Connecticut-born Benedict Arnold; it took place in New London and Groton in 1781, killing dozens of people and burning New London to the ground.

Aside from these four raids, the American Revolution had less immediate political and physical impact on Connecticut than on its neighbors. Connecticut continued to support the colonial cause throughout the war with a constant flow of troops and money under the guidance of Governor Jonathon Trumbull. Although the threat of having the Connecticut charter revoked was nearly 100 years old in the 1770s, it remained a motivating force throughout the Revolution.

Following the war, Connecticut became part of the newly formed United States, although it was internally governed under the 1662 charter until 1818.

Abigail B. Chandler

See also: Connecticut (Chronology); Connecticut River; King Philip's War; New Haven; Puritanism. *Documents:* Fundamental Orders of Connecticut (1639); Connecticut Blue Laws (1650).

Bibliography

Calloway, Colin G. *First Peoples.* Boston: Bedford/St. Martin's, 1999.

Roth, David M., and Freeman Meyer. *From Revolution to Constitution, Connecticut History 1763–1818.* Chester, CT: Pequot, 1975.

Taylor, Robert. *Colonial Connecticut.* Millwood, NY: KTO, 1979.

Van Dusen, Albert. *Puritans Against the Wilderness, Connecticut History to 1763.* Chester, CT: Pequot, 1975.

Connecticut River

The Connecticut River, the longest river in New England, flows just over 400 miles from its origins in the mountains of New Hampshire, near Canada, into the Atlantic Ocean near the town of Saybrook, Connecticut. A sandbar at the mouth of the river kept any significant urban development from occurring near its juncture with the Atlantic, though European settlements of some consequence did spring up farther upriver.

The physical history of the Connecticut River began about 11,000 years ago, when the last glaciers receded. The human history began shortly thereafter, when Paleo-Indians moved into the area in pursuit of game. When Europeans—specifically a Dutch fur trader named Adriaen Block—explored the river in 1614, the region was home to a number of Native American communities, including the Narragansett and the Niantic.

From 1614 until the 1630s, the Connecticut River was the center of a fur trading network between the Dutch, operating out of New Amsterdam, and their Native American neighbors. In the 1630s, increasing immigration of both English settlers (from Plymouth and the Massachusetts Bay Colony) and Pequots gradually forced the Dutch out of the picture. The English settlement at Windsor in 1633 marked an early effort to thwart the Dutch. In 1636, Thomas Hooker brought his congregation to the Connecticut River Valley and founded the town of Hartford. By the end of that year, around 1,000 English people lived in five settlements along the river.

The Pequot moved into the area at approximately the same time as the English, and the two groups almost immediately clashed. In the main action of what became known as the Pequot War (1637–1638), English Puritans burned Mystic Fort, a fortified Pequot village on the nearby Mystic River. Hundreds of Native American noncombatants lost their lives, and the English, spurning acceptable rules of combat, offered no quarter to those attempting to surrender. After the Pequot War, new English settlements continued to grow in the Connecticut River Valley. In a move that would be considered genocidal by twenty-first-century standards, the English sold many of the surviving Pequots into slavery in the West Indies and proclaimed that to identify oneself as Pequot was illegal.

Almost four decades later, Metacom's (King Philip's) War (1675–1676) touched the Connecticut River Valley. Frustrated by English land greed and renewed missionary vigor, the tribal leader Metacom led a coalition of Wampanoags, Nipmucs, and Narragansetts against Plymouth colony. The conflict soon spread to the west and expanded to pit Metacom's forces against the English and their native allies. Because native peoples fought on both sides of the conflict, one historian has called Metacom's War a "civil war."

The Massachusetts towns of Deerfield, Hatfield, Northampton, and Springfield, all lying near the Connecticut River, came under attack. When the ferocious fighting subsided, many English settlements took more than a decade to rebuild—Northfield, for instance, was not resettled until 1714. Many Native American communities were permanently destroyed; some Native Americans took refuge among the Five Nations (who had nominally aided the English cause). The conflict also produced one of the most famous of the "Indian captivity narratives," that of Mary Rowlandson. The intensity of the fighting and the extent of the casualties have rarely been rivaled in North America, and one of the results of the conflict was that the English asserted their dominance over the Connecticut River Valley.

During Queen Anne's War, in the first decade of the eighteenth century, the Connecticut River Valley was again the site of conflict, this time, between the English and the French, although each side boasted Native American allies in the war. As the English slowly conquered more territory from their French and Native American neighbors, settlements in the Connecticut River Valley prospered and expanded farther to the north. This halting and uneven process continued throughout the Revolutionary and early Republican periods in the history of the United States.

Matthew Jennings

See also: Connecticut; Connecticut (Chronology); King Philip's War.

Bibliography

Bacon, Edwin M. *The Connecticut River and the Valley of the Connecticut: Three Hundred and Fifty Miles from Mountain to Sea, Historical and Descriptive.* New York: G. P. Putnam's Sons, 1911.

Hard, Walter. *The Connecticut. Rivers of America Series.* New York: Rinehart, 1947.

Steckl, William F., and Evan Hill. *The Connecticut River.* Middletown, CT: Wesleyan University Press, 1972.

Constantinople, Fall of

The capture of Constantinople by Turkish Muslims (Ottomans) in 1453 accelerated the age of oceangoing exploration. The Portuguese were interested in circumventing the overland trade routes to Asia as early as 1420, hoping to gain direct access to lucrative spices, silks, gold, porcelain, cotton, and opium. But with Christians controlling Constantinople up until 1453, the Venetians and Genoese enjoyed protection and monopolized Eastern trade. After 1453, Turkish middlemen did not sever European commerce, but they cut into already shrinking Italian profits.

Europe's primary conduit to the outside world shifted from Venice, still a power in the Aegean and Adriatic seas, to the Iberian Peninsula and more northerly ports. Portugal navigated around Africa's Cape of Good Hope and Cape Agulhas in 1487, and, by the 1510s, they had colonies along India's Malabar Coast and in the East Indies (or Spice Islands).

The Romans had control of the critical spot on the Bosporus Straits at the end of the classical age. With Rome in decline, the center of its empire shifted east. The city of Byzantium, renamed after Emperor Constantine in 330 C.E., became the cosmopolitan heart of Europe during the Middle Ages—the center of Eastern Orthodox Christianity and the nexus of an international trade in slaves, timber, furs, fish, wheat, wine, and salt. It commanded the allegiance of the Roman Empire until the eleventh century, but after the Crusades a schism developed between the eastern and western realms. By the end of the fourteenth century, the population of Constantinople had declined, and the Turks controlled Anatolia (Asia Minor) across the straits.

The Ottomans crossed the Dardanelles and defeated the Bulgarians, Bosnians, and Serbians at Kosovo in 1389. Christian Europe was too splintered to offer them effective resistance in the fifteenth century. Only the Sunni Turks' preoccupation with Persian Shiites to the east delayed their seizure of Constantinople. Led by Sultan Mehmed II (who maintained a network of spies in Europe, as well as a force of Christian mercenaries), the Turks assaulted the barricaded citadel for seven weeks during the spring of 1453, beheaded Constantine IX, and renamed the city Istanbul. Further expansion on the Balkan Peninsula followed throughout the 1460s, and the Ottomans controlled Egypt and western Arabia by the end of the century.

After 1453, Venice retained an active Middle Eastern trade through the port of Alexandria, but Genoa's geographic position and military weakness made its situation more precarious, as Constantinople's fall severed its connection to the Levant and Black Sea. Columbus, born in Genoa in 1451, grew up in a port whose soldiers had fought at Constantinople and whose economic survival now depended on navigational breakthroughs. It was the Portuguese, however, led by Prince Henry and John II, who capitalized on the relative decline of the Venetians. The Portuguese were still unable to undersell the Arabs and Venetians, but their Asian colonies were profitable, and some Venetians even began to sail under Prince Henry's charters. The Portuguese also took pride in promulgating Christianity. In 1453, Pope Nicholas V sanctioned a crusade against Islam, which emboldened explorers and even helped rationalize the African slave trade (although most African captives were not Muslims).

While Muslims gained territory in Eastern Europe and Asia, Christians reasserted their control over the Moors (Muslims) in Spain, expelling them from the peninsula by 1492. Hoping to upstage Portugal, the Castilian monarchy granted Columbus ships to seek a western route to China, a scheme he had failed to sell to the Portuguese, French, and English. When New Spain yielded gold and silver to currency-starved Europe, England, France, and the Netherlands followed Spain's lead to America.

European expansion resulted from cultural, technological, and economic forces independent of the fall of Constantinople; however, the disruption of trade patterns in the eastern Mediterranean hastened those developments. In addition, there were two more indirect ways that the events of 1453 impacted European (and thus colonial American) history.

First, the Ottoman takeover benefited from the spread of gunpowder from China to western Asia, anticipating developments that would revolutionize European weaponry and fuel expansion. Second, Muslim encroachments into central Europe affected the Protestant Reformation. If the Turks had not threatened Vienna in the sixteenth century, the Vatican could have cracked down more readily on Protestants and German princes allying themselves with Martin Luther. Because of the Turkish threat, the Holy Roman Empire could not afford to alienate those rulers, making it more lenient toward a movement that contributed to British colonization of the Americas.

Cameron Addis

See also: Exploration; Trade.

Bibliography

Parry, J. H. *Europe and a Wider World, 1415–1715*. London: Hutchinson, 1966.
Runciman, Steven. *The Fall of Constantinople, 1453*. Cambridge, UK: Cambridge University Press, 1969.

Continental Congress, First

The First Continental Congress was the colonies' reaction to Parliament's passage of the Coercive Acts of 1774. The Coercive Acts, characterized by American colonists as the Intolerable Acts, culminated almost a decade of political unrest that began with the Stamp Act crisis in 1765. These acts were intended to assert British authority in the colonies. The first of these laws, the Boston Port Bill, closed Boston Harbor to all commerce until the city compensated the East India Company for property destroyed during the Boston Tea Party. Bostonians refused to pay for the tea and organized committees of correspondence to petition the other colonies for support.

The Coercive Acts caused a significant rise in political awareness and activity throughout the thirteen colonies, and most responded favorably to the call for a colonial congress. Fifty-five delegates arrived in Philadelphia, Pennsylvania, to attend the First Continental Congress; only Georgia did not send a delegation. Congress convened in Carpenter's Hall on September 5, 1774, and Peyton Randolph of Virginia was elected to preside over the body. In order to preserve colonial unity, it was decided that each colony would receive an equal vote.

Congress was principally concerned with two issues, establishing the nature and extent of colonial rights and determining the best method to protect these rights. The delegates were divided into two com-

Fifty-five delegates to the First Continental Congress, representing every colony except Georgia, convened at Carpenter's Hall in Philadelphia from September 5 to October 26, 1774. They gathered in response to the Coercive Acts and other British efforts to assert authority. *(Atwater Kent Museum of Philadelphia, Pennsylvania/Bridgeman Art Library)*

mittees. The trade committee examined the British commercial system to identify oppressive trade regulations. The grand committee, fundamentally the more important of the two, determined the colonies' rights, identified when their rights had been violated by Britain, and proposed action to defend these rights.

Committee deliberations were interrupted in mid-September when Paul Revere rode into Philadelphia with the Suffolk Resolves, which had been adopted in Massachusetts after British general Thomas Gage fortified Boston Neck. These resolves represented the most drastic opposition taken against British authority. They denounced the Coercive Acts and urged resistance by withholding tax payments and organizing a colonial militia. The Suffolk Resolves confronted Congress with a dilemma. Congress opposed open conflict with Brit-

ain, preferring a negotiated settlement, but it also feared appearing too conservative and losing its leadership position. Congress, therefore, unanimously endorsed the Suffolk Resolves but warned Massachusetts not to form an independent government or take offensive military action.

After endorsing the Suffolk Resolves, Congress returned to its agenda and remained in committee for the next few weeks. On October 14, Congress adopted the Declaration of Rights, which stated that colonial rights rested on three pillars: the laws of nature, the British constitution, and the colonial charters. Congress then turned its attention to defending these rights within the imperial system. Debate centered on what form of trade embargo should be imposed against Britain. The Massachusetts delegation favored an immediate stoppage to all trade, while several Southern colonies opposed any ban on the export of tobacco, rice, or indigo.

The First Continental Congress culminated with the adoption of the Association of 1774 on October 20. The Association imposed a ban, to begin on December 1, on all British imports and on the consumption of East India Company tea. The prohibition on American exports to Britain, Ireland, and the West Indies was scheduled to begin on September 10, 1775, after the tobacco crop was harvested. Rice was excluded from the ban.

To enforce the Association, Congress called for the election of committees in every town, city, and county in the colonies. These committees were authorized to inspect customs house records and publish the names of offenders in the local newspaper. Association violators were socially and economically ostracized from the community.

The Association of 1774 represented the beginning of the movement to replace British authority in the American colonies. The local committees that enforced the Association supplanted British government and became revolutionary institutions, the means by which colonial authority was exercised at the local level. The Association was ultimately a failure due to the fact that it did not accomplish its primary objective, British imperial reform. It was, however, the most successful system of economic coercion ever devised by the colonies. In 1775, British imports decreased to a fraction of the previous year's totals.

After adopting the Association, the First Continental Congress concluded its business by drafting a petition to the king, as well as addresses explaining its action to the people of America, Britain, and Quebec.

Congress dissolved on October 26 with the understanding that, if necessary, a second Continental Congress would convene on May 10, 1775.

Thomas Nester

See also: Coercive Acts (1774); Politics and Government (Chronology); Politics and Government (Essay); Revolutionary War.

Bibliography

Jillson, Calvin, and Rick K. Wilson. *Congressional Dynamics: Structure, Coordination, and Choice in the First American Congress, 1774–1789.* Stanford Studies in the New Political History. Stanford, CA: Stanford University Press, 1994.

Marston, Jerrilyn Greene. *King and Congress: The Transfer of Political Legitimacy, 1774–1776.* Princeton, NJ: Princeton University Press, 1987.

Rakove, Jack N. *The Beginnings of National Politics: An Interpretive History of the Continental Congress.* New York: Alfred A. Knopf, 1979.

Continental Congress, Second

The First Continental Congress adjourned in October 1774 after agreeing to call a second gathering if circumstances warranted. Following the Battles of Lexington and Concord in April of 1775, the delegates met again at Philadelphia on May 10. Although lacking any legal authority, the Second Continental Congress saw no alternative. It began to govern.

Presiding was John Hancock, new to the Congress, in the stead of Peyton Randolph, a Virginia attorney, who was ill. Some delegates were veterans of the First Continental Congress, but some were new—notably Thomas Jefferson and Benjamin Franklin. Absent was the Pennsylvania conservative Joseph Galloway. Although all colonies sent delegations, Georgia's arrived only in the fall.

Initially, Congress was conservative. Most believed that reconciliation was still possible. A handful assumed that the time for reconciliation had passed—John and Samuel Adams, Richard Henry Lee, Franklin, perhaps Hancock and Jefferson—and the radicals slowly began to dominate such conservatives as John Dickinson. The issue was irrelevant to the business of the Congress, though. Its initial purpose was the redress of grievances, not determining the possibility of independence. What it did, it did of necessity.

On June 15, Congress took charge of the army outside Boston. John Adams wanted George Washington as commander in chief to gain Southern support for what was primarily a Northern-based conflict. Adams had some doubts about Washington after his mismanagement of the military campaign around New York. Still, Washington had the best military reputation in the colonies, he had good judgment and self-control, and he was commander of the Virginia militia. He even wore his uniform to the Congress's sessions.

The selection of Washington converted the New England army into a continental army. Under Washington were four major generals—Charles Lee, Israel Putnam, Philip Schuyler, and Artemas Ward. Lee, who had experience as a British officer and had lobbied for the position of commander in chief in Philadelphia, was the only alternative to Washington. Support for Lee ended, however, when the British surprised and captured him in New Jersey in December of 1776. Washington's major Christmas triumph at Trenton, New Jersey, came shortly thereafter.

Even as it prepared to wage war, Congress denied any intent to be disloyal to the British Crown. Its so-called Olive Branch Petition to the king, prepared by John Dickinson and John Jay, was almost fawning. Congress expressed loyalty to the king and disapproval of the actions of his ministers and Parliament. The messenger, Richard Penn, was a Tory.

Congress sent addresses to the people of Great Britain, Ireland, and Canada. It also issued $2 million in currency, proclaimed a day of fasting and prayer, and authorized the creation of governments of the states. The next major document, the *Declaration of the Causes and Necessity of Taking Up Arms*, was stronger than the Olive Branch Petition. It raised the possibility of independence unless England restored American rights.

Congress was never able to solve the problems of raising money for arms, supplies, and soldiers' pay. It could issue paper money by fiat, and it could borrow domestically and abroad. But neither its money nor the state currencies had backing. The continental and state currencies depreciated rapidly, fueling high inflation. And while Congress could enact nonbonding resolutions, it could pass no laws. It could ask the states for men, money, and materials, but the states could refuse, and many did.

In late May of 1776, Congress attempted, unsuccessfully, to bring French Canada in as the fourteenth state. It also authorized an invasion of Canada, in order to forestall Canadian invasion of the colonies.

In June, Richard Henry Lee presented a resolu-

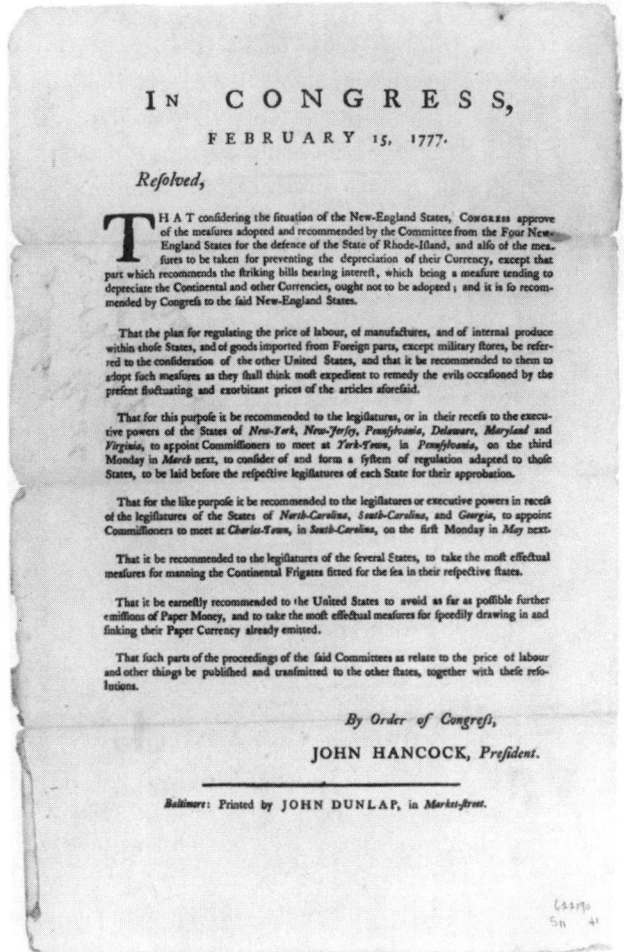

A 1777 broadside reports on developments at the Second Continental Congress, which first convened as a governing body in May 1775 after the start of the Revolution. The Congress directed the war effort and adopted both the Declaration of Independence and the Articles of Confederation. *(Library of Congress, LC-USZ62-66969)*

tion calling for independence. Public opinion by this time had shifted. Congress passed the petition and directed Jefferson to rework it into the Declaration of Independence.

Needing a stronger central authority to prosecute the war, in July 1776, Congress began considering the Articles of Confederation. Adopted in November 1777, the Articles were finally ratified in 1781.

Meanwhile, Congress had sent Silas Deane to France in March 1776. He managed to get French aid in supplies, arms, and experienced military officers. Arthur Lee and Benjamin Franklin joined him later, and, together, they cemented the 1778 Franco-American Alliance.

Regional conflict hampered the work of the Congress. Political alignments reflected sectional differ-

ences, with the Southern colonies opposing the Northern ones, and the middle states providing the balance, favoring one side, then the other, depending on the specific issue.

Members of Congress also had to worry about the real risk of attack by British armies. They relocated their deliberations several times between 1776 and 1778. From Philadelphia, Congress went to Baltimore, back to Philadelphia, then on to Lancaster and then York, Pennsylvania, before returning again to Philadelphia in 1778. After the war, Congress continued its itinerant ways, meeting in Princeton, New Jersey, Annapolis, Maryland, and Trenton, New Jersey. In 1785, it finally settled in New York, where it remained until 1789.

John H. Barnhill

See also: Adams, John; Adams, Samuel; Dickinson, John; Jefferson, Thomas; Lee, Richard Henry; Politics and Government (Chronology); Politics and Government (Essay); Revolutionary War; Washington, George. *Documents:* Letters between Abigail Adams and John Adams (1776); The Declaration of Independence (1776).

Bibliography

Burnet, Edmund C. *The Continental Congress.* Westport CT: Greenwood Publishing, 1975 (reprint of 1941 edition).

Henderson, H. James. *Party Politics in the Continental Congress.* New York: McGraw-Hill, 1974.

Montross, Lynn. *The Reluctant Rebels: The Story of the Continental Congress, 1774–1789.* New York: Harper, 1950.

Rakove, Jack N. *The Beginnings of National Politics: An Interpretive History of the Continental Congress.* New York: Alfred A. Knopf, 1979.

Coode's Rebellion

Coode's Rebellion, named after its leader, planter John Coode, was an anti-Catholic uprising that occurred in Maryland in 1689. The uprising was largely in response to the Glorious Revolution of the previous year in England, in which the authoritarian Catholic monarch James II was overthrown and replaced by the Protestant monarchy of William and Mary.

The 1680s were a time of radical change and unrest in many of Britain's North American colonies. There were protests in Massachusetts against the decision to annul the Massachusetts Bay charter, which had granted the colony a certain degree of self-rule. Instead, a more centrally controlled government was established for all of New England, one headed by a Crown-appointed governor named Edmund Andros.

The decade was also a troubled one in England, especially after King James II rose to power and began to establish more thorough Crown control over Parliament and local governments. The fact that he practiced his Catholic faith openly and persecuted Anglican bishops made resentment even greater. When his wife gave birth to a son in 1688, fear swept many sectors of the English government that a Catholic monarchy was being permanently established in the predominantly Protestant country. In 1688, parliamentary leaders, backed by the army and the public opinion, forced James II into exile and made his Protestant daughter Mary (she had been born to James II's first wife, who was a Protestant) and her husband, the Dutch Protestant Prince William, the joint monarchs of England.

The news of this Glorious Revolution, as it was called, emboldened Protestant leaders in the colonies to overthrow what they saw as James II's tyranny. In Massachusetts, the government of Andros was overthrown. In Maryland, there was also an uprising. The so-called Protestant Association, led by Coode, quickly removed the officials appointed by the Catholic proprietor of the colony, Lord Baltimore.

Still, the conflicts between Catholics and Protestants in the only Catholic-dominated colony in British North America were long-standing ones. These were aggravated by a sagging market for the colony's main crop, tobacco, and a perception among small farmers and the poor and middle classes that they were being overtaxed by Catholic governing officials.

The Protestant Association ruled the colony for two years, until Parliament imposed a royal government and made the Church of England the official church in Maryland. This state of affairs continued until 1715, when Charles Calvert, Lord Baltimore, died and was replaced by his son Benedict Calvert. As Calvert was a convert to the Anglican Church, London restored Maryland to his control, under which it remained until the American Revolution.

Penny M. Sonnenburg

See also: Glorious Revolution; James II; New England, Dominion of; William III of Orange and Mary II.

Bibliography

Carr, Lois Green, and David William Jordan. *Maryland's Revolution of Government, 1689–1692.* Ithaca, NY: Cornell University Press, 1974.

Craven, Wesley Frank. *The Colonies in Transition: 1660–1713.* New York: Harper and Row, 1968.

Hall, Michael G., Lawrence H. Leder, and Michael G. Kammen, eds. *The Glorious Revolution in America.* Chapel Hill: University of North Carolina Press, 1964.

Copley, John Singleton (1738–1815)

John Singleton Copley used realism and deft characterization to become one of the best portrait painters of the eighteenth century and the foremost American artist of the colonial era.

Born in Boston on July 3, 1738, Copley learned to paint and engrave from his stepfather, Peter Pelham. A successful mezzotint engraver from London, Pelham died in 1751. Forced to earn a living, Copley copied one of Pelham's engravings to the point of plagiarism to produce his first work, *Reverend William Welsteed* (1753). Copley's first known painting is a portrait of tavern keeper Mrs. Joseph Mann (1753).

Boston had no schools that offered art instruction, and much of the population still clung to old Puritan ideas that held most forms of painting to be either blasphemous or frivolous. As a result, Copley was largely self-taught. He studied anatomy and theories of art, while making numerous copies of engravings of history paintings on mythological themes, including *Galatea* (1754), *The Return of Neptune* (1754), and *The Forge of Vulcan* (1754). The colonists valued art chiefly as a means of recording likenesses and had little interest in this type of art.

Intensely concerned with economic security and desirous of social advancement, Copley turned his focus to portraiture. In the next few years, he copied heavily from popular English portraits to produce saleable items for the American market. By the age of 21, he had become the foremost portraitist in the colonies.

Combining bold colors with the dramatic use of light and shadow, Copley avoided the stiff, flatly colored, crudely drawn likenesses that most colonial artists churned out. He developed a style that gave painted human figures the look of three dimensions. He also had a rare gift for observing unconscious personal mannerisms. His paintings featured precise contours, occasional sharp dissonances of color, and a smooth finish that neatly concealed all signs of brushwork. Another characteristic of Copley's distinct style is his attention

John Singleton Copley is regarded as the first great American portrait painter, but his romanticized historical works, including *Watson and the Shark* (1778), are among his best-known paintings. *(The Detroit Institute of Arts, Michigan/Founders Society purchase, Dexter M. Ferry, Jr., fund/Bridgeman Art Library)*

to textiles and the vast variety of shiny, filmy, coarse, and fine effects that fabrics can provide.

Much of Copley's popularity derived from the veneer of elegance that he gave to his subjects, as well as his talent for capturing individual character. The warmth and hospitality of Mrs. Ezekiel Goldthwait is clearly revealed in her portrait (1771), as is the bloom in the face of benign Mrs. Thomas Boylston (1766). Copley's sitters probably chose the pose and costume they liked best from a variety of English aristocratic prints the artist showed them, since his works employ the props, clothing, and settings typical of eighteenth-century English mezzotints.

As the years passed, Copley added profitable sidelines. He painted miniatures on copper and ivory, which were intended more as keepsakes than likenesses. About 1763, he began a ten-year infatuation with pastels. Pastels were an attractive alternative to oils, because portraits were created using cheaper materials and took less time to complete but still satisfied buyers. Copley would use pastels for his 1769 self-portrait.

As tensions rose in the years before the Revolu-tion, Copley kept aloof from any appearance of sympathy with a political faction in the belief that politics brought neither pleasure nor advantage to an artist. He painted both Tories and revolutionaries, including Paul Revere and John Hancock. While he never publicly declared his sympathies, his 1769 marriage to Susanna Farnham Clarke did link Copley to a prominent loyalist family. Copley's friendly relations with both sides made him the choice as mediator between revolutionary leaders in Boston and the agents of the East India Company during the tea tax protests. His efforts proved futile, however, and the worsening situation soon made neutrality impossible for him to maintain.

In 1774, a mob gathered outside Copley's Beacon Hill mansion to demand that he turn over a loyalist friend. Fearing he would be forced to surrender his friend or have his house pulled down and his family murdered, Copley managed to escape and fled to England.

While political turmoil had triggered his flight, his exile also gave Copley the opportunity to better his skills to match England's sophisticated standards. He became the first American painter on record to take up residence abroad at the instigation of European colleagues, who had been impressed by his 1766 exhibition of *Boy with a Squirrel*. Copley also is believed to be the first American painter to exhibit abroad. In England, Copley continued to refine his work, and the Royal Academy of Arts rewarded his efforts by electing him to full membership in 1779.

Bitter and frustrated in his later years by financial difficulties and a waning reputation, Copley died in London on September 9, 1815.

Caryn E. Neumann

See also: Art, Fine; Arts, Culture, and Intellectual Life (Chronology); Arts, Culture, and Intellectual Life (Essay).

Bibliography

Flexner, James Thomas. *John Singleton Copley*. New York: Fordham University Press, 1993.

Frankenstein, Alfred. *The World of Copley, 1738–1815.* New York: Time-Life, 1970.

Corn

"If maize [corn] were the only gift the American Indian ever presented to the world," noted environmental historian Alfred Crosby, "he would deserve undying gratitude, for it has become one of the most important of all foods for men and their livestock." Corn is the third most important food crop in the history of humankind, following rice and wheat.

Corn's origin has caused many scholarly arguments. Until recently, most botanists believed that corn was developed in the Valley of Mexico by Amerindians, who, 7,000 years ago, began to systematically select the best specimens of the wild grain teosinte, causing teosinte to evolve into corn. Scientific experiments, however, have caused some scholars to dispute this explanation.

The discovery in 1954 of fossil corn pollen more than 80,000 years old in Mexico, along with subsequent botanical experiments, proved that teosinte was involved in the miracle that became corn, but did not itself evolve into corn. Its pollen fertilized wild corn, creating a natural hybrid, whose seeds were larger and did not scatter so easily. This spontaneous cross breed-

ing first took place in the Peruvian Andes about 4,000 years ago and spread south, "taming" all wild corn over the course of the next 2,000 years. Amerindian food gatherers no doubt appreciated the new hybrid corn and selected it for planting over its wild relative, speeding up the process of evolution. Gradually, trade and population movements brought corn to many parts of the Americas where climate permitted its cultivation and the native peoples engaged in agriculture.

By the time Europeans arrived in the Americas in 1492, hundreds of varieties of hybrid corn from five major groups—dent, flint, flour, sweet, and pop—were being grown throughout the continent. More versatile and adaptable than either rice or wheat, corn could be grown in the North, in the South, and even in regions with little water—the Hopis developed a type with a long taproot that, while spindly-looking, produces extensive crop yields. Most importantly, corn grows into nourishing food in just three months.

The first written mention of corn was made on

Among the Iroquoian farming peoples, the cornfields were the domain of women. It was the females of the tribe who planted and weeded the crops, kept away the birds (as seen here), and harvested the corn. *(Engraving by Seth Eastman, provided by Prints Old and Rare, Pacifica, California)*

October 16, 1492, when Christopher Columbus noted in his *diario* that it grew on Fernandina (in the Bahamas), but he called the grain millet. Columbus's son Ferdinand clarified this, writing that the Tainos had "a grain resembling panic grass that they call maize and is most tasty, boiled, roasted, or ground into flour." Spaniards transplanted corn to Spain, where documents mention it being cultivated by 1498. It spread to Italy by 1554, where corn quickly replaced millet and sorghum as the grain of choice for polenta, the thick porridge that was the staple food of Italian peasants. Egyptians soon were cultivating vast fields of corn, and it continued to spread across the Middle East. In fact, in many regions of the world, corn is known as "Turkish wheat" or "Syrian wheat," which indicates how early it was established in those regions.

Today, corn is primarily known as animal feed throughout Europe, but it also is a staple food for the poor not only in Spain and Italy but also in Southern France, Portugal, and the Balkans (Yugoslavia, Hungary, and Romania are among the largest corn producers in the world). Corn also helps to feed the populace in northern and southeast China; China is second only to the United States in quantity of corn production. The hill people of India, and those in the country's north and northwest, also eat a prodigious quantity of corn, as do all of the peoples of Indonesia and nearby islands. Many Africans outside of Egypt raise corn, too, particularly those from Nigeria east to the middle of the continent.

Unfortunately, the Central American technique of nixtamalization, whereby corn is prepared with wood ashes or lime, which enhances the availability of the grain's protein and vitamin content, was not exported along with the seed crops. Therefore, people outside the Americas who rely on corn as a staple food tend to suffer from pellagra and other vitamin deficiencies.

Living first among the Tainos, Spanish colonists ate corn as a boiled or roasted vegetable and as *arepa*, a thick corn bread. After conquering the Aztecs and Incas, however, they discovered many new ways to eat corn, among which were hundreds of varieties of tortillas, tamales, and dumplings, various types of *atolli* (nonalcoholic drinks) and *chicha* (beer), and *pinolli*, a toasted corn carried by travelers.

Like the Central and South American colonists, North American colonists also owe thanks to the Native Americans and their corn for their nourishment—indeed, for their very survival. The U.S. tale of the first Thanksgiving recognizes this. Native Americans of the Woodland culture taught French, Dutch, and English colonists how to plant corn, dropping four kernels and a fish head for fertilizer into each hole poked with a stick into a prepared mound. Unfortunately, the newcomers did not adopt the natives' companion planting method of growing corn with squash and beans. The beans replenish the nitrogen used by the corn, while the corn stalks provide poles for the beans, and the wide leaves of the low-growing squash keep weeding to a minimum.

North American colonists also did not show their thanks for very long. As French food historian Maguelonne Toussaint-Samat notes:

> In their eagerness to dispute possession of a land which belonged to neither of them, the French and English agreed on only one point: the Indians were more vulnerable to the destruction of their maize stores than the destruction of their villages.

Lynne Guitar

See also: Agriculture; Columbian Exchange; Grain.

Bibliography

Coe, Sophie D. *America's First Cuisines*. Austin: University of Texas Press, 1994.

Colón, Ferdinand. *The Life of the Admiral Christopher Columbus by His Son Ferdinand.* Translated by Benjamin Keen. New Brunswick, NJ: Rutgers University Press, 1959.

Crosby, Alfred W., Jr. *The Columbian Exchange: Biological and Cultural Consequences of 1492.* Westport, CT: Greenwood, 1973.

Galinat, Walton C. "Maize: Gift from America's First Peoples." In *Chilies to Chocolate, Food the Americas Gave the World*, edited by Nelson Foster and Linda S. Cordell. Tucson: University of Arizona Press, 1992.

Josephy, Alvin M., Jr., ed. *America in 1492: The World of the Indians Before the Arrival of Columbus.* New York: Alfred A. Knopf, 1992.

Toussaint-Samat, Maguelonne. *History of Food.* Translated by Anthea Bell. Malden, MA: Blackwell, 1997.

Coronado, Francisco Vázquez de (1510–1554)

The late 1530s and early 1540s witnessed a remarkable series of encounters between Spanish explorers and native North Americans. In the Southeast, Hernando de Soto cut a path of death and destruction through parts of ten future states. Juan Rodríguez Cabrillo sailed and charted over 1,000 miles along the Pacific coast. And, in the Southwest, Francisco Vázquez de Coronado led a huge expedition from 1540 to 1542, which traveled from the northern part of New Spain into present-day Arizona, New Mexico, Texas, Oklahoma, and Kansas.

Coronado was born in Salamanca, Spain, in 1510. Since he was the second of four sons, and the family estate had already been promised to his older brother, his chances for advancement at home were slim. In 1535, he moved to Mexico as part of Viceroy Antonio de Mendoza's retinue. Through his relationship with the viceroy, Coronado gained the governorship of Nueva Galicia, which contained parts of the modern Mexican states of Sinaloa and Nayarit and most of Jalisco.

Inspired by the incredible journey of Cabeza de Vaca, in 1538, Mendoza and Coronado sent the Franciscan Fray (Father) Marcos de Niza at the head of a small exploring party, which contained Cabeza de Vaca's famous slave Esteban, through the unknown territory to the north. Esteban was killed at Cíbola—a Zuni town—but Marcos returned to tell a fantastic story, comparing the material wealth of New Mexico with that of Mexico and Peru.

It is now likely that Fray Marcos never actually visited Cíbola, fearing his fate would be the same as Esteban's. On his glowing recommendation, however, Coronado outfitted a much larger expedition. It consisted of 300 Spaniards, more than 1,000 conquered Native Americans from throughout Mexico, and about 1,500 horses. A group of Franciscans, led by Fray Marcos, accompanied the expedition as well. Many of the young Spaniards, including Coronado, had never engaged in a journey of reconnaissance or conquest before.

Upon reaching Cíbola, Coronado was shocked by the discrepancy between Marcos's description and the actual situation; he branded the Franciscan a liar and sent him back to Mexico. Coronado's large army proceeded to attack and subdue the town, which was turned into a base of operations for future exploration.

One Spanish party seized a Hopi pueblo. When

In this depiction by nineteenth-century artist Frederic Remington, the Spanish conquistador Francisco Vázquez de Coronado leads a massive expedition north from New Spain in search of gold. The Spanish traveled throughout the American Southwest, but the legendary cities of gold were nowhere to be found. *(Private Collection/Bridgeman Art Library)*

they heard word of a great river to the west, another party struck out in that direction. Although they came upon the Grand Canyon, they did not find anything they termed of value there. Other members of the Coronado expedition explored the vast territory to the east, including the pueblos of New Mexico.

During the winter of 1540–1541, Coronado moved his headquarters to the Rio Grande near Albuquerque, where already tense relations with the Pueblo people took a turn for the worse. Tired of having their food, clothing, and women appropriated by the Spanish, the Pueblo revolted. The Spanish, led by Coronado's first lieutenant, García López de Cárdenas, retaliated by burning the pueblo at Arenal, smoking out the inhabitants, and burning them at the stake. Some thirteen native towns were destroyed, but the Pueblo people still refused to submit.

In the spring of 1541, Coronado moved his main force to the northeast, in search of an allegedly rich kingdom called Quivira, in present-day Kansas. Coronado relied on the word of a native of that country, whom the Spanish called the Turk. The expedition wound its way through the plains of West Texas, Oklahoma, and Kansas, finding no cities of note, and no visible signs of the country's alleged wealth. As it turned out, the Turk had been instructed by the Pueblo to lead Coronado's army to a place where it would starve to death. Discouraged, the Spanish strangled the Turk and then retraced their steps back to the south.

The expedition was deemed a failure, and Coronado spent years defending his actions in Mexico City. He died there in 1554, perhaps as the result of a riding injury sustained on the expedition. His right-hand man Cárdenas was tried in Spain for crimes against the American natives, and he died in prison.

Although Coronado did not succeed in finding huge inland empires or great wealth, he did increase Spanish knowledge of the Southwestern region immensely. In the process, however, the Spanish irreparably damaged their reputation and relationship with the Pueblo people.

Matthew Jennings

See also: Exploration; Spanish Colonies on Mainland North America (Chronology).

Bibliography

Flint, Richard, and Shirley Cushing, eds. *The Coronado Expedition to Tierra Nueva: The 1540–1542 Route Across the Southwest.* Niwot: The University Press of Colorado, 1997.

Weber, David J. *The Spanish Frontier in North America.* New Haven, CT: Yale University Press, 1992.

Cortéz, Hernando (1485–1547)

Of impoverished origins, Hernando Cortéz was the Spanish conquistador who, beginning in 1519, led a small force of Spanish soldiers against the Aztec Empire of Mexico. With his native allies, mostly consisting of Aztec subject peoples, Cortéz vanquished the mighty Aztecs in a two-year campaign. In the process, he became the ruler of a vast territory, stretching from the Caribbean to the Pacific. Intrigues at the Spanish court of Charles V, however, led to Cortéz's dismissal as governor of Mexico, and he was forced to return to Spain to defend his reputation.

Cortéz was born in 1485 to a noble, but poor, family in the Extremadura region of Spain. At the age of 14, he was sent to study at the University of Salamanca, Spain's finest, where he earned a reputation as intelligent but also ruthlessly ambitious and quarrelsome. Upon graduating, Cortéz first gravitated toward a military career. In 1503, at the age of 19, however, he became convinced by tales of Christopher Columbus's journeys to the Western Hemisphere to set sail for Hispaniola—the base of Spain's incipient American empire.

After working as a farmer and legal official for a half-dozen years, he joined Diego Velázquez's expedition to conquer the island of Cuba. Rising through the ranks, Cortéz became mayor of the Cuban capital at Santiago; he also received a *repartimiento*, or gift of land with native peoples as slaves. An able administrator, Cortéz soon won the respect of Velázquez, who chose him in 1518 to lead an expedition to establish a settlement on the eastern coast of the mainland, near present-day Tabasco, Mexico.

Early the following year, Cortéz set sail with six ships and 300 men. Known for his diplomatic abilities, he soon won over the local natives, gaining intelligence from them about a great inland empire. He then sailed up the coast, establishing the city of Veracruz as his base of operations. While Cortéz had not received his government's approval to conduct warfare, he soon turned his 300 settlers into a cohesive military unit. To ensure their loyalty, he burned his ships, making it impossible for anyone to return to Hispaniola or Cuba.

To survive, he told his men, they would have to conquer the territory.

Cortéz's expedition used a mixture of force—backed by horses, guns, and armor—and diplomacy with the native peoples they encountered as they marched inland. Those who resisted were attacked; those who cooperated, many of them disgruntled subject peoples of the Aztecs, were incorporated into the Spanish force. In November 1519, Cortéz entered the Aztec capital of Tenochtitlán, with several hundred Spaniards and about 1,000 Tlaxcaltecs, the Aztecs' chief enemies. There, he was greeted with great respect by the emperor Montezuma II, who may have believed Cortéz an incarnation of the god Quetzalcoatl. Fearing a trap, Cortéz made Montezuma II his prisoner.

Meanwhile, other Spaniards began to hear of Cortéz's success and started to plot against him. In 1520, an expedition from Cuba led by Pánfilo de Narváez landed in Mexico. Cortéz quickly defeated Narváez's forces and made the survivors part of his own army. During his absence, however, the Aztecs had risen in rebellion, laying siege to the Spanish garrison at Tenochtitlán. With great loss of life to the Spaniards, Aztecs, and Tlaxcaltecs, Cortéz managed to lift the siege and move his forces out of the city. After a period of regrouping, he marched again on Tenochtitlán in December 1520.

Following eight months of siege laying and street fighting, Cortéz had once again conquered the Aztec capital. He became absolute ruler of Mexico, rebuilding the city and renaming it Mexico City. Still, he remained restless, setting off on an ill-fated, two-year expedition to conquer Central America in 1524. While away, underlings seized his property and began to abuse his Aztec subjects.

All of this news eventually reached Spain, where members of the court had convinced Charles V that Cortéz, 8,000 miles distant, had too much power and was likely to establish Mexico as his own independent kingdom. To counter this talk, he sent five lengthy letters pledging his loyalty. An envoy was sent to investigate, but he died soon after arriving, leading to rumors that Cortéz had him poisoned.

In 1528, Cortéz felt compelled to return to Spain, with a fabulous treasure in tow. Impressed, Charles V did not punish him, but he did not give him the governorship of Mexico that Cortéz so desired. Instead, Charles V offered him lowlier titles and property in Mexico.

Upon his return to the New World, Cortéz settled on his plantations near Cuernavaca, about 30 miles south of Mexico City. Legal problems over land and titles continued to plague him. He returned to Spain, where he died in 1547.

James Ciment

See also: Aztec; Montezuma II; New Spain; Spanish Colonies on Mainland North America (Chronology).

Bibliography

Johnson, William Weber. *Cortéz*. Boston: Little, Brown, 1975.
Prescott, William Hickling. *History of the Conquest of Mexico*. 3 vols. Chicago: Hooper, Clarke, 1843.

Cotton

Cotton clothing is as old as civilization. It clad the people of Egypt, India, and China long before the Christian era. Cotton fabrics from Muslim countries appeared in Italy and Spain in the first century. Moorish Spain cultivated cotton in the ninth century, and Peruvians and Mexicans used cotton for garments and tapestries in pre-Columbian times.

Cotton was not significant during the colonial period, either economically or socially. Long-staple Sea Island cotton was valued, because it was easy to clean and made a high-quality, fine thread, but it could be grown only in a few places. Short-staple cotton, the variety best suited to the greater part of colonial North America, required a great deal of labor—it often took a full day to clean a single pound. Consequently, colonists usually dressed in fabric woven from linen (made from flax) and sheep's wool.

The Spanish made the first European effort to produce cotton commercially in the New World, in Florida in 1556. But the attempt failed, because the land was poorly drained and rains were excessive. In 1607, the English at Jamestown encountered similar difficulties in growing cotton as a viable commercial crop. Early seventeenth-century settlers in the South grew cotton to make a coarse cloth for household use, not commerce.

The first decades of colonial life were a struggle for subsistence, and the cash crop that took hold was tobacco, not cotton. American cotton was labor-intensive and not really suited for the primitive technology of the English textile industry. Then, the Industrial Revolution in England began in textiles, formerly a cottage industry. In 1760, the English cotton trade employed only 40,000 people, and its value was

The first cotton mill in America was established by Samuel Slater in Pawtucket, Rhode Island, in 1793—the same year Eli Whitney invented the cotton gin. Cotton production skyrocketed in the following decades, as did the slave population. *(Smithsonian Institution, Washington, DC/Bridgeman Art Library)*

only around 600,000 pounds. Exports were growing, however, rising in value from 23,253 pounds in 1701, to 45,986 pounds in 1751, and 200,354 pounds in 1764. Even so, the 1764 value of cotton exports was but one-twentieth of the value of wool exports. At the time, only coarse cloth was made in England; the technology was not yet capable of handling finer fabrics, which were supplied through imports from Continental Europe.

Late in the eighteenth century, American farmers began specializing in cash crops as surpluses became possible. Long-staple Sea Island cotton became one of the cash crops in the lowlands and islands of South Carolina and Georgia, two of the places where slavery was most common. More important Southern crops at the time were rice, sugar, flax, and hemp.

Sir Richard Arkwright established the first water-powered spinning mill in 1771 at Cromford, Derbyshire, England. American inventor Eli Whitney developed the concept of the cotton gin in 1793, which made it possible to clean short-staple cotton much more easily. With the new technology, the volume of the cotton trade had increased threefold by 1803, and cultivation expanded of short-staple cotton, which was suitable for cultivation in many more places than long-staple cotton.

The increase in cotton crops led to a massive increase in slavery in the American South—from 750,000 slaves in 1790, when the United States pro-

duced 3,000 bales of cotton, to 1 million slaves ten years later, when production totaled 75,000 bales, and 4.5 million slaves on the eve of the Civil War, when the country produced over 3.8 million bales of cotton.

John H. Barnhill

See also: Agriculture; Clothing; Columbian Exchange; Furnishings; Slavery, African American.

Bibliography

Bruchey, Stuart, ed. *Cotton and the Growth of the American Economy, 1790–1860.* New York: Harcourt, Brace and World, 1967

Kane, Nancy. *Textiles in Transition.* New York: Greenwood, 1988.

Toynbee, Arnold. "Lectures on the Industrial Revolution in England." 1884. http://socserv.mcmaster.ca/~econ/ugcm/3ll3/toynbee/indrev.

Von Tunzelmann, George N. "Time-Saving Technical Change: The Cotton Industry in the English Industrial Revolution." *Explorations in Economic History* 31:1 (1995): 1–27.

Cotton, John (1584–1652)

John Cotton was probably the single most important figure in the consolidation of Massachusetts Congregational Church polity, or the "New England Way."

Born in 1584 in Derby, England, Cotton was educated first at Trinity, and then at Emmanuel College, where he underwent religious conversion to Congregationalism in 1609. After receiving his bachelor of divinity degree in 1612, he accepted the vicarship of St. Botolph's Church in Boston, Lincolnshire. By that time, he was well ensconced in English Puritan circles, with connections to the Earl of Warwick and the Massachusetts Bay Company. In addition, within his own congregation Cotton drew together a group of Puritan parishioners to hold communion privately, a harbinger of his later commitment to the Congregational Church.

While at St. Botolph's, John Cotton did not fully conform to the liturgy of the Church of England, which drew the ire of Church authorities. Tension was only intensified when radicals in his parish smashed the church's stained-glass windows in an act of religious iconoclasm. In the early 1630s, King Charles I and William Laud (the bishop of London until 1633, then archbishop of Canterbury) began a more rigorous campaign to root out nonconformity. As a result, in 1632, Cotton was summoned before the Court of High Commission, but he instead went into hiding. Rejecting flight to the more tolerant Netherlands, Cotton opted for emigration to the Massachusetts Bay Colony. There, he became co-pastor with John Wilson at the First Church of Christ in Boston. Cotton's talents as a preacher quickly provoked a revival within the Boston church, resulting in an influx of new members.

Cotton was also an important voice in several of the debates swirling around the new colony. Reversing his previous criticism of the Salem church for its quasi-separatist practices, in a 1636 sermon, he defended the practice of limiting access to the sacraments to church members. He also helped establish the use of conversion narratives as a test for church membership and took a lead role in opposing Roger Williams.

While crucial to the establishment of New England church polity, these events paled when compared to the Antinomian Controversy. By 1636, several New England ministers had begun to question Cotton's doctrinal orthodoxy. Both Cotton and his opponents were Calvinists and believed in double predestination: that God had chosen (or "elected") certain individuals for salvation through a free gift of grace and had chosen the rest for eternal damnation, based purely upon His own inscrutable will. All the ministers equally agreed that receiving God's grace would lead one to comport oneself morally. Cotton differed with the other ministers as to whether good works could be used as evidence that one had, in fact, received grace and was, therefore, among the elect. Cotton argued that good works could not be trusted without a sense of a true saving faith in Christ (that is, one's works could be taken as evidence of salvation only after one had become certain of the experience of grace through other means).

Anne Hutchinson, who had been a frequent auditor of Cotton's sermons in England and had followed him to the New World, always maintained that her views on salvation were consonant with those preached by Cotton. Cotton himself was at first unaware how greatly they differed. He finally came to understand Hutchinson's views, and when the authorities in the colony moved against her and her followers, Cotton officially repudiated her. He managed to work out a theological compromise with the other ministers at the 1637 synod and personally pronounced Anne Hutchinson's excommunication from the Boston church.

Although tainted by the Antinomian Controversy, Cotton's reputation revived during the 1640s through his apologetics in response to English and Scottish Presbyterian attacks on Congregationalism. This debate between English and New England Puri-tans had begun in manuscript form during the late 1630s. By 1642, with the English Civil War in full swing and after the convening of the Westminster Assembly to reform the Church of England, this debate entered the press. Most prominently, in 1644, Cotton published *The Keyes of the Kingdom of Heaven*, to which the Scottish Covenanter Robert Baillie responded with a scathing attack on Cotton and Congregationalism in *A Dissuasive from the Errours of the Time*.

The argument continued in the press until the late 1640s, but, by then, the failure to achieve a religious settlement in England had made the question of church polity all but irrelevant. Beginning in 1646, nonetheless, Cotton participated in the synod that produced the Cambridge Platform, which crystallized New England's church polity. John Cotton died in December 1652.

Kenneth A. Shelton

See also: Massachusetts Bay Colony; Ministers and the Ministry; Puritanism.

Bibliography

Emerson, Everett. *John Cotton*. Rev. ed. Boston: Twayne, 1990.

Sargent, Bush, Jr., ed. *The Correspondence of John Cotton*. Chapel Hill: University of North Carolina Press, 2001.

Ziff, Larzer. *The Career of John Cotton: Puritanism and the American Experience*. Princeton, NJ: Princeton University Press, 1962.

Covenants

A covenant is a formal agreement, symbolizing a bargained-for promise that is binding for both parties. While the dominant twenty-first century use of the word "covenant" may refer to agreements that deal with the exchange of goods and services or the sale of land, in colonial America, it was often used to refer to religious promises between two or more individuals. In the example of Puritan settlers in Massachusetts, we may see that the underlying principles of religious covenants were applied to civil, political, and familial relationships.

In 1628, Puritans seeking religious freedom and economic prospects set sail from England, landing in Plymouth, which had been settled first by the Pilgrims, a separate group of Puritans, in 1620. The following year, the merchants involved in this endeavor received a royal charter as the Massachusetts Bay Colony. John

Winthrop, the most prominent member of this venture, organized the initial segment of what was later to be known as the Great Migration of Puritans who no longer believed that they could practice their religion freely in England. In 1630, more than 1,000 Puritan men and women immigrated to Massachusetts, the majority settling in the Boston area. By 1643, Boston had become the largest town in the English-speaking colonies, with a population of nearly 20,000.

The establishment of many New England communities was the result of collective written agreements, the most famous of which was part of the Plymouth "Mayflower Compact." The idea of such compacts, while previously conceptualized by political philosophers, had never come to fruition before the New England Puritans. To the colonists, the civil covenants embodied their desire to live in small communities where cohesion and participation were integral to daily life.

Central to the Puritans' beliefs was the idea that they were in a special relationship with God. They believed that God had entered into a covenant with them and that they were chosen for a special mission in the New World. As John Winthrop had explained, "Thus stands the cause between God and us: we are entered into Covenant." The settlements that were established in the colony were to reflect this special position, acting as an example to the rest of the world, "a city upon a hill." By living up to this ideal, the community would retain God's favor, experiencing peace, prosperity, harmony, and happiness. If, however, individuals failed to live up to their special commission, they would surely experience the wrath of God.

In turn, the Puritans promised one another that they would live together in harmony, working toward communal goals. A leading Puritan clergyman, John Witte, Jr., made the following observation in 1624:

We are by nature covenant creatures bound together by covenants innumerable and together bound by covenant to our God. Such is our human condition. Such is this earthly life. Such is God's creation. Blest be the ties that bind us.

These "innumerable covenants" included at least four between individuals: a national covenant, a political covenant, an ecclesiastical covenant, and a family covenant. The key to the success of covenant relationships was that they be entered into willingly. Puritans believed that meaningful obedience to civil and scriptural law was the result of voluntary submission, not coercion.

The most prominent covenant was the civil covenant. Through this covenant, individuals were obligated to preserve godly beliefs and values, both adopting and advocating godly morals and mores. Individuals were expected to live in the service of God, neighbor, and community. Embracing this ideal of a civil covenant, the leaders of the Massachusetts Bay Colony transformed the nature of the original charter to reflect a community based on mutual consent.

Even the manner by which land was granted in Massachusetts reflected their communal ideals. Unlike the Southern colonies of Virginia and Maryland, where headrights were granted to individual applicants who settled their lands at a distance from one another, in Massachusetts groups of men collectively applied to the General Court for land grants. The men who received such grants were responsible for determining how it would be distributed. They began by surveying the land and plotting the area where houses and churches would be established. Only then would families be given individual parcels, which were scattered outside the town center for farming.

The political covenant was tripartite: God, individuals, and political or civil leaders. Within this paradigm, political leaders were to lead by example, encouraging citizens to live up to their obligations under the national covenant. The Puritans believed that, under the political covenant, political leaders and the people were responsible for the other's obligations before God and man. When individuals failed to live up to their responsibilities, it was the duty of the leaders to impart discipline, discipline that might ultimately result in banishment or death if the delinquent individual failed to amend his or her behavior. If the civil leaders failed to perform their duties under the political covenant, the people were responsible for protesting the behavior. If the leaders were unwilling to appropriately discharge their duties, the people could unseat them from office.

Early in the 1630s, Winthrop and other local leaders, exercising their political responsibility, began to issue edicts in an attempt to improve the colonial government. True to their Puritan beliefs, these official orders had moral overtones, demonstrating the interrelationship between church and state. Church attendance was mandatory for all colonists, regardless of church membership. Immoral conduct such as blasphemy, gambling, drunkenness, lascivious entertainment, and sexual misconduct was to be severely punished. Premarital sex, as evidenced by a child being born to a couple less than nine months after their wedding, would result in pecuniary fines and public humiliation. Those convicted of having sexual relations with members of the same gender might be hanged. In addition, commercial restrictions were enforced to ensure the just price of goods and prevent individual profiteering. Most people favored such laws and were willing to abide by them.

Congregationalist Puritans also embraced ecclesiastical covenants. It was believed by these Puritan groups that biblical scriptures required every national community to establish and maintain institutional churches. The social structure of Puritan churches required congregation members to meet together to grant formal consent to new church policies. The ecclesiastical covenant also required congregational members to undertake certain spiritual and moral obligations, vowing before God and one another that they would do so. These obligations included preaching the Gospel, administering the sacraments, and caring for those members of the community who were sick or destitute. The church was also responsible for educating political leaders in the Word of God, admonishing or removing those who were not abiding by these guidelines.

The final type of contract was the family or marital contract. A marital contract might be entered into willingly by a man and a woman, but, ultimately, it was the creation and commandments of God that instituted the arrangement. God created humans to be social creatures, seeking the companionship of others. He commanded mankind to "be fruitful and multiply" (Genesis 1:28), designing men's and women's bodies with the physical capability to do so.

When entering into a marriage under the provisions of the church, husband and wife affirmed their fidelity to one another and pledged to abide by the laws that God had established for marital relations. If they satisfied the terms of this covenant, God, in turn, would see that the family prospered. If a husband or wife failed to keep their vows, God would set his wrath upon the entire family. Married couples played an important role in the community, as they were to nurture and inculcate their children with love for God and respect for the authority of the church and the law.

The covenant principles upheld by Puritan communities were also based upon the idea that man, having free will, was able to choose how he would act. Once selecting that course, however, he was obligated to perform that act, regardless of the potential outcome. Thus, an individual was free to enter into contracts with others within the community, but once doing so,

he was bound to fulfill the bargained-for responsibility that accompanied that contract.

The Puritans' belief in the absolute obligation to stand by one's word was based on three premises. First, the act of breaking a promise was perceived as being a sin. Secondly, failing to fulfill one's obligations, and thereby defeating the other party's expectations, was to demonstrate a lack of respect and love for that individual. Finally, and perhaps most importantly, the Puritans believed that social cohesion and harmony were dependent upon each member of the community adhering to the covenants that he or she entered into voluntarily.

Without this stability, society would effectively break the original covenant that it had with God. As a consequence, the community would lose God's favor, and social deterioration would be the inevitable result.

Joann M. Ross

See also: Massachusetts Bay Colony; Puritanism.

Bibliography

Black's Law Dictionary, ed. Bryan A. Garner. 7th ed. St. Paul: West Group, 1999.

Brack, Oscar Theodore, and Hugh Talmage Lefler. *Colonial America.* 2nd ed. New York: Macmillan Company, 1968.

Breen, Timothy H., and Stephen Foster. "The Puritans' Greatest Achievement: A Study of Social Cohesion in Seventeenth-Century Massachusetts." *Journal of American History* 60:1 (1973): 5–22.

Gillon, Steven M., and Cathy D. Matson. *The American Experiment: A History of the United States.* Boston: Houghton Mifflin, 2002.

Middleton, Richard. *Colonial America: A History, 1565–1776.* 3rd ed. Oxford, UK: Blackwell, 2002.

Norton, Mary Beth, David M. Katzman, David B. Blight, Howard P. Chudacoff, Thomas G. Paterson, William M. Tuttle, Jr., and Paul D. Escott, eds. *A People and a Nation: A History of the United States.* 6th ed. Boston: Houghton Mifflin, 2001.

Witte, John Jr. "Blest Be the Ties That Bind: Covenant and Community in Puritan Thought." *Emory Law Journal* 36 (1987): 579–601.

Creek

The Creek Indians moved into present-day Alabama and Georgia from the west. They are known today as members of the Muskogee Nation, a highly organized, unified community that counts about 40,000 members. During the colonial period, however, an individual

Creek's identity was rooted in his or her particular town. Prolonged exposure to Europeans forced the Creek (the name is probably of English origin) to reshape their identity in order to effectively resist the cultural and territorial effects of colonization.

The Creek numbered about 15,000 in 1685, when serious English colonization was just beginning. The tribe's population initially dropped dramatically as a result of disease. Over time, however, an increasing number of Native Americans began to consider themselves Creeks, and, in 1790, after a century of interacting with the English, their population had recovered to approximately the same level as it had been 100 years earlier.

The Creek spoke variants of the Muskogean language, some of which were mutually unintelligible. By the time they met the English, the Creek peoples had also divided into Lower Towns and Upper Towns. The Lower Towns were located on the Chattahoochee, Ocmulgee, and Flint rivers, and the Upper Towns were on the Coosa, Tallapoosa, and Alabama rivers. In the colonial period, the Upper Towns preferred trading with the Spanish and French, while the Lower Towns dealt primarily with the English, first out of Charles Town and later out of the fledgling colony of Georgia. In addition, following a division in their society, Creek towns were classified as "red" or "white." This determined the towns' responsibilities in warfare: red for war, white for peace.

Each Creek town (or *talwa*) was fiercely independent, so the confederacy remained relatively loose throughout the colonial period. Creek kin groups, or clans, were matrilineal (clan identity passed through the mother) and matrilocal (husbands moved near their mothers-in-law). Town councils advised the leaders (*micos*) on political, social, and military matters. *Micos* could not act independently of their counselors, though they did conduct diplomacy between Creeks and foreigners, and they controlled access to surplus food in the town's granary.

The Spanish under Hernando de Soto moved through Creek country, leaving the Creek to deal with the devastating effects of European-introduced disease. Creek interaction with the English lasted longer and was more complex. Since the English did not move into Creek country in large numbers until the middle of the eighteenth century, most Creek interaction with the English took the form of trade. From the founding of South Carolina in 1670, Creeks gradually came to depend on English trade goods. Trade with the English had benefits but also serious consequences.

The trade between the Creek towns and the English consisted of a wide range of items. Cloth, deerskins, firearms, alcohol, and Native American slaves were most common. Creek men extended their hunting season and expanded their hunting territory in an effort to satisfy English demands for deerskins. Creek men, sometimes accompanied by English traders and other allied Native Americans, terrorized the missions of Spanish Florida as they raided for slaves in the opening decade of the eighteenth century. Creek women incorporated English manufactured goods into their homes, changing Creek domestic life. Creeks also held African slaves, and this reshaped Creek notions of property and power.

Creek relations with the English were for the most part peaceful, mainly because Creeks did not want to cut off their access to trade goods, and because the English posed little threat to the Creeks' relationship with the Spanish. The Creek did participate in the opening phase of the Yamasee War (1715–1717) by killing the English traders living in their towns, but they did not, on the whole, endorse the policy of removing the English entirely. The founding of Georgia in 1733 as a buffer between Spanish and English America brought the Creek and English even closer together. In fact, the loose construction of Creek identity led to an increasing number of biracial leaders.

In 1739, the Creek and English signed the Treaty of Coweta, which drew a line between Creek and English territory. The imaginary line failed to stop white encroachment, however. The Creek struggled to maintain cultural and political autonomy and to retain as much of their land base as they could. They grew to respect British colonial officials but despise Anglo-American settlers. Still, the Creek remained basically neutral during the American Revolution.

In the aftermath of the conflict, Creeks faced a new and deadly threat: an aggressive, expansionist American republic. Their response was increasing centralization in government. They also continued to lose land, and were forcibly removed to Indian Territory in the 1830s, after decades of bitter conflict with white settlers.

Matthew Jennings

See also: Native American–European Conflict; Native American–European Relations; Native Americans.

Bibliography

Braund, Kathryn Holland. *Deerskins and Duffels: Creek Indian Trade with Anglo-America, 1685–1815.* Lincoln: University of Nebraska Press, 1993.

Green, Michael D. *The Politics of Indian Removal: Creek Government and Society in Crisis.* Lincoln: University of Nebraska Press, 1982.

McIntosh, Kenneth W. "Creek (Muskogee)." In *Encyclopedia of North American Indians*, edited by Frederick E. Hoxie. Boston: Houghton Mifflin, 1996.

Crime

In the early seventeenth century, the most common crimes in the North American colonies were crimes against people, property, and the public order. Crimes such as disturbing the peace, public intoxication, fornication, lying, and idleness were relatively common in all of the colonies, regardless of whether those colonies were founded for religious, political, or economic reasons. Cheating, dice, clog dancing, forgery, blasphemy, perjury, and coin clipping (the act of slicing off tiny slivers of silver or gold from the edges of coins and then melting those slivers down into bullion) were also crimes with which the early colonial leaders were forced to contend.

It should be noted that the majority of the men and women who committed crimes during this early period of colonization were by no means career criminals, nor were they the desperate poor (so common in Western Europe at the time) who committed crime only in order to survive. In a country where unemployment was not a problem and where land and food were both readily available, there was little reason to risk running afoul of the law. When first-generation colonists turned to crime, that turn had more to do with personality, disposition, temptation, and peer pressure than it did with any economic necessity.

Consequently, the vast majority of the crimes committed by colonists in the early seventeenth century were either relatively minor moral lapses, such as drinking too much or falling asleep in church, or petty crimes of opportunity, such as stealing a pair of stockings from a clothesline. In fact, the items most often stolen from early colonial households were silver, linens, and silks. There were exceptions, however, with Stephen Hopkins, a Pilgrim of the London contingent and onetime assistant governor of Plymouth colony, being one of the most obvious. During the course of an illicit career that spanned more than thirty years, Hopkins was found guilty of mutiny, assault and battery, disorderly conduct, price fixing, breach of contract, and illegal sale of alcohol. The nature and number of the crimes he committed successfully, crimes for which he was never brought to trial, are open to speculation.

More serious crimes—murder, burglary, robbery (the colonial equivalent of mugging), vicious assault, rape, treason, sedition, and arson—also occurred in all of the colonies, but the frequency with which those crimes occurred depended largely on locale. The murder rate, for example, was twice as high in Maryland as it was in Massachusetts in the seventeenth century, and the rate of morals offenses was higher in New England at that time than it was anywhere else. That does not mean, however, that residents of the Middle and Southern colonies never worried about immorality, nor is it to say that violence was unknown north of New York. On the contrary, a morals offense such as profaning the Sabbath—an offense usually associated with the New England colonies, where sin and crime were conflated—occurred in Virginia just as it did in Plymouth and Massachusetts Bay. In fact, the first Sunday law passed in North America, a law that required every man and woman to attend church on the Sabbath both in the morning and in the afternoon (on penalty of fine, whipping, or death), was passed not in New England but in Virginia in 1610.

Similarly, while homicide was by no means a daily occurrence in early-seventeenth-century New England, murders did happen, and many were so violent and gruesome as to be noteworthy even by modern standards. There appears in the church records of the Plymouth colony a coroner's jury report from 1648, which gives the following brief account of how Alice Bishop, for apparently no reason whatsoever, murdered her 4-year-old daughter, Martha, while the child was sleeping peacefully in her bed.

[In] the house of said Richard Bisops, wee saw at the foot of a ladder which leadeth into an upper-chamber, much bllod [blood]; and going up all of us into the chamber, wee found a woman child, of about foure years of age, lying in her shifte uppon her left cheeke, with her throat cut with divers gashes crose wayes, the wind pipe cut and stucke into the throat downward, and a bloody knife lying by the side of the child, with which knife all of us judge, and the said Allis hath confessed to five of us att one time, that shee murdered the child with the said knife.

Though a particularly horrific example of colonial murder, the Bishop case is also a precursor of sorts to what would become a curious trend in violent crime in colonial New England. In Massachusetts between 1674 and 1774, women accounted for fully one-third of all those accused of murder, and more than three-quarters of those women were charged with killing their own children.

Colonial Crime at the End of the Seventeenth Century

From the early years of colonization to roughly 1650, crimes such as drunkenness, idleness, and fornication far outnumbered more serious crimes such as theft and vicious assault. By the end of the 1670s, however, violent crimes and property crimes were occurring in the colonies almost as frequently as were victimless crimes, and the rates of both were on the rise. This was not due to any appreciable increase in the number of people who were committing crimes—in fact, the number of criminals operating within the colonies remained relatively constant between 1651 and 1680—nor was it a result of any radical increase in the inherent criminality of the colonists. Rather, the increasing crime rate that characterized the North American colonies in the last thirty years of the seventeenth century was due, in large part, to the rapidly changing nature of colonial life itself. The urbanization and increasingly cosmopolitan nature of many colonial towns coupled with ever-increasing class stratification in both urban and rural areas, as well as an ebbing sense of divine mission and communal responsibility, provided fertile ground for the growth of social deviance.

Long-established urban areas such as Boston and Philadelphia were no longer the quaint hubs of small-town colonial life; they were rapidly becoming thriving commercial centers that cultivated and catered to the needs and desires of foreign merchants, traders, and travelers. And the more urban and commercial those towns became, the more dependent they became on a large lower class—a service class—made up of men and women whose only job was the provision of whatever labor or assistance the towns' various visitors required. Even though many of those visitors were rowdy sailors, pirates (who operated with the knowledge and protection of local officials), and refugee strangers from the hinterlands, the people who comprised the service class

upon whom they relied were politically and socially irrelevant, and they knew it. Many were convicted criminals transported from England, runaway servants, or indentured servants whose terms of indenture had expired and who could not procure good farmable land of their own; the only stake they had in the New World was the money they could squeeze out of it. For them, there was no chance for full participation in society, and so playing by society's rules was not a priority.

To make matters worse, these newly transformed urban areas were perfect havens for criminals of every sort. All manner of bloodletters and thieves enjoyed the anonymity afforded by urban congestion, and they were assisted in the plying of their trades by dimly lit streets, the absence of any police force (in the modern sense) to stop them, and easy access to rural provinces, which made managing successful getaways all the easier. In Boston, New York, and Philadelphia, crime had been more of a nuisance than a problem in the years before those towns became thriving seaports. By 1690, however, the number of assaults, arsons, burglaries, murders, and thefts in all three towns had risen considerably. In fact, according to the records of the Massachusetts Bay Colony's Court of Assistants, the number of murders in Massachusetts tripled over the course of the seventeenth century, going from three in the years between 1630 and 1640 to nine in the years between 1673 and 1683.

As these urban centers grew, so did the appetites of their inhabitants for all manner of unseemly diversions. Brothels and pubs were abundant in seaside towns from Massachusetts to Carolina, and such morals offenses as drunkenness, sexual promiscuity, and unruly behavior became more and more common the closer the seventeenth century came to its close. Even Newport, the quietest and most respectable of all the early towns (it didn't get involved with shipping until 1675), was having trouble controlling its drunkards by mid-century, and by 1680, the "whores of Boston" were internationally renowned.

It should not be supposed that vice was limited only to city dwellers or to members of the urban lower classes. Captain Thomas Bradnox, for example, a Maryland justice of the peace, not only was known as one of the heaviest drinkers in Kent County but also was given to swearing and disturbing the peace when he was drunk. Similarly, John Barnes, a landholding merchant of the Plymouth colony, was an uncontrollably heavy drinker, and he was disenfranchised for drunkenness in 1659.

Colonial Crime in the Eighteenth Century

Crime had gone from a nuisance in the early days of colonization to a serious colonial problem by the end of the seventeenth century. Between 1700 and the coming of the American Revolution, it went from being a serious problem to a veritable plague. According to Carl Bridenbaugh, "instances had occurred of nearly every known offense against society" even before the eighteenth century had reached its midpoint. By 1715, there were so many pickpockets, burglars, and shoplifters operating in Boston that one colonial observer noted scarcely a night went by without some kind of crime being perpetrated. Philadelphia, infamous by 1720 for its pirates and highwaymen, was plagued by all manner of crimes, both victimless and violent. But the changes in the frequency, variety, and severity of the crimes being committed in eighteenth-century colonial North America were not really changes at all; rather, the rising crime rate and escalating violence after 1700 were simply a continuation of the general trend in deviant behavior. The real changes occurred in the nature of crime; it was becoming organized and intercolonial.

Although ordinary street crimes and petty crimes of opportunity were still the most commonly committed offenses in eighteenth-century colonial North America, crime in all of the colonies showed traces of organization as early as 1663. The organized underground networks of thieves and fences that had operated so successfully in places such as London's Whitechapel district had been unknown in the colonies prior to that time. By 1700, however, such criminal groups had begun appearing in both rural and urban areas. By 1750, they were in full swing. Some gangs operated without a single base of operations, roving from one unsuspecting neighborhood to another, pilfering and plundering as they went. Others showed an extraordinary degree of sophistication and organization. One gang of thieves in particular, with a base in the Carolina backcountry and associates in every colony, had developed a system of theft and transportation that made detection and suppression of their illicit activities a serious problem for colonial authorities. The goods pilfered by the gang in the South were sent to their accomplices in the North for distribution, and the goods pilfered in the North were, likewise, sent to the South. That way, stolen property was never resold in the area from which it came, thereby lessening the possibility of detection.

Counterfeiters and con men were similarly sophisticated, organized, and intercolonial. Con men such as Tom Bell (a Harvard-educated ne'er-do-well who made a living impersonating the son of one colony's leader while visiting the prominent families of another colony) generally worked alone. Counterfeiters such as Peter Long and John David, on the other hand, frequently operated in gangs with associates in numerous locations and made use of various underground networks for the distribution of their coins and notes, as well as for the provision and maintenance of safe houses and workshops.

By one colonial newspaper's estimation, there were more than 500 counterfeiters scattered throughout the colonies by 1768; in 1773, counterfeit currency had become such a problem in colonial Virginia that business there almost completely shut down. Owen Sullivan, one of the most infamous, prolific, and mobile colonial counterfeiters, based his gang (the Dover Money Club) in Dover, New York, but lived and worked with counterfeiters all over New England. Over the years, many of Sullivan's associates were brought to justice, and, when four of them were apprehended in Newport, Rhode Island, in 1755, they admitted to having printed bogus currency valuing 50,000 pounds from plates supplied to them by Sullivan. Sullivan himself was brought to justice and hanged in 1756.

Con men, while infinitely more flamboyant, never impacted colonial society to the extent that the counterfeiters and thieves did. Still, their exploits made great copy and went a long way toward making crime and the criminal lifestyle seem attractive, something it had not been before the eighteenth century.

Conclusion

For many living in Western Europe in the early seventeenth century, it seemed that their society was being overrun by vice, iniquity, and crime. Impoverished farmers and homeless serfs were flooding into England's urban areas, and entire neighborhoods in cities such as London and Bristol were swarming with petty criminals of all varieties.

Those who promoted the English colonization of North America used the public's fear of crime as yet another way to make life in the colonies appear as an attractive alternative to life in the mother country. Those prototypical travel agents portrayed the colonies as havens of safety and virtue, as places free from the sin and wickedness of the Old World, as a world in which honest, hardworking men and women could live without fear of being victimized by highwaymen, con artists, lewd women, and thugs. It was an effective selling strategy.

While some of the early colonists were utopians, none of them truly believed they could create a society completely free of crime, vice, and violence. They knew crime would be a part of their lives in the New World as it had been a part of their lives in the Old, but they were confident they could keep it to manageable levels, levels far below those of the countries they were leaving.

To a large extent, they were successful. Crime in the early North American colonies was far from widespread. Even with the waning of the strict moral codes set forth by the first colonial generation, increasing secularism, and the urbanization of many of the seaports, crime never became a problem of the same magnitude as in Western Europe. The majority of colonists were law-abiding people, who lived according to their moral traditions and middle-class values. Crime, then as now, was the exception, rather than the rule.

Jay R. Hopler

See also: Debt and Debtor's Prison; Gambling; Prisons and Punishment; Prostitution; Riots.

Bibliography

Barck, Oscar Theodore, Jr., and Hugh Talmage Lefler. *Colonial America.* New York: Macmillan, 1958.

Bridenbaugh, Carl. *Cities in Revolt: Urban Life in America, 1743–1776.* New York: Capricorn, 1955.

———. *Cities in the Wilderness: The First Century of Urban Life in America, 1625–1742.* New York: Capricorn, 1964.

Browning, Frank, and John Gerassi. *The American Way of Crime.* New York: G. P. Putnam's Sons, 1980.

Cohen, Daniel A. "A Fellowship of Thieves: Property Criminals in Eighteenth-Century Massachusetts." *Journal of Social History* 22:1 (Fall 1988): 65–92.

Erikson, Kai T. *Wayward Puritans: A Study in the Sociology of Deviance.* New York: John Wiley and Sons, 1966.

Powers, Edwin. *Crime and Punishment in Early Massachusetts, 1620–1692: A Documentary History.* Boston: Beacon, 1966.

Purvis, Thomas L. *Colonial America to 1763.* New York: Facts on File, 1999.

Scott, Kenneth. *Counterfeiting in Colonial America.* New York: Oxford University Press, 1957.

Semmes, Raphael. *Crime and Punishment in Early Maryland.* Montclair, NJ: Patterson Smith, 1970.

Cromwell, Oliver (1599–1658)

Few individuals in history are as controversial as Oliver Cromwell. General, politician, religious zealot, deposer of king and Parliament, and ultimately the lord protector of England until his death in 1658, to some he was a great man, to others a tyrant. One certainty, however, is that he was one of the most important individuals in the history of Britain and in the foundation of European settlement in the New World.

Born in Huntingdon, England in 1599, Cromwell studied at nearby Cambridge University. He initially earned his living through farming until sometime around 1628, when he became a devout Puritan following a religious conversion experience. The Puritans were an English Protestant sect that sought to simplify the Church of England through strict adherence to Calvinist theology and discipline. Throughout his life, Cromwell was guided by a Puritan sense of dedication and an unswerving belief that he was God's chosen vessel. He first became a member of Parliament in 1628 but played only a minor role in national politics until 1640.

It was the English Civil War that lifted Cromwell from obscurity, and at the heart of the conflict was religion. The Church of England began quarreling with the Puritans, and this division became more pronounced during the reign of Charles I (1625–1649), when laws were passed compelling Puritans to conform to Anglicanism or face legal censure. Because of this, beginning in 1630 as many as 20,000 Puritans immigrated to America from Britain, settling mainly in the New England colonies. By 1642, the unpopular Charles I, besieged by an invading Scottish army and accused of pro-Catholic sentiment, was stripped of most of his royal power by Parliament, and war between the king and Parliament ensued.

Cromwell rushed to defend Parliament, and, despite a lack of military experience, he became one of the greatest generals in history. Within two years, he raised and trained his own army and inflicted significant defeats on the royalist forces (called Cavaliers). Eventually, he was granted command of all of Parliament's troops (called Roundheads). He remolded them into a powerful fighting force known as the New Model Army, and at the Battle of Naseby in 1645, he inflicted a crushing defeat on Cavalier forces. Within a year, Charles I had no recourse left but surrender.

Under Oliver Cromwell in the 1650s, the British Protectorate proved important to colonial prospects in North America. His military success over Holland and seizure of Jamaica from Spain were vital to the growth of the British Atlantic economy. *(York Museums Trust [York Art Gallery], United Kingdom/ Bridgeman Art Library)*

Parliament was split on the proper form of government for England, with the Presbyterians, supported by many Scots, advocating a constitutional monarchy under Charles I, while Cromwell and the army feared retribution upon the king's return. Threatened with chaos, Cromwell decisively broke the deadlock by defeating the Scottish army, purging Parliament of 110 members, and bringing Charles I to trial. Charles I was convicted and executed in 1649.

Cromwell, then, took the place of the monarch. As leader of the army and the most powerful man in the country, he was happy to leave the governing of England to the members of Parliament who remained following the purge. But they ruled poorly, and Cromwell felt obliged to disband them by force in 1653. Within five years, he had deposed both king and Parliament, and, in their place, he created the Instrument

of Government—the only written constitution in Britain's long history. It made Cromwell lord protector of the realm for life.

Cromwell's fifteen years in power were marked both by great victories and by great tragedies. He was successful in his war against Holland (1652–54) and seized Jamaica from Spain, both important events in the development of the Atlantic economy. Yet, in 1649, he led an army to Ireland to settle the decade-old Catholic rebellion, and, at Wexford and Drogheda, he routed the Irish armies, slaughtering many of the surrendering troops and shipping the prisoners off to Barbados. So brutal was Cromwell's suppression of Ireland that even though he was there only nine months, the oath "The curse of Cromwell on you" is still uttered today. In 1651, he turned to Scotland and defeated a Scottish-royalist army, bringing an end to the English Civil War.

The years of the Commonwealth saw Cromwell rule as the virtual dictator of England. He became increasingly unpopular with the majority of English citizens, who longed for a return to traditional government. In an effort to secure stability, Cromwell was offered the title of king but declined, choosing instead to proffer his untrained son as his heir apparent. This proved disastrous, for after the elder Cromwell's passing in 1658, his son was forced out. Within two years, Parliament recalled Charles II, the son of the slain king, and restored the monarchy.

The historian John Buchan best summed up Cromwell's life and legacy:

> A devotee of law, he was forced to be often lawless; a civilian to the core, he had to maintain himself by the sword; with a passion to construct, his task was chiefly to destroy . . . the most English of . . . figures, he spent his life in opposition to the majority of Englishmen; a realist, he was condemned to build that which could not last.

Yet even in the New World, Cromwell's influence was enormous. His victories over Holland and Spain allowed Britain to more fully develop the Atlantic colonies, and public reaction to his Puritan zeal, following Charles II's restoration in 1660, hastened nonconformist immigration to America. Beyond this, Cromwell sanctioned the execution of Charles I based on the claim that he had broken his covenant with the English people; Cromwell believed that a leader who breaks a covenant may legitimately be overthrown. This Puritan concept of the covenantal nature of government would come to influence the founding of a number of American colonies, including Massachusetts and Connecticut.

Todd E. A. Larson

See also: Charles I; Charles II; English Civil War; Puritanism.

Bibliography

Buchan, John. *Oliver Cromwell.* Boston: Houghton Mifflin, 1934.

Davis, J. C. *Oliver Cromwell.* New York: Oxford University Press, 2001.

Gaunt, Peter. *Oliver Cromwell.* Cambridge, UK: Blackwell, 1996.

Morrill, John, ed. *Oliver Cromwell and the English Revolution.* New York: Longman, 1990.

Cuba

Cuba is the largest of the Caribbean islands, situated on the northwestern end of the Antilles arc of islands. The main island covers about 40,500 square miles and runs 777 miles from northwest to southeast.

In pre-Columbian times, the population numbered in the tens of thousands and comprised several different peoples, the hunters and gatherers living in the far west being the longest established. They had been displaced from the eastern part of the island between 1000 and 1200 C.E. by the Taino, an Arawakan people, who had migrated from the Orinoco River basin in South America along the Antilles islands chain.

The Taino people lived in villages, practiced advanced agriculture, fished, had started ranching, and were able potters. Although most of their culture was lost during the European colonization, some elements were taken over by the Spanish—including words such as *tobaco* (tobacco) and *huracán* or *cacique* (local leader), but also such items as the canoe and the *hamaca* (hammock).

Cuba was the second island Christopher Columbus set foot on during his first voyage. When he arrived, on October 27, 1492, he believed it to be Japan. After talking with Taino inhabitants, he referred to it as "Colba"—the Taino word for "cultivated area" or "green"—a term that later developed into "Cuba."

Spanish settlement, however, started on the neighboring island of Hispaniola and did not begin on Cuba until 1510. Development was then propelled by the discovery of gold deposits, but the heyday was short and ended about 1520, as the deposits turned out to be unsatisfying.

The main Spanish force had set off to conquer the Central American mainland, and they used Cuba only as a base of operations. Concurrently, the rebellion of the native peoples against their brutal so-called pacification intensified and ended only in the 1530s, when the native tribes had been vastly diminished by European diseases. In 1544, 3,000 colonists, 1,000 indentured natives, 800 black slaves, and about 5,000 free natives lived in Cuba.

Due to its geopolitical benefits, the island was given a key role within the Spanish empire around 1560. It guarded the Straits of Yucatán in the west, as well as the Straits of Florida in the north (which served as the entrance from the Atlantic to the Gulf of Mexico) and hence the route of the Spanish ships carrying Mexican and Peruvian silver. The ships had to gather annually in Havana on the northeastern coast of Cuba to form a fleet, known as the Carrera de Indias, before crossing the Atlantic, heading for Seville. Havana's role in this resulted in a rapid growth of the city and its suburbs, where by 1700 about 80,000 of the approximately 130,000 Cuban inhabitants lived.

In addition, a two-part economy developed. The west became a center of commerce and maritime craftsmanship; the east supplied the harbor with cattle, grew tobacco, and devoted itself to the trade in contraband with the English and the French. These European powers used the "forbidden back door"—the Windward Passage, southwest of Cuba—to enter the Caribbean Sea and infiltrate Jamaica and western Hispaniola (Saint-Domingue).

By the time of the French Bourbon's accession to the Spanish throne in 1713, the Spanish empire and its silver bullion trade had been overshadowed by the rising English and French empires and their successful plantation economies. Administrative, military, and economic reforms were initiated but not carried out decisively before 1762, when the British invasion of Havana came as a shock. Possession of Cuba was returned to Spain in 1763 as compensation for losing Florida, and it became a trial ground for further reform efforts concerning the Hispanic-American world.

Cuban population growth further accelerated during the eighteenth century, and in the 1774 census, 96,400 white, 30,800 free colored (mestizos, mulattos, and freed slaves), and 44,300 enslaved inhabitants were counted. The slave population increased at a rate greater than that of the other segments of society, indicating

A Spanish possession since the early 1500s, Cuba was captured by British forces in 1762, by which time it offered prospects for great wealth in sugar. The British held Cuba for only ten months, however, as the island was returned to Spain in the Treaty of Paris. *(The Stapleton Collection/Bridgeman Art Library)*

that the Cuban economy and society underwent a fundamental change.

From 1740 to 1790, in response to the declining bullion trade and the social and ecological crises besetting the British sugar-producing colonies of Barbados and Jamaica, the Cuban elite developed sugar plantations on a large scale, ousting small farmers and largely eliminating Cuba's subsistence agriculture. This development was boosted by the political breakdown of the main sugar producer in the islands, Saint-Domingue, between 1792 and 1804.

In the 1810s and 1820s, the Spanish colonies in America, apart from Cuba and Hispaniola (now the Dominican Republic), revolted and gained their independence from Spain. The Spanish Crown proved extremely obliging to the Cuban elite in ceasing limitation and control of the slave trade. Based on an ever harsher exploitation of slave labor until 1886, Cuba became the world's main sugar producer in the nineteenth century and remained a Spanish colony until 1898.

Alexander Engel

See also: Caribbean (Chronology); Slavery, Caribbean; Sugar; Tobacco.

Bibliography

Gott, Richard. *Cuba: A New History.* New Haven, CT: Yale University Press, 2004.

Johnson, Sherry. *The Social Transformation of Eighteenth-Century Cuba.* Gainesville: University of Florida Press, 2001.

Cumberland Gap

In colonial times, the Cumberland Gap was the pass through which the Ohio River Valley could be reached most directly from southern Virginia and the Carolinas. It lies midway in the central range of the Appalachian Mountains, which separate the Atlantic seaboard from the Mississippi watershed by a succession of steep ridges, extending 150 miles inland along a 600-mile corridor from Pennsylvania to Georgia.

For approximately 120 miles, straddling the present-day boundary between Virginia and Kentucky, and then into northeastern Tennessee, the chief barrier to westward travel consists of two precipitous ridges—Cumberland Mountain on the south and Pine Mountain on the north—running parallel at intervals varying from 9 to 15 miles. The elevation of these rugged mountains exceeds 3,500 feet above sea level near the gap. Where Virginia, Kentucky, and Tennessee now intersect, a deep cleft penetrates Cumberland Mountain to about 1,600 feet above sea level. Another notch bisects Pine Mountain 10 miles to the north, beyond which several tributaries of the Kentucky River meander in a protracted descent toward the bluegrass plateau below.

During seasonal migrations to natural salt licks, herds of bison, deer, and other large animals gradually stamped out a well-worn trace (up to 5 feet wide) between these mountain gaps and the rolling meadows of central Kentucky. In the course of stalking game, Native Americans also discovered this highly useful route, marked it with directional symbols, and eventually lengthened its course northeastward to the Ohio River. The improved trail served as a major artery for long-distance hunting, trade, and warfare by Cherokees from Tennessee and Shawnees from Ohio, who called it the Warriors' Path.

Anglo-Americans remained unaware of the twin notches at Cumberland and Pine mountains, much less of their geographical significance, for most of the colonial period. Gabriel Arthur, a Virginian, almost certainly traversed those passes in June 1674 with Shawnees, as probably did James Salling, another Virginian, with Cherokees in 1730. But they left no maps or detailed accounts by which other white explorers might retrace their steps across the Appalachians. As later colonists probed the forest primeval of southwest Virginia to barter furs with Native Americans or to seek sites for farmsteads, they gradually became aware that tantalizingly close to the farthest frontier outposts

As dramatized in this nineteenth-century painting by George Caleb Bingham, the frontiersman Daniel Boone blazed a trail through the Cumberland Gap in the 1770s. The passage launched thousands of pioneers on their journeys west. *(Washington University, St. Louis, Missouri/Bridgeman Art Library)*

lay a key gap through which a quick crossing might be made over the mountains.

The Loyal Land Company sent Thomas Walker in 1750 to survey a tract of 800,000 acres in Virginia's western territory for its investors to claim. Walker reached Cumberland Mountain on April 13 and penned the first written description by any British subject of the gap's precise location and surrounding terrain. He referred to the defile as "Cave Gap," a title he possibly learned from isolated pioneers on the Holston River, just over two weeks' travel eastward.

On April 17, Walker found the headwaters of a large river—called the Shawnee by Native Americans—flowing southwest from the Pine Mountain narrows, and he named it for the duke of Cumberland, who had crushed Scotland's Jacobites at Culloden in 1745. Over the next generation, the surrounding highlands—which Walker always designated by the Shawnee name Wasioto (or Ouasioto, meaning "place of plentiful deer")—also became known as the Cumberlands, and Cave Gap was subsequently renamed Cumberland Gap.

Cumberland Gap first assumed a significant role in western expansion from 1761 to 1772, when Daniel Boone, Elisha Walden, Richard Skaggs, James Knox, and other woodsmen led parties of "long hunters" (so called because they went off into the wilderness for long periods of time) through the mountains over the old buffalo trace. They accomplished an extensive reconnaissance of central Kentucky's geography while living off the land for periods of up to eighteen months. In spring 1775, Boone and thirty axemen cleared and widened a 200-mile trail through the pass and along the Warriors' Path from modern Kingsport, Tennessee, to Boonesborough, Kentucky. The widened trail became known as the Wilderness Road.

The Cumberland Gap served as the sole Southern avenue by which Virginians and Carolinians could reach the bluegrass region. The Ohio River was a superior route for moving west, however, since this waterway could be traveled not only in much less time but also with far more possessions than was possible on the Wilderness Road. The latter overland route was not improved to accommodate wagon traffic until late 1796.

While the majority of the Ohio Valley's settlers came by flatboat from Pittsburgh, an enormous overland migration still passed through the Cumberland Gap. Perhaps 30,000 Easterners had trudged westward through the pass by 1789. Another 70,000 probably followed in their footsteps to the Ohio country during the 1790s.

Thomas L. Purvis

See also: Appalachia; Boone, Daniel; Kentucky.

Bibliography

Burns, David M. *Gateway: Dr. Thomas Walker and the Opening of Kentucky.* Middlesboro, KY: Bell County Historical Society, 2000.

Chinn, George M. *Kentucky: Settlement and Statehood, 1750–1800.* Frankfort: Kentucky Historical Society, 1975.

Kincaid, Robert L. *The Wilderness Road.* New York: Bobbs-Merrill, 1947.

Currency

Money, like skilled labor, was in short supply in colonial America. Because the British forbade the minting of coins in North America, official coins were rare. Even as late as 1775, there were seventeen different forms of money being used in North Carolina alone. In fact, most purchases were obtained on credit, with the expectation that payment would come later.

As a result, legal tender came in many forms as people tried to come up with a medium of exchange. Currency adopted by the colonists included wampum and furs. Wampum was a form of Native American money made of pieces of clamshell strung together in lengths varying from a few inches to 6 feet. Furs, including beaver pelts, were worth 10 shillings a pound in 1631.

According to Glyn Davies, in 1637, Massachusetts declared "white wampum legal tender for sums up to one shilling, a limit raised substantially in 1643." And, in 1664, Peter Stuyvesant "arranged a loan in wampum worth over 5,000 guilders for paying the wages of workers constructing the New York citadel." In 1760, J. W. Campbell built a factory for assembling wampum in New Jersey; this factory remained in operation for 100 years.

Other forms of legal tender included cash crops such as tobacco, rice, indigo, wheat, or corn. Tobacco leaves were used, as well as tobacco "notes," which could be exchanged more easily than leaves. Adopted in Virginia in 1727, this form of currency remained legal for more than 200 years. Unfortunately, at times tobacco's overabundance created a depressing effect on

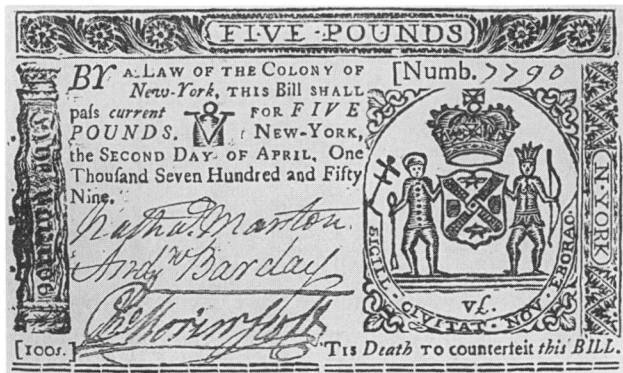

Paper currency in colonial America was hard to come by, differed from colony to colony, and fluctuated drastically in value. This five-pound note was issued in New York in 1759. *(Brown Brothers, Sterling, Pennsylvania)*

the value of its exchange. Cut nails were also used in many places, with 100 nails equaling 10 pence.

Foreign money, especially French or Spanish, was commonly used throughout the colonies, but it was spent most often on imported goods, because importers refused to accept anything but hard coin. In fact, the English word "dollar" came from a Germanic word, "thaler," which identified a large silver coin minted during the fifteenth century in Austria. In English, the word came to be used to identify any silver coins of similar size, particularly Spanish coins. The Spanish dollar, often called a "piece of eight" because it was cut into eight pieces or bits in order to make change, formed the most common basis for calculating the value of other money. It normally equaled 4 shillings 6 pence in British sterling. It was also the price of most buckskins; thus the term "buck" came to mean a dollar.

Other early coins were minted in spite of the British ban, but they varied in size, denomination, and value. In Massachusetts, the silver Pine Tree shilling was minted from 1652 to 1684 in the first colonial mint opened in Boston. Because the die for the coin was never altered, this coin always bore the same date.

Massachusetts Bay was the first colony to issue paper currency, doing so when it was faced with the need to pay soldiers as they returned from fighting in Quebec. In defiance of English law, other colonies soon followed suit. These notes were also known as "bills of credit" and implied to their holders that they could be redeemed at a later time for gold or silver. The notes were used to pay taxes and could be used as legal tender, but their value fluctuated greatly, to the point where some depreciated so much as to be worthless.

In 1718, petitioners to the General Assembly in Philadelphia sought to make produce the basis of official transactions, but their petition was denied. By 1720, however, with a depression looming, Jonathan Dickinson, a merchant and politician, and Thomas Griffitts, a merchant, recognized that without some kind of proper currency, the colony would continue to suffer economically. In 1721, Francis Rawle published a pamphlet encouraging the circulation of paper money as a way to stimulate the economy. As a result, the assembly passed Pennsylvania's first paper money act in 1723, releasing 15,000 pounds in bills of credit. The assembly later enacted three more paper-money laws.

The lack of a common currency eventually gave rise to conflict and disagreement. In 1740, *A Discourse Concerning the Currencies of the British Plantations in America, Especially with Regard to Their Paper Money*, written by William Douglass, appeared in Boston. In it, Douglass asserted:

> Silver itself is a Merchandize, and being the least variable of all others, is by general consent made the Medium of Trade . . . a trading Country must have regard to the universal commercial Medium, which is Silver; or cheat, and trade to a Disadvantage. It is true, that in some Countries of Europe Billon (a base mixture of Metals) is used for small Change, but not as a Medium of Trade. . . . There can therefore be no other proper Medium of Trade, but Silver, or Bills of Exchange and Notes of Hand payable in Silver at certain . . . Periods. . . . The British Plantations have not only varied, from Sterling, but have also very much varied from one another; to the Confusion of Business, and Damage of the Merchant.

Another early advocate of a common currency was Benjamin Franklin, who published his *Modest Enquiry into the Nature and Necessity of a Paper Currency* in 1729. In this discourse, Franklin applauded the efforts of the Pennsylvania Land Bank, which released a series of notes as well as loans "in the form of paper money secured by mortgages on the property of the borrowers." This kind of early bank was not the same as institutional banks of today; in fact, the term "bank" simply meant the batch of bills issued to the borrower. It wouldn't be until Alexander Hamilton introduced the concept of a national bank in 1790 that banking would take on greater importance.

Franklin also appeared before Parliament in London in 1766 in an effort to convince the British government that the colonies needed an official currency. The Crown's refusal to consider the matter became a constant source of tension and a factor in provoking the American Revolution.

Introduction of the American Dollar

It was the colony of Maryland that first introduced the dollar as its unit of paper money; in prior years, because its neighboring colonies had given greater exchange to their paper currency, Maryland suffered in the exchange. In 1767, Maryland began printing paper money in $1 units, as well as in multiples and fractions of a dollar. The value of the money was backed by the Spanish dollar.

Though still confusing, this uniform system was the first of its kind and provided the colony's citizens with a fairly stable form of exchange. Maryland even used secret marks on its currency as a way of deterring counterfeiting, although this did not prove very successful. In 1770 and 1774, Maryland reissued its currency, using the same denominations and designs.

The face of the Maryland $1 note carried the name of the engraver, Thomas Sparrow, along the top border and the initials of Jonas Green, the printer, on the back. This formal monetary unit survived until the Revolutionary War. In 1775, the dollar designation was adopted by the Continental Congress, and, in 1792, it was adopted by the U.S. Congress.

With the American Revolution, funding for supplies and troops became an important issue for the colonies. Early in the war, the Continental Congress took out huge loans from France and Spain, totaling $9 million. It also began issuing paper dollars, called "continentals." Backed by little more than good faith, the millions of continentals in circulation were worth not even one-fortieth of their original value by 1780, and Congress had to accept payments due from individual states in the worthless notes. To make matters worse, individual states began printing their own paper money despite protests by Congress, eventually releasing more than $200 million in currency.

By 1781, a coin shilling was worth seventy-five times more than a paper shilling, and one state, Massachusetts, voted to outlaw paper money, requiring all debts to be paid in coin. This move especially hurt farmers, and many had to sell their farms. Discontented farmers demanded tax relief and a moratorium on debt collection. When these demands were ignored, Daniel Shays, a former captain in the Continental army, led a ragtag army of farmers in a revolt, often called Shays'

Rebellion. Though the rebellion was put down, it resulted in a push to make the new federal government stronger and more capable of providing economic relief and direction.

A national coinage system was established in 1785, but few coins appeared before 1793. The first coin struck for the United States was the Fugio cent. On one side, thirteen circles represented the new union; on the other side was the image of a sundial and the word "fugio," to show that "time flies." The motto "Mind your business" was also stamped on the coin. Later, this motto was changed to "In God we trust," as suggested by Ben Franklin.

Gail L. Jenner

See also: Banks and Banking; Currency Act (1764).

Bibliography

Douglass, William. "Discourse on the Currencies of the American Plantations." 1740. University of Virginia. http://etext.lib.virginia.edu/users/brock/webdoc2.html.

Newman, Eric P. "The Earliest Money Using the Dollar as a Unit of Value." http://www.chicagocoinclub.org/projects/PiN/ted.html.

Purvis, Thomas L. *Revolutionary America, 1763 to 1800.* New York: Facts on File, 1995.

Currency Act (1764)

Also known as Grenville's Continental Currency Act, this bill was passed by Parliament in 1764. It was enacted to control the rapidly increasing intercolony inflation plaguing the British Empire as a direct result of the French and Indian War (1754–1763) and to reduce the massive provincial debts accrued during the war, mainly in Virginia.

Written primarily at the prompting of British merchants with the hope of preventing individuals in the American colonies from paying debts with depreciated colonial currency, the act prohibited all of the colonial governments from issuing paper money as legal tender. All currency already circulating was supposed to be immediately retracted by the colonial governments through the use of recall dates on any outstanding issues of circulating currency.

Institution of the act created serious monetary shortages in the colonies at the exact time that Grenville's Sugar Act cut off the flow of specie into the colonies from the West Indies trade. Although following on the heels of the Sugar Act, the Currency Act added little to colonial irritation until after the colonies had united in protest against the Stamp Act.

Incidentally, currency scarcity was a continual problem in the colonies. British currency was so limited that most colonies in the New World had to depend instead on Spanish milled dollars or to simply print their own currency. The imbalance of trade between England and the colonies prevented the acquisition of hard currency from outside sources. While usage of paper currency printed within the colonies sometimes led to inflation and hardship for creditors, its lack was a privation for everyone. Interestingly, prior to the Currency Act, Parliament had issued numerous prohibitions against the issuance of paper money in the colonies, but none aroused much opposition. The most significant of these prohibitions had been the Currency Act of 1751, but it applied solely to New England.

Seeing the Currency Act as tantamount to reducing the colonial economy to one of barter, many colonials believed the act (like the Stamp Act) was part of a systematic attempt by factions within Parliament to "enslave" the colonies. Since the act was not a means of taxation, the colonists did not try to nullify it as a measure beyond the power of Parliament, as they did with the Sugar Act. Instead, they closed all local courts in the colonies.

To some extent, the court closures were the most effective action possible, since they often raised the value of money, while limiting the payment of debts by preventing their collection, thus reducing demands for money. With most creditors of colonial debtors being British merchants, court closures ensured the participation of these individuals in the repeal of the Currency Act, the Stamp Act, and the Sugar Act.

Solomon K. Smith

See also: Banks and Banking; Currency.

Bibliography

Greene, Jack P., and Richard M. Jellison. "The Currency Act of 1764 in Imperial-Colonial Relations." *William and Mary Quarterly,* 3rd series, 18 (1961): 485–518.

McCusker, John J., Russel R. Menard, and Peter J. Albert. *The Economy of Early America: The Revolutionary Period, 1763–1790.* Charlottesville: University Press of Virginia, 1988.

Morgan, Edmund S., and Helen M. Morgan. *Stamp Act Crisis: Prologue to Revolution.* Chapel Hill: University of North Carolina Press, 1995.

D

Dartmouth, Lord (1731–1801)

Known to his contemporaries as "the good Lord Dartmouth," William Legge, second earl of Dartmouth, was a philanthropist and statesman who played an important role in precipitating the American Revolution.

Legge's life was characteristic of a man born into the wealth and privilege of eighteenth-century England's landed elite. Born on June 20, 1731, he was educated at Westminster School and Trinity College, Oxford. Following his education, Legge and his stepbrother, Frederick North, went on a grand tour of the Continent, which, during the eighteenth century, was considered an essential part of the maturation process of all young gentlemen.

Legge remained abroad from 1751 to 1754 and visited such places as the University of Leipzig, Venice, Florence, and Paris. Upon his return to England in the spring of 1754, Legge became engaged to Frances Nicholl, daughter of Sir Charles Gunter Nicholl. The two were married in January 1755 and had nine children.

In 1750, Legge had succeeded his grandfather as earl of Dartmouth, and, on May 31, 1754, he took a seat in England's House of Lords. Although he was not particularly interested in politics—preferring to focus on his family and philanthropic work—Lord Dartmouth quickly gained a reputation as a staunch Whig and made governmental stability a primary concern.

In 1765, Lord Rockingham invited Dartmouth to become a member of his newly formed Whig government. Dartmouth accepted the position of first lord of trade on July 19, 1765. During his year as president of the Board of Trade, Dartmouth was faced with the controversy surrounding the historic Stamp Act, and he played a critical role in arguing for its repeal.

Dartmouth's actions during the Stamp Act crisis became well known among his contemporaries and gained him a considerable reputation as someone who was sympathetic to the plight of the colonists. An example of these actions was his supporting a measure that required colonial assemblies to pay reparations to individuals who suffered losses during the Stamp Act riots. Throughout his political career, however, Dartmouth remained loyal to Parliament and to the principles of the Declaratory Act, which bolstered the legislative authority of the English government over its colonies.

Dartmouth resigned as president of the Board of Trade on July 30, 1766, amid the intense political infighting that emerged in the wake of the Stamp Act crisis. Frustrated at his lack of power, Dartmouth made a bid for a secretaryship, but the man who had replaced Lord Rockingham, Sir William Pitt, first earl of Chatham, would not support such a move. Dartmouth temporarily removed himself from politics.

In 1772, Dartmouth obtained the coveted secretaryship. He became secretary of state for the colonies in yet another new government led by his stepbrother, Lord North. As secretary of state, Dartmouth became a member of the innermost circle of royal advisers and intimately tied to the affairs of the colonies. Although he remained sympathetic to the demands of the colonists, Dartmouth viewed their acts of protest, especially the Boston Tea Party and its aftermath, as a "most unwarrantable insult to the authority of this Kingdom," and made it his priority to secure "the dependence of the colonies." As tensions mounted and it became increasingly apparent that Parliament would not be able to ensure colonial dependence, Dartmouth decided once again to remove himself from politics and resigned his post as secretary of state in 1775, but this did not mark the end of his political life.

Dartmouth remained involved in English government in various advisory capacities for the next seven

William Legge, second earl of Dartmouth, served in the British government as secretary of state for the colonies from 1772 to 1775. While sympathetic to the plight of the colonists, he regarded their acts of defiance as "unwarrantable." *(Coram Foundation, Foundling Museum, London, United Kingdom/Bridgeman Art Library)*

New Hampshire, which, after 1769, became known as Dartmouth College. Lord Dartmouth died on July 7, 1801.

Michael A. Rembis

See also: Board of Trade; Stamp Act (1765).

Bibliography

Bargar, B. D. *Lord Dartmouth and the American Revolution.* Columbia: University of South Carolina Press, 1965.

Thomas, P. D. G. *British Politics and the Stamp Act Crisis: The First Phase of the American Revolution, 1763–1767.* Oxford, UK: Clarendon, 1975.

Daughters of Liberty

Daughters of Liberty were women who took actions to support resistance to Britain before and during the American Revolution. There was no official organization, although the name was obviously intended to be a parallel to the Sons of Liberty. Throughout the war, an individual woman might refer to herself as a "daughter of liberty" in private correspondence, especially when helping the war effort through home manufacturing and her role as a consumer.

There are three public forms of action usually attached to the idea of Daughters of Liberty. The first and largest set of public actions was a series of public spinning demonstrations held during the boycotts of British trade goods used to protest the Stamp Act, Townshend Duties, and Tea Acts. A successful boycott required colonists to find other sources for imported goods. Women felt "Nationly" as they turned to home manufacturing to fill the demand for cloth all over the colonies. Between 1768 and 1770, New England women held at least forty-six spinning meetings, with over 1,644 women participating. About two-thirds of these documented demonstrations took place in 1769. Many more people participated as observers, and newspapers reported on the events in detail.

Women combined benevolence and religion with their patriotism. Thirty of the demonstrations were held in the homes of clergy, and, in almost every case, women donated products of their labor to the minister or the poor. Many of the women equated liberty not only with freedom from political bondage but also with freedom from the bondage of sin.

A second, related use of the term Daughters of Liberty referred to women who refrained from use of

years. He received the title of lord privy seal—a post with significantly less responsibility than secretary—on November 10, 1775, and continued to support the government of his stepbrother, Lord North, until its demise in 1782, at which time Dartmouth gave up the privy seal.

Throughout his life, Dartmouth remained a pious and philanthropic family man. His biographer, historian B. D. Bargar, describes Dartmouth as a "sincerely pious Anglican" and argues that Dartmouth sought to reform the Anglican Church "from within" by engaging in numerous good works. Perhaps Dartmouth's most well-known act of philanthropy was his direct involvement in the creation of the Indian Charity School in

boycotted goods. Milcah Martha Moore of Philadelphia recorded a long verse in her commonplace book that included these lines:

> If the Sons (so degenerate) the Blessing despise,
> Let the Daughters of Liberty, nobly arise,
> And tho' we've no Voice, but a negative here,
> The use of the Taxables, let us forbear.

In Boston, 536 "Mistresses of Families" signed a pledge in 1770 to totally abstain from tea to "save this abused Country from Ruin and Slavery." The most famous group of women to sign a pledge were the 51 women of Edenton, North Carolina, who promised in 1774 to follow the resolves of the provincial congress and to do everything they could to support the public good. This declaration was widely publicized and satirized in newspapers. One British cartoonist turned that event into a satirical woodcut, depicting the women as mannish, immoral, and neglectful of women's duties. Women in Charles Town, South Carolina, signed a similar declaration.

Throughout the War for Independence, women continued to see a patriotic role for themselves through their roles as consumers and producers. Both officially and unofficially, women tried to prevent merchants from charging outrageous prices for scarce goods. Between 1776 and 1779, women participated in at least thirty-seven actions in five states, protesting price gouging, and women led the actions in one-third of these cases.

As "A Daughter of Liberty, living in Marblehead" complained in 1779, "We cannot get bread nor yet meat, We see the world is nought by cheat." She then went on to call for repentance from sin as a way of bringing the war to an end. The understanding of what it meant to be a Daughter of Liberty often linked both restraint from luxury and personal piety to patriotism.

Home manufacturing and restraint from luxury blended in the third major public action taken by women. In 1780, Esther DeBerdt Reed published a call (*The Sentiments of an American Woman*) to women to put aside "vain ornaments" and donate the money they would save to a fund for American troops. Thirty-six Philadelphia women responded by forming a group to solicit funds for soldiers. The effort spread beyond Pennsylvania both through newspaper accounts and letters the women sent to the wives of governors of other states. The women raised $300,000 from 1,600 contributors in Pennsylvania. Those in New Jersey and Maryland raised about $32,000 more, and Virginia efforts were equally successful.

At George Washington's request, the money raised was not given directly to the soldiers; instead the women used the funds to buy cloth and make shirts and stockings. It was a fitting demonstration of women's support of the war and their organizing skill as the conflict entered its critical later stages.

While not officially calling themselves Daughters of Liberty, the group continued on in the spirit of the term. Their actions serve as a capstone to women's support of independence through supportive manufacturing and selective consumption.

Joan R. Gundersen

See also: Politics and Government (Chronology); Politics and Government (Essay); Revolutionary War; Women.

Bibliography

Gundersen, Joan R. *"To Be Useful to the World": Women in Revolutionary America, 1740–1790.* New York: Twayne, 1996.

Kerber, Linda. *Women of the Republic: Intellect and Ideology in Revolutionary America.* Chapel Hill: University of North Carolina Press for the Institute of Early American History and Culture, 1980.

Norton, Mary Beth. *Liberty's Daughters: The Revolutionary Experience of American Women, 1750–1800.* Boston: Little, Brown, 1980.

Ulrich, Laurel Thatcher. " 'Daughters of Liberty': Religious Women in Revolutionary New England." In *Women in the Age of the American Revolution,* edited by Ronald Hoffman and Peter J. Albert. Charlottesville: University Press of Virginia for the Capitol Historical Society, 1989.

Death and Dying

Death in epidemic proportions was an ever-present reality for the residents of colonial America. Without significant medical and mortuary institutions to shelter them from the effects of the grim reaper, early Americans were forced to confront death and its aftermath head-on, with fewer pretensions and illusions than people living in modern industrialized societies.

Since mortality rates were significantly higher than in contemporary America, the frequency with which one might have to face the death of a close relative was much greater. In the early years of settlement, particularly in the South, rare was the individual who lived to adulthood without losing one or both parents. Infant mortality rates were staggering; many never lived past their first year. Even in the New England colonies, where death rates were lowest, one in four children died before reaching adolescence, and households typically lost three children out of the average nine born to Puritan couples.

In fact, colonial mortality statistics, high as they were, greatly underestimate the actual frequency of death. These calculations did not include children under a year of age, those stricken down during that portion of life when one is most vulnerable and susceptible to disease.

Coping with Death

The ways in which colonial communities dealt with and memorialized death, burial, and grieving were largely determined by their cultural and religious backgrounds. Residents of all the British and European colonies, including Africans, as well as the Native American inhabitants of North America, subscribed to a form of fatalism. All regarded man as being at the mercy of forces over which he had little control. Even in the eighteenth century, the "Age of Reason," popular fatalism held sway over the Enlightenment rationalism of colonial elites.

For European colonists in the seventeenth and eighteenth centuries, death almost always occurred in the home, in the midst of one's family. Except in urban settings, professional doctors were rare, especially in the earlier century. Medical and mortuary establishments, both of which play a significant role in removing the dying process from the ordinary experience of people today, did not exist. Relatives and neighbors supervised the care of the dying and the interment of the physical remains after death. In backcountry settlements or in isolated homesteads in the South, families had to be self-reliant in these mournful duties. Where close communities thrived, as in Puritan New England, neighbors and clergy played a more important role.

During the American colonial period, cultural attitudes toward death in the Western world were in a state of transition; Americans of European descent took part in this change, albeit at a slower pace. Religious leaders, especially Protestants, began to place greater emphasis on the edifying and dramatic aspects of the death scene. Christians could learn lessons from the ways in which both fellow believers and the unchurched faced death. Facing death without fear and with a firm faith in God was considered a sign of the dying person's sincere belief and served as an example to the survivors. Family members gathered around the deathbed, often

literally in a circle, to witness the event, lend support and comfort, and mark their own mortality.

Native Americans and African Americans

The religious beliefs of Native Americans and African Americans were different from Christianity. In animistic religious traditions, the spirits of the deceased are believed to go on living in a parallel spirit world after death. Items from the deceased's life were often interred with the body for use in this spirit realm.

Before Christianity was introduced to African slaves in the colonies, their traditional funerals were elaborate, and the graves decorated with gifts or possessions of the dead. African religious beliefs commonly included ancestor worship, and such practices were important to maintaining good relations with the world of spirits. Of course, African religious traditions could not be re-created in America in their complete form, but many practices lingered on.

Also related to the loss of a family member, "mourning wars" were a practice among Native Americans of the Iroquois Confederacy. Since the population of tribal cultures was small and the economy was a subsistence one, the deaths of individuals, especially in epidemics or warfare, were sorely felt by surviving members of the tribes.

Native Americans did not follow the Europeans' practice of total war, in which the enemy was driven away or destroyed. Their own style of warfare instead avoided massive casualties. Raids against other tribes were meant to take captives and demonstrate bravery, not to exterminate the enemy. Such a war would mean the loss of too many of one's own warriors and endanger the survival of the group. In mourning wars, the Iroquois sought to replace tribal members who had been lost to disease or in battle; captives taken in such wars were adopted into the tribe and frequently given the names of the dead.

In a very real sense, European settlers brought death with them to the New World in the form of epidemic diseases. These unseen weapons proved to be their greatest tool of conquest of the Native Americans, albeit unconsciously wielded. Deadly pathogens such as smallpox, diphtheria, measles, whooping cough, and scarlet fever had long plagued the populations of Europe. To the Native Americans, long sheltered from the epidemics that had ravaged Eurasia, the coming of white settlers to their lands meant a demographic disaster. Smallpox, especially, was a mass killer, bringing a painful and gruesome death to most and leaving survivors scarred and disfigured for life. Entire tribal cultures were wiped out within decades, and vast areas depopulated. Traditional Native American funerary customs were disrupted, as the survivors often fled without burying the dead, leaving the dying to endure their death alone.

By the time the English arrived, epidemic diseases introduced by the Spanish or European fisherman sojourning on the Atlantic Coast of North America had done their deadliest work among the native peoples of the continent. Early New England settlers found entire villages abandoned, with unburied bodies lying as stark testament to the terror inspired in survivors by the scope of the catastrophe. When new outbreaks of disease occurred among the native population, Englishmen interpreted this as a sign of divine approval of their mission to seize the land from its original inhabitants.

Unlike the Native Americans, the European settlers in the New World encountered no new diseases, except perhaps gonorrhea, but they continued to be plagued by those familiar to them, albeit in less epic proportions. Malaria and various fevers were common, especially in the Southern climes. Periodic outbreaks of smallpox occurred among whites as well. When disease or illness struck, colonists typically resorted to purgative cures, such as bleeding, to cure the suffering patient. These remedies, based on a faulty understanding of human physiology and the causes of disease, did little more than further weaken the dying person. Traditional folk remedies, which were also regularly employed, at least had the advantage of doing no harm.

Chesapeake Region

The early Chesapeake was a deathtrap, with mortality rates exceeding 40 percent, on average, during the seventeenth century. The humid climate and the marshy terrain that surrounded Jamestown were conducive to disease and bred malaria, fevers, and dysentery. Especially in summer, streams and shallow wells ran low, and the brackish water, when consumed, caused the proliferation of the microbes that bring dysentery and typhoid fever.

Out of the initial 104 settlers who came to Jamestown in 1607, only thirty-eight survived after the fevers, dysentery, and starvation took their toll. There were no farmers among the original group, as the settlers assumed that nature and servile native peoples would feed them. Expecting to find gold, the gentle-man adventurers of Jamestown instead found mostly misery and death.

During the "starving time" of the winter of 1609–1610, things became so desperate that at least one man resorted to cannibalism, killing his wife and using her as a source of food. John Smith, by this time safely in England, quipped darkly, "A dish such as salted wife I have never heard of." Authorities in the colony burned the offending husband at the stake. Another man, found guilty of stealing food, was chained in public and left to starve to death as a lesson to others.

One English writer compared Jamestown to a slaughterhouse. If it was, then the Virginia Company continuously fed it new victims. The company transported 10,000 settlers to the colony between 1607 and 1622, of which only 20 percent were still living by 1623. Only dreams of tobacco fortunes and headright land grants kept the colony afloat by attracting new immigrants. (A headright was a grant of 50 acres of land given to every colonist residing in Virginia—most were given two headrights—as well as to new settlers paying their way to Virginia and to wealthy landholders in Virginia who paid the way for impoverished immigrants.)

Gradually, the population of Virginia grew healthier. The early months of a new immigrant's stay in the colony were a time of seasoning, when the local diseases attacked the body of the newcomer en masse. After a month or so of prostration, if he or she survived, the new Virginian acquired a level of immunity and passed this advantage on to his or her offspring. The population of the colony was also expanding inland to healthier locales, where there were running streams rather than stagnant swamps. By the end of the seventeenth century, the population was increasing through natural growth rather than immigration.

Mortality still remained exceedingly high in the Southern colonies throughout the colonial era. This was especially the case in the lowcountry regions of Georgia and South Carolina, where planters fled the unhealthy rice lands, with its hosts of mosquitoes, for the comforts of Charles Town in the summer months. African slaves, who had no such escape, were hit especially hard during acclimation. One quarter typically died within their first year in America.

As a consequence of the great frequency of death, families in the Southern colonies were sundered more often than in either England or New England. Households commonly consisted of children from two or more unions. Very few children reached adulthood with both birth parents still living. Children who grew up facing the likelihood that they would be separated from parents by death developed a hardened worldview. Parents, realizing they might not always be around for their offspring, encouraged children (at least male children) to develop independent, self-reliant outlooks and strong-willed, individualistic characters.

Although undoubtedly fatalistic, white Virginians in the colonial period were less preoccupied with death than their New England cousins, who commonly used the fear of death as an inducement to greater religious devotion and frightened their children into obedience to God with assurances of death's inevitability. Thoughts of death and dying and the morbid fears in which Puritans seemed to revel were noticeably absent from the correspondence and journals of Chesapeake planters.

In a region where the Anglican Church was dominant, Southerners were less devout and more worldly, for many of their religious duties consisted of outward conformity to a ritualistic faith. They read from the prayer book on Sunday, but during the week, they engaged in worldly pursuits such as card playing, dancing jigs, and gambling on horse races—activities the pious Puritans would condemn. "Eat, drink, and be merry, for tomorrow we die" might have been their motto.

For the Virginia Anglican, death was inevitable, but the loss of a loved one, or indeed the prospect of dying oneself, was something to be contemplated with stoic reserve rather than morbid brooding. Southerners mourned and grieved their loss, but, at least before the Great Awakening, they engaged in little introspection about death and its meaning for the future of their own soul. With the coming of revivalist religion, and its emphasis on salvation and the afterlife, Southerners, particularly the yeoman farmers who joined New Light churches, became more preoccupied with such matters.

New England

The Chesapeake region and New England region present a stark contrast in the experience of death during the colonial period. While only a minority of early Virginians lived to their 45th year, New Englanders who lived to see adolescence commonly survived into their 70s.

One of the primary reasons was that New England's colder climate and overall elevated topography discouraged the rampant spread of disease so common in marshier areas. While parts of New England did breed disease, these areas were a smaller percentage of the Northern colonies; as in the South, some wealthy residents in these vicinities were able to spent time in healthier places, such as along the coast, during the heat of summer.

The Southerners' stoic resignation in the face of death also was vastly different from the New England fascination with death. The Calvinist belief in predestination made Puritan Congregationalists insecure about the state of their souls and eternal destination. They brooded over their own mortality and the great question posed by the grave's yawning chasm: "Am I one of God's elect?"

Rather than shelter their young from death, parents forced even small children to face death squarely in the face, to look into open graves, and to meditate on Bible passages that prescribed death as the lot of all humanity. Describing the outlook of New Englanders, Harriett Beecher Stowe wrote of the "unutterable . . . melancholy, which regarded human existence itself as a ghastly risk, and, in the case of the vast majority, an inconceivable misfortune."

New England funerary sculpture featured grim reminders of these sobering facts in the forms of grinning death's heads. In the face of inevitable death and probable damnation, the best that devout New Englanders could do was to use these facts to redouble their efforts at service to God, in hopes of the unlikely redemption of their souls.

Rituals of Death

Funerals in early colonial America were invariably simple and hastily organized affairs, rendered so by the necessity of quickly interring the unembalmed corpse. Indentured servants and African slaves were often buried by their masters without ceremony, sometimes in unmarked graves. For members of their own family, Southern planters sometimes staged elaborate funerals in order to substantiate their social status. But most early Americans could not afford such excess, and Puritans thought it vanity.

In the South, family burial grounds were most common, as few of the sprawling, plantation-centered neighborhoods had public cemeteries. But in New England, where towns were tightly knit communities, public burial grounds were far more common. Among all European colonists, outward signs of grief were thought to be inappropriate. Families sought to main-

The first colonial cemetery in America was located on Burial Hill in the Plymouth Colony. The oldest gravestone carries the date 1681, but tradition holds that passengers of the *Mayflower,* including Governor William Bradford, were buried there earlier. *(Brown Brothers, Sterling, Pennsylvania)*

tain an outward reserve, and they considered weeping openly unseemly.

In the eighteenth century, as the population increased and society developed, funerals did become more elaborate, complete with black armbands, coffin trimmings, and processions to the gravesite. Social gatherings after the funeral became occasions for conspicuous displays of wealth for the rich. Poor families often incurred debt to pay for services and to hire well-known ministers to deliver the sermon.

In addition to the prevalent attitudes, customs, and rituals of death in New England and the South, other regional and religious variations existed. For instance, Quakers in the middle colonies regarded death as a friend, not something to be feared or abhorred by those who discovered their Inner Light. Mourners reflected upon the life of the deceased solemnly rather than morbidly.

Backcountry residents of the frontier regions were more likely to be Presbyterian than Anglican. In a violent society plagued by constant threat of attacks by natives or local feuds, they most valued courage in the face of death. Mourners observed the deathwatch and the wake after death, and they regarded viewing, or even touching, the corpse as an important form of taking leave of a family member. Funerals were always held in the home of the stricken family, and neighbors "laid out" the body for public viewing.

Colonial Americans had much in common in their experience and attitudes toward death. Throughout the colonies, Americans shared fatalistic beliefs, the practice of a deathwatch, relatively simple funeral rites, and reserved mourning customs. All religious denominations regarded death and dying as principal occasions for reinforcing socially held norms and building character: stoic resignation in the South, sanctified grimness in New England, and courage in the backcountry. Death was a spectacle, to be closely attended, with lessons to teach the living.

David Ballew

See also: Disease; Malaria; Orphans; Smallpox; Syphilis; Widows and Widowers.

Bibliography

Ariès, Philippe. *The Hour of Our Death.* Translated by Helen Weaver. New York: Alfred A. Knopf, 1981.

Coffin, Margaret M. *Death in Early America: The History and Folklore of Customs and Superstitions of Early Medicine, Funerals, Burials, and Mourning.* Nashville, TN: Thomas Nelson, 1976.

Fischer, David Hackett. *Albion's Seed: Four British Folkways in America.* New York: Oxford University Press, 1989.

Hawke, David Freeman. *Everyday Life in Early America.* New York: Harper and Row, 1988.

Jackson, Charles O., ed. *Passing: The Vision of Death in America.* Westport, CT: Greenwood Press, 1977.

Kupperman, Karen Ordahl, ed. *Captain John Smith: A Select Edition of His Writings.* Chapel Hill: University of North Carolina Press, 1988.

Mitford, Jessica. *The American Way of Death.* New York: Simon and Schuster, 1963.

Rumford, Beatrix T. "The Role of Death as Reflected in the Art and Folkways of the Northeast in the Eighteenth and Nineteenth Centuries." Master's thesis, State University of New York at Oneonta, 1965.

Taylor, Alan. *American Colonies.* New York: Viking, 2001.

Debt and Debtor's Prison

Debt and insolvency were taken very seriously in early America. Personal and business debt in the colonial era was often viewed as a moral failing. Business insolvency was seen as the result of excessive speculation. Personal insolvency was taken to be a sign of overconsumption or laziness, a sin related to greed or sloth. In either case, not paying one's legally contracted debts was considered akin to stealing.

American laws concerning debt and bankruptcy were closely modeled on those of England. The first British bankruptcy law was passed in 1570, during the reign of Henry VIII. It was motivated by the fact that the debtors' prisons were filled to capacity. This law, however, did not solve the problem. In 1705, the Statute of Anne Bankruptcy Act allowed for the execution of persons who had accumulated excessive or fraudulent debt, the latter a result of misrepresenting one's assets and liabilities to the lender.

Early American bankruptcy laws were designed for the relief of the creditor rather than as a safety net for the debtor. As such, the penalties were harsh and unforgiving. A debtor in colonial times could be imprisoned and have his property seized and liquidated, as well as be made to endure the public punishment of the pillory, where he might have one or both ears nailed to the frame or cut off entirely.

Debtor's prisons were especially unpleasant places and, in many cases, worse than regular prison. The government fed and clothed felons and criminals but not debtors; debtors had to feed themselves or get friends or family to support them. In some cases, debtors who had no hope of repayment would commit crimes that would result in their being moved to regular prison facilities.

Overcrowded and lacking in sanitation facilities, these "gaols" were hotbeds of typhus and other diseases, and many people died while incarcerated. In addition to the debt owed, the guilty also were expected to pay for their confinement. Because many debtors could not support their families on the outside, wives and children could sometimes be found living in cells with debtors.

Detention acted as a guarantee that the guilty would appear for the court date and not try to hide assets. There were two ways to get out of debtor's prison. The debtor could offer assets equal to the debt owed as security or find someone to post bail and act as guarantor for the debt. Upon ultimately settling their obligations, debtors were usually allowed to keep a few personal and necessary items for themselves and their families, including bedding and nonluxury clothing.

In contrast to regular prison, debtors' prisons were more likely to contain numbers of well-educated people. In the 1790s, the debtors in the New York jail formed an internal government modeled after that of the fledgling United States, complete with a legal structure, judges, and other officers. Some debtors also sponsored newspapers composed and published from within, in an attempt to raise public consciousness about the treatment of debtors.

Because there was a strong moral component behind the criminality of debt, there were also predictable regional differences in interpreting what a condition of debt meant. In the South, debt was not necessarily a sin, but it was definitely considered ungentlemanly. In New England, attitudes toward debtors contained a strong moral dimension. The more commercial-minded middle colonies were probably the most lax in terms of punishing debtors; as merchants understood, the essence of business was debt, and harsh penalties might discourage entrepreneurial activity. Not surprisingly, New York State became one of the first in the nation to eliminate imprisonment for non-fraudulent debt after the Revolution.

The American Revolution and, more importantly, the commercial revolution of the early nineteenth century led to a gradual change in the attitude toward imprisonment for debt. By the middle of the nineteenth century, most states had outlawed the practice. Although, under the Constitution, bankruptcy law came under the jurisdiction of the federal government, it was not until 1800 that Congress passed its first bankruptcy statute.

Anna Gersh

See also: Class; Crime; Prisons and Punishment; Property and Property Rights.

Bibliography

Coleman, Peter. *Debtors and Creditors in America: Insolvency, Imprisonment for Debt, and Bankruptcy, 1607–1900.* Madison: State Historical Society of Wisconsin, 1974.

Mann, Bruce H. *Republic of Debtors: Bankruptcy in the Age of American Independence.* Cambridge, MA: Harvard University Press, 2002.

Deism

Deism asserts the primacy of human reason and experience over and above spiritual knowledge based on special revelation. Born during the Enlightenment, Deism was spurred by the intuitional observations of Francis Bacon, the scientific discoveries of Isaac Newton, and the philosophical queries of John Locke. Taken together, these ideas were called New Learning.

Bacon formulated a philosophy of induction in which knowledge began with experience and observation, whence broad generalizations and abstractions were drawn. Isaac Newton discovered a set of natural laws on which the workings of the universe were based. John Locke claimed that knowledge was based on intuition and experience, and that, with the aid of human reason, clarity of thought was possible. The principles of New Learning formulated by Bacon, Newton, and Locke presented a picture of the world that operated on natural and observable laws. While most of the early advocates of New Learning were not hostile to the concept of God, the underlying assumptions and the implications of this system opened the door to a universe in which God was relegated to a creative, yet disinterested, role.

Deism elicited significant consideration in such an intellectual climate and after a wave of notoriety in Britain took root in the North American colonies. British Deism began in the seventeenth century with Lord Herbert of Cherbury, whose *De Veritate* (On truth) advanced core ideas of Deistic thinking. Cherbury argued for God's existence; for reverence, worship, and awe toward the deity; for a moral and ethical life; and for the reality of eternal life. Another early English Deist, Charles Blount, advanced similar ideas but focused specifically on living an ethical life. British Deism was further bolstered by the writings of John Toland, whose influential *Christianity Not Mysterious* (1696) pushed for a more logical understanding of Christianity and largely rejected supernatural revelation. Anthony Collins continued the assault on traditional Christianity, and his *Grounds and Reasons of the Christian Religion* (1724) questioned the biblical theme of prophecy and rejected Jesus's claims to divinity. Similarly, Thomas Woolston's *Discourses on the Miracles of Our Savior* (1727–1729) sought to uproot biblical accounts of miracles. Matthew Tindal's *Christianity as Old as the Creation* (1730) essentially collated the views of his predecessors and issued such a comprehensive account of Deistic thinking that this work became known as the "Deist Bible."

While Deists such as Toland and Collins were known in the North American colonies, John Tillotson and William Wollaston were most popular among educated colonists. Tillotson and Wollaston argued that reason was the arbiter of truth and that God was best worshiped with the mind.

Deism first gained a foothold in the North American colonies with the decline of Calvinism, a rigid theological system that emphasized the absolute sovereignty of God in matters of salvation. As the seventeenth century gave way to the eighteenth century, Calvinism received a decisive blow with the religious revivals of the 1740s known as the Great Awakening. Factions emerged as the fires of revival settled and rational religion gained notoriety with the writings of influential Boston ministers such as Charles Chauncy and Jonathan Mayhew. Deistic thinking was less widespread throughout the middle colonies, although clearly visible, and did not make significant ripples in the Southern colonies.

While the more radical forms of French Deism (as in the writings of Voltaire) remained silenced until after the American Revolution, Benjamin Franklin was influenced by French philosophy and helped to popularize a liberal and rationalistic view of the world. Such modes of thought helped to liberate religious claims from distinct references to God and Jesus, all the while providing a foundation and impetus for the North American colonies to declare independence from Britain. This helps to explain why Thomas Paine's *Age of Reason* received considerable endorsement. Thus as Calvinism was supplanted by rationalism and as distinct threads of Deistic thought helped to shape American independence, rational religion gained a prominent place in North American culture.

Following the American Revolution, Thomas Jefferson became a leading advocate of Deism, and at the dawn of the nineteenth century, Deism was subsumed under Unitarianism and Universalism, broad systems of Christian thought that placed a premium not only on rationalism but also on ethical living. Deism was critical to the development of North America, because it upheld the necessity of rational religion, while laying claim to a distinct system of ethics.

Phillip L. Sinitiere

See also: Arts, Culture, and Intellectual Life (Essay); Jefferson, Thomas; Religion (Chronology); Religion (Essay).

Bibliography

May, Henry F. *The Enlightenment in America*. New York: Oxford University Press, 1976.

Morais, Herbert M. *Deism in Early Eighteenth Century America*. New York: Columbia University Press, 1934.

Walters, Kerry S. *The American Deists: Voices of Reason in the Early Republic*. Lawrence: University Press of Kansas, 1992.

———. *Benjamin Franklin and His Gods*. Chicago: University of Illinois Press, 1999.

———. *Rational Infidels: The American Deists*. Durango, CO: Longwood Academic, 1992.

Delaware

The influences of neighboring Pennsylvania and Maryland converged with the social, political, and economic forces of the colonial Atlantic world to shape the unique colonial history of the Three Lower Counties on the Delaware, one of the two official names of Delaware during the colonial period.

Dominion

On the basis of Henry Hudson's voyage past the Delaware Bay in 1609, Dutch merchants established a few trading posts along the Delaware River in the 1630s. Soon thereafter, the New Sweden Company and colony, established by Dutch merchants who received a charter from the king of Sweden, established more settlements and trading posts along the west bank of the Delaware. Through the 1650s, Swedish and Dutch officials in Delaware quarreled over claims to the area, but neither power proved willing or able to marshal the resources needed to make its claims stick.

During the period of Swedish and Dutch rule, Delaware was home to a few thousand Native Americans and no more than 1,000 Swedes, Dutch, and Finns, along with perhaps 100 African slaves and servants. Perhaps 1,000 more Dutch, Scandinavians, and Africans lived in the scattered trading settlements in the Delaware River valley, extending northward as far as present-day Burlington, New Jersey.

Dutch claims to Delaware came to an end in 1664, when an English fleet forced Dutch officials in New Amsterdam to recognize English claims to the regions surrounding the Hudson and Delaware Rivers. From 1664 to 1681, Delaware nominally fell under the governance of James Stuart, Duke of York, but English officials paid little attention to the sparse settlements in Delaware. In 1681, King Charles II granted William Penn a charter for the colony of Pennsylvania, and Penn requested that the duke of York transfer his somewhat dubious claim to Delaware to Penn. The duke of York accommodated Penn's request, and the Three Lower Counties now came under the jurisdiction of Penn's colony.

In November 1682, Penn called on the property holders of Delaware to hold elections for delegates to meet and form a new colonial government with Pennsylvania. The representatives accepted Penn's offer and passed the Act of Union. Delaware's three counties now fell officially under the government of Pennsylvania. Ethnic and religious differences, compounded by commercial rivalries, frayed relations between Delaware and Pennsylvania, and the joint government soon proved unsatisfactory to both parties.

In 1704, Penn and representatives from Delaware reached an agreement whereby Delaware gained its own representative assembly, while Penn or his appointees would continue as governor of the colony. This arrangement lasted through 1776, when the counties of New Castle, Kent, and Sussex on the Delaware declared their independence from Great Britain and adopted the name Delaware.

Peoples, Settlement, and Development

The economic, social, and political forces of the colonial Atlantic world shaped the settlement and development of Delaware. When European trade and disease decimated Native American populations, native nations such as the Iroquois and the Susquehannocks launched wars for captives against smaller tribes, including Delaware's Lenni Lenape. In order to protect themselves from more powerful native peoples and the Europeans, the Lenni Lenape traded their land for European goods and then migrated to the interior, where they incorporated themselves into other tribes. By 1700, few Lenni Lenapes remained in Delaware.

The commerce and politics of the colonial Atlantic world also shaped the experiences of Europeans and Africans in Delaware. Planters sought the labor of Europeans and enslaved Africans to address their labor needs. Middle-class families from Maryland and Britain also came to Delaware for land. And Delaware farmers and planters, using free and unfree labor, grew products for sale in the wider Atlantic world.

The more heavily populated and commercially powerful colonies of Pennsylvania and Maryland shaped social and economic life in colonial Delaware. In many ways, northern Delaware was an extension of the middle colony of Pennsylvania, with small farmers, artisans, and merchants settling the northern county of New Castle. The Swedes, the Dutch, the non-Quaker English, and the few African slaves of New Castle produced grain for Philadelphia merchants. With the beginnings of the great Scots-Irish migration to the colonies in the early 1720s, large numbers of Scots-Irish indentured servants and families appeared in New Castle County, as did Quaker families from Pennsylvania, adding to New Castle's ethnic and religious diversity.

The streams that flowed into the Christiana and Delaware Rivers around Wilmington encouraged merchants to erect mills. By the 1740s, Wilmington had become an important destination for the wheat, corn, and flour produced by Delaware's laborers.

The southern counties of Kent and Sussex were much like the Chesapeake colony of Maryland, which bordered them to the south and west. Because Dutch merchants and Swedish officials had difficulty attracting settlers to Delaware, early on they turned to indentured and enslaved Africans to address their labor shortage. Although slavery was an important social and economic institution in Delaware during the colonial period, it never grew to the importance that it did in the Chesapeake colonies. Southern Delaware's population of enslaved Africans peaked at around 30 percent in the early 1700s, compared to the 40, 50, and sometimes 60 percent in heavily enslaved areas of Virginia and Maryland.

After the English established dominion, slavery grew slowly in Delaware. It was only after 1710 that planters began following the farmers who had left Maryland for Delaware over the previous half century. As these planters and farmers in the lower counties developed commercial ties with Philadelphia, they shifted production away from tobacco to grains. Delaware planters' heavier reliance on less labor-intensive crops such as wheat explains in part why slavery was far less established in the lower counties of Delaware than in neighboring Maryland.

The large numbers of indentured servants from Scotland and Ireland who arrived in Delaware beginning in the 1720s further lessened planters' and farmers' need for African slaves. From the 1720s through the 1760s, the size of Delaware's unfree white population rivaled the size of its unfree black population. Delaware, befitting its place as a colony in between, straddled the line that separated societies with slaves (such as Pennsylvania) from slave societies (such as Maryland and Virginia), where the number of slaves was much higher and the institution more central to the society's economy, political order, and culture.

The majority of white families in southern Delaware engaged in farming, supplementing family labor with the labor of indentured servants and perhaps one or two African slaves. Despite the numerical majority of small farming families, the few planters who owned larger plantations, which were worked by twenty or more slaves, tended to dominate social, economic, and political life in southern Delaware.

Governance: Social and Political Authority

The hundred, a unique political unit falling somewhere between the townships of Pennsylvania and the counties of Maryland, formed the basis of government and community in Delaware. In the southern counties, wealthy planters who solicited the support of middle-class property holders directed political life. In northern New Castle County, with fewer slaves and planters, both merchants and farmers were more active in politics.

The Amstel House, dating to the 1730s, is one of several colonial and federal buildings still standing in New Castle, Delaware, a thriving center of trade that served briefly (1776–1777) as the state capital. *(Courtesy of the New Castle Historical Society)*

Throughout Delaware, freeholders elected prominent and wealthy men to some local offices, while the governor, acting on the recommendation of the assembly, appointed judges and justices of the peace. Voters in each county elected tax assessors and sheriffs, who together with the justices of the peace governed the counties. Widespread ownership of land by European men, combined with a liberal-voting requirement, meant that most free white men in Delaware had the right to participate in local and colonial government. They did so infrequently, however, and remained generally satisfied with the governing classes, freeing Delaware from the political strife that plagued other colonies.

In Delaware as a whole, widespread ownership of land allowed white males to create self-governing communities of property holders, with property holders responsible for governing their dependents. In southern Delaware, with its large, unfree population, hierarchy and subordination shaped social relationships. Planters dominated southern Delaware's rural society of gentry planters, yeoman farmers, free but propertyless whites, white indentured servants, and enslaved Africans. Ideally, the patriarchal family head governed all of his dependents: his wife, children, slaves, and servants.

In northern Delaware, the greater Quaker presence, combined with the smaller unfree population, meant less emphasis on hierarchy and subordination. Consequently, in northern Delaware, women enjoyed greater authority in the family and in community institutions such as churches.

As in the rest of British North America, ownership of land provided families with some independence and economic security, and white families in Delaware made acquiring land their overriding goal. Enslaved African Americans, denied opportunities for independence, sought to create and maintain extended families to provide some security against the vagaries of life.

They also sought greater personal freedoms within the institution of slavery through the process of subtle negotiations with masters.

With independence, Delaware maintained its dual identity as a place in between Pennsylvania and the Chesapeake states. Northern Delaware became an important manufacturing center beginning in the early 1800s, while the southern counties remained overwhelmingly rural and agricultural.

Finally, slavery, perhaps more than any institution, illuminates the effect of Northern and Southern influences on Delaware. Like Maryland and Virginia, Delaware never abolished slavery. But like Pennsylvania, Delaware largely managed to eradicate the institution by the time of the Civil War, as slavery declined in importance through the nineteenth century. On the eve of the Civil War, as few as 1,000 African Americans remained enslaved in Delaware, even though the legislature had taken no legal steps toward gradual emancipation.

John Craig Hammond

See also: Delaware (Chronology); Lenni Lenape (Delaware); Swedes. *Document:* Founding of New Sweden (1700s).

Bibliography

Essah, Patience. *A House Divided: Slavery and Emancipation in Delaware, 1638–1865.* Charlottesville: University Press of Virginia, 1996.

Munroe, John A. *Colonial Delaware: A History.* Millwood, NY: KTO, 1978.

———. *History of Delaware.* Newark: University of Delaware Press, 1979.

Williams, William H. *Slavery and Freedom in Delaware, 1639–1865.* Wilmington, DE: Scholarly Imprints, 1997

Delaware River

From its source in east-central New York, the Delaware River flows southward from mountainous terrain to the gentle hills of the lower Delaware Valley and then into Delaware Bay. Navigable by oceangoing vessels to Trenton, the river forms boundaries between Pennsylvania and New York, Pennsylvania and New Jersey, and New Jersey and Delaware.

The colonies of the Delaware River Valley grew and prospered during the eighteenth century, and the river served as an important avenue of commerce in colonial America. By the mid-1700s, Philadelphia had emerged as one of the leading commercial centers in the colonial Atlantic world, while the population of the Delaware Valley had grown in both size and diversity.

In 1610, Captain Samuel Argall, an Englishmen who sailed into Delaware Bay while searching for supplies for the fledgling Virginia colony, named the bay for Lord de la Warr, governor of the Virginia colony. It would not be until the 1680s, however, that the English began to settle along the river in large numbers. In the intervening years, the region's native population, the Lenni Lenape, engaged in trade with the Dutch and Swedes, who erected several small trading settlements along the lower Delaware. The Lenni Lenape relied on trading, mixed farming, and the Delaware River Valley's abundant fish and wildlife.

After the English conquest of the Dutch colony of New Netherland in 1665, King Charles II began issuing charters that would establish the colonies of Pennsylvania, New Jersey, and Delaware. In 1682, a group of Quaker investors purchased West New Jersey from an English nobleman. In that same year, Charles II granted William Penn a charter for the lands on the west bank of the Delaware River. The Quaker presence profoundly impacted the historical development of the Delaware River Valley.

Quakers believed in the spiritual equality of all people before God, and Penn insisted that Quakers recognize Native American land claims and negotiate with them fairly. In 1682, the 5,000 or so Lenni Lenape remaining in the lower Delaware Valley agreed to sell Penn large amounts of land in southeastern Pennsylvania. In 1771, painter Benjamin West immortalized Quaker–Native American relations in *William Penn's Treaty with the Indians.* Hostilities with other Native Americans and Europeans, along with the effects of overhunting and disease, had weakened the Lenni Lenape over the previous half century. In order to gain security for their remaining lands, as well as European goods, the Lenni Lenape sold Penn large tracts of land in eastern Pennsylvania.

In later treaties, colonists, in conjunction with the powerful Iroquois, were far less scrupulous in their dealings with the native peoples of the Delaware Valley. As the European population of Pennsylvania continued to grow, Penn's heirs negotiated the infamous "Walking Purchase" treaty of 1737, which forced the Lenni Lenape to cede much of their remaining lands on the west bank of the River. By midcentury the rapid growth of the European population had forced most of the native peoples of the Delaware Valley inland to the Susquehanna and Ohio valleys.

Penn's promise of religious toleration, good government, and generous land terms attracted numerous European emigrants to the region. In addition to large numbers of English and Welsh Quakers, Protestants from present-day Germany and French Huguenots also settled in the region, joining the Dutch, Scandinavians, and non-Quaker English who tended to settle along the lower Delaware. In the 1720s, Scots-Irish Presbyterians began moving to the region in large numbers. Ethnic and religious diversity, if not tolerance, became the defining feature of the colonies of the Delaware River Valley.

The climate of the region favored the production of grain and livestock over the more profitable but far more labor-intensive tobacco, which dominated the Chesapeake colonies. Except in the lower counties of Delaware, the settlers of the Delaware Valley failed to develop a plantation economy, and with it the more pronounced differences in wealth and freedom characteristic of the South. Family farms dominated the rural economy of the region. Still, farmers, along with merchants and artisans, used the labor of indentured European servants and African slaves.

Merchants dominated the commercial centers of the river: Philadelphia, Wilmington in Delaware, and Burlington in West Jersey. During the eighteenth century, Delaware Valley merchants became the prime suppliers of lumber, grain, and salted fish and meat for the plantation colonies in the Caribbean. Trade with England and continental Europe was equally brisk. The abundance of timber along the upper Delaware allowed Philadelphia to become an important shipbuilding center in the British Empire. The furnaces along the upper Delaware, like those at Durham, became important sources of pig iron. The colonial economies of the Delaware River Valley thrived under protective British mercantilism.

The American Revolution brought important changes to the Delaware River Valley. As pacifists, many Quakers refused to participate in colonial resistance against British policy, or the war that followed. Consequently, Quakers lost much of their political power in Pennsylvania and New Jersey to groups such as the Scots-Irish, who had come to resent Quaker dominance. After American independence was won, the two dominant features of the colonial Delaware River Valley, ethnic diversity and phenomenal economic growth, continued to define the region.

John Craig Hammond

See also: Delaware; Delaware (Chronology); New Jersey; Pennsylvania; Philadelphia.

Bibliography

Bridenbaugh, Carl. "The Old and New Societies of the Delaware Valley in the Seventeenth Century." *Pennsylvania Magazine of History and Biography* 100:2 (1976): 143–72.

Illick, Joseph. *Colonial Pennsylvania: A History*. New York: Charles Scribner's Sons, 1976.

Weslanger, C. A. *The Delaware Indians: A History*. New Brunswick, NJ: Rutgers University Press, 1972.

De Soto, Hernando (c. 1500–1542)

Hernando de Soto has been characterized alternately as a vicious murderer and a noble adventurer. He was born around 1500, the son of Francisco Mendez de Soto, a nobleman of Jerez de los Caballeros, and Doña Leonor Arias Tinoco, a noblewoman from the city of Bajadoz. Little is known of his life in Spain. De Soto gained fame as a result of his participation in the Spanish conquest of the Americas.

At the age of 14, de Soto joined the expedition of Pedro Arias de Ávila, then engaged in the conquest of Panama. He spent the next nine years raiding villages for food, gold, and slaves. In 1523, de Soto, along with his partner Juan Ponce de León, assisted in Cordoba's conquest of Nicaragua. For his services, de Soto received land in Nicaragua, interest in mines, and Native American laborers and slaves. By 1530, de Soto was one of the wealthier men in León, Nicaragua, making a small fortune in the shipping and slave trading industry there.

In 1530, de Soto further increased his fortune by joining in the conquest of Peru. He served as lieutenant governor of Cuzco from 1534 to 1535. Returning to Spain, he tried, unsuccessfully, to be appointed head of government for various territories in Central and South America. De Soto did succeed in marrying into a family with extensive Central American connections, when he wed Isabel de Bobadilla, under whose father de Soto had fought in Panama.

De Soto finally received a royal contract to explore the interior of La Florida, which included most of the southeastern United States. Rumors abounded that precious gold and gems could be found in inland mountains, and, in May 1539, de Soto, at the head of a column of 600 men and 240 horses, landed at Tampa

The Spanish explorer Hernando de Soto is credited with "discovering" the Mississippi River in May 1541, somewhere south of present-day Memphis. His party had landed in Florida two years earlier and plundered native settlements on its way north. *(Private Collection/Bridgeman Art Library)*

Bay. De Soto's party spent the next few years exploring the American Southeast and exploiting its Native American inhabitants.

Though scholars continue to debate de Soto's precise route, the general outline is as follows. De Soto's party wound up the Gulf Coast of Florida, through Georgia and South Carolina, across the Smoky Mountains in North Carolina and Tennessee, southeast through Georgia and Alabama, and then west through Mississippi and Arkansas. After de Soto's death, his party continued to explore in Texas, Mississippi, and Louisiana.

De Soto's tactics were harsh and effective. No matter what kind of welcome he received, he would capture several prominent Native Americans and hold them hostage to ensure adequate provisions for his men and horses, as well as to guarantee safe passage through hostile territory. The 1530s and 1540s were a time of rapid change for Native Americans in the Southeast, as larger polities (Mississippian chiefdoms) declined and modern tribal identities were formed. De Soto sought to capitalize on the shifting political landscape, and his march through the Southeast brought Native American cultures face-to-face with the horrors of conquest. De Soto apparently was given to hunting Native Americans for sport, feeding them to dogs, and severing the noses and hands of those who were uncooperative.

Native Americans in the Southeast resisted de Soto in a number of ways. The most common form of resistance was to abandon a town and employ guerrilla tactics to harass the expedition. Native American resistance slowed de Soto down and weakened his force but did not stop him. De Soto's firepower and willingness to subdue native peoples propelled the party along a winding trail thousands of miles in length. As historian David Weber put it, "de Soto and his men left a trail of shattered lives, broken bodies, ravaged fields, empty storehouses, and charred villages."

De Soto did experience setbacks, however. At Mabila, in central Alabama, de Soto came under attack by Tuscaloosas, and the casualties on both sides were heavy. De Soto had an opportunity to head for the Gulf of Mexico and safety. Not having found the massive fortune he sought, he instead chose to press on with the remnants of his army. De Soto's army was further weakened by a surprise attack in Chickasaw country.

De Soto took ill and died in May 1542. His body was allegedly sunk in the Mississippi River in an effort to convince local natives that he was not human. De Soto's journey through the American Southeast from 1539 to 1542 paved the way for future Spanish exploration and settlement. At the same time, it demonstrated the horrors of European civilization to the region's native peoples.

Matthew Jennings

See also: Exploration; Mississippi River; Spanish Colonies on Mainland North America (Chronology).

Bibliography

Hoffman, Paul E. "Hernando de Soto: A Short Biography." In *The De Soto Chronicles*, edited by Lawrence Clayton, et al. Tuscaloosa: University of Alabama Press, 1993.

Weber, David J. *The Spanish Frontier in North America.* New Haven, CT: Yale University Press, 1992.

Wright, J. Leitch. *The Only Land They Knew: American Indians in the Old South.* 1981. Reprint, Lincoln: University of Nebraska Press, 1999.

Detroit

The site that would become the city of Detroit, a flat plain on the Detroit River, was probably first inhabited around 6000 B.C.E. These early inhabitants had verifiable contact with both the Copper People and the Mound Builders, who left three small mounds in the area. By 1600, the region was home to the Huron, Ottawa, Chippewa, Fox, Sac, Miami, and Potawatomie tribes, but warfare between the Huron and the five Iroquois nations had devastated several settlements and severely reduced the population by the time of European contact along the river.

The first Europeans to see Detroit were probably French coureurs de bois, voyageurs seeking new sources of furs. In 1625, French explorer and interpreter Étienne Brûlé mapped Lake Erie from Georgian Bay on the orders of Samuel de Champlain. Other French explorers continued to pass by the area en route to Lake Erie from Sault Sainte Marie, and named it literally "the strait"— Detroit.

Permanent settlement came in 1701, when Antoine Laumet de Lamothe Cadillac convinced Louis XIV that the region needed a chain of fortifications in the fur trading lands, both to keep out the British and to exert French control over the native peoples in the area. Cadillac called the area "Detroit du Pontchartrain," although the "du Pontchartrain" was soon dropped from common use. Cadillac brought over his own wife and encouraged the establishment of permanent farms and a Roman Catholic parish, St. Anne's, which is the second-oldest continuously functioning parish in the United States. Protected by a log stockade, the French settlers farmed winter wheat, oats, and corn, and they traded in beaver, muskrat, and deerskins. While they initially lived on narrow "ribbon" land allotments along the river, over time, the settlement developed orchards that produced a well-known brandy.

Because of its remote location, Detroit was not involved in the French and Indian War, but surrendered to British general Jeffery Amherst on September 8, 1760, under the terms of Montreal's capitulation. British settlers and agents of the British army did not arrive in Detroit to take possession until 1761, after which the fort and its inhabitants were prime targets in the rebellion of Chief Pontiac and his supporters against the British. Major Henry Gladwin of the 80th Light Foot Regiment defended the settlement against a two-month siege, which ended on October 31, 1763. Despite the slaughter at Bloody Run of the relief force sent to aid Detroit, it was the only British fort in the region that did not fall to Pontiac during the war.

During the American Revolution, Detroit was a convenient and strategic launching point for British raids into Pennsylvania, Kentucky, and New York. Detroit's lieutenant governor, Henry Hamilton, and his military commander, Captain Richard Lernoult, fearing attack from George Rogers Clark, rebuilt the stockade in the eighteenth-century "snowflake" pattern popularized by Vauban and engineered in Detroit by Captain Henry Bird. Other partisan activities, particularly among the loyalist Iroquois tribes, gained Hamilton the reputation of a "hair-buyer," or giver of bounties on scalps, but it is probably undeserved American propaganda. Although Detroit was given by treaty to the United States in 1783, it remained in British hands as a Native American trading center and was so attached to British Canada that it elected two members to the provincial council in 1791.

In 1794, the battle of Fallen Timbers placed American authority close enough to Detroit to finally claim the city and the surrounding region for the United States, although the British garrison withdrew across the straits to Fort Malden only in 1796. The border between the two remained a sore point, with the British encouraging runaway slaves to escape to Canada, and the British commander of the Great Lakes, Commodore Alexander Grant, refusing to move from his house at Grosse Point, which had become American territory, until his death in 1813.

In 1805, a catastrophic fire destroyed most of the original French structures in Detroit. But the disaster allowed the town to be rebuilt largely in brick, on a system of plazas copied from Pierre L'Enfant's plan for the U.S. capital.

The War of 1812 saw Detroit used as a natural base for attacks on Fort Malden. In a dramatic turn of events, cannonades from the British caused Governor William Hill to surrender Detroit to the British, for which he was later court-martialed. The British occupation was extremely uncomfortable for the people of Detroit, who suffered food shortages and martial law. This situation lasted until Commodore Perry's victory on the Great Lakes in September 1813 and the defeat of British land forces at the Battle of the Thames.

In the postwar opening of the Old Northwest, Detroit became the capital of the Territory of Michigan and a gateway for westbound travelers. It was aggressively advertised to settlers after the opening of the Erie Canal in 1825, and steamboat travel and advantageous land acts soon made Detroit a growing American city.

Margaret Sankey

See also: Fortifications; French; French and Indian War; Pontiac.

Bibliography

Bald, F. Clever. *Detroit's First American Decade, 1796–1805.* Ann Arbor: University of Michigan Press, 1948.

Mason, Philip P. *Detroit, Ft. Lernoult and the American Revolution.* Detroit, MI: Wayne State University Press, 1964.

Peckham, Henry Howard. *Pontiac and the Indian Uprising.* Detroit, MI: Wayne State University Press, 1994.

Russell, Nelson Vance. *The British Regime in Michigan and the Old Northwest, 1760–1796.* Northfield, MN: Carleton College Press, 1939.

Woodford, Arthur. *This Is Detroit: 1701–2001.* Detroit, MI: Wayne State University Press, 2001.

Woodford, Frank, and Arthur Woodford. *All Our Yesterdays.* Detroit, MI: Wayne State University Press, 1969.

Dickinson, John (1732–1808)

A leading figure in colonial politics during the later half of the eighteenth century, John Dickinson was a conservative revolutionary who personally reflected the tortured loyalties that bound the Mid-Atlantic colonies to Great Britain. Regardless of his divided political sentiments, Dickinson ably served both Delaware and Pennsylvania in many different positions, partaking in both sessions of the 1774 and 1775 Continental Congress and the Constitutional Convention of 1787.

John Dickinson was born on November 8, 1732, on Maryland's Eastern Shore. His family was part of the Quaker elite, and John's father, Samuel Dickinson, was a well-respected judge and landowner. This early high status enabled John to receive an extensive education in his early years, despite his constant poor health. In 1750, Dickinson moved to Philadelphia to pursue legal studies under John Moland, who was among the leading lawyers in the Pennsylvania colony. After spending two years under Moland's tutelage, from 1754 to 1757, Dickinson continued his training in London at Middle Temple, the most prestigious center of legal training in the British Empire. Following the completion of his coursework and training, Dickinson returned to Philadelphia and joined the bar in 1757.

In part due to his family's immense property holdings in Delaware, Dickinson was elected to the state assembly in 1760, where he became speaker for a year. Political office in Pennsylvania called, however, and Dickinson was nominated and elected to serve in the state assembly in 1762. Serving for three years, he was a strong supporter of the Proprietary Party, which was led by the Penn family and was conservative in supporting traditional society and elite elements of Pennsylvanian society.

Dickinson was constantly at odds with Benjamin Franklin, who was the leader of the opposing Royalist Party, which garnered its support from the Pennsylvania backcountry and German Americans (then known as Dutch) who resented Quaker control over the colony. When the issue of changing the colony's charter to a royal one arose in late 1763, Dickinson led the Proprietary Party in denouncing it, arguing the colony would be at the mercy of the British ministry and the colonists' traditional rights as Englishmen would be violated or ignored. Dickinson's strong statements and efforts led to his electoral defeat in 1765 and a five-year absence from the state assembly.

It was during the period from 1765 to 1770 that John Dickinson wrote his *Letters from a Farmer in Pennsylvania*, which gained him enormous recognition throughout the colonies. Dickinson was stirred to action after his involvement and leadership in the Stamp Act Congress, which met in 1765, arguing in his letters that the act was unconstitutional because of the lack of representation for the colonies in the House of Commons. Hence, Dickinson's *Letters* stressed the rights the colonists had as English citizens, particularly in regard to taxation, and the need to protect the public liberty. During this period of popular success, Dickinson married Mary Norris, daughter of wealthy merchant Isaac Norris, in July 1770 and further solidified his standing in elite society.

Later that fall, Dickinson was elected again to a seat in the Pennsylvania Assembly, and he served until 1776. During this time, Dickinson found himself allied with the vocal Presbyterian Party, which sought to preserve colonial rights, particularly during the after-

The patriot John Dickinson, portrayed here by Charles Willson Peale, served Delaware and Pennsylvania in several capacities before and after the Revolution, but he was best known as the author of *Letters from a Farmer in Pennsylvania* (1765–1770), a series of anti-British political tracts. *(Courtesy of Historical Society of Pennsylvania Collection, Atwater Kent Museum of Philadelphia/Bridgeman Art Library)*

math of the Intolerable Acts of 1774. He was selected to attend the First Continental Congress, which met in the fall of 1774. Serving for only a brief period, he penned a petition to King George III, which urged the king to listen to the colonists.

When the Second Continental Congress met in 1775 after the battles of Lexington and Concord, Dickinson was opposed to seeking independence, and instead stressed reconciliation and moderation in dealing with Great Britain. He voted against the Declaration, declaring that it was premature. This move caused long-term tensions with John Adams and other leading New Englanders.

Dickinson resigned from the Pennsylvania Assembly in 1776 and refused to serve in the Continental Congress, instead fighting as a private at the battle of Brandywine in 1777. He was elected president of Delaware in 1782, a position he held until 1785. A delegate from Delaware to the 1787 Constitutional Convention,

he offered strong support for ratification with his *Letters of Fabius*.

In the 1790s, Dickinson became increasingly critical of George Washington's pro-British policy, and he strongly supported Thomas Jefferson and the Republican Party in the election of 1800. After an extended illness, he died in Wilmington, Delaware, on February 14, 1808.

Peter Bratt

See also: Continental Congress, First; Continental Congress, Second; Revolutionary War.

Bibliography

Flower, Milton E. *John Dickinson: Conservative Revolutionary*. Charlottesville: University Press of Virginia, 1983.

Jacobson, David L. *John Dickinson and the Revolution in Pennsylvania: 1764–1776*. Berkeley: University of California Press, 1965.

Power, Susan M. *Before the Convention: Religion and the Founders*. Lanham, MD: University Press of America, 1984.

Diplomacy (Foreign Affairs)

Since the British first settled North America in the early 1600s, the American colonists had, for the most part, governed themselves. This arrangement had worked well for the colonies and the mother country for over a century, but the end of the French and Indian War (1754–1763) brought about a departure from the status quo. In fact, the issues of taxation and representation, which arose after the war, were the main concerns of diplomacy between the colonies and England in the period up to 1776.

The French and Indian War had served to remove France from the North American continent, but it had also greatly depleted the British national treasury. In an attempt to make the colonies help pay for the cost of the war and for the administration of Britain's new territorial possessions, Parliament passed a series of controversial taxes, which were viewed as unjust by colonists and ultimately led to a defiance of the mother country. The most notable example of this new policy was the Stamp Act, which was a tariff placed on all printed materials. Under the Stamp Act, instead of paying taxes to a local legislature, the colonies were now ordered to pay the tax directly to England. The main objection to the tax did not reside in the amount of the tax. Rather, outrage among the colonists stemmed from the fact that they had not been consulted in the matter.

Benjamin Franklin, perhaps the most world-famous American colonist of his time, had been in England since 1757 on a mission representing the legislature of Pennsylvania in a taxation dispute. To Franklin's chagrin, the president of the Privy Council, Lord Granville, informed him that, in the opinion of the king's advisers, King George III was the supreme legislator for the colonies. This did not sit well with Franklin, and he expressed his disagreement. Franklin replied to Granville that the king did not have such power. Instead, Franklin insisted, legislatures had the right to pass laws with the king's consent. After Franklin's speech, Granville reiterated that Franklin was mistaken. Consequently, Franklin left the meeting appalled by the inequality with which British subjects in the colonies were regarded.

When, in 1765, the Stamp Act was passed by Parliament without the consent of the colonists, Franklin protested and lobbied in London for the repeal of the new law, but he found little support for his efforts. Likewise, in North America many colonists penned petitions to Parliament requesting that the Stamp Act be repealed, but the pleas were ignored. Daniel Dulany, Jr., a Maryland lawyer, gave credence to the colonial protest when he wrote that, according to British law, Parliament had a right to impose external taxes on the trade of the colonies, but that it did not have a right to impose internal taxation. As a form of protest, colonial leaders proposed more drastic measures than petitions and organized a boycott of all British goods. By 1766, British businessmen back in England began to feel the brunt of the boycott and begged Parliament for relief. Parliament relented, and the Stamp Act was repealed that same year.

King George III, among other British leaders, held the belief that the removal of France from North America might encourage the colonists to rebel. Since British protection against a French threat would no longer be necessary, independence might seem like an attractive alternative to the colonists. Consequently, the king felt that there was a greater need to keep the colonies under tighter control than ever before, and both Parliament and the king felt that taxation was an effective way of doing so. Not surprisingly, the same day in 1766 that the Stamp Act was repealed, the Declaratory Act was passed. According to the Declaratory Act, Parliament claimed the right to continue to pass any laws for the colonies that it deemed necessary. Colonial defiance of British law led to stronger military control, but, ironically, stronger control only seemed to push the colonists to further rebellion.

One year later, Parliament passed a new set of taxes called the Townshend Duties, which placed a tariff on a variety of imports. Immediately, colonists again organized a boycott of all British goods, and mobs gathered to protest. In an attempt to restore order, British troops were shipped to the colonies by the thousands. On March 5, 1770, the protests, coupled with the strong military presence in Massachusetts, culminated in tragedy. As the troops arrived to quell a riot in progress in Boston, the crowd began harassing the troops. In retaliation, the troops fired on the crowd, killing five civilians. The Boston Massacre, as it came to be called by the colonists, led to the repealing of most of the Townshend Duties with the exception of the tax on tea.

Encouraged by their success in getting tariffs repealed, colonists now took on the tea tax. Once again, Franklin unsuccessfully pleaded in London on behalf of the colonists. In protest of the tax, Bostonians, disguised as Native Americans, boarded British ships and dumped their cargo of tea overboard. News of the 1773 Boston Tea Party spread across the colonies and led to copycat tea parties in New Jersey, New York, Rhode Island, and South Carolina.

In 1774, relations between Britain and the colonies went from bad to worse. In London, Franklin discovered some letters written by royal governor Thomas Hutchinson, dated 1772, which asked Parliament to take stronger measures against the colonists. Franklin mailed copies of the letters to the colonies, hoping to make Hutchinson the scapegoat for all the past troubles between the colonies and the mother country, and he asked the Privy Counsel for Hutchinson's removal. To Franklin's surprise, however, it was he who was reprimanded for leaking the private letters of a government official and fomenting trouble. Having fallen from grace in the eyes of many in Britain, Franklin left the mother country and returned to the colonies. After the departure of this important ambassador, matters continued to worsen with Parliament passing the Coercive Acts (1774), which were called the Intolerable Acts by colonists.

One of the Coercive Acts, the Boston Port Bill, authorized the closing of the port of Boston until the town paid for the tea that had been destroyed half a year earlier. Since the Boston economy was primarily based on trade, the closing of the port hurt all of Boston

In January 1774, Benjamin Franklin (kneeling), the agent of Massachusetts to the British government, was reprimanded by London's Privy Council for his role in the "Hutchinson Affair." He returned to America committed to the cause of independence. *(Brown Brothers, Sterling, Pennsylvania)*

economically. Also, General Thomas Gage became the military governor of Massachusetts, placing the colony under military rule, which defied the Massachusetts charter of self-government. Another of the acts underlined British duplicity in legal treatment by allowing British officials accused of crimes in the colonies to be tried in England.

Further enraging the colonists, the Quartering Act authorized General Gage to quarter soldiers in privately owned Boston taverns, uninhabited houses, and other buildings. Britain deemed this action as a practical solution to the shortage of housing for the thousands of troops that had recently been shipped to the colonies. However, this intrusion upon private property upset the colonists so much that it would later appear as a grievance in the Declaration of Independence and as a protection in the American Bill of Rights.

As a whole, the Coercive Acts were so offensive to the colonists that, as a direct reaction, the leaders of the colonies gathered at the First Continental Congress

in 1774. George Washington, Patrick Henry, John Adams, and Benjamin Franklin were among the delegates who met to bring organizational strength to the rebellion. After some debate, the delegates came to a compromise, agreeing to unite in defense of Massachusetts and the other colonies, which meant that the time had come for them to arm themselves against military aggression. As a conciliatory measure, the delegates also agreed to send a new petition directly to the king, affirming their continued loyalty.

Parliament and the king saw the Continental Congress as an illegitimate body that was not to be recognized or negotiated with. The British felt that the colonists were conveying betrayal, rather than loyalty, through their recent actions. Consequently, after 1775, the British continued to reinforce the troops in the colonies, and the colonists continued to arm themselves.

On April 19, the British army found out that the rebels had a storehouse of arms and gunpowder at Concord near Boston, and they proceeded to seize it. The storehouse, however, was under rebel guard, and an exchange of fire between both groups led to the battle of Lexington and Concord. Although not a major battle, it had major significance as the first skirmish of the rebellion. One month later, the Second Continental Congress met and drew up plans to establish the Continental army and appointed George Washington as commander in chief.

As the rebellion progressed, more and more colonists began to feel that a break with England was unavoidable. For example, by 1775, John Adams believed that petitions were a waste of time. A few others, however, still sought reconciliation. John Dickinson convinced Congress to bypass Parliament and send the Olive Branch Petition directly to the king. After the king heard about the high British casualties in battles such as Bunker Hill, however, negotiations were far from his mind. He drove the point home by declaring the colonists enemies of Great Britain and outside his protection. The defiance that the colonists had exhibited had firmly convinced the king that force was the only way to crush the rebellion.

In 1776, the civil disturbance between the colonies and the mother country was transformed into a full-scale war for independence. Understanding that the colonies could not hope to defeat Great Britain without foreign aid, the delegates had created the Committee of Secret Correspondence in late 1775 and appointed Benjamin Franklin as the chair.

At the time, France seemed the most likely nation to approach for aid, as the French government, wanting revenge for the loss of its North American territories to the British in the French and Indian War, was eager to begin discussions with the colonists. In fact, the French had placed secret agents in the colonies as early as 1770 to report on the state of the ongoing rebellion. To the delight of the colonists, the Comte de Vergennes, foreign minister under King Louis XVI, wasted no time in sending agent Julien-Alexandre Achard de Bonvouloir to North America to meet with the Committee of Secret Correspondence. Bonvouloir reported back to France that the colonists were, in fact, seeking independence. Greatly encouraged, Vergennes recommended to King Louis to approve secret aid to the colonies. On April 6, the Continental Congress voted to open American ports to all nations, and the next month France began to secretly ship arms, ammunition, clothing, and tents to the colonies. France, however, was reluctant to publicly commit itself to the fight as long as the colonists pledged loyalty to the British king.

To convince France and other European countries of the sincerity of its desire for independence, Congress asked Thomas Jefferson to begin drafting the Declaration of Independence in June. After undergoing a few revisions by members of Congress, the Declaration was finished on July 2, 1776, and was formally approved and signed two days later. Heavily influenced by the British philosopher John Locke, the document set out to justify the colonists' cause of independence to Britain and the world. Interestingly, in the Declaration, Jefferson makes King George III the scapegoat of all past troubles between the colonies and the mother country. Finally, the document declares that the colonies would henceforth be called the "United States of America," which would exist free and independent. In light of this new status, all political ties between Great Britain and the newly created United States were dissolved. From that point on, these states would have the right to wage war, make peace, enter into alliances, and regulate trade.

As a way of putting teeth into the declaration, in September Congress appointed Arthur Lee, Silas Deane, and Benjamin Franklin to a commission to France. John Adams proposed that the three agents seek continued aid and recognition from France without entering into a military alliance. By early 1777, however, the war was going badly for the colonists. It became painfully obvious to the Americans that a military alliance with France was necessary.

This alliance did not occur until 1778, after Franklin convinced France that the colonies would be forced to surrender to Britain if France did not commit to an alliance. Shortly after the alliance was formalized, France declared war against Great Britain, and French troops were sent to North America. The war would drag on for another five years. Ultimately, the French alliance was perhaps the greatest determinant in winning American independence.

Rolando Avila

See also: Military and Diplomatic Affairs (Chronology); Military and Diplomatic Affairs (Essay).

Bibliography

Bailey, Thomas A. "The Colonial Backdrop." In *A Diplomatic History of the American People*. Englewood Cliffs, NJ: Prentice Hall, 1980.

Bemis, Samuel F. "America: The Stakes of European Diplomacy (1492–1775)." In *A Diplomatic History of the United States*. New York: Henry Holt, 1955.

———. *The Diplomacy of the American Revolution*. Bloomington: Indiana University Press, 1957.

Clarke, Ronald W. *Benjamin Franklin: A Biography.* New York: Random House, 1983.

Dull, Jonathan R. *A Diplomatic History of the American Revolution.* New Haven, CT: Yale University Press, 1985.

———. *The French Navy and American Independence: A Study of Arms and Diplomacy, 1774–1787.* Princeton, NJ: Princeton University Press, 1975.

Hutson, James H. *John Adams and the Diplomacy of the American Revolution.* Lexington: University Press of Kentucky, 1980.

Morris, Richard Brandon. *The Peacemakers: The Great Powers and American Independence.* New York: Harper and Row, 1965.

Savelle, Max. *The Origins of American Diplomacy: The International History of Anglo-America, 1492–1763.* New York: Macmillan, 1967.

Stinchcombe, William C. *The American Revolution and the French Alliance.* Syracuse, NY: Syracuse University Press, 1969.

Stourzh, Gerald. *Benjamin Franklin and America Foreign Policy.* Chicago: University of Chicago Press, 1954.

Disease

The public health crisis that emerged in America's early history can, in part, be traced to precipitating conditions in England. The practice of "enclosure," essentially land ownership, caused about half the rural peasantry of England to lose their lands between 1530 and 1630. The newly displaced population flocked to the cities in hopes of relief. London grew from 120,000 in 1550 to 200,000 by 1600, and that population was nearly doubled by 1650.

The result was a dramatic increase in urban crime, poverty and disease. Lack of fresh water and necessary sewage techniques made cities hotbeds of virulence. Parliament responded to the growing concern by criminalizing poverty. Vagrants were whipped, thieves were hanged, and debtors were jailed, but these measures only increased the anxiety of the population and did nothing to manage the health crisis.

Diseases from Europe

A partial solution was to send these poor to the colonies to work. Conditions in England made this as attractive to the homeless poor as it was to the wealthy; promises of milk and honey in the New World were readily accepted by all. The long journey to America on cramped ships with little attention to sanitation made an excellent host for the growth of disease. In fact, the arrival of ships would be one of the colonists' first clearly identifiable sources of disease.

Ships from Europe bringing soldiers from Germany and emigrants from Germany and other parts of Europe, as well as ships from Africa bringing slaves, were virtual incubators of disease. Smallpox, yellow fever, dysentery, and measles were just a few of those associated with the arrival of these ships. The cramped quarters forced individuals to spend the long journeys literally trapped in their own waste. Drinking water was "black, thick with dirt, and full of worms," according to one German emigrant, and lice and spiders were everywhere. The dead were thrown overboard, but many went unnoticed for long periods in the stinking, dark, confined holds of the ships. Yellow fever, also known as "stranger's disease" is thought to have originated in Africa, where it is endemic, and brought via the West Indies, where the first slave ship, a property of the Dutch West India Company, collected its unfortunate cargo and delivered them to America in 1626.

The most feared of the recurring ship-borne epidemics was smallpox. It was a highly contagious virus characterized by fever, intense headache, and eruptions of dark, red pustules all over the body. Because of its easily identifiable characteristics, excellent documentation is available in historical records. When first introduced to the population, the death toll would often reach upwards of 30 to 50 percent of those infected.

In the 1720s variolation was introduced to combat the deadly disease. In this early form of inoculation, healthy persons were infected by inserting the pus from a sick person into a small incision. The best results gave the healthy person a lesser form of the illness and left him or her with immunity to it, although early experiments were also known to trigger outbreaks. Overall, however, variolation was considered a great success, and was responsible for shrinking the death toll from 10 to 50 percent to 1 to 5 percent. Reverend Cotton Mather and Benjamin Franklin were ardent supporters of variolation.

Sanitation and Disease

Early colonists were ill prepared for the sanitation challenges of their new home. Not only were ships importing sickness from all over the world, but lack of necessary sanitation technology and knowledge, combined with the immediate demands of survival, made sanitation concerns a low priority. Public health was seen as the responsibility of the community and church. Early colonial cities were filthy places. People threw their waste in the streets, and most sanitation was managed with the use of pigs, goats, and turkey buzzards. These left their own waste, along with that of horses, which were used by everyone for transportation.

Diphtheria (caused by infected milk), dysentery and other intestinal diseases (known as "flux"), and common colds, which often resulted in pleurisy or pneumonia, killed many more people than epidemics. In the Southern colonies, malaria was endemic and was referred to as part of the "seasoning" process or quartile fever due to the predictability of its appearance in the population.

Disease killed more than half the members of the original Jamestown colony and decimated native populations, who had no immunity. In 1587, Thomas Harriot wrote of the colonists' visits to native villages in his *Briefe and True Report of the New Found Land of Virginia,*

> we sought by all meanes possible to win them by gentlenesse but that within a few dayes after our departure from every such Towne, the people began to die very fast, and many in short space. . . .

Native American populations—including the Iroquois and Susquehannock in the east; the Huron, Chippewa, and Potawatomi along the Sandusky River and around the southern shores of the Great Lakes; and the Catawba, Sioux, and Cherokee farther south—all suffered the devastating effects of these new diseases.

The number one killer of colonial women, however, was childbirth. In the Plymouth colony, one out of every thirty births resulted in the mother's death. In other areas, this mortality rate was even higher.

Realizing the relationship between foul odors and ill health, early city planners began to institute laws against the use of animals as waste management. In 1670, Charles Town (which later became Charleston, South Carolina) passed an ordinance against "swine running free" and ordered property owners to cut their "stinking weeds." By the 1680s, New York and Boston hired public scavengers and began to arrange for garbage removal by contract, and, in 1691 New York created the first commission on street cleaning. In 1712, Charles Town hired America's first health officer, Commissioner Gilbert Guttery, who, having by this time established a link between incoming ships and epidemics of yellow fever and smallpox, was empowered to board ships to investigate the health of the crew and cargo before allowing them to disembark.

Medicine

With the exception of Anton van Leeuwenhoek's invention of the microscope in 1674 and variolation nearly a century later, understanding that the presence of disease was somehow related to sanitation and that quarantine could occasionally manage outbreaks was the upper limit of early colonial medical knowledge. The prevailing medical theory was that disease was the result of some imbalance in one's "humors" or fluids. Cures consisted of various methods of manipulating the levels of one's humors.

Bleeding and "puking and purging" complemented an exhaustive list of recipes with ingredients that included salt pork, spider eggs, gunpowder, brimstone, hot ashes, cat's blood, dried toad, virgin's hair, and tobacco, to name only a few. Some of these recipes were meant to be taken internally; others were used externally in the form of poultices, meant to draw out disease through the flesh. Early colonists' chances of survival were often better if they did not seek relief from the medical doctors of the day.

The lack of certain knowledge in colonial medicine frequently rendered doctors impotent for much beyond simple comfort of the sick. In the absence of effective male medical professionals, much of colonial health care was practiced by women. In seventeenth-century New England, 24 percent of medical practitioners were women. Women served as surgeons, physicians, nurses, and midwives until their practices fell under the suspicion of the town fathers. Considering the materials used in established medical practice, which often had harsher effects on the body, it is ironic that so many of these women ended up being accused of witchcraft. We know about some of the remedies they used, because those convicted of witchcraft were forced to surrender their property to the town.

No discussion of colonial disease would be complete without addressing the popular suspicion in recent years that smallpox was used as a way to exterminate the native population. According to some historians, an early example of unintentional biological warfare was when the disease was passed along with gifts from the English.

Frustrated by Native American requests for provisions in exchange for their cooperation, a practice sustained by the French, the English believed the way to manage the indigenous population was by dominance through punishment—or even extinction. In a series of letters written during the summer of 1763 between General Jeffery Amherst and his officers, as well as correspondence between Amherst and Colonel Henry Bouquet, this idea is discussed specifically to "put a most Effectual Stop to their very Being." While the specific causes of disease were unknown, it could not escape anybody's attention that the native peoples died in large numbers from diseases that Europeans died of in far fewer numbers.

There is no doubt that life during the colonial era of this country was riddled with difficulty. Limited technology, a lack of information, and a firm, albeit naive, belief in the divine providence of a just cause conspired to complicate the matter of settlement for everyone involved. We can, however, thank those early Americans for innovations in sanitation and public health, including sewer works and inoculation, which might never have come into being if not for their sacrifices.

Anna Gersh

See also: Death and Dying; Malaria; Smallpox; Syphilis.

Bibliography

Castillo, Susan, and Ivy Schweitzer, eds. *The Literatures of Colonial America: An Anthology.* Malden, MA: Blackwell, 2001.

"Colonial Diseases and Cures." http://homepages.rootsweb .com/~sam/disease.html.

Hawke, David Freeman. *Everyday Life in Early America.* New York: Harper and Row, 1989.

A History of Public Health in South Carolina. South Carolina Department of Health and Environmental Control. 2001. http://www.scdhec.gov/administration/history/.

"Jeffrey Amherst and Smallpox Blankets." http://www.somsd .k12.nj.us/~chssocst/ssgavittus1amherstsmallpox.htm.

Morris, Richard B. *Encyclopedia of American History.* New York: Harper, 1953.

Quinn, Arthur. *A New World: An Epic of Colonial America from the Founding of Jamestown to the Fall of Quebec.* Boston: Faber & Faber, 1994.

Taylor, Alan. *American Colonies.* New York: Viking, 2001.

Ward, Harry M. *Colonial America 1607–1763.* Englewood Cliffs, NJ: Prentice Hall, 1991.

Dominicans

The Dominicans (Order of Friars Preachers) are Catholic friars belonging to a religious order founded in 1215 by the Spanish priest Santo Domingo de Guzmán (St. Dominic). Preaching and saving souls through peaceful example, teaching, and writing have been the order's goals from its inception. The Dominicans also are defined by their passion for justice.

The first Dominicans in the Americas, Fray Pedro de Córdoba, the vice provincial, along with Antonio Montesino and Bernardo de Santo Domingo, landed in 1510 in Santo Domingo, capital of today's Dominican Republic. Their church complex included a university dedicated to St. Thomas Aquinas. Established in 1538, it was the first university in the Americas and offered courses in theology, philosophy, law, and medicine (it is now called the Universidad Autónoma de Santo Domingo). Most importantly, from the moment they landed, the Dominican friars dedicated themselves to the salvation of the native people of the island, the Taino.

In order to save the Tainos' souls, the Dominicans first had to save their lives. The Taino were subjected to a system called *encomienda*, whereby, as protected vassals of the Spanish Crown, they were "commended"—whole villages at a time—into the hands of individual Spaniards on Hispaniola. The Spanish *encomenderos* were under royal mandate to feed and clothe their native subjects and teach them Catholic doctrine and Christian ways. (The natives could not be bought or sold, but the Crown could take them away and

The first Dominicans in the Americas arrived in the early sixteenth century. Members of this Roman Catholic order, shown here conducting a baptism, were dedicated to the salvation of native peoples throughout South, Central, and North America. *(Museo Nacional de Historia, Mexico City, Mexico/Giraudon/Bridgeman Art Library)*

commend them to a different Spaniard at will.) In theory, *encomienda* was a mutually beneficial system, wherein the grateful Taino would grow and prepare their *encomenderos'* food, construct their roads and buildings, mine gold, and perform any other required labor. The disruption of the Tainos' traditional lifestyle, however, especially the disruption of their planting and harvesting cycles, physical abuse by their *encomenderos*, and diseases resulting from contact with Europeans and their imported animals, decimated their population in a relatively short time.

In 1511, on a Sunday just before Christmas, Fray Antonio Montesino mounted the pulpit and gave an impassioned sermon. He spoke out, on behalf of all the Dominican friars in Santo Domingo, against the *encomienda* system, threatening the resident Spaniards that if they did not release their commended Native Americans, their sins would no longer be absolved in confession. Panicked Spaniards complained to Governor Diego Colón (Christopher Columbus's elder son), who ordered the friars to rescind their threat, but the following Sunday Montesino gave an even more impassioned anti-*encomienda* sermon, encouraging the salvation of the Native Americans through a mission system.

One *encomendero*, Bartolomé de las Casas, took the message to heart. He gave up his Native American slaves and, in 1515, he took holy vows and became the most outspoken of all the Dominicans against the *encomienda* system. Las Casas earned the title of royal protector of the natives for his decades of sacrifice and multiple volumes of writing in defense of the indigenous peoples of the Americas.

The fame of Las Casas surpassed that of his superior in Santo Domingo, Pedro de Córdoba, from whom he appears to have gotten his inspiration. Sometime before 1521, de Córdoba wrote *Doctrina Cristiana para instrucción e información de los indios por manera de historia*, the first manual on how to convert the native peoples to Christianity. Printed in Mexico in 1544, it stressed that the native peoples and Spaniards were equals in the eyes of God and that the natives must be peacefully evangelized, not forced into labor nor robbed of their property and goods.

Hundreds of Dominican friars actively evangelized among the Native Americans throughout South, Central, and North America, refusing military protection because it negated their peaceful mission. Fray Montesino left Santo Domingo to join Lucas Vázquez de Ayllón's expedition in 1526, along with Fray Antonio de Cervantes and Fray Pedro de Estrada, to establish a town on the North American mainland in today's South Carolina.

In the late 1530s, Fray Luis de Soto and Juan de Gallegos accompanied Hernando de Soto's brutal and destructive exploration party through today's Florida, Georgia, the Carolinas, Tennessee, Alabama, Mississippi, Arkansas, Oklahoma, and Texas. Fray Luis Cancer and two others were killed at Tampa Bay on June 24, 1549. In 1553, at least four Dominican friars were martyred on the Gulf Coast of Texas near the Rio Grande. Most of the Dominican friars of the early colonial era, however, sacrificed their lives anonymously. Today, there are active Dominican orders in ninety-two countries of the world.

Lynne Guitar

See also: Catholic Church; Franciscans; Jesuits; Missions; Religion (Chronology); Religion (Essay).

Bibliography

Bedouelle, Guy. *In the Image of Saint Dominic.* San Francisco: Ignatius, 1994.

Hinnebusch, William A. *The Dominicans: A Short History.* New York: Alba House, 1975.

Rubio, Fray Vicente. *Fray Pedro de Córdoba, Padre de los Dominicos de América.* Santo Domingo: Segunda Etapa, 1988.

Drake, Sir Francis (1540–1596)

Born in Devonshire, England, in 1540, Sir Francis Drake came from a seafaring family. His uncle, Sir John Hawkins, was among the first of the "sea dogs," English ship captains who raided Spanish and Portuguese holdings in Africa and the New World on behalf of their country and their queen, Elizabeth I. While Hawkins was content with harassing the slave trade, his nephew was far more ambitious.

In 1572, Drake devised a plan to attack Nombre de Dios, a Spanish port on the Caribbean coast of Panama. Twice a year, Spanish treasure ships sailed out of Nombre de Dios, loaded with silver from the mines of Peru. While Drake's attack failed to capture much treasure, the trip won him a reputation for daring in his own country, and struck fear throughout the Spanish empire, where he became known as "The Dragon."

In 1577, Drake sailed from England with 164

men in five ships on an expedition that would take him into the Pacific Ocean by way of the Straits of Magellan. Drake later reported that Elizabeth I planned the trip herself to interfere with Spanish trade in the Far East. As the fleet entered the Straits of Magellan, Drake changed the name of his flagship from the *Pelican* to the *Golden Hind*. The ships passed through the straits in just three days and headed north into the Pacific. A storm hit and continued for three weeks, scattering the fleet 600 miles to the southwest. Drake lost three ships in the storm, and, after another squall, the fourth ship, the *Elizabeth,* became separated from the *Golden Hind* and sailed for home.

With only eighty men and one ship remaining, Drake pressed on. He had already discovered Cape Horn, and he now continued north, attacking Spanish ships and colonial towns in Chile, Peru, and Mexico. Drake sailed out of Spanish territory and continued up the West Coast of North America. He probably sailed close to Vancouver Island and may even have made it all the way to the Arctic Circle.

Drake and his crew returned south to California, where they spent the summer with native peoples. Finally, they set sail for the Spice Islands; there, the local sultan proposed an alliance with the English against the Portuguese. With his ship laden with gold, silver, gems, and now cloves, Drake headed around Africa for home, arriving in England in September 1580.

Drake's treasure amounted to 300,000 pounds, which was quickly stored in the Tower of London. Queen Elizabeth I used part of the treasure to pay off her foreign debt. She invested another 42,000 pounds in the Levant Company; profits from this company were later used to establish the British East India Company. For his services, Drake was knighted and received 10,000 pounds from the take, with his crew dividing another 10,000 pounds among themselves.

Drake later served as vice admiral of the English fleet that defeated the Spanish Armada. In 1596, he died of a fever while raiding Spanish pearl fisheries in Puerto Rico and was buried at sea off the coast of Panama.

Mary Stockwell

See also: Exploration; Piracy.

Bibliography

Thomson, George Malcolm. *Sir Francis Drake.* New York: Morrow, 1972.

Dulany, Daniel, Jr. (1722–1797)

Daniel Dulany, Jr., is best known for his legal arguments against the 1765 Stamp Act. A prominent lawyer and politician, as well as the scion of one of the most powerful families in Maryland, Dulany considered himself in the political mainstream and spent his life seeking to mediate disputes. He did not support revolution and, shocked by the violence of anti-British mobs, remained neutral throughout the colonial crisis.

Dulany was born on June 28, 1722, in Annapolis, Maryland, the eldest son of a large landowner and prominent lawyer. He received an English education, attending Eton and Clare College, Cambridge, where he studied until 1742. He then entered Middle Temple and, in 1746, was called to the bar, a distinction rarely accorded to a colonist. Upon returning to Maryland in 1747, Dulany established a law practice that primarily served planters and merchants in Anne Arundel and Prince George's counties. He also became a major landowner when his father gave him lots in Frederick Town and western Maryland totaling 14,000 acres.

Dulany's political career began in 1751 when he won a seat in the lower house of the Maryland General Assembly as a delegate from Annapolis. In the wake of King George's War, the French moved into Ohio country, and tensions rose throughout the English colonies. In this climate of fear, a Catholic scare began in Maryland. Dulany was Protestant, but his nephews were Roman Catholic, and he feared for their safety, as well as the maintenance of a just and fair society. He fought repeatedly in the Maryland assembly against attempts to persecute Catholics, seeing one bill that condemned them as the first step toward extreme anti-Catholic legislation that was already being discussed among the legislators. In 1754, by opposing a bill that confiscated all lands held by priests and in trust for priests, he lost much of the support of his constituents. He declined to run for reelection that year, but he was returned to his old seat in the 1756 election.

The prominent position of the Dulany family helped boost the young lawyer's political career. The proprietor of Maryland, Frederick Calvert, sixth Lord Baltimore, wanted to keep the influential Dulany family on his side in the ongoing struggle between the proprietor and the lower house. In 1761, Baltimore named Dulany provincial secretary. Although considered to be the most brilliant attorney in Maryland, Dulany closed his law office in 1763 to devote all his energies to the management of his lands and his growing political career. He saw himself as a political moderate, despite his close ties to Britain and Lord Baltimore, and attempted to mediate the burgeoning colonial dispute.

During the Stamp Act crisis of 1765, Dulany wrote a widely circulated pamphlet, *Considerations on the Propriety of Imposing Taxes in the British Colonies for the Purpose of Raising a Revenue by Act of Parliament,* that attacked the tax—which placed fees on newspapers, playing cards, and a host of official documents—on constitutional grounds. In the pamphlet, Dulany recognized the right of Parliament to control trade but drew a sharp distinction between laws designed to be regulatory and those created to raise revenue. He noted that the tax fell on those who could least afford to pay it, namely, the residents of a poor province, and particularly hurt the poorest of the poor by targeting mortgagors, debtors, and defendants. He argued that while the people in England could complain to the local representative about disagreeable legislation, the people of Maryland and the other American colonies did not have that opportunity.

The violence of the opposition to the Stamp Act cooled Dulany's anti-British ardor. While he opposed the tax, he found mobs and the collapse of societal order to be far more disagreeable. Later in 1765, his *Right to the Tonnage* took a more conservative position in local politics, and Dulany would never again oppose the right of Britain to impose a tax upon its colonies.

Dulany spent the Revolution divided between the loyalists, many of whom were family members, and the patriots. His neutrality cost him both considerable wealth and much of his power. He retired from politics and spent the remainder of his years occasionally practicing law until his March 17, 1797, death in Baltimore.

Dulany proved typical of many of the propertied men of the Revolutionary era. Unwilling to quietly acquiesce to unfair treatment from the British government, he also did not favor any method of protest that disrupted the order of colonial society. While Dulany helped form public opinion in favor of revolution, he did not support such radicalism.

Caryn E. Neumann

See also: Catholic Church; Dulany, Daniel, Sr.; Maryland; Maryland (Chronology); Stamp Act (1765).

Bibliography

Land, Aubrey C. *The Dulanys of Maryland: A Biographical Study of Daniel Dulany, the Elder (1685–1753) and Daniel Dulany, the Younger (1722–1797).* Baltimore: Maryland Historical Society, 1955.

Dulany, Daniel, Sr. (1685–1753)

Daniel Dulany, Sr., emerged as the quintessential colonial American success story. He rose from indentured servitude to become one of the largest landowners and most politically powerful men in Maryland. The family he founded, subsequently led by his namesake son, would play a major role in the history of Maryland until the Revolution.

Daniel Dulany was born in Queen's County, Ireland, in 1685. He attended, but did not graduate from, the University of Dublin and then decided to emigrate to Maryland in 1703. Lacking money to pay for the voyage, he followed a common strategy and became an indentured servant bound to the ship's captain. Dulany's subsequent successes would convince him of the merits of indentured servitude, and he promoted it strongly. His enthusiasm did not minimize the dangers faced by such immigrants; knowing their vulnerability, he became a staunch advocate of shipboard sanitary measures designed to reduce the number of travelers who succumbed to disease on the long sea journey.

Once in Maryland, Dulany found a distinguished local lawyer and planter in Charles County, Colonel George Plater, who agreed to redeem him from the captain in exchange for three years of clerking in his law office. Dulany proved to be adept at law and was admitted to practice in Charles County in 1709. In 1716, he went to London to continue his legal studies for a time and became one of the few colonial lawyers admitted to Gray's Inn, one of the four Inns of Court that constituted England's center of legal learning. Returning to the colonies as one of the best legal minds in Maryland, Dulany moved his practice from Charles County to Prince George's County before advancing in 1720 to the provincial courts in the capital of Annapolis.

While achieving personal success, Dulany also hungered for political accolades. He began to acquire the offices that would make him the founder of a powerful political dynasty. In 1720, Dulany was named attorney general, a post that he held until 1725 and then again from 1734 to 1744. In 1722, the voters of Annapolis elected Dulany to the lower house of the General Assembly. He was reelected to every successive assembly until 1742.

Maryland's inhabitants were in a unique position among the American colonists because after years of neglect, the new proprietor of the settlement, Charles Calvert, fifth Lord Baltimore, fully intended to use his nearly kinglike power. When the proprietor exercised his charter right to veto legislation or when he issued by fiat new rules for the colony, his opponents accused him of violating their rights as Englishmen. In *The Right of the Inhabitants of Maryland to the Benefit of the English Laws* (1728), Dulany became the first to launch a legal challenge against Baltimore. His argument, based on the belief that colonists had equal rights with the residents of England to the benefits and protection of English statutory and common law, would be echoed in later colonial protests against the British. At the time, Dulany's citing of English constitutional rights as embodied in the Magna Carta and his appeal to natural law to define fundamental liberties were boldly original. He soon became a leader of the Anti-proprietary or Country Party, which sought to extend English statute law to Maryland to replace arbitrary rule by Baltimore.

Dulany may have been motivated to challenge Baltimore because, as a member of the General Assembly, he feared that his power and influence would be diminished. In any event, his antagonism toward the proprietor did not last long. In 1742, he accepted an appointment from Baltimore to become a member of the Governor's Council of State, which constituted the upper house of the General Assembly.

Dulany's success at law brought him wealth, prominence, and social acceptance. He also acquired the means to become one of the largest entrepreneurs in Maryland. Dulany made vast numbers of loans, emerging as one of the colony's major moneylenders. He played an active role in the slave trade, profiting both from the sale of slaves and from lending money to those who purchased them. He also speculated in land on a large scale, investing mostly in property in the sparsely settled western portions of the colony. Upon his death in Annapolis, on December 5, 1753, Dulany had amassed one of the greatest fortunes in North America.

Dulany's life epitomizes the promise of the New World. Rising from servitude to become one of the most influential men of his generation, he played a major role in shaping colonial Maryland.

Caryn E. Neumann

See also: Dulaney, Daniel, Jr.; Maryland; Maryland (Chronology).

Bibliography

Land, Aubrey C. *The Dulanys of Maryland: A Biographical Study of Daniel Dulany, the Elder (1685–1753) and Daniel Dulany, the Younger (1722–1797).* Baltimore: Maryland Historical Society, 1955.

Dunmore, Lord (1732–1809)

John Murray, fourth earl of Dunmore, was the royal governor of Virginia from 1770 to 1776. Of noble birth, he was descended from the Stuart line. In 1761, he was one of sixteen Scottish peers elected to Parliament.

Selected to be the governor of New York in 1770, Dunmore arrived there with his family on October 19, 1771. Although well received in New York, he was promoted to the post of governor of the Virginia colony as successor to Governor Botetourt, who had died on October 15, 1770.

Initially, Dunmore was popular in Virginia. His newborn daughter was named after the colony, leading the province to adopt her as its own. In her honor, provincial leaders named two new counties Dunmore and Fincastle (the second of his titles). Yet the honeymoon did not last long. In 1773, Dunmore responded to rising patriot sentiment by dissolving the House of Burgesses after that body considered forming a committee of correspondence, an institution already adopted in other colonies. The following year, when the Burgesses established a day of mourning for the Boston Port Bill, Dunmore again dissolved the body.

On numerous occasions while governor, Dunmore showed great interest in frontier affairs involving Native Americans and possessed a genuine concern for the security of frontier settlements. Yet Dunmore (through agents) instigated a frontier crisis with the native peoples, resulting in a military expedition to the Ohio Valley. The confrontation, possibly conceived to divert Virginia's revolutionary spirit, began early in 1774, when Dr. John Connolly, a representative for Dunmore, occupied Fort Pitt and attacked nearby Native American villages in retaliation for recent raids on frontier settlements in Virginia. While Connolly's actions seem geared toward starting a full-scale war with local tribes, he claimed that he was trying to defuse ongoing antagonism between Virginia and Pennsylvania concerning disputes over the ownership of the region.

Although regional hostility remained constant, a series of violent acts forced open conflict. First, a party led by Captain Michael Cresap killed one Native American and captured another near the junction of Yellow Creek and the Ohio River at Logan's Camp (also known as Baker's Cabin) on April 27, 1774. Three days later, Daniel Greathouse enticed some Native Americans to his house, plied them with alcohol, and then murdered six of them. While responses varied, most were like that of a half-breed named Logan. Angered by the murder of his brother and sister at Baker's Cabin, Logan, once an extraordinarily faithful translator for the English, took thirteen scalps in attacks on nearby homesteads and traveling merchants.

On June 10, Governor Dunmore organized the militia in the tidewater region and sent them to Fort Pitt, where he established a military headquarters. Little happened in the next month, but in early August, Major Angus McDonald raided Shawnee villages on the Muskingum River. A month later, Dunmore led a force of 2,000 militiamen down the Ohio River, while Colonel Andrew Lewis took a second column of more than 1,000 down the Kanawha River with the expectation that the two groups would reassemble inside Indian Territory.

The Ohio tribes—particularly the Shawnee, Miami, Wyandots, and Ottawas—under the leadership of Chief Cornstalk rallied about 1,000 warriors to attack Lewis before he rejoined Dunmore. In a major engagement at Point Pleasant, Lewis defeated the Native Americans on October 10, forcing the native alliance to collapse. Shortly afterward, the tribal leaders came to Dunmore suing for peace.

Although tension between Dunmore and Virginia briefly eased after his return from Ohio, events outside the colony drove the two entities toward an inevitable confrontation. Reacting to the closure of Boston and the subjugation of Massachusetts, the Virginia convention put the militia into a posture of defense. Dunmore countered the Assembly's move with a series of blunders that forced a crisis. The first error occurred in the middle of the night on April 20, when Dunmore seized the provincial powder supply at Williamsburg. Two weeks later, Patrick Henry raised militiamen in Hanover County and marched on the capital. Concerned by the threat of war, Dunmore reimbursed the province 330

pounds for the powder on May 4, defending his action by saying that he was protecting the colony from a rumored slave revolt. Later, Dunmore recanted and declared Henry an outlaw. With tension reaching a boiling point, Dunmore fled the capital for the safety of a warship patrolling the Chesapeake Bay.

From the warship, Dunmore conducted raids and military operations for the remainder of his time in Virginia. In retaliation for the looting and burning of a British sloop, he sent naval forces to destroy Hampton on October 24–25. On November 7, Dunmore declared martial law in Virginia and offered to free slaves and indentured servants willing to join his military forces in Norfolk. The colonists defeated these forces at Great Bridge on December 9. The loyalists and former slaves were loaded aboard nearby transports and evacuated to Gwynn Island. On January 1, 1776, Dunmore ordered warships to fire on Norfolk, destroying most of the town. The remainder of Dunmore's forces remained at Gwynn Island until early July, when the colonials forced them to abandon this post as well.

Defeated and weak from disease, Dunmore sent his ragtag group of refugees and military forces to Bermuda, while he returned to England by way of New York. Upon his return to England, the Crown rewarded Dunmore for his services as royal governor of Virginia and his efforts to retain control of the colony by making him governor of the Bahamas.

Solomon K. Smith

See also: Army, British; Native American–European Conflict; Revolutionary War.

Bibliography

Selby, John E. *Dunmore*. Williamsburg: Virginia Independence Bicentennial Commission, 1977.

———. *The Revolution in Virginia, 1775–1783*. Williamsburg, VA: Colonial Williamsburg Foundation, 1988.

Thwaites, Gold, and Louise Phelps Kellog, eds. *Documentary History of Dunmore's War*. Madison: Wisconsin Historical Society, 1905.

Dutch

During the colonial period, the Dutch played a role in the settlement of North America. More importantly, Dutch expansion intensified the economic development of Europe and the Atlantic world.

Dutch Expansion

The Dutch became part of European expansion while under the control of Spain. At the time of the 1579 creation of the United Provinces, which marked partial independence from Spain, the Dutch possessed substantial practical experience in oceanic trade, which they soon turned to their own benefit.

After gaining independence, the Dutch displaced Antwerp as the major trading center of Europe, and, by 1597, Dutch merchants had made their first voyage to Asia. Their goal was to supplant Portuguese dominance in the Asiatic trade, and, as part of this successful endeavor, they were introduced to the trans-Atlantic slave trade.

In the seventeenth century, Dutch expansion and economic development occurred in two separate, but intertwined, regions and through two joint-stock companies. The first area was the Indian Ocean trade, where the Dutch East India Company successfully struggled to define a place for itself; the second involved the Atlantic Ocean and the Dutch West India Company. In 1602, the Dutch state created the well-funded East India Company, controlled by seven governing boards, each representing a province. The company's success stemmed from its ability to send out well-armed and well-supplied fleets, as well as from its position in the much-desired Indian Ocean trade.

Instead of trying to take on the Portuguese and English directly, the Dutch focused on establishing trade enclaves close to the supply of spices. This hurt the Portuguese, who controlled commercial centers rather than production points. The company took control of Jakarta and renamed it Batvia, and this became the major trading center from which the Dutch expanded. To avoid conflict with Mughal, English, and Portuguese fleets, the Dutch followed a new route to Asia that involved sailing to Australia and then heading north. Their success in this region made them important and successful middlemen.

As the Dutch worked to establish themselves in the lucrative Indian Ocean trade, they also played a vital role in the development of the plantation complex in the Americas. In the 1500s, the Netherlands was the center of European sugar distribution, and, as sugar production developed in the Americas, especially in Brazil under the Portuguese, the Dutch became involved through financial investment. Although planters still relied on slave labor from Africa, Dutch capital modernized sugar production through new technology.

By the early 1600s, the Dutch, along with the English, began to challenge the position of the Spanish and Portuguese in the Americas. One of the results of these efforts was the Dutch seizure of part of Brazil (modern Suriname) from the Portuguese. The Dutch West India Company then sought to expand its role in the American carrying trade.

From this base, the Dutch played an important role in expanding sugar production in the West Indies, especially after the capture of Curaçao. Again, their position as middlemen gave the Dutch great economic power throughout the Atlantic world. At the same time, their focus upon shipping and exchange—traditional middlemen activities—made them less concerned with colonization.

Dutch in New Netherland

Dutch activities in North America centered on their colony of New Netherland, which lay along the Hudson River from Manhattan inland to modern Albany. Initial Dutch claims in North America came from an English explorer, Henry Hudson, whom the Dutch East India Company had hired in 1609 to search for a Northwest Passage to the Far East. Hudson, traveling on the *Half Moon*, claimed the land along the river for the Netherlands, but on his return to Europe, he stopped in England, where officials seized his ship and challenged Dutch claims.

Dutch merchants saw an opportunity to become involved in the fur trade, and the Dutch States-General in 1614 incorporated the New Netherland Company and granted it a monopoly on trading rights along the Hudson River. Most of the company's activity occurred at Fort Nassau, near Albany, but its failure to create a permanent settlement caused its grant, which expired in 1618, not to be renewed. In 1621, the joint-stock West India Company took control of the Dutch claims along the Hudson.

The Dutch West India Company established two main settlements: New Amsterdam on Manhattan Island and Fort Orange near Albany. The first settlers in both were not Dutch; instead, they were French-speaking Belgians called Walloons. The company was more interested in the short-term profits of the fur trade than the long-term profits of settlement and ignored colonization while working to develop a trading relationship with the Iroquois Confederacy.

In 1626, Peter Minuit took control of the colony and quickly brought stability to it by focusing the settlement on the island of Manhattan, which his pre-

The Stadthuys in New Amsterdam (today's New York City) served as the Dutch town hall from 1654 to 1699. Adjacent to the large stone building, at what was then the corner of Pearl Street and Coenties Slip, was the slave market. *(New-York Historical Society, New York/Bridgeman Art Library)*

decessor, Willem Verhulst, had purchased for 60 guilders in trade goods. The Dutch used this purchase to defend their claims to the land from English challenges. In his purchase, Verhulst established the policy that all land the Dutch acquired from the local Native Americans would come through purchase or negotiation and not from expropriation.

Minuit successfully centralized the colony, and, after his removal from office in 1631, the company worked to develop ways to entice settlers into the region. From this, they developed the patroonship system. Each patroon who brought over fifty settlers would receive his own manor along the Hudson River. The patroon would possess great power over his holdings, but while many patroonships were planned, only one, Rensselaerswyck, was actually created. By the late 1630s, the patroonship idea had come to little, and the company began granting more liberties and freedoms, especially economic ones. While this increased freedom expanded economic activity, it did little to increase the number of settlers.

For the next two decades, the colony suffered from

several unpopular governors and from increasing conflict with various neighboring English settlements. In modern Connecticut, the Dutch lost territory to the English, but, to the north, a Dutch-sponsored Iroquois army defeated the Hurons, thus drawing the Great Lakes fur trade away from Montreal to New Netherland.

While Dutch relations with the Iroquois remained stable, under the leadership of Willem Kieft, relations with other tribes deteriorated. Kieft worked to acquire more Native American land, along with the ability to tax indigenous peoples. This led to Kieft's War (1643–1645), the first of three wars against the local Algonquin tribes, which, while brutal and deadly, did not diminish Native American resistance to Dutch settlement. A truce occurred briefly in 1642, but in 1643, the Iroquois attacked the Algonquin along the lower Hudson River, and Kieft, eager to demonstrate his ability as a military leader, led a group of soldiers who massacred eighty people at Pavonia. This caused the Algonquin to unite and wreak devastation throughout the Dutch and English settlements of the region. In reaction, the Dutch fortified New Amsterdam (in the process, constructing a wall on what would become Wall Street). In March 1644, the Dutch attacked the Algonquin at Stamford, where they killed all but eight of 700 warriors. Both sides agreed to peace in 1645.

In 1647, Peter Stuyvesant arrived to replace Kieft, and during his seventeen-year period in office (1647–1664), the colony grew and prospered. One of his most important reforms involved granting local governments more power, but as the colony flourished, it became a growing threat to English interests in North America.

During Stuyvesant's governorship, the Peach War of 1655 began when a Dutch farmer killed a native woman who was stealing peaches. In reaction, 2,000 Native Americans attacked New Amsterdam, causing the Dutch to attack local villages. A fragile peace was soon established.

The final war with the native peoples of the region, the Esposus War (1658–1664), occurred when Native Americans attempted to halt Dutch advances onto their land. The war resulted in an important Algonquin defeat, after which they lost much of their land to the Dutch. In 1667, an English fleet sailed into New Amsterdam's harbor, causing Stuyvesant to surrender the town without firing a shot. But the Dutch and English continued to struggle for control of the territory as a whole, and, in 1673, the Dutch recaptured the land during the third Anglo-Dutch War, only for it to be restored to the English the following year.

The three Anglo-Dutch Wars (1652–1654, 1665–1667, and 1672–1674) diminished Dutch resources and hurt their global position. During this struggle between England and the Netherlands, England passed a series of Navigation Acts designed to curtail Dutch economic power.

The transformation of Dutch New Amsterdam into British New York did not end Dutch influence in the region. During the seventeenth century, New Amsterdam was one of the colonies' most culturally diverse settlements, and it included Walloons, Germans, Norwegians, Englishmen, Native Americans, and African slaves. The British authorities did not force out the Dutch settlers of New Amsterdam, and New York grew not only because of British economic development but also because of its continued ties to the Dutch economy. The settlers of New Amsterdam proved capable of creating a place for themselves within New York.

Ty M. Reese

See also: Dutch West India Company; Fort Orange; Hudson, Henry; New Amsterdam; New Netherland; New York; New York and New Netherland (Chronology); New York City; Stuyvesant, Peter; William III of Orange and Mary II.

Bibliography

Boxer, C. R. *The Dutch in Brazil, 1624–1654.* Oxford, UK: Oxford University Press, 1957.

———. *The Dutch Seaborne Empire, 1600–1800.* New York: Alfred A. Knopf, 1965.

Condon, Thomas J. *New York Beginnings: The Commercial Origins of New Netherland.* New York: New York University Press, 1968.

Israel, Jonathan I. *The Dutch Republic: Its Rise, Greatness and Fall, 1477–1806.* Oxford, UK: Clarendon Press, 1995.

Kammen, Michael. *Colonial New York: A History.* New York: Scribner, 1975.

Dutch West India Company

The Dutch West India Company (West-Indische Compagnie) was a joint-stock company endowed with a monopoly of Dutch business in the Atlantic. Although its success was shorter-lived than that of its famous counterpart in the Eastern hemisphere, the Dutch East India Company (Vereenigde Oost-Indische Compagnie), the West India Company essentially contributed to the development of the Atlantic economy and the colonization of the North American mainland.

The West India Company was founded on July 1, 1621, by governmental edict, whereas the East India Company had started in 1602 as a private merger. Consequently, the state's influence on the governing board of the West India Company was comparatively large, reflecting the political aim in creating this company: to destroy and take over the Spanish and Portuguese trade by conquering their strongholds and settlements. Portugal shared a joint monarchy with Spain from 1580 to 1640, while the Protestant Netherlands had revolted to get out of Spanish Hapsburg's Roman Catholic empire.

The chartering of the West India Company did not initiate Dutch business in the Atlantic, but focused and enforced action, as in 1621 a truce between Spain and the Netherlands had ended. Thus, attacking the Iberian merchants meant not only economic warfare, but also recovering the flow of overseas goods formerly received from the Iberian colonies that had made the Netherlands Europe's main commercial hub.

The seizure of Portuguese territory in eastern

Brazil (Bahia) in 1624 was ended a few months later by Spanish forces. In 1628, the West India Company captured a Spanish silver fleet, providing funds for another conquest. This time, the occupation of northeastern Brazil (Pernambuco), accomplished between 1630 and 1634, lasted longer. As the Brazilian economy was relying on sugar plantations based on slave labor, the Dutch now had to engage in the slave trade. They had already tried this before, but despite driving the Portuguese out of the gold trade on the West African coast, they could not capture the main slave-trading fortress before 1637.

This was the turning point, for the West India Company quickly gained control over the Gold Coast. Enslaving 23,000 people and shipping them to the Americas over the next thirty-five years, the company became the main slave trader of the mid-seventeenth century. But as successful as the brutal slave trade proved to be, the Brazilian occupation proved disappointing in the end. Dutch immigrants stayed away, and the estates remained in the hands of rebellious Portuguese. Although the West India Company massively increased sugar production by establishing proper trading networks, it had to surrender the colony in 1654.

The main Dutch settlement on the North American mainland met a similar fate. In 1609, Henry Hudson, on behalf of the East India Company looking for a western passage to India, missed his way and sailed inland on a waterway later named the Hudson River. Other Dutch expeditions followed. In 1623, the West India Company decided for a settlement in New Netherland, as it would be their only promising possession out of Spanish reach. In 1626, New Amsterdam was founded on an island called Manna-hata on land bought from Native Americans in exchange for goods worth 60 guilders (later mistakenly equated to $24).

New Amsterdam developed into a commercial foothold, rather than a nucleus of a pervaded territory, as the Dutch decided to focus on commerce instead of agriculture. Yet the fur trade was less profitable than expected, so no decisive measures were taken to defend New Amsterdam against the surrounding English colonies, not even when it was invaded in 1664. The town was surrendered without a fight by Governor Peter Stuyvesant. The Dutch recaptured the place in 1673, but they gave it back in 1674 in exchange for the recognition of Suriname as a permanent Dutch colony. New Amsterdam, renamed New York in the 1660s, remained English.

Apart from some small islands such as Curaçao, Suriname remained the only Dutch colony in the Western Hemisphere. Yet this did not diminish the West India Company's presence in the Atlantic, as it maintained its grip on the slave trade. Dutch Atlantic business shifted toward multilateral trade, supplying other colonial powers with slaves and transferring colonial produce to Europe.

Around 1650, the English were able to rapidly build up a sugar plantation economy on Barbados. This so-called sugar revolution marked the transition to a market-oriented Atlantic economy focusing on slave-labor-based growing of tropical crops.

In the onset of mercantilism, the main colonial powers ensured the exclusion of other nations from trade between their colonies and Europe. It was at this point that their small basis of colonies proved fatal to the Dutch. The West India Company was ousted from the slave trade by English competition, went bankrupt, was refounded with a far smaller amount of capital in 1674, and lost its monopoly even on the Dutch slave trade in 1738. It was finally dissolved in 1794.

Alexander Engel

See also: Dutch; Fort Orange; New York City; Slave Trade; Trade.

Bibliography

Emmer, Piet C. "The Dutch and the Making of the Second Atlantic System." In *Slavery and the Rise of the Atlantic System*, edited by Barbara L. Solow. Cambridge, UK: Cambridge University Press, 1991.

———. "The Dutch West India Company, 1621–1792: Dutch or Atlantic?" In *Companies and Trade: Essays on Overseas Trading Companies During the Ancien Régime*, edited by Leonard Blussé and Femme Gaastra. The Hague: Martinus Nijhoff, 1981.

Page, Willie F. *The Dutch Triangle: The Netherlands and the Atlantic Slave Trade, 1621–1664*. New York: Garland, 1997.

General Index

Biographical Index

Geographical Index

Colonial America

An Encyclopedia of Social, Political, Cultural, and Economic History

Volume Three

Edited by James Ciment

With an Introduction by
Michael Zuckerman, University of Pennsylvania

SHARPE REFERENCE

an imprint of M.E. Sharpe, Inc.

SHARPE REFERENCE

Sharpe Reference is an imprint of M.E. Sharpe, Inc.

M.E. Sharpe, Inc.
80 Business Park Drive
Armonk, NY 10504

Cover Photo: Tontine Coffee House, c. 1797 (oil on linen), Francis Guy (1760–1820) / © New York Historical Society, New York, United States; www.bridgeman.co.uk.

Maps: Adapted by Carto-Graphics from the following sources:

Kwame Anthony Appiah and Henry Louis Gates, Jr., eds., *Africana: The Encyclopedia of the African and African American Experience* (New York: Basic Books, 1999). See map: Volume 3, page 788.

Geoffrey Barraclough, ed., *The Times Atlas of World History,* 6th edition (Maplewood, NJ: Hammond, 1982). See maps: Volume 1, pages xlii, xliii, 15, 214; Volume 2, pages xx, xxi; Volume 3, pages xx, xxi; Volume 4, pages xx, xxi, 850; Volume 5, pages xx, xxi.

James Ciment, ed. *Encyclopedia of American Immigration* (Armonk, NY: M.E. Sharpe, 2001). See map: Volume 1, page 55.

James Henretta, et al. *America's History.* 2nd edition (New York: Worth Publishers, 1993). See maps: Volume 1, pages xli, xlii, xliii, 59; Volume 2, pages xix, xx, xxi, 327, 362; Volume 3, pages xix, xx, xxi, 581, 738, 788; Volume 4, pages xix, xx, xxi; Volume 5, pages xix, xx, xxi.

Mary Beth Norton, et al. *A People and a Nation.* 6th edition (Boston: Houghton Mifflin, 2001). See maps: Volume 1, pages xliv, xlv; Volume 2, pages xxii, xxiii, 324; Volume 3, pages xxii, xxiii, 812; Volume 4, pages xxii, xxiii.

Library of Congress Cataloging-in-Publication Data

Colonial America: An encyclopedia of social, political, cultural, and economic history/James Ciment, editor.
  p. cm.
  Includes bibliographical references and index.
  ISBN 0-7656-8065-3 (Set: alk. paper)
  1. United States—Civilization—To 1783—Encyclopedias. I. Ciment, James.

E162.C68 2005
973.2′03—dc22   2003023235

Printed and bound in the United States of America

The paper used in this publication meets the minimum requirements of
American National Standard for Information Sciences
Permanence of Paper for Printed Library Materials,
ANSI Z 39.48.1984.

MV (c) 10 9 8 7 6 5 4 3 2 1

Publisher: Myron E. Sharpe
Vice President and Editorial Director: Patricia Kolb
Vice President and Production Director: Carmen Chetti
Executive Editor and Manager of Reference: Todd Hallman
Senior Development Editor: Jeff Hacker
Project Editor: Laura Brengelman
Program Coordinator: Cathleen J. Prisco
Text Design: Carmen Chetti and Jesse Sanchez
Cover Design: Jesse Sanchez

Contents

❧ ～ ❧

iii

Indexes

List of Maps

Topic Finder

Biographies

Religion

Bible
Bradford, William
Calvinism
Catholic Church
Christ and Christianity
Covenants
Cromwell, Oliver
Deism
Dominicans
Edict of Nantes, Revocation of
Education
Education, Higher
Edwards, Jonathan
English Civil War
Franciscans
God
Great Awakening
Huguenots
Hutchinson, Anne
Jesuits
Jews
Las Casas, Bartolomé de
Marquette, Jacques
Mather, Cotton
Mather, Increase
Methodist Church
Ministers and the Ministry
Missions
Of Plymouth Plantation
Pietism
Pilgrims
Praying Towns
Presbyterianism
Puritanism
Quakers
Reformation
Religion (Chronology)
Religion (Essay)
Religions, African
Religions, Native American
Sermons
Serra, Fray Junípero
Shakers
Slave Communities and Culture
Whitefield, George
Williams, Roger
Witchcraft and Witch Trials

Spanish Colonies

Acapulco
Armada, Spanish

Borderlands, Spanish
Cabrillo, Juan Rodríguez
California
Canary Islands
Caribbean (Chronology)
Caribbean Sea
Catholic Church
Charles V
Columbian Exchange
Columbus, Christopher
Coronado, Francisco Vázquez de
Cortéz, Hernando
Cuba
De Soto, Hernando
Dominicans
Ferdinand and Isabella
Florida
Franciscans
Government, Spanish Colonial
Hispaniola
Jamaica
Jesuits
King George's War
Las Casas, Bartolomé de
Menéndez de Avilés, Pedro
Mexico City
Missions
Mississippi River
Native American–European Conflict
Native American–European Relations
New Mexico
New Orleans
New Spain
Philip II
Piracy
Ponce de León, Juan
Precious Metals
Puerto Rico
Queen Anne's War
Santa Fe
Serra, Fray Junípero
Slavery, Caribbean
St. Augustine
Texas
Tordesillas, Treaty of (1494)
Vespucci, Amerigo

Women and Gender Issues

Adams, Abigail
Alexander, Mary Spratt Provoost
Anne, Queen

Maps

ARCTIC OCEAN

BERING
SEA

INUIT

ALEUT

TLINGIT

HAIDA

TSIMSHIAN

SALISH

NOOTKA

PACIFIC

OCEAN

INUIT

DENE

DOGRIB

CHIPEWYAN

CREE

BLACKFOOT

KOOTENAI

CROW

NEZ
PERCE

CHEYENNE

PAIUTE
SHOSHONE

POMO

YOKUT

UTE

NAVAJO

PUEBLO HOPI PUEBLO
PAPAGO

APACHE
PUEBLO

COCHIMI
PIMA

ZACATEC

Zacatecas
TOLTEC
Guadalajara
Tenocutitúan
(Mexico City)
NAHUATL
(AZTEC)
Acapulco

INUIT

Hudson
Bay

ASSINIBOINE

OJIBWA
(CHIPPEWA)

DAKOTA
(SIOUX)

PAWNEE

IOWA

ARAPAHO

KIOWA

COMANCHE

Rio Grande
River

COAHUILTEC

Gulf of
Mexico

MIXTEC
ZAPOTEC
Guatemala

CREE

SAUK

OTTAWA
POTAWATOMI

ILLINOIS

ALGONQUIN

HURON
IROQUOIS

SHAWNEE

NATCHEZ

CHOCTAW

Vera Cruz

MAYA

MISKITO

INUIT

NASKAPI

MONTAGNAIS

MICMAC

ABENAKI

MOHAWK
ONONDAGA
CAYUGA
SENECA
ONEIDA
ERIE
SUSQUEHANNOCK
LENNI LENAPE (DELAWARE)

POWHATAN

TUSCARORA
Roanoke (English, 1587)

CHEROKEE
CHICKASAW

YAMASEE
CREEK
St. Augustine

CALUSA
SEMINOLE

LUCAYO

Havana
CIBONEY
ARAWAK

Mérida

BEOTHUK

NARRAGANSETT
PEQUOT

ATLANTIC

OCEAN

SUB TAINO
TAINO
Santo Domingo

ARAWAK

CARIB

CARIBBEAN SEA

CUNA
GUAYMI Panama

Spanish

0   500   1000 Miles

0   500   1000 Kilometers

North America, 1600. The above map shows the multiplicity of native peoples on the North American continent in 1600, as well as the extensive Spanish presence in Mexico, Central America, the Caribbean, and southwestern portions of what is now the United States. Note that the English colony of Roanoke mysteriously disappeared shortly after its establishment in 1587. *(Carto-Graphics)*

North America, 1700. The above map shows the presence of European colonial powers on the North American continent circa 1700. Note that the presence of Europeans varied: British holdings in the Hudson Bay region were little more than claims on maps, while settlements along the Atlantic seaboard of what is now the United States included tens of thousands of European settlers and African slaves, as well as the remaining native peoples. *(Carto-Graphics)*

ARCTIC OCEAN

BERING
SEA

INUIT

ALEUT

INUIT

INUIT

DENE

Hudson
Bay

TLINGIT

DOGRIB

INUIT

HAIDA

CHIPEWYAN

NASKAPI

TSIMSHIAN
Disputed
by Russia
and Spain

CREE

MONTAGNAIS

BEOTHUK

SALISH

BLACKFOOT

NOOTKA

KOOTENAI

ASSINIBOINE

CREE

ALGONQUIN

MICMAC

Quebec

NEZ
PERCE

CROW

OJIBWA
(CHIPPEWA)

Montreal

ABENAKI

Halifax

HURON

PACIFIC

CHEYENNE

DAKOTA
(SIOUX)

SAUK

OTTAWA

MOHAWK
ONONDAGA
CAYUGA
SENECA

Boston

NARRAGANSETT

PAWNEE

IROQUOIS
TUSCARORA

PEQUOT

OCEAN

POMO

PAIUTE

SHOSHONE

IOWA

POTAWATOMI
ERIE

ONEIDA
New York

SUSQUEHANNOCK

Philadelphia

YOKUT

UTE

ILLINOIS

Ohio River

Baltimore

LENNI LENAPE (DELAWARE)

POWHATAN

ARAPAHO

SHAWNEE

ATLANTIC

NAVAJO

KIOWA

CHEROKEE

OCEAN

PAPAGO

PUEBLO
HOPI PUEBLO

Santa Fe

CHICKASAW

Charles Town

APACHE
PUEBLO

COMANCHE

NATCHEZ

YAMASEE

COCHIMI

PIMA

CREEK

St. Augustine

COAHUILTEC

CHOCTAW

New Orleans

CALUSA

ZACATEC

Gulf of
Mexico

SEMINOLE

LUCAYO

British

Zacatecas

CIBONEY

Havana

SUB TAINO

ARAWAK

British

TOLTEC

Guadalajara

ARAWAK

TAINO

CARIB

Mexico City

Vera Cruz

Mérida

French

Santo Domingo

French

NAHUATL
(AZTEC)

MIXTEC

MAYA

CARIBBEAN SEA

Dutch

Acapulco

ZAPOTEC

MISKITO

CUNA

GUAYMI

Spanish
British
French
Russian

0   500   1000 Miles
0   500   1000 Kilometers

North America, 1775. The above map shows the presence of European colonial powers on the North American continent on the eve of the American Revolution. Note that some regions—particularly in the heart of Mexico and along the Atlantic seaboard of what is now the United States—were more heavily populated by colonists than other areas. *(Carto-Graphics)*

European Settlement Areas, Eastern North America, 1650. The above map shows the thin line of European settlements along the Atlantic seaboard and the St. Lawrence River Valley. At the time, the total European and African populations in the British colonies stood at about 50,000, with a few thousand more in the Dutch, French, and Spanish colonies. *(Carto-Graphics)*

British Colonies, Mainland North America, 1765. By 1750, British settlements on mainland North America had pushed westward to the eastern edge of the Appalachian Mountains. The population of the thirteen colonies in 1750 was roughly 1.2 million, including about a quarter of a million slaves. *(Carto-Graphics)*

Colonial America

Volume Three

N

Natchez

Located on a high bluff overlooking the lower Mississippi River in present-day Mississippi, colonial settlement at Natchez existed on the far fringes of the colonial Atlantic world. Consequently, claims to Natchez and its surrounding hinterlands shifted between Native American and European powers through the eighteenth century. In 1798, the United States incorporated "Natchez Country" into the newly formed Mississippi Territory.

The Natchez Indians who inhabited the bluff were descendants of larger, more centralized nations of the lower Mississippi Valley, which had fragmented into a host of smaller tribes and nations in the 1500s because of disease, warfare between native peoples, and Spanish raids. Like other native nations in the lower Mississippi Valley, the Natchez engaged in mixed agriculture, hunting, and the small-scale trading of deerskins. In the late 1600s, English traders operating out of Charles Town, South Carolina, arrived in the area. This led to a dramatic growth in the deerskin trade and intense competition between Native Americans, who now sought to expand their hunting grounds at the expense of their rivals.

In 1714, French colonial officials made a concerted effort to erect a settlement, fort, and trading post at Natchez to expand their influence in the lower Mississippi Valley. Strategically located between Canada and the Illinois Country to the north, Louisiana and the Gulf Coast to the south, and the Native Americans and fur trade of the lower Mississippi Valley, Natchez became an important trading center in the 1720s. Over 300 Africans, many of whom were slaves, 400 Europeans, and perhaps 1,600 Natchez Indians lived in Natchez during this period. Joining them were scores of native and European traders, who periodically met at Natchez to barter and exchange. In addition to the nearly 50,000 deerskins passing through Natchez annually in the mid-1720s, the Natchez District's mixed population produced substantial quantities of wheat and tobacco, along with smaller amounts of rice, indigo, cotton, tar, and silk for exchange at Natchez or downriver in New Orleans.

In 1728, Sieur Etcheparre De Chepart, an ambitious commandant, assumed command of the French fort at Natchez. Relations between the French and the Natchez rapidly deteriorated after Chepart ordered the natives to evacuate a village where he planned to establish a tobacco plantation. A group of Natchez chiefs negotiated a settlement allowing them to remain in their village until harvest. To show their gratitude, they promised that each family would provide the French commandant with a "basket of corn and a fowl" at the end of the harvest.

The Natchez then quickly laid plans to revolt against the French and drive them from the area. With the assistance of African slaves, the Natchez planned to "cut off the French to a man." On November 28, 1729, the Native Americans arrived in Natchez—ostensibly to pay tribute to the French commandant. At day's end, 145 Frenchmen, 36 women, and 56 children lay dead, while 300 African slaves and 50 French women and children became Natchez captives.

This massacre effectively ended French plans to build plantations around Natchez. It also led to the demise of the Natchez people by the 1740s. The French joined with the Choctaw nation—who welcomed the chance to destroy this rival—to wage war against the Natchez Indians, forcing them to give up their settlements around Natchez. By the 1740s, the French and Choctaws had effectively destroyed the Natchez.

After the Natchez Rebellion, the settlement on the bluff remained sparsely inhabited. From the 1730s through the 1750s, most of the French colonists in the lower Mississippi Valley lived between New Orleans and Point Coupee to the south. The French maintained a garrison of fifty or so troops among the roughly fifty families who remained at Natchez. Native and European traders sometimes traded with the soldiers and settlers, but the small settlement remained but a shadow of the thriving trading center of the 1720s.

In 1763, Britain gained control of Natchez from the French as a result of the Great War for Empire, incorporating the region into the province of West Florida. The British offered large land grants to encourage settlement, and the Anglo-American and enslaved African population around Natchez grew steadily. With the onset of the American War for Independence, the British encouraged loyalists to settle around Natchez, and many brought slaves with them. By 1780, perhaps 5,000 loyalists and 1,200 slaves inhabited Natchez and the surrounding plantations.

In 1783, Spain claimed control of the disputed Natchez region under the Treaty of Paris. Hoping to counteract American claims on the region, the Spanish encouraged American settlement and loyalty to the Spanish government by providing generous land grants, bounties for staples such as tobacco, and free access to the slave trade. Under Spanish rule, Anglo-American planters laid the groundwork for the rapid expansion of a plantation society. The introduction of Eli Whitney's cotton gin in 1793, which Natchez planters copied in 1795, spurred this expansion.

The 1795 Treaty of San Lorenzo ceded the lands north of the 31st parallel to the United States, bringing Natchez and the newly created Mississippi Territory under American control in 1798. The plantation economy around Natchez grew steadily, though Choctaw resistance, the constant threat of war and disorder from the Spanish and British, and uncertainty over land claims slowed the migration of American planters. American victory in the War of 1812 weakened the native nations of the old Southwest, while solidifying American power in the lower Mississippi Valley.

After 1815, planters from the Atlantic states poured into Natchez and the Mississippi Territory. The expansion of their plantations finally led to the forced removal of the Choctaws in the 1830s, during the presidency of Andrew Jackson. By then, Natchez's stately mansions, thriving slave markets, and grand plantations had made it the epitome of the antebellum cotton kingdom.

John Craig Hammond

See also: French Colonies on Mainland North America (Chronology); Native American–European Conflict; Native American–European Relations; Native Americans.

Bibliography

Clayton, James D. *Antebellum Natchez.* Baton Rouge: Louisiana State University Press, 1968.

Usner, Daniel H. *American Indians in the Lower Mississippi Valley: Social and Economic Histories.* Lincoln: University of Nebraska Press, 1998.

———. *Indians, Settlers, & Slaves in a Frontier Exchange Economy: The Lower Mississippi Valley before 1783.* Chapel Hill: Published by the University of North Carolina Press for the Institute of Early American History and Culture in Williamsburg, Virginia, 1992.

Native American–African American Relations

The centuries-long interaction between African Americans and Native Americans is one of the least researched and least understood chapters in American race relations. Native American–African American relations in the West, particularly in the nineteenth and twentieth centuries, have been the subject of serious scholarly inquiry. The colonial period, however, remains woefully understudied as compared to ethnic divisions within the white population, African-European relations, and interactions between Native Americans and European Americans.

Africans were among the earliest explorers of North America. Esteban, a slave in the service in the service of the Spanish, accompanied Cabeza de Vaca on his overland journey from Florida to Mexico. In fact, Africans accompanied nearly all of the Spanish expeditions through the American Southeast. They served as slaves alongside Tainos on Hispaniola as early as 1510. Native Americans and Africans also worked side by side in the mining operations of Spanish Mexico.

Outside of Latin America, the North American Southeast was the only place where large numbers of Africans, Native Americans, and Europeans came together for an extended period of time. The attitudes of Native Americans toward African Americans varied widely, from friendliness to tentative acceptance to outright hostility, depending on the tribe and the historical context of the contact. For example, in 1752, Catawbas expressed great resentment at the presence of a single African American in their nation. Native Americans were also employed as a sort of police force, keeping Carolina's growing slave population from running away to Spanish Florida and freedom.

From the earliest European explorations and slave imports, Native Americans and Africans came together in large numbers. While little studied by historians, relations between the two groups are known to have included marriage, as between this African American man and native woman in Mexico. *(Museo de America, Madrid, Spain/Giraudon/Bridgeman Art Library)*

In many cases, whites tried to keep Native Americans and African Americans separated, fearing that Native Americans could turn African Americans against their white owners and that African Americans could interfere with their plans to dominate the local native tribes. In addition, in many places, such as South Carolina, an English minority coexisted with large populations of Native Americans and African Americans, both of which had justification to hate the English. So it made good political sense to separate the two as much as possible. In 1758, outgoing South Carolina governor James Glen explained to incoming governor William Lyttelton that "it has always been the policy of this government to create an aversion in them [Native Americans] to Negroes."

In spite of white attempts to separate them, Native Americans and Africans, particularly in the Southeast, did form bonds, whether through intermarriage or through shared work experience. The segregationist policies of the late nineteenth and twentieth centuries, however, have made relations between African Americans and Native Americans even harder to uncover.

Southern Native Americans, already suffering from racial prejudice, did not wish to be subjected to Jim Crow laws and went to great lengths to prove that they were not of African ancestry.

The best place to look for the relationship between Africans and Native Americans is in colonial slave quarters. During the early years of English colonization, most African imports were men, while the typical Native American slave was a female. One early colonial tract boasted that a man of modest means could succeed in Carolina with 150 acres of land, one male African slave, and one female Native American slave. Since the Church of England rarely sanctioned slave marriages, whatever the ethnicity of the parties, records of Native American–African intermarriage are few and far between. The English did use the term "zambo" to describe the offspring of these unions.

The cultural influence of Native Americans on African Americans is hard to gauge, especially in cases where similar practices—such as making baskets and canoes—existed in both cultures prior to contact. But Africans brought rice culture to the American South, and, in doing so, changed the diet and agricultural practices of Native Americans. In return, some types of foods that today fall under the category of "soul food," such as grits and corn bread, can be traced to Native Americans, as can a wide range of folk medicines made of native plants and animals. In addition, excavations on slave cabins have unearthed an astounding array of artifacts of both Native American and African origins, such as pipes, bowls, and beads, which indicate an expansive exchange of material culture.

Some Native Americans, particularly the Creek and Cherokee, owned African slaves, although the practice was never particularly widespread. Some groups, such as the Seminole of Florida, did not force African slaves to labor on plantations, but rather allowed them to live in autonomous communities so long as they paid tribute to the Seminole. Interracial communities (also known as "triracial isolates"), which blended African American, Native American, and white heritages, such as the Shinnecock, Montauk, and Mashpee in the North and Lumbee, Melungeon, and Brass Ankle in the South, further testify to the lasting interaction between these groups.

Though the history of African-Native interaction has yet to be written in any comprehensive way, the preliminary findings threaten to change traditional conceptions of colonial life. One of the main shifts will likely be the recognition that, in addition to maintaining cultural practices from West Africa, African slaves in the Southeast were profoundly influenced by Native Americans.

Matthew Jennings

See also: African Americans; Native Americans; Native Americans and Slavery; Slavery, African American.

Bibliography

Forbes, Jack D. *Africans and Native Americans: The Language of Race and the Evolution of Red-Black Peoples.* 2nd ed. Urbana: University of Illinois Press, 1993.

Foster, Laurence. "Negro-Indian Relationships in the Southeast." Ph.D. dissertation, University of Pennsylvania, 1935.

Littlefield, Daniel F., Jr. *Africans and Creeks: From the Colonial Period to the Civil War.* Westport, CT: Greenwood, 1979.

Porter, Kenneth Wiggins. "Relations Between Negroes and Indians Within the Present Limits of the United States." *Journal of Negro History* 17 (1932): 287–367.

Willis, William S. "Divide and Rule: Red, White, and Black in the Southeast." *Journal of Negro History* 48:3 (July 1963): 157–76.

Native American–European Conflict

Although Europeans and Native Americans interacted in many different ways over their centuries of colonial contact, the most striking and, arguably, the most pervasive was in the context of warfare. Colonial wars touched every part of North America east of the Mississippi and occurred from the beginnings of European colonization in the Caribbean and Mexico through the era of the American War for Independence.

Sixteenth Century: Wars of European Conquest

Native American–European conflicts in the 1500s were generally affairs of military conquest, but, on occasion, smaller conflicts broke out. Trade, which would become a leading cause of conflict between cultures in the centuries to come, was not really a factor at this early date.

The most famous conflict of the sixteenth century was Hernando Cortéz's conquest of central Mexico between 1519 and 1521. Cortéz had superior technology in the form of muskets, but their effect in combat was extremely limited, especially when facing an enemy as numerous as the Aztec people. Rather, Cortéz owed his success to the alliance of other enemies of the Aztec, particularly from the city of Tlaxcala. Epidemic diseases from Europe that swept through Tenochtitlán also aided the Spanish. After initially being repelled by a superior Aztec force, Cortéz regrouped and returned, conquering the Aztec easily.

Other campaigns conducted farther to the north were much less spectacular, perhaps because other Spaniards failed to follow Cortéz's lead. Juan Ponce de León—in search of gold, slaves, and a magical "fountain of youth"—landed near Tampa Bay with only a small party of Spanish invaders (without the aid of native allies) and was promptly shot. He returned to Cuba, where he died of his wounds.

Similarly, Hernando de Soto wrought havoc throughout the southeastern portion of what would later become the United States. He succeeded in spreading disease and terrifying native populations wherever he went, but he failed to find much treasure and lost his life in the process. Native peoples, most of whom still fought in a style reminiscent of the Mississippians (limited goals and prolonged skirmishes, with a heavy

An etching from the 1580s (based on the first-hand account of colonist John White) depicts the Native American village of Pomeiooc near the Roanoke settlement. While surrounded by poles stuck in the ground, native settlements in the region were poorly fortified and vulnerable to attack. *(Brown Brothers, Sterling, Pennsylvania)*

emphasis on surprise), succeeded in pushing the explorer out of their respective territories. A pitched battle took place at Mabila, a fortified town in central Alabama in 1540. While the Spanish suffered many casualties, they did manage to repel a force of Tuscaloosas.

Francisco Vásquez de Coronado encountered similar problems in his expedition into the American Southwest. Unable to find gold or allies, he marched as far north and east as Kansas but was forced to return with little to show.

It bears mentioning that the Spanish rarely intended genocide. They would have preferred that Native Americans remain alive and labor for them in mines, missions, and farms. Unfortunately, disease, warfare, slavery, and dislocation disrupted native lifeways so severely that genocide was often the result. The clearest example of this was the island of Hispaniola, which may have boasted a population of millions before the Spanish invasion. After less than a century of colonization, it was left with a native population of zero.

1600 to 1675: Wars for Trade and Territory

In the 1600s, new forms of violence erupted for new reasons. Trade became increasingly important as a cause of war. Also, in North America, Native Americans and Europeans, particularly the English, had begun to compete for land and resources. Over the course of the seventeenth century, conflicts flared in Canada, Virginia, and New England. The Southeast experienced a slightly lower level of violence, if only because smaller numbers of Europeans had settled in the region. Pennsylvania's frontier also largely escaped violence because of small native populations and the diplomacy of William Penn in the colony's earliest years.

From 1603 to 1615, Samuel de Champlain established alliances with the Huron in the St. Lawrence Valley, believing that both groups could profit from the fur trade. He was right, but his actions had deadly consequences for the Huron. The Iroquois, who were becoming the major military power in the region (especially after they had been armed by the Dutch), conducted a series of operations in Huronia in the 1640s that almost entirely eliminated the Huron.

Like most people, the Iroquois also went to war for cultural reasons. Through "mourning wars," the Iroquois sought to avenge the deaths of relatives and clan members who had been victims of war or disease. Often, captives were adopted into the Iroquois tribe. In the "Beaver Wars," the Iroquois killed many Hurons, adopted many, and sent the remainder fleeing to the Great Lakes region. As a result of the conflict, the Iroquois became the preeminent Native American group in the Northeast.

The Powhatan in Virginia encountered a different kind of enemy. In the late sixteenth and early seventeenth centuries, Powhatan, a paramount chief, had come to control most of the eastern half of Virginia through diplomacy and intimidation. In 1607, the English appeared at Jamestown, and Powhatan adopted them, he believed, as another tributary village. The English, however, did not recognize this and began to settle outside of the area given them by Powhatan; they also pressed native means of subsistence by stealing corn and other resources. In order to teach the English how to behave, the Powhatan conducted a series of raids from 1610 to 1614. More serious conflict erupted in 1622 and 1644, when the Powhatan (in these cases, under the leadership of Opechancanough, Powhatan's brother) again tried to stop English expansion and curb

English abuses. In these conflicts, the English used the attacks as pretexts for wars of extermination. What they lacked in military power they made up for in cruelty.

In New England, the English settlement at Plymouth in 1620 posed little threat to Massasoit, the Wampanoag leader, and, for a time relations in the area were peaceful. But the settlement of tens of thousands of zealous Puritans on Massachusetts Bay in the decades that followed presented a more significant threat.

Tensions flared in 1636 and 1637 in the Connecticut River Valley. The Pequot had been among the more powerful native groups in the region but had fallen on hard times and run afoul of the English, who were spreading into the valley to trade and farm. This proved a lethal combination, and the combined forces of Plymouth, Massachusetts Bay, the Wampanoag, and the Narragansett attacked the Pequot. The main action involved the wholesale slaughter of 500 to 1,000 Pequot noncombatants at a fort on the Mystic River in 1637. Puritans horrified their allies by setting fire to the fort and killing men, women, and children as they ran out. The treaty that stopped the war provided for the remaining Pequot to be dispersed among other tribes and sold into slavery. They were also no longer allowed to use the term "Pequot" to describe themselves.

The lessons of the seventeenth century were clear to both Native Americans and Europeans. Europeans, in most cases, had to use Native American allies to accomplish their goals of obtaining trade and territory. Native Americans, for their part, realized that they could not remain isolated and independent. They needed European firearms and therefore allied with one of the competing colonial powers in increasing numbers. The term "Indian war" does not apply to any of the conflicts over North America in the colonial period. The native peoples fought on both sides of these battles.

1675 to 1783: Wars for Survival, Wars for Empire

The end of the seventeenth century brought another major shift to conflict between Native Americans and Europeans. By this time, a permanent presence of Europeans on the Eastern seaboard of America had been achieved. As European power increased, Native Americans made tough choices about their allies, whom they would fight, and when they would fight—all with a mind to surviving the colonial onslaught. The battles over Virginia, New England, and the Southeast reflect this shifting colonial reality. As the eighteenth century progressed, England and France, and finally England's colonies, squared off against one another in a battle for the heart of North America.

Bacon's Rebellion has been portrayed as playing a number of roles in the drama of colonial Virginia. It has been cast as a race war, a battle over patronage, and a fight between the tidewater establishment and the underrepresented backcountry. Its relation to Anglo–Native American conflict is of more importance to the current discussion.

Virginia and its native neighbors had been at peace since the 1640s. Increased English settlement and disgruntlement among the native peoples exploded into a vicious war in 1675 and 1676. A group of Doeg Indians, upset with a crooked planter, began to attack white settlements on the frontier. Neighboring planters launched a retaliatory strike against the Doeg, but they killed some Susquehannocks (who had been allied with Virginia). The Susquehannock responded in kind, striking settlements on the western edge of Virginia and Maryland. Frontier planters, under the leadership of Nathaniel Bacon, raised a sizable army and began to attack any Native Americans they could find. The results were devastating, and though Bacon's Rebellion failed to reform Virginia government, it made one fact abundantly clear: Even if the king and the governor preferred peaceful relationships, colonists could annihilate Native Americans.

At approximately the same time as Bacon's Rebellion, King Philip (Massasoit's son, Metacom) was inspiring Native Americans to fight English encroachment, both physical and cultural, in southern New England. By 1675, the Puritans numbered 60,000 and had taken an increased interest in converting the native peoples to Christianity. Young Wamapanoag men in particular had grown increasingly uncomfortable with the English. The years between 1637 and 1675 witnessed a lengthy period of peace between the English and the Wamapanoag. In 1675, however, Metacom's forces attacked the English settlements at Plymouth. Soon, other native communities saw the chance to inflict pain on the English, and the conflict exploded into a regional war.

Native Americans dominated the early stages of the war, destroying a number of towns on the Massachusetts frontier. In 1676, food shortages, as well as an alliance between New York and the Mohawks, convinced most Native Americans to give up the fight. Metacom himself was killed in the summer of that year. This was basically the last gasp for the native peoples of southern New England. Many sought refuge among the Iroquois. Still others went to live in "praying towns"—early reservations set up for the purpose of Christianizing natives.

The Southeast, which had largely escaped conflict in the late seventeenth century, became a bloody battleground in the early eighteenth century. Native Americans found themselves wedged in between three European rivals. The crumbling Spanish Empire maintained a presence in the form of missions in central Florida and the Gulf Coast. The French controlled Louisiana, and the English at Charles Town had established a wide-ranging trade in deerskins, firearms, native slaves, and cloth.

In the early decades of the eighteenth century, several major wars broke out. The Tuscarora War (1711–1715) erupted when the Tuscarora, upset by the expansion of North Carolina, struck settlements along the Neuse River, killing 130 Swiss, German, and English colonists. Although North Carolina's colonial forces were unable to respond, South Carolina sent an army of 500 Native Americans and a handful of whites and African Americans to stop the Tuscarora. This attack succeeded in capturing slaves and plundering several Tuscarora towns. Later, in 1712, a larger force of Cherokees fighting with South Carolina defeated the Tuscarora. The defeated Tuscarora migrated northward to New York, where they became the Sixth Nation of the Iroquois in 1722.

In 1715, the Yamasee, and in fact most of the native peoples in the Southeast, launched a furious assault on South Carolina. The war began because English settlements were expanding and Carolina traders were driving the Yamasee more and more into debt. The Yamasee and Creek managed to drive the line of settlement to within 30 miles of Charles Town, but the English and their Cherokee allies fought back. The Yamasee retreated to the protection of Spanish Florida.

Imperial conflict began to reshape the Southeast early in the eighteenth century. Chickasaws who were allied with the Carolina traders fought French-allied Choctaws. Joint Carolina-native armies seriously weakened the Spanish mission system in 1704, when they burned Apalachee, its most prosperous province, and carried hundreds of mission natives off into slavery.

The Seven Years' War—which, in America, lasted from 1754 to 1763 and was known as the French and Indian War—expanded on earlier types of war, but it was also a new kind of conflict. Although the war erupted in America, it originated in London and France, where the two major imperial powers forced a show-

down over North America, and it was fought all over the world.

The French had become worried that they were losing the continent of North America to Great Britain. In the 1750s, they and their native allies (mainly from the Great Lakes region) began to assault frontier outposts in the Ohio River Valley. These early attacks were a great success, and, by 1754, a joint French-native venture had established Fort Duquesne (present-day Pittsburgh). The British Empire struck back, though their initial attempts at retaliation were ineffective. In 1755, for instance, a major British army was routed by a much smaller French and Native American force near Fort Duquesne.

Native Americans at the outskirts of Virginia and Pennsylvania seized the opportunity to block colonial expansion. At one point, the fighting ranged within about 30 miles of Philadelphia, the largest English city in America. To sum up, 70,000 French colonists and their native allies had attacked British North America, with a population of around 1.5 million, and had beaten them badly.

Native Americans played a crucial role in turning things around for the British. William Pitt, the new British prime minister, began to pour extraordinary amounts of money and resources into the conflict. The Iroquois, who had remained neutral, were persuaded to join the British. After 1759, the Iroquois-British alliance won major victory after major victory, taking Montreal and Quebec by the early 1760s and finally forcing the French to surrender their claim to North America.

The last "Indian war" of the colonial period was the War for Independence, and it was a disaster for Native Americans. A few groups sided with the Americans, but most native communities, sensing that an independent America would overrun what remained of their land, sided with the British. In the aftermath of the war, it made no difference what side Native Americans had fought on. The American Revolution spurred a new wave of white settlement in the Ohio River Valley, the Midwest, and the South, and this expansion brought with it a new wave of violence.

Matthew Jennings

See also: Bacon's Rebellion; Beaver Wars; French and Indian War; Furs; Military and Diplomatic Affairs (Chronology); Military and Diplomatic Affairs (Essay); Militias; Native American–European Relations; Native Americans; Revolutionary War; Tuscarora War; Yamasee War.

Bibliography

Calloway, Colin G. *New Worlds for All: Indians, Europeans, and the Remaking of Early America.* Baltimore: Johns Hopkins University Press, 1997.

Gleach, Frederic W. *Powhatan's World and Colonial Virginia: A Conflict of Cultures.* Lincoln: University of Nebraska Press, 1997.

Jennings, Francis. "Wars: Colonial Era." In *Encyclopedia of North American Indians,* edited by Frederick E. Hoxie, 668–70. Boston: Houghton Mifflin, 1996.

Nash, Gary B. *Red, White and Black: The Peoples of Early North America.* Upper Saddle River, NJ: Prentice Hall, 2000.

Native American– European Relations

Native America in 1500 was a stunningly diverse place. Native peoples had adapted to their environment for more than 10,000 years. They formed complex societies with their own worldviews, methods of exchange, and expressions of spirituality and art. Varying greatly in size, these societies included the small, kin-based communities of the Plains and autonomous villages in the Eastern woodlands; centralized mound-building cultures along the Mississippi and in the Southeast; and large tributary empires such as that of the Aztec in Mexico's central valley.

Europeans, who first arrived in significant numbers in the sixteenth century, brought sweeping historic changes to these native communities. However, the speed and depth of the changes varied enormously, depending on when, where, and under what circumstances Native Americans met Europeans. By the end of the eighteenth century, colonial America had been thoroughly reshaped by the interaction between diverse groups of Native Americans and Europeans.

Early Contact

Although some Native Americans—such as the Taino, Aztec, Timucuan, and Pueblo peoples—met European explorers face to face, many more groups experienced their early presence through new trade goods and the diseases brought unwittingly by the Europeans. Disease was a serious killer of Native Americans throughout the colonial period, but perhaps never more so than in the earliest years of contact. Some estimates place the population of North America north of the Rio Grande at 5 to 7 million in 1492. By 1900, this number was around 250,000.

While disease colored interaction between Europeans and Native Americans, it was not the only factor that brought about the precipitous decline in native populations. The short- and long-term effects of colonization—dislocation, war, and psychological trauma—should not be overlooked.

Early contacts between Native Americans and Europeans ran the gamut from peaceful trading partnerships to skepticism of each other's intentions and outright warfare. The Spanish were the first Europeans to take a serious interest in North America. Having successfully emerged from the *Reconquista* (their campaign to remove the Moors from the Iberian Peninsula), they demonstrated a burning desire to convert natives to Christianity at the same time as they exhibited a lust for conquest and treasure.

The first attempts by the Spanish to explore and colonize north of the Rio Grande can be seen as little more than a series of miserable failures. In Florida, Ponce de León searched fruitlessly for gold and slaves and was shot and mortally wounded by local natives in 1521. In 1528, Pánfilo de Narváez's voyage to the Gulf of Mexico ended in tragedy: most of his party died and a handful of survivors walked overland for six years until they reached Mexico.

The *entradas* of Francisco Vázquez de Coronado in the Southwest (1540–1543) and Hernando de Soto in the Southeast (1539–1542) were larger and more adequately funded. They fared slightly better but did not improve the sorry state of Native American–Spanish relations in North America. De Soto, for instance, would move through various chiefdoms in search of gold, taking headmen and women hostages, looting graves, and shooting resisters or throwing them to war dogs as examples. He faced not only constant harassment, but, in 1540 at Mabila (in central Alabama), he nearly lost a pitched battle to Tuscaloosa warriors. Coronado pushed his way through Pueblo country and reached western Kansas in search of mythical golden cities. Finding none, he battled his way back to Mexico.

If the Spanish were mainly concerned with extracting precious metals and using native labor to do it, the French were mainly concerned with removing another sort of wealth: beaver fur. Accordingly, early contacts with the French in Canada were somewhat less hostile. Jacques Cartier traveled up the St. Lawrence River from 1534 to 1541 and established a fur trade that would profit the French and the tribes that joined them for many years.

French traders, and later settlers, were overwhelmingly men. They established themselves in native communities and, with their native wives and partners, created a substantial number of biracial offspring, known in Canada as the Métis people. Although there were intimate physical relationships between Europeans and natives in all parts of North America, they were far more common in areas settled by the French and Spanish.

Planting Colonies and Missions

As the sixteenth century gave way to the seventeenth, Europeans came to America in increasing numbers and with a wider range of goals. For native-white relations, the most important of these was the founding of permanent European colonies in North America, often on the basis of religion. And as these settlements expanded, violence often erupted along their frontiers.

Under Juan de Oñate, the Spanish moved across the Rio Grande into Pueblo country in 1598. They established the colony of New Mexico at the intersection of two long lines of pueblos and spread out into the surrounding native communities. New Mexico had little to offer in terms of material wealth, but the densely populated area was of great interest to the Jesuits and, later, the Franciscans, who sought converts among the Pueblo. Although there were periods of peaceful interaction, mistrust and hostility were more common. Native leaders assumed, correctly, that the Spanish priests were trying to alter their traditional religions, and they often reacted violently. The Pueblo Revolt, a reaction against increased religious and secular supervision, drove the Spanish out of New Mexico between 1680 and 1693.

In the first decade of the seventeenth century, the French planted a colony at Quebec. Although the French did not become a large colonial presence in terms of settler population, they interacted with a wide range of Native American peoples through their fur trade and missionary activities. The Jesuits operating in New France, for instance, were slightly more tolerant of native religions and were able to win a large number of nominal converts to Catholicism. The Dutch, working out of New York, maintained basically friendly relations with Native Americans, particularly the Iroquois, because they wanted to cut into the French fur trade.

The English colonies in the Chesapeake and New England, both established in the first half of the seventeenth century, were more bent on dominating local native populations than converting them or engaging them in trade. Although trade networks did operate out of Plymouth, Massachusetts Bay, and Virginia and the colonists occasionally tried to convert Native Americans, these colonies were very different from their Spanish and English counterparts.

Early English efforts to colonize North America, such as that at Roanoke in the 1580s, were failures. In 1607, however, Jamestown was founded on the peninsula between the James and York Rivers, feeding Chesapeake Bay. The tiny group of colonists posed little threat to Powhatan, and relations were generally peaceful. After a few years, however, the colonists began to press local Native Americans for food and land, and violence ensued. From 1610 to 1614 and in 1622, 1644, and 1676, white Virginians battled their neighbors for control of the area's rich farmland. By 1700, Virginia was a wealthy plantation colony, driven by the labor of African slaves and the production of tobacco.

Similarly, Plymouth, founded in 1620, posed no threat and offered a potentially valuable ally to Massasoit, sachem, or chief, of the Wampanoag, so he welcomed the fledgling colony. But the Massachusetts Bay Colony, which attracted tens of thousands of settlers, did pose a threat. The Puritans, believing themselves to be God's "elect," had few qualms about dispossessing Native Americans.

In 1637, the Pequot War opened the Connecticut River Valley for settlement. In 1675 to 1676, a large coalition of Native Americans led by Massasoit's son Metacom (or "King Philip") punished the Puritans. An alliance of the Puritan colonies, New York, and the Mohawks ended the threat and essentially ended Native American resistance to English colonization in New England. One of the causes of the outbreak of King Philip's War was the increasing reliance of the area's native peoples on Christian cultural and religious guidance. White New Englanders had made some modest attempts to convert the Native Americans, mainly by moving them into "praying towns." But young Wampanoag men resented these missionary efforts and the expanding power of the Puritan settlements.

Violence marred Anglo-Native American relations throughout eastern North America, but it was not the only way in which the groups interacted. In South Carolina, for instance, traders established a profitable exchange that would continue for several decades. And in Pennsylvania, William Penn's Quaker beliefs brought to the area a period of cooperation known as the "Long Peace." Of course, in the eighteenth century, both of these colonies would engage Native Americans in brutal wars.

Spreading out from Charles Town in the 1670s and 1680s, Carolina's formidable network of traders provided the region's Native Americans with trade goods, which they could no longer get from the fragile and dilapidated Spanish mission system. A brisk trade in cloth, deerskins, firearms, and native slaves fanned out from Carolina to the Creek, Cherokee, Chickasaw, Catawba, and Yamasee. The trade was conducted on uneven terms, though, and soon many Native Americans, particularly the Creek and Yamasee, had fallen into debt. In 1715, Native Americans throughout the Southeast killed the English traders living in their villages and pushed back the effective line of English control.

As mentioned above, William Penn, a prominent Quaker who founded Pennsylvania in 1682, established peaceful relations with his native neighbors. Although there were many complex reasons this occurred, the two most important were the fact that the region's native population (which had been thinned by disease) feared Iroquois raids, and that Penn's Quaker beliefs prompted him to treat his native neighbors with respect, signing treaties and paying them for land. As Pennsylvania expanded in the 1730s, Penn's heirs found it difficult to control settler violence, and the situation deteriorated through the middle of the eighteenth century.

Building Empires

The Spanish had met overwhelming numbers of Native Americans who refused to let them to settle. The French had established a small colonial presence in Canada, and the English had exploited native depopulation and rivalries to found colonies in the early colonial period.

By 1700, though, several large expansionist colonies and an increasingly tense rivalry between England and France would come to characterize native-white relations. And the rapid expansion of British North America in the eighteenth century—by the 1750s, the population of the thirteen colonies had reached 1.5 million—would alter native-white relations significantly.

Many Native American communities, such as the Tuscarora of North Carolina and the Delaware (Lenni Lenape) of Pennsylvania, were forced from their homelands entirely. Others, like Catawbas in South Carolina and numerous smaller groups in New England, re-

signed themselves to the domination of a nonnative majority and began to integrate themselves into colonial life.

During the eighteenth century, even powerful nations like the Creek and Cherokee in Georgia and South Carolina, respectively, were forced to evacuate and to cede or sell pieces of their homelands. Although they tried to maintain cultural autonomy as they lost political autonomy and military power and they, like other Native Americans, continued to play an important role in eastern North America, North America was, in fact, becoming increasingly English. The Seven Years' War, or the French and Indian War as it was known in the colonies, all but completed the shift.

In the 1750s, France and its native allies (mainly from the Midwest and the Great Lakes region) began to attack British settlements and outposts in the Ohio River Valley. These hostilities led to the establishment of Fort Duquesne, present-day Pittsburgh. Britain and France basically decided to force each other into a final showdown for North America, though the fight spread around the globe as well. The British fared poorly at first, but their fortunes reversed under the able leadership of William Pitt (the new prime minister). Sensing the turning tide, the Iroquois gave up neutrality and formed an alliance with the British. After the Treaty of Paris in 1763, France gave up its North American empire, leaving Britain as the sole colonial power.

Tribes that had been accustomed to playing the European powers off against one another no longer had that option, and the British knew that. Jeffery Amherst, the commander of British forces, also stopped distributing gifts to allied natives.

The 1760s saw two native revivals that cut across tribal lines. Followers of Pontiac and Neolin, or the "Delaware prophet," rejected European culture, and the rebellion that bears Pontiac's name removed the British from many of their western outposts. In 1763, the British reconciled with Native Americans and promised to protect them from encroaching settlers. The Proclamation of 1763 drew a line along the top of the Appalachian Mountains and declared everything west of the line Native American lands.

The 1763 proclamation did little to stop the Anglo-American movement westward, however; by 1768, Britain had ceded control of Native American affairs back to the colonies. To make matters worse, by the Treaty of Stanwix, the British and Iroquois ceded a wide swath of land belonging to the Shawnee, Delaware, and Cherokee.

In the American War for Independence, most native communities, though not all, sided with the British. In the wake of the stunning British defeat, the newly created United States government treated all Native Americans as defeated enemies and dealt with them harshly.

Matthew Jennings

See also: Furs; Military and Diplomatic Affairs (Chronology); Military and Diplomatic Affairs (Essay); Native American–European Conflict; Native Americans; Trade. *Document:* John Eliot and His Work with Native Americans (1670).

Bibliography

Calloway, Colin G. *New Worlds for All: Indians, Europeans, and the Remaking of Early America.* Baltimore: Johns Hopkins University Press, 1997.

Mancall, Peter H., and James M. Merrell, eds. *American Encounters: Natives and Newcomers from European Contact to Indian Removal, 1500–1850.* New York: Routledge, 2000.

Nash, Gary B. *Red, White and Black: The Peoples of Early North America.* Upper Saddle River, NJ: Prentice Hall, 2000.

Richter, Daniel K. *Facing East from Indian Country: A Native History of Early America.* Cambridge, MA: Harvard University Press, 2001.

Native Americans

Any meaningful account of colonial America must recognize the crucial role of Native Americans in the struggle for the continent. Until the last half of the eighteenth century, the eastern portion of North America was above all else native land.

The First Americans

The origins of the first Americans are still hotly debated in some circles, but the most widely accepted theory is that Asia's population expanded into North America over the Bering Strait land bridge between 40,000 and 10,000 B.C.E. These Paleo-Indians relied on big game hunting, as well as gathering, and they probably lived more or less as equals in small bands that ranged over large areas. By 8000 B.C.E., however, many large game animals—including mastodons, mammoths, and camels—had become extinct. Archaeologists debate whether climatic changes or overhunting brought about their demise. The habitable portion of North America contained perhaps 100,000 people during this period; it seems unlikely that such a small, dispersed population could hunt several species to extinction. (Of course, European Americans brought the passenger pigeon to extinction rapidly by repeatedly killing off the youngest generation.)

By 8000 B.C.E., glacial ice was also no longer a factor for most of North America, and many of the landscape's present-day physical features and animals were in place. Paleo-Indians began to hunt smaller, less mobile creatures, such forest-dwelling deer or fish that repeatedly migrated to the same place. Paleo-Indian population and population density rose dramatically during this period (sometimes referred to as the Archaic period). People living in the Mississippi watershed also began to plant crops such as squash at roughly this time. Eventually, large, sophisticated societies grew from these humble beginnings.

The Mississippian culture, with major cities at Cahokia (near present-day East St. Louis), Spiro, and Natchez, dominated the eastern half of North America. By 1100 C.E., Cahokia was home to a complex, stratified society of 20,000 people. In the Southwest, by roughly 1250, a group called the Anasazi had planned and constructed twelve large towns and hundreds more informal villages, constituting a formidable trading empire.

From 1400 to 1600, these large, centralized societies declined and smaller, decentralized polities, often multiethnic and multilingual, replaced them. These are the forerunners of the Native American communities that met Europeans in the fifteenth and sixteenth centuries. Native American societies were strikingly diverse, speaking hundreds of mutually unintelligible languages, subscribing to widely varying belief systems, and inhabiting virtually every part of North America's plains, forests, deserts, mountains, and grasslands. They are often divided into broad language groups like Algonquian, Iroquoian, Muskogean, and Siouan; many modern tribal names date from the period of European colonization.

It is important to recognize that Native Americans were undergoing drastic cultural shifts in the period leading up to their "discovery" by Europeans. One of the most common mistakes in colonial history is to assume that native societies were static, simply waiting for Europeans to enter their land so that history could begin.

Discovering Europeans

Although contact with Europeans themselves became more common throughout the colonial period, most

North America Indian Tribes, 1492. A wide diversity of native peoples lived in North America at the time of their first encounter with Europeans. The above map shows the major regions and tribes of North American Indians in 1492. *(Carto-Graphics)*

Native Americans discovered Europeans through trade goods and disease. Because they had remained isolated from European and African diseases, the native peoples had no immunity to them. Smallpox was a particularly lethal killer. The estimates of Native American population and depopulation vary widely, but even modest estimates suggest that the population north of the Rio Grande before 1492 was over 5 million. By 1900, only 250,000 Native Americans lived in this area.

While disease was *one* factor in this tragic decline,

it was not the only factor. Dispossession, relocation, and centuries of colonial rule also drastically reduced the Native American population. In some areas, such as southern New England, more than 75 percent of the Native American population died within the first few decades of English settlement.

As noted above, Native Americans also discovered European trade goods, alcohol, and firearms. At first, native groups adapted European trade goods into their own ways of life. For instance, copper kettles were of

Beginning in Paleo-Indian times, native peoples up and down the Atlantic coast of North America relied on fishing as a primary means of sustenance. This illustration depicts Virginian natives during the sixteenth century. *(Brown Brothers, Sterling, Pennsylvania)*

great value not as cookware but as sources of copper, pieces of which were worn as a sign of prestige in some communities. As the colonial period progressed, Native Americans began to use European goods in European ways. They often became dependent on these goods and on trade with nearby European settlements, and were drawn into the expanding Atlantic economy.

The French and Spanish made inroads into North America in the sixteenth century, and the English followed in the late sixteenth and early seventeenth centuries. These earliest contacts were little more than reconnaissance missions and had minimal impact on native cultures.

The major exceptions were the native people, usually young men, who were carried back to Europe as trophies or in the hope that they could learn European languages and become interpreters. In 1534, Jacques Cartier kidnapped two sons or nephews of the St. Lawrence Iroquoian chief Donnacona. The Spanish explorers Pedro Menéndez de Avilés and Lucas Vásquez de Ayllón both used native interpreters.

After their initial coastal contacts, European explorers, missionaries, and armies began to move farther inland. There, they met a wide range of native cultures. The Spanish in the Southeast, for instance, witnessed centralized Mississippian cultures before their decline. Hernando de Soto, who cut a path of destruction across the Southeast between 1539 and 1542, stayed at Cofitachequi, a chiefdom near present-day Camden, South Carolina. The French established close ties with the villages of Huronia, in Ontario. Both the French and Spanish claimed native converts, but the extent to which native peoples accepted Christianity is unclear and still debated.

The sixteenth century brought an increasing number of fur traders to French Canada. These men had little effect on native ways of life, though they did encourage Native Americans to hunt for beaver more extensively. They also fathered many biracial children, known as Métis.

One of the long-standing myths of this early period of contact is that Native Americans believed the European explorers had supernatural powers; most of the evidence to support this comes from the explorers' own records. If the natives did initially think this way about the Europeans (because they came from the sea and seemed immune to smallpox), close contact with them probably soon changed their minds.

The seventeenth century saw the planting of several colonies on North America's Eastern seaboard and an increase in the interaction between Native Americans and their new neighbors. Native Americans continued to understand themselves and the newcomers in terms deeply rooted in their American past.

An example of this is the way that Powhatan, a paramount chief in control of the eastern half of Virginia, dealt with the English who settled at Jamestown in 1607. Powhatan treated the English colony as another village in his realm. He demonstrated his power by kidnapping John Smith and adopting him into the world of the Powhatan. When the English overstepped their bounds or pressed the Powhatan for food, Powhatan reacted violently. Even after the settlement of Jamestown, Virginia was still Powhatan territory.

European involvement also had a serious impact on Huron-Iroquois relations. The Huron had allied with the French, accepting Jesuit missionaries in their settlements and becoming major power brokers as a result of their involvement in the fur trade (their access to furs from the Great Lakes region ensured their position). The Iroquois, armed by the Dutch, turned European colonization to their advantage by taking furs from Huron traders and captives to the Dutch at Fort Orange (present-day Albany, New York). The Iroquois (an alliance between the Cayuga, Onondaga, Seneca, Mohawk, and Oneida) increased their power as a result of colonization. By 1649, the Iroquois had destroyed the Huron as a political entity. Some were adopted into Iroquois villages, and others scattered to the Great Lakes. The Iroquois also began to distribute wampum (southern New England shell beads) to neighboring tribes in an effort to cement alliances.

Most Native American communities with close Euro-American contacts did not fare so well in the seventeenth century. The Pequot, for example, were a relatively powerful tribe that controlled the Connecticut River Valley. The Puritans at Massachusetts Bay and Plymouth, looking for new farmland and noticing a decline in the Pequot population, launched a genocidal war against them in 1637. The main action of the Pequot War took place at a fort on the Mystic River: the Puritans set fire to the fort and put between 500 and 1,000 Pequots (mainly noncombatants) to the sword as they fled the flames. The peace treaty that ended the war forced the Pequot to renounce their identity.

It bears mentioning that Native Americans fought on both sides of the two major conflicts over New England, the Pequot War and the much more devastating King Philip's War (1675–1676).

Living with Europeans

By the eighteenth century, it had become clear to many Native American communities, particularly those east of the Mississippi and in New Mexico, that Europeans were to be a permanent physical presence on the landscape, for better or worse. Native Americans adapted to this fact in a variety of ways, and they found it increasingly difficult to hold onto their cultural identity, land, and political autonomy as the colonial period progressed.

Three trends are crucial to understanding the eighteenth-century plight of Native Americans east of the Mississippi. English and French imperial power was expanding rapidly, English settlements were experiencing a population boom all along the Eastern seaboard, and only the most powerful Native American groups, or those best positioned to play the European powers against one another, would survive the period with any semblance of autonomy.

The case of the Tuscarora, an Iroquoian-speaking, sedentary farming tribe who lived in North Carolina, demonstrates the problems faced by Native American during this time. They had become dependent on the goods offered by English traders operating out of both Carolinas, and, in the first decade of the 1700s, they were further squeezed by the founding of English and Swiss/German colonies on the Neuse and Cape Fear Rivers. They struck back violently, killing 130 settlers in a single, swift attack in 1711. The military forces of North Carolina did not offer much resistance, but the combined forces of the colony of South Carolina, its Yamasee allies, and the Cherokee defeated the Tuscarora. By 1722, most of the Tuscarora had retreated to New York, where they joined the Iroquois and became the Sixth Nation.

The Creek in the Southeast and the Iroquois in the Northeast both survived the colonial onslaught. Although both had become dependent on European goods, each of these native powers was in an ideal position to play the Europeans off one another to its own advantage. The Creek and Iroquois were also willing and able to absorb the refugee populations of defeated tribes.

The Seven Years' War, known in America as the French and Indian War, would all but destroy Native American diplomatic options. The conflict erupted in 1754, during a prolonged period of explosive European (particularly English) population growth. The population of the thirteen colonies grew from 250,000 in 1700 to 1.6 million in 1760, placing extraordinary new pressure on Native America.

In the early 1750s, seeking to regain lost trade, the French and their native allies began to attack British frontier posts. By 1754, they had beaten the British out of the Ohio River Valley and established Fort Duquesne (present-day Pittsburgh, Pennsylvania).

By the middle of the eighteenth century, both England and France had recognized the importance of controlling North America, so they decided it was time for a final showdown for the entire continent (or at least its eastern half). Both nations poured men and resources into the conflict. The early years of the war saw decisive French victories. The British were forced to give up their western posts, and Native Americans allied with the French destroyed settlements in the western parts of Virginia and Pennsylvania (at the low point of the war, the fighting came within 30 miles of Philadelphia). The Iroquois managed to remain neutral in the early years of the war, although the Seneca did aid the French in some of their campaigns.

The year 1758 was pivotal. The British, through the masterful diplomacy of Sir William Johnson and the renewed interest in the war shown by the new prime minister William Pitt, were able to convince the Iroquois to join their side. They pushed the French out of the Ohio Valley and eventually went on to the heart of French Canada, taking Montreal and Quebec. The Treaty of Paris, signed in 1763, effectively removed the French from North America. By the terms of the Proclamation of 1763, the British drew a line (along the top of the Appalachians) that would separate North America into Native and Anglo-American spheres.

The Proclamation of 1763 was a miserable failure, and not just because Native Americans and Anglo-Americans already lived on both sides of the line. It infuriated American colonists, who wanted to retaliate against Native Americans and secure lands on which they had been speculating for a number of years. To make matters worse, Native Americans could no longer use European conflict to their advantage.

If the French and Indian War was bad for Native Americans, the American Revolution was a total disaster. Some Native Americans fought on both sides, though most groups—fearing American expansionism—sided with the British.

After the war, it mattered little what side specific Native American communities had fought on. Native Americans were considered hostile foreigners in their own land, and they suffered mightily at the hands of the young American republic. Although many tribes survived the eighteenth century, they faced an uncertain, and likely gloomy, future. Native Americans would reinvent themselves repeatedly in the years following American independence; they would rely on a variety of strategies to cope with the harsh political realities they faced.

Some trends of Native American life in the colonial period deserve mention here. The population of native North America declined catastrophically as a result of exposure to European diseases and colonial dislocation. Still, Native American communities survived two centuries of intense colonial pressure by adapting to their rapidly changing political environment. Equally remarkable is the fact that some Native Americans survived with their tribal identities intact, albeit in altered forms.

Matthew Jennings

See also: Abenaki; Arawak; Aztec; Beaver Wars; Brant, Joseph; Brant, Mary "Molly"; Captivity (by Native Americans); Carib; Cayuga; Cherokee; Chickasaw; Choctaw; Creek; Erie; French and Indian War; Furs; Hopi; Huron; Iroquois Confederacy; Lenni Lenape (Delaware); Massasoit; Maya; Missions; Mohawk; Mohegan; Montezuma II; Natchez; Native American–African American Relations; Native American–European Conflict; Native American–European Relations; Native Americans and Slavery; Navajo; Oneida; Onondaga; Opechancanough; Ottawa; Pequot; Philip, King (Metacom); Pocahontas; Pontiac; Powhatan; Powhatan Confederacy; Praying Towns; Pueblo; Race and Ethnicity (Chronology); Race and Ethnicity (Essay); Religions, Native American; Seminole; Seneca; Squanto; Taino; Tuscarora; Tuscarora War; Yamasee; Yamasee War; Zuni. *Documents:* The Constitution of the Iroquois Nations (c. 1570); John Eliot and His Work with Native Americans (1670); Captivity Narrative of Mary Jemison in the 1750s (pub. 1824).

Bibliography

Calloway, Colin G. *New Worlds for All: Indians, Europeans, and the Remaking of Early America.* Baltimore: Johns Hopkins University Press, 1997.

Gleach, Frederic W. *Powhatan's World and Colonial Virginia: A Conflict of Cultures.* Lincoln: University of Nebraska Press, 1997.

Mancall, Peter C., and James H. Merrell, eds. *American Encounters: Natives and Newcomers from European Contact to Indian Removal, 1500–1850.* New York: Routledge, 2000.

Richter, Daniel K. *Facing East from Indian Country: A Native History of Early America.* Cambridge, MA: Harvard University Press, 2001.

Trigger, Bruce G., and Wilcomb E. Washburn, eds. *The Cambridge History of the Native Peoples of the Americas,* Vol. 1, *North America,* Part One. Cambridge, UK: Cambridge University Press, 1996.

Native Americans and Slavery

The relationship between Native Americans and slavery is complicated. Native Americans held war captives (though mainly for social purposes, not as laborers), Native Americans were enslaved by Europeans, and Native Americans enslaved Africans. The second two practices had more in common with the way people generally conceive of slavery.

Native Americans' enslaving of Africans occurred mainly in the South, particularly among interior agricultural nations such as the Creek and Cherokee, although it did not become widespread until after the War for Independence. Except in certain areas on the Northwest Coast, however, Native Americans did not place monetary value on slaves or exchange them as property.

The European practice of enslaving Native Americans was integral to the way both the Spanish and English approached colonization. The French also practiced native slavery on a small scale but gave it up around the turn of the eighteenth century. After the first few decades of settlement, the Spanish began to use different methods to force the labor of Native Americans, while the English relied more on indentured servants from Europe and slaves from West and West Central Africa.

The arrival of the Spanish at Española (Hispaniola) in 1492 not only signaled the end of the isolation between the Americas and the Europe but also began the European practice of enslaving Native Americans. Columbus and his men enslaved the Taino they met, as well as other native Caribbean peoples.

Mainland Native Americans came face to face with this threat as Spanish sea captains raided coastal tribes for slaves. The journeys of Ponce de León in Florida in 1513 and Hernando de Soto throughout the entire Southeast in 1539 to 1542 were not only treasure-seeking missions and military expeditions. Both men enslaved Native Americans as they passed through.

Some forces within the Spanish Empire worried about the effects that slavery might have on indigenous people in the Americas. The most vocal critic of enslaving natives was Bartolomé de las Casas, a priest who had witnessed the destruction wrought by Columbus's men in the Caribbean. In 1542, las Casas wrote his *Short Account of the Destruction of the Indies,* a forceful denouncement of the practice of enslaving native people. Spaniards eventually abandoned the outright enslavement of native peoples in favor of the more subtle coercion of the *encomienda,* a tribute system that basically required Native Americans to labor for individual landholders or the Catholic Church. The largest of these was granted to Hernando Cortéz, who controlled the labor of 23,000 families in Oaxaca. To the native peoples laboring in the fields or mines of prominent Spaniards or on mission churches, the differences between slavery and encomienda must have seemed slight.

Slavery Under the English

Although slavery had not been practiced in England for hundreds of years, and in spite of the fact that official English policy frowned on the enslavement of Native Americans (after all, it was part of the "Black Legend" of Spanish colonialism, which said the Catholic Spanish were particularly cruel in the Americas), English colonists all along the Atlantic coast captured, sold, and used Native American slaves from the earliest years of settlement. English colonial America suffered from a chronic labor shortage and a widespread hatred of the native peoples, and these conditions allowed for a flourishing slave trade between English colonies and a system of native slave labor within them.

In 1622, Powhatans under the leadership of Opechancanough attacked the outlying settlements of Jamestown in what colonists and more than a few historians have referred to as the "Massacre of 1622." The aftermath of the attacks more closely resembled a massacre, however, as angry colonists lashed out against the Powhatan. A tract published in London, titled in part *The Barbarous Massacre in Time of Peace and League, treacherously executed by the native infidels,* argued that some good could come of the violence: "the Indians, who before were used as friends, may now most justly be compelled to servitude in mines, and the like, of whom some may be sent for the use of the Summer [Caribbean] Islands."

After conflicts with Native Americans in 1622, 1644, and 1676, Virginians took native people as slaves. Although most of these slaves appear to have been exported to the West Indies to support the growing sugar industry, some stayed in Virginia to labor on tobacco plantations.

In New England, the situation was strikingly similar. Following the Pequot War of 1637–1638 and King Philip's War in 1675–1676, New Englanders sold large numbers of defeated Native Americans into slavery in the Carolinas and the West Indies. A small number even made their way to England. The kidnapping of individual Native Americans also occurred, though this method of enslavement is harder to trace.

A survey of the English colonies in the seventeenth century would have found Native American slaves in every one. The Middle colonies had the lowest numbers of native slaves, while New England and the South had the highest. By the turn of the eighteenth century, South Carolina's population of native slaves would dwarf that of all the other mainland colonies.

Carolina and the Native Slave Trade

It would be an understatement to say that the arrival of the English and the subsequent establishment of the slave trade disrupted Native American life in the Southeast. From its modest beginnings at Charles Town in 1670, the English slave trade grew to a wildly profitable, competitive industry that exploited the region's Native Americans to an extreme degree.

One of the consequences of contact with Europeans was the increasing demand by the native peoples for access to English trade goods, particularly firearms, manufactured cloth, and rum. In return, the English demanded deerskins and slaves. The terms of exchange were rarely, if ever, equal, and Native Americans often soon fell into debt to Carolina traders, forcing them to extend hunting seasons and expand hunting territories.

Native Americans also found that they could profit by selling war captives to the English; they could profit even more by raiding enemy groups for slaves. Tribes allied with the English, or at least armed with English rifles, forayed far to the west in search of slaves. One scholar estimates that the Choctaw lost over 2,000 people to slave raiders armed by Carolina traders. Although English colonial policy outlawed enslavement of the native peoples, this edict was unenforceable.

The Yamasee, who by the 1680s had moved into the sphere of the English at Charles Town, were famous for wreaking havoc on neighboring communities of independent Native Americans or those allied with the Spanish. Thomas Nairne, the chief Indian trader operating out of Carolina, undertook a slave-raiding expedition with the Yamasee that captured 30 or so slaves. The account left behind by Nairne indicates that, by the early years of the eighteenth century, slave raiding had become a reasonably precise science. The Yamasee knew exactly where unsuspecting natives could be found and were able to capture large numbers of them at once with a relatively low risk of casualties. During the Tuscarora War (1711–1715), native South Carolinians fighting in the army of John Barnwell captured Tuscarora slaves at a rate that upset the white command, not because they disapproved of the practice, but because they wanted slaves for themselves.

Besides being exported from Charles Town, Native Americans were forced to labor alongside indentured servants and growing numbers of Africans in the rice plantations of South Carolina. During the late seventeenth and early eighteenth centuries, up to 25 percent of plantation labor may have been provided by Native American slaves. Working and living alongside African American slaves, these Native Americans exerted a profound influence on the development of African American culture.

Native American slavery declined throughout the eighteenth century in English America, largely because of the massive importation of African slaves. Although some Native Americans, particularly Southern groups like the Cherokee and Creek, would eventually adopt white racial attitudes toward African Americans and acquire their own plantations, this development, by and large, occurred in the 1780s, after the American War for Independence.

Matthew Jennings

See also: African Americans; Native Americans.

Bibliography

Gallay, Alan. *The Indian Slave Trade: The Rise of the English Empire in the American South, 1670–1717.* New Haven, CT: Yale University Press, 2002.

Lauber, Almon Wheeler. *Indian Slavery in Colonial Times Within the Present Limits of the United States.* New York: Columbia University, 1913.

Perdue, Theda. "Slavery." In *Encyclopedia of North American Indians,* edited by Frederick E. Hoxie. New York: Houghton Mifflin, 1996.

———. *Slavery and the Evolution of Cherokee Society, 1540–1866.* Knoxville: University of Tennessee Press, 1979.

Wright, J. Leitch. *The Only Land They Knew: American Indians in the Old South.* Lincoln: University of Nebraska Press, 1999.

Nature

See Environment and Nature

Navajo

The Navajo's origin story tells of their eternal presence in the region where the Holy People ordered the universe and charged them with maintaining that order. Archaeologists, however, postulate that the Navajo, or Dine people, as they call themselves, migrated from the northwestern parts of the continent to their current home in the Southwest.

The Navajo remain tied to the native peoples to the north through their Athapaskan language. One of only two groups in the Southwest of Athapaskan origin, the Navajo reached the region sometime between 900 and 1500 C.E. Their migration was long and gradual, following the front range of the Rocky Mountains southward into northern New Mexico. Their arrival prompted a general reshuffling of the native peoples in the region. The territory they chose as their homeland (Dine'tah) was a vast, sprawling region marked off by their four sacred mountains: the San Francisco Peaks to the west, Mount Taylor to the south, Blanca Peak to the north, and Hesperus Peak to the south. Essentially a hunting people, the Navajo learned from their Pueblo neighbors and fully adapted to their new environment in the centuries before Spanish contact. Adaptability was central to the Navajo character, for the great strength of the Navajo has been their ability to learn from others and incorporate new methods into their culture.

In the 1540s, an expedition led by Francisco Coronado lumbered through the region. This expedition gave the Spaniards their first contact with the *Apaches de Nabajo.* The Spaniards referred to all Athapaskan-speaking peoples as Apache and then located them geographically. The first contact between Navajos and Spaniards occurred at the base of Mount Taylor and was initially friendly, but fighting soon erupted as a result of the Spaniards' desire to retain some Navajo captives obtained from the Hopi.

With Spanish settlement came new pressures on the Navajo people. The Navajo adopted little Spanish culture, evidenced by the lack of Navajo names in baptismal records and the lack of Spanish words in their vocabulary. Spanish livestock, however, was another story. Because of their sedentary lifestyle and large territorial holdings, the Navajo readily accepted the new animals into their culture, completely remaking their economy. In true Navajo fashion, the people created new traditions that told of how the Holy People had given them the livestock, thus negating the Spanish influence. In this way, relations between the Navajo and the Spanish remained cordial until 1680.

In 1680, a native revolt, designed to overthrow the Spanish, erupted in the region. The Navajo were ready participants, as throughout the seventeenth century the Spanish had been unable to control their growth and cultural independence. When the Spanish regained control over the region in 1692, the Navajo were flooded with refugees from the Pueblo tribes. The arrival of the Pueblo in Navajo territory brought together the two roots of historic Navajo culture, the Athapaskan-Apachean and the Anasazi-Puebloan. Navajo culture was again transformed. Spanish stock-raising supplanted agriculture, and pottery and weaving techniques became more advanced as a result of the Pueblo influence.

Intermittent warfare with the Spaniards marked Navajo society until sometime around 1716, after which a gradual peace was forged, as both Spaniards and Navajos found a new enemy in the Ute. Once peace with Spain was secured, the Navajo faced new pressures that tested their culture's flexibility. In the face of severe drought and increasing attacks from the Ute, the Navajo abandoned their Puebloan traits and began to raise livestock in widely dispersed communities.

In expanding their territory, Navajos came into contact with Spanish settlement in the region. As a result, in 1774, war with the Spanish resumed, when the Navajo drove Spanish settlers from eastern portions of their territory. Their success in war with the Spanish demonstrates the strength of the new Navajo way of life that developed during this period. Now secure, the Navajo continued to expand their territories, moving into areas left vacant by the Spanish.

Held together socially by a vast ceremonial system designed to restore the universe to harmony, the Navajo absorbed, traded with, and raided other peoples, always learning from various groups in the region. Despite their adaptability, the Navajo had little knowledge of the onslaught that lay ahead. Despite the massive toll taken by disease, Spanish imperial policy, missionary work, and other crises caused by contact, the Navajo continued to believe that they could retain the order the Holy People had given to the universe.

Todd Leahy

See also: Native American–European Conflict; Native American–European Relations; Native Americans; New Mexico; Spanish Colonies on Mainland North America (Chronology).

Bibliography

Iverson, Peter. *Dine: A History of the Navajos*. Albuquerque: University of New Mexico Press, 2002.

Milner, Clyde, Carol O'Connor, and Martha Sandweiss, eds. *The Oxford History of the American West*. New York: Oxford University Press, 1994.

Sturtevant, William, ed. *Handbook of North American Indians*. Vol. 10. Washington DC: Smithsonian Institution, 1983.

Navigation Acts (1651–1733)

Although England established its first shipping regulations in the fourteenth century, trade between England and the American colonies was still duty-free as late as 1642. Under mercantilist, or pre-free market capitalist, theory, trade with the colonies was encouraged, while trade with rival nations was to be limited as much as possible.

The first navigation act came as an attempt by Oliver Cromwell, under the British Commonwealth, to counter the Dutch carrying trade (transporting goods of another country), which was more efficient than and threatened to overwhelm British shipping interests. The Navigation Act of 1651 required all imports from Asia, Africa, and America to be brought in English-owned vessels. European goods could travel on ships of the producing country, the receiving country, or, again, on ships belonging to English people. Colonial goods also had to enter England on English ships or on those of the originating country.

This act damaged New England's interests, because Northern colonial products were similar to those produced in England. As suppliers of raw material and receivers of finished goods, the Southern colonies benefited from the limitation on trade in Southern products, such as tobacco, ship's stores, and rice. Northerners adjusted because the act was ignored or only loosely enforced. The real intent of the act was to hurt the Dutch—colonial feelings did not matter—and it did lead to the first Anglo-Dutch war.

The next act, in 1660, required colonial trade on English vessels only; defining colonial ships as English, the act helped develop Northern shipping. This act hurt the Southern colonies by enumerating the items the colonies could and could not trade outside English territory. Restricted items included wool, sugar, tobacco, and cotton. Over time, modifications to the

Navigation Acts expanded the list of enumerated items. Even worse, this act imposed a duty on exports to England. The act of 1672 extended this tax to inter-colonial trade in restricted items. The impact of these taxes on trade among the colonies and with Europe or the West Indies could have been disastrous, but again enforcement was mostly nonexistent.

Other acts came into being in 1661, 1662, 1663, 1670, and 1673. The act of 1663 required all shipments to the colonies to pass through England. On the other hand, colonial commodities did gain preferential treatment—monopolies or tax exemptions. Tobacco was an American monopoly, while the West Indies had tariff protection against the French sugar interests. State subsidies were also English policy, designed to guarantee a steady supply of critical items such as ship's stores.

The most unpopular act was the Molasses Act of 1733. It increased tariffs on sugar and molasses from the French West Indies. Trade for these items was the New England way of getting rid of its surplus flour, lumber, livestock, and fish; the English Corn Laws barred these items from England, and there was no other market. The risk of economic disaster was real but enforcement was lax. Still the acts galled. And the protected British West Indian sugar was too expensive. The New Englanders kept their French West Indian trade by smuggling. The British began enforcing their restrictions after the French and Indian War, thirty years after New Englanders had begun smuggling in response to the Molasses Act. Seemingly arbitrary seizures of vessels increased the hostility of the colonials. The Navigation Acts limped along until they finally were repealed in 1849, and the mercantilist policy was replaced by free trade.

The English oversight and enforcement efforts proved ineffective, making the situation worse. In England, the Board of Trade and Plantations, charged with enforcing the act, came into being only in 1696 and proved somewhat more effective. Still, enforcement was nearly impossible when oversight was weak. Lawbreakers connived with the local customs officials and possibly the governor, and admiralty court juries refused to convict their neighbors, maybe fellow smugglers. Smuggling was a popular pastime in Britain, with an estimated 40,000 or so smugglers of Indian tea and French silk.

The British adoption of the mercantilist philosophy meant that inevitably conflict would arise. The colonies became more substantial and independent, less willing to accept trade deficits and restrictions on their livelihoods, and reluctant to make sacrifices for the good of the mother country with no reciprocal benefit. Britain's difficulties were only made worse by her bad habit of forgetting the colonies in favor of more immediate business, such as the British Civil War, the Glorious Revolution, and wars with the Dutch and French. Benign neglect became merely neglect, and when the British tried to re-establish a strong subordinate status after the French wars, it was too late. People accustomed to ignoring or working around the multiple Navigation Acts had no compunction about resisting new laws, which were inconsistently applied and frequently repealed under colonial pressure.

John H. Barnhill

See also: Board of Trade; Economy, Business, and Labor (Chronology); Economy, Business, and Labor (Essay); Mercantilism; Merchants; Trade; Transportation, Water.

Bibliography

Kammen, Michael. *Empire and Interest; The American Colonies and the Politics of Mercantilism.* Philadelphia: Lippincott, 1970.

McCusker, John J. *Mercantilism and the Economic History of the Early Modern Atlantic World.* Cambridge, UK: Cambridge University Press, 2001

Navy, British

During the colonial period, Britain's navy was transformed from a small and provisionally organized and financed entity into the largest, most complex, and most powerful maritime force in the world. Although the navy did not officially adopt a policy for North America until the middle of the eighteenth century, it proved effective through most of the period in both defending Britain's Atlantic trading empire and laying siege to the holdings of other European nations. Its resources were strained by the American Revolution, to the extent that Britain temporarily lost command of the sea, though the British Navy reclaimed oceanic supremacy by century's end.

Seventeenth Century

Prior to the mid-seventeenth century, England did not possess a navy that was operable during both war and peacetime. Although several specialized warships were built during and after the reign of Henry VIII, financial constraints and major competition from well-established naval powers slowed the growth of the English navy except in times of war or threatened invasion, as in the case of the encroaching Spanish Armada in 1588.

At the end of the English Civil War, Parliament passed the Navigation Acts and devoted considerable resources to establishing a large standing navy for the protection and enlargement of the nation's maritime trade. Aimed primarily at the Dutch, the premier naval power in Europe, these measures led to three wars between the two countries in the seventeenth century. England fared well in the first (1652–1654), and although the navy enjoyed only a few successes in the second (1665–1667) and the third (1672–1674), the conflicts served to reduce the Dutch to a secondary naval power. Apart from sending a force to capture New Netherland (renamed New York) in 1664, the navy fought its campaigns mainly in domestic waters.

Following the Dutch wars, France became England's principal maritime rival. English naval dockyards and the victualing (provisioning) of ships were substantially improved, allowing the navy to cruise in distant waters. A struggle in parliament soon ensued over the projected role of the navy. The Whig government believed it was unnecessary for the navy to have a formal presence in North America, as England's colonies experienced only sporadic threats. The navy's chief concern there was the protection and administration of the Newfoundland fisheries. The navy's main squadrons were stationed in the Mediterranean, on the French Atlantic coast, and in the English Channel to support land-based campaigns on the Continent, blockade French ports, and defend England from possible invasion. The ascendancy of the British navy was sealed in 1692, with its destruction of the core French fleet in the Battle of Barfleur in 1692. At century's end, the British navy consisted of 170 ships, compared to just 40 in 1600.

Eighteenth Century

Under a Tory government, the navy began to operate farther afield, though its activities in North America remained intermittent. British naval forces eventually took the French base at Port Royal, Nova Scotia, renamed it Annapolis Royal, and strengthened its fortifications. A failed amphibious assault on Quebec in 1711 by a large force led by Admiral Hovenden Walker marked the end of the short-lived attempt to extend the navy's reach to North American waters. The colonies lacked adequate facilities to sustain the navy for extended campaigns, and the potential gains did not yet outweigh the costs. This changed by midcentury, as the value of colonial trade to Britain increased and required protection and the navy became more reliant on North America as a source of seamen and products such as timber, pitch, and tar.

The impetus for the British navy's heightened presence in North American waters was the renewed threat of the French after 1744. Although France was active in fortifying Louisbourg and Quebec and rebuilding its naval fleet earlier in the century, Britain did not establish a corresponding naval base in the northern region of the continent. Instead, Britain focused its energies on protecting its Southern colonies of South Carolina and Georgia from possible Spanish attack. The navy was also active in the West Indies, as a squadron under Admiral Vernon captured the Spanish port of Porto Bello during the War of Jenkins' Ear (1739–1743), followed by a failed siege of Cartegena.

In 1745, Britain responded to the French threat in the northern part of America by commissioning Captain Peter Warren the commander in chief of a North American squadron. French forces advanced on Canso, Nova Scotia, that year, but they were held at Annapolis Royal, Nova Scotia, by troops and naval vessels from New England. Warren's fleet united with the New England force and laid siege to Louisbourg, which fell after seven weeks. When Louisbourg was returned to France in 1749, Britain recognized the strategic importance of having a North Atlantic naval base to counter future French hostility in the region and chose Chebucto (renamed Halifax) for its location.

North America became the chief arena for British and French conflict during the French and Indian War (known as the Seven Years' War in Europe). Large squadrons of the British Navy were sent there, and the fleet achieved several major victories with the valuable assistance of a strong colonial force of privateers. In 1755, the navy assisted an expedition from Massachusetts against French forces at Chignecto, which drove the French from the Bay of Fundy. While the navy convoyed a force under the command of Braddock to attack the French on the Ohio, it also moved a squadron into the Gulf of St. Lawrence under Admiral Boscawen to prevent French reinforcements from arriving in Quebec. The latter action failed, however, as the force did not arrive in time. Further missed opportunities resulted in the building of a royal dockyard at Halifax in 1758. The British immediately reaped the rewards, for part of the North American squadron wintered in

The British Navy—the world's most powerful maritime force—suffered its worst defeat of the American Revolution in September 1779, when the colonial *Bonhomme Richard,* commanded by John Paul Jones, forced the surrender of the HMS *Serapis* off the English coast. *(Guardian Royal Exchange Insurance Collection/Bridgeman Art Library)*

Halifax and arrived off Louisbourg three months earlier than in the previous year to effectively blockade the fortified town and attain victory.

The British navy pursued the same strategy against Quebec the following year, as its vessels arrived in the Gulf of St. Lawrence before the French and deprived the city of much needed supplies and reinforcements. The navy bombarded the city during the months prior to Wolfe's victory on the Plains of Abraham, forcing much of the population to flee outside the walls and destroying most of the city's infrastructure. The British conquest of New France was ultimately achieved by Admiral Hawke's devastation of the heart of the French fleet at Quiberon Bay later that year and the arrival of a British squadron at Quebec in the spring of 1760 with supplies for its forces. British naval victories in Guadeloupe (1758), Martinique (1761), and Havana (1762) also hastened the end of the war and the French regime in North America.

Between 1763 and 1775, the British navy became more active in North America. This was made possible by the existence of a colonial support system that provided crews, provisions, and a host of ancillary services. The navy supported large numbers of troops now stationed in the colonies and conducted coastal surveys of the continent's northeastern coast. The navy was also directed to enforce a series of parliamentary acts designed to reduce smuggling and tax colonial trade through the imposition of new customs duties. Naval seizures of colonial trading vessels created friction between colonial merchants and Crown officials and generally helped foment anti-British sentiment. Customs commissioners and other Crown representatives sought refuge aboard navy vessels during the Stamp Act crisis in 1765. Colonial animosity against the navy was made still worse by its part in enforcing the Townshend Acts in 1768. Greater use of the press also increased the colonists' resentment of the navy and sparked riots in several ports. The navy became a direct symbol of British tyranny in America, especially after it closed the port of Boston in 1773 and attempted to enforce the Intolerable Acts.

Britain's navy proved unprepared for war in the summer of 1775 and was quickly overwhelmed, as naval vessels became the refuge for governors and other royal officials while attempting a blockade of the entire Atlantic coastline with only thirty warships. During the American Revolution, the British navy proved most effective in the raid and capture of key ports such as New York and Newport in 1776, Savannah in 1778, and Charles Town in 1780. It could not, however, manage a successful blockade of the Chesapeake or New England and thus did not heavily impact the war on land. This was due in part to a large and well-developed colonial merchant marine that was quickly converted into an aggressive and resolute privateering fleet. As Continental privateers expanded their operations overseas to attack British merchant shipping and supply lines, the British navy was forced to allocate resources closer to home and assemble costly and time-consuming convoys.

The British navy faced a different war once France entered the conflict in 1778, followed by Spain (1779) and Holland (1780). Its role changed from supporting a war of occupation and conquest to fighting a major European maritime war. The navy lost its numerical superiority by 1780 and was forced to keep most of its battleships in domestic waters and the Mediterranean. The failure of Admiral Graves's squadron to control the Chesapeake in September of 1781 led to French occupation of the bay and General Cornwallis's surrender to the Continental army at Yorktown weeks later.

Britain soon recovered her naval strength. Although this came too late to save the American colonies, it did enable Britain to retain those farther north and in the West Indies, the Mediterranean, and the British Isles. Britain again became the world's leading naval power, which allowed the nation to resume its imperial ambitions and commercial expansion all over the world well into the nineteenth century.

Michael F. Dove

See also: Armada, Spanish; Army, British; Atlantic Ocean; Caribbean (Chronology); French and Indian War; King George's War; Queen Anne's War; Revolutionary War; Trade; Transportation, Water.

Bibliography

Black, Jeremy, and Philip Woodfine, eds. *The British Navy and the Use of Naval Power in the Eighteenth Century.* Leicester, UK: Leicester University Press, 1988.

Harding, Richard. The *Evolution of the Sailing Navy, 1509–1815.* New York: St. Martin's, 1995.

Kennedy, Paul M. The *Rise and Fall of British Naval Mastery.* London: A. Lane, 1976.

Rodger, N.A.M. The *Wooden World: An Anatomy of the Georgian Navy.* London: William Collins Sons, 1986.

Stout, Neil R. *The Royal Navy in America, 1760–1775.* Annapolis, MD: Naval Institute Press, 1973.

Syrett, David. *The Royal Navy in American Waters, 1775–1783.* Aldershot, Hants, UK: Scolar Press, 1989.

Negro Election Day

Negro Election Day was a festival in the Dutch colony of New Amsterdam whereby the African American community chose its unofficial leaders.

Most early colonial settlement was located along lucrative seaports or large river valleys. This commonsense approach to establishing villages not only promoted much needed trade connections, but it also provided entranceways for European immigrants wanting to move to the New World. After the New England colonies had firmly planted roots, the move to settle began in what were known as the Middle colonies—New York, New Jersey, and Pennsylvania—and the most unique of these was New York.

New York only became an English colony in 1664, long after the Dutch had settled New Amsterdam (New York City) and New Netherland (New York). It began in 1609, when the Dutch East India Company, on a classic exploration search, sent Henry Hudson to the New World to find a Northwest Passage to the Orient. Sailing along the Atlantic coast, he took a side trip up a large river, but found it dwindled down to a stream. While Hudson failed to discover a route to the Orient, the river that now bears his name became a productive fur trading post, which the Dutch needed to show a profit from their exploration.

Even though this was the first non-English colony to be established in early America, it was New Netherland's fundamental diversity that made it different from its neighboring English colonies. Although relatively few in number, its early settlers embraced immigrants from Holland, Sweden, France, and Germany and also—most importantly—from Africa. When the Dutch West India Company attempted to mimic the success of the earlier East India Company, it began not only importation but also the transportation of a new commodity—blacks from Africa, who transplanted their unique customs and culture to New Netherland. Some of these people eventually won their freedom. This introduced a different type of hierarchy not seen in the other colonies. As New Amsterdam's population increased, its culture became more diverse, allowing foreign traditions and customs to become an important part of the city's daily life.

The lowest rung of a seaport's social hierarchy contained free and bound workers. Free laborers were mainly young white men and women—journeymen artisans, sailors, fishermen, domestic workers, seamstresses, and prostitutes. While the ranks of unfree workers included mostly apprentices and indentured servants doing menial labor in shops and on the docks, black men and women also made up a substantial part of the bound labor force. Although the vast majority of African slaves who were imported by the Dutch West India Company in New Netherland were sold to Southern plantations, some were bought by urban merchants and craftsmen. Laboring as porters at the docks, assistants in craft shops, or servants in wealthy households, colonial black residents made up almost 20 percent of New York City's population. As the percentage of black residents of New York, as well as the 10 percent in the other Middle colonies increased, limitations on blacks were put into place, as white society feared the African traditions and did not understand the importance of maintaining them.

The character of slavery in Northern seaports changed decisively during the mid-eighteenth century. At that time, warfare in Europe required the service of many who might otherwise have become immigrants, thus limiting the supply of white indentured servants. The colonial cities therefore imported larger numbers of Africans. These newcomers brought to urban black culture not only a labor force but also a new awareness of a common West African past. This culture made an impact as African traditions were tolerated and appeared most vividly in annual festivals, likened to those held in West Africa.

Initially, these festivals occurred only in New Amsterdam. Black men and women paraded in their masters' clothes or mounted on their horses. A special, albeit unofficial, election followed, during which the participants chose their own black kings, governors,

and judges, who then conducted a special court session to settle minor disputes among white and black members of the community.

"Negro Election Day," with its temporary reversal of roles, was not intended to challenge the established racial order. This toleration and recognition of a different culture gave the black community of New Amsterdam a sense of importance, even if for only one day. This festival eventually spread to other colonial seaports, but it never became as important as it was in Dutch New Amsterdam and, later, English New York City.

Penny M. Sonnenburg

See also: African Americans; Free Blacks; Slave Communities and Culture; Slavery, African American.

Bibliography

Archdeacon, Thomas J. *New York City, 1664–1710: Conquest and Change.* Ithaca, NY: Cornell University Press, 1976.

Goodfriend, Joyce D. *Before the Melting Pot: Society and Culture in Colonial New York City, 1664–1730.* Princeton, NJ: Princeton University Press, 1992.

New Amsterdam

Sharply contrasting the bustling metropolis that later emerged on Manhattan Island, New Amsterdam was a small, neglected outpost in the sprawling Dutch empire. From the 1620s through 1664, New Amsterdam served as the main town and trading post for the scattered Dutch settlements in New Netherland.

The Dutch West India Company, which governed the colony of New Netherland, settled the town with artisans, soldiers, sailors, merchants, and traders from throughout Northern Europe, and slaves from West Africa, the Caribbean, and South America. Diversity became the defining characteristic of New Amsterdam. Though the inhabitants were diverse, they also were few. Only 1,500 settlers lived in New Amsterdam and its immediate hinterland in 1664, when a largely uncontested English conquest established the new town and colony of New York.

After the Dutch secured independence from Spain in 1609, they quickly established colonies and trading outposts in Asia, Africa, Brazil, and the Caribbean. They also extended their burgeoning commercial empire to the Hudson, Connecticut, and Delaware River

New Amsterdam, the name of New York City during the Dutch colonial period, is viewed at the lower end of Manhattan Island in 1653, the year in which its first municipal government was created. *(Brown Brothers, Sterling, Pennsylvania)*

Valleys of North America. Dutch traders, hoping to tap into the fur trade with the Iroquois and other tribes, established Fort Orange at present-day Albany in the 1610s. In 1625 the Dutch West India Company established New Amsterdam at the tip of Manhattan Island to protect the valuable trade upriver, to produce food for Dutch colonies in the Caribbean, and to provide naval stores and a provisioning station for the Dutch fleet.

Sometime in the spring of 1626, a company official "purchased" Manhattan Island. As the Native Americans understood matters, they had sold nothing to the Dutch West India Company, and they probably understood the transaction as a rental or lease agreement. The Dutch overlooked the technicalities lost in the cultural translation; confident that they "owned" Manhattan, they went about establishing the semblance of a town. By the fall of 1626, the settlers had erected thirty log homes, a fort, a secure countinghouse for trade, and a mill that also doubled as a church. Within two years, perhaps 250 settlers lived at New Amsterdam.

The town's population grew slowly over the next two decades. Prosperity at home meant that few Dutch men and women had any reason to emigrate to North America, and periodic and often deadly Native American wars deterred settlement. After a few years of

trading, those few who did go to New Amsterdam usually returned home with their profits. Dutch imperial officials turned to the displaced groups, who had moved to the Netherlands over the past half-century to escape wars or religious persecution. Families of Flemings, Walloons, Scandinavians, Jews, Germans, and French Protestants all answered the Dutch West India Company's call for colonists in New Amsterdam, but again, only in limited numbers.

Already well-experienced in the slave trade, the Dutch West India Company and individual settlers turned to slave labor to address the town's chronic shortage of laborers, especially agricultural workers. Many of the slaves carried to New Amsterdam had been exposed to European languages and cultures in West Africa and the Caribbean. This background enabled them to integrate themselves into New Amsterdam's Dutch culture, while their concentration in the town and its hinterland allowed them to forge a distinct African-Dutch culture. Many became fluent Dutch speakers, married and baptized their children in Dutch churches, and took Dutch names, all the while retaining African cultural practices. Slaves could gain "half-freedom," which allowed them to work for wages and own property, in exchange for annual payments to the Dutch West India Company. By 1664, men and women of African descent accounted for one-fifth of the town's population, and perhaps a fifth had purchased their own freedom.

During its brief history, New Amsterdam served as the main town and trading post for the Dutch settlements and plantations along the banks of the Hudson River, Dutch traders upriver at present-day Albany, and Puritans and other English settlers on Dutch-controlled Long Island. Despite its prime location and the advantages of slave labor, New Amsterdam never became a bustling commercial center like Boston or Philadelphia. The overstretched Dutch West India Company concentrated its resources on potentially more lucrative adventures—raiding Spanish gold ships, competing with Portuguese sugar colonies, and capturing trading forts on the African coast—resulting in the neglect of New Netherland. Yet the failure of New Netherland ultimately stemmed from the unwillingness of ordinary Dutch men and women to settle in the colony.

The small population of New Amsterdam and New Netherland left it vulnerable to English imperial ambitions. When four English warships arrived in the harbor in August of 1664, the people of the town surrendered rather than see the town destroyed. In 1667, the Dutch formally ceded New Netherland to the English. Like its predecessor, colonial New York was characterized by diversity, and the Dutch continued to play an important role in colonial affairs. The two countries, however, continued to battle over the city until the English seized it in 1674.

John Craig Hammond

See also: Cities; Dutch; New Netherland; New York; New York and New Netherland (Chronology); Stuyvesant, Peter.

Bibliography

Burrows, Edwin G. *Gotham: A History of New York City to 1898*. New York: Oxford University Press, 1999.

Goodfriend, Joyce D. "Burghers and Blacks: The Evolution of Slave Society at New Amsterdam." *New York History* 59 (1978): 125–44.

Rink, Oliver A. *Holland on the Hudson: An Economic and Social History of Dutch New York*. Ithaca, NY: Cornell University Press, 1986.

New Bern

In 1710, Baron Christophe von Graffenried led a group of Swiss and German Palatine settlers to the confluence of the Trent and Neuse Rivers at the lower edge of North Carolina's Outer Banks. There, they founded the town of New Bern (named after the Swiss capital) on land von Graffenried supposedly purchased from the Tuscarora Indians.

The early settlers suffered from debilitating diseases, a warm, humid climate, lack of adequate supplies, and constant conflicts with the local natives, especially the Tuscarora. The Tuscarora complained about the colonists' encroachment on their homelands but received no redress of grievances. In frustration, they attacked the settlers, triggering the Tuscarora War in the Carolinas from 1711 to 1715. The North Carolina militia burned several native villages and traded sieges with the Native Americans before the Tuscarora finally made peace and moved to New York to join the Iroquois confederation.

New Bern, the second oldest town in North Carolina, enjoyed a quiet existence as a modestly successful port town through the early and mid-eighteeenth century. It exported a variety of crops, but its main exports were lumber and naval stores. Tar, pitch, turpentine, resin, and shingles all left the swamps and long-leaf pine forests surrounding the town and made their way to England in the holds of merchant ships.

The port town enjoyed a surge in prestige and prosperity when, in 1770, Royal Governor William Tryon chose New Bern as the site of the colony's first permanent capital. He commissioned Tryon Palace, designed by English architect John Hawks, as the governor's residence and capitol building. After becoming the capital, New Bern developed the nickname "the Athens of North Carolina" for its cultural institutions. The colonial capital became the home of the first printing press, the first newspaper, and the first incorporated school in the colony.

In the days leading up to the American Revolution, New Bern played a significant role. The Sons of Liberty, led by Cornelius Harnett, held meetings here that defied the Stamp Act and subsequent parliamentary acts. In 1775, patriots drove Josiah Martin, the royal governor, from the capital, forcing him to seek refuge first in Fort Johnston and then finally on board a British warship. The military hardships of the war itself came to New Bern in August 1781, when Major James Craig led a British force of nearly 300 redcoats and 300 Tories from Wilmington to New Bern. On August 19, they entered the town, burned property and outlying plantations, and then returned to Wilmington.

After the Revolution, New Bern became the first

place in North Carolina and the third place in America to celebrate Independence Day. North Carolina's capital moved to Raleigh in 1792, but New Bern enjoyed increasing prosperity as a thriving port town into the nineteenth century.

Judkin Browning

See also: North Carolina; North Carolina (Chronology); Ship's Stores.

Bibliography

Beaumont, Sarah. *Colonial New Bern.* Raleigh, NC: Capital Printing Company, 1901.

Taylor, H. Braughn, ed. *Guide to Historic New Bern, North Carolina.* New Bern, NC: New Bern/Craven County American Revolution Bicentennial Commission, 1974.

Watson, Alan D. *History of New Bern and Craven County.* New Bern, NC: Tryon Palace Commission, 1987.

New England, Dominion of

Comprising all the English colonies of North America from north and east of the Delaware River, the Dominion of New England was created by James II in 1685. It was part of a larger plan developed in the late seventeenth century to re-establish royal control in England and the emerging British Empire, especially the American colonies.

The resolution to combine New England into a single province created a centralized political power and placed it in the hands of one royal governor and council appointed by the king. Local assemblies within the individual colonies ceased to exist, with control over the colony diverted to the governor and council. This centralized government held complete executive and legislative authority over the people who lived within its jurisdiction, a vast region stretching from New Hampshire to New Jersey.

On taking office, the new government caused turmoil among the local inhabitants by providing freedom of worship to everyone, restricting the number of traditional town meetings to once a year, actively enforcing the Navigation Acts, and issuing land grants only in the king's name. After James II's removal and William and Mary's ascendance to the throne in 1688, the duration of the Dominion effectively ended.

Although the life span of the Dominion was short, it spawned sporadic but decisive reactions in the American colonies. In New York and Massachusetts, local leaders staged revolts partly to protest the expansion of royal authority in the new governor and partly in support of the largely peaceful Glorious Revolution of 1689, which brought William of Orange to the throne.

In Boston, after they received news of the accession, it took nearly three weeks for local elites to raise a popular revolt on April 18, 1689. Boston's revolt, justified by a number of reasons, essentially destroyed the entire Dominion of New England. Regardless of the motivation behind the revolt, the result was that Sir Edmund Andros, the royal governor of the Dominion, was officially deposed and the old charter of Massachusetts restored.

By the end of 1689, every colonial assembly in New England had been reinstated. Expediency, unfair preferential treatment, the ascension of William and Mary, and imitation of Massachusetts all led to the revival of the old charters in every colony of New England except New York. Being a proprietary colony of James II, New York had no charter to restore. Here, a popularly supported revolt under the direction of local leaders like Jacob Leisler raised the militia and forced Francis Nicholson, the lieutenant governor in charge of New York, out of the region.

Unfortunately, subsequent events led to the execution of Leisler, the limitation of the new Massachusetts charter, and the exoneration of both Andros and Nicholson. Despite efforts to restore the past, the economic and political autonomy of the early days of the Northern colonies did not return.

Solomon K. Smith

See also: Andros, Sir Edmund; Glorious Revolution; Leisler, Jacob. *Document:* Commission of Sir Edmund Andros for the Dominion of New England (1688).

Bibliography

Barnes, Viola F. *The Dominion of New England: A Study in British Colonial Policy.* New Haven, CT: Yale University Press, 1923.

Johnson, Richard R. *Adjustment to Empire: The New England Colonies, 1675–1715.* New Brunswick, NJ: Rutgers University Press, 1981.

Lovejoy, D. S. *The Glorious Revolution in America.* New York: Harper and Row, 1972.

New Hampshire

The first settlement in New Hampshire was the result of a 6,000-acre land grant to David Thomson in 1622. Thomson and a small group of settlers arrived aboard the *Jonathan* on April 16, 1623, and began a settlement at Odiorne's Point. Although some of the colonists remained, Thomson abandoned the colony and his claim to it. In 1629, the Crown granted the same land to Captain John Mason, who named his holdings New Hampshire, after his home county in England.

The exact territory encompassed by Mason's grant was indistinct owing to multiple grants of the same territory in a short period of time. In addition to Mason's grant, the Crown awarded Mason and Ferdinando Gorges the lands called Laconia, which bordered New Hampshire on the north and west. A third grant, the Squamscott Patent, went to Edward Hilton, one of the original settlers who arrived with Thomson. Yet another grant given to Mason, Gorges, and several others, the Pascataway Patent, encompassed much of the same territory.

In 1691, Samuel Allen purchased Mason's original land grant, but Allen failed to obtain approval from the settlers, and the Privy Council voided the transaction in 1739. In 1746, John Tufton Mason, the legal heir, sold all claims to New Hampshire to a group of twelve Portsmouth citizens, finally settling the disputes over who owned the patent.

Most of New Hampshire's population resided in one of four towns in the colony until the middle of the seventeenth century. Originally settled in 1623, Portsmouth was incorporated as a town in 1631 and served as the government center for the colony. Dover, the original 1623 location, was established by Thomson. Exeter was begun by Massachusetts exile John Wheelwright in 1638, and Hampton was founded by the Bay Colony under the guidance of Reverend Stephen Bachiler.

Government

For much of its early history, New Hampshire was intricately linked with Massachusetts. By 1643, the colony's four towns had willingly placed themselves under the jurisdiction of Massachusetts. This arrangement continued until disputes over the land grants prompted the Crown to establish New Hampshire as a separate royal colony in 1679.

With the establishment of New Hampshire as a royal colony, John Cutt of Portsmouth was named president of the Council, which served as the colony's executive body and was composed of nine men, six appointed by the Crown and three appointed by the king's six appointees. A legislative body known as the Assembly was made up of delegates elected from the towns. The king retained the power to veto the Assembly's actions.

The colonial government adopted New Hampshire's first legal code, nearly identical to Massachusetts law, in 1680. It provided for the definition and punishment of fourteen capital crimes, a court system, trial by jury, and a militia. It also defined voters as Protestant males over the age of 24 and owning a taxable estate worth 20 pounds.

In 1685, James II took over the reorganization of the New England colonies that had been begun by his brother, Charles II. Under this plan, all of the Northern colonies became the Dominion of New England and subject to a royal governor. Edmund Andros became the governor and established a central government at Boston. During this time, Andros exerted absolute authority. New taxes were imposed, and town meetings were forbidden. Churches were prohibited from collecting tithes to pay their ministers' salaries.

Andros was removed from power in 1689, when the colonists received word that the overthrow of James II was imminent. New Hampshire returned to its earlier arrangement with Massachusetts, requesting its government and protection. That arrangement lasted until a royal charter in 1691 again recognized New Hampshire as a separate colony.

Warfare

Much of New Hampshire's history is marked by wars with the native peoples. This began with King William's War in 1689. New Hampshire was positioned on the frontier of the dispute over the Canadian border. Its towns were attacked by French troops and their native allies, and the colony's men fought with the English.

A brief period of peace followed until the outbreak of war again in 1702. Queen Anne's War renewed the hostilities with France and again subjected New Hampshire to native raids throughout the colony. Again, men and money were contributed.

Following this conflict, New Hampshire enjoyed

a relatively lengthy period of peace until local issues between the colonists and Native Americans again embroiled them in war. The series of battles that took place between the English and the French and their native allies during 1724–1725 was known as Dummer's War, after William Dummer, governor of the Massachusetts Bay Colony.

King George's War, fought in the American colonies from 1744 to 1748, disrupted the peace once more. A regiment from New Hampshire was involved in the capture of Louisbourg, a French stronghold that guarded Canada. Following this, a brief period of quiet reigned until the French and Indian War began in 1754. As it had in the previous wars, New Hampshire contributed its resources to the defense of England. Following the conclusion of this armed combat, New Hampshire would not fight again until the American Revolution began in 1775.

Economy

New Hampshire grew quickly. By 1763, its population had reached roughly 30,000, and, in 1761, it boasted 61 towns. A rapid expansion between 1760 and 1775 generated another eighty-six new townships. This growth stemmed primarily from new populations, including a large number of Scots-Irish settlers. In addition, the Privy Council's decision to fix the boundary between New Hampshire and Massachusetts in 1740 increased the colony by 3,500 square miles.

The economy boasted three sectors. Maritime vocations bolstered much of the economy, and an abundance of fish spurred the growth of fisheries. Trade, too, was an important ingredient in the colonial economy. Furs and fish were traded, but New Hampshire's primary trade came from its involvement in slavery; large purchases of sugar produced by slaves in the West Indies were distilled into rum and exported to Europe. Shipbuilding also flourished in New Hampshire. In addition to the building of the ships, a variety of industries associated with ships developed, including the manufacture of rope walks and sails, and commerce in imported goods.

Lumber was also important to the economy. Raw lumber for building was exported in significant amounts. Maple sugar became a popular export as colonists learned how to produce it from the abundant trees. New Hampshire also became the leading producer of ships' masts, due to the availability of large timber from which to create the massive center beams. As a result, the state eventually acquired a near monopoly on ships' masts for all of New England. Finally, a small business and professional class, including some printers and lawyers, also contributed to the economy.

Society

New Hampshire did not place the emphasis on religion that some colonies did. From its inception, a number of denominations—Anglicans, Puritans, Quakers, Baptists, and Presbyterians—resided there. The outbreak of revival in the 1730s, known as the Great Awakening, did affect the colony. George Whitefield, the popular evangelist who spread the revivals throughout the colonies, visited New Hampshire in 1740 and 1744. This religious fervor resulted in the founding of Dartmouth College in 1769.

Because of its close association with Massachusetts, New Hampshire adopted a similar emphasis on education. Towns were required to maintain public schools. Dartmouth College, while initially meant only to train Native Americans as missionaries to their own people, soon became an institution of higher education.

American Revolution

New Hampshire quickly became involved in the Revolutionary movement that led to independence. In 1773, the colony established a standing Committee of Correspondence that operated throughout the war. The following year, the colonial assembly voted to dissolve the royal government. This body would meet throughout the war to decide on contributions to the war effort and work out a new plan of government.

In December 1774, a group of New Hampshire men seized Fort William and Mary and the stores of weapons it housed. These weapons were distributed to towns throughout the colony and were eventually used in the war.

The committee met in January 1775 to approve the actions of the Continental Congress and conduct other business related to the war effort. At the fourth meeting of the committee, conducted just after the outbreak of war in May 1775, the body voted to establish a provincial post office system and an army of 2,000 men. New Hampshire was able to contribute men with considerable military experience to the war effort. In July, the colonial assembly established the First Provincial Congress to govern the colony.

In addition to fighting the war against England, New Hampshire also worked to revamp its frame of government. Under the new system that emerged after the Revolution, the franchise was expanded to include all taxpayers, and the property requirements for office-holders were significantly reduced. Each town was granted one assemblyman per 100 freemen in the House of Representatives. Members of this lower legislative body were responsible for electing the upper house, known as the Council. All state officers were elected by both legislative bodies, in part, because the new government made no provision for an executive officer. There was also no established judicial system.

New Hampshire was the first state to establish a separate government, and, on June 15, 1776, it declared its formal independence from England. While the Provincial Congress had acted quickly, the voters were not so quick to accept the new government. A series of constitutional conventions beginning in 1778 worked to revise the government. A new constitution was finally approved and put into effect in July 1784.

Tonia M. Compton

See also: New Hampshire (Chronology); Portsmouth, New Hampshire.

Bibliography

Daniell, Jere R. *Colonial New Hampshire: A History.* Millwood, NY: KTO, 1981.

Fry, William Henry. *New Hampshire as a Royal Province, Studies in History, Economics and Law*, Vol. 29, No. 2. New York: Columbia University, 1908.

Squires, James Duane. *The Granite State of the United States: A History of New Hampshire from 1623 to the Present,* Vol. 1. New York: American Historical Company, 1956.

Van Deventer, David E. *The Emergence of Provincial New Hampshire, 1623–1741.* Baltimore: Johns Hopkins University Press, 1976.

New Haven

New Haven is a port city located in New Haven County, in southern Connecticut, where the Quinnipiac River and other small rivers flow into Long Island Sound. When the first Europeans arrived in the seventeenth century, the Quinnipiack Indians were inhabiting the area. They were semi-sedentary, hunting wild animals such as deer and fowl, harvesting shellfish and scaled fish, and collecting roots, nuts, and fruits. They also cultivated corn, beans, and squash to supplement their diet.

In 1638, Theophilus Eaton and the Reverend John Davenport left Boston with a company of about 500 Puritans and sailed into New Haven harbor. After learning that the Mohawk and Pequot tribes were threatening the Quinnipiack and other tribes in the area, the Puritan colonists purchased land from Momauguin, the leader of the Quinnipiack, offering a small assortment of European goods and protection against raids by other native peoples.

The colony had no official charter, so the colonists met on June 4, 1639, to establish a government and church polity similar to the Massachusetts model. The following year, they renamed the settlement New Haven, and, by 1641, the town had grown to about 800 settlers. Built on a grid of nine squares, the central grid was designated the "market place," a public area now called The Green. The colony soon expanded to include a series of detached settlements along Long Island Sound, such as Guilford, Branford, Milford, and Stamford; Southold, on the eastern end of Long Island; and settlements as far away as present-day Salem, New Jersey.

With New Haven's fine natural harbor, the first settlers had predicted that their town would grow into a prosperous, commercial seaport. The sudden decline in the number of new immigrants coming to New England and Boston's predominance in commercial trade with Britain, however, hampered any prospect of New Haven becoming a commercial hub in the Atlantic world. After failing to establish a direct trade route to England in 1646, the settlement evolved into a small agricultural seaport town, overshadowed by the commercial seaports of Boston and New Amsterdam.

During the British Civil Wars, New Haven supported the parliamentary side; after the restoration of Charles II, it became the refuge of three regicide judges, Edward Whalley, William Goffe, and John Dixwell. John Davenport, as it was later revealed, hid the regicides in a cave on West Rock, where they eluded the king's officials. After changing their identities, Whalley and Goffe settled in Hartford and then Massachusetts, and Dixwell settled in New Haven.

It was around this time that Charles II gave his brother James, the Duke of York, the lands between the Delaware and Connecticut Rivers. After James seized New Amsterdam in 1664, the New Haven Colony, fearing a union with New York under the rule of a Catholic regent, reluctantly agreed to merge with the colony of Connecticut under the Charter of 1662. With the establishment of the Dominion of New England in 1688, James annulled the colony's charter, but it was reinstated by William and Mary following the Glorious Revolution in 1689.

At the turn of the century, a small group of Puritan congregationalists founded a college for training the ministry. Having opened its doors at Killingsworth (now Clinton) in 1702 as the Collegiate School, five years later, the college moved to Saybrook (now Old Saybrook). In 1716, the college was relocated to New Haven. After receiving a large benefaction from Elihu Yale in 1718, it was renamed Yale College. During the colonial period, Yale expanded its studies and eventually gained recognition as one of the world's leading universities.

Although New Haven was not as prosperous or as strategic as the seaports of Boston, New York, Philadelphia, and Charles Town, it was nonetheless raided by British and Hessian forces during the American Revolution and occupied for a brief period. The patriots of New Haven, including the old Reverend Naphtali Daggett, put up a brave fight, but they were overwhelmed by the strength of the British, who routed them and left the town partially burnt. After the Revolution, the Connecticut Assembly appointed Roger Sherman, New Haven's mayor, to the Constitutional Convention at Philadelphia. As one of the framers of the U.S. Constitution, Sherman was the delegate who put forth the Connecticut Compromise, an alternative to the Virginia Plan, whereby smaller states were to receive equal representation in the upper house. The proposal was accepted, and the idea of unicameral legislature was abandoned in favor of a bicameral congressional government.

As a commercial and agricultural center during the eighteenth century, New Haven grew into a relatively prosperous town. By the end of the colonial period, it had about 3,500 inhabitants and was, together with Hartford, the co-capital of Connecticut, a position it maintained until the second half of the nineteenth century.

With Eli Whitney's invention of the cotton gin in 1793, and with his firearms and ammunition company, the city emerged as a leading manufacturing center during the early republic. In 1808, James Brewster introduced the first assembly line at his famous New Haven carriage factory, and other industries and businesses flourished in the area.

The city, moreover, took a leading role in the abolition movement. It is well known for the Amistad incident of 1839, in which nearly fifty African Mendi slaves, captured by the Spanish, were given safe passage back to Africa by the Federal District Court in New Haven.

Michael Sletcher

See also: Connecticut; Connecticut (Chronology); Yale College.

Bibliography

Atwater, Edward Elias, ed. *History of the City of New Haven to the Present Time.* 2 vols. New York: W. W. Munsell, 1887.
———. *History of the Colony of New Haven to Its Absorption into Connecticut.* Meriden, CT: Journal, 1902.
Calder, Isabel MacBeath. *The New Haven Colony.* New Haven, CT: Yale University Press, 1934.
Osterweis, Rollin Gustav. *Three Centuries of New Haven, 1638–1938.* New Haven, CT: Yale University Press, 1953.
Shumway, Floyd, and Richard Hegel. *New Haven: An Illustrated History.* Woodland Hills, CA: Windsor Publications, 1987.

New Jersey

Benjamin Franklin supposedly described New Jersey as a "barrel tapped at both ends." Because of its location between Pennsylvania and New York, the importance of the Hudson and Delaware Rivers to colonial commerce, and the influence of Philadelphia and New York City, Franklin was largely correct. European settlers entered New Jersey through the ports of its more famous neighbors, and much of New Jersey's commerce depended on merchants in Philadelphia and New York.

As in the other Middle colonies, ethnic and religious diversity characterized settlements in New Jersey. East Jersey's diversity mirrored that of New York and West Jersey's diversity mirrored that of Pennsylvania. Despite the important influences of New York and Pennsylvania, a unique history nonetheless characterized colonial New Jersey.

Dominion

Henry Hudson explored the Delaware Bay and the Hudson River in 1609, laying the basis for Dutch claims to lands in the Delaware and Hudson River Valleys. Beginning in the 1610s, the Dutch West India Company financed settlements in New Netherland. The great majority of Europeans who settled in New Netherland, however, favored settlement in the Hudson Valley in what would become the English colony of New York. Until the 1660s, the Dutch presence in Jersey remained minimal, confined to a string of forts,

The Georgian-style Ford Mansion in Morristown, New Jersey, which served as General George Washington's military headquarters in the winter of 1779–1780, is one of that state's great landmarks of the Revolutionary War. *(Courtesy of Morristown National Historical Park)*

trading posts, and settlements along the Delaware River and a few Dutch settlements across the Hudson River from New Amsterdam.

In the 1650s, England began to challenge Dutch commercial superiority, and, in 1664, King Charles II of England granted his brother James Stuart, Duke of York, a colony stretching from the Connecticut to the Delaware Rivers. Shortly thereafter, an English fleet forced the Dutch governor of New Netherland to recognize English claims to "New York," establishing English dominion over what would become New York, New Jersey, Pennsylvania, and Delaware.

The Duke of York promptly granted the part of his claim that would become New Jersey to two nobles as a reward for their support of the Stuart family. As proprietors of New Jersey, Lord John Berkeley and Sir George Carteret enjoyed the rights to all of New Jersey's lands, along with the exclusive right to govern the colony. In 1676, after Quaker investors purchased Berkeley's claim, Berkeley and Carteret divided the colony into the provinces of East and West Jersey, and

ownership of West Jersey soon devolved into the hands of over 100 Quaker shareholders. On Carteret's death in 1682, his heirs sold his claims to groups of speculators. By 1685, the East Jersey Proprietors, a small group of Scots who aimed to recreate the near feudal system of social, political, and economic relations of Northern Scotland in East Jersey, assumed control of Carteret's half of the Jersey colony.

Confusion over who possessed rightful claims to govern the Jerseys launched politics into a state of constant confusion. Puritans, Dutch, and other settlers refused to recognize the legitimacy of the proprietors' governments, a situation compounded by the constant infighting among the proprietors themselves. Finally, in 1702, English officials pressured the various proprietors and investors to cede their claims to govern the Jerseys to the Crown, though the proprietors and shareholders retained the rights to their Jersey land claims. New Jersey then became a royal colony, governed by a Crown-appointed governor, an executive council, and an elective assembly. Reflecting the earlier division of the colony, New Jersey had two colonial capitals, Perth Amboy in the east and Burlington in the west, with the yearly assembly alternating between the two.

Peoples, Settlement, and Development

Perhaps 10,000 Lenni Lenapes occupied New Jersey at the time of European contact. Like many Woodlands peoples, the Lenni Lenape lived in semipermanent agricultural villages and spent part of the year hunting, fishing, and trading.

In the early 1600s, New Jersey Indians began trading with Dutch and Swedish outposts along the Delaware and Hudson Rivers. But even prior to the appearance of European traders along the Delaware, disease and war with the Iroquois of upstate New York decimated their population. Many Lenni Lenapes responded to these pressures on their population by joining other native nations and tribes in Pennsylvania and New York. The colony's European population had swelled to nearly 14,000 by 1700, placing further pressure on the native population. The Lenni Lenape continued to sell land—often under duress—and to move out of the colony in hopes of incorporating themselves into other tribes and consolidating their power. By 1763, fewer than 1,000 Native Americans lived in New Jersey.

Close proximity to Pennsylvania and New York shaped European settlement patterns in East and West Jersey. Many Quakers called West Jersey home, as did small enclaves of Dutch, Swedish, and Finnish settlers, remnants of the brief period of Dutch and Swedish colonization along the lower Delaware. Beginning in the 1720s, after entering the colonies at the port of Philadelphia, significant numbers of Germans and Scots-Irish Presbyterians settled in West Jersey.

East Jersey was even more diverse. Beginning in the 1660s, many of the inhabitants of New Netherland—a motley assortment of Flemings, Walloons, French Huguenots, German Protestants, Dutch, and their African and African American slaves—spilled over into East Jersey from New York. Non-Quaker English, New England Puritans, Scottish, and Scots-Irish emigrants also settled in East Jersey. Finally, Quakers and Baptists seeking refuge from religious persecution in New England added to the religious diversity of East Jersey. In the 1720s, the Great Awakening—a series of religious revivals—arose amid this potent religious and ethnic brew, adding to the colony's religious diversity.

The importance of religion in colonial New Jersey profoundly affected the lives of women, particularly Quakers and Puritans. Over time, they used their place in religious life to gain greater authority in the church and family.

New Jersey was the most diverse colony in terms of both religion and ethnicity, even more than its diverse neighbors, New York and Pennsylvania. Diversity did not necessarily lead to the creation of a cohesive culture, however. New Jersey's ethnic and religious groups tended to settle in homogeneous communities, allowing them to preserve many features of their culture and institutions. Similarly, the concentration of New Jersey's African and African American population in two northeastern counties allowed for the creation and preservation of a distinct, Northern African American culture.

Most white Jersey families sought ownership of land, and they expected to provide a landed inheritance for all of their children. New York and Philadelphia merchants' demand for Jersey's agricultural products created a prosperous economy that allowed most European families to obtain the land that alone provided independence and economic security. To supplement family labor, they turned to free and unfree labor of indentured servants and, in northern Jersey, enslaved Africans and African Americans. Often unable to gain their freedom during the colonial period, slaves instead forged extended family ties and sought greater personal freedoms within the institution of slavery.

Politics and Authority

Most of the European population could reasonably expect to own land at some time in their lives, and, with it, the right to participate in their own governance. The ethnically and religiously homogenous townships that dotted New Jersey were essentially self-governing, run by local notables with the consent of the freeholders, the property-holding adult white men of the community. In most cases, the freeholders selected prominent locals of similar ethnic and religious backgrounds to govern their communities and represent their interests in the colonial assembly. The assembly spent much of its time acting on local petitions, trying to mediate, often unsuccessfully, disputes between various landed, commercial, and political interests.

Leading local men and the electorate shared a host of common interests, ranging from resistance to the

Anglican Church, resistance to the royal governor, and resistance to the proprietors, who claimed large portions of the colony on the basis of the proprietary charters. Politics was especially important in East Jersey, as local leaders and the freeholders sought to defend the values and interests of their communities against groups with conflicting values and interests, such as the proprietors. The relationship between the electorate and leading local men remained complex and deferential, but local leaders actively sought the support of the "people," in part to shore up their own political influence against the governor, the proprietors, and other officeholders.

In West Jersey, wealthy Quaker merchants centered in Burlington exercised considerable economic and political power. In East Jersey, proprietors who held tracts of land measured in the thousands and tens of thousands of acres sought to use their wealth, influence, and political power to create a more hierarchical society. In doing so, they generated sustained conflicts that pitted small landowners and locally prominent men against the "gentlemen" proprietors.

Conflicts over land titles had sporadically plagued East Jersey since the 1660s, when Puritan farmers rebelled against proprietors who tried to claim Puritan lands around Elizabethtown and Newark. Beginning in the 1740s, the problem spread, as the proprietors began to challenge the legitimacy of land titles throughout northern Jersey. In some cases entire townships found their land deeds contested by proprietors and land companies, and, by 1745, upwards of 500,000 acres of Jersey land titles came under suspicion. Actual settlers, who had purchased their land in good faith and then made settlement and improvements, faced the prospect of proving the legitimacy of their titles in costly court cases against well-funded proprietors.

Small farmers, and in some cases their wives, joined with local leaders in land riots to retain possession of their land and protect their community from threatening outside forces. The land rioters' objective was to retain possession of the title to their lands by intimidating the proprietors and their agents, forestalling court hearings, preventing the enforcement of evictions, and preventing resettlement of seized lands. By and large, the land rioters succeeded in defending their land titles from the proprietors.

The unique history of colonial New Jersey continued to shape events during the Revolution and in the early national period. Some great landholders became loyalists, while many land rioters became patriots, sustaining political divisions through the early national period. Finally, prosperity and diversity, fed by prox-imity to New York City and Philadelphia, continued to characterize the state.

John Craig Hammond

See also: New Jersey (Chronology); New York; New York City; Pennsylvania; Philadelphia.

Bibliography

Hodges, Graham Russell. *Root & Branch: African Americans in New York & East Jersey, 1613–1863.* Chapel Hill: University of North Carolina Press, 1999.

Lurie, Maxine N. "New Jersey: The Unique Proprietary." *Pennsylvania Magazine of History and Biography* 111:1 (1987): 77–97.

McConville, Brendan. *These Daring Disturbers of the Peace: The Struggle for Property and Power in Early New Jersey.* Ithaca, NY: Cornell University Press, 1999.

Pomfret, John E. *Colonial New Jersey: A History.* New York: Scribner's, 1973.

Wacker, Peter O. *Land and People: A Cultural Geography of Preindustrial New Jersey, Origins and Settlement Patterns.* New Brunswick, NJ: Rutgers University Press, 1975.

New Mexico

By the time a Spanish expedition crossed the Rio Grande into what is now New Mexico, Pueblo Indians had been living in a string of settlements from El Paso to Taos for more than three centuries. The story of colonial New Mexico is, at its core, the struggle of autonomous Pueblo villages to resist Spanish military force and cultural conquest from 1540 to 1846, when the United States took control of the region.

The Rio Grande Valley was home to between sixty and seventy independent native communities, totaling less than 40,000 people, when Francisco Vázquez de Coronado approached it from Mexico in 1540. The independent pueblo was the main unit of political organization, and the pueblos had relatively little contact with one another. The Pueblo peoples of New Mexico spoke at least five mutually unintelligible languages (Tiwa, Tewa, Piro, Tano, and Keresan), and each language was broken down further into dialects. The Pueblo were farmers, who had mastered the skill of raising crops in a harsh, unforgiving climate.

Like Hernando de Soto, who was cutting a path of destruction through the Southeast at the same time, Coronado had no system of conquest. He moved through Pueblo country with 300 Spanish soldiers and

Christianized native servants. After establishing a base camp near modern-day Albuquerque, Coronado required local Tiwas to furnish his army with food, clothing, and women. Not surprisingly, the Tiwa resisted Coronado's demands; Coronado responded by burning 200 of the native people at the stake. Ten of twelve Tiwa villages were ultimately abandoned as a result of the fighting with the Spanish; the remaining two were conquered. Although Coronado left New Mexico as soon he learned that there was no treasure to be had, the Spanish gained a reputation for violence among the Pueblo.

In 1598, Juan de Oñate brought a different style of Spanish colonization to New Mexico. After declaring all of New Mexico to be under Spanish rule, he assembled Pueblo leaders at several locations along the Rio Grande to inform them of the benefits of Spanish rule. Chief among these benefits were peace, justice, new crops, livestock, and trade. Oñate also indicated that if the Pueblo would submit to the Catholic Church, they could avoid an eternity of suffering.

Spanish records indicate that the Pueblo agreed on the spot to become servants of the Spanish Crown and the church; however, Oñate's tenure as governor of New Mexico was marked by constant violence between the Pueblo and their Spanish masters. When Oñate's own nephew was killed in a surprise attack, the governor responded ferociously. Spanish forces overwhelmed the people of Acoma Pueblo, killing 500 men and 300 women and children. Some 80 men and 500 women and children stood trial; many of these had their feet cut off, and all were forced into twenty years of servitude. Powers in Mexico City eventually brought Oñate up on charges of cruelty and adultery.

New Mexico's native people were caught in a conflict between the colony's civil and ecclesiastical authorities. Various governors tried to reduce the power of the missions. The more the Pueblo people worked on missions, the less they could contribute to the colony's labor supply, thereby robbing the colony's government of valuable resources. Missionaries and governors accused each other of using native labor for personal gain. In reality, both sides abused the Pueblo, and, between 1630 and 1680, the situation deteriorated rapidly. Missionaries embarked on a new program to crush native religion by force. At the same time, warfare between the Pueblo and Apache was intensifying.

All these forces came to a head in the Pueblo Revolt of 1680. The Pueblo began the revolt by killing missionaries and all the Spaniards they could find. Then, they laid siege to Santa Fe. Within a matter of days, all the missions had been destroyed; and half of the forty or so priests and hundreds of Spanish colonists had been killed. The surviving Spanish colonists left for El Paso, where they stayed for twelve years. The Pueblo Revolt marked the first time that Pueblo peoples from different regions had acted in concert toward a single goal.

The Spanish reconquest of New Mexico began in 1692. Eventually, Spain did regain control of the Pueblo. Still, the first half of the eighteenth century was marked by factional strife between the various pueblos and simmering conflict between the Spanish and the Pueblo people. Missionaries reconsidered their attempt to quell native religion, and they stopped confiscating ceremonial objects. In the second half of the eighteenth century and beyond, Spain's influence on New Mexico, and indeed its influence in the Americas as a whole, markedly declined.

Matthew Jennings

See also: Borderlands, Spanish; Santa Fe; Spanish Colonies on Mainland North America (Chronology).

Bibliography

Simmons, Marc. *New Mexico: A Bicentennial History.* New York: W. W. Norton, 1977.

Spicer, Edward H. *Cycles of Conquest: The Impact of Spain, Mexico, and the United States on the Indians of the Southwest, 1533–1960.* Tucson: University of Arizona Press, 1962.

Weber, David J. *The Spanish Frontier in North America.* New Haven, CT: Yale University Press, 1992.

New Netherland

New Netherland was a prominent Dutch colony in North America in the early seventeenth century. The Dutch sought to trade for furs with native peoples and established trading posts at the mouth of the Hudson River (New Amsterdam) and 150 miles upriver (Fort Nassau). In 1664, England seized the colony and renamed these settlements New York and Albany, respectively.

Algonquin Indians had moved into the area that became New Netherland by 1000 C.E., and Iroquois Indians had entered the region around 1300 C.E. By the early seventeenth century, the Algonquin occupied the lower Hudson River Valley, while the Mohawk of the Iroquois League occupied the upper Hudson River region.

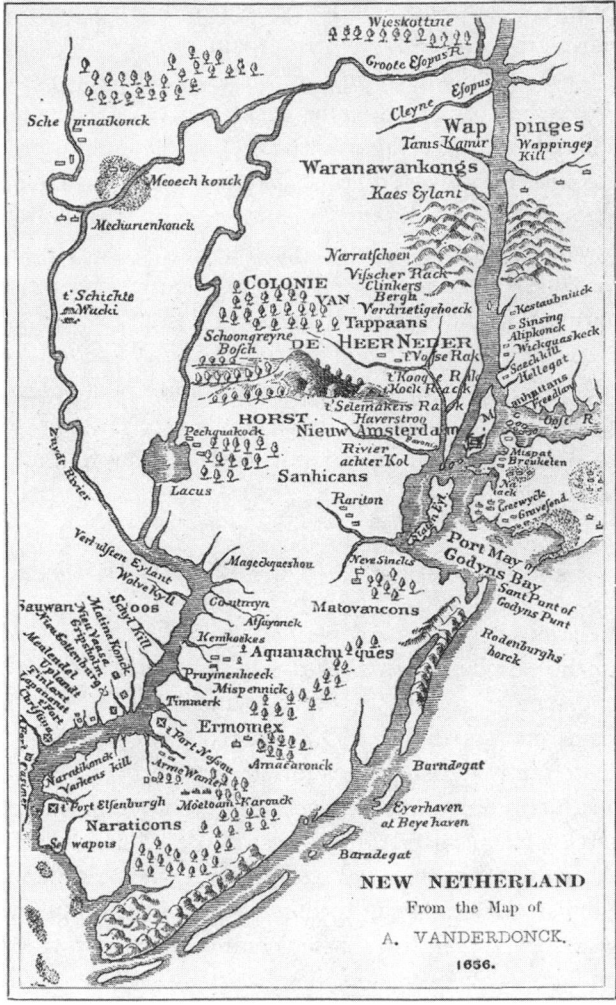

NEW NETHERLAND
From the Map of
A. VANDERDONCK.
1656.

The Dutch colony of New Netherland—mapped here in 1656, eight years before its capture by the English—extended from northern Delaware and New Jersey through Manhattan Island and up the Hudson River to modern-day Albany. *(Brown Brothers, Sterling, Pennsylvania)*

Dutch Colonization

The Netherlands were a leading economic power by the early seventeenth century, and Dutch colonization efforts in America emphasized commerce over extensive settlement. In 1609, Englishman Henry Hudson, employed by the Dutch, sailed his ship the *Half Moon* up the river to be named for him. Within a year, the Dutch began trading trinkets, guns, and alcohol with the native peoples along the Hudson River for furs. In 1614, the Dutch established Fort Nassau (Albany) on the river. Prominent Dutch traders tried to control the early fur trade in the region.

In 1621, the Dutch government granted a charter to the West India Company allowing the company to monopolize trade and shipping in the Dutch regions of the Americas and West Africa and to establish military and civil bodies to oversee its holdings. The company sought to populate its North American territory to counter English and French claims to the region. In 1624, it brought thirty French-speaking Walloons from southern Belgium to the Hudson River Valley and founded the colony of New Netherland. Because the Dutch economy was prosperous at this time, few Dutch settlers wanted to go to America. Thus, New Netherland contained an ethnically diverse population from its inception, a primary feature of the colony throughout the period of Dutch control. Cornelis Jacobsz May became the first director-general of New Netherland in 1624. The company re-established Fort Nassau as Fort Orange and ordered the construction of Fort New Amsterdam (later New York City) at the mouth of the Hudson on Manhattan Island. By 1625, New Amsterdam contained about 270 colonists, Fort Orange 30. Most of the early settlers were Walloons, but others were Dutch, German, Scandinavian, and African.

The company granted extensive power to the director-general and allowed very little political participation by the colonists. Willem Verhulst succeeded May as director-general in 1625, and Peter Minuit succeeded Verhulst a year later. In 1626, Minuit purchased Manhattan from the Manhate Indians (also known as the Rechgawawank) for trinkets valued at 60 guilders (about 24 dollars or the equivalent of several thousand dollars today). The Mohawk Indians supplied the Dutch with beaver pelts for trade, and this became a leading commodity of New Netherland. Although the Dutch government granted the company a monopoly on trade, colonists almost immediately began trading illegally with the Native Americans.

The Dutch government remained concerned at New Netherland's small population and, in 1628, adopted the first patroonship plan. It granted patroons—wealthy men willing to sponsor colonial settlement—large tracts of land along the Hudson River if they brought sixty immigrants to New Netherland within three years. The 1629 Charter of Freedoms and Exemptions increased the incentives offered to patroons by allowing them access to the fur trade.

Several men took advantage of this plan, but, by 1636, only Kiliaen van Rensselaer retained his patroonship. The others became discouraged and returned their lands to the company. Rensselaer established Rensselaerswyck near Fort Orange. Most of the settlers in New Netherland during this early period were single men, as Rensselaer offered skilled workers and professionals wages that were higher than those in Holland.

The West India Company brought eleven African slaves to the colony in 1626. Slave importations, most from the Dutch colony of Curaçao, became a key part of the region's economy, as New Netherland relied on slave labor more than any other North American colony in the first half of the seventeenth century. By 1640, New Amsterdam contained roughly 100 Africans—a third of its total population. The company allowed slaves to live on their own and required payment for work performed. These relatively independent slaves learned the Dutch language, purchased property, and established families in New Netherland. In some cases, the company freed its slaves, particularly less productive, aging slaves, and a free black population developed.

Black residents could sue in Dutch courts, marry, baptize their children into the Dutch Reformed Church, and fight in defense of the colony. As the company's control over the colony weakened, individual settlers began importing slaves directly from Africa in 1655. These slaves had fewer liberties than the company slaves and encountered greater barriers to gaining their freedom. Although Dutch slave traders resold many slaves to Virginia and Maryland colonists, many remained in New Netherland. By the English takeover in 1664, one fifth of New Amsterdam's population was African. Of the city's 375 black residents, 75 were free.

The company recalled Minuit in 1631. Jansen Kroll replaced him but remained only a year; he was succeeded as director-general by Wouter van Twiller in 1633. Van Twiller's drunken behavior and poor accounting practices convinced the company to replace him with Willem Kieft in 1638. Kieft was the most dictatorial of these men but saw dramatic population growth during his tenure because the Dutch government issued the Freedoms and Exemptions Act of 1640, promising 200 acres to each colonist who brought five Europeans to New Netherland. The colony's European population doubled between 1638 and 1643.

Relations between local natives and the Dutch soured under Kieft, and war broke out in the early 1640s. Kieft angered the Algonquin people in 1639 by imposing a tax on them, and he overreacted to a few native raids in the summer of 1641 by attacking Algonquin villages. In 1643, Kieft and his men massacred more than 100 friendly natives. In response, the Algonquin attacked outlying farms. By its end in 1645, the war had claimed the lives of 200 colonists and approximately 1,000 Native Americans, including women, children, and the elderly. Many surviving colonists moved to fortified New Amsterdam.

In 1646, the company recalled Kieft, and Peter Stuyvesant became director-general in 1647. Stuyvesant's tenure was fraught with conflict. He fought with colonists over taxes and political participation, with the company over religious toleration, with the Dutch government over judicial matters, and with Rensselaerswyck over trade in the Fort Orange area. The authoritarian Stuyvesant began extensive reforms in New Netherland, including the creation of strict fire codes, price controls on bread, and enforcement of laws against smuggling and liquor sales to the native peoples. He also required attendance at Sunday religious services.

Relations with New England

Relations between New Netherland and New England to the east deteriorated as the colonies spread toward one another and as the home countries engaged in a series of wars in the 1650s and 1660s. Overlapping Dutch and English land claims in America became such an acute problem that leaders signed a 1650 agreement setting the border 10 miles east of the Hudson River. Although this line was generous to New England, English settlers began to move across it within a few years. Several English Puritan communities had formed on Long Island also, and these insisted that Stuyvesant allow them town meetings. He ignored their demands, but such attitudes spread to Dutch settlements and further undermined his authority.

Stuyvesant encountered other problems as well. New Sweden seized a Dutch fort on the Delaware River in 1654. The following year, Stuyvesant led 600 men against the Swedes, who peacefully agreed to Dutch rule. While Stuyvesant was absent, Algonquin Indians attacked the farms of several colonists. The ensuing war caused much property damage and cost the lives of fifty colonists and sixty natives. Stuyvesant hurried back to end the conflict and recover hostages. He banned the creation of outlying settlements and fortified the defenses of New Amsterdam.

By 1664, New Netherland's population was approximately two-thirds Dutch. The colony also contained English, German, French, Finnish, and Jewish settlers. This diverse population had little loyalty to the company or the Dutch government, and many colonists disliked Stuyvesant's authoritarian rule. That year, King Charles II of England granted the region to his brother, James, Duke of York. James sent four ships under Colonel Richard Nicolls to New Netherland demanding its surrender. Although Stuyvesant wanted to resist, he received no support from the townspeople. Focused on trade, they held little allegiance to the Netherlands. When Nicolls informed them that they would retain commercial and political rights, they agreed to English rule, and James renamed the colony New York. New Amsterdam became New York City and Fort Orange became Albany.

Dutch influences remained in New York after the English takeover. Place names such as Breukelyn (Brooklyn) and Haerlem (Harlem) continued with only slight modification. Most settlers stayed in the colony, as did Stuyvesant. During a subsequent English-Dutch war, the colony briefly reverted to Dutch rule in 1673. The following year, the Dutch signed a treaty surrendering all claim to New York forever.

James E. Klein

See also: Dutch; Fort Orange; New Amsterdam; New York; New York and New Netherland (Chronology); New York City. *Document:* Rights and Privileges of Patroons (1629).

Bibliography

Berlin, Ira. "From Creole to African: Atlantic Creoles and the Origins of African-American Society in Mainland North America." *William and Mary Quarterly* 53:2 (April 1996): 251–88.

Kammen, Michael. *Colonial New York: A History.* New York: Charles Scribner's Sons, 1975.

Rink, Oliver A. *Holland on the Hudson: An Economic and Social History of Dutch New York.* New York: Cornell University Press, 1986.

New Orleans

Although the French explored the area that now encompasses coastal Louisiana as early as 1682, settlement of Louisiana did not begin until 1718, when Pierre le Moyne, Sieur d'Iberville, founded the city of New Orleans. Despite the richness of the Louisiana territories, France never exploited the region to its fullest, leaving New Orleans and most of Louisiana a sparsely settled backwater.

Although it was not the first French settlement in the region, New Orleans became its capital in 1722, since it controlled access to the largest water route into the American interior. The original layout of New Orleans was a gridiron (see plan on page 608) that fell within a bend of the Mississippi River. This area, now called the Vieux Carré, or French Quarter, formed the main city limits until the nineteenth century.

The Louisiana colony was first proprietary and then a corporate colony before becoming a royal province in 1732. The population of French Louisiana was remarkably diverse, ranging from French settlers and soldiers to German immigrants to Native American slaves and hunters and, finally, African slaves, who, by the early 1730s, clearly outnumbered the Europeans colonists. The settlers around New Orleans raised tobacco and indigo as cash crops, but the main economy depended on the work of a combined group (European, Native Americans, and African), who farmed, herded, fished, hunted, and traded with nearby natives for deerskins.

Spain won control of the city after the Seven Years' War (known as the French and Indian War in America), and it remained in their possession until 1800, when it was ceded back to France. In 1803, New Orleans was sold to the United States by Napoleon Bonaparte as part of the Louisiana Purchase. In 1815, British military forces under General Edwin Pakenham attempted to seize New Orleans, but they were defeated by Andrew Jackson and a combined force of frontier militiamen, Creole aristocrats, free blacks, and pirates.

Like other Southern cities, New Orleans experienced a substantial growth in its population of mulattos and other free persons of color, which became a serious problem due to the inability of its white leaders to deal fairly with racial issues. Although New Orleans had always had a very diverse population, the result was the nineteenth-century emergence of highly delineated segregation. Those with white skin held the top tier, while blacks, regardless of condition, were pushed to the bottom. Mulattos became a virtual third caste within society, precariously stationed in an ambiguous position somewhere in between, not quite white and not quite black.

Most free blacks and many mulattos were skilled artisans (blacksmiths, carpenters, cobblers, and so on), farmers, or common laborers. Others supported themselves and their families as fishermen or hunters. A few New Orleans mulatto families became quite rich, generally operating businesses—such as stores, hotels, and barbershops—that served whites exclusively. Some free blacks, like Cyprien Richard, even became slaveholders.

Solomon K. Smith

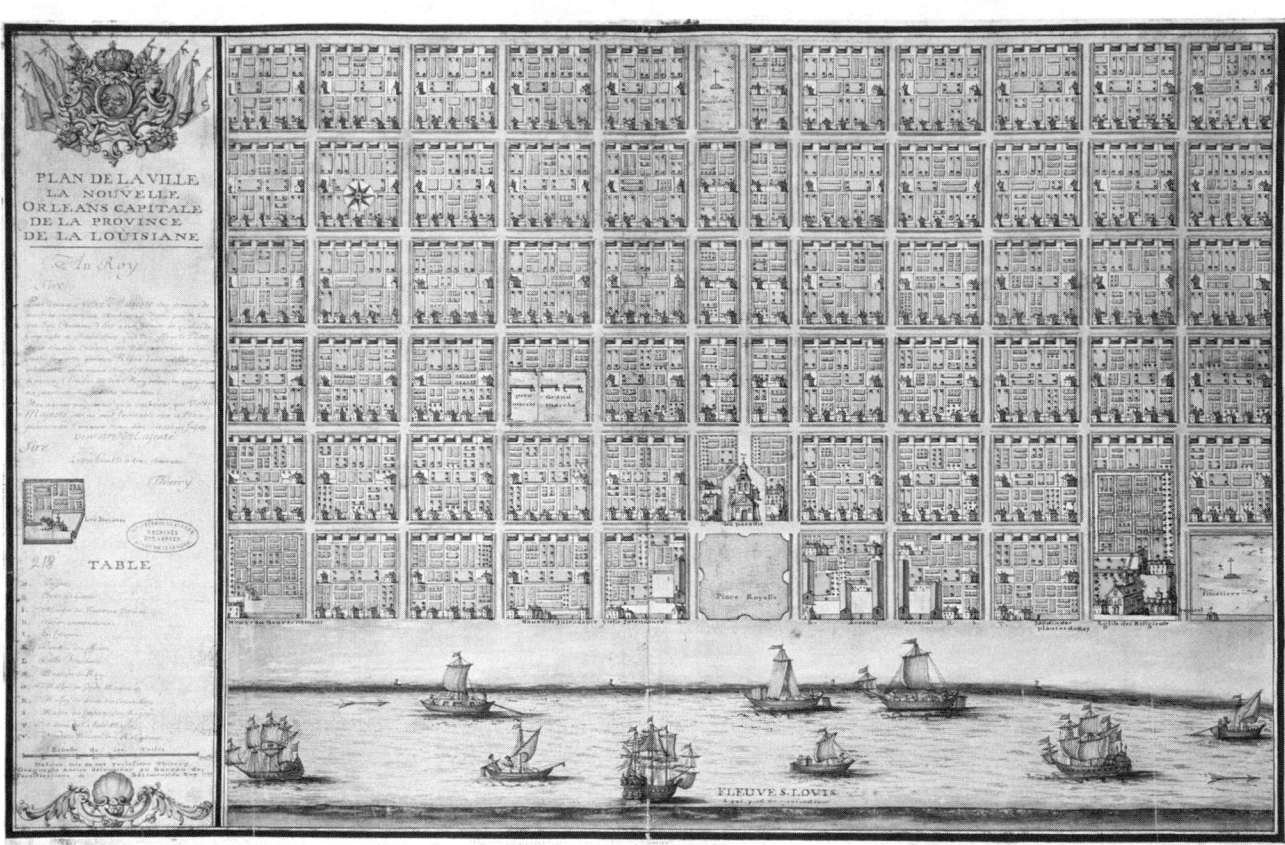

French colonial New Orleans was one of America's first planned cities, laid out by military engineers in 1718. The simple rectilinear pattern remains visible today in the Vieux Carré, or French Quarter. *(Giraudon/Bridgeman Art Library)*

See also: French; French Colonies on Mainland North America (Chronology); Louisiana; Mississippi River; Spanish Colonies on Mainland North America (Chronology).

Bibliography

Ingersoll, Thomas N. *Mammon and Manon in Early New Orleans: The First Slave Society in the Deep South, 1718–1819.* Knoxville: University of Tennessee Press, 1999.

Montero de Pedro, Jose, marques de Casa Mena. *The Spanish in New Orleans and Louisiana.* Translated by Richard E. Chandler. Gretna, LA: Pelican, 2000.

Usner, Daniel H. *Indians, Settlers, & Slaves: In a Frontier Exchange Economy.* Chapel Hill: University of North Carolina Press, 1992.

New Spain

Of the Spanish viceroyalties established in the New World, New Spain and Peru, founded in 1535 and 1543, respectively, were the longest lasting.

The term "viceroyalty" designates an area ruled by a viceroy, who acts on behalf of the king in matters of government. Columbus, for instance, was the first viceroy of the Indies, but that position's power was sapped by the Council of the Indies. New Spain's viceroy also answered to the Council, and two viceroyalties were carved out during the eighteenth century—New Granada and La Plata.

The area known as New Spain—the modern nation of Mexico, a huge chunk of Central America, Spanish possessions in the Caribbean, and a large swath of the American Southwest and Florida—was home to hundreds of distinct Native American societies. These ranged from autonomous villages and chiefdoms to the massive state of Mexico centered at Tenochtitlán in Mexico's central valley.

Native Life and Conquest

Native life in the area that would become New Spain was extraordinarily diverse. In the thirteenth and fourteenth centuries, the Valley of Mexico was the site of a struggle for power between several rival peoples.

The Mexica people (often referred to as the Aztecs) came from the north to central Mexico sometime in the thirteenth century. After serving as mercenaries to Culhuacan and settling on land (Tenochtitlán) controlled by the Tepaneca, the Mexica rose to power through a series of marriage-based alliances, as well as success in trade and warfare.

By the middle of the fourteenth century, most groups in the region spoke the Nahuatl language, the language of the Mexica. Although they spoke similar languages, each Nahua polity retained its own elaborate musical and literary tradition, which helped to solidify its separate ethnic identity.

The Mexica developed a vast tributary empire at the same time as they adopted the strict social hierarchy that characterized the *altepetl* (Nahua polities). In this sense, the Mexica were not particularly innovative; they borrowed various practices from other neighboring groups and used them to their advantage. Society was divided into classes of nobles and commoners, and these divisions were apparent in education, work, and military service. Commoners could climb the social ladder through good marriages and military prowess.

The sacred center of Tenochtitlán was a stunning complex of pyramids, temples, royal palaces, and libraries. The city itself was constructed on a series of islands in a shallow lake and was home to approximately 200,000 residents at the time of the conquest. In comparison, Spain's largest city, Seville, had a population of around 70,000. The Mexica constructed a series of causeways and aqueducts to facilitate travel around Tenochtitlán and to bring fresh water to its residents. In the reign of Montezuma II (1502–1520), Aztec politics, religion, and economy were closely interrelated. All three would be permanently altered by contact with the Spanish in the 1510s.

The conquest of Mexico by the Spanish under Hernando Cortéz began in 1519 and was completed by 1521. In 1519 Cortéz led an unauthorized expedition from Cuba to the mainland. He, along with the soldiers under him, hoped that success would legitimate their actions. Using disgruntled Nahua allies, superior military technology, horses and war dogs, and a devastating smallpox epidemic, a relatively small Spanish force brought down the Aztec empire. They replaced the Aztec nobility with a Spanish ruling class—throwing Aztec priests and nobles to war dogs in many cases— installed Christian religious symbols in place of indigenous ones, and forced enslaved Nahuas to construct a cathedral and palace.

In 1535, the viceroyalty of New Spain was created to deal with the administrative problems brought on by the rapid expansion of the Spanish empire. The position of viceroy was given to Antonio de Mendoza, whose high social rank was intended to bring order to the chaos of the region, which had lapsed into a contest between several conquistadors.

By the time English colonies were founded on the East Coast of North America, Spanish viceroys presided over a large, land-based empire centered at Mexico City, which was home to a massive cathedral, a university, and a publishing house. From this base, New Spain would continue to grow throughout the colonial period, eventually encompassing much of the southwestern United States.

Exploration and Expansion

In the sixteenth century, Spanish expeditions fanned out from Mexico City to the south, west, and north. Most of these expeditions were undertaken in an effort to exploit New Spain's precious metals.

The earliest northern efforts, by Nuño de Guzmán and Francisco Vázquez de Coronado, failed to find any gold or silver. The second half of the sixteenth century was more productive. By the 1670s, silver strikes at Zacatecas, Guanajato, and San Luis Potosí had pushed silver production in New Spain past that of Peru. Native laborers and African slaves were brought north to work in and around the mines, and new cities appeared. Still, most of the wealth generated by the mines was funneled through Mexico City, which dwarfed other cities in New Spain in size and importance.

Society in New Spain was diverse. Most early African and Spanish immigrants were men, and many took native wives. Within a few generations, the result was a large class of mestizos and other mixed-race peoples, who contributed immensely to the development of a distinctly Mexican culture and what would eventually become the nation's character. Spanish and *criollo* (creole) officials encouraged native participation in religious festivals such as Corpus Christi and the ceremonies that accompanied the arrival of new viceroys. Throughout the colonial period, skin color continued to determine one's opportunities to a certain extent, but occupation, income, and cultural characteristics became more important over time.

In the seventeenth century, as central Mexico and outlying silver-producing areas grew in wealth and refinement, Spain began the slow, uneven process of exploring its northern frontier and exploiting the native people there. In 1598, Juan de Oñate took possession of New Mexico in an elaborate ceremony, but neither that colony nor other territories like Florida brought any real wealth to the Crown or to the individual nobles involved.

Northern New Spain remained firmly in native hands, though Franciscans, along with smaller numbers of Jesuits and soldiers, maintained tiny outposts throughout the region. Franciscans were particularly skilled at settling in the midst of large, sedentary native communities such as those of the Pueblo. The government of New Spain saw little economic opportunity in New Mexico, Arizona, Texas, and California. Missionary sects had more success in converting the native peoples in these frontier areas, as the missionaries did not have to compete with mine owners or ranchers.

As elsewhere, native people selected which parts of European religion to accept and which to reject and often made room in their indigenous worldviews for European saints and gods. In one partial exception to this rule, Pueblo Indians responded to a crackdown on their indigenous religion by rising up against the Spanish. The Pueblo Revolt of 1680 forced the Spanish to move south of the Rio Grande for more than a decade, while a retaliatory expedition returned to reconquer the area.

The wealth generated by New Spain encouraged other European nations, most notably France and England, to recognize the importance of overseas colonies. In the eighteenth century, northern New Spain was one of several entities competing for land and resources in North America. The French colony of Louisiana and English traders from Charles Town encroached upon Spanish soldiers and missionaries, but the English, in particular, were able to offer more trade goods and better prices than their Spanish counterparts. In the opening decade of the eighteenth century, the easternmost portion of New Spain was devastated in a series of attacks by the English and their native allies.

Mexico's fertile, populous central valley and the mining and agricultural areas that surrounded it continued to produce great wealth for the Spanish Crown. The portion of New Spain that exists within the borders of today's United States never prospered in the same way. Still, Spain exerted a cultural influence, particularly in the Southwest, which would be felt for centuries to come.

In the late eighteenth century, during the reign of Charles III, Spain attempted to modernize the institutions of its far-reaching empire. Collectively, these plans were known as the Bourbon reforms. Within New Spain, the reforms rankled elite and popular forces alike.

In the first decades of the nineteenth century, a new generation of New Spain's elites channeled their frustrations into a revolutionary movement that would eventually lead to the creation of the modern nation of Mexico.

Matthew Jennings

See also: Mexico City; Spanish Colonies on Mainland North America (Chronology).

Bibliography

Cheetham, Nicholas. *New Spain: The Birth of Modern Mexico.* London: Victor Gollancz, 1974.

Gibson, Charles. *The Aztecs Under Spanish Rule: A History of the Indians of the Valley of Mexico, 1519–1810.* Stanford, CA: Stanford University Press, 1964.

Meyer, Michael C., and William H. Beezley, eds. *The Oxford History of Mexico.* New York: Oxford University Press, 2000.

Weber, David J. *The Spanish Frontier in North America.* New Haven, CT: Yale University Press, 1992.

New York

People of various ethnicities and races have influenced the culture, politics, and economics of the region that is now New York State. Before the arrival of Europeans, various native peoples lived there; some spoke dialects of a similar language, while others spoke completely different, though distantly related, languages. In terms of their economy, some native peoples fished, while others hunted game and gathered plants. Politically, they organized at the village level, rather than on a regional or larger level. When Europeans arrived, they added to this already existing diversity of languages, economic arrangements, and politics.

Native Peoples in New York

The history of the peopling of New York begins around 5000 B.C.E. Around this time, native peoples of the Paleolithic Age lived in a region that today encompasses New York, New Jersey, Delaware, Pennsylvania, and Connecticut. The cultures of the Iroquois and Algonquins, the two native groups encountered by the Europeans upon their arrival, date to the twelfth century.

Algonquian-speaking peoples lived along the coastal plain and river valley areas of New York. Their origins are uncertain, although archaeologists and ethnographers believe that some Algonquian languages are related to the Muskogean language family of the southeastern United States. Algonquian-speaking peoples were the first to meet Europeans, and many died because of European diseases, as well as in the English and Iroquoian conquest of their lands.

Most Algonquian-speaking peoples lived near bodies of water and survived by fishing and gathering plants. Those who lived in the coastal plain spoke dialects of Algonquian, which made communication among them possible. They built canoes to trade and communicate with other native peoples and also used walking trails to exchange furs, pottery, baskets, and food.

Iroquoian-speaking peoples were the other large Native American population at the time of the Europeans' arrival. They lived in the lower Great Lakes and St. Lawrence Valley regions. Iroquoian-speaking peoples spoke distantly related languages within the Iroquoian language family. Around 1000 C.E., they established settlements along the St. Lawrence River Valley. Mainly, they hunted and gathered plants, but they also raised corn. In the fourteenth century, colder temperatures made it more difficult to grow maize. It also led to a scarcity of good farmland, as well as other natural resources, which, in turn, resulted in competition and frequent wars among the native peoples.

As for their political organization, Iroquoian-speaking peoples were more formally organized than Algonquian-speaking peoples. Iroquoian-speaking peoples organized village councils, which included a representative from each clan in the village. Archaeologists believe that the Five Nations—which included the Seneca, Cayuga, Onondaga, Oneida, and Mohawk—formed an alliance known as the Great League of Peace and Power at some time in the late fifteenth century. (In the early eighteenth century, the Tuscarora, a people from farther south, became the sixth nation to join the alliance.)

The word "peace" in the league's name referred to the importance of good relations between villagers and with outsiders, while "power" referred to the spiritual strength created by uniting the various villages, clans, and peoples. The Great League's main body was the Grand Council. Headwomen from each clan chose the fifty male sachems who served on the council. The Grand Council maintained peace but was not a political body with a unified foreign policy or a central government.

After the arrival of the Europeans, the Iroquois quickly became the most powerful group of native peoples. In 1642, the Iroquois began a war with the Huron to the north and west. Since they had access to English firearms, which the Huron did not, they were soon victorious.

By the late seventeenth century, the Five Nations had organized a confederacy to handle their diplomatic and military affairs. This organization formed a permanent alliance with the English under the leadership of Governor-General Sir Edmund Andros, an alliance known as the Covenant Chain, which the two parties agreed to in 1677. Yet, each group interpreted the meaning of the Covenant Chain differently. The Iroquois believed that it recognized Iroquoian autonomy. The English believed that it established their sovereignty over the Iroquois peoples, thus lessening concern that the Iroquois might form an alliance with the French.

Arrival of the Dutch in New York

The Englishman Henry Hudson set sail for the Dutch East India Company in 1609, hoping to find a Northwest Passage to the Orient. Instead, Hudson reached what is today New York, sailing up the river which today bears his name. By 1621, a group of Dutch merchants had formed a national joint-stock company, the Dutch West India Company, whose early economic ventures in New Netherland brought little economic success. Throughout New Netherland's existence, the threat of English expansion always loomed as the English tried to establish trading posts along the Hudson and Connecticut River Valleys and protested that the entire North American seaboard belonged to them.

In order to make their claim to the Hudson River Valley and its trading opportunities more secure, the Dutch West India Company sent a group of thirty Walloon families, French-speaking exiles from the Southern Netherlands, to settle in New Netherland in 1624. Between 1624 and 1625, a total of 300 colonists from throughout Northern and Western Europe settled in New Netherland, 270 in New Amsterdam, and 30 at Fort Orange (near Albany). The Dutch had trouble attracting immigrants from the Netherlands, since there was no extensive religious persecution or high unemployment there. Many Dutch people also believed that the political rights offered in the colonies were not as favorable as those in the Netherlands.

Around 1626, a labor shortage led to the Dutch West India Company's decision to buy African slaves in order to guard its livestock, perform farm labor, help load and unload ships, and work on military projects. The company granted slaves "half freedom" after many years. This status enabled slaves to marry, own property, and travel freely throughout the colony. They also could testify in court cases against free whites. In exchange for this status, slaves had to pay the company a yearly sum. By 1664, about 700 of the colony's nearly 9,000 people were of African descent.

As a result of the limited economic success of the company's fur-trading ventures, the Dutch government encouraged the establishment of subcolonies—patroonships—along the Hudson in 1629. Patroons were also granted special fur-trading rights. The patroonships were largely unsuccessful, with the exception of Kiliaen van Rensselaer's Rensselaerswyck.

After 1639, the West India Company officials extended trading privileges to all settlers. A year later, the company offered 200 acres to each colonist who brought five people with him. As a result of these administrative changes, New Netherland's population went from 1,000 to almost 2,000 between 1638 and 1643. Yet the New Netherland settlement was never as attractive to the Dutch as other Dutch settlements in Asia, Brazil, and the West Indies.

Beginning in 1639, relations with native peoples in the area grew tenser. Unfortunately for the Algonquin, the Dutch saw them as obstacles to settlement. The Algonquin also looked upon the Dutch unfavorably because of Dutch zeal to occupy Algonquin lands and the Dutch practice of letting their livestock roam free, often leading to the trampling of the Algonquins' unfenced cornfields. The Dutch were more careful not to antagonize the Iroquois, since they were essential to the fur trade. Rather than negotiate with the Algonquin, Governor-General Kieft decided to go to war with them. By 1645, their superior weapons and alliances with other native peoples helped the Dutch to defeat the Algonquin.

The English Navigation Act of 1651 forbade foreign ships to engage in English trade at sea, an action that the Dutch saw as a direct reference to them. The following year, the first of three English-Dutch wars began. New Netherland did not participate in this first war, which was fought abroad. In 1663, English competition with the Dutch in Africa and their perception that Dutch trading activities in New Netherland violated the 1660 English Navigation Act led to another war between the two countries.

In March 1664, King Charles II gave his brother James, the Duke of York, a land grant in North America that included Long Island and the lands along the Hudson River, on the western side of the Connecticut River, and on the eastern side of Delaware Bay. The residents of New Netherland surrendered to the En-

glish, because they did not have the weapons or the food supplies to sustain another war effort. James never visited the colony, and the lack of English defense contributed to the Dutch recapturing it in 1673. After the English mounted an attack in 1674, however, English rule in the colony was permanently established.

English Assume Control of New York

Richard Nicolls, the first English governor of the colony, enforced a group of laws known as the Duke's Laws, initially designed for the Long Island and Westchester settlements. The laws' main components did not allow for an elected assembly or town meetings, but they did mandate religious toleration and kept some Dutch political systems in place.

Meanwhile in Albany, settlers sought to maintain their position in the fur trade. Therefore, they were not as interested as the rest of the colony in antagonizing the French to the north, with whom they traded. Albany residents further resented the privileges granted to New York City merchants, such as a 1678 law that gave these merchants a monopoly over the export trade and a 1684 law that made New York City the single entry port of the colony. Colony officials appeased Albany merchants by granting them a monopoly over the fur trade in 1686.

In 1688, a royal decree by James II made New York part of the new Dominion of New England, whose central headquarters was Boston. When word reached the colony of King James II's overthrow in 1689, the colonists, already anxious because of a rumored French-Native American conspiracy against them and the diminished power of their colony, reacted by rebelling against Lieutenant Governor Nicholson.

After Nicholson fled to England, Jacob Leisler eventually became the commander in chief of the colony. When the English sent a new governor in 1691, Leisler's refusal to immediately step down for the new governor led the Crown to charge him with treason, a charge for which Leisler was executed.

Between 1691 and 1710, English colonists were cautious in their relations with their French counterparts. New Yorkers had chosen not to engage in the English-French wars—King William's War from 1689 to 1697 and Queen Anne's War from 1702 to 1713—because of the colony's poor fortifications and the heavy costs that would be involved. The French, in turn, sent no military expeditions of their own against the English for fear of antagonizing their Iroquois allies. Around 1701, the Iroquois negotiated treaties with the British and French that maintained the Iroquois' neutrality in any British-French conflicts. The British did attempt to send expeditions to fight against the French in Canada in 1709 and 1711, but both expeditions were unsuccessful.

Politically, two factions dominated the colony around the middle of the eighteenth century. In 1709, Lewis Morris organized an interest group consisting primarily of Hudson Valley farmers, New York City artisans, and small traders in Albany and New York City. Morris was able to unite these various interest groups by promising better roads, land laws, and cheap money to farmers; he also offered traders import protection, subsidies for local production, and peddler restrictions. Finally, he agreed to impose more taxes on the wealthy.

Robert Hunter, governor from 1710 to 1720, sided with Morris's faction, granting artisans, shopkeepers, and yeoman farmers special rights, as well as protection to religious dissenters and the Dutch population. In 1720, Adolph Philipse and Peter Schuyler began organizing wealthier merchants in New York City and Albany, large landowners, prominent Angli-

cans, and poorer freemen. William Burnet, Hunter's successor, also formed a coalition with Morris's group, which led to tense relations with the Philipse-Schuyler group.

These two factions came to be referred to as the Court (Philipses) and Country (Morrisites). The Court party was known as a cosmopolitan interest, involved in overseas, intercolonial, and slave trades and in political dealings with native peoples. Conversely, the Morris group was known as provincial and interested in creating a strong intracolonial economy. Although other political parties existed, these two were the most influential in their time.

In 1734–1735, colonial politics shifted with the arrest of John Peter Zenger, printer of the *New York Weekly Journal,* a newspaper that Morrisites had recently established. Governor Cosby, political enemy of the Morrisites, had Zenger arrested for libel and the newspaper burned. A jury acquitted Zenger; his landmark case helped establish the idea of a free press and the legitimacy of the public's right to criticize their government officials.

Once the British had defeated the French in the French and Indian War in 1763, white settlers began encroaching even more on Native Americans' lands. In

Fort Ticonderoga, dating to 1755, commanded a strategically important water route in upstate New York. It was the object of bloody fighting during the French and Indian War and became a vital Northern defense for colonial forces in the American War for Independence. *(Library of Congress, HABS, NY, 16-FOTI,1-2)*

1768, a meeting between 3,100 native peoples and several intercolonial delegations granted the English most of central and southwestern New York. In turn, the native peoples received goods valued at 10,460 pounds, recognition of tribal lands located within the territorial domain granted by the English, and an agreement that the boundary line separating British from native lands would be respected. The treaty ultimately provided the native peoples little protection, since British government officials could not control the westward expansion of white settlers and speculators.

When the British government decided to impose new imperial policies on its North American colonists in the 1760s, many became incensed at the lack of consideration of their rights. Artisans and mechanics, in particular, began speaking for their own interests instead of relying on elites to do so. Eventually, they formed a group known as the Sons of Liberty, whose goal was to promote a united colonial front against the mother country's harsh policies.

In 1777, after the colonists had won their independence, New York's congress created a constitution that granted common men more rights than had been granted them under the English. Some of the major components of this constitution included abolishing manorial assembly seats, but with an assurance that royally granted lands were still legal; keeping the political system of a governor, lieutenant governor, and bicameral legislature, but allowing the popular election of the executive and upper houses; and lowering the property qualifications to vote in assembly elections.

Throughout the colonial period, the residents of the province of New York constantly experienced social, economic, and political upheavals. For native peoples, the increasing European presence meant a greater loss of land and autonomy, especially after the French were driven from the area. The black slave population in the province was never as large as that in the Southern colonies, yet slaves formed an important part of the province's labor force, especially in New York City. While the Dutch and English were the only European powers to establish governments in the colony, the colony's population came from many other European countries, including France, Germany, Sweden, Scotland, and Ireland. The story of colonial New York, then, is one in which these different groups sought to maintain their distinct cultures as much as they sought to adapt to new cultures, economic opportunities, and political systems.

Lisa Y. Ramos

See also: Fort Orange; New Amsterdam; New Netherland; New York and New Netherland (Chronology); New York City.

Bibliography

Bonomi, Patricia U. *A Fractious People: Politics and Society in Colonial New York.* New York: Columbia University Press, 1971.

Kammen, Michael. *Colonial New York: A History.* New York: Scribner's, 1975.

Kierner, Cynthia A. *Traders and Gentlefolk: The Livingstons of New York, 1675–1790.* Ithaca, NY: Cornell University Press, 1992.

Klein, Milton M. *The Empire State: A History of New York.* Ithaca, NY: Cornell University Press, 2001.

Lustig, Mary Lou. *The Imperial Executive in America: Sir Edmund Andros, 1637–1714.* London: Associated University Press, 2002.

Richter, Daniel K. *The Ordeal of the Longhouse: The Peoples of the Iroquois League in the Era of European Colonization.* Chapel Hill: Published by the University of North Carolina Press for the Institute of Early American History and Culture in Williamsburg, Virginia, 1992.

Rink, Oliver A. *Holland on the Hudson: An Economic and Social History of Dutch New York.* Ithaca, NY: Cornell University Press, 1986.

New York City

Although New York City was a small settlement throughout most of the seventeenth century, by the end of the eighteenth century, it had grown in importance. From a small Dutch trading post that struggled to compete with the English colonies in the early 1600s, over the next 100 years, New York City gradually grew into the economic and political center of a young United States.

The native peoples who lived in the New York City area when the Europeans arrived were the Rechgawawank, known as the Manhate to Europeans. In 1626, Peter Minuit purchased Manhattan Island from the Manhate for 60 guilders in goods, or the equivalent of about 24 dollars (several thousand dollars in today's money).

Arrival of the Dutch

New York City's beginnings date to 1625, when Amsterdam merchants of the Dutch West India Company set up a trading post at the mouth of the Hudson River and named it New Amsterdam. For the first thirty years, the colony was more a trading post than a full-fledged settlement. Company officials ran the colony of New Netherland very strictly, granting few political rights to members of the community. With the arrival of Director-General Peter Stuyvesant in 1647, the colony finally began to take the form of a permanent, organized settlement. In 1653, he granted New Amsterdam settlers the right to form a city government.

Early on, the colony attracted a diverse group of Europeans, from Walloons—French Protestants who first sought exile in the Spanish Netherlands (what is today Belgium)—to Sephardic Jews from Brazil. Few Dutch citizens immigrated to New Amsterdam, because socioeconomic and political conditions were not as desperate in the Netherlands as they were in the countries from which most of the other immigrants came. By the end of the seventeenth century, however, Dutch settlers still outnumbered English and French settlers, although the English and French made up a sizable 40 percent of the colony's population.

Since most European immigrants chose to work for themselves, and the Dutch West India Company needed laborers to work on its behalf, slavery quickly became a part of New Amsterdam's economy. In 1626, the company brought eleven black slaves to the settlement. Black slaves in New York City enjoyed half-freedom: they could marry, own property, and testify against whites in courts. By 1664, blacks—both slave and free—made up about 20 percent of New Amsterdam's population.

Takeover by the English

The English Duke of York assumed power over New Amsterdam and the colony of New Netherland in 1664, renaming the colony New York. During the first thirty years of English rule, New York City entered a new phase of development, marking the end of a strong Dutch influence. Although Dutch merchants managed to retain power over the settlement's economic affairs in 1677, English and French merchants were in control of New York's economic affairs by 1703. Some Dutchmen still retained their positions of wealth during the early English period; however, Dutch people of the middling rank saw their opportunities for socioeconomic advancement quashed.

While the French began arriving in large number in the 1680s and had established a cultural base by founding the Église Française à la Nouvelle York in 1688, English immigration in the 1680s had slowed. The English did not form a church of their own until

1697, when they established Anglican Trinity Church (although another English group, the Quakers, had organized a small number of meetings by this time). It took longer for the English to form a culturally cohesive group because of strife between Crown officials and English settlers in the colony. In addition, unlike the Dutch and French populations, the English population included a greater variety of religious groups.

The years 1689 to 1691 mark a significant turning point in the history of New York City. After the fall of Charles II in the Glorious Revolution of 1688, Jacob Leisler assumed power in the city, primarily representing a group of Dutch residents. In many ways, the rebellion of New York City residents was a response to the loss of Dutch power after the English takeover of New Amsterdam.

Leisler was able to gain the support of many of these Dutch by promising that William of Orange's ascension to the English throne would force the English to give up New York. Leisler, however, was removed from power in 1691 by the new monarchs, William and Mary. This event marked the defeat of New York's Dutch and reflected the final loss of strong Dutch political influence in the colony.

Slavery and Race

In the early eighteenth century, under the British, the slave trade boomed. Male slaves composed 15 percent of the manual labor force and 20 percent of New York City's population in 1703. Free blacks tended to live on farms north of the city's center, and black slaves typically served as domestic servants in white households.

Significantly, the slave trade expanded even after slave revolts in 1712 and 1741. The 1712 revolt—in which some twenty slaves killed nine white people—led to the creation of stricter slave laws, severely curtailing slaves' rights. In 1741, white New Yorkers blamed black slaves for a number of fires and robberies and came to believe that slaves were planning a huge conspiracy. As a result, almost 100 slaves were tortured, hung, burned, or resold into slavery in the West Indies.

In contrast to the fewer rights given black slaves under English rule, members of minority religions were given more rights. The English allowed Lutherans, Quakers, and Jews to hold services, a right not granted them under the Dutch. By 1695, all of these groups were worshiping in their own churches.

Under the rule of Lord Cornbury in the early years of the eighteenth century, the British worked toward

This 1767 map of New York City, by British Army surveyor Bernard Ratzen, is believed to be the most accurate of the pre-Revolutionary War period. Open land was still plentiful in lower Manhattan. *(Brown Brothers, Sterling, Pennsylvania)*

assimilating the Dutch and French to the English language and the Anglican religion. Besides schools, Cornbury turned to the Anglican Society for the Propagation of the Gospel in Foreign Parts to promote his assimilationist policy. Since, from 1702 to 1726, the Dutch Reformed Church was not allowed to offer classes to Dutch children, the Dutch heritage lost much of its influence. By the middle of the eighteenth century, most Dutch people spoke English as their first language.

As for the French Huguenots, by 1720 they had suffered a severe rift within their church, and, by 1730, many had left the church. This contributed to their assimilation into English culture, as did their tendency to marry outside their group. As for the British population, the early eighteenth century saw the rise of the Presbyterian and Baptist Churches. The Anglican Church grew, too, taking in many of the French Huguenot population and some of the Dutch.

Political rule in New York City became more fractious in the 1730s. During this period, a common form of political protest was the publishing of political pamphlets. In 1735, the rights of the publishers of these pamphlets came into question when printer John Peter Zenger was arrested for libel; he was later acquitted in a landmark case for freedom of the press. Political leaders during this period also began appealing to the large group of artisans in the city. In the elections of 1733 and 1734, artisans were able to elect many of their own to city office. This era, then, demonstrated a greater level of political participation among the white male population and established the idea of a government's power being vested in the people.

In 1765, New York City was in a precarious state. Not only had British imports decreased, but grain prices had skyrocketed and land prices had taken a dip. Thus, when the British government passed the Stamp Act that same year, the first tax ever on the American colonies, New York's residents reacted by opposing this act and subsequent English measures. This opposition served to unify many of the American colonists, as the English suddenly began imposing what the colonists viewed as unfair and restrictive policies.

Whether under Dutch or English rule, New York

City was important to the Dutch and English empires in the North American mainland. For many Europeans who came to settle there, it represented the most tolerant community in the seventeenth century and a place to seek economic opportunities in the eighteenth century. For the Africans who lived in New York City, both slave and free, opportunities decreased with time; they had enjoyed greater liberties in the seventeenth century under Dutch rule than they did in the eighteenth century under the British.

Lisa Y. Ramos

See also: New Amsterdam; New Netherland; New York; New York and New Netherland (Chronology).

Bibliography

Archdeacon, Thomas J. *New York City, 1664–1710: Conquest and Change.* Ithaca, NY: Cornell University Press, 1976.

Goodfriend, Joyce D. *Before the Melting Pot: Society and Culture in Colonial New York City, 1664–1730.* Princeton, NJ: Princeton University Press, 1991.

Kammen, Michael. *Colonial New York: A History.* New York: Oxford University Press, 1975.

Nash, Gary B. *The Urban Crucible: The Northern Seaports and the Origins of the American Revolution.* Cambridge, MA: Harvard University Press, 1986.

Rothschild, Nan A. *New York City Neighborhoods: The 18th Century.* San Diego, CA: Academic Press, 1990.

Tiedemann, Joseph S. *Reluctant Revolutionaries: New York City and the Road to Independence, 1763–1776.* Ithaca, NY: Cornell University Press, 1997.

Newfoundland

In the sixteenth century, England's first North American possession, the island of Newfoundland, marked the northwestern edge of the known world to Europeans. Its Grand Banks was one of the world's richest breeding grounds for codfish, and it became the site of an international fishery. Settlement of the island began in the early seventeenth century, initiating a lengthy dispute among English fishing interests. The fishery also fueled English-French imperial rivalry over the island. By the early eighteenth century, England had assumed sole possession of Newfoundland.

Within a decade of Giovanni Caboto's (John Cabot's) voyage to Newfoundland in 1497, fishing vessels from Spain, Portugal, and France conducted a migratory fishery in its waters. Between 1530 and 1600, the Basques operated cod, seal, and whale fisheries off Newfoundland and Labrador. Although Europeans did not settle the island, some erected temporary structures and encountered the island's native inhabitants. The Beothuk, an Algonquian-speaking people numbering between 500 and 700, lived by hunting, gathering, and fishing. Over the colonial period, as meetings with Europeans became more frequent and hostile, the Beothuks gradually withdrew to the interior.

In 1583, Sir Humphrey Gilbert claimed Newfoundland for Queen Elizabeth I. By the early seventeenth century, the Iberian fisheries declined and were superseded by those of the English and the French. The English practiced a "dry fishery" (as opposed to the European "green" or "wet" fishery whereby ships returned directly to Europe from the fishing grounds with a heavily salted catch), which required the presence of shore stations to lightly salt and sun-dry the catch prior to returning home. Attentions turned to year-round settlement of the island, which prompted a bitter and long-standing debate in England between the West Country migratory (or ship) fishing interest and the resident fishing interest.

English policy toward settlement in Newfoundland was noncommittal for much of the colonial period, and although the resident fishery was not officially encouraged, the English government realized that some settlement was necessary to protect its claim over the island. Several officially sponsored attempts at colonization occurred in the first half of the seventeenth century, the first one being John Guy's colony at Cuper's Cove (Cupids) in 1610. Others followed, including George Calvert's (Lord Baltimore) colony of Avalon between 1619 and 1625. Frustrated by the colony's lack of progress, Lord Baltimore abandoned the settlement and founded a new colony in Maryland. The most successful of the colonies was David Kirke's Ferryland, which functioned between 1638 and 1652. Although these all failed to become self-sufficient and profitable for their investors and officially came to an end, many settlers remained. By 1670, English settlement on the island was firmly established.

Competition from France

England's main competition in Newfoundland was France. In 1662, France established a settlement at Plaisance (Placentia) on the southwest coast of the Avalon Peninsula to conduct a dry fishery. Its strategic location between New France and Europe made it a useful supply base and port for French naval and merchant vessels. The imperial contest to control the valuable fishery led to several conflicts in Newfoundland, especially during King William's and Queen Anne's Wars. France relinquished its claim to Newfoundland in 1713, though the French continued to enjoy fishing rights between Cape Bonavista and Pointe Riche. These rights were later confirmed by the Treaty of Paris in 1763, which also ceded to France the south coast islands of St. Pierre and Miquelon.

By the early eighteenth century, the island was increasingly visited by trading vessels from Ireland and New England. Ireland was the main provider of victuals to Newfoundland after 1650, though during wartime and by midcentury, the "coasters" from New England largely assumed this function. Although the New Englanders were criticized for spiriting away fishermen from the island, settlement increased and expanded along the south and west coasts of the island as Newfoundland received an influx of Irish laborers after 1720.

Increased trade, population growth, and ensuing tensions between English Protestants and Irish Catholics encouraged Britain to create civil institutions in Newfoundland. In 1729, Henry Osborne, a naval commodore, was appointed the island's first governor and commander-in-chief. Possessing full civil and military authority, he divided the island into six districts and appointed justices of the peace and constables. In 1730, a jail and a courthouse were built in St. John's, making the town the official judicial center of the island. Missionaries from the Church of England opened schools, and the island's economy diversified to include sealing, furring, and salmon fishing. The migratory interest gradually supported settlement, as West Country merchants became concentrated on the island and operated importation and supply businesses.

The island experienced a period of prosperity between 1763 and 1775, as it was fully brought into the British trading system. A customs house was built in 1766, indicative of Newfoundland's position at the apex of a triangular trade between New England and the West Indies. Despite initial hardships in 1775, the American Revolution ultimately assisted Newfoundland's development. In the absence of New England traders, Newfoundland merchants looked to Bermuda and Canada for supplies and sent their own vessels to the West Indies. The drain of settlers to New England ended and the resident population was further encouraged by the war's lengthy disruption of the migratory fishery. However, growing numbers of British and Miqmaq settlers and increased exploitation of resources had a devastating effect on the island's remaining Beothuk, who ceased to exist as a people by 1829.

Between 1750 and 1790, Newfoundland's permanent population more than doubled, from 7,000 to close to 17,000. By the close of the eighteenth century, Newfoundland had received a new constitution, its first chief justice, and a supreme court. The economic and strategic value of the island's fisheries and trade continued to invite settlers and traders from all over the Atlantic world.

Michael F. Dove

See also: Canada; Fish and Fisheries; Vikings.

Bibliography

Head, C. Grant. *Eighteenth Century Newfoundland.* Toronto: McClelland and Stewart, 1976.

Major, Kevin. *As Near to Heaven by Sea: A History of Newfoundland and Labrador.* Toronto: Viking, 2001.

Matthews, Keith. *Lectures on the History of Newfoundland, 1500–1830.* St. John's, Newfoundland, Canada: Breakwater, 1988.

O'Flaherty, Patrick. *Old Newfoundland: A History to 1843.* St. John's, Newfoundland, Canada: Long Beach Press, 1999.

Newport

Newport, Rhode Island, was one of British North America's largest cities before the War for Independence.

Long before the English town was founded in 1639, the island of Aquidneck was home to the Narragansett and Wampanoag peoples, who seemed to have fought over it regularly. Giovanni da Verrazano, sailing for France, spent a couple of weeks there in 1524 and praised the location, but no immediate European settlement followed. In the 1630s, while New England was in the throes of its Antinomian Controversy, William Coddington led a group of refugees from Massachusetts Bay to the mouth of Narragansett Bay and there founded Newport.

Early Newport society, like early New England society in general, was fairly stratified, and Coddington, a failed merchant with pretensions to the gentry class, envisioned himself at the top. Merchants and artisans were drawn to the economic opportunities provided by the harbor, and the way the land was divided gave the middling class decent-sized farms and the gentry massive estates that they rented out to tenants. Although Newport was founded by a small, tightly knit group of outcasts from the larger Bay Colony, there were Baptists, Quakers (George Fox, the founder of Quakerism, visited Newport in 1672), and, later, a small Jewish population living alongside the Puritans. Importantly, and unlike the Massachusetts Bay Colony, Newport's civil and religious institutions were almost completely separate, and a remarkable tolerance for various sects existed. Not surprisingly, Massachusetts Bay residents looked down on Rhode Island—sometimes referring to it as Rogue's Island—as a backward and sinful place.

Newport grew rapidly and became something of a commercial center during the eighteenth century. Merchants operating out of Newport were plugged into the Atlantic world through their connections to Boston, London, Holland, West Africa, Charles Town, and the West Indies. They oversaw a profitable trade in rum, lumber, provisions, and livestock, and they imported sugar, flour, molasses, and other food products as well as cloth and other supplies. In 1731, Governor Joseph Jencks reported to the board of trade that Newport had approximately 4,640 residents living in 400 houses. The merchant fleet boasted between seventy-five and eighty-five boats. Newport's population continued to grow in terms of population and importance to Atlantic trade, and by the time of the War for Independence, it was among the largest cities in British North America.

Some time in the early eighteenth century—the precise date is unclear—Newport began to trade directly with West African nations for slaves. Typically, though not always, slaves from West Africa would be taken to the West Indies, and molasses from the West Indies would be taken to Newport and used in the production of rum. Interestingly, two outspoken opponents of slavery, Ezra Stiles and Samuel Hopkins—the former a future president of Yale and the latter one of Jonathan Edwards's brightest students—both preached in Newport during the colonial era. Newport's fortunes were tied to Atlantic trade, including the slave trade, yet it also produced eloquent attacks on that trade.

In the middle of the eighteen century, Newport's trade suffered as a result of international conflict. The Seven Years' War hurt Newport particularly—though it benefited smugglers and privateers at first, since its merchants had previously operated in both the British and French West Indies. New taxes in the 1760s made it difficult and unprofitable to trade with the French; therefore there was considerable support for independence in Newport.

With George Washington's Continental army otherwise occupied, the British under Clinton took Newport without a fight in December 1776. Occasion-ally, state militias from New England would attack British forces with little effect. In the summer of 1778, a larger national army and a French naval squadron attacked Newport, but bad weather prevented them from taking it. In 1779, the British left, deciding to concentrate on the war in the South. The French under Rochambeau arrived the next summer, effectively ensuring that Newport would not fall back into British hands.

Newport remained an important commercial center in the nineteenth century, though it never fully escaped the shadow cast by Boston and other towns in the region, such as New York, which grew much more rapidly.

Matthew Jennings

See also: Cities; Rhode Island; Rhode Island (Chronology).

Bibliography

Coughtry, Jay Alan. "The Notorious Triangle: Rhode Island and the African Slave Trade, 1700–1807." Ph.D. thesis, University of Wisconsin, 1978.

James, Sydney V. *Colonial Rhode Island: A History.* New York: Charles Scribner's Sons, 1975.

McLoughlin, William G. *Rhode Island: A Bicentennial History.* New York: W. W. Norton, 1978.

Newspapers and Journals

During the eighteenth century, British North America witnessed the rise of a new form of print that was to radically alter the way information was disseminated to society. Printing presses had already been established throughout several of the colonies, and, by 1700, six printers had set up shop throughout several colonial cities.

Before the eighteenth century, printers focused on publishing religious, theological, and, to a lesser extent, political, legal, and educational materials in the form of books and almanacs. New periodical forms, however, had developed in Restoration England, and these soon proved influential in America.

The *London Gazette* was a weekly publication that gained an extensive readership throughout England by the end of the seventeenth century. In 1690, a Boston printer named Benjamin Harris published America's first attempt at this kind of a newspaper, entitled *Publick Occurrences.* The newspaper was immediately suppressed

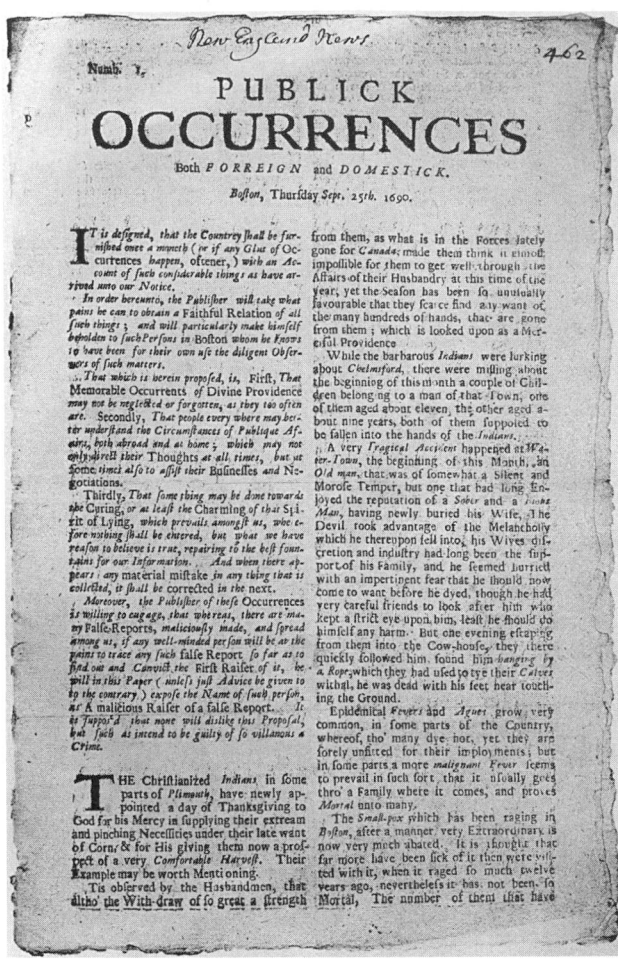

The first newssheet in America, called *Publick Occurrences,* was published in Boston on September 25, 1690. Intended as a monthly, the publication was suppressed by the colonial government and never appeared again. *(Brown Brothers, Sterling, Pennsylvania)*

by the government of Massachusetts for publishing information considered too critical of the government.

The desire for a weekly publication remained strong, and in 1704, John Campbell, another Boston printer, began publishing the *Boston News-Letter,* which lasted for nineteen years. Soon after, other printers began publishing newspapers in the major urban centers across the colonies, and, by 1750, a total of twelve newspapers had been established.

Newspapers treated their readers to a multitude of different topics. The major focus of most eighteenth-century newspapers was political and diplomatic news. Printers published an extensive amount of material about European affairs, since wars, diplomatic intrigues, and political debates seemed to be of primary interest to readers. By the second half of the eighteenth century, however, other types of information competed for space.

An increase in economic activity made newspapers quite valuable to shopkeepers and merchants, who advertised their wares and services to a growing consumer public. Printers encouraged this advertising, since they found it to be a lucrative supplement to their earnings. Religious material in the form of debates, devotional and promotional literature, and advertisements offered opportunities to those in search of spiritual enrichment. While the subject matter was diverse, the limited space provided by newspapers of the time prevented any extended analysis of one particular subject. Most newspapers normally consisted of four pages per issue, with two to four columns on each.

As newspapers proliferated in the colonies, another influence from England contributed to the rise of a second type of periodical. The *Gentleman's Magazine,* first published in London in 1731, offered readers a more comprehensive array of literary articles that allowed authors to go into greater depth than they could in newspapers. Magazines were lengthy by comparison, with the number of pages per issue ranging on average from ten to fifty. Many of the articles published in magazines reflected the growing influence of Enlightenment thinking, where rational thought spilled over into political, scientific, economic, and religious essays. Convinced that there was a similar demand for magazines in America, several printers attempted to meet this need. In February 1741, Andrew Bradford and Benjamin Franklin, both printers from Philadelphia, respectively published the first two magazines in America within three days of one another: Bradford's *American Magazine, or A Monthly View of the Political State of the British Colonies,* and Franklin's *General Magazine, and Historical Chronicle, for All the British Plantations in America.*

Although printers compiled the material for newspapers and magazines, they depended heavily on outside resources. Many printers subscribed to other periodicals and had no compunction in borrowing articles and information generously from their competitor's pages. European periodicals in particular became an important source of verbiage for American periodicals, as the desire for European material remained strong in the United States through the end of the eighteenth century. Printers also published personal letters, many of which were deliberately written for public display. Local authors provided printers with a vast array of material, most of which was printed, since many of these authors were also the subscribers and financial supporters of these same periodicals.

Table 1. Growth of the Newspaper Industry over the Eighteenth Century

Year	Number of Newspapers
1700	0
1725	4
1750	12
1775	48
1800	197

Sources: Thomas Purvis, *Colonial America to 1763* (New York: Facts on File, 1999), 258–59; Thomas Purvis, *Revolutionary America 1763–1800* (New York: Facts on File, 1995), 277.

The rise in the overall numbers of periodicals throughout the eighteenth century attests to their increasing popularity. Tables 1 (above) and 2 (below) illustrate the growth of periodicals during this era. In the year 1700, not a single newspaper or magazine had been published in North America. By the end of the century, that changed dramatically, with over 200 periodicals circulating throughout the various states. This rapidly growing industry was responding to a surge in reader demand. According to one estimate, approximately 15 percent of all adult white males subscribed to some form of periodical by the end of the century, creating a higher per capita readership of periodicals than anywhere else in the Atlantic world. The normal circulation size of periodicals ranged from the low hundreds to just over a thousand.

Printers faced an arduous journey in publishing a periodical. Once publication of the periodical began, the distribution process suffered trials and tribulations at several levels. Readers often complained about lateness in the arrival of their periodicals. In turn, printers lamented over their inability to collect the money owed to them by subscribers. Additional factors contributed to the interruptions of regular delivery, including problems with paper supply, poor weather conditions,

Table 2. Growth of the Magazine Industry over the Eighteenth Century

Year	Number of Magazines
1700	0
1755	2
1800	14

Sources: Thomas Purvis, *Colonial America to 1763* (New York: Facts on File, 1999), 259; Thomas Purvis, *Revolutionary America 1763–1800* (New York: Facts on File, 1995), 278.

and labor shortages. The failure rate of many periodicals, in particular magazines, attests to the inability of many printers to overcome these numerous obstacles. Most magazines published in the eighteenth century, for example, never made it past their first year of publication.

Regardless of the poor success of periodical publishing, many printers still tried to make a go of it. Printers worked hard at meeting the demands of their readers by appealing to the eye, offering diverse subject matter, and trying to control publication costs. To boost their sales, printers offered incentives, including bulk sales at a discounted price, or reduced rates for those who agreed to subscribe long-term. Since collecting subscription payments was unpredictable, they tried other things to supplement their income. Advertisements became essential to a periodical's survival, particularly newspapers, and by the end of the eighteenth century, it had become an integral part of such publications.

A periodical's success also depended on it being affordable to as many people as possible. Prices varied, but generally periodicals cost between 15 and 20 shillings a year to subscribe. This price proved costly for the common person, so most subscribers were among the wealthy.

Although subscribers tended to belong to the upper ranks of society, printers still hoped that people of more modest means would have access to periodicals. Literacy rates in New England were fairly high, with almost universal literacy for white males by the end of the eighteenth century. The rates for white males in the South were slightly lower, with about two-thirds literate by the end of the century. Although literacy among females was lower than that of men, rates were still high compared to those in other nations, with some 60 percent of women in New England being literate and about 30 percent of those in the South.

For those who did not subscribe, there were various ways of gaining access to magazines and newspapers. One was through circulating libraries, where periodicals became an important part of their holdings. Taverns and coffeehouses also provided free access to periodical literature, as innkeepers subscribed to newspapers and magazines in an effort to draw in customers. Also, people often came across periodicals through personal relationships, as many shared their copies of newspapers and magazines.

Most printers also tried to branch out beyond the cities in order to expand their readership. Overall, successful printers were the ones who marketed their periodicals in any way possible to ensure an adequate number of readers.

Newspapers and magazines had become a vital form of communication by the end of the eighteenth century. As American society matured, periodicals filled a growing need for information, with newspapers providing more of the political and economic content and magazines the cultural, religious, and literary material. For those who could not afford to buy books or other expensive printed items, periodicals offered greater access to information than ever before. The words of one author from the *The Philadelphia Monthly Magazine* (January 1798) rang true to many: "among all the modes [of communication] that have been devised for that purpose, no one has been so effectual as that of periodical performances."

Keith Pacholl

See also: Art, Cartoons, and Broadsides; Arts, Culture, and Intellectual Life (Chronology); Arts, Culture, and Intellectual Life (Essay); Franklin, Benjamin; Language; Literature; *Poor Richard's Almanack;* Reading and Literacy; Zenger, John Peter. *Documents:* The Trial of Peter Zenger (1735); Maxims from *Poor Richard's Almanack* (1739); Newspaper Account of the Boston Massacre (1770).

Bibliography

Brown, Richard. *Knowledge Is Power.* New York: Oxford University Press, 1989.

Clark, Charles. *The Public Prints: The Newspaper in Anglo-American Culture, 1665–1740.* New York: Oxford University Press, 1994.

Copeland, David. *Colonial American Newspapers.* Newark, NJ: University of Delaware Press, 1997.

Mott, Frank. *A History of American Magazines.* Cambridge, MA: Harvard University Press, 1957.

Pacholl, Keith. "Bearers of the Word: Religion and Print and Early America." Ph.D. diss., University of California, Riverside, 2002.

Purvis, Thomas. *Colonial America to 1763.* New York: Facts on File, 1999.

———. *Revolutionary America 1763–1800.* New York: Facts on File, 1995.

North, Lord (1732–1792)

Although actually the Second Earl of Guilford by inheritance, Sir Frederick North was best known by the courtesy title of Lord North. The honorary title was given to North when he became prime minister, and he used it until his father's death in 1790.

Born April 13, 1732, North attended Eton and Oxford, an education that provided him with good social and political contacts, who proved helpful to him when he entered Parliament at the age of 22. As the representative for the town of Banbury, North remained in Parliament for nearly forty years. The Duke of Newcastle made him lord of the treasury in 1759, a position he held under both John Stuart Bute and George Greenville until 1765.

North was a natural politician who rose through the government, first entering the Privy Council and becoming paymaster general in 1766, then being made chancellor of the exchequer in 1767. He became prime minister in March 1770, a post he held for the next twelve years. This was a time of unprecedented turmoil for the British Empire, and North had few friends by the time his ministerial position ended.

Although a man of notable intelligence and undeniable ability, North, while prime minister, allowed himself to be placed into the unenviable position of pawn between king, Parliament, and the colonies. Private letters between North and the king reveal that there was the intimacy and confidentiality of friendship between them, which possibly explains the compliance of North. As minister, North was in a difficult position. It was his task to defend measures he neither created nor approved. This required him to engage in debates in the House of Commons with some of the ablest orators of the period, particularly Charles J. Fox and Edmund Burke, with little or no support except from a few champions of the Crown, who were paid for their help.

While North's time as prime minister lasted twelve years, the American Revolution was certainly the most important event during his service, and he was one of the main participants in the action. In the past, critics and some historians have wrongfully charged North with pushing the colonies toward independence, but this is not entirely the case. In nearly every circumstance where North presided over legislative activities placing him at odds with the colonies, he was following the orders of the Crown. Nevertheless, North's first act as head of the government was the retention of the tea duties. Later, in 1774, North introduced the Boston Port Bill.

After the war erupted, North counseled the king to sue for peace and reconciliation with the colonies. North might have succeeded, but outside forces swayed

Sir Frederick North, commonly known as Lord North, served as British prime minister from 1770 to 1782 and is remembered for his role in losing the American colonies. He resigned after the British surrender at Yorktown. *(San Diego Museum of Art, San Diego, California/Bridgeman Art Library)*

the king. Of questionable mental stability, the king was persuaded by his advisers that it would be better to wage war—even though, by 1779, many considered it impossible to win—than to let another Whig-dominated government come to power. Having heard about the surrender of Cornwallis at Yorktown, North resigned from his position as prime minister in March 1782.

Lord North re-entered politics in April 1783, when he formed a coalition with his former political opponent Charles J. Fox. North and Fox shared the position of secretary of state under the premiership of the duke of Portland, but the coalition ministry collapsed in December 1783, when Fox's East India bill was rejected by Parliament.

Suffering from failing eyesight, North dropped entirely out of public life. Although completely blind by 1789, he made a final political appearance in Parliament to offer his support to the Regency bill. He died in London on August 5, 1792.

Solomon K. Smith

See also: Boston Port Bill; Revolutionary War.

Bibliography

Thomas, Peter D. *Lord North.* New York: St. Martin's, 1976.
Valentine, Alan C. *Lord North.* 2 vols. Norman: University of Oklahoma Press, 1967.
Whiteley, Peter. *Lord North: The Prime Minister Who Lost America.* London: Hambledon Press, 1996.

North Carolina

In 1524, Giovanni da Verrazano, a Florentine captain in French employ, first explored the North Carolina coast near Cape Fear, writing descriptive journals of the unexplored lands. Sir Walter Raleigh financed several unsuccessful expeditions between 1584 and 1590 to settle the Roanoke Colony, on the Outer Banks, in the name of England. Yet North Carolina would receive its first permanent European settlers from the Virginia colony, established first at Jamestown in 1607. The settlers moved south into the Currituck and Albemarle Sound regions in the mid-seventeenth century.

In 1663, King Charles II granted Carolina land to eight noblemen proprietors. These men had survived the civil wars with their property intact; they generally supported the king and were rewarded by an appreciative Charles II. North and South Carolina became separate colonies in 1691. Factions and squabbles developed between the proprietary forces and the antiproprietary residents and became so divisive that, in 1729, both colonies abandoned their proprietary claims and became royal colonies.

Unlike its neighbor to the south, which grew wealthy raising rice and importing slaves, North Carolina grew slowly and modestly. Most of the residents were subsistence farmers, living on dispersed farms and raising moderate amounts of tobacco, corn, cattle, and swine. The most profitable products in colonial North Carolina were naval stores (tar, pitch, and turpentine) and lumber. Only a very few wealthy planters lived along the rivers near the coast.

Although the tempestuous Outer Banks along North Carolina's coastline and the lack of natural harbors prohibited much sea travel, early port cities such as Bath and New Bern were established in the late seventeenth and early eighteenth centuries. The myriad coves and stormy waters served as havens for pirates, most famously Blackbeard, who eventually died at the hands of the British navy in Pamlico Sound in 1718.

Early colonial expansion beyond the coast led to a conflict, known as the Tuscarora War, with the native Tuscarora between 1711 and 1715. The Tuscarora and various other tribes had lived along the coast of North Carolina before being challenged by the encroaching Europeans. Their defeat in the war led them to move to New York. European settlers would encounter other proud tribes, such as the Cherokee and Catawba, in the Piedmont and mountainous regions of the colony to the west.

Although most of the early settlers were English, several came from other parts of Europe. Christopher von Graffenreid settled the town of New Bern with many Swiss and German Palatine immigrants in 1710. Highlanders fleeing unrest and economic crisis in Scotland settled along the Cape Fear River in the middle decades of the eighteenth century. Beginning in the 1730s, Scots-Irish and German immigrants began coming down the frontier trails all the way from Philadelphia and settled along the North Carolina frontier, in the plains of the western Piedmont and mountains and valleys of the Appalachians. North Carolina also became a haven for unique religious sects, as Quakers settled along the Eastern seaboard and Moravians clustered in the Piedmont.

In the years leading up to the Revolution, economic and social differences between the settlers in the western regions and the predominantly English settlers in the east led to conflict. The centralized system of government favored the eastern aristocrats and prompted western outrage at what they deemed unfair taxes, fees, and lack of judicial redress. Calling themselves Regulators, several disgruntled farmers marched east to demand their rights. After years of threats and conflict, Governor William Tryon crushed a Regulator army on May 14, 1771, at Alamance Creek, near Hillsborough, effectively ending the movement.

When Parliament passed the Stamp Act in 1765, North Carolina's Sons of Liberty, led by Cornelius Harnett, instigated protests and forced the governor to refuse the stamps. North Carolina patriots continued to be active in protests in the early 1770s, often coming into conflict with Josiah Martin, the new royal governor; in 1775, they forced Martin to take refuge aboard a British warship. As the Revolutionary War began, 3,000 loyalist Scottish Highlanders rallied and marched from Cross Creek (modern Fayetteville) toward Wilmington to rendezvous with a British army en route by sea. Patriot militia routed them at the Battle of Moore's Creek Bridge on February 27, 1776. British leaders abandoned their plans to defeat the Southern colonies

for several years. On March 15, 1781, the Redcoat army of Lord Cornwallis fought to a bloody draw with a colonial army under General Nathaniel Green at Guilford Court House. This battle and subsequent lack of supplies and support forced Cornwallis to abandon North Carolina and move to Yorktown, Virginia, where he would be forced to surrender his army.

After the war, North Carolina's independent-minded population vigorously debated the Constitution and initially rejected it, fearing a strong central government. But after the promise of a Bill of Rights, the state finally joined the new nation by ratifying the Constitution on November 21, 1789—becoming the twelfth state to do so.

Judkin Browning

See also: New Bern; North Carolina (Chronology); Ship's Stores.

Bibliography

Connor, R.D.W. *The Colonial and Revolutionary Periods, 1584–1783.* In *History of North Carolina,* vol. 1. Chicago: The Lewis Publishing Company, 1919.

Powell, William S. *North Carolina: A Bicentennial History.* New York: W. W. Norton, 1977.

———. *North Carolina Through Four Centuries.* Chapel Hill: University of North Carolina Press, 1989.

Northwest Passage

Although the idea of a Northwest Passage—a sea route cutting through the American continent to Asia—may seem absurd today, this dream arose and remained a propelling force for many years, justifying continued exploration by Spain, France, and England. The backbone of the search for a Northwest Passage was the desire to open lucrative trade with China. A number of explorers searched for the passage—some finding only disaster or death. While the passage was never found, their search produced several side effects.

Sixteenth-century colonial America was dominated by Spain. With the explorations of Christopher Columbus, who sailed under the Spanish flag, Spaniards initiated the exchange between America and the Old World that continues to this day.

In 1497, King Henry VII, more than ten years after dismissing Columbus's request for money, chose John Cabot to look for a passage to the Indies across the North Atlantic. Cabot managed to reach the tip of Newfoundland. Believing he had found Asia, he excit-

The English mariner Sir Martin Frobisher was one of a number of explorers who became convinced of the existence of a Northwest Passage, secured the financial backing to find it, and failed to do so. He made three attempts in the 1570s. *(Photo by Archive Photos/Getty Images)*

edly rushed back to England to gather a small follow-up fleet with which to continue his explorations. In 1498, hurrying headlong toward disaster, he disappeared and was not heard from again.

Meanwhile, about 3,000 miles to the south, Columbus reached the shore of mainland Venezuela. In less than a year, another Spanish expedition landed about 600 miles farther south—a feat found to be so significant that it prompted the Portuguese to send Amerigo Vespucci to carry out additional investigations.

The rise of cartography in the sixteenth century caused some to speculate that several large masses of land were scattered in the western Atlantic. Speculation among cartographers was that these masses were connected to each other but not to Asia. The searchers for the Northwest Passage were apparently undaunted by geographical facts that were rapidly becoming apparent. The focus, but not the search, was altered as the question arose as to how much water existed between this large land mass named America (in honor of Amerigo Vespucci) and Asia.

In 1519, this question prompted King Charles I of Spain to finance Ferdinand Magellan's expedition to circumnavigate the globe. With several starts and stops along the way, the travelers finally arrived at the Pacific Ocean in late November 1520. After a journey of almost four months across the Pacific, Magellan reached the Philippines, where native tribesmen killed him. What was left of the expedition managed to continue into the Indian Ocean; in 1522, the remaining explorers made it back to Spain with a boatload of spices.

Looking at what was gained and lost, Magellan's expedition appears to have been a disaster. It started out with five ships and 250 men, only to limp back with one ship and 18 men. The geographic information gained and brought back by the survivors, however, was invaluable. There was no longer any doubt that America was a continent unto itself and that it was separated from Asia by an unfathomably enormous body of water—the Pacific Ocean.

In 1524, France sent Giovanni da Verrazano on a scouting expedition to the New World. His mission was to explore the Atlantic coast from North Carolina to Canada and ferret out the ever-elusive Northwest Passage. Verrazano returned unsuccessful from his mission. Eleven years later, France probed farther north. Jacques Cartier voyaged up the St. Lawrence River, but his luck was no better.

England did not intend to be left behind in the exploration race, though it entered it a bit late, in the sixteenth century under Spain's shadow. As early as the mid-1500s, Martin Frobisher got Queen Elizabeth I's attention. Frobisher's ease at performing slaving voyages to West Africa, privateering raids in the Atlantic, and fighting forays in Ireland was enough for the queen to become interested in sponsoring his explorations. So much so that, in 1576, he sailed on yet another search for a Northwest Passage to Asia, an all-expense-paid trip funded by Elizabeth I herself.

Frobisher sailed north of Labrador and returned to England with an Eskimo (complete with kayak) and a massive stone that was easily mistaken for gold ore. The queen, thrilled, gave him money for two more voyages in 1577 and 1578, from which he managed to haul back close to 2,000 tons of this unique black rock. Poor Frobisher was not able to maintain his prestige when, on closer inspection, the minerals he had brought home turned out to be "fool's gold." He thus became the fool, his reputation ruined.

In the early 1600s, the English navigator Henry

Hudson, sailing for the Dutch, also sought the elusive Northwest Passage, searching the bay and the river that currently bear his name. In 1611, his starving and frustrated crew mutinied and left Hudson, his son, and seven crew members in an open boat; none of them was ever heard from again.

In the 1630s, English explorers Luke Fox and Thomas James also explored Hudson Bay in a vain attempt to find the passage. The last major effort during the colonial era was led by British explorer Samuel Hearne in the early 1770s.

The search for the Northwest Passage never bore fruit, and the explorations finally ended. What came in their place was the realization that there were riches to be found in America, and the shift from exploration to colonization began in earnest. Spain, France, England, and others began the race to settle the New World.

Several major attempts to find a passage to the west were again made by various European countries in the nineteenth century. The first success came in the early twentieth century, with the 1903–1906 expedition of Norwegian explorer Roald Amundsen, the first man to reach the South Pole.

Penny M. Sonnenburg

See also: Canada; Exploration; Transportation, Water.

Bibliography

Parry, J. H. *The Age of Reconnaissance.* Cleveland: World Publishing, 1963.

Quinn, David B. *North America from Earliest Discovery to First Settlements.* New York: Harper and Row, 1977.

Of Plymouth Plantation

Of Plymouth Plantation stands as one of the most famous and important journal histories produced during the colonial period. Its author, William Bradford, was a separatist who journeyed with his congregation from the village of Scrooby, England, first to the Netherlands and then to America (in the famous *Mayflower* pilgrimage). After the death of the Plymouth colony's first governor in 1621, Bradford was elected governor and remained the dominant political personage in the colony until his death in 1657.

Although clearly intended as a history, the journal was not published during the colonial period. Instead, the manuscript passed down through Bradford's heirs and eventually was deposited in Thomas Prince's library in the eighteenth century. Cotton Mather, Nathaniel Morton, and Thomas Hutchinson all used the journal as a source for their own histories of New England. After vanishing during the American Revolution, the journal reappeared in the John Williams Library in London; it was finally returned and deposited in the Massachusetts State House in 1897. The historian Samuel Eliot Morison was able thereby to publish the first complete transcription from the original manuscript in 1952, which remains the definitive edition to this day.

Bradford wrote within traditional English Protestant historiography. This approach drew heavily on John Foxe's *Book of Martyrs* and saw history in millennial terms. The Protestant Reformation, accordingly, constituted the restoration of the true church away from the control of the Pope (who was identified as the Biblical Antichrist). In this context, England served as a bulwark of Protestantism. Bradford, therefore, began his narrative with the revival of the church from "Anti-Christian apostasy" under the Church of Rome and continued through the Marian Martyrs and the restoration of Protestantism under Queen Elizabeth I. As a

Puritan, however, Bradford believed that the Elizabethan church remained only half reformed, and he explained how this resulted in the rise of Puritanism. The persecution of the Puritans led some of them to the conclusion that the Church of England was hopelessly corrupt and that separation from it was therefore required. At this point, the story narrows to Bradford's church, and God's providence (understood earlier in the grand sweep of world events) became merely an interpretive tool for individual blessings and misfortunes. Indeed, Bradford exhibited little sense of a special divine mission or place within Christian history for the Plymouth colony.

The narrative moves swiftly through the escape of the Scrooby congregation to the Netherlands and the subsequent discussion of plans to relocate to America. Here, the second theme of Bradford's history entered: the colony's financial difficulties with the London adventurers (investors) who provided the capital for the expedition. As the colonists sat shivering and starving on the coast of Massachusetts, the company began to wonder aloud why the settlers were not sending back any marketable commodities. In addition, the original plan for the colony had been that everyone would work toward a common stock, which would then be divided up among the stockholders after seven years. Thus provisions were also grown and distributed communally. Desperate to increase food production, in 1623, Bradford dispensed land to individual householders to work for their own subsistence, which appears to have solved the problem.

A third major theme was the colony's relationships with the various Native American groups. The first hesitant encounters with the native peoples occurred while the Pilgrims were still scouting the coast. Upon settlement, two English-speaking natives, Samoset and Squanto, appeared and used their linguistic skills to become middlemen. They produced generally pacific relations for the colony, an alliance with the chief

William Bradford's *Of Plymouth Plantation,* a journal of the colony from the Pilgrims' landing in 1620 to his death in 1657, is one of the most important historical and literary works of the colonial era. (*© North Wind Picture Archives*)

Massasoit, and access to the economically crucial beaver trade.

As Plymouth became allied with certain Native American groups, the colony found itself drawn into inter-tribal rivalries. At the same time, Plymouth joined an alliance of the other New England colonies after 1630. This alliance coordinated military action during the Pequot War (a war they fought alongside the Narragansett in 1637–1638) and subsequent diplomatic action during a period of rising hostility toward the Narragansett, which was itself born out of hostilities between the Narragansett and (then Plymouth allies) the Mohegan.

By the end of the journal, a degree of pessimism had crept into Bradford's tone. Profane and scandalous individuals (especially servants) seemed to abound. Most famously, Bradford recounted the discovery, conviction, and execution of a young man for bestiality, an event that capped a correspondence between Plymouth and the ministers of Massachusetts concerning the increasing instances of sexual transgression.

Almost as if reflecting this despair, the manuscript ends abruptly, with visit of an English privateer to Massachusetts in 1646. Immediately following the end of the narrative is a passenger manifest for the *Mayflower.* Thus the story comes almost full circle.

Kenneth A. Shelton

See also: Bradford, William; Pilgrims; Plymouth.

Bibliography

Bradford, William. *Bradford's History of the Plymouth Settlement, 1608–1650.* Edited by Harold Paget. New York: E. P. Dutton, 1920.

———. *Of Plymouth Plantation, 1620–1647.* Edited by Samuel E. Morison. New York: Alfred A. Knopf, 1952.

Miller, Perry, and Thomas H. Johnson, eds. *The Puritans, A Sourcebook of Their Writings.* New York: Harper and Row, 1938.

Oglethorpe, James (1696–1785)

Born on December 22, 1696, into a wealthy and prominent family, James Edward Oglethorpe became a noted eighteenth-century politician, soldier, colonizer, and social reformer. As a teenager, he was lured by the prospect of military service and the potential for glory and advancement that it offered. He joined the army of the Holy Roman Empire in its fight against the Turks and, as an aide-de-camp to Prince Eugene of Savoy, participated in the successful siege of Belgrade in 1717.

After proving himself on the battlefield, Oglethorpe returned to England and embarked on his political career. In 1722, he was selected to the English House of Commons from the borough of Haslemere. He would hold this seat continuously for the next three decades.

In Parliament, the young Oglethorpe cast his social and political nets widely. He championed the cause of impressed sailors and led a celebrated investigation into debtor prisons. Oglethorpe also invested money in the Royal African Company, but within a few

James Oglethorpe founded the Georgia colony as a haven for debtors and Protestant dissenters. He is commemorated with this bronze statue by Daniel Chester French in Savannah, the site of his first settlement in 1733. *(Library of Congress, LC-D416-695)*

years of this financial move he reversed himself and became an ardent opponent of slavery. In 1730, he and other leading gentlemen proposed the establishment of a new British colony in America that would provide a haven for the nation's poor and simultaneously serve as a strategic buffer against French and Spanish territorial expansion along the Atlantic Coast. The new settlement—established by charter in 1732 and named Georgia in honor of the king—therefore represented a convergence of Oglethorpe's military and philanthropic impulses.

Oglethorpe in 1732 announced that he would accompany the first shipload of Georgia settlers over the Atlantic. By following through on this pledge, Oglethorpe became the only member of the board of trustees to ever visit Georgia. Although he was granted very limited official authority, he nevertheless became the de facto governor of the fledgling colony, directing nearly every aspect of Georgia's military defenses and civil administration. He personally chose the location

for the first town, Savannah, and is generally considered to be the colony's founder.

Because the initial wave of settlers had little experience in operating a government, they were at first grateful for Oglethorpe's strong leadership. They commonly referred to him as "Father," a term that reflected not only their affection for him but also their understanding of his strict sense of discipline. Constables and judges frequently deferred to Oglethorpe's immense stature and prestige. Within a few years, however, a segment of the colony's population grew unhappy under Oglethorpe's stern rule. Many residents blamed him for the colony's initial prohibition on slave ownership, a policy that retarded Georgia's economic development. Concerns over Oglethorpe's role in America were also raised by several trustees in London, who feared that their suddenly famous and powerful colleague might pursue an agenda contrary to the interests of the trust as a whole. Leading trustees fretted about the endless stream of expenditures arriving from the new colony, which threatened to bankrupt them. Numerous large promissory notes arrived over with Oglethorpe's signature but contained no explanation for the expense.

Slowly but steadily, Oglethorpe's assumed authority was shifted to regularly appointed officials until, in 1738, the trust instructed him to confine himself to his duties as general of the forces of South Carolina and Georgia. In any case, these duties absorbed all of his attention after the outbreak of the War of Jenkins' Ear in 1739. General Oglethorpe mounted a failed campaign against the Spanish outpost of St. Augustine in 1740, but he redeemed himself by soundly defeating a counterattack by a numerically superior force two years later. After a second unsuccessful attempt to capture St. Augustine, Oglethorpe returned to England permanently in 1743.

In his later career, Oglethorpe could not maintain the heights to which his involvement in Georgia had propelled him. He faced a court martial for his unit's lackluster performance in the Jacobite rebellion of 1745. Although he was acquitted, the stain on his reputation may have contributed to the loss of his parliamentary seat in 1754.

Shortly after the outbreak of the Seven Years' War in 1756, the British government denied his request for a battlefield command. Unwilling to sit out the fighting, Oglethorpe adopted a pseudonym and campaigned with the Prussian army.

Until his dying day, Oglethorpe expressed support for the rights of American colonists, even in the face of growing rebellion. In 1785, at the age of 88, the elderly statesman paid his respects to John Adams, the United States's first ambassador to Great Britain. On June 30 of that year, James Oglethorpe died, bringing to a close his half-century relationship with America.

Andrew C. Lannen

See also: Georgia; Georgia (Chronology); Savannah. *Document:* Oglethorpe's Vision for the Founding of Georgia (1733).

Bibliography

Inscoe, John C., ed. James *Edward Oglethorpe: New Perspectives on His Life and Legacy.* Savannah: Georgia Historical Society, 1997.

Spalding, Phinizy, and Harvey H. Jackson, eds. *Oglethorpe in Perspective: Georgia's Founder After Two Hundred Years.* Tuscaloosa: University of Alabama Press, 1989.

Ohio Country

The land that England's North American colonists called the Ohio Country began at the Ohio River Valley and extended north toward Lake Erie. The Appalachian Mountains and Allegheny River marked the eastern edge of the region, while the Miami River offered a western boundary.

Probably no other part of the North American interior came to have more symbolic and strategic importance than the Ohio Country, prompting the Native Americans to give it their own name, the Middle Ground. To the east of the region lived the Five (later Six) Nations of the Iroquois Confederation, and farther to the east lived the English colonists. To the west and north lived the Algonquin and the French.

Because of the nearly constant fighting that went on between competing Native American groups and between competing European nations, the Ohio Country did become the middle ground for two centuries of violence. King William's War (1689–1697), Queen Anne's War (1702–1713), King George's War (1744–1748), the French and Indian War (1754–1763), Pontiac's Rebellion (1763–1766), and the American War for Independence (1775–1783) all involved the Ohio Country.

At the conclusion of the American War for Independence, the Native Americans could no longer take advantage of European divisiveness in order to preserve their own interests, and white settlers began to see all native people of any tribe as the last remaining obstacle to settlement of the region. The United States then began a process of removing the indigenous people that ultimately left the Ohio Country completely open to white settlement by 1843.

The Fur Trade

Much of the early conflict over this area had to do with the fur trade. For example, the Five Tribes of the Iroquois (Mohawk, Onondaga, Cayuga, Oneida, and Seneca) began trading beaver furs to the French in exchange for metal axes and knives, brass cooking pots, wool blankets, guns, gunpowder, lead, and liquor. The goods were so beneficial to the Iroquois' life that they had hunted down most of the beaver in central New York by the 1640s. Between 1649 and 1654, they used their new weapons to fight and win the "Beaver Wars" against the Erie Indians.

The Iroquois who then settled in the northeast of the Ohio Country became known as the Mingo. Their Beaver Wars initiated 100 years of complex negotiations, shifting alliances, mutually beneficial trade relations, and vicious warfare among all the tribes of the Middle Ground, which became home to the Wyandot (north), Delaware (southeast), Shawnee (south), Miami (west), and Ottawa (northwest).

By the 1750s, cheaper goods, which were easier to supply from the British colonies, coupled with British successes during King George's War, had diminished the appeal of French goods and led most of the Ohio Country native peoples to become British allies. In response, Canadian governor Marquis de la Galissonière sent an expedition under Pierre-Joseph de Céloron de Blainville to expel the British and chastise the natives. Céloron's men and native allies burned the Miami trading town of Pickawillany, killing women, children, and British traders and also brutally murdering Pianguisha, a Miami leader also known as "Old Briton" or "La Demoiselle."

When the British did not offer protection to their Native American allies, the Miami, Delaware, and Shawnee returned to their old French allegiances. Events like these convinced the Ohio Country natives that both the French and the English cared more about controlling the land than about honoring their agreements.

Settling the Ohio Country

Meanwhile, the intensifying global conflict between the French and English found traction in the Ohio Country, where the fur trade had become the most important bargaining chip in the power struggle between the European and Native American groups living around the region. The French seized several English trading posts and built fortifications such as Fort Duquesne (present-day Pittsburgh, Pennsylvania). The English Crown granted 200,000 acres of Ohio Country land to the Ohio Company, formed by investors from Virginia to sell Ohio Country land to settlers.

In 1750, the Ohio Company sent Christopher Gist to survey their lands, and, in 1753–1754, they sent one of their investors, George Washington, with Gist and some Virginia militiamen to attack Fort Duquesne. Washington failed, but the fighting quickly spread throughout the entire Ohio Country and became part of the French and Indian War (known as the Seven Years' War in Europe).

A later expedition under General Edward Brad-dock, which included Washington and the famous frontiersmen Daniel Boone and John Finley, also failed. During the American Revolution, Boone led the Americans' fight against the British and their Native American allies in the Ohio Country; he was captured and adopted by the Shawnee (from whom he later escaped).

The Treaty of Paris at the end of the French and Indian War ceded to the English all French claims to the Ohio Country. The agreement upset the native peoples greatly, since they themselves had never been conquered. Furthermore, the English Parliament issued the Proclamation of 1763, which promised the native peoples that white settlers would remain east of the Allegheny Mountains, but Native Americans felt that Britain failed to enforce it. Worse, the British believed they had made the Native Americans into English subjects and treated them with increasingly heavy-handed policies.

As the Native Americans had become dependent on European weapons and supplies, their situation became desperate. In response, many joined a militant cultural movement led by the Delaware prophet Neolin, who called on his people to return to traditional ways and a mixture of Christianity and Native American spirituality. They also followed the Ottawa war chief Pontiac, whose ingenious tactics seriously threatened the Ohio frontier from 1763 to 1766.

In part due to resentment over the Proclamation of 1763, the colonists revolted and won their independence in the War for Independence. After the war, the Confederation Congress of the United States of America passed the Northwest Ordinance of 1787, which incorporated the Ohio Country into the Northwest Territory. Eventually, the state of Ohio, along with significant parts of Indiana, West Virginia, and Pennsylvania, were created from the Ohio Country.

Ryan L. Ruckel

See also: Exploration; French; French Colonies on Mainland North America (Chronology); Mississippi River.

Bibliography

Hatcher, Harlan. *The Buckeye Country: A Pageant of Ohio.* New York: H. C. Kinsey, 1940.

Hinderaker, Eric. *Elusive Empires: Constructing Colonialism in the Ohio Valley, 1673–1800.* Cambridge, UK: Cambridge University Press, 1997.

Hurt, R. Douglas. *The Ohio Frontier: Crucible of the Old Northwest, 1720–1830.* Bloomington: Indiana University Press, 1996.

White, Richard. *The Middle Ground: Indians, Empires, and Republics in the Great Lakes Region, 1650–1815.* Cambridge, UK: Cambridge University Press, 1991.

Oliver, Andrew (1706–1774)

A prominent American royalist, Andrew Oliver was a member of the General Court and the Council. He also served as a stamp official, a provincial secretary, and the lieutenant governor of Massachusetts in the years preceding the American Revolution. His firm commitment to the British Crown allowed him to advance in colonial government, but his intense loyalism ultimately led to his demise.

Born in Boston on May 28, 1706, Andrew Oliver hailed from a long line of successful merchants, officers of government, and ecclesiastical leaders in New England. Oliver's first colonial ancestor, Thomas Oliver, arrived in Boston in 1632, serving as an Elder in the church, while his own father, Daniel, was a member of the Council. Upon his graduation from Harvard in 1735, young Andrew was chosen as a member of the General Court. In later years, following in the footsteps of his father, he became a member of the Council. Family connections, especially to his brother-in-law Governor Thomas Hutchinson, helped gain him the appointment of secretary of the province in 1756.

When the British Parliament passed the Stamp Act in 1765, Oliver accepted a position as a distributor of stamps in New England, despite American opposition to the proposed tax. Although his appointment allowed him to gain more prestige among his fellow royalist colleagues, it caused a major drop in his popularity among the residents of Boston. As a result of his decision to accept the office, he narrowly avoided losing his seat on the Council.

In the months preceding the enactment of the Stamp Act, many colonial patriots united in violent opposition to the legislation. On August 14, 1765, a mob operating in conjunction with the Sons of Liberty hanged an effigy of Oliver on the "liberty tree" in Boston. Later that evening, the group destroyed a structure being built as the stamp commissioner's office; the following morning, they forced Oliver to publicly sign a pledge swearing that he would never serve as a stamp distributor anywhere in the colonies. Weeks later, on hearing of Oliver's rumored intentions to take up a post as a stamp official, the Sons of Liberty once again compelled him to swear an oath before a justice of the peace, under the same liberty tree, that he would never be directly or indirectly involved in any attempt to collect stamp duties from the colonists.

Although most Americans condemned Oliver for his actions during the Stamp Act crisis, the events of the period gained him new respect among his royal superiors. In October 1770, Oliver was rewarded for his devotion by being appointed lieutenant governor of Massachusetts.

In this position, Oliver once again drew the ire of American patriots when letters he wrote to his secretary of treasury fell into the hands of Benjamin Franklin. In this correspondence, Oliver recommended the dispatch of British troops to the colonies and the criminal prosecution of several prominent American patriots, including Samuel Adams. The intercepted letters were published in various newspapers and were presented to the assembly. Americans throughout the colonies, and especially in New England, demanded Oliver's resignation from office.

Oliver, however, died on March 3, 1774, before his forced removal. His death was a cause of celebration for many American patriots. A coffin, rope, and gallows were exhibited in one of the nearby public offices as one last expression of American opposition to the ministry of the loyalist Andrew Oliver.

Throughout his life, Andrew Oliver was a devoted civil official, unwavering in his loyalty to his government. Although these attributes might have drawn praise and support at any other time, loyalty and devotion to the British Crown in the years leading to the American Revolution appeared traitorous to many colonists. Despite his abilities, attributes, and rich heritage as a governmental leader, Oliver's unwavering loyalty to what most Americans deemed an oppressive regime led to his ultimate reputation as a foe to the American cause of liberty. This reputation was further entrenched after his death, as his sons, William and Andrew, became prominent figures on the side of the royalists during the Revolutionary War.

Aaron F. Christensen

See also: Loyalists; Revolutionary War; Stamp Act (1765).

Bibliography

Collier, Christopher. *The American Revolution, 1763–1783.* New York: Benchmark, 1998.

Morgan, Edmund S., and Helen M. Morgan. *The Stamp Act Crisis: Prologue to Revolution.* Chapel Hill: University of North Carolina Press, 1953.

Shipton, Clifford Kenyon. *Andrew Oliver, Lieutenant Governor of Massachusetts.* Cambridge, MA, 1943.

Oñate, Juan de (c. 1552–1626)

Juan de Oñate gained fame for leading a mission that "rediscovered" New Mexico and established a lasting Spanish presence in the Southwest through the late sixteenth and early seventeenth centuries. Like previous conquistadors, Oñate could be ambitious and brutal, but he also presaged a new era of Spanish government, one that would be characterized more by rules and regulations than by brute force.

Don Juan de Oñate y Salazar was born to Cristóbal de Oñate and Doña Catalina de Salazar in Zacatecas, Mexico, probably in 1552. His father, an ethnic Basque,

had arrived in the Americas in 1524, in time to participate in the round of conquests that followed the fall of Tenochtitlán. He received several valuable *encomiendas* (grants of people and land), participated in the founding of Zacatecas, and rose to the post of lieutenant governor of Nueva Galicia.

The elder Oñate maintained diverse holdings in mines, stock ranches, farms, and a sugar refinery, and he displayed his military prowess during the Mixton War (1540–1542). His elite status called for frequent trips between the mining city of Zacatecas and the colonial capital at Mexico City. His son Juan was exposed to the world of colonial officials, as well as to the more feudal world of the conquistadors.

In the 1570s, Oñate began to participate in the ongoing conflict with the Zacateco and Chichimeca. ("Chichimeca" was a generic term the Spanish applied to many northern tribes they perceived as uncivilized.) The young conquistador led expeditions around Zacatecas, and he also accumulated a sizable fortune through running the family mines and making new silver strikes in the area. His marriage to Isabel de Tolosa Cortéz

Juan de Oñate, the last of the Spanish conquistadors to explore the New World, followed the Colorado River to the Gulf of California in 1604. On the way back, he left an inscription on a sandstone bluff at El Morro in western New Mexico. (© *North Wind Picture Archives*)

Montezuma, who was descended from the conquistador Hernando Cortéz and the penultimate Aztec emperor, further improved his position.

In 1595, Oñate signed a contract for the exploration of New Mexico with Viceroy Luis de Velasco of New Spain. The main goal of the expedition was to discover a route to the ocean, either Atlantic or Pacific, and good ports. Also, special care was to be taken to convert, not harm, native peoples in the process, as stipulated by the Orders for New Discoveries enacted in 1573. As reflected in these regulations, missionary orders, especially the Franciscans, had gained new power over the process of colonization in the second half of the sixteenth century.

The expedition of around 500 people, including 130 Spanish soldiers, finally left for New Mexico in 1598. After establishing a base of operations at San Juan (in northern New Mexico), Oñate immediately set out to find the Pacific coast. In 1601, he tried for the Atlantic. Vastly underestimating the size of North America, he made it to present-day south central Kansas before turning back. Finally, in 1604–1605, Oñate made his way down the Colorado River to the Gulf of California. On the return voyage, he signed the massive El Morro rock outcropping. (In addition to Puebloan petroglyphs and signatures left by American settlers and soldiers, Oñate's inscription is a popular attraction today at El Morro National Monument.)

Juan de Oñate's reputation as an explorer was beyond reproach, but his tactics as governor offended his Pueblo hosts and the viceregal government in Mexico City. Hungry Spanish soldiers began to press the Pueblos for corn and clothing, and the people of Acoma fought back, killing several soldiers, including Oñate's nephew. Oñate decided to make an example of the Acoma Pueblos; a retaliatory raid killed 800 Pueblos, and those who survived were enslaved or mutilated. The surviving children of Acoma were placed in the custody of the Franciscans, a slight nod to the Orders for New Discoveries. These brutal actions put a temporary halt to Pueblo resistance, but it picked up again in the years that followed. Further compounding Oñate's problems was the fact that he had spent most of his money on far-reaching expeditions, hoping to get rich quickly, and had failed to set up a workable base of operations.

Oñate's actions led to his replacement in New Mexico. He spent his remaining years, and what was left of his personal fortune, trying to rebuild his damaged reputation, first in Mexico City, and later in Spain. He succeeded to some extent and earned appointment as the king's mine inspector, although he was permanently banished from New Mexico due to his abuse of the native peoples. Don Juan de Oñate died while inspecting a mine back in Spain in 1626.

Matthew Jennings

See also: Exploration; New Mexico; New Spain; Spanish Colonies on Mainland North America (Chronology).

Bibliography

Simmons, Marc. *The Last Conquistador: Juan de Oñate and the Settling of the Far Southwest.* Norman: University of Oklahoma Press, 1991.

Weber, David J. *The Spanish Frontier in North America.* New Haven, CT: Yale University Press, 1992.

Oneida

The Oneida people, one of the five Iroquois nations, emerged as a distinct linguistic and cultural group around 1400. By the time of early European contact in the 1620s, the Oneida may have numbered as many as 3,000, established in a rich and vast territory. Their hunting grounds stretched approximately from present-day Utica, New York, to Lake Oneida and from the St. Lawrence River to Lake Ontario, bordered on the east and west by the Unadilla River and present-day Binghamton, New York.

Early Dutch and French explorers recorded visits to probable Oneida villages, which were palisaded and contained large longhouses that housed extended clans. The Oneida were accomplished fishermen and hunters, living on salmon and deer, as well as cultivated maize, squash, and beans.

As with many other native peoples, however, the coming of the Europeans brought the Oneida exposure to disease and new technology. Smallpox and other epidemics may have halved the Oneida population, while the introduction of gunpowder weapons and the fur trade revolutionized native life. The fur and skins trade resulted in a scarcity of beaver and deer, forcing the Oneida to expand their hunting grounds. This, in turn triggered problems with neighboring tribes and fostered a dependence on European trade goods such as firearms, alcohol, and metal pots and tools. The Oneida also became involved in warfare between the Algonquin/French and the Iroquois/British, which was endemic during the 1650s. The situation was complicated by the conversion of some Oneidas to Catholicism, which tied them to France, while others converted to Anglicanism.

During the colonial wars of the late seventeenth century, the Oneida attempted to remain neutral, but, in 1696, they were attacked by Frontenac as potential allies of the British. Several villages were destroyed, and the population was further depleted. To make up the demographic loss, the Oneida took in refugees from other tribes and frequently adopted captives or remnants of other tribes such as the Tuscarora or Yamasee. Despite this, the Oneida people were increasingly scattered, as some retreated into Canada while others moved south into the Ohio Valley.

The mid-eighteenth century brought continuing waves of epidemic disease, which further weakened the Oneida, and political pressure threatened to split the tribe just as it increasingly pushed the American colonies away from Great Britain. Sir William Johnson, a British Indian agent, was particularly successful at cultivating the ginseng trade among the Oneida, binding some to Great Britain. On the other side, the arrival of the Congregational missionary Samuel Kirkland drew other Oneidas to the colonists' cause. Kirkland, who had failed in an earlier mission to the Mohawks, skillfully identified significant cleavages among the Oneida, caused by the rising power of the warriors over the shamans and elders and by hopelessness due to the failure of traditional ways to protect the Oneida from disease and defeat. Kirkland's fire-and-brimstone Puritanism drew in many converts, who eschewed alcohol, embraced radical Protestantism, and attempted to settle as farmers.

The American Revolution completed this split among the Oneida. The southern Oneida peoples, influenced by William Johnson, followed Johnson's brother-in-law Joseph Brant into the British camp. The northern Oneida sided with New York colonists, even going so far as to supply volunteers for the Tryon County militia. Oneida warriors fought with the militiamen to relieve Fort Stanwix and were ambushed at Oriskany Creek in August 1777 by Joseph Brant. In this battle, colonists were amazed to see several Oneida women fight fiercely alongside their husbands.

Oneida who had connections in the south provided intelligence and took part in the harassing of General Burgoyne's troops on their disastrous march to Saratoga. The Native Americans probably contributed crucially to the victory by significantly weakening the British forces before the battle. There also is a strong Oneida tradition relating how the tribe sent much-

needed corn to the starving army at Valley Forge, although this is difficult to corroborate.

Unfortunately, those Oneida fighting with the Americans also were used against the Onondaga, relatives and former allies of the Oneida, in a deadly raid by General John Sullivan. Although Sullivan requested and received officer's commissions for many of the native leaders, the resistance of the Oneida to join the attack was compounded by a retaliatory raid by Brant in July 1780, which destroyed the main Oneida village and left hundreds homeless. General Philip Schuyler grudgingly housed the refugees in barracks at Schenectady, New York, while the Oneida warriors attached to the Americans harried a loyalist invasion of the Mohawk Valley in 1781.

After the war, although treated as allies of the victorious colonies and reimbursed $5,000 for their destroyed village, the Oneida were quickly squeezed by expansionist New York. New York manipulated the sale of Oneida land, which became three counties in 1784, despite a suit by the state of Massachusetts claiming that the sale was illegal under provisions of the Articles of Confederation; the case was later settled out of court. In 1788, New York allowed speculators to "lease" large tracts of Oneida lands for 999 years, again in contravention of state legislation, ostensibly to protect the Oneida tribe from fraudulent offers from land companies.

In 1795, the new federal government, led by Timothy Pickering, attempted to block New York's further attempts to buy or lease lands in the hands of the Oneida. It was forced to give up in the face of intransigent state officials, who continued to cut land deals with individual Oneidas, even though the land the natives were selling often did not belong to them as single owners.

Steadily, Oneida land in New York was reduced to a fraction of what the tribe had been guaranteed by postwar agreements, and many Oneida began to leave the state for the Ohio Valley or Canada. Even institutions such as the Oneida Academy, established to educate Oneida children, had become bastions of the New York white elite by the 1820s.

With these disappointments, most of the remaining Oneida followed Reverend Eleazer Williams to a settlement in Wisconsin, where a new town at Duck Creek was founded in 1825. New York, which had in 1838 promised to pay the selling Oneida annuities, left the new settlement stripped of this security and instead paid off the whole amount of the land sale in a lump sum in 1839.

Margaret Sankey

See also: Iroquois Confederacy; Native American–European Conflict; Native American–European Relations; Native Americans.

Bibliography

Campisi, Jack. *History of the Oneida Indians.* Seymour, WI: Seymour Community Schools, 1972.

Campisi, Jack, and Laurence M. Hauptman, eds. *The Oneida Indian Experience.* Syracuse, NY: Syracuse University Press, 1988.

Richards, Cara. *The Oneida People.* Phoenix, AZ: Indian Tribal Series, 1974.

Onondaga

The Onondaga are one of the founding nations of the Iroquois Confederacy, a long-standing alliance between the Five Nations of the Iroquois. The confederacy, which originally included the Onondaga, Cayuga, Seneca, Oneida, and Mohawk, expanded in 1722 to include the Tuscarora. The peoples of the Iroquois Confederacy conceived, and continue to conceive, of themselves as families arranged around a single longhouse. The Onondaga, or "People on the Mountain," were located in the geographic center of the Iroquois country, which, in colonial times, stretched across much of northern New York, Pennsylvania, and southern Ontario.

In mythic times, Tadodaho, a furious Onandaga war chief, was soothed by Hiawatha, the founder of the Great League of Peace and Power. In recognition of Tadodaho's conversion, the Onondaga played a role in Iroquois politics that outweighed their small population. The Onondaga were "firekeepers," who would host and moderate meetings between the major chiefs of the Five Nations.

Clan structure and kinship were extremely important in colonial-era Onondaga society, and the clans themselves were divided into two "moieties," or sides, which sat on opposite sides of the fire during diplomatic councils. Within Onondaga villages, as in other Iroquois villages, political life was not exclusively the domain of men. Since women were often in charge of village life while men were away for extended periods, conducting trade, diplomacy, and war, they assumed no small measure of political power in Onondaga villages. Iroquois women also played an important role in

the mourning war (a war in which enemy captives were taken to replace dead kin) by determining when it had reached its conclusion.

The onset of European colonization brought significant changes to Onondaga country. Like the other Iroquois nations, the Onondaga allied themselves loosely with the Dutch in an effort to facilitate trade in beaver pelts. It eventually became clear, however, that the French and English would be the major European players in the colonization of the Northeast, and many native communities adjusted their diplomacy to deal with this emerging reality.

The Iroquois were particularly adept at playing the English and the French off one another to maintain their autonomy and position as the main native power brokers of the Northeast. The Onondaga were longtime advocates, and perhaps even architects, of Iroquois neutrality, although this did not save them from a devastating attack by the French and their Algonquin-speaking allies in 1690. In a series of councils in 1700, the Onondaga helped craft a workable Iroquois foreign policy, one of which recognized that the Iroquois had become dependent on European goods and could no longer resist either the French or the English. (The end of the so-called Beaver Wars of the seventeenth century did allow the Iroquois to rebuild and regroup.)

As the eighteenth century progressed, the carefully constructed Iroquois policy of neutrality became increasingly difficult to maintain. The Onondaga still maintained control of their day-to-day lives, but their external affairs were more firmly in the hands of Euro-Americans. The unfolding of the American War for Independence hammered this point home.

As they had previously, the Onondaga people struggled to main their autonomy and neutrality, although the fighting threatened to tear apart the Six Nations of the Iroquois. American forces, believing that Onondaga were supporting the British war effort, attacked the Onondaga. Such offensive action prefigured a new era in which native peoples could not remain neutral.

Following the war, the Onondaga entered into a treaty relationship with the state of New York, which significantly reduced the tribe's land base to 7,300 acres near Syracuse. Some Onondagas relocated to Ontario. In 1815, the prophet Handsome Lake, who, in the early 1800s, had developed a new religion that many Onondagas continue to practice, died and was buried outside the Onondaga longhouse at Nedrow, New York.

The Onondaga in the early twenty-first century

have steadfastly maintained that the treaties they signed with New York were not legitimate, thus forming the basis for one of the largest unsettled land claims in the United States. In both Canada and the United States, Onondaga people have continued their role as the fire keepers for the Six Nations Iroquois.

Matthew Jennings

See also: Iroquois Confederacy; Native American–European Conflict; Native American–European Relations; Native Americans.

Bibliography

Bradley, James W. *Evolution of the Onondaga Iroquois: Accommodating Change, 1500–1655.* Syracuse, NY: Syracuse University Press, 1987.

Mohawk, John C. "Onondaga." In *Encyclopedia of North American Indians,* edited by Frederick E. Hoxie, 443–44. Boston: Houghton Mifflin, 1996.

Richter, Daniel K. *The Ordeal of the Longhouse: The Peoples of the Iroquois League in the Era of European Colonization.* Chapel Hill: University of North Carolina Press, 1992.

Opechancanough (c. 1545–c. 1646)

In order to understand the impact of Opechancanough's rise to power, one must first have an understanding of the relationship that existed between the native peoples and the colonists in the early Virginia colony. When Powhatan decided to retire, he assigned the leadership role of the Algonquin to Opechancanough, his brother. Powhatan's timing was most prudent, since he made this decision as the Virginia colonists were succeeding in the cultivation of the only crop that they were willing to work at—tobacco. Powhatan's confederacy took on a different demeanor, which strained the already tenuous interaction between the colonists and the natives. Their contacts began as a broad exchange of information and trade, but they were always marked by tension. The colonists had arrived in the New World with the attitude that they were special, and they fully expected friendliness and help from the native population.

The early Virginia colonists depended heavily on Native American support as they struggled to establish themselves and become acclimated to a new world. What the colonists did not realize was that they had begun to settle in the middle of one of the most powerful Native American tribes on the continent— the Powhatan, a confederacy of Algonquin tribes.

The first years at Jamestown were brutal for the English, even though the natives had taught them how to cultivate food crops as well as medicinal herbs. With disease and starvation running rampant in the colony, limiting the number of those able and willing to work the fields, the colonists were forced to depend heavily on the Powhatan. The English demanded food from them—food that the Powhatan knew the colonists could easily have grown themselves, had they not been preoccupied with the constant search for riches with as little labor as possible. This pressure forced the Native Americans both to produce food for themselves and to try to meet the demands of the colonists. Resentment grew as this reliance became expectancy; this, in turn, provided the fuel not only to ignite the anger of the natives as a group but also to damage the previously amicable relationship between John Smith and Powhatan. This animosity made Jamestown a dangerous place for both Native Americans and English.

In 1613, the English unwisely captured Pocahontas, Powhatan's favorite daughter, and brought her back to Jamestown as a captive. In a short period of time, John Rolfe, a most influential colonist, fell in love with her and asked the English authorities and her father for permission to marry her. Both the authorities and Powhatan reluctantly agreed, and the first Anglo–Native American marriage in Virginia's history took place.

This union of two people would not be enough to unify the natives and the colonists. Still, cultural interaction continued and was facilitated by native people living among the English as day laborers. This exchange worked both ways, as settlers, in turn, fled to outlying Native American villages, seeking to escape autocratic English rule and the demands of tobacco planters.

Opechancanough's rule saw a new period of increased violence, as the tobacco planters demanded more and more land to cultivate their crop. A growing population placed more pressure on the Native Americans, as more and more people moved up the Chesapeake, pushing the natives off the land they had held under Powhatan's rule. The newcomers also introduced diseases that the native people were ill equipped to cope with, thus decimating their population. Opechancanough quickly realized that he would have to employ a different strategy in order to save his people.

Opechancanough now embarked on a program of aggression and spiritual renewal within his tribe. He depended heavily on Nemattanew, a war captain and religious prophet, who also provided a humorous interlude for the English, as he dressed up with feathers as though he fully intended to fly. Nemattanew proved dangerous to some of his people, as he managed to convince them that he was immortal and, if they rubbed their bodies with a special ointment, they would be immune to musket fire.

March 1622 saw Opechancanough preparing for a unified attack on the Virginia settlements. Plans were accelerated as the English, in retribution for a settler's death, murdered Nemattanew; his murder was the trigger that set off the combustible atmosphere that came from years of white expansion and pressure on native hunting lands. Two weeks later, the famous Native American assault took place and dealt the colony a staggering blow. One of the casualties was John Rolfe, and his death proved the final blow for the Virginia Company of London, which declared bankruptcy and turned over control of the colony to the English Crown.

By 1640, Virginia had grown to over 8,000 residents. The colony continued to grow, and, by 1662, the population had swelled to 25,000. This force had the ability to reduce the Native American population to numbers that would no longer be considered dangerous to the Virginia colonists and the ever-increasing number of people desiring Virginia as their new home.

Penny M. Sonnenburg

See also: Jamestown; Native American–European Conflict; Native American–European Relations; Native Americans; Powhatan; Powhatan Confederacy.

Bibliography

Crosby, Alfred W., Jr. *The Columbian Exchange: Biological and Cultural Consequences of 1492.* Westport, CT: Greenwood Publishing, 1972.

Jennings, Francis. *The Invasion of America: Indians, Colonialism and the Cant of Conquest.* Chapel Hill: University of North Carolina, 1975.

Orphans

The possibility of losing one or both parents was common to all children in the early modern period. Parents of both sexes could die of sickness or be killed while working under unsafe conditions. Women often died in childbirth. The transition to North America brought additional complications, especially in the Southern colonies, where the climate was particularly unhealthy for Europeans.

In most circumstances, a child losing one parent could rely on his or her circumstances remaining relatively unchanged. Wills usually provided for the continued support of the family, and bereft spouses often remarried. Most importantly, the surviving parent continued to serve as a protector and an advocate for his or her children. By contrast, orphaned children were left without personal protection or advocacy, and few laws existed to protect their rights until they came of age.

While being left orphaned was traumatic for all children, the financial backgrounds of their parents had a strong impact on their futures. In addition, cultural differences between colonists and regions could dictate how orphans were treated. Children orphaned within close-knit religious communities, such as the Quakers or Mennonites, were often absorbed into other families. These groups looked on all members as being part of the same family; orphaned children were considered part of this extended family and readily adopted. Settlers living in isolated areas, such as the Virginia backcountry, also simply adopted orphans into their families, as towns were too scattered to provide much support.

Under the best of circumstances, wealthy parents left wills specifying who was to care for their children and how they were to be cared for until they came of age. Plans for education, dowries, and other uses of the inheritance could be spelled out. Unlike poor children, wealthy siblings left orphaned could usually rely on not being separated; however, advocacy still remained an important question for wealthy orphans. Until the orphan came of age, the guardian had the right to manage the child's lands or money. Many children saw their inheritances squandered before they reached adulthood. Guardians also could arrange and sign marriage contracts, sometimes arranging for the orphan to marry one of the guardian's children, thus maintaining ongoing control over his or her inheritance.

Poor children left orphaned had few options. If they were lucky, they were adopted by a family member or neighbor and regarded as a full member of the family. In most cases, they were regarded as little more than servants, with no hope of inheriting land or gaining a dowry against marriage.

Another problem was that the transition to North America often broke down family connections. First-generation indentured servants in all parts of the colonies were most likely to be unable to provide their children with extended family members. If orphaned, such children would become dependent on local authorities for survival. Although towns were expected to support their own poor, few rules existed to regulate this support. In addition, most towns had residency rules. If a homeless woman died in childbirth, there was no requirement for the town to provide for the child following her death.

Small towns commonly "bound out" poor orphans. The family who requested the least amount of money from the town for looking after the child would be granted custody. Usually, the child was looked on as a servant. Young children, unable to provide much in the way of labor or personal defense, were often vulnerable. Older children, capable of more skilled work, could be assigned to work off any debt left behind by their parents. The yearly renewal of these indentures offered some hope for transition if a child—particularly if he or she was placed with an abusive family—but children had little say over these decisions.

Larger towns in the Northern and Middle colonies began organizing almshouses in the late seventeenth century. By 1865, Boston had an almshouse where various programs were established to train inmates for future work. Girls were taught to work as domestic servants, boys as laborers. The most common trade in 1740 was "picking oakum," or recycling old rope, along with shoemaking, mop making, spinning wool for mops, and candlewicking.

Although orphanages became more common in the nineteenth century, they were usually as poorly regulated as the colonial almshouses. Organized, federal protection for orphans did not come into existence until the early twentieth century.

Abigail B. Chandler

See also: Child Rearing; Children; Family; Inheritance; Law and Courts; Widows and Widowers. *Document:* Probate Inventory of a Plymouth Colony Estate (1672).

Bibliography

Pollock, Linda A. *Forgotten Children.* Cambridge, UK: Cambridge University Press, 1983.

Sommerville, C. John. *The Rise and Fall of Childhood.* Beverly Hills, CA: Sage Publications, 1982.

Otis, James (1725–1783)

James Otis, a leader of colonial Massachusetts politics and an early contributor to the rhetoric of the American Revolution, was born in Barnstable, Plymouth Colony, on February 5, 1725. His family had gained some prominence throughout the region: His father James Otis, Sr., served in the Massachusetts House of Representatives, despite a lack of formal education.

James Otis, Jr., graduated from Harvard in 1743 and completed his master's degree in 1746. Following his formal training, Otis studied under attorney Jeremiah Gridley and was admitted to the Plymouth Colony bar. Following that, he began his own practice in Barnstable. He practiced law there for two years before moving to Boston in 1750. In addition to his work as an attorney, Otis handled his father's business affairs in Boston and became generally engaged in commerce. He married Ruth Cunningham, the daughter of an affluent Boston merchant, in 1755.

The following year Otis began his tenure as the advocate general of the vice-admiralty court. He resigned his position with the court in 1760 in protest of the writs of assistance issued by the Massachusetts superior court. These writs allowed customs officials to search vessels at will for smuggled goods. Otis presented a lengthy and eloquent argument against the writs of assistance before the high court. The writs, Otis argued, were a violation of common and natural law and trampled on human rights. Otis further declared that any act of Parliament that so impeded the natural rights of the colonists was invalid. Otis's argument against the writs of assistance helped to establish the basic groundwork of the division between Parliament and the colonies. His declaration of the writs as unconstitutional raised the fundamental question of how much authority Parliament had and to what extent that body could exercise sovereign powers.

Otis's argument against the writs of assistance moved him to the forefront of the infant Revolutionary movement. In 1761, Otis was elected to the colonial assembly; in 1764, he was chosen to head the Massachusetts committee of correspondence. The author of numerous pamphlets and letters that outlined the issues of the Revolution, Otis drafted a concise argument against Parliament's efforts at taxation in *The Rights of the British Colonies Asserted and Proved.* Otis opposed later acts of the British Parliament, declaring the Sugar Act a law that taxed the colonial population without their consent.

Otis served as a member of the Stamp Act Congress in 1765, narrowly losing the post of presiding officer to his fellow Massachusetts representative Timothy Ruggles. Although Otis was widely supported by a radical faction within the Congress, the group as a whole tended to adopt a moderate voice of opposition. It declared that the provision of the Stamp Act that granted greater jurisdiction to the vice admiralty courts violated the right to trial by jury.

In 1766, Otis was elected speaker of the Massachusetts colonial assembly, an honor that was disallowed him by the veto of Bernard, the royal governor. The position went instead to Thomas Cushing, one of Otis's followers. Governor Bernard continued his attack on Otis, negating the election of his father, James Otis, Sr., to the Massachusetts Council.

In 1767, Otis attacked the Townshend Acts, another of Parliament's efforts to tax the colonies. He chaired a Boston town meeting that called on the local inhabitants to begin manufacturing a variety of articles—including clothing, furniture, sugar, liquor, cheeses, and jewelry—so as not to consume those items taxed by the Townshend Acts. Together with fellow Revolutionary Samuel Adams, Otis convinced the Massachusetts assembly to adopt the Circular Letter, a document that declared the colonial position and rejected the idea that the colonies could be adequately represented in Parliament. The letter was sent to the speaker of every other colonial assembly in an effort to regain the type of cooperation and harmony that had been evident at the time of the Stamp Act crisis.

Otis's political and philosophical thought helped to shape the ideology of the American Revolution. In 1769, he was attacked by a British customs official and sustained severe injuries. The resulting skull fracture damaged his brain and incapacitated him mentally. After an incident in which he vandalized the State House, Otis was declared insane, and his brother Samuel was named his guardian.

The following year, Otis was removed from public life. He spent the rest of his years at the homes of family friends, no longer recognizable as the strong political force he had once been. On May 23, 1783, Otis was struck by lightning and died instantly.

Tonia M. Compton

See also: Revolutionary War; *Rights of the British Colonies Asserted and Proved, The* (1764); Stamp Act (1765); Townshend Acts (1767). *Document:* Rights of the British Colonies Asserted and Proved (1764).

Bibliography

Gipson, Lawrence Henry. *The Coming of the Revolution, 1763–1775.* New York: Harper & Row, 1954.

Middlekauff, Robert. *The Glorious Cause: The American Revolution, 1763–1789.* New York: Oxford University Press, 1982.

Sheedy, Jack. "James Otis, Jr. . . . The first Barnstable patriot," Summerscape '98, a supplement to the *Barnstable Patriot.* http://www.barnstable-patriot.com/sscape/jotis.html.

Ottawa

Ottawa, the capital city of Canada, is located in southern Ontario, on the Quebec border, at the confluence of the Ottawa, Gatineau, and Rideau rivers. When the first Europeans arrived in the early seventeenth century, the Algonquin Indians inhabited the area. They were semi-isedentary, hunting wild animals such as deer and fowl; harvesting shell and scale fish; collecting roots, nuts, and fruits; and cultivating corn, squash, and beans to supplement their diet.

With the arrival of the French in the early seventeenth century, the Algonquins became middlemen in the fur trade. By the middle of the century, however, they were forced to leave the region by the Huron and Iroquois, who were fighting for control of the fur trade market.

On June 4, 1613, the French explorer Samuel de Champlain, who was searching for a Northwest Passage to the Orient, ventured up the Ottawa River, which the Algonquin then called Kichesippi (the Great River), and which the Europeans later called the Ottawa River (after the local Outaouais tribe). After coming across the present-day site of Ottawa, Champlain stopped to admire the Rideau and Chaudière falls and set up a temporary camp before traveling farther west.

The camp, which was by no means a permanent settlement, became a stopping point for explorers, fur traders, missionaries, and soldiers for the next 185 years. Natural obstacles, such as the Chaudière Falls and treacherous rapids, forced travelers to portage their canoes and set up camps on the north and south sides of the river.

No permanent settlement existed in the area until Philemon Wright and a group of colonists from Massachusetts migrated northward in 1800 and settled on the north side of the river (now Hull, Quebec). They called the settlement Wright's Town. There, they built houses and a mill, and farmed the land. When France blockaded the European ports during the Napoleonic Wars and denied the British timber imports from the Baltic States, Wright and the other colonists built a raft and conveyed timber down the Ottawa River to Quebec City, establishing the lucrative timber trade of the Ottawa Valley.

In 1857, Queen Victoria was asked to settle a dispute between Kingston, Toronto, Montreal, Quebec City, and Ottawa as to which city should become the capital of the United Province of Canada. She chose Ottawa, probably because of its mixed French and

English population, as well as its geographic and strategic location on the border of Ontario and Quebec—a decision that was reaffirmed during confederation in the British North America Act of 1867.

Since confederation, Ottawa has remained the capital city of Canada. It is now the fourth-largest city in the country—after Toronto, Montreal, and Vancouver.

Michael Sletcher

See also: Native American–European Conflict; Native American–European Relations; Native Americans.

Bibliography

Brault, Lucien. *Ottawa, Old and New.* Ottawa: Ottawa Historical Information Institute, 1946.

Ross, A. H. D. *Ottawa, Past and Present.* Toronto: Musson Book, 1927.

Taylor, John H. *Ottawa: An Illustrated History.* Toronto: J. Lorimer, 1986.

Woods, Shirley E. *Ottawa: The Capital of Canada.* Toronto: Doubleday Canada, 1980.

P

Paine, Thomas (1737–1809)

Thomas (Tom) Paine was a leading voice for independence in the American colonies. His widely read pamplet *Common Sense* helped turn the colonies' dispute with Great Britain into a movement for independence and revolution. Paine's writings, with their sustained attacks on the excesses of hereditary government and calls for greater political power for the middle classes, played an important role in the late-eighteenth-century transition from monarchy and colonialism to republican government and independence.

Born in 1737 in the market town of Thetford, England, to a Quaker corset maker and the daughter of an Anglican attorney, Paine attended a local grammar school until the age of 13. He apprenticed with his father and then moved to London in 1756, where he continued working in trades. After marrying and losing his first wife to a difficult childbirth in 1760, Paine obtained a position as a tax official with the help of his Anglican grandfather.

From his upbringing in Thetford, to his experiences in London, and his service as a tax official in Sussex and Lewes, Paine witnessed firsthand the glaring social, economic, and political inequalities that marked British life. It was these issues that so consumed him during the American Revolution. After arranging a separation from his second wife, Paine returned to London, where he met for the second time with Benjamin Franklin, received a letter of introduction, and set sail for Philadelphia in September 1774.

In the spring of 1775, the conflict between Britain and the American colonies took a turn for the worse as British regulars clashed with Massachusetts militiamen at Lexington and Concord. The colonies were now engaged in an armed rebellion against Britain, but few colonists wanted independence, hoping instead to resolve the conflict peacefully and remain part of the British Empire. Paine disabused his fellow colonists of this hope, beginning in January 1776, when *Common Sense* first appeared in Philadelphia. Within three months, an unprecedented 120,000 copies of the fifty-page pamphlet had circulated throughout the colonies.

A brilliant polemic denouncing monarchy and hereditary government, *Common Sense* was written expressly for a popular audience. Unlike most essayists of the American Revolution, Paine spoke to his betters, his equals, and his inferiors all at the same time, in the same tone, and with the same message. He asserted that the laboring and middling ranks of society should have a greater political role, thus helping legitimatize political action during the American Revolution.

Common Sense also contained a ringing plea for independence. The ongoing British efforts to put down the rebellion in New England made reconciliation between Britain and the American colonies impossible, claimed Paine. The colonies had to become independent and sever their ties with the king, Parliament, and the entire British Empire: "everything short of that" would be "mere patchwork."

Common Sense's call for independence, however, did not speak to the difficulties of war. In the months following the Declaration of Independence, the Continental army suffered a series of defeats and withdrawals, and support for the war slipped. Paine responded with *The American Crisis,* a series of essays first issued in December 1776, at the war's low point.

"These are the times that try men's souls," began the first *Crisis* letter, which reminded the now-independent colonists of the high cost of independence and liberty. "The summer soldier and the sunshine patriot will, in this crisis, shrink from the service of their country; but he that stands it *now,* deserves the love and thanks of man and woman. Tyranny, like hell,

The pamphleteer Thomas Paine, whose *Common Sense* (1776) aroused pro-independence sentiment, also wrote a series of essays, *The American Crisis,* during the war. "These are the times that try men's souls," it began. *(Brown Brothers, Sterling, Pennsylvania)*

is not easily conquered," explained Paine as he implored Americans to support the war effort.

During the war, Paine continued writing additional *American Crisis* essays and other pamphlets. He served with the army in 1776 and 1777, served as secretary for the Continental Congress's Committee on Foreign Affairs, and, in 1781, served as an unofficial assistant for an American diplomatic mission to France. Paine also remained active in Pennsylvania's and Philadelphia's turbulent wartime politics, serving on various city committees charged with addressing wartime problems and shortages, and clerking for the Pennsylvania assembly.

The states of New York and Pennsylvania, the national government, and prominent Revolutionaries like George Washington all acknowledged Paine's important contributions to the effort to secure American independence. Pennsylvania granted him 300 pounds, Congress granted him $3,000, and New York granted him a 300-acre farm in New Rochelle.

In the 1790s, Paine became embroiled in the struggles between the Federalists and Republicans in the United States, as well as in the transatlantic debates spawned by the French Revolution. *Rights of Man* (1791, 1792) was well received by American Republicans. His *Age of Reason* (1795), however, with its deistic attacks on organized religion and orthodox Christianity, garnered him a reputation as an atheist infidel, and Paine fell out of favor with many of his adopted countrymen.

Paine returned to the United States in 1802, after nearly a decade in England and France. He eventually settled on his farm in New Rochelle, where he died on June 8, 1809.

In 1805, Paine's bitter antagonist, John Adams, wrote a tribute. Adams deplored Paine's ideas about society and government, but he admitted "I know not whether any man in the world has had more influence on its inhabitants or affairs over the last thirty years than Tom Paine."

John Craig Hammond

See also: *Common Sense* (1776); Revolutionary War. *Document: Common Sense* (1776).

Bibliography

Foner, Eric. *Tom Paine and Revolutionary America.* New York: Oxford University Press, 1976.

Foner, Philip S. *The Complete Writings of Thomas Paine.* 2 vols. New York: Citadel, 1945.

Kaye, Harvey J. *Thomas Paine: Firebrand of the Revolution.* New York: Oxford University Press, 2000.

Patriots

A long-standing term in Anglo-American political culture, "patriotism" signified legitimate political opposition to government corruption; "patriots" withheld loyalty to the current state and strove to restore it to an imagined, virtuous, and pure past. In the early eighteenth century, patriots were public men loyal to the state but critical of specific government policies. Patriots were thus critics and reformers rather than vocal defenders of government policy.

By the late eighteenth century, patriotic rhetoric became the hallmark of political radicalism, leading the politically conservative Samuel Johnson to remark famously in 1775 that patriotism "was the last refuge of a scoundrel." By the 1770s, the term "patriot" had become so linked to British radicals that political conservatives used it to defame their political opponents. It was not until the late nineteenth century that those in authority coopted the rhetoric, stripped its long association with political criticism and reform, and used it instead to press for popular approval of government actions.

Patriotism was considered a male virtue, although women did occasionally claim this trait for themselves. A patriot demonstrated love of his country by remaining vigilant, making sure that government bodies remained true to universal principles and respected the rights of the governed. Patriots exhibited virtue by upholding the common good at the expense of individual self-interest through either military or civic service. Assuming that power frequently led to corruption, patriots were expected to curb political injustices by raising critical voices against their own government. Patriots thus remained loyal to their country's permanent ideals, not to specific party interests or government factions; their task was to ensure that particular administrations remained true to abstract moral standards and defended the rights of all Britons.

The oppositional meaning of the term emerged in British politics during the 1720s from three sources. Its first meaning was derived from both Greek political thought and Italian Renaissance humanism, popularized by Machiavelli in Italy and Bolingbroke in England. This tradition upheld the virtues of a balanced constitution and emphasized the patriot's need to fight political corruption, defined as the undue influence of any one branch of the state over the others. The second tradition looked toward an imagined Saxon past, in which a perfect constitution had secured liberty to all. Patriots used this idealized history to urge men to reform the present state in its image. The third source held the greatest sway over American minds. English Protestants held deep convictions that England was an "elect" nation, like ancient Israel, chosen specially by God to be the birthplace of liberty.

These three sources came together in the early-eighteenth-century British mind to make England the natural home of liberty and virtue, blessed with a balanced constitution that was in constant danger from power-hungry and corrupt men. When such men gained influence, the political opposition had a patriotic duty to rise up in defense of their collective liberties and guard against political slavery.

American Revolutionaries found in this oppositional language a powerful means of asserting their critiques of George III's rule and legitimating their Revolution. In the mid-eighteenth century, the word gained popularity among radical Whigs, who emphasized the patriot's duty to protect personal liberty from all forms of political tyranny. From the mid-1760s on, patriots specifically opposed George III, depicting him as a corrupt tyrant, whose administration threatened individual virtue and liberties. While simultaneously critiquing George III's administration, Revolutionary patriots upheld what they claimed were the true ideals of the British constitution, a political system based on ideals of natural rights and individual sacrifice for a common good. Patriot ideology drew directly from a British radical tradition that included such thinkers as John Locke, John Milton, John Hampden, Algernon Sydney, John Wilkes, and Thomas Paine.

In addition, the term "patriot" retained very strong moral and religious implications to American Revolutionaries. Revolutionary reformers—like their British forebears—used the term to signify their critique of the British government, reminding American colonists that they had a collective moral duty to God to vigorously guard their constitutional rights.

By the American Revolution's outbreak, American patriots were also expected to promote more democratic and egalitarian ideals. For example, in 1777, Virginia's Reverend John Hurt defined "patriot" as encompassing "the idea of a public blessing . . . a power of doing good, exerted and extended to whole communities; and resembles" that universal and benevolent "providence which protects and supports the world."

Americans' patriotism was rooted in their belief that they possessed unalienable rights as both freeman and as Protestants, and that their patriotic loyalty was to God first and the British king second. Such an understanding gave their radical political ends moral legitimacy.

Karen O'Brien

See also: Boston Tea Party; Committees of Correspondence; Lexington and Concord, Battles of; Loyalists; Militias; Revolutionary War; Sons of Liberty.

Bibliography

Cunningham, Hugh. "The Language of Patriotism, 1750–1914," *History Workshop Journal* 12 (1981): 8–33.

Hurt, John. *The Love of Our Country. A Sermon Preached before the Virginia Troops in New Jersey.* Philadelphia: Styner and Cist, 1777.

Karsten, Peter. *Patriot Heroes in England and America.* Madison: University of Wisconsin Press, 1978.

Samuel, Raphael. *Patriotism: The Making and Unmaking of British National Identity.* London: Routledge, 1989.

Patroons

A patroon was a landowner in North American colony of New Netherland in the seventeenth century. *Patroon* is a Dutch word for patron or master, and patroons had all the rights, privileges, and obligations of feudal lords, including a degree of legal authority over those who lived on their lands.

After the Englishman Henry Hudson sailed the *Half Moon* into New York harbor on behalf of the Netherlands, he reported his findings to his employer, the Dutch East India Company. The Estates General of the United Netherlands gave the New Netherland Company a monopoly on exploration and commercial development of the colony of New Netherland. The company developed a fur trade, but the government wanted increased settlement to counter its rival, England.

In 1623, a new charter company, the Dutch West India Company, settled thirty Walloon families on homesteads in lower Manhattan, on the western shore of Long Island, in Albany, and along the Delaware and Connecticut Rivers. As colonization was still too slow, in 1629, the company and government jointly issued the Charter of Freedoms and Exemptions.

The charter excepted Manhattan from the patroon system. In the rest of the New Netherland, individuals, with the permission of the governor and council, could claim large tracts of land. All they had to do was pay for transportation to the New World and settlement costs on their land for fifty adults within four years. They would then be patroons, with rights to claim up to 16 miles of riverfront on one side of a river or 8 miles on both sides, and as much contiguous property as the patroon wanted. To get more than the maximum 16 miles of waterfront, however, the patroon had to bring in more settlers. His land thus grew in proportion to the numbers of settlers beyond the original fifty.

On his land, the patroon had full title, legal authority, and absolute inheritance rights. His tenants could fish, hunt birds, or mill grain only with his permission. To enforce his rule, the patroon had the right to appoint magistrates and officers in any town he chose to establish.

The patroon was to establish and document local government compatible with the Dutch government's and the company's rules. He had to select a deputy who met with the company director and council. And each estate had to provide an annual report to Manhattan for transmission to Amsterdam. Patroons also had to provide the people on their land with a teacher, a minister, and a medical person.

The patroon had claim to a tenth of all products of his land. Rent was 500 guilders per year (approximately $200), and the tenants had to provide both quitrent (fixed rent) and some food products such as fowl and butter.

The most successful patroonship was the Rensselaerwyck, which eventually controlled counties near Albany, Rensselaer, and part of Columbia. Others were the Van Cortlandt manor, which included 85,000 acres, and the Livingston manor, which totaled 160,000 acres. Staten Island was totally the property of Cortnelis Melyn. Thomas Pell had Pelham, while Lloyd's Neck belonged to James Lloyd. Fordham and Scarsdale were patroonships as well.

The patroon administered justice through a court system he established. Settlers on his territory did have the right to appeal his decisions to the director and council on payment of up to fifty guilders (about $20).

For the first decade, the members of the patroon's colony were exempt from customs and taxes. On the other hand, they could not leave the colony except by written consent of the patron, and the company promised to apprehend runaways. The company also promised to provide slaves, but at its convenience. And it demanded that all settlers outside of Manhattan had to compensate Native Americans appropriately for any land the settlers acquired.

The company barred patroons from trading in furs, a company monopoly, except in territories where the company had no presence. Manufacture of woolen, cotton, or linen cloth, and weaving in general were prohibited, because they competed with Dutch industry. Punishment could include banishment.

Within the limits, patroons could trade from Florida to Newfoundland, but they had to clear their cargoes through Manhattan and pay a 5 percent duty to the company before shipping cargo to Holland. Patroons also could fish and sell their catch to neutral countries; the duty was three guilders per ton. The company also provided defense against all enemies, "outlandish and inlandish," and it fortified Manhattan.

In 1664, the Dutch lost New Netherland to the English, but the English recognized all Dutch titles. Because land was so abundant, many settlers rejected the patroon lands. For a small price, they could acquire native lands without all the rules of the patroon system. The attempt to maintain a feudal land system in an area of virtually unlimited land had little chance of success, and it was gradually phased out.

John H. Barnhill

See also: Dutch; Land and Real Estate; Landlords; New Netherland. *Document:* Rights and Privileges of Patroons (1629).

Bibliography

Kammen, Michael. *Colonial New York: A History.* New York: Charles Scribner's Sons, 1975.

Rink, Oliver A. *Holland on the Hudson: An Economic and Social History of Dutch New York.* New York: Cornell University Press, 1986.

Paxton Boys

The Paxton Boys were a group of *banditti*—allegedly lawless frontier settlers—from central Pennsylvania. Violence between the native peoples and colonists on Pennsylvania's frontier spun out of control in 1763. In December of that year, the Paxton Boys went on a rampage, massacring twenty peaceful Native Americans at Conestoga and Lancaster.

In early 1764, the now 500-man-strong Paxton Boys marched on Philadelphia to kill 140 Moravian Indians who had taken refuge there and to make their grievances known to the Quaker-dominated Pennsylvania government. In February, Benjamin Franklin and nearly 700 troops and militiamen stopped the Paxtons' march at Germantown, just outside the city, after officials pledged to hear the marchers' grievances and grant amnesty for their actions.

By the early 1750s, British colonists had begun expanding into western Pennsylvania and the Ohio Valley. British expansion worried the native peoples and the French, who claimed the region as their own. The Great War for Empire—which included the French and Indian War (1754–1763), also known as the Seven Years' War (1756–1763)—erupted in this milieu of competing empires, colonial settlers, and concerned Native Americans when Virginians led by George Washington tried to destroy the French Fort Duquesne at the forks of the Ohio River in 1754.

By 1760, the victorious British were laying claim to the entire trans-Appalachian West and Canada. British authorities failed, however, to make a permanent peace with the various native tribes and nations, halt colonists' encroachments on Native American lands, or stop aggression against the native peoples.

Furthermore, the war started a cycle of indiscriminate violence between European settlers and Native Americans in the Pennsylvania backcountry, dissolving already weak relations between the two. In the spring of 1763, natives launched Pontiac's Rebellion, a series of attacks on British forts and colonial settlements across the entire trans-Appalachian frontier.

The settlers on the Pennsylvania frontier, many of whom were Scots-Irish Presbyterians, responded by escalating their attacks on any Native American who happened to cross their path. After a few minor skirmishes in the woods and an attack on native peoples in the Wyoming Valley of Pennsylvania, the Paxton Boys grew frustrated at their inability to stop native attacks. The refusal of the Quaker-dominated colonial government to send troops to western Pennsylvania to assist the settlers in their war against the native tribes infuriated central Pennsylvanians even further.

In December 1763, fifty or so armed settlers from Paxton, Pennsylvania (present-day Harrisburg), turned their fury against a peaceful band of Conestoga Indians living on a small reservation outside Lancaster. After the Paxton Boys slaughtered six natives on their reservation, colonial officials locked fourteen remaining Conestogas in the Lancaster jail to protect them from further violence. The jail and colonial officials proved no match for the infuriated Paxtons, who broke into the jail and murdered the Conestogas. Their outrage against the native peoples and colonial officials who had failed to provide for frontier defense was not yet spent.

In early 1764, a force of some 500 Paxton Boys began their march on Philadelphia. In Philadelphia were two groups whom the Paxton Boys targeted for their vengeance: Quakers and Native Americans. The Quakers were the politicians, who refused to provide money for backcountry defense, while sponsoring the "Friendly Association," a Quaker organization that protected Native American lands and defended native rights against white settlers. That colonial officials were allegedly sheltering 140 Moravian Indians in the city outraged the Paxtons.

Panic ensued when reports of the Paxton Boys' march on Philadelphia reached the city. In order to protect the city from the "Christian white savages," Benjamin Franklin organized a militia company for the city's defense and headed to Germantown to meet these "lawless people." The Paxtons backed down in the face of 700 troops and militia, along with promises that colonial officials would work to restore order to the frontier.

The Paxton affair signified the near-total collapse of native-colonial relations in the period between the Great War for Empire and the American Revolution. As colonial settlements continued to push westward into Native American lands, colonial and imperial officials proved unwilling or unable to meet the demands of the native peoples that the settlers be removed and frontier *banditti* be punished for violence against natives. Similarly, tribal chiefs proved unable to restrain younger warriors, who insisted on attacking white settlements so as to halt white expansion and exact revenge for violence committed against their people. After 1760, the Pennsylvania backcountry became the scene of intense, indiscriminate violence.

The Paxton affair also reflected the growing religious, ethnic, regional, and political rifts in late colonial Pennsylvania. Distrust between Scots-Irish Presbyterians in central Pennsylvania and Quakers in eastern Pennsylvania grew after 1740, erupting during the Paxton affair. This event also had important ramifications for the American Revolution in Pennsylvania. Native peoples in western Pennsylvania sided with the British, who pledged to halt white settlement and expansion, while hostilities between the Scots-Irish and the Quakers became the defining force in Pennsylvania politics during the American Revolution.

John Craig Hammond

See also: Native American–European Conflict; Ohio Country; Pennsylvania.

Bibliography

Dunbar, John, ed. *The Paxton Papers*. The Hague: M. Nijhoff, 1957.

Merrell, James H. *Into the American Woods: Negotiators on the Pennsylvania Frontier*. New York: W. W. Norton, 1999.

Vaughan, Alden T. "Frontier Banditti and the Indians: The Paxton Boys' Legacy, 1763–1775." *Pennsylvania History*, 51:1 (January 1984): 1–29.

Peddlers

As colonial settlement grew and the frontier was pushed westward, agricultural areas expanded faster than urban areas. For many people living on the frontier, and even for those in more established regions, markets, urban shops, and country stores were not always close by. Peddlers, often called hawkers or chapmen, brought sought-after wares to settlers' doorsteps and played an important role in colonial economic and social development, especially in New England.

While colonial farmers have often been portrayed as living within a subsistence economy, their survival was, in fact, tied to a market economy. The long distances between most frontier homes and a market, however, meant that farmers were not willing to make the difficult, time-consuming journey when they needed only a few items.

Peddlers, with their traveling stores, were a welcome sight for those living in more isolated areas, as they provided easy access to necessary goods. Most peddlers did not deal in large items, because their horses and wagons could carry only a limited weight. Instead, they hawked such smaller products as books (including chapbooks, or small anthologies of writings, hence the name "chapman"), combs, buttons, needles, kitchen implements, and medicines. The peddler also brought with him news and gossip, and he provided fresh company to lonely frontier families.

While peddlers served an important economic and social role, they were also generally disliked. Although consumers welcomed the opportunity presented by the peddlers, they resented having to pay a higher price for the goods because of the convenience of the system. Many local merchants used this argument against peddlers; they also contended that these itinerant salesmen sold inferior goods, although many peddlers obtained their goods from the same merchants who openly criticized them. For the owners of urban and country stores, peddlers were competitors, who forestalled isolated farmers and their families from coming to their stores, where these shoppers usually made large purchases.

Other negative stereotypes of peddlers included connecting them to criminal networks, and many goods hawked by peddlers were assumed to be stolen. Other peddlers were accused of purchasing their goods on credit but never returning to pay for them.

These issues—including competition, crime, and debt—caused most colonies to regulate peddlers' activities. A South Carolina law of 1737 ordered that each peddler needed to be licensed to legally practice his trade. In 1765, Connecticut passed a law that required each peddler to pay an annual fee of 20 pounds. In 1767, New York outlawed peddlers and established a fine of 5 pounds for anyone caught hawking goods; this decision was later reversed, when it became clear that peddlers served an important role. After the return of peddlers to New York, it was decided to create a

Peddlers played a vital economic and social role by supplying needed goods to remote areas and—like these hawkers of tea water—more specialized commodities in urban areas. In either case, peddlers also facilitated the exchange of news and gossip. *(Brown Brothers, Sterling, Pennsylvania)*

licensing system with a fee of 8 pounds per horse and a fee of 5 pounds per wagon or sledge.

Colonial peddlers have not received the same amount of historical attention as larger urban-based merchants. Yet by moving within the ever-changing boundaries of settlement and connecting the settlers of these regions with the larger market economy, they played a vital role in colonial expansion and in the continued growth and development of the American economy.

Ty M. Reese

See also: Merchants; Trade.

Bibliography

Bridenbaugh, Carl. *Cities in Revolt: Urban Life in America, 1743–1776.* New York: Alfred A. Knopf, 1955.

McCusker, John J., and Russell R. Menard. *The Economy of British America, 1607–1789.* Chapel Hill: University of North Carolina Press, 1985.

Penn, William (1644–1718)

William Penn was born on October 14, 1644. His father, an English naval officer, had married Margaret Jasper Vanderscure on June 6, 1643. As a child, Penn was quiet and introspective. He saw little of his father, who was generally away at sea, and spent most of his childhood secluded in the family home with his mother.

Penn had little formal education. He attended the

Chigwell Free Grammar School for less than a year. In 1656, the family moved to an estate in Ireland. King Charles II rewarded his father's loyalty with a knighthood in 1660. Sir William was also given a royal commission in the Navy and a larger Irish estate. The family then returned to London.

At the age of 16, Penn enrolled in Christ Church College at Oxford. An avid reader and quiet by nature, he disliked the Oxford climate and left after just two years. In July 1662, Penn traveled to France, where he attended school at Saumur, a Protestant seminary, returning to London after two years. His father enrolled him in law school at Lincoln's Inn, the "finishing school" for well-to-do gentlemen.

When war with Holland erupted, Penn's father was returned to active service, and he took William with him on his flagship. The king's brother, James Stuart, the duke of York, accompanied the Penns. After a time, Penn was sent to London with dispatches for Charles II and then returned to law school. Despite several victories in the war, rumors of the duke's incompetence surfaced, and the elder Penn claimed for himself the blame being placed on the duke, thus damaging his own reputation. His actions cemented a lifelong friendship with the royal family, a connection that would serve Penn well in later years.

Penn as a Quaker

In 1667, Penn left Lincoln's Inn, traveling to Ireland to settle a lawsuit over the family estate. Penn also served as a military aide during the insurrection of disgruntled soldiers at Carrickfergus, action in which he distinguished himself. His success spurred him to pursue a career in the military, but he was denied a position in the army. It was during this time that Penn became a Quaker. He had long been acquainted with Quaker beliefs, but it was while he was in Ireland, under the influence of Thomas Loe, a disciple of the Society of Friends' founder George Fox, that Penn converted.

Penn quickly became a defender of his fellow Quakers and their beliefs. His publication of *Sandy Foundations Shaken,* a pamphlet that was part of an ongoing debate with Thomas Vincent, a Presbyterian minister, resulted in his imprisonment in the Tower of London for libel. Refusing to recant, Penn remained in prison for seven-and-a-half months until his father petitioned the Privy Council for his release. Penn authored 150 books and pamphlets over the course of his life, writings in which he consistently argued for tol-

eration of nonconformity. Penn believed that a person's conscience belonged only to God, a belief for which toleration was an absolute necessity.

On April 4, 1672, Penn married Gulielma Maria Springett. They had seven children, four of whom died in infancy. Only Springett, Letitia, and William (Billy) survived to adulthood.

In 1675, Penn became a trustee for the colonial venture in New Jersey. While this was not a wholly Quaker colony, many members of the sect were involved in its ownership and settling. Penn helped to frame the constitution for the colony in a document entitled "Concessions and Agreements."

Founding of Pennsylvania

Inspired by his work with the New Jersey colony, Penn formally requested an American land grant from the king on June 1, 1680. His father's loyalty to the royal family and the unpaid debt owed him aided Penn's request, and on March 4, 1681, Charles II approved the patent for Pennsylvania. Penn became the sole proprietor of roughly 45,000 square miles of unexplored land in the American colonies. The patent was geographically imprecise, leaving Penn unsure of exactly what land he owned, and resulting in a prolonged dispute over the southern boundary.

Penn began his "holy experiment" with grandiose ideas of religious freedom and financial success. He began selling land subscriptions of 5,000 acres, hoping to establish a colony of prosperous Quakers. Only 41 subscriptions of that size were sold at the cost of 100 pounds each, a number far short of his original goal of 100 subscribers. In the absence of wealthy investors, Penn sold 430 subscriptions to smaller investors, at an average of 750 acres. Most of these subscribers were skilled laborers, though the number included some professional men, two teachers, three doctors, and seven single women. These investors immigrated almost immediately.

For his capital city Penn envisioned what he called the "city beautiful" plan, an ideal that proved unrealistic. Investors were slated to receive a bonus grant of 10 acres in the city lot in order to build townhouses. Penn sought to avoid the crowded and polluted conditions of European cities. No homes were to be built closer than one-quarter mile from the waterfront. The city was to have two large open squares and smaller ones in every quarter. Two main highways as well as several smaller streets were to provide a grid on which to organize the city. Streets that ran north and south

William Penn, a prominent English Quaker, spent seven months in prison and wrote scores of books and pamphlets on religious toleration. Finally obtaining a land grant in 1681, Penn founded the colony of Pennsylvania. *(Private Collection/Bridgeman Art Library)*

were to be identified by numbers, while those running east and west were to be named after types of trees. Given the limited financial means of most of his investors, Penn eventually reduced the size of the land bonuses, as well as allowing for the establishment of smaller back streets that would accommodate the less affluent.

In 1681, as Penn was drafting the frame of government for Pennsylvania, his mother died. Penn had been close to his mother and was now orphaned, his father having died in 1670. During this time Penn relied heavily on his advisers in Pennsylvania. Early in 1682 he dispatched Captain William Markham to the colony to determine a site for the capital and establish friendly relations with the native population. Penn himself arrived in the colony late in 1682.

Penn in Pennsylvania

During his tenure there, Penn and the elected colonial assembly adopted his Frame of Government (later known as the Charter of Liberties), the basis of Penn-

sylvania law for nearly a century. Among its provisions were universal manhood suffrage, and fair and open trials for those accused of a crime. The law also opened the colony to persons from all religions, with no threat of persecution.

The government of the colony consisted of a governor with limited powers and a deputy governor. The Provincial Council, a seventy-two-member body, proposed legislation. The General Assembly could have up to 500 members and had as its responsibility the approval or defeat of legislation proposed by the council. One-third of the members were elected each year and each served a term of three years. The governor held the power to veto legislation.

In addition to establishing a working government, Penn also labored to achieve good relations with the native peoples in the area. Penn was convinced that no minorities should suffer persecution, as the Quakers had in England. As part of his effort, Penn purchased the land of Pennsylvania from the Native Americans and instructed officials to treat them as equals. Penn also insisted that negotiators utilize translators. Peaceful relations with the Susquehannock, Shawnee, and Lenni Lenape resulted from Penn's efforts; Penn also gained a reputation of courage among the native population.

Penn returned to England in 1684, his primary goal being the resolution of Pennsylvania's southern boundary. When James II assumed the throne in 1685, the dispute was settled, with the territory in question being equally divided, half going to Lord Baltimore and the other half reverting to the Crown. Penn spent many years as an active member of the royal court, his influence evident in the 1687 royal proclamation that declared liberty of conscience for all. Penn's favor with the court disappeared when William of Orange overthrew the Stuart dynasty.

Penn's Final Years

In 1692, Penn's wife died. Five years later, he married Hannah Callowhill, a fellow Quaker from Bristol. Hannah gave birth to seven children, four of whom died very young. The surviving children—John, Thomas, and Richard—would all play roles in the American colony. In 1699, Penn, Hannah, and Letitia sailed to Pennsylvania, where the first of his children with Hannah was born. John Penn was the only one of Penn's children to be born in America.

During his second visit to the colony, Penn successfully concluded the 1701 treaty with the Potomac

Indians, establishing commercial relations with them through authorized representatives. In 1701, when he learned that legislation to return the proprietary colonies to the Crown had been introduced in the House of Lords, Penn returned to London. During this time, he also faced charges from his financial adviser, Phillip Ford, who had embezzled much of Penn's income and tricked him into signing a document transferring the ownership of Pennsylvania to Ford.

In October 1712, Penn suffered a stroke, followed by a second one four months later. The resulting paralysis left him unable to attend to the business of running the colony, a role that his wife Hannah assumed. Penn died six years later on July 30, 1718.

Tonia M. Compton

See also: Native American–European Relations; Pennsylvania; Pennsylvania (Chronology); Quakers. *Document:* Pennsylvania Charter of Privileges (1701).

Bibliography

Dunn, Mary Maples. "The Personality of William Penn." In *The World of William Penn,* edited by Richard S. Dunn and Mary Maples Dunn. Philadelphia: University of Pennsylvania Press, 1986.

Geiter, Mary K. *William Penn.* New York: Longman, 2000.

Powell, Jim. "William Penn, America's First Great Champion for Liberty and Peace." The Religious Society of Friends. http://www.quaker.org/wmpenn.html.

Wildes, Harry Emerson. *William Penn.* New York: Macmillan, 1974.

"William Penn." Virtualology Museum of History. http://www.williampenn.org.

Pennsylvania

In modern American mythology, Pennsylvania represents a distinctive part of the American tradition. If New England provided the sense of destiny and mission, and Virginia contributed unfettered capitalism and individualism, Pennsylvania offered liberty, tolerance and diversity.

With this central role, Pennsylvania has contributed mightily to the development of both colonial and modern American society since its founding in 1682. To understand what factors played such major roles in shaping Pennsylvania, one must begin by examining the founder of the colony, William Penn.

Quakers

Son of a prominent admiral in the British navy, William Penn grew up in a prosperous, elite family. The stability and harmony of his childhood was not replicated in the broader context of the English nation during this period, as the English Civil War (1641–1649) and the resulting Protectorate of Oliver Cromwell caused deep divisions within English society. Catholics and proponents of a high church were driven into hiding or exile, while Protestant dissenters from the Church of England, such as Puritans and Quakers, multiplied in number and political power at the end of Cromwell's reign. With the collapse of the Protectorate in 1661 and the Restoration of King Charles II in the same year, civil war and military strife ceased, but the devastation of property, lives, and society was to be felt in the years to come, well unto the Glorious Revolution of 1689.

Quakers were among the most notorious Protestant dissenters during this period. Denying traditional religious authority, Quakers instead followed the authority of the "inner light"—that is, they believed that the Holy Spirit is present and works in the minds of living believers as it did in Jerusalem during the life of Jesus. Preaching a doctrine of tolerance, humility, simplicity, and love, Quaker evangelists were present throughout England, arguing for freedom of religion and tolerance for all Protestant believers.

The British civil authorities and Church of England responded harshly to such pleas, jailing large numbers of Quakers for refusing to attend Anglican services. Nearly 10,000 Quakers languished in jail during the 1660s, yet this effort to quash the Quaker faith failed as its membership rose throughout England. Preachers like George Fox persisted in spreading Quaker doctrine despite the threat of imprisonment and freely offered their words to all who would listen.

In 1660, William Penn, a student at Oxford University, accepted Quaker teachings and refused to attend Anglican services at college. This action infuriated Penn's father, who promptly sent his son on a grand tour of Europe to get radicalism out of his system. This effort failed, and, by 1667, William was jailed for publicly supporting the Quaker cause. Over the next decade, Penn was repeatedly harassed for his efforts to promote religious liberty in Great Britain.

By the 1670s, however, Penn's fortunes changed. In an effort to gain broader political support, King Charles II pushed for religious tolerance and started to cultivate Penn's favor. While this alliance can be explained as the result of politics, the king owed William's now-deceased father a fortune, as the senior Penn had given him loans to support his lavish lifestyle. When the king offered grants of land in cancellation of his debts, he found the right man in William Penn, as the latter sought a site in North America where Quakers could settle and enjoy religious freedom. In 1681, Charles II granted Penn control over the lands from Maryland to New York—an area soon named Pennsylvania in the proprietor's honor.

True to his Quaker principles, Penn established a constitution for his new colony that provided for religious liberty. He also actively promoted his new holdings to those in England and throughout Europe who sought a safe haven from the war-torn continent and marauding armies as well as a refuge from the religious intolerance that had been widespread since the early days of the Reformation.

Founding of Pennsylvania

With the launching of William Penn's colony, settlement quickly commenced. A large portion of the 10,000 Quakers who arrived in Pennsylvania before 1700 began their journey from the North Midlands region of England. In time, this region provided the elites of Pennsylvania's colonial society, as these first families intermarried and pursued close business and political alliances. Along with these Quakers, nearly an equal number of settlers came from the northern regions of Germany and Scotland, which had long suffered from a lack of economic opportunity and the heavy hand of war. To say that diversity is an essential part of Pennsylvanian history is an understatement; this pluralism provided both opportunity and conflict from the beginning.

Opportunity was available for the new colonists for a variety of reasons. First, the natives who lived in the Delaware River Valley—the Lenni Lenape or Delaware tribe—had been weakened by disease and were small in number and influence. Although this condition explains part of the reason for amicable relationships between the natives and newcomers, the fair and even-handed treatment that William Penn gave to the Lenni Lenape provided for long-standing peace and made warfare a foreign concept in the region for nearly sixty years. New settlers in Pennsylvania were also blessed by a relatively temperate climate and extremely fertile soil, which allowed for a long growing season. Finally, the stated tolerance in religious affairs saved Pennsylvania from some of the conflicts that marked the New England and Virginia colonies.

Despite these opportunities, discord arose among the settlers of Pennsylvania. Non-Quakers resented Penn's favoring of the group via choice land tracts and property in Philadelphia. The Quaker elites frowned on the Presbyterians and Reformed farmers from Scotland and Germany who sought to ignore land claims that Penn had established. All agreed, however, that as a proprietor, William Penn retained too much political power, limiting the legislature's say in colonial affairs, and they refused to pay the rents that Penn charged for use of his lands.

By the time of Penn's death in 1718, he was heavily in debt owing to a lack of return on his colony. He lamented that his dream had been taken over by "brutish" settlers intent on having their own way, resulting in the "harmonious society ruined."

By 1723, the colony of Pennsylvania had fulfilled some of Penn's hopes but dashed others. The colony was indeed a haven of religious tolerance. As a result, a heterogeneous mixture of Protestant groups and sects arrived in the Delaware River Valley. With all this diversity, however, these groups quickly found plenty to disagree about, especially issues of land and representation in the Pennsylvania Assembly, which had gained much power in 1700. The existing system of representation favored the established Delaware Valley region, which was heavily settled by Quakers (especially Philadelphia), over the rapidly expanding Presbyterian and Reformed population in the backcountry of the colony. This geographic and religious division remained until the early 1800s. Colonial politics in Pennsylvania often became nasty; the politics of the region became even more confrontational over the issue of the Penns' powers.

Hence, the Quaker elite, which was overrepresented in the assembly, divided into "proprietor" and "antiproprietor" factions. The Proprietor Party tended to be conservative in religious and cultural matters, strongly supportive of the Penn family's administration of the colony, and drawn from the Quaker merchant elites. The Antiproprietary Party was made of landholders who resented the taxes on the land, were strongly supportive of immigration to the region, and were hostile to the Penns' control over Pennsylvania.

Into this situation, in 1723, stepped Benjamin Franklin, the man who would define Pennsylvania like no other for the next sixty years. Fleeing from both an oppressive brother and a lack of economic opportunity in Boston, Franklin quickly established himself in the printing business in Philadelphia. Over the next ten years, he learned the trade, honed his love of science and invention, traveled to England, and formed nu-

The city of Bethlehem in eastern Pennsylvania (later a center of steel manufacturing) was founded in 1741 by Moravian exiles from Europe. The Pennsylvania colony, William Penn's "great experiment" in religious freedom, also attracted other pacifists such as Quakers and Amish. *(Library of Congress, LC-USZ62-43546)*

merous well-placed connections on both sides of the Atlantic.

By 1732, Franklin began publishing the *Poor Richard Almanack,* as well as the *Pennsylvania Gazette,* and these publications made him a well-known and wealthy man. Certainly his invention of the Franklin stove did much to gain him renown as an inventor, but the fact that this device also filled his pocket with money should not be ignored. Franklin was all things: a man of enlightenment, reason, creative ability, and keen awareness of the bottom line. In short, Franklin is best understood as a reflection of his times, during which Pennsylvania saw both continuity and transformation.

Growth of Pennsylvania

Between 1725 and the commencement of the French and Indian War in 1754, the population of colonial Pennsylvania exploded. While the population of 1715 was a mere 70,000, it grew to nearly 430,000 settlers by 1760. Although a high natural birth rate and economic prosperity explain part of this growth, the sheer number of immigrants to the region must also be taken into account. Nearly 150,000 Scots-Irish and Germans filled the western region of the colony, expanding Pennsylvania's border to the Susquehanna River.

While the countryside saw a large increase, Philadelphia also witnessed a dramatic expansion, doubling in population to 23,000 by the eve of the American Revolution. This growth occurred partly because the town became a center of transatlantic trade, but it was also due to the growth of an artisan class that provided goods and services to the elite families of the colony in many different ways.

Finally, many indentured servants did their term of service in Philadelphia; likewise, the number of African slaves in the town increased drastically and amounted to 9 percent of the population by 1750. The world of Pennsylvania and Ben Franklin from 1725 to 1754 was one of expansion, growth, and diversity in many respects.

With these changes in the makeup of Pennsylvania society, other changes in the colony reflected general trends in the British colonies of North America. By 1750, Pennsylvania was losing the egalitarianism that had marked the colony since its founding. The richest 10 percent controlled nearly 40 percent of the wealth, up from nearly 20 percent from 1715. In contrast, the middling artisans of Philadelphia saw their average yearly income decline from 30 to 23 pounds over the same period. Hence, economic opportunity was decreasing in the urban areas and inching closer toward the situation in Boston, where a few elite merchants increased their control over the wealth, power, and politics of the community throughout the eighteenth century.

With the idea and reality of social harmony and equality rapidly disappearing, many Quakers gradually withdrew from social and political activity. Their almost total absence after the end of the French and Indian War allowed for other groups, primarily the Anglicans, to gain control over the colony, as well as the levers of society. This shift was displayed most prominently in the legislative battles of the Pennsylvania Assembly, which had remained divided between the Proprietor and antiproprietor parties until the crisis of the 1760s. The latter party increasingly advocated royal control over Pennsylvania, arguing that the needs of colonial merchants and commerce would be served without the tiresome burden of Penn family control.

The leading advocates of this new platform were Ben Franklin and Thomas Galloway. Their vicious campaign against proprietor control gained them friends in Great Britain and the Pennsylvanian backcountry, as the new settlers resented the favored status of the native tribes in the region.

French and Indian War

The French and Indian War commenced with George Washington's failed offensive against the French near present-day Pittsburgh in 1754. Part of a global struggle, known as the Seven Years' War, whose main theater was in Europe, the French and Indian War was the final colonial struggle between the British and French for global mastery.

In North America, the French gained the upper hand quickly, as British regulars under the command of Braddock were annihilated in 1755, not far from where Washington had met defeat nearly a year earlier. The failure of British offensives in Pennsylvania's backcountry, along with spectacular French success along the New York frontier, led to a reassessment of British war efforts by late 1757.

With the accession of William Pitt, the elder, as prime minister and architect of British global strategy, the focus of the global conflict shifted to North America, and Pitt demanded increased colonial support for the imperial cause. The pacifist heritage and continued Quaker presence in Pennsylvania hindered British efforts to mobilize the militia and severely limited the colony's contribution to the war effort.

Within Pennsylvania society, the lack of Quaker support for the British caused deep division along religious and regional lines. The pacifist groups, which included most Quakers, Amish, and Moravians, lived in the long-inhabited Delaware River Valley, where there were no hostile Native American tribes nearby. The situation in the backcountry stood in stark contrast to that in the eastern regions, as the French and their allies threatened the Scots-Irish Presbyterians and Reformed Germans. Not surprisingly, these backcountry groups deeply resented the failure of the elites to provide an effective defense, and a group of such disgruntled citizens called the Paxton Boys marched upon Philadelphia when the colony failed to settle a dispute between settlers and natives after Pontiac's Rebellion in 1763.

Briefly stated, while the British and colonial efforts against the French resulted in a decisive victory on the Plains of Abraham in 1759, the conflict revealed deep divisions in Pennsylvania society. The diversity and pluralism that marked Pennsylvania from its beginning yielded bitter fruit well after the commencement of the war in 1763.

The efforts of British colonial administrators to pay for the immense burden of empire following the expensive conflict dominated the next and final epoch of colonial Pennsylvania. Over the 1760s, administration after administration of the British government sought to pay for the French and Indian War by increasing the tax burden on the American colonies through a variety of import and trade taxes.

In Pennsylvania, the long-prevailing political divisions between the Proprietors and the royalists led by Benjamin Franklin continued well into this period. The Proprietor forces, led by John Dickinson, opposed British efforts to gather taxes by arguing that without colonial representation in the English Parliament, these new fees and dues encroached on the colonists' personal liberties. Interestingly, Franklin supported many of the British taxes, arguing that imperial control over Pennsylvania was simply better than being under the thumb of the Penn family.

In the 1770s, as the conflict with Britain approached, Pennsylvania remained deeply divided along the ethnic, religious, and regional lines that had ruptured during the French and Indian War. When the Congress gathered in Philadelphia declared independence in 1776, the Pennsylvania delegation remained split, as Dickinson abstained and Franklin vocally pressed for independence along the lines of his Albany Plan of 1754.

When British forces defeated Washington at the battle of Brandywine Creek in the fall of 1777 and occupied Philadelphia two weeks later, many of the Quaker elite welcomed British soldiers into their homes and left with the British forces when the town was evacuated in the spring of 1778. The diversity, tolerance, and liberty that had marked the Pennsylvania of William Penn was supplanted by bitter and deep division by the time of the American Revolution.

Peter Bratt

See also: Delaware River; Fort Duquesne; Franklin, Benjamin; Germans; Lenni Lenape (Delaware); Penn, William; Pennsylvania (Chronology); Philadelphia; Susquehanna. *Document:* Pennsylvania Charter of Privileges (1701).

Bibliography

Fischer, David Hackett. *Albion's Seed: Four British Folkways in America.* New York: Oxford University Press, 1991.

Illick, Joseph E. *Colonial Pennsylvania: A History.* New York: Charles Scribner's Sons, 1976.

Pequot

The Pequot lived along the lower reaches of what became the Thames and Mystic Rivers in southeastern Connecticut. They inhabited two fortified towns and an unknown number of small settlements along the coast and on small islands lying close to shore, with trade and kinship connections to Long Island.

The tribe developed as close relations of the Mohegan. A legend about the tribe's origins, probably incorrect, has the Pequot "invading" New England from the west, and the Mohegan, under Uncas, seceding from them in the mid-1630s. The close kinship connections between these two tribes, who together had about 16,000 people in 1600, not only blurred their differences but also helped the Pequot challenge the

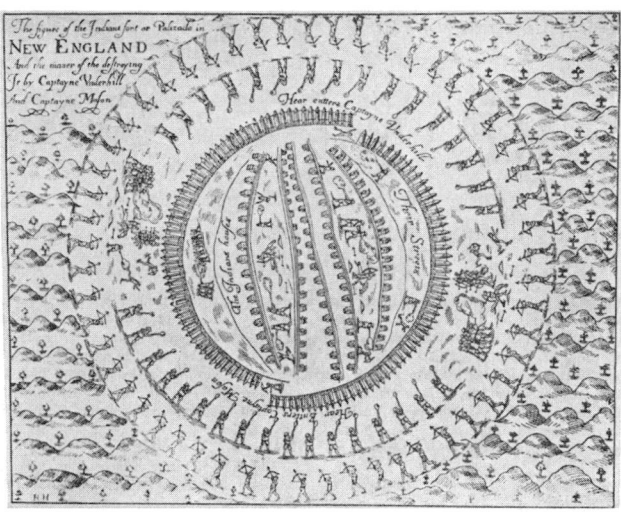

The Pequot War of 1637 was the first significant conflict between native peoples and European colonists in New England. This period engraving depicts a Pequot fort in Connecticut surrounded by colonial musketeers and an outer ring of Mohegan allies. *(New York Public Library, New York)*

Narragansett for access to the fur trade with the Dutch in the 1620s. Unfortunately, those connections and the upheaval created by the trade also lay the groundwork for the intertribal politics that, after the ambitious Uncas became the Mohegan sachem, resulted in the 1637 war that nearly wiped out the Pequot.

The 1633 smallpox epidemic decimated coastal native peoples, including the Pequot, but left the rival Narragansett relatively undisturbed. The Pequot tried to strike at the resulting Dutch-Narragansett trade axis but only angered both groups, resulting in a Dutch raid in 1634 that killed their chief sachem. In desperation, Sassacus, the new Pequot sachem, approached Boston for help and offered the town a trading post along the Connecticut River in exchange for arranging a truce with the Narragansetts. The Bay Colony agreed to arrange the truce, but instead of the trading post, the colonists asked for and received tribute from and title to the whole Connecticut Valley. They also demanded custody of those suspected of killing John Stone, an English sea captain, and his crew.

This imposed agreement became a step along the road to the Pequot War, as English settlements quickly sprouted and the Pequot began to feel besieged within their territory. Tribal leaders found their situation increasingly tenuous as they tried to meet the continued English demands to turn over Stone's murderers, compete with the Narragansett, and maintain the allegiance of outlying villages. Sassacus began to lose power as some of his sachems, such as Wequash, began to strike out on their own or even join with Uncas's Mohegans, who were increasingly allied with the colonists.

In early 1636, the English built Fort Saybrook at the mouth of the Connecticut River, signaling that they intended to become a permanent power in the area. That summer, the Pequot were blamed when trader John Oldham was found murdered on his ship; in August, Massachusetts dispatched an expedition under John Endecott to obtain revenge for Oldham. Negotiations went nowhere, and the English raids accomplished little but drive the tribe into war, as the Pequot began raiding settlements and killing isolated colonists. Sassacus also sought to establish an alliance with the Narragansett against the English, but he failed, as that tribe instead formed an uneasy alliance with Massachusetts.

The Pequot continued to hit English outposts and, in February 1637, tried to cut off Fort Saybrook. As winter turned to spring, Pequot raids intensified. On April 23, they attacked Wethersfield and killed nine colonists. This led Connecticut and Massachusetts to mobilize, raise an army, and seek the assistance of Plymouth, the Mohegan, and the Narragansett. On May 26, this force attacked and destroyed the Pequot fort on the Mystic River, using surprise, fire, and ruthless slaughter to kill about 650 inhabitants, mostly women and children, since Sassacus and his main body of warriors were at the other Pequot fort at Weinshauks.

The English tactics and massacre of the Pequot horrified their native allies. Many Narragansetts left, leaving the Puritan-Native American force vulnerable. But the Pequot, who were shocked by their defeat and blamed Sassacus, were unable to agree on a single course of action. Some fled to Long Island or Block Island, and others sought refuge with the Narragansett, who competed with the Mohegan to "adopt" the greatest number of Pequot and increase their power in the region.

The largest group, with about 300 men led by Sassacus, headed west to join the Mohawk but were closely followed by Mohegan bands and a fresh colonial force. On July 14, another major battle, at a swamp west of modern New Haven, resulted in the capture of 180 Pequots and the killing of many more. Sassacus escaped with his brother and other Pequot sachems and finally reached Mohawk country. There, he and his party were set upon and slaughtered by those he had hoped would provide refuge.

After the Pequot War

The Pequot tribe was declared extinct as part of the 1638 Treaty of Hartford. Because the Puritans initially insisted that the survivors join a "friendly" tribe, about 800 were incorporated into the Mohegan; another 440 lived under Narragansett authority (which would later become the Eastern Pequot); and about 400 remained nominally under Mohegan control around the Thames River and Niantic Bay.

Within five years, Connecticut settlers, anxious about Mohegan ambitions, allowed the reconstitution of two Pequot groups under the leadership of Wequash and Robin Cassasinamon, who had been English allies. Their bands would, over the next few decades, become the Stonington or Lantern Hill (eastern) and Mashantucket (western) Pequot communities. Ironically, Uncas's continued efforts to "enlist" members of the two bands in his tribe enabled the Pequot survivors to obtain more autonomy and power—although under English domination.

When the Pequot and their English neighbors complained of Mohegan raids, Puritan leaders in the new United Colonies rebuked Uncas and arranged autonomy and reservations for Wequash and Cassasinamon in exchange for tribute paid to Uncas. In 1651, the colony gave land to Cassasinamon's band at Noank, which had been part of the original Pequot territory. In September 1654, the commissioners of the United Colonies declared the Pequot remnants under their protection and a year later "appointed" Wequash and Cassasinamon community leaders. They also issued rules that included an end to traditional ceremonies. In 1658, the Pequot got Connecticut colonists to recognize their right to additional land at Mashantucket (near Stonington) and persuaded the colonies to give them access to the wampum shell beds on Long Island.

When King Philip's War broke out in 1675, the Pequot men fought for the English in independent units and as scouts with the Connecticut militia. When the war ended, the Pequot were allowed to resettle in peace. The smaller eastern band made their home on 280 acres claimed by both Massachusetts and Connecticut but granted by both to the Pequot group. The western band soon faced problems with a conflict over community leadership as well as efforts by the town and colony to take their lands at Noank, although they were still allowed to fish and hunt there.

After making the move to Mashantucket, two distinct communities developed, one associated with Cassasinamon, the other under Daniel and then Schadab. As with the Mohegan, efforts by Connecticut authorities to choose the Pequot sachem, favoring Daniel and Schadab rather than Cassasinamon, failed to unite the tribe and left at least half very unhappy with the province.

During the early 1700s, about 325 Pequots lived at Mashantucket and about 150 at Lantern Hill, both probably maintaining residence and subsistence patterns very similar to those of a century earlier. Slash-and-burn cultivation of maize, hunting, and seasonal movements to the coast (at Noank) continued. At Mashantucket, the only archaeological evidence of European ways is apple orchards and pig bones.

During the eighteenth century, the Pequot population on the reserves declined steadily as men died in the colonial wars or as they moved away to work as laborers or seamen and the colonists encroached on their reserves. As with the Mohegan, members of the tribe resisted Christianity until the Great Awakening offered a sense of spiritual equality and renewal; after 1740, native Christian preachers and teachers like Samuel Ashbow at Mashantucket and Edward Nedson at Stonington became Pequot leaders. At Mashantucket, the embrace by some of evangelical Christianity, along with long-standing political conflict over tribal leadership resulted in the formation of separate "conservative" and "reform" groups. The latter established a nuclear settlement, Indiantown, with about twenty-five families, who increased their use of animal husbandry and began to build farms and framed houses. The remaining "conservative" Pequots, about fifty, continued to live on small, scattered homesteads, in very small framed houses or traditional wigwams, without farm implements or fencing.

In total, about 200 western Pequots remained at Mashantucket by the middle of the century, whereas the smaller eastern band retained only about forty members, mostly women. In March 1773, reformers from the two Pequot bands, along with five other southern New England tribes—Narragansett, Montauk, Niantic, Farmington, and Mohegan—made plans to create a new Christian Native American community, Brothertown, among the Oneida of New York, far from their shrinking homelands. Indiantown was abandoned by 1795, suggesting that its residents were part of this Brothertown movement. By the end of the century, the two Pequot groups were approximately about the same size, each comprising about fifty residents.

Daniel R. Mandell

See also: King Philip's War; Massachusetts Bay Colony; Native American–European Conflict; Native American–European Relations; Native Americans; Philip, King (Metacom).

Bibliography

Cave, Alfred. *The Pequot War.* Amherst: University of Massachusetts Press, 1996.

De Forest, John W. *History of the Indians of Connecticut, From the Earliest Known Period to 1850.* Hartford, CT: William Jason Hamersley, 1851.

Hauptman, Laurence M., and Wherry, James D., eds. *The Pequots in Southern New England: The Rise and Fall of an American Indian Nation.* Norman: University of Oklahoma Press, 1990.

Philadelphia

Beginning in 1774, Philadelphia hosted the First Continental Congress and two years later witnessed the signing of the Declaration of Independence in the Pennsylvania State House. More than a decade later, American statesmen gathered in the same city to draft the Constitution. In short, no city performed a greater role in giving birth to the United States of America. As the largest, most diverse, and most economically vibrant entrepôt in North America, Philadelphia could rightfully claim to be the metropolis of the British American colonies and of the new American nation.

William Penn conceived of Philadelphia as a commercial and administrative center for his new colony, which had been awarded a charter in 1681 by King Charles II as a partial payment for a debt owed by the Crown to Penn's father. Penn pledged to give city lots in Philadelphia to the first group of investors in proportion to the total amount of land they purchased in the country. This generosity was intended as an incentive for settlers to sign on to Penn's project in the early phases of planning. Penn, as the chief proprietor, elected to name the city Philadelphia, or City of Brotherly Love, in light of his vision of the colony as a haven of toleration for religious dissenters. Penn's coreligionists in the Religious Society of Friends, also known as the Quakers, formed a large contingent of the First Purchasers of Pennsylvania land, and Philadelphia became home to a wealthy cadre of Quaker merchants.

Unlike most colonial towns, Philadelphia began with a blueprint, with William Penn and other planners as architects. Part of their design for the city, wedged between the Delaware and Schuylkill Rivers, included city blocks arranged in a grid, four major public squares, and a central square for the city hall. Penn instructed his planners to include space in house lots for "Gardens or Orchards or fields, that it may be a greene Country towne." Settlement proceeded, though not without controversy, as Penn and his First Purchasers squabbled for years over the assignment of town lots. Nevertheless, on the eve of the Enlightenment, Penn's design became a model of urban planning for the English-speaking world.

By the time Philadelphia received its first charter of incorporation in 1701, reports held that nearly 7,000 people resided in the city and its adjacent suburbs—a number historians believe to be too large. More reliable figures exist for later periods. Historians place Philadelphia's population just prior to the Revolution at 24,000, and nearly three times that by 1800. This rapid growth made Philadelphia the largest city in the early republic. As a consequence of this dynamic growth, Philadelphia was wracked by political struggles throughout its early history. Penn's decisions as proprietor triggered factional disputes between those supportive of his policies and those opposed to them. Quakers and Church of England adherents disputed matters of religion, as well as the distribution of political offices, which seemed to favor wealthy Quaker merchants.

The most politically influential group of Philadelphians were wealthy merchants like Isaac Norris, Jonathan Dickinson, and Edward Shippen, who had built great commercial empires by the 1720s and left their imprint on the city's social and cultural life. Their wealth enabled them to live far above the standard of most urban laborers, in affluent districts like Society Hill, and their lifestyle expanded to include lavish mansions, expensive imported furniture, decorative arts, and many other cultural refinements associated with the English landed and mercantile elite. The economy the merchants helped to build enticed thousands of immigrants to the Delaware River Valley region, and by 1776 Philadelphia hummed with activity. Artisans, laborers, shopkeepers from a variety of ethnic backgrounds, and a sizable free black community contributed to the diverse makeup of the city and began to make their presence felt in civic affairs.

By midcentury, Philadelphia served as a major hub of institutional governance and social reform in the colonies, which encouraged and channeled new forms of political and social activism. Philadelphia hosted the Philadelphia Yearly Meeting of the Society of Friends beginning in 1681, which was the largest

The Old State House in Philadelphia was built in 1735, by which time the municipal population exceeded 10,000. By the 1750s, Philadelphia had become the largest city and leading economic center in the North American colonies. *(Brown Brothers, Sterling, Pennsylvania)*

and most influential of the yearly meetings in the colonies. Philadelphia also served as home of Christ Church, one of the largest of the Church of England congregations in British North America, which played a strategic role in forming the national Protestant Episcopal Church following the American Revolution. Presbyterians could also conceive of Philadelphia as the center of gravity for colonial Presbyterianism, as the first presbytery, synod, and General Assembly were all held in the city. Thus, Philadelphia served as the epicenter of religious development in early America, as the religious organizations of the Old World entered the colonies and became formal religious denominations.

The religious diversity and vitality of Philadelphia helped to stimulate two of the largest social and cultural movements of pre-Revolutionary America, evangelicalism and abolitionism. When William Tennent, Sr., founded the "Log College" for ministerial training near Philadelphia, he initiated a sequence of events that led to the schism of Presbyterianism into "Old Sides" and "New Sides," fueled by the appearance of the English revivalist George Whitefield in Philadelphia in 1739. New Side Presbyterianism contributed to the development of evangelicalism, which historians of religion describe as a strain of Protestantism that stresses the importance of conversion experiences, personal piety, and the authority of the Bible. In another vein, Quakers at the 1754 Philadelphia Yearly Meeting were the first at a yearly meeting to officially denounce slavery. The Quakers also provided many of the leaders of the colonial abolitionist movement, including John Woolman and Anthony Benezet.

Benezet helped to organize the first antislavery society in colonial America in 1775, enlisting the help of such luminaries as Benjamin Franklin and Benjamin Rush. This impulse to reform society and improve humanity grew out of the peculiar dynamics of Philadelphia urban life. As a principal hub of commercial activity, Philadelphia was situated at a crossroads on the North American seaboard for the circulation of people, goods, and ideas around the Atlantic rim, including Western Europe, Great Britain, West Africa, the Caribbean, and elsewhere.

Men like Benjamin Franklin, a printer and newspaper publisher, helped to connect Philadelphia with the main currents of Enlightenment thought. Franklin helped to form the first scientific organization in America, the American Philosophical Society, in 1743, and his subsequent research on optics and electricity placed Philadelphia among a select group of eighteenth-century cities that were transforming the landscape of human knowledge. In 1751, Franklin helped to organize the first university in America, Philadelphia's University of Pennsylvania, which prefigured other Philadelphia "firsts" in the fields of science and medicine, including the first major hospital (1755) and first American medical college (1765).

Clearly, Philadelphia was at the forefront of major social, religious, intellectual, cultural, and political change in pre-Revolutionary America. Thus, it served as an unofficial "capital" of the colonies before the War for Independence. As such, it was the natural choice for the meeting of the First Continental Congress, formed in 1775 to discuss and respond to the British government's decision to close Boston Harbor and alter the Massachusetts Bay Colony's charter following the Boston Tea Party.

In early 1776, a Philadelphia printer published Thomas Paine's *Common Sense,* which made the case for independence and swelled the ranks of Americans calling for a constitutional separation from Great Britain. The Continental Congress approved this measure on July 2, 1776 and, two days later, accepted Thomas Jefferson's Declaration of Independence, which was written at his rented house at Seventh and Market Streets. During the War for Independence, Philadelphia had strategic value for both the defending American forces and their British foes. General William Howe dislodged the Congress from its seat at Philadelphia in 1777, which he hoped would divide the colonies at their economic and administrative linchpin. General George Washington understood the value of Philadelphia to the patriot cause and engaged the British army at several points in the Philadelphia environs.

Encamped at Valley Forge near Philadelphia during the winter of 1777–1778, Washington transformed his band of citizen soldiers into a disciplined fighting force and demonstrated its capability in the Battle of Monmouth in New Jersey. From this point on, the British military had to contend with a much more determined, more motivated, and more effective American army.

After the Revolution, Philadelphia retained its status as the center of intellectual and political life for the new nation, but only for a generation. Soon, the nation's capital would move to New York City and then to a new federal district on the Potomac River in Maryland. New York City would also overtake Philadelphia as the largest city in the United States in the 1810 census.

Nevertheless, Philadelphia played a large role in

shaping American culture in such diverse areas as the decorative arts, painting, literature, industrial technology, and medical research. It also built institutions that became national models in the fields of mental health, criminal rehabilitation, and poor relief. As the nation's leading city in its formative period, Philadelphia was witness to and helped to shape the important political, intellectual, and cultural developments that gave birth to the United States of America.

Jeffrey B. Webb

See also: Cities; Delaware River; Franklin, Benjamin; Native Americans; Penn, William; Pennsylvania; Pennsylvania (Chronology); Susquehanna.

Bibliography

Bushman, Richard L. *The Refinement of America: Persons, Houses, Cities.* New York: Vintage Books, 1993.

Nash, Gary B. "City Planning and Political Tension in the Seventeenth Century: The Case of Philadelphia," *Proceedings of the American Philosophical Society* 112:54–73.

———. *Urban Crucible: Social Change, Political Consciousness, and the Origins of the American Revolution.* Cambridge, MA: Harvard University Press, 1979.

Roach, Hannah Benner. "The Planting of Philadelphia: A Seventeenth-Century Real Estate Development," *The Pennsylvania Magazine of History and Biography* 92:3–47 (1968): 143–94.

Rothman, David J. *Discovery of the Asylum: Social Order and Disorder in the New Republic.* Boston: Little, Brown, 1971.

Weigley, Russell F., ed. *Philadelphia: A 300-Year History.* New York: W. W. Norton, 1982.

Philip, King (Metacom; c. 1638–1676)

Born circa 1638, Metacom (later King Philip) was the second of three sons of Massasoit, the chief sachem of the Wampanoag tribes. He grew up in a rapidly changing world in which the careful peace engineered by Massasoit with the English colonists in Plymouth was fraying in the face of English expansion and the cultural strains that came with the introduction of Christian missions to the native population.

Massasoit, sachem of tribes that had been weakened by European diseases and warfare with the more powerful Narragansett, accepted nominal submission to Plymouth in order to gain the colonists' power against his regional rivals and access to European goods. Unfortunately, as Plymouth grew more established and powerful, its inhabitants no longer saw nominal submission as sufficient. And the Wampanoag, with little but land to barter for money and trade goods, had already lost much of their best hunting and agricultural land.

When Massasoit died in 1660, his eldest son Wamsutta became chief sachem and commemorated the occasion by asking the Plymouth General Court to choose European names for himself and his younger brother. The settlers chose Alexander for Wamsutta and Philip for Metacom, names they used for the rest of their lives, usually with the titles "Prince" or "King" as a European courtesy.

Alexander was sachem for only two years, dying in 1662 after a visit to Josiah Winslow. His death was probably from a fever he had contracted during his visit, although Philip, Alexander's wife, and many Wampanoags believed that he had been poisoned. Philip, the new sachem, vowed to revenge his brother.

Philip was a gifted leader, using the traditional role of the sachem to forge alliances among the Wampanoag, as well as with regional rivals. Many of these connections were made through his family, including the marriages of Philip's sisters and his own marriage to Wootonekanuske, a sister of Alexander's powerful wife, the female sachem Weetamoo of the Pocasset. Through these ties, Philip continued to keep the peace, despite the expansion of Rhode Island and Plymouth into Philip's own base of power, Mount Hope (later Bristol, Rhode Island), and accelerating conflict over native access via easements to the land they had sold colonists.

In 1671, after learning that Philip had been entertaining regional tribal leaders, perhaps with a view to taking action against Plymouth, the colony demanded that he sign another treaty, acknowledging total sovereignty of the English, including the English king and English laws. Philip had no choice but to sign, since Massachusetts, Rhode Island, and Connecticut backed Plymouth and refused to intercede. This humiliation undermined Philip's authority with the Wampanoag. His position was further weakened when his friend and secretary, an English-raised, "praying Indian" named John Sassamon, left Philip's service after a disagreement to serve as the minister to a missionary settlement.

In December 1674, soon after visiting Philip at Nemasket, Sassamon was found dead of unknown causes under the ice of Assawompsett Pond. Earlier that fall, Sassamon had tried to convince Josiah Winslow that the Wampanoag were threatening the colony, but he had been brushed off. His death spurred suspicions of murder at the hands of three of Philip's entourage. On March 1, three Wampanoag, including Philip's councilor Tobias, were indicted for the murder and tried by the Plymouth General Court, which demanded jurisdiction as Sassamon was a Christian and all were under English law. Philip appeared voluntarily to deny any involvement, and the prosecution relied on a single native witness.

A jury of twelve Englishmen and a separate consulting jury of six Christian Native Americans found all three guilty, and they were executed over Philip's protests in June 1675. It is unknown if Philip had a hand in the murder, if his men took matters into their own hands, or if there had been a murder at all.

In the aftermath of the trial, a group of young Wampanoag men raided the settlement at Swansea after refusing Philip's plea for arbitration of outstanding land issues and legal jurisdiction problems. This raid triggered what became known as King Philip's War. Philip probably never led his men directly in battle because of a badly scarred hand injured by an exploding gun in childhood, but he directed their retreat to and escape from the Pocasset swamp. His solid tactical thinking saved his people at Nipsachuck Hill, again through an unexpected retreat. Badly diminished by disease, the Wampanoag took refuge in New York until evicted by Governor Edmund Andros in March 1676.

Philip sadly returned to Mount Hope, where a Plymouth force led by Benjamin Church captured his wife and son. In a subsequent attack on the encampment on August 12, 1676, one of Church's men, a Pocasset named Alderman, shot and killed Philip. The body of the sachem was decapitated and quartered before being sent to Plymouth, where his body was left unburied in the local woods and his head remained on display for twenty years. Philip's wife and son were sold into slavery in the West Indies, where they both died.

Margaret Sankey

See also: King Philip's War; Massachusetts Bay Colony; Native American–European Conflict; Pequot.

Bibliography

Drake, James. *King Philip's War: Civil War in New England 1675–6.* Amherst: University of Massachusetts Press, 1999.

Kawashima, Yasuhide. *Igniting King Philip's War.* Lawrence: University Press of Kansas, 2001.

Leach, Douglas. *Flintlock and Tomahawk: New England in King Philip's War.* New York: Macmillan, 1958.

Philip II (1527–1598)

King of Spain (1555–1598) and King Consort of England (1554–1558), Philip II was born in May 1527. The son of Holy Roman Emperor Charles V and Isabella of Portugal, Philip was raised to rule the Habsburg family's vast domains in Europe and the New World. From his earliest childhood, he was educated for kingship and prepared to assume control of the largest empire in the world, serving several times as his father's regent in Spain and touring the Netherlands and Italy.

Philip's first two marriages, to his cousins Maria of Portugal (1543–1544) and Mary I of England (1554–1558) were meant to establish Spain as the leading Catholic power in Europe and assure its position on the Atlantic coast. In 1555, on Charles V's retirement, Philip II inherited Spain, Naples, the Netherlands, and Spain's overseas empire, while the Austrian branch of the family inherited the Holy Roman Empire.

A hands-on administrator, Philip II improved Spanish bureaucracy by centralizing it in a permanent capital, Madrid, and in his palace complex at El Escorial, and by appointing capable and efficient men, like Francisco de Toledo, to positions of power in the Americas. Fascinated by his empire, Philip II took great interest in native cultures, preserving Aztec and Mayan art and manuscripts in his archives, supporting ethnographic and botanical studies, and ordering a geographic and cultural survey, known as the "Forty-Nine Questions," beginning in 1576. Unfortunately, Philip II's propensity for micromanaging, combined with slow communications with the empire, hampered innovation or initiative on the part of his viceregents and his Council of the Indies in Madrid. On his personal orders, Spanish explorers claimed Florida in 1564 and the Philippine Islands in 1570.

The enormous wealth of the Spanish Empire, with one-fifth paid directly to the king, made Philip II immensely powerful in Europe and financed his commitments to the rest of his lands. Throughout his reign, Philip II juggled threats on all sides. He led a coalition against the Ottoman Empire in the Mediterranean, put down the Morisco Revolt within Spain in 1568, and, in 1580, engineered the dynastic takeover of Portugal on the death of King Sebastian. His most draining campaigns centered on the Protestant-led revolt of the Netherlands, which turned into a grueling guerilla war lasting into the reigns of Philip's son and grandson.

A pious Catholic, Philip II felt compelled to

impose orthodoxy on his own realms, going to great expense and suffering personal unpopularity because of his support for the Inquisition. He also used his special authority to appoint bishops and missionaries in order to support reformers like Bartolomeo de las Casas, who argued for the humane treatment of Mexicans, and favored St. Teresa of Avila's Carmelite reforms.

Philip II's last two marriages, in 1559 to Elizabeth of Valois (who died in 1568) and Anna of Austria in 1570 (she died ten years later), were arranged in an attempt to hold together his European authority in the face of increasing difficulty. Spain's huge spending on defense and suppression of the Dutch Rebellion led by William of Orange pushed the Crown toward bankruptcy—a precarious situation made worse by the lack of a state bank and the inflation caused by the influx of gold and silver from America. Philip II, as instigator and financier of the Catholic League led by the Guise brothers, involved Spain in the bloody Wars of Religion in France. In 1588, he launched the Spanish Armada in a failed attempt to unseat Elizabeth I of England, his former sister-in-law.

Even the Ottoman Empire continued to loom, having recovered quickly from Philip II's naval triumph at Lepanto in 1571. Precious convoys of wealth from China, South America, and Mexico were constantly menaced and taken by such English privateers as Francis Drake, adding to Spanish financial instability. Realizing the already unwieldy nature of his empire and the dangers of over expansion, Philip II issued the 1573 Ordinance on Discovery and Populations, banning additional conquests. By the 1580s, he also had abandoned large-scale development of Florida.

Although a brilliant and pragmatic monarch, Philip II left behind a structure of government, infrastructure, and empire that seriously handicapped Spain in the sixteenth century and initiated a period of decline in comparison with England and France. Philip II died on September 13, 1598, at the Escorial and was buried as a Franciscan monk. He was succeeded by his only surviving son (by Anna of Austria), Philip III.

Margaret Sankey

See also: Politics and Government (Chronology); Politics and Government (Essay); Spanish Colonies on Mainland North America (Chronology).

Bibliography

Kamen, Henry. *Empire: How Spain Became a World Power.* New York: HarperCollins, 2003.
Parker, Geoffrey. *The Grand Strategy of Philip II.* New Haven, CT: Yale University Press, 1998.
Williams, Patrick. *Philip II.* Basingstoke, Hampshire, UK: Palgrave, 2002.

Piedmont

Conceived in the broadest possible geographic terms, the Piedmont region extends from the Hudson River Valley in New York to central Alabama and comprises the foothills of the Appalachians. As it relates to American history before 1776, however, people usually define the Piedmont as consisting of the combined backcountry of the colonies of South Carolina, North Carolina, and Virginia. In fact, this Piedmont region served as a sort of laboratory of colonization, in which English planters, diverse native communities, African and African American slaves, and non-English European immigrants (mainly the Scots-Irish) lived in close proximity and often came into conflict.

Native settlement in the Piedmont had occurred by 10,000 B.C.E. On the eve of European colonization, several paramount chiefdoms in the Mississippian tradition had risen and fallen, leaving smaller, autonomous tribes in their wake. These were the predecessors of colonial-period communities like the Catawba, Monacan, Tuscarora, and Cherokee. Most native groups practiced corn and squash agriculture in addition to hunting, fishing, and foraging for wild food. In many cases, agriculture provided for settlement in large villages.

Although the Spanish under Hernando de Soto brought a fair amount of death and destruction to the Piedmont's inhabitants, they did not establish permanent settlements in the region. But in the late seventeenth and eighteenth centuries, immigrants from English colonies did just that, with disastrous effects on the region's native peoples. By the time of the War for Independence, many native groups had been dispossessed or weakened by disease. The presence of expanding English colonies, first in Virginia and later in the Carolinas, exerted new pressures on the area's native groups.

Although some English planters moved from the Atlantic coast into the Piedmont region, many chose to remain in what they considered to be more "civilized" areas surrounding Charles Town and Williamsburg. This reluctance, combined with the fact that river-based travel was difficult in the Piedmont, prevented the development of large towns in the region for much of the eighteenth century.

Migration to the backcountry or Piedmont occurred in two streams. In Virginia, larger landholdings were more common, as were African slaves and tobacco plantations, spurred on by the colony's more extensive network of navigable rivers. A new generation of Virginia planters grew to prominence in the Piedmont.

Farther to the south, the Carolina backcountry was also populated by some immigrants from the East, but a large number of Scots-Irish and Germans descended into the region, following what was known as the Great Wagon Road. Their landholdings were often smaller than those in Virginia, and these yeoman farmers tended to focus on livestock and cereal grain agriculture. While nonnative settlement remained minuscule in the Piedmont, the area's population exploded in the middle of the eighteenth century.

The population increase in the backcountry sometimes spurred conflict with older, more established areas. The conflict between eastern and western Virginia was more subdued. Bacon's Rebellion of 1676 had some of these trappings, but it was more about patronage than political representation; in any event, Bacon's own plantation was not really in the Piedmont region.

South Carolina and North Carolina's Piedmont regions both were the sites of violent Regulator movements in the 1760s. Frustrated by their lack of representation in the colonial legislatures and the dearth of courts and public officials, backcountry residents took the law into their own hands in what has been viewed in some instances as vigilantism and in others as effective political protest. One prominent scholar has shown that the people ordering the violence were planters trying to bring order to the backcountry, not just a disorganized mob.

The War for Independence brought more violence to the Piedmont region. Supporters and opponents of the actions of the Continental Congress waged what amounted to a civil war against each other—in some instances, burning each other's homes and property. Additionally, British and American forces moved back and forth across the region, particularly in the war's later stages leading up to the surrender of Lord Cornwallis at Yorktown.

Although the Piedmont was an important region in colonial America, it would really come into its own after the War for Independence. Cotton agriculture would spread through the region in the late eighteenth and early nineteenth centuries.

Matthew Jennings

See also: Appalachia; Environment and Nature; North Carolina; South Carolina; Tidewater; Virginia.

Bibliography

Billings, Warren E., John E. Selby, and Thad W. Tate. *Colonial Virginia: A History.* White Plains, NY: KTO, 1986.
Coggeshall, John M. *Carolina Piedmont Country.* Jackson: University Press of Mississippi, 1996.
Lefler, Hugh T., and William S. Powell. *Colonial North Carolina: A History.* New York: Charles Scribner's Sons, 1973.

Pietism

More a way of believing than an organized religious movement, Pietism originated in seventeenth-century Germany.

In the century after Luther had begun the Protestant Reformation, intellectual disputes splintered the church. In the German states, the Reformation brought on the Thirty Years War, which ended with the nation in ruins. A Lutheran minister, Philipp Jakob Spener, wanted to comfort the people by emphasizing the mystical side of Luther's teachings, the need for a personal Christian experience, and a new birth.

The mystical element had roots in both Roman Catholicism and the Anabaptist movement. The idea of a personal relationship with God came from the Anabaptist belief that God offers the "inner light" of the Holy Spirit as the guide to salvation. Anabaptists, who suffered persecution for their beliefs, disdained excessive dependence on the written word, and their inner light sometimes led them to millennialism.

Spener wanted Christians to follow their faith with their hearts rather than dispute it with their minds, but he was not a millennialist. The pietism he envisioned incorporated lay ministries, small-group Bible studies, individual lives devoted to prayer and the study of the Bible, right living, a "heart-felt" faith, and a "new birth." Pietists were a priesthood of the true believers, with no need for a formally educated and separate priesthood. Even though they rejected a trained priesthood, they did not reject education in itself. Rather, they shifted theological education's emphasis away from analysis, interpretation, and explication toward a more practical and personal education that enhanced the personal, internal, religious experience.

Spener also called for a change from attacking nonbelievers and the heterodox to practicing a sympathetic and kind approach. In addition, he felt that preaching had to sacrifice pleasing rhetoric if that was what it took to convey to the new Christian what faith meant and how it was revealed in Christian life.

Pietism worked well with most other traditions. Spener was a Lutheran, English Puritans incorporated Pietism into their Calvinism, and John Wesley used Pietist emphases from the Moravians in his Methodism. English Independents and Quakers were of the Anabaptist Pietist tradition, as were the German Mennonites and the Amish. Latter-day Hussites, the German Brethren and Moravians, also immigrated to the Middle colonies.

Pietism was perhaps as vital as Calvinism in American Protestantism. For instance, Cotton Mather had Pietist tendencies. Pietism was as important as Puritanism to Jonathan Edwards, who emphasized that the indwelling of the Holy Spirit would manifest itself in outward signs in a true Christian. Staring in 1749, the Great Awakening was to a good extent a Pietist revival movement. Its most prominent preacher, perhaps the most inspiring revivalist of all time, George Whitefield, also displayed Pietist leanings.

Pietists who had personal experiences of Jesus Christ had an urge to share that relationship with others, and that urge often became a commitment to evangelism. Count Leopold von Zinzendorf founded the Moravian Missionary Society in Germany, which sent hundreds of missionaries to America. Several colonies were actually founded on Pietist principles. The Baptist Roger Williams founded Rhode Island; Quakers George Fox and William Penn founded New Jersey and Pennsylvania.

Pietists could be within or outside the church. Churchly Pietists include the Lutheran Henry Melchoir Muhlenberg, while the separatists include the Moravian Count Zinzendorf, Johann Conrad Beissel of the Ephrata Cloisters, Johann Kelpius who came from a Philadelphia religious community; and Ernst Christian Hochman von Hohenua of the Brethren.

Pietists also influenced Universalists such as Dr. George de Benneville, who gathered the believers in his Olay, Pennsylvania, house church. Other Universalist leaders came from Methodist or Baptist Pietism. Pietism reached into the hills and rural areas of New England due to the revivalism of Caleb Rich, Isaac Davis, and Adams Streeter.

The Pietist "inward turn" was integral to the individualism that characterized America. The inward turn also influenced the transcendentalist writers Ralph Waldo Emerson and Henry David Thoreau. It brought respectability to emotion, in contrast to the emphasis on intellect and rationality that had characterized the philosophies of such Enlightenment revolutionaries and deists as Benjamin Franklin and Thomas Jefferson.

Pietism was vital to the Baptists and Presbyterians after the Second Great Awakening. The early national period saw a revival of the Great Awakening that had slumbered through the Revolution's dominant enlightenment thinking. The old Pietist impulse reemerged as inner commitment, bearing fruit in outward expression—abolitionism, educational reform, women's suffrage—and all efforts to bring society more in line with the Christian values given to each individual through a personal experience of God.

John H. Barnhill

See also: Christ and Christianity; Germans; Religion (Chronology); Religion (Essay).

Bibliography

Balmer, Randall Herbert. *Blessed Assurance.* Boston: Beacon Press 1999.

Brown, Dale W. *Understanding Pietism.* Grand Rapids, MI: Eerdmans, 1976.

Crowner, David, and Gerald Christianson, ed. and transl. *The Spirituality of the German Awakening.* New York: Paulist, 2003.

Erb, Peter C., ed. *The Pietists.* New York: Paulist, 1983.

Spener, Philipp Jakob. *Pia Desideria.* 1675. Translated by Theodore G. Tappert. New York: Fortress Press, 1964.

Pilgrims

Perhaps no group of Early American colonists is as widely known—and as misunderstood—as the Pilgrims. While most American schoolchildren can tell the basic story of these settlers, their story often has been oversimplified into an inaccurate myth. The motivations, experiences, and legacy of the Pilgrims extend well beyond the tradition of Thanksgiving Day.

Pilgrims in England and the Netherlands

The Pilgrims traced their roots to Puritan England of the late 1500s. Puritans had traditionally dissented from the theology and control of the Church of England, believing that the Church's practices needed to be reformed and "purified."

By the turn of the seventeenth century, a particularly devout group of Puritans became convinced that the Church of England was so corrupt that its ills would infect even those righteous members who remained within the fold. These believers despaired of reforming the Church from within. In 1604, at Scrooby, England, they declared themselves "the Lord's free people." Withdrawal from the Church of England, these Scrooby Pilgrims believed, would allow them both to remain unblemished in the sight of God and to work for the Church's reform and salvation.

Nonseparating Puritans condemned their separatist Pilgrim brethren, considering their actions heresy. As a result, the new separatists found themselves theologically and physically persecuted to an astounding degree. By 1607, their afflictions had become so great that the Scrooby Pilgrims fled to the Netherlands for sanctuary.

As the Pilgrims settled into their new home, they eventually formed a comfortable and even prosperous community in and around the town of Leyden. The Netherlands of the seventeenth century was a region where commerce, trade, finance, and education were all thriving pursuits; accordingly, it attracted immigrants from across Europe. The atmosphere of tolerance that prevailed was no doubt attributable to the healthy economy, the abundance of educated citizens, and the frequent contact between native Dutch and immigrants, as well as among the immigrant groups themselves. Certainly such a culture must have seemed refreshing and welcoming to the former "heretics" from England.

Most of the Pilgrims took full advantage of the absence of persecution that had been their lot in their homeland, and they became widely engaged in business, academia, and social affairs in Leyden. Some Pilgrims were employed in shops, banks, or in other phases of commerce. A few took the opportunity to become students or professors. And a number of Pilgrims engaged in the local textile industry, becoming weavers and sellers of cloth.

Word of the group's success and peaceful existence spread and attracted a steady stream of Pilgrims from England. Still, there was a growing sense among the Pilgrims that they were becoming "too Dutch" and losing their identity as Englishmen. Some also worried that material success was dimming the spiritual mission that had originally driven the group from their homeland.

The Pilgrims' past experience made it clear that returning to their homeland was not an option. Instead, in July 1620, a group of Leyden Pilgrims left on the ship *Speedwell* for England to complete negotiations with the Virginia Company. By September 16, they were joined by English Pilgrims and set sail on the *Mayflower,* bound for the New World.

Pilgrims in the New World

The Pilgrims' arrival in North America was not an auspicious beginning. Although they survived the long and difficult journey with one more Pilgrim than had left England (one adult had died, but two babies were born on the voyage), the *Mayflower* landed, not in Virginia territory, but far to the north, on Cape Cod in Massachusetts.

The group immediately realized that their location left them without legal authority from the king to settle in the New World. Nevertheless, they decided to remain where they had landed; after a brief, month-long sojourn at the tip of Cape Cod, they established a settlement at Plymouth, Massachusetts. The founders of this new settlement signed the Mayflower Compact to create a framework for self-governance.

The first winter at Plymouth was a harsh one, leaving over half the new colonists dead by the spring of 1621. Soon, however, local Native Americans came to the settlement's rescue. Samoset and Squanto, who

The 90-foot, 180-ton *Mayflower*, a converted merchant ship, had been used in the French wine trade before being chartered for the Pilgrims' 1620 voyage to America. This model is housed at the Science Museum in London. *(Science Museum, London, United Kingdom/Bridgeman Art Library)*

both spoke some English, aided the Pilgrims by teaching them how to plant corn, showing them productive fishing and hunting areas, and pointing out edible plants. These two protectors also helped the Pilgrims establish a good relationship with the Wampanoag chief Massasoit, in whose territory the group had settled. By the fall of 1621, the settlers were sufficiently established in their new land to observe a day of thanksgiving. That observance has come to be an American tradition.

Most of the Pilgrims who came on the *Mayflower* were of lower- or middle-class economic backgrounds. Elder William Brewster served as the group's preacher, but the fact that he was a layman, not a minister, prevented him from administering the sacraments. An Anglican priest had been sent to Plymouth in the early 1620s, but he was soon dismissed because his theology was found unacceptable.

Even in the absence of a pastoral leader or a formal church, the Pilgrims seem to have remained remarkably observant in their religious faith. By most accounts, Pilgrims in America were content with daily piety rather than seeking to break new theological ground. Their relief from persecution because of their religious beliefs, along with this everyday religiosity, allowed them to pursue the ideals of the Mayflower Compact in creating "a body politick" based on mutual respect and the pursuit of the common good.

Perhaps because of their reputation as heretics and dissenters, the Pilgrims never attracted large numbers of immigrants to their new home in Plymouth Colony.

Daily Life of American Pilgrims

While it is easy to romanticize the Pilgrims' life as one that mirrors our legends of that first Thanksgiving, it is important to remember that these settlers were strangers in a strange and unsettled land. Hard work, homesickness, and fear were ongoing features of life for the Pilgrims.

When the first Pilgrims and those who followed them arrived in the New World, they came to a land that was heavily forested and all but unknown to white Europeans. As with any groups setting out to frontier areas, the Pilgrims faced the immediate necessity of establishing shelter from the elements, from wild animals, and from potentially hostile natives. Land had to be scouted to determine its fitness as a site for settlement; once a tract was chosen, the timber had to be cleared away and the ground leveled to create a suitable building site. Driven both by the impending winter and the scarcity of tools, the earliest Pilgrims built small huts and houses from the trees felled in clearing the area. Later settlers may have enjoyed more time for their task, but the difficulty and danger of raising massive beamed roofs and other components was still formidable.

In conjunction with the building of dwellings, the settlers had to quickly determine means by which they could supply themselves with food. Although some food had been brought over from England, the necessity of becoming self-sufficient was immediately evident. The Pilgrims had to scout out good fishing and hunting areas and to learn over time what crops could be grown in this new and unfamiliar land. In addition, the differences in plant life between the New World and the Old made it necessary for settlers to learn which plants could or could not be safely eaten.

Everyone—men, women, and children—worked long and hard in the settlement at Plymouth. Many historians have pointed to the value of their Puritan faith for these Pilgrims. Without a sense of divine assistance and the righteousness of their enterprise, the difficult circumstances of life in North America would likely have been unbearable. Religious observances such as days of fasting and prayer, along with regular preaching and church meetings, must have played an essential part in maintaining the Pilgrims' emotional and mental strength for the harshness of the life that confronted them daily. Still, it seems logical that they also must have experienced homesickness for family members and for the ways of life that had been left behind in England and the Netherlands.

William Bradford

By far the most widely remembered Pilgrim is William Bradford. Attracted to the Scrooby Pilgrims as a young Englishman, Bradford went first to Amsterdam and, later, to Leyden with them in the early 1600s.

His father having died before Bradford was a year old, he was trained by his uncles to be a farmer. Still, his natural curiosity went beyond matters of crop planting and animal husbandry, and his was an intelligent and inquiring mind. In addition to becoming relatively prosperous as a weaver in Leyden, Bradford took the opportunity to read and educate himself. When the *Mayflower* set sail in 1620, he was one of the leaders who had helped plan the voyage and negotiate with English businessmen to arrange financial backing for the trip and settlement.

For many historians, William Bradford has come to personify the Plymouth colony. A devout Separatist, he also took his place in colonial civil affairs, winning election as the colony's governor a total of thirty times.

Bradford's legacy is also that of his massive volume *Of Plymouth Plantation*. Written between 1630 and 1647, this book discusses virtually every aspect of life in the Pilgrim settlement and colony, from the styles of dress and descriptions of housing to relations with the Native Americans; from matters of theology to descriptions of local plants and animals; and from character sketches of local personalities to discussions of weather and crops. *Of Plymouth Plantation* remains an invaluable source of information on this early period of colonial life, and most historians point to it as the definitive record of the Pilgrim experience in North America.

Barbara Schwarz Wachal

See also: Bradford, William; Mayflower Compact; Plymouth; Puritanism. *Document:* The Mayflower Compact (1620).

Bibliography

Abrams, Ann Uhry. *The Pilgrims and Pocahontas: Rival Myths of American Origins.* Boulder, CO: Westview, 1999.

Bartlett, Robert M. *The Faith of the Pilgrims: An American Heritage.* New York: United Church Press, 1978.

Bradford, William. *Of Plymouth Plantation, 1620–1647: The Complete Text.* Notes and introduction by Samuel Eliot Morison. New York: Alfred A. Knopf, 1952.

Dillon, Francis. *The Pilgrims.* New York: Doubleday, 1975.

Seelye, John D. *Memory's Nation: The Place of Plymouth Rock.* Chapel Hill: University of North Carolina Press, 1998.

Piracy

The early colonial period in American history witnessed the "golden age" of piracy. In the mid-sixteenth century, England, the Netherlands, and France were struggling to overtake Spain and Portugal in the race for trade and empire. These challenger nations, by the licensing of entrepreneurs, through state sponsorship, or simply by turning a blind eye to pillage, let privateer and pirate ships sail free.

In the seventeenth century, piracy was, for the most part, conducted in the Caribbean basin, where the primary targets were the rich Spanish galleons laden with gold and silver from the Mexican and South American mainland. The men, and occasionally women, who perpetrated these raids, at times with the blessing of their national governments, were English, French, and Dutch as well as sometimes renegade Span-

ish, Portuguese, and African pirates, who took part in the predations at sea.

The pirates of the seventeenth century operating out of the Caribbean basin were called buccaneers, so named from the French *boucan,* which means to roast or dry meat over an open fire, since these men hunted and feasted on the feral cattle and pigs that roamed the sparsely inhabited Caribbean isles. Since the early 1600s, the European states had a policy on the seas of "no peace beyond the lines," which meant that while trade was for the most part carried out peaceably in European waters, all ships outside these lines of amity were fair game. Thus, the bellicose tradition of mixing trade and plunder was applied in the Atlantic and Caribbean regions.

By the end of the seventeenth century, several types of piracy were in existence: officially sanctioned piracy (privateering), commercial piracy, and marauding. These were not mutually exclusive and the career of any given pirate could encompass all three categories. During wartime, European nations issued official commissions, or letters of marque, to individual mariners and ships in support of marauding missions. In times of peace, the commissions were called letters of reprisal, which allowed an aggrieved subject of the prince to steal from those subjects who had stolen from him on prior occasions. Since there were not as yet any formal methods of insurance in place, letters of reprisal were a crude way of compensating for losses at sea and provided many opportunities for abuse. They also illustrate the weak institutional structure of international relations at the time.

Commercial piracy was fostered by local merchant communities that were suffering from an unfavorable balance of trade and a lack of hard currency. Colonial merchants, often with the support of the local government, sponsored pirate voyages in addition to offering buccaneers sanctuary and trading opportunities. While in port, the pirates exchanged goods, spent their booty at the local taverns and inns, repaired and re-equipped their ships, and purchased services of all kinds before heading back out to sea. In return, the townspeople acquired various cargoes, mostly Spanish commodities, as well as prized "pieces of eight" and other forms of cash. In the Caribbean islands, Port Royal, Jamaica, was the first to earn a reputation as a pirate haven. At the turn of the century, the mainland ports of New York, Philadelphia, Boston, Newport, and Charles Town likewise became favored hubs of pirate activity.

The third form of piracy, marauding, not only took place along the Atlantic seaboard but also ex-

Edward Teach, better known as Blackbeard, was an English pirate notorious for terrorizing ships in the West Indies and off the Carolina coast until his death in 1718. His treasure is said to be buried somewhere along the Eastern seaboard. *(Library of Congress/Bridgeman Art Library)*

American pirates, including Edward Teach, otherwise known as Blackbeard, who was killed in a battle off the Outer Banks of North Carolina in 1718.

As pirates grew more and more violent, thereby alienating previously sympathetic states, merchants, and ship owners, they were systematically hunted down and exterminated. The colonial governments continued to commission privateers to attack British shipping during the Revolutionary War.

Kevin P. McDonald

See also: Caribbean (Chronology); Crime; Drake, Sir Francis; Spanish Colonies on Mainland North America (Chronology); Transportation, Water.

Bibliography

Johnson, Charles. *A General History of the Robberies and Murders of the Most Notorious Pirates.* 1724. Guilford, CT: Lyons, 2002.

Lane, Kris E. *Pillaging the Empire: Piracy in the Americas, 1500–1750.* Armonk, NY: M. E. Sharpe, 1998.

Rediker, Marcus. " 'Under the Banner of King Death': The Social World of Anglo-American Pirates, 1716 to 1726." *William and Mary Quarterly,* 3rd Ser., 38:2 (April 1981): 203–27.

Ritchie, Robert. *Captain Kidd and the War Against the Pirates.* Cambridge, MA: Harvard University Press, 1986.

Pitt, William (1708–1778)

tended to the Pacific and Indian Oceans, thousands of miles from the American mainland, while the organized marauders maintained their bases of operation in the colonial ports noted above. In the Pacific region, these pirates pillaged Spanish ships making the Acapulco-to-Manila run, as well as raiding coastal towns. The most spectacular of these raids took place in 1671, when Henry Morgan and a group of predominantly English buccaneers sacked the Spanish port of Panama City.

The most famous Anglo-American pirate was William Kidd, who was tried and executed in London in 1701. Kidd was married to a wealthy New York widow and lived in a house on Wall Street for a number of years before turning pirate in the Indian Ocean. He had been legally commissioned in New York and London as a privateer and proclaimed his innocence until the end, but international politics involving the Indian Mughal, King William III, and the powerful East India Company conspired to cause his downfall. In addition to Kidd, there were a number of other infamous Anglo-

William Pitt, British statesman, was educated at Eton and Oxford. Following four undistinguished years in the army, he entered Parliament, where he allied with the opponents of Prime Minister Sir Robert Walpole.

Pitt first entered American affairs following the War of Jenkins' Ear (1739–1743), a conflict with the Spanish in Georgia and the Mediterranean. In a mocking indictment of Walpole's humiliating peace treaty with the Spanish, Pitt called the agreement "a stipulation of national ignominy." His vociferous criticism propelled him through the ranks of the opposition and struck a chord with the public.

Pitt was kept from office only until 1745, when King George II was forced to appoint him paymaster of the forces to prevent the resignations of his ministers. After a decade of robust service, Pitt was dismissed in 1755 for disagreements with his political masters over the massive British war against France and her allies. It was at this juncture, at the age of 46, that Pitt married Lady Hester Grenville, with whom he had two daughters and three sons, including his namesake William, who later became prime minister.

As France grew stronger and British defeats became disturbingly more frequent, Pitt, whose calls for rearmament had been ignored during the previous years of peace, was eventually appointed secretary of state in 1756, or prime minister, and he immediately took command of the war effort. For the next four years, he pursued an ambitious, aggressive program of military campaigns designed to deprive France of all her colonial possessions and contain her in Europe. These campaigns, which in America became known as the French and Indian War, were truly global in scope, encompassing India, Europe, the West Indies, and North America.

In the American theater, Pitt concentrated resources on Louisbourg and Quebec, two fortified French settlements that guarded the St. Lawrence River. In July 1758, Louisbourg fell to a force of 14,000 regulars under General Jeffery Amherst, opening the St. Lawrence to the British navy and cutting off interior settlements from French reinforcement. Soon afterward, General Abercromby, using a mixed force of colonists and natives, captured Fort Duquesne, proudly renaming it Pittsburgh. After the fall of Quebec to General Wolfe in the spring of 1759, the remaining French outposts found themselves surrounded and the French governor of Canada soon surrendered. This collapse sealed British hegemony in North America, simultaneously uniting the European territories and opening the vast prairie lands to the west to English settlement.

During these years, news of British victories in theaters across the globe seemed to flood London. In 1759 alone, Pitt's *annus mirabilis,* British armies won critical engagements in Minden, Guadeloupe, Lagos, and Quiberon Bay. When George II died in 1760, his son inherited an empire that stretched from Canada to India. But the new king had little respect for Pitt's achievements and forced his resignation in 1761, filling the cabinet with his own favorites. Confined to the back benches, Pitt nevertheless spoke out against the Treaty of Paris, signed in 1763, which, he believed, offered too many concessions to the vanquished French.

Pitt never regained real power. Dogged by manic depression, which kept him confined to his home for months on end, his postwar career was a series of minor recoveries punctuated by long periods of absence and decline. But having fought so hard to secure North America, the rising crisis in that region always commanded his attention. In 1766, he publicly denounced the Stamp Act, a duty on commercial goods designed

to pay for the cost of the recent war. While asserting Britain's claim to sovereignty over the colonies, Pitt argued that taxation should proceed only with colonial consent, as "Americans are the sons, not the bastards, of England."

After a brief return to the premiership in 1766, which was abruptly curtailed by illness, Pitt, now Lord Chatham, was forced to watch from the sidelines. But when, in 1774, the government proposed the closure of the port of Boston in response to the Boston Tea Party, Pitt boldly protested such excessive retribution and warned that unless friendly relations resumed soon, "we, not they, shall be undone."

In January 1775, Pitt offered his own solution to the current impasse. Arguing that the only way to rebuild trust was to remove fear and resentment from the bosoms of the colonists, he proposed the immediate removal of troops from Boston, the establishment of independent judges, and the introduction of trial by

The British statesman William Pitt, the elder, known as "the Great Commoner," led his nation to preeminent status on the international scene. In the Western Hemisphere, he wrested control of Canada from the French and advocated conciliation with the American colonies. *(Brown Brothers, Sterling, Pennsylvania)*

jury. He also recognized the colonies' right to consent to taxation and the utility of the Continental Congress as a political conduit. Despite support from several major figures in Parliament, this "Provisional Act" was defeated by sixty-eight votes to eighteen. Further proposals met similar fates.

The great statesman died on May 11, 1778, at the age of 70.

Richard Bell

See also: French and Indian War; Politics and Government (Chronology); Politics and Government (Essay); Revolutionary War.

Bibliography

Peters, Maria. *The Elder Pitt.* New York: Longman, 1998.
Plumb, J. H. *Chatham.* London: Collins, 1953.
Sherrard, O. A. *Lord Chatham and America.* London: Bodley Head, 1958.

Plantations

A plantation can be defined as an organized system of agricultural production in which large amounts of land are brought under cultivation for the purpose of attaining economic gain. In most cases, plantation owners grow a single crop, commonly referred to as a "staple" or "cash" crop, which they then sell on both the local and global markets.

In colonial North America, plantation agriculture played a critical role in the economic, political, social, and cultural development of five Southern colonies—Maryland, Virginia, North Carolina, South Carolina, and Georgia—where plantation owners concentrated their efforts on the production of three main crops: rice, tobacco, and cotton. The type of crop a planter grew depended on local climate, soil conditions, available labor, and market conditions. Planters in Maryland, Virginia, and most of North Carolina grew tobacco, while those located on the coastal regions of South Carolina and Georgia grew rice. As more and more planters migrated inland, cotton production became increasingly important, especially in Georgia and the Carolinas.

The first plantations were located in Virginia. John Rolfe's introduction of tobacco to Virginia in 1613 and the creation of the "headright" system shortly thereafter led to a flood of newcomers to the colony. Under this new system, prospective landowners were promised 50 acres of land for every person whose passage to the New World they financed. The result, at least in part, was the emergence of a small group of wealthy planters who owned large tracts of land that were cultivated by a continuous stream of indentured servants.

The length of one's servitude was limited, however; by the mid-seventeenth century, agricultural production in Virginia was increasingly influenced by a burgeoning group of newly freed servants. Although a small group of wealthy planters continued to dominate Virginia society, most Southern planters were actually poor farmers, who owned approximately 100 acres of land each and lived in modest wooden houses. They had no servants or slaves, and their crops were usually laid out in haphazard fashion. This would all change by the beginning of the eighteenth century.

During the last half of the seventeenth century and the beginning of the eighteenth century, the influx of indentured servants to the colonies declined dramatically, while the importation of slaves from Africa increased. The amount of land under cultivation also increased. The founding of Maryland (1632), the Carolina colonies (1663), and Georgia (1732) greatly expanded the amount of land available for plantation agriculture and, in turn, generated a tremendous demand for laborers.

In an effort to shore up their position atop the social and political hierarchy and create a seemingly endless labor supply, Southern colonial leaders institutionalized a system of chattel slavery based on race, permanently altering plantation agriculture. By 1700, slave owners dominated Southern society.

Masters, Slaves, and Plantation Architecture

Slave owners' domination of Southern society permeated every aspect of plantation agriculture, including the layout and design of the plantation itself. By the mid-seventeenth century, wealthy planters began building very large, well-ordered plantations with carefully constructed homes and outbuildings that reflected their own tastes, values, and attitudes. Many wealthy slave owners modeled their plantations after English manorial estates, complete with formal gardens and extensive stretches of fenced, neatly cultivated land.

In many ways, a neat, well-ordered plantation became symbolic of a planter's dominance over nature and society. By maintaining a strict hierarchical order,

Orton Plantation, built about 1725 on the Cape Fear River in coastal North Carolina, was a leading producer of rice. Plantation farming was vital to the development of Southern colonies. *(Library of Congress, LC-G602-CT-[043])*

slave owners were able to bolster their power and authority over a labor force that continually resisted domination. Over the course of the colonial period, the plantation became a site where complex social relations were played out on a daily basis and often were manifested in the physical appearance of the plantation.

The central focus of a large plantation was the master's home, commonly referred to as the Big House. Situated atop the highest land available to the planter, the Big House loomed over the other buildings and the outlying fields, and it was the center of activity for the master and his family. It was a showplace, where the master and his family displayed their wealth and power and entertained guests.

Situated on lower ground, either behind or beside the Big House, were quarters for those slaves who worked in and around the house. Slave quarters stood in neat rows and the individual buildings usually were nothing more than a single-room cottage with a chimney and a couple of small windows. Made of wood or stone, with tile or shingle roofs, some slave cottages also had a small front porch. Slave quarters for field

hands generally were of the same type, but these were located farther away from the Big House, near the fields.

In between the slave quarters and the Big House was the yard. Elderly slaves and certain slave women and men—those who were pregnant, nursing, injured, or disabled—performed most of the household chores in the yard. They used large cast-iron kettles and washtubs to make soap and do the wash. They also watched over slave children, who were kept in the yard while their parents worked the fields.

Surrounding the yard were numerous outbuildings, including the kitchen, poultry shed, dairy, smokehouse, icehouse, and various other storage sheds. As the eighteenth century progressed, it became increasingly common for plantation owners to build separate kitchens, not only to avoid unpleasant heat, odor, noise, and the danger of fire, but also to maintain a sense of physical space between the slaves and their masters.

Most plantation owners raised chickens, turkeys, ducks, geese, and pigeons, which they kept in small coops or "houses" located near the kitchen. Other meats, such as pork, were preserved and stored in a smokehouse. A large plantation usually cured and stored about

2 tons of pork each year. Hogs that were slaughtered, quartered, salted, and dried over a smoldering fire in autumn were butchered into usable cuts in spring.

Another important outbuilding was the icehouse. Evidence suggests that Virginia planters used icehouses as early as 1665. These tended to be located away from the other buildings and built at least partly underground, where temperatures remained cooler and more constant. During the winter months, planters would gather large chunks of ice and place them inside the icehouse, where they would then be packed in grass or sawdust. Ice stored in this manner tended to last most of the year.

Scattered throughout the plantation were other important outbuildings, such as craft shops, barns, and stables. In most cases, very large plantations had slaves who were skilled artisans—carpenters, coopers, blacksmiths, tanners, shoemakers, spinners, and distillers—who required their own shops.

Perhaps the most important items on the plantation were the equipment and buildings used to produce the crop. Tobacco plantations in Maryland, Virginia, and North Carolina used tobacco presses, while plantations located in coastal South Carolina and Georgia had winnowing houses. A tobacco press was nothing more than a screw-operated bolt set in a heavy wooden frame. Slaves inserted dried tobacco leaves into the press and turned the bolt to compress them. Most tobacco presses were large enough to accommodate a hogshead of tobacco, which was a barrel 4 feet tall and 2½ feet in diameter. A single hogshead held between 1,000 and 1,300 pounds of tobacco.

Winnowing houses, used in the production of rice, were slightly more complex. A winnowing house was a small, square room raised approximately 10 feet off the ground. After the rice was dried, threshed, and pounded, it was passed through a grate built into the floor of the winnowing house, which would filter out the grain. The process of pounding and winnowing was repeated until the rice was clean.

Plantation Work Rhythms

Plantation slaves generally worked from dawn until dusk and used the evening hours to meet their own needs and the needs of their kin. Slaves planted the labor-intensive crops in the spring, tended them throughout the summer, and harvested them in autumn. Slaves spent the winter months preparing for the next planting season and tending to the daily tasks necessary to maintain the plantation. Despite an extremely demanding work schedule and an often unaccommodating—and in some cases brutal—master, plantation slaves forged extensive kin networks and made time for religious worship, singing, storytelling, and other forms of cultural expression.

Masters spent their days organizing the work force; keeping an inventory of equipment, buildings, produce, and slaves; and acquiring the items necessary to keep the plantation running smoothly. They disciplined slaves, oversaw their medical treatment and their daily comings and goings, and, in some cases, chaperoned important social events such as, weddings, births, funerals, and religious services. The master's gaze was not omnipresent, however, and much of the slaves' daily lives—their relationships, celebrations, meetings, and numerous acts of resistance—went undetected. In addition to managing his workforce, the master also cared for his own family and entertained his guests.

Plantations and Southern Society

Although owners of modest plantations and poor farmers occupied much of the Southern landscape during the colonial era, the term "plantation," evokes the expansive holdings of a wealthy planter. By 1750, the notion that a plantation was a well-ordered, well-constructed country estate belonging to a wealthy gentleman was firmly entrenched in the popular culture. Such plantation owners, in turn, held a tremendous amount of social, economic, political, and cultural authority, but that authority was not absolute.

Slaves and poor and middling white planters continually challenged Southern society's ruling elite. Their unrest would lead, at least in part, to uprisings such as Bacon's Rebellion (Virginia, 1676) and the Stono Rebellion (South Carolina, 1739), as well as the emergence of the Regulators in North and South Carolina during the early eighteenth century.

Michael A. Rembis

See also: African Americans; Agriculture; Cotton; Indentured Servitude; Indigo; Laborers, Rural; Land and Real Estate; Planters; Rice; Slavery, African American; Slavery, Caribbean; Tobacco.

Bibliography

Durant, Thomas J. Jr., and J. David Knottnerus, eds. *Plantation Society and Race Relations: The Origins of Inequality.* Westport, CT: Praeger, 1999.

Horn, James. *Adapting to a New World: English Society in the*

Seventeenth-Century Chesapeake. Chapel Hill: University of North Carolina Press, 1994.

Joyner, Charles W. *Down by the Riverside: A South Carolina Slave Community.* Urbana: University of Illinois Press, 1984.

Vlach, John Michael. *Back of the Big House: The Architecture of Plantation Slavery.* Chapel Hill: University of North Carolina Press, 1993.

Wood, Peter H. *Black Majority: Negroes in Colonial South Carolina from 1670 through the Stono Rebellion.* New York: Alfred A. Knopf, 1974.

Planters

The term "planters" usually refers to an Anglo-American landowner holding twenty or more slaves during the colonial and antebellum periods of American history. This definition should not be taken as hard and fast, however, since other murky categories such as "large landowners," "great planters," and "middling planters" cloud the picture. Before 1776, this elite social class was most relevant to the development of Southern colonies and the Caribbean, though some arguments could be made for the inclusion of the mid-Atlantic colonies.

Interestingly, because slavery did not exist in England or elsewhere in Great Britain, the category of "planter" seems to be unique to the New World. Planters from the Chesapeake, the lower South, and the Caribbean varied in their methods of pursuing wealth, but all relied on the labor of African slaves.

As the eighteenth century progressed, some planters, particularly in Virginia's tidewater region, became enamored with patriotic thought, which in part explains why they so fervently supported the movement toward independence. Planters also held a large percentage of colonial America's wealth and exerted a great deal of its political influence.

Birth of the Planter Class

Sugar plantations, worked by men and women in various conditions of servitude, had existed in the Mediterranean and off the coast of West Africa for some time before the English began to colonize the Americas. The earliest English experiences with plantation agriculture in the New World occurred in the Caribbean and in Virginia. Virginia, begun in 1607 as a trading venture, had failed miserably on that score.

In the decades that followed, Virginia's farmers had recognized the profitability of tobacco, which was coming into vogue in England in the first half of the seventeenth century. One should not take this fact to mean that a planter class appeared in Virginia overnight. Rather, as the seventeenth century progressed, the English gentry began to rely more heavily on slave labor and eventually placed themselves at the head of a racial caste system, with a large African labor force at the bottom. Drawing on examples from Ireland, the Mediterranean, and Portuguese and Spanish New World colonies, the English established plantations on Barbados as well, though these focused on sugar production.

Sugar, which was becoming increasingly popular in England, made Barbadian planters some of the richest men in the Americas. The first planters on Barbados intended to reproduce English institutions, including English common law, as faithfully as possible. By the second half of the seventeenth century, however, they had created a way of life totally centered on sugar production and its attendant African slavery. The planter class in Barbados, which in some ways was a

The "planter class," Anglo-American landholders and slave owners, were the social and economic elite of the Southern colonies and the Caribbean during the colonial and antebellum periods. *(Yale Center for British Art, Paul Mellon Collection, New Haven, Connecticut/Bridgeman Art Library)*

model for later settlements, was relatively small in size, but what it lacked in numbers it made up in cohesion and power. Land was increasingly concentrated in their hands, and less well-off white farmers were slowly squeezed out of the islands.

Within a matter of decades, the planters of Barbados, Jamaica, and the Leeward Islands had come to completely dominate Caribbean society, exceeding the role of the gentry in England. The English Caribbean planters gained a reputation for violence, excess, and moral profligacy. In fact, many planters on the islands managed their estates from abroad as absentees.

Late in the seventeenth century, a third planter class emerged in South Carolina's low country. The existence of a planter class hinged on the development of a single profitable staple crop. In the case of South Carolina, this crop was rice. South Carolina was a sort of middle ground between the planting classes of Virginia and Barbados. South Carolinian planters were richer than Virginia planters but their wealth paled in comparison to that of the West Indian elite.

American planters also positioned themselves at the head of a large, restive labor force, but the slave-to-master ratio was never as high in the South as it was in the Caribbean. And, unlike some planters in the islands, absenteeism was rare in colonial South Carolina rice plantations. Rice plantations were more profitable and less healthy than Chesapeake tobacco plantations, but less profitable and healthier than Caribbean sugar plantations.

Life as a Planter

As mentioned previously, some planters were more hands-on than others in their management of their plantations. This was particularly the case in the Chesapeake, where the quality of a man's tobacco was intimately tied to his status among fellow planters and even his masculinity. Virginia's leading planters prided themselves on the quality of their crops and often personally supervised the various stages of planting, cutting, and curing. Rice planters probably felt many of the same pressures.

Still, planters had more free time than anyone else in colonial America, and their lives reflected a level of luxury that was extraordinarily rare. The great planters in America did not have centuries of tradition supporting their claims to dominance, as did the English aristocracy. Rather, they had in the span of a few generations shoved their way to the top of colonial society. They found ways to express their power and social status, from building imposing frame houses and brick estates to educating their children in England and importing English luxuries, including carriages, clothing, and fine housewares.

Diaries like that of William Byrd II, one of Virginia's wealthiest men, give students of colonial history an extraordinary glimpse into the lives of planters. Byrd's secret diary reveals his passion for the finer things. Alongside entries detailing the intricacies of Virginia politics—in which Byrd was a major player—and the minutiae of running a large plantation, there appear references to wine and spirits, rich food, music, and sex. As the eighteenth century progressed, in fact, the concept of "refinement" became increasingly important, and planters strove not only to outclass their social inferiors but also to adopt sophisticated English styles ever more faithfully and rapidly. The widespread drinking of tea is just one example. Planters also engaged in a variety of leisure activities. The most popular in Virginia and South Carolina were cardplaying, horseracing, and cockfighting. Activities like these sometimes crossed class lines, though planters made the contests more exciting and aristocratic by wagering exorbitant sums.

In the Southern colonial legislatures, the wealthiest planters ran the show. They expected to be put into office by their social inferiors, and more often than not, they were. Southern planters viewed themselves as an aristocracy and believed that just as their families, smallholding neighbors, and slaves owed them deference and obedience, they had certain paternalistic obligations to those groups as well. The trend of returning the same small group of men to the legislature time and again continued through the era of the American Revolution.

Planting and Revolutionary Ideology

Planting a staple crop such as rice or tobacco on a large scale and living a comfortable, stylish life necessitated going into debt. In both the Chesapeake and South Carolina, planters borrowed in order to bring more acreage under the plow, finance the purchase of slaves, and import increasingly fine things from Europe.

Yet even as planters tried to emulate English styles in the middle of the eighteenth century, they grew aware of their differences from England. In fact, some of the wealthiest members of colonial society were ardent patriots during the imperial crises of the 1760s and 1770s. The reasons for this Revolutionary fervor lie in the mentality of the great planters in the decades before the Revolutionary War.

It would not be accurate to argue that planter debt or the rituals surrounding the production of tobacco and rice brought about the War for Independence. One could assert, however, that the rising debts of the planters in combination with the mentality of men whose identity was so tightly wrapped up in their agricultural production made them particularly susceptible to the tenets of "country thought"—sometimes referred to as republicanism or radical opposition. "Country thought" refers to a group of ideas floating around in eighteenth-century England, many of which stressed personal liberty and autonomy, emphasized civic virtue, and attacked unbalanced government or military government as inherently corrupt.

From this perspective, the debt incurred to sustain profitable agriculture was also a threat to a planter's liberty and manhood. T. H. Breen has argued that it was precisely because of the culture of planting tobacco that the planters of Virginia's tidewater were early converts to the cause of independence; these same men, including Patrick Henry, George Washington, and Thomas Jefferson, formulated an American brand of country thought with its roots deep in tobacco agriculture.

In the years after the War for Independence, planters continued to wield power, but some of the democratic impulses of the Revolution also seeped into colonial legislatures. In South Carolina, for instance, a number of artisans and mechanics—the muscle of Charles Town's Revolutionary movement—were elected to public office. Overall, the early state governments of the South and, to some extent the national government, were dominated by the planting class.

Matthew Jennings

See also: Landlords; Plantations.

Bibliography

Billings, Warren M., John E. Selby, and Thad W. Tate. *Colonial Virginia: A History.* White Plains, NY: KTO, 1986.

Breen, T. H. *Tobacco Culture: The Mentality of the Great Tidewater Planters on the Eve of Revolution.* Princeton, NJ: Princeton University Press, 1985.

Dunn, Richard S. *Sugar and Slaves: The Rise of the Planter Class in the English West Indies, 1624–1713.* Chapel Hill: University of North Carolina Press, 1972.

Weir, Robert M. *Colonial South Carolina: A History.* Millwood, NY: KTO, 1983.

Plymouth

The Pilgrims who settled the Plymouth Colony were a varied people bound together by a common religion. The Pilgrims sought religious freedom from the Anglican Church. They objected to the corruption of the Anglican Church and separated from it, forming their own church. This strain of separatism was strongest in Scrooby, England, where a church was begun under Richard Clyfton. The original members of the Scrooby group included William Brewster and William Bradford.

In 1607, the Scrooby separatists departed England and fled to Holland to avoid persecution by the English government. The government viewed the separatists as treasonous and was aggressive in its efforts to destroy the movement. The Scrooby separatists eventually settled in Leyden, Holland, which appealed to the fledgling church because of the country's policy of religious toleration.

While safe from persecution in Leyden, church members became dissatisfied with their exile and, by 1617, had resolved to journey to the English colonies in the New World. Limited economic and social opportunities as well as the difference in languages prohibited Leyden from becoming a permanent home to the Pilgrims.

The Pilgrims decided to settle near the colony of Virginia, close enough to settled territory for protection yet distant enough for them to exercise religious freedom. In 1617, the church sent two agents to London to negotiate with the Virginia Company. Their agents were successful in securing approval of their statement of religious beliefs from the King and the Privy Council, but they failed to secure a land patent in Virginia.

Joint-Stock Company

In 1619, Thomas Weston, a London merchant, became the promoter of the Leyden congregation. Weston had ties to the Leyden church because Edward Pickering, his agent, had married one of its members. On July 1, 1620, under Weston's leadership, a joint-stock company was formed, and the funds were divided into shares. An investment of 10 pounds bought a single share.

The terms of the company were to continue for seven years, and all profits generated by the company would remain in the common stock. At the end of the seven years, all capital and profits were to be divided among the shareholders. All land, houses, and goods would be included in the division of funds. These terms were harsher than what the settlers had originally agreed to. The provision including houses and goods in the division of profits was especially troubling. The company also required settlers to work for seven days a week rather than the five days agreed upon by the church.

The Leyden congregation rejected these terms of settlement. The company's financial backers engaged Robert Cushman to work with the settlers, and it was not until 1621 that he was able to gain their approval of the settlement agreement.

The joint-stock company survived until 1627. The final dissolution of the company resulted in the interest in the colony being sold to the settlers. Under the terms of the liquidation, fifty-eight settlers, the "Purchasers," were involved in the division of property. Single men received one share, which equaled a set amount of property. Heads of families received one share per member of the household. Livestock, housing, and land were all included in the liquidation scheme, with the meadows remaining common areas. Eleven men personally assumed the company's 1,800-pound debt in exchange for a six-year monopoly on trade with the natives.

First Years

The company was plagued by financial difficulties; these delayed departure of the voyage until August 1620. When the ships finally left England, they were short of supplies and dangerously late in attempting the ocean crossing. The *Speedwell,* overloaded and leaky, was forced to return to Plymouth, accompanied by the *Mayflower.* Then, both groups, a total of 102 passengers, crowded onto the *Mayflower* for the voyage.

On November 11, 1620, the *Mayflower* landed at Provincetown Harbor, well north of its destination in Virginia. The settlers spent a month exploring the area for the best place to settle and, on December 16, arrived at Plymouth Bay.

The first winter in Plymouth was severe and resulted in the deaths of nearly half the company. Spring brought the first native visitors. Samoset, a member of the Massasoit tribe, ventured into the settlement in March. He introduced them to Squanto, one of the few remaining Patuxet Indians; the two men helped the

settlers, teaching them how to plant and harvest corn. Squanto lived in Plymouth until his death in 1622.

In November 1621, the *Fortune* arrived from England, bringing thirty-six new settlers and a land patent. John Pierce was named the grantee for the land. The terms of the patent included 100 acres per person, 1,500 acres for public purposes, freedom to trade and fish along the coast, and the authority to make laws. The patent did not specify land boundaries.

Settlers continued to arrive in the early years of the colony. Many did not share the Pilgrims' religious convictions but had paid their own way to the settlement. The "particulars" were free to work for themselves, but they were shut out of Plymouth government and the Native American trade. Emigration to Plymouth in large numbers continued throughout the 1630s. There was little growth in the colony between 1640 and 1650, but after that period of stability the push for expansion and land resumed. The result was a colony whose boundaries grew ever closer to those of the Native American population. By 1675, the Plymouth Colony boasted a population of 7,500 in an area of 1,600 square miles.

Housing in the Plymouth Colony was generally modest. In the initial stages of settlement, small, crude cottages provided the most basic shelter. As the colony became more settled, solid-frame homes covered with clapboards became the rule. These small one-and-a-half-story homes were the center of family life. Families tended to be small nuclear groups composed of a husband, wife, and their children. Many households also included servants, who, in the early years of settlement, were usually hired or indentured, as slavery existed only on a very small scale. Plymouth's social life revolved around the church.

Church

John Lyford was the first minister at Plymouth. Initially embraced by the colony, he was banished from Plymouth in 1625 because of his opposition to Governor Bradford. Plymouth would not obtain another minister until 1629, when Ralph Smith arrived; his tenure was short-lived, too. John Reyner occupied the pulpit at New Plymouth from 1629 until 1654.

The church was supported by Plymouth's civil government, although there was no specific legislation supporting the church until 1650, when the General Court passed laws punishing slander of the church or

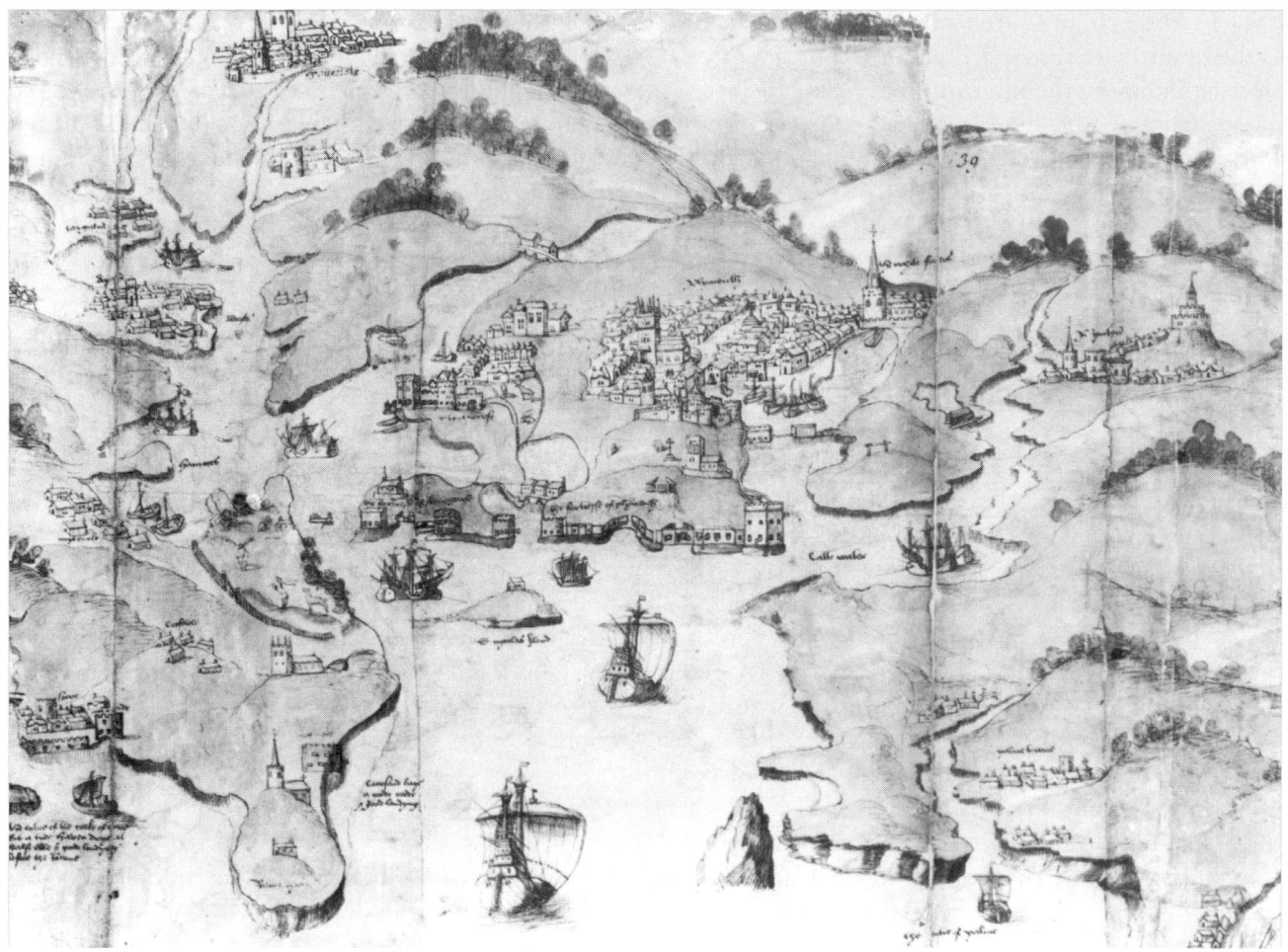

An early visitor to Plymouth gave the following description: "the harbour is not only pleasant for air and prospect, but most sure for shipping, both small and great, being land-locked on all sides. The town is seated on the ascent of a hill. . . ." *(Private Collection/Bridgeman Art Library)*

its minister. In 1651 legislation requiring church attendance was adopted.

Local churches exercised much control over their own governance. They elected their own ministers and established the conduct of the worship service, as well as sitting in judgment of local members brought before them. This self-determination extended to the exercise of the Half-way Covenant, whereby the children of members of the church could be admitted to church membership without professing a conversion experience.

The Plymouth Colony, like most of its New England neighbors, experienced a decline in religious unity during the mid-seventeenth century. There was also a marked decline in the numbers of church members throughout the colony. Membership in the church was restricted to those who professed a conversion experience; their testimony of conversion was given before the church members, who decided whether or not to extend membership to the candidate.

In order to bolster flagging church memberships, a number of ministers throughout the New England colonies, particularly in Massachusetts, advocated the adoption of the Half-way Covenant. But churches in the Plymouth Colony generally rejected this compromise.

Efforts to suppress Quakerism provide another example of the increasing religious splintering that occurred. Quakers had first arrived in Plymouth in 1656, and the following year legislation to suppress them was passed by the General Court. In 1658, severe punishments, including whippings, were meted out to some Quakers. The persecution of Quakers continued until an order from the Crown in 1660 required that all Quakers be sent to England for trial.

In 1668, John Cotton was elected and ordained as the minister for the New Plymouth church. Cotton's election indicated the Pilgrims' move from their separatist stance to the more moderate Puritan view of working within the established church to make it better.

Government

When the *Mayflower* landed at Provincetown in November 1621, the settlers agreed to a contract of government known as the Mayflower Compact. Such a document was necessary because the patent the joint-stock company had secured from the Virginia Company was invalid, given that they had failed to settle within the specified boundaries. John Carver was chosen as the first governor; his death shortly after their arrival resulted in the election of William Bradford as governor.

The governor and the General Court were the primary organs of government for the colony. The term *freeman* was used to denote citizenship, though there was no legislation to define what constituted a freeman until 1668. Freemen were allowed to vote and hold office in the colony. Legislation in 1656 required that those who wished to obtain the status of freemen first gain the approval of the freemen in their town before submitting their names to the General Court. In 1668 legislation established freemen as those who met minimum land ownership requirements.

The year 1665 brought about the establishment of a uniform local court system. Select courts were established in every town and were composed of three to five men elected by the town and confirmed by the General Court. These courts had full authority over civil suits in amounts up to 40 shillings. In addition, the select courts heard lawsuits between English settlers and Native Americans that resulted from English livestock damaging the natives' crops.

In 1685, county courts were established in the colony and a new edition of *Colony Laws* was published, with significant revisions to the 1636 codification of colonial law.

Economy

Plymouth's economy was limited by its geographic location. The lack of good port facilities limited trade. Additionally, Plymouth's settlers lacked the necessary capital and contacts with English commercial circles to expand their economy.

The Plymouth economy was influenced by the sea. Fish and whale oil were popular exports, though the trade was generally only coastal rather than transatlantic. Shipbuilding and associated trades were also important in Plymouth. There also was limited success with ironworks and some local industries, including grain and sawmills.

Agriculture was primary to the colony. Communal grazing lands supported a variety of livestock. Edward Winslow, one of the original colonists, made several trips between England and the Plymouth Colony. In 1624, he returned to the colony with three heifers and a bull for the entire community. This livestock would prove to be essential. With the arrival of the Puritan settlers at Massachusetts, the sale of livestock to colonists there became a major source of revenue. An additional source of revenue for the colonists was the export of beaver skins to England.

The government regulated the economy. The primary ways it exercised this power were through setting general prices and wage levels and by granting monopolies that served the best interest of the public as a whole.

King Philip's War

The settlers of the Plymouth Colony initially enjoyed a peaceful relationship with the Wampanoag and Massasoit Indians. A period of mild unrest in 1662 marked the first disruption in that relationship. Plymouth's policies required payment to the native peoples for every purchase of their lands; the growth of the colony in the second half of the seventeenth century led to greater purchases of Native American lands in the 1660s. Settlers' livestock often harmed the native peoples' crops, as the white settlements grew closer to native villages. This increased proximity also resulted in efforts to proselytize the western Native American population.

In 1671, King Philip (Metacom), the Wampanoag chief, was forced into signing a peace treaty. The establishment of a white community near the Wampanoag village at Mount Hope had resulted in escalated conflict between settlers and the native peoples. In the treaty that King Philip signed, he acknowledged himself as subject to the king of England and the law of Plymouth. Despite the treaty, unrest continued to grow and ultimately led to the outbreak of war.

In 1675, Wampanoag and Narragansett Indians began conducting raids on communities throughout Plymouth in response to the decade of unrest that had preceded the war. The colony's militia attempted to trail the natives and attack them in order to protect the colony. The militia, however, lacked experienced military leadership and spent most of a year blundering throughout the countryside in a disorganized attempt to locate Philip's warriors. The war spread throughout the New England colonies and was not settled until the militia destroyed King Philip's camp and killed him in the summer of 1676.

Final Years

Plymouth's status as an English colony meant that it was subject to changes that were the result of English politics. The restoration of King Charles II to the throne in 1660 brought a degree of uncertainty to the colony. While Plymouth had obtained a general land grant, the colony had never obtained a royal charter that specified its boundaries. In 1665, the king sent royal commissioners to visit the New England colonies. Plymouth requested of these commissioners that they petition the king for a royal charter on their behalf, but the colonists failed to take the more aggressive action of sending their own envoy to request the charter.

In 1677, the Plymouth Colony, without a royal charter, petitioned the king for the rights to the Mount Hope lands that were occupied by the Wampanoag but were now viewed as open to English settlers in the aftermath of King Philip's War. Three years later, Governor Josiah Winslow received a letter from Henry Coventry, the secretary of state for the American colonies, indicating that the Crown would grant the colony's request for title to the Mount Hope lands. Secretary Coventry also indicated that the king would respond favorably to a request from the colony for a royal charter.

Winslow died later that year. His successor, Thomas Hinckley, continued the colony's efforts to obtain a royal charter but again failed to take any aggressive action. In 1685, Plymouth's efforts to obtain a charter were invalidated by the Crown's decision to reorganize the New England colonies. King James II implemented a plan that consolidated the colonies into the Dominion of New England and appointed Edmund Andros the general governor. Authority under the new Dominion was centralized at Boston. The New England colonies chafed under this arrangement, and the news of the overthrow of James II in 1688 resulted in the overthrow of Andros in Boston the next year. Plymouth reverted to its former colonial government structure.

Plymouth's autonomy continued until King William III undertook a reorganization of Massachusetts in 1691. Under this plan, Plymouth was annexed to the Massachusetts Bay Colony and its citizens became subject to that colony's authority. The Plymouth Colony as a separate entity ceased to exist; however, its legacy of religious freedom and success despite overwhelming odds continued.

Tonia M. Compton

See also: Massachusetts Bay Colony; Mayflower Compact; Pilgrims. *Document:* The Mayflower Compact (1620).

Bibliography

Demos, John. *A Little Commonwealth: Family Life in Plymouth Colony.* New York: Oxford University Press, 1970.

Langdon, George D., Jr. *Pilgrim Colony: A History of New Plymouth 1620–1691.* New Haven, CT: Yale University Press, 1966.

McIntyre, Ruth. *Debts Hopeful and Desperate: Financing the Plymouth Colony.* Plymouth, MA: Plimoth Plantation, 1963.

Rutman, Darrett B. *Husbandmen of Plymouth: Farms and Villages in the Old Colony, 1620–1692.* Boston: Beacon Press, 1967.

Pocahontas (c. 1594–1616)

Although myth and speculation surround Pocahontas, the famous storybook "Indian princess," there is a substantial amount of recorded fact regarding the favorite daughter of the powerful Algonquin Chief Powhatan.

Born around 1594, Matoaka (nicknamed Pocahontas, meaning "playful" or "naughty one") met the legendary John Smith of Jamestown, Virginia, in 1607, in her father's village of Werowocomoco on the north shore of the Pamunkey River (now called the York River). Lively, intelligent, and resourceful, the young Pocahontas was described by one Englishman in 1610 as

> of a coulour browne, or rather tawnye . . . round-faced, with the fore part of her grosse and thick black hair shaven close, and the very long thicker part being tied in a pleate hanging down to her hips.

Whether the precocious 12-year-old saved Smith from a violent death at the hands of her father has never been substantiated. The tale was not recorded until after Pocahontas traveled to London years later. The young Pocahontas, however, did bring gifts of food and supplies to the starving men and boys of Jamestown. Still, of the original 104 Englishmen deposited on the

The fabled Pocahontas, daughter of the chief Powhatan, converted to Christianity, married John Rolfe, and traveled to London in 1615 as Lady Rebecca Rolfe. She was feted at court but died before returning home. *(Brown Brothers, Sterling, Pennsylvania)*

shores of the James River in May and June 1607, only forty were alive in late December, when another ship returned with seventy to a hundred more settlers, including two women.

At first Chief Powhatan (whose real name was Wahunsonacock) opposed settlement by whites on his lands. Chief of the thirty-plus tribe confederacy of Powatanas—a thriving agricultural and fishing nation totaling between 9,000 and 15,000 people—he had been given an ominous prophecy by one of his shamans that foretold the destruction of the Powatanas. In spite of this fear, Chief Powhatan eventually feasted and entertained the ambitious and feisty John Smith. He also befriended Jamestown's settlers, at least for a time.

In 1609, after being badly injured in a gunpowder accident, John Smith returned to England. He would not see Pocahontas for another seven years. In the meantime, Pocahontas married Kocoum, "a captainne of Powhatan." There is some indication that she bore a child (a girl) at this time, but many believe the child died.

By 1612, relations between the settlers and the Powatanas had deteriorated. Captain Samuel Argall, fearing an attack by several of the disgruntled tribes and acting in retaliation for the capture of eight Englishmen, tricked and then kidnapped the unsuspecting Pocahontas. During her captivity, Pocahontas met and married the widowed John Rolfe, the man credited with planting and commercializing the first tobacco crop in America. This crop became so important that its export later ensured Jamestown's survival; in 1617, some 50,000 pounds of cured tobacco was exported to England.

Whether the young woman fell in love with Rolfe or whether the marriage was part of her conditional release, however, is not clear. It is known that Pocahontas converted to Christianity, was baptized Rebecca, and married John Rolfe on April 5, 1614. Reluctantly, Powhatan gave his consent, along with a large piece of property. This union represented a great alliance for the English, ensuring peace with the Powhatan. The peace, unfortunately, would come to a quick end after Powhatan's death in 1618.

One year after John Rolfe and Pocahontas were married, Pocahontas gave birth to a son, Thomas. Not long after that, the young family traveled with Sir Thomas Dale back to London. Sir Thomas Dale hoped to secure more funding and more settlers for Jamestown; Rolfe hoped to secure a trade agreement for his expanding tobacco crop. Accompanying them on this voyage were Pocahontas's sister Matchanna and her husband Tomocomo, as well as several other Powhatan men and women.

In England, Pocahontas was viewed as a princess and eagerly received at the court of King James I. She also was reunited with John Smith. But after several months in England, Rolfe was anxious to return to America. The group was to set sail in March 1616, but Pocahontas fell ill and the ship's departure was delayed.

Pocahontas died in Gravesend, England, at the age of 22. The church record reads: "1616 March 21, Rebecca Wrolfe, Wyffe of Thomas John Wrolfe Gentleman, a Virginia Lady borne was buried in ye Chancell. Entered by Rev. Nicholas Frankwell." The gravesite was later destroyed when the church had to be rebuilt.

Although John Rolfe returned to Jamestown, young Thomas Rolfe remained in England to be raised by Rolfe's family. Incredibly, the descendants of Pocahontas, who derive from this son, include many distinguished Americans, including Thomas Jefferson Randolph, the grandson of President Thomas Jefferson.

Gail L. Jenner

See also: Jamestown; Native American–European Relations; Native Americans; Powhatan; Powhatan Confederacy; Rolfe, John; Smith, John; Women.

Bibliography

Abrams, Ann Uhry. *The Pilgrims and Pocahontas: Rival Myths of American Origin.* Boulder, CO: Westview Press, 1999.

Allen, Paula Gunn. *Pocahontas: Medicine Woman, Spy, Entrepreneur, Diplomat.* San Francisco: Harper San Francisco, 2003.

Cassidy, James J. Jr., ed. *Through Indian Eyes: The Untold Story of Native American Peoples.* New York: Reader's Digest, 1995.

Ponce de Léon, Juan (1460–1521)

A Spanish explorer, Juan Ponce de Léon conquered and settled the island of Puerto Rico. He is most famous for his futile and ill-fated search for the legendary fountain of youth in Florida.

Born into a powerful and noble Spanish family in 1460, Ponce de Léon was appointed a page at the court of Ferdinand of Aragon as a youth. He was also part of the military expedition that conquered Granada in Southern Spain in 1492, ending the 700-year-long Moorish presence on the Iberian Peninsula.

His career as an explorer may have begun just after that, as he was believed to be a member of Christopher Columbus's second expedition to the Western Hemisphere. By 1502, Ponce de Léon found himself living in Hispaniola, the base of the Spanish empire in its earliest years, where he served as a captain and provincial governor of the eastern half of the island under Governor Nicolás de Ovando.

When rumors came back of gold on the nearby island of Puerto Rico, Ponce de Léon organized an expedition that explored and conquered the island from 1508 to 1509. He also established Puerto Rico's first settlement at Caparra, just outside modern San Juan. Appointed governor of the island, he was soon removed by rivals and returned to Hispaniola.

Encouraged by the Spanish government, Ponce de Léon followed up on a new rumor of the existence of a fountain of youth on Bimini Island in the Bahamas. Once again outfitting an expedition with his own money, he erred in his navigation and landed in Florida around Easter 1513, near the present-day city of St. Augustine. He named the territory Florida, after the Spanish word for the Easter holiday, *Pascua Florida.*

Continuing on his search for the fountain of youth, he sailed down the Atlantic coast of the Florida Peninsula, through the Florida Keys, and up the Gulf Coast. His expedition proving fruitless, he returned to Puerto Rico and eventually Spain. There, he won the court's approval to serve as military governor of Bimini and Florida in 1514.

It took Ponce de Léon seven years to raise a second expedition for Florida, and he finally sailed there in 1521. Landing at Charlotte Harbor on the peninsula's Gulf Coast, he encountered hostile members of the Seminole tribe and was wounded by an arrow. Retreating to Cuba, he died in Havana later that year.

James Ciment

See also: Exploration; Florida; Puerto Rico; Spanish Colonies on Mainland North America (Chronology).

Bibliography

Fuson, Robert H. *Juan Ponce de León and the Spanish Discovery of Puerto Rico and Florida.* Blacksburg, VA: McDonald & Woodward, 2000.

Pontiac (c. 1720–1769)

Little is known about the early life and career of Pontiac, an Ottawa war leader most closely associated with a series of frontier attacks known as Pontiac's Rebellion. Euro-American recreations of his life in the eighteenth and nineteenth centuries made him one of the country's most famous Native Americans, a symbol of fierce resistance to European colonization, and a leader of a racial struggle for the Great Lakes region.

Pontiac's legacy is more complex and interesting than the two-dimensional portrayals allow. It deserves to be understood within the context of mid-eighteenth-century America.

Setting the Stage: North America in 1760

The Great Lakes region was in a state of turmoil in 1760. The French had evacuated the region and were in the process of losing North America to the British entirely, leaving their thousands of native allies in the lurch. Native communities through the Ohio River Valley and the Great Lakes, many of whom were already refugees from earlier conflicts, struggled to come to grips with the new political reality of native life in America. There would no longer be two imperial powers that Native Americans could play off against one another. Furthermore, the region's native peoples had failed to create any sort of confederation that could prevent or slow Anglo-American expansion. The British who were moving into the region did not treat the native peoples on the same terms as the French had.

The British who occupied the former French forts and trading posts were under the orders of Major General Jeffery Amherst, who stopped reciprocal gifting and restricted the sale of powder. Native peoples had generally viewed the French as symbolic "fathers," but the British did not behave according to these long-established rules. They were intent on conquest.

At approximately the same time, Neolin, also known as the "Delaware prophet," began to preach a message of pan-American Indian unity and rejection of European culture that appealed to many Native Americans, including Pontiac. Neolin had a vision of heaven that contained only native peoples. He proclaimed that at one time, the native peoples had direct access to heaven, but that their path had been blocked because of their increasing contact with white people and dependence on them. Borrowing from Christianity, Neolin advocated a return to the "old ways." His message was taken up by many different Native Americans, however, and, in fact, led away from tradition.

Pontiac accepted the teachings of Neolin, but he modified them slightly: he focused Neolin's mistrust of white people in general more tightly on the British. He also mediated Neolin's desire for Native Americans to give up white ways. Pontiac was a war leader, to be sure, but he was also a deft politician, who was able to bring together different strands of anti-British sentiment.

Pontiac's Rebellion

Rising anti-British feeling among Native Americans allowed diverse groups of Senecas, Shawnees, Delawares, and various Algonquin villages to set aside former differences. In the winter of 1762, war belts traveled throughout Indian Country as Native Americans prepared for war against the British.

In the spring of 1763, war came. The Ottawa laid siege to Detroit, while other natives destroyed all of the British outposts in the Ohio River Valley. The native warriors failed to take the three largest British installations—at Detroit, Fort Niagara, and Pittsburgh—but they inflicted a great deal of real and psychological terror. By the end of the summer, they had killed several thousand settlers, traders, and British soldiers. When

news of the situation reached London, Parliament sent reinforcements and passed the Proclamation Act, a last-ditch effort to avert conflict along the colonial frontier. The British had fought the native forces to a stalemate, and though sporadic fighting continued for a couple of years, no territory changed hands and the loss of life lessened considerably.

Both sides of the Anglo-Native American conflict resorted to brutal tactics during Pontiac's Rebellion. Pontiac seized a British captain under a flag of truce; an Ojibwe leader later tortured the captain to death as revenge for a nephew's killing. Jeffery Amherst, commander of British forces and a confirmed hater of Native Americans, ordered his soldiers not to take any prisoners; he also gained notoriety for sending smallpox-infected blankets into native villages.

The results of Pontiac's Rebellion were not decisive in favor of either the native peoples or the British. Native Americans had failed to evict the British from the Great Lakes and the Ohio River Valley, as the British retained their three key military strongholds. On the other hand, the British had set out to subjugate the Native Americans and subject them to colonial rule, and they had failed in that mission. Both sides gradually moved away from their hard-line positions (Amherst, for example, returned to England and was chastised for his brutality) and began to seek a meaningful, lasting peace in the years after the rebellion.

Pontiac's Life After the Rebellion

Pontiac's role in regional tribal affairs continued after the rebellion fizzled. Although he had lost influence among the native peoples near Detroit for failing to destroy the fort, he gained prestige elsewhere for his leadership abilities and political skills. In the Wabash and the Illinois country, for instance, he became an important man; tribes in these areas had no desire to settle with the British.

Pontiac traveled widely, enlisting new allies to resist British policies. Although he often claimed to represent the French, he more clearly represented Algonquin resistance to British colonial rule. Some of the British came to view Pontiac as possessing almost superhuman powers. After the Shawnees agreed to terms with the British in 1764, Pontiac began seriously to consider peace with the British.

Pontiac's reputation as a skillful negotiator increased when he mediated a dispute between the Kickapoo and the Shawnee. In 1765, the Kickapoo attacked a group of Shawnees who were acting as a British trader's escort, killing several of them. The Shawnee threatened to go to war over the incident, but the natives of the Illinois Country called in Pontiac to smooth over the differences between the groups. He did so masterfully, and in the process went from being a war leader to being a chief. Interestingly, the number of native peoples loosely allied with Pontiac increased after his famous rebellion.

Pontiac's reputation and power had grown, but he had fashioned himself as the leader of a vast native empire stretching across the current Midwest. In reality, his power was much more limited. Also, he began to behave recklessly and arrogantly, prompting a French trader to predict in 1766 that he would be dead within a year. This ominous prediction was not off by much.

Pontiac stabbed an Illinois leader, which set in motion the chain of events that would end his life. He lost influence among the Ottawa themselves, and, by 1768, he was living in exile among the Illinois. The most famous American Indian of his generation was without a home. In 1769, a nephew of a Peoria chief killed Pontiac in Cahokia, a French village near present-day East St. Louis.

Pontiac's life and death demonstrate the limits of chieftainship in the Great Lakes region in the 1760s. He was able to draw people to him with an anti-British message cobbled together from many different strains of thought. He took part in the cross-cultural revival/uprising that bears his name and, for a time, believed himself to be the leader of a gigantic Native American empire. Pontiac expanded his own role far beyond what was expected or even desired from an Ottawa war leader. In the end, his self-aggrandizement cost him his life.

Matthew Jennings

See also: Great Lakes; Native American—European Conflict; Native Americans; Ohio Country.

Bibliography

Nash, Gary B. *Red, White and Black: The Peoples of Early North America.* Upper Saddle River, NJ: Prentice Hall, 2000.

White, Richard. *The Middle Ground: Indians, Empires, and Republics in the Great Lakes Region, 1650–1815.* Cambridge, UK: Cambridge University Press, 1991.

———. "Pontiac." In *The Encyclopedia of North American Indians,* edited by Frederick E. Hoxie. Boston: Houghton Mifflin, 1996.

Poor Richard's Almanack

Famous for such pithy sayings as "Early to bed and early to rise, makes a man healthy wealthy and wise," *Poor Richard's Almanack* was published annually by Benjamin Franklin from 1732 to 1758. Franklin began the almanac when, as a rising Philadelphia printer, he lost his lucrative almanac printing business to competitors. Franklin responded by creating his own almanac and selling it to the public under the name of Richard Saunders, also known as Poor Richard.

Almanacs were extremely important in colonial America and were surpassed in sales only by the Bible. They provided something valuable for everyone. A basic calendar helped avoid confusion over dates at a time when, because England had not yet joined other European countries in adopting the Gregorian calendar, colonial calendars disagreed with the calendars followed elsewhere. Almanacs included the phases of the moon and the changes in the tides (information needed by travelers and mariners) and forecast the weather for farmers while simultaneously—and sometimes controversially—giving astrological predictions and mysterious home remedies for various afflictions. Prosaic information such as the dates that court would be in session stood alongside entertaining pieces such as predictions of fantastic events, amusing sayings, and the occasional bawdy verse (or two). Though *Poor Richard* was not the most popular almanac in colonial America—its sales peaked at 10,000 per year versus the 50,000 to 60,000 sold by the leading publication—it did have a devoted following across the colonies and generated a healthy income for Franklin.

Much of the almanac's success stemmed from the popularity of Poor Richard. More than simply a pseudonym for Franklin, Poor Richard was a fully developed literary character, one of the many created by Franklin over his lifetime. Almanacs typically began with a preface expressing the warm greetings of the author, who presented himself as a polymath—an astrologer, mathematician, and all-around wise man rolled into one. Franklin used the prefaces to bring Poor Richard to life. In the first almanac, Poor Richard read the stars and predicted the death of rival almanac maker Titan Leeds, provoking a running controversy. When Leeds responded abusively, Poor Richard countered in the next almanac by claiming that since Leeds was always a gentleman he must be dead, with someone else shame-

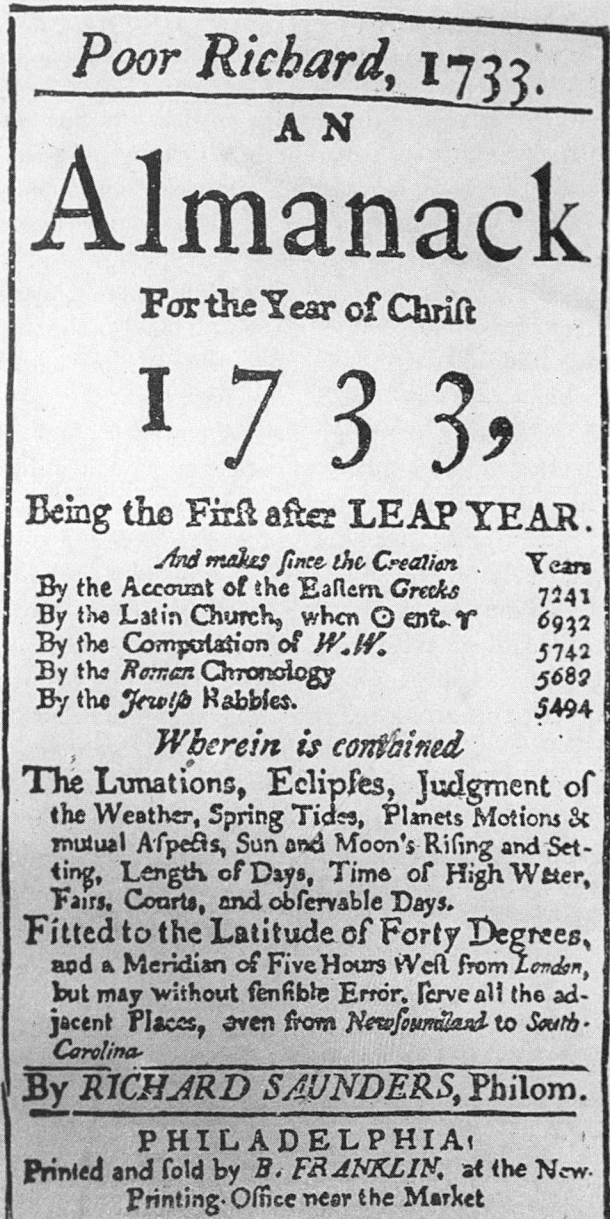

Benjamin Franklin's enormously popular *Poor Richard's Almanack,* published annually from 1732 to 1758, was full of homespun wisdom, pithy common sense, and practical information. *(Brown Brothers, Sterling, Pennsylvania)*

fully writing the almanac under an assumed name. Franklin also entertained by offering readers a glimpse into Richard's squabbles with his wife, Bridget. The two characters exchanged humorous barbs from one almanac preface to another, with Richard complaining of his wife's pretensions to gentility and Bridget criticizing her husband's habit of airing her faults in public.

Over time, Franklin downplayed the comedy and increasingly turned to supplying practical knowledge.

More and more, *Poor Richard* also encouraged the virtues of thrift and industry through proverbial wisdom. In 1748, Franklin expanded the almanac from twenty-four to thirty-six pages, changed the name to *Poor Richard Improved,* and allotted more space to essays providing useful information on topics such as farming techniques, cooking recipes and home remedies, money-making strategies, and especially science.

Occupied by other affairs, Franklin left publication of the almanac to others after 1758 (a version of *Poor Richard's Almanack* continued to appear afterward). Franklin departed with one of his most famous performances. He created a new character, the sagacious Father Abraham, to expound the wisdom of Poor Richard on the value of thrift and industry. Encompassing the numerous proverbs on these virtues included in the almanac over the years, and presented in the form of "as Poor Richard says," this preface quickly achieved wild popularity. Reprinted profusely in America and abroad as "The Way to Wealth," it has been seen as the epitome of an American philosophy of material success and as a classic of American literature.

On the whole, much of what appeared in *Poor Richard's Almanack* was not original with Franklin, since he borrowed freely from others. Richard Saunders was the name of a deceased London almanac maker, and the moniker *Poor Richard* was taken from the title of another publication, *Poor Robin's Almanack.* The characters of Richard and Bridget as well as the trick of predicting his rival's death were patterned after the satiric writings of Jonathan Swift.

Even the famous aphorisms, although frequently seen as the insights of Franklin, usually expressed commonly known folk wisdom. Franklin, however, used his fine-tuned ear to give these sayings the perfect ring. For example, in Franklin's hands the saying "Fresh fish and new come guests smell, by that they are three days old" became the much more memorable "Fish & visitors stink in three days."

David Head

See also: Franklin, Benjamin; Newspapers and Journals.

Bibliography

Brands, H. W. *The First American: The Life and Times of Benjamin Franklin.* New York: Doubleday, 2000.

Franklin, Benjamin. *The Papers of Benjamin Franklin.* Edited by Leonard W. Labaree. Vols. 1–7. New Haven, CT: Yale University Press, 1959–1964.

Meister, Charles W. "Franklin as a Proverb Stylist." *American Literature* 24 (1952–1953): 157–66.

Population and Demographics

At the end of the sixteenth century, encouraged by the colonization of Ireland, England was interested in extending its reach. Another factor was that war with the Spanish and the expenses associated with colonizing Ireland had left the realm financially depleted.

Following the example of the French and Spanish, England subcontracted the work of colonization to a few highly motivated promoters, who became known as the West Country Men. These men included Sir Richard Grenville, Sir Francis Drake, and Sir Walter Raleigh, among others. The West Country Men secured investment by drawing attention to the serious problem of overpopulation that was plaguing England, especially the urban centers, at the time. England's population was 3 million in 1500, 4 million in 1600, and 5 million by 1650.

The constantly expanding gap between rich and poor, encouraged by critical legislation like the enclosure acts, which forced thousands of subsistence farmers into poverty and ultimately into the urban centers in an effort to find work, frightened the wealthy (a mere 5 percent of the population). The West Country Men sold the colonization plan on the basis of the theory that this growing population of poor people might well create problems that could not be controlled by legislation. Additionally, colonization would provide opportunity for all, while simultaneously lifting England's financial burdens by sending the poor overseas.

Early English colonization efforts also involved the West Indies. Two of the most pivotal settlements in the New World, however, were the Massachusetts Bay Colony and the Chesapeake Bay Colony, both of which continue to influence population distribution in America to this day.

Chesapeake Bay and the Middle Colonies

Initial voyages to the New World were generally unsuccessful. The first colonists were a mix of a few enthusiastic middle-class adventurers, looking for the vast wealth promised by the stories of Spanish expeditions, and a far larger proportion of lower-class emigrants seeking to escape the brutality of the English law code.

After an initial exploratory mission a year earlier, the first colony was established at Roanoke Island, in Virginia in 1586. This famed "Lost Colony" had vanished by the following year due to disease, trouble with indigenous peoples, the Spanish, and other problems.

The first successful Virginia colony was the settlement at Jamestown in 1607, but it also had serious problems getting started. Of 105 initial settlers, only thirty-two survived after the first seven months, the high mortality rate being attributed to starvation and disease. Aided by supplies from England, assistance from the native peoples, and a mandatory work program initiated by John Smith, the colony established agricultural success with the introduction of tobacco production, the single most influential factor in its population growth. Virginia would continue to lead the colonies in both population growth and wealth generation through the end of the eighteenth century.

By 1620, over 1,700 colonists had been shipped to Smith's Chesapeake Bay Colony. Of these, only 350 had survived. The early settlers were plagued by starvation due to failed get-rich-quick schemes; diseases including smallpox and malaria; and chronic troubles with native peoples. New settlers continued to arrive, but their life expectancy was only forty-five years.

Two major policy changes during this time transformed the Virginia colonies into successful enterprises. First, the near-bankrupt Virginia Company surrendered control of the lands and laborers to the colonists. The idea of private property was very attractive to members of the English middle class, who could not expect to own property in overcrowded London.

In addition, the Virginia Company initiated a program called "headright," which offered fifty acres of land to emigrants who could pay their own passage and an additional fifty acres for any servant they brought with them. This attracted a more stable and skilled middle class hoping to establish homesteads. By this time, communities had been established, and news of life in the New World had reached England. Later settlers had the benefit of knowing what lay ahead.

The native population of Virginia in 1607 was estimated at near 24,000. By 1669, it had dwindled to 2,000. Fear and frustration with the indigenous peoples inspired legislation to curb their numbers. Landowners were given license to shoot any Native Americans caught trespassing on their lands. Since the native peoples did not acknowledge land ownership, this was viewed by them as yet another unwarranted assault and provoked hostilities. Diseases, including smallpox and the common cold, for which they had no immunity, further culled the native population. Driven inland, coastal tribes, like the Pequot and the Paspahegh, steadily declined. Inland populations, however, continued to cause problems for the colonists through the eighteenth century.

Between 1620 and 1630, the tobacco boom inspired increased immigration, and the population grew rapidly. From a slim, near-starving 350 settlers in 1616, the population of Virginia exploded, reaching nearly 13,000 by midcentury. At this time, the mortality rate continued to be high. Hard work and disease due to poor sanitation took 25 percent of the population yearly.

In 1650, African slaves comprised only 2 percent of the population. It was much cheaper for a Virginia farmer to purchase an indentured servant. Between 1625 and 1640, 15,000 indentured servants had immigrated to Virginia. As land became scarce due to the headright program and profits grew from tobacco, purchasing slaves became more desirable. Indentured servants would be set free and expect severance pay in the form of land, goods, and/or money. Slaves, on the other hand, were considered property. African slaves were also better accustomed to the demands of farm labor and the hot climate of the American South, and so made more cost-effective workers. By 1770, African slaves made up 13 percent of the population, and by the time of the American Revolution, slaves comprised 45 percent of Virginia's total population.

New Netherland in the Hudson River Valley and New Sweden in the Delaware River Valley did not experience the same growth rate as the more southern and northern colonies. Despite the relatively mild climates and fertile soil in these colonies, the Dutch and Swedish simply did not have the same impetus to leave their homes as did the English. In 1660, New Netherland had only 5,000 colonists, compared with 25,000 in Chesapeake Bay.

New England

Farther north, the first settlements of the Plymouth and Massachusetts Bay Colonies, experienced similar difficulties getting started but benefited from the cooler weather and faster-running waters, which provided a less hospitable environment for disease. The Mayflower carried religious "separatists," or Pilgrims, who had originally left England for Holland, but fearing its vulnerability to Spain and concerned about their children taking up Dutch ways, sought a new refuge in North America. Also on the *Mayflower* were Captain Miles Standish, the ships' officers and crew, indentured servants, and hired artisans; all totaled fewer than 150

people. A long, starving winter and disease killed half the settlers the first year.

Although the Plymouth Colony's initial growth was slower, the fact that the *Mayflower* colonists arrived in family units and shared a common faith that encouraged hard work and community allowed the population to grow naturally. This was augmented by a low, natural mortality rate—only 5 percent from disease—and a relatively long life expectancy of seventy years, if one survived childhood. The arrival of new settlers and the establishment of family farms whose goal was self-support created slow but steady growth. By 1630, about 1,500 colonists lived in the Plymouth Colony.

Between 1630 and 1640, the Great Migration brought many more families to New England. The most successful of the New England colonies was the Massachusetts Bay Colony. By 1660, Massachusetts was home to 20,000 inhabitants of a total New England population of 33,000.

Unlike the Southern colonies, emigrants to New England came seeking a combination of religious freedom and economic opportunity. The lack of a big cash crop like tobacco kept most New Englanders in comparatively modest lifestyles. Most servants came with the families they worked for in England. By 1700, less than 5 percent of the population was indentured and only 2 percent were slaves.

Continued Growth

The population of the American colonies continued to expand in all directions. From 1700 to 1775, population increased steadily at a rate of 3 percent per year. The biggest obstacles for the colonists were in some ways self-generated. Brutal policies with regard to the native peoples and political and legal favoritism for the wealthy and well-connected created an environment of fear and distrust. This motivated Native American hostility and caused dissension among the lower classes and slaves, especially early in settlement. It is interesting to consider how the population might have looked had the colonists attempted to assimilate rather than conquer.

The first American census was taken in 1790. The total population of the sixteen American colonies totaled 3,893,874. The most populous was Virginia, with a total population of 747,550, of which 292,627 were slaves. Pennsylvania followed, with a total population of 433,611, but only 3,707 of these were slaves. The least populous colony was Delaware, with just over

59,000 inhabitants, followed by Rhode Island with 69,112. Only three colonies—Massachusetts, Maine, and Vermont—were without slaves at the time of the census, as they had abolished the institution of slavery.

Population growth everywhere is driven by the ability of the inhabitants to sustain themselves, given available resources. The colonists brought with them a powerful entrepreneurial spirit and were driven by a self-determination that continues to inform the American consciousness to this day. The success and power of this country is rooted in these fundamental ideals.

We should keep in mind, however, that these ideals would not have sustained the colonists without the help of the native peoples. The Native Americans not only helped feed the starving and ill-prepared first settlers but also gave them their biggest cash crop in tobacco and with that the means to build a nation.

Anna Gersh

See also: Children; Cities; Class; Death and Dying; Disease; Marriage and Divorce; Race and Ethnicity (Chronology); Race and Ethnicity (Essay).

Bibliography

Quinn, Arthur. *A New World: An Epic of Colonial America from the Founding of Jamestown to the Fall of Quebec.* Boston: Faber & Faber, 1994.

1790 Census Data. http://fisher.lib.virginia.ed/cgi-local/censusbin/census/cen.pl?year=790.

Taylor, Alan. *American Colonies.* New York: Viking, 2001.

Ward, Harry M. *Colonial America 1607–1763.* Englewood Cliffs, NJ: Prentice Hall, 1991.

Portsmouth, New Hampshire

The earliest inhabitants on the site of Portsmouth were most likely bands of Pigwacket and Piscataqua natives, and their first meetings with English traders and fisherman were largely peaceful exchanges. Early English forays into the region were sporadic and carried out by small parties, and, as such, did not pose a serious threat to native cultures. Natives along the coast served as middlemen between interior tribes and the English in a small-scale fur trade.

For most of its early history, New Hampshire was divided between Puritan immigrants, including some who had been exiled from the much larger Massachusetts Bay Colony, and a mix of adventurers, farmers, and fisherman who concentrated more on turning a profit than creating a utopian society. By 1640, there were four towns in the region that would become New Hampshire. In Strawbery Banke (later, Portsmouth), the older class of adventurers held sway, while Puritans controlled Exeter and Hampton. Hilton's Point (today's Dover) was home to a large population of fishermen, although the town's inhabitants shifted between Puritanism and the more worldly concerns of making money. Throughout the seventeenth century, the Puritan leadership of Massachusetts Bay claimed New Hampshire and tried to annex it—with help from inside the four towns—but, in 1679, the Crown declared the two colonies separate.

Portsmouth depended on Atlantic trade; for this reason, town life was very much oriented toward the sea. A flourishing trade developed in naval stores, and demand for New England's white pine masts and spars spiked in the years of maritime conflict between the English and the Dutch. Naval products were not the only way to make a living in Portsmouth. Farming remained key, and, as the local economy picked up, speculation in real estate also provided early settlers with a way to wealth.

Neighboring Puritans would criticize the Piscataqua River region for fostering a culture of degeneracy, drunkenness, and prostitution, but Portsmouth was not entirely devoid of religious feeling. On several occasions, leading Congregationalists tried to woo preachers from Massachusetts, and they, in turn tried, and failed to establish a church. There were too many people indifferent to religion, but in 1671, a Congregational Church was established.

The establishment of royal government brought a new set of problems to Portsmouth. The royal lieutenant governor, Edward Cranfield, succeeded only in alienating all of the people who had governed previously by punishing smugglers and attempting to curb the power of the church. Another experiment in colonial control, the short-lived Dominion of New England, further muddied the waters of colonial politics. Some of Portsmouth's leaders decided to rejoin Massachusetts, while others withheld payment of taxes to voice their concerns about such a move. Massachusetts's 1691 charter did not include the four New Hampshire towns, so the colony remained effectively independent.

Portsmouth continued to prosper in the eighteenth century as Britain emerged as the world's foremost naval power. Sail makers and rope manufacturers joined mast producers and lumber mills to drive the town's economy forward. Portsmouth became home to a large class of artisans who worked in and around the shipyards. Although local trade was important, Portsmouth remained intimately tied to the larger Atlantic world.

Ships made in New Hampshire took regular trading voyages to the West Indies and England. Farmers in the area surrounding Portsmouth had increased access to imported goods, including salt, sugar, molasses, and rum.

The upheavals of the eighteenth century had a profound effect on Portsmouth. As in other colonies, a small, but vocal Sons of Liberty movement rose in opposition to the Stamp Act of 1765. The Portsmouth Sons of Liberty pressured the stamp collector to resign, and the governor had little desire to provoke unrest by enforcing the act. The Townshend Duties that followed the Stamp Act were a different story, and royal officials and some Portsmouth residents did not oppose the taxes nearly strenuously enough for the Sons of Liberty.

The crisis leading up to the War for Independence revealed deep divisions in Portsmouth. The governor pressed for legislation to control unrest, but the colonial legislature ignored his requests, prompting him to adjourn, and later dissolve, the House of Representatives. The Portsmouth Committee of Correspondence was instrumental in coordinating colony-wide resistance to royal policies, as well as intercolony resistance.

In the wake of the fighting at Lexington and Concord, New Hampshire's already weak royal government fell apart. Meeting at Portsmouth, the House of Representatives took measures to separate from England. The war itself took place entirely outside of New Hampshire's borders, though the state did contribute significantly to the Revolutionary cause.

Matthew Jennings

See also: New Hampshire; New Hampshire (Chronology).

Bibliography

Daniell, Jere R. *Colonial New Hampshire: A History.* Millwood, NY: KTO, 1981.
Heffernan, Nancy Coffey, and Ann Page Stecker. *New Hampshire: Crosscurrents in Its Development.* Rev. ed. Hanover, NH: University Press of New England, 1996.

Potomac River

The Potomac River stretches 290 miles from western Maryland to the Chesapeake Bay, forming the present border between Virginia and Maryland for much of its length. As the river nears the Chesapeake, it forms the border between Washington, D.C., and Virginia. Including the north and south forks of its main tributary, the Shenandoah, the Potomac has two impassable cataracts (with the first only 10 miles north of Washington, D.C., and the second just above Cumberland, Maryland) and a drainage area of 5,960 square miles.

Although the water above the first cataract comes directly from the mountains, below that point the water is brackish for most of its length, becoming saltier as it nears the Chesapeake Bay. The average rise and fall of the tide is approximately 3 feet. A flourishing estuary, the Potomac River basin supports an enormous and extraordinarily diverse ecological system.

Europeans officially discovered the river in 1608, when Captain John Smith visited the northern Chesapeake and recorded the fact that the Powhatan name for the river was Patawomec, although the Chesapeake Bay and many of its tributaries had been explored unofficially by the Spanish as early as 1497. Various Native American nations of Algonquin origin plied the waters of the Potomac for countless generations before the arrival of the Europeans; they lived mainly along the banks of its 170-mile-long tidal reaches. Until 1634, the native peoples were the sole occupants of the banks and surrounding region of the Potomac, rather carelessly guarding their territory from the incursions of warrior raiding parties or European explorers and traders. Native villages and cornfields were scattered along the forested shores of both sides of the river, while the waters of the river itself attracted deer and offered a plentiful supply of oysters, fish, and waterfowl. After the settlement of Maryland in 1634, a constant stream of Europeans invaded the once idyllic waters of the Potomac.

The seventeenth and eighteenth centuries saw massive changes in population along the Potomac, as Native Americans were driven from the region and replaced by English colonists establishing vast tobacco plantations. The initial English settlements started below the first set of falls, but European settlement quickly expanded upriver and displaced the native peoples.

During these early years, in the absence of serviceable roads, the Potomac served as a highway from one settlement to another. The Potomac as a thoroughfare allowed for the reliable transportation of goods (particularly furs, grain, and tobacco) to the Chesapeake, with a return of people and supplies back into the interior. The passage of people upriver was especially important, since it provided a labor source for agriculture and allowed for the movement of settlers to interior regions such as the Ohio Country. Since cataracts obstructed passage directly to the Chesapeake, most transportation went only to and from the cataracts. People portaged their goods around these obstacles and picked up new transport on the other side.

No matter how high up the river one lived, waterfront property was essential, since the river was the only viable way to move goods. This situation made land near the banks particularly valuable and therefore expensive, with questions of ownership and usage sometimes leading to violent confrontations. When the Chesapeake and Ohio Canal bypassed the falls in 1828, direct navigation was opened up as far upstream as Cumberland, Maryland.

Solomon K. Smith

See also: Maryland; Transportation, Water; Virginia.

Bibliography

Beitzell, Edwin W. *Life on the Potomac River.* Berryville: Virginia, 1979.
Gutheim, Frederick. *The Potomac.* New York: Rinehart, 1949.
Stephan R. *Commoners, Tribute, and Chiefs: The Development of Algonquian Culture in the Potomac Valley.* Charlottesville: University Press of Virginia, 1993.

Powhatan (c. 1540–1618)

Powhatan was the most powerful man in eastern Virginia, or Tsenacommacah, when Jamestown was founded there in 1607. Powhatan was the father of Pocahontas and the brother of Opechancanough, leader of the 1622 and 1644 attacks on English Virginia.

The term "Powhatan" may also refer to the Native Americans under the rule of Powhatan, the Powhatan Confederacy, or the specific village of Powhatan, near the site of present-day Richmond, Virginia. Most of the information we have concerning Powhatan and the related Native Americans of late-sixteenth- and early-seventeenth-century Virginia comes from archaeological studies of the region and first-hand accounts left behind by the English.

Powhatan was born between 1540 and 1550. He inherited the inner coastal plain between the James and Mattaponi Rivers. Conservative estimates place the number of people under Powhatan's control between 13,000 and 15,000. Powhatan was born in the village that came to be known as Powhatan.

Powhatan expanded his inheritance through conquest, taking villages along the James and York Rivers. In the years just prior to 1607, Powhatan was still conquering tribes farther to the east and north. His territory eventually stretched over much of eastern Virginia, based on the James, York, and Rappahannock Rivers, and included coastal tribes such as the Chesapeakes. Powhatan tried to persuade neighboring villages by intimidating them with the threat of violence. If that failed, he was willing to use force to accomplish his goals. He is known to have conquered the Kecoughtan people, at the mouth of the James River, by 1596 or 1597. Power appears to have been more concentrated in Powhatan than was common among other Algonquian-speaking tribes, though he did possess the same kind of authority the English expected of a king, or that the Native American communities of the Southeast expected of their chiefs.

Politically, Powhatan ruled over about thirty separate villages; though all of the villages were linguistically similar, there were significant local variations in custom and culture. Each village had its own *werowance,* who governed with Powhatan's approval. If the local *werowance* ran afoul of Powhatan, he could be replaced with a more suitable man, in some cases a brother or son.

In addition to the political power Powhatan held over his various subjects, he was often personally connected to the villages. He solidified his hold on the region by marrying women from the various villages. Typically, Powhatan would keep a wife until she bore him a child. The wife and child would then return to their village of origin until Powhatan called for the child some years later. Powhatan was said to have a dozen temporary wives at once, and about a hundred by the time the English arrived at Jamestown. Powhatan's empire had been expanding throughout his adult life. The arrival of the English stemmed this tide and began a gradual reversal of the process.

When the English came to the peninsula between the James and York Rivers in 1607, they settled on the eastern edge of Powhatan's territory. This provoked two responses from the Powhatan people, who were evidently interested in determining the motives of the English and their military strength. A small party of English colonists ventured up the James River to Powhatan; they were warmly received by Parahunt, Powhatan's son, and seemed to establish friendly relations through the exchange of gifts and trade goods.

POWHATAN
Held this state & fashion when Capt. Smith was deliuered to him prisoner 1607

The powerful Algonquin chief Powhatan—portrayed here in Captain John Smith's *Generall Historie of Virginia*—headed a confederacy of native tribes in the Virginia Tidewater when English settlers established Jamestown in 1607. *(Brown Brothers, Sterling, Pennsylvania)*

At roughly the same time, 200 men had attacked the fort at Jamestown, killing ten colonists. Further minor assaults occurred over the span of a week. A tentative peace was reached when the Powhatan claimed that they had not made the attacks and that they could stop the aggressors. John Smith was captured and adopted into Powhatan society through a complex series of rituals, one of which involved being rescued from death by Pocahontas, which was probably more of a performance than an actual near-execution.

Through the bond formed with John Smith, the military leader of the Jamestown colony, Powhatan believed he had adopted Jamestown as another subordinate village; in exchange for being allowed to remain in Virginia, the English would provide Powhatan with two cannons and a grindstone. The English did not understand the terms of the exchange and never provided the cannons or stone; they had their own ideas about colonization and conquest, most of which ran at cross-purposes with Powhatan's plans. Moreover, shortly after his adoption, John Smith left Virginia and Powhatan faced a new colonial government, one that understood even less clearly the terms of the agreement between Powhatan and Smith.

In 1608, Smith returned to Virginia, and in October, Powhatan demonstrated again his feelings of superiority toward the English. King James I had sent Powhatan some gifts and a crown, which Powhatan was invited to Jamestown to receive. Powhatan's alleged response was

> if your king have sent me presents, I also am a king, and this [is] my land. Eight days I will stay to receive them. Your father is to come to me, not I to him; nor yet to your for fort: neither will I bite at such a bait.

The English ended up bringing the gifts to Powhatan, but problems arose when Powhatan was supposed to kneel to receive the crown. He steadfastly refused to submit to the English, and it was only by force that the English were able to bend Powhatan enough to place the crown on his head. Although English recorders speculated that Powhatan did not understand the importance of the crown or of kneeling to receive it, the more likely scenario is that Powhatan understood precisely what was going on and wanted no part of it.

Powhatan's problems were compounded by the fact that English settlements began to expand into the James River valley in 1610. Although Jamestown was weak and Powhatan could have wiped out the colony if he had chosen to do so, he did not—perhaps recognizing that the English could provide valuable assistance against other villages that Powhatan wanted to control. Jamestown also began to receive regular shipments of supplies and people from England.

The expansion of the colony was cause for alarm to Powhatan, and the first Anglo-Powhatan War, which lasted from 1610 to 1614, did little to slow the spread of the English into Powhatan's territory. Scholars have debated whether the actions of the Powhatan and the English actually constituted a state of war. It may be more accurate to say that the Anglo-Powhatan relationship soured and that both parties began to behave more aggressively, weakening the chances of any lasting peace between the two groups.

In 1610, Powhatan's personal life was also in crisis; he had apparently developed serious feelings for one of his wives and was refusing to send her and his child away, causing a small political incident. Hostilities between the English and the Powhatan ceased temporarily when Powhatan allowed his daughter Pocahontas to marry John Rolfe, a Virginia planter.

In the long run, the arrival of the English, their refusal to play by Powhatan's rules, and their eventual ability to feed themselves spelled disaster for Powhatan. The world into which he had been born was rapidly changing, and his people began to look elsewhere for answers. Opechancanough, his brother, assumed practical leadership of the Powhatan people, and Powhatan remained chief in title only.

The year 1617 brought more bad news. Pocahontas had died in England, and an epidemic, perhaps smallpox, wiped out many of the Powhatan. Retiring from public life, Powhatan died a year later in 1618. He had consolidated his power over most of eastern Virginia by the start of the seventeenth century but had watched his control slip away when he could not control the pace of English settlement.

Matthew Jennings

See also: Jamestown; Native American–European Relations; Native Americans; Opechancanough; Pocahontas; Powhatan Confederacy; Virginia; Virginia (Chronology).

Bibliography

Gleach, Frederic W. *Powhatan's World and Colonial Virginia: A Conflict of Cultures.* Lincoln: University of Nebraska Press, 1997.

Rountree, Helen C. *Pocahontas's People: The Powhatan Indians of Virginia Through Four Centuries.* Norman: University of Oklahoma Press, 1990.

———. *The Powhatan Indians of Virginia: Their Traditional Culture.* Norman: University of Oklahoma Press, 1989.

Powhatan Confederacy

By the time the English established their colony at Jamestown in 1607, the native villages under the chief Powhatan numbered around thirty. These communities ranged across much of eastern Virginia.

Whether or not a confederacy existed under Powhatan's leadership has been a matter of contentious debate within the scholarly community. Some scholars insist that to use the term *confederacy* is improper, since Powhatan gained control of Virginia through violence and intimidation. Others argue that the term does not imply willing acceptance of Powhatan's rule, but rather that the villages were linked and their residents often acted in concert. Apart from the squabble over terminology, it is more important to consider Powhatan culture and political structures and how these forces shaped the colonization of early Virginia.

Powhatan—born between 1540 and 1550—inherited the position of paramount chief and quickly expanded the territory under his control throughout the late sixteenth and early seventeenth centuries. Although he expanded his territory by conquest, his position was hardly analogous to that held by Queen Elizabeth I in England. He was not a monarch and did not have "subjects" in the traditional sense.

Powhatan's territory, Tsenacommacah, was split up into various districts. The districts were broken down into individual villages and other types of settlements. Each village had its own *werowance,* or chief, often the leader of the tribe before Powhatan arrived, who served at Powhatan's discretion. Powhatan also placed relatives—because of matrilineal inheritance these were more often siblings than children—in positions of power throughout his growing empire.

The nature of Powhatan society prevented the chief from making all but the largest strategic decisions in the governance of his people. Most affairs were handled at the local level by officials with tributary ties to Powhatan. Powhatan could also not act independently of the advice of his priests and councilors.

Chiefs did play large roles in Powhatan ceremonial life, presiding over the rituals that transformed boys into men and celebrated the ripening of the first of the year's corn. The chiefs' prominence in events like these, when they were honored by their wives, priests, and ordinary people, probably led the English who met them to inflate their role in their peoples' everyday lives. Chiefs also acted as stewards for tribal lands and fulfilled other political duties.

When the English arrived at Jamestown, Powhatan's empire in eastern Virginia was at the height of its power. The English had superior technology and were every bit as expansionist and nationalist as the Powhatan. They also had fewer people and a propensity for dying of starvation and disease. Moderate estimates place the Powhatan population at the time between 12,000 and 14,000; Powhatan tried to incorporate the English into his empire at the same time the English tried to expand theirs into Virginia.

Powhatan went about this task in a culturally specific way. His forces captured John Smith and took him on a tour of Powhatan territory. Smith met various native military and political leaders from throughout eastern Virginia, including Powhatan and his brother

Opechancanough. While Smith's perceptions were colored by his Englishness, his writings show him to be a keen observer of Powhatan society.

Smith's life was threatened three times, finally and most famously by Powhatan. In this instance, one of Powhatan's daughters—Pocahontas—intervened. It is unclear whether the danger facing Smith was real or ritual, but most scholars believe he was the unknowing party to a ceremony through which Jamestown became another village tributary to Powhatan.

The English did not behave like subjects of Powhatan, however. They acted aggressively, pressing their Native American neighbors for food, fur, skins, and territory. As a result, the English and the Powhatan fought each other sporadically from 1610 to 1614. More destructive attacks, led by Opechancanough, occurred in 1622 and 1644.

The end of the Powhatan Confederacy is hard to place. Powhatan himself retired from public life in 1617 and died a year later. The paramount chieftancy was no longer in place as of 1650. Algonquin resistance to English colonization continued well into the seventeenth century, but white colonists overran their settlements almost entirely in the 1676 fighting associated with Bacon's Rebellion. By 1700, most Native Americans still remaining in Virginia lived on reservation-type lands.

Matthew Jennings

See also: Jamestown; Native American–European Relations; Native Americans; Opechancanough; Powhatan; Virginia; Virginia (Chronology).

Bibliography

Gleach, Frederic W. *Powhatan's World and Colonial Virginia: A Conflict of Cultures.* Lincoln: University of Nebraska Press, 1997.

Rountree, Helen C., ed. *Powhatan Foreign Relations, 1500–1722.* Charlottesville: University Press of Virginia, 1993.

———. *The Powhatan Indians of Virginia: Their Traditional Culture.* Norman: University of Oklahoma Press, 1989.

Praying Towns

The term "praying towns" generally refers to Christian Native American villages set up by the Massachusetts Bay Colony between 1651 and 1674, although similar settlements were also created in the seventeenth century by the French in Canada and by native converts on Martha's Vineyard and in New Plymouth during the same period. Since Europeans believed in a close connection between church and state, those efforts brought colonial political influence along with the Gospel. In addition, missionaries believed that natives needed to be "civilized" as well as Christianized and created the mission towns for that purpose.

Puritan leaders in Massachusetts believed that mission communities would allow them to isolate and control potential converts in order to completely change native ways. Their envoy, Reverend John Eliot, learned Algonquian from a Pequot War captive. He was spurned in his first effort, preaching to the Massachusett sachem, but, in 1647, he gained the support of Waban, head of Nonantum (modern Newton). The Puritan minister drew a curious and anxious crowd that grew at each of his five visits, and he convinced many to embrace "civilized" life and Protestantism. The native converts wore English clothes, cut their hair, and forswore many old customs.

In 1651, Waban and Eliot founded the first Praying Town, Natick, along the edge of Nipmuck territory. Natives who went to live there gained material assistance, education, and deeper connections to the colonists and their powerful god. Residents were required to follow a legal code designed to force them into English social and political patterns, including gender roles and monogamy. At the same time, pre-mission community leaders (like Waban) became leaders in the praying towns, and they enforced a traditional regard for community peace and stability, although Eliot and English magistrates supervised the native courts and reviewed all major decisions.

Not all Europeans demanded that native converts embrace wholesale change. The French Jesuits preferred to work with village leaders, and (after initial failures) the few mission towns that they set up were largely governed by native chiefs and did not require their members to give up all of their customs. Among the English, the Mayhews, who owned Martha's Vineyard, asked Christian Native Americans to remain loyal and pay tribute to their leaders. In New Plymouth, Richard Bourne and John Cotton followed the pattern set by Mayhew, permitting converts to maintain many traditions not tolerated by Eliot's followers. They gained enough support to create a Christian American Indian village at Mashpee and small churches scattered around Cape Cod and the villages west of Plymouth.

The praying towns helped spark King Philip's War. By 1674, Eliot had created a network of seven praying towns, and, that year, he brought Native American Christian leaders to seven Nipmuck towns farther west, alarming many native sachems. John Sassamon, one of Eliot's most prominent converts, became secretary to Metacom (King Philip) but earned his enmity when he warned the English that the Wampanoag sachem planned war. In February 1675, Sassamon's body was found under pond ice; those accused of his murder were three of Metacom's advisers, and their trial was clearly aimed at the sachem.

A few months later, the terrible war erupted. The "praying Indians" rejected Metacom and asked to join colonial forces, but they were deeply suspected of treachery and were confined to Deer Island in Boston Bay in the fall. Native Americans on Cape Cod and the Vineyard, on the other hand, managed to remain in their villages and out of the conflict. When Massachusetts finally approved native enlistment, the praying Indians contributed critical scouting skills. As the war ended, they were released from Deer Island.

Most of the few Native Americans who remained in Massachusetts soon resettled Natick and three other praying towns. These groups (ironically) increased their autonomy, particularly after Eliot died in 1690, and provincial laws barred the sale of their lands without permission of the assembly. A decade later, when Massachusetts annexed New Plymouth, the Native American residents of the praying towns there obtained similar protections. But throughout the eighteenth century, these remaining communities were battered by changes in the colonial economy; by the terrible effects of epidemics, alcoholism, and indebtedness; and by the loss of men in wars or to migratory labor.

The survivors adapted by teetering along the line between isolation from colonial society and culture and immersion in it, seeking to satisfy their needs in the new environment while maintaining critical boundaries against white settlers. By the time of the American Revolution, only a handful of such towns remained, led by native ministers, who preached in the Wampanoag language and were largely acculturated to English ways.

Daniel R. Mandell

See also: Christ and Christianity; King Philip's War; Missions; Native American–European Relations; Native Americans; Religion (Chronology); Religion (Essay); Religions, Native American.

Bibliography

Axtell, James. *The Invasion Within: The Contest of Cultures in Colonial North America.* New York: Oxford University Press, 1985.

Gookin, Daniel. "Historical Collections of the Indians of New England." *Collections of the Massachusetts Historical Society,* 1:1 (1792): 141–226.

Mandell, Daniel R. *Behind the Frontier: Indian Communities in Eighteenth-Century Eastern Massachusetts.* Lincoln: University of Nebraska Press, 1996.

Precious Metals

The quest for gold and silver played a large role in the European colonization of the Americas, particularly in its earliest stages. Columbus noted in the diary of his first voyage that the people he met wore gold jewelry; this observation, combined with the mistaken belief that he had reached a land near Asia, led Ferdinand and Isabella to commission a second voyage.

Relations between the Taino and the Spaniards soon soured, when Columbus as governor instituted a tributary system whereby each Taino over the age of 14 was required to turn in a certain amount of gold. The Taino and other native peoples around the Gulf of Mexico died quickly in the Caribbean gold mines.

From the enslaved mine workers, the Spanish heard rumors of an inland native empire with large stone cities and vast amounts of gold. In Mexico's central valley, Hernando Cortéz took it upon himself to conquer the Aztecs. Successful conquistadors were able to keep a good deal of their plunder, but a fifth had to go to the Spanish Crown. As a portent of troubles to come, French pirates also stole much of the gold that the Spanish had stolen from the Aztecs as it made its way toward Spain in 1523.

A similar war of conquest led by Pizarro felled the Inca empire of Peru. Within a matter of years, the extraction of precious metals, whether through plunder or mining, had filled Spanish treasure ships and made the Spanish empire the largest and most powerful in the world. In North America, many tribes managed to lure Spanish explorers out of their territory with fantastic tales of gold-rich civilizations. These rumors propelled Spanish exploration of vast areas of the interior, without, however, their discovering up the precious metals they sought.

Ultimately, silver mining, though less romantic than the search for gold, provided a surer source of income for Spain. By the end of the seventeenth century, imperial bureaucrats had begun to equate control over American resources with much of the success of Spain itself. This administrative shift coincided with the expansion of silver mining in New Spain (roughly Mexico) and Peru.

Silver mining had a dramatic impact on the form of Spanish society in the Americas. Significant numbers of African slaves were imported to work in the silver mines, and native people from all over New Spain were brought to mining towns, not only to mine ore, but also to provide various services that cropped up around the mines. The Spanish drew on medieval (and earlier) experience with mines on the Iberian Peninsula as they constructed a network of mines in the Americas. They also succeeded in tying the mining industry into the developing Spanish Atlantic commercial world.

The English were not immune to gold fever, and the earliest adventurers at Jamestown spent an inordinate amount of time searching for precious metals in the Chesapeake. This futile gold hunt was one factor that contributed to the Jamestown colony's disastrous early years.

From 1500 to 1650, the Spanish-American empire exported more than 180 tons of gold and 16,000 tons of silver, a fifth of which went to the Spanish Crown, accounting for 25 percent of its revenue. Spain's wealth drew attention from other European nations, which, according to the tenets of mercantilism, were in constant competition for a finite amount of trade. England, France, Holland, and Portugal all launched devastating raids on Spanish treasure ships. Piracy and smuggling spread newfound Spanish wealth throughout Europe. Francis Drake earned the favor of Sir Walter Raleigh and Queen Elizabeth I with his daring raids on Spanish treasure ships and Atlantic colonies.

The rapid influx of such a huge amount of hard currency also had mixed effects on the development of the Spanish economy at home. It experienced crippling inflation and slow growth in manufacturing relative to the rest of Europe. Dutch, English, and French manufacturers picked up the slack, ushering in a new period of economic prosperity.

Matthew Jennings

See also: New Spain; Spanish Colonies on Mainland North America (Chronology).

Bibliography

Stein, Stanley J., and Barbara H. Stein. *Silver, Trade, and War: Spain and America in the Making of Early Modern Europe.* Baltimore: Johns Hopkins University Press, 2000.

Taylor, Alan. *American Colonies.* New York: Viking, 2001.

Presbyterianism

The term "presbyterianism" can refer to many things. It can refer to a form of church government that is structured around elders (from the Greek *presbuteros*) or a theological system based on covenant theology and the sovereignty of God. It may also refer to a church movement that began with the Reformation and continues to the present day.

Although there are many heroes of the Continental Reformation, John Calvin is most widely associated with the Presbyterian form of church government. Calvin was a French theologian who fled to Geneva to avoid persecution. There, he took the helm of the Reformation in Switzerland and initiated his Presbyterian form of government in both church and state. Calvin envisioned two types of elders: (1) ruling elders, who had the primary task of governance; (2) teaching elders, who were to preach and teach the word of God. A systematic presentation of Calvin's doctrine can be found in his *Institutes of the Christian Religion.*

Under Calvin's influence, Presbyterian theology emphasized God's sovereign reign over against his creation. God's righteousness and goodness were contrasted to man's utter depravity. In this view, apart from God's grace and love, humanity is unable to restore itself to wholeness. Only through God's predestination are individuals redeemed by the incarnation and atonement of Jesus Christ, God's only son. Just as Adam is the representative (federal head) of all of humanity in its sinfulness, Jesus Christ is the representative (federal head) of humanity's salvation.

John Knox, a Scot, spent some time with Calvin in Geneva. Although he did not possess Calvin's theological rigor and political genius, Knox was solely responsible for the introduction of Presbyterianism into Scotland. Knox wrote the first *Book of Discipline* and the *Directory of Worship,* which are the foundational texts for Presbyterian order and worship today. Knox also organized the first General Assembly in Scotland. Knox was the primary vehicle for the Reformation in Scotland, whereby Roman Catholicism was replaced by Presbyterianism in the latter part of the sixteenth century. Today, the Presbyterian movement in Scotland is known as the Church of Scotland.

Many Scots migrated to Ireland in early part of the seventeenth century and brought along their Presbyterian theology and form of church government. A presbytery was formed in Ulster in 1642, and by the end of the next decade, five presbyteries existed in Northern Ireland. In 1681, the presbytery of Laggan authorized Francis Makemie to receive a call to the ministry from a colony on the Eastern shore of Virginia. Later, in the early 1700s, economic, political, and religious hardships initiated a migration of Scots-Irish to America. By 1776, over 250,000 Scots-Irish had made the trip across the Atlantic to the New World. There was no specifically Presbyterian colony, but Presbyterian churches were scattered throughout the Middle colonies by the beginning of the nineteenth century.

Makemie, considered the founder of American Presbyterianism, was instrumental in forming the first presbytery of the early colonies around 1706. Presbyterianism was quickly being established in this region, so that, by 1717, four presbyteries gathered together to form the first Synod of New York and Philadelphia. In 1729, they adopted the Westminster Confession of Faith; in May 1789, four regional synods (New York and New Jersey, Philadelphia, Virginia, and the Carolinas) held their first general assembly. All of this occurred despite a schism that lasted from 1741 to 1758.

Although modern Presbyterians draw from a variety of confessions and catechisms, the Westminster Confession of Faith and Shorter and Longer Catechisms have remained at the center of American Presbyterianism. The impetus for the confession and catechisms came out of the restructuring of the Church of England by the Puritans. The desire was to have an English church that was Calvinistic in theology and Presbyterian in government.

The English Parliament convened the Westminster Assembly in 1643 in Westminster Abbey. This assembly comprised 121 ministers (or "divines"), ten members of the House of Lords, twenty members of

The First Presbyterian Church in Philadelphia is believed to have originated when founder Francis Makemie organized a congregation there in 1698. The building itself was erected in 1704 and redesigned with a classical temple facade in the last years of the century. *(Yale University Art Gallery, New Haven, Connecticut/Bridgeman Art Library)*

the House of Commons, and eight influential Scotsmen. It was overwhelmingly Presbyterian. The assembly was convened to advise Parliament in the restructuring of the Church of England and to navigate a clear theological path among Catholicism, Arminianism, and Anabaptist tendencies. The confession and catechisms were delivered to Parliament in 1647. The assembly continued to meet until 1649. Although the work of the assembly never was fully adopted in England, the Scottish General Assembly accepted the Westminster Confession and Catechisms in 1647.

Today, there are several Presbyterian denominations in the United States. The largest is the Presbyterian Church (U.S.A), which has over 2.5 million members and over 11,000 congregations.

Robert Leach

See also: Anglican Church; Reformation; Religion (Chronology); Religion (Essay).

Bibliography

Book of Confessions: Study Edition. Louisville, KY: Geneva, 1996.

Drury, Clifford Merrill. *Presbyterian Panorama.* Philadelphia: Presbyterian Church in the United States of America, 1952.

Hanzsche, Wm. Thomson. *The Presbyterians: The Story of a Stanch and Sturdy People.* Philadelphia: Westminster, 1934.

McKim, Donald. *Introducing the Reformed Faith.* Louisville, KY: Westminster-John Knox, 2001.

Smylie, James H. *A Brief History of the Presbyterians.* Louisville, KY: Geneva, 1996.

Torrance, Thomas F. *Scottish Theology from John Knox to John McLeod Campbell.* Edinburgh, UK: T&T Clark, 1996.

Prisons and Punishment

On the eve of the European invasion of North America, the various aboriginal nations each possessed their own set of laws and norms dictating proper behavior. Early European immigrants, including the Spanish, Dutch, French, and English, brought with them their distinct legal systems. English forms of punishment eventually predominated in most of North America, although colonial criminal law differed from justice in England in several important ways.

Criminal law in England at the beginning of the seventeenth century distinguished between serious crimes (felonies) and less serious offenses (misdemeanors). A wide variety of punishments existed in England, most which relied on the public shaming of offenders.

The stocks, branding, whipping, and mutilation were imposed to embarrass the wrongdoer in the hope that he or she would not reoffend. The goal of punishment was not to reform prisoners but to frighten them into behaving lawfully. If the offender had committed only a minor offense, or if the convict was wealthy, a shaming punishment might not be imposed; instead, such offenders sometimes paid a fine.

Persistent offenders often faced transportation or the death penalty. From 1718 to 1775, the English courts sentenced approximately 50,000 felons to transportation, whereby they were shipped to America and sold as indentured servants. The English criminal law of the eighteenth century, often referred to as the "Bloody Code," prescribed capital punishment for upwards of 160 felonious offences by the 1760s, though many convicts received reprieves through benefit of clergy, transportation, or royal pardon.

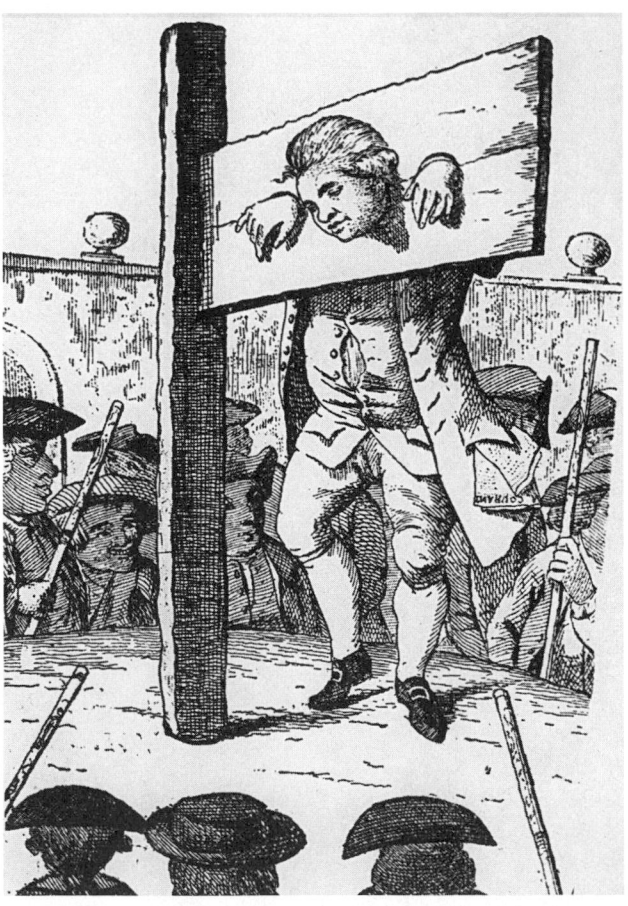

Confinement in stocks, sometimes for extended periods, was a common punishment in colonial America, especially in Puritan New England. Those convicted of what were considered serious crimes, including moral offenses, were thus subjected to public shame and ridicule. *(Brown Brothers, Sterling, Pennsylvania)*

Punishment in America

In the first permanent English settlement at Jamestown, Virginia, established in 1607, the Virginia Company established a form of military law to enforce order. The "Lawes Divine, Morall, and Martiall" (1611) imposed harsh sanctions for many crimes, including economic crimes. For example, Virginia law imposed capital punishment for colonists who left without permission. Death was also the sanction for seamen who entered Virginia and sold goods at prices below those prescribed by the colony's government. After the creation of a House of Burgesses in 1619, Virginians ended their short but harsh experience with martial law.

The American colonies received the full spectrum of punishments employed in England. In small colonial communities, shaming punishments were especially important. Usually very public in nature, they were intended to cause humiliation such that the offender would not again step out of line. Warnings and fines were the weakest forms of punishment employed for small offenses. More serious crimes led to the use of the stocks, the pillory, or whipping. For offenders deemed likely to reoffend, communities employed more permanent shaming punishments such as mutilation (for example, the cutting off an offender's ear). Adulterers might be required to permanently wear the letter "A" denoting their crime, while a murderer could have an "M" branded on his or her hand. Repeat offenders could also be banished.

As in England, the death penalty was the ultimate form of punishment, with hanging the standard method of inflicting death. Murder and rape were usually capital crimes. The early leaders of the colonies also imposed the death penalty for several crimes that in England were not capital offenses, though, for the most part, the colonial courts actually hung few people for these offences. For example, Massachusetts made adultery a capital offense, but executions for adultery ended by the mid-seventeenth century. Similarly, the courts of New England ended hangings for buggery after 1673. Despite the extension of capital punishment to a few additional crimes, the colonies inflicted the death penalty less frequently than did authorities in England. Before 1660, Massachusetts executed fifteen people; and prior to the American Revolution, Pennsylvania executed only ninety-four people.

Incarceration was not an important form of punishment during the colonial period. The notion that separating criminals from the general population would lead to reform was a foreign idea; instead, it was thought important that a criminal should be exposed to the censure of his or her fellow citizens. Therefore, the penitentiary was not developed until the nineteenth century.

Jails, however, existed during the colonial period. For example, the first Boston jail opened in 1635. By 1776, each of the 14 counties in Massachusetts was required to have a jail. Jails were typically small and unimpressive structures that served a variety of functions. They held debtors and prisoners awaiting trial or punishment. Jails were intended to coerce compliance rather than to apply sanctions or rehabilitate. Living conditions in these jails were deplorable. Often overcrowded, they typically kept inmates in communal rooms with few amenities and little heat or food. Houses of correction supplemented jails, confining vagrants and paupers.

Punishment and Religion

Religion was an important feature of crime and punishment in colonial America, probably even more so than in England. Many of the religious dissenters who migrated to America, such as the Puritans of New England and the Quakers of Pennsylvania, were especially interested in enforcing religious norms. Most of the colonies therefore made little distinction between sin and crime.

Early Puritan legal codes demonstrate the importance of religion in the justice system of colonial America. The 1648 *Laws and Liberties of Massachusetts* dictated that heresy and blasphemy were crimes, that Jesuits entering the colony were to be expelled, and that Anabaptists who continued to hold their beliefs were to be banished. In addition, Massachusetts had strong laws against Quakers, hanging two Quakers in 1659. The Sabbath was also taken seriously and enforced by the criminal law. Fines could be imposed for skipping church services, for example. The connection between religion and the criminal law was perhaps most graphically illustrated in the *Laws and Liberties of Massachusetts,* which included a Biblical citation supporting each of the code's capital offenses.

The courts acted as the secular arm of the churches, prosecuting individuals for sexual crimes such as adultery, sodomy, buggery, and fornication. The punishments for some of these crimes were serious, especially during the seventeenth century, when, for example, buggery was a capital offense in Puritan New England. Courts also frequently prosecuted less serious sexual offenses. Unmarried couples convicted of fornication were fined, whipped, or placed in stocks. Religious offenses also existed outside of New England. For example, Virginia imposed penalties for failing to attend church and applied the death penalty to those convicted of rape, sodomy, larceny, murder, or sacrilege.

The Demographics of Punishment

Most of those punished in colonial America were poor men. Offenders were typically laborers, slaves, servants, and poor freeholders, not ministers of religion or wealthy merchants. In eighteenth-century New York, men were accused in 94.4 percent of violent crimes and 73.9 percent of thefts. Similarly, in Massachusetts, women committed only 19.7 percent of serious crimes between 1673 and 1774. African American slaves consistently faced especially harsh punishment. In the South, masters and overseers brutally punished many minor offenses summarily on the plantation, frequently with the whip. Slaves also faced more frequent execution than whites; as a result, capital punishment was more common in the South than in the North. From 1706 to 1784, the courts of Virginia sentenced 555 slaves to death. Harsh punishment of slaves was not limited to the South, however; it also occurred in the North. For example, prosecutions for an alleged slave conspiracy in New York in 1741 led to the execution of over thirty slaves.

Women, while constituting a relatively low percentage of all offenders, were disproportionately punished for certain crimes. Most charges of infanticide, for example, were levied against women. Women were also more frequently charged with witchcraft than were men. Witchcraft was a crime in England, and the 1648 *Laws and Liberties of Massachusetts* made witchcraft a capital offense in the colony. Witchcraft trials were most common in the North, the most notorious being the 1692 witch trials in Salem, Massachusetts, when twenty people—most of whom were women—were executed.

By the eighteenth century, there was a shift away from directing punishment at sin. Colonial society was changing as immigrants continued to enter the colony and cities and towns grew in size. The old elites faced greater difficulties in controlling the population through traditional shaming punishments. The colonies increasingly placed more emphasis on property offenses and less on moral ones. In addition, in the years preceding the Revolution, English officials utilized the criminal law to limit political dissent; for example, officials used the law of treason to punish those who challenged English authority.

Changing ideas about the value and purposes of punishment stirred in the late eighteenth century, though the most significant alterations in punishment did not occur until after the American War for Independence. The Italian Marquis de Beccaria, in his 1766 *Essay on Crimes and Punishment,* reflected and encouraged a growing compassion for those convicted of wrongdoing. He also maintained that the certainty, not the severity, of punishment was the key to deterrence. Criticism from commentators such as the Englishman John Howard slowly emerged about the deplorable state of jails. Such ideas about punishment ultimately led to the construction of the large nineteenth-century American penitentiaries, where it was hoped that inmates would be reformed by serving long prison sentences.

R. Blake Brown

See also: Crime; Debt and Debtor's Prison; Law and Courts.

Bibliography

Beattie, J. M. *Crime and the Courts in England, 1660–1800.* Princeton, NJ: Princeton University Press, 1986.

Chapin, Bradley. *Criminal Justice in Colonial America, 1606–1660.* Athens: University of Georgia Press, 1983.

Friedman, Lawrence M. *Crime and Punishment in American History.* New York: Basic Books, 1993.

Greenburg, Douglas. *Crime and Law Enforcement in the Colony of New York, 1691–1796.* Ithaca, NY: Cornell University Press, 1974.

Hull, N. E. *Female Felons: Women and Serious Crime in Colonial Massachusetts.* Urbana: University of Illinois Press, 1987.

Johnson, Herbert A., and Nancy Travis Wolfe. *History of Criminal Justice.* 2nd ed. Cincinnati, OH: Anderson Publishing, 1996.

Proclamation of 1763

At the conclusion of the French and Indian War, known as the Seven Years' War in Europe, the British extended their rule across French Canada and into Florida through the 1763 Treaty of Paris. In this process, they encountered significant problems with Native Americans, who had preferred French colonial policy and mistrusted British intentions.

After suppressing Pontiac's Rebellion, the British needed to formulate a plan to keep the peace on the frontier and maintain the loyalty of the Native Americans. The Proclamation of 1763 was issued by King George III on October 7 from his court in London on the advice of Secretary of State Lord Egremont and

President of the Board of Trade Lord Shelburne. It attempted to mandate a solution to Native American mistrust and establish British rule over the new lands. A limit to settlers spreading over the Appalachians had already been implemented by Colonel Henry Boquet in 1761; that decision provided a useful model for the proclamation.

The proclamation formally annexed the French islands of Cape Breton and St. John's; expanded the colony of Georgia between the Alatamaha River and St. Mary's; and set up four new imperial government units in East and West Florida, Quebec, and Grenada (the Caribbean Grenadines), including all the associated royal officials and their powers. Veterans of the French and Indian War were granted land, preferably in the three new continental British possessions, based on their ranks, ranging from field-grade officers receiving 5,000 acres to a private soldier's claim of 50 acres.

The proclamation also forbade further British settlement west of the Appalachians or beyond the headlands of the rivers flowing into the Atlantic Ocean, effectively keeping the white population on the East Coast. Those lands to the west were considered the possessions of the "Indians," and all but royal officials were forbidden to grant claims or to purchase any of it, as Native Americans were under the personal protection of the British monarch.

The proclamation stirred heated feelings amongst the colonists, many of whom had quickly taken advantage of the peace to buy up western land claims that were now worthless. Colonial celebrities—such as Washington, Franklin, George Mercer, and the Lee family—were heavily invested in land speculation in the rich Ohio Valley, and their fortunes suffered because of the royal decision.

Colonists believed that the king and his ministers wanted to keep the settlers close to the coastline because this made them easier to tax and police, although Shelburne hoped that the westward limit would help to encourage the settlement of Quebec and Florida. The colonists were also angered by the privileged position granted to Native Americans, including additional royal regulation of the fur trade and the prohibition of the sale of rum or rifled weapons to the tribes. Royal Indian agents threatened the trade conducted by colonists and cut off their ability to make quasi-legal land transactions.

For the British, the Proclamation of 1763 made good sense. It offered the tribes proof that Britain would honor its claims to essential hunting grounds and protect them from fraud and underhanded business deal-

ings—both were much-missed protections under the French royal officials. Ideally, the proclamation also would encourage the colonists to settle in underpopulated areas of the Eastern seaboard before pushing inland to areas where there would likely be conflict with Native Americans.

The Proclamation of 1763 was meant as a temporary halt to colonial expansion, pending investigation and governmental regulation. It was followed up in 1764 by a more precise drawing of the western boundaries of the individual colonies, largely the work of the northern and southern Indian agents Sir William Johnson and John Bruce, along with elaborated rules for colonial dealings with Native Americans. The problem was that settlers already in the forbidden areas refused to leave, while new immigrants crossed the borders in spite of the proclamation, triggering continual problems with the tribes, as their promised lands were encroached on. More fraudulent deals also took place for the purchase of land.

The British responded by stepping up their presence in the former French chain of frontier forts and constructing more defensive works along the line of the proclamation. The expense of these fortifications, which seemed pointless to the colonists without the French as an enemy, triggered many of the tax demands that fueled the American Revolution.

Margaret Sankey

See also: Appalachia; French and Indian War; Land and Real Estate; Maps and Surveys; Ohio Country.

Bibliography

Abernethy, Thomas. *Western Lands and the American Revolution.* New York: Russell and Russell, 1959.

James, Alfred P. *George Mercer of the Ohio Company: A Study in Frustration.* Pittsburgh: University of Pittsburgh Press, 1963.

Johnson, Cecil. *British West Florida, 1763–1783.* Hamden, CT: Archon, 1971.

Property and Property Rights

The concepts of property and property rights in colonial America reflected common law patterns established in England. Property was categorized as either real property or personal property. Simply put, real property was land, but it also included anything growing on, attached to, or erected on the land that could not easily be removed without causing injury to the land. All other property was considered "personalty," or personal property. Of the two categories of property, real property was given more economic and legal significance.

In 1290, England's Statute Emptores established the principle in common law that land should be freely alienable, allowing it to be transferred or conveyed from one person to another. This statute, along with subsequent legislation, was based on four separate theories: (1) land should be available for its highest and best use; (2) land owners should be able to sell property, utilizing the profits acquired therefrom; (3) land owners should be encouraged to make improvements to the land, but they will not do so if there is no opportunity to sell the property later for a profit; and (4) creditors should be able to reach the property interests of debtors who are in default.

There were three recognized restraints on alienation in common law: disabling restraints, forfeiture restraints, and promissory restraints. A disabling restraint prevented a person from receiving property, a grantee, from transferring his interest in that land to another. Any attempts to do so would be considered null and void. If land were subject to a forfeiture restraint, any attempt to transfer or convey the land would result in the land being forfeited by the present owner in favor of a previously appointed recipient. Additionally, a grantee could willingly enter into a promissory restraint in which he would promise not to transfer his interest in land.

Settlers in colonial America often placed additional restraints on the use and ownership of property. Landownership, when associated with community membership, required owners to utilize their land in a manner consistent with communal views of appropriate land use. In such cases, landowners ran the risk of losing the right to their property if they did not use the land in a manner deemed appropriate by the community in which they lived.

In many New England towns, for instance, individuals owning parcels of land within the town limits were required to erect structures on them on penalty of losing the land. Several colonies insisted that owners of land suitable for waterwheel sites build mills or risk losing the land to someone who was willing to construct a mill for the public good.

In New York City, landowners were subject to fines if they failed to remove poisonous or foul-smelling weeds from the areas surrounding the front door of their homes. In one New Hampshire town, landowners were required to cut down trees on their property that offended their neighbors. In contrast, residents of Pennsylvania were required to plant foliage to improve the aesthetic value of their property.

Individuals as Property Owners in Colonial America

Upon arriving in colonial America, English settlers found an abundance of fertile and inexpensive land that could be acquired quite easily. It would be inaccurate, however, to say that all people immigrating to the American colonies were able to own property of their own. The right to own property was often tied to one's religious beliefs, social status, race, and gender.

Availability and distribution of land was intertwined with political patronage and nepotism, and the stability of ownership was often precarious. Following the Spanish and Indian Wars, for example, higher taxes were imposed to cover the immense war debt. Small-scale Southern farmers were the hardest hit by this legislation. Finding it difficult to remain competitive in agricultural markets, they were forced to sell their holdings to large plantation owners at prices far below the land's actual value. The scene was thus set for the emergence of an economy based on elitist planters and tenant farming.

Regional differences also played a significant role on property ownership. In New England, where communal goals were elevated above the interests of the individual, land ownership bore a direct relationship to an individual's character. Land was sold only to a town's male residents, and then only if such men were able to pass religious and moral tests administered by the town fathers. Such tests were designed to ensure godliness among the town's inhabitants and to foster solidarity within the group. Still, land distribution in the New England colonies was perhaps the most comprehensive, providing the majority of male settlers the opportunity to own a share of the available land.

Immigrants to other colonies often did not find it as easy to become landowners. In agricultural regions like the colonies of Virginia and Maryland, indentured servitude was one way by which laborers could eventually acquire property of their own. Working six days a week, often ten or fourteen hours each day, the life of an indentured servant was a hard one. Like slaves, they could be disciplined or even sold by their masters, and they faced severe punishment if they attempted to run away. Once an indentured servant fulfilled his obligations, however, he might be rewarded with money, livestock, corn, tobacco, tools, and, sometimes, land of his own. Thus, indentured servitude afforded many men the opportunity for social and economic mobility.

There were two categories of individuals in colonial America who were prohibited from entering the world of property ownership and control of land: slaves and married women. Unlike indentured servants, Africans who were brought to the American colonies as slaves did not have the hope of earning their freedom and acquiring property of their own. Rather than earning the right to own individual property, they themselves were viewed as a commodity that could be bought and sold. Generations would pass before such individuals would gain their freedom by manumission or by buying their freedom from their masters. Only then would they be able to count themselves among other members of the landed population. There were some early examples of successful free blacks owning land, but these were exceptions.

Married women were also legally handicapped, unable to act independently of their husbands in matters of property ownership and control. Some legal protections of a woman's and her children's rights did apply on the death of the husband.

Property Rights within the Marital Relationship

The marital property system in British common law supported the interest of the patriarchal landed class to keep estates intact and under the control of a single male. Under this system, a married woman was to be supported and maintained, but she was not entitled, by and large, to exercise the power of ownership. Her property relationship to her husband was one of dependency. This is the marital property system that was adopted by the majority of states in America.

Under this system, a woman ceased to be considered a separate legal person at the time of marriage. Husband and wife were considered one, and that one was the husband. Except for clothes and ornaments, all personal property owned by the wife at the time of marriage or acquired thereafter, including her earnings (if any), became the property of her husband.

In addition, a husband had the right of possession to all his wife's lands during the marriage, including land acquired during the marriage. That right was alienable by the husband and reachable by his creditors. The wife also had the duty of rendering services within the home. In exchange for all of this, and a marriage vow to obey her husband, the wife received the benefit of the husband's support and protection.

The wife's previously held real and personal property came under the husband's control upon marriage under what was termed an Estate by the Marital Right. After the marriage and until issue was born of the marriage, the husband was entitled to the use and occupation of the wife's land, as well as to the rents and profits that resulted, so long as the marriage was not dissolved by divorce or death.

Once live children were born to the marriage, the husband's estate in the land became one of "Estate by Curtesy." Should he survive his wife, he would enjoy use and benefit of the land for the duration of his life.

If a wife survived her husband, the control of her previously held property was returned to her. She also was entitled to dower, which amounted to one-third of all property that her husband had owned at any time during the marriage. In addition, she could be a beneficiary of his will, because such a bequest would not take effect until after his death, when she regained her legal existence as a single woman.

Joann M. Ross

See also: Class; Inheritance; Land and Real Estate; Landlords; Marriage and Divorce; Plantations; Tenant Farming; Widows and Widowers.

Bibliography

Black's Law Dictionary, 7th ed. Edited by Bryan A. Garner. St. Paul, MN: West Group, 1999.

Dukeminier, Jesse, and James E. Krier. *Property.* 4th ed. New York: Aspen Law & Business, 1998.

Freyfogel, Eric T. "Land Use and the Study of Early American History." *Yale Law Journal* 94 (January 1985): 717–42.

Gillon, Steven M., and Cathy D. Matson. *The American Experiment: A History of the United States.* Boston: Houghton Mifflin, 2002.

Middleton, Richard. *Colonial America: A History, 1565–1776.* 3rd ed. Oxford, UK: Blackwell, 2002.

Moynihan, Cornelius J. *Introduction to the Law of Real Property: An Historical Background of the Common Law of Real Property and Its Modern Application.* St. Paul, MN: West Group, 1962.

Norton, Mary Beth, David M. Katzman, David B. Blight, Howard P. Chudacoff, Thomas G. Paterson, William M. Tuttle, Jr., and Paul D. Escott, eds. *A People and a Nation:*

A *History of the United States.* 6th ed. Boston: Houghton Mifflin, 2001.

Prostitution

Commercialized vice appeared early in colonial America. Prostitution was most often connected to urban, maritime, and, especially, wartime societies. Prostitutes plied their trade individually in nearly every community, ranging from the large to the small. During times of war, it was common for prostitutes to follow the army, sometimes in groups as large as several hundred. Most of these prostitutes were probably widows who turned to selling themselves for lack of other employment, but the trade certainly attracted all types of women.

The patronage of ladies of pleasure encouraged the opening of disorderly, or bawdy, houses in most cities. Some towns like Boston were infamous for the number and openness of their bawdy houses. In addition, mariners' wives often worked the streets near Boston's waterfront.

In other cities, prostitution was limited to specific areas, like the platform at the Battery in Manhattan, where the streetwalkers were known to openly ply their trade. New York was said to have many prostitutes but no bawdy houses. In Charles Town, the many women of ill report, most of them cast-outs from England's Newgate prison, candidly approached men nightly on the streets.

There were many variations of the bawdy house. Dorcas Griffiths of Boston was caught operating a bawdy house in the back of a grocery store, using a liquor license as a cover. Also in Boston, for over twenty years, Hannah Dilley rented out rooms in her husband's house to whores and even procured work for them. Prudence Sherrald was able to run her bawdy house openly in Philadelphia, because city officials, military officers, and city elites commonly frequented it. Newport had the only establishment run by a black woman, a Madam Juniper. Elsewhere, it appears that bawdy houses were run exclusively by whites.

The men who frequented prostitutes were not limited to the lower sorts or to sailors and soldiers. Many respectable colonials consorted with these women. Lawyers, sea-officers, journeymen, gentlemen, merchants, apprentices, and various officers of the government patronized the most respectable bawdy houses in a town. The most notable (or rather notorious, considering the details he documented in his secret diary) person known to frequently associate with prostitutes was the famed diarist and planter, William Byrd II of Virginia. Even Increase Mather, son of the famous New England preacher Cotton Mather, was once caught during a raid at a Boston bawdy house.

In Puritan New England, legislative attempts to regulate disorderly conduct within private homes were difficult to enforce. Since employing a host of officials to keep close watch on each home and make presentments for each infraction was impossible, persecution depended on informers. Since the indictment of prostitutes depended on an informer who would be exposing his own crime, however, legal prosecution of prostitutes was often frustrated. Unless prostitutes were caught in the act, officials generally charged them with entertaining of lewd, dissolute, and disorderly persons, or for pandering.

Prostitution plagued Boston from the 1650s onward, as documented by such early accounts as the prosecution of Alice Thomas and the mid-eighteenth-century trial of Hannah Dilley. In 1759, prostitution had become such a problem in Boston that officials received the authority to bind guilty women as indentured servants for up to five years.

Communities sometimes destructively rioted against houses of ill repute. A Boston mob destroyed a bawdy house in 1734, and this happened again in 1737, under the direction of some well-meaning magistrates. In New York, mobs routed prostitutes from various sections of the city numerous times in the colonial era.

Such attacks, efforts at regulation, and prosecution do not appear to have substantially curtailed the activities of prostitutes and disorderly houses. Prostitution was certainly one of the contaminants of urban life; however, it only touched a relatively small segment of the population.

Solomon K. Smith

See also: Crime; Marriage and Divorce; Sex; Syphilis.

Bibliography

Bridenbaugh, Carl. *Cities in Revolt: Urban Life in America, 1743–1776.* New York: Oxford University Press, 1955.

Mayer, Holly. *Belonging to the Army: Camp Followers and Community during the American Revolution.* Columbia: University of South Carolina Press, 1996.

Stansell, Christine. *City of Women: Sex and Class in New York, 1789–1860.* Chicago: University of Illinois Press, 1987.

Providence

Providence, Rhode Island, was founded in 1636 by the banished minister Roger Williams and a group of refugees from the Puritan Massachusetts Bay Colony. In the first half of the 1630s, Williams had been at the center of controversies in Boston, Plymouth, and Salem, where he broke with the Church of England. The Massachusetts legislature—still associated with the Anglican Church—tried to have him shipped off to England. Williams fled to Narragansett Bay, where, with the permission of the Narragansett sachems who controlled the land, he and a small band of followers founded Providence. Through the 1640s, the population of Providence remained under 500.

Spiritually speaking, Providence was not unique among New England settlements. The Plymouth Colony, for instance, had split from the Church of England. Providence remains fascinating because of its thoroughgoing critique of the way the Puritans conducted their religion. Church attendance was not compulsory, and the church could receive no support from the government. Williams believed that the church could remain pure only if it stayed away from community matters. Besides various sects of Puritanism, Providence was home to a fractious Baptist congregation as well.

Williams also admitted, which other Puritans could not, that the Narragansetts' religion was suitable to them and did not belong to a particularly foul category; he viewed indigenous religions as no worse than flawed versions of Christianity. During the eighteenth century, Providence, and Rhode Island in general, was home to a large number of small religious groups that had splintered from larger communities and each other over and over again. Not surprisingly, there has been a tendency to lift up Roger Williams as an early example of American separation of church and state, or a visionary in native–white relations.

Providence was governed in a very strange way for colonial America. According to a 1644 patent obtained by Roger Williams, settlers could form their own government, decide issues, and enact laws by majority vote as long as these laws did not run afoul of Parliament. Other groups, such as William Coddington's antinomian followers at Newport, disliked the arrangement. When Massachusetts Bay and Plymouth tried to annex the land, however, most English people in Rhode Island sided with Williams's patent. This did little to keep the colony from breaking apart into its

A S.W. view of the BAPTIST MEETING HOUSE, Providence, *R.I.*

The Baptist Meeting House, a landmark of colonial Providence, was constructed in 1744–1745. The congregation, organized by Roger Williams in 1639, is believed to be the first of its denomination in America. *(Library of Congress, LC-USZ62-31789)*

original factions (Newport, Providence, and a few other settlements of Puritan outcasts). Williams's land policy, which included generous allotments for all newcomers, also fell apart when earlier generations of settlers complained.

Throughout the seventeenth and into the eighteenth century, Providence struggled against other towns in Rhode Island over land. In the first decade of the eighteenth century, these controversies receded, and migration and cultivation increased throughout Rhode Island. In the 1680s, Rhode Island would become part of the Dominion of New England, which was administered by the British Crown under the auspices of Sir Edmund Andros.

During King Philip's War, which destroyed several English towns and all but destroyed the region's native peoples, the septuagenarian Roger Williams commanded a militia of fewer than thirty men while the other inhabitants of Providence fled south to Aquidneck Island and the relative safety of Newport. The warriors recognized that Williams was a good man and had never intended any harm to the area's native peoples, but King Philip's War was a complex and broad conflict, and the Narragansett spared Williams's negligible force and put Providence to the torch.

The economy of colonial Providence remained small but diverse. Merchants in Providence relied mainly on Boston and Newport, and later Philadelphia and New York, for access to goods and therefore were only peripherally a part of the growing Atlantic commerce. As roads extended into the backcountry, Providence's economy expanded beyond farming to commercial endeavors. The Brown family took the lead in this regard, launching trade with Bristol and London in the decades before the War for Independence. Water-powered mills also provided a measure of balance to the colonial economy.

While Newport was devastated by the Revolutionary War, Providence escaped relatively unscathed and took the lead in the new state's commerce. Still, Providence remained secondary to Boston, New York, and Philadelphia.

Matthew Jennings

See also: Rhode Island; Rhode Island (Chronology).

Bibliography

James, Sydney V. *Colonial Rhode Island: A History.* New York: Charles Scribner's Sons, 1975.
McLoughlin, William G. *Rhode Island: A Bicentennial History.* New York: W. W. Norton, 1978.

Public Houses

See Inns and Taverns

Pueblo

The Pueblo Indians describe their emergence from the underworld as having been like a maize shoot sprouting from the earth. Established in a number of compact settlements on the semiarid Colorado plateau of northern Arizona and New Mexico, the pueblo developed a society based on agriculture and distinctive arts and crafts held together by a comprehensive worldview and ceremonial system.

The men of every pueblo considered their town to be the center of the universe and placed the main kiva at the center of a sacred space that extended outward in the four cardinal directions, upward to the four skies, and downward to the underworld. Rain was their central preoccupation, but all forces were balanced and represented in Pueblo society. Maintaining that balance was the charge of the Pueblo people. The Pueblo form a nation in the Southwest, despite divisions based on location, ecology, language, and social institutions.

Dating back over 1,000 years, the Pueblo settlement at Acoma is one of the oldest surviving communities in what is now the United States. Despite their ancient presence in the region and their cultivated respect for continuity and tradition, the Pueblo's culture was not static. In the years prior to Spanish occupation, the Pueblo had learned to live in the region through raiding, war, immigration, and, most often, vast trade networks. When the Spanish arrived, the Pueblo people, who conceived of their society as unfolding according to a preordained plan, were thrown into disarray.

The first information Spaniards obtained concerning the Pueblo came from Álvar Núñez Cabeza de Vaca's expedition, which traversed the area in 1528. Inspired by their accounts, Fray Marcos de Niza, accompanied by native guides and an African slave named Esteban, who had been with de Vaca, led an expedition into Pueblo territory. Met with hostility, the expedition returned to Mexico. Undeterred, the Spaniards launched another expedition under Francisco Vázquez de Coronado in 1542. Seeking vast riches, Coronado returned to Mexico disappointed, and no expedition visited the Pueblo for the next forty years.

Small Spanish expeditions returned to Pueblo territory by the 1580s; however, in 1598, Don Juan de Oñate led 400 Spaniards and Mexican Indians northward into the upper Rio Grande Valley. The stability of Pueblo society and culture, as well as Pueblo achievements in architecture, agriculture, and crafts, aroused Spanish admiration, but contact led to conflict.

Ill equipped for life in the Rio Arriba, the Spaniards placed heavy demands for food and tribute on the Pueblo people. This prompted rebellions by the Tompiro, Tiwa, and Acoma in December 1598. The Spaniards crushed the rebellions, and, for the next seventy years, the Pueblo toiled under an oppressive system,

The Pueblo settlement at Acoma, New Mexico, is the oldest continuously inhabited community in the United States, dating back nearly 1,000 years. The mission church, seen here, was begun in 1629. *(Denver Public Library, Western History Collection, Jesse Logan, N-67)*

providing tribute and personal service to the Spaniards. Their settlements secure, the Spaniards dispatched missionaries to the various pueblos, where suppression of native religious practices emerged as a point of contention.

By 1680, the Pueblo had suffered droughts, overtaxing demands for tribute, increasing raids by their nomadic neighbors, and the suppression of their religion. Seeking to free themselves, they devised a plan to expel the Spanish from their territory. Pueblo leaders planned to (1) cut Santa Fe off from outlying communities, (2) send word to the Pueblo in the north and south of the fall of the capital, and (3) attack before the annual supplies from Mexico arrived in the territory. The revolt exploded throughout the Pueblo territory, resulting in the deaths of twenty-one of the thirty-three Franciscan friars there and 400 colonists. The remaining Spaniards fled back to Mexico. Thus, the revolt provided the Pueblo with an intermission of independence.

In 1692, just twelve years after their expulsion, the Spaniards returned with a new colonial system. Gone were the harsh tribute and labor demands, and the assaults on Pueblo religion were tempered by moderation. By 1700, the Pueblo and Spanish had developed a tenuous peace. The Pueblo became allies to the Spanish as raids from neighboring peoples increased in frequency. The Spanish ended the prohibition against trading guns, and enlisted the Pueblo in the defense of the occupied territories on the Rio Arriba.

The Pueblo peoples' desire for peace and harmony led them to declare truces during the summer and fall. During these truces, vast trading fairs were held among the Native Americans. Sensing an opportunity, the Spaniards gave government sanction to these fairs in an effort to open communication with the hostile groups.

Spanish protections ensured, the Pueblo began to recover some of their lost prosperity. By 1800, they had gained a secure position in provincial society.

Todd Leahy

See also: Missions; Native American–European Conflict; Native American–European Relations; Native Americans.

Bibliography

Gutierrez, Ramon. *When Jesus Came the Corn Mothers Went Away: Marriage, Sexuality, and Power in New Mexico, 1500–1846.* Stanford, CA: Stanford University Press, 1991.

Milner, Clyde A., II, Carol A. O'Connor, and Martha A.

Sandwiess, eds. *The Oxford History of the American West.* New York: Oxford University Press, 1994.

Sturtevant, William, ed. *Handbook of North American Indians.* Vol. 10. Washington, DC: Smithsonian Institution, 1978–2001.

Puerto Rico

As one of the first areas of the New World to be "discovered" by Spain, Puerto Rico has a long and complex colonial history. Christopher Columbus's party landed on the shores of *Burenquen* (or *Borinken*), as its native inhabitants called it, on November 18, 1493, during his second voyage in search of a western route to Asia.

At the time, the central Caribbean island was home to an estimated 70,000 Tainos, whose sedentary, agriculturally oriented society was organized around *cacicatos* or chiefdoms. Their immediate ancestors were the Arawak-speaking peoples of northern South America, who began settling the Caribbean archipelago some 500 years prior to the arrival of the Europeans.

Claiming the island for the Spanish Crown, the Europeans named it San Juan Bautista (Saint John the Baptist). Later, it was renamed Puerto Rico or Rich Port, in the mistaken belief that it contained vast quantities of mineral wealth.

In 1505, Vicente Yanéz Pinzón, captain of the *Niña,* one of the three caravels that accompanied Columbus on his first voyage to the Americas, secured a *capitulación* or agreement to undertake the colonization of Puerto Rico. However, the prospects of acquiring additional fame and riches elsewhere consumed most of his energies. He sent only a shipment of goats and

Christopher Columbus landed on Puerto Rico on his second voyage to the New World in November 1493 and claimed the island for Spain. Natives called it Borinquén; Columbus dubbed it San Juan Bautista. This map dates to 1599. *(Royal Commonwealth Society, London, United Kingdom/Bridgeman Art Library)*

pigs in preparation for a future settlement before his contract expired. Not much later, Juan Ponce de León, who gained royal benefaction by successfully putting down a native uprising at nearby Hispaniola (today the Dominican Republic and Haiti), began the Spanish colonization of the island.

Ponce de León landed on the southwestern coast of Puerto Rico in 1508. From the start, the Spaniards sought out the *Borinqueños* for their knowledge of the island, especially for information about potential sources of gold. Relations quickly soured as the Iberians established *repartimientos* and *encomiendas,* dividing up the natives among themselves in order to expedite their conversion to Christianity and assure a steady supply of workers. Led by the *cacique* Agueybaná the Brave, the Taino rebelled against their oppressors in 1511 but failed to dislodge them. The subsequent destruction of their ecological base of survival—coupled with forced labor, epidemics, warfare, and deculturation—all but decimated the native inhabitants. Despite the demographic catastrophe, the southwestern villa of San Germán reported some 2,000 "Indians" at the start of the nineteenth century.

In the absence of indigenous workers, the Spaniards stepped up their requests for *licencias* or royal permits for importing the "more sturdy" Africans. Available figures show that enslaved Africans comprised the bulk of the island's work force as early as 1530. Over 6,000 were imported to Puerto Rico between 1540 and 1600 to work in military installations, private homes, alluvial mining, pearl fisheries, and *haciendas* or agricultural estates. Along with the Iberians and Amerindians, the Wolofs, Mandingas, Fulas, Fantis, Ashantis, Yorubas, and Congolese, among other African ethnic groups, also contributed significantly to Puerto Rico's multiethnic makeup.

Following the exhaustion of Puerto Rico's placer deposits, shortages of capital and labor crippled the colonial economy. The number of sugar mills in operation, for instance, shrank from eleven in 1582 to seven in the 1630s. Faced with declining fortunes, many of the resident Iberian colonists fled hastily to Mexico and Peru, hoping to start anew in the mainland mineral enclaves. Their exodus almost depopulated the island, which, by about 1650, was effectively on the fringes of Spanish exploration, trade, and immigration in the Americas. In fact, relatively few Spanish colonists immigrated to the Hispanic Caribbean between 1600 and the last third of the eighteenth century.

In 1700, Puerto Rico possessed an estimated 6,000 inhabitants, although it is likely that countless escaped slaves, illegal traders, castaways, and pirates eluded census takers by taking up residence on the periphery of Spanish colonial control. After the Bourbons came into power in Spain in 1701, the Spanish Crown became increasingly concerned about the scanty population, military weaknesses, and impoverished economic conditions in the Hispanic Caribbean. Although the region had been a political liability and a drain on the royal coffers, requiring annual subsidies from the treasury of New Spain, the Crown considered it a key strategic link in the imperial order. The Bourbons gradually restored Spanish authority in Puerto Rico during the second half of the eighteenth century by revamping its defenses, congregating the dispersed population into towns, encouraging immigration (including slave trading), redistributing land among commercial farmers, fostering the production of cash crops, and promoting commerce.

As a result of these changes, Puerto Rico's population swelled from about 45,000 in 1765 to 136,000 in 1794. During the same interval, the number of enslaved Africans tripled from 5,037 to 17,508. These developments helped set the stage for Puerto Rico's gradual transition from a military post and penal colony of subsistence farmers to a leading exporter of tropical staples, especially sugar and coffee, in the next century.

Jorge L. Chinea

See also: Caribbean (Chronology); Ponce de León, Juan; Slavery, Caribbean; Spanish Colonies on Mainland North America (Chronology).

Bibliography

Carrión, Arturo Morales, ed. *Puerto Rico: A Cultural and Political History.* New York: W. W. Norton, 1983.

López, Adalberto, ed. *The Puerto Ricans: Their History, Culture, and Society.* Rochester, VT: Schenkman, 1980.

Monge, José Trías. *Puerto Rico: The Trials of the Oldest Colony in the World.* New Haven, CT: Yale University Press, 1997.

Punishment

See Prisons and Punishment

Puritanism

Puritanism was not a social, political, or economic movement. Rather Puritanism was an attempt by Protestants in the sixteenth and seventeenth centuries to reform and *purify* the Church of England based on their understanding and application of scripture.

The sixteenth century was a time of great political and social change, and these changes dovetailed with religious life in England. Certainly, the movement had social, political, and economic repercussions and therefore cannot be seen solely as a matter of religion. Puritanism can be divided into two branches: (1) English Puritanism, which aimed to reform the Church of England, bringing it more into line with Presbyterian theology and church polity; and (2) American Puritanism, which transported the ideals and aspirations of the movement to the New World.

English Puritanism

As a reform movement, Puritanism had it roots in the earth-shaking German and Swiss reformations of Martin Luther, Ulrich Zwingli, and John Calvin. These three religious figures spoke out against the papal abuse of authority and were in favor of a return to the biblical understanding of church and church governance. King Henry VIII broke formal ties with the Roman Catholic Church because the papacy was unwilling to annul his marriage to Catherine of Aragon, his Spanish wife, who had been unable to give him an heir. In 1534, the English Parliament, in the Act of Supremacy, established the Church of England and appointed the king as the earthly head of the church.

Henry VIII died in 1547 and his son Edward took the throne. Archbishop Thomas Cranmer instituted church policy and oversaw spiritual matters in England. Cranmer revised the prayer book, permitted clergy to marry, published a doctrinal statement called the Forty-Two Articles, and generally initiated Protestant reform.

The death of King Edward VI in 1553 brought his half-sister Mary to the throne. A devout Catholic, she was determined to bring Roman Catholicism back to England. For her brutality in dealing with Protestants who resisted her, she earned the nickname "Bloody Mary." It is reported that in her reign she martyred nearly 300 reformers, including women, children, and even expecting mothers. Archbishop Cranmer was burned at the stake on March 21, 1556. Many Protestants fled to the Continent, especially Geneva, and were influenced by Calvin's preaching. After Mary's rule came to an end in 1558 and her sister Elizabeth took the throne, these Protestants brought Calvin's theology back to England.

Queen Elizabeth I tried to steer England's religious life carefully between Romanism and Protestant-

"Puritan" was originally a derogatory term for sixteenth-century separatists from the Church of England, who called for greater purity in faith and politics; they later adopted the name themselves. American Puritans founded their theocratic settlement as "a modell of Christian charity." *(New York Historical Society, New York/Bridgeman Art Library)*

ism, in the tradition of King Henry VIII. This ecclesiastical diplomacy is often called the Elizabethan Settlement. Elizabeth's first order of business was to reinstate Henry's Act of Supremacy and Act of Uniformity in 1559. Elizabeth established herself as the only supreme head of the church and ordered the *Book of Common Prayer,* with a few concessions for Catholics, back into worship services. Unfortunately, this only had the effect of alienating both religious groups. The Catholic Church excommunicated her in 1570. It is at this point that we see the emergence of Puritans, who were protesting relics of Romanism still found in the Church of England. In 1572, some anonymous Puritans circulated a document entitled *Admonition to Parliament,* demanding that England's religious polity be purified of all Romanism and established as Presbyterian, not Episcopalian. Elizabeth appointed Matthew Parker as Archbishop of Canterbury to suppress the Puritan movement and maintain uniformity in her church. Elizabeth's sovereign rule came to an end in 1603 and James I took the throne.

In 1604, King James I called the Hampton Court Conference to discuss the Church of England. James I had been raised a Presbyterian, but to everyone's amazement he was sympathetic to the Episcopalian form of church government because it elevated the king. This frustrated Puritan reformers; in addition, by 1604, James I was requiring all pastors to subscribe to the Thirty-Nine Articles (a shortened version of the Forty-Two Articles). James I is best known for having sponsored a leading English translation of the Bible, the King James Version in 1611. The first group of Puritan dissidents left England in September 1620, sailing on the *Mayflower* to the New World in hopes of establishing a theologically and politically *pure* church.

Succeeding James I was his son, King Charles I. Charles I made William Laud Archbishop of Canterbury, and Laud re-established and enforced a fixed standard of worship. Laud also initiated the Star Chamber, which suppressed the Puritans and the Calvinis doctrines. This was more than many Puritans could bear, and a second group left for the Massachusetts Bay Colony in 1630. Laud and Charles I also attempted to impose their ecclesiastical restrictions on the Scots. This inflamed the Scots' Presbyterian sympathies. In 1638, they formed a National Covenant that pledged the Church of Scotland to Presbyterianism. Civil War broke out in England in 1642 and eventually Charles I and the Church of England were defeated. Charles I was executed in 1649. For a short time, Puritans were in control of church life in England. It was during this period that the Westminster Assembly of 1643 was convened by the Long Parliament to reform the Church of England by writing the Westminster Confession of Faith and the Westminster Catechisms.

Oliver Cromwell was thrust into the political spotlight by his army. Four years after Charles I's death, Cromwell dismissed Parliament and made himself Lord Protector of England. For a moment, a Puritan Commonwealth was firmly established in place of the monarchy. A group known as Triers was set up by Cromwell to examine clergy for their fitness for the ministry. Cromwell governed the church for only seven years, until his death in 1658. Charles II returned from exile in Ireland and restored the monarchy to England in 1660.

The Savoy Conference of 1661 was convened to rewrite the *Book of Common Prayer.* About twelve Anglicans and twelve Presbyterians, plus a handful of assessors, met in vain to revise the text. Very few concessions were made, especially to Richard Baxter's desire for an alternative service book and for the ordination of Presbyterian ministers. In 1662, King Charles II sanctioned the fourth Act of Uniformity, which forever committed England to the *Book of Common Prayer* and the Episcopal form of church government.

American Puritanism

The first group of Puritans, or Pilgrims, landed in Plymouth (modern-day Massachusetts) on December 20, 1620, and established the Plymouth Colony in New England. Upon landing, forty-one persons composed The Mayflower Compact, which was a religious and social covenant that ordered religious and political life in the Plymouth. William Brewster acted as their ruling elder and teacher, William Bradford as their governor, and Miles Standish as their military leader. That year, the harsh winter killed half of the original group.

This group of Puritans is known as the separatists, or independents, because they separated from the Church of England. They saw the established church as corrupt and impure and saw themselves as isolationists, because they wanted to isolate themselves from those outside of their covenant community.

The area north of Plymouth, in Salem, was settled by a group of Puritans who were not concerned about separating themselves from the Church of England but rather wanted to remain united to England and to reform the church from within. They were able to secure a charter from King Charles I, which enabled them, in a sense, to incorporate their group as a business, to occupy a territory, and to form a civil court to rule. On October 29, 1629, the Massachusetts Bay Company was inaugurated with the election of company officers. John Winthrop was elected as governor. In March 1630, Winthrop and a group of about 1,000 settlers left England for the New World. While aboard the *Arabella*, Winthrop addressed his fellow settlers and admonished them to enter into a covenant with God to participate in and maintain a godly community. The hope for this community was to establish an English populace in America. Salem proved to be an inadequate center for the commonwealth, so Winthrop tried setting up a civil center in Charles Town before finally settling on Boston.

The first winter was uncommonly cold and nearly 200 settlers died. In the spring, another 200 returned to England. Yet the theological and ideological hope of the New World was impressively inviting to English Puritans, so that by 1640 more than 18,000 dissidents had made the voyage across the Atlantic.

In this early stage of American Puritanism, the political structure was primarily theocratic. Only church members could vote and hold civil office. Despite having suffered religion persecution in England, both the Puritans and Pilgrims did not practice religious toleration. This was to protect the covenant community from outside influences and competing theologies and ideologies. Baptists, Quakers, and eventually, in some regions, Catholics were restricted and censured.

The Puritans valued education next to religion. As early as 1636, they founded a college at Cambridge that eventually became Harvard University. In 1647, the General Court of the Massachusetts Bay Company passed the Old Deluder Satan Act, which required townships of fifty or more families to appoint a teacher who was to teach all children to write and read. Townships of 100 or more families were to establish a grammar school to prepare youth for the university.

Puritan Theology

One of the hallmarks of Puritanism is the theological theme of transformation. At the center of the Puritan idea was the impetus to transform the Church of England by purifying her of all ungodliness. This included transforming the liturgy, prayer books, worship, and government.

William Perkins was one of the first notable theologians to write extensively about the transforma-

tion of English religious and social life during the reign of Queen Elizabeth I. Perkins was a great influence on William Ames, who picked up where Perkins left off by writing about the transformation of church polity. Ames also is well known for his refutation of Roman Catholic criticisms of the Protestant Reformation. Two of Ames's greatest works are *The Marrow of Theology* (1623) and *Cases of Conscience* (1630).

Commitment to the written and preached Word of God, as presented in the Holy Scriptures, is not only a characteristic of the Reformation but is honed and sharpened in the Puritan movement. Preachers such as Richard Sibbes, Thomas Goodwin, and John Owen brought Puritan theology and ideals to the populace. Puritans believe that the Bible is the ultimate authority of the church and the life of the believer. This may have been in reaction to the Catholic notion that the papacy is the earthly authority of the Church. Either way, the Bible played the dominate role in shaping the life and thought, law and practice of Puritan magistrates, clergy and laity.

Puritans placed theological emphasis on a personal conversion experience. This was one way in which church officers could tell the redeemed, or elect, from those not redeemed. To become a member of Puritan church one would have to testify to one's personal conversion and give evidence of true repentance, the turning from sin to God. In Puritan America this became of prime importance, because church membership was a prerequisite to voting and holding public office. Puritans were particularly interested in proving that the individual's conversion was predetermined by God, not achieved by themselves. Theologically speaking, the believer was elected, or chosen, by God to be saved.

Richard Baxter was probably the greatest pastor and evangelist of the Puritan movement. He is noted as having been instrumental in the conversion of an entire town, Worcestershire, England. Baxter was too poor to attend university, yet he published 186 books and became known as one of the movement's greatest thinkers. Not only was he remembered for his fidelity as a pastor, but he also was known for his commitment to church unity and peace; he sought to find a middle ground amid some of the movement's greatest theological controversies. Baxter spent time in prison under James II; he was released and survived the Revolution of 1688.

The second wave of immigration to America in the early 1600s did little to boost church membership and attendance in the Bay Colony. In fact, by 1650, only about 17 percent of those living in the colony were members of a church. Part of this was due to the Puritans' insistence on the articulation of a personal conversion experience for church membership. As a means of boosting membership roles and to define baptism, Puritans allowed for partial membership (called the Half-way Covenant). Basically, they permitted the baptism of children of parents who had been baptized yet were not full members of a church. These children and their parents were half-members and were subject to the governance of the church but could not vote or participate in the Lord's Supper.

A Puritan was expected to exhibit certain evidences of salvation. One of these was the pursuit of holy living according to the commandments of Scripture. A pious life was sure evidence of a believer's salvation. For example, the Lord's Day (Sabbath) was set aside for the worship of God and the fellowship of believers. Businesses and recreational activities ceased on Sundays. Puritans were also expected to devote themselves to daily prayer and the reading of Scripture. Two mechanisms for purifying the community were the practice of self-examination and the confessing of one's sins to another believer, sometimes in a conference or meeting.

The Puritans had a sophisticated system not only of personal ethics but also of social ethics and communal living. At the center of most Puritan towns would be a common area and meetinghouse, the latter typically used for religious worship and business meetings. The idea was to provide space were people could get together, commune, and promote the common good.

Puritans were also asked to covenant or contract with one another. This was done to promote the notion that individuals do not exist as islands but rather in relation to each other. By covenanting with God and each other, Puritans were encouraged to love and care for one another by practicing wise stewardship of their wealth and material possessions.

Closely tied to charitable living was the Puritan emphasis on vocation and calling from God. People living in a community were believed to be called by God to provide a particular function or service in the community. Puritans were admonished to live out their religious convictions in their work. This is sometimes referred to as the Puritan work ethic. Everyone had a function in society and everyone was responsible for supporting and upholding those in need.

Lasting Impressions

John Owen is said to have been the greatest systematic theological thinker of the Puritan movement. He was an adviser to Oliver Cromwell, who in 1651 made him dean of Christ Church and later vice-chancellor of Oxford University. Not only did Owen sit on England's parliament, he was one of Cromwell's Triers and a participant of the Savoy Conference. Jonathan Edwards also influenced New England theology. He wrote *The Freedom of the Will* (1754) and *Original Sin* (1758), which defended the idea of God's sovereign act in the salvation of the individual. John Milton (*Paradise Lost*) and John Bunyan (*The Pilgrim's Progress*) are two noted Puritan authors who put the movement's ideals into prose and poetry.

By the dawn of the eighteenth century, Puritanism was winding down. War with Native Americans, the influx of other Protestant and Catholic settlers, issues of religious freedom, the Salem witch trials, and many other issues all contributed to the weakening of the Puritan ideal in New England. Puritanism lives on today in the theology and ideology of the Reformed, Presbyterian, and Congregational Churches around the world.

Robert Leach

See also: Boston; Christ and Christianity; Massachusetts Bay Colony; Pilgrims; Religion (Chronology); Religion (Essay). *Documents:* A Modell of Christian Charity (1630); The Trial of Anne Hutchinson (1637); Psalm 23 from *The Bay Psalm Book* (1640).

Bibliography

Carden, Allen. *Puritan Christianity in America: Religion and Life in Seventeenth-Century Massachusetts.* Grand Rapids, MI: Baker, 1990.

James, Sydney V., ed. *The New England Puritans.* New York: Harper and Row, 1968.

Lloyd-Jones, D. M. *The Puritans: Their Origins and Successors.* Edinburgh, UK: Banner of Truth Trust, 1987.

Neal, Daniel. *The History of the Puritans.* Vols. 1–3. Minneapolis, MN: Klock & Klock, 1979.

Packer, J. I. *A Quest for Godliness: The Puritan Vision of the Christian Life.* Wheaton, IL: Crossway, 1990.

Rutman, Darrett B. *American Puritanism: Faith and Practice.* Philadelphia: J. B. Lippincott, 1970.

Quakers

Starting in the late 1680s, Quakers began to migrate to the British North American colonies in large numbers. By the middle of the eighteenth century, they had become one of the most influential Protestant sects in the New World. Their struggle for religious liberty in Britain and New England, their work in establishing the colonies of New Jersey and Pennsylvania, and their protests against slavery gave them a prominent role in shaping American political culture and social mores.

The English Civil War and Interregnum (1642–1660) spurred the creation of new religious sects, having been energized by far-reaching debates over political and religious authority in Britain. This included such transitory groups as the Seekers, the Ranters, and the Fifth Monarchy Men but also groups soon to become a permanent part of English Protestantism, namely Baptists and Quakers.

The Quakers grew out of the radical wing of Puritanism, a movement that sought a thorough reform of the Church of England along Calvinist lines. Puritans, and later Quakers, stressed liturgical simplicity, personal self-discipline, and the work of the Holy Spirit. Quakers departed from the Puritans on the means by which the Holy Spirit accomplishes this work. Puritans held that the Spirit works principally through Scripture, while Quakers thought the Spirit could communicate directly. Soon, Quakers came to understand the Spirit as an inner light given to believers to guide them along their spiritual journey. Without creeds, churches, or paid clergymen, Quakers sought to recreate the primitive Christianity of the New Testament in seventeenth-century England.

Quakers found early converts among separatist Puritans and Baptists in the English North and West Country, Wales, and the cities of London and Bristol. Separatist Puritans in Nottinghamshire, Leicestershire, and Derbyshire were among the first to exhibit traits that would come to be associated with Quakerism in the 1650s, which included spontaneous meetings of believers driven to heights of spiritual ecstasy by the Holy Spirit. These men and women referred to themselves as "friends," thus giving the movement its eventual name, the Religious Society of Friends.

Quakerism was spread through these counties in the English midlands and northwest by such itinerant ministers as George Fox, William Dewsbury, and James Naylor. In the hands of George Fox, as recorded in his influential *Journal,* the movement acquired many of its distinctive beliefs and practices. Fox understood the Christian faith to preclude paying homage to presumed superiors, so Quakers were enjoined to use *thee* and *thou* in addressing everyone, regardless of social position, and to refuse to tip their hats to the rich, the well born, and the powerful. Also, Quakers were to dress and act in a plain style, lest anyone show the sin of pride through refinement in clothing and demeanor.

These early teachers brought Quakerism into ill repute among Anglicans, since they echoed the social and economic radicalism of civil war groups such as Levellers and Diggers. Quakers responded to their critics by channeling the movement through a system of weekly, monthly, quarterly, and yearly meetings and winning strategic converts among the gentry and nobility. Notably, meetings for business involved both men and women, and their acceptance of the spiritual authority of women became a Quaker distinction. Margaret Fell and William Penn provided examples of affluent, well-born men and women who could practice Quakerism while nevertheless preserving the fabric of the English social order. In fact, William Penn's role in organizing the colonies of West New Jersey and Pennsylvania testified to a new outlook within the movement, one geared toward building institutions and contributing to the development of the English colonial system.

Quakers in the Colonies

Quakers actually entered the colonies much earlier than 1682, the traditional founding date for Pennsylvania. At the movement's inception, in the early 1650s, Quakers came to New England in an effort to protest the residual religious "forms" that Puritans allegedly carried with them to Massachusetts Bay, Connecticut, and Plymouth Colony. Like their English counterparts, colonial Quakers accused the Puritans of supporting a hireling clergy, practicing idolatry in the form of images and altarpieces, and encouraging spiritual deadness through written creeds and theologically sophisticated sermons.

Officials in New England persecuted Quakers through imprisonment, banishment, and execution, most spectacularly in Massachusetts Bay between 1659 and 1661, when four Quakers were hanged. Many Quakers found refuge in Rhode Island, where Roger Williams had established a haven for persecuted sectarians and dissenters ever since his own banishment from Massachusetts Bay over twenty years earlier. But the main body of colonial Quakerism was centered on the Delaware Valley region, as large numbers of persecuted Quakers arrived in the 1680s and 1690s to help realize William Penn's vision of a "holy experiment" in the New World.

In 1681, Pennsylvania Quakers organized the Philadelphia Yearly Meeting. This meeting was composed of representatives from lower-level weekly, monthly, and quarterly meetings. Thus, the Quaker form of church government most closely resembled the presbyterian system advocated by English Puritan reformers in the 1640s. The Philadelphia Yearly Meeting took up weighty issues of policy for the expatriate Quaker community, including the issues of wealth and worldliness, Quaker and non-Quaker intermarriage, war and peace, and slavery. The advices of the yearly meeting stand as a record of Quaker engagement with the world, a catalogue of the Quaker struggle to resolve several key tensions that emerged within the sect. These efforts entailed an ongoing battle to bridge the gulf between the inward and outward aspects of life and to create social standards within a sect that otherwise stressed individual conscience. Friends received these advices in their monthly meetings and sometimes used them as instruments of discipline for errant followers.

Discipline aside, Pennsylvania Quakers actively promoted the principles of religious freedom and toleration and worked to eliminate forms of oppression that they believed violated the teachings of Jesus. Penn's early charters for the colonies, such as the West Jersey Concessions and the Frame of Government of 1682 (Pennsylvania), provided for freedom of religion. This placed Penn in rare company in seventeenth-century England as a lawmaker committed to a written constitution enshrining the principle of religious toleration for all sectarians and dissenters. Gradually the idea of religious toleration gained traction, leading to the Act of Toleration (1689) in England and maturing in the U.S. Constitution's First Amendment guarantee of religious liberty.

The Quaker-led campaign against religious oppression dovetailed with their campaign against war. Quakers believed that war stemmed from a lust for power. They also stood against oath taking of any sort, which complicated their relationship to the state in general.

By the 1660s, Quakers had developed a Peace Testimony that forbade followers from participating in war or supporting it in any way. This position interfered with their efforts to provide for the defense of the colony of Pennsylvania during the War of the Spanish Succession, when French raiding parties threatened coastal and estuary settlements along the Atlantic seaboard.

Finally, in 1756, the Peace Testimony prompted

The "meeting" is the heart of Quaker practice. The term is used to designate the gathering of adherents for worship, monthly congregational meetings for fellowship and the transaction of business, and the high-level administrative unit of the Society of Friends. *(Museum of Fine Arts, Boston/ Bridgeman Art Library)*

many Quaker legislators to withdraw from the Pennsylvania Assembly so that the colonial government could prepare unimpeded for another war with France. As such, the Quaker principle of pacifism rendered the sect a minority party in the legislature for the first time since the start of the eighteenth century, and there it would remain for the rest of the colonial period.

Quakers and Social Reform

But Quakers did not withdraw from public life altogether. They remained at the forefront of social reform despite their abdication from power in Pennsylvania government. They were instrumental in developing state-of-the-art educational institutions in Pennsylvania, promoting criminal justice reform, and providing for the relief of the poor. For example, the Friends' Alms House in Philadelphia (1729) became a model of charity for the disadvantaged; when joined with the Bettering House (1767), it offered the Atlantic world a new vision of philanthropy and benevolence.

Perhaps Quakers are best known for their leadership in another area of social reform, antislavery. Prominent Quaker ministers John Woolman and Anthony Benezet were the best-known antislavery reformers in the colonial world. The efforts of Quaker antislavery activists won the Philadelphia Yearly Meeting the distinction of being the first organized religious body to denounce slavery (1754), and Benezet organized the first antislavery society in America (1775).

All told, Quakers made up less than 2 percent of all religious adherents at the time of the American Revolution, and therefore they influenced the direction of American politics, society, and culture out of proportion to their numerical strength in early American history. The cumulative legacy of Quaker efforts to eliminate oppression and liberate the human spirit in the seventeenth and eighteenth centuries gave the denomination a distinct identity.

An epilogue to this colonial experience might be found in the women's movement prior to the U.S. Civil War. After being banned from the World's Anti-Slavery Convention in London because of her gender, Quaker reformer Lucretia Mott helped Elizabeth Cady Stanton organize the first women's rights convention at Seneca Falls, New York, in 1848.

Jeffrey B. Webb

See also: Penn, William; Pennsylvania; Pennsylvania (Chronology); Religion (Chronology); Religion (Essay). *Document:* Protest of German Quakers Against Slavery (1688).

Bibliography

Barbour, Hugh. *The Quakers in Puritan England.* New Haven, CT: Yale University Press, 1964.

Levy, Barry. *Quakers and the American Family: British Settlement in the Delaware Valley.* Oxford, UK: Oxford University Press, 1988.

Marietta, Jack D. *The Reformation of American Quakerism, 1748–1783.* Philadelphia: University of Pennsylvania Press, 1984.

Nash, Gary B. *Quakers and Politics: Pennsylvania, 1681–1726.* Princeton, NJ: Princeton University Press, 1968.

Tolles, Frederick B. *Meeting House and Counting House: The Quaker Merchants of Colonial Philadelphia, 1682–1763.* Chapel Hill: University of North Carolina Press, 1948.

Quebec Act (1774)

Passed by Parliament on June 22, 1774, the Quebec Act attempted to secure the political allegiance of Britain's new Catholic Canadian subjects—acquired as a result of the Seven Years' War with France—by offering them broad civil and religious rights. Responding to the petitions of French Canadians (who were angered by their harsh treatment under appointed British Protestant magistrates) and the urgings of Guy Carleton, governor of Canada, Parliament adopted the bill's liberal provisions.

The Quebec Act extended the boundaries of Quebec north to Hudson Bay territory, east to the Labrador coast, south to the Ohio River, and west to the Mississippi. It combined French Canada's customary legal code relative to property and civil rights with English criminal law, and it granted Canadian Catholics—the traditional spiritual and military foes of Protestant New Englanders—religious toleration and political emancipation. Catholics were allowed to practice their religion freely in exchange for their allegiance to Great Britain. The act did not, however, provide Canadians with an elective assembly. American colonists viewed this omission as proof that Parliament intended to establish tyranny in all its North American colonies.

While to modern eyes the act appears enlightened in its toleration of religious outsiders, in colonial estimations it "proved" that the king was in league with diabolical forces. Colonists viewed the act—together with the Episcopate controversy (1767–1770) and the Coercive, or Intolerable, Acts (1774)—as proof that Britain intended to establish in America the Catholic faith, institute political absolutism, and thereby destroy

American Protestants' traditional political rights and religious liberties.

Reactions to the Quebec Act were fast and furious. In 1774, the first Continental Congress responded with a list of grievances supporting a boycott of British trade. Some Southern colonists were angered by the limits the act placed on land acquisitions west of their borders. Settlers eager to move into these Ohio territories did not want to reside in a Catholic colony. Many others inveighed against the act for purely religious reasons. Up and down the Atlantic coast, ministers preached inflammatory sermons against it.

Typical was the reaction of Ezra Stiles, a Congregationalist minister in Rhode Island, who railed against it

> for establishing the Romish Idolatry over two Thirds of the Territories of the British . . . and thereby exciting a Jubilee in Hell and throughout [the] Pontificate, and this with the direct view & Design of employing the Arms of Papists as such against protestant Puritans. . . . This obliging Token of Friendship from the Bench of Bishops will not be very soon forgotten by the Puritans of America.

The act had the power of uniting disparate Protestant colonists behind an ostensibly moral issue. Contemporary observers remarked that this bill, more than any other act of Parliament, inflamed the passions of colonials against the Crown and propelled them closer to revolution.

The colonial uproar that followed passage of the Quebec Act confounded Britons, who instead celebrated the liberal religious provisions it granted. But to American colonists, the act violated the historic rights of Protestant subjects. Colonists who had fought in the French and Indian War (the Seven Years' War in Europe) had been motivated largely by a British patriotism that defined itself as both anti-French and anti-Catholic.

Most Anglo colonists interpreted the annals of British history through a Protestant lens, reading their national past as a struggle of Protestant forces against papal foes over the survival of British constitutional liberties. Indeed, in protests associated with the Stamp Act, colonists burned effigies of the pope alongside those of stamp collectors. Anti-Catholicism also lurked deep in popular political culture. In annual Pope's Day celebrations (Guy Fawkes Day in England), revelers rejoiced that a seventeenth-century Catholic plot to blow up Parliament had been exposed.

Furthermore, Americans viewed the Quebec Act as a direct attack on their own civil liberties. While many did not actually fear that Catholicism would become firmly established in the American colonies, the act appeared to set an alarming precedent. By establishing Catholicism in *one* of its colonies, colonists feared that Parliament was asserting a right to establish a religion in *any* of its colonies, removing the right of individual colonies to regulate themselves.

The act also renewed fears that the Church of England aimed to place Anglican bishops in its American colonies, thus establishing Anglicanism and directly attacking the colonists' religious liberties. To the colonial mind, it was a slippery slope from the removal of religious liberties to the termination of all liberties and, hence, to political slavery. The Quebec Act did, however, help ensure Canadian loyalty to Britain during the American Revolution.

Karen O'Brien

See also: Canada; Catholic Church; French; Revolutionary War.

Bibliography

Coupland, R. *The Quebec Act: A Study in Statesmanship.* Oxford, UK: Clarendon Press, 1925.

Neatby, Hilda M. *The Administration of Justice Under the Quebec Act.* London: Oxford University Press, 1937.

Noll, Mark A. *Christians in the American Revolution.* Washington, DC: Christian University Press, 1977.

Stiles, Ezra. "April 10, 1775, Stiles to Richard Price." Richard Price Papers, American Philosophical Society Library, London.

Quebec City

One of the oldest European settlements in the New World, Quebec City was named after an Algonquian word meaning "place where the river narrows." Its powerful influence and strategic location on the north shore of the St. Lawrence River invited several sieges over the colonial period, as Quebec City evolved from a trading post into the heart of New France and finally into a British colony.

In 1535, when French explorer Jacques Cartier visited the area where Quebec City later took root, about 500 St. Lawrence Iroquois inhabited the nearby village of Stadacona. Cartier claimed the region for France. He left the St. Lawrence area the following year, after many of his crew had perished from cold, starvation, and scurvy. Two unsuccessful attempts to settle the area followed shortly thereafter, one by Cartier in 1541 and the other by Sieur de Roberval in 1542–1543.

When Samuel de Champlain arrived in the region in 1608, Stadacona had disappeared, possibly due to disease and intertribal warfare. Champlain established a fur trade with the Algonquin and Montagnais nations and built a dwelling to serve as a fort, a residence, and a storage depot for trade goods. This was erected at the foot of Cap-aux-Diamants, a promontory overlooking the St. Lawrence River and the future site of the walled upper town of Quebec. In 1615, missionaries of the Recollect Order joined the small settlement to spread Christianity to the area's native populations.

In 1627, the French Crown appointed the Company of New France (Company of One Hundred Associates) to oversee expansion of the settlement from trading post to town. This expansion was interrupted between 1629 and 1632, when English privateers led by the Kirke brothers captured and governed the town until the Treaty of Saint-Germain-en-Laye returned it to France. Between 1627 and 1663, the population increased from 72 to 550. The Jesuits established their headquarters in the town in 1633 and founded a college there in 1635. The church of Notre-Dame-de-la-Paix was built atop Cap-aux-Diamants, as was Château Saint-Louis, the governor's residence and administrative center for the colony. The Ursuline Convent was founded in 1639 to educate French and native girls. The town's first hospital, the Hôtel-Dieu de Quebec, was built in 1644.

In 1663, the French Crown assumed direct control of New France and sent a military governor to Quebec City. Additional administrators, troops, and agents for merchants in France bolstered the city's population. The city also became the religious center of the colony, as Bishop François Xavier de Laval-Montmorency founded the Séminaire de Québec in 1663. A decade later, Quebec City became the diocese for all of French North America. The city's lower and upper towns became increasingly differentiated, as the former spread along the river and remained the residential and com-

Called "the jewel of New France," Quebec was founded by Samuel de Champlain on the St. Lawrence River in 1608, making it the oldest city in Canada. It later became the political, religious, and commercial center of the colony. *(Brown Brothers, Sterling, Pennsylvania)*

mercial district while the latter was fortified and contained administrative and religious institutions. In the eighteenth century, the city's fortifications were strengthened and its port facilities expanded to accommodate an increase in domestic and foreign trade.

Sir William Phips's unsuccessful attack on the city in 1690 prompted Governor Frontenac to begin construction of the Royal Battery. The city survived another siege in 1711, when Sir Hovenden Walker's squadron of ships and some 8,000 troops suffered heavy losses on the reefs of the St. Lawrence River estuary. Britain's last siege of Quebec City came in 1759. A two-month naval bombardment destroyed most of the city's major buildings and wrought considerable suffering upon its civilian population. This was followed by General Wolfe's victory over the Marquis de Montcalm's force in a pitched battle on the Plains of Abraham, which lay behind the walled city. Both generals died in the battle and the French retreated to the city, which conditionally surrendered to the British five days later. With the help of naval reinforcements, the British retained control of Quebec City in 1760 in the face of a French siege. Although the French and Indian War (known as the Seven Years' War in Europe) officially ended with the Treaty of Paris in 1763, the fall of Quebec City signaled the end of the French regime in North America.

In 1763, the population of Quebec City was about 8,000. Under British rule, it remained the administrative center of the region, and its commerce was greatly increased through its exports of wheat and timber throughout the British Empire. In 1775, a colonial American force under Richard Montgomery and Benedict Arnold failed to take the city, which held out under Governor Guy Carleton until British reinforcements arrived.

Britain passed the Constitutional Act in 1791, which divided the Province of Quebec into Upper and Lower Canada. Quebec City, with a population of close to 10,000, became the capital of Lower Canada. The city continued to perform a central role in the British colony and to function as the heart of French settlement in North America.

Michael F. Dove

See also: Canada; French; French and Indian War; French Colonies on Mainland North America (Chronology).

Bibliography

Greer, Allan. *The People of New France.* Toronto: University of Toronto Press, 1997.

Trudel, Marcel. *Introduction to New France.* Toronto: Holt, Rinehart and Winston of Canada, 1968.

Young, Brian, and John A. Dickinson. *A Short History of Quebec.* Montreal: McGill/Queen's University Press, 2003.

Queen Anne's War

From 1702 to 1713, Great Britain waged war alongside the Dutch and several German states against France and Spain. This general war in Europe, also known as the War of the Spanish Succession, had far-reaching consequences for colonial British America. Many territories formerly owned by France and Spain reverted to British control, and Great Britain emerged as the dominant commercial power in the Atlantic world. With the concluding Peace of Utrecht, a new international order was fashioned that would carry the important Atlantic powers through the remainder of the eighteenth century.

In many ways, Queen Anne's War was a continuation of King William's War. In the earlier conflict, William III joined with his fellow countrymen, the Dutch, to preserve his title to the throne of England, Scotland, and Ireland against French efforts to derail the Protestant succession and elevate a pro-French Catholic to power. Having won this conflict, William III solidified his alliance with the Dutch and turned his attention to the matter of the Spanish-held Netherlands. The point at issue in 1701 was whether Louis XIV of France, along with other members of his ruling family, the Bourbons, would be able to control the possessions of Spain in the Netherlands, Italy, and the New World. Therefore William III, along with his Dutch counterparts, persuaded several key German states to join in an offensive campaign to wrest control of the Spanish kingship from the Bourbon family, and to wrest control of the Spanish Netherlands, Milan, Naples, Sicily, and the Spanish colonies from French and Spanish forces.

William III died unexpectedly in 1702, so leadership of the conflict passed to his successor, Queen Anne, and her commanding general, the Earl of Marlborough. In the war's early phases, the allies pushed into the Spanish Netherlands and took control of strategic points along the Meuse River in France. Meanwhile, German forces captured several key objectives on the Rhine River, which separated the two powers. Thus the allies were positioned to invade deep into France by means of the major rivers in Northern Europe.

Fortunes turned against the allies when France persuaded Bavaria to join its cause in 1703, and together they defeated alliance forces in the upper Rhine, subsequently moving to pressure Vienna. The German states in the alliance were therefore led to request support for a campaign to relieve Vienna, which was reluctantly agreed to by Marlborough. This ultimately brought the British their greatest victory in the European campaign, when Marlborough defeated French and Bavarian forces at Blenheim, along the Danube River in Bavaria.

With this victory, Britain was emboldened to pursue broader goals in the war. Earlier, Britain desired segmentation of the Spanish possessions in Europe and the New World, a rather limited aim. After Blenheim, Britain, along with new allies Portugal and Savoy, wanted to see the Crown of Spain fall into the hands of the royal family of Austria, the Hapsburgs. This led Britain to engage in a new strategy of moving onto Spain itself by means of the Atlantic seaboard and Mediterranean basin. In 1704, the English navy took possession of Gibraltar, at the mouth of the Mediterranean Sea off the coast of Spain. By 1708, the British were in control of Minorca, off the southern coast of France. Victories at Barcelona (1705) and Madrid (1706) enabled the alliance to put a Hapsburg in possession of eastern Spain, though not in control of it all, while allied successes in the Spanish Netherlands, especially at Ramillies (1706) and Oudenarde (1708), weakened the French position in the north.

Peace negotiations, which started in 1709, foundered in the face of determined allied efforts to force unacceptable terms on Louis XIV. That same year, Marlborough had won an appallingly gruesome victory at Malplaquet, but, by that time, most parties had grown tired of the conflict. The alliance disintegrated over the terms to be dictated to France, especially trading rights in Spanish America, and England ultimately made a separate peace with France in 1712.

The Dutch saw that further aggression would be fruitless without English assistance and agreed to the terms of the 1713 Peace of Utrecht. This agreement formally ended the war by recognizing Philip V's control of Spain and Spanish America, though with the proviso that the Crowns of Spain and France should forever be separated. The Netherlands reverted to Hapsburg control, along with Sardinia, Naples, and Milan. Great Britain won title to Nova Scotia, Newfoundland, Hudson Bay, and several French possessions in the West Indies, along with Gibraltar and Minorca.

In the colonies, Queen Anne's War took the form of French privateering up the Atlantic coast and native raids along the frontier. In several colonies, the war became a stimulus to the formation of militias, which were to become important later in the colonial period. In Pennsylvania, the pacifist Quaker governing party was forced to withstand vociferous criticism of its management of colonial defense.

In the end, the war brought to the British exclusive trading rights with Spanish possessions in the New World. These trading privileges, along with its territorial acquisitions, were instrumental to Britain's rise as a major commercial and military power in the eighteenth century. Thus endowed, Great Britain was positioned for global dominance in the nineteenth century.

Jeffrey B. Webb

See also: Anne, Queen; Military and Diplomatic Affairs (Chronology); Military and Diplomatic Affairs (Essay); War.

Bibliography

Barthorp, Michael. *Marlborough's Army, 1702–11*. London: Osprey Publishing, 1980.

Boles, Laurence Huey Jr. *The Huguenots, the Protestant Interest, and the War of the Spanish Succession, 1701–1714*. New York: Peter Ling, 1997.

Demos, John. *The Unredeemed Captive: A Family Story from Early America*. New York: Vintage Books, 1994.

Hattendorf, John B. *England in the War of the Spanish Succession: A Study of the English View and Conduct of Grand Strategy, 1702–1712*. New York: Garland Publishing, 1987.

Jarrett, Derek. *Britain: 1688–1815*. New York: St. Martin's, 1965.

Shennan, J. H. *International Relations in Europe, 1689–1789*. New York: Routledge, 1995.

Quincy, Josiah, Jr. (1744–1775)

Josiah Quincy, Jr., lawyer and patriot leader, was born in 1744 in Boston and raised in nearby Braintree. He graduated from Harvard in 1763, returning in 1766 to collect a master's degree and to deliver one of the first English orations, on the subject of patriotism. Speaking in the aftermath of the Stamp Act, Quincy's speech drew on the writings of the great English Whigs John Trenchard and Thomas Gordon; it suggested the origins of a political philosophy that would guide him for the next decade.

Quincy soon took up the law and trained in the Boston office of Oxenbridge Thatcher. Before long, Quincy was handling the bulk of the firm's business and, when Thatcher died, the young lawyer assumed the remainder. Although he had never been formally "admitted to the Gown," by 1766 Quincy was practicing before the Inferior Court; by 1767, he had built one of the largest practices in Boston.

His financial independence assured, in October 1769, Quincy married Abigail Phillips, the daughter of a leading local merchant, who became the "Dear Partner" of his life. Together, they had two children. Their son Josiah Quincy would become a congressman, president of Harvard College, and a popular mayor of Boston.

Quincy had long believed that Thomas Hutchinson had been responsible for blocking the formal ratification of his legal credentials, so when, during the 1760s, antagonism toward the colonial administrator began to escalate, Quincy led the charge to unseat him. Under various pen names, Quincy caricatured his nemesis as a "rapacious Grasper of Sovereignty, elated with a Plentitude of Power" and soon extended his criticisms to Hutchinson's associates, "these venal hirelings," and the imperial policies they were perceived to be supporting. Through a series of newspaper articles published in the *Boston Gazette,* he advised the local government of the bloody consequences of continued imperial abuse of the colonists: "In defense of our civil and religious rights," Quincy warned in 1767, "we dare oppose the world." Such fighting talk quickly established Quincy as the voice of radical Boston Whigs.

Following the Boston Massacre, Quincy made a bold decision to defend the soldiers accused of unsanctioned murder. Together, John Adams and Quincy argued a brilliant defense that resulted in the acquittal of these hated symbols of British cruelty. While Quincy's actions seemed counterintuitive to many commentators, in fact, they demonstrated to London the maturity of the colonial system of justice and thus the considered seriousness of American objections to the pattern of British administration.

Throughout 1770 and 1771, Quincy continued his newspaper attacks on British North American policy and began encouraging patriot measures, such as the nonimportation agreement. In 1772, he was appointed to the Committee of Correspondence, an important patriot group whose members included James Otis, Jr., and Samuel Adams. It had been established to coordinate patriot action with other groups in other colonies. In this office, he left Boston in early 1773 on

Dubbed the "Boston Cicero" by John Adams, Josiah Quincy was a prominent attorney and outspoken patriot. He both won acquittal for the British soldiers involved in the Boston Massacre and helped incite the Boston Tea Party. *(Brown Brothers, Sterling, Pennsylvania)*

a mission to build contacts in the Southern colonies. The journey was also supposed to ameliorate the symptoms of tuberculosis Quincy had recently developed. While the expedition did little to improve his deteriorating health, Quincy returned to Boston in May, having successfully cultivated valuable alliances with political and commercial leaders from Pennsylvania to South Carolina.

Not yet 30 years of age, the young attorney, despite his slight frame and persistent frailties, now found himself at the center of the conflict with the colonial administration. Using his oratorical gifts (John Adams famously dubbed him the Boston Cicero), he incited local men to board ships in the harbor and turn the tea into the sea.

Throughout 1774, Quincy continued his campaign against Hutchinson. He argued that the governor bore sole responsibility for the ongoing crisis, having "done more general mischiefs and committed greater public crimes than his life can repair or his death satisfy."

When the British responded to the Tea Party by closing the port of Boston, Quincy published a stinging indictment of the legality of this punishment. He argued that the Boston Port Bill had been used to condemn the town without a formal hearing and disproportionately punished in a manner that precluded redress.

In September 1774, Quincy traveled to England to gain intelligence for the Continental Congress of Parliament's intentions toward North America. He met with Lords North, Dartmouth, and Shelburne, but he was unable to broker any substantive reconciliation.

In the spring of 1775, Quincy sailed for Boston. Already in the last stages of consumption, he died as his ship tied up in Gloucester harbor, only a mile from shore.

Richard Bell

See also: Boston Massacre; Hutchinson, Thomas; Revolutionary War; Stamp Act (1765).

Bibliography

McFarland, Philip James. *The Brave Bostonians: Hutchinson, Franklin, Quincy, and the Coming of the American Revolution.* Boulder, CO: Westview, 1998.

Quincy, Josiah. *Memoir of the Life of Josiah Quincy, Junior, of Massachusetts: 1744–1775.* 2nd ed. Boston: J. Wilson, 1874.

Shipton, Clifford K. "Josiah Quincy." In *Sibley's Harvard Graduates,* vol. 15. Boston: Massachusetts Historical Society, 1970.

R

Raleigh, Sir Walter (1554–1618)

Sir Walter Raleigh remains one of the most vibrant and fascinating figures in English colonial history. He was born in 1554 at a farmhouse called Hayes Barton, in Devon. His father, Walter Raleigh, was of noble birth but relatively modest means. His mother, Katherine, belonged to one of the more prosperous families in the West Country.

Not much is known of Raleigh's early life, though like other boys of his social standing, he likely learned from a tutor how to read and write in English and Latin. Raleigh was his father's fifth son, and as such he could expect very little as far as his inheritance was concerned. His father did manage to send him to Oxford, where he probably studied for a year before heading off to the religious wars in France from 1569 to 1574.

Upon his return from France, Raleigh took up study at the Inns of Court, though he apparently had little interest in becoming a lawyer. He and his older half-brother, Sir Humphrey Gilbert, had more exciting plans. They proposed in 1577 to take to sea in an effort to capture Spanish ships, sell them to the Dutch, and use the proceeds to attack Spanish colonies in the Americas. Although Queen Elizabeth was not impressed at first by the idea of attacking the Spanish, she eventually granted Gilbert permission to seek out territories not occupied by Christian princes or people for six years. Their mission was allegedly a colonizing venture, but the real mission was privateering, and in this both Raleigh and Gilbert failed.

Raleigh went to Ireland in 1580 as part of large English force sent to crush a rebellion there. Raleigh's behavior in Ireland, though it may seem vicious, was unexceptional in the eyes of the English. Raleigh participated in the wholesale slaughter of 600 men at Fort Smerwick. He also wholeheartedly advocated the destruction of Irish crops, Irish livestock, and Irish people. In addition, he seems to have purposefully put himself in harm's way, apparently so he could extricate himself with a feat of unnecessary bravery. Raleigh, though he hated the Irish as much as anyone, saw little opportunity for money or glory in Ireland, and he chafed under the leadership of Lord Grey, his superior officer there.

As legend has it, when Raleigh met Queen Elizabeth for the first time, he spread a new cloak on the ground to prevent her from stepping in a puddle. This story is probably not true, but it points to the larger fact that Raleigh made an immediate positive impression on the queen. Raleigh's image at court was that of a flashy outsider, and Elizabeth was apparently impressed with his intellect and wit.

In 1583, Raleigh interceded with the Queen on behalf of his half-brother Gilbert who, still working on the old patent of exploration, intended to found a colony in North America. Raleigh also supplied a new ship and bought stock in Gilbert's company. The expedition did claim Newfoundland for England, but it also claimed Gilbert's life, for he drowned on the return trip.

During this period, Raleigh continued to accumulate gifts from the queen. He received several substantial manors and a large financial gift in the form of the "Farm of Wines," a monopoly under which every wine maker in England had to pay Raleigh a fee. Elizabeth also gave Raleigh a license to export cloth, another highly profitable plum. Raleigh began to acquire clothes, jewels, and a serious desire to colonize North America. In 1584, Queen Elizabeth granted Raleigh permission to explore and claim territories, reserving 20 percent of any gold and ore he might find for the British Crown.

Under the sponsorship of Queen Elizabeth I, the dashing courtier, military commander, and writer Sir Walter Raleigh organized the first, failed attempt to establish a settlement in North America, the Roanoke Colony, in the 1580s. *(National Portrait Gallery of Ireland, Dublin, Ireland/Bridgeman Art Library)*

The Lost Colony and Its Aftermath

Until Sir Walter Raleigh came on the scene, England had primarily viewed North America as an obstacle to effective exploration, the goal of which was to discover a speedy route to the Far East. Raleigh changed this by focusing on America itself. Raleigh's motives for colonizing are not precisely clear; he likely hoped to find treasure, raid Spanish colonies, and explore simply for the sake of exploration.

The first voyage to North America undertaken on Raleigh's behalf was a smashing success, particularly in the area of public relations. Two well-equipped ships financed by Raleigh and commanded by members of his household sailed from Plymouth in April 1584. They stopped in Puerto Rico for a new supply of food and water, then sailed north to an island off the coast of present-day North Carolina, where they stayed for six weeks. The expedition returned to London with two

Native Americans, who became instant celebrities. Raleigh was elected to Parliament in the same year. Raleigh, together with Arthur Barlowe (one of the captains of the voyage) and both Richard Hakluyts, Senior and Junior, tried to muster support for an even more extensive colonizing expedition.

The second expedition was to include 500 men; reinforcements were to follow. Thomas Harriot and John White were tapped to study the region's native peoples, mainly Algonquian speakers. In April 1585, at least seven ships containing about 600 men sailed for Virginia. After some trade, piracy, rough weather, and adventures at sea, the colony at Roanoke was established in the summer of 1585. Supplies were short, though, so only 100 men remained and the rest returned to England.

Throughout the winter of 1585–1586, the colonists struggled to eke out a living in an unfamiliar environment. They explored their surroundings, establishing friendly relations with some tribes and leaning on others for food and supplies. Not surprisingly, relations with Wingina, the nearest tribal leader, went sour. In June 1586, the colonists killed Wingina and beheaded him. This hostile situation resulted in the abandonment of this first Roanoke colony.

Raleigh collected the accounts of the first colonists and decided to outfit another expedition, intending that this second party would have less of a military character and would settle near Chesapeake Bay. Under the leadership of John White, the group, which included women and children, sailed in 1587. After a few weeks, responding to the colonists' worries over supplies, White returned to England, promising to return soon with the needed goods; however, he was not able to return until 1590. He discovered the colony abandoned, the fort ransacked, and the word "CROATOAN" carved into one of the posts.

What happened to the colonists at Roanoke stands as one of the great mysteries in early American history. They may have fallen victim to an attack by Native Americans or been adopted into neighboring tribes. Their fate is wrapped in legend and folklore. Some of the Jamestown settlers claimed to have heard Powhatan boasting that he had killed them when his armies invaded the island. In the later seventeenth and early eighteenth centuries, explorers claimed to have seen fair-skinned, blue-eyed Native Americans on the coast of Virginia. The loss of the colony stung Raleigh, who still believed that an English settlement could thrive there.

Raleigh in the Tower and Eldorado

In 1588, Sir Walter Raleigh was at the height of his power and prestige. By 1592, he had been disgraced, dismissed from Elizabeth's court, and imprisoned in the Tower of London. Although he was never formally charged, it seems likely that his crime lay in offending the queen by concealing from her his marriage to Elizabeth Throckmorton, a maid of honor in Queen Elizabeth's court.

While in the Tower, Raleigh continued to conduct his business, which, in fact, was booming. Ships belonging to Raleigh had captured the Portuguese ship *Madre de Dios,* which was until then the richest single prize ever brought into an English port. Raleigh, from his cell, secured Elizabeth's share of the booty and thereby secured his release from the Tower.

Raleigh, who was still banned from court, believed that an expedition to Guiana could win back the queen's favor. In 1595, therefore, he set out in search of Eldorado, a mythical kingdom of gold thought to exist somewhere in the Americas. Raleigh finally reached the Orinoco River and sailed up it with a small fleet of rowboats, but he never found Eldorado. His adventures did raise his standing in the eyes of some English people, but the queen largely ignored his expedition. Raleigh undertook a number of military missions against the Spanish, including an abortive attack on Cadiz, but never regained the prestige of his early years at court.

Upon Elizabeth's death in 1603, James I took over the English throne and began to replace Elizabeth's court with his own. This did not bode well for Raleigh, who was brought up on charges of treason and, following a sham trial, once again imprisoned in the Tower of London. He remained a prisoner there for thirteen years, until he was released in order to secure financing for another voyage to the jungles of South America, where Raleigh's party clashed with a group of Spanish explorers.

Raleigh was accused of trying to start a war between England and Spain. He was beheaded in London in October 1618. The massive, Anglocentric *History of the World* he had been writing while imprisoned remained unfinished.

Raleigh's relevance to colonial America deserves note. He was one of the leading men of Elizabethan England and spent much of his life and fortune encouraging, financing, and participating in colonization schemes. He financed the Roanoke colony, which, although it failed, paved the way for more successful experiments at Jamestown.

Matthew Jennings

See also: Exploration; Roanoke Colony; Tobacco. *Document:* A Call for English Colonization of America (1584).

Bibliography

Coote, Stephen. *A Play of Passion: The Life of Sir Walter Raleigh.* London: Macmillan, 1993.

Gleach, Frederic W. *Powhatan's World and Colonial Virginia: A Conflict of Cultures.* Lincoln: University of Nebraska Press, 1997.

Milton, Giles. *Big Chief Elizabeth: The Adventures and Fate of the First English Colonists in America.* New York: Farrar, Straus and Giroux, 2000.

Winton, John. *Sir Walter Raleigh.* New York: Coward, McCann & Geoghegan, 1975.

Reading and Literacy

During the medieval and early Reformation periods in Europe, the ability to read or write belonged primarily to clerics and wealthy members of the nobility. In contrast, the seventeenth and eighteenth centuries saw the first moves toward a predominantly literate population on both sides of the Atlantic. The reasons for these changes were both religious and social. As in England and throughout Europe, a wide range of literacy existed in the North American colonies.

Southern Colonies

The first permanent English settlement in North America was the Jamestown colony, founded in 1607. Although the Anglicans who settled Chesapeake, Virginia, and the Catholics who settled Maryland had very different religious ideas, they shared similar cultural standards. The leaders of both colonies came from wealthy families in England, accustomed to controlling everything and everyone around them. Literacy for the masses was feared and carefully controlled. Coastal North and South Carolina functioned in much the same way. In all four colonies, wealthy men had a literacy rate of close to 100 percent. In contrast, only 30 percent of indentured servants could at least sign their names and only 1 percent of African American slaves could do so. Likewise, only 25 percent of women, even wealthy women, were literate.

As a means of controlling literacy, education was carefully managed. Slaves were subject to the strictest laws and could have a finger amputated for learning to read. While grammar schools were rare, the region founded universities equal to those in England. A planter's son could be taught at home and then sent on to the College of William and Mary in Williamsburg, Virginia. Unlike other parts of North America, even yeoman farmers' children had few options for an education. The best they could hope for was literate parents.

To limit the spread of books, Virginia's governor, Lord Culpeper, ordered that all printers be subject to the "king's pleasure" in the 1670s. The first printer in Maryland, William Nuthead, was ordered in 1693 to print only blank bonds for fear that he might circulate subversive broadsides.

Backcountry Literacy

Literacy in the western backcountry of Virginia, Maryland, North Carolina, and South Carolina was also low. The region was settled predominantly by indentured servants and Scots-Irish emigrants who were well enough off to afford passage to North America but too poor to afford land near the coast. Literacy for the population as a whole stood at about 30 percent at the time of the American Revolution.

Unlike other regions, literacy was not linked to religion. Faith was spread through the spoken rather than the written word. This emphasis is evident even among literate settlers. In the early 1750s, four out of five titles found in personal libraries were secular rather than religious. In contrast to the Scots-Irish communities, Protestant German and French settlers also created small pockets of literacy throughout the backcountry.

The primary reasons for illiteracy in the West, unlike the coastal South, stemmed more from cultural differences than from strict laws. Literacy today and in the other English colonies is defined by the ability to read or write. In contrast, literacy in the backcountry was defined by oral tradition. A man or woman who could remember stories, ballads, and the lore of cooking and herbs without written text was not illiterate by backcountry standards. They were also carrying on the traditions of hundreds of years in Ireland and Scotland.

New England

The southern New England colonies—Massachusetts, Connecticut, and Rhode Island—saw the highest standards of literacy in North America. All three were settled by the Puritans. A product of the Reformation, they sought to improve, or purify, both Anglicanism and English society. Most of the Puritans came from East Anglia, a part of England that was already known for its high literacy rates. A core tenet of their faith was the belief that all church members should be able to read the Bible for themselves. They also made the first English translation of the Bible in the 1550s. Their Bible was outlawed in England in the early seventeenth century by James I, leading to the need to emigrate.

Once the Puritans were settled in New England, laws designed to promote literacy throughout society were quickly passed. In 1647, the Massachusetts Bay Colony passed a law called the "Old Deluder Satan Act," requiring every town of fifty families to have a schoolmaster and every town of 100 families to keep a grammar school. Connecticut passed similar laws in 1650. In contrast, Plymouth Colony, much poorer than its Massachusetts counterpart, saw lower levels of literacy in the early seventeenth century. By the outbreak of the American Revolution, the literacy rate among men in all three colonies was close to 90 percent. Despite these efforts, some women, servants, and poorer members of society were left uneducated. Near total literacy was not achieved until well into the nineteenth century.

While Massachusetts, Connecticut, and Rhode Island had very high standards of literacy, this was not the case for all of New England. For instance, literacy was far less common in Maine, despite the fact that it was a part of Massachusetts for most of the colonial period. Maine was settled by a combination of trappers and traders and people who left the Plymouth Colony. It also remained a frontier settlement well into the eighteenth century. Vermont and New Hampshire saw similar settlement patterns. Northern New England also had a stronger French Catholic influence than southern New England. The strong urge toward literacy was a mark of the reformist Protestant religions rather than Catholicism. Despite this, Maine, New Hampshire, and Vermont still shared more regional similarities with the rest of New England than with other colonies.

Middle Atlantic Colonies

The primary English settlement group in the Middle Atlantic region of New York, Pennsylvania, Delaware, and New Jersey was a religious group known as the Quakers. Although knowledge was important to the Quakers, they also had a strong dislike of hierarchy. Children were usually educated at home rather than in organized schools. Literacy was also less prized by the Quakers than the Puritans. While a Pennsylvania law passed in 1683 required that all children be taught how to read in school, it also required them to learn a useful trade. Education beyond the grammar school level was less common. By 1776, Pennsylvania had founded only one university.

The Middle Atlantic colonies also comprised the most ethnically diverse populations of the North American colonies. New York was initially settled by the Dutch, bringing with them a Protestant interest in

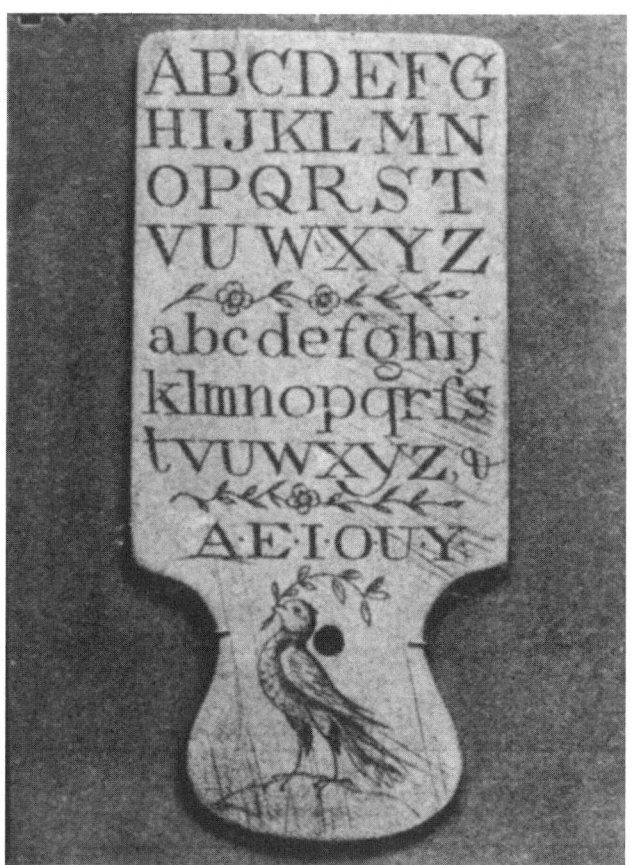

The hornbook, a kind of reading primer for children, was one of a proliferation of teaching tools that contributed to the spread of literacy in the colonies. A sheet of vellum or parchment displaying the alphabet was attached to a paddle-shaped board. *(Brown Brothers, Sterling, Pennsylvania)*

literacy. In 1700, some 80 percent of men and 60 percent of women in Holland were literate. This emphasis remained despite Anglican control of New York after 1664. Dutch-language books and newspapers continued to circulate in the colony. A New York bookseller in 1702 stocked a wide selection of secular and religious books in Dutch.

Farther south, Swedish and Finnish settlers moved into Delaware. By 1675, Sweden had literacy rates similar to those of Holland and New England. Germans brought similar codes with them to Pennsylvania. As most Quaker laws allowed other settlers to create their own schools, the European and Quaker colonists had little influence on one another.

Overall, the Middle Atlantic colonies float somewhere between the Chesapeake and New England. Like the Puritans, literacy was important to most of the people settling there. Unlike the Puritans, they demonstrated a less aggressive interest in spreading it, leading to lower literacy rates. There were also larger gender gaps in literacy in the Middle Atlantic region. At the time of the American Revolution, literacy for men in all four colonies stood at about 65 percent. Literacy for women was closer to 40 percent.

Wealth and Literacy

Those who had wealth and power in the colonies were usually also able to read and write. Literacy was not, however, an absolute necessity for success or survival.

In 1651, William Phips was born in modern-day Woolwich, Maine, to parents who may or may not have been able to read. Throughout his life, Phips was dependent on others around him (most likely his wife, Mary Spencer Phips) for assistance in reading and writing. In 1691, Phips became governor of the Massachusetts Bay Colony and was also knighted. While Phips is an exception rather than the rule, the fact that he received this honor indicates a great deal about the colonial period. That is, universal literacy was still a foreign concept.

Measuring Literacy

Identifying and defining literacy in the colonial period often requires different measures and standards than those customarily used today. A common indication of literacy is the ability to sign a document such as a will or deed. If a signer was unable to write his or her name, a mark was used instead. However, a full signature should not always be taken as a total indication of literacy, as some people learned to sign their names without being able to write anything else. It was also possible that a person using a mark to sign a document possessed some reading skills.

The books owned by a settler can be another indication of literacy. Many people learned to read the Bible but nothing else, using a familiarity gained in church to follow the words. A settler who possessed other books as well was most likely fully literate.

Abigail B. Chandler

See also: Child Rearing; Children; Education; Libraries; Literature; Newspapers and Journals.

Bibliography

Amory, Hugh, and David D. Hall. *A History of the Book in America.* Cambridge, UK: Cambridge University Press, 2000.

Fischer, David Hackett. *Albion's Seed.* New York: Oxford University Press, 1989.

Lockridge, Kenneth, A. *Literacy in Colonial New England.* New York: W. W. Norton, 1974.

Real Estate

See Land and Real Estate

Recreation

See Sports and Recreation

Reformation

The word *reform* (from the Latin *reformāre*) simply means to change something by making it better. In referring to *The Reformation* proper (or Protestant Reformation), we are describing the ecclesiastical protest of the Roman Catholic Church during the sixteenth century. The enormity of this religious event and its far-reaching implications for the world is second only to the inauguration of the Christian church in the first century.

Europe was ripe for such a change, for the Reformation occurred in the heart of the Renaissance, a cultural reformation of art, science, literature, political and social thought, and technology. The feudal system was slowly waning while the middle class was waxing as a social and political force. It was in this spirit of cultural change that Johann Gutenberg invented a process of printing with movable type, which was essential to the success of the Reformation. For example, because of Gutenberg's invention, Desiderius Erasmus was able to publish his Greek New Testament in 1516, which marked a decisive return to the Scriptures.

Many figures are associated with the Reformation, but three pillars emerge as foundational. Martin Luther was a Catholic monk who, while striving for his own salvation, also became caught up in a struggle against the abuses in the Roman Catholic Church. He specifically attacked the selling of indulgences, a moneymaking scheme concocted by the papacy whereby an individual could, in effect, win "pardon" for a temporal sin by buying off the Church. Luther outlined his criticisms in his "Ninety-five Theses," which he posted on the door of the castle at Wittenberg, Germany, in October 31, 1517. The theses were translated, printed, and widely distributed and are considered to mark the beginning of the Protestant Reformation (or, more specifically, the Lutheran Reformation).

Ulrich Zwingli, a Catholic priest, launched the Reformation in Switzerland. He was a close associate of Erasmus and was influenced by the Greek New Testament. Zwingli began his religious reform not by composing theses but by preaching expository sermons in his parish in Zurich. The result for both priest and parish was a return to a more primitive Christianity and a rejection of papal doctrines that lacked scriptural support. Zwingli's reform quickly spread to neighboring areas around Zurich and, by the early 1500s the Swiss Reformation was well under way.

John Calvin was born in Picardy, France, in 1509, and—like Luther and Zwingli—was trained for the priesthood. At some time during his studies in France, Calvin underwent a conversion, probably under the influence of French reformers or his professors. He then began to study Scripture and the theology of the Reformation. In 1536, he published the first edition of his most widely acclaimed work, *The Institutes of the Christian Religion,* which was the first systematization of reformed theology. Later, Calvin became the religious leader in Geneva and therefore continued Zwingli's Swiss Reformation. More than Zwingli or Luther, Calvin has had the greatest impact on the Protestant churches in Europe and America.

From centers in Germany and Switzerland, the

The Protestant Reformation was a reaction to the perceived excesses of the Catholic Church in sixteenth-century Europe. Two central figures, Martin Luther and John Calvin, are portrayed in this engraving. Protestantism was brought to America by the Puritans. *(Bibliotheque de l'Histoire du Protestantisme, Paris, France/Bridgeman Art Library)*

ideals and theology of the Reformation spread to Scotland, England, the Netherlands, and France. Scotland became Presbyterian, and England become Anglican. The Puritans, who struggled for church reform in England and hoped to work their religion into all aspects of life, transported Protestantism to America in the 1600s.

Although the principles of the reformation are widely debated, a few basic protests of the reformers are significant:

The first protest was aimed at the abuse of papal authority. The reformers rejected not only the selling of indulgences and a merit-based system of penance but also the elevation of the pope as the head of the church. For the reformers, Jesus Christ was the only authority over the church.

The reformers championed a return to the authority of Scripture (*sola Scriptura*) as the only rule for the life and work of the church. They advocated that the Bible be translated into common languages so that all could engage in its study.

The reformers also protested the exclusivity of the priesthood and argued that all of God's people have a divine calling to a particular vocation. This idea worked itself out in the laity's involvement in church ministry.

Finally, salvation of the individual was seen as a gift from God that could come only by God's grace through faith (*sola fide*). The idea that people could be saved by their own works or merits was rejected.

Robert Leach

See also: Catholic Church; Christ and Christianity; Religion (Chronology); Religion (Essay).

Bibliography

Gonzalez, Justo. *From the Protestant Reformation to the Twentieth Century.* Nashville, TN: Abingdon Press, 1988.

Hillerbrand, Hans. *The Protestant Reformation.* New York: HarperCollins, 1968.

Schaff, Philip. *History of the Christian Church.* Vol. 7, *The German Reformation: The Beginning of the Protestant Reformation up to the Diet of Augsburg 1517–1530.* Peabody, MA: Hendrickson, 1996.

———. *History of the Christian Church.* Vol. 8, *The Swiss Reformation: The Protestant Reformation in German, Italian, and French Switzerland Up to the Close of the Sixteenth Century 1519–1605.* Peabody, MA: Hendrickson, 1996.

Regulators

In the middle of the eighteenth century, the backcountry of the Carolinas was filling up with wave upon wave of immigrants. Colonial political leaders, oriented toward the colonies' eastern areas, often drew up gigantic, inconvenient counties, forcing those who inhabited the backcountry to travel many miles to participate in government or lodge complaints about taxation and other matters. The backcountry was equipped with few courthouses and jails, and crime, particularly cattle theft, was widespread.

The western portions of the two colonies had been entirely dominated by the older, established eastern portions. Colonial governors stationed in the eastern regions appointed relatives and friends to posts in the western counties, further widening the gap between the more settled East and the frontier West. As a response to these inequalities, "Regulator" movements sprang up in both North and South Carolina in the 1760s.

South Carolina's Regulation Movement

People living in South Carolina's backcountry had a long list of complaints against the colonial government. There were no courts, so people had to travel all the way to Charles Town to deal with legal issues. They were also underrepresented in the colonial legislature.

In 1766, a crime wave inundated the Carolina backcountry. Roving bands of criminals harassed the population and often used coercion and torture to learn the whereabouts of money or valuables. Tavern keepers and store owners were particularly susceptible to this sort of violence; if they refused to aid or supply the gangs, they ran the risk of having their stores and taverns burned, occasionally with them inside. A few of the outlaws were captured and sent to Charles Town for trial. Six were convicted, but five of these were pardoned by a newly appointed governor, desirous of beginning his administration on a generous note.

In 1767, these gangs of criminals picked up where they had left off. Across the colony, individuals took matters into their own hands. Soon local people began to fight back against the outlaws. A sort of civil war broke out in the backcountry between people looking to "build communities and those who wanted to destroy them," as one historian has put it. As reports of the violence and vigilantism reached Charles Town, the governor, viewing the vigilantes as an unruly mob, ordered them to return to their homes. This action further demonstrated how out of touch the Charles Town government was with the backcountry.

By October 1767, the vigilantes had taken on a more regular form and had grown in strength. It is important to note that the Regulators were often drawn from the backcountry's leaders; until relatively recently, historians tended to consider them a sort of frontier rabble. In fact, they were almost all property owners, and their leaders were wealthy, slave owning planters. They craved law and order, and in late 1767, they sent their requests, twenty-three of them in all, to the colonial legislature. The Regulators demanded courts, courthouses, jails, and schools. They also berated the legislature for its recent purchase of a statue of William Pitt.

The legislature responded by creating two companies of rangers (deputizing the Regulator forces already in the field) and a circuit court system for the backcountry. By 1768, the Regulators, now paid by the colony, had hunted down many outlaws in both North and South Carolina, sent them to trial, and witnessed the execution and branding of some of the more notorious among them.

With the outlaws dispatched, the Regulators turned their attention to other groups, such as vagrants and poor people. In 1768, they established the Plan of Regulation, an essentially reactionary document. The Regulators controlled South Carolina from Cherokee territory to within 50 miles of the coast. They performed a variety of services, from tracking down husbands who had abandoned their families to collecting debts.

The Regulators legitimized their position at the top of backcountry society, and though they did secure additional seats in the colonial legislature for the region, they began to rub some people the wrong way. They abused their power and often used their authority to settle personal scores. The Regulator movement in South Carolina was swept up in the larger movements both toward and away from independence from Great Britain in the 1770s.

Regulation in North Carolina

Regulation in North Carolina took a tone similar to the process that occurred in South Carolina, with one major exception: It was much more violent.

The inequalities faced by backcountry settlers in North Carolina were not as gross as those in South Carolina, but the region was terribly underrepresented in the legislature and bore the burden of unfair taxation. A group of concerned settlers drafted a document in 1766 known as Regulation Advertisement Number One, which sought to balance these inequalities and grab the attention of the colonial government. Authorities largely ignored the petition, and, in 1768, a formal Regulation movement took hold. The North Carolina Regulators agreed not to pay their taxes until the government recognized the unfairness of the situation and did something to address backcountry grievances.

The grievances of backcountry folks in North Carolina also had to do with the conduct of local officials, whom they viewed as irretrievably corrupt. No local officials in the rapidly expanding western part of the colony were popularly elected; they were all appointed by the colonial government, stationed near the coast at New Bern. Frontier dwellers also resented the fact that many local officials held multiple offices and drew multiple salaries. Another bone of contention between the colonial government and the backcountry Regulators was the mansion being constructed by Governor Tryon. Known as the "Palace," it was built under the supervision of John Hawks, a leading English architect, at a cost of 15,000 pounds to the taxpayers of the colony.

In 1768, the Regulators drew up Regulator Advertisement Number Four, which delineated their plan of action more clearly. They resolved not to pay taxes and not to pay local officials' fees. The Regulators also agreed to meet periodically as a sort of alternative legislature and to pool resources to defray necessary expenses.

In 1771, the British governor of North Carolina, William Tryon, put down a revolt by backcountry "Regulators" over the oppressive rule and corruption of local officials and the use of taxes to build a new governor's mansion. *(Brown Brothers, Sterling, Pennsylvania)*

Rioting followed the 1768 petitions, and several Regulator leaders were jailed for allegedly inciting the riots. Interestingly, the rioters targeted local officials, whom they saw as particularly corrupt. In South Carolina, the initial movement was directed against criminals; in North Carolina, the Regulators attacked the government. Their leading followers promptly stormed the jails and freed those who had been imprisoned, setting up a showdown with Governor William Tryon.

In 1771, Tryon raised a militia force of about 1,500 to march into the backcountry and restore order by putting down the Regulators. The Regulators, with about 2,000 men, met the militia in the brief battle of Great Alamance Creek, in which a handful of men on each side were killed. Six Regulators were eventually caught and hanged, but most of the rest received pardons. Many Regulators chose to emigrate from North Carolina to the far west, to what would eventually become the state of Tennessee.

The Regulator movement in the Carolinas was one of a number of conflicts between established Eastern colonial governments and their unhappy subjects in the backcountry. Like the Paxton Boys movement in Pennsylvania, it demonstrated the tension between the frontier and the coast. It also illustrated the conflict that could arise when areas in the West grew more rapidly than those in the East.

Matthew Jennings

See also: Crime; North Carolina; North Carolina (Chronology); South Carolina; South Carolina (Chronology); War.

Bibliography

Edgar, Walter. *South Carolina: A History.* Columbia: University of South Carolina Press, 1998.

Klein, Rachel N. *Unification of a Slave State: The Rise of the Planter Class in the South Carolina Backcountry, 1760–1808.* Chapel Hill: University of North Carolina Press, 1990.

Lefler, Hugh T., and William S. Powell. *Colonial North Carolina: A History.* New York: Charles Scribner's Sons, 1973.

Reich, Jerome. *Colonial America.* 4th ed. Upper Saddle River, NJ: Prentice Hall, 1998.

Religions, African

African religions had a profound impact on the development of a distinct set of African American cultures in British North America, and their long-lasting effects are just beginning to gain the scholarly attention they deserve. The years to come will likely shatter many preconceived notions concerning African religions in colonial America. One trend is already apparent: Africans in America retained African religious traditions in one form or another for a much longer time than scholars had previously assumed.

Some African slaves had been exposed to some aspects of Christianity through their dealings with European and African Christians in Africa, so the process of religious change had deep roots. Before 1776, particularly in the years of the Great Awakening, many African Americans began to adopt some of the tenets of Christianity. They did so on their own terms, according to their own distinct historical experiences.

Religion in West and West Central Africa

Most African slaves came to mainland North America from West and West Central Africa, two vast and diverse regions. African religions in these two areas varied widely in how they explained the concepts of good and evil, salvation and creation, and how they viewed prophecy and possession. Still, most African religions shared a common set of underlying principles.

Most West Africans did not draw a formal line between the natural and the supernatural; they believed that ancestor spirits, responsive to the needs of their living relatives, could affect their daily lives. The supernatural world was revealed to human beings through various means, including revelation and divination. During the sixteenth and seventeenth centuries, Europeans believed in revelation as well, but Africans and Europeans disagreed about the methods of receiving revelation and what specific revelations could be taken to mean. In many communities, illness or conflict was tied to problems in the spirit world. Most cultures believed in a creator (some had multiple creators), but creators and other "high gods" were not as relevant in day-to-day life as more localized spiritual beings.

African religions were pluralistic and dynamic, practical and adaptable. These characteristics gave African religions a fluidity and resiliency. This allowed African people to fit in new beliefs and deities in accordance with their particular situation, in this case, plantation slavery in the Americas.

In the sixteenth and seventeenth centuries, there were several sorts of revelation. Augury and divination relied upon the study of worldly events to define otherworldly intentions. One wide-ranging form of divination was the Yoruba tradition of Ifa, in which cowry shells were tossed on a special board. In the pattern made by the shells, the diviner found answers to specific questions. Similar divination rituals in other parts of Africa used teeth or bones to prophesy in a similar way. Dream interpretation was another way in which people gained access to the spirit world. People with special gifts also could hear voices or receive visions. The most intense form of revelation was possession. Spirits were capable of possessing animals, people, or objects to reveal their presence.

Mediums in Angola and Kongo were revered for their ability to convey the wishes of spirits. In Kongo, the *nganga ngombo* (spirit medium) would stand entranced in the middle of a ring of singers and deal with their spiritual concerns. In Angola, the *xingila* would enter a trance induced by clapping, drumming, and dancing. Although priests and mediums were powerful, their continued power was not assured; if they failed to produce results, they might lose their positions of esteem. Continuous revelation prevented any one African religion from gaining orthodox status and contributed to the multiplicity of religions.

Early European observers dismissed many African religious forms as witchcraft and the work of the devil. In fact, African religions and Christianity did not meet for the first time on American plantations. Many Africans had been exposed to Christianity in Africa. While the word "conversion" does not adequately describe the process that took place, some Africans had already begun to pick and choose Christian precepts and saints that appealed to them. This process would accelerate and expand in the Americas.

African Religions in America

Few events in human history have had the devastating impact of the trans-Atlantic slave trade. In the four centuries of the trade, more than 15 million people were forcibly removed from Africa; of these, approximately 10 million arrived alive in the Americas. In the slave fortresses and on the slave ships, Africans struggled against nearly impossible odds to maintain their faiths, at the same time as they cobbled together new religious identities with people from other parts of Africa. Africans from areas with strong localized religious tendencies, such as Senegambia, came into contact with people who worshipped more universal deities, such as the Aja nation on the Slave Coast.

Once settled on plantations, new bonds of community were forged from distinct ethnic identities.

Slaves imported to Catholic areas proved particularly adept at merging Catholic saints with African deities. "Voodoo," whose name is derived from "vodu," the Dahomean word for "god," is just one of several belief systems derived from mixed African and European heritage. This should not be confused with "hoodoo," which was much more common in North America, and properly refers to a set of religious practices based on remembered West Central African traditions, not necessarily a well-defined system of belief.

The Carolina low country and the Chesapeake possessed the largest slave populations in British North America. In both of these areas, hoodoo and conjuring were extremely important to transplanted Africans. Slaves called on spirits and spiritual knowledge for a variety of reasons; they used traditional remedies to heal the sick, and they also relied on sorcery to harm their enemies, both black and white.

Slaves who had accesses to the world of charms and poisons were feared and revered in slave communities. White masters' fears of being poisoned by their slaves loomed large and were not unfounded. Slaves suspected of poisoning met harsh fates, including torture and death throughout North America.

Slaves also decorated their cabins and created art objects with items and patterns that could welcome positive spirits and ward off negative ones. Folk medicine and conjuring were closely related in the Southern colonies, and slave doctors, nurses, and midwives who could heal were valued by their African compatriots and English masters alike.

Funerary practice was extremely important to natives of West and West Central Africa, as it marked the passage from the world of the living to the world of the dead, and it remained so to Africans living in the American colonies. African funeral traditions lived on throughout the South. Many slaves believed that death returned them to their ancestral homelands in Africa, and funerals sometimes turned into celebrations, complete with long processions, music, and drinking alcohol. The dead sometimes were dressed in African clothing and beads and were occasionally buried under mounds of glass, potsherds, and seashells. This type of grave was used in the Carolina low country throughout the colonial period and beyond.

When African Americans did turn to Christianity on a large scale, during the era of the Great Awakening—roughly the 1730s and 1740s—they made it fit their worldview and coexist with the belief systems they already had in place. Christianity held few benefits for the first generations of African Americans, and most continued to rely on an amalgam of beliefs derived from their experiences in Africa and as part of the slave trade. These practices lived on, although Christianity played an increasingly important role as more Africans were born in America over the course of the eighteenth century.

African Americans also put their own spin on the evangelical movements of the Great Awakening. Slave preachers, recognizing the redemptive and revolutionary aspects of some parts of Christian teaching, exhorted their congregations tirelessly. African American Christianity relied on the great physical expressiveness of older forms in combination with new revelations brought by the Bible and other religious texts. Occasionally, members of the congregation would fall into trancelike states, perhaps reflective of ancient practices; similarly, African Americans relied on the ring shout and the choreographed call-and-response pattern during their church services.

Slaves were particularly enthusiastic about the implications of Christian baptism, which many believed would make them free in a literal sense, as this had been the case in some colonies in the early years of slavery. This interpretation ran against the view of the masters and could lead to violence.

Most African American Christians continued to mix African notions with Christian teachings throughout the colonial period. Some even applied a millennial reading to the Revolutionary events of the 1770s.

Matthew Jennings

See also: African Americans; Religion (Chronology); Religion (Essay); Slave Communities and Culture; Slavery, African American.

Bibliography

Gomez, Michael A. *Exchanging Our Country Marks: The Transformation of African Identities in the Colonial and Antebellum South.* Chapel Hill: University of North Carolina Press, 1998.

Morgan, Philip D. *Slave Counterpoint: Black Culture in the Eighteenth-Century Chesapeake and Lowcountry.* Chapel Hill: University of North Carolina Press, 1998.

Sobel, Mechal. *Trabelin' On: The Slave Journey to an Afro-Baptist Faith.* Princeton, NJ: Princeton University Press, 1988.

Thornton, John. *Africa and Africans in the Making of the Atlantic World, 1400–1800.* 2nd ed. Cambridge, UK: Cambridge University Press, 1998.

Religions, Native American

Native American religions have always been philosophically and socially complex, as well as intimately tied to the historical experiences of the communities that espouse them. For instance, many Native Americans would insist that their people had no "religion," as the term is understood by nonnatives. Some would argue that native belief cannot be separated from the everyday experiences of individual Native Americans and their collective experience of ritual life.

Several crucial differences between Native American religions and European religions led early Europeans to misinterpret or disparage native beliefs. Native peoples conceived of sacred power in a spatial way: certain places were extraordinarily sacred, and the ways in which things were arrayed in space was fundamentally important. The beliefs of native communities were often tied to specific features of their surrounding landscape, and certain lakes and mountains took on special significance for those who lived near them. Time tended to be a more important concept to European religions, which also were readily transferable across space.

Secondly, native religions place great emphasis on communal ceremonial practice. Vine Deloria, a leading native scholar, has argued that Native Americans participate in ceremonies not for their own benefit, but for the good of the community as a whole. Consequently, individual transgressions could harm the spiritual well-being of the entire community.

Creation

Every native community has its own creation story and culture heroes, although there is considerable variance among these narratives. Iroquois-speaking peoples believed that the world was created on the back of a turtle. Other groups saw their origins in the sexual union of the sun and moon, or a first man and woman. In both the Southwest and Southeast, native peoples spoke of traveling on long journeys underground and emerging as human beings.

Stories of cultural heroes are just as varied. In one widely known example, Iroquois people told early Europeans of twin brothers, one of whom worked hard to make the world habitable and fertile, and the other who worked at cross purposes with the first. The world existed in tension between good and bad forces as a result of the brothers' eternal struggle.

Many native communities told tales to their youth as a way of imparting cultural values. For instance, trickster stories, featuring characters like Fox and Coyote, who could change form in order to trick humans and teach a lesson, gave native parents a way to teach their children some of life's lessons.

Architecture and Objects

Native American architecture reflected beliefs about society and religion. Two spectacular examples are the Aztec capital city of Tenochtitlán and the Mississippian mound complex at Cahokia. At each of these sites, native people constructed massive ceremonial centers reflective of their respective worldviews.

The Aztec understanding of the universe focused on a central place, their capital city. Fittingly, they built a huge stone pyramid topped by a temple. Warehouses, schools, and palaces ringed the sacred site, and from this position, the Aztecs reckoned their place in the world. The giant earthworks at Cahokia (near present-day East St. Louis, Illinois) were also set apart as the special domain of priests and chiefs.

Native art objects like pipes, masks, and flutes underscore the performative aspects of religious celebrations and rituals. These objects, by and large, were meant to be used, to be seen in motion, and to inform native peoples' understanding of themselves and their world. The physical appearance of a sacred object was considered inseparable from its function. Masks in particular, used throughout North America, were meant to be worn during religious performances. Dance and music were important to native religious expression and remain so.

Rituals

The stages of Native American life were often delineated by religious rituals. Among many peoples, puberty rites marked the transition to adulthood. These rites differed according to the sex of the participants, but most taught young women the roles of wife and mother and taught men their culturally appropriate role.

In many cultures, isolation and fasting accompanied this process. Ojibwe boys, for instance, were led into the woods to fast and wait for a vision or dream. The dream received could serve as a lifelong spiritual guide.

Of course, vision quests were not only for young men. People throughout North America engaged in the practice to assuage grief or in an effort to obtain shamanic powers. Shamans practiced throughout North America, although their role varied from culture to culture. Some inherited their spiritual gifts, while others earned them. Often, Shamans advised tribal leaders.

Aspects of Native American religions and related worldviews appeared in many activities that at first glance do not seem particularly religious. Hunting, fishing, and agriculture gave many peoples a context in which to express their religious beliefs. In the Pacific Northwest, Kwakiutl belief stressed the interdependency of animals and human beings; hunters killed game animals during the summer, then during winter ceremonials paid homage in various dances and rituals, often disguised as game animals. Such beliefs and practices were not at all uncommon. Success in hunting or warfare could be an indication of spiritual blessing.

Seasonal cycles, crucial to effective agriculture, played an important role in many Native American religions. Corn was especially valued. The legend of the Cherokees' Selu, the Corn Woman, is the most famous example. Selu's children conspired to kill her. At her request, they dragged her bleeding body over the ground; wherever her blood fell, corn grew.

Arrival of Europeans and Change

In the era of European colonization and Christianization, Native American religions underwent significant changes. In certain areas, particularly New Spain and New France, European missionaries achieved remarkable success in converting native peoples to Catholicism.

Jesuits operating in Canada and Franciscans throughout the American Southwest and Southeast set up a number of populous missions. Franciscans were particularly adept at settling in the midst of large, sedentary native communities and integrating themselves—to the extent possible—into the everyday lives of the native peoples.

Of course, how much native parishioners chose to accept of the new faith was up to them. Generally, native communities incorporated the Christian God and saints into their indigenous religious practices, which they maintained as integral parts of their cultural life. Efforts by Europeans to force complete religious conformity was more likely to meet resistance and could lead to violence, as was the case in New Mexico's Pueblo Revolt of 1680.

The English were not as interested in converting North America's native populations to Christianity. Notable exceptions were the "praying towns" established by John Eliot in seventeenth-century Massachusetts.

Adapted religious forms also served as means by which the native peoples could confront European colonialism. In the 1760s, Neolin, a prophet among the Lenni Lenape (also known as the Delaware) exerted great influence among eastern Native Americans. Neolin used the tactics of evangelical Christianity to spread a pan-native, anti-white message. He believed that whites and Native Americans had been created as separate races of people and that white people had obstructed the indigenous peoples' access to heaven. To remedy the situation, he preached, native peoples should band together and reject the trappings of Euro-American life.

Neolin's teachings inspired the widespread anti-British campaign known as Pontiac's Rebellion. They also laid the groundwork for later revivalist movements, the most striking of which took hold among the Shawnee in the early nineteenth century and in Handsome Lake's religion in Iroquois country.

Matthew Jennings

See also: Native Americans; Religion (Chronology); Religion (Essay). *Document:* John Eliot and His Work with Native Americans (1670).

Bibliography

Carmody, Denise Lardner, and John Tully Carmody. *Native American Religions: An Introduction.* New York: Paulist, 1993.

Deloria, Vine. *God is Red: A Native View of Religion.* 2nd ed. Golden, CO: Fulcrum Publishing, 1994.

Gill, Sam D. "Religious Forms and Themes." In *America in 1492*, edited and with an introduction by Alvin M. Josephy, Jr. New York: Alfred A. Knopf, 1992.

Tinker, George E. "Religion." In *Encyclopedia of North American Indians*, edited by Frederick E. Hoxie. Boston: Houghton Mifflin, 1996.

Revere, Paul (1735–1818)

Paul Revere, silversmith and Revolutionary patriot, was born in Boston in 1735 to a family of French Huguenots. When his father died in 1754, Revere inherited a thriving silversmith's shop. After a brief tour of duty as lieutenant in the French and Indian War, Revere returned to business. In 1757, he married Sarah Orne ("Sary"), with whom he had eight children.

Over the next decade, Revere diversified his business to encompass surgical instruments, copper engravings, music sheets, carved picture frames, and even dentistry items. But it was his work in silver that remained the core of his business. By the eve of the Revolution, he was the most respected silversmith in New England, producing everything from shoe buckles to commemorative tankards for customers of all social ranks.

During the 1760s, as the local economy slackened and tensions with Britain grew, Revere became increasingly active in political affairs. He joined several working-class Whig political organizations, including the North Caucus Club and the more exclusive Long Room Club. In 1765, he became one of the first members of the Sons of Liberty, a fraternity that led local opposition to the Stamp Act.

In 1770, Revere put his engraving skills to work for the Whig cause, publishing a controversial engraving condemning the Boston Massacre. This incendiary piece distorts the actual, complex events of that March night into a picture of a cruel, calculated slaughter. Three years later, in May 1773, his wife Sarah died; Revere remarried, wedding Rachel Walker, who bore him eight more children.

By this time, Revere had become the de facto leader of the town's artisan class and thus was instrumental in the planning and execution of the Tea Party in Boston harbor in December 1773. For the next two years, he served as an express rider for the Committee of Safety in Boston, an anti-British organization. In its service, he made more than a dozen rides to New York, Philadelphia, and towns north of Boston, delivering news of the Suffolk Resolves, the Boston Port bill, and other developments to pockets of Whig resistance.

It was his ride from Charlestown to Lexington on April 18, 1775, that won him a place in the national memory. Immortalized and falsified in Longfellow's nineteenth-century poem, Revere's "midnight ride" was part of a coordinated attempt to warn John Hancock and Samuel Adams that the British, currently occupying Boston, were headed toward patriot bases in Lexington and Concord. Revere's warning gave patriot leaders just enough time to spread the alarm throughout the countryside, initiating the rapid formation of militias in many towns.

Refused a position in the Continentals, Revere spent several years as a major in the Massachusetts army.

Paul Revere—patriot, fabled nightrider, and master silversmith—lived to the age of 83. After the war, he designed and printed the first Continental currency, manufactured cannons, and pioneered the production of copper plating. *(Library of Congress/Bridgeman Art Library)*

He helped defend Boston harbor, escorted prisoner-of-war transports, and participated in an operation to liberate Newport, Rhode Island, from British occupation.

In one disastrous campaign in 1779, Revere tried to engage the British in Penobscot Bay, Maine—a maneuver that led to the worst patriot naval defeat of the war. Revere was unjustly court-martialed and subsequently acquitted, though not before being forced to leave the service.

Revere's business interests continued to expand after the war as he searched for new outlets for his talents. He opened a hardware store, became involved in the manufacture of gunpowder, and secured the contract for the production and engraving of the first Continental currency and the official seal of the colonies. In 1789, he established a foundry to manufacture bells and cannons; by 1794, he had secured lucrative defense contracts to provide howitzers, mortars, and naval artillery. In 1800, he invented a new way of rolling sheet copper and was soon supplying copper to cover the dome of the rising statehouse, the cornerstone of which he had laid in 1795.

Now in his 60s, Revere was a prominent civic leader. He was elected as first president of the Massachusetts Charitable Mechanic Association and of Boston's first board of health. He also served as a Suffolk County coroner for six years and was a member of several philanthropic committees.

In his later years, he increasingly traded on his wartime feats. Because of his patriotic deeds and more recent success with his iron foundry, he took to calling himself "the Old Founder" and reportedly wore uniforms of the Revolution every day until his death in 1818 at the age of 83.

For decades, Revere had successfully spanned the political chasm that threatened to separate artisans from the elites. He may be most usefully remembered not as a leader but as a communicator and an organizer, without whom the Revolution might often have faltered.

Richard Bell

See also: Art, Cartoons, and Broadsides; Artisans; Boston Massacre; Lexington and Concord, Battles of; Revolutionary War.

Bibliography

Fischer, David Hackett. *Paul Revere's Ride.* New York: Oxford University Press, 1994.

Forbes, Esther. *Paul Revere & the World He Lived In.* Boston: Houghton Mifflin, 1942.

Revolutionary War

The American Revolution began as a series of protests against British mercantile policies, which evolved over time into the broader, violent War for Independence (1775–1783) fought for civil and religious rights. Early protests (1763–1773) were not aimed at establishing national independence; rather, they were intended to pressure the Crown and Parliament into granting colonists specific political and economic concessions.

Until late 1775, many colonists upheld conciliation as a laudable, attainable goal, and considered political independence a radical and doomed proposition. After the outbreak of armed violence in Massachusetts in April 1775, however, colonial protests changed quickly into social revolution. Drawing on deep-rooted ideas about moral government, the rights of the governed, and the obligations of rulers, common people appropriated much elite rhetoric to further their own political ends.

By the war's end, many men and women—free as well as enslaved—clamored for an end to traditional social and class privileges, attempting to turn the Revolution's abstract ideals of rights and liberties into actual political practice. While the war did preserve rights long enjoyed by white male colonists—freedom of religion, local representation, and the right to own property—it did not expand them wholesale to new groups. Women, blacks, and Native Americans enjoyed few liberating changes, and the achievement of national independence preserved many legal racial and gender inequalities.

Pre-War Colonial Developments

When viewed in 1760—the year a young, inexperienced, and politically naive George III became king of Great Britain—a united colonial rebellion appeared almost unthinkable. For starters, the North American colonies seemed more divided than united.

As late as 1775, many colonists would have agreed with Connecticut minister Robert Ross's claim that "it was doubtless expected, from Colonies so different in climate, trade, and *religion,* that they would never agree, but contend and jar, and so break into pieces among themselves." For example, orthodox New England Calvinists were deeply suspicious of more religiously tolerant Rhode Island; Connecticut engaged in a heated dispute with Pennsylvania over control of Wyoming Valley lands; and civil war broke out between western and eastern North Carolina in 1771.

The social and cultural commonalities that did exist between colonies seemed to bind them close to the British Crown. Free colonists were mainly of English descent and proudly asserted their English identity and the inherited rights that they believed such a heritage guaranteed. American colonists also relished all things British and fashioned themselves as English cosmopolitans, greedily purchasing the latest British consumer goods. Colonists were also overwhelmingly Protestant and thus shared with their transatlantic English counterparts the assumption that they belonged to a specially blessed, elect nation. American colonists understood that they were subjects of the most powerful, largest empire in the history of the Western world, and such an identity conferred upon them a large measure of national pride.

The benefit of historic hindsight, however, unearths developments that point if not to the inevitability of the Revolution at least to ways of understanding how it came about. Most colonists worked as farmers and many owned their land, which granted white male colonists a measure of economic and political independence unknown in England. Whereas only a very small minority of Britons could vote, fairly widespread colonial property ownership meant that a large percentage of America's white male population enjoyed suffrage. Thus, many male colonists had a hand in determining the makeup of the representative local assemblies that made laws and levied taxes. As a result, white male colonists held different assumptions about local government and enjoyed a more direct relationship to it than did their contemporaries across the Atlantic.

Prior to 1763, the political meaning of membership in the British Empire remained largely symbolic in the colonies. Most colonists could go for years without encountering an imperial officer. In addition, appointed royal governors held very little ruling power, as they were often beholden to the will of the colonial legislature. And while the king held the right to veto any colonial law, he rarely, if ever, did so. Local governments maintained control over taxation, and weak, often very inefficient imperial officers enforced the few customs duties and trade regulations that governed colonial economic life.

This loose imperial administrative system led to very different assumptions about the nature of the relationship between Crown, Parliament, and the American colonies. Colonists praised the loose structure of imperial rule, identifying parliamentary supremacy over the king with the ascendancy of colonial assemblies over royal governors. Over time, colonists developed the idea that all Britons had the right to representative government and that they were more beholden to local representatives—whom they elected—than they were to Parliament, in which they had no direct vote. Parliament and king disagreed, however; custom, they argued, and not constitution, informed such erroneous colonial assumptions.

In reality, Parliament did maintain ultimate authority over all British subjects—and this meant the authority to tax—even if it did not always choose to exercise its powers. Through the revenue and billeting acts of the 1760s and early 1770s, Parliament asserted the British belief in its sovereignty over all subjects.

Early Protests, 1763–1770

Breaking from the pattern set by earlier Hanoverian kings, who had governed the North American colonies loosely and without a large imperial presence, the new King George III aimed to play an active role in government administration. His political miscalculations toward the colonies began almost immediately. Victory in the Seven Years' War (1756–1763) had left Britain deeply in debt and in need of massive funds to support the 7,000 regular soldiers now stationed in America. With George III's support, Britain's Chancellor of the Exchequer George Grenville decided that American subjects should be taxed to support this large—and by most Americans unwanted—military presence.

Both the decision to maintain a permanent military force in the colonies and to directly tax colonists in order to pay for their own defense were key in setting off the string of events that would eventually culminate in American independence. While colonists accepted the right of representative assemblies in local governments to assess taxes, they did not believe that Parliament enjoyed the same authority. By taxing them without American representation and against Americans' wishes, colonists believed that Parliament wielded an arbitrary and potentially abusive authority.

The presence of thousands of redcoats in their cities and along western borders seemed to support their suspicions. Rather than see a standing army as guarding their liberties—or protecting them against foreign foes, as Parliament claimed—colonists feared that the occupying army aimed to force them and their assemblies into tame submission.

Such fears were born of experience. Britain had always left colonial defense up to the colonists themselves. Furthermore, the one war in which large numbers of British troops had been sent to defend colonists—the Seven Years' War, or French and Indian War, as it was known in the colonies—had resulted in the expulsion of France from Canada. The events of recent past, then, contradicted parliamentary assertions. Colonists were convinced that such acts endangered their collective rights and liberties, and they argued this first through petitions and later through boycotts, street demonstrations, and armed rebellion.

Initial colonial protests targeted specific Acts of Parliament, however, and in no way urged revolution. The Sugar Act (1764), the first revenue act passed by Parliament, targeted imports and toughened custom methods. Mainly because it threatened colonial merchants' profits, the act initiated a flurry of petitions by the colonial gentry but no mass movement.

The Stamp Act (1765) targeted items such as playing cards and marriage licenses—likely to be used by nonelite Americans—and thereby widened the scope of protest to include ordinary people. Large numbers pledged to boycott British goods and support instead local manufactures. Extralegal groups such as the Sons of Liberty organized to enforce such pledges. Resistance soon moved into the streets, where people paraded, burned effigies, and attacked Customs houses.

Faced with large-scale popular protests, members of Parliament repealed the act. Before long, however, they tried again, this time passing the equally unpopular Townshend Acts (1767). The heat of resulting protests led the British government to dissolve multiple colonial legislatures—in the eyes of many colonists, the very basis of their political liberty.

In 1770, the physical threat suggested by British soldiers became reality when confused troops opened fire on jeering Boston crowds, initiating what became known as the Boston Massacre. Small though it was in the annals of massacres—it left five Americans dead—its effects were huge. The killings inflamed the pens of talented colonial propagandists, who, in turn, provoked intense popular reactions throughout the colonies by publishing a steady stream of partisan sermons, pamphlets, and newspapers.

By taking to the streets in response to British policies and atrocities, ordinary colonials exercised the traditional plebeian belief that each man had the right to life and property, defined as the fruits of his own labor. Following the notions of John Locke, they believed that in return for political loyalty, government had a moral responsibility to provide for the safety, liberty, and well-being of all its subjects. High taxes, they feared, might reduce subjects to the status of debtors, resulting in the loss of their land, and land was the foundation of colonial personal and political independence.

Worse, they feared that Parliament consciously meant to reduce them to slavery. To a slaveholding society, such fears were a powerful motivator. Blacks, both free and unfree, experienced daily the harsh reality that their labor could be stolen; their lot reminded whites of the inhumane realities of bondage. Some colonists also viewed their political troubles with England as God's judgment on them for owning slaves. Many common people, black as well as white, combined a political rhetoric concerned with liberty and property with religious language informed by Christian egalitarianism to propel their own movements for egalitarian civil rights.

Moving Toward War, 1770–1775

Political events and popular sentiment soon culminated in armed resistance and revolution. Samuel Adams, a radical Bostonian, initiated a committee of correspondence (1772)—first between separate Massachusetts

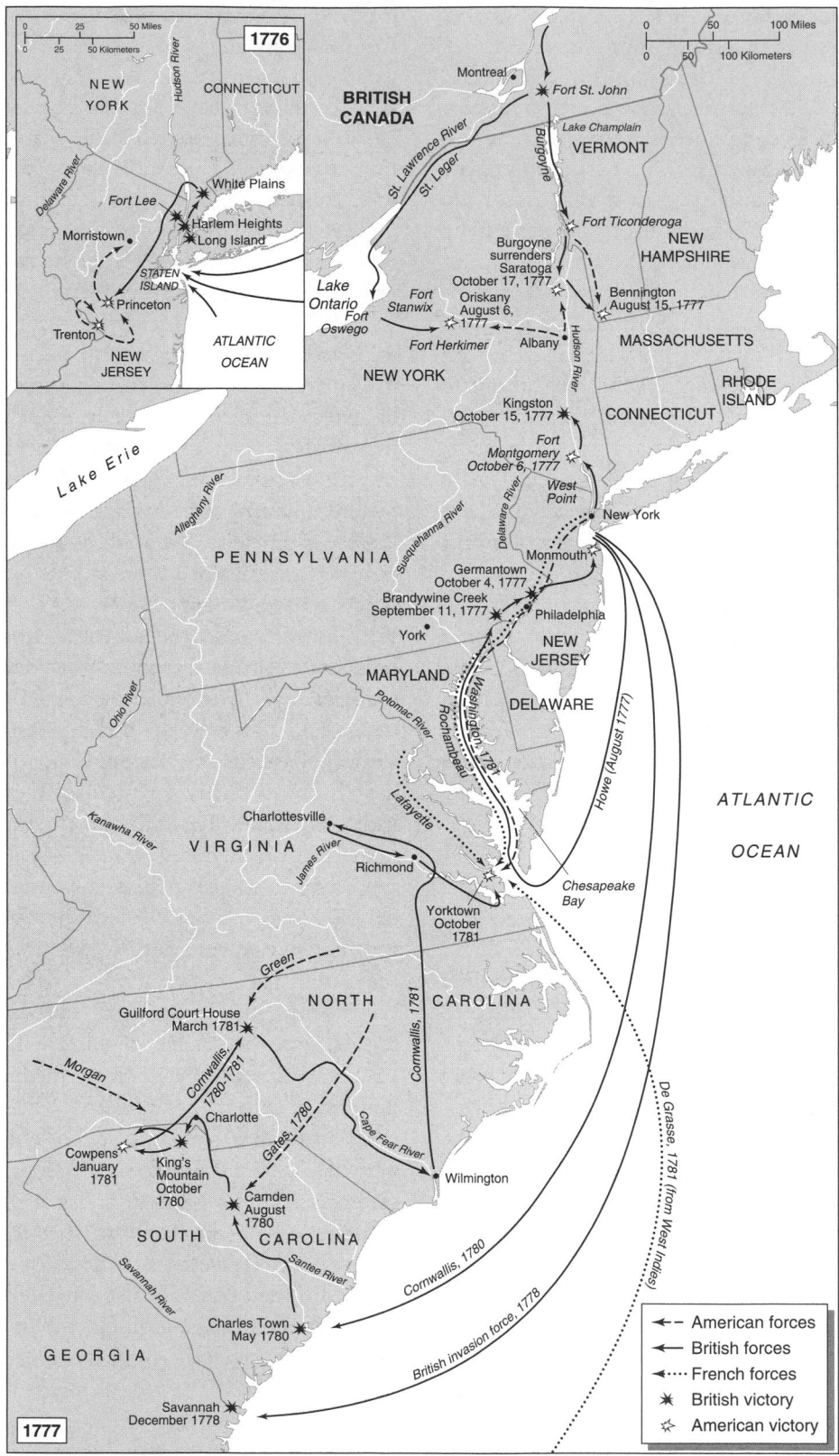

Revolutionary War, 1775–1781. The Revolutionary War was a wide-ranging conflict that stretched from Lower Canada to Georgia. While the British won most of the battles in the South, their losses in the North and their inability to destroy rebel forces led to an admission of defeat after the Battle of Yorktown in October 1781. *(Carto-Graphics)*

towns, later between separate colonies—to keep Americans abreast of British Crown encroachments on their liberty. Passage of the tough, retaliatory Coercive Acts (1774) convinced colonists that their worst fears were being realized: George III and his ministers aimed to reduce the colonies to absolute political dependence. The Quebec Act (1774) angered ordinary men and women more than any other, convincing many Protestants that Parliament aimed to take away their traditional religious liberties.

Local protests, through print, correspondence, and cross-colony organizing, became joined in a colonies-wide resistance movement. Local committees of correspondence organized the first Continental Congress (1774), which not only agreed to halt commerce with Britain but, more importantly, became the first legitimate representative body of all the colonies. Although only the most radical members publicly advocated complete independence, many were slowly coming to believe that armed rebellion was imminent.

The War for Independence, 1775–1783

On April 19, 1775, armed rebellion broke out in Concord and Lexington, Massachusetts, between British soldiers and untrained American militias. In May 1775, the second Continental Congress met to assess the dire situation: America was fighting perhaps the strongest European force; political and religious differences still split colonists; and America lacked an army, leadership, and a central government. Despite these looming problems, Congress authorized the formation of the Continental army and placed George Washington at its head.

The Revolutionary movement gained considerable momentum with the January 1776 publication of Thomas Paine's radical pamphlet *Common Sense.* Paine raised the democratic hopes of many common colonists by urging them to break with tradition, criticize their beloved British constitution, and view their rebellion as a deeply moral struggle for national independence. Enjoying more popular authority than either the Continental army or Congress, Paine tapped the democratic aspirations of the many. After much debate, Congress finally voted for independence on July 2, 1776.

Initially, British military victory seemed assured. They had a regular army, the ability to raise revenue, experienced officers, and the support of thousands of American loyalists and Native Americans. The British also tried to win the loyalty of enslaved blacks, promising them freedom in return for military service. Some joined the British, but many blacks recognized that the British government had condoned their enslavement in the first place. They instead embraced the opportunity provided by wartime disruptions and fled to freedom in Canada.

British attempts to enlist slaves also enraged many white colonists, turning formerly lukewarm patriots into Revolutionaries. The challenges of transporting troops and supplies across the Atlantic, the need to occupy a vast territory, and the depth of popular commitment to the Revolution further tipped the scales closer to American victory and ensured a long, hard military struggle.

Recruiting American soldiers the first year was easy; mobilizing men became progressively harder as supplies, pay, food, and patience grew increasingly scarce. While Continental troops performed well at Bunker Hill in 1775, by the fall of 1776, hopes for American victory had grown dim. New York City remained under British control, and attempts to invade British-controlled Canada had failed miserably.

In the summer of 1777, American troops won a stunning victory at Saratoga, where the British surrendered over 5,800 troops to American forces. As a result, France allied herself with the Americans, providing desperately needed monetary and military support.

After 1779, the war moved southward into its most violent phase, appearing more as a bloody guerilla war and less as a moral struggle for rights. By 1780, the situation had grown so dire that a string of troop mutinies occurred, and a lack of new recruits gave leaders cause to worry. Finally, in 1781, a decisive American and French victory at Yorktown secured the surrender of General Cornwallis and 6,000 British troops. Formal peace was achieved diplomatically in 1783.

Revolution's Domestic Legacy

While liberating for common white men, the Revolution had mixed results for other Americans. Nonelite white men entered local politics in increasing numbers, property ownership increased as frontier lands opened up for white settlement, and aristocratic pretenses were attacked openly.

The Revolution also nationalized radical political movements that had once been localized. These political and social benefits, however, were distributed unevenly. A postwar economic depression forced many poor sol-

In the Siege of Yorktown, the last major confrontation of the Revolutionary War, American and French forces surrounded 6,000 British troops led by General Charles Cornwallis on the Virginia peninsula and forced their surrender on October 19, 1781. *(Chateau de Versailles, France/Lauros/Giraudon/Bridgeman Art Library)*

diers to sell their land bounties, earned through military service, to predatory speculators.

Women, blacks, and Native Americans also failed to reap the benefits of a supposedly democratic revolution. While small numbers of middle-class women saw an expansion of educational opportunities, the lives of the majority were still bounded by home and marriage. Women could not own property; they lacked important legal rights and in marriage became completely dependent on their husbands. Male independence was, in many ways, defined by the dependence of the individual's family.

Blacks fared even less well. Although emancipations increased after the Revolution and some blacks gained freedom by fleeing to Canada or joining the British forces, slavery was retained under the Constitution and strengthened in the years following independence. And while some treaties and accommo-

dations were made with Native Americans, the new American nation often violently and unfairly removed the native peoples from their lands.

Karen O'Brien

See also: Army, British; Boston Massacre; Boston Port Bill; Boston Tea Party; Bunker Hill, Battle of; Coercive Acts (1774); *Common Sense* (1776); Continental Congress, First; Continental Congress, Second; French and Indian War; Lexington and Concord, Battles of; Loyalists; Military and Diplomatic Affairs (Chronology); Military and Diplomatic Affairs (Essay); Native American–European Conflict; Navy, British; Patriots; Quebec Act (1774); Sugar Act (1764); Tea Act (1773); Townshend Acts (1767); War. *Documents:* Townshend Revenue Act (1767); The Boston Port Act (1774); A Case for Non-Interference by Parliament (1775); Petition of London Merchants for Reconciliation with the Colonies (1775); *Common Sense* (1776); The Declaration of Independence (1776).

Bibliography

Breen, T. H. "'Baubles of Britain': The American and Consumer Revolutions of the Eighteenth Century." *Past and Present* 119 (May 1988): 73–104.

Calloway, Colin G. *The American Revolution in Indian Country: Crisis and Diversity in Native American Communities.* New York: Cambridge University Press, 1995.

Frey, Sylvia R. *Water From the Rock: Black Resistance in a Revolutionary Age.* Princeton, NJ: Princeton University Press, 1991.

Morgan, Edmund S. *The Birth of the Republic, 1763–1789.* Chicago: University of Chicago Press, 1956, 1977.

Norton, Mary Beth. *Liberty's Daughters: The Revolutionary Experience of American Women, 1750–1800.* Ithaca, NY: Cornell University Press, 1996.

Ross, Rev. Robert. "A Sermon, in Which the Union of the Colonies Is Considered and Recommended, and the Bad Consequences of Divisions Are Represented." New York, 1776.

Royster, Charles. *A Revolutionary People at War: The Continental Army and American Character, 1775–1783.* Chapel Hill: University of North Carolina Press, 1979.

Young, Alfred F., ed. *Beyond the Revolution: Explorations in the History of American Radicalism.* DeKalb: Northern Illinois University Press, 1993.

Rhode Island

In the late sixteenth century, Rhode Island was home to five Native American tribes: the Narragansett, the Wampanoag, the Niantic, the Pequot, and the Nipmuc. Of these tribes, only the Narragansett had lands solely within the modern borders of Rhode Island, stretching along the edges of Narragansett Bay. The Wampanoag lived in Massachusetts and eastern Rhode Island, the Niantic and Pequot tribes in Connecticut and southwestern Rhode Island, and the Nipmuc in Massachusetts and northern Rhode Island. All of these tribes were members of a larger Algonquin confederation and spoke languages similar to the other Algonquin tribes.

Prior to European contact, the total Native American population in Rhode Island was approximately 10,000 people. Following exposure to European diseases in 1616 and 1617, the total Native American population fell to approximately 4,000.

First European Encounters

The first known European exploration of Rhode Island was a voyage made in 1524 by Giovanni da Verrazano, an Italian explorer. In 1614, the Dutch explorer Adriaen Block met with the Narragansett tribe. Both men may have contributed to the colony's English name. Verrazano described the shape of an island in Narragansett Bay as being similar to the shape of the island of Rhodes in Greece. Block noticed red clay on islands in the bay and called them *Roodt Eylandt,* meaning "Red Island" in Dutch.

In the early 1630s, an English minister named William Blackstone moved to North America. Seeking solitude, he started a farm near modern-day Boston. On hearing about the Puritans' search for land, he invited John Winthrop and his followers to settle near him. Soon afterwards, Blackstone decided to move farther south in search of more permanent solitude. In 1634, he established a farm called "Study Hill" in northeastern Rhode Island. Blackstone occasionally preached to his neighbors, but he never formed an organized congregation. He continued to live on his farm until his death in 1675.

Although Blackstone was the first English settler in Rhode Island, the colony was not firmly established until the arrival of Roger Williams in 1636. Like Blackstone, Williams was a minister from the Massachusetts Bay Colony. Unlike Blackstone, Williams actively sought leadership of his own religious congregation. In late fall of 1635, he was exiled by the leaders of Massachusetts Bay for his "dangerous opinions" on religion, political rule, and English treatment of Native Americans.

Following his exile, Williams spent the winter with a Wampanoag community on the eastern side of Narragansett Bay. In the spring, he purchased land on the Seekonk River from the Wampanoag. Governor Edward Winslow of Plymouth Colony informed him that he was living on Plymouth land and suggested that he move farther west. In June of 1636, Williams purchased land from the Narragansett on the other side of the Seekonk River. Shortly afterward, he was joined by his wife, children, and some of his followers. They founded a town they called Providence and drew up a fellowship to determine laws of governing.

Other towns began to be founded in Rhode Island, all of them by religious dissidents from the Massachusetts Bay Colony. Anne Hutchinson, William Coddington, and John Clarke founded Portsmouth on the north end of Acquidneck Island in 1638. Coddington, Clarke, and their followers then broke away from Portsmouth to found Newport in 1639. Following several years of wrangling with the Massachusetts Bay Colony, the Plymouth Colony, and the existing Rhode Island towns,

Like other settlements in Rhode Island, Newport was founded (in 1639) by religious dissidents from the Massachusetts Bay Colony. By 1730, as seen here, the town flourished in shipping and the Triangle Trade. *(Brown Brothers, Sterling, Pennsylvania)*

Samuel Gorton founded Warwick in 1643. Although Hutchinson, Coddington, and Clarke had spoken with Roger Williams about obtaining land from the Narragansett tribe, the four towns existed as separate entities rather than a unified colony, making them vulnerable to control from Massachusetts Bay.

In 1644, England was ruled by a Puritan-dominated Parliament, rather than the Crown. Encouraged by this, Providence, Portsmouth, and Newport agreed to send Williams to England to obtain official recognition. A patent was granted, and the Rhode Island towns were united. The patent defined Rhode Island's boundaries and extended religious freedom to all of its people. The first General Assembly of the colony met in 1647, and official laws were drawn up.

As Rhode Island's religious freedoms became better known, the colony became a refuge for members of other religions. In 1656, a community of Jews settled in Newport. They were followed in 1657 by Quakers fleeing persecution in Boston.

By 1660, England was again under Crown rule. Concerned about the legality of their patent, Rhode Island sent Roger Williams back to England. In 1663, Charles II granted an official charter to the "Colony of Rhode Island and Providence Plantations." Like the

patent, the charter granted religious freedoms, as well as a great deal of self-rule.

King Philip's War began in 1675 between the Wampanoag and their English neighbors in southeastern Massachusetts. Although Rhode Island had always had good relations with their Wampanoag and Narragansett neighbors, the colony was drawn into the war. A major battle took place at a Narragansett village in the Great Swamp in northeastern Rhode Island. An army of British colonists led by Governor Josiah Winslow of Plymouth Colony and Captain Benjamin Church from Rhode Island destroyed the village late in 1675. In March of 1676, the Narragansett began preparing to attack Providence. Roger Williams met with Canonchet, the Narragansett chief, in the hope of a diplomatic intervention. He was unsuccessful, and Providence was nearly destroyed.

In July of 1676, a troop of men led by Benjamin Church attacked the Native American leader King Philip (also known as Metacom) near his home at Mount Hope, Rhode Island. King Philip was killed, along with hundreds of his tribe. Following this event, the war ended in southern New England, although it continued for another two years in Maine and New Hampshire.

Despite granting royal charters to Connecticut in 1662 and Rhode Island in 1663, the British Crown remained concerned about controlling the Puritan colonies of New England. In 1684, King James II revoked Massachusetts Bay Colony's charter. Shortly afterwards, he created the Dominion of New England. Consisting of Massachusetts Bay, Plymouth, New Hampshire, and Maine, the Dominion was governed by Sir Edmund Andros.

Connecticut and Rhode Island both hoped to remain independent but were annexed to the Dominion in 1687. Like Connecticut, Rhode Island was able to hide its charter. Following the Glorious Revolution in England, Massachusetts revolted, and Governor Andros was imprisoned. Shortly afterward, Rhode Island began reasserting its independence, arguing that its charter was still valid, because it had never been revoked. In 1690, the colony regained recognition by the British Crown.

Coming of the Revolution

The earliest signs of the American Revolution in Rhode Island were protests in 1765 against the Stamp Act, followed by more protests against the Townshend duties in 1767. In 1772, the British war ship *Gaspee* was assigned to patrol Narragansett Bay for smugglers avoiding the duties. When Rhode Islanders protested, the British threatened to hang anyone who resisted being searched. Captain Benjamin Lindsey organized a group of men who burned the *Gaspee* to the waterline. Shortly after the Revolutionary War officially began with the Battle of Lexington and Concord in 1775, Rhode Island sent troops under the command of Nathaniel Greene to Massachusetts.

The colonies began plans for a separate country with the 1774 convening of the Continental Congress in Philadelphia. Rhode Island sent two representatives, Stephen Hopkins and Samuel Ward. The two were also sent in June of 1775, when the Continental Congress met for a second time. Following the creation of the Continental army, Hopkins argued for the creation of a navy as well. The Continental navy was organized in December 1775 under the command of Esek Hopkins, Stephen Hopkins's younger brother. On May 4, 1776, Rhode Island became the first colony to declare itself fully independent of Britain. The other colonies quickly followed.

In December 1776, the war arrived in Rhode Island when Sir Henry Clinton captured Newport. Two years later, the British still controlled the city. When the French joined the Americans in 1778, they planned to retake Newport. An American force under General John Sullivan would attack the British from the east; a French fleet under Count d'Estaing would attack from the west. Before they were able to begin the attack, a British fleet under the command of Admiral Richard Howe appeared in Narragansett Bay. The French sailed away, and a storm damaged both the American and English fleets. D'Estaing returned to Boston, leaving Sullivan alone to face the British. On August 29, 1778, Sullivan unsuccessfully fought a large group of British soldiers in the Battle of Rhode Island. Shortly afterward, he retreated, leaving the British still in command of Newport. Eventually, the British left Newport of their own accord in October 1779.

Although the remainder of the war was fought south of Rhode Island, the colony continued to support the colonial cause with troops, money, and supplies. Following the end of the Revolution in 1781, Rhode Island resisted becoming part of the United States, as it feared it would be powerless against larger states. In 1787, Rhode Island was the only state not to send delegates to the Constitutional Convention.

Rhode Island eventually agreed to ratify the Constitution and became the thirteenth state in 1790. It was ruled under the terms of its 1663 charter until a state constitution was written in 1843.

Abigail B. Chandler

See also: Newport; Providence; Rhode Island (Chronology); Williams, Roger.

Bibliography

Calloway, Colin G. *First Peoples.* Boston: Bedford/St. Martin's, 1999.

James, Sydney. *The Colonial Metamorphoses in Rhode Island.* Hanover, NH: University Press of New England, 2000.

———. *Colonial Rhode Island.* New York: Charles Scribner's Sons, 1975.

Withey, Lynne. *Urban Growth in Colonial Rhode Island.* Albany: State University of New York Press, 1984.

Rice

English planters began cultivating rice along the southeastern coast of colonial North America in the early seventeenth century. Evidence suggests that settlers attempted to grow rice in Virginia as early as 1609 and that, by the early eighteenth century, Englishmen, mostly from Virginia, were growing rice in North Carolina as well. Early English settlers grew rice primarily for their own consumption, not export, especially in Virginia, where tobacco cultivation dominated the economy.

By the 1690s, rice cultivation had spread to South Carolina, where African slaves primarily from the Upper Guinea Coast played a critical role in the production of rice as a cash crop intended for export. Africans brought an intimate knowledge of the production of many types of rice with them to the New World and often helped their English overseers and masters, who did not have as much experience growing rice, create and maintain expansive rice plantations.

African slaves introduced many sophisticated soil- and water-management techniques to coastal South Carolina that made large-scale rice production possible. The hollow cypress logs—known as "trunks" or "plugs"—that planters used to control the flow of water through embankments were an African innovation. Africans also most likely brought the red-colored rice found in early South Carolina. By no means was every slave in South Carolina brought from the rice fields of West Africa. There were, however, hundreds who were. As the eighteenth century progressed, thousands of slaves in South Carolina became much more familiar with the planting, hoeing, processing, and cooking of rice than their English owners.

Each year, slaves repeated an intense planting, growing, and harvesting process that was critical to the production of rice. In the spring, slaves harrowed and plowed the land in preparation for planting. Then, during the first week of April, they sowed the rice seed by hand, using a small hoe. Slaves then flooded the field, barely covering the seeds (sprout flow). When the grain sprouted, slaves drained the field and allowed the rice to grow for approximately three weeks.

During the first week of May, slaves removed any grass growing among the sprouts with a hoe and flooded the field again (point flow). After a few days, they slowly drained the field, exposing the top half of each plant. The water was left at this level until the plant was able to stand on its own (long flow). Slaves then drained the field completely and removed any weeds. Again, after approximately three weeks, usually by end of June or the beginning of July, they flooded the field once again, gradually adding more water until the plants were completely submerged (lay-by flow). They then kept the field flooded for the next two months.

Rice planted during the first week of April was usually ready to be harvested by the first week of September. In September, slaves drained the field and cut the rice with large sickles called rice hooks. They then laid the rice on the ground and allowed it to dry overnight. The next day the rice was shipped by flatboat to the threshing yard.

During the colonial period, threshing was most often done by beating the rice stalks with flails. Slaves also used the mortar-and-pestle technique, which they brought with them from Africa, to remove rice grains from their husks. Several slaves, usually women, cleaned the grain a little bit at a time by placing it in a wooden mortar and beating it with a wooden pestle. In October, slaves "fanned" the threshed grain in wide, flat winnowing baskets made from an African design.

Rice production increased dramatically in South Carolina after 1705 and was critical to the colony's development. Plantation owners exported large quantities of rice throughout the world. By 1739, South Carolina had exported 764,280 barrels or 143,986 tons of rice. From the 1750s through the late nineteenth century, South Carolina remained America's leading rice producer.

The production of rice in South Carolina would not have been possible without African slaves. They provided the knowledge and experience as well as the labor necessary for large-scale rice cultivation. The importance of slaves to rice production led to a rapid rise in South Carolina's slave population. By 1740, approximately 40,000 Africans were living in South Carolina, versus approximately 20,000 whites. Although the production of cotton eventually eclipsed the production of rice in South Carolina, the culture that emerged on the coastal rice plantations made a lasting impression on South Carolina's landscape, economy, and society.

Michael A. Rembis

See also: Agriculture; Food and Diet; Plantations; Slavery, African American; South Carolina.

Bibliography

Carney, Judith A. *Black Rice: The African Origins of Rice Cultivation in the Americas.* Cambridge, MA: Harvard University Press, 2001.

Joyner, Charles W. *Down by the Riverside: A South Carolina Slave Community.* Urbana: University of Illinois Press, 1984.

Littlefield, Daniel C. *Rice and Slaves: Ethnicity and the Slave Trade in Colonial South Carolina.* Baton Rouge: Louisiana State University Press, 1981.

"Rice Cultivation in Georgetown County." http://www.cr.nps.gov/nr/twhp/wwwlps/lessons/3rice/3facts1.htm.

Wood, Peter H. *Black Majority: Negroes in Colonial South Car-*

olina from 1670 through the Stono Rebellion. New York: Alfred A. Knopf, 1974.

Rights of the British Colonies Asserted and Proved, The (1764)

Written by the famous Massachusetts lawyer James Otis, Jr., *The Rights of the British Colonies Asserted and Proved* was a direct response to the Stamp Act, passed by the British Parliament earlier in the year. The central theme of this document is the necessity of colonial representation in Parliament, especially if Parliament desired to tax the colonies. A corollary to Otis's arguments was that American colonists had the same rights as Englishmen.

Otis opened his treatise with a brief history of Anglo-Saxon liberties, a common theme in pre–Revolutionary War documents. A discussion on the English Bill of Rights follows, where Otis claimed that, since the ascension of William and Mary to the English throne, the colonies had constantly praised the English Constitution. He also stated that the colonies had repeatedly demonstrated their loyalty to the Crown in wars and in their "affection and reverence" for their mother country. Thus, because of these displays, the colonists had more than demonstrated their loyalty and Englishness; therefore they possessed the same rights as all English subjects.

Otis argued that the colonists' rights derived from more than just acts of loyalty and fealty. The rights he believed the colonists possessed came from the same sources as English liberties—namely, natural law, common law, and acts of Parliament. As a result of sharing these rights, "Every British subject born on the continent of American, or in any other of the British dominions," possesses "all the natural, essential, inherent and inseparable rights of our fellow subjects in Great Britain." Furthermore, Otis argued that after the 1688 settlement, no one held that these rights were confined only to the English isle. After stating his argument in these stark terms, Otis then listed six fundamental rights of all Englishmen that specifically related to the Stamp Act controversy. All six of these rights concerned the limits or boundaries of the authority and power of a legislative body, in this case Parliament. Of these six, the second enumeration, the unalterable form of the supreme national legislature and the permanence of a

subordinate legislature, Otis went into some detail. It is in this section that Otis first lays out his belief that the colonists, as Englishmen, had the right to be represented in Parliament. Just because the colonies had subordinate legislatures did not mean that they could not be so represented. And by being represented, their taxation would be more lawful and acceptable. Thus, Parliament might actually have the authority to tax the colonies, provided that the colonies were not deprived of representation.

Along with his reliance on English history and law, Otis depended heavily on the sanctity of property to buffer his argument. He argued that liberty could not exist when property could be taken, through taxation, without some form of consent. Taxing the colonies without any form of representation meant depriving them "of one of their most essential rights, as freemen," and, if it continued unabated, it would lead to the deprivation of all civil rights and slavery.

Otis also made a distinction between prohibitions of trade and taxation. Although liberty could still be enjoyed with prohibitions on trade, it could not survive under taxation without representation. Otis argued that once this "barrier of liberty" was destroyed, it would never be restored. In Otis's estimation, the loss of other liberties was also occurring. The common law guarantee of a jury trial had succumbed in cases concerning the admiralty, hence, a colonist's "peculiar privilege of an Englishman" and his property was left to the fate of one person.

Otis also defended the colonists' rights to have legislatures. He refuted charges that to have subordinate legislatures was treasonous and calculated only as a way of gaining independence from Great Britain. No colonists, claimed Otis, had made that claim; in fact, the colonials were so well versed in the English Constitution that they understood that their local governments were secondary to Parliament and would therefore never want any other government. Furthermore, the existence of colonial legislatures would actually help Parliament to remain informed of the general needs of the colonials while at the same time allowing the colonies to administer to their local needs and concerns.

Otis's *Rights of the British Colonies Asserted and Proved* relied on that famous theme of the Revolution, "No taxation without representation." His essay went through several quick editions in both England and the colonies. So popular and convincing was its argument that the Massachusetts legislature endorsed it, as did radicals in England. Although Otis may be better known for his attack on the Writs of Assistance, his

Rights of the British Colonies Asserted and Proved ranks as one of the most important pre-Revolutionary War documents.

Aaron N. Coleman

See also: Otis, James; Revolutionary War.

Bibliography

Bailyn, Bernard. *Ideological Origins of the American Revolution.* Cambridge, MA: Harvard University Press, 1967; reprint, 1992.

Brennan, Ellen E. "James Otis: Recreant and Patriot." *New England Quarterly* 12 (1939): 691–725.

Colbourn, Trevor. *The Lamp of Experience: Whig History and the Intellectual Origins of the American Revolution.* Chapel Hill: University of North Carolina Press, 1965.

Tudor, William. *The Life of James Otis of Massachusetts.* New York: Da Capo, 1970.

Riots

Throughout the history of British North America, riots and uprisings played a role not only in the attempt to re-create Europe in America but also in the creation of a new social, economic, and political system. As Europeans traveled to British North America, they attempted to re-create what they had known in Europe in the New World. The European settlers thus brought with them specific social, economic, political, and cultural ideas that were adapted to their new environment and shaped their lives.

Throughout British North America, from 1607 to independence, there were both small and large riots that occurred for a variety of reasons. Many riots were local responses to changing circumstances, as colonists attempted to maintain traditional securities and a stable life. In others, people sought to overturn existing political systems or, in the case of slaves, to gain their freedom.

While riots were a common feature of colonial society, none created great change. Nevertheless, all provide insight into the changing local, regional, and imperial situations.

Seventeenth-Century Rioting

During the seventeenth century, as the colonies developed and expanded, there were two major riots that marked transitions in the development of Virginia and New York. These were the two most important politically based uprisings until those of the American Revolution.

The first was Bacon's Rebellion, which occurred in Virginia in 1676. By the 1670s, Virginia suffered from a growing population of economically depressed individuals—former indentured servants—as well as declining tobacco prices and increasing taxes. These factors combined created social instability. In 1675, a squabble occurred between Virginian freemen and the Susquehannock Indians. Governor William Berkeley reacted to the situation by proposing the construction of a series of frontier forts, but those living on the frontier were unhappy with this plan. At this point, Nathaniel Bacon took command of a frontier militia preparing to attack all the local tribes.

For the most part, Bacon's militia was driven by the desire for more land. This group soon found itself in conflict with the coastal Tidewater elite, led by Berkeley, resulting in the militia's march on, and burning of, Jamestown. Before this social and political struggle could intensify, Bacon died, and the rebellion came to an end.

Berkeley soon regained control of Virginia and in the process executed twenty-three men before he was recalled to England. The rebellion did lead to the creation of a new series of treaties with the native peoples in the area, in turn opening more land to white settlement. After the rebellion, there was a distinct transition from the use of indentured servants to the utilization of slave labor.

The second of these riots was Leisler's Rebellion, which occurred in the context of England's Glorious Revolution in 1688. The seeds of the rebellion were planted in 1664, when the English captured New Amsterdam and turned it into New York while allowing the already established Dutch inhabitants to remain. When news reached the colonies of the removal of James II and his replacement by William and Mary, most of the colonies accepted the change. In New York, Jacob Leisler captured the government and became governor in the name of the new king and queen.

In 1691, the king finally appointed a new governor for New York, but Leisler refused to give up power. He was charged with treason and executed, along with his son. This seizure of power by Leisler, to the detriment of the old elite, caused a division in New York politics between the Leisler and anti-Leisler factions, creating problems for years to come.

What can be seen in both of these uprisings are attempts on the part of emerging factions to gain some type of political power. Riots with political motives would move into the background for most of the eighteenth century, only to re-emerge in the 1760s.

Moral Economy and Rioting

The most common form of rioting in British North America evolved out of what historians have termed "the traditional moral economy." In England and other parts of Europe, the traditional social structure created contractual obligations between the various groups. While the lower class accepted the power of the upper, the upper reciprocated by working to ensure the stability of the lower. This meant that in times of crisis— be it famine, plague or war—the two classes were interdependent and supported one another.

Thus, in times of famine, the upper class set the price of food to a level that ensured the survival of the poor. The vast majority of riots that occurred in the colonies did so in the context of this moral economy, as the local population reacted to any adverse changes. As the colonies were brought into the larger market economy of the Atlantic world, these riots became common, bringing about changes that challenged the stability of the colonists' lives. Shortages of food also led to food riots, sometimes called bread riots, which occurred in both Europe and British North America. The interdependence of the rich and the poor, however, led to the concept of a "just price" that would ensure the survival of all.

As a market economy developed and as British North America became increasingly tied to it, the idea of a just price came under challenge. In the 1770s, as the American crisis led to war, food riots became very common as the military demanded food, and merchants, seeing an opportunity to profit from this, raised their prices. The underlying purpose of most food riots was to show that the people were unhappy and that local officials needed to intervene.

Food riots are interesting in that both sides understood their roles and responsibilities and because the majority of the participants were women, the ones primarily responsible for feeding their families. While women were still relegated to a traditional domestic role, and where the idea of coverture, or the subsuming of a woman's legal identity in that of her husband's upon marriage, gave their husbands total power over them, women still developed a way of becoming active and gaining an indirect political voice.

Along with food riots, numerous other riots occurred throughout British North America. In 1763 and 1764, as the French and Indian War came to a close, regular soldiers rose in rebellion over changes in how they would be paid for their services. In an attempt to save money, the British army made many changes that negatively affected the rank and file. Like the participants in the bread riots, the soldiers resisted, because they saw that these changes would make their situation worse.

Another important form of rioting concerned the urban reactions to the press gangs of the Royal Navy. The Royal Navy possessed the tradition and right to impress sailors into service but, as most sailors knew the horrors of service in the Royal Navy, they actively and at times violently resisted the numerous press gangs.

While the European colonists rose up in reaction to situations that negatively affected them, another group that rioted to improve their position within colonial society were African slaves. They were in the worst position in that they lacked freedom and were relegated to lifetimes of toil. In response to their condition, slaves developed numerous ways to resist the institution of slavery. Rioting, or rebellion, was the most visible means of resistance. Because of the threat of punishment, it was the least chosen means of resistance. The most famous examples of slave uprisings in British North America included the slave revolts of 1712 and 1741 in New York City and the Stono Rebellion of 1739, along with numerous smaller riots.

All examples of rioting in British North America centered on the desire of various groups, reacting to what they saw as detrimental changes, to protect or improve their place in colonial society.

Ty M. Reese

See also: Cities; Crime; Food and Diet; Revolutionary War.

Bibliography

Gilje, Paul. *Rioting in America.* Bloomington: Indiana University Press, 1996.

———. *The Road to Mobocracy: Popular Order in New York City, 1763–1834.* Chapel Hill: University of North Carolina Press, 1987.

Nash, Gary. *The Urban Crucible: Social Change, Political Consciousness and the Origins of the American Revolution.* Cambridge, MA: Harvard University Press, 1979.

Pencak, William, ed. *Riot and Revelry in Early America.* University Park: Pennsylvania State University Press, 2002.

Roanoke Colony

In late July 1587, Governor John White and his party of eighty-nine men, seventeen women, and eleven children arrived at Roanoke Island, just inside the Outer Banks of North Carolina's coast. Financed primarily by Sir Walter Raleigh, the expedition was the second attempt to settle the region.

In 1584, a reconnaissance expedition to the Outer Banks, by Philip Amadas and Arthur Barlowe, had brought back two natives, Manteo and Wanchese, and had revealed the land to be suitable for colonization. Raleigh financed an expedition in 1585, led by Sir Richard Grenville, to establish an English garrison on Roanoke under the direction of Governor Ralph Lane. Such naturalists and artists as White and Thomas Harriot lived with the garrison from July 1585 to June 1586, collecting much information about the region and its inhabitants. In late July 1586, they returned to England on board Sir Francis Drake's ships, bringing positive word of an attractive and fertile land but also one of limited resources, poor harbors, and devastating storms. Raleigh subsequently financed the White expedition for 1587.

White's party intended to establish not a military garrison but an independent settlement in the Chesapeake area—a settlement that would be self-sufficient and live in harmony with the Chesapeake Indians. On the trip across the Atlantic, White and Simon Fernandes, the Portuguese pilot and a former pirate, argued repeatedly. When they arrived at Roanoke to consult with a garrison left there by Grenville in late 1586, Fernandes forced the entire party off at Roanoke.

Although they were concerned and disappointed, the colonists set about repairing the cottages and fort left behind by the previous expedition. They had brought back Manteo, who offered advice and then returned to his native settlement of Croatoan, near Cape Hatteras, not far away. Soon after their arrival at Roanoke, Elinor Dare, White's daughter and wife of his fellow settler Ananias Dare, gave birth to the first English person born in America—a baby girl they named Virginia Dare.

After unloading their supplies, the colonists decided that White should return to England to make sure that more supplies would be sent as soon as possible. White reluctantly agreed. Before leaving, White and the colonists determined that in his absence, the main body of the colonists would try to establish a settlement 50 miles inland (toward the Chesapeake area), while a small contingent would remain in Roanoke to meet White on his return.

White left in late August and arrived in England on November 8, 1587. He immediately met with Raleigh and asked that a relief force be organized. Raleigh initially assured him that supplies would be sent with all due speed. However, escalating conflicts with Spain (the Spanish Armada attacked in 1588) delayed White's return. He tried to send two pinnaces to Roanoke in 1588, but they were beset by French privateers and failed in their mission. When White finally did return to Roanoke in 1590 (as a passenger aboard Captain Abraham Cocke's man-of-war *Hopewell*), the colonists had disappeared; the only trace of the settlers was the word CROATOAN inscribed on a tree.

White believed the inscription signaled that at least some of the colonists had taken refuge with Manteo and his people at Croatoan. He asked that Cocke sail the 60 miles to the native settlement, but he encountered hostility from the crew. They were anxious to return to England to collect their prize money from recently captured goods and wished to leave the tempestuous seas of the Outer Banks, which had already caused several deaths by drowning.

The *Hopewell* suffered more damage from the weather and barely made it back to England on October 24, 1590. White could not persuade the otherwise preoccupied Raleigh to finance another venture to find the colonists, and he never returned to North America. Although the Roanoke colonists were never heard from again, White died convinced that they had still been alive in 1590.

Based on various forms of circumstantial evidence, some scholars speculate that the colonists had established settlements near the Chesapeake but Powhatan destroyed them shortly before the settlement of Jamestown in 1607. No conclusive evidence of this has been found. Roanoke finally became known in legend as the "Lost Colony," and the fate of the Roanoke colonists remains shrouded in mystery.

Judkin Browning

See also: Exploration; Raleigh, Sir Walter; Virginia; Virginia (Chronology).

Bibliography

Durant, David N. *Raleigh's Lost Colony.* New York: Atheneum, 1981.

Hudson, Marjorie. *Searching for Virginia Dare: A Fool's Errand.* Wilmington, NC: Coastal Carolina Press, 2002.

Quinn, David Beers. *Set Fair for Roanoke: Voyages and Colonies, 1584–1606.* Chapel Hill: University of North Carolina Press, 1985.

Rolfe, John (1585–1623)

Born in Norfolk, England, in 1585, to landowners John Rolfe and Dorothea Mason of Heacham Hall, little is known about the younger John Rolfe until he joined the Virginia Company in 1608 and sailed for America with his first wife, whose name is unknown. The ship on which they were traveling, the *Sea Venture,* was shipwrecked on the island of Bermuda, a story that later inspired Shakespeare's *The Tempest.* While marooned, Rolfe's wife gave birth to a daughter, named Bermuda, and he helped to break down the wrecked *Sea Venture* into three smaller vessels for the settlers' escape. Although the family reached Virginia by May 1610, both wife and daughter died shortly after their arrival.

Personally addicted to nicotine, Rolfe, an amateur Jacobean alchemist and chemist, conducted extensive agricultural experiments on the native tobacco plants in an attempt to establish a profitable staple crop for the colony. Unsatisfied by the results of his experiments, he smuggled in precious seeds of Spanish Orinoco tobacco, which yielded a crop of valuable leaves for export.

Established as one of Virginia's wealthiest landowners, Rolfe became smitten with another Virginia celebrity, Pocahontas, or Matoaka, daughter of Powhatan. She was living as a carefully held hostage at Jamestown after acting as a liaison between the English and her powerful father. Rolfe was concerned about his strong attraction to a non-Christian woman, and he wrote extensively to Sir Thomas Dale and the Virginia Company's authorities asking for instructions and approval of his courtship. When Pocahontas converted to the Church of England in 1613, taking the name Lady Rebecca, he wasted no time in courting her and gaining permission from Powhatan for them to wed at Jamestown on April 5, 1613.

This marriage regularized relations between the settlers and the Powhatan Confederacy. It further enriched Rolfe by bringing him land near Varina, as well as the expertise of an established tobacco growing culture. In 1616, he was promoted to recorder-general of the colony of Virginia, and he became a father again with the birth of his son Thomas.

That same year, the Virginia Company brought Rolfe and his family back to England on a promotional tour to recruit more settlers and gain investors in the growing tobacco market. Rolfe was offended by his treatment during the trip. His wife, now referred to as "Lady Rebecca," was given the status of visiting royalty at the court of James I; however, Rolfe was still considered a commoner, which necessitated embarrassing differences in their social presentation. Rolfe complained frequently about her stipend, their lodgings, and his seating at official events.

The Rolfes made a short visit to his brother and relatives in Norfolk, but he was anxious to return to his plantations. Before they could return to North America, Pocahontas became ill, probably from smallpox; she died at Gravesend in March 1617. Leaving young Thomas behind with his brother Henry, Rolfe returned to Virginia.

Shortly after his homecoming, Rolfe married Jane Pierce, a widow, by whom he had a daughter, Elizabeth, in 1620. Although it was often reported that Rolfe died in the March 1622 attack on Jamestown by the Powhatan, he survived that conflict and died sometime in 1623.

Rolfe left substantial property, including 1,700 acres at Mulberry Island and Varina, as well as his original land grant, to Thomas Rolfe, who never saw his father again and moved to Virginia only after 1640. Thomas Rolfe's many descendents formed a substantial bloc within the elite first families of Virginia. As grandchildren of Pocahontas, they necessitated exemptions in Virginia's laws against nonwhite property ownership and marriages.

All historical records concerning John Rolfe's daughter Elizabeth after the age of four were lost. Historians do not know if she survived to adulthood or left any heirs.

Margaret Sankey

See also: Jamestown; Pocahontas; Powhatan; Powhatan Confederacy; Smith, John; Virginia Company. *Document:* The Jamestown Settlement (1607–1609).

Bibliography

Allen, Paula Gunn. *Pocahontas.* San Francisco: HarperCollins, 2003.

Barbour, Philip. *Pocahontas and Her World.* Boston: Houghton Mifflin, 1970.

Price, David. *Love and Hate in Jamestown.* New York: Alfred A. Knopf, 2003.

Rowlandson, Mary (1637–1711)

The author of the first captivity narrative in American history and only the second American woman to publish, Mary Rowlandson spent three months in 1676 as the prisoner of the Narragansetts during King Philip's War. Her best-selling *The Soveraignty and Goodness of God* (1682) provides a valuable perspective on the conflict that slowed New England's growth for a generation.

Born to farmers John and Joan White in Somerset County, England, in 1637, Rowlandson crossed the Atlantic with her parents as part of the great migration of Puritans. She arrived in Salem, Massachusetts, in 1639 and settled on her father's tract of land about 6 miles outside of town. The small, isolated community of late-arriving Puritans subsequently separated from Salem and formed the town of Wenham. Her family then moved to the frontier town of Lancaster, about 50 miles away.

In Lancaster, Rowlandson married minister Joseph Rowlandson around 1656. With this marriage, Rowlandson rose in status to become the most prominent woman in town and the only one entitled to the honorific "mistress" instead of "goodwife." The loss of status that Rowlandson later suffered during her captivity would be a recurrent theme in her biography.

A bold, independent, and pious woman, Rowlandson had borne at least three children by 1676. In that year, her husband went to Boston to plead for troops to defend Lancaster from expected native attacks by Metacom (King Philip) and his supporters. About 400 Narragansetts, Nipmucs, and Wampanoags from a large intertribal encampment at the Nipmuc town of Menameset about 25 miles to the south attacked Lancaster on February 10, 1676.

When English soldiers arrived, the Rowlandsons' garrison house soon stood engulfed in flames, while fourteen townspeople lay dead and twenty-three had been taken away as captives. By the end of March, English would flee Lancaster as too difficult to defend. Joseph Rowlandson remained in Boston and declined a position as army chaplain in order to devote his energies to securing the release of his family.

Mary Rowlandson then entered upon three months of captivity with her three children. Her infant Sarah died in her arms soon after their capture, while Rowlandson became separated from the other two when her captor sold her to another Narragansett. She may have decided to write her story as a means of dealing with the trauma of these events and of understanding the experience in Puritan terms.

In an era when women very rarely published, Rowlandson was likely prompted to seek an audience as part of Increase Mather's project to demonstrate the role of divine providence in the shaping of human lives and events. *The Soveraignty and Goodness of God* is a typical captivity tale in that it is the story of a morally pure white woman, who confronts the hellish terror of life among savages. The account is divided into twenty removes for the twenty occasions when Rowlandson and her captors broke camp and traveled. Biblical references are included to show that God was testing Rowlandson and her fellow colonists through the medium of a destructive war.

Rowlandson's captor Quinnapin was married to the squaw sachem Wetamoo of the Pocasset Wampanoag, and this placed the Puritan under the control of one of the most politically powerful Native American women. Despite this, Rowlandson refused to recognize Wetamoo's status and reacted angrily when the native people treated her as just another servant. Throughout the work, Rowlandson portrays natives as savages and Europeans as civilized people with chaste motives. Her blatant biases do not make the book a useful guide for Native American history but do show the refusal of Puritans to adjust to another culture.

As the war gradually turned in the colonists' favor, Rowlandson was ransomed and rejoined her family in Boston. In 1677, Joseph agreed to serve as minister at Wethersfield, Connecticut, and he capitalized on his wife's fame to secure a salary that made him one of the highest-paid clergymen in New England. He did not enjoy his status long, however, leaving Rowlandson a widow in 1678.

Her status and money ensured that Mary Rowlandson did not remain single for long. Within the year, she married wealthy landowner Samuel Talcott, also of Wethersfield. Widowed again in 1691, she died in January 1711.

Rowlandson's book became a best seller in colonial New England and has been continually in print since 1770. One of the rare autobiographies of a colonial woman, it provides valuable insight into Puritan thought, as well as instruction about the cultural tensions that led to King Philip's War.

Caryn E. Neumann

See also: Captivity (by Native Americans); Literature; Native American–European Relations; Women.

Bibliography

Breitweiser, Mitchell Robert. *American Puritanism and the Defense of Mourning: Religion, Grief, and Ethnology in Mary White Rowlandson's Captivity Narrative.* Madison: University of Wisconsin Press, 1990.

Salisbury, Neal, ed. *The Sovereignty and Goodness of God by Mary Rowlandson.* Boston: Bedford, 1997.

Royal African Company

Over the course of eighty years (1672–1752), the Royal African Company played an integral role in the transatlantic slave trade. Chartered in England by Charles II as a joint-stock company in 1672, the Royal African Company conducted trade along the coast of Africa from the Senegal River to Angola. The establishment of slave forts in these regions facilitated the company's trade and provided protection from rival nations.

During the first two decades of its existence, the Royal African Company maintained a monopoly of the slave trade. The company controlled the English trade to the West Indies and the English colonies in North America until 1698. In addition to its trade monopoly with the English colonies, the company also received the Spanish *asiento,* granting it exclusive rights to supply the Spanish colonies with slaves.

Although the Royal African Company maintained a monopoly of the English and Spanish trade, it faced competition from other European trading companies. Prior to 1672, Denmark, France, Holland, Portugal, and Sweden each established chartered companies to engage in the slave trade from Africa.

As a complex business, the slave trade from Africa required considerable organization on both sides of the Atlantic. Ships departed from prominent ports such as Bristol or Liverpool carrying trade goods for sale along the West African coast. Trade goods included an assortment of items such as beans, beer, brass, candles, chairs, cider, copper, earthenware, glasses, gunpowder, guns, haberdashery, kettles, salt, and textiles.

These items were traded for enslaved Africans.

The Royal African Company also purchased ivory, gold, and various exotic woods; however, enslaved Africans comprised 40 percent of the Royal African Company's trade in Africa. Captive Africans were transported to the West Indies or North America, where they were sold. The proceeds of these sales, along with items procured in Africa and plantation cash crops from the colonies, were then brought back to England.

In 1698, Parliament opened the slave trade to any English subject who could pay the 10 percent ad valorem tax on all goods and slaves exported out of Africa. The Royal African Company received the proceeds of this tax to pay for the maintenance of its forts in Africa. As English subjects, American merchants received licenses to participate in the slave trade, provided that the Royal African Company received the prescribed 10 percent of their profits.

The Chesapeake colonies, Middle colonies, New England colonies, and low-country colonies developed different economies and labor needs. In the Chesapeake colonies of Virginia and Maryland, African slave labor replaced the labor of white indentured servants on tobacco plantations during the 1680s. Prior to this time, the majority of Africans who came to the Chesapeake colonies arrived from the West Indies through the Atlantic trade with the British Caribbean. By 1686, seven Royal African Company ships with over 1,400 slaves had arrived in Virginia. The number of Africans imported into the Chesapeake continued to increase; during the first four decades of the eighteenth century, 39,000 slaves entered Virginia.

The Royal African Company also provided slaves to New York, following the Dutch cession of New Amsterdam to the British in 1664. Slaves for the New York market also arrived in New Jersey, which did not impose an import duty on slaves. Most African slaves brought to the New York area were used to work the large estates along the Hudson River. Africans also were employed as servants, artisans, cooks, and coachmen.

During the eighteenth century, most British slave ships were built in the American colonies. In this context, Massachusetts and Rhode Island developed a thriving lumber industry and maintained productive shipyards for the trade.

Rum production also flourished in the New England colonies. The expansion of New England merchants in the trade made American-produced rum an important commodity for trade with African rulers, particularly during the 1690s, when wars in Europe disrupted the traditional trade routes of the Royal African Company.

In the years preceding its dissolution, the Royal African Company provided slaves for the expanding rice plantations of South Carolina. Between 1735 and 1740, the company imported 11,000 slaves from Angola and the Gambia region to meet the colony's labor demands.

The company's subsequent bankruptcy and reorganization diminished its capacity to control the trade from Africa. In 1752, the Royal African Company was dissolved.

Karen B. Bell

See also: Joint-Stock Companies; Slave Trade; Slavery, African American; Slavery, Caribbean; Trade; Triangle Trade.

Bibliography

Coughtry, Jay. *The Notorious Triangle: Rhode Island and the African Slave Trade, 1700–1807*. Philadelphia: Temple University Press, 1981.

Davies, Kenneth Gordon. *The Royal African Company*. New York: Longmans, Green, 1957.

Kullikoff, Allan. "The Origins of Afro-American Society in Tidewater Maryland and Virginia, 1700–1790." *William and Mary Quarterly* (April 1978): 226–59.

Reiss, Oscar. *Blacks in Colonial America*. North Carolina: McFarland & Co., 1997.

Wood, Peter H. *Black Majority: Negroes in Colonial South Carolina from 1670 through the Stono Rebellion*. New York: W. W. Norton, 1974.

Rush, Benjamin
(1745–1813)

Benjamin Rush, physician, patriot, and reformer, was educated in the household of Samuel Finley, his maternal uncle, and at the College of New Jersey (later Princeton) under the tutelage of Samuel Davies. Finley's discipline and Davies's Presbyterian gospel of public duty instilled in Rush a deep piety and commitment to social welfare that stayed with him throughout his life.

Rush received his bachelor of arts degree in 1760 and soon sailed for Europe to attend Edinburgh's prestigious medical school. After receiving his medical degree in 1768, Rush returned to the colonies and set up in practice in Philadelphia. In 1769, he was appointed professor of chemistry at the College of Philadelphia; he was the first native-born American to hold that position.

Dr. Benjamin Rush was one of the leading men of science and social reformers of his time. He founded America's first free dispensary, wrote its first chemistry textbook and first treatise on mental illness, and was an early advocate of women's education. *(The Stapleton Collection/Bridgeman Art Library)*

Thus equipped with a small income and good prospects and imbued with a zealous urge to improve his city and his world, Rush turned his attention to politics and the growing tensions with Great Britain. As early as 1769, he was arguing privately for economic autonomy and domestic production as the surest path to liberty. Going public in 1773, he coauthored a newspaper piece appealing to readers to keep East Indian tea out of American ports. After Lexington and Concord, he began encouraging his friend Thomas Paine to compose a persuasive tract to argue the case for political independence, suggesting the title *Common Sense*.

Rush served as Pennsylvania's delegate to the second Continental Congress (1774) and signed the Declaration of Independence (1776). That same year, he married Julia Stockton, the daughter of family friends and fourteen years his junior. In 1777, he was named surgeon general of the Middle Department of the Continental army and served diligently until he resigned, after criticizing General Washington's failure to improve medical conditions in the field.

Returning to private practice and college teaching, Rush became deeply disillusioned by the way the republican experiment was unraveling in postwar Philadelphia. A lower-class group of self-proclaimed "egalitarians" had seized control of state government, instituting a unicameral legislature that Rush perceived as a seat of arbitrary power more dangerous than monarchy. To heal the wounds of such factionalism and to revive his dream of a republican utopia, Rush set about creating a network of voluntary associations that encompassed prison welfare, health care, temperance, exercise, Sunday schools, missionary societies, and African church organizations.

In addition, Rush cared passionately about the state of female education in the new United States, advocating that ladies should be sufficiently educated "to concur in instructing their sons in the principles of liberty and government." To train a generation of young ladies to bring up good-citizen sons, Rush established the Young Ladies' Academy in Philadelphia, a model imitated nationally, where students studied reading, writing, bookkeeping, arithmetic, geography, history, vocal music, Christian religion, and Bible reading. Rush's mission to educate the future of the republic also extended to the men of the Pennsylvania backcountry and culminated in the foundation of Dickinson College in Carlisle in 1783.

As a teacher of medicine, Rush was the most influential physician in America. His son estimated that 2,872 students were registered in his medical classes between 1779 and 1812 at the College of Philadelphia and the University of Pennsylvania (from 1792). He was the author of a popular syllabus on chemistry and published several important medical treatises on cholera, dropsy, measles, cancer, tuberculosis, and dengue.

During the yellow fever epidemic of 1793, which claimed one in ten of his fellow Philadelphians, Rush worked tirelessly to treat the sick and prevent the spread of the disease. His insightful efforts to improve public sanitation won him many endorsements, but his seemingly indiscriminate bloodletting proved deeply controversial and led to claims that he was contributing to the death toll.

Overall, however, Rush's medical contributions were more positive. In 1786, he had established the nation's first free dispensary, and he sponsored many preventive programs, including a course of smallpox inoculations and, later, vaccinations. And as a result of his advocacy for humane treatment of the insane and his authorship of the first comprehensive medical treatise on mental illness, Rush is justly called the Father of American Psychiatry.

As his reputation grew, Rush was appointed to several honorary positions, such as treasurer of the U.S. Mint in 1797 and scientific adviser to the Lewis and Clark expedition in 1803. Mixing in increasingly lofty circles, it was Rush who finally healed the ancient rift between John Adams and Thomas Jefferson.

In the spring of 1813, the doctor, by now Philadelphia's first citizen, fell ill. After bleeding himself twice, he died five days later at his home.

Richard Bell

See also: Revolutionary War; Science.

Bibliography

Goodman, Nathan. *Benjamin Rush, Physician and Citizen, 1746–1813.* Philadelphia: University of Pennsylvania Press, 1934.

Hawke, David Freeman. *Benjamin Rush; Revolutionary Gadfly.* Indianapolis, IN: Bobbs-Merrill, 1971.

Kloos, John. *A Sense of Deity: The Republican Spirituality of Dr. Benjamin Rush.* Brooklyn, NY: Carlson, 1991.

S

Saint-Domingue

The French colony of Saint-Domingue, situated in the western third of Hispaniola, was the main overseas component of the French Empire. It developed into the world's most prosperous colony of the eighteenth century. Saint-Domingue should not be confused with Santo Domingo, which refers to the Spanish colony on the eastern part of Hispaniola or its main city, after which both the Spanish and the French colonies were named.

In the course of the French Revolution, Saint-Domingue (then renamed Haiti) gained independence as the second state of the New World after the United States. This is a unique and meaningful case, as it is the only example before the twentieth century of the governmental power of a colonized country being passed to the most deprived social group—in this case, former slaves and poor free persons of African descent.

The Emergence of the Colony, 1630–1720

The colony of Saint-Domingue was born out of anarchism. Originally the Spanish had colonized Hispaniola from 1492 onward, virtually extinguishing its Arawak population within years. The city of Santo Domingo, founded on the southeast coast, became the earliest center of the Spanish-American empire before the focus moved to the American mainland and to the Cuban naval base of Havana. The Windward Passage—between Hispaniola and Cuba, its northwestern neighbor—and the vicinal coasts of both islands were under weak control of the authorities, as the urban footholds of Spanish power—Havana and Santo Domingo—were situated on the opposite coasts of the respective islands. This lack of official control encouraged traffic in contraband between the coastal Spanish inhabitants and the French and English buccaneers. To repress this illegal commerce, the Spanish decided to withdraw from western Hispaniola in 1605. This move, on the other hand, gave the pirates the opportunity not only to use the Windward Passage as a forbidden back door to the Caribbean but also to establish footholds there.

At first, around 1630, settlement focused on Tortuga Island, in front of the northwestern coast of Hispaniola. Settlers trickled into the main island from the 1650s onward. In 1670, Cap François (today Cap-Haïtian) was founded on the northern coast and developed into the island's main city, only in the late eighteenth century to be rivaled by Port-au-Prince, the capital of Saint-Domingue, or Haiti, since 1749.

In the beginning, both French and English pirates took seats on Hispaniola, but this coexistence, just like the rather anarchic disposition of the settlements, quickly came to an end. The French government had established colonies in Guadeloupe, Martinique, and some smaller Caribbean islands since the 1620s and had even appointed military governors to Tortuga since 1642. But only in the 1660s did Jean Baptiste Colbert, appointed secretary of finance by Louis XIV, intensify colonization in the New World. A new French West India Company was advised to enforce settlement on the main island of Hispaniola. Bertrand d'Oregon, governor from 1665 to 1676, contributed most to turning the piracy settlement into a formal French colony. The country was divided into northern, western, and southern departments, following the mountain chains stretching from east to west.

Later on, the head of the colony's administration became twofold, as in 1705—formally in 1719—the military governor was joined by an *intendant,* a delegate of the French government. Although the governor focused on military concerns and the intendant on financial matters, they shared in leading the administration and thereby controlled each other.

Before the first intendant arrived, military conflict with Spanish and English forces occupied the governor's attention. Even though the land was ceded by the Spanish to the French in the Treaty of Ryswick in 1697, the outbreak of the War of the Spanish Succession in 1702 revived fighting between the European powers in the Caribbean, until the Treaty of Utrecht was signed 1713. In the following years, the focus shifted from the military to the economic development of Saint-Domingue.

The Unfolding of Economy and Society, 1720–1790

Even in the seventeenth century, the coarse commerce of piracy was not the only economic activity on Saint-Domingue. The settlers cultivated land for self-supply and also grew tobacco for sale. This crop was encouraged by the authorities, but around 1720 the growing of tobacco was ousted by a modern plantation economy.

The main product was sugar. Saint-Domingue contributed the lion's share of sugar production to the annual yield of about 65,000 tons, which put the French colonies ahead of the British, making them the market leaders around 1760. At first, indigo took second place in Saint-Domingue's foreign trade. By the 1780s, output had stagnated and the dyestuff had fallen back to third place, but Saint-Domingue still provided about 1,000 tons, or half of the world's production.

A rapid extension of coffee cultivation between 1765 and 1780 more than tripled the annual yield to nearly 40,000 tons, or two-thirds of the world's produce. Cacao also was grown until about 1740, and cotton became a fourth major product of Saint-Domingue, with about 500 tons in the late 1760s and 1,000 tons around 1790.

Thus, the economic relevance of the colony was enormous. Consequently, after losing the Seven Years' War, the French government ceded the whole of Canada to the British to secure possession of Saint-Domingue in 1763.

In 1789, some 2.5 million acres of land were cultivated on about 7,800 plantations. The plantation economy was the most effective but also a cruel preindustrial system of production, an intense single-crop agriculture relying on the exploitation of slave labor. Saint-Domingue is a very illuminating example of the plantation system, as nowhere else did it generate such vast economic growth and have such grave consequences for the composition of the society.

By 1790, between 500,000 and 700,000 slaves were living in Saint-Domingue, more than in the whole of the United States at that time. Slaves constituted about 20 percent of the U.S. population, but 90 percent of Saint-Domingue's. The small layer of about 60,000 free people again stratified. The bottom half was made up of the so-called *affranchis,* mulattos and freed slaves. The upper half was formed by the *petits blancs* ("small whites") and the richest and most powerful *grands blancs* ("big whites"). Three-quarters of the whites and two-thirds of the black slaves had not been born in Saint-Domingue. This indicates the extent to which the growing economy affected the fabric of this society.

The same goes for the gender imbalance of these classes: About 60 percent of the slaves and even 80 percent of the whites were male. The overabundance of white men emboldened prostitution—55 percent of the free colored people were female—and encouraged interracial sexual relations. This was the main reason for the growing number of affranchis, who had accounted for no more than a third of the free population until the 1760s. Their imminent outnumbering of the white population increased social tension, especially as, in contrast to whites and slaves, nearly all free colored people had been born in Saint-Domingue but could gain no social standing or even political participation in their country.

The Haitian Revolution, 1790–1804

The tremors of the French Revolution, starting in 1789, tempted different social groups in Saint-Domingue to improve their position. Analogous to the French National Assembly, an assembly of the free people of the colony was allowed. Still, to what degree the free colored people should participate remained controversial.

Completely excluded by the grands blancs, the affranchis revolted, to no avail, in 1790. When, on the other hand, the French government tried to pacify the mulattos by granting civil rights to the wealthiest among them in 1791, the whites objected and fighting flared up again.

More seriously, a slave rebellion broke out in August, involving up to 80,000 slaves by November. To obtain allies against the rebellion, the government gave civil rights to all affranchis in 1792. But the disintegration of the country continued, especially when, in 1793, French, Spanish, and British forces arrived. Different factions of the rebels allied with different European powers.

The former slave Toussaint L'Ouverture joined the slave revolt sweeping the French colony of Saint-Domingue (later Haiti) in 1791. He rose to a position of power and ultimately led the nation to independence—making it the first in Latin America to attain that status. *(Bibliotheque Nationale, Paris, France/Roger-Viollet, Paris/Bridgeman Art Library)*

In 1794, during the most radical phase of the French Revolution, slavery was abolished in all French colonies. This caused François Dominique Toussaint-L'Ouverture, a former slave and the most successful rebel leader allied with the Spanish, to change sides and unite with the French forces. By 1795, the Spanish troops had been expelled; by 1799, the British occupiers had withdrawn; and, in 1801, even the Spanish part of Hispaniola was taken.

Toussaint-L'Ouverture was a charismatic and able but also rigid and sometimes cruel politician, and he ousted both white and colored rivals for power. With French consent, he enacted a constitution and made himself lifetime governor general in 1801; however, Napoleon wanted to re-establish slavery in all overseas parts of his empire. Toussaint-L'Ouverture was placed under detention in 1802 and died in France in 1803.

The fear of slavery again empowered a rebellion. An army of blacks and mulattos, led among others by the former slave Jean-Jacques Dessalines, succeeded in definitively driving the French from the island. On January 1, 1804, Dessalines declared Hispaniola independent and became its emperor later that year.

The Europeans and the United States showed little sympathy for the new state. It became a bogey also for the colonial elite, as it proved that the colonial social order could be turned upside down. Hence, this case had an enormous impact on the process whereby the Latin American colonies became independent.

War had devastated the cultivated land, and both international isolation and internal struggles hampered economic recovery, so the richest land of the Caribbean developed into one of the poorest. And the colonial name of Saint-Domingue vanished.

The new state, soon again limited to the western part of Hispaniola, was renamed Haiti, the original Arawak expression for the island, meaning "mountainous." This indicates the difficulty of finding a national identity, as the Arawaks had been extinguished well before the French set foot on the island or the coming of the displaced blacks who formed Haitian society.

Alexander Engel

See also: Caribbean (Chronology); French; Hispaniola; Slavery, Caribbean; Sugar.

Bibliography

Crouse, Nellis M. *The French Struggle for the West Indies, 1665–1713.* New York: Octagon, 1966.

Geggus, David Patrick. *Slavery, War and Revolution: The British Occupation of Saint Domingue, 1793–1798.* Oxford, UK: Oxford University Press, 1992.

———. "Sugar and coffee cultivation in Saint Domingue and the shaping of the slave labour force." In *Cultivation and Culture: Work Process and the Shaping of Afro-American Culture in the Americas,* edited by Ira Berlin and Philip Morgan. Charlottesville: University Press of Virginia, 1993.

McClellan, James E., III. *Colonialism and Science. Saint Domingue in the Old Regime.* Baltimore: Johns Hopkins University Press, 1992.

Ott, Thomas. *The Haitian Revolution, 1789–1804.* Knoxville: University of Tennessee Press, 1973.

Salem

The site of the largest and most infamous witch hunt in American history, Salem was the first town settled by nonseparating Puritans in Colonial America. Despite the witch hysteria and the religious and civil turmoil caused by the separatist Roger Williams, Salem's growth as a commercial seaport propelled the Massachusetts city to the forefront of colonial politics during the Revolutionary era.

Three years after the separatist colony of Plymouth was established in 1620, a group of farmers, fishermen, and trappers landed at Cape Ann, Massachusetts, on a quest for riches. Having little success, most of the company returned to England within five years. Led by Roger Conant, the remaining settlers found sheltered, fertile land at the mouth of the Naumkeag River. Their settlement, which was called Naumkeag in 1626, was renamed Salem in 1629 for the Hebrew word *shalom,* or peace.

The New England Company, which was granted permission to settle and govern the area, sent Captain John Endecott, a Dutch war veteran, to preside over the new town. Under his leadership, the first nonseparatist Congregational Church in Massachusetts was founded at Salem on July 20, 1629.

Because of its location, Salem was the destination for John Winthrop's fleet. Only a few weeks after their arrival in June 1630, however, Winthrop and his followers moved to the more sheltered and spacious bay. Although the Salem Church had not separated from the Church of England, its acceptance of the separatist Roger Williams as a member in 1633 and as minister

Best known as the site of the witch trials of 1692, Salem, Massachusetts, was the first town settled (in 1626) by non-separating Puritans in colonial America. It became a fishing, building, and maritime trade center in the eighteenth century. (© *Peabody Essex Museum, Salem, Massachusetts/Bridgeman Art Library*)

in 1635 raised a stir among the religious and civil leaders throughout the colony. As minister, Williams insisted that the king's land patent in New England was invalid and that civil government had no authority over religious affairs. The members of his congregation agreed with these claims. Their support, however, waned, as Williams boldly claimed that all churches outside of Salem were not pure and must be renounced as false. Having lost the support of his congregation, in October 1635, the General Court ordered Williams to leave the colony. His removal to Rhode Island in January, however, did not mark an end to the civil and religious turmoil that would later engulf this settlement.

By the beginning of the 1690s, the diverging interests of the people of Salem Village, which had recently been established as an independent settlement from Salem Town, led to an outbreak of witch hysteria unparalleled in American history. Factions within the village emerged, as people expressed either support for or opposition to Samuel Parris, their new minister. The opposition between these factions, normally split along economic and social lines, was heightened when, in January 1692, a group of girls began to show symptoms of what village leaders believed to be demonic possession. Accusations of the practice of witchcraft were directed at factional opponents and especially at women who defied traditional norms for their class and gender.

A special court was convened in Salem Town to try the suspected witches. On June 2, 1692, Bridget Bishop, accused of being a witch, was condemned; she was executed by hanging eight days later. This first execution brought new fervor to the episode; accusations and arrests spread through the village and to the surrounding towns. As additional "witches" were condemned and executed, anxiety swept through the colony. In an attempt to avoid the punishment of death, accused witches began to confess and even to implicate others. Hundreds were arrested and imprisoned, and numerous ministers, civil leaders, and lay people began to oppose the proceedings of the court.

By late October, Governor Sir William Phips suspended the trials and eventually pardoned all remaining prisoners. The witch craze ultimately claimed the lives of almost two dozen men and women. Although apologies and monetary restitution were later made, the events of 1692 remain a dark mark on Salem's history.

Despite these events, Salem developed into a major fishing, building, and maritime trade center during the eighteenth century. Its commercial successes and population growth thrust Salem into the spotlight during the Revolutionary period.

In 1774, a provincial congress was organized in the town, and two months before the hostilities at Lexington and Concord, skirmishes between Americans and British soldiers broke out on Salem's streets. During the war, Salem's fleet captured or sunk over 450 British vessels. When the United States was finally organized after the Revolution, Salem was the sixth-largest city in the new country.

Aaron F. Christensen

See also: Massachusetts; Puritanism; Trade; Witchcraft and Witch Trials. *Documents:* The Salem Witch Trial of Susanna Martin (1692); Thomas Brattle on the Salem Trials (1692); A Poem Recalling the Hanging of a Relative due to the Salem Witch Trials (in 1692; pub. 1857).

Bibliography

Boyer, Paul, and Stephen Nissenbaum. *Salem Possessed: The Social Origins of Witchcraft.* Cambridge, MA: Harvard University Press, 1974.
Demos, John Putnam. *Entertaining Satan: Witchcraft and Culture in Early New England.* New York: Oxford University Press, 1982.
Morgan, Edmund S. *The Puritan Dilemma: The Story of John Winthrop.* Boston: Little Brown, 1958.

Santa Fe

Santa Fe was, and remains today, the capital of New Mexico, which was the most populous and successful settlement on New Spain's northern frontier. The Spanish settled Santa Fe around 1608, when Juan de Oñate, the first Spanish colonizer of New Mexico, began to move some of his settlers south from San Gabriel. In 1610, Pedro de Peralta, the governor of New Mexico, made Santa Fe an official villa and the capital of the colony.

Pueblo Indians already lived in Santa Fe when the Spanish settlers moved there. In fact, Spaniards forced the Pueblos to labor as part of the *repartimiento,* in which the native peoples were made to work on public projects. In this manner, the Pueblo built Santa Fe for the Spanish settlers.

For decades, Spaniards and Native Americans continued to live together in Santa Fe and northern New Mexico with intermittent conflict. Missionaries in New Mexico labored to convert the native peoples to Christianity, and these missionaries' repression of native religion and treatment of the natives were harsh at times. The missionaries and government officials also quarreled with each other and fought over native labor. Sometimes, the Pueblos were able to play the two sides off against one another to negotiate better treatment.

In the 1660s and 1670s, drought led to crop failure, livestock deaths, and famine. The Apache and Navajo, who also were suffering from the drought, made more raids on the Pueblo. As a result of these difficulties, many Pueblos abandoned Christianity and returned to their native religion.

A San Juan Pueblo Indian named Popé organized most of the Pueblos in a coordinated revolt that occurred on August 10, 1680. Pueblos killed about 400 of 2,500 settlers in New Mexico, but the natives largely directed their anger toward missionaries and religious objects, killing twenty-one of thirty-three missionaries and destroying churches. Many Spanish survivors fled to Santa Fe and continued to fight, until they realized they could not win and fled to El Paso on September 21, 1680.

The Pueblo peoples maintained control of Santa Fe and northern New Mexico for about a decade, until Diego de Vargas reconquered the region in 1692 and 1693. When the Spaniards returned, they lessened demands on the native peoples for labor and allowed them more religious freedom.

The nonnative population of Santa Fe increased throughout the eighteenth century. In 1750, the population of Santa Fe included 965 nonnatives and 570 natives. By 1790, Santa Fe consisted of 2,997 nonnatives and 598 natives.

From the time the Spaniards first arrived, Native Americans became part of Spanish households. Many of these native peoples were *criadas,* or servants, who had been taken in war by Spaniards or rescued from Plains Indians, who were holding them captive. These *criadas* were raised in Spanish households and taught Christianity. Some were adopted into families formally or as godchildren. Treatment of servants ranged from incorporation as family members to sheer cruelty.

The high number of female servants contributed to the unbalanced sex ratio of the Santa Fe population. There were more women in Santa Fe than men, making Santa Fe an unusual settlement on the frontier of New Spain, where men more often outnumbered women.

The late 1800s saw major changes affecting Santa Fe. In 1786, Spanish officials negotiated a peace with the Comanche, which led to relative peace for several decades and allowed settlers to expand beyond the town limits. Government reforms, known as the Bourbon reforms, increased money circulation and regulated taxes more accurately, stimulating the economy of New Mexico. Settlers in northern New Mexico traded in Chihuahua, as well as at Taos with Plains Indians.

After Mexican independence in 1821, Santa Fe became the locus of an international trade route known as the Santa Fe Trail. Starting in Missouri, American merchants brought manufactured products to trade for mules and silver in Santa Fe. Many merchants who participated in this trade became wealthy. The trade also changed Santa Fe and New Mexico, because of the influx of foreigners and manufactured goods.

During the United States–Mexican War from 1846 to 1848, Stephen Kearney took Santa Fe and New Mexico with little fighting, but within months there were various challenges to American control. Following the war, New Mexico became a permanent part of the United States, and Santa Fe remained the capital of New Mexico.

Amy Meschke

See also: New Mexico; Spanish Colonies on Mainland North America (Chronology).

Bibliography

Brooks, James F. *Captive and Cousins: Slavery, Kinship, and Community in the Southwest Borderlands.* Chapel Hill: University of North Carolina Press, 2002.

Frank, Ross. *From Settler to Citizen: New Mexican Economic Development and the Creation of Vecino Society, 1750–1820.* Berkeley: University of California Press, 2000.

Weber, David J. *The Spanish Frontier in North America.* New Haven, CT: Yale University Press, 1992.

Savannah

In early 1733, James Oglethorpe scouted a location for Georgia's first permanent settlement. He selected an elevated site on Yamacraw bluff, several miles upstream from the mouth of the Savannah River. The new town drew its name directly from the nearest major geographic landmark: Savannah.

The settlement's street plan was distinctive, calling for sizable public squares at frequent intervals. Today, these are still the town's most recognizable and celebrated decorative features. In the colonial era, they were used for a variety of practical purposes—markets,

Savannah, Georgia, a major Southern port just above the mouth of the Savannah River, was laid out in 1733 by James Oglethorpe into forty-lot wards, each centered on an open square. Beyond the downtown wards were gardens and farms for every colonist. *(Brown Brothers, Sterling, Pennsylvania)*

public gatherings, and even places of refuge in times of war for people in outlying villages.

Physically, Savannah's location appeared ideally suited to promote economic growth. The nearby native population offered opportunities for trade, and the waterfront could hold an estimated 400 vessels at once. However, Savannah was economically stagnant during its early years. The Native American trade quickly shifted westward to the town of Augusta.

Additionally, the Savannah River's depth near the Atlantic Ocean proved unpredictable; even experienced pilots grounded ships surprisingly often. Many merchants adopted the awkward expedient of loading or unloading a portion of their cargoes on the coast in order to reduce the draft of their ships as they entered the river.

Another difficulty was that Savannah held little attraction for merchants during its first two decades. As late as 1760, the town was a motley collection of 200 or so wood buildings, and an aura of impermanence hovered over it. The close proximity of the prosperous port at Charles Town meant that most goods imported into early Georgia passed through South Carolina. The leading Savannah merchant house of Habersham and Harris did most of its buying and selling in the neighboring province rather than London.

The situation did not change until Georgia experienced its first prolonged economic expansion in the 1760s. In 1761, only 41 ships cleared Savannah's harbor. A decade later—driven by a developing plantation society and booming rice exports—that number had jumped to 217 vessels, as the young port began to emerge as a worthy destination in its own right.

Savannah's newfound prosperity was reflected in its population and improved physical appearance. From an initial seeding of 114 settlers in 1733, it had grown to a bustling seaport of some 3,500 inhabitants by the eve of the American Revolution. The once empty waterfront was now lined with tidy warehouses holding valuable commodities bound for destinations throughout the Atlantic world.

Just as Savannah's economy was slow to develop, so, too, was its culture. Early shipments contained few books other than tracts intended to foster obedience and industry in the colonists. Education was largely in the hands of private tutors. By the 1740s, Savannah took a few important developmental steps. The Bethesda Orphanage and school instructed parentless children in theology and the classics, and an informal public lending library was run out of the Savannah rector's residence. Two other libraries soon developed. Savannah achieved its first true literary landmark with the 1763 launch of the *Georgia Gazette,* the province's first regular newspaper.

The population was not large or cosmopolitan enough, however, to sustain the arts. Plays and performances entertained residents from time to time, but Savannah never had a permanent theater. In some ways, Georgia's cultural life stayed undeveloped as compared to cities in other colonies.

The one realm in which Savannah consistently excelled was political agitation. As the province's capital and major trade center, the town became the focal point for opposition to various policies implemented by British authorities. During the first two decades of Georgia's existence, a group of town residents, referred to derisively as "malcontents," led an effective lobbying campaign in America and England against the Georgia Trust's restrictive policies on the ownership of land and slaves.

Two decades later, the town experienced riots in opposition to the 1765 Stamp Act, though these did not approach the ferocity of demonstrations in other parts of America. In ensuing years, however, Savannah's Sons of Liberty branch protested new imperial taxes more vehemently than did people in other areas of the colony.

During the American Revolution, Savannah was again the center of political conflict over the province's future. A British expeditionary force captured the city in 1778 and tried to use it as a base to reassert royal control over the colony as a whole. This strategy achieved decidedly uneven results until the English permanently withdrew in 1782. The new state was left to find its own way in the infant American nation.

Andrew C. Lannen

See also: Georgia; Georgia (Chronology).

Bibliography

Davis, Harold E. *The Fledgling Province: Social and Cultural Life in Colonial Georgia, 1733–1776.* Chapel Hill: University of North Carolina Press, 1976.

Weeks, Carl Solana. *Savannah in the Time of Peter Tondee: The Road to Revolution in Colonial Georgia.* Columbia, SC: Summerhouse Press, 1997.

Science

The European discovery of America was contemporary with the early modern scientific revolution, and America and science interacted from the beginning. America was a subject of interest to European scientists from its discovery, but it was not until the eighteenth century that the colonies developed self-sustaining scientific communities of their own.

Impact of America on European Scientific Knowledge

In addition to a mass of fascinating new data, America presented a fundamental challenge to the worldview of early modern European natural philosophers, whose "scientific revolution" corresponded chronologically with the first two centuries of colonization. The basic intellectual problem, once it was realized that the Americas were not an extension of Asia, was the lack of awareness shown both by Greek and Roman classical writers and by the Bible.

There were attempts to graft classical and biblical knowledge onto the Americas. Some suggested that the Native Americans were the ten lost tribes of Israel, and even though that was never a majority opinion among European thinkers, nearly all agreed on the necessity of fitting them into the biblical framework of descent from the sons of Noah. Some argued that America could be found in the Bible, or that various places in the New World were named after biblical figures. But Europeans gradually became aware that America was not dealt with specifically either by the classics or the Bible. The myriad of new plant and animal species encountered eventually made much of classical natural history, as well as geography, obsolete. Amerigo Vespucci specifically pointed out the abundance of new species not mentioned by the ancient Roman natural historian Pliny the Elder.

European expansion became the standard example for those who argued that modern civilization had advanced beyond the classical world. The would-be intellectual revolutionary Francis Bacon specifically compared himself to Columbus, and the frontispiece of his *Great Instauration* (1620) showed a ship sailing past the Pillars of Hercules, the western limit of the Mediterranean and a symbol of the limits of ancient knowledge.

The initial impact, intellectual and otherwise, of the New World discoveries was greatest by far in Spain, which received most of the new information. Spanish investigators dominated sixteenth-century New World natural history, producing a long series of works of which the earliest notable example is Gonzalo Fernández de Oviedo y Valdés's *Natural History of the Indies* (1526). The most complex debates on New World peoples and subjects in the sixteenth century were carried on in Aristotelian terms in the very conservative Spanish universities, particularly the University of Salamanca. The Spanish debate on the status of the Native Americans was the last major European intellectual debate to be framed entirely in Aristotelian terms.

European attitudes toward indigenous scientific knowledge varied. In all places, specifically local knowledge of geography, natural history, and local diseases was valued. The importation and cultivation of new crops—tobacco, tomatoes, corn, potatoes, and chocolate—required some appropriation of indigenous knowledge. The Mayan and Aztec calendars provoked curiosity and respect from European chronologists. But indigenous knowledge received little study in the more theoretical and abstract areas of natural philosophy, and interest in indigenous knowledge declined in the course of colonization.

Natural History

Much Spanish writing on the New World was translated into other European languages. The disciplines most transformed by the new knowledge were those of natural history, botany, and zoology. New natural knowledge came to Europe in a flood, particularly from the only recently encountered lands of the West. All kinds of previously unknown plants and animals had properties that had to be worked out with some help from indigenous informants but little from the ancient authorities.

Medicine was another local science drawing on both European and indigenous sources of knowledge. Colonial medicine was particularly important in the tropics, where diseases occurred that had no European precedents. Europeans were particularly interested in the medical properties of strange plants, and many of the scientific explorers and knowledge gatherers sent from Europe were physicians, such as Francisco Hernández, the Spanish physician who led a scientific survey of Mexico from 1571 to 1577.

Europeans were sometimes carried away with enthusiasm over the medical potential of foreign plants. For example, tobacco, a New World plant, was hailed as a wonder drug. It was claimed that it could cure migraine, cold stomach, kidney pain, hysteria, gout, toothache, worms, scabies, nettles, burns, wounds from poisoned arrows, and gunshots. Tobacco was also viewed as psychologically beneficial in calming the mind and making men more attractive to women.

In European colonial possessions, the creation of an exhaustive natural history both inventoried a colony's natural resources and made a textual claim on it. The production of such natural histories, however, required a substantial commitment of resources both to the collection of knowledge and to its publication in book form. Hernández's ambitious and state-sponsored natural history of Mexico was never published in its complete form, and the proposed natural history of Virginia that Thomas Harriot was involved in never got past its initial stages due to poor financing and the general shakiness of the English position in Virginia.

The tradition of European investigation of the natural history of foreign lands continued throughout the early modern period, although the predominantly medical interest of many of the early naturalists faded by the late seventeenth century in favor of a less use-oriented view. Curios, dried plants, and stuffed animals from foreign lands became the subjects of an international trade, mostly centered in Amsterdam during the seventeenth century and appealing to European collectors and museums.

While natural history specimens flowed from America to Europe, American scientists suffered both from intellectual isolation and from the difficulty, if not impossibility, of obtaining scientific equipment. The most important original scientist produced in the seventeenth-century British colonies, the physician and alchemist George Starkey of Bermuda and Harvard College, emigrated to England in part because of the dearth of laboratory equipment in New England.

Science in the Colonies

As Europeans established permanent settlements in the New World, the institutions and practices of European intellectual life went with them. Institutions such as the University of Mexico City or Harvard University mostly taught an Aristotelian curriculum, adapting to new intellectual currents with some time lag relative to Europe. But colonial institutions and groups could never compete with their counterparts in Europe as generators of new knowledge.

English science in the New World differed from French and Spanish in not being state-sponsored. Much English science, Harriot's *A Briefe and True Report of the New Found Land of Virginia* being the most notable example, was produced by individuals or groups hoping to promote colonization. As such, it had a promotional aspect.

What intensified English science in the Americas was the founding in 1660 of the Royal Society for the promotion of natural knowledge—a London-based organization with state sponsorship but financial and organizational independence. The first colonial admitted was John Winthrop, Jr., who was visiting London at the time. Winthrop was a practitioner of medicine and alchemy, and he brought the first telescope to New England. Over the period from 1660 to 1783, fifty-three colonials would be admitted as fellows (although twenty were colonial governors admitted primarily for their political prominence), and over 260 letters from colonials were published in the Royal Society's journal

Philosophical Transactions. Colonial fellows benefited from not having to pay admission fees or dues until 1753, when the society's financial needs caused the exemption to be abolished. (Difficulties in communication could still lead to problems, as when Cotton Mather was wrongly accused of falsely passing himself off as a fellow because his name did not appear on printed lists of fellows.) The Royal Society also sent lists of "queries" with persons journeying to the colonies in hopes of gathering information systematically.

Colonial scientists in the seventeenth century were a heterogeneous lot, but two groups prominently represented were physicians and ministers. Physicians were the group with the most education in the sciences, and ministers like Cotton Mather, in addition to a high level of education and a habit of reading, viewed science in terms of "natural theology." Mather's *The Christian Philosopher* (1721) was one of many works using the properties of the created world to exalt the glory and providence of God. In the eighteenth century European colonies in the Americas developed their own scientific communities and institutions, which increasingly claimed independence from their European peers.

Natural history continued to be the quintessential colonial science. The immediate fieldwork of natural history could only be carried out on the spot, either by colonial residents or by visitors from the metropolis. Colonial residents joined networks of correspondence and exchange, but usually as subordinates. European scientists were particularly interested in animals and plants unique to the New World, and some of them touched off scientific controversies.

It was debated in both Europe and America whether rattlesnakes had the power of charming or "fascinating" their prey, or whether the pouch of the female opossum was actually a womb. (Opossums, the only marsupials known to European science before the discovery of Australia, presented several problems in classification.)

British collectors such as James Petiver or Hans Sloane (who had come to Jamaica as physician to the governor and written a book on its natural history) established networks of contacts in the Americas from whom to receive specimens for their collections. The London Quaker merchant Peter Collinson was a correspondent of the leading mid-eighteenth-century colonial scientists and served as their agent in London. John Bartram of Philadelphia, despite his lack of formal training, parlayed his connections with Sloane and other English collectors into a leading position in American

botany. Mark Catesby, by contrast, was an Englishman commissioned to bring back specimens from the colonies, as well as to write a natural history.

Eighteenth-Century Science

The eighteenth century, with the expansion of astronomy and cartography, also saw the spread of observatories and programs of observation outside Europe, since it was often necessary or beneficial that astronomical phenomena, such as the transits of Venus, be viewed from many places on the globe. The need to establish the exact location of isolated ports and islands spurred scientific endeavor. However, colonial astronomy and surveying still filled the traditional colonial role of providing data for compilation and analysis in Europe.

Science in the colonies was practiced in institutions and settings resembling Europe's. Like British universities, colonial universities switched from an Aristotelian curriculum to a Newtonian one. A key moment was the founding of the Hollis professorship in Mathematics and Natural Philosophy at Harvard in 1727. Its first two incumbents, Isaac Greenwood and the astronomer John Winthrop, Jr., did much to spread advanced physics, astronomy, and mathematics in New England. At Yale, Thomas Clap, president of the university from 1745 to 1766, also promoted modern science in the curriculum.

The universities were not the most dynamic centers of western science in the eighteenth century; however, scientific societies were. British America's first enduring scientific society was the American Philosophical Society, founded in Philadelphia in 1768. (A similar phenomenon took place in French colonies. Saint-Domingue had a private group with some public support, the Circle of Philadelphes founded in 1784. It eventually received a royal charter.) Many of the medical societies and library companies formed in the mid-eighteenth century also had scientific interests. Informal groups of persons interested in science existed in many colonial cities. The influx of Scottish physicians and those with Scottish education particularly encouraged the growth of science. A popular scientific culture began to emerge, with public lectures and demonstrations and the publication of books on science. Many of the lecturers, like Benjamin Franklin's friend Ebenezer Kinnersley, were showmen, as well as educators.

A powerful motivation for the foundation of colonial scientific institutions was economic development. The French founded a network of botanical gardens in their island colonies of Mauritius, Reunion, Saint-Domingue, and Guadeloupe, hoping to acclimate economically productive crops, as coffee was acclimated in the French Caribbean colonies. France was building on a long tradition of active botanical investigation of the New World, dating back to Samuel Champlain's sending of American plants to Paris in the early seventeenth century. French colonial gardens often employed botanists trained at the Royal Botanical Garden in Paris and reported back to it. Britain lagged behind France botanically, setting up a centralized system only after the American Revolution with the founding of Kew Gardens.

The Spanish also turned to a more aggressive approach to the resources of their empire in the late eighteenth century, sending the Royal Botanical Expedition to Mexico in 1787. The leading scientific center of Spain's American Empire was Mexico City, which received a Royal Botanical Garden in 1788 and a Royal Mining College in 1792.

In the eighteenth century, colonial residents began to be independent voices in Western science. The botanists John Clayton of Virginia and Dr. Alexander Garden of Charles Town (after whom the gardenia is named) were respected correspondents and colleagues of European botanists, not persons principally valued for their collecting ability, like John Bartram.

Colonial scientists also made their presence felt in new fields. One reason for Benjamin Franklin's fame was that he was the first colonial scientist, born and resident in a colony, to make an important original contribution to experimental physics. This led to his acceptance as a peer by Europe's leading scientists. Franklin was fortunate to be working in a relatively young field, where there was not a great deal of previous literature or mathematized theory to master.

The disadvantage of colonial isolation for more theoretically inclined physicists can be seen in the work of Franklin's New York contemporary Cadwallader Colden. Colden's *An Explication of the First Causes of Action in Matter; and the Cause of Gravitation* (1745) showed little awareness of work in mechanics and physics since Newton, and the book was harshly reviewed when it appeared in Europe.

Colonial scientific communities began, by the late eighteenth century, to emphasize their separateness from Europe. The study of local natural history could contribute to the sense of a separate colonial identity, as could scientific disputes with Europeans. Mexican naturalists attacked the Royal Botanical Expedition's at-

tempt to impose the "European" Linnaean system of classification on Mexican plants.

Particularly important for New World natural historians was defending the Western hemisphere from European scientists like the Comte de Buffon and Cornelius de Pauw, who claimed it inferior to the Eastern hemisphere. Buffon pointed to cases where New World animals were smaller than those of the Old World, as pumas were smaller than lions, to argue that the New World's climate and humidity produced generally inferior fauna. This argument was also given a racist twist, as Native Americans were considered inferior to Old World people, Europeans in particular; some went even further to assert that Europeans inevitably degenerated in the Americas. This aroused the pride of New World scientists. Thomas Jefferson defended the fauna of the New World from the aspersions of Buffon and others in *Notes on the State of Virginia* (1785).

Resentments between colonial and European scientists and the desire to build an independent scientific culture could easily lead to support for political independence. Both Franklin and Jefferson combined support for American independence with contributions to an independent American science.

William E. Burns

See also: American Philosophical Society; Clocks and Timekeeping; Disease; Education, Higher; Environment and Nature; Exploration; Franklin, Benjamin; Maps and Surveys; Rush, Benjamin; Science and Technology (Chronology); Technology; Wright, Susanna. *Document:* A Report on the Kite Experiment (1752).

Bibliography

Bell, Whitfield J. *Patriot-Improvers: Biographical Sketches of Members of the American Philosophical Society.* Two volumes. Philadelphia: American Philosophical Society, 1997–1999.

Gerbi, Antonello. *The Dispute of the New World: The History of a Polemic, 1750–1900.* Revised and enlarged edition. Translated by Jeremy Moyle. Pittsburgh: University of Pittsburgh Press, 1973.

———. *Nature in the New World: From Christopher Columbus to Gonzalo Fernández de Oviedo.* Translated by Jeremy Moyle. Pittsburgh: University of Pittsburgh Press, 1985.

Grafton, Anthony, with April Shelford and Nancy Siraisi. *New Worlds, Ancient Texts: The Power of Tradition and the Shock of Discovery.* Cambridge, MA: Belknap Press, 1992.

Hindle, Brooke. *The Pursuit of Science in Revolutionary America.* Chapel Hill: University of North Carolina Press for the Institute of Early American History and Culture in Williamsburg, Virginia, 1956.

Stearns, Raymond Phineas, *Science in the British Colonies of America*. Urbana: University of Illinois Press, 1970.

Scots-Irish

Although there were Scots-Irish in the colonies in small numbers during the seventeenth century, the major influx came in the eighteenth century, beginning in 1718 and lasting into the 1770s. Throughout the period, numbers waxed and waned, depending on conditions in Ireland, but immigration halted only for the American Revolution, 1775 to 1783, and it resumed after the war.

The Scots-Irish are a distinct group from the coincident migrations from Ireland of Anglicans, Quakers, and Catholics. The predominant religion of the Scots-Irish was Presbyterianism. Scots-Irish were those who were born in or lived in Ireland but whose ancestral or personal origins were in Scotland. Other names for the Scots-Irish include the Ulster Scots and Irish Presbyterians. From the first arrivals in 1718 through the end of the century, approximately 250,000 Scots-Irish immigrated to the United States, half the number who came in the nineteenth century.

Background

In the early seventeenth century, Scottish settlers began entering Ulster in the north of Ireland, when King James I gave Catholic land to English and Scottish Protestants in an attempt to control the territory. The migration of the Scots to Ulster continued through the seventeenth and eighteenth centuries.

The Scots planters in the 1630s became increasingly alienated by the Stuart religious policies, when the king established the Church of Ireland as the official church. Although the Presbyterians had tried to adapt their ecclesiastical system to the demands of the Stuart policy, with only moderate success, they found increasingly that the two were incompatible. Furthermore, a strong Scottish evangelical movement concerned them, as did the persecution of the English Puritans, who emigrated in 1620.

When James I died in 1625, Charles I, his son, proved an aggressive defender of his church, imposing new taxes and threatening to take church lands, as well as dealing harshly with the Covenanters, as those Scots who signed the National Covenant to uphold the Presbyterian religion were called. Charles I's behavior led

to the English Civil War, and he was beheaded in 1649. The Stuart rule gave way to the Commonwealth of Oliver Cromwell. In 1690, England and France went to war.

Meanwhile, in Ireland, Thomas Wentworth, Earl of Stratford, became lord deputy. New bishops, who were severely anti-Presbyterian, came into office. The locals contacted settlers in Massachusetts and received sufficient encouragement that some attempted to migrate in pursuit of religious freedom. Unfortunately, on this occasion, their ship, the *Eaglewing,* proved unable to withstand stormy weather, so the migration was delayed.

In the seventeenth and eighteenth centuries, Ireland was tumultuous—with rebellion, the Cromwellian Interregnum, and the Battle of the Boyne in 1690, when William of Orange, with French assistance, bested the Catholic James II. Rebellions occurred in 1798 and 1803. Repression, unrest, higher rents, disabilities—the Scots-Irish had ample reason to leave their homeland. And when a congregation's minister led the way, they emigrated.

Although the colonies were strongly anti-Catholic, they held no animosity toward Presbyterians or other nonconformists. These sorts were allowed to enjoy religious freedom and to prosper, as long as they were not too conspicuous in their peculiarities and avoided the strongly religious colonies of New England.

Migration

There were multiple waves of migration from Northern Ireland to America. The high tides were in 1717–1718, 1725–1729, 1740–1741, 1754–1755, and 1771–1775.

The reasons for the large migrations in the eighteenth century included high rents and religious persecution. Most came freely, but there were also indentured servants and deported prisoners. Others arrived with the British army and opted to settle instead of returning. Ministers naturally took the lead in some migrations, collecting their flock from one or more Irish towns or parishes and bringing all to the colonies to cluster together in the new settlement.

The Scots-Irish presence in the colonies began in the seventeenth century, but the first major migration was the group led by Reverend James McGregor in 1718 from County Londonderry to Boston. This group founded Londonderry, New Hampshire. Most Scots-Irish, however, settled in waves from Pennsylvania through Virginia and the Carolinas. Even so, there was a Scots-Irish presence in all thirteen colonies.

The first movement in 1717–1718 opened the path. It came on the heels of drought years, bad crops, and high prices. Also influencing the decision to move was the practice of rack renting. Under this practice, once a lease expired, the landlord would raise the rent and lease to the highest bidder. In the seventeenth century, rents were usually reasonable—supply exceeding demand. In the eighteenth century, as more immigrants came to Ulster and land became scarce, landlords took the upper hand. The rack rents uprooted families that had been on the same lease for a generation, maybe two.

Those who immigrated in 1717 sent back reports to those who would follow. They reported on their cold welcome in Boston and other unanticipated problems. Or they reported from their entry points on the Delaware River that Pennsylvania was the place to be. By 1720, emigration from Ulster to America meant mostly hitting the Delaware ports and moving west. The pattern persisted for fifty-eight years. This was the Great Migration, with a vast majority of immigrants entering at Philadelphia, New Castle, or Chester.

So large that it seemed capable of emptying Ulster of all Protestants, the second wave, that of 1725–1729, caused Parliament to look into the causes of migration. The immigrants cited rack rents as the determinant, but there also was the fact that their lives were wretched: they were living in poverty, without enough food for their families. At the same time, government restrictions on commerce and manufacturing precluded the development of alternatives. Add taxes at relatively exorbitant rates, a scarcity of hard money, and rack rents were the final blow.

Worst of all was the short wave of immigration of 1740–1741. In the former year, famine—not to be confused with the great potato famine that hit Catholic Ireland in the middle years of the decade—struck Ireland. The famine caused the deaths of an estimated 400,000 people and generated a decade of exodus.

Within the colonies, this was the first time that the Scots-Irish moved away from Pennsylvania. Heading southwest through the Great Valley, the new immigrants (and some old) settled the fertile Shenandoah Valley of Virginia, which had a southern opening to North and South Carolina.

The fourth migration took place in 1754–1755. It came about due to another drought in Ulster and strong government propaganda in the colonies. North Carolina enjoyed a succession of aggressive recruiters in

the governor's mansion. These governors directed their sales pitches to Ulster and Scotland. Two of them were Ulstermen themselves. All they had to do to sway a drought-stricken Ulsterman was point to the successes of the Scots-Irish in America.

On the down side, this is when the frontier Scots-Irish first encountered the Native Americans. The French and Indian War of 1754–1763 created havoc on the frontier, discouraging not only new immigration but old settlers as well. At the time, Ulster was experiencing an economic recovery so great that the places of the colonial migrants were taken by southern Irish and Scots. Ulster's population exploded, pressing resources and creating the precondition for the next migration, just waiting for the next depression.

By 1770, famine had returned to Ulster, and population pressures had led to the division and subdivision of farms until the plots produced too little to sustain the families living on them. This time, the specific blow was the expiration of the leases on the Antrim estate of the Marquis of Donegal. Rack rents were so extreme as to result in large-scale evictions of long-tenured families. Over the three years that followed, 100 vessels sailed from Northern Ireland, carrying 25,000 to 30,000 Ulster Protestants.

Canadian Settlement

Migrations also occurred between Canada and the other colonies. Farmers who failed owing to bad location moved on. Land was free or cheap.

Farming was a compatible occupation with the Scots-Irish heritage. Some participated in the trade in rum, sugar, and tobacco, matching their occupations to their region. Presumably, at least some held slaves.

In Canada, as in points south, English politics and wars with France influenced migration. In the mid- to late eighteenth century, Canada's speculators made generous land offerings that proved a strong attraction. Arthur Dobbs attracted migrants to both Canada and the Carolinas. Alexander McNutt had 800,000 acres of Nova Scotia ripe for settlement until the Privy Council, fearing the impact on Ulster's population, placed a five-year moratorium on migration to Nova Scotia. Thomas Desbrisay was noted for making claims for his lands that were, if not fraudulent, extremely close.

Scots-Irish migrants to the Canadian colonies had the problem that much of the settlement was Catholic, the result of the French era. Protestants and Catholics were not exactly the warmest of friends, and Presbyterians were skeptical about moving into Catholic areas.

After 1760, the British government actively recruited Protestants into the Catholic areas, but the Revolution halted that effort.

A number of loyalists migrated to Canada during the American War for Independence. Some returned, some did not, and some migrated from eastern Canada to more hospitable places. After the war, migrations into Canada continued from the east and south. By 1791, Canada was home to 80,000 British and twice that number of French. Canada would become Anglicized only during the Napoleonic Wars.

Life in America

In the 1720s and 1730s, many Scots-Irish settled in Pennsylvania. From Pennsylvania, some moved on to Virginia and the Carolinas, and their descendents settled Georgia, Kentucky, and Tennessee in the 1780s and 1790s.

Generally, the Scots-Irish migrated in family groups and settled near other members of their extended families. Immigration may have been simultaneous or separate. Again, some people came with their congregations.

The establishment of the early settlement units provided family links for subsequent migrants. Even though the home situation eased in the early eighteenth century, because harvests were better, rents remained high, tenure was uncertain, and tithes to the state church continued to gall. With encouragement from those who prospered in the colonies, the draw was difficult to resist.

Emigrants in the eighteenth century had no passenger ships; these did not become available until the nineteenth century. Cargo vessels were the only option, and the newly independent United States in 1783 made Ulster a virtually free-trade partner. Increased trade meant increased opportunity for travel.

Indentures before 1770 tended to be younger, single laborers who worked for their passage in dangerous, difficult jobs. They may have sojourned in England for a time, trying to amass the price of passage.

The end of the war altered the type of immigrant, increasing the number of families who came and reducing the level of poverty among the migrants. Eighteenth-century incentives remained strong, as land speculators and governments promised land. Options ranged from South Carolina to Prince Edward Island, Canada.

Once in the colonies, the new immigrants naturally gravitated to New York and the other port cities. They could then take a coastal vessel down to the Carolinas or migrate west.

Scots-Irish tended to migrate to some of the more troubled places in the colonies. They had a strong reputation as tenacious fighters, which made them especially attractive to the Eastern governments in search of a well-defended Western frontier. They also had a strong and deep faith that included a commitment to education (the uneducated could not master the arguments of the Presbyterian religious scholarship and therefore could not understand and participate in their faith). As early as 1716, William Tennent established a log college at Neshaminy, Pennsylvania. And the College of New Jersey, later Princeton, opened in 1746. Scots-Irish eventually moved into the professions, politics, and the presidency.

Throughout the fifty-eight years since the Glorious Revolution, when a Protestant monarchy returned to the throne of Britain, religion had played a role, although not a decisive one. Not coincidentally, while the Church of England and the Catholic churches held onto their members, the Presbyterians headed for the colonies.

All thirteen colonies had Scots-Irish settlers. The principal path—thus, the area most settled by Scots-Irish—was through Pennsylvania, the Valley of Virginia, and the Piedmont of the Carolinas. Presbyterians did settle elsewhere, but many of them were English, Welsh, or Scottish. It should be remembered that by 1717, the Scots and the Scots-Irish were two distinct nationalities, the Scots-Irish having adapted to Irish living over generations.

The Scots did migrate in large numbers during the eighteenth century, matching only 20 to 25 percent of the Scots-Irish total. The Scots had a different history and different path, most coming as criminals or indentured servants prior to the Act of Union in 1707 and as Englishmen seeking to escape from poverty thereafter. Also, they had their troubles, their evictions, enclosure, and the breakup of the clans. The Scots reacted to America differently, too. They avoided fighting the native peoples, frontier trading, and pioneering. They were Eastern-oriented merchants, generally loyalists in the Revolution. Although sharing Presbyterianism and a Scottish heritage, the Scots were not at all the Scots-Irish.

Over time, the Scots-Irish assumed a new character, as did other groups. As the Scots had become Scots-Irish over generations in Ulster, so the Scots-Irish over generations on the frontier, in the backwaters away from the tamer Americans, became Americans themselves. Eventually, some began to lose their Presbyterianism, as they mingled and intermarried with Methodists and Baptists. Still, through it all, they contributed to the settlement of the colonies by taking on the hard jobs in the backwaters—breaking the soil, clearing the wilderness, safeguarding the English, Germans, and Scots in the East.

The Scots-Irish participated in both the French and Indian War and the American Revolution, generally supporting the patriots in opposition to the British Crown. They also fought the Eastern-dominated governments, as in the case of the various mid-eighteenth-century regulator movements. When governments in the eastern parts of the colonies passed hard money requirements for the payments of taxes, skimped on military protection, and imposed other decisions that harmed their interests, those on the frontier—including the Scots-Irish—protested and rebelled. They also insisted on having a say not just in the colonies' defense, but in their development as well.

The Scots-Irish provided a much-needed barrier between the wilderness to the West and the coast-hugging civilization developing on the Eastern seaboard. Their self-reliance and willingness to fight when necessary also forced a leveling that eventually brought increased democracy to the colonies.

John H. Barnhill

See also: Appalachia; Immigration; Piedmont.

Bibliography

Betit, Kyle J. "Colonial Scots-Irish Immigrants: The Irish Records." http://scripts.ireland.com/ancestor/magazine/articles/iha_scotsus1.htm.

Hewitson, Jim. *Tam Blake & Co.: The Story of the Scots in America.* Edinburgh, UK: Canongate, 1995.

Leyburn, James G. *"The Scotch-Irish: A Social History.* Chapel Hill: University of North Carolina Press, 1962.

Orr, Brian. "Emigration—The Ulster-Scots (Scots-Irish): What made them seek a better land?" *The Irish At Home and Abroad* 2:1, 1994/1995. http://www.tartans.com/articles/plantation3.html.

Seminole

The Seminole Indians came into being as the result of a number of historic forces in the eighteenth century. Their history began when groups of native peoples, attempting to relieve the pressure exerted by expanding English plantations, moved into southern Georgia and Alabama and eventually northern Florida.

The Seminole peoples were offshoots of the Creek—or Muskogee—nation, but they did not all speak Muskogee. Many relied on their indigenous languages, while adopting some of the Creeks' cultural practices. Still others remained culturally independent, but historic circumstances made them Seminole as well.

As English plantations and the attendant Native American slavery expanded into Creek territory at the end of the seventeenth century, they uprooted a diverse array of native communities, many of whom formed the basis for the later Seminole tribes. The first Seminoles were Muskogee migrants from the Chattahoochee River region on the border between Georgia and Alabama, though later immigrants came from throughout Creek country and beyond. The "proto-Seminoles" were the survivors of the warfare, disease, and dispossession that accompanied both Spanish and English colonization in the Southeast. Florida had been all but depopulated by the process in the sixteenth and seventeenth centuries. Diverse groups of Yuchis, Alabamas, Tallassees, Yamasees, Hitchitis, and Oconees came together gradually to form the early modern Seminoles.

The name *Seminole* comes from a Creek word that means "runaway" and has connotations of wildness. As African slaves fled Carolina plantations, many of them ended up in northern Florida, living in autonomous black towns among the region's natives. By 1800, Europeans had taken to calling all of Florida's non-white peoples Seminole.

The Seminole and Muskogee shared many cultural traits, including a matrilineal clan structure, town-based government, and the creation of larger political networks—paramount chiefdoms and confederacies. In their civil government, Seminoles attempted to avoid open disputes and focused on rule by consensus, even if occasionally consensus was a long time in coming.

Seminoles farmed, fished, hunted, and gathered wild plants for food. They also participated in a profitable trade with British companies and individuals operating in the region. Seminoles provided deerskins in exchange for items of European manufacture, including cloth, tools, knives, firearms, and ammunition. Like other tribes, the Seminoles managed to use European products in their own culturally specific ways, but they came to be dependent on traders.

The year 1763 was pivotal for Native Americans in North America. The end of the French and Indian War ensured that Britain and its colonies would dominate affairs in the eastern half of the continent. The Seminole had traded with French, Spanish, and Anglo-American factors, but, increasingly, they were surrounded by British Americans. A decade or so later, the Seminole were again free to trade with both Britain and Spain, as well as the newly created American states of Georgia and South Carolina.

In the American Revolution, many Seminoles sided with the Americans, while the Creeks, more likely to be Muskogees, generally sided with the British. The war also heightened African American immigration to Seminole country, as some slaves used the disruption of the war to strike out for freedom, while others earned their freedom by aiding the military efforts of the British and occasionally the American Revolutionaries. Some black Seminoles reached the highest levels of Seminole society, and their legal status within Seminole towns is hard to ascertain. More acculturated Creeks and Seminoles did own black slaves in the English style.

In the early nineteenth century, though few Seminoles had participated in the Creek Wars, General Andrew Jackson invaded Spanish Florida and burned Seminole towns and the towns of their neighbors of African descent. In the 1820s, facing pressure from the United States—which gained Florida in 1821—some Seminoles began to consider moving to lands west of the Mississippi. Most Seminoles chose to remain in Florida, and the result was the Second Seminole War (1835–1842), which was the longest and costliest of the United States' nineteenth-century Indian Wars.

By the 1840s, most Seminoles lived in Indian Territory, where they re-established their culture and government. Several hundred Seminoles remained in Florida's swamps, and others, under Wildcat and John Horse—the leader of a black town—migrated to northern Mexico.

Matthew Jennings

See also: Native American–European Conflict; Native American–European Relations; Native Americans.

Bibliography

McReynolds, Edwin C. *The Seminoles.* Norman: University of Oklahoma Press, 1957.

Sattler, Richard A. "Seminole." In *Encyclopedia of North American Indians,* edited by Frederick E. Hoxie. Boston: Houghton Mifflin, 1996.

Wright, J. Leitch, Jr. *Creeks and Seminoles: The Destruction and Regeneration of the Muscogulge People.* Lincoln: University of Nebraska Press, 1986.

Seneca

Known as the "Keepers of the Western Door," the Seneca Nation of Indians was the most numerous tribe in the Iroquois Confederacy during the colonial period. One of the original Five Nations, the Seneca played a vital role both in the protection of the Confederacy from outsiders, as well as in controlling the lucrative fur trade between the French and English traders during the colonial period.

Estimates of the Seneca population vary widely. Some historians put the figure at around a couple of thousand in the late 1600s, while others say it was closer to 5,000. Almost all agree, however, that it fell dramatically in subsequent decades, to anywhere between 600 and 2,000 by the end of the American Revolution.

A complex set of factors contributed to this loss in numbers, including but not limited to disease, warfare, and economic strains caused by fluctuations in the fur trade. Although the Seneca had the largest population of all the Iroquois, they had the fewest number of council chiefs (known as sachems). Yet no one tribe dominated the council, as council chiefs had to vote as a unanimous group in order to be heard. As the Keepers of the Western Door, two of the Seneca sachems were responsible for alerting the Confederacy to possible threats from neighboring tribes, as well as informing the council as to the status of the several tributary tribes of the Iroquois.

The tribe consisted of eight clans, or families, to which each member claimed affiliation. Senecas were members of the Bear, Turtle, Wolf, Beaver, Snipe, Hawk, Heron, and Deer clans. Clans rotated membership in the councils, and each council member would assume the name of the predecessor from his clan. Handsome Lake (Skanyarioh), for example, was the name of the council member of the Turtle Clan.

The Seneca occupied most of what is now the western portion of New York, residing in villages in parts of Livingston, Ontario, and Monroe Counties. Yet the main concentration of Seneca villages was split into two groups, the eastern and western tribes, a division that existed before the formation of the Iroquois Confederacy. These villages were moved every ten to twenty years, for both economic and environmental reasons.

While the Seneca encountered immigrants from many parts of Europe during the colonial period, missionaries and fur traders dominated the bulk of the

The Seneca chief Red Jacket, or Sagoyewatha, earned his English name for wearing the British uniform during the American Revolution. He later made peace with the new U.S. government. *(Library of Congress, LC-USZ62-128675)*

interactions between the tribe and whites. As the westernmost tribe of the Iroquois and because of their experience and expertise in trapping furs, the Seneca consolidated their hold over the fur trade in western New York. Thus, the tribe dealt heavily with French, Dutch, and, later, English traders. The Dutch presence in western New York was limited, however, and, by the early sixteenth century, the French were the primary European buyers of beaver pelts and other furs.

Relations between the French and the Seneca were not always amicable, as the tendency of French merchants to trade with neighboring tributary tribes strained relations, leading to war between the French and the Seneca in 1686. The French were victorious in this encounter, enabling them to secure their hold as the major trading partner of the Seneca. This alliance would last throughout the French and Indian War.

While several missionaries attempted to establish a foothold in Seneca villages, their efforts during the

sixteenth and seventeenth centuries were largely ineffectual and short-lived. The Seneca resisted most attempts by Jesuit missionaries to gain converts among the tribe. In 1688, the Jesuits formed their first permanent mission in the area, yet relatively few Native Americans were willing to convert.

During the early part of the eighteenth century, English traders began to have an increased presence in the Seneca fur trade. The Seneca proved adept at balancing the trade between both French and English interests, remaining powerfully neutral during most disputes between the two. Yet the outbreak of the French and Indian War in North America all but forced the Senecas to choose sides. Primarily because of their long-standing ties with the French, many of the Seneca warriors fought alongside French troops in their campaigns against the British.

With British victory came changes in the nature of trade. The free trade that had existed prior to the outbreak of war was now controlled through British outposts, where English garrisons could regulate the flow of goods. Although the Seneca were not pleased with this new arrangement, as their participation in Pontiac's Rebellion shows, English promises to keep land-hungry settlers off the natives' land were welcomed by the tribe. Yet in the years preceding the American Revolution, English settlers continued to ignore the treaties between the Seneca and the English that forbade them to encroach on Iroquois land.

When the war began, the whole of the Iroquois Confederacy chose to remain neutral. As the war raged on, however, the Iroquois began to see more and more battles fought near or on their settlements. Convinced that the Revolutionary soldiers were the same men who desired their lands, the Seneca sided with the British; this alliance proved disastrous to the Seneca after the war.

Although the Seneca had never actually been defeated in battle, the newly formed United States government viewed them as a defeated people. This status put the Seneca at a disadvantage in negotiating later treaties, whereby they tried to hold onto what little land they had left.

Craig Miller

See also: Iroquois Confederacy; Native American–European Conflict; Native American–European Relations; Native Americans.

Bibliography

Francello, Joseph A. *The Seneca World of Ga-No-Say-Yeh.* New York: Peter Lang, 1989.

Jennings, Francis. *The Ambiguous Iroquois Empire.* New York: W. W. Norton, 1984.

Wallace, Anthony F. C. *The Death and Rebirth of the Seneca.* New York: Vintage Books, 1972.

Sermons

As early as 1630, John Winthrop wrote *City Upon a Hill*, which portrayed the role of religion in everyday colonial life. "Therefore lett us choose life, that wee, and our Seede, may live; by obeyeing his voyce, and cleaveing to him, for hee is our life, and our prosperity." The phrase "city upon a hill" was used to describe the new settlement, with "the eies (eyes) of all people" upon them as they forged a new life in a new land.

With such words, the Pilgrims and Puritans laid a foundation for their new world. Since their principal spokesmen were ministers, emphasis was placed upon not only themselves and their religion, but also their role in a new destiny for the New World. What they wanted to do was to create for themselves and their descendants a heaven on earth, a community in which they could worship and live in a way they believed to be correct, without any interference. The Bible would then be cited as the sole authority for law and everyday life, and anyone who dared to disagree with its doctrine, or presented different ideas, would be promptly banned (examples included Roger Williams and Anne Hutchinson) or worse.

Because drama and novels were viewed as evil diversions, the printed works of the period were religious in nature. It is not surprising, then, that sermons and various theological works remained the most prevalent form of writing. The most prolific writer of all was Cotton Mather, who published approximately 450 books and pamphlets, all based on his religious beliefs and various sermons.

Another early minister and writer was Jonathan Edwards, who is famous for his frightening, powerful sermon, "Sinners in the Hands of an Angry God." Edwards's rigid Puritan experience and the strong Calvinist beliefs of many, coupled with his sense of duty, placed him in a situation where he had to defend the strict and gloomy new force of Calvinism from the forces of liberalism that were beginning to spring up around him.

If God should let you go, you would immediately sink, and sinfully descend, and plunge into the bottomless gulf. . . . The God that holds you over the pit of hell, much as one holds a spider or some loathsome insect over the fire, abhors you, and is dreadfully provoked. . . . he looks upon you as worthy of nothing else but to be cast into the bottomless gulf.

Such sermons as these had an enormous emotional impact, enough to send entire congregations into hysterical fits of weeping and expressing bitter remorse. After a period of time, such rigid and bitter denunciations of people who had sinned alienated some from the very source of Calvinism that Edwards was attempting to defend.

Early ministers were totally committed to the salvation of their listeners, and this is the primary theme throughout all of their messages. Furthermore, there is a strong consistency in these sermons that effectively links the ministers of the early 1600s with those of the later 1770s. For instance, there are very few true doctrinal differences between the great ministers such as John Cotton and Jonathan Edwards. Their sermons were a primary force in creating a cohesive culture that moved toward self-identity and independence. Those sermons reflect the piety and passions of a people whose culture would ultimately form the fertile soil for creation of the American nation.

Although the core of their sermons remained consistent, changes made over time reflected an adjustment to a changing environment. The principal themes remained at all times those of personal piety and liberty. These themes are linked by a shared sense of cultural and religious destiny, the "city set on a hill" mission, in which New England would fulfill the goal of Calvin's Geneva to create the perfect society so that the Kingdom of God might be fully realized on earth.

The New England preacher, more than the statesman or soldier, was the preeminent power in the colonial period. His sermon was both religious and political, reflecting a conceptual marriage of church and state. There were multiple connections between religious and political thinking in early American life, and the sermon played a pivotal role in the development of that life.

The sermon was also an excellent educational experience. Sunday morning might be a time to hear the latest news or see old friends and neighbors, but it was also an opportunity for many to sit under a man of God who had spent many hours preparing for a two-, three-, or even a four-hour sermon. Many a colonial pastor, such as Jonathan Edwards, spent eight to twelve hours daily studying, praying over, and researching his sermon. Colonial sermons were filled with the fruits of years of study and were designed to appeal not only to the emotions and will, but also to the intellect.

As Daniel Boorstin has noted, the sermon was one of the chief literary forms in colonial America. Realizing this, listeners followed sermons closely and would often discuss them later with family and fellow congregants. Thus, without ever attending a college or seminary, a churchgoer in colonial America could gain an intimate knowledge of biblical doctrine, church history, and classical literature. Often, a sermon was later published, and listeners could review what they had heard previously.

Arthur E. Chapman

See also: Bible; Christ and Christianity; Ministers and the Ministry; Religion (Chronology); Religion (Essay).

Bibliography

Boorstin, Daniel. *The Americans: The Colonial Experience.* New York: Random House, Vintage Books, 1958.

Morison, Samuel Eliot. *The Intellectual Life of New England.* Ithaca, NY: Cornell University Press, 1965.

Stout, Harry S. *The New England Soul: Preaching and Religious Culture in Colonial New England.* New York: Oxford University Press, 1988.

Serra, Fray Junípero (1713–1784)

Fray (Father) Junípero Serra established more than twenty Franciscan missions in California in the late eighteenth century. His legacy is a complex one of missionary work, personal conviction, courage, violence, and the destruction of the cultures of California's native peoples.

While Pope John Paul II beatified Serra in 1987, many native Californians oppose Serra's progression toward sainthood, citing his record of cruelty to their forebears. Others, including academics, have criticized the beatification as well. Serra's supporters claim he was simply a man of his times.

Junípero Serra was born on Mallorca, a Spanish island in the Mediterranean, in 1713. Though not wealthy, he attended religious schools and displayed an aptitude for the life of the mind. While still in his teens, he was ordained as a priest. From the late 1730s

The Spanish missionary Fray Junípero Serra has been called the Apostle of California for his work there in the late 1700s, including the founding of twenty-one Franciscan missions. He was beatified in 1987. *(Courtesy of University of Southern California, on behalf of the USC Specialized Libraries and Archival Collections)*

to 1749, Serra was a professor of philosophy. He gave up a prestigious academic post to seek converts and a martyr's death in the Americas.

Serra's arrival in Mexico was remarkable for the fact that he insisted on walking from the port at Vera Cruz to Mexico City. In the 1750s, Serra worked at various jobs in and around the colonial capital. The expulsion of the Jesuits in 1767, and especially their arrest and removal from Baja California, landed the Franciscan Serra an appointment as head of the new missions. Serra managed the religious aspects of the colonization of Alta California (the present-state of California), while Captain Gaspar de Portolá attended to more secular and military matters.

Even in the late eighteenth century, Europeans had little understanding of the geography of the interior of North America. As such, England, Spain, Holland, and Russia all maintained claims to the continent's Pacific coast. Of these nations, Russia posed the most immediate and serious threat to Spanish expansion in the region. In the late 1760s, Serra's Franciscans and Portolá's soldiers and sailors struck out to the north in an effort to gain native converts and stop Russian encroachment.

Serra was legendary for his cruelty, not only to native people, but also to himself. He believed in a severe form of Christianity: he wore coarse shirts with bits of metal that irritated his skin, flogged himself until he drew blood, burned himself with a candle, and insisted on walking everywhere, aggravating his ulcerous legs. As if these self-inflicted punishments were not enough, Serra also suffered from asthma and generally poor health.

Serra, like other Spanish colonizers before him, failed to grasp the subtleties of native culture, especially concerning the importance of gifts and reciprocity. Serra insisted on intimidating native people to bring them into line with the new mission order. He relied on heavy-handed tactics such as whippings, burnings, and executions to achieve his goals. In 1775, some Ipais repaid Serra's cruelty by killing their priest at San Diego and burning the mission. Other native communities followed suit.

The second half of the eighteenth century witnessed a conflict between secular and religious forces over which group would control Spanish colonization. At the time, Spain was engaged in a massive overhaul of its colonial empire, known as the Bourbon reforms. California, which was becoming a financial liability, was an experiment in a new form of colonization that combined Spanish settlements with missions and native communities. (Earlier efforts generally segregated the Spanish and Native Americans.)

In the late eighteenth century, California was a densely populated region, but concentrating native people in missions intensified the effects of European diseases, and the native population dropped precipitously. Missions were supposed to take on a smaller role in the process of colonization, but they became the defining feature of the developing society. They were intended (misguided as it sounds now) to help native peoples, but ended up with disastrous effects. Their bringing natives together in large numbers and exposing them to European diseases led to epidemics that killed many of these native peoples.

While these calamities cannot be blamed on the rigid policies of Junípero Serra, he molded the missions of California—including San Diego, San Gabriel, San Juan Capistrano, San José, San Francisco, San Luis Obispo, and Monterey. By the time of his death in 1784, Serra had overseen the founding of several important missions that accounted for nearly all cattle and grain production in California and boasted a native population of just less than 5,000.

Matthew Jennings

See also: California; Franciscans; Missions; Native American–European Relations; Spanish Colonies on Mainland North America (Chronology).

Bibliography

Costo, Rupert, and Jeannette Henry Costo, eds. *The Missions of California: A Legacy of Genocide.* San Francisco: Indian Historian Press, 1987.
Tinker, George E. *Missionary Conquest: The Gospel and Native American Cultural Genocide.* Minneapolis, MN: Fortress Press, 1993.
Weber, David J. *The Spanish Frontier in North America.* New Haven, CT: Yale University Press, 1992.

Servants, Domestic

"Domestic servants" are those who do most of their work in the home. Domestic help throughout the colonial period came predominantly from three sources: contracted indentured servants, redemptioners, and African slave labor, which had been introduced to the American colonies by the early decades of the seventeenth century.

Indentured servants offered their services to a master in exchange for passage to America, and sometimes convicts (or vagrants) from England were "sentenced" to do service in America. An indentured contract was a written agreement between the servant and the master. The servant would sign on, usually for a term between four and seven years, and work for the master for that period of time. On completion of the contract, servants became "free" and received clothing and usually a sum of money ("freedom dues") or other means to make a start for themselves. Approximately one-half to two-thirds of white immigrants coming to colonial America were indentured servants.

The redemptioners were individuals who had no pre-established contract prior to arriving in America; they usually paid a portion of their own passage. Redemptioners were given a certain amount of time, once arriving in America, to establish a contract before they were "sold" to the highest bidder to pay for the remainder of their passage. If the redemptioner was able to make a contract, it was usually less than that of an indentured servant, because it was based on the remaining amount of money owed.

The third group bound to servitude was the slaves. Although slaves predominantly worked in the fields, house slaves operated as domestic help. Slavery was

Irish Servants.

JUST ARRIVED, *in the* Ship JOHN, *Capt.* ROACH, *from* DUBLIN,

A NUMBER of HEALTHY, INDENTED MEN and WOMEN SERVANTS:

AMONG THE FORMER ARE,

A Variety of TRADESMEN, with some good FARMERS, and stout LABOURERS: Their Indentures will be disposed of, on reasonable Terms, for CASH, by
GEORGE SALMON.

Baltimore, May 24, 1792.

From the early eighteenth century until well into the nineteenth century, hundreds of thousands of Irish immigrants in America took work as domestic servants. *(National Park Service Statue of Liberty National Monument)*

drastically different than indentured (or contracted) servitude. Unlike indentured servants, whose term of contract was set, the law bound slaves to an owner for life and required the slave to work at whatever task was ordered.

Domestic servants, both indentured and slaves, were found in all thirteen colonies throughout the colonial period. When the number of indentured servants declined in the late seventeenth century, colonial households relied on slave labor and paid domestic help. Following the American Revolution, the slave labor system became more common in the South, and the free labor system became the norm in the North. For example, domestic service was a position readily available to free black women in Northern states.

Women as Domestic Servants

Domestic service work has traditionally been a female occupation, because it is work done in the home. In the colonial period, the only substantial group of women wage earners worked as domestic servants; the majority of them were unmarried or widowed women. Domestic servants were often women who worked in temporary situations during hard times. Domestic service positions required little training and little capital investment, making them suitable situations for those who were unable to pursue more lucrative work. Because the apprenticeship system was essentially closed to women, domestic service became one of their only means of gainful employment.

Young girls also worked as domestic servants, and female domestic servants usually remained in service

until they married and established their own households. Because there was a fear of idleness in colonial America (as also in England), children as young as 8 and usually from the poorest class were sometimes "bound out" as servants to learn the lessons of industrious and useful labor. Children's contracts usually required that they work until the age of majority, and many guaranteed some provision for schooling.

Wages and compensation for domestic servants varied throughout the thirteen colonies. Indentured servants were usually compensated only by their passage to America, room and board for their term of service, and a small sum of money and suit of clothing after the completion of the contract. In some cases, an indentured servant might receive additional wages while serving out the contract, but this was rare. Wages for free laborers who worked as domestic servants were normally only basic subsistence, but they did receive room and board while employed. House slaves received no wages.

Laws and Domestic Servants

There were few laws in colonial America that dealt specifically with domestic servants; rather, there were general laws dealing with servants of all types. Labor legislation existed in all thirteen colonies and had a twofold purpose.

On the one hand, laws protected the servant from cruelty by the master. For example, servants' contracts that bound them in a particular colony could not be sold out of that colony without the servant's consent. Masters were required to provide adequate food, clothing, and lodging for their servants and to care for their servants when they became ill. The law also protected servants from cruelty, especially bodily maiming (although servants could be disciplined). Servants could sue in court for violations of the law and, if victorious, could have their contracts terminated and thus become free.

On the other hand, laws protected the master's capital investment in the servant. The law guaranteed a master's right to retrieve servants if they ran away. In some cases, additional time was added to the original contract when the servant returned. There were stiff penalties (ranging from fines to beatings) for anyone harboring a runaway servant, and incentives (usually monetary) were given to individuals who assisted in the return of runaways. In addition, there were special laws for female servants. They were barred from marrying without the permission of the master, and those who became pregnant faced additional time added to their contracts.

Slaves faced the strictest penalties under the law, because they were considered property and thus had virtually no legal rights. The laws against runaway slaves were the strictest. Many colonies made provisions under the law to return fugitive slaves to their owners, often with a monetary reward to the person assisting in the return. Slaves found without a written pass were suspected of being fugitives and returned promptly to their owners. Punishment for running away was usually harsh. Unlike indentured servants, slaves could not sue in court and were not protected under the law.

Life as a domestic servant was hard. The colonial household was a place of production, meaning that all subsistence products used in the home were made in the home. This was different from the situation in the industrialized household, where many necessary items were produced in factories and bought in stores.

Servants' main responsibilities were cooking and cleaning, both arduous tasks. With no indoor plumbing, servants had to carry in buckets of water to cook and clean. Ashes from a wood-burning stove kept the servant constantly busy trying to keep the home clean.

Servants were also responsible for tasks such as sewing, weaving, spinning, knitting, tailoring, preserving food, and gardening. They made such household items as soap, candles, medicines, and cheese. In addition, domestic servants were not confined to household tasks. They also worked in the fields to produce subsistence crops for the household.

The servant fell under the discipline of the master and mistress of the house. For example, in Puritan New England, parents were encouraged to discipline not only their children but also their servants in order to maintain a moral family structure for all who lived in the household.

Social Status of Domestic Servants

Domestic servants also fell low in the hierarchy of status. Domestic work was considered unskilled labor, because it required little formal training. It also did not require the period of apprenticeship that accompanied the skilled craft positions usually reserved for males. Within the household, servants knew that their place was below the master, mistress, and children. Colon-

ists brought this view with them from England and used it to legitimize the low social status of servants in America.

The existence of slavery in the American colonies also contributed to the stigma of servitude. Although there was a distinct difference between servant and slave (especially concerning the law), slavery was generally associated with any type of servitude.

Immigration had a similar effect. By the 1710s, German and Irish immigrants began coming to America. Many of the newly arriving immigrants became domestic servants, a trend that continued well into the nineteenth century. The negative attitude toward immigrants in general reinforced the stigma of domestic work.

Also contributing to this negative image were continuing problems between masters and servants. Routinely, servants complained of ill treatment and hard work, and masters complained of ungrateful and inefficient servants. In many cases, both were correct.

With the beginning of the factory system in the late eighteenth century, new opportunities for wage work were opened to women. Skills such as sewing, spinning, and weaving became important to the textile factories. In addition to taking jobs in the factories, women began using their domestic skills to do piecework in their own homes. Even with the new opportunities, domestic service work continued to be the largest employer of women and girls throughout the nineteenth and early twentieth centuries. Increasing immigration in the mid-nineteenth century introduced a new group of single and poor women from Ireland and Germany who would become domestic servants. These positions continued to be associated with unskilled labor and to carry the stigma of hard work, low pay, and dissatisfaction.

Lisa Guinn

See also: Class; Housing; Indentured Servitude; Laborers, Urban; Slavery, African American.

Bibliography

Hofstadter, Richard. *America at 1750: A Social Portrait.* New York: Vintage Books, 1973.

Morgan, Edmund S. *American Slavery, American Freedom: The Ordeal of Colonial Virginia.* New York: W. W. Norton, 1975.

Salmon, Lucy Maynard. *Domestic Service.* New York: Macmillan, 1901.

Servants, Indentured

See Indentured Servitude

Seven Years' War

See French and Indian War

Sex

Sex played a significant role in the fabric of colonial society. Contrary to popular images, early Americans were a lusty lot. Puritans, falsely portrayed as the most sexually repressed of Americans, celebrated sexuality within the confines of marriage. Other groups, notably early Southerners and African Americans, sometimes observed fluid definitions of marriage and engaged in premarital sex and serial monogamy. Meanwhile, colonial courts prosecuted a number of cases of what were deemed sexual transgressions.

To the Puritans, marriage only officially took place after a church ceremony, and sex only took place within marriage. They wholeheartedly promoted active sex lives between husbands and wives, both to populate New England and to discourage illicit, nonmarital unions. Ministers hoped that a strong sexual marital relationship would remove the temptation of adultery.

Sex was so essential in the lives of Puritans that a wife could divorce her husband for failing to satisfy her sexually. New England courts held that a women had a right to expect sexual satisfaction in bed and that a man who failed to provide such contentment had failed as a husband. Marital sexuality did have limits, though. Puritan teachings warned that marital sex could become illicit if a husband and wife allowed their desire for each other to surpass their love of God.

The first generation of Puritan settlers only engaged in debates over sexuality with nonbelieving outsiders, who occasionally chose to shock their devout neighbors with public displays of lewdness. As time passed, however, the sons and daughters of the original settlers developed different ideas about marriage.

Additionally, long-standing popular traditions condoned premarital sex, and these beliefs proved stronger than official dogma in shaping sexuality. Many couples dated the start of their marriages to the time of

their commitment to one another and engaged in sexual relations in the belief that they were doing so within the marital bond. The Puritan fathers disagreed.

Scores of women, including those holding church membership, were prosecuted in seventeenth century New England courts for bearing children outside of wedlock. At the same time, more and more New Englanders were appearing before church congregations and in court, charged with lewd speech, fornication, adultery, bigamy, rape, incest, sodomy, and bestiality. Many of these people were caught in the act, because Puritans believed that they had a right to keep a sharp eye on the activities of their neighbors in order to guarantee that everyone behaved in a proper manner.

The distance between settlements in colonial America and the distance between the New World and the Old made it easy for some to begin extramarital relationships without detection. Colonists were notoriously lax in following the legal requirement that one marriage be dissolved before entering into a new one. Additionally, the requirements for official separation were difficult. The simple declaration that a marriage had failed would not dissolve it. If one spouse claimed adultery, the guilty parties would suffer public condemnation, as well as physical punishment.

In the Southern colonies, sexuality was much less restricted for a number of reasons. The ratio of men and women was severely skewed, and women were in short supply. Restricting sexuality only to marriage deprived most young men in the South of any access to a legal sexual relationship. However, unmarried indentured servants who engaged in sexual relations could find themselves charged in court as economic and moral liabilities. Pregnancy left a servant unable to perform her duties and therefore deprived her master of labor that he had purchased.

Marriage in the South also proved difficult to achieve, because many communities lacked both clerics and established governments. Unlike colonists in the North, some couples in these circumstances entered into relationships that were recognized as legitimate marriages by their peers.

For African Americans, sexuality often involved continuing African patterns of serial monogamy or polygamy. Whites interpreted such behavior as being rooted in an animalistic and depraved nature. The depiction of blacks as incapable of sexual loyalty was further reinforced by the practice of separating husbands and wives in slave sales.

The refusal to recognize the humanity of blacks, combined with a notion of white male privilege, also contributed to the widespread rape of slave women by masters and overseers. Masters had no legal requirement to recognize slave marriages, and many did not do so.

Caryn E. Neumann

See also: Marriage and Divorce; Prostitution; Syphilis.

Bibliography

D'Emilio, John, and Estelle B. Freedman. *Intimate Matters: A History of Sexuality in America.* New York: Harper and Row, 1988.

Godbeer, Richard. *Sexual Revolution in Early America.* Baltimore: Johns Hopkins University Press, 2002.

Shakers

A Protestant communal sect that came to America from Great Britain in 1774, the Shakers experienced considerable persecution for their unusual beliefs. Under the guidance of Mother Ann Lee, the congregation (also known as the United Society of Believers in Christ's Second Appearing) shocked their neighbors in upstate New York by advocating celibacy, practicing pacifism, and allowing women to share leadership duties.

The Shakers began in Manchester, England, in 1746 as a splinter group from a Quaker community. Known as the "Shaking Quakers" for the tremors that members experienced during worship, the group soon became the target of considerable harassment for their radical beliefs and their acceptance of Ann Lee, a woman, as their leader, which proved especially troubling to laypeople and authorities alike.

Ann Lee had sought comfort among the Shakers after the deaths of all her children, and she became convinced that God had claimed her offspring as punishment for engaging in the sin of sex, the same act that had resulted in the banishment of Adam and Eve. Consequently, Lee viewed marriage as the root of all evil, and she promoted celibacy as a means of growing closer to God. Sexual intercourse was solely given to humans for reproduction, Lee argued, and the inability to use it only for this purpose had made us base and animal-like.

While imprisoned for attacking the established Church of England, Lee had experienced a revelation that led the Shakers to believe that she was the second coming of Christ, the vital female component of God the Father-Mother. About 1772, she became the official leader of the small congregation.

As persecution of the Shakers increased, a small group composed of Lee, her brother, niece, and husband, and five others followed her vision of a holy sanctuary in the New World to New York City in May 1774. The group worked at odd jobs before relocating in late 1776 to an area northwest of Albany known as Niskeyuna (subsequently named Watervliet).

The views of the Shakers were so unusual that they met with considerable harassment in the New World as well. They held services in an open space with an altar in the middle so that ecstatic experiences and dancing could become a part of the worship service. Such excessive behavior was frowned upon by other Christian denominations and played a not inconsiderable role in establishing the Shakers' radical reputation.

Perhaps most controversially, the Shakers held to an ideal of gender equality based on their belief that God incorporates both masculine and feminine characteristics. The congregation created parallel male and female leadership positions in an attempt to live as close to God's ideal as possible. Pairs of trustees governed temporal concerns, including the sales and purchase of goods, legal disputes, and other interactions with the outside world. Deacons and deaconesses oversaw specific tasks such as kitchen work and industries, such as farming or the production of medicinal products. While the positions rotated among the membership, the Shakers still divided along traditional gender lines to complete work-related tasks.

The Shakers sought to create a truly selfless and spiritual society. They emphasized simplicity in dress and lifestyle, creating a style of furniture in the process that became an American classic. They also suppressed individuality and created communal alternatives to the family system. All property was shared, and biological kinship relations were abandoned in favor of a village-wide family of brothers and sisters. Preferring first-person religious experiences, they did not rely heavily on written doctrines, although they did draw guidance from the Bible and the personal writings of Lee.

Horrified and angered by the strange newcomers, other residents of New York persecuted and physically attacked many of the Shakers, including Lee, for being radical, English, and pacifistic. The leaders of Albany, all patriots quick to discriminate on the basis of religion, demanded that the Shakers swear loyalty to America. Uninterested in patriotism or politics, Lee forbade her followers to fight anyone for any cause. As followers in Christ's footsteps, Lee proclaimed, the Shakers would never aid or abet the sins of war and bloodshed.

The survival of the congregation remained in

The first community of Shakers in America was founded in 1776 by "Mother" Ann Lee in an area northwest of Albany, New York, known as Niskeyuna (later renamed Watervliet). *(Brown Brothers, Sterling, Pennsylvania)*

considerable doubt until a wave of religious revivalism called the New Light Stir swept across New England between 1776 and 1783, bringing in new converts from other radical groups and allowing the Shakers to proselytize safely. The little village in New York soon swelled with new recruits.

The Shakers emerged as one of America's most durable and successful communal experiments by virtue of their longevity, with 6,000 members in 19 communities at their peak between 1830 and 1840. As interest in utopian social movements faded, the Shakers declined significantly. By the end of the twentieth century, only a handful of members remained in the two last surviving settlements.

Caryn E. Neumann

See also: Quakers; Religion (Chronology); Religion (Essay).

Bibliography

Campion, Nardi Reeder. *Mother Ann Lee: Morning Star of the Shakers.* Hanover, NH: University Press of New England, 1990.

Gidley, Mick, and Kate Bowles, eds. *Locating the Shakers: Cultural Origins and Legacies of an American Religious Movement.* Exeter, UK: University of Exeter Press, 1990.

Stein, Stephen J. *The Shaker Experience in America.* New Haven, CT: Yale University Press, 1992.

Ship's Stores

The term "ship's stores," or "naval stores" as they were commonly known during the colonial era, included a number of materials used in the construction and maintenance of wooden ships. As such, naval stores included, but were not limited to, tar, pitch, rosin and hemp, turpentine, masts and ship timbers, potash, pearlash, lime, and iron. Since European navies were made up entirely of wooden vessels until the late nineteenth century, naval stores were important materials in both Europe and the American colonies. Because of the importance of naval vessels to the economic, political, and military salience of the European powers, their need to build and maintain navies created an insatiable demand for naval materials.

Europe was not devoid of the resources needed to produce naval stores, but after hundreds of years of use, the supply of those materials had become limited or required trade with other nations. Although the Baltic and eastern Slavic states were main European sources for naval stores, trade in these supplies was almost entirely monopolized by the Crown of Sweden. Taking advantage of their monopoly, the Swedes forced many European nations to trade under disadvantageous conditions, such as the transport of naval materials only by Swedish or Dutch ships and the setting of exorbitant prices.

When wars erupted, supplies of naval stores often became uncertain, and safe reliable transport was nearly impossible. The customary practice of mercantilism compounded the situation. The Swedes generally requested currency in exchange for their naval stores, which put those who traded with them in opposition to the mercantile system, since they needed to sustain and expand their currency supplies in order to maintain a strong nation.

Therefore, a desire to procure reliable and inexpensive resources for the production of naval stores outside of Europe was among the major reasons that England (as well as other European powers, for that matter) became interested in colonizing North America. With abundant supplies and uncertain ownership claims, North America offered numerous opportunities for European nations to avoid dependence on the Swedish naval stores monopoly. Not surprisingly, then, these materials were among the first marketable commodities that the colonists sent back to Europe.

Unlike other industrial activities, the production of naval stores required little more than the ownership of land possessing an abundance of resources and a labor force to procure the materials. Colonial America had an abundant supply of natural resources, but labor was always in short supply.

While every European nation involved in the settlement of America promoted the production of naval stores, successful production became widespread only in the English colonies. The main reason for this was the commitment of the British government, through its Board of Trade, to promote this commerce. On numerous occasions during the colonial era, the Board of Trade sent orders and directives to the colonial governors to build naval stores production facilities and to limit lumbering activities that were not in support of industries producing naval stores. Since the many

colonial governments could not build such facilities and the policing of lumbering was nearly impossible, the Board of Trade pushed legislation in Parliament and the colonial assemblies that allowed for the issuance of bounties and other subsidies to promote construction and operation by private interests.

While these practices were useful, labor shortages within the colonies still set limits. To remedy the labor problem, the British government supplemented the emigration of workers from the Palatine States to special settlements, such as Newburgh (New York), New Bern (North Carolina), the Schoharie Valley (New Jersey), and the Great Valley (Pennsylvania), which were originally set up exclusively for naval stores production.

Solomon K. Smith

See also: Navy, British; New Bern; Trade; Transportation, Water.

Bibliography

Knittle, Walter A. *Early Eighteenth Century Palatine Emigration: A British Government Redemptioner Project to Manufacture Naval Stores.* Philadelphia: Dorrance & Company, 1937.

Malone, Joseph J. *Pine Trees and Politics: The Naval Stores and Forest Policy in Colonial New England, 1691–1775.* Seattle: University of Washington Press, 1964.

McCusker, John J., Russel R. Menard, and Peter J. Albert. *The Economy of Early America: The Revolutionary Period, 1763–1790.* Charlottesville: University Press of Virginia, 1988.

Sint Eustatius

Commonly known as Statia, Sint Eustatius is a tiny island of just over 8 square miles located at the southern end of the Dutch Windward Islands in the central Caribbean. Volcanic in origin, the saddle-shaped island has a small agricultural valley in the center bounded by cliffs to east and west and hills to the north and south. The soil is thin and standing water nonexistent, while the relative dryness of the savannah climate was exaggerated early on by the effects of deforestation.

Statia has only one town, Oranjestad, divided into a residential Upper Town on the cliff top and the commercial Lower Town along the beach. Despite its small size, Oranjestad was one of the foremost trading centers in the eighteenth-century Atlantic world, dealing in tropical produce, European goods, and African slaves. Undiscriminating multinational trade created political tension in a mercantilist age, however, and

Statia changed hands twenty-two times between 1636 and 1816, as France and England tried either to control or to shut down this prosperous Dutch trading hub.

While there is evidence of prehistoric settlement on Statia 1,200 years ago, the island was uninhabited when it first was sighted by the Spanish in about 1493. Small, dry, and without a native labor source, Statia held little interest for the Spanish. The first European venture occurred in 1629, when a French expedition tried and failed to establish a permanent colony on Statia. Like the French, the Dutch were looking for footholds in the Caribbean, and, in 1636, the Dutch West India Company established a small, fortified settlement intended to provide agricultural products for the European market. Statia was particularly valued for its defensible size and its location close to two Dutch islands, just over 2 miles from England's St. Kitts and Nevis and close to the French sugar islands with which Statia eventually conducted most of its trade.

Statia began as a tobacco colony, but, by mid-century, Statians had expanded plantation production to include sugar and then cotton, coffee, ginger, and indigo. In 1662 there were 1,174 inhabitants (71 percent of whom were slaves), a figure that increased again by half by 1741. As well as shipping its own produce, Statia increasingly traded in the products of neighboring islands, often illegally, and began to refine muscavado sugar from other islands.

Bolstered by very low customs duties, and as Statia's soil fertility declined, multinational commerce by the eighteenth century had surpassed local agriculture in importance. Sheltered but without a good harbor, Lower Town lacked conventional wharfs, and most goods were offloaded at anchor onto small boats and brought to the beach. This labor occupied the island's slave majority, who were less necessary for the dwindling plantations. By the 1770s, nearly six hundred warehouses lined the beach, and a remarkable average of 2,700 ships came to the port yearly, peaking at 3,551 ships in 1779. Business was so brisk that goods were piled in the open outside the full storerooms, and Statia was known as the Golden Rock, the busy town being described as a great fair.

The community that formed in Statia consisted of a stable core of prosperous long-term residents and their slaves, who were increasingly living alongside a more mobile immigrant population. The profits Statia generated by the 1730s brought a multinational group of merchants (usually unmarried) from some two dozen countries and colonies; these newcomers facilitated the existing international illicit trade. The diversity of the island's population was remarkable, including Jewish, Anglican, Catholic, and Lutheran communities alongside the Dutch and trading in goods from all over the globe. Increasingly, Statian merchants and ships traded with the mainland American colonies, becoming their principal supplier of tea by 1770 and a steady supplier of gunpowder. It was from Statia that the United States received the first foreign salute to its flag on November 16, 1776.

After 1776, Statia's continued illicit trade in armaments to America touched off Britain's anger with the Dutch and with English merchants trading with the rebel colonies through Statia. By 1775, Britain had vessels stationed off Holland's coast to intercept Statian trade, while British privateers stopped Dutch vessels in the Caribbean from 1777.

To prevent Holland from joining the League of Armed Neutrality, which would have given the Dutch powerful allies in its defense of neutral countries' rights in wartime trade, Britain declared war on Holland in December 1780. Immediately a squadron under Admiral Sir George Rodney sailed for Statia, seizing the island on February 3, 1781. Rodney captured vast amounts of goods, sent away English merchants operating there, and deported one-third of the Jewish merchants. The loss of trade for the Dutch was substantial, but much of the material auctioned off by Rodney was bought back by its former owners, and trade briskly resumed in the 1790s.

By the 1820s, however, American commerce had altered patterns of Caribbean trade to the exclusion of Statia. The little island rapidly fell into the economic decline in which it remains.

Neil Kennedy

See also: Caribbean (Chronology); Dutch; Slavery, Caribbean; Sugar.

Bibliography

Goslinga, C. C. *The Dutch in the Caribbean and in the Guianas, 1680–1791.* Assen, Netherlands, and Dover, NH: Van Gorcum, 1985.

Klooster, Wim. *Illicit Riches: Dutch Trade in the Caribbean, 1648–1795.* Leyden, Netherlands: KITLV, 1998.

Slave Communities and Culture

From the early seventeenth century to the American Revolution, African American slaves innovatively created new communities and cultures by combining the common elements of their African traditions with new influences from white colonial society. By doing so, they found a measure of dignity, assertiveness, and independence in the midst of oppression.

Regions

Slavery in the colonies can be broadly divided by four geographic regions: the New England colonies of Connecticut, Massachusetts, New Hampshire, and Rhode Island; the Middle colonies of Delaware, New Jersey, New York, and Pennsylvania; the Chesapeake colonies of Maryland, North Carolina, and Virginia; and the low country of Georgia and South Carolina. Although slavery was legally practiced everywhere, it varied in extent from region to region.

The economy of the North was largely based on commercial trade and small-scale agriculture, although slave labor still played a significant role. In urban centers like New York, Providence, and Boston, slaves worked as domestic servants and artisans and in maritime industries. Their numbers increased throughout the colonial period at a steady, if not spectacular, rate. By the end of the eighteenth century, African American slaves comprised nearly 20 percent of the population of New York City.

Slaves also lived on the farms of Long Island, New Jersey, and Delaware, tending stock and raising corn and wheat; many had done the same work in Africa and were brought to the colonies for that reason. Throughout the rural North, the majority of slaves lived in groups of no more than two or three families and represented only a small percentage of the population. Even the largest Northern estates had no more than sixty or seventy slaves, at most, one-third the number found on the major plantations of the South. By the 1750s, slaves represented less than 10 percent of the North's overall population; it was in the South that this population would experience its greatest growth.

Slavery in the Chesapeake and low country colonies began with a few Africans helping to clear the land for permanent settlements. Once this frontier period ended, however, the institution of slavery virtually exploded. Southern economies were based on the cash crops of tobacco, wheat, corn, rice, indigo, beef, timber, and naval stores, all of which required large numbers of slaves. Other slaves labored as artisans, domestic servants, boatmen, teamsters, and dock workers. Indeed, just about any labor-intensive job that needed to be done in the Southern colonies was done by African American slaves.

The slave population growth was so massive that blacks outnumbered whites in many counties, as well as in the colonies of South Carolina and Georgia. The greatest number, however, were in Virginia, where the slave population grew from a few dozen in 1625 to nearly 12,000 by the turn of the century. The Chesapeake also had a large white population, however, so slaves remained a demographic and cultural minority. Although each individual plantation was predominantly black—most had between ten and twenty slaves—cultural contact and exchange between the races (including Native Americans) was still common. White society was a constant, if not always welcome, force in the slaves' lives.

By contrast, the low country's high mortality rates (caused by the harshness of the environment, rampant disease, and the hard labor involved in rice production), even higher importation rates, and a small white population meant that most slaves there had only occasional contact with white society. Although the Atlantic slave trade slowed after the 1739 uprising known as the Stono Rebellion, blacks remained in the majority. These slave laborers were generally left alone on the plantations with only a few trusted white overseers, while the slaveholders themselves lived in healthier climates.

Slave culture in the low country therefore retained a stronger African flavor than anywhere else in the colonies. Only in the multiethnic city of Charles Town did slaves become intimately familiar with white society. Even there, the large black population fostered the existence of a distinct, independent slave culture.

The creation of this distinct culture actually began on the other side of the Atlantic, centuries before North America was colonized. In economic centers such as Timbuktu and Dakar, trade was facilitated by the use of Arabic and *lingua francas,* dialects based on the structural similarities of West African languages and eventually including European linguistic elements introduced by traders on the Atlantic coast. This process continued, albeit under much harsher circumstances, when African slavery was introduced to North America in 1619.

The slaves came from a variety of regions, including Ghana, Senegambia, the Congo, and the British West Indies, and were compelled to forge new communities based on racial identity rather than ethnicity. Yet it was their American-born children who ultimately did the most to create new cultures from the traditions of the past and the realities of the present. The labor and living conditions of slave communities, although brutal, were still healthy enough that their numbers grew primarily through childbirth rather than the slave trade. By the time of the American Revolution, foreign-born slaves were a minority.

Shared language was the first cultural element to appear in slave communities as the unwilling immigrants looked for ways to communicate with each other. Slaves in the isolated, overwhelmingly black low country combined various African tongues and some English words into a new language called Gullah. Their counterparts in North Carolina also created a Creole dialect, but they could usually speak English as well. The slave dialects of New England and the Chesapeake, on the other hand, contained some African words and grammar structures but were close enough to English that most whites could understand them. Although the "Africanness" of each regional dialect depended on local demographics, a distinctively African American way of speaking could be found everywhere. Slaves did not resist learning English when it was to their advantage, but they did not abandon the old ways either. In fact, some elements of their dialect, including words such as "okay," "banjo," and "yam," were absorbed into English.

The Slave Family

The most important institution in slave communities was the family. Some African-born slaves initially tried to marry within their ethnic group, but they were rarely able to do so. Other family traditions such as polygamy and bridal dowries also largely disappeared, victims of the slaves' limited marriage choices and dowries. Even traditional nuclear families were in peril of being broken apart at any time, since slaveholders had no legal obligation to sell family members together. Some families never lived in the same household; a slave who married someone from a neighboring plantation would only be able to see his or her spouse at holidays and during time off on Sundays.

As a result, the slaves' definition of family was often based as much on personal relationships as it was on bloodlines. Africans who had come over on the same slave ship shared a deep bond. Plantation communities, which were large enough to contain multiple households but small enough so that everyone knew each other well, were really extended families where everyone not related by blood was still an "aunt," "uncle," or "cousin." When parents and children were sold apart, members of the extended family quickly assumed parental responsibilities; there were no orphans in the slave community.

On most plantations, slaves lived in a collection of small huts known as "slave row." Though crudely built by uninterested masters, the slaves themselves organized, cleaned, and decorated their homes in traditional ways. The physical arrangement of many slave rows, for example, resembled that of West African villages. This became the center of the slaves' culture, their refuge away from the master's watchful eye. Many also tended small gardens, raising crops for personal consumption or for sale at local markets; some rural communities, in fact, became dependent on these gardens, since white landowners were focused on producing cash crops.

Within the slave community, religious leaders and skilled artisans—carpenters, blacksmiths, and others—occupied the highest level of the social hierarchy. These positions were usually dominated by men, although a great deal of influence was held by powerful matriarchs or by women skilled in the textile crafts. Domestic servants and slaves of mixed ancestry sometimes enjoyed a higher status, based on favorable treatment from the master, and those who were most familiar with white society also had an advantage over more recent immigrants, particularly in regions with large white populations.

For the most part, however, distinctions based on gender, place of birth, skill level, and complexion were mitigated by the fact that all slaves, regardless of their personal characteristics, were still slaves and still relegated to the lowest level of society. The world that the slaves created for themselves had room for all of these disparate groups.

Appearances

In this world, personal appearance and demeanor were an important form of self-expression and resistance. Slaves were issued Western-style clothing made from cheap, drab-colored cloth and were unable to reproduce most West African fabric patterns. They still created their own aesthetic, using brightly colored garments that had been produced by artisan women using plant dyes, as well as the old clothes of their masters. Through this they retained the African tradition of visual liveliness, in which bold colors are arranged to create a vibrant appearance.

Slaves also took care in arranging their hair into braids, wraps, shaved patterns, and long Afros, despite the fact that they had little time for personal grooming. Women often covered their hair with vividly colored bandannas, which served both form and function, since they added to a woman's personal appearance and also protected her head from the sun.

Even the body language of slaves—the positioning of one's hips, eyes, head, and hands—was important. In many African societies, a stiff posture was seen as a symbol of death, while flexed joints symbolized vitality. Body movement became a means to retain old traditions and quietly assert one's humanity without being directly confrontational.

For example, the practice of turning one's head to the side or rolling the eyes upward (now known as "rolling" or "cutting" eyes), which was used in African societies to show displeasure, took on an added meaning in America. Slaves were required to show deference to whites by not looking them in the eye, and cutting eyes seemingly satisfied white authority but also subtly challenged it.

Naming practices also show the slaves' retention of old traditions and creation of new ones. During the seventeenth and early eighteenth century, parents often gave their children African names that could be easily disguised as English words: Cudjo became Joe, Phiba became Phoebe, and so on. The common African practice of naming children after honored ancestors or based on which day of the week they had been born also continued in the colonies; some slave parents chose to use the English equivalent, so children might be given such names as Sunday or Wednesday. Masters might have found these names odd, but they rarely knew the hidden meaning behind them. Other names such as Quashie (Kwasi) and Cuffee (Kofi) had no English equivalent but could be easily pronounced by whites.

In short, naming practices were a way for African Americans to quietly assert their humanity in the face of ridicule or hostility. By the Revolution, however, many slaves had biblical or British names, since they identified themselves as African Americans rather than as members of separate ethnic groups.

Religion

From the early colonial period, religion played a central role in the culture of slave communities throughout the colonies. African slaves arrived in the Americas with a wide variety of faiths, including Islam and many indigenous belief systems, and many slaves practiced these beliefs without interference. Most masters were indifferent or hostile to their slaves' spiritual concerns, believing that blacks were culturally or racially incapable of receiving the Christian gospel, that Christianity would give them a danger-ous sense of self-worth, or that conversion might be legal grounds for freedom.

Organizations like the Society for the Propagation of the Gospel in Foreign Parts tried to evangelize among the slaves but were handicapped by language barriers and limited resources. Finally, the slaves themselves saw little point in embracing the faith of their oppressors, especially since Christianity was used to justify slavery and white supremacy. Not surprisingly, the few slave conversions that took place were in New England and urban areas.

Christianity did take a greater hold in slave communities during the mass revivals of the 1740s known as the Great Awakening. Thousands were attracted to the newer Baptist and Methodist denominations, whose exuberant style of worship was similar to their African traditions and whose focus on personal, heartfelt conversion rather than a formal theology provided them with the opportunity to become preachers. Like other aspects of slave culture, however, their religion was far different from what white society had intended. African Americans rejected the notion that God had ordained them to be inferior, obedient servants; they instead created an antislavery theology, using biblical stories of the Hebrews' escaping from bondage and then defeating enemy forces much larger than their own. For the most part, however, Christianity did not take hold in slave communities during the colonial period. By the end of the Revolution, only a small percentage of African Americans were Christian.

Most slaves practiced a folk religion centered on the belief that the real world and the spirit world were one and the same. It was thought that the dead continued to interact with the living; the black Christian practice of "catching the Holy Ghost" originated from this belief. Many slaves also believed that illness and misfortune were caused by an affront to the gods, a failure to properly honor one's ancestors, or the harmful intervention of a conjurer: one who had been blessed at birth with the ability to affect the natural world through the spirits. Conjurers became prominent members of the slave community, called on to heal illness, win the affections of a desired mate, provide spiritual assistance for a planned escape from slavery, and perform a number of other services. They were psychiatrists, doctors, spiritual leaders, and magicians for their communities, even to those who professed Christianity. In a confusing world, where punishment and mortality often seemed arbitrary, the notion that unseen forces could be used for both good and evil offered slaves a feeling of comfort and control.

Festivals

Music and dance also played a prominent role in the lives of the slaves. The sounds they created were again a blend of cultures, using African instruments such as the drum and kalimba alongside European instruments like the banjo, gourd, and fiddle. Satirical songs and dances, whose lyrics and structure mocked the pretensions of white society, were especially popular.

Festivals also were celebrated. In North Carolina, the Christmas holidays were recognized with a celebration known as John Canno. During the festivals of Election Day in New England and Pinkster Day in New York State and New Jersey, slaves put on their best clothes, sang and danced through the streets, and elected black "governors." Those elected became leaders within the slave community for the following year, settling minor disputes between slaves, and sometimes even imposing punishments, although only in cases where no whites or free blacks were involved.

Whites tolerated or even encouraged these festivals, seeing them as a useful way to release tension in an oppressed, politically weak group. Although many black governors were owned by powerful whites, their authority was not simply a by-product of the master's influence. These men carried real influence in the slave community by virtue of their intelligence, physical strength, or even the status that they had once held in Africa. Election Day and Pinkster Day were thus one of the slaves' best opportunities to enjoy cultural independence and a small measure of power.

A Cultural Blend

Africans arrived in the colonies disoriented, physically weak, and condemned to spend their lives struggling with the daily brutality and humiliation of being coerced laborers from a despised racial group. In spite of these obstacles, they created a culture that blended familiar traditions into a pan-African whole and combined it with borrowed elements from white society.

This enabled them to strengthen their communities, preserve something of their African past, assert their humanity, and make sense of their world. Their efforts would help to shape popular American culture and lay the foundation for the next 200 years of African American life.

David Broadnax, Sr.

See also: African Americans; Native Americans and Slavery; Plantations; Religions, African; Slavery, African American; Slavery, Caribbean.

Bibliography

Berlin, Ira, and Ronald Hoffman, eds. *Slavery and Freedom in the Age of the American Revolution.* Charlottesville: University Press of Virginia, 1983.

Hoffer, Peter Charles, ed. *Africans Become Afro-Americans: Selected Articles on Slavery in the American Colonies.* New York: Garland Publishing, 1988.

Morgan, Kenneth. *Slavery and Servitude in Colonial North America: A Short History.* New York: New York University Press, 2001.

Wood, Betty. *The Origins of American Slavery: Freedom and Bondage in the English Colonies.* New York: Hill and Wang, 1997.

Slave Rebellions

African American slaves engaged in countless rebellions and other acts of resistance during the colonial era. Although they were ultimately unsuccessful in overthrowing slavery, their constant low-level resistance, fugitivism, and armed rebellion was a constant thorn in the side of the slave regime.

Slave culture itself was inherently subversive, although not in ways that could be easily detected by whites. This culture was strongly influenced by West African traditions, especially in Charles Town, the Georgia Sea Islands, and other areas with large African-born populations. Folk stories about the trickster character Bre'r (short for "brother") Rabbit and real-life slaves who got the upper hand on whites through cunning and deception were circulated throughout slave communities. Songs such as "Many Thousand Gone," Swing Low, Sweet Chariot," and "Go Down, Moses" carried a double meaning, speaking overtly of religious concerns but secretly carrying messages about freedom. The story of Moses and the Israelites' escape from Egyptian bondage was of particular importance in these songs and in African American Christianity generally. These elements and others created a climate of rebellion in slave communities.

Low-level, everyday rebelliousness was the most common form of slave resistance. One common tactic was stealing from the master; slaves did not consider this immoral, since their own coerced labor had produced the master's wealth. Arson and destruction of farm implements was also frequent. So many buildings and farm tools were destroyed that slaveholders began using brick instead of wood for construction and developed the steel "negro hoe," which was much more difficult to break than a traditional wooden hoe. Other forms of daily resistance included working slowly, feigning illness or pregnancy, arson, self-injury, poisoning, and even killing oneself or one's children. The men, women, and children who performed these acts did not take the more drastic step of running away or rebelling openly, but they nevertheless found other ways of resisting slavery and asserting their humanity.

Escape

Next to low-level resistance, running away was the most common form of slave rebelliousness. This struck a blow against the slave regime, but it also took the even bolder step of elevating the rebel to freedom. The decision to run away was usually a carefully calculated one. Some fugitives took to the main roads, pretending to be free blacks, slaves on legitimate errands, or (in the case of extremely light-skinned blacks) white travelers. The majority, however, were forced to take more arduous paths through the wilderness, where they fought hunger, exposure, and slave catchers. Most were caught or returned voluntarily within less than two weeks. Young men made up the largest number of fugitives, but women, families, and even entire plantation communities sometimes escaped as well. In all cases, the flight to freedom was a cooperative effort, as slave communities and free blacks (and some sympathetic whites as well) provided fugitives with food, supplies, and hiding places along the way.

The destination of fugitives varied over time and place. Although slavery was legal in all thirteen colonies and fleeing to the North was no guarantee of freedom, many fugitives nevertheless headed for Boston, New Bedford, and other Northern cities that were known for protecting runaways. Other urban areas were favored as well, since fugitives could blend in with their large free black populations. Some fugitives headed for Florida, where Spanish officials had promised freedom to any runaway who converted to Catholicism and aided them against the English.

Later, an even greater conflict would encourage fugitivism and other forms of rebellion on an unprecedented scale. During the American Revolution, thousands of slaves fled to British lines in Virginia and Staten Island, where they served as laborers, scouts, and soldiers in hopes of being freed by the British after the war. Thousands more fled to Northern cities, doubling the fugitive population in Philadelphia and quadrupling it in New York. After the Revolution, Northern slavery would never be the same, in part because of the efforts of fugitive slaves.

Petit marronage and *grand marronage* (from the Spanish word *cimarrón,* which originally referred to cattle that had escaped from their owner) were additional forms of slave resistance. Petit marronage was the act of temporarily running away to escape from physical punishment, to gain relief from the drudgery of slave labor, to visit other maroons (slaves engaged in marronage), or to negotiate with their masters for better treatment. Slaves may have been subjugated, but through petit marronage they were able to assume at least a small amount of power over their masters. Those who engaged in grand marronage, on the other hand, had no intention of ever returning to their masters or even living as free blacks in white society. These maroons—many of whom had been born free in Africa—sought to create independent societies in unsettled regions apart from white interference.

Maroon communities were commonly located in the mountains of North Carolina, marshes along the southern Atlantic coast, and the Great Dismal Swamp, a wetland on the Virginia/North Carolina border. The harshness of these environments, along with constant harassment from white militias, made it difficult for maroons to establish permanent settlements. Most were forced to move constantly and survive on food and supplies that they or their friends had stolen from nearby settlements. For a number of African Americans, however, living as free people in the wilderness was better than living as slaves on the plantation.

The success or failure of maroon communities was partly determined by whether local Native Americans chose to help them, ignore them, or side with whites against them. In some cases, maroons settled in Native American villages and became valued members of their societies. The most famous example of this occurred in the 1750s when a group of fugitive slaves and Creek Indians fled from Georgia to northern Florida and joined with natives in a biracial society known as the Seminole (from the Creek word for "runaway"). Combining Native American knowledge of the land with West African agricultural and military techniques, the Seminole successfully resisted white encroachment for nearly a century. Another successful maroon community was established near Savannah during the Revolution, when several hundred maroons formed an alliance with the British Army and waged a guerrilla war against the colonists from their large stockaded village.

Rebellion

The most direct but least frequent form of slave resistance was open rebellion, in which the slaves sought to overthrow their masters and then either flee elsewhere or completely topple the slave regime. In some instances, rebellions broke out spontaneously as a response to physical or sexual assault; scores of masters and overseers were injured or killed by slaves who suddenly rose up in self-defense. More common, however, were premeditated rebellions in which the target was slave society as a whole, not any specific individual. Even in these moments, however, rebels usually did not harm whites who were perceived as sympathetic, including Quakers, Catholics, French nationals, and anyone who had individually established good relations with them.

Premeditated rebellions could be inspired by rumors of imminent emancipation, the presence of free blacks, economic depression, or international conflicts. Combinations of these forces in fact led to large waves of slave resistance during the 1730s, the Seven Years' War, and the Revolution. It was more common, however, for slave rebels to act without any external influence, responding to nothing more than the oppressive brutality of their slave existence.

Colonial America's first slave rebellion took place in 1526, at the mouth of South Carolina's Pedee River, when a small group rebelled against their Spanish masters and fled into Native American territory. When the Spanish left for the Caribbean, America's first slave rebels also became its first permanent, non–Native American settlers. Slaves in the English settlements later carried on this tradition; in 1663, an alliance of slaves and white indentured servants formed the first major insurrectionist plot in British North America. The colonial legislatures attempted to prevent additional incidents by banning slaves from carrying anything that could be used as a weapon, from congregating without white supervision, or from interacting with Native Americans, but these efforts were not successful.

Northern cities quickly became a common site of slave rebellions. In 1638, a small uprising took place in Boston. Slaves and Native Americans in the New York area staged rebellions in 1709 and again in 1712, setting fire to buildings and killing a total of sixteen whites. After the second uprising, twenty-one rebels were tortured and killed, while many of New York's other 2,000 slaves fell victims to random violence and harsher restrictions. This wave of terror was repeated in 1741 after a series of mysterious fires. Although it is still unclear whether slaves actually started the fires, several were accused of conspiring to commit mass arson and to poison the water supply, and hundreds more were executed, beaten, or banished from New York.

Other urban waves of destruction attributed to slave rebels took place in Boston and New Haven between 1721 and 1723, in Annapolis in 1739, and in Burlington, Pennsylvania, in 1741.

The most violent slave rebellion of the colonial period took place in 1739 at Stono, South Carolina. An African-born slave named Cato or Jemmy led twenty men and women to an armory on the Stono River near Charles Town; there, they captured weapons and began marching toward Florida, attracting eighty more slaves to their cause by beating messages on drums. The rebels were initially successful in driving off the militia, but after marching about 12 miles, they stopped to rest and thus gave their attackers time to regroup and re-engage them. In the end, between seven and twenty-five whites and about fifty slaves were killed either in the fighting or the subsequent criminal trials.

These events had such a traumatic effect on white South Carolinians that many of them seriously considered completely abolishing slavery, even though slaves made up over half the colony's population and were the backbone of its economy. Slavery would ultimately survive this crisis, but so did slave resistance.

In the end, all of colonial America's slave revolts failed to overthrow the institution. Many plots were betrayed by fellow slaves seeking freedom, financial reward, or white favor. Sheer demographics were an even greater problem; slaves never amounted to more than one-third of the colonial population, and most lived in small groups on isolated plantations. The white population was heavily armed, quick to respond to any real or imagined threat of insurrection, and unrepentant about punishing suspected rebels with torture or painful execution.

Nevertheless, slave resistance persisted throughout the colonial era, fundamentally affecting American society. It was a severe hindrance to the slave regime and the entire colonial economy. It shaped relations between European powers and between African Americans, white colonists, and Native Americans. Finally, it helped lead to the end of slavery in the North and the abolition of the international slave trade after the Revolution.

David Broadnax, Sr.

See also: African Americans; Slave Communities and Culture; Slave Trade; Slavery, African American; Slavery, Caribbean.

Bibliography

Aptheker, Herbert. *American Negro Slave Revolts.* New York: Columbia University Press, 1983.

Berlin, Ira. *Many Thousands Gone: The First Two Centuries of Slavery in North America.* Cambridge, MA: Belknap Press, 1998.

Franklin, John Hope, and Alfred A. Moss, Jr. *From Slavery to Freedom: A History of African-Americans.* New York: McGraw-Hill, 2000.

Frey, Sylvia R. *Water from the Rock: Black Resistance in a Revolutionary Age.* Princeton, NJ: Princeton University Press, 1991.

Genovese, Eugene D. *From Rebellion to Revolution: Afro-American Slave Revolts in the Making of the Modern World.* Baton Rouge: Louisiana State University Press, 1979.

Price, Richard, ed. *Maroon Societies: Rebel Slave Communities in the Americas.* Baltimore: Johns Hopkins University Press, 1979.

Thornton, John. *Africa and Africans in the Making of the Atlantic World.* New York: Cambridge University Press, 1992.

Slave Trade

The slave trade was an integral part of the mercantilist economic structure that operated among the colonies in North America. The early settlers initially attempted to enslave native peoples, a venture that proved unsuccessful. The introduction of African slavery provided a necessary labor source.

Until the late seventeenth century, slavery accounted for a relatively small portion of colonial laborers, as the indentured servitude of both whites and blacks was more common. By the dawn of the eighteenth century, however, slavery had become the dominant system, and the traffic in slaves was growing to match the demand.

Origins of the Slave Trade

African slaves first became commodities in international trade through Portuguese exploration. In 1441, Portuguese traders brought back to their country ten African natives; the captives, a gift for Prince Henry, had been abducted as curiosities rather than for sale. Just three years later, however, Portuguese traders returned with a cargo of 235 Africans as slaves. These captives were distributed among the regent of Portugal and the church.

The growth of sugar plantations in Portuguese colonies such as Brazil spurred a demand for cheap labor that was met by African slaves, and the Portuguese continued to control the slave trade through the sixteenth century. A series of papal bulls gave Portugal exclusive rights in Africa, thereby sanctioning the enslavement of its native peoples. In 1518, Portugal's King Charles V granted the governor of Bresa a monopoly on the annual shipment of 4,000 African slaves to the West Indies, evidence of how quickly the slave trade had grown.

By the eighteenth century, the slave trade had become an important and well-developed part of imperial and colonial economies. England, Portugal, and France were the primary nations involved, shipping well over half of the slaves traded from Africa during this time.

Throughout the 1700s, the English dominated the slave trade, primarily because of their preeminence as a maritime power. English traders had access to the necessary resources, both naval and financial. The continued growth of the English colonies and the strength of British manufacturing also served as assets.

Operation of the Slave Trade

The slave trade began in the interior regions of Africa. Most of the men and women who were captured and sold into slavery came from limited areas along the western coast of Africa, including Benin, the Gold Coast, Gambia, and Guinea. Captives were chained together in a coffle. The thirty to forty chained men and women were forced to march to the coast, often carrying goods to be traded, and it took several days to reach the slave trade ships.

As the slave trade grew, fortresses were established along the African coast to provide housing for the Europeans involved and to hold slaves until ships arrived with traders to purchase them. Fortresses such as Portugal's Elmina, in Ghana, included dungeons that housed 150 to 200 people at a time. The captives were fed twice a day and were subject to inhumane conditions for as long as three months before being sold to a ship's captain.

After being purchased, the slaves were packed into the holds of ships to be transported to the colonies in what was known as the Middle Passage. These ships were designed specifically to carry large numbers of human cargo, and slaves were chained together and stuffed into small spaces that prevented them from standing upright. The close quarters and lack of care resulted in diseases such as scurvy and dysentery among the captives. Historians estimate that the mortality rate for slaves subjected to the Middle Passage was as high as 13 percent. By the end of the seventeenth century,

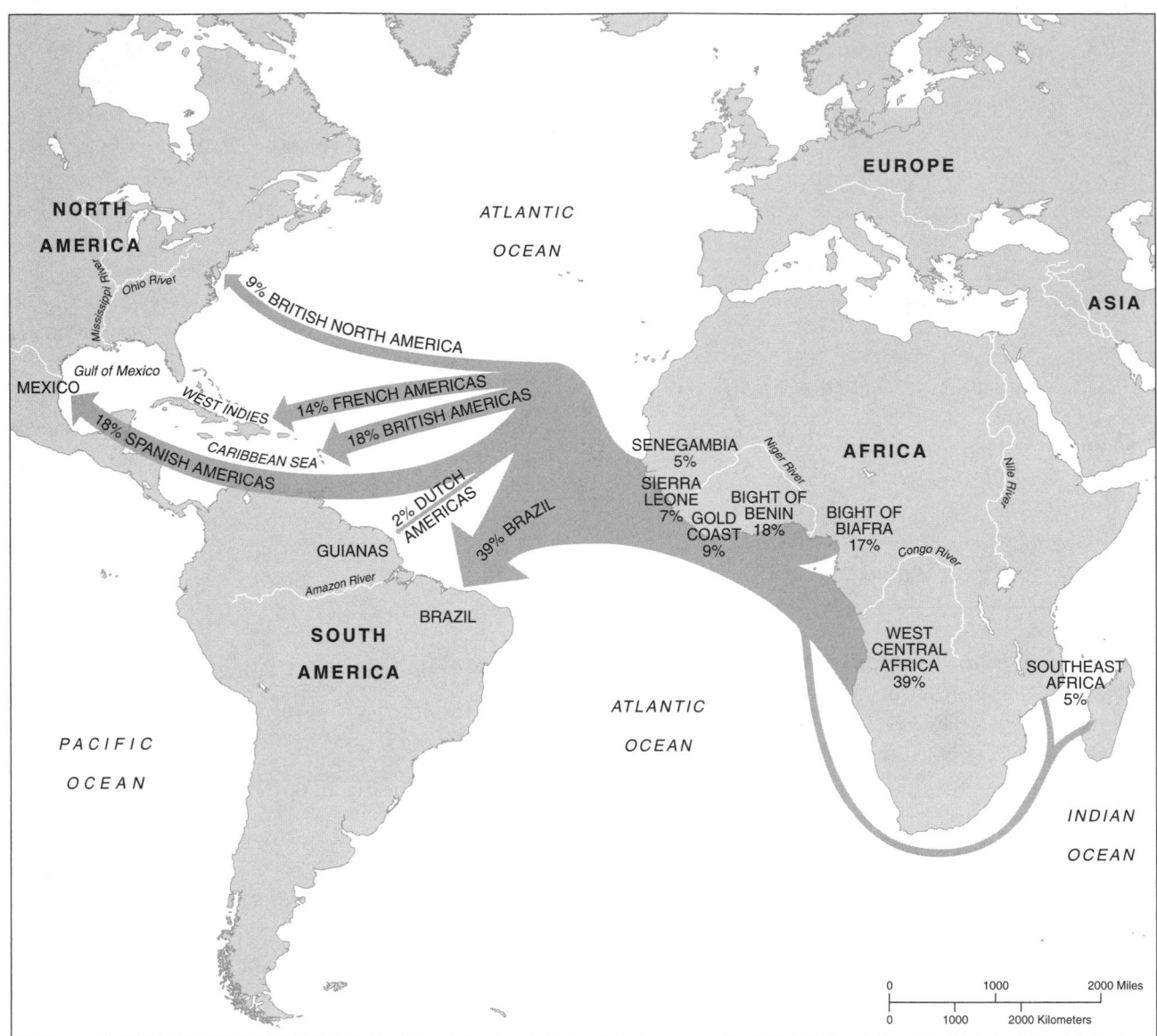

Trans-Atlantic Slave Trade, 1510s–1860s. The Trans-Atlantic slave trade was an enormous enterprise that lasted for more than three centuries. Slaves came largely from West and Central Africa, and most were destined for Brazil and the Caribbean. Less than 10 percent were shipped directly from Africa to Britain's colonies on mainland North America and, after 1776, to the new United States. *(Carto-Graphics)*

however, British slavers improved conditions so that the mortality rate dropped to as little as 3 percent.

In 1747, the average length of a round-trip slaving voyage from New York was 232 days. This included eight to nine weeks to reach Africa, around sixteen weeks spent trading to obtain slaves, and an additional eight to nine weeks for the return voyage. Slave voyages presented those engaged in the trade with a number of risks. Water travel, though improved by the advances of the seventeenth century, was still a dangerous undertaking as ships were sometimes unable to sustain the hardships of a lengthy voyage. In 1766, the slave

ship *Nancy* sank after springing a leak. Its captain, crew, and cargo of 59 slaves managed to reach Barbados in the ship's lifeboats. Such instances were not isolated and often did not end so fortunately.

In addition, colonial slave traders were the targets of slave ships from other countries. In the late eighteenth century, several New York slave ships were attacked by French privateers and forced to surrender their human cargoes.

Another peril of the slave trade was the possibility of slave insurrections. It was not uncommon for the captives to organize rebellions on board the ship and attempt to gain their freedom. In 1760, Captain John Nicoll's ship *Agnes* fell victim to a slave uprising; the rebellion resulted in Nicoll killing the 40 slaves involved. On the New York schooner the *Catherine*, slaves on board organized an uprising and took over the ship.

Slaves were traded in the colonies as part of the triangular trade, the three-pronged process of exchanging goods that grew out of the expansion of the European colonies. The triangle began in Africa, where large numbers of ships waited off the coast to receive cargoes of slaves. Captives were purchased for a variety of goods, including guns and gunpowder, cloth, kettles, knives, shells (used as currency), and rum. Having obtained their cargoes, the slave ships generally sailed for the West Indies, where the slaves were sold and the ships were loaded with cargoes of raw sugar. From there, the ships traveled to New England, where the sugar was sold. New cargoes of rum and manufactured goods were loaded, and, bearing these items that could be exchanged for slaves, the ships then returned to the coast of Africa.

In reality, transatlantic trade was not this simple. But the sequence of exchanging manufactured goods for African slaves, whose labor provided the raw materials that went into making items in high demand, generally applies to the colonial slave trade.

Slave Trade Numbers

The overall numbers of Africans subjected to enslavement is a matter of debate among historians. Estimates of the total range from 9.5 million to 11.7 million Africans forcibly transported via the slave trade. The largest numbers of slaves were shipped from Africa during the course of the eighteenth century, and it is estimated that as many as 6.1 million slaves were taken from Africa during this time. Imports to North America during the eighteenth century number just over 194,000.

Most of the African slaves who were shipped to the New World were sent to colonies in the Caribbean and South America. Only 400,000 slaves were sent directly to the American colonies; this amounted to roughly 5 percent of the slaves who came from Africa. Many slaves were later sent to the mainland colonies from island plantations in the West Indies.

In 1672, English merchants established the Royal African Company of England, a group of merchants and investors that maintained a monopoly on the slave trade until the mid-1690s. The Company established seventeen slave "factories," fortresses for the processing of slaves, on the western coast of Africa, employing 200 to 300 workers. From 1672 to 1713, the company engaged in roughly 500 slave voyages, purchasing 125,000 slaves; the 100,000 who survived the journey were sold in the British West Indies. Once the slave trade was opened to competition from other merchants, lower prices resulted in greater numbers of slaves being imported directly to the colonies.

Colonial Slave Traders

Colonial settlers and merchants also engaged in the slave trade. The first black laborers had arrived in Virginia in 1619 on a Dutch ship that sailed to Jamestown. That year, the earl of Warwick and Virginia's Captain Samuel Argall embarked on a voyage that included slaves. In 1630, another ship arrived in Virginia with slaves to sell. By 1636, the Northern colonies had begun their connection, when colonists at Marblehead built a ship, the *Desire,* to engage in the slave trade with the West Indies.

The number of black slaves in North America remained small throughout much of the seventeenth century. In 1650, only 2,000 blacks lived in the American colonies. By 1700, that number had escalated to 31,000 blacks, nearly all of them slaves.

Over the next fifty years, the slave trade became a prominent business in New England. By 1770, Rhode Island had 150 ships involved in the slave trade, and colonial legislation recognized the importance of this commerce to the local economy. Massachusetts tax laws benefited slave ships that docked at ports in the colony, allowing for a refund of the taxes imposed on importers of slaves. Other colonies established similar laws. In New Jersey, however, the tax on slaves was established as a means of prohibiting the importation of enslaved laborers into the colony.

New York's legislation was an attempt to encourage the importation of slaves directly from Africa by establishing a three pound tax on slaves imported from anywhere but the African coast. Although the slave trade constituted only a small portion of New York's entire overseas trade during the colonial period, New York served as an important point of entry. From 1700 to 1715, nearly 500 slaves entered the colonies via New York, with over half of them coming from other colonies and roughly 200 arriving directly from Africa. Between 1715 and the start of the American Revolution, New York served as the starting point for at least 120 slave voyages.

From its beginning, South Carolina was a slave

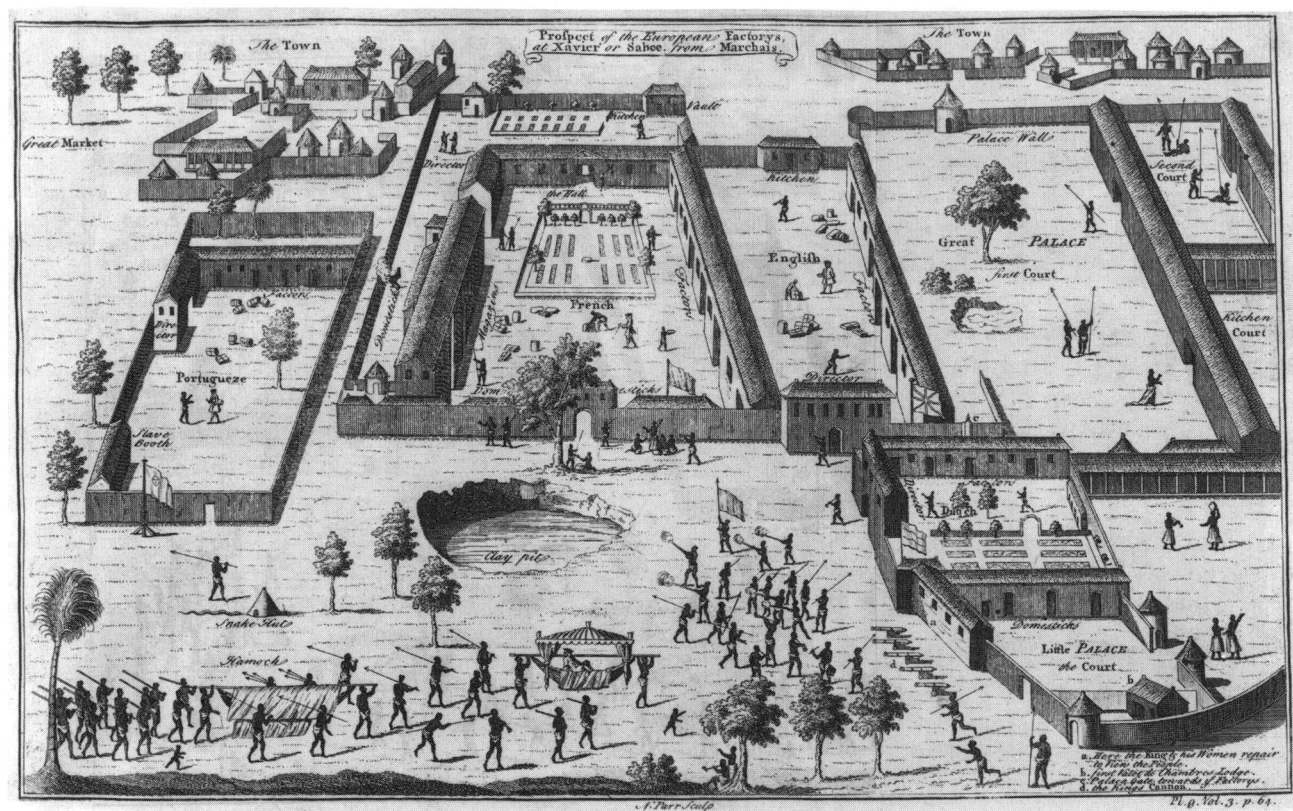

The African slave trade originated in the interior regions of the continent, where natives were captured and marched in chains to sprawling compounds—such as this one in Nigeria in 1746—along the western coast to await shipment. *(Library of Congress, LC-USZ62-106828)*

colony; the establishment of large rice plantations increased the need for laborers and solidified the colony's position on slavery. During the eighteenth century, the colony purchased large numbers of slaves. In 1724, Joseph Wragg, captain of a slave ship, arrived with a shipment of 142 slaves, and at least four other slave ships stopped in South Carolina, bringing a total of 734 African slaves to the colony that year. Samuel Wragg, Joseph's brother and an agent for the colony, reported that, by 1726, South Carolinians purchased 1,000 slaves annually. He went on to make a contract with the Royal African Company, establishing the purchase of 300 slaves from Gambia to be sent to the colony.

In South Carolina, slave ships that arrived were generally arranged for by a local merchant, who would take responsibility for selling the slaves once they arrived in port, often including them as just another commodity in an existing import businesses. Henry Laurens was among the chief participants in South Carolina's slave trade in the eighteenth century; in 1755, Laurens reported that his business dealt with 700 slaves in that year. Laurens and fellow merchants

who participated in the slave trade were generally members of the colonial elite, a position that gave them access to useful information regarding finances and crops.

Colonial traders rarely paid cash for the slaves they purchased from ship captains, and rarely received cash from the men and women who purchased slaves. In the early days, South Carolina merchants often paid for their cargoes in rice, and planters usually purchased their slaves on credit, paying the merchants in crops after the harvest. The extension of credit was a risky move for the merchants, and Laurens recommended to those wanting to become involved in the slave traffic that they hold a reserve of 10,000 pounds sterling.

The slave trade could be an extremely profitable business. In the last forty years of the eighteenth century, British slave traders received a total of 60 million pounds for the slaves they sold. The average profit for slave voyages during this time was nearly 10 percent, a significantly higher profit margin than the return on investment in colonial plantations.

Merchants who imported slaves sought to obtain those individuals who would be most marketable. In

South Carolina, for instance, merchants preferred slaves from Gambia and the Gold Coast, as they were most in demand in the colony. Traders also preferred cargoes largely consisting of young men, generally not over the age of 25, and young women under the age of 20. Young male slaves brought the highest profit margin.

The prices of slaves who arrived as part of the triangular trade varied from colony to colony and also depended on broader economic issues. In South Carolina, as in the other Southern colonies, which were the largest consumers of slave labor, prices were determined by such variables as taxes imposed on importation by the colonial government, the success or failure of crops, the availability of new land, the demand for slaves in other colonies, and wars occurring locally or in Europe.

From 1651 to 1675, slaves sold for an average of 5.26 pounds. In the last quarter of the seventeenth century, the average price dropped to 3.67 pounds as a result of increased availability of slaves in the colonies. Fifty years later, in 1751, the price for male slaves in South Carolina was around 250 pounds; female slaves were valued at around 200 pounds. In the next few years, the demand for slaves led to a jump in prices, and, in 1755, young men were selling for as much as 330 pounds. The demand drew slave traders to the colony and again resulted in a flooded market, bringing the price back down to 260 pounds for a male slave.

Banning the Slave Trade

Despite interruptions caused by the American Revolution, the slave trade to the new United States would flourish into the late eighteenth and early nineteenth centuries. But the tide of national and world opinion was running against it.

The slave trade became a source of debate at the Constitutional Convention in 1787. Most Northerners wanted to ban it; many Southerners wanted to keep it open. Ultimately, a compromise was reached. Article I, Section 9 of the Constitution prohibited Congress from banning the trade for twenty years. In 1807, Congress did just that, and the United States prohibited the importation of slaves after January 1, 1808. This followed a similar move by the British Parliament the year before.

Given the high value of slaves—especially after their importation was banned—smuggling continued. Ultimately, the importation of slaves into the United States did not end until slavery itself was destroyed in the Civil War.

Tonia M. Compton

See also: Dutch West India Company; Royal African Company; Slavery, African American; Slavery, Caribbean; Trade; Triangle Trade. *Document:* On Being Brought from Africa to America (early 1770s).

Bibliography

Blackburn, Robin. *The Making of New World Slavery: From the Baroque to the Modern, 1492–1800.* London: Verson Press, 1997.

Brinkley, Alan. *American History: A Survey.* 9th ed. New York: McGraw-Hill, 1995.

Donnan, Elizabeth. "The Slave Trade into South Carolina Before the Revolution." *American Historical Review* 33:4 (1928): 804–28.

Lovejoy, Paul E. "The Volume of the Atlantic Slave Trade: A Synthesis." *Journal of African History* 23:4 (1982): 473–501.

Lydon, James G. "New York and the Slave Trade, 1700 to 1774." *William and Mary Quarterly*, 3rd ser., 35:2 (1978): 375–94.

Pope-Hennessy, James. *Sins of the Fathers: A Study of the Atlantic Slave Traders, 1441–1807.* New York: Barnes and Noble, 1967.

Spears, John R. *The American Slave Trade: An Account of Its Origin, Growth and Suppression.* Port Washington, NY: Kennikat, 1900.

Slavery, African American

By the 1640s, colonists found themselves in a crisis situation: there was a distinct shortage of labor in the New World. The settlers had been quick to recognize the agricultural potential of the land they had come to. Realizing this potential, however, was a goal that would prove highly labor-intensive. Furthermore, the land in the Middle and Southern colonies was particularly suited for producing cotton, rice, indigo, and especially tobacco—all labor-intensive crops.

Europeans did not arrive in sufficient numbers in the late seventeenth century to fill the need for this labor, and attempts to either hire or enslave Native Americans as field workers proved unsatisfactory. As a result, talk turned increasingly toward adapting the system of African slavery that had been so widely used in the Caribbean islands and Latin America.

As early as the sixteenth century, Africans had been brought from West Africa to work in Spain's New World colonies, and the Portuguese had brought slaves from Angola and Zaire to Brazil even earlier. Between 1433 and 1488, it is estimated that from 500 to 1,000

African slaves were imported annually to Portuguese colonies in the Western Hemisphere. Large shipments of African slaves began to arrive at the sugar cane plantations of Hispaniola (modern-day Haiti) in 1502. It has been estimated that, by the end of the 1500s, some 80,000 African slaves were being brought to the Spanish colonies each year.

In light of this history, it is probably not surprising that American colonists began to consider importing slave labor by the late 1600s. Spain's and Portugal's relative successes in the enterprise, along with the widespread beliefs that Africans possessed almost superhuman physical strength and were genetically well suited to heavy labor in hotter climates than those of the Europeans' homelands, made the enslavement of African laborers an attractive solution to the colonies' need for workers. In addition, Africans' skin color was seen as a bonus by potential slaveholders: their blackness would make them stand out from their white fellows and make it more dangerous for them to attempt to escape.

Slave-Master Relations in the American Colonies

With the institutionalization of black slavery in the colonies, the relationship between masters and slaves became more rigid than that between masters and their indentured servants. Virginia led the colonies in slave ownership in 1756; the 120,000 slaves there comprised one half of the colony's population. In some regions, particularly areas of the Chesapeake tobacco country and virtually everywhere in South Carolina, blacks far outnumbered whites. Majority rule, then, was not in white colonists' best interests.

Instead, the dynamic between masters and African American slaves was based on power and fear, and, as a result, laws were quickly enacted to address the master-slave relationship. Colonial slave codes were heavily based on similar laws that had existed for decades in Caribbean slave culture. Although slave codes varied somewhat from one colony to the next, the effect was overwhelmingly uniform: African slaves were effectively redefined, and they were now legally considered to be property rather than human beings.

Under the slave codes, African Americans could not bear arms, they were forbidden to move about freely, and their rights to freely assemble or to seek legal redress were eliminated. The killing or maiming of one's own slaves was legalized as a "property right"; injuring or killing a slave owned by another was prosecuted as a crime against that owner's property. Rules for maintaining order among slave populations mandated various forms of punishment for misbehavior, such as guidelines that required whipping any slave who attempted to strike a white person. It is important to realize that such slave codes were in force in all of the colonies, although harsher laws were more prevalent in Southern areas.

Daily Life of Colonial Slaves

Daily life for any settler in colonial America was a difficult proposition, and African Americans' hardships were only exacerbated by the rigors of slavery. Nevertheless, slaves were able to develop a meaningful sense of community within the larger colonial society. The family was the traditional unit of society within African life, and slaves generally retained a strong sense of family, even within captivity. Although one's immediate family members might not have been present in a given setting, the slaves' world generally established a type of family unit within the slave quarters.

Males were usually considered dominant figures within slave life, although the restrictions imposed by slavery meant that slave men were less dominant than in their native situations. Slave women were by no means invisible or even marginalized within the family dynamic. In fact, because of necessities frequently imposed on them by their men's inability to act, slave women often were empowered within the family structure.

An important component of slave life was religious practice. Tribal religions often involved veneration of the ancestors and worship of nature. Some scholars have speculated that many Africans would have been exposed to the tenets of Islam prior to their removal to the colonies, and there are scattered references in early colonial records to slaves who prayed to a god named Allah. Missionaries had gone to western areas of Africa as early as the sixteenth century in an attempt to replace "paganism" with Christianity. The fact that this missionary activity overlapped with the slave trade both temporally and geographically may explain the fact that the Christian message was ignored by most Africans. However, the failure of these missionaries to convert natives in Africa did not deter missionary efforts towards African slaves within America. Records exist showing that as early as the 1620s and 1630s, Christian missionaries were attempting to evangelize "the black heathens" within the colonies.

Early religious outreach efforts toward African Americans were led by members of the Society of Friends. Quakers would continue to be among slaves' most outspoken advocates until the early 1800s. As early as 1700, Quakers established "meetings" (the denomination's name for their local congregations) specifically directed toward free and enslaved blacks. However, as the century wore on and the fear of blacks' rebellion plots grew among whites, many localities outlawed such meetings.

From the mid-eighteenth century through emancipation, African Americans formed a significant component of the growing Baptist and Methodist denominations. The first independent black congregation in the colonies, Silver Bluff Baptist Church, was established in the early 1770s in South Carolina. However, it was the exception rather than the rule, even among the Baptist and Methodist denominations. Fear of assembling and empowering slaves meant that there were few recognized clergy among colonial churches, and there were no blacks in any positions of church leadership.

This denial of formal organizational power did not preclude the establishment of informal, often secretive, networks based on social, religious, and even political grounds. The Stono Rebellion of 1739 made colonists feel vindicated in their fears of slaves' plots to overthrow their white masters. However, even these fears rose and fell over time and between one area and another. In 1702, for example, substantial numbers of enslaved and free blacks fought to defend various colonial strongholds against Native American and, at some times, French attackers. Well into the mid-1700s, in some regions, black indentured servants could reduce their terms of service by offering comparable amounts of time in military service to their colonies. During this same period, Virginia and South Carolina allowed indentured African Americans to enlist in their respective militias, and, in some cases, even slaves were allowed to serve.

By the time of the Revolutionary War, the need for troops loyal to the colonial position was desperate, so much so that both free and enslaved African Americans were called upon to serve their new nation. Several thousand slaves, mostly from the Northern colonies, were granted manumission and were freed following their service in the cause of the Revolution.

Barbara Schwarz Wachal

See also: African Americans; Agriculture; Cotton; Equiano, Olaudah; Free Blacks; Indentured Servitude; Laborers, Rural; Laborers, Urban; Native American–African American Relations; Native Americans and Slavery; Negro Election Day; Plantations; Planters; Religions, African; Rice; Slave Communities and Culture; Slave Rebellions; Slave Trade; Slavery, Caribbean; Tobacco. *Documents:* Virginia Slave Laws (1660s); Protest of German Quakers Against Slavery (1688); The Demand for Slavery in Georgia (1743); Slave Petition to the Governor, Council, and House of Representatives of the Province of Massachusetts (1774).

Bibliography

Hoffer, Peter Charles, ed. *Africans Become Afro-Americans: Selected Articles on Slavery in the American Colonies.* New York: Garland Publishing, 1988.

Morgan, Kenneth. *Slavery and Servitude in Colonial North America: A Short History.* New York: New York University Press, 2001.

Noel, Donald L., ed. *The Origins of American Slavery and Racism.* Columbus, OH: Merrill Publishing, 1972.

Reiss, Oscar. *Blacks in Colonial America.* Jefferson, NC: McFarland, 1997.

Schneider, Dorothy. *Slavery in America: From Colonial Times to the Civil War.* New York: Facts on File, 2000.

Wood, Peter H. *Strange New Land: Africans in Colonial America.* New York: Oxford University Press, 2003.

Slavery, Caribbean

African slave trading was a long-standing practice when the Portuguese reached West Africa. Between the tenth and fourteenth centuries, a trans-Saharan trade flourished, comprising mostly females bought as servants, agricultural workers, or concubines. Iberians got their slaves through Ceuta, Morocco.

When the Portuguese arrived in West Africa in the mid-fifteenth century, they dealt directly with the slavers, trying to satisfy a new market for slaves on the sugar plantations on the Atlantic islands of Madeira and São Tomé. The discovery that the New World contained prime sugar-producing land was a major stimulus to the slave trade.

Sugar

Sugar was rare and expensive in Europe when Muslims controlled the market. The Atlantic islands were a godsend for Europeans with a sweet tooth. Between 1441 and 1888, as many as 12 million mostly West and West Central Africans became slaves in the Americas. About two-thirds of all slaves worked in the sugar colonies.

The transatlantic slave trade was a key component of the development of colonial America under the mercantilist/capitalist economy. When, in the early seventeenth century, the British, French, and Dutch entered the Americas, their labor source was indentured servants, usually young European males who contracted for some or all of the cost of their passage and keep in return for three to seven years of labor. By the late seventeenth century, the need to produce tobacco, sugar, indigo (used to make blue dye), and rice demanded more labor than indenture provided. By the middle of the eighteenth century, the three largest slave colonies in the New World were Jamaica, Saint-Domingue, and Brazil. The principal money crop was sugar.

Sugar was highly profitable, returning about 10 percent on investment; in exceptional years, such as that in Barbados in the 1650s, it brought in 40 to 50 percent. Plantations varied in size by location and time. In 1680, the average Barbadian plantation had 60 slaves; Jamaica in the 1830s averaged about 150. Slave populations ranged from about one-third in late-eighteenth-century Cuba to 90 percent in Jamaica in 1730, Antigua half a century later, and Grenada in the 1830s.

Slaves were isolated from the white culture to emphasize the difference between the two. Slave codes, such as the Barbados Slave Act (1661), specified capital crimes as rape, arson, murder, assault, and theft of anything valued at greater than a shilling. Lesser crimes brought punishments including whipping, branding, and nose slitting. Castration was practiced if not officially sanctioned. The Barbadian code was a model for other English Caribbean colonies. Jamaican observers noted punishments including rubbing melted wax into lash wounds, amputations, impaling, and burning alive. Drawing and quartering was an option on Nevis.

In all cases, overseers checked cabins twice monthly for stolen goods and weapons, and slaves had to have a pass to visit off the plantation. The brutal culture allowed Sunday for rest, but otherwise slaves worked six ten- or twelve-hour days. During harvest, the shifts could be much longer. Commonly the rations were meager. Work and hunger were the norm.

Slave Culture

Slave culture retained some elements of African culture in the indifference and absence of owner imposition of white cultural values, including Christianity. Even when encouraged, Christianizing seemed to many owners to be a breaking down of the white-black barrier. Segregated slaves developed an African-English patois and established African customs in music, dance, funerals, and marriages that incorporated the various African practices of the many cultures thrown together. They also considered rebellion.

In a society where slaves outnumbered whites four to one, slave risings occurred often enough to keep the planters alert. Between 1640 and 1713 seven slave revolts produced death for white and black alike. Several other would-be revolts were aborted before they could cause damage. Slave rebellions occurred in Demerara in 1823 and Jamaica in 1831.

Jamaica was a hotbed due to the presence of escaped slaves, known as maroons, from the former Spanish plantations. Maroons were rebels hiding in the mountains and providing sanctuary for escapees from the English plantations. Jamaica was unusual; more commonly, there were fewer hiding places and no outlaws to provide support. Relative peace was the case in Barbados, Antigua, and St. Kitts and Nevis.

In Guyana, the first slaves were brought by Dutch settlers and traders in the early seventeenth century. Although the Dutch never developed extensive plantations, they took the slave trade from the Portuguese in the 1630s. The edge was only temporary, with the French and English vying for the trade in the 1640s, and Danes, Swedes, and Germans also entering the trade. The largest traders in the eighteenth century were the British, Portuguese, and French.

Slavery in Guyana was typically field slavery, which meant long hours along with inadequate clothing, shelter, and food. Slaves received little medical attention, and they were often punished severely and exploited sexually. Slavery was a lifetime status, changeable only by death, running away, or manumission. In 1825, Demerara-Essequibo had only forty-four manumitted slaves and a slave population nearing 72,000. Berbice had eleven in a slave population of 21,000.

Emancipation

Slavery was sanctioned and encouraged by European governments and churches. Not until the second half of the eighteenth century did Enlightenment thinkers such as Jean-Jacques Rousseau, in France, began speaking seriously and strongly of applying concepts expressed as liberty, equality, and fraternity. In England, the humanitarian movement had its origins in the strong evangelical movement that arose at the same time.

Britain outlawed slavery through the Somerset case in England in 1772 and the Knight case in Scotland in 1778. These cases involved only 14,000 to 15,000 slaves in both England and Scotland, which had a large if not surplus supply of free labor. Where slavery was more integral to the economy, specifically in the Caribbean, abolition was more difficult.

British antislavery efforts became more organized with the formation in 1787 of the Society for the Abolition of the Slave Trade. Leaders such as Thomas Clarkson, William Wilberforce, and Granville Sharp focused their attacks initially on the slave trade, not slavery itself. They campaigned to sensitize the public to the nature of the trade while simultaneously working for parliamentary action. In 1807, Parliament outlawed the slave trade for all British nationals and subjects. Emboldened by this success, the society sought next the abolition of slavery. Finally, in 1833, Parliament abolished slavery effective August 1, 1834.

Aside from humanitarian considerations and the pressure from abolitionists, Parliament's reluctant abolition rested on four considerations. First, the government had attempted since 1823 to convince Caribbean officials and owners to ameliorate the abysmal conditions of the slaves. Government recommended the outlawing of the flogging of women, the end of using the whip in the field, religious instruction and recognized marriages for all slaves, shorter working days, better clothing and food, and compulsory manumission. Planters in the Caribbean strongly opposed these reforms, especially in Jamaica and Barbados. But the planters lost their clout when the sugar economy began declining in the 1830s due to soil exhaustion and tumbling prices. Britain's economic interest in the West Indies waned with the decline of the sugar economy.

At the same time, the English saw value in Africa, as a provider not of slaves but of raw materials and markets for Britain's industrial revolution. Africa provided oils and cotton, and it bought manufactured goods. Africans were more valuable as producers and consumers in Africa than in the Caribbean as underconsuming, underproducing slaves. Economic pragmatism was a significant factor in changing Britain's longstanding policy.

There were other considerations as well, especially fear. Some in Britain believed that continuing slavery would increase the incidence of uprisings, which could result in a significant loss of property and lives.

A final factor leading to abolition was politics. Electoral reform in 1832 brought to power a reform majority in Parliament. The reformers enacted partial abolition in 1834, a transition "apprenticeship," and total abolition in 1838.

John H. Barnhill

See also: African Americans; Caribbean (Chronology); Equiano, Olaudah; Indentured Servitude; Plantations; Planters; Religions, African; Slave Rebellions; Slave Trade; Sugar.

Bibliography

"African American World." http://www.pbs.org/wnet/aaworld/reference/articles/slavery.html.

Beckles, Hilary, and Verene Shepherd, eds. *Caribbean Slavery in the Atlantic World.* Princeton, NJ: Markus Wiener, 2000.

Mariners Museum. "Captive Passage: The Transatlantic Slave Trade and the Making of the Americas." http://www.mariner.org/captivepassage/arrival/arr009.html.

McDonald, Roderick A., ed. *West Indies Accounts; Essays on the History of the British Caribbean and the Atlantic Economy in Honour of Richard Sheridan.* Kingston, Jamaica: The Press, University of the West Indies, 1996

Paquette, Robert L., and Stanley L. Engerman, eds. *The Lesser Antilles in the Age of European Expansion.* Gainesville: University Press of Florida, 1996.

Sandiford, Keith Albert. *The Cultural Politics of Sugar: Caribbean Slavery and Narratives of Colonialism.* New York: Cambridge University Press, 2002.

Stinchcombe, Arthur L. *Sugar Island Slavery in the Age of Enlightenment: The Political Economy of the Caribbean World.* Princeton, NJ: Princeton University Press, 1995.

Smallpox

A highly contagious disease unknown in the New World prior to the arrival of Columbus, smallpox scarred and killed vast numbers of people during the colonial period. It spread only through direct human contact with infected bodily fluids or infected objects, such as bedding or clothing. With no effective treatment available, the only effective prevention practiced in this era was isolation from infected persons and inoculation with a small amount of the smallpox virus.

Smallpox, derived from the Latin word for "spotted," refers to the raised bumps that appear after a person has been infected with the variola virus. Variola major is the most common form of the disease, with an overall fatality rate historically of about 30 percent. It is this form that struck most New World victims.

The disease in its early stages presented symptoms similar to those of influenza, specifically an intense headache and backache, fever, vomiting, and general malaise. Some people also experienced anxiety, but patients with this symptom, typically Native Americans, often succumbed before the appearance of the distinctive rash associated with the disease.

By the fourth day of disease, the first smallpox sores appeared in the mouth, throat, and nasal passages. At this point, the patient became contagious. Over a twenty-four-hour period, the rash gradually extended to the skin surface, covering the victim in raised pustules that concentrated on the soles of feet, palms of the hands, face, forearms, neck, and back. On some victims, the rash caused subcutaneous hemorrhaging from the gums, eyes, nose, and other orifices. As the rash progressed in the mouth and throat, drinking became difficult and dehydration followed. After two weeks, scabs formed and encrusted most of the body, making any movement painful.

Death commonly occurred between ten and sixteen days and disproportionately claimed the very young and very old. For those who did recover, all symptoms disappeared after about thirty days. Survivors, including future United States president George Washington, suffered from unsightly scarring and occasionally blindness, but they also had a lifelong immunity to the disease.

While smallpox is an age-old killer, the infection rate among populations with no prior exposure to the disease approached 80 percent, with a correspondingly high mortality rate that often exceeded 50 percent. It appeared to be more deadly among Native Americans, with twenty-three recorded epidemics prior to 1775. These epidemics caused the destruction of entire native villages with no one left even to bury the bodies.

Other factors worsened the Native American death rate. With everyone ill, no one remained to provide sustenance. Famine and dehydration claimed victims, while healing practices took additional lives. A popular remedy for illness, the sweat bath, exacerbated the effects of a high fever. On emerging from a sweat lodge, Native Americans would immerse themselves in the coldest and deepest part of a river. Badly weakened by the pox, many were unable to swim and drowned.

Colonists, just as desperate to find relief from the pox, also utilized sweat lodges, as well as fasting, bleeding, blistering, vomiting, and an array of medicines, including laxatives and mercury. The most effective approaches, however, were isolation and inoculation.

In 1647, the Puritan settlers of the Massachusetts Bay Colony implemented a quarantine to keep ships from spreading the disease and later ordered a red flag to fly outside infected households. During the 1721 Boston outbreak, which had a 15 percent fatality rate, 900 of the city's 10,700 colonists fled into the surrounding hills. Flight, although popular, did not offer the immunity of inoculation.

The deliberate implantation of live variola in an incision on a patient's hand or arm triggered a milder form of smallpox but did not lessen the infectious properties of the disease. While some colonists objected to those who attempted to circumvent God's will by inoculation, many others were angered by the introduction of smallpox in areas that were not experiencing outbreaks. Riots broke out at inoculation hospitals, and various legislatures enacted regulations to block the procedure in an effort to maintain public health and the peace. Even where the practice was known and permitted, the expense of inoculation placed it beyond the means of most Americans. Few workers could afford either its price or the weeks spent convalescing afterwards.

A notable smallpox outbreak in 1775–1782 affected the outcome of a number of battles during the American Revolution, and epidemics continued to rage after the war. In the late twentieth century, a successful vaccination program eliminated the disease worldwide, but variola remains a cause for concern as a possible agent of bioterrorism.

Caryn E. Neumann

See also: Death and Dying; Disease; Malaria.

Bibliography

Fenn, Elizabeth A. *Pox Americana: The Great Smallpox Epidemic of 1775–82.* New York: Hill and Wang, 2001.

Fenner, F., et al. *Smallpox and Its Eradication.* Geneva: World Health Organization, 1988.

Williams, Nathaniel. *The method of practice in the small-pox, with observations on the way of inoculation: Taken from a manuscript of the late Dr. Nathaniel Williams, of Boston in N. E.: Published for the common advantage, more especially of the country towns, who may be visited with that distemper.* Boston: S. Kneeland, 1752.

Smith, John (1580–1631)

More than any other figure, Captain John Smith deserves credit for the survival and early success of the Jamestown Colony. Although he was not a stockholder in the Virginia Company, company officials gave Smith a leadership role in the initial expedition in 1607 because of his previous military experience. At a time of severe emergency in the struggling English settlement, Smith took charge of the governing council, much to the chagrin of the gentlemen adventurers who made up the bulk of Jamestown's early population.

The military discipline and order that Smith put in place most likely saved the colony from extinction, but it raised dissent among the colonists, who had him replaced a little more than a year later. The colony soon missed Smith's leadership skills and the discipline he had imposed. During the "starving time" of the winter of 1609–1610, the Jamestown settlers suffered terribly.

John Smith's greatest failing was in Native American relations. Contrary to the romantic mythmaking he himself encouraged, his bombastic policies toward the tribes of the Powhatan Confederacy set Jamestown and the Virginia colony on a course for recurrent conflict with its native neighbors.

Early Years

The future governor of the Jamestown colony was born to a humble but respectable yeoman farming family in Lincolnshire, England, in 1580. In his youth, John received some schooling and served as an apprentice to Thomas Sewell, a merchant in Willoughby-by-Alford, Smith's hometown. But the young John Smith longed for adventures "beyond the sea." When his father died in 1596, he jumped at his first opportunity to live the adventurous life of a soldier. In 1597, at the age of 17, he joined a group of English volunteers fighting against the Spanish in the cause of Dutch independence.

After fighting for two years in the Low Countries, Smith returned briefly to England before setting off again in 1600 as a mercenary in an Austrian expedition against the Turks. During this campaign, he was promoted to captain.

We have only Smith's own swashbuckling account of his adventures in Europe and Turkey to draw upon for knowledge of this segment of his life. In his autobiography, *The True Travels, Adventures, and Observations of Captaine John Smith* (1630), he describes fighting duels against the Turkish champion, his capture in Transylvania, and his subsequent escape from captivity in Turkey. Smith claimed that the Pasha's wife fell in love with him and aided his escape—not the last time the charity of a well-wishing female would intervene on his behalf, if Smith's accounts can be believed. After his escape, he traveled through Russia and Europe to Morocco before returning to England in 1604 or 1605.

The legendary Captain John Smith, portrayed here in an engraving from his *Description of New England* (1616), is rightly credited with founding the first permanent English colony at Jamestown. *(Private Collection/Lauros/Giraudon/ Bridgeman Art Library)*

Smith did not remain long in England before he again sought travel and adventure. He became interested in the colonization movement then being promoted in England as a means of relieving the surplus population and furthering the economic interests of the mother country.

Because of his military experience and no doubt due to his propensity for self-promotion, the Virginia Company chose Smith to be a member of its first expedition to Virginia. Along with 143 others, Smith set sail for America and was present when the colonists founded Jamestown on May 13, 1607.

In Jamestown

The English settlers at Jamestown struggled to survive in the early period of the colony's existence. Disease, malnutrition, and attacks by the natives diminished the population by more than 50 percent in the first year. After constructing a palisade fort and naming the settlement after their monarch, the English at Jamestown seemed unable or unwilling to work together for survival. Many refused to work or were too sick to do so.

Promoters of colonization in England had misinformed prospective colonists that the native peoples, docile and childlike as they were supposed to be, would willingly give the Europeans food out of their abundance. So the colonists concentrated their efforts on exploring the region and looking for gold. John Smith himself led several of these expeditions, and he was one of the first to make contact with the Powhatan Indians.

Though exceptional in many ways, John Smith shared the Englishman's ethnocentric appraisal of the natives. Like others, he regarded the indigenous peoples as inferior and available to be used for the purposes of the white settlers. The Eastern woodland tribes lived just above subsistence level and did not possess the reserves to feed additional hungry adventurers. When the local tribes balked at the amount of food the Englishmen demanded, Smith led punitive expeditions against them to seize the supplies. These early clashes did more than anything else to set English–Native American relations in the Chesapeake down a path of significant conflict in later years.

The tribes near Jamestown were part of the Powhatan Confederacy, which consisted of more than thirty tribes led by a "great chief," Powhatan himself. Initially, Powhatan regarded the English at Jamestown as insignificant and gave them food out of pity. Soon, however, the native peoples discovered that the settlers possessed firearms and metal implements, and Powhatan sought to make the English into subordinate allies in his struggle against his inland enemies. This was most likely the aim behind the capture and "trial" of John Smith.

In late 1607, when Smith led a group exploring the region near Jamestown, a hunting band from one of Powhatan's tribes attacked the Englishmen. The other colonists were killed, but the natives presented Smith to Powhatan as a captive.

In his *Generall Historie of Virginia, New England, and the Summer Isles* (1624), Smith described what took place next as a trial in which he was sentenced to death. He claimed that he was rescued by the intervention of Pocahontas, Powhatan's 11-year-old daughter. For the Powhatan people, this ritual display of mercy probably signified that Smith was to become a subordinate chief, with obligations of loyalty to their chief. The import of the ceremony was apparently lost on Smith, however, as he attributed his rescue to the girl's personal regard.

After spending the summer of 1608 in further explorations, during which time he gathered information that would later be used to complete his detailed map of Virginia, Smith returned to Jamestown. During his absence, Captain Christopher Newport had assumed leadership of the colony. Native American relations had deteriorated even further, and several tribes had become openly hostile. Disease, coupled with the lack of effective leadership, also had taken a heavy toll on the settlement. When Newport returned to England, Smith became president of the council, which made him, effectively, governor of Virginia.

To save the colony from impending disaster, Smith ordered the unruly colonists to work and established a regimen that the highborn gentlemen resented. Forcing them to farm and dig wells made Smith none too popular; however, he threatened to banish and let starve anyone who refused to engage in productive labor. He also dispersed the colonists into smaller settlements in the interior, in order to move them away from the unhealthy swamps around the James River. During Smith's tenure as leader of the colony, a semblance of order and stability was restored, and the death rate declined significantly due to the dispersal of the population and relocation to healthier areas.

It is unfortunate that Smith continued the practice of using force and intimidation against the native populations. In later years, after he had left the colony, Powhatan would drive the English back inside their palisade and lay siege to the settlement. The result was the "starving time" of the winter of 1609–1610, during which the bulk of the population of the colony died and several even resorted to cannibalism. Safely at home in England, on being informed of one colonist's cannibalism of his wife, John Smith quipped darkly, "[of a] dish such as salted wife I never heard."

Downfall from Power

In 1609, the Virginia Company dispatched a new group of colonists to Virginia, along with a new governor to replace the unpopular Smith. Smith himself was badly injured in a gunpowder explosion in October, and he returned to England to recover from severe burns. There, he remained a staunch promoter of Jamestown, although he became a harsh critic of the Virginia Company and the leaders it chose to guide the struggling colony.

Smith's only additional voyage was a brief trip in 1614, sponsored by a group of London merchants, to promote colonization and trade in New England. Afterward, he published a tract entitled *A Description of New England* (1616), maintaining that Northern lands of the North American seaboard would make a more successful ground for colonies than Virginia. He argued that a successful colony should pursue the steady development of agriculture and industry, rather than pinning its hopes on instant riches as the early Virginians had.

Smith continued to spend his remaining years as an ardent proponent of colonization. In all, he wrote and published eight books on the topic, as well as two works on seamanship. He died on June 21, 1631, and is buried in St. Sepulchre's Church in London.

David Ballew

See also: Jamestown; Pocahontas; Powhatan; Powhatan Confederacy; Rolfe, John; Virginia Company. *Document:* The Jamestown Settlement (1607–1609).

Bibliography

Barbour, Philip J. *The Three Worlds of Captain John Smith.* Boston: Houghton Mifflin Company, 1964.

Morgan, Edmund S. *American Slavery, American Freedom.* New York: W. W. Norton and Company, 1975.

Smith, John. *The Complete Works of Captain John Smith.* 3 vols. Edited by Philip J. Barbour. Chapel Hill: University of North Carolina Press, 1986

Vaughan, Alden T. *American Genesis: Captain John Smith and the Founding of Virginia.* Boston: Little, Brown, and Company, 1975

Sons of Liberty

Giving a voice and participation to the average American colonist, the Sons of Liberty were actively involved in violent resistance to the Stamp Act of 1765. Opposition to British legislation by such rebellious and independent groups would do much to bring about the American Revolution.

In an effort to defray the expense of the Seven Years' War and the cost of maintaining troops and forts along the American frontier, the British Parliament began taxing the colonies in the early 1760s. It was in North America, after all, that the British Empire had acquired such debt. Proposed taxes in the colonies,

much to their surprise, however, were widely resisted by politicians and ordinary citizens alike.

Following the unsuccessful Sugar Act of 1764, Parliament proposed a tax that would raise revenue in the colonies by taxing everyday paper goods such as books, documents, and newspapers. This Stamp Act, which was not an uncommon form of taxation in England, brought about violent mob reactions in the American colonies.

Unlike the Sugar Act of the previous year, the proposed tax, which was to become effective November 1, 1765, affected every colonist and brought up constitutional arguments against laws imposed from outside the colonies. The proposed legislation was seen as a symbol of British tyranny over the colonies.

In response, during the early summer of 1765, a group of workers, tradesmen, artisans, and lawless seamen, known as the Loyal Nine, began agitating against the Stamp Act. After changing their name to the Sons of Liberty, when Isaac Barré referred to Americans by this title in a speech against the act in the House of Commons, the organization began to use coercive measures and mob violence to destroy the new legislation.

Although the Sons of Liberty often resorted to lawless mob activity, most of the emerging groups throughout the colonies were under the leadership of upper-class merchants and politicians. These leaders, such as Samuel and John Adams of Boston, who had much to lose if such an act were passed, anonymously organized the actions of the groups. Even radical leaders were occasionally threatened, as unruly mobs made up of members of the Sons of Liberty spun out of control.

One of the first widely known acts carried out by

The Sons of Liberty Bowl, a cherished symbol of the struggle for independence, was commissioned of Paul Revere by members of the secret organization in 1768. It honored an act of defiance by the Massachusetts legislature against the Townshend Acts. *(Museum of Fine Arts, Boston/Bridgeman Art Library)*

the Sons of Liberty took place on August 14, 1765, when Andrew Oliver, a stamp distributor, was hung in effigy on the "liberty tree" in Boston. The rowdy mob later ransacked the structure that was being built as the stamp office and forced Oliver to publicly resign his position as a stamp official. Less than two weeks later, on August 26, the mob spent an entire night demolishing Governor Thomas Hutchinson's home.

The Sons of Liberty became so intimidating—burning effigies, destroying property, and threatening lives—that they were able to force the resignation of all stamp agents in the colonies before the act ever took effect. Local officials were unwilling to respond to these violent mob actions for fear of their lives.

As resistance to the Stamp Act mounted, correspondence and coordination of defiant actions took place throughout the colonies. Beyond simple violence directed toward British leaders and institutions in the colonies, the Sons of Liberty took it upon themselves to coerce American merchants and ordinary citizens to comply with nonimportation and nonconsumption agreements. Their efforts, especially in enforcing economic sanctions against the British, led many English merchants to join the clamor for the repeal of the Stamp Act.

When the Stamp Act did take effect in November, Americans went about their business largely ignoring the new legislation. The ineffectiveness of the act, together with its condemnation by most British merchants, led to its repeal just months after it was enacted.

Although the Sons of Liberty movement broke up after the repeal of the Stamp Act, it was revived again in 1767 in response to the Townshend Revenue Acts. Many members continued in active correspondence and in organizing resistive efforts against British legislation, until the group finally disbanded for good in 1783.

Despite its short history, the Sons of Liberty provided a way for ordinary Americans to express their opposition to British policies in the colonies. The radical response to the Stamp Act and ultimate victory of the Sons of Liberty in pressuring Parliament to repeal the act gave its members experience from which they would draw throughout the American Revolutionary crisis.

Aaron F. Christensen

See also: Committees of Correpondence; Patriots; Revolutionary War.

Bibliography

Maier, Pauline. *From Resistance to Revolution: Colonial Radicals and the Development of Opposition to Britain, 1765–1776.* London: Routledge & Kegan Paul, 1973.

Morgan, Edmund S., and Helen Morgan. *The Stamp Act Crisis: Prologue to Revolution.* London: Cumberlege for the North Carolina University Press, 1953.

Walsh, Richard. *Charleston's Sons of Liberty: A Study of the Artisans, 1763–1789.* Columbia: University of South Carolina Press, 1959.

Soto, Hernando de

See De Soto, Hernando

South Carolina

By the time of the American War for Independence, South Carolina was a prosperous plantation colony. It was home to some of the wealthiest men in America and to one of the colonies' most refined cities, Charles Town (it became Charleston late in the eighteenth century). South Carolina was also the home of a large population of African and African American slave men and women.

Through slightly more than a century of serious English colonial activity, a small, relatively harmonious planter elite had clawed its way to the top of a society wracked by divisions of class and race. The dominance of English planters was far from assured in the colony's early years. Both Spanish and English forces claimed the area, which was, of course, largely controlled by native peoples. The story of South Carolina's colonial development is a story of halting, uneven Spanish and English colonization, native and African American resistance, and intercultural violence.

Native Life and Spanish Incursions

For much of South Carolina's colonial history, the region was mostly native land. When armies of Spaniards began to wind through South Carolina in the sixteenth century, they came upon large paramount chiefdoms, the main one being that of Cofitachequi, near present-day Camden. In the years before European colonization, the world of the Mississippian chiefdoms was already changing, and the arrival of the Spanish sped up these changes. Across the Southeast, large chiefdoms were dispersing into smaller groups of autonomous villages and bands, the tribes that would face the full force of English settlement in the late seventeenth and eighteenth centuries.

Native life in South Carolina was strikingly diverse. Scores of different languages were spoken, and these spanned a number of linguistic groups: Siouan, Iroquoian, Muskogean, and Algonquian. Tribes ranged in size from tiny enclaves along the resource-rich Atlantic coast to more numerous inland nations such as the Cherokee and Creek.

Most native peoples in South Carolina lived in permanent or semipermanent villages centered around agriculture. Beans, corn, and squash were the main crops. Agriculture and domestic life were the exclusive province of women, while men engaged in a separate sphere of activities, including hunting, warfare, trade, and diplomacy. The clan was the basic unit of native society, and through one's clan—an association almost always passed down through the mother—one gained access to a wide-ranging network of kin. Clan membership guided marriage choices and prescribed punishments for crimes. Numerous and often complex ceremonies accompanied many different aspects of native life.

In the first half of the sixteenth century, Spanish conquistadors and explorers began to spread out from their base of operations in the Caribbean. From 1539 to 1542, largely as a result of Cabeza de Vaca's reports of his improbable journey and exaggerated riches in the interior Southeast, Hernando de Soto launched an exploratory probe, an *entrada*, into the area.

In what later would become South Carolina, de Soto's army came across the paramount chiefdom of Cofitachequi, ruled by a woman, the "Lady of Cofitachequi." Upon his arrival in Cofitachequi, de Soto appears to have received treatment befitting a dignitary. Following protocol established at other points in the entrada, however, he took several Cofitachequis hostage to ensure safe passage through the chiefdom. Although he found the pearls of Cofitachequi irregular and small, he also ordered his soldiers to raid a burial site and remove a large quantity of pearls from the body cavities of deceased natives. Thus, de Soto's party soon wore out its welcome.

The Spanish never succeeded in establishing a colony in the interior of South Carolina, although Franciscans established some missions in the Sea Islands. Nevertheless, diseases introduced to South Carolina by European explorers devastated native communities; when the English began to colonize the area in the closing decades of the eighteenth century, they entered a shattered world.

English Beginnings in South Carolina

Founded in 1670, South Carolina was a relatively late addition to the English colonial world. To the north, Virginia and Massachusetts Bay were growing and prospering. In the Caribbean, Barbados was flourishing as a result of a booming sugar trade. Charles II's restored monarchy had advanced English colonization throughout the Americas, adding New York and securing Jamaica.

Prominent men who had remained loyal to the king began to call in favors, and Anthony Ashley Cooper—who would soon become Lord Shaftesbury—led a renewed drive to plant an English colony in the American Southeast. To aid in this task, Shaftesbury drew up the Fundamental Constitutions, a series of guidelines that would set up a utopian, hierarchical society in South Carolina. It bears mentioning that Shaftesbury's personal secretary was John Locke, though what effect the philosopher actually had on these guidelines is unknown.

It was established that Shaftesbury and a handful of elites would govern South Carolina as lords proprietors. As it turns out, however, the actual English settlement of South Carolina did not resemble the

This list of English land grants in the new colony of South Carolina begins in 1674 with 1,070 acres for Lady Margaret Yeamans, wife of the governor. *(New York Public Library, New York)*

orderly structure laid out in the Fundamental Constitutions.

South Carolina quickly attracted disaffected gentry from other parts of the empire, most notably Barbados. Shaftesbury's plan called for town-based settlement to avoid the chaos and violence that marred Virginia's early years, but planters snapped up as much riverfront property as they could afford.

Traders began to exploit divisions between coastal tribes, taking native slaves, arming some tribes against others, and generally increasing the native peoples' dependence on European tools and trade goods. The end of the seventeenth century witnessed the demise of several coastal tribes. Some native Carolinians displaced by the English sought refuge with the Spanish at St. Augustine or with the Creek and Cherokee. Others remained close to the English at Charles Town for protection.

Early South Carolina was a rugged society on the edge of the English empire. Because of this, a rough sort of equality occurred, not by design, but out of necessity. Slaves and masters labored, sometimes alongside one another, to clear fields, raise cattle, and produce naval stores. Roaming cattle wreaked havoc on native fields and exacerbated tensions between Native Americans and white people.

Native reactions to the threat of colonial encroachment were complex and varied among different tribes. During the Westo War (1680), the Tuscarora War (1711–1715), and the Yamasee War (1715–1717), Native Americans fought both alongside and against the English invaders. In the first decade of the eighteenth century, as an offshoot of a larger colonial conflict (Queen Anne's War), a combined force of English and Yamasee destroyed the missions of Spanish Florida, carrying off hundreds of slaves and further weakening Spain's position in the region.

As damaging as the Yamasee War was to native and nonnative South Carolinians, the tribe's defeat brought a tenuous peace, as the Yamasee and their allies moved to the periphery of the colony. The estimated native population "east of the mountains" of South Carolina dropped from 10,000 in 1685 to 5,100 in 1715. As the eighteenth century progressed, the number of Native Americans in South Carolina continued to drop as a result of disease, emigration, and violence; by 1790, the native population totaled closer to 500.

While the early economy of South Carolina was diverse and other crops, especially indigo, grew well there, around the turn of the eighteenth century, rice emerged as the colony's most profitable staple. Rice agriculture affected colonial society in two crucial ways. First, it brought huge profits to a small group of planters. On the eve of the War for Independence, nine of the North American colonies' ten wealthiest men were South Carolina rice planters. The county surrounding Charles Town was almost four times wealthier than any other mainland county.

The second primary effect of rice agriculture was to increase South Carolina's reliance on slave labor. White planters utilized African expertise and labor to produce rice, preferring slaves who had previous experience in rice cultivation. Slaves from the region between the Senegal and Gambia Rivers in West Africa were particularly prized, although traders and planters often had to settle for slaves from other regions.

In the first half of the eighteenth century, the colony's black population skyrocketed. South Carolina was more African than English as early as 1708, and this trend continued throughout the colony's history. One early settler, Samuel Dyssli, famously noted that South Carolina was "more like a negro country than one settled by white people."

The large number of Africans had a profound effect on colonial society at large, in terms of cuisine and speech patterns. The task system of slave labor, whereby slaves were assigned certain tasks and given free time upon their completion, allowed for the development of a distinctly African American culture. Slaves created a world apart, structuring their communities according to their own traditions and creating a vibrant society independent of that of their masters. Slaves in South Carolina negotiated a space for themselves in colonial society and also attained a level of autonomy unknown anywhere else in British North America.

Proprietary government in South Carolina failed miserably. From the beginning of English settlement, individual planters resisted the constraints placed on them by the lords proprietors. A powerful faction of Barbadians settled along Goose Creek and essentially ran South Carolina's council and Commons House of Assembly. The proprietors did not understand the situation on the ground in colonial South Carolina, and the Goose Creek men resisted any attempt by them to exert control over the colony.

The proprietors insisted on religious tolerance, but the Goose Creek men fought to establish the Anglican Church. The proprietors wanted orderly, town-based settlement, but white South Carolinians spread out along the coastal rivers in an effort to secure as much fertile plantation land as possible. The proprietors insisted on treating Native Americans fairly in trade and land negotiations, but white South Carolinians treated the native peoples horribly, inciting wars between tribes, enslaving the losers, and driving the winners into increasing debt and dependence. In addition, the proprietors had hoped to recoup their investment by a monopoly over the trade in deerskins, but the Goose Creek men kept the profits, which were substantial, for themselves.

In what has been described as the "Revolution of 1719," the lords proprietors relinquished their weak grip on South Carolina. By the end of the 1720s, the Crown had bought out the proprietors, and the transition to royal government was complete.

A Mature Colonial Society and Independence

The Yamasee War and the Revolution of 1719 allowed the Goose Creek men and like-minded white Carolinians to rid themselves of two forces they perceived as holding them back: Native Americans and the proprietors. Colonial society in South Carolina was developing along lines that favored owners of large plantations, worked by large numbers of black men and women.

In 1739, slaves at Stono, just outside of Charles Town, rose up against their masters in one of the largest slave rebellions ever undertaken in American history. Twenty or so Angolans, under the leadership of a black man maned Jemmy (some sources spell the name Jemy), attacked a store early on a September Sunday morning. The attackers quickly overpowered and killed the shopkeeper and began to distribute arms and powder to slaves on nearby plantations. By afternoon, between 60 and 100 slaves were on the march. Their destination is not known, but it was probably Spanish St. Augustine, which had offered fugitive slaves refuge in the past. A hastily assembled white militia put down the rebellion, and many of the participants were executed.

A new slave code enacted in 1740 assuaged some of the planters' fears, but it was not strictly enforced. Generally speaking, planters were frightened of their slaves, so they put a system in place that would keep slaves frightened of them as well. Though slaves would continue to resist their masters in small ways on a day-to-day basis, for the rest of the colonial period, they would not again mount so direct a challenge.

For most of its history, South Carolina had developed as a British colony on its own, a beneficiary of the British policy known as "benign neglect." In the middle of the eighteenth century, Great Britain took a renewed interest in the management of its empire and sought to profit from it.

The French and Indian War (known in Europe as the Seven Years' War) did not affect South Carolina as much as it did other colonies. South Carolina did, however, undertake an ill-conceived campaign against the Cherokee that accomplished little, apart from poisoning relations between the two groups for decades.

Reaction against the Stamp Act in South Carolina was particularly vociferous, and a passionate Sons of Liberty movement grew up in Charles Town. Yet the movement toward independence revealed deep divisions in South Carolina's society. Not only had coastal planters and politicians fought with a rising class of backcountry planters in the Regulator movement of the 1760s, they also had fought among themselves.

In 1775, the royal governor moved his offices to a ship in Charles Town harbor, essentially turning the city over to the Revolutionaries. Loyalist and patriot militias ranged through the backcountry. Many of South Carolina's slaves used the confusion of the fighting to seek their freedom, either by joining the British or running away.

Throughout the Revolutionary War, British and American forces alternately controlled the crucial port at Charles Town, while rival militias ravaged the Piedmont and the upcountry. In 1780, Charles Town fell to the British, but an American victory at Cowpens forced the British to abandon the city in 1782.

After the fighting ended, South Carolina's planters were in a delicate position. Their economic fate was in the hands of British creditors and trading houses, and many wanted a quick return to business as usual. On the other hand, their political fate was in the hands of the victorious Revolutionaries. Although loyalists in South Carolina received leniency in most cases, the protection of private property, including plantations and slaves, trumped other political concerns.

In the nascent government of the United States, South Carolina took on a large role for such a small state. South Carolina's immense wealth and its leading citizens' reputation for fiery oratory would give the state a prominent part in the formation of the federal government.

Matthew Jennings

See also: Charleston; Locke, John; Plantations; Planters; Rice; Slavery, African American; South Carolina (Chronology).

Bibliography

Edgar, Walter. *History of South Carolina.* Columbia: University of South Carolina Press, 1998.

Littlefield, Daniel C. *Rice and Slaves: Ethnicity and the Slave Trade in Colonial South Carolina.* 1981. Urbana: University of Illinois Press, 1991.

Merrell, James H. *The Indians' New World: Catawbas and their Neighbors from European Contact through the Era of Removal.* Chapel Hill: University of North Carolina Press, 1989.

Sirmans, M. Eugene. *Colonial South Carolina: A Political History, 1663–1763.* Chapel Hill: University of North Carolina Press, 1966.

Weir, Robert M. *Colonial South Carolina: A History.* Millwood, NY: KTO, 1983.

Wood, Peter H. *Black Majority: Negroes in Colonial South Carolina from 1670 through the Stono Rebellion.* New York: W. W. Norton, 1974.

Spanish Armada

See Armada, Spanish

Spanish Colonial Government

See Government, Spanish Colonial

Sports and Recreation

Sports and recreation were a part of colonial American life in every region and for men of every ethnicity and social class, although social status often determined what sorts of sports a man played. Sports served a variety of functions, including military training, reinforcing hierarchy, and allowing elite men to compete in a relatively safe environment. Women participated in certain recreational activities, such as music making and dancing, but blood sports and athletic competition were almost without exception male avocations.

Before the arrival of Europeans, the native peoples of North America played a variety of games and sports. In the Southeast, many tribes played ball games akin to lacrosse; in the Northeast, Five Nations Iroquois were renowned for their matches. Teams representing villages or clans would struggle to get possession of a small deerskin ball in their netted sticks, then hurl or carry the ball into a goal. Play was rough, and some tribes used the exercise to accumulate the skills necessary for combat. Often, spring ceremonies, like the Green Corn, would conclude with large ball games.

Southeastern Native Americans also played a game called chunkey, in which two men would compete to cast poles near to a thrown stone. Chunkey was not as violent as the ball game, but players still competed intensely, both players and onlookers wagered extravagantly on the contest, and humiliation and scorn were the loser's lot.

The English brought their own forms of sport and recreation to America. In New England, people engaged in all sorts of games, much to the chagrin of Puritan authorities, who were constantly legislating against various diversions. Games that involved gambling and drinking, such as cards, dice, shuffleboard, and horse racing, were frowned upon. Militia companies, however, were required to engage in regular sports; as with the native peoples, these sports helped keep them fit and enhanced training.

Individuals were also encouraged to ice skate and engage in other respectable sports. The Boston game—an early form of American football—was imported from English villages and thrived in New England. Some Puritan moralists disapproved of the rough team game, but once it was regulated, towns, academies, and colleges began to engage in the sport with official approval. The Massachusetts game—also known as the New England game or bittle-battle—featured many of the characteristics of modern baseball, including a pitcher, a batter, and four bases.

Southern sporting life was determined by region and class. Southern colonies were much more stratified than their Northern counterparts, and deep societal divisions appeared in people's recreational choices. Elites in Virginia and the Carolinas participated in horse races and cockfights. Lower-class people were legally barred from competing in horse races, although they did watch and wager, sometimes enjoying liquor provided by their betters. Elite men used the races as an excuse to display their wealth, often through high-stakes wagers. Lower-level, well-to-do Virginians imported the red fox for their hunts. And, as in New England, men of various classes engaged in games with cards and dice.

Poorer Southerners and slaves competed in their own forms of recreation. One of the more gruesome forms was the gander pull, popular in the backcountry. Contestants would ride by a gander—with a greased neck, suspended upside-down from a tree branch—at a full gallop, and attempt to rip the animal's head off. Children learned to compete in blood sports from an early age. In one contest known as "muzzling the sparrow," young men, hands tied behind their backs, held a small bird by the wing with their teeth. The object of the game was to bite the sparrow's head off.

Music and dancing were two recreational activities enjoyed by men and women together, although the forms varied according to class, race, and region. Every culture that came to America brought its own folk dances and music. Dances accompanied important social occasions, such as weddings and holidays, in many communities.

Among upper-class Virginians, daughters and sons were schooled from an early age in music and dance, since their level of refinement correlated with opportunities for a good marriage. Virginia's gentry class took dance very seriously.

Sports and recreation played an important role in American colonial life, whether the participants were male or female, native or nonnative, slave or free, elite or common. In fact, many of the contests in which colonial Americans engaged reflected the tensions of class, race, and gender that underlaid much of life in Britain's North American colonies.

Matthew Jennings

See also: Child Rearing; Children.

Bibliography

Fischer, David Hackett. *Albion's Seed: Four British Folkways in America.* New York: Oxford University Press, 1989.

Hudson, Charles. *The Southeastern Indians.* Knoxville: University of Tennessee Press, 1976.

Struna, Nancy L. *People of Prowess: Sport, Leisure, and Labor in Early Anglo-America.* Urbana: University of Illinois Press, 1996.

Squanto (c. 1590–1622)

Squanto (the anglicized version of Tisquantum) was born in Patuxet, a village of 2,000 Wampanoags on Plymouth Bay in present-day Massachusetts, around 1590. During his life, he lived as a member of the Wampanoag tribe, as a slave to a sea captain, as a free

Squanto, an Indian of the Patuxet tribe, was a guide, interpreter, and friend of the Puritan settlers at Plymouth Colony. He taught them how to grow crops using fish as fertilizer and helped arrange a peace treaty with area natives. *(Private Collection/Bridgeman Art Library)*

man both in Spain and in England, and finally among the English Pilgrims at Plymouth.

The Wampanoag at Patuxet integrated themselves into the colonial world by trading extra corn and furs with explorers they viewed as friendly and warding off those they perceived as hostile. In 1614, John Smith, of Virginia fame, arrived in Patuxet. Smith initially fought with the native peoples, but he later made peace and returned to England. He left a ship behind to fish for cod under the leadership of Thomas Hunt.

Hunt lured about twenty Native Americans on board and then took off for Spain. When Hunt reached Málaga, he began selling his captives as slaves, a process some priests forced him to abandon. It appears that they intended to convert Squanto and the others to Christianity. Squanto disappears from the documentary record at this point.

In 1617, Squanto resurfaced in London. He lived with John Slany, the treasurer of the Newfoundland Company for a time. He studied the English language and English culture, and he gradually became convinced that someone associated with English colonization could return him to Patuxet. On an expedition to Newfoundland, Squanto got to know Thomas Dermer (the two had met previously in 1614, when Dermer served under John Smith on his fateful voyage to Patuxet). Back in England, Dermer introduced Squanto to Sir Ferdinando Gorges, a principal colonizer of New England during the early seventeenth century. Gorges recognized that Squanto could be of great assistance.

The New England to which Squanto returned in 1619 was profoundly different from the place he had left behind in 1614. His own village, Patuxet, no longer existed, owing to recent disease epidemics. In fact, many of the coastal communities lost up to 90 percent of their population. Stunned survivors regrouped into different communities and struggled to meet the challenges of their new world. The Wampanoag found it more and more difficult to resist incursions and tribute demands by the Narragansett, their powerful neighbors to the west.

Squanto's particular skills served the Dermer party well in 1619, when he eased the Wampanoag Chief Massasoit's concerns about the English. When the party returned the next year, the response was more hostile. Dermer was killed in a clash with the Wampanoag on Martha's Vineyard, and Squanto was captured and brought to the Pokanoket, a community among the Wampanoag and the home village of Massasoit.

In 1620, a group of English religious refugees arrived at Plymouth Bay. During the well-documented "starving time" that winter, half of them died. In the spring, Massasoit dispatched a series of emissaries to the English. The most knowledgeable was Squanto.

Squanto's assistance to the English at Plymouth would prove invaluable. He taught them how to plant corn using fish as fertilizer, but also, more importantly, he secured a treaty that would ensure peace between the Pokanoket, the Nemasket, and the struggling Plymouth Colony. During this same time, Squanto came to live with the English at Plymouth, where he continued to make treaties and assist the colonists.

Diplomatic intrigues diminished Squanto's usefulness to the English. In 1621, the Pilgrims invited a second Native American, a Pokanoket named Hobbamock, to live with them. Squanto seems to have inflated his prestige in English society when dealing with Massasoit and his prestige with Massasoit when dealing with the English. As a result, he ran afoul of both groups and required English protection against Massasoit. In 1622, Squanto died of a fever.

Many accounts of the Pilgrims include the story of how Squanto helped the English; his legacy has been reduced to that of simply a friendly native. His real story is more complex and dramatic than that. Squanto bridged worlds that today seem oceans apart, although they were not all that distinct during the colonial period. His story proves that a single person could move between them.

Matthew Jennings

See also: Pequot; Pilgrims; Plymouth.

Bibliography

Kupperman, Karen Ordahl. *Indians & English: Facing Off in Early America.* Ithaca, NY: Cornell University Press, 2000.

Salisbury, Neal. *Manitou and Providence: Indians and Europeans, 1500–1643.* New York: Oxford University Press, 1982.

———. "Squanto (Tisquantum)." In *The Encyclopedia of North American Indians,* edited by Frederick E. Hoxie. Boston: Houghton Mifflin, 1996.

St. Augustine

In 1565, Menéndez de Avilés founded St. Augustine, one of two precariously established Spanish footholds in what would later become the United States. Initially, a small, insignificant outpost along Florida's Atlantic coast, St. Augustine remains the oldest European urban center in the present-day United States.

Basically a fortified military post with little economic importance, St. Augustine served Spain as one of the last naval bases and defensive positions for the galleons of the Spanish treasure fleet as they made their yearly trip to Spain. Since even in a bad year, the treasure fleets carried considerable cargoes of gold and silver, they persistently attracted official and unofficial raids from pirates and privateers of English, Dutch, and French origin. But the treasure fleet was not the only target. St. Augustine was besieged on numerous occasions throughout its history (once even drawing the attention of Francis Drake); it was last occupied by foreign invaders in 1702.

St. Augustine at its founding was supposed to be an important part of the Spanish empire, but its value had diminished by the end of the sixteenth century. The Spanish decision to establish St. Augustine came

A massive stone fortress built in St. Augustine, Florida, in 1672, Castillo San Marcos (later renamed Fort Marion) guarded that early Spanish settlement from English aggression and protected the sea route for treasure ships returning to Spain. *(Library of Congress, LC-D4-13354)*

as a direct result of attempts by other European nations to build colonies in North America, particularly the French, who had built a small Huguenot town in northern Florida in 1564. After eliminating the French presence, Avilés planted the St. Augustine colony in an extremely advantageous position.

Situated on a peninsula that jutted out into Matanzas Bay, the rectangular walled town was surrounded by a series of palisades on one side and water on the others. With only one exposed land approach, Avilés set up three parallel lines of defense to protect the city walls. As a last-ditch protection for the city gate, the Spanish consecutively built nine wooden forts; these were all destroyed by invading forces, until they were finally replaced in 1672 by the stone ramparts of the Castillo de San Marcos.

At the end of the French and Indian War (known as the Seven Years' War in Europe), St. Augustine and west Florida were transferred from Spanish ownership

to the British. Still only sparsely populated, the city nearly doubled in size with the arrival of a British garrison. After the American Revolution, St. Augustine again changed hands, when the British returned it to Spain, an ally of the United States, in 1783 as part of the Treaty of Paris.

Never expanding beyond the size of approximately four hundred structures during most of its history, St. Augustine, like most settlements in the New World, was a cosmopolitan mixed-race community. Under the Spanish, the town was dominated by individuals of Spanish mainland descent but also included Africans, Native Americans, various Europeans from nations allied with Spain, and people from the Caribbean and coastal Latin America. When the city was transferred to Britain at the end of the French and Indian War, the already diverse population of St. Augustine was expanded to include English, Scots, Scots-Irish, French Huguenots, and Americans.

Beyond the military garrisons and civil servants that composed nearly half of the population, occupations in St. Augustine varied very much as they did in other colonial settlements. There were merchants, Native American traders, planters, shoemakers, chain makers, cabinetmakers, butchers, bakers, innkeepers, storekeepers, blacksmiths, haberdashers, ship's caulkers, carpenters, goldsmiths, surveyors, millwrights, joiners, machinists, stonecutters, brick makers, chair makers, hostlers, lawyers, physicians, day laborers, hunters, slaves, servants, and even a few prostitutes. Religious institutions were also ubiquitous, since the Spanish established a Catholic monastery early on and the British brought Protestant ministers.

Solomon K. Smith

See also: Florida; Menéndez de Avilés, Pedro; Spanish Colonies on Mainland North America (Chronology). *Document:* The Founding of St. Augustine (1565).

Bibliography

Gold, Robert L. *Borderland Empires in Transition: The Triple-Nation Transfer of Florida.* Carbondale: Southern Illinois University Press, 1969.

Manucy, Albert. *Sixteenth-Century St. Augustine.* Gainesville: University Press of Florida, 1997.

Wright, J. Leitch. *British St. Augustine.* St. Augustine, FL: Historic St. Augustine Preservation Board, 1975.

St. Kitts

The lush island of Saint Christopher, or St. Kitts, is located among the closely grouped cluster of the Leeward Islands in the northeastern Caribbean. Club-shaped St. Kitts is just 68 square miles in size and is positioned like an exclamation point with its twin island, Nevis, offset to the south. Both islands are volcanic in origin. In the 1600s, St. Kitts offered the best land in the Leewards, with plentiful rain and fertile soil but high rates of erosion when deforested. Dominated by the aptly named Mount Misery, about half the land area was suitable for cultivation, mainly the hill slopes and coastal plain.

Developed simultaneously by the French and English for the first century after its discovery, the joint occupation of St. Kitts irritated relations between the two nations. As a result, the island changed hands seven times between 1666 and 1713, and substantial economic success came only after European peace. Relative to its size, in the mid-eighteenth-century St. Kitts was the richest British colony and a place where sugar was indeed king.

St. Kitts was visited by the English in 1585 and 1622, but, like the Spanish before them, they were discouraged by the determined resistance of the native Carib Indians in that area. In 1624, Sir Thomas Warner formed a tobacco colony in St. Kitts, diverting the Caribs with a combination of treaty and treachery. The need to defeat the Caribs and fend off a Spanish attack in 1629 required the English to cooperate with the French, who had occupied the northern and southern ends of St. Kitts in 1625. This left French Saint Christopher with the better harbor at Basseterre and the English with the best farmland. Once these hostilities had ended, offshoot settlements from St. Kitts developed rapidly in Nevis, Montserrat, and Antigua, with labor provided by English and Irish indentured servants.

When the value of tobacco declined during the 1630s, a period of attempted agricultural diversification slowly gave way to the cultivation of sugar cane. The process took time, as capital was scarce and waited on the development of both local government institutions and local land ownership (rather than tenancy), both of which encouraged investment in plantations and increasingly in African slaves.

The joint occupation was problematic, however; disruptive warfare meant enormous losses in goods and laborers for planters. The English lost the island to the French in 1666, 1689, and 1706, before securing sole control under the Treaty of Utrecht in 1713. The peace brought new investment, and half of the French land went to Scottish planters and investors.

In 1687, Dr. Hans Sloane wrote that the English in St. Kitts were healthier than those on other islands, owing to the cooler temperature, although four yellow fever epidemics between 1648 and 1793 took their toll. In 1678, the white population was 1,897; it had risen to only to 2,377 by 1745 and dropped to 1,900 in 1774. In contrast, the black population rose from 1,436 in 1678 to 19,174 in 1745 and 23,462 in 1774, with most of the gain coming after the 1720s. Unlike the male-dominated early days, by 1678, there were nearly equal numbers of men and women in both the black and white populations. The growth and stability of St. Kitts was reflected in sugar exports, which increased from less than 1,000 tons in the 1600s, to 4,437 tons in 1725 and to 8,789 tons by 1748.

The rise of the plantation system and sugar monoculture made St. Kitts dependent on external sources

Brimstone Hill Fortress, located atop a volcanic peak on the island of St. Kitts, was one of the largest colonial military enclaves in the Caribbean. In 1782, French troops laid siege and forced the British to surrender. Today, the rebuilt complex is a national park. *(Library of Congress, LC-USZ62-45296)*

of food and supplies, as well as on slave labor. It also forced out white small farmers as estates were enlarged. The dominant planter elite modeled their social and cultural behaviors on London. In general, they did not develop strong local creole identities or sympathies, as their counterparts did in America, though poorer whites often did.

Used to having a powerful commercial lobby in London, the Leeward Island planters protested against the Stamp Act of 1765, complaining that it was inexpedient (rather than unconstitutional) because of their dependence on now-disrupted American trade. There was little chance the British West Indian colonies would join the rebel Americans, though, because of elite cultural affinities with Britain and the islands' dependence on British capital, markets, and protection from foreign threat and slave revolt.

For the planters of the Leeward Islands, the American Revolution brought shortages of food and supplies and indebtedness. The war ruinously disrupted com-

mercial relations both legal and illegal. With the Royal Navy hindered by the loss of American supply routes and delayed overly long in the capture of Dutch Sint Eustatius, the Count de Grasse, a French admiral, captured St. Kitts, Nevis, and Montserrat early in 1782. While the planters in each place capitulated quickly, in St. Kitts they did nothing to help the British garrison fighting in their defense, the planters being furious over the trade losses they suffered with Sint Eustatius's capture and wary of damage to their estates.

At the end of the war, planters in St. Kitts tried to rebuild trade on the old terms but were denied by Britain. A series of hurricanes between 1780 and 1786, disruptions in the French colonies, and the inadequacy of supplies from Canada, however, meant that renewed trade by the British West Indies with the United States was both essential and inevitable.

Neil Kennedy

See also: Caribbean (Chronology); Slavery, Caribbean; Sugar.

Bibliography

Dunn, Richard. *Sugar and Slaves: The Rise and Fall of the Planter Class in the English West Indies, 1624–1713.* New York: W. W. Norton, 1973.

O'Shaughnessy, Andrew. *An Empire Divided: The American Revolution and the British Caribbean.* Philadelphia: University of Pennsylvania, 2000.

St. Lawrence River

The St. Lawrence River runs more than 600 miles from its source in the Great Lakes to the Gulf of St. Lawrence and the Atlantic Ocean. The river was the site of early French–Native American interaction in the sixteenth and seventeenth centuries, and eventually the St. Lawrence River Valley became home to the government of New France.

In the worldwide conflict of the Seven Years' War (known in North America as the French and Indian War), the St. Lawrence was pivotal in the massive struggle for control of the continent. France lost its grip on the river, and the ultimate result was the removal of the French as a colonizing power in North America.

In the sixteenth century, the St. Lawrence was home to large towns of Iroquoian-speaking Native Americans. The Iroquois sustained such large settlements, because they hunted and gathered to supplement their agricultural production. In 1541, Jacques Cartier attempted to found a settlement on the river. This early colonial venture was marked by mistrust between the French and their Iroquois hosts, biting cold, and disease. The colony failed miserably.

French, Basque, English, and Portuguese fishermen and traders, who explored the area, discovered the two items that would eventually drive the colonization of the St. Lawrence and Great Lakes region: beaver pelts and fish. In the meantime, the increasing presence of the French upset the delicate native political balance. The Huron and Algonquin peoples allied themselves with the French against the Five Nations Iroquois, and the Iroquois, armed by the Dutch in the Hudson Valley, attacked the French and their allies. The fur trade, driven by the beaver hat rage in Europe, also placed pressure on native communities, which began to range farther from their traditional hunting grounds to satisfy European traders' seemingly endless demand.

In 1608, Samuel de Champlain founded the colony of New France at Quebec. This and other French settlements established in the early years of the seventeenth century tended to be all-male endeavors. The St. Lawrence was frozen for nearly six months of the year, and the region had a limited growing season for crops, but it did offer access to the vast interior and high-quality furs. The French and their Native American neighbors embarked on a campaign against the Iroquois, which, though militarily successful, resulted in the destruction and dispersal of the Huron villages when the Five Nations retaliated later in the 1640s and 1650s.

In 1663, the French Crown assumed control of Canada from the Company of New France, a fur-trading enterprise, and large-scale colonization got off to a slow start. The activities in which the company engaged did not require a large settler population. Also, there were not as many economic "push" factors driving French men and women to Canada as there were for the English settlers farther south, as France was not undergoing the same dramatic commercialization of the countryside.

In the 1660s, the French population of New France was only 3,000, while the population of New England and the Chesapeake topped 85,000. Its development subsidized by the Crown, Canada began to grow, although many indentured servants brought there returned to France when their indentures were up.

Canada remained primarily a trading venture, although agricultural exports helped local farmers. Nominal French control of the interior of North America branched out from a narrow base along the St. Lawrence River from Quebec to Montreal. The French, not primarily interested in settlement, allied themselves with a network of native traders that stretched out along the river systems of the Midwest.

The French hold on the St. Lawrence River Valley was tenuous, but that fact did not prevent them from attempting a massive reorganization of their empire in the 1750s. This project brought the French into conflict with the populous, aggressively expansionist Anglo-Americans in the Ohio River Valley, with devastating results for French rule in Canada.

In 1758, a huge British fleet captured the fortress at Louisbourg, which protected the mouth of the St. Lawrence. In 1759, General James Wolfe faced Louis-Joseph de Montcalm, a French general, on the Plains of Abraham, outside Quebec. After a brief battle, the French broke ranks and retreated to Quebec. Both commanders died in the battle, and Quebec fell shortly thereafter. In 1760, Montreal suffered a similar fate.

The French and Indian War resulted in France's

final abandonment of the St. Lawrence River Valley. In the aftermath of the war, the British were particularly cruel to the inhabitants of Acadia, forcing their evacuation. When Britain's other mainland colonies broke away in 1776, Canada remained part of the British Empire.

Matthew Jennings

See also: Canada; Cartier, Jacques; Exploration; French; French Colonies on Mainland North America (Chronology); Furs; Great Lakes; Montreal; Quebec City; Transportation, Water.

Bibliography

Eccles, W. J. *France in America.* Rev. ed. East Lansing: Michigan State University Press, 1990.

Richter, Daniel K. *Facing East from Indian Country: A Native History of Early America.* Cambridge, MA: Harvard University Press, 2001.

Taylor, Alan. *American Colonies.* New York: Viking, 2001.

St. Louis

Named in honor of King Louis IX, St. Louis was first established as a fur trading post by Pierre Laclede, a member of Mexent & Laclede Fur Company, and Auguste Chouteau, his 13-year-old associate, in 1764. The site they selected was ideal: 18 miles south of the confluence of the Mississippi and Missouri Rivers. It had both river access and a bluff to protect it from the river's flooding.

While Laclede returned to New Orleans, Auguste began construction of the small village. A year later, Laclede returned to St. Louis with Auguste's mother, Marie Chouteau, and her three children. The primitive settlement consisted of little more than two granaries, a bakery, a maple sugar works, and a church. But St. Louis grew quickly, as its location served to make it the "gateway" city for the ever-increasing north-south commerce that traveled the Mississippi River.

In 1768, the Spanish built a fort on the nearby banks of the Missouri River. This was replaced in 1780 with Fort San Carlos and other fortifications within St. Louis. During the American War for Independence, the city came under attack by the British with allied natives. In the only Revolutionary battle fought west of the Mississippi, outnumbered Spanish troops under Governor Fernando de Layba, along with colonial militia and slaves, succeeded in defending the city.

By the time of the Louisiana Purchase in 1803, St. Louis had grown to more than 1,100 people and had become a bustling river landing. When President Thomas Jefferson appointed Meriwether Lewis and William Clark to lead the expedition that would explore the territory, St. Louis was the jumping-off point.

When the explorers returned to St. Louis on September 23, 1806, they had completed a journey of 7,689 miles. Clearly, St. Louis was the link connecting the eastern and western halves of the country. Moreover, Lewis and Clark's extensive observations and descriptions of the animals they had seen, in particular the vast numbers of beaver and muskrat, spurred the flow of trappers to the region. As a result, St. Louis became the most important stop for traders and trappers alike.

In 1817, steamboats replaced keelboats as a more efficient mode of transportation, and, to keep up with the traffic, stone wharves and warehouses had to be built. Politically St. Louis became a hotbed of dissension: the French, whose claims to the region dated to the 1680s, resented the newcomers. Disagreements over land titles and mining claims arose. Hunters and squatters, disregarding treaties with the Native Americans, moved onto the natives' lands. In addition, traders resented the increased number of federal regulations being placed on trade with the native peoples.

Regardless of the tension, however, St. Louis was a market city of importance in and well beyond the colonial period. Large boats docked at its wharves, while smaller vessels navigated the shallower stretches of river with their loads of grain, lumber, furs, and salt pork.

In 1849, with the California gold rush, came the miners and emigrants, bent on crossing the plains as quickly as possible. St. Louis was once again the gateway city, providing the starting point for many headed to the West. Unfortunately, that same year, cholera, arriving with the emigrants, spread through the city, killing hundreds. Then, a steamboat exploded while docked at one of the crowded levees and fire spread to the center of the city. Before the fires were extinguished, more than a dozen blocks of city buildings were destroyed. One of the few buildings to survive the fire was the Old Cathedral, which had been built on the original site of the first church. But St. Louis quickly rebuilt, this time with brick and iron rather than wood. The city was destined to become a major manufacturing center, host to the World's Fair and the Olympic Games in 1904, site of the nation's first gasoline station, and the future home of Fortune 500 companies.

Even in its infancy, fur trader and entrepreneur Pierre Laclede foresaw the success St. Louis would experience. In his journal of 1763, he wrote, "I have found a situation where I am going to form a settlement which might become hereafter one of the finest cities in America."

Gail L. Jenner

See also: French; French Colonies on Mainland North America (Chronology); Louisiana; Mississippi River.

Bibliography

Billon, Federic Louis. *Annals of St. Louis in its early days under the French and Spanish dominations, 1764–1804.* 1886. Reprint, New York: Arno: 1971.

Peterson, Charles E. *Colonial St. Louis: Building a Creole Capital.* Tucson, AZ: Patrice, 1993.

Stamp Act (1765)

Faced with the costly aftermath of the French and Indian War in North America, the members of the ministry of Prime Minister George Grenville were extremely concerned about the enormous British national debt. This amount strained the ability of the Crown to lay any further tax on the British Isles without risking violent protest.

By 1764, efforts to raise revenues through the tightening of existing customs regulation and the Sugar Act had been unsuccessful. British documents and newspapers had carried stamps since 1689, and the tax had been a reliable source of revenue for the government. The delegates to the Albany Congress of 1754 had even considered a stamp tax to finance their plan of union.

Grenville had probably been considering a Stamp Act in the American colonies since 1763. He proposed it to the House of Commons on March 9, 1764, primarily so that Parliament could affirm its ability to tax the colonies. He stipulated, however, that the colonies had a year in which to propose an alternate source of revenue. This offer to the colonies of finding a means to tax themselves was immediately suspect, as colonial agents could not get Grenville to give them any solid procedure by which they could offer such plans or have them approved. Meanwhile, the Earl of Halifax, as secretary of state for the South, surveyed the colonial governors via a circular letter, inquiring about the many documents that might need to carry a stamp.

Although the colonists protested through their agents, including Benjamin Franklin, there was little organized resistance by the time the measure came to the House of Commons in February 1765. Drafted by

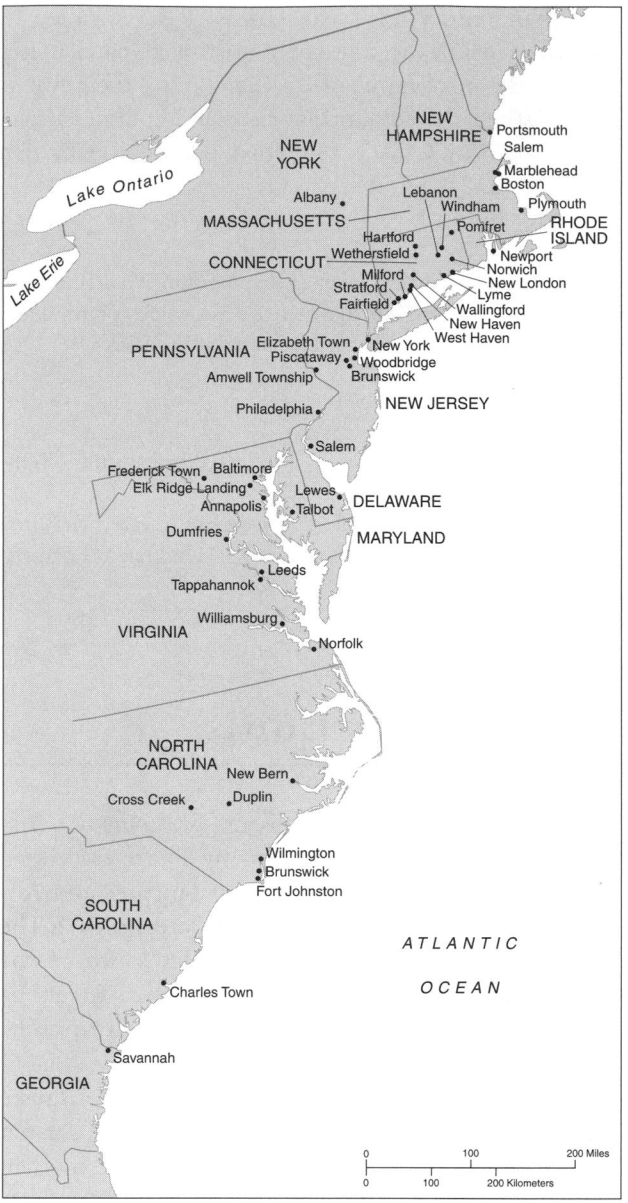

Stamp Act Demonstrations, 1765. Historians site the widespread demonstrations throughout the colonies against the Stamp Act, a British law imposing fees on a host of commodities and services. These demonstrations mark the beginning of organized colonial opposition to British rule. *(Carto-Graphics)*

Thomas Waltey of the Treasury, the schedule of stamp duties covered all printed material and legal documents, including playing cards, newspapers, diplomas, and ship clearances. The fees were generally far lower than those that residents of England already paid, with the exception of the fees for matriculation certificates and professional *bona fides,* with the purpose of discouraging lower-class Americans from gaining them.

Members of the House of Commons voiced no

dissent on their right to tax in this manner, although two members, Colonel Isaac Barré and General Henry Conway, protested the tax as unjust and a hardship for the colonies. Barré's speech gave rise to the phrase "Sons of Liberty." After refusing to hear colonial petitions against the measure, the House passed the fifty-five resolutions of the Stamp Act on February 7, 1765, and decreed that the act would take effect on November 1, 1765.

In the colonies, reactions were extremely negative. Pamphlets, most famously Daniel Dulany, Jr.'s *Considerations on the Propriety of Imposing Taxes,* attacked the House of Commons for taxation without representation. Grenville answered with "virtual representation," that is, he maintained that colonists were represented by Parliament as a whole.

In May, Virginia's House of Burgesses voted a resolution against the measure, and Rhode Island passed laws allowing civil servants to disregard the requirements for stamps. Massachusetts began a circular letter of protest in June, inviting all the colonies to send delegates to a Stamp Act Congress in New York to plan a course of action. Colonists resented not just the tax itself, but also the fact that the stamps had to be paid for in cash, a situation that pinched those not living in the population centers, who primarily dealt in a barter economy. Additionally, many saw the tax on printed material to be a measure meant to promote censorship.

Representatives of nine of thirteen colonies attended the New York meeting in October 1765; Virginia, New Hampshire, North Carolina, and Georgia did not send delegates. Canadian colonies and the Caribbean islands declined to participate in the protest. Despite voting that the House of Commons had the right to legislate for the colonies, the delegates denied it the right to tax. Although bold, this means of defiance meant little when royal officials in America planned to use the stamps, even if colonial subjects didn't.

A more violent response came from the Sons of Liberty. Formed in Boston the summer of 1765, this group's name and organization spread throughout the colonies by August, when it began terrorizing distributors of the stamps. Using mob action, the Sons of Liberty burned officials in effigy, assaulted them and looted their houses, and intimidated men in every colony into resigning their commissions to distribute the stamps. These activities were particularly disruptive in Boston, where the governor had to take refuge in Castle William, a fort on an island in Massachusetts Bay.

When the Stamp Act went into effect on November 1, there was no one willing to distribute the stamps, and the Sons of Liberty forced higher colonial courts to function without stamps. Planning ahead, merchants sent their ships out before November. In the short term, stopping colonial trade hurt the Caribbean colonies and Britain far more than the rebellious Americans. Merchants in Britain also reported that the colonies had signed nonimportation agreements, which threatened to further cripple British business.

By July 1765, Grenville's government had fallen, and it was replaced by one led by the Marquis of Rockingham. He disliked the Stamp Act and was willing to consider repeal. Under continued lobbying from London merchants and colonial agents, as well as testimony from military experts about the slim chances of enforcing the act short of a military occupation, the

On November 7, 1765, the publishers of the *Pennsylvania Gazette* (Benjamin Franklin and David Hall) printed this sheet without a name, date, or masthead to avoid punishment for not using imported, stamped paper as required by the Stamp Act. *(Library of Congress, rbpe 34604500)*

House of Commons repealed it on February 21, 1766. Rockingham, however, paired the repeal with the passing of the Declaratory Act, reserving Parliament's right to tax the American colonies.

The Stamp Act showed that the colonies could use unified action, especially economic boycotts. It also allowed extremists to take control of the political debate, thereby promoting the careers of key figures like Patrick Henry, Richard Henry Lee, and James Otis, Jr. These radicals would soon win the support of many colonists, as tensions with Great Britain escalated toward the Revolution.

Margaret Sankey

See also: Grenville, George; Politics and Government (Chronology); Politics and Government (Essay); Revolutionary War.

Bibliography

Bullion, John. *A Great and Necessary Measure: George Grenville and the Genesis of the Stamp Act.* Columbia: University of Missouri Press, 1982.

Morgan, Edmund, and Helen Morgan. *The Stamp Act Crisis.* Chapel Hill: University of North Carolina Press, 1953.

Thomas, Peter David. *British Politics and the Stamp Act Crisis.* Oxford, UK: Clarendon Press, 1975.

Stuyvesant, Peter (c. 1610–1672)

Peter Stuyvesant ruled the Dutch colony of New Netherland as director-general or governor from 1647 until 1664, when England seized the colony and renamed it New York. Born about 1610, Stuyvesant was intensely loyal to the Dutch West India Company, which employed him, and he was a devout member of the Dutch Reformed Church. He directed the company's holdings on Curaçao from 1638 until 1646.

In 1644, a cannonball crushed his right leg during an assault on the Spanish colony of St. Martin. Enduring intense pain, Stuyvesant continued the assault for twenty-eight days but ultimately withdrew due to a lack of support from his men. Surgeons amputated the leg, and Stuyvesant wore a wooden leg thereafter.

Arrival in New Amsterdam

In 1647, Stuyvesant arrived in New Amsterdam as the West India Company's director-general of New Neth-

erland. He faced a very diverse population in the colony, as it had drawn settlers from different regions of Europe—France, Belgium, Germany, and Scandinavia. Further, the company had shipped African slaves to the region since 1626; some of these Africans had gained their independence, giving New Netherland a sizable free black population. Several Native American groups also resided along the Hudson River, notably the Mohawk and several Algonquin tribes.

Conflict dominated Stuyvesant's tenure in New Netherland. His authoritarian ways upset many, but he did effect significant changes in the colony. The colonists disagreed with the taxes he imposed and wanted greater political participation. Company officers in Holland disagreed with his intolerant religious views. Rensselaerswyck, a prosperous community on the upper Hudson, resented Stuyvesant's attempts to increase the company's control of that region's trade in beaver fur.

Much of the tension between the colonists and the director sprang from the lack of political authority in New Netherland towns. Dutch charters did not allow popular political participation, in stark contrast to the English communities of New England. As the population of the English colonies grew, some of these colonists settled on the north shore of Long Island, and they insisted on town meetings and voting rights similar to those in New England. Stuyvesant held few elections in New Netherland. Incumbent local officials nominated their successors to the director, who made the final selection.

In 1649, several New Amsterdam residents, calling themselves the Nine Men, made formal complaint about Stuyvesant's opposition to local control. The company ordered him to create a New Amsterdam Court of Justice. He did so in 1653, but disallowed popular elections, instead appointing men to this body.

Stuyvesant also strengthened the position of social elites in the colony, when he created greater and lesser burgher rights. The former applied to those who held high civil, military, or ecclesiastical offices and to settlers who paid 50 guilders (approximately 20 dollars). Lesser burgher rights went to those born in the city, those who had lived there for eighteen years, and merchants who paid a fee of 20 guilders to the company. Only those possessing greater burgher rights were eligible for public office.

Stuyvesant initiated several reforms and increased the regulation of New Netherland. He revised fencing laws to reduce property damage by livestock. He enacted strict fire codes and appointed fire wardens to inspect poorly built chimneys. He enforced existing

Peter Stuyvesant was the last governor of the Dutch colony of New Netherland (later New York), to 1664. Stuyvesant's right limb had been shattered by a cannonball years earlier, and he wore a wooden leg, which he ringed with bands of silver, earning him the nickname "Old Silver Leg." *(Brown Brothers, Sterling, Pennsylvania)*

laws against selling liquor to the native peoples and made certain that settlers promptly paid natives for services rendered. He enforced smuggling laws and imposed an excise tax on imported liquor to pay for repairs to Fort New Amsterdam.

To reduce food shortages and raise revenue, he created price controls on bread and required permits to slaughter animals for meat. He also imposed controls on alcohol production in the colony and created laws to discourage excessive consumption. He closed all taverns at 9 P.M. and imposed stiff penalties for Sunday drinking and knife fighting. He even ordered drivers to walk their wagons through New Amsterdam streets to reduce the danger to pedestrians.

In 1658, he established the Rattle Watch, a rudimentary police force of nine men who patrolled New Amsterdam and pursued criminals. Each carried a rattle or a wooden clapper to sound the alarm. Stuyvesant also established primary schools in several communities, including Brooklyn, Flatbush, and Harlem.

Stuyvesant, then, greatly increased the regulation of economic and social activity. The West India Company ended its monopoly of trade in the colony in 1647, however, and company officers often negated his decrees when colonists complained.

Stuyvesant and Religion

True to his religious convictions, Stuyvesant required attendance at Sunday religious services. The director's strict adherence to the Dutch Reformed Church created friction with colonists and company officers.

In 1652, the director attempted to prohibit Quakers and Anabaptists from preaching in the colony. Two years later, he refused Lutheran settlers' request to bring a Lutheran minister to New Netherland. Receiving complaints about the director's obstinate behavior, company officials informed Stuyvesant that they supported his position but urged him to exercise leniency toward nonbelievers. When a group of Jewish settlers located in New Netherland in 1654, Stuyvesant sought to ban them from the colony. The company rejected his request and ultimately adopted a policy of religious freedom.

Stuyvesant engaged in considerable military activity as director. In 1654, the governor of New Sweden seized the Dutch Fort Casimir on the Delaware River. Stuyvesant, preoccupied with rising hostilities between New Netherland and New England, did not respond until the following year, when he led a force of 600 men against the Swedes. The 400 outnumbered Swedish settlers surrendered and agreed to Dutch rule.

While Stuyvesant was absent from New Amsterdam, a war party of 1,900 Algonquins passed through New Amsterdam, seeking to attack rival native groups at the eastern end of Long Island. They stopped on Manhattan Island and rested in Hendrick van Dyck's peach orchard. Inexplicably, van Dyck shot a native woman and so enraged the Algonquin that they redirected their enmity toward the Dutch, and the Peach War ensued.

The Native Americans moved throughout New Amsterdam, breaking into houses and setting some buildings afire in a search for van Dyck. The chiefs attempted to calm the situation, but the colonists, emboldened by liquor, attacked the natives and drove them from the city. In the following days, the Algonquin burned and pillaged settlements along the Hudson, taking survivors as hostages. Stuyvesant hurried back to lead the Dutch forces against the natives. By the war's end later that year, fifty colonists and approximately sixty Native Americans were dead, five hundred head of cattle were missing, and thousands of bushels of corn had been destroyed.

To guard against future attacks, Stuyvesant banned the creation of outlying settlements, banned Native Americans from New Amsterdam at night, and called for corporal punishment of those selling liquor to the native peoples. These measures ended native attacks on New Amsterdam, but such conflicts continued in other Dutch communities. The colonists fought wars with the natives from 1659 to 1660 and from 1663 to 1664.

Tensions between New Netherland and New England had grown steadily as their settlements expanded. In 1650, Stuyvesant signed an agreement that placed the border between the two colonies at a line 10 miles east of the Hudson River. Although this line was generous to New England, English settlers soon began to move across it.

England and the Netherlands went to war from 1652 until 1654 and again in 1660. These conflicts further increased hostilities between the colonies.

In 1664, English King Charles II, ignoring Dutch claims to New Netherland, granted all land between the Connecticut and Delaware rivers to his brother, James, Duke of York. James assembled an invasion fleet of four ships, which put into Gravesend Bay at the mouth of the Hudson River late in August 1664. Stuyvesant sent a messenger out to learn of their intentions. Colonel Richard Nicolls, the English commander, demanded the surrender of New Amsterdam.

Stuyvesant called for the defense of the city but received no support from the populace. They had grown weary of his authoritarian rule and held little loyalty to the West India Company or to the Dutch government. Their greatest concern was commerce and, once informed that Nicolls would allow them to retain their political and property rights, they agreed to surrender. Dominie Megapolensis, the colony's leading Dutch Reformed cleric, went to Stuyvesant and convinced him that capitulation was the best option.

On September 8, 1664, the Dutch soldiers marched out of the fort, the English marched in, and New Netherland became the English colony of New York. The English government assumed the company's administrative duties, and Nicolls replaced Stuyvesant as governor. The company directors recalled Stuyvesant to Amsterdam in 1665 to explain his failure to defend the colony. By that time, the Dutch government had become disenchanted with the company's mismanagement and discounted its charges against Stuyvesant.

Stuyvesant became amenable to English rule, and he continued to live in New Amsterdam, now renamed New York City; Governor Nicolls sought advice from him regularly. Despite his injury in 1644, Stuyvesant remained in good physical condition until his death in 1672. He was buried on Manhattan Island in the chapel he had built on his farm a decade earlier.

James E. Klein

See also: Dutch; New Amsterdam; New York City.

Bibliography

Berlin, Ira. "From Creole to African: Atlantic Creoles and the Origins of African-American Society in Mainland North America." *William and Mary Quarterly* 53:2 (April 1996): 251–88.

Kammen, Michael. *Colonial New York: A History.* New York: Charles Scribner's Sons, 1975.

Kessler, Henry H., and Eugene Rachlis. *Peter Stuyvesant and His New York.* New York: Random House, 1959.

Rink, Oliver A. *Holland on the Hudson: An Economic and Social History of Dutch New York.* Ithaca, NY: Cornell University Press, 1986.

Sugar

Sugar was the most important commodity of the Atlantic trade in colonial times. The art of sugar making was first known in India and Persia, the first written evidence dating from 500 C.E. By the time of the Arabian expansion in the seventh century, sugar cultivation spread on the Mediterranean coast, but consumption and even knowledge of it remained extremely rare in most parts of Europe until the time of the Crusades in the twelfth century. Then, however, sugar became an inevitable part of European diet and nutrition culture—as medicine, spice, decorative material, sweetener, and, finally, as a staple food.

At first limited by its price to the aristocracy and even then reserved for special occasions, it became available to the lower classes and was consumed in ever larger quantities over the course of the centuries. Until the utilization of the sugar beet in the nineteenth century, sugar could only be extracted from the sugar cane; therefore, this ever-increasing European consumption depended on non-European production.

To compensate for the decreasing Arabian production in the Mediterranean, the cultivation of sugar cane was introduced to Atlantic islands near Europe in the fifteenth century, when the Portuguese captured São Tomé and the Spanish occupied the Canary Islands.

Although the bullion trade became the primary objective of Iberian economic activities in the Americas after 1492, the suitable climate of the newly seized colonies also led to an expansion of sugar cane cultivation. Early attempts by the Spanish bogged down, but the introduction of the crop to Portuguese Brazil proved very successful. Brazil outstripped the production of the Atlantic islands and the Mediterranean to become the main producer of sugar in the sixteenth century.

Turning sugar cane into sugar is a highly integrated and labor-intensive process. By immediately milling the chopped cane, juice is extracted and then immediately boiled in order to reduce it. Reaching supersaturation, sucrose crystallizes, leaving residual juice, so-called molasses. The crystals can be further refined to attain different types and qualities of sugar; from the molasses, rum can be distilled. The need for an instant, frictionless procedure was the reason for combining the growing and processing on a single site and for relying on easy-to-direct coerced labor. Hence the slave labor–based colonial plantation system was developed by the Europeans only to handle the sugar production.

Yet the Brazilian plantation economy was not fully developed until the occupation by the Dutch West India Company in the 1630s and 1640s. The Dutch overcame the commercial imperfections of the system by providing economically adequate imports of slaves and building up trading networks to connect the production firmly with the European markets of consumption. The annual sugar output reached 23,000 tons around 1640.

The success of the Dutch inspired English planters to build up sugar plantations in Barbados. Relying on Dutch commercial know-how, a nearly complete transition of the island's economy was accomplished in just a few years, around the 1650s. Output doubled between 1651 and 1655 to nearly 8,000 tons.

This remarkable development is known as the "sugar revolution," and the result exemplified a new type of colonial business. It marks the transition from the so-called First Atlantic System—an Atlantic economy created by Spain and Portugal, focusing on the South American mainland, state-dominated, and devoted mainly to the transfer of bullion, with only a secondary interest in plantations—to the more capital-intense Second Atlantic System—created by the Netherlands, England, and France, dominated by market-orientated private merchants, and focusing on

Caribbean plantation colonies to supply Europe with tropical crops.

In this new economy, sugar production has remained far more important than the growing of other crops such as coffee and indigo, even until today. For decades, the English colonies led the market with an annual output of about 20,000 tons around 1700 and 40,000 tons in the 1730s and 1740s. The share of Barbados decreased in favor of the northern Leeward Islands, mainly Jamaica. The French grew 10,000 to 20,000 tons at the beginning of the eighteenth century and, expanding cultivation on Saint-Domingue and overtaking Britain, 75,000 tons around 1760. By 1800, all Caribbean islands together delivered about 250,000 tons of sugar annually, nearly all of it consumed in Europe.

Cuba, which had provided a considerable share of the sugar crop since the late 1770s, contributed about 30,000 tons to the total. But when Saint-Domingue left the world market after gaining its independence in 1804, the Spanish colony of Cuba was the only remaining larger Caribbean island determined to enforce slave labor. The fact that Cuba then gained undisputed market leadership within just three decades shows the tight and reciprocal connection between preindustrial sugar production and the exploitation of slave labor.

Alexander Engel

See also: Agriculture; Caribbean (Chronology); Plantations; Slavery, Caribbean; Trade.

Bibliography

Higman, Barry W. "The sugar revolution." *Economic History Review* 52:2 (2000): 213–36.

Mintz, Sidney W. *Sweetness and Power: The Place of Sugar in Modern History.* New York: Viking Penguin, 1985.

Watts, David. *The West Indies. Patterns of Development, Culture and Environmental Change Since 1492.* Cambridge, UK: Cambridge University Press, 1987.

Sugar Act (1764)

The Sugar Act of 1764, also known as the Plantation Act and American Revenue Act, replaced the Molasses Act of 1733, which had proven ineffective in raising needed revenue for the British Empire. In contrast to its predecessor, the Sugar Act contained strict enforcement guidelines. Also, unlike previous taxation attempts, the Sugar Act, for the first time, taxed the colonies directly. Consequently, the passage of the Sugar Act (and the later Stamp Act) led to widespread protests in Colonial America.

Great Britain's victory in the French and Indian War (known as the Seven Years' War in Europe) had both costs and benefits for the empire. On the one hand, the French defeat allowed Britain to claim new territory in North America. On the other, great financial resources were consumed during the war, which had almost doubled Britain's national debt. Furthermore, maintaining the new lands required a continued and considerable expense. Consequently, taxation seemed an attractive solution to King George III and his advisers.

Taking charge of the king's financial affairs in April 1763, First Lord of the Treasury George Grenville began an investigation into the American customs service; he found that corruption and smuggling had rendered it extremely inefficient. For decades, the Molasses Act had been ignored by the colonists, and the British government had made little effort to enforce it. In an attempt to rectify the situation, Grenville replaced many customs agents, issued stern orders to colonial officials, and sent the British navy to patrol the coasts.

Once effective measures for enforcement were in place, however, Grenville began to question the amount of the tax. Aware that molasses was imported to the colonies in great quantities by rum distillers, Grenville feared that if it were enforced, the existing Molasses Act, which charged a duty of sixpence per gallon of molasses, would place an unbearable burden on the colonists. For this reason, Grenville abolished the Molasses Act and replaced it with the Sugar Act, which cut the duty on molasses in half but raised the tax on sugar and added a duty on Madeira wine.

Furthermore, under the Sugar Act, cargo had to be bonded before it was loaded on a ship. If a customs agent discovered unbonded products, he had the right to seize the goods and the ship. This provision led to the seizure of colonial ships, including the *Liberty,* which was owned by John Hancock, and the *Ann,* which was owned by Henry Laurens.

The colonists immediately questioned the validity of the Sugar Act. Traditionally, the colonists had not questioned Parliament's power to regulate trade for the benefit of the mother country. However, since the colonists had always taxed themselves, they viewed the new policy of direct taxation as an overstepping of parliamentary power. Public protests began, and the political slogan "no taxation without representation," became popular. Many colonial leaders opposed the

tightening of British control over the colonies and sent letters of protest, which, for the most part, went unheeded. Widespread outrage over the controversial new tax and a perceived lack of political power led to unifying movements throughout most of the colonies.

As a form of protest against the Sugar Act, the later Stamp Act, and other tax measures, a boycott of all British goods was enforced in Boston, Philadelphia, and New York. For the next few years, colonists brewed native sage and sassafras and abstained from British tea. They wore homemade clothing instead of British fashions.

By 1766, the effects of the boycott began to take hold in Britain, and British businessmen began to plead with Parliament for relief. During this time, the king fired Grenville over an issue of office appointments and replaced him with the Marquis of Rockingham. Rockingham, who was more sympathetic to the views of the colonists than Grenville, responded by persuading Parliament to repeal the Stamp Act and lower the sugar tax from 3 pence to 1.

Ironically, the revenue collected under the Sugar Act contributed considerably less than 1 percent to the British annual budget. Yet, it was an extremely significant measure, since it was the first of a long line of new tax measures that ultimately led to colonial rebellion, the Revolution, and finally American independence.

Rolando Avila

See also: Grenville, George; Sugar; Trade.

Bibliography

Bacon, Raymond H. "Rhode Island and the Sugar Act of 1764: An Early Effort at Colonial Unity." Master's thesis, Rhode Island College, 1970.

Blankinship, Blanton Coy. "The Sugar Act in the Colonial South, 1764–1767." Master's thesis, Louisiana State University and Agricultural and Mechanical College, 1981.

Johnson, Allen S. "The Passage of the Sugar Act." *William and Mary Quarterly.* 3d Series. 16:4 (October 1959): 507–14.

Miller, John Chester. "The Quest for a Colonial Revenue: The Sugar Act." In *Origins of the American Revolution.* Stanford, CA: Stanford University Press, 1991.

Surveys

See Maps and Surveys

Susquehanna

Running through central Pennsylvania, the colonial Susquehanna River Valley lay between the Delaware River Valley to the east, the land of the Iroquois and New York to the north, and the Ohio Valley and the Great Lakes region to the west. Pennsylvania and Iroquois officials recognized the great commercial and strategic value of a region that bordered so many different colonies and empires, and shared control of it through the 1750s. Both encouraged numerous groups of Europeans and Native Americans to settle in the Susquehanna, and Iroquois and Pennsylvania officials promoted trade, accommodation, and peace between the groups who settled there. After 1750, however, this long but fragile peace fell apart. The region plunged into two decades of war that ultimately drove the Susquehanna's indigenous peoples into the Ohio Country, opening the entire valley to settlement by European Americans.

In the early 1600s, upwards of 6,000 Susquehannocks, whom John Smith called a "great" and "well proportioned" people, controlled the Susquehanna Valley. But in the 1660s, Iroquois warriors launched mourning wars (wars to obtain captives to replace dead kin) against the Susquehannock after they had spurned the Iroquois's overtures to join their confederacy. Within two decades, the valley was devoid of human settlement except in the far lower reaches.

When William Penn established Pennsylvania in 1682, he immediately laid plans to extend his patent to the lower Susquehanna Valley. At the same time, the Iroquois who lived north of the Susquehanna Valley hoped to resettle the area with dependent native nations that would serve as a buffer, protecting them from colonists in New York and their native enemies, the Cherokee and Catawba. Pennsylvania similarly encouraged displaced Native Americans to resettle the region, hoping to profit from the fur trade, and to establish a barrier between the settlements on the Delaware River and the French and Native Americans to the west.

Pennsylvania and the Iroquois agreed to share control of the Susquehanna Valley, formalizing their alliance in treaties signed in 1701 and 1736. The Pennsylvania government assumed responsibility for European settlers, missionaries, and traders, and the Iroquois claimed the exclusive right to speak for the various native tribes and nations who settled there. A host of displaced native peoples—the Delaware, sur-viving Susquehannocks, the Shawnee who had retreated to the Ohio Country, displaced Chesapeake tribes like the Conoy, displaced New England tribes like the Mahican, and a host of smaller bands—settled in the Susquehanna Valley under the auspices of the Iroquois and Pennsylvania. In the 1720s, European settlers, mainly German Protestants and Scottish and Irish Presbyterians, began establishing farms and settlements in the lower Susquehanna Valley.

Historians have long noted the importance of diversity in colonial Pennsylvania, and the Susquehanna Valley was its most diverse part. Routine meetings to settle issues of trade and land trade might involve representatives from a dozen Native American nations, mediators and negotiators from Pennsylvania and Iroquois nations, and scores of missionaries, traders, interlopers, and transients. Often, these meetings would be conducted in five or six languages. At one 1753 meeting, a Shawnee spoke, a Nanticoke translated his words into English, a German missionary then translated the English into German, and two Native Americans then translated the German into Delaware and Mahican. Meanwhile, an official acting for the Iroquois and the Pennsylvania government, versed in any number of languages, silently observed to ensure that the proceedings accorded with their interests.

Conflicting interests, dislike, and distrust often threatened to produce violence between Native Americans and European settlers. But the diverse peoples of the Susquehanna Valley had shared interests, too, and Iroquois and Pennsylvania officials worked hard to remind them that peace and trade benefited all. Through the 1750s, Pennsylvania and Iroquois negotiators maintained a carefully constructed peace, largely freeing the Susquehanna Valley from the wars and violence that plagued so many other frontiers in British North America.

By the 1750s, however, these negotiators found it increasingly difficult to contain the distrust that had long simmered between native peoples and Europeans. When the French and Indian War spilled over from the Ohio Valley in 1756, the entire region descended into war and chaos. In the 1760s, Ohio and Susquehanna natives joined Pontiac's Rebellion in an effort to push back white settlement.

In the 1770s, the American War for Independence brought another round of war. Much like the Iroquois mourning wars of the 1660s and 1670s, the Revolutionary War ravaged the upper Susquehanna Valley, again leaving it largely devoid of human settlement.

In the 1780s, American land speculators and settlers moved in. Unlike their predecessors, they did not invite the region's displaced Native American nations to join them.

John Craig Hammond

See also: Pennsylvania; Pennsylvania (Chronology); Philadelphia.

Bibliography

Mancall, Peter C. *Valley of Opportunity: Economic Culture Along the Upper Susquehanna, 1700–1800* Ithaca, NY: Cornell University Press, 1991.

Merrell, James H. *Into the American Woods: Negotiators on the Pennsylvania Frontier.* New York: W. W. Norton, 1999.

———. "Shamokin, 'The Very Seat of the Prince of Darkness': Unsettling the Early American Frontier." In *Contact Points: American Frontiers from the Mohawk Valley to the Mississippi, 1750–1830,* edited by Andrew R. L. Cayton and Fredrika J. Teute. Chapel Hill: University of North Carolina Press, 1998.

Swedes

The early 1600s was a time when Sweden was a world power, whose troops had fought successfully in Germany, Poland, the Baltic, Russia, and Denmark. Inspired by the riches garnered by other European powers from their overseas colonies, Sweden also wanted to spread its influence to the New World. In 1637, Swedish, Dutch, and German stockholders formed an alliance—the New Sweden Company—whose primary purpose was to capitalize on the fur and tobacco trade in North America. It was the responsibility of the company to replenish the royal treasury with riches from beyond the Atlantic.

Peter Minuit approached Sweden with stories of treasures to be found in the New World and touted his success at establishing Dutch colonies. He was not a novice colonizer, as he had struggled for seven years to make Dutch New Netherland a profitable fur trading and farming center. After those years of struggle, he was replaced and returned home, leaving behind his only significant act, that of purchasing Manhattan Island for an estimated 24 dollars worth of trinkets.

Minuit and Samuel Blommaert, a copper and brass merchant from Amsterdam, had bought some land in the Delaware Valley. After several unsuccessful attempts to convince the Dutch to form a new settlement on the Delaware, Minuit traveled to Sweden and, using his persuasive skills, was hired to start Sweden's

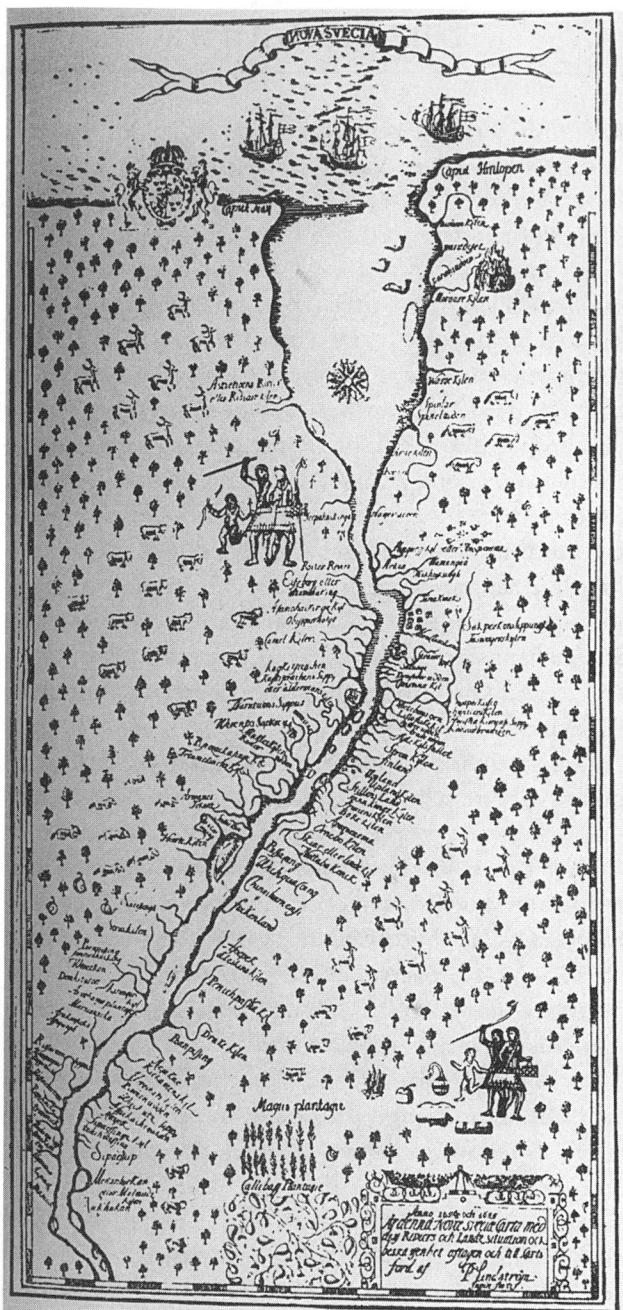

At its peak in 1654, the New Sweden colony dominated the territory along 60 miles of the Delaware River in what is now New Jersey, Pennsylvania, and Delaware (southeast at top). The Dutch took control the following year. *(Brown Brothers, Sterling, Pennsylvania)*

new colony. Toward the end of 1637, the company's first expedition, led by Minuit, sailed from Sweden in two ships, the *Kalmar Nyckel* and the *Fogel Grip.*

After a rough and seemingly interminable crossing, these two ships reached the Delaware River in early 1638. At the mouth of the Brandywine Creek, the first Swedish colonists established Fort Christina, named in honor of the Swedish queen. With the backing of Dutch merchants, Sweden, itself a powerful and prosperous European nation, founded New Sweden on the west bank of the Delaware River.

Much like Fort Orange on the Hudson, Fort Christina specialized in fur trading with the native peoples. Because the trading post lost money, the Dutch investors lost interest and sold their part of the company to their Swedish partners and the Swedish Crown.

The company was reorganized in 1643 and dispatched farm families to raise provisions, livestock, and tobacco. Some of the families were Swedes, but most came from Finland, then under Swedish rule. Highly skilled at farming in heavily forested Sweden and Finland, the colonists adapted quickly, introducing some frontier techniques that became classically "American," including the construction of log cabins. The log cabin became a legacy that played an important role in American life for over 200 years.

Since they were so few in number—roughly 300 to 400 men, women, and children—the New Sweden colonists were unable to defend the land when violently confronted by their Dutch neighbors. In September 1655, the Dutch governor, Peter Stuyvesant, appeared with seven warships and more than 300 armed men. Bribed by the Dutch, the Swedish commander quickly surrendered himself and left by ship for home. Most of the colonists remained and accepted Dutch rule.

For over ten years, the Delaware settlements grew modestly to about 500 colonists, as new Dutch settlers joined the Swedes and Finns. This was still not enough, as the colony had become stretched too thin to hold both the Delaware and the Hudson against the English.

Penny M. Sonnenburg

See also: Delaware. *Document:* Founding of New Sweden (1700s).

Bibliography

Munroe, John A. *Colonial Delaware: A History*. Millwood, NY: KTO, 1978.

Weslanger, C. A. *Dutch Explorers, Traders, and Settlers in the Delaware Valley, 1609–1664*. Philadelphia: University of Pennsylvania Press, 1961.

Syphilis

In the colonial era, syphilis was also known as the French disease, the French pox, the Spanish disease, and yaws. Archaeological evidence suggests that Native Americans suffered from syphilis prior to Columbus's voyage, and fifteenth-century European sources corroborate these findings. The evidence, however, remains inconclusive, and the origin of syphilis remains one of medicine's unsolved mysteries.

Forms of endemic syphilis may have existed in Europe prior to 1492. Syphilis, however, was most likely unknown in the Old World before that time, for contemporaries discussed it as a new disease; once it appeared, it spread virulently throughout Europe, Africa, and parts of Asia.

Soldiers engaged in continental warfare, especially the armies of French King Charles VIII (who died of syphilis in 1498), contributed heavily to its initial European spread. By the early sixteenth century, sailors had carried it to nearly every port city; death frequently followed contraction of the disease in the first half-century of European infection. By the seventeenth century, the disease had lost some of its ferocity and was marked by periodic remission.

Early American colonists often confused two related but distinct diseases caused by *Treponema pallidum*: endemic (nonvenereal) syphilis and venereal syphilis. Endemic syphilis, transferred though fluid mediums such as saliva, was common to rural areas characterized by poor sanitation and close living quarters. In advanced stages, it often caused loss of the nose and palate. Venereal syphilis was—and is—transmitted through genital contact. Syphilis also could be passed from a mother to her unborn child.

Both diseases carried the same symptoms, making diagnosis difficult. Symptoms included fevers, rashes, genital ulcers, ulceration of the mouth and uvula, gummy tumors, lymph gland swelling, bone inflammation, and agonizing muscle pain. No one, however, knew its exact cause, and many confused the disease with gonorrhea. Indeed, over the course of the seventeenth and eighteenth centuries, little progress was made in treating or preventing the spread of the disease.

The disease was fairly widespread among white colonists, slaves, and Native Americans by the eighteenth century. Syphilis was also common among the British, French, and provincial troops, who fought in the many colonial wars, which may have contributed to its spread. By midcentury, more libertine and cosmopolitan men accepted the affliction as a consequence of sexual activity. Colonial newspapers and imported British periodicals carried ads promising "cures" for venereal diseases, as did local surgeons.

Syphilis even became something of an eighteenth-century political joke. Pointed references to syphilis and other venereal diseases, often used to mock or defame political opponents, can be found in both the colonial and English press. Imported broadsides, novels, and prints included references to syphilis in colonial political culture. Colonists, too, used accusations of syphilitic infection to insult local politicians, often insinuating that the afflicted suffered from moral laxity—or a passionate, robust sexual nature.

William Byrd II of Westover, for example, remarked in 1728 in his diary that the disease was so common in North Carolina that "it ceases to be a Scandal." He sneered that the ruling house of burgesses had made a motion that "a Man with a Nose shou'd be incapable of holding any Place of Profit in the Province."

Literate eighteenth-century Britons could learn about the disease and its treatment in over 100 published works. Home remedies circulated widely, and colonial treatments were generally harsh and unsuccessful. Mercury was administered most frequently and to the best effect, but its toxicity often led to excessive drooling, loss of hair and teeth, and sometimes death. Other treatments included bleeding, baths, fumigation, and poultices. The most famous American treatment was credited to a Virginia slave named James Papaw, who, in 1729, earned his freedom by making his concoction public.

By the end of the eighteenth century, thanks to advances in the printing of illustrations, syphilis was again a fashionable topic. Medical treatises published in Europe were translated into English and became popular in both England and America, prompting an interest in new clinical research.

While syphilis was treated as something of a laughing matter during the Restoration years, as the century progressed, the disease was no longer cause for laughter. Especially after the French Revolution, syphilis became associated increasingly with women and prostitution, and political commentators used it as a metaphor for moral corruption and a want of public virtue.

Karen O'Brien

See also: Disease; Prostitution; Sex.

Bibliography

Crosby, Alfred W., Jr. *The Columbian Exchange: Biological and Cultural Consequences of 1492.* Westport, CT: Greenwood Press, 1972.

Merians, Linda E. "Introduction," in Merians, ed., *The Secret Malady: Venereal Disease in Eighteenth-Century Britain and France.* Lexington: University Press of Kentucky, 1996.

Oriel, J. D. *The Scars of Venus: A History of Venereology.* London: Springer-Verlag, 1994.

Parramore, Thomas C. "The 'Country Distemper' in Colonial North Carolina." *North Carolina Historical Review* 48:1 (January 1971).

General Index

F

Q

Biographical Index

Geographical Index

C

Colonial America

AN ENCYCLOPEDIA OF SOCIAL, POLITICAL, CULTURAL, AND ECONOMIC HISTORY

Volume Two

EDITED BY JAMES CIMENT

WITH AN INTRODUCTION BY
MICHAEL ZUCKERMAN, UNIVERSITY OF PENNSYLVANIA

SHARPE REFERENCE
an imprint of M.E. Sharpe, Inc.

SHARPE REFERENCE

Sharpe Reference is an imprint of M.E. Sharpe, Inc.

M.E. Sharpe, Inc.
80 Business Park Drive
Armonk, NY 10504

Cover Photo: Tontine Coffee House, c. 1797 (oil on linen), Francis Guy (1760–1820) / © New York Historical Society, New York, United States; www.bridgeman.co.uk.

Maps: Adapted by Carto-Graphics from the following sources:

Kwame Anthony Appiah and Henry Louis Gates, Jr., eds., *Africana: The Encyclopedia of the African and African American Experience* (New York: Basic Books, 1999). See map: Volume 3, page 788.

Geoffrey Barraclough, ed., *The Times Atlas of World History,* 6th edition (Maplewood, NJ: Hammond, 1982). See maps: Volume 1, pages xlii, xliii, 15, 214; Volume 2, pages xx, xxi; Volume 3, pages xx, xxi; Volume 4, pages xx, xxi, 850; Volume 5, pages xx, xxi.

James Ciment, ed. *Encyclopedia of American Immigration* (Armonk, NY: M.E. Sharpe, 2001). See map: Volume 1, page 55.

James Henretta, et al. *America's History.* 2nd edition (New York: Worth Publishers, 1993). See maps: Volume 1, pages xli, xlii, xliii, 59; Volume 2, pages xix, xx, xxi, 327, 362; Volume 3, pages xix, xx, xxi, 581, 738, 788; Volume 4, pages xix, xx, xxi; Volume 5, pages xix, xx, xxi.

Mary Beth Norton, et al. *A People and a Nation.* 6th edition (Boston: Houghton Mifflin, 2001). See maps: Volume 1, pages xliv, xlv; Volume 2, pages xxii, xxiii, 324; Volume 3, pages xxii, xxiii, 812; Volume 4, pages xxii, xxiii.

Library of Congress Cataloging-in-Publication Data

Colonial America: An encyclopedia of social, political, cultural, and economic history/James Ciment, editor.
    p. cm.
  Includes bibliographical references and index.
  ISBN 0-7656-8065-3 (Set: alk. paper)
   1. United States—Civilization—To 1783—Encyclopedias. I. Ciment, James.

E162.C68 2005
973.2′03—dc22
                                2003023235

Printed and bound in the United States of America

Publisher: Myron E. Sharpe
Vice President and Editorial Director: Patricia Kolb
Vice President and Production Director: Carmen Chetti
Executive Editor and Manager of Reference: Todd Hallman
Senior Development Editor: Jeff Hacker
Project Editor: Laura Brengelman
Program Coordinator: Cathleen J. Prisco
Text Design: Carmen Chetti and Jesse Sanchez
Cover Design: Jesse Sanchez

Contents

List of Maps

VOLUME 2

Topic Finder

Biographies

Religion

Maps

North America, 1600. The above map shows the multiplicity of native peoples on the North American continent in 1600, as well as the extensive Spanish presence in Mexico, Central America, the Caribbean, and southwestern portions of what is now the United States. Note that the English colony of Roanoke mysteriously disappeared shortly after its establishment in 1587. *(Carto-Graphics)*

North America, 1700. The above map shows the presence of European colonial powers on the North American continent circa 1700. Note that the presence of Europeans varied: British holdings in the Hudson Bay region were little more than claims on maps, while settlements along the Atlantic seaboard of what is now the United States included tens of thousands of European settlers and African slaves, as well as the remaining native peoples. *(Carto-Graphics)*

North America, 1775. The above map shows the presence of European colonial powers on the North American continent on the eve of the American Revolution. Note that some regions—particularly in the heart of Mexico and along the Atlantic seaboard of what is now the United States—were more heavily populated by colonists than other areas. *(Carto-Graphics)*

European Settlement Areas, Eastern North America, 1650. The above map shows the thin line of European settlements along the Atlantic seaboard and the St. Lawrence River Valley. At the time, the total European and African populations in the British colonies stood at about 50,000, with a few thousand more in the Dutch, French, and Spanish colonies. *(Carto-Graphics)*

British Colonies, Mainland North America, 1765. By 1750, British settlements on mainland North America had pushed westward to the eastern edge of the Appalachian Mountains. The population of the thirteen colonies in 1750 was roughly 1.2 million, including about a quarter of a million slaves. *(Carto-Graphics)*

Colonial America

Volume Two

E

East India Company

The English East India Company (EIC) was chartered under Queen Elizabeth I in 1600 to raise capital for voyages and trade to the East Indies (Indian Ocean). This private company had twenty-four directors, who were elected by the shareholders, and was modeled after a number of preexisting smaller Dutch corporations that eventually merged into the Vereenigde Oost-Indische Compagnie (VOC) in 1602. These English and the Dutch companies were unique in their initial separation between the ownership of capital and its management by a professional class of merchants and salaried administrators; the emerging principles of capitalism were found in the constitutions of these chartered trading companies.

Over the course of the colonial period, these rival trade companies would grow into wealthy and powerful corporations that monopolized the East Indies trade within their respective nations. The Dutch West Indies Company, which founded the colony of New Netherland, was modeled on the VOC, and a number of English companies operating in the Americas, including the Hudson's Bay Company, were modeled on the EIC.

Although the EIC was a privately chartered joint-stock company, it had important political ties with Parliament and the Crown, since Parliament had the right to control and confirm monopoly grants. In addition, over time, the company became obligated to make substantial financial loans to the state in return for its monopoly trade status. Even though it was privately owned, the EIC was very much wedded to English state interests.

The crucial difference between trade in the East and that with the Americas was the existence of powerful states and economic interests in the Indian Ocean basin. The Portuguese had been the first Europeans to establish significant trade networks in the region, entering the Indian Ocean in the early sixteenth century with cannons blazing in what had previously been a peaceful trade zone. The Portuguese were able to establish a Europe-wide monopoly in the spice trade, but the Dutch soon entered the region, refusing to recognize Portuguese claims. The English and French were not long in following, and all the European nations operating in the region established similar trade companies, though the Dutch and English ones were by far the most successful.

The Indian Ocean had a structural unity created by the periodic rhythms of the monsoon winds and by economic interdependence between one region and another. Cotton textiles from India were vital for the purchase of pepper and spices in the Indonesian archipelago, and precious metals imported from the Middle East, East Africa, Japan, and eventually the Spanish Americas supplied monetary liquidity, which helped the wealthy and powerful centralized empires in Asia to function efficiently. This preexisting trade network induced the European bureaucratic companies to follow the natural contours of commercial geography and design a coordinated system of operations directed from London and Amsterdam stretching from the Red Sea and the Persian Gulf to the South China Sea.

Although they maintained their own respective national monopolies, the Dutch and English companies competed fiercely and, at times, violently against one another, as well as against the older Portuguese Estado da India and the various incarnations of the French East India Company (the Compagnie Française des Indes Orientales, Compagnie des Indes, and Compagnie Française des Indes) in a global competition for markets and resources that was similar to the various European colonial and trading ventures in the Americas. Until the eighteenth century and perhaps later, however, the Asian ventures were much more profitable.

The principle of joint-stock capital, the national

To all and Singular...

FACSIMILE OF GRANT OF ARMS TO THE "NEW" EAST INDIA COMPANY, DATED 13 OCT. 1698.

The dominance of the English East India Company was briefly challenged by the charter of a parallel firm, the New East India Company, in 1698. The two companies merged in 1702 to become the world's largest trading enterprise. *(Guildhall Library, Corporation of London, United Kingdom/Bridgeman Art Library)*

monopoly, and integrated organization in Asia were innovative elements that were not widespread in European commerce at the time. The capital market in Europe developed after 1600 almost in parallel with the growth of trade to Asia and the rising fortunes of the various East India companies. The most significant impact of the companies lay in the public acceptance of the notion that the corporate financial liabilities were, in fact, the assets of others, and investment and capital accumulation were at once effected through this mechanism. The capital transactions of the EIC and VOC at the height of their commercial activity in the first half of the eighteenth century were comparable to the role played by national institutions such as the Bank of England and the Bank of Amsterdam.

The EIC became indirectly involved in North American colonial affairs whenever North American colonists attempted to circumvent the EIC trade monopoly in the Indian Ocean region. Merchants from New York, for example, began a trade network with Anglo-American pirates based on Madagascar in the late seventeenth and early eighteenth centuries. After a series of successful and spectacular raids, these pirates, who sometimes flew the English colors, became a problem in the Indian Ocean trade region, and the Mughal emperor of South Asia, refusing to distinguish between English pirates and English merchants, threatened to dismiss the EIC from the lucrative inter-Asian trade.

The EIC subsequently pressured the members of Parliament, among whom sat many shareholders, to take action against the North American colonies. Pressure came to bear on the North American and colonial administrators and merchants, who supported the pirates through the granting of privateering commissions and the fencing of pirate goods. As a result, a number of colonial governors were recalled, and at least one infamous pirate based in New York, Captain William Kidd, was tried and executed.

Kevin P. McDonald

See also: Board of Trade; Boston Tea Party; Joint-Stock Companies; Tea; Tea Act (1773); Trade.

Bibliography

Chaudhuri, K. N. *Trade and Civilization in the Indian Ocean: An Economic History from the Rise of Islam to 1750.* Cambridge. UK: Cambridge University Press, 1985.

Furber, Holden. *Rival Empires of Trade in the Orient, 1600–1800.* Minneapolis: University of Minnesota Press, 1976.

Edict of Nantes, Revocation of

On October 22, 1685, the absolutist monarch Louis XIV of France revoked the Edict of Nantes and thereby formally ended the last pretense of legal protection for the civil and political rights of French Protestants. Called Huguenots (possibly meaning "confederates"), French Protestants faced open persecution at the hands of troops called dragoons, sent into Protestant communities and homes to enforce either religious conversion or prison sentences and worse. Between 100,000 and 200,000 Huguenots escaped to England, Germany, Holland, Switzerland, and some eventually fled to British North America. Official intolerance hurt the prestige of both the Catholic Church and the French Crown, and the revocation interrupted Huguenot emigration to underpopulated New France.

With the Edict of Nantes, in April 1598, King Henry IV had brought an end to the fierce religious warfare within France that erupted in 1562. The edict introduced the novel principle that subjects should be free to worship as Catholics, or as Huguenots within restricted boundaries, without the state prescribing religious belief to its subjects. From the 1660s on, Louis XIV rolled back protections offered by the edict. In 1685, he declared that, since he believed the greater part of the French population had now embraced Catholicism, the edict was unnecessary.

The persecution of French Huguenots encompassed the full range of social classes, from the nobility, legal professionals, and merchants to booksellers, tradesmen, and farmers. Consequently, the escape of Huguenot families to Protestant Europe had a considerable negative impact on the French economy. In contrast, their resettlement in European and colonial American cities often reinvigorated commerce and trades in those places by introducing new networks of transatlantic capital, credit, information, and affiliation. There was also a cultural impact to the resettlement, as Huguenot printers and booksellers helped spread regional or national literatures across Europe, translating English and French literature and Italian and German scholarly periodicals. The resulting interchange of ideas and correspondence between peoples and languages brought a cosmopolitan stamp to the thought and literature of the eighteenth-century Atlantic world.

Between 1550 and 1620, French Huguenots had attempted to form New World colonies without success; after that time, individual Huguenots made their own way to British North America and New France. As a result of the increased persecution in France, symbolized by the revocation of the Edict of Nantes, between 1680 and 1700, around 2,000 Huguenots migrated to the British colonies. They were attracted by promotional pamphlets promising religious tolerance and material gain, particularly from William Penn's Pennsylvania, although very few of these immigrants actually went there. Most settled in New York, South Carolina, and New England.

Several hundred more Huguenots and their descendants migrated to North America colonies from Europe during the eighteenth century, with smaller numbers in Nova Scotia and western Florida. The number of American Huguenots has often been exaggerated, a result of both their substantial success and the fact that their migration supported dominant Puritan narratives about America as a Protestant haven for Europe's persecuted.

The 1680s migration was the first substantial body of colonists to come to British North America from the European continent, and they formed, for a time, distinct communities where they settled. But these migrants were mainly young adults, and most were childless when they arrived. Persecution and resettlement had taught them the advantages of blending in, and, within two generations, most Huguenots had been assimilated into American society, joining Anglican, Presbyterian, Baptist, or Dutch Reformed churches and intermarrying with English, Scots-Irish, and Dutch.

In the beginning most of the Huguenot congregations were dependent on financial support either from former Huguenots or from Huguenot communities well established elsewhere, particularly in London. Still, small Huguenot congregations in New York and Charles Town retained the French character of the religious observances until the French and Indian War and the American Revolution made this cultural separateness more difficult to sustain.

The Huguenot migrants who chose agricultural occupations settled together in rural communities such as New Rochelle and New Paltz in New York and in short-lived Huguenot settlements in Massachusetts and Rhode Island. Huguenot merchants and tradesmen established themselves in such major ports as New York, Charles Town, and Boston. In these places, a number of Huguenots and their descendants rose to social, political, and economic prominence, including the Faneuils, Bowdoins, Manigaults, DeLanceys, and Laurens. Through civic and religious participation, and by their industry, charity, and display, these families became instrumental in the formation of the political and commercial culture of eighteenth-century America.

Neil Kennedy

See also: French; French Colonies on Mainland North America (Chronology); Huguenots; Louis XIV; Religion (Chronology); Religion (Essay).

Bibliography

Butler, Jon. *The Huguenots in America: A Refugee People in New World Society.* Cambridge, MA: Harvard University Press, 1983.

Davies, Horton, and Marie-Hélène Davies. *French Huguenots in English-Speaking Lands.* New York: Peter Lang, 2000.

Education

Education in colonial North America varied greatly between Spanish, French, and English colonies. In Spanish and French areas, education was largely provided by the church or by missionaries and mostly directed at natives, as there were fewer European settler families. In the British colonies of mainland North America, where the population of settlers continued to grow through the seventeenth and eighteenth centuries, education was largely for the benefit of their children and was conducted in individual households.

Even within the British colonies, however, there was much variation. Literacy and learning were more heavily emphasized in New England than in the colonies of the mid-Atlantic and the South. Still, there was one constant of colonial education, regardless of where it occurred, and that was an emphasis on piety and practicality.

British North America

A general absence of schools and teachers meant that most children in Britain's North American colonies were educated at home. Parents, grandparents, older siblings, and other relatives living under the same roof served as instructors. Moreover, it was not just the biological children who were taught, but any servant children in the household as well.

The curriculum consisted of three general areas of learning. The first was basic skills—reading, writing, and a little simple arithmetic. Primers, imported from England early in the colonial era and later written and published in the colonies, were used for the first two skills, along with the Bible. Arithmetic usually consisted of knowledge passed on from father to son. That is, while girls often received teaching in basic reading and writing, numbers learning was generally reserved for boys.

The second area of the curriculum consisted of piety, teaching Christian morality, and basic knowledge of the Bible. The third focus was vocational. Since the vast majority of colonial residents lived and worked on the land, vocational education consisted of basic agricultural and homemaking skills, the former taught to boys by their fathers and the latter to girls by their mothers. This started at a very young age—sometimes as early as three or four—and largely meant learning by doing, whether that involved birthing cows or churning butter.

For urban and some rural children, particularly boys, apprenticeship in a craft served as a form of education. Parents usually paid to have their children placed with a craftsman—the better paying the craft, the higher the fee. As part of the bargain, the craftsman also got the labor of the child. In return, the apprentice would receive training in the particular craft, basic instruction in literacy and piety, and room and board.

Wealthier residents of the Britain's North American colonies, notably planters in the Chesapeake region or South Carolina, had other options. Some hired tutors to live on the plantation, and a few sent their children, usually sons, to England for an education. Virtually no education was offered to African American slaves beyond instructing them in the tasks they were to perform as adults.

New England was the first region of British North America to move in the direction of more formal education for children. Puritan theology, which emphasized the basic sinfulness of human nature, did not see children as later generations of Americans came to—as innocent creatures who could be corrupted by bad influences. Instead, Puritans viewed even infants as tainted by original sin and saw all small children as depraved, since they had not yet had a chance to learn the word of God. Thus, it was especially important that children become literate so that they could read the Bible on their own.

As early as 1642, the commonwealth of Massachusetts ordered parents and the masters of apprentices to provide the children under their guardianship with an education in reading, religion, and civics. Five years later, the commonwealth passed the "Old Deluder Satan Act." Under that law, all townships with fifty to one hundred households were required to hire someone to teach reading and writing, so that children could read their Bibles and, as the law's name implied, not fall prey to Satan's wiles. For towns with over one hundred households, the law required that the curriculum include Latin grammar so that boys would be ready to attend a university. In addition, the citizens of Boston founded the nation's first secondary school, the Boston Latin School, in 1635.

The colonies of the mid-Atlantic—notably New York and Pennsylvania—lacked the religious uniformity and centralized theocracy of New England. Indeed, as these middle colonies drew immigrants from many parts of Europe, there was no common language and no common religious denomination. Formal schooling was largely provided by the local churches and parishes.

In rural areas, there were also so-called dame schools, run by a local woman, who was paid by local residents to offer a rudimentary education in reading and writing. Most students who attended dame schools did so a few months a year for a few years, generally in the winter when they were not needed for farm work. While there were some attempts in both Pennsylvania and New York to set up public schools in the larger towns and cities, sectarian disputes arose. By the beginning of the eighteenth century, the burden of education had once again fallen on local churches.

In the Southern colonies, where most people lived scattered on isolated farms and plantations, rather than clustered in villages, formal education was even more rudimentary than in the middle colonies. When they did not hire private tutors, a few wealthier planters in more-settled areas established small private schools. For boys, these academies offered Latin, alongside basic grammar and arithmetic. For girls, academy education also included elaborate rules of etiquette alongside instruction in basic letters.

For the middling class and the poor, there was virtually no formal education available in the rural South. In 1642, however, Virginia did pass a "poor law," which established "workhouse schools" for the children of the indigent that emphasized vocational training and moral teaching. While discipline was strict in all colonial schools—with frequent use of corporal punishment—the regimen of the workhouse schools was particularly harsh, and many students ran away.

In all the colonies, private academies emphasized intellectual learning—ancient languages, philosophy, and theology—aimed at preparing students for college in the colonies or, more rarely, university in Europe. This kind of education was increasingly seen, however, as impractical by the rising merchant class of eighteenth-century colonial cities from Charles Town to Boston. Many merchants began to hire tutors to educate their sons in the more practical matters of mathematics, science, business, history, navigation, and modern languages.

Eventually, this new, practical education became formalized in what were called "new academies." Perhaps the first and best known of these academies was the Philadelphia Academy, founded in that city by Benjamin Franklin and other practical-minded citizens in 1751. At first for boys exclusively, these academies soon added "female departments," which eventually became separate "female academies," offering instruction in the fine and domestic arts.

French and Spanish North America

Education in both Spanish and French America was largely administered by the Catholic Church or by missionaries connected to various Catholic brotherhoods, such as the Jesuits and Franciscans. Because so few Spanish or French women came to the colonies, making for few settler families, most education was oriented toward either Native American or mixed-race children.

The very first schools established in the Western Hemisphere by Europeans were in Mexico in the 1520s, set up under Franciscan tutelage. Because the schools consisted of native children, the friars taught in the native language. The curriculum consisted of basic reading, writing, and arithmetic, as well as the Catholic catechism. Special schools were also established for abandoned mestizo children, the offspring of Spanish fathers and native mothers. In general, however, schools in New Spain—in both Mexico and what is now the southwestern United States—were few and far between. Literacy was exceptionally low among Native Americans and mestizos in Spain's North American colonies.

A similar pattern developed in colonial Canada under the French. Native American and mixed-race children, or Métis, were largely educated in mission schools, including those run by the Jesuit and Ursuline orders, the latter an order of nuns. The first mission school in Quebec was founded in Trois-Rivières in 1616. As with schools in Spanish America, the emphasis was on basic literacy and the Catholic liturgy, with the goal of training Native American missionaries to advance the conversion of native Canadian peoples.

As most French settlers lived on isolated farms, there was little in the way of formal education in rural areas. In towns and cities, however, the French tried to recreate the school system that existed in France. This system tended to be more centralized, whether under government or church control, and it emphasized intellectual training in Latin, Greek, and philosophy for university preparation. As in New Spain, however, the vast majority of natives and settlers in New France received no formal education.

Education for a New Republic

The American Revolution represented a significant break in the education offered in Britain's North American colonies. Temporarily, the war disrupted formal schooling. In its wake, American educators began to emphasize more practical education.

In addition, schools—both private and public—became centers for inculcating citizenship values. Thomas Jefferson and some of the other founders firmly believed that an educated citizenry was essential to the proper functioning of a republic. Education for the children of middling and lower-class Americans became increasingly widespread in the new country, with the broad exception of the rural South.

James Ciment

See also: Arts, Culture, and Intellectual Life (Essay); Child Rearing; Children; Education, Higher; Reading and Literacy. *Document:* A Tutor and his Pupils (1773–1774).

Bibliography

Cohen, Patricia Cline. *A Calculating People: The Spread of Numeracy in Early America.* Chicago: University of Chicago Press, 1982.

Cremin, Lawrence. *American Education: The Colonial Experience, 1607–1783.* New York: Harper & Row, 1970.

Lockridge, Kenneth. *Literacy in Colonial New England.* New York: W. W. Norton, 1974.

Education, Higher

As a central energizing force in the American experience, higher education in the British North American colonies started out following English and Continental European models, but it eventually developed distinctive American characteristics. Among the colleges established between 1607 and 1775, all, with one exception, set out to train ministers in the predominant religion of the respective colonies. Yet, almost from the beginning, they also endeavored to educate all students in the humanities and sciences, as well as in the "useful arts."

Harvard

New England Puritans believed that every person should read sufficiently well to comprehend the Bible. In 1636, the Great and General Court of the Colony of Massachusetts Bay authorized creation of a college to be located at Newtown (renamed Cambridge in 1638). The college was to emphasize divinity studies, and its purpose was to train ministers for Congregational parishes in the colony.

The school was named Harvard in 1638 when John Harvard, a young clergyman, bequeathed his library and one-half of his estate to the fledgling institution. Following the appointment of Henry Dunster as president in 1640, Harvard added a library and two other buildings. After the execution of Charles II in January 1649, the General Court authorized Harvard to offer degrees in 1650, ignoring the established English practice of obtaining royal permission to grant college degrees. This was one of the early examples of the colonies exercising independent initiatives in contravention to established practices of the mother country.

The curriculum at Harvard, modeled after curricula in English and European universities, was designed to turn out learned clergymen and gentlemen. Latin and Greek were at the core of the four-year course of study, while rhetoric, logic, mathematics, and philosophy (which included natural physics, astronomy, mental ethics, economics, and political science) were the attendant subjects required of all students. Harvard began with four students and one teacher. During the seventeenth century, the school enrolled an average of twenty to fifty students per year, most from New England, although the college also accepted students from Virginia, New Netherland, and Bermuda.

William and Mary

The more open plantation structure of Southern society, and the frequent "troubles" with the native peoples, were two of many reasons that Southern colonists failed, after several attempts, to establish an early college in the South. In February 1693, however, Governor Sir Edmund Andros obtained a charter from the Crown to establish a college in Virginia, named the College of William and Mary after the reigning king and queen.

The Reverend James B. Carr, the Anglican commissary for Virginia and conveyor of the charter to the colony, was named the first president of the new college. It was located on a remote tract of land between the James and York Rivers known as the "Middle Plantation," later to be renamed Williamsburg. The mission of the college was to prepare ministers in the Anglican tradition, following the model established in Scottish universities, with a two-year bachelor's degree program and a four-year master's degree, with courses in divinity, philosophy, languages, and other "good arts and sciences," as directed by the charter.

The construction of the main edifice—designed by Christopher Wren and, since the early twentieth century, known as the Wren Building—began in 1695. Recurring fires and other mishaps, along with the

The Christopher Wren Building (named for its architect) at the College of William and Mary in Williamsburg, Virginia, is the oldest academic building in continuous use in the United States. It was completed in 1699. *(Brown Brothers, Sterling, Pennsylvania)*

unfortunate appointment of a disinterested faculty, delayed the firm establishment of the college as a viable institution of learning until 1726.

Yale

Traditionalist Puritan leaders, troubled by the tendency toward modern science and a lessening of religious stringency at Harvard, felt the need for an institution that adhered to traditional Congregationalism. Not long after the establishment of William and Mary in the South, New England saw its second college in 1701, when Yale College began as a Puritan school in the home of its first rector, Abraham Pierson, in Killingworth (now Clinton), Connecticut.

In 1707, the school moved to Saybrook (now Old Saybrook), and, in 1716, it moved finally to New Haven. It was renamed Yale College in 1718, after Elihu Yale, a Boston-born English merchant in the British East India Company, donated to the college nine bales of goods valued at over 562 pounds, 417 books, and a portrait and coat of arms of King George I. Yale followed a traditionalist, Puritan curriculum for a generation, devoted to "upholding and propagating the Christian Protestant religion by a succession of learned and orthodox men."

College of New Jersey (Princeton)

In a move to counter the conservative philosophy at Yale and also to counter opposition to the Great Awakening by both Harvard and Yale, moderate Presbyterians in New Jersey sought to continue the tradition of a Presbyterian institution. The Log College, operated by William Tennent, an Edinburgh-educated Presbyterian minister, was located in Bucks County, Pennsylvania. When Tennent died in 1745, there was consternation that the Log College supplying of Presbyterian ministers in the middle colonies would come to an end. The denomination's leaders proposed a new college for the middle colonies, applying for a charter in 1745.

Presbyterians disapproved of Harvard and Yale's opposition to the new religious revivals of George Whitefield, yet they also were uncomfortable with the restrictive limitations of the Log College curriculum. They envisioned a college with a more modern approach. The charter was eventually granted by acting governor John Hamilton, an Anglican with rather liberal views, to a board of trustees, all Presbyterians, who

directed that the new college would be operated by "well disposed and public spirited persons" and that the mission of the college would be to offer the arts and sciences, a seminary to prepare ministers of the Gospel, and instruction "useful in the learned professions."

Named the College of New Jersey, and created under the sponsorship of the New York Synod, the school was originally located in Elizabeth. In October 1747, upon the death of its first president, Jonathan Dickinson, the college moved to the parsonage of Aaron Burr, local Presbyterian rector of Newark and the college's second president. In 1753, the FitzRandolph family donated 10 acres of land in Princeton, where the College of New Jersey established a permanent home in 1756. Although dominated by Presbyterian trustees, the college was open to adherents of all recognized religions, reflective of the eighteenth-century movement away from the traditionalist philosophies at Harvard and Yale.

Although officially the College of New Jersey, it was commonly referred to as Princeton College, or Nassau Hall, the name of its main building. At the college's sesquicentennial celebration in 1896, the name was officially changed to Princeton University.

University of Pennsylvania

The development of higher education in the colonies took a radical turn when, in 1749, Benjamin Franklin, prominent Philadelphia author and publisher, wrote a tract entitled *Proposals Relating to the Education of Youth in Pensilvania*. Lamenting the lack of an academy of higher learning in Pennsylvania, Franklin submitted a startling proposal to the people of that colony. Quoting such luminaries as Locke and Milton, he recommended establishing a secular academy offering courses in modern vernacular languages, mathematics and commerce, and local, colonial, and universal history and geography. "Students should be taught everything useful and everything ornamental," he wrote. He also recommended regularly scheduled periods of physical activity, a well-stocked library, and an atmosphere in which the boarding scholars "diet together, plainly, temperately and frugally."

The mission of the academy was to prepare students not primarily for the ministry—although students could choose that course of study if they wished —but for careers in business, science, and public service. In addition, Franklin suggested that students aiming for different careers take courses suitable for each career. This was a significant departure from the "one curriculum for all students" philosophy that dominated the other colonial colleges. The Philadelphia Academy, as it was named, was thus America's first liberal arts college.

In 1751, a charter was granted by the Pennsylvania Legislature, a board of trustees was appointed by Franklin, and classes began later that year. The Academy was renamed the College of Philadelphia in 1755. The curriculum was modified by the Reverend William Smith in 1756 to include the study of the classics, ancient as well as modern languages, philosophy, history, mathematics, science, and the useful arts. In 1765, John Morgan established America's first medical school at the college, and, in 1779, the name was officially changed to the University of Pennsylvania, the new nation's first university.

King's College (Columbia)

By the early eighteenth century, New York and New Jersey Anglicans had been considering the establishment of an Anglican college in the North for many years. Lewis Morris of New Jersey began drawing up plans as early as 1704, but financing problems and interparish rivalries competing for authority over, and the location of, such a college delayed any agreement until 1754, when New York City Anglicans forged a compromise. They were granted a charter by George II, and a board of trustees was formed.

All factions agreed to follow the model established by the Philadelphia Academy for religious liberty; in addition, the new institution, called King's College, would have a seminary for the training of Anglican clergy. A curriculum was established based on ancient and modern languages, history, logic, mathematics, and the sciences, as well as husbandry and commerce. The college opened for eight students in July 1754 in a schoolhouse attached to Trinity Church at Broadway and Wall Street in lower Manhattan, and the first classes were taught by Reverend Samuel Johnson.

The college grew rapidly, and, in 1767, a medical school was established. The college closed in 1776 because of the Revolutionary War and reopened in 1884 as Columbia College. It was renamed Columbia University in 1896.

College of Rhode Island (Brown)

The College of Rhode Island, another product of the Great Awakening, was chartered in 1764 by the Baptist

denomination. The Baptists gained a foothold in New England in 1639, twenty-five years after their founding in the Netherlands by British Separatists, when Roger Williams, who had earlier converted to the religion, established the first Baptist church in Providence. Another parish was established in Newport in 1644.

The Baptists rejected the more cerebral intellectualism, the ecclesiastical authority, and the close ties between church and state of the Congregational, Anglican, and Presbyterian denominations. Instead, they favored a more emotional, personal devotion to the written word of the Bible, a commonsense identity, and a complete reliance upon faith.

Having established a successful Baptist preparatory school in New Jersey in 1756, the Philadelphia Baptist Association began to search for a suitable location for a college. Denomination leaders in Rhode Island, where the first Baptist church was founded, welcomed the idea. Ezra Stiles, the Congregational rector at Newport, and James Manning, Baptist emissary to Rhode Island, drew up the plans for a "liberal and catholic" institution for the province. A charter was granted by the Rhode Island legislature in 1764, providing for a board of trustees composed of Baptists, Congregationalists, Anglicans, and Quakers. The mission of the college was to prepare a succession of men for a life of "usefulness and reputation" through instruction in the "vernacular languages, the arts and sciences."

The college was located in the parsonage of James Manning at Warren, Rhode Island, and it began with one student, William Rogers. By 1769, the college had eleven students, each paying $12 per year tuition. Seven students graduated that year. In 1770, the cornerstone was laid on the first college building, now University Hall, modeled after Nassau Hall at Princeton, and was constructed by Nicholas Brown and Company, owned by the Brown brothers, from a prominent Rhode Island family.

During the Revolution, the British seized the college building and used it as a barracks. Later, the Continental Congress established it as a hospital for French troops. In 1782, the college regained possession and began repairs on the wartime damage, and, in 1783, John Brown offered to pay half of the cost of a new library. The first commencement after the war, in 1786, included among the graduates Nicholas Brown Jr., who became a trustee of the college five years later. After creating Brown and Ives, Rhode Island's largest mercantile company, Brown donated a total of $160,000 to the college over the course of his life until his death in 1841. Following his first donation, $5,000 in 1804, the trustees renamed the college Brown University at Providence, in the State of Rhode Island and Providence Plantations.

Queen's College (Rutgers)

Under New Jersey Governor William Franklin, the illegitimate and estranged son of Benjamin Franklin, Queen's College, named in honor of Charlotte of Mecklenburg, queen consort of George III, was granted a charter by the Crown on November 11, 1766. Its mission was to provide "useful learning and true religion" to the youth of New Jersey and neighboring provinces, and to prepare young men for "an able and learned" ministry in the Dutch Reformed Church.

A board of trustees was appointed, and, after obtaining funding and appointing a faculty, the board established a location at New Brunswick in 1771. In November of that year, one sophomore and five freshmen met in the Sign of the Lion, a downtown tavern. The teacher was 18-year-old Frederick Frelinghuysen, stepson of the college president. In 1774, 19-year-old Matthew Leydt became the first graduate.

The college struggled through the Revolution with sporadic instruction, fell on hard times, and closed in 1795. The trustees raised $12,000 over the next ten years and reopened the college in 1807. The school closed again in 1812 because of economic depression and the coming war with England, reopening in 1825.

That year, the college was renamed Rutgers, after Colonel Henry Rutgers, a Revolutionary War hero who was lauded for his "Christian values" but who was also known for his generous philanthropy. In 1826, Colonel Rutgers donated to the college a $200 bell and the interest on a $5,000 note. Upon his death in 1830, he donated one-third of his estate to charities but, for unknown reasons, not one cent to Rutgers College.

In 1864, the Dutch Reformed Church severed its affiliation with the college. Rutgers became a university in 1924, and, in 1945, the legislature declared Rutgers the state university of New Jersey.

Dartmouth

Dartmouth College, the last of the colonial colleges, was granted a charter on December 13, 1769, by George III. The charter went to Eleazar Wheelock, who established the institution at Hanover, New Hampshire, to educate and instruct "the youth of the Indian tribes," as well as "English youths and others." Wheelock, a Congregational minister, had formerly operated Moore's Charity School at Lebanon, Connecticut, a school for Native American boys, which he wished to expand into a college. He secured the assistance of William Legge, second earl of Dartmouth; Samson Occom, a Mohegan Indian and former student who raised considerable funds for the project; and John Wentworth, royal governor of New Hampshire, who donated 10 acres of land at Hanover.

Wheelock's mission to educate Native American youth did not succeed. So the college proceeded to follow a liberal and useful arts curriculum and to prepare young men for the Congregational ministry. In 1815, Dartmouth experienced a sensational series of events. A newly elected Republican-dominated legislature declared the original Dartmouth charter invalid, because it was issued by a king who was eventually deposed. A new board of trustees was appointed, and the college was renamed Dartmouth University, taken over by the state, and declared a state university. The deposed board of trustees, led by former president Francis Brown, commenced an action in the New Hampshire courts, demanding the return of the Dartmouth College seal, its charter, records, account books, and the keys.

Denied justice in New Hampshire courts, the board appealed to the federal courts on the basis of the contracts clause of the Constitution (Article I, section X, clause 1). The board argued that no state may impair the obligations of a contract and that the original charter issued by George III was not only valid at the time but currently valid. The board further argued that Dartmouth was a private institution perpetually free from interference by the state of New Hampshire. The case went before the Supreme Court in 1819, with Daniel Webster, a Dartmouth alumnus (class of 1801), representing the Dartmouth trustees. It has become a part of American legend that on the final day of his oral argument before the Court, Webster, with choking voice and quivering lips, brought tears to the eyes of the justices when he pleaded,

> Sirs, you may destroy this little institution. It is weak. . . . I know it is one of the lesser lights in the literary horizon of the country. You may put it out. But if you do so, you must carry through your work. You must extinguish, one after another, all those great lights of science which, for more than a century have thrown their radiance over our land. It is sirs, as I have said, a small college, and yet there are those who love it!

The Court's decision in *Dartmouth College vs. Woodward,* issued by John Marshall, stands as a landmark decision in American constitutional law. It declared that the original charter of 1769 was valid, regardless of the results of the Revolutionary War. The decision was a strong, affirmative interpretation of the contracts clause. It established the doctrine that private institutions, duly chartered, may conduct their affairs according to the charter, and that the states may not subsequently impair the obligations of contracts once the contracts are complete.

Role in the Colonies

In addition to becoming an educated clergy, which was the career choice of approximately half of the graduates of the nine colonial colleges prior to the Revolution, the graduates also became the leaders of business, commerce, politics, and, late in the colonial era, medicine and law. Many of the members of the Stamp Act Congress and the Continental Congresses, as well as the signers of the Declaration of Independence and the Constitution, were graduates of these nine colleges.

A case can be made that one of the manifestations of the American movement away from loyalty to the mother country was the tendency by some of the colleges to ignore existing rules and practice of obtaining charters from the king, by instead obtaining charters and eventually the power to offer degrees from the colonial government. Although the colleges began with structures based on English and European models, by the 1770s, these institutions had become distinctly American. They would provide a sturdy foundation for the modern American system of higher education to come.

James R. Belpedio

See also: Arts, Culture, and Intellectual Life (Essay); Education; Harvard College; King's College; William and Mary, College of; Yale College. *Document:* Founding Colleges in America (1754).

Bibliography

Boorstin, Daniel. *The Americans: The National Experience.* New York: Vintage Books, 1965.

Brubacher, John Seiler, and Willis Rudy. *Higher Education in Transition: A History of American Colleges and Universities.* New Brunswick, NJ: Transaction, 1997.

Cowley, W. H. *International and Historical Roots of American Higher Education.* New York: Garland, 1991.

Lucas, Christopher J. *American Higher Education: A History.* New York: St. Martin's Griffin, 1996.

Rudolph, Frederick. *The American College and University.* Athens: University of Georgia Press, 1990.

Tewksbury, Donald G. *Founding of American Colleges and Universities Before the Civil War.* New York: Teachers College, 1932.

Edwards, Jonathan (1703–1758)

Jonathan Edwards was perhaps the most influential clergyman in colonial America. He is often credited with initiating the Great Awakening, and his extensive writings constitute an insightful and seminal body of colonial religious and intellectual thought.

Early Life and Early Career

Jonathan Edwards was born in 1703, in East Windsor, Connecticut. He was the only son among the eleven children of Reverend Timothy Edwards and Esther Edwards, the daughter of influential Puritan clergyman Solomon Stoddard. After being tutored by his parents, the young Edwards enrolled at the age of 13 at Yale College. While at Yale, he read widely in the works of Sir Isaac Newton and John Locke; his interests besides theology were far-flung and included spiders, atoms, rainbows, and the workings of the human mind.

Following his graduation from Yale in 1720, Edwards remained in New Haven to continue his theological studies. He was licensed to preach in the Presbyterian Church in 1722 and earned his Master of Theology degree the following year. After leading a Presbyterian congregation in New York for two years, Jonathan Edwards returned to Yale as a tutor.

The year 1727 was an important one for Jonathan Edwards. In July, he married Sarah Pierpoint, a granddaughter of the noted Puritan minister Thomas Hooker; eventually, they would have eleven children together. That same year, Edwards accepted a position as assistant minister to his grandfather Solomon Stoddard in Northampton, Massachusetts. Stoddard died only two years later, leaving the young minister in charge of a congregation that consisted of prominent merchants and political leaders.

This group had been comforted by a liberal theology and Stoddard's ability to compromise. By comparison, Edwards was a less conventional thinker than

The Congregational minister Jonathan Edwards of Connecticut was perhaps the most original religious thinker and influential clergyman of the colonial period. His orthodox sermons aroused the religious spirit of the Great Awakening. *(Brown Brothers, Sterling, Pennsylvania)*

Edwards' thinking during the years of his schooling and early ministry.

For Edwards, the will was not a separate mental or emotional faculty or ability; rather, the will was the expression of basic human motivations. Because all mankind inherited sinful natures in Adam's fall, Edwards believed that human nature would never exhibit itself in a free will turned toward goodness and morality. He held that free will could only be turned toward God after God Himself undertook to change the individual's heart as an act of divine grace.

Edwards also believed that he and his contemporaries were living in the dawn of the millennium, at which time the kingdom of God would come on earth and require each person to account for himself at a day of judgment. Accordingly, Edwards believed that the ideal church, composed as a body of true believers redeemed by God's grace, should strive toward perfection and thus be found righteous at the last judgment. As a result, he broke with the teachings of his grandfather, who had offered the sacrament of the Lord's Supper to all socially upstanding members of the community. Edwards believed that the church had a responsibility to maintain stricter standards; he preached that only those who were regenerate sinners and who had professed their acceptance of God's grace should be allowed full communicant membership in the church.

Great Awakening

During his early years at Northampton, Edwards focused his preaching particularly on the youth and young adult members of his congregation, and he instilled this group with a sense of yearning for a more personal, individualized religious experience. Before Stoddard's death, the Northampton church had undergone what he had described as several "seasons of revival"; therefore, his grandson found a fertile field when, in late 1734 and early 1735, he undertook the preaching of a series of sermons on the topic of justification by faith. In response, the Northampton church underwent a remarkable period of spiritual self-examination and renewal, and many emotional conversions occurred.

While confusion and some dissent among the older parishioners greeted Edwards's early efforts, word of the transformation of the Northampton congregation quickly spread. The news and similar activity soon spread, first to Suffield, South Hadley, and Hatfield, Massachusetts, then to East Windsor, Lebanon, and New Haven, Connecticut. It ran through the Connecticut River Valley and to the Long Island Sound.

his grandfather had been. His theology, which soon came to be known as "Edwardseanism," had developed in his youth as a product of his attempts to apply Enlightenment thought to traditional Calvinism. In 1731, Edwards made a stirring speech in Boston in which he championed orthodox Puritanism. The next few years served to solidify this attitude within his preaching and writing.

Edwards's Theology

Jonathan Edwards had been one of the first thinkers in America to read John Locke's *Essay Concerning Human Understanding* in 1717. The question of man's free will in light of Edwards' own strong Calvinist belief in predestination was one that engaged the minister for all of his life. He was convinced that merely an intellectual grasp of the gospel was insufficient. Instead, for an individual to truly experience the Word of God, he must possess empirical knowledge—that is, he must experience it firsthand. In addition, a sense of millennialism, of apocalypticism, and of pietism all informed

At the same time, itinerant preachers were spreading a similar evangelistic message of personal spiritual accountability throughout New England. While such a fever pitch of emotion understandably could not last forever, a genuine sense of expectancy spread throughout the colonies in response to this evangelistic fervor. The belief that a meaningful spiritual life could only be coerced from the colonists by means of jeremiadic preaching—that is, a listing of all of the benefits offered by a divine Providence, followed by a longer list of all the colonists' shortcomings, accompanied by a recitation of evils to come unless the people changed their sinful ways—was supplanted by evangelism, or literally, the "good news" of personal salvation, which would lead to an individual's right relationship with God.

For a time, evangelism and itinerant preaching became something of a cottage industry in colonial America. Many of the long-established churches in New England decried the presence of evangelists, questioning their sincerity and the efficacy of their preaching. Others were disturbed by the lack of decorum and propriety they believed such charismatic preaching induced. Many questioned the actual value of conversions experienced in the heat of emotion and disorder, arguing instead that true recognition of God's work within a sinner's heart could only come through long reflection, prayer, and assistance by a respectable minister of the established church hierarchy. In many communities, laws were passed banning itinerants the right to assemble makeshift congregations at revival meetings or, in some cases, even to enter a community unless the itinerant preacher had been invited by a licensed minister of an established congregation. The dangers of the Great Awakening seemed clear to mainline churches. They saw that emotional and charismatic preaching offered an interesting change from the daily routine of difficult settlement life and that it was also a powerful draw for those who had regularly attended the established churches in a region. Congregational Church ministers were quick to apprehend the possibility: not only might their pews become permanently vacant because former members would decide to abandon their church homes for this new, entertaining preaching, but their collection plates might well become similarly depleted. Interestingly, Jonathan Edwards shared some of his fellow ministers' concerns; still, he was reluctant to completely discount the value of revivalistic religion, pointing out that the more intense forms of worship might be needed to reach some particularly unrepentant sinners' hearts and that many lives were being perma-

nently changed for the good in the wake of such evangelism.

Departure and Writings

Jonathan Edwards enjoyed an extended successful tenure at the Northampton church in the years 1728–1750. However, by the mid-1740s, some members of the congregation began to be bothered by Edwards's extreme orthodoxy. Disagreements came to a head by 1750, when Edwards tried to discipline the children of several prominent families in the church for looking at a "bad book," a midwives' manual they had obtained. At last, the congregation made it clear that Edwards's resignation was expected.

Ironically, his departure from the Northampton church marked the beginning of an exceptionally productive time for Edwards. He was assigned the duties of preaching to the whites and Native Americans at the mission church in the frontier settlement of Stockbridge, Massachusetts. While at Stockbridge, Edwards embarked on a period of intense study and contemplation and produced some of his most deeply philosophical theological texts, including *Freedom of the Will* (1754) and *The Nature of True Virtue* (1765).

Edwards's Stockbridge writings captured the attention and approval of many scholars and ministers. He was invited to serve as president of the College of New Jersey (now Princeton University) in 1758. After serving only two months in that office, he died as the result of a reaction to a smallpox inoculation.

Barbara Schwarz Wachal

See also: Bible; Christ and Christianity; Ministers and the Ministry; Puritanism; Religion (Chronology); Religion (Essay); Sermons; Whitefield, George.

Bibliography

Aldridge, Alfred Owen. *Jonathan Edwards.* New York: Washington Square, 1964.

Davidson, Edward H. *Jonathan Edwards: The Narrative of a Puritan Mind.* Cambridge, MA: Harvard University Press, 1968.

Scheick, William J. *The Writings of Jonathan Edwards: Theme, Motif, and Style.* College Station: Texas A&M University Press, 1975.

Smith, John Edwin. *Jonathan Edwards: Puritan, Preacher, Philosopher.* South Bend, IN: University of Notre Dame Press, 1992.

Townsend, Harvey G., ed. *The Philosophy of Jonathan Edwards from His Private Notebooks.* Westport, CT: Greenwood, 1974.

Elizabeth I (1533–1603)

Born September 7, 1533, Elizabeth I was the only child of Henry VIII of England and his second wife, Anne Boleyn. Anne's pregnancy had added urgency to Henry VIII's break with the Catholic Church, and his disappointment at the birth of a second daughter was intense.

Elizabeth's early life was traumatic and unpredictable, as Anne Boleyn was beheaded for adultery and Henry VIII married four more times. He disinherited Elizabeth as a bastard, then, in 1544, restored both his daughters to the succession after their brother Edward VI. Elizabeth, who had been educated by the best Renaissance scholars and raised as a Protestant, lived precariously under both of her siblings. She was a political marriage prize for Thomas Seymour, but he was executed by his brother for treason. She became a rallying point for Protestants during the reign of Mary I, and Sir Thomas Wyatt's using her as a figurehead for his rebellion against Mary nearly cost Elizabeth her life for treason as well.

On November 17, 1558, she inherited the throne and a country torn by religious and financial troubles. Few other monarchs wanted to recognize Elizabeth I as the legitimate heir, and only the support of her former brother-in-law, Philip II of Spain, prevented French pressure from replacing her with Mary Stuart of Scotland. Using herself as a diplomatic object, Elizabeth I

Queen Elizabeth I established Great Britain as a major European power, with an unparalleled navy and vast trade network. In North America, she supported voyages of exploration and settlement. *(Private Collection/Bridgeman Art Library)*

entertained marriage proposals from the rulers of Europe, balancing England carefully between France and the Hapsburgs of Spain and Austria. She also attempted to steer a middle course in religion, keeping sumptuous forms of worship in the Church of England while admitting Calvinist teachings in the Thirty-nine Articles. One of her great strengths was using the talents of skilled advisors such as Sir William Cecil and Sir Francis Walsingham, who created the British intelligence service. She also creatively financed her court based on medieval and royal prerogatives.

With France and Spain unwilling to confront England directly, Elizabeth I encouraged privately financed voyages of exploration and discovery, investing in the sailings of Drake and Raleigh under the pseudonym Bess Tudor. Elizabeth I's astrologer, alchemist, and occultist, Dr. John Dee, constructed an elaborate justification for English claims on the New World, based on King Arthur, adventures of semimythological Welsh princes, and the real voyage of John Cabot. Although the explorations of Sir William Gilbert failed to establish a colony in Newfoundland, and Sir Walter Raleigh's first attempt at colonizing the land he claimed for the queen at Roanoke failed, enthusiasm ran high for exploration. Men like Martin Frobisher braved the far northern reaches of the Atlantic in search of an Arctic passage to Asia. Private companies, such as those founded to trade with Muscovy and the Levant, made fortunes for English businessmen and encouraged interest. More practically, the armed merchantmen served as a privately financed navy for England, operating under letters of marque against Spain and France as privateers.

Despite the image of Elizabeth I as a glorious and successful Protestant champion, her reign began to encounter serious problems. In 1570, the pope excommunicated the queen, inspiring a wave of assassination plots. Foreign affairs, including the Dutch revolt, the seizure of power by Presbyterians in Scotland, and religious wars in France, necessitated an expensive and long-term English campaign for the Crown to reassert its power in the British Isles and overseas.

Threats to the throne endangered Elizabeth I's tolerant religious policy, as she was besieged by radical Protestant demands for state security. One of the most consuming commitments of Elizabeth I's reign was the shiring of northern Ireland by English settlers, who set in motion the Anglicization of Ireland as a colony and began centuries of conflict between the Church of England colonists and earlier Roman Catholic landowners, beginning in the 1580s with a savage guerilla war.

After Mary Stuart of Scotland was executed in 1586 for participating in an assassination plot, England was open to an invasion from Spain. Philip II, no longer constrained by Mary's claim to the throne, launched the Spanish Armada against Elizabeth I. England, with almost no standing army, prepared for invasion, and prevailed because of a combination of luck in the form of a devastating storm, which scattered the armada, and the skill of the queen's privateer captains, who defeated the remaining vessels. The last years of Elizabeth I's reign saw a codification of national legend, with England as the rightful ruler of the Atlantic, and Elizabeth I as "Gloriana," all encouraged by artists and writers such as Sir Philip Sidney and William Shakespeare.

As the queen aged with no heir and the economy slumped at the turn of the century, ambitious courtiers plotted for the succession. Elizabeth I died at Richmond Palace on March 23, 1603, having launched England as a confident, Protestant, seafaring nation. She was succeeded by Mary Stuart's son, the Protestant James VI of Scotland, who was crowned James I of England.

Margaret Sankey

See also: Armada, Spanish; Politics and Government (Chronology); Politics and Government (Essay).

Bibliography

Brimacombe, Peter. *All the Queen's Men: The World of Elizabeth I.* New York: St. Martin's, 2000.

Hartley, T. E. *Elizabeth's Parliaments.* Manchester, UK: Manchester University Press, 1992.

Jenkins, Elizabeth. *Elizabeth the Great.* New York: Coward-McCann, 1958.

Loades, David. *Elizabeth I.* London: Hambledon and London, 2003.

English

Even though they entered the race for American colonies at a comparatively late date, the English made up for lost time by founding a number of successful colonial ventures and spreading their cultural influence and institutions throughout North America and the Caribbean. Where the English came from, where they went, and what they did when they got there was, for many decades, the only narrative of colonial American history.

Recent scholarship has fostered a renewed interest in other colonial stories, including those of Native Americans, African slaves, the Dutch, the French, and the Spanish. Still, the English, in part due to their large numbers, in part because of fortuitous historical circumstances, came to dominate the eastern half of North America before 1776. After 1776, the American empire, featuring many of the characteristics of the British Empire that preceded it, spread Anglo-American people and institutions far to the west.

English people came to what would eventually become the United States in four waves. These waves of immigration established four "culture hearths," from which distinct British identities and practices would spread out in North America. Nearly all the immigrants spoke English and shared a basic set of British legal traditions and Protestantism, but they differed in their social status and region of origin. Differences in the American setting amplified regional distinctions in speech, architecture, cuisine, and other areas.

In the 1630s, huge numbers of Puritans moved from East Anglia to Massachusetts, planting Puritan cultural imperatives, which would take root throughout the Northeast. In the decades that followed, a small number of elite royalists migrated to Virginia, bringing large numbers of rural laborers and indentured servants from the south of England. Framing the turn of the eighteenth century was a migration of people from the North Midlands and Wales to the Delaware Valley, where they established Pennsylvania, New Jersey, and Delaware. The last large influx was from the fringes of Britain. Right up until the onset of the American Revolution, thousands of immigrants from Scotland and Ireland flooded the Appalachian backcountry, displacing Native American communities.

Any effort to delineate culture in colonial America must come with the caveat that cultures evolve over time due to new influences and people's choices. Even when viewed in freeze-frame, there are areas of overlap between cultural groups. Broad generalizations are necessary to span the long period of time (from Roanoke in 1585 to Lexington in 1775) and space (from the Caribbean to Canada) covered by the English colonial experience.

British Culture in the Seventeenth Century

English colonization in North America got off to an inauspicious start. A colony funded by Sir Walter Raleigh in Roanoke disappeared, and the Jamestown colonists died in droves. The Pilgrim Separatists who lived at Plymouth were more successful, but their impact on America's popular imagination has far outstripped their actual influence.

In what has been termed the "Great Migration," tens of thousands of English Puritans left East Anglia for Massachusetts. Driven by the belief that they were God's chosen people and facing increasing persecution at home, they strove to create a perfect society in America. Their desire to live holy lives governed many aspects of early English society in Massachusetts. In accordance with their religious beliefs, their East Anglian heritage, and their middle-class social status, the English Puritans set out to build their holy city. They moved to Massachusetts in families, settled in orderly towns devoted to farming or fishing, and weeded out dissenters.

In Virginia, wealthy Cavaliers displaced by the English Civil War, along with indentured servants, established a different sort of society. Governor William Berkeley recruited well-to-do planters for the colony, rewarded them with large estates and positions of influence, and essentially crafted a rigidly hierarchical society based on plantation agriculture. The Virginia Cavaliers, nearly all of them Anglican, settled in a dispersed fashion along the Chesapeake region's rivers and grew tobacco. At the lowest level of English society were numerous English indentured servants. Most of these unfortunate individuals were young men who signed away their freedom for a period of seven years to labor in fields of Virginia. As the seventeenth century progressed, African slaves gradually replaced white indentured servants.

The Delaware Valley exhibited yet another set of English cultural traits. Quakers came from the North Midlands of England and Wales and moved to the Delaware Valley in family units, although not quite at the same rate as their neighbors in New England. Most Quakers were from the lower middle class, their proprietor, William Penn, being a notable upper-class exception. Penn's vision, his "holy experiment," influenced the region in countless ways. There was no military establishment, and commerce and agriculture existed in harmony. While not all of the colonists in the Delaware Valley were Quakers, most appreciated their values, especially their concept of inner light, a spiritual goodness implanted in every human being.

The fourth culture hearth, the Appalachian backcountry, was colonized last, by Scots, Irish, Scots-Irish, and English immigrants from other outlying areas of Britain. This last migration was gigantic, numbering more than a quarter of a million people over a half-century. Unlike the other waves of immigrants, the backcountry colonists, as a group, seem not to have viewed themselves as a chosen people or participants in a holy experiment. Most, whether Catholic, Presbyterian, or Anglican, were trying to escape terrible economic conditions at home. It is a cliché that the backcountry was a rough, violent place, populated by warriors of Celtic extraction. It is true that little government was initially established and that backcountry residents fought among themselves and against their Native American neighbors.

Mature English Colonial Societies

Each of the four culture hearths exerted influence over other new settlements. Massachusetts spawned orderly, town-based, western settlement. Puritans also left the colony—or were forced out for heretical teachings—to found and populate other colonies. Plantation agriculture, and the sort of hierarchical, slave-based society it engendered, expanded south from the Chesapeake and north from Barbados to flourish in coastal areas of North and South Carolina, with tobacco production around Albemarle Sound and rice production on the Ashley and Cooper river systems.

Even as the Delaware Valley and the Mid-Atlantic region became diverse, ethnically and economically, areas first colonized by Quakers continued to demonstrate a discernable Quaker influence; indeed, their very diversity should be viewed as the legacy of the Quakers. The backcountry settlements grew in size and influence throughout the colonial era. In some areas, this entailed conflict between established coastal authorities and more recently settled areas to the west, as happened during the Regulator crises in North and South Carolina and the Paxton Boys uprising in western Pennsylvania.

British-based cultural and political institutions emerged throughout colonial North America. English people transplanted English common law and modified it to fit their American situation. Generally speaking, colonial assemblies in the seventeenth century were weak and were expected to bend to the will of Parliament, the monarch, and royally appointed governors and councils. In the eighteenth century, following the example of the English House of Commons, the colonial lower houses claimed financial authority and power over governors and councils. American assemblies, and the colonies themselves, developed with a minimum of royal oversight. Some scholars have referred to this as a policy of "salutary" or "benign neglect."

The English and French North American empires collided in the French and Indian War (known in Europe as the Seven Years' War) from 1754 to 1763; one of the results was the removal of the French government from the colonial scene. The Ohio Valley was now fair game for the spread of English culture, much to the dismay of the Shawnee and other tribes.

In the wake of the massive global conflict, Great Britain faced crippling debt, postwar depression, and the burden of defending a vast new empire. In response, Britain attempted to rein in its colonies; these attempts were met with stubborn popular, commercial, and legislative resistance. Still, most Anglo-Americans, even on the very brink of the American War for Independence, identified themselves as English and petitioned Parliament for relief based on their rights as English people.

The regional distinctions, with their deep roots in colonial experience, lived on in the newly formed United States as separate regional cultures. The most obvious were the Yankee culture in the North and the planter culture in the South. The four broad categories of Englishness continued to exert influence into the early republic and beyond, although newly created Americans sought to craft their own distinct national identity.

Matthew Jennings

See also: Race and Ethnicity (Chronology); Race and Ethnicity (Essay).

Bibliography

Fischer, David Hackett. *Albion's Seed: Four British Folkways in America.* New York: Oxford University Press, 1989.

Middleton, Richard. *Colonial America.* 2nd ed. Oxford, UK: Blackwell, 1996.

Taylor, Alan. *American Colonies.* New York: Viking, 2001.

English Civil War

The English Civil War of 1642–1646 was fought between King Charles I of England and Parliament over fundamental questions of control of church and state. The king lost the war and was executed in 1649.

Outbreak of Civil War

Charles I succeeded to the thrones of England, Scotland, and Ireland upon the death of his father, James I, in 1625. Greatly dissatisfied with his early English Parliaments, Charles I governed England on his own, beginning in 1629, for an eleven-year period known as his personal rule. But in the summer of 1640, the king's Scottish subjects, alienated by his attempts to forcibly alter their Presbyterian Church, successfully invaded northern England and demanded a payment to withdraw. Charles I had no choice but to convene Parliament for assistance.

Those summoned to London in November 1640, at the start of what would become known as the Long Parliament, were almost unanimous in their determination to ensure that the king would never again rule without them, and they forced Charles I to agree to a number of laws that effectively limited his sovereignty. However, as the parliamentary opposition, headed by John Pym, called for greater innovations in the governance of church and state, a reaction set in among the more moderate members of the Commons and Lords. Rebellion by Catholics in Ireland in late 1641 further complicated the situation, for Parliament would not entrust the king with the command of an army to put down the rebellion.

In January 1642, Charles I tried to arrest Pym and other opposition leaders. His failed attempt demonstrated that he was willing to use force against his political opponents, and the resultant uproar in London caused the king to abandon his capital. Negotiations throughout the first half of 1642 failed to resolve the crisis.

On August 2, 1642, as recorded in the journal of the House of Lords, Parliament declared that England stood in "imminent danger . . . by reason of a malignant party prevailing with his Majesty." Both houses, therefore, had no recourse but to issue a call to arms to defend "the true Religion, the Laws and Liberties of the Kingdom, and the Power and Privilege of Parliament." Thus Parliament declared war on the king, who countered with his own call to arms at Nottingham on August 22.

Charles I was fighting to maintain not only his royal prerogatives in governing the state but also his role as supreme governor of the Church of England. He believed in the Anglican episcopate and rituals, as opposed to the Puritans, who led his parliamentary opposition and wanted to further reform the church, "root and branch." The king's followers—called royalists or, pejoratively, Cavaliers—predominated in the north, parts of the Midlands, the West Country, and Wales. The parliamentarians—derogatorily labeled rebels or Roundheads by their opponents—controlled London and its wealth, the navy, and the richer shires in the center, the east, and the southeast. Nevertheless, even after the formal declarations of hostilities, most of the English people still hoped for a negotiated settlement to avoid a fratricidal war.

In fact, neither king nor Parliament thought that the war would be protracted. Each side believed it would be victorious in the first major military encounter and would then be able to dictate peace terms to its defeated opponent. Parliament's lord general, Robert Devereux, Earl of Essex, led his forces northwest from London that fall, intent on stopping the king from marching south from Yorkshire, where he had been recruiting. The two armies, numbering about 14,000 men each, met at Edgehill in Warwickshire on October 23, 1642. Charles I was in the field, as was his cavalry commander, his 22-year-old nephew Prince Rupert, already a veteran of the Continental wars. Despite the prince's sweeping cavalry charge, the battle of Edgehill ended in a draw.

That winter, the parliamentary leaders in London and the king at his headquarters in Oxford set in motion plans for a protracted conflict, as both sides commissioned local nobles and gentry to build up regional armies. Both sides also engaged in an intense war of words, producing and distributing countless propaganda pamphlets and news sheets aimed at winning public opinion.

Campaigns of 1643–1644

Charles I's queen, Henrietta Maria, had left England in early 1642, taking with her the royal jewels, which she pawned on the Continent to raise money for her husband's cause. On her return voyage, the queen safely landed on the coast of Yorkshire in February 1643. The men and supplies she brought with her aided the northern royalists, led by William Cavendish, Marquess of Newcastle, in their struggle against the local parliamentary forces raised by Lord Ferdinando Fairfax and his son, Sir Thomas. At the end of June, the Fairfaxes were expelled from the heart of Yorkshire; the queen was able to journey south to be reunited with her husband at Oxford.

In the West Country, royalists under the command of Sir Ralph Hopton held off Sir William Waller's parliamentary forces at Lansdown, north of Bath, on July 5. On July 13, with cavalry reinforcements from Oxford, Hopton decisively defeated Waller at Roundway Down in Wiltshire. Those losses in the field left two parliamentary strongholds, Gloucester and Bristol, vulnerable to royalist attack. Rupert quickly set off to capture Bristol, which surrendered on July 26, thus giving the royalists a much-needed port and manufacturing center. Charles I besieged Gloucester in August, but a relief army under Essex forced the king to raise the siege on September 6. On their return east, the two armies had an indecisive encounter at Newbury in Berkshire on September 20 before marching off, the king to Oxford, Essex to London.

The royalist victories in 1643 had led John Pym and his colleagues to seek additional military support for their cause, just as the king was bringing back some of the English troops from Ireland to bolster his forces. Pym achieved a major coup when he negotiated an alliance with the Scots. In return, on September 25, the House of Commons subscribed to the Solemn League and Covenant, whereby they promised to adopt a Presbyterian system of church government, although not everyone in England would favor such a religious settlement. John Pym, having accomplished this last service in Parliament's cause, died on December 8.

On January 19, 1644, the Scots army crossed the border into England. A new joint executive, the Committee of Both Kingdoms, was formed in London to direct military operations in the field. The royalist north was again endangered, and the Marquess of Newcastle had to withdraw to the walled city of York, where he was besieged by three allied armies in June. Joining the Scots were the Fairfaxes, who had rebuilt their army, and the Eastern Association, led by William Montagu, Earl of Manchester, and his cavalry commander, Oliver Cromwell. The king sent Prince Rupert to the relief of York and then took the field to defeat Waller at Cropredy Bridge, north of Banbury, on June 29.

Rupert broke the siege of York by approaching from the north and surprising the besiegers, who expected a relief attempt from the west. But the prince believed his uncle wanted him to bring the enemy to battle despite his inferior numbers (18,000 versus 27,000 troops). The ensuing battle of Marston Moor, fought west of York on July 2, was one of the largest battles ever fought on English soil. After three hours of desperate struggle, the royalists were broken, with over

The Battle of Marston Moor on July 2, 1644, one of the largest and bloodiest battles ever fought on the nation's soil, was the decisive confrontation in the English Civil War. More than 4,000 men were killed on the plains of Yorkshire. *(Harris Museum and Art Gallery, Preston, Lancashire, United Kingdom//Bridgeman Art Library)*

4,000 killed. York and the north were lost to the king, and Parliament had a new hero, Cromwell, whose cavalry had played a decisive role in the allies' victory.

At this juncture, London was hopeful that an end of the war might soon be achieved. But Charles I still had his field army. In early September, after a dogged pursuit, he delivered a major blow to Parliament's lord general, Essex, at Lostwithiel in Cornwall. Subsequently, the parliamentary armies of Essex, Manchester, and Waller failed to encircle the king on his return march east. At the second battle of Newbury, on October 27, the outnumbered royalists managed to hold off their opponents until nightfall, when they marched away to the safety of Oxford. A year that had begun with high hopes for Parliament's cause ended on a triumphant note for the royalists.

The New Model Army and the End of the War

In December 1644, the House of Commons decided that its armies must be restructured to ensure victory in the field. Only after months of negotiations, however,

did the House of Lords concur with the formation of the New Model Army, to be composed of the armies of Essex, Manchester, and Waller. On April 3, 1645, these commanders were removed by the Self-Denying Ordinance, "for the discharging of the Members of both Houses from all offices, both military and civilian." The one exception made was for Cromwell, who sat in the Commons but was appointed lieutenant general of horse of the New Model Army, which was to be commanded by Sir Thomas Fairfax.

Charles I left Oxford in May and had to decide on his strategy for the new campaign season. His queen had left England for the safety of her native France, and his 14-year-old heir, Charles, prince of Wales, had been sent to the loyalist West Country. The king then fatefully decided to split his forces. He and Rupert, now commander in chief, would march north, while 3,000 of his cavalry were sent west. In the meantime, Fairfax and the New Model Army had been directed on various inconclusive missions by the Committee of Both Kingdoms. Only when the king surprised the parliamentary stronghold of Leicester in the Midlands on May 31 did the committee give Fairfax permission to proceed as he saw fit. Fairfax immediately set off in pursuit of the king's army.

On June 14, the New Model Army, numbering 14,000–17,000 men, encountered the king's 10,000 men at Naseby in Northamptonshire. Despite their inferior numbers, the seasoned royalist infantry held its own, but the parliamentary cavalry, led by Cromwell, proved to be the deciding factor. In the end, the king's army was totally broken, with over 4,000 of his infantry captured. The king, however, did escape to Wales, where he began recruiting new forces.

Fairfax was determined to bring the war to an end as quickly as possible. There was a growing war-weariness in the country, and popular self-defense forces, called Clubmen, had arisen in many locales against the depredations of both armies. The New Model Army marched west, carefully avoiding any confrontations with the Clubmen en route, and defeated the last major royalist field army at Langport in Somerset on July 10. But rather than pursue the fleeing royalists farther west, Fairfax concentrated on cutting them off by capturing a series of royalist strongholds, among them Bristol, which Prince Rupert surrendered on September 10. The war wound down that winter as the New Model Army again turned west, where Hopton surrendered the king's last forces in March 1646, but not before sending the prince of Wales out of the country. With his son safely away, Charles I surrendered himself on May 5 to the Scottish army. The civil war had come to an end.

But the long-sought peace did not bring a final resolution to the contentious questions concerning state and church in England. Instead, a more radicalized New Model Army—made up of men such as Cromwell, who wanted independent congregations—began to part ways with its nominal commander, Parliament. Fairfax remained lord general through the royalist uprisings in 1648, which he and Cromwell put down, but he played no part in the trial and execution of Charles I in January 1649. Nor would he lead the New Model Army against his former allies the Scots when they supported Charles II, which led to Fairfax's resignation in 1650. Cromwell then assumed control not only of the New Model Army but also of the English state until his death in 1658. Yet even Cromwell could not formulate a permanent form of government, and, in 1660, the Stuart monarchy was restored.

Because of distances and the lapse of time in communications, the newly founded British North American colonies played no direct role in the civil war. The Puritans of New England favored the parliamentary cause, while the royal colony of Virginia remained loyal to Charles I. The Virginia House of Burgesses even condemned the king's execution, but not until October 1649, some nine months after his death.

Florene S. Memegalos

See also: Charles I; Charles II; Cromwell, Oliver; Puritanism.

Bibliography

Clarendon, Edward Hyde, Earl of. *The History of the Rebellion and Civil Wars in England Begun in the Year 1641.* 6 vols. Edited by W. Dunn Macray. Oxford, UK: Clarendon, 1888.

Gardiner, S. R. *History of the Great Civil War, 1642–1649.* 4 vols. London: Longman, Green: 1901–1904. Reprint, London: Windrush, 1987.

Kenyon, John. *The Civil Wars of England.* London: Weidenfeld and Nicolson, 1988.

Prall, Stuart E. *The Puritan Revolution and the English Civil War.* Malabar, FL: Krieger, 2002.

Roots, Ivan. *The Great Rebellion: 1642–1660.* London: B. T. Batsford, 1966.

Wedgwood, C. V. *The King's War, 1641–1647.* London: Collins, 1958.

Enlightenment

The intellectual movement that followed the scientific revolution of the seventeenth century is known as the Enlightenment. The Enlightenment is usually understood as a primarily French movement in ideas, but there also was a Scottish and a German Enlightenment.

The major ideas of the Enlightenment embraced freedom, optimism, reason, independence, tolerance, secularization, and change. The political ideas that Enlightenment theorists propagated were those of liberty, democracy, and the sovereignty of the people. The Age of Enlightenment or Age of Reason brought to educated Europeans and their American counterparts a new worldview based upon science, reason, and Deism. Deists subscribed to a view of God as something like a watchmaker, who created the world and set it in motion, then let it run on its own laws.

The thinkers of the Enlightenment, who were known as philosophes, applied the laws of nature and science to society. The formative influences of the Enlightenment derived from the English may be found in the work of scientists Isaac Newton and Francis Bacon and philosopher John Locke. Newton and his disciples taught that the universe was a self-regulating system

The seventeenth-century English philosopher John Locke, a forerunner of the Enlightenment and the American experiment in government, advanced a political philosophy that stressed individual rights, the social contract, and limited state authority. *(Brown Brothers, Sterling, Pennsylvania)*

in which there was nothing but matter. The laws of this self-regulating universe could be discovered, and humans could exploit these to their own advantage. Lockean liberalism stressed individual rights, the social contract, and limited government; the role of government was to protect individual rights, and property was power. Democracy, however, was not a part of the Lockean system. Bacon, the father of the scientific method, stressed empiricism.

Jefferson claimed to have been most influenced by the works of these three men. Scholars of the American Enlightenment most commonly refer to it as "moderate" in the sense that the Americans did not subscribe to the more radical views of French Enlightenment thinkers such as Jean-Jacques Rousseau and even Voltaire. Rousseau was too democratic, while Voltaire was too antireligious for the American temperament.

Although the French Enlightenment thinkers did not constitute the primary influence on the American colonists, they nevertheless did have an impact. From Charles de Montesquieu, the Americans inherited the political ideas of checks and balances and the separation of powers. The American Constitution is based on these premises. The religion of Voltaire, or Deism, a natural religion based on understanding God through reason, became the religion of Jefferson and, with some modifications, Benjamin Franklin as well.

The American Enlightenment is usually dated as occurring between 1765 and 1815. Most scholars are in agreement that the American patriots were primarily sons of the Scottish rather than the French Enlightenment. The most important of the Scottish Enlightenment thinkers were David Hume, Adam Smith, Adam Ferguson, and Francis Hutcheson. Hume and Smith provided Americans with the view that the modern laissez-faire market, with its encouragement of individualistic economic practices, produced happiness for the greatest number. At the same time, the Scottish thinkers bequeathed to the Americans the ideas that individuals have rights because they are God-given. Civic morality, which was an important concept for the Americans, came from the Scottish school. Americans were also deeply influenced by the commonsense philosophy of the Scot Thomas Reid, which stated that all men were equal not because they were physically the same but because they were endowed by God with a common moral sense.

Although they read his works, Americans were not entirely in agreement with Hume because of his skepticism. However, they were great admirers of Francis Hutcheson. Hutcheson was a moral philosopher at the University of Glasgow from 1730 until his death in 1746. In his course of moral philosophy, he included a study of human nature and inquired into what constituted the greatest good and happiness of humanity, together with an account of natural law and human behavior as it was before governments existed. His major work, *A System of Moral Philosophy* (1755), dealt with contracts and rights and provided advice on how to conduct oneself as a citizen. Hutcheson argued that moral distinctions are intuitive, rather than arrived at by reason. He stressed the doctrine of the greatest happiness for the greatest number, anticipating utilitarianism. Hutcheson also believed in religious freedom, economic liberty, and the reform of representative institutions.

In addition to the Scots and the French, the Americans drew upon the ideas of the Italian jurist Cesare Beccaria, who stressed the reform of criminal law. In 1764, Beccaria published his major treatise, *On Crimes and Punishments*. In this work, he stressed common Enlightenment themes such as individual rights and the greatest happiness for the greatest number and applied them to the judicial system. He argued that no one could be proclaimed a criminal until he was found guilty, and he wrote against the death penalty as a punishment. In addition to Beccaria, the Dutch natural rights theorist Hugo Grotiu, whose views on the laws of nature and principles of civil government also influenced Jefferson. Grotius stressed man's natural rationality and sociability, two key concepts of the Enlightenment.

The works of the Swiss jurist and professor of natural and civil law J. J. Burlamaqui were also read by the Americans. He wrote *The Principles of Natural Law* (1747) and *The Principles of Political Law* (1751), in which he attempted to prove the existence of a natural law by tracing its origins to God, human reason, and moral character.

Americans relied a great deal on classical authors when forming their political system. The return to classical political theory and especially republican ideology constitutes another trait of the Enlightenment. Homer, Cato, Pliny, Seneca, Livy, and Justinian were all cited in revolutionary literature. Jefferson read the classics, but he was selective: the political histories of Rome were his preference.

A leading scholar of the American Revolution, Bernard Bailyn, argues that the British libertarian thinkers John Trenchard and Thomas Gordon were as important as Locke in providing Americans with the political ideas that founded their nation. In the 1720s and 1730s, both wrote political pamphlets in England, which were reproduced in colonial newspapers. Their major work, *Cato's Letters or Essays on Liberty, Civil and Religious, and Other Important Subjects* (1720–23) was published anonymously. Their principal ideas dealt with corruption in government. They were antiaristocratic, attacked high-church pretensions, and were critical of the way English politics functioned. They believed in civil liberties and opposed divine right monarchy and the passive obedience to government, which, they argued, must be accountable to the people. The 144 letters provide a compelling theoretical basis for freedom of conscience and freedom of speech. Virtually half the private libraries in the American colonies contained bound volumes of *Cato's Letters.*

The most representative American Enlightenment thinkers, who, unlike their European counterparts, were also practicing politicians, were Thomas Jefferson, John Adams, and Benjamin Franklin. Jefferson's pamphlet *A Summary View of the Rights of British America* (1774) was his earliest contribution to the colonial debate. In this work, Jefferson stressed many Enlightenment ideas, such as natural rights. Politically, he denied parliamentary authority over the colonies, recognizing no tie with the mother country except the king. Jefferson drafted the American Declaration of Independence with amendments by John Adams and Benjamin Franklin, linking Enlightenment principles directly to the situation in the colonies. To fight for American independence was to fight for a government based on popular consent in place of a government based on monarchy.

John Adams never wrote a comprehensive treatise of political theory or Enlightened ideology. In addition to his letters, his ideas can be found in his numerous tracts such as *Thoughts on Government* (1776) and the Novanglus papers (1774–75). Adams favored the British Enlightenment thinkers over the French, although he did read the French philosophers. From the British, he was indebted for his views on republican government, as a government "of laws, and not of men." Here Adams meant that there would be little room for abuse in the conduct of government, for the law would have precedence over men's actions. Adams came up with a doctrine he called "social happiness," meaning that the government would operate according to Newtonian science—on its own laws—and bring order and stability to society.

In addition to his dedication to science and his belief in Deism, Franklin is responsible for the worldview of American liberal ideology, in which the moral and intellectual improvement of the individual led to an increase in wealth and success for the community. In other words, the material progress of the individual and society would mean its overall moral progress.

Much of Franklin's Enlightenment ideology is contained in his *Autobiography* (composed between 1771 and 1788 and first published by his grandson William Franklin Temple in 1818). In Part II, Franklin "conceived of a project for arriving at moral perfection," a kind of scientific method for morality, in which he listed thirteen virtues: temperance, silence, order, resolution, frugality, industry, sincerity, justice, moderation, cleanliness, tranquility, chastity, and humility. These words summarize the American interpretation of the Enlightenment.

Leigh Whaley

See also: American Philosophical Society; Deism; Science; Science and Technology (Chronology).

Bibliography

Bailyn, Bernard. *The Ideological Origins of the American Revolution.* Cambridge, MA: Belknap Press, 1992.

May, Henry F. *The Enlightenment in America.* New York: Oxford University Press, 1976.

Mayer, Donald H. *The Democratic Enlightenment.* New York: G. P. Putnam's Sons, 1976.

Pole, J. R. "Enlightenment and the Politics of American Nature." In *The Enlightenment in National Context,* edited by Roy Porter and Mikulas Teich. Cambridge, UK: Cambridge University Press, 1981.

Environment and Nature

To the first Europeans who encountered, conquered, and settled it, North America appeared to be largely in a state of nature. Outside of Mexico and the American Southwest, there were few large native cities or towns. Along the Atlantic seaboard of what is now the United States and Canada, thick forests covered the land almost to the edge of the sea.

While many Native American groups farmed, their agricultural practices tended to be less intensive than European farming, giving the impression that much of the continent remained unsettled and unused. This impression contributed to European attitudes that the native inhabitants did not rightfully have possession of the continent, and, therefore, that the land could be seized and settled upon by Europeans.

Caribbean

To the first Europeans, the Americas presented a greatly varied topography and climate, as well as a vast array of flora and fauna. The Caribbean, first encountered and settled by Spaniards in the early sixteenth century, consists of small and large islands, many quite mountainous. Most of these tropical islands enjoy abundant rainfall and, at first encounter, were heavily covered in rain forest, although a few were desert-like, owing to the vagaries of the trade winds.

The Caribbean islands are roughly divided into two groups: the Greater Antilles, consisting of the four large islands of Cuba, Hispaniola (the Dominican Republic and Haiti), Jamaica, and Puerto Rico, and the Lesser Antilles, including dozens of smaller islands. The latter can be subdivided into the southerly Windward Islands (from Guadeloupe south to Trinidad) and the northerly Leeward Islands (from the Virgin Islands

south to Montserrat); these names come from their relative exposure to the predominant trade winds.

Within just a few decades of the arrival of the Spanish, the large native population that inhabited the Caribbean was almost completely eliminated. Some natives died at the hands of Spanish conquerors, but most were overcome by the diseases the Europeans inadvertently brought with them.

By the eighteenth century, many of the smaller islands—as well as Jamaica and the western half of Hispaniola—had been seized by the British, French, and Dutch. On the smaller islands, much of the native forest was stripped away to make room for sugar plantations. On the larger islands, large parts were also converted from rain forest to monoculture.

Mexico and the American Southwest

Spain was also the original conqueror and colonial master on the North American mainland in the regions now known as Mexico and the American Southwest. This vast realm, encompassing roughly 1.5 million square miles, presented an extraordinary diversity of climate and topography to the early Spanish conquistadores, missionaries, colonial administrators, and settlers. Along the Gulf of Mexico, there is a broad, flat plain, roughly 100 miles in width, that eventually gives way to the Sierra Madre Orientale mountain range. This coastal plain is tropical and subtropical in climate, and it is quite humid and rainy. Unlike many of the Caribbean islands, however, the Europeans found this region to be largely devoid of thick forest and covered instead in heavy scrub and low-lying bush. Much of this area was later converted by the Spanish to sugar, tobacco, and indigo plantations, as well as to cattle ranches.

The interior of Mexico, where the majority of the pre-Columbian native population lived, consists of a vast highland valley, several hundred miles in length, several dozen miles in width, and mostly above a mile in altitude. The valley experiences a subtropical climate and is semi-arid. The Aztecs and earlier civilizations in the Valley of Mexico utilized extensive irrigation systems to make up for the lack of water, and the Spanish followed suit.

Northward from the Valley of Mexico, the topography becomes more broken, with long mountain ranges, stretching largely north to south, interspersed with river valleys, the most notable being the one formed by the Rio Grande. In addition, the northern stretches of New Spain, as the country's mainland North American colony was called, were exceptionally arid and presented desert-like conditions. Much of the region experienced—and continues to experience—less than ten inches of rain annually, with frequent extended droughts.

Atlantic Seaboard

With the exception of Florida, which was administered by the Spanish and experiences a climate similar to the Caribbean (although its marshy south and flat, forested north were quite different in appearance from the Caribbean islands), the Atlantic seaboard of North America bore the closest resemblance, in both climate and flora, to Western Europe. The climate ranged from temperate to continental and included abundant precipitation, although temperatures at the same latitude tended to be colder in North America than in Western Europe. And while individual species varied, both areas had thick forests of deciduous and evergreen trees.

The topography was also not all that different. Again, while the specifics varied, the general contours were recognizable. Numerous rivers ran from interior, relatively low mountain ranges to the sea. In Pennsylvania, New York, and southern New England, there were wide river valleys, surrounded by low-lying mountains. To the south, the many rivers flowed from the interior Appalachian Mountains, across the Piedmont, a wide flat plateau, to the coastal plain, or tidewater, region.

There were, however, significant differences. For one thing, North America is much colder than most of Western Europe, since it does not enjoy the warming effect that the tropical waters of the Gulf Stream bring to the eastern North Atlantic. Latitude for latitude, temperatures differ enormously between Western Europe and the eastern part of North America. The Pilgrims, for example, were shocked by, and unprepared for, the severity of their first New England winter. They had expected milder weather, since Plymouth, Massachusetts, where they first settled, is at the same latitude as northern Spain, which enjoys an almost subtropical climate and is more than 600 miles south of the region around Plymouth, England, from which they originally hailed.

While the thick forests of eastern North America appeared similar to those of Europe, their extensiveness awed the newcomers. Over the millennia, and particularly since the late Middle Ages, Western Europeans had cut down much of their forests, leaving large patches here and there but nothing like the blanket of trees that stretched endlessly from the sea to the mountains and beyond in the New World. Gradually, the settlers cut back the forests of the Atlantic seaboard, but the task was so daunting that early farmers merely girdled the trees, stripping them of bark so that they would die and their leaves would fall off, allowing sunlight to reach the crops planted amid the dead trunks.

Canada was even more extreme. While the St. Lawrence Valley of Quebec, where the French first settled in the early seventeenth century, was well watered and enjoyed summers long enough for European-style agriculture, its climate was colder than any experienced in Western Europe outside of Scandinavia. It was also thickly covered in forests of maple and evergreen.

As a result, the French were occupied largely in fur trapping and trading with the natives. Settlers in the area did not engage in widespread agriculture until well into the eighteenth century.

Views About Nature

Several impressions struck the earliest Europeans to explore North America. The first was its appearance as a wilderness. Christopher Columbus and other Spaniards who first encountered the islands of the Caribbean were so amazed by their abundant flora and fauna and so enamored by their gentle tropical climate that the explorers believed they had encountered some kind of lost Eden. By contrast, Hernando Cortéz and the conquistadores of New Spain did not encounter a wilderness at all, but a thickly settled, intensively farmed valley, punctuated by numerous towns and cities. They had no illusions that they had found a landscape still in a state of nature.

The French and English who first settled North America, however, believed they had encountered just such a wilderness. For one thing, the native population was much more sparsely settled than Europeans were in their home continent. Eastern woodland Native Americans engaged in slash-and-burn agriculture. That is, they would burn down a section of forest, plant their crops for a time, and—when the soil was played out—move to a new section of forest to repeat the cycle. This, of course, meant that large portions of the countryside were either not farmed or in recovery from an earlier farming cycle. In either case, they appeared as if they were not being used or had been abandoned, an appearance contributed to by the fact that the native population was in decline, having been decimated by European diseases.

These factors led English settlers to believe that much of the countryside was theirs for the taking. In this, and in their belief that the regions they were encountering were still in a total state of nature, they were mistaken. Even where the forests remained, they had been affected by the native peoples, who often burned off areas to form meadows for animals, making game easier to hunt.

Another impression the earliest English settlers had was one of abundance. In this, they were not mistaken. The forests were thick with game throughout the Atlantic seaboard region. The fishing grounds off the coast were so rich that European ships had been sailing thousands of miles to reach them as early as the mid-sixteenth century. Early Puritan chroniclers talk about sea coves so full of lobsters one could walk across on their backs and rivers dense with fish. The thick forests, while a bane to farmers, offered seemingly unlimited building material, fuel, and ship stores.

At the same time, however, many early European settlers were terrified by the untamed wilderness at their doorsteps, seeing it as a dangerous landscape, both physically and morally. The wilderness was easy to get lost in and full of predatory creatures, and the climate could kill, especially in the mid-Atlantic, New England, and Canadian colonies.

The wilderness was also a terrifying place in moral terms. Unlike contemporary Americans, European settlers—especially the Puritans—saw a state of nature as a place where the devil lurked. Entering that realm exposed one not only to physical dangers but to the chance that one might be morally corrupted as well. Bolstering that belief was the behavior of the Native American, who appeared to live in a sinful state of nature, where false gods were worshipped, bodies were exposed, and sexuality was freer than was considered moral by Europeans.

It would take a century or two before European settlers of eastern North America—now citizens of an independent United States—would come to embrace nature, seeing in the frontier experience a unique identity for themselves.

James Ciment

See also: Agriculture; Bartram Family.

Bibliography

Cronon, William. *Changes in the Land: Indians, Colonists, and the Ecology of New England.* New York: Hill & Wang, 1983.

Merchant, Carolyn. *The Columbia Guide to American Environmental History.* New York: Columbia University Press, 2002.

Whitney, Gordon G. *From Coastal Wilderness to Fruited Plain: A History of Environmental Change in Temperate North America, 1500 to the Present.* New York: Cambridge University Press, 1994.

Equiano, Olaudah (1745–1797)

In 1789, the English reading public had their first opportunity to read an account of slavery from the perspective of a former slave in the American colonies, Olaudah Equiano. He described the terror of capture, the horror of the Middle Passage, and the aspirations of the enslaved for freedom.

Equiano was born in 1745 into the Ibo tribe in the prosperous agricultural village of Isseke in what is now Nigeria. Slave traders captured Equiano, along with his sister, when he was only 11. After several months' travel, during which time he was traded multiple times and separated from his sister, he arrived at the coast and was sold to European slave traders. Equiano then endured the horrors of the Middle Passage across the Atlantic Ocean.

After a few days on the West Indian island of Barbados, he was taken to Virginia, where he was sold to a tobacco planter named Campbell. In 1757, Michael Pascal, an English naval officer, purchased the 12-year-old and renamed him Gustavus Vassa after a sixteenth-century Swedish king.

Equiano accompanied Pascal with English forces in their conflict against France in the French and Indian War, participating in the successful 1758 siege of Louisbourg, a fortress on Cape Breton Island in Canada. Besides becoming a skilled sailor, while a slave for Pascal, Equiano also learned to read and write and was baptized in the Church of England. In 1763, Pascal sold Equiano to Robert King, a Quaker slave trader living on Montserrat in the West Indies. King permitted Equiano not only to earn money but also to invest in trading voyages between the West Indies and Geor-

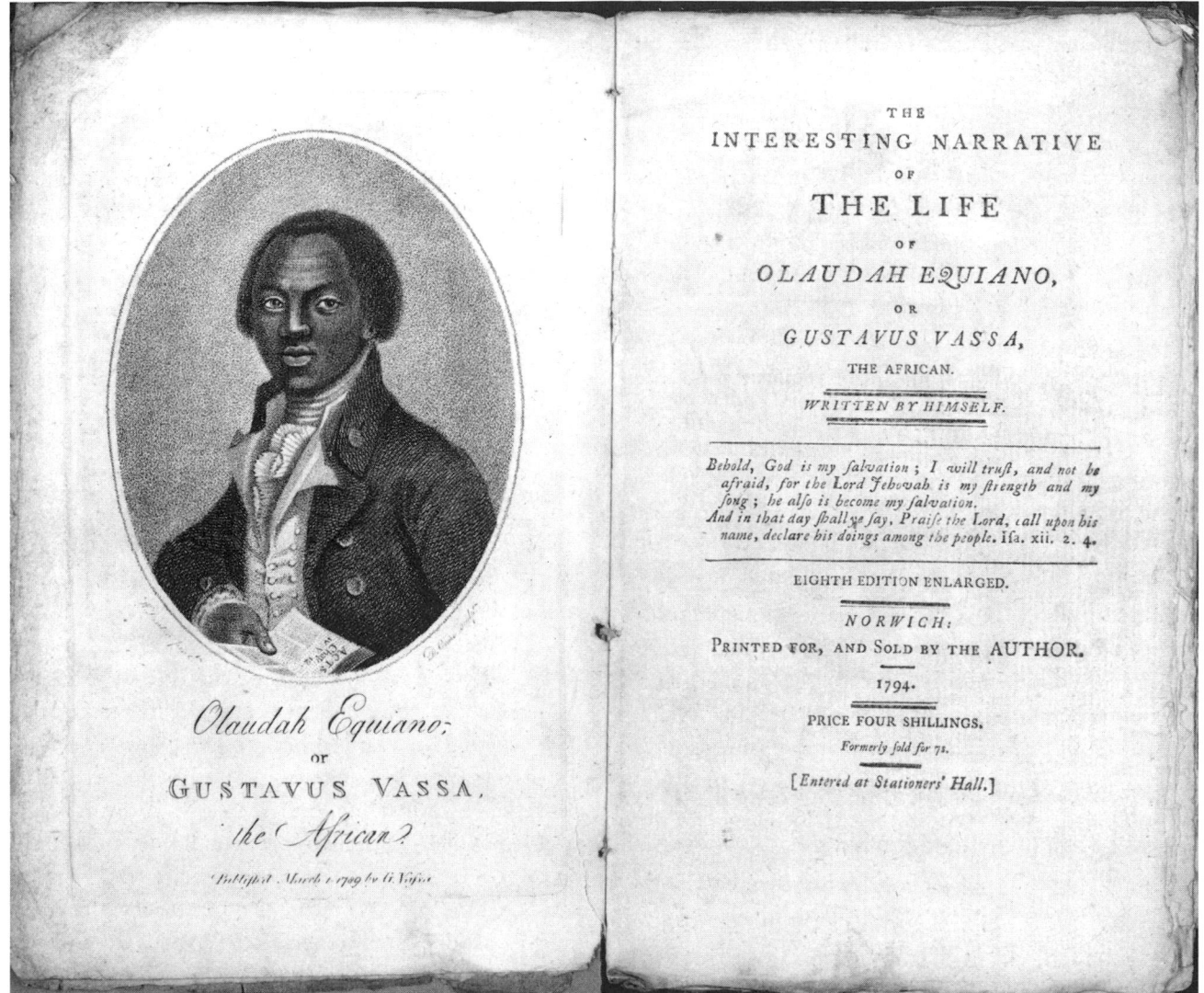

The Interesting Narrative of the Life of Olaudah Equiano, or Gustavus Vassa, the African (1789) was a first-hand account of his capture by slavers, the Middle Passage, and ten years of enslavement. Equaino became a prominent figure in the English antislavery movement. *(Library of Congress, LC-USZ62-54026)*

gia and South Carolina. In three years, he earned enough to buy his freedom.

Equiano continued to work for King for a couple of years before returning to London in 1768. Over the next three decades, he continued to travel. From the Arctic (where he participated in a quest to find a Northwest Passage) to Turkey, Genoa, Spain, Nicaragua, Pennsylvania, New York, and England, Equiano saw much of the Atlantic and Mediterranean worlds. In those locales, he held a variety of jobs. He was a hairdresser, a merchant, a personal servant, an author, and a lecturer.

Although a free man, Equiano only slowly took up the antislavery cause. For two years, he worked with Robert King in the slave trade, and, in the mid-1770s, he was an overseer on a slave plantation in Nicaragua. The brutality he had experienced and facilitated, along with a profound spiritual conversion in 1774, led Equiano to seek ways first to ameliorate the condition of slaves and then to attack the slave trade and slavery itself.

After the Anglican Church rejected his offer to serve as a missionary to Africa in 1779, Equiano took up his pen against slavery. He published letters and reviews critical of proslavery advocates, particularly West Indian planter James Tobin, challenging Tobin's assertions of black inferiority. Equiano was briefly involved in a project to relocate poor blacks from

England in Sierra Leone, and, in 1788, he submitted an antislavery petition to the queen. He came to advocate interracial marriage as a solution to the multitude of problems associated with differences of color. This was not just a rhetorical effort. Equiano married Susan Cullen, an Englishwoman, in 1792, and the couple had two daughters.

Yet it was his 1789 autobiography that made Equiano a truly influential figure in the antislavery crusade. Entitled *The Interesting Narrative of the Life of Olaudah Equiano, or Gustavus Vassa, the African. Written by Himself,* the book was part spiritual narrative, part adventure tale, and part travel account. Most importantly, it was a powerful indictment of the slave trade and slavery, drawing upon his experiences as both a victim and one who, for a time, contributed to the horrors of the pernicious labor system. Before his death in 1797, Equiano's autobiography became a bestseller. Going through eight editions in England, the book was translated and appeared in five other nations. For eight years, Equiano traveled throughout the British Isles campaigning against slavery and selling his book, and his efforts attracted support for the growing campaign to end the English slave trade.

Besides his becoming one of the most effective antislavery voices in England, Equiano's autobiography became the prototype of a new literary genre, the slave narrative, which became very important in America. By the time of the American Civil War, there were, including Frederick Douglass's classic *Narrative of the Life of Frederick Douglass,* over a hundred such narratives. These works told of a cruel system of bondage and stood as testimony to the widespread urge for freedom among slaves.

Larry Gragg

See also: Slave Trade; Slavery, African American. *Document:* On Being Brought from Africa to America (early 1770s).

Bibliography

Allison, Robert J. "Olaudah Equiano: An African in Slavery and Freedom." In *The Human Tradition in Colonial America,* edited by Ian K. Steele and Nancy L. Rhoden. Wilmington, DE: Scholarly Resources, 1999.

Equiano, Olaudah. *The Interesting Narrative of the Life of Olaudah Equiano, Written by Himself.* Edited by Robert J. Allison. Boston: Bedford/St. Martin's, 1995.

Gates, Henry Louis, Jr., ed. *The Classic Slave Narratives.* New York: New American Library, 1987.

Erie

Almost no documentary evidence exists concerning the Erie people. Scholars have had to reconstruct their culture using a combination of archaeological information and characteristics of nearby, linguistically related tribes, such as the Huron and the peoples of the Iroquois League—the Cayuga, Seneca, Onondaga, Oneida, and Mohawk.

Until the middle of the seventeenth century, the Erie lived along the shore of Lake Erie between the present-day cities of Buffalo, New York, and Erie, Pennsylvania. The Five Nations Iroquois, the Huron, the Erie, and a handful of tribes belonging to other language groups seem to have developed out of an Iroquois culture centered in southern Ontario. The Erie's tribal history is closely intertwined with those of other Iroquoian-speaking peoples.

When the French became aware of their presence in the early seventeenth century, the Erie were a loose confederacy of three villages centered in present-day New York State. Like other Iroquois, the Erie constructed longhouses, practiced corn agriculture in semipermanent settlements, and managed to build up a sizable population, perhaps between 8,000 and 12,000 by the 1640s. This figure is based on French estimates placing Erie military strength between 2,000 and 3,000 warriors. As in other Native American cultures in the area, Erie men were responsible for hunting and warfare, and women seem to have been the primary farmers.

The destruction of the Erie people as a distinct culture has its roots in the complex pattern of warfare and resource competition that had begun before European colonization and disease, but these latter factors accelerated the tribe's demise. In the seventeenth century, a series of devastating wars erupted as tribes competed for access to European trade in furs, firearms, and other goods. Iroquoian-speaking peoples also engaged in "mourning wars." In a typical mourning war, warriors took up arms to take captives in an effort to seek revenge for or to replace deceased kin. This sort of warfare was intended to restore balance and harmony by offering condolence to the aggrieved party. This ancient practice took on new meaning as disease repeatedly swept through Iroquois country, placing new strains on the system, as all of the Iroquoian speakers sought to replace a large number of relatives. Two particularly devastating epidemics occurred in 1637 and 1639–41.

The stakes also rose as Europeans became involved in the region. Between 1643 and 1647, the western Iroquois battled the Hurons annually, resulting in heavy casualties. During the middle of the seventeenth century, wars became longer-lasting and more deadly. In the 1640s, the Iroquois systematically destroyed the Huron confederacy, killing hundreds of people, adopting others into their confederacy, and sending thousands of refugees into the Great Lakes region. By 1649, the remaining Hurons had been defeated or dispersed. Other groups dispersed in like fashion were the Petun by 1650, the Neutral Nation by 1651, and the Wenro by 1638.

In the 1650s, the Iroquois turned their attention toward the Erie, with disastrous results for the latter. The Iroquois had obtained firearms and become skilled in their use. By contrast, the more isolated Eries were poorly armed. As Iroquois demand for furs and captives increased, the Five Nations began to attack the Erie, whose significant population, combined with their linguistic and cultural similarities to the Five Nations, must have made them ideal candidates for adoption. Additionally, Erie villages were situated in such a way that Iroquois wanting to reach hunting territories in Ohio and the Great Lakes had to travel through them.

A concerted campaign against the Erie commenced in 1654, and, by 1657, they had ceased to exist as a distinct political entity. Some individual Eries lived among the Five Nations, while others dispersed, perhaps reconstituting themselves as part of the Westo tribe of the Carolinas. One group of Eries did manage to survive until they surrendered to the Senecas in the 1680s.

The Erie's history demonstrates the disastrous consequences of colonization for some Native American groups and the rising power of the Iroquois confederacy during the seventeenth century. Eries also participated in the Iroquois settlement of the Ohio River Valley in the early decades of the eighteenth century.

Matthew Jennings

See also: Native American–European Conflict; Native American–European Relations; Native Americans.

Bibliography

McConnell, Michael N. "Erie." In *Encyclopedia of North American Indians*, edited by Frederick E. Hoxie. Boston: Houghton Mifflin, 1996.

Richter, Daniel K. *The Ordeal of the Longhouse: The Peoples of the Iroquois League in the Era of European Colonization.* Chapel Hill: University of North Carolina, 1992.

Exploration

Sustained European exploration to the North American continent began in the late fifteenth century. At that time, Western European nations began sending expeditions to the North and South American continents. The most important European objectives in what they called the New World included finding specie, converting Native Americans to Christianity, growing crops for export (which depended on the exploitation of the labor of Native Americans and Africans), developing new markets for European goods, and establishing permanent European settlements in the Americas.

The first people to arrive in North America were hunters from Asia searching for game. Between 40,000 and 20,000 years ago, they crossed into Alaska from Siberia via a land bridge that spanned the Bering Strait at the time. By the time Christopher Columbus arrived in the New World in 1492, between 7 million and 18 million native people lived in the part of North America north of Mexico, with twice as many living in the rest of North America. Rather than a virgin land, pre-Columbian North America was a continent with numerous, complex indigenous societies.

Christopher Columbus was not the first European to arrive in North America. Norsemen are believed to have visited and settled present-day Newfoundland, Baffin Island, and Labrador sometime in the eleventh century. The first European thought to have sighted part of the North American continent was Bjarni Herjolfsson in 986. Leif Eriksson, another Norseman, landed in Newfoundland in 1000. The Norse are not credited with the Old World's discovery of North America, however, since settlements did not mark the beginning of sustained contact between the Americas and Europe.

The Portuguese and the British also claim to have sent out western expeditions between 1431 and 1492, which may have led to other European sightings of or landings in the Americas before Columbus. The Portuguese even argue that João Fernandes of the Azores landed in the Americas shortly before Columbus, but this account has not been corroborated. In addition, the British claim that British fishing ships from Bristol began fishing along the Newfoundland coast as early as 1482.

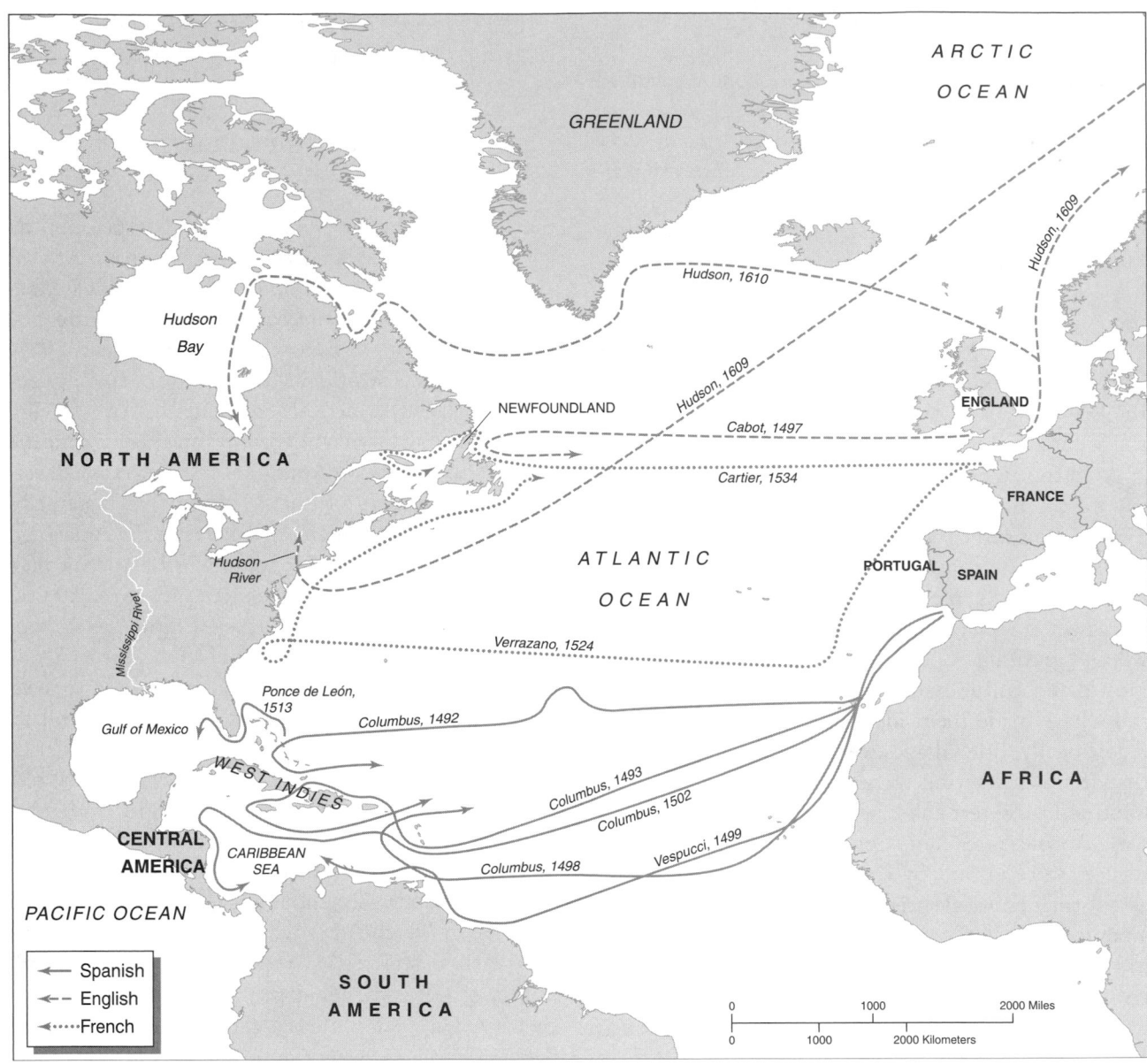

Atlantic Exploration, 1492–1609. During this period, Spanish, English, and French explorers charted various routes across the Atlantic Ocean. The Spanish largely concentrated on routes to the Caribbean and South America, while the English and French focused on routes to the North American mainland. *(Carto-Graphics)*

Even if the British, Portuguese, and Scandinavians sighted and visited the Americas before Columbus, several qualities distinguish Columbus's expeditions from all earlier ventures. One difference is the royal backing Columbus received. Moreover, unlike the small fishing expeditions of the British and Scandinavians, Columbus's expeditions were carefully planned and documented so that later European adventurers could replicate them. Finally, another major difference was that news of Columbus's voyages spread rapidly throughout Europe, while news of the earlier expeditions had not.

Christopher Columbus's arrival on one of the outer islands of the present-day Bahamas—which he named San Salvador but which the local inhabitants, the Tainos, referred to as Guanahaní—on October 12, 1492, marked the beginning of sustained contact between Europe and the Americas. Columbus never realized the vast impact that his New World expeditions had. When he died in 1506, he thought that he had simply landed in parts of the Asian continent.

The writings of Amerigo Vespucci, an Italian merchant who wrote about his two voyages to South America in 1499 and from 1501 to 1502 as part of Spanish and Portuguese expeditions, helped popularize the idea of the discovery of a "New World." Amerigo Vespucci, unlike Columbus, believed that Columbus had discovered a continent between Europe and Asia previously unknown to Europeans and the rest of the world.

Spanish Exploration in North America

Among the earliest Spanish expeditions to the North American mainland were Juan Ponce de Léon's expeditions in 1512–1513 and 1521 and Pánfilo de Narváez's in 1528. Both expeditions began their journey in present-day Florida. Ponce de Léon's expedition, although often portrayed as carried out in search of a fountain of youth, was, in fact, in search of gold and slaves. Ponce de Léon was not well received by the native peoples he met, and he died in 1521 after having engaged in battle with a group of natives.

Narváez's 1528 expedition from Santo Domingo to the Gulf Coast of North America in search of gold was even more ill-fated. Some 600 men were reduced to just 80 after a series of shipwrecks stranded them on the Texas coast. An arduous overland journey back to Mexico killed off all but four members of the original expedition.

They were received quite differently, at least through part of their travels, than Ponce de Léon's expeditions had been. No doubt, part of the reason was that this small band of explorers could not risk making enemies of the native peoples they met, as the larger Ponce de Léon expedition could. According to one of the expedition members, Álvar Núñez Cabeza de Vaca,

The innovative cylindrical projections of Flemish cartographer Gerardus Mercator in the latter half of the sixteenth century, collected in his landmark *Atlas* (1595), coincided with the peak of early European exploration. *(The Stapleton Collection/ Bridgeman Art Library)*

the Native Americans he and his fellows met as they traveled through Texas and on to Mexico regarded the Europeans as godlike people or "children of the sun."

Another Spaniard who visited the North American mainland in search of gold was Hernando de Soto, who traveled through the U.S. Southeast from 1539 to 1542. De Soto and his men began their expedition in Florida, and they saw the Savannah River, the southern Appalachians, the Gulf of Mexico, the Mississippi River, and parts of eastern Oklahoma during their travels. Having read the accounts of earlier Spanish expeditions, de Soto knew that some Native Americans regarded the Spanish as godlike. He tried to use this knowledge to his advantage upon encountering new groups of native peoples, claiming that he and his men were also "children of the sun." This strategy proved of little advantage to de Soto, as he and his men meant resistance from Creeks, Choctaws, and Chickasaws they encountered during their travels. De Soto responded with a brutal campaign of destruction and murder.

One of the reasons that the Spaniards faced resistance from native peoples was because they carried weapons with them in their expeditions to find gold and slaves for the Spanish Crown. This militaristic approach often made the very first encounters between native peoples and the Spanish explorers especially violent ones.

Besides using a militaristic approach, the Spanish and later Europeans were able to conquer the indigenous peoples they encountered largely through the diseases brought from Europe, which proved deadly to many natives. Native Americans did not have antibodies to protect them from smallpox, influenza, and other illnesses. In some cases, whole communities were completely wiped out by these diseases, the diseases sometimes reaching native communities even before Europeans did.

The Spanish also sent expeditions to the New World to establish settlements. In 1565, they established St. Augustine in Florida. In 1568, Spanish Jesuit missionaries set up missions in Georgia and South Carolina. And in the early 1570s, the Spanish tried and failed to establish a mission in Virginia. In addition to Spanish Jesuits, Spanish Franciscan missionaries also explored the North American mainland. Above all, Franciscan missionaries came to convert the native peoples to Christianity and to use them as laborers for the colonies the Europeans hoped to establish. After Juan de Oñate's successful establishment of a settlement in present-day New Mexico in 1598, Spanish Franciscan missionaries soon arrived and converted many eastern Pueblos to Christianity.

English Exploration in North America

The earliest English expedition to the North American mainland was John Cabot's expedition to find a Northwest Passage to the Indies. Cabot was an Italian whose actual name was Giovanni Caboto. He landed on Newfoundland in 1497 and claimed it for England. The Spanish argued, however, that the Treaty of Tordesillas, which essentially divided ownership of the New World between Spain and Portugal, meant the territory Cabot claimed actually belonged to Spain. Despite these Spanish claims, the English continued to send expeditions to the New World.

John Cabot died during his second voyage to North America. In 1508, his son Sebastian also sailed for England in search of a Northwest Passage to the Indies. Sebastian Cabot sailed along the coastline of North America from Cape Hatteras to near the Arctic Circle, but he, too, failed to find a Northwest Passage. For almost seventy years, the English monarchy sponsored no voyages to the New World. Not until Martin Frobisher's expeditions, again seeking a Northwest Passage in 1576, 1577, and 1578, did the English monarchy seriously begin to sponsor New World ventures again. In 1578 and 1580, the English sent two more expeditions to the New World. These expeditions were different from the Cabots' and Frobisher's, because they were colonizing expeditions. The 1578 expedition was led by Humphrey Gilbert, the 1580 expedition by Walter Raleigh. Both failed because of a lack of supplies and England's war engagements back home.

Between 1497 and the early sixteenth century, the English did participate in smaller ventures in the New World. During this time, the British and Portuguese formed an alliance to explore North America, an alliance that yielded little benefit for either. These largely fishing expeditions were made up primarily of sailors and merchants from Bristol, England, although the expeditions were often led by Portuguese pilots. Small business ventures rather than large national ventures, these voyages are important because they were the first contacts between Europeans and native peoples in the northeastern part of the North American continent.

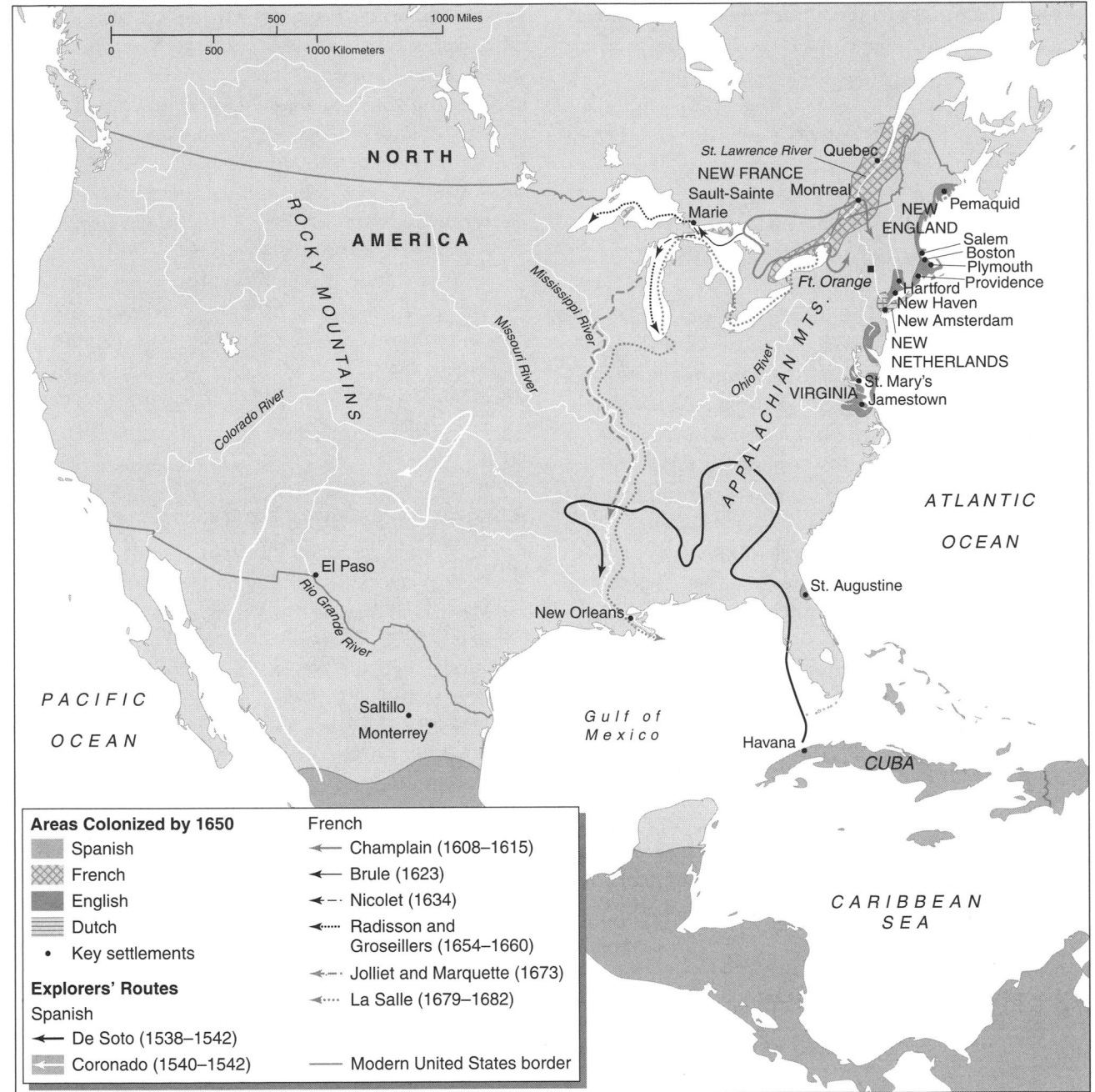

North American Exploration, 1500–1700. While the British settled the Atlantic seaboard, the interior of North America was largely explored by the French and Spanish. The above map shows the routes and dates of major European expeditions that explored the continent in the sixteenth and seventeenth centuries. *(Carto-Graphics)*

In many ways, the immense success of Spanish exploratory and Catholic religion expeditions in the New World in the early sixteenth century convinced the English that they had to increase their own colonization efforts. The English wanted to counter the Spanish Catholic influence in the New World with their Protestant influence, and they also wanted to be able to compete economically and politically with the Spaniards.

The establishment of the first permanent English settlement in Jamestown in 1607 offers an example of how the English planned to settle the New World. The English plan was to have the Virginia colony produce enough foodstuffs and other raw materials for itself and additional food and materials for export to England, in exchange for which the colonists would receive clothing and other goods. England's colonization plan was not particularly successful because the English colonists could trade with local Native Americans in order to obtain food and other goods.

Dutch Exploration in North America

Like the English, the Dutch viewed the success of the Spanish in the New World as a threat, and they, too, refused to acknowledge Spanish claims to all of North America. Unlike the English and Spanish, however, Dutch expeditions to the New World focused more on commerce than on setting up colonies.

During most of the seventeenth century, the Dutch were regarded as the most successful nation then engaged in world commercial trade. Eventually, Holland did establish a colonial presence in the New World in what is today's Delaware, New Jersey, Pennsylvania, New York, and Connecticut. Henry Hudson, an Englishman sailing for the Dutch East India Company, landed in this region in 1609.

Hudson had intended to visit Captain John Smith in Virginia, but he was blown off course and landed in the present-day mid-Atlantic region. He sailed the river that came to be named for him for 150 miles before turning back to England. Because Holland was not really interested in colonization, it eventually let its claims in North America shrink to a few settlements and ports on the Hudson River.

French Exploration in North America

French exploration to the New World began with the expedition of Giovanni da Verrazano in 1524. Verrazano also hoped to find a Northwest Passage to China, like many other explorers before and after him; however, his expedition landed in North Carolina. He then sailed north another four months, eventually spending most of his time along the Maine coast. In 1534, Jacques Cartier also set sail with the hopes of finding a Northwest Passage to China. His expedition reached Newfoundland and other nearby territories.

In 1535, the French monarchy once again sent Cartier on an expedition to discover a Northwest Passage to the East. On this expedition, Cartier explored the Labrador coast and came upon the North American waterway now known as the St. Lawrence River. Navigating upstream, he found two large native towns, Stadacona (present-day Quebec) and Hochelaga (present-day Montreal). In 1541, Cartier once again sailed to the North American continent; this time he brought with him hundreds of colonists, whose arrival did not sit well with the Stadaconans.

Another French expedition, this one led by Jean-François de La Rocque, Sieur de Roberval, sailed for North America in 1542. Roberval's expedition set up a colony of 200 colonists in Newfoundland. These two colonizing expeditions failed due to French encroachment on Native American lands, which led to some French colonists being killed by the natives. The spread of scurvy among the colonists and a lack of food supplies also contributed to the failure of the colonies.

The French also attempted to settle in other parts of the North American continent. A Huguenot colony had been set up in Florida in the sixteenth century, but the Spanish destroyed it in 1565. By the mid-sixteenth century, the French monarchy had lost interest in sponsoring expeditions to North America. Due in part to war back in France, the French turned their attention to domestic matters. In the 1580s, however, French interests in the New World were once again rekindled because of their interests in exploiting the fur and fishing trades in the areas around Newfoundland.

In 1603, the French monarchy gave Pierre de Gua, Sieur de Monts, the right to settle La Cadie (Acadia). The pilot of de Monts's expedition was Samuel Champlain. This expedition established a colony along the Bay of Fundy. However, the colonists soon succumbed to disease and the cold of winter and abandoned the site. They eventually founded the first permanent French settlement, which they called Port Royal.

Champlain launched a second expedition to the North American continent in 1608. He decided to establish a settlement on the St. Lawrence River instead of in Acadia, because he realized that the fur trade along the St. Lawrence would help sustain a colony. Champlain established Quebec on the banks of the St. Lawrence River, where the native village of Stadacona was located. Champlain did not settle down in Quebec, however; he was too busy in his continued search for a Northwest Passage to the East, visiting the Ottawa River, the Georgian Bay of Lake Huron, and the Iroquois (Richelieu) River.

Conclusion

While European exploration in the area of North America north of Mexico did not yield the Northwest Passage to the East that so many European countries—France, England, the Netherlands, and Spain—sought, it did lead to the establishment of trading networks, permanent European colonies, and the exchange of ideas between the native peoples of the New World and Europeans. Yet relations between these two groups were also often volatile, with Native Americans attacking European colonies. Often, this was in response to European encroachment, often backed by armed might, which was driven by the ongoing search for riches, land, labor, and souls.

Lisa Y. Ramos

See also: Boone, Daniel; Cabot, John; Cabrillo, Juan Rodríguez; Cartier, Jacques; Columbus, Christopher; Coronado, Francisco Vázquez de; De Soto, Hernando; Drake, Sir Francis; Hakluyt, Richard; Hudson, Henry; Humboldt, Alexander von; Jolliet, Louis; La Salle, René Robert Cavelier, Sieur de; Maps and Surveys; Marquette, Jacques; Menéndez de Avilés, Pedro; Oñate, Juan de; Ponce de León, Juan; Raleigh, Sir Walter; Tordesillas, Treaty of (1494); Verrazano, Giovanni da; Vespucci, Amerigo. *Documents:* Columbus's Letter Announcing His Discoveries in the New World (1493); John Cabot's Discovery of North America (1497); Marquette's Travels on the Mississippi (1673).

Bibliography

Axtell, James. *Beyond 1492: Encounters in Colonial North America.* New York: Oxford University Press, 1992.

———. *The Invasion Within: The Contest of Cultures in Colonial North America.* New York: Oxford University Press, 1985.

Gleach, Frederic W. *Powhatan's World and Colonial Virginia: A Conflict of Cultures.* Lincoln: University of Nebraska Press, 1997.

Hussey, W. D. *Discovery, Expansion and Empire.* Cambridge, UK: Cambridge University Press, 1954.

Johnson, Donald. *La Salle: A Perilous Odyssey from Canada to the Gulf of Mexico.* New York: Cooper Square, 2002.

Nobles, Gregory H. *American Frontiers: Cultural Encounters and Continental Conquest.* New York: Hill and Wang, 1997.

Sale, Kirkpatrick. *The Conquest of Paradise: Christopher Columbus and the Columbian Legacy.* New York: Alfred A. Knopf, 1992.

Family

The role of the family was central to European society throughout the early modern period. For many people, self-identity and government were determined by their family rather than by their nation or country. Although national and religious differences had their impacts on family life, certain aspects of family structure were consistent among different countries and religions. These aspects were then transplanted to the North American colonies. While early settlement had some disruptive effects on the traditional European family structure, it still was predominantly intact at the time of the American Revolution.

Most seventeenth- and eighteenth-century families were part of larger households. These larger households included a nuclear family of father, mother, and children at the core. They also might include persons from what today would be considered the extended family, such as grandparents, and the children of deceased siblings of the parents, as well as step- and half-children from previous marriages where a spouse had died. In addition, the colonial household might include non-family members. In the countryside, this might include farm laborers and household servants, both child and adult. In the cities, additional household members might be servants and apprentices. The household then functioned as an economic unit, consuming as one, and producing what it needed for its own purposes and for sale on the market.

Family Members

The household was represented legally, financially, and politically by the head of the household. In most cases, the head was the husband, father, or master. In the case of his death, this position could be taken by his wife or by an oldest son. If the household could not financially survive, it was dissolved. The second member of the household was usually the wife. She ensured that all members of the household were fed and clothed.

Ideally, the husband and wife formed a united pair, sharing responsibilities and leadership roles. They also worked to provide fair treatment and support for all members of their household. That this ideal did not always exist is demonstrated by court records on both sides of the Atlantic. Husbands and wives took each other to court for lack of material support, for beating, for infidelity, and various other causes.

The next in order were underage children. Their parents were expected to provide them with food, shelter, and some form of religious upbringing. They were also expected to provide them with some means of survival as adults, whether through apprenticeships, education, or inheritance. Again, ideals and reality were not always the same. If their parents were in debt, children could be bound out as indentured servants to provide support for themselves or for their families. In some cases, children were abandoned outright.

Other members of the household are harder to define. Grown children, both single and married, sometimes lived with their parents. Although not the head of the household, an adult man living with his parents could represent himself legally. Usually, he was waiting to acquire land of his own, whether inherited from his parents or purchased.

Other potential family members in the household included nieces, nephews, cousins, and the parents' younger siblings. A younger sister, left orphaned, might live with her brother and sister-in-law until she married. Ideally, she would gain skills to help her with a household of her own, although her work also could be exploited by a family needing extra household help.

Finally, older parents often lived with their grown children, depending on them for financial support. And while a son might inherit the family home when his father died, his mother usually inherited a lifetime share in one or two rooms.

Servants occupied an even more ambiguous role. On the one hand, they were not members of the family and were presumably unable to inherit land or goods. In addition, they often had family ties of their own. On the other hand, they were considered legal members of the household in which they worked. They were listed on the tax roles of the head of the household, and he was responsible for feeding and clothing them.

For families with only a few servants, these boundaries became even more blurred. Living in close quarters, servants were easily absorbed into the family dynamics. Large households on both sides of the Atlantic were even more complicated, especially on the slave-owning Southern plantations.

Migration to the Colonies

While family life remained stable in the Northern colonies during early settlement, the experience of colonization in the South initially served to upset family and household bonds. Only the wealthy were able to move their families to the Southern colonies as complete groups. Once there, the warm Southern climate proved disastrous for initial settlement, and mortality rates were far higher than in the Northern colonies. Only one in three marriages lasted more than ten years without one or both partners dying. Nearly a quarter of all children died before reaching the age of 1, and 50 percent died before age 20.

By the 1680s, family life finally had begun to stabilize for wealthy Southern families. As the native-born population was better able to survive the Southern climate, both parents stood a better chance of surviving together.

Like their Anglican counterparts in England, Southerners placed a strong emphasis on family bonds. They also emphasized the importance of hierarchy within the family, as well as in the larger realm of the household. Due to the isolation of Southern plantations, the Southern household became more important than the community—even more so than in the more closely settled Northern colonies.

Would-be colonists, too poor to afford the cost of passage, arrived as indentured servants, trading seven years of service for the journey to North America, a parcel of land, some tools and clothing, and sometimes dues in the form of cash. While most servants were free or enslaved single men and, in some cases, women, families occasionally agreed to take their chances with indentures. Once they had arrived, women were only allowed to keep children under the age of 2 or 3. Other children were taken as servants to separate plantations or farms. Unlike adults, their indentures could last anywhere from seven to twenty years, usually until they were adults.

A woman who became pregnant while still indentured had few choices. Ideally, the father of the child would purchase the rest of her indenture, and they would marry. In most cases, however, the child's father was either unable or unwilling to marry. The new mother's indenture would then be extended for a longer period, and the child would also be indentured.

Family life after an indentureship was again balanced between the ideal and reality. If a couple could acquire land of their own, they had the hope of raising a family and establishing a household. Most of these families settled in the backcountry regions of western Virginia, the Carolinas, Kentucky, and Tennessee. Colonists unable to obtain land of their own usually had no choice but to remain servants permanently. Whether or not they could raise families in this context was dependent on the willingness and generosity of the head of the household.

African Americans

More than any other group in the colonies, African Americans were caught in the distinction between family and household. Initially, most were brought to the Southern colonies as indentured servants. Like their white counterparts, they had the hope of finishing their indentureships and gaining farms and households of their own. Unlike their white counterparts, Africans did not take the Atlantic passage by choice, and many of these families were broken up.

Throughout the colonial period, free African Americans earned their livings either with small farms in the backcountry or as laborers in the cities. While they did not face the possibility of their families being split apart by their owners, they were nearly always on the edge of society. Most kept documentation of their free status with them at all times, concerned that they could be seized and sold into slavery.

By the 1670s and 1680s, permanent servitude for African Americans was fully established. On a small farm, slavery was little different from servitude, aside from the permanence of the situation. On a larger plantation, these two positions had very different ramifications.

With the exception of household workers, most slaves lived isolated from the family who owned the plantation. Legally, they were part of the household; however, they were not members of the household as family. While church- or state-ordained marriage was usually forbidden between slaves, family groups still emerged. Hunting, fishing, and small gardens were encouraged, allowing family members to provide some food of their own. Where possible, individual traditions brought from Africa could be incorporated into their life as a family.

Ideally, husband, wife, and children were able to live on the same plantation. Reality, however, dictated that many lived on separate plantations. The possibility of family members being sold even farther away was constantly present. Another tension on family life was the abuse of African American women by their white owners, bringing half-white, half-African American children into the family.

Religious Groups

The Northern colonies were predominantly settled by groups of religious dissenters, whether the Pilgrims and Puritans in New England or the Quakers and Moravians in the Mid-Atlantic colonies. Dutch colonists in New York shared similar Protestant beliefs. While families traveled as complete units, they also saw themselves as being part of the larger, religiously defined assembly.

Unlike the Southern colonists, the expensive Atlantic passage to the Northern colonies was usually shared among the entire group. The few indentured servants were less likely to be members of the religious gathering and usually had indentured themselves in the hope of financial improvement. In the event of the group's being unable to pay for the full passage, settlers able to finance their own way were also invited. A breakdown of the passengers on board the *Mayflower* demonstrates colonists falling into all three categories.

Once having arrived in North America, if one or both parents did not survive the first few difficult winters, there were aunts, uncles, cousins, or grandparents to serve in their place. In many ways, the united family group was able to continue much as it had in England or Europe.

Once established, the balance between family, household, and group had somewhat different results in the North than in the South. Both the Puritans and the Quakers maintained the right to survey the activi-

ties of their members. Actions that placed the group in jeopardy, whether physical, social, or religious, were usually punished by banishment from the group. No similar parallels can be found in the Southern colonies, where individual families played a larger role.

Despite this emphasis on community, writings by many of the Puritan leaders indicate an interest in family life. Like other European social groups, the husband was the head of the family and the household and had the final say in all matters. He was responsible for ensuring the religious and financial well-being of his household.

At the same time, the Puritans placed great emphasis on creating the perfect family. As a means of achieving this goal, courtship prior to marriage was an important ritual, determining whether or not the man and woman were truly suited to each other. After marriage, husbands and wives were encouraged to be affectionate to each other and to their children. Furthering the Puritans' interest in family life, single members of the community were encouraged or required to live within established households. Despite this emphasis on family life, the reasoning behind it still led back to the greater good of the community. Only by creating the perfect family could the Puritans realize their goal of creating the perfect society.

Like the Puritans, the Quakers looked to the larger religious community rather than to the individual family. Few distinctions were drawn between family members by blood or family members by religion. A fellow Quaker was referred to as "brother" or "sister." Common terms used to describe the community were "brethren of one family" and "a family of God." When a couple decided to marry, it was as much a community decision as a personal one.

Despite this emphasis on community, individual families functioned very much as their European counterparts did. The family was headed by the husband, and children were expected to obey and honor their parents. The differences lay in the belief that all members of the family and community were equal before God. Unlike the Puritan, Anglican, and Catholic faiths, women were also allowed to speak in meetings. A part of the Quaker belief also was an emphasis on love between husbands and wives, parents and children, family and community.

Native Americans

Throughout the entire colonial period, European settlers came in contact with Native American communities and their very different definitions of family life. Like the Europeans, these tribes were patriarchal. Most, but not all, governing was done by male members of the tribe.

Unlike the Europeans, many tribes, including the Iroquois and Mohawk, were matrilineal and matrilocal. Family lineage was traced through the mother's side rather than the father's. After marriage, the couple usually lived with the wife's family rather than the husband's. While some tribes, such as the Abenaki, were patrilineal, women still played a larger role in tribal politics than they did in European society.

Tribes were customarily organized into family clans. Within these families, identity and custom were passed on through oral tradition. One of the traditions of the Mohawk was the belief that family members killed in battle, whether fighting other Native Americans or Europeans, had to be replaced by captives. In 1704, the group of Mohawk, Abenaki, and French who attacked Deerfield, Massachusetts, brought two Mohawk women with them, seeking new family members among the captives. Once adopted into a tribe, captives were considered full family members.

Similar to Quaker customs, marriages were as much about the tribe and family clans as they were about the couple. Despite the importance of these ties, compatibility between partners was considered essential. Some tribes required a period of celibacy after marriage, which put off conceiving children until the couple had established their ability to live happily together. Others did not hold formal marriage ceremonies until several months after the couple had lived together.

A woman or man unhappy in the match was able to dissolve the bond without penalty. If she had left her parent's dwelling space, she returned home. If her husband had come to her parents' home, he returned to his family. While many European observers took this as an example of Native American society being less constrained, it demonstrates a need for social stability within tribes in order to survive.

While the experience of settlement in North America changed nearly all aspects of life for European colonists, traditional definitions of family and household remained largely intact throughout the colonial period. These same definitions also remained constant beyond the American Revolution.

By contrast, family life was permanently disrupted for African Americans and Native Americans. African American families were initially broken up by the Atlantic passage and later by the strictures of slav-ery. European disease destroyed many Native American families and tribes, and, following colonization, surviving tribes were encouraged to follow the traditional European model for family life.

Abigail B. Chandler

See also: Child Rearing; Children; Housing; Indentured Servitude; Marriage and Divorce; Orphans; Sex; Slave Communities and Culture; Widows and Widowers; Women. *Document:* Raising Colonial Children (1699).

Bibliography

Berkin, Carol, and Horowitz, Leslie. *Women's Voices, Women's Lives.* Boston: Northeastern University Press, 1998.

Calloway, Colin G. *First Peoples.* Boston: Bedford/St. Martin's, 1999.

Fischer, David Hackett. *Albion's Seed.* New York: Oxford University Press, 1989.

Gordon, Michael. *The American Family in Social-Historical Perspective.* New York: St. Martin's, 1973.

Norton, Mary Beth. *Founding Mothers & Fathers.* New York: Alfred A. Knopf, 1996.

Shammas, Carole. *A History of Household Government in America.* Charlottesville: University Press of Virginia, 2002.

Ferdinand (1452–1516) and Isabella (1451–1504)

Ferdinand of Aragon and Isabella of Castile created the foundations of the modern Spanish state. Through their sponsorship of Christopher Columbus, they also initiated Spain's American empire.

Ever since Muslims from North Africa had established themselves in the Iberian Peninsula in the early eighth century C.E. by defeating the Christian Visigothic kingdom, various centers of Christian resistance had emerged and been engaged in a centuries-long struggle, the *Reconquista,* to recapture the peninsula. In the High Middle Ages, Moorish Spain had been an important cultural center and point of contact between the Islamic world and Christian Europe. But by the fifteenth century, the Iberian Christian kingdoms—Castile, Aragon, Portugal, and Navarre—had won back the peninsula with the exception of the Moorish kingdom of Granada, on Castile's southeastern border.

It was into this still-divided Iberian world that Isabella was born in 1451 to King John II Trastamara of Castile. During the reign of Isabella's half brother, Henry IV, civil war erupted, and Isabella became the

Queen Isabella and King Ferdinand welcome Christopher Columbus in Barcelona upon his return from the New World in April 1493. His first voyage marked the beginning of Spain's empire in the Americas. *(Brown Brothers, Sterling, Pennsylvania)*

rallying point for the discontented Castilian nobles. To secure peace, Henry IV recognized his half sister as his heir in 1468, thus setting aside his daughter, Juana la Beltraneja, whose legitimacy had been questioned.

To strengthen her political position, Isabella arranged to marry her second cousin, Prince Ferdinand, born in 1452 to King John II Trastamara of Aragon. Since Henry had not sanctioned the marriage, Ferdinand had to secretly enter Castile in 1469 to claim his bride. Upon Henry's death in 1474, Isabella had herself crowned queen of Castile with her husband named as king consort, which meant that if Ferdinand outlived his wife, he could not be king of Castile in his own right.

Isabella's claim to the throne did not go unchallenged. Her dispossessed niece, Juana, put in a rival claim with the military backing of the king of Portugal. But by 1479, Isabella and Ferdinand's forces had triumphed in the field, and, that same year, Ferdinand inherited Aragon upon his father's death. The dynastic union of the two largest Iberian kingdoms was now achieved, although both kingdoms would continue to be governed by their own laws throughout the sixteenth

and seventeenth centuries. The monarchs had to rebuild royal authority, but the Crown of Aragon remained contractual in nature, which meant that the king's authority was limited by representative assemblies (*cortes*). In Castile, however, the larger state with a richer economy based on wool exports, the monarchs exercised more absolute control.

In 1482, Ferdinand and Isabella initiated a campaign against the last Moorish kingdom, which culminated ten years later, on January 2, 1492, with their triumphal entry into the city of Granada. Among those who witnessed this epochal event was Christopher Columbus, who had arrived in Castile in 1486 seeking sponsorship for a voyage to find new trade routes to the east by sailing west. Isabella's resources had been tied up in the Granada war, but with the war's completion— and despite her advisers' negative evaluation of Columbus's proposal—the queen decided that Castile would finance the Genoese explorer. On August 3, Columbus set sail into the uncharted waters of the Atlantic, and on October 12, 1492, he made his historic landfall in the Caribbean.

While Columbus's royal sponsors sought new

trade routes and territorial expansion, they also envisaged the spread of Christianity. For the Catholic Monarchs (*los reyes catolicos*), as Pope Alexander VI titled them for the successful completion of the *Reconquista,* religious uniformity had been an aim from early in their reign. In 1478, they had received the right from the papacy to hold a royal Inquisition to investigate *conversos,* those who had converted from Judaism to Christianity but were suspected of secretly reverting in faith. In 1492, the monarchs called for the conversion or the expulsion of all Jews from Castile, and, in 1502, the Muslims of Granada were given the same choice. Ferdinand and Isabella had achieved outward religious conformity in Castile, but at the cost of uprooting vital segments of their people.

On his four voyages Columbus did open new lands for conversion and laid the groundwork for Spain's overseas empire. Prior to his death in 1506, he explored beyond the islands of the Caribbean, reaching the coasts of South America and Central America on his last two voyages. In 1503, a *Casa de Contratación* (house of trade) was founded in Seville to control New World trade. By 1508, Spain controlled the island of Hispaniola, which would be used as a base for further exploration and colonization. In 1513, Juan Ponce de León explored Florida, and Vasco Núñez de Balboa reached the Pacific Ocean by crossing the Isthmus of Panama.

Ferdinand also increased Spain's power within Europe by annexing Naples to the Crown of Aragon in 1504 and the kingdom of Navarre to Castile in 1512. He forged dynastic alliances through the marriages of his five children. His youngest daughter, Catherine, became the first wife of Henry VIII of England. However, the monarchs' only son, Juan, who had married in 1497, died that same year. Their eldest daughter, Isabella, died in childbirth in 1498, and her infant son lived just two years.

With Queen Isabella's death in 1504, her second daughter, Juana, married to Philip of Hapsburg, became queen of Castile. After Philip's sudden death in 1506, Juana, known as La Loca, was judged mentally incapable of ruling. Instead, Ferdinand became regent of Castile from 1507 until his death in 1516, when the kingdoms of Spain and Spain's growing American empire passed to his eldest grandson, Charles of Hapsburg.

Florene S. Memegalos

See also: Charles V; Columbus, Christopher; Exploration; Spanish Colonies on Mainland North America (Chronology). *Document:* Columbus's Letter Announcing His Discoveries in the New World (1493).

Bibliography

Edwards, John. *The Spain of the Catholic Monarchs 1474–1520.* Oxford, UK: Blackwell, 2000.

Fernandez-Armesto, Felipe. *Ferdinand and Isabella.* New York: Taplinger, 1975.

Rubin, Nancy. *Isabella of Castile, the First Renaissance Queen.* New York: St. Martin's, 1991.

Fish and Fisheries

Fisheries were critical to both the subsistence and economies of colonial North America. French, Portuguese, Spanish, and English fishermen were visiting the fisheries off Newfoundland as early as the sixteenth century, while various Native American tribes were using the same sites much earlier.

Although fishing was a major part of the economy for the coastal areas of most of the American colonies, it was the bastion of the New England economy. Poor, rocky soil dominated the region, while the nearby waters of the Grand Banks were abundantly populated with cod, mackerel, and halibut. Generally, merchants from Boston controlled the market, selling the best fish down the Atlantic coast for flour and tobacco. Mediocre-grade fish went to southern Europe in trade for wine and salt, while the lowest-grade fish was shipped to the sugar-producing islands of the Caribbean as food for slaves. The dependence on fishing spurred the development of other businesses in New England, particularly shipbuilding and its related industries, shipping and transport services, as well as various commercial and financial activities.

While many nations harvested the abundant fisheries of North America, their methods differed a great deal, depending on the market and the availability of salt. If salt was readily available at reasonable prices, then fishermen produced extraordinarily salty fish that was then sold to northern European markets, where people were accustomed to heavily pickled foods. Called the green fishery method, it required that large vessels troll the deep offshore waters in search of fish, which were liberally salted onshore and carried wet in the belly of the ship to market. When salt was expensive or not plentiful, fishermen used the dry fishery method. Smaller vessels plied the waters closer to the coast to catch lesser cod, which was lightly sprinkled with salt and dry-cured to rock hardness onshore in the open air. Fish preserved using the dry fishery method went

The abundant fisheries of the northern Atlantic, especially off the coasts of Newfoundland (pictured here) and New England, were the primary source of subsistence and the economic foundation of colonial North America. *(The Stapleton Collection/ Bridgeman Art Library)*

exclusively to markets in warm climates, where the lower moisture content reduced the likelihood of spoilage. Because both methods depended on landing onshore, fishermen established themselves in every part of coastal North America, where productive inshore fisheries, suitable harbors, and plentiful timber reserves adjoined one another.

Since fishing expeditions meant long periods away from home, vessels carried everything needed for the voyage in their holds: salt, water and provisions, fishing equipment, various materials needed for repairing and maintaining the ship, nails and boards for constructing small fishing boats, and a wide variety of tools. Life on board fishing vessels was uncertain and harsh, but a successful voyage could bring huge profits for all involved—from fishermen and ship captains to investors ashore.

With so many peoples visiting the abundant fisheries of the Grand Banks, it should be no surprise that a great deal of tension arose concerning fishing rights. Although the long-standing rivalry between Britain and France created an unending strain, Britain received overall control of the fisheries at the end of the Seven Years' War, or the French and Indian War, as it was known in the colonies.

After the American Revolution, the former colonies acquired the right to fish along Newfoundland and Nova Scotia through the Treaty of Paris, but these rights were revoked with the outbreak of the War of 1812 and never officially restored. The United States and Canada would squabble for nearly 100 years before joint usage was finally agreed upon in 1910.

Solomon K. Smith

See also: Atlantic Ocean; Food and Diet; Newfoundland.

Bibliography

Bailyn, Bernard. *The New England Merchants in the Seventeenth Century.* Cambridge, MA: Harvard University Press, 1955.

Lydon, James G. "Fish for Gold: The Massachusetts Fish Trade with Iberia, 1700–1773." *New England Quarterly* 54:4 (1981): 539–82.

Vickers, Daniel. *Farmers and Fishermen: Two Centuries of Work in Essex County, Massachusetts, 1630–1850.* Chapel Hill: University of North Carolina Press, 1994.

Florida

The story of the colonization of Florida differs significantly from that of the thirteen colonies that eventually fought the American War for Independence. As English colonies, East and West Florida were too underdeveloped, too underpopulated, and too dependent on Great Britain to break away in 1776. In 1783, as stipulated by the Treaty of Paris, Florida reverted to Spanish control, and it did not become a territory of the United States until 1821.

Early Florida

The first Floridians arrived around 10,000 B.C.E. They were hunter-gatherers whose diet consisted of small animals, plants, nuts, and shellfish. By the time they encountered Europeans, they had developed a number of diverse, complex societies. On the eve of colonization, Florida's Native Americans began to construct temple mounds, evidently a practice adopted from other southeastern Native Americans. They also grew their food and had established complex trading networks with local and far-off native communities. Some large, centralized cultures existed, but these seem to have been more common elsewhere in the Southeast.

Spanish interest in Florida began in 1513, when Juan Ponce de León, a veteran of the *Reconquista* and the campaigns on Hispaniola and governor of the fledging colony of Puerto Rico, explored along the coast. Incidentally, the name Florida, bestowed by Ponce de León, refers to the day he came ashore between St. Augustine and the St. Johns River, the Feast of Flowers at Easter time.

In the sixteenth century, Spanish Florida encompassed the interior region between present-day Tampico, Mexico, and Philadelphia. Ponce de León encountered hostile Native Americans wherever he went. In 1521, he returned to Florida to plant a colony after subduing Caribs in the lower Antilles, only to be wounded by natives. He returned to Cuba, where he died.

Pánfilo de Narváez's 1528 expedition to Florida fared even worse. He left Santo Domingo with 600 men and searched for gold rumored to be near Tampa Bay and present-day Tallahassee, but found nothing. Working without tools (their original ships were lost), they constructed makeshift vessels. All of the boats sank in a storm off the Texas coast, and the eighty survivors began the long overland trek to Mexico. Eight years later, four men, including Cabeza de Vaca, the treasurer of the expedition, reached Mexico City.

Hernando de Soto's *entrada,* a treasure-seeking expedition of 600 men lasting from 1539 to 1542, was also a failure. By the 1540s, the Spanish had failed to find mineral wealth in Florida and had run afoul of the region's Native Americans, who numbered around 350,000 during the early years of Spanish colonization. Consequently, the Spanish had basically given up ever turning a profit on Florida, though they had tentative plans to create a few military outposts. French interest in the area prodded the Spanish to speed up these plans. In 1562, Jean Ribaut led a group of Huguenots (French Protestants) to the St. Johns River, where they traded peacefully before moving north to Port Royal (now in South Carolina) to plant a colony. Ribaut returned to France to resupply, and the Spanish hurried their efforts to plant their own colony and destroy that of the French.

Under Pedro Menéndez de Avilés, a Spanish fleet left from Cadiz at around the same Ribaut left France. Menéndez de Avilés founded St. Augustine in 1565 and took off shortly thereafter. Finding Fort Caroline poorly defended, he marched overland and took it easily, killing 138 Frenchmen. He later found the remainder of the French party and killed most of them, although he did spare ten who turned out to be Catholic.

The French gave up any hope of establishing colonies in Florida, and the Spanish reinforced the fortress at St. Augustine. This fortification, Castillo San Marcos, still stands today and was never taken in battle, although Sir Francis Drake did destroy the entire town around it in 1586. In the wake of English attacks, the Spanish decided to maintain a minimal military presence and expand missionary activity among the Native Americans.

Mission Life

The main feature of colonial life in Florida under the Spanish was the mission. These were multipurpose

Founded by the Spanish in 1565, St. Augustine in northeastern Florida is the oldest city in the United States. The parish, also the oldest, was established in 1594; the present cathedral, built in the Spanish Mission style, dates to 1797. *(Library of Congress, LC-D4-13352)*

frontier institutions, which served both secular and religious functions. The missions' goal was to persuade the Native Americans to accept Catholicism and allegiance to the king of Spain. The mission system in Florida reached its peak in the 1630s, when forty-four Franciscan missions had been planted among a population of Native Americans that by then numbered less than 50,000. After 1650, the mission system declined slowly.

The most successful missions were those along the Atlantic Coast between present-day Savannah and St. Augustine and those established across northern Florida in a line extending west into the region now known as the Panhandle. Soldiers and missionaries were the main Spanish populations in Florida, and there were fewer European settlers than in other American colonies. Spanish Florida was divided into four mission districts: Guale, Timucua, Apalachee, and Apalachicola.

Florida's native peoples lived in towns centered around circular public spaces, which occasionally functioned as ball courts. Most towns included a number of round buildings with domed roofs. Although early missionary efforts usually consisted of a short speech, the erection of a cross, and the priest moving on to another community, later missionaries stayed in the villages, supervising the construction of churches and friaries.

By the 1670s, the missions in the Apalachee district (near present-day Tallahassee) were the most populous and prosperous in Florida. At their height, these missions were home to 8,000 baptized Native Americans, or about three-quarters of the Christian natives in Florida. The newer missions in Apalachicola, farther to the west, were failing, however, and soon the other mission provinces would be subject to a new threat: English settlers.

The Eighteenth Century

The English founded the colony of Carolina at Charles Town in 1670. The same year, the Spanish in Madrid relinquished their claim to areas north of Port Royal, hoping to stave off English raids. At first, the threat to the Spanish missions was more perceived than real, although the Spanish and English skirmished indecisively throughout the late seventeenth century. By 1700, South Carolina was an aggressive, expansionist plantation colony that desired to trade with Native Americans in deerskins, firearms, alcohol, cloth, and (most unfortunately for natives associated with the missions) slaves.

In 1702, Governor James Moore, as part of the larger imperial conflict known as Queen Anne's War, struck St. Augustine with a force of 600 white colonists and 600 Native American allies. Although he destroyed the town, he failed to take the fortress, where the entire population of the town huddled with the garrison for two months. Spanish forces sailed from Cuba to reinforce the beleaguered fort. Moore's force retreated to Charles Town, where Moore lost his post for failing to take the Spanish fort.

In 1704, Moore led a devastating raid into Apalachee, killing hundreds and enslaving more than 1,000 native people. The province of Apalachee never recovered. Native Americans had revolted in Apalachicola province, so the western half of Florida reverted to native control, save for a few military outposts. Over the next few decades, the English would wear down the provinces of Guale and Timucua as well, and their new colony of Georgia (1733) would pinch Spanish designs on Florida even more tightly. English traders were able to provide better trade goods more regularly and were always willing to arm Native Americans who were willing to enslave their neighbors.

Trade difficulties between the British and the Spanish in the Caribbean brought about the War of Jenkins' Ear in the late 1730s and early 1740s. English forces under James Oglethorpe failed once again to capture the fortress at St. Augustine, and the two forces fought to a stalemate. The Spaniards could not get rid of Georgia, and the English seemed unable to remove the Spanish from Florida. France (in Canada and Louisiana) and England (along the Atlantic seaboard and beyond) were winning the contest for North America, and it mattered less and less that the Spanish hold on to forts at St. Augustine and Pensacola.

During the Seven Years' War (or French and Indian War, as it was known in North America), France—and to a lesser extent Spain—attempted to halt the Anglo-American advance across the continent of North America. They were unsuccessful, and Florida became two British colonies by the terms of the Treaty of Paris, signed in 1763.

During the American War for Independence, the Spanish were able to recapture West Florida. In the talks that followed, the Spanish got both Floridas back, and held them, though mainly on paper, for several decades. Americans gradually moved into the area, and a series of diplomatic moves in the early years of the nineteenth century made Florida a territory of the United States. Florida became a state in 1845.

Matthew Jennings

See also: De Soto, Hernando; Menéndez de Avilés, Pedro; Ponce de León, Juan; St. Augustine; Spanish Colonies on Mainland North America (Chronology). *Document:* The Founding of St. Augustine (1565).

Bibliography

Gannon, Michael, ed. *The New History of Florida.* Gainesville: University Press of Florida, 1996.

Taylor, Alan. *American Colonies.* New York: Penguin Putnam, 2001.

Tebeau, Charlton W. *A History of Florida.* Coral Gables, FL: University of Miami Press, 1971.

Food and Diet

Trade and exploration in the sixteenth, seventeenth, and eighteenth centuries led to enormous changes in the production and consumption of food all over the world. Explorers and settlers in both North and South America brought new foods home to Europe; from there, they were introduced to other parts of the world. In turn, colonists introduced European foods and cooking methods to the Americas.

Some of the foods that traveled to Europe, Africa, and the Far East during the colonial period remain familiar there today, including corn (maize), turkeys, maple syrup, and cocoa beans. Others became integral to European and Asian foodways—tomatoes in Italy, potatoes in Ireland, chiles in India.

Other foods are less well known, largely because they had little impact on Europe. One example is the manioc or cassava root. Native to the Caribbean region, it flourishes in humid environments but also can survive a drought. It was made into flour and, if fermented, a sweet liquor. Two early grains also cultivated in South America were amaranth and quinoa, both of which contain large amounts of protein. Once wheat cultivation became common, these grains became less important.

Native American Foods in South America

Prior to European contact, South America was populated by hundreds of different tribes, each with its own culinary traditions. Diets varied widely from region to region, usually based around a primary ingredient. The coastal lowlands and Caribbean used manioc, dried and ground into flour for bread. Manioc was supplemented with fruits, fish, and small animals. Mexico, Central America, and the lower parts of the Andes used corn. The Aztecs ate corn formed into tortillas and filled with chiles, poultry, or fish. Andean natives toasted, popped, or cooked their corn, mixing it with chiles. The higher parts of the Andes mountains relied on the potato, as it could survive a wider temperature range. Other foods widely consumed in South America were beans, pumpkins, squash, tomatoes, jicama, and the cocoa bean. Trade flourished between regions, bringing potatoes to the lowlands and peppers to the mountains.

The arrival of the Spanish in the early 1500s brought drastic changes to the region. Accustomed to the seasonal nature of life in Europe, settlers wrote enthusiastic letters home about the availability of fresh food throughout the year in a tropical climate. Although they adapted to the new foods of South America, they emphasized cultivation of their own familiar foods, including wheat, rice, peaches, cherries, and asparagus, and cattle for beef, milk, and butter. While these European foods were initially prized in the New World, they became commonly available. The Spanish also encouraged the growth of food, both European and American varieties, for export. Although South American tribes already had established trade routes in place for foodstuffs between geographical regions, the Spanish extended them. In Peru and other places, potatoes, beans, bananas, sugar, quinoa, wheat, and other produce traveled between mountains and coastal basins by llama.

By the late 1500s, the Spanish were firmly established throughout Mexico and other parts of the continent. They also had come into contact with tribes in the southwestern part of North America, and tried their traditional food. Many of the natives had died from disease or warfare; the remaining population lived in places too isolated for contact or had been forced into working for the Spanish. The diet of the latter group now relied on European foods, especially wheat and beef. The Spanish also settled in Florida and the American Southwest, where similar exchanges of foodstuffs occurred.

Native American Foods in North America

As in South America, foodways in North America varied widely across the continent. Native American cultures and food production were customarily influenced by their surroundings, although a complex trade network allowed for exchange between regions.

Tribes living on the West Coast of North America had a predominantly hunter-gatherer lifestyle prior to the arrival of European settlers. Their food supplies revolved around the seasons—fishing and gathering nuts in the warmer months and hunting in the cooler months, when meat could be more easily stored. Unlike their Aztec counterparts, tribes in the Pacific Northwest relied on salmon, which provided both sustenance and a focus for annual ceremonies. In the Southwest, a series of groups evolved over time, the Anasazi eventually amalgamating with the Pueblo tribes encountered by the Spanish. Like the Aztec, their sophisticated culture focused on the cultivation of corn. Moving farther east, tribes on the Great Plains relied on the buffalo as their primary food and ritual source, and their methods of hunting were affected by Spanish introduction of the horse in the early 1500s. Tribes in the Northeast obtained food through a variety of methods, some foods actively cultivated, others hunted. Most lived in settled, if periodically mobile, communities. Foods native to their region include the cranberry, maple syrup, wild rice, and various wild game.

All of these tribes saw drastic change during the colonial period. Most suffered from diseases introduced by European settlers. Their food sources were hunted or pushed away by farming. Differences in land use and food production also caused friction between Native Americans and Europeans. A European family defined its farm as a set plot of land, possibly adjoined by other set plots of land. While their use of the land changed from season to season, it was always the same land. In contrast, many tribes moved from place to place within a larger region, fishing by an ocean or river in the spring, hunting in a forest in the fall. These different conceptualizations of land use often led European colonists to believe Native Americans were trespassing on their lands.

European American Foodways

The foodways developed by British settlers in North America reflect two factors: the immediate impact of their new homes and the lasting impact of their own traditions. Although new foods had a profound change on many colonists, the need to maintain familiarity remained the stronger influence. Whenever possible, they tried to introduce the British crops they were accustomed to. When this was not possible, they adapted their own cooking methods to the new ingredients. As a result, distinctive regional styles of food preparation quickly emerged, often mimicking regional styles home in Britain.

The Puritans who settled Massachusetts came largely from East Anglia, in the southeastern corner of England. Although they were known for a simple diet, diaries and letters indicate a broad interest in the food on their tables. They were largely prosperous and well educated. Living so close to Europe, they were also likely exposed to many different styles of cooking. Unlike in other parts of England, the primary method of preparing food in East Anglia was baking. This tradition is evident in many of the New England foods that first emerged in the colonial period: beans baked overnight for the Sabbath, pies, and breads. Most villages built standing ovens to be used by residents too poor to have bake ovens built inside their own chimneys. As wheat did not grow well in New England, a common bread was "thirded bread," made from a blend of wheat, corn, and rye, designed to stretch the wheat as far as possible. Other foods adapted and adopted by settlers in New England include maple syrup, cranberries, squash, mussels, lobster, and codfish.

Foodways in the Chesapeake region of Virginia and Maryland were less homogeneous than in New England. Both colonies were voluntarily settled by wealthy aristocrats and poor indentured servants and involuntarily settled by African slaves. The planters' families came predominantly from southwestern England, a region known for its fried and simmered foods, a tradition reflected in Virginia's fried chicken, for example. Once the colonies were established, the planters were also wealthy enough to afford to import whatever foodstuffs were not immediately available, including wheat flour, spices, and wines. New World foods such as the potato did not appear on wealthy families' tables until after they had become popular in England and Europe. In contrast, indentured servants ate a diet far more reflective of the region they lived in, based heavily on local corn and pork. While pigs were introduced to the Chesapeake, the meat was easily processed through salting and/or smoking, an important necessity in the Southern heat. Slaves had a similar diet, supplemented whenever possible with whatever

African foodstuffs could be obtained. Examples of these foods are yams, okra, plantains, black-eyed peas, and watermelon. In time, all of these foods became integral to planter-class diets—perhaps a reflection of who was doing the cooking.

The first English settlers in the mid-Atlantic region were predominately Quakers from northern Britain and the Midlands. Like the Puritans, the Quakers placed a strong emphasis on simplicity in their diet. However, also like the Puritans, the Quakers brought traditions of their own to the New World. Boiling was the most popular way of cooking in northern England, probably a reflection on a region where a fire would be kept burning for warmth for long periods of time. Steamed puddings and dumplings were common, and an entire meal could be prepared in one pot. Soup provided a liquid base, pudding was tied into a bag and lowered into the soup, and vegetables could be tied into a bag or placed in a jug and suspended as well.

Foodways in the region also reflected a strong influx of German, Dutch, and Scandinavian colonists. All three groups introduced an emphasis on spiced, sweet foods largely unknown in northern England. The modern cookie stems from Dutch and German tradition; English settlers were more apt to prepare a cake or pudding for a dessert. A popular means of preserving fruit in the Mid-Atlantic was by boiling it down to a thick sauce called a "butter" or "cheese." Apples, plums, pears, and lemons were all treated in this way. This method fits in well with the northern England tradition of boiling; however, it was also common among the German settlers. It is likely that the two groups exchanged variations on this theme.

Initially, French traders, explorers, and missionaries brought very few traditions to North America. They were predominantly interested in gaining furs or converts, and they recognized that the most effective means of doing this was to live among the Native American tribes. In time, French communities developed in Quebec and on Cape Breton Island. These colonies could be loosely compared with the Chesapeake region: the wealthy could afford to live like their counterparts at home in France, while the poor learned to adapt to eating local foods. Salt cod was a constant staple, and potatoes, able to withstand weeks of fog and rain, became another.

The northeastern soup known as chowder derived from French settlers on Cape Breton. The French word for a soup pot or cauldron is *chaudière*, and, on the northern coast of France in the seventeenth century, a fish stew was known as a *chaudree*. Early chowders were made with salt cod, onions, potatoes, and sea biscuits, ingredients readily available in maritime Canada. In time, chowder also gained milk to become the dish known today as New England fish chowder.

After the Acadian expulsion of the late eighteenth century, many French colonists settled in Louisiana. There, the proximity to South and Central America led to the development of the Cajun culinary tradition, using local tomatoes, chiles, and cooking techniques. The word "Cajun" was derived originally from the word "Acadian," but very little Cajun cooking resembled the Acadian tradition brought from Canada. Despite a long and flourishing culinary tradition of their own at home, French settlers showed a greater willingness to experiment with new flavors and ideas.

Despite these regional distinctions, there were similarities in foodways all over the Atlantic world. Increased trade had brought a new range of ingredients to England and Europe. Popular dishes in the seventeenth century still showed a medieval sensibility, mixing as many flavors as possible together. Gervase Markham's 1623 *Country Contentments* includes a recipe for chewet pie, calling for chopped chicken, suet, currants, dates, raisins, mace, cinnamon, ground cloves, grated orange rind, sugar, and candied caraway seeds. Similar recipes are found in other books of the period.

Vegetables were rarely eaten raw and were usually combined with other ingredients. Breads were usually leavened with barm, a foam found on the top of barrels of beer. European settlers brought these traditions with them to the New World, adapting them to local ingredients where needed.

New Eating Habits

By the end of the eighteenth century, increased trade had made exotic ingredients even more widely available. Cookbooks also had become an important part of English and German life, making it easier for a housewife or palace chef to attempt a new dish. Trade had brought greater prosperity and wealth as well. A larger middle class was slowly emerging on both sides of the Atlantic, and there was also an increased emphasis on gentility. On the eve of the American Revolution, colonists and Europeans alike longed for matched plates, tea and liquid chocolate services, and the ability to serve people their own food individually, rather than from a common dish.

At same time, food also reflected the influences of the Great Enlightenment and the move toward a classical simplicity. While spices were now more widely available, emphasis was placed on a single flavor rather than several. A chicken pilau recipe from the manuscript cookbook of Mrs. Frances Bland Tucker Coulter in Virginia calls for rice, butter, ground cloves, chicken, bacon, and pepper.

A transition toward simplicity also was created by the American Revolution. Boycotting imported tea, sugar, and other goods, patriotic colonists relied more heavily on replacements available in North America. While citizens of the United States did go back to drinking tea after the war, the emphasis on relatively simple fare continued into the nineteenth century.

Abigail B. Chandler

See also: Agriculture; Alcohol; Coffee; Columbian Exchange; Corn; Fish and Fisheries; Grain; Inns and Taverns (Public Houses); Kitchens, Colonial; Livestock; Sugar; Tea. *Document:* Colonial Recipe for Apple Tansey (1754).

Bibliography

Baker, James. "English Yeoman Foodways at Plimoth Plantation." In *The Plimoth Plantation New England Cookery Book*, edited by Malabar Hornblower. Boston: Harvard Common Press, 1990.

Black, Maggie. *A Taste of History: 10,000 Years of Food in Britain.* London: British Museum, 1993.

Calloway, Colin G. *First Peoples.* Boston: Bedford/St. Martin's, 1999.

Fernandez-Armesto, Felipe. *Near a Thousand Tables.* New York: Free Press, 2002.

Fischer, David Hackett. *Albion's Seed.* New York: Oxford University Press, 1989.

Slive, Daniel J. *A Harvest Gathered: Food in the New World.* Providence, RI: John Carter Brown Library, 1989.

Super, John C. *Food, Conquest, and Colonization in Sixteenth-Century Spanish America.* Albuquerque: University of New Mexico Press, 1988.

Tannahil, Reay. *Food in History.* New York: Stein and Day, 1973.

Fort Duquesne

Fort Duquesne was located at the confluence of the Ohio, Monongahela, and Allegheny rivers, in present-day Pittsburgh, Pennsylvania. It was one of a series of fortifications constructed by France along Lake Erie and at the headwaters of the Ohio River in the period leading up to the French and Indian War.

France and Britain both claimed sovereignty over the Ohio territory and hoped to control its resources

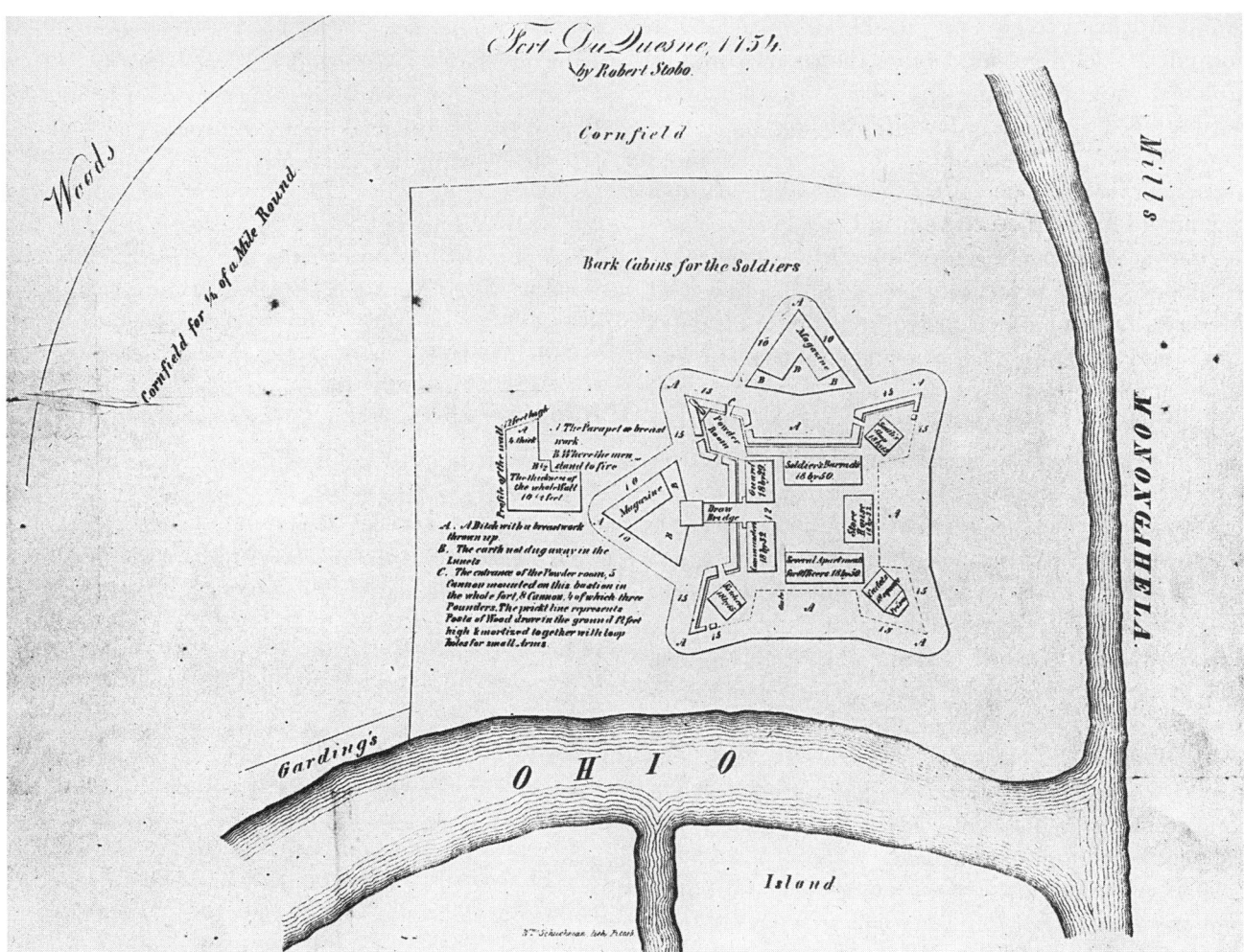

Fort Duquesne, as diagrammed in 1754, the year of its construction, was located at the confluence of the Ohio, Monongahela, and Allegheny rivers—the site of downtown Pittsburgh today. The fort was built during the French and Indian War to help protect frontier settlers. *(Brown Brothers, Sterling, Pennsylvania)*

and the trade with local Native American tribes. An imperial dispute arose when Anglo-American settlers, land speculators, and traders threatened French dominance in the Ohio Valley. This greatly concerned France. The Ohio River system served as the vital transportation and communication artery between the St. Lawrence River in New France and the Mississippi River in Louisiana.

The construction of French fortifications was most disturbing to the Ohio Company, a British land speculating firm that claimed 200,000 acres in the region. Virginia governor Robert Dinwiddie, an Ohio Company investor, assumed responsibility for defending British (and his own) interests in the valley. The governor sent 21-year-old George Washington, of the Virginia militia, to Fort LeBoeuf, located between the forks of the Ohio River and Lake Erie, to demand that the French withdraw from the region. They refused, and

the Virginia militia began constructing Fort Prince George at the forks of the Ohio River in February 1754.

Two months later, Captain Claude-Pierre Pecaudy de Contrecoeur arrived at the site of the partially completed fort with more than 600 French soldiers and Native American warriors and demanded the Virginians' surrender. Vastly outnumbered, the militia accepted the French terms and abandoned the fort.

Contrecoeur renamed the fortification in honor of New France's governor-general, Marquis Duquesne, Sieur de Menneville, on April 18, 1754, and the French replaced the flimsy stockade structure with a more formidable earthen square. In May, Washington's attack on a French reconnaissance party provoked Fort Duquesne's garrison. In retaliation, the French laid siege to the hastily constructed Fort Necessity, driving the British completely from the Ohio Valley by July.

At London's behest, colonial representatives convened in Albany, New York, in the spring of 1754 to formulate a defensive strategy for the western frontier. Colonial infighting hampered the Albany Congress, which failed to provide for any defense, and forced London to assume responsibility for countering France's incursions. Major General Edward Braddock was dispatched to America on November 25, 1754, with two regiments of British regulars, the 44th and the 48th. Braddock's mission was to drive the French from four locations encroaching on British territory in the north and west: Forts Duquesne, Niagara, Saint-Frederic, and Beausejour.

Braddock led the advance on Fort Duquesne. The general's contempt for the colonial militia, Native American allies, and North American frontier warfare tactics jeopardized his mission from the outset. He shunned Native American warriors, mistakenly believing that European-style tactics would prevail in the wilderness. Braddock approached Fort Duquesne from the south, cutting a difficult road north from Virginia. The vastly outnumbered French ambushed and decisively defeated Braddock's column before it reached the fort. Significantly, Native Americans constituted the majority of the French force. Braddock was killed and the remnants of his army retreated to Philadelphia, leaving the frontier unprotected.

Fort Duquesne's garrison now assumed the initiative and encouraged Ohio Native Americans to raid along Pennsylvania's western frontier. They ravaged British settlements and forced panicked colonists to flee east, seeking refuge in Philadelphia. By October 1755, native raiders reached within 70 miles of Pennsylvania's capital.

In 1757, Secretary of State William Pitt assumed control of Britain's flagging war effort and planned new assaults against the French strongholds. Brigadier General John Forbes was charged with the assault on Fort Duquesne. Central to the new British strategy was neutralizing the Ohio native tribes.

The Easton Conference, held during the fall of 1758, allayed Native American fears of British designs on their lands. The colonists stated that they did not intend to settle beyond the Allegheny Mountains and only wanted to evict the French from the region and revive trade. French trade had been hampered by the British naval blockade, and the Ohio tribes accepted the British guarantees, costing France a crucial ally and source of manpower.

With the Ohio natives neutralized, Forbes constructed a road west from Carlisle, Pennsylvania. The French used harassing raids in a failed attempt to delay the British advance. Vastly outnumbered, Captain François-Marie Le Marchand de Lignery destroyed Fort Duquesne before retiring on November 23, 1758. The British, still miles away, occupied the remains of the fort the following day and began constructing Fort Pitt.

Thomas Nester

See also: Braddock, Edward; Fortifications; French Colonies on Mainland North America (Chronology); Military and Diplomatic Affairs (Chronology); Military and Diplomatic Affairs (Essay); Pennsylvania; War.

Bibliography

Anderson, Fred. *Crucible of War: The Seven Years' War and the Fate of Empire in British North America, 1754–1766.* New York: Alfred A. Knopf, 2000.

Nester, William R. *The Great Frontier War: Britain, France, and the Imperial Struggle for North America, 1607–1755.* Westport, CT: Praeger, 2000.

O'Meara, Walter. *Guns at the Forks.* Englewood Cliffs, NJ: Prentice Hall, 1965.

Fort Orange

The Dutch West India Company built Fort Orange in 1624. Encompassing a hill some 700 feet above the west bank of the Hudson River and facing the ruins of Fort Nassau, this large square structure with palisaded walls stretched 500 feet in length.

Later known as Albany, Fort Orange was originally founded as a trading post, although it rarely housed more than twenty-five traders and an equal number of mercenary soldiers employed by the Dutch West Indian Company. In the 1630s, the company brought eight refugee families from the Spanish Netherlands to Fort Orange to provide labor and to grow food for the garrison. Two years later, however, they were relocated to Manhattan Island, both for their own safety and to protect the company's fur trading interests.

Through its intense participation in the fur trade, Fort Orange played an important role in changing the distribution of power in the region, especially the future of the Five Nations of the Iroquois Confederacy. For neighboring Native Americans, the establishment of Fort Orange was a major element in the shift from the use of traditional tools to European trade goods and weapons. Until 1624, Native Americans in the region had to get such goods from the French in Canada, leaving them at a disadvantage as compared to their

Algonquian and Huron rivals in the North, who were in closer proximity to the French.

Access to Dutch goods from Fort Orange sparked the Mohawk-Mohegan War, which lasted from 1624 to 1628, although growing Mohawk political, military, and demographic forces also spurred hostilities. In 1626, in an effort to protect their position, the Dutch mistakenly intervened in the Mohawk-Mohegan war. Commissary Daniel van Krieckenbeeck, a senior trader who worked on the Hudson for five years, sided with the Mohegan. Armed with muskets, Krieckenbeeck and six other traders accompanied a Mohegan war party. Before reaching the Mohawk camp, the war party was ambushed. Krieckenbeeck and three of his companions were killed. Some reports suggest that one Dutchman was roasted and eaten by the victorious Mohawk.

The Mohawk won the war and drove the Mohegan northeast of Fort Orange. With only one native power in the region, the growing trade monopoly of the Dutch West India Company on the upper Hudson River was countered by the Mohawk's control over access to the Dutch. Although they feared the Mohawk were placing a stranglehold on their trade, the traders at Fort Orange were powerless to stop them.

Nevertheless, trade at Fort Orange flourished. Some 5,788 skins were purchased in 1625, 10,000 in 1628, and nearly 30,000 in 1633. Although guns were exchanged, the majority of the Dutch trade involved metal goods such as hatchets, knives, hoes, and kettles, as well as wampum. The rapid expansion of trade at Fort Orange led to intensified trapping in Mohawk territory, severely depleting beaver populations by 1640. After that time, the local trade primarily depended on Mohawk capture of Huron and Algonquin fur convoys en route to Quebec.

During the second Anglo-Dutch War, Peter Stuyvesant surrendered the colony of New Amsterdam to Sir George Cartwright. The Dutch colony became the British colony of New York, and Fort Orange became Albany. Both remained in British hands until the American Revolution, when they sided with the rebels.

Solomon K. Smith

See also: Dutch; Dutch West India Company; Fortifications; New Netherland; New York; New York and New Netherland (Chronology).

Bibliography

Innes, J. H. *New Amsterdam and Its People*. New York: New York University Press, 1969.

Kammen, Michael. *Colonial New York: A History*. New York: Charles Scribner's Sons, 1975.

Steele, Ian. *Warpaths: Invasions of North America*. New York: Oxford University Press, 1994.

Fortifications

The construction of fortresses to hold territory was an established part of European war in the early modern period. European powers applied this practice to their colonial territories. Forts could be constructed from wooden palisades (suitable for small outposts), earthworks, bricks, stone, or a combination of materials. Some coastal forts used tabby, a concrete made from oyster shells. On one occasion during Pontiac's Rebellion, a British unit attacked by Native Americans in western Pennsylvania used bags of flour to temporarily fortify their position—creating a "flour-bag fortress."

Forts with wooden palisades were easier and cheaper to build than stone or earthworks, and also easier for a retreating force to destroy. Since large guns could not be mounted on the wall, however, such forts could not be defended against artillery. Forts near bodies of water that could support naval guns were especially vulnerable, and hence these were usually made of stone.

Types and Functions of Fortified Places

Fortresses in the Americas varied greatly in size and function. Some were built to withstand attacks by Native Americans, insurrectionary slaves, or small parties of whites, and some, particularly in the eighteenth century, were built to withstand besiegers by land or water equipped with artillery. Fortresses protected cities, trading posts, waterways, and passes. They protected ports from attack by sea, as Castle William stood guard over Boston. One of the reasons that the Chesapeake was a perpetual security headache was that its mouth was too wide for the guns of a fort to cover.

In addition to providing defense against military attack, fortresses served as bases for armies or raiding parties, both European and Native American. They were secure storehouses for trade goods or food. They also psychologically intimidated Native American or settler populations. Fort Albany, built by Sir Edmund Andros in 1676, after the English takeover of New York, stood on the heights above the Dutch town of

Albany, providing a constant reminder of English power.

Fortified places varied in the number of people they could hold, from a few people to a garrison of several hundred soldiers. Some larger fortifications resembled small cities. At the other extreme, even a private house could be fortified. Fortified houses appeared as early as the Spanish settlement of Mexico. The classic examples of fortified private dwellings in British American colonies occurred in the Caribbean, where slave-owning planters lived in constant apprehension of slave revolts. The largest single house in the seventeenth-century British colonies was Colbeck Castle in Jamaica, literally a castle laid out with attention to defense and gun emplacements.

Fortresses and Society

Fortification was expensive, requiring a considerable commitment of labor and materials that was sometimes in danger of being reassigned to other projects. The original fortress at Plymouth, a wooden palisade enclosing settlers' houses and a blockhouse, was later cannibalized for its wood, which was used for more houses. Shortly after the Dutch purchase of Manhattan, the Dutch West India Company's ambitious plan for Fort New Amsterdam at its southern tip had to be considerably cut back when the governor of the colony, Peter Minuit, diverted laborers and building materials to building houses for the colonists. The hastily built fortress had to be reconstructed in 1633, but many of the workers sent over from the Dutch Republic were drafted into the colony's military forces, and the work was finished by the company's slaves. Even then, the expert Dutch builders and engineers had to sue the company for their wages. Nor did the expense of a fortress stop when building was completed. A fortress was useless unless garrisoned, and establishing a permanent fort meant a long-term commitment to adequately man it.

Expense was not the only reason colonists did not always welcome fortification. They sometimes saw a fortress not merely as protection from Native Americans or rival colonists but as a way for the central government to exert its power over local communities. In Virginia, Governor William Berkeley's plan to build a chain of nine fortresses along the frontiers of Virginia aroused considerable opposition from frontiersmen, who feared that the central colonial government would prevent them from waging war on local Native Americans. The

fortresses, which were never built, were one of the factors precipitating Bacon's Rebellion.

Quakers opposed fortification as they did other warlike activities; even the construction of a redoubt to protect Philadelphia from privateers was preceded by a heated debate. The Swedish traveler Peter Kalm, visiting Wilmington in 1748, observed that such was the fear of privateers that even the Quakers were helping fortify the town. He noticed that many Quakers did not actually work on the defenses, but aided financially and helped get things ready.

National Styles in Fortification

Native Americans had been fortifying themselves in both wood and stone long before the arrival of Europeans, and continued to do so. Iroquois towns, surrounded by double or triple wooden palisades and other defenses, were referred to as "castles" by Europeans. The Narragansett of Rhode Island built several forts, including an elaborate wooden fort in the Great Swamp, which, in 1675, was destroyed by the colonists, who took heavy casualties in doing so. Another impressive Narragansett fort was the stone fort known as Queen's Fort. Both these fortresses show evidence that native peoples incorporated European ideas about fortification into their own military tradition.

English settlers came from a country where fortresses were relatively little used. Most British American cities were originally unfortified or lightly fortified, which gave them greater geographic flexibility as opposed to being confined in heavy fortifications. Among the few exceptions were New York (originally Dutch), Charles Town, and Savannah.

Continental Europeans were experienced in fortress building, and they constructed the most impressive strongholds in North America. The great stone fortress of San Marcos at the Spanish town of St. Augustine was built from 1672 to 1687 on the site of previous wooden forts to protect Spanish Florida from English aggression. San Marcos was built in the classic square shape, with bastions extending from the corners to enable gunners to attack besiegers at any point. It held dozens of cannons and hundreds of soldiers, and withstood attacks from James Moore in 1702 and James Oglethorpe in 1740.

One of the few early attempts to build an elaborate, European-style fortress in British North America was Old Saybrook, built during the 1630s. The engineer Lion Gardiner led the project under the governor of Connecticut, John Winthrop Jr. The fortress was never completed.

The French were the great fortress builders of colonial America. France had the best engineers and the most advanced techniques. British forts were built somewhat haphazardly, with little central direction. Until the eighteenth century, French forts followed lines south and west from the mouth of the St. Lawrence, south and west through the Great Lakes, and down the Mississippi.

Eighteenth-Century Fortification

The height of fortification in colonial America was in the decades preceding the French and Indian War, as the French and British staked out their claims and prepared themselves for conflict over the interior of North America. Following the Peace of Utrecht in 1713, France built a new fortress, Louisbourg, on Cape Breton Island at the mouth of the St. Lawrence. Incorporating the latest in European fortress design, Louisbourg hung as a perpetual threat over New England. The capture of the fortress by New England troops, aided by a small British fleet, in King George's War (part of the War of the Austrian Succession, as it was called in Europe) was a celebrated achievement, partly due to French ineptitude in allowing the Americans to capture usable guns from the outlying Grand Battery. The decision of the British government to hand the fortress back to France in return for concessions in India as part of the peace settlement provoked great resentment among colonists, although the British established a fortified base at Halifax in Nova Scotia to keep Louisbourg in check. This was a common pattern in this period, as new French fortresses inspired British responses, and vice versa. The young George Washington was in charge of a project to build twenty-one small frontier fortresses for protection against the French and their Native American allies, although all of these proposed fortresses were not built.

The French fortification system met its end during the French and Indian War. Louisbourg was taken again in 1758 by British regular forces under the command of Jeffery Amherst. This time, the fortress was destroyed. The following year, the French themselves destroyed the limestone Fort Saint-Frederic on the narrows of Lake Champlain rather than let it fall into English hands. Fort Saint-Frederic had been a base for numerous armies and raiding parties, French and Native American, against New York and New England.

The colonies lacked the educational system to produce masters of fortification engineering. The British army had brought its own specialists to design and supervise the construction of its American fortresses. This colonial lack was felt keenly at the outset of the American Revolution, although American craftsmen made a partially successful effort to fortify the territory held by the rebels. In the end, it was necessary for the Continental army to employ European specialists, mostly French officers, for its engineering work.

William E. Burns

See also: Fort Duquesne; Fort Orange; Military and Diplomatic Affairs (Chronology); Military and Diplomatic Affairs (Essay); St. Augustine; War; Weaponry.

Bibliography

Grant, Bruce. *American Forts: Yesterday and Today.* New York: Dutton, 1965.

Malone, Patrick. *The Skulking Way of War: Technology and Tactics Among the New England Indians.* Lanham, MD: Madison, 1991.

Rink, Oliver A. *Holland on the Hudson: An Economic and Social History of Dutch New York.* Ithaca and New York: Cornell University Press, 1986.

Steele, Ian. *Betrayals: Fort William Henry and the Massacre.* New York: Oxford University Press, 1990.

———. *Warpaths: Invasions of North America.* New York: Oxford University Press, 1994.

Franciscans

The Franciscan friars are members of a Catholic religious order founded by St. Francis of Assisi in 1208 and officially recognized by Pope Innocent III in 1209. (The female complement of the order, the Poor Clares, was begun in 1212.) The Franciscans' goals are to teach and evangelize as Jesus's apostles did.

The Franciscan friars were instrumental in the spread of Christianity and European influence across today's Mexico and southwestern United States. Franciscan friars accompanied many of the early Spanish conquistadors and played a key role in the spread of Spanish settlement in the New World, especially into today's Texas and California, where they established missions and presidios.

The earliest Franciscans in the Americas sailed to the island of Hispaniola and founded the first monasteries in the New World in the cities of Concepción de la Vega and Santo Domingo. The famous Taino cacique

The Franciscan mission in Trampas, New Mexico, dating to 1700, is one of the best preserved in the Southwest. Franciscan friars played a vital role in the spread of Spanish frontier settlements in the region. *(Library of Congress, USW3-015112-E)*

Enriquillo (who led a successful rebellion against the Spaniards from 1519 to 1534) was educated in the Santo Domingo monastery as a boy, and Bartolomé Colón, Christopher Columbus's brother and the founder of Santo Domingo, was buried there. The Franciscans' fame on Hispaniola, however, was eclipsed by that of the Dominican friars. Their main impact was in New Spain—Spanish Mexico.

Twelve Franciscans arrived in Mexico in May 1524, at Hernando Cortéz's request, to convert the Native Americans. Thirty-five years later, there were 300 of them at eighty Franciscan missions. Franciscans were the most frequent administrators of the Holy Offices of the Inquisition in Mexico City and Lima, Peru (both founded in 1569), and later in Cartagena (1610). Franciscans, aided principally by Juan de Zumárraga (he was the first archbishop of Mexico and brought the first printing press to the Americas), founded the College of Santiago Tlatelolco near Mexico City for the express purpose of training the sons of Native American chiefs to be priests, but their goal was opposed by most Spaniards; from 1555 to 1591, laws were promulgated that specifically prohibited the ordination of Native American priests.

One Franciscan friar, Vasco de Quiroga, used his own money to found a series of missions in Michoacán (he was later made bishop of the region), which were based on the ideas in Sir Thomas More's philosophical novel *Utopia.* Here, Native Americans were taught a wide array of technical skills, such as masonry, carpentry, ironwork, and tanning, and European-style weaving, textile dyeing, ceramics, animal husbandry, and agriculture, in addition to reading, writing, and Christian doctrine. All lands were held communally, and the

Native Americans received social benefits, including hospital care and freedom from abuse. These missions set the pattern for those that would follow.

Among the many Franciscan missions and presidios throughout Texas and California were the Alamo, built in 1744 as the chapel of the Mission San Antonio de Valero (founded in 1718), and San José, San Juan, Concepción, and Espada (the latter was originally called San Francisco de los Tejas), along the San Antonio River in east Texas. The missions of Baja California were founded by a group of friars led by Junípero Serra and included San Diego de Alcalá (1769), Monterey (1770), San Francisco de Asis (in 1776, San Francisco was a presidio, built along with Mission Dolores), and Santa Barbara (1786). Santa Barbara's church design has been traced to a reprint of an architecture book originally published in 27 B.C.E. that one of the Franciscans had in his possession, and of all the California missions, Santa Barbara was the only one that remained in the hands of the founding Franciscan order.

There were also the missions of San Antonio de Padua and San Gabriel Arcángel (1771), San Luis Obispo (1772), San Juan Capistrano (1776), Santa Clara (1777), San Buenaventura (1782), Santa Cruz (1791), San José and San Fernando Rey de España (1797), and San Luis Rey de Francia (1798), among others. The last California mission was founded by General Mariano Vallejo and Friar José L. Quijas in Sonoma, not only to evangelize the Native Americans there but also to stop Russian infiltration (the Russians had built Fort Ross, just to the north). The mission system was abolished by the Mexican government after its independence from Spain in 1834.

The most famous individual Franciscan, without doubt, was Bernardino de Sahagún. Born Francisco Rivera in 1500, Sahagún took the name of his Spanish hometown when he took holy orders. He arrived in Mexico with nineteen other Franciscan friars in 1529 and devoted fifty years of his life to the study of the principal native language Nahuatl, Aztec culture, and history. His most important written work is the *Historia General de las Cosas de la Nueva España* (general history of the things of New Spain), which was highly criticized in its time because it explains the conquest of Mexico from the Aztecs' point of view.

Lynne Guitar

See also: Catholic Church; Dominicans; Jesuits; Missions; Religion (Chronology); Religion (Essay).

Bibliography

Brown, Walden. *Sahagún and the Transition to Modernity*. Norman: University of Oklahoma Press, 2000.

Castañeda, Carlos E. *Our Catholic Heritage in Texas*. 7 vols. New York: Arno, 1976.

Jackson, Robert H., and Edward Castillo. *Indians, Franciscans, and Spanish Colonization: The Impact of the Mission System on California Indians*. Albuquerque: University of New Mexico Press, 1995,

McCarty, Kieran. *Before They Crossed the Great River: Cultural Backgrounds of the Spanish Franciscans of Texas*. Austin: Texas Catholic Historical Society, 1992.

Phelan, John L. *The Millennial Kingdom of the Franciscans in the New World: A Study of the Writings of Gerónimo de Mendieta, 1525–1604*. Berkeley: University of California Press, 1956.

Short, William J. *The Franciscans*. Wilmington, DE: Michael Glazier, 1989.

Franklin, Benjamin (1706–1790)

Benjamin Franklin lived an extraordinary life. He has been called "the first American" by several historians, because he fulfilled the American dream and was such an influential figure in colonial America and in the formation of the United States. He went from rags to riches and from obscurity to world renown. His industry, thrift, and ability to make friends contributed enormously to his success. Franklin was a man of many talents and many occupations, but his most notable roles included printer, author, inventor, scientist, statesman, and diplomat.

Childhood and Apprenticeship

Franklin, one of seventeen children, was born on January 17, 1706, into a pious Puritan family in Boston, Massachusetts. His father, Josiah, who had immigrated to North America from England in 1682, was a soap and candle maker. Franklin's mother, Josiah's second wife, was named Abiah. Franklin held a deep admiration and respect for both of his parents. Josiah taught the young boy how to read; considering his tenth son a tithe for the church, he sent him at the age of 8 years old to begin his education as a minister at Boston Grammar School. The expense proved too difficult for the elder Franklin to bear, however, and he transferred the boy to George Brownell's school, where he studied writing and arithmetic. The young Franklin excelled in writing, but he did poorly in math. After two years, his father could no longer afford to keep him in school, so he brought him back home to work in his soap and candle shop.

Benjamin Franklin hated the smell of the hot wax and the boiling soap, but he obeyed his father and learned his trade. After the boy had spent two years cutting wicks, pouring hot wax into candle molds, and running errands, his father recognized that he was unhappy and asked him what he wished to do instead. Now 12, Franklin informed his father that he longed for a life at sea. Disapproving, his father instead set him up as an apprentice with his half-brother James, a printer. The young man accepted his father's judgment and threw himself into his work. He set type and ran the press. Before long, he mastered the printing trade. In 1721, James, with Benjamin's help, started the weekly *New England Courant*, the fourth newspaper established in colonial America.

Benjamin Franklin read many books on a variety of subjects, but his intellect was mostly stirred by the secular views of Sir Isaac Newton, John Locke, and other writers of the Enlightenment. Consequently, from an early age, Franklin had fused his Calvinist earnestness and work ethic with the new secular philosophies of common sense and personal freedom. Without his brother's knowledge, Franklin wrote clever pieces, using the pen name "Mistress Silence Dogood," sliding them under the newspaper's door. To Franklin's delight, his brother liked the essays and often published them. In 1722, James was arrested for printing political criticism, which the authorities found offensive. This did not deter Franklin. The 16-year-old concealed his status as an apprentice and ran the paper on his own.

After his incarceration, James found out that Franklin was, in fact, his mystery writer, and he refused to print any more of the articles. To make matters worse, James became increasingly jealous of his brother's superior talent and began to beat him. In 1723, determined to endure his brother's abuses no longer, Franklin ran away to Philadelphia at the age of 17. He arrived in the city with only a Dutch dollar and a copper shilling in his pocket. Before long, he had demonstrated his skills and gained employment in Samuel Keimer's print shop.

With his knack for making friends, Franklin befriended Sir William Keith, the governor of the province. Keith was so impressed with Franklin that he encouraged him to start his own printing shop. Since Franklin's father was unable to provide him with the

As a statesman, diplomat, scientist, inventor, civic leader, writer, and printer, Benjamin Franklin—portrayed here by Charles Willson Peale in 1789, the year before his death—was the voice and embodiment of the American character. *(Atwater Kent Museum of Philadelphia/Bridgeman Art Library)*

means to do so, Keith promised to sponsor him and sent Franklin to England to buy the necessary equipment. Unfortunately for Franklin, he arrived in London to discover that the letters of credit that Keith had promised had not been sent. Franklin spent the next year and a half working in London printing houses and sowing some wild oats. His indulgences were so great that he fell into debt. Thomas Denham, another of Franklin's new friends, provided a way for him to escape his creditors and paid for Franklin's passage back to colonial America. Franklin's debt to Denham was forgiven when Denham died.

In 1726, Franklin returned to America and resumed work at Keimer's shop. In 1728, however, he formed a business partnership with Hugh Meredith, a fellow worker in the print shop. With financial support from Meredith's father, the men purchased *The Pennsylvania Gazette* from Keimer in 1729. One year later, the Franklin-Meredith partnership fell apart, and Franklin borrowed money from friends to buy out

Meredith. In 1730, at the age of 24, he became the sole owner of the print shop and the newspaper.

That same year, Franklin formed a common-law union with Deborah Read Rogers, who was married but had been deserted by her husband (upon her husband's death, she married Franklin). They had two children together: Francis Folger, who died at age 4, and Sarah. Franklin also had two illegitimate children: an older son named William and a daughter.

Poor Richard's Almanack

In 1732, Franklin began to publish the annual *Poor Richard's Almanack*, which was a huge success. Franklin printed a new issue every year for twenty-five years (1732–1757), and it sold about 10,000 copies annually. In it, Franklin included information about the weather, some recipes, and a calendar of important dates. Most people, however, read it for its funny stories and commonsense phrases, which could be applied to everyday life. Examples include the familar, "Early to bed, early to rise, makes a man healthy, wealthy, and wise," "Haste makes waste," and "A penny saved is a penny earned."

The paper made Franklin famous in the colonies. It became common practice for colonists to quote the wise phrases in the paper by saying, "as Poor Richard says . . ." Eventually, the *Almanack* reached England, and it was translated and printed in France as well. Success led to more success for Franklin. He became the official printer of Pennsylvania, New Jersey, Delaware, and Maryland.

As his wealth and influence in the colonies continued to grow, Franklin started a lending library, established a volunteer fire department, and promoted a volunteer militia. After his son Francis died of smallpox, Franklin encouraged parents to inoculate their children against the dreaded disease.

His interest in science led him to document his scientific inquiries and experiments. He invented many items, such as a chair that turned into a ladder that could be used to reach books on a shelf. He also invented a very efficient stove, which, before long, was in great demand. Even though he was in a position to profit from his inventions, he chose not to. For Franklin, the satisfaction of knowing he had improved people's lives was payment enough. Besides, the printing business had already made him quite wealthy.

In 1748, Franklin retired at the age of 42. Retirement, however, did not mark the end of his contributions to society. In fact, Franklin, who lived to be 84, remained extremely active during the next forty-two years. He believed that exercise was a key to good health, and he exercised often by swimming, walking, and lifting weights.

Scientific Endeavors

Franklin's scientific endeavors increased after retirement. He made a crude electric battery, which he hoped could be used to cook food. Observing the ocean currents, he discovered that the Gulf Stream, which was warmer than the rest of the water around it, could be located by dipping a thermometer into the ocean.

He conducted an experiment using different-colored cloth patches on the snow. To his surprise, darker colored patches sank deeper in the snow than lighter ones. Consequently, Franklin discovered that darker colors absorb more heat than lighter colors.

While previous street lamps had burned out often, Franklin's new square funnel design burned all night. He grew tired of the inconvenience of needing one pair of glasses to see up close and another pair to see objects far away; his solution was to invent bifocals. Franklin, a violinist and song writer, invented a new instrument called a glass harmonica, which became very popular and was used both in the colonies and in Europe. In order to reach books on a shelf without the use of a ladder, Franklin invented an extended, artificial arm.

His most famous experiment, however, was that of flying a kite during a lightning storm. Although extremely dangerous, the experiment proved the presence of electricity in lightning. Franklin saw a practical application for his discovery. He encouraged people to place a rod on their house so that lightning would hit the rod instead of the home, thereby saving it from fire. More than any other experiment, this particular one gained Franklin world fame. British scientists awarded him a medal, and, even though he had very little formal schooling, his accomplishments gained him the respect of many important and educated people. A number of scientists called him "Dr. Franklin," and intellectuals referred to him as the "darling of the Enlightenment."

Besides improving life for others with his inventions, Franklin also sought to improve himself. He taught himself to read French, Spanish, Italian, and Latin. He made up thirteen rules, which he followed religiously. He worked on putting one of the rules into practice for one week, and then he went on to the next one. After he had completed all of them, he started over with the first one again. His rules included, "Don't eat or drink too much," "Don't waste anything," and "Don't hurt anyone."

Franklin recognized his own brilliance and believed that it was his duty to continue to use his talents in order to improve the world around him in as many ways as he could. For example, in 1737, he became postmaster in Philadelphia. His reforms in mail delivery were so successful that he was appointed deputy postmaster general (1753–1774) for all of the colonies.

Also, in 1751, Franklin established an academy that later became the University of Pennsylvania. That same year, he was instrumental in building the Pennsylvania Hospital, which was the first general hospital in the colonies.

Politics

By 1751, Franklin had become convinced that he could best effect change in the colonies by entering politics. He ran for an assembly seat and won. In this position, he proposed a plan of union for the colonies at the Albany Congress, but it was rejected by the British government.

During the French and Indian War (1754–1763), Franklin served as a general in the British army. He raised troops, built forts, and protected the colonists from the French and their Native American allies; however, a domestic dispute led to Franklin being recalled to the political arena. He returned to his assembly position to find that the war had produced a strain between the Penns, the founders and rulers of Pennsylvania, and the inhabitants of the colony, who accused the Penns of not paying enough to fund the war effort. In 1757, the Pennsylvania Assembly sent Franklin to England to plead its case.

Patriot in England

Franklin and his son William sailed to England together. Once there, Franklin was thrilled to be surrounded by adoring fans, and his celebrity status as America's greatest scientist and inventor led to many social invitations. William entered law school and immersed himself in English high society. Franklin's circle of friends in high places contributed to his son's appointment as royal governor of New Jersey. In addition, Franklin's mission was a success. In 1760, the British governor ordered the Penns to pay their fair share of the war expenses.

His mission accomplished, Franklin returned to America, but problems between the Penns and Pennsylvanians persisted. By 1764, popular sentiment supported ousting the Penns from Pennsylvania.

Consequently, Franklin returned to England with a new mission, which was abandoned when more pressing needs arose shortly after he arrived.

This time, strained relations between the colonies and the mother country were to keep Franklin in England for much longer. The French and Indian War had created a financial strain on the British treasury, and King George III, for the first time, supported taxing the colonists directly in order to raise needed revenue. The Stamp Act (1765), for example, placed a tariff on all printed materials. The colonists were in an uproar over what they perceived to be a violation of their rights. Since they did not have representation in Parliament, they did not feel that Parliament had a right to tax them directly. "No taxation without representation" became a new popular political slogan in America. Franklin spoke for the colonists in British newspapers and in Parliament.

Franklin's life in England between 1765 and 1775 was spent as an advocate for colonial rights. As British-American relations worsened, personal relations between Franklin and his son also deteriorated. In 1774, William informed his father of the death of Franklin's wife of forty-four years, blaming him for it. Furthermore, Parliament wished to make Franklin a scapegoat for all the troubles between the colonies and the mother country and accused him of being a troublemaker.

Franklin, who had fallen in love with England, reluctantly left for home. By the time he arrived in Philadelphia, the first battles of the American Revolution at Lexington and Concord (1775) had already occurred. Franklin never looked back. From that point on, he shed his allegiance to England and became a formidable revolutionary.

American Revolution

During the American Revolution, Franklin served as an American agent in France. Perhaps his greatest service to America was convincing France to aid the colonists. (Without France's aid, victory would have been far more difficult, if not impossible.) In 1781, Franklin was appointed commissioner to negotiate peace terms with Britain. Having done so, he later served as a delegate to the Constitutional Convention in 1787.

In the years that followed, Franklin urged the colonies to ratify the Constitution, and he supported the inauguration of the new government. Perhaps only George Washington did more than Benjamin Franklin to free the United States from England.

One of the greatest and most enlightened thinkers in the colonies, Franklin's efforts helped set the United States on a firm constitutional foundation. He died on April 17, 1790.

Rolando Avila

See also: Art, Cartoons, and Broadsides; Artisans; Arts, Culture, and Intellectual Life (Chronology); Arts, Culture, and Intellectual Life (Essay); Diplomacy (Foreign Affairs); Enlightenment; Franklin, William; Military and Diplomatic Affairs (Chronology); Military and Diplomatic Affairs (Essay); Newspapers and Journals; Philadelphia; *Poor Richard's Almanack;* Revolutionary War; Science; Science and Technology (Chronology). *Documents:* Maxims from *Poor Richard's Almanack* (1739); Advice to a Young Tradesman (1748); A Report on the Kite Experiment (1752); Correspondence of Benjamin Franklin (1752, 1753, 1769).

Bibliography

Brands, H. W. *The First American: The Life and Times of Benjamin Franklin.* New York: Anchor, 2002.

Currey, Cecil B. *Road to Revolution: Benjamin Franklin in England, 1765–1775.* Garden City, NY: Anchor, 1968.

Dull, Jonathon R. *Franklin the Diplomat: The French Mission.* Philadelphia: American Philosophical Society, 1982.

Isaacson, Walter. *Benjamin Franklin: An American Life.* New York: Simon & Schuster, 2003.

Jennings, Francis. *Benjamin Franklin: Politician.* New York: W. W. Norton, 1996.

Labaree, Leonard Woods, and Edmund Sears Morgan, eds. *The Autobiography of Benjamin Franklin.* New Haven, CT: Yale University Press, 2003.

Morgan, Edmund Sears. *Benjamin Franklin.* New Haven, CT: Yale University Press, 2002.

Van Doren, Carl. *Benjamin Franklin.* New York: Viking Press, 1938.

Franklin, William (c. 1730–1814)

William Franklin, born between September 1730 and March 1731, was the illegitimate son of Benjamin Franklin. He was raised in Philadelphia by his stepmother, Deborah Read Rogers Franklin, and his father, who made certain that his son received a formal education. William Franklin studied under Theopholis Grew in 1738 and at Alexander Annand's classical academy from 1739 to 1743.

After completing his studies at the academy, young Franklin worked in his father's print shop. The vocation did not suit him, however, and, in 1746, Benjamin Franklin arranged for William to serve as an ensign in one of the Philadelphia companies raised for service during King George's War. Military life suited William Franklin, and he ascended to the rank of captain before the end of hostilities.

Not content in Philadelphia, Franklin joined Conrad Weisner's expedition over the Allegheny Mountains in 1748. This was the first British expedition into the Ohio River Valley. Franklin enjoyed the wilderness and spent the remainder of his life, to no avail, attempting to profit on Western lands.

Franklin returned to Philadelphia in the early 1750s and, with his father's assistance, began his government career. He served as clerk to the justice of the peace and postmaster general of Philadelphia before Benjamin Franklin appointed him controller of the North American postal system. The outbreak of the French and Indian War brought Franklin back to the Pennsylvania frontier. He served as his father's aide de camp and field secretary as they attempted to bolster Pennsylvania's western defenses in the face of unremitting Native American depredations.

Franklin accompanied his father to London in 1757. He acted as Benjamin Franklin's aide and confidant while also engaging in legal work at Middle Temple. Throughout his early career, Franklin actively supported his father's political positions through pamphlet writing, a skill that served him well in later years.

While living in London, Franklin fathered his own illegitimate child, William Temple, who was born sometime after 1759. He also courted and married Elizabeth Downes, the daughter of a wealthy Barbadian planter, in 1762. When Franklin left England, he returned to the colonies, with experience and political connections. Shortly after his return, he was appointed royal governor of New Jersey. The young governor had his work cut out for him. New Jersey remained a politically divided colony even after its unification in 1702. As evidence of this factionalism, Franklin was sworn into office in each of the colony's two competing capitals in 1763.

Franklin's first decade as governor proved rather successful. He managed to steer a moderate course, reconciling sectional differences and defending the king's interests without offending the assembly. Prior to the Revolution, New Jersey remained one of the more conservative colonies, and the governor managed to sidestep controversial acts passed by Parliament. Parliament repealed the Stamp Act before Franklin faced serious political opposition, and British troops were removed from New Jersey to satisfy opponents of the Mutiny Act. The Coercive Acts, however, ruptured Franklin's relationship both with the citizens of New Jersey and with his father.

The governor diligently defended the British Crown and detested political extremism. He believed that rapprochement with England was desirable and opposed the extralegal bodies then forming in the colonies and subverting the Crown's authority. Franklin communicated updates on colonial activities to London, and he encouraged the New Jersey assembly to seek a separate peace with Britain.

Franklin's actions came to the attention of the Continental Congress, which viewed him as a serious threat. In 1776, he was arrested and imprisoned in Connecticut. His lax incarceration permitted him correspondence, the freedom of the town, and rides in the countryside. Franklin used these liberties to maintain contact with other loyalists and to encourage local farmers to abandon the rebellion. In 1777, the same year that his wife died, Franklin was restricted to solitary confinement for eight months.

Later exchanged for Governor John McKinly of Delaware, Franklin continued to actively support the British war effort from New York. He organized loyalist refugees and successfully petitioned for the establishment of the semiautonomous Board of Associated Loyalists in 1779. The board gathered intelligence on rebel strength and activities, conducted raids, and organized New York's defenses. Most importantly, Franklin and the board acted as the political voice of the loyalist population.

Franklin was implicated in the loyalists' execution of a rebel prisoner, and, in 1782, he departed America for the last time. He lived the remainder of his life in exile in England, where he continued to assist loyalists, helping them submit claims to the British government for losses sustained during the Revolution. In 1788, Franklin married his landlady, Mary D'Evelyn, but he remained estranged from his family until his death in 1814.

Thomas Nester

See also: Franklin, Benjamin; Loyalists.

Bibliography

Randall, Willard Sterne. *A Little Revenge: Benjamin Franklin and His Son.* Boston: Little, Brown, 1984.

Skemp, Sheila L. *Benjamin and William Franklin: Father and Son, Patriot and Loyalist. The Bedford Series in History and Culture.* Edited by Natalie Zemon Davis and Ernest R. May. Boston: Bedford/St. Martin's, 1994.

———. *William Franklin: Son of a Patriot, Servant of a King.* New York: Oxford University Press, 1990.

Free Blacks

The status of free blacks varied throughout colonial America. Not all blacks who arrived in America came as slaves. The status of the first blacks who arrived in 1619 is unclear, but it is likely that they were indentured servants, bound to service for a set term and then set free to make their own way. The same was true of later arrivals as well. It was not until the late seventeenth century that the majority of blacks who came to the colonies arrived as slaves.

Population

It is difficult to determine how populous free blacks were in the colonies. They were not counted for purposes of taxes, census, or military service, nor were they generally included in church records. It is estimated that before 1770, approximately 5 percent of northern blacks were free. Larger pockets of free blacks appeared in some colonies; in 1764, as many as 40 percent of Massachusetts blacks may have been free. In the Southern colonies, fewer than 5 percent of blacks were free. As slavery became more prominent, the population of free blacks decreased. The first census to record the free black population came in 1790, and it reported some 13,000 freedmen living in the New England states.

Enslaved blacks were able to obtain their freedom in a variety of ways. Masters sometimes chose to free their slaves through manumission, with freedom beginning upon the master's death. In order for manumission to be recorded by the court, a manumission deed was required, a document that generally necessitated a monetary fee and some knowledge of the legal system. A high proportion of slaves freed in this manner were mulattos, children, and women.

A less common means of obtaining freedom was through self-purchase. Some slaves were able to earn cash (usually by working on their own after completing their required labor) and pay their master for their freedom. At times, freedom brokers were involved in the process. Whites would buy slaves from their masters, with money that the slaves had earned themselves, and then free them. Slaves who attempted to gain their freedom in this manner were subject to the honesty of the whites who helped them, and some found themselves still enslaved, despite having paid the price of their purchase.

The most common way for a slave to obtain freedom was by running away. Cities with larger populations of free blacks provided anonymity for fugitive slaves. Runaway slaves occasionally settled into established maroon communities, settlements deep in the frontier areas, where the inhabitants were generally all runaway slaves.

The colony of Louisiana differed from the British colonies. Before the introduction of sugar and the entrenchment of slave labor, a labor shortage prompted the Spanish Crown to promote the development of a free black class to fill middle-class working positions and defend the colony. This free black population grew from just 97 in 1771 to 315 three years later. Free blacks in colonial Louisiana were able to attain a measure of success by working for wages and operating business enterprises, and through inheritances from whites and other free blacks. Their ability to acquire marketable skills and their ties to the white community helped to promote the importance of free blacks in the colony.

Some free blacks even owned slaves. This was more often a case of purchasing relatives after obtaining their own freedom, although some free blacks did mimic the white practice of chattel slavery in an effort to identify with white society.

Laws Governing Free Blacks

The free black population presented a dilemma for colonial leaders. Free blacks hovered in a status somewhere between slave and white. Their color relegated them to an inferior social status, but their freedom prevented them from being controlled like the slave population. In South Carolina, whites sought to eliminate the nebulous category of free blacks through the 1740 Negro Act, a law that assumed all blacks were slaves. As slavery became more firmly entrenched in the colonies, the presence of free blacks proved even more troublesome for whites, resulting in a series of laws throughout the colonies designed to restrict the free black population. That colonial leaders had difficulty categorizing free blacks is evident in the fact that most laws designed to govern them were found in the slave codes.

Throughout the colonies, free blacks were prevented from serving as soldiers in local militias. Both Connecticut and New Hampshire excluded free blacks entirely. Massachusetts required free blacks to serve in the militia; however, they were relegated to such menial tasks as repairing highways and cleaning city streets rather than drilling and preparing for battle with the regular militia. Only in times of alarm were free blacks allowed to perform other duties, but even those were limited by the commanding officer and might not have included bearing weapons. Additionally, most colonies passed laws that prohibited free blacks from bearing weapons. Pennsylvania required free blacks to obtain a special license in order to own a firearm. Virginia and South Carolina boasted similar provisions; generally licenses were awarded only to those living in frontier areas.

Other typical laws that governed free blacks included punishments restricting freedom. Free blacks who loitered could be bound out for service as apprentices; the children of indigent free blacks were also subject to forced apprenticeship. Trade between free blacks and slaves was prohibited without the consent of the slave's master, and free blacks faced severe fines and penalties for harboring fugitive slaves.

Social and Living Conditions

Laws, including those that prevented free blacks from assembling in companies and disallowed the sale of liquor to them, also restricted their social life. Marriage between free blacks and whites was forbidden; in Pennsylvania, free blacks who violated that law could be sold into slavery for life. Many colonies required free blacks to obtain a pass in order to travel outside the limits of the town in which they lived and imposed a curfew as early as 9 P.M. Free blacks were also prevented from entertaining slaves in their homes.

Many colonies established laws that prevented free blacks from owning property. New York and New Jersey had specific provisions that restricted them from owning real estate, and Virginia's laws prohibited free blacks from owning slaves. South Kingstown, Rhode Island, prevented free blacks from owning horses, sheep, and other domestic animals. A 1717 Connecticut law was likely the most severe example of regulations that restricted property ownership: Free blacks were prohibited from living in any town in the colony, purchasing land, or carrying out business; the provisions of the law were retroactive.

Upward mobility also was limited. A free black rising to a position of prominence threatened the white population. Whites sought to limit black employment to the type of menial labor that denoted subservience. There were no public schools for free blacks, and economic opportunities were also minimal. Free blacks competed with whites for jobs and were often denied jobs because of their color. Excluded from skilled labor positions, free blacks struggled to make their livelihood doing the same type of work that slaves did, working on farms or as domestic servants, signing on as sailors, and involving themselves in various trades.

In matters of health care and material provisions, slaves often fared better than did the free black population. The lack of good employment led to miserable living conditions, particularly in the cities, where free blacks tended to cluster. Because they could afford no better, their homes were those available to the lowest-income population, and creature comforts were nearly nonexistent. Free blacks often made their homes in alleys and on riverfronts or docks. In 1742, over 7 percent of Boston's black population was free but living in the almshouse. Free blacks also lacked the protection that a white master could provide and were often subject to violent attacks.

Despite the best efforts of the white population to restrict free blacks and relegate them to a status that closely resembled slavery, there were stories of success. Captain Paul Cuffee prospered on the seas and became a prominent New England merchant. Emanuel Bernoon was the owner of a successful oyster house, and Lucy Terry Prince gained renown as a poet and storyteller.

The American Revolution affected the free black population in numerous ways. Northern free blacks sought to join the war effort. The ideas of the Revolution stood in direct contrast to the practice of slavery and led to the eventual demise of slavery in the Northern states and considerable numbers of manumissions in the Upper South, increasing the free black population. The idea of freedom spread. Many slaves served in the British army, having been told they would gain their freedom at the war's end. After the war, the British removed most of those slaves to Nova Scotia and gave them their freedom. Virginia and Maryland also both saw large jumps in their population of free blacks, which numbered nearly 30,000 in 1790.

After the Revolution, those blacks who remained enslaved found the idea of freedom more concrete. Yet the reality of freedom remained more difficult to obtain, as slavery became firmly entrenched in American law.

Tonia M. Compton

See also: African Americans; Slavery, African American.

Bibliography

Greene, Lorenzo Johnston. *The Negro in Colonial New England.* New York: Atheneum, 1969.

Hanger, Kimberly. "Patronage, Property and Persistence: The Emergence of a Free Black Elite in Spanish New Orleans." In *Against the Odds: Free Blacks in the Slave Societies of the Americas,* edited by Jane G. Landers. Portland, OR: Cass, 1996.

Newman, Debra. "Black Women in the Era of the American Revolution in Pennsylvania." *Journal of Negro History* 61:3 (1976): 276–89.

Olwell, Robert. "Becoming Free: Manumission and the Genesis of a Free Black Community in South Carolina, 1740–90." In *Against the Odds: Free Blacks in the Slave Societies of the Americas,* edited by Jane G. Landers. Portland, OR: Cass, 1996.

Piersen, William. *Black Yankees: The Development of an Afro-American Subculture in Eighteenth Century New England.* Amherst: University of Massachusetts Press, 1988.

Wiecek, William. "The Statutory Law of Slavery and Race in the Thirteen Mainland Colonies of British America." *William & Mary Quarterly* 34:2 (1977): 258–80.

Wright, Donald. *African Americans in the Colonial Era.* Wheeling, IL: Harlan Davidson, 2000.

French

The French presence in the Americas was tenuous from start to finish, because France failed to attract sufficient population to the regions it claimed. Strong central control reduced autonomous decision making in French colonies, and the location of many colonies in undesirable or dangerous areas discouraged immigration. Despite centuries of effort, when France fought Britain for empire between 1690 and 1763, the superior British presence ended French aspirations in the New World.

When the Italian John Cabot explored parts of North America in 1497 and 1498 for England, the only French there were the fishermen off Nova Scotia and Newfoundland who traded sporadically with the Native Americans. French trinkets bought American furs, but the government of France had greater aspirations; it wanted gold and silver to match what the Portuguese and Spanish had found to the south.

A quarter century passed before France began explorations to the north—Giovanni da Verrazano sailed up the East Coast for France in 1524, and Jacques Cartier explored the coast and the St. Lawrence River in three trips between 1534 and 1541. Cartier returned to France after finding the St. Lawrence River impassable above Montreal. A weak settlement founded by Cartier failed, and France forgot the northern lands for another sixty years.

To the south, Jean Ribault led the French effort to establish a presence at the St. Johns River (in present-day northern Florida) in 1562. Ribault also established a colony at Charlesfort (South Carolina) that failed. René de Laudonniére established a fort at La Caroline on the St. Johns in 1564. The Spanish destroyed the fort, establishing St. Augustine in the process. When Ribault tried to remove the Spanish, the French forces proved too weak to compete with even the overextended Spanish. A toehold in Brazil, part of the general European rush of the second half of the century, proved equally tenuous.

While the French government turned its attention away from the New World, French fishermen continued their small but regular fur trade with the Native Americans. When, in the late sixteenth century, beaver hats became fashionable, the French government built on the trade the fishermen had established. As good mercantilists, the French tried to establish royal monopolies over the trade, but they did not back the royal licenses with manpower and other resources. Each of the several late-sixteenth- and early-seventeenth-century efforts to establish a profitable fur trade failed. A veteran of a failed colony in Acadia, Samuel de Champlain, took colonists to Quebec, established the first permanent French settlement in 1608, and became the "father of New France."

Once New France gained a toehold on the continent, small French parties used the waterways to penetrate the interior for exploration and trade. Etienne Brûlé was the first European to see Lake Superior. Champlain himself was the first European to discover Lake Champlain in 1609, and he explored Huronia in 1615.

The French colony itself struggled. In 1629, Quebec's near-starving citizens fell to the English, who returned Quebec during the later peace, allowing New France to survive, if not prosper.

The French approach to colonial development was flawed. The emphasis on the fur trade and the feudal land system—in which landowners were vassals of the king, and those who worked the land were vassals of the landowners—hampered growth. The English system allowed more autonomy, even in New England, with its early insistence on settlement by town unit. New France also lacked representative government.

In addition, the colony faced hostile Iroquois, who resented Champlain's taking the side of the Huron in the Huron-Iroquois wars. In 1648–1649, the Iroquois bested both the Huron and the French Jesuits, and this tribe continued to threaten the colonists of sparsely populated New France until nearly the end of the seventeenth century.

French weakness in attracting colonists contrasted with English strength. In 1650, England had ten self-sufficient colonies with a population of 52,000. By 1666, New France still had only 3,215 inhabitants. By the time of the French and Indian War, the English colonies had 1.7 million people. Yet France persisted in expanding the domain of New France, if not its population.

French explorers continued to probe deeper into the continent. When La Salle reached the mouth of the Mississippi River in 1682, France claimed lands blocking the English colonial frontier from the Great Lakes and Ohio River Valley to the Gulf of Mexico. It was a claim that was more impressive on the map than in reality. For instance, French Louisiana claimed the watershed of the Mississippi, but France had people only in Mobile and New Orleans.

As the two empires expanded, French borders reached those of the English. Expanding French territory and growing English populations meant conflict with French explorers and trappers. From the establishment of the Hudson's Bay Company in 1670, trading wars were just parts of the larger wars for empire. French trappers Pierre Troyes and Pierre le Moyne, Sieur d'Iberville, took the battle to the Hudson's Bay Company and almost drove the English out of the fur region in the late eighteenth century.

At the same time, the Anglo-French wars began: King William's War (in Europe, the War of the League of Augsburg), 1689–1697, Queen Anne's War (War of the Spanish Succession), 1702–1713, King George's War (the colonial portion of the War of the Austrian Succession), 1744–1748, and the French and Indian War, 1754–1763 (in Europe, the Seven Years' War, 1756–1763). When Wolfe defeated Montcalm at Quebec, the French were effectively eliminated as a major power on the North American continent.

The French still maintained a strong presence in the Caribbean, where they had served as privateers and merchants from the sixteenth century. In the first fifty years of the seventeenth century, they established tobacco colonies at St. Christopher, Martinique, and Guadeloupe. King Louis XIII authorized slavery in the

French West Indies in 1636. The French also colonized St. Croix in 1650. The tobacco islands faded with the opening of highly profitable plantations on the sugar islands, the most important of which was Saint-Domingue (western Hispaniola), founded in 1664.

The Caribbean was inhospitable. Mosquitoes attacked white rulers and black slaves equally, bringing yellow fever, malaria, and other diseases that were often fatal. But the Caribbean also meant wealth for young, ambitious Frenchmen willing to risk an early death. Slaves, of course, had no choice. They also had to endure insufficient food and brutality. Many of them had some immunity to the tropical diseases, but that did not keep them from dying from dysentery, influenza, and other diseases made deadly by malnutrition and lack of medical treatment.

By the 1730s, the Caribbean colonies were about 10 percent European, 5 percent mulatto, and 85 percent African. By 1780, Saint-Domingue had half a million slaves. Revolutionary France freed the slaves, but Napoleon reinstituted slavery until 1848, when the rise of beet sugar made sugar cane colonies less profitable and slavery economically less important.

In South America, France had Guiana. In 1604, while the Spanish and Portuguese were loading American gold into European coffers, the French sent their first expedition to Guiana. Because the Dutch and English were there, too, Henry IV authorized settlement; however, as before, France's effort was too weak.

Two decades later, the Rouen Commercial Company sent twenty-six settlers to establish a village at Sinnamary; these settlers later united with others at Cayenne. In 1643, the governor was so bad that first his officers and then the native peoples rose against him; the latter, being stronger, destroyed the colony.

In 1656, a Dutch force of sixty refugees from Brazil seized French Guiana and established a sugar-exporting colony. A French force of 1,200 retook the colony in 1663–1664. Over the next 100 years, the French, Dutch, and English competed for the area, with the French losing it to the English in 1667 but taking it back in 1676. By 1763, Guiana had become important, since France, having lost much territory after the French and Indian War, had no significant American empire. Guiana remained the largest French possession.

Louis XV, king of France, needed a base from which to control slave rebellions on his remaining islands, and he sent 14,000 French settlers to Kourou, north of Cayenne. After 10,000 died in the first two years, the survivors relocated to the Îles du Salut (Salvation Islands), where malaria was less prevalent. By

the time of the French Revolution and emancipation, Guiana had 10,000 slaves, 500 free blacks, and 1,500 Europeans.

The French presence in the Caribbean fluctuated with the fortunes of war. The American Revolution brought St. Lucia back, but it didn't come close to recapturing the losses of the French and Indian War. Disaster struck in 1791, when the slaves rose up in Saint-Domingue, the jewel of the empire. Under first Toussaint L'Ouverture and then Jean-Jacques Dessalines, the slaves bested French, Spanish, and English forces and, finally, won independence as Haiti in 1804. In the meantime, France was again at war with England, losing its colonies, regaining them in the peace, only to lose them again when the war resumed. Napoleon decided that Louisiana was probably not a viable investment for France, so he sold it to the United States in 1803.

Being of no economic benefit, Guiana seemed a good location for a prison; the first political prisoners began arriving in 1795 and quickly died due to the unhealthy environment. The prison idea dwindled until 1852, when Louis Napoleon decided to build a penal colony to replace the prison ships off the French coast. Once again, half of the prisoners died within the year, and the prison camp soon closed. Eventually, the prisons relocated to relatively healthful locations, but for eighty years, well into the twentieth century, Devil's Island and other sites killed prisoners at a high rate.

French population in the Americas never matched French ambitions. Colonies were established and faded. When the colonial period ended, the French had little more than a handful of Caribbean islands and disease-ridden prison colonies to show for their efforts.

John H. Barnhill

See also: Acadians; Canada; Cartier, Jacques; Champlain, Samuel de; Detroit; Edict of Nantes, Revocation of; Fort Duquesne; French and Indian War; French Colonies on Mainland North America (Chronology); Furs; Huguenots; Jolliet, Louis; La Salle, René Robert Cavelier, Sieur de; Louis XIV; Louisiana; Marquette, Jacques; Montcalm, Louis-Joseph; Montreal; Native American–European Relations; New Orleans; Quebec Act (1774); Quebec City; Saint-Domingue. *Documents:* Marquette's Travels on the Mississippi (1673); The French and the Fur Trade (1724).

Bibliography

Eccles, William John. *The French in North America: 1500–1783.* East Lansing: Michigan State University Press, 1998.
"French Colonial Empire." http://www.wikipedia.org/wiki/French_Colonial_Empire.

Garner, Ray. "A High Price in Human Lives Was Paid for French Wealth from the Caribbean," 2000 Research Review, University of Alabama in Huntsville. http://www.uah.edu/News/2000rr/french.html.

Hart, Jonathan. *Representing the New World: The English and French Uses of the Example of Spain.* New York: St. Martin's, 2001.

"The History of Canada." http://www.linksnorth.com/canada-history/thefounding.html.

Holbrook, Sabra. *The French Founders of North America and Their Heritage.* New York: Atheneum, 1976.

Miles, Alexander. *Devil's Island: Colony of the Damned.* Berkeley, CA: Ten Speed, 1988.

Miquelon, Dale Bernard. *Dugard of Rouen: French Trade to Canada and the West Indies, 1729–1770.* Montreal: McGill-Queen's University Press, 1978.

Munford, Clarence J. *The Black Ordeal of Slavery; Slave Trading in the French West Indies, 1625–1715.* Lewiston, NY: Edwin Mellen, 1991.

National Park Service. "European Exploration of the Southeast and Caribbean." http://www.cr.nps.gov/seac/outline/07-exploration/index.htm.

French and Indian War

The Seven Years' War, known in America as the French and Indian War, established British supremacy over most of North America. As a result of its defeat, France ceased to be a colonial power in North America.

The impact of this conflict on Native Americans was more ambiguous. Large, interior nations, which had previously been able to play the English and French off each other for their own diplomatic game, now faced not only increasing white settlement in their lands but a powerful, far-reaching bureaucracy that cared more about the maintenance of its overseas empire than the promises it made to the native peoples.

It would not be an exaggeration to call the Seven Years' War a global conflict. In addition to the fighting in Europe and North America, French and British interests battled in India, Africa, the Philippines, and the Caribbean.

Prelude to War

Though the French and English had fought over North America off and on for several decades, the French and Indian War eclipsed all of these conflicts in terms of the amount of destruction and the finality of its result. Throughout the late seventeenth and early eighteenth centuries, France and England jostled for territory, access to profitable trade, and alliances with powerful Native American nations, such as the Creek, Cherokee, and Iroquois. Roughly concurrent with this fighting was an explosion in the population of British America. In 1700, a quarter of a million people lived in the English colonies; in 1750, this number had grown to 1.2 million, and, by 1760, the population had reached 1.6 million. This rapid growth was due in large part to Scots-Irish and German immigrants, who moved into the American backcountry throughout the eighteenth century. Speculation in land, the formation of land companies, and the speedy settlement of frontier territory brought the English, French, and Native Americans into new kinds of contact with one another. English colonies were no longer tiny outposts along the Eastern seaboard; rather, they were turning into large, profitable, and well-populated colonies.

The implications of rapid colonial development were not lost on the French, who sought to secure Native American allies against British expansion through the early 1750s. The French intended to capitalize on their strengths in the Ohio Valley and the Great Lakes, areas as yet unsettled by the British. They constructed a number of forts in the Ohio Valley and encouraged the Iroquois, Shawnee, and Delaware to join them against the English. Most Native American groups approached by the French were reluctant to fight the English, who provided them with more goods and cheaper prices than the French. In 1752, in an effort to change that situation, French soldiers and allied Native Americans attacked English trading posts and replaced them with their own forts.

Matters came to a head in Virginia in 1754, when the British governor of Virginia, Robert Dinwiddie, sent men under the young George Washington to kick the French out of Fort Duquesne, a recently constructed stronghold near the Forks of the Ohio (near present-day Pittsburgh). On the way, Washington erected Fort Necessity; his defeat of a small French patrol in turn incited the larger French force to surround his encampment and force his surrender. The remnants of Washington's army straggled back to Virginia.

The English response to the French threat was not particularly encouraging. Colonial leaders and representatives of the Iroquois gathered at the Albany Congress in 1754. This was a halfhearted attempt to forge a bond between the different English colonies and draw the Iroquois into the English camp. The congress accomplished little, other than to prove that agents of different colonial land companies were already carving

The French and Indian War began on July 3, 1754, with a defeat by the French of British colonial troops at Fort Necessity, a small stockade in the mountains of southwestern Pennsylvania. The colonials were commanded by 22-year-old George Washington. *(Fort Necessity National Park)*

up Iroquois territory by signing questionable deals with minor polities.

In Europe, British and French officials were already busy planning an all-out war for North America. In 1755, the British sent Edward Braddock and 2,200 men to capture Fort Duquesne. Meanwhile, the French sent 3,000 men to Louisbourg and Quebec. Braddock's campaign proved disastrous to the British. A force of around 1,000 French and Native Americans ambushed Braddock's regulars 10 miles from the fort, killing or wounding about half the men, including Braddock, who died of his wounds four days after the battle; the French forces suffered minimal casualties of their own.

Braddock's arrogance and unwillingness to use Native American allies (only eight scouts accompanied the expedition) in his campaign was a major factor in this disaster. One Native American scout recalled that Braddock treated the natives like animals and ignored their advice.

British Losses and the Turning of the Tide

In the wake of Braddock's defeat at Fort Duquesne, the Lenni Lenape and Shawnee renewed their efforts against colonial settlements in western Pennsylvania, Virginia, and Maryland. By the spring of 1756, 700 colonists had been killed or captured. Thousands more fled to the relative safety of the East. These raids aided the French cause greatly, and a combined force of French regulars, colonials, and Native Americans took Oswego, on Lake Ontario (in 1756), and Fort William Henry (in 1757) under the leadership of Governor General Pierre de Rigaud de Vaudreuil and General Louis-Joseph Montcalm. The situation was so desperate in Pennsylvania that the governor was said to have considered allowing hostile Native Americans to pass through Pennsylvania unharmed if they would stop attacking Pennsylvania and instead concentrate their efforts on the Virginia frontier.

Raids continued elsewhere along the frontier, from New York to Georgia. Morale in the English colonies was painfully low. The British colonies were divided among themselves, and 70,000 French Canadians and their allies were whipping a population of a million and a half supported by the British army. The British hoped to be able to persuade the major interior nations of the Iroquois, the Lenni Lenape, Shawnee, Cherokee, Creek, and Choctaw, to join their side, or at least to remain neutral. At this point, the English colonies were entirely dependent upon Native American support.

In 1756 and 1757, Britain's luck improved, and the tide of the war began to turn as the result of a number of factors. By paying Mohawk mercenaries some 32,602 pounds, the British ensured that they would at least quiet attack by the Lenni Lenape, even if they did not join the side of the English. In 1759, the Mohawks chose the English because of their proximity to fur traders at Albany, their attachments to Sir William Johnson, and the large amount they were paid. British victories had also convinced the Mohawks that they were likely to win the war.

The Iroquois played the war perfectly, in terms of politics. They maintained neutrality until it was clear that their best interest lay in supporting the British. The sad footnote to this is, of course, the fact that the Iroquois were much more powerful when they could play the English and French off each another. The situation they faced in 1763 offered no such option.

Meanwhile, back in England, poor conduct of the war had forced a change in government. William Pitt became prime minister in 1757, and he took a fierce interest in the prosecution of the war. Though the war had spread to Europe in 1756, Pitt continued to pour money and men into North America, believing it to be the heart of the conflict. Though he was probably correct in this belief, it led to wild spending that would catch up with Great Britain in the decades to come. One of Pitt's most successful policy shifts came when he stopped the practice of requiring American colonies to provide troops and supplies and began to reimburse them. The colonies pursued the war with renewed vigor.

In 1758, Britain fielded an army of 45,000, half regular troops and half colonials, against a French force of 6,800 regulars and 2,700 colonials. Both sides had Native Americans supporting them, but the sheer number of troops involved made this a European fight. After poor Canadian harvests in 1757 and 1758, the French forces in North America were starving and morale was low. British units now employed colonial and Native American scouts, and some infantry units trained with rifles and tomahawks instead of muskets. Add to this the fact that the British were winning the war at sea and the French were losing interest in Canada and focusing more intently on the conflict in Europe, and it is not hard to see why the British made significant gains in 1758 and 1759.

In 1758, a British army approached Fort Duquesne for the third time. This time, after the Lenni Lenape deserted to reestablish trade with Pennsylvanians, the French abandoned the fort, blowing it up upon their retreat. The British built Fort Pitt, which was ten times larger than Duquesne, on the site. Also in 1758, the British under General Jeffery Amherst captured Louisbourg, the fortress that controlled access to the St. Lawrence River and Quebec beyond. In 1759, forces under General James Wolfe attacked Quebec and met the army of Montcalm in a pitched battle. The French retreated to Quebec. Both Montcalm and Wolfe were fatally wounded in the battle, but Quebec was now in British hands. In 1760, British forces surrounded Montreal, forcing Vaudreuil to abandon the city and surrender all the remaining French forts in North America.

Although the war was effectively over in North America, the British war machine was still in high gear. The British had mastered the art of financing, organizing, and executing overseas wars. They had used this prowess to take Martinique and other sugar-rich islands from the French in the Caribbean, take Manila and Havana from the Spanish, and assert themselves as the dominant European power in India. The Treaty of Paris, signed in 1763, recognized British supremacy in North America. It also returned the more profitable sugar islands to the French, gave Spanish Florida to the British in exchange for Havana, and French Louisiana to the Spanish. One could argue that, in the case of the North American interior, European powers did not have the authority to simply swap lands. In 1763, it mattered little to native peoples in the Mississippi River Valley whether France, Great Britain, or Spain "owned" the land.

Aftermath

The removal of the French from North America brought about an unfortunate situation for most of the native peoples of the Ohio River valley, the Southeast, and the Great Lakes region. The rise of Anglo-American power spelled disaster for many of these tribes.

The Cherokee were among the first to recognize their dire situation. In 1759, in response to South Carolinian deer poaching and land grabbing, the Cherokee killed about thirty settlers. When South Carolina's governor called for the killers, the Cherokee responded by offering one French scalp or prisoner for every dead Carolinian. The governor rejected the offer; instead the Carolinians seized and killed a negotiating party of twenty-two native chiefs. Until 1760, British regulars, Carolina volunteers, and Cherokee fought back and forth across the frontier. In 1761, a peace treaty was signed, and, in 1766, a formal boundary was drawn between South Carolina and the Cherokee.

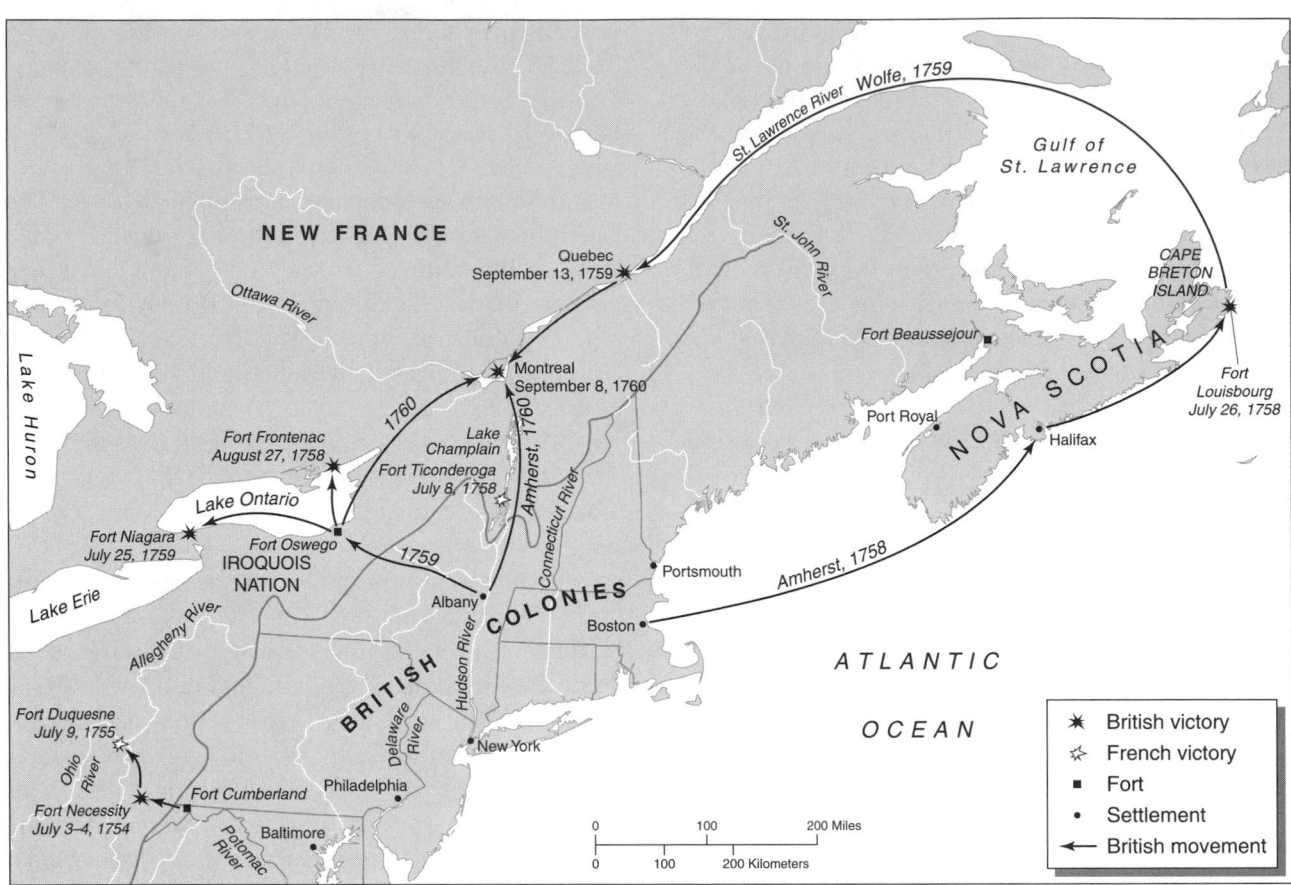

French and Indian War, 1754–1763. With its victory in the French and Indian War, the British gained control over virtually all of mainland North America east of the Mississippi River. *(Carto-Graphics)*

In the Great Lakes and Ohio River Valley, a different situation existed. There was no single dominant Native American nation, such as the Cherokee, but rather networks of basically autonomous villages; historian Richard White described the colonial situation there as a "middle ground." In the decades before the French and Indian War, neither Native Americans nor the European settlers could entirely impose their will in the region. The result of this situation was a tenuous peace, based on trade, between Europeans and natives. The removal of the French from the situation and the presence of serious British military power in the form of the army of General Jeffery Amherst complicated the situation. Amherst viewed the British as conquerors and the Native Americans as subjects; he intended to reward those who had helped the British and punish those who had not. Ignoring the diplomatic traditions that had existed in the middle ground, Amherst quickly retook Western forts, outlawed the giving of gifts to Native Americans, and restricted the sale of gunpowder to them as well.

The British disregard for the promises they had made (only a minor stockade at Fort Pitt and a speedy withdrawal from native lands) was an insult to native peoples in the Great Lakes and Ohio River Valley. In 1763, fed up with poor British behavior, Native Americans, following Pontiac, took every British fort in the West, except for Forts Niagara, Detroit, and Pitt. Pontiac's Rebellion, as the event became known, developed slowly. The region's Native Americans were unable to forge any lasting pan-Indian identity during this time period, and for this reason, Pontiac's Rebellion was really a series of loosely linked revolts rather than the mass uprising that some historians have made it out to be. By 1766, the revolts had been stymied, and things had returned to normal. However, the fragile middle ground would be irrevocably lost when white Americans moved into the region en masse after the War for Independence.

More traditional interpretations leap from the end of the French and Indian War to the beginning of the War for Independence thirteen years later. It is true that

Great Britain's massive postwar debt led to increased taxation on the American colonies. Still, the story is not complete if it ignores the challenges faced by Native Americans in the wake of France's departure from North America.

The end result of the multiracial, multicontinental war, so far as colonial America is concerned, was the establishment of British supremacy and the removal of France from the picture. This massive, rapid shift in power affected Native Americans and English colonists profoundly, and forever altered the human landscape of the continent.

Matthew Jennings

See also: Acadians; Army, British; Canada; French; French Colonies on Mainland North America (Chronology); Louisiana; Military and Diplomatic Affairs (Chronology); Military and Diplomatic Affairs (Essay); Montcalm, Louis-Joseph; Native American–European Conflict; Navy, British; Quebec City; Revolutionary War; Wolfe, James.

Bibliography

Anderson, Fred. *Crucible of War: The Seven Years' War and the Fate of Empire in America.* New York: Alfred A. Knopf, 2000.

Hindraker, Eric. *Elusive Empires: Constructing Colonialism in the Ohio Valley, 1673–1800.* Cambridge, UK: Cambridge University Press, 1997.

McConnell, Michael N. *A Country Between: The Upper Ohio Valley and Its Peoples, 1724–1774.* Lincoln: University of Nebraska Press, 1992.

Nash, Gary B. *Red, White, and Black: The Peoples of Early North America.* 4th ed. Upper Saddle River, NJ: Prentice Hall, 2000.

Taylor, Alan. *American Colonies.* New York: Penguin Putnam, 2001.

White, Richard. *The Middle Ground: Indians, Empires and Republics in the Great Lakes Region, 1650–1815.* Cambridge, UK: Cambridge University Press, 1991.

Furnishings

While both regional and national distinctions were common, furniture styles in North America followed an evolution similar to Europe's throughout the colonial period. Although the challenges of early settlements did place some limitations on furniture ownership, wealthy colonists often transported furniture with them. Through these importations and the skills of joiners or furniture makers, colonists were able to keep up with their European counterparts.

Also similar to what occurred in Europe, furniture styles moved gradually from the upper to the middle and lower classes. Unlike Europe, working-class and middle-class families in the colonies were able to gain direct knowledge of other traditions through contact with their neighbors.

Dwellings

Most colonists initially lived in one-room dwellings. In the northern colonies, this room centered around the hearth. In the Southern colonies, the hearth was smaller and used predominantly for heat in the winter; cooking was commonly done in a separate shelter. Otherwise, all activities required by the family took place in this room. A loft overhead provided extra storage or sleeping space. Most houses were initially built using wattle and daub for walls and thatch for the roof in both North and South. The wattle and daub was later encased in sawed boards for a more fire- and weather-resistant dwelling.

The first piece of furniture in a house was usually a chest. While these chests served the practical purpose of transporting smaller items from Europe, the chests belonging to wealthier settlers also reflect styles of the time. Furniture of the early seventeenth century was heavy and ornate, similar to carved woodwork of the medieval period. The carving was done by specialized, trained craftsmen called "turners." Other items of furniture found in early houses included beds, stools, tables, and benches or "forms." A high-backed bench called a settle was designed to keep drafts from circulating behind its occupant. Immigrants from mainland Europe brought the custom of cupboard beds with them, beds literally built into the wall; this style also was adopted by the Pilgrims, who had lived in Holland. All of these items could be made in the New World, and only wealthier colonists would transport them.

After a second room was built, the two chambers were each used for specific purposes. The first room was referred to as the hall and was used as kitchen, workroom, and sleeping space for younger members of the family. Furniture in it had to be easily adaptable and easily moved. A rough bed frame or tabletop was often designed to fold against the wall. As a fire burned in the room every day of the year, items also had to be resistant to smoke damage. The family stools and benches would remain in the hall.

The Federal style, as represented in this drawing room at the Baltimore Museum of Art, typified American furniture design, interior decoration, and architecture from about 1780 to 1820. *(Baltimore Museum of Art, Maryland/Bridgeman Art Library)*

Bedding

The second room was called the parlor. The couple's bed, referred to as the "best" or "great" bed, was moved into the parlor. Similar to the chests, a wealthy family could afford a bed with extensive carving. They typically had high headboards and some form of canopy, again to protect against drafts. The linens or "bed furniture" were often the most valuable item in the house. Cloth remained expensive throughout the entire colonial period, and linens were often heavily embroidered. Keeping the bed in the parlor served to both preserve and display it, as fires were lit in the parlor only as needed. Even after a house gained a second floor and more chambers, this bed remained on the ground floor.

Another item of furniture possibly found in a parlor was a cupboard or cabinet. Similar to the chests,

these were heavily carved. Contact with Dutch and German settlers brought the tradition of painting the chests with geometric designs and bright colors. Like the bed, the cupboard was used to display whatever belongings the family possessed, such as pewter, porcelain, or glassware.

Upstairs chambers were used predominantly for storage or sleeping. As they rarely had fireplaces, they were unheated through the winter months and could be almost unlivable. Trundle beds, small beds made to tuck under larger ones, were rarely found in upstairs chambers. Their frequent presence in the parlor probably indicates a child's sleeping space, keeping the child close to parents and whatever warmth was available from the hearth. Further extensions to the house on the ground floor were used as a separate summer kitchen, dairy, or stillroom, depending on the needs of the family.

These traditions and choices of furniture continued throughout the seventeenth century. Primary distinctions in style came from smaller items: carpets from the Middle East, more dishes, more cloth. By the early eighteenth century, however, changes in European furniture had begun to sweep over the Atlantic. Transglobal trade was prospering, and Europe was now influenced by styles from the Far East. Europeans also had begun to look back to the classical period and its flowing lines, symmetry, and balance. The eighteenth century also saw the growth of larger gaps between rich and poor, rural and urban. Farm families often continued with the same furniture and traditions, unwilling or unable to change.

Houses in the eighteenth century continued the evolution toward rooms and furniture used for separate purposes. While the idea of a parlor, a room set aside with the family's best possessions, continued, wealth was now displayed differently. Furniture was prized for its comfort and genteel atmosphere. A family that had put its money into linens a generation back might now consider a specialized table and tea service for its parlor. Other new furniture for the parlor could include an upholstered wing chair, daybed, or embroidered fire screen. While these items were found across the colonies, regional styles remained evident. A chair made in Philadelphia was distinguished by its short, stumpy back legs and gracefully carved front legs. Chairs made in Newport, Rhode Island, had rounded shoulders and often a shell carving as part of the back.

Where the upper chambers of a house in the seventeenth century were used simply for sleeping or storage, the eighteenth century saw bedrooms become rooms for living as well as sleeping. New items of furniture were clothes presses or chests of drawers, to hold the expanded wardrobes made possible by the greater availability of cloth. Dressing tables with matching benches also became common. Linking furniture in both parlor and bedroom together was the concept of a room arranged en suite, all of the pieces made to match. This indicated wealth enough to purchase all of the furniture at once. It also indicated a close, ordered environment very different from that of the centuries before.

Probate Inventories

Establishing what items of furniture were found in colonial households is done largely through probate inventories. When the head of a household died, his (or, in some cases, her) possessions were listed and valued in a probate inventory. Any debts owed were taken from the total value. The remaining amount was divided between the heirs, according the wishes of the deceased. Probates were customarily done a room at a time, making it possible to reasonably assess how each room was furnished and what it was used for. Probates written thirty or forty years apart for a father and son can indicate changes in the family's finances.

While probates are invaluable, they also have their limitations. Different regions and periods used different terms for some items. A bow-back chair could also be referred to as a rush-seat or crooked-back chair in 1760s New England. In the 1790s, the term "bow-back" referred to a Windsor chair. Items such as portraits not assigned monetary value by whoever was doing the probate would also not appear. Although most women's belongings were automatically subsumed into their husband's estates on marriage, some women were able to have their belongings remain legally separate. These items, such as a spinning wheel or chest, may not have appeared in probates done of their husband's belongings.

Evolution in furniture styles also indicate broader changes in society. The small houses and limited furniture of the early settlements reflected the challenges of life in the colonies. They also reflect a period barely out of medieval society. Most people in Europe were accustomed to living close together, often with their animals beside them. Once a family was established in the colonies, its life could continue very much as it had in Europe.

In contrast, the eighteenth century brought changes to all of the Atlantic world. As financial prosperity grew, so did definitions of privacy, ownership, and personal comfort. The possibility of a separate bedroom for a married couple was a new concept on both sides of the Atlantic.

Abigail B. Chandler

See also: Art, Fine; Art, Folk; Artisans. *Document:* Probate Inventory of a Plymouth Colony Estate (1672).

Bibliography

Fitzgerald, Oscar P. *Three Centuries of American Furniture.* Englewood Cliffs: Prentice Hall, 1982.

Kirk, John T. *American Furniture & the British Tradition to 1830.* New York: Alfred A. Knopf, 1982.

Sweeney, Kevin. "Furniture and the Domestic Environment in Wethersfield, Connecticut." In *Material Life in America, 1600–1860,* edited by Robert Blair St. George. Boston: Northeastern University Press, 1988.

Furs

The trade that resulted after furs were discovered in North America occurred quite unexpectedly and naturally in 1580. Around Newfoundland and in the Gulf of St. Lawrence, fisheries, whaling ventures, and sea hunts employed at least 400 vessels and about 12,000 men. The fisheries were not under any one nation's control but were mostly a mix of French, Basque, Portuguese, and English. With this mix and the number of men involved, temporary camps had to be established in order to perform daily duties. As these men settled in and began to look for firewood, fresh water, and space to sun-dry their fish or render whales into oil, they came in direct contact with Native American hunters. These hunters captured the mariners' attention, because they wore attractive furs: beaver, fox, otter, lynx, and martin.

These furs had become scarce in Europe, due to overhunting, and they commanded high prices for making fashionable goods. Native Americans were eager to trade their pelts for manufactured European goods such as beads, kettles, and knives. The native people not only performed the hard work involved in hunting and killing the animals, they also treated the furs. This provided the traders with an immediate profit without the necessity of taking the time or trouble to prepare furs for shipment.

Even though fishing was valuable, the fur trade turned out to be vastly more profitable. This simple barter relationship required nothing more than bringing goods desired by the Native Americans across the Atlantic, anchoring a few ships in a sheltered bay, and waiting for traders to arrive with pelts. Large settlements were not required, and by 1630, the French had a name for what New France had become—a *comptoir,* a storehouse for the skins of dead animals.

The fur trade illustrated the pervasiveness of Native American–white interaction. The barter arrangement benefited both groups as each profited in its own way. The colonists received valuable furs for inexpensive European products, while the Native Americans got invaluable trade goods in exchange for readily acquired animal pelts.

The demand for furs prompted Native Americans to become even more efficient hunters and trappers. Hunting parties became larger, and, in some cases, farming tribes shifted their villages to be closer to trade routes and waterways. Furthermore, tribal organization altered somewhat; small groups merged in order to control more territory, as the hunting began to reduce the supply of furs nearer to their homes.

By the end of the seventeenth century, there were no longer enough beavers to meet French demand, due to overhunting. This forced Native Americans to replace beaver pelts with less desirable deerskins and other furs. The French had to accept these replacements if they wished to maintain the loyalty of these people.

While the coastal barter traders multiplied, their goods became cheaper, more widespread, and demystified. The Native Americans came to appreciate these goods more for their utility than for their shine. They valued the superior strength and cutting edge of metal arrowheads, axes, knives, and hatchets, and their use as both tools and weapons. These items eased strain and reduced workload, just as metal kettles aided cooking. Metal hoes also facilitated the tilling for maize, beans, and squash, and these were the food supplies that the English sought as they began their own settlement along the coast of the New World.

Although animal pelts had appeared plentiful to early French traders, other European countries had to depend on other trade goods as the animals were overhunted and eventually became relatively scarce.

Penny M. Sonnenburg

See also: Canada; French; Native American–European Relations; Trade.

Bibliography

Bailey, Alfred G. *The Conflict of European and East Algonkian Cultures, 1504–1700: A Study in Canadian Civilization.* Sackville, New Brunswick, Canada: Tribune Press, 1937.

Parkman, Francis. *Pioneers of France in the New World.* Boston: Little, Brown and Company, 1865.

Gage, Thomas
(c. 1719–1787)

Born in late 1719 or early 1720, Thomas Gage was commander in chief of British forces in the American colonies from 1763 to 1775.

The son of a member of the House of Commons and a viscount in the Irish peerage, Gage received a balanced education and was commissioned as an ensign before he was 20. He developed friendships with other future famous British officers such as James Wolfe, John Burgoyne, and William Howe. Gage steadily advanced through the ranks before purchasing a major's commission in 1748; he was promoted to lieutenant colonel in 1751.

Known as "Honest Tom," Gage was a popular officer when his regiment left for America as part of General Edward Braddock's expeditionary force in 1754. Gage led the advance guard of Braddock's army on July 9, 1755, when combined French and Native American forces ambushed and decisively defeated them near the Monongahela River, mortally wounding Braddock in the process. Gage demonstrated remarkable personal courage in the engagement, continuing to rally his men, despite being wounded.

In 1758, Gage again received a wound while leading General James Abercromby's advance guard in an unsuccessful attempt to capture Ticonderoga from the French under the command of the Marquis de Montcalm. After the engagement, Gage was temporarily promoted to brigadier general. He married an American girl, Margaret Kemble, and became commander of Albany, New York. In September 1760, Gage assumed the title of military governor of Montreal. Though disdaining both French Catholics and Native Americans, Gage excelled at the position and earned a quick promotion to major general in 1761.

In 1763, the government named him commander in chief of British forces in North America, and Gage relocated to New York City. During his decade of residence in New York, he enjoyed both the professional respect of his officers and men and personal fulfillment, as he fathered six children by his wife. When the Stamp Act crisis broke out in 1765, Gage removed troops from the frontier and redistributed them among the Eastern seaboard port cities, but he managed to adeptly handle difficulties as they arose without engendering much lasting furor.

After Gage made a brief trip home to England in 1773, the government appointed him governor of Massachusetts as well as commander in chief on April 2, 1774. Gage returned to a seething cauldron of discontent in Boston created by Parliament's passage of the Boston Port Bill, which closed off the harbor to commerce until the citizens had repaid the debts from the Boston Tea Party. On April 19, 1775, after a year of constantly rising tensions, Gage ordered British troops to seize stockpiles of munitions the colonists had stored in Concord. A confrontation with colonists on the Lexington green led to the first shots being fired in what would become the Revolutionary War. Concealed colonists shot at the British troops on their return march from Concord, causing tremendous casualties.

Gage urgently requested reinforcements and received them in June 1775, when several thousand British troops arrived along with Generals William Howe, John Burgoyne, and Henry Clinton. When colonists fortified Breed's Hill, overlooking Boston, Gage approved an attack plan designed by Howe. On the afternoon of June 17, 1775, Howe led British soldiers to a costly victory over the colonists in the battle of Bunker Hill. Deeming him unequal to the crisis, Parliament recalled Gage to Britain on September 26, 1775, replacing him with William Howe.

In the ensuing years, Gage lived in modest wealth, raising his large family. Although he had not been a

Thomas Gage served as commander in chief of British troops in North America from 1763 to 1775 and was governor of Massachusetts at the start of the American Revolution. He was recalled to London after the Battle of Bunker Hill. *(Brown Brothers, Sterling, Pennsylvania)*

brilliant commander, he had distinguished himself as a competent and courageous officer, and he always remained popular with those under his command. He died after a prolonged illness on April 2, 1787.

Judkin Browning

See also: Military and Diplomatic Affairs (Chronology); Military and Diplomatic Affairs (Essay); Revolutionary War.

Bibliography

Alden, John Richard. *General Gage in America: Being Principally a History of His Role in the American Revolution.* Baton Rouge: Louisiana State University Press, 1948.

Anderson, Fred. *Crucible of War: The Seven Years' War and the Fate of Empire in British North America, 1754–1766.* New York: Alfred A. Knopf, 2000.

French, Allen. *General Gage's Informers; New Material upon Lexington and Concord. Benjamin Thompson as Loyalist and the Treachery of Benjamin Church, Jr. A Study by Allen French.* Ann Arbor: University of Michigan Press, 1932.

Gambling

Reflecting the fascination with games of chance in the mother country, settlers in all the English colonies gambled. Rich and poor alike participated, and few condemned the contests. Critics did raise concerns about the consequences for participants, but those apprehensions more often led to regulatory laws than efforts to eliminate gambling. Ironically, amid the attempts to restrict gaming, its most popular form, the lottery, contributed significantly to the funding of a large number of public works projects throughout the colonies.

Seventeenth-century English people embraced a wide variety of games of chance. In homes and taverns across the land, as well as in exclusive gaming houses in London, they gambled on card and dice games and bought lottery tickets. Horse racing and cockfighting particularly attracted high-stakes wagers from upperclass gamblers. Immigrants to the colonies in North America took along with them this widely shared attraction to gaming.

Gambling had many appeals for colonists. Most assuredly saw it as nothing more than a pleasing pastime, an opportunity for convivial evenings with friends at the local tavern. Others enjoyed the competition inherent in wagering on contests such as horse races. Virginia planters, for example, through heavy betting on quarter horse racing, reflected the aggressive individualism that helped them succeed in the competitive Atlantic tobacco market. Gambling undoubtedly appealed to some because it offered a hope for economic gain that otherwise eluded them. For the civic-minded, taking a chance on a lottery ticket offered not only a small chance for a prize but also a way to raise funds to benefit schools, churches, or other worthy public ventures.

From taverns in New England villages and middle-colony towns to Southern plantations and isolated backcountry settlements, colonists bet on dice and card games, billiards, and shuffleboard. In the late colonial period, the heaviest gambling appears to have occurred in Charles Town, South Carolina. There, it was not uncommon to see servants, slaves, and even entire plantations lost at card games. Betting on horse races occurred throughout the late seventeenth and eighteenth centuries in Massachusetts, New York, the Carolinas, and Virginia. Begun as simple sprints along dirt roads, by the mid-eighteenth century, horse races had become well-organized events at circular tracks. Beyond the wagers between contestants, increasingly, there were side bets involving spectators.

Present from the earliest years of English settlement, the lottery was the most popular form of gambling in the colonies. The Virginia Company of London, which established the first permanent English colony in 1607, quickly came to depend upon lotteries for much of its funding. Merchants used them to dispose of inventories, and landowners sometimes resorted to them to sell real estate. Most often, however, local and provincial governments used lotteries for public purposes. Although unwilling to pay higher taxes, colonists eagerly bought chances on lotteries that funded the construction of schools, colleges, churches, forts, bridges, poorhouses, jails, lighthouses, and streets throughout the colonies.

Gambling did not develop unchallenged. Many critics raised concerns about the growing participation in games of chance. To New England clergymen, the chief danger of wagering on games, besides the ruinous losses suffered by gamblers, was the waste of precious time and neglect of duty. Critics in the Southern colonies worried more about the disorder associated with gambling, including fighting and fraud, as well as the impact of heavy gaming losses on the local economy. Some observers concluded that the poor were most harmed by gambling, believing that it not only impoverished their families but also destroyed their work ethic. Others, especially in the South, worried that heavy stakes wagering carried the potential to ruin many gentry families and, as a consequence, diminish the stability of planter society.

These concerns inevitably led to laws restricting and occasionally prohibiting gambling. While gambling was not an illegal activity under English common law, colonial legislatures did make attempts to outlaw it. In 1646, Massachusetts passed the first colonial law to prohibit gambling, making gaming illegal in public houses. Most New England colonies followed their lead, reflecting a shared concern that gambling in taverns too often led to idleness. Other jurisdictions, especially the Quaker-dominated government of Pennsylvania, also prohibited certain forms of gambling for a time, and in 1769, the British government ruled that royal colonies could no longer authorize lotteries without Crown approval. Yet enforcement of such prohibitions was often lax.

The ambivalence evident in policing gambling in the colonies was due to the absence of a sustained movement against gambling per se. Most felt if the abuses involved in gambling could be eliminated and the worst consequences for problem gamblers could be checked, then gambling could continue. Moreover, there was a general recognition that gambling in the form of buying lottery tickets was a relatively painless way of supplying essential public services.

Larry Gragg

See also: Crime; Debt and Debtor's Prison; Inns and Taverns (Public Houses). *Document:* Connecticut Blue Laws (1650).

Bibliography

Breen, T. H. "Horses and Gentlemen: The Cultural Significance of Gambling Among the Gentry of Virginia." *William and Mary Quarterly* 34:2 (1977): 239–57.

Ezell, John. "The Lottery in Colonial America." *William and Mary Quarterly* 5:2 (1948): 185–200.

Findlay, John M. *People of Chance: Gambling in American Society from Jamestown to Las Vegas.* New York: Oxford University Press, 1986.

George I (1660–1727)

George I, king of Great Britain and Ireland, was the first of the Hanoverian line to become a British monarch. Following the death of Queen Anne, the last of the Stuarts, George Louis came to London from Germany, where he held the title of elector of Hanover.

Born on May 28, 1660, George had traveled to England at the age of 20 on a diplomatic mission, but he was abruptly recalled by his father to be married to his cousin Sophia Dorothea. The union produced two children, the future King George II and the future mother of Frederick the Great of Prussia, but it ultimately proved an unhappy one, with suspicion of infidelity on both sides.

In 1694, Sophia began a semipublic intrigue with Count Philip von Königsmark, a dashing Swedish adventurer. Her plans to elope were shattered, however, when the count suddenly vanished. Rumors circulated that he was murdered by parties loyal to George, although no corroborating evidence has ever been produced. The couple divorced soon afterward, and Sophia was put under house arrest in Hanover until her death in 1726. George's treatment of his ex-wife served to alienate him from his son and heir, initiating a pattern of father-son hostility that would characterize the entire Hanoverian dynasty.

As a young man, George enjoyed a memorable career in the German imperial army, distinguishing himself at Vienna in 1683 and during the capture of Neuhäusel in Hungary in 1685. By the 1690s, he had developed a reputation for preferring fighting to learning and gambling to politics.

When, under the provisions of the Act of Settlement (1701), he became British monarch in 1714, George I, whose English was faltering at best, devoted scant attention to matters of government, preferring instead to delegate responsibility to a trusted group of Whig ministers. In 1718, his ministers entered into the Quadruple Alliance with France, the United Provinces (Netherlands), and the Holy Roman Empire, a valuable agreement that contained Spain's imperial aspirations and guaranteed the Hanoverian succession.

Despite the importance of his cabinet's business, the king's attendance at its weekly meetings was progressively more infrequent. In consequence, his ministers became ever more powerful. Viscount Charles Townshend was preeminent until 1717, while, from 1721, it was his brother-in-law Sir Robert Walpole, first lord of the Treasury, who presided at these meetings and directed the course of British foreign and domestic policy. Walpole is justly considered the first British prime minister, a term initially used to mock his position as the king's favorite. It was, it seems, a lucky accident of history that the king's poor English and his lack of interest in politics conspired to produce the foundations for parliamentary democracy—a system of party politics largely insulated from royal interference that centered power in a prime minister as the leader of the dominant party.

Walpole's supremacy was reinforced by his skillful handling of the South Sea bubble in 1720. Established in 1711, the South Sea Company provided loans to the government to relieve the national debt. Its share price soon soared, and speculators poured millions into the company in the hope of a quick profit. By July 1720, the company's shares had become vastly inflated, and confidence in the company's ability to realize its potential crashed almost overnight. The share price tumbled, and hundreds of prominent financiers—and thousands of small investors—were ruined. Many court officials were implicated in this crash, which appeared to much of the public as a deliberate attempt to defraud investors. Parties on all sides clamored for restitution, and Walpole launched a public inquiry that eventually restored the public's faith. In gratitude, George I appointed him chancellor of the exchequer, thereby securing Walpole's control of the House of Commons. Walpole had become indispensable.

George I himself seemed anything but indispensable. His lavish lifestyle made him unpopular, and his continuing mistreatment of his well-respected son only added to public resentment. When his first grandson was born in 1717, George I refused to let his son name the boy's godparents. A family row ensued, culminating when George I expelled the prince and princess from court, taking legal charge of the boy and his other grandchildren. This action only served to create a center of opposition to the king, based around his son's counter court at Leicester House in Westminster. Several attempts to unseat George I followed over the next decade (including attempts to restore the Stuart dynasty), all of which Walpole successfully anticipated and thwarted.

On June 11, 1727, en route to Hanover, George I suffered a stroke and died at the age of 67. Never really accepted as an Englishman, he was buried in Hanover and succeeded by his son and namesake.

Richard Bell

See also: Politics and Government (Chronology); Politics and Government (Essay).

Bibliography

Hatton, Ragnhild. *George I.* New Haven, CT: Yale University Press, 1978.

Plumb, J. H. *The First Four Georges.* New York: John Wiley and Sons, 1967.

George II (1683–1760)

George II, king of Great Britain and Ireland, was born on November 10, 1683, the only son of George I and Sophia Dorothea. Following his parents' acrimonious divorce, the prince was brought up by his grandparents in Hanover and educated in European history and languages, subjects at which he apparently excelled.

In 1705, he married Caroline of Ansbach, with whom he had three daughters and a son. George was a small, dapper man with a great respect for the military. Accordingly, in 1708, he fought for the British-Hanoverian alliance at Terbank and later distinguished himself in a daring assault at the battle of Oudenarde.

After following his father to London in 1714 and assuming the title of Prince of Wales, young George

The reign of England's King George II (1727–1760) was marked by military successes and strategic acquisitions throughout the colonial world during the Seven Years' War, known as the French and Indian War in North America. *(Guildhall Art Gallery, Corporation of London, United Kingdom/Bridgeman Art Library)*

quickly won much public admiration for his command of English and his taste for British life. His father, who became more unpopular with every passing year in Britain, reacted violently, even considering a plan to kidnap the prince and ship him off to North America. Such animosity was entirely mutual; the prince's early, forced separation from his mother fed a lifelong loathing of his father, a resentment soon fueled by opposition groups in Parliament, who sought to further their own causes by allying with the future king.

Consequently, many hoped that the death of George I in 1727 would signal a new era in British politics. In fact, the accession of George II (then 44) initially did little to change the status quo. Sir Robert Walpole, George I's most senior minister, was able to maintain his powerful position, due, in large part, to his alliance with Queen Caroline, whose political judg-

ments informed her husband's. Indeed, despite the customary infidelities, George II doted on his wife, an intelligent woman with a considerable knowledge of philosophy and theology.

Relations with his children, however, were never as intimate. George II's oldest son, Frederick, grew up to be a typical Hanoverian heir—bitter, argumentative, and angry at his father's excesses. By 1737, Frederick had begun, as his father had done, to entertain opposition politicians at his counter court at Leicester House in Westminster. When Frederick died in 1751, interest quickly turned to Frederick's 13-year-old son, George.

The king, meanwhile, had had his eyes on political matters. Throughout the 1730s, Spain had been angrily protesting Britain's ties to Atlantic piracy. Following Captain Robert Jenkins's famous anatomical evidence of Spanish retaliation (an ear sliced off by his Spanish captors), the bellicose king, no longer moderated by Caroline, who had died of a ruptured womb in 1737, pushed Britain into war in 1739. Walpole, who had devoted his career to peace at all costs, struggled on for three years, but he resigned in 1742 as it became clear to him that the war with Spain (now allied with France) could not be quickly won.

The conflict soon encompassed the Austrian succession, and, in 1743, the king himself led his troops to victory at the battle of Dettingen, the last British monarch to do so. Charles II's victory gave many in Parliament hope that Britain might win and perhaps even profit from the conflict. By the mid-1740s, a young parliamentarian named William Pitt had become the most vocal proponent of this point of view, proposing nothing less than a global war against France and her allies, designed to cripple France's trading empire and revive British commerce. Well supported by businessmen in London and the other port cities, Pitt soon became difficult for the king to ignore. In 1745, Pitt was made paymaster of the forces, and, in 1756, he became prime minister.

George II's reluctant support of Pitt initiated an escalation of the smoldering conflict with France. Over the next four years, Pitt's military operations in theaters across the colonial world secured for Britain valuable commercial and strategic territories. One by one, Martinique, Guadeloupe, Dakar, and Bengal all surrendered to King George II.

In North America, historians have credited George II himself with the decision to deploy colonial militia, rather than British regulars unfamiliar with the local terrain, against the French and Native American forces in the forested interior. Such tactics, in tandem with more traditional assaults on fortified settlements, led to the fall of Louisbourg, Quebec, and Montreal and eventually the collapse of the French colonial empire throughout Canada.

Before the conclusion of Pitt's worldwide struggle, however, the 77-year-old king began to fail. On the morning of October 25, 1760, Charles II died of heart failure, in the midst of the most successful military campaign in British history. He was buried at Westminster alongside his queen and succeeded by his 22-year-old grandson, George III.

Richard Bell

See also: King George's War; Politics and Government (Chronology); Politics and Government (Essay).

Bibliography

Chenevix Trench, Charles P. *George II*. London: Allen Lane, 1973.

Plumb, J. H. *The First Four Georges*. New York: John Wiley and Sons, 1967.

George III (1738–1820)

George III, the eldest son of Frederick, Prince of Wales (son of George II and Caroline of Ansbach), and Augusta of Saxe-Gotha, was born June 4, 1738, at St. James, London. Although in line for the throne, the constant feud between his parents and grandparents caused George to be isolated at home and tutored by Francis, Lord North.

When Frederick died in 1751, George became Prince of Wales and the focus of his grandfather's attention. During this period, George was heavily influenced by his widowed mother's household steward, the Earl of Bute, who stressed the political works of Bolingbroke in the prince's education. As an eligible young aristocrat, George was romantically linked to a Quaker, Hannah Lightfoot, and a distant cousin, Lady Sarah Lennox, but these relationships were abandoned upon the death of his grandfather, George II.

George III, the first of the Hanoverian dynasty to be born in Britain and to be a native English speaker, ascended the throne on October 25, 1760. As a young and popular monarch, he presided over the end of the Seven Years' War (known as the French and Indian War in colonial America), which left Britain an enormously powerful empire. Inherently dignified, the king brought formality back to the raucous court life, especially after his marriage to Charlotte of Mecklenburg-Strelitz, with whom he had fifteen children. Studious and serious, George collected the books that later became the core of the King's Collection of the British library. He also patronized innovations in technology (establishing the Longitude Prize) and agriculture, endorsing the latter so enthusiastically that he was given the nickname "Farmer George" by the press.

George III's education had primed him to assume the throne as a king who was above political parties and deeply attached to the concept of royal prerogative. These beliefs led him to overturn the longstanding monopoly of British politics by the Whigs and instead seek cabinets of loyal "king's friends," including leaders of the Tory party, who had been excluded for more than a generation from real power. He began this process in 1762, forcing out William Pitt and replacing him with his old tutor, the Earl of Bute, backed up by Henry Fox, managing the House of Commons.

The financial and colonial crises of the 1760s saw a series of prime ministers, including Grenville, Rockingham, Pitt (as the Earl of Chatham), and Grafton, before the king settled on the son of his old governor, Lord North. From 1770 to 1782, North was a loyal supporter of the king and mirrored his views on America. Far from a disconnected monarch, George, a product of the generation that feared Jacobite rebellion, had an aversion to the American colonies forming an alternate parliament or defying royal prerogative or Parliament's authority. George III was also an inveterate enemy of John Wilkes, a radical and advocate of colonial rights, finding Wilkes an obscene affront to royal dignity.

The siege of Yorktown and the intense debate over continuing the war against the American colonies saw the collapse of North's government, much to the king's dismay. George III, however, was far from helpless in his powers. He manipulated the vote on the 1782 India Bill and, the following year, called an election in order to organize the electoral victory of William Pitt, who once again headed the ministry.

By 1788, the king was suffering seriously from an illness that had begun to plague him as early as 1765, sending him into the custody of doctors who bled, purged, and otherwise tortured him back to health the subsequent year. Modern research points to the hereditary disease porphyria, which poisons the body with uric acid, as the source of his so-called "madness" rather than a mental illness. The progression of this disease may be an explanation for his cycles of illness and recovery.

On July 9, 1776, a mob of angry colonists toppled and smashed an equestrian statue of King George III in the city of New York. Pieces of the gilded lead were melted down for bullets to be used against British troops. *(Bonhams, London, United Kingdom/Bridgeman Art Library)*

When the French Revolution broke out in 1789, George III, although no longer as popular as he had been as a young ruler, retained the loyalty of his people. This was despite the poor behavior of his children (leading to the Royal Marriage Act to regulate their affairs with Catholics, actresses, and foreigners), violent feuds with his sons, and increasing isolation from the public. The wars against revolutionary France, however, caused Pitt to raise taxes substantially and enforce a Sedition Act and the suspension of habeas corpus, measures that caused many subjects to blame the king personally for curtailing their liberties. On May 15, 1800, an assassin shot at the king in his box at Drury Lane Theater; the king, either asleep or with great calm, ignored the attempt. George III continued to play a role in politics, refusing to endorse Catholic emancipation when it was suggested in 1801 and using his patronage to form a voting bloc in the House of Commons.

In 1810, the king's illness reappeared. He was declared permanently insane and replaced by his eldest son, George (IV), as regent. Blind, miserable, and in constant pain, George III lived on until 1820, dying on January 29. Reviled by Americans as a tyrant for his refusal to accept their demands for representation and equal rights as British subjects, George III is affectionately remembered by his subjects in Britain as a long-serving monarch, who restored dignity to the monarchy and gave the British their triumphs in 1763 and 1815.

Margaret Sankey

See also: Politics and Government (Chronology); Politics and Government (Essay); Revolutionary War.

Bibliography

Ditchfield, G. M. *George III: An Essay in Monarchy.* New York: Palgrave Macmillan, 2002.

Hibbert, Christopher. *George III: A Personal History.* New York: Basic Books, 1998.

Lloyd, Alan. *The King Who Lost America.* Garden City, NJ: Doubleday, 1971.

Georgia

Established in 1733, Georgia was the last British mainland colony founded before the American Revolution. Other contemporary colonization schemes had stalled in the imperial bureaucracy during the approval process, but a small group of energetic and ambitious individuals steered the Georgia project to fruition. The royal charter appointed these gentlemen trustees for the new settlement for a period of twenty-one years.

Trust members were drawn from the military, political, philanthropic, commercial, and religious elite of English society. The most prominent among the initial group were James Oglethorpe, widely considered the founder of Georgia, and Viscount John Percival (later the earl of Egmont), who served as the governing corporation's first president.

The corporation carefully screened prospective settlers in order to weed out undesirables. Berths on the initial settlement voyage were reserved for individuals and families judged to be part of the "deserving poor" of England. These consisted mostly of unemployed artisans or displaced tenant farmers whose financial distress was due more to external conditions than to character defects. Others were persecuted foreign Protestants seeking shelter in a place free from the Catholic Church's influence. Georgia would provide these unfortunates a second chance, while at the same time reducing the size of the mother country's impoverished, discontented underclass.

Choosing colonists based on proven economic failure, however, created difficult administrative problems for the trustees. Few of the initial settlers were qualified to participate in running the colony, and Georgia stood out from the other colonies because it was designed without a representative assembly of any kind. By offering to accompany the first wave of settlement, Oglethorpe temporarily solved the leadership void. He took nearly every civilian and military duty upon his shoulders. Oglethorpe chose the site of Savannah, which would soon become the capital of Georgia. He negotiated peaceful land cessions from local Native Americans, and he diplomatically explained the nature of the new British presence to hostile commanders of French and Spanish forces in Louisiana and Florida, respectively. At the same time, he prudently laid out a series of defensive fortifications in case diplomacy failed to keep the peace. In taking these actions, Oglethorpe clearly exceeded the powers expressly granted to him by the trustees. These steps benefited Georgia in the short run but masked serious administrative deficiencies that would later cause unrest.

The trustees wanted to closely regulate the behavior of Georgia's inhabitants, placing restrictions on property to prevent colonists from growing too prosperous and independent. Land ownership was capped at 500 acres, with the typical settler receiving only 50 acres. Land grants contained clauses preventing the mortgage or sale of the land. Upon a landowner's death, the property could pass only to the eldest male heir. If only female heirs existed, the land would revert to trust control. A widow or daughter had to petition for case-by-case exemptions from this policy in order to inherit property from the estate of a deceased husband or father. Such exemptions were commonly granted, but uncertainty over the transfer of farms between generations caused some Georgia inhabitants to delay their clearing or cultivating efforts. Why should a landowner invest time and money, when the work of a lifetime might be taken away from his children? Trust officials contended that the land restrictions were necessary to ensure a sufficient supply of adult male militiamen, but colonists countered that the unusual and burdensome regulations violated their rights as Englishmen.

By far the most controversial measure in colonial Georgia was the passage in 1735 of a law prohibiting the ownership or use of slaves in the province. The trustees justified it as a practical measure, emphasizing how the presence of a large slave population weakened military defenses and led to the risk of slave revolts. Slavery also was seen as encouraging laziness in masters.

Colonists did not share these views; instead, they saw the law as an undue and illegal infringement on their economic and legal rights. Pointing to the plantation labor system that dominated nearby provinces as a model for development, Georgians complained that trust policies damaged the new province's economy by preventing farmers from acquiring the necessary labor for agricultural improvement. After unrealistic early predictions of success, by the 1750s, the port of Savannah acted as little more than a subsidiary of the port of Charles Town, South Carolina. Were the trustees keeping Georgia poor, some inhabitants posed, in order to better control it?

In the late 1730s and 1740s, discontented settlers, including several Savannah government officials, launched a concerted petition campaign to abolish

Georgia's restrictive property and slavery regulations. The trustees—relying on dubious information that portrayed the petitioners as a tiny faction—dismissed the proslavery advocates as a handful of lazy "malcontents." The frustrated colonists took their case to the English public. They published a series of scathing pamphlets describing Georgia as a complete wasteland devoid of towns, people, or hope. These propaganda pieces portrayed Oglethorpe as a malicious tyrant and charged his fellow trustees with gross incompetence. The campaign against the trustees culminated in a House of Commons investigation into Georgia's administration. Although the findings vindicated trust policies, the victory was generally irrelevant, as the trustees found it nearly impossible to enforce their unpopular policies in Georgia and so began a slow retreat. Most land restrictions were lifted in 1749, the slavery ban was removed in 1750, and the corporation finally surrendered its charter entirely to the Crown in 1752—a full year before its scheduled expiration.

Because of Georgia's lack of development and population, friendly relationships with local Native Americans were an absolute necessity. The province likely could not have survived a major conflict with the powerful Creek or Cherokee. To limit tensions, colonial and imperial officials strove to limit white interaction with Native Americans by regulating trade with Native Americans and preventing private land purchases from tribes. These policies improved relations to the point that many Native American warriors fought for the English in the War of Jenkins' Ear. Inevitably, though, the European desire for profit and expansion led to episodes of tension between colonists and Native Americans, and these served to illustrate the Georgia government's lack of military strength. In the name of maintaining the peace, Colonial authorities sometimes ignored violent flare-ups involving the deaths of whites trading with the tribes.

The end of trustee government (1732–1752) and the onset of royal rule (1752–1776) led to major transformations in Georgia's society and economy. The Crown established a colonial representative assembly, giving inhabitants some input into their province's future for the first time. Gone were the restrictions on property accumulation and slave ownership. Georgia eagerly embraced the plantation system prevalent in other Southern colonies. Elites began amassing large plantations worked by dozens of African slaves. Royal governor James Wright ensured that settlers would not run out of fertile land anytime soon by securing peaceful cessions of Native American lands in 1763 and 1773 that totaled over 4 million acres. Trade from Savannah increased throughout the 1750s and 1760s, moving the young port out from under the shadow of the more established Charles Town to the north. As a result of these developments, the colony began a slow but steady climb toward economic prosperity.

A tightening of imperial administration after 1763 soon crushed residents' newfound hopes. Because of its precarious defensive position, Georgia's initial reactions to increased colonial regulation were mild—for example, it was the only province to successfully enforce the 1765 Stamp Act, if only for a day. Despite this hesitance, Georgia residents viewed the new measures as an attack upon their rights and liberties. By 1775, confronted with example after example of what they saw as London's stubborn refusal to acknowledge the validity of colonial reasoning, many Georgians agreed with residents of other North American colonies that they could no longer live under British rule. A provincial council steadily usurped the powers of the royal government, and then imprisoned Governor Wright in January 1776. He, however, escaped his captors a few weeks later and took refuge with the British navy.

During the early years of the American Revolution, Georgia's economic and military weakness meant that it could contribute little in the way of money or manpower to the overall American cause. British warships operating off the Atlantic severely damaged trade, which was devastating for a province that relied on imports to provide many necessities of life. In December 1778, a British expedition easily conquered Savannah and the surrounding area. The following years saw rebel and Tory partisans engaged in a bitter struggle for control over the rest of Georgia, which did not end until the British abandoned Savannah in July 1782.

Due to its late founding, Georgia frequently lagged far behind other colonies politically, economically, and culturally. Perhaps with the goal of negating this dubious distinction, in 1788, Georgia moved quickly to ratify the Constitution of the United States, becoming the fourth state to join the new union.

Andrew C. Lannen

See also: Georgia (Chronology); Oglethorpe, James. *Documents:* Oglethorpe's Vision for the Founding of Georgia (1733); The Demand for Slavery in Georgia (1743).

Bibliography

Abbot, W. W. *The Royal Governors of Georgia, 1754–1775.* Chapel Hill: University of North Carolina Press, 1959.

Coleman, Kenneth. *Colonial Georgia: A History*. New York: Charles Scribner's Sons, 1976.

Davis, Harold E. *The Fledgling Province: Social and Cultural Life in Colonial Georgia, 1733–1776*. Chapel Hill: University of North Carolina Press, 1976.

Reese, Trevor R. *Colonial Georgia: A Study in British Imperial Policy in the Eighteenth Century*. Athens: University of Georgia Press, 1963.

Germans

German-speaking immigrants came to British colonial North America in two main phases. Germans were present in some of the earliest seventeenth-century settlements and formed a sizable portion of the massive influx of colonists that arrived in the middle decades of the eighteenth century. Between 1683 and 1783, what had been a small but steady movement of Germans exploded. About 125,000 German speakers arrived during this 100-year span, increasing the total German population of the colonies to approximately 200,000.

German-speaking colonists, unlike the Dutch, French, and Spanish, did not generally run into direct conflict with the English. Germans in America built strong local support networks and communicated ideas through religious and commercial means across the various boundaries that divided colonial life. Even though they maintained distinct cultural traits and their language, they adopted English political culture as a way to further their communities' interests.

Early German Interest in North America: Wealthy Men and Refugees

The first wave of German migration was really more of a steady stream of unconnected individuals. As it did for their English counterparts, social class determined the German-speakers' colonial experience to a great extent. Some men of means paid their own way and occupied positions of power in the colonies. Peter Minuit of New Netherland is one famous example. German artisans labored in the Jamestown colony with the support of the Virginia Company.

Most of the early German immigrants to North America came from the North German territories. Other seventeenth-century Germans came to the colonies for religious reasons. Throughout the region that would become Germany, the seventeenth and early

eighteenth century was a time of serious religious upheaval. The Thirty Years' War, the War of Palatine Succession, and the War of the Spanish Succession tore through the German-speaking world and shifted the point of origin for emigration farther to the southwest. The War of the Spanish Succession, in particular, drove German settlers en masse to the Americas.

For more radical people of the Reformed faith, the experience of the 1709–1710 conflict also led to

German mercenaries called Hessians (because many hailed from the principality of Hesse-Kassel) constituted about one-third of the British fighting force in the American Revolution. Thousands of Hessians stayed behind after the war and became citizens of the new United States of America. *(The Classical Gallery, Virginia/Bridgeman Art Library)*

British North America for specific reasons—they became increasingly mistrustful of Catholicism and France and began to admire British liberties and political institutions. Of course, the new relationship between German and English-speaking American colonists was beneficial to both parties; in exchange for the right to settle on the periphery of the expanding British Empire, the Germans—most of whom ended up in the mid-Atlantic region—provided a buffer between profitable English settlements and New France. In marked contrast with the later generations of immigrants, the religious radicals of this period were usually absorbed relatively rapidly into English communities.

Eighteenth-Century Migration: Economic Motivations and Cultural Autonomy

In the early part of the eighteenth century, Germans increasingly came to the American colonies for economic reasons. They also came in much larger numbers and did not blend in as seamlessly as their predecessors, inciting mistrust on the part of their English neighbors.

The main recipient of the new influx was the backcountry of the tolerant Quaker colony, Pennsylvania. From Philadelphia, German-speaking communities sprang up in Virginia and Maryland; Charles Town, South Carolina, served as the center of the German community in the Southeast—the famed "Pennsylvania Dutch" were neither confined to Pennsylvania nor mainly Dutch in origin.

Some early eighteenth-century settlers came to New York, but troubles—fueled by language differences—resulted when the settlers' concept of rights ran afoul of their requirement to produce naval stores for the governor. Bad publicity resulted, and the flow of immigrants was redirected to Pennsylvania.

Most German-speaking colonists migrated to America in families, and many were guided through the early steps of the process by immigrants who had arrived earlier. Although some were indentured servants and a few were wealthy merchants, most occupied the middle rungs of society, working as artisans and smallholding farmers.

German immigrants created sweeping support and communications networks not only between themselves in the American colonies but reaching across the Atlantic to continental Europe as well. Merchants, recruiters, and immigration agents known as "newlanders" competed with one another for the growing trans-Atlantic trade in German-speaking migrants. Missionary societies and the Lutheran community in London sent money, literature, and medicine to German immigrants in the colonies. The pietist university at Halle, founded in 1694, was especially active in this regard. More radical strains of German Protestantism, outside of this mainstream support network, faced challenges in funding their colonial ventures.

Perhaps the most famous German settlement in British colonial America was Germantown, founded in 1683 on a 43,000-acre tract a short distance from Philadelphia. Germantown, led in its early years by Francis Daniel Pastorius, was noteworthy for its distinctly German characteristics. The Germantown colonists, almost entirely artisans and farmers, began to produce flax and linen shortly after their arrival. They brewed beer and distilled spirits. They also set up a paper mill—the first in Pennsylvania—and later a printing press that distributed German reading material throughout the colonies. As early as 1701, a fair had been established, serving to distribute German crafts to eager colonists. Quakers among the German colonists also protested the slaveholding practices of their English counterparts in the colony.

Not all German settlements were so peaceful. In the Shenandoah Valley, groups of Irish and Germans (both Catholic and somewhat despised by their English neighbors) commonly rioted on each other's saints' days. Germans displayed St. Patrick with potatoes around his neck, and the Irish returned the "compliment" by stringing St. Michael up with a sauerkraut rope. Such exhibitions often ended in violence.

In the eighteenth-century phase of migration, many ordinary German speakers sought to better their economic position, which necessitated movement between English and German spheres. Germans continued to speak their own dialects among themselves, but those oriented toward the marketplace picked up some English in an effort to blend into the world of Atlantic commerce. Legal and economic language was a strange blend of English and German, heavy on the English— "ein Bill of Sääl," "ein Freeholder," and "der Cort" are some examples that have little to do with the German words describing the same items and institutions. Church services continued to be conducted in German, as did school lessons. Of course, tavern discourse was almost always conducted in the native tongue as well.

As Germans emerged as a force in British colonial America, they hung on to old cultural traits at the same time as they modified their lifestyles to mirror those of their English neighbors. From spare homes of the southwestern German style, they moved into increasingly elaborate dwellings. While they produced many goods for English domestic use and catered to English tastes, items for their own use still reflected German sensibilities. They sold tinware, but preferred their own utensils to contain pewter. Similarly, their plates and home decorations used red, green, and yellow extensively, while the items they produced for sale were more plain. Clothing colors and styles also varied according to nationality. As German tavern culture spread out from Philadelphia, non-Germans began to appreciate some of the German-style cuisine, including scrapple, a fried cake of pork and cornmeal.

Germans did not pick up every English whim. They preferred coffee to tea, for instance. In fact, in the middle of the eighteenth century, German-American cultural forms blossomed. Hand-painted birth, marriage, and death certificates, along with house blessings and other forms of folk art, could be found throughout the colonies and were widely used in the mid-Atlantic region and the growing backcountry.

Over the course of the eighteenth century, in an effort to secure their descendants' future financial stability, German-speaking peoples accepted English legal and political forms, allowing them to participate more fully in the larger economy. English clerks and officials, and some English-speaking German elected officials, began to replace German teachers, ministers, and merchants as the intermediaries between German communities and the larger American colonial world. Still, they continued to sing German songs, both religious and secular, relied on time-honored folk medicine, including herbs and conjuring, and participated in a vibrant, distinctly German culture.

By the time of the American Revolution, German-speaking people were present in every colony, yet they were viewed with suspicion by many of their Anglo-American neighbors. They sought economic and religious security in many of the same ways as their English counterparts but remained in separate ethnic enclaves, even after most German colonists had begun to speak English. Although their cultural impact on colonial America was immense, it would only be a slight generalization to say that German Americans shied away from political action on a national scale in the late eighteenth century.

Matthew Jennings

See also: Immigration; Language; Pennsylvania; Pennsylvania (Chronology). *Document:* Protest of German Quakers Against Slavery (1688).

Bibliography

Kuhns, Oscar. *The German and Swiss Settlements of Colonial Pennsylvania: A Study of the So-Called Pennsylvania Dutch.* 1900. New York: Eaton & Mains, 1914.

O'Connor, Richard. *The German-Americans: An Informal History.* Boston: Little, Brown and Company, 1968.

Roeber, A. G. " 'The Origin of Whatever Is Not English Among Us': The Dutch-Speaking and the German-Speaking Peoples of Colonial British America." In *Strangers Within the Realm: Cultural Margins of the First British Empire,* edited by Bernard Bailyn and Philip D. Morgan. Chapel Hill: University of North Carolina Press, 1991.

———. *Palatines, Liberty, and Property: German Lutherans in Colonial British America.* Baltimore: Johns Hopkins University Press, 1993.

Glorious Revolution

In 1689, Englishmen forced the abdication of King James II and invited William of Orange to occupy the throne. This event, known as the Glorious Revolution, marked a watershed period in British history.

William's ascension confirmed the Protestant character of the English state, ended a prolonged period of constitutional upheaval and religious violence in the seventeenth century, energized the Whig faction in English politics, and established, once and for all, the principle of parliamentary supremacy in the English government. Because of the importance of the constitutional and political changes during this time, the Glorious Revolution profoundly affected the British-American colonies as well.

Origins

The Glorious Revolution began amid controversy surrounding the kingship of Charles II and his heir apparent, James, Duke of York, in the 1670s and early 1680s. The chief issue in dispute was James's religion, Roman Catholicism. Parliament demanded that the king be Protestant; pressure thus began to build to change the succession, passing over James in favor of another member of the royal family with a clear Protestant commitment. The effort to exclude James from the succession

William of Orange (later King William III) summons the Convention Parliament in 1689 at the invitation of both houses following the forced abdication of James II. The accession of William and Mary later that year ended the bloodless Glorious Revolution. *(Brown Brothers, Sterling, Pennsylvania)*

was spearheaded by a group of political leaders in Parliament called Whigs. The Exclusion Crisis ended in 1685, when James actually became king, though not before various plots to prevent this from happening had been exposed and defeated.

James II's actions as king worsened the situation. He swept justices and county officials from their posts, appointing his personal favorites, and made attempts to rig the English electoral system to ensure a pro-king Parliament. He also made it clear that he wished to return the Church of England to Roman Catholicism, appointing Catholics to high positions at the major universities and eliminating legal restrictions on Catholic citizens. James II's use of his royal powers infuriated many citizens, and when he produced a male heir in 1688, Whigs and their political opponents in Parliament, the Tories, came together secretly to plot James II's removal from office.

This required an alternative to James II, whom the leaders of the Glorious Revolution found in William of Orange. William was nephew to Charles II and James II and had married James II's eldest daughter Mary. William had excellent credentials as a leader of European Protestantism in his position as stadholder in the Netherlands; therefore, English parliamentary leaders sent word to him that they and the rest of the nation would support an invasion designed to dislodge James II.

In late 1688, William assembled an invasion force and, by early November, landed a large army on English soil. James II responded to this threat by fleeing to France. Parliamentary leaders met in early 1689 and declared that James II had abdicated the throne, inviting the next legitimate heir, James II's daughter Mary, to be queen. She agreed to rule only as long as her husband, William, was made king; Parliament gave its assent.

William and Mary's coronation brought about several important constitutional changes. First, they agreed to a document called the Bill of Rights (1689).

This established, once and for all, the principle of parliamentary supremacy over the monarch. William and Mary pledged not to suspend parliamentary statutes, enact new forms of taxation, or maintain a standing army in peacetime without the consent of Parliament. They also agreed to respect the right to trial by jury, free elections, and freedom of speech. Finally, the Bill of Rights stipulated that no Roman Catholic could ever occupy the throne. On another front, Parliament passed the so-called Toleration Act (1689), which gave freedom of worship to Baptists, Quakers, Independents, and other religious dissenters (though not Unitarians or Roman Catholics). The Bill of Rights and Toleration Act were joined by the Triennial Act (1694), which required the king to call new parliamentary elections at least once every three years. Taken together, these acts are known as the "Revolution Settlement," a landmark development in the advance of individual rights and the concept of limited government.

Such a momentous change in the constitutional arrangements between people, Parliament, and king in England quite naturally had an effect on the British-American colonies. The Glorious Revolution triggered political violence in Boston, New York, and Maryland in 1689, not to mention political controversy in most other colonies as well. But these rebellions and controversies were as much the product of long-simmering grievances of colonists as the ripple effect of the sudden transfer of power in England. Indeed, leaders of these rebellions protested policies dating back to 1660 and beyond, especially the ill-fated efforts of Charles II and James II to reorganize the colonies in the early 1680s. The Glorious Revolution merely gave the occasion for these resentments to boil over into organized resistance and violent action.

In Boston, colonists nursed bitterness against James II for revoking the Massachusetts Bay Colony charter in 1684 and, two years later, forming the Dominion of New England. These changes represented the culmination of royal policy, beginning in 1660, aiming to redesign the colonial system. England encouraged the Puritan colonies to become more tolerant toward members of the Church of England and religious dissenters like the Quakers, to produce more revenue for the mother country, and to take more responsibility for defense of the colonies against France. But James II took a more forceful position.

By revoking the Massachusetts Bay charter, he hoped to end the practice of self-government that made the Puritan colony so difficult to control. The new government went forward with a Crown-appointed president and council, and, more importantly, no colonial assembly. This enraged Puritan leaders, but further outrages were to come. James II brought all the Puritan colonies together with New York and New Jersey under one political jurisdiction—the Dominion of New England—with Governor Edmund Andros at its head. The stage was set for full-scale insurrection.

Bostonians linked the unpopular Dominion with James II's arbitrary policies of 1684. When news of his abdication arrived, they staged an uprising against Governor Andros and his officials in April 1689. These rebels also were energized by suspicions that Andros was secretly conspiring with French Catholic officials in Canada. Having taken Andros and his trusted aides captive, rebels gained credibility by including Cotton Mather and the aging Simon Bradstreet (a former governor) in the proceedings.

Eventually, the Dominion of New England was dissolved, and Massachusetts Bay won a new charter that restored the representative assembly, but retained a royal governor with veto power over colonial legislation. Significantly, voting rights under the new charter were based not on religious affiliation but on property, and religious toleration was extended to Protestant dissenters. These reforms ultimately weakened the Puritan influence over the Massachusetts Bay Colony.

Glorious Revolution and Leisler's Rebellion

In New York, the Glorious Revolution produced a large-scale uprising known as Leisler's Rebellion. Like the Boston rebellion, this sprang from earlier disagreements between colonists and England. New Yorkers were frustrated when James II failed to implement a proposed plan of government for New York, which would have given the residents a permanent legislative assembly and secured many of the traditional rights of British subjects. Instead, the king placed New York into the Dominion of New England under Governor Andros, which, of course, provided for exclusive royal control and no colonial assemblies. In late May of 1689, the New York militia seized the English garrison in the colony in the wake of news of William's invasion of England, James II's abdication, the Boston rebellion against Andros, and French–Native American maneuvering against frontier settlements. The militia's action forced Andros's lieutenant governor, Francis Nicholson, to flee for his life. Jacob Leisler, a militia captain, was appointed commander in chief, giving the insurrection its name.

Leisler and his trusted aides never achieved the credibility that the rebel leadership earned in Massachusetts Bay. Wealthy English and Dutch merchants in New York and Albany were galled by his policies of ending trade monopolies and imposing taxes. Furthermore, Leisler determined to end the French Catholic threat against the frontier once and for all, which led to a spectacular failure to take Canada by force. Frustrations with Leisler's management of public affairs came to a head in 1690, and the colony's elite welcomed William's decision to deny recognition to Leisler's government. Newly appointed royal officials, under the governorship of Henry Sloughter, imprisoned Leisler's supporters and eventually ended the rebellion with Leisler's execution on charges of treason in May 1691.

The Glorious Revolution in England occasioned political upheaval in Maryland as well. For decades, disgruntled settlers complained about the privileges reserved for the proprietary family, the Calverts. The faith of the proprietary family, Roman Catholicism, added religious fuel to these economic and political tensions. When English parliamentary leaders made James II's Catholicism an issue in the succession crisis of the 1680s, and when the arch-Protestant William replaced James II in 1689, the opportunity arose for Protestant Marylanders to press their case against proprietary rule. John Coode, an anti-proprietary assembly leader from the early 1680s, organized the so-called Protestant Association and took the colonial capitol and proprietary estates by force. In 1691, King William ratified the results of Coode's Rebellion by invalidating the proprietary charter and bringing Maryland under royal control.

Insurrections in Maryland, New York, and Boston proved to be only the most immediate and visible consequence of England's Glorious Revolution for the British-American colonies. The event brought about a centralization of colonial administration, including the creation of the Board of Trade in 1696, and initiated a decades-long pattern of conflict between English and French colonists, along with their Native American allies.

Most importantly, the Glorious Revolution gave colonists first-hand experience with the constitutional questions that wracked England for much of the seventeenth century. Drawing from this experience, later colonists began to think more critically about the status of the colonies within the British Empire and the foundational principles of government. These thoughts would mature as justifications for rebellion against England in 1776.

Jeffrey B. Webb

See also: James II; Politics and Government (Chronology); Politics and Government (Essay); William III of Orange and Mary II.

Bibliography

Greene, Jack P. *Peripheries and Center: Constitutional Development in the Extended Polities of the British Empire and the United States, 1607–1788.* Athens: University of Georgia Press, 1986.

Hall, M. G., et al., eds. *The Glorious Revolution in America.* Chapel Hill: University of North Carolina Press, 1964.

Jarrett, Derek. *Britain, 1688–1814.* New York: St. Martin's, 1965.

Lovejoy, David S. *The Glorious Revolution in America.* Middletown, CT: Wesleyan University Press, 1987.

Reich, Jerome R. *Leisler's Rebellion: A Study of Democracy in New York, 1664–1720.* Chicago: University of Chicago Press, 1953.

Tully, Alan. *Forming American Politics: Ideals, Interests, and Institutions in Colonial New York and Pennsylvania.* Baltimore: Johns Hopkins University Press, 1995.

God

As the weary Mayflower passengers made their way onto the shores of Cape Cod, according to William Bradford, they "fell upon their knees & blessed ye God of heaven, who had brought them over ye vast & furious ocean." He went on to add that nothing could sustain the people but "the Spirit of God and His Grace."

John Winthrop, founder of the Puritan settlement at Massachusetts Bay in 1630, made clear to his followers that "the God of Israel is among us. . . . He shall make us a praise and glory, that men shall say of succeeding plantations: 'The Lord make it like that of New England.' "

More than 100 years later, Alexander Hamilton wrote, "The sacred rights of mankind are not to be rummaged for among old parchments or musty records. They are written, as with a sunbeam, in the whole volume of human nature, by the hand of the divinity itself; and can never be erased or obscured by mortal power."

Finally, in 1780, Samuel Cooper declared that the "everlasting maxims" of equality and freedom were "confirmed . . . by the instructions, precepts, and examples given us in the sacred oracles [i.e., the Bible]; . . . and that they come from him who hath made of one blood all nations to dwell upon the face of the earth."

This belief in God as the great provider or sustainer and the great designer of freedom directed the footsteps of most of those drawn to the shores of colonial America. To conceive of American principles without the influence of these religious ideals is impossible. Indeed, the Great Migration, which lasted from 1630 to 1643, saw the emigration of 20,000 people to New England and 45,000 to the Southern colonies or the West Indies, most motivated by the desire to exercise freedom of religious choice. Men such as Bradford, Winthrop, Thomas Hooker, Charles Chauncy, John Cotton, and John Davenport, who abandoned England for the rugged shores of America, believed that people should not have to conform to the rigors of an established church. Unfortunately, under King Charles I, and especially under the archbishop of Canterbury, William Laud, protesters and reformers were imprisoned, fined, branded, even tortured. They had little choice but to flee.

The history of their revolutionary thinking, however, had its roots in the Protestant Reformation of the sixteenth century. Martin Luther, by posting his ninety-five protests against the Roman Catholic Church, challenged the order of life as it had been lived for hundreds of years. He maintained that people had to be free to enter into a relationship with God, that the Church could not control that relationship, and that every man had the right to act according to his own conscience. Luther believed that only God has authority over conscience, that human laws have power only over life and property or those things that are "external upon earth."

John Calvin, like Luther, also believed that people's minds and hearts could not be controlled by civil governments or rulers. In his famous series of texts, *Institutes of the Christian Religion,* he outlined the limits of royal authority and the right of individuals to "disobey ungodly magistrates."

Calvin's words exerted tremendous influence on other thinkers. Theodore Beza, Calvin's successor, wrote *The Right of Magistrates,* justifying armed revolt. According to President John Adams, Hubert Languet's *Vindiciae Contra Tyrannos* (The legal claim against tyrants), appearing in 1579, helped lay the foundation for American political theory. In succeeding decades, other Christian ideologists, including John Knox, John Ponet, Christopher Goodman, Johannes Althusius, Samuel Rutherford, and John Locke, produced political writings that defended the right of the people to overthrow tyranny whenever necessary. Thomas Jefferson and his colleagues later used Locke's and Rutherford's theories in defending their rejection of King George III.

Another theological document that influenced American's founding fathers was the Westminster Confession of 1656. This text was second only to the Bible in importance in pre-Revolutionary New England, with more than 5 million copies in print. In fact, James Madison, also known as the "father of the Constitution," integrated many of the Westminster Confession's principles into the Constitution.

The colonists' belief in God was an important element in their lives. Likewise, the impact of that belief on the development of this country's philosophical roots is something that cannot be underestimated. It forms the cornerstone of American democracy.

Gail L. Jenner

See also: Bible; Christ and Christianity; Great Awakening; Ministers and the Ministry; Missions; Religion (Chronology); Religion (Essay); Sermons.

Bibliography

Amos, Gary, and Richard Gardner. *Never Before in History: America's Inspired Birth.* Dallas, TX: Haughton, 1998.

Gorges, Ferdinando (1566–1647)

Sir Ferdinando Gorges was born in Wraxall, Somerset, in 1566. He gained prominence in England as an Elizabethan war hero and advocate of North American settlement. Despite forty years of backing charters and companies that received North American lands from the British Crown, Gorges never saw any of his lands in North America.

In 1605, along with Sir John Popham, Sir Thomas Gates, and Sir Raleigh Gilbert, Gorges petitioned King James I for charters incorporating the London and Plymouth Companies. The charters were granted on April 10, 1606, giving the London company lands from North Carolina to New York and the Plymouth Colony, present-day New England. Neither company was to settle within a hundred miles of the other. In 1607, the Plymouth Company attempted a permanent settlement at the mouth of the Kennebec River. Despite the failure of the Popham Colony in 1608, Gorges remained obsessed with settling Maine.

In 1621, Gorges formed a group called the Council for New England and was granted a royal charter. His new lands ran between Philadelphia and the south coast of Newfoundland, overlapping the rival Plymouth Company's claim. The London Company took the case to the Privy Council and to Parliament, where it was debated until 1628 and Charles I's dissolution of Parliament. Gorges's charter remained legal until 1639.

During its approximately twenty-year existence, the Council for New England had a very different status from other companies. Gorges served as governor, subject only to the English Crown. His potential citizens answered to him rather than to the Crown or Parliament. Another distinction given to Gorges was the ability to give out land charters of his own. The Pilgrims initially applied to the London Company for a charter south of the Hudson River. When they landed on Cape Cod, they sent home to England for a new charter from Gorges's council.

In 1629, the group of religious dissidents known as the Puritans applied directly to Charles I for a charter, as they did not want to be under Gorges's rule. Charles I granted their charter, and they began the New England Company. Their Massachusetts Bay Colony ran from the Charles River to the Merrimac River. The Puritans also expressed an interest in the land farther east around the Kennebec River.

In 1630, concerned about the spread of the Massachusetts Bay Colony, William Bradford, governor of Plymouth, applied for a charter with better terms from Gorges. The original charter had allowed each settler 100 acres of land, unclaimed by the council around Plymouth after three years of settlement. The new charter granted the Pilgrims land on either side of the Kennebec and the exclusive right to trade on the river.

Gorges and the Pilgrims had a unique relationship in a period marked by constant religious tension. Gorges was a wealthy Anglican, and the Pilgrims had separated from the Church of England. The Pilgrims' religious beliefs were closer to those of the Puritans, but their land interests were in conflict. The Puritans were wealthy enough to obtain land charters of their own; the Pilgrims needed Gorges's support in England. By backing their requests for land, Gorges chose to ignore the Pilgrims' religion in favor of their obedience and support.

In 1637, the Council for New England announced that the Massachusetts Bay Colony's charter was illegal and demanded that King Charles I assert more control over the Puritans. The Puritans, in turn, refused to surrender their charter, and New England was thrown into an uproar. In 1639, Charles I dissolved the Council for New England and granted Gorges a new charter, this time to the Province of Maine. Gorges's latest charter limited his geographic control but strengthened his immediate power.

Gorges granted more charters in the 1640s, including one between Cape Porpoise and the Kennebec River to Alexander Rigby and George Cleeves. This become a semidependent province called Lygonia, which lasted from 1646 to 1652. Lands around the Saco and York rivers were also given as grants.

Gorges died in 1647, leaving the Province of Maine without leadership or control. Although the province declared itself an independent region and elected a governor, the Massachusetts Bay Colony was able to claim Maine with the help of Oliver Cromwell's backing in England.

After his restoration to the English throne, Charles II returned control of Maine to Gorges's grandson, Ferdinando Gorges II. In order to help document his claim to Maine, Gorges II reprinted his grandfather's accounts regarding his land acquisitions. In 1677, the younger Gorges sold his lands to the Massachusetts Bay Colony for 1,270 pounds.

Abigail B. Chandler

See also: Land and Real Estate; Massachusetts Bay Colony; Pilgrims.

Bibliography

Baxter, James Phinney, ed. *Sir Ferdinando Gorges and His Province of Maine. Including the Brief Relation, the Brief Narration, His Defence, the Charter Granted to Him, His Will, and His Letters.* Boston: Prince Society, 1890.

Duncan, Roger. *Coastal Maine.* New York: W. W. Norton, 1992

Preston, Richard Arthur. *Gorges of Plymouth Fort.* Toronto: University of Toronto Press, 1953

Government, Spanish Colonial

The basis for the Spanish empire was mercantilism, a highly controlled, political/economic system, in which colonies were established to funnel wealth into the mother country, deprive political rivals of wealth, and maintain power at the expense of colonial rivals.

The basis for this empire's economy was the *encomienda* system, under which the Crown gave land and the residents on that land to specific individuals. Under this system the landholders created huge and highly profitable estates with laborers in virtual peonage, and some of these peasants were virtually worked to death. The *encomiendas* raised some European plants and animals, but it did not grow crops that competed with Spanish products such as grapes, olives, and hemp.

As of 1600, the Spanish colonial empire encompassed what was known as New Spain and Peru. The former stretched over the mainland from the Isthmus of Panama north. It also included the West Indies and Venezuela. Peru encompassed all Spanish territory south of New Spain, except Venezuela and Brazil, which were the property of Portugal. Each colony's governor was a viceroy, responsible solely to the Spanish king.

In Spain, the Council of the Indies advised the

The governor of each colony in New Spain was a powerful viceroy, responsible solely and directly to the Spanish crown. The governor's palace on the island of Dominica was typically lavish. *(The Stapleton Collection/Bridgeman Art Library)*

king on colonial matters and handled colonial correspondence. It also served as an appeals court for the *Casa de Contratación,* the House or Board of Trade, which, from its 1503 establishment in Seville, served as the clearinghouse for all trade with the New World. It controlled the movement of goods, passengers, and missionaries in the mercantile effort to maximize the flow of wealth to the Crown. A bureaucracy commonly wrote new rules for each new situation rather than working from precedent.

The *audienca* was the Spanish court of justice. Originally a court of appeals, by the late fifteenth century, it was administrative, as well as judicial, and handled both civil and criminal cases. The court was divided into districts with at least four judges in each district. Early in the sixteenth century, territorial and regional *audiencas* replaced the somewhat arbitrary and inconsistent administration of the conquistadores.

The colonial *audiencial pretorial* was an executive and legislative body, the core of colonial administration. The main organ of royal authority, it oversaw colonial administrators and had the right to appeal to the Council of the Indies. Initially, it protected the rights of individuals, but it became corrupt and inefficient during the seventeenth and eighteenth centuries.

The *alcalde* was the principal local judge and administrator. An elected official, he presided over the town council and served as mayor and sheriff. In extreme cases the *alcalde* was the sole representative of the royal law in his assigned region. Also serving as administrators of parts of the province were the *corregidores*; royally appointed, they were responsible for larger areas than the *alcalde* were.

The lowest administrative element was the *cabildo,* the city council. It came into being in the early sixteenth century as an equivalent of the Castilian *ayuntamiento* (its original name). This was the only Spanish institution open to Creoles or Spaniards born in the colonies, and it consisted of elected administrators, usually landowners, who oversaw the affairs of its region. Heading the *cabildo* was the *alcalde* or mayor. Assisting the *alcalde* in judicial affairs were the *alcaldes ordinaries.* The *cabildo* distributed land, taxed, provided police service, and oversaw trade, as well as public facilities such as hospitals and jails. The *cabildo* had emergency powers to select a governor, lieutenant governor, or captain general. Over the centuries, it became appointive, proprietary, and hereditary. Corruption and inefficiency characterized the *cabildo* after the seventeenth century.

When the Bourbon kings replaced the Hapsburgs

in the early eighteenth century, they sought to reverse the ruin brought about by the Hapsburgs' foreign and domestic policies. They restructured the economy and the government, centralizing power at home and modernizing colonial government in order to increase taxes and establish more direct military control. New Spain was structured into twelve *intendencias.* The *intendentes,* who ruled these areas, were subordinate to the commandant general in Mexico City, who reported directly to the king, bypassing the viceroy. Liberalized commercial policies and greater worker freedom resulted in increased migration and economic growth.

The *audiencia* and viceroyalty increasingly took the powers of the *cabildo* as administration centralized. When colonial independence movements began early in the nineteenth century, the *cabildo* was often the focal point of efforts to attain self government. This was because it was a tradition-rich, civil institution that was both accessible and convenient for the nationalists.

John H. Barnhill

See also: Borderlands, Spanish; California; Cuba; Hispaniola; Mexico City; Missions; New Mexico; New Spain; Politics and Government (Chronology); Politics and Government (Essay); Puerto Rico; Spanish Colonies on Mainland North America (Chronology); Texas.

Bibliography

Fisher, Lillian Estelle. *The Intendant System in Spanish America.* Berkeley: University of California Press, 1929.

Kamen, Henry. *Empire: How Spain Became a World Power, 1492–1763.* New York: HarperCollins, 2003.

Parry, J. H. *The Spanish Theory of Empire in the Sixteenth Century.* Cambridge, UK: Cambridge University Press, 1940

Wortman, M. L. *Government and Society in Central America, 1680–1840.* New York: Columbia University Press, 1982.

Grain

Grains have been a mainstay source of food for humans for centuries. So it should be no surprise that such items were central to the economies of the American colonies, whether produced for local use or for export.

While Native Americans were familiar with the different types of grains found on the continent (barley, buckwheat, millet, oats, rye, and wheat), they did not bother to exploit these crops because of their dependence on corn (maize). Thus, the first widespread use of grains as staple crops can be attributed to European settlements, with the people of each nation bringing their own European varieties to America rather than utilizing what could be found there (corn is the major exception to this rule). Since each region had different climates, ecosystems, and settlement patterns, each region relied on its own group of staple crops. In New England, English East Anglican settlers grew wheat, rye, and oats; the Middle colonies focused their agricultural production on similar grains and other foodstuffs; Virginia and Maryland grew corn and wheat; and South Carolina grew rice.

Early on, the production of grains and foodstuffs derived from grains became essential to the economies of the American colonies, as well as to the economies of many Europe nations and their colonies outside of North America. Grains and foodstuffs from the colonies supported the existence of cash crop production, especially sugar, which occurred in most British, French, and Dutch colonies in the West Indies. North American crops also supplied food to various European nations, including Britain, Holland, France, and Italy. Earnings from these exports financed the importation by colonists of various goods they could not produce themselves, which drove economic and industrial growth in Europe (particularly Britain).

More importantly, grain production was indispensable to the development of the American colonies. Urban areas in the America colonies, such as New York City and Boston, could not have existed without crop surpluses within those same colonies, while other cities such as Philadelphia and Baltimore depended heavily on the exportation of grain and foodstuffs. The wealth of cash crops in the Southern colonies also would have been impossible without access to reliable sources of food for workers, whether they were grown as supplemental crops or imported.

While grain production could be found throughout the American colonies, the highest levels of production occurred in the Middle colonies (present-day Pennsylvania, Delaware, New Jersey, and New York). Because grains were notorious for depleting the soil, American farmers developed an endless variety of agricultural systems in order to replenish their lands while maintaining yearly yields.

In New England, farmers alternated several years of grain with several years of clover. In New York, many farmers used a rotation of corn and potatoes, barley (or peas), wheat, and grass. They also recommended a rotation of corn, wheat, and pasture, or corn, wheat, and three years of clover. Many Middle-colony farmers divided their farms into ten fields of equal size, using four for pasture, four for clover and hay, and two for wheat. A Maryland farmer recommended a three-field system, which started with grain, went to hay or clover, and ended as pasture.

George Washington had a relatively conservative rotation system, setting aside three fields for clover or grass, one of corn and potatoes, two of wheat, and one of buckwheat (which he used as pasture). Other Virginians were less conservative and utilized one of two systems: one field of wheat and clover used alternately, the clover being pasture, the other using corn, oats, and clover, with the last being pasture. Regardless of the system followed, grains were essential to every agricultural community in early America.

Solomon K. Smith

See also: Agriculture; Corn; Rice; Trade.

Bibliography

Gras, Norman S. *A History of Agriculture in Europe and America.* New York: F. S. Crofts, 1940.

Klingaman, David. "The Significance of Grain in the Development of the Tobacco Colonies," *Journal of Economic History* 29:2 (1969): 268–78.

McCusker, John J., Russel R. Menard, and Peter J. Albert. *The Economy of Early America: The Revolutionary Period, 1763–1790.* Charlottesville: University Press of Virginia, 1988.

Great Awakening

The Great Awakening was a period of intense spiritual examination and renewal in the life of colonial America. Marked by charismatic preaching, enthusiastic conversion experiences, and intense controversy, the Great Awakening set a tone of evangelical revivalism that has been a recurring phenomenon in American Protestantism for over 250 years.

Origins of the Great Awakening

Scholars and theologians variously define the period of the Great Awakening. Some argue that the phenomenon began as early as 1720 and extended through the frontier evangelism in the West and South as late as the 1760s. Most agree, however, that the movement's peak occurred during the decades of the 1730s and 1740s. The roots of the movement can be traced to the evangelicalism that grew from pietism brought to the col-

onies by German immigrants during the 1720s. This German movement was marked by extremely pious behavior, highly emotional church services, and the sense of having a mystical union with God. Its appeal was, therefore, much more one of sentiment and the heart than of the intellect and the mind. In addition to these German pietist roots, a simultaneous return to pietism was observed in the 1720s among New England Puritans, whose religious heritage began in a pietistic separation from the Church of England in the 1580s.

Three highly influential ministers were responsible for introducing this pietism into local congregations during the 1720s. Dutch Reformed minister Theodore Jacob Frelinghuysen brought his highly charismatic preaching to churches in New Jersey and Pennsylvania, where German immigrants were notably open to his message. The father and son William and Gilbert Tennent created a similar stir within Pennsylvania churches at the same time, directing their message especially to Scottish and Irish immigrants. Frelinghuysen and, to a lesser degree, the Tennents had all been influenced by German pietism and employed it in their preaching. Many scholars see this activity as a precursor to the actual Great Awakening.

Jonathan Edwards and George Whitefield

Many trace the beginnings of the Great Awakening itself to the preaching of Jonathan Edwards in the Connecticut River Valley in the early 1740s. Edwards, a Congregational minister at the Northampton church established by his grandfather, Solomon Stoddard, became interested in the pietistic movement as it had been employed by Frelinghuysen and the Tennents. Strongly grounded in the Puritanism of his ancestors, Edwards spent much of his career formulating a reconciliation between Calvin's concept of original sin and man's innate depravity and the emerging Enlightenment notions of man's reason and free will.

In 1734 and 1735, Jonathan Edwards undertook a series of sermons in which he warned his congregation to consider the eternal consequences of their earthly behavior and called upon the faithful to devote their lives solely to the power and control of God's will. In doing so, Edwards stated what would become the core of Great Awakening preaching: the belief that sinful man can only be redeemed as a result of Christ's crucifixion and that one must undergo an emotionally charged conversion experience to validate his or her

The latter phases of the Great Awakening saw a rapid expansion of the Baptist and Methodist denominations in the South and along the Western frontier. Circuit-riding preachers and camp meetings were effective in spreading the evangelical fervor. *(Bibliotheque Nationale, Paris, France/Bridgeman Art Library)*

submission to the will of God. A number of itinerant traveling ministers soon appeared throughout the colonies to preach a message similar to Edwards's, although their approaches varied widely. By 1739, the mood of revivalism was such that the English preacher George Whitefield made a visit to evangelize the colonies.

George Whitefield had undergone a personal conversion experience following his study of numerous German pietist tracts. A colleague of John Wesley, Whitefield was a successful revivalist in England before coming to evangelize the colony of Georgia in 1739. Whitefield was noted for his eloquent preaching from memory, his highly charismatic style, his extravagant physical gesturing, and his extensive use of Biblical metaphors in sermons. He also made shrewd use of techniques that had previously been restricted to business enterprises, including buying newspaper space to advertise upcoming speaking engagements and distributing inexpensive, simplified tracts to restate his spoken

message. While some questioned whether it was his spiritual message or his showmanship that drew so many listeners, Whitefield had many imitators throughout the colonies. During his fifteen-month stay in America, Whitefield preached to thousands of colonists, eventually visiting Charles Town, Philadelphia, New York City, and Boston.

Difficulties Faced by Evangelists

Although his tour was a resounding success, Whitefield and other itinerant preachers were not universally acclaimed across the colonies, and their presence was particularly unwelcome to established ministers of traditional denominations. Part of the difficulty arose from theology. Whereas evangelists and revivalists preached the consequences of unholy living, the terrors of eternal damnation, the observable effects of even hidden sins, and hopes of the imminent millennium as reasons for both individual and collective conversion, more conservative ministers and their flocks in the Presbyterian and Congregationalist traditions found it difficult to reconcile this theology with their reliance on Calvinism, particularly the doctrines of special election and the perseverance of the saints.

Further, the extreme emotionality and high theatrics of many revivalists and their listeners were perceived as unseemly by many conservatives. Chief among these critics was the Boston minister Charles Chauncy, who ridiculed the tales of converts' fainting, speaking in tongues, shouting, and other physical antics while in the throes of conversion. As a practical matter, many ministers of the more staid tradition felt threatened by the spectacle provided by their rivals' fiery style of preaching. Certainly, the sheer entertainment value of such displays in the settlers' harsh day-to-day existence cannot be underestimated.

In addition, the physical venues of many revivals—at tent meetings, camp meetings, and open-air revival gatherings, which sometimes lasted several days—were often criticized by traditionalists, especially those of the formal "high-church" heritage. Many mainline critics pointed out that religious enthusiasm proclaimed during public and showy conversion experiences quickly faded once the novelty had worn off and the itinerant preacher had left an evangelized area. As for the evangelists, many of them followed George Whitefield's lead and turned this controversy to their advantage, inviting people to come hear their message and decide for themselves. Many colonists did just that and added to the resounding success of the revivalists' trade.

Threats to Tradition

On a more pragmatic level, revivalists were seen as a threat to the stability and authority of established church hierarchies. Traditional churches had to address the immediate problem of a loss of membership. Although some new converts, whose souls had been redeemed by the efforts of itinerant evangelists, went on to form new, strict, and pious sects of their own, it was more common for new converts simply to stop attending any organized church, relying for their spiritual refreshment on occasional visits to camp meetings or revivals. While church fathers often genuinely worried about such former members' souls, the more pressing concern was the fact that such defectors usually considered themselves beyond the control of church leaders and posed a threat to social order within the colonies. Additionally, by challenging the authority of the established churches, such former members impaired the

churches' ability to impose taxes crucial to their own perpetuation.

From the traditional churches' standpoint, action was called for. The Connecticut legislature outlawed appearances and speaking engagements by itinerant preachers, unless these preachers were invited by the minister of an established congregation. Similar laws were passed in most of the colonies in an attempt to limit evangelists' access to speaking venues and, by extension, to the colonists themselves. While a complete discussion of the topic is beyond the scope of this article, many scholars have pointed to the legal maneuverings by both sides of this controversy as the origin of the eventual doctrine of the separation of church and state.

Within the established colonial denominations, the Great Awakening led to a number of splits and schisms. In Virginia, the Church of England was recognized as the legal church of the colony. As in so many cases, wealth was equated with control in the Virginia church, with the result that landed and moneyed tobacco planters often punished ministers who disparaged the planters' vices. As the Great Awakening dawned in Virginia in 1743, a bricklayer named Samuel Morris and a number of like-minded church members withdrew from the Anglican fellowship, preferring instead to invite a series of itinerant revivalists to minister to them. Although Morris and his friends suffered harassment at the hands of the state and church officials, they held fast to their denial of the Church of England.

George Whitefield's tour of the Middle colonies in 1739 and 1740 led to an even more drastic division within the Presbyterian and Dutch Reformed churches. Many of these churches' members heard and welcomed the preaching of Whitefield and other evangelists. They valued their Presbyterian or Reformed heritage, but they believed that new times called for new ways of preaching and for a contemporary message. Accordingly, they were drawn to the revivalists' assurance of God's grace that would follow a personal conversion experience. Such a notion, however, was in direct conflict with the traditionalists' more conservative doctrine of total depravity and with the belief that one was unable to know whether or not one was part of God's elect. Borrowing from the Quakers the concept of being able to discern God's will by means of an "inner light," the pro-evangelism factions of the Presbyterian church and the Dutch Reformed church declared that they were living in a new land in new times that required a "new light." The terms "New Light" and "Old Light" were applied to these denominations to indicate to which faction and which set of beliefs—liberal or conservative, modern or traditional—a given congregation subscribed. A similar schism occurred within the Congregational Church in New England, although this denomination remained united until 1754, much longer than their Presbyterian and Dutch Reformed counterparts. (On the other hand, the Philadelphia Synod of the Presbyterian Church had already split along similar lines during the 1720s as a result of disagreements arising over Gilbert Tennent's preaching.)

The process of schism was traumatic for mainline churches. Friends and even members of the same family often found themselves on opposing sides of the controversy. Even those who had no church affiliation prior to undergoing conversion as a result of Great Awakening evangelism engaged in the debate. When conservatives ridiculed the enthusiasm of the revivalists and their converts, these believers condemned their tormentors as unrepentant and unconverted sinners and often invited them to "see the light" via an evangelist's preaching. While conservatives insisted on orthodox doctrine and the conventional liturgy, new converts argued for the legitimacy of pious experience and spontaneous preaching. In broader cultural terms, the Great Awakening pointed out growing differences within the emerging American society, and it frequently challenged culturally accepted norms.

Great Awakening and Social Class

Perhaps the major discrepancy pointed out by the evangelical movement dealt with wealth. Wealth and the established Protestant churches had traditionally been closely tied, arguably as far back as the wake of the Reformation. Within the colonies, the theocratic nature of early governance also implied economic advantage. The church was supported by taxation of the citizenry, and the requirement of an educated clergy also implied that those so employed were men of some wealth and social standing. On the other hand, evangelists who preached in the Great Awakening were almost never trained theologians, ministers, or scholars. Instead, they relied on their personal talents when addressing, persuading, and convincing their audiences. These revival leaders also relied on their own conversion experiences to guide them as they tried to make new converts. What itinerant preachers lacked in formal schooling, they compensated for with their spiritual earnestness; what they lacked in dignified robes

and ornate churches was balanced by their personal enthusiasm and conviction that they were doing the true work of God.

The issue of social class drove much of the spread of the Great Awakening. As major denominations split over ideological issues, money generally stayed the conservative course: Old Light church members were usually the more wealthy and socially established members of their communities, while New Light groups usually attracted younger (hence, often less wealthy) supporters. These same lines often defined memberships in terms of other social categories that were frequently tied to wealth. Thus, divisions within church groups over Old versus New Light thinking often broke down communities as urban or rural, natives or new immigrants, creditors or debtors. Itinerant preachers were quick to recognize the disinheritance of persons in rural areas, new immigrants, and the poor, and they were quick to direct their messages of inclusion and love to those colonists who were often made to feel like outcasts.

By extension, preachers of the Great Awakening effectively questioned the motives that underlay the very founding of the colonies, as well as the direction in which the colonies would proceed in the future. No matter how much Old Light churches might protest that they and their forefathers had been sent by God on an errand into the wilderness, such a notion was difficult to reconcile with the greed and commercialism that many revivalists and New Lighters saw and deplored in their adopted homeland.

As an alternative, evangelists and their followers offered not pomp and ceremony, but rather a welcoming spiritual home for the disenfranchised, an atmosphere they believed was much more attuned to the communal ethic of an agrarian America that the earliest settlers had envisioned. In effect, the evangelists, revivalists, itinerants, and their followers were seeking the egalitarianism that would eventually become crystallized as one of the foundations of American belief.

Subsidence of the Awakening

As might be expected, the fever pitch of revivalism could not continue at uniformly high levels. There were certainly peaks and ebbs in the tide of religious enthusiasm in most communities. Often, itinerant preachers would be invited to return to areas where more pious converts were alarmed by their neighbors' backsliding into sin. By the early 1750s, the extended fervor of the

Great Awakening had ended in New England and the Middle colonies.

Over the following three decades, the enthusiasm and excitement of those earlier days was shifted toward the South and along the Western frontier. The Baptist and Methodist denominations experienced extensive growth in this period and posed some of the same threats to established churches their predecessors had. Both groups were known for their attempts to reach the unchurched, no matter how remote their location, and the Methodist circuit-riding preacher became an icon of these far-flung congregations. Baptists were known for their outspokenness on matters of wealth and race, as witnessed by their refusal to turn a blind eye toward wealthy planters' vices and by their denial that slavery was justified by African Americans' innate intellectual and moral inferiority. Both Baptists' and Methodists' efforts in the wake of the Great Awakening form an important chapter in their denominations' histories.

As for the Great Awakening as a whole, this period of intense spiritual awareness and renewal laid the foundations for the emerging nation's interest in and struggle with religious matters. The extreme enthusiasm of revivalism, which had caused such a stir, became yet another fiber in the thread of colonial history. As the Revolutionary War approached, colonists' attention turned to matters of nationalistic, not religious, fervor. Still, the sense of piety, of personal accountability, and of wanting to be right with one's God set the tone for innumerable revivals of religious and spiritual fervor that have continued to this day.

Barbara Schwarz Wachal

See also: Baptists; Bible; Christ and Christianity; Edwards, Jonathan; God; Methodist Church; Ministers and the Ministry; Religion (Chronology); Religion (Essay); Sermons; Whitefield, George. *Document:* On the Death of the Rev. Mr. George Whitefield (1770).

Bibliography

Bumsted, J. M., ed. *The Great Awakening: The Beginnings of Evangelical Pietism in America.* Waltham, MA: Blaisdell, 1972.

Bushman, Richard L., ed. *The Great Awakening: Documents on the Revival of Religion, 1740–1745.* New York: Published by Atheneum for the Institute of Early American History and Culture at Williamsburg, Virginia, 1970.

Clark, Stephen R. L. *God's World and the Great Awakening.* New York: Oxford University Press, 1991.

Cowing, Cedric B. *The Great Awakening and the American Revolution: Colonial Thought in the 18th Century.* Chicago: Rand McNally, 1971.

Gaustad, Edwin S. *The Great Awakening in New England.* Gloucester, MA: P. Smith, 1965 [c. 1957].

Harlan, David. *The Clergy and the Great Awakening in New England.* Ann Arbor, MI: UMI Research Press, 1980.

Lambert, Frank. *Inventing the "Great Awakening."* Princeton, NJ: Princeton University Press, 1999.

Pollock, John. *George Whitefield and the Great Awakening.* New York: Doubleday, 1972.

Tracy, Joseph. *The Great Awakening: A History of the Revival of Religion in the Time of Edwards and Whitefield.* Carlisle, PA: Banner of Truth Trust, 1976.

Great Lakes

The Great Lakes—Huron, Ontario, Erie, Michigan, and Superior—had basically taken on their current size and shape by about 12,000 B.C.E. They formed as the result of glaciers continually advancing and retreating, and finally receding and melting to provide one of the earth's largest freshwater systems. It has been estimated that the Great Lakes contain half of the world's supply of fresh water.

The human history of the Great Lakes began when small bands of Paleo-Indians moved into the region between 7000 and 4500 B.C.E. During the colonial period of American history, the Great Lakes region was in constant flux as native peoples in the interior of the continent struggled to survive a tide of native refugees from the Atlantic seaboard and European settlers.

A diverse array of native peoples inhabited the region from the fifteenth to the eighteenth century. Algonquian speakers, Iroquoian speakers, and Siouan speakers constituted most of the population, but striking diversity existed within each of these broad categories. Because of the different climates and physical settings in the region, four basic subsistence patterns emerged, though many groups employed a combination of these practices.

Around Lake Ontario and in present-day Illinois, Michigan, and Wisconsin, people depended on domesticated plants—mainly corn, beans, and squash—for their survival. In forests where wild game abounded, groups such as the northern Ojibway, Cree, and Assiniboine hunted moose, caribou, bear, and smaller game as well. In the small lakes to the south and west of Lake Superior, the Menominee, Ojibway, Winnebago, and Dakota harvested wild rice. Finally, the southeastern Ojibway, Ottawa, and Huron developed cultures centered around fishing, particularly lake trout and whitefish.

European colonization affected the Great Lakes rather indirectly at first. Apart from a few fur trading outposts and scattered Jesuit missions, few European settlers arrived in the Great Lakes region in the seventeenth century. As the Five Nations Iroquois came into contact with Europeans, and became dependent on European trade goods, they pressured neighboring native communities with their newly acquired firearms. From 1641 to 1701, the Iroquois carried out a series of devastating attacks on the Wenro, Huron, Erie, Neutral Nation, and other tribes in the Great Lakes region. Many of these tribes were dispersed. Refugees fled to the Illinois country, were adopted by the Five Nations Iroquois, or moved even farther west, which sometimes brought them into conflict with the Dakota.

The Iroquois continued to raid several hundred miles away from their homeland but were eventually driven back by the French and their native allies in 1680. In 1687, the French and their allies defeated the Seneca in a canoe battle on Lake Erie. By 1701, the Iroquois were forced to sue for peace, and negotiated terms at Onondaga, Albany, and Montreal. The Montreal peace treaty included more than twenty tribes.

From 1720 to the 1760s, the French were the dominant colonial power in the Great Lakes, but a small French treasury, affairs in Europe, and a relatively small number of settlers combined to deflate serious French efforts at exploration and expansion in the region. Missionaries continued to spread into Illinois country along the Mississippi River and worked in and around Detroit as well. The French policy of trying to concentrate as many Native Americans as possible around Detroit exacerbated tensions, and in the years that followed, the French, Illinois, and other groups attempted to exterminate the Wisconsin-based Mesquakie. By 1740, the Mesquakie had been dispersed. The real demographic tragedy of this period was the depopulation of Illinois country. Constant raiding and warfare had reduced the Illinois population from 6,000 to 2,000 by 1763.

Richard White has famously described the Great Lakes region as a sort of "middle ground": a territory in which neither Europeans nor Native Americans had enough power to dictate terms. According to this model, the various European outposts and autonomous—often multiethnic—villages existed in a state of rough equality. The Seven Years' War, known in America as the French and Indian War, helped to collapse the middle ground and establish a new imperial power

in the Great Lakes. The end result of the war was the French abandonment of continental North America. As the British moved into the region and tried to maintain peace between land-hungry Anglo-American settlers and their neighbors, they touched off a series of conflicts collectively known as Pontiac's Rebellion.

The Great Lakes would continue to be the site of turmoil in the late eighteenth and early nineteenth centuries, as the new United States exerted increasing pressures on Native American groups to assimilate or move out of the way.

Matthew Jennings

See also: Exploration; Furs; Mississippi River; Ohio Country; Transportation, Water.

Bibliography

Tanner, Helen Hornbeck, ed. *Atlas of Great Lakes Indian History.* Norman: University of Oklahoma Press, 1987.

White, Richard. *The Middle Ground: Indians, Empires, and Republics in the Great Lakes Region, 1650–1815.* Cambridge, UK: Cambridge University Press, 1991.

Green Mountain Boys

The Green Mountain Boys were originally organized as a local self-defense organization for settlers in the "New Hampshire Grants" of what is today part of Vermont. As part of the colonial militia, they played a crucial role in the opening moves of the American Revolution at the frontier of New England.

In the 1750s, New Hampshire Governor Benning Wentworth received royal permission from George II to issue grants to land in the Green Mountains, which was claimed by Massachusetts, New York, and New Hampshire. Wentworth made a fortune from land speculators and settlers. Many of the settlers were ambitious younger sons from Connecticut and Massachusetts, who bought the claims cheaply and founded more than sixty settlements, including Bennington, Marlboro, and Wilmington.

Unfortunately, New York sought and achieved a conflicting royal decision from George III giving that colony legal authority over the area in 1766. New York speculators then sold the land, and conflicting titles began to surface in the New York courts. Meanwhile, New York sheriffs arrived to dispossess earlier settlers or demand payment to the land's new owners.

The response among the settlers was the formation

Monuments to Ethan Allen and the Green Mountain Boys are found in village squares throughout New England. The exploits of this legendary band of armed irregulars include the capture of Fort Ticonderoga in 1775. *(Brown Brothers, Sterling, Pennsylvania)*

of the Green Mountain Boys in 1770. Led by the extended family of Ethan and Ira Allen, Seth Warner, Remember Baker, and Robert Cochrane, these men established local committees of safety, a warning system to alert the settlers to the approach of the authorities. The "boys" acted as the mobile force of the community.

Although they have gained the status of Robin Hood–like folk heroes, their actions often included burning out rival settlers, killing livestock, and harassing or humiliating New York officials. Notable clashes included Ethan Allen's offer to top New York's 20 pound bounty on him as an outlaw, as well as the group's killing and dismembering a dog named "Tryon" after the New York governor. They also beat offenders with birch branches, rescued arrested members of the group from the sheriffs, and raised funds to contest the cases in court.

In 1771, the Green Mountain Boys forced a *posse comitatus* of 300 men from Albany County to retreat from the farm of John Breckinridge. In 1773, they refused a truce from Governor Tryon by attacking and destroying a settlement at Rupert, fighting a contingent of veteran officers of the 42nd Highland Regiment, who had chosen the area as their land grant.

When the American Revolution broke out, the Green Mountain Boys were ambivalent about their participation. They had used a lawyer notorious for his Stamp Act distributor position in their cases against New York, and they balanced their distrust of the royal government against their antagonism toward their neighboring colonies. They recognized, however, the chance to swing opinion in their favor and gain leverage with their neighbors to support the independence of Vermont as a separate entity.

Ethan Allen and the group volunteered to take Fort Ticonderoga, a key point in the British control of the region and a gateway to Canada. Despite deep hostility toward the New York militia contingent and dislike of Connecticut officer Benedict Arnold, who had been sent to lead the attack, the May 10, 1775, assault on Ticonderoga was a success. Subsequently, however, an attack led by Allen and Arnold on British-held St. John failed.

The Green Mountain Boys, with their knowledge of the region, proved invaluable to the 1775 invasion of Canada and siege of Montreal. Allen and a few of the men also took part in a disastrous independent attack that led to Allen's capture and imprisonment until 1778. In his absence, Seth Warner was authorized by the Continental Congress to organize official regiments—the Green Mountain Regiment and the Vermont Rangers (under Colonel Samuel Herrick)—and to pay participants back wages for the Ticonderoga and Montreal campaigns.

The Green Mountain Boys disliked being led by any but their own chosen officers and often carried out their threat to go home when their settlement were threatened. But their sharpshooting, tracking, and guerilla skills were highly valued by the Continental army.

As an organized unit of the American military, the Green Mountain Boys saw significant action at Montreal, the Battle of Valcour Island, the American retreat from Fort Ticonderoga in July 1777, and the Battle of Hubberdton, a little-known delaying action against Burgoyne's invasion. They also fought in the Vermont mountains against Hessian *Jaeger* troops, a skirmish that won Arthur St. Clair crucial time to set up the Battle of Bennington. The men subsequently took part in the Battle of Bennington and both battles of Saratoga, turning back the British march south.

The Green Mountain Boys' participation in the Revolution won their cause, Vermont's independence, and status and respect, if not support, among neighboring colonies. Many of them were crucial in Vermont's 1777 declaration of independence, adoption of a constitution, and campaign for eventual statehood in 1791.

Margaret Sankey

See also: Military and Diplomatic Affairs (Chronology); Military and Diplomatic Affairs (Essay); Militias; New Hampshire; Revolutionary War; Vermont.

Bibliography

Alderman, Clifford Lindsey. *The Gathering Storm.* New York: Julian Messner, 1970.

Dexter, Warren W. *Vermont: Wilderness to Statehood, 1748–1791.* Rutland, VT: Academy, 1989.

Jellison, Charles A. *Ethan Allan: Frontier Rebel.* Syracuse, NY: Syracuse University Press, 1969.

Grenville, George (1712–1770)

While prime minister of Great Britain from 1763 to 1765, George Grenville attempted to remedy England's financial woes by imposing new taxes upon the American colonies. His policies, including the Sugar and Stamp Acts, contributed greatly to the development of revolutionary thought by creating anger and unrest among the colonists.

Born in 1712 at Westminster in London, Grenville attended Eton before entering Christ Church, Oxford University, in 1730. After additional studies at Inner Temple and Lincoln's Inn, he was called to the bar in 1735. Grenville entered Parliament in 1741 as member for the tiny borough of Buckingham. A formidable speaker and debater, he also displayed a talent for financial stringency and administrative efficiency in a House of Commons perennially concerned with the growth of public expenditure.

In 1744, Grenville joined Henry Pelham's government but was dismissed by the Duke of Newcastle's administration in 1755, only to be brought back into the government in 1756 as treasurer to the navy. In 1761, Grenville was appointed leader of the House of Commons. In April 1763, his financial acumen prompted George III to name him prime minister.

Grenville devoted much of his short ministry to the growing problem of America colonial policy. The British public debt had mushroomed during the Seven Years' War with France, much to the consternation of Britons, including Grenville. He believed that the expenses of maintaining the American colonies placed too great a burden upon the mother country and hindered its prosperity. In 1759, he voiced opposition to the extravagant war policies of William Pitt. In 1761, he supported peace negotiations with France because the war had cost Britain too much in terms of lives and money. As prime minister, Grenville aimed to deny France any foothold that could provide an excuse for future hostilities or threaten British trade, but his chief focus became reduction of the national debt.

The conquest of Canada, French Acadia, and the Floridas in 1763 created the dilemmas of administering these prizes and securing the new territory. Before Grenville took office, the Commons voted to keep an expensive army in the colonies and approved the principle of a colonial contribution for its support. Grenville did agree that the colonists should pay their share of their administration and defense, but he consistently opposed any measure that would increase expenses. To no avail, he had opposed the Proclamation of 1763, banning white settlement beyond the Appalachians, on the grounds that it would lead to the cost of employing an army to keep Native Americans and colonists separated. Grenville was left with the responsibility of devising a means to balance the budget.

England had traditionally imposed regulations to promote trade and encourage colonial development. Grenville changed this policy to regulate trade as a means of raising revenue and exploiting colonial holdings. To defray the expenses of defense, the Sugar Act of 1764 imposed a tax upon sugar, indigo, coffee, and cloth imported into America. While this measure triggered protests in the colonies, the 1765 Stamp Act tax on paper goods enraged Americans even more.

Grenville took steps to improve the administration of the colonies but again succeeded only in driving the colonists further from Britain. The 1764 Currency Act addressed the belief that an increase in the supply of paper money lessened the value of the currency. With this law, Grenville forbade the issuance of paper money in all the colonies south of New England, creating a chronic shortage of specie that forced the colonists to use alternative methods of exchange. The 1764 American Duties Act targeted smuggling by setting up a new court under an English judge. By situating this court in the garrison town of Halifax, Nova Scotia,

Grenville expected to end the local pressures that had led judges and juries to acquit smugglers. Unfortunately, the practical problems of transporting witnesses to Nova Scotia discouraged use of the court, and acquittals continued unabated.

George III had chosen Grenville to take over his government, but the king grew to heartily dislike his minister. An overbearing man with a hectoring manner, Grenville disagreed with the king over the conduct of everyday government business. Having lost royal support, he tendered his resignation on July 10, 1765. Grenville spent the remainder of his days as a member of Parliament and died in November 1770.

Grenville's ministry aimed to strengthen Britain but only succeeded in weakening the mother country's influence over her American colonies. His administration can only be categorized as a failure.

Caryn E. Neumann

See also: Currency Act (1764); French and Indian War; Politics and Government (Chronology); Politics and Government (Essay); Stamp Act (1765); Sugar Act (1764).

Bibliography

Bullion, John L. *A Great and Necessary Measure: George Grenville and the Genesis of the Stamp Act, 1763–1765.* Columbia: University of Missouri Press, 1982.

Lawson, Philip. *George Grenville: A Political Life.* Oxford, UK: Clarendon, 1984.

H

Hakluyt, Richard (c. 1551–1616)

Richard Hakluyt the Younger (hereafter Richard Hakluyt), one of the staunchest advocates of English colonization in the Americas, was born in 1551 or 1552 in Herefordshire. His cousin Richard Hakluyt the Elder, for whom he was named, spurred the young man's interest in geography. Hakluyt studied geography at Oxford, receiving his bachelor's degree in 1574 and a master of arts degree in 1577.

Hakluyt spent his adult life compiling and publishing accounts from English, French, Spanish, Portuguese and Dutch explorers, such as John Cabot, Giovanni da Verrazano, and Jean Ribaut. He made a comfortable living from the publication of his works, the patronage of wealthy clients, and several positions within the Church of England.

In 1582, Hakluyt published *Divers Voyages Touching the Discoverie of America*, which touched on many of the themes of his later work. He not only published accounts of voyagers, but also focused his inquiries squarely on America and provided a list of American commodities and detailed instructions for establishing colonies. Finally, *Divers Voyages* made Hakluyt's nationalist and expansionist tendencies clear.

Hakluyt spent the years between 1583 and 1589 in France, gathering information concerning America and publicizing and collecting money for English colonial expeditions. There, he formulated the idea for his most important work. Hakluyt had heard and read the insults of the French, namely, that the English were lazy and incompetent colonizers; these affronts prompted Hakluyt to "publish the maritime records of our own men, which are hitherto scattered and buried in dust."

To this end, in 1589, Hakluyt published the first volume of *The Principall Navigations, Voyages, and Discoveries of the English Nation. The Principall Navigations* did not focus solely on America or on recent expeditions. Hakluyt drew on what he viewed as a long tradition of English exploration, dating back to King Arthur's conquests of Ireland, Norway, and Greenland. Hakluyt believed firmly in the supremacy of English institutions and English people and in their abilities as colonizers. Hakluyt thought that all people, once they had been educated in the virtues of English civilization, would happily accept the protection of the English Crown. If *Divers Voyages* marked Hakluyt's transformation to professional geographer, his second major work made him England's most famous geographer, as well as an adviser to Sir Walter Raleigh and Queen Elizabeth.

Hakluyt's influence on the early English colonization of America is unmistakable. He advocated the conversion of Native Americans to Christianity, and, in fact, viewed conversion as an essential part of colonization. Moreover, colonies played an important role in strengthening England itself. American colonies could provide Christianity to "savage" peoples, protect England's interests abroad, and provide gainful employment for those put out by the rapid and tumultuous social changes occurring in England. Poor, displaced English subjects, he thought, would make clothes for the freezing natives of North America. Richard Hakluyt's view of colonization was supremely idealistic; he believed that violence would not play any part in England's colonial project.

Although he never visited America himself, and in spite of the fact that his peaceful vision of English colonization was far from the violent truth of Roanoke and Jamestown, Richard Hakluyt was a crucial player in every English colonizing expedition to America in the late sixteenth and early seventeenth centuries. He maintained close contact with Sir Humphrey Gilbert (an early martyr to the cause of English colonialism),

Sir George Peckham (another early promoter of colonization), Sir Walter Raleigh (a patron of his), and Thomas Harriot (chronicler of the first Roanoke expedition). In addition, he served as a director of the Virginia Company, though it is unclear what role he took in planning that colony. Hakluyt also corresponded with the French geographer Mercator and kept abreast of the latest developments in his field until his death in 1616.

Hakluyt's works appealed to a nation eager to make up lost ground against the Spanish and French in the race to colonize the Americas. They reflect the expansionist and nationalist tendencies of late-sixteenth- and early-seventeenth-century England.

Matthew Jennings

See also: Exploration; Virginia Company. *Document:* A Call for English Colonization of America (1584).

Bibliography

Kupperman, Karen Ordahl. *Indians and English: Facing Off in Early America.* Ithaca, NY: Cornell University Press, 2000.

Oberg, Michael Leroy. *Dominion and Civility: English Imperialism and Native America, 1585–1685.* Ithaca, NY: Cornell University Press, 1999.

Parks, George Bruner. *Richard Hakluyt and the English Voyages.* New York: American Geographical Society, 1928.

Halifax

In 1749, Britain founded Halifax, Nova Scotia, to counter French fortifications, establish an important economic settlement, and assimilate the local French population, known as Acadians. While Halifax became an important military center, it did not succeed in encouraging Acadian assimilation, and boom-and-bust cycles defined its economy in the colonial period.

The 1713 Treaty of Utrecht transferred mainland Nova Scotia from the French to the English. To protect the approaches to the St. Lawrence River and the heartland of New France, the French constructed a massive fortress, Louisbourg, on Cape Breton Island (Ile Royale). While a force of New Englanders captured Louisbourg in 1744, two factors soon increased British anxiety over their control of Nova Scotia.

The first was a failed French invasion of the colony in 1746. The French sent a fleet to capture the capital of Nova Scotia, Annapolis Royal. Weather played havoc with the invasion, however, and though ships arrived at the large harbor at Chibouctou (the native peoples, the Mi'kmaq, called the place *chebookt* meaning "chief

harbor"), the invasion failed. Second, in 1748 a new treaty returned Louisbourg to France.

In England, the Duke of Bedford responded by calling for an intensive effort to make Nova Scotia a bulwark against the French. Bedford wanted a comprehensive program of settlement and economic development at key points around the Nova Scotia coast. Such settlements would have the secondary benefit, Bedford thought, of assimilating the Mi'kmaq and the Acadians.

In 1749, 2,500 people from England arrived in Chibouctou. The majority of these settlers had recently been released from the armed forces; others were artisans such as carpenters. Edward Cornwallis, a 37-year-old army officer, commanded the new colony. Cornwallis changed the name of the settlement from Chibouctou to Halifax in honor of Lord Halifax, the chief officer of England's Board of Trade and Plantations. The settlers quickly built dwellings and defenses, including a palisade, five wooden forts, and three batteries, to defend against a sea borne invasion.

The Mi'kmaq viewed these developments with alarm. Cornwallis responded by treating the Mi'kmaq with contempt. He did not recognize their sovereignty and refused to negotiate for fishing and hunting rights. The Mi'kmaq were traditional allies of the French, and violence soon erupted between the natives and the British settlers. Cornwallis responded by offering 10 pounds for every Mi'kmaq scalp. Despite mobilizing a force of New England "Indian fighters" to combat the Mi'kmaq, the Halifax settlers remained unable to move freely beyond the fortifications.

This hostile relationship with the Mi'kmaq also affected the settlement of "foreign Protestants" brought from the Upper Rhine Valley in the early 1750s. The British wanted to place them close to the Acadians, but fear of Mi'kmaq attack required that most be settled in Lunenburg, within easy reach of Halifax.

In 1752, Cornwallis resigned. A number of the early Halifax settlers moved to New England. Business people and professionals from the American colonies, who saw an opportunity to take advantage of government spending in Halifax, replaced them. Such spending increased markedly during the Seven Years' War (known as the French and Indian War in North America), which began in 1756. The new governor of Nova Scotia, Charles Lawrence, along with Governor William Shirley of Massachusetts, wanted to attack the French at Louisbourg. Military expenditures soon flooded into Halifax as the British built a new fort and established a naval yard.

Overcrowding, disorder, drinking, and brothels defined wartime Halifax. In 1758, 22,000 military personnel were in Halifax in preparation for an attack on Louisbourg, but the bustle was short-lived. In 1758, Louisbourg fell, followed by Quebec in 1759, and Montreal in 1760. The French defeat in northern North America substantially reduced Halifax's military importance, and, as a result, the city's population shrank to 3,685 by 1767.

After Governor Lawrence died in 1760, power rested with a small group of powerful merchants, despite the establishment of an elected assembly in Nova Scotia in 1758. Joshua Mauger, who had created his vast wealth through West Indies trade, smuggling with Louisbourg, and a monopoly over the local production of rum, was the most influential of these men. Although merchants like Mauger became very wealthy, most people in Halifax suffered from the decrease in British expenditures in the city during the mid-1760s. Poverty was common, and most people visiting Halifax found it a small, crude settlement.

The American War for Independence brought renewed prosperity to Halifax. Some people in Halifax identified with the complaints of the American colonists, and there was a chance that Nova Scotia might join the thirteen colonies. Nova Scotia, nevertheless, remained within the British sphere. This was, in large part, due to Britain's substantial military presence and the fact that many Halifax merchants saw business opportunities for themselves if they backed the mother country.

R. Blake Brown

See also: Acadia, Nova Scotia; Canada; French and Indian War.

Bibliography

Fingard, Judith, Janet Guildford, and David Sutherland. *Halifax: The First 250 Years*. Halifax: Formac Publishing Company, 1999.

MacNutt, W. S. *The Atlantic Provinces: The Emergence of Colonial Society, 1712–1857*. Toronto: McClelland Stewart, 1965.

Upton, L.S.F. *Micmacs and Colonists: Indian-White Relations in the Maritimes, 1713–1867*. Vancouver: University of British Columbia Press, 1979.

Hamilton, Alexander (c. 1755–1804)

Alexander Hamilton, merchant, lawyer, soldier, statesman, and first secretary of the treasury, was born on the island of Nevis, in the British West Indies, on January

A leader of the Federalist party and an advocate for a strong central government, Alexander Hamilton served as the first U.S. secretary of the treasury. He established sound fiscal policies and financial credit for the young nation. *(Brown Brothers, Sterling, Pennsylvania)*

11 in either 1755 or 1757. He was the illegitimate son of a poor Scottish merchant of aristocratic descent, James Hamilton, and a French Huguenot physician's daughter, Rachel Fawcett Lavine. In 1765, his father abandoned the family; three years later, his mother died.

Hamilton, who had recently been apprenticed as a clerk to a firm of New York merchants, excelled in the pursuit of commerce and was soon left in charge of the firm. Recognizing his talents, friends raised enough funds to send him to Barber's Academy in Elizabethtown, New Jersey, and, in the autumn of 1773, he went to New York City to study at King's College (now Columbia University).

Hamilton was a successful student, but his studies were soon interrupted by the Revolutionary events in North America. Throwing his support behind the American cause, he wrote several pro-Whig pamphlets in 1774 and 1775, supporting the colonists' grievances. Receiving a commission as an artillery captain in 1776, he participated in some of the fiercest fighting of the war, including the battle of Trenton, where he and his men prevented the British from crossing the Raritan River.

In February 1777, Hamilton was promoted to the rank of lieutenant colonel, and he served as George Washington's aide-de-camp, a position he held for the next four years. In July 1781, he took a field command position under the marquis de Lafayette. Later that year, at the battle of Yorktown, he led an assault on a British garrison, which he captured with little loss of life.

Hamilton married Elizabeth Schuyler, the daughter of a well-connected, aristocratic New York family, in early 1781 and resigned his military commission in November of that year. He subsequently moved with his family to Albany, New York, where he studied law. He opened a practice but soon became involved in politics.

In July 1782, he was elected by the New York legislature to the Continental Congress, and, in April 1786, he won a seat in the state legislature and represented New York at the convention in Annapolis, Maryland. At the convention, he, together with James Madison and John Dickinson, pushed through a resolution calling for another convention in Philadelphia the following May to address problems facing the nation.

Intended as a convention for the alteration and improvement of the Articles of Confederation, the Philadelphia convention took on a new life and became a gathering place for the framing of a new constitution. Hamilton, who was one of three delegates representing New York, played a small role in the proceedings. He gave one major speech, endorsing a strong federal government in which the executive and members of the Senate would be elected for life, members of the legislature would be elected for three-year terms by universal manhood suffrage, and members of the Supreme Court would be appointed for life.

While Hamilton's role was small at the Philadelphia convention, his role in the state ratification process was much larger. Collaborating with James Madison and John Jay, he wrote fifty-six of the eighty-five essays in *The Federalist Papers*, a persuasive series of arguments in favor of the new Constitution.

After the state ratifications of the Constitution and while serving another term in the Continental Congress, Hamilton was appointed by President Washington as the first secretary of the treasury. He set to work immediately, establishing a financial program to support public credit and promoting manufacturers. In order to stabilize the nation's debt, Hamilton put together a funding scheme, whereby the entire foreign debt was to be refinanced in Holland at lower interest rates and domestic debt, both federal and state, was to be funded by public tax money at the federal level. Hamilton, moreover, proposed the creation of a national bank; Congress passed the bank charter, and Washington signed it into law on February 25, 1791.

Hamilton's economic program, together with his pro-British stance and opposition to the French Revolution, eventually brought him into conflict with Thomas Jefferson and James Madison, who went so far as to accuse Hamilton of being a monarchist. The quarrel escalated, with Jefferson resigning as secretary of state in December 1793, and it subsequently led to the formation of the first political party system in the United States—the Federalists and the Democratic-Republicans.

In January 1795, Hamilton, satisfied with his achievements, resigned from the cabinet to improve his own financial situation. He resumed his law practice in New York City, while maintaining his influence in both federal and state politics. President Washington and other officials in the cabinet continued to seek his advice on matters of policy.

In 1796, Hamilton used his political influence to oppose John Adams's election to the presidency. When that effort failed, he secretly used his influence in Adams's cabinet to affect policy. During the 1800 presidential election, Hamilton again used his influence to oppose Adams; when Jefferson and Aaron Burr tied for the presidency, he threw Federalist support behind Jefferson, as he distrusted Burr even more.

Hamilton's aversion to Burr reemerged in 1804, when he used his influence to prevent Burr from being elected governor of New York. Infuriated, Burr challenged Hamilton to a duel. Early in the morning of July 11, 1804, the two men met at Weehawken, on the New Jersey shore of the Hudson River, where the first shot hit Hamilton and mortally wounded him. He died the next day, leaving behind a wife and seven children.

Michael Sletcher

See also: Politics and Government (Chronology); Politics and Government (Essay); Revolutionary War; Washington, George.

Bibliography

Cooke, Jacob Ernest. *Alexander Hamilton: A Biography*. New York: Scribner's, 1982.

Flaumenhaft, Harvey. *The Effective Republic: Administration and Constitution in the Thought of Alexander Hamilton*. Durham, NC: Duke University Press, 1992.

Hecht, Marie B. *Odd Destiny: The Life of Alexander Hamilton*. New York: Macmillan, 1982.

McDonald, Forrest. *Alexander Hamilton: A Biography*. New York: W. W. Norton, 1979.

Miller, John Chester. *Alexander Hamilton: Portrait in Paradox*. New York: Harper, 1959.

Mitchell, Broadus. *Alexander Hamilton*. 2 vols. New York: Macmillan, 1957–1962.

Hancock, John (1737–1793)

John Hancock is the least known of the founders of the United States. He was born in Braintree (now Quincy), Massachusetts, in 1737, the son and grandson of ministers of the Congregational Church. Orphaned at age 9, young John was adopted by his wealthy uncle, merchant Thomas Hancock. Thomas provided John with a good education—the younger Hancock attended Boston Latin School and Harvard, from which he graduated in 1754 at the age of 17.

He worked for his uncle in his mercantile business until the older man died in 1764, at which time, John

The Boston merchant John Hancock (portrayed by John Singleton Copley), known as the first signer of the Declaration of Independence, was also one of the wealthiest men in the colonies. *(Brown Brothers, Sterling, Pennsylvania)*

inherited his wealth and his business. John Hancock was reputed to be the wealthiest man in the colonies.

Hancock acted in many ways to serve the rebel cause during the revolutionary period. Before the Revolution, Hancock, a businessman, was one of the strongest opponents to the Stamp Act, a tax on paper items, including newspapers, imposed by the British on the colonists in 1765. At this time, he entered the opposition to the mother country, although he did not demand outright independence. With Samuel Adams, Hancock led a protest group, called the Sons of Liberty or Liberty Boys, against the Stamp Act.

In June 1767, after the English passed the Townshend Acts, which imposed duties on items such as glass, lead, paper, and paint, Hancock refused to allow English custom officers on his ships. Other merchants followed suit.

Between 1769 and 1771, Hancock was a member of the Massachusetts General Court, as well as chairman of the Boston town committee formed after the Boston Massacre to investigate this incident. In 1768, his ship *Liberty,* which had been allegedly smuggling Madeira wine into the province, was seized by British customs officers—an act that Hancock protested as unconstitutional. General Thomas Gage, whose duty was to enforce the Coercive Acts, ordered that Hancock and Adams be sent to England to stand trial. Paul Revere went on his famed midnight ride primarily to inform the two rebels about their imminent arrest. Thanks to his warning, they escaped to Philadelphia.

On October 14, 1774, Hancock was elected president of the Massachusetts Provincial Congress and chairman of the Committee of Safety. This body voted to raise 12,000 troops in the province of Massachusetts and elected Hancock as a delegate to the Second Continental Congress. He served as president of the provincial congress until 1775.

John Hancock is probably most remembered from this period as the first signatory of the Declaration of Independence. This came about because he was the president of the First and Second Continental Congresses from 1775 to 1777. In addition, he served in the war as a major general and commander of the Massachusetts militia that fought at Rhode Island. He was instrumental in repairing French–American relations, which ensured the defeat of the British in the American War for Independence.

Although Hancock supported declaring independence from the British later than many others, John Adams still admired Hancock. In a letter Adams wrote to William Tudor in 1817, he reminisced about Hancock being "radically generous and benevolent" and "an example to all the young men of the town."

After the Americans declared their independence from England, Hancock continued his political life, serving in a variety of important roles that helped to shape the young nation. As a member of the Massachusetts Constitutional Convention of 1780, he assisted in acquiring the state's approval of the Constitution in 1788. In 1787, he was a delegate to the Federal Convention, where he recommended the amendments that would later become the Bill of Rights. The first governor of Massachusetts, Hancock served the people of the state for nine one-year terms, from 1780 to 1785, and again from 1789 to 1793.

Hancock was a private man, and not much is known about his personal life. He did not marry Dorothy (Dolly) Quincy until 1775, when he was 38. She came from a well-established and wealthy New England family. The couple had two children: a daughter, who died as an infant, and a son, who died at age 9 from a skating accident.

Never a very healthy man, Hancock died at the age of 56 on October 18, 1793. He was mourned by many Americans. At least 20,000 attended his funeral procession.

Leigh Whaley

See also: Adams, Samuel; Boston; Continental Congress, Second; Merchants; Revolutionary War; Sons of Liberty; Stamp Act (1765).

Bibliography

Fowler, William M., Jr. *The Baron of Beacon Hill: A Biography of John Hancock.* Boston: Houghton Mifflin, 1980.

Proctor, Donald J. "John Hancock: New Soundings on an Old Barrel." *Journal of American History* 64 (1977): 652–77.

Unger, Harlow Giles. *John Hancock: Merchant King and American Patriot.* New York: John Wiley and Sons, 2000.

Harriot, Thomas
(1560–1621)

Thomas Harriot was the first English scientist to visit and write about North America. Of obscure background, Harriot graduated from Oxford in 1580. At Oxford, he would have been exposed to the geography lectures of Richard Hakluyt, a leading promoter of British interests in America.

After graduation, Harriot made his way to London, where he became involved with a circle of men interested in exploration, navigation, and cartography. He applied his exceptional mathematical and astronomical knowledge to navigation problems, conducting classes in applied mathematics for sea captains and other seafarers and improving navigational techniques and instruments. He devoted some fruitless effort to the classic problem of early modern navigators: the determination of the longitude, or east-west position, of a ship at sea, a problem not fully solved until the eighteenth century.

In 1582 or 1583, Harriot met Sir Walter Raleigh and acquired his patronage, moving into the top floor of Raleigh's residence at Durham House in late 1583. In 1585, Harriot crossed the Atlantic to Raleigh's first, ill-fated colony in Roanoke. (There is inconclusive evidence that he also may have sailed on the preliminary voyage the year before.) While there, he mapped the shoreline and some of the interior, learned some of the Algonquian language, and devised a simple phonetic alphabet for it. He made extensive notes on the natural history of the region, the society and customs of the Native Americans, and its prospects for colonization, in hopes of writing an encyclopedic treatment of the area on his return. Unfortunately, many of Harriot's notes, maps, and charts were lost in the abandonment and evacuation of the colony in 1586. He returned with the rest of the colonists that July and published a much shorter work than he had originally planned.

A Briefe and True Report of the New Found Land of Virginia (1588) was the first published description in English of what was to become the mid-South colonial region, as well as a promotional piece for Raleigh's continuing plans for a colony. Harriot was familiar with some of the previous scientific and medical literature on the New World produced by Spanish writers, such as the physician Nicolás Monardes, whose work was available in English translation as *Joyfull Newes out of the New Founde Worlde.* In addition to discussion of the natural history and geography of the proposed colonial site, Harriot discussed potentially profitable New World crops, including corn, squash, and tobacco. Like many in Raleigh's circle, he became an avid tobacco smoker. (He eventually died of cancer, and is often claimed to be the first recorded smoker to die of it.)

Harriot also experimented with the growing of European crops in America and claimed that oats, barley, and peas could all be grown there successfully. His promoter's optimism can be seen in his claim that tropical crops, such as sugar and bananas, could also be grown in the region and that viticulture was a possibility. Harriot also discussed the mineral resources of the region, claiming that alum and saltpeter were available and that copper, silver, and iron could be mined. Other exploitable resources included furs, silkworms, sassafras, and civet cats.

He noted the lack of metal weapons among the native peoples and surmised that the English could defeat them with little difficulty, after which the natives could be easily brought under English sovereignty and Christianized. Claiming to have conversed with their priests, he depicted their religion as very similar to Christianity. He also claimed that the Native Americans were overawed by the power of the English and that this led them to believe the English God must be more powerful than their own.

A Briefe and True Report was widely circulated in England and Europe. In 1589, it was included in the first edition of Hakluyt's *An Account of the Principal Voyages and Discoveries of the English Nation*. It also attracted the attention of a Flemish publisher, Theodore de Bry, who was particularly interested in publishing work on America. In 1590, Harriot's work came out in English, German, French, and Latin editions, becoming one of the first and most influential texts introducing America north of the Spanish possessions to European readers. De Bry's versions included engravings based on the paintings of John White, who had accompanied Harriot to Roanoke.

Before his death in 1621, Harriot also wrote a history of the Roanoke expedition, probably to defend Raleigh from his critics. The history was never published and is now lost.

William E. Burns

See also: Exploration; Native American–European Relations; Roanoke Colony.

Bibliography

Fox, Robert, ed. *Thomas Harriot: An Elizabethan Man of Science.* Aldershot, Hants, UK; Burlington, VT: Ashgate, 2000.

Shirley, John W. *Thomas Harriot: A Biography.* Oxford, UK: Clarendon, 1983.

Stearns, Raymond Phineas. *Science in the British Colonies of America.* Urbana: University of Illinois Press, 1970.

Harvard College

The institution that was to become Harvard College was established in 1636 by the General Council of the Massachusetts Bay Colony. The first college to be founded in North America, it was intended to imitate the nature and purpose of many of the first Puritans' English alma maters. The council appropriated 400 pounds—almost half the tax levy for that year—to establish a college that would educate the colony's future ministers, teachers, professionals, and public servants.

The site of the first college building was an ox pasture in what was to become Cambridge. This secluded address was chosen because Cambridge was free of antiacademicism of the kind that Anne Hutchinson was stirring up in nearby Boston. When a young, undistinguished pastor from nearby Charlestown bequeathed his library of 329 books and half of his estate to the college in 1638, it was named Harvard in his honor.

Stability was not easily ensured, however. Within a year of the bequest, the administration had dismissed the first master on charges of "cruel and barbarous beatings" of students, and the college was forced to close. The college languished for almost a year before the Board of Overseers appointed Henry Dunster as president, an event that could justly be considered the second founding of Harvard College.

By the time Dunster resigned in 1654, Harvard had become an internationally recognized university with several campus buildings and a growing endowment, administered under a legal charter. By 1650, the year when the college graduated its first American-born student, the class size had risen from a handful to close to fifty students from throughout New England.

Five years later, buoyed by the college's success, John Eliot and Dunster began an ill-fated experiment to bring Native Americans to Harvard in hopes of converting and "civilizing" them. While their efforts produced a Bible printed in the Algonquian language, the Indian College only served a handful of Native American students, most notably John Sassamon, whose English education cost him his life and initiated King Philip's War (a wide-scale conflict between the colonists and Native Americans of New England). In 1665, with only one fully graduated student to its name, the Indian College was disbanded.

By 1767, when Paul Revere made this copperplate engraving of the campus, Harvard was already a venerable institution of higher learning. The oldest college in North America, Harvard was founded in 1636. *(Reproduction by Joshua Chadwick, Library of Congress, LC-USZ62-96223)*

For the next 100 years, the college focused its efforts on educating the colony's future leaders. Emphasizing the study of liberal arts over theology, the rigorous colonial curriculum (based upon the medieval trivium and quadrivium) offered a progressive schedule, which began with Latin, Greek, Hebrew, logic, and rhetoric and culminated in advanced study of physics, philosophy, and mathematics with the option of studying divinity at the master's level.

Students, however, had other ideas about the purpose of a Harvard education. By the early eighteenth century, the region's newly prosperous port cities were sending growing numbers of their sons to Cambridge in the hope of creating young gentlemen. Thinking of their education in terms of fashion, refinement, and proper manners, Harvard students of the new century seemed to place their academic interests second to their extracurricular pursuits. When a fire destroyed Harvard Hall, a list of claims for replacement items included pipes, tobacco, liquors, punch bowls, glasses, and tea sets. Only one Bible was reported as lost.

The students' taste for luxury made them vocal opponents of the series of British tax levies that precip-

itated the American Revolution. In indignant response to the Tea Act and the Townshend duties on paper, seniors voted to abstain from tea drinking and insisted that their degrees be printed on domestically manufactured paper by the patriot newspaper presses.

In October 1775, the students temporarily relocated to Concord so that the college buildings could be requisitioned to use its lead roofing for patriot bullets and to provide a billet for more than 1,500 Continental army soldiers. While many students and alumni fought in the conflict, including General Artemas Ward (class of 1748), it was with the pen rather than the sword that Harvard's sons made the most difference. Men such as James Bowdoin (class of 1745) and John Adams (class of 1755) served among the first generation of governors and legislators in the new republic.

The disruptions caused by the Revolution served to temporarily depress enrollments, but, by the 1780s, the college was already firmly established. A faculty of nine, a library of 5,000 items, and a continuous building program made Harvard an intellectual institution of imposing stature.

In 1780, the authority of Harvard's administration was guaranteed in perpetuity by the Massachusetts constitution. This set the stage for the college's almost unchecked nineteenth-century expansion, during which Harvard became one of the nation's pre-eminent universities and a serious rival to the European colleges from whose roots it had sprung.

Richard Bell

See also: Boston; Education, Higher; Puritanism. *Document:* Founding Colleges in America (1754).

Bibliography

Bailyn, Bernard. "Foundations." In *Glimpses of the Harvard Past.* Cambridge, MA: Harvard University Press, 1986.

Morison, Samuel Eliot. *The Founding of Harvard College.* Cambridge, MA: Harvard University Press, 1935.

———. *Three Centuries of Harvard College.* Cambridge, MA: Harvard University Press, 1936.

Henry, Patrick (1736–1799)

Patrick Henry was elected to the Virginia House of Burgesses in 1765, at age 29, and he promptly aroused controversy by opposing the Stamp Act. Some called it treason, but Henry earned his reputation as a defender of colonial rights. *(Brown Brothers, Sterling, Pennsylvania)*

Patrick Henry was born in Hanover County, Virginia, on May 29, 1736, the second son of John and Sarah Henry. At the age of 18, he married Sarah Shelton, who was only 16 years old. Henry's father attempted to help him start a business as a shopkeeper, but it went bankrupt shortly thereafter.

Henry decided to study law, and he passed the bar exam by his mid-20s. He first gained public recognition in 1763 as a lawyer involved in the litigation surrounding the famous Parson's Cause controversy. He argued that the British Crown was compelled to accept all laws passed by the Virginia legislature, as long as these laws were good and just.

In 1765, in his first year as an elected member to the Virginia colonial assembly, the House of Burgesses, Patrick Henry became the center of controversy over his opposition to the Stamp Act. On May 30, 1765, as business was winding down for the day, Henry arose and offered seven resolutions, which challenged the right of Parliament to tax the colonies. His resolutions attacked the constitutionality of the act, demanded that the tax go unpaid, and even went so far as to assert that anyone who complied with the Stamp Act would be "deemed an enemy to his Majesty's colony."

To some members of the House of Burgesses, Henry's position was treasonous, and they threatened to censure his actions. Although only five of his resolutions passed (and the fifth was later rescinded), word of Henry's seven resolutions soon reached the other twelve colonies, where they were reprinted in their entirety. As a result of his Stamp Act resolutions, Henry's reputation as the defender of colonial rights was established.

As conflict with Britain loomed on the horizon, Henry insisted that Virginians make all necessary preparations in the event of hostilities. On March 23, 1775, a meeting took place among Virginian leaders to decide what actions the colony should take in the wake of increasing tensions. At this meeting, Henry uttered the following words that solidified his radical reputation:

> The question before the House is one of awful moment to this country. For my own part, I consider it as nothing less than a question of freedom or slavery. . . . I know not what course others may take; but as for me, give me liberty or give me death.

When Henry received word that the governor of Virginia, Lord Dunmore, had seized the colony's supply of gunpowder from Williamsburg to prevent the colonials from using it, he immediately mobilized the local militia in response. This mobilization occurred the same day as the battle of Lexington and Concord, on April 19, 1775.

With the opening of hostilities in 1775, the House of Burgesses elected Henry to serve as a member of the Continental Congress. He returned to Virginia in 1776, where he played an important role in the creation of that state's constitution in May of that year. The state rewarded Henry's patriotic contributions by electing him Virginia's first governor under the new constitution; Henry would go on to serve a total of four terms in this position.

During the constitutional crisis of the late 1780s, Henry harbored suspicions over the attempt to strengthen the federal government. Upon hearing about the secret discussions taking place during the constitutional convention of 1787, Henry was reported to have said in disgust, "I smell a rat."

He used his energies to argue vociferously against the new constitution and became a leader of the anti-federalist movement in Virginia in the hope of preventing its passage. Henry believed that the new government was simply too powerful and that the proposed constitution appeared to be too "perilous and destructive" to individual liberties. In addition, he argued that this centralized government would have "no checks, no real balances" and that "such a government is incompatible with the genius of republicanism." Unfortunately for Henry, his efforts were largely unsuccessful, and the Constitution was ratified in 1788.

After the constitutional crisis of the late 1780s, Henry stepped away from an active public life. George Washington attempted to appoint him as secretary of state in 1795, but he declined the offer. Even in the last year of Henry's life, President John Adams appointed him as a diplomat to France, but, by then, Henry's health had deteriorated so much that he declined the appointment. After battling an extended illness, Henry passed away on June 6, 1799, at the age of 62.

Keith Pacholl

See also: House of Burgesses; Politics and Government (Chronology); Politics and Government (Essay); Revolutionary War; Virginia.

Bibliography

Axelrad, Jacob. *Patrick Henry: The Voice of Freedom*. Westport, CT: Greenwood, 1975.

Beeman, Richard. *Patrick Henry: A Biography*. New York: McGraw-Hill, 1974.

Mayer, Henry. *A Son of Thunder: Patrick Henry and the American Republic*. New York: Franklin Watts, 1986.

Hispaniola

Hispaniola (Española), a large Caribbean island between Cuba and Puerto Rico, became the setting for one of the most influential events in human history when Christopher Columbus waded ashore in 1492 and claimed the land for Spain. The island continued to play a pivotal role in history, as it split into two of the most profitable sugar colonies in the Atlantic. The French sugar colony at Saint-Domingue also was the setting of a successful slave revolt, which resulted in the creation of the modern nation of Haiti.

When Christopher Columbus became the first European to set foot on Hispaniola in 1492, it was already home to more than 300,000 Taino Indians. Spanish colonization destroyed the Taino with surprising rapidity. The Taino had no resistance to European diseases, and by 1548 only 500 remained alive. Disease, however, was only one of a number of factors that contributed to the destruction of the Taino. Spanish troops forced Native Americans to labor on plantations and mines, often maiming or killing those who refused. Many Taino refugees abandoned their villages and starved to death in the mountains. The Spanish did not intend to wipe out the Taino; they would have preferred that they stayed alive as a labor pool, but the effects of Spanish colonization on Hispaniola were genocidal. From Hispaniola, the Spanish branched out over the Western Hemisphere, continuing to bring disease and Catholicism to other native peoples in North, Central, and South America.

As early as 1493, the Spanish had planted sugar on Hispaniola, but Spanish settlers and planters were more interested in the mainland and the extraction of precious metals. By the 1660s, the Spanish had abandoned the western third of Hispaniola, and the French had established the colony of Saint-Domingue on the island. By the 1680s, Saint-Domingue was home to 2,000 African slaves, 4,000 white settlers, and a steadily developing sugar industry.

It would be hard to overestimate the importance of sugar to the Atlantic economy during the seventeenth and eighteenth centuries. Sugar drove a wide-ranging trade in gold, firearms, slaves, and rum and drew people from West Africa, Europe, the Caribbean, and North America into trade with one another. Spain's power in the Caribbean had diminished significantly by the start of the eighteenth century, and England, France, and the Netherlands competed violently for supremacy.

Sugar production in Saint-Domingue required large numbers of slaves. Slaves under the labor regime of sugar production were treated harshly; sugar planting was, in fact, so profitable that planters often found it cheaper to purchase slaves, work them to death, and purchase new ones. Profit margins in the rice and tobacco regions of Carolina and the Chesapeake were slimmer, and conditions for slaves were slightly better.

After 1713, Saint-Domingue's sugar industry had reached maturity. By 1735, Saint-Domingue sugar was more plentiful, cheaper, and better than the sugar produced anywhere else in the Caribbean. Although business was booming, living conditions for slaves in Saint-Domingue were deplorable. They faced disease, the prospect of death from exhaustion, and a vicious labor regime.

In 1791, slaves in Saint-Domingue rebelled against their masters. The revolt stands alone among New World slave uprisings in terms of the numbers of slaves involved, the level of its violence and destructiveness, and its ultimate success. Slaves in Saint-Domingue took advantage of an unstable political situation (a veritable civil war between supporters of the king and the French assembly) and their overwhelming numerical majority—they outnumbered whites 450,000 to 30,000, with 25,000 mixed race persons—to strike against the colony's best sugar plantations.

Toussaint L'Ouverture, an educated freedman who had purchased his freedom in 1776, rose to the fore of the revolution. He consolidated his power by defeating the more radical aims of rebel slaves, biracial elites, and armies sent by Britain and Spain to capitalize on the situation. In 1802, Napoleon succeeded in capturing Toussaint, who died in a French prison. Napoleon failed to regain Saint-Domingue, however, and after two years of fierce fighting, Haiti was declared an independent republic under the leadership of Jean-Jacques Dessalines in 1804.

The Haitian Revolution had a profound effect on other slave regimes, which tightened restrictions on slaves and sought new alliances between poor whites and planters. Today, Hispaniola is divided between the modern Republic of Haiti and the Dominican Republic.

Matthew Jennings

See also: Caribbean (Chronology); Columbus, Christopher; Saint-Domingue; Slavery, Caribbean.

Bibliography

Klein, Herbert S. *African Slavery in Latin America and the Caribbean*. New York: Oxford University Press, 1986.

Nash, Gary B. *Red, White, and Black: The Peoples of Early North America.* Upper Saddle River, NJ: Prentice Hall, 2000.

Taylor, Alan. *American Colonies.* New York: Penguin Putnam, 2001.

Hooker, Thomas (1586–1647)

The Puritan minister Thomas Hooker was a central figure in the settlement of Connecticut. Born July 7, 1586, in Marfield in Leicestershire, England, he attended Emmanuel College, receiving his master of arts degree in 1611.

In 1618, Hooker became rector of St. George's in Esher. While he served there, Joan Drake, the wife of a patron of the church, fell into a deep spiritual melancholy and became convinced that she was damned. Hooker was part of a team of ministers sent to treat her, and it was his pastoral technique that ultimately prevailed.

Not only did this success give a boost to Hooker's career, but the arguments he had used became his pastoral methodology. Like many English Puritans, he preached covenant theology, which understood Calvinist predestination in terms of a contract between God and the believer, wherein God both set the requirements for salvation and fulfilled them. In addition, while staying in the Drake house, Hooker met and married one of their maids.

From 1626, Hooker held the position of lecturer at Chelmsford in Essex, until, in July 1630, certain of his parishioners presented him to the Court of High Commission for nonconformity. Protected for a time in the household of the Earl of Warwick (a figure important in the early history of the Massachusetts Bay Company), the following summer, Hooker received an invitation from the English congregation in Amsterdam to become an assistant to their minister, John

Hooker walk through the wilderness 1636

The Reverend Thomas Hooker led members of his Puritan congregation from Massachusetts to the Connecticut River Valley in 1636 and helped found the colony that became Hartford. *(Library of Congress, cph 3c01098)*

Paget. Hooker's incipient Congregational leanings (in particular, his desire to test the beliefs and behavior of parents who presented their children for baptism) caused Paget to reject him in what became an acrimonious intra-church fight.

Hooker stayed with fellow Puritan minister Hugh Peter at Rotterdam, and together they managed the publication of Congregational theorist William Ames's *Fresh Suit Against Ceremonies*, an attack upon the English *Book of Common Prayer*. Hooker briefly returned to England and then (one step ahead of the law) boarded the *Griffin*, bound for New England, along with fellow Puritan ministers John Cotton and Samuel Stone. Arriving in September 1633, Hooker and many of his former congregants settled at Newtown (present-day Cambridge). Shortly thereafter, he was an important voice in mediating a dispute between Massachusetts governor John Winthrop and deputy governor Thomas Dudley.

Hooker and his congregation did not remain in Newtown long, due to a lack of grazing land and a clash of egos between Hooker and John Cotton. In 1636, they sold their land to a newly arrived group of settlers headed by Thomas Shepard (who subsequently married Hooker's daughter) and moved to the Connecticut River Valley at what became Hartford, Connecticut.

There, Hooker's church, by applying only a test of behavior and doctrinal knowledge for admittance to membership rather than a narrative of one's personal experience of receiving saving grace, differed slightly in practice from those in the Massachusetts Bay Colony. He also played a part in the formulation of the Fundamental Orders, the Hartford colony's constitution (though his exact role is unclear), and gave a sermon in which he defended the right of people to choose their magistrates.

Hooker remained a prominent voice in intercolonial affairs. He returned to Massachusetts in 1637 to take part in the proceedings against Anne Hutchinson and was a moderator, along with Peter Bulkeley, of the 1637 synod that met to deal with the crisis. He also promoted an alliance of the New England colonies to face the threat of the Pequot.

In 1643, Hooker and John Cotton moderated an assembly at Harvard to deal with the development of Presbyterianism in the town of Newbury. The year before, he had been invited, along with several other ministers, to attend the Westminster Assembly in England, which met to restructure the Church of England. Recognizing that the assembly was dominated by Presbyterians, he declared that he had no wish to travel 3,000 miles in order to agree with three men.

New England's ministry, nevertheless, still wished its views to be heard in the "great debate," and Hooker was convinced to write a defense of New England church practices. He complied by writing *A Survey of the Summe of Church Discipline*, a response to the Scottish Covenanter Samuel Rutherford's *Due Plea for Presbyteries*. The first copy was lost at sea, and Hooker refused to risk letting another copy out of his possession, which meant that the work was published only after his death in 1647.

Kenneth A. Shelton

See also: Connecticut; Connecticut (Chronology); Massachusetts Bay Colony; Ministers and the Ministry; Puritanism.

Bibliography

Bush, Sargent. *The Writings of Thomas Hooker: Spiritual Adventure in Two Worlds*. Madison: University of Wisconsin Press, 1980.

Shuffelton, Frank. *Thomas Hooker, 1586–1647*. Princeton, NJ: Princeton University Press, 1977.

Winthrop, John. *Winthrop's Journal, "History of New England," 1630–1649*. Edited by James Kendall Hosmer. New York: Charles Scribner's Sons, 1908.

Hopi

The Hopi country lies on the southern escarpment of Black Mesa, a highland about 60 miles wide, located in northeastern Arizona. Many scholars believe that people have occupied the Black Mesa for at least 10,000 years. Archaeological research presents a clear development from the early period to the lifestyle, technology, architecture, and agriculture seen on the three Hopi mesas today.

Hopi mythology holds that the Hopi entered this world through a hole in the bottom of the Grand Canyon, to the west of their villages. When a Hopi dies, he or she returns to this area to enter the world below. As their origin myth demonstrates, all Hopi life is based on equilibrium, both social and individual; reciprocities are designed to conciliate the supernatural powers to obtain rains, ensure good harvests, health, and peace.

The prominent features of Hopi society are a distinctive Pueblo lifestyle and language, although some dialectical differences exist among the communities. The foundation of Hopi life was the cultivation of corn, beans, squash, and cotton. To the Hopi, corn was their mother, with the people drawing life from the plant as a child does from its mother. Contact with the Spaniards would alter this lifestyle, but Hopi agriculture allowed this native people to persist in a harsh, dry environment.

The Hopi established vast trade networks across the region, trading with the Navajo for sheep and wool, with the Havasupai for buckskin, and with the Zuni and eastern Pueblo for turquoise and other goods. In times of severe drought, however, the Hopi lifestyle was attractive to their less sedentary neighbors, who frequently raided Hopi pueblos in search of vital resources. Raids from neighboring native peoples had forced the Hopi to defensive positions on Black Mesa, which would enable the Hopi, the westernmost Pueblo people, to staunchly resist European influence.

Spanish contact began with the Coronado expedition, though Spaniards were never numerous in Hopi country. Awatovi was the first town in Hopi territory visited by the Spaniards. After a brief skirmish, a gift exchange occurred, and the Spaniards continued on their way. European contact was limited to sporadic, widely spaced military expeditions and a few Franciscans who lived among the Hopi. The first Franciscan mission was established at Awatovi, where the inhabitants initially resisted conversion but later acquiesced in response to a reported miracle: a cross placed upon the eyes of a blind Hopi youth by Father Porras restored the child's sight.

From their base at Awatovi, the Franciscans established four *visitas*, or local chapels, across the Hopi country. These areas saw only occasional visits by priests, but some residents of Awatovi began to exhibit aspects of Christian zeal. Although the religious effect on the Hopi remained small, the material effect was

The Hopi ("peaceful") Indians, a pueblo-dwelling people on the Black Mesa in northeastern Arizona, relocated their villages to defensive positions in remote areas to resist intrusion by neighboring tribes and the Spanish. *(Brown Brothers, Sterling, Pennsylvania)*

great, as domestic animals, new food plants, and European goods flowed into the country with the annual pack trains moving north from Mexico.

In 1680, the Hopi were willing participants in the anti-Spanish revolt that swept all of the Pueblo peoples. Because of their location, little is known of the events in the Hopi towns during the revolt. When Diego de Vargas returned to the area in 1692, however, he found that Hopi country had become a refuge for the irreconcilables among the Pueblo of the east, those who could not bring themselves to submit to Spanish domination. Continuing their resistance to the Spanish invasion, the Hopi sacked Awatovi, the only Hopi pueblo to return to Christianity following the 1680 revolt, in 1700.

The following year, the governor at Santa Fe sent a military expedition to punish the Hopi for the destruction of Awatovi. Allied with the Ute, Havasupai, and Navajo neighbors, the Hopi repelled the Spaniards. Militarily defeated, the Spaniards dispatched the Franciscans to return the Hopi to the Christian fold. All Franciscan attempts failed, and, in 1741, the king of Spain assigned the Jesuits to the Hopi territory. For

their part, the Jesuits answered the call by dispatching no one to the area.

The military defeat of the Spaniards and continued resistance to Catholicism provided the Hopi with greater group cohesion. Rather than destroying their identity, the arrival of the Spanish in their territory heightened Hopi identity.

By 1750, the only contact the Hopi had with the Spanish was the expeditions passing through Hopi territory on their way to the Colorado River and the Grand Canyon. In 1800, the Hopi remained isolated on their mesas. Their brave stand against the Spanish allowed them to continue to live by the tenets of their culture.

Todd Leahy

See also: Native American–European Relations; Native Americans; Navajo; New Mexico; Spanish Colonies on Mainland North America (Chronology).

Bibliography

Milner, Clyde, Carol O'Connor, and Martha Sandweiss, eds. *The Oxford History of the American West.* New York: Oxford University Press, 1992.

Sturtevant, William, ed. *Handbook of North American Indians.* Vol. 9. Washington, DC: Smithsonian Institution Press, 1983.

Horses

Originally a native of North America, the horse species and its close relations became extinct during the end of the last Ice Age for reasons that still remain unclear. North America would remain unoccupied by these majestic animals until the sixteenth century, when European explorers reintroduced them to their "New World."

Spain is given credit for bringing horses back into the Western Hemisphere, aboard shipping vessels headed by Christopher Columbus. Evidence for this exists in letters written by the king and queen of Spain to their personal secretary, Fernando de Zafra, directing him to arrange competent horsemen for the journey.

The first place in the Western Hemisphere that horses would once again call home was the island Spaniards referred to as Española (later Hispaniola). Explorers brought the Paso Fino breeds with them as they ventured onto the islands of Puerto Rico, Jamaica, and Cuba between 1509 and 1511. Using these four islands as their home bases, the Spaniards continually returned from travels to the mainland continents of Central and North America in order to replenish their supply of horses from this original stock of animals, as few stallions would be transported from Spain after the first thirty years of expeditions.

Hernando de Soto brought the first group of horses onto North American mainland in 1539. He brought more than 600 men, along with their 237 horses, to the present-day location of Tampa Bay, Florida, in order to colonize the area and search for gold. Known for their excessive violence and cruelty, these conquerors set out to march through Native American territories, capture chiefs, and hold hundreds of native people for ransom. De Soto began his conquests by traveling north through the present-day states of Georgia and the Carolinas, crossing the Great Smoky Mountains, and heading south again through Georgia and Alabama.

During October 1540, Native Americans, following the Choctaw chief Tuscaloosa, ambushed de Soto's men at Mabila, a town located just south of present-day Montgomery, Alabama. Horses captured by these Native Americans are said to be the early ancestors of the Chickasaw breed.

In spite of their successful defense against the natives, de Soto's men and their horses retreated north, crossing the Mississippi River and exploring the Arkansas region. As the Spaniards persisted in their explorations, so did the horses they brought with them. During the sixteenth and early seventeenth centuries, the horse population in North America rapidly increased. In fact, it was during this period that a fast-growing, wild horse population was born, a result of animals that were left to roam the countryside and breed.

The Spaniards were not the only settlers who recognized the advantages of bringing horses to the New World. When English colonists immigrated to Jamestown, Virginia, in 1607, they brought eight horses along with them. Horses, after all, would serve many useful purposes to any group of explorers or settlers. Not only did they provide a means of transportation, but the more docile mares also worked alongside settlers to help clear the land for homesteads and plowed fields for planting. In times of confrontation with Native Americans, the Spanish conquistadors and English settlers depended on their horses to help lead them to victory. For the settlers at Jamestown, the animals provided one additional benefit—they served as food for the starving colonists during the famine that nearly destroyed the colony in its first years.

Over the centuries, many of the horse breeds that were popular during the colonial period have become extinct. One such breed, the Narragansett Pacer, named for the Narragansett Bay area of Rhode Island in which the animals were bred, introduced Europe to a new, exclusively American breed of horse during the eighteenth century. These animals, most likely a cross between English and Dutch horses brought over between 1629 and 1635, enjoyed a reputation of being the best saddle horses known anywhere in the world. George Washington owned one, which he raced in 1768; the English philosopher Edmund Burke begged a friend to send him a pair of these horses; and it is believed that Paul Revere rode a Narragansett on his famous ride.

In the days before the "Wild West" was settled by white settlers of European descent, it was Rhode Island that was known as "horse country." In large part, the origin of this reputation can be traced back to John Hull, treasurer of the Massachusetts Bay Colony. After purchasing land west of Narragansett Bay from a local tribe, Hull had the territory fenced off and set aside for horse farms. Some of the horses from the breeding farms that were established on this land were sold to the seacoast colonies and the Caribbean Islands to work on plantations. Those that remained in the American colonies were in high demand throughout the eighteenth century.

Rhode Island was made all the more popular by being the only New England colony to permit horse racing. The competition at these events encouraged breeders to seek continual improvements to their stocks. This practice often resulted in a change in characteristics of certain breeds and eventually in the creation of new breeds altogether.

Aubrey L. Muscaro

See also: Agriculture; Columbian Exchange; Livestock; Transportation, Land.

Bibliography

"A Chronological History of Humans and Their Relationship with the Horse." The International Museum of the Horse. http://www.imh.org/imh/kyhpl1a.html.

Johnson, John J. "The Introduction of the Horse into the Western Hemisphere." *The Hispanic American Historical Review* 23:4 (November 1943): 587–610.

House of Burgesses

The London Company created Virginia's General Assembly in 1619 in an effort to bring increased stability and prosperity to the fledgling colony. On July 30, 1619, Virginia's new governor, Sir George Yeardley, his six councilors, and twenty elected representatives, commonly known as burgesses, held their first meeting in a Jamestown church.

Initially, the burgesses held little actual power. Councilors assisted in creating bills, they managed the affairs of the burgesses, and their approval was necessary for any act to pass into law. Over the course of the seventeenth century, however, the burgesses gradually asserted their legislative prerogatives and ultimately formed a distinct political body, separate from the council and the governor, which came to be known as the House of Burgesses. England first recognized the House of Burgesses in 1639, and, by mid-century, the house was regularly disciplining its own members. It had also established a standing committee to oversee elections, created its own rules of conduct, and gained control of the appointment of its speaker and clerk, the two most important officers of the house. By 1666, Governor William Berkeley openly recognized the House of Burgesses's exclusive right to raise public funds.

Freeholders from various counties, which the General Assembly began to create in the 1630s and 1640s, elected representatives to the House of Burgesses. By February 1752, there existed forty-six counties and four boroughs—one each for the college, Jamestown, Norfolk, and Williamsburg—in colonial Virginia. Between 1752 and 1772, the General Assembly created fifteen additional counties, including Berkeley, Dunmore, and Fincastle.

Virginia's sixty-one counties and four boroughs elected hundreds of burgesses. As many as 399 different individuals served in the House of Burgesses between 1750 and 1774. In fact, only five burgesses, all of whom represented the well-established counties in Virginia's Tidewater region, served the entire period between 1752 and 1774.

Several factors accounted for turnover in the house. Generally, burgesses died, accepted a position that made them ineligible to serve in the house, lost at the polls, declined to run, or, in some cases, were expelled. Expulsion from the house was actually quite rare; there are only three known cases during the period between 1750 and 1774.

Burgesses usually gained the support of their constituency by serving as county clerk, sheriff, coroner, surveyor, tobacco inspector, customs collector, or naval inspector. Most burgesses—approximately three-fourths of the total—served as either vestrymen (church officials) or justices of the peace. Although there is no indication that anything resembling political parties existed in colonial Virginia, burgesses did support various familial and economic interests.

Once elected, burgesses swore an oath of supremacy and allegiance to the British Crown and took a test oath stating they had taken Holy Communion according to the rites of the Anglican Church. Burgesses then began a legislative process that closely resembled the practices and procedures of the English House of Commons. The House of Burgesses initiated all legislation, including revenue bills. It drew up resolutions, and it sent petitions to the king.

For their services, burgesses received travel expenses and ten shillings for each day's attendance at the general assembly. They were also made exempt from any arrests or attachments, except treason, during legislative sessions and for ten days before and ten days after each session.

Burgesses tended to come from Virginia's middle and upper classes. Virtually all of them had at least some connection to the production of tobacco, although many considered planting a secondary occupation.

Burgesses were also lawyers, merchants, and land speculators, and some had interests in mining and manufacturing. The most powerful burgesses were wealthy and tended to be related to Virginia's most prominent families. They were of British origin, and most were Anglicans. They had attained a high level of education and tended to be quite experienced in local politics. They also came from areas of Virginia that had been settled for at least one generation. By 1752, approximately one-fifth of the members—those who were the most powerful—handled most of the business of the house, providing it with a continuity of leadership that began in the 1720s and continued until the Revolution.

On May 26, 1774, partly in response to the Boston Port Act, Governor Dunmore dissolved the General Assembly. The leaders in Williamsburg had received word on May 17, 1774, that Boston harbor would be closed effective June 1 and had decided that the time for action had arrived. The House of Burgesses ceased to exist, but its form would rise once again, after the Revolution, as the Virginia legislature.

Michael A. Rembis

See also: Assemblies, Colonial; Bacon's Rebellion; Politics and Government (Chronology); Politics and Government (Essay); Virginia; Virginia (Chronology).

Bibliography

Billings, Warren M., John E. Selby, and Thad W. Tate. *Colonial Virginia: A History.* White Plains, NY: KTO, 1986.

Greene, Jack P. "Foundations of Political Power in the Virginia House of Burgesses, 1720–1776." *William and Mary Quarterly* 16 (3rd ser. 1959): 485–92.

———. *The Quest for Power: The Lower Houses of Assembly in the Southern Royal Colonies, 1689–1776.* Chapel Hill: University of North Carolina Press, 1963.

Griffith, Lucille. *The Virginia House of Burgesses, 1750–1774.* Rev. ed. Tuscaloosa: University of Alabama Press, 1970.

Housing

In the course of colonial history, housing developed from primitive temporary structures to a wide range of styles, materials, and class and regional differences. The earliest colonial housing was very primitive, in keeping with the poverty of the early colonists.

One common temporary solution to the housing problem in both Virginia and New England in the early seventeenth century was digging a rectangular hole in the ground about 7 feet deep, walling it with timber, flooring it with planks, and putting a wooden roof over the whole. During the first settlement of Philadelphia, some people lived in "caves" dug into the banks of the Delaware River. (These persisted as homes for the very poor or criminals into the eighteenth century.) This phenomenon of cheap temporary shelters was repeated in the subsequent expansion of the colonial frontier.

Eighteenth-century settlers of the backcountry also built temporary structures. These huts (also called "English wigwams") were constructed of animal skins, bark, or sod. Despite their name, the structures had European, as well as Native American precursors.

The Early American House

Even when more permanent structures began to be built, many colonists did not put much effort into them, perhaps believing that they would have the opportunity to better themselves by moving again. These were usually one-room buildings, a story or a story and a half high.

Early colonial houses were based on English models, though English houses themselves varied between the different regions that the colonists came from. The general trend in the first few decades of settlement was for housing patterns to settle down into a few types, as some English types ceased to be built.

More-enduring houses, with waterproof foundations, rather than just posts driven into the ground, began to appear in New England after 1650 and in the Chesapeake around 1700. Whereas earlier houses were built mostly by those who planned to dwell in them, these houses were more likely built by specialist craftsmen. The most common construction material in the seventeenth century was America's abundant wood, particularly oak. (There were only a dozen or so brick houses in seventeenth-century New England.) To avoid the expense of nails, many houses were held together with dried wooden pegs known as "treenails."

Clapboard houses, common in English-settled areas, were built around four wood posts pounded into the ground at the corners. The standard size of the single room was around 18 by 20 feet. Walls were wattle and daub, clad on the outside with short planks or clapboards, about 5 or 6 feet long, placed horizontally. In fact, the common use of clapboards distinguished Anglo-American architecture from that of England, where wood was scarce. Even a small house required as much as a ton of wood.

The Tate House outside Portland, Maine, exemplifies the center-chimney Georgian style prominent in New England late in the colonial period. The symmetrically designed exterior was covered with clapboards for warmth. *(Library of Congress, HABS, ME, 3-STROWA, 1–8)*

Houses in the North developed steeper roofs, which the snow could slide off easily. At first, roofs were often made of thatch or sod, but, eventually, the use of shingles, which minimized the fire hazard, became common. (Thatch roofs disappeared by about 1670.) White pine and fir were used for shingles, but cedar, due to its lightness and durability, was the most popular material—so popular as to rapidly deplete the stock of cedar trees. The lightness of cedar shingle roofing contributed to the American tendency to build houses with very thin walls without much load-bearing capacity. Clay tiles nailed to the roof were also used and, in the eighteenth century, replaced shingles in many areas. They offered still better protection from fire. Benjamin Franklin was among those who recommended tile roofing for fire protection.

The windows of early colonial houses were slits designed to minimize the loss of heat; sometimes they were covered with translucent paper or cloth rather than glass. Heat loss was further minimized through the use of shutters. External privies were ubiquitous and chamber pots rare until the eighteenth century.

Additions to the house, if necessary, often took the form of lean-tos, one-story wooden structures attached to the back of the building. (These were an American innovation without English precedent.) Lean-tos could be used for cooking or storage. A few houses, belonging to the wealthiest members of the community, were distinguished by enclosed and gabled two-story "porches."

The log cabin, a much snugger and better-built alternative to the clapboard house, was introduced to America by the Swedish colonists of Delaware. It had little effect on the building practices of Anglo-Americans until the settlement of Pennsylvania, when German and British settlers copied the houses of their new Swedish neighbors. From there, the log cabin diffused through the settlement of the backcountry in the eighteenth century.

Another local variation in housing was the stone-ender, a form of house common in Rhode Island, which, unlike some other areas in New England, had access to good stone for building and lime suitable for mortaring. The stone-ender featured a massive stone chimney that furnished most of the wall on one end of the building. The separation of the chimney from the wooden part of the house meant that stone-enders had considerably less risk of burning than all-wooden buildings.

The interior layout of most early American houses was simple. The bulk of the ground floor was taken up by a single large, multifunction room, called a hall. This room was used for cooking, eating, working, and praying, and sometimes for sleep. As people prospered, they added a second room, or parlor. This room was used for visitors and to provide the master and wife of the household with a separate sleeping area. In eighteenth-century New England, the parlor became a necessity for all those aspiring to respectability. One-room houses became a mark of poverty, and rooms became more functionally differentiated. The lean-to also became a more integral part of the house. The combination of the two rooms and the lean-to led to the classic New England saltbox house, so called because its shape resembled that of a salt container of the time. The one-room house persisted for much longer in the South, where poor, white, independent farmers thought it no disgrace.

Some of the most shoddily built housing in the colonies was that inhabited by slaves, particularly field workers on plantations, who lived in small groups in simple wooden huts with dirt floors, close to where they worked. Many slaves, particularly on small farms, lacked any dedicated housing and slept in barns or tobacco houses. Where African Americans, whether free or enslaved, were able to build their own houses, they often incorporated some African features, such as central rooms measuring 12 by 12 feet, pounded dirt floors, and palmetto-leaf thatching.

Heating the Home

One of the great problems with early colonial houses was heating them, a problem exacerbated by the coldness of the winters compared with those in Britain. Early colonists took advantage of the bountiful supply of wood to build large, centrally located fireplaces, twice the size of those they had known in England. In addition to the tendency of fireplaces to send much of their heat up the chimney, heat also escaped through the many cracks and other openings in the walls. If a person was not close to the fire, he or she often derived little warmth

from it, and fireplaces and open hearths were also dangerous for children.

The fireplace's insatiable hunger for wood contributed to deforestation and meant that much of the household's daily labor was spent chopping down trees and preparing wood for the fire. This was a task whose burden increased over time, as people exhausted the timber resources close to their dwellings and had to go farther and farther afield for wood. (A supply of wood was a common perquisite of ministers. Samuel Parris, later to become infamous as a leader of the Salem witch hunt, had bitter disputes with his parishioners for years over what he alleged was their failure to keep his house adequately supplied with firewood.)

Firewood was particularly a problem for cities, given their population concentrations. Boston, which had no native timber, was perpetually bedeviled by a shortage of wood and, after 1730, turned to importing coal from Britain. New York City had to pass strict laws regulating the fees that could be charged for hauling wood, in order to prevent exploitation by haulers during the winter.

America's firewood situation improved with the development of better houses, and eventually the introduction of the more efficient stove for heating. German colonists are often credited with bringing heating stoves to America. They spread only slowly to the Anglo-American population—Benjamin Franklin pointed out that stoves had the disadvantage of not allowing people to see the flames. He combined a visible fire with the heating advantage of the stove in his "Pennsylvania Fire Place."

Since a fire was necessary for cooking even on hot days, early colonists in the South faced the problem of dissipating heat during the summer. One solution was to put the fireplace at the end of the house rather than at the central location common in northerly climes. Eventually, many Southerners physically separated the kitchen from the rest of the house.

Urban Housing

Urban houses differed in several ways from rural dwellings. In seventeenth-century America, some of the few truly rich people lived in cities, and sometimes they had large houses with several rooms. From its founding, Philadelphia broke with the tradition of American timber houses and built its dwellings mostly of brick. Brick houses in Philadelphia were both taller—some extending to three stories—and more cramped than wooden houses in New England. Brick offered less vulnerability to fire—a constant danger, particularly in large cities—than wood.

Although wooden houses predominated at first, the Dutch built much of their housing in New Amsterdam in brick or stone. Dutch houses also put the gable end to the street, while the broad front of the house faced an alley. The Virginia Assembly, prompted by governor William Berkeley, enacted in 1662 a requirement that each county support the building of a brick house in Jamestown as part of a program to expand and modernize the capital of the province. The program was unsuccessful due to the general indifference of Virginia planters to urban centers.

The cities also had large populations of poor, who were housed in crowded wooden buildings in back alleys, vulnerable to epidemic disease and fire. A calamitous fire, such as the one that swept Boston in 1679, sometimes led a town to replace its destroyed wooden housing stock with brick. Severe weather could have the same effect. Charles Town, whose houses originally were wooden and built in the manner of the West Indies, where its colonists originated, with high ceilings and large windows to minimize heat, suffered a severe hurricane in 1713. As a result of the damage, the South Carolina Assembly ordered that subsequent building be in brick, although this requirement was frequently ignored. Charles Town had a distinctive, French-influenced style of brickwork, a contribution of the town's large Huguenot population.

Although some bricks were imported from England, most bricks used in colonial buildings were American-made. Some areas, such as tidewater Virginia, boasted clay deposits that made excellent bricks. Bricks were also recycled as old buildings fell into ruin or were demolished. Ivor Noel Malcolm, an archaeologist specializing in colonial Virginia, has estimated the size of the average eighteenth-century colonial American brick measured 8¾ by 4 by 2⅝ inches. Seventeenth-century bricks were slightly smaller.

As brick and stone houses became more common, cheaper wooden housing dropped in status. The mid-eighteenth-century Swedish traveler Peter Kalm, describing the town of New Brunswick, pointed out that many of the houses had only one brick wall, facing the street, while the rest of the building was of wood. Someone passing through rapidly, he claimed, might think most of the town brick. Wooden housing held on longest in New England.

The Georgian House

As the colonies prospered in the eighteenth century, rich Americans increasingly followed the latest European fashions in architecture and furnishings, as in other areas. In the seventeenth century, economic differences among Americans had been expressed principally in the size rather than the style of their houses. The classically influenced Georgian style of eighteenth-century England provided a way to distinguish between houses by style rather than size.

The English Georgian house found many American imitators, beginning with wealthy men who immigrated from England, such as Peter Sergeant of Boston and Richard Whitpaine of Philadelphia. Official residences were also trendsetters—the Governor's Palace in Williamsburg, Virginia, built by Alexander Spotswood in the early eighteenth century, introduced classically influenced Palladian architecture to the Chesapeake and was widely imitated.

The grand house of the late seventeenth and eighteenth centuries was marked by brick construction, painted clapboards, and large, symmetrically arranged sash windows with ornamental wooden frames and crown glass rather than inferior "broad glass" windows with lead casements. Staircases were broad, straight, and unenclosed. Rooms were laid out in a symmetrical pattern. The front room was transformed into a parlor, without bedding or work tools, and given over to the best-quality furniture and display items. The huge central fireplaces of the seventeenth century were abandoned in favor of smaller, more efficient fireplaces. Such seventeenth-century features as tall gables and overhanging second floors disappeared, sometimes through remodeling of existing structures.

The Georgian house required more book knowledge of classical architectural forms than did previous housing styles. Books of patterns were commonly used. These books were imported from England. Among the first published in America (although originating in England) was Abraham Swan's *A Collection of Designs in Architecture*, printed in Philadelphia in 1775. The Georgian style's basis in texts, rather than the experience of individual builders and the customs of local communities, meant that it had more uniformity across the colonies, and between the colonies and Britain, than had previous American building styles.

Like the homes of the English gentry on which they were modeled, American Georgian homes, often built on the top of a hill or other prominent position for lesser folk to see and admire, proclaimed both the owner's high social status and participation in an elite transatlantic culture. Sometimes, a Georgian facade, visible to the public, concealed a non-Georgian house. Other architectural features that became more popular in elite and middle-class houses of the eighteenth century were open verandas and porches.

Artisans and Architects

The need for housing in the settled areas of the colonies led to the development of construction industry of carpenters, joiners, bricklayers, and stonecutters. The most expert of these workers found their services in high demand, with towns or individuals actively seeking to recruit them. Skilled workers also emigrated from England and Europe.

Professional architects did not exist in America, but many American gentlemen learned architecture and applied their knowledge to their own residences. Two of the best-known examples are Thomas Jefferson's Monticello and George Washington's modifications to Mount Vernon.

The most active gentleman architect was Peter Harrison (1716–1775) of Newport, Rhode Island, a merchant and customs officer by profession. Although most of the buildings Harrison was known for were public, he also worked on several private residences. The most notable was governor John Wentworth's mansion in Wolfeborough, New Hampshire.

William E. Burns

See also: Artisans; Bathing and Hygiene; Family; Furnishings; Inheritance; Kitchens, Colonial; Servants, Domestic. *Document:* Probate Inventory of a Plymouth Colony Estate (1672).

Bibliography

Bridenbaugh, Carl. *Cities in the Wilderness: The First Century of Urban Life in America, 1625–1742.* 2nd edition. New York: Alfred A. Knopf, 1955.

Deetz, James. *In Small Things Forgotten: The Archaeology of Early American Life.* New York: Doubleday, 1977.

Hawke, David Freeman. *Everyday Life in Early America.* New York: Harper and Row, 1988.

Hume, Ivor Noël. *Guide to the Artifacts of Colonial America.* 2nd edition. Philadelphia: University of Pennsylvania Press, 2001.

Kennedy, Roger G. *Architecture: Men, Women and Money in America, 1600–1860.* New York: Random House, 1985.

Wolfe, Stephanie Grauman. *As Various as Their Land: The Everyday Lives of Eighteenth-Century Americans.* New York: HarperCollins, 1993.

Hudson, Henry (c. 1560–c. 1611)

Henry Hudson was an early-seventeenth-century English explorer who captained four voyages in search of a shorter passage to the Far East. Very little is known about Hudson's early life. He was most likely born in the 1560s or 1570s to a London family that possibly owned shares in the Muscovy Company.

From his youth to the command of his first voyage in 1607, Hudson probably worked aboard a variety of ships, where he gained important maritime experience, which fueled his rise through the ranks to commander. From 1607 to 1611, Hudson commanded four voyages, three for England and one for the Netherlands.

Hudson's first command was for the ship *Hopewell* of the Muscovy Company. It appears that in this period, Hudson was an acquaintance of Richard Hakluyt, who recommended his abilities to the company. The goal was to discover a Northwest Passage that could expedite the voyage from Europe to the Far East, ensuring a constant, and quicker, flow of profitable spices, silks, and other commodities to Europe. Hudson believed, as did others in Europe, that if they sailed far enough north, the temperature would increase and the icepack would disappear.

The *Hopewell* left England in April but had problems with the ship's compass, which many of the crew perceived as a bad omen. By June, they had reached the Greenland coast and then began their voyage back to England.

In April 1608, the *Hopewell*, again commanded by Hudson, sailed from England. Instead of resuming the search for a Northwest Passage, the *Hopewell* sailed in search of a northeast route around the icepack. The *Hopewell* made it north of modern Norway, where the crew and captain believed they spotted a mermaid. But by August, the crew was becoming restless. To avoid a mutiny, Hudson agreed to return to England. On his return, the Muscovy Company was dissatisfied with the results of Hudson's two voyages and decided not to give him command of another.

The Dutch East India Company had heard of

Hudson's voyages and his abilities, however, and its leaders started to negotiate with him to command one of their vessels in the continued search for a shorter route to the Far East. Hudson accepted, and, in April 1609, the *Half Moon (De Halve Maen*, in Dutch) sailed from the Netherlands.

When no northeast route was found, Hudson decided, and the crew concurred, to search for a Northwest Passage. In July, the *Half Moon* arrived at Newfoundland, where Hudson set foot upon American soil for the first time. The members of this expedition then continued south and, by early August, had arrived at Cape Cod. They continued on to Delaware Bay and, by September, had turned north again and were near Sandy Hook. The *Half Moon* expedition then sailed up what came to be known as the Hudson River, still in hopes of discovering a Northwest Passage. After 150 miles, they decided that it was a false lead and began their return voyage.

Hudson, as an employee of a Dutch company, claimed much of the land he encountered for the Netherlands. His voyage and land claims set the foundations for the Dutch colony of New Netherland. In November, Hudson decided to land in England rather then continue to the Netherlands, but he encountered problems in England because of his service to a foreign state. Hudson was able to avoid serious punishment for his Dutch voyage, and, in 1610, he sailed under the British flag on the *Discovery*.

On his final voyage, Hudson entered into what would become Hudson Bay and explored it, again in search of the elusive Northwest Passage. Because of the extended time spent exploring, the *Discovery* wintered in the bay. It was a harsh winter for the crew; by spring, the men were ready to return to England, but Hudson wanted to remain and continue his search. With this, the crew mutinied. Hudson, his son, and a few crewmen were placed in a boat and set adrift. They were never seen again.

Hudson's fame continues today mainly because of the importance of the bay and river that carry his name. While his voyages provided some land claims for the English in the Americas, his one non-English voyage allowed the Dutch to create an important early settlement in North America.

Ty M. Reese

See also: Canada; Exploration; Hudson River.

Bibliography

Saffer, Barbara. *Henry Hudson: Ill-Fated Explorer of North America's Coast*. Philadelphia: Chelsea House, 2001.

Hudson River

The Hudson River is a 115-mile long body of water that flows through New York. Once thought to be the route to the fabled Northwest Passage, the river provided colonial explorers and settlers with the only navigable waterway from the Atlantic seaboard through the Appalachian mountain barrier. As various powers sought control of North America, the river became one of the most hotly contested waterways on the continent.

The Hudson River, estimated to be about 75 million years old, begins at Lake Tear of the Clouds at an elevation of 4,322 feet on the southwestern slopes of Mount Marcy in the Adirondack mountain range, and it ends at New York City. Befitting one of the great North American rivers, it has been known by many names. To the Iroquois, it was the Cohohatatia or "place to catch shad." To the Lenni Lenape and the Mohican, the river bore the names of Muhheckunnuk, meaning "great waters constantly in motion" and Mahicannittuck, or "place where the Mohican dwell."

The exact date of European discovery of the river

The English navigator Henry Hudson and his crew sailed aboard the *Half Moon*, a small vessel with a shallow draft, on his third and most fruitful voyage in 1609. It was during this voyage that Hudson explored the river that would take his name. *(Brown Brothers, Sterling, Pennsylvania)*

is open to debate. Many Europeans probably saw the waterway without leaving any documentation of their discovery of it. Norse, Portuguese, English, and Dutch ships searching for fish are known to have traveled widely in North America, but the fishermen aboard these vessels did not leave traces of their presence.

In 1524, the Florentine explorer Giovanni da Verrazano became the first documented European to explore the river in his search for the Northwest Passage. The Florentine sailed past the mouth of the river, poked into several inlets in the lower New York bay, and then stopped navigating the waterway when unfavorable winds began to blow. He named it Grande Rivière and also referred to it as the "River of Steep Hills" when describing the waterway to the King of France.

English-born Hudson proved more persistent than Verrazano. Hudson earned credit for the discovery of the body of water on September 4, 1609 while captaining the Dutch ship *Half Moon*. Hudson, working for the Dutch West India Company, hoped to find the Northwest Passage to China. He abandoned this hope upon discovering the shallowness of the waters of the river above present-day Castleton. Hudson continued to explore, in the hope that the river might offer a lead to the Western Sea or Pacific Ocean, believed to be somewhere in that vicinity. He dropped anchor at Albany and sent the ship's long boat upriver. In this manner, Hudson and his crew discovered the full expanse of the river.

Hudson called the river the Manhattes, from the tribe at its mouth; however, to add to the confusion, the Dutch also used several other names for the waterway. In 1611, they named it the Mauritius River after Prince Maurice of Nassau, but occasionally they used the name Nassau River, also in honor of the prince. Generally, the Dutch referred to river as the Groote or Great River, in testament to its importance in their lives. About 1659, the river also appears on several maps as the Norumbee.

The Hudson River Valley offered an incredible amount of natural wealth. Oak, chestnut, and hickory trees filled the shores along the river, while low-lying land held vast green meadows with rich soil. Explorers reported seals splashing on the rocks of the river, as well as salmon, sturgeon, and cod so plentiful that they could be caught without a net. Fur-bearing animals, such as beaver, were also in great supply. Settlers flocked to the valley to take advantage of this bounty, and the Hudson River Valley became one of the most attractive areas for settlement in North America.

Riverways were the roads of choice in colonial America and the Hudson served as a vital highway for both civilians and the military. The Dutch peppered the coasts, inlets, and estuaries of the Hudson with forts to guard against other land-hungry Europeans and the Native Americans. In 1674, the Treaty of Westminster gave the Hudson to the British, who then erected their own fortifications.

When the Americans took control of the river during the Revolution, their presence at the fort at West Point would deny the narrows of the Hudson to the British. As the key to New York City, Fort Albany, and the Atlantic seaboard, the Hudson River became the most heavily fortified and contested strategic route in American military history.

Caryn E. Neumann

See also: Dutch; Fort Orange; Hudson, Henry; New Amsterdam; New Netherland; New York; New York and New Netherland (Chronology); New York City; Patroons; Transportation, Water.

Bibliography

Keegan, John. *Fields of Battle: The Wars for North America.* New York: Alfred A. Knopf, 1996.

Keller, Allan. *Life Along the Hudson.* New York: Fordham University Press, 1997.

Huguenots

Huguenots, French Calvinistic Protestants, who lived in France during the sixteenth and seventeenth centuries, were persecuted for various reasons. The Protestant Reformation was started in Germany in 1517 by Martin Luther, who "protested" the abuses of the Roman Catholic Church. From Germany, Luther's reform spread all over Europe, including France, not only because religious reform was needed, but because a cultural renaissance in the arts, sciences, and political and social thought was already underway.

The Huguenots were most influenced by Luther's predecessor, John Calvin, who was born in Picardy, France. Calvin published his protestant treatises in *Institutes of the Christian Religion* (1536), a work dedicated to King Francis I of France. In that same year a general edict was issued calling for Calvin's general removal.

Around 1555, the first home Huguenot church was founded on Calvin's teachings, and, by May 1559,

As many as 30,000 Huguenots (French Calvinist Protestants) were slaughtered by Catholic mobs in the St. Bartholomew's Day Massacre of August 24, 1572. Hundreds of thousands would emigrate to America over the next century. *(Bibliotheque Nationale, Paris, France/Giraudon/Bridgeman Art Library)*

the Synod of Paris was convened and the French Protestant Church was formalized.

With the coronation of Francis II and the rise of the Guise family, however, the Huguenots were persecuted. This sparked the Wars of Religion (1562–1594), which were an intermittent series of civil wars marked by the 1572 Massacre of St. Bartholomew, in which 30,000 Huguenots were slaughtered.

It is important to note that while religious beliefs were central to conflict between Huguenots and Catholics, politics and family power struggles also contributed. The Edict of Nantes was signed in April 1598 by Henry IV, a Huguenot descendant who proclaimed himself to be Catholic. Henry IV's desire was to end the Wars of Religion, grant free exercise of religion to Huguenots, and restore a general sense of peace to France. At that time, the prevailing idea in Europe was that religious conformity was necessary to maintain

civil and ecclesiastical peace. Henry IV broke new ground in church/state relationships by having the state less directly involved in matters of the church.

Henry IV's edict remained in effect for nearly eighty-seven years, but, in October 1685, Louis XIV revoked it and reinstituted Catholicism as the state religion of France. This meant a resumption of persecution of the Protestants. Thereafter, nearly 300,000 Huguenots immigrated to America, England, Holland, Ireland, Prussia, and South Africa. Nearly a century later, in November 1787, Louis XVI issued the Edict of Toleration, which ensured civil and ecclesiastical rights for Protestants, including the right to marry.

One might think that the Pilgrims were the first Protestants to seek refuge in North America, but, in fact, a group of Huguenots landed near St. John's River in Florida in 1562. The Spanish were jealous of this attempt at colonization, particularly by Huguenots. In

June 1565, Pedro Menéndez de Avilés was dispatched from Cadiz with eleven sailing ships carrying an army of over 1,000 men to seize the coastal settlement and claim it for Spain and the Roman Catholic Church. Arriving in Florida, he established a fort south of the St. John's River in a harbor Menéndez named St. Augustine. Menéndez led a troop of about 500 men across land to the French colony and attacked it, killing about 140 Protestants. Others were given the option of conversion to Catholicism or slavery.

During the late 1600s, and for another 100 years, many Huguenots migrated to America. Most settled in New York, Pennsylvania, Virginia, and the Carolinas; they intermarried and their numbers grew rapidly. They provided a necessary balance to agrarians already settled in these colonies, filling a need for medical professionals, bankers, merchants, artisans, and craftsmen. They therefore had considerable influence on early colonial life.

By the middle of the eighteenth century, more than 15,000 Huguenots had immigrated to the New World, mostly around Charles Town, South Carolina. By the end of the eighteenth century, most Huguenots had lost much of their Huguenot identity as they assimilated into colonial life. In fact, many Huguenots became Anglicans.

Robert Leach

See also: Edict of Nantes, Revocation of; French Colonies on Mainland North America (Chronology); Religion (Chronology); Religion (Essay).

Bibliography

Butler, Jon. *The Huguenots in America*. Cambridge, MA: Harvard University Press, 1983.

Gray, Janet Glenn. *The French Huguenots*. Grand Rapids, MI: Baker Book House, 1993.

Holt, Mack P. *The French Wars of Religion, 1562–1629*. Cambridge, UK: Cambridge University Press, 1995.

Kingdon, R. M. "Why Did the Huguenot Refugees to the American Colonies Become Episcopalian?" *HMPEC* 49 (1980): 317–35.

Humboldt, Alexander von (1769–1859)

The German Romantic Alexander von Humboldt was the most important European scientist to travel in Spanish America in the colonial period. His works introduced generations of Europeans to Latin America.

Born to a noble Prussian family in 1769, Humboldt was educated at two of Germany's leading institutions, the University of Göttingen and the Mining College of Freiberg. Humboldt desired to travel. He was frustrated in his hope to accompany Napoleon Bonaparte in his invasion of Egypt, so he and his friend Aim Bonpland, a French botanist, planned an expedition to Spanish America. This presented many difficulties. Spain was at war with Britain, and the Spanish government, was notoriously jealous of its extensive American holdings. Although Spain had sent out a number of scientific expeditions, including that of Francisco Hernández in 1571 and the Royal Botanical Expedition of 1787 (the latter was a group of scientists with the mission of cataloging the natural resources of Mexico), much of Spanish America still remained to be systematically examined by European scientists.

With some difficulty, Humboldt managed to obtain a royal commission to collect specimens for the king's museum and to make geographical and astronomical observations. Leaving Spain in June 1799, Humboldt's expedition dodged the British blockade of Spanish ports and survived a shipboard typhoid epidemic.

The expedition landed in Venezuela. From there, Humboldt and Bonpland explored up the Orinoco, finding many new specimens and observing Native American life. (Humboldt mistrusted the common assumptions of European superiority to Native Americans.) After spending the winter of 1800–1801 in Cuba—where close observation reinforced Humboldt's hatred of slavery—the two set out again, this time along the Andes.

There was much to see in the mountains and adjoining regions. Humboldt greeted America with a rapturous enthusiasm characteristic of the Romantic period but uncharacteristic of European scientists, many of whom viewed the nature of the New World as innately inferior to that of the Old World. Humboldt devoted much of his natural history studies to refuting that claim, praising the size, vigor, and activity of New World animals and even such geological features as volcanoes. His observations of different plants found at different elevations contributed to his later development of plant geography. He climbed Chimborazo, then thought the highest mountain in the Americas, and observed Inca remains.

The expedition then went to Mexico, where Humboldt enjoyed the company of educated people and indulged his growing interest in pre-Columbian American history and archaeology. There was less exploration to be done in Mexico than in South America but still plenty to occupy Humboldt's energies. He climbed more volcanoes (a major interest of his), visited silver mines and other features of interest, and established the latitude and longitude of many Mexican locations. Before leaving the country, he declined an offer of a position in the Mexican government.

From Mexico, Humboldt and Bonpland went to the United States by way of Cuba. In the United States, Humboldt was treated as a scientific celebrity and admitted to the American Philosophical Society. He visited Thomas Jefferson at Monticello and discussed the future of the Americas with Jefferson and other American statesmen, returning to Europe in 1804.

The scientific fruits of Humboldt's and Bonpland's expeditions in South America and Mexico were enormous. They discovered and collected thousands of species, and Humboldt produced the first accurate maps of the continent, with the aid of the state-of-the-art instruments he brought from Europe. Humboldt's publications also laid the foundations for the study of pre-Columbian America, the greatness of which he brought to European attention. The years following his return to Europe were marked by a steady stream of publications. Humboldt wanted to disseminate what he had learned of the Americas in Europe, and he was also financially pinched, as the Humboldt family lands suffered greatly during the Napoleonic wars.

The bulk of Humboldt's labors went into the vast, thirty-volume report on his travels in Spanish America. On specific parts of this work, he had the collaboration of other scientists, including Bonpland and the German astronomer Jabbo Oltmanns. But most of it was Humboldt's, including three of the most celebrated sections, the single-volume *Essay on the Geography of Plants* (1807), which set forth his theories on the influence of height, latitude, temperature, and rainfall on the distribution of plants; the four-volume *Political Essay on the Kingdom of New Spain* (1811), the first elaborate and accurate statistical and geographical description of Mexico; and the seven-volume *Personal Narrative* (1815–1826), which recounted Humboldt's experiences from 1799 to 1804. Charles Darwin found the *Personal Narrative* an inspiration in his own scientific journey to South America.

William E. Burns

See also: Exploration; Germans.

The German naturalist and explorer Alexander von Humboldt explored the Spanish colonies of South and Central America from 1799 to 1804. He collected large quantities of data and specimens indicative of the flora, fauna, geology, climate, and ethnography. *(Brown Brothers, Sterling, Pennsylvania)*

Bibliography

Crosland, Maurice. *The Society of Arcueil: A View of French Science at the Time of Napoleon I.* Cambridge, MA: Harvard University Press, 1967.

De Terra, Helmut. *Humboldt: The Life and Times of Alexander von Humboldt, 1769–1859.* New York: Alfred A. Knopf, 1955.

Gerbi, Antonello. *The Dispute of the New World: The History of a Polemic, 1750–1900.* Revised and enlarged edition, translated by Jeremy Moyle. Pittsburgh: University of Pittsburgh Press, 1973.

Huron

"Huron" is a term of French provenance referring simultaneously to various Native American ethnic communities. Its etymological origin remains uncertain. In the Middle Ages, "huron" was slang for unrefined person. Yet, in 1639, a Jesuit missionary suggested that a Frenchman first applied this designation to a group of Northern Iroquois fur traders, whose distinctive hairstyle reminded him of *hures* (wild boars).

From the mid-1620s to 1650, the French primarily applied the term "Huron" to five allied tribes of Northern Iroquois origin: the Attignawantan, the Attigneenongnahac, the Tahontaenrat, the Arendarhonon, and the Ataronchronon. These groups called themselves "Wendat," meaning "islanders." Their intertribal alliance was, in many ways, comparable to the League of the Iroquois. At contact, the Huron counted some 20,000 members. Their adjacent tribal territories extended between Georgian Bay and Simcoe Lake in present-day south-central Ontario, Canada.

The Huron shared a typically Northern Iroquois lifestyle, being sedentary and practicing slash-and-burn agriculture. Noticing the existence of cultural similarities between the Huron and their Northern Iroquois neighbors in Ontario, the French extended this particular denomination to other regional groups. To the immediate southwest of the Huron proper were the Huron of the Tobacco Nation, so called for their extensive use of the native plant. Farther south were the Neutral Huron, who observed a nonpartisan position in the war between the Huron and the Iroquois.

In the early 1600s, French explorer and colonial administrator Samuel de Champlain came to view the Wendat as essential partners in the development of the fur trade. The Huron were indeed on friendly terms with many nomadic peoples to the north, promising the French a nearly inexhaustible access to high-quality beaver pelts. In 1615, Champlain negotiated an alliance with the Wendat, opening a period of close contact between both peoples. As Champlain had expected, Huronia quickly became a major gateway in the expanding fur trade. At the height of the trade, the Huron may have supplied the French with as many as 10,000 beaver pelts annually. Benefiting from their alliance with the French and their pivotal position in the fur trade, the Huron enjoyed unprecedented ascendancy in the Great Lakes region. Their language, for instance, became a lingua franca in the trading zone extending from the Ottawa Valley to the shores of Green Bay, Wisconsin.

Huron commercial, diplomatic, and political supremacy was short-lived. Dependence on trade goods made the Huron vulnerable to French cultural hegemony. Champlain and his counterparts insisted on Christianizing their native allies and pressured the latter to accept missionaries in their villages. The clergymen's uncompromising attitude toward their hosts' culture fostered factionalism between Native American converts and traditionalists. By the1630s, waves of European infectious diseases also wrought havoc among the Huron. Lacking immunity to these exotic pathogens, the Huron population dwindled to less than 10,000 individuals in the late 1640s.

These internal disruptions were magnified by the growing power of the Iroquois. Supplied with Dutch guns, the Iroquois accelerated their onslaught on the divided, less armed, and ailing Huron throughout the 1640s. In March 1649, the Iroquois launched a daring attack against the Wendat, who abandoned their homeland within two weeks. Some survivors fled to neighboring tribes, while others surrendered to their enemies.

Many Huron converts settled briefly on Christian Island in Georgian Bay. But, by 1650, famine and Iroquois war parties forced these survivors to disperse, and 300 of them elected residence near Quebec City. In time, these exiles settled in Lorette, where their descendents still reside today. Despite continuing Iroquois attacks and French pressures to assimilate, the Huron of Lorette have preserved their ethnic distinctiveness.

After dispersing the Huron, the Iroquois successfully turned their weapons against the other Native Americans allied with the French in the Great Lakes region. In 1650, the Huron of the Tobacco Nation and a small contingent of Huron refugees in their midst began an exodus westward to escape the Iroquois onslaught. In the early eighteenth century, this mixed ethnic community settled in the Detroit region. By then, the French had begun to designate this tribe as "Huron."

While counting no more than 500 individuals, this Northern Iroquois group gained tremendous diplomatic influence in the Northeast. Around 1720, for instance, they assumed great authority in the intertribal alliance that bound them to the Chippewa, the Ottawa, and the Potawatomie. After the fall of New France in 1763, English and later American authorities adopted the term "Wyandot" as a standard designation for this people.

Christophe J. M. Boucher

See also: Furs; Great Lakes; Native American–European Conflict; Native American–European Relations; Native Americans.

Bibliography

Boucher, Christophe J. M. "The Legacy of Iouskeha and Tawiscaron: The Western Wendat (Wyandot) People to 1701." Ph.D. dissertation, University of Kansas, Lawrence, 2001.

Heidenreich, Conrad. *Huronia: A History and Geography of the*

Huron Indians, 1600–1650. Toronto: McClelland and Stewart, 1971.

Sioui, Georges E. *Huron-Wendat: The Heritage of the Circle.* Vancouver: University of British Columbia Press, 1999.

Tooker, Elizabeth. "Wyandot." In *Handbook of North American Indians.* Vol. 15, *Northeast,* edited by Bruce G. Trigger. Washington, DC: Smithsonian Institution Press, 1978.

Trigger, Bruce G. *The Children of Aataentsic: A History of the Huron People to 1660.* Reprint, Kingston, Ontario, and Montreal, Quebec: McGill-Queen's University Press, 1987.

Warrick, Gary A. "A Population History of the Huron-Petun." Ph.D. dissertation, McGill University, Montreal, Quebec, 1990.

Hutchinson, Anne (1591–1643)

Anne Hutchinson's willingness to speak out against what she perceived as corruption within the church and society of her day led to ostracism from her community. Today, she is widely remembered as a heroine of religious freedom and an early feminist.

Background

Anne Hutchinson was born in Alford, Lincolnshire, in England in 1591, the daughter of Francis and Bridget Marbury. Her father, a deacon at Christ Church, Cambridge, was jailed for a year when he dared to speak out against ministers in the Church of England whom he believed had earned their positions via political maneuvering rather than by merit. He later served successfully within the Anglican church, but his outspoken opinions influenced his daughter to take an early and deep interest in matters of theology and church polity. Educated by her father and allowed full range of his library, Anne often questioned the principles and policies of organized religion.

Following her marriage to merchant William Hutchinson, the young homemaker retained a strong interest in spiritual matters. The entire family was sympathetic to the emerging Puritanism and particularly approved of the sermons of John Cotton, who echoed the preaching of Francis Marbury. As persecution of Puritans in England grew, many emigrated to the New World colonies. William and Anne Hutchinson, their children, and Cotton were among those who came to the Massachusetts Bay Colony in 1634.

Life in the colonies was difficult, and the Hutchinsons underwent the hardships of day-to-day life that

Colonial religious leader Anne Hutchinson was banished from the Massachusetts Bay Colony in 1637 for challenging Puritan doctrine and authority. Her willingness to speak out earned her an enduring reputation as both a champion of religious freedom and an early feminist. *(Private Collection/ Bridgeman Art Library)*

all the settlers encountered. The family was well respected among their neighbors, and Anne, the mother of fifteen children, was known for her skills as a midwife. In addition, she retained her interest in the preaching of John Cotton, although she became increasingly concerned with the stringency of the religious hierarchy in Boston.

Hutchinson began to host Thursday afternoon meetings at her home, which were attended by local women. Initially, these gatherings were devoted to discussion of Cotton's recent sermons, to reading and discussion of the Scriptures, and to prayer. Although Puritans believed that women were inferior beings, their souls were considered of equal value to those of men. Accordingly, the church fathers viewed Hutchinson's leadership of such gatherings as an acceptable and even desirable "women's work," because such discussions might spiritually enlighten and elevate the presumably less-capable members of the society.

As word of these meetings spread, an increasing number of Bostonians expressed interest in them. Soon, groups were meeting at the Hutchinson home twice each week, and men as well as women began to attend. Sometimes, as many as eighty people would gather on a given afternoon to hear Mrs. Hutchinson's lecture. Her audience included magistrates and scholars as well as common citizens. Governor Henry Vane was a friend and frequent visitor during her meetings.

Increasingly, Hutchinson's comments focused on her interpretation of and agreement with Cotton's reliance on the covenant of grace—the notion that God's elevation of the Elect was based on His goodness and grace rather than on any actions that might be taken by humans in an attempt to earn salvation. Hutchinson also began to address her concerns that some Boston churchmen were becoming too concerned with an emphasis both on a covenant of works and on church rules and regulations.

In hindsight, one might argue that Hutchinson's difficulties with the Puritan establishment in the New World can be traced to the journey from England. Perhaps unwisely, she predicted to several voyagers the exact date of their landing in the colonies, a matter of some conjecture in virtually all seafaring trips at the time. She attributed this clairvoyance to the power of the Holy Spirit. Initially, John Cotton, upon hearing of this claim of direct communication from God, was sufficiently alarmed to deny the Hutchinson family membership within his new congregation.

Although Hutchinson made the requisite public disavowal of her statements, saying that she had been guilty of "wrong thinking," it is doubtful that she recanted in her heart. Rather, she made the appropriate formal amends to allow her household to join the social and religious community, almost assuredly with the understanding that she had just experienced the oppression of those who had fled to a new land precisely to avoid oppression. This irony could not have escaped the woman's sharp notice, and it undoubtedly played into her later pronouncements regarding what she considered the illogical and unnecessary constraints imposed on virtually every aspect of community life by the Boston church hierarchy.

Accordingly, when the talk at the Hutchinsons' Bible meetings turned increasingly toward criticism of the church establishment, members of that establishment became alarmed. Their alarm grew as Hutchinson became more insistent that God revealed himself directly to all believers, not just to a select few clergy who could pass on the message (with their own modifications) to their parishioners.

Clearly, with her mounting criticism and her personal popularity, this woman represented a threat in the eyes of the Boston Puritan hierarchy. In addition, as she attracted larger groups to her lectures, she began to expound on the differences she saw between John Cotton's and her own view of the covenant of grace as compared with the covenant of works. Hutchinson drew a distinction between the Church's increasing reliance on works and what she termed "preparation." Preparation, she believed, was every believer's duty to do good works—not as a means of earning salvation, but rather as a thank-offering of law-abiding obedience to God's will in humble response to the gift of His grace. As a consequence, her attitude became increasingly separatist, with many listeners interpreting her remarks as a call to break from the established Puritan church in the colony.

Winthrop and Hutchinson

One of those who was most disturbed by Anne Hutchinson's burgeoning popularity was her neighbor minister John Winthrop. In 1637, Hutchinson's follower Henry Vane lost the colonial governorship to Winthrop, who wasted no time in having charges brought against her. Interestingly, the initial complaint concerned her activity as a woman rather than as a religious agitator. In this complaint, Anne Hutchinson was charged with taking part in activity "not fitting for [her] sex."

Aside from the content of her message, the significance of Hutchinson's actions cannot be overstated. While her initial meetings were approved because they helped to educate and strengthen her sisters in their faith, by widening the scope of her activity—by speaking to groups of women and men, by going beyond mere explanations of John Cotton's sermons, and by engaging in independent commentary and criticism—she became an increasing threat to the authority of the men in power in the church and the colony. Winthrop and others recognized this threat to the integrity of the Puritan way of life in the New World, and they brought charges against this woman to put her back into her proper place.

At her hearing before a panel of magistrates, Hutchinson displayed the characteristic strength she had learned as her father's daughter. She responded to the initial charges of violating the Fifth Commandment by her refusal to defer to the church fathers. She denied violating her appropriate sphere by turning to Scripture passages that upheld the role of women in speaking on spiritual matters.

The panel then charged her with antinomianism, saying that she was teaching that man can be saved by faith alone and therefore he was not bound to follow colonial church leaders' interpretations of proper behavior. Hutchinson responded that she believed both faith and obedience to church rules were necessary, if those rules were made and enforced in good faith. However, she told the court, she was able to discern between true and false preaching, and it was her duty to pass this insight along to those who looked to her for spiritual guidance. When questioned as to how she could draw these distinctions, she answered, "By an immediate revelation by the voice of [God's] own spirit to my soul."

Hutchinson's testimony created a sensation and sealed her fate. By avowing her ability to receive direct communication from God, she echoed the basic claim of Quakers to follow an "inner light," a claim that had long subjected members of that group to charges of heresy. Her mentor, John Cotton, quickly dissociated himself from Hutchinson. Despite similarities in many of their beliefs, Cotton was quick to realize that her problems could damage his own credibility. As a result of her quest for freedom of religion and freedom of thought, Hutchinson brought down the wrath of the Puritan establishment upon herself.

Anne Hutchinson was excommunicated from the Puritan fellowship in the Massachusetts Bay Colony and was banished from the territory, lest her boldness further infect her neighbors. Along with her family and some sixty followers, Hutchinson relocated to the more tolerant colony of Rhode Island, and her group is counted among the founders of Portsmouth.

Following her husband's death in 1642, she and her children moved to Long Island. The following year, all of the Hutchinson family, except for a 10-year-old daughter, was slaughtered in a massacre by a native tribe.

Barbara Schwarz Wachal

See also: Massachusetts Bay Colony; Puritanism; Religion (Chronology); Religion (Essay); Rhode Island; Women. *Document:* The Trial of Anne Hutchinson (1637).

Bibliography

Augur, Helen. *An American Jezebel: The Life of Anne Hutchinson.* New York: Brentano's, 1930.

Battis, Emery John. *Saints and Sectaries: Anne Hutchinson and the Antinomian Controversy in the Massachusetts Bay Colony.* Chapel Hill: Published by the University of North Carolina Press for the Institute of Early American History and Culture at Williamsburg, Virginia, 1962.

Bremer, Francis J., ed. *Anne Hutchinson, Troubler of the Puritan Zion.* Huntington, NY: R. E. Krieger Publishing, 1981.

Lang, Amy Schrager. *Prophetic Woman: Anne Hutchinson and the Problem of Dissent in the Literature of New England.* Berkeley: University of California Press, 1987.

Rimmer, Robert. *The Resurrection of Anne Hutchinson.* Buffalo, NY: Prometheus Press, 1987.

Williams, Selma R. *Divine Rebel: The Life of Anne Marbury Hutchinson.* New York: Holt, Rinehart and Winston, 1981.

Hutchinson, Thomas (1711–1780)

Thomas Hutchinson, politician and public servant, was the great-grandson of Anne Hutchinson and the son of a wealthy merchant and local councilman. Following four years at Harvard College and a mildly rebellious youth, Hutchinson settled down to the serious business of fulfilling his family's expectations. He became an apprentice to his father's business and, in 1734, married Margaret Sanford, who came from a respectable family in Rhode Island. For two decades, they enjoyed a happy marriage, producing three sons and two daughters. After Margaret died in 1753, Hutchinson never remarried.

Hutchinson first entered politics as a representative in the Massachusetts House in 1737. In the House, Hutchinson fought against proposals for a land bank (1740) and instead pressed the cause of hard money, eventually stabilizing the colony's currency and securing a refinancing of its public debt (1749). That cause cost Hutchinson his seat in the House and his position as Speaker, but he was immediately elected to the General Council. In this capacity, he spent much of the next fifteen years meeting with Native American delegations around the Northeast, most notably at the Albany Congress in 1754, where he advocated for Benjamin Franklin's plans for greater colonial cooperation.

Throughout the 1750s, Hutchinson's growing reputation for scrupulous honesty won him office after office. By 1760, he was serving as both chief justice and lieutenant governor, a monopoly that led many critics to question his ability to do duty to each of his salaried posts. Nevertheless, by 1763, Hutchinson was

A leader and symbol of the loyalist movement in pre-Revolutionary Massachusetts, Thomas Hutchinson served as the colony's royal governor from 1771 to 1774. In June 1774, he left for England and never returned. *(Massachusetts Historical Society, Boston, Massachusetts/Bridgeman Art Library)*

the most important man in Massachusetts politics, with an exemplary record.

As lieutenant governor, he disapproved of Parliament's ambitious plans to raise revenue through colonial taxation, arguing that it would harm Anglo-American commerce. However, he upheld the Crown's authority to tax the colonies, a stance that many mistakenly conflated with a pro-Stamp Act position. Public resentment of those hated duties brought a mob to Hutchinson's home in 1765. Led by Ebenezer Mackintosh, they tore his elegant mansion to the ground, carrying away personal possessions worth 3,000 pounds.

No doubt affected by the sacking of his home, Hutchinson's pro-British posture hardened over the following years. While he remained critical of specific British policies toward North America, Hutchinson became increasingly convinced that strong, decisive action was needed if Parliament was to establish its supremacy and quell the rising tide of colonial civil disobedience. "I wish the good of the colony," he wrote in a 1769 private letter that he would come to deeply regret, "when I wish to see some further restraint of liberty, rather than the connexion with the parent state should be broken."

In 1770, Hutchinson became embroiled in the aftermath of the Boston Massacre. Summoned to calm the crowd, the lieutenant governor promised an immediate public inquiry and swift justice. Two skillful patriot lawyers, John Adams and Josiah Quincy, were appointed to represent the soldiers at trial, a shrewd move that served to legitimate the proceedings and which resulted in the soldiers' controversial acquittal for murder.

When Hutchinson inherited the governorship in 1771, it seemed as if calm had been restored to Massachusetts. But in 1773, Samuel Adams published several letters from Hutchinson's private correspondence, which Franklin had illicitly acquired from colleagues in London. The letters called for parliamentary supremacy and were falsely construed by his enemies in the House as evidence that Hutchinson and his brother-in-law Andrew Oliver had conspired to "advance themselves to posts of Honor and Profit, not only to the Destruction of the Charter and Constitution of this Province, but at the Expense of the Rights and Liberties of the American Colonies."

Whatever had been left of Hutchinson's reputation now lay in tatters. Ever dutiful, he tried to enforce Parliament's Tea Act of 1773 and insisted that the East India Company's tea cargoes be unloaded on Boston's docks. A mob thought otherwise and, disguised as Native Americans, boarded the ships and tossed the tea into the harbor.

In London, his repeated calls for decisive action were finally heeded in 1774 when Parliament passed the Coercive Acts, providing for the closure of the port of Boston and replacing Hutchinson with General Thomas Gage. Hutchinson immediately sailed for England for an audience with George III and settled there to wait out the war. Fully intending to return to a subdued and loyal colony, in 1776 he published a careful rebuttal of the Declaration of Independence.

As the war continued, Hutchinson's homesickness grew. He died of apoplexy in London in 1780, after forty-three years spent fulfilling his father's prophecy of the rewards of a life of service: "Depend upon it . . . if you serve your Country faithfully you will be reproached & reviled for doing it."

Richard Bell

See also: Massachusetts; Politics and Government (Chronology); Politics and Government (Essay); Revolutionary War.

Bibliography

Bailyn, Bernard. *The Ordeal of Thomas Hutchinson*. Cambridge, MA: Harvard University Press, 1974.

Shipton, Clifford K. "Thomas Hutchinson." In *Sibley's Harvard Graduates*, vol. 8. Boston: Massachusetts Historical Society, 1951.

Walmsley, Andrew Stephen. *Thomas Hutchinson and the Origins of the American Revolution*. New York: New York University Press, 1999.

Hygiene

See Bathing and Hygiene

I

Immigration

In the race for successful colonization of the New World, more than a mere presence was essential. Rapid population growth and the ability to attract and retain immigrants separated the winners from the losers.

Spanish Colonies

The Spanish presence in North America dated from the early sixteenth century. Juan Ponce de León discovered Florida in 1513. Five years later, Cabeza de Vaca explored Texas, New Mexico, and Arizona. Other explorers followed, traveling the Mississippi and Colorado rivers at midcentury.

Settlement followed quickly. In 1526, Lucas Vázquez de Ayllón founded the first European settlement in present-day Florida. Called San Miguel de Guadalupe, it was located somewhere along the coast in Georgia or South Carolina. Like the later English efforts in Virginia, the colonists, who came from the Caribbean islands, fell prey to malaria and other diseases. About two-thirds of the 600 settlers (including Ayllón) died before the 200 or so survivors returned to the West Indies in 1527.

The following wave of Spanish migration consisted of about 200,000 people, who established around 200 settlements. These included St. Augustine, Florida, which, in 1565, became the first permanent settlement by Europeans in territory that would later become the United States. The Spanish also established Santa Fe, Albuquerque, El Paso, and many California towns from San Diego to San Francisco. From these settlements, the Spanish were able to mine gold and silver for transport to Europe. What they were not able to do was attract immigrants in sufficient numbers.

During the sixteenth century, Spain used St. Augustine as its North American military headquarters. In 1763, Spain lost Florida to Britain after the French and Indian War (known as the Seven Years' War in Europe) but got it back twenty years later.

The legend of the Seven Cities of Cíbola brought Francisco Vázquez de Coronado to an exploration in 1540–1542, which included present-day New Mexico, Arizona, Texas, Oklahoma, and Kansas. Although the expedition found no gold, it gave Spain a claim to what would be called New Mexico. Settlement began in 1598 with the arrival of Spanish missionaries to the Pueblo. These settlers established Santa Fe in 1609–1610.

After decades of harsh Spanish treatment, the Pueblo rose in 1680, killing 400 Spaniards and taking Santa Fe. The Spanish retook Santa Fe in 1692. At the same time, in 1682, Franciscan friars built their first two missions in Texas, and Spanish missions were established throughout central, east, and southwest Texas by 1731. Unfortunately, Texas attracted few colonists; as late as 1793, there were only about 7,000 settlers there. Spanish settlement in California began in 1769, but California also failed to attract many settlers. Rather, it was a land of Franciscan missions and Spanish presidios.

The Spanish colony in Florida proved too weak and underpopulated to withstand the encroachment of other European settlers. The government of the United States began negotiating for purchase of some or all of Florida, and, finally, in 1821, it came under American control. With the floodgates of settlement open, English settlers quickly outnumbered the Spanish.

When westward expansion in the early nineteenth century became a concern for Spanish governors, they attempted to limit trade between the Northern colonies and the United States. In doing so, they thought to control the influx of Anglo-Americans. As had the French, Dutch, and Swedes, they failed.

Swedish and Dutch Colonies

The Swedish presence dated from the establishment in 1638 of Fort Christina on the Delaware River near Delaware Bay. Under Peter Minuit, the Swedes traded in furs and tobacco. After years of conflict with both the Dutch and English, the Swedish settlement fell in 1655 to Peter Stuyvesant, who renamed it Altena.

In 1609, the Dutch West India Company vessel *De Halve Maen (Half Moon)*, skippered by the Englishman Henry Hudson, entered what would become known as the Hudson River, and the first Dutch trading post was established at Fort Orange in 1614. The first families in New Netherland arrived only a decade later. With exclusive trading rights, the company sought to attract a large contingent of settlers to its post on Manhattan, but even the offer of free land along the Hudson River was not enough to entice settlers. Under the eighteen-year administration of Peter Stuyvesant, starting in 1646, the population grew from 2,000 to 8,000. That was not enough, for, in 1664, all of Stuyvesant's New Netherland fell to a superior English force.

French Colonies

The French also came to the New World, establishing a few cities and gaining a toehold in Latin America and the Caribbean, but mostly exploring the wilderness of New France, the vast unknown from Quebec to the Gulf of Mexico. Establishing sufficient population to support French settlements would prove impossible, and the result was the loss of New France, with the eventual loss as well of Louisiana.

In 1562, a French attempt to colonize Florida failed. In 1607, the British destroyed the small settlement of Port Royal, Acadia. In 1608, Samuel de Champlain founded Quebec, establishing a permanent French presence. And in 1617, the first *habitant,* or settler, family claimed land near the city of Quebec; New France had its first immigrants. Ten years later, the Compagnie de la Nouvelle-France came into being as a fur trading and colonization venture; in 1663, the company lost its contract because it couldn't attract the required number of immigrants. That same year saw the arrival of the *filles du roi,* 775 potential brides, only half of whom got married. In 1665, of a 1,300-man regiment sent to quell the Iroquois, 400 soldiers opted to remain in New France after their service was over and begin families. In 1685, New France had a population of 10,275. New England, in contrast, had about 160,000.

Champlain explored northern New York, but the French expansion began only sixty years later with the explorations of Jacques Marquette and Louis Jolliet down the Mississippi River in 1673. René-Robert Cavelier, Sieur de La Salle, sailed the Mississippi to the Gulf of Mexico, claiming Louisiana for the French king. French settlements included Detroit, St. Louis, and New Orleans. The southern part of New France was blessed with fertile soil and a warm climate, well suited for farms and plantations. Founded in 1718, New Orleans quickly became a busy port. New France was open only to Catholics, so French Protestants (Huguenots) had to settle in the English colonies. French missionaries and priests were active in the Mississippi Valley.

From that point until France's loss in the French and Indian War, the French presence slowly shrank, territory after territory falling to the English, exemplified by the deportation of 12,000 French Canadians from newly British territory to Louisiana, Acadians becoming Cajuns.

By the mid-eighteenth century New France boasted a population of 80,000. But this population was spread over many miles; the English, numbering 1.5 million, were clustered along the Atlantic seaboard in their thirteen colonies. War between the two groups of settlers began in 1754. Initial French successes gave way to English victories. With the fall of Montreal in 1760, New France was no more.

English Colonies

English explorers of the sixteenth century were looking for a passage to the Indies. Over time, English governments shifted their interest to colonies as an outlet for surplus population, a source of raw materials for developing industries, and a market for finished goods. King James I gave a group of merchants permission to settle Jamestown, Virginia, in 1607. Initially, the project drew adventurers hoping to make easy fortunes in the New World. Other English found the colonial venture attractive as a way to flee religious persecution.

By 1650, Virginia was home to 15,000 colonists from the James to the York and Rappahannock rivers. The coast was becoming crowded, so an inland push commenced. By 1685, Virginia's population was 60,000.

In the North, Massachusetts overcame initial difficulties, and, by 1630, more than 1,000 Puritans lived in Boston. English pressure against critics of the established Anglican Church sent an additional 20,000 Puritans to Massachusetts over the next decade. From the time of Henry VIII, Catholics and Protestants had fought bloody battles in England. Some Protestants wanted to purify even the Anglican Church, which was too ritualistic for these hard-line Puritans. Rejected at home, they decided to build their Protestant model society in the New World.

Maryland was established in 1632 by Lord Baltimore, George Calvert, as a haven for Catholics suffering under the English Protestant Interregnum. Calvert had explored Newfoundland, but the winter was severe there, and Virginia rejected him. Calvert returned to Ireland, sending his son and 300 settlers to Maryland; the colony remained the property of the Calverts, though freemen had the right to consult on laws.

Pennsylvania was William Penn's purchase from Charles II in 1681. The Quaker Penn wanted a colony of peace for all creeds and nationalities. Settlers began to come to Philadelphia in 1682.

As among other groups of people, there were significant regional differences among the English settlers who came to America. Historian David Hackett Fischer finds the origin of American sectionalism in the waves of British migration. According to Fischer, the culture of the Northeast is strongly defined by the 21,000 East Anglian Puritans who settled Massachusetts between 1629 and 1641 and spread out from there to New England and, later, along the northern border of the United States.

A different culture arose from the immigration of 45,000 English from the Saxon south and west of England between 1642 and 1679; this regional difference crossed class lines, including both gentry and indentured servants. In the middle states, the predominant influence came from the 23,000 North Midlands Quakers who settled Delaware between 1675 and 1725.

A final group settled the mountainous South. These were the 250,000 Scots-Irish, Scots, and border English, who came through Pennsylvania and through the Appalachian backcountry all the way to Georgia. Their descendants pushed the frontier and their values across the continent.

Before 1650, Englishmen migrated to the North American colonies because of a mix of economic and political and religious reasons. James I, a divine-right monarch, thought he answered to God, not Parliament. His conflicts with Parliament exploded under Charles I into civil war, which the parliamentary Roundheads won after seven years. England was also undergoing

economic dislocation due to enclosure (the transfer of communal lands to private ownership), which drove workers out into a world where inflation was rampant. The colonies were attractive, especially the sugar islands, where large fortunes were to be made for relatively small investments. And the mainland colonies seemed empty, with fertile land for the taking.

Some immigrants came as families. Usually, these were religious dissenters, such as the Puritans and Quakers, or they were uprooted by the periodic depressions common in Britain. These immigrants came more to the Northern colonies, where they received land, Northern land being less profitable, or so the Crown believed. Families of immigrants moved to towns, promoting urban growth, unlike in the Southern colonies, where they scattered across rural areas. The colonies were also a good place to send debtors and other criminals and ease the overcrowding of British prisons.

Many new immigrants came to the English colonies as indentured servants, a reciprocal arrangement of benefit to both landowner, who needed the labor, and immigrant, who was short of money. After a landowner paid a servant's passage, the indentured servant would work to repay the cost, normally for seven years. Sometimes, owners also were granted land by the government or private companies, generally 50 acres for each indentured servant. Indentured servants tended to be young, unmarried men, both poor and middle-class.

Indentures were predominant in Virginia, Maryland, the Carolinas, Jamaica, and Barbados. Because of the high death rate in these colonies due to the unforgiving climate and servants failing to acclimatize in time, the demand for labor persisted. And indentured servants sometimes faded into the wilderness, breaching their contracts and becoming part of the general populace. A better, more controllable, source of labor was African slaves, who were brought to the colonies in large numbers.

Non-English Immigration to English Colonies

Through the seventeenth century, the English dominated the colonies. Everywhere but in New York, English culture was the norm. With the coming of the eighteenth century, other cultures competed, brought to the colonies by Swiss, Swedes, Africans, Scots-Irish, Germans, and others.

The usual trigger for a wave of immigration was an adverse event in Europe—a drought or famine, a persecution, a recession. Immigration slowed for about thirty years while Europe was embroiled in the War of the Spanish Succession, or Queen Anne's War, as the English called it. After 1710, a massive wave of Scots-Irish and German immigrants flooded the colonies.

William Penn was the first to encourage German immigration. From the establishment of Germantown in 1683, the German population of Pennsylvania grew, until by 1775, it had reached 100,000, roughly one-third of the colony's population. Another German migration came in response to persecution in the Rhineland in 1708; these Germans settled the Hudson Valley of New York. By 1775, Germans were in Virginia, western Maryland, and North Carolina. German settlements along the Eastern seaboard stretched as far north as Maine.

The largest non-English ethnic group to immigrate to the American colonies before the Revolution was the Scots-Irish. From Ulster in Northern Ireland, these immigrants had settled along the New England frontier as early as 1713. New Englanders frowned on them, and the Scots-Irish turned to the more receptive Pennsylvania. Moving west, they settled near what would be Pittsburgh. Generally, they made good frontier settlers, being rugged, largely without fear, and willing to fight. Virginia encouraged them to settle on its frontier from the 1730s. They continued south through the Carolinas and into Georgia.

Not to be confused with the Scots-Irish, the Scots migrated in large numbers during the mid-eighteenth century. Their motivation was a desire to escape pervasive, grinding poverty in Scotland. In the dozen years prior to the American Revolution, approximately 25,000 Scots migrated to the colonies. Scots tended to avoid the frontier; they became stereotyped as passive rather than active or belligerent, as were the Scots-Irish.

Other groups settled in smaller numbers. The Dutch were mostly in what became New York, and the Swedes were in the Delaware Valley. Swiss established Beaufort, South Carolina, in 1732. Huguenots had a presence in South Carolina and southern Virginia early in the eighteenth century.

Between 1600 and 1800, about 2.3 million Africans were brought to the colonies as slaves. They came primarily, but not solely, into the Southern colonies. Numbers from 1761 showed only 41,000 in the North from Delaware to New Hampshire, while 284,000 lived in the South. Maryland and Virginia had nearly 60 percent of all slaves, with North Carolina, South Carolina, and Georgia being home to another 30 percent.

John H. Barnhill

See also: Dutch; English; French; Germans; Indentured Servitude; Language; Race and Ethnicity (Chronology); Religion (Essay); Scots-Irish; Swedes. *Documents:* A Call for English Colonization of America (1584); Gottlieb Mittelberger on Immigration to the Colonies (c. 1750).

Bibliography

Bannon, John Francis. *The Spanish Borderlands Frontier, 1513–1821.* New York: Holt, Rinehart and Winston, 1970.

Barkan, Elliott Robert. *A Nation of Peoples: A Sourcebook on America's Multicultural Heritage.* Westport, CT: Greenwood, 1999.

Fischer, David Hackett. *Albion's Seed: Four British Folkways in America.* New York: Oxford University Press, 1989.

Gibson, Charles. *Spain in America.* New York: Harper and Row, 1966.

Hoffer, Peter Charles. *The Peopling of a World: Selected Articles on Immigration and Settlement Patterns in British North America.* New York: Garland, 1988.

Takaki, Ronald T. *A Different Mirror: A History of Multicultural America.* Boston: Little, Brown, 1993.

Taylor, Alan. *American Colonies.* New York: Penguin, 2002.

Indentured Servitude

The Americas appeared to have unlimited potential as a source of wealth. The biggest problem was finding enough workers to tap that potential. The earliest efforts to exploit native labor, especially in Latin America, quickly exhausted the indigenous population. A replacement source of labor was vital. Options ranged from immigration to forced migration. Somewhere in the middle, an interim arrangement in the heavily labor-dependent colonies, was the indentured servant.

All colonial powers—Spanish, English, French, and Dutch—used indentured labor to grow their tobacco, various spices, and indigo, a plant used to make blue dye. An indenture is a mortgage, in this instance, a promise of labor in return for passage, food, and shelter. It may have been a written contract, legally enforceable, with a duration ranging from four to seven years. Indentured servants could be African, but they were most often young European men.

Indenture came to the colonies over time: Virginia and Barbados introduced the practice in the 1630s and 1640s, Jamaica in the 1660s, South Carolina in the 1690s. The French introduced indenture to Saint-Domingue, Martinique, and Guadeloupe from the 1660s through 1680s.

An indenture was a contract of labor in return for passage and upkeep for a period of four to seven years, after which workers were generally granted the means to start their own farms or businesses. Immigrant indentured servants were a primary source of labor throughout the Americas. *(Private Collection/Michael Graham-Stewart/Bridgeman Art Library)*

Leaving Europe

Indentured laborers had a reputation as riffraff, beggars, and thieves; instead they were a broader representation of the working classes of England. Their backgrounds ranged from desperate poverty to middle-class status. Some had no particular skills, while many had experience in textile work or other trades, as well as farming.

Generally, they were not among those who left England during the sixteenth century for religious reasons. Those people tended to migrate to the Northern colonies. In the South and the Caribbean, where most indentured laborers were, the motivation was survival or economic improvement. The English enclosure movement—in which communal land came under private ownership—and other dislocations had forced many laborers, farmers, and home textile workers, among others, to emigrate in search of work. By the time they were ready to sign on, they had probably been forced from their birthplace, ranging farther and farther afield in search of a living, eventually ending up in one of England's growing cities.

Often, the only alternative to indenture was the workhouse, a harsh and primitive home to the homeless waif, the vagrant, the general loser in society's ruthless obeisance to the wealthy and powerful. And workhouse life was no guaranteed refuge from indenture overseas. Early on, the government figured out that it could clear its prisons and workhouses of society's detritus and help the mercantile economy at the same time. The solution was shipping them to the New World, at first, under the Virginia Company. If all went well, the landless vagabond would become a landowner, a taxpayer, a contributor to society rather than a burden. If not, mortality was high. There were abuses, too, with English traffickers rounding up misfits and shipping them to the colonies against their will.

As many as three-fourths of the migrants to the Caribbean (especially Barbados and Jamaica) and the Chesapeake Bay area were indentured servants—mostly young and unmarried men, some with previous experience in service, some unskilled, and some skilled. Bachelors were supposed to be more focused on the labor expected by their masters, and men always outnumbered women in the Chesapeake Bay area and the Caribbean during the seventeenth century.

Single men also were the majority of the immigrants to Virginia, Maryland, the Carolinas, Barbados, and Jamaica. These colonies were run privately by Crown-chosen investors, generally loyal Anglicans, who took risks for the chance to profit from colonial trade. With their milder climates, these colonies appeared to have great profit potential and a better chance of fulfilling the mercantilist ideal of colonies supplementing home economies, rather than competing with them, as Northern colonies would.

Virginia and Maryland attracted 120,000 indentured servants in the seventeenth century. Mostly they were between the ages of 15 and 24, with a ratio of six men to each woman in 1635, shifting to a ratio of three men to each woman by the century's end. Most came from London, southeast England, and the area from the Thames Valley to the West Country. Their backgrounds ranged from common labor to skilled artisans, farmers, and yeomen, and occasionally gentlemen. Driving them to seek a new start were English population growth, enclosure of farmland, and bad times in the cloth industry.

In 1619, the Virginia Company promised a headright of 50 acres for each servant finishing a contract, but the company failed to make clear that the headright went to the person paying transportation, not necessarily to the servant. With this amount of land on offer for each passenger to Virginia, the early immigrant who paid the passage of a family and servants could amass a goodly holding just by getting them across the ocean. Fares could be 6 to 9 pounds in currency or 120 pounds of tobacco. The master paying for new workers could easily hire an agent to take care of the details.

Fifteen was the legal age for making a labor contract. Some sailed with no contract, hoping to strike a deal on arrival; these risked sale by the ship's captain to anyone he chose. In the Caribbean, indentured laborers usually went through the auction process on arrival, going to the highest bidder, often with the dirtiest work.

Throughout the colonies, indentured servants endured hard physical toil in difficult conditions under the watchful eye of an overseer; he was accountable only to the owner in Europe, who desired simply a positive return on investment. Those servants who did live through their term of indenture later blended in with the general population.

Costs and Benefits

As late as 1671, the mortality rate was 80 percent. The voyage to the Chesapeake was difficult, sailing first to the Azores, then west to Virginia. Between 1620 and 1680, something on the order of 35 percent of the women and half of the men died on the voyage. With killers including dysentery, smallpox, malaria, and other contagious diseases, life expectancy was 40 years. In 1644, the Eastern shore's population was 340; by 1662, it was only 707.

Mortality was high, but indentured immigrants kept coming. Perhaps they had no knowledge of death rates; perhaps they had no livable alternative. Perhaps they believed the promises, the lies, about folks getting rich in tobacco and sugar. If they knew the dismal truth that most would not succeed to any great extent, they ignored it.

Although recruiters made Virginia sound like paradise, with a sure rise of the indentured laborer to landholder in a matter of time, not all found it to be quite such a paradise. In 1623, Richard Frethorne, working near Jamestown, wrote his parents an urgent plea to either redeem him or send him food. He had just experienced a bloody Native American incursion that came as retaliation for the behavior of the Jamestown settlers, and Frethorne was among the settlers afraid to leave the fort for food. Clearly, sixteen years into the settlement, life in Virginia was far less than the Eden promised by the promoters.

Prospects picked up after 1625. Between then and the end of the 1650s, the tobacco market boomed, creating a great demand for labor. Immigrants came to Virginia at a rate of 2,000 per year. As many as three quarters of the white colonists in Virginia and Maryland began their New World adventure as dependent laborers. Land was cheap, and start-up costs, mainly for tools and equipment, were low. Even starting at the bottom, a man with a willingness to work hard, be thrifty, and avoid legal troubles, plus a touch of good luck, could become a landowner, perhaps even a solid citizen and community leader.

Whether or not the majority made the climb, there were enough to inspire others to dream and strive. When the major labor source became slavery in the last years of the seventeenth century, struggling indentured servants could at least feel superior to black laborers.

Indentured Servitude Versus Slavery

Despite their legal status as contracted free individuals, servants could find their treatment indistinguishable from that of slaves. Masters could abuse servants, especially women, and would sometimes provide food, shelter, and clothing only sufficient to sustain life marginally. Abused as servants, some indentures became abusers themselves when they were older.

Sometimes, the indentures could be chained together, put on the block at public market, and auctioned to the highest bidder, just like slaves. Also like slaves, they had to carry documentation to prove their status—slaves had to have permission to roam, and previously indentured servants had to prove they had finished their contract.

There were legal restrictions in the South. Seventeenth-century laws restricted masters' "barbarous" treatment of servants; however, permitted punishments included the ball and chain, as well as whipping. Laws also limited servants' "unapproved" marriages and fornication. Such laws often differentiated among Native Americans, slaves, and indentured servants, as well as between the baptized and unbaptized, and Christians and "heathens."

More often, conflict occurred between servant and master than between slave and servant, who often ran away together. That they escaped together is not surprising, because seventeenth-century slaves and servants lived similar lives. They worked side by side, ate together, and often shared sleeping quarters.

The pattern persisted at least until Bacon's Rebellion in 1676. Nathaniel Bacon and the governor, William Berkeley, disagreed on Native American policy, with the Easterner taking the position that friendly

Native Americans should be left alone. Bacon believed all Native Americans were a threat. When Bacon defied the governor in the east and fought Native Americans anyway, his men were both black and white, raising the specter among the Eastern elites of a united underclass, a threat to their security. The result was a clearer distinction in the status and treatment of slaves and indentured servants, even when they worked side by side.

No matter how similar their lives, there was one critical difference: one was free and one was not. Although it was not always the case in the early years, with at least some of the first black laborers being indentured rather than enslaved, from the middle of the seventeenth century, slavery became the normal state for blacks. After 1662 in Virginia, and later in other colonies, the child of a slave mother was a slave—bondage in perpetuity. Slavery was a matter of capture, an involuntary state of forced servitude, whereas indentured laborers made and consented to a contractual arrangement, maintaining the right of control over themselves and their labor.

When conditions became too unbearable, indentured servants ran away. The numbers of runaways are only speculation in the absence of documentation. Still, it is clear that governments regarded it as a serious problem. The eighteenth-century *Virginia Gazette* carried hundreds of advertisements trying to retrieve runaways, both servants and slaves. Punishments were as severe as those for runaway slaves and could be as many as twenty, thirty, or more lashes. Also, runaways faced extensions to their contracts that could be twice the length of the original term. Servants could at least hope that their first sentence would be only a warning; slaves were assured that their punishment would be swift and severe.

Indentured Servitude in Colonial Canada

Indenture was practiced as far north as Nova Scotia. Slavery also occurred there, as in all colonies, and loyalists fleeing the Revolution brought their slaves. For black Nova Scotians, however, indenture was more common. It came as a punishment in lieu of a fine or a means of freeing a debt, the same as in the tobacco and sugar colonies. Punishment and treatment were the same as for slaves. Many black loyalists during the Revolution were in serious poverty, and they sold themselves into indenture.

The 1784 indentured population of Shelburne was 125, about 10 percent of the total black population. Abuses, even at this late date, were the same as the ones that plagued the system at the outset. Masters indentured blacks, collected their rations, and kept their supplies—they were in effect getting paid to receive free labor.

Another abuse of the system was to free the indentured servant just short of the completion of the contract, thus avoiding the required end-of-contract payment. Or it was possible to make an oral agreement for one term and then get an illiterate servant to unknowingly sign on for a longer term.

Some black indentured servants were smuggled to the West Indies and sold into slavery. Failure to keep any paperwork often forced the courts to decide for the white master or the black servant—an easy choice when the word of a black meant little.

Servitude or Slavery

Although it lasted through the colonial era, indenture was not fully satisfactory. It alleviated population pressures in England by providing agricultural work for the displaced. As the labor market moved overseas, so did the workers. Eventually, the agricultural market, especially the plantations, became the province of slaves.

In the eighteenth century, as slaves took over unskilled labor, indentured servants had to develop more skills as artisans and mechanics. Ironworkers, textile workers, shipbuilders—these were the skilled laborers a master would pay passage for, not another field hand. These immigrants tended to be older, and, with time, they would start families or bring theirs over from Europe.

John H. Barnhill

See also: Agriculture; Immigration; Laborers, Rural; Slavery, African American.

Bibliography

Digital Collections Program, Industry Canada. "Slavery in Nova Scotia." http://collections.ic.gc.ca/blackloyalists/story/prejudice/slaves.htm.

Leyburn, James G. *The Scotch-Irish: A Social History.* Chapel Hill: University of North Carolina Press, 1962.

Olson, James Stuart. *The Ethnic Dimension in American History.* New York: St. Martin's, 1979.

Takaki, Ronald. *A Different Mirror.* Boston: Little, Brown, 1993.

Indigo

Indigo was the most important textile dyestuff in history. It provides a blue dye, but it is also a main component to achieve greens and the color most difficult to dye, which is black. One reason for indigo's importance is its superior color fastness compared to other natural dyestuffs, an especially useful characteristic when dying textiles often exposed to dirt. This is why workers traditionally wore blue (giving rise to the term "blue collar") and why blue jeans—created as working clothes in mid-nineteenth century—are this color.

The term "indigo" refers not only to the dyestuff itself but also to plants of the genus *Indigofera*, from which the dyestuff is made. Another important crop for that purpose is woad, the sole European source for blue dyestuff in the Middle Ages.

In the late sixteenth and early seventeenth centuries, indigo proved to be an excellent commodity for the early transcontinental trade of the Europeans—in this case mainly for the East India companies. As the dyestuff could be gained in a near-pure form from the plant, it had a very high value-to-weight ratio, like spices or bullion. Even in the late eighteenth century, a pound of ordinary indigo was ten to twenty times more valuable than a pound of ordinary coffee or refined sugar. So, even with the cost of transport, which was moderate when compared to that of bulkier goods such as wheat, non-European indigo proved to be highly competitive with woad, ousting it from the European market in the course of the seventeenth century.

As in the case of coffee, the tropical crop indigo was suitable for growing on slave-labor-based plantations. This highly efficient but cruelly exploitative preindustrial system had been developed to meet the needs of labor-intensive crop production in the colonies. When the price of tobacco fell due to the massive extension of tobacco cultivation in Virginia in the mid-seventeenth century, many tobacco planters decided to become indigo planters.

Plantations in Central America and the Caribbean supplied much of the world demand for indigo, a vital textile dyestuff, until the mid-1700s. Production, which relied on slave labor, was then begun in South Carolina (depicted here) as well. *(The Stapleton Collection/Bridgeman Art Library)*

In the late eighteenth century, approximately 2,000 tons of indigo reached the world market annually. About 300 tons of it, held to be the finest quality, was grown in Guatemala. Venezuela and Brazil provided less; the most prosperous Caribbean colony, Saint-Domingue, yielded three times more. However, indigo cultivation on Saint-Domingue had already reached its peak by around 1730, when the extension of sugar growing and the booming coffee market began to put dyestuff production in the shade. Beneficiaries of this development were planters in South Carolina.

The individual credited with starting South Carolina's indigo production in the mid-eighteenth century is Eliza Lucas Pinckney. Born in the West Indies, she immigrated to South Carolina with her family in 1738, at the age of 16. She was entrusted with the management of her father's plantations near Charles Town and experimented successfully with growing the indigo plant in that environment. In 1744, she married Charles Pinckney, a man of great influence in South Carolina, who promoted the distribution to other planters of the seed she had grown. From the 1750s to the 1790s, South Carolina supplied on average about 300 tons of indigo annually to the world market.

Although the study of Eliza Lucas Pinckney's letters and diaries leave no doubt about her impressive personality and commitment, there is more to the development of Carolina indigo production than the endeavors of a single person. Others—such as her neighbor Andrew Deveaux—also promoted the growing of indigo. And the macroeconomic circumstances were favorable, with French production of dyestuff in decline.

The War of Jenkins' Ear (1739–1743) and the Seven Years' War (1756–1763) cut off the British textile industry from the French and Spanish dyestuff supply, stimulating the expansion of cultivation in Carolina. After 1763, the planters secured protection from the British Parliament. A bounty on Carolina indigo and then a duty on foreign indigo imported to England were established, keeping the American dyestuff competitive.

In 1776, the independence of the thirteen colonies ended the preferential position of Carolina indigo in Britain. From the 1780s on, cultivation in British India was recommenced and intensified, ousting all other producers from the market. Indigo production in South Carolina ceased in the late 1790s, and Saint-Domingue indigo left the world market in 1804. Until the inven-

tion of synthetic indigo in 1897, British India was nearly the sole supplier of the dyestuff.

Alexander Engel

See also: Agriculture; Clothing.

Bibliography

Balfour-Paul, Jenny. *Indigo.* London: British Museum, 1998.
Coon, David L. "Eliza Lucas Pinckney and the Reintroduction of Indigo Culture in South Carolina." *The Journal of Southern History* 42:1 (1976): 61–76.
Sharrer, G. Terry. "Indigo in Carolina, 1671–1796." *The South Carolina Historical Magazine* 72:1 (1971): 94–103.

Inheritance

"Inheritance" has been defined by the third edition of *Ballentine's Law Dictionary* as "the taking of property by descent or intestate succession." When property passes by operation of law, it is said to have passed by the law of intestate succession.

Common Law

Inheritance in the colonies (except for New Amsterdam, where inheritance was governed by Dutch law) was governed by English common law. Common law is judge-made law; the written opinions of judges in earlier cases would be used as precedents in later cases.

Common law had different rules for the inheritance of real property and personal property. Real property is land, whereas personal property could be livestock, slaves, furniture and furnishings, farm and business equipment, crops, and cash. If a person died without a will and owned real or personal property, the property passed by the laws of descent and distribution.

The law of primogeniture (from the thirteenth century) provided that all the land and personal property of the deceased passed by operation of law to the eldest son, subject to the rights of the deceased's widow, who was entitled to dower, which amounted to one-third of the estate, plus the income from the estate for her lifetime. Upon the death of the widow of a decedent who died without a will, her one-third interest also passed by operation of law to their eldest son.

Entailment required that property, usually real property, be passed on to an established order of heirs. Upon the death of a property owner, the property passed to the eldest son. If the eldest son had died, the land would pass to the next eldest son. If there were no male heirs, property would pass to the single daughters or to the husbands of those married, in equal parts. If there were neither sons nor daughters living, the estate would pass to the eldest grandson. Illegitimate children could not inherit under common law.

If a married man died without children, his property would pass to his widow for her lifetime. Such a widow could apply to the county court for a new patent on the land. Once she received the patent, she was free to sell it, give it away, or bequeath it in her will.

The property of an unmarried man who died without a will passed to his eldest brother. The property of those who died without heirs, and that of widows who failed to obtain a new patent, went to the colony by the doctrine of escheat. The property of convicted felons could not be passed to their heirs, and no beneficiary who had been convicted of a felony could inherit. Such property also was forfeit to the colony through escheat.

The doctrines of primogeniture and entailment ensured that large parcels of land were not broken up into smaller plots. One benefit to the British Crown and colonial officials was that there were fewer persons from whom taxes had to be collected.

Representative of the Estate and Guardian

Under a will, the personal representative of the estate is called an executor. The appropriate colonial court would appoint an administrator for estates where there was no will. The court would require the posting of a bond with surety by administrators and executors who were not excused from bond in the will. The surety would be financially liable for any loss caused by the personal representative. It was the duty of the personal representative of the estate to marshal the assets of the estate; to advertise for creditors, to file an inventory of the assets and liabilities of the estate with the court; and to ensure that the property passed correctly.

When the estate was ready to be closed, the personal representative would ensure that all debts and taxes of the deceased were paid from the assets and that all specific bequests in a will were paid. Once the court approved the personal representative's final accounting, the court would release him and the sureties on his bond and would order the administrator or executor to execute deeds to the heirs and close the estate. Upon the death of an executor, the court was empowered to appoint his successor.

If the beneficiary of an estate was under 21 years of age and no guardian was named in the will, it was necessary for the court to appoint a guardian to take possession of the property. Generally, a boy at age 14 and a girl at age 12 could request that a particular person be appointed his or her guardian.

Changes in Inheritance

There were exceptions to all of these rules at one time or another in all of the colonies. Drastic changes were brought about by the American Revolution (1776–1783). Thomas Jefferson introduced bills in the Virginia legislature to abolish entailments, to do away with the preference for males, and to abolish the doctrine of primogeniture. This began the breakup of large estates in Virginia.

Thereafter, each of the new states amended its law to provide that a father or mother, other sons and daughters, brothers and sisters, and their respective heirs could inherit. In addition, illegitimate children were given inheritance rights through their mother.

Edward F. Butler, Sr.

See also: Children; Family; Law and Courts; Orphans; Property and Property Rights; Widows and Widowers. *Document:* Probate Inventory of a Plymouth Colony Estate (1672).

Bibliography

American Jurisprudence Proof of Facts, 2nd series. Rochester, NY: Lawyers Co-Operative, 1974.

Ballentine, James A. *Ballentine's Law Dictionary.* 3d ed. San Francisco: Bancroft-Whitney, 1969.

Howe, Henry. *Historical Collections of Virginia.* Baltimore: Clearfield, 1993.

Kimbrough, Robert T. *Summary of American Law.* Rochester, NY: Lawyers Co-Operative, 1974.

Moynihan, Cornelius J. *A Preliminary Survey of the Law of Real Property.* St. Paul, MN: West, 1940.

Vogt, John, and T. William Kethley, Jr. *Will and Estate Records in the Virginia State Library: A Researcher's Guide.* Athens, GA: Iberian, 1987.

Inns and Taverns (Public Houses)

Inns and taverns were among the first buildings constructed in colonial America. From the beginning, they ranged in style from the very elegant to the mean and nasty, catering to everyone from society's upper elites to the lowest laboring classes.

In the urban taverns that served an elite and middle-class clientele, men (and occasionally women) gathered on a regular basis to read and exchange news, transact business, argue over political issues, and share a cordial drink with friends. Rowdy dramshops along the waterfront in the port towns catered to mariners and sailors, who constituted between one-tenth and one-quarter of the male population. Rural taverns, often situated on the main road, hosted mixed company, which included local residents, as well as travelers who needed a night's lodging, a hot meal in winter, or a cool drink in summer. Whether rural or urban, elegant or seedy, taverns and inns played a central role in colonial American society, competing from the outset with the church as the most popular public space.

Until the middle of the eighteenth century, when "pubs" (public houses) became separate commercial entities, taverns served as inns and were run in buildings designed as private residences. The amenities offered were basic: most had one barroom, where customers sat around a single table, normally drinking from pewter tankards but sometimes sharing from a communal bowl. By the middle of the eighteenth century, tavern keepers began to provide a regularly scheduled "ordinary," or bill of fare.

Travelers looking for lodging could expect to share a bed, sometimes with a stranger and generally in rooms close to the bar and the proprietor's family. Some tavern owners, or publicans, performed small favors for their customers in return for a fee, including keeping packages, delivering messages, renting horses, and making small loans.

Despite the fact that licensed taverns were required to display a sign, it was often difficult to tell the difference between a reputable house and a seedy one. In the larger cities (Philadelphia, Boston, New York), taverns drew together customers from a wide variety of backgrounds in conditions of forced intimacy.

Boston

In colonial times, most public and private business, including legal, administrative and mercantile activities, was conducted in taverns. Such was the case in Boston, the largest colonial port, which erected its first tavern in 1634 but did not build the public Town House until over two decades later. Even after its erection in 1657, nearby taverns such as the Blue Anchor were the preferred sites for court hearings and assembly and legislative sessions, most likely because of the convenience of heat and light provided by the tavern keepers during the harsh winter months, thereby avoiding the expense of duplicating these services in the Town House. Justices traveling on a circuit did not always arrive together, and to heat and light the courthouse for an extended period was quite costly. In addition, the taverns provided lodging, food, and drink to justices and their servants and escorts.

Colonial authorities followed English precedent in the careful licensing of such establishments and enforcing provisions. As early as 1634, the Massachusetts General Court forbade any person to operate an unlicensed public house, and enforced rules against disorder, gambling, sale of alcohol on the Sabbath or to youths and Native Americans, and extension of credit to sailors without permission from the captain. The court also set curfews and price and quality controls. The colonial laws governing taverns and drinking behavior rarely mentioned women. Married women were expected to fulfill their duties to their husbands and children and refrain from squandering their time drinking in taverns. On the other hand, a high proportion of tavern licensees were themselves women. Of the fifty-four taverns operating in Boston in 1690, twenty-four were licensed to women.

In Boston, the largest colonial town at the beginning of the eighteenth century and one with a strong puritanical bent, the inns and taverns were thus carefully regulated. Complete regulation, however, was impossible. Even in the upper-class establishments, trouble sometimes ensued, as in 1728, when a quarrel at the Royal Exchange ended in a duel and the death of an aristocratic youth.

New York

The colony of New York fostered an even more hospitable climate for alcohol consumption. Between 1653 and 1664, during Dutch rule, there were seventeen inns and taverns operating in New Amsterdam, which did not yet boast a population of 2,000 people. After the English seized control, the number of official inns and taverns doubled by 1680 as the population increased.

As in Boston, the taverns and inns were sites of commercial transactions as well as government business, and they required official licenses from the local government. The Dutch governors Kieft and Stuyvesant, however, reported numerous problems with unlicensed houses, indicating the hard-drinking nature of the early colonists. Problems with unlicensed taverns continued after the English takeover, and taverns were a perennial problem in New York and some of the other colonies because of alcohol abuse.

New York City lawmakers initially allowed Native Americans and blacks access to taverns until 1680, when a law was passed forbidding them to enter. The penalty for violating this law was set at 5 pounds, a clear indication that the authorities took this issue seriously. After the slave conspiracy of 1712, city authorities identified the taverns as seedbeds of antiwhite conspiracy. Nonetheless, New York continued to maintain a reputation as a hard-drinking town, and taverns were allowed to serve alcohol after 3 P.M. on Sundays, a liberty not allowed in most of the other colonies. In addition, widows were granted free licenses to run dramshops in order to help them gain a decent living.

For the lower classes, taverns proliferated, and it was at these establishments that most of the lawlessness took place. One infamous tavern, called the Dog's Head in the Porridge Pot, catered to the "scum of society" in slovenly surroundings and was the site of numerous brawls.

Philadelphia

Philadelphia, like New York, was a rowdy colonial port town with more public houses per capita than Rotterdam or Paris. Within a year of the first Quaker settlers' arrival in 1682, two Philadelphians were keeping taverns in caves dug into the Delaware riverbank. By 1686, there were at least six taverns in operation, and, by 1756, there were 101 licensed premises.

Philadelphians occasionally and inconsistently applied British distinctions between different types of public houses—inn, tavern, and alehouse—to their tavern trade, and the city's stock of public houses tended to uniformity in size, tone, and service. Unlike New York, however, innkeepers successfully petitioned for the suppression of unlicensed dram shops and tippling houses in 1720.

Taverns remained an important part of political life throughout the eighteenth century, and on the day John Adams arrived in Philadelphia to attend the First Continental Congress, he was met by a delegation of prominent Philadelphians who whisked him away to the City Tavern. Washington, arriving a few days later, likewise dropped into the tavern before he bothered to visit his lodgings.

Coffeehouses and Public Houses

Taverns in Boston began facing competition from coffeehouses, the first of which opened in 1676, following the London model, and which quickly became the center of mercantile activity. Coffeehouses that opened in New York tended to develop into taverns, offering food and lodging as well. The Black Horse Tavern, owned and operated by Johannes D'Honneur, was one such example. Committees of the Assembly regularly met at the Black Horse, which became the de facto social headquarters of the popular party. Lawyer and statesman Andrew Hamilton lodged there during the Peter Zenger trial and was given a magnificent banquet. Another tavern, Todd's, was the preferred meeting place of the court faction and aristocracy.

Competition induced tavern owners to provide beds, food, and service of superior quality. Fairly steady and dependable patronage encouraged them to introduce innovations and improvements, and public regulation prevented many abuses for which there was no remedy in the backcountry. The cost of setting up as an innkeeper in the towns, including the expense of the license fees and equipment, made it a business enterprise of some magnitude, attracting mainly those with capital and social standing. Furthermore, the varied patronage of town populations fostered the existence of many types of public houses to cater to the needs, tastes, wallets, and morals of a wide range of people. Alternatively, the vices and disorders that flourished in the tavern tap rooms and grog shops were likewise intensified in the towns, especially along the waterfront, where they constituted one of the prominent social problems faced by colonial communities.

In the eighteenth century, the tavern continued as an important public institution and as a focus for business, social, and recreational life. The tavern grew in importance as the temporary homes of itinerant shows and exhibitions and continued as a favorite place for playing games such as backgammon, cards, dice, bowling, shuffleboard, and billiards, as well as the occasional cockfight. Taverns also became the headquarters for clubs designed for all classes, and their number increased with the growth and expansion of each colonial community. As their number increased, a marked improvement in quality and reliability of food and drink ensued. The "liquor problem," however, continued apace, and no satisfactory solution could be found.

Thus, colonial inns and taverns were conceived early on as public institutions that should provide all needed services and be carefully regulated by law to prevent the usual sorts of abuses relating to alcohol, which each colony and town met with varying degrees of success. After the construction of the first American hotels in the 1790s, which grew out of the existing fine inns that catered to more elite clientele, taverns and pubs became the refuge for the lower and middle classes.

Kevin P. McDonald

See also: Alcohol; Food and Diet; Gambling; Transportation, Land. *Document:* The Journal of Sarah Kemble Knight (1704).

Bibliography

Bridenbaugh, Carl. *Cities in the Wilderness: The First Century of Urban Life in America, 1625–1742.* London: Oxford University Press, 1971.

Conroy, David W. *In Public Houses: Drink and the Revolution of Authority in Colonial Massachusetts.* Chapel Hill: University of North Carolina Press, 1995.

Salinger, Sharon V. *Taverns and Drinking in Early America.* Baltimore: Johns Hopkins University Press, 2002.

Thompson, Peter. *Rum Punch and Revolution: Taverngoing and Public Life in Eighteenth-Century Philadelphia.* Philadelphia: University of Pennsylvania Press, 1999.

Irish

See Scots-Irish

Iron

Deposits of iron, whether found in bog or mineral form, are located in every section of North America. Prior to the American Revolution, iron mining was conducted on a broad scale, since iron was needed to supply British iron manufacturing operations, which, in turn, supplied the colonies with finished goods. After 1800, British-made iron goods became too expensive or were no longer available, so iron manufacturing operations sprang up in most regions of North America, attracting industrialists, mercantilists, and, eventually, agriculturalists.

Iron extraction enterprises varied by the source. Where located, the mineral form of iron could be inexpensively mined. Because bog iron differed in consistency from mineral iron, it was often expensive to extract and offered uncertain profits. Early production methods were primitive—ore was mined, melted in charcoal-heated furnaces, and then puddled, forged, and smelted. As manufacturing techniques progressed, wrought iron, cast iron, and eventually various grades of steel were produced.

All production methods required large labor forces in order to mine the ore, supply fuel for the fires, and maintain the furnace. Labor varied by region. Most occupations at iron settlements were strenuous and thus principally male employments, with labor supplies in the North primarily dependent on free wage labor. A mixture of slave and free labor could be found in the central region, while slavery dominated the South. Employment opportunities at iron mines and manufacturing sites varied a great deal by skill. Regardless of location, iron settlements were economically important, because they stimulated the construction of transportation networks and supplied materials for other industries.

Iron mining was key to the development of settlements throughout America. It was particularly vital to central and northeastern Alabama (especially Birmingham), northwestern Georgia, eastern Tennessee, the Kanawha River Valley of West Virginia, and various regions of the Carolinas, Virginia, Pennsylvania, Maryland, New Jersey, New York, Massachusetts, Maine, New Hampshire, Rhode Island, and Connecticut.

Solomon K. Smith

See also: Artisans; Manufacturing; Tools.

Bibliography

Bealer, Alex W. *The Art of Blacksmithing.* Edison, NJ: Castlebooks, 1995.

McGaw, Judith A., ed. *Early American Technology: Making and Doing Things from the Colonial Era to 1850.* Chapel Hill: University of North Carolina Press, 1994.

Tryon, Rolla M. *Household Manufactures in the United States, 1640–1860.* New York: Augustus M. Kelley, 1966.

Iroquois Confederacy

The Iroquois Confederacy is a group of six Native American nations that have acted as a single nation, with a few exceptions, since well before the arrival of Europeans in North America. Though the term "Iroquois Confederacy" usually refers to a specific political arrangement reached in the late seventeenth century, here it refers both to that political entity and to the League of the Iroquois, a cultural association between the various members.

The Mohawk, Seneca, Cayuga, Oneida, and Onondaga nations were the original members. In 1722, Tuscaroras displaced from North Carolina moved north and joined the Confederacy. English colonists commonly referred to the Iroquois Confederacy as the Five Nations or Six Nations. Interestingly, the name "Iro-

In this painting by Frederic Remington, a French explorer addresses a council of Iroquois Indians. Most villages in the Iroquois Confederacy, located in what is now upstate New York, felt they had little choice but to trade heavily in French goods. *(Museum of Fine Arts, Houston, Texas/Hogg Brothers Collection, Gift of Miss Ima Hogg/Bridgeman Art Library)*

quois" is derived from an Algonquian word meaning "real adders." The people of the Iroquois Confederacy call themselves, as they did in the colonial period, Haudenosaunee, or "people of the longhouse."

Legendary Beginnings

Modern anthropologists trace the roots of the Iroquois Confederacy to the late fifteenth century; some Iroquois oral traditions place the founding several centuries earlier. In any event, the Iroquois Confederacy predates English and French expansion into North America and likely the first tentative Spanish and Portuguese explorations of the Americas as well. Since the alliance predates written records of colonization, it is necessary to rely on Iroquois legends to discern its origins.

Early stories often refer to the Iroquois Confederacy as the "Great League of Peace and Power." In this conceptualization, power and peace were broadly defined. Power referred to both the spiritual and secular power that came from joining clans and villages together in alliances. Similarly, peace was not only the

peace among the Five Nations of the Confederacy; it was the way people and villages should deal with each other. When it came to dealing with outsiders, whether Native American or European, peace often seemed a secondary objective. Demonstration of the league's power usually took precedence.

At some time in the distant past, perhaps during the fifteenth century, all of the Iroquois were at war, both internally and externally, with devastating results for all those concerned. Hiawatha, a former Onondaga chief, lost all of his daughters to the fighting; this awful series of events drove him mad and caused him to abandon village life for the forest. In the forest, he encountered a supernatural being, Deganawidah, the Peacemaker. Deganawidah showed Hiawatha how to mourn properly by performing the first condolence ceremony, a practice that would ease his suffering. The condolence ceremony was the center of the Gospel of Peace and Power, which Deganawidah wanted Hiawatha to spread throughout Iroquois country. If the people accepted Deganawidah's teachings, violence would become unnecessary.

The people did not accept the gospel immediately. One major stumbling block was the opposition of Tadodaho, an Onondaga war chief and sorcerer. He was known as an extremely violent man; his rage had made him insane and, it was said, twisted snakes into his hair. Deganawidah, Hiawatha, and a coalition of Mohawks, Oneidas, Cayugas, and Senecas combed his hair and gave him words of condolence. This calmed Tadodaho, and his opposition faded. Another version of the story has Deganawidah and Hiawatha offering Tadodaho the leadership of the combined Five Nations, and a female chief bestowing the honor upon him. Tadodaho and Hiawatha joined other disciples of the Gospel of Peace and Power and spread Deganawidah's message throughout Iroquois country. Reciting the Deganawidah epic in its entirety or performing a proper condolence ceremony is no small undertaking. Each can last several days.

It is important to note that the Gospel of Peace and Power was not the special reserve of the Iroquois Confederacy. Indeed, the gospel formed the basis for diplomatic negotiations and trade talks with other Native Americans and Europeans. Strict rules governed how these meetings took place. Reciprocity and persuasion were valued above coercion and brashness. Reciprocity was crucial in many Iroquois relationships, whether in village society or in tribal or national politics.

The arrival of Europeans in Iroquois country brought two significant changes. The first was a group of new technologies, which both improved the range of available gifts and increased the deadliness of war. The second was disease, which killed thousands of Iroquois. The Iroquois Confederacy found it increasingly difficult to balance the desire for peace with the imperatives for war (to punish poor or unequal gifting and offer condolence to the relatives of the dead) as they met Europeans.

Covenant Chain

Relations between the Five Nations and their neighbors had, like many others, seen periods of both peace and war. The new pressures exerted on the Five Nations by the arrival of Europeans took their toll, though, and in the middle of the seventeenth century, the Five Nations undertook a series of military campaigns against adjacent Native American communities. Economic motives, particularly the search for furs, can only partially explain the ferocity with which the Iroquois lashed out between 1630 and 1660. The Beaver War between the Huron and the Five Nations in the early 1650s sheds some light on the subject.

When the Five Nations swept through the depleted Huron country, they captured or killed every band of Hurons they could find, whether the Huron had furs or not. It is likely that the Five Nations were seeking to restore the balance upset by the overwhelming numbers of dead. Captive taking was as important as, if not more important than, economics, as far as the motivation to go to war was concerned.

The Iroquois relationship with Europeans began with the establishment of trading relations with the Dutch in New Netherland. In the 1610s, the Iroquois Confederacy began to acquire trade goods from the Dutch in exchange for beaver pelts. The exchange had relatively little impact on either party at first. The Five Nations extended their winter hunting season slightly, perhaps, and worked new materials into their preexisting arts and crafts. Relations during this early period developed along reciprocal lines that would have been familiar to the Five Nations. Trade and peaceful relations went hand in hand, just as they did between the members of the Iroquois Confederacy. The Five Nations also placed great importance on maintaining trade relations with the same person. For instance, when Jacob Eelckens, a Dutch trader, fell out of favor with colonial authorities and was forced to leave the colony in 1623, the Five Nations's relations with the Dutch began to sour. In later decades, war and inflation further weakened the Iroquois Confederacy's relationship with the Dutch.

The Iroquois Confederacy's interaction with the French began on somewhat shaky footing. The first direct contact between the Confederacy and the French was in 1609, when a Mohawk military expedition fought Samuel de Champlain. Fifteen years of intermittent warfare ensued. The Iroquois and France reached a peace agreement in 1624, but the treaty did not last long. A more lasting peace came in 1665–1667, and it brought with it a new wrinkle in the relationship between the French and the Iroquois Confederacy.

Jesuit priests inundated Iroquois territory; some villages received them openly, some were more hostile, and many were ambivalent. The varying degrees of hospitality prefigured intravillage conflict over the acceptance of the newcomers. The brand of Christianity preached by Jesuits had little in common with the principles of Deganawidah's Gospel of Peace and Power, but, compared to Puritan missionaries, the Jesuits were willing to meet the Five Nations halfway.

Iroquois Catholicism in the seventeenth century was a syncretic faith with roots in older non-Western traditions. Many men and women of the Iroquois Confederacy left to join mission communities such as the one at Kahnawake.

Most villages in the Iroquois Confederacy, whether or not they became primarily Catholic, did recognize their need for European trade goods, which in the 1660s and 1670s were usually supplied by the French. They may have not approved of their increasing dependence on French trade, but they had little choice in the matter.

In the 1670s, however, relief appeared in the form of a new English political entity, New York, which had been taken from the Dutch in the 1660s. The English were more than willing to work with anti-French factions in Iroquois country. The Iroquois Confederacy was also positioned to play a pivotal role in two of the major conflicts of English colonial America, King Philip's War (1675–1676) and Bacon's Rebellion (1676). Mohawks aided the English against their Algonquin enemies by attacking Philip's winter camp. Around the same time, Susquehannock refugees from Bacon's Rebellion in Virginia moved into Iroquois country.

The Iroquois Confederacy emerged at the end of the seventeenth century as the preeminent Native American nation in the region. It had gained new trade partnerships with the English and swelled its ranks with former Mahican and Algonquin enemies. During this period, Governor Andros of New York began to establish a series of ties with local Native American communities, known as the Covenant Chain. The Iroquois Confederacy was the crucial link in the chain, and the alliance served it well; in the 1670s, its borders were well defended and it had easy access to English trade goods. The Covenant Chain also inspired, or at least allowed for, attacks on the French and their allied Native Americans.

The Covenant Chain itself revolved around an intricate series of rituals that bound Iroquois to English in the same way that the League of Peace and Power bound Mohawk to Onondaga. The reciprocal language and rites associated with the Covenant Chain reinforced the bond in both Iroquois and English minds. Just as Onondaga was the seat of the Confederacy, Albany was the seat of the Covenant Chain. New Yorkers and Iroquois offered condolences to each other and exchanged gifts.

Invigorated by the development of the relationship with the English, the Iroquois Confederacy chased most of the Jesuits from their territory. The Confederacy also embarked on a new series of wars, both for captives and for furs. These new wars took Iroquois warriors far from home and increased both their reputation as fierce fighters and the hatred of them among tribes such as the Illinois, Miami, Ojibwe, and Fox. They also ranged into the Carolinas in their never-ending search for pelts and captives.

During the 1684 peace talks, some Iroquois began to resent the presence of both Anglophile and Francophile factions within the Confederacy. This group, the neutralists, tried to convince the various members of the Five Nations that they relied too heavily on Europeans; they should take care of their own needs. During the 1680s, even through a war with France beginning in 1687, all three factions—those for the French, those for the English, and those for Iroquois independence—were present, though the Anglophiles and neutralists were the strongest. In the 1690s, though, the political winds shifted again when France invaded Iroquois country. The Iroquois Confederacy suffered a number of serious defeats. These, combined with a smallpox epidemic, led to a resurgence of the movement to make peace with the French. Both French and English authorities seized on the opportunity to try to win over the Iroquois Confederacy, which, although weakened, could still prove a valuable ally and source of furs.

Neutralists, under the banner of the great orator Teganissorens, used the opportunity to advance their case. They recognized that the Confederacy would likely remain dependent on European trade goods, whether French or English. Their main goal was to slow the tide of cultural and political dependence, to avoid entangling alliances with either European power.

The first decade of the 1700s severely tested the Iroquois Confederacy. All three factions vied for the soul of the Confederacy, and eventually the neutralists won. Although their victory was in part due to the war-weariness of France and England, it allowed the Iroquois Confederacy to play the two colonial powers off each other in an effort to build a lasting peace. The French and English both disregarded the Confederacy's guiding principle of reciprocity; however, their nearly equal levels of strength allowed the Iroquois to regroup.

England and France fought a series of wars in North America in the first half of the eighteenth century, but none of them required a significant revision of the policy of Confederacy neutrality. The French and Indian War, known in Europe as the Seven Years' War, would change all of that. The Iroquois Confederacy remained neutral in the early years of the war but eventually was won over to the English side. The practice of playing the English and French off each other, which had served the Confederacy so well, became less and less of an option. The English began paying Mohawk warriors handsomely for their services; the Mohawks had also developed close ties to Sir William Johnson, the British superintendent of northern Native Americans, who had married a Mohawk woman. Perhaps the most decisive factor was that the English had begun to win the war. Iroquois leaders examined the political situation, and decided to back the English.

The American Revolution and Beyond

The American Revolution presented a similar challenge to the Iroquois Confederacy, but the end results were more damaging. Religious divisions, between Mohawks who were members of the Church of England and Oneidas who were Congregationalists with ties to Boston, forced a split in the Confederacy. Most of the Six Nations followed the lead of the Mohawk chief Joseph Brant in siding with the British. The Oneida and Tuscarora sided with the Americans.

In the wake of the surprising American victory in 1783, it made little difference which side various Native American communities had chosen. The new American national government had no role for Native Americans; however, the Iroquois Confederacy is sometimes given credit for influencing American representative government and the Constitution of 1787.

Whether American governmental leaders knew about the intricacies of the Iroquois Confederacy or not would be difficult to prove. In any event, the Confederacy continues to meet today. The Grand River Council in Canada is the primary Iroquois body that deals with the Canadian government, and the Grand Council at Onondaga performs a similar function for Six Nations people in the United States. The Iroquois Confederacy has survived in some form for 500 or more years, and it has allowed Six Nations people to retain their distinct identity in the face of great adversity.

Matthew Jennings

See also: Cayuga; Mohawk; Native American–European Conflict; Native American–European Relations; Native Americans; Oneida; Onondaga; Seneca; Tuscarora; Tuscarora War. *Document:* The Constitution of the Iroquois Nations (c. 1570).

Bibliography

Jennings, Francis. *The Ambiguous Iroquois Empire: The Covenant Chain Confederation of Indian Tribes with English Colonies from Its Beginnings to the Lancaster Treaty of 1744.* New York: W. W. Norton, 1984.

Mohawk, John C. "Iroquois Confederacy." In *Encyclopedia of North American Indians,* edited by Frederick E. Hoxie, 298–302. New York: Houghton Mifflin, 1996.

Morgan, Lewis Henry. *League of the Ho-Dé-No-Sau-Nee or Iroquois.* 1851. Reprint, New York: Dodd, Mead, 1904.

Richter, Daniel K. *The Ordeal of the Longhouse: The Peoples of the Iroquois League in the Era of European Colonization.* Chapel Hill: University of North Carolina Press, 1992.

Isabella, Queen

See Ferdinand and Isabella

Jamaica

Colonial rule of Jamaica began under the Spanish when Christopher Columbus discovered the island on his second voyage in 1494. Arawak Indians, the original inhabitants of the island, gave Columbus a hostile reception, but they soon began to trade fresh provisions for Spanish trinkets.

Following its initial discovery by Columbus, Jamaica remained under Spanish control for the next 150 years. Spain introduced pigs, goats, cattle, various citrus fruits, bananas, and plantains to the island.

Spanish hopes for gold were never realized in Jamaica, and, consequently, the Spanish government took little interest in the island. The Spanish governor of Jamaica ruled fairly independently of the Spanish Crown. Toward the end of Spanish rule, this independence fostered financial and governmental ineptitude, creating violent conflicts between the governor and the Catholic Church, weakening the colony at an inopportune time.

On May 10, 1655, an English fleet under the command of Admiral William Penn accompanied by an army of 2,500 men under General Robert Venables appeared in what is now Kingston Harbor, on the southeastern coast of Jamaica. Penn and Venable's primary mission from the lord protector, Oliver Cromwell, had been to wrest control of Hispaniola from the Spanish. Having failed miserably in that operation, they turned their sights on Jamaica, where only 1,500 Spanish lived. This mission, a part of Cromwell's "Western Design," was an attempt to disrupt Spanish commercial control of the West Indies and establish strategic English military and commercial outposts in the region.

The Spanish settlers on Jamaica offered little resistance. They buried their treasures, stripped the capital, St. Jago de la Vega, of any valuables, and scattered northward into the interior of the island. Reluctantly, Spain ceded Jamaica to England in 1655.

The last half of the seventeenth century saw the initial formation of colonial government, commercial development, and slave culture in Jamaica, which set the foundations for its tremendous economic growth in the eighteenth century. Political institutions were similar to those in other British colonies. A royal governor ruled alongside an elected assembly of landed or commercial elite, which fashioned laws in accordance with the island's needs.

Trade under the Spanish had developed poorly and was limited to only limited raw materials, such as mahogany, animal hides, and animal grease. English settlers and government officials quickly realized the potential of Jamaica to produce export crops, although early attempts to cultivate cash crops such as tobacco, indigo, and cocoa proved unsuccessful. In contrast, sugar plantations, following the Barbadian model, enjoyed early and long-lasting success. Sugar soon became Jamaica's chief product, with exports to England and Ireland growing from 1,154 tons in 1676, to 4,874 tons in 1700, and in excess of 17,000 tons in 1748, with sugar produced by over 600 plantations by 1750.

Large-scale sugar production required a large labor force. Arawaks were no longer available, having been completely eliminated under Spanish rule through slavery and disease. Attempts at utilizing indentured servants from England proved inadequate. Spain had introduced chattel slavery of Africans to the island, and the dramatic development of sugar plantations by the English in the last half of the sixteenth century encouraged the further development of the slave trade.

Jamaica soon became a center for the Atlantic slave trade. Between 1702 and 1808, at least 830,857 slaves were imported into Jamaica, with perhaps 194,287 reexported to other British, Spanish, or French colonies. For most of the eighteenth century, there were at least ten slaves for every free white in Jamaica. Given

The port towns of Jamaica were prominent in the Atlantic sugar and slave trade during the seventeenth century. Port Royal was the preeminent merchant and shipping center until its destruction in the great earthquake of June 7, 1692. *(British Library, London, United Kingdom/Bridgeman Art Library)*

of Jamaica reflected its growing importance as a center of Atlantic trade in sugar and slaves. Port Royal was the principal mercantile and shipping center until its destruction in an earthquake in 1692. Kingston was established in 1693, and, during the eighteenth century, it was the island's chief port and largest city (the third largest city in British America). St. Jago de la Vega (or Spanish Town) remained the island's capital and principal administrative center.

As the island was settled and planters desired ports closer to their plantations, other harbors grew in importance. Montego Bay, Savannah La Mar, and Port Antonio joined Kingston as free ports in 1758, and these became key centers of commerce during the colonial period.

Douglas Mann

See also: Caribbean (Chronology); Slavery, Caribbean; Sugar.

Bibliography

Black, Clinton. *Story of Jamaica from Prehistory to the Present.* London: Collins, 1965.

Dunn, Richard. *Sugar and Slaves, The Rise of the Planter Class in the English West Indies, 1624–1713.* Chapel Hill: University of North Carolina Press, 1972.

the imbalance between free whites and African slaves, and the inherent brutality of chattel slavery, it's no surprise that slaves often attempted to rebel. Major, though unsuccessful, uprisings of this period include the Maroon Wars (1725–1739; 1795–1797) and Tacky's Revolt (1760).

Because Jamaica devoted its agriculture to the production of sugar, it needed to import its material and staple goods from England and colonial North America. Prior to the American Revolution, Jamaica enjoyed a close commercial relationship with the North American colonies. Receiving mostly sugar and rum from Jamaica, colonial North American merchants supplied the island with fish, corn, rice, other necessary foodstuffs, and wood products. The American Revolution severed these relationships, and supplies from England became more expensive. This, coupled with the drop in sugar prices, caused a financial decline in Jamaica.

During the colonial period, the principal towns

James I (1566–1625)

Born June 19, 1566, in Edinburgh Castle, James I was the only son of Mary Stuart, Queen of Scotland, and Lord Henry Darnley, her second husband. When Mary fled the county after Darnley's death and her third marriage to James Hepburn, Earl Bothwell, the nobles of Scotland proclaimed the year-old child as James VI of Scotland.

Raised as a Presbyterian by a clique of John Knox supporters, the young king deeply resented his manipulation by powerful nobles and the Scottish kirk, and he asserted his independence upon gaining his legal majority. Married to Anne of Denmark in 1589, James VI had three children by 1600, making him an even more attractive heir to the English throne of Elizabeth I, which he inherited upon her death on March 24, 1603.

Now King James I of Great Britain, he moved south to London, where he confounded the expectations of his new subjects. Calvinist Protestants expected his support, as did Catholics, who looked to his wife Anne, a Catholic convert. Instead, James I wholeheartedly

The first Stuart king of England, James I granted the Virginia Company a charter for the Jamestown settlement in 1606, encouraged disgruntled Puritans to join the Plymouth Colony, and ordered the execution of Sir Walter Raleigh in 1618. *(Brown Brothers, Sterling, Pennsylvania)*

supported the Church of England. He issued the Book of Sports, a declaration that recreational activities were acceptable on the Sabbath, which infuriated English Puritans, and commissioned the so-called King James translation of the Bible (1611), an edition that was strongly nationalistic and orthodox. James I turned completely away from Catholic supporters after the failed 1605 plot by Guy Fawkes to assassinate the king and his family at the opening of Parliament with a huge gunpowder explosion.

Ignoring the demands of Parliament to support Protestants in Europe, James I chose to make peace with Spain, a move that allowed him to develop England's American colonies. Under his rule, the Virginia Company gained a charter for the settlement at Jamestown, and he encouraged dissatisfied Puritans to join the Plymouth Colony. Although he personally loathed tobacco and published a pamphlet against it, James I nevertheless supported the Virginia Company's efforts to expand and recruit more settlers to grow this crop.

Parliament clashed continually with James I over his refusal to enter the Thirty Years' War in Europe, even to save his son-in-law Frederick V of the Palatinate. James I was even willing to execute Elizabeth's favorite, Sir Walter Raleigh, for antagonizing Spanish colonies in South America, an act that many Englishmen saw as a betrayal of the nation's maritime accomplishments.

Although he made important attempts to modernize the British monarchy, James I was often compared unfairly to Elizabeth I, who had left her successor a larger-than-life-image and huge debts to contend with. In 1610, unable and unwilling to live on and run his administration from the monarch's private income, James I proposed that Parliament guarantee him an income of tax revenue in return for his giving up disliked royal prerogatives, like the granting of monopolies and single-item customs revenue. When Parliament refused, James I raised money by creating the title of baronet and selling it to ambitious gentry families.

James I was particularly attracted to the idea of divine-right kingship, and he wrote a treatise on it for the instruction of his son. The king used his own funds to establish London as a Renaissance court, patronizing European artists and supporting William Shakespeare, who wrote *Macbeth* in tribute.

In his later years, James I suffered increasingly from porphyria, a hereditary and painful chemical imbalance, and overindulged in food and drink, often to disgusting excess. Having done his duty and provided an heir, James I, who was by preference homosexual, favored a series of male courtiers, culminating in the creation of George Villiers as Duke of Buckingham in 1623.

Despite his unpopularity at the time of his death, James I had personally united England and Scotland, prevented English colonies from becoming targets in a Catholic-Protestant European conflict, attempted to reform medieval royal finance, and promoted Britain as a cultural center of the Northern Renaissance. Mocked as "the wisest fool in Christendom," James I died at Theobald's Park, Hertfordshire, on March 27, 1625.

Margaret Sankey

See also: Bible; Politics and Government (Chronology); Politics and Government (Essay); Virginia Company.

Bibliography

Croft, J. Pauline. *King James*. New York: Palgrave, 2003.

Lee, Maurice. *Great Britain's Solomon*. Urbana: University of Illinois Press, 1990.

McElwee, William Lloyd. *Wisest Fool in Christendom*. Westport, CT: Greenwood, 1974.

James II (1633–1701)

Born October 14, 1633, at St. James's Palace, James II was the second surviving son of Charles I of Great Britain and his wife Henrietta Maria of France. A child during the English Civil War, James went into exile after his father's execution and spent the years before the Restoration training with the armies of France and Spain.

At the court of his sister, Mary Stuart, Princess of Orange, he contracted a 1659 secret marriage with her English lady-in-waiting, Anne Hyde, by whom he had two daughters, Mary and Anne. In 1660, his brother, Charles II, was restored to the British throne and brought James back with him as Duke of York and Lord High Admiral.

In these positions, James took a keen interest in the navy, founding a naval library and instituting the policy of part-time officers on half-pay as an efficiency measure. He was also deeply involved in colonization, acting as the head of numerous private trading companies, including the Hudson's Bay Company, Royal African Company (whose primary business was selling slaves from West Africa), and Scotland's Royal Adventurers Trading into Africa. He frequently used royal resources to protect and advance his private fortune. At James's urgings, Charles II ordered the seizure of New Amsterdam during his wars with the Dutch, turning the colony, renamed New York, over to James as sole proprietor in 1664.

James and Anne Hyde alarmed Charles II and the nation by announcing their conversion to Roman Catholicism in 1669, sparking a political firestorm. Three parliaments attempted to exclude James from the succession to the throne, but they failed because of Charles II's skillful political manipulation. Deeply unpopular because of his beliefs, James went into exile in the Netherlands and then into a lower-profile job as High Commissioner of Scotland from 1679–1682. After the death of Anne Hyde, James married Italian Catholic princess Maria Beatrice d'Este in 1673, further agitating anti-Catholic feelings.

Upon the death of Charles II, who died without a legitimate heir, James II became king on February 6, 1685. His political opponents accepted his accession, expecting him to have a short reign and be succeeded by one of his Protestant daughters. Instead, James II embarked on an alarming program, including a Declaration of Indulgence, allowing dissenting Protestants (including Quakers like his friend William Penn) and Roman Catholics to hold offices and commissions in the army and navy. He also installed Catholics in local governments and in the universities at Oxford and Cambridge.

When these actions ignited a revolt led by Charles II's illegitimate son, the Duke of Monmouth, James II had the insurrection put down brutally. He allowed Judge George Jeffreys to punish the rebels with death sentences and transportations to the Caribbean, penalties widely seen as excessive and tyrannical.

In enforcing his edicts, James II arrested and tried seven Church of England prelates who refused to read the Declaration of Toleration from the pulpit. In the colonies, James II installed Sir Edmund Andros as governor of a combined Dominion of New England, after voiding the charters of Connecticut, Massachusetts, New Jersey, and Rhode Island. He also made the colonists suspicious that he intended to work with Catholic France.

Events came to a head in June 1688 when Maria Beatrice gave birth to a living son. James II's enemies could no longer expect him to pass the throne to his daughters and made the momentous decision to send for his son-in-law, William of Orange for help. The army defected to William when he arrived in Torbay, England, and James II fled London for exile in France in December 1688. James II insisted that he never vacated the throne, but he was considered to have abdicated, and Parliament replaced him with his elder daughter Mary and her husband William III.

With aid from Louis XIV of France, James II invaded Ireland in an attempt to regain his throne in 1689–1690. He was defeated at the Battle of the Boyne by William III and returned to exile at St. Germain, where he and Maria Beatrice raised their son James and a daughter, Louisa Maria.

After James II died on September 6, 1701, his son and his grandson (also named James) would launch repeated attempts to regain the British throne—most notably, rebellions in 1715, 1719, and 1745. They led a movement named for him, Jacobitism, after the Latin version of James, Jacobus.

Margaret Sankey

See also: Glorious Revolution; Politics and Government (Chronology); Politics and Government (Essay).

Bibliography

Callow, John. *Making of James II: The Formative Years of a Fallen King.* Thrupp, Stroud, UK: Sutton, 2000.

Miller, John. *James II.* New Haven, CT: Yale University Press, 2000.

Webb, Stephen Saunders. *Lord Churchill's Coup.* New York: Alfred A. Knopf, 1995.

Jamestown

In 1606, a group of English gentry, merchants, and adventurers formed the Virginia Company of London and petitioned King James I to grant them permission to establish a colony in North America. In December of that year, 144 Englishmen boarded the *Susan Constant, Discovery,* and *Godspeed* and began the long journey to the New World.

The colonists arrived in the Chesapeake Bay in April 1607. Three weeks later, in May 1607, they landed on a small peninsula 60 miles up the James River from the coast and immediately began constructing a fort. They named their settlement Jamestown.

A Hostile Environment

The early settlers at Jamestown did not fare well. The voyage from England alone claimed thirty-nine lives. Once they landed, the colonists faced attack from the native peoples, who viewed them with a combination of suspicion and fear. The English settlers and the natives, who were led by their chief Powhatan, skirmished repeatedly throughout May and June 1607. The settlers' situation was made more precarious by disease, which, by September, had claimed an additional fifty lives.

Distracted by the attacks of hostile natives, disease, and their own bickering and plotting, the settlers failed to cultivate the crops necessary to sustain them through the winter. They would have faced certain death had Powhatan and his people not come to their aid in the autumn of 1607. The Native Americans brought corn to Jamestown, which they traded for axes, swords, pots, and other goods. They also allowed Captain John Smith to travel upriver to trade. Even with this help, only thirty-eight settlers survived their first year at Jamestown.

Despite extreme hardship brought on at least in part by their own negligence, the settlers at Jamestown

The fort at Jamestown, the first permanent English settlement in America, is depicted in this artist's rendition. Excavations on the island—including part of the original fort uncovered in 1996—have enabled researchers to trace and reconstruct a number of buildings at the settlement site. *(Courtesy of APVA Preservation Virginia)*

endured. An English ship carrying a fresh food supply and 120 additional colonists arrived in January 1608. By fall 1609, there were 500 colonists living in Jamestown. That would change, however, by spring 1610. Rather than fend for themselves, the colonists had decided early on to obtain the bulk of their corn from the Native Americans and to rely upon England for the rest of their supplies. Although the forests and rivers abounded with game, fish, and waterfowl, the settlers again failed to store enough food for the winter. Many colonists starved, and others resorted to cannibalism, theft, and desertion to stay alive.

When Lieutenant Governor Thomas Gates and 175 new colonists arrived in Jamestown in June 1610, they encountered sixty weary settlers and a severely depleted food supply. Gates and the remaining settlers were preparing to abandon Jamestown for good, when the colony's new governor, Thomas West, baron de la Warr, came sailing up the James River with 300 additional setters.

Despite their experience during the brutal winter of 1609–1610, the colonists still remained reluctant to plant crops. When yet another governor, Sir Thomas Dale, arrived in the colony in May 1611, he found that nothing had been planted except for a few private gardens. Instead, settlers spent their time bowling in the streets and raiding and destroying nearby Native American villages. It became evident early in these first years of Jamestown's settlement that colonists were both unable and unwilling to produce the food necessary for survival.

A number of factors contributed to the colonists' lack of productivity. Many settlers were simply too sick to work. Virginia's warm, moist climate and the unsanitary condition of the fresh water in and around Jamestown provided a breeding ground for deadly diseases such as dysentery, typhoid fever, and malaria. The settlement was also plagued with a lack of organization and discipline, which stemmed largely from the social position of the colony's settlers. An odd combination of English gentlemen and their servants had migrated to Jamestown to make their fortune, and neither group was willing to sacrifice for the common good of the community. Both gentlemen and servants also lacked many of the skills necessary for survival.

In 1609, the king placed complete control of the colony in the hands of a local governor named Thomas West, appointed by the London Company, who, although assisted by a council, would act more like a military commander than a governor. A series of harsh laws, known as the "Lawes Divine, Morall, and Martiall," were also instituted. Neither measure proved overly effective. Jamestown continued to flirt dangerously with its own demise for the next twelve years.

Tobacco, Native Americans, and a Royal Colony

Life for Jamestown settlers improved somewhat when John Rolfe imported a mild strain of tobacco from the West Indies into the colony in 1613. Gentlemen and servants alike had found the treasure for which they had been looking. Tobacco grown in Virginia brought such a good price in England that settlers began growing it in the Jamestown streets. By 1619, Jamestown had exported 10 tons of tobacco to Europe and was becoming something of a boomtown.

Organizational changes made by the London Company also made life more tolerable for colonists. In 1612, in an effort to minimize risk, raise capital, and increase migration to Virginia, the London Company issued a new charter that declared it a joint-stock company. By 1619, the company had replaced martial law in the colony with English common law and formed the House of Burgesses, a representative assembly elected by the colony's inhabitants.

In the 1610s, the company began to allow settlers to own land. Under the new headright system, a colonist would receive 50 acres of land for each person whose passage to Virginia he financed. A flood of newcomers poured into Jamestown and the surrounding wilderness, placing a tremendous strain on the already fragile settlement.

Faced with a dwindling local food supply and disintegrating relations with the colonists, the native chief Opechancanough, who had succeeded his brother Powhatan upon his death in 1618, led an attack against Jamestown in March 1622. The Native Americans killed 347 settlers, nearly one-third of the total population, and completely destroyed most of the smaller outlying settlements.

The attack failed to oust the colonists from Jamestown, but it succeeded in gaining the attention of the king, who launched a royal investigation into the affairs of the London Company. Among other things, investigators found that disease and gross mismanagement, not Native American raids, was the primary cause of the extremely high mortality rate in Jamestown.

In 1624, with only 1,200 settlers still alive out of the 6,000 sent over since 1607, King James I revoked the London Company's charter and made Virginia a royal colony. The king allowed Jamestown's House of Burgesses to remain intact. All new laws, however, had to be cleared by the king's bureaucrats. The king also had the power to appoint Virginia's royal governor, and Virginia would remain a royal colony until 1776.

Bacon's Rebellion and the End of Jamestown

By 1619, the Jamestown export business was going so well that colonists were able to afford to import two new groups that dramatically affected life in Virginia: African servants and women. Settlers indentured twenty Africans from a Dutch trading vessel passing through Chesapeake Bay in 1619. They also financed the passage of ninety women from England. In all, about 1,000 new settlers, most of them white male servants from England, came to Jamestown each year between 1622 and 1640. The population grew to 5,200 by 1634 and 8,100 by 1640. Despite a continuing high death rate, a steady stream of newcomers enabled Jamestown to survive.

By 1639, tobacco had become the colonies' chief export, with Jamestown alone exporting 750 tons of tobacco. The same year, residents constructed their first brick church, and, in 1642, Sir William Berkeley became governor of Virginia. Until 1660, many former servants, white and black, managed to acquire land. Some former servants even served on county courts and in the House of Burgesses. But by 1665, tobacco overproduction had led to a drop in price to one penny per pound, and upward mobility became increasingly difficult. The richest 15 percent of settlers, who, because of the headright system had always had a distinct advantage over other settlers, acquired much of the social and political power in Virginia.

Many newcomers, such as Nathaniel Bacon, felt as though they were being systematically excluded from politics, as well as valuable trade opportunities. When Bacon arrived in Virginia in 1674, he managed to get himself appointed to the Governor's Council, in part because he was Governor Berkeley's cousin by marriage, but Bacon had been excluded from the valuable fur trade on Virginia's western frontier. To Bacon and other newcomers, Berkeley's decision to restrict the fur trade to all but a few of his closest associates looked like favoritism.

Berkeley's decision not to attack Native Americans on the frontier, some of whom were hostile, also angered Bacon and other newcomers, who were forced to live on the western edge of English settlement. Ignoring Berkeley's orders, Bacon gathered a group of frontiersmen and indiscriminately slaughtered numerous Native Americans, then turned on Governor Berkeley and his inner circle in Jamestown. In September 1676, following several confrontations with local Native Americans and with Governor Berkeley, Bacon and his followers marched on Jamestown and burned it to the ground. Bacon died of dysentery in October 1676, and his rebellion quickly collapsed.

Jamestown, which had also lost its status as the mandatory port of entry for Virginia in 1662, never fully recovered from Bacon's Rebellion. In 1699, Virginians abandoned Jamestown for good and moved their capital to Williamsburg.

Michael A. Rembis

See also: Pocahontas; Powhatan; Powhatan Confederacy; Rolfe, John; Smith, John; Tobacco; Virginia; Virginia (Chronology); Virginia Company. *Document:* The Jamestown Settlement (1607–1609).

Bibliography

Billings, Warren M., John E. Selby, and Thad W. Tate. *Colonial Virginia: A History.* White Plains, NY: KTO, 1986.

Bridenbaugh, Carl. *Jamestown, 1544–1699.* New York: Oxford University Press, 1980.

Geiter, Mary K., and William A. Speck. *Colonial America: From Jamestown to Yorktown.* New York: Palgrave Macmillan, 2002.

Horn, James. *Adapting to a New World: English Society in the Seventeenth-Century Chesapeake.* Chapel Hill: University of North Carolina Press, 1994.

Morgan, Edmund S. *American Slavery, American Freedom: The Ordeal of Colonial Virginia.* New York: W. W. Norton, 1975.

Rountree, Helen C., and E. Randolph Turner III. *Before and After Jamestown: Virginia's Powhatans and Their Predecessors.* Gainesville: University Press of Florida, 2002.

Jay, John (1745–1829)

John Jay, one of the best legal minds in colonial New York, became a reluctant supporter of the Revolutionary cause. A conservative Anglophile, he liked the law and order established by Great Britain. As one of New York's delegates to the First Continental Congress, he opposed moves toward resistance and war.

Jay was born in New York City on December 12, 1745, to Peter Jay, a prosperous merchant, and Mary

Van Cortlandt, a member of one of the great Dutch patroon, landed families of the Hudson River Valley. Family ties, particularly to his French Huguenot grandfather, played a major role in shaping Jay's political beliefs.

The Huguenots were Protestants, who challenged the authority of the Catholic Church. By doing so, they inadvertently challenged royal authority, since the French church and French monarchy supported each other. For attacking the rights of kings, Jay's grandfather was imprisoned in the fortress at St. Malo. He escaped and fled by ship to America. As a consequence, Jay was a pious Protestant who distrusted both the Catholic Church and the French nation that had persecuted his forebear. The Jay and Van Cortlandt families would be among the minority of New York aristocrats who sided with the Whigs during the Revolutionary War.

Jay's elite family also influenced his choice of a profession. After graduating from King's College (now Columbia University) in 1764, Jay settled immediately upon the elite profession of law. He next managed to find a rare apprenticeship at a time when the lawyers

A lawyer and Anglophile from New York, John Jay became a reluctant but staunch supporter of the Revolutionary cause, an accomplished foreign diplomat, and the first chief justice of the United States (1789–1795). *(Brown Brothers, Sterling, Pennsylvania)*

in the province were trying, with considerable success, to restrict the numbers of entrants into the legal field to protect the livelihoods of those already admitted to the bar. In 1764, Jay became a law clerk in the office of Benjamin Kissam, a prominent Tory. As a clerk, Jay mastered the techniques of draftsmanship, pleading, and legal research. After completing four years of this apprenticeship, he was admitted to the New York bar in 1768.

Jay enjoyed a successful law practice, earning about 1,000 pounds annually in the years before the Revolution. He attempted, without success, to obtain a position as a jurist in 1772 and 1774. Being on the bench would have provided Jay with increased social and professional status. It would also have meant that he would not have had to work so hard to obtain business, thereby enabling him to spend more time with his wife and family. On April 28, 1774, Jay married Sarah Van Brugh Livingston, a member of another powerful Dutch clan and the daughter of a future governor of New Jersey. The couple, who were known to be very devoted to each other, had seven children.

Jay retired from the active practice of law in 1774. Along with a desire to spend more time at home, he probably found his energies consumed by political demands. In 1774, he was elected to the Committee of Correspondence in New York City. He served as a delegate to both the First Continental Congress in 1774 and the Second Continental Congress in 1775.

Jay drafted the Second Continental Congress's *Address to the People of Great Britain*, justifying the actions of the American Revolutionaries. In the address, he denounced Parliament for claiming the right to tax the colonists without their consent and proclaimed that Americans would "never consent to be hewers of wood or drawers of water."

Described by his contemporaries as being scrupulously honest in fiscal matters, Jay was a stickler for law and order. He feared that independence from Great Britain would be followed by mob rule, and he certainly did not lead the push for revolution. After opposing the Declaration of Independence, however, he chose to support the patriot cause.

His willingness to compromise with enemies made Jay one of the most influential Founding Fathers, and he became president of the Continental Congress in 1778. He joined with Benjamin Franklin in negotiating the peace treaty with Great Britain and later coauthored the *Federalist Papers* with Alexander Hamilton and James Madison. In 1789, Jay became the first chief justice of the Supreme Court.

He may be best known for the unpopular 1794 Jay's Treaty, which failed to guarantee America's rights as a neutral on the high seas (protecting American ships from warring British and French fleets), although it did ensure continued peace with Britain. As governor of New York from 1795 to 1801, Jay was noteworthy for abolishing slavery in the state.

Upon his wife's death in 1801, Jay retired from politics. He returned to his home in Bedford, New York. There, he pursued various intellectual, as well as agricultural, interests, and became president of the American Bible Society. He died at his home on May 17, 1829.

Caryn E. Neumann

See also: Continental Congress, First; Continental Congress, Second; Politics and Government (Chronology); Politics and Government (Essay); Revolutionary War.

Bibliography

Johnson, Herbert A. *John Jay: Colonial Lawyer.* New York: Garland Publishing, 1989.
Smith, Donald L. *John Jay; Founder of a State and Nation.* New York: Teachers College Press, 1968.

Jefferson, Thomas (1743–1826)

Thomas Jefferson was born in Shadwell, Virginia, on April 13, 1743. Jefferson's earliest memory, at the age of 3, was of a 50-mile trek on horseback with a family slave through the Virginia wilderness, as the Jefferson family relocated to a plantation that Peter Jefferson, his father, was to manage. Peter Jefferson became a wealthy planter in his own right, and Jane Randolph Jefferson, Jefferson's mother, held high social standing; both of these parental characteristics would be of benefit to Jefferson's education and career.

From an early age, Jefferson exhibited a keen mind and engaged in self-study by reading books. At the age of 9, he began his formal education with a Scottish minister and teacher, the Reverend William Douglas. Well versed in classical languages, Jefferson enrolled in William and Mary College at the age of 17, where he took classes in science, mathematics, rhetoric, philosophy, and literature.

After college, Jefferson studied law under George Wythe, also a teacher of John Marshall and Henry Clay. Wythe cultivated a love of British liberties in Jefferson, who, after concluding his formal studies, practiced law on the Virginia circuit. While traveling on the circuit, Jefferson met his future wife, Martha Wayles Skelton, a wealthy widow and daughter of a prosperous Virginia lawyer. The two married on January 1, 1772, and lived in Monticello, which was on Jefferson's Virginia plantation. In 1782, however, Martha Jefferson died during the birthing of their sixth child.

Jefferson, a tall and slender man, always stood and walked straight with his shoulders square. He was very formal, bowed to everyone he met, and preferred to be called by his last name. Unlike other gentlemen of his day, however, he never wore a white wig. Instead, he sported his own reddish brown hair. He never claimed affiliation with any organized religion because he was a devout Deist. Jefferson is sometimes regarded as a contradictory man, since he had a great love of liberty yet never freed any of his slaves. Furthermore, in recent years, DNA testing has supported the view that Jefferson fathered several children with Sally Hemings, one of his slaves.

Jefferson loved music, played the violin, and liked to sing. His voice was thin and he never developed into much of a public speaker, but he was always eloquent with his pen. For example, as a member of the Virginia House of Burgesses from 1769 to 1774, he seldom spoke, yet he wrote a pamphlet titled *A Summary View of the Rights of British America* (1774), in which he questioned British colonial policies and supported colonial rights. His pamphlet so impressed other colonials that it gained him a seat in the Second Continental Congress (1775–1776).

In keeping with his shy manner, Jefferson was seldom heard to utter an audible comment in the congressional proceedings; however, his ability to write led John Adams to recommend Jefferson as author of the Declaration of Independence in 1776. In this document, which was greatly influenced by the works of the British philosopher John Locke, Jefferson attempted to justify the colonial point of view in the struggle for independence.

Besides being an effective writer, Jefferson was also an architect, an inventor, and an agriculturalist, and he continued to serve the newly independent United States in various capacities after 1776. During the American Revolution, Jefferson served as governor

Of all his achievements, Thomas Jefferson chose three to be inscribed on his gravestone: "author of the Declaration of American Independence, of the Statute of Virginia for religious freedom, and Father of the University of Virginia." *(Brown Brothers, Sterling, Pennsylvania)*

of Virginia from 1779 to 1781, and he drafted the Statute of Virginia for Religious Freedom, which called for the separation of church and state.

After the war, Jefferson served for a second term in the Continental Congress from 1783 to 1785 and as U.S. minister to France from 1785 to 1789. During President George Washington's first term in office, Washington appointed Jefferson secretary of state in 1790.

From 1797 to 1801, Jefferson served as vice president under President John Adams. During Adams's presidency, the passage of the Alien and Sedition Acts prompted Jefferson to write the Kentucky Resolutions, which emphasized states' rights as found in the U.S. Constitution.

In 1801, Jefferson became the third president of the United States, and he held this office until 1809. As president, he oversaw the acquisition of Louisiana from France, which more than doubled the size of the United States at that time.

After his retirement from politics, Jefferson set up the curriculum, selected the faculty, and designed the buildings for the University of Virginia. Jefferson

died on July 4, 1826, the fiftieth anniversary of the Declaration of Independence.

Rolando Avila

See also: Continental Congress, First; Continental Congress, Second; Politics and Government (Chronology); Politics and Government (Essay); Revolutionary War. *Document:* The Declaration of Independence (1776).

Bibliography

Axelrod, Alan. *The Life and Work of Thomas Jefferson.* Indianapolis, IN: Alpha, 2001.

Bowers, Claude Gernade. *The Young Jefferson, 1743–1789.* Boston: Houghton Mifflin, 1945.

Gordon-Reed, Annette. *Thomas Jefferson and Sally Hemings: An American Controversy.* Charlottesville: University Press of Virginia, 1997.

Miller, John Chester. *The Wolf by the Ears: Thomas Jefferson and Slavery.* New York: Free Press, 1977.

Peterson, Merrill D. *Thomas Jefferson and the New Nation: A Biography.* New York: Oxford University Press, 1970.

Jesuits

The Jesuits are members of the Society of Jesus, a Roman Catholic order founded in 1540 by Ignatius Loyola. As missionaries and educators, the Jesuits participated in the European colonization of the Americas and Asia.

Ignatius Loyola, born in 1491 into a noble Basque family in northern Spain, was trained as a courtier and a soldier. Severely wounded in battle in 1521, Ignatius underwent a lengthy convalescence, during which time he began to read about the lives of the saints. He thus became inspired to give up his soldiering to lead a life in imitation of Christ. As he followed his new calling, he made notes on his spiritual experiences, which he would later incorporate into a handbook to guide others, known as *The Spiritual Exercises.*

Ignatius initially hoped to live in the Holy Land but managed only a brief visit there in 1523–1524. Back in Spain, he decided that to "help souls" he needed a formal education, and so he attended the universities of Alcalá and Salamanca before receiving an M.A. at Paris in 1535. Ignatius gathered about him a small group of like-minded men, who, with the approval of Pope Paul III, were all ordained priests in 1537. Although their continued hope to work in the Holy Land did not materialize, this small company received papal authorization in 1540 as the Society of Jesus. Its members were to carry out various works at the Pope's bidding, including the establishment of foreign missions and the education of the young. Ignatius was elected the first father-general of the order, and, by the time of his death at Rome in 1556, the society had ten provinces—the basic administrative units—and a hundred religious houses. Ignatius Loyola was canonized in 1622.

The Society of Jesus quickly established itself throughout Europe and became part of the Counter-Reformation, the movement to win Protestants back to Catholicism. On their foreign missions, the Jesuits provided pastoral care for Europeans abroad and worked to convert the natives. Portugal was one of the first colonial powers to emerge in the sixteenth century, and King John III in 1540 asked the Pope to send Jesuits to his trading stations in Southeast Asia. One of Ignatius's original companions, Francis Xavier, went to India and set up a major missionary station at Goa, so India became one of the first provinces of the order. Xavier traveled extensively in the region and began a mission in Japan in 1549. In South America, Portugal's colony of Brazil had an organized Jesuit province by 1553, while Spanish America had Jesuit missions in New Granada (Colombia), Chile, Peru, Ecuador, Paraguay, and Mexico (which included California).

In the seventeenth century, France became a colonial power in North America, beginning with the explorations of Samuel de Champlain, who founded the city of Quebec in 1608. From the start, the Jesuits were an important part of the French colonial mission, as they moved from the Atlantic coast down the St. Lawrence River to the Great Lakes, and eventually down the Mississippi. The published record of their encounters with the natives and their explorations, known as *The Jesuit Relations,* became a unique source document for colonial French Canada. As educators, the Jesuits of New France established a college at Quebec in 1635, and they also became known for their work with recording Native American languages. The French-trained Jesuit Jacques Marquette had been working extensively with the Huron, but in 1673 he set off with Louis Jolliet on a voyage of discovery down the Mississippi River. They were the first Europeans to travel and chart the upper Mississippi from Wisconsin to its confluence with the Arkansas River.

England was also an emerging colonial power in the seventeenth century, although the English colonies were Protestant and not open to Jesuit missions. The one exception was the colony of Maryland, granted by King Charles I to the Calvert family, who were Catho-lics. Cecil Calvert arrived in Maryland in 1634, accompanied by five Jesuits who set out on a mission to convert both Protestants and the Native Americans along the Chesapeake Bay and the Potomac River. The Catholic predominance did not last, especially after the firm establishment of a Protestant monarchy in England when the Catholic monarch James II was driven from the throne in 1688. There followed in 1692 penal laws in Maryland against Catholics and Jesuits.

Two more significant events affected the Jesuit presence throughout North America. With Britain's victory over France in the French and Indian War (known as the Seven Years' War in Europe), French Canada and all lands east of the Mississippi River passed to Britain in 1763. The Jesuit missions in these regions could no longer be sustained. Then, in 1773, the papacy officially suppressed the entire Society of Jesus.

In the eighteenth century, the Catholic families of Maryland sent their sons to be educated in Europe. John Carroll was one such young man, and, in 1753, he had entered the Jesuit order while studying abroad. Back home in Maryland, he conducted private services, but he could no longer follow his Jesuit vocation after the 1773 suppression. An active patriot during the Revolution, John Carroll became the first Catholic bishop in the new republic. The Catholic academy he founded in 1789—Georgetown University, in the District of Columbia—became a major Jesuit institution of higher education when the Society of Jesus was restored by the papacy in 1814, a year before John Carroll's death.

Florene S. Memegalos

See also: Catholic Church; Dominicans; Franciscans; Missions; Religion (Chronology); Religion (Essay).

Bibliography

Aveling, J. C. H. *The Jesuits.* New York: Stein and Day, 1982.

O'Malley, John W. *The First Jesuits.* Cambridge, MA: Harvard University Press, 1993.

Thwaites, Reuben Gold, ed. *The Jesuit Relations and Allied Documents: Travels and Explorations of the Jesuit Missionaries in New France, 1610–1791.* 73 vols. Cleveland, OH: Burrows Brothers, 1896–1901.

Jews

In September 1654, the *St. Charles* sailed into the port at New Amsterdam. Twenty-three tired and bedraggled passengers disembarked to establish the first Jewish settlement in colonial America. They arrived penniless, with simply the clothes on their back and a few personal items. Unable to pay the captain of the boat, Jacques la Motte, three of them were held in a form of indentured servitude until the outstanding debt for passage was paid.

These voyagers were widely traveled. Their previous residence had been in what is now the Brazilian city of Recife, in the state of Pernambuco, a former Dutch colony that had been recaptured by the Portuguese in January 1654. These newcomers were only able to remain in Pernambuco a short time under Portugal's watchful eye.

South America was not their first home, for these were Sephardic Jews, whose origins were in the Iberian Peninsula. There had been a thriving Jewish community in Iberia consisting of scholars, professional men, and traders. In 1478, this community was victimized by the persecution inherent in the Spanish Inquisition, which forced Spain's Jews to become either conversos

(Christians) or marranos (nominal converts who continued to secretly observe and preserve their Jewish practices and traditions). With only those two choices, many chose to flee, hence their voyage and settlement in Brazil.

The Jews' home in Pernambuco was more tolerant of their faith but still placed limits on their civic activities. As long as they could practice their religion, however, the only complaint they appeared to have was being unable to serve in the town's defense forces.

When the Portuguese recaptured Pernambuco in 1654, the results were disastrous for the Jewish community. Some residents headed to the homes of friends and relatives in French and English Caribbean colonies, where only light restrictions on religious practice existed. Others went to Dutch outposts, including New Amsterdam.

New Amsterdam was considered a haven even though the governor, Peter Stuyvesant, was neither the epitome of tolerance himself nor a strong proponent of

Dedicated in 1762, Touro Synagogue in Newport, Rhode Island, is the oldest Jewish house of worship in the United States and the only one still surviving from the colonial era. (© *John T. Hopf, Congregation Jeshuat Israel*)

it in general. The Dutch West India Company pressured him to give Jews the right to "travel and trade to and in New Netherland and live and remain there, provided the poor among them shall . . . be supported by their own nation."

At times, Stuyvesant refused to acquiesce. For instance, in 1655, he denied Salvador Dandrada, Jacob Cohen, and several other Jews the right to trade at Fort Orange and along the Delaware River, areas where gentile merchants were allowed exclusive trade rights. Stuyvesant further exacerbated the situation when he refused Dandrada's application for the right to purchase a home in the city.

In response, New Amsterdam's Jewish community sought aid from their friends in old Amsterdam, who sent orders the next year forcing Stuyvesant to allow the Jews to trade and buy real estate. This enabled them to form strong community ties, but they were still not allowed to open retail shops, become craftsmen, or hold public worship services. Shortly thereafter Asher Levy and Jacob Barsimson were able to win the right to serve in the local militia rather than paying the enlistment tax, as they had previously been required to do. Ultimately, they gained the full rights of citizenship, despite Stuyvesant's protests.

The Dutch colony of New Netherland was eventually taken over by the English. This 1664 change in colonial leadership did not force the Jewish community—mostly Sephardim, or Jews of Iberian origin, with a small percentage of Ashkenazim, or German Jews—to disperse to find refuge. Although the new government was not necessarily supportive of Jewish religious beliefs, it acknowledged the importance of the Jewish presence, which provided a commercial force in the port towns and contributed to the diversity that steered the colonies away from their economically limited, soil-based agricultural mind-set and practice.

Members of the Jewish community focused on maintaining a cohesiveness, which not only reinforced their religious beliefs but their traditions as well. This communal strength later supported Ashkenazic migration from Russia, Poland, and the Balkans, more than a century after the colonial period had ended in North America.

Penny M. Sonnenburg

See also: Religion (Chronology); Religion (Essay); Rhode Island.

Bibliography

Baseler, Marilyn C. *Asylum for Mankind: America 1607–1800.* Ithaca, NY: Cornell University Press, 1998.

Feingold, Henry L. *Zion in America: The Jewish Experience from Colonial Times to the Present.* New York: Hippocrene, 1974.

Johnson, Sir William (1715–1774)

Born in 1715 in Smithtown, County Meath, Ireland, William Johnson was the eldest of the eight children of Christopher Johnson and Anne Warren, a minor Anglo-Irish gentry family, tenants of the Earl of Fingal. Although the family arranged for Johnson to read law and serve as a local magistrate, his options in Ireland were limited. He called upon his maternal uncle, Admiral Sir Peter Warren, for aid in emigrating to America in 1737.

With twelve families of Irish tenants, Johnson moved to Warren's large land grant at Warrensburg, near Schenectady, New York. By 1741, he had acquired 1,000 acres of his own, built an imposing fortified house, Mount Johnson, and peopled the land with

Sir William Johnson was a New York fur trader, land speculator, and loyalist. With strong ties to the region's Iroquois peoples, he acted as their spokesman and intermediary with the colonial government. (*Brown Brothers, Sterling, Pennsylvania*)

Scotch and Palatine settlers. He took one of these settlers, Catherine Weissenburg, as a common-law wife, and with her he had three surviving children. (She died sometime around 1758.)

Johnson soon became a key link between settlers, the government in Albany, and the Iroquois tribes, particularly the Mohawk, who dominated the region. Through open-handed credit and his friendship with the Mohawk sachem Hendrick (Tiyanoga), Johnson became both a wealthy fur trader and spokesman for the Mohawk, who called him Waeraghigaguy, "the man who understands great things."

With this link to the Mohawk, Johnson provided crucial aid to the British in King George's War by delivering the support or neutrality of the Six Nations and working out prisoner exchanges with French-allied tribes in Canada. He was rewarded with the title Colonel, but he increasingly irritated the Dutch authorities in Albany with his demands for the curtailment of the rum trade and fair treatment of the Native Americans under his patronage.

In furtherance of this, Johnson stage-managed the Mohawk appearance at the Albany Congress of 1754, holding back their arrival to inconvenience the meeting, then putting forth demands for limits on land sales, and calling for his appointment as Royal Indian Agent. Although the Congress moved on to discussing colonial union, the Board of Trade named Johnson as Indian Agent North in 1755.

During this period, Johnson built a grand neoclassical estate, Johnson Hall. Sometime around 1759, the Mohawk woman Mary "Molly" Brant, sister (or perhaps half-sister) of the warrior and leader Joseph Brant, became his acknowledged consort and mother of a second family of his children.

When the French and Indian War broke out, Johnson once again delivered Iroquois support, as well as that of his many tenants, joining the attempt to fortify Crown Point. Despite being wounded in the thigh, he also commanded the Battle for Fort George in September 1755 against General Dieskau. In 1759, Johnson's 1,000 men joined the Battle of Niagara, and Johnson himself took over command when Brigadier General John Prideaux was wounded early in the fight. Johnson was rewarded with only the second baronetcy given to an American for delivering one of the few successes of the early years of the war.

After the war, Johnson was both extremely powerful and one of the most hated men in the colonies. Albany politicians resented his influence with the British, while colonists tried to defy British strictures against moving farther west, a policy Johnson enforced with a view to preserving the Mohawk and their Iroquois neighbors. Tarred as Irish, a "Squawman," and a tool of royal policy for his support of colonial taxation, Johnson chose to become an independent power in the Mohawk Valley. Victims of the Paxton Boys, a group of frontier whites in Pennsylvania who attacked Native Americans, fled to him for protection in 1763, and Johnson joined in the suppression of Pontiac's Rebellion almost as a feudal vassal of the Crown.

In 1769, George III rewarded Johnson with 99,000 acres of land, which he settled with Irish and Highlander Scottish emigrants. Strongly loyalist, Johnson promoted the Church of England to his settlers and the Mohawk. He also engaged in paternalistic policies such as providing schools, roads, investment for agricultural experiments, and local justice.

On July 11, 1774, Johnson was addressing a group of Iroquois sachems, persuading them not to join Cresap's Rebellion against the colony of Virginia, when he collapsed and died. His death had a significant influence on the coming American Revolution, as it made possible the seizure of Fort Ticonderoga, a site otherwise guarded by his influence. It also splintered the Iroquois, especially tribes like the Cayuga and Oneida.

Johnson's estate was destroyed by colonists during the war. His white and Mohawk family members scattered to British protection in Canada, where his descendents reside today.

Margaret Sankey

See also: Albany Congress (1754); Native American–European Relations.

Bibliography

Flexner, James Thomas. *Lord of the Mohawks.* Boston: Little, Brown, 1979.

Hamilton, Milton. *Sir William Johnson: Colonial American.* Port Washington, NY: Kennikat, 1976.

Igneri, David. *Sir William Johnson: The Man and His Influence.* New York: Rivercross, 1994.

Joint-Stock Companies

During the late fifteenth century European commercial classes were swiftly rising and gaining prominence. The emergence of new trade networks challenged countries that previously had been dominant in trade, spurring some to try to participate in and expand these networks and develop others. Furthermore, European population growth put a strain on previously abundant resources, such as land and food, making overseas expansion absolutely necessary. For these reasons, Spain, England, France, and the Netherlands undertook exploration and colonization attempts, which would shape the future of the New World.

In the fifteenth century, Spain took the lead not only in exploring but also in colonizing the Americas. Conquest and success came easily, a result of divisiveness among the native peoples, combined with the devastating effects of European disease on the indigenous population. The early part of the sixteenth century was a reactionary time as the other key countries battled for dominance of the seas and markets. The sixteenth century witnessed the rise of the Dutch merchant fleet, one of the largest in the world. The Dutch were able to capture most of the Far Eastern business that Portugal had previously monopolized. In addition, they were able to infiltrate Spain's Caribbean stronghold.

This rise in European commercialism brought with it new ways for merchant companies to finance their ventures, including what can be viewed as a rudimentary form of the modern-day corporation: joint-stock companies. Wealthy people with extra capital pooled their resources and invested money in risky enterprises. The only protection agreed upon was that operation as a group limited the participants' involvement to the monies that they were willing to invest. The earliest and most important of these Dutch joint-stock companies were the Muscovy Company, the Levant Company, and the East India Company.

England was quick to recognize the value of such a company structure. In September 1605, two groups of English merchants petitioned James I for a license to explore and colonize Virginia. This resulted in the formation and organization of two joint-stock companies, one controlled by London merchants and the other by a group from the Plymouth and Bristol areas. The idea was that the London Company was to colonize southern Virginia, while the Plymouth Company was given colonization rights to northern Virginia. Although both were officially still considered under the control of the Royal Council for Virginia, James I himself appointed prominent people to high positions within these companies. These were people who he felt were the most qualified to be stockholders of these companies while still reporting directly to the council. While these appointees were considered to be under royal control, their presence provided the over-

seas companies and their colonies with unintentional independence.

England's first attempts were not the successes that had been envisioned, with early efforts such as the settlement of Roanoke failing. Competing Dutch and Spanish colonial ventures, population pressure within England's own borders, and the desire of England's merchants and gentry for new markets led to the supplanting of joint-stock companies by proprietary companies and royal charter companies. These ultimately provided company stockholders with more financial security and the companies with better control of overseas colonies.

Penny M. Sonnenburg

See also: Mercantilism; Merchants; Trade; Virginia Company.

Bibliography

Kupperman, Karen Ordahl. *Roanoke: The Abandoned Colony.* Totowa, NJ: Rowman and Allanheld, 1984.

Martin, John Frederick. *Profits in the Wilderness: Entrepreneurship and the Founding of New England Towns in the Seventeenth Century.* Chapel Hill: University of North Carolina Press, 1991.

Jolliet, Louis (1645–1700)

Louis Jolliet (also spelled Joliet) was a French Canadian explorer. In 1673, he gained fame as the leader of the first European expedition to extensively explore the Mississippi River.

Jolliet was born in 1645 in Beauport, outside of Quebec, in present-day Canada. He received Jesuit training in Quebec but left the seminary in 1667 and traveled to France for unknown reasons. He returned to New France in 1668 to become a fur trader with the Native Americans.

While Jolliet journeyed across the Atlantic Ocean and back, King Louis XIV of France was busy trying to solidify his empire. Part of this plan involved making his North American colony more economically viable, a task left to the new intendant, Jean Talon. Talon sent Louis Jolliet's brother, Lucien, on an expedition to Lake Superior to find copper mines. When Lucien disappeared, Louis Jolliet emerged as an unlikely replacement to be Talon's principal explorer.

Talon selected Jolliet to lead an expedition to find the great river that Native Americans called "Messipi," a waterway that the French thought might lead to the Gulf of Mexico, the Gulf of California, or Hudson Bay.

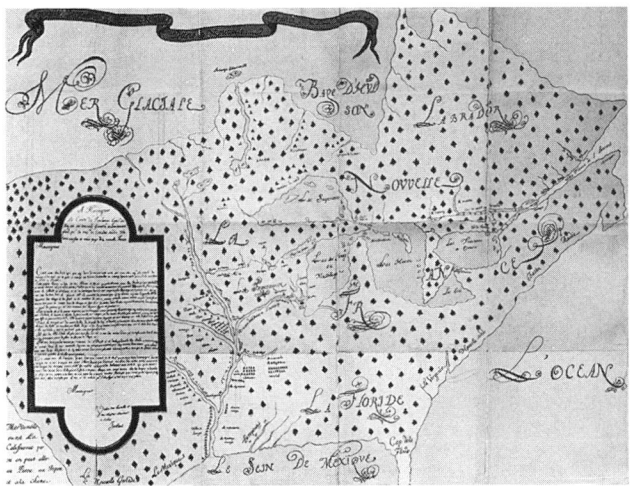

In 1673, the French Canadian Louis Jolliet led the first expedition by white men to explore and chart the Mississippi River. His original map was lost in a canoe accident, but he was able to reconstruct the major elements from memory. *(Brown Brothers, Sterling, Pennsylvania)*

Whatever the case, the successful mapping of this river would boost the economy of New France. Jolliet's selection as leader for this expedition also stemmed from his Jesuit training. Because Jesuits in the Great Lakes region resisted encroachment by fur traders, Jolliet's Jesuit connection and the addition of the Jesuit father Jacques Marquette to the party eased this potential conflict.

The journey to find the Mississippi River's mouth began on May 17, 1673. Jolliet, Marquette, and five oarsmen set off from Saint-Ignace across Lake Michigan in two canoes. They carried with them writing and drawing equipment, navigation tools, and plenty of furs. The furs were important, because the explorers financed the trip themselves, and the furs could be used to trade with Native Americans along the way, either for provisions or for profit. The group journeyed into Green Bay, up the Fox River, and across Lake Winnebago to where the Fox River resumed. At the end of the Fox River, with the help of Mascouten Indians, the party portaged their canoes to the Wisconsin River and paddled for the Mississippi, which they reached on June 17, 1673.

Two hundred miles south, the explorers encountered a group of Illinois. Jolliet's previous experience with Native Americans and Marquette's knowledge of native languages made this meeting a peaceful one, especially when it became clear that the French were enemies of the Iroquois, who perpetually threatened smaller tribes. Jolliet was disappointed to find out that the Illinois would not become future partners in the fur trade and knew little of the lower Mississippi.

Shortly after leaving the Illinois behind, the party passed the mouths of the Missouri and Ohio rivers. By this time, Jolliet knew that the river emptied to the south and that the Missouri might be worth exploring as a passage to the West. He also worried about confronting Spanish explorers or their Native American allies as he continued south.

An encounter with Quapaws in July, just south of the mouth of the Arkansas River, convinced Jolliet to return to New France. The explorers struggled to convince the Quapaws that they had peaceful intentions. Once the French party had accomplished this, the Quapaws warned Jolliet that violent bands of native peoples roamed the southern Mississippi. Additionally, the presence of Spanish articles of trade among the Quapaws indicated that Spanish explorers and the mouth of the Mississippi were both close. The group, having determined where the river emptied, began its long journey back up the Mississippi on July 17.

Another meeting with the Illinois persuaded Jolliet to follow the Illinois River to present-day Chicago instead of the longer route they had originally followed. The group paddled up the west coast of Lake Michigan before settling in Green Bay for the winter. When Jolliet left for Montreal in spring, Marquette remained in Green Bay. A disastrous mishap just outside Montreal cost Jolliet his map, journal, and almost his life. He later recounted his findings from memory, but some detail was lost.

After 1674, Jolliet's career involved service for New France in Canada. He went to Hudson Bay in 1679 to chart English movements, and he was given the island of Anticosti in the Gulf of St. Lawrence for his service. He explored Labrador in the early 1690s and became royal hydrographer of New France in 1697. Jolliet died in 1700.

Thomas F. Jorsch

See also: Exploration; French; French Colonies on Mainland North America (Chronology); Marquette, Jacques; Mississippi River. *Document:* Marquette's Travels on the Mississippi (1673).

Bibliography

Delanglez, Jean. *Life and Voyages of Louis Jolliet (1645–1700)*. Chicago: Institute of Jesuit History, 1948.
Severin, Timothy. *Explorers of the Mississippi.* New York: Alfred A. Knopf, 1968.

Journals

See Newspapers and Journals

K

Kentucky

In the native Cherokee language, the land called *Ken-tah-teh* meant "tomorrow" or "the land where we will live." True to its name, this territory would come to symbolize the promise of the new nation, its raw potential and seemingly endless supply of natural resources. It was, in the colonial era, a place of struggle: first between white settlers and native inhabitants, and, once the indigenous peoples had been driven from the land, between settlers and land speculators, who hoped to turn Kentucky and its frontiersmen's dreams for independence into profit.

Kentucky's allure was irresistible for land-starved farmers deprived of agrarian independence in the East. Although "long hunters" forayed into the wilderness west of the Appalachian Mountains in the early eighteenth century, permanent migration did not truly begin until the last half of that century. By 1775, the trans-Appalachian traffic caused one Virginia minister to wonder, "What a buzzel is amongst people about Kentuck?"

Kentucky had become known, in the words of Steven Channing, as an "Eden of the West." This myth of Kentucky was, according to Channing, the myth of America itself: a place of endless possibility and resources, where opportunity awaited any man brave enough to make the journey.

One such man was Kentucky's legendary explorer, Daniel Boone. Himself a long hunter, Boone first entered the region in 1767 and stayed for over two years. He returned home to North Carolina with the beginnings of a reputation for adventure and resourcefulness that would blossom a few years later. After losing a son to the Shawnee in 1773, Boone himself was captured, but he so endeared himself to his captors that they refused the ransom offered by the British for his return. Boone later returned from his stay with the Shawnees.

In 1778, during the American Revolution, he fended off a siege at Boonesborough by natives allied with the British, thus ensuring Kentucky's future in the new republic.

Kentucky, like the rest of the Ohio Valley, was the locus of several important colonial economic and political rivalries. France and Britain struggled there for control of the continent, while trappers and traders competed for Native American allegiances and access to trade routes and hunting grounds. France sent Jesuit priests, traders, and soldiers into the area to make claims on the territory and win crucial native allies. Britain, on the other hand, focused its imperial efforts on land speculators. These companies identified large parcels of land to sell for settlement, and although these initial efforts would fail to produce any large-scale migration, they did succeed in opening up the land west of the Appalachians to exploration. They also ignited a controversy over who had rights to this land that would define Kentucky at the end of the colonial era and beyond.

The Transylvania Company, like its predecessor, the London Company, which had founded the colony of Virginia centuries before, was part of such a speculating scheme. Led by Richard Henderson, several North Carolinians formed the land company in 1774 to purchase large tracts of land from the Cherokee for settlement. Although the Cherokee ceded much land in exchange for goods brought to the area by Henderson and his comrades, not all were happy with the trade. Dragging Canoe, Chief Attakullakulla's son, prophesied that now "a dark cloud hung over the land." Dragging Canoe was himself killed a year later in the two decades of fighting that would ensue between Native Americans and settlers for control of Kentucky.

In addition to native hostilities, the Transylvania Company experienced competition from Virginians wishing to make claims in Kentucky. In 1775, the two groups competed for rights to the land called Kentucky in the Continental Congress. Virginia had long desired rights to the land lying beyond its western border but, not having a charter from the Crown, was unable to pursue its title. Once independence was declared, and Virginia became a state, its dominion could legitimately be extended into Kentucky. This desire for land and wealth was as much a precipitant of the American Revolution as a desire for liberty or independence, and, as such, Kentucky became both "a cause of the Revolution and its child."

After the war, Kentucky's settlement preoccupied many of those charged with drawing up the blueprints for the new nation. The remaining Native Americans, always relatively few in number, were driven out, and land speculation intensified. The democratic dreams of this "good poor man's country" eroded in the accumulation of large estates, tenancy, and the depletion of native fauna due to overhunting.

Carole Emberton

See also: Appalachia; Boone, Daniel; Cumberland Gap; Ohio Country.

Bibliography

Channing. Steven A. *Kentucky: A Bicentennial History.* New York: W. W. Norton and Company, 1977.

Friend, Craig Thompson, ed. *The Buzzel About Kentuck: Settling the Promised Land.* Lexington: The University Press of Kentucky, 1999.

Kieft's War

Kieft's War of 1643 to 1645 substantially weakened the Dutch position in the New World. It began as an attempt by Willem Kieft, director general of the Dutch settlement of New Netherland, to remove the Native Americans who threatened the economy of the young colony. It ended with one of the bloodiest massacres of Native Americans in colonial history and the flight of many settlers back to Europe.

In the 1630s, the Dutch West India Company struggled to maintain its colony, which had been formed to conduct trade on the eastern shoreline of America. The United Provinces States General placed pressure upon the company to populate the settlement or lose it, while smugglers within the colony threatened the company's profits. To save the settlement, company directors choose a new representative with a reputation for discipline, merchant Willem Kieft. Upon his arrival

in 1638, Kieft tightened company control of the government and imposed measures to curtail smuggling.

Over the next four years, the stability that Kieft created led to a fourfold increase in the European population of New Netherland. To prosper and avoid being overwhelmed by the rapidly expanding English colonies to the northeast and southwest, the Dutch needed to expand. However, tensions with Native Americans rose as the Dutch moved into closer proximity to the various tribes in the region. Kieft worsened matters in 1639 by forcing Native Americans to pay a tribute, ostensibly for Dutch protection against external tribal enemies.

In 1640, Dutch settlers seeking retribution for stolen swine killed several Raritans. In the following year, the Raritan attacked the Staten Island settlement and killed four settlers while destroying two homes. The Dutch refrained from a retaliatory attack but offered bounties for dead Raritans. To formulate Native American policy, Kieft formed an advisory Council of Twelve, and after the murder of another settler by a native, he sought advice on whether war should be declared. The council recommended that no action be taken against the native peoples since the Dutch settlements were widely spread and the colony still numerically weak.

The few surviving accounts of the war differ as to Kieft's conduct. One colonist declared that the confrontational Kieft was committed to the belief that nearby tribes needed to be removed and exterminated. After meeting individually with Kieft, the council members were persuaded to agree to immediate retaliation. Another colonist suggests that extremists may have intimidated Kieft into ordering attacks. This account is given some credence by the fact that one extremist, Maryn Adriaessen, who led the attack on Corlear's Hook, subsequently tried to assassinate Kieft on March 21, 1643. There is no disagreement about the fact that settlers frightened for their safety began to push Kieft to attack.

Conflicts among Native Americans also set off the war. In the winter of 1642–1643, Mohicans demanded tribute from Wickquasgecks and Tappans, who then sought refuge within the Dutch encampment. About 500 of these Native Americans moved to the presumed safety of the Dutch settlement at Pavonia with members of the Hackensack tribe, while another group went to Corlear's Hook.

Meanwhile, Kieft received a petition from three members of the council, who demanded an immediate attack upon the Native Americans to avenge the earlier attacks upon the Dutch. Soldiers under the command of Jeuriaen Rodolff attacked Pavonia, while Adriaessen led his forces to Corlear's Hook on the night of February 25, 1643. Records disagree about the brutality of the assaults and the numbers of Native Americans killed. About eighty Native Americans are generally believed to have died at Pavonia. One Dutch witness reported that adult Native Americans were thrown into the river and prevented from returning to land, while children were torn away from their mothers and hacked to death before their parents. Perhaps forty Native Americans died at Corlear's Hook in a similar orgy of violence. Kieft's orders apparently directed the commanders of the expedition to take prisoners while sparing women and children, but these orders were not obeyed. According to one colonist, Kieft later thanked and rewarded the troops for their conduct, but another Dutch account has him apologizing for the attack.

Kieft achieved a truce in April, but this did not last. Outnumbered by the Native Americans, the New Netherland colony barely managed to survive, with many colonists fleeing back to Europe. Kieft became a scapegoat for the colony's troubles, and in 1647, the Dutch West India Company recalled him. He died in a shipwreck en route to the Netherlands, and his papers sank with him.

Kieft's legacy is mixed. While conflict may have been inevitable in light of European expansion, the brutality of Kieft's War nearly toppled the colony of New Netherland and forever tarnished the Dutch image.

Caryn E. Neumann

See also: Dutch; Dutch West India Company; Military and Diplomatic Affairs (Chronology); Military and Diplomatic Affairs (Essay); New York; War.

Bibliography

Rink, Oliver A. *Holland on the Hudson: An Economic and Social History of Dutch New York.* Ithaca, NY: Cornell University Press, 1986.

Winkler, David F. "Revising the Attack on Pavonia." *New Jersey History* 116:3–4 (1998): 2–15.

King George's War

King George's War was the name for the American phase of the larger European conflict known as the War of the Austrian Succession (1740–1748). Some historians also include the War of Jenkins' Ear (1739–1743) as part of this larger conflict. The War of the Austrian Succession began as an Anglo-Spanish conflict over the terms agreed in the Treaty of Utrecht, by which the British gained access through the *asiento* (patent, or exclusive trading relationship) to Spanish colonies in the Americas.

Since 1714, the British had abused the terms of the treaty by continuing to smuggle, as well as through such subterfuges as offloading multiple cargoes over the deck of a single ship per year, thereby bringing in more cargoes than was specified in the treaty. For their part, the Spanish harassed and detained British ships while searching for contraband, creating incidents such as the one in 1731 in which Captain Robert Jenkins of the *Rebecca* lost his ear to Spanish customs agents during an on-deck brawl off Cuba. Jenkins's ear, preserved in alcohol, added to the public furor about Spanish abuses when it was displayed during hearings in the House of Commons, and this incident led to a declaration of war by the British in 1739.

The Anglo-Spanish conflict was largely fought at sea, using privateers. It included the dispatch of Commodore George Anson with a fleet to the Pacific with the mission of capturing the Manila treasure convoy. He succeeded in 1743 and returned to England with a large amount of Spanish gold for the British treasury. A British assault on the Spanish city of Porto Bello, Panama, was a disaster, with large numbers of casualties from wounds and malaria, but it left a lasting impression on its American participants, including Lawrence Washington, who later named his plantation Mount Vernon in honor of the operation's commander, Admiral Edward Vernon.

In the new colony of Georgia, Governor James Oglethorpe took the opportunity presented by the war to lead the colonial militia, reinforced by British soldiers, in a 1740 attack on St. Augustine, a Spanish fortress where runaway Georgia slaves had been sheltered and from which the Spanish launched raids on the frontier. The attack failed, but in 1744, Oglethorpe successfully defended St. Simon's Island against an invasion by St. Augustine's governor, Manuel Monteano, and preserved the southern border of Georgia.

The War of the Austrian Succession had broken out in Europe in 1740, when the British, Dutch, Sardinians, and Saxons supported the succession of Maria Theresa to the throne in the Austrian Empire against the claims of the Bavarians, French, and Prussians. Key battles were fought in Western Europe by traditional military forces at Dettingen and Fontenoy. The French attempted to split British forces by backing the Jacobite rebellion of 1745 in Scotland, a campaign that ended with the battle of Culloden in 1746. It spurred a large wave of Scots emigration to the Southern American colonies, especially Virginia and North Carolina, throughout the 1740s and 1750s.

When the French entered the war in 1744, they staged an attack on a British position in Nova Scotia, destroying the fort and taking prisoners back to Louisbourg on Cape Breton Island in Nova Scotia. This war is sometimes referred to in New England as Governor Shirley's War because of the attack then launched by Governor William Shirley with the Massachusetts militia on the French fortress at Louisbourg. Shirley's men, led by William Pepperrell, took Louisbourg in 1745, giving the British control of French Canada. In the American backcountry, the Huron and Mohawk, allies of the French, fought the Iroquois, led by British Indian Agent Sir William Johnson around Albany and Saratoga. The British and French armies also fought for possession of key fortresses in India, with the British surrendering Madras to the French.

The war ended with the Treaty of Aix-la-Chappelle (Aachen) in 1748. The European border changes were extensive, with Prussia keeping Silesia, and France gaining Lorraine while acknowledging Austrian possession of Tuscany. In the colonies, Britain exchanged Louisbourg for Madras, canceling out all the gains of the colonial campaigns. New Englanders were deeply disappointed in the terms of the treaty. They complained so vociferously that the British government reimbursed Massachusetts for the Louisbourg campaign and awarded Pepperrell a baronetcy.

The treaty did nothing to settle the borders of the French and British possessions in North America. New Englanders became immediately suspicious of French military activity in the Ohio and Allegheny Valleys, which would lead to another outbreak of war in 1754.

Margaret Sankey

See also: George II; Military and Diplomatic Affairs (Chronology); Military and Diplomatic Affairs (Essay); War.

Bibliography

Chapin, Howard. *Privateering in King George's War.* Providence, RI: E. A. Johnson, 1928.

Ivers, Larry. *British Drums on the Southern Frontier.* Chapel Hill: University of North Carolina Press, 1974.

Rawlyk, George. *Yankees at Louisbourg.* Orono: University of Maine Press, 1967.

Williams, Glyndwr. *Prize of All the Oceans.* New York: Viking, 2000.

King Philip's War

King Philip's War, or Metacom's War, was a series of battles in southern New England between the British, along with their native allies, and the Wampanoag and their allies in 1675 and 1676. The war had its origins in the ongoing struggle between Puritan New England and the Native American communities that surrounded it for much of the seventeenth century.

The roots of King Philip's War can be traced to the beginning of English settlement in southern New England, where religious refugees under William Bradford founded the Plymouth Colony in 1620. Upon their arrival, these first colonists secured the alliance of Massasoit, sachem of the Wampanoag and father of Metacom (known as King Philip). Massasoit sought allies against the Narragansett of present-day Rhode Island, who were at the time of English settlement the most powerful group in southern New England, controlling a large territory and about 4,500 warriors.

Throughout New England, a series of events exerted pressure on Native American communities in the seventeenth century. Disease devastated the population of nearly every tribe. The Massachusett people, for instance, lost about 90 percent of their population in a sixty-year period. The terms of exchange between colonists and Native Americans were also shifting. A flourishing trade in beaver pelts and wampum marked stabilized relations between the two groups, but when demand for furs decreased in Europe and wampum currency was devalued, colonists began to take more and more land from their neighbors. Complicating matters was the 1661 death of Massasoit, who had been a remnant of older, more stable times.

By the 1660s, the English were no longer a tiny outpost on the fringe of Wampanoag country. Plymouth and Massachusetts Bay were home to tens of thousands of English Puritans who had developed a fearsome militia system. Another factor contributing to the deterioration of a once-peaceful relationship was an increasing English insistence on converting Native Americans to Christianity. Though all of these factors were present in the years leading up to King Philip's War, it bears mentioning that peace, not war, was the normal relationship between Native Americans and the English in southern New England.

William Goffe, a Cromwellian who had signed the death warrant of Charles I and later fled to New England, was said to rally the residents of Hadley, Massachusetts, against an attack by the natives during King Philip's War. *(Brown Brothers, Sterling, Pennsylvania)*

Massasoit's oldest son, Wamsutta (whom the English dubbed Alexander), assumed leadership of the Wampanoag, and soon ran afoul of Plymouth. He was accused of discussing war with the Narragansett and of selling land to the renegade colony of Rhode Island. An armed guard captured him and brought him to Plymouth for questioning. Upon his return, he took ill and died.

The Wampanoag, and Philip in particular, believed that Wamsutta had been poisoned. At the age of 24, Philip was elevated to sachem; he subsequently took the English title of king. Within five years, he, too, had offended English sensibilities and was accused of plotting against Plymouth in collusion with the Dutch and French. The years 1671 to 1675 saw what one historian has called a "cold war" mentality develop among both the English and Native Americans.

In 1675, three Wampanoags stood trial in Plym-

outh for the murder of John Sassamon, a Christian Native American who functioned in both the Wampanoag and English colonial worlds. The Wampanoags asserted their innocence but were sentenced to death. All three were hung, but one rope broke, and the man fell to the ground, only to be shot a month later by Plymouth authorities. This farcical trial touched off King Philip's War.

Civil War in New England

It makes sense to conceive of King Philip's War as a civil war. The people engaged in killing each other in 1675 and 1676 knew each other relatively well. Native American and English worlds had overlapped to a great extent, and separating ally from enemy was a daunting task for those on both sides of the conflict.

On June 20, 1675, a group of Wampanoags looted English homes in Swansea and set two on fire. The English settlers raised an army of 200 men to protect the town. The Puritans at Boston assembled three separate negotiating parties, dispatching one to Nipmuc territory (which was deserted, an indication that something was amiss), one to travel to Rhode Island (where Roger Williams could help defuse any situation with the Narragansett), and one to meet with Philip. On June 23, colonists defending Swansea shot another looter dead; on June 24, Wampanoags killed nine Swansea colonists. While the English skirmished around Swansea, Philip traveled to other Wampanoag villages to muster support for in the rapidly growing conflict.

The conflict spread quickly to other colonies. Narragansetts began to probe Rhode Island, and Nipmucs attacked Mendon, in Massachusetts Bay. Philip's growing army met a combined force of English and Mohegans on July 30, but English bumbling allowed Philip to escape to the west, effectively spreading the war to the Connecticut River Valley and Maine. Through the summer and fall of 1675, Wampanoags and their allies outmaneuvered English forces, burning houses and then retreating into the woods. At Springfield, Massachusetts, on October 5, Nipmucs and Agawams burned 300 homes before being chased off. What had begun as a relatively minor series of skirmishes was escalating into a full-scale war.

By December, the colonies of Massachusetts Bay, Plymouth, and Connecticut had assembled an army of 1,000 men. This large force was intended to make the Narragansett turn over Wampanoag refugees. The colonial army did succeed in laying siege to a fortified village, killing 600 Narragansetts in what became known as the Great Swamp Fight. The immediate result of this battle was to draw the Narragansett into the war, but it also weakened the colonial army, so that it had to stop for the winter.

Early 1676 was the high-water mark for the Wampanoag in their battle against the English. The frontier towns of Lancaster and Groton were attacked with great success, forcing their abandonment. Native ambushes struck militia companies in Massachusetts and Rhode Island. Narragansetts burned part of Providence, including Roger Williams's home. Eleven frontier towns had been abandoned by colonists, and one more had become nothing more than a military base.

Around this time, the English shifted tactics to great effect; instead of seeking to engage their enemies in pitched battles, they struck at supply lines and food stores. They began to capture small bands of "rebel" natives. The English also employed the assistance of other native peoples at an increasing rate. Moreover, even if forces loyal to Philip were able to force the abandonment of a town, they paid dearly in terms of lives and food lost.

In June 1676, the Puritans launched another combined offensive. By this point, most of the Native American combatants seem to have tired of war and retreated. In southeastern Massachusetts, on August 12, King Philip was shot and killed by a Native American known as Alderman, a former ally working with Benjamin Church and the Puritans. Resistance to the English melted away following Philip's death.

Aftermath and Interpretation

To be sure, King Philip's War devastated New England. Some writers have estimated that it took the colonies decades to recoup the losses suffered in a single year of fighting. Whole towns had to be rebuilt and resettled. This may be true, but the region's native peoples fared far worse after the war. An estimated 3,000 Native Americans, of a population of 20,000, lost their lives in battle or English massacres. Those who survived faced harsh retribution from the English, who mistrusted even those Native Americans who had fought alongside them during the war.

Almost as interesting as the events of King Philip's War are the volumes of literature about it. While it was still occurring, Puritans struggled to discern God's will in the progress of the conflict, and spilled a lot of ink on the subject. Some of the veterans, notably Benjamin Church, published their accounts after the war. Mary Rowlandson, captured at Lancaster, wrote perhaps the most famous of the Native American captivity narratives, *The Soveraignty and Goodness of God*.

King Philip's War took on a mythic importance in the United States in the nineteenth century. Through the play *Metamora; or, the Last of the Wampanoags*, Americans reconstructed the events of 1675–1676 to serve a variety of purposes, including the justification of Native American removal in the antebellum period.

The lasting significance of King Philip's War has also been subject to various interpretations. Between 1990 and 2000, four monographs appeared on the conflict. King Philip's War has been viewed as the initial shot in a long war between Anglo-Americans and Native Americans. It also has been viewed as an American first, where both combatants and noncombatants were annihilated.

Matthew Jennings

See also: Connecticut; Massachusetts; Military and Diplomatic Affairs (Chronology); Military and Diplomatic Affairs (Essay); Native American–European Conflict; War.

Bibliography

Bourne, Russell. *The Red King's Rebellion: Racial Politics in New England, 1675–1678*. New York: Atheneum, 1990.

Drake, James D. *King Philip's War: Civil War in New England, 1675–1676*. Amherst: University of Massachusetts Press, 1999.

Lepore, Jill. *The Name of War: King Philip's War and the Origins of American Identity*. New York: Alfred A. Knopf, 1998.

Malone, Patrick M. *The Skulking Way of War: Technology and Tactics Among the New England Indians*. Lanham, MD: Madison, 1991.

Schultz, Eric B., and Michael J. Tougias. *King Philip's War: The History and Legacy of America's Forgotten Conflict*. Woodstock, VT: Countryman Press, 1999.

King's College

King's College was officially opened on July 17, 1754. The idea of founding a college in the province of New York, however, goes back to 1704.

In 1704, Lewis Morris, of New Jersey wrote to the secretary of the Society for the Propagation of the Gospel in Foreign Parts. In his letter, he requested that the society petition the British Crown for 32 acres of land located in New York. Trinity Church had already requested this land, to no avail. Wanting to build a college there, the church hoped that the society's request might be taken more seriously. The land was finally given over to Trinity Church in 1702 or 1703. Trinity officials asked the governor, Lord Cornbury, where on that parcel they should build a college. But Lord Cornbury never responded to them, and they dropped the matter.

The idea of opening a college in the colonies interested the English once again in 1728. Having received approval for opening a college in Bermuda, Bishop Berkeley left England for the islands in 1729. He never arrived there; his ship made it to Rhode Island instead. While in New England, Berkeley decided that New York was a better location for a college. He then requested permission to open a college on the North American mainland instead of Bermuda, mentioning New York as a possible location. Soon after, though, he returned to England at the request of a friend, and no one else pushed for the establishment of a college until years later.

In 1746, the New York General Assembly approved a measure to raise 2,250 pounds through a public lottery for the colony in general, as well as for the establishment of a college. By 1751, several lotteries had raised nearly 3,500 pounds, and these monies were used to pay for ten trustees, who had to decide where to situate the college. Trinity Church proposed the college be built on any of the unused portion of the 32 acres it had acquired almost fifty years earlier. The trustees decided to use the church's land, but controversy over this choice soon erupted.

Trinity Church was a Church of England (or Anglican) church; furthermore, seven of the ten trustees who formed the board of governors of the college were Anglicans, and some were vestrymen at Trinity Church. These facts, along with a proposal by these seven trustees that the board of governors of the college would always maintain an Anglican majority, created a strong opposition to the college. Led by William Livingston, the opposition sought approval of the college not by a royal charter but by the General Assembly. In essence, the opposition feared the Anglican affiliation of many of the individuals associated with the college would lead to the suppression of dissenting religious views held by students and faculty.

Thanks to the assistance of Lieutenant Governor James Delancey—whose family happened to be feuding with the Livingstons—the English government finally chartered King's College on October 31, 1754, by which time classes had already been in session for three months. Reverend Samuel Johnson, an Anglican clergyman, became the first president of King's College in July 1754. Johnson was the only instructor that year,

and the subjects he offered included Greek, logic, metaphysics, and ethics. Eight students began their studies that summer in the Trinity vestry room. At the college's first commencement, on June 21, 1758, five of the members of the first entering class graduated, along with three transfer students.

Construction of a building for the college was completed in June 1760. In the beginning, however, King's College trustees failed to find significant financial backing. Finally, in 1767, the college acquired valuable real estate near the Hudson River, which helped stabilize its financial situation.

The Revolutionary War interrupted studies at the college and eventually helped lead to its redesign. In 1776, there were no students admitted, and the college's building became a military hospital, although the board of governors continued to meet occasionally during the war. On May 1, 1784, the trustees dissolved King's College and formed Columbia College in its place.

King's College lasted only thirty years, from 1754 to 1784. During that time, it attracted students from influential families, including George Washington's stepson, John Parke Custis. The college also prevailed in the face of significant political controversy and financial challenges.

Lisa Y. Ramos

See also: Education, Higher; New York City. Document: Founding Colleges in America (1754).

Bibliography

Arrowsmith, Robert. *Columbia of Yesterday, 1754–1897*. Reprinted from the *Columbian*. Staten Island, NY, 1926.

Coon, Horace. *Columbia: Colossus on the Hudson*. New York: E. P. Dutton, 1947.

A History of Columbia University, 1754–1904. New York: Columbia University Press, 1904.

Loth, David. "King's College Controversy." *American Heritage* 5:1 (1953): 14–17.

Kitchens, Colonial

The 200 years of European settlement leading to the American Revolution saw many changes in how colonists ate. Initially, most settlements struggled simply to provide enough food for their inhabitants. In time, challenges instead came from new foods and new ideas about food preparation.

Family life and domestic chores in colonial America revolved around the kitchen. The open hearth, dating to the early seventeenth century, was the most important feature and the center of activity. *(Brown Brothers, Sterling, Pennsylvania)*

Similar to their European counterparts, women in the early seventeenth century cooked over open hearths. A poor family cooked and lived in the same room. A wealthy family would have additional rooms. Both Northern and Southern colonists tried to isolate their kitchens at the back of the house to minimize the risk of fire. When possible, Southern families built a separate building for cooking; Northerners usually did not, so that the kitchens also would serve to help heat the house.

Most hearths began with a pole made of green wood, suspended inside the chimney. Greenwood poles were easily available, but a cook had to watch the pole carefully as it would dry out and break after a few months, plunging the meal into the fire. The next step up was an iron bar, again suspended over the fire. Chains hung off the bar or pole. For a low simmer, the pot was hung from the top of the chain and moved down to the hot flames as needed. Ideally, a cook wanted a crane arm, an iron bar that swung out from the side of the chimney. Crane arms were safer and gave far more control over cooking.

Nearly all colonists brought at least one or two cast-iron pots from Europe. The first hung over the fire for cooking and heating water. Women with only one pot could lower smaller jugs or puddings tied in cloth into this pot and cook two or three dishes at once. The second pot usually had legs and a flat lid and was called a bake kettle or Dutch oven. Hot embers were raked onto the hearth, and the pot was set on top of the embers with bread, cake, or pie inside. The lid, loaded with more embers, was placed on top. A hooked tool was used to lift the lid, which had a small handle. The embers would be changed once or twice during the cooking time. The bake kettle could be used on fires both inside and out of the home.

Wealthier and more settled colonists acquired other utensils. A spit, an iron bar placed on top of two andirons in front of the fire, was used for roasting meat. A family unable to afford a spit or andirons suspended meat on strings from the bar over the hearth, spinning it to provide an even heat. A griddle (a flat iron pan) could be hung from the bar for cooking flat breads. A spider pan (a frying pan on legs) was used over hot embers, similar to the bake kettle. Toasters held two slices of bread in an iron frame. They were set in front of the fire and swung round to allow both sides to brown. A mulling iron, a long iron poker, was kept buried in the hot embers below the flames. It could be plunged into a mug or pitcher to instantly heat the contents. Most kitchens were also equipped with various smaller utensils, graters, and mortars and pestles.

Larger houses often had a bake oven, a hollow space in the chimney next to the hearth. A separate fire was kindled in the bake oven and allowed to burn for two hours or more. The hot embers were raked out and the oven quickly doused with a damp broom to prevent sparks. Food was placed inside the oven, and a wooden or iron door was set in front of it. The heat from the bake oven lasted for several hours, and most families would do a week's baking in a day.

Many communities also provided a freestanding outdoor bake oven for residents. It worked in the same way as the indoor ovens. Used by those who didn't have their own oven, it also allowed families to pool their limited supplies of firewood for baking.

By the late eighteenth century, food preparation had begun to change in Europe. While the open hearth remained the most common way of cooking food until the early nineteenth century, new adaptations circulated on both sides of the Atlantic. The tin kitchen or reflector oven became common in the 1760s. It had a curved tin back and was open in the front. A spit was suspended across the front, and meat was placed on the spit. With the open side placed facing the fire, the heat from the fire hit the curved back and was reflected back toward the meat, roasting it.

A French method of cooking spread first to England and French Canada and then to the English colonies. Iron mesh baskets, holding hot coals, were lowered into the top of a hollow brick box built against a wall. A trivet was set on top of the coals, providing an even heat for cooking. This method evolved into the closed cookstoves of the nineteenth century.

The colonial period saw a constant need to adapt to new dishes and ingredients. For example, oats grew easily in the rough soil and harsh climate of the outer British Isles and were regarded as a dietary mainstay for much of Scotland, Ireland, and Wales. In contrast, neither wheat nor oats grew well in the parts of the New World that were first settled, so the colonists instead learned to grow corn from their Native American neighbors. However, they continued to prepare corn in the same way as they had prepared oats, pound-

ing and simmering it into mush. Corn was also ground and made into flat cakes. It could be baked on a board held up to the fire or in a bake kettle or oven. Other new foods were squash, beans, maple syrup, cranberries, blueberries, and new types of fish and game. Again, colonists were introduced to these foods by Native Americans.

Trade in the colonial period also brought many changes. Spanish explorers in sixteenth-century South America came across two new foods, the potato and tomato, and brought them home to Europe. By the end of the eighteenth century, both vegetables had traveled back across the Atlantic to North America. Plantations in the Caribbean made sugar and molasses available. Trade worldwide brought spices and other exotic foods, such as subtropical and tropical fruits, to colonial seaport towns. For the most part, these items were still only available to the rich, but many settlers knew of them.

A gradual rise in literacy and printed materials led to the writing of several cookbooks in England over the course of the colonial period. Some of the most common British cookbooks of this period include Gervase Markham's *The English Huswife* in 1615, Eliza Smith's *The Compleat Housewife* in 1727, and Hannah Glasse's *The Art of Cookery Made Plain and Easy* in 1747. Like the others, Markham's book advised women on subjects such as cooking, dairying, brewing, baking, and distilling. The records of the Virginia Company indicate that at least one copy of Markham's book was brought to Virginia by 1620.

In time, however, colonial women began voicing complaints about these British cookbooks, as they did not offer information about ingredients available in North America. While some foods had adapted well to traditional methods, the women wanted additional suggestions and advice. The first attempt to address this problem was in 1742. William Parks, a printer in Williamsburg, edited out all references to British ingredients and reprinted Eliza Smith's *The Compleat Housewife*.

Finally, in 1796, a woman named Amelia Simmons published a book titled *American Cookery*. Although many of her recipes were borrowed directly from British books of the period, she included such American ingredients as cornmeal, pumpkin, and pearlash (an early forerunner of baking soda, made from wood ash). Simmons's book was an instant success and led to several British cookbooks being rewritten for their American audiences.

The early years of colonial exploration and settlement occurred at the very end of the medieval period. Most people in Europe were still living the same way as their ancestors. By the late eighteenth century, Europe had seen nearly 300 years of extensive exploration and trade. Food cooked anywhere in the colonies was influenced by two patterns of change: the circumstances of the New World and the ideas sweeping across the Atlantic as part of the Enlightenment.

Abigail B. Chandler

See also: Food and Diet; Furnishings; Housing; Servants, Domestic. *Document:* Colonial Recipe for Apple Tansey (1754).

Bibliography

Baker, James. "English Yeoman Foodways at Plimoth Plantation." In *The Plimoth Plantation New England Cookery Book*. Boston: Harvard Common, 1990.

Black, Maggie. *A Taste of History: 10,000 Years of Food in Britain.* London: British Museum, 1993.

Bullock, Helen. *The Williamsburg Art of Cookery.* Richmond, VA: Dietz, 1966.

Gilgun, Beth. *Tidings from the 18th Century.* Texarkana, TX: Rebel, 1993.

Wilson, Mary Tolford. "The First American Cookbook." In *A Facsimile of "American Cookery," 1796.* New York: Dover, 1958.

Laborers, Rural

Colonial America was overwhelmingly rural. In fact, just before the American Revolution, more than 90 percent of the population could be considered rural. Rural laborers, whether enslaved, indentured, or free, raised the crops and livestock that drove the economies of many Atlantic colonies. Their experiences are crucial to understanding what life was like for ordinary people in Britain's North American mainland colonies. The experience of colonial rural labor varied according to region, crop, and whether one was free or not.

Chesapeake Region

The earliest white rural laborers were indentured servants in the Chesapeake. In the seventeenth century, most of the labor on tobacco plantations was performed by indentured servants from England, Scotland, and Ireland. Indentured servants usually traded a period of time—four to seven years was a typical term of indenture—for their passage to North America.

The life of indentured servants was materially comparable to that of slaves during the same period—both faced harsh labor in a new, often deadly, disease-ridden environment, and both could be punished by the lash. Slaves, of course, could not generally look forward to freedom or landownership, though some Africans—most famously Anthony Johnson—in the Chesapeake did rise through the ranks of colonial society to work their own plantations.

Servants in Virginia lived short, hard lives. Criminals and debtors were sometimes assigned to Virginian masters, but as the seventeenth century progressed, most were "volunteers." All, however, were fleeing increasingly hard times for the landless poor of the British Isles. Of the 120,000 people who immigrated to the Chesapeake region before 1700, 90,000 were indentured servants. It is not a coincidence that indentured servants seized on the opportunities presented by Bacon's Rebellion—a revolt of poor frontier farmers against the planter elite nearer the coast—although this 1676 fray was not primarily a class revolt.

Gradually, tobacco planters phased out indentured servitude in favor of slavery. This mirrored an earlier transformation on the sugar island of Barbados. Slaves had been too expensive for most of the earliest generation of planters, and servants were readily available. As conditions improved in England, the pool of available laborers willing to undergo the rigors of indentured servitude dried up, and these rural laborers were replaced by African slaves.

As rural laborers, slaves presented some advantages over indentured servants. They served for life, could produce more labor, and because of their racial and cultural separateness ensured that few poor white Virginians would join them should they rise up.

Slave life in Virginia was closely regulated by the planter class, and, as dark skin came to be associated with servitude, planters regulated the lives of free people of color as well. Planters severely punished rebelliousness and other infractions, using violence to ensure their slaves produced as much profit as possible. New laws were also enacted curtailing the meager concessions that slaves had achieved and to keep masters from freeing their slaves. In the words of one scholar, Virginia had gone from a "society with slaves" to a "slave society."

This slave society supported the labor-intensive production of tobacco, a series of arduous tasks that lasted all year. Tobacco was planted in flats, transferred to hills, weeded, topped, primed, suckered, cut, cured, and finally packed in barrels for transport. One worker could manage as much as 3 acres of tobacco, which could produce between 1,500 and 2,000 pounds of the valuable crop.

Carolinas

In the early years of South Carolina, most rural labor was performed by African slaves. Slaves worked at a variety of jobs, including clearing forests and herding cattle. After the introduction of rice in the last decade of the seventeenth century, however, most slaves were forcibly employed in the production of South Carolina's cash crop.

It seems likely that Africans from the rice-producing region between the Senegal and Gambia rivers taught Carolina's planters how to grow rice using the tides. Growing rice, while not necessarily less arduous or dangerous, was a different sort of work than growing sugar and tobacco, and most Carolina planters used the task system, as opposed to the gang system, to organize their slaves. Slaves were assigned a series of tasks to perform each day, and when those tasks were complete, they had the remainder of their time to themselves. Many helped family members or friends complete their tasks or tended gardens of their own.

This sort of autonomy had its benefits—slaves developed a vibrant culture quite apart from that of their masters and held on to remembered African traditions much longer. Nevertheless, both the climate and the work involved in growing rice placed harsh demands on their bodies. Though mortality rates were not as high as in the Caribbean sugar colonies, the semitropical disease environment of the region claimed the lives of many slaves.

New England

For the most part, New England was settled by families. Each member of the family performed his or her duty to keep the household running smoothly. Generally, the men and boys would labor in the fields and barns, while women performed essential domestic tasks in the house and garden. Though imported servants and slaves did exist in colonial New England, most rural labor was performed by free white people.

In New England, the absence of any highly profitable staple crop combined with the religious imperatives of Puritanism to keep farms to a size that could be managed by a single family with minimal outside assistance. Even near the bottom of the social ladder, free people could, and did, own their own family farms.

Compared to the "starving time" that marred the Virginia colony's earliest laborers, rural laborers in Massachusetts lived longer lives of higher quality. The ethic of community ran strong among New England's Puritans, and some jobs, such as overseeing herds of swine and inspecting fences, were passed around communally. Town selectmen would even make community-wide decisions regarding when to plant and when to harvest.

Middle Colonies

Pennsylvania was once famously described as "the best poor man's country in the world." Rural laborers in southeastern Pennsylvania benefited from the area's fertile valleys and diverse mix of livestock raising and cereal grain production. Once their indentures were up, servants in this area could realistically look forward to land ownership and even some modicum of economic success.

A similar situation obtained in other parts of the Delaware River Valley. Like their neighbors in New England, farmers in the Mid-Atlantic region produced beef, pork, and grain for export, to feed West Indian slaves, American colonists in other regions, or even people in Europe.

Impact of Slavery

As the eighteenth century progressed, the maturation of colonial societies along the Eastern seaboard led to new challenges for rural laborers. Greater numbers of slaves, many imported directly from Africa, labored on increasingly large plantations in the Chesapeake, the Carolinas, and Georgia.

The slave population also began to reproduce itself around this time. This should not be taken to mean that slave life in the Middle colonies was stable and healthy. It was healthier than work on a sugar plantation, but that was cold comfort to slaves knee-deep in a swamp tending to rice plants. The wealth produced by these plantation slaves was awesome. By the 1770s, some 100 million pounds of tobacco, 60 million pounds of rice, and 1 million pounds of indigo were exported to England each year.

Some white laborers who chose not to compete with Southern slave labor packed their belongings and moved farther into the backcountry, hoping to own their own farms. Good farming land was increasingly scarce along the coast, forcing second sons of the gentry to strike out on their own. In New England, this movement occurred in the form of new towns being settled. The rural clusters and isolated farms that marked the Mid-Atlantic colonies and the Southern colonies, respectively, fanned out to the west as well.

During the second and third quarters of the eighteenth century, native-born fortune seekers were joined by a massive influx of British settlers (really a mix of English, Irish, Scots, and Scots Irish) and Germans (from the western states along the Rhine). Within a matter of decades, the immigrants had dispossessed Native Americans of the land and transformed it thoroughly. The rapid rise of the backcountry often bred conflict between newly settled counties and older, more powerful coastal areas.

American Revolution

The American Revolution may have begun in coastal cities, but the success of the Americans in their fight against Great Britain depended in large part upon their ability to survive without imported goods. Rural production made this possible.

Rural laborers were deeply divided during the struggle for independence. Many recent immigrants sided with Great Britain, as did thousands of African American slaves, hoping to parlay their loyalty into freedom.

While the American Revolution disrupted the lives of countless rural workers, for many, it was a temporary disruption. Most great planters of the South held on to their property, and the rural models established in the colonial period continued to spread across the continent during the early years of the American republic.

Matthew Jennings

See also: Agriculture; Class; Economy, Business, and Labor (Chronology); Economy, Business, and Labor (Essay); Indentured Servitude; Slavery, African American; Tenant Farming.

Bibliography

Danbom, David B. *Born in the Country: A History of Rural America.* Baltimore: Johns Hopkins University Press, 1995.
Fischer, David Hackett. *Albion's Seed: Four British Folkways in America.* New York: Oxford University Press, 1989.
Hofstadter, Richard. *America at 1750: A Social Portrait.* New York: Alfred A. Knopf, 1971.
Taylor, Alan. *American Colonies.* New York: Viking, 2001.

Laborers, Urban

As the British North American colonies developed during the seventeenth and eighteenth centuries, urban areas and the laborers who toiled within them played a vital role in the social, economic, political, and cultural development of the colonies.

The first group brought to colonial America to fill the demand for urban and rural labor were indentured servants. This was a contractual labor system whereby Europeans, usually poor but not always, entered into a contract that paid for their voyage to the New World; to pay off this debt, they agreed to work for their master for a set number of years. For most of the seventeenth century, indentured servants were mainly utilized as agrarian laborers. As the use of slaves expanded in the eighteenth century, more indentured servants, from the British Isles and continental Europe, filled the labor needs of the growing urban areas.

While an apprenticeship system did not fully develop in colonial North America, mainly because of the labor scarcity, indentured servants did fill the need in this traditional manufacturing system. Some of the indentured servants arrived with already acquired skills and therefore quickly proved valuable, while others negotiated the specific skill they would acquire through their servitude.

As the eighteenth century commenced and the colonies developed, the work these indentured servants engaged in expanded. Not only were they employed as unskilled physical laborers, but they also constructed the buildings, housing, and infrastructures of these urban areas while manufacturing finished goods. As the colonies developed, the range of commodities that were in demand also expanded, thus creating a need for workers with even more specialized skills. One example concerned the expanding demand for printed materials, especially newspapers, and many print shops employed indentured servants.

A second group of urban laborers, usually studied within their agrarian context, were African slaves. By the middle of the seventeenth century, as the flow of indentured servants slowed and the flow of slaves increased, African slavery became the second labor system to develop within colonial North America. The scarcity of labor, especially the need for workers to make the land productive, helps to explain the utilization of African slaves, but this demand for workers existed beyond the plantation.

In urban areas, African slaves engaged in various tasks. In ports, slaves worked as watermen, as porters, and at other jobs requiring hard physical toil, such as loading and unloading commodities from ship to shore and vice versa, as well as moving them within and beyond the city. Throughout ports and inland urban

Foremost among urban free wage laborers in the colonies were skilled craftsmen—such as coopers, shown here—who most often acquired their skills through the guild system. Apprentices learned from master craftsmen and worked as journeymen until they had saved the capital to start their own shop. *(Brown Brothers, Sterling, Pennsylvania)*

areas, slaves primarily filled unskilled physical jobs, but they also participated as skilled laborers. Some slaves worked for their master within his shop, while others were taught specific skills. The masters, usually skilled craftsmen, saw slavery as a way to meet their labor needs while guaranteeing themselves a long-term skilled employee.

In many ports, especially those in the South, slaves also directly participated in maritime ventures. During the winter, when there was little plantation work, many slaves served as sailors for short trading voyages throughout the Americas. Other slaves were more permanent sailors, toiling on vessels that traveled the world, and some slaves even served as sailors on vessels participating in the trans-Atlantic slave trade. In some cases, slaves became highly skilled pilots and navigators whose ability and knowledge allowed ships to safely enter and exit specific ports. In the New England colonies, slaves also were included on many fishing voyages.

The presence of slaves working in these urban areas meant that these slaves interacted and lived with the other laborers within the port on a daily basis. This interaction created a diverse, urban working class within the North American colonies.

The cultural diversity within this class of urban laborers can be seen in the Great Negro Plot of 1741 in New York City. While this attempt to burn the city to the ground has traditionally been viewed as a slave uprising, research has shown that a great variety of urban laborers, including free and unfree, white and black, participated in, and were punished for, this uprising.

The final group of urban laborers to develop was free wage laborers. Much of our understanding of these laborers has been influenced by the belief that colonial North America was the best poor man's land—wages were higher there, therefore life was better. Free wage laborers in the colonies can be broken down into the following categories: skilled, unskilled, and maritime.

The early skilled craftsmen who arrived in the colonies had acquired their knowledge and skills through the guild system and therefore brought along this system of labor training. The guild system was designed not only to train skilled laborers but also to protect the secrets of the trade. By reducing or limiting the number of people employed in any one trade, guilds were able to protect their place within the market.

At the top of the guild system was the master craftsman, who was highly skilled and owned his own shop. A good colonial example was Benjamin Franklin, who not only owned his own print shop, within which he employed journeymen and apprentices, but also provided capital to his most talented journeymen to start their own businesses. Below the master craftsman was the journeyman, who, while highly trained and skilled, lacked the capital to start his own business and therefore continued to work for his master as a wage laborer. At the bottom was the apprentice, who began his training in his early teens and did not become free—that is, achieve journeyman status—until his early 20s.

Most masters were selective about the apprentices they accepted, and after negotiation with the parents, a contract was drawn up. In some instances money changed hands, but most often, in exchange for teaching the youth the trade, the master received the apprentice's labor wage-free. The master was required to provide his apprentices with the basic necessities of life, and sometimes the apprentices were allowed access to education. The master oversaw the apprentices' upbringing to make them productive members of the community.

While this traditional mode of manufacturing established itself in many urban areas, the major problem involved the lack of labor coupled with the abundance of land. Many masters found it hard to acquire free apprentices and therefore turned to different types of bound labor. In some cases, masters purchased the contracts of indentured servants; in others, they bought slaves. It was not until the second half of the eighteenth century that an adequate supply of free wage laborers began to develop. Wage labor rose in importance because of the increasing number of indentured servants becoming free, continued migration to the colonies, and changes in production and the market economy. As free wage labor developed, urban laborers—male and female, white and black—filled a multitude of skilled and unskilled jobs.

As the coastal ports expanded, workers were needed to create the port infrastructure and to manufacture commodities, build ships, move commodities, and serve as sailors, among other endeavors. Alongside these free wage laborers lived and worked sailors. While some sailors remained transient, most had home ports, which they returned to and lived in until their next voyage.

During the second half of the eighteenth century, the growing urban laborer population participated significantly in the events surrounding the American Revolution. Some free laborers met the local voting requirements and became politically active. And their life and work in urban areas meant that they had access to the information and new ideas flowing throughout the Atlantic world.

During the American crisis, urban street mobs played an important role in publicly resisting what the colonists saw as increasing British tyranny. The mob—composed mainly of the lower class and usually dominated by free and unfree urban laborers—protested the Stamp Act, intimidated tax collectors, and was blamed for the Boston Massacre. By this time, urban laborers were beginning to develop a common consciousness that allowed them to act as a group.

Ty M. Reese

See also: Artisans; Cities; Class; Economy, Business, and Labor (Chronology); Economy, Business, and Labor (Essay); Servants, Domestic.

Bibliography

Hodges, Graham Russell. *New York City Cartmen, 1667–1850.* New York: New York University Press, 1986.

Innes, Stephen, ed. *Work and Labor in Early America.* Chapel Hill: University of North Carolina Press, 1988.

Morris, Richard B. *Government and Labor in Early America.* New York: Columbia University Press, 1946.

Rediker, Marcus. *Between the Devil and the Deep Blue Sea: Merchant Seaman, Pirates, and the Anglo-American Maritime World, 1700–1750.* New York: Cambridge University Press, 1987.

Smith, Billy. *The "Lower Sort": Philadelphia's Laboring People, 1750–1800.* Ithaca, NY: Cornell University Press, 1990.

Land and Real Estate

The indigenous peoples of colonial America viewed land in terms of its productiveness to those cultivating it, but otherwise they attached no value to the land. Thus, land had no recognizable market value, and the idea of hoarding land for years or decades before utilization was unheard by the natives. Ownership was limited to immediate usefulness, and, even then, ownership was a collective concept, not an individual one.

This set of cultural beliefs was challenged, however, with the coming of European settlers.

Upon arriving in colonial America, English settlers found an abundance of fertile land that could be acquired quite easily and inexpensively. Agriculture quickly became the primary economic pursuit in the colonies. It has been estimated that at least 90 percent of the settlers made their livelihood from farming or farm-related endeavors. As a result, land became the chief symbol of wealth in most colonies.

To fully understand the agrarian economy of the colonies, it is necessary to place it within the political social atmosphere of the time. Availability and distribution of land were forever intertwined with political patronage and nepotism. Based upon the right of discovery, the king was believed to be owner and lord of all land within his empire. He exercised unlimited control over the distribution of land grants to his subjects. Such grants were made to investment companies, individual proprietors, and relatives.

The manner by which the recipients of royal land grants disposed of the land varied from colony to colony, but it generally fell into three categories: Some land was sold, some was given away, and the remaining portions were leased to tenant farmers. Regional differences in land use were the result of climatic, agricultural, and even religious variances.

Southern Colonies: Virginia and the Carolinas

The Southern colonies, particularly Virginia and the Carolinas, were unique in several ways that set them apart from the rest of colonial America. First, Southern agriculture was commercial in nature, with exportation a central goal. The proceeds from the sale of the three staple exports—tobacco, rice, and indigo—were used to acquire commodities not available locally. Second, land holdings were, by comparison, far larger than other regions. Plantations of several thousand acres, while not the norm, were certainly evident in the South. Even the acreage owned by the average Southern planter far exceeded that held by his counterparts in the Middle colonies and New England. A final distinction was the ever-increasing reliance on slave labor to work the land.

From the very beginning, colonizers in Virginia were preoccupied with the desire to amass vast estates. Encouraging immigration to the region, the Virginia Company introduced a new system of land distribution, the headright system, which offered a settler 50 acres of land for each person he would bring to the colony. Later, after the Virginia Company lost its charter, this policy was continued by the British Crown. The system was ripe for abuse, however, and allotments were made for imaginary inhabitants. In this manner, estates measuring several thousand acres were evident by 1650. Records indicate that by 1704, there were twenty-five men whose estates totaled at least 5,000 acres. Within fifty years, the size of the great plantations exploded in size, ranging from 30,000 to 100,000 acres.

The plantation economy of colonial Virginia was built on the interrelationship of these ever-growing large estates, tobacco, and slavery. Prior to the Revolutionary War and the creation of new states, Virginia was a vast region that exceeded all of New England in size. Unassigned land was available to those savvy enough to manipulate the political system and gain land grants for themselves. Tobacco, an immensely popular commodity in Europe, became the premier cash crop. The richness of the region's soil and the temperate weather created an ideal environment in which to grow tobacco, and the intricate network of waterways within the colony made access to Atlantic trade routes accessible to individual plantation owners. The success of the tobacco industry was dependent on slave labor. After approximately 1619, the slave trade became an integral part of the economic and social framework of colonial Virginia. In fact, by 1776, slaves represented 40 to 60 percent of the colony's population.

The history of the Carolinas in colonial America in many ways paralleled that of Virginia. Geographically, the area was immense and exceeded the length of New England and the Middle colonies of New York, Pennsylvania, New Jersey, and Delaware. In 1629, King Charles I granted the entire region to Robert

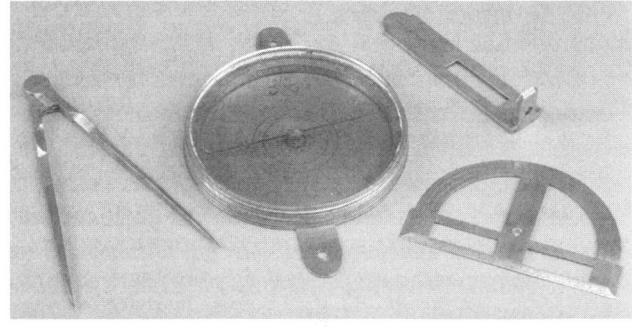

No implement or equipment was more vital to the settlement, charting, and development of the American frontier than a surveyor's tools, such as these seventeenth-century brass instruments. *(Courtesy of Historical Society of Pennsylvania Collection, Atwater Kent Museum of Philadelphia/Bridgeman Art Library)*

Heath, who named the area Carolina after his benefactor. Unfortunately for Heath, King Charles II rescinded his patent in 1663 and divided the region among eight English lords.

A charter was established that divided these eight grants into sections of 12,000 acres, to be governed by lord proprietors who received profits from the sale of land as well as quitrents—monetary payments made by tenants similar to rent in lieu of feudal services. In turn, the land was further divided and sold to commoners, who could divide the land yet again and sell it to others. When the colonial assembly objected to paying the quitrents, the lord proprietors divided the region into two separate territories in an attempt to control the rebellion. The two territories were reunited briefly in 1691, but, in 1712, they were divided once more and became known as North and South Carolina.

In the early decades, the land not held by the lord proprietors was distributed fairly evenly among the other colonists. Following the wars with the Spanish and natives, however, higher taxes were imposed to cover the immense war debt. Smaller farmers were the hardest hit by this legislation. Finding it difficult to remain competitive in agricultural markets, many were forced to sell their holdings to large plantation owners at prices far below actual value. The scene was thus set for the emergence of an elitist planter economy.

Unlike the planters of North Carolina, who, like Virginia planters, made their fortunes in tobacco, South Carolina planters invested in rice and, later, indigo. Introduced shortly before 1700, rice was seen as an easy crop to cultivate; success required nothing more than a steady supply of slave labor and someone to oversee them. To keep up with demand for rice, planters imported thousands of slaves to fulfill the need for manual labor. Slaves were arriving in the colony at such a tremendous rate that they outnumbered whites by about two to one by the 1730s.

The assemblies of South Carolina and North Carolina appealed to the king in 1719 and 1729, respectively, asking that the territories be made a royal province. The Privy Council agreed, buying the property rights from the lord proprietors. The land acquired became public land, under the control of royal governors and councils, who had control over the disbursement of the land and often allocated the most desirable portions to themselves. The players may have changed, but the game of land distribution stayed the same.

Middle Colonies: New York and Pennsylvania

The land system in the Middle colonies was a hybrid of New England and the Southern colonies. Land was generally allocated by land grants from the king to companies and proprietors. The average size of an individual's holding was between 100 and 200 acres and was sold for as little as 5 pounds for the total acreage in the seventeenth century. By the eighteenth century, however, this price had increased at least threefold. In New York, estates as large as 12,000 acres were owned by such families as the Van Cortlandts, Pells, Livingstons, Beekmans, and Van Rensselaers.

Unlike the agrarian societies that were developed in the South, the Middle colonies were unable to sustain a plantation-based economy and had to look elsewhere for stability. Colonial New York, where harsh winters prevented the successful cultivation of tobacco, rice, or indigo, provided a fine example of urban commerce and urban aristocracy. Originally founded by the Dutch, the region that would later be known as New York was created as a commercial operation for the exportation of animal furs. The Dutch West India Company was so dismayed at the slow development of the colony that, in 1629, it offered a reward of a vast estate to any man responsible for bringing fifty adult settlers to the region. These men, called patroons, would hold perpetual lordship over the tenants on their land. The patroons' tenants would be subject to a more severe version of the quitrents system; not only were the rates higher, but default was certain to result in eviction from the land.

In 1664, the English, under Charles II, successfully usurped the colony from the Dutch. Charles II granted control of the territory to his brother, the Duke of York, who would later become King James II. The English did not disturb the feudal patroon system, but renamed the land holdings "manors." What followed was a series of unsavory land purchases from Native Americans, as well as unscrupulous land grants, from which royal governors would reserve for themselves a prime share of the land being allocated. It was the rare honest royal governor who abhorred the apparent unjust dealings and appealed to Parliament, contending that the development of New York was being impeded because immigrants were settling in other colonies where freehold land was available.

By the opening years of the eighteenth century,

there was little land left to allot in the colony of New York. An English victory in the French and Indian War temporarily alleviated this problem, however, as vast new territory became available to the north.

The history of New York thus presents a picture of entanglement between politics and ownership of land. Those landholders with the largest estates clearly had familial ties with those seated as governors or council members. Members of these select families tightened ranks through a series of marital alliances and commercial endeavors.

The origins of Pennsylvania began in 1681 when Charles II granted a great tract of land to William Penn as repayment for a debt owed to Penn's father. The boundary of the land grant met Maryland in the south and New York in the north, and extended westward beyond what had been explored up to that time. The land, which was to be held in free and common tenancy, was to be distributed as Penn saw fit. While Penn was sole proprietor of this vast region, he did not have the resources to personally fund settlements there. To aid in this task, he enlisted the assistance of a group of wealthy Quakers, or the Free Society of Traders, with members purchasing tracts of 10,000 acres. In exchange, they negotiated special privileges that included exemption from paying quitrents and the right to develop the choicest property in the new city that Penn was planning, Philadelphia.

Settlement of Pennsylvania spread rapidly as new immigrants arrived. By the middle of 1683, the colony was home to more than 3,000 people, many of whom were English, Irish, Welsh, Dutch, and German. Within five years, the population had grown to an amazing 12,000 people, a fantastic feat when one considers that it took Virginia nearly thirty years to reach a comparable number. As these settlers discovered, Penn structured the division of land judiciously. Property, widely distributed, was available for a low price, and safeguards were established so that no one person could accumulate a vast estate. Toleration of personal and religious beliefs attracted merchants and artisans from English settlements on both sides of the Atlantic. Similarly, Quakers, seeking religious freedom, arrived, bringing with them well-established trade connections. Soon, Philadelphia was rivaling Boston as a commercial port.

One of the factors that aided in the development of Pennsylvania was Penn's desire to treat the indigenous peoples fairly. Penn learned to speak the native Lenni Lenape language, established strict trade rela-tions, and forbade the sale of alcohol to Native Americans. A noted pacifist, Penn upheld a policy of negotiating proper treaties with indigenous peoples, paying 1,200 pounds for the first land settled along the Delaware River. These policies attracted to the area many native people who wished to escape harsh dealings with other English colonists. Relations between the two cultures continued to flourish thanks to the Quaker convictions of generosity and love.

Geography was also instrumental in the development and continued existence of Pennsylvania. With New York to the north, Maryland to the south, and mountains along its western border, the colony's settlers did not have to fear attacks from external forces seeking to usurp their land.

New England Colonies

Settlers in the New England colonies acquired land in one of several ways. The first was actual occupancy, or squatting, which was utilized before local governments were established and was evident in such towns as Boston, Salem, New Haven, and Hartford. Notably, however, such landowners came under the jurisdiction of subsequently formed legislatures.

Early settlers also purchased land directly from Native Americans, particularly in Connecticut and Rhode Island. As colonial governments were established that required legislative involvement in land transactions, this method was abandoned.

The final and most prevalent method of land acquisition was by means of a grant from the colonial legislature. Under this method, towns were plotted and tracts were surveyed before individual ownership was granted.

The vast majority of New England land granted by the legislature was given to large groups or communities. The towns that resulted held communal goals above individual economic ones. To ensure godliness among the town's inhabitants, land was only distributed to those who passed religious and moral tests administered by the town fathers. Promoting solidarity, land was sold only to town residents and only if there was a consensus of the town fathers. These settlers found that the climate and geography made the exportation of staple crops virtually impossible. The earliest New England settlers, therefore, established a local economy that combined livestock grazing, production of essential crafts, and trade-related services.

Massachusetts, the quintessential New England

colony, was settled mainly by members of Puritan congregations. In the fall of 1620, 102 people set sail from England on the famed *Mayflower,* which was to land hundreds of miles farther north than anticipated, in an area they called Plymouth. Unprepared for the harsh winter conditions they encountered, only half of the passengers were still alive when spring arrived. In 1628 another group of Puritans arrived to launch the colonial enterprise that would come to dominate New England. The following year, the merchants involved in this endeavor received a royal charter as the Massachusetts Bay Colony.

The Massachusetts Bay Colony attracted additional Puritans who no longer believed that they could practice their religion freely in England. They sought reform of the Church of England, but thought it more prudent to pursue such change from a distance in the colonies. John Winthrop, the most prominent member of this venture, organized the initial segment of what was to later be known as the "Great Migration." In 1630, more than 1,000 Puritan men and women moved to Massachusetts, the majority settling in the Boston area. By 1643, nearly 20,000 of their fellow believers had joined them, making Boston the largest town in the English-speaking colonies.

Central to the Puritans' beliefs was the idea that they were in a special relationship with God. They believed that God had entered into a covenant, an agreement or contract, with them and that they were chosen for a special mission in the New World. In turn, they promised one another that they would live together in harmony, working toward communal goals. The leaders of the Massachusetts Bay Colony transformed the nature of the original charter to reflect a community based on mutual consent.

The manner by which land was granted in Massachusetts also reflected the Puritans' communal ideals. Unlike the Southern colonies of Virginia and Maryland where headrights were granted to individual applicants who settled their lands at a distance from one another, in Massachusetts, groups of men collectively applied to the General Court for land grants.

The men who received such grants were responsible for determining how they would be distributed. They began by surveying the land and plotting the area where houses and churches would be established. Only then would families be given individual parcels scattered outside the town center for farming. True to the social hierarchy that had existed in England, parcels of land were allotted according to social status. While those who had been lower on the social ladder in England received less desirable parcels, it is notable that every man did receive land.

Later, when people began to move beyond the territorial limits of the Massachusetts Bay Colony into other areas of New England, such as Connecticut and New Hampshire, the same process of land grants was maintained. This practice is what truly set these settlers apart from other English settlements.

Joann M. Ross

See also: Agriculture; Economy, Business, and Labor (Chronology); Economy, Business, and Labor (Essay); Inheritance; Laborers, Rural; Landlords; Plantations; Property and Property Rights; Tenant Farming. *Document:* Probate Inventory of a Plymouth Colony Estate (1672).

Bibliography

Brack, Oscar Theodore, and Hugh Talmage Lefler. *Colonial America.* 2nd ed. New York: Macmillan, 1968.

Freyfogel, Eric T. "Land Use and the Study of Early American History." *Yale Law Journal* 94 (January 1985): 717–42.

Friedenberg, Daniel M. *Life, Liberty, and the Pursuit of Land: The Plunder of Early America.* New York: Prometheus, 1992.

Gillon, Steven M., and Cathy D. Matson. *The American Experiment: A History of the United States.* Boston: Houghton Mifflin, 2002.

Hoffer, Peter Charles. *Law and People in Colonial America.* Baltimore: Johns Hopkins University Press, 1992.

Middleton, Richard. *Colonial America: A History, 1565–1776.* 3rd ed. Oxford, UK: Blackwell, 2002.

Norton, Mary Beth, David M. Katzman, David B. Blight, Howard P. Chudacoff, Thomas G. Paterson, William M. Tuttle, Jr., and Paul D. Escott, eds. *A People and a Nation: A History of the United States.* 6th ed. Boston: Houghton Mifflin, 2001.

Landlords

The relationship between a landlord and his tenants in colonial America was patterned on the common law pattern established in England. The acquisition of land was intimately entwined with political favor and patronage. Land was the chief form of wealth in the American colonies.

The king was presumed to be the owner and lord of all land within his provinces. As such, it was his right and responsibility to grant allotments to his subjects. Such grants were made to companies that invested in land speculation and to individual proprietors. Land speculators generally sectioned off and sold the land they were given. Individual proprietors, however, often divided the land and became landlords, leasing the land to tenant farmers as a means of continuing income.

The landlord-tenant relationship involved a landowner granting a lease to a tenant for a designated period of time, during which the tenant gained the right of possession, physical control, and the right to exclude others from a particular tract of land. The form of lease was designated a periodic tenancy, a tenancy for a fixed term, or a tenancy at will. A periodic tenancy was a lease for a determined duration of time that continued for succeeding periods until either the landlord or the tenant terminated it; a month-to-month lease provides a contemporary example. A tenancy for a fixed term was a lease that would last for a predetermined amount of time that could be designated by days, weeks, months, or years. A third, but less common, tenancy was a tenancy at will, in which no specific time framework was established, but which lasted as long as both landlord and tenant desired. The English Statute of Frauds (1677) required that all leases for more than three years be in writing if they were to be enforceable.

In colonial America, most leases were primarily agricultural in nature and focused little attention on the quality of buildings erected on the land. The duties of the landlord reflected this emphasis. A landlord had a duty to deliver the right of possession to his tenant at the beginning of the tenancy, but without specific terms in the lease, he had no other obligations to the tenant.

If a previous tenant remained on the land beyond the date that a subsequent tenant's lease was to commence and the landlord did not remove the prior tenant within a reasonable period of time, the landlord would be in default on the lease. In such a case, the new tenant had two options. The first was to affirm the lease, refuse to pay rent for the time that he was not in possession, and recover the cost of finding alternate accommodations. The tenant also could choose to terminate the lease and seek to recover damages from the landlord. The measure of damages could include the cost of renting other premises in excess of the rent specified in the lease, the cost of ousting the prior tenant, and any reasonably anticipated loss caused by the delay of acquiring possession.

Similarly, a landlord had no duty to provide habitable premises or to repair or maintain the leasehold once a tenant took possession. The prevailing idea of *caveat lessee*, "let the lessee beware," was based on the rationale that a prospective tenant was able to protect himself by inspecting the premises before entering the lease. Even if a landlord fraudulently warranted that the premises were habitable, a tenant who discovered a defect was still obligated to pay rent. The tenant's only recourse was to sue the landlord for damages.

An exception existed for hidden or latent defects of which the landlord was aware. If such defects or dangerous conditions were known to the landlord but not easily discoverable by the tenant, the landlord had a legal duty to disclose the defects, but not to repair them. Additionally, if the lease included an express promise by the landlord to make repairs, the landlord would be liable for any injuries that resulted from his negligent breach of this obligation.

Thus, property rights in colonial America clearly favored the landlord and often appeared hard-hearted regarding the plight of tenants. The law required a landlord to tender possession of the leasehold to a legal tenant, but included no provision regarding the condition of such premises. After the Revolution and the opening up of lands in the West, the balance of power would shift somewhat away from the landlord to the tenant.

Joann M. Ross

See also: Land and Real Estate; Patroons; Planters; Tenant Farming. *Document:* Rights and Privileges of Patroons (1629).

Bibliography

Dukeminier, Jesse, and James E. Krier. *Property.* 4th ed. New York: Aspen Law and Business, 1998.

Friedenberg, Daniel M. *Life, Liberty, and the Pursuit of Land: The Plunder of Early America.* New York: Prometheus, 1992.

Moynihan, Cornelius J. *Introduction to the Law of Real Property: An Historical Background of The Common Law of Real Property and Its Modern Application.* St. Paul, MN: West Publishing, 1962.

Language

Numerous languages have always been spoken in the Americas. In fact, scholars estimate that when Europeans arrived in the Americas in the fifteenth century, as many as 2,000 native languages existed. Of these languages, 329 were spoken by native peoples on the North American mainland. Once Europeans began sustained contact with the peoples of the Americas in the fifteenth century, they contributed more languages to the already multilingual New World.

Some of the most common European languages on the North American mainland during the colonial era were Spanish, English, French, Dutch, and German. The European importation of African slaves also brought West and Central African languages to the mainland and its coastal islands. These African languages often combined with English to form creole languages. Such languages had the grammar and sentence structure of West and Central African languages; their vocabularies contained primarily English words, though African languages influenced the pronunciations of these words. This kind of melding occurred with other languages as well.

Native American Languages on the Colonial North American Mainland

Linguists believe that the many Native American languages that existed on the North American mainland at the time of European contact fit into twelve language stocks. These include Na-Dene, Salishan, Penutian, Uto-Aztecan, Yuman, and Coahuil in the West; Eskimo-Aleut in the northernmost tip; Siouan and Caddoan in the Midwest; and Algonquian, Gulf, and Iroquoian in the East. These language stocks are as different from each other as Indo-European languages are from Semitic languages. Furthermore, related languages within each larger language stock can differ from each other as much as English does from Russian.

Certain geographic regions had more linguistic diversity than others. On the West and Northwest Coasts, the languages spoken in the colonial era were distantly related. In the Midwest and on the East Coast, the languages spoken were more closely related. Thus, Native American peoples living near each other often spoke mutually unintelligible languages.

When Europeans encountered native peoples on the North American mainland, they often classified distinct tribes as members of one nation because of their close proximity to each other, similar societal organization, or shared language. But in the earliest years of contact, native peoples identified more with their villages than with fellow language-speakers or those living in the same region.

In the mid-sixteenth century, for instance, Francisco Vázquez de Coronado mistakenly identified all of the native peoples of what is now New Mexico as Pueblos. At that time, however, they spoke seven languages—Keresan, Piro, Tano, Tewa, Tiwa, Tompiro, and Towa—and did not think of themselves as members of a common Pueblo nation. Thus, upon first contact with each other, Europeans often misunderstood many Native Americans' notions of societal organization and group identity.

Native peoples also communicated in other ways besides speaking. Plains Indians, who lived in today's Midwestern United States and the southern part of Canada, communicated using sign languages, which consisted of hundreds of signs and allowed them to communicate with Plains peoples who spoke other languages. When the Europeans arrived, native peoples from distinct villages came into even closer contact with each other.

In order to trade goods, many Native Americans learned trade jargons, which consist of a minimal vocabulary and could only be used in certain contexts. These terms were typically derived from Native American languages. For instance, Chinook, Choctaw, and Comanche trade jargons became the languages of commerce in different regions of the North American mainland. Native peoples also borrowed words from European languages to explain unfamiliar customs, animals, and objects such as "Christmas," "horse," "cat," "cow," "book," and "gun."

By the end of the colonial period, many Native Americans had begun using European languages as their main means of communication, as European domination made learning their languages necessary for survival. By the mid-eighteenth century, the Massachusett people of New England spoke primarily English. During the same period, Calusas in Florida were speaking predominantly Spanish.

Some of the first Native American words adopted by Europeans include the following, from peoples in the West Indies: "canoe," "hammock," "maize," and "hurricane." Since most of the Europeans' first contacts were with Native Americans who spoke one of the forty to fifty Algonquian languages, most native words incorporated in the English language come from these languages.

Some of the most common words adopted by Europeans referred to places or natural features; many American rivers, such as the Mississippi, Ohio, and Yukon Rivers, carry Native American names. During most of the eighteenth century, however, as tensions between Europeans and the native peoples mounted, Europeans avoided adopting native words into their languages.

African Languages on the Colonial North American Mainland

African slaves on the North American mainland brought many distinct languages with them. Generally, they came from West Africa and represented such African peoples as the Ashanti, Fulani, Ibo, Mandingo, and Yoruba. Their languages were as distinct and mutually unintelligible from each other as were the various Native American languages. When transporting African slaves across the Atlantic Ocean, European slave traders used this diversity of languages among African peoples to their advantage. On slave ships, slave traders separated slaves with similar ethnic and language backgrounds, since they feared that keeping these slaves together might result in their plotting an uprising.

Those slaves who survived the horrendous voyage across the Atlantic found themselves working on plantations with other Africans of different ethnic backgrounds who spoke different languages, but they soon began to identify with their fellow slaves despite these ethnic and linguistic differences. Over time, a more global African identity replaced some slaves' previous distinct African identities. Slaves were more likely to lose much of their African cultures in regions with few slaves and where slaves worked in households in close contact with their owners, such as New England and the Mid-Atlantic.

In South Carolina and the Georgia Low Country, however, where slaves greatly outnumbered whites on the rice and indigo plantations, they were able to maintain more aspects of their cultures, and they created a creole English influenced by West and Central African languages. Some of the first slaves taken to South Carolina and Georgia already spoke a West African creole, which had been created by British slave traders and local African traders and was also used as a common language between Africans of different ethnic backgrounds along the West African coast. This language became the basis for Gullah.

An example of the continued influence of African languages on the North American mainland was the slave practice of giving African names to their children. Many children were given African names based on the days of the week, months, and seasons.

European Languages on the Colonial North American Mainland

Spanish

When the Spaniards became the first Europeans to maintain sustained contacts with native peoples on the North American mainland at the end of the fifteenth century, they brought with them a language already influenced by other cultures. Moors and Jews in Spain who spoke Arabic and Ladino, respectively, had already contributed to the vocabulary, grammatical structure, and pronunciation of Spanish. As a result, the Spaniards were not completely opposed to adopting Native American words into the Spanish language. In fact, the Spaniards allowed Nahuatl, the Aztec language, to continue to be used for religious and governmental functions for many years after they conquered Mexico.

While the Spaniards adopted many Aztec words, including "coyote," "chocolate," and "chile," Spanish also became a common language among native peoples who spoke different languages. In New Mexico, members of one Pueblo community used Spanish when trading with another Pueblo community that spoke a different language. At different times, the Spaniards sent settlement expeditions to New Mexico, Texas, and California, and these communities developed distinct Spanish dialects because of their isolation from each other and from the older settlements in central Mexico.

English

By 1660, English settlers on the colonial North American mainland numbered 70,000; there were 5,000 Dutch settlers and 3,000 French settlers. By 1700, the English and African populations numbered 250,000, and the French and Spanish populations numbered 7,500. Early on, then, English became the dominant language.

The English used the English language in their quest to civilize and Christianize native peoples. Seventeenth-century Puritans also hoped that by teaching Native Americans to speak English, they could use them as translators and not have to learn to speak native languages themselves, which many viewed as difficult. Even so, seventeenth-century Puritans did not generally view Native American languages as inferior.

Puritans, like other Europeans at that time, believed that all languages were corrupt forms of one original language that God had given Adam in the Garden of Eden. It was not until the late seventeenth and early eighteenth century, when the thinker John Locke popularized the idea that languages were essentially human creations, that the English and other Europeans began to view their languages as refined and Native American languages as savage.

French

While the French never established large settlements on the North American mainland in comparable numbers to English settlements, French Catholic missionaries, mostly Jesuits, achieved greater success than English Protestant missionaries in converting the native peoples. A key reason for the Jesuits' success was their willingness to teach Native Americans about religion in their own languages, which the Jesuits felt was easier than teaching them French. Because of this approach to conversion, the Jesuits produced many grammar books, dictionaries, and prayer books in native languages.

Another group of Frenchmen, traders, also communicated with native peoples in local languages. In the seventeenth century, those traders who refused to trade only in French forts were known as coureurs de bois. They visited Native American villages in the Great Lakes region and in Illinois country, using trade jargons based on native languages. Many traders learned this jargon through their marriage to Native American women. The children of such mixed unions, the Métis, often spoke both Native American and European languages, and frequently they served as mediators between the French and native peoples.

Some of the first intermediaries for the French, however, were Native Americans taken to France by early French explorers. For example, Jacques Cartier took two sons of an Iroquois chief to France in 1534. After a year in France, they returned to North America. A French-Iroquoian dictionary was based on communications between Cartier and the two Iroquois.

Dutch

Another European power that established an empire on the colonial North American mainland was the Netherlands. The Dutch engaged primarily in trade on the mainland and were not as interested in converting the native peoples to Christianity as the Spanish, French, and English were. Instead, relations between Dutch colonists in the Mid-Atlantic region and local Native American tribes tended to be tense and violent.

In the seventeenth century, the Dutch colony of New Netherland was known as the most ethnically diverse and religiously tolerant colony in North America. A French observer remarked that, in 1643, he heard eighteen languages—European, African, and Native American—being spoken there. But there were fewer Dutch immigrants overall, mostly because economic pressures in Holland were not as severe and did not propel as many people to the New World. Therefore, Dutch never became as influential as English.

As the result of a series of military defeats, the Dutch had to cede New Netherland to the English in 1667 (they briefly regained it in 1673 before finally losing control of it in 1674). Once under British rule, the New Netherland colonists resisted such rule because the British did not allow the use of Dutch in courts, imposed English common law on them, and carried out other measures that limited the New Netherland colonists' rights. These ethnically diverse peoples soon began to identify as a Dutch people in defense against this stern English rule. It was not until the mid-eighteenth century that they finally began to assimilate English ways and speak the English language.

German

In the eighteenth century, Germany and Switzerland also began sending large numbers of immigrants to the North American mainland. About 90,000 to 100,000 German-speaking immigrants came to the mainland in the eighteenth century from regions such as Palatine, Alsace, Baden, Bavaria, Hesse, and Switzerland. Settling predominantly in Pennsylvania, they were called "Pennsylvania Dutch" because they spoke Deutsch (German).

These immigrants often learned little English, although, in many cases, it did not matter because they settled near other German speakers. They sustained their language by publishing books, newspapers, and almanacs in it. Germans also settled in other parts of the North American continent. Many cities across today's Eastern United States still carry German names, such as Herkimer and New Berlin (both in New York), Fredericksburg (Virginia), and New Bern (North Carolina).

Diversity and Uses

While English was the most common language spoken by American colonists by the time of the Revolutionary

War, it was simply one among hundreds of other languages heard in the sixteenth, seventeenth, and eighteenth centuries on the North American mainland. Native American peoples, immigrant Europeans, and African slaves also created jargons and creole languages in order to communicate with each other.

Language in colonial North American history was a tool of conquest and a form of resistance, a means of negotiating cultural differences and of facilitating trade. Ultimately, the languages of colonial North America produced the English spoken in the United States today.

Lisa Y. Ramos

See also: Arts, Culture, and Intellectual Life (Chronology); Arts, Culture, and Intellectual Life (Essay); Immigration; Literature.

Bibliography

Brandes, Paul D., and Jeutonne Brewer. *Dialect Clash in America: Issues and Answers.* Metuchen, NJ: Scarecrow, 1977.

Calloway, Colin G. *New Worlds for All: Indians, Europeans, and the Remaking of Early America.* Baltimore: Johns Hopkins University Press, 1997.

Conklin, Nancy Faires, and Margaret A. Lourie. *A Host of Tongues: Language Communities in the United States.* New York: Free Press, 1983.

Cutler, Charles L. *O Brave New Words! Native American Loanwords in Current English.* Norman: University of Oklahoma Press, 1994.

Gray, Edward. *New World Babel: Languages and Nations in Early America.* Princeton, NJ: Princeton University Press, 1999.

Hoffecker, Carol E., et al., eds. *New Sweden in America.* Cranbury, NJ: Associated University Presses, 1995.

Nash, Gary B. *Red, White, and Black: The Peoples of Early North America.* 4th ed. Upper Saddle River, NJ: Prentice Hall, 2000.

Opala, Joseph A. *The Gullah: Rice, Slavery, and the Sierra Leone–American Connection.* Freetown, Sierra Leone: USIS, 1987.

Taylor, Alan. *American Colonies.* In *The Penguin History of the United States,* edited by Eric Foner. New York: Viking Penguin, 2001.

La Salle, René Robert Cavelier, Sieur de (1643–1687)

Like John White and Walter Raleigh with the "Lost Colony" at Roanoke, René Robert Cavelier, Sieur de La Salle, did not succeed in establishing a viable colony. Still, as with the early voyages to Roanoke, La Salle's voyage to the Gulf of Mexico paved the way for colo-

Seeking the mouth of the Mississippi River, the French explorer René Robert Cavelier, Sieur de La Salle, and his expedition reached what is now Matagorda Bay, Texas, in early 1685. They missed their destination by about 400 miles. *(Brown Brothers, Sterling, Pennsylvania)*

nization, in his case, the establishment of Louisiana. In claiming the Mississippi River Valley for France, and naming the region Louisiana in honor of his king, La Salle advanced the cause of French colonization immeasurably, and the accounts of his expedition have taught generations of scholars about the native peoples of the Lower Mississippi Valley. La Salle's vision was certainly impressive, but the man himself was noted for his fierce temper and paranoid tendencies.

La Salle was born in Rouen in 1643. Although trained for life as a priest, he gave up his religious training and, in 1667, sailed to Canada, where he received a large estate and prospered as a result of the fur trade. His fur-trading activities brought him into close proximity with the Iroquois, and he picked up the basics of the Seneca language from a band camped on his land.

La Salle, who had been obsessed with China from a young age, may have come to believe that the Ohio River, which his native clients claimed flowed into a great sea, was the same as the Colorado and, therefore, could prove to be the elusive passage through North America. In 1669, La Salle set out with a small group of Senecas and two priests to explore the Ohio River country. The party gradually splintered, and, after being abandoned near the site of Louisville by everyone except Nika, his Shawnee slave interpreter and guide, La Salle returned to Montreal in the dead of winter. (It is also possible that La Salle spent the winter trading in western Iroquois country. There is little firsthand evidence of his early journeys, and the secondary sources are often contradictory.)

La Salle's hardships convinced the novice explorer, who by this point had been joined by Henri de Tonty, that the Ohio River was not part of a passage. He instead concentrated on finding a passable way from the Great Lakes to the Mississippi River. To this end, he spent 1679 and 1680 trading and exploring in the Great Lakes and the Illinois country, cementing an Illinois–French alliance and racking up considerable debt in the process.

La Salle is best known for two dramatic voyages undertaken in the 1680s. In 1682, the explorer and his fleet, half-French and half-native, floated down the Illinois River to the Mississippi and then all the way to the Gulf of Mexico. The French explorers were not particularly impressed by the Mississippi (which they called the Colbert), though they did make contact with many native groups in the region, including the Quapaw, Choctaw, Chickasaw, and Natchez. In April 1682, the party reached the Gulf of Mexico, and La Salle performed an elaborate ceremony, during which he claimed possession of the entire region for Louis XIV, naming it Louisiana in his honor.

In 1684, La Salle undertook to discover the mouth of the Mississippi from the Gulf of Mexico, and he landed with soldiers and craftsmen at Matagorda Bay (in present-day Texas) to found a colony and look for the great river's mouth, which he had missed by about 400 miles. The search lasted for two years, and resentment against La Salle and his violent nephew Crevel de Moranger boiled over. In March of 1687, La Salle, his nephew, his slave Nika, and Moranger's servant Saget were killed by disgruntled members of the colonizing party. Only a handful survived the Matagorda expedition.

La Salle advanced the cause of French colonization in the Illinois and Mississippi River Valleys. His failure to establish a lasting colony at the mouth of the Mississippi should probably be attributed to the nature of the Mississippi delta, rather than any shortcomings on his part. Future French colonizers would build on La Salle's legacy in the years that followed. In the 1990s, the wreck of La Salle's ship, the *Belle*, was discovered in Texas, sparking renewed interest in the discoverer and French colonization in North America.

Matthew Jennings

See also: Exploration; French; French Colonies on Mainland North America (Chronology); Mississippi River; Ohio Country.

Bibliography

Galloway, Patricia K., ed. *La Salle and His Legacy: Frenchmen and Native Americans in the Lower Mississippi Valley.* Jackson: University Press of Mississippi, 1982.

Muhlstein, Anka. *La Salle: Explorer of the North American Frontier.* Translated by Willard Wood. New York: Arcade Publishing, 1994.

Osler, E. B. *La Salle.* Don Mills, Ontario: Longman Canada, 1967.

Wood, Peter H. "La Salle: Discovery of a Lost Explorer." *William and Mary Quarterly* 89:2 (April 1984): 294–323.

Las Casas, Bartolomé de (1474–1566)

Born in Seville, probably on August 24, 1474, Bartolomé de las Casas was the son of baker Pedro de las Casas and his wife, Isabel de Sosa. His father's family was descended from *conversos,* former Spanish Jews, and, during his childhood, his father and three uncles accompanied Christopher Columbus's second voyage to the New World as entrepreneurs.

Las Casas attended Latin school in Seville and Grenada and was present as part of the militia to put down the 1497 Morisco revolt. Intrigued by his family's connection to the New World, especially his short ownership of a slave boy (freed by royal command in 1500), las Casas, having taken minor orders with the Dominicans and been tonsured in the Catholic Church, sailed for Hispaniola (Española) in 1499 alongside his father.

In the new world, Bartolomé las Casas acted as a soldier, while putting down a native revolt in Higuey (1502–1506). During a visit to Rome in 1506, he took formal vows as a priest. Like many Spanish settlers, however, las Casas was more concerned with his land allotment in Hispaniola, given to him by Diego Columbus, than with the spiritual welfare of his native workers, who mined gold and farmed his *encomendia* (a land grant, which also included rule over its peoples).

Although repelled by the massacres during the conquest of the island, he continued to behave as a

Bartolomé de las Casas, one of the first Spanish missionaries in the Americas, is called the Apostle of the Indies for his advocacy of just treatment for native peoples. *(Archivo de Indias, Seville, Spain/Mithra-Index/Bridgeman Art Library)*

conquistador himself until 1514, when he was scolded harshly by his own confessor, a Dominican priest, who refused him absolution until he attended to his spiritual obligation to his native slaves. This crisis of faith proved a turning point in las Casas's life. He sold his properties and returned to Spain with a mission to reform the treatment of natives and push for their evangelization.

Back in Spain, las Casas studied law at the Collegio de San Gregorie, adding legal heft to his arguments in favor of abolishing the *encomendia* system and establishing free native communities. He found powerful patrons, including Archbishop Francisco Ximines de Cisneros and Jean de Sauvage, but was continually blocked by equally powerful conquistador landowners and their representatives in Spain, including several Catholic orders. Although unable to impress Ferdinand of Aragon, las Casas found favor with his royal successors, Holy Roman Emperor Charles V, and the young heir to the throne, Philip II of Spain.

With royal backing, las Casas returned to the New World with a plan to found a model community at Cumana, Venezuela. His Franciscan friars were scattered in a storm, and the local landowners fiercely resisted aiding the community, despite being ordered to do so. In the chaos surrounding the *communeros* revolt, the plan foundered, and las Casas retreated to the Dominican monasteries at Santo Domingo in 1522 and then Puerto de Plata in 1526.

At the monasteries, he began his massive *Historia de las Indias* and *Apologitica Historia*, which outraged Spanish landowners by insisting that the natives were not lesser beings and that they should not be enslaved on the false premise of their inferiority. His *Historia,* using many documents in the library of Diego Columbus, is an indictment of the violent takeover of the New World by the Spanish, as well as a rich, though exaggerated, ethnographic view of native life, including the medicinal use of plants, religious rituals, languages, and social customs. Setting off the conquistadors again by insisting that they return the loot taken from the conquest of Peru, he further antagonized them by refusing absolution to slave owners. He also made inspection trips to dioceses in Mexico and Puerto Rico in 1531–1532.

Despite royal connections, las Casas was a deeply unpopular figure among the Spanish in America. His bishopric in Chiapas, an appointment from Philip II, was a disaster repeated in 1537 in Guatemala, when the local Europeans refused to accept him as their spiritual authority. He, in turn, refused them his services as a priest until they reformed and allowed him to form communities of free natives. This resistance on the part of the Spanish in America ran counter to stated royal and papal policy of peaceful conversion and evangelizing the native population. Las Casas was forced to return to Spain unsuccessful.

Institutionally, las Casas did get the Council of the Indies overhauled in 1540–1541, after years of petitioning and royal audiences. Its new members agreed with his plans for instructing the natives and prosecuting corruption in the Spanish administration. What should have been his greatest triumph, the 1542 New Laws of the Indies, which categorized the natives as subjects, not slaves, and ended the *encomendia* system, was blunted by the protests of the conquistadors, who were able to bend the new laws and force Philip II to allow similar exploitation under new forms of indenture.

At the end of his life, las Casas was still writing, endlessly revising his histories and writing pamphlet after pamphlet decrying the treatment of the native peoples. These received wide distribution, as did the transcript of his five-day debate with Juan Ginés de Sepúlveda before the royal theological council.

Bartolomé de las Casas died sometime before July 20, 1566, when he was buried at the Convent of Stocha in Madrid. A revered figure among native Catholics in the Americas, the Dominican priest was one of the first historians and ethnographers of the New World. He also was one of the few Europeans of his time who spoke for the rights of the native people.

Margaret Sankey

See also: Catholic Church; Government, Spanish Colonial; Native American–European Relations; Spanish Colonies on Mainland North America (Chronology).

Bibliography

Frede, Juan, and Benjamin Keen, eds. *Bartolomé de las Casas in History.* DeKalb: Northern Illinois University Press, 1971.
Hanke, Lewis. *Bartolomé de las Casas: An Interpretation of his Life and Writings.* The Hague: Martinus Nijhoff, 1951.
Traboulay, David. *Columbus and Las Casas.* New York: Rowman and Littlefield, 1994.

Law and Courts

It would be a mistake to assume that law in early America begins with the transplantation of European legal forms across the Atlantic. Like all human communities, native societies had, over the course of centuries, developed ways of regulating behavior and settling disputes.

Although there was wide variation between native peoples, most native legal apparatuses were intimately connected to an individual group's system of clans and kinship. Clans were generally charged with punishing crimes—including murder and adultery—and the retaliatory aspects of clan-based law have been emphasized by many scholars.

Gradually, as native peoples came into contact with various sorts of Europeans, they were forced to confront alien legal forms. On rare occasions, Native Americans were able to turn European American laws to their advantage, but more often the application of these laws resulted in losing their land and sovereignty. Tribal law today remains a complex tangle of indigenous, local, state, and federal statutes.

The colonial American legal system was never a coherent whole. Each colony in British North America was basically responsible for the creation of its own legal system. Because of this, the law and courts in early America were a confusing hodgepodge of different applications of English legal theory, adapted for use in a variety of American settings. Most ordinary colonists knew little about English law; a few highly educated men knew slightly more. In England, a complex of courts—both civil and religious—regulated community life; most people dealt with the law through the person of the justice of the peace.

The first colonial laws were the charters granted to various colonizing companies for establishing English colonies in the Americas. These charters combined feudal social ideas with forward-looking ideas about profit and capitalism; they also compacted private law and public law into a single document. As it turned out, most of the charters had relatively little effect on the systems of law and courts that developed in the colonies.

Roots of American Law

Virginia's disastrous early years demonstrate some of the problems with English colonial law. Granted to a private company, the early colony at Jamestown was failing miserably to turn a profit, and in fact was proving quite deadly for its inhabitants. Sir Thomas Dale, charged with the task of turning things around for the company, implemented a code of "Lawes Divine, Morall, and Martiall," a strict system of discipline designed to bring order to the chaotic Chesapeake.

As English Virginia grew and expanded, particularly after Opechancanough's coup of 1622, it became clear that the planters, not the company, were in charge; they began to revise the legal system to suit their needs. Accordingly, most of the cases heard by Virginia's early courts were related to servitude. Indentured servants routinely received longer terms of service for various infractions, including running away and getting pregnant. They could also sue their masters after being treated unfairly—for instance, not receiving proper "freedom dues" upon release from their indentures. As such servants were gradually phased out in favor of Africans who were slaves for life, the legal system changed. Eventually, African slaves would not be allowed to sue or own their own land.

The Puritans of Massachusetts were familiar with legal persecution; church authorities in the first half of the seventeenth century had mounted increasingly aggressive campaigns against the reform-minded sect. The Puritans were also extremely legalistic in their outlook. They viewed the Bible as a source of law, but their statutes were closer to English jurisprudence. Still, not everyone who moved to New England was a Puritan. Court records indicate that adultery, absence from church, and other crimes were committed regularly.

Nathaniel Ward's "Body of Liberties," written in 1641, codified many of the Puritans' ideas regarding law and order. Rights were to be protected (especially in the case of men and property), and accused persons could expect a fast jury trial. All male church members were given the status of "freeman," meaning they could vote and hold office. Ministers, although powerful, were forbidden from holding office. Civil courts in the Bay Colony closely resembled English local courts.

The early Massachusetts and Virginia legal systems differed from English law in some key aspects. Ordinary men had a hand in the creation of the law. This made American courts and laws more open and simple than the complex tangle of British courts, each of which had its own special protocol to follow. Colonial law also blurred the line between public and private law; this line had been hard and fast in England. In a sense, the colonies were projects in reforming a legal system that had become out of touch with the people it was supposed to serve.

It also bears mentioning that American colonial law severely limited the rights of both single and married women. Married women had the status of *femme covert*, which meant that their legal existence was subsidiary to that of their husbands.

Court Day

In colonial America, court day served a variety of legal and social functions. The hierarchical nature of colonial society was on display when people from all of society's ranks gathered in and around the courthouse. In highly stratified colonies like Virginia, the divide between rich and poor was most striking as the rich competed in horse races and wagered on cockfights, while poorer whites and slaves watched or participated in their own forms of recreation. The earliest county courts were often held in the homes of wealthy men, and men of means served as justices. As time passed, separate buildings were designated as courthouses, but they reflected, in many ways, the internal divisions of colonial society.

Courts in the late seventeenth and early eighteenth century varied from colony to colony, depending on the date and circumstances of the colony's establishment. Rhode Island, for instance, borrowed some English laws, but its courts were communal, and its judges were elected, reflecting that colony's relatively egalitar-

ian roots and the vision of Roger Williams. In South Carolina's early years, all cases were heard in the colonial capital of Charles Town, which was the cause of no small amount of bitterness among backcountry planters and farmers. New Haven's early courts focused more on the Bible than the mandates of English law.

Under Peter Stuyvesant's administration, town government and the legal system developed along Dutch lines in New Amsterdam. Even after the English took over, they kept the Dutch court system, provided that the courts remained loyal to the English.

Pennsylvania is a special case in colonial legal history. William Penn's Frame of Government combined elements of older colonial plans and charters, but he infused them with a particularly Quaker flavor. Specific rights were guaranteed, while other colonies' laws generally referred to a vague body of rights claimed by all English people. Penalties for misconduct were slight in comparison with the harsh criminal codes of other colonies. The Quakers had been subjected to persecution in both Old and New England, so the various statutes enacted in Pennsylvania guaranteed protection from illegal search and seizure and opened up the government to people of all Protestant persuasions.

Court proceedings in British North America were marked by their accessibility and simplicity. Lawyers and nonlawyers—professionally trained lawyers were rare in the colonies—argued their cases in a plain style. Individual lawyers would occasionally insert bits of Latin or artful pieces of English law into their pleading, but simplicity was the rule.

The majority of cases were decided in one or two meetings of the court, even at the level of the colonial supreme court. Most courts in colonial America had general jurisdiction, meaning they could hear all sorts of cases, not just cases regarding a specific branch of law, since American colonial law did not really have the various branches and subdivisions that characterized English law. Litigants who were dissatisfied with the outcomes of their cases could appeal to higher courts, provided they had the means to do so.

For most of the seventeenth century, American courts and legislatures operated independently of England. Ordinary colonists created legal systems that suited their needs and eschewed the formality of the English legal process. The eighteenth century witnessed increasing British oversight of the colonies and closed with a massive uprising against new forms of imperial control.

The eighteenth century also saw the development

of a class of professional lawyers. Litigation grew more popular, and complex, driving the demand for lawyers higher and higher. American lawyers trained, or "read," under the tutelage of older, more experienced practitioners.

One striking difference between the colonial legal systems and that of England was the existence of slavery in America. Slavery had vanished from England, and so American slave law was basically an American creation. Over a period of decades, slavery came to be legally associated with brown skin, and the aftershocks of that decision far outlived the colonial period. Laws and courts severely curtailed all sorts of slave activity, including the use of firearms, meeting in large groups, and moving from plantation to plantation. The legal protection of slavery is a clear-cut example of how early Americans, in this case white planters, could affect the law to suit their needs.

The aftermath of the Seven Years' War (known in North America as the French and Indian War) brought about crises on several levels. In a legal sense, the British government, newly rejuvenated, yet facing postwar debt and depression, sought to define the status of the colonies in an expanding empire. New forms of taxation raised howls of protest from colonial merchants, planters, artisans, and lawyers. Many Americans convinced themselves that armed resistance to the new policies was not only legal but necessary to protect long-held legal rights.

After the War for Independence, the new American states built on the laws and courts established by their colonial predecessors, with important adjustments. Unlike England, the new American republic was a federal system, with state courts and federal courts having jurisdiction over different types of crimes and civil matters. Still, the unique Anglo-Saxon mix of statutory law and common law has prevailed on this side of the Atlantic to the present day.

Matthew Jennings

See also: Crime; Debt and Debtor's Prison; Inheritance; Land and Real Estate; Orphans; Prisons and Punishment; Widows and Widowers; Zenger, John Peter. *Documents:* The Trial of Anne Hutchinson (1637); The Trial of Peter Zenger (1735).

Bibliography

Chase, Anthony. *Law and History: The Evolution of the American Legal System.* New York: New Press, 1997.

Higginbotham, A. Leon, Jr. *In the Matter of Color: Race and the American Legal Process: The Colonial Period.* New York: Oxford University Press, 1978.

Hoffer, Peter Charles. *Law and People in Colonial America.* 1992. Rev. ed. Baltimore: Johns Hopkins University Press, 1998.

Pencak, William, and Wythe W. Holt, Jr., eds. *The Law in America, 1607–1861.* New York: New York Historical Society, 1989.

Lee, Richard Henry (1732–1794)

Richard Henry Lee was born on January 20, 1732, at Stratford Hall in Westmoreland County, Virginia, to Thomas and Hannah Lee. The Lees were one of the most influential families in Virginia, and Thomas had become one of the largest landholders in the colony.

In December 1757, Richard Henry Lee married Anne Aylett, who bore him four children before her death in 1768. A year later he remarried, this time to Anne Pinckard, and their union resulted in five additional children. Lee resided at Stratford Hall until his own estate, Chantilly, was finally completed in the early 1760s.

Lee's public career began in his early 20s, when he was first appointed as justice of the peace for Westmoreland County in 1755. In 1758, the county elected him as its representative to the House of Burgesses, and there he began a long and prestigious career.

As the imperial crisis with Great Britain worsened throughout the 1760s, Lee joined in opposition to various British policies that he perceived to be violations of colonial rights. In protest against the 1765 Stamp Act, Lee coauthored the Westmoreland Resolves, which outlined the dangers of the act and advised citizens against paying the tax. In 1767, Lee confronted the Townshend Acts, duties that Parliament had placed upon an assortment of imported items. Joining with other members of the House of Burgesses, Lee signed a list of resolves that called for Virginians to enter into an association designed to boycott British goods until the duties were repealed.

In 1773, Lee helped to organize one of the first committees of correspondence in the colonies, designed to share information and coordinate American protests and actions against British policies. When the First Continental Congress met in 1774, Lee was one of the seven delegates chosen by Virginia to attend the meeting at Philadelphia.

Lee believed that reconciliation would be possible only if King George III and Parliament were willing to acknowledge the unfairness of prior British legislation and recognize American protests. It became clear to Lee that such recognition was not forthcoming, and, by early 1776, he was convinced that the only recourse left to the colonists was independence. On June 7, 1776, Lee proposed to Congress a resolution that outlined the case for independence:

> Resolved, That these United Colonies are, and of right ought to be, free and independent States, that they are absolved from all allegiance to the British Crown, and that all political connection between them and the State of Great Britain is, and ought to be totally dissolved.

Throughout the war, Lee served on numerous committees and became renowned for his tireless energy. In 1779, finally exhausted by his efforts, Lee returned home to Virginia to convalesce. His convalescence proved short-lived, however, as he was elected to the Virginia state legislature in 1780.

In 1784, Lee was back in Congress, this time as its president, in which capacity he served until November 1785. Lee declined to participate as a delegate in the Philadelphia constitutional convention in 1787 for health reasons. In spite of his absence, he believed that the work of the convention was critical, and in a letter to John Adams expressed how "the present federal system . . . has been found quite inefficient and ineffectual."

Upon hearing the results of the convention, however, Lee believed that the delegates had gone too far in empowering the new government. Drawing upon his experience of the pre–Revolutionary War days, Lee warned about possible encroachments upon personal liberties and demanded that a bill of rights be attached to the Constitution to ensure the protection of these liberties. In fact, Lee refused to sit as a delegate on the Virginia ratifying committee because of his concerns over the Constitution without a bill of rights. Thus, as Lee watched from the sidelines, Virginia narrowly ratified the Constitution by a vote of 89 to 79.

Whatever concerns Lee might have had with the new government were put aside when he was chosen as one of Virginia's two senators under the new Constitution. As a senator, he worked vigorously to have a bill of rights added to the Constitution. His work paid dividends when Congress voted that twelve amendments be attached to the Constitution, ten of which were later ratified by the states.

Lee continued to work hard as a senator until his health again took a turn for the worse in 1792. He

The scion of a prominent Virginia family, Richard Henry Lee introduced the resolution in the Second Continental Congress on June 7, 1776, that called for American independence. It was adopted on July 2. *(Library of Congress, LC-USZ62-92331)*

returned to his home at Chantilly, where he was at last able to enjoy retirement from public life and spend time with his family. On June 14, 1794, Richard Henry Lee passed away quietly at his home, to be mourned by a nation who praised him for his efforts toward procuring independence and a bill of rights on behalf of all Americans.

Keith Pacholl

See also: Continental Congress, First; Continental Congress, Second; House of Burgesses; Revolutionary War; Stamp Act (1765).

Bibliography

Ballagh, James Curtis, ed. *The Letters of Richard Henry Lee.* New York: Da Capo Press, 1970.

Chitwood, Oliver Perry. *Richard Henry Lee: Statesman of the Revolution.* Morgantown: West Virginia University Library, 1967.

Matthews, John Carter. *Richard Henry Lee.* Williamsburg: Virginia Independence Bicentennial Commission, 1978.

Legge, William

See Dartmouth, Lord

Leisler, Jacob (1640–1691)

In New York City, on May 16, 1691, Jacob Leisler suffered a treasoner's gruesome execution for his leadership role in the bloodless rebellion that upended the colony of New York in 1689. He has been described as everything from a common man's hero to a foreigner turned resentful by exclusion from the colony's economic and political center.

In fact, the dramatic final turn in Leisler's life was rooted in a complicated mix of cultural, religious, economic, and political factors that stretched across the Atlantic world. Leisler's career demonstrates both the considerable openness of the English colonies to foreign Protestants within their communities and the multiethnic tension that often boiled just under a seemingly tolerant surface.

Early Years

Born in the German states in 1640, Jacob Leisler was raised in the predominantly Lutheran city of Frankfurt. His father was an orthodox Calvinist minister to French Huguenot congregations in exile, who continued Leisler's grandfather's legacy of compassion for fellow Calvinists persecuted by Spanish and French Catholicism. In the midst of the religious and political turbulence of the region, the younger Leisler witnessed firsthand the displacement of the persecuted, but he also received the exceptional education available to the son of a prosperous family.

Coming from a long line of magistrates, Leisler was able to draw upon a legacy of lessons in the vital strength of established legal systems, in the importance of civic duty, and in the value of supporting networks between orthodox Protestant communities. Following his father's death in 1653, Leisler was sent to military school to further his education in tactics, law, and languages. This military path led him in turn to Amsterdam, where the family had numerous contacts.

In 1660, Leisler sailed for the Americas as an officer with the Dutch West India Company; he was 20 years old and second in command of troops being sent to the colony of New Netherland. Drawing on the privileges he gained as an officer, within three years he was also operating in the profitable deerskins and tobacco trade, developing transatlantic commercial contacts from Boston to Amsterdam.

In 1663, Leisler married Elsie Tymens, an indebted widow eight years his senior with four children; the couple would have two sons and five daughters of their own between 1664 and 1676. Through Elsie's mother, Leisler gained access to a prominent New Amsterdam merchant family, the Loockermans, while his name provided that family with the luster of a European pedigree, one with a coat of arms.

England Seizes New Netherland

When England seized the colony of New Netherland in 1664, the generous terms negotiated between the Dutch and the English meant that not only could Leisler continue his commercial ventures largely uninterrupted, but he also could extend his operations and contacts into the English Atlantic world. From New York, Leisler expanded his commercial involvement in a wide range of products, from salt and sugar to servants and slaves, and became the greatest New York dealer in Chesapeake tobacco.

By the 1670s, Leisler owned, in full or in part, at least a half dozen vessels registered in several colonies, and he was among the wealthiest men in New York. He was also one of the principal property owners in the city, in addition to owning land in England and continental Europe. After the mid-1670s, Leisler increasingly concentrated on England's triangular trade, dealing in West Africa, the West Indies, and on to England, where he enlarged his commercial connections, solidifying those associations with his children's marriages.

Transatlantic journeys still held dangers, though, and, in 1677, Leisler and two stepsons were captured along with his ship by Algerian corsairs. In an indication of Leisler's importance, New York's governor raised a public collection for the group's ransom, but Leisler's own large ransom came first from a European source.

His social and economic prominence meant that Leisler was sought out for civic, military, and juridical positions within the colony, but he shunned political office. His religious convictions persuaded him that civic rather than political duty was the best means to preserve both honest action and the Protestant faith.

Fearing unnecessary suffering, Leisler had supported capitulation to the English in 1664, but, in 1673, when the English lost New York during the Third Anglo-Dutch War (and before it was reclaimed the next year), Leisler supported the Dutch occupation for the religious conservatism it signaled. After following the expelled Dutch governor back to Holland, Leisler returned to New York the next year and resumed his elite status, though he continued to remain out of political office.

By the 1680s, the colony was experiencing heightened challenges stemming from taxation and land policy, and from tensions related to the arrival of increasing numbers of Quakers, Native Americans, Jews, and French Huguenots. A 1683 act to naturalize all foreign Christians in New York threatened to overwhelm the Dutch majority with a heterogeneous society, which would challenge the Dutch New Yorkers' commercial power that Leisler and his colleagues represented. The annexation of New York to the new Dominion of New England also posed a mercantile threat, since the transfer of public records to Boston greatly hindered local commercial operations.

Most distressing for orthodox Calvinists such as Leisler, however, was the toleration of Catholics encouraged by the colony's proprietor, the duke of York, and a series of his governors. The European interests and orthodox Calvinism of Leisler's group made Catholic advances in Europe seem especially alarming, particularly with the coronation of the Catholic duke of York as King James II in 1685.

The response in the colony to England's Glorious Revolution was swift and was tied both to regional reactions and to Dutch New Yorkers' support for the new monarchs, William and Mary. Amid rumors of a massive French and Native American attack on Albany, in April 1689, Bostonians seized Governor Edmund Andros and declared the dominion defunct. These actions excited communities around New York City to denounce the local authority of Lieutenant Governor Francis Nicholson and elect new political representatives.

On May 31, the city militia seized the fort and, on June 8, commissioned Leisler, a militia officer, as captain of the fort. Within two months, he accepted the position of commander in chief of the province, apparently with a sense of reluctant obligation. The delegates established a Committee of Safety to govern the province, with Leisler at its head. England's Privy Council and King William empowered Nicholson (who had fled to England) to resume control of the colony, and, in his absence, granted power to those who had acted to preserve the peace, which became the basis for Leisler's claim of authority.

For nearly two years Leisler's government conducted legitimate business, maintaining order and commerce within the colony in the interests of traditional community liberties. But it also exiled and imprisoned political opponents. As Leisler grew increasingly suspicious and arbitrary, he relied on his son-in-law Jacob Milborne, who was part of a family of Presbyterian radicals in England and Bermuda and connected to transatlantic networks of radical Protestants.

Within the colony, only Albany, lying north on the Hudson River, was powerful enough to resist Leisler. Albany's residents worried that his rebellion would endanger relations with their Iroquois allies. Although the town was predominantly Dutch, the leading merchants and military men there formed the Albany Convention, an independent ruling body that fought off Leisler's control. A French and Native American raid on Schenectady on February 8, 1690, which left over sixty dead, pushed aside Albany's opposition to New York City.

During the period of the rebellion, the provisional colonial governments did try to cooperate with each other, in part for their security and in part as a show of their loyalty and value to the new king. In June 1689, two delegates from Connecticut came to New York to help the insurgents declare loyalty to William. Leisler entered into friendly correspondence with Maryland, although the latter was unwilling to lend soldiers to defend New York's frontier. More assertively, in May 1690, delegates from New York, Massachusetts Bay, Plymouth, and Connecticut agreed to a joint invasion of New France. Without imperial support, the assault collapsed, but it was part of an increasing regional involvement of New York, which would continue after 1691.

In 1690, King William appointed Henry Sloughter as governor of the colony. Although Sloughter didn't arrive for fourteen months, Captain Richard Ingoldsby arrived early the following year, demanding that Leisler surrender the fort on Sloughter's behalf. Citing a technicality regarding Ingoldsby's commission, Leisler refused. When Sloughter arrived himself on the evening of March 19, 1691, Leisler again refused, claiming that, in the interest of safety, he would not surrender the fort until morning. For these actions, he and nine others were charged with treason against the Crown.

Leisler's Trial

The trial lasted for eighteen days. In terms of familiarity with English law and political thought, it was heavily weighted in the prosecution's favor, particularly as Leisler and Milborne refused to recognize the court's authority. Two of the men were acquitted, but the other eight were convicted and sentenced to death. A month later, Leisler's and Milborne's sentence was carried out. The other six rebels obtained a reprieve and were pardoned by the Crown in 1694.

In 1695, both Leisler's and Milborne's bodies were exhumed by supporters and given proper burial, the two having been pardoned posthumously by an act of Parliament. Though the bodies were put to rest, the divisions in New York between the Leislerian faction and its opponents would continue to underscore the colony's political life. Often exaggerated now, this factionalism was usually not clear-cut, and it became of less concern than matters of economic decline and frontier defense.

Since it was directed more or less into the political arena, in the long run, factionalism legitimized the structure and operation of government in the colony. Leislerians forged new connections to Holland and to English Whigs, and they learned to use the language of English liberties in protecting their interests within the empire.

Neil Kennedy

See also: Dutch; Germans; Glorious Revolution; New York City.

Bibliography

Kammen, Michael. *Colonial New York: A History.* New York: Oxford University Press, 1975.
McCormick, Charles. *Leisler's Rebellion.* New York: Garland Publishing, 1989.
Voorhees, David W. "The 'Fervent Zeale' of Jacob Leisler." *William and Mary Quarterly* 51:3 (July 1999): 447–72.

Lenni Lenape (Delaware)

The Lenni Lenape, also known as the Delaware, spoke a language in the larger Algonquian family of languages in colonial times, when they lived along the Delaware River and its tributaries, including parts of the present-day states of Delaware, New Jersey, and Pennsylvania. They played a large role in the development of those three English colonies, and their subsequent splintered migration left Delaware or Lenni Lenape communities throughout the United States and Canada.

As with many other Native American groups, the central political unit of Lenni Lenape life was the village. Within basically autonomous villages, men hunted alone and women farmed in groups; the major exception to this rule was the fall deer kill, when many Lenni Lenapes worked together. Lenni Lenapes inherited clan membership through their mothers. Additionally, Lenni Lenapes moved inland from large, agriculture-based villages and seaside fishing towns to hunt every fall.

The Lenni Lenape's *gamwing* (big house rite) has sparked much interest among anthropologists and historians. Each fall, principal towns hosted this large ceremony to give thanks and to pray for success in the hunt. The *gamwing* exemplified the gender roles of Lenni Lenapes, since corn and meat (female and male pursuits) were both venerated.

In the years leading up to the arrival of Europeans, the Lenni Lenape were wedged in between the peoples living on the Susquehanna River and the Five Nations Iroquois. The Dutch encountered the Lenni Lenape in

Chief Lappawinsoe and his Lenni Lenape (Delaware) peoples were tricked out of half a million acres of land by the Pennsylvania colonial government in the "Walking Purchase" of 1737. *(Private Collection/Bridgeman Art Library)*

the first half of the seventeenth century, and the two groups began to trade in beaver pelts and items of European manufacture. The Dutch, mainly interested in commerce, had little reason to settle on Lenni Lenape territory, and they initially built only a sparsely populated series of trading forts along the river. When their territory was granted to the duke of York, the Lenni Lenape faced a new sort of threat: prolonged contact with land-hungry English people. The duke of York also began to make grants in what is now New Jersey, and English settlements expanded rapidly. The Lenni Lenape experienced successive waves of English settlement, and the tribe was decimated by fatal disease epidemics.

The trend toward dispossession reversed itself, or at least slowed down, when the colony of Pennsylvania took root in Delaware Bay in the 1680s under the visionary leadership of William Penn. Penn was a Quaker who saw his colony as a "holy experiment," promising religious tolerance and peaceful relations with the region's native peoples. By and large, Penn succeeded in his goal, and Lenni Lenapes and Pennsylvanians enjoyed what has been termed "the Long Peace."

Penn's descendants were not so evenhanded in their disposition toward the Lenni Lenape, and in the infamous "Walking Purchase" of 1737, they defrauded the native peoples out of their last remaining settlements on the Delaware River. By the terms of the Walking Purchase deed (itself based on questionable legal grounds), Pennsylvania was to gain title along a line that a man could walk in one day. Colonial officials cheated, hiring three runners to follow a trail that had been blazed earlier. The result was that the Lenni Lenape ceded much more territory than they had intended, and were effectively dispossessed of their homeland.

The French and Indian War divided the Lenni Lenape's loyalties between the English and French. Some villages remained neutral, while others seized the opportunity to raid English farms in New Jersey and Pennsylvania. As it became clear that the English would win the contest for North America, the Lenni Lenape moved back into their camp, although some warriors participated in the attack on Fort Pitt during the larger conflict known as Pontiac's Rebellion.

During and after the War for Independence, the Lenni Lenape splintered and scattered. Some moved multiple times, to Indiana, Missouri, and then Oklahoma, or to Indiana, Texas, and then Oklahoma. Still others ended up in Wisconsin, Kansas, or the Grand River Reserve of the Six Nations in Ontario. In 1992, many of the scattered tribal members met together and formed the Delaware Nation Grand Council of North America.

Matthew Jennings

See also: Native American–European Relations; Native Americans; Penn, William; Pennsylvania; Pennsylvania (Chronology).

Bibliography

Miller, Jay. "Delaware." In *Encyclopedia of North American Indians*, edited by Frederick E. Hoxie. Boston: Houghton Mifflin, 1996.

Weslager, C. A. *The Delaware Indians: A History.* New Brunswick, NJ: Rutgers University Press, 1972.

León, Juan Ponce de

See Ponce de León, Juan

Lexington and Concord, Battles of

As the first military engagement between the British army and the colonial American militia, the battles of Lexington and Concord were the "shot heard 'round the world," igniting the political protest of the colonists into armed rebellion.

This two-pronged engagement began with a plan for 700 British regulars, under the command of Colonel Francis Smith, to move quickly out of Boston and seize important colonial political leaders, including Samuel Adams and John Hancock, at Lexington, as well as a large power magazine located at Concord. The British assembled the night of April 18 on Boston Common, then marched out about 10 P.M., intending to arrive at Lexington by dawn.

Colonial leaders within Boston, alarmed by troop movements and expecting a military move by General Thomas Gage, commander in chief of British forces in America and military governor of Massachusetts, checked in with their intelligence sources. The colonists learned that two British soldiers had talked about a raid on Lexington and Concord; the information was then confirmed by a source close to Gage, possibly his American wife, Margaret Kemble Gage. On this information, riders, including Paul Revere, Dr. Martin Herrick, William Dawes, and Dr. Samuel Prescott, among

British forces under Colonel Francis Smith retreat from Concord, Massachusetts, after the first day of fighting with colonial militia on April 19, 1775. By the time they reached Boston, the British had suffered 273 casualties. *(Brown Brothers, Sterling, Pennsylvania)*

others, fanned out along the roads to alert the local militias and locate British roadblocks and patrols.

Because of these warnings, the British advance force under Major John Pitcairn encountered armed militia when he arrived in Lexington at 5 A.M. Pitcairn ordered the militia to disarm, but they only dispersed across Lexington Green. During the confusion, a shot rang out, probably from behind a stone wall or from Buckman's Tavern. (Historians strongly suspect Samuel Adams as the provocateur and source of the shot.) The British responded with a volley and bayonet charge into the militia, killing eight and wounding nine, while one British regular was wounded. Allowing the troops a triumphant volley, Pitcairn proceeded to Concord, where at 7 A.M. he again encountered militia, this time arrayed on the high ground near North Bridge.

Pitcairn's troops searched Concord, finding only three cannons and some shot because the townspeople had ample warning to hide their supplies. Furious, he cut down Concord's liberty pole and allowed the soldiers to search house to house, looting in the process. As a parting gesture, Pitcairn set afire the cannons' gun carriage, in the process accidentally setting fire to the courthouse; the British soldiers and townspeople worked together to put out the blaze. The smoke alerted the militia, now 500 strong, who encountered a small British force on the bridge. While retreating to the main body of troops, one of the British regulars let off his musket, triggering a volley, and the militia responded in a firefight in which four British officers and five soldiers were killed. Pitcairn and Smith decided to return to Boston before their men ran out of ammunition and were trapped.

Fighting spread as the British retreated the 18 miles back to Boston, followed by increasing numbers of militiamen led by Brigadier General William Heath, who fired at them from behind stone walls and houses along the route. The British particularly resented that the militia targeted British wounded in carts; one militiaman, Ammi White, hatcheted a wounded regular to death. At Lexington, the British encountered a relief force under Brigadier General Hugh Percy, who escorted the retreating British troops back to Boston, sending out flanking parties and pouring artillery fire on the attacking militia as they traveled. The Royal Welsh Fusiliers covered the end of the British line, walking backward most of the way. Percy avoided being trapped by fresh militiamen when Colonel Timothy Pickering held back the Marblehead militia from surrounding the British retreat column, for reasons that are still unclear.

Reaching safety in Boston under the guns of the HMS *Somerset*, which was moored in the Charles River, the British discovered that in contrast to the militia, which lost 49 men and had 39 wounded, they had taken losses of 73 dead, 174 wounded, and 26 missing. The battles, though small in scale, hardened opposition on both sides: The British were convinced that the colonists were savages and rebels, the militia that the British were thugs and looters. The colonists also became more confident in their ability to take on regular troops.

In essence, these battles signaled the start of the armed Revolution. They also concentrated both British strength and the colonial militia around Boston, where vicious partisan fighting would continue within and outside the city for nearly a year, until British troops withdrew from the region in March 1776.

Margaret Sankey

See also: Adams, Samuel; Army, British; Gage, Thomas; Hancock, John; Military and Diplomatic Affairs (Chronology); Military and Diplomatic Affairs (Essay); Militias; Revere, Paul; Revolutionary War.

Bibliography

Fischer, David Hackett. *Paul Revere's Ride.* New York: Oxford University Press, 1994.

Hallahan, William. *The Day the American Revolution Began.* New York: William Morrow, 2000.

Tourtellot, Arthur Bernon. *Lexington and Concord.* New York: W. W. Norton, 1963.

Libraries

As the colonial period progressed, so did the capabilities of the printing press. Books became increasingly more common on both sides of the Atlantic. A literate colonist could choose from titles both religious and secular, including novels, cookbooks, agricultural manuals, and political treatises. By the turn of the seventeenth century, several colonists had begun to create libraries, usually hoping to enrich their communities. These libraries fell into several categories, including personal, social, university, and clerical.

While New England had the highest ratio of libraries per capita, they were found in all thirteen colonies, as well as the Western lands settled by the Spanish. While French Jesuit priests traveled with their own book collections, the largely trade-based form of French colonization was not conducive to the creation of libraries. By the time of the American Revolution, there were 308 known libraries in the colonies.

The foundation of libraries in New England followed patterns similar to those in the other colonies. Initially, they were the result of philanthropic donations. In 1638, John Harvard donated his collection as the foundation of a library for Harvard College. In 1656, John Keayne donated books for a public library in Boston. In the eighteenth century, libraries created by groups of settlers emerged, including the Redwood Library in Rhode Island in the 1740s. Most of these were social or subscription libraries, collections owned by a specific society or association. An individual could buy a share in the society and so gain borrowing privileges. Unlike the libraries donated by one person, these libraries had both a wider selection and a larger patron base.

The most unusual library in New England was one created by John Eliot in the 1660s. As a means of Christianizing the Massachusett tribe, he set up a press and printed religious works in their own language. When the press finished its run in 1730, it had created a collection of twenty-eight volumes. In total, New England founded 120 libraries during the colonial period.

Libraries had the most uneven growth in the Southern colonies of Virginia, Maryland, and the Carolinas. Coastal planters such as William Byrd II and Robert Carter amassed huge selections of books, comparable to or surpassing the libraries of Northern universities. They also willingly sponsored libraries for their own universities and churches. Thomas Bray, an Anglican clergyman, established as many as thirty-four parish libraries in Maryland. However, these libraries were rarely available to settlers from other social classes. In addition, settlement in the South revolved around scattered plantations and farms. Even if libraries had been open to a wider selection of the population, they would have been difficult to maintain and to use in the backcountry.

In contrast to the South, the Middle Atlantic colonies of New York, Pennsylvania, Delaware, and New Jersey had the advantages of several cities and a critical mass of highly literate settlers. In 1731, Benjamin Franklin and some of his friends banded together

Benjamin Franklin and friends founded the Library Company of Philadelphia—the first subscription library in America—in November 1731. It was another year before the books arrived and the library actually opened. The initial membership fee was 40 shillings. *(Library of Congress, LC-D418-28058)*

to create the Library Company of Philadelphia. Their first published catalog in 1754 listed 317 books. Another circulating library was founded in Philadelphia in 1769 by Thomas Bradford.

Records indicate that women borrowed nearly as many books from libraries as men. They also indicate that fiction was the most popular choice for borrowers. While Dutch colonists in New York do not appear to have organized formal libraries, their personal collections were extensive. German Mennonites brought similar collections to Pennsylvania. By the end of the eighteenth century, the Middle Atlantic colonies had founded eighty-three libraries.

Libraries in the Spanish colonies, which became Florida, New Mexico, and California, were scarcer than in the Eastern states. They were largely religious and housed in either convents or missions. Of the seven that have been documented, one was in Florida, two in New Mexico, and four in California. A private library also was founded in Florida in the 1680s but did not survive. There also are records of smaller, personal libraries as early as the 1640s.

While only four libraries were founded prior to 1691, by the end of the eighteenth century, there were hundreds more. The largest growth took place between 1696 and 1700, with forty-seven founded. The second half of the eighteenth century had a steady increase of approximately fifteen to twenty new libraries created each year, until the outbreak of the American Revolution.

Abigail B. Chandler

See also: Arts, Culture, and Intellectual Life (Chronology); Arts, Culture, and Intellectual Life (Essay); Education; Education, Higher; Franklin, Benjamin; Literature; Reading and Literacy.

Bibliography

Amory, Hugh, and Hall, David D. *A History of the Book in America.* Cambridge, UK: Cambridge University Press, 2000.

Gilmore, William J. *Reading Becomes a Necessity of Life.* Knoxville: University of Tennessee Press, 1989.

McMullen, Haynes. *American Libraries Before 1876.* Westport, CT: Greenwood, 2000.

Literacy

See Reading and Literacy

Literature

The literature of colonial America is primarily English in its origin. Like most of colonial life, it is reflective of the English roots of most of the colonists. While differences can be observed between the literature of the Northern colonies and that of the South, and between various periods within the colonial era, the overall, similar topics and themes reflect the prevailing concerns and attitudes of the era as a whole.

New England and the Middle Colonies: Life and Literature

New England and, to a lesser degree, the Middle colonies were heavily settled by Puritan immigrants. Not surprisingly, then, a strong Puritan influence is evident in the literature of these Northern colonies, particularly that written early in the colonial era. In terms of forms, topics, and ideology, Puritanism undergirds virtually all English-language colonial literature produced north of the Mason-Dixon Line.

Puritans in England had been particularly critical of the arts and entertainment, which they believed to be frivolous. Many of these same beliefs came across the sea with the new settlers. Accordingly, humor, dramas or theatrical plays, and fictional works, including short stories and novels, are virtually unknown in Northern colonial literature. Instead, sermons, essays, and treatises, on moral and ethical topics, and other "useful" nonfiction are the norm. Letters, journals, and diaries also were written, usually to convey moral or practical information to the anticipated reader. Such works might contain useful observations concerning the land, plants, and animals in a given location, descriptions that might be used to inform newcomers or attract prospective settlers.

In some cases, poetry was the chosen form of expression, particularly for official, commemorative, or memorial occasions. Often such poetry was religious in nature, expressing adoration for God and his Creation. Writing poetry was also one of the limited creative options available to colonial women, although few had time in their busy daily lives to engage in it. (Presumably, this "feminine" form of literary production would have been considered harmless by the Puritan leadership.) Sometimes, ministers employed poetry to convey Biblical truths, reminders for thanksgiving, or warnings against ungodly conduct. Various psalters, or rudimentary hymnbooks, were used in worship services to aid in the congregational recitation of Scripture. Initially, music and song were forbidden in Puritan worship, although these constraints eased somewhat with the passage of time.

Regardless of the form or style of the text, it is important to recognize the underlying reliance on religious thought in Northern writings of the colonial period. Even when examining what might seem to be a piece of mundane correspondence, for instance, one is quickly struck by the reference to Puritan concerns: a colonist writing to a friend in England was as likely as not to include references to God's providence in the new land, to his new community's responsibility to plant the kingdom of heaven in the wilderness, or to signs of God's grace to His undeserving and sinning children. The pervasive nature of Puritan ideology finally waned with time, particularly in the Middle colonies, with the arrival of immigrants from Germany and other non-Anglican European nations.

Physical surroundings in New England and the Middle colonies also played a part in the production of literature. Arriving in a literal wilderness meant long hours of hard manual labor for early colonists. Even after settlements became established with the passage of time, most Northern colonists lived in rural settings. Usually, colonists' days began at sunrise and ended at sundown, and constant manual labor engaged men, women, and children. It is little wonder, then, that comparatively little literature was produced in the early days of New England and the Middle colonies. The surprise is, rather, that any was produced at all.

Given the importance that Puritans placed on Bible reading by individual worshippers, literacy was emphasized even during the harsh and labor-filled days of the early settlement period. And, indeed, literacy rates were higher in New England than in colonies farther south or even in England, for that matter. At a higher level, the need to train clergy in secular and spiritual leadership led to a precocious development of institutions of higher learning. Harvard College, for example, was founded in 1636, just six years after the Puritans first settled in Boston.

Puritans, indeed, saw themselves as God's chosen people in the New World, and they believed their primary and overwhelming duty was to live as devout members of the Elect. As a consequence, much literature of the Northern colonies throughout the period strove to present moral guidance. Even with the approach of the Revolutionary War, the prevailing concern of establishing God's kingdom in the New World formed the basic framework of literature from New England and the Middle colonies.

Southern Colonial Life and Literature

While most early colonists in the Southern colonies also came from England, important differences from New England and the Middle colonies existed in the region from Maryland southward. From the late 1600s onward, increasing numbers of immigrants to the South came from non-English homelands, both in Europe and in Africa, bringing with them a variety of non-Puritan religious traditions. In addition, the physical environment and the emerging economy of the South (including the pervasive presence of slavery) were major points of contrast to life in the Northern colonies.

Southern writers, though not bound by their Northern brothers' Puritan compulsion to be "useful," nonetheless produced a large body of purposive literature. Sermons, tracts promoting settlement in the region, nature studies, and essays and treatises on scientific and education topics were written and published. Humor, however, often in the form of satire, was far more apt to be created by a Southern author who would not have to face censure from a Puritan theocracy.

The difference in religious composition is reflected in the style and content of those texts that addressed spiritual themes. Sermons would often focus on the practical, everyday application of scriptural themes rather than on constant anxieties over depravity and election. The variety of religious denominations and traditions in the region (Roman Catholics, Lutherans, Presbyterians, Methodists, Quakers, and others) led to tolerance for various theologies; this tolerance, often to the point of general disinterest in religious matters, is evident in Southern colonial literature and stands in stark contrast to rigid New England Puritanism.

Although an overt theology is not evident in all Southern literature, the writings from the colonial period do reflect Southerners' shared sense of mission with their fellow colonists in New England and the Middle colonies. Like their Northern counterparts, most Southerners lived in rural areas, and most farmed, an occupation that grew with the emergence and expansion of tobacco culture early in the colonial period. The climate and terrain of the Southern colonies—not to mention the use of slave labor for the continual work required to raise a crop—made daily life somewhat easier in this area, however, allowing, in turn, more leisure time for the process of writing.

A number of colonial-era texts document the traditional world of gracious Southern life. One component of this life involved widespread literacy among white males, a characteristic that grew throughout all the colonies as time went on. Another was a widespread interest in the fine arts and the sciences, both of which flourished in the absence of Puritan mandates against "frivolous pursuits" and questioning the unknowable ways of God. As a consequence, a decidedly belletristic strain quickly became ingrained as a hallmark of Southern gentility.

While the overwhelming evils of the slave system in America need not be recounted here, the presence of Africans in the colonies did provide an important contribution to the literature of the New World. Folklore, folk tales, songs, superstitions, religious rituals and beliefs, and other traditions were all part of slave life. Although this oral tradition was not put down in writing until the late nineteenth and the twentieth centuries, it would certainly have been known among most white writers in the colonial South. It is difficult to say how much of this African contribution is directly evident in colonial literature, but it certainly forms an important part of the backdrop against which authors were writing.

Evolution of Colonial Literature

Astounding changes and progress occurred in colonial America between the time of the Pilgrims' arrival and the Revolutionary War. As life in the colonies changed, so did literature.

As colonists became more settled, marginally greater leisure allowed more time for reflection and writing. Letters, diaries, journals, and descriptive narratives were created in increasing numbers. In the South, as labor-intensive and nutrient-robbing tobacco crops left once-rich farms drained of productivity, planters moved westward and southward to seek new land. This movement to the frontier engendered a spirit of exploration and expectation that is evident in Southern writings of the time; a similar sense can also be found in the frontier texts of those New England and Middle colonies settlers who decided to expand to the west.

Literature produced toward the end of the colonial period bears the hallmarks of Enlightenment thought. While topics and interests of previous years often persisted, these later texts view such interests through the lens of reason, often critically questioning previously held "truths." New England Puritanism largely gave way to Deism, and Enlightenment thought encouraged writers to seek deeper meaning in empirical knowledge. By the dawn of the Revolution, colonial literature had a firm foundation from which to address the growing crisis with Britain.

Major Works

Much of the colonial literature studied today falls into the category of religious writings. Of this body of work, the first example is John Winthrop's sermon "A Modell of Christian Charity" (1639), given aboard the ship *Arabella* before it landed in the New World. Winthrop's notion of the English colonists serving as God's representatives on an errand into the wilderness was widely shared by his contemporaries. It formed one of the foundations of the establishment of the new society, as did his exhortations to Puritans to consider themselves "a city upon a hill," an example of godly living for all nations. Other famous sermons of the colonial period include Michael Wigglesworth's epic 1662 poem/sermon, "Day of Doom," which warned his Puritan flock against the terrors of being unprepared on Judgment Day; Jonathan Edwards' "A Divine and Supernatural Light" (1734), in which he explained the mystery of God's grace in terms of human understanding; and Edwards' "Sinners in the Hands of an Angry God" (1741), another fire-and-brimstone sermon aimed at frightening wayward Christians back into goodness to avoid judgment at the whim of a wrathful and righteous God.

Much of the colonial literature that survives is in the form of poetry. Wigglesworth's *Day of Doom* was widely circulated and was quite popular in its day. Another minister, Edward Taylor, undertook poetic art for his own edification rather than for publication. By the mid-1680s, Taylor began what would become two series of private *Preparatory Meditations.* These poems, beautifully written and filled with vivid descriptions and figures of speech, reveal the tensions Taylor himself felt between man and God as he prepared to receive and administer the sacraments.

Two colonial women also created poetry that has enjoyed a resurgence of interest in recent years. One, Anne Bradstreet, came from England with her parents and husband to escape persecution for their Puritan faith. Although her father Thomas Dudley and husband Simon were leaders in their community, daily life and

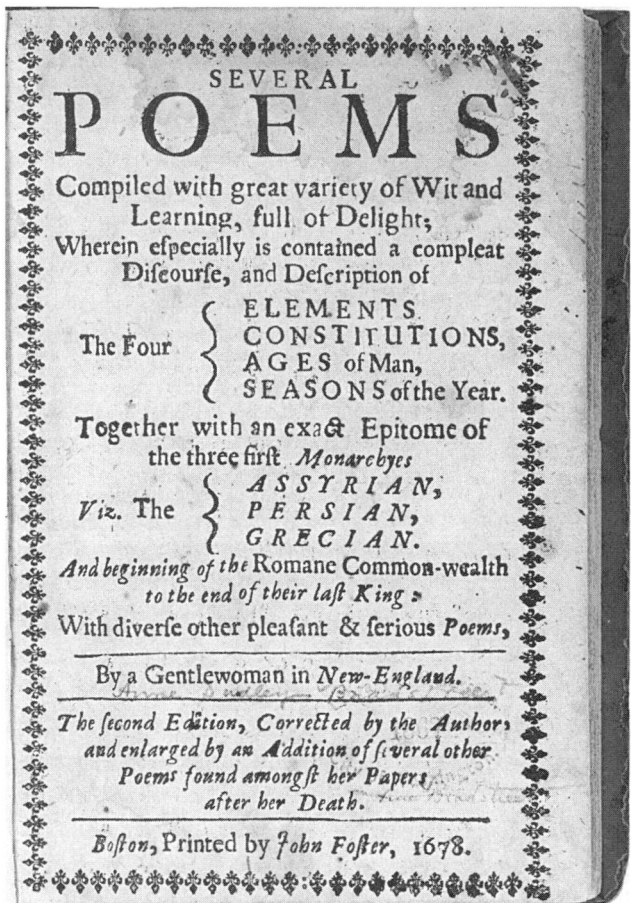

The Massachusetts Puritan Anne Bradstreet is widely regarded as the first American poet of note. Her *Tenth Muse Lately Sprung Up in America* appeared in 1650. *Several Poems,* which contained much of her best work, was published in 1672, six years after her death. *(Rare Book and Special Collections Division, Library of Congress)*

child rearing in the harsh conditions of colonial America were not easy for Anne, who was often left to manage on her own when Simon was required to be away on business. Nevertheless, she had been well educated by her parents and had read widely as a child in classic and contemporary literature in her father's library. Not surprisingly, she found the writing of poetry to be a comforting and enjoyable release for her feelings in the midst of a difficult life in a new land. Much of Bradstreet's poetry, written from the mid-1640s through the 1660s, is imitative of works she had read, but she provides a valuable picture of the life of a colonial Puritan woman. Her poems cover topics as diverse as religious worship and adoration, mourning for a family house that burned, grief over a grandchild who died in infancy, and the joys of married love.

The other woman poet was Phillis Wheatley, a young slave woman from Boston. She earned international renown with the 1773 publication of a volume of her verse, *Poems on Various Subjects, Religious and Moral.* Although the poems are highly derivative of her favorite writers' works, the volume is generally remembered for its value as the accomplishment of a colonial woman and as the first volume of works published by an African American.

Probably the two most widely remembered works of colonial literature form bookends for the period: William Bradford's *Of Plymouth Plantation,* written from 1630 to 1647, and Benjamin Franklin's *Autobiography,* written during the 1770s. Despite the different times in which they lived and the theological beliefs the authors held, there are remarkable points of comparison between these two texts. Both offer extensive practical and empirical information to interested readers, sometimes dealing with the most mundane matters. While they ascribe natural and spiritual phenomenon to different sources, both the Puritan Winthrop and the Deist Franklin are convinced of a superior power at work in the affairs of man. These authors discuss their own experiences as men in positions of leadership within their local communities and colonial America as a whole, and they strive to create texts that will be—in the best Puritan sense of the word—"useful" to future generations. Bradford's and Franklin's books are usually pointed to as the most valuable historical and cultural texts of their respective time periods.

American colonial literature was a diverse field of endeavor, with constraints of time, energy, leisure, religious guidelines, and even gender combining to inspire many variations over the years of the colonial period. While the volume of such works may seem small compared to other eras, the quality of those texts that have survived offer modern readers fascinating insights into life during the founding days of the nation.

Barbara Schwarz Wachal

See also: Arts, Culture, and Intellectual Life (Chronology); Arts, Culture, and Intellectual Life (Essay); Bradford, William; Bradstreet, Anne; Education; Education, Higher; Edwards, Jonathan; Franklin, Benjamin; Libraries; Reading and Literacy; Taylor, Edward; Theater; Warren, Mercy Otis; Wheatley, Phillis; Winthrop, John; Wright, Susanna. *Documents:* A Modell of Christian Charity (1630); Upon the Burning of Our House (1666); A Poem Recalling the Hanging of a Relative due to the Salem Witch Trials (in 1692; pub. 1857); Captivity Narrative of Mary Jemison in the 1750s (pub. 1824); Evangeline, A Tale of Acadie (in 1755; pub. 1847); On the Death of the Rev. Mr. George Whitefield (1770).

Bibliography

Gunn, Giles, ed. *Early American Writing.* New York: Penguin, 1994.

Nelson, Dana D. "Reading the Written Selves of Colonial America: Franklin, Occom, Equiano, and Palou/Serra." *Resources for American Literary Study* 19:2 (1993): 246–59.

Scheick, William J. *Authority and Female Authorship in Colonial America.* Lexington: University Press of Kentucky, 1998.

Ziff, Larzer. *The Literature of America: Colonial Period.* New York: McGraw-Hill, 1970.

Livestock

Livestock—cattle, hogs, sheep, and chickens—arrived with the first European settlers. It was common for farmers in many areas to allocate nearly nine-tenths of their land to animal pasture rather than crops, providing more butter and meat for their tables and wool for their homespun clothing. Since most farmers had very fertile land, livestock and grain excesses were common. And, as urban populations grew exponentially throughout the colonial era, foodstuff surpluses became increasingly important.

The 25,000 to 30,000 people in mid-eighteenth-century Boston, Salem, Providence, and similar towns relied exclusively on local farmers who provided meat, butter, and other foodstuffs. Planters living near the small but growing towns of Williamsburg and Annapolis fattened cattle and hogs for quick sale, supplying residents in each city with nearly 300,000 pounds of meat a year.

The planters who had left Barbados to settle South Carolina came to America expecting to produce goods for exportation and turned to satisfying the growing demand for salted pork and beef in the West Indies. Within ten years of settlement, Carolinians had thousands of hogs and cattle, with the richest men owning several hundred of each. Slaves and servants drove some animals back to pens at night, but most livestock remained in the woods, necessitating a semi-annual roundup. Once captured, the animals were driven to Charles Town, where they were butchered and sent to the islands. As rice replaced cattle in the South Carolina low country, herders moved to the upcountry of the colony and to Georgia. In the 1760s and 1770s, Georgia cattlemen produced thousands of barrels of salted meat each year for export.

Livestock was essential to settlement. Former servants and laborers in the seventeenth-century Chesapeake bought livestock even before they built houses. When a family set up a farm, they purchased a cow or two, a few swine, and some dunghill fowl. Early in the seventeenth century, cattle were scarce, but by mid-century they were plentiful. Cattle herds grazed the open range, and hardy swine lived off the forests. Mid-Atlantic and Southern farmers acquired horses, while New Englanders bought oxen.

Chesapeake fathers, godparents, and other relatives often gave children livestock as gifts. Throughout the colonies, daughters of both middling class and poor men received livestock as part of their dowries. Animal ownership did not ensure subsistence and market crops, but at least the new family could plow fields and put eggs, milk, butter, and meat on their table. The new farm family then cleared the land and planted crops so they could pay off the debts accrued from livestock purchase.

Livestock caused innumerable tensions between whites and Native Americans. As white farmers took over the land, they altered the topography, permitting their cattle and hogs to forage in fields and woods in competition with animals hunted by Native Americans or even in the native's unfenced cornfields. To preserve the available food for their livestock, colonists killed animals like deer that Native Americans relied on for subsistence. When Native Americans killed roaming livestock for meat—not recognizing them as private property—the colonial farmers became furious. Some rich farmers hired natives and poor whites to tend their livestock. The white herdsmen, dependent on the money earned tending animals, resented the competition of the natives and sometimes reacted violently.

As lands became more settled and hunting diminished, many Native Americans turned to livestock husbandry. By the middle of the late seventeenth century, Native Americans living among settlers in New England, Long Island, and the Hudson Valley were herding livestock. They particularly liked pigs, because the animals required little care and could be hunted when left to their own devices. King Philip, the Pequot sachem, raised huge numbers of hogs in the 1660s, setting them to graze on Hog Island. This eventually led to war because Portsmouth farmers also used the island. Native Americans also sold pork in Boston, often procuring firearms in return.

The few native residents who remained in the Tidewater region of the Chesapeake turned to herding to support themselves. William Taptico, the last leader of the Wicomico tribe in Virginia, raised sheep, milk cows, and hogs during the 1710s.

In times of war, soldiers often drove off vast numbers of livestock to keep the animals from being used by their enemies, or they simply confiscated the animals for their own use. During the American Revolution, the patriots regularly ordered the removal of livestock to safe havens out of reach of the British army.

From March 1777 through 1780, livestock was relocated from the New Jersey coast; from the Wilmington, Delaware, area, Darby Creek, Pennsylvania, and Kent County, Maryland; from parts of the Eastern Shore of Maryland; and from the North Carolina coast. This removal of livestock caused great hardships for local residents, who depended on the animals for milk, meat, plowing, and transportation.

Solomon K. Smith

See also: Agriculture; Horses.

Bibliography

Anderson, Virginia DeJohn. "King Philip's Herds: Indians, Colonists, and the Problem of Livestock in Early New England," *William & Mary Quarterly* 51 (1994): 6001–6024.

Kulikoff, Alan. *From British Peasants to Colonial American Farmers.* Chapel Hill: University of North Carolina Press, 2000.

Oakes, Elinor F. "A Ticklish Business: Dairying in New England and Pennsylvania, 1750–1812." *Pennsylvania History* 47 (1980): 195–212.

Locke, John (1632–1704)

John Locke was an English scholar, physician, and political theorist whose writings influenced American Revolutionary thought in the eighteenth century.

Locke was born in Wrington, Somerset, in 1632. His father's active support of Parliament in the English Civil War of 1642–1646 helped young Locke gain admission to the prestigious Westminster School in London in 1647 and to Christ Church College, Oxford, in 1652. He received his master's of arts degree in 1658, the same year that Oliver Cromwell, lord protector of England, died.

After the Restoration of King Charles II in 1660, Locke remained at Christ Church as a tutor. In his university years, he developed an avid interest in the new experimental science of innovators such as his friend Robert Boyle, a pioneer in chemistry and one of the founders of the Royal Academy of Sciences, which Locke himself would join.

After serving on an English diplomatic mission to Germany in 1665, Locke returned to Oxford to study medicine. Through his practice, he befriended and gained the patronage of Anthony Ashley Cooper, one of Charles II's inner court circle. In 1663, the king had made eight of his favorites, including Lord Ashley, lords proprietors of the Carolina colony, and Locke drew up the Fundamental Constitutions of that colony. The result, ratified in 1669, granted most governing powers to wealthy landowners in an archaic feudal-type order. But the colonists who eventually settled there refused to work in serflike capacities for the landholders, and the experiment in constitutional feudalism quickly failed. In the part of the colony that would later form North Carolina, farmers rose in rebellion in 1677. To the south, smallholders and planters—many of them coming from Barbados—eventually formed their own government.

Locke benefited from Lord Ashley's rise in power, for his patron, created earl of Shaftesbury, became lord chancellor of England in 1672. But when Charles II's secret pro-Catholic dealings with France became public knowledge, Shaftesbury broke with the king and became a leading member of the opposition party, known as the Whigs. Locke continued in government as secretary to the Council of Trade and Plantations until 1675.

The ensuing crises that befell Charles II's reign greatly affected John Locke's career and writings. The Popish Plot of 1678–1679, a false but sensational tale of a vast Catholic conspiracy against the king, fed into the Exclusion Crisis of 1679–1681. Shaftesbury was among those who wanted to force King Charles II to exclude his Catholic brother James, duke of York, from the succession. Charles II refused and eventually triumphed in Parliament. Shaftesbury left England in 1682 and died abroad. Locke, considered a Whig writer, also thought it prudent to leave England in 1683.

It was during his self-imposed exile in the Dutch Republic that John Locke wrote several important works, published at later dates. One of the most influential was *Essay Concerning Human Understanding* (1690), in which Locke explained that knowledge comes from what is perceived by the senses and the mind's reflection on these perceptions. He also wrote *Letter on Toleration* (1689) and *Thoughts Concerning Education* (1693).

While Locke was abroad, James II came to the throne in 1685 and quickly antagonized the nation with his pro-Catholic policies and attempts to circumvent parliamentary law. In 1688–1689, the political elite of England replaced James II with his daughter, Mary, and her husband, William, Prince of Orange, an event known as the Glorious Revolution. John Locke was in the same party with Mary when she sailed from Holland to England in 1689, and, in 1690, his *Two Treatises of Government* was published. Under the new regime, Locke served in government again, and, from 1696 to 1700, he was an important member of the Board of Trade. He died in 1704.

Locke's most influential political work, *Two Treatises of Government*, actually originated during the Exclusion Crisis. In the early seventeenth century, Sir Robert Filmer had written a work in support of the divine right of kings, entitled *Patriarcha*. It was published only in 1680, however, when it was used as a counterargument against Shaftesbury and the Whigs, who wanted to alter the succession. Locke in turn wrote a refutation of *Patriarcha*, which became the *First Treatise*. This entire work was probably written prior to his 1683 exile. Upon his return to England in 1689, he prepared the manuscript for publication, although the three editions put out during his lifetime (1690, 1694, 1698) were published anonymously.

Locke, in a preface, tied *Two Treatises* to the events of 1688–1689. He explained he was writing "to establish the throne of our great restorer, our present King William—to make good his title in the consent of the people." It is in the *Second Treatise* that Locke explained the origin, extent, and purpose of civil government. For Locke, an empirical scientist, natural laws exist not just for the physical world but also for human institutions. Natural law is universal and can be discovered by human reason.

Like his fellow English theorist Thomas Hobbes, Locke believed that humans form governments to live better lives. But Hobbes in *Leviathan* (1651) argued that life was so brutal in a "state of nature" that people enter into a contract with a ruler who is given absolute power. Locke instead held that people in the state of nature are more reasonable. Also by natural law, prior to the existence of government, people have the right to life, liberty, and property. It is to protect these rights that they enter into a contract to form a government. If that government breaks the contract and fails to protect the people's natural rights, the governed have a right to rebel and replace it.

Locke's ideas gained influence in the later eighteenth century among America's leading political thinkers and became a theoretical basis for the Revolution. Thomas Jefferson, in the Declaration of Independence, echoes Locke when he writes of men's rights to "life, liberty, and the pursuit of happiness . . . that whenever any form of government becomes destructive of these ends, it is the right of the people to alter or abolish it, and to institute new government."

Locke's ideas also influenced the writers of the U.S. Constitution in such areas as limitations on executive power and the protection of individual rights against any arbitrary exercise of power.

Florene S. Memegalos

See also: Arts, Culture, and Intellectual Life (Essay); Child Rearing; Children; Jefferson, Thomas; South Carolina; South Carolina (Chronology).

Bibliography

Locke, John. *Two Treatises of Government.* Edited by Peter Laslett. Rev. ed. Cambridge, UK: Cambridge University Press, 1988.

Yolton, John W. *John Locke, an Introduction.* Oxford: Blackwell, 1985.

———, ed. *John Locke: Problems and Perspectives, A Collection of New Essays.* Cambridge, UK: Cambridge University Press, 1969.

Long Island

Prior to European settlement, Long Island was inhabited by twelve Native American tribes. These tribes included the powerful Setuket near Stony Brook, the Matinecock on northern Long Island, the Montauk on Montauk Point, and the Manhanset on Shelter, Ram, and Hog Islands. All of these tribes belonged to the Mohegan nation. Like many Northeastern native peoples, the Long Island tribes suffered greatly from European diseases in the early seventeenth century.

In 1609, the Dutch explorer Henry Hudson met with the Canarsee tribe in western Long Island. Following his voyage, Hudson claimed New York for Holland. A formal charter was granted to the West India Company in 1621, and New Netherland became a colony in 1623. The colony claimed all the land between the Delaware and Connecticut Rivers.

Dutch settlement in western Long Island continued to spread throughout the 1620s and 1630s. Towns spread across the region, although most settlers lived on scattered farms. The first organized church was built in 1654 and was followed by various schools in 1661. As in the rest of New Netherland, Dutch language and culture flourished. Unlike most of the English colonies, religious toleration was encouraged, and western Long Island had small numbers of Jewish, Quaker, and Anabaptist settlers.

Charles I granted Long Island to the Earl of Sterling in 1635. Although this action was protested by the Dutch, their objections did not prevent English colonists from moving to eastern Long Island in the late 1630s. Most of these settlers were from New England, seeking new towns in which to practice their own interpretation of the Puritan faith. In addition, the Earl of Sterling sold grants of land to royalists fleeing the English Civil War, thereby creating an Anglican minority.

In 1664, England claimed the rest of Long Island and New York by granting the region to King Charles II's brother, James. Following a lengthy dispute, the Dutch agreed in 1667 to cede New York to the British in exchange for Surinam. Although New York City itself remained Dutch in character throughout the seventeenth century, Long Island became ever more English. In 1683, the Charter of Liberties joined Long Island to Staten Island and divided the district into three sections modeled after Yorkshire in England.

Although rarely directly affected by the various colonial wars of the late seventeenth and eighteenth centuries, Long Island contributed both soldiers and financial support to King Philip's War, King William's War, Queen Anne's War, and the French and Indian War. In contrast, the American Revolution was felt directly by the region.

The first signs of the war were financial and cultural. By the late eighteenth century, maritime industries and trade provided the primary source of income for Long Island. The boycott of British goods resulting from protests against the Sugar Act, the Townshend duties, and other acts had a financial effect on commerce. The cultural and religious divisions between Puritans and Anglicans became bitter political divisions between patriots and loyalists. By 1776, the war itself had arrived in Long Island.

The Continental army moved to New York City and began fortifying Brooklyn Heights in the spring of 1776 under the direction of General Nathaniel Greene. In June, the British fleet anchored off Long Island, planning to drive the Continental army from New York and take over Brooklyn Heights. On August 22, General William Howe landed 20,000 troops at Gravesend Bay. Within a week, he had seized all of western Long Island. Hundreds of American soldiers were killed, wounded, or taken prisoner. Washington withdrew from New York City to Harlem Heights on September 12. There, he hoped to regroup the Continental army and prepare for another attack. Three days later, the British took New York City and Long Island.

British rule on Long Island had a devastating effect on the region. Howe's attack on Gravesend Bay had destroyed dozens of farms in Kings and Queens counties. Each winter, the British garrison in New York City required Long Islanders to provide thousands of cords of wood, leaving almost no trees behind by the end of the war. American officers taken prisoner in 1776 were given parole and boarded with Long Island families. The Continental Congress was charged for their board, a total sum of nearly $30,000.

Although General Charles Cornwallis surrendered to Washington in October of 1781, the British did not leave New York and Long Island until November of 1783. True prosperity did not return to the region until the whaling boom of the early nineteenth century.

Abigail B. Chandler

See also: New York; New York and New Netherland (Chronology).

Bibliography

Bliven, Bruce. *New York.* New York: W. W. Norton, 1981.
Wilson, Rufus. *Historic Long Island.* New York: Ira J. Friedman, 1969.

Louis XIV (1638–1715)

The long-awaited eldest son of Louis XIII of France and Anne of Austria, Louis XIV, the "God-given," was born September 5, 1638, twenty-three years after his parents' marriage. Louis XIII died in 1643, leaving his son under a regency of Anne of Austria and her advisor, Cardinal Mazarin.

Louis XIV's most powerful childhood memory was of the Fronde (1649–1653), a rebellion of the French nobility and urban elite, which drove the royal family from Paris and soured the young king on trusting the nobles and the city of Paris. In 1659–1660, France ended the last military outbreak associated with of the Thirty Years' War with the Treaty of the Pyrenees, securing its diplomatic prestige and a Spanish bride, Marie-Thérèse of Austria, for Louis XIV.

The seventy-two-year reign of France's Louis XIV, the "Sun King," was the longest in European history (1643–1715). The nation's colonies, like almost everything else in French life, were controlled from the palace at Versailles. *(Chateau de Versailles, France/Lauros/Giraudon/Bridgeman Art Library)*

In 1661, Mazarin died, and Louis XIV announced that he would be his own first minister, handling state affairs directly. With excellent advice from Jean-Baptiste Colbert and Michel Le Tellier, the king made significant progress in reforming France's corrupt tax system and modernizing its army. Louis XIV concentrated the nobles around his lavish court at Versailles, which became a cultural center for Europe, and sent *intendants*, or royal governors, into the provinces to represent his will. All of this boded well for a centralizing and reforming monarchy that might fundamentally alter France's still-feudal fiscal system and tame its independent nobles.

Louis XIV inherited France's colonies in the Caribbean and New France (at that time, confined to eastern Canada), which he treated as provinces of France, naming strong *intendants* such as Louis de Frontenac, and insisting that only loyal, Roman Catholic settlers emigrate. Because of his policy, French colonies were entirely controlled from Versailles and given no self-government or economic opportunities outside the royal monopolies.

Under his reign, Jacques Marquette and Louis Jolliet explored the Mississippi, and Pierre le Moyne, Sieur d'Iberville, began settlement in Louisiana, but these were not profitable ventures for the monarchy. The colonies also were never used as "safety valves" for France's religious minorities or prisoners, as Britain's were, leaving the French colonies in Canada underpopulated and difficult to defend.

Louis XIV was fundamentally a medieval monarch; he wanted to glorify his reign rather than truly modernize the French government and its bureaucracy. In 1668, he embarked on the first of a series of expensive European wars. France had the military engineer Sébastien Vauban, who fortified the border cities at enormous expense, and the marquis de Louvois, who raised huge armies for the king. In the long run, the four decades of war, beginning in 1668, unified France's enemies in Germany and bankrupted the treasury for little actual gain.

Louis XIV's effort to enforce the will of the late Charles II of Spain and place his grandson Philip of Anjou on the Spanish throne turned into the War of the Spanish Succession (1701–1714). This ended with France winning a treaty that offered it less than Louis XIV's enemies had offered him to desist in 1700, before the war started.

Although Louis XIV lived a luxurious life with his mistresses, he was also deeply committed to the cause of Roman Catholicism, especially the Gallican Church under his authority in France. After the death of his queen, Marie-Thérèse, Louis XIV secretly married his children's governess, the marquise de Maintenon, who pushed him toward a more austere and religious life. This resulted in his persecution of a Catholic sect, the Jansenists, who believed in predestination, and the revocation of the 1598 Edict of Nantes, which guaranteed toleration for Protestants, in 1685. Protestant refugees, having been "dragooned" by French soldiers and driven from their homes, flooded into Britain, the Netherlands, and overseas colonies such as South Carolina, bringing with them cash and valuable trade skills.

Louis XIV is regarded as the "Sun King," a magnificent monarch who placed France at the center of Europe as a cultural and diplomatic power. Unfortunately, his huge expenditures on war and his treatment of nobles as courtiers rather than administrators laid the foundations for crisis later in the century, and his colonial policy stifled expansion and autonomy in French territory.

The government Louis XIV constructed with himself at the center worked until his death on September 1, 1715. He was succeeded by his great-grandson, the underage Louis XV.

Margaret Sankey

See also: Edict of Nantes, Revocation of; French; French Colonies on Mainland North America (Chronology).

Bibliography

Ashley, Maurice. *Louis XIV and the Greatness of France.* New York: Free Press, 1946.
Goubert, Pierre. *Louis XIV and Twenty Million Frenchmen.* New York: Pantheon, 1970.
Hatton, Ragnhild. *Louis XIV and His World.* New York: Putnam, 1972.
Lynn, John. *The French Wars 1667–1714.* Oxford, UK: Osprey, 2002.

Louisiana

Recognizing the great strategic importance of the Mississippi River Valley, the French began establishing the colony of Louisiana around 1700. Though the boundaries of colonial Louisiana were largely undefined, the area included present-day Louisiana and the Mississippi Valley as far north as the Missouri River.

French Louisiana was really two colonies. The bulk of European settlers and African slaves clustered around New Orleans and its surrounding plantations, while French traders and soldiers stationed forts and posts along the Mississippi River and its tributaries. Louisiana was only marginally incorporated into the colonial Atlantic economy until the 1780s, when French planters and Spanish officials established a viable plantation economy. This set the stage for the explosive growth of slavery with the sugar and cotton boom of the 1790s.

In the 1540s, Hernando de Soto led a Spanish expedition through the lower Mississippi Valley. De Soto's expedition was a violent one, and it also introduced devastating diseases, which led to the collapse of the complex native civilizations of the lower Mississippi Valley. When a French and Native American expedition from Canada explored the region in the 1670s, they encountered only "Petites Nations," descendants of survivors of de Soto's raids, who had collected themselves into small tribes. Over the next three decades, some of these tribes would form the Choctaw, Creek, and Chickasaw, powerful confederacies that competed with the Natchez for supremacy in the lower Mississippi Valley.

Outside of New Orleans, French Louisiana was little more than a string of forts and trading posts existing at the sufferance of the native peoples. These posts, located at places like Natchez and St. Louis, strengthened alliances built on trade and tribute between the French and the Mississippi Indians, providing the French with their one viable export from Louisiana, deerskins. More powerful Native American nations like the Choctaw welcomed these alliances, using French dependence to their own advantage. Less powerful tribes could not dictate terms to the French and often entered into these alliances to protect themselves from enemy tribes. Despite the protection afforded by alliances, war and disease eventually devastated these small tribes. The population of the Petites Nations, for example, declined from over 20,000 in 1685 to 4,000 in 1730.

French efforts to establish a plantation economy in Louisiana began in 1717 when the French government granted the Company of the West a charter to establish a colony in the lower Mississippi Valley. It established a main town at New Orleans and offered land grants in the vicinity. From 1718 to 1730, the company also provided over 5,000 Europeans and 6,000 Africans for labor; in 1719, it was renamed the Company of the Indies. Merchants and officials engaged in the fur trade, smuggling, and sometimes piracy, while those with plantations produced small crops of rice, cotton, tobacco, and naval stores.

In the early years, the plantation economy languished. Louisiana rice, indigo, and tobacco were inferior, pricey, and heavily dependent on subsidies from the French government, and Louisiana planters could not compete with English colonies like Virginia and South Carolina, which produced the same staples. Slave and Native American resistance also thwarted attempts to create a plantation society. The Natchez Indian Rebellion of 1729, in which several hundred slaves either participated or were captured, hastened the end of French efforts to establish a plantation society in Louisiana. In 1731, the French Crown took control of the colony from the Company of the Indies, but did little to promote emigration or economic development.

An exchange economy involving merchants, traders, planters, farmers, slaves, and Native Americans emerged in the aftermath of the plantation regime's collapse. Louisiana planters and merchants began provisioning the sugar islands of the Caribbean, producing timber, naval stores, and cattle. With no staple crop demanding a regimented labor system, planters increasingly let slaves provide for themselves. Slaves used these opportunities to claim greater control over their own lives by hiring themselves out, working for wages, and producing goods for the New Orleans market. Some managed to purchase their own freedom, leading to the growth of a small, but significant, class of free blacks and mulattos in New Orleans.

In 1763, France transferred control of Louisiana to the Spanish. Spain's main interest in Louisiana was to create a buffer colony protecting the far more lucrative province of Mexico. Spanish policies, nonetheless, nurtured the slow growth of slavery in the 1780s and 1790s. In the mid-1790s, the invention of the cotton gin and the slave rebellion in Haiti led to a plantation revolution in Louisiana.

North of New Orleans, planters established cotton plantations. South of New Orleans, planters fleeing the slave rebellion in Haiti brought to Louisiana the capital and expertise needed for sugar production. By 1803, when the United States acquired the Louisianas, French planters and Spanish officials were well on their way toward creating a thriving plantation society.

John Craig Hammond

See also: Acadians; French; French Colonies on Mainland North America (Chronology); Mississippi River; New Orleans; Spanish Colonies on Mainland North America (Chronology).

Bibliography

Berlin, Ira. *Many Thousands Gone: The First Two Centuries of Slavery in North America*. Cambridge, MA: Belknap Press, 1998.

Hall, Gwendolyn Midlo. *Africans in Colonial Louisiana: The Development of Afro-Creole Culture in the Eighteenth Century*. Baton Rouge: Louisiana State University Press, 1992.

Usner, Daniel H. Jr. *Indians, Settlers, & Slaves in a Frontier Exchange Economy: The Lower Mississippi Valley Before 1783*. Chapel Hill: University of North Carolina Press, 1992.

Loyalists

In the years leading to the American Revolution, colonists found themselves divided into three distinct factions concerning their view of the British Empire. These three sectors—the patriots, the loyalists, and the neutrals—viewed American independence from different perspectives. The loyalists were also referred to as Tories, based on their alignment with the conservative

A cartoon of 1775 depicts a Virginia loyalist being forced to sign a document by a club-wielding mob of patriots, as another loyalist is being led toward the gallows. Loyalists were treated with increasing harshness as the Revolution approached, and they were finally declared traitors. *(Library of Congress, LC-USZ62-9488)*

party in Britain. The conservative stance promoted the power of the church and the prestige of the monarchy.

In 1776, between 20 and 30 percent of the colonial population remained openly loyal to the British monarchy. These loyalists were largely people who still found the idea and spirit of the British Empire to be the most desirable situation in the New World. This appeal was due to Britain's historical, cultural, and economic ties with the colonies.

Convinced that American prosperity, growth, and stability were dependent on British ruling authority, supported by a monarchical government, loyalists were in all sectors of colonial society. The most dedicated loyalists were royal officials of all levels, urban lawyers, and wealthy merchants with commercial ties to England. Loyalism extended into the religious realm based on the early-eighteenth-century grants of religious liberty to groups such as the Palatine Germans in New York and the French Huguenots in the Carolinas. Some were considered loyalists simply due to their engaging in opposition politics with leading patriots.

The backcountry farmers in the Carolinas tended toward loyalism because of resentment of the power of the lowland gentry. Southern slaves expressed their resentment against the white slave-owning class. Lord Dunmore's promise of eventual freedom for slaves led many thousands of blacks in Virginia to join the loyalists, while many in South Carolina fled to Charles Town, finding refuge with the British army when the city was occupied during the Revolution.

Assuming the British would win the war, many Native Americans—most importantly, the powerful Iroquois Nation—established strong economic ties to the empire. Even in the New England towns at the heart of the fracas, such as Concord, Massachusetts, had a small, silent core of loyalists who refused to condone armed revolution. For many colonists, the idea of confronting what they believed to be a strong British military was overwhelming. If this was not dissuasive enough, others doubted the survival of a new, young nation in a world dominated by competing empires. Therefore, enclaves of loyalism based on different reasons existed everywhere in colonial America.

While rebellion against England was still uncertain, the loyalists were most active between 1774 and 1776. Every major city had a few loyalist printers, who produced newspapers and pamphlets. Loyalists in New York City circulated literature in 1776 titled "A Declaration of Dependence." In the backcountry areas where printed material was not yet available, rallies and speeches took the place of print culture.

In 1775, loyalists' worst fears were realized, when the First Continental Congress passed a resolution that declared loyalists to be traitors, subject to varying degrees and forms of punishment. Throughout the war, approximately 7,000–8,000 loyalists fled to England, while some 28,000 found refuge in Canada. But many chose to remain in America through the close of the Revolution and adjust to the changing politics of their individual communities.

Penny M. Sonnenburg

See also: Continental Congress, First; Patriots; Revolutionary War.

Bibliography

Kammen, Michael. *Empire and Interest.* Philadelphia: Lippincott, 1970.

Middlekauff, Robert. *The Glorious Cause: The American Revolution, 1763–1789.* New York: Oxford University Press, 1982.

Nash, Gary B. *Race and Revolution.* Madison, WI: Madison House, 1990.

M

Madeira

See Azores and Madeira

Maine

Initially populated by a variety of Algonquian-speaking native peoples, Maine was fought over by the French and English for much of the seventeenth century, before being absorbed into the Massachusetts Bay Colony in 1691.

The earliest inhabitants of Maine were members of a larger, Algonquian-speaking group of tribes called the Wabanaki (the name means "people of the dawn"). Their lands ran west to the Hudson River, north to the Saint Lawrence, east to Newfoundland, and south to the Long Island Sound. Within Maine, these tribes were known as the Abenaki, Penobscot, Passamaquoddy, Maliseet, and Micmac. While the Wabanaki came in close contact with both French and English, their relations with the Europeans varied widely.

Maine was visited by several European explorers, including Giovanni da Verrazano in 1534, James Rosier in 1602, and Sir Humphrey Gilbert in 1605. Based on their accounts, Captains George Popham and Raleigh Gilbert attempted the first permanent settlement in New England in 1607. The colonists built a fort at the mouth of the Kennebec River, explored Casco Bay, and attempted trade with neighboring Abenaki. Frigid weather and Popham's death resulted in the colonists' decision to abandon the settlement and sail home to England in their pinnace, the *Virginia* (the first ship built by Europeans in the New World).

Although the Popham colony had failed, neither the French nor the English lost interest in Maine. Both countries wanted to control Maine's rivers and the easy access they provided to Canada. They also wanted Maine's rich resources of furs, timber, and fish. Seasonal fishing camps were set up along the Maine coast, with men fishing through the summer and returning home to Europe for the winter. The Pilgrims were supplied by camps in the Damariscotta region during their first difficult year at Plymouth.

In 1629, following a treaty between England and France, Maine was divided into two parts. The land between the Piscataqua and Kennebec rivers was called the Province of Maine and was claimed by England. The eastern stretches of the Maine coast were called Acadia and were considered French territory.

Funding for settlement in the New World was provided by companies, usually formed by noblemen, speculators, and explorers. A wealthy English nobleman named Ferdinando Gorges was granted a royal charter in 1621 and formed his own company, calling it the Council for New England. Although his lands stretched from Philadelphia to Newfoundland, Gorges primarily focused his attention on Maine. Unlike most charters of the period, Gorges's gave him almost total control over his lands, including the right to grant smaller charters as he saw fit.

In 1630, Gorges granted William Bradford and the Plymouth Colony land on both sides of the Kennebec, as well as the exclusive right to trade on the river. By the 1640s, settlers from Plymouth had become an active presence in the Kennebec region. Lands between Cape Porpoise and the Kennebec River were given to Alexander Rigby and George Cleeves in 1643 and became a semidependent province called Lygonia. More lands around the Saco and York rivers also were given as grants. In 1647, Gorges died, leaving the Province of Maine without government. It promptly declared itself an independent region and elected Edward Godfrey, a settler who lived near the York River, as governor.

At the same time, the Puritans of Massachusetts

Bay Colony also began claiming Maine. With Gorges dead and fellow Puritan Oliver Cromwell on the rise back home in England, the Puritans were able to redraw their boundaries to 3 miles north of the Merrimac River in 1650. This placed New Hampshire and most of Maine within the boundaries of the Massachusetts patent. While southern Maine capitulated, New Plymouth settlers resisted Puritan claims by obtaining bills of sale from their Abenaki neighbors as proof of ownership. All of these claims were put into dispute by the outbreak of King Philip's War in 1675. Plymouth's land in both Maine and Massachusetts was fully absorbed into Massachusetts Bay Colony in 1691.

French interest in Maine stemmed around trade and missionary work. Initially, the French set up seasonal fishing camps in the Penobscot Bay area. As their knowledge of Maine increased, they began trading up and down the rivers, and trading posts were established far into the Maine wilderness. For the most part, the French traders' relations with the Micmac, Maliseet, Abenaki, and Penobscot tribes were positive. Unlike the English, they had little interest in permanent settlement on Native American land. Another important Native American–French relation grew from the Jesuit missions. Jesuit missionaries spent years with their adopted tribes, converting members to Christianity, describing their surroundings, and gaining fluency in the native languages. In 1671, France laid claim to lands around the Kennebec, arguing that the English settlers living there would prefer French rulership to Puritan. Although nothing came of this claim, it serves as indication of further French interest in southern Maine.

King Philip's War began in 1675 between the Wampanoags and their English neighbors in southeastern Massachusetts. The Wampanoags feared total English control over their lands and hoped to drive them out. They were gradually joined by other tribes, including the Wabanaki in Maine. Another cause for war in Maine, beyond land, was a law reiterated by the Massachusetts General Court in 1675, stating that no guns or ammunition could be sold to Native Americans. The French, an active presence in the Penobscot Bay region, supported the Wabanaki by supplying them with weapons and other supplies.

In the summer of 1676, just as the war was ending in Massachusetts, towns and settlements up and down the Maine coast were attacked. Most survivors fled to the relative safety of Massachusetts. Peace in Maine was finally declared in 1678 under the Treaty of Casco.

This relative peace settled over Maine until the outbreak of King William's War in 1689 and Queen Anne's War in 1702. As in the wars fought in Europe, these were battles between English and French over imperial control, though these conflicts were further complicated by Native American interests. The patterns of attack were similar to those of King Philip's War, with a series of raids on English settlements, and the line of the line of attack moved back and forth constantly. When treaties for both wars were signed in Europe, these resolutions had little or no immediate effect on the residents of Maine.

By the end of Queen's Anne's War in 1714, most Native Americans living along the coast had died due to war or disease. In 1763, under the terms of the Treaty of Paris, France ceded all claims to Maine, Newfoundland, and Nova Scotia. The English were permanently established in Maine.

Over the next few years, settlements continued to grow along the coast. At this time, Maine's primary industries consisted of fishing, timber, and shipbuilding. The region was still governed and owned by Massachusetts Bay Colony, although local government thrived.

Somewhat similar in its progression to King Philip's War, the conflicts of the American Revolution began in Massachusetts and then spread north. Following the battles of Lexington and Concord, several Maine towns began forming militias. Maine sent numerous men to the war effort, including troops under Benedict Arnold, who marched to Quebec in late 1775. Maine ships were also used as privateers during the war, frequently capturing British merchants.

As in the other colonies, the question of being a patriot or loyalist was hotly debated within Maine. Unlike Massachusetts, Maine had a relatively strong Anglican presence. The presence of British settlements and troops in Nova Scotia and New Brunswick also had an impact on the region's loyalties. Most Mainers were accustomed to living balanced between Massachusetts to the south and the Maritimes to the east, trading wherever the price was best.

During the Boston occupation of 1775, the British became desperate for firewood. Vice Admiral Samuel Graves in Boston commissioned a Machias sea captain named Ichabod Jones to sail home with a load of supplies and trade them for wood. When the merchant ships and armed schooner arrived in Machias on June 2, the local Sons of Liberty captured them in the first naval battle of the Revolution. Shortly afterward, the British sent several ships to attack Machias in retaliation. Similar British raids took place up and down the Maine coast throughout the rest of the Revolution, including attacks on Falmouth, Damariscotta, and Southwest Harbor.

The only full engagement between the British and American navies in Maine was the Penobscot Expedition of 1779. Hoping to gain control of Penobscot Bay, British troops under the command of Brigadier General Francis McLean began building a fort outside Castine. A small fleet of American ships sailed from Boston, and more men marched overland. McLean called for reinforcements from Halifax, and the Americans were beaten. The British occupied Castine for much of the rest of the war.

At the close of the American Revolution, the Maine coast was heavily settled, but little was known about its interior. Acres of Maine had been given as bounty to Revolutionary War soldiers, and floods of settlers were preparing to head inland. Maine was declared officially part of the new state of Massachusetts in 1776. It remained so until 1821, when Maine was admitted to the Union as a separate state under the terms of the Missouri Compromise.

Abigail B. Chandler

See also: Massachusetts; Massachusetts (Chronology).

Bibliography

Bourke, Bruce. *Twelve Thousand Years: American Indians in Maine.* Lincoln: University of Nebraska Press, 2001.

Clark, Charles. "The Founding of Maine, 1600–1640." *Maine Historical Society Quarterly* 18:3 (1978): 55–62.

Duncan, Roger. *Coastal Maine.* New York: W. W. Norton, 1992.

Leamon, James. *Revolution Downeast.* Amherst: University of Massachusetts Press, 1993.

Reid, John. "French Aspirations in the Kennebec-Penobscot Region." *Maine Historical Society Quarterly* 23:1 (1983–1984): 85–92.

Malaria

Malaria is a parasitic disease transmitted from one human to another by the bite of infected anopheles mosquitoes. When a human is bitten by a female mosquito looking for a blood meal, the *Plasmodium falciparum* protozoa (the most common bacteria associated with malaria in American history) enter the bloodstream and travel to the liver, where they multiply. When the protozoa reemerge into the bloodstream,

symptoms such as fever, headache, back pain, chills, sweats, nausea, vomiting, diarrhea, and cough appear. By the time a patient shows symptoms, the parasites have already reproduced, clogged blood vessels, and ruptured blood cells. An untreated *Plasmodium falciparum* infection ultimately can lead to renal failure, pulmonary edema, coma, and even death.

The periodic fevers characteristic of malaria were initially associated with climate and geographic location. Many European writers believed that the effluvia, or exhalations, from marshes and swamps caused the disease. These atmospheric poisons came to be called by the Italian term *mal'aria,* or "bad air."

Malaria's seasonal nature was not lost upon the colonists, who recognized that the disease would flare up annually in almost epidemic proportions. In 1723, a missionary wrote that the malarial illnesses held "one from the beginning of August to the latter end of December." By the middle of the century, those wealthy enough to afford it began to travel during the fever months to places such as the more salubrious seaside city of Newport, Rhode Island. However, this practice may have been more hazardous, because it did not give such individuals an opportunity to acquire any immunity.

Native Americans also had little immunity to the disease, because malaria was unknown in the Americas prior to the arrival of Europeans. Along with smallpox and measles, malaria was the major killer of Native Americans during the colonial period.

Malaria itself, however, usually does not cause death on its own. More often, the disease weakens the individual's resistance to other diseases that he or she otherwise would have warded off if healthy. Anemia, loss of energy, susceptibility to infection, and chronic invalidism are common characteristics of victims of malarial fever. Although the majority of those infected probably did not die directly of malaria, being weakened from periodic malaria attacks would have made them especially susceptible to other, more lethal diseases.

As with other diseases, malaria also preys on those who are most vulnerable. In the colonial period, infant mortality rates were very high due to their early exposure. Furthermore, young women who contracted malaria often suffered miscarriages and premature labor.

The specter of malaria had a profound impact upon the social, cultural, and political development of the early colonies. Of primary importance was the establishment of a plantation economy in the Southern colonies and the growing dependence of the region's population upon slave labor. The sudden rise of profitability in rice planting had encouraged the importation of slaves to the New World. Unfortunately, African slaves brought with them not only experience with rice culture but also a less deadly form of malaria, *Plasmodium vivax,* which in combination with the already virulent *Plasmodium falciparum* resulted in worsening health conditions for the white population in the Southern colonies.

In the last decades of the seventeenth century, the white population actually experienced a decline in population, while the black population began to become self-sufficient and stable. This population growth, coupled with the fact that black slaves who possessed only one copy of the gene for sickle-cell anemia had greater resistance to malaria (as opposed to individuals who had two copies of the gene and frequently had symptoms of the anemia itself), further justified slavery on a massive scale in those colonies that practiced plantation agriculture.

Though there is no cure for malaria, the primary means of combating the symptoms is the administration of quinine. During the colonial era, the effects of quinine on malaria were not fully understood, though Peruvian bark or cinchona bark, which is a source of quinine, was one of the treatments used—if not always effectively.

Dr. Benjamin Rush, a signer of the Declaration of Independence and a member of the Constitutional Convention, experimented with cinchona bark but wrote that "in every case in which I prescribed the bark, it was offensive to the stomach . . . [it produced] a paroxysm of the fever so violent as to require the loss of 10 ounces of blood to moderate it." As this suggests, other treatments applied included bleeding, as well as opiates and mercury. In many cases, the treatments were almost worse than the disease.

Jeffrey Heeren

See also: Death and Dying; Disease; Smallpox.

Bibliography

Cassedy, James H. *Medicine in America: A Short History.* Baltimore: Johns Hopkins University Press, 1991.

Numbers, Ronald L., and Todd L. Savitt, eds. *Science and Medicine in the Old South.* Baton Rouge: Louisiana State University Press, 1989.

Poser, Charles M., and George W. Bruyn. *An Illustrated History of Malaria.* New York: Pantheon, 1999.

Manufacturing

Throughout the colonial period, manufacturing never achieved an economic importance remotely approaching that of agriculture. The development of colonial manufacturing was limited by both economic and political factors.

Labor and capital were scarce and expensive in America as compared to Britain and Europe, and the ease of obtaining land in the New World drew off much of the potential labor supply for industry into agriculture. The colonies were subject to British economic regulations, which often discouraged colonial manufacturers out of fear that they would compete with British manufacturers of the same goods. At the same times, colonists were unable to use tariffs to help their own industries, although individual colonies could and did grant monopolies and subsidies to encourage particular enterprises. What industry did emerge was usually small-scale and often based on household production.

Manufacturing in the First English Colonies

The most industrially minded of the early colonization companies was the Virginia Company, which wanted to diversify the economy of the Virginia colony beyond tobacco monoculture. The company's ambitious plans included ironworks, silkworm cultivation, and silk manufacture. Dutch and Polish workers were imported for the first colonial glassworks, founded in 1608; after its failure, a second attempt was made with Italian workers. (Importing experienced continental European workers, rather than relying on local workers, was common for founders of colonial manufacturing enterprises.) These manufacturing efforts were unsuccessful for a number of reasons, including Native American attacks and other disasters that struck the colony and the ever-present lure of quick wealth in tobacco. The technical problems involved in such industries also proved more formidable than first thought.

The Massachusetts Bay Company was somewhat more cautious—and more successful—in founding industrial enterprises. The first large-scale American cloth enterprise was founded in 1638, as twenty Yorkshire families with textile experience were settled in Rowley, Massachusetts, and a fulling mill was established. The following year, a glassworks was set up at Salem. In the 1640s, John Winthrop Jr., an enthusiast for science and

The first ironworks in America dates to the mid-1600s, but the arrival of a viable manufacturing sector awaited the fuller development of the economy in the eighteenth century. Even then, the British often suppressed the expansion of ironworks and other competitive industries in the colonies. *(New York Public Library, New York)*

technology who later became the first American member of the Royal Society, attempted to establish an ironworks, first at Braintree and then at Lynn. The works produced wrought iron suitable to be made into bolts, nails, and tools. Despite the technical ingenuity of the project, high labor costs and other economic factors eventually brought it to a halt.

Another of the largest American manufacturing efforts in the seventeenth century began around 1688, when the first large colonial pottery was set up in Burlington, New Jersey. The proprietor of New Jersey, physician Daniel Coxe, claimed to have spent about 2,000 pounds on the plant and planned to export stoneware to the neighboring colonies, as well as Barbados and Jamaica. The project was abandoned shortly afterward, when Coxe sold his interest in New Jersey.

Local, Household, and Plantation Manufacturing

More modest manufacturing activities serving local needs emerged in the first decades of colonization, and persisted throughout the colonial period. Kilns for the manufacture of crude earthenware appeared shortly af-

ter colonization, and home-based industry was common in the American colonies, as it was in Britain and Europe.

In textiles, the most important category of expenditure in household goods, domestic American household production coexisted with imports from Europe. The two most important textiles in colonial America were wool and linen, the latter being made from the flax plant. (Not all American flax was processed locally; much of it was exported to Ireland, the center of fine linen production.) In addition to use as clothing or bedding, textiles were also used to make sacks, wagon covers, and other essential items.

Textile production was generally a gendered activity. Women spun wool or flax into yarn. In New England and the Chesapeake in the early eighteenth century, women also took over weaving, previously a task performed by men. In the Middle colonies, however, where many male weavers from continental Europe emigrated, weaving remained a man's trade.

In all cases, spinning was a much more widely dispersed trade than weaving. Studies of wills and inventories in Chester County, Pennsylvania, a center of flax culture, from 1773 to 1776 reveal that two-thirds of the households possessed spinning wheels, while less than 8 percent owned looms.

Much of the cloth and garments produced by Americans were either worn by members of the household or exchanged with neighbors as part of a local barter economy. By the period immediately before the American Revolution, capitalist production for the market had begun to transform household textile manufacture. The development of communication and transportation networks between colonial communities in the eighteenth century also enabled more centralized household production. Certain communities were identified with a particular kind of manufactured good, which was then sold over a wide area. For instance, Germantown, Pennsylvania, became known for "Germantown stockings," of which many thousands of pairs were made annually. Lynn, Massachusetts, was a center of shoemaking.

While women worked on household textile production, European and Native American men found productive ways to occupy themselves during periods when the demands of agriculture were low. They availed themselves of America's abundance of trees to make potash from wood ash, cedar roofing shingles, and barrel staves of red and white oak, although the barrels themselves were made by specialists known as coopers. (In addition to their use in American storage and shipping, barrels and casks were also exported to the West Indies.) Gourds were dried and made into containers and vessels.

Among specialized local producers were shoemakers, who, unfortunately, left few records. In New England and the Middle colonies, blacksmiths made items as varied as nails, door hinges, andirons, simple locks, latches, tongs, trivets, wrought-iron candlesticks, pothooks, horseshoes, and harness parts.

The slaveholding societies of the colonial South followed a different pattern. Much of the limited manufacturing that took place was carried out by slaves, often providing only necessary goods for a plantation and its owners rather than items intended for trade. Southern blacksmiths, for example, whether indentured servants or, increasingly, slaves, made a more limited range of goods than their Northern counterparts, and many Southerners imported the iron products they needed.

The vast majority of slaves' work was in the areas of agriculture and domestic service, but slaves were also spinners, weavers, tanners, shoemakers, coopers, wheelwrights, and cabinetmakers. Slaves were industrial laborers as well. Maryland and Virginia iron foundries in the eighteenth century relied on slave workers. In the North, some Pennsylvania iron enterprises used slave labor and petitioned for a reduction of the tariff on slaves in 1727.

Expansion of Manufacturing

The development of the American economy in the late seventeenth and eighteenth centuries led to the expansion and diversification of manufactures. The growth of printing meant that printers had to have paper. The first American paper mill was constructed at Germantown, Pennsylvania, in 1690. The limiting factor for American papermakers was the shortage of rags, the basic material for paper in the eighteenth century.

Another industry that emerged in the eighteenth century was coppersmithing. This had little to do with the opening of American copper mines, the first being established near Simsbury, Connecticut, in 1705. American copper mines usually exported their ore to England to be refined. American coppersmiths then imported the refined copper in the form of sheets, which they made into teapots, warming pans, bells, and brass surveying instruments. Like blacksmiths, coppersmiths also recycled metal goods.

In addition to the establishment of new industries, old ones continued to grow. In 1739, German immigrant Caspar Wistar, using German workers, built the most successful colonial glass factory in Alloway, New Jersey. Wistar was also one of the few early American buttonmakers.

Britain and Colonial Manufacturing

In the seventeenth century, British authorities' principal motivation for regulating American production was to retain the American and West Indian markets for British manufacturers. A 1699 law forbade the export of raw wool, yarn, and finished fabrics from the colonies by ship, as well as the transportation of these materials by horse or cart from one colony to another. In fact, few American manufactured goods could compete with British products at this point, although the colonial shipbuilding industry had begun to establish itself as a force.

When it came to the development of American industry, British authorities preferred shipbuilding to the establishment of a colonial textile industry. The board of trade refused to intervene against colonial shipbuilders, when so requested by Thames shipwrights in 1724. The board feared that suppressing colonial shipbuilding would force Americans to develop an export textile business to pay for imports from Britain. British industrialists were also concerned about the lure of America's high-wage economy for their most skilled workers. The development of American ceramics was pronounced enough that the English pottery magnate Josiah Wedgwood was concerned about both the potential emigration of his company's skilled craftspeople and the possible loss of the American market.

Britain did not oppose all American manufactures. It did support American industries that complemented rather than competed with British industries or those that filled British needs. For instance, Britain encouraged the colonies to produce naval necessities, such as pitch and turpentine. Policy also could be influenced by different interests. British iron producers attempted to suppress colonial competition, while manufacturers who used iron welcomed colonial supplies.

The Royal Society of Arts, a group founded in London in 1754 that included some American members, particularly encouraged a revival of the old project, going back to the Virginia Company, of an American silk industry. Silk was a product Britain itself could not effectively produce. The society concentrated its efforts on the far Southern colonies, particularly Georgia, where it cooperated with the colony's proprietors. A group of Italian silk workers was established at a Savannah filature, where the silk cocoons would be wound into thread. Although the workers successfully produced silk thread, the project proved economically unviable and was abandoned by 1771. South Carolina silk was even less successful. The Society had more success in encouraging the development of the colonial potash industry, an effort encouraged by Parliament, which lifted the tariff on American potash in 1751.

Politicization of Manufacturers

Although colonial manufacturers had always had to reckon with the British government's insistence that home industries not be harmed by colonial ones, the question of manufacturing was even more politicized during the decades before the American Revolution. Repressive British legislation, such as the Townshend Acts, was answered with a series of nonimportation movements, designed to discourage Americans from paying for British goods and to encourage American manufactures. In 1767, a Boston town meeting coupled a call to lobby Parliament to repeal the acts with a call for American authorities to provide bounties for do-

mestic manufactures. This call was heard from many other quarters as well.

The effort to promote American manufacturing in the decades before the Revolution took many forms. In New England and Pennsylvania, there was an attempt to revive and expand domestic spinning. Ministers, newspaper proprietors, and local societies for the promotion of arts sponsored spinning bees and competitions for young women, often imbued with a patriotic flavor. More than sixty spinning parties were reported in local New England newspapers in the 1760s. These meetings usually took place at ministers' houses and were put forth as examples of women's patriotism.

Harvard students flaunted their patriotism by appearing at commencement in outfits entirely American in origin (although America had always produced much of its own clothing). Patriotic colonists in New England, New York, and Pennsylvania were encouraged not to eat lamb, so as to increase the supply of wool. The duty on the importation of paper also led to efforts to encourage the gathering of rags for use by colonial papermakers.

Other efforts to strengthen American industry were on a larger scale and organized on a more capitalistic basis. The earliest surviving American porcelain was made at Southwark in Philadelphia from 1770 to 1772 by the firm of Gousse Bonnin and George Anthony Morris. Bonnin, the leader of the venture, the American China Manufactory, associated his enterprise with American liberty and patriotism, pointing out that Philadelphians were spending 15,000 pounds a year on imported porcelain. He recruited English workers and produced soft-paste porcelain in the manner of the English Bow factory. The firm's failure may have been due to a deliberate effort to sabotage it by dumping British and Dutch porcelain on the American market, although labor difficulties also contributed to its woes. Despite the efforts of Bonnin and other ceramicists, American ceramics were still not of the quality to compete with Wedgwood and other leading British producers—efforts to duplicate Wedgwood's popular creamware or queensware in America were unsuccessful—and imports continued to dominate the market.

There also were several attempts to address the needs of American shipbuilders for sailcloth and cordage by encouraging Americans to raise hemp. The Society for the Promotion of Arts, Agriculture, and Oeconomy (also known as the New York Society of Arts) was founded in New York in late 1764 by merchants of the city's patriot faction. It focused principally on the development of linen manufacture. The Society succeeded in employing 300 people in the industry and attracted the unfavorable notice of the Board of Trade.

Philadelphia's American Philosophical Society was less successful in its alliance efforts with Philadelphia merchants and the Pennsylvania legislature to promote the silk industry. The society also requested that clays be submitted to it to determine the best deposits for different kinds of ceramics, offered premiums for rags for papermaking, and supported one of the few American glassmakers attempting to make a superior product, Henry William Stiegel.

Stiegel founded a glassworks at Manheim, Pennsylvania, in 1768. He planned to manufacture the highest-quality glass, known as flint glass, and the society gave its official approval. One important advantage of flint glass was its superior optical qualities, which the American Philosophical Society, the country's leading scientific organization, was in a position to certify. The society's efforts were in vain, however, as high labor costs and foreign competition forced Stiegel to close his glassworks in 1774.

Another, more effective Philadelphia organization was the United Company of Philadelphia for Promoting American Manufactures, headed by Benjamin Rush. Founded in 1775, it concentrated on textiles and soon employed 700 people. This company survived until the occupation of Philadelphia by the British in 1777.

The British response to the development of American industry in the late eighteenth century concentrated particularly on textiles, the basis of the British export economy—in 1772, woolen textiles comprised over 30 percent of British exports to the thirteen colonies. In 1766 and 1768, the Board of Trade required colonial governors to submit reports on all colonial manufactures established since 1734, though most governors described the manufacturing activity in their colonies as negligible. In 1774, Parliament prohibited the export from Britain of tools used in textile manufacture.

Benjamin Franklin, in an interview before the House of Commons, had pointed out that colonists might produce their own manufactured goods if Britain imposed tariffs on exports to America. Therefore, textile manufactures, along with other products of British industry, were omitted from the Townshend duties of 1767. As with the restriction of other freedoms, the quarrels between Britain and the colonies over regulating manufactures contributed to the outbreak of the American Revolution.

William E. Burns

See also: Artisans; Economy, Business, and Labor (Chronology); Economy, Business, and Labor (Essay); Laborers, Urban.

Bibliography

Hindle, Brooke. *The Pursuit of Science in Revolutionary America.* Chapel Hill: University of North Carolina Press for the Institute of Early American History and Culture in Williamsburg, Virginia, 1956.

Hood, Adrienne D. "The Material World of Cloth: Production and Use in Eighteenth-Century Rural Pennsylvania." *William and Mary Quarterly,* 3rd series, 53 (1996): 43–66.

Hood, Graham. *Bonnin and Morris of Philadelphia: The First American Porcelain Factory, 1770–1772.* Chapel Hill: University of North Carolina Press for the Institute of Early American History and Culture in Williamsburg, Virginia, 1972.

Hume, Ivor Noël. *A Guide to Artifacts of Colonial America.* New York: Alfred A. Knopf, 1970. 2nd edition. Philadelphia: University of Pennsylvania Press, 2001.

McCusker, John J., and Russell R. Menard. *The Economy of British America, 1607–1789.* Chapel Hill: University of North Carolina Press for the Institute of Early American History and Culture in Williamsburg, Virginia, 1985.

Mulholland, James A. *A History of Metals in Colonial America.* University: University of Alabama Press, 1981.

Ulrich, Laura Thatcher. *The Age of Homespun: Objects and Stories in the Creation of an American Myth.* New York: Alfred A. Knopf, 2001.

York, Neil Longley. *Mechanical Metamorphosis: Technological Change in Revolutionary America.* Contributions in American Studies, no. 178. Westport, CT: Greenwood, 1985.

Maps and Surveys

Maps of the Americas made by Europeans and colonists progressed from crude outlines, based on dead reckoning and observation, to precise works reflecting the efforts of professional surveyors and cartographers.

Early Maps

European expansion in the fifteenth and sixteenth centuries was accompanied by a rising concern with accurate mapping, which was complicated by the difficulty of reconciling several accounts into a single map. The *Casa de Contratación,* founded in 1503 to oversee and regulate Spanish movements to the New World, emphasized accurate cartography and navigation. In 1512, the "royal pattern," a continuously updated cartographic pattern, was established. The Spanish could not maintain a monopoly on New World cartographic information, however, and maps circulated widely in the sixteenth century.

The first published map to include the word "America" and to depict North and South America with a continuous coastline was the German scholar Martin Waldseemüller's *Cosmographica* (1507). New World maps also were included in the first known atlas, Abraham Ortelius's *Theatrum Orbis Terrarum* or *Theater of the World* (1570).

Latecomers to the New World, the English were also latecomers to New World mapping. The first published map of the New World originally produced (as opposed to maps that were adapted from Continental ones) by an English cartographer was John White's map, which was included in the 1590 edition of Thomas Harriot's book *A Briefe and True Report of the New Found Land of Virginia.* John Smith was another early English mapper.

Maps and Politics

Maps served many functions in colonial society. One of the most significant functions was expressing—and advancing—political claims. The French cartographer Guillaume Delisle published a technically excellent *Map of Louisiana and the Course of the Mississippi* (1718), which was particularly influential in its treatment of the Gulf of Mexico. The map also aggressively advanced the French position in North America, restricting the English holdings in the Southeast to the territory east of the Alleghenies. (French cartographers had the advantage over English of much more knowledge of the interior of North America.) Herman Moll fired back in 1720 with *A New Map of the North Parts of America Claimed by France*, minimizing French claims and expanding English ones.

Politically speaking, the most important map produced in the colonial era was one by Dr. John Mitchell. The first edition of the map appeared in London in 1755, with the title *A Map of the British and French Dominions in North America.* Sponsored by the Lords Commissioners for Trade and Plantations, the Mitchell map precisely delineated the maximum extent of English claims, even to the Pacific. The fourth edition of this map, published in 1775 after the British conquest of Canada in the French and Indian War, was titled *A Map of the British Colonies in North America with the Roads, Distances, Limits and Extent of the Settlements.* This map later became the cartographic basis of the

territorial negotiations between Britain and America at the conclusion of the Revolutionary War.

In addition to being used in political struggles between empires, maps also influenced what happened within nations. Poor understanding of local geography meant that grants of land made in London often had vaguely defined boundaries or overlapped with other grants. Colonies produced maps that supported their boundary claims against those of their neighbors.

Maps also made economic claims. New York officials, in communicating with the government in England, used deceptive maps that showed easy access from New York to Iroquois country, claiming that this meant the government should put more resources into the colony to support the fur trade with the Native Americans of the North.

A map also helped to reinforce ownership. The second Lord Baltimore, proprietor of Maryland, rewarded the Prague-born Augustine Herrman with a manor of 13,000 acres for his map *Virginia and Maryland as It Is Planted and Inhabited This Present Year 1670* (1673).

Surveying

Mapping was part of the Europeans' great endeavor to know the strange new lands. Mappers drew on Native American knowledge, as well as their own observations and European cartographic techniques. As more land in the Americas was conquered, settled, and explored by Europeans, there was an increased need for accurate, or at least mutually agreeable, boundary lines to demarcate individual properties.

The work of surveyors included establishing boundaries, laying out towns, plotting the course of roads, dividing properties between heirs or purchasers, and a host of other tasks. Surveying had developed in Europe in the mid-sixteenth century as a mathematical and astronomical discipline. In America, surveyors were handicapped, relative to their European counterparts, by the dense woods in some areas, which made taking a long view difficult if not impossible. European surveyors often used church spires, usually the highest point in a village or town, as a landmark; again, this was impossible in less developed parts of the colonies.

The bulky theodolite, a standard tool for taking the azimuth in Europe, was less popular in America, where the more portable circumferentor or surveyor's compass was better adapted. The first basic text specifically adapted for American surveying, John Love's frequently reprinted *Geodaesia, or the Art of Surveying and Measuring of Land Made Easy* (1688), recommended against the theodolite based on Love's surveying experience in Jamaica and North Carolina.

Simple surveying, establishing property lines, was a common profession for landowners and sons of the landowning class, the most famous example being George Washington. Surveying also could be a lucrative profession: In Virginia, surveyors were allowed to charge forty pounds of tobacco per 100 acres surveyed. In addition to these private surveyors working for landowners, individual colonies also appointed surveyors general for government work, and some counties did the same. An early example was Richard Norwood, employed by the Bermuda Company to survey its newly acquired islands in 1610. Thomas Holme, surveyor general of Pennsylvania, planned and laid out the city of Philadelphia.

Important eighteenth-century surveyors general included Cadwallader Colden in New York and Nicholas Scull and William Parsons in Pennsylvania. In Virginia, the position of surveyor general was a perquisite of the College of William and Mary.

Late-Colonial-Era Mapping and Surveying

The growing sophistication of American surveying helped improve cartography. The mid-eighteenth century saw an outburst of maps published by professional surveyors. Peter Jefferson and Joshua Fry's *Map of the Inhabited Parts of Virginia* (1754), commissioned by the colonial government, was a frequently reprinted example and one of the sources of John Mitchell's map. Jefferson was a leading Virginia surveyor (and Thomas Jefferson's father), and Fry was a former professor of mathematics and natural philosophy at William and Mary who had previously worked with Jefferson tracing the border between Virginia and North Carolina in 1747. The Welsh-born Lewis Evans was another significant American surveyor, mapper, and cartographer, who created *General Map of the Middle British Colonies in America* (1755).

Despite the growing sophistication of American cartographers, however, printing maps was a different matter. Because of superior skills and technology, the best maps of America continued to be published in London or elsewhere in Europe throughout the colonial period. In fact, many of the most expert surveyors and cartographers in the decades preceding the American Revolution continued to be immigrants or visiting experts from Europe.

The most famous and technically most sophisticated boundary line drawn in colonial America, the Mason-Dixon Line, which established the boundary of Pennsylvania and Maryland, was named after two Englishmen. The boundary between the original royal grants to the Calverts of Maryland and the Penns of Pennsylvania had never been clear, leading to a dispute that lasted for many decades. American surveyors lacked the technical skill to resolve the issue, and English surveyors had the advantage of impartiality between the contenders. The astronomer Charles Mason and the surveyor Jeremiah Dixon, along with their equipment, came from England to Philadelphia in November 1763.

Before getting to the main business of tracing the Maryland–Pennsylvania boundary, the two Englishmen fixed the southern limit of Philadelphia and traced the boundary between Pennsylvania and Delaware. They began their main task in 1765, accompanied by axemen, clearing a corridor about 10 yards wide and employing a recently invented instrument, the zenith sector, which the Mason-Dixon expedition had introduced into American surveying. They faced bad weather, geographical barriers, including the Susquehanna River and the Blue Ridge Mountains, and suspicion from local Native Americans. The line, over 233 miles long, was concluded on October 9, 1767. Mason and Dixon's effort raised the level of American surveying.

The British acquisition of Florida following the French and Indian War (known as the Seven Years' War in Europe) led to a burst of surveying and cartographical activity, at first more associated with the British government in London than with American cartographers. The German immigrant William Gerard de Brahm, a surveyor and military engineer, had already produced important maps of the Southern colonies, beginning with the frequently reprinted *Map of South Carolina and a Part of Georgia* in 1757. Appointed surveyor general for the new Southern Department, de Brahm and his assistant, the Dutchman Bernard Romans, surveyed the coasts of Florida in the 1760s and early 1770s. Romans established contacts with American scientists and mariners and combined natural history with cartography, publishing the *Concise Natural History of East and West Florida* in 1775.

William E. Burns

See also: Exploration; Land and Real Estate; Property and Property Rights; Vespucci, Amerigo.

Bibliography

Bedini, Silvio. *With Compass and Chain: Early American Surveyors and Their Instruments.* Frederick, MD: Professional Surveyors Publishing Company, 2001.

Cumming, William P. *The Southeast in Early Maps: With an Annotated Check List of Printed and Manuscript Maps of Southeastern North America During the Colonial Period.* Chapel Hill: University of North Carolina Press, 1958.

Gronim, Sara Stidstone. "Geography and Persuasion: Maps in British Colonial New York." *William and Mary Quarterly,* 3rd series, 58 (2001): 373–402.

Hughes, Sarah S. *Surveyors and Statesmen: Land Measuring in Colonial Virginia.* Richmond: Virginia Surveyors Foundation, 1979.

Schmidt, Benjamin. "Mapping an Empire: Cartographic and Colonial Rivalry in Seventeenth-Century Dutch and English North America." *William and Mary Quarterly,* 3rd series, 54 (1997): 549–78.

Wilford, John Noble. *The Mapmakers.* 2nd ed. New York: Vintage Books, 2001.

Marquette, Jacques (1637–1675)

Father Jacques Marquette, also known as Père Marquette, was a French explorer and Jesuit missionary. He spread Christianity among Great Lakes Native American tribes from 1666 to 1675 and accompanied Louis Jolliet as chaplain on the first European expedition to extensively explore the Mississippi River.

Jacques Marquette was born on June 1, 1637, to a prominent family at Laon in the north of France. He entered a Jesuit school at Nancy in 1654. Marquette studied and taught at various Jesuit schools in France, where he earned mediocre marks but gained expertise in many languages. He dreamed of overseas missionary work in the pattern of his role model, the great Jesuit proselytizer Francis Xavier.

Marquette realized his dream in 1666 when he received orders to become a missionary in New France, France's North American colony. Three weeks after arriving in Quebec, Marquette traveled to the Jesuit mission at Three Rivers, where he began a course of study that resulted in his mastery of six native dialects. In 1668, he began working for the Ottawa mission at Sault Sainte Marie, and he succeeded Father Claude Allouez at La Pointe in Chequamegon Bay in 1669. Unpleasant relations with the Sioux forced Marquette and his converts to flee to the St. Ignace mission at Mackinac in 1671.

While imbued with a strong work ethic and a devout sense of mission, Marquette met with limited missionary success among the native peoples. Generally, only the very young, elderly, or ill accepted Christian baptism. Other efforts to convince Native Americans to become less nomadic, plant fields, and save surplus food for famine times also yielded discouraging results.

Despite the small number of converts, Marquette enjoyed as much or more success than other missionaries. The efforts of Jesuit missionaries such as Marquette also made for amicable relations between most Native American tribes and the French. The Jesuit practices of accepting native culture, learning native languages, and living among the native population created a sense of trust between the two cultures. This allowed for a flourishing fur trade and less direct hostility as compared to other European colonization efforts.

In 1673, Marquette further satisfied his yearning to spread Christianity to people who had never encountered it when he agreed to be chaplain on Louis Jolliet's expedition to explore the Mississippi River and discover its mouth. On May 17, 1673, the two men, accompanied by five oarsmen, set off across Lake Michigan from St. Ignace. They traveled to Green Bay and through Wisconsin, arriving at the Mississippi River on June 17, 1673, thus becoming the first Europeans to explore the river at any significant length.

They followed the waterway south until they were a few miles downstream of the mouth of the Arkansas River. Their journey ended there after an encounter with a village of Quapaws. At first hostile toward the Europeans, the Native Americans befriended the party after a native translator was found who communicated with Marquette in the Illinois dialect. Convinced that they were close to the mouth of the Mississippi River, and that the river definitely flowed south into the Gulf of Mexico and not west to the Gulf of California, the explorers turned back to avoid entanglements with the Spanish.

Marquette's duties on the adventure included translating, spreading the word of God, being a symbol of goodwill (it was believed that the "black robes," as they were known, had a peaceful reputation among native peoples), and keeping a detailed journal. Since a canoe accident destroyed Jolliet's journal and forced him to recount his trek from memory, Marquette's

The French Jesuit missionary Jacques Marquette accompanied Louis Jolliet as a chaplain on his exploration of the Mississippi River, the first by white men, in 1673. *(Brown Brothers, Sterling, Pennsylvania)*

journal became the only original account of the expedition; it was published in 1681.

The arduous return journey began on July 17, 1673. Instead of retracing their steps, the group was convinced by a band of Illinois encountered on the return trip to travel the shorter route up the Illinois River to present-day Chicago. Winter's approach eventually halted the group at Green Bay, where Marquette took ill. Realizing that he would not survive the trip back to Montreal, he received permission to return to work with the Illinois, which he did until his health failed again.

Marquette died at the mouth of the Père Marquette River at present-day Ludington, Michigan, on May 18, 1675, as he endeavored to return to St. Ignace. Christianized Native Americans exhumed his remains two years later and interred them at Mackinac.

Thomas F. Jorsch

See also: Exploration; French; French Colonies on Mainland North America (Chronology); Jesuits; Mississippi River. *Document:* Marquette's Travels on the Mississippi (1673).

Bibliography

Severin, Timothy. *Explorers of the Mississippi.* New York: Alfred A. Knopf, 1968.

Thwaites, Reuben G. *Father Marquette.* New York: D. Appleton, 1902.

Marriage and Divorce

Marriage was a common state for most people in the seventeenth and eighteenth centuries, whether European, African American, or Native American. The primary differences between these marriages lay in how the marriage ceremonies were conducted and the specific roles of the two spouses once married.

English, Dutch, and Scottish Traditions

The original thirteen colonies were governed by English law, derived from Anglo-Saxon tradition. Following settlement, each colony then modified English law to create its own marital codes.

Marriage was seen as a choice made by both partners. As part of that choice, the woman agreed to have her legal identity become part of her husband's. This act was called *coverture* and the wife was referred to as a *feme covert*—terms borrowed from the archaic French still used in English law. Her husband became owner of all her property, both land and movable (as objects were called). He also received the right to manage and collect rents on any property she owned.

Any children resulting from the marriage could not inherit land from their mother until their father's death. If the husband consented, however, a marriage contract written before the ceremony could specify property to remain in the woman's possession. Wealthy families often did this as a means of protecting their investment in a dowry.

In eastern Virginia, Maryland, Georgia, and the Carolinas, the process of being married in the Anglican church often took several weeks or months. Following engagement, the marriage was officially announced by calling the banns in church on three successive Sundays. The ceremony was conducted in the church and was followed by a celebration and the consummation of the marriage. All five components were considered necessary for the wedding to be legal. Vows could not be taken during Lent, Advent, or the three weeks prior to the Feast of Saint John.

Marriage among Quakers in the Mid-Atlantic colonies also followed a specific process. Quakers were expected to marry other members of the Quaker faith. They also could not marry first cousins or, sometimes, even second cousins. Finally, the couple had to be approved by the community. As a result of these restrictions, many Quakers chose not to marry. The average marital age was also higher than among other cultural groups.

Once the marriage was approved, the wedding

Marriage for the Puritans of New England—like that between Dr. Francis Le Baron and Mary Wilder of Plymouth—was a civil contract rather than a religious one. The couple established a covenant between themselves and the state. *(Library of Congress, LC-USZ62-12716)*

was officially announced to the community. During the ceremony, the group gathered together in silence. As was common to Quaker religious meetings, the members were given time to speak upon the marriage as they wished. Finally, the couple declared their intention to marry in their own words. After the marriage, they settled in their home and continued their lives as part of the Quaker community.

According to the Pilgrims and Puritans of New England, marriage was a civil contract rather than a religious one. Courtship was usually a lengthy process in order to enable the couple to become fully acquainted. Following courtship, the couple agreed to form the marriage as a covenant between themselves and the state. As in the other cultural groups, the service was followed by a meal. While the civil marriage custom was unique among English colonists, similar practices were conducted in the Protestant low countries, where the Pilgrims had lived prior to coming to North America. Dutch colonists in New York also conducted civil marriages.

Marriages in unsettled areas all over the colonies reflected the customs of their inhabitants. As legal and religious officials were rare, marriage could be as simple as having the man and woman agree publicly to live together. Regardless of who officiated, marriages were usually occasions for much celebrating. Scottish and Scots-Irish colonists often followed the Scottish tradition of "handfasting," by which the couple would agree before two witnesses to live together for a year and a day. If they were content with the agreement at the end of this time, they would seek out official religious or legal status. If not, they were free to separate.

French and Spanish Traditions

The other two countries primarily involved in European colonization of North America were France and Spain. Both took their code of law from Roman tradition, which recognized the husband and wife as separate persons who could continue to own property separately after marriage. Any property acquired during the marriage was owned jointly, and land was passed down to their heirs. Despite these legal protections, French and Spanish households functioned very much as English households did, with the husband or head of the household making the primary decisions.

These laws were employed in the regions settled by the French and Spanish: Florida, Louisiana, California, Acadia, and Quebec. Following the acquisition of

Louisiana in 1803, the United States allowed local property customs to continue.

Another difference between France, Spain, and England was the Catholic tradition of celibacy for monks, nuns, and priests. Several religious groups settled in the French and Spanish colonies, setting up communities similar to their European counterparts. Following their captivity by the French during the colonial wars of the early eighteenth century—including Queen Anne's War, King George's War, and the French and Indian War—some English women chose to live as Catholic nuns in New France rather than to marry.

African American and Native American Marriage

As formal, legal marriages were usually forbidden between African American slaves, weddings between slaves often followed traditions brought from Africa. One such custom consisted of the couple leaping over a broom together in the presence of other slaves. If possible, the ceremony was followed by a celebration of some form.

Native American marriage customs varied from tribe to tribe. These marriages followed a formal process and had to be sanctioned by other members of the tribe. As in most cultural groups of the period, marriage was as much about the community as it was about the couple.

Divorce

While divorce was not impossible under English law, it was almost unheard of in the Southern colonies. Physical separation was possible for wealthy women who could appeal to the courts for separate maintenance by their husbands in cases of abuse or neglect. In 1681, William Fitzhugh sought a legal separation for his abused sister-in-law, Rose Blackston. The separation was denied, and she eventually eloped with another man in 1697. Poor women were dependent on their family or friends for help, although sheltering a runaway wife was grounds for punishment.

Divorce was also almost nonexistent among the Quakers and the various European Protestant sects living in the Mid-Atlantic colonies. Settlers in the backcountry colonies, where formal marriages were less common, were more likely to desert a bad marriage, provided that it was financially possible.

In contrast, divorce under certain conditions was allowable in the colonies of Connecticut, Massachusetts, and Rhode Island. A married person seeking divorce had to be able to clearly prove willful desertion, adultery, bigamy, or impotence to a court of law.

Bigamy and desertion were relatively easy to prove, and most successful divorce cases involved either situation. Desertion was defined as three years of neglect of duty or seven years' absence. In 1680, Elizabeth Wade Stevens successfully demonstrated that her husband, Thomas Stevens, already had wives in Boston, England, and Barbados. She was given a divorce and granted the right to marry again. A common penalty for divorce was to require that neither party marry again.

Demonstrating adultery or impotence as grounds for divorce required personal testimony and so was much harder to prove. Martha and John Hewitt of Plymouth Colony were married in 1667. Shortly afterwards, it became evident that Martha Hewitt was four or five months pregnant. Faced with fornication charges, John Hewitt refused to acknowledge paternity. Circumstantial evidence suggested that Martha Hewitt's father, Christopher Winter, was the father of the child. In March of 1668, Martha Hewitt and Winter were brought to court in Plymouth County on an incest charge. Citing lack of concrete evidence, the case against Winter was dropped, and his daughter was whipped for fornication before marriage. In June of 1669, John Hewitt attempted to divorce his wife Martha on grounds of adultery. As the charge against her father had never been conclusively proven, the divorce suit was turned down.

Following a rejected divorce suit, Massachusetts colonists had the same options as their counterparts in the other colonies. Wealthier colonists could set up separate households in one form or another. Desertion was another possibility, leaving the other spouse to appeal again for divorce after the required seven years waiting period. Most, like John and Martha Hewitt, were left to make the best of a bad situation. In nearly all cases of separation or divorce between European colonists, the husband maintained ownership of land and house and was given custody of the children.

As formal marriages were rare between African Americans, divorce usually consisted of the couple simply agreeing to separate. A couple also might be parted because one member had been sold to a different plantation. Most Native American tribes allowed for divorce as a means of maintaining stability within the tribe. The couple quietly agreed to separate, and their lives continued without penalty. As the United States became a country, both African Americans and Native Americans became more subject to marital codes and practices based on European laws and traditions.

Abigail B. Chandler

See also: Child Rearing; Children; Family; Inheritance; Sex; Widows and Widowers.

Bibliography

Calloway, Colin G. *First Peoples*. Boston: Bedford/St. Martin's, 1999.

Cott, Nancy. *Public Vows: A History of Marriage and the Nation*. Cambridge, MA: Harvard University Press, 2000.

Fischer, David Hackett. *Albion's Seed*. New York: Oxford University Press, 1989.

Mary I (1516–1558)

Mary Tudor, born February 18, 1516, in London, was the only surviving child of Henry VIII of England and his first wife, Catherine of Aragon. As the heir to the English throne, Mary received a careful education supervised by the Spanish humanist Vives, during the course of which she developed a deep Roman Catholic piety and began to take great pride in her descent from Ferdinand and Isabella of Spain.

Until the beginning of Henry VIII's divorce proceedings in 1529, Mary was treated as princess of Wales, with a court at Ludlow. As a desirable royal bride, she was courted by Francis I of France and Charles V of the Holy Roman Empire. After Henry's marriage to Anne Boleyn, however, Mary was declared a bastard and became a servant in her stepsister Elizabeth's household. Throughout her exile, Mary continued to be a practicing Roman Catholic. She also was protected by Charles V's ambassador and supported by many English people, who had loved Catherine of Aragon and respected Mary as the king's legal daughter.

Jane Seymour, Henry VIII's third wife, reconciled Mary and her father. She also persuaded Mary to acknowledge the Act of Succession recognizing Henry VIII as head of the church. In 1544, shortly before his death, Henry VIII restored both of his daughters, Mary and Elizabeth, to the succession, after their brother Edward. Mary had close and affectionate ties to her younger brother, and her position throughout his reign remained privileged, despite attempts by the Seymours and John Dudley, duke of Northumberland, to hide her Catholicism and curtail her popular charitable donations. When Edward VI died in 1553, Northumberland and leading Protestants attempted a coup on behalf

Queen Mary I is known as "Bloody Mary" for her execution of Protestants in the mid-sixteenth century, yet her efforts to restore Catholicism to England ultimately proved unsuccessful. Nor did she advance the nation's colonial interests or sea trade for fear of intruding on Spanish claims. *(Brown Brothers, Sterling, Pennsylvania)*

of Lady Jane Grey, who ruled for nine days before Mary rallied support in England's central counties and marched on London to overthrow Jane in July 1553.

As queen, Mary I enjoyed early support from even Protestant subjects, who acknowledged her as Henry's daughter and looked forward to her reign, especially after she retained most of the council, making the government inclusive and widely representative. The new queen also moved slowly to restore Catholicism, retaining the Act of Supremacy placing herself at the head of the church in England, and making no move to reverse the dissolution of the monasteries and sale of church property. However, Mary I inherited a huge debt of 700,000 pounds from Edward VI's reign and confronted poor harvests across England.

In 1554, Mary I married her cousin Philip II of Spain, son of Emperor Charles V. In response, Sir Thomas Wyatt and several thousand Protestants rebelled in favor of her younger sister, Elizabeth. The rebels were crushed when Mary I led troops out of London against them. The queen ordered the execution

of Wyatt, as well as Jane Grey, her husband, Guildford Dudley, and the duke of Suffolk for their part in the rebellion.

The return of Cardinal Reginald Pole to England with absolution from the pope saw the return of medieval heresy laws and their swift implementation. Mary I burned as heretics more than 300 English subjects, including Archbishop Thomas Cranmer, while hundreds of Protestant families fled to Calvinist Geneva. The burnings were quickly memorialized in John Foxe's *Book of Martyrs,* which became a classic colonial text, propagandizing anti-Catholicism and the villainy of Queen Mary I and the Spanish.

Much to the disappointment of the English merchant community, Mary I did not advance English sea trade and colonial interest for fear of infringing on Spanish claims, nor did she push England to fight for more of the wealth of the Americas. Instead, the Spanish involved Mary I in declaring war on France in January 1557. English campaigns in France were a fiasco, losing England's last continental possessions, Ham, Guines, and the port at Calais.

Mary I suffered two false pregnancies, the second probably an ovarian tumor. At the time of her death on November 17, 1558, having failed to join England to Spain, produce an heir, or restore Catholicism to the nation, she was succeeded by her half sister, Elizabeth I.

Margaret Sankey

See also: Catholic Church; Politics and Government (Chronology); Politics and Government (Essay).

Bibliography

Erickson, Carolly. *Bloody Mary.* Garden City, NY: Doubleday, 1978.

Loades, David. *Mary Tudor: A Life.* Oxford, UK: Blackwell, 1988.

Ridley, Jasper. *Bloody Mary's Martyrs.* New York: Carroll and Graf, 2002.

Mary II

See **William III of Orange and Mary II**

Maryland

Maryland's founding represented an early example of a shift in English colonial policy. While joint-stock companies had established colonies such as Virginia and Massachusetts Bay, England's King Charles I granted Cecilius Calvert, Lord Baltimore, a proprietary charter for the colony of Maryland. The Calvert family remained proprietors of the colony until the American Revolution, except for a period from 1691 until 1715, when the British Crown administered Maryland as a royal colony.

Throughout its existence, the colony witnessed a power struggle between the elected colonial legislature and proprietary officials. Although there was some ebb and flow in this contest, in general, the proprietor maintained a strong hold on the colony until the 1770s.

Origins of European Settlement

In 1632, King Charles I awarded land on both sides of Chesapeake Bay to the Calvert family. At the time of the grant, a diverse Native American population resided in the area. The Doeg, Mattawoman, Choptico, Patuxent, and Piscataway comprised a confederation on the western shore of the bay; the Nanticoke, Choptank, Pocomoke, and Wicomico resided on the eastern side; and the powerful Susquehanna lived at the north end of the bay. All told, at least 8,000 Native Americans lived in the region in the 1630s.

In the second half of the seventeenth century, these various populations declined sharply as many died from European diseases such as smallpox. As the number of Native Americans shrank, Europeans drove them from the land to establish farms for the cultivation of tobacco. By 1700, the European immigrant population controlled the bay area.

In 1634, Leonard Calvert, Lord Baltimore's brother, sailed into the Chesapeake as the first governor of Maryland. On board also were twenty gentlemen, most of whom, like the Calverts, were Roman Catholic, and approximately 130 artisans and laborers, most of whom were Protestant. They established the colony's first capital, St. Mary's, along the western shore. Lord Baltimore envisioned Maryland as a refuge for England's persecuted Catholics, but also as a profitable venture.

Catholic emigration to the colony remained slight, and the Protestant population soon dominated Maryland. To protect the Catholic minority, Baltimore drafted the Act Concerning Religion in 1649, which ensured religious freedom. Although limited to Christians, it was an early expression of religious toleration in European North America.

Agriculture

Taking their cue from Virginia, early Marylanders began growing tobacco for sale in Europe. Lord Baltimore initially encouraged the creation of large medieval manors, but the availability of land in Maryland created staffing problems for these large estates, as tenants left to establish their own farms.

In 1640, Lord Baltimore adopted the headright system to spur population growth: the proprietor granted 100 acres of land for each man, another 100 acres if he brought his wife, and fifty acres for each child brought to the colony. Colonists could gain additional acres if they brought indentured servants. In return for passage to America, these servants worked for the planters for some number of years, often four, at the end of which the planters provided them with freedom dues—that is, land, tools, and seed, and/or money to purchase these. Many servants did not live until the end of the indenture due to diseases such as malaria and dysentery. As planters relied on indentured servant labor, slavery was rare in Maryland in the seventeenth century.

Government

In 1635, Maryland settlers called for a representative assembly. The Calverts reluctantly agreed and formed the House of Delegates. Beginning in 1639, all free men became eligible to elect members to this body, which became the lower house of the legislature. The governor collected a group of advisors, which evolved into the colonial council or upper legislative house. Initially, wealthy Catholics and Protestants sat on the council, while less wealthy Protestants dominated the assembly.

Despite the toleration act, early Maryland experienced considerable religious tension. In 1688, while England was in revolution, the smaller planters seized the colony in the name of King William and Queen Mary. Maryland became a royal colony in 1691, and the Anglican Church became its official church in 1702. Catholics lost the right to vote and worship in public.

In 1715, the fourth Lord Baltimore joined the Anglican Church and regained the proprietorship of Maryland. During royal rule, the assembly had increased its power at the expense of the governor. Gradually, the proprietor and his governor reasserted their control over the colony, culminating in the fifth Lord Baltimore's trip to Maryland in 1732. During this visit, the proprietor stripped the assembly of much of the legislative power it had assumed during the previous fifty years. Although this initially produced some grumbling, a rebound in the price of tobacco between 1740 and 1770 sparked the Maryland economy and quieted discontent.

Population

Maryland's population remained small and egalitarian through much of the seventeenth century. The colony contained few women, hindering natural population growth. By 1675, Maryland contained roughly 13,000 colonists.

The first Africans arrived in Maryland in 1642. Their legal status seems to have been similar to that of indentured servants. Slavery only began to develop as an institution in late seventeenth-century Maryland, and adoption of slave labor was slow. In 1697, slaves comprised just 10 percent of the colony's 30,000 non-Native American inhabitants.

In the eighteenth century, a permanent economic and social elite formed in the colony. Many of these gained their riches from tobacco production and added to that wealth by purchasing slaves. By 1710 Maryland contained 8,000 slaves, and, by 1762, slaves constituted 30 percent of the total population. Most slave owners had fewer than five slaves, though a few large plantations had more than 100. Maryland's free black population remained quite small and could not vote, hold office, or testify in court.

After 1700, Maryland saw considerable growth. Annapolis had become the capital in 1694, Scots-Irish and German immigrants established inland settlements, and bay area towns such as Chestertown, Joppa, and Baltimore prospered.

While Maryland's total population and the number possessing moderate wealth grew, wealthy elites dominated colonial offices until the American Revolution. The colonists loosely adhered to the social deference common in Europe; however, Maryland elites increasingly distinguished themselves from their social counterparts in England. The influx of women augmented the natural birthrate, and the adoption of slavery created a fixed social elite.

Wars

Beginning in 1754, the French and Indian War (known as the Seven Years' War in Europe) resurrected religious tension in the colony as some suspected Maryland Catholics of aiding Catholic France against them. The war also afforded the assembly an opportunity to assume greater control of the colonial budget, arguing that additional funds would strengthen the colony against French attack. In fact, Maryland provided little assistance to the British war effort.

Like other British colonies, Maryland experienced the distinct change in British imperial policy following the end of the French and Indian War in 1763. Most Marylanders were hardly bothered by the Sugar Act and Currency Act of 1764, but they loudly protested the Stamp Act of 1765. Assemblymen led demonstrations at which colonists burned in effigy the royal stamp distributor. Local chapters of the Sons of Liberty formed to coordinate protests. Daniel Dulany, Jr., published an inflammatory pamphlet asserting that Parliament had erred when it issued the Stamp Act.

Opposition to parliamentary rule in Maryland was less than in other colonies. Protestors belatedly drafted a nonimportation agreement in 1769 and, a year later, formed the Baltimore Association to enforce adherence to this agreement. The relative quiet of the early 1770s ended in 1774 when colonists learned that Parliament had closed Boston Harbor. A new nonimportation association formed, and, in October of that year, Marylanders burned the ship *Peggy Stewart* and its cargo of tea.

Anti-British radicals created an illegal convention to administer the colony, created Committees of Correspondence, and named delegates to the Continental Congress. For the next two years, Maryland experienced dual government as the convention legislated for the colony, and the governor, Robert Eden, continued to direct colonial officers. In 1775, the convention created a militia to defend the colony against the British military. Governor Eden left Maryland in June 1776 as fighting increased throughout the colonies.

After the Revolution

Following the Declaration of Independence, Maryland held a constitutional convention to create a state government. Men owning fifty acres of land or property worth 40 pounds were given the opportunity to select delegates to this convention. The constitution they produced resembled in structure the colonial government minus the proprietor. It also reflected the conservative nature of the delegates.

All white men possessing property worth at least 20 pounds could vote, but only those worth 500 pounds could hold office in the lower house of the new state legislature. Seats in the upper house, in the executive council, as delegates to the Continental Congress, and as local sheriffs were open only to those worth 1,000 pounds, and the governor's chair was available only to those worth 5,000 pounds. Finally, the convention did not ask Maryland voters to ratify the constitution but issued the document as already in force.

The less affluent agreed to these restrictions because the first state assembly designated as legal tender for all debts the paper money that had already lost a portion of its original value. This eased payment of debts for the poor, and they acquiesced to the state constitution.

James E. Klein

See also: Baltimore; Calvert, Cecilius; Calvert, George (First Lord Baltimore); Catholic Church; Chesapeake; Maryland (Chronology).

Bibliography

Burnard, Trevor. *Creole Gentlemen: The Maryland Elite, 1691–1776.* New York: Routledge, 2002.

Land, Aubrey C. *Colonial Maryland: A History.* Millwood, NY: KTO, 1981.

Linck, Joseph C. *Fully Instructional and Vehemently Influenced: Catholic Preaching in Anglo-Colonial America.* Philadelphia: Saint Joseph's University Press, 2002.

Morgan, Philip D. *Slave Counterpoints: Black Culture in the Eighteenth-Century Chesapeake & Lowcountry.* Chapel Hill: University of North Carolina Press, 1998.

Massachusetts

From its inception, Massachusetts was a uniquely religious settlement. The impetus behind the founding of the Massachusetts Bay Company in 1629 was the belief that the Anglican Church of England was corrupt and should be purified. John White, a leading Puritan, secured the royal charter for the company, gaining rights to lands in New England that had earlier been held by the Dorchester Company.

Establishing the Bay Colony

There were 110 original investors in the Massachusetts Bay Company, and John Winthrop, a prominent Puritan, joined their ranks a year later. Some members of the company, under the guidance of Winthrop, moved to gain control of the settlement; they voted to transfer the land patent and government to those who actually settled the colony rather than to all investors. Under these new rules, Winthrop was elected governor.

In the spring of 1630, the Puritans departed for their colony with a fleet of eleven ships, including the *Arabella,* which transported Winthrop to the colony. Over 1,000 passengers and significant amounts of supplies and livestock made the journey. The colonists arrived in New England in June and July and began to build Winthrop's "city upon a hill," a community that would exemplify Christian values.

The colony experienced rapid growth, attracting mostly Puritan settlers, who numbered between 1,000 and 2,000 each year. This rapid expansion encroached on Native American lands, and, in 1637, the Bay Colony's inhabitants found themselves engaged in war with the Pequot. The war resulted in the near extinction of the tribe.

A similar pattern of expansion into Native American lands precipitated the 1675–1676 King Philip's War. The Wampanoag in Plymouth Colony joined with the Narragansett, Pocumtuck, and Nipmuc in Massachusetts, raiding colonial settlements. Because the conflict affected its frontier, Massachusetts joined with Plymouth Colony in its effort to end raids by the natives. In the course of the war, three Massachusetts towns were burned. The white colonists successfully subdued the tribes after chasing them throughout New England, finally capturing and killing the Wampanoag leader Philip in 1676.

Society

The colonists who populated Massachusetts were mostly from the middle and lower ranks of English society, a group composed of yeoman and tenant farmers, as well as skilled artisans. Servants immigrated to Massachusetts, as did a fair number of the gentry. Much of the colony was composed of white settlers; however, Native Americans and African Americans were also members of Massachusetts society.

The first blacks arrived in Massachusetts as early as 1633; by 1680, there were between 100 and 200 black residents in the colony. In 1715, it was home to 2,000 blacks in an overall population of 96,000. Slavery in Massachusetts was low as compared to other colonies, largely due to the lack of a labor-intensive crop that required numerous workers. Massachusetts residents were well aware of the presence of blacks in their community, however, and established extensive laws to govern black residents' behavior.

By the 1770s, when this map was drawn, nearly a century had passed since the termination of the Puritan commonwealth. Religious influences in the Massachusetts Bay Colony had waned in favor of a commercial spirit and thriving trade economy, and the population exceeded 250,000. *(Library of Congress, g3760 ar088100)*

The colonists placed a great emphasis on the importance of education in the community. In 1636, they established Harvard to provide the necessary education for ministers. Education of children was also of primary importance. In 1647, the General Court adopted legislation that required all towns with 50 or more families to provide for the education of the town's children by supporting a public school. Larger towns, those with 100 families or more, were required to establish more extensive grammar schools that included training in Latin.

This emphasis on education resulted in high literacy rates throughout Massachusetts. A result of this widespread literacy was the establishment of a printing press in Cambridge, begun in 1638. In 1640, the press produced *The Bay Psalm Book*.

Religion

The Puritans worked diligently to build a Christian colony, and there was little room for dissent within the community. In 1635, the Puritans faced a conflict with Roger Williams, the minister at Salem. Williams called for absolute separation of church and state, and he also believed that the Puritans should separate from the Anglican Church. Williams was brought before the General Court and subsequently banished from the colony. Other dissenters faced similar punishments.

In 1636, Anne Hutchinson began holding prayer meetings in her home and claimed that she heard directly from God. John Wheelwright, a Boston minister who supported Hutchinson, publicly challenged the religious and political leadership of the colony.

Wheelwright and Hutchinson were both banished in 1637.

Despite the emphasis on religion during its formative years, devotion to the church waned as the colony developed. The second and third generations of Puritan settlers joined the church in far fewer numbers than had their ancestors.

In 1662, several ministers met to discuss the declining church membership. In an effort to bolster shrinking congregations, they voted to extend the Halfway Covenant to churches. This compromise allowed the children of church members to become members in their own right, without presenting evidence of their conversion to the congregation for approval. It was left up to the local churches to decide whether or not they would accept this policy. In this, as in their ability to elect their own clergy and manage their own affairs, church members exercised autonomy.

The accusations of witchcraft at Salem in 1692 are perhaps the best-known religious episode in the colony's history. Samuel Parris, the local minister, was at the center of the fray. His daughter and her friends claimed that they had been attacked by witches and began naming their tormenters. In the ensuing furor, hundreds of people in Salem and nearby towns were accused of being witches.

The hysteria prompted Governor Phips to appoint a special court to try the accused. Twenty villagers were executed, having been convicted of practicing witchcraft. Accusations of witchcraft continued until the General Court disbanded the special court later that year, but the episode left its mark on the colony.

In the wake of the Salem witch trials, and with increasing numbers of non-Puritans and non–church members in the colony, secularism increased through the late seventeenth century. This decline in the importance of religious faith was challenged by a revival movement that began in 1734. Known as the Great Awakening, this increased religious fervor spread from Massachusetts throughout much of colonial North America. Sparked by the preaching of Jonathan Edwards, the revival was fueled by the young English preacher George Whitefield.

The revival meetings that characterized the Great Awakening were marked by boisterous, emotional sermons that elicited equally passionate responses from the congregation. This ardor in worship and repentance contrasted with the traditionally dignified order of services in the Puritan churches. Reactions to the revivals resulted in a split of many congregations. Those who accepted the new religious fervor came to be known as "New Lights," while the traditionalists were referred to as "Old Lights." This breach of church congregations resulted in plural churches in many Massachusetts towns.

Government

The colony's charter provided a framework for the government that included an executive in the form of a governor, a deputy to the governor, a board of advisers known as magistrates, and the members of the company, the freemen. These constituted the colony's General Court. Although initially a select few, in 1632, freemen were defined as all male heads of household who were also church members. In 1634, they began electing town delegates to represent the communities in establishing colonial laws.

The General Court not only set wages and prices on goods but also passed laws requiring church attendance and sumptuary laws intended to maintain the social hierarchy. In 1690, the General Court approved the introduction of paper money; in 1751, it authorized the return to hard money.

In 1685, James II undertook a reorganization of the New England colonies begun by his brother, Charles II. This plan gathered all of the New England colonies under the Dominion of New England and the rule of a royal governor, Edmund Andros. Andros established a central government in Boston and proceeded to exert absolute authority. New taxes were imposed. Town meetings, excepting the annual election of officers, were forbidden. And churches were prohibited from collecting tithes to pay ministers' salaries.

In April 1689, following the news that James II would soon be replaced by William and Mary, Massachusetts citizens formed the Council for the Safety of the People. This ad hoc group overthrew the Dominion leadership and reinstated colonial rule.

Massachusetts continued to operate under the established colonial system until 1691, when King William issued a new charter, consolidating the Bay Colony and Plymouth Colony under the rule of a royal governor. The new charter restored the Massachusetts General Court as a legislative and judicial body. It also provided for deputies in the legislature's lower house to nominate members of the upper house, known as the Governor's Council. In addition, the Puritan church and Harvard were allowed to remain; the charter, however, instituted an official policy of religious toleration. King William appointed William Phips as the first royal governor. Phips, a Massachusetts resident and

Puritan, was a follower of Increase Mather, who led the Boston church.

In the early part of the eighteenth century, Massachusetts maintained a steady rate of growth, a stable economy, and domestic peace. When called upon to support the English efforts against the French in King George's War, however, the colonists responded with little hesitation. In 1745, Massachusetts deployed 4,000 men and successfully captured the French settlement at Louisbourg, a major victory that allowed the British to control access to Canada.

Massachusetts again supported an imperial war in 1754 with the French and Indian War (the counterpart to the Seven Years' War in Europe). The treaty that ended the war in 1763 prohibited westward expansion for the colony. In addition, the superior attitude of the regular British troops offended the volunteer militia companies who fought alongside them. These issues would find expression in Revolutionary Massachusetts in the 1770s.

Economy

The Massachusetts economy developed around agriculture and maritime trade. In addition, shipbuilding and its associated trades served as a mainstay of its economy.

Much of the land was split into family farms that produced crops such as corn and wheat. Agricultural surpluses were shipped primarily to the West Indian colonies of Barbados and St. Kitts. In exchange, Massachusetts imported sugar, tobacco, salt, indigo, cloth, and household goods. Large amounts of the sugar imported to the colony were converted into rum; by 1750, Massachusetts boasted more than sixty distilleries and exported over 2 million gallons of rum.

As families grew and towns expanded, it became harder to obtain land. By the eighteenth century, there was little room for Massachusetts to grow, given its French and Native American neighbors. This lack of opportunity for growth frustrated later generations and further fed the rebellion against England.

Revolutionary Massachusetts

Revolutionary activity in Massachusetts centered on the question of taxation and representation. The first spark of rebellion began with the Stamp Act of 1765. Boston's response was the Braintree Instructions, a listing of the ways in which the act violated the rights of Englishmen. Drafted by John Adams, the Braintree Instructions declared that the taxes imposed would drain cash from the colony and that it violated the principles of the Magna Carta by taxing freemen without their consent. Adams also objected to the enforcement of the tax by a single judge of the Vice-Admiralty Court. This response to the Stamp Act was adopted throughout Massachusetts.

Boston residents also reacted with actions that included vandalizing the home of the royal governor, Thomas Hutchinson. Hutchinson was a native of Massachusetts, but his friendships with English officials, his connections to the Anglican Church, and his wealth all separated him from the colonial activists. He soon became a symbol of all that was wrong with English control of the colony.

Further violence included the 1770 Boston Massacre, in which British troops fired into a mob and killed an 11-year-old boy and several others. This was followed by the Boston Tea Party, Massachusetts's response to the Crown's decision to grant a monopoly on tea imports to the colonies to the nearly bankrupt East India Company. While this decision actually lowered the price that colonists would pay for tea, it was interpreted as another attempt at illegal taxation and a threat to American tea merchants. When ships carrying 45 tons of tea docked at Boston Harbor, a group of radicals known as the Sons of Liberty disguised themselves as Native Americans, marched aboard the ships, and dumped the tea, valued at more than 10,000 pounds, into the harbor.

The destruction of property brought Massachusetts to the forefront of England's response to colonial rebellion. The Crown ordered the Boston ports closed until the tea had been paid for. Other acts, known in Massachusetts as the Coercive Acts, included a nullification of the 1691 Massachusetts charter and a requirement that the colonists quarter British soldiers. The Coercive Acts significantly expanded the power of the royal governor and his appointees, and limited towns to one meeting annually—if it was approved by the governor.

In the summer of 1774, Massachusetts's committees of correspondence framed the colony's reaction to the Coercive Acts. The response urged the governor's appointees to resign their positions, requested citizens to gather in order to prevent courts from sitting, and recommended that town militias be activated and military supplies stockpiled. The first shots of the American Revolution were fired in Massachusetts at Lexington and Concord on April 19, 1775.

At the same time as the colonies declared their independence, Massachusetts residents also sought reforms in their own government. After years of attempts to revise the state constitution, in the spring of 1779, a constitutional convention was held, and Massachusetts voters approved a new government framework in 1780.

The basic form of government, drafted in large part by John Adams, included an upper legislative body known as the Senate, whose members were chosen annually and apportioned according to the local tax districts. Initially, senators were required to own land valued at 300 pounds or more or a combination of personal and real property worth 600 pounds.

Each incorporated town was allotted one delegate in the lower house of the legislature. In order to be eligible for this office, delegates were again required to be property owners, although the requirement was substantially lower than that for the Senate. In addition, the state agreed to pay for one round-trip journey to the legislative session in order to ensure widespread participation. All elected officials served terms of 1 year.

The governor was required to be a Massachusetts freeholder with property valued at 1,000 pounds. As defined, the position of governor was a weak one. The governor's powers were limited to the ability to call and dismiss the legislature, command the state militia, and veto legislation. Massachusetts elected its first governor, John Hancock, under the terms of the new state government, in 1780.

Tonia M. Compton

See also: Boston; Connecticut River; Massachusetts (Chronology); Massachusetts Bay Charter; Massachusetts Bay Colony; Pilgrims; Plymouth; Puritanism; Revolutionary War. *Document:* Slave Petition to the Governor, Council, and House of Representatives of the Province of Massachusetts (1774).

Bibliography

Andrews, Charles McLean. *The Colonial Period of American History.* Vol. 1, *The Settlements.* New Haven, CT: Yale University Press, 1934.

Brown, Richard. *Massachusetts: A Bicentennial History.* New York: W. W. Norton, 1978.

Faragher, John Mack, et al. *Out of Many: A History of the American People.* 3rd edition. Upper Saddle River, NJ: Prentice Hall, 2000.

Main, Gloria. "The Standard of Living in Colonial Massachusetts." *The Journal of Economic History,* 43:1 (1983): 101–108.

Twombly, Robert C. "Black Puritan: The Negro in Seventeenth-Century Massachusetts." *William and Mary Quarterly,* 3rd series, 24:2 (1967): 224–42.

Massachusetts Bay

For most of its human history, the area that became known as the Massachusetts Bay was Native American territory. The native peoples who came to the bay area, following game as glaciers receded, built sophisticated cultures based on its physical characteristics and animal life. English settlement on the bay dates from the early years of the seventeenth century. By the late eighteenth century, Massachusetts Bay was the location of one of colonial America's largest cities.

Although they were mainly Algonquin, the native peoples of southeastern New England spoke a number of distinct languages, many of which were mutually unintelligible. The Massachusett, Wampanoag, and Nauset established semipermanent villages and relied on the rich marine life of the bay for food and other resources. In precolonial times, the bay was home to large numbers of cod, herring, haddock, giant tuna, and swordfish. Closer to shore, clams, scallops, and some oysters could be obtained as well. Generally speaking, deep-sea fishing was a male task, while women, also in charge of agriculture, gathered shellfish.

Just prior to English colonization, particularly between 1616 and 1619, European disease decimated native populations. The Massachusetts were hit particularly hard; about nine in ten Massachusetts may have died in the epidemics. At the time he encountered the Pilgrims, Wampanoag sachem Massasoit presided over a shattered world.

Forays by Giovanni da Verrazano and Esteban Gómez—the latter a Portuguese mariner in the employ of Spain—along the Massachusetts coast in the 1520s piqued European interest in the region but did not alter native lifeways significantly. The same cannot be said for intensive English efforts at colonization, which began about a century after the earliest European explorations. Beginning with the small band of separatist Pilgrims led by William Bradford that established Plymouth in 1620, English interest in, and immigration to, the land surrounding Massachusetts Bay continued to grow. The Massachusetts Bay Company, a joint-stock trading venture, eventually came to be dominated by Puritans, whose troubles in England seemed more serious every day. The leadership of the company obtained a liberal charter from Charles I, which gave them a great deal of local decision-making power, and they made it even more liberal by removing it to New England.

On the shores of Massachusetts Bay, under the guidance of John Winthrop, the Puritans set about the business of establishing a holy example for the Anglican Church: a "city upon a hill." While the dream of establishing a godly society eluded Puritan leaders, the towns they founded, such as Rockport, Salem, and Boston, grew rapidly. In a period known as the Great Migration, roughly 10,000 Puritans came to the Massachusetts Bay Colony between 1630 and 1640, along with about 10,000 other settlers. Many thousands more followed them as the seventeenth century progressed. Englishmen fished the waters of the bay, and a fledgling shipbuilding industry took hold. In the marshes that grew alongside the bay, cattle grazed, further sustaining the remarkable population explosion.

While seaside towns founded by the English prospered, native communities in the Massachusetts Bay area suffered correspondingly. Native peoples struggled at first to survive as autonomous political entities, but after King Philip's War (1675–1676), as sovereignty vanished, cultural survival and ethnic identity became more important than political independence.

Boston became one of the most important English seaports in the Americas. It counted 3,000 inhabitants by the 1660s; the population approached 20,000 on the eve of the War for Independence. While English capital had financed the earliest shipbuilding and mercantile ventures, Americans operating out of Boston and Salem took over these activities as settlements expanded.

In the 1760s and 1770s, Boston became a hotbed of American Revolutionary activity. Reinvigorated by the global successes of the Seven Years' War (1756–1763), the English Parliament attempted to tighten the reins of its expanded empire, with disastrous effects. The Stamp Act riots of 1765 and the furor over the Townshend Duties brought Bostonians of many different social groups together in protest against what they perceived as new and unfair forms of taxation.

The Sons of Liberty first organized in Boston in the 1760s. Massachusetts Bay itself became a symbol of protest when Revolutionaries, dressed as Mohawks, dumped three ships' cargoes of East India Company tea into Boston Harbor. Following independence, American fishing and shipping operations continued to expand in the region, prompting commercial and industrial growth well into the nineteenth century.

Matthew Jennings

See also: Boston; Cape Cod; Fish and Fisheries; Massachusetts Bay Colony; Transportation, Water.

Bibliography

Labaree, Benjamin Woods. *Colonial Massachusetts: A History.* New York: KTO, 1979.
Salisbury, Neal. *Manitou and Providence: Indians, Europeans, and the Making of New England, 1500–1643.* New York: Oxford University Press, 1981.

Massachusetts Bay Charter

The Massachusetts Bay Colony emerged from the pretext of a joint-stock trading enterprise called the Massachusetts Bay Company. It gained its legality in 1629 when King Charles I issued the Massachusetts Bay Charter at the behest of a group of Puritan merchants.

The founders of the company selected John Winthrop, a prosperous Puritan lawyer, to lead the endeavor, sending more than 1,000 men, women, and children across the Atlantic in 1630. Since the charter required the Massachusetts Bay Company to maintain a home office in England, Winthrop and the other company leaders decided to take the charter with them to New England, in order to transfer the entire government of the colony to Massachusetts Bay, where they hoped it would ensure local, but more importantly Puritan, control.

Upon arrival in Massachusetts Bay, the founders effectively translated the company charter into a plan for government, a process that took nearly 14 years to complete. By transferring the Massachusetts Bay Company charter to America, an English trading company evolved into a provincial government and initiated a unique project of colonization.

Power within the company rested with the General Court, which was responsible for the election of a governor and his eighteen assistants. The General Court consisted of the shareholders, commonly referred to as freemen, because they had the freedom of the company. Of those who went to America, only a few besides Winthrop and his assistants initially had such status and freedom. While this suited these select few, more than 100 settlers petitioned for freeman status shortly after the colony was established. Rather than risk trouble, the inner group invited applications and finally admitted 118 in 1631. Afterward, provisions were made such that only church members, a limited category, could become freemen.

Originally, the General Court consisted of one

house, composed of company members who had the power to pass laws and levy taxes. It acted as the supreme legislative and judicial authority in the colony. In 1634, the colony had grown large enough to make reliance on membership cumbersome, and the composition of the General Court became limited to just two or three representatives from each township. In 1644, the government established by the charter was further altered when the General Court was expanded into a two-house legislature, which set the deputies and assistants to the governor in a separate house from the elected town representatives. With establishment of a bicameral legislature, all legislative decisions required a majority in both houses for passage.

Thus, over an extended period, the Massachusetts Bay Company underwent a metamorphosis that took it from trading corporation to the governing body of a commonwealth. Church membership replaced stock ownership as the criteria for becoming a freeman, later called a voter. The General Court, like Parliament in England, became a representative body composed of two houses: The House of Assistants roughly corresponded to the House of Lords, and the House of Deputies was comparable to the House of Commons. Although the charter remained unchanged, the performance under the charter was entirely different from original expectations.

Solomon K. Smith

See also: Boston; Massachusetts Bay Colony; Politics and Government (Essay); Politics and Government (Chronology); Puritanism; Winthrop, John.

Bibliography

Collier, Christopher. *Pilgrims and Puritans, 1620–1676.* New York: Benchmark, 1998.

Peters, Ronald M. *The Massachusetts Constitution of 1780: A Social Compact.* Amherst: University of Massachusetts Press, 1978.

Taylor, Robert J. *Massachusetts: Colony to Commonwealth.* Chapel Hill: University of North Carolina Press, 1961.

Massachusetts Bay Colony

The Massachusetts Bay Colony was founded by a group of Puritans in 1630. Puritans had come under increasing religious prejudice in England. Eventually, prominent members of the group dominated the Massachusetts Bay Company, a joint-stock, colonizing venture. In 1629, the company received a liberal charter from King Charles I, just before he dissolved Parliament. In 1630, the company moved its charter, its headquarters, and hundreds of people to the shores of Massachusetts Bay.

John Winthrop was elected governor of the company and colony; he would serve in that capacity for many of the colony's formative years, until his death in 1647. Discontented colonists from the Massachusetts Bay Colony later broke off to form several other New England colonies during the seventeenth century. Thus, the influence of the original colony was widely felt in the northern region of English North America.

Massachusetts Bay under Puritan rule was a strict, moral colony, and many of the colony's leaders believed that God had formed a special covenant with the Puritan community. This sentiment was reinforced by John Winthrop's "Modell of Christian Charity" speech delivered aboard the *Arabella.*

In the new colony, full church membership was restricted, and, initially, only full church members could vote and hold office. It would be a mistake to label this form of government a theocracy, however. While ministers were powerful, they were forbidden from holding office in Massachusetts.

The main unit of government in Massachusetts Bay was the town. Town, congregation, and family were all extremely important to early colonists. The Puritan way did not deal particularly well with dissent, and several colonists, most notably Roger Williams and Anne Hutchinson, ran afoul of the authorities and were banished. Puritans soon came to view Native Americans as agents of the devil and, accordingly, fought the Pequot War (1637–1638) in a strikingly vicious manner.

As the seventeenth century progressed, hard-core Puritans comprised a smaller and smaller portion of the population, and a vigorous merchant class began to assert itself. The Congregational Church was also undergoing changes, exemplified by the Half-way Covenant of 1662, which extended some privileges to people who had not undergone a conversion experience. The economy of the Massachusetts Bay Colony was diverse, but fishing, shipbuilding, and trade were three of the main activities.

The Massachusetts Bay Colony was the chief beneficiary of what has been termed the "Great Migration," in which tens of thousands of Puritans immigrated in a matter of decades. As the Massachusetts Bay Colony expanded westward, it exerted pressures on native communities, and a series of wars, the most devastating being King Philip's (Metacom's) War (1675–1676), which permanently disrupted native life in the region.

In the 1680s, Massachusetts Bay was one of the colonies included in the Dominion of New England. The Dominion was an attempt by James II and others in the English government to exert a new level of control and extract a new level of profit from American colonies. This met fierce opposition in Massachusetts; Dominion government essentially ended when rebels in Boston imprisoned Sir Edmund Andros, the Dominion's governor.

In 1691, the Massachusetts Bay Colony received a new royal charter that gave it control over the former Plymouth Colony, adding many miles of new territory and increasing the population of the larger colony. Massachusetts continued to move farther away from the Puritan ideals upon which it had been founded and closer to the "Yankee" commerce-oriented ethic that would dominate the late eighteenth and nineteenth centuries.

The eighteenth century saw Massachusetts assert itself as a crucial part of England's overseas empire. Throughout the century, Massachusetts was a battleground in the ongoing conflict between the French, the English, and native peoples allied with both groups. In King George's War, Massachusetts forces took the massive French fort at Louisbourg, only to see it returned as part of the peace settlement. In the aftermath of the French and Indian War, Massachusetts became a hotbed of anti-English sentiment and eventually led the movement toward independence.

Massachusetts activists, the Sons of Liberty, led the protests against the 1765 Stamp Act and famously rejected the Tea Act of 1773 by disguising themselves as Mohawks and dumping British tea into the harbor. It is not surprising that Massachusetts was an early advocate of independence. In 1775, fighting broke out between British and Massachusetts forces at Lexington and Concord, signaling the beginning of the American Revolution.

Matthew Jennings

See also: Boston; Massachusetts Bay Charter; Puritanism; Winthrop, John.

Bibliography

Labaree, Benjamin W. *Colonial Massachusetts: A History*. Millwood, NY: KTO, 1979.

Morgan, Edmund S. *The Puritan Dilemma: The Story of John Winthrop*. 2nd ed. New York: Longman, 1999.

Massasoit (d. 1661)

Massasoit was considered one of the great sachems (chiefs) of the seventeenth century. A Wampanoag leader, he allied himself with the settlers in Plymouth upon their arrival in 1620. Throughout his life, he fought with the English settlers against other native tribes, thus affording protection not only for his own people but also for the fledgling settlers. Along with other great chiefs of the time, however, he resisted the missionary attempts at converting the Native Americans and saw those attempts as threats to his people's survival.

Plymouth, different from most other colonies, often paid the Native Americans for the land taken from them. This unique breed of colonists ordinarily settled around Native American villages, because the native peoples had invited them. This commonsensical approach to the indigenous population lessened encroachment on the colonists by other tribes or Europeans wanting to settle in the same area. In this friendly atmosphere, it is not surprising that Massasoit signed a nonagression treaty with the Pilgrims, which he honored until his death.

Much legend surrounds the events that preceded the treaty between Massasoit and the Pilgrims, including the part played by Squanto, the Native American translator and liaison with the Pilgrims. The true extent of the part he played in the story of their initial survival—that is, the legend, in which the friendly, ever helpful native taught the settlers how to raise corn and provided them with much-needed food—is uncertain. Squanto's importance to the Pilgrims may indeed have been somewhat exaggerated, however, as he was serving as an agent of Massasoit.

The Pilgrims were a quick study when it came to the native peoples' agricultural practices, and their first harvest, in 1621, was bountiful. While it may be true that there was a celebration of that harvest—a feast to which Massasoit and other Wampanoags were invited—as well as a ceremony, historians note that the simple celebration has been given religious overtones that were not apparent at the original event. It is true that the foods present, including pumpkins, turkeys, corn, and squash, were indigenous to the Americas and were surely provided by the local tribe or at the very least grown with their aid.

In any case, the event itself proved to be premature, as the harvest was good but not sufficient to

Massasoit, "great Sachem of the Wampanoags, Protector and Preserver of the Pilgrims, 1621," is memorialized in a statue that overlooks the harbor in Plymouth where the Pilgrims landed. *(Library of Congress, LC-D419-14 DLC)*

support the addition of the thirty-five new settlers who arrived in November 1621. Once again, short rations forced the Pilgrims to rely on the generosity of Massasoit for the food they needed to survive.

Massasoit died in 1661, but his legacy continued as his sons, Wamsutta and Metacom (who also was known as King Philip), presided over the Wampanoag and continued to honor the treaty Massasoit had signed with the colonists. This was not an easy task, as the tribe's position was rapidly deteriorating.

A period of resentment toward white authority began when Wamsutta died under suspicious circumstances while he was being questioned by Plymouth authorities about a possible uprising. Conflict and increasing tension between the colonists and the Native Americans finally led to Metacom's declaring an all-out war on the Plymouth Colony in 1675. Decades of

peaceful relations, as well as a long-honored coalition, came to an end.

Penny M. Sonnenburg

See also: Native American–European Relations; Native Americans; Pilgrims; Plymouth; Squanto.

Bibliography

Langdon, George D. *Pilgrim Colony: A History of New Plymouth 1620–1691.* New Haven, CT: Yale University Press, 1966.
Nash, Gary. *Red, White, and Black.* Englewood Cliffs, NJ: Prentice Hall, 1974.

Mather, Cotton (1663–1728)

Cotton Mather was one of the most influential Puritan clergymen and perhaps the most controversial public figure of his day.

The oldest of twelve children, Cotton Mather was born in Boston in 1663. Bostonians of the day likely saw him as the heir apparent to a colonial dynasty: Mather's grandfathers were the illustrious Puritans Richard Mather and John Cotton, both of whom had been instrumental in the founding of the Massachusetts Bay Colony, and his father was Increase Mather, a Boston minister and the first president of Harvard College.

Tutored in classical languages and Hebrew as a child, Mather entered Harvard at the age of 12. His youth and his family's prominence made him an easy mark for older students, and their teasing left him miserable. In addition, a stutter made the ministry seem out of reach. In his early days at Harvard, then, Mather began to study science and medicine.

As the young man's stutter disappeared over time, he returned to study for the ministry, although he remained actively interested in medical and other science throughout his life. Perhaps this fascination was reinforced by his misfortune in marriage and family life: His first two wives died at relatively young ages, and his third wife became insane; only two of his fifteen children lived longer than Mather himself.

Public Life and Controversies

Following his graduation from Harvard with a master's degree in 1681, Cotton Mather served as an assistant to his father at Boston's Old North Church for the next forty years. While Mather was known to be an eager and industrious minister, often writing as many as five sermons each week, he is more widely remembered for his participation in and commentaries on various political activities of his day and for his writings.

Mather entered the ministry at a time of changing attitudes toward Puritan teachings. As early as the 1630s, rigid Puritanism had come under attack from some merchants who found its reliance on strict interpretations of Old Testament pronouncements concerning commerce to be too restrictive. Adhering to the letter of the Pentateuch was increasingly seen as damaging to New World business and trade with England. By the time the Massachusetts Bay Colony had its charter revoked in 1684 and then restored in 1691, the merchants had allied their interests into a formidable bloc of power.

The new colonial charter contained two drastic changes from earlier Puritan rule: First, the voting franchise was now based on property ownership rather than on church membership. Second, religious toleration was imposed, in contrast to the former Puritan habit of charging "heresy" against anyone who questioned ecclesiastical authority or preaching or who failed to observe any of the myriad laws and restrictions imposed by the hierarchy. Against this backdrop of greater religious freedom, Increase and Cotton Mather came to their own prominence in Boston church life.

Cotton Mather was not well suited to these changing times. In his youth and early ministry, Mather was one of those who strove to strengthen Puritan faith and practice in the colonies. At the same time, beginning early in his career and continuing throughout his life, Mather carried on correspondence on religious, scientific, and other topics with various church leaders, scientists, physicians, and other professionals from around the world. Although he never left his native New England, Mather was probably exposed to more ideas and points of view than virtually any other leading member of colonial society. His native intelligence, coupled with his continual exposure to new ideas, made him somewhat open to the growing spirit of ecumenism as new immigrants from different lands came to the New World. But he remained firmly convinced that the Puritan theocracy he had grown up with was the only way in which God's kingdom could exist in America, and he was in the forefront of those calling for Puritanism's reinforcement and renewal, not its demise.

Such an attitude set Cotton Mather at odds with many of his contemporaries. Further exacerbating this conflict was Mather's personality. As a child of family and privilege, Mather early became convinced of his

Cotton Mather was renowned as a man of letters and science, as well as a Puritan minister. He produced more than 400 published works, the most celebrated of which is *Magnalia Christi Americana* (1702), an ecclesiastical history of New England. *(Brown Brothers, Sterling, Pennsylvania)*

own special status within New England life. By most accounts (including his own words among his voluminous writings), Mather was self-centered, arrogant, and spoiled. Such traits may be found in many men of brilliance, but they are usually tempered by a willingness to engage in dialogue with those holding other opinions or positions within society; Mather evidenced no such willingness. True to his Puritan roots, he seems to have been convinced that there was only one legitimate worldview, one that held Mather himself at the center, with the success or failure of God's plan for His people in the New World resting squarely upon the shoulders of Cotton Mather. Mather's personality was such that he almost never entertained ideas other than his own, and his dismissal of others was rarely tactful. If someone disagreed with his Puritan vision, that person was dismissed out of hand as being an instrument of Satan.

Not surprisingly, these personal traits of arrogance and egocentricity were damaging to Mather as a pastor and as an influential leader in the community. Unlike Mather, other prominent ministers who emerged from colonial New England were able to mix compassion and empathy with their brilliance and were accessible to and beloved by their congregations. In contrast, Mather felt himself to be far above fraternizing with his flock; in fact, many of his diary entries refer to his parishioners in such extremely derogatory terms as "insignificant lice," "silly people," and "foolish." In part, Mather's arrogance can be attributed to his belief in the Puritan tradition that New England's highest privilege was to be ruled by the godly, among whom he considered himself. But his inability to recognize that times were changing and that changes were required on his part if he were to earn a position of influence in the new culture resulted in his failure to be the religious or civic leader he had hoped to be.

Literary Works

Cotton Mather was undoubtedly the most widely read man in America in his day. At a time when an established colonial minister's library might respectably contain fewer than 30 volumes, Mather's consisted of over 3,000 books. During his lifetime, he himself produced over 400 published works, although many of these were short, cheap volumes, which often took advantage of public interest in some current community event (for example, an execution of a criminal might prompt Mather to publish an essay warning against sin). His topics ranged from folklore to science to his primary concern, theology. An examination of Mather's works reveals that though he had a gift for the craft of writing and studied many new ideas his philosophical rigidity left him lacking in the willingness to reconsider his worldviews. Of all his writings, two stand out as being particularly worthy of comment.

Wonders of the Invisible World (1693) addressed the widespread interest in and fear of witchcraft of the day. It recounts the events of the Salem witch trials of the previous year as Cotton Mather and his father Increase had been present at those trials. Both Mathers had been among those calling for severe prosecution of the accused witches, although to their credit, as the trials continued and the hysteria escalated, both came to urge caution and to denounce the reliance on "spectral evidence" (tales of ghosts and evil spirits inhabiting those accused of being witches) that formed the basis of many convictions. *Wonders* also gives an account of a variety of old wives' tales, superstitions, and other mystical happenings in the colonies. Such stories were widely circulated and fed into most colonists' fears of evil lurking within the New England forests and wilderness.

The massive *Magnalia Christi Americana* (1702) combines history and biography to tell the stories of eminent colonial personages. While it sometimes slips into extremes of praise, this useful work does provide factual information about many of the leading men and founders of colonial America. Its running theme is one that would come to be repeated often through American history: Even men from humble beginnings could undertake the Lord's work and, by careful dedication to godly works, rise to prominence in the New World.

Barbara Schwarz Wachal

See also: Massachusetts Bay Colony; Mather, Increase; Ministers and the Ministry; Puritanism; Sermons.

Bibliography

Mather, Cotton. *Magnalia Christi Americana: or, The Ecclesiastical History of New-England from Its First Planting in the Year 1620 unto the Year of our Lord, 1698.* Reprint, New York: Arno Press, 1972.
Middlekauf, Kenneth. *The Mathers: Three Generations of Puritan Intellectuals, 1596–1728.* New York: Oxford University Press, 1971.
Silverman, Kenneth. *The Life and Times of Cotton Mather.* New York: Harper and Row, 1984.

Mather, Increase (1639–1723)

Increase Mather was a highly visible figure in colonial Boston. The son of influential Puritan minister Richard Mather and the father of Cotton Mather, Increase Mather had a considerable influence on New England culture as a Congregational minister, author, and ambassador. Mather's view of himself as the heir of the founders of New England is evident in his legacy of pursuing orthodoxy. Yet his was an orthodoxy tempered by a pragmatism developed in response to the changing times in which he lived.

By the turn of the eighteenth century, Boston's church leadership was largely in the hands of Increase Mather and his son Cotton. Increase Mather had assumed the pastorate of Dorchester Church from his father Richard. In 1664, he began a fifty-year tenure as the pastor of Boston's Second, or Old North, Church. The following year, he was named president of Harvard College, a position he would hold until 1701, when he was ousted in conjunction with the rise of a new merchant class within New England church life.

A true Congregationalist, Increase Mather opposed the formation of ministerial alliances and associations, believing that such groups would serve only to reduce the traditional independence of each individual church. Likewise, as an orthodox Puritan, Mather was a longtime opponent of Solomon Stoddard and others who favored a policy of open communion, arguing that the practice eroded the foundation of the church. Still, for all his orthodoxy, Mather was something of a pragmatist. For example, although he originally opposed the Halfway Covenant—allowing for the baptism into the faith of the children of parents who had not undergone the full conversion experience in adulthood—he eventually reversed his opinion, publishing his ideas in *The First Principles of New England* in 1675.

Like many of his contemporaries, Increase Mather published a number of tracts, pamphlets, and other pieces. His religious texts included sermons, devotional pieces, ecclesiastical treatises, and various works discussing and defending church polity. He also published several records of New England history, including accounts of the Native American wars. Among his most influential writings were those that reflected the combined political and religious aspects of New England culture. Probably Mather's most important published work addressed the intersection of politics and religion in the Salem witch trials of 1692.

Like most New Englanders and virtually all of his colleagues in the clergy of his day, Increase Mather was a firm believer in the dangers of witchcraft. As a leader of the Massachusetts Bay Colony, he was heavily involved in the trials resulting from the widespread hysteria attending reported supernatural activity in Salem, Massachusetts, in 1692. Unlike many of his contemporaries, however, Mather and his son Cotton became increasingly troubled as the prosecution, punishment, and public opinion grew more violent. As a consequence of his belief that the court was acting improperly, Increase Mather worked both publicly and behind the scenes to bring the trials to an end. His *Cases of Conscience Concerning Evil Spirits* (1692) was a record of his observations on the American experience with witchcraft.

Mather's reputation for moderation, as well as his leadership within colonial life, led to his involvement in a more overtly political capacity. In 1684, the charter of the Massachusetts Bay Colony was revoked by the Crown. Increase Mather was appointed as an ambassador to the royal court and sent to London in 1688 to negotiate a new charter with the Catholic king James II. As part of the negotiations that continued into the reign of William III, the appointment of a royal governor was decreed, and William Phips, the candidate favored by Mather, was appointed to the post. By 1691, a new charter was granted to the Massachusetts Bay Colony, although it differed materially from the original charter. In addition to its provision for a royal governor, the new charter based the franchise on property ownership rather than church membership.

Despite his pragmatism and his recognition that times were changing, Increase Mather retained a deep sense of loyalty to the basic Puritan orthodoxy of his forefathers. He was particularly distressed with the changes he saw taking place at Harvard College as that institution's ecclesiastical mission shifted, in part, in response to the rising merchant culture. As a result, he and others founded Yale College in 1701 in the hope that this new institution would become the home of orthodoxy that Harvard once had been.

Barbara Schwarz Wachal

See also: Massachusetts Bay Colony; Mather, Cotton; Ministers and the Ministry; Puritanism; Sermons.

Bibliography

Hall, Michael G. *The Last American Puritan: The Life of Increase Mather, 1639–1723.* Middletown, CT: Wesleyan University Press, 1988.

Lowance, Mason I. *Increase Mather.* New York: Twayne, 1974.

Murdock, Kenneth Ballard. *Increase Mather, the Foremost American Puritan.* New York: Russell & Russell, 1966 [c. 1925].

Maya

Long before European conquest, the Maya had built one of the great Native American civilizations. The Maya people lived in what is now southern Mexico, Guatemala, Honduras, and Belize. No single Maya city-state dominated the entire region. Rather, each one had its own capital and surrounding, subject towns. Warfare and trade caused the power of various Maya city-states to expand and contract over time. The history of the Maya can be divided into three periods: preclassic (2000 B.C.E.–200 C.E.), classic (200–900), and postclassic (900–1540).

The early Maya practiced slash-and-burn agriculture. While this method produced high yields initially, it quickly exhausted the soil and forced the Maya to move to new fields. By the classic period, the inhabitants of growing Maya cities demanded more food. This

El Caracol, the tenth-century Mayan observatory at Chichén Itzá in Mexico's Yucatán Peninsula, testifies to the sophistication of that civilization long before European contact. The Spanish did not take control of the Yucatán until the 1540s. *(Chichén Itzá, Yucatán State, Mexico/Bridgeman Art Library)*

led to the development of techniques to increase agricultural production. For example, the Maya drained swamps and riverbanks to create elevated fields near cities. They also built irrigation canals and reservoirs when needed. At other times, they constructed terraces on mountainsides for farming.

Improved agricultural techniques allowed the Maya to develop large cities. During the classic period in particular, significant urbanization occurred. The largest Mayan cities had more than 50,000 inhabitants. Each served as a political and religious center for the surrounding countryside. Examples of monumental architecture could be found in these cities, where large pyramids often served as sites for the many Mayan rituals and ceremonies. Limited technology meant that construction of these monuments required the mobilization of thousands of workers.

Among the largest cities was Tikal, located in the Petén jungle of present-day Guatemala. Tikal, established at least as early as 292 C.E., was one of the earliest settled Maya sites. The city possessed six great pyramids, including the tallest Maya structure (known to archaeologists simply as "Temple 4"), which was 230

feet high. Tikal also had reservoirs, artificial lakes, palaces, and ball courts.

Mayan society was divided between nobles, a middle class, and commoners. The members of the elite nobility served as political rulers and religious leaders, positions that were closely intertwined. Merchants and artisans comprised a middle group. Some merchants grew wealthy from long-distance trade; urban artisans made luxury items such as jewelry, ceramics, and other handcrafted products. Commoners worked mainly in agriculture, cultivating their own lands, as well as those of the elite. They produced crops such as corn, beans, and other vegetables to sustain Mayan society. There was one more class below the commoners—that of the slaves, which was generally made up of war captives and criminals.

The Maya made many important advances in learning and culture. They developed a complex calendar system, including a 365-day calendar, as well as a 260-day ceremonial calendar. They made key contributions in mathematics and astronomy and understood the concept of zero and place value.

The Maya also had written literature, using a form

of hieroglyphics, although only four pictorial manuscripts have survived. The Maya also inscribed pillars, facades, and stairways, where they often recorded historical events. The importance of writing among the Maya placed scribes near the top of society.

Europeans succeeded in conquering the Maya, as they did other indigenous groups in the New World. The conquest of the Maya was different from other conquests, however, in that the Spanish had to subjugate each region one by one, causing the process to take nearly 200 years in some areas. By the late 1520s, the Spaniards had conquered Chiapas in southern Mexico, but it took them several campaigns and twenty years to conquer Mexico's Yucatán Peninsula. Spaniards arrived in Guatemala in 1524, fighting with the Quiche Maya and then conquering other Maya groups there. The longest holdout was the Petén area and its dense forests. Many Maya from other regions fled there to escape Spanish conquest.

After the Spanish conquest, the Maya did not always readily accept Spanish rule. The most significant Maya uprising against the Spanish came in 1712 with a widespread revolt in Chiapas known as the Tzeltal Maya Rebellion. The root cause of the rebellion, which included both Tzeltal and Tzotzil Maya, was religion. Traditional religious beliefs persisted in the region, which alarmed the Spanish Catholic religious officials. The Spanish sought to end native religious practices, and a dispute developed over the recognition of Native American sightings of the Virgin Mary.

In 1712, thirty-two Mayan towns revolted, declaring Spanish authority void and creating their own indigenous priesthood and civil hierarchy. The next year, however, the Spanish put down the Mayan revolt. While the Mayan people survived, and continued to survive, as an ethnic group with their own language and customs, the existence of an independent Mayan political entity ceased.

Ronald Young

See also: Native American–European Conflict; Native Americans; New Spain; Spanish Colonies on Mainland North America (Chronology).

Bibliography

Burkholder, Mark, and Lyman John. *Colonial Latin America.* 5th ed. Oxford, UK: Oxford University Press, 2003.

Coe, Michael. *The Maya.* 6th ed. New York: Thames and Hudson, 1999.

Sharer, Robert. *The Ancient Maya.* 5th ed. Stanford, CA: Stanford University Press, 1994.

Mayflower Compact

A small separatist group of people in England, known as Pilgrims, were persecuted because of their religious beliefs. Some of them sought relief by emigrating to Leyden, Holland, but they became concerned about liberal attitudes there leading some of their children to loosen their ties to the church. Therefore, they decided to relocate to the New World, where they hoped to be able to practice their faith freely.

After a difficult Atlantic crossing on the ship *Mayflower,* the Pilgrims were faced with a different challenge: There would be no civil authority on land for them to answer to. Many passengers had hired themselves out as indentured servants, promising to work for seven years to pay for their passage, and some thought that, since they were outside the bounds of English law, they could assume their freedom as soon as they landed.

In response, the leaders of the Pilgrim group created what became known as the Mayflower Compact, a document designed to be their rule and guide to life and living in the New World. The Mayflower Compact became the official constitution of Plymouth Colony, lasting until Plymouth merged into the Massachusetts Bay Colony in 1692. The first American state paper, it provides the original statement of the principles of American democracy as we now know and understand them. For the first time in world history, a group of men of their own free will agreed to be governed by themselves according to the will of the majority.

The Compact expresses four major themes: a deep faith and belief in God and His divine guidance; a deep loyalty to England and the king, even though its signers had been persecuted and exiled in their homeland; a mutual regard for one another as equals in the sight of God; and an intent to establish just and equal laws upon which would be built a truly democratic form of government.

The Pilgrims believed in God, and, believing in God, they believed in the equality of all men before God. Therefore, without precedent, they made all men equal before the law. Here then is the birth of popular constitutional liberty, foreshadowing the Declaration of Independence, the Bill of Rights, and the Constitution.

The Mayflower signers were very careful to recognize King James I as their lawful sovereign. Although the King of England was also the head of the church, they had come to the conviction that religion was a

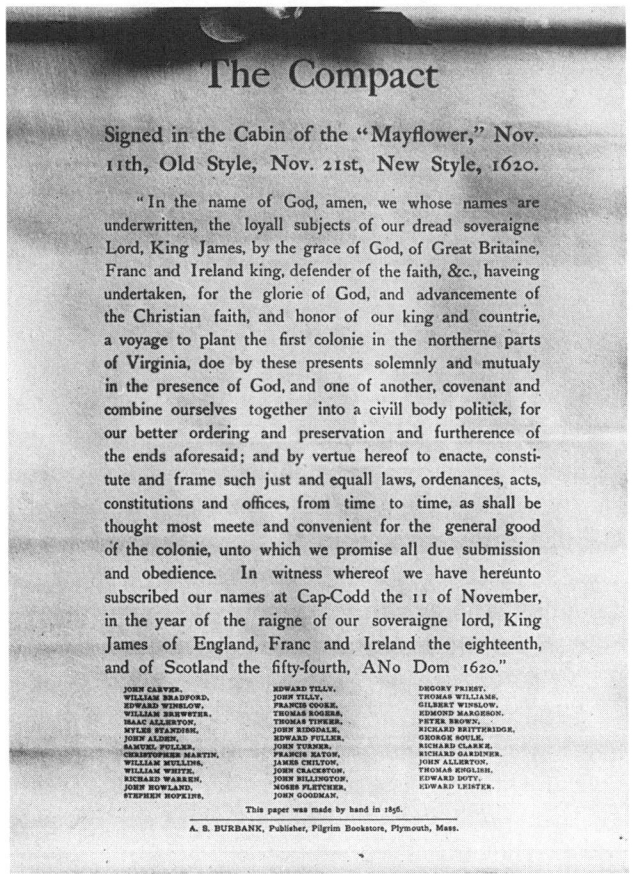

The Compact

Signed in the Cabin of the "Mayflower," Nov. 11th, Old Style, Nov. 21st, New Style, 1620.

"In the name of God, amen, we whose names are underwritten, the loyall subjects of our dread soveraigne Lord, King James, by the grace of God, of Great Britaine, Franc and Ireland king, defender of the faith, &c., haveing undertaken, for the glorie of God, and advancemente of the Christian faith, and honor of our king and countrie, a voyage to plant the first colonie in the northerne parts of Virginia, doe by these presents solemnly and mutualy in the presence of God, and one of another, covenant and combine ourselves together into a civill body politick, for our better ordering and preservation and furtherence of the ends aforesaid; and by vertue hereof to enacte, constitute and frame such just and equall laws, ordenances, acts, constitutions and offices, from time to time, as shall be thought most meete and convenient for the general good of the colonie, unto which we promise all due submission and obedience. In witness whereof we have hereunto subscribed our names at Cap-Codd the 11 of November, in the year of the raigne of our soveraigne lord, King James of England, Franc and Ireland the eighteenth, and of Scotland the fifty-fourth, ANo Dom 1620."

JOHN CARVER,	EDWARD TILLY,	DEGORY PRIEST,
WILLIAM BRADFORD,	JOHN TILLY,	THOMAS WILLIAMS,
EDWARD WINSLOW,	FRANCIS COOKE,	GILBERT WINSLOW,
WILLIAM BREWSTER,	THOMAS ROGERS,	EDMOND MARGESON,
ISAAC ALLERTON,	THOMAS TINKER,	PETER BROWN,
MYLES STANDISH,	JOHN RIGSDALE,	RICHARD BRITTERIDGE,
JOHN ALDEN,	EDWARD FULLER,	GEORGE SOULE,
SAMUEL FULLER,	JOHN TURNER,	RICHARD CLARKE,
CHRISTOPHER MARTIN,	FRANCIS EATON,	RICHARD GARDINER,
WILLIAM MULLINS,	JAMES CHILTON,	JOHN ALLERTON,
WILLIAM WHITE,	JOHN CRACKSTON,	THOMAS ENGLISH,
RICHARD WARREN,	JOHN BILLINGTON,	EDWARD DOTY,
JOHN HOWLAND,	MOSES FLETCHER,	EDWARD LEISTER.
STEPHEN HOPKINS,	JOHN GOODMAN,	

This paper was made by hand in 1896.

A. S. BURBANK, Publisher, Pilgrim Bookstore, Plymouth, Mass.

The Mayflower Compact, signed by forty-one male passengers on November 1, 1620, was a statement of democratic principles that served as the official constitution of Plymouth Colony. Although copies survive, the original document has never been found. *(Brown Brothers, Sterling, Pennsylvania)*

matter of individual conscience and belief, having made that logical step from the search for religious freedom to the discovery of political freedom.

In time, the Pilgrims' democratic ideals spread to other colonies. Their example gradually softened the restrictive and intolerant government of the Massachusetts Bay Colony. By the time the more free and tolerant Plymouth Colony was absorbed into the Massachusetts Bay Colony, the latter was ready to open privileges to all.

The Compact was an agreement signed by all the men on board, including the indentured servants, promising to abide by laws that would be drawn up and agreed upon by all male members of the community. Women were not allowed to participate in the governing process.

The Mayflower passengers were not men of wealth and position, nor were they a homogenous group, coming, as they did, from various walks of life and religious backgrounds. Many of them were strangers to the Ley-

den flock, and less than half were members of the Church of Leyden. Differences of opinion would certainly occur, and dissensions were bound to arise. But there was no one to whom they could appeal. Wise leadership proposed a document that would bind them all to submit to "such a government and governors as we should by common consent agree to make and choose."

As soon as the document was completed, the entire company was called together to hear it read aloud. Once the Compact was signed, those who signed it became legal voters and proceeded to elect a governor. Their choice was John Carver, America's first democratically elected leader.

Arthur E. Chapman

See also: Bradford, William; Pilgrims; Plymouth.

Bibliography

Wish, Harvey, ed. *William Bradford of Plymouth Plantation.* New York: Capricorn, 1962.

Menéndez de Avilés, Pedro (1519–1574)

Pedro Menéndez de Avilés was born in Asturia, Spain, in 1519, the same year in which Hernando Cortéz began his conquest of the Aztecs in Mexico's central valley. Menéndez was a poor nobleman, which probably influenced his decision to leave Spain to seek wealth in the New World. Little is known of Menéndez's early career, but he served the Holy Roman Emperor Charles V admirably against the French in the Bay of Biscay. Menéndez's area of expertise was naval conflict, and he also earned membership in the prestigious Order of Santiago.

After dealing with accusations of smuggling in 1563, Menéndez was contracted by Philip II in 1565 to discover and settle North America in his name. Menéndez would receive the titles of governor, captain general, and *adelantado*, and, if he fulfilled the terms of the contract (including the founding of two cities), he would receive land and the title of marquis. In theory, the area under the control of Menéndez stretched from present-day Canada to Mexico, though in practice, it was much smaller.

Because of their success in extracting wealth in Mexico and Peru, the Spanish did not focus their attention on colonizing in the present-day United States. Spain's great treasure fleets did, however, attract the attention of English and French sea captains, and Menéndez's colony in Florida would protect shipping lanes. In addition, Menéndez had the general authority to convert the region's Native Americans and attack any Europeans who might encroach on the Spanish claim. The first European threats were the French forts Charlesfort (built on Port Royal Sound in 1562) and Caroline (established on the St. Johns River in 1564). It bears mentioning that both of these were Huguenot (French Protestant) enterprises.

Traditionally, scholars have asserted that the Spanish came to North America to plunder, the French came to trade, and the English came to settle. In the case of Florida, as elsewhere, these distinctions are too simple, and they do not convey the reality of the colonial situation. Menéndez had an expansive, visionary plan for Spanish Florida. It would include agriculture, livestock, fishing, naval stores, and shipbuilding industries.

In the summer of 1565, Spanish and French fleets raced across the Atlantic to shore up their defenses in

The Spanish seaman Pedro Menéndez de Avilés was commissioned by King Philip II to establish a colony in Florida, where he landed in 1565 and founded the settlement of St. Augustine. *(Brown Brothers, Sterling, Pennsylvania)*

Florida. The French under Jean Ribaut reached Florida first, but their small colony provided little resistance against the larger Spanish undertaking. Menéndez sailed from Cadiz with eleven ships and over 1,000 men. Though he was delayed, and the size of his fleet was diminished, by severe weather, he managed to reach St. Augustine in September. After a brief naval battle near Fort Caroline, Menéndez sailed south, where he founded St. Augustine, the first permanent European settlement in what is now the United States. Local Timucuans, under the guidance of Seloy, provided materials and manpower to build a Spanish fort.

When a storm weakened the French fleet, Menéndez took the opportunity to attack Fort Caroline. The assault was a total surprise to the French, whose forces were divided and ill. Menéndez captured the fort and renamed it San Mateo, executing most of its defenders. Between 150 and 300 Frenchmen had been shipwrecked away from Caroline, and Menéndez caught them south of St. Augustine. The French offered to give up their weapons in exchange for their lives, to which Menéndez replied that if they did so, "I should deal with them as Our Lord should command me." The surrendering French troops were executed. Though this was not in keeping with the European code of warfare, Menéndez viewed it as necessary to keep Native Americans and the French Protestants—whom Menéndez thought shared similarly satanic beliefs—from allying against the Spanish.

Pedro Menéndez de Avilés envisioned a transcontinental Spanish American empire. At the time of his death due to typhus in 1574, Spanish Florida was but a weak outpost that remained on the periphery of the Spanish Empire.

In the years following, the English under Sir Francis Drake would destroy the town of St. Augustine, though not its fort, the massive, stonewalled Castillo San Marcos. Spanish Florida would continue to spark Native American uprisings and lose money for the Crown in the decades to come.

Matthew Jennings

See also: Military and Diplomatic Affairs (Chronology); Military and Diplomatic Affairs (Essay); New Spain; St. Augustine; Spanish Colonies on Mainland North America (Chronology); War.

Bibliography

Gannon, Michael, ed. *The New History of Florida.* Gainesville: University Press of Florida, 1996.

Tebeau, Charlton W. *A History of Florida.* Coral Gables, FL: University of Miami Press, 1971.

Weber, David J. *The Spanish Frontier in North America.* New Haven, CT: Yale University Press, 1992.

Mercantilism

Mercantilism was the dominant economic theory of the colonial era. Most early mercantilists assumed that the basis for national wealth was bullion, a finite resource, and that nations competed to gain bullion at their rivals' expense. Mercantilism assumed an activist government and a self-sufficient country.

British mercantilism was defined by Thomas Mun of the British East India Company in the 1620s. Mun agreed with the general notion that the mercantile nation should develop domestic or colonial sources for all of its needs—agricultural products, raw materials, and finished goods. It needed a strong merchant marine, preferably armed, to control colonial trade.

For orthodox thinkers, trade meant especially the bullion trade for mercantilist nations fortunate enough to have gold and silver mines. Previously, British mercantilism had entailed a significant amount of state-sponsored piracy. Mun eased the pressure to acquire hard metal by pointing out that, for those without direct access to bullion, a favorable balance of trade was a means of acquiring the wealth of other mercantilists. Mun argued that bullion outflows could be beneficial if they resulted in favorable trade balances. This approach reduced but did not eliminate the fixation with bullion as the basis of national economic health.

Control of trade predated mercantilism. In medieval Europe, local governments assessed tolls or tariffs on goods entering or leaving their areas of control. Under mercantilism, the internal trade barriers between different parts of a country gave way to centralized government and international trade controls.

The major mercantilist powers were England, France, Holland, and Spain. All attempted to restrict colonial trade to the home country. These nations wanted colonies that could provide materials and products needed in the home country. In return, they wanted colonies that needed products made in the home country, as well as colonies that operated at a deficit.

Colonies received subsidies for production of raw materials, while restrictions and penalties were placed on manufactures that competed with the home country. Manufacture of these products for local use was acceptable, unless it interfered with the market for European imports. Colonial trade with other European nations was permissible when it brought advantage to the home country, in the form of bullion or a favorable trade balance.

Navigation Acts

Control of colonial trade came through the Navigation Acts. These acts, effective mostly during the seventeenth and eighteenth centuries, restricted imports and exports to intra-colonial shipping. This approach promoted a larger merchant marine, and the sale of shipping services enhanced the balance of trade.

These British acts required that ships have crews made up of three-fourths British citizens or colonists. The Navigation Acts also itemized or enumerated products that had to pass through British ports to the benefit of British reshippers and the British government, which had an easier time collecting import duties. While, on balance, British interests were served by the acts, they also could be mutually beneficial. While controlling England's sources of grain, salt, and other items, tariff walls kept European competition from harming nascent colonial ventures—tobacco for Europe and iron for colonial use, for instance. And subsidies from England were always a possibility for the colonials.

British legislation could hurt the colonies, as in the case of the Corn Laws of 1666, which banned colonial grain shipments. As British law had banned colonial manufacture, these prohibitions effectively ended the New York woolen and linen industries, which had supplied about three-fourths of the colony's needs, in the late seventeenth century. Northern manufacture of hats and iron also struggled against British restrictions.

Colonies benefited because the Navigation Acts restricted foreign competition. New England was able to establish a shipbuilding industry. South Carolina got indigo subsidies. North Carolina got subsidies for ship's stores—pitch, tar, turpentine, and lumber. American goods were competitive in Britain because British tariffs increased the prices of comparable French and other European goods.

Of course, all these tariffs meant that British and colonial consumers had to pay more than they would have otherwise for British goods and other goods transshipped through Britain. This cost the South more than New England or the Middle colonies. Unfinished products from the South were monopolized by England,

and the finished goods it needed had to pass through British ports. New Englanders had Caribbean markets, legal or not, and they had little compunction about smuggling.

New Englanders really had objected to the Molasses Act of 1733, which increased duties on French West Indian sugar and molasses, protecting British Caribbean sugar interests. The French Caribbean was New Englanders' outlet for lumber, livestock, flour, and fish in the aftermath of the Corn Laws. The colonists would have been more irate if British authorities had enforced the laws, but again enforcement was lax.

Enforcement

Britain's colonial enforcer was the Board of Trade and Plantations, established only in 1696. The board was noted for lax enforcement, and its principle contribution to colonial affairs was to promote lawbreaking, contempt for officialdom, and occasional connivance of customs officials, maybe even an occasional governor, with the lawbreakers. The Admiralty Courts established to increase adherence to the laws were no better; local juries were reluctant to convict their neighbors of offenses they engaged in themselves.

Until the end of the French and Indian War (known as the Seven Years' War in Europe), the controls were tolerable, because they were not enforced. When the British government attempted to recover the costs of the war, however, friction ensued. Prior to the war, colonials had a lighter tax burden than residents of England. The English thought that the colonials should pay a fair share of the war debt, as well as the new costs of administering the enlarged empire. Parliament began enforcing the old acts and imposing new ones.

The acts were sound from a mercantilist perspective, providing for the well-being of the mother country and compensating for colonies that might prove a drain on the home government. The Sugar Act of 1764 attempted to protect the struggling sugar economy of the British West Indies by taxing foreign sugar and molasses (highly important to New England). The Currency Act of 1764 limited the power of the colonies to issue paper money. The Stamp Act of 1765 was simply for revenue, requiring a stamp on legal documents.

Other objectionable acts of the period were the Quartering Act of 1765, the Townshend Acts of 1767, and the Tea Act of 1773. Colonists also objected to the Quebec Act of 1774, which attempted to control the frontier and cut costs. Its actual effect was to disturb colonials who wanted to settle on Native American and old French lands, as well as compete in the area set aside for the Hudson's Bay Company.

The new laws gave the Middle colonies and New England a better appreciation of older Southern grievances about the burdens of mercantilist policies. Boycotts and other resistance became popular. When resistance led to repeal of the Townshend and Stamp Acts, colonists learned that stubbornness worked. The British, on the other hand, decided that a stronger colonial administration, with troops to back it, might be in order.

On the financial side, mercantilism worked nicely. Trade in 1772 was three times what it was in 1702. Shipping in 1788 was over a million tons. On the eve of the American Revolution in 1776, only one-third of British trade was within Europe; in 1700, the reverse had been true. The West Indian trade mushroomed as well, with a fivefold increase in exports and a fourfold increase in imports.

In 1759, New England's balance of trade was a negative 561,000 pounds. Obviously, New Englanders could not afford to sustain such deficits for any length of time. Many were compensating off the books by means of the timeworn custom of smuggling. But overall British mercantilism seemed to bear out Mun's deemphasis of bullionism.

Mercantilism and the Revolution

Although the colonies became increasingly lucrative over time, the British government still maintained a focus on European affairs. Mercantilism was, after all, a system wherein European governments competed with one another. Colonies were secondary—merely additional resources to be counted in the competition.

Mercantilists failed to realize that colonies could have interests, too. This European focus led to salutary neglect, which allowed the colonies to develop their own economies and interests. When Britain finally turned its focus back to its colonies, because it wanted to exploit them again, through enforcing the navigation acts and levying new charges, colonial interest had already diverged.

John H. Barnhill

See also: Board of Trade; East India Company; Economy, Business, and Labor (Chronology); Economy, Business, and Labor (Essay); Merchants; Trade.

Bibliography

Ekelund, Robert B., and Robert D. Tollison. *Politicized Economies: Monarchy, Monopoly, and Mercantilism.* College Station: Texas A & M University Press, 1997.

Kamman, Michael G. *Empire and Interest: The American Colonies and the Politics of Mercantilism.* New York: Lippincott, 1970.

Wallerstein, Immanuel M. *Mercantilism and the Consolidation of the European World-Economy, 1600–1750.* New York: Academic Press, 1980.

Merchants

Merchants in the colonial era provided a variety of services that were crucial to the economic well-being of the American colonies. To obtain goods, they operated ships that occasionally participated in smuggling and privateering. With cash in short supply, they commonly bartered for goods and traded everything imaginable. As the primary source of financing in small communities, they also offered credit. In times of war, they supplied the troops with all the necessities. Although merchants played a part in nearly every economic transaction, they were still a minority in an American population that remained overwhelmingly rural throughout the colonial era.

Merchants received a slow start in the Americas partly because of the religious background of many of the New England colonists. The Puritans regarded trade as a morally dangerous field of endeavor. Rather than take advantage of his economic position and seek the most money that he could obtain for a product, the Puritan merchant was expected to be content with merely a just price for his merchandise. A shopkeeper who pursued unseemly profits ran the risk not only of antagonizing his neighbors but also of being brought before a Puritan court of law. By the late seventeenth century, religious beliefs had weakened; at the same time, a capitalist spirit and merchant class developed.

Early Merchants

The first merchants who appeared did so in port cities as elements of the triangle trade. Largely a private endeavor, this began with manufactured items from Europe that were sent to Africa for the purchase of slaves. The slaves were transported to the Americas, in the infamous "Middle Passage," to be exchanged for the products of slave-operated plantations. These cash crops, such as indigo or tobacco, were then transported to Europe to complete the triangle. Northern merchants participated heavily in the triangular trade, while Southern merchants more often carried on direct trade with England.

Another variation on this trade in New England involved merchants who sent rum to Africa to buy slaves, who were sold for molasses in the West Indies. The molasses would be transformed into rum in New England distilleries. The process would then repeat. The various forms of triangle trade eventually involved everything that could be profitably traded, including indentured servants.

Most merchants did not engage directly in the triangle trade. Only a very few, such as Thomas Hancock of Boston, were wealthy export-import traders in large cities. Many more merchants were small storekeepers, who engaged in a range of transactions, including serving as intermediaries between the large merchants in the cities and the smaller ones in the remote areas.

In the North, the key to prosperity was trade, because the soil did not support cash crops such as tobacco, and merchants accordingly focused entirely on merchandising. In the South, particularly in the Chesapeake region, the owners of large plantations typically operated stores for the benefit of the surrounding growers. These large planters often carried a hundred or more debtors on their books.

Merchants in remote areas or on the Western frontier frequently also farmed a small plot of land to help make ends meet. Such men were usually the only source of goods from the outside world, apart from the rarely seen traveling peddler. These storekeepers provided an essential service for an area by accepting crop surpluses from neighboring farmers in exchange for the few manufactured goods that a rural family required but could not produce. They were also the only cash buyers of farm surplus and the only source of credit.

Most of the articles sold by merchants throughout the colonies were items used in the production of clothing—textiles, buttons, sewing needles, and so on—and farm equipment. These merchants also dealt in basic household items, and their wares included weapons, tools, kitchen implements, and the like.

Merchants typically operated their stores as sole proprietorships. The shortage of skilled labor meant that a merchant would perform every task in the store. Larger merchants might have an apprentice or two to sweep the floors and tend the fire. They also might have an assistant to tend the books and assist the occasional customer. Even the large stores did not see an abundance of activity. A busy merchant like Thomas Hancock might have twelve transactions on a typical day. In this preindustrial era, many merchants closed the store after lunch and did not reopen until the next day.

In time, colonial merchants presided over a stream of commerce that ran from the farms of the trans-Appalachian west across the Atlantic seaboard to England and Europe and often to Latin America and the islands of the Caribbean. As the colonies grew, demand for goods also increased. To meet the increasing American appetite, some merchants, particularly in New England, gradually were drawn into illegal trade and pirating.

New England merchants typically owned a share in a ship to divide the risks of transporting merchandise across the Atlantic and to the Caribbean. Since they served markets outside of the British Empire, these ships had more opportunity to sneak into a French or Spanish port to pick up goods in violation of British mercantile policy.

Pirating also offered an appealing way of acquiring goods. In addition, the British licensed private ships to prey on ships that traded with the enemy, a practice known as privateering. These privateers attacked French and American ships, usually in Caribbean waters. By 1759, forty-eight privateers had been commissioned in New York alone.

Merchants conducted overseas trade with the help of foreign merchants, who acted as agents for American exporters. The agents accepted goods on consignment, often items sold on a commission basis by the American merchant, and disposed of the products when the best price could be obtained in the local market. The agent then remitted the proceeds of the sale, after deducting his own commission, in either bills of exchange or return cargo.

The primitive transportation system of the colonies made the cost of many products prohibitively expensive. In an age when ships sailed only as fast as the wind blew, it took a month or more—and much money—to ship goods from England to America. The lack of roads in the Americas also meant that shipping goods from a port city to the frontier could take six weeks, adding an additional cost. Freighting might add as much as 20 percent to the original cost of an item.

The prices that merchants charged varied with the terms of individual transactions. The lowest prices were offered for cash sales. On credit sales, markups might reach 100 to 200 percent above the merchant's cost, depending upon the length of credit offered.

Customers routinely expected credit for their purchases. Terms of six months to one year were common, and longer periods were negotiable. A 6 percent interest charge was usually assessed on overdue accounts, but merchants seldom made vigorous efforts to collect the unpaid balances. Often outstanding accounts would remain unpaid for years. This reluctance to pursue debtors was both the result of a combination of communication delays and the chronic shortage of specie that afflicted the colonies.

A persistent shortage of hard money required even the large merchants in the port cities to accept payment for goods in kind. As business grew, the variety of items acquired in trade also grew. Thomas Hancock, for example, operated a general store not only to sell the manufactured goods he imported but also to dispose of additional items he accepted in exchange for these imports. Like most of his port city merchant peers, Hancock sold textiles, clothing, hardware, rum, and tea among his many wares.

Wars and Trade

During the various wars in the Americas, the range of goods available through merchants helped the British war machine. In the absence of a central quartermaster to organize military purchases, individual British commanders negotiated contracts with merchants to provision their armies with food, clothing, and other essential gear. The merchants also assisted the soldiers by offering payday loans. The slow communication of the era meant that some soldiers ran out of money before receiving their pay. Merchants bought the future wages of soldiers, at a discount, in exchange for providing immediate cash.

Until the eve of the American Revolution, merchants rarely cooperated with each other outside of partnerships. In 1761, the merchants of Boston, Newport, and Providence formed the first monopoly in America in an attempt to form a pool to regulate prices and restrict output of spermaceti candles and other whale products. The venture failed.

Boycotts of British goods had more success. The periodic boycotts that occurred between 1765 and 1774 brought temporary unity among patriot merchants. Neutral and loyalist merchants, estimated to be more than 60 percent of all merchants, did not join these Revolutionary efforts.

Caryn E. Neumann

See also: Board of Trade; Economy, Business, and Labor (Chronology); Economy, Business, and Labor (Essay); Mercantilism;

Trade. *Document:* Petition of London Merchants for Reconciliation with the Colonies (1775).

Bibliography

Findlay, Ronald. *The Triangular Trade and the Atlantic Economy of the Eighteenth Century.* Princeton, NJ: International Finance Section, Department of Economics, Princeton University, 1990.

Pusateri, C. Joseph. *A History of American Business.* Arlington Heights, IL: Harlan Davidson, 1984.

Schlesinger, Arthur M. *The Colonial Merchants and the American Revolution.* New York: Atheneum, 1968.

Metacom

See Philip, King

Methodist Church

In contrast to Roman Catholicism and Protestant denominations that came to America with the first settlers, American Methodism grew out of the First Great Awakening that swept through the colonies during the 1730s and 1740s. Because the Great Awakening separated rigorous religious tradition from spirituality and biblical truth, new groups of believers formed all over, each seeking greater understanding and fulfillment in its members' relationship with God.

An outgrowth of the Anglican (Episcopal) Church, or Church of England, the first Methodist meeting was held in New York City, in the sail loft of a Manhattan rigging house. Five people attended this meeting, organized by Philip Embury.

Two individuals who affected the establishment of this new denomination were John Wesley, an ordained Anglican priest, and George Whitefield, a dynamic preacher and Anglican evangelist. Arriving in the colonies during the 1730s, each developed an enthusiastic following, and people swarmed to hear them preach their transformational message. This asserted that all men and women were equal before God and thus did not require any kind of intermediary—such as a priest or minister—to stand between them and God or interpret the Bible.

Indeed, coupled with the emerging egalitarianism that was developing during the years leading up to and following the American War for Independence, the Methodist message attracted hundreds, then thousands, of followers. While there were approximately 50 to 60 Methodist congregations in 1780, by 1820, there were more than 2,700. After 1820, that number multiplied dramatically, and approximately one of every thirty-six Americans declared himself or herself to be a Methodist.

Francis Asbury, born in England in 1745, became the first Methodist bishop in America. During the Revolutionary War, he tried to remain neutral. But as he had ties to England, he eventually sided with the loyalists. He was able, however, to mediate many of the differences that were arising between the Northern and Southern Methodists. Traveling extensively, he crossed from one end of the country to the other many times. It is estimated that Asbury traveled more than 300,000 miles in twenty-four years. When illness finally overtook him, he had to give up much of his ministry. Asbury died in 1816 at the age of 71.

During the War for Independence, other Methodists also found it hard to remain neutral. John Wesley had urged preachers to refrain from taking a political stand, but that led many to view Methodists as Tories. The perception was unfortunate, since most Methodists believed in individual freedom of conscience and choice.

Methodism also supported the establishment of missions. This outreach garnered new members among the middle class, the poor, and other overlooked populations all over America and abroad. Itinerant preachers traveled the countryside, inviting all to participate in lively camp meetings. The meetings became as much social events as religious ones, especially for those who lived in rural areas. Hymn singing took on great importance at these revivals, and several new hymnals were published, including three volumes by John Newton, whose best-known hymn is "Amazing Grace."

As a result of its democratic tenets and its bold style of worship, slaves and free African Americans flocked to the newly established church. Moreover, Methodists, like Baptists, readily appointed black preachers and incorporated black members into their congregations. John Marrant, the first African American missionary to successfully minister to the Native Americans, converted a number of the Cherokee and was ordained as a Methodist minister in London in May 1785.

Another African American, Richard Allen, was born a slave in Philadelphia in 1760 and eagerly adopted Methodism at age 17. His master, also a Methodist, allowed Allen the opportunity to earn his freedom when he chose to become an itinerant preacher. Though he preached to white and blacks alike, racism was still

The first Methodist Episcopal church in America was built in New York City in 1768 by Barbara Heck and her cousin, Philip Embury. A Wesleyan convert from Ireland, Embury had started preaching there a few years earlier. *(Museum of the City of New York/Bridgeman Art Library)*

a dividing issue, so he founded Bethel Church, a congregation of African Americans, in 1793. It wasn't long before other black congregations formed, and, in 1816, these congregations joined together to form the African Methodist Episcopal Church. Richard Allen served as its first bishop.

In 1780, the American Methodists, like the Quakers, declared that slavery was "contrary to the laws of God, man, and nature." By 1785, the Methodist Church urged its members to free any slaves they owned. Of course, this declaration met with great resentment in the South, so that by 1800, the church withdrew its outspoken opposition.

American Methodism also supported the practice of speaking in tongues, as well as belief in miracles and dreams. These mystical elements of Christianity had long been repressed in other sects and denominations, but they contributed greatly to the religious and spiritual revival that led to the establishment and growth of the Methodist Church.

Gail L. Jenner

See also: Bible; Christ and Christianity; Religion (Chronology); Religion (Essay). *Document:* On the Death of the Rev. Mr. George Whitefield (1770).

Bibliography

Amos, Gary, and Richard Gardner. *Never Before in History: America's Inspired Birth.* Dallas, TX: Haughton, 1998.

Wigger, John H. *Taking Heaven by Storm: Methodism and the Rise of Popular Christianity in America.* New York: Oxford University Press, 1998.

Mexico City

Mexico City, today one of the largest cities in the world, was at the center of a monumental struggle between Europeans and native peoples in the sixteenth century. It has served alternately as the capital of the ancient Mexican empire, the central city in Spain's North American colonies, and Mexico's modern-day capital.

Mexico City's Metropolitan Cathedral, the largest in Latin America, was begun in 1573 with stone from ruined Aztec temples and completed in 1675. It introduced the European baroque and neoclassical architectural styles to New Spain. *(Library of Congress, LC-USZC4-6810)*

Mexico's central valley, which had been inhabited for thousands of years before conquest, was, in the 1500s, the center of a populous, powerful society. Spanish soldiers and their native allies were able to conquer the Mexica, an indigenous group of Nahuatl speakers, in the 1520s, and put a new colonial regime in their place. Mexico City, built on the site of Tenochtitlán, served as a center from which the Spanish could administer their expanding New World empire while they tried to recreate Spanish institutions in the Americas.

In the thirteenth century, the Valley of Mexico was divided into a number of rival city states, of which the Aztecs were one—technically speaking, these were the Mexica. The Mexican state expanded through warfare and intimidation. By the early-sixteenth-century reign of Montezuma II, it encompassed both central and southern Mexico in a vast tributary empire.

Tenochtitlán, the center of the Mexican empire, was built on a group of islands in a shallow lake and was home to about 200,000 residents. The Mexica had also constructed a number of causeways, bridges, and aqueducts to facilitate travel through the huge city and to bring fresh water to its many residents. The city's sacred center featured a number of large stone buildings, including the massive main temple. Like the Castilian society it was about to encounter, Mexican society engaged in intensive agriculture, maintained a strict social hierarchy, including dynastic rulers, and believed in comparable religious systems.

The arrival of the Spanish under Hernando Cortéz in 1519 brought an end to Tenochtitlán. The city itself was the site of several bloody battles, including the Spanish ambush at the feast of Huitzilopochtli. Using a fortuitous combination of epidemic disease and aggrieved native allies, Cortéz was able to conquer Tenochtitlán by 1521. The Spanish enslaved or killed many of the defeated Mexica—feeding priests and nobles to their war dogs was not uncommon—and forced their newly captured slaves to construct a cathedral and palace for Cortéz out of the ruins of their city. The atrocities committed by the Spanish during the conquest are documented in the accounts gathered by conscientious priests, who interviewed subsequent generations of Nahuatl speakers. A notable example of such an account is the Florentine Codex, compiled by Bernardino de Sahagún.

After the conquest, the newly constructed Mexico City became a center of Spanish culture in the Americas, as well as an administrative center from which the Spanish could conduct the business of empire. To this end, Mexico City became the site of the first printing press (1539), the first cathedral (construction began in 1530), and the first university (1551) on the mainland.

Colonial Mexico City was a diverse and intriguing place. Enslavement of the native peoples was abolished in 1542, but they continued to be treated as second-class citizens, and African slaves began to appear in greater numbers. Several social and racial strata existed, partly the result of a dearth of Spanish women in the region and the lower status accorded to *criollos*, or Spaniards born in the New World.

Shortly after the conquest, Franciscan missionaries began to arrive, and other religious orders, including the Augustinians, Dominicans, and Jesuits, followed. The priests, apart from constructing churches and instructing their native parishioners, also helped to develop a distinctly Mexican culture, a hybrid of Spanish and indigenous traditions. The Christians' success was aided by the reported appearance of the Virgin Mary to a Native American in 1531.

Mexico City continued to be the backdrop to a number of crucial social, religious, and economic developments, as Mexico worked out its own national identity. Following the upheavals of the 1810 independence movement, Mexico City became the capital of the modern nation of Mexico.

Matthew Jennings

See also: Aztec; New Spain; Spanish Colonies on Mainland North America (Chronology).

Bibliography

Gibson, Charles. *The Aztecs Under Spanish Rule: A History of the Indians in the Valley of Mexico, 1519–1810.* Palo Alto, CA: Stanford University Press, 1964.
Lockhart, James. *We People Here: Nahuatl Accounts of the Conquest of Mexico.* Berkeley: University of California Press, 1993.
Taylor, Alan. *American Colonies: The Settling of North America.* New York: Viking Penguin, 2001.

Militias

The colonies developed militias for their own defense. Britain could not afford to provide sufficient numbers of His Majesty's troops. Constantly in debt, the mother country also was too far away to justify sending its army to protect the sparsely populated colonies.

In the Crown's opinion, if colonists wanted to journey to an unknown wilderness, they should be prepared to provide for their own defense. Lacking the tax base to support a professional army of their own, colonists turned to the age-old means of local protection—the militia.

Duties of the Militia

The militia provided more than an affordable means of protection. It was also an important aspect of the burgeoning republican philosophy guiding the American colonists. The citizen-solider ideal, long an important aspect of Western philosophy, influenced the founding of colonial America as it had the Greek city-states.

Participation in the militia was understood to be part of a colonist's social contract. An individual, in return for his membership in the society, was obligated to render service unto the community. One way in which this obligation could be fulfilled was through militia service. Colonists were skeptical of a standing, professional army, but a voluntary militia that was locally based and could not be sent into service beyond the local community proved acceptable.

Although all able-bodied men, ages 16 to 60, were expected to serve in their local militias, class biases influenced the militias' organization and the quality of service one was expected to perform. Wealthy, elite units, usually cavalry, served in contradistinction to the common foot soldier, who was most likely from the poorer classes. Foot soldiers were required to provide their own weapons, and many could not. Therefore, it was not uncommon for militiamen to be forced to perform some kind of public service in return for their arms, much like the English working class who were compelled to labor in workhouses in return for charity. In fact, by the time the minutemen began to wage their

At the start of the Revolutionary War, each colonial militia had its own regimental colors and standard. The Philadelphia Light-Horse Troop carried this regimental flag into several major battles. *(New York Public Library, New York)*

uphill battle against British regulars for independence, the ranks of the colonial militias shared more in common with the impressed vagabonds, who comprised the bulk of European armies, than the colonists would have admitted.

Despite the simplicity of its legal organization, the colonial militia was anything but static. The composition, as well as the performance, of militias depended largely on their location. New England found it easier to fill the muster rolls and maintain the militia, due to its concentrated population, than did the more sprawled-out settlements of the Southern colonies. Virginia, for example, experienced a fitful history of militia organization.

In the early days, when men were still starving, it was difficult to convince them of their obligation to serve. Whereas Boston could draft large numbers of men when Native American wars necessitated it, Jamestown could not. When it tried, as it did in the months leading up to Bacon's Rebellion, the colonial government suffered a breakdown. Virginians, it seemed, might be compelled to fight if the potential profits were large enough, and Nathaniel Bacon convinced them that they were. Thus, the Virginia militia, in many ways, resembled European mercenary armies more than the citizen-soldiers of Sparta or even Plymouth.

South Carolina provides another interesting counterpoint to New England. With a more scattered population than either New England or the Chesapeake, the colony faced constant problems in readying its militia to defend against Spanish and Native American encroachments. Although the militia had rallied to save the colony during the Yamasee War in 1715, the colony's assembly reported with apprehension only five years later that South Carolina's 2,000 militiamen were spread over nearly 150 miles. This was still a problem in 1738, when the colony's lieutenant governor, William Bull, reported to the assembly that an effective militia seemed "Inconsistent with a Domestick or Country Life."

South Carolina's biggest problem, however, was not its sparsely populated backcountry. Slavery had become the most formidable obstacle to organizing an effective militia in the Southern colonies. As the black population grew, and in South Carolina began to surpass the white population, the idea of arming blacks became increasingly unpopular, especially after the Stono Rebellion in 1739. The threat of a slave insurrection would continue to loom over the South, preventing Carolinians from arming their slaves and inspiring stringent restrictions on their mobility.

As a result, the majority of able-bodied men in South Carolina were precluded from militia service. Perhaps even more importantly, this caused the Southern militia, particularly in South Carolina where a black majority existed, to become primarily a means of policing and controlling slaves rather than a means of defense. Later, during the antebellum period, the Southern militias would develop into slave patrols as the focus of law enforcement and military organization in the South turned to defending and protecting the institution of slavery.

African Americans and the Militia

Because it posed an ideological affront to the citizen-solider ideal, blacks' inability to serve in the militia might have been a foregone conclusion. African Americans did, however, make a significant impact on the colonial military. Both Massachusetts and Connecticut allowed blacks to enlist in their militias periodically, and, in 1707, the former required slaves to enlist and aid in building roads. Rhode Island also allowed both slaves and free blacks to serve. Even colonies that barred arming slaves and free blacks allowed members of both groups to participate in various forms of military labor or as musicians.

During the Revolution, African Americans fought on both sides. Thousands of slaves won their freedom from the British; the results for those who fought in the war on behalf of the colonists proved less profitable. While some black militiamen were rewarded by individual states, such as New Jersey, with freedom and even land grants, the march from militia service to citizenship was more gradual and indirect. It would take nearly a century—and another war—for black military service to pave a solid road to freedom.

Professional Army Versus Militia

Professional soldiers held notoriously low opinions of the American militiamen. As Daniel Boorstin notes, the American militia was "a most unmilitary outfit by European standards."

Rarely in the history of the colonies had the militias been trained by professional soldiers. The British, understandably, if unwisely, mocked the colonial militias' ragtag assemblage. Even General George Washington thought them an undisciplined lot and frowned upon their desire to elect their own officers. Such democratic impulses apparently had no place within the Continental army.

It was perhaps the French public who became the American militiamen's most outspoken supporters. Their long-standing animosity toward the British made them the colonists' natural allies, and their fascination with America's frontiersman mythology translated into admiration for the minutemen. The French thought every American was an ace with a musket. Their legendary skill with weaponry was matched in the French mind only by their unbridled patriotism. French writers waxed poetic about the hardships militiamen endured— no shoes, ragged clothing, harsh weather, and scarcity of food. France's own burgeoning republicanism no doubt contributed to the glorification of the American cause and the lengths to which its citizen-soldiers would go to obtain independence.

Hardened French soldiers like Lafayette, however, dismissed the militia as "only armed peasants who have sometimes fought," and doubted their ability to fight effectively, much less win a war against Britain. For victory, according to Lafayette, the expertise of professional soldiers was required, and the militia would "be useful only to . . . make noise, and frighten" the enemy.

Still, the colonial militia emerged from the Revolution with a legendary reputation. They had seen considerable action and contributed successfully at the Battle of Saratoga and later at Cowpens. While Army officers on all sides remained reluctant to give much credit for the American victory to the militia, the image of the minutemen, patriots driven by a deep and abiding desire for liberty, endured. The history of the colonial militia remains a complicated one, despite the appealing simplicity of this image.

Carole Emberton

See also: Bunker Hill, Battle of; Lexington and Concord, Battles of; Military and Diplomatic Affairs (Chronology); Military and Diplomatic Affairs (Essay); Native American–European Conflict; Revolutonary War; War.

Bibliography

Boorstin, Daniel J. *The Americans: The Colonial Experience.* New York: Random House, 1958.

Murphy, Orville T. "The French Professional Soldier's Opinion of the American Militia in the War of the Revolution." *Military Affairs* 32:4 (February 1969): 191–98.

Quarles, Benjamin. *The Negro in the American Revolution.* New York: W. W. Norton, 1961.

Shy, John W. "A New Look at Colonial Militia." *William & Mary Quarterly* 3rd ser. 20:2 (April 1963): 175–85.

Whisker, James B. *The American Colonial Militia: The New England Militia, 1606–1785.* Vol. 2. Lewiston, NY: Edwin Mellen Press, 1997.

Mining

See Iron; Precious Metals

Ministers and the Ministry

Ministers who came to the New World in the late seventeenth and early eighteenth centuries landed in a turbulent and disorienting environment. There were various congregations scattered about, competing religious sects, an inadequate number of ministers, and hardly any of the supports for the ministerial authority found in the Old World, such as bishops or consistories to ordain and discipline ministers. Outside New England, there was no theological education or dependable salaries, and no assurance of continuity in any parish. Yet ministers came to the New World with their hopes and the energy to minister to these diverse groups of people with different religious needs, and they attempted to nourish and build a moral base for society, politics, and commerce.

In 1607, Jamestown, Virginia, became the first successful English colony established in America. The Virginia Company of London sponsored these first visionary settlers with the primary purpose of making a profit for the company. These nascent Virginians brought to the New World their Protestant religious institution, known as the Church of England (Anglican Church) and later as the Episcopal Church. (The Church of England had emerged from the 1534 Reformation that occurred during Henry VIII's reign.) Anglican priests began to minister to the colonists and, to some degree, to Native Americans.

Both the Pilgrims and Puritans saw the Church of England as corrupt and too papist. The Pilgrims did not think it possible to reform the Church of England, so they completely separated from England and its state church. In 1620, the Pilgrims obtained a land grant from the Virginia Company and established a colony in Plymouth, Massachusetts.

Some powerful Puritans held stock in the Massachusetts Bay Company, and, under the leadership of John Winthrop, they landed in New England in 1630. The Puritans also sought to reform the Anglican Church. They wanted to discard priestly vestments and the order of worship required by the *Book of Common Prayer*, reserve the Sabbath for worship only, recognize only the sacraments of baptism and communion (called the Lord's Supper), and install a congregational form of government instead of government by the bishops. With this emphasis upon the involvement of the laity in church government, the Puritans became known as the Congregational Church.

While the Puritans had no confidence that their reforms could happen in seventeenth-century England, they did not separate completely from England, as did the Pilgrims. Instead the Puritans came to America with a mission to build "a city upon a hill" to demonstrate the model for a Christian society, and then take that model back to England as the foundation for a new society.

Virginia and New England

Before 1680, there was little public religious life in the colonies except for that supported by the colonial governments. New England and Virginia recognized only the Congregational Churches and the Church of England, respectively, and these churches received tax money to support their ministers and ministry. Ministers functioned as spiritual leaders, teachers, and counselors. Between 1680 and 1770, however, religious diversity upended these two established colonial churches.

As the cultivation of tobacco expanded in Virginia, so did the landowners' prosperity and their appetite for land. The ambition for wealth conflicted with regular church attendance, and Virginians struggled with the importance of religion in their society; ministers had little support from the prosperous squires. In 1680, more than half of the thirty-five parishes in Virginia had no minister, and many had no church building. It took a concentrated effort under the leadership of James Blair, agent of the Anglican bishop in London, to renew the Anglican Church. In the 1690s, Blair led a campaign of church building, new taxes, and laws outlining church administration, which lasted well into the 1720s.

Two issues troubled the Anglican Church about Virginia: the clergy's independence from the squires, who made up the majority of the vestry and controlled the clergy's salaries, and the proposal to appoint an American bishop who would govern the Anglican churches and ordain ministers. This salary issue, called the Parson's Cause, peaked in the 1740s. Ministers were often immigrants without local support and so had to ingratiate themselves to powerful persons. At the same time, without tenure and a guaranteed salary, they could not be independent of the landowners. In 1749, the Virginia legislature approved an act that guaranteed ministers tenure from the time they arrived in the parish. The ministers accepted this law as their charter of independence and aggressively defended it.

The possibility of a colonial bishop appointed by the London Anglican bishop lingered until the eve of the Revolution. By this time, clergy and squires alike feared a curtailment of their liberties by a British bishop. The Anglican Church had been struggling with dissenters, principally the Baptists, and there was a call to renewal among the Anglican churches to begin with the local parishes and their program of worship.

In Virginia, one had to attend church at least once every fourth Sunday. In many areas, however, parishioners did not have the opportunity to attend services overseen by an ordained clergyman every week, because of the scarcity of ministers. The population was scattered across large plantations instead of being largely concentrated in towns and cities, and so ministers often had to travel a circuit of 60 to 100 miles or more, sometimes over rivers and through swamps. These challenges took their toll on a minister's health, morale, and effectiveness.

When the minister was present, he presided over

a worship service structured according to the *Book of Common Prayer.* Ordinarily, the minister preached a sermon based on the biblical texts for the day and remained available for visiting with the parishioners after the service. Relying on the stretched resources of these itinerant ministers, the parish sometimes appeared more symbolic than central to life in Virginia.

In New England, the Great Migration of the 1630s and 1640s attracted more than 20,000 newcomers to the area. The Great Migration was more than just a movement of people across the Atlantic Ocean; this well-planned immigration had a religious dimension to it. The Puritans saw themselves as leaving behind a corrupt, vicious, and dying Old World, to build God's "city upon a hill" in the New World. These people had committed to a new society based on biblical teachings, and they felt obliged to become a model for others.

John Winthrop, a stockholder in the Massachusetts Bay Company and its designated leader, preached a sermon, "A Modell of Christian Charity," on board the *Arabella.* He exhorted the Puritans to observe the covenant, a mutual agreement between them and God. It was believed that if the people were obedient and faithful, they would be favored by God, but if they disobeyed the covenant, they would experience a calamity. The Puritans believed that every event had a cause and that any tragic event, such as drought, a town fire, illness, or pestilence, was the result of breaking the covenant. Ministers interpreted these experiences through scripture and demanded strict obedience to the covenant.

The Puritans chose John Calvin, the Reformation theologian, as the source of their theology. Calvin emphasized the sovereignty of God, the belief that no event happens except by the will of God, as well as the doctrine of predestination. Predestination taught that God had chosen a selected group of people, who would receive forgiveness of their sins and upon death would enter heaven. Those who were baptized and who searched for forgiveness had to adopt a life of piety, examine the biblical teachings and apply them to their lives, and attend church with the hope that one day they would feel confident of their election. With this confidence in their election, then they would publicly "claim" their conversion before the congregation. These converts then became "saints" with the right to vote on church and public issues.

Such practices led to an emphasis upon seeking new knowledge of the scriptures and following the guidance of the minister. Ministers had a heavy responsibility to study the Bible and its commentaries in order to teach and lead the people to an assurance of conversion. Puritans expected their ministers to be educated and able to interpret the Bible, and they opened Harvard University in 1636 with this aim. Later, some Puritans felt that Harvard had strayed from orthodoxy, and so they established Yale College in 1701.

Attendance at church was mandatory, and an absentee could be fined. Puritan meetinghouses were plain—no padded pews or religious icons, nothing to distract the worshiper from concentrating on the Word of God. The church represented the nucleus of Puritan life positioned in the center of town. The typical worship service included prayers, readings from the Bible, communion, and a sermon that followed a strict logical pattern: text, explanation, and then application.

Puritans appreciated a good, lively, thought-provoking sermon. As the spiritual leader of the community, ministers used several types of sermons— Sunday sermons (which could be up to two hours in length), Thursday sermons, election-day sermons, fast-day sermons, and special-occasion sermons—and they also conducted weekly catechism classes for the youth. Thursday sermons often were teaching sessions on some topic of interest to ministers and adult churchgoers, such as prophetic texts in Daniel and Revelation. These sermons provided an opportunity for the congregation and other ministers to hear sermons on difficult topics.

In New England, the average weekly churchgoer could hear approximately 7,000 sermons in his or her lifetime, which totaled 15,000 hours of concentrated attention to the Word. The Puritan communities had no competing public voices of a different viewpoint; the sermon was the only regular voice of authority.

By 1660, New England ministers had begun to notice a decline in church attendance and were concerned that the Congregational churches might lose influence in their communities. Factors that influenced this decline included increasing commercial activities, population growth that increased the numbers of non-Puritans, and the movement westward for land by the second and third generations, which allowed them independence from their parents. Many Puritan congregations watched the children of older members ignore the churches or reject them outright.

The ministers began to preach "jeremiads," sermons of complaint and remorse for the "falling away" from biblical teachings, emphasizing the need to repent and reclaim the covenant. Because of the paucity of new members, some ministers established the Half-way Covenant. This allowed children of baptized members to be baptized with the expectation that these children would eventually claim their own conversion and become full members of the church. Until then, these unconverted children could not participate in communion or vote on church matters, privileges granted only to the converted "saints."

Not all Puritans accepted the Half-way Covenant because they thought it compromised the experience of conversion; however, Solomon Stoddard, pastor of the Northampton church, effectively used the Halfway Covenant to gain new more members. Stoddard allowed anyone of good character to take communion and assumed that such participation would aid in the quest for conversion. After Stoddard's death in 1729, his grandson Jonathan Edwards, a theologian and philosopher, became pastor of the Northampton church.

First Great Awakening, Religious Diversity, and Revolution

In 1734, Jonathan Edwards noticed that something distinct and strange had happened in his Northampton community. This "Surprising Work of God" became known as "The First Great Awakening." While Edwards was preaching one Sunday about what he saw as the sins of the town's youth, the congregation suddenly became emotional and penitent and sought forgiveness for their sins. Without discarding his belief in God's sovereignty, Edwards understood this phenomenon as God's special work, affecting this generation. The emotion seemed to be necessary for people to have confidence in their salvation, although Edwards did not think that conversion stood alone on emotional demonstrations. He stressed that a change of mind was not the same as a change of heart, which implied deep feeling, a new direction for one's life. He concluded that one experiences both a mental and an emotional change in conversion.

To complement Edwards's unusual experience in Northampton, other ministers who related more to the common people became popular. England's George Whitefield, an Anglican minister, attracted large audiences in the South and New England. He preached the possibility and necessity of individual conversion for anyone with faith in God. Those who heard Whitefield praised him for his sermons' common language, his extemporaneous prayers, and his ability to establish strong rapport with his audiences.

In the Middle colonies, William Tennent Sr. and his four sons popularized the message of individual conversion by faith. A Scotsman, Tennent came to Pennsylvania and opened a one-room schoolhouse called the Log College in 1730. His son Gilbert's most famous sermon, "The Danger of an Unconverted Ministry," specifically addressed the question of who was best qualified to interpret biblical truth. For the Tennents, only the converted minister, regardless of education, had the necessary qualification to interpret the Bible.

Emotional demonstrations during these revivalistic services prompted a disagreement between the "Old Lights" and "New Lights." The New Lights, such as Edwards, Whitefield, and the Tennents, accepted the combination of faith and emotion as authentic conversion experiences in those who changed their lives. The more traditional Old Lights rejected these emotional conversions as shallow in commitment and without enough substance to sustain the faith. Charles Chauncy of Boston's First Church represented the Old Lights' rational position, which primarily focused on "understanding" and strict clerical control over congregations. Edwards responded that the interconnections of thought and emotion were such that neither existed without the other. But even Edwards admitted that it was easier for converts to talk like saints than to act like saints.

The First Great Awakening brought Christianity to many Americans who otherwise might not have had the opportunity to hear they could decide for themselves whether or not to become a Christian. It also raised questions about the qualifications for the ministry. One had to ask what level of education ministers really needed and whether the experience of conversion alone was enough. This upheaval over ministerial authority received more attention as different denominations gained more members.

From the 1740s on, the role of the minister as the authoritarian figure in the colonies depended on what denomination people selected as the home for their religious faith. Ministers also contributed to the ideas and emotions that fueled the Revolutionary War.

In 1750, even before Great Britain tightened its control over colonial trade, Jonathan Mayhew, pastor of Boston's affluent West Church, proclaimed the duty of resisting a tyrannical government in his sermon "Discourse Concerning Unlimited Submission." He called upon Christians everywhere to stand up for justice when it was in jeopardy. If governments existed for the purpose of protecting the rights and future of the people, then nothing good could result from a government that demanded its citizens submit when that government ruled in a way that was not best for the people.

In 1770, other ministers denounced the Boston

Massacre, when British soldiers fired into a crowd, killing five colonists. One minister, John Lathrop of Old North Church, pronounced God's condemnation of this murder and characterized it as akin to that of Cain murdering his brother Abel, as written in Genesis 3:10. Ministers felt obligated not to ignore this act of treachery and proclaimed that if Britain did not change its policies of violence, then it should not rule these colonies.

James A. Denton

See also: Bible; Christ and Christianity; God; Great Awakening; Religion (Chronology); Religion (Essay); Sermons.

Bibliography

Ahlstrom, Sydney. *A Religious History of the American People.* New Haven, CT: Yale University Press, 1972.

Anderson, Virginia DeJohn. *New England's Generation: The Great Migration and the Formation of Society and Culture in the Seventeenth Century.* Cambridge, UK: Cambridge University Press, 1991.

Bonomi, Patricia U. *Under the Cope of Heaven: Religion, Society, and Politics in Colonial America.* New York: Oxford University Press, 1986.

Butler, Jon. *Becoming America: The Revolution Before 1776.* Cambridge, MA: Harvard University Press, 2000.

Gaustad, Edwin, and Leigh Schmidt. *The Religious History of America: The Heart of the American Story from Colonial Times to Today.* Rev. ed. San Francisco: HarperCollins, 2002.

Isaac, Rhys. *The Transformation of Virginia, 1740–1790.* New York: W. W. Norton, 1982.

Smith, John E., Harry S. Stout, and Kenneth P. Minkema, eds. *A Jonathan Edwards Reader.* New Haven, CT: Yale University Press, 1995.

Stout, Harry S. *The New England Soul: Preaching and Religious Culture in Colonial New England.* New York: Oxford University Press, 1986.

Missions

Each of the major colonial powers—England, France, and Spain—saw in North America a prime opportunity to spread Christianity. In fact, Christianity became one of the tools of conquest in some parts of the Americas.

The ways in which each nation went about spreading the Christian faith varied dramatically. Accordingly, native peoples responded to European missionaries in different, culturally specific ways. Occasionally, tribes in close proximity to European settlements accepted missionaries as a way to lessen the impact of coloniza-tion on their communities. Other groups resisted missionaries' efforts from the outset, and some Native Americans incorporated aspects of Christianity into their own worldviews.

Spanish Missions

The Spanish were the first group of Europeans to missionize in the Americas. Franciscans (members of the order of St. Francis of Assisi) arrived in 1493 on Columbus's second voyage. In 1523, two years after the conquest of Mexico's central valley, Franciscans are noted as working in New Spain. A 1526 Spanish edict required that two priests accompany any exploration party in the Americas.

In the mid-sixteenth century, following run-ins with colonial officials and settlers in Mexico, the Franciscans moved into more remote areas of the empire, including Florida and New Mexico. The Royal Orders for New Discoveries, issued in 1573, declared that spreading Christianity was the primary motivation for colonizing and outlawed conquest. Accordingly, missionaries, now the spearhead of Spanish colonization, were to enter new lands first and pacify the native population with the Gospel.

In 1573, Franciscans began serious mission work in Florida, and, by 1598, they were constructing missions among the Pueblo peoples of New Mexico. Jesuits worked briefly in native communities in Florida and present-day Arizona, but the bulk of missionary work in Spanish America was performed by Franciscans.

The process of establishing missions was accompanied by rituals, intended to demonstrate the power of the priests. In 1629, at Cíbola, a Zuni pueblo, the colonial governor and a handful of accompanying soldiers kissed the friars' feet. A priest then announced that he had come to free the Zunis from their ignorance. Since their refusal to accept missionaries in the time of Coronado had resulted in war, Zuni leaders decided to accept a missionary among them. The missionaries in New Mexico became convinced that they were on their way to destroying native religion entirely and building a new republic of Christian peoples. The 1680 Pueblo Revolt, largely a response to Spanish religious intolerance, proved them wrong.

In Florida—the current state and parts of present-day Georgia, South Carolina, and Alabama—the Franciscans established missions in existing Native American villages. By 1675, there were four mission provinces in Florida: Guale, Timucua, Apalachee, and Apalachicola. In mission towns, Native American men

English missionaries like John Eliot shared the conviction of Spanish and French counterparts that their particular brand of Christianity was superior. Puritan missionary efforts reflected their emphasis on literacy and education. *(Brown Brothers, Sterling, Pennsylvania)*

and women were expected to adopt Spanish modes of dress and agriculture as a way to prove that they were moving toward civilization as the Spaniards defined it. The Franciscans worked diligently to dismantle Native American cultures, and they tried especially hard to convert native leaders and children, believing that these groups could turn the tide in the Franciscans' favor.

As elsewhere, native peoples chose to accept Christianity on their own terms, selecting pieces of the doctrine that meshed with their own cultural perspectives and rejecting tenets that did not. Some native communities went along with the missionaries, hoping to gain access to a new realm of spiritual power. Tribes that moved regularly could spend part of their time in the missions and then relocate when the priests' demands became too burdensome.

The missions struggled against the effects of disease and slave raids by the English, which led to the decline of the mission provinces over the following decades. The missionaries also became less important as the Spanish began to rely more heavily on soldiers to colonize North America.

By the eighteenth century, the Spanish missions, driven by the Franciscans and funded by the Crown, had brought about a great number of conversions in Florida and New Mexico. To what extent the people who lived on the missions actually accepted Christianity is harder to define.

French Missions

The French, broadly speaking, began their North American colonies as commercial ventures. The early explorers, such as Jacques Cartier, preached their own versions of Christianity, but there is no evidence that Catholic priests were involved in their efforts. By the seventeenth century, the French were relying on a mix of trade and Catholicism to colonize

In 1608, the French under Champlain moved into the St. Lawrence River valley and founded Quebec. From this base, the French would send out hundreds of missionaries into Iroquois lands, the Great Lakes, and North America's vast interior. The Jesuits, who arrived in 1625, were the primary, but not sole, missionary order in New France. The Recollects (Franciscans) worked throughout the colony as well.

Jesuits working in New France faced chronic difficulties in manpower, supplies, and stability from one administration to the next. New France also faced continual raids from the Five Nations Iroquois, who, at that time, were loosely affiliated with the Dutch at Albany. Conversely, without its Native American population, New France would have been little more than a name on a map.

Missionary activity, and pretty much all colonial activity, in New France was closely connected to the fur trade, which developed first in the Iroquois lands and later in the Great Lakes. To facilitate trade and conversion, the French formed a close bond with the Huron, an Iroquoian-speaking group, though not one of the Five Nations. The French missionaries perceived the Huron as particularly receptive targets. Other Iroquois, Algonquins, and Montagnais, however, were thought to be more hostile to the gospel.

Like the Spanish Franciscans farther to the south, French missionaries believed that native lifeways needed to be replaced with European ones in order to facilitate conversion to Christianity. The native peoples of New France were expected to participate in Catholic institutional life by enrolling in religious schools. Some Native American boys and girls were sent to French families in Quebec—and even France—to receive their Christian education.

By the middle of the seventeenth century, seminaries were failing for lack of students, and the Jesuits adopted a new approach, one more recognizable to students of colonial history. The Jesuits began to work closely with the fur trading company, and they began to educate Native American adults, as well as children.

The Jesuits also came to understand that Christianity was not wholly incompatible with a wide range of native faiths, and sent missionaries out alone or in small pairs to live with bands of Native Americans. Both sedentary and nomadic missions were to be set apart from French colonial society, largely because of the perceived bad influence of French settlers.

The result of the shift in policy was that the French were able to reap fur trade profits from a huge chunk of North America, while using little in the way of French military force or European settlers. At mission communities, Jesuits also allowed Native American men and women some leeway in practicing a syncretic form of Catholicism; native rituals coexisted with, and took on new meaning from, Catholic ceremonies.

English Missions

The English entered North America after the Spanish and the French. They, too, were confident that their own particular form of Christianity was superior to those in Europe and far superior to the religions practiced by Native Americans.

For decades, scholars wrote that the English, French, and Spanish modes of colonization were fundamentally different. It was believed that since the Spanish and French were interested in conquest and the fur trade, they were more concerned with religion's pacifying effects; as the English were settlers, and their industrious farms expanded into Native American territory, they left no room for compromise with native religions. Recent scholarship has shown that the English *were* concerned about the natives' spiritual well-being.

The first and most famous English missionary efforts spread from the Puritan colonies at Plymouth and Massachusetts Bay. The English, like other Europeans, found North America's indigenous population sorely lacking the accoutrements of civilization. The Puritans did believe that the Native Americans could be educated out of their backwardness, although the conversion process might be long and arduous. As in the Spanish and French mind-sets, the natives had to quit acting so much like natives if serious religious reeducation was to take place.

In the 1640s, John Eliot and his associates helped to establish towns of "praying Indians," most notably Natick, near some English settlements. From this privileged vantage point, Native Americans in New England could learn about civilized life in preparation for their conversion. John Eliot also translated the Bible into Algonquian and published a series of fictional dialogues between native people concerning the basic tenets of Puritan faith. Literacy and education were crucial aspects of English Puritan faith, and their missions reflected these goals. Over time, missionary efforts suffered as English settlements expanded and placed new pressures on native communities. Tensions boiled over in the 1670s during King Philip's War, a bloody conflict that divided New England along racial lines.

Comparing Missionary Efforts

Every missionary endeavor in North America must be seen as a combination of forces. Europeans varied in their approach to native peoples. The Spanish came first and were the most aggressive and successful in converting Native Americans to a European faith, in this case, Roman Catholicism. The French and English who followed were neither as determined to convert nor as thorough in their missionary efforts. The Jesuits, who spearheaded the French effort, were a determined group, but they suffered from a lack of money, missionaries, and government support. The English, while not entirely unconcerned with native conversion, were the weakest of the three main European colonizers as far as missionary work was concerned.

As for Native American acceptance of European missionary ideas, the record is mixed. Generally, native peoples tended to pick and choose, adopting those pieces of European religion they admired, while at the same time striving to maintain their political independence and, later, their cultural autonomy.

Matthew Jennings

See also: Christ and Christianity; Dominicans; Franciscans; God; Jesuits; Native American–European Relations; Religion (Chronology); Religion (Essay); Serra, Fray Junípero; Spanish Colonies on Mainland North America (Chronology).

Bibliography

Axtell, James. *The Invasion Within: The Contest of Cultures in Colonial North America.* New York: Oxford University Press, 1985.

Weber, David J. *The Spanish Frontier in North America.* New Haven, CT: Yale University Press, 1992.

Mississippi River

The Mississippi River, which flows from northern Minnesota to the Gulf of Mexico, is the fourth-longest river on earth. It also has one of the largest drainage areas, ranking behind only the Congo and the Amazon. Just before and during the colonial period of American history, the Mississippi was at the heart of the largest Native American civilization north of Mexico, a crucial piece of France's North American empire, and one of many areas that Native Americans, the French, and the English struggled to control during the eighteenth century.

The human history of the Mississippi River began thousands of years ago when Paleo-Indians migrated into the region. Between 700 and 1250, the city of Cahokia flourished on the Mississippi River in what is now present-day Collinsville, Illinois, across the river from today's St. Louis. Cahokia, a theocracy, exacted tribute from tens of thousands of people in the surrounding area. It also participated in, and perhaps exerted some control over, trade networks that stretched across North America. Cahokian agriculture consisted of corn, beans, and squash, and these foodstuffs were supplemented by hunting and fishing.

Cahokia was the largest of what have been labeled Mississippian cultures. From 700 to 1400 (and beyond, in a few cases), paramount chiefdoms in the Mississippian mold dominated much of North America. Perhaps overextended or facing food shortages, Cahokia began to decline around 1150, and, by 1250, was all but abandoned. Smaller polities, ones that more closely resembled historic-era tribes, were the main political entities along the Mississippi River when Europeans arrived several hundred years later. Natchez, another Mississippian center on the river, was a notable exception: it retained elements of Mississippian culture into its encounter with the French.

The Spanish maintained a lukewarm interest in the Mississippi River. De Soto crossed the river in his 1539–1542 *entrada*, and his body may have been sunk in the river. The French, however, were the first Europeans to seize on the Mississippi's importance as a piece of their colonial empire. At the end of the seventeenth century, the French, trying to counter British endeavors on North America's Atlantic coast and Spanish colonies throughout the Americas, began to explore the region near the mouth of the river. Pierre Le Moyne d'Iberville established Biloxi in 1699, for instance. Marquette, Jolliet, and La Salle also tried to increase French awareness of the region to promote French trade and the Catholic Church. Along the upper Mississippi and in the adjoining Great Lakes region, the fur trade flourished, while farther south a wider range of economic activities occurred.

By the early eighteenth century, the river was at

the center of a contest among the French, English, and Native Americans for control of the region. Matters came to a head when traders operating out of Carolina armed the Chickasaw. The resulting conflict left 1,800 Chickasaws dead and another 500 enslaved. The French were able to secure alliances with many of the tribes along the Mississippi River in the early eighteenth century, as they were doing at approximately the same time in the St. Lawrence River valley.

One often-overlooked component of the French North American empire is Illinois country. Though its French population was smaller than those at Montreal, Quebec, and New Orleans, a substantial number of priests, soldiers, and settlers were moving through the region by the middle of the eighteenth century. Towns that were founded primarily as missions and for trading purposes (such as Cahokia/Fort St. Louis and Kaskaskia) were becoming agricultural settlements peopled by a mix of French laypeople, clergy, and Native Americans of various tribes. Since neither Native Americans nor Europeans could control the region, one scholar has labeled it a "middle ground."

The fragile middle ground collapsed in the wake of the French and Indian War. The French gave up their North American possessions. The native peoples living along the Mississippi River were faced with an aggressive, expansionist set of colonies and, later, an American nation intent on displacing tribes to the west of the Mississippi. The Mississippi River took on symbolic meaning in Jacksonian America as the dividing line between the white and Native American worlds.

Matthew Jennings

See also: French; French Colonies on Mainland North America (Chronology); Louisiana; New Orleans; Ohio Country; St. Louis.

Bibliography

"Cahokia." In *The Encyclopedia of North American Indians*, edited by Frederick E. Hoxie. Boston: Houghton Mifflin, 1996.

Ekberg, Carl J. *French Roots in the Illinois Country: The Mississippi Frontier in Colonial Times.* Urbana: University of Illinois Press, 1998.

Usner, Daniel H., Jr. *Indians, Settlers and Slaves in a Frontier Exchange Economy: The Lower Mississippi Valley Before 1783.* Chapel Hill: University of North Carolina Press, 1992.

Moctezuma

See Montezuma II

Mohawk

The Mohawk were a branch of the Iroquoian language group in North America and one of five founding members of the Iroquois Confederacy. Their villages lay northeast of Lake Erie in what is now upstate New York. Because of their easternmost position in the lands of the confederacy, the Mohawk were known as the "Eastern Doorkeepers." Mohawk was the name applied to the people by their Algonquin enemies; their real name is Kanien'Kehake, meaning "The People of the Flint."

Like other Eastern woodlands native peoples, the Mohawk practiced a mixed subsistence economy— hunting and gathering, supplemented by agriculture. Labor was divided between the sexes, with women doing the farming and food gathering while men hunted and fought as warriors. Households and clans were matrilineal. Clan mothers had great power over the domestic sphere and even wielded significant influence over the tribal leadership.

The main factor that enhanced the influence and power of the Mohawk in the region was their development, along with the other Iroquois Five Nations, of a more complex political and diplomatic structure. According to Iroquois traditional lore, it was the Mohawk leader Hiawatha who established the Great League or Confederacy. This probably occurred in the early sixteenth century. Prior to this, there were numerous and destructive wars between the Five Nations. Hiawatha also allegedly established the main diplomatic instrument for preventing such conflicts—the condolence ceremony, whereby ritual and tribute settled blood feuds before they escalated into war. Once they were at peace with one another, the Iroquois turned their aggressions outward.

Young Iroquois warriors were always eager to earn the prestige that came with victory in battle. In addition to honor, warfare also brought captives who replenished the tribe's population, and, according to Native American religious beliefs, enhanced the tribe's spiritual power.

By the seventeenth century, the need for captives was more pressing because diseases brought to North America by Europeans were rapidly diminishing the population of the native peoples. Clan mothers demanded more captives to replace those in their communities lost to smallpox and other epidemics. Tribal leaders complied by attacking their Algonquin neighbors and other Iroquoian-speaking tribes that were not part of the league. However, these conflicts, called "mourning wars," were trivial compared to the much greater intertribal wars that resulted from the expansion of the European fur trade in the Great Lakes region.

The French were the first Europeans to establish trading settlements in the region, founding Quebec in 1608. Their presence had an instant effect on the native population. French traders formed alliances with the Algonquian-speaking peoples north of the Great Lakes. The Huron, an Iroquoian tribe, broke with the Five Nations and joined the French trading bloc. The allies of New France were the most able hunters of the region and had access to the richest hunting grounds for beaver, but the men of the Five Nations were the better warriors. Effectively shut out of the fur trade, the Mohawk and their Five Nations brethren began attacking trading parties of French-allied neighbors, seizing fur-laden canoes on their way to Quebec. With superior weapons provided by French traders, the enemies of the Mohawk began to turn the tide and defeated the Mohawk in 1609.

Disaster for the Five Nations Iroquois was averted when a new European power entered the colonial arena in North America. In 1614, the Dutch established a permanent trading colony at New Amsterdam and built Fort Orange on the Hudson River near Mohawk lands. The Dutch became the principal rival to the French on the St. Lawrence River for access to the furs of the Great Lakes. The Iroquois Confederacy established trading ties with the Dutch, who could supply them with the weapons their enemies to the north received from New France. The region now became a battleground between the two commercial-military alliances.

During the intense and ferocious "Beaver Wars" that ensued, the Mohawk became the military arm of the Dutch trading empire. As the easternmost member of the league, the Mohawk became middlemen, providing Dutch guns and other manufactured goods to the Five Nations. As their own importance within the confederacy was enhanced, the Mohawk led fierce attacks on the Algonquin and Huron allies of the French. The desire for access to lucrative trade was reinforced by the need to replace their own growing losses to war and disease with captives. The Five Nations crushed the Huron, destroying entire villages and adopting the surviving women and children. In doing so, they also cemented their own central position in the European trading system.

In the 1660s, new challenges confronted the Iroquois. The English conquered the Nations' trading partners, the Dutch. Commercial rivals, the Susque-hannock and Mahican, succeeded in beating back Iroquois assaults. Furthermore, French reprisals against Mohawk villages had begun to take a heavy toll on the tribe's population. According to some estimates, the Mohawk lost six out of every ten warriors. Never again would the tribe be as dominant as it was in the 1640s. To escape these attacks, many Mohawks fled to Canada and joined "praying Indian" villages supervised by the Jesuits.

During the eighteenth century, the Mohawk and the confederacy adapted and recovered their central position in the fur trade. They adopted a strategy of playing the British and French against one another to negotiate more generous trade concessions. By remaining neutral in Anglo-French conflicts, the Iroquois hoped to have the best of both worlds. The fall of New France in 1763 irreparably undermined this strategy.

During the American Revolution, the Mohawk, led by their chief, Joseph Brant, split with the Five Nations and gave their support to the British. When the colonists won the war, it spelled doom for the Mohawk in their traditional homeland. After the war, remaining members of the tribe relocated to Canada, where the British government rewarded them for their support with land.

David Ballew

See also: Iroquois Confederacy; Native American–European Conflict; Native American–European Relations; Native Americans.

Bibliography

Axtell, James. *The Invasion Within: The Contest of Cultures in Colonial North America.* New York: Oxford University Press, 1985.

Nash, Gary. *Red, White, and Black: The Peoples of Early North America.* 4th ed. Upper Saddle River, NJ: Prentice Hall, 2000.

Trigger, Bruce G., and Wilcombe E. Washburn, eds. *The Cambridge History of the Native Peoples of the Americas.* Vol. 1, *North America.* New York: Cambridge University Press, 1996.

Mohegan

The Mohegan Indians lived along what became the Thames River in southeastern Connecticut and developed as close relations of the Pequot people. In 1600, the population of the two tribes totaled about 16,000.

In 1626, Uncas, son of the Mohegan sachem,

married the daughter of Tatobem, the Pequot sachem. While this cemented their connections in the fur trade, it laid the groundwork for future conflict. Uncas began to contest Pequot authority, and, when the Dutch killed Tatobem in 1634, he and others "defected" to the Narragansett. When the English established Fort Saybrook, Uncas saw an opportunity to gain power in the region.

In 1636, Uncas offered to help the English fight against the Pequot, and, in May 1637, he joined the force that attacked Mystic Fort, killing many and scattering the survivors. As the campaign continued, Uncas sought to gather as many as of his people as possible to build up Mohegan power, and his became the leading Native American group in eastern Connecticut. New conflicts erupted with the Narragansett, led by Miantonomo, as the two tribes became rivals.

In 1638, the English colonists summoned Uncas and Miantonomo to a conference in Hartford. The resulting treaty required both to submit disputes to the English. Soon, rumors, possibly orchestrated by Uncas, convinced the English that Miantonomo was forging a hostile alliance with the feared Mohawks. In July 1643, when simmering hostilities flared into war and the Mohegan captured Miantonomo, the Puritans authorized his execution and promised to protect Uncas against retribution.

Miantonomo's death did not result in peace. In February 1644 and May 1645, Narragansett war parties hit Mohegan villages, retreating only when the English intervened. The Mohegan, in turn, battled Narragansett allies, including the Pocumtuck and Nipmuc in western and central southern New England. Uncas also continued to pressure Pequot remnants and to gain dominance over the Montauk on eastern Long Island.

While this warfare gradually came to an end, the colonists continued to suspect Uncas's independence (he barred Puritan missionaries) and aggressive ambitions. Yet the Mohegan remained loyal military allies, and, at the outbreak of King Philip's War, they offered their assistance. As in the Pequot War, the Mohegan provided important support for English forces and carried out their own attacks on the enemy. After the war, the elderly Uncas and his son, Owaneco, reconfirmed their allegiance to Connecticut. Uncas died around 1685.

At the turn of the century, about 600 Mohegans remained, but their lands were shrinking rapidly. Tensions emerged as Connecticut began giving white settlers grants of land never sold by the tribe. In 1703, Owaneco accused the assembly of land fraud, and, two years later, the Mohegan filed suit against the colony. In 1707, a royal commission ruled in favor of the tribe. Connecticut appealed to the Privy Council, where the case died.

Additional tensions developed in 1720, when New London colonists reported hearing gunshots and seeing threats in the faces of their Mohegan neighbors. The Mohegan sachem assured the governor that his people were simply building a fort against Mohawk attack. But the colonists remained fearful; three years later, they limited how far Native Americans could travel from their villages. Connecticut authorities also intervened in Mohegan politics to ensure that their favorite, Ben Uncas II, became sachem.

From this point on, most Mohegans added their objection to the colony's meddling to their anger over its land grab. The tribe renewed its pleas against Connecticut in the 1730s. While the initial verdict in 1738 favored the colony, appeals continued the case for thirty-five years.

The Mohegan, like other Connecticut tribes, initially resisted English religion and culture. But gradually, as the land filled with colonists who reshaped the environment and economy, these Native Americans began adopting Anglo-American ways. Some became interested in Christianity, particularly after 1740, when the Great Awakening offered a sense of spiritual equality and renewal. Several graduated from Eleazar Wheelock's Indian school, including the famed Samson Occom, who became a tribal leader.

By the mid-eighteenth century, festering political conflicts and the religious awakening drove a growing wedge between conservatives and reformers, resulting in the division of the Mohegan into two villages, Johnstown and Benstown. At the former, men led by Occum began to build farms, fence land, and plow fields. Both groups called public meetings and wrote petitions to the legislature to discredit their opponents, weakening the tribe overall.

In spring 1773 came the final rejection of the tribe's land case, and Occum and other Native American reformers began to lay plans for a new community among the Oneidas in New York. While the war interrupted their plans, afterward many left for Brothertown. Only 200 Mohegan remained in Connecticut by 1790, when the last 2,300 acres they controlled as a tribe were divided up into individual plots for families.

Daniel R. Mandell

See also: Native American–European Conflict; Native American–European Relations; Native Americans.

Bibliography

De Forest, John W. *History of the Indians of Connecticut, From the Earliest Known Period to 1850.* Hartford, CT: William Jason Hamersley, 1851.

Salisbury, Neal. *Manitou and Providence: Indians, Europeans, and the Making of New England, 1500–1643.* New York: Oxford University Press, 1982.

Weinstein, Laurie. "Land Politics and Power: The Mohegan Indians in the Seventeenth and Eighteenth Centuries." *Man in the Northeast* 42 (1991): 9–16.

Montcalm, Louis-Joseph (1712–1759)

Louis-Joseph, marquis de Montcalm-Gozon de Saint-Véran, commander of French troops in North America, defeated the British in several key battles early in the French and Indian War. But his loss at the Battle of Quebec in September 1759—in which he was killed—signaled the end of French rule in Canada. *(Library of Congress, LC-USZ61-239)*

Louis-Joseph, marquis de Montcalm-Gozon de Saint-Véran, was born February 29, 1712, at Château de Candiac, his family's estate. Of a distinguished lineage of military men, Montcalm received a strong classical education as a youth before joining his father's regiment in 1727. With delicate health as a child, Montcalm grew robust, though of slight build, as a soldier. He first saw action in 1733 at the sieges of Kehl and Philipsburg.

In 1735, his father died, and Montcalm, the only heir, returned to Candiac to manage the estate between campaigns. He married Angélique-Louise Talon de Boulay in 1736, and they had ten children, six of whom survived childhood.

During the War of the Austrian Succession, Montcalm served as a captain in Bohemia in 1741, where his meritorious service earned him appointment as a Knight of St. Louis. Later, as colonel of the Auxerrois Regiment in Italy, he was badly wounded and captured by the Austrians at the Battle of Plaisance (Piacenza) in 1746. Upon his parole in France, Louis XV promoted him to brigadier general. In a later battle, he was again wounded, but recovered, and after the Peace of Aix-la-Chapelle in 1748, he returned to Candiac and his wife, children, and mother, with whom he maintained a strong attachment throughout his life.

On January 25, 1756, Louis XV appointed Montcalm as commander of North American troops. Though not the most brilliant or heralded general in France, Montcalm was a proven, experienced, and competent professional officer. Passionate and quick-tempered, he was also quick to regain his composure, and calm and courageous in battle. He sailed from Brest at the head of nearly 1,200 French regulars on April 3, arriving in Canada on May 13.

Once in North America, Montcalm maintained a tense, combative relationship with Governor-General Pierre de Rigaud de Vaudreuil de Cavagnial, marquis de Vaudreuil. Vaudreuil and Montcalm came into conflict over strategy and the proper use of colonial militia and their Native American allies. Montcalm disdained the discipline and fighting character of the colonial militia, and he distrusted the Native Americans. He adhered to a European view of civilized warfare and considered the natives' styles of warfare as uncivilized, barbarous, and lacking in strategic soundness. His failure to take advantage of Native Americans' talents and skills, so successful in the North American wilderness, severely hindered French attempts to maintain a substantial presence on the continent.

Shortly after landing in Canada and marshaling his forces, Montcalm dispatched troops and trusted subordinates to defend Forts Carillon, Frontenac, and Niagara on the Canadian frontier in order to allow him security to assume the offensive. In his first campaign, he captured Oswego on August 14, 1756. He then attacked Fort William Henry, at the foot of Lake Champlain. Using European siege tactics, he forced the fort to capitulate on August 19, 1757. Perhaps his most glorious victory occurred at Ticonderoga on July 8, 1758, when his greatly outnumbered troops, well fortified in trenches and behind an elaborate abatis, delivered a crushing defeat to 15,000 British soldiers.

In 1759, while overwhelming British forces captured outlying French forts, Montcalm consolidated his greatly outnumbered troops at Quebec. Situated high on bluffs overlooking the river, Montcalm skillfully repulsed several assaults ordered by British General James Wolfe. From June 28 to September 12, the French frustrated British attempts to take the city. Montcalm hoped to keep the British at bay until the onset of Quebec's early winter forced them to withdraw. He wished to avoid an open-field battle, because he recognized the disciplined, highly trained British Redcoats had an enormous advantage over his mélange of provincial troops, Native American allies, and assorted French regulars.

On September 13, in a clever maneuver, the British sailed past Quebec and scaled the heights behind the town. At dawn, Montcalm learned to his dismay that nearly 4,500 British troops were arrayed in line of battle on the Plains of Abraham in the city's rear. Because the British cut off his supply lines, Montcalm had to meet them in a field battle. Failing to wait for potential reinforcements from his aide, Bougainville, who had 3,000 troops a few miles in the British rear, Montcalm attacked impetuously and suffered a decisive defeat.

As he tried to rally his retreating troops at the city's gate, Montcalm was mortally wounded in the groin and leg. He died the next morning. Quebec formally surrendered on September 18, hastening the end of French resistance in North America.

Judkin Browning

See also: Canada; French; French and Indian War; French Colonies on Mainland North America (Chronology); Military and Diplomatic Affairs (Chronology); Military and Diplomatic Affairs (Essay); Quebec City; Wolfe, James.

Bibliography

Anderson, Fred. *Crucible of War: The Seven Years' War and the Fate of Empire in British North America, 1754–1766.* New York: Alfred A. Knopf, 2000.

Lewis, Merriwether Liston. *Montcalm, the Marvelous Marquis.* New York: Vantage, 1961.

Parkman, Francis. *Montcalm and Wolfe.* Boston: Little, Brown, 1902.

Montezuma II (1466–1520)

The last ruler of the Aztecs, Montezuma II ruled over an empire that was at the height of its power when he ascended to the throne in 1502. Seventeen years later, Montezuma II greeted the Spanish conquistador Hernando Cortéz at his capital Tenochtitlán. After attempting to buy off Cortéz, he was imprisoned by the Spanish conquistador and eventually killed by his own people (so Spanish accounts tell it), ending his reign and causing the downfall of his empire.

The Aztecs had migrated to the valley of Mexico following the fall of the Toltec Empire in the late twelfth century, founding their capital at Tenochtitlán in 1325. Over the next two centuries, the militaristic Aztec gradually conquered much of modern-day Mexico and northern Central America, forcing other native peoples to pay tribute or face destruction.

Technically proficient, highly organized, and adept militarily, the Aztecs also were much resented by their subject peoples. The Aztecs ruled over an uneasy empire and their religion reflected that fact. Periodically, they engaged in invasions against other peoples to obtain human sacrifices to propitiate gods, who constantly threatened to bring down destruction on the empire.

Montezuma II, the ninth emperor of the Aztecs, ascended the throne upon the death of his uncle in 1502. Like many of his predecessors on the throne, Montezuma II was commander of the empire's army and led many of its expeditions against neighboring peoples. He also was a highly religious man and had a fatalistic streak. When Cortéz arrived in 1519, Montezuma II may have believed him to be an incarnation of Quetzalcoatl, an Aztec god who, legend had it, would be white, hirsute, and come from the east. The bearded Cortéz fit the bill, and Montezuma II lavished great gifts on him in hopes of winning the man-god's favor.

Suspicious of a trap, the Spanish conquistador had Montezuma II imprisoned and forced the Aztecs to offer even more treasure. When Cortéz abandoned the capital to fight off a rival Spanish expedition in early

1520, the Aztecs rose up; however, they were subsequently reconquered, and their capital was destroyed.

By seeming to have subjected himself so easily to such a small force of Spaniards—Cortéz commanded but 300 or so men, along with about 1,000 native allies—Montezuma II lost the respect of his people. While trying to rally them against Cortéz during the latter's absence in June 1520 (again, according to Spanish accounts), Montezuma II was attacked with spears and arrows. He died three days later.

James Ciment

See also: Aztec; Cortéz, Hernando; Native American–European Conflict; Spanish Colonies on Mainland North America (Chronology).

Bibliography

Collis, Maurice. *Cortés and Montezuma.* New York: New Directions, 1999.
Prescott, William Hickling. *History of the Conquest of Mexico.* 3 vols. Chicago: Hooper, Clarke, 1843.

Montreal

Montreal, Canada's second largest city, is located in the Hochelaga Archipelago in southern Quebec, near the confluence of the St. Lawrence and Ottawa rivers. When the first Europeans arrived in the sixteenth century, the Huron inhabited the region, including a village on the island of present-day Montreal, which they called Hochelaga. The Huron were hunters and farmers, living in long bark-covered houses and surviving on fish, beaver, and deer, as well as corn, squash, and beans.

In 1535, the French explorer Jacques Cartier, while searching for a Northwest Passage to the Orient, came across the island of Hochelaga, and the Huron led him to the top of a small mountain. Cartier named it Mont Royal and planted a cross in honor of King François I. Cartier later returned to France. In 1611 the explorer Samuel de Champlain, who thought about establishing a colony or trading post on the island, abandoned the project after hostilities broke out between the Huron, Algonquin, and Iroquois.

In 1642, Paul de Chomeday, Sieur de Maisonneuve, and forty colonists arrived in New France and founded a colony on the island, which they first called Ville Marie and later renamed Montreal. Under the direction of the Société de Notre Dame, Maisonneuve

and his fellow colonists also sought to convert Native Americans in North America to Catholicism. In the early years, the settlement suffered many hardships, largely from Iroquois raids. With the growth in the fur trade in the seventeenth century, it became an important trading center and gateway to the western interior of Canada. Fur traders converged on Montreal, using it as a hub for exploring and establishing trading posts in the Great Lakes area and the Mississippi Valley.

At first, New France was governed by a private company, but, in 1663, King Louis XIV took possession of the French settlements, including Montreal, and declared New France a royal colony. While natives had originally brought pelts to European trading centers, the liberalized laws governing the fur trade that were enacted in 1652 had led to the emergence of a new class of European voyageurs, otherwise known as coureurs de bois (woods runners), whose numbers were ever increasing during the second half of the seventeenth century. With the emergence of the coureurs, the supply of furs quickly outgrew European demand, and Louis XIV was forced to limit the number of annual coureur outings from Montreal and other French settlements in 1681. In 1696, he made another attempt at curtailing the supply side of the market and issued a decree restricting trade to settlements along the St. Lawrence River.

In the eighteenth century, Montreal continued to prosper as the center of the fur trade. By the start of the French and Indian War in 1754, the city had about 4,000 inhabitants of French descent.

Under the command of General James Wolfe, the British defeated the French army on the Plains of Abraham at Quebec City. Having retreated to Montreal, where the British forces surrounded them, the French surrendered the city, with little bloodshed, in 1760. Three years later, after signing the Peace Treaty of Paris at Montreal (1763), they relinquished the city and the rest of French Canada to the British, who renamed the former French colony the province of Quebec. Under British rule, the French retained their laws, religion, and language and developed a unique cultural identity within this British colony.

In the third quarter of the eighteenth century, tensions between the American colonists and the British came to a climax. In November 1775, the Americans sent two military expeditions into the Province of Quebec in the hope of winning French support for the Revolutionary cause. While Benedict Arnold laid siege to Quebec City, General Richard Montgomery marched

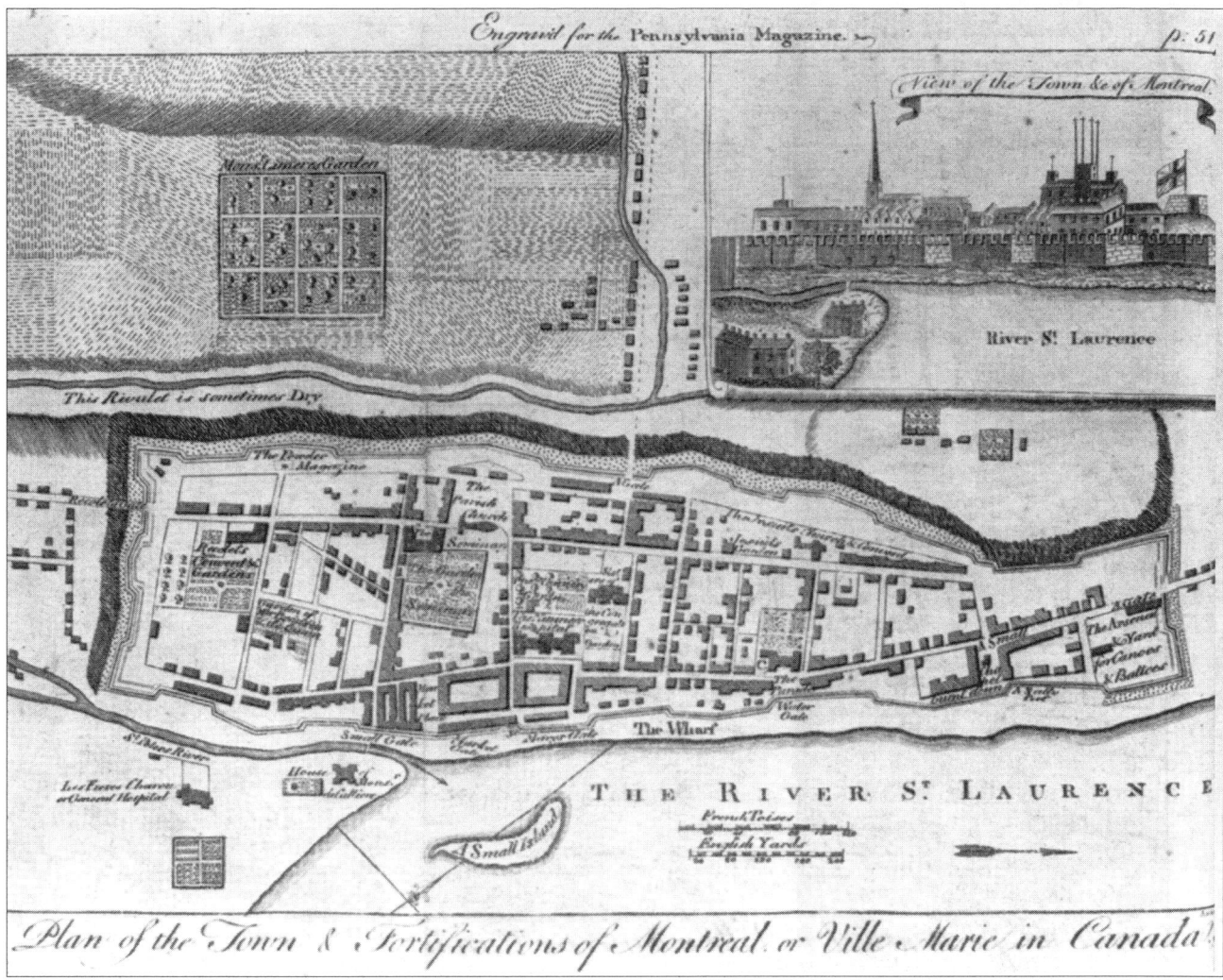

Montreal was founded in 1642 as Ville Marie on an island in the St. Lawrence River. It was renamed in the seventeenth century for Mont Royal, around which it had been expanded and fortified. *(Library of Congress, LC-USZ62-45558)*

down the Richelieu River and captured Montreal. French support for the American cause, however, did not materialize. After a failed diplomatic mission, which included Benjamin Franklin, Samuel Chase, and Charles Carroll, the Americans left the city on June 6, 1776. For the remainder of the war, Montreal and the rest of French-speaking Canada were allied with the British cause.

After the Revolution, Montreal prospered as a French and English city within the British Empire. The British North America Act of 1867 established the Canadian confederation of united provinces under a self-governing Canadian Parliament. Montreal emerged as the second-largest city in Canada and the city with the largest French-speaking population outside of France.

Michael Sletcher

See also: Canada; Champlain, Samuel de; French; French Colonies on Mainland North America (Chronology).

Bibliography

Atherton, William H. *Montreal, 1535–1914.* 3 vols. Montreal: S. J. Clarke, 1914.

Cooper, John Irwin. *Montreal: A Brief History.* Montreal: McGill-Queen's University Press, 1969.

Rumilly, Robert. *Histoire de Montréal.* 5 vols. Montreal: Fides, 1970–1974.

Murray, John

See Dunmore, Lord

Murray, Judith Sargent (1751–1820)

Judith Sargent Murray helped establish the first Universalist church in America, but she is best known for her discussion of gender roles and advocacy of expanded economic, social, and political opportunities for women. She was a noted poet and essayist in an era when women rarely published.

Born in 1751 to a prosperous and socially prominent merchant family in Gloucester, Massachusetts, Judith Sargent displayed signs of great intelligence at a time when women were valued more for beauty and social charms than brains. She read widely, including the work of female authors gaining popularity in Europe, and toyed with the idea of becoming a professional writer. Although she sought to improve her mind by obtaining an education in the classics, her parents insisted that she instead learn traditional female arts like cooking and sewing, a decision that left her angry and embittered. In 1769, Sargent married merchant John Stevens and, in 1776, joined him in becoming involved with the controversial Universalist religious movement.

Sargent held to the Puritan religion of her ancestors until the new faith of Universalism emerged with an egalitarian message that gave her a framework in which to define and defend her belief that men and women were spiritual and intellectual equals. While Universalists believed that all humans were tainted with sin, they stirred controversy by challenging the notion of predestination. All people would be saved from damnation, not just a select few, because Christ had died for the sins of everyone.

Writing in 1776, she argued that if God did not differentiate between men and women, then differing gender definitions were mere artificial constructions. In January 1778, she signed the articles of association creating the first Universalist church in America, thereby inviting the scorn of most members of the Gloucester community. Her steadfast belief in God's support of her actions meant that this criticism, though severe, had little personal impact upon her.

Sargent's rejection of the established church led her to question other social and intellectual conventions. As she subsequently declared, any argument based on "the despotism of tradition, the prejudices of education, and the predominating sway of revered opinions" was never again quite as persuasive. Once Sargent defied her community over the explosive topic of religion, she found it easier to take issue with other concerns, especially when she was convinced that she was acting in accordance with God's word.

Encouraged by other Universalists, especially Reverend John Murray, to share her thoughts on gender relations, she began to write for a public audience. By 1784, she regularly sent essays and poems to a select number of New England magazines, but she remained uncomfortable about becoming a public woman and nodded to conventional mores by employing the pseudonym Constantia. Sargent wrote on a wide variety of subjects, often discussing politics, manners, religion, marriage, the education of women, women's attributes as breadwinners, and motherhood.

Sargent's life changed dramatically as her husband's business gradually failed because of the poor trading conditions during the American Revolution. A tepid patriot who was shocked at the lack of civil liberties accorded loyalists, she now had another reason to dislike the conflict. Most New Englanders of this time considered financial setbacks to be evidence of moral failure, and a humiliated Sargent became too ashamed to appear in public. Stevens attempted to resuscitate his career but died in 1787 before doing so.

John Murray, an old friend and the man most responsible for bring Universalism to America, had been boarding in the Stevens household, and Judith married him in 1788. After losing a son in infancy, she bore a daughter in 1791who survived to adulthood.

Murray encouraged his wife to publish, and, in 1795, under her own name, Judith Sargent Murray began a short-lived career as a playwright with two comedies, both of which appeared briefly on the stage in Boston. In 1798, she published *The Gleaner*, a three-volume collection of her writings that included both old and new essays, as well as poems and both of her plays.

Following her second husband's death in 1815, Murray published her last work, *Life of John Murray, by Himself: With a Continuation by Mrs. Judith Sargent Murray*. She died at her daughter's home in Natchez, Mississippi, in 1820.

Caryn E. Neumann

See also: Christ and Christianity; Religion (Chronology); Religion (Essay).

Bibliography

Fields, Vena Bernadette. *Constantia: A Study of the Life and Works of Judith Sargent Murray, 1751–1820.* Orono: University of Maine Press, 1931.

Harris, Sharon. *Selected Writings of Judith Sargent Murray.* New York: Oxford University Press, 1995.

Skemp, Sheila L. *Judith Sargent Murray: A Brief Biography with Documents.* Boston: Bedford, 1998.

Music

Refined, "high culture" music along European lines was a very late arrival to the seaboard cities of colonial British America. Instead, early music in Colonial America was a musical patchwork, as each native and immigrant culture contributed its own musical sensibilities, instruments, and styles.

These various musical traditions affected each other in countless ways. Yet, by 1776, it would still be difficult, if not impossible, to identify a unique, unified, American musical style. It makes more sense to imagine a number of loosely affiliated American "musics" at the crossroads of three continents: America, Europe, and Africa.

Native Music

Native American culture before and during the colonial period was predominantly oral. Music was passed from generation to generation in much the same way as were religion and other cultural forms. Indeed, the divisions between religion, artistic expression, and everyday life among many native peoples were not nearly as sharp as they were among the newcomers from Europe.

Most of the written accounts of early Native American music come from the biased writings of European observers. Early accounts, whether from Cabeza de Vaca in the Southeast or Le Jeune in Huron country, vary widely in their assessments of native music. Interestingly, in their range of descriptions—from savage, chaotic, and wild to unrefined yet graceful—accounts of native music parallel European ideas about native peoples themselves.

One thing is clear from oral traditions across the centuries and written accounts alike: music was, and remains, fundamentally important to Native Americans. Its performance has traditionally accompanied major life events, religious ceremonies, and more mundane activities as well.

Each individual native community used music in ways that reflected that particular group's historical experiences; some songs were even the property of certain tribal members or clans and reserved solely for their use. Music was sung and played on flutes, trumpets, gourds, and drums. Often, the tones being sung indicated the meaning of the songs, sometimes in conjunction with words, sometimes not.

By their very nature, the myriad musical cultures of North America were extremely adaptable to change. Thus, Native American music today reflects centuries of interaction with European and African music, while, at the same time, remaining a marker of identity and strength for indigenous peoples throughout North America.

Religious Influences

The first European music in the Americas expressed the dual economic and religious nature of the project of colonization. At the same time as soldiers, sailors, farmers, and traders brought early music emphasizing secular themes, Spanish and French missionary activities brought European religious music to the colonies.

Roman Catholic worship in the sixteenth through eighteenth centuries stressed routine, and services were designed to impress native and nonnative parishioners alike. Early in establishing their missions, priests worked hard to incorporate native choir members into religious services. By 1528, natives were singing Latin hymns in and around Mexico City; similar services, though on a much less grand scale, were taking place in Spanish Florida by the late 1550s and early 1560s. Mexico City, with its massive cathedral, became a center of religious music in the Americas for both Native Americans and Spanish.

Although the French and Spanish colonial aims and destinations were different, a similar musical pattern developed in New France. French missionaries, however, were willing to incorporate native cultural forms into their services to a greater extent than the Spanish.

The first English settlers in America were not particularly interested in spreading their various sects of Protestantism to adjacent Native American communities. In New England, music was a matter of individual and community spiritual health. In Plymouth and the Massachusetts Bay Colony, colonists sang God's praise from a very small variety of psalters.

Disputes occasionally arose over the proper translations of religious texts, and the Puritans, ever legalistic, would not tolerate license with the scriptures. One result of these disputes was *The Whole Booke of Psalmes Faithfully Translated into English Metre*, also known as the *Bay Psalm Book*, which was published in

Cambridge, Massachusetts, in 1640. Various incarnations of the *Bay Psalm Book* were in use well into the eighteenth century.

Puritans "lined out" their hymns, mainly in unison, with one singing leader calling out the lines and the congregation echoing them. Eventually, a schism developed between "lining out," or "Old Way" singing, and "Regular Singing," simply singing the songs as written. Old Way singing faded from the scene exceedingly slowly, and variations existed in remote territories into the twentieth century. As Regular Singing rose to prominence, singing schools developed, and soon, choirs began to form. By the end of the colonial period, the American colonies had begun to produce composers, the most notable of whom was Boston's William Billings.

Not all Anglo-Americans were of a Calvinist bent, and Anglicans, whose carefully prescribed liturgical calendar resembled that of the Catholics, contributed a great deal to colonial American music. The Anglicans were not opposed to the great expense of church organs, nor to hiring expensive professionals from Europe to play them. Particularly well-off Anglican churches spared no expense: Charles Theodore Pachelbel, son of the great Johan Pachelbel, played at St. Philip's in Charles Town, South Carolina, from 1737 to 1750.

German-speaking Protestants, with none of the worries of the Puritans concerning elaborate arrangements or the corrupting effects of musical instruments, also transported an elaborate musical culture with them from continental Europe. They disseminated their music throughout the areas in which they settled.

Music at Home and on the Plantation

Not all early American music was religious in nature. Each cultural group had its own folk music, and these songs, some of which are still around today, accompanied the home and social lives of white colonists.

The British Isles, for instance, had an ancient tradition of ballad singing, which made its way across the Atlantic and was dispersed throughout the backcountry. Sometimes, ballad writers would alter lyrics to ancient tunes to make them more relevant to life in America; "The Trappan'd Maid" complained about a servant's lot in Virginia, for instance.

American events also formed the subject matter for songs like "The Death of General Wolfe," which celebrated the sacrifice of the hero of the French and Indian War. Fiddle tunes and dancing music, almost entirely imported from Europe, also lightened many of the burdens associated with rugged colonial life.

The peoples who encountered one another in colonial North America all underwent a cultural transformation. Perhaps none was as significant as the transition of various groups of Africans into African Americans over the span of several generations. One of the ways in which diverse African peoples established an identity that allowed them to survive and thrive culturally under the most miserable physical conditions was music. African cultures were not destroyed by the Middle Passage and slavery. Instead, they were broken down, altered, and rebuilt in an effort to form a new African American cultural identity, of which music was a crucial part.

The music made by black Americans varied widely from region to region. Throughout North America, Africans took up European instruments such as the violin and French horn, although they modified the instruments and the way they were played to their own musical ideas. African slaves also made drums, flutes, xylophones, and other instruments, including a predecessor of the modern banjo, much the same way as they had in Africa. A uniquely African American form of fife-and-drum music is still performed today.

Skilled African musicians entertained at social events for their masters, but also for members of their own community. African slaves used music and dance to express their feelings about the institution of slavery, their masters, and a variety of life experiences. Perhaps the most famous African American contributions to early American music are the work song and the spiritual. Some of these satirized the cultures of the colonies' elite. Many used the call-and-response patterns familiar to students of black music throughout the transatlantic world. African Americans farther to the north fell under the influence of Anglo-American musical forms to a greater extent than their Southern cousins.

In the middle of the eighteenth century, elites in colonial America began to undergo a process that some scholars call refinement. In colonial cities on the Eastern seaboard, well-to-do Americans began to emulate European culture, and music was one of the areas they found lacking. Over the course of the eighteenth century, concerts and the places in which they were performed became increasingly elaborate.

A class of professional composers and musicians was slow to develop in colonial America. Still, colonial Americans of every race and ethnicity made music and performed it in a variety of secular and religious settings.

Matthew Jennings

See also: Arts, Culture, and Intellectual Life (Chronology); Arts, Culture, and Intellectual Life (Essay); Theater.

Bibliography

Crawford, Richard. *America's Musical Life: A History.* New York: W. W. Norton, 2001.

Josephy, Alvin M., Jr., ed. *America in 1492: The World of the Indian People Before the Arrival of Columbus.* New York: Alfred A. Knopf, 1992.

Rath, Richard Cullen. "African Music in Seventeenth-Century Jamaica: Cultural Transit and Transition." In *William and Mary Quarterly* 50:4 (October 1993): 700–26.

Wright, Louis B. *The Cultural Life of the American Colonies, 1607–1763.* New York: Harper and Row, 1957.

General Index

Biographical Index

Geographical Index

Colonial America

AN ENCYCLOPEDIA OF SOCIAL, POLITICAL, CULTURAL, AND ECONOMIC HISTORY

Volume Four

EDITED BY JAMES CIMENT

WITH AN INTRODUCTION BY
MICHAEL ZUCKERMAN, UNIVERSITY OF PENNSYLVANIA

SHARPE REFERENCE
an imprint of M.E. Sharpe, Inc.

SHARPE REFERENCE

Sharpe Reference is an imprint of M.E. Sharpe, Inc.

M.E. Sharpe, Inc.
80 Business Park Drive
Armonk, NY 10504

Cover Photo: Tontine Coffee House, c. 1797 (oil on linen), Francis Guy (1760–1820) / © New York Historical Society, New York, United States; www.bridgeman.co.uk.

Maps: Adapted by Carto-Graphics from the following sources:

Kwame Anthony Appiah and Henry Louis Gates, Jr., eds., *Africana: The Encyclopedia of the African and African American Experience* (New York: Basic Books, 1999). See map: Volume 3, page 788.

Geoffrey Barraclough, ed., *The Times Atlas of World History,* 6th edition (Maplewood, NJ: Hammond, 1982). See maps: Volume 1, pages xlii, xliii, 15, 214; Volume 2, pages xx, xxi; Volume 3, pages xx, xxi; Volume 4, pages xx, xxi, 850; Volume 5, pages xx, xxi.

James Ciment, ed. *Encyclopedia of American Immigration* (Armonk, NY: M.E. Sharpe, 2001). See map: Volume 1, page 55.

James Henretta, et al. *America's History.* 2nd edition (New York: Worth Publishers, 1993). See maps: Volume 1, pages xli, xlii, xliii, 59; Volume 2, pages xix, xx, xxi, 327, 362; Volume 3, pages xix, xx, xxi, 581, 738, 788; Volume 4, pages xix, xx, xxi; Volume 5, pages xix, xx, xxi.

Mary Beth Norton, et al. *A People and a Nation.* 6th edition (Boston: Houghton Mifflin, 2001). See maps: Volume 1, pages xliv, xlv; Volume 2, pages xxii, xxiii, 324; Volume 3, pages xxii, xxiii, 812; Volume 4, pages xxii, xxiii.

Library of Congress Cataloging-in-Publication Data

Colonial America: An encyclopedia of social, political, cultural, and economic history/James Ciment, editor.
    p. cm.
    Includes bibliographical references and index.
    ISBN 0-7656-8065-3 (Set: alk. paper)
    1. United States—Civilization—To 1783—Encyclopedias. I. Ciment, James.

E162.C68 2005
973.2′03—dc22
2003023235

Publisher: Myron E. Sharpe
Vice President and Editorial Director: Patricia Kolb
Vice President and Production Director: Carmen Chetti
Executive Editor and Manager of Reference: Todd Hallman
Senior Development Editor: Jeff Hacker
Project Editor: Laura Brengelman
Program Coordinator: Cathleen J. Prisco
Text Design: Carmen Chetti and Jesse Sanchez
Cover Design: Jesse Sanchez

Contents

iii

Indexes

List of Maps

VOLUME 4

Topic Finder

Religion

Maps

North America, 1600. The above map shows the multiplicity of native peoples on the North American continent in 1600, as well as the extensive Spanish presence in Mexico, Central America, the Caribbean, and southwestern portions of what is now the United States. Note that the English colony of Roanoke mysteriously disappeared shortly after its establishment in 1587. *(Carto-Graphics)*

North America, 1700. The above map shows the presence of European colonial powers on the North American continent circa 1700. Note that the presence of Europeans varied: British holdings in the Hudson Bay region were little more than claims on maps, while settlements along the Atlantic seaboard of what is now the United States included tens of thousands of European settlers and African slaves, as well as the remaining native peoples. *(Carto-Graphics)*

North America, 1775. The above map shows the presence of European colonial powers on the North American continent on the eve of the American Revolution. Note that some regions—particularly in the heart of Mexico and along the Atlantic seaboard of what is now the United States—were more heavily populated by colonists than other areas. *(Carto-Graphics)*

European Settlement Areas, Eastern North America, 1650. The above map shows the thin line of European settlements along the Atlantic seaboard and the St. Lawrence River Valley. At the time, the total European and African populations in the British colonies stood at about 50,000, with a few thousand more in the Dutch, French, and Spanish colonies. *(Carto-Graphics)*

British Colonies, Mainland North America, 1765. By 1750, British settlements on mainland North America had pushed westward to the eastern edge of the Appalachian Mountains. The population of the thirteen colonies in 1750 was roughly 1.2 million, including about a quarter of a million slaves. *(Carto-Graphics)*

Colonial America

Volume Four

T

Taino

The Taino were the first Amerindians to meet and have sustained contact with Europeans. It was the Taino who watched curiously when Christopher Columbus planted the Spanish flag and dubbed their island San Salvador on October 12, 1492.

Often referred to as Island Arawaks, the Taino's population and cultural core was the island they called Quisqueya, today Hispaniola, shared by the Dominican Republic and Haiti. The Taino also populated Puerto Rico and eastern Cuba, had colonies in the Bahamas and Jamaica, and had established trade routes that extended throughout the Caribbean to Florida and the Yucatán. *Taino* comes from *nitaíno,* which is what they called out when European ships approached, perhaps signifying that they were "nobles," the word's most frequently accepted meaning. It is more likely, however, that they meant that they were not cannibals.

One thing we know for certain is that Taino was *not* a collective name that they used; they identified themselves by individual *yucayeque* (population center) and by *cazicazgo,* the extent of a region under the control of a particular *cacique* (chief). Their languages were significantly different from cazicazgo to cazicazgo but mutually comprehensible, which has led to the as-yet-unresolved debate whether the Guanahatabey (also called Ciboney) of northeastern Hispaniola and Cuba were a separate people from the Taino. Their agricultural base and techniques of cultivation were slightly different from cazicazgo to cazicazgo, and designs of both domestic and elite products varied too, but Tainos' spiritual beliefs and practices appear to have been relatively uniform and widespread.

The Taino's most advanced agricultural features arose in western Hispaniola, where they dug irrigation channels, and in the northern valleys, where they constructed fields called *conucos* with knee-high mounds of soil 8 to 9 feet in circumference. Here, they intercropped yucca, beans, squash, peppers, corn, sweet potatoes, peanuts, and other tubers. The conucos required only occasional weeding and pest removal, and there was no need to build storage sheds, for the main crop, yucca (also known as casaba or manioc), could be left in the ground until needed. Cultivated crops, in combination with wild foods and protein gathered from seas, rivers, and lakes, gave the Taino a stable food base, which allowed the populations to expand exponentially—their yucayeques averaged 500 to 1,000 inhabitants.

The typical yucayeque had many *bohios* (conical straw houses) centered around a *batey* (plaza and playing field), upon which the cacique's *caney* (house/temple) faced. The porch of the caney is where the sacred *cohoba* ceremony took place, wherein the cacique inhaled hallucinogenic powder that allowed him to communicate with his *zemies,* or spirit guides. The plaza was the site of the Taino's *areitos,* communal song and dance ceremonies, as well as their ballgame, which was both sport and religious ritual.

The Taino in the Boca Chica region of eastern Hispaniola brought pottery making to "a new height of ceramic art . . . characterized by elaborate modeled-incised designs, many of which appear to be representations of zemies." The term "zemi" (or "cemi") encompassed dual concepts, for it denoted a spiritual double who gave advice and protected humans and was also the physical symbol of that spiritual being. There were thousands of zemies, representing the broad pantheon of the Taino's legendary gods and culture heroes, plus deceased ancestors and nature spirits. Just about every object used by the Taino, both utilitarian and ceremonial, was decorated with carvings, paintings, or weavings of the zemies and their symbols. Taino wore elaborate jewelry honoring their zemies and decorated their bodies with painted-on multicolored zemi symbols. Some sported permanent tattoos.

The Taino people, who watched as Columbus landed on Hispaniola in 1492, were the first Amerindians to have sustained contact with Europeans. *Caciques* (chiefs) wore elaborately embellished costumes and sat on carved ceremonial seats called *dujos*. (Musee de l'Homme, Paris, France/Bridgeman Art Library)

Spanish chroniclers generally described the Taino as "naked," but all of them wore jewelry and zemi symbols, leg bands and armbands. Married women wore a cotton loincloth called a *nagua*—the more noble they were, the longer the nagua.

Caciques dressed far more elaborately, especially for ceremonial occasions. They had brilliant cotton capes embroidered with parrot feathers; carved gold-and-pearl-embellished masks, crowns, and pendants; and elaborate belts. While all the other Tainos sat on the ground, caciques sat on elaborately carved and polished wooden *dujos* (ceremonial seats). Caciques had elaborately decorated canoes, too, some of which could hold hundreds of people; when on land, caciques were often carried about on litters. Some caciques were buried in caves, which were frequently decorated with petroglyphs and pictographs, or at other prestige burial sites. Their corpses were accompanied by elaborate grave goods, among which might be the buried-alive body of a favorite wife.

Taino cultural development was abruptly halted with the arrival of the Spaniards, Africans, and their animals—all brought along germs and viruses to which the Amerindian peoples had no inbred immunities. Disease combined with exploitation caused a drastic decline in the Taino population. An estimated 90 percent of the original 2 million died within two genera-

tions. Today, descendants of those Tainos who survived are attempting to make a comeback.

Lynne Guitar

See also: Caribbean (Chronology); Native American–European Conflict; Native Americans.

Bibliography

Colón, Ferdinand. *The Life of the Admiral, by His Son Ferdinand.* Translated by Benjamin Keen. New Brunswick, NJ: Rutgers University Press, 1959.

Columbus, Christopher. *The Diario of Christopher Columbus's First Voyage to America, 1492–1493.* Abstracted by Fray Bartolomé de las Casas. Edited by Oliver Dunn and James E. Kelley, Jr. Norman: University of Oklahoma Press, 1989.

Fernández Méndez, Eugenio. *Art and Mythology of the Taíno Indians of the Greater West Indies (Arte y Mitología de los Indios Taínos de las Antillas Mayores).* San Juan, Puerto Rico: Ediciones El Cemi, 1979.

Guitar, Lynne. "Documenting the Myth of Taíno Extinction." In KACIKE: The Journal of Caribbean Amerindian History and Anthropology (December 2002). http://www.kacike.org.

Martyr D'Anghiera [de Angleria], Peter [Pedro]. *De Orbe Novo: The Eight Decades of Peter Martyr D'Anghiera.* Translated by Francis Augustus MacNutt. New York: Burt Franklin, 1970.

Rouse, Irving. *The Taínos: Rise and Decline of the People Who Greeted Columbus.* New Haven, CT: Yale University Press, 1992.

Stevens-Arroyo, Antonio M. *Cave of the Jagua: The Mythological World of the Taínos.* Albuquerque: University of New Mexico Press, 1988.

Taylor, Edward (c. 1644–1729)

Edward Taylor has been called America's first important poet—though many scholars would give this title to Anne Bradstreet—but his work was not published until the twentieth century. In 1937, while working in the Yale University Library, Thomas H. Johnson discovered Taylor's manuscripts. The works first appeared in print in 1939.

Little is known of Edward Taylor's early life. He was probably born in Coventry, England, in about 1644 and had migrated to New England by 1668, where he stayed briefly as a guest of Increase Mather.

Taylor matriculated at Harvard College and graduated from that institution in 1671 with his roommate and friend Samuel Sewall, the famous judge. While at school, Taylor was made a student butler, usually a position reserved for responsible, older undergraduates. He was also one of four students chosen to speak before the president and fellows during his senior year.

From Harvard, Taylor moved to Westfield, on the frontier near Northampton and not far from Connecticut, in 1671. At the end of the first year of his service as a minister, the town voted to keep him on, although King Philip's War (1675–1676) prevented his ordination until 1679. Taylor served the congregation as both pastor and physician, a dual role that was not uncommon in Puritan Massachusetts, remaining at Westfield for the rest of his life.

Academic and career successes aside, Taylor's personal life seems to have been fraught with tragedy. He and his first wife, Elizabeth Fitch, had seven children between 1675 and 1688. None of these children outlived their father, and Elizabeth herself died in 1689. In 1692, Taylor married the daughter of a Hartford judge, with whom he had six children, all of whom reached adulthood, though only one male descendant carried on the family name. Taylor dealt with his losses in the poem "Upon Wedlock and the Death of Children," lamenting the "branches" taken from his tree.

Taylor served his congregation ably for a long time. Samuel Sewall remarked that he once preached a sermon in Boston worthy of St. Paul's famed Preaching Cross in London. His tombstone in Westfield praises him as an "Aged, Venerable, Learned, & Pious Pastor . . . Served God and his Generation Faithfully for Many Years."

An inventory of Taylor's estate taken after his death in 1729 showed him to be in possession of a substantial library. It was not at all uncommon for Puritan pastors to accumulate large libraries, but this library was one of the largest in the area where Taylor preached. His library included many expensive works rare in New England, a collection of seventeenth-century schoolbooks, and books that aided Taylor's practice of medicine. It also contained books by Cotton Mather, Increase Mather, and Samuel Sewall, which indicate that Taylor kept up his reading in current affairs.

As mentioned above, Taylor's considerable skill as a poet did not become known until more than two centuries after his death. Taylor's will specifically instructed that none of his 400 pages of accumulated manuscripts ever be published. In accordance with Taylor's wishes, his grandson Ezra Stiles, president of Yale, deposited the unopened manuscripts in the university library.

The themes of Taylor's poetry are predictable enough for a man raised on seventeenth-century Puritanism: God's power, man's painful march to sainthood, and deep love for Christ. What sets his poems apart from many other works produced in colonial America is his style. He avoids the plain style, favoring rhetorical flourish and high-minded analysis of scripture. Following English models, he also modified love poetry to serve religious ends.

Taylor's central work is a series of loosely connected poems that explains most of the tenets of Puritan faith. Taylor called the work *God's Determinations Touching His Elect: And The Elects' Combat in Their Conversion, And Coming Up To God and Christ: Together With The Comfortable Effects Thereof*. While other Puritan poets, particularly Michael Wigglesworth in his *Day of Doom*, focused on the triumph of the church at the end of the world, Taylor focused on the individual's personal journey to sainthood in a way that could be compared to the works of some of the metaphysical poets then working in England. In addition to the lengthy *God's Determinations*, Taylor wrote a number of shorter *Sacramental Meditations*, which were, in essence, autobiographical treatments addressing Taylor's love for Christ.

Matthew Jennings

See also: Literature.

Bibliography

Davis, Thomas M. *A Reading of Edward Taylor*. Newark: University of Delaware Press, 1992.

Johnson, Thomas H., ed. *The Poetical Works of Edward Taylor*. Princeton, NJ: Princeton University Press, 1939.

Miller, Perry, ed. *The American Puritans: Their Prose and Poetry*. New York: Columbia University Press, 1956.

Tea

Originally imbibed for its medicinal properties, tea has not only been an important commodity and widely consumed beverage throughout the world but also—of particular relevance to the American colonies—the main ingredient of a domestic ritual in Great Britain. Of the kinds of tea annually exported from China, black and green are the main types. Separated by quality in an ascending order of fineness, black is divided into bohea, congou, and souchong; while green could be either singlo or hyson. On occasion, China exported small quantities of pekoe (the finest black) along with twankay and hyson skin (medium-quality greens).

During the seventeenth century, the tea trade was haphazard and fragmented. Tea was procured by sailors and employees of the East India Company (EIC) for private trade to supplement their salaries, having little influence on Chinese production. Traders generally bought small quantities at varying prices wherever they went in Asia, carried it home in ships with other goods, and sold it privately or through auctions. Conversely, the Chinese tea trade was extensive and highly organized, albeit overwhelmingly domestic. Until demand for tea increased in Europe and became linked to elites, few merchants bothered to engage solely in the tea trade. Yet even when the EIC gained a monopoly on British tea importation and started shipping large amounts of tea to England and Europe, it hardly affected the regular direct trade of China.

There were many reasons for the rise of tea consumption after 1680. Tea was more profitable than coffee for existing networks of wholesalers and local retailers selling to households in Britain and the colonies. Since tea was consistently available at an affordable price, families of limited means were accustomed to drinking it rather than coffee. As a result, tea consumption became customary, leading to a vastly expanded domestic market. In Britain, the American colonies, and large parts of Europe, tea consumption became a central part of every meal and a domestic ritual, where tea and sugar were served with certain other foods. Although initiated among the upper classes, the ritual was primarily a cultural phenomenon that eventually transcended class distinction.

Tea consumption came to represent a healthy lifestyle that offered a morally sound alternative to the drinking of alcohol, which had previously been the most common beverage. The theoretical justification for drinking tea (derived from this context of health) emphasized balance and moderation.

Another reason tea consumption was tied to respectability was that its physical equipment (tea services and china) tended toward refinement on a small scale, as opposed to a costly, conspicuous display of wealth. As a result, tea consumption was firmly established in the home and became so embedded in the culture of respectability that it could not become unfashionable. An increase in the number of people who wanted to think themselves respectable meant a demand for the commodities used in this ritual.

The importance of smuggling to the development of the European tea trade cannot be overestimated—not merely for its detraction from legitimate trade and profits but by contributing significant innovations in trade while promoting economic growth. Tea smugglers developed more efficient means of transportation, took advantage of international facilities of capital and credit, and invaded established channels of legal distribution; in short, they expanded markets beyond the norm. Focusing on isolated markets like those on the coast and rural regions, smugglers introduced tea to areas far removed from the influence of the fashionable world. After 1760, tea smuggling was so prevalent that the practice threatened legal trade, alarming the government and legal traders.

In 1767, the British Parliament laid a tax, part of the Townshend Duties, of three pence a pound on all tea imported into the American colonies. Although tea could still be sold more cheaply in the colonies than in England even with the new tax, the Townshend Duties caused problems in the colonies. While the revenue act of 1767 taxed tea, it also placed duties on glass, white lead, painters' colors, and paper. Revenue from the Townshend Duties was to be used for the administration of the duties and the support of civil government within the colonies, while the residue, if any, was to be appropriated by Parliament for the defense of the colonies.

Prior to 1767, the colonial customs service and that in the British Isles were under the direction of a single board in London. The Townshend Acts created a separate board in America under the control of the king. Established in Boston, the American customs commission managed all American port officials, who could search and seize anything, utilizing a new search warrant to be issued by colonial courts.

Previously, imperial taxes in America were collected at local ports, local costs for collection deducted, and the net balance transmitted to London. But now colonial officials had new reason to enforce imperial duties, because they were paid based on the basis of how much revenue was collected. Since the prime minister selected officials to administer the new system, it allowed Lord North and his associates to use the system for political patronage.

Solomon K. Smith

See also: Boston Tea Party; East India Company; Tea Act (1773); Trade.

Bibliography

Brewer, John, and Roy Porter. *Consumption and the World of Goods*. New York: Routledge, 1993.

Mui, Hoh-cheung, and Lorna H. Mui. "Smuggling and the British Tea Trade before 1784." *American Historical Review* 74 (October, 1968): 48–73.

Smith, Woodruff D. "Complications of the Commonplace: Tea, Sugar, and Imperialism." *Journal of Interdisciplinary History* 23 (Autumn, 1992): 259–78.

Tea Act (1773)

When Parliament approved the Tea Act on May 10, 1773, it triggered a sequence of events that led to a crisis in the British Empire. First Lord of the Treasury Frederick North had urged its passage to save the financially troubled East India Company, England's largest. Yet colonists in America saw it as part of a plan to deprive them of their liberties.

Since its victory over France in the Seven Years' War in 1763, the English government had sought ways to fund the escalating costs of maintaining its expanded empire in North America. In the face of growing resistance to taxation at home, British ministers concluded that they must raise revenue in the colonies. However, most colonists, who believed that only representatives they had elected could impose taxes, viewed parliamentary taxes—as they did the 1765 Stamp Act and the 1767 Townshend Duties—as evidence of a developing plan to take away their rights. Protests and boycotts by colonists led to the repeal of most of those taxes.

The remaining tax was a three-pence-per-pound levy on tea, a commodity widely consumed in North America. Many colonists, however, purchased smuggled tea imported from Dutch sources, a circumstance that contributed heavily to the growing financial crisis facing the East India Company. Dwindling sales in the colonies, which reputedly consumed nearly 5 million pounds of tea annually, and a saturated domestic market left the company with a surplus of nearly 18 million pounds of tea in early 1773. Making matters worse, company ships were bringing an additional 8 million pounds from China. Since tea sales represented about 90 percent of the company's revenue, it was near bankruptcy. When company directors petitioned the government for both a loan and a request for reduced taxes on their tea exports, they found a receptive ear in Lord North.

He developed and pushed through Parliament a plan not only to save the ailing company but also to raise revenue in the colonies and confirm the right of the English government to tax the colonists. He supported the request for a government loan and a reduction in some of the taxes the company had to pay. When some members of the House of Commons also argued for an elimination of the remaining Townshend Duty on tea, North refused. Retaining that duty, he maintained, was an essential part of the government's plan to raise money to pay the salaries of English officials in the colonies. Moreover, he saw the duty as an important symbol of British sovereignty, specifically Parliament's right to tax the colonies.

North emerged victorious and the East India Company received a government loan of 1.4 million pounds and permission to ship their tea directly to the colonies. The company would not only avoid paying the tax normally collected in England but also the requirement that it sell its tea at public auction to merchants who, in turn, would sell it to merchants in the colonies. The company could select its own merchants, or consignees, in the colonies and further reduce the cost of the tea. Although the tea continued to carry the three-pence-per-pound Townshend Duty, the total price to American consumers would drop by nearly 50 percent, making it cheaper than smuggled Dutch tea. In September, the company shipped over 1,200 chests of tea destined for four colonial ports.

Opposition to the Tea Act developed first in Philadelphia and New York, where merchants, who had become dependent upon smuggled tea, faced a significant loss of business. They argued that the legislation creating a monopoly for the East India Company represented a precedent that would destroy all foreign trade. Others worried that the British were engaging in a cynical ploy to deceive the colonists, with cheap tea, into relinquishing their principled opposition to taxation without representation.

Tea consignees in New York City, Philadelphia, and Charles Town, South Carolina resigned in response to threats from mass meetings. The most notable resistance to the act occurred in Boston, where activists tossed the cargo from three tea ships into the harbor on December 16, 1773.

In response, the British government, early the following year, passed a series of measures to punish Boston and the Massachusetts Bay colony. Besides closing the port of Boston, these Coercive Acts limited town meetings, provided for the quartering of British troops in empty public buildings, and gave the Crown the power to select members to the provincial council. Called the Intolerable Acts by colonists, the punitive legislation persuaded twelve colonies to send delegates to a Continental Congress in Philadelphia in 1774, a step that eventually led to the Revolution.

Larry Gragg

See also: Boston Tea Party; East India Company; Revolutionary War; Tea; Trade.

Bibliography

Labaree, Benjamin Woods. *The Boston Tea Party.* New York: Oxford University Press, 1964.

Thomas, Peter D. G. *Tea Party to Independence: The Third Phase of the American Revolution, 1773–1776.* Oxford, UK: Clarendon Press, 1991.

Technology

Colonial American technology blended early modern European technologies with indigenous American and African elements, all adapted to the material conditions of the Americas. Some materials, most notably wood, were abundant in America but scarce in Europe, while labor, abundant in Europe, was scarce in America. Although colonial America was not a particularly dynamic society technologically, it shared in technological changes in the Western world, as well as showing its own local peculiarities.

Multicultural Origins of Colonial Technology

Many aspects of growing New World crops such as corn and tobacco were obviously dependent on Native American knowledge, although the scale at which the colonists operated was often far vaster than that of the indigenous inhabitants. Native Americans also pioneered the tapping of maple trees and the production of maple sugar. Another area where colonists borrowed Native American techniques was tree felling. Rather than chopping down trees, many of the colonists used a common Native American procedure called "girdling," which involves cutting or burning a circle through the bark around the tree and then leaving it to die and eventually fall.

Enslaved African Americans also brought technical skills with them. The early cultivation of rice in South Carolina relied on the knowledge and skills enslaved West Africans brought about growing, processing, and irrigating the crop. The English colonists also learned from previous European colonizers. For example, some of the techniques for growing and preparing tobacco were learned from the Spanish, the first colonizers to grow this plant.

Immigrants and migrant workers from other parts of Europe enriched the technology of the English colonies. The importance of Continental workers for industrial technology can be seen as far back as the first ventures of the Virginia Company, the most technologically minded of the early colonization companies, when the first Polish and Dutch and then Italian glassmakers were brought in to get the glassworks up and running. The first sawmill in Massachusetts Bay was built by Danish immigrants. The early eighteenth-century iron industry in Virginia involved the immigration of German and Swiss miners and ironworkers.

The technology of Continental immigrants changed domestic life, as well as American industry. Log cabins were introduced by Swedish settlers, who came to the Delaware Valley in 1638. German immigrants introduced several technical innovations of general use, such as the deep or "Conestoga" wagon, with a far greater carrying capacity than the English cart, and the long rifle.

British settlers favored inefficient open hearths for both cooking and heating, using wood lavishly, while Germans introduced the far more energy- and fuel-efficient technology of the stove. This innovation only slowly diffused to the Anglo-American population, and early stove designs were open to improvement. Both of the two great physicists produced by colonial America, Benjamin Franklin and Benjamin Thompson (best known by his later title of Count Rumford), were fascinated with the problem of efficiency in fireplaces and stoves, and they originated stove designs.

Technology and the American Environment

For power technology, the colonists used (besides direct animal and human muscle power) a technology widely used in Europe since ancient times: the mill. Mills were particularly suited for America due to the shortage of labor and the presence of easily exploited quick-running streams. Although windmills were used from an early period, the most common form of mill was the water mill. All three forms of water mill—the horizontal mill with the wheel on its side; the undershot mill with the water running along the bottom to turn the mill; and the most efficient, the overshot mill, with the water

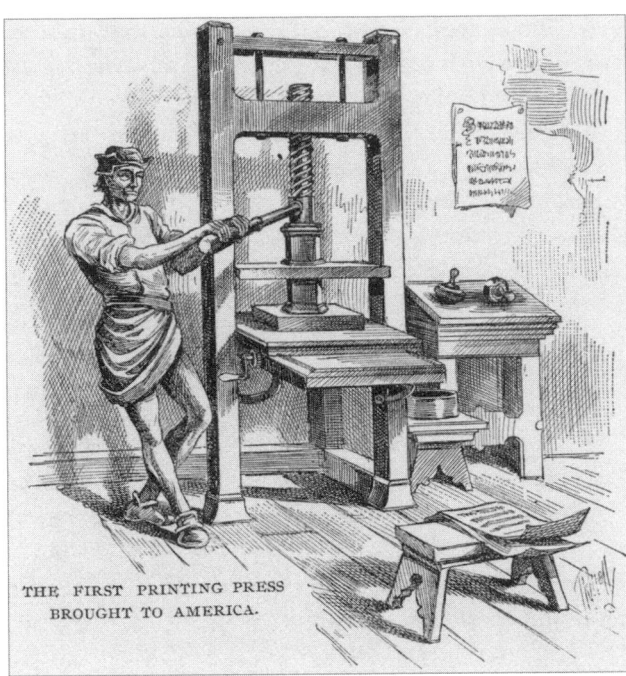

THE FIRST PRINTING PRESS BROUGHT TO AMERICA.

The first printing press in British North America dates to 1638 and the arrival of Stephen Daye in Massachusetts. Dye set up the colonies' first printing plant, the Cambridge Press, and began publishing a broadside called *The Freeman's Oath*. (© North Wind Picture Archives)

running along the top of the mill—appeared in colonial America.

Mills had many uses. Two of the most important were grinding grain (gristmills) and cutting lumber into boards (sawmills). Sawmills, which used straight saws rather than the later circular saw, wasted considerably more wood than did sawyers cutting lumber by hand (sawdust also polluted mill streams when not properly disposed of), but they were much faster. The abundance of wood in early America and the demand for boards meant that speed was more important than efficiency.

Another use of mill power was fulling woolen cloth, that is, pressing cloth to increase its weight and bulk. Fulling mills, mostly animal-powered, were found in New England from the 1640s, spreading to the mid-Atlantic and Southern states after 1700. Animal-powered mills also crushed bark for tannin, and, by the mid-eighteenth century, mills were grinding tobacco into snuff. Thousands of mills dotted the colonial landscape, to the point that a shortage of millwrights became a problem.

Although many aspects of European technology could be transplanted to the Americas with little change, the differing American environment prompted modifications and innovations. A good example of how the material conditions of colonial life and the colonial economy shaped technology is the invention and spread of the zigzag fence.

Fencing land was important both for practical reasons of protecting crops from animals and for ideological reasons—"enclosing" agricultural land was essential to claiming it as property. Early settlers built the kinds of fences they had known in Europe—vertical wooden posts set into the ground, with crossbeams nailed to them. (They made little use of hedges or stone fences at first.) The problem with these fences was that they required a good deal of labor to build, as well as plenty of nails, which were scarce.

The zigzag, worm, or snake fence, pioneered on the Chesapeake, took advantage of two things America had in abundance: land and wood. Zigzag fences piled rails on top of each other in a zigzag formation. They were held together by slanted stakes at the corners. The fences took up a lot of space and required a lot of wood, but they did not require nails and could be built quickly, since no postholes were needed. They could also be taken down quickly and moved if the need arose. Zigzag fences eventually became the most common type of wooden fence outside of New England, which stubbornly stuck to post fences in an area where land was scarcer. (The New England stone fence emerged late in the colonial period, partly as a response to deforestation.) The bountiful supply of wood also led early settlers to use wooden pegs in construction rather than expensive hand-wrought metal nails.

The inventor of the zigzag fence is not recorded, and many of the improvements and adaptation of European technology to American conditions were originated by persons now unknown; however, there are some known innovators in the seventeenth century. The first American mechanical patent was issued by the Massachusetts Bay Colony to Joseph Jenks in 1646, giving him exclusive rights to his innovations in sawmills and a mill for making scythes for fourteen years. Despite this early example, patents never became a standard way of rewarding technological innovation in colonial America. Most inventors sought to sell their products directly or to be awarded a cash prize by a colonial legislature or, later, a scientific society.

Industries

The most important communications technology of the early modern period was the printing press. The first printing establishment in British North America was founded in Cambridge, Massachusetts, in 1638. (The

British colonies were actually latecomers to printing, as the earliest surviving Spanish American printed text, from Mexico City, dates from nearly a century earlier.) The first printing press in Pennsylvania was established in 1685, and the Philadelphia printing industry dominated eighteenth-century American publishing.

The limitations of the American market meant that colonial American printing was not technically advanced by European standards. Americans seeking the services of fine printers and bookmakers—cartographers looking for printers for their maps, for example—continued to turn to London printers. By contrast, cheap publications with a ready local market, such as almanacs and newspapers, poured in torrents from American presses.

Printers also branched out into other technological activities, such as papermaking, but the presses themselves still usually had to be imported. Type fonts also had to be imported from England. The Connecticut silversmith and counterfeiter Abel Buell presented a prototype font to the American Philosophical Society in 1769, but the first successful American commercial type foundry did not appear until after the Revolution.

Probably the most complex technological objects in the preindustrial world were ships. From modest beginnings, shipbuilding became a major industry in the eighteenth-century British colonies, with major centers of production in Boston and Philadelphia joined by Virginia after about 1740 and Charles Town after about 1760.

Access to wood made America a natural for shipbuilding (and for supplying material to ships built elsewhere, such as the tall pine trees that made masts for the ships of the Royal Navy), but it took some time to learn how to use unfamiliar woods. For example, some early American ships were built with red oak, which does not resist water damage as effectively as white oak. American ships also were built with connecting dowels, or "treenails," made of another American wood, locust, rather than oak.

Eighteenth-Century Improvements

By the early eighteenth century, the growing wealth, population, and sophistication of the colonies meant that technology had become more ambitious and complex. A growing class of technological specialists included surveyors, navigators, clockmakers, almanac writers, and the builders of scientific instruments. Private schools and teachers catered to men desiring some familiarity with technical mathematics, and the subject even began to creep into the university curriculum.

The colonies were now able to plan and carry out large engineering projects, such as the 1,600-foot-long wharf built at Boston from 1710 to 1713 and the later Newport wharf, which was over 2,000 feet long. Merchant interests pressed for further infrastructure improvements, including the improvement of harbors, dredging of channels, and building of roads.

The founding in 1754 of the Royal Society of Arts, a London group devoted to improving technology and agriculture by offering prizes for innovations, gave American technology a boost similar to that given American science by the founding of the Royal Society in the seventeenth century. American members of the Society of Arts included leading scientists like Franklin and the Charles Town natural historian Dr. Alexander Garden. Franklin and other colonial American scientists shared with the Society of Arts a belief in the fundamentally utilitarian orientation of science.

America's first successful scientific society, the Philadelphia-based American Philosophical Society, over which Franklin presided, emphasized science's technological applications. Of the six original standing committees, two were devoted to technological improvement: the committee on mechanics and architecture and the committee on husbandry and American improvements. The society also advised on technical problems, such as the ambitious project to construct a canal between the Chesapeake and the Delaware River. The canal was not built until several decades later, and, at the time, Franklin, among others, urged the promoters to get expert engineers from Europe.

The Virginia Society for the Promotion of Usefull Knowledge, founded in 1773, took an even more explicitly utilitarian stance than the American Philosophical Society. John Hobday, the inventor of a threshing machine, was awarded a gold medal shortly after the society's foundation. The Virginia Society, however, was swept away in the turmoil of the Revolution.

The Reverend Jared Eliot, a Connecticut clergyman, sought to introduce some of the improvements in agricultural technology associated with the English writer Jethro Tull to America. Eliot's series of six essays, *Essays on Field-Husbandry in New England* (1748–1759), advocated the use of a drill-plough, a machine for planting seeds evenly along rows rather than scattering them by hand. Eliot's son-in-law Benjamin Gale, a member of the Society of Arts and the American Philosophical Society, won a medal from the Society of Arts for an improved drill-plough in 1770; however, use of the drill-plough did not catch on until the early nineteenth century. Eliot also published a book on extracting iron from black sand, for which he won a medal from the Society of Arts at a time when Britain wanted to increase colonial iron production.

Development of American technology acquired a political edge in the period following the end of the French and Indian War (known as the Seven Years' War in Europe), as Americans believed that domestic manufactures would lessen the colonies' economic subjugation to Great Britain. The New York Society of Arts, founded in 1763 by businessmen from the city's "patriot" faction, was less concerned with technological innovation in general than with the specific goal of fostering an independent linen industry in the city.

British concern with American technological development varied in different economic sectors. The general pattern was for the British to encourage the manufacture of materials that could then be finished in Britain. Thus, pig and bar iron were encouraged, but not steel.

The production of potash (potassium carbonate), a chemical made from wood ash with a variety of commercial uses, was also encouraged by the British in the late colonial period. American settlers had been making potash for their own use since the earliest settlements—it was used in soap making, glass making, and the preparation of saltpeter from gunpowder. The British Parliament, facing a shortage, lifted the tariff against colonial potash in 1751. This brought about a boom in the first American chemical industry. By 1770, the colonies were exporting 2,000 tons of potash to Britain annually, about two-thirds of Britain's consumption.

In the years immediately preceding the Revolution, Americans took little notice of the technological advances made in Britain, which was then in the early stages of the industrial revolution. (Nor did the British encourage colonial industrialization.) There were only three steam engines in the colonies, and these were of the older and less efficient Newcomen type. Christopher Colles, an Irish immigrant who operated in Philadelphia and New York, tried to promote steam engines and gave lecture courses at the American Philosophical Society on hydraulics and pneumatics in 1772, but he had little success. In 1774, Colles went to New York City, where he promoted a plan to pipe water into the city through hollow logs. The plan garnered some support but was cut short by the American Revolution.

Americans were interested in emulating the canal-building movement transforming the internal communications of Great Britain. In addition to the Chesapeake-Delaware Canal, there were plans to build a canal connecting Beaufort and the Neuse Rivers in North Carolina and one connecting the James and York Rivers in Virginia. Despite these and several other canal plans, no substantial transport canals were built before the American Revolution.

War has always been a spur to technological innovation, and the American War for Independence was no exception. David Bushnell, a young Yale student, invented and built a one-man submarine for use against the British. It was an effective submarine but an ineffective weapon. Less dramatic but more influential was the Rhode Island metalworker Jeremiah Wilkinson's development of a process for making nails out of cold iron rather than forging them.

One technological problem that was never completely solved during the war was that of gunpowder. Despite the efforts of some of America's sharpest minds, including Benjamin Rush, the Continental army remained dependent on imported gunpowder.

William E. Burns

See also: Artisans; Clocks and Timekeeping; Manufacturing; Science; Science and Technology (Chronology); Tools; Weaponry.

Bibliography

Carney, Judith A. *Black Rice: The African Origins of Rice Cultivation in the Americas.* Cambridge, MA: Harvard University Press, 2001.

Goldenberg, Joseph A. *Shipbuilding in Colonial America.* Charlottesville: University Press of Virginia for the Mariners Museum, Newport News, 1976.

Grasso, Christopher. "The Experimental Philosophy of Farming: Jared Eliot and the Cultivation of Connecticut." *William and Mary Quarterly,* 3rd ser., 50 (1993): 502–28.

Hindle, Brooke, ed. *America's Wooden Age: Aspects of Its Early Technology.* Tarrytown, NY: Sleepy Hollow Restorations, 1975.

———. *The Pursuit of Science in Revolutionary America.* Chapel Hill: University of North Carolina Press for the Institute of Early American History and Culture in Williamsburg, Virginia, 1956.

Kebabian, Paul B., and William C. Lipke, eds. *Tools and Technologies: America's Wooden Age.* Burlington: University of Vermont for the Robert Hull Fleming Museum, 1979.

McGaw, Judith A., ed. *Early American Technology: Making and Doing Things from the Colonial Era to 1850.* Chapel Hill: Published by the University of North Carolina Press for the Institute of Early American History and Culture in Williamsburg, Virginia, 1994.

York, Neil Longley. *Mechanical Metamorphosis: Technological Change in Revolutionary America.* Westport, CT: Greenwood Press, 1985.

Tenant Farming

Although it may seem surprising, due to the abundance of land in North America, tenancy was found everywhere in the colonies. Since many coastal regions were occupied, sons of poor men were unable to acquire land and form households where they were born unless they leased the land. In frontier areas, wealthy individuals who had money and political power procured millions of acres of undeveloped land through speculation, grants from provincial governments, or inheritance. Speculators leased excess land to tenants rather than sell it as small parcels for profit.

During the early years of settlement, for example, Dutch landlords in New Amsterdam enticed some families by offering low rents for long terms—generally for several generations. In 1705, one-third of the householders in Virginia's Prince George county were tenants, but, as nearby frontiers had come under cultivation by the 1770s, the proportion increased to more than half. Most families in southern Maryland and Virginia's Northern Neck rented land in the 1780s.

Increased population density changed the character of tenancy. With most land developed by the 1750s, landlords usually rented land for short periods and charged substantial rents, amounting to a third or even half of a single worker's crop. Tenants in these areas could barely afford the high rents, as they rarely accumulated much savings. Short-term tenancy grew in regions like the Hudson River Valley, where tenancy was already common, and in places tied to growing for urban markets such as southeastern Pennsylvania. Frontier landlords commonly granted leases at nominal rents for several generations. In return, tenants were required to improve the land by building structures and planting orchards.

Although tenants lived autonomously, they depended on landlords for land, building materials, tools, and often for marketing their crops. Most tenants paid a portion of their crop as rent, since they owned little other property. The richest tenant might own a horse, a little livestock, and live in a small house, but few had outbuildings like kitchens to improve their standard of living. Most tenant farmers did not stay in the same neighborhood for more than a few years, usually they moved away in search of land or other opportunities.

Markets complicated the dependence of tenants upon landlords. Each party tried to gain wealth from the land, but landlords could raise rents at will and dispose of the land whenever they wanted. Since tenants were dependent on landlords, good weather, and markets, many received charity from local officials. Common types of relief, often provided by or at the direction of county court justices, were exemptions from taxation, cash payments, and donations of food or manufactured goods. Church vestries also provided indigent childcare and paid medical expenses for poor.

The children of tenants received little help from their poor parents, whether the parents were alive or dead. Middle-aged tenants usually had estates valued at less than 45 pounds, leaving their beneficiaries with only a small sum after debts were paid. Even when tenants could add an inheritance to accumulated property, they rarely had enough money or collateral to buy a slave or a tract of land.

The most frugal tenant could only amass the money necessary to buy a 50-acre plot after benefiting from five years of good crops, high market prices, and saving more than half of each year's profits. This was a very difficult task, however, since tenants paid taxes and needed to purchase manufactured goods and subsistence items with their profits. Some former tenants escaped their hardship by moving to either a raw frontier or a rapidly developing area.

Most farmers tried to avoid tenancy, seeking instead economic independence. Whenever rich men threatened to secure land tenure, farmers and their sons resisted dependency, sometimes violently. Tenancy-related revolts occurred in the Hudson River Valley, New Jersey, Virginia, Maryland, and Pennsylvania. From revolts, wealthy landowners learned that secure land tenure for farmers ensured the social peace they desired, while attempting to collect rents yielded only small amounts of money or caused rebellion. Since land was abundant, most landowners sold off undeveloped land, deciding instead to retain their economic power by granting credit.

Solomon K. Smith

See also: Agriculture; Class; Laborers, Rural; Land and Real Estate; Property and Property Rights.

Bibliography

Bliss, Willard. "The Rise of Tenancy in Virginia." *Virginia Magazine of History and Biography* 108 (1950): 427–41.

Kim, Sung Bok. *Landlord and Tenant in Colonial New York: Manorial Society, 1664–1775.* Chapel Hill: University of North Carolina Press for the Institute of Early American History and Culture in Williamsburg, Virginia, 1978.

Stiverson, Gregory. *Poverty in a Land of Plenty: Tenancy in Eighteenth Century Maryland.* Baltimore: Johns Hopkins University Press, 1981.

Tennessee

Tennessee, which was for most of the colonial period an over-mountain extension of North Carolina, became the sixteenth state of the Union in 1796. Roughly rectangular in shape, Tennessee is geographically divided into three sections—east, middle, and west—by the Cumberland Plateau and the northwesterly-flowing portion of the Tennessee River. Colonial Tennessee was a land of overlapping frontiers: Multiple Native American groups claimed all or some of the territory for hunting or dwelling, while English, French, and Spanish explorers and traders competed for access to and control of native trade and lands.

The first Tennesseans arrived more than 12,000 years ago, and, by the time of European contact in the sixteenth century, Tennessee was home to several distinct groups of Mississippian Indians or frequently visited by them. The state's name likely derives from Tanasi (also spelled Tanasee), a Cherokee town.

The advent of Europeans and their diseases wreaked havoc on Native American populations. By the early eighteenth century, disease and warfare had taken their toll. The Cherokee would be the only natives with permanent settlements in the Tennessee territory, although the Chickasaw still claimed hunting grounds in middle and west Tennessee.

Spanish explorer Hernando de Soto's visit in the spring of 1540 marked the first European presence in the state (including the first black visitors—both free and enslaved Africans). The Spanish would have little

In the winter of 1779–1780, settlers James Robertson and John Donelson led a party of 300 settlers into middle Tennessee and built a fort on the Cumberland River. Fort Nashborough, as it was called, later became the settlement of Nashville, chartered as a city in 1806. *(Courtesy of the Tennessee State Library and Archives)*

other direct contact in the state, though their presence in Florida, as well as their later control of the Mississippi River port of New Orleans, guaranteed they would remain important to early Tennessee settlers. In 1673, English trader-explorers James Needham and Gabriel Arthur from the Virginia colony entered east Tennessee, while French explorers Jacques Marquette and Louis Jolliet stopped along the Mississippi River at the Chickasaw Bluffs.

As the French and English competed for Native American alliances and control of Tennessee, trade was the weapon of choice, though violence was ever-present. The French established trading networks mostly in the west but also into the Cumberland Basin at French Lick (near present-day Nashville). English traders entered Tennessee from the southeast. The native peoples sold not just animal pelts but also other natives as slaves into the coastal settlements or the West Indies.

English advantages in the supply of trade goods successfully bound the Cherokee to them during most of the Anglo-French contests for North America. English victory in the Cherokee War of 1760 began a treaty-war-treaty cycle that continued into the nineteenth century, eventually ending with the Cherokees' forced removal to the west of the Mississippi River under President Andrew Jackson of Tennessee.

The desire for land—whether for hunting, farming, or selling for profit—is the constant theme in Tennessee's early history. The Proclamation of 1763, declaring Tennessee officially off limits to British-American colonists, did little to stop the flow of British settlers over the mountains for hunting or settlement. "Long hunters" like Daniel Boone—so called because of the lengthy hunting trips over the mountains into the Tennessee and Kentucky territories—came back armed with more than just animal pelts. They also returned with tales of bountiful lands to encourage settlement and with information for their land-speculating partners, who planned to profit from such expansion.

The first permanent Anglo settlers arrived in the late 1760s. One of the biggest speculators, Richard Henderson of North Carolina, formed the Transylvania Company, and, in the 1775 Treaty of Sycamore Shoals, purchased 20 million acres of present-day Tennessee and Kentucky from Cherokee factions aligned with Attakullakulla ("the Little Carpenter"). Eager to exploit his new purchases, Henderson financed the land and river voyages of James Robertson and John Donelson's group of 300 settlers into middle Tennessee, where they founded Nashborough (later Nashville) in 1779–1780. Speculators, surveyors, and lawyers would become prominent political and social leaders in early Tennessee.

In violation of both the British Proclamation and existing treaties between colonial governments and the Cherokee, settlers in northeastern Tennessee bound themselves together into the extralegal Watauga Association (1772–1778) and crafted their own land agreements with factions of Cherokee leaders. During the American Revolution, when Tennessee settlers felt exposed to the British and their Cherokee allies, Watauga settlers sought annexation from either North Carolina or Virginia, and, in 1777, became Washington County, North Carolina.

The move for local self-governance remained dormant for only a short time. When North Carolina was slow to cede its western lands to the newly formed United States, local settlers designated themselves the State of Franklin in 1784 and petitioned for admission as the fourteenth state in the Union. Rebuffed, they disbanded and returned to North Carolina, becoming the federal "Territory Southwest of the River Ohio" in 1790 and achieving statehood as Tennessee in 1796.

Charles A. Israel

See also: Appalachia; Exploration.

Bibliography

Aron, Stephen Anthony. *How the West Was Lost: The Transformation of Kentucky from Daniel Boone to Henry Clay.* Baltimore: Johns Hopkins University Press, 1996.

Faragher, John Mack. *Daniel Boone: The Life and Legend of an American Pioneer.* New York: Henry Holt, 1992.

Finger, John R. *Tennessee Frontiers: Three Regions in Transition.* Bloomington and Indianapolis: Indiana University Press, 2001.

Satz, Ronald N. *Tennessee's Indian Peoples: From White Contact to Removal, 1540–1840.* Knoxville: University of Tennessee Press, 1979.

Texas

Spain founded and settled Texas as a buffer against French encroachment in Louisiana. Throughout the Spanish and Mexican periods, the settler population remained small, as the indigenous peoples controlled most of Texas.

In 1519, Alonso Alvarez de Pineda led an expedition to explore the lands along the Gulf of Mexico coast from Florida to Texas. In the next decade, Álvar Núñez Cabeza de Vaca accompanied the Pánfilo de Narváez expedition to Florida and then sailed along the shores of the Gulf Coast. Many in the expedition died before the survivors of the expedition landed ashore on Galveston Island off the Texas coast in 1528.

Cabeza de Vaca and Esteban, a black slave, wandered around Texas for years, sometimes being held captive by the native peoples. In 1536, the two men found some Spaniards, who took them to Mexico. Cabeza de Vaca's stories about his journeys increased Spanish interest in the lands north of New Spain. Francisco Vázquez de Coronado's expedition passed through Texas in 1540–1541.

The next major expeditions into Texas did not occur until after 1685, when René Robert Cavalier, Sieur de La Salle, trying to initiate a French colony at the mouth of the Mississippi River, landed at Matagorda Bay and built Fort St. Louis on Garcitas Creek. After several attempts, a Spanish expedition led by Alonso de Léon discovered the ruins of the fort, which had been attacked by Karankawa Indians. The French attempt to settle Louisiana prompted Spanish officials to occupy Texas.

Missionaries first settled East Texas to work with the Caddo Indians. In 1690, Franciscan missionaries founded missions San Francisco de los Tejas and Santísimo Nombre de María. The missions failed by 1693, as the native peoples, ravaged by smallpox, no longer supported the missionaries. Also, the isolated missions had difficulty obtaining supplies. Missionaries wanted to reoccupy the area, and the French neighbors in Louisiana supported the Spanish venture for trade reasons. In 1716, Captain Domingo Ramón led the expedition that founded four missions and the presidio (fort) San Francisco de los Dolores. The East Texas

The Nuestra Señora de Loreto presidio and Espíritu Santo de Zuñiga mission, know as La Bahía, was an important Spanish settlement in Goliad, southern Texas. The area was a main passage from Mexico to other Texas missions and settlements. *(Library of Congress, HABS, TEX, 88-GOLI,4)*

settlements grew slowly, and the settlers carried on illegal trade with nearby French colonists.

In 1718, Governor Martín de Alarcón founded presidio San Antonio de Béxar and Mission San Antonio de Valero, later called the Alamo. From 1720 to 1731, four missions opened in the San Antonio area, including San José y San Miguel de Aguayo, San Francisco de la Espada, Nuestra Señora de la Purísima Concepción, and San Juan Capistrano. All of these missions except for San José were transferred from the East Texas mission field. The civil settlement grew in 1731, when fifty-five Canary Islanders moved to San Antonio.

San Antonio remained a small, marginal settlement that subsisted on agriculture, ranching, and trade with the native peoples and merchants from other parts of New Spain. Apache and Comanche raids hurt the settlement for years and prevented expansion. Native hostilities continued until the Comanche peace of 1786 brought relative peace to the area and allowed for some expansion. The missions began secularization in the late eighteenth century, and most became parish churches.

Another important mission field, presidio, and settlement in present-day Texas was at Goliad. In 1722, the Spanish founded the presidio Nuestra Señora de Loreto and mission Espíritu Santo de Zuñiga, known as La Bahía. The Spanish did not consider this area part of Texas, but it was the main entryway from Mexico to the Texas settlements.

The Spanish also tried but failed to establish missions and forts among Tonkawas in the 1740s and among the Lipán Apaches at the San Sabá River in the 1750s. The Apaches would not stay at Mission Santa Cruz de San Sabá, and within a year, in 1758, Comanches and other Apache enemies destroyed the mission.

Meanwhile, the East Texas settlements were barely surviving. In 1773, the Crown ordered East Texas settlers to move to San Antonio. The settlers petitioned to move back to East Texas, and under Antonio Gil Ybarbo, they eventually settled Nacogdoches. The East Texas settlements continued to have close ties to Louisiana.

The independence wars that began in the 1810s with Father Miguel Hidalgo's revolt hit Texas hard. In the 1812 invasion of Texas, Bernardo Gutierréz de Lara and American participants took San Antonio and killed Governor Manuel Salcedo. In 1813, the Spanish army reclaimed San Antonio and executed those suspected of siding with the rebels. The region was devastated by the decade of fighting when Mexican independence was finally achieved in 1821.

During the Mexican period, large numbers of Anglo-American settlers moved into Texas, changing the makeup of the colony. Texas became independent of Mexico in 1836.

Amy Meschke

See also: Borderlands, Spanish; Spanish Colonies on Mainland North America (Chronology).

Bibliography

Chipman, Donald E. *Spanish Texas, 1519–1821.* Austin: University of Texas Press, 1992.

De la Teja, Jess F. *San Antonio de Béxar: A Community on New Spain's Far Northern Frontier.* Albuquerque: University of New Mexico Press, 1995.

Weber, David J. *The Mexican Frontier, 1821–1846: The American Southwest under Mexico.* Albuquerque: University of New Mexico Press, 1982.

Thayendanegea

See Brant, Joseph

Theater

While some plays were written and produced in North America during the colonial period, most were imported directly from England, scripts and actors alike. Initially, the rigors of early settlement did not encourage playwriting or acting. Later on, acting was too precarious a profession to risk unknown plays or actors.

In the English-speaking colonies, Shakespeare was the most popular playwright, more so than in England at the time. The first known Shakespeare production in North America was *Romeo and Juliet*, performed in New York by an amateur group in 1730. By the outbreak of the Revolution, nearly 500 performances of Shakespeare's plays had been staged in the colonies. Other popular plays were George Lillo's *George Barnwell*, George Farquhar's *The Recruiting Officer* and *The Beaux' Stratagem*, and John Gay's *The Beggar's Opera*. Despite the long Atlantic passage, a new play opening in London usually reached the colonies within three to seven months.

Most of these plays were followed by an "afterpiece," usually a lighthearted farce or a musical performance. Although Virginia and Maryland were the most accepting of the theater, plays were performed in nearly

Early Plays, Venues, and Companies

The first known play to be performed in an English colony was *The Bare and the Cubb* on August 27, 1665, in a tavern on the eastern shore of Virginia. Although the play was deemed a success, one member of the community, Edward Martin, complained of heresy. The three actors in the play, Cornelius Watkinson, Philip Howard, and William Darby (also author of the play), were summoned to the county court. There, the magistrates requested that the defendants perform the play and found them "not guilty of fault." Martin was then requested to pay the court costs. It is not known if there were any repeat performances.

Other early plays include a production of Benjamin Coleman's *Gustavus Vasa* in Cambridge, Massachusetts, in 1690 and the *Pastoral Colloquy* in Williamsburg, Virginia, in 1702. The first play to be printed in the colonies was Robert Hunter's *Androboros, a B{i}ographical Farce in Three Acts* in 1714. It was written as a satire of the Anglican Church and was probably never performed.

In 1716, William Levingston began raising funds to build the first organized playhouse in Williamsburg. The first play to be performed there was part of a public entertainment in honor of the birthday of King George I. In time, Levingston's fortunes were reversed and his theater fell into disrepair.

Most professional actors in the seventeenth and eighteenth centuries were members of traveling companies. The first attempts to organize such a company in the colonies began in Philadelphia under the management of Walter Murray and Thomas Kean. The only play known to have been performed by them in Philadelphia was the political drama *Cato*. After mixed reviews, the company moved to New York, where they opened with a performance of *Richard III*. Eventually, they relocated to Williamsburg, where the company finally folded in 1752.

Shortly afterward, the first fully professional company sailed from London to Williamsburg, calling itself the London Company of Comedians. Run by Lewis and Sarah Hallam, the company included the Hallams' three children and ten other English actors. Although they were refused a license to perform, the Hallams decided to stay in Williamsburg and become permanent members of the community. Eventually granted a license, they began acting, promising only the most moral

Mercy Otis Warren was a prolific playwright, poet, and historian of the revolutionary period. Her work—including the dramatic satires *The Adulateur* (1773), *The Defeat* (1773), and *The Group* (1775)—commented on current events and supported the patriot cause. *(Museum of Fine Arts, Boston/ Bridgeman Art Library)*

all of the colonies. Local amateur productions were also more apt to receive acceptance than touring professional ones.

The French and Spanish also brought their own theatrical additions to North America during the colonial period. Passion plays, dramatic representations of the life and death of Jesus Christ, had long been a part of Catholic Europe. By 1526, the Spanish were using such plays to convert Native Americans to Christianity. Likewise, Jesuit priests in Canada had started to employ similar methods by 1606. Once these French communities were permanently established, they also began importing plays and actors from France, just as the English were doing to the south.

Among the other European immigrants, the Dutch and German colonists generally regarded plays with tolerance, if with the opinion that money could be better spent elsewhere. After the British acquisition of New York, plays became more common in that colony.

plays. In time, they traveled among Virginia, Pennsylvania, New York, and South Carolina.

After Lewis Hallam died in 1755, the company was taken over by David Douglass. The troupe gradually gained acceptance throughout the colonies, in part because it changed its name in 1763 to the American Company of Comedians. It also was the first professional group to perform a play written by an American, Thomas Godfrey, Jr.'s *The Prince of Parthia*. After waiting out the American Revolution in Jamaica, the American Company returned to the United States and continued touring throughout the 1790s.

Overcoming Opposition

During the colonial period, opposition to the theater was widespread, especially in the Northern colonies. Massachusetts, New York, Pennsylvania, New Hampshire, and Rhode Island all passed numerous laws against acting. Initially, these rules reflected the sensibilities of the Puritans and Quakers, who hoped to rebuild England in the colonies without England's faults. They regarded the theater as immoral, leading to vices such as idleness, prostitution, and gambling.

As the theater became more respectable, later rulings in the Northern colonies reflected different concerns. Many colonists were suspicious of English acting companies, seeing them as little more than propaganda for the English throne. Likewise, lawmakers did not want money going to English enterprises that were not part of their community. They also did not want the poorer members of their communities spending money on unnecessary items, such as play tickets. Most Northern colonies were centered around cities and towns, making plays more accessible to all members of society. In contrast, Southern colonies had relatively few cities and many outlying plantations and farms, isolating the rural poor and slaves from potential temptation.

These prohibitions culminated in an act passed on October 20, 1774, by the Continental Congress encouraging frugality and economy in the face of impending war. As part of this rule, professional theater was officially banned for the duration of the war. The only plays to be put on by a professional company during the Revolution were in Maryland, the one state that voted against the ruling.

Despite this ruling, amateur acting and playwriting thrived during the Revolution on both sides, loyalist and patriot. Most productions were political, consisting of satire, propaganda, or both. Among the patriots, one of the most prolific writers was the historian and poet Mercy Otis Warren. Examples of her work include *The Adulateur*, *The Defeat*, and *The Group*. All of her plays commented directly on recent events and took place in Boston, sometimes thinly disguised as the mythical country Upper Servia. Passages from her plays were also published in such patriotic publications as *The Massachusetts Spy*.

Plays produced on the opposite side were usually done by British soldiers. Bored with long occupation of American cities, they used plays as a means of demonstrating their cause, as well as for providing entertainment. General John Burgoyne, leader of the troops occupying Boston in 1775–1776, wrote and produced a farce titled *The Blockade of Boston* in 1775. Remembering the 1774 ruling, Burgoyne frequently sent handbills announcing his productions to George Washington, John Hancock, and other members of the Continental Congress as a way of goading them.

Following the British soldiers' withdrawal in 1776, an anonymous parody titled *The Blockheads; or the Affrighted Officers* circulated in Boston. Plays were also written by loyalists as a way of demonstrating their political support for the British cause; such works included Jonathan Sewall's *A Cure for the Spleen* in 1775. Attempting to bridge the gap between patriots and loyalists was the work of Robert Munford. His 1775 *The Patriots* urged for pacifism and reason rather than the blind patriotism demonstrated by those on both sides of the conflict.

While the plays written during the Revolution are more recognizable as political propaganda than as drama, they represent the first true body of such work created in America. Following the war, acting companies again returned to the familiar imports from England, their incomes still too precarious to chance any unknowns. Playwriting independent of English influence did not become part of theater in the Unites States until the 1850s.

Abigail B. Chandler

See also: Arts, Culture, and Intellectual Life (Chronology); Arts, Culture, and Intellectual Life (Essay); Literature; Music; Warren, Mercy Otis.

Bibliography

Brown, Jared. *The Theater in America During the Revolution.* Cambridge, UK: Cambridge University Press, 1995.
Davis, Peter A. "Puritan Mercantilism and the Politics of Anti-Theatrical Legislation in Colonial America." In *The American Stage: Social and Economic Issues from the Colonial*

Period to the Present, edited by Ron Engle and Tice L. Miller. Cambridge, UK: Cambridge University Press, 1993.

McDermott, Douglas. "The Theater and Its Audience: Changing Modes of Social Organization in the American Theater." In *The American Stage: Social and Economic Issues from the Colonial Period to the Present,* edited by Ron Engle and Tice L. Miller. Cambridge, UK: Cambridge University Press, 1993.

Rankin, Hugh F. *The Theater in Colonial America.* Chapel Hill: University of North Carolina Press, 1965.

Tidewater

The term "Tidewater" usually refers to the areas of Virginia between the fall line and the Atlantic coast. Technically, the Tidewater region ends where the inland waterways cease to be tidal. The area includes Chesapeake Bay and environs and extends about 100 miles from the coast. Four major rivers feed the bay: the James, Rappahannock, York, and Potomac. The Tidewater in the seventeenth century was the site of some of the most important events in American colonial history; in the eighteenth century, the planters living in the Tidewater adopted a Revolutionary stance that set them on a collision course with Great Britain.

In the closing decades of the sixteenth and the beginning of the seventeenth century, Powhatan built up, through strong-arm diplomacy and outright conquest, a paramount chiefdom that covered most of eastern Virginia. Autonomous Algonquin villages, which were settled communities based on corn agriculture, would offer tribute to Powhatan in exchange for protection against outside attacks and also to prevent Powhatan from turning on them. The birth of the English colony of Jamestown in his world gave Powhatan little cause for concern, and he adopted John Smith into the Tidewater through a complicated series of rituals, culminating in the famous rescue of Smith by Pocahontas, Powhatan's daughter.

As pathetic as the settlement at Jamestown was, it supplanted Powhatan as the main power broker in the Tidewater within a couple of decades. Early attempts to turn a profit from surface mining and trade failed, but tobacco agriculture did not. Eventually, tobacco turned into the Tidewater's staple crop, with small farms and larger plantations spreading out beyond Chesapeake Bay.

Tobacco cultivation was hard on land and labor. The indentured servants who initially worked in the fields gave way to African slaves as the seventeenth century progressed. A Dutch ship brought the first Africans to Virginia, and while their legal status may have been slightly murky, the legal status of Africans in late-seventeenth- and eighteenth-century Virginia was crystal clear. They and their children were permanent chattel, or movable property. A rigid, caste-like system grew to maturity in the Tidewater's tobacco-producing areas.

At the pinnacle of this Tidewater plantation society were the great planters. In addition to dominating the region economically and culturally, they controlled Tidewater politics tightly. Their fathers and grandfathers had worked the land in the Tidewater and struggled to survive in a harsh and alien environment, but by the eighteenth century many of the leading planter families, such as the Byrds and Carters, had begun to establish themselves as a new American aristocracy, one whose powers in Virginia surpassed those possessed by the English aristocracy across the Atlantic. This class of men shared one defining characteristic: they were first and foremost tobacco planters, and this label carried a fair amount of cultural baggage in eighteenth-century Virginia.

Crop masters, as the very best referred to themselves, presented themselves as perfectly independent, skilled agriculturalists who took great pride in their ability to produce quality tobacco. They claimed to know precisely when to plant, sucker, cut, and cure tobacco plants. Their tobacco plantations—requiring large investments in capital, land, and slaves, as well as their extravagant lifestyles, amounting to a blatant attempt to copy the English aristocracy—ran much of the Tidewater into massive debt.

Not surprisingly, the great planters of the Tidewater were susceptible to political philosophies that were fairly radical in England. The ideas have a variety of names—country thought, opposition philosophy, and republicanism to name a few—but they all shared a deep-rooted belief in personal autonomy, civic virtue, and the corrupting influence of political power.

When the tobacco market slowed in the 1760s and early 1770s, the great Tidewater planters saw their personal autonomy, their virtue, and, to some extent, their masculinity eroding, and they took extraordinary steps to stop it. The Tidewater provided some of the most able defenders of American liberty, both in terms of philosophy, in the person of Thomas Jefferson, and military guidance in the person of George Washington.

After the American War for Independence, the Tidewater continued to be important, as the newly created United States struggled to put together a government and a national identity.

Matthew Jennings

See also: Environment and Nature; North Carolina; Piedmont; South Carolina; Virginia.

Bibliography

Billings, Warren M., John E. Selby, and Thad W. Tate. *Colonial Virginia: A History.* White Plains, NY: KTO, 1986.

Breen, T. H. *Tobacco Culture: The Mentality of the Great Tidewater Planters on the Eve of Revolution.* Chapel Hill: University of North Carolina Press, 1985.

Gleach, Frederic W. *Powhatan's World and Colonial Virginia: A Conflict of Cultures.* Lincoln: University of Nebraska Press, 1997.

Timekeeping

See Clocks and Timekeeping

Tobacco

Tobacco, used extensively for curing and in religious and sociopolitical rituals by native peoples across the Americas, was introduced to Europeans in 1492—though they got its name wrong. As tobacco burned its way into our modern history, spreading rapidly across Europe, Asia, and Africa, doctors extolled its virtues as a medicinal panacea, while popes denounced it as the "devil weed" and world leaders encouraged its spread in order to tax it and add to their treasuries. Tobacco use rose, spiraling upward like the evocative smoke of the burning herb, then began plummeting to smoldering ashes as, in the last half of the twentieth century, its use was irrevocably linked to cancer.

Discovery and Cultivation by Native Americans

The tobacco plant and its derivative products were called *cohiba* or *cohoba* by the Taino, the natives of the Greater Antilles who introduced it to Christopher Columbus and his crews. Spain's Royal Historian Gonzalo Fernández de Oviedo y Valdés wrote in the 1530s that it was the hollow inhaler tubes used by the Taino that were called *tabaco,* the name other Spaniards mistakenly understood to be the herb itself.

Tobacco was growing wild in South America by 6000 B.C.E., and the plant belongs to the Solanaceae family (nightshade), specifically to the genus *Nicotiana,* which contains more than 100 species. By the time Christ was born in the Near East, tobacco had spread across most of the Americas, where native peoples chewed its leaves, drank it as a tea, rubbed it onto their bodies, or inhaled it in all manner of medicinal preparations and curing rituals. Above all, however, Native Americans cherished tobacco as a sacred intoxicant that eased communication not only among men but also between this world and the world of the spirits.

By the time Europeans arrived in the Americas, native peoples as far north as today's Montreal were growing vast quantities of tobacco, "on which they set great value," wrote Jacques Cartier. Columbus and Cartier, among others, recorded that Amerindians used tobacco in many religious ceremonies, took tobacco with them whenever they traveled (it was as important as food), gave tobacco as prestige gifts, and shared tobacco as a key part of many of their social rituals—for example, some North American Indians smoked a *calumet* (peace pipe) before negotiations.

Tobacco's value among Amerindian peoples can also be seen by the way the herb entered their creation myths. Among the Taino, for example, a gob of spittle laden with tobacco juice grew on the back of Demivan Caracaracol, causing so much pain that his brothers broke the hump open with an axe, releasing a female turtle. (Turtles are a common Amerindian symbol for fertility and the creation of the world.) The Hurons also connect tobacco to females and fertility (although it appears that only the men used it), saying that once, long ago, the land was barren until the Great Spirit sent forth a female savior, who created potatoes wherever she touched her right hand, corn with her left, and tobacco where she sat to rest.

The Cuban scholar Fernando Ortiz, in his magnum study *Cuban Counterpoint: Tobacco and Sugar,* hypothesizes that the smoking of tobacco was a later development among the Amerindians than chewing it or inhaling its powder. Keeping the fire away from the smoker's mouth requires more advanced technology than a hollow reed. Mayans may have been the first to develop the cigar, for the earliest archaeological record we have of smoking is a Mayan vessel from 600–1000 C.E. that was discovered in Uazactun, Guatemala. It depicts a roll of tobacco leaves tied with string—and the word the Mayans used for smoking was *sik'ar.*

First Europeans to Use Tobacco

The first European to smoke a cigar was Rodrigo de Jérez, who was sent by Columbus, along with Luis de Torres, on November 2, 1492, to explore inland Cuba. It is said that Jérez enjoyed smoking so much that he took some cigars home with him to Spain. The smoke coming from his mouth and nostrils made him appear so demonic that his neighbors denounced him to the Inquisition, and he spent some three to seven years in a dungeon (accounts vary). By the time he came out, other sailors had spread the habit of chewing, inhaling, and smoking tobacco across the Iberian Peninsula.

It was the medicinal value of tobacco, however, that really spread its use across the Old World. In 1571, a Spanish physician named Nicolás Monardes wrote *Joyfull News out of the New Founde Worlde*. The book was a compilation of Amerindian cures, including tobacco as a curative for thirty-six different ailments, ranging from wounds and open ulcers to toothaches, lockjaw, rheumatism, worms, bad breath, insomnia, and all manner of colds and respiratory problems. (In the following century, it would also be hailed as a protection against plague.) Medicinal tobacco was used as a poultice, ingested as a tea, or inhaled as snuff.

In Europe, inducing sneezing by inhaling various powders was a popular curative. Tobacco quickly replaced powdered pepper, myrrh, sneezewort, white hellebore, and spurge, for it had a soothing effect, relieving the sufferer's worries about his or her illness. Oviedo

The tobacco plant is indigenous to the Americas; native peoples have been smoking and chewing its leaves for millennia. The Spanish carried it back to Europe, and smoking—both for pleasure and medicinal purposes—became widespread there in the sixteenth century. *(Private Collection/ Bridgeman Art Library)*

noted, however, that tobacco made people oblivious to their pain but did not cure them. He also noted that Africans, who were taken to the Indies as slaves, soon took to growing tobacco around their homes to smoke when they finished work, saying that it relieved their tiredness.

Imperial Spain held a monopoly on tobacco sales until 1556, when a clergyman named André Thevet took seeds from Brazil to France. Although it appears that tobacco was growing in Portugal as early as 1512, it is not listed among Lisbon's market items until 1558.

Tobacco did not become popular in France until the French ambassador in Lisbon, Jean Nicot, wrote to Queen Catherine de Medici in 1559 lauding tobacco's curative properties. He sent some to the French court, recommending it for the queen's migraine headaches. Today, the genus of the herb still bears his name, as does tobacco's addictive alkali substance.

Tobacco in England's North American Colonies

Shortly after tobacco reached France, Sir John Hawkins and his sailors introduced pipe smoking to England. Documents indicate that Sir Francis Drake brought back the first plant specimens in 1573, but they made little impact, for smoking tobacco remained principally a sailor's habit until 1586. That was when colonists returning from the Virginia Colony were seen disembarking at Plymouth and smoking tobacco in pipes. It caused quite a sensation among the upper classes of England, especially when it became known that Sir Walter Raleigh himself was a pipe smoker. Just before he lost his head on the executioner's block in 1618, Raleigh smoked one last pipeful of tobacco. Some claim that the pipe was still clamped in his mouth when the axe came down. Ralph Lane, the first governor of the Virginia Colony, is credited with inventing the long-stemmed clay pipe used by Raleigh, although Native Americans had been using such pipes for centuries.

All American schoolchildren learn the story of the first permanent English settlement in America and how Jamestown would have been lost had it not turned to raising tobacco as an export crop. Captain John Smith, the colony's leader, was imprisoned by the Powhatans; according to his account, the native princess Pocahontas spoke up for him and saved his life. Pocahontas married John Rolfe, another of the Jamestown colonists, whom she showed how to plant, care for, cure, ferment, and age tobacco. Rolfe planted seeds from

Trinidad and the Orinoco River regions, which were not as bitter as the standard variety grown by the native peoples along the Chesapeake.

The new tobacco's potential as a commercial crop was tremendous—there were already 7,000 shops selling tobacco in and around London by 1614, the year that the Jamestown colonists broke the Iberian monopoly by exporting a shipment to England. Ten years later, the Jamestown colonists sold 200,000 pounds of tobacco in London; in 1638, some 3 million pounds; and by the 1680s, more than 25 million pounds per year.

Most of the work of the Virginia Assembly during the early decades of the colony dealt with laws and taxes regulating the tobacco trade, including those concerning the indentured servants and African slaves required for the labor-intensive crop. In 1676, Virginia's Governor Berkeley learned the hard way that the colonists would not support tobacco taxes that they considered to be too high—the ensuing Bacon's Rebellion was a foretaste of the American Revolution.

By the mid-1700s, the Middle colonies of North America were exporting half of the world's production of tobacco and had become dependent on African slave labor. Tobacco had become, very literally, a "cash crop," whose leaves were used as cash. When a private ship arrived carrying ninety English women to be wed in Jamestown, the colonists paid with 120 pounds of tobacco per woman. Tobacco set the monetary standard in the colonies for more than two centuries, for its value was relatively stable. Each colony had its own currency, which was not always recognized by the others, but goods and services could still be traded in terms of the cost in gold of a pound of tobacco.

In recognition of tobacco's importance to the American economy and to the American Revolution, all "continental money" that was printed throughout the Revolution bore the stamp of a tobacco leaf. In fact, the Revolution was known as the Tobacco War along the East Coast because one of the causes was resentment against heavy taxes levied on tobacco by the British. Tobacco also was used as collateral to secure the loans from France with which the colonists financed the Revolution.

Back in France and England, pipe smoking had spread from sailors to the working class during the seventeenth century, so aristocrats switched to snorting snuff. Queen Charlotte (for whom Charlottesville, Virginia, and Charlotte, North Carolina, are named), wife of King George III of England, was known as Snuffy Charlotte, because she was so fond of it. "Dandies" at the royal courts carried exquisite snuff boxes decorated with cameos, miniature paintings, and jewels—and lace handkerchiefs to wipe away the brown slime that dripped from their noses as a result of their addiction.

Spanish nobles preferred smoking cigars, a habit that Napoleon Bonaparte and Lord Wellington's troops spread back to their home countries after the invasion of Spain in 1808. Spaniards and Portuguese had already introduced cigar smoking to Asia, Turkey, and Russia.

Hostility to Tobacco

The first to speak out against the "devil weed" were the popes of the 1600s, who forbade Catholic clergy and the faithful from using it because of its close connection with Amerindian "demonic" rituals and because the sneezing caused by taking snuff was considered to be too closely related to sexual ecstasy. Addiction to tobacco, however, proved stronger than the repeated threats of excommunication.

In 1603, King James I of England wrote "A Counterblast to Tobacco," the first antismoking report in history. When he needed tax revenue, he still ended up encouraging the increased use of tobacco in England.

Napoleon Bonaparte, too, was against the rising use of tobacco (although he is said to have snuffed up to 7 pounds of it a month), but he was cognizant of its importance to his treasury. He wrote to his advisers, "This vice brings in 100 million francs each year. I will certainly forbid it at once—as soon as you can name a virtue that brings in as much revenue."

Tobacco has a unique place in American colonial history. There was no other agricultural product that could even approach it in terms of its acceptance across a wide range of social categories, its use as a political tool, its utility for an incredible number and variety of practical applications and cultural rituals, and—perhaps most important of all—the revenues that it brought to its growers, manufacturers, distributors, and vendors, as well as in the form of taxes over the centuries. Tobacco is frequently touted as the reason colonists in North America were so expansionist, so greedy to take over more and more Native American territory, for tobacco quickly drained the soil of its nutrients, requiring "unspoiled" land.

Tobacco is fundamentally linked to the history of African American slavery, as well as to the causes of Bacon's Rebellion and the American Revolution. Tobacco set the monetary standard in the North American colonies for more than 200 years, and it continues to have a major influence on the South's income today.

Unfortunately, tobacco is also unique in that no

other American agricultural product has fallen so fast and so far. Today tobacco is intimately linked with precedent-setting records for damage suits against the industry that produces and sells products known to cause cancer. Perhaps this is the real "Montezuma's revenge."

Lynne Guitar

See also: Agriculture; Jamestown; Plantations; Raleigh, Sir Walter; Slavery, African American; Trade; Virginia Company. *Document:* Tobacco Growing (1775).

Bibliography

Borio, Gene. "The History of Tobacco, Part I (to 1676)." http://www.historian.org/bysubject/tobacco1.htm.

———. "The History of Tobacco, Part II." http://www.historian.org/bysubject/tobacco2.htm.

"A Brief History of Jamestown, VA." http://www.tobacco.org/History/Jamestown.html.

Monardes, Nicolás. *Joyfull News out of the New Founde Worlde.* Translated by John Frampton Marchant. London, 1577.

Ortiz, Fernando. *Cuban Counterpoint: Tobacco and Sugar.* Translated by Harriet de Onis. Durham, NC: Duke University Press, 1995.

Oviedo y Valdés, Gonzalo Fernández de. *Historia general y natural de las Indias. Biblioteca de Autores Españolas.* Vols. 117–21. Madrid: Gráficas Orbe, 1959.

Tools

Colonial Americans used and modified the culture of tools and tool making they had inherited from Europe. Tools were indispensable to a variety of economic activities and represented a considerable capital investment. The economic value of tools can be seen in probate inventories that carefully describe not only specific tools but even parts of a tool, such as metal harrow teeth.

Agricultural Tools

Early immigrants from England came with standard agricultural tools. These included the hoe, the forked hoe, and the spade for tilling; the sickle for harvesting; the flail for winnowing; and bill hooks for removing underbrush, as well as weeding tongs and shovels. Rather than making the entire shovel of metal, the usual practice was to make the body of the shovel of wood and sheath it with metal.

Plows began to appear in the 1630s and 1640s and were usually heavy, requiring several teams of oxen to draw them. Given the expense of a plow and oxen, many farmers could not afford them and either continued to hoe or hired a plow from a wealthier neighbor. Colonists originating in different parts of Europe would bring different styles of plow or other equipment. For example, English-derived plows had a flat ploughshare, a wooden coulter to cut the soil ahead of the plowshare, and two handles; Dutch farmers in America used "hog plows" with a pyramidal ploughshare, no coulter, and one handle. The lighter Dutch plow took less animal power to pull and worked better on good soil, while the English plow took much more power to pull but was more effective on poor and rocky soil. Most American plows remained heavy and inefficient until the development of the shovel plow, named after its shovel-shaped ploughshare, in the mid-eighteenth century.

Although the first tools were imported, there soon emerged local American tool making carried out by farmers themselves or by blacksmiths. Some smiths in centers of population came to specialize in tool making. The best tools were usually those imported from England, but most farmers could not afford them. The growing prosperity of the colonies meant that good tools became more widely distributed in the eighteenth century. Their quality also improved. For example, metal spades nailed to wooden handles replaced the seventeenth-century metal-sheathed wooden spades.

The most popular tool for harvesting grain in the areas of English settlement was the sickle, a curved metal blade with a short wooden handle. It required bending over to grasp the grain plant by hand and then swinging the sickle to cut it. Dutch farmers in New York and New Jersey used a device called a mathook, which in conjunction with the *sith*, or Flemish scythe, enabled them to harvest more efficiently without bending over. By the end of the colonial period, the cradle scythe, a much more efficient but heavier device, had come into use for grain harvesting in New England. The cradle scythe had a long straight blade at the end of the handle, with four wooden "fingers" about the same length as the blade and parallel to it. When wielded by a skilled practitioner, the cradle scythe not only cut grain more quickly than the sickle but also laid it out in a way that made for easy binding into sheaves.

The late eighteenth century and the time of the American Revolution saw much interest on the part of society's leaders in better agricultural tools as part of the overall movement for "improvement." The newly

The early colonial iron industry could not support shipbuilding or other heavy manufacturing, but it was valuable in the production of pots and pans, nails and bolts, and basic hand tools. *(Brown Brothers, Sterling, Pennsylvania)*

founded American Philosophical Society heard papers on ideas for upgrading tools.

One particularly vexatious problem that cried out for a solution was associated with the threshing of grain. The basic threshing tool was the flail, which had existed unchanged for many centuries. Two pieces of wood were held together by a strap. The thresher held one piece and swung the other at the grain. It was exhausting and slow work. (The alternative was threshing by having heavy-hoofed animals walk over the grain, which also was slow and produced unclean grain.)

There were several attempts to mechanize threshing. In 1770, the General Assembly of Pennsylvania awarded a man named John Clayton (not the Virginia botanist of the same name) a patent for a threshing machine, but the machine proved ineffective. The Virginia Society for the Promotion of Usefull Knowledge, shortly after its founding in 1773, awarded a gold medal to John Hobday, inventor of a threshing machine that he claimed was capable of threshing 120 bushels in a day.

The most publicized new tool of the time was the seed drill, introduced by the Englishman Jethro Tull and then improved by Connecticut clergyman Jared Eliot, the foremost American promoter of the "new agriculture." Assisted by Thomas Clap, the president of Yale College, and Benoni Hylliard, a local wheelwright, Eliot made several improvements to the drill-plough. Eliot's version of Tull's seed drill combined a plough with a mechanism for the planting of seeds that produced more even planting than would be possible by hand. Despite the interest they attracted, the new machines had as yet little impact on the practice of farming.

Woodworking Tools

Nearly as important as agricultural tools were woodworking tools. Colonial America was rich in wood, particularly at the early stages of colonization, and the early colonists built an enormous amount from scratch. In 1622, the Virginia Company recommended that each immigrant family come equipped with two broadaxes, two felling axes, two steel handsaws, one whipsaw, two hammers, two augurs, six chisels, two stocked braces, three gimlets, two hatchets, two froes, nails, and a grindstone. If all this equipment were actually brought along, it would have represented a substantial portion of an immigrant family's economic outlay.

No woodworking tool was more important to the development of America than the axe. Axes show up very early in the European invasion of North America, as small axes and hatchets were common trade goods of Europeans dealing with Native Americans. These axes were traded to the natives by Spanish, French, and English traders. They were known as Biscayan axes if they were Spanish and as Hudson Bay axes if they were English. Given the Native Americans' lack of sharp metal tools, axes were quite valuable in exchange.

The "felling axe" for chopping down trees was among the most common axes used by the settlers themselves, and it underwent substantial improvement in the British colonies from its European original. The American felling axe developed by shortening the blade and creating a heavier (and sometimes steel-reinforced) poll, on the opposite side of the handle of the blade, to counterbalance the weight of the blade and make the axe easier to swing; it also made the reverse of the blade a more effective hammer. The body of the blade of the American felling axe was composed of iron—charcoal iron being useful for this purpose—with a steel cutting wedge as wide as 1.5 inches welded on. When the edge dulled, it was replaced by welding a sheet of steel on one side of the axe, a process known as "steeling" the axe.

Another common kind of axe was the hewing or "goosewing" axe, with the handle bent away from the blade to enable the user to chop wood without having his hand strike the wood. Goosewing axes often had the maker's name inscribed on them, while felling axes did not. The mortising or "posthole" axe, with the blade at right angles to the haft, was used to chop the square mortises into wood for making a mortise-and-tenon joint.

Although axes were made in America, many fine woodworking tools used by carpenters, joiners, cabinetmakers, turners, and other workers in wood continued to be imported from Britain. (One exception was the plane, the most common woodworking tool, which was often made by woodworkers themselves out of maple with a metal blade.) The average master woodworker spent 10 to 20 pounds on tools. Woodworkers sometimes supplemented their income by selling imported tools, and the Continental Congress was concerned by how the Revolutionary War's severing of economic ties to Britain would adversely affect the American economy by ending the import of British tools.

Some Americans took up commercial toolmaking. Among the earliest was Francis Nicholson of Wrentham, active in the first half of the eighteenth century and specializing in joiners' and carpenters' planes.

Textiles

Another important class of tools, those used in textile manufacturing, changed very little in the colonial period. Spinning wheels were uncommon in the early phases of colonization but much more common later. They were divided into two types, the "walking wheel" for spinning wool into yarn and the foot-operated treadle wheel (also known as the Dutch, linen, or foot wheel) used for spinning flax. Both types of spinning wheels were made of wood, and their operation was quintessentially "women's work."

Once spun, yarn was gathered and measured by hand on wooden reels known as "niddy-noddys." There were also hand-cranked reels. The thread was then woven into cloth on wooden looms.

Spinning took on a political aspect during "homespun" campaigns, when Americans were encouraged to wear American-made clothes rather than imports from Britain. The mechanization of textile manufacturing, which would revolutionize the American economy, occurred only after the American Revolution.

William E. Burns

See also: Agriculture; Artisans; Iron; Manufacturing; Technology.

Bibliography

Cohen, David Steven. *The Dutch-American Farm.* New York and London: New York University Press, 1992.

Kauffman, Henry J. *American Axes: A Survey of Their Development and Their Makers.* Brattleboro, VT: Stephen Green Press, 1972.

Kebabian, Paul B., and William C. Lipke, eds. *Tools and Technologies: America's Wooden Age.* Burlington: University of Vermont for the Robert Hull Fleming Museum, 1979.

McGaw, Judith A., ed. *Early American Technology: Making and Doing Things from the Colonial Era to 1850.* Chapel Hill: Published by the University of North Carolina Press for the Institute of Early American History and Culture, Williamsburg, Virginia, 1994.

Ruttman, Darrett B. *Husbandmen of Plymouth: Farms and Villages in the Old Colony, 1620–1692.* Boston: Published for Plimoth Plantation by Beacon Press, 1967.

Ulrich, Laura Thatcher. *The Age of Homespun: Objects and Stories in the Creation of an American Myth.* New York: Alfred A. Knopf, 2001.

Tordesillas, Treaty of (1494)

Christopher Columbus's 1492 voyage on behalf of the Spanish Crown caused serious diplomatic problems because of previous Portuguese explorations in the South Atlantic and Indian Oceans. Papal bulls issued in 1452 and 1454 by Pope Nicholas V gave the Portuguese the right to subjugate any infidels they encountered in the course of their explorations and vaguely defined Portugal's possessions as those lands on Africa's "south coast and east side." Additionally, a bull issued in 1481 gave spiritual jurisdiction over all new discoveries to the Portuguese Order of Christ, the religious organization founded by Prince Henry the Navigator.

Until Spain's sponsorship of Columbus, the Portuguese had been unchallenged in their voyages down the coast of Africa and in their claims to the Azores, Madeira, and Cape Verde islands. A subsequent treaty between Spain and Portugal, signed in 1487, confirmed Portugal's possession of the "Indies" and the "seas as far as the Indies."

Upon Columbus's arrival in Seville to report his discovery and claiming of Hispaniola, Ferdinand and Isabella of Spain dispatched ambassadors to Pope Alexander VI, appealing to his authority as head of the Roman Catholic Church to validate Spanish claims and define Spanish and Portuguese spheres of exploration. The pope, a Spaniard, quickly issued three papal bulls over the summer of 1493, giving Spain Columbus's discoveries and defining the line between Spain and Portugal's claims as 100 leagues (1 league equals 3 miles) southwest of the Azores and Cape Verde islands. Portuguese King Jao II was furious. The pope's decision defined no westward limit, thus cutting into Portuguese claims in India, and limiting Portuguese navigation to routes around the Cape of Good Hope.

Instead of relying on the Vatican's pronouncements, the Spanish and Portuguese monarchies exchanged ambassadors in order to arrange a state treaty to address the problem. The Spanish accredited Garcia de Carvajal and Rodrigo Maldonado de Talavera, an expert on Columbus's original proposal to cross the Atlantic, while Portugal sent Ruy de Sousa and Arias de Almadana.

On June 7, 1494, in the Castilian town of Tordesillas, the signatories agreed to a treaty that specifically excluded the papacy from the negotiations and reserved authority for dividing discoveries to the nations claiming them. These terms were meant to cover all present and future territorial claims as well as those under discussion. The line of demarcation was set at 46 degrees 37 minutes west, or 370 leagues west of the Cape Verde islands, a significant difference from the 1493 papal bull. The two nations also agreed to dispatch a joint surveying party within ten months.

Although this provided an immediate solution to rival claims, the Treaty of Tordesillas was still sufficiently vague to cause enduring problems, especially after Portugal claimed Brazil in 1500. Spain and Portugal hotly contested the point from which the 370-league line was to be measured: the most westward Cape Verde island or the center island in the chain, a specific point that affected Portuguese settlements in the western part of Brazil (where surveying a border in the middle of the Amazon rainforest was nearly impossible). Claims on the Molucca Islands were also at issue. In addition, extension of the line of demarcation into the Eastern Hemisphere divided Asia, allotting China to Portugal and Japan to Spain.

The Vatican was incensed at being left out of the treaty, and Pope Julius II did not approve the agreement until 1506. The treaty remained in force, despite British and French exploration and settlement, until the two Iberian powers dissolved it by mutual agreement in 1761.

Margaret Sankey

See also: Columbus, Christopher; Exploration; Military and Diplomatic Affairs (Chronology); Military and Diplomatic Affairs (Essay); Spanish Colonies on Mainland North America (Chronology).

Bibliography

Harrisse, Henry. *The Diplomatic History of America: Its First Chapter, 1452–1493–1494.* London: B. F. Stevens, 1897.

McAlister, Lyle N. *Spain and Portugal in the New World, 1492–1700.* Minneapolis: University of Minnesota Press, 1984.

Traboulay, David M. *Columbus and Las Casas: The Conquest and Christianization of America, 1492–1566.* Lanham, MD: University Press of America, 1994.

Townshend, Charles (1725–1767)

Author of the 1767 duties that bore his name, Charles Townshend was an aristocratic English statesman who rose to prominence through his often unscrupulous behavior. The taxes he proposed levying on the colonies led to active resistance against English rule, doing much to bring about the American Revolution.

Born on August 29, 1725, the second son of Charles Viscount Townshend, young Charles was educated at Leyden University in Holland. Upon his return to England, he sat on behalf of Great Yarmouth in Parliament from 1747 to 1761. Over the course of his political career, Townshend was able to make a name for himself by allying with any group or individual offering him the best chance for future success. His shifting allegiances earned him the nickname "weathercock" among friends and opponents alike.

By 1749, Townshend had been given a commission on the Board of Trade. While serving in that capacity, the young upstart distinguished himself in a debate over proposed changes to the marriage law. His political future seemed bright indeed as he was made lord of admiralty in 1754 and appointed treasurer of the chamber two years later under William Pitt, the new secretary of state.

True to his nickname, Townshend shifted his allegiance from Pitt to the new secretary of state and John Stuart, Earl of Bute, and he was awarded the post of secretary of war in 1761, which allowed him to be active in the conduct of government business in the House of Commons. After resigning this last position, he was appointed president of the Board of Trade in

February 1763. When Grenville succeeded Bute in April, Townshend refused a post after his nominee failed to win a commission in the new administration. Although he later accepted the position of paymaster general, which he continued to hold through Rockingham's ministry, he was an outspoken critic of both administrations.

In 1766, Townshend became part of William Pitt's cabinet as his chancellor of the exchequer. Due to ill health, Pitt was unable to keep his subordinates under close watch. As the new chancellor, Townshend used his post to get a substantial share of a public loan and to rise above many of his colleagues, seizing leadership of the cabinet.

The problem of raising revenue from the colonies to defray the expenses of maintaining British troops and forts on the Western frontier fell squarely on the shoulders of Charles Townshend, as a leader in the new administration. Despite its best efforts, Parliament had never been able to levy an effective tax in the colonies. The Stamp Act of 1765 was repealed before it had yielded any profits. The revenue acts proposed by Townshend in May 1767 would include a port duty on glass, lead, painters' colors, paper, and tea, establish a custom's commission to oversee the laws of trade, and suspend the New York Assembly until it complied with an earlier quartering act. Parliament, desperate for money and hoping that Americans would respect this new tax, passed the Townshend Revenue Acts on June 29, 1767.

The provisions of the new acts infuriated Americans. Money gained from the taxes was to be used against Americans by paying the salaries of colonial governors and judges who were independent of the assemblies. Americans were also fearful of Townshend's reorganization of the custom's office. Over the several preceding decades, custom officials residing in England often delegated their duties to agents in the colonies, who were easily bribed by American smugglers. The new Customs Commission would put a stop to smuggling and be easily corruptible, as those officers seizing a vessel were entitled to one-third of the profits from the sale of the cargo. These officers also were given blanket search warrants, known as Writs of Assistance, which Americans rightfully considered an invasion of privacy. Finally, by dissolving the legislative functions of the New York Assembly, Parliament, in the eyes of many, was overstepping its bounds in an effort to gain supreme authority over the colonies.

To most Americans, the Townshend Revenue Acts

England's Chancellor of the Exchequer Charles Townshend (portrayed by Sir Joshua Reynolds) sponsored the eponymous legislation in 1767 that imposed duties on goods imported into America and sparked colonial protests. *(Private Collection/Philip Mould, Historical Portraits Ltd., London, United Kingdom/Bridgeman Art Library)*

exemplified the carelessness of parliamentary legislation. Like the Stamp Act before it, the proposed measures were immediately resisted. Riots took place in colonial towns, nonimportation associations were formed, and royal officials were scoffed at. The economic sanctions and other forms of resistance led, by April 12, 1770, to a repeal of all these duties except the tax on tea.

Despite his many abilities, Charles Townshend's career was marred by inconsistency of character, untrustworthiness, corruption, and, in the end, failure. On September 4, 1767, before the duties that bore his name were ever enacted, he died of typhus at the age of 42.

Aaron F. Christensen

See also: Board of Trade; Townshend Acts (1767). *Document:* Townshend Revenue Act (1767).

Bibliography

Forster, Cornelius P. *The Uncontrolled Chancellor: Charles Townshend and His American Policy.* Providence: Rhode Island Bicentennial Foundation, 1978.

Namier, Sir Lewis Bernstein. *Charles Townshend, 1725–1767.* New York: St. Martin's, 1964.

Thomas, Peter David Garner. *The Townshend Duties Crisis: The Second Phase of the American Revolution, 1767–1773.* New York: Oxford University Press, 1987.

Townshend Acts (1767)

In the aftermath of the Stamp Act Crisis, the British government continued to face a looming debt from the Seven Years' War and political pressure to prove Parliament's ability to tax the American colonies.

From 1766, William Pitt, Earl of Chatham, headed the ministry, with Charles Townshend at the Exchequer, or finance ministry, and two supporters of the Marquis of Rockingham, General Henry Conway and Lord Shelburne, in the cabinet. Rockingham was also sympathetic to colonial interests. This was a deliberate coalition of men, some of whom, like Pitt, had supported the repeal of the Stamp Act, and others, like Conway, had been long-time colonial sympathizers. Townshend suffered a severe financial defeat at the hands of Rockingham, however, whose supporters forced a 20 percent reduction in the customary land tax from 4 shillings to 3 shillings in February 1767. Thus, the need for revenue became more crucial than ever.

In March 1767, Townshend proposed a new set of colonial taxes on a range of luxury items, using the argument that the Stamp Act had been an internal tax, but that the new proposal was external, covered under the Declaratory Act, and charged only on items purchased willingly by the colonists as imports. Townshend also gambled that the items themselves—fruit and wines from Spain and Portugal, tea, paint, pane glass, and paper—were likely to affect only the wealthy, avoiding agitating the level of society that had protested the Stamp Act.

Eventually, merchants lobbied successfully for the removal of the wine and fruit from the act, arguing that the proposal contradicted the Navigation Acts by allowing Iberia to trade directly with America. Thus, on June 29, 1767, Townshend presented his new tax bill to the House of Commons, which, thinly attended at the end of the spring session, passed it without much debate.

News of the new taxes reached America during the summer recess of the colonial assemblies, restricting protests to personal appeals and petitions. In London, despite the fierce presentations of pamphlets by Benjamin Franklin and Arthur Lee, who wrote as Junius Americanus, the entire issue was overshadowed by the outrageous political maneuvers of John Wilkes and his bids to reenter the House of Commons.

In America, radicals like Samuel Adams attempted to organize boycotts like those that had pressured for a repeal of the Stamp Act. Merchants and many of the Southern colonies, however, did not come out in enthusiastic support, although some patriots showed their affiliation by letting their houses go unpainted and refusing tea. London merchants, who had found expanded European markets during the 1765 boycotts, were not badly hurt by these early protests and did not add their voices to those of the colonists for repeal.

What really began to threaten colonial leaders were a series of associated bills presented by Townshend and passed by the House of Commons. Revenue from the new taxes would not go to pay the war debt or the costs of garrisoning the army in America, but to make colonial officials independent from the legislatures. Additionally, there would be three new Admiralty courts to prosecute smuggling without juries in Charles Town, Philadelphia, and Boston, as well as Halifax, and an American-based Board of Customs Commissioners in Boston. Writs of Assistance, a kind of general warrant used by customs collectors in New England, would be expanded throughout the colonies; these were feared as an excuse to arrest without cause and hold colonists indefinitely.

Massachusetts, its assembly back in session in October, voted a resolution endorsing boycott and defiance; it subsequently sent this resolution out as a Samuel Adams-authored circular letter to the other colonies. When instructed to rescind the document, the assembly voted refusal and was dismissed by the London ministry. Members of the assembly who had voted to obey the government's orders were harassed and turned out of their seats.

Meanwhile, all of the other colonies voted support for the circular letter, although their actual commitment was lukewarm, since some already taxed to pay their officials and they were not adversely affected by the taxes. In Pennsylvania, lawyer John Dickinson published a series of *Letters from a Farmer in Pennsylvania* in the *Pennsylvania Gazette* between December 1767 and February 1768, arguing that although Britain could regulate imperial trade, no tax, internal or external, could be levied on the colonies without their consent, a more stringent position than previously presented to the British authorities.

Townshend, who died unexpectedly of typhus on September 4, 1767, did not live to see his policies enforced. He was succeeded at the Exchequer by Lord North.

The ministry, appalled by Massachusetts's defiance, moved 4,000 troops into Boston—significantly, two regiments recently employed in Ireland to put down a tax protest on malt—and dispatched naval patrols to Boston Harbor. Samuel Adams advocated resistance to the troops, but they landed without incident and took up garrison duty in the resentful city, which was required to quarter and feed them. This situation led directly to the Boston Massacre of 1770, as colonial dissatisfaction took the form of riots over seized ships (John Hancock's smuggler, *Liberty*, was taken) and harassment of customs officials, leading to more hostile relations with the troops.

Moved by Dickinson and Adams and by fear of the growing enforcement powers of the government in London, increasing numbers of colonists signed non-importation agreements against *all* British goods, which eventually convinced merchants to lobby the ministry in 1770. All but one of the Townshend Acts were repealed on April 12, 1770. For the British politicians involved, the action was less attributable to colonial pressure than to internal British politics, as Lord North used the repeal to establish his new cabinet. Significantly, the tax on tea, the least lucrative of the items, was kept as a symbolic proof of Parliament's power to levy taxes on the colonies.

Margaret Sankey

See also: Board of Trade; Mercantilism; Revolutionary War; Townshend, Charles. *Document:* Townshend Revenue Act (1767).

Bibliography

Barrow, Thomas C. *Trade and Empire: The British Customs Service in Colonial America, 1660–1775.* Cambridge, MA: Harvard University Press, 1967.

Sosin, Jack M. *Agents and Merchants: British Colonial Policy and the Origins of the American Revolution, 1763–1775.* Lincoln: University of Nebraska Press, 1965.

Thomas, Peter David Garner. *The Townshend Duties Crisis: The Second Phase of the American Revolution, 1767–1773.* New York: Oxford University Press, 1987.

Trade

After 1492, Spain instituted an economic system of transatlantic trade between the mother country and its colonies known as mercantilism. Under this system, all trade was regulated for the benefit of the parent country. Columbian exchange (trade between the "Old World" and the "New World") proved to be very profitable for Spain. Gold, silver, and other precious resources fortified the Spanish Empire for more than a century.

The defeat of the Spanish Armada in 1588, however, encouraged other European countries to challenge Spain's position in the Americas. The British sent a group of colonists to the North American continent, but the venture was a complete failure. The Roanoke colony mysteriously vanished without a trace. Britain's second attempt, at Jamestown, however, was a success and secured a firm footing for continued British colonization of the North American Eastern coast.

British Colonies

Jamestown was founded in 1607. Had it not been for a friendly local Native American tribe sharing their food with the settlers and teaching them how to plant crops, it, too, would have failed and might not have led to a third attempt to colonize the Americas. These ventures were, after all, great financial investments made by private citizens with the king's permission. Unlike the Spanish, however, the British did not find an abundant supply of precious metals. Instead, John Rolfe learned from Native Americans how to cultivate tobacco, a plant native to the Western Hemisphere, and he began shipping it to England. By 1620, tobacco had become very popular in England and was in high demand. It quickly became the South's chief crop.

In general terms, the Northern colonies prospered through shipbuilding, fishing, and trade, because neither the cold climate nor the hard, rocky ground was particularly conducive to agriculture. On the other hand, the Southern colonies had an economy based on agriculture, because the environment was appropriate for growing rice and tobacco. In the years that followed, the colonial economy became much more diversified, and Great Britain continued to capitalize on it. England purchased over half of all the crops that the colonies produced for market. Also, almost all imports to the colonies came from England.

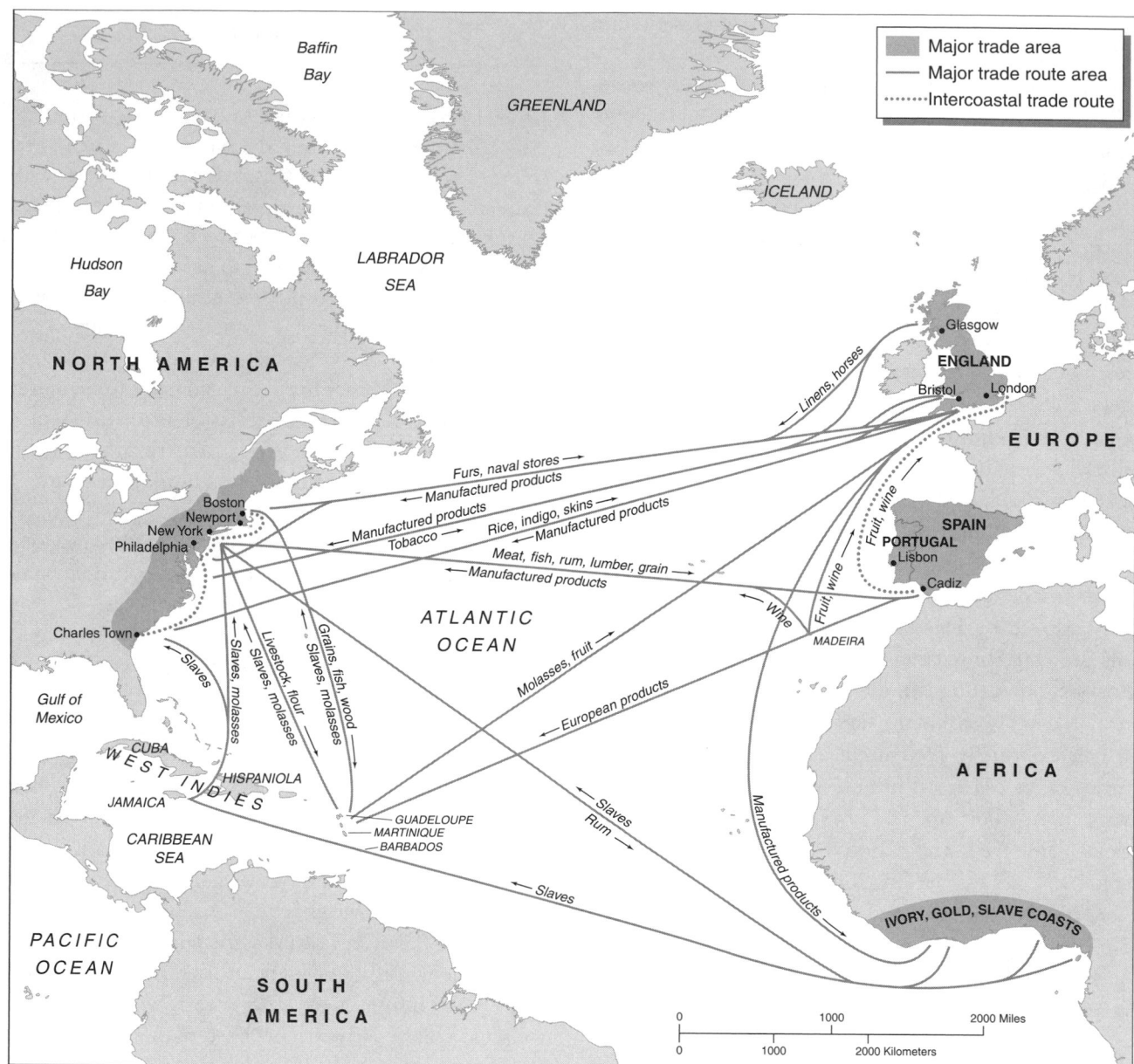

Trans-Atlantic Trade, 1700. The so-called Triangle Trade between Europe, Africa, and North America was, in fact, a far more complicated set of routes by 1700. A variety of goods were being traded between many different regions. *(Carto-Graphics)*

By 1770, the main exports of the New England colonies were fishing-related products (dried fish, pickled fish, and whale products) and wood. The main exports in the Middle colonies were grains and grain-based products (rice, wheat, and flour), wood products, and iron. The Chesapeake colonies provided most of the tobacco and some grains as well. In the lower Southern colonies, agricultural products made up most of the tradable items, which included grains, indigo (a blue, plant-based dye), and wood.

French Colonies

Since the early 1600s, the French had built a sizable fortune based on the fur trade. In the 1700s, the British also sought to cash in on fur, and they began to do some trapping in disputed French/British territory. The military clash that followed announced the coming of the French and Indian War (1754–1763). After the war, the British victory afforded the colonists the ability to venture into newly acquired territory in search of furs.

Furs were also bought from Native Americans, who traveled to the colonial frontier to trade. However, for various reasons, including a diminished supply of the most sought-after beaver furs, the colonial fur trade was never as prosperous as the French enterprise had been. The fur trade, which had been of major economic importance to the French in North America, accounted for only a small percentage of all British colonial trade.

Just like the Spanish, the British North American colonial system followed the rules of mercantilism, which were aimed at enriching the mother country. According to the general guidelines, the colonies were to supply England with raw materials such as tobacco, indigo, furs, grain, and timber. Furthermore, the colonies were expected to purchase English manufactured goods such as glass, clothes, dishes, weapons, and tools.

In order to gain greater control over colonial trade, Parliament passed a series of laws known as the Navigation Acts. The Navigation Act of 1651 stated that all goods sent to England or its colonies had to be transported by British-made ships. The purpose of the law was to minimize the possibility of other European nations benefiting from British colonial trade. The Navigation Act of 1660 stated that certain enumerated items not produced in England (such as tobacco, cotton, indigo dye, and sugar) could only be traded with England and its colonies. This measure sought to get rid of any competition for coveted colonial goods. The Navigation Act of 1663 (Staple Act) stated that all European imports to the colonies had to pass through English ports. Under this act, ships carrying goods from Europe to America had to dock in England and pay a duty before being allowed to proceed. Because of this act, England became the center for colonial trade. With the Navigation Act of 1673 (Plantation Act), England, which already controlled imports, began to control exports as well. The latest act required that ships leaving colonial ports pay a tax on enumerated goods.

In 1675, King Charles II organized the Lords of Trade, a small group of advisers who were charged with overseeing British trade. In 1696, the Board of Trade, which replaced the Lords of Trade, was created by King William III. Its function was to enforce the Navigation Acts. Many colonial merchants, however, found the acts too restrictive and unfair, and they ignored them whenever possible. Consequently, smuggling—importing or exporting goods illegally—was common. While these limits on trade frustrated some colonial businessmen, they went a long way toward boosting the colonial

From the early 1600s, British colonialism in North America was based on trade, as depicted in this engraving of the West Indies by Theodore de Bry. The aim of the mercantile system was to enrich the mother country with supplies of sugar, tobacco, indigo, cotton, and other raw materials. *(Library of Congress/Bridgeman Art Library)*

shipbuilding industry. The increase in colonial ship acquisition led to an increase in colonial trade. In the last part of the seventeenth century, colonial merchants developed a series of trade routes known as the triangular trade. Triangular trade (not literally triangular in shape) was responsible for the transporting of slaves, goods, and ideas found in books and newspapers. Most of these routes fell within the guidelines of mercantilism, but some did not.

Triangular Trade

In a very common triangular route, colonial ships carried rum and iron from New England to Africa. Once in Africa, the cargo was traded for slaves and gold, which were then shipped to the British-held West Indies, where they were traded for sugar and molasses. Finally, the sugar and molasses were shipped to New England and made into rum, and the process started all over again. A second frequent route involved the shipping of colonial grain and lumber to the West Indies, where they were traded for sugar, molasses, and fruit. These goods were then taken to England and traded for manufactured items, which would be shipped to New England.

On occasion, however, colonists strayed from governmental mandates and engaged in smuggling. According to British trade laws, for example, colonists were to buy sugar and molasses only from the West Indies. The demand for these items was so great, however, that colonial merchants sometimes illegally purchased them from the French, Dutch, and Spanish.

The Spanish and the Portuguese were the first to import slaves into the Americas. It has been estimated that, before 1700, Spain and Portugal shipped over 1.5 million slaves to South America. In 1619, a Dutch ship introduced slaves to North America, and, by 1660, when the supply of indentured servants began to wane in the British colonies, slave labor began to look like an attractive alternative. A large labor force was required for growing tobacco in the Southern colonies and producing sugar in the West Indies. Also, as opposed to indentured servants who were bound to service for seven years, slaves could be bound for their entire lives. Furthermore, indentured servants came to the colonies when they chose to come, but slaves could be imported at will to meet the labor demands of any given time.

The first African slaves were captured in wars among African states and then sold to Europeans. By 1700, however, most slaves were kidnapped from the interior of Africa and transported to the African coast by powerful African kingdoms, such as the Dahomey.

The British slave trade, which lasted more than a century, became a very profitable business, and by 1740 more than 40 percent of the population of the Southern British colonies was of African descent. It has been estimated that over 2 million Africans were transported to the British colonies, and almost 12 million were transported by Europeans to North and South America during the existence of the slave trade.

Mercantile System

Early on, the British colonists lacked the means of manufacturing finished goods. Consequently, the colonists imported most of their finished goods from England and Europe. However, the mercantile system put the colonies at a disadvantage and usually left them with a trade imbalance.

After 1660, for example, England raised taxes on New England fish, flour, wheat, and meat in order to protect merchants in England who sold the same products. New England timber, furs, and whale oil, however, were not placed under the heavy burden of taxation. Consequently, New England colonies could still trade, but their trade was kept from its full potential. Basically, the system worked as England intended. New England bought more from England than they sold. The colonies

attempted to use triangular trade to combat the trade imbalance, but trade legislation continued to give England the advantage.

Even under the trade imbalance, however, many colonial businesses prospered, and, even under the yoke of mercantilism, many colonists began leaning toward self-sufficiency by making products in their homes. In order to protect the sale of English-made goods, Parliament passed laws that restricted manufacturing in the colonies. Colonists were allowed to make goods for their own personal use, but they were prohibited from selling these goods anywhere else, including England or any other colony. In 1699, for example, Parliament passed the Woolen Act, which prohibited the colonies from sending wool to England or to other colonies. The Iron Act (1750) kept the colonists from making their own iron. Because of this act, the colonists had to send their raw iron to England and buy finished iron products from English iron mills.

Trade made the colonies what they were: agricultural centers, commercial centers, and, overall, industrious centers. The mercantile system worked well for England. It provided ready markets for English-made goods, and it supplied the mother country with raw materials not available in England. It was no wonder that England spared no expense in the defense of the colonies during the French and Indian War or that England could not stand to lose the North American colonies during the American Revolution.

Trade transformed the colonists from dependent subjects to independent and industrious citizens. Before the American Revolution, colonists thought of themselves primarily as members of the British Empire. Many felt allegiance only to their own colony and mother country. There was little sense of a unified colonial entity. Many differences divided the colonies, and many rivalries existed.

In the midst of all this, the economics of trade within the colonies created the first real bond among them. Because each colony belonged to a distinct regional economy, each region had something unique to offer another region. For example, fish from the New England colonies was readily exchanged for flour from the Middle colonies, indigo from the lower South was traded with all of the other regions, and so on. In fact, in the eighteenth century, even though foreign trade was more profitable, domestic trade accounted for greater volume. As the American Revolution approached, the economic bonds that existed for over a century became the seed from which political and military bonds grew.

The French and Indian War had a profound effect on colonial trade laws, and trade regulation became a major factor in bringing on the crisis of revolution. The expense of waging the French and Indian War and maintaining troops in North America after the war had to be addressed, so taxes were raised in England. Furthermore, King George III and his ministers believed that the colonists should share the monetary burden of their own defense. Consequently, for the first time in colonial history, Parliament taxed the colonies directly.

In 1764, the Molasses Act (1733), which was often ignored by the colonists, was replaced by the Sugar Act. The Sugar Act, which placed a tax on a variety of foreign products such as textiles, wines, and coffee, cut the sixpence per gallon duty on sugar in half. Lord of the Treasury George Grenville hoped that the reduction of the tax would discourage smuggling and remove the temptation to bribe customs officers. Another notable distinction between prior trade laws and the Sugar Act was that the new act was rigorously enforced. The Stamp Act (1765), which also taxed the colonists directly, placed a tariff on all printed materials, including newspapers, pamphlets, almanacs, bonds, leases, deeds, licenses, insurance policies, college diplomas, dice, and playing cards. This act angered all sectors of colonial society.

Colonists found the new laws unbearable and sent petitions to Parliament, led protests, and organized boycotts. In 1770, a Boston demonstration against the new trade regulations got out of hand and culminated in the Boston Massacre. In 1773, colonists boarded three ships in Boston harbor and flung the tea cargo overboard rather than pay the tea tax. As the crises worsened, Thomas Jefferson drew up the Declaration of Independence (1776), which declared the colonies an independent nation free, among other things, to regulate its own trade.

Rolando Avila

See also: Board of Trade; Boston Port Bill; Dutch West India Company; East India Company; Joint-Stock Companies; Mercantilism; Merchants; Native American–European Relations; Navigation Acts (1651–1733); Royal African Company; Slave Trade; Transportation, Land; Transportation, Water; Triangle Trade; Virginia Company.

Bibliography

Barrow, Thomas C. *Trade and Empire: The British Customs Service in Colonial America, 1660–1775.* Cambridge, MA: Harvard University Press, 1967.

Caruthers, J. Wade. "Influence of Maritime Trade in Early American Development: 1750–1830." *American Neptune* 29:3 (1969): 199–210.

Davis, Ralph. "English Foreign Trade, 1700–1774." *Economic History Review*, 2nd ser., 15 (1962): 285–303.

Deyle, Steven. "By Far the Most Profitable Trade: Slave Trading in British Colonial North America." *Slavery & Abolition* 10:2 (1989): 107–25.

Emert, Phyllis Raybin. *Colonial Triangular Trade: An Economy Based on Human Misery.* Lowell, MA: Discovery Enterprises, 1995.

Jones, Alice Hanson. *Wealth of a Nation to Be: The American Colonies on the Eve of the Revolution.* New York: Columbia University Press, 1980.

Lawson, Murray G. *Fur: A Study in English Mercantilism.* Toronto: University of Toronto Press, 1943.

Price, Jacob, and Paul G. E. Clements. "A Revolution of Scale in Overseas Trade, 1675–1775." *The Journal of Economic History* 47:1 (1987): 1–43.

Shepard, James F. "Commodity Exports from the British North American Colonies to Overseas Areas, 1768–1772: Magnitudes and Patterns of Trade." *Explorations in Economic History* 8:1 (1970): 5–76.

Shepherd, James F., and Gary M. Walton. *Shipping, Maritime Trade, and the Economic Development of North America.* Cambridge, UK: Cambridge University Press, 1972.

———. "Trade, Distribution, and Economic Growth in Colonial America." *Journal of Economic History* 32:1 (1972): 128–45.

Steele, Clarendon. *Politics of Colonial Policy: The Board of Trade in Colonial Administrations, 1696–1720.* Oxford, UK: Clarendon Press, 1968.

Trade, Triangle

See Triangle Trade

Trade, Board of

See Board of Trade

Transportation, Land

One challenge facing early American colonists was maintaining communications across a space much larger than that which they had known in England or Europe. Attending Sunday services, carrying goods to market, or even courting could involve many miles of travel.

Although travel by water took up much of the need, many Americans did not own boats or live close to navigable waterways and therefore had to travel on land. Colonial Americans, like their native predecessors and contemporaries, were willing to travel long distances by foot, although as forests were cleared and more horses were brought to the colonies, those who could afford it traveled on horseback.

The paths used by the colonists often followed older Native American routes. One native pathway that became a major thoroughfare in early colonial America was the Bay Path, which went from Cambridge to Springfield, Massachusetts, and the Connecticut River. Paths were marked by blazes, sections cut out of bark of trees along the way—hence the term "trailblazing." These bright patches showed the traveler the way.

Roads

Although initial efforts at colonization often followed waterways, subsequent expansion took colonists into areas more difficult of access as traffic grew heavier. Road building, rather than trailblazing, became a necessity, and many new roads were laid out by surveyors rather than following native trails. In most of colonial America, however, roads remained poor or virtually nonexistent. They frequently crossed private property, making it necessary to dismount and mount to open and close gates. Passage in wheeled vehicles over rocky country was jarring and unpleasant. Roads were also unmarked, making it easy for people to get lost. Bridges were uncommon owing to their expense, and crossing bodies of water was generally accomplished by ferries or fords.

Differences between governments also hindered communications. A plan to institute a postal service between Boston and New York during the Second Dutch War came to nothing, partly because there was no road between these two major cities, one English and one Dutch. Once roads were built, they had to be maintained, and this responsibility fell to the local authorities. The British government took no responsibility for the state of roads, and even provincial assemblies usually deferred to local bodies.

Labor was found for road maintenance by means of a draft, a method with a long tradition in Europe. For example, in Pennsylvania, where roads were somewhat better than in the rest of the colonies, before 1762, all male inhabitants were legally required to spend a few days each year on roadwork. In 1762, a system was established whereby men could buy their way out of the obligation, and that money was used to hire laborers.

Despite the poor quality of the roads, early American travelers had some advantages over their European contemporaries (and many European roads were just as bad). Early America had little "highway robbery," although natives might attack travelers in some times and places. Farmhouses often offered hospitality in areas lacking inns or taverns. Travelers were essential in circulating news to isolated farmers in a society without mass communications.

Vehicles

By the eighteenth century, Americans could travel in wagons, in carriages, and—during the winter—on sledges and sleighs. (Winter travelers also benefited from snowshoes, a Native American invention.) With the exception of some coaches, all of these vehicles were American-made.

Coaches were the most prestigious of vehicles, restricted to persons of the highest social status. The earliest coach to be mentioned in the British colonies was that which, Anthony Colve, the governor of New Netherland, presented to Sir Edmund Andros, the incoming governor as the colony passed from Dutch to British rule. Some of the first to be seen in America were vehicles of state employed by colonial governors sent from England, from whom they diffused to the American upper classes.

Private coaches remained restricted to the elite; the Massachusetts tax list of 1753 includes only six. Of somewhat lower status was the two-wheeled calash. Another vehicle, the chaise, or as it became known in America, the "shay," was a light two- or four-wheeled carriage; it was introduced between 1710 and 1730.

All of these horse-drawn vehicles were largely urban phenomena, except for a few owned by wealthy rural Southern planters. One evidence of the spread of coaches and other vehicles in the South is that while the Virginia ferry law of 1702 mentioned only rates for people and horses, the revision of the law in 1720 added rates for two- and four-wheeled vehicles.

As bearers of status, these coaches and other vehicles were not designed in merely functional terms. Strict Puritans suspected them as worldly vanities and sometimes went through agonies of conscience about purchasing them. Riding a coach or carriage on the Sabbath was felt to be particularly damnable.

Use of horse-drawn vehicles was not restricted to individual owners and their families. Stagecoaches and other forms of public transportation emerged in the early eighteenth century. By 1716, there was a fortnightly run between Boston and Newport, although it lasted only a few years. Regularly scheduled wagon-based transit began in New Jersey, building on the freight wagons that traveled between the coast and the Delaware River.

By 1750, there was a regular New York–Philadelphia run, traveling by land and water and taking about three days. Philadelphia-Chesapeake lines emerged in the 1760s, taking various routes to different endpoints, although over time Baltimore dominated. The first successful New England stage route was between Boston and Portsmouth in 1761, and a Boston–New York stage route was finally established in 1772. In addition to these intercity routes, there were also local routes in the areas of Boston, New York, and Philadelphia.

Wagons and Carts

Not only people but also goods moved overland in horse-drawn vehicles. Wagon and cart technologies differed between the various European groups that settled in North America. English settlers made greater use of carts, Germans of wagons. The Swedes had a unique practice of using cross sections of tree trunk as cartwheels.

One vehicle that originated in America and came into widespread use in the late colonial period and beyond was the Conestoga wagon, named for the Conestoga River Valley in Lancaster County, Pennsylvania. The term appears in the early eighteenth century and was originally applied to the wagons that farmers used to take their goods to Philadelphia. (A Conestoga Wagon Inn had appeared on Philadelphia's Market Street by 1750.) The defining features of the Conestoga wagon included a cloth cover held up with eight to twelve wooden hoops, a curved body with an upswept front and back, wheels with a diameter of 54 inches or greater, and wooden axles. The manufacture of these wagons was concentrated in southeastern Pennsylvania, and it seems to have originated in the German farmer community. The necessity of protecting farm produce from the weather in the four-day journey from Lancaster to Philadelphia encouraged covering the wagon. The Conestoga received wider exposure in 1755, when General Braddock hired over 150 farm wagons for the advance against Fort Duquesne. Increasing use of wagons led to the widening and smoothing of roads to accommodate them.

Whether they arrived in cities in wagons or on boats, once there, goods were frequently maneuvered through narrow, winding streets on carts. Carts and their operators were vital to the commerce of colonial America. The profession of cartman carried some status beyond that of most workers. New York City's cartmen were, from 1695, freemen of the city and held some lower municipal offices. Another mark of the status claims of New York cartmen was that, in 1677, African Americans were barred from being cartmen, although they could work for cartmen as employees or slaves. Cartmen did not freely negotiate their fees. The Common Council of the city regulated the size of carts and cartmen's charges, particularly for hauling firewood.

Roads and War

The increasingly technological wars of the British, French, and their Native American allies in the eighteenth century created an incentive for road building. Wide roads were necessary to move large bodies of regular troops, along with their supplies and siege cannon.

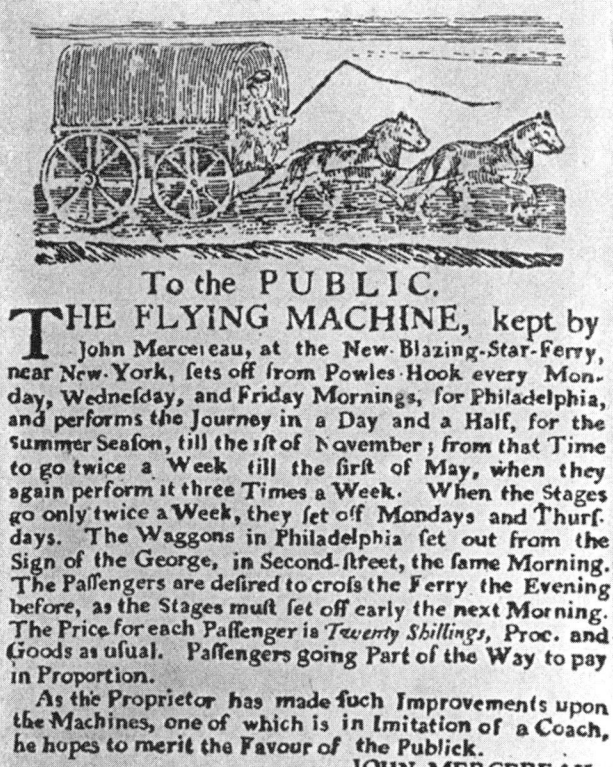

Advertised as "The Flying Machine," John Mercereau's stage wagon cut the travel between Philadelphia and New York to a day and half in 1771. *(Brown Brothers, Sterling, Pennsylvania)*

Another force driving the improvement of roads in the midcentury was the improvement of the postal service after British authorities finally established such a service covering all the continental colonies in 1751. (The postal service itself was considered to be contributing to the military organization of the colonies.) Benjamin Franklin, appointed co-deputy postmaster in 1753, was particularly active, traveling extensively through the Northern colonies, inspecting post offices, and suggesting new routes and procedures. He devised a crude cyclometer that he hitched to the back of his chaise in order to measure the distances along the roads, and he laid out milestones and encouraged others to do so.

Improvement of transportation and land communication between the colonies was one force tending to colonial unity before and during the Revolution. The publication of a full atlas of America's roads, however, waited until 1789, several years after the Revolution, when Christopher Colles's *A Survey of the Roads of the United States of America* was published.

William E. Burns

See also: Agriculture; Economy, Business, and Labor (Chronology); Economy, Business, and Labor (Essay); Exploration; Horses; Inns and Taverns (Public Houses); Merchants; Peddlers; Trade; Transportation, Water. *Document:* The Journal of Sarah Kemble Knight (1704).

Bibliography

Hawke, David Freeman. *Everyday Life in Early America.* New York: Harper and Row, 1988.

Hodges, Graham Russell. *New York City Cartmen, 1667–1850.* New York: New York University Press, 1986.

Holmes, Oliver Wendell, and Peter T. Rohrbach. *Stagecoach East: Stagecoach Days in the East from the Colonial Period to the Civil War.* Washington, DC: Smithsonian Institution Press, 1983.

Shumway, George, Edward Durrell, and Howard C. Frey. *Conestoga Wagon 1750–1850: Freight Carrier for 100 Years of America's Westward Expansion.* York, PA: Early American Industries and George Shumway, 1964.

Wolfe, Stephanie Grauman. *As Various as Their Land: The Everyday Lives of Eighteenth-Century Americans.* New York: HarperCollins, 1993.

Transportation, Water

Transportation by water was central to the colonial experience, from Christopher Columbus to the British Armies carried to America in the Revolutionary War.

The Americas were inaccessible by land from Europe, so every first-generation colonist's experience of America began with a long ocean voyage. Sea transportation played only a slightly less prominent a role in the lives of the American-born colonists. Communication, trade, and visits to Europe and to the West Indies depended on ships.

Given the cheapness of transportation by water as compared to that by land, America's economic development was largely dependent on her access to markets, sources of goods, and emigrants by water. Although few of the original settlers were seamen, British Americans themselves developed from relatively early times an active shipbuilding industry and vigorous ports. Fishing, whaling, and merchant shipping (the last encouraged by the Navigation Acts) absorbed the labor of many colonists.

Crossing the Ocean

The early colonization of America benefited from both navigational and design improvements in European ships; it also posed new challenges. The magnetic compass, used to find the direction of a ship, was already in general use in the late medieval period.

The *Casa de la Contratación,* founded in 1503 to regulate Spanish movement to and from the New World, trained pilots and captains in the arts of cartography and navigation, systematizing the information Spanish captains gathered from the Americas. The *Casa de la Contratación* was part of a larger European movement to make navigation a more textual body of knowledge, as opposed to something passed down orally. The Spanish also hoped to enforce their early monopoly over the New World by restricting their European rivals' access to navigational and cartographic information. This strategy did not succeed.

Crossing the ocean was dangerous and unpleasant, particularly in the early decades of colonization. Ships were overcrowded, unsanitary, and often full of rats and disease. The diet was poor, consisting on British ships mainly of easily preserved foods such as biscuit and salt beef, although sometimes live animals were brought on board and slaughtered during the voyage or ocean fish were caught and eaten.

Conditions improved during the eighteenth century with the exception of voyages bringing convicts and, above all, slave voyages. Slave ships were notorious for disease. The death toll among sailors was high, even higher than among the slaves on some voyages. Storms were also very dangerous.

The lightweight birch bark canoe, used by native peoples to travel the lakes and rivers of the continent's interior, was adopted by Europeans. It proved indispensable in the exploration and settlement of the frontier. (© *Peabody Essex Museum, Salem, Massachusetts/Bridgeman Art Library*)

One factor that particularly improved transoceanic voyages was the gradual replacement, during the seventeenth century, of the old southern route, in which ships sailed to the Caribbean and then up the coast of North America. Instead, the new route went directly across the Atlantic, approximately on the great circle that was the shortest distance. While it could take three to four months to reach America by the old route, a journey by the new outbound route might take only seven to eight weeks, depending on the weather. The return crossing to Britain was shortened even more by the Gulf Stream and prevailing westerly winds.

Given the value of goods transported across the sea, security for water-borne trade and travelers (there were no "passenger ships" in the early modern period) was always a problem. Piracy diminished rapidly after about 1720, but merchant vessels were subject to the depredations of enemy warships and privateers during the frequent wars of the period.

In 1664 and 1673, much of the Chesapeake tobacco fleet was destroyed by the Dutch. The Chesapeake's wide mouth, impossible to cover with guns, made it a security nightmare. The solution eventually adopted for the Chesapeake tobacco trade was the formation of an annual "convoy" of 150 to 200 ships, escorted by vessels of the Royal Navy from the Chesapeake to England. The transatlantic convoy system had actually been pioneered by Spain, who used it to transport the year's haul of precious metals (hence the term "plate fleet"). It worked fairly well to protect the tobacco ships, but other traders were still vulnerable, as was all trade to the West Indies.

Ships and Shipbuilding

Shipbuilding emerged from modest beginnings to become one of colonial America's most important industries. Building ships was a top concern of the early colonization companies. The cod fishery, central to the early Massachusetts economy, and trade across the Atlantic, along the coast, and to the Caribbean all required vessels, which could be created locally given North America's abundance of wood.

The first vessel built in the English colonies of North America was the *Virginia*, a 50-foot pinnace built by colonists of a short-lived colony at the mouth of the Kennebec in Maine in 1607. A pinnace was usually a coasting vessel, movable under either oars or sails but capable of ocean voyaging. The colony was abandoned the next year, but the *Virginia* sailed between Virginia and London for twenty years before being wrecked on the Irish coast.

In 1622, the Virginia Company sent out Captain Thomas Barwick and twenty-five ship's carpenters to construct small vessels for coasting. Barwick died shortly after he arrived, though, and the plan came to nothing. There was a more successful effort at Plymouth, where a ship's carpenter was sent in 1624.

The leading shipbuilding colony in the early seventeenth century was New England. The New England Company sent six shipwrights to Salem in 1629 to build shallops, small undecked vessels, for fishing. John Winthrop's bark (a small decked sailing ship built for fishing and coastal trade) *Blessing of the Bay* was launched on July 4, 1631. New England was building oceangoing ships in the 1630s; the 60-ton *Rebecca* was launched from Medford in November 1633 and the 120-ton *Desire* from Marblehead in 1636. The General Court of Massachusetts exempted ship's carpenters from militia training in 1639. The development of the colonial iron industry further aided shipbuilders, although cordage and sailcloth would continue to be imported until the American Revolution.

The centers of New England shipbuilding in the late seventeenth century were Charlestown, Salem, Salisbury, Portsmouth, and particularly Boston. Boston was not advantageously situated for access to the wood and iron shipbuilders needed, but its capital and good harbor facilities enabled it to dominate the trade. Connecticut also acquired a shipbuilding industry, centered in New London. The largest merchant ship ever produced in colonial America—720 tons—was built by the New London shipwright John Jeffrey and launched in 1725.

New England shipbuilders were building not only for local needs, but for British shippers as well. They had an advantage over their English competitors both in the supply of wood and also in their design. English shipbuilders were still building dual-use ships, capable of being used as cargo ships or warships. This meant that English ships, unlike the Dutch *fluyts* or flyboats, were not designed for optimum carrying capacity. (The *Susan Constant,* leader of the Jamestown expedition, had so little capacity for carrying supplies that she had been obliged to stop in the West Indies for food and water on the way to North America.) New England ships were pure cargo ships, capacious in comparison.

New England shipbuilding was further stimulated by the need to replace the considerable English losses in the War of the League of Augsburg (King William's War) and the War of the Spanish Succession (Queen Anne's War). Other foreign markets for American ships included the French and Spanish West Indies, as well as Spain and Portugal. So successful was the New England shipbuilding industry that some English mercantilists worried that it would drain wealth from the mother country.

The second major shipbuilding center to emerge was Philadelphia; William Penn encouraged shipwrights to settle in his new colony. The late seventeenth

century saw a boom in Philadelphia shipbuilding, which completely dominated the industry in Pennsylvania and the Delaware Valley. By the early eighteenth century, Philadelphia was second only to Boston as a builder of ships.

The types of ships Americans built were also changing. The pinnace disappeared in the late seventeenth century, to be replaced by the sloop. The sloop, a single-mast vessel of Dutch origin, came in two main forms: small vessels between 20 and 40 tons that specialized in coastal trade and West India traders of 50 tons or more. Unlike the pinnace, the sloop was a pure sailing vessel.

By the early eighteenth century, Boston was by far the leading harbor in the British Empire outside England, with a 1,600-foot wharf constructed between 1710 and 1713. (A 2,000-foot wharf was later built at Newport.) New York, with a merchant fleet composed mainly of sloops, was a distant second. Although shipbuilding, along with the rest of the economy, slumped after Queen Anne's War, the American shipbuilding industry was still a formidable competitor to that of Britain. In 1724, the master shipwrights of the Thames, the center of British shipbuilding, petitioned the Board of Trade to restrict American shipbuilding, claiming that the emigration of British shipwrights to the Americas would threaten the home industry. The board refused to intervene. By 1730, one-sixth of the British merchant fleet was built in the colonies; on the eve of the American Revolution, about one-third of British-registered tonnage was built in America, and ships ranked fifth in value among exports from the thirteen colonies.

The mid-eighteenth century saw new shipbuilding centers emerge outside New England and Philadelphia and the two-masted schooner replace the sloop. The poet Ebenezer Cooke, representing the view of some Maryland leaders, had called for the establishment of a Chesapeake shipbuilding industry in his 1730 *Sot-Weed Redivivus.* Even though Chesapeake shipbuilding had been relatively modest, there was already an extensive industry, concentrated in Norfolk and Annapolis, devoted to refitting and repairing ships in harbor. Chesapeake shipbuilding took off after the late 1740s, and by the end of the colonial period Maryland and Virginia combined had replaced Philadelphia as the second largest shipbuilding center in America after Boston. Southern shipbuilders specialized in large oceangoing ships and fast sloops and schooners. Charles Town, where 17 ships were launched between 1760 and 1774, had the largest average tonnage of any American shipbuilding center, and Georgia, where shipbuilding was just starting, had the second largest.

Paradoxically, as much as town establishments loved water-borne trade, they were suspicious of the sailors who were necessary for it. Sailors epitomized the transient population, the "mobility" in the eighteenth-century sense. Sailors were a distinct group, easily recognizable by their rolling gait, weathered skin, distinctive clothing, and tattoos. The sections of towns near the docks that catered to sailors—with cheap lodgings, taverns, entertainment, and brothels—epitomized the nonrespectable. Groups of sailors on leave were perceived as a possible source of crime and riot and had a reputation for brawling and blasphemy.

These suspicions were not without a basis in fact; sailors were prominent among the riotous crowds at the opening of the American Revolution. Sea captains and British authorities were also concerned about the propensity of sailors to desert, either in pursuit of higher pay on another ship or to settle in America as farmers or workers. (This was particularly easy in the decentralized Chesapeake.)

Inland Waterways

There was much travel and transport on fresh waters, as well as on the sea. The vast majority of the early colonists lived in proximity to either the sea or a river or stream. The comparative cheapness of transporting goods over water was a boon to the domestic, as well as the export, American economy; however, personal transportation was a more complex matter. Many ordinary Americans could not afford boats and often lacked the skills to sail them.

Some colonists turned to a Native American invention that impressed many Europeans, the dugout canoe. *Canoe*, deriving from the indigenous people of Hispaniola, was the first native word adopted into European languages. A canoe could be made from the trunks of several different kinds of trees, although red cedar was widely preferred for its lightness and durability. The canoe's opening was either burned or hacked out of the wood. Another Native American device adopted by settlers was the birch bark canoe. The usefulness of bark boats was enhanced by their lightness but limited by their fragility. Canoes, both dugout and bark, were particularly indispensable for explorers and traders; since they were paddled rather than sailed, they required less specialized skill to use. The expansion of

the French in the interior of America, as well as that of their rivals the Iroquois, depended on the use of canoes.

Many other types of craft were used in America's waterways. Black slaves in South Carolina used shallow boats adapted from West African designs for fishing and transportation. Ferries in the Chesapeake area included flat-bottomed boats rowed, poled, or pulled through shallow waters and small sailing ships or "package boats" for deeper waters.

No area was more shaped and dominated by water transport than the Chesapeake—a region particularly rich in rivers, stream and inlets. Early visitors were much impressed by its many waterways, some comparing the newly encountered land to the Netherlands, with the hope that it would become as wealthy. The ease of moving hogsheads of tobacco by water, a process far easier on the tobacco than land transport, was essential to the development of the Chesapeake tobacco industry. The ability to anchor ships in fresh water helped protect them from the worm (*Teredo navalis*) that attacked ships' bottoms.

Transportation in the Chesapeake depended on the ability to cross water. Therefore boating skills and boats were widely distributed among the population, particularly in the eighteenth century, and roads often served merely to link ferries. The ease of transporting goods and people from plantations directly to ships on the bay also slowed the development of urban centers in the region.

The further expansion of the colonies in the eighteenth century meant that inland water transportation assumed an even more prominent role. The last decades of colonial rule saw a concerted effort to improve internal waterways by means of canals. Americans were aware of the active canal building going on in England and saw canals as a route to economic development.

The leaders in these projects were usually urban commercial interests. Philadelphia was the most active center of canal promotion. Thomas Gilpin, a Quaker merchant and member of the American Philosophical Society, was the most vigorous promoter of a canal connecting the Delaware with the Chesapeake. Philadelphia merchants subscribed 140 pounds to surveying possible routes, while Baltimore merchants charged the Philadelphians with planning to divert trade from their city. The scheme was supplemented by another plan to connect the Susquehanna and the Schuykill Rivers.

These proposed canals led to much activity by the American Philosophical Society, the Pennsylvania Assembly, and Philadelphia merchants. Benjamin Franklin, in London, wrote to Samuel Rhoads, a member of the assembly, suggesting that it would be better to hire an experienced English canal builder rather than letting Americans try to build it themselves. Neither canal was actually built until the early nineteenth century.

William E. Burns

See also: Board of Trade; Columbian Exchange; Dutch West India Company; East India Company; Economy, Business, and Labor (Chronology); Economy, Business, and Labor (Essay); Exploration; Merchants; Navigation Acts (1651–1733); Navy, British; Northwest Passage; Piracy; Ship's Stores; Slave Trade; Trade; Transportation, Land; Triangle Trade.

Bibliography

Goldenberg, Joseph A. *Shipbuilding in Colonial America.* Charlottesville: University Press of Virginia for the Mariners Museum, Newport News, 1976.

Hawke, David Freeman. *Everyday Life in Early America.* New York: Harper and Row, 1988.

Hindle, Brooke. *The Pursuit of Science in Revolutionary America.* Chapel Hill: University of North Carolina Press for the Institute of Early American History and Culture in Williamsburg, Virginia, 1956.

McCusker, John J., and Russell R. Menard. *The Economy of British America, 1607–1789.* Chapel Hill: University of North Carolina Press for the Institute of Early American History and Culture in Williamsburg, Virginia, 1985.

Middleton, Arthur Pierce. *Tobacco Coast: A Maritime History of Chesapeake Bay in the Colonial Era.* Newport News, VA: Mariners Museum, 1953.

Rediker, Marcus. *Between the Devil and the Deep Blue Sea: Merchant Seamen, Pirates, and the Anglo-American Maritime World.* Cambridge, UK: Cambridge University Press, 1987.

Triangle Trade

The term "Triangle Trade" describes the economic exchange between Europe, Africa, and the Americas from the beginning of the sixteenth to the end of the eighteenth century. The concept focuses on the transatlantic slave trade and includes the movement of commodities from Europe to West Africa, where European slavers exchanged the commodities for slaves. From Africa, vessels transported the slaves to the Americas to be sold. After selling the slaves, the slavers loaded their vessels with cash crops and other goods for the voyage back to Europe. It was within the Triangle Trade that the colonists of British North America created opportunities to profit and expand their economic options.

The Triangle Trade began in Europe, where European slavers outfitted their vessels with crews, commodities, and supplies. The various commodities that the slavers carried to West Africa came from Europe, the Americas, and the Far East. The slave traders needed to carry the proper commodities; if they did not, the African slave traders would not do business with them, or they would demand more in exchange for each slave.

Most of the 15 million African slaves carried to the Americas went to the West Indies or into Central and South America, with North America serving as a secondary market. Many of the slaves brought to North America first lived on West Indian sugar plantations.

When the slavers arrived in West Africa, they could sail along the coast, purchasing small lots of slaves and thus increasing their travel time. They also could sail to one of the numerous slave-trading centers, where they could purchase large numbers of slaves and shorten their voyage. In West Africa, the textiles and alcohol (including rum) manufactured in the Americas, as well as tobacco and various other goods, were combined into an assortment and then exchanged for slaves. Once full of human cargo, the vessel sailed from West Africa to the Americas. This was known as the Middle Passage, during which approximately 20 percent of the slaves died; numerous ships experienced small or large slave uprisings.

Once in the Americas, the ship typically underwent a quarantine period to avoid the introduction of disease. This gave the captain time not only to advertise the impending slave auction but also to prepare the slaves for auction by utilizing various tricks to make them appear healthier than they were. Once the slaves had been sold at auction and handed over to their new owners, the vessels were prepared for their return to Europe.

Some ships returned with only their profits and ballast, but the majority carried American commodities. Most of these cargoes, because of the mercantile ideas of the time, were cash crops. The major cash crops were tobacco and sugar, plus rum and molasses, but the ships also carried naval stores, furs, grains, rice, indigo, precious stones and metals, and other natural resources. The flow of American cash crops to Europe allowed the American colonists to purchase a wide variety of European manufactured or re-exported commodities.

While mercantilism and the Navigation Acts restricted the participation of British North America in the Triangle Trade, the colonists soon found ways to profit both within and without the system. New England merchants found that they could profit not only through the fur trade but also through the carrying trade. Some colonists reacted to the limitations of the Navigation Acts by smuggling, which proved highly profitable, and they soon became adept at it.

The American colonists sent ships throughout the Atlantic world to exchange various commodities for others. From the Middle colonies, they acquired staple crops that they carried to the West Indies, where they traded the food they brought—needed there because the plantations produced only sugar—for molasses. They then carried the molasses back to New England, where they distilled it into rum, which could be traded anywhere. In Rhode Island, merchants became directly involved in the Triangle Trade by sending vessels to West Africa to participate in the slave trade.

The Triangle Trade provides a simplified explanation not only of the transatlantic slave trade but also of the economic interaction between Europe, Africa, and the Americas. The problem with the system for the American colonists was that its design and regulation ensured that most of profits flowed back to Europe, as when the Americans traded inexpensive raw materials for expensive finished goods. While the Atlantic economy was not as simple as a triangle—actually, it was made up of numerous interconnected triangles—the Triangle Trade concept summarizes the primary pattern of seagoing commerce at the time.

Ty M. Reese

See also: East India Company; Royal African Company; Slave Trade; Trade; Transportation, Water.

Bibliography

Hancock, David. *Citizens of the World: London Merchants and the Integration of the British Atlantic Community, 1735–1785.* New York: Cambridge University Press, 1995.

Tuscarora

When they first met European settlers in Virginia and North Carolina, the Tuscarora Indians had been in the area for many years, although their Iroquoian language suggests that they may originally have moved into the region from the north. The Tuscarora were the largest single native group in North Carolina, and they occupied much of the present state.

In 1701, John Lawson, surveyor general for Carolina and the region's foremost white expert on Native Americans, placed the number of Tuscarora warriors at around 1,200, which would have indicated a total population of over 5,000. Their numbers were almost certainly higher in the sixteenth century, before they faced the ravages of European disease.

The Tuscarora established permanent settlements based on corn agriculture, hemp gathering, and the maintenance of orchards. Among many Native American groups, and the Tuscarora were no exception, agriculture was considered largely women's work. Hunting and warfare were the exclusive domain of men.

In the winter, the Tuscarora removed to hunting camps. Tuscarora political life in the colonial period appears to have been highly centralized. Because of their location between expanding white settlements and interior nations, and as a result of their looming military presence, the Tuscarora became middlemen in the flourishing Anglo-Indian trade in rum, furs, skins, and firearms.

The European settlement of North Carolina, and particularly the founding of the Swiss-German settlement at New Bern in 1709 by Baron Christophe von Graffenried, posed a new set of problems for the Tuscarora. Prior to New Bern, white, largely English settlement had occurred north of their territory in Virginia and south of their territory in South Carolina. The Tuscarora also became victims of white abuse, both by individual settlers and the overall unequal terms of trade. To make matters worse, white settlements had begun to encroach on Tuscarora land.

Native Americans allied with the traders at Carolina compounded the Tuscarora's problems by continually raiding for slaves to satisfy Carolinian and West Indian demands. By 1711, the situation had deteriorated, and the southern Tuscarora decided to attack white settlements in the conflict that came to be known as the Tuscarora War.

The Tuscarora War was the defining event of the tribe's history in the colonial period. The Tuscarora succeeded in terrorizing the English and Germans of North Carolina, killing 130 of them in the initial attack. North Carolina, essentially paralyzed by fear—the colony already had a relatively weak military—asked Virginia and South Carolina for help. South Carolina responded by immediately sending an army of 500 Native Americans, mainly Yamasees, under the command of John Barnwell into Tuscarora country, where they burned several of the main towns, killing men and enslaving women and children.

The main Tuscarora force held out, though it was weakened significantly when Tom Blount, the accommodationist leader of the Northern Tuscarora, chose the English side in the conflict. He betrayed King Hancock, the Southern Tuscarora leader, to the English, who killed him. In 1713, South Carolina sent an army of 1,200 Native Americans under the command of James Moore to finish the job. Starving and powerless, the Tuscarora abandoned their homeland. A treaty was signed in 1715, officially ending the war.

In 1722, the first Tuscarora refugees made their way into Iroquois territory, where they were accepted by the Five Nations Iroquois, becoming the Sixth Nation. The process by which the Tuscarora made it to New York is not well known, but they continued to arrive until 1804.

In the American War for Independence, the Tuscarora and Oneida sided with the colonists, while most Native Americans remained neutral or actively supported the British cause. After the Treaty of Paris and the establishment of the United States, the new American government made no distinction between allied and enemy native nations. Some Tuscarora towns were among those burned by American forces in the aftermath of the war.

The Tuscarora rebuilt their homes, which were again destroyed by the British during the War of 1812 and once again rebuilt. The construction of a reservoir in the 1950s flooded much of their land, but their resistance to the project united Native Americans from many different tribes in the early beginnings of the Red Power movement. The Tuscarora maintained a strong cultural identity through all of the challenges they faced in the colonial period and beyond.

Matthew Jennings

See also: Iroquois Confederacy; Native American–European Conflict; Native American–European Relations; Native Americans; Tuscarora War.

Bibliography

Landy, David. "Tuscarora." In *Encyclopedia of North American Indians*, edited by Frederick E. Hoxie. Boston: Houghton Mifflin, 1996.

Rights, Douglas LeTell. *The American Indian in North Carolina.* Durham, NC: Duke University Press, 1947.

Tuscarora War

The Tuscarora War of 1711 to 1715 pitted the Tuscarora of North Carolina against the newly created Swiss and German settlement at New Bern. The end result of the conflict was the demoralization and defeat of the Tuscarora, who emigrated to join the Five Nations Iroquois in 1722.

The Tuscarora had been living in North Carolina and Virginia for many years when the colonies of Virginia (1607) and South Carolina (1670) were founded. The tribe's population is estimated to have been over 5,000 in 1701. They lived in settled agricultural communities in the Tidewater region, though their hunting territory was farther inland.

As European settlers came to the region in increasing numbers, the Tuscarora became brokers of a flourishing trade in alcohol, fur, and deerskins between interior Native American nations and the English colonies on the coast. The establishment of New Bern in 1709 by Baron Christophe von Graffenried and his many followers posed a serious new threat to Tuscarora power in the region.

Like other tribes, the Tuscarora had been subjected to abuses by traders operating out of Virginia and South Carolina. They were often cheated and occasionally captured and sold into slavery, particularly by natives in league with the traders at Charles Town.

By 1711, the Tuscarora had had enough, and they struck back violently. In the initial stages of the war, the Tuscarora scored two decisive victories. They were able to capture John Lawson, surveyor general of Carolina, and the Baron von Graffenried himself. Although de Graffenried bargained for his life, Lawson quarreled with one of the Tuscarora leaders, Core Tom, and was put to death. The first swift attack took the lives of more than 100 English and German colonists and threw all of North Carolina into disarray. North Carolina, with few white settlers and a weak military, called on South Carolina and Virginia for assistance.

Virginia did nothing, citing poor finances and a recently signed treaty with some northern Tuscarora villages. South Carolina dispatched an army of thirty whites, led by John Barnwell and a multiethnic force of 500 Native Americans, consisting primarily of Yamasees. During 1712, Barnwell's army inflicted serious damage on the Tuscarora. On January 30, for instance, at a palisade called Fort Narhantes, Barnwell's men stormed a Tuscarora stronghold, killing all the men inside. Barnwell lamented that the natives fighting with him took most of the plunder and slaves, writing that "only one girl we got."

Barnwell met the Tuscarora again at Catechna, a fortified town. The situation here was more complex, and Barnwell, his forces depleted by deserters, sued for peace and the release of white prisoners. Upon his return to New Bern, he expected to be commended for his performance, but no commendation came. Barnwell did, however, profit by selling some native peoples, assembled under the pretense of peace, into slavery.

A larger force of South Carolinians, this time accompanied by around 1,000 Native Americans, including many Cherokees, arrived in North Carolina in 1713. The Tuscarora people's morale had flagged significantly when King Hancock (also known as Hencock) was enticed into negotiations with Tom Blount, the accommodationist chief of the Northern Tuscarora. Blount betrayed Hancock to the English, who promptly executed him.

James Moore's expedition destroyed any hope of the Tuscarora remaining in North Carolina. At Catechna, Moore's forces crushed the Tuscarora, killing around 600 and taking almost 400 into slavery. This ended any effective Tuscarora resistance at the same time as it opened up large areas of central North Carolina for European settlement. In fact, by the end of the colonial period, North Carolina had witnessed remarkable growth.

Though a handful of Tuscarora accepted English domination and remained in North Carolina on reservations, the majority slowly made their way north. In 1722, the first Tuscarora arrived in the north and became the Sixth Nation of the Iroquois, joining their distant linguistic cousins. By 1800, there were hardly any Tuscaroras still living in North Carolina.

The Tuscarora War, however, should not be seen as simply a race war or a contest between Euro-Americans and Native Americans for territory. Native Americans fought on both sides of the conflict for a variety of reasons. Also, the Tuscarora, though defeated, managed to maintain a distinctly Tuscarora identity.

Matthew Jennings

See also: Military and Diplomatic Affairs (Chronology); Military and Diplomatic Affairs (Essay); Native American–European Conflict; Tuscarora; War.

Bibliography

Milling, Chapman J. *Red Carolinians.* 2nd ed. Columbia: University of South Carolina Press, 1969.

Nash, Gary B. *Red, White and Black: The Peoples of Early North America.* 4th ed. Upper Saddle River, NJ: Prentice Hall, 2000.

Rights, Douglas LeTell. *The American Indian in North Carolina.* Durham, NC: Duke University Press, 1947.

Vasa, Gustavus

See Equiano, Olaudah

Vermont

The first state admitted into the Union after the original thirteen colonies, Vermont was sparsely settled by whites during the colonial period. It served primarily as a natural trade route between the English colony of Massachusetts and the French colony of Quebec, and it became a zone of conflict for the two European empires and their Native American allies.

In the years immediately preceding European settlement, the Abenaki (also spelled Abnaki), an Algonquian-speaking tribe, were the original inhabitants of the area. In response to the formation of the powerful and aggressive Iroquois Confederation in the late sixteenth century, the various tribes of New England formed an Abenaki confederation as a defensive measure, with the Vermont region forming their northwestern frontier.

In 1609, French explorer Samuel de Champlain, based in Quebec, became the first European to travel the region, and the large lake that forms the northwestern boundary of the present-day state bears his name. Champlain and other French explorers also gave the state its name: Vermont, from "vert" (green) and "mont" (mountain), for the mountainous landscape thickly forested with conifers. (During the period under British colonial rule, the region was also known as the "New Hampshire grants" after London charters granting the territory to New Hampshire.)

In 1666, the French established the first permanent European settlement here, on the Isle La Motte in Lake Champlain. At the same time, Jesuit missionaries—living among the native inhabitants—helped create economic and political alliances between the French and the Abenaki. On behalf of the French and their own interests, the Abenaki continually skirmished with the English in the far south of Vermont.

In 1724, settlers from English-speaking New England and Dutch-speaking New York founded their first permanent settlements in Vermont. The English settled at Pownal in the far southwestern corner of the present-day state; the Dutch erected Fort Dummer on the Connecticut River near what is now Brattleboro in the southeast corner of the state. The establishment of these towns coincided with intensified warfare with the Abenaki, decimating the latter's ranks and forcing most of the survivors to migrate northward to Quebec, where they eventually settled, largely near the town of Saint-François-du-Lac.

By the time of the American Revolution, the English-speaking population of Vermont had grown to roughly 20,000. And many Vermont settlements were named after the Connecticut and Massachusetts towns from which most of the settlers came.

The fact of English settler domination also was confirmed politically by the 1763 Treaty of Paris, which ended the French and Indian War between France, Britain, and various Native American tribes. While English possession was confirmed by the treaty, Vermont remained disputed between the colonies of New Hampshire and New York.

The vast majority of Vermonters of the colonial period—with their roots in New England—resented New York's claims. Fiercely independent small-hold farmers, Vermonters feared the introduction of land speculators and the large estate-type farming typical of New York's Hudson River Valley. As for New Hampshire's claims, that colony was isolated from the most populated region of Vermont by the daunting Green

Mountains. Thus, during the confusion of the American Revolution, Vermonters took it upon themselves to fight for their independence, not just from England but from other colonies as well.

In 1770, a local farmer and politician named Ethan Allen organized a militia, popularly known as the Green Mountain Boys, to defend the territory against outside incursions. At the beginning of the American Revolution in May 1775, the Green Mountain Boys helped capture the British fort at Ticonderoga. After a poorly organized attempt to capture Montreal, Allen himself was held prisoner by the British until 1778; however, his followers continued the fight to secure Vermont's independence.

In January 1777, delegates representing the various towns of the region met at Westminster. Citing the recently held Second Continental Congress at Philadelphia, where the thirteen colonies had declared their independence from Britain, the delegates declared Vermont an independent republic. They went on to declare the "arbitrary acts of the crown . . . null and void," which meant that Crown grants to New York and New Hampshire, giving them control over Vermont, were "totally dissolved." And they stated that the inhabitants of the region "are at present without law or government, and may be truly said to be in a state of nature; consequently, a right remains to the people of said New Hampshire Grants to form a government best suited to secure their property, well being and happiness."

The fierce independence of the Vermont settlers continued after the American Revolution. They maintained their nominal independence from the new United States until they could secure a guarantee that their territory would not be subsumed into New York State. When that assurance was finally made, Vermonters surrendered their claims to full sovereignty and joined the Union as the fourteenth state in 1794.

James Ciment

See also: French; Green Mountain Boys; New Hampshire; New York.

Bibliography

Fisher, Dorothy Canfield. *Vermont Tradition: The Biography of an Outlook on Life.* Boston: Little, Brown, 1953.

McGrory, Klyza, and Stephen C. Trombulak. *The Story of Vermont: A Natural and Cultural History.* Hanover, NH: University Press of New England, 1999.

Morrissey, Charles T. *Vermont, a Bicentennial History.* New York: W. W. Norton, 1981.

Verrazano, Giovanni da (c. 1480–c. 1528)

The Italian explorer Giovanni da Verrazano led France's first official voyage of discovery to the coast of North America and produced the first topographical description of a continuous voyage along the East Coast of the continent. In his valuable commentary on the indigenous people the voyagers encountered on that coast, Verrazano proved himself a highly educated and sophisticated observer, producing a remarkably objective and detailed account of the experience. In two more voyages, Verrazano searched for a path to Asia as an alternative to the Portuguese-dominated route around Africa, and he sailed to the Cape of Good Hope and Cape Horn before looking for a western passage in the Gulf of Mexico.

Although associated with Florence, Italy, by himself and contemporaries, it is more likely that Verrazano was born during the 1480s in Lyons, France, among the Florentine business community there. Undoubtedly, he received a gentleman's education in Florence before working as a commercial agent in the silk and spice trade in the eastern Mediterranean. He may have joined Thomas Aubert's French voyage to Newfoundland in 1508, and he saw Ferdinand Magellan in Portugal in 1517, but little more is certain.

His experience and knowledge of the difficulties in competing with the Portuguese in the Asian trade led Verrazano and his cartographer brother Girolamo to the court of King Francis I of France by 1523, where they proposed a voyage of exploration due west from the Madeira Islands. From contemporary knowledge, Verrazano was aware that he would not land immediately on the east coast of Asia, but he hoped to find passage westward through the largely unknown area between Newfoundland and Florida. Fearing Portuguese reprisals, Francis I contributed only the use of four ships, and the voyage was financed largely by Florentine businessmen in Lyons. Reduced to fifty men and a single vessel, the *Dauphine*, and detained by storms and the outbreak of the Franco-Spanish war, Verrazano sailed from France on January 1, 1524, and reached North America in late March.

Declaring that he was witness to a new land never before seen, Verrazano arrived on the coast somewhat south of Cape Fear, North Carolina, where fires on the shore indicated human occupation. Without landing,

As portrayed in this seventeenth-century ceramic, the Italian navigator Giovanni da Verrazano, in the service of France, sailed up the east coast of North America in 1524, discovering New York and Narragansett bays. His explorations also produced a topographical map and valuable commentary on indigenous peoples. *(New-York Historical Society, New York/ Bridgeman Art Library)*

Verrazano sailed 50 leagues to the south, searching for a port. Fearing that he was approaching Spanish Florida, he returned north and landed near his initial sighting.

Verrazano's admiring descriptions, taking up one-third of his report, give the first ethnological details of the indigenous people of southeastern North America and indicate a potential for courteous interaction. Farther up the coast, he encountered numerous other groups, who offered food and information about local anchorages, and he carefully noted variations in physique, dress, diet, behavior, and housing. Similarly, Verrazano's report indicates a deep appreciation for the landscape; he named the Chesapeake Bay area Arcadia for its fruitfulness and beauty, and praised, in particular, sites he called Refugio (Narragansett Bay) and Angoulême (New York Bay).

After lengthy and agreeable encounters in the latter two places, the *Dauphine* sailed north along a less hospitable coast. The hostility and suspicion with which the Abenaki of Maine regarded Verrazano suggests that Native-European trade relations had already been soured by kidnappings and insufficient gifts from earlier European explorers and fishermen. Indeed, Verrazano himself had kidnapped a native boy farther south to bring back to France.

Verrazano continued with little further comment north to Newfoundland before sailing for France. On the return voyage, he calculated the extent of known exploration of the eastern coast of the Americas and suggested that this new continent might be larger than Asia.

On his return, Verrazano found his king, Francis I, distracted by war and his investors discouraged by his lack of commercial discoveries. Disappointed, Verrazano gave a copy of his brother's map of his explorations to King Henry VIII of England, who was provoked into sending a voyage in 1527.

Under arrangements made with French investors in 1526, Verrazano undertook two more voyages, poorly documented, with a more purely commercial goal of opening French trade with Asia. The first voyage, in 1526, with three ships, followed Magellan's route down South America's eastern coast but failed to round the stormy Cape Horn; the ships headed due east to the Cape of Good Hope, which, also proving impassable, forced a retreat by way of Brazil.

This 20,000-mile voyage over fifteen months was followed in 1528 by an expedition of five ships seeking a western passage through the Isthmus of Panama. On an island beach somewhere off the Gulf of Darien, Giovanni da Verrazano was killed by indigenous people, who were probably hostile due to prior Spanish raids.

In the 1860s, doubt was cast on Verrazano's achievements by a number of scholars, who questioned his reports and revived a scurrilous version of his death. This controversy was overturned within a generation, particularly with the discovery and publication in 1909 of an original copy of his lost report to Francis I, which restored Verrazano's fame. In 1964, his name was given to what was then the world's longest suspension bridge, connecting Brooklyn and Staten Island, thus honoring his achievements.

Neil Kennedy

See also: Exploration; Hudson River.

Bibliography

Quinn, David Beers. *Explorers and Colonies: America, 1500–1625.* London: Hambledon Press, 1990.

Wroth, Lawrence. *The Voyages of Giovanni da Verrazzano, 1524–1528.* New Haven, CT: Yale University Press, 1970.

Vespucci, Amerigo (1454–1512)

Amerigo Vespucci has two continents named after him, North and South America. His contributions to the discovery and exploration of these continents have been the subject of a historical controversy that began during his lifetime and continues to the present day. Scholarly opinions of his accomplishments vary widely, from accounts that brand him a liar who never visited the Americas to narratives that rank him among the foremost navigators and explorers of his age.

Vespucci was born in Florence in 1454, the third son of a prosperous family, which boasted an ambassador, a banker, and a bishop. Vespucci's family was on good terms with the powerful Medici family, and Amerigo worked for Lorenzo di Pier Francesco de Medici's trading house. Amerigo worked twenty years in the commercial house in Florence, and, in 1491, he was transferred to Seville to work under Juanoto Berardi in the merchant banking and ship chandlery business.

When Juanoto Berardi died in 1495, Vespucci took over the Medici operations in Seville. From this post, he outfitted Christopher Columbus's third voyage to the New World. It was around this time that Vespucci went to sea for the first time, and the merchant navigator became embroiled in controversy shortly thereafter.

In 1499, Vespucci helped to finance and accompanied Alonso de Ojeda's expedition to the Indies, but he got off the ship in Hispaniola and returned to Seville ahead of Ojeda. Once in Seville, Vespucci wrote about the voyage as if Ojeda were not even present. His account garnered him an appointment to accompany Gonçalo Coelho of Portugal in his exploration of Brazil.

In the fall of 1501, Coelho's fleet reached the coast of Brazil. In contrast to Pedro Álvarez Cabral's landing

The early Italian explorer Amerigo Vespucci was the first to identify the Western Hemisphere as a "new" continent rather than part of Asia. In 1507, a German mapmaker designated the region he had explored as "America." *(Brown Brothers, Sterling, Pennsylvania)*

of 1500, relations with the people of Brazil were tense, and in some cases hostile. The fleet did not find great mineral wealth, but it did collect wood, parrots, monkeys, and a few native Brazilians.

Vespucci wrote two accounts of Coelho's voyage—which he claimed as his own third voyage, although it was not really *his*, and was his second voyage, in any event—known as the *Lettera* and *Mundus Novus*. Both of these were published in Florence around 1505. These documents resulted in Amerigo Vespucci's name being associated with the continent of South America and ultimately led to his lasting fame.

In his writings, Vespucci made claims that were clearly exaggerated. For example, he assessed his own skills as a navigator quite positively: "Though a man without practical experience, through the teaching of the marine chart for navigation, I was more skilled than all the shipmasters of the whole world" (from Samuel Eliot Morison's account). Vespucci, again giving credit to himself, and not the captain of the voyage, goes on to describe an incredible journey. Vespucci's achievements as a navigator must be taken with a grain of salt, but his descriptions of the Guarani of Brazil rival Columbus's early accounts in terms of their attention to ethnographic detail.

If Amerigo Vespucci made most of his discoveries as an observer and not as a captain himself, why do two continents bear his name? The answer, in part, can be traced to the nature of Columbus's and Vespucci's accounts. Vespucci played up native sexuality, while Columbus left it out of his account. This, among other factors, gave Vespucci's letters a wider readership. Vespucci also emphasized the newness of the lands he visited. Columbus conceived of the islands he had come across as part of Asia and did not see or describe much of continental America.

It was geographer Martin Waldseemüller, a professor at Saint-Dié in Lorraine, who first used the name America to describe South America, and eventually it was used to represent both of the newly discovered continents. Waldseemüller's map and Vespucci's *Mundus Novus* were in wide circulation among influential men, and the name stuck. Vespucci's false claim that he had visited the American mainland in 1497, before Columbus, was thus enshrined. By the time Vespucci's claims were proven false, the term "America" was already widely used.

Amerigo Vespucci died in Seville in 1512. His writings continued to excite controversy and interest in the new discoveries long after his death.

Matthew Jennings

See also: Exploration; Maps and Surveys.

Bibliography

Arciniegas, Germán. *Amerigo and the New World: The Life & Times of Amerigo Vespucci.* Translated by Harriet de Onís. New York: Alfred A. Knopf, 1955.

Morison, Samuel Eliot. *The European Discovery of America: The Southern Voyages.* New York: Oxford University Press, 1974.

Pohl, Frederick J. *Amerigo Vespucci, Pilot Major.* New York: Columbia University Press, 1944.

Vikings

Five centuries before Columbus, the Vikings, a seafaring people from Northern Europe, became the first Westerners to discover and colonize North America. During their brief stay, they left no lasting influence. Their presence was largely forgotten until recent archaeological discoveries revived interest in the Viking experience in North America.

Scholars dispute the origin of the word *Viking*. In the old Scandinavian language, *vik* meant a "bay" or "inlet." Vikings might have been so named because this word would describe where most harbored their boats. Britons called the Vikings *Norsemen*, which in old English meant "men from the north," the direction from which the Vikings approached Britain.

Much of what is known about the Vikings comes from archaeological study, but documentary sources also exist. Epic Scandinavian stories called *sagas* reveal much about Viking culture.

The Vikings originated in Scandinavia in the area of present-day Denmark, Norway, and Sweden. Over many years, what had originally been small communities of Neolithic farmers, hunters, and fishermen evolved into Iron Age feudal kingdoms. Viking culture reached its peak between the ninth and eleventh centuries. During this period, the Vikings, who had always depended on the sea for food, owing to the short growing seasons of the cold North, became a seafaring power.

As seafarers, the Vikings excelled at shipbuilding. From thick Scandinavian forests, Viking shipwrights built stout, deep-drafted vessels known as *knorrs* to haul cargo around the seas and fjords of Scandinavia. They also built sleek "long ships." These lengthy (60- to 90-foot), shallow-drafted, open boats had high sterns and prows carved to resemble mythical creatures, such as dragons. Along the side rails, a crew, numbering as

The L'Anse aux Meadows archaeological site in northern Newfoundland—a Norse settlement dating to 1000 C.E. and discovered in 1960—provides conclusive evidence that the Vikings were the first Europeans to discover and colonize America. *(Parks Canada/J. Steeves/H.01.11.01.26[14])*

many as ninety, would display their colorful round wooden shields. A single mast with a square sail or oar power drove the craft. The Vikings' navigational skills were as advanced as their ships, and both enabled the Scandinavians to range throughout Europe and beyond.

While many voyages were for trade, many others were in search of loot. During the idle months between planting and harvest, farmers and sailors became fearsome warriors, as the Vikings mounted expeditions to raid settlements and monasteries throughout the continent and in the British Isles. Their pagan religion glorified accomplishments in battle, and this, coupled with the prospect of gaining wealth, made them highly motivated, often merciless foes. Traveling ever farther seeking new places to sack, the Vikings reached as far east as Russia and as far south as Spain. The British Isles were a favorite target. Here, as elsewhere, many Vikings who came as raiders settled as colonizers.

Overpopulation and internal political dissent in Northern Europe also drove Vikings to seek new lands. Some headed west across the treacherous North Atlantic. In the late 800s C.E., Vikings colonized Iceland. Here around 930, clan leaders seeking to create a type of representative assembly established the *althingi,* which remains the world's oldest active parliamentary body.

Around 982, the son of a Norwegian exile living in Iceland named Eric the Red led a group of Vikings even farther west to colonize a large, ice-laden island earlier sighted by wayward sailors. Eric called the place Greenland so as to tempt potential settlers with visions of rich pasture.

Eric's son Leif was also an explorer. The "Saga of Eric the Red" also relates Leif Ericsson's exploits, which occurred around 1000 C.E. The saga tells that Leif and his party, sailing farther west of Greenland, found inviting coastal lands full of lush meadows, thick forests, and streams teeming with fish. Here they wintered before returning home. The saga further relates that Tyrkir the German, a member of the party, once ventured from the settlement and discovered wild grapes growing in the forest. This earned the place the name Vinland, or "land of grapes."

On his return, word of Leif's good fortune attracted other explorers. Around 1010, Thorfinn Karlsefni led over 150 colonists from Greenland in search of Vinland. The party passed thick forests and desolate sandy beaches before settling for the winter in a sheltered bay. The next spring, they settled near a wide river in an area farther south that had grapes. Life might have been good here but for worsening relations with the native peoples, whom the Vikings referred to as *skraelings.* For unknown reasons, these people went from being trading partners to being hostile adversaries. Greatly outnumbered, the Vikings abandoned their efforts to colonize the place.

The location of Vinland is much disputed. Various sites from New England to Labrador have been suggested, but none quite fits the descriptions of the land given in the sagas. What is not disputed, however, is that Vikings did indeed reach and colonize part of the coast of the North American continent 1,000 years ago.

In 1960, researcher Helge Ingstad discovered the remains of a Viking settlement dating from 1000 C.E. at L'Anse aux Meadows in Newfoundland, Canada. The excavated site revealed several dwellings, workshops, and an iron forge. It also established conclusively that the Vikings were the first Europeans to discover America.

Charles H. Wilson III

See also: Exploration; Newfoundland.

Bibliography

Graham-Campbell, James, ed. *Cultural Atlas of the Viking World.* New York: Facts on File, 1994.

Ingstad, Helge. *Westward to Vinland.* Translated by Erik J. Friis. New York: St. Martin's, 1969.

Wahlgren, Erik. *The Vikings and America.* Ancient Peoples and Places series. London: Thames and Hudson, 1986.

Virginia

The first permanent settlement in America was Jamestown, Virginia, chartered in 1606. With this settlement—one of two company-established colonies, the other being the Plymouth Colony—its sponsors, the London Company's investors, hoped to make substantial profits while extending England's boundaries across the sea. The region making up the Virginia colony was larger than most European nations; thus, it was an important territory to conquer. As it turned out, however, Jamestown proved to be an investment disaster, although it ultimately succeeded as an English Crown colony. It also set the economic stage for much of the South.

A few days before Christmas in 1606, three small ships—the *Susan Constant, Godspeed,* and *Discovery*—set sail from London. The captain of the best ship was Christopher Newport, and his passengers included the famous soldier-adventurer John Smith. Other organizers included Ferdinando Gorges, a seasoned navigator, and Richard Hakluyt, at one time the historiographer of the East India Company, who was connected with the cathedral at Bristol and had sought permission from Sir Walter Raleigh to establish a Protestant settlement in the New World (although neither Gorges nor Hakluyt joined the voyage).

The ships' crews included merchants, traders, and landed gentry, individuals anxious to realize a profit but lacking in practical skills. This oversight became an important issue later on, as the group was ill prepared for the hardships it would face in the wilderness. In April 1607, the three vessels encountered a series of storms along the east coast of North America. Seeking protection, the voyagers entered the lower end of the Chesapeake Bay and soon came to the mouth of a wide river, which they named the James, after their king.

They sailed upriver to where the water was deep enough to allow them to drop anchor. Unfortunately, the location later proved to be near a marsh infested with malaria-carrying mosquitoes. But it was here that the adventurers founded Jamestown. In celebration of their safe arrival, Parson Robert Hunt nailed a board between two trees, a spot from which he read the Episcopal service every day and twice on Sunday.

In one of the colony's first political actions, Edward Wingfield was elected president; this, however, proved to be the first of many poor choices made by these settlers. Wingfield was not a practical man and could not lead effectively. When Wingfield later returned to England, the settlers elected John Ratcliffe as leader, again a poor choice. Ratcliffe was more interested in developing his own empire than in developing the settlement.

The men did begin work on a fort approximately an acre in size. A palisade encircled the triangular fort, with its longest side facing the river. At each point of the triangle stood a small cannon. The men also built a handful of thatched houses and a small church within the fort's boundary; these buildings later proved to offer little protection against the harsh winters and rainy summers. The settlers also began clearing land for planting English wheat. They did not, however, dig wells but drank water straight from the dirty river—another problem that came back to haunt the newly established community.

Meanwhile, Captain Newport and John Smith led an expedition upriver. Passing several Algonquin villages, they met Chief Powhatan, the infamous father of young Pocahontas who later befriended John Smith and the men of Jamestown. Careful not to offend the chief or his tribe, Newport and Smith offered small gifts, including looking glasses, beads, and little bells. Smith, who became part of the governing council, was one of the few people to recognize the importance of good relations with the native peoples. He learned the local dialects and also mapped and explored the area around the Chesapeake Bay, as well as the Potomac and the Rappahannock Rivers.

While this group was gone, the fort was attacked by another band of natives. Several men were wounded, and only by retreating to the ships still anchored nearby were they able to escape. Cannon fire scared off their attackers.

In June, as the fort neared completion, Newport and his crews departed for England, leaving only the smallest ship behind along with approximately 100 men and boys. Newport's ships carried a cargo of timber, some worthless rocks the adventurers hoped contained gold, and the herb sassafras, used as a medicine for fevers.

Because the Virginia colony project began as a commercial enterprise, the governing corporation's interest in profits overruled the welfare of the people who were a part of it. Even if every colonist died, the corporation believed it could and would survive. Stockholders in the corporation admitted new members, elected officers, and wrote bylaws. In this way, the company ruled the colony much like a sovereign state. It could impose taxes, coin money, and even regulate

A 1606 map of Virginia, as described by Captain John Smith, shows the Chesapeake Bay, Potomac River, and other familiar geographic features. A vignette of the native leader Powhatan appears at the upper left. *(Library of Congress, LC-USZ62-116706)*

trade. It also had a treasury and was responsible for the colonists' defense.

One important aspect of the charter provided that those who ventured to settle in the colony remained Englishmen. As such, they retained all the attendant rights and privileges, even though they were no longer living on British soil.

Religion

In addition to being given political power, the London Company was also assigned the job of spreading Protestantism. The colonizers were to propagate "the Christian religion to such people as yet live in darkness and miserable ignorance of the true knowledge and worship of God," in order to "bring the infidels and savages, in those parts, to human civility." Although they were not as fervent in this part of their mission as the Puritans in their quest for religious freedom, the religious intent of the Virginia founders was among their primary motivations. Church doctrine served as the foundation for law, and the church's creed became the measure of a godly man.

After a prayer "said by Mr. Bucke, the Minister, that it please God to guide and sanctifie all our proceedings," the initial order of business for the first Virginia Assembly, held in 1619, was to enact a number of laws mandating church attendance on the Sabbath, as well as tax support for the clergy and church. One law declared that "all persons whatsoever upon the Sabbath days shall frequent divine service and sermons, both forenoon and afternoon."

Even in 1624, laws were passed declaring that "there shall be in every plantation, where the people use to meete for the worship of God, a house or room sequestred for that purpose, and to be for any temporal use whatsoever" and that "whosoever shall absent himselfe from divine service any Sunday without an allowable excuse shall forfeite a pound of tobacco, and he that absenteth himselfe a month shall forfeit 10 pound of tobacco."

The Virginia colony, however, attracted many because of the opportunity it offered to start a new life. Initially, the Virginia Company hired settlers for a term of seven years, but these workers could not own land. The corporation provided tools and supplies, while profits went back to the company. This proved the least successful of all the company's enterprises, however, because it offered little incentive to the workers. After ten years, only a handful of laborers still operated under this plan. In 1614, the company implemented several reforms; one of these gave 50 acres to those who chose to work for the company.

In addition, 100 acres of deeded land were offered for a price to those who could afford it. Investors could choose to travel to Virginia and work the land or hire other laborers to take their place. In the second scenario, the investor received not only his original allotment of land but also a second 100 acres for every laborer he could persuade to sail with him to Virginia. These holdings were subject to an annual tax or "quitrent" of 2 shillings per 100 acres.

A third kind of enterprise undertaken by the corporation was the granting of larger tracts of land in return for "meritorious" service. This reward was reserved for individuals who had worked as officers of the company or were substantial investors. Many of these estates later grew into enormous plantations.

After the first expedition returned to England, disaster struck the small settlement. The summer was unbearably hot, and the flimsy shelters did not protect the men from sudden storms. Food spoiled, and the few chickens that had survived the ocean voyage did not last long. In addition, because no cattle or sheep had been brought over, there was no butter or milk or easily obtained meat. The remaining sources of food included oysters, crabs, fish, and roasted squirrels. Before long, the men were suffering from disease, and many died.

By autumn, half of the original settlers were dead, and those who remained quarreled continuously. Governor Dale, in an effort to contain the conflict, hanged, shot, or broke men "on the wheel" as punishment for crimes. John Smith also wrote that there was "no talke, no hope, nor worke, but dig gold, wash gold, refine gold, load gold." The foolishness of the men caused Smith to impose strict order and to demand work in exchange for food. It was during this first winter that Pocahontas brought food to the starving settlers, helping them survive.

When the second expedition finally arrived, just after the New Year, it again brought more "gentlemen" and several goldsmiths, much to the horror of John Smith. Two women also arrived, "Mistresse Forest [Forrest] and Anne Buras [Burroughs], her maide." Mistress Forrest soon married John Layden in a church wedding. Their child, Jamestown's first, was born the next year. They named their daughter Virginia.

A third expedition once more brought gentlemen, a few tradesmen, some soldiers, and more women, many of whom arrived sick and exhausted. Unfortunately, many had died en route to Jamestown; fever had killed adults, as well as infants born during the voyage. Only a few sheep and goats survived the crossing, and John Smith, once again angered by the company's ignorance, wrote:

> When you send again, I entreat you rather send but thirty carpenters, husbandmen, gardeners, fishermen, blacksmiths, mason, and diggers up of trees' roots, well provided, than a thousand such as we have. . . . Nothing is to be expected thence, but by labor.

In 1609–1610, the colony faced its third winter. Although there were now 700 inhabitants, the settlement again barely survived. After that season, known as "the starving time," the remaining population numbered only 60. Most died from disease and starvation. In 1609, John Smith, injured by exploding gunpowder, was forced to return to England. He would later make two more voyages to the New England region. Finally, in 1616, he compiled his observations in a document called the "Countrie of Massachussetts, which is the Paradise of all those parts."

Introduction of Tobacco

In spite of the bitter failure of the first years, Jamestown's fate turned around in 1613. There were several reasons for the settlement's eventual survival, the most important being the introduction of a crop that became highly successful: tobacco. Although little money could be made by raising corn or grain, tobacco, "the obnoxious weed," grew easily in the Virginia climate. With its popularity soaring in Europe, much of it having come from the Spanish West Indies, fortunes were quickly made in Virginia, as much as $75,000 a year. Interestingly enough, King James I detested tobacco, declaring that it was "loathesome to the eye, hateful to the nose, harmful to the brain, dangerous to the lungs."

John Rolfe, one of Virginia's first settlers, is credited with discovering a method of curing tobacco that contributed to its economic success in the young colony. In no time, it became the economic backbone of Virginia. In 1616, accompanied by his Native American wife, Pocahontas, Rolfe traveled to England to pursue the commercial distribution of tobacco. His marriage to Powhatan's favorite daughter was seen as a great alliance for Virginia. Even James I received Pocahontas as "royalty." Pocahontas died before she was able to return to her homeland.

The second element that helped to ensure Virginia's survival was the influx of workers, "indentured servants" bound to serve for ten years in return for the cost of their passage to the colonies. Most of these bond servants were poor; many were abducted off the streets of English cities or lured aboard, only to discover their destiny too late. Others were deported convicts. The last group of workers was slaves, the first of which were brought by a Dutch ship in 1619. Although some Africans came as indentured servants, it was not long before they were kept as slaves. This influx of ready and cheap labor was seen as a great benefit to the large and growing tobacco plantations.

The third component that helped to stabilize Virginia also came in 1620–1621, when the London Company sent approximately 100 young women, "agreeable persons, young and incorrupt." These women were "sold with their own consent to settlers as wives at the cost of their transportation." These first women faced tremendous hardships as they carved out homes for themselves and their children. Thus, within thirty years, the first "native-born" Virginians took their place in history.

In spite of Virginia's eventual success as a colony, it was deemed a commercial disappointment by its initial investors. Facing bankruptcy, the London Company's charter was finally abolished in 1624 by James I. After that, Virginia's affairs were managed by a governor appointed by the Crown, aided by a small council also selected by the king. The Virginia House of Burgesses, America's first legislative body, still had

Virginia Company

a voice and passed laws, but these were subject to approval by either the governor or the king.

This shift became an important point of contention with the colonists, who saw themselves as independent of England's authority. They resented the British Crown's interference and intolerance, and their discontent grew as the years went by. Clearly, the seeds of a desire for self-determination had been sown when the first colonists stepped off at Jamestown.

It is interesting to note that of all those who settled and rose to the top of Virginia's social ladder, in the end, only three families "derived from English houses of historic note." Three others "derived from minor gentry." The rest descended from merchants, adventurers, entrepreneurs, indentured servants, and slaves.

Virginia continued as one of the most important colonies and later became one of the most important states in the new union. Four of the first five presidents were from Virginia, and four other presidents were born in Virginia. Virginia also became the heart of the Southern Confederacy, its army led by Virginian Robert E. Lee.

In 1800, Virginia was the most populous state, with more than 885,000 residents; it remained so until the 1820s, when New York surpassed it. Tobacco remained its most important cash crop, and slavery became the means by which it was produced. In fact, in 1860, roughly 39 percent of Virginia's 1.2 million people were slaves. Today, Virginia is the twelfth most populous state, with about 6.2 million residents.

Gail L. Jenner

See also: Jamestown; Piedmont; Tidewater; Tobacco; Virginia (Chronology); Virginia Company; Williamsburg. *Documents:* Virginia Slave Laws (1660s); John Clayton's Report on Virginia (1688).

Bibliography

Athearn, Robert G. *American Heritage Illustrated History of the United States: The New World.* Vol. 1. New York: Choice Publishing, 1988.

Breen, T. H. *Tobacco Culture: The Mentality of the Great Tidewater Planters on the Eve of Revolution.* Princeton, NJ: Princeton University Press, 2001.

Morgan, Edmund. *American Slavery, American Freedom: The Ordeal of Colonial Virginia.* New York: W. W. Norton, 1975.

Thane, Elswyth. *The Virginia Colony.* London: Crowell-Collier, 1969.

Vaughan, Alden T. *American Genesis: Captain John Smith and the Founding of Virginia.* Boston: Little, Brown, 1975.

The Virginia Company of London was granted a charter in April 1606 by King James I of England. The stated purpose of the company, composed mostly of London financiers and rural gentry, was to plant colonies along the coast of North America between the 34th and 41st degrees of latitude. Some supporters wanted to forestall colonization by English Catholics or Spain; others believed that Virginia might have deposits of gold.

The Company's mission, financed in part by lotteries, was conceived as a long-range project rather than a quick raid on the area's resources. Investors agreed not to take any dividends for the first seven years. The company also received new charters in 1609 and 1612, and it was eventually assigned a belt of territory that extended across North America to the Pacific Ocean.

The Virginia Company sent out its first colonizing expedition of three ships under the leadership of John Smith in December 1606, instructing its colonists to maintain good relations with the local natives, then dominated by chief Powhatan. The expedition, poorly prepared for the rigors of life in the New World, proved unsuccessful. Despite the public relations coup of the visit of Powhatan's daughter Pocahontas, a Christian convert, to London and the beginnings of tobacco cultivation, subsequent ventures also failed to prove economically rewarding. By the late 1610s, therefore, the company was increasingly troubled.

The Virginia Company was not merely an economic organization. It also presented its mission in religious terms, sponsoring and publishing sermons given to meetings of shareholders and emphasizing the duty of converting natives and planting Protestant Christianity in North America. (The great poet and preacher John Donne spoke before the company in 1622.) Unlike the sponsors of the early New England colonies, the Virginia Company, whose board included the archbishop of Canterbury and several bishops, was allied with the episcopal hierarchy of the Church of England. There was even an attempt to found a college at Henrico for the Christian education of Native American men.

The company also sponsored promotional literature, including John Smith's *A True Relation . . . of Virginia,* pamphlets by London writers, and even ballads. The literature emphasized both Virginia's economic possibilities and God's care for the colonists. News about the struggles and disasters of the early colonists (often seen as the work of Satan) was not widely disseminated, for fear that it would discourage further colonization.

Between 1615 and 1619, the company became involved in a struggle between the court-connected London financier Sir Thomas Smythe and an aristocratic faction led by Sir Edwin Sandys (a member of the company's council since 1607), his brother the poet George Sandys, and the Earl of Southampton. Unlike Smythe, Edwin Sandys and Southampton were considered political opponents of the king. Sandys succeeded in acquiring control of the failing company in April 1619, and the Sandys faction tried to revitalize the settlement by actively recruiting thousands of colonists in England, which was then undergoing a severe economic depression. (Many of these new colonists quickly died once they had reached Virginia.)

The Sandys faction also tried to reorganize the colony on the basis of representative government. This replaced the system of almost absolute military rule by company governors, including the notoriously corrupt and tyrannical Samuel Argall, appointed governor in 1617. The new system divided power between a governor and council appointed by the company in London and "burgesses" elected from Virginia towns and plantations on a relatively wide franchise. Sir Francis Wyatt, a Sandys relation, was chosen as governor late in 1620. He was accompanied to Virginia by his close friend George Sandys in the recently created post of treasurer of the colony, to which he had been appointed on May 2, 1621. Wyatt and Sandys had ambitious plans to establish self-sustaining agriculture and even industry in the new colony.

The Sandys leadership was handicapped by lack of business experience and limited knowledge of the situation in America. Soon after 1620, the company came under fierce attack in both Virginia—where the native attack of March 22, 1622, had resulted in the deaths of over 300 colonists—and London, where Edwin Sandys had to contend with the king's fury.

There was rampant factionalism within the company itself, largely resulting from Sandys's own mismanagement. The government was also suspicious of the colony's overly democratic political arrangements. A trial before the court of King's Bench in May 1624 resulted in the company's dissolution and the Crown's takeover of Virginia as the first English Royal Colony in the Americas (although its representative institutions were left intact). Sporadic attempts to revive the Virginia Company continued until 1640.

William E. Burns

See also: Jamestown; Joint-Stock Companies; Rolfe, John; Smith, John; Tobacco; Trade. *Document:* The Jamestown Settlement (1607–1609).

Bibliography

Canny, Nicholas, ed. *The Oxford History of the British Empire.* Vol. 1, *The Origins of Empire. British Overseas Enterprise to the Close of the Seventeenth Century.* Oxford, UK, and New York: Oxford University Press, 1998.

Ellison, James. *George Sandys: Travel, Colonialism and Tolerance in the 17th Century.* Cambridge, UK: D. S. Brewer, 2002.

Miller, Perry. *Errand into the Wilderness.* Cambridge, MA: Harvard University Press, 1956.

Wabanaki

See Abenaki

War

During the seventeenth and eighteenth centuries, colonial America saw protracted fighting between the great powers of Europe on the one hand and the American colonists and Native Americans on the other. European powers, namely France and Great Britain, exported their continental conflicts to America, and colonists fought to gain more land and defend themselves against Native American attacks. The struggles between France and England climaxed during the Seven Years' War, known as the French and Indian War in the colonies, when British victories largely drove the French from North America. Several years later, the British would themselves be humiliated in North America, with their defeat in the War of American Independence.

Warfare in colonial America took place against a backdrop of changes in European warfare collectively known as the "Military Revolution." This concept, articulated by two historians, Michael Roberts and Geoffrey Parker, refers to the period from 1500 to 1800, when gunpowder weapons came to dominate battlefields around the world. During that period, Europeans integrated firearms into their armed forces and developed large professional armies capable of wielding such weapons to maximum effect on the battlefield. In addition, European navies successfully adopted heavy cannon and married them to sturdy sailing ships that would allow Europeans to project their power around the globe.

Weaponry

In small arms and artillery, gunpowder weapons superseded older missile weapons such as the bow and arrow and the trebuchet. Firearms offered infantry forces a way to kill heavily armored opponents and were easier to learn to use as compared to the longbow, or the couched lance. New weapons required new tactics, and European leaders turned to the example of the ancient Romans for ways to fight that stressed linear formations and discipline. Over time, linear tactics became more effective and required greater discipline, contributing to the rise of large standing armies in Europe.

Early firearms were heavy and unreliable, and their smoothbore barrels offered little in terms of accuracy at any distance. Also, their slow rates of fire and reload meant that musketeers required the support of large numbers of pikemen—infantrymen who wielded long spears to attack or to keep cavalry at bay. These linear formations often required revision when they were employed in the woods of America, where sharpshooters could play a large role and cavalry was far more limited in scale than in Europe. Yet linear formations remained essential to warfare in colonial America; despite popular mythology, the Americans won their War for Independence not with eagle-eyed killers blasting away at the British from a distance, but with the well-trained and disciplined Continental army, organized along European lines.

Heavy cannon easily blasted through the high thin walls of medieval castles, which led to the development of a new style of fortress design known as *trace italienne*. Those new fortresses replaced the castles of the Middle Ages with low, thick, angular walls, designed to deflect incoming artillery and draw attackers into a lethal crossfire. Square and round towers were replaced by bastions, angular features designed to offer mutually supportive fire. Such new fortresses spread throughout

Europe and later throughout the world, as they offered a superb means of defense when constructed with stone but still provided protection when constructed only with earth and wood. The Castillo de San Marcos in St. Augustine, Florida, is an excellent example of this kind of defensive structure.

The discovery of how to employ gunpowder weapons at sea also proved to be of great importance to Europeans. Large, sturdy ships built to survive the storms of northern waters also served as solid platforms for cannon. Broadsides fired from such ships provided an enormous volume of firepower from a mobile platform able to carry a nation's power around the globe. The English in particular enjoyed great success at sea; English ships served as the "wooden walls" of their country and allowed British forces unprecedented mobility. The combination of land and sea forces offered the British tremendous operational flexibility, which they would exploit often in the Seven Years' War and the American War for Independence.

In addition to the so-called military revolution, broader changes were under way in early modern Europe that also spread to North America. The Protestant Reformation and the Catholic Counterreformation spawned a vast array of conflicts within and between European countries that would profoundly affect the course of settlement and warfare in North America. Puritans, the iron-willed Calvinists of England, originally settled in Massachusetts to create a "City upon a Hill," which was intended to serve as a model reformed society. During the first half of the seventeenth century, anti-Puritan sentiment in England helped increase the number of settlers traveling to New England, and the poor performance of the Protestant forces in the early stages of the Thirty Years' War also spurred immigration. A growing population helped make Massachusetts and, indeed, all of New England into a military power of increasing potency. In addition, Protestant pirates and privateers from England and the Netherlands preyed on the ships and settlements of the Spanish empire in Central and South America.

Eighteenth-century warfare took place in the age of the flintlock firearm, and both muskets and rifles were employed by combatants. The term "flintlock" refers to the way in which the weapons are fired: on pulling the trigger, a hammer bearing a small piece of flint strikes the steel lid of a pan containing a small amount of gunpowder, which then ignites the main charge of black powder in the barrel of the weapon, propelling a lead ball out of the barrel and toward its target.

Muskets are smoothbore weapons that can be loaded quickly and can accept a bayonet, but they have a very short range. During the eighteenth century, flintlock muskets served as the main weapon of soldiers, but small numbers of soldiers and many civilians carried rifles. Unlike smoothbore muskets, the barrels of rifles contained grooves called *rifling* that caused the ball to spin when fired, offering far better range and accuracy. Those grooves made rifles far slower to load, however, and meant that any units of riflemen would be extremely vulnerable to a swift counterattack or to troops on horseback. In addition, black powder caused rifles to foul rapidly, requiring them to be cleaned often, and rifles could not accept a bayonet without damaging the barrel of the weapon.

Categories of War

War in colonial America can be divided into two broad categories: war between Europeans and war between Europeans and indigenous opponents.

War with Native Americans

In fighting Native Americans, the English employed the same sort of brutality they had used against the Irish for centuries. Anglo-Saxons had a long heritage of brutality toward the Irish. Atrocities traditionally thought to have begun during the Elizabethan conquest can be dated back to the twelfth century as well: at Waterford in 1170 the English killed seventy prisoners and threw their bodies over a cliff; fifteen years later, Irish raiding into Meath were put to the sword, and over a hundred heads were sent back to Dublin. And Oliver Cromwell famously slaughtered the Catholic Irish garrison at Drogheda in 1649. The English often viewed their Irish opponents as inhuman savages, a common theme that runs through American attitudes toward Native Americans and African Americans and through English attitudes toward the Irish. Edmund Spenser's *View of the Present State of Ireland* provides an excellent example of the escalating anti-Irish rhetoric of the late sixteenth century. English colonists would employ similarly aggressive methods in waging war against their Native American opponents.

Native Americans generally waged war by raiding settlements and then disappearing into the forest rather than confronting the colonists in battle. Therefore the colonists sought either to bring the native warriors out to fight or to destroy their ability to do battle by burning the natives' crops, supplies, and villages—

This rare engraving, dating to the 1770s, is one of the first depictions of a soldier in the Continental army. The legend calls it an "accurate depiction." *(Brown Brothers, Sterling, Pennsylvania)*

often with a high toll in civilians. Colonists confronted Native American guerrilla warfare in a simple and brutal way: by crushing their opponents' logistical apparatus, and forcing them either to fight or to starve. This attack on the means by which an opponent might wage war forms a cornerstone of the American way of fighting and has often reappeared in American wars. Sherman's march to the sea is a particularly vivid example.

King Philip's War, the greatest of the wars between the colonists and the native peoples, occurred in 1675–1676, when the Wampanoag sachem Metacom formed an alliance of several tribes to attack Puritan colonies in New England. Metacom, known to the English as King Philip, enjoyed enormous early success against the colonists. Both sides waged ruthless attacks that proved extremely destructive and did not spare civilians. Eventually, English arms ground the Wampanoag and their allies down, and the war came to an

end when King Philip was finally hunted down and killed by his adversaries. The Puritan victory ended the Native American threat to New England.

War Among Europeans

Conflict between Europeans and American colonists often occurred in the coastal areas of North America. During the colonial period, water served as the main route of transportation. Ships were, of course, needed to transport goods and people to and from the mother country, and they also served as the best means of transportation from one colony to another. Port cities were, therefore, of tremendous importance during wars between European powers, as was control of the seas. During the French and Indian War, Britain and France fought for several years for control of the St. Lawrence River. In the American War for Independence, ports such as Boston, Philadelphia, and New York all served as important centers for major campaigns.

The British ability to mount conjoint operations, demanding close coordination between the army and the navy, allowed them to strike with surprise and overwhelming force at a specific point, while forcing the Continental army to prepare to confront an attack along an extended coastline. British success in New York in 1776 came about because of British skill at mounting operations of this kind. Yet when the British lost control of the sea, as they did in the Chesapeake Bay in 1781, disaster resulted. When the British army headed by Lord Cornwallis retreated to Yorktown in 1781, a French fleet prevented its escape by sea. The Continental army, led by George Washington, laid siege to Yorktown and eventually forced Cornwallis to surrender.

During the seventeenth and eighteenth centuries, Britain and France waged a number of wars against each other as the British sought to organize European coalitions to oppose the growth of French power in Europe. During these years, France fielded a huge standing army and sought to expand her already vast power. All of the major wars—the Nine Years' War (1689–1697), the War of the Spanish Succession (1701–1714), the War of the Austrian Succession (1740–1748), the Seven Years' War (1756–1763, known in America as the French and Indian War), and the American War for Independence (1775–1783)— saw fighting between the two sides in North America, with fighting growing in scale and intensity as the eighteenth century progressed. French settlements in North America were largely centered in Canada, along the St. Lawrence River, while British colonies stretched along a narrow strip of land from Massachusetts to Georgia.

The Seven Years' War was the last major struggle between France and England for control of North America. Conflict first erupted in what is today western Pennsylvania, where a British column under General Edward Braddock was defeated in 1755. Much fighting also took place in upstate New York, near Lake Champlain, in the area that controlled the land approaches from New York to the St. Lawrence River. The British finally won a decisive victory at Quebec on September 13, 1759, when the small army of General James Wolfe defeated the army of the Marquis de Montcalm on the Plains of Abraham outside the city. When Montreal surrendered the following September, the British had gained effective control of North America.

That death grip on North America would be short-lived. By the mid-1770s, British policies drove many colonists into open rebellion against the Crown. In the American War for Independence, which followed, British forces enjoyed tactical successes and performed well when in close contact with the Royal Navy. Yet the British failed to strike with the necessary vigor to win the war. Colonial forces, led by General George Washington, gradually improved over time from the undisciplined militia that confronted the British early in the war to the professional army that received the British surrender at Yorktown in 1781.

Mitchell McNaylor

See also: Army, British; Beaver Wars; Bunker Hill, Battle of; English Civil War; Fortifications; French and Indian War; Kieft's War; King George's War; King Philip's War; Lexington and Concord, Battles of; Military and Diplomatic Affairs (Chronology); Military and Diplomatic Affairs (Essay); Militias; Native American–European Conflict; Navy, British; Queen Anne's War; Revolutionary War; Tuscarora War; War of Jenkins' Ear; Yamasee War.

Bibliography

Anderson, Fred. *Crucible of War: The Seven Years' War and the Fate of Empire in British North America, 1754–1766.* New York: Alfred A. Knopf, 2000.

———. *A People's Army: Massachusetts Soldiers and Society in the Seven Years' War.* Chapel Hill: Published by the University of North Carolina Press for the Institute of Early American History and Culture in Williamsburg, Virginia, 1984.

Black, Jeremy. *European Warfare, 1660–1815.* New Haven, CT: Yale University Press, 1994.

———. *Warfare in the Eighteenth Century.* London: Cassell, 1999.

Cave, Alfred A. *The Pequot War.* Amherst: University of Massachusetts Press, 1996.

Clinton, Henry, Sir. *The American Rebellion; Sir Henry Clinton's Narrative of His Campaigns, 1775–1782, with an appendix of original documents.* New Haven, CT: Yale University Press, 1954.

Commager, Henry Steele, and Richard Morris, eds. *The Spirit of 'Seventy-Six: The Story of the American Revolution as Told by Participants.* Indianapolis, IN: Bobbs-Merrill, 1958.

Duffy, Christopher. *The Military Experience in the Age of Reason.* New York: Atheneum, 1987.

Gipson, Lawrence Henry. *The British Empire before the American Revolution.* 15 vols. Caldwell, ID: Caxton Printers, 1936–1970.

Higginbotham, Don. *The War of American Independence: Military Attitudes, Policies, and Practice, 1763–1789.* New York: Macmillan, 1971.

Leach, Douglas Edward. *Flintlock and Tomahawk: New England in King Philip's War.* New York: Macmillan, 1958.

Lee, Henry. *Memoirs of the War in the Southern Department of the United States.* New York: University Publishing Company, 1870.

Mackesy, Piers. *The War for America, 1775–1783.* Cambridge, MA: Harvard University Press, 1964.

Malone, Patrick M. *The Skulking Way of War: Technology and Tactics Among the New England Indians.* Lanham, MD: Madison, 1991.

Martin, Joseph Plumb. *Private Yankee Doodle: Being a Narrative of Some of the Adventures, Dangers, and Sufferings of a Revolutionary Soldier.* Boston: Little, Brown, 1962.

Parker, Geoffrey. *The Military Revolution: Military Innovation and the Rise of the West, 1500–1800.* Cambridge, UK: Cambridge University Press, 1988.

Parkman, Francis. *France and England in North America.* 2 vols. New York: Literary Classics of the United States, 1983.

Philips, Kevin P. *The Cousins' Wars: Religion, Politics, and the Triumph of Anglo-America.* New York: Basic Books, 1999.

Rogers, Clifford J., ed. *The Military Revolution Debate: Readings on the Military Transformation of Early Modern Europe.* Boulder, CO: Westview Press, 1995.

Royster, Charles. *A Revolutionary People at War: The Continental Army and American Character, 1775–1783.* Chapel Hill: University of North Carolina Press, 1979.

Shy, John. *A People Numerous and Armed: Reflections on the Military Struggle for American Independence.* New York: Oxford University Press, 1976.

Steele, Ian Kenneth. *Betrayals: Fort William Henry and the Massacre.* New York: Oxford University Press, 1990.

———. *Warpaths: Invasions of North America.* New York: Oxford University Press, 1994.

War of Jenkins' Ear

In April 1731, Spanish authorities stopped and boarded the British merchant ship *Rebecca* as it sailed near the coast of Cuba. After an inspection of the vessel's cargo and paperwork, the *Rebecca's* commander, Captain Robert Jenkins, was pronounced guilty of smuggling. As punishment, his captors sliced off one of his ears. This seemingly minor event had explosive consequences. During testimony to a committee of the House of Commons seven years later, Jenkins produced a handkerchief and carefully unfolded it to reveal his preserved ear. His punishment was condemned as barbaric and prompted howls of public outrage.

Throughout the 1720s, tensions between England and Spain had risen as the former expanded its commercial grip on the Atlantic and the latter attempted to limit foreign trade with its colonial possessions. When diplomatic overtures failed to bring about a peaceful resolution to trade issues, Great Britain, in October 1739, declared war on Spain—launching the War of Jenkins' Ear.

Just a month after the declaration of war, Admiral Edward Vernon mounted an assault on the lightly defended town of Porto Bello on the Isthmus of Pan-

ama and captured it easily in a single day. Vernon became an instant celebrity in England and the New World. Commemorative medals honoring his victory sold at brisk rates to an adoring public. Hoping to duplicate his success on a larger scale, Vernon in 1740 began planning an attack on the heavily fortified city of Cartagena. Leaders in England reinforced him with an army under the command of General Thomas Wentworth, and every American colony except Georgia and South Carolina was required to send troops to support the expedition.

When Vernon launched the offensive in early 1741, his force of 9,000 men included some 3,500 American colonials. The expedition arrived near Cartagena in March, and the disaster was officially under way. Vernon urged a rapid assault, but Wentworth counseled patience. While the two officers quarreled over tactics, disease carried death and demoralization through the ranks. When the British strike against the city finally came three weeks later, the Spanish repulsed it with heavy losses to the attackers. The British, having

1. Spanish Guarda Costa boarding Capt. Jenkins's Ship and Cutting off his Ear.

The War of Jenkins' Ear in 1739 was triggered in part by an incident eight years earlier: Spanish naval authorities boarded a British merchant ship near Cuba, confiscated its cargo, and cut off the ear of Captain Robert Jenkins as punishment for smuggling. *(Private Collection/Bridgeman Art Library)*

decided that the city could not be captured, evacuated the remnants of their force on April 17, 1741. No more than 600 of the 3,500 Americans survived the ill-fated campaign.

The other significant military operations during the War of Jenkins' Ear occurred along the disputed Florida-Georgia border. British General James Oglethorpe, leading a combined force of nearly 2,000 Georgia and South Carolina troops, launched an attack on the Spanish garrison at St. Augustine in 1740. Early successes against outlying positions gave the general hope for a quick victory, like Vernon's at Porto Bello. The initial plan called for simultaneous land and sea assaults against the St. Augustine fortifications so as to overwhelm the outnumbered defenders. When a sea attack proved not feasible, however, Oglethorpe unsuccessfully struggled to find an alternative means of capturing his target. Plagued by internal bickering and a lack of direction, the army laid half-hearted siege to the town for about a month before retreating. Oglethorpe attributed the campaign's failure to insubordination on the part of the South Carolina troops, but they placed the blame on the general's indecision and lack of vision. The resulting controversy caused ill feeling between the two provinces for decades.

Back in Georgia, Oglethorpe braced for a Spanish counterattack. He had less than 700 men at his disposal and could expect no assistance from the now embittered South Carolinians. In the summer of 1742, a Spanish invasion force numbering nearly 2,000 moved to attack Frederica, the southernmost settlement in Georgia. After a few minor yet sharp engagements in which the Spanish army received the worst of the exchanges, the Spanish commander's confidence began to waver. Sensing this hesitation, Oglethorpe fed rumors to the enemy camp that a strong reinforcing army from South Carolina was about to land behind the invaders, and that a force under Admiral Vernon was about to attack the weakened garrison at St. Augustine. Although he had a clear numerical superiority, the Spanish general became convinced that English forces outnumbered his own and ordered a panicked retreat—leaving behind supplies and artillery in his haste to escape.

In 1743, Oglethorpe again mounted an unsuccessful offensive against St. Augustine. This marked the final clash in the colonial conflict known as the War of Jenkins' Ear.

Andrew C. Lannen

See also: Georgia; Military and Diplomatic Affairs (Chronology); Military and Diplomatic Affairs (Essay); Oglethorpe, James; War.

Bibliography

Ferling, John. *Struggle for a Continent: The Wars of Early America.* Arlington Heights, IL: Harlan Davidson, 1993.

Leach, Douglas Edward. *Arms For Empire: A Military History of the American Colonies in North America, 1607–1763.* New York: Macmillan, 1973.

Warren, Mercy Otis (1728–1814)

A patriot woman of letters during the American Revolution and its aftermath, Mercy Otis Warren penned countless pieces of correspondence, poems, plays, essays, and a three-volume history of the American Revolution. She was among the most significant intellectuals of the Revolution, male or female.

Mercy Otis Warren and James Warren, her husband, descended from the earliest settlers of Massachusetts. She lived in Barnstable, Plymouth, and Milton, Massachusetts. The third of thirteen children, in her childhood she learned both the domestic arts and a partial college preparatory curriculum.

Warren was an adept student. Both her husband and her brother, James Otis, Jr., a Harvard graduate, encouraged her to develop her considerable intellect, and her family's wealth gave her the means to do it. Her belief in Providence and the early republican activism of her brother James inspired her to write on public issues to an extent unusual for women of the era. Her role model was Catharine Macaulay.

Warren corresponded with many of the leading lights of the Revolutionary era, including George Washington and Thomas Jefferson. Her most extensive and meaningful correspondents, however, included Elbridge Gerry, John and Abigail Adams, and Macaulay. Letters to Macaulay focused on politics and their shared opposition to Tory traditions. Her relationship with John Adams tended toward the tempestuous, and they did not communicate at all for several years after Adams savaged Warren's history of the Revolution. The Gerry-Warren correspondence displayed the republican values they shared during the Revolution, their concern with what they saw as the counterrevolution of the Federalist era, and their pleasure at what they saw as the restoration of republican values under the Jeffersonians. Warren's writings to Abigail Adams ranged widely from discussions of childhood education to the work of Molière.

Warren was perhaps the first American woman to

write plays. She focused on political themes and was most noted for a trilogy about the American Revolution. The first of these, *The Adulateur* (1772), attacked "Rapatio," who represented the prominent Tory Thomas Hutchinson, as the overseer of an evil system of political corruption. "Brutus," his opponent, championed resistance to the colonial system. In its sequel, *The Defeat* (1773), the Hutchinson character's malevolence increased. Warren urged the good men of the resistance to practice the virtue that she believed necessary for sound government. In the final play of the trilogy, *The Group* (1775), Warren satirized British efforts to undermine the chartered rights of the citizenry of Massachusetts to elect the upper house of its legislature.

Warren also wrote a large number of political, philosophical, didactic, and spiritual poems. Perhaps most notable was her first poem, "The Squabble of the Sea Nymphs" (1774). Written at the request of John Adams, it alluded to the Boston Tea Party and contrasted the perfidy of Tories with the justice of the patriot cause. Similar works followed. A common theme in her poems was the virtue of self-sacrifice. Although her poems display a keen and educated mind, Benjamin Franklin rightly judged her as "a mediocre poet at best."

From the perspective of the historian, Warren's most significant work was her three-volume *History of the Rise, Progress and Termination of the American Revolution*, which featured a florid and Manichean style that reflected its times. Warren hoped that the work would "teach philosophy by example," as Bolingbrook once said. Her political philosophy in the *History* is in the "old republican" tradition of the radical Whig, anti-Federalist, and Jeffersonian continuum.

Her history emphasized what she saw as the eternal battle between popular liberty and the dangerous power of arbitrary and unrepresentative government. Liberty alone could not sustain a republic, however. In her view, republican government was unstable and tended toward despotism. Reason and the virtue of self-sacrifice were necessary to stave off this degeneration.

When she wrote the work in the 1780s and 1790s, her hopes for the long-term prospects of the American republican system already had begun to wane. She believed that the self-sacrifice that had marked the Revolution had given way to selfishness, faction, and greed, and that the consolidation of government represented by the Federalists did not bode well for the future of liberty. Publication may have been delayed to 1805 to coincide with the reelection of an administration sympathetic to her views.

John Adams began to viciously attack the *History*

in 1807, and, in 1808, Warren's husband died. She nevertheless maintained her spirits and carried on with her intellectual life until her death in 1814. That she accomplished so much, despite her considerable duties as a devoted wife and mother of five children, made her life all the more noteworthy.

David M. Fitzsimons

See also: Arts, Culture, and Intellectual Life (Chronology); Arts, Culture, and Intellectual Life (Essay); Literature; Theater.

Bibliography

Richards, Jeffrey H. *Mercy Otis Warren.* New York: Twayne, 1995.

Warren, Mercy Otis. *History of the Rise, Progress, and Termination of the American Revolution.* Edited by Lester H. Cohen. 2 vols. Indianapolis, IN: Liberty Classics, 1988.

———. *The Plays and Poems of Mercy Otis Warren.* Edited by Benjamin V. Franklin. Delmar, NY: Scholar's Facsimiles, 1980.

Zagarri, Rosemarie. *Mercy Otis Warren and the American Revolution: A Woman's Dilemma.* Wheeling, IL: Davidson, Harlan, 1995.

Washington, George (1732–1799)

George Washington served as commander in chief of the Continental army during the American War for Independence, presided over the convention that drafted the U.S. Constitution, and was the first president of the United States of America.

Born on February 22, 1732, in Westmoreland County, Virginia, Washington grew up in the Northern Neck of Virginia. He received little in the way of formal education, particularly in comparison with contemporaries such as John Adams. Yet his youth and later military service gave him a firm practical foundation in the art of being a Virginia gentleman, which would serve him well in later life. In his youth, he worked as a surveyor, developing an interest in land speculation that would last his entire life.

Washington inadvertently ignited the French and Indian War in 1754, when, while serving as a lieutenant colonel in the Virginia militia, he and a party of militiamen attacked a band of French troops. Among those Frenchmen killed in the attack was Ensign Joseph Coulon de Villiers de Jumonville, a French diplomat, carrying a message that ordered the English to abandon the Ohio Valley. Several months later, a larger French

A 1779 portrait by Charles Willson Peale honors General George Washington and his victory at the Battle of Princeton. He wears a blue sash, designating his rank as commander in chief of the Continental army. *(Pennsylvania Academy of the Fine Arts, Philadelphia/Bridgeman Art Library)*

Burgesses, in which he would serve until 1774. He married a wealthy widow, Martha Custis, in 1759. They would have no children. Two years later, after the death of his sister-in-law, he inherited Mount Vernon, his late brother Lawrence's plantation.

In the years leading up to the American Revolution, Washington devoted himself to developing his plantation and opposing Britain's measures to exert more control over her American colonies. That opposition grew stronger over the years, and in the 1770s, Washington was elected to the First and Second Continental Congresses.

Military Career

Washington appeared at the Second Continental Congress in his Virginia militia colonel's uniform, advertising his military experience to a Congress in search of a commanding general. John Adams nominated Washington as commander of the Continental army, and he accepted in June 1775. He took command of a force arrayed around Boston. This force lacked any professional training and knew little of the military arts. Nevertheless, with the arrival of heavy siege cannon from New York, Washington managed to drive the British from Boston in March 1776.

Despite the auspicious beginning of 1776, the year took a darker turn when the British moved against New York City that summer. Washington was hammered by the British at Long Island and Manhattan Island and was eventually forced to retreat to New Jersey. He divided his raw forces in the face of the enemy and was saved from total annihilation only by the lethargy of General Sir William Howe, the British commander.

December 1776 saw a rapid revival of patriot fortunes. On Christmas Day, 1776, Washington led the Continental army across the Delaware River to attack an outpost of Hessian mercenaries in British service, taking more than 900 Hessian prisoners. On January 3, 1777, Washington struck at a British army at Princeton, New Jersey, in a brilliant stroke that allowed him to hit the British and then slip away.

During the 1777 campaign, Washington tried to protect the young nation's capital of Philadelphia against attack from General Howe, but without success. From late 1777 into 1778, the Continental army wintered at Valley Forge, Pennsylvania. During that winter, Washington, with the help of Prussian drillmaster Friedrich von Steuben, worked to shape a truly professional army from his rough recruits. The two men set

force captured Washington and his men; they forced him to sign a paper, written in French, stating that he had assassinated the French diplomat.

During the 1755 campaign, Washington accompanied British General Edward Braddock's expedition against Fort Duquesne in modern-day Pennsylvania. On July 9, he was present as a force of French soldiers and their native allies ambushed and devastated Braddock's column. Washington performed well and survived the battle with his hide and reputation intact. Later in the war, he commanded the Virginia Regiment as a colonel, attempting to defend the Virginia frontier. He resigned in December 1758.

Washington began his political career in July 1758, when he was elected to the Virginia House of

about training their men in precision drill, which would allow them to perform linear evolutions on the battlefield and stand fast against British regulars, enabling the Continental army to meet the British on the field of battle and beat them on their own terms. On June 28, during the 1778 campaign, Washington's newly trained troops won a minor victory against the British rear guard at Monmouth Court House.

For the next several years, Washington defended the Hudson Highlands of New York against British attack. The Hudson served as a bridge between the Middle colonies and New England: if the British captured it, then they could sever the links between the colonies and defeat them one by one. On July 16, Washington ordered a bold night attack at Stony Point, New York, capturing a British garrison that guarded a crossing point on the Hudson River. The following year, Washington narrowly avoided disaster when he inspected the defenses of West Point, New York, and uncovered Benedict Arnold's plot to betray West Point to the British just as it threatened to come to fruition.

In 1781, Washington executed the plan that would win the war for the patriot cause. With French naval and military support, Washington cornered a British army at Yorktown, Virginia. Then his army besieged the city. With the French fleet preventing an evacuation such as the one that took place at Boston in 1776, Washington could hammer away at Yorktown, reducing it by a formal siege. The British surrendered on October 19, 1781.

For the next two years, Washington and the Continental army resided in Newburgh, New York. There, Washington took steps to prevent the destruction of the American Revolution by military coup. His force of character prevented the American Revolution from turning to a military dictator like Cromwell or Napoleon. On December 23, 1783, Washington resigned his command of the army and retired to Mount Vernon, earning the title of American Cincinnatus, after the Roman farmer called to save the Roman republic, who achieved victory and then retired to his farm.

Washington's retirement did not signal a total retreat from public life. In 1787, he served as president of the Constitutional Convention, lending it his incomparable prestige. After the ratification of the Constitution, Washington became the first president of the United States of America, chosen by unanimous vote of the electoral college.

Washington appointed the first Cabinet, with Alexander Hamilton serving as secretary of the treasury, Thomas Jefferson as secretary of state, and Henry Knox as secretary of war. He chose the site of the new national capital, in the city that would become Washington, D.C. During his two terms in office, Washington faced the difficult diplomatic problem of dealing with the French, at that time in the throes of their own violent national revolution. In 1794, Washington suppressed the so-called Whiskey Rebellion of farmers in western Pennsylvania, who opposed taxes on distilled spirits.

Once again, in 1797, Washington showed his character by leaving the presidency after serving two terms. His was a rare act in world history and one that helps to make the case for American exceptionalism: How many other countries have been blessed with a leader who could retire at the height of his powers?

In his farewell address to the nation, Washington emphasized the need to avoid the factionalism of political parties and the entanglements of international alliances. He enjoined the American people to remember that: " 'Tis substantially true, that virtue or morality is a necessary spring of popular government. The rule extends with more or less force to every species of free Government." Washington died at Mount Vernon on December 14, 1799.

Mitchell McNaylor

See also: Army, British; Continental Congress, Second; French and Indian War; Maps and Surveys; Planters; Revolutionary War.

Bibliography

Brookhiser, Richard. *Founding Father: Rediscovering George Washington.* New York: Free Press, 1996.

Cunliffe, Marcus. *George Washington: Man and Monument.* London: Collins, 1958.

Dalzell, Robert F., and Lee Baldwin Dalzell. *George Washington's Mount Vernon: At Home in Revolutionary America.* New York: Oxford University Press, 1998.

Ferling, John E. *Setting the World Ablaze: Washington, Adams, Jefferson, and the American Revolution.* New York: Oxford University Press, 2000.

Flexner, James Thomas. *Washington: The Indispensable Man.* Boston: Little, Brown, 1974.

Freeman, Douglas Southall. *George Washington: A Biography.* 7 vols. New York: Charles Scribner's Sons, 1948–1957.

Higginbotham, Don. *George Washington and the American Military Tradition.* Athens: University of Georgia Press, 1985.

Marshall, John. *The Life of George Washington.* 1838. Reprint edited by Robert Faulkner and Paul Carrese. Indianapolis, IN: Liberty Fund, 2000.

McDonald, Forrest. *The Presidency of George Washington.* Lawrence: University Press of Kansas, 1974.

Smith, Richard Norton. *Patriarch: George Washington and the New American Nation.* Boston: Houghton Mifflin, 1993.

Spalding, Matthew, and Patrick J. Garrity. *A Sacred Union of Citizens: George Washington's Farewell Address and the American Character.* Lanham, MD: Rowman and Littlefield, 1996.

Washington, George. *Writings.* New York: Literary Classics of the United States, 1997.

Wills, Garry. *Cincinnatus: George Washington and the Enlightenment.* Garden City, NY: Doubleday, 1984.

Weaponry

The possession and use of weapons constituted an important aspect of life during the colonial period. Weapons provided the colonists with a measure of security, as well as a means of survival by hunting. As Europeans expanded their presence in the New World, they developed a deep-seated appreciation for personal ownership of these valuable tools. Weapons gave them the independence to maintain themselves and their families, free from any of the typical restrictions they had lived under in Europe.

The native peoples of the New World did have a number of truly effective and efficient weapons that were in use throughout the New World. The weapons that the first Europeans had to face ranged from the blowguns of the South American area to the atlatl, or throwing stick, used in the area now known as Mexico, and other weapons designed for closer hand-to-hand combat. The weapons of the native peoples often served a variety of purposes—from cutting and piercing to use primarily for defense and even for symbolic or ritualistic purposes.

The Spanish and Portuguese explorers encountered the blowgun, which hurls a dart, frequently tipped with poison, from a tube propelled by the lungs of the firer. The Yagua Indian of the Peruvian Amazon used these weapons. Since these natives wore grass skirts, the Spanish believed them to be female warriors, thereby naming the Amazon River for the Greek myth of Amazon women warriors.

American Indian warriors initially used bows and arrows, war clubs, tomahawks, lances, and knives during battle with their enemies. Their bow design was much shorter than the longbow used by Europeans, as the natives did not engage in the longer-distance warfare common in Europe. Arrowheads were made of flint and bone, metal only coming into use well after Euro-

pean contact. The native warriors were highly skilled, and it was said that an experienced warrior could fire twenty arrows in the time it took a settler to fire and reload a single-shot musket—a feat easily demonstrated by English longbowmen of the period.

The head of the tomahawk was made of stone and was usually employed in close-quarter fighting. It could be thrown as well. However, most of the literature describing a thrown weapon involved the use of a metal head, which would have been obtained through trade with the Europeans in the later days of exploration. Stone knives also were occasionally employed in a similar way to tomahawks, being secured crossways with dried animal tendons. Knives also could be thrown or used for stabbing or cutting.

Warriors also carried lances or spears of various lengths; each was tipped with a point of chipped stone or bone. Like the Europeans, these frequently would be decorated with artistic designs or feathers. The lance could be thrown and, after horses were introduced, it became a weapon similar to that used by Europeans.

There also were a number of ritual weapons, used in special ceremonies or to inspire younger warriors by their use in combat. Some of the "coup sticks" were works of carved art, decorated with basket-like weavings on the handle and colorful feathers. To "count coup" would enable the user to add to the decorations for his exploits in battle, and thereby add to his reputation as a warrior. In advanced age, the warrior could use this device in a variety of spiritual ceremonies designed to keep his memory alive or to inspire younger warriors to feats of courage.

Longbows

The weaponry of the period may be classified into two general types: weapons that were designed to throw or hurl something else, such as bows, muskets, rifles, and cannons, and weapons used more directly, such as swords, knives, and axes. There also were weapons that were some combination of both.

Since everyone had to use an axe and a knife in daily life, these tools were common. In the British and French colonies of North America, they merged into a new tool, the tomahawk, rather similar to what we call a hatchet today. The primary difference was in the design, which allowed the tomahawk to be thrown as a missile, as well as to be used as a hand axe.

The very first of the projectile weapons to appear in the New World were the crossbow and matchlock. The earliest records indicate that some distances were measured in terms of "crossbow shots," that is, the expected distance a bolt or arrow could be hurled from the crossbow. The early explorer Álvar Núñez Cabeza de Vaca noted that he used the metal pieces from his crossbows to manufacture nails when he and his men attempted to build boats in an effort to return from the North American mainland to Spanish outposts in Cuba in 1528. Hernando de Soto had a group of crossbowmen with him when he crossed the Mississippi, and Francisco Vázquez de Coronado and Estévan Juan Carrillo noted that when they explored the Southwest, they carried a number of crossbows as well.

A crossbow was sometimes made of horn, but was typically steel, and the bowstring was made of hemp or flax. The crossbow would be attached to a stock, pivoting on an axle of iron or a heavy cord. The arrow, bolt, or quarrel would be placed in a groove on the top of the stock, which would be lined with brass, iron, or horn. Preparing this device to be fired was difficult because the bow would not easily bend. Another tool, frequently called a crannequin, was then developed to allow the bow to be bent back into a cocked position by use of a gear and rack. A simple windlass was also used, as was a simple lever, which was called a "goats foot," due to the appearance of the fork, which fitted over the stock. Once the bow was drawn into firing position, the bolt, arrow, or quarrel would be placed into the groove. The weapon was ready to be fired by pressing on a trigger release, which would, in turn, release the bowstring. Crossbows such as this would be expected to fire effectively and accurately up to 350 yards.

When fired, the power of the crossbow was truly incredible. In modern test firings, it has been found to be fully capable of penetrating wood planks three-quarters of an inch thick at a range of 60 yards. Such a fearsome weapon fully suited the needs of combating men in heavy armor. But for use in the colonies against Native Americans or for hunting, the power of the crossbow was ill suited because of its slow rate of fire (due to the long period of time required to reload) and its considerable weight.

By the time of the colonization of the New World, the use of longbows in Europe had begun to disappear, and there is little evidence to confirm that these were used on the American continent, although they may have been. By the middle of the sixteenth century, the crossbow had declined in use throughout Europe, as well as in the colonies. The latest reference to this weapon was in an inventory conducted by Ponce de Leon in 1596.

Organized artillery regiments and the use of carronades (light, short-barrel pieces suited for naval warfare) were introduced by the British in the early 1700s. Various artillery pieces and other ordnance are depicted in this etching of 1779. *(Library of Congress, LC-USZ62-45362)*

Firearms

The weapon of choice, ideally, was one that allowed the hunter or attacker to be some distance from the target. The solution to this need was the development of the smoothbore musket in the 15th century. This early projectile firearm became the most important arm of the early explorers and colonists, but a weapon such as this was also valuable to Europeans.

All early firearms were also known as smoothbores, meaning that the barrel or bore was smooth and the shot (projectile) was, typically, a lead ball. These weapons used coarse black gunpowder as a propellant and very fine-quality gunpowder as part of the ignition system. The ignition system of these weapons had a mechanical flint striking against steel (flintlock), which would throw sparks into a small pan filled with gunpowder. This would ignite the gunpowder and thereby allow a flame to enter the barrel through a small port from the pan. The gunpowder in the barrel would then be ignited and would explode, creating a large volume of gas, which would propel the ball out of the barrel. Loading these weapons was through or down the barrel; hence all were labeled as muzzleloaders.

Matchlocks were an important projectile weapon during the early 1600s. These devices worked by an action that would bring a lighted match into direct contact with the priming powder. To confuse matters, matchlocks were frequently and interchangeably named arquebuses, calivers, and muskets. Because of the confusion in terms, it is not easy to determine exactly what type or style of matchlock is referred to in early accounts. It appears that the term "arquebus" was also applied to a wide variety of firearms, although, at a later date, the term became associated with a wheel lock, as opposed to a matchlock. In very general terms, an arquebus would be lighter than a musket and could be fired without a rest or support.

A "caliver" appears to have been the forerunner of our current term "caliber." It also denoted a firearm that was lighter than a musket and could be fired without a support or rest. The term "musket," however, has almost always meant a heavy military firearm. At first, this would have been a matchlock, which was so heavy that a forked rest was absolutely necessary to keep the barrel steady when firing. This device would frequently weigh around 20 pounds, with a barrel of about 8 to 10 gauge (that is, the diameter of the projectile). This heavy weapon would then require up to 2 ounces of powder per charge, which thereby greatly increased the total weight carried by each individual.

Around 1650, the overall weight of the musket was reduced to about 16 pounds and the caliber made standard at 10 gauge. This then meant that "musket bore" became a standard of measure. It is interesting to note that the standard musket ball was a 12 gauge, substantially smaller in diameter than the musket's caliber. Using a smaller ball would have eased loading, because the barrel would foul after several discharges, reducing the actual bore, but it also increased the musket's unreliability with regard to accuracy.

The actual operating system of the matchlocks was simplicity in itself. There was a forked holder for the match mounted on the outside of the lock, which became known as the serpentine. This was, in turn, attached on the inside of the lock to a lever (sear). This

lock would then pivot in the center on the inside of the lock plate. The trigger, which looked like a crossbow trigger, was attached to the end of the lock opposite the serpentine. An upward pressure on the trigger, working through the sear, depressed the serpentine, which held the match in an arc toward the flash pan, which held the priming powder. The match would ignite the powder, which would set off the charge in the barrel by means of a small hole from the pan into the interior of the barrel. There would also be a small spring fastened to the lock that put a force on the sear, keeping the serpentine away from the pan and avoiding accidental discharges. A hinged cover on the pan could be closed when not firing. The match itself was a loosely braided cord soaked in saltpeter so that it would burn at a measured rate, which was about 4 to 5 inches an hour.

Simple though this action was, the challenge of loading this device was indeed daunting. Such a long and difficult task, which was also somewhat hazardous, could be made worse by misfirings, or discharging without intent to fire.

A Virginia sentinel in 1611 would be required to

shoulder his piece, both ends of his match being alight, and his piece charged, and primed, and bullets in his mouth, there to stand with a careful and waking eye, until such time as his Corporal shall relive him.

As with any other necessary device or tool, matchlocks would undergo a long series of changes and alterations, finally developing many of the features of the later flintlock firearms. Some of the earliest examples of matchlocks came to the New World with the very first expeditions, and in these accounts they are usually referred to as arquebuses.

The word "musket" did not appear until the 1540 account of the Coronado expedition. But by the year 1578, muskets clearly were in use in Spanish Florida. For a period of about 150 years, the matchlock saw service throughout the colonies, but it was not the principal projectile weapon for about half of that time. By the last quarter of the seventeenth century, its use had effectively disappeared in the colonial areas.

There are several important reasons for the matchlock's decline. It was slow, it was very heavy, it required the user to carry additional weight in powder, and it was inaccurate. Another disadvantage was the lighted match, which could cause an accidental discharge or could even ignite the additional powder being carried by the shooter. This occurred to Captain John Smith in 1609, when a lighted match set off loose powder in his pocket and caused severe burns.

Although flame and this weapon should not ever be in close proximity, it was absolutely necessary to have a ready nearby source of fire to relight the match, should it go out. In addition, it was extremely difficult to keep the match burning on wet or very windy days. Usually, such weather conditions would render the matchlock totally useless, except as an awkward club. The final major drawback was that, during the hours of darkness, a lighted match could literally be a "dead" giveaway to any observant opponent. The only real advantage, in fact, of the matchlock was that when its shot hit its target, the damage would be awesome.

Around 1520, a much safer and reliable system of ignition, known as the wheel lock, was developed. Only fifty years later, the snaphaunce (an early flintlock, *snaphaunce* is a Dutch term meaning "snapping cock") was created, and, after 1600, other primitive flintlocks began to appear. But it was not until about 1720 that the wheel lock really started to replace the matchlock in the colonies.

The wheel lock operated essentially like a modern cigarette lighter: a spark is created by having a wheel spin against a piece of pyrite (flint). This simplicity in firing was duplicated in the loading and firing. To load, a wheel is wound against a spring. Then, a charge is loaded into the barrel (as in any muzzle loader), the pan is filled with priming powder, and the frizzen, or hammer, is closed. The weapon is now ready to fire by pulling the trigger. When the trigger is pulled, the spring action begins turning the wheel, and a shower of sparks is produced, igniting the priming powder.

Since early accounts seldom provided specific information as to exactly which type of weapon ignition system was being used, we cannot be certain whether a wheel lock or matchlock was in use. To further complicate matters, the term "firelock" was applied equally to both of these weapons, as well as to the musket that replaced them, the flintlock.

The move from matchlock to flintlock was generally similar in all the colonies. By 1624 or 1625, the matchlock was definitely a tool of the past. A census of that period indicated that out of a total of 1,089 firearms, only 47 matchlocks were found. When Thomas Matthew described Bacon's Rebellion of 1676, he noted that his men had flintlocks, since matchlocks were no longer used in the Virginia colony.

In 1673, the Massachusetts General Court ordered its agent, Hezekiah Usher, to purchase 500 "new snaphances or fire lock muskets" in England for its use. Then, in 1677, the Plymouth General Court outlawed the matchlock as an unacceptable weapon. The colony of New Haven determined that only flintlock firearms were acceptable as public arms in 1649. New Haven then enacted a law in 1664–1665, recognizing that only flintlock arms were serviceable weapons. Such actions caused rapid conversions from match- to flint-ignition systems.

There are at least six types of flint-ignition firearms: the snaphaunce, English lock, dog lock, Scandinavian snaplock, miquelot lock, and standard flintlock. Although all of these weapons were used in the various colonies, it is the flintlock, which began reaching the colonies in large numbers by 1660, that is of primary interest.

For over 200 years, the flintlock was the dominant type of firearm; as a result, there were a number of rather minor variations in design and manufacture. To be able to determine the exact type of flintlock under consideration requires real familiarity and the handling of many actual specimens.

The development of the various types of wheel locks and flintlocks aided in the development of several additional types of firearms. These included such weapons as the long fowler, fusil, musketoon, petronel, carbine, blunderbuss, and pistol. Of these, the pistol first appeared sometime after 1520; it was a wheel lock dag, that is, a long, heavy device with straight grips, which was rather popular with sixteenth-century cavalry. This design was also used with flintlock pistols until sometime after the beginning of the seventeenth century, when curved grips came into being.

One of the earliest reports of pistols in the colonies comes from Ralph Lane's report concerning the English colony on Roanoke Island in 1586. The number of references then increases rather quickly, starting with Captain John Smith. He used some form of a French snaphaunce pistol in the well-documented fight with Native Americans in 1607 that resulted in his capture by Powhatan and later meeting Pocahontas.

By 1611 in Virginia, all targeteers, or those who adjusted guns for targeting practice, were required to have either wheel lock or flint pistols, along with their swords and targets. The military census of Virginia in 1624–1625 revealed that there were fifty-five pistols of various types in that colony. In Pilgrim Hall at Plymouth, there is an example of an early dog lock pistol that belonged to John Thompson, who settled there in 1622.

The carbine was a rather popular weapon in

seventeenth-century English colonies. As it was shorter and lighter, it was widely used by both infantry and cavalry, as well as by civilian hunters. In order of popularity, it was second only to the musket itself. The listing of "public arms" in Maryland in 1678 shows a total of 177 carbines and 613 muskets.

Of all the early types of firearms, perhaps the most interesting is the blunderbuss. By the seventeenth century, the blunderbuss, an effective short-barreled gun of large caliber, was almost always a flintlock. This weapon was designed to spray projectiles at very close range, much like a shotgun today. This device has been popularized to such an extent that some believe that it was a widely used firearm in the English colonies, but it was seldom used before the eighteenth century. In the 1678 military inventory of Maryland, out of 791 arms listed, there is only one blunderbuss.

Another interesting firearm was the long fowler. Used exactly as the name implies, it was an important hunting gun, as well as a weapon. The extended length and rather heavy breech provided for an extensive range, but that same length meant that the long fowler was very unwieldy. There are several early references to these firearms since the Massachusetts Bay Colony settlers carried with them (in their own words), "6 long ffowlinge peeces wth musket boare, 6 foote long ½" and "6 longe ffowling peeces wth musket boare 5–½ foote longe."

Edward Winslow of Plymouth recommended to those considering relocation to his colony, "Bring every man a musket or fowling piece. Let your piece be long in the barrel." Some of these firearms were as long as 7½ feet in length, which meant that they had to be fired from a stand with supports. Most fowling pieces appeared in the Hudson Valley of New York, where their use would be natural because of the annual migration patterns of ducks and geese in that area.

To summarize, all the colonies used matchlock firearms during the first half of the seventeenth century, rapidly changing to flintlock as they sought the best firearms available. As a result, the colonies were years ahead of Europe in accepting this new type of weapon, which better fitted the actual needs of the people using them.

Since the early colonists' weapon of choice would be one that would allow the hunter or attacker to be some distance from the target, the firearm was the obvious solution. This does not mean that firearms were the only weapons used, however; edged weapons were necessary as well.

Once the distance from the target was removed and the struggle became hand to hand, the firearms of the day were useless, except as clubs. They took too long to recharge (load) and were excessively heavy. Since the use of the bayonet, which converts a firearm into a polearm, did not come into common usage until the American Revolution, the explorers and colonists had to carry separate weapons to fill this need.

A few groups during the earliest of years, including the Spanish lancers, some targeteers, and pikemen, did not use firearms at all. But the reliance on edged weapons gradually disappeared, as they were not practical in typical woodland combat.

Swords and Knives

Of all the edged weapons available during this period, the most common was the sword. Every man, while on military duty, had to carry a sword, even when equipped with a firearm. Therefore, every warrior had to be familiar with its use.

It should not be surprising to find that in inventories of estates, there would be more swords than firearms and that more examples of this weapon would survive to today. As early as 1608, Captain John Smith was able to report that there were more swords available than men to carry them, and, in 1618, the "Committee for Smythes Hundred in Virginia" recommended that forty swords and daggers be provided for the thirty-five men soon to arrive from England.

Unfortunately for us, there was a wide range and variety of swords available, and America's forefathers used the term "swords" in such a generic way as to make it impossible to be accurate in identifying references to specific types. The early Spanish carried the dominant of the two principal types used throughout the sixteenth century: the double-edged cutting sword, which had been developed from earlier ages, and the rapier. It is difficult to distinguish references between the two until the art of fencing developed much later; it was then that the rapier came to be used for thrusting as opposed to cutting. With this change, the rapier blade changed as well, becoming longer, narrower, more rigid, and with only a rather rudimentary edge.

Determining the date of manufacture of these edged weapons is difficult, but there is a general rule that may be applied: If the hand guard is somewhat simple and the pommel is larger with a short grip, it may be an older-style sword.

During the middle of the seventeenth century, a

smaller version of the sword was created in France, and, by the eighteenth century, this small sword had become popular throughout all of Europe. This was a light weapon that was practical for civilian use, since it emphasized speed and dexterity, instead of the formal and rather ponderous thrusts and parries of the rapier. Small swords were only used for thrusting, at first with a hexagonal blade, but finally, with the more familiar triangular shape, with all sides being concave. This provided the effect of having three sides or three edges to the blade and increasing strength and rigidity without adding any weight.

One of the earliest proofs of such small swords being used in the colonies is a 1564 painting of Frenchman Jacques Le Moyne engaged in combat with Native Americans in Florida. In the 1597 account of Captain Don Luis de Velasco, who was serving with Don Juan de Oñate's expedition, it was noted the he carried with him "a sword and a gilded dagger with their waist belts." One would suppose that this was a rapier, as he also took with him "one broadsword with shoulder belt."

Samuel de Champlain gives us his own drawing of his famous combat in 1609 with Native Americans; he is plainly wearing a swept-hilted sword, supported by a waist belt. Captain John Mason of Connecticut carried a 32-inch straight, double-edged blade during the Pequot War. His sword is 1¾ inches wide at the hilt and bears a badly worn inscription, recorded as "Veni Vidi Vici." Another famous surviving sword, a cup-hilted rapier, belonged to Captain Miles Standish of the Plymouth Colony.

A different type of sword, rather popular in colonial America, was of a short, single-edged design, which became popularized as a cutlass. This weapon quickly assumed a wide variety of names, including cutlash, cutilax, curtle axe, and cutlace. As this device quickly became the standard for the foot soldier throughout the period, it became more commonly known as a "hanger." This was because it "hung" on the side of the soldier by a shoulder strap. Numerous references to this weapon may be found throughout all colonial records.

Another rather unique term for a variation of this blade was known as the falchion. This was also a short, single-edged cutting sword but with a heavier blade, often with a clipped point. Because it was not to be used for thrusting or stabbing but for cutting, no point was needed. One of the earliest references to this weapon was in a report by William Simmonds, who said that

Captain John Smith carried a falchion with which he fought Paspahegh on Glass House Point in 1609. In 1644, John Winthrop described a falchion as the tool used to execute a Native American.

For the man mounted on the back of a horse, none of these swords would be satisfactory. As a result, one will find numerous references to another type of sword known as a "horseman's sword." Such swords were commonly very long, straight, double-edged, and frequently basket-hilted. The Spanish were especially fond of this design and even adapted the cup hilt into their rapiers.

Swords used during the colonial period were manufactured in cities still known today for their fine-quality steel products: Solingen and Toledo, for example, as well as Valencia and Milan. These blades would be shipped to the various colonies, where the hilts would be designed and fabricated by local artisans. Unfortunately for the master artisan sword makers of these early manufacturing centers, as their fame grew, so grew the forging of their marks and names. So blatant was this forgery that there are examples of blades bearing the marks not only of Solingen, but those of Toledo and Valencia as well.

In the colonies, swords were not the all-around type of cutting tool needed for purposes other than simple cutting or thrusting. As a result, the colony of Connecticut in 1675 directed that "Ten good and serviceable hatchets be provided in each county for the use of the army, and ten soldiers to carry them instead of swords." Those carrying hatchets would become known as "pioneers," cutting the way for the rest of the force following them. Due to the flexibility of the hatchet, it quickly grew in popularity, and the colonists begin to abandon their heavier, more awkward swords for this lighter and more adaptable tool. Economics also played a major role, since a sword, imported from Europe, would be a very costly alternative to a device more easily manufactured nearby. The hatchet also had the advantage of dual purpose, since it had numerous domestic applications. Because many colonists were required to furnish and provide their own weapons when they served in the militia, the versatile hatchet found its place in history.

To complement the weapon arrangement of the day, the constant companion of the sword and hatchet was the dagger. Colonial references to daggers abound. Miles Standish and his force totally depended upon the use of daggers when they eliminated troublemakers in a locked room in Wessagusset. Velasco noted his "gilded dagger" on the 1597 expedition, and forty daggers were requested to be a part of the arms order for thirty-five men to be sent to Smythes Hundred in 1678.

Because of the number of rapiers throughout the colonies, it may be assumed that there would have been at least an even number of daggers as well. The two worked together because of the European development of a special style of fencing involving the use of both. When employed in this fashion, the dagger became known as the left-hand dagger, as this was the hand holding it.

The left-hand dagger developed into two types: the poignard and the main gauche. The poignard was also known as a quillon dagger, due to the style of its cross-guard. This cross-guard was of a simple style, usually with curved quillons, pointing back toward the point. Daggers with straight quillons and with wider, more triangular knuckle bows became known as main gauche daggers.

Polearms

The sword, dagger, and hatchet were joined by still another type of edged weapon that saw widespread service throughout the colonies. This weapon was the polearm. Unlike their references to other devices previously discussed, the early colonists were very specific when mentioning these weapons.

The polearms utilized in the colonies were the lance, halberd, partizan, bill, pike, and half-pike. A lance was the primary offensive weapon of the mounted soldier, and it was a special spear designed to be used from horseback. A lance would usually be 10 to 14 feet in length with a steel, leaf-shaped head attached to the shaft by either a socket or a tang driven into the wooden shaft. The shaft would ideally swell to its widest point just before the grip. On occasion, just before the grip, a medal shield, known as a vamplate, would be added to protect the hand. The Spanish introduced the lance into their colonies, and it remained popular there until about 1600, but its use never truly developed in any of the other colonial areas.

A typical weapon noted in almost all colonial records was the halberd, which was a polearm with an axe head balanced with a beak or fluke and topped off with a spear point. The butt end of the pole would be typically enclosed with an iron or brass cap, known as the ground iron, butt cap, or foot. Used on occasion as a combat weapon, the halberd was typically carried by noncommissioned officers as a symbol of their rank, or as a ceremonial arm. In the Jacques Le Moyne painting of Native Americans in Florida during 1564, a halberd with a concave blade is present. The 1578 inventories of the Spanish forts in Florida also recorded the presence of halberds.

Strachey's Martiall Lawes of 1611 for Virginia indicates that sergeants had to carry halberds when in garrison, but that they should be abandoned for firearms when in the field. The records of the Pequot War (1637–1638) indicate that halberds were actually used in combat, and the settlers of Massachusetts Bay Colony purchased three halberds for their sergeants. In the report of expenses for the costs of King Philip's War, "Pole axes" are noted. And, in 1689, Governor Leisler of New York threatened to run one of the councilors through with a halberd.

The partizan, about 6 or 7 feet in length with the head at one point and one or more branches at the base, was typically a weapon used by officers. Basically, this would describe any short spear used by an officer during the colonial period. In 1628, colonists preparing for the trip to found the Massachusetts Bay Colony purchased "2 partizans, for capten & lieftenant (sic)."

Another type of polearm was the bill, or, as it was sometimes called, the brown bill, due to the browned finish of its blade. It had evolved from the farming tool of the same name. The bill had a hook-shaped blade with a cutting edge on the concave side along with a variety of spikes and projections on the opposite side. Bills were rather common in England, but there is only one report of them in the colonies. The Virginia Company petitioned the King for arms from the Tower of London after the Massacre of 1622. Among the arms requested and received were 1,000 brown bills, of which 50 were diverted to Bermuda, the remaining 950 finding their way to Jamestown in 1623.

The most popular of all polearms in the colonies was the pike. The full pike and half pike are identical except for their respective lengths. A typical full pike would have a shaft ranging from 14 to 16 feet, and the corresponding half pike would be half that. The preferred wood for the shaft was ash, and the head would be either leaf or diamond shaped. There was some variation in the design of the head, but this was not typical. There would also be long, slender metal straps known as langets, which would be tied to the head end of the shaft to prevent the head from being cut off by an axe or sword. Since the opposite end of the pike was designed to be braced in the ground, it was a common practice for that end to be pointed as well. Frequently, a pointed metal cup would be fitted there to add in the bracing.

Almost every colony has left us records of pikes, beginning as early as the report of Alvaro Flores in 1578 on the status of Spanish forts. Captain John Smith reported in 1609 that the colony at Jamestown had more pikes and swords than men to use them. The Massachusetts Bay Colony brought sixty pikes and twenty half pikes with them, almost as many as the muskets they carried. Plymouth Colony required that every town provide one half pike for every four men. The colony of New Netherland, differing from the other colonies, often noted the half pike (but not the full pike), since that was its weapon of choice from 1633 to 1673.

The heavy dependence upon the pike would be a normal extension of European tactics, since the use of pikemen was the bulk of all infantry forces during the sixteenth and the beginning of the seventeenth century. But in the New World colonies, different tactics were required. As the pike was found to be ineffectual against the Native Americans, their use was soon abandoned. In 1675, the General Court of the Massachusetts Bay Colony determined that

> Whereas it is found by experience that troopers & pikemen are of little use in the present war wth the Indians . . . all pikemen are hereby required . . . to furnish themselves wth fire armes (sic).

Connecticut, however, continued to use pikes until the end of the period, and pikes remained in use solely for ceremonial purposes for many years.

The development of weapons in Europe and the colonies began to diverge as demand met the very real needs of the colonists and explorers. The sword was replaced with the hatchet or tomahawk, and the dagger changed into an all-purpose knife, instead of the rather specialized types so popular in Europe. The use of lances was only popular in the Spanish colonies, and the halberd and partisan became useful only as symbols of rank. With a few exceptions such as Connecticut, the pike was not widely used as a weapon in the colonies.

Although many weapons originally came to the colonies from Europe, the colonists were years ahead of Europeans in the development and use of firearms. This was especially true of the rifle, a new type of weapon that better fitted the actual needs of the American people.

Arthur E. Chapman

See also: Army, British; Military and Diplomatic Affairs (Chronology); Military and Diplomatic Affairs (Essay); Militias; Navy, British; Technology; War.

Bibliography

Gill, Harold B., Jr. *The Gunsmith in Colonial Virginia*. Williamsburg, VA: Colonial Williamsburg Foundation, 1974.

Gluckman, Arcadi. *United States Muskets, Rifles and Carbines*. Harrisburg, PA: Stackpole, 1959.

Laubin, Reginald, et al. *American Indian Archery*. Civilization of the American Indian Series, No. 154. Norman: University of Oklahoma Press, 1991.

Peterson, Harold L. *Arms and Armor in Colonial America, 1526–1783*. Mineola, NY: Dover, 2000.

Taylor, Colin F. *Native American Weapons*. Norman: University of Oklahoma Press, 2001.

West, Benjamin (1738–1820)

Historical painter to king of England George III and president of the Royal Academy, Benjamin West was the "most prominent artist in the English-speaking world" in his day. West was praised by continental European painters such as Jacques-Louis David, the painter of the French Revolution. In fact, David was moved to tears when West's name was mentioned. An American neoclassical painter who made his career in England, West was the first American-born painter to attain international fame.

West was born into a family of nine children in rural Pennsylvania, near Springfield (now Swarthmore), on October 10, 1738. He was the tenth and last child of John West and Sarah Pearson. Thomas Pearson, his maternal grandfather, had been a friend of William Penn, founder of the colony. The two men had come to Pennsylvania together. West's father has been variously described as a businessman, a cooper, a tinsmith, a hosier, and an innkeeper. Although West grew up among the Quakers, he was not a member of the Society of Friends.

Apparently West was encouraged by his family to paint at a young age. When he was ten years old, he learned how to mix colors from the local natives. His first white instructor was William Williams, a minor American artist whom West met in 1747. Williams taught him the rudiments of the palette, brushes, and colors.

In 1756, West came to the attention of the Reverend William Smith, the first provost of the College

The work of Pennsylvania-born neoclassical artist Benjamin West created a sensation throughout Europe when he visited in the 1760s. He later served as "historical painter" to Britain's King George III and became president of the Royal Academy. *(Brown Brothers, Sterling, Pennsylvania)*

of Philadelphia, which later became the University of Pennsylvania. From Smith, he learned as much of the classics as a painter needed at this time. Although known as a history painter, West began his career by painting portraits. The portraits of the Morris children, dating from about 1752, are his earliest.

His earliest historical painting and the only extant one from the colonial period is *The Death of Socrates* (c. 1756), which West painted at the age of 18. This painting was commissioned by inventor and gunsmith William Henry, who had read the story of Socrates' death to West. The painting has been described as "naïve, awkward and provincial," but it did demonstrate West's potential.

West left America in 1760 for economic and professional reasons. He could get much better prices for his paintings in Europe, and there he could view the great works of the masters at first hand. Before leaving America, he became engaged to Elizabeth Shewell, telling her that he would not be away for more than three years. After touring and painting in Italy for

three years, however, West decided to visit England for a short time; apparently he was already contemplating not returning to America. In 1764, he had a successful showing of three paintings at the Society of Artists in London, and this triumph convinced him to remain there. West's fiancée joined him in London, where they were married in September 1764.

During his early years in London, West focused on portraits, and they provided him with a great deal of his income over the next twenty years. Many of these portraits were of Americans who visited London, including William Allen, the mayor of Philadelphia and later chief justice of Pennsylvania, and his daughter, Anne Allen.

West began painting for King George III in 1768, a patron he had for more than thirty years. Between 1768 and 1801, he completed approximately sixty paintings for the king. In 1772, George III appointed West "historical painter to the king," a position that came with an annual stipend of 1,000 pounds. West succeeded Sir Joshua Reynolds as president of the prestigious Royal Academy in 1792, a post he held except for a single year (1803) until his death.

West's most renowned paintings, all completed during his time in London, are *Agrippina Landing at Brundisium with the Ashes of Germanicus* (1768), *The Departure of Regulus from Rome* (1769), *The Death of General Wolfe* (1771), and *William Penn's Treaty with the Indians* (1772). *The Death of General* Wolfe was a controversial painting at the time, because West clothed his figures in contemporary rather than classical dress.

West died in 1820 at the age of 81. In terms of lasting legacy, West became best known as the American who painted *The Death of General Wolfe* and as a neoclassical artist who influenced many generations of American artists.

Leigh Whaley

See also: Art, Fine; Arts, Culture, and Intellectual Life (Chronology); Arts, Culture, and Intellectual Life (Essay).

Bibliography

Abrams, Ann Uhry. *The Valiant Hero. Benjamin West and Grand-Style History Painting.* Washington, DC: Smithsonian Institution Press, 1985.

Alberts, Robert C. *Benjamin West: A Biography.* Boston: Houghton Mifflin, 1978.

Erffa, Helmut von, and Allen Staley. *The Paintings of Benjamin West.* New Haven, CT: Yale University Press, 1986.

Evans, Grose. *Benjamin West and the Taste of His Times.* Carbondale: Southern Ilinois Press, 1969.

Galt, John. *The Life, Studies and Work of Benjamin West, Esq.* 2 vols. London: Cadell & Davies, 1816–1820.

West India Company

See Dutch West India Company

Wheatley, Phillis (c. 1754–1784)

Phillis Wheatley arrived in colonial Boston as a slave from Africa in 1761. Bought by Susannah Wheatley, the wife of a prosperous Boston tailor, "for a trifle," the young girl soon exhibited an innate intelligence that would make her the toast of the colonies and of London.

Like many slaves in the Northern colonies, she was put to work as a domestic servant. Within a year of her arrival, the little girl had learned to speak English remarkably well. Recognizing her abilities, her owners arranged for her to be educated by tutors and themselves. Soon, young Phillis Wheatley was more educated than many white children in Boston. She studied astronomy, geography, and world history, and she showed a gift for understanding and discussing complicated passages of Scripture. Early on, she was excused from doing her regular household chores, and eventually, the Wheatleys also removed her from the company of other African Americans in the household and the neighborhood.

Not surprisingly, young Phillis Wheatley was quite a conversation piece and a curiosity among colonial society. She quickly became known as a brilliant and graceful conversationalist within her master's Boston circle, and she was usually expected to accompany her owners on their social rounds. Although she might be encouraged to join in parlor conversation, she was nevertheless subjected to segregation, usually taking her meals in the host's kitchen with the servants rather than at table with the white guests.

Likely as a result of her frequent isolation from both white and black companionship, and of the free time she enjoyed because of her exemption from work, Wheatley spent much of her time reading her master's collection of books. She was particularly fond of poetry, and the English poet Alexander Pope was her favorite. Wheatley began writing poems for her own amusement, and, by the age of 13 (doubtless with her owner's assistance), she had her first work published.

Following the death of the popular evangelist, the broadside publication of her poem "On the Death of the Rev. Mr. George Whitefield, 1770" was widely reprinted throughout the colonies and in Whitefield's native England. In 1773, 19-year-old Phillis Wheatley sailed for London at the invitation of the Countess of Huntingdon, the evangelist's patron. In London, she was widely hailed as the "Sable Muse" and was the guest of honor at numerous gatherings of various poets, authors, intellectuals, and government officials. Only Susannah Wheatley's illness back in Boston, which required her favorite slave's hasty return to care for her mistress, interfered with plans for the young poet to be presented at court to King George III.

On her return voyage, the young slave woman carried copies of a volume of her poems published in London, *Poems on Various Subjects, Religious and Moral.* Underwritten by the countess, this first published work by an African American required a preface including a sworn testimony of eighteen leading Bostonians verifying that the verse was indeed the product of Phillis Wheatley's own creative genius.

The poems in this volume were generally derivative of the poetry Wheatley had read and loved. Her topics reveal an awareness of social and political events of the day, and the poems indicate the decidedly white sensibilities that formed her experience. Even the poems that address her own experiences as an African American ("On Being Brought from Africa to America," "To S. M. A Young African Painter, on Seeing His Works") are careful to reflect the prevailing notions of white supremacy of the day.

Following her owners' deaths, Phillis Wheatley was freed. She married a free African American, John Peters, and had three children, all of whom died in childhood. As a free woman, Wheatley was, for the first time, exposed to the necessity of supporting herself. Because she had been coddled by Susannah Wheatley, she found herself unaccustomed to doing the menial work that was available to her.

As her health failed and she felt the burdens of her unaccustomed work, Wheatley attempted to have a new volume of her literary works published. She advertised for subscribers to her "Poems & Letters on various subjects, dedicated to the Right Hon. Benjamin Franklin Esq.," but the proposed work did not attract sufficient interest among investors to underwrite the cost of publication.

Wheatley had only one more poem published

after her *Poems on Various Subjects*—a piece she wrote and sent to General George Washington. Interest in her works and life was renewed with the advent of academic work in African American studies and women's studies in the late twentieth century.

Barbara Schwarz Wachal

See also: African Americans; Literature. *Document:* On Being Brought from Africa to America (early 1770s); On the Death of the Rev. Mr. George Whitefield (1770).

Bibliography

Robinson, William H., ed. *Critical Essays on Phillis Wheatley.* Boston: G. K. Hall, 1982.

———. *Phillis Wheatley and Her Writings.* Boston: G. K. Hall, 1984.

Wheatley, Phillis. *The Collected Works of Phillis Wheatley.* Edited by John Shields. New York: Oxford University Press, 1998.

Whitefield, George (1714–1770)

George Whitefield was born in 1714 into a family of moderate means. From early childhood, he was adept at public speaking and dramatic performances. He also demonstrated the prodigious memory and keenness of wit that marked his adulthood. By the time Whitefield entered Oxford at the age of 17, he was already proficient in Latin and Greek. It was at Oxford that Whitefield embraced religion with a passion. He joined the Holy Club, a student group led by John and Charles Wesley.

In his mid-20s, Whitefield began preaching an enthusiastic and emotionally charged brand of Christianity anywhere in England that he could gather an audience, advertising himself and his meetings by distributing flyers and handbills. His dramatic performances moved many listeners to renew their spiritual devotion; however, many conservative clergymen in the Church of England viewed the young preacher's emotional appeal with distaste and prevented him from speaking at their churches. Finding his access to Anglican churches limited, Whitefield instead turned to open-air preaching. This approach proved so successful that he soon drew crowds approaching 100,000 souls.

Whitefield soon turned his eyes toward America, where the Wesleys had gone as missionaries in 1735. Although his Oxford compatriots had mixed success in the young Georgia colony, they urged him to follow their example. Whitefield decided to see Georgia with his own eyes and to find out what role the New World might play in his future.

After a brief trip in 1738, Whitefield left England the following year for an extended stay in America. Near Savannah, he founded Bethesda Orphanage, an institution that would not only care for the material needs of parentless children but also inculcate a passion for worship. After laying the foundations of Bethesda, Whitefield spent the next two years traveling from Georgia to Maine, stopping at many points in between.

Wherever Whitefield went, people gathered to listen. Through a mixture of drama and force of will, he impressed on his listeners a desire to experience spiritual renewal. People traveled for days to hear him speak. A 1741 sermon in Boston reportedly drew a crowd of 20,000—a total greater than the city's population. Whitefield's relentless schedule led him to average more than ten gatherings per week, and his presence usually touched off waves of conversions and religious revivals in the surrounding area. His evangelical Calvinism impressed even the most skeptical listeners. According to witnesses, Whitefield's powerful voice alone—free from the histrionics that would characterize later revivals—could make people weep.

Whitefield's popularity helped fuel the print revolution in the American colonies. Newspaper publishers who reprinted his sermons were rewarded with increased circulation. Whitefield further boosted print sales by writing autobiographical pamphlets, which lacked the obscure and learned allusions that often made similar works inaccessible to the general public.

Whitefield's ministry had its greatest impact in the Northern colonies, with their Puritan background. While his influence was not nearly so strong in Southern provinces, his message did tend to create divisions throughout the British settlements. Whitefield attacked what he saw as the complacency and excessive rationalism of the eighteenth-century Church of England. In England and America, he saw signs of a society afflicted with spiritual decay. He accused Anglican ministers of neglecting their divine mission to convert souls—both white and native—to the Lord's cause.

His criticisms of contemporary religious practice helped create a lasting split among the American clergy. "New Lights" tended to embrace religious fervor as the cornerstone of a full Christian life. "Old Lights," however, feared that the new emotionalism might degenerate into zealotry or derangement, and they strongly defended traditional elements of Anglican worship.

When Whitefield ended his first extended tour of the colonies in 1741 and departed for England, he left behind settlements rejuvenated with holy devotion. Whitefield and other itinerant ministers, such as Gilbert Tennent and James Davenport, helped to maintain a spiritual movement that would soon become known as the Great Awakening.

Whitefield carried his message to America a total of seven times in his life. It was in 1770, on the last of these journeys, that the great missionary passed from the world, having delivered 18,000 sermons that touched the lives of millions of listeners.

Andrew C. Lannen

See also: Great Awakening; Ministers and the Ministry; Religion (Chronology); Religion (Essay); Sermons. *Document:* On the Death of the Rev. Mr. George Whitefield (1770).

Bibliography

Lambert, Frank. *"Pedlar in Divinity": George Whitefield and the Transatlantic Revivals, 1737–1770.* Princeton, NJ: Princeton University Press, 1994.

Stout, Harry S. *The Divine Dramatist: George Whitefield and the Rise of Modern Evangelicalism.* Grand Rapids, MI: William B. Eerdmans, 1991.

Widows and Widowers

Mortality rates for both men and women were high in Europe during the early modern period. Men frequently were killed while working under unsafe conditions. Women often died in childbirth. Both sexes were subject to disease and the lack of adequate or effective medical treatment.

The move to North America added further complications, especially in the Southern colonies where the climate was particularly unhealthy for European settlers. Until the 1680s, only one in three Southern marriages lasted for more than ten years without one or both partners dying. While Northern colonists had fewer climate risks, mortality rates remained high compared to modern times.

Despite the uncertainty of survival and the brevity of so many marriages, letters and journals surviving from the period indicate deep attachment between spouses. A tombstone in Essex, Massachusetts, remembers one husband's "amiable consort," an affectionate reference to a dearly loved wife. Beyond this grief, the death of a spouse had very different legal and financial implications for men and women.

English Colonies

Most married couples divided labor between them, the man responsible for the financial support of the family, the woman attending to domestic tasks and running the household. As all property and possessions belonged to the husband, the household of a man whose wife died remained intact. There was no probate inventory, no assessment of the estate. If she had been married before and had children from that marriage, her belongings would usually go to those children. (In most cases, this was decided as part of a premarital contract.) Otherwise, all property would remain in the widower's possession, whether the deceased wife had brought it into the marriage or not.

If possible, an unmarried daughter, female cousin, or sister would step into the wife's role of overseeing the domestic side of the household. Another option was to hire a housekeeper. In most cases, these were short-term solutions, since the man usually remarried.

If his new wife was previously unmarried, family life usually continued very much as it had before. If his new wife had been widowed, especially if she had minor children from her first marriage, the family became an extended one. Most families of the period had children with various combinations of parents. Children left orphaned could also be adopted into a new family.

The procedures and decisions required of a widow were far more complicated. The first task for most women was to oversee the probate of her husband's estate, assessing his property and possessions, collecting any money owed and ensuring that any debts were paid. Her role was to ensure that his wishes were carried out and his belongings legally disposed. While many men arranged for assistance in the form of trustees or overseers, placing their wives as executors of the estate was a logical choice. Only 11 percent of men dying in Maryland in the seventeenth century did not make their wives the executors of their estates.

A wife was familiar with how the household had been run and was responsible for any minor children. Most women were also familiar with the process of probate, having seen mothers, sisters, or female friends undertake similar tasks. The job did not, however, guarantee a widow control over her husband's possessions.

The original thirteen colonies were governed by English law, derived from Anglo-Saxon tradition. According to English law, any property or possessions brought by the woman to the marriage automatically became part of her husband's estate. While some marital contracts maintained a separate, legal right to land owned by the wife before marriage, these were rare. In most cases, they were written at the request of a widow remarrying who wished to protect her children's interests.

Following the death of a male spouse, women were entitled to the "widow's dower" or "widow's third," a law passed as a means of providing for women left without financial support. This included the right to use one-third of her husband's real estate at the time of his death, regardless of how much of it she had brought to the marriage. While she could not sell the land, she could rent it out, farm it, or sell anything produced from it. If the real estate consisted of the house her husband had owned, she had the right to a portion of it, usually one or two rooms. Again, she could live there or rent the space out, but she could not sell it. She also was entitled to a third of his personal possessions, following any sales for debt.

If a man died without a will, the widow's third was automatically assigned to her. If a man wished to leave his wife more than her third, it had to be clearly identified in his will. After her death, her share usually reverted to her husband's heirs, usually the couple's children. If they did not have children, it would go to other male members of his family. If the widow remarried, her share became part of her second husband's estate, although, again, she could safeguard her own children's interests in a premarital contract.

After the estate had gone through probate, the widow was able to undertake her new life. If she was deemed the head of a household, she could now be taxed. She could enter into contracts, for herself and for her children, and she could write a will, providing for her children. While remarriage was an option, it did not necessarily happen immediately or at all.

The future circumstances of a widow's life were usually dictated by her financial status. While a poor woman was entitled to a third of her husband's estate, it was a third following the payment of any outstanding debt. If she had adult children, her best hope was that they would be able to maintain her in some way. If she had underage children, the household was usually broken up. If family or friends could not assist her, she and the children became dependent on the town and colony for support. Most communities had rules outlining eligibility for such assistance.

The future of a woman from a wealthier family also may have depended on whether or not her children were of age. If she had an adult son, it was likely that he had inherited the house she and her husband had lived in. While he was required to give her space to live in the house, she had no say in how the household was run.

If a relatively well-off widow's children were underage and it was financially possible, she could continue to run the household herself. When this happened, the family was usually from the merchant class, and the woman also took on running the family business. She would post an announcement in the local paper that she was continuing her husband's work and hope that his usual customers would return.

In 1735, Benjamin Franklin's sister-in-law Ann Franklin began running her husband's printing shop in Newport, Rhode Island. She published the *Newport Mercury*, Benjamin Franklin's almanacs, and various other documents. The wife of a Maryland blacksmith, Jane Burgess, took over her husband's shop in 1773. While such roles gave women very different responsibilities than was common at the time, the usual implication of these actions was that they were safeguarding their children's inheritances until such children were of age.

French and Spanish Colonies

The French and Spanish colonies, including Louisiana, Acadia, New Mexico, and California, followed Roman tradition for deciding law and custom. Under Roman law, a woman had separate claim to any real estate brought to the marriage. During the marriage, the husband could manage the property and spend its income, but it returned to her or her heirs following his death. A widow also was able to keep any personal property brought to the marriage such as clothing, dishes, and tools. She was able to sell or trade these items without her husband's consent or dispose of them as she wished in her own will.

While these rights were greater than those granted to English women, they did not necessarily reflect a greater interest in protecting a French or Spanish woman's ownership of personal property. Often, they were used to protect her family's personal and legal interests. Having invested in her dowry prior to her marriage, her family wanted to maintain control over this investment. These early established legal differences posed challenges as former French and Spanish colonies became part of the United States following the American Revolution.

By the early nineteenth century, medical improvements had led to a drop in mortality rates for both men and women. Most spouses could expect to raise their own children to adulthood. As a result, the concept of the family as a complete, unifying group gained in importance throughout the nineteenth century.

Abigail B. Chandler

See also: Family; Gender Issues (Chronology); Gender Issues (Essay); Inheritance; Marriage and Divorce; Property and Property Rights. *Document:* Probate Inventory of a Plymouth Colony Estate (1672).

Bibliography

Brown, Kathleen. *Good Wives, Nasty Wenches & Anxious Patriarchs.* Chapel Hill: University of North Carolina Press, 1996

Dayton, Cornelia Hughes. *Women Before the Bar.* Chapel Hill: University of North Carolina Press, 1995

Norton, Mary Beth. *Founding Mothers & Fathers.* New York: Alfred A. Knopf, 1996

Wilkes, John (1725–1797)

An eighteenth-century English radical, John Wilkes's libel of King George III caused the rise of the "Wilkes and Liberty" campaign, as the radical segments of London's middle and lower class struggled to protect their freedoms from what they saw as growing political tyranny. Wilkes also became a hero to many American patriots. He was frequently toasted at banquets, and his name was mentioned in political speeches.

Wilkes was born on October 17, 1725, to a malt distiller. His marriage to a wealthy landowner, Mary Meade, in 1747 gave Wilkes the economic freedom to carouse with friends—resulting in his divorce in 1757—and later to become involved in political activities, eventually leading to his election as a member of Parliament from Aylesbury.

Coinciding with Wilkes's election was King George III's appointment of the Earl of Bute as prime minister. This upset many members of Parliament, who felt that Bute was not qualified to serve in this position. Wilkes quickly became Bute's most vehement critic; his criticism became even more vehement when, in June 1762, he created *The North Briton,* his own newspaper, to further attack George III and Bute. Wilkes was soon arrested for seditious libel, but his case was dismissed because of his status as a member of Parliament. The episode increased Wilkes's reputation as a protector of English liberties.

In the colonies, silversmith and future patriot Paul Revere celebrated Wilkes's criticism of the king and Bute by creating a punchbowl weighing 45 ounces and holding 45 gills (half-cup servings), after the issue number of *The North Briton* in which the allegedly seditious article appeared. At a banquet, other future patriots, including James Otis, Jr. and John Adams, drank 45 toasts from it. Indeed, throughout the colonies, the number 45 became symbolic of resistance to tyranny.

Back in England, Wilkes found himself in more trouble. After engaging in a duel, for which Parliament declared him not immune, Wilkes fled to France. Debts there forced his return to England in 1768, where he ran for the Middlesex parliamentary seat. He won easily, but before he could take his seat, he was arrested and transferred to the King's Bench Prison to await trial. Wilkes's arrest created protest throughout London, with the crowd most often gathering on St. George's Field near the prison. There were sympathy protests throughout the colonies as well.

A London journalist and member of Parliament, John Wilkes was a leader of political radicalism in eighteenth-century Britain. He stirred controversy with his attacks on King George III and called for reform in the 1760s. *(Philip Mould, Historical Portraits Ltd., London, United Kingdom/Bridgeman Art Library)*

On May 10, 1768, a well-organized crowd of 15,000 arrived at St. George's Field to await the start of Wilkes's trial. The authorities feared that the crowd might try to rescue Wilkes; therefore, the Riot Act was read, but the crowd refused to disperse. As the situation worsened, the troops opened fire and killed seven protestors, making the St. George's Field Massacre a rallying point for London radicalism.

As the mob took to the streets, Wilkes was found guilty and sentenced to twenty-two months in prison, as well as a 1,000-pound fine. The guilty verdict caused Wilkes to lose his seat in the House of Commons. He was reelected three times by the voters of Middlesex, but each time, Parliament overturned the election results. After his third reelection, Parliament appointed Colonial Henry Luttrell as the Middlesex representative.

The Middlesex supporters of Wilkes formed the Bill of Rights Society to protest his situation, while also developing a radical reform program. Through the Bill of Rights Society, Wilkes' supporters tied their cause to that of the American colonists involved in their own struggle with English tyranny.

In April 1770, Wilkes was released from prison, and, while his parliamentary ban kept him out of the House of Commons, he remained politically active. He became increasingly interested in supporting the cause of freedom of the press. When Parliament tried to prevent newspapers from publishing its proceedings, Wilkes resisted. When two of his printers were arrested for having printed the proceedings, crowds again gathered in support of Wilkes and his cause. This time, the government decided to release the two printers.

In 1774, Wilkes returned to politics, being elected lord mayor of London. He was subsequently elected to represent Middlesex in the House of Commons and continued to work to reform England's political system.

During the American Revolution, Wilkes persisted in his radicalism and pushed for reform; however, his views changed as he grew older. In the 1790 election, the Middlesex voters decided that he was no longer radical enough to suit them, and he lost the election. With this, he retired from politics. Wilkes died in December 1797.

Ty M. Reese

See also: George III; Politics and Government (Chronology); Politics and Government (Essay).

Bibliography

Rude, George. *Wilkes and Liberty: A Social Study of 1763 to 1774.* Oxford, UK: Clarendon Press, 1962.
Thomas, Peter David Garner. *John Wilkes: A Friend to Liberty.* Oxford, UK: Clarendon Press, 1996.

William and Mary, College of

The College of William and Mary was the second college to be founded in North America. Its royal charter, awarded in 1693, laid out two aims: the study of divinity required to train a minister and the general education required to become a gentleman. James Blair, a Scottish cleric, was appointed president and left London with a generous endowment of 2,000 pounds, as well as 20,000 acres of land. He was also entitled to the revenue derived from taxes on tobacco and furs on these lands in order to establish his college somewhere in the royal colony of Virginia.

Blair chose Middle Plantation, a struggling settlement that, when the first college building was completed in 1698, was renamed Williamsburg. Following the destruction of the capitol in Jamestown in 1699, Blair and Governor Francis Nicholson relocated the seat of government to Williamsburg.

Although well-equipped with a royal charter, a sizable endowment, and a campus, the college lay bereft of any students or faculty and operated as little more than a grammar school for boys until 1705. A half-hearted attempt to establish an Indian school was failing, and local gentry continued to send their sons abroad to be educated. It was only in the 1720s, as the second generation was followed by the third, that Virginia's elite began to realize the benefits of local higher education.

By 1729, the college had finally secured sufficient faculty and students to allow the transfer of administrative control from the trustees to the faculty. With his authority now assured, President Blair set to work on the curriculum. After completing their courses in the Grammar School, boys entered the School of Philosophy, where they followed a curriculum heavily reliant on English and Scottish models: rhetoric, logic, and ethics were followed by advanced study in physics, metaphysics, and mathematics. Students might then proceed to the graduate School of Divinity before being confirmed as Anglican ministers.

One innovation in the undergraduate syllabus was the provision that students would not confine themselves solely to the study of classical philosophers. By the time President Blair died in 1743, the works of Locke, Newton, and other modern thinkers were also being taught to a student body that numbered around sixty annually.

This diet of natural law and natural rights clearly had a profound effect on students passing through the college in the mid-eighteenth century, and ultimately this royal endowment produced many gifted patriot-politicians. Thomas Jefferson (class of 1762), for one, looked back on his studies with Professor William Small, the pioneer of the lecture system, as the most formative period in his intellectual life. Moreover, the proximity of the colonial legislature provided a useful laboratory in which to observe and participate in political life. By the time of the Revolution, the House of Burgesses was nearly full of William and Mary men; at the Continental Congress, 16 of the 33 delegates, including the congress's president, had been educated at the college.

As the only American college to have been founded by royal charter, William and Mary benefited from a unique position in colonial politics for much of the eighteenth century. A succession of bishops of London filled the office of chancellor and used this office to bring many Anglican clergy to the college as faculty. The president of the college also served as the head of the church in Virginia, an imperial bond that tied the authority of the college to the fortunes of the Anglican church in the colony and, by extension, to the reputation of the British Crown itself.

Thus, while William and Mary had benefited academically and financially from its imperial associations, growing anti-British sentiment after midcentury quickly put the college's future in jeopardy. In 1775, two of the college's six professors fled to England, while three more left to join the Continental army. Thirty-seven students also joined the army, while many others organized militia companies. In 1777, the remaining faculty wisely appointed their patriot chaplain, the Reverend James Madison (second cousin of the future U.S. president), to the office of president, a move that surely saved the college from a sacking. Instead, the college was briefly closely and occupied by both sides, first as a hospital and then as a barracks.

The loss of its English endowment meant that the college faced dire financial circumstances after the Revolution. In 1779, President Madison took action, closing the costly Grammar and Divinity Schools and

replacing them with the more lucrative preprofessional Schools of Law and Medicine, thereby creating the first university in North America. Alongside this structural reorganization came a political reorientation. The nationwide expansion of Phi Beta Kappa, a Greek letter fraternal organization that had begun among William and Mary students in 1776, was emblematic of the college's distinctive turn away from the motherland toward a future tied to Virginia and to the new United States.

Richard Bell

See also: Education, Higher; Williamsburg. *Document:* Founding Colleges in America (1754).

Bibliography

Godson, Susan H., et al. *The College of William & Mary: A History.* Vol. 1. Williamsburg, VA: King and Queen Press, 1993.

Kale, Wilford. *Hark upon the Gale: An Illustrated History of the College of William and Mary.* Norfolk, VA: Donning, 1985.

Morpurgo, J. E. *Their Majesties' Royall Colledge: William and Mary in the Seventeenth and Eighteenth Centuries.* Williamsburg, VA: College of William and Mary, 1976.

William III of Orange (1650–1702) and Mary II (1662–1694)

Born at the Hague, November 4, 1650, William III of Orange was the posthumous son of William II of Orange and his wife, Mary Stuart (daughter of Charles I of England). Educated at Leyden, he was kept out of power until 1670, when the pressure of war with France caused the Dutch to accept him as their captain general and then stadholder, a position that had become hereditary to the Orange family. William quickly showed himself a skillful and dedicated soldier, who resisted invasion by both Louis XIV and his British allies.

In 1677, to seal a treaty with Charles II, William married his niece Mary, the eldest daughter of James II by his first wife Anne Hyde. Mary had been born in St. James's Palace, April 30, 1662, and had been educated as an English Protestant gentlewoman rather than a potential queen. Happy in the Netherlands, William and Mary's world changed in 1688, when the birth of

James II's son, potentially a Catholic king, prompted disgruntled English politicians and nobles to invite William to come to England to take the throne.

Although the military and Parliament supported William, he was unwilling to accept the throne as a conquest, nor did he wish to rule as a prince consort by right of his wife. Instead, Parliament invested them jointly as king and queen. They responded with the Declaration of Rights, which limited the power of the monarch and served as a model for the later American Bill of Rights, and an agreement with the Scottish Parliament to allow Scotland to remain Presbyterian and retain its independent government.

With Britain's resources, William III was able to continue his wars against Louis XIV's France, which quickly spilled over into Scotland and Ireland when the French backed a force to restore James II to the throne. William III was in command of the army at the Battle of the Boyne, and he continued the campaign in the Netherlands as head of the League of Augsburg until the Treaty of Ryswick in 1697.

William III's expensive and time-consuming wars allowed much of British government to be taken up by professional politicians and required the development of infrastructure suitable to an emerging world power. In 1694, the Bank of England opened for business, giving the king a centralized financial system superior to any other in Europe. Mary II took little part in government and served uncomfortably as the sovereign when William III went overseas to fight.

Colonial possessions were of great concern to William and Mary. The Revolution of 1688 had sparked great changes in colonial government, including the breakup of the Dominion of New England and the removal of the charter for Maryland from the possession of the Catholic Calvert family. Additionally, the Crown had to put down a pro-Dutch faction in New York led by Jacob Leisler and to reissue the Massachusetts Charter to combine Plymouth and Massachusetts Bay as a single entity. The War of the League of Augsburg spilled over into North America as King William's War, in which French-backed Native Americans raided the Massachusetts frontier and Governor William Phips of Massachusetts seized Acadia.

Mary II, deeply concerned for the spiritual welfare of the colonists, advocated an American Episcopal bishop and endowed the College of William and Mary in Virginia. She died of smallpox on December 28, 1694. William III never remarried or had children.

In 1696, William III implemented the Navigation Act, which installed a bounty system for needed naval stores and staple products and allowed royal officials to issue writs of assistance as the equivalent of search warrants to trap smugglers and tax evaders. William III's government, a group of Whigs known as the Junto, engaged Captain William Kidd to track down the pirates. Kidd's own piracy later became a source of deep embarrassment to the Crown.

William III, never popular in England, died on March 8, 1702, after contracting pneumonia while recovering from a riding accident. Jacobites, supporters of James II and his descendents, often toasted the mole into whose hole the king's horse had fallen. As one of his last political acts, William III had signed into law the Act of Settlement, which passed the throne to his cousin and sister-in-law, Mary II's younger sister Anne.

Margaret Sankey

See also: Glorious Revolution; Politics and Government (Chronology); Politics and Government (Essay).

Bibliography

Hamilton, Elizabeth. *William's Mary.* New York: Taplinger, 1972.

Hoake, Dale, and Mordechai Feingold eds. *The World of William and Mary.* Stanford: Stanford University Press, 1996.

Robb, Nesca. *William of Orange: A Personal Portrait.* New York: St. Martins, 1962.

Williams, Roger (c. 1602–1683)

Roger Williams's views on the separation of church and state and his fair dealings with Native Americans have ensured his place among the most forward-thinking people of his age. Williams based his life upon his religion as he understood it, and his politics and philosophy were subsumed by passionate faith. Biographers, most notably George Bancroft, tend to emphasize the aspects of his beliefs that modern readers find agreeable. But Williams's life was more complex than his legend or these writings let on.

Roger Williams was born in between 1602 and 1606 in Smithfield, England, a bustling commercial area on the northwestern side of London. From an early age, religion was the most important thing in his life. Though the precise date is unknown, Williams experienced a life-changing conversion early in life. Separatist sentiment was strong in and around Smithfield, and it is not surprising that Williams latched on to a particularly strong version of Separatist faith.

As a young man, Williams worked as a stenographer for Sir William Coke, a famous lawyer. His connection to Coke paved his way to study at Cambridge from 1624 to 1628. Following his formal education, Williams became pastor at the manor house of Otes, about ten miles outside of London. In 1629, he married Mary Barnard, and, in 1630, wary of the increasing persecution of Puritans and Separatists, the couple sailed for New England.

From 1631 to 1635, Williams worked as a farmer and pastor, all the while engendering controversy for his radical views. Williams fought relentlessly to keep religious practice pure and free from the influence of the Church of England. He questioned the right of the English king to grant land in America and the wisdom of allowing magistrates to rule on religious matters.

While he was the pastor at Salem, Williams forced a showdown with the Massachusetts Bay Colony authorities. Believing in the absolute autonomy of individual congregations, he refused to submit to directives from the colony's leaders. Williams's headstrong behavior resulted in his banishment from the Massachusetts Bay Colony in 1635. Before he could be shipped back to England, however, he struck out for the edge of the Plymouth colony, eventually arriving at the site of present-day Providence.

Providence, the settlement founded by Williams, attracted about 100 Separatists and other outcasts in its first four years of existence. Best known were Anne Hutchinson and her followers, who also moved to the area following their banishment from the Massachusetts Bay Colony. Rhode Island continued to grow, and, while not all of its residents were of the same mind as Williams, they enjoyed the colony's prime location and tolerance for diverse viewpoints.

In 1643, Williams sailed to England to secure Rhode Island's patent. There, he obtained a patent that included language separating religious and civil authority completely. It also combined Providence, Portsmouth, and Newport under one colonial government.

While in London, Williams wrote and published his most famous work, *The Bloudy Tenent of Persecution.* In this document, Williams advanced the ideas that every person and religious group was entitled to religious liberty as a fact of nature and that governments should play no role in the enforcement of religious laws. He supported his radical views with passages from the Bible.

From 1654 to 1657, Williams served as president

Banished from Puritan Massachusetts, Roger Williams founded the colony of Rhode Island on the principles of religious tolerance, separation of church and state, and representative democratic government. *(Brown Brothers, Sterling, Pennsylvania)*

of Rhode Island's general assembly. From this post, he was able to deal with factional problems that had plagued Rhode Island since its inception, relying on his skills as a politician.

Williams was fascinated by his Narragansett neighbors, and his *Key into the Language of America,* published in 1643, has proven to be extremely useful in reconstructing the native world of Rhode Island in the seventeenth century. The book, intended to serve as a guide for converting the Narragansett to Christianity, is packed with thorough ethnographical observations. Williams was primarily interested in Narragansett culture as a means to conversion, but he also found religious significance for the English in their dealings with native peoples.

When he no longer served Rhode Island in an official capacity, Williams continued to guide the colony from behind the scenes, until deteriorating health forced his retirement from public life in the 1670s. Roger Williams died in early 1683.

Matthew Jennings

See also: Puritanism; Rhode Island; Rhode Island (Chronology).

Bibliography

Chupack, Henry. *Roger Williams.* New York: Twayne, 1969.

Garrett, John. *Roger Williams: Witness Beyond Christendom, 1603–1683.* New York: Macmillan, 1970.

James, Sydney V. *Colonial Rhode Island: A History.* New York: Charles Scribner's Sons, 1975.

Williamsburg

"The establishment of the first city government in Virginia was of primary importance in American political history." These are the words spoken by Governor John G. Pollard in 1932. Colonial Williamsburg played a significant role in the cultural, educational, and architectural history of Virginia.

The town of Williamsburg, Virginia, originally known as Middle Plantation, was founded by John Page, a planter who arrived from England in 1650. Williamsburg was named in honor of King William III. Page was a wealthy and powerful Virginian who convinced Virginia officials to move the capital from Jamestown to Williamsburg after a fire destroyed Jamestown.

Page devoted his life to the promotion of Williamsburg. He donated the land for the most important church in the town, Bruton Parish Church, and he helped to establish the College of William and Mary. Page would serve in several important capacities in Virginia's colonial government: colony officer, high sheriff, and member of the Governor's Council, the upper house.

Williamsburg was created by an act of the General Assembly in 1699. Francis Nicholson, the governor at the time, and his executive council appointed a governing board of directors composed primarily of landowning gentlemen. These officials were appointed rather than elected during the first 170 years of the town's history.

The city of Williamsburg, Virginia (pictured around 1740), was founded as Middle Plantation in 1633 and became the permanent capital of the colony in 1699. It remained the political and cultural center of Virginia for the next 80 years. *(Library of Congress, LC-USZ62-2104)*

Governor Nicholson designed the town. He is responsible for making a boulevard out of Duke of Gloucester Street and for the "capitol," in which the House of Burgesses met. In addition, between 1699 and 1722, most of the historic and stately buildings of Williamsburg were built: the first capitol, the courthouse, the theater (1716–1717, the first in America), and, in 1720, the Governor's Residence.

In 1722, King George I granted Williamsburg a royal charter incorporating the town. Williamsburg would now have a local government composed of a mayor, a recorder, six aldermen, and a twelve-member council known as "Common Hall." It was an unelected government and could send one representative to the House of Burgesses.

Colonial Virginia had a population of 23,000 by 1750, or about one-fifth of the entire colonial population. Approximately 3,000 of these inhabitants lived in Williamsburg, a town made up of some 300 homes. Slaves, mostly household servants, made up about half of the town's population. The town occupied an area of about a square mile; its population increased to about 4,000 with the political season, when the lower house, the House of Burgesses, was in session. The British influence, personified by the governor, was evident in the style and fashion favored by the townspeople. Williamsburg had an air of sophistication and a refinement not found elsewhere in the colonies.

The College of William and Mary, the second college to be founded in America, was an important and integral part of colonial life in Williamsburg. (Harvard College, the first, was founded in 1636.) In September 1693, the Virginia Assembly decided to create an educational institution that would educate the state's elite males, who would serve the town as doctors, lawyers, or ministers. In February 1693, therefore, the colonial legislature asked Reverend James Blair to petition King William III and Queen Mary II for a charter for the college. Blair traveled to England and returned with the charter. During the first thirty-five years of its existence, the college operated as "grammar school" for Williamsburg's elite, educating boys from ages 12 to 15.

The College also had a school of divinity, a school of philosophy, and an Indian school. The Indian school educated and "Christianized" Native American boys. The college rarely had more than sixty students and was primarily a training institution for Anglican ministers. British-born Anglican ministers controlled the college and transmitted their values of loyalty to the mother country to the town. The college was unapologetically loyalist, and college and town politics were intrinsically connected.

In 1779, the Reverend James Madison, a cousin of the founding father by the same name, became president of the college. His goal was to reorganize the college by eliminating the grammar school and instruction in divinity. Thomas Jefferson is one of the college's most famous graduates. He arrived at William and Mary in 1760 at the age of 16 and enrolled in the School of Philosophy, where he remained for two years before embarking on the study of law.

During the years preceding the Revolution, Williamsburg was one of the most significant political centers in the colonies. In 1765, from the state capitol, legislator and patriot Patrick Henry delivered his famous speech against the Stamp Act in which he spoke the famous words "Give me liberty or give me death." This pronouncement resulted in the resignation of the local stamp agent. Both British and French forces spent time in Williamsburg during the war.

In 1780, the capital of Virginia was moved to Richmond, and Williamsburg became a small college town. Between 1927 and 1935, under the sponsorship of John D. Rockefeller, the town of Williamsburg was restored to resemble its colonial state and is today a popular living history museum.

Leigh Whaley

See also: Virginia; Virginia (Chronology); William and Mary, College of.

Bibliography

Greenspan, Anders. *Creating Colonial Williamsburg.* Washington, DC: Smithsonian Institution Press, 2002.

Maccubbin, Robert P. *Williamsburg, Virginia: A City Before the State, 1699–1999.* Williamsburg, VA: City of Williamsburg, 2000.

The Restoration of Colonial Williamsburg in Virginia. Architectural Record. New York: F. W. Dodge, 1935.

Winslow, Josiah (1629–1680)

Born in 1629 to Edward Winslow and his second wife, Susanna White, Josiah Winslow grew up in Marshfield, Massachusetts, a town founded by his father, Governor William Bradford's chief diplomat and negotiator with local Native American tribes.

As a young man, Winslow attended Harvard University, but he did not take a degree, which was usual for those not entering the ministry. Instead, Winslow became a soldier, managing his family's property, while advancing in the Plymouth militia, assuming command of the forces at Marshfield in 1652. A solid citizen and man of property, Winslow married Penelope Pelham, a Bostonian of impeccable family, sometime around 1657.

Continuing his political rise, Winslow attained a Marshfield magistracy, then joined Plymouth's War Council in 1658. The following year, upon the death of Miles Standish, Winslow became overall commander of the Plymouth militia. He also served from 1659 until 1672 as Plymouth's delegate to the United Colonies, which various New England settlements had created for mutual consultation.

Throughout his life, Winslow's interests were primarily military and centered on the colony's immediate neighbors, the Native American tribes with whom his father had carried out diplomatic and trade agreements. In 1662, Winslow, acting as a major in the militia, took part in the controversial apprehension of Wamsutta, the son of Massasoit, leader of the Wampanoag, an Algonquian-speaking tribe of eastern Massachusetts.

Wamsutta had sold land to settlers from outside of Plymouth, a breach of a long-standing land policy that directly affected Winslow, one of several important Plymouth leaders with investments in local land. Wamsutta died of a fever at Winslow's house en route to Plymouth, sparking rumors of coercion and murder, especially among the followers of Wamsutta's brother, King Philip (Metacom).

In 1672, the death of Governor Thomas Prince brought Winslow election to the governorship of Plymouth, the first American-born leader of an English settlement. Still primarily a military man rather than a theocrat, Winslow sponsored the building of public schools and unsuccessfully instructed the Plymouth churches to formulate a toleration policy for Quakers and other dissidents.

Winslow's expertise as a military commander was put to the test in 1675, when King Philip's War began in June with attacks on Plymouth's outlying settlements, including Winslow's home at Marshfield. Requesting aid from the Massachusetts Bay Colony and other New Englanders, Winslow created an army of perhaps 1,000 men and was awarded overall authority as commander in chief of the United Colony Troops.

In December 1675, Winslow led this army to Wicklow, Rhode Island, where he established a base to use in attacking the Narragansett, a people he believed were rendering crucial aid to the Wampanoag. On December 19, he and his men devastated the main Narragansett village, eliminating them as a potential threat to Plymouth. Rather than remain in the captured village, Winslow insisted on an exhausting march back to Wickslow in brutal winter conditions, during which many of the wounded colonial militiamen died. Despite his victory in what would become known as the "Great Swamp Fight," Winslow was heavily criticized for the high casualties and his decision to retreat to Wicklow rather than recover and regroup his army.

As a postwar governor, Winslow had to confront the heavy financial and political fallout of the hostilities. A comfortable rather than prosperous colony, Plymouth now faced heavy and unpopular taxes that endangered its independence within New England. To add to the problem, Winslow found himself justifying the war to King Charles II of England, who was displeased that Plymouth had failed to renew its royal charter following the English Civil War. Winslow did succeed in charming the king's emissary, Edward Randolph, who suggested a united New England under Winslow's governorship.

Winslow died in office on December 18, 1680, at his Marshfield estate. He was succeeded as governor by his deputy, Thomas Hinckley.

Margaret Sankey

See also: Bradford, William; Native American–European Relations; Pilgrims; Plymouth.

Bibliography

King, H. Roger. *Cape Cod and Plymouth Colony in the Seventeenth Century.* Lanham, MD: University Press of America, 1994.

Langdon, George D. *Pilgrim Colony.* New Haven, CT: Yale University Press, 1966.

Leach, Douglas Edward. *Flintlock and Tomahawk.* New York: W. W. Norton, 1966.

Stratton, Eugene Aubrey. *Plymouth Colony: Its History and People.* Salt Lake City: Ancestry Publishing, 1986.

Winthrop, John (1588–1649)

John Winthrop was one of the major figures of colonial American life. A devout Puritan and a shrewd politician, Winthrop did much to establish an orderly society based on both justice and mercy in the New World; his ideology and actions led to the establishment of what we venerate as the American tradition.

Early Life

Born the son of a country gentleman in Suffolk, England, in 1588, John Winthrop enjoyed a comfortable life. Following two years of studying law at Trinity College at Cambridge University, Winthrop returned home as the steward and justice of the peace of his father's estate. Although Winthrop's journals describe his youth as "wild and dissolute," by the time of his return home, the 18-year-old was married and had clearly begun to develop a sense of his inherited Puritanism.

Like many Englishmen in the early seventeenth century, Winthrop was increasingly alarmed by the growing sense of the Anglican church's oppression of dissent. By the mid-1620s, ministers who refused to adhere strictly to all Anglican tenets were being silenced in growing numbers. It was clear that religious intolerance was on the rise.

Economic conditions in England were also difficult by the end of the 1620s. Winthrop, who by then had seven children and a wife to support, was also a landlord with responsibility for his tenants and his own servants as well. Later in the decade, his family's previously successful cloth business was sinking under the weight of higher prices and rising taxes; similarly, the profits from his sizable grain acreage were being eroded by the government's heavy-handed financial policies. Further, Winthrop's dismay at the dishonesty he perceived at court was widely known, a fact that—in addition to his open and devout Puritanism—likely led to the loss of his attorney's license, although no official reason for its revocation was given.

Such conditions of growing intolerance and oppression in England led many citizens to consider leaving their homeland for the New World. In 1629, Winthrop was elected the first governor of the newly formed Massachusetts Bay Company.

Settlement in America

In March 1630, Winthrop and some 700 colonists set sail for America. While at sea aboard the *Arabella,* John Winthrop delivered his now-classic sermon, "A Modell of Christian Charity." In this sermon, Winthrop articulated the moral code for a godly society in the New World. His exhortation that the colonists must create a righteous society that would be "a city upon the hill" formed the foundation of an ideal of American exceptionalism that has endured.

The *Arabella's* landing at Salem, Massachusetts, on June 12, 1630, must have presented something of a shock to Winthrop and his companions. While the emigrants recognized they were going to an unsettled land, the degree to which sufficient housing and provisions were in short supply doubtless made some question their decision to leave England, no matter what the repressions there.

Soon Winthrop and other leaders moved the seat of the Puritan settlement to Boston; here, a civil government based upon the royal charter was soon established. Two distinctions in this early government of the Massachusetts Bay Colony are noteworthy: First, a theocracy established the joint rule of both civil and church authorities (as opposed to the later American evolution of a separation of church and state). Second, by autumn of 1630, a system was developed that allowed freemen (citizens), rather than only the company's stockholders, the power to elect the colony's leaders.

Creating New England Society

Winthrop was truly a leader in the creation and establishment of New England society. He served as governor of the Massachusetts Bay Colony for all but a few years between his arrival in 1630 and his death in 1649; Winthrop also wielded considerable influence as a member of the Council of Assistants in those few years when he did not win reelection. Accordingly, his vision of New Englanders as God's chosen people—a vision shared by most of his fellow Puritan settlers—was the driving force behind the colony's new life.

While Winthrop did attempt to strike a balance between the authority of the governor and the interests of the governed, it is important to keep in mind the strong religious component of colonial New England life. Both civil and church leaders were quick to point out passages of Scripture that commanded obedience to those in positions of authority.

As a result, there quickly arose a deep intolerance for those whose ideas threatened the Puritan utopia envisioned by Winthrop and his followers. For example, Anne Hutchinson's Scripture study meetings were initially greeted with approval by Winthrop and the Puritan fathers as a useful way of instructing the women who attended. As word of Hutchinson's gatherings spread and men began to attend with their wives, however, those in authority grew uneasy.

When Hutchinson began to express increasingly liberal ideas in her lectures, expounding upon the sermons of Puritan minister John Cotton, and then began to emphasize the individual's need to rely on his or her own "inner light" for appropriate spiritual guidance in the Christian life, Winthrop stepped in. Not only could this new society not tolerate such heretical ideas, he could not allow the authority of the ruling theocracy to be usurped. Significantly, as a woman speaking in public on such topics, Hutchinson was even more of a threat to the underlying patriarchy as well. The ensuing Antinomian Controversy, which raged from 1636 through 1638, condemned Hutchinson, her family, and many of her followers as heretics and resulted in many of these colonists' persecution and eventual excommunication from the established church, as well as their banishment from the Massachusetts Bay Colony.

It was not only Puritan dissent within the colony that concerned Winthrop. In 1643, the governor demanded the capture of the radical Puritan preacher Samuel Groton in Rhode Island and ordered him and his followers brought to Boston for trial and sentencing on charges of heresy. By 1646, Presbyterians faced heavy persecution in the Massachusetts Bay Colony as a result of their advocacy of more liberal rules concerning church membership.

It is interesting to note that, by the 1640s, officials in England were loosening many religious strictures and were becoming somewhat more tolerant in matters of dissent. However, the geographical distance of the Massachusetts Bay Colony from England, combined with the founders' and leaders' view of their own role as the traditional "nursing fathers" of Puritanism and orthodoxy, resulted in the colony's isolation from any shift toward more liberal viewpoints on religious matters.

While many of Winthrop's attitudes may be difficult to understand, it must be remembered that he and his fellow leaders were driven by two strong impulses that reinforced each other. Foremost was the vision of a Promised Land in the wilderness. The sense of God's protection, sanction, and commission in the unknown of the new land was coupled with a sincere belief that the colonists—particularly their leaders—would be called to account for their actions in God's behalf at the Judgment Day. Combined with this inclination was a desire to establish not a social and cultural democracy, but rather a gentrified society.

Thus, Winthrop hoped to actualize in the Massachusetts Bay Colony the ideal of a somewhat benevolent oligarchy in which each individual had a role to play within the social hierarchy. While all levels of society, Winthrop believed, would necessarily be interdependent, there was no question in his mind but that each person should accept his or her prescribed place and perform his or her prescribed duties within the hierarchy.

By 1645, with the Massachusetts Bay Colony well established in the new land, Winthrop could comfortably write on the differences between natural and civil liberty, saying that the latter could be "maintained and exercised in a way of subjection to authority." However, by that time, Winthrop had been defeated in two gubernatorial elections by colonists who found his methods arbitrary and unacceptable. In addition, the rising importance of Boston as a seaport contributed to the decline in popularity of Winthrop's ideas. As commerce and contact with the world outside the Massachusetts Bay Colony grew, so too did the colony's worldview. Such exposure rendered Winthrop's ideology largely obsolete by the end of the decade, and, by the time of the governor's death in 1649, the once-despised notion of dissent was becoming increasingly linked in the popular mind to the concept of progress.

John Winthrop's *Journal* offers scholars interesting information on early Massachusetts history, as understood by a man who helped shape much of it. Yet even without reading the written text left by Winthrop, it is clear that his influence pervades much of what Americans have come to consider their heritage.

Barbara Schwarz Wachal

See also: Boston; Massachusetts; Massachusetts (Chronology); Massachusetts Bay Colony; Ministers and the Ministry; Puritanism. *Document:* A Modell of Christian Charity (1630).

Bibliography

Bremer, Frances J. *John Winthrop: America's Forgotten Founding Father.* New York: Oxford University Press, 2003.

Dunn, Richard S., James Savage, and Laetitia Yeandle, eds. *The Journal of John Winthrop, 1630–1649.* Cambridge, MA: Harvard University Press, 1996.

Morgan, Edmund S. *The Puritan Dilemma: The Life of John Winthrop.* Boston: Little, Brown, 1958.

Winthrop, John. *Life and Letters of John Winthrop.* Reprint, New York: DaCapo Press, 1971.

Witchcraft and Witch Trials

The men and women who traveled to the New World as settlers brought with them a set of social customs and religious beliefs that played a primary role in the development of the British colonies. Among the religious beliefs that these settlers, particularly the Puritans, espoused was a conviction that supernatural powers operated in the world they lived in. The God they worshiped was part of that supernatural world. Their cosmology also included the devil, other evil spirits, and witches.

The widespread belief in witchcraft was evident in colonial laws and the trials of witches that occurred during the period. The prosecution of suspected witches was common in the course of the seventeenth century; however, the hysteria of the Salem witch trials seems to have largely ended the practice of subjecting accused witches to criminal prosecution.

Beliefs About Witchcraft

The concepts of magic and witchcraft were commonly accepted in Europe and the New World. Physical events were interpreted as signs, either good or bad, according to the prevailing religious beliefs and superstitions. The presence of evil spirits was viewed as a direct result of the conflict between good and evil in the supernatural world. Just as God must battle Satan, so too, those people who were part of God's elect found themselves embroiled in an earthly battle with evil, typically in the form of a witch.

Witchcraft was motivated, in the minds of the colonists, by *maleficium*—that is, those who practiced black magic sought to purposely inflict evil upon the men and women with whom they lived. *Maleficium* might be manifested in any number of ways, from minor afflictions to major devastation. Colonial laws similarly defined witchcraft, implying that witches were in close fellowship with the devil or other "familiar spirits." One colony declared the crime of witchcraft to be "giving entertainment to Satan."

The signs of such an association with the devil could, according to the prevailing belief system, be found in any number of ordinary occurrences, including the death of an animal, loss of a crop, spoiling of a batch of beer, or coming down with an illness. These common afflictions became associated with witchcraft when those who were subject to such troubles accused another settler of causing the problem through magic. Disastrous events, such as wars or widespread drought or famine, could also be attributed to the evil intentions of a witch in the community.

Witchcraft was specifically addressed in colonial laws, and most of these laws were adopted in the mid-seventeenth century. Between the years of 1636 and 1647, Plymouth, Massachusetts, Connecticut, Rhode Island, and New Haven adopted such legislation. All of the New England colonies, as well as Virginia and Maryland, prescribed the death penalty as punishment for those convicted of practicing witchcraft. Massachusetts law not only required the execution of convicted witches but also punished those who consulted witches; the consequences of doing so ranged from banishment to death.

Equally important were the colonial laws that allowed settlers to sue for slander those who accused them of witchcraft. New England records report at least twenty-six such cases, most occurring in Massachusetts.

"Typical" Witches

Colonists believed that any of their fellow settlers had the potential to be witches. Historians have discovered that men and women accused of witchcraft shared similar characteristics, including commonalities in gender, age, marital status, and family.

Women were most commonly accused of practicing evil magic. In New England, 80 percent of those accused were women. Prior to 1640, no men were accused of witchcraft, and only twenty-two men were subject to such allegations during the colonial period.

The typical witch was not only female but also middle-aged, usually between the ages of 40 and 60. In New England, nearly half of all those accused of witchcraft fell in this age range. Stereotypical witches were also usually married. Of those accused in New England, 79 percent were married and another 10 percent were widowed. Single or divorced women were generally not susceptible to such allegations.

Nearly one in six of the accused women in New England had no children, a status that was not typical of women in colonial society. Many of those who did have children had what were considered small families for the time, with fewer than six children. A number of those who faced witchcraft complaints had borne children who died before reaching adulthood.

Another characteristic of the typical witch was the social position she occupied. Few women of the highest social order were subjected to such allegations. Most accused witches came from the lowest ranks of society. These women also engaged in occupations that made them susceptible to charges of practicing magic. In particular, women who practiced some sort of medicinal work, such as midwifery, often found themselves implicated.

A final common factor among those most likely to be accused of engaging in witchcraft practices was a record of previous accusations of other crimes. Forms of assaultive speech, such as slander, were chief among the disturbances that such women had been accused of. In New England, at least twenty of the women facing prosecution for witchcraft had previously been accused of or convicted for verbal aggression. Theft was another common previous accusation. Other offenses included lying, physical assault, sexual misbehavior, and, in one case, arson.

Accusations of Witchcraft

There were numerous reasons why certain colonists accused others of witchcraft. Some allegations of witchcraft were leveled against others as a result of conflict between the parties. Other times, accusations of witchcraft could be used as a means of blackmail for achieving a specific goal such as ownership of a coveted property. The juries who decided the cases rejected most accusations of witchcraft that stemmed from such personal motivations.

Many times, however, charges of practicing magic stemmed from a fervent belief in the supernatural as the reasonable explanation for events that had occurred. Children were often the accusers of witchcraft, the supposed innocence of youngsters lending weight to the charges.

The accusers who leveled charges of witchcraft often exhibited what they claimed were outward signs of the evil worked upon them by the accused. The evidence they produced varied, depending on the supposed action of the witch. Afflicted individuals might exhibit a range of physical manifestations, including seizures, hysteria, and muteness. They also might report a loss of appetite or experiencing sensations of being cut, bitten, or pinched. Oftentimes, those suffering from the afflictions of a supposed witch were young

children, whose parents brought the formal charges; the victims of such affliction were generally female. In cases where witchcraft hysteria overwhelmed populations, such "symptoms" could quickly spread to other sufferers, particularly if the accused witch was nearby.

Witchcraft Trials

Before a trial began, a suspected witch was often subjected to a series of tests meant to ascertain whether or not he or she was a witch. One such test required a thorough search of a woman's body, looking for physical evidence of fellowship with evil spirits (called familiars) in the form of witch's teats. These were believed to be evidence of the witch's familiars, who were sent out to do her bidding and received sustenance from her body by sucking on the nipple-like mark. Typically, women of standing in the community were gathered to examine the body of a female suspect.

Another test for the presence of a witch was the ancient practice of having the accused, along with several others in a crowd, touch the victim. If the victim was able to distinguish the touch of his or her supposed tormentor, it was believed to be evidence that the latter was a witch.

A third test administered was the water test. The accused witch was bound hand and foot and then thrown into a body of water. It was believed that a guilty person would float, being assisted by the devil; the innocent sank. Other extralegal tests for witches included the requirement that the accused recite a passage of scripture without error. Such a task, it was believed, could not be completed by someone associated with evil.

Prior to indictment for witchcraft, the legal process required the gathering of formal evidence. This was generally obtained through the depositions of witnesses of the events or people associated with the afflicted and the accused. The depositions, in combination with the results of the above tests, were presented as evidence for indictment, which was followed by a formal trial with the verdict to be determined by a jury. The trials allowed for testimony on both sides of the case. Many cases brought before juries resulted in the acquittal of the accused. For those convicted of witchcraft, the punishment was death by hanging.

While the most famous instance of widespread hysteria over witchcraft occurred in Salem, Massachusetts in 1692, accusations and trials of witches began earlier in the century. Prior to the trials at Salem, there were nearly 100 incidents of witchcraft accusations or

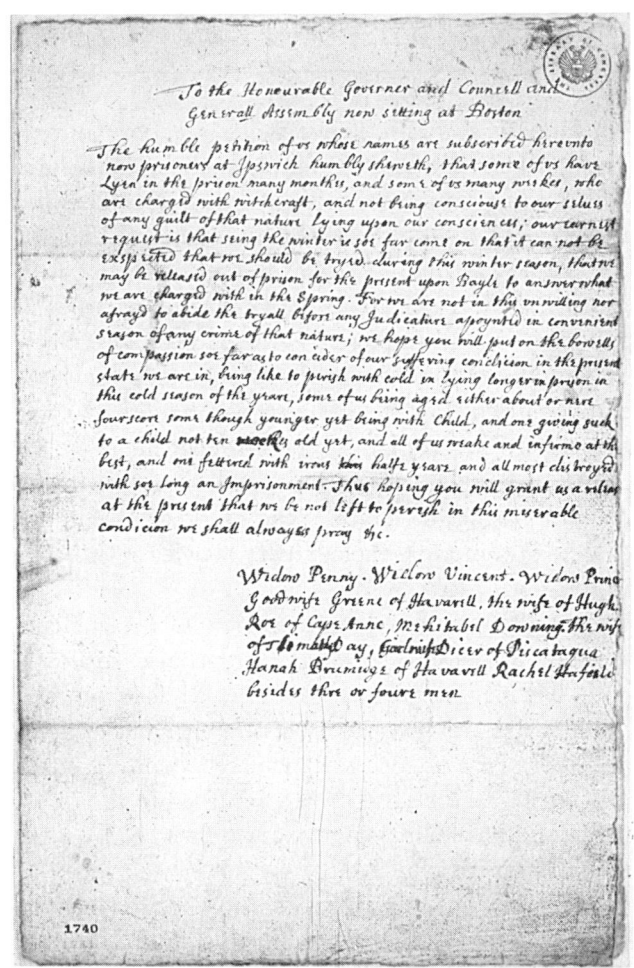

A petition by ten women accused of witchcraft in Salem, Massachusetts, appeals for their release on "bayle," lest they "perish with cold." Some are "fettered with irons," and all are "weake and infirme." Hundreds had been arrested. *(Library of Congress, LC-MSS-12021-1)*

trials, with about 80 percent occurring after 1648 and resulting in the executions of more than two dozen people. Others were punished for their involvement with magic by banishment and whippings.

The series of trials for witchcraft that occurred in Salem are the best documented of the colonial era. The episodes began with the accusation of witchcraft by several young girls in Salem, who began experiencing fits that were believed to be the work of witches. After the girls began naming their tormentors, trials began, and six women were subsequently convicted and hanged.

During this time, at least forty-eight other people in the community claimed to be possessed, and accusations flew throughout the small village. The girls and others in the village accused hundreds of residents of practicing magic. Some of the accused confessed to the practice of witchcraft, no doubt hoping to save their lives and property. This decision proved wise, as the authorities determined that those who admitted their evil practices would not be hanged.

Throughout the course of the witchcraft hysteria that spread through much of the colony, nearly 200 people were accused of being witches; almost 75 percent of those accused were women. By the time the trials ended, a total of thirteen women and seven men had been convicted of practicing witchcraft and had been executed, among them George Burroughs, a minister. Giles Corey refused to enter a plea to the charge of bewitching and was pressed to death. Others died while in prison awaiting their trials.

The frenzy of witchcraft accusations eventually reached the highest levels of society, with the governor's wife and the prominent minister of Boston's Old South Church being named as witches. It was accusations of this nature that finally prompted Governor Phips to declare an end to the trials, though these later claims were generally not considered to be serious. The validity of the accusations and trials was addressed by Increase Mather in his essay *Cases of Conscience*, recognizing that the charges of witchcraft were, in many cases, lies. This denunciation of the panic that had gripped the community served to effectively eliminate future witch hunts.

Witchcraft Trials in Other Colonies

Although the widespread agitation that encompassed the colony of Massachusetts generally resulted in the demise of accusations of witchcraft, during this same time period other colonies remained susceptible to similar charges being leveled against its settlers. This was particularly true in Connecticut; however, charges of witchcraft were not new in the colony. In the 1659s, at least two women were executed after being convicted of being witches. In 1662, a supposed coven of witches was tried in Hartford; the result was the execution of four women and the fleeing of many who were associated with the convicted. During the 1692 Salem crises, several women were tried in Connecticut courts, although there were no executions as a result of the trials.

Nearly ninety 90 percent of the witchcraft trials in the seventeenth century were held in one of the Northern colonies. In cases where executions occurred, 95 percent of such punishments were meted out in the Puritan communities of New England. Common beliefs about witchcraft and magic, however, resulted in the accusation of witches in the Southern colonies as well.

In Virginia, most cases dealing with witchcraft were slander cases brought against persons who had leveled accusations of the practice of black magic. In 1655, Thomas Godby's wife, Ann, was brought before the court on charges of slander for having accused other women in the community of witchcraft. The court ruled against the Godbys and fined them 300 pounds of tobacco and the court costs. In Princess Anne County, John and Anne Byrd charged defamation of character against a neighbor who had accused them of afflicting him through their interaction with the devil; the Byrds' charges were dropped.

In other cases, Virginians faced accusations of witchcraft at trials. In 1656, William Harding was sentenced to ten lashes and banishment from the colony after being found guilty of practicing sorcery. Grace Sherwood was accused of being a witch in 1705. Her body was searched for physical evidence, but when none was found, she was subjected to the water test, during which she floated. Sherwood was held over for trial; however, the officials involved in the case seemed uncertain how to proceed, and the case was eventually dropped.

Tonia M. Compton

See also: Crime; Prisons and Punishment; Salem; Women. *Documents:* The Salem Witch Trial of Susanna Martin (1692); Thomas Brattle on the Salem Trials (1692); A Poem Recalling the Hanging of a Relative due to the Salem Witch Trials (in 1692; pub. 1857).

Bibliography

Booth, Sally Smith. *The Witches of Early America.* New York: Hastings House Publishers, 1975.

Demos, John Putnam. *Entertaining Satan: Witchcraft and the Culture of Early New England.* New York: Oxford University Press, 1982.

Drake, Frederick C. "Witchcraft in the American Colonies, 1647–62." *American Quarterly* 20:4 (1968): 694–725.

Godbeer, Richard. *The Devil's Dominion: Magic and Religion in Early New England.* Cambridge, UK: Cambridge University Press, 1992.

Karlsen, Carol F. *The Devil in the Shape of a Woman: Witchcraft in Colonial New England.* New York: Vintage Books, 1989.

Taylor, John M. *The Witchcraft Delusion in Colonial Connecticut, 1647–1697.* Williamstown, MA: Corner House Publishers, 1984.

"Witchcraft in Virginia." *William and Mary College Quarterly Historical Papers* 1:3 (1893): 127–29, 2:1 (1893): 58–60.

Wolfe, James (1727–1759)

On January 2, 1727, James Wolfe was born into an important British military family at their Kent estate. Along with his younger brother, he was educated with the aim of being commissioned into the army. In 1741, he became a second lieutenant in the 1st Marine Regiment. Wolfe took part in the Ghent campaign as an adjutant, and he was present at the Battle of Dettingen. He impressed the Duke of Cumberland, the commander in chief, sufficiently to be promoted to first lieutenant, then captain of the 4th Foot in 1744. Recalled to Britain in November 1745 because of the Jacobite Rising, he served at the Battle of Falkirk and as aide-de-camp to General Henry Hawley at Culloden in April of 1746.

Wolfe impressed his superior, General Henry Hawley, in helping suppress the Jacobite Rising in 1745. Hawley then further groomed Wolfe by promoting him to staff officer and ordering him to coordinate raids from Fort Augustus against the remaining Jacobites. In the fall of 1746, Wolfe returned to the continental theater as a major and was wounded badly at the Battle of Maastricht.

Despite his stellar record and the patronage of Cumberland, Wolfe had few opportunities once the War of the Austrian Succession ended in 1748. Although he was a solid member of the establishment because of his family connections, Wolfe did not have the financial resources or the aristocratic weight to secure a command. Instead, he ran day-to-day operations for Edward Cornwallis, the absentee colonel of the 20th Foot, who was lieutenant governor of Nova Scotia. In his free time, Wolfe studied classical military treatises and new drill books from Prussia, being particularly fascinated by the new tactic of using mixed skirmishers against columns of troops, which he experimented with in the training of his own regiment.

The chance for action finally occurred in 1757, when he took part in an amphibious assault on Isle d'Aix, Rochefort, France, under Sir John Mordaunt. The operation was a fiasco, and Wolfe both infuriated his superiors and gained the respect of his peers by refusing to criticize Mordaunt at his court-martial. Promoted to rapidly to lieutenant colonel of the 67th Foot, then brigadier general, Wolfe received orders to embark for North America as a subordinate to General Jeffery Amherst. Wolfe took part in the siege of Louisbourg, commanding an artillery battery responsible for

The death of General James Wolfe is dramatized in a famous painting by Benjamin West. Wolfe died at the Battle of Quebec in September 1759, as did his adversary, France's General Montcalm. The British victory secured Canada from the French, and Wolfe was lionized as a martyr. *(Private Collection/Phillips, Fine Art Auctioneers, New York/Bridgeman Art Library)*

both bombarding the walls of Louisbourg and destroying French ships off the coast. When Louisbourg surrendered in November 1758, Wolfe ignored Amherst's orders and returned to London in order to beg a European command from Ligonier. When refused, he volunteered to lead the siege of Quebec.

Having received this command, Wolfe embarked for Canada as part of a three-pronged attack on the French at Fort Niagara, Fort Ticonderoga, and Crown Point, and his key objective, the fortified city of Quebec. Wolfe had his pick of junior officers and assigned Isaac Barré as his adjutant general and Guy Carleton as his quartermaster. Arriving in May 1759, Wolfe conducted extensive reconnaissance of the area on both sides of the St. Lawrence around Quebec and destroyed French settlements to aid in the siege. By September, the pressure of soon losing naval support, due to the winter freezing of the river, pushed him to attack. On September 13, Wolfe and his men, including militia contingents from New England, crossed the St. Lawrence

before dawn and, landing at the Foulon Road, marched on Quebec in thin, two-rank rows for frontage as they crossed open fields. The Marquis de Montcalm, the French commander, ordered his troops out of the city to meet the British on the Plains of Abraham. Wolfe, taking an observation position to the right of the line, was wounded three times, and he died on the field. A deserter from the 60th Foot was later court-martialed and executed for Wolfe's death, but some of the three shots were undoubtedly fired by French snipers. Wolfe died early in the battle, but his subordinates carried the day against the French, and the city of Quebec surrendered on September 18, 1759, securing Canada for the British.

Wolfe was lionized as a martyr and depicted as the savior of British North America, but his real influence lay in studying and disseminating Prussian tactics such as alternate firing and bayonet drill. In 1768, his *Instructions to Young Officers* was printed and thereafter sold briskly throughout the rest of the century. Wolfe's legacy was not a heroic death on the Plains of Abraham but the lasting foundation for British army training and the fierce discipline that delivered victory in the Napoleonic Wars.

Margaret Sankey

See also: French and Indian War; Montcalm, Louis-Joseph; Quebec City.

Bibliography

Fregault, Guy. *Canada: War of the Conquest.* Translated by Margaret Cameron. Toronto: Oxford University Press, 1969.

Parkman, Francis. *Montcalm and Wolfe.* Boston: Little, Brown, 1924.

Reid, Stuart. *Wolfe: The Career of General James Wolfe from Culloden to Quebec.* New York: Sarpedon, 2000.

Women

The lives of women of European descent in the colonial Americas had much in common with those of women in Europe. They were subordinated within patriarchal institutions and subject to their fathers, husbands, and, when outside those family relationships, the men of church and state, who were also styled as "fathers."

In much of Europe, married women could not own property in their own names and were legally represented by their husbands. Often, women's daily lives were taken up with domestic concerns, keeping house or caring for children—in the case of unmarried women, perhaps as servants, mistresses, or even nuns (who frequently ran schools for girls and tended to the domestic needs of male and female religious orders alike). Women's work did vary greatly, however, according to their class and location.

Life in the colonies created opportunities, interactions, and relationships that differed from those found in Europe. Many women were able to participate in politics, commerce, religion, and intellectual life, thus going beyond traditional roles.

European colonization of the Americas had a negative impact on indigenous women and on African women brought to the New World as slaves, but here, too, victimization is not the only story. Tensions between tradition and change, limitations and opportunities, mark the experiences of women in the Americas during the colonial period.

Native American Women

When Christopher Columbus first set foot in the West Indies, what would come to be known as the Americas were inhabited by millions of people from thousands of native cultures, about half of whom, we can assume, were women. At the beginning of the European presence in the Americas, the enterprise of exploration and colonization was almost wholly undertaken by men, although the land and its native inhabitants were frequently characterized as feminine in ways that helped justify conquest and had very real consequences for the women and men who lived here.

During the early years of encounter and conquest, native women sometimes served as translators and go-betweens. This may have reflected their secondary and thus nonthreatening status in both the cultures they bridged. Doña Marina, often known as "La Malinche," and Pocahontas are the two most famous such women.

Because of the paucity of European women in the colonies during the sixteenth century, sexual relations between European men and native women also played an important role in shaping the power dynamics of conquest and of gender relations for generations to come. Ranging from rape and forced concubinage to marriage and consensual intimacies, these relations ranged from basely exploitative to highly beneficial financially and socially to the women involved.

Likewise, conquest had a mixed effect on native women's social and economic roles. Women were often forced to accommodate themselves to the sexual division of labor imposed by Europeans, which differed from their preconquest roles. This usually involved a loss of traditional prestige and power. For instance, some women who were traditionally responsible for planting and harvesting were pressured to confine their labors to domestic tasks that Europeans deemed more feminine. Others were required to undertake the bulk of tribute labor or were forced into personal service.

As a consequence, women's social and familial roles were disrupted, and the tribal power they had once held was sapped, rendering them as legally disempowered as European women. There are also examples of native women using the colonial legal systems to sue for redress and petition for rights traditionally unavailable to them. For some women, these changes provided new opportunities to participate in trade in urban centers and gain other kinds of cultural power by negotiating the borders between Native American and European cultures.

For the most part, however, conquest and colonization had a devastating impact on Native American women, both through the effects that disease and armed conflicts had on individuals and communities and through transformations in their social roles. By gaining cultural knowledge and participating in shaping New World communities that were rooted in cultural exchange and personal interactions, some native women adapted and thrived, thereby helping to shape colonial society as a whole. And some, like Weetamoo, the widow of Wamsutta and an important sachem in her own right, asserted themselves as tribal and military leaders in resistance to European incursions.

African American Women

African women are known to have been in the Spanish and Portuguese colonies as early as 1535, when a slave name Margarita accompanied conquistadors in an expedition to conquer Chile. They were also present in the British, Dutch, and French colonies at least as early as 1619. Almost all of these women came unwillingly.

Some 30 to 40 percent of the 3.5 million Africans forcibly transported to the Americas throughout the colonial period were women. Most served as slaves or indentured servants, though communities of free blacks also existed. As servants or slaves, black women's work crossed traditional gender boundaries—they worked in house and field alike, belying European notions of women's proper place, while uncovering the white colonists' dehumanizing attitude toward Africans.

Whether a black woman, free or slave, was in an urban or rural area also influenced her experiences of family and community. In cities, enslaved women were more acculturated, since they often inhabited households with few or no other servants and were isolated from larger communities of Africans. Some enslaved women in cities were able to earn money through cooking, sewing, and vending enterprises in which they agreed to pay their masters a set fee, while keeping profits that exceeded that fee. By doing so, such women were sometimes able to purchase their freedom and the freedom of their children and other family members. In areas where farm labor was organized on a task basis, as in South Carolina (enslaved laborers were assigned tasks that needed to be completed but were not required to work particular hours), women also might engage in forms of economic enterprise outside their assigned tasks. In both cases, such opportunities were limited by the power of masters and the bias of laws, forces that often worked against free blacks as well, despite their putative independence.

Enslaved African women were frequently exploited sexually by white owners for pleasure and economic advantage. This was especially true once laws such as the one passed in Virginia in 1662 declared "all children born in this country shall be held bond or free only according to the condition of the mother."

Enslaved women in the Americas were more likely to experience some kind of family life, especially among female family members, than enslaved men, who were often separated from their parents and children alike. And because of their ties to children and older family members, women were less likely to attempt escape.

In North America, the number of Africans in the colonies remained relatively low until later in the seventeenth century, when they were allowed to marry and become free landowners. During the late seventeenth century and throughout the eighteenth, the number of blacks both born in and brought to the Americas soared, as economic and social practices, along with supporting laws and ideologies, institutionalized slavery.

The experiences of black women in the Americas during the colonial period were more varied than is often recognized. But the institutionalization of slavery in the colonies increased the legal and social restraints placed on both free and enslaved blacks at the same time that the population of black women in the Americas was increasing dramatically.

European-American Women

Thirty Spanish women accompanied Columbus on his third voyage to the Caribbean in 1478. By 1540, European women were present in most Spanish-American cities, but their numbers did not begin to swell until the 1560s. Women from France, England, and the Netherlands did not begin to settle in North America until the seventeenth century.

In New France and New Spain, sexual relations between European men and native and African women created mixed-race populations categorized as Métis or mestizos. However, enduring colonial stability was seen by most Europeans to depend on the presence of European women, who would enable settlements to grow through natural increase, rather than continued immigration or the official recognition of mixed-race populations.

Many of the first European women to arrive in the Americas came as part of attempts to stabilize settlements through the development of European families. Sometimes early male settlers arrived with their wives or had their wives or fiancées follow them across the Atlantic. Single women also came as indentured servants or explicitly as future brides. It was not until the settlement of the Massachusetts Bay Colony that women and families participated in the development of a new colony at its beginnings. New England was the first successful colony the settlement of which was not primarily motivated by dreams of conquest and economic exploitation.

Gender imbalance benefited early female colonists, who could afford to be selective in choosing husbands. Because of high mortality rates, women frequently accrued sizable fortunes through successive husbands, gaining a degree of wealth, social eminence, and political power that would have been less accessible to them in Europe. Nonetheless, as wives and servants, women were legally subordinate to their husbands and masters and still at the mercy of double standards that governed their sexuality and judged their behavior.

The hardships of life in the new settlements forced many women to participate in farming and other forms of physical labor that were largely men's work in Europe, making their traditional household duties more difficult. Also, infant mortality rates were high throughout the colonial period—most women suffered the deaths of children either personally or through losses among family and friends.

As with family roles, legal status, and economic opportunities, there was much continuity between women's religious lives in Europe and in the Americas, but the New World also provided opportunities rarely available before. Religious beliefs and practices provided spiritual sustenance and avenues of community involvement and self-expression for numerous women, but Catholics and Protestants alike tended to reinforce patriarchal authority, particularly by silencing women's public voices on religious matters. There are myriad examples of women facing such silencing in the early colonies. Anne Hutchinson and Sor Juana Inés de la Cruz are just two of many women to be silenced for speaking or writing publicly about religious matters.

The project of converting Native Americans to Christianity and spreading the word of God in the New World, a project that was both heartfelt and useful as a way to justify and raise funds for colonization, allowed many women to skirt the limits placed on women's public speech. Nuns who came to the Americas to establish convents, schools, and hospitals were often motivated by missionary zeal, a zeal they wrote about

in letters and reports that drew attention (and funding) to their endeavors. Quaker women—including Mary Fisher, Anne Austin, Elizabeth Hooton, and Joan Vokins—were among the most adventurous of the early women missionaries to the Americas, seeing colonial settlements and not just "heathen" communities as important targets for their preachings. These women also were some of the most prolific writers.

Social experiments founded on religious dissent, such as the Massachusetts Bay Colony, allowed women to express their own dissent, even in the face of silencing from patriarchal forces. Arguably, the participation of Anne Hutchinson and other women in the Antinomian Controversy was enabled by their experience of Puritan challenges to social and political control of religion in England.

The violence of the frontier and other elements of colonial life led to more dramatic expressions of religious belief, such as the captivity narrative of Mary Rowlandson and the testimony of women and girls during the witchcraft trials of the late seventeenth century. Various popular spiritual movements of the seventeenth and eighteenth centuries put "feminine" enthusiasm in the foreground, attracting numerous women.

Restrictions

Women were largely excluded from formal education throughout the colonial period. John Winthrop famously observed of the studious and ailing wife of the governor of Hartford,

> if she had attended her household affairs, and such things as belong to women, and not gone out of her way and calling to meddle in such things as are proper for men, whose minds are stronger, etc., she had kept her wits, and might have improved them usefully and honorably in the place God had set her.

Few women had access to more than a rudimentary education, both because they were women and because of the limited educational available to anyone not of the more privileged classes. In Catholic colonies, girls might have access to convent schools, such as the one established by the Ursulines in Quebec in 1639 for both the daughters of French colonists and native girls, or to schools taught by *beatas* in Spanish-ruled countries. Although women's educational opportunities were limited throughout this period, these expanded during the eighteenth century as literacy increased, print culture changed the intellectual landscape of the colonies, the number of female entrepreneurs opening schools increased, and women's education became linked to colonial self-determination.

In the early years of the United States, the ideology of "republican motherhood" encouraged women's education so that mothers could raise well-educated, patriotic children. Women's roles as teachers of young children and older girls at home, as well as in convent and grammar schools, led to an increased focus on their intellectual development, worldly success, and educational opportunities that helped give rise to later feminist movements.

Just as education for women was limited in the Americas as in Europe, women were less frequently encouraged and recognized as poets, writers, and artists than men throughout the colonial period. Those who were recognized were usually treated as rare exceptions, as the title *Tenth Muse*, given to Anne Bradstreet and Sor Juana Inés de la Cruz, two of the best-known American women poets of the seventeenth century, attests.

Nonetheless, women like Bradstreet were successful in male-dominated literary and intellectual circles during the seventeenth century, and recognition of such women increased throughout the eighteenth century. For evidence of rich artistic cultures flourishing outside the publishing world and other avenues of official recognition, we also can look to forms of artistic expression that often do not register in male-centered histories, such as quilts, diaries, and letters, as well as literary salons and circulating commonplace books.

In exploring the ways in which gender shaped the lives of women in the Americas, issues of family and reproduction are some of the first concerns, as we have seen. Domestic roles and life experiences related to marriage and childbirth were shaped by the rigors of colonial life, patterns in women's immigration from Europe and Africa, and relationships among different races and classes in New World societies and economies. Indeed, the colonies themselves were shaped by these forces—issues of sex and gender did not only affect individuals.

Colonial America also provided new opportunities for women outside their prescribed roles, whether they were of European, African, or Native American descent. Women participated in religious missions, social experiments, educational reforms, and artistic expression, all linked to the growth of European colonies in the New World.

Tamara Harvey

See also: Child Rearing; Children; Family; Food and Diet; Furnishings; Gender Issues (Chronology); Gender Issues (Essay); Housing; Kitchens, Colonial; Marriage and Divorce; Servants, Domestic; Widows and Widowers. *Document:* Raising Colonial Children (1699).

Bibliography

Berkin, Carol. *First Generations: Women in Colonial America.* New York: Hill and Wang, 1996.

Hewitt, Nancy A. *A Companion to American Women's History.* Oxford, UK: Blackwell, 2002.

Socolow, Susan Migden. *The Women of Colonial Latin America.* Cambridge, UK: Cambridge University Press, 2000.

Wright, Susanna (1697–1784)

Susanna Wright, poet and scientist, was born August 4, 1697, in Warrington, England. Her parents, Patience Gibson and John Wright, moved to Chester, Pennsylvania, in 1714. Susanna Wright stayed in England to complete her schooling and then joined her family in America. She continued to study throughout her life, and her letters demonstrate fluency in French and competency in Italian and Latin. Gifted in many fields (including as a water-colorist), she was a leading intellectual figure in colonial Pennsylvania.

Wright's unmarried state was no protection from heavy household responsibilities. When her mother died in 1722, she took responsibility for her father's household and raising her seven younger brothers and sisters, as single adult women were expected to serve their families in such roles. Later, she helped with her brother James's family. In her role as housekeeper and surrogate mother, Wright supervised all the heavy chores of a colonial household, including domestic manufacture of cloth and clothing, care of livestock, and food preparation and preservation.

Her father, John Wright, began traveling to the frontier as a Quaker preacher to the native peoples. In 1724, he stayed with the Native Americans at Shawana Town in the Susquehanna Valley. Two years later, when the natives moved to Conestoga Indian Town, John Wright, Susanna Wright, Robert Barber, and Samuel Blunston purchased about 1,000 acres in the area.

John Wright received a patent to operate a ferry in 1730, and the area became known as Wright's Ferry. The Wrights' house also served as an inn, which Susanna ran. In 1738, Susanna Wright designed Wright's Ferry Mansion for her brother.

In 1745, Wright finally achieved the independence of her own household, when widower Samuel Blunston, a close family friend, willed her a life interest in his nearby property. She lived on that property until her death.

With interests in nature and access to her father's books on medicine, Susanna Wright became a skilled herbalist, who prepared and prescribed medicine for her neighbors. She also regularly corresponded with other leading Pennsylvania scientists, including James Logan and Benjamin Franklin. Her scientific experiments extended to agriculture, including silkworm cultivation. Wright won a 1771 prize offered in Philadelphia for the person cultivating the most silkworms, and Benjamin Franklin presented Queen Charlotte with a piece of Wright's silk, which was then made into a court dress. The Philadelphia Library Company has preserved a piece of her homespun silk.

John Wright was a justice of the peace and a longtime member of the Pennsylvania Assembly. Neighbors turned to Susanna Wright in her father's absence. She drafted wills, deeds, and indentures for neighbors unable to write. Through her scribe's duties, she had became involved in politics and elections in 1742, and she succeeded Samuel Blunston as prothonotary after his death. Greatly respected by her neighbors, she also settled local disputes.

Wright wrote regularly throughout her life but did not keep copies of her own work. As a result, scholars can only find a small sample of her writings. That work shows great skill in blending spiritual and intellectual concerns, and at least two poems reveal a strong voice for equity for women. Her poems were often addressed to women and used ordinary life events to make profound observations.

Wright gained literary fame as a poet by circulating her work in manuscript form. Her correspondents shared her writings with others and, in turn, sent her their own work. Manuscript circulation was an accepted part of the eighteenth-century literary world. Friends might copy poems into journals or keep a copy before sending the work on to others. For example, Wright's poems were used as texts for girls studying at Quaker schools in Philadelphia. She became part of a lively intellectual circle of friends that included a number of other women poets, including Elizabeth Graeme Fergusson, Hannah Griffitts, and Deborah Logan. The largest known group of Wright's poems is in a manuscript commonplace book kept by Milcah Martha Moore, who used the book to create her own selective anthology of materials she read.

Wright's reputation grew. In her later years, many people made the trip to Wright's Ferry to meet her, including Dr. Benjamin Rush. He noted in his journal that he had met "the famous Suzey Wright a lady who has been celebrated Above half a Century for her wit— good Sense & valuable improvements of mind." Susanna Wright died on December 1, 1784, in Pennsylvania.

Joan R. Gundersen

See also: Arts, Culture, and Intellectual Life (Chronology); Arts, Culture, and Intellectual Life (Essay); Literature; Science.

Bibliography

Blecki, Catherine La Courreye. "Susanna Wright's 'The Grove.'" *Early American Literature* 38:2 (2003): 239.

Blecki, Catherine La Courreye, and Wulf, Karin A., eds. *Milcah Martha Moore's Book : A Commonplace Book from Revolutionary America.* University Park: Pennsylvania State University Press, 1997.

Cowell, Pattie. "'Womankind Call Reason to Their Aid': Susanna Wright's Verse Epistle on the Status of Women in Eighteenth-Century America." *Signs: Journal of Women in Culture and Society* 6:4 (1981): 795–800.

Shields, David S. *Civil Tongues and Polite Letters in British America.* Chapel Hill: University of North Carolina Press, 1997.

Y

Yale College

Established in 1701 by a group of ministers to combat the latitudinarianism, or tolerance of various religious doctrines, of Harvard in nearby Massachusetts, Yale was Connecticut's first college. For sixteen years, this "Collegiate School" had no fixed campus and operated out of private homes in Hartford, Saybrook, and New Haven. It was only in 1717, when the colony's General Assembly granted the college the sum of 500 pounds to build its first college house, that New Haven, the colony's largest urban center, was selected as the school's permanent home.

In its early decades, the college benefited enormously from the money-raising efforts of Jeremiah Dummer, Connecticut's agent in London. In 1714, Dummer endowed the college library with 800 books he had personally solicited from their authors. This gift—which contained sought-after works by Locke, Newton, Halley, Steele, Raleigh, Chaucer, Milton, and Bacon—at one stroke transformed the college's library into the finest in New England. Four years later, Dummer persuaded Elihu Yale, a wealthy Londoner who had made his fortune as governor of Madras, to donate 417 books and goods worth 562 pounds. This endowment—the largest single donation from any private group or individual until well into the nineteenth century—secured the patron's posterity when the college renamed itself in his honor later that year.

Although staffed mostly by young Harvard graduates, Yale quickly took New England higher education in a new direction. While the curriculum was built around the traditional subjects being taught at Harvard and in England, Yale soon acquired a reputation in science and divinity. By the 1720s, the new science and philosophy of Newton and Locke was being taught; and by the 1750s, owing to the enthusiasm of President Thomas Clap, Yale became the first college to demand knowledge of arithmetic as a condition of admission. Clap procured scientific instruments for the college, including a frictional electrical machine donated by his friend Benjamin Franklin, and built an orrery to show the movement of the planets.

While never a Calvinist seminary, Yale graduated a large number of ministers, particularly in its first four decades, and frequently fell prey to religious controversy. In 1722, accusations of Arminianism—the brand of antiauthoritarianism that fed Methodism—were leveled at several faculty and tutors, forcing their swift departure from New Haven. Twenty years later, as much of New England embraced the "New Light" radicalism of the Great Awakening, the administration came under fire for its condemnation of Arminian apologists like George Whitefield and James Davenport. Insisting on Calvinist orthodoxy, the college expelled students who refused to apologize for their New Light sympathies or attended unauthorized meetings. Facing religious criticism on all sides, President Clap, a man selected for his conservative Calvinism, soon moved to establish Yale's own college church, the first in America, to insulate his students from the false religions swirling outside its doors. In 1745, he also amended the college charter to establish the college as a perpetual corporation, legally autonomous and protected from outside religious or political influence.

Following the excitement of the Great Awakening, student–administration relations only worsened. Unconnected disciplinary infractions slowly escalated into a series of riots in the 1750s, as the authoritarian Clap sought to keep control of a college population expanding faster than the resources necessary to provide for it. In 1764, students poisoned the food at the underfunded commons to protest the bland, repetitive diet of bread, salted pork, and milk. Poor commons, rising tuition charges, and excessive restrictions on personal liberty fueled rebellions that by the 1760s seemed nearly continuous. In 1766, when two tutors

A Front VIEW of YALE-COLLEGE, and the COLLEGE CHAPEL, NEW-HAVEN.

Yale College was founded as the Collegiate School in Connecticut in 1701. The first campus building in New Haven, its permanent home, dates to 1717. The institution was later renamed for its first major benefactor, Elihu Yale. *(Brown Brothers, Sterling, Pennsylvania)*

resigned after their windows were smashed and their lives threatened by students angry at maladministration, Clap was finally forced to leave. The college nearly closed while the trustees scrambled to restore order.

The appointment of acting President Naphtali Daggett inaugurated a decade of reconciliation during which students and faculty came together in anti-British sentiment. Following the Townshend Duties in 1769, the Yale senior class voted to appear at commencement entirely in homespun and used their graduation speeches to argue against "the Unconstitutional measures of the British Parliament." In 1775, students formed their own militia company, and, over the next six years, Yale's sons came to form half of the field officers in the Connecticut militia.

By 1775, Yale had long since assumed equal status with "Mother Harvard." It had graduated more students in seventy-odd years than Harvard had managed in almost twice that time. Yale's graduates—ministers, doctors, and a growing number of lawyers—were assuming positions of power all over the new nation. They also had been influential in founding most of the seven colleges established during the Great Awakening,

making Yale's nineteenth-century progressive leadership a model for American higher education for a long time to come.

Richard Bell

See also: Arts, Culture, and Intellectual Life (Essay); Education, Higher; New Haven. *Document:* Founding Colleges in America (1754).

Bibliography

Oviatt, Edwin. *The Beginnings of Yale 1701–1726.* New York: Arno Press, 1969.

Tucker, Louis Leonard. *Puritan Protagonist: President Thomas Clap of Yale College.* Chapel Hill: University of North Carolina Press, 1962

Warch, Richard. *School of the Prophets: Yale College, 1701–1740.* New Haven, CT: Yale University Press, 1973.

Yamasee

The Yamasee Indians are most closely associated with a single event in the history of the colonial Southeast—the Yamasee War. Apart from their role in the years leading up to this war and its aftermath, not much research has been done on Yamasee origins and culture. Usually, they exist primarily in historical literature as foils to English colonization.

The Yamasee, like most seventeenth- and eighteenth-century tribes, were multiethnic. That is to say, people speaking different languages and adhering to different cultural practices could consider themselves Yamasee. This obstacle to identification is compounded by the fact that it was usually Europeans, with limited ethnographic skills, who were doing the classifying. From 1650 to 1715, the Yamasee lived near, essentially among, both the Spanish and English in the Southeast. They fought alongside and against both of those colonies. They dispersed as a distinct political unit in the aftermath of the Yamasee War, but in the 1950s, a group previously identified as Altamaha Cherokee began working to reassert their Yamasee identity. Currently, the tribe is not recognized by Georgia, South Carolina, or the U.S. government.

The language and culture of the Yamasee have been the source of much controversy about their identity. Since they drew on populations throughout the Southeast, they spoke their own indigenous languages; however, they also communicated with each other and the outside world using a trading language, or lingua franca. This should hardly be surprising, since recent scholarship about the Creek, Choctaw, and Catawba suggests that these groups were essentially multiethnic as well. The Yamasee first appear in written historical records in 1663, when a Franciscan friar operating north of St. Augustine noted their arrival, though not their area of origin. They seem to have been able to understand the language of the Creek, itself a hodge-podge of Muskogean tongues.

From the 1660s to the 1680s, the Yamasee were loosely associated with Spanish colonization in Florida. They did not participate to the same extent as other groups. The Yamasee avoided joining mission communities. They also resisted Spanish attempts to alter their culture and force them to pay tribute and labor obligations. The fact that the number of people considered to be Yamasees grew rapidly indicates that the group readily accepted refugees from neighboring communities.

In the mid-1680s, the Yamasee emigrated en masse from Spanish Florida to just outside of Charles Town; at the time of their remove, they may have numbered in the thousands. The English colony at Carolina provided trade goods and firearms, which the Spanish friars were more reluctant to do. The English also had little interest in converting the Yamasee and did not hold their non-Christian status against them. The push factors also should not be overlooked: in the 1670s and 1680s, the Spanish made new attempts to draft Yamasee into their labor force and urged participation in mission life.

Over time, the Yamasee became among Carolina's staunchest Native American allies. They participated in military actions alongside the Carolinians in 1702, 1704, and 1710. In 1702, Governor James Moore launched an attack on St. Augustine. Moore's force of Yamasees, Creeks, and Apalachicolas destroyed the town but failed to take the stone fort.

In 1704, having lost his post, Moore and his army of natives struck Apalachee, a more prosperous mission province to the west. The attack resulted in a stunning defeat for the Spanish and mission natives. Several hundred perished, and over a thousand were carried off as slaves.

In 1711, the Tuscarora attacked the fledgling colony of North Carolina, and the Yamasee again aided the South Carolinians. A force of 500 Native Americans, mostly Yamasees, served with John Barnwell and later with James Moore, Jr., in another campaign. The Yamasee again made off with numerous slaves for sale at Charles Town.

The Yamasee War (1715–1717) is sometimes referred to as the earliest pan–Native American uprising in North America. Upset by traders' abuses and encroaching white settlement and livestock grazing, a broad coalition of Native Americans—including Creeks, Yamasees, and members of smaller tribes—killed white traders in their villages and then turned on a terrified English populace. The English threw together an army of mercenaries, servants, slaves, and militiamen to counter the initial attack. Eventually, the Carolinians enlisted the assistance of the Cherokee, a powerful interior nation, and defeated the Creek and the Yamasee. In the aftermath, the Yamasee scattered throughout the Southeast. Many returned to Spanish Florida, whence they continued to harass the English for years.

While Yamasee history may be manipulated to serve a variety of purposes, new archaeological evidence is continually being unearthed. The recovery of more Yamasee artifacts and the creative use of historical documents, combined with the continued assistance of the Altamaha Cherokee, may provide increasing certainty about Yamasee culture in the years to come.

Matthew Jennings

See also: Native American–European Conflict; Native American–European Relations; Native Americans; Yamasee War.

Bibliography

Milling, Chapman. *Red Carolinians.* 2nd ed. Columbia: University of South Carolina Press, 1969.

Nash, Gary B. *Red, White and Black: The Peoples of Early North America.* 4th ed. Upper Saddle River, NJ: Prentice Hall, 2000.

Shrager, Bradley. "Yamasee Indians and the Challenge of Spanish and English Colonialism in the North American Southeast, 1660–1715." Ph.D. diss. Evanston, IL: Northwestern University, 2001.

Yamasee War

The Yamasee War was the pivotal conflict in determining whether the North American Southeast would be Native American or English land. It broke out when a pan–Native American coalition attacked traders and outlying white settlements on Good Friday, 1715, and petered out in 1717 when the Cherokee entered the war on the English side, forcing the Yamasee to scatter among Spanish missions and other Southeastern native communities and forcing the Creek to negotiate peace.

As in most conflicts, there is no single explanation for the outbreak of hostilities between the English and their neighbors. The Yamasee had been close allies of the Carolina colony, participating in slaving raids against the Spanish and their allied mission natives in 1702 and 1704. The Yamasee also played a major role in the subjugation of the Tuscarora during the Tuscarora War (1711–1715). The Yamasee had been pushed out of Spanish Florida by renewed forced labor drafts and increasing cultural pressure from the missions, and they were drawn toward Carolina by more plentiful opportunities for trade and the acquisition of firearms.

Traditional interpretations of the war suggest that unscrupulous traders operating out of Carolina angered the Yamasee sufficiently to cause war, but more recent theories point to a wide array of factors, of which trade debts were merely one. The Yamasee had been among the prime movers in the far-reaching Native American slave trade that grew in the Southeast in the late seventeenth and early eighteenth centuries. It was their very effectiveness as slave raiders and providers of deerskins that brought the Yamasee into conflict. They, and other groups who had occupied Port Royal before them, had likely overhunted fragile deer populations and overraided nearby native communities. By 1715, they had essentially outlived their usefulness to the shrewd English colonists.

The Yamasee also inhabited what was considered prime agricultural land, which may seem confusing, considering its swamp-like qualities. Carolina was becoming a rice producer, and Yamasee lands were ideal for the purpose. The colony's government recognized as much when it set apart some land for the Yamasee in an effort to curtail white settlement. The colonial government in South Carolina was not totally in the dark about rising tensions and, in the early eighteenth century, it made a number of moves to halt trading abuses and regularize relations with the Yamasee. However, the colonial government was weakened by factionalism, and, in any event, the damage had already been done. In April 1715, the Yamasee, Creek, Cherokee, and Chickasaw, together with numerous smaller tribes, killed the traders in their villages, including Thomas Nairne, the newly appointed South Carolina Commissioner of Indian Affairs.

In the next phase of the war, there is little evidence to indicate that the Creek, Cherokee, or Chickasaw participated. The Yamasee, with help from smaller native groups, began to attack white plantations, driving the effective line of white control back toward Charles Town. The colonists, fearing that they were facing an alliance of Creek, Cherokee, and Chickasaw (which certainly could have destroyed the colony), threw together an army of indentured servants, mercenaries, militiamen, and slaves. Other colonies, sensing the gravity of the situation, chipped in with munitions, food, supplies, and armed men.

In fact, the Creek, Cherokee, and Chickasaw had no desire to crush what they viewed as a valuable trading partner. They made it clear that they intended peaceful relations with the English. An agreement to end hostilities was made in late 1717.

After this conflict, the Yamasee scattered among many Southeastern tribes. Some stayed in Florida, and from there launched raids against ever-expanding English plantations. The Carolina border was not entirely secure until the settlement of Georgia.

Historians have speculated since the eighteenth century about French or Spanish involvement in the Yamasee War. While both European powers could have benefited from a successful campaign, France's hold over the Lower Mississippi Valley was very tenuous. Spanish Florida was crumbling, and it does not seem likely that the Spanish could have incited the attack. They welcomed refugees and were never sad to see a few English Protestants get killed. Hypothesizing in this manner also takes away from the fact that, in 1715, the Yamasee were perfectly capable of conducting their own affairs by assembling a coalition to fight abuses.

The long-term result of the Yamasee War was to ensure that Carolina would continue to trade with Creek, Chickasaw, and Cherokee, forgoing peaceful relations with smaller tribes, while currying favor with more powerful ones. Although it took some time, the areas around Charles Town also began to produce the rice that would eventually make South Carolina North America's most African and wealthiest colony.

Matthew Jennings

See also: Military and Diplomatic Affairs (Chronology); Military and Diplomatic Affairs (Essay); Native American–European Conflict; Native Americans; War; Yamasee.

Bibliography

Gallay, Alan. *The Indian Slave Trade: The Rise of the English Empire in the American South, 1670–1717.* New Haven, CT: Yale University Press, 2002.

Milling, Chapman. *Red Carolinians.* 2nd ed. Columbia: University of South Carolina Press, 1969.

Yeomanry

The yeomanry originally designated a group of small, independent commercial farmers in England, who, during the course of the seventeenth century, ceased to exist as a result of industrialization and enclosure. In colonial America, "yeomanry" referred to a class of small farmers, who owned their own land, grew their own food, and produced goods for the market.

The term is a broad one that encompassed several different kinds of farmers. Many yeomen owned relatively small plots of land, 100 acres or less, while others owned larger tracts. Some yeomen owned slaves, some did not. All yeomen, regardless of their position, relied on the labor of their wives and children to make their farms viable and assumed authority over them.

The yeoman class also exhibited differences in various parts of the country as a result of relations with other social groups. In the North, yeomen defined themselves, in part, by their struggle against large-scale capitalists to maintain their economic security and independence. In the South, yeomen contended for control of the state with planters, although they shared with them an ideal of local self-sufficiency and joined with them to avoid peonage, or economic dependency on large landholders.

Land

The yeomanry formed out of the struggles over land that occurred during the seventeenth century. Many colonists came to the New World seeking land of their own, and they successfully acquired property through warfare with Native Americans or grants from colonial authorities. By the latter half of the eighteenth century, between two-thirds and three-quarters of white, male householders were freeholders who owned land in places as diverse as Connecticut, eastern Massachusetts, Long Island, New York, and Tidewater, Virginia.

Yeoman farmers consolidated their position as free landowners during the Revolutionary period. The concept of independent landholding was dear to yeomen who, when threatened with the loss of land tenure, were known to petition legislatures and to riot. To them, landholding signified security, independence from economic subservience, and freedom from dependence on other men for land or wages.

The Whig gentlemen who led the American Revolution understood that to mobilize yeoman farmers, who constituted a significant portion of the population needed to fight the war for independence from Great Britain, they would have to appeal to their fears of losing their land. Revolutionary leaders spoke to the yeomanry of the English ministers as cunning men, who, in Samuel Adams's words, were threatening to "take away your Barn and my house" and, according to John Adams, intended to tax land and property and "reduce the country to lordships" by remaking yeomen into tenant farmers and wage laborers.

The success of these appeals depended on previous relations between yeoman and gentlemen. Where anti-British Whig gentlemen landowners had protected the property rights of yeomen—for example, in New Jersey, eastern Pennsylvania, and eastern Carolina—yeomen often joined the cause. In places where yeomen perceived gentlemen landowners as enemies who ignored their interests—Vermont and the Carolina backcountry, for instance—they backed the British.

Those yeomen who had supported and fought in the Revolutionary War realized their position of strength and demanded an active role in the formation of public policy in exchange for military service. They argued that their position as property owners made them independent, freethinking men, and therefore guaranteed them political rights. Furthermore, they contended that the new government should be a democracy, consisting of property owners, who could not only express their views through elected representatives but could assert their will through other, more direct means.

Political Ideology

The radical Revolutionary rhetoric of the yeoman farmer provided the foundation for the creation of a powerful and durable political ideology, usually referred to as "Jeffersonian agrarianism." Following the Revolution, Americans debated the terms of the new political and social order. The Federalists, led by Alexander Hamilton, favored a strong central government and the holding of political power by the landed few. The Republicans, led by Thomas Jefferson, believed in the primacy of local government and a primarily agrarian national economy.

The Republicans were determined that there would be no aristocracy in America. They envisioned an ideal society, a republic based on small, independent producers (i.e., the yeoman farmer). In such a republic, every man would be able to acquire skills and independence, and his independent, industrious lifestyle would provide the basis for fulfilling civic obligations. They believed that the best kind of social order for establishing this kind of polity was one in which the majority of the country's white, adult males retained their independence as property owners.

This view reflected the belief that only truly free men could be entrusted to choose representatives and to judge their performance. Jefferson further contended that only widespread landholding could create an independent social group capable of preventing the seizure of power and corruption of the republic by wealthy merchants, lawyers, and gentlemen. At one time, Jefferson even drafted legislation that would have given all free men in Virginia 75 acres of land upon marriage.

Economics

Besides serving as an icon for the nation's political ideals, the yeoman farmer also provided the inspiration for the development of economic and moral ideals. As an independent producer, the yeoman represented the basic source of wealth for the nation, providing its inhabitants with agricultural produce, minerals, and other commodities.

The figure of the yeoman farmer also represented morality to many thinkers and writers, who associated a life working the soil with virtue. In their view, the rural atmosphere created a better person, one more honest, industrious, and immune to the temptations of luxury.

The independent, industrious, and upright yeoman farmer became the preeminent symbol and hero of the agrarian eighteenth century. As economic and technological change brought challenges to the agrarian way of life, Americans debated the role of industry and agriculture in society. Within this context, the yeoman farmer as a noble cultivator and free citizen gained currency, and the idea of a republic of virtue populated by noble cultivators acquired mythic proportions. The "yeoman dream" became a foundational ideology that referred to the American ideal of traditional success: personal, moral, financial, and religious achievement open to all, regardless of class or occupation.

The yeoman dream resonated not only in the political arena, but in the economic, social, and cultural realms, and it came to be celebrated by various writers and spokespeople in the eighteenth century and the first half of the nineteenth century. Literary representations of the myth of the yeoman included James K. Paulding's *The Backwoodsman* (1818) and Timothy Flint's *Recollections of the Last Ten Years* (1826), both of which portray agrarian democratic utopias set in the West.

Lydia Maria Francis Child extolled the yeoman dream in her periodical, *Juvenile Miscellany* (1820s–1834), which provided a mixture of fact and fiction and aimed to inculcate good behavior in young readers. Writing under the pen name Peter Parley, the popular children's author Samuel Griswold Goodrich portrayed America as the last refuge of the yeoman dream. Both Child and Parley emphasized that the competence and independence of a yeoman society could be attained by any American, if pursued in a moral fashion.

Farmers' magazines naturally praised the yeoman dream, but labor periodicals also publicized the agrarian ideal of traditional success. Labor journalists adapted the image of the yeoman farmer to create for their readers the image of a competent, independent, and moral yeoman mechanic, who would one day be the master of his own shop. Rural journalists, intellectuals, spokespeople for immigrants, and others also united around the ideal of traditional success, offering their own models, all based on the yeoman.

Marjorie L. Hilton

See also: Agriculture; Class; Laborers, Rural; Land and Real Estate; Planters; Tenant Farming.

Bibliography

Burns, Rex. *Success in America: The Yeoman Dream and the Industrial Revolution.* Amherst: University of Massachusetts Press, 1976.

Kulikoff, Allan. *The Agrarian Origins of American Capitalism.* Charlottesville: University Press of Virginia, 1992.

Liddle, William D. " 'Virtue and Liberty': An Inquiry into the Role of the Agrarian Myth in the Rhetoric of the American Revolutionary Era." *South Atlantic Quarterly* 77: 1 (Winter 1978): 15–38.

Z

Zenger, John Peter (1697–1746)

John Peter Zenger was a mildly successful, but constantly in debt, printer in New York. He was little known until he became involved in a struggle between rival city political factions that led to his arrest on a charge of criminal libel. His subsequent trial has become a part of American legend related to freedom of the press.

Zenger was born in the Rhine Valley of Germany in what is now Bavaria in 1697. His family immigrated to New York as part of a group of 3,000 Germans sent by England's Queen Anne in a scheme to produce naval stores for the English navy. As indentured servants, the immigrants were obligated to pledge seven years of service to their masters in return for freedom and a grant of land. The plans went awry, however, when many of the refugees, including Zenger's father, died in the harsh conditions of the transatlantic voyage. His mother, Johanna, was left with three children in a strange land with no means of support.

The young Zenger, age 13, attempted an apprenticeship with a cobbler that never took hold, and, in 1811, he was apprenticed to William Bradford, New York's most prominent printer. After eight years, upon completion of his contract, he married Mary White of Philadelphia and settled in Chestertown, Maryland. The marriage produced a son, John, but Mary died soon after, and Zenger moved back to New York. He married Anna Catherine Mulim on September 11, 1822. In 1825, he went into partnership with William Bradford, his former master, leaving the firm in 1826 to open a shop of his own on Smith Street.

New York politics in the 1720s and 1730s was a volatile affair, dominated by ambitious, even greedy, merchants, traders, bankers, and lawyers, who joined factions to compete for profits and government favors. The arrival of Governor William Cosby in 1632 added fuel to the political fires when he removed Lewis Morris as chief justice during a suit brought by Cosby against Rip Van Dam, who had served as interim governor before Cosby's arrival. Cosby wanted half of Van Dam's salary, but Morris sided with Van Dam's lawyers, James Alexander and William Smith. Cosby promptly removed Morris and appointed James Delancey to replace him on the bench.

Morris allied himself with Alexander and Smith and several other prominent New Yorkers to form the "Popular Party" in vocal opposition to the governor. They needed an outlet for their criticism of Cosby, but the existing newspaper and official paper of record in New York was Bradford's *New York Gazette,* and it was controlled by the governor and his supporters.

Morris and Alexander decided that they would start a newspaper. They approached Zenger, who had previously printed several broadsides for the People's Party. He agreed to print what would become the voice of political opposition, the *New York Weekly Journal.* Alexander became managing editor and chief writer, while his cohorts, Van Dam, Morris and others, provided much of the political content in columns, as well as letters to the editor, most of which soundly criticized Governor Cosby and his appointees, charging arrogance, graft, and corruption.

Zenger, a German immigrant with a limited education and a tradesman's understanding of the English language, probably understood little of the politically oriented screed that he printed. Nevertheless, the *New York Weekly Journal* became the first truly free press in the American colonies. It stood out from the usual fare delivered up by colonial newspapers, which were timid publications that reprinted news and stories from England and published government notices and official records, announcements of the arrivals and departures of merchant ships and their cargoes, and merchant's advertising.

Much of the prevailing understanding of freedom of the press was rooted in the ideas expressed in John Milton's *Areopagitica.* Published in 1644, it defended the idea that government must not enforce prior restraint upon publishers by way of licensing presses. This was Milton's appeal to Parliament to void the Licensing Order of June 16, 1643, requiring authors to submit their works to appointed government censors prior to publishing them.

The other popular view of press freedom was included in the ideas expressed in *Cato's Letters,* a series of essays published anonymously in England by Thomas Gordon and John Trenchard between 1720 and 1723. The essays established a compelling foundation for freedom of the press and speech by condemning both prior restraint, as well as subsequent prosecution of articles that criticized government authority. *Cato's Letters* were perhaps the most widely read and discussed series of publications in the colonies. These and Milton's work were undoubtedly major points of reference during Zenger's arrest and trial.

Alexander, as chief writer for the *New York Weekly Journal,* stated a philosophy of freedom of the press justifying the paper's attacks on the government. He explained that it was the duty of the press to act as a check on government actions and power, both exercised with legal impunity, by providing punishment with the "lash of satire" to those government officials who would not otherwise suffer punishment for their actions.

At first, the administration ignored the *New York Weekly Journal,* but as the rhetoric against Cosby increased, both in volume and sarcastic intensity, the governor sought a remedy. This resulted in a formal charge of seditious libel against Zenger, who, as printer of the newspaper, was legally responsible for the articles. Under common law, seditious libel was the serious criminal act of holding the king or his agents in the government up to public ridicule. Moreover, the truth of the libel could not be used as a defense at trial. The fact of the libel itself was proof of guilt.

Unable to convince a grand jury to indict Zenger, Cosby was able to convince the governor's council to respond to the political attacks. On November 6, 1734, the council ordered that four issues of the *New York Weekly Journal* be confiscated and publicly burned. Eleven days later, on November 17, 1734, Zenger was arrested and detained, pending a formal charge, which finally came down as "information" issued by Attorney General Richard Bradley in January 1735.

A formal charge by prosecutor's information was not unusual in the colonies. Fortunately for Zenger, the information contained the word "false" in its reference to the seditious statements. This would provide his attorney a basis for his defense later at trial.

Zenger was ably defended by Alexander and Smith, but they were soon disbarred in an unrelated dispute with the court. Alexander then retained Andrew Hamilton of Philadelphia, regarded by many as Pennsylvania's most accomplished defense attorney. Hamilton surprised the court at the opening of Zenger's trial, on August 4, 1735, by announcing that he was representing the accused.

The prosecutor's case was a simple explanation of the facts of the criminal libels. The printed pages were the evidence. Hamilton began his defense by admitting that Zenger had, in fact, printed the words, but he stated that Zenger had the right to print the truth. He eloquently argued that the decision of the jury, rather than that of a panel of judges, ought to decide this case. The prosecution reiterated that the admission of facts by Zenger proved his guilt, and argued that the law recognized that if the libels were true, the truth was an aggravation of Zenger's guilt because it brought even greater shame and public ridicule upon the governor. Hamilton countered that Zenger was free to print something as long as it was true.

Following closing arguments and Chief Justice Delancey's instructions that the fact of the libels were sufficient for a guilty finding, the jury retired "for a short time." It returned with a contrary verdict of not guilty. Zenger was released from custody the following day.

His acquittal caused an immediate sensation among the public at home, as well as in England. The case, however, established no legal precedent, as a jury's verdict does not change the law. Furthermore, the jury's decision was a clear case of jury nullification. The facts of the case, as well as established law, pointed to a finding of guilt, yet the jury disregarded both facts and law and found Zenger not guilty. The Zenger trial had little impact on law; however, it had great impact on the political views of American colonists. By and large, the colonists regarded the trial results as an eminently sensible and logical ingredient of basic freedom and a necessary means of holding the powers of government in check.

Within a short time after his trial, Zenger, capitalizing on political friendships, obtained government contracts to publish official notices. When Cosby died in 1736, the Popular Party formed by Alexander and Lewis disbanded, so there was no further need for a newspaper to broadcast their opposing viewpoints. The *New York Weekly Journal* became the newspaper of record for New York in 1737 and became, like most other colonial newspapers, a far cry from the critical voice of opposition that it was in 1734. Zenger died at age 49 in 1746. His wife Anna and son John continued publishing the *New York Weekly Journal* until 1751. Zenger eventually became known as the patron saint of American newspaper publishers.

There were no other major prosecutions of criminal libel brought during the remainder of the colonial period, with the notable exception of the William McDougall trial in 1770–1771, which ended with the death of the Crown's principal witness. Colonial legislatures, however, continued the practice of licensing colonial presses and punishing publishers for violating their contracts; thus, they applied both prior restraint and subsequent punishments to individual publishers for publishing information that reflected badly on legislators. Not until the establishment of speech and press freedom clauses in the first state constitutions and, subsequently, the establishment of the First Amendment guarantee of a free press in the Bill of Rights in 1791, did the concept of freedom of the press become widely recognized in the United States. Moreover, there is ample evidence that those state and national protections were aimed at prior restraint only and not at subsequent prosecutions.

James R. Belpedio

See also: Law and Courts; Newspapers and Journals. *Document:* The Trial of Peter Zenger (1735).

Bibliography

Botein, Stephen. *"Mr. Zenger's Malice and Falsehood": Six Issues of the New-York Weekly Journal, 1733–1734.* Worcester, MA: The American Antiquarian Society, 1985.

Finkelman, Paul, ed. *A Brief Narrative of the Case and Tryal of John Peter Zenger, Printer of the New York Weekly Journal.* St. James, NY: Brandywine Press, 1997.

"John Peter Zenger." *Encyclopedia of World Biography.* Farmington Hills, MI: Gale Group, 1998.

Joyce, William, et al. *Printing and Society in Early America.* Worcester, MA: The American Antiquarian Society, 1983.

Levy, Leonard W. "Did the Zenger Case Really Matter? Freedom of the Press in Colonial New York." *William and Mary Quarterly,* 3rd ser. (1960): 35–60.

———. *Emergence of a Free Press.* New York: Oxford University Press, 1985.

Zuni

Situated just west of the continental divide, the town of Zuni sits on the banks of the Zuni River, a tributary of the Little Colorado. The Zuni's relative isolation from the rest of the Pueblo Indians and their unique colonial experience resulted in the development of a distinctive Zuni culture.

A highly secretive people, the Zuni's social, religious, and political system—with its connections to the kinship and clan systems—has defied interpretation by scholars since the nineteenth century. In the most general terms, Zuni society was matrilineal. With a backbone of religious and ceremonial organizations tied to kinship designations, it revolved around religious leaders, who acted as a unit, rather than as individuals.

European interaction with the Zuni began in violence. In 1539, the Zuni met and killed Esteban, a North African who had been a companion of Álvar Núñez Cabeza de Vaca's ill-fated expedition. Esteban arrived at Zuni in advance of the expedition, which was headed by the Franciscan Fray (Father) Marcos de Niza. Fearing for his own safety, Marcos returned to Mexico without entering the city.

Despite the hostility of the Zuni, Marcos's reports prompted more Spanish exploration. When Francisco Vázquez de Coronado passed through Zuni on his return trip to Mexico in 1542, he left behind several Mexican Indians, who were still there when Antonio de Espejo visited the area forty years later.

Zuni contact with Europeans remained sporadic throughout the sixteenth century. When Juan de Oñate led an expedition into their territory in 1598, however, he was greeted warmly. Oñate's expedition soon left the Zuni, as Spanish colonization efforts focused on the Rio Grande Valley.

The first mission to the Zuni began in Hawikuh in 1629. By 1632, the church was built, and a new mission was opened in Hanola (present-day Zuni). The Pueblo Revolt expelled the Spanish in 1680, causing the Zuni missions to lose their friars. When Diego de Vargas reestablished Spanish control in 1692, he found that the Zuni had carefully guarded the ritual objects taken from the churches. Their behavior was the only instance of such action in the area.

At the time of the de Vargas expedition, the Zuni

had abandoned five of their six towns and returned only to the town of Zuni. To some degree, the complex nature of Zuni society may be due to the consolidation of these previously autonomous towns.

After 1692, the Zuni saw no Spanish presence, as colonial effort again focused on the Rio Arriba. Unlike their neighbors in the Rio Grande Valley, the Zuni were not visited by secular Spaniards until 1700, when three exiles from Santa Fe entered the region with three new priests. The three settlers were killed in 1703, apparently for aggressive behavior, thus ending the secular presence. These settlers constituted the last secular Spanish settlement in the Zuni area until Spanish-speaking communities were founded in the 1860s, about 30 miles to the east.

The Franciscan friars, however, continued their residence among the Zuni throughout the eighteenth century. Despite the friars' best effort, the Zuni proved a determined people, who protected their religious ceremonies with their lives; they often performed their ceremonies underground or outside of town, always beyond the prying eyes of their local padre. Finding the Zunis too resistant to their efforts, the Franciscans finally abandoned their missions in 1820. With the departure of the Franciscans, the Spanish presence among the Zuni people ended.

Despite the limited Spanish presence among them, the Zuni adapted some aspects of the colonizers' culture. Like other native peoples, the Zuni incorporated the introduction of these European ways into their own culture, myths, and legends. The heritage of nearly three centuries of Spanish contact included a few metal tools, agricultural products such as wheat, livestock such as sheep and goats, and a variety of concepts and practices that the Zuni altered to fit their belief structure, such as a secular government with parallel religious leadership.

Although the Spanish influence was minimal, it was significant. The Zuni constructed a complex and secretive society, which evolved, in part, in response to their contacts with the Spaniards, who had attempted to put an end to Zuni religious practices. The Spaniards had failed to realize that any change in the Zuni religion would amount to the end of the Zuni culture. While the Zuni developed a social system that incorporated elements of the colonizers' society, they still maintained the integrity of their own religious and cultural mores.

Todd Leahy

See also: Native American–European Conflict; Native American–European Relations; Native Americans.

Bibliography

Davis, Nancy. *The Zuni Enigma.* New York: W. W. Norton, 2000.

Milner, Clyde A., II, Carol A. O'Connor, and Martha A. Sandweiss, eds. *The Oxford History of the American West.* New York: Oxford University Press, 1994.

Sturtevant, William, ed. *Handbook of North American Indians.* Washington, DC: Smithsonian Institution Press, 1983.

Chronologies

Arts, Culture, and Intellectual Life

1624

John Smith publishes *The Generall Historie of Virginia, New-England, and the Summer Isles.* The best known of all of his works, this contains the story of Smith's imprisonment by Powhatan and his subsequent rescue by Pocahontas, one of the most enduring legends in American history.

The period of Smith's literary productivity spans twenty-three years—from the earlier publication of *A True Relation of . . . Virginia* (1608), to the publication of *Advertisements for the Unexperienced Planters of New England* (1631). As noted by Norman S. Grabo and Russel B. Nye in *American Thought and Writing, Volume I: The Colonial Period,* Smith's writings "form the first substantial body of literary work done in and about America."

1630

William Bradford begins writing *Of Plymouth Plantation.* Ostensibly a history of the Plymouth Colony, it is also intended to be a record of God's workings in the New World and an interpretation of God's divine plan for His Puritan saints.

Bradford will work on the manuscript until 1650, but he will never complete it. The manuscript will disappear at the time of the American Revolution, during the British occupation of Boston, and not surface again until 1855, when it will be found in the library of the Bishop of London. Bradford's work will be published the following year and returned to America in 1897.

1636

Harvard University is founded as Harvard College in Cambridge, Massachusetts.

1638

Stephen Daye and Elizabeth Glover establish the first printing press in North America in Cambridge, Massachusetts. In the first year of operation, the press produces the colonies' first two imprints. The first, *The Freeman's Oath,* is only one paragraph long; the second is *An Almanac Calculated for New England by Mr. Pierce, Mariner.*

Upon Glover's death in 1643, the press will become the property of Henry Dunster, her second husband and president of Harvard. Dunster will waste no time in allying the press closely with the college, and it will become the foundation for the publishing house known since 1913 as Harvard University Press.

1640

Elizabeth Glover's printing press produces *The Whole Booke of Psalmes Faithfully Translated into English Metre,* also known as *The Bay Psalm Book.* A collaborative translation of the Hebrew psalms of David by some of the most influential Puritans in the Massachusetts Bay Colony, *The Bay Psalm Book* provides an accurate, affordable, plainspoken alternative to the Sternhold-Hopkins Psalter of 1562, the psalm book most commonly used by the Plymouth Colony Pilgrims and the English Puritans.

The Bay Psalm Book is the first book to be both written and printed in North America. It also is one of the three most commonly owned books in seventeenth-century New England—the Bible and *The New England Primer* (1690) being the other two.

1641

In Boston, William Read paints the first colonial portrait. The subject of the portrait is the governor of Massachusetts, Richard Bellingham.

1650

The Tenth Muse Lately Sprung Up in America; or Several Poems Compiled with Great Variety and Wit, etc., by Anne Bradstreet, is taken to England by Bradstreet's brother-in-law, Reverend John Woodbridge, and published without her knowledge or consent. *The Tenth Muse* is the first book of poetry published by anyone, man or woman, living in the colonies of British North America. The poems in this collection are linguistically and rhetorically accomplished; they are, however, for the most part, conventional and derivative, more products of Bradstreet's poetic influences than they are of her individual poetic voice.

A second, revised edition of *The Tenth Muse,* titled *Several Poems Compiled with Great Variety of Wit and Learning, Full of Delight,* will be published in 1678, six years after the author's death. As Pattie Cowell comments in her essay on Bradstreet, which appears in the fourth edition of *The Heath Anthology of American Literature,* edited by Paul Lauter, "this later work . . . develops from the conventional public verse of the first edition to more private themes of family, love, nature, sorrow, faith, and resignation."

1662

The Reverend Michael Wigglesworth, minister to the town of Malden, Massachusetts, publishes *The Day of Doom; or, A Poetical Description of the Great and Last Judgment.* Inspired by a dream he had ten days after the death of his father, *The Day of Doom* is an epic poem in which Wigglesworth describes Judgment Day in vivid detail and illustrates the urgent need for repentance, as well as the promise of redemption. The poem is an instant best-seller; the entire press run of the first edition (1,800 copies) is sold out within the year.

As popular and accomplished as it is, *The Day of Doom* is not Wigglesworth's only poetic achievement; indeed, it is not even his only best-seller. His next work, *Meat Out of the Eater or Meditations Concerning the Necessity, End, and Usefulness of Afflictions unto God's Children, etc.* (1669), will fall just shy of equaling *The Day of Doom*'s success and popularity.

1665

The first play performed in North America, *The Bare and the Cubb,* by William Darby, is presented in Accomac County, Virginia. The play shocks local residents; one in particular, a man named Edward Martin, files a charge of public wickedness against Darby, Cornelius Watkinson, and Philip Howard, the three men responsible for the play's production. So that their innocence or guilt can be properly determined, the accused are ordered to perform the play, in full costume, before the local magistrate. The magistrate, seeing nothing untoward in the performance, dismisses all charges against the three men and orders their accuser to pay the court costs.

1670

In Boston, John Foster creates the first art print ever produced in colonial America. As David Bjelajac demonstrates in *American Art: A Cultural History,* the print is done in a straightforward, unadorned style that mirrors the reputed preaching style of its subject. The woodcut depicts the Reverend Richard Mather, dressed in the stark black raiment of the scholarly divine, holding a small pair of reading glasses and pointing to a book he holds open in his left hand. The woodcut is created a year after Reverend Mather's death, possibly as a frontispiece to a biography written by his son, Increase Mather.

John Foster will go on to construct Boston's first press in 1675 and to produce, in 1677, *A Map of New England,* the first map ever printed in America.

1682

Edward Taylor, minister to the town of Westfield, Massachusetts, and one of colonial America's greatest poets, begins composing *Preparatory Meditations Before My Approach to the Lord's Supper.* As Alan Shucard explains in *American Poetry: The Puritans Through Walt Whitman,* Taylor composed these meditations on human depravity, God's goodness and mercy, and the hope for God's grace "every other month for 43 years [as a way] to prepare himself spiritually for the next Lord's Supper, or Eucharist."

Although his most remarkable achievement, *Preparatory Meditations* is not Taylor's only contribution to American poetry. In addition to writing *God's Determinations Touching His Elect: and the Elects Combat in Their Conversion, and Coming Up to God in Christ Together with the Comfortable Effects Thereof* (c. 1685), he also will compose love poems, elegies, Biblical paraphrases, meditations, lyrics, and the 20,000-line *Metrical History of Christianity.*

Mary White Rowlandson publishes *The Soveraignty and Goodness of God, Together with the Faithfulness of His Promises Displayed; Being a Narrative of the Captivity and Restauration of Mrs. Mary Rowlandson.* A detailed account of her abduction by, her treatment at the hands of, and her eventual release from a band of Algonquin natives during King Philip's War, the book is one of the earliest best-sellers written in North America and the first one written by a woman. In the first year alone, Rowlandson's *Narrative* goes through four printings. Along with John Smith's story of his capture and imprisonment by Powhatan and his subsequent rescue by Pocahontas, Rowlandson's *Narrative* is one of the most important contributions to the American genre of the captivity narrative.

1684

An issue of the *London Gazette* is reprinted in Boston, marking the first time a newspaper is produced in America.

1690

The New England Primer is published in Boston. Part reader, part spelling book, part religious/historical text, it combines literacy with moral and religious instruction in an attempt to provide young Puritans with the tools necessary to ensure the continued viability of their individual spiritual lives—and, by extension, the continued viability of the spiritual life of the community—while simultaneously placing that individuality in the context of culturally sanctioned behavior. *The New England Primer* is hugely popular, and it will sell nearly 5 million copies by 1830.

In Boston, Benjamin Harris prints *Publick Occurrences.* This would have been the first monthly news publication printed in colonial America. Unfortunately, Harris fails to acquire the proper licenses, and publication of *Publick Occurrences* is halted after only one issue.

1693

The College of William and Mary is founded.

1695

Dinah Nuthead, upon the death of her husband, William, assumes control of the printing press he had established in St. Mary's, Maryland, ten years earlier. She becomes North America's first female printer. (Although Elizabeth Glover was the first woman to establish a printing press in North America, her son and her late husband's apprentice handled the press's day-to-day operation. Dinah Nuthead was the first woman in North America who actually set the type and ran the press herself.)

1701

Yale University is founded as the Collegiate School of Connecticut.

1702

Cotton Mather publishes *Magnalia Christi Americana; or The Ecclesiastical History of New England from its First Planting,* the most celebrated of his more than 400 published works. The *Magnalia* contains a history of New England, biographies of various colonial authorities and Puritan divines, a history of Harvard College, descriptions of the state of the churches, accounts of providential occurrences, and descriptions of the "Wars of the Lord."

1704

John Campbell, postmaster of Boston, begins publishing the *Boston News-Letter,* North America's first newspaper published on a regular basis. Since his readers are more interested in European news and gossip than they are in what is happening in the colonies, Campbell dedicates the *Boston News-Letter* primarily to goings-on overseas.

1707

Robert Feke, the first great native-born American painter and the first painter to evolve a uniquely American style of painting, is born in Oyster Bay, Long Island. Unlike more traditional artists such as John Smibert, who received formal artistic training in Europe, Feke will rely on instinct, intuition, and natural ability to compose his paintings, not on any formal artistic theory. As a result, his paintings will be endowed with a realism and clarity that is lacking in Smibert's work, and Feke's paintings will become more popular with the colonists, who are, themselves, unschooled in the particulars of art and art history.

In 1741, Feke will paint his masterpiece, *Isaac Royall and His Family.* The painting will bear a striking resemblance to Smibert's *The Bermuda Group—Dean George Berkeley and His Family,* and it will be obvious that Feke used it as a model for his own work.

1708

Henrietta Dering Johnston emigrates with her husband from Ireland to South Carolina. Johnston is the first female painter to work in the North American colonies. She is also the first American pastelist.

1710–1735

A small group of Hudson Valley artists known as the Patroon Painters—so-called because they make their livings painting the portraits of New York's wealthy, upper-class landowners, or "patroons"—ply their talents from New York City to Albany. The Patroon Painters are native-born American artists, who have neither the luxury of formal artistic training nor the benefit of any great masters with whom study is possible. Instead, they rely for inspiration and instruction on mezzotints imported from England; as a result, most of the paintings attributed to the Patroon Painters are little more than local versions of European originals.

1714

The first play printed in North America is published. Written by Robert Hunter, the governor of New York, *Androboros; A Biographical Farce in Three Acts,* is a satire in the tradition of Jonathan Swift. In *Androboros,* Hunter lampoons the machinations of colonial politics, ridicules New York's local government, and mocks his political adversaries.

Some of Hunter's most biting satire is reserved for the play's title character, Androboros, a treacherous rabble-rouser, who ends up falling victim to the very trap by which he intends to ensnare the Keeper. The Keeper is a barely disguised depiction of Governor Hunter himself, while Androboros is a thinly disguised portrait of Francis Nicholson, one of Hunter's most reviled enemies. The play is never produced.

1716

William Levingston, a successful merchant, builds the first American playhouse on the Palace Green in Williamsburg, Virginia. His indentured servants, Charles and Mary Stagg, help him in this venture; in addition to being Levingston's servants, they are also actors and dancing masters.

Plays are performed here until the playhouse eventually falls into a state of neglect and is converted into a town hall in 1745.

1719

William Brooker succeeds James Campbell as postmaster of Boston and begins publishing the *Boston Gazette,* the second regularly published newspaper established in British North America. Almost identical to the *Boston News-Letter* in both style and content, the founding of the *Boston Gazette* creates America's first competitive newspaper market.

1721

The first music textbook printed in North America, *A Very Plain and Easy Introduction to the Whole Art of Singing Psalm Tunes,* is published in Massachusetts by Reverend John Tufts. By 1682, with those who could read music firmly in the minority, the practice of psalm singing in the colonies lacked even a modicum of regularity and had become, in many places, a cacophonous, ear-splitting din. Tufts's *Introduction,* it is hoped, will restore a degree of musical literacy to the colonies; the textbook also is intended to put an end to the musical butchery caused by "lining out." This system of psalm singing is described by Thomas L. Purvis in *Colonial*

America to 1763 as that by which a precentor "who [is] typically a church elder, [sings] a psalm line by line, with pauses in between each that [allow] the congregation to repeat the stanza in his meter and melody."

After losing the printing contract for William Brooker's *Boston Gazette,* Benjamin Franklin's brother, James, begins publishing *The New England Courant,* the third regularly produced newspaper established in the American colonies. Unlike the stiff and torpid reporting that characterizes the *Boston News-Letter* and the *Boston Gazette,* the *New England Courant* is designed to entertain, amuse, and stimulate readers. Benjamin Franklin, writing under the pseudonym of Silence Dogwood, frequently contributes satirical essays to the *Courant,* and he will briefly assume the paper's editorship, when his brother is jailed on contempt charges in 1722.

1727

Now in Philadelphia, Benjamin Franklin establishes the Junto, a combination intellectual society and mutual improvement club. According to the rules Franklin drafts to govern the society, meetings are to be held every Friday evening, and members are required to arrive at those meetings prepared to discuss and debate the moral, political, and philosophical questions that had been posed at the previous week's meeting and to raise new questions for discussion the following week. Members are also required to write and present an original essay on a topic of their choosing once every three months. Franklin's Junto remains active for forty years, longer than any other colonial American society of its kind.

North America's first circulating library—the Philadelphia Library Company, established by Franklin in 1731—will be a direct result of the Junto. In 1743, the Junto also will become the foundation upon which Franklin will build the American Philosophical Society, North America's first scientific association.

1728

Peter Pelham's portrait of Cotton Mather is the first mezzotint produced in North America.

1729

William Burgis creates *The Boston Lighthouse,* North America's first maritime print. It depicts a British ship anchored near the first colonial lighthouse.

Scottish-born John Smibert, the first professional artist to achieve success in America, opens a studio/art gallery in Boston. A member of the group led by Dean George Berkeley to establish a college in Bermuda, Smibert decides to stay in the colonies after the group receives word that Parliament has cut off the college's funding. It is for *The Bermuda Group—Dean George Berkeley and His Family*, the painting of those involved in the ill-fated project for which Smibert is best known.

One year later, Smibert will hold an art exhibition in his Boston studio that will be the first such exhibit ever held in America. He will retire in 1746, after having completed more than 250 portraits.

1732

Benjamin Franklin first publishes *Poor Richard's Almanack* under the pseudonym Richard Saunders. Richard Saunders is more than just a pseudonym, however; he is a persona. The adages attributed to this fictional henpecked stargazer—such proverbs as "It is hard for an empty sack to stand upright," and "Keep thy shop, and thy shop will keep thee" that Franklin intersperses among the usual weather forecasts and important dates—are what makes Franklin's almanacs more popular than any others published in the colonies. By Franklin's own account, *Poor Richard's Almanack* will sell an average of 10,000 copies a year over the next twenty-five years.

1735

Flora, or Hob in the Well, the first opera performed in North America, is presented in the courthouse in Charles Town, South Carolina, as is the Thomas Otway tragedy, *The Orphan.* So successful are these performances, a theater will be constructed in 1736 to better accommodate the audiences; unfortunately, the New Theatre in Dock Street lasts only four years, burning down in 1740.

Gustavus Hesselius, a Swedish-born artist who has been living in colonial North America since 1711, paints the portraits of two Lenni Lenape (Delaware) chieftains, Lapowinsa and Tishcohan. As Wayne Craven states in *American Art: History and Culture,* these portraits are "the first lifesize [sic], bustlength [sic] images of Native Americans painted by a white artist in colonial America."

1738

John Singleton Copley, the greatest native-born colonial American painter, is born in Boston. As a portraitist, Copley is unsurpassed. He has the ability to idealize his subject's features without sacrificing the person's individuality, as well as to render a truthful representation of the person without the result being coarse or unpleasant. It is this ability to strike a delicate balance between the ideal and the real that makes him, by 1766, one of the most sought-after portraitists in colonial America.

In 1765, *Boy with a Squirrel,* Copley's portrait of his stepbrother, Henry Pelham, introduces his work to an admiring international audience, when it is entered in the annual exhibition of the Society of Artists in London.

1741

North America's first two magazines appear in Philadelphia. The first, Andrew Bradford's *American Magazine, or A Monthly View of the Political State of the British Colonies,* makes its debut on February 13; Benjamin Franklin's *General Magazine, and Historical Chronicle, For All the British Plantations in America* appears three days later. Both magazines rely heavily on their

British predecessors and counterparts for inspiration, and both are primarily concerned with political issues.

At least half of the *American Magazine*'s total page count is devoted to news of the proceedings of various colonial assemblies, with articles on such topics as colonial history, foreign politics, money, religion, and the weather accounting for the other half. By contrast, political news comprises only one-third of Franklin's *General Magazine;* the remaining space is devoted to articles on religion and finance, as well as to such things as historical sketches, poetry, dialogues, and current events. The *American Magazine* lasts for only three issues; the *General Magazine* lasts for six.

1745

Dr. Alexander Hamilton (not to be confused with the Alexander Hamilton who served as George Washington's Secretary of the Treasury) founds the Ancient and Honorable Tuesday Club in Annapolis, Maryland. The club functions as a kind of cultural training ground, a place where affluent and would-be affluent members of colonial American society go to learn how to behave like sophisticates. Club members discuss all things of cultural interest, from literature and painting to architecture and musical compositions.

Robert Feke paints a portrait of Brigadier General Samuel Waldo to commemorate the role Waldo played in the New England militia's victory over the French at Louisbourg, Nova Scotia. Feke's portrait of Waldo is one of the first three paintings done in North America explicitly to commemorate the deeds of great men. The other two portraits, both done by John Smibert, are of Sir William Pepperrell and Sir Peter Warren, both of whom, along with Waldo, led the Louisbourg campaign.

1746

Princeton University is founded as the College of New Jersey.

1749

The first professional American theater company begins performing European plays in Philadelphia. Headed by Walter Murray and Thomas Kean, the troupe moves to New York City in 1750, where they perform at the First Nassau Street Theatre until 1751. From New York, the company moves south, performing in Williamsburg and various other towns in Virginia and Maryland. Unable to compete with the theatrical company led by Lewis Hallam, the Murray-Kean troupe dissolves shortly after Hallam's arrival in the colonies in 1752.

Benjamin Franklin publishes *Proposals Relating to the Education of Youth in Pensilvania.* In this pamphlet, he asserts the importance of education to both familial and communal well being, laments that Pennsylvania does not possess a college or academy for the education of its youth, argues for the necessity of establishing such an institution, and suggests a curriculum.

Franklin's *Proposals* will lead to the establishment of the Philadelphia Academy in 1751. In 1755, the Philadelphia Academy will become the College of Philadelphia; in 1791, the school will become known as the University of Pennsylvania.

1754

Columbia University is founded as King's College in New York City.

Jonathan Edwards publishes *A Careful and Strict Enquiry into the Modern Prevailing Notions of that Freedom of the Will, Which is Supposed to be Essential to . . . Praise and Blame,* his masterwork. In *Freedom of the Will,* Edwards argues that the nature of the human will is of the utmost importance, because people are not predisposed to either good or evil deeds, even though they are born already in a fallen state. According to Edwards, human beings do not possess free will but are, nonetheless, free to do that which their wills allow. It is this freedom, and no other, that has been granted to the human race. *Freedom of the Will* is hailed immediately as a major philosophical treatise, and it is adopted as a textbook by several colleges, including Yale, Edwards's alma mater.

1755

Thomas Johnston produces *A Prospective Plan of the Battle Fought Near Lake George on the 8th of September 1755,* the first engraving of a historical event ever produced in America.

1762

The St. Cecelia Society, the first organization in North America devoted entirely to secular music, is formed in Charles Town, South Carolina. The society is composed primarily of amateur performers, though professional musicians are also engaged on a seasonal basis. The society will regularly offer concerts until its dissolution in 1912.

1764

Brown University is founded as the College of Rhode Island.

Two plays dealing explicitly with the circumstances of the Paxton Rebellion are published anonymously. In December 1763, angered by concessions made to Native Americans and by the inability of the colonial authorities to protect them and safeguard their interests, a group of fifty settlers, known as the Paxton Boys, from Pennsylvania's western provinces, had attacked the peaceful native village of Conestoga and slaughtered the inhabitants. The following January, when colonial authorities attempted to arrest those responsible, the Paxton Boys were joined by 550 of their fellow frontiersmen in a march on Philadelphia. Only Benjamin Franklin's skillful negotiations with the leader of the rebels, Lazarus Stewart, averted a murderous disaster.

Both plays about these events, *The Paxton Boys* and *A Dialogue, Containing Some Reflections on the Late Declaration and Remonstrance, of the Back-Inhabitants of the Province of Pennsylvania,* treat the Paxton Rebellion with derision and contempt and encourage American settlers to remain loyal to the British Crown. The rebels, as well as those colonists who are sympathetic to their cause, are portrayed as cowardly and treacherous, while good citizens are shown to be those men and women who are still loyal British subjects. *The Paxton Boys* is the first American play to feature Native Americans as characters.

1766

Rutgers University is founded as Queen's College in New Brunswick, New Jersey.

The Southwark Theatre, North America's first permanent theater, opens in Philadelphia.

Major Robert Rogers publishes *Ponteach, or the Savages of America,* the first American play to feature a Native American as the leading character and the first play written with a uniquely American theme. While Rogers in *Ponteach* (pronounced Pontiac) presents Native Americans as noble, benevolent human beings, whose rebellions against the British are justified, he depicts his fellow colonists as cruel, greedy, amoral thugs. The traders cheat the native peoples and get them drunk, the hunters kill them for amusement, the military is completely indifferent to their plight, and the colonial authorities steal from them. Rogers even portrays members of the clergy as being rapacious and conniving in their dealings with the indigenous peoples of North America.

It is this pro-native/anti-British colonial slant that marks *Ponteach* as a significant ideological shift in American playwriting. By finding fault with the manner in which the indigenous peoples are treated by the British and by suggesting that their rebellion is understandable, perhaps even defensible, Rogers, a former major in the British army, is the first colonial playwright even to imply that any kind of rebellious behavior against the British government might be justified. *Ponteach* is never performed.

1767

David Douglass's American Company presents *The Prince of Parthia* at the Southwark Theatre in Philadelphia. Written by Thomas Godfrey, Jr., *The Prince of Parthia* is the first play written by a native-born American playwright ever to be performed on the American stage by a professional theater company. It is the story of an evil prince (Vardanes) who convinces his father (King Artabanus) to imprison his brother (Arsaces) because he resents his brother's skill on the battlefield and because his brother has won the love of a woman (Evanthe) for whom both he and his father lust. A third brother (Gotarzes) learns of the plot and attempts to free Arsaces; although he is successful, word that Arsaces has been killed reaches Evanthe, and she kills herself. Unable to live without her, Arsaces, too, commits suicide, leaving Gotarzes to pick up the pieces. Hopelessly tedious and dull in the extreme, the play is performed only once.

Thomas Forrest (under the pseudonym Andrew Barton) writes *The Disappointment, or the Force of Credulity,* the first comic opera composed in North America. As George O. Seilhamer explains in *History of the American Theatre: Before*

the Revolution, *The Disappointment* satirizes the popular colonial belief that Blackbeard (Edward Teach) hid his pirate booty on the banks of the Delaware River, near Cooper's Point, and that he killed a prisoner and buried him with the loot so that the man's ghost would guard the area and frighten away treasure hunters. Consequently, any report of anything even remotely supernatural happening in the vicinity of Cooper's Point is enough to get the superstitious and the gullible running for two things: their shovels and someone with a knowledge of the black arts, who can help them find the exact spot where the treasure is buried and cast a spell of protection around the area to ward off the angry ghost.

The existence of such a colorful myth, along with the presence of such unbelievably gullible people, is fertile soil, indeed, for the playing of practical jokes. It is one of these jokes, played by Forrest himself on his tailor and a printer named Ambruster, that supplies the play's subject matter. Though the first performance of *The Disappointment* is scheduled to take place at Philadelphia's Southwark Theatre on April 20, the performance is canceled and never rescheduled. In fact, the play is never produced. It does, however, mark the first appearance of an Irish character in an American drama.

1769

Dartmouth College is founded in Hanover, New Hampshire.

1771

Benjamin Franklin begins work on his *Autobiography*. The most important and influential of his many and varied literary compositions, the *Autobiography* is divided into three sections. As David M. Larson notes in his essay on Franklin, which appears in the fourth edition of Paul Lauter's *Heath Anthology of American Literature,* "the first section tells the story of Franklin's youth and young manhood in Boston and Philadelphia, viewing the protagonist, the young Franklin, as though he were a character in a novel. . . . The second section . . . recounts Franklin's youthful attempt to achieve moral perfection [and] the third section . . . portrays the adult Franklin's use of the principles of conduct that he discovered in the first section and enumerated in the second [and] focuses on his rise to prosperity, his scientific studies, and . . . his work as philanthropist and politician." Franklin will work on his *Autobiography* until 1788, but he will never actually complete it.

1772

Mercy Otis Warren, the most prolific writer of pro-American independence propaganda plays, publishes *The Adulateur: A Tragedy as it is Now Acted in Upper Servia.* It is the first of her three dramas that satirize colonists still loyal to the British Crown and portray British officials as greedy, dishonest hypocrites; *The Defeat* (1773) and *The Group* (1775) are the other two.

Mrs. Warren is particularly fond of lampooning the

governor of Massachusetts, Thomas Hutchinson, who is not only perceived to be a treacherous British loyalist, but is also the man the patriots blame for the Boston Massacre and the Boston Tea Party. In both *The Adulateur* and *The Defeat,* Hutchinson is portrayed as a despicable traitor, who will do anything for money and power and who has no love or concern for the common people.

By the time *The Group* is published, Hutchinson has been called back to England, so Warren is forced to find other targets for her vicious wit. As it happens, Hutchinson's brother and father-in-law are still very much on the political scene, and she attacks them with as much vehemence as she did their unfortunate relative. Two weeks after *The Group* is published in Boston, the Revolutionary War begins. As S. E. Wilmer points out in *Theatre, Society and the Nation: Staging American Identities,* it is a war the play both predicts and encourages.

1773

Phillis Wheatley publishes *Poems on Various Subjects, Religious and Moral,* the first book ever published by an African American. Published in London, this collection of thirty-nine poems is Wheatley's second volume of poetry. In 1772, she tried to publish a volume containing twenty-eight poems on such topics as morality, piety, American patriotism, and race (her poem "Thoughts on Being Brought from Africa to America" was to have appeared in that volume), but she failed to secure the number of subscribers necessary for publication. Her third volume of poetry, which will contain thirty-three poems and thirteen letters, will meet a similar fate in 1779. The first American edition of *Poems on Various Subjects, Religious and Moral* will appear in Philadelphia in 1786, two years after Wheatley's death.

Jay Hopler

Economy, Business, and Labor

1497

An Italian sea captain in English service, John Cabot (Giovanni Caboto), discovers cod fisheries off the coast of America. The news spreads rapidly in Europe.

1501

King Henry VII of England grants a monopoly of American trade to some Bristol and Portuguese merchants.

1512

The Spanish government gives a charter to Juan Ponce de Léon's expedition authorizing the taking of Native American slaves.

1521

A Spanish slave-raiding party lands in present-day South Carolina, kidnapping natives to work in the Caribbean.

1543

The Spanish government ineffectively bans enslavement of Native Americans in its New World possessions.

1562

The English captain John Hawkins lands in West Africa to take on a cargo of slaves destined for the Spanish colonies in America. This is the first English slave-trading voyage. British involvement in the African slave trade will be marginal until the 1640s.

1573

The Spanish Crown issues the "Orders for New Discoveries." These orders establish the legal regime under which New Mexico will be colonized; they envision an economy based on *encomiendas* (grants of land and local rule), as well as exacting tribute from Native Americans.

1576–1578

The English sailor Martin Frobisher makes his first voyage to the Arctic in 1576 in search of the Northwest Passage. He returns with what he believes is gold ore.

In 1577, Frobisher makes a second voyage to the Arctic. In addition to more "gold ore," his return cargo includes enslaved Inuits, who die shortly after arriving in England. The following year, Frobisher sails once more to the Arctic; however, his "treasure" is revealed to be worthless iron pyrite, or fool's gold.

1582

The Spanish government sends African slaves to work in St. Augustine, Florida.

1586

Returned Virginia colonists introduce tobacco smoking to English society. (Previously, only sailors had smoked tobacco.)

1606

The Virginia Company is chartered by James I.

1607–1608

The English colony of Jamestown is founded in 1607. The following year, a glassworks is built at the colony.

1612

John Rolfe introduces the cultivation of mild, "Spanish" tobacco with seeds smuggled from the Caribbean to Jamestown. This tobacco will prove far more valuable as an export than the harsher local variety, and it will become the foundation of the Chesapeake tobacco trade.

1614

A group of Amsterdam merchants, organized as the New Netherland Company, receives a charter from the States-General of the Dutch Republic granting a monopoly for four fur-trading voyages to the recently explored area of the Hudson River. The profitable venture, which includes the establishment of a permanent trading post at Fort Nassau (south of present-day Albany), increases interest in the area among Dutch merchants.

The Spanish king, Philip III, requires, on pain of death, that all Spanish colonial export tobacco be shipped to Seville. The problems this creates for the Spanish tobacco trade help open the door for exports from the Chesapeake.

The earliest exports of tobacco from Virginia are recorded.

The first saltworks in the British American colonies is established in Virginia.

1619

The first slave ship to arrive in British North America lands at Jamestown. The Dutch vessel sells twenty African slaves to the colonists, who treat the slaves similarly to indentured servants.

1620

The first tannery in the British North American colonies is founded at Jamestown.

1621

The Dutch government charters the West India Company to control trade with West Africa and the Americas.

1622

Native American attacks on the Virginia colony destroy early Virginia industries. Virginia's trade will now be based almost entirely on tobacco.

1624

The Virginia Company's charter is revoked.

King James I of England establishes a royal tobacco monopoly.

1626

Eleven slaves arrive in the first importation of slaves into New Netherland.

1628

The New England Company is organized.

1629

To encourage colonization, the Dutch West India Company sells patroonships, combining quasi-feudal rights over large territories with the right to trade fur, fish, and other commodities.

The New England Company sends six shipwrights to Salem to build fishing vessels. This is the beginning of commercial shipbuilding in New England.

1632

In Paris, Father Gabriel Sagard, a missionary of the Recollect order, publishes an account of his journeys among the Huron. To encourage investment in the area by French businessmen, he describes the copper mines of the Lake Superior region, although he does not claim to have seen them himself.

1638

By early October, the first printing business in British America is in operation in Cambridge, Massachusetts.

The first large-scale American textile business is founded at Rowley, Massachusetts.

1643

John Winthrop, Jr., then visiting England, creates a Company of Undertakers of the Iron Works in New England. Winthrop returns to the Massachusetts Bay Colony with financial backing, materials, and a company of skilled workers.

1644

Construction begins on a blast furnace for smelting iron ore in Braintree, Massachusetts. The General Court of Massachusetts issues Winthrop a monopoly on iron manufacture.

1645

The Jesuit missionary Father Lallemant learns of the salt springs of the Onondaga people in what is now upstate New York.

1646

The first American mechanical patent is issued by the Massachusetts Bay Colony to Joseph Jenks. It gives him exclusive rights for fourteen years to his improvements in sawmills and scythes.

1647

The first known export (from Massachusetts to the West Indies) of live horses from the British American colonies occurs.

1650

The Iroquois, whose principal European trading partners are the Dutch, are victorious over the French-allied Huron in the so-called Beaver Wars. This establishes them as the dominant Native American force in the fur trade, forcing French-Canadian fur traders farther west.

1651

The English Parliament's First Navigation Act requires that all goods imported into England be carried in English vessels. The principal target of this legislation is the Netherlands.

1652

The Massachusetts General Court votes to establish a mint in Boston; it also incorporates a company to provide water to the city.

1653

The Royal Navy begins buying masts for its ships in New England.

1660

A new navigation act passed by the British Parliament requires that all goods imported or exported from the colonies must be carried in British or colonial vessels. It also mandates that sailors and merchants be English and requires the colonists to export some goods—such as sugar, tobacco, and wool—only within the British Empire.

The Royal Company of Adventurers into Africa, a British group involved in the slave trade and other African trades, is chartered.

1662

A modification to the Navigation Act requires that merchant vessels be built within the British Empire to avoid paying duties.

1663

Governor William Berkeley of Virginia publishes *Discourse and View of Virginia*, advocating that the colony develop a more diverse economy with less reliance on tobacco.

The Staple Act requires that most products destined for the colonies that are produced in Europe (outside Britain) first pass through England to be loaded onto ships from Britain or the colonies.

The Royal Company of Adventurers into Africa receives a new charter. Unlike the 1660 document, it specifically mentions the slave trade. The company is unsuccessful in breaking into the Dutch-dominated market.

1667

Much of the Virginia tobacco fleet is seized by the Dutch, who are at war with the British.

1670

The Hudson's Bay Company is founded.

1672

The Royal African Company, an English slave-trading group, is established. Unlike previous groups, it is dominated by businessmen rather than courtiers, and it will prove to be more successful.

1673

Still at war with Britain, a Dutch fleet seizes half of the Virginia tobacco fleet and scatters much of the rest. The Dutch also shut down the Newfoundland fishing ground.

The British government imposes duties on goods shipped between colonies.

Jesuit missionaries Louis Jolliet and Jacques Marquette discover coal deposits in the Illinois region.

1675

The Governor and Council of New York charter a joint-stock company, the New York Fishing Company, for developing the regional fishing industry.

1676

At a Quaker meeting in Rhode Island, William Edmundson attacks slavery. His speech is the first known Quaker protest against slavery in America.

1677

In New England, the British colonists' victory in King Philip's War is followed by enslavement of many of the surviving natives.

1680

The Pueblo revolt in New Mexico destroys the *encomienda* system and leads Spanish authorities to decrease their use of forced native labor.

1682

William Penn, governor of the new colony of Pennsylvania, charters a joint-stock company, the Free Society of Traders in Pennsylvania, with substantial endowments of land. Although the society eventually erects factories and mills on some of its land, it proves to be a failure.

1684

The French government orders its Canadian colony to send Iroquois prisoners to France to serve as galley slaves. This is the only known case of a European government demanding Native American slaves for labor in Europe.

1685

The governor of New York licenses Captain Johannes Rosenboom to trade with the western New York Native Americans; this is in defiance of French claims over the area.

1688

The Boston mint is closed by order of the English government.

The first large colonial pottery works is set up at Burlington, New Jersey, by the governor, Daniel Coxe. The effort is short-lived.

1690

William Rittenhouse and William Bradford construct the first paper mill in the colonies at Germantown, Pennsylvania.

This year also marks the approximate beginning of large-scale cultivation of rice for export in South Carolina.

1692

Arnout Viele, a Dutchman in English service, makes the first fur-trading expedition from Albany to Native American settlements in the Ohio Valley.

1693

Jesuits in French North America petition the governor of Canada to halt the trade in enslaved natives, which they claim hinders efforts at conversion. The governor accedes to their request, but the new prohibition is initially ineffective.

1696

The Board of Trade, a department of the British government to oversee trade with the colonies, is founded.

A parliamentary act establishes vice-admiralty courts in America.

The first known slave to be imported directly from Africa arrives in South Carolina.

South Carolina enacts an extensive slave code modeled on Barbadian slave law.

1697

Massachusetts fixes the value of the Spanish dollar at six shillings. Spanish dollars are widely used throughout the colonies as currency.

1698

A parliamentary act ends the Royal African Company's monopoly on the African slave trade.

To combat smuggling, the British government requires that tobacco imports be in hogsheads rather than shipped loose in bulk.

1699

To protect markets for English-made woolen goods, British law forbids the export of raw wool, yarn, or fabric from the colonies to England. The law also forbids the use of a horse, cart, or carriage to move these goods from one colony to another.

1700

The Massachusetts judge Samuel Sewall, involved in a legal case over a slave promised freedom by his master, publishes *The Selling of Joseph*, one of the first American tracts against slavery. Sewall stops short of advocating abolition, instead calling for the end of slave importations from Africa.

The Pennsylvania Money Act values a Spanish dollar at nearly eight shillings, hoping to attract specie.

1702

The first evidence appears of London-style coffeehouses—the Pennsylvania, Carolina, and New England Coffee Houses—devoted to meetings of foreign traders with North American colonists.

1704

The Board of Trade, accepting the Massachusetts valuation, fixes the value of the Spanish dollar in the colonies at six shillings. This is known as the proclamation rate and is ignored in some of the colonies.

Former South Carolina governor James Moore, with the backing of the South Carolina Assembly, invades Spanish Florida with a private army of Englishmen and Creek Indians, taking thousands of Native American slaves, mostly women and children.

1705

The first copper mine in British America is opened near Simsbury, Connecticut.

The Virginia Slave Code incorporates a number of previous laws relating to slavery and establishes that conversion to Christianity does not free a slave.

Parliament's new bounties on such naval stores as tar, pitch, and turpentine lead to a rapid expansion of this industry in the pine-rich Carolinas. The Carolinas soon surpass New England as the leading producer of naval stores.

1706

The growth of the South Carolina rice industry leads Parliament to add rice to those commodities that colonies are forbidden to export outside of the British Empire.

1707

The Act of Union between England and Scotland opens up Britain's American colonies to Scottish trade and emigration.

1708

Valuation of the Spanish dollar in the colonies at six shillings is confirmed by parliamentary statute.

1710

Work begins on a new, 1,600-foot wharf in Boston's harbor. It will be completed in 1713.

1711

A force of Creeks, Chickasaws, and South Carolinians invades the Choctaw country, capturing and enslaving several hundred Choctaws.

1712

Captain Christopher Hussey of Nantucket locates schools of sperm whales in the North Atlantic, a discovery that begins the deep-sea sperm whale trade.

The French government hands over control of Louisiana to a private trading company headed by the financier Antoine Crozat.

A slave uprising in New York City results in the death of ten white colonists and the burning of many buildings. After the uprising is suppressed, nineteen insurgents are executed.

1713

Following the War of the Spanish Succession, Britain receives the *asiento*, the right to import slaves into Spanish America.

Copper is discovered on the Schuyler estate in New Jersey. One of America's most productive copper mines will be sited there.

1714

The succession of the Hanoverian ruler George I to the British throne leads to hostility between Great Britain and Sweden, which is at war with Hanover. This increases British demand for colonial iron and naval stores, products previously imported from Sweden.

The Land-Bank controversy in Boston begins with the publication of *A Projection for Erecting a Bank of Credit in Boston, New-England. Founded upon Land Security*. Several other pamphlets follow.

1716

An anonymous Boston publication, *Some Considerations Upon the several sorts of Banks*, argues that the solution to the town's economic depression is a public works program and government loans to encourage new industry.

English immigrant Thomas Rutt sets up a bloomery forge (a small forge that produces wrought iron) in the Manatawny region of Pennsylvania. Rutt will go on to be a leader in the establishment of the Eastern Pennsylvania iron industry.

1717

The Company of the West, a group headed by the Scots-French financier John Law, takes over Louisiana.

1718

Indigo cultivation begins in Louisiana.

1719

Colonel Alexander Spotswood sets up a blast furnace (used for smelting iron) near Fredericksburg in Virginia, the beginning of the Virginia iron industry. He encourages the immigration of German iron workers.

The Company of the West changes its name to the Company of the Indies. As rumors of gold and diamonds found in Louisiana circulate in Paris, the price of company stock skyrockets.

1720

Approximate date of the founding of the Principio Company, colonial America's largest ironworks. Located in Maryland, it principally serves the British market. Although most of the investors are English, they include Augustine Washington, George Washington's father. Slaves perform much of the work, at first in unskilled and later in skilled positions.

The campaign for a land bank in Boston revives with the publication of John Colman's *The Distressed State of the Town of Boston Considered*. Edward Wigglesworth responds with *A Letter from One in the Country to his Friend in Boston*, advocating hard money and tight credit.

When no gold or diamonds are found in Louisiana, the collapse of the "Mississippi Bubble" in Company of the Indies stock forces John Law to leave France, relinquishing control of the company.

1721

The Puritan minister John Wise publishes *A Word of Comfort to a Melancholy Country* under a pseudonym, advocating paper money and easy credit as beneficial to the rural population.

Another minister, Thomas Paine, replies in *A Discourse Shewing that the Real First Cause of the Straits and Difficulties of this Province of the Massachusetts Bay is its Extravagance, and not Paper Money, and also what is a Safe Foundation to Raise a Bank of Credit on, and what not*. Paine attacks extravagance and vanity, particularly among the lower classes, as the real source of Massachusetts's economic problems.

1722

The White Pines Act, intended to reserve trees for masts for the Royal Navy, requires a permit to fell white pines with a diameter over 24 inches unless on private land.

1723

Frenchman Philippe Renaut establishes a lead mine on the west bank of the Mississippi.

1724

The Carpenters' Company of the City and County of Philadelphia is founded. This association of master carpenters and house builders establishes uniform rates for their work.

The master shipwrights of the Thames petition the British government to restrict colonial shipbuilding. Parliament, influenced by English merchants who use colonial-built ships, refuses to intervene.

Parliament's bounty on naval stores expires. The industry quickly collapses in South Carolina, but it persists in North Carolina.

1729

The Quaker merchant Ralph Sandiford's *Mystery of Iniquity*, one of the earliest antislavery writings, is published.

Publication of Benjamin Franklin's *A Modest Enquiry into the Nature and Necessity of a Paper-Currency*, advocating paper money for Pennsylvania. Franklin is appointed the printer of the currency.

Parliament restores some bounties on naval stores.

1730

Prohibitions on exporting rice outside the British Empire are relaxed. This benefits South Carolina rice planters, who develop markets in Southern Europe.

1731

The Baltimore Company is formed. A Maryland group planning to build ironworks, mostly to supply the British market, it will become one of the largest colonial iron manufacturers.

Failure of the Company of the Indies leads to the French government resuming direct rule of Louisiana.

1732

The British Parliament's Hat Act restricts colonial hat makers by limiting each master hat maker to two apprentices and by banning the export of colonial hats. Passed at the behest of London hatters fearing competition, this act proves to be ineffective.

Upon the petition of a group of investors, the Connecticut Assembly charters the New London Society United for Trade and Commerce, originally as a joint-stock trading company, which issues notes. Shortly afterwards, the society is suppressed by the Connecticut government.

1733

The British Parliament's Molasses Act heavily taxes colonial imports of sugar, molasses, and rum from outside the British Empire. The act's goal is to protect British Caribbean sugar from competition with cheap French colonial sugar, but it is easily circumvented.

1734

The Library of the Carpenters' Company of Philadelphia is founded; it is a repository of works on building design, most printed in England.

1735

Slavery is prohibited in the new British colony of Georgia.

The first American insurance company, the Friendly Society for the Mutual Insurance of Houses Against Fire, is founded in Charles Town, South Carolina. It will collapse after being unable to pay for the damage caused by the great Charles Town fire of 1740.

1737

In Boston, an anonymous author publishes *A Proposal to Supply the Trade with a Medium of Exchange and to Sink the Bills of other Governments*; it advocates a Land Bank.

1738

In Boston, the physician William Douglass publishes *An Essay concerning Silver and Paper Currencies, more especially with regard to the British Colonies in New England*, advocating "hard money."

1739

The German immigrant Caspar Wistar builds a successful colonial glass factory, using German workers, in Alloway, New Jersey.

Eliza Lucas begins to experiment with indigo cultivation at her father's plantation in South Carolina.

In the Stono slave rebellion in South Carolina, about twenty whites are killed before the rebellion is suppressed.

In December, a scheme for a Land Bank to issue notes backed by real estate is put forth in the Massachusetts General Court.

Two French traders, Pierre and Paul Mallet, arrive in Santa Fe, New Mexico. The Spanish colony, exploited by a cartel of Chihuahua merchants who control trade between New Mexico and Mexico, attempts to establish a connection with the French North American trading network. The Spanish Crown will suppress this trade by 1753.

1740

In the aftermath of the Stono Rebellion, South Carolina establishes a comprehensive slave code with an emphasis on controlling the movement of slaves through a system of passes. The South Carolina code will become a model for other colonies.

The first type foundry in colonial North America is established at Germantown, Pennsylvania. It produces type for German-language presses.

The Massachusetts opponents of the Land Bank put forth a scheme for a bank, the Silver Bank, to issue notes backed by silver. Both the Land Bank and Silver Bank begin to issue notes.

In Boston, William Douglass's *A Discourse Concerning the Currencies of the British Plantations in America, Especially with Regard to Their Paper Money* is published anonymously. Douglass compares the different currency schemes of the colonies, condemns the idea of a Land Bank, and recommends the Silver Bank.

An anonymous paper-money advocate responds to Douglass in *An Inquiry into the nature and uses of money; more especially of the bills of Publick Credit, Old Tenor. Together with a proposal of some proper Relief in the present exigence. To which is added a reply to the Essay on Silver and Paper Currences.*

Another anonymous Boston pamphlet, *A letter from a Country Gentleman at Boston to his friend in the Country*, advocates a Land Bank.

1741

A lengthy trial and investigation into an alleged "slave conspiracy" in New York City leads to the execution of 29 blacks and four whites, with the transportation of many others.

The Massachusetts Land Bank controversy continues with the publication of the anonymous *A letter to—Merchant in London concerning a late Combination in the province of the Massachusetts-Bay in New England to impose or force a private-Currency called Land-Bank-Money*, which brings forth various replies and vindications.

The British Parliament declares both the Land Bank and the Silver Bank illegal. This act extends the 1720 Bubble Act's prohibition of forming joint-stock companies from Britain itself to the colonies.

1744

Benjamin Franklin gives a model Franklin stove to the iron founder Robert Grace; he helps publicize the new stoves when they are built.

In South Carolina, Eliza Lucas harvests her first successful production crop of indigo.

1746

An Address to the Inhabitants of North Carolina on the Want of a Medium in Lieu of Money is published in Williamsburg, Virginia.

1747

A land speculation company, the Ohio Company, is organized in Virginia to claim lands west of the Appalachians.

1749

The British Parliament agrees to subsidize colonial indigo.

1750

The British Parliament passes the Iron Act, encouraging iron imports from America by removing duties on bar and pig iron. To protect British iron businesses, Parliament also forbids colonial enterprises from constructing mills for slitting or rolling iron or making steel. The lifting of the tariff is followed by an increase in American iron exports to Britain, but the prohibitions prove difficult to enforce.

Welsh shoemaker John Adam Dagyr arrives in Lynn, Massachusetts. He will introduce improved techniques for making high-quality shoes and begin Lynn's career as America's shoemaking center.

Around this time, Scottish immigrant Edward Pattison settles in Berlin, Connecticut. He will introduce tinsmithing to the colonies, and Berlin will become the center of colonial tin manufacture.

In Georgia, the ban on slavery is lifted.

1751

Sugar cane is introduced as a new crop in Louisiana.

The Society for Encouraging Industry and Employing the Poor is founded. This Boston group sets up a linen factory to employ poor Boston women and children in spinning, while advertising in Ireland for skilled male weavers. Despite support from Boston's elite, the operation never becomes self-sustaining and collapses by 1759.

The British Parliament removes the tariff from American potash (potassium carbonate), leading to expansion of the industry.

As part of a plan to return the New England colonies to specie currency, Parliament's Currency Act prohibits these colonies from issuing additional bills of credit or passing legal tender laws.

1752

The Sterling ironworks is established in Orange County, New York.

Benjamin Franklin takes the leading role in founding the Philadelphia Contributorship for the Insurance of Houses from Loss by Fire.

1753

The Susquehanna Company, a land speculation company, is formed to press claims to the Wyoming Valley in northern Pennsylvania.

Obadiah Brown of Providence establishes a spermaceti (whale oil) candle works at Tockwotton, Rhode Island.

1754

First mention of a rice-pounding mill in a South Carolina plantation sale.

The Quaker John Woolman denounces slavery in *Some Considerations on the Keeping of Negroes*.

1755

The Schuyler, New Jersey, copper mine, confronted with flooding in its deep shafts, imports from England the first steam engine in America to pump out the water.

1759

Opening of the one of the few lead mines in the British colonies, along the Great Kanawha River in Virginia. Investors include the lieutenant governor of Virginia, Francis Fauquier, and several leading Virginians.

1760

A Philadelphia group of master shoe craftsmen forms the Cordwainers' Fire Company, combining the functions of a trade group and a volunteer fire company.

1761

The United Company of Spermaceti Candlers, an association of candle makers in Boston, Providence, Newport, New York, and Philadelphia, is formed to fix the price for spermaceti and allocate the available spermaceti among its members.

1762

In Boston, Thomas Hutchinson's *A Projection for Regulating the Value of Gold and Silver Coins* and Oxenbridge Thatcher's *Considerations on Lowering the Value of Gold Coins within the Province of Massachusetts Bay* are published.

1763

A New York Society of Arts is formed with the goal of fostering an independent American linen industry.

Boston merchants form a Society for Encouraging Trade and Commerce to oppose the renewal of the Molasses

Act, due to expire in 1764. The society becomes the central organization of the Boston mercantile community.

An artisans' group, the Ancient and Honorable Mechanical Company of Baltimore, is founded.

1764

Parliament's Currency Act forbids the issuing of bills of credit as money, as well as the reissuing of existing bills. It also establishes a new, superior vice-admiralty court in Nova Scotia with an English judge and jurisdiction over all the British colonies in North America.

Parliament's Revenue Act, usually referred to as the "Sugar Act," replaces the Molasses Act of 1733. The new act lowers the duty on molasses, but heavily taxes sugar, coffee, wine, and other luxury goods in order to support the British Army in America. It also more closely regulates American exports to Britain in general. The Act is more strictly enforced than the Molasses Act, and arouses great resentment among the colonists.

1765

The British Parliament passes the Stamp Act, imposing a tax on printed matter in the colonies.

Efforts to establish hemp in the colonies intensify as Parliament establishes a bounty on it. Edmund Quincy's *Treatise of Hemp Husbandry* is published by command of the Massachusetts Assembly. It contains material on European and American hemp raising, including an account of a large hemp-raising project at Salem, Massachusetts.

Tench Francis's *Considerations on a Paper Currency* is published.

1766

Antonio de Ulloa, the new Spanish governor of Louisiana (which France had ceded to Spain in the Treaty of Paris in 1763), arrives in New Orleans. He will attempt to reorient the economy of the colony from that of the French Empire to the Spanish.

The Philadelphia Quaker schoolteacher Anthony Benezet publishes *Caution and Warning to Great Britain and her Colonies on the Calamitous State of the Enslaved Negroes in the British Dominions*, an influential denunciation of slavery.

Colonial resistance prompts the British Parliament to repeal the Stamp Act.

1767

The British Parliament imposes the Townshend duties on imports to the colonies including lead, paper, glass, and tea.

The Commercial Conduct of the Province of New York Considered, by "A Linen Draper," is published. It advocates the establishment of manufacturing.

1768

Henry William Stiegel founds a glassworks at Manheim, Pennsylvania, planning to manufacture the highest quality glass yet made in America.

The New York Chamber of Commerce, the first such organization in the English-speaking world, is organized and will receive a patent from the Crown in 1770. The chamber turns its attention to regulating the values of the various currencies in circulation in New York.

A revolt in New Orleans forces out the Spanish governor, Antonio de Ulloa. The rebels protest against the policy of orienting Louisiana to the Spanish economy and claim that Ulloa will force them to drink Spanish wine instead of Bourdeaux.

1769

Abel Buell establishes the first American English-language type foundry in Killingworth, Connecticut.

Isaac Doolittle of New Haven is the first American to build a printing press.

Disagreements over the membership fee and other matters in the Carpenters' Company of Philadelphia lead to a split and the creation of a new group, the Friendship Carpenters' Company, with a much lower entrance fee.

A new Spanish governor, Alejandro O'Reilly, reestablishes Spanish control over New Orleans and Louisiana. He forbids commerce with foreign ports and expels many foreign merchants.

1770

The Townshend Duties are repealed, except for the tax on tea.

Alejandro O'Reilly attempts to end the slavery of the Native Americans held by French colonists in Louisiana contrary to Spanish law. Although some are freed, O'Reilly's efforts are mostly unsuccessful.

1771

Master tailors of Philadelphia meet at Carpenters' Hall to form the Taylors' Company of Philadelphia. They plan to fix prices and limit the wages paid to journeymen.

1773

Parliament's Tea Act provides for the shipping of the British East India Company's unsold tea directly to the colonies. This act is protested in the colonies as undercutting American tea importers and reinforcing the tea tax. Tea ships are turned away from major American harbors, and the Boston Tea Party protests the tax on tea.

A chamber of commerce is organized in Charles Town.

1774

Economic failure forces Henry William Stiegel to close his glassworks.

The British Parliament forbids the export to America of tools and machines used in textile production.

Parliament's Boston Port Act (one of the "Intolerable Acts") closes the port of Boston.

The First Continental Congress passes several measures to encourage American manufactures. It also prohibits imports from Britain and promises to discontinue the importation of foreign slaves.

1775

The United Company of Philadelphia for Promoting American Manufactures, which concentrates on textiles, is founded.

Cabel Fox establishes a business to make lampblack for printers' inks in Germantown. The high-quality product eventually becomes known as "Germantown lampblack."

The Continental Congress issues orders to standardize the muskets being manufactured for the Revolutionary War, although manufacturers frequently ignore the specifications.

John Murray, Earl of Dunmore, royal governor of Virginia, offers freedom to slaves willing to fight on the British side in the American Revolution.

1776

The Second Continental Congress passes a resolution against slave importation.

American rebels adopt the Spanish peso as currency.

The Continental army's need for lead to make ammunition leads the Virginia government to take over the Kanawha River mines.

The Scottish professor Adam Smith's *The Wealth of Nations* includes criticism of slavery and British policy towards America.

1777

The British occupation of Philadelphia ends the United Company of Philadelphia for Promoting American Manufactures.

The constitution of Vermont (at the time a district of New York) prohibits slavery.

1778

French entry into the Revolutionary War diverts the Royal Navy from attacks on American shipping, leading to a revival of American international trade.

1780

Pennsylvania passes a law for gradual emancipation of its slave population.

1781

On December 31, Congress incorporates the Bank of North America.

1783

Trade with Great Britain is restored after the Treaty of Versailles ends the Revolutionary War.

William E. Burns

Gender Issues

1607

Three vessels from a division of the English Virginia Company make landfall in the Chesapeake Bay, founding Jamestown, the first permanent, surviving English settlement in North America. Of the 108 original members of the expedition, none were women.

Pocahontas, whose real name is Matoaka, is taken and held hostage by the English at Jamestown in retaliation for the capture of Englishmen by her Algonquin tribesmen. John Smith claims that Pocahontas saved his life by intervening with her father, the powerful chief Powhatan, in 1607. While a prisoner, she agrees to marry John Rolfe, perhaps to serve her father's interests by using the marriage to forge an alliance with the English. She becomes a Christian, takes a Biblical name (Rebecca), and travels with Rolfe to England, where she dies as she is preparing to return to America. Her life is an example of one of the critical gender roles both European and Native American women played during the colonial period—that of being given in marriage to seal strategic political, military, and business relationships pursued by male family members.

1620–1621

In an effort to encourage the men of Jamestown to settle down and make them more serious about their profit-generating work, the Virginia Company sends more than 150 women for them to marry. Many of these women are widows or orphans who have little prospect of a secure and happy life without a marriage to a man with property, and they have been recruited because they are healthy and used to hard work. The men of the colony pay the expense of their passage by giving the ships' captains 150 pounds of choice tobacco. For the most part, the women go to work with their husbands on the outlying tobacco farms.

Separatists (Pilgrims) aboard the *Mayflower* found Plymouth Plantation. Of the original 102 passengers, eighteen are women, all married and accompanying their husbands on the voyage. Two of the women give birth either en route or close to the time of landfall, and a third woman has given birth just prior to the voyage and is nursing her child. On the ship the women make clothes and cook, and once they arrive, their first task is to find a way to do the laundry. While the Pilgrim men and some of the crew go to search for a place to build the settlement, the women and children remain on the ship. Of the married women, only four survive the winter, and therefore must assume the cooking and cleaning responsibilities for the entire colony. When the ship *Fortune* arrives in November 1621, these same women will also serve the needs of most of its passengers, as only a few of the new arrivals are women.

1637

The heresy trials of Anne Hutchinson begin. Hutchinson believes she received personal revelations during the 1634 voyage to Massachusetts Bay Colony with her family. Later, with the encouragement of her minister, John Cotton, she leads a regular, large gathering in her home to discuss church doctrine and the Bible. Her followers begin to contradict the Puritan leadership, even refusing to participate in a war against the Pequot Native Americans, and Hutchinson is brought to trial. Though, on the surface, the trials are about Hutchinson's religious views, they are also about containing her within prescribed gender roles. Cotton withdraws his support, and Hutchinson is judged by Governor Winthrop as "a woman not fit for our society" and "an American Jezebel." She is exiled, even though she is pregnant with her sixteenth child. She, her family, and a group of about sixty followers go to Rhode Island.

1639

The first divorce decree in North America is handed down in Massachusetts.

1641

Massachusetts adopts the "Body of Liberties," part of which declares that husbands should not beat their wives.

1643

Anne Hutchinson, now a 51-year-old widow, moves her fourteen children to an area of Long Island she has purchased from the Dutch, who claim to have bought it from local Native Americans. She and all but one of her children are killed by Algonquin natives the following year.

Goody Armitage is licensed in Massachusetts Bay to own and run an inn, but she is not allowed to serve as its bartender. She is an example of the many kinds of occupations women are beginning to hold, such as barbering for both men and women and running a slaughterhouse.

1648

Margaret Reed Brent asks for the right to vote. She is the first woman in the English colonies to do so. A Catholic, she had emigrated to Maryland from England with her sister and brothers, from whom she acquired 1,000 acres. As a major landowner, Brent serves herself and others as an attorney and frequently appears before the Maryland General Assembly. As he lies dying, Maryland's governor, Leonard Calvert, asks Brent to oversee the selling of his estate to pay the colony's militia. The soldiers had saved the colony by putting down a rebellion but are now becoming mutinous themselves due to the lack of pay. Brent solves the problem through the bold move of selling both the governor's estate and his cattle, for which she gains even greater approval from the General Assembly.

Brent then asks the Assembly for two votes, since she is both a landowner and Lord Baltimore's designated representative, but the Assembly refuses. It was not unusual at the time for women to serve as their own attorneys and to serve as proxy voters for men, usually their husbands, who might have to be absent; likewise, it was normal for male property owners to have a vote. Brent is interesting because she represents all of these categories at once, but she is not given even one vote. She is also an example of the importance of class distinctions, since she does not seek voting rights for all women but rather for herself as a female member of a class that generally already has such privileges. In response to the Assembly's rejection, Brent moves to Virginia in 1650.

1649

The Maryland Toleration Act allows Christians of "any sect" to live and speak according to their convictions. The act uses some of the earliest gender-neutral language, referring to "person or persons" and saying "his or her religion" and "his or her consent."

Massachusetts law considers midwives, physicians, and surgeons to have equal legal standing.

1650

America's first published book of poetry is Anne Dudley Bradstreet's *The Tenth Muse Lately Sprung Up in America*. Unknown to Bradstreet, her work had been taken to London by her brother-in-law in order to get it published. Despite being a mother of eight children, Bradstreet is criticized by other family members for not sticking to needlework, which is considered more in line with her traditional gender role.

1656

Mary Fisher and Ann Austin arrive in Boston. They are part of the first group of Quakers to arrive in America, but Fisher and Austin are promptly banished to the West Indies by the Puritans. Of the fifty-nine in the original Quaker party, twenty-six are women, and all but four of them are unmarried.

Founded in England by George Fox and Margaret Fell as the Religious Society of Friends, the Quakers refuse to tip their hats and speak with deference to their social superiors (including the king) because they argue that God recognizes no social distinctions among people. They support women's separate but equal ministerial status with men and encourage women to preach because they believe God communicates with each person individually by means of an "inner light." They refuse to serve in militia or even pay religious taxes during the English Civil War because they practice nonviolence, and, in 1652, they make the first formal declaration against American slavery.

1660

By 1660 there are 20,000 Quakers in Britain, and many are going out as missionaries. Almost universally despised because of their disavowal of traditional gender, racial, religious, and social hierarchies, Quakers are commonly beaten or put to death. Mary Dyer is hanged in Boston because she insists on practicing Quakerism. One of the few supporters of Anne Hutchinson, she had followed Hutchinson into exile and eventually traveled to England where she became a Quaker. Attracted to the Quakers' radical views on gender roles, Dyer converts and then returns to America to participate in the "Lamb's War" against Puritan civil and religious authority in Massachusetts. Knowing they will almost certainly be killed, such Quakers as Dyer persist in practicing Quakerism in Massachusetts, repeatedly returning after being deported, until the Puritan leadership feels compelled to execute them to prevent their ideas from spreading. Dyer's execution and that of others will eventually contribute to Parliament's decision to revoke the charter of the Massachusetts Bay Colony in 1684.

1662

Virginia law clarifies the issue of what racial identity should be assigned to children born from the union of English men and black women by declaring the child to be of the same race as its mother.

1675

The year-long war known as King Philip's War begins in June of this year. King Philip is a Wampanoag Indian, whose real name is Metacom and whose father is none other than Massasoit, the Native American who helped the Pilgrim settlers to survive the first cruel winter. Among the Native American leadership is a woman named Wetamoo, who deeply hates the English because she believes they poisoned her husband (Massasoit's son) some ten years earlier. She has replaced her husband as the sachem of the Pocasset band of the Wampanoag, but only about two dozen of her 300 warriors survive the war, and she falls during an escape attempt and drowns. Her head is put on public display at

Taunton, Massachusetts. Metacom is also beheaded; his head is displayed at Plymouth, and his family is sold into slavery and sent to the West Indies. Interestingly, the most complete account of Wetamoo's life is by Mary Rowlandson, who had been captured and given to Wetamoo.

1676

Nathaniel Bacon leads a rebellion of backwoods Virginia farmers, along with their women, servants, and slaves. Frustrated in their efforts to attain land and provide for their families, Bacon's "army" defeats Governor Berkeley's militia and burns down Jamestown. Bacon's sudden death from illness, however, contributes to the eventual defeat of this rebellion. Wealthier men set about passing laws that sharply restrict the ability of the landless, women, servants, and slaves to challenge propertied authority, even making gossip a crime. This may have been because spreading rumors was one of the colonial woman's primary means of having a political impact.

Bacon's Rebellion might be seen as a conflict made of different ideas about gender. An eastern Virginia man had to have property, wealth, and the obedience of his social inferiors, all of which he secured through laws. The western Virginia man respected few authorities outside of his own family, whose honor he protected through independent action and violence when necessary.

Kateri Tekakwitha flees the Mohawk tribe where she has been growing up. Her Algonquin-Christian mother had been captured by the Mohawk and taken for a wife. Orphaned by a 1660 smallpox epidemic that left Tekakwitha horribly scarred and partially blind, she later responds to Jesuit missionaries and is baptized a Catholic. Her Mohawk tribesmen are so disapproving that they stone her, and she is nearly killed. She escapes by herself in a canoe by night, eventually arriving at Sault St. Louis on the St. Lawrence River. There, a village of Christian Native Americans takes her in. Tekakwitha becomes known as the "Lily of the Mohawks," a saint to whom local Native Americans pray for miracles, even after her death at the age of 24. She is nominated for beatification in the 1930s.

1682

The Quakers found Pennsylvania. Women and men are considered nearly equal in the Society's hierarchy, and that hierarchy itself is intended to be limited. Women are ordained as ministers and allowed to preach, and Quaker women are involved in leadership and decision-making on issues that relate to other Quaker women, including marriages. The Quakers may be the only sect of the day that holds these views. Many nineteenth-century American reformers will have some kind of Quaker heritage.

1690

Some thirty Boston women receive a license to cut lumber and manufacture fertilizer.

1692

In January, the Salem witchcraft trials begin. Tituba, a Caribbean-African slave girl, tells witchcraft stories to a group of English girls in Salem, Massachusetts, at or near the home of her master, Reverend Samuel Parris. Parris's daughter, Betsy, and her friends then begin acting strangely. When it is suggested they have been "bewitched," the girls begin naming several local people, especially women and including Tituba, as witches. A number of arrests are made and trials begin. Tituba confesses and is sold for an amount equal to the cost of keeping her in prison. Others are eventually set free, but six others, including Bridget Bishop and Rebecca Nurse, are hanged in the summer. Nurse is a 71-year-old mother of eight who had been at odds with the community and has some sort of birthmark. Bishop is in her late 50s or early 60s; married three times and widowed twice, she has no children.

Of the 141 people eventually charged, several die in jail and a total of twenty others (thirteen women and seven men) are executed by September. More trials continue until the spring of 1693, when the governor forces them to stop. A significant number of the accused are old, eccentric, infirm, or have disputes with other members of the community over property and class issues. This illustrates the importance both of gender and class in the kinds of social judgments that could be made about someone in colonial Massachusetts.

1693

The College of William and Mary is founded. It is the second college in North America and is open only to men, despite being named in part for Mary II, Queen of England.

1695

After her husband's death, Dinah Nuthead continues his printing business in St. Mary's and Annapolis, Maryland. Licensed by the General Assembly and approved by the governor, she is the first of several female printers in the English colonies in North America, although she herself never learns to read or write. No item turned out by her press has yet been located, and it is not known for how long she continued to print. She may have been unable to locate a journeyman printer who could help her continue the business.

1697

In March, Hannah Dustin, Mary Neff, and a young boy escape from their Native American captors by butchering nearly a dozen natives who are asleep with their family. Neff is a midwife and Dustin is a mother of twelve. They have been force-marched nearly 100 miles and, in a practice common to both white settlers and the native peoples, the natives killed Dustin's baby daughter by smashing her skull against a tree. The Massachusetts General Assembly gives the three escapees a reward in pounds sterling for the scalps they present.

1700

Records indicate that, especially in the Southern colonies, it is not at all uncommon for women to be pregnant before they are married. Most affected, however, are indentured servant women, who are generally forbidden to marry under the terms of their contracts. Some 20 percent of these seventeenth-century women will have children without being married.

The French construct a fort at Detroit. Because French settlements of this type consist of male soldiers, trappers, and priests, there is often a high degree of cohabitation between the French and Native Americans. This facilitates the French "going native," as opposed to the English settlements' ability to preserve English culture and language through the cohesiveness of the English family. That is, traditional gender roles may be stretched by frontier pressures, but they are still preserved by the family structure in English settlements.

1704

Sarah Kemble Knight makes a six-month business trip from Boston to New York. She goes on horseback and travels alone in the winter, although she is a widow and a mother. Her account of her travels, *The Journal of Madame Knight*, will be published in 1825. Knight looks after her husband's estate and becomes a wealthy shopkeeper, which indicates she is an astute businessperson as well as a clever writer of the picaresque genre. Colonial women of this time quite commonly work side by side with their husbands and manage "male" affairs when the men are away or dead.

1709

Henrietta Johnston becomes America's first female commercial artist when she begins drawing portraits for wealthy Charles Town, South Carolina, residents. Perhaps born in France as Henrietta de Beaulieu, her innovative pastel techniques and the high quality of her work allow her to support her family, something her second husband cannot fully accomplish with his ill health and low pay at St. Philip's Anglican Church. Her skills will become even more important after Reverend Johnston's drowning in 1716, and she is among the first artists in the world to use pastels.

1711

The British expand the slave trade in the city of New York by opening a slave market on Wall Street. Conditions are so deplorable that an African woman protests by murdering her master and his family. She is burned at the stake.

The famous Madame Montour interprets for an Albany meeting of Iroquois with the governor of New York. Born of mixed French and Native American heritage, Montour is rumored to be the captured daughter of Canada's French governor. She has been raised as an Iroquois and has married the powerful Oneida chief Carandowana ("Big Tree"). Gifted with languages and skilled in negotiating, Montour will be energetically courted by both the French and the English through the 1740s. Through her efforts, the Iroquois become more closely allied with the English and cancel their plans to mount a war against the settlers of North Carolina.

1716

Midwives in the colony of New York receive official licenses.

1726

An English court rules that William Penn's second wife, Hannah Callowhill Penn, can keep her husband's remaining lands and title to Pennsylvania, which she desires to will to her children. The suit, which has dragged on since Penn's death in 1718, is brought by the oldest son of Penn's first wife and would result in transfer of the lands and title to someone living in England. Members of the Penn family will continue to govern Pennsylvania until the Revolution, but Hannah will die within a week of the decision. This is perhaps one of the most significant examples of the kinds of gender-based property disputes common throughout colonial America.

1727

The first convent in North America is founded by Ursuline nuns in New Orleans, a settlement founded by the French in 1718. Though the Ursulines are based in Italy, they will serve the French colony by opening a hospital, a school, and an orphanage. They also look after the so-called casket girls, who have been sent from France to marry Frenchmen in colonial Louisiana. "Casket" is an English corruption of the French *cassettes*, which refers to the large hope chests that the girls bring with them. Filled with home-starting necessities and serving as dowry, the chests improve the girls' bargaining position in marriage arrangements, while their marriages will ensure the most enduring French cultural presence in the whole Mississippi Valley.

1730

Deborah Read Rogers arranges a common-law marriage with Benjamin Franklin. Read's husband is missing and presumed remarried and or dead in the West Indies, but without proof, she cannot legally marry another man.

1738

In one of the most stunning examples of how the pressures of colonial life can reveal the full range of the gender role women can fill, Eliza Lucas Pinckney, at age 16, assumes control of her family's plantation near Charles Town, South Carolina. Her father is recalled to the island of Antigua in the West Indies for military service during one of Britain's wars with Spain and France. When he is made governor there, Eliza is left to care for her younger sister and their sickly mother. By the time she marries a widowed judge, Charles Pinckney, in 1744, she has taught her sister and two of their black slaves how to read and write and has single-handedly revolutionized the agricultural industry of South Carolina by developing a hybrid variety of the indigo plant. The war has greatly increased the demand for the blue dye made from indigo, whereas it has stifled the colony's primary export, rice. Pinckney's letters and journals describe daily life and gender relations in great detail. Her sons will become generals and heroes of the Revolutionary War: Charles, a framer of the Constitution, and Thomas, the ambassador to Spain and Britain who negotiates the critical 1795 Treaty of San Lorenzo ("Pinckney's Treaty"). Eliza Lucas Pinckney may be the first European agriculturalist, male or female, in North America.

1749

John Cleland's novel *Fanny Hill* includes lesbian sex, but suggests it as a way that women might prepare for hetero-sexual intercourse in marriage. Other books, such as *The Ladies' Dispensatory* (1740), offer sexual advice, usually cautioning that lesbianism, like masturbation, could lead to health problems or even death. Although male homosexuality is well documented and severely punished for its perceived betrayal of the male gender role, female homosexuality is not considered to be such a threat and is rarely documented.

1757

An example of the gender differences between Native Americans and Europeans is a meeting between the Cherokee chief Attacullaculla and male officials from South Carolina. The chief criticizes the Carolinians, arguing that all men are born of women, so women should be allowed into the important councils. As with many Native American societies, Cherokee ancestry is traced through the female, not the male line, and property belongs to mothers and daughters instead of the men. Young married couples join the woman's family, not the man's, and women commonly hold leadership positions as shamans.

1764

In the court case *Davey v. Tyner*, the colonial Pennsylvania Supreme Court supports the existing "joint deed system of conveyance" by which a married woman's property is somewhat protected. A wife must give formal verbal consent to a justice of the peace before her property can be sold.

1765

Mary Jemison marries the Seneca chief Hiakatoo. Jemison was born on a ship bound for America. When she was 15 years old, her family was killed by Native Americans in Pennsylvania. This is her second marriage to a Native American, and she has chosen not to live as a white woman. Her skill with languages and her attractiveness to the Seneca (who

call her Deh-he-wa-mis, or "Pretty One") bring her an exalted position as a negotiator in the Lake Erie region. She bears a dozen children and dies on her own large estate in 1797 at the very old—for the colonial period—age of 90.

William Blackstone's *Commentaries on the Laws of England* builds upon the earlier work of Edward Coke (1620s) and Matthew Hale (1670s) in validating the application of English common law to emerging legal issues. Common law depends on precedent, that is, the decisions made by past judges and juries. New cases are compared to the older ones, and, unless the details can be shown to be significantly different, the old ruling applies to the new case. Thus, common law seems to strengthen traditional views and slow the pace of cultural change. One aspect of Blackstone's *Commentaries* is his extended definition of the term "coverture," or property laws for women, to include other forms of female identity. An example is whether women can testify against their husbands if, in the eyes of coverture law, they are not two separate people but one married entity. Blackstone's ideas will set the terms of debate on gender issues for the next two centuries.

1772–1775

Mercy Otis Warren publishes her trilogy of plays anonymously between 1772 and 1775. *The Adulateur, The Defeat,* and *The Group* are all satires of British rule that use feminine imagery to describe the innocence of the American colonies, but male imagery to show British buffoonery. Her later history of the Revolution will "speak volumes" for the quality of the female mind.

1773

Phillis Wheatley leaves Boston for London, where her book of poetry will be published under the title *Poems on Various Subjects, Religious and Moral*. Since her arrival in Boston as a slave from Gambia in 1761, Wheatley has been warmly received and often not treated as a slave because of her charming personality and widely popular poetry. Even before her book is published, she has been recognized as the first African American poet. However, her fortunes decline, and she is largely forgotten after her master and mistress die, leaving her in poverty.

1774

"Mother Ann" Lee is freed from prison in England and emigrates with her husband and a few other male disciples to New York. As a member of a Quaker splinter group known as the "Society of Believers" or "Shaking Quakers," she is imprisoned for preaching on the feminine qualities of God. She has a vision in which she sees herself as the feminine Second Coming of Christ. She and her disciples found a communal, pacifist, utopian community on a farm in New York, where they are persecuted during the Revolution as loyalists.

Fifty-one North Carolina women sign the "Edenton Resolution," wherein they declare they will neither drink tea nor wear clothing made in England until England repeals the Intolerable Acts. This is an example of two important ways in which women aid the revolutionary cause—they organize support and they police the colonials' boycotts of English goods.

From September 5 through October 26, the Daughters of Liberty in Philadelphia open their families' homes to the delegates to the First Continental Congress. Abigail Adams's correspondence with her husband John will offer one of the most studied examples of gender relationships within the family of an American founding father and future president.

1776

In March, the first month of assembly for the Second Continental Congress that year, Abigail Adams writes these famous words to her husband as he deliberates on the system of laws for the new country being born in revolution: "Remember the Ladies, and be more generous and favourable to them than your ancestors. Do not put such unlimited power into the hands of the Husbands. Remember, all men would be tyrants if they could. . . . Emancipating all nations, you insist upon retaining absolute power over Wives. . . . If particular care and attention is not paid to the Ladies, we are determined to foment a Rebellion, and will not hold ourselves bound by any Laws in which we have no voice or Representation."

1778

On June 28, "Molly Pitcher" (Mary Ludwig Hays McCauley) earns her nickname by carrying water to her soldier husband and other Continental soldiers of his company who are suffering from the heat at the Battle of Monmouth, New Jersey. When her husband is wounded or collapses from the heat, she mans an artillery piece of the 7th Company of Pennsylvania Artillery until the battle's end. Before the war and her marriage, she had been a domestic servant. She receives a pension from the Pennsylvania legislature in 1822, and her story becomes even more widely known.

1779

Margaret Cochran Corbin receives the first soldier's pension ever granted to a woman, as the Continental Congress recognizes her for her bravery and sacrifice during the ongoing Revolutionary War. As so many other women have done, Margaret accompanied her husband when he enlisted in the Continental army. During the Battle of Harlem Heights, New York in 1776, after her husband was killed, she assumed his post, firing an artillery piece until she was nearly killed by cannon fire. Receiving severe wounds to her face and upper body, Corbin lost the use of one arm but she will be considered a regular soldier in the Continental army until her discharge in 1783 at the end of the war.

Her example of heroism is also symbolic of the gender role filled by women throughout the colonial period. During this period, women undergo extreme difficulties in order to support their husbands' endeavors and assume many male-role responsibilities (though not all of their rights) when their husbands are removed from the scene.

1780

The Ladies Association of Philadelphia is organized by Esther De Berdt Reed, the First Lady of Pennsylvania. The Ladies Association quickly becomes the largest revolutionary-era volunteer women's organization, spreading from New Jersey to South Carolina and taking in more than $7,000 in gold, mostly by going door to door. The women provide crucial assistance to George Washington's soldiers, much of which is sent by way of Martha Washington.

1782

Deborah Sampson Gannett becomes the first American woman to enlist on her own in the Continental army. Dressed like a man and resembling the many adolescent boys who have been recruited, she takes the name Robert Shurlieffe (although various sources state his name as Shurtleff, Shirtliffe, and Shurtliffe) and sees action in several battles until she is wounded at Tarrytown, New York. When she is taken to the hospital, her ruse is uncovered, and George Washington himself discharges her in 1783. After the war, she receives a pension and travels as a lecturer, telling exaggerated stories of her military exploits.

Ryan L. Ruckel

Military and Diplomatic Affairs

1453

The Turks capture Constantinople, destroying the last vestiges of the Byzantine Empire. The loss of that city will leave Eastern Europe and much of the Mediterranean vulnerable to Turkish attack.

The Hundred Years' War, fought principally between England and France, finally comes to an end. The war has ravaged the French countryside as the warring armies preferred to stage large-scale raids into enemy territory rather than fight pitched battles.

1469

King Ferdinand and Queen Isabella marry, joining the Crowns of Castile and Aragon.

1492

Catholic forces capture Granada, the last Muslim stronghold in Spain. This ends the *Reconquista,* the 700-year-long struggle to evict Muslims from the Iberian Peninsula.

Christopher Columbus discovers the Americas.

1494

Charles VIII of France invades Italy, inaugurating the Hapsburg-Valois Wars, which will last until 1559. The French army employs gunpowder artillery with great success against the medieval defenses of the cities of Italy. These cities traditionally had been defended by thin, high walls, which served well against medieval siege tactics. Against heavy cannon, however, such walls cannot stand.

Thus, the French campaign eventually inspires a massive change in European defensive architecture, the development of *trace italienne,* or Italian-style, fortifications. Such defenses consist of low, thick, angled walls, arranged to offer interlocking fields of fire against an opponent. Such defenses will become essential in Europe and in America.

1517

Martin Luther nails his Ninety-Five Theses to the castle church door in Wittenberg, Germany. His action will spark the Protestant Reformation and lead to two centuries of religious warfare between Protestants and Catholics.

1519

Hernando Cortéz's expedition arrives in Tenochtitlán, Mexico.

1520–1521

Aztec forces drive Cortéz and his Spaniards from Tenochtitlán. Cortéz captures the city after a three-month siege.

1532–1533

The Spanish conquistador Francisco Pizarro leads 180 men in the conquest of the Inca Empire of Peru.

1540

Ignatius Loyola founds the Society of Jesus. The Jesuits will serve as the spiritual envoys of the Counter Reformation that will seek to destroy Protestantism and spread Roman Catholicism around the world.

1547

King Henry VIII of England dies, and Edward VI becomes king.

1553

King Edward VI dies, and Mary I becomes queen of England. During her brief reign, she attempts to undo the English Reformation.

1554

Mary I of England marries Philip II of Spain.

1557

The English lose control of the port of Calais in France early in the Anglo-French War of 1557–1559.

1558

Upon the death of Mary I, Elizabeth I succeeds to the throne of England.

1559

The treaty of Cateau-Cambrésis ends the wars between France and Spain for control of Italy.

1565

Turkish forces under the command of Suleiman the Magnificent besiege but fail to take the Christian stronghold of Malta in the central Mediterranean.

Spanish forces begin building a fortress, the Castillo de San Marcos, at St. Augustine, in what will become Florida.

The fortress provides a classic example of the *trace italienne* fortress design in the New World.

1585

English settlers unsuccessfully attempt to found a colony at Roanoke in what later will be North Carolina.

1588

A British fleet thwarts the Spanish Armada in the English Channel, attacking the 130 Spanish warships from long range and damaging them through superior naval gunnery. In early August, the British attack the Armada with fire ships, forcing the fleet to flee and disperse. Prevailing winds force the Spanish northward. While attempting to escape by sailing around Scotland, the Armada falls prey to storms and loses almost half its total strength.

1598

The Edict of Nantes, issued by Henry IV of France, grants limited religious liberties to French Protestants, known as Huguenots. The edict also establishes several Protestant havens inside deeply Catholic France. Later French rulers will restrict Protestant liberties, and the edict will be revoked in 1685.

1600–1603

English military leader Lord Mountjoy suppresses the Earl of Tyrone's Rebellion in Ireland. The Spanish had supported the rebellion in part as a response to English attacks on Spanish outposts in the Caribbean and South America.

1603

Queen Elizabeth I dies. James VI of Scotland is crowned King James I of England.

1605

The Gunpowder Plot, a scheme by Catholics to blow up the British Parliament, is discovered before it can be executed.

1607

The Jamestown colony is founded by English adventurers in Virginia. Because of its location in a swampy area on the York-James peninsula, Jamestown is plagued by all manner of mosquito-borne illnesses. Many settlers will be lost to disease and starvation before the colony begins to thrive.

1609

Beginning of the Twelve Year's Truce between the Spanish and the Dutch, temporarily ending the conflict between the two sides over the territory that is now Belgium.

1618–1648

On May 23, 1618, Bohemian Protestants, fearing the intentions of the Catholic Holy Roman Emperor, throw several of his representatives out a window. This event, the so-called Defenestration of Prague, helps to ignite the conflict known as the Thirty Years' War, which will devastate much of Central Europe.

1620

Religious separatists known as Pilgrims settle at Plymouth in what is today Massachusetts. Before disembarking from their ship the *Mayflower*, the Pilgrims sign the Mayflower Compact, the first document in British North America to espouse the principles of self-government.

1622

The Powhatan Indians attack the colonial inhabitants of Wolstenholme Town, the main settlement of the Martin's Hundred Plantation, downriver from Jamestown, Virginia. Fifty-eight out of approximately 140 settlers are killed, and another twenty are taken prisoner.

1623

Portsmouth, the first settlement in what is now New Hampshire, is founded.

1624

A Dutch colony is established on Manhattan Island.

England, prompted by a failed attempt of Prince Charles to marry the Infanta of Spain, declares war on Spain.

1626

British forces attempt to capture the Spanish port of Cadiz and fail.

1627

British forces, led by the Duke of Buckingham, attempt to intervene on the Île de Rhé, near the beleaguered Huguenot city of La Rochelle, and fail. The English forces were attempting to support fellow Protestants oppressed by the Catholic French King Louis XIII.

1628

La Rochelle, a Protestant stronghold, falls to the forces of the French Cardinal Richelieu after a fourteen-month siege.

The British Parliament passes the Petition of Right, a critical document in the development of rights and liberties for the people of England.

1629

The Massachusetts Bay Company, a joint-stock company, is chartered by the English Crown to settle lands in New England.

1629–1640

In an attempt to rule without Parliament, King Charles I turns to a variety of dubious schemes to raise money without legislative approval. British custom provides that the imposition of taxes requires the consent of Parliament, but Charles I hopes to cover his expenses by other means. War with Scotland finally forces him to call a session of Parliament in an attempt to raise more money.

1630–1643

Fearful of Catholic influence in England and of Catholic military success on the Continent, English Puritans begin to flee to New England in what has been called the Great Migration. They hope to create an ideal Protestant community.

1631

On May 31, Imperial troops sack the Protestant city of Magdeburg, part of the principality of Saxony in present-day Germany, in one of the most brutal atrocities of the Thirty Years' War.

In the Battle of Breitenfeld, Germany, King Gustavus Adolphus of Sweden defeats the Imperial army commanded by Count Johannes Tilly in the first major Protestant victory in the Thirty Years' War.

1632

In the Battle of Lützen, Germany, King Gustavus Adolphus defeats Count Albrecht von Wallenstein in a major setback for Imperial forces. Gustavus Adolphus is killed during the battle.

1633

William Laud becomes Archbishop of Canterbury. Seen by many in England as pro-Catholic, or at least not Protestant enough, Laud persecutes Puritans, causing their migration to New England and sparking events leading to the English Civil War.

Maryland is founded.

1635

Connecticut is founded.

1636

Roger Williams founds Providence in what will later become Rhode Island.

1637–1638

The Pequot War is fought between the English colonists of New England and the Pequot Indians. The colonists crush the Pequot by surrounding their principal village, setting it afire and killing those who attempt to escape.

1638

Colonists from Sweden settle in Delaware.

1639–1640

Charles I's attempts to force the Church of England's *Book of Common Prayer* upon Scotland in the so-called Bishops'

Wars provoke staunch resistance. Scottish forces eventually invade northern England and force Charles I to pay an indemnity in exchange for peace.

1640

King Charles I calls the Long Parliament, given its name to distinguish it from the Short Parliament of April and May 1640. Charles I calls both parliaments to help him raise money to put down rebellions by the Scots; the Long Parliament will sit until 1653.

1641

A rebellion in Ireland breaks out in October.

Parliament passes the Grand Remonstrance, a list of grievances against Charles I.

1642

Charles I withdraws from London, and the English Civil War begins between royalist and parliamentary forces.

1643

Parliamentary forces make league with Scottish Covenanters against the king. (The Scottish Covenanters were Presbyterians who pledged to maintain their own form of church government and worship.)

The French army defeats a Spanish army at the battle of Rocroi, France.

1644

The Battle of Marston Moor in England ends in victory for Parliament.

1645

The British Parliament executes William Laud, the Archbishop of Canterbury, and it reorganizes its troops into the New Model Army. This army wins the Battle of Naseby, effectively defeating the royalist cause in the Civil War.

1646

The royalist stronghold of Oxford surrenders. Charles I surrenders to the Scots, who later turn him over to Parliament, ending the first round of the English Civil War.

1648

Charles I allies with the Scots and launches the second Civil War. He is once again defeated. Oliver Cromwell defeats the Scots at the battle of Preston.

The Treaty of Westphalia ends the Thirty Years' War.

1648–1653

A civil war, called the *Fronde*, erupts in France, as aristocrats make a final attempt to preserve their power in the face of growing monarchical consolidation.

1649

King Charles I is tried and executed by Parliament. Executive authority is assumed by Oliver Cromwell, who adopts the title of Lord Protector of the Commonwealth.

1649–1650

Oliver Cromwell and his army conquer Ireland. After capturing the town of Drogheda, they massacre Irish Catholics.

1650

Cromwell defeats Scottish Covenanters at the battle of Dunbar, Scotland.

1651

Cromwell wins the battle of Worcester, in the English Midlands, ending an attempt to bring Charles II to the throne.

1652–1654

The First Dutch War is fought between Britain and the Netherlands over trade and control of the sea lanes of Europe.

1655

English forces capture the island of Jamaica in the Caribbean.

1659

The Treaty of the Pyrenees finally ends the Franco-Spanish conflict that broke out during the Thirty Years' War.

1660

King Charles II takes the throne of England.

1664

The Dutch transfer New Amsterdam to the English, who rename it New York.

1664–1667

The Second Dutch War is another conflict between Britain and the Netherlands over colonies and trade.

1667

The British navy is crushed by the Dutch at the battle of Medway on the English River Thames.

1670

The Secret Treaty of Dover promises French aid to help Charles II retain his throne, if he openly converts to Roman Catholicism.

1672–1674

The Third Dutch War is the final conflict between England and the Netherlands over trade and colonies. Various colonies—including Suriname, some East Indian islands, and New Netherlands (New York)—are exchanged between the two countries as a result of the three wars.

1675–1676

King Philip's War is a brutal war fought in New England between English colonists and Native Americans. While native warriors achieve some success and destroy several colonial towns, the war ends when Metacom, known to the colonists as King Philip, is killed.

1676

Virginian Nathaniel Bacon leads an uprising, known as Bacon's Rebellion, against the colonial government of Virginia. Under Bacon's leadership, poor whites, as well as blacks, attempt to overthrow the wealthy elite who dominate Virginia. The rebellion is eventually defeated.

1678

The Popish Plot, a fictitious but widely believed conspiracy of Jesuits to assassinate King Charles II, is fabricated by an Anglican clergyman named Titus Oates. Dozens of Catholics are executed as a result.

1679

The Exclusion Crisis breaks out as Protestant nobles attempt to block James the Duke of York's succession to the throne.

1681

Pennsylvania is chartered.

1683

The Rye House Plot, an alleged conspiracy by Whig opponents to overthrow Charles II, fails. It leads to the execution of Algernon Sidney, whose *Discourses* will greatly influence the founding fathers of the United States.

1685

King Charles II of England dies and is succeeded by his brother James II.

King Louis XIV of France revokes the Edict of Nantes, leading to widespread violence against the Huguenots and to large Huguenot migrations to the North American colonies.

The Duke of Monmouth rebels against James II. His forces are crushed at the battle of Sedgemoor, in southwest England, by an army commanded by John Churchill, later Duke of Marlborough. Monmouth's followers are executed or transported to the Caribbean.

1686

Sir Edmund Andros becomes governor of the Dominion of New England and later attempts to seize the charter of Connecticut. Three years later, after receiving word of the Glorious Revolution, the colonists will overthrow and imprison Andros.

1688

In the Glorious Revolution, William of Orange lands in England in November. James II flees a month later.

1689

The Convention Parliament proclaims that James II has abandoned the throne and offers it to William of Orange and his wife Mary, the daughter of James II.

The English Bill of Rights confirms the supremacy of the British Parliament and effectively ends the idea of the divine right of kings in England. After 1689, the power of Parliament will increase.

The Nine Years' War (also called the War of the League of Augsburg), known in America as King William's War, begins, pitting the Dutch and the English against the French and those loyal to James II, known as the Jacobites.

1690

Forces under King William III defeat a Jacobite army in Ireland at the Battle of the Boyne.

A French and Native American force raids Schenectady, New York.

The British capture Port Royal, Acadia (modern-day Nova Scotia).

1691

The French recapture Port Royal, Acadia.

1697

The Treaty of Ryswick ends the Nine Years' War.

c. 1700

In European armies, the flintlock musket and the socket bayonet begin to supersede the old combination of matchlock musket and pike. The flintlock offers a more reliable ignition system for firearms. The socket bayonet allows a soldier to convert his musket into a short pike without sacrificing the ability to fire his weapon. These advances increase the effectiveness of European infantry formations.

1701–1714

The War of the Spanish Succession is fought to prevent Louis XIV from joining the Bourbon Crowns of France and Spain. English, Dutch, and Austrian armies will battle against the French, primarily in the elaborately defended area of the Spanish Netherlands and the northeastern border of France. Fighting also breaks out in Spain and in Austria, and takes place sporadically around the globe.

1702

King William III dies. Anne, daughter of James II, becomes Queen of England.

1704

Anglo-Austrian forces, led by the Duke of Marlborough and Prince Eugene of Savoy, defeat the French at the battle of Blenheim.

British troops capture Gibraltar.

The French and their native allies raid and burn Deerfield, Massachusetts.

1706

Marlborough defeats another French army at the battle of Ramillies. The dazzling victory allows for the rapid conquest of four cities in the ensuing campaign: Ostend, Menin, Dendermonde, and Ath.

1707

The Act of Union, voted on by the parliaments of both countries, formally joins England and Scotland.

1708

Marlborough and Prince Eugene of Savoy defeat the French at the battle of Oudenarde. They follow up that victory by besieging and capturing the French city of Lille, one of the strongest and most elaborately defended cities on the French border.

A British naval expedition seizes Minorca.

1709

Marlborough and Prince Eugene of Savoy win the Battle of Malplaquet, a bloodier and less decisive victory over the French than those achieved earlier in the war.

1710

British colonists capture Port Royal, Acadia (Nova Scotia).

1711

A British naval expedition against Quebec fails.

Queen Anne removes the conservative Duke of Marlborough from his command of the allied army and brings him back to England. Marlborough had been charged with misuse of public funds. His removal is a sign of the waning of Tory power during Anne's reign.

1713

The Peace of Utrecht ends the War of the Spanish Succession.

1714

Queen Anne of England dies without issue, bringing an end to the Stuart dynasty. George I, the first of England's Hanoverian kings, is crowned in order to ensure a Protestant succession.

1715

Unsuccessful Jacobite uprising in Scotland of pro-Catholic supporters of James II, the pretender to the British Crown.

1718

The French found New Orleans on the Mississippi River.

1727

George I dies. George II is crowned King of Great Britain.

1733

Georgia is founded by James Oglethorpe as both a debtor's colony and a bulwark against the threat from Spanish Florida.

1733–1735

The War of the Polish Succession, a general European conflict over who would rule in Poland, leads to more Russian influence in that Eastern European country.

1739

The War of Jenkins' Ear erupts between Britain and Spain. The conflict between the two nations will be subsumed into the larger European conflict known as the War of the Austrian Succession.

South Carolina slaves launch the Stono Rebellion, but fail to win their freedom.

1740–1748

In the War of the Austrian Succession (the American portion is known as King George's War, 1744–1748), much of the fighting takes place in Europe after Frederick II of Prussia's seizure of the rich Austrian province of Silesia.

1741

A combined force of colonial and British troops, transported and supported by the Royal Navy, besieges the Spanish colonial city of Cartagena in South America. Military ineptitude and mosquito-borne illnesses take a heavy toll on the attacking force. The British withdraw without taking Cartagena.

1743

The Battle of Dettingen is the last battle in history in which a British monarch leads national forces into battle. It results in the defeat of the French in the War of the Austrian Succession.

1745

English colonists, with British naval aid, capture Louisbourg, Nova Scotia. The British government will return it to France at the Treaty of Aix-la-Chapelle. The capture of a major fortress was a dramatic coup and a great boon to the colonists' military pride; Britain's willingness to bargain it away in peace negotiations leaves many colonists bitter and resentful.

The Battle of Fontenoy results in a French victory and the conquest of Flanders.

1745–1746

"Bonnie Prince Charlie," Prince Charles Edward Stuart, leads a Jacobite uprising from Scotland. Although the Jacobites briefly invade England, they return to Scotland and are annihilated by the forces of George II at the battle of Culloden on April 16, 1746.

1746

Russia and Austria conclude a defensive alliance.

1748

The treaty of Aix-la-Chapelle ends the War of the Austrian Succession and allows Prussia to keep Silesia.

1754

The royal governor of Virginia dispatches a small force under George Washington to confront French expansion into the Ohio territory. A skirmish between troops led by George Washington and those led by Coulon de Jumonville sparks the outbreak of the French and Indian War (known as the Seven Years' War in Europe, it will last until 1763).

Washington surrenders Fort Necessity, effectively handing control of the Ohio Valley to France.

At the Albany Congress, Benjamin Franklin promotes a plan for a union of the colonies, but he fails to secure approval for it.

1755

British General Edward Braddock's expedition to capture Fort Duquesne is defeated, when the British force marches into a well-prepared French and Native American ambush. Braddock is mortally wounded, and the British army retreats.

The first deportation of Acadians from Nova Scotia by the British takes place.

1756

The French capture Minorca from the British, although they later return it in the Treaty of Paris.

Austrian diplomat Wenzel von Kaunitz completes a diplomatic revolution in Europe by concluding a defensive alliance with Austria's traditional enemy, France.

The Seven Years' War breaks out in Europe, with France, Russia, and Austria facing off against Great Britain and Prussia. The war begins when Prussia preemptively attacks her neighbor Saxony.

1757

A French army led by the Marquis de Montcalm captures the British garrison of Fort William Henry in upstate New York. Montcalm's Native American allies later massacre the garrison as it returns to British territory following the terms of a surrender agreement.

East India Company forces, led by Robert Clive, win a major victory at Plassey, Bengal, India.

1758

The second deportation of Acadians by the British occurs.

French forces under the Marquis de Montcalm successfully defend Fort Carillon on Lake Champlain against a British attack.

The French fortress of Louisbourg, which guards the entrance to the St. Lawrence River and the heart of French North America, falls to a British amphibious force. The British also capture Fort Frontenac, seizing control of Lake Ontario.

The British take Fort Duquesne, in modern-day Pennsylvania, and rename it Fort Pitt.

1759

A large British army commanded by General James Wolfe lands near the French stronghold of Quebec. For several weeks, Wolfe tries to take the city but fails. Eventually, he moves his army upriver of Quebec, engages the French in battle, and defeats them on the Plains of Abraham on September 18. Although Wolfe dies in the battle, the French are compelled to surrender Quebec.

The British capture Fort Niagara.

Major General Jeffery Amherst takes Fort Carillon; the British rename it Fort Ticonderoga.

Amherst captures Fort St. Frédéric; the British rename it Crown Point.

Duke Ferdinand of Brunswick defeats the French at the battle of Minden.

The British win a naval victory at Quiberon Bay off the French coast.

1760

Major General Amherst captures Montreal from the French.

George III becomes king of Great Britain.

1761

French forces in Pondicherry, India, capitulate to the British.

1762

Tsarina Elizabeth of Russia dies. The new tsar, Peter, quickly makes peace with King Frederick II of Prussia. The removal of the Russian threat allows Frederick to escape destruction.

British capture Havana, Cuba, which they later return to Spain in the Treaty of Paris.

British forces capture Manila in the Philippines, but word of the victory does not reach Europe until after the signing of the Treaty of Paris.

1763

The Treaty of Paris ends the Seven Years' War. Britain gains Canada and control of all the land from the Appalachians to the Mississippi, except New Orleans. King Frederick II maintains control over Silesia.

Although the British have crushed the French in North America and India, the war leaves them with a massive war debt. Britain's efforts to tax its American colonies will serve as a major point of friction and contribute to the outbreak of the American War for Independence.

The Proclamation of 1763 forbids British settlers from moving west of the Alleghenies. The measure is intended to stave off future conflict between colonists and Native Americans. It does not achieve that goal, however, and only fuels American resentment of arbitrary British rule.

In the aftermath of the French and Indian War, Native Americans can no longer exploit tensions between the French and the British to their advantage. In Pontiac's Rebellion, Native Americans stage a massive uprising; it will take two years for the British to quell.

1765

Parliament passes the Stamp Act as a measure to raise revenue to help pay off the debt incurred during the Seven Years' War and to support its troops.

Parliament enacts the Quartering Act, forcing colonists to supply food and shelter to British troops. Another money-saving measure by Parliament, the Quartering Act offends colonists as a display of arbitrary rule. To colonists schooled in the standing army debate of the late seventeenth and early eighteenth centuries, troops quartered in private homes are a sign of impending tyranny.

1768

Britain sends two regiments of soldiers to Boston.

1770

British soldiers, harassed by a Boston mob, fire into a crowd of civilians. They kill five colonists and wound others, in an incident that becomes known as the Boston Massacre.

1772

Prussia, Austria, and Russia partition about one-third of Poland.

1773

In the Boston Tea Party, patriots dressed as Native Americans board British ships and throw tea into Boston Harbor to protest taxes.

1774

The British Parliament closes the port of Boston. General Thomas Gage takes command of British troops in Boston.

In Lord Dunmore's War, the royal governor of Virginia leads an expedition into the Ohio River valley against the Shawnee. The Virginians win a major battle at Point Pleasant and then conclude the Treaty of Camp Charlotte with the Shawnee, ending the war.

1775

Boston silversmith Paul Revere's famous ride alerts colonists of an impending British raid into the Massachusetts countryside to seize patriot leaders and weapons. The battles of Concord and Lexington take place the following day, when colonists resist the attempted raid.

Lord Dunmore orders the seizure of the gunpowder stored in Williamsburg's magazine. He also declares he will arm any slave and indentured servants who will fight with him against the nascent rebellion, giving them their freedom in exchange for military service. Later, he and his family flee to a British ship anchored off the Virginia coast.

George Washington receives the appointment as commander-in-chief of the Continental army.

Britain wins a Pyrrhic victory at Bunker Hill, near Boston.

On New Year's Eve, a patriot army, commanded by Benedict Arnold, Richard Montgomery, and Daniel Morgan, assaults the British in Quebec. The attack fails after the colonists suffer grievous losses.

1776

British forces abandon Boston to the Continental army and sail away to the north to regroup and refit.

Washington moves the Continental army south to defend New York City.

The Battle of Long Island takes place. The British victory leads to British occupation of New York City for the duration of the Revolution.

British troops, supported by the Royal Navy, outmaneuver and destroy Washington's army in New York. Washington barely manages to evacuate his troops from Manhattan; he retreats into Pennsylvania.

On Christmas Day, Washington launches a surprise attack on a garrison of Hessian soldiers at Trenton, New Jersey. The Hessians, German mercenaries in the pay of the British, had neglected their defenses in favor of holiday festivities. Washington captures almost the entire garrison, securing a major tactical victory and a much-needed boost to patriot morale after months of defeats.

1777

The British plan a three-pronged offensive to win the war: One force will invade New York from Canada; another will move north from New York City; a third army, commanded by General Sir William Howe, will sail south from New York and move on Philadelphia.

The Battle of Brandywine and the Battle of Germantown lead to the British capture of Philadelphia.

On October 19, the British army in upstate New York, commanded by General John Burgoyne, is compelled to surrender by Continental troops after the British lose the Battle of Saratoga. The American victory at Saratoga inspires the French government to join the war against Great Britain.

1778

In February, France and the rebelling colonies conclude an alliance committing France to support openly the American War for Independence.

British troops capture Vincennes in what is now Indiana.

1778–1779

The War of the Bavarian Succession is fought between Austria and Prussia.

1780

The Battle of Camden, South Carolina, leads to a British victory, giving the British an important base of operations.

Benedict Arnold, now in British service, leads a raid into Virginia, targeting Richmond and Charlottesville and sending Virginia Governor Thomas Jefferson running for safety.

1781

The battle of Cowpens, South Carolina, results in a psychologically important American victory.

French victory in the naval battle off the Virginia cape severs Lord Cornwallis's seaward escape route from Virginia.

The Franco-Colonial siege of Cornwallis's army trapped at Yorktown eventually results in a British surrender. The defeat of Cornwallis effectively ensures the colonists' victory in the American War for Independence.

1783

On September 3, the United States and Great Britain finally sign the Treaty of Paris, ending the American War for Independence.

Mitchell McNaylor

Politics and Government

1492

In August, Christopher Columbus sails from Palos, Spain, on his first voyage of discovery. Approximately two months later, he lands on an island in the Bahamas.

1494

Pope Alexander VI draws a line of demarcation on a map of the New World, splitting the territories between Spain and Portugal.

1499

Following the dismissal of Christopher Columbus, Francisco de Bobadilla is selected to govern Hispaniola.

1512

The Spanish Crown dictates the Laws of Burgos to colonists in the New World. It is the first code of laws to regulate Spanish treatment of the natives.

1519–1523

Hernando Cortéz defeats the Aztecs and consolidates his hold over the valley of Mexico. In 1523, he becomes the official governor of New Spain.

1524

The Council of the Indies, based in Spain, is established to have supreme authority over the Spanish colonies and to administer them.

1527

The first *audiencia* is established in Mexico City, followed by one in Santo Domingo and in other Spanish settlements. These governing bodies are under the authority of the viceroys and are made up of a president, judges, a Crown prosecutor, and lesser officials.

1535

Conquered Mexican territories become the Viceroyalty of New Spain. Hernando Cortéz is selected to lead the colony.

1540

Francisco Vázquez de Coronado leads a Spanish expedition throughout the American Southwest in search of gold, en-countering the Hopi and other native peoples. Afterward, Spanish friars and priests set up missions throughout the area.

1542

The New Laws of the Indies are dictated by Charles V to the Spanish colonies, providing better treatment for the natives. The rights granted are judged by the colonists to be too pro-native, resulting in revolt and the repeal of the laws in the Viceroyalty of New Spain and the Viceroyalty of Peru.

1556

Charles V abdicates as ruler of the Netherlands and Spain and as Holy Roman Emperor in favor of his son, Philip II.

1568

In Europe, revolts begin throughout the Low Countries (the Netherlands) against Philip II of Spain.

1570

Five independent tribes—the Cayuga, the Mohawk, the Oneida, the Onondaga, and the Seneca—form the Iroquois League. The League has a confederate structure, which will be influential in the later creation of the Articles of Confederation, because America's founding fathers will study the Iroquois form of government.

1581

The Dutch declare independence from Spain, but Spanish forces continue their attempts to retake the Low Countries.

1584

Sir Walter Raleigh receives a charter from Queen Elizabeth I of England to colonize North America. Raleigh's five attempts at establishing a settlement on Roanoke Island, in what later will become North Carolina, all fail.

1606

King James I of England grants a charter to the Virginia Company to establish a colony in Virginia.

1607

A ship reaches the shores of Virginia carrying 105 colonists from England. They will establish the colony of Jamestown.

1608

A French colony, led by Samuel de Champlain, is established at Quebec.

1609

A Spanish colony is established in New Mexico at Santa Fe.

1613

The Dutch establish a small trading post on Manhattan Island.

1619

The Virginia House of Burgesses, the first legislative assembly to meet in America, conducts its first session at Jamestown. Twenty-two burgesses represent eleven plantations throughout the colony.

1620

On November 11, near Cape Cod, settlers aboard the *Mayflower* sign the Mayflower Compact. This self-government plan for the colony will take effect when the passengers disembark.

The Pilgrims land at Plymouth, Massachusetts, on December 21.

1624

The Virginia Company's charter is revoked, and Virginia becomes a royal colony.

1626

Peter Minuit of the Netherlands purchases Manhattan Island from the Canarsee Indians.

1627

Cardinal Richelieu of France organizes the Company of One Hundred Associates (*Compagnie des Cent-Associés*) in order to settle New France. The new company is given jurisdiction over all French lands between Florida and the Arctic, and the company is granted a monopoly over all trade except for fishing.

1629

King Charles I of England dismisses Parliament and rules as an absolute monarch. As a result, many English subjects leave for the American colonies.

1630

John Winthrop leads more than 900 Puritan colonists to establish Boston in the Massachusetts Bay Colony.

1635

In September, Roger Williams is banished from Salem by the Massachusetts General Court, because his religious views are deemed unacceptable by the Puritans. The following month, Williams is banished from the entire Massachusetts Bay Colony for religious dissent. He will found Providence and the colony of Rhode Island.

1637

In November, Anne Hutchinson is banished from the Massachusetts Bay Colony by the Massachusetts General Court for her heretical beliefs and threat to the Puritan theocracy. She, along with her family and a group of followers move to Rhode Island, where they establish a democratic community.

1641

The "Body of Liberties" legal code, based on the Old Testament, is adopted in the Massachusetts Bay Colony.

1643

The New England Confederation is formed for mutual protection by the colonies of Connecticut, New Haven, Plymouth, and Massachusetts Bay.

1644

A group of eleven slaves successfully petitions the government of New Amsterdam for their freedom.

1647

Peter Stuyvesant becomes director general of the colony of New Netherland, as well as colonies in the Caribbean (Aruba, Bonaire, and Curaçao).

1649

King Charles I of England is beheaded. Oliver Cromwell and his forces begin to assert control over England, Ireland, and Scotland.

Maryland's Assembly passes the Toleration Act, which guarantees freedom of worship and lauds religious tolerance.

1650

The Hartford Treaty is signed, setting a boundary between New Netherland and New England.

1660

Parliament restores the monarchy and Charles II becomes king of England.

The Navigation Act of 1660, the first of many laws governing trade and navigation in the American colonies, goes into effect. It mandates that only English-built ships with crews that are two-thirds English will be allowed to trade with the colonies. Also, mercantilist policies are enacted requiring that certain goods (indigo, sugar, and tobacco) be shipped to Britain only.

1663

King Louis XIV assumes personal control of New France, making it a royal colony.

The charter of Rhode Island incorporates religious freedom.

1664–1674

The Navigation Act of 1663 goes into effect on March 25. It requires that all imports shipped to the British colonies from other countries come through ports in Britain and be transported on British ships.

A British naval squadron accepts the surrender of New Amsterdam, renaming the colony New York. The Dutch recapture the colony briefly in 1673, but it is ceded back to Britain in 1674.

1676

Dissidents—angered by high taxes and low tobacco prices, and resentful of government officials—rebel and begin to raid local Native American tribes. Led by Nathaniel Bacon, the rebellion exposes deep discontent among the colonists. In September, Jamestown is burned to the ground by Bacon and his followers.

1682

William Penn, the founder of Pennsylvania, lands near Chester, Pennsylvania.

1685

The Edict of Nantes is revoked, prompting almost 200,000 Huguenots to leave France for other European countries and the North American colonies.

1687

Throughout the Spanish colonies, leadership posts within the *audiencias* are largely put up for sale, allowing wealthy colonists to participate in the colonies' legislative affairs.

1688

Quakers in Philadelphia pass legislation against slavery.

1690

The first paper money is issued in the colony of Massachusetts, prompted by the need to pay soldiers fighting a war in Quebec.

1700

King Philip V ascends to the throne of Spain. He is the first Bourbon ruler of the Spanish Empire.

1701

William Penn grants the Charter of Privileges to his colony of Pennsylvania. It establishes a unicameral legislature and a policy of religious freedom.

1733

Georgia is settled as a penal colony and a haven for debtors. It is initially established with a ban on slavery.

1735

The printer of the *New York Weekly Journal*, John Peter Zenger, is acquitted on charges of seditious libel. This ruling sets one of the first freedom-of-the-press precedents in the colonies.

1750

The Georgia colony revokes its laws against slavery.

1754

The *Pennsylvania Gazette* contains the first recorded American political cartoon. Created by Benjamin Franklin, the cartoon attacks the fragmentation of the colonists regarding frontier defense.

Delegates from different colonies meet at the Albany Congress to decide upon a common policy toward the Iroquois.

The French and Indian War begins. It is the North American phase of the Seven Years' War in Europe (1756–1763).

1760

King George II dies, and George III ascends to the British throne.

1761

Thomas Hutchinson is selected to be the chief justice of Massachusetts.

British forces in Boston without warrants begin to search colonists' homes for smuggled goods.

1762

Louisiana is ceded to Spain by France as a result of the Treaty of Fontainebleau.

1763

Under the terms of the Treaty of Paris, France cedes its North American territories (Canada and areas east of the Mississippi River) to Britain. This effectively ends the French and Indian War in the colonies.

1764

The Sugar Act is passed by the British Parliament on April 5, placing taxes on foreign sugar, increasing taxes on coffee, indigo, and wines from the island of Madeira, and banning the importation of French wines and rum.

In June, the Massachusetts Assembly creates the first Committee of Correspondence. It works to inform all the colonies about the revolutionary events taking place.

In Britain, the Currency Act is passed on September 1, forbidding the colonies from issuing their own currency.

1765

On March 22, the British Parliament passes the Stamp Act, which requires that goods, documents, and services be notarized and taxed in the American colonies. Revenue from the tax helps to maintain the British armies stationed in America. Three days later, Parliament passes the Quartering Act, which requires the American colonies to provide barracks and provisions for British troops.

In response to the Stamp Act, Patrick Henry issues a diatribe against it at Virginia's House of Burgesses on May 29. He states, "If this be treason, make the most of it." The next day, the House of Burgesses legislates its Virginia Resolves, which attack the Stamp Act because it taxes colonists without representation in Parliament.

On August 28, colonists who are against the Stamp Act burn the records of a vice-admiralty court in Boston.

Delegates from nine colonies meet on October 7 to hold the Stamp Act Congress, which enacts a Declaration of Rights and Grievances. The declaration denounces taxation without representation.

1766

In February, Benjamin Franklin writes an unauthorized letter to the British in defiance of the Stamp Act. The legislature of Georgia also acts in resistance to the Stamp Act; the legislature is subsequently dissolved by the royal governor.

On March 7, the British Parliament passes the Declaratory Act, which states that Parliament has the right to enact laws governing the American colonies. Eleven days later, the Stamp Act is repealed, but Parliament cites the Declaratory Act, stating that all future laws concerning the colonies are lawful.

1767

The Townshend Acts are approved by the British Parliament. These acts place import taxes on manufactured products shipped to America.

1768

American assemblies are forced to disband by British administrators in the colonies.

1769

Thomas Hutchinson takes his new post as governor of Massachusetts.

1770

In February, Alexander McDougall is put in jail for printing subversive flyers in New York.

On March 5, the British military is unable to disperse a mob of colonists in Boston peacefully. The violence that results will become known as the Boston Massacre. Five colonists die and others are wounded.

On April 12, the Townshend Acts, which imposed taxes on certain goods that colonists import, are repealed.

On November 27, the Boston Massacre trials begin to decide the fate of the eight British soldiers and one officer involved in this incident. All are acquitted on the basis of

self-defense, except for two privates, who are branded on their left thumbs and released.

1772

On June 9, colonists from Rhode Island attack and burn the Royal Navy schooner *Gaspee* while it is caught in ice.

1773

The Tea Act is passed by the British Parliament on May 10. It grants the East India Company a monopoly on the tea trade.

On June 5, the Boston Committee resolves to form the Solemn League and Covenant, agreeing to cease all trade with Great Britain.

Committees of Correspondence from Virginia and Massachusetts condemn the Tea Act on October 16.

Patriots, dressed as Native Americans, board British ships in Boston Harbor on December 16. They dump more than 300 crates of tea overboard in protest of the taxes on tea and the East India Tea Company's monopoly on the trade. This event becomes known as the Boston Tea Party.

1774

On January 3, Governor William Tyson of New York enforces the boycott of tea, saying that tea will not land in New York except by "point of the bayonet."

One of the Coercive Acts, the Boston Port Bill, goes into effect on March 31. It orders the closure of Boston Harbor until reparations are made for the tea lost during the Boston Tea Party.

Lord Dunmore, governor of Virginia, dissolves the Virginia House of Burgesses.

General Thomas Gage arrives in Boston to take the position of military governor on May 13.

The establishment of the Quebec Act on May 20 widens the divide between Canada and the American colonies. This act, which attempts to ensure French Canadians' allegiance to the Crown by expanding Quebec's territory, changes the oath of allegiance process for public officials and allows for the practice of Catholicism.

Along with the Quebec Act and the Boston Port Bill, the Massachusetts Government Act (which annuls the Massachusetts Colony's charter and gives the British governor complete authority) and the Administration of Justice Act (which allows the British governor to move trials to another colony or to Britain) are effectively instated. Together, these acts become known as the Coercive Acts or Intolerable Acts.

On June 2, military governor Thomas Gage declares martial law in Massachusetts.

The Continental Congress meets for the first time in Philadelphia on September 5. Joseph Warren of Boston, Massachusetts, calls for a ban on British goods. And the Suffolk Resolves, which attack and void the Coercive Acts by stating that Parliament does not have authority over the

American colonies without colonial representation, are adopted.

In October, the Continental Congress passes a Declaration and Resolves stating that only colonial legislative bodies may enact legislation for the colonies. The Congress also enacts the Continental Association in order to suspend commerce with Britain. And it asks colonists to forgo such expensive activities as horse racing, cockfighting, and gambling, in order to concentrate on the current situation.

1775

In January, the City of Philadelphia's Committee agrees to support the Provincial Congress. Governor William Franklin of New Jersey, Benjamin Franklin's son and a staunch loyalist, pleads with the General Assembly of New Jersey to remain associated with the king. The Provincial Congress of South Carolina takes control of the colonial treasury. And the Assembly of New York chooses not to consider measures taken by the Continental Congress.

In early February, delegates from New Jersey state that they will support the king if liberties previously held by colonists are returned. The Second Massachusetts Provincial Congress holds its first meeting in Cambridge; it condemns anyone assisting the British army in and around Boston.

On February 9, the king and Parliament of Britain declare that Massachusetts is in a state of rebellion. Later in February, imports from Pennsylvania are banned in Britain.

Patrick Henry addresses the Virginia Convention on March 23, promoting resistance against Britain. His speech includes his famous statement, "Give me liberty, or give me death."

New York's Colonial Assembly holds its final meeting. General Thomas Gage, royal governor of Massachusetts, is ordered to arrest members of the Massachusetts Provincial Congress on April 14.

On April 19, the American Revolution begins with the engagements at Lexington and Concord, Massachusetts. The famous "shot heard 'round the world" is fired. The Massachusetts' Provincial Congress enacts the creation of a militia.

The first referendum in U.S. history is disapproved when Massachusetts voters vote against their constitution on May 16. Ten days later, the Continental Congress declares a new name for the American colonies, the United Colonies of America.

In June, the Continental Congress approves the creation of a Continental army of around 20,000 troops. George Washington is appointed commander in chief of the Continental army.

On July 6, the Continental Congress approves the distribution of Colonel John Dickinson's *Declaration of the Causes and Necessity of Taking Up Arms*; the document attempts to justify the colonists' right to defend themselves. (Thomas Jefferson originally had composed a similar document, but his version was deemed too militant.)

The Continental Congress's Olive Branch Petition, a last offer to find a solution to the differences between the colonies and the Crown, is sent to the king on July 15. This petition requests that he end his military activities in the colonies. A few days later, the Continental Congress selects delegates to reach agreements with Native Americans.

On August 18, the Provincial Congress of New York suggests that areas around New York City should be fortified. King George III of Britain proclaims the American colonies are rebelling, and he declares the revolt will be put down by force. The *Pennsylvania Gazette* publishes a story that tells how Parliament plans to try rebels from the colonies in England for their offenses.

In September, the Massachusetts Assembly requires that representatives take oaths of allegiance. The Continental Congress establishes a secret committee to deal with spies and espionage in the impending war. King George III officially refuses the requests of the Olive Branch Petition; British military activity in the colonies will continue.

In November, Lord Dunmore, royal governor of Virginia, promises to emancipate slaves who fight for the British and loyalist forces during the war; he also declares martial law throughout the colony. Montreal is occupied by invading American forces, but colonists there are not convinced to join the American rebellion. On November 28, the Continental Congress enacts the creation of the American Navy; the following day, the Congress establishes a secret committee to control and seek out foreign assistance.

On December 3, the first Navy Jack of the United States Navy is flown aboard the USS *Alfred* on the Delaware River. Five days later, colonial forces led by Benedict Arnold begin the siege of Quebec City, Canada. Later in December, the British Parliament allows for the confiscation of vessels owned by "rebellious" American colonists.

Esek Hopkins is selected to be the first commodore of the American Navy. General George Washington proposes the enlistment of African Americans in the Continental army.

1776

Common Sense by Thomas Paine is published on January 10. The pamphlet supports American independence, attacks the ideas of hereditary monarchies, and describes the future economic benefits of independence. Later in January, the Continental Congress allows for the enlistment of black soldiers.

The Continental Congress authorizes privateering against British ships on March 19. On April 6, it moves to suspend the slave trade and opens all ports to any nation except for Britain.

On May 2, King Louis XVI of France sends military supplies to the American army.

A convention of delegates from all over Virginia vote in favor of independence on May 6; the state's delegates at the Continental Congress are informed to vote that way at the Congress as well. Virginia delegate Richard Henry Lee proposes independence at the Continental Congress on June 7, proclaiming, "These united colonies are, and of right ought to be, free and independent states."

On June 10, the Congress creates a War and Ordnance Board to oversee the military matters of the American colonies. The following day, it appoints a committee to create a draft of the Declaration of Independence; the committee appointed by the Continental Congress selects Thomas Jefferson to compose the first draft.

Also in June, Virginia passes the Declaration of Rights, which guarantees certain rights to citizens and is a precursor to the Bill of Rights. The Continental Congress adopts the predecessor to the modern flag of the United States, containing thirteen red and white stripes and thirteen stars on blue. The Congress starts to print paper money, and it declares that loyalists are guilty of treason against the united American colonies.

On June 27, Thomas Jefferson completes his first draft of the Declaration of Independence. It is read at the Continental Congress the next day.

On July 2, the Continental Congress passes a resolution calling for independence from Great Britain. On July 4, the Declaration of Independence is adopted by the Continental Congress unopposed; it is read publicly for the first time on July 8 in Philadelphia.

On September 9, the United Colonies are renamed the United States by the Continental Congress. On September 20, Pennsylvania approves its Declaration of Rights, which guarantees certain rights and freedoms to the state's citizens, and it ratifies its constitution.

On December 27, the Continental Congress gives General George Washington dictatorial powers to be used during urgent war decisions.

1777

In January, slaves in Massachusetts petition for their freedom before the legislature. The Declaration of Independence is reprinted, containing the signatures of all the signers.

In March, Congress votes to buy blankets for soldiers in the Continental army.

In April, the General Court of Massachusetts votes in favor of a referendum on the state constitution.

Vermont, then a district of New York state, abolishes slavery in July.

On September 19, the Continental Congress is forced to flee from Philadelphia as British troops advance to occupy the city. The Congress reconvenes on September 27 in Lancaster, Pennsylvania. Lancaster serves as the country's capital for three days, after which the capital moves to York, Pennsylvania.

The Articles of Confederation, the United States' first plan of government, is agreed upon by the Continental Congress. The plan will not be completely ratified by the states until 1781.

1778

In early January, France puts forth an offer of alliance with the American states.

In March, the British Parliament agrees to start negotiations with the colonies. Shortly thereafter, France notifies Great Britain about its new alliance with the American colonies. American diplomats in France are officially received by King Louis XVI as allies.

On April 16, British delegates sail for America to offer terms of peace. Congress ratifies the alliance with France in May.

In June, the General Assembly of Rhode Island stops enlisting enslaved blacks.

In July, the Continental Congress adopts the Articles of Confederation. The united colonies are officially referred to as the United States of America for the first time.

In September, Benjamin Franklin is sent to Paris as the American representative to France.

1779

Congress authorizes a $100 bounty for enlistment in the Continental army.

Thomas Jefferson is elected governor of Virginia.

1780

In March, Pennsylvania passes the Emancipation Act, ending slavery throughout the state.

In August, an American diplomat, sent to negotiate an alliance with the United Provinces of the Netherlands, is captured at sea by the British.

In December, General George Washington writes to Congress requesting money for his suffering army. Meanwhile, the Netherlands ally with the American states in their war against Britain.

1781

In February, Congress legislates the establishment of the departments of Finance, War, and Marine. General Cornwallis proclaims an invitation to loyalists to assist in the suppression of the rebellion.

The Articles of Confederation are officially ratified on March 1, providing the United States with its first plan of government.

A prisoner exchange agreement between the Continental and British armies is signed on May 3 in Pegues Place, South Carolina.

In August, Robert Livingston becomes the first secretary of foreign affairs.

In November, John Hanson is elected to the presidency of the United States, under the Articles of Confederation.

1782

In January, loyalists from the United States start leaving for Nova Scotia, New Brunswick, and the Bahamas. The number of loyalists who leave is believed to exceed 100,000, including over 15,000 slaves.

In June, Congress adopts the country's official seal. The Great Seal of the United States is used by General George Washington on a document authorizing a prisoner exchange with the British on September 16.

In November, preliminary peace terms are agreed upon by delegates of the United States and Britain, signaling the end of the Revolutionary War.

1783

Portugal recognizes the independence of the United States.

U.S. troops threaten to mutiny if they do not receive their back pay.

On September 3, the Treaty of Paris is signed, officially ending the Revolutionary War.

General George Washington gives his last orders to the Continental army on October 2; the army is disbanded a month later. In December, General George Washington resigns from his post as commander in chief of the Continental army and returns to his home at Mount Vernon, Virginia.

1784

In January, the legislature of Connecticut enacts a program of gradual emancipation.

Later in January, Congress approves the Treaty of Paris, in which Great Britain recognizes the independence of the American states.

In February, trade with China officially opens when the *Empress of China* sails from New York to Canton.

In April, Native Americans, supported by the British, raid and pillage settlements throughout the Ohio Valley in violation of the Treaty of Paris. Congress prohibits slavery in the Northwest Territory.

In July, amendments to the Articles of Confederation are rejected by Rhode Island legislators.

In August, a group of counties in North Carolina attempts to secede from the state, but their calls for statehood are refused by Congress.

In October, slaves who fought during the Revolutionary War for the Continental army are emancipated in Virginia.

In November, the United States agrees to a peace treaty with the Iroquois.

Congress moves the nation's capital to New York City on December 24.

1785

John Adams voices his concerns over Britain's failure to comply with the Treaty of Paris and demands that Britain withdrawal from American soil.

Thomas Jefferson proposes a standard national currency system. A few days later, the Mount Vernon Conference on interstate navigation and commerce is held. It proves a precursor to the conventions that will eventually abandon the Articles of Confederation.

1786

Virginia adopts Thomas Jefferson's Statute for Religious Freedom, which establishes that religious beliefs are solely the individual's concern and that a separation between state and religion should exist.

Congress approves the dollar as the monetary standard.

The Annapolis Convention (a precursor to the Constitutional Convention the following year) is called to reform interstate trade regulations.

1787

Massachusetts farmers led by Daniel Shays attempt to take over an arsenal at Springfield, Massachusetts, on January 25, but they fail. The group, angered by a lack of paper money, high taxes, and fear of debtor's prison, leads a short rebellion, which forces many people to view the Articles of Confederation as an inefficient and problematic governmental system.

In February, the Continental Congress calls for another meeting in May to revise the Articles of Confederation. In May, delegates convene in Philadelphia to discuss the revisions; George Washington is elected to preside over the Constitutional Convention. Edmund Randolph presents the Virginia Plan to the Convention, calling for a bicameral legislature with representation based upon population.

On July 13, Congress, still under the Articles of Confederation, passes the Northwest Ordinance, which proposes Congress's eventual creation of three to five states in the Northwest Territory.

In September, Elbridge Gerry and George Mason put forward a proposal on the topic of a bill of rights. Thirty-nine of forty-two delegates who attended the Constitutional Convention in Philadelphia sign the Constitution of the United States, and it is sent to Congress for approval. Congress reaches an agreement to send the Constitution to the states for ratification on September 28.

On October 27, Alexander Hamilton, James Madison, and John Jay publish the first of their Federalist Papers in a New York newspaper. The essays argue for the passage of the Constitution.

Delaware ratifies the Constitution on December 7; it is the first state to do so. Pennsylvania ratifies the Constitution on December 12, and New Jersey does so on December 18.

1788

More states ratify the Constitution: Georgia (January 2), Connecticut (January 9), Massachusetts (February 6), Maryland (April 28), South Carolina (May 23), and New Hampshire (June 21). Although Rhode Island had voted against ratification (April 24), the required number of states to approve the Constitution has been reached.

On July 2, Congress is notified that the Constitution has achieved the required number of state approvals for ratification.

On August 2, North Carolina's first attempt to ratify the Constitution fails.

The last session of Congress under the Articles of Confederation is held on October 12.

1789

In February, Delaware prohibits slavery. Electors unanimously vote George Washington to power as the first president of the United States under the Constitution.

In March, the new national government under the Constitution goes into official operation.

George Washington states that becoming president is like "a culprit going to the place of his execution." He is inaugurated as the first president of the United States at Federal Hall in New York City on April 30.

Arthur Holst

Race and Ethnicity

58,000–10,000 B.C.E.

Groups of Paleo-Indians migrate into the Americas, most likely from Asia, though other theories exist as to their origins. Over time, they begin to differentiate into regional subcultures. These are the distant ancestors of colonial-period Native Americans.

750–1550 C.E.

The Mississippian culture, with major cities at Cahokia (near present-day East St. Louis), Spiro, and Natchez, dominates the eastern half of North America. By 1100, Cahokia is home to a complex, stratified society of 20,000 people. In the Southwest, by roughly 1250, a people known as the Anasazi have constructed twelve large towns and hundreds more villages, constituting a formidable trading empire.

1492

Christopher Columbus, a Genoan sailing for King Ferdinand and Queen Isabella of Spain, reaches San Salvador in October and inaugurates a new era of contact—and conflict—between ethnic groups. Columbus immediately begins to search neighboring Caribbean islands for gold and treasure; he also enslaves several of the Taino people he encounters.

1494

The Treaty of Tordesillas divides the New World between Spain and Portugal, the preeminent naval powers of the fifteenth and sixteenth centuries.

1510

The Spanish bring the first African slaves to Española (Hispaniola). Europeans have been enslaving Africans for decades on sugar-producing islands off the coast of Africa and in the Mediterranean, but this marks the earliest stages of the transatlantic slave trade, which will disrupt millions of lives on three continents.

1513

Juan Ponce de León, allegedly in search of the "fountain of youth," but more likely in search of gold and slaves, lands near present-day Daytona Beach and names the "island" he believes he has landed on Florida. Ponce de León's first meeting with Native Americans is an attack the Spanish suffer at the hands of Ais Indians. Ponce de León's fleet continues up the west coast of Florida, where it meets resistance from the Calusa Indians. Following Hernando Cortéz's encounter with the Aztec, Ponce de León returns to Florida in 1521 and begins constructing buildings in a location lost to history. He is shot, and dies of his arrow wound in Cuba.

1521

Relying on superior technology, surprise, disease, and an alliance of anti-Aztec native peoples, Cortéz conquers the Aztec Empire of central Mexico. In the major battle of the campaign, Cortéz's army lays siege to the Aztec capital at Tenochtitlán (a city of 200,000; Seville's population at the time was 70,000). The Spanish capture, hold hostage, and eventually execute the ruler Montezuma II. They also feed the surviving Aztec priests to the Spanish war dogs.

1534–1541

In the Northeast, Jacques Cartier travels up the St. Lawrence River, trading and establishing generally friendly relations with that region's Native American population.

1539–1543

Hernando de Soto's *entrada* into what is now the southeastern United States represents one of the earliest Spanish attempts to explore and exploit the region. De Soto and a column of about 600 men travel through the Southeast in search of gold and treasure. His routine involves taking leading Native American men hostage and holding them in exchange for provisions, women, and safe passage through hostile territory. De Soto eventually falls ill and dies; his body is allegedly sunk in the Mississippi River. Half of his expeditionary force limps back to Mexico.

1540–1542

Francisco Vázquez de Coronado invades what is now the southwestern United States in search of the Seven Cities of Gold, legendary cities of fabulous wealth. The Pueblo Indians, upset with Spanish rape and plunder, first revolt, then send the Spanish farther north with rumors of gold and silver. Coronado's army reaches as far north as present-day Kansas; realizing that no gold is to be found in the region, the Spanish return to punish the Pueblos again.

1565

Spanish and French forces clash on Florida's Atlantic Coast. Pedro Menéndez de Avilés defeats French Protestant forces under Jean Ribaut, and France gives up its claim to Florida. St. Augustine is founded.

1587

Backed by Sir Walter Raleigh, Governor John White and 115 men, women, and children arrive at Roanoke (off the coast of North Carolina) in the summer. Virginia Dare is born; she is the first English child born in North America.

John White returns to England for supplies. By the time of his return in 1590, the colony has disappeared. White discovers destroyed buildings, a ransacked fort, and the word "Croatoan" scratched into one of the stockade posts. Though search parties look for the colonists in the late sixteenth and early seventeenth centuries, they are never found. Various theories about the colonists' disappearance are that they were assimilated into local tribes, killed by local native peoples, or killed during the Powhatan's conquest of the area in the early 1600s.

1598

Don Juan de Oñate crosses the Rio Grande at the site of present-day El Paso and begins the formal colonization of New Mexico. When he reaches present-day Albuquerque, which the Spanish call Santo Domingo, he addresses the assembled leaders of the Pueblo people. Oñate explains the benefits, both secular and religious, of submitting to the Spanish, and all of the leaders agree that they will submit.

The Spanish set up their headquarters at a Tewa pueblo they call San Juan, forcing the Indians to provide them with housing, labor, food, and clothing. The Spanish and Pueblo people remain crowded together in the area until about 1608, when Oñate starts to move the capital to Santa Fe. Oñate also seeks a route to the Pacific Ocean and manages to reach the Gulf of California in 1604 or 1605.

The Pueblos of Acoma attack the Spanish, killing eleven colonists, including Oñate's nephew. In retaliation, Oñate's forces attack Acoma, killing 500 men and 300 women and children. He also takes about 80 men and 500 women and children captive; their punishments range from terms of servitude to maiming.

1607

Settlers at Jamestown establish the first permanent English colony in North America. Relations with the Powhatan people are peaceful at first, as the English pose no immediate threat to the natives. Poor preparation and a poor location (in a swamp) cause much grief to the English, as more than half of the original settlers die.

1608–1627

Samuel de Champlain, continuing his earlier efforts, founds the colony of New France when he secures the alliances of a number of native peoples and builds a fortified trading post at Quebec in 1608. In 1609, the French and their allies battle the Iroquois.

By 1627, only eighty-five men will live at Quebec. French interest in New France remains low, although a handful of Jesuits and fur traders make inroads in the Northeast and Great Lakes regions.

1610–1614

A series of conflicts subsequently known as the Anglo-Powhatan Wars begins in Virginia. These pit the newly arrived English colonists against a group of Native Americans led by a chieftain named Powhatan. The wars are actually more of an extended series of raids, which break out as the English move beyond their stockade at Jamestown and press the Powhatan to supply them with corn.

1614

Pocahontas, a daughter of Powhatan who had been held captive at Jamestown, marries John Rolfe, an English planter. The intercultural marriage brings about a brief period of peace between the English and Powhatan.

1619

The first shipment of Africans arrives in mainland North America when a Dutch ship unloads twenty "Negars" at Jamestown, Virginia. Although their legal status is not precisely clear, and some of them do end up serving out indentures and being freed, the majority of Africans in Virginia during the colonial period are slaves.

1620

The Pilgrims, religious refugees from England by way of the Netherlands, land at Plymouth, in present-day Massachusetts. Squanto, a Wampanoag translator and guide, aids the colonists and helps to eases tensions between the English and Massasoit, the local Pokanoket sachem.

1622

Ever-expanding English settlements in Virginia prompt Opechancanough (Powhatan's brother, who replaced him as leader of his people) to launch an attack on outlying settlements. The attacks are an astonishing success, killing 347 English colonists, although Opechancanough does not pursue the fight back to Jamestown. The retaliatory strike by the English is equally vicious and many Powhatan people are killed. The end result of this conflict is that new areas are open for white settlement.

1632–1649

French Jesuits establish missions and convert Hurons in present-day Ontario. The Huron, and other native peoples, accept baptism on their own cultural terms, and many add the Europeans' God to their spiritual understanding of the world. The priests' records, published as *The Jesuit Relations*, will become indispensable tools for historians and anthropologists seeking to reconstruct North America's native past.

1636

Roger Williams, banished from the Massachusetts Bay Colony in 1635, founds Providence, Rhode Island. Williams advocates tolerance of Native American religions and the purchase of Indian land.

1637–1638

Ostensibly upset over the killing of trader John Stone (who had been banished from the Massachusetts Bay Colony), the United Colonies of New England send a force to punish the Pequot of the Connecticut River Valley. In the main action of the Pequot War, the English and their Narragansett and Wampanoag allies set fire to a major village on the Mystic River (also known as Mystic Fort). As the village burns, Pequot noncombatants, mainly old men, women, and children, run for their lives, only to be put to the sword by the English. Estimates of the dead range from 400 to 900; the native people who survive are sold into slavery. By the terms of the treaty that stops the fighting, the Pequot are forced to submit to the English in every way, and their tribe is effectively dissolved.

1641

Massachusetts is the first North American colony to officially recognize African slavery and give it legal sanction. By the end of the colonial period, slavery exists in all thirteen of Great Britain's North American colonies, whether in the North or the South.

1644

Opechancanough, leader of the 1622 attack on Virginia, strikes the English again. This fighting results in a treaty between the two groups, although the treaty will be rendered meaningless in the decades to come, as tens of thousands of English settlers flock into Powhatan territory.

Also in 1644, eleven African slaves in New Amsterdam petition for their freedom. The Council of New Netherland frees the slaves, since they have served the colony for an extended period of time.

1649

Weakened by disease and famine, the Huron villages of Ontario are all but destroyed by Iroquois war parties in a series of conflicts known collectively as the Beaver Wars. The surviving Hurons join other villages throughout the Great Lakes, and many Hurons are adopted into the villages of their former enemies, the Iroquois.

1651

Anthony Johnson, a free African (one of the original black settlers at Jamestown), receives 250 acres of land in Northampton County, Virginia. Johnson becomes master of his own plantation. Though this will never be common, it happens more often in slavery's early years. As the seventeenth century progresses, white Virginians turn increasingly to African slavery and begin to divide their society sharply along racial lines.

1662

A Virginia law mandates that children should follow the condition of their mother; therefore, the children of slaves become slaves.

1664

Maryland enacts a law preventing miscegenation between Africans and English people. Other colonies add similar laws throughout the colonial period, reflecting a fear of race mixing.

1674–1677

During this three-year stretch, the English and the Iroquois come to an agreement known as the Covenant Chain, through which each group can increase its power. The Iroquois receive special trade privileges from the English so long as they remain allied to the English and provide security against the Algonquin. The Covenant Chain benefits both the English and the Iroquois but spells disaster for Native American peoples who are not part of the chain. The Iroquois step up raids, particularly in the Illinois country.

1675–1676

King Philip's War rages in New England. King Philip, a native leader also known as Metacom, upset with biased colonial policies and the encroachment of English farm animals in Wampanoag hunting lands, begins a series of raids, which soon escalate into full-blown war. Other Native Americans, not necessarily acting in concert with Metacom, succeed in destroying several English towns and pushing the line of settlement back. The tide of the war turns dramatically when the Mohawk join the side of the English (thanks to their relationship with New York), and the Iroquois's participation is another major factor in deciding the war for the English. Metacom and his allies are fighting on two fronts, and, in 1676, Metacom himself is shot by a fellow Native American, acting on behalf of the English.

1676

Nathaniel Bacon, one of the wealthiest planters in Virginia, heads a rebellion against Native Americans and his cousin, Governor William Berkeley. Fighting erupts when a party of Doeg Indians begins raiding white farms on the James River as retaliation for crooked trading practices. Bacon takes matters into his own hands and slaughters a group of Susquehannocks, who have been allied with Virginia for decades.

1680

The Pueblo, chafing under Spanish civil and ecclesiastical authority, rebel. Led by Popé, a Tewa who suffered physical abuse at the hands of the Spanish, the Pueblo lay aside traditional rivalries in order to cast off the Spanish. The Spanish who survive the initial attack hole up at Santa Fe, where they face a numerically superior Pueblo army. The Spanish are able to fight their way out of Santa Fe, although they have to retreat all the way to the present site of El Paso, Texas. The Pueblo kill 200 of the 1,000 Spanish colonists and half of the forty or so priests. This is one of the greatest setbacks the native peoples have yet inflicted on European colonization in North America. New Mexico reverts to Pueblo control for more than a decade.

1682

William Penn founds the colony of Pennsylvania as a refuge for Quakers fleeing persecution in England. Penn, through intermediaries, establishes peace with the Lenni Lenape (called the Delaware by the English) and other smaller tribes.

Eventually, the Quaker colony is surrounded by a ring of Native American groups that have migrated from as far away as South Carolina. Though Penn has practical reasons for this—namely, his desire to protect his colony against Iroquois and French attacks, he also makes a point of purchasing Native Americans' lands, and word of Pennsylvania's fair treatment of natives spreads. The period between the 1680s and the 1740s comes to be known as the "Long Peace."

Mary Rowlandson, who was held captive by Native Americans after a raid on Lancaster, Massachusetts, during King Philip's War, publishes *The Sovereignty and Goodness of God*, the first and most popular example of a genre known as "captivity narratives."

1688

In the Germantown Protest, a group of Pennsylvania Quakers denounces slavery and the slave trade at one of their monthly meetings.

1699

Virginia passes a law declaring that free African Americans are required to leave the colony, but the law generally goes unenforced.

1700–1701

The Iroquois establish peace with both France and Britain. They will continue to play the two powers off each other until the late stages of the French and Indian War, when trading ties and the diplomacy of Sir William Johnson, coupled with British military success, force them to abandon the French and ally themselves with the English.

Also in 1701, John Lawson, officially the surveyor general of the young Carolina colony, travels extensively in the Southeast. His *New Voyage to Carolina* spurs English interest in the region.

1708

A small slave revolt takes place on Long Island; seven whites are killed. For their role in the uprising, two African American male slaves and a Native American slave are killed, and one African American woman is burned alive.

The African population of South Carolina surpasses the colony's white population. Slaves are used for a variety of tasks, but they are most concentrated in rice production.

1711

Fed up with unscrupulous traders and the establishment of a German and Swiss colony at Neuse-Bern (present-day New Bern, North Carolina), the Tuscarora Indians attack English farms, killing over 100 colonists. North Carolina, already weak and sparsely settled, requests help from its neighbors. South Carolina responds by sending two expeditions; both are led by white men but consist largely of Native Americans (Yamasee, Creek, Cherokee, and Catawba). In 1713, Captain James Moore's army storms the main Tuscarora town of Nooherooka, killing hundreds. Moore's force kills 166 male captives deemed unsuitable for slavery and sells about 400 women and children into slavery. In the aftermath of the war, most Tuscarora leave North Carolina for the Northeast; once there, they become the Sixth Nation of the Iroquois in 1722.

1712

A slave revolt grips New York City. Nine whites lose their lives, and twenty-one slaves are executed.

1715

On Good Friday, the Yamasee and Creek attack plantations and farms outside of Charles Town, South Carolina, killing about 400 colonists. They were driven to anger by continuing white encroachment, crooked traders, and extensive slave raids. Most of the English people in the colony retreat to the vicinity of Charles Town. Eventually, the Yamasee run low on firearms, and the fighting slows. Carolina also recruits Cherokees, along with some Catawbas and Tuscaroras, to fight Yamasees and Creeks. By 1717, the English have made a peace treaty allowing the Yamasee to keep the lands west of the Savannah River (today the border between South Carolina and Georgia) and keeping white settlement to the east.

1720–1735

The French wage a series of genocidal wars against the Fox Indians of Wisconsin and Illinois. Their goal is to annihilate the Fox people entirely.

1730

The township of Natick, Massachusetts, formerly a "Praying Town" set aside for Native Americans, is taken over by white settlers.

1732

South Carolina attempts to ban the import of African slaves. Planters are fearful that a substantial black majority will lead to a slave uprising and the loss of life and property.

1733

Georgia is founded by a group of high-minded Englishmen. The trustees initially forbid slavery within the colony, fearing its effects on white working men. By the 1750s, however, Georgia's settlers have basically replicated South Carolina's society, which continues to be built on African slave labor and plantations.

1737

Pennsylvania fraudulently acquires 1,200 square miles of territory formerly belonging to the Lenni Lenape; this is known as the "Walking Purchase." The Lenni Lenape agree to sell as much land to the colony as a man could walk in a day and a half. William Penn's sons send scouts ahead to blaze a trail, and set up a relay team of walkers who race about 60 miles into Lenni Lenape territory.

The Lenni Lenape find themselves caught between hostile Iroquois and Pennsylvania forces. Penn's "Long Peace" and the dream of harmonious race relations have ended.

1739

A group of approximately sixty African slaves takes up arms against their masters outside of Charles Town, South Carolina. Led by a slave known as Jemmy (some sources spell the name Jemy), a group comprised primarily of Angolans strikes out for the Spanish colony at St. Augustine, Florida, and freedom. Along the way, the rebellious slaves kill about twenty whites, although they spare a shopkeeper known to be kind to his slaves.

The suppression of this rebellion, which later would become known as the Stono Rebellion, is quick and the revenge ruthless. The colony's militia captures the rebels and decapitates the leaders, placing their heads on pikes, one per mile, on the road from the battlefield to Charles Town. After the Stono Rebellion, a new, harsh slave code is enacted; this code becomes the model for other Southern colonies farther west.

1741

City leaders in New York uncover what they believe to be a "Great Negro Plot." Africans, by this time, approximately one-fifth of the city's population, reportedly intend to burn New York City and kill all of its white residents. One

hundred fifty-four blacks and twenty-four whites are arrested in the conspiracy.

1742

The Cherokee and Iroquois sign a peace treaty, putting a halt to many years of mutual raiding and competition for resources.

1751

The Catawba and the Iroquois agree to a peace treaty at Albany, New York. The Iroquois Confederation (the Cayuga, the Mohawk, the Oneida, the Onondaga, the Seneca, and the Tuscarora) has become the major Native American power brokers in eastern North America.

1754–1763

During the French and Indian War, the American theater of the Seven Years' War, the British and French vie for control of North America. Initially, the British fare poorly, suffering humiliating losses at Fort Duquesne and along the frontier, where French-allied natives torment colonists. Eventually, under the leadership of William Pitt, the Elder, the British pump more money and supplies into the war effort. Sensing a British victory, the Iroquois break their policy of neutrality to join the English. The war ends with a massive victory for the English, and the French abandon North America altogether.

Concurrent with the larger French and Indian War, white Carolinians, from 1759 to 1761, incite an ineffective war against the Cherokee, a powerful interior nation of Native Americans.

1763

Native Americans throughout the Ohio River Valley and the Great Lakes region follow the lead of Pontiac, an Ottawa leader, and rebel against the English. Native Americans seize all but two of the British forts in the West. Eventually Pontiac loses what influence he had been able to build. He is killed in 1769 by a Peoria man.

1770

Anthony Benezet, a Philadelphia Quaker, opens a school specifically for African Americans.

1775

African Americans are officially excluded from the Continental army. The Continental Congress approves the measure. Lord Dunmore, British governor of Virginia, proclaims that all slaves who leave their masters to serve the British will receive their freedom. It is unclear exactly how many slaves take him up on this offer. Worried about Dunmore's proclamation, General Washington changes his mind and allows his officers to enlist free black soldiers and sailors.

1776–1783

One of Thomas Jefferson's earliest drafts of the Declaration of Independence accuses King George III of carrying out the slave trade and inciting slaves to revolt. The section concerning slavery, which Southern delegates find repugnant, is stricken from the document.

The American War for Independence presents a new set of challenges to African Americans and Native Americans. Native Americans, fearing that an American victory will mean further dispossession, for the most part side with the British. In the aftermath of the war, it matters little to the fledgling American republic which side Native Americans chose. The whites mostly believe that the native peoples have no place in American society.

Many African Americans find their freedom as a result of the War for Independence. Some join British forces, some simply leave for Canada, and others join the Americans. Those who fought for both the British and American sides are granted their freedom.

In the North and upper South, particularly in Maryland and Virginia, some masters, living up to their revolutionary ideals, manumit their slaves. The experience of slaves in the Deep South, however, changes little, whether one's master had been patriot or Tory.

Matthew Jennings

Religion

Prior to the Arrival of Europeans

Before native peoples encountered Europeans in the Caribbean and beyond, they had created remarkably diverse and complex systems of belief. Some major differences between European and native religions would lead Europeans to disparage native worldviews and even dismiss them as the work of the devil.

In many native cultures, particular places were extraordinarily sacred, and the way things were arranged in space was extremely important. Certain lakes and mountains possessed great spiritual power for groups that lived near them. European faiths, based on a linear concept of time, were transferable across great distances. Early Europeans who came to the New World, generally speaking, would be unable to grasp the intimate connection between the natural and supernatural worlds that was a hallmark of many Native American belief systems.

1492

Citing economic and religious imperatives, Christopher Columbus persuades King Ferdinand and Queen Isabella of Spain to finance a voyage west across the Atlantic. Columbus perceives himself as a messenger of God, sent to save the souls of peoples ignorant of Catholic christianity.

1537

Bartolomé de las Casas, an early defender of native people and critic of Spanish atrocities, is vindicated when Pope Paul III issues *Sublimis Deus*; this papal bull declares that Native Americans are human beings, and, as such, are not to be enslaved. The slavery of indigenous peoples slowly ends, but the *encomienda* system of natives being forced to labor for Europeans will continue.

1565

In a particularly vicious attack, Pedro Menéndez de Avilés eradicates a small colony of French Protestants settled near the St. John's River in northern Florida. Although the French ask for clemency, Menéndez executes the men, sparing only a handful who pledge allegiance to the Catholic Church.

1584

In consultation with Sir Walter Raleigh, Richard Hakluyt the Younger lays out a plan for English colonization. Hakluyt and Raleigh stress the necessity of spreading Protestant Christianity to counter the teachings of Rome, which have been spread by Catholic explorers and missionaries.

1595

Natives on St. Katherine's Island (off the coast of Georgia) rebel against their Spanish missionaries, citing the friars' complete disregard for their indigenous religion.

Don Juan de Oñate begins the Spanish colonization of New Mexico. Friars accompanying his expedition establish several missions among the Pueblo Indians and write scathing indictments of Oñate's treatment of the native peoples.

1607

The first Anglican parish is formed at Jamestown, Virginia. Richard Hakluyt is named honorary rector.

1614

Alexander Whitaker, rector of the second Anglican parish in Virginia, at Henrico, performs marriage rites for John Rolfe, a planter, and Pocahontas, the daughter of the paramount native chief, Powhatan.

1619

The newly formed Virginia House of Burgesses takes initial steps toward establishing the Anglican Church as the official church of Virginia. Establishment means that the Anglican Church would be the only legally sanctioned church and would be supported by taxpayers' money. Throughout the seventeenth century, a severe shortage of clergy will plague the Anglican Church in most parts of colonial America.

Also in 1619, the first Africans arrive in Virginia on a Dutch slave ship. They are the first of around 400,000 Africans eventually transported to British North America. The slaves come from a variety of religious backgrounds, including Christianity, Islam, and a number of local and national religions.

1620

The separatist Pilgrims arrive at Plymouth under the leadership of William Bradford. The original 102 passengers on board the *Mayflower* are religious refugees. Dismayed at what they viewed as the liturgical excesses of the Church of England, they had left England for Leyden, Holland, in 1607.

After several years, concerned that their children were beginning to adopt the Dutch language and culture, they decided to embark for the New World.

The Pilgrims' sparsely populated colony in Plymouth will remain independent until 1691, when it will be subsumed under the new charter of the much larger Massachusetts Bay Colony.

1625

Jean de Brébeuf, a Jesuit missionary to New France, arrives in Huron territory. There, he will labor for more than a decade, learning the Huron language and culture, despite his minimal success in securing converts to the Catholic faith. Brébeuf will be captured by the Five Nations of the Iroquois during the wars of the 1640s and slowly tortured until he dies.

1629

The Dutch Reformed Church is established as the official church of New Netherland. In theory, this precludes any other churches from gaining a foothold in the colony; in practice, as in Amsterdam, the proscription is barely enforced, because the company charged with settling the area does not want to drive off potential colonists.

Peter Stuyvesant, who guides the colony through the 1660s, will not approve of such lax policies. His harsh treatment of a group of Jewish settlers and a Quaker who had been holding secret meetings in his home will earn Stuyvesant stern rebukes from the management of the Dutch West India Company.

1630

The first wave of the Puritan Great Migration arrives in Massachusetts. This movement will transplant tens of thousands of English Dissenters to New England. Immediately, the Saints, as they call themselves, attempt to set up a godly community under the leadership of John Winthrop. Winthrop's "Modell of Christian Charity" speech, delivered onboard the *Arabella,* encourages the Puritans to set an example, to act as "a city upon a hill," in order to correct the excesses and corruption of the Church of England. Continuing persecution of Puritans by Archbishop William Laud and others in England swells the colony's population.

1632

King Charles I grants Maryland to Cecilius Calvert, Second Lord Baltimore. Calvert, the owner of the first proprietary colony in English North America, intends his Chesapeake claim to serve as a safe haven for displaced English Catholics. He invites both Catholics and Protestants to move to his colony and instructs Catholics to conduct their rites as privately as possible to preserve harmony among the colonists.

In the early 1640s, Protestants will seize control of the government and expel the Jesuits, but lawful authority will soon be restored. Maryland's 1649 Toleration Act (England would pass a similar measure half a century later) guarantees all Christians the right to worship as they see fit. In 1655, William Claiborne, a Protestant rebel, will gain control of Maryland and bar Catholics from office; by 1660, Calvert's authority will be restored. Even as Anglican planters rise to dominate the colony in the eighteenth century, Maryland will remain the focal point of Catholicism in the colonies.

1635

Roger Williams runs afoul of the authorities in Massachusetts Bay Colony by preaching a radical separatist message and questioning the right of an English king to deed what is essentially native land to the Puritans. He is banished, but, following a warning from John Winthrop, Williams escapes and eventually establishes the colony of Rhode Island.

Founded on the principle of religious toleration, Rhode Island soon becomes a haven for exiles from Massachusetts Bay. Government in Rhode Island will be totally separate from religion, except to restore order should religious quarrels arise. Not surprisingly, Sephardic Jews will find Rhode Island's tolerant religious climate to their liking and begin to migrate there in the seventeenth century.

1636

Harvard College is founded in Cambridge, Massachusetts. Education is of primary importance to the Puritans, and this is true not only of Biblical instruction. Students at Harvard must know Latin and Greek upon matriculation, and their curriculum stresses knowledge of the Greek and Roman classics, as well as the traditional arts and sciences.

1637

The Antinomian Controversy rocks the religious establishment in the Massachusetts Bay Colony. Anne Hutchinson, a knowledgeable interpreter of Scripture, is charged with accusing Puritan ministers of preaching a covenant of works (as opposed to a covenant of grace) and with other censored behavior. She is banished and moves first to Rhode Island and then to Long Island, where she and most of her family lose their lives in a native attack.

1638

A small community of Swedish Lutherans settles at the site of present-day Wilmington, Delaware, where they establish a colony known as Fort Christina and a church (known today as "Old Swedes' Church").

1641

A band of Ojibwe invite Isaac Jogues, a Jesuit who had arrived in Quebec in the 1630s, to establish a mission among them at Sault Sainte Marie. On a trip to Quebec, Jogues is captured by the Iroquois. He will later be released and return to France. In 1646, after returning to North America, Jogues finally achieves martyrdom for trying to convert Native

Americans, when he dies at the hands of a Mohawk war party.

1673

Jacques Marquette, a long-serving Jesuit fluent in several Native American languages, and explorer Louis Jolliet travel the Mississippi River in search of a way to the Pacific. Their explorations form the basis for France's claim to the vast Mississippi River Valley.

1676

Kateri Tekakwitha, the daughter of an Iroquois chief and an Algonquin Christian mother, also known as the "Lily of the Mohawks," converts to Christianity at the age of 20. She quickly gains fame by depriving herself of food, wounding her flesh, and praying constantly. She will die in 1680 and will be beatified by Pope John Paul II 300 years later.

1680

In response to a crackdown on indigenous religious practice and increased efforts at conversion, the Pueblo peoples, under the leadership of the shaman Popé, rise up against and nearly vanquish the Spanish in New Mexico. The surviving Spaniards flee to El Paso and points south, while New Mexico reverts to native control for a decade.

1682

Pennsylvania is established on the Delaware River by the wealthy Quaker William Penn as a haven for his co-religionists. Quakers have been widely persecuted in both England and New England for their radical beliefs. Penn's liberal 1682 Frame of Government declares a policy of religious toleration and respect for local tribes as well. In this way, Penn hopes to set his "holy experiment" apart from the failures that have wracked other English colonial projects.

The capital, Philadelphia, will remain under Quaker control for several decades, while the western portion of Penn's huge land grant will be settled mainly by Presbyterians, Lutherans, and members of the German Reformed Church.

1685

King Louis XIV of France revokes the Edict of Nantes, suspending the rights of French Protestants, or Huguenots, to practice their religion. About 500 Huguenots, many of them skilled at various trades, will move to Carolina (then constituting both North and South Carolina) by 1700 as a result.

1690

Father Damian Massanet establishes the first Spanish mission at San Francisco de los Tejas (in present-day Texas).

1692

The witch trials scandalize the town of Salem, Massachusetts. Puritans, fearing they have let down the moral standards of their ancestors, begin to search for scapegoats. Widowed and older women, along with a handful of men, are accused of engaging in witchcraft and sorcery. The furor eventually subsides—after the governor's wife is accused—but not until more than two dozen alleged witches have been put to death. One of the judges involved, Samuel Sewall, will publicly apologize for his role in 1697.

1698–1701

The English clergyman Nicholas Bray founds two organizations designed to spread the teachings of the Anglican Church in the North American colonies: the Society for Promoting Christian Knowledge and the Society for the Propagation of the Gospel.

1701

Yale College is founded in Connecticut to train that colony's next generation of preachers. As at Harvard, in addition to religious studies, students undergo a rigorous program of liberal education in the classics, arts, and sciences.

1740

George Whitefield, the famed itinerant revivalist from England, embarks on his second tour of British North America. His visit coincides with a marked evangelical upsurge in the colonies, known as the Great Awakening. Whitefield occasionally preaches in churches, but he usually speaks to large meetings outdoors. He enthusiastically advocates a religion of the heart and argues that human feelings and emotion are central to the experience of religion. His visit has an especially profound effect on New Englanders.

The Great Awakening converts many believers to the Baptist and Methodist forms of Protestantism in America, although most itinerant preachers stress that the feelings in one's heart should overcome loyalty to any specific denomination. The Great Awakening also inspires the conversion of a large number of slaves and free blacks, who, in the years that follow, will build their own churches on evangelical models.

Meanwhile, the Great Awakening divides colonial society between Old Lights (those who mistrust the revivalists) and New Lights. (It used to be fashionable to argue that the New Lights spawned the Revolutionary movement, but there was not much hard evidence to support the claim. It is possible, however, to argue that the fire of the Great Awakening brought Americans of various denominations together and may have sparked some recognition of a continent-wide identity.)

1741

In a sermon titled "Sinners in the Hands of an Angry God," and delivered at Enfield, Connecticut, Jonathan Edwards terrifies the congregation with a graphic description of what awaits them in hell. He famously compares human beings' fate with that of a spider dangling from a thread over a flame. Even Edwards, however, like Tennent, Whitefield, and other moderate revivalists, fails to go far enough in the eyes of more radical preachers.

Late 1750s

Neolin, also known as the Delaware Prophet, preaches a pan-native message among the Lenni Lenape (Delaware) people. Among his followers, who receive a revivalistic message that shuns European civilization, is an Ottawa war leader named Pontiac. Neolin argues that native people and white people were created to be separate and that native communities must undergo a cleansing to remove European influences from their villages. Later nativistic revivals, most notably that of Tenskwatawa, the Shawnee prophet, will build on this theme of repudiating white culture and its damaging effects on native lifeways.

1766

A number of Moravians arrive in North Carolina and establish the community of Wachovia. The Moravians are intensely devout pacifists. Although they practice slavery, they accept their slaves as spiritual equals.

1767

Thomas Bradbury Chandler, a New Jersey Anglican, argues forcefully in his published sermon *Appeal to the Public* that America requires Anglican bishops to perform vital ecclesiastical functions in the colonies. His claim that episcopacy and monarchy go hand in hand, and that republicanism can destroy both, is not well received outside the strongly Anglican Middle colonies. Chandler will leave for England in 1775.

1760s–1770s

Father Junípero Serra establishes a string of missions among the native peoples of California, stretching from San Diego in the south to San Francisco in the north. Because of his brutal tactics and the fact that he has been beatified, Father Serra remains a focus for criticism of the Catholic Church's treatment of Native Americans.

1791

The thirteen new states ratify the First Amendment to the United States Constitution, both guaranteeing religious freedom and banning state establishment of religion.

Matthew Jennings

Science and Technology

1503

The Spanish king Ferdinand of Aragon founds the *Casa de Contratación,* a repository of navigational and cartographical knowledge.

1507

Martin Waldseemüller's *Cosmographica* is the first published map to include the word "America."

1512

The "royal pattern," a continuously updated cartographical chart, is established at the *Casa de Contratación.*

1519

Martín Fernández de Enciso's *Summa de Geografia* is published. It is the first attempt to indicate the Americas in relation to European geography in book form.

1520

Hernando Cortéz, conqueror of Mexico, addresses the first of five letters to King Charles I of Spain that add greatly to European knowledge of the American mainland. These letters continue until 1526.

1526

The first Spanish book on the natural history of the New World, Gonzalo Fernández de Oviedo y Valdés's *Natural History of the Indies,* is published in Seville.

1529

In a letter dated July 8, the Italian-born explorer Giovanni da Verrazano describes part of the coast of North America to King Francis I of France.

1534

The French explorer Jacques Cartier searches for the Northwest Passage. He will repeat his unavailing effort in 1536.

1537

Pope Paul III issues the bull *Sublimis Deus,* declaring that natives of the Americas are human beings with souls, not animals.

1538

The first university in the New World is founded at Santo Domingo to train priests.

1540

This is the year of the earliest surviving printed sheet from the Americas, a *Manual for Adults,* which was written in Spanish and printed in Mexico City.

1550

The Dominican missionary Bartolomé de las Casas and the Spanish humanist Juan Ginés de Sepúlveda debate at Valladolid on whether the inhabitants of the New World are natural slaves in the Aristotelian sense. Ginés de Sepúlveda upholds the position that Native Americans are natural slaves; las Casas opposes it. The debate is inconclusive, but las Casas's position eventually wins out intellectually over Sepúlveda's views among Spanish thinkers.

1551

The first university on mainland North America is founded in Mexico City by the Spanish to train priests.

1555

Richard Eden's *The Decades of the Newe Worlde or West India, Conteyning the Navigations and Conquestes of the Spanyards* is published in London. It includes a translation of a large part of Oviedo's earlier work, as well as discussion of Spanish mining techniques.

1569

A Seville physician, Nicolás Monardes, who never crossed the Atlantic, publishes *Two Books, of Which One Treats All the Things Found in the Western Indies Which Are of Medical Use and the Other Treats the Bezoar Stone.* Drawing on information available regarding Native American practices, as well as his own experiences, he paints the New World as full of wonderful cures for Europeans' ailments. Monardes later adds sections to his influential work, which is published in Latin translation in 1574.

1570

The reform of the Spanish Council of the Indies leads to an effort to systematically gather natural and geographical information.

The first medical book published in the New World is *Medical Works*, by Francisco Bravo, in Mexico City.

The Antwerp map seller and cartographer Abraham Ortelius publishes *Theater of the World*, the earliest atlas. It shows North America as a wide continent rather than a narrow barrier between Europe and Asia (as it was previously shown by Waldseemüller and others). The frontispiece adds a personification of America as a goddess to the traditional three figures of Asia, Europe, and Africa.

1571

The Spanish physician Francisco Hernández arrives in Mexico with a royal commission to carry out scientific exploration. He will return to Spain in 1577; his work is never to be published in complete form.

1577

An English translation of Monardes's book, *Joyfull Newes out of the New Founde Worlde, Written in Spanish by Nicholas Monardes Physician of Seville and Englished by John Frampton, Merchant,* is published.

1580

John Florio's English translation of Jacques Cartier's accounts of his voyages is published as *A Short and Briefe Narration of the Two Navigations and Discoveries to the Northweast Partes Called New Fraunce.*

1588

Based on his experiences in Sir Walter Raleigh's Roanoke colony, Thomas Harriot publishes *A Briefe and True Report of the New Found Land of Virginia*. It includes discussion of the prospective colony's natural history, economic resources, and geography.

1589

The first edition of Richard Hakluyt's collection *Principall Navigations, Voyages, and Discoveries of the English Nation* is published. It includes a number of accounts relating to America.

1590

Harriot's *Briefe and True Report* is published in English, French, German, and Latin. It includes the first significant published map of the New World, created by an English cartographer, John White. The edition spreads knowledge of North America in continental Europe.

1602

The first English account of coastal New England, John Brereton's *A Briefe and True Relation of the Discoverie of the North Part of Virginia*, is published.

1610

The French explorer Samuel de Champlain sets up an experimental garden in Quebec to investigate acclimating European crops in North America. He will also ship New World seeds and plants back to Paris.

1612

John Smith's *A Map of Virginia with a Description of the Countrey* is published.

1616

John Smith's *A Description of New England* is published. It includes the first detailed and reasonably accurate map of the New England coast.

1625

Reverend Samuel Purchas publishes a collection of travel narratives, *Purchas His Pilgrimes*, which includes accounts of North America.

1634

William Wood's *New England's Prospect* is published. It combines descriptions of New England's topography and natural history with promotion of colonization in the area.

1635

The French physician Jacques-Philippe Cornuti publishes, in Latin, *Canadian Plants*. Based on plants sent to Paris by French explorers, the well-illustrated work is the most scientifically advanced treatment of New World plants to date.

1636

Harvard College is founded, primarily to train ministers. It offers courses in the classics, science, philosophy, and theology.

1638

The first printing business in British America is in operation by early October in Cambridge, Massachusetts.

1639

The first British-American almanac is published in Cambridge, Massachusetts. The author is a sea captain, William Pierce.

1646

The first American mechanical patent is issued by the Massachusetts Bay Colony to Joseph Jenks. It grants him an exclusive right for fourteen years to his improvements in sawmills and scythes.

1650

The New England alchemist George Starkey, frustrated with the paucity of available laboratory equipment, relocates to England. There, he becomes a leading chemist.

1657

Richard Ligon's *A True and Exact History of the Island of Barbadoes* is published. Ligon discusses natural history, concentrating on crops of actual or potential economic value. As one of the few books about the Caribbean available in English, it will influence subsequent studies.

1662

The Royal Society, a group for the promotion of natural knowledge, is chartered by King Charles II on July 15. Among its members is the American John Winthrop, Jr. On July 16, Winthrop gives a talk on the preparation of pitch in New England, the first paper at the Royal Society by a colonist.

1672

John Josselyn's *New-England's Rarities Discovered* is published. Along with his later *An Account of Two Voyages to New-England* (1674), Josselyn's work constitutes the most complete natural history of New England produced in the colonial era.

The first book in English devoted to West Indian botany, *The American Physitian* by the naval physician William Hughes, is published. This work goes beyond scientific description to discuss medical and economic uses of American plants.

1678

The English clergyman and natural historian John Bannister arrives in Virginia. Until his death in 1692, he will carry on an active correspondence with the Royal Society and many of England's leading natural historians. While Bannister publishes nothing in his lifetime, many later scientists and writers will make use of his manuscripts and collections.

1680

Thomas Brattle of Harvard College telescopically observes a conspicuous comet, which has since been referred to as the Great Comet of 1680. Brattle's records eventually find their way to Isaac Newton, who praises their accuracy in *Mathematical Principles of Natural Philosophy* (1687).

1682

Another great comet, named after Edmund Halley, attracts much interest in America. Halley will later publish *Synopsis on Cometary Astronomy* (1705), claiming that this comet had and would continue to return approximately every seventy-six years. His theories will prove true in 1758.

1683

Increase Mather publishes *Kometographia, or a Discourse Concerning Comets*, exhibiting familiarity with the scientific literature on comets. He leads the formation of the Boston Philosophical Society, the first scientific society in British America. The first meeting is April 30. The society's history is largely unknown, but it seems to have become defunct by the end of 1685.

1687

In September, Hans Sloane leaves England as the newly appointed physician to the governor of Jamaica. He will return to England in 1689 with an enormous natural history collection from the Caribbean.

1688

The Reverend John Clayton, who lived in Virginia from 1684 to 1686, sends the first of six letters on Virginia's natural history and geography to the Royal Society. Dated May 12, it is read at the society meeting on May 16. The letters will continue through May 22, 1694.

John Love publishes the first surveying manual adapted to New World conditions, the frequently reprinted *Geodaesia, or the Art of Surveying and Measuring of Land Made Easy.*

1693

The College of William and Mary is founded.

1696

Sloane publishes *Catalog of Plants of the Island of Jamaica* in Latin. Its usefulness is enhanced by cross-references to other works of Caribbean botany.

1701

A new school, later to become Yale College, is founded at Saybrook, Connecticut.

1705

The French monk and government agent Charles Plumier publishes the eight-volume *American Botany.*

1708

Thomas Robie of Harvard begins publishing an almanac series, *An Ephemeris of the Coelestial Motions.* Several volumes will include discussions of scientific topics, disseminating Newtonian physics to a popular audience.

The Philadelphia physician Christopher Witt establishes a botanical garden at Germantown, Pennsylvania.

1711

Cotton Mather starts gathering accounts of American curiosities to send to *Philosophical Transactions*, the journal of the Royal Society.

1718

French cartographer Guillaume Delisle publishes a *Map of Louisiana and the Course of the Mississippi*, combining advanced cartographic technique with aggressive support of French territorial claims.

1719

On December 11, a spectacular aurora borealis appears over New England. Along with the English aurora of 1716, it will inspire pamphlets by Cotton Mather, Thomas Robie, and the Reverend Thomas Prince. Robie and Prince emphasize that auroras can be explained by natural causes and are not divine signs. Mather attempts to balance natural and providential causes.

1720

The first pharmacopoeia (list of medicines) published in British America, the *Pharmacopoeia Londinensis*, is printed at Boston. It is a reprint of a seventeenth-century English work.

Herman Moll responds to Delisle's *Map of Louisiana* with *A New Map of the North Parts of America Claimed by France* supporting English territorial claims.

1721

During a smallpox epidemic in Boston, Cotton Mather and Dr. Zabdiel Boylston introduce inoculation, only recently known to Europeans. Mather draws on information both from *Philosophical Transactions* and from questioning his slave Onesimus and other African Americans about African inoculation practices. Mather's advocacy sets off a major controversy, and, in November, an opponent of inoculation throws a bomb (which fails to explode) into his house. He also publishes *The Christian Philosopher*, an ambitious attempt to present current science, as he understands it, in the framework of Puritan theology.

1722

Mark Catesby arrives in Charles Town, South Carolina, on May 3. With both English and American patronage, he collects natural history specimens, seeds of American plants for English gardens, and information to write a natural history of the area. He will sail for the Bahamas in 1725 and return to London with his discoveries the following year.

1726

Dr. Zabdiel Boylston publishes *An Historical Account of the Small-Pox Inoculated in New-England*, vindicating his and Cotton Mather's pro-inoculation activity. On a visit to London, Boylston is admitted to the Royal Society on July 7.

He speaks to the Royal Society and the Royal College of Physicians on his experiences with smallpox inoculation.

1727

The London merchant Thomas Hollis endows the Hollis Professorship in Mathematics and Natural Philosophy at Harvard with 1,200 pounds and a gift of scientific equipment. The first holder of the chair is Thomas Robie's pupil Isaac Greenwood, who arrives from England and gives a series of public lectures on experimental philosophy, beginning in January. Greenwood will do much to promote scientific awareness in New England.

1728

John Bartram, the so-called "Father of American botany," establishes a botanical garden in Kingessing, Pennsylvania.

1729

On May 22, Mark Catesby submits the first of the five parts of the first volume of his *Natural History of Carolina, Florida, and the Bahama Islands*. The final installment of this first volume is presented to the Royal Society on November 23, 1732.

Isaac Greenwood publishes the first mathematical textbook by an American, *Arithmetick Vulgar and Decimal*. It will not be as successful as European imports.

1731

The octant, a navigational instrument, is independently invented by John Hadley in England and Thomas Godfrey, Sr., in Pennsylvania. The coincidence sets off a series of unsubstantiated charges of stealing the idea made by Americans against Hadley.

Benjamin Franklin and his associates found the Library Company of Philadelphia. A general-interest institution, it will acquire many scientific books and a collection of scientific instruments.

1733

Founded in the new city of Savannah, the Trustees' Garden is the first public garden devoted to agricultural research in British America. Unfortunately, due to neglect, this garden will disappear by 1748.

1735

The first part of the second volume of Catesby's *Natural History* is submitted to the Royal Society on January 20. The whole work will not be completed until April 16, 1747.

1736

Dr. William Douglass, an opponent of smallpox inoculation in 1721 (he had since accepted the practice), leads the formation of the Boston Medical Society, which is devoted to advancing medical knowledge. Douglass also publishes a clinical study of the recent New England scarlet fever epidemic, *The Practical History of A New Epidemical Eruptive Military Fever, with an Angina Ulcusculosa, Which Prevailed in Boston, New England, in the Years 1735 and 1736.*

1737

America's first commercial botanical garden and nursery is established at Flushing, New York, by the French Huguenot settler Robert Prince. His descendants will continue to own it until 1869.

1738

A smallpox epidemic rages in Charles Town, South Carolina. A Scottish doctor, James Kilpatrick, inoculates about 800 people before the practice is outlawed.

Isaac Greenwood loses his position at Harvard due to drunkenness.

1739

On January 2, Isaac Greenwood's former pupil and astronomer John Winthrop, Jr., takes the Hollis Chair at Harvard. He will hold the chair until his death, introducing differential and integral calculus into the curriculum.

A French military party discovers a deposit of fossils, including a mastodon, at Big Bone Lick on the Ohio River in the present-day state of Kentucky.

The Dutch botanist Johann Friedrich Gronovius's *Flora Virginica* is published. It is based on a manuscript by the Virginia botanist and collector John Clayton. A second volume appears in 1743.

1740

The College of Philadelphia, later the University of Pennsylvania, is founded.

Around this time, Benjamin Franklin devises the Pennsylvania Fire Place or Franklin stove, a device for heating rooms more efficiently by minimizing the escape of heated air.

1742

A spectacular shooting star arouses the Reverend Thomas Clap's interest in meteors, to which he will devote much of his scientific career.

1743

The first American Philosophical Society is founded in Philadelphia. It will last until 1746.

1744

Benjamin Franklin gives a model Franklin stove to the iron founder Robert Grace, which helps publicize the invention.

1745

Thomas Clap becomes president of Yale College, a position he will hold until 1766. He reorganizes the curriculum to place more emphasis on science.

Cadwallader Colden publishes *An Explication of the First Causes of Action in Matter, and the Cause of Gravitation*, a work of physical theory that attracts some notice, mostly unfavorable, in Europe.

In Philadelphia, Dr. Thomas Cadwallader publishes his *Essay on the West-India Dry Gripes*, discussing cases of lead poisoning caused by the use of lead pipes in distilling West Indian rum.

1746

The College of New Jersey, later Princeton University, is founded.

1748

In September, a Swedish disciple of the great botanist Carl Linnaeus, Peter Kalm, arrives in North America. Kalm will gather plants in Pennsylvania, New York, New Jersey, and New France, and meet many American botanists, natural historians, and other scientists before leaving for Sweden in February 1751.

The clergyman-physician Jared Eliot publishes the first of six short treatises, *Essays on Field-Husbandry in New England.* The last pamphlet in the series, which adapts the new agricultural ideas of the Englishman Jethro Tull and other "improvers" to New England, will be published in 1759.

The Charleston Library Society is founded in South Carolina.

1749

Benjamin Franklin's friend Ebenezer Kinnersley commences a tour of the colonies that will last until 1753. An electrical demonstrator, lecturer, and showman, Kinnersley disseminates Franklin's electrical theories.

A medical society is organized in New York City.

The surveyor Lewis Evans publishes *Map of Pensilvania, New-Jersey, New-York, and the Three Delaware Counties.*

1750

A group called the Young Junto starts meeting in Philadelphia to discuss scientific questions, among other issues.

1751

Benjamin Franklin publishes *Experiments and Observations on Electricity*, putting forth his electrical theory and suggesting the use of pointed metal rods to protect buildings from lightning.

The British Parliament removes the tariff from American potash (potassium carbonate), a substance derived from burning wood and used in soap manufacture, glassmaking, dyeing, and bleaching. This leads to expansion of the American industrial chemical industry.

1752

In June, Benjamin Franklin's famous experiment with a kite and key establishes that lightning is a form of electricity.

The Pennsylvania Hospital is founded in Philadelphia.

Along with Britain, the colonies switch from the Julian calendar to the Gregorian calendar. Eleven days are expunged from the calendar following September 2.

Two surveyors, George Heap and Nicholas Scull, publish *A Map of Philadelphia and Parts Adjacent, with a Perspective View of the State House.*

1753

On July 5, for financial reasons, the Royal Society withdraws the exemption from fees previously extended to fellows from the colonies.

On November 30, the Royal Society awards Benjamin Franklin the Copley Medal, its highest honor.

The Philadelphia professor Theophilus Grew publishes a textbook, *The Description and Use of the Globes, Celestial and Terrestrial.*

1754

The Royal Society of Arts is founded. Also known as the London Society for the Arts, this group is devoted to improving technology in Britain and its colonies by circulating technical information and offering prizes for new ideas.

King's College in New York, later Columbia University, is founded.

Joshua Fry's and Peter Jefferson's *Map of the Inhabited Parts of Virginia* is published. It will go through several more editions in England and France.

1755

Dr. John Moultrie organizes a Charles Town medical society, the Charles Town Faculty of Physick, becoming its first president. It is oriented more to improving physicians' economic status than to advancing medical science.

On November 18, an earthquake shakes New England. On November 26, John Winthrop, Jr., gives a lecture in the Harvard chapel, setting forth the natural explanations of earthquakes and rebuking those who ascribed them to God's anger. The talk is published as *A Lecture on Earthquakes* and sets off a controversy between Winthrop and Thomas Prince that lasts into the next year.

The first edition is published of Dr. John Mitchell's government-sponsored *A Map of the British and French Dominions in North America.*

Lewis Evans's *General Map of the Middle British Colonies in America* is published.

1756

On April 29, Benjamin Franklin is admitted as a fellow of the Royal Society. On July 15, it is unanimously agreed that fees be waived for those from the colonies.

The Jamaica physician Patrick Browne publishes *Civil and Natural History of Jamaica*, the first book in English to apply Linnaeus's system of botanical classification based on the number and arrangement of a plant's sexual organs to American plants.

1758

William Small becomes professor of mathematics at the College of William and Mary. Before moving back to England in 1764, Small will become Thomas Jefferson's instructor, impressing him favorably.

1759

The Lancaster Library Company is founded in Lancaster, Pennsylvania. It is modeled on the Philadelphia Library and includes a museum and collection of scientific equipment.

1760

The English natural historian John Ellis, with the approval of Linnaeus, Europe's arbiter of botanical names, names the cape jasmine after his correspondent, the botanist and physician Alexander Garden of Charles Town. The plant is now known as the gardenia.

1761

The first of two transits of Venus across the face of the sun in the mid-eighteenth century occurs on June 6. These rare phenomena provoke worldwide bursts of scientific activity. The transit is not visible in the thirteen British colonies, but John Winthrop, Jr., leads a group of observers to Newfoundland in a trip financed by the Massachusetts Assembly with instruments on loan from Harvard. Winthrop subsequently publishes *Relation of a Voyage from Boston to Newfoundland, for the Observation of the Transit of Venus, June 6, 1761.*

1762

The Pennsylvania Hospital Library, the first medical library in British North America, is founded.

William Shippen delivers a course of anatomy lectures in Philadelphia with the hopes of founding a medical school. He also promotes "man-midwifery," the supervision of births by male surgeons rather than female midwives.

John Bartram explores the interior of South Carolina in search of new plants.

Jared Eliot publishes *An Essay on the Invention, or Art of Making Very Good, if Not the Best Iron, from Black Sea Sand.*

1763

The London Society of Arts awards Eliot a gold medal for his success in extracting iron from sand. The society also sends James Stewart to New England to encourage the potash industry.

A New York Society of Arts is formed with the goal of fostering an independent American linen industry.

Two Englishmen, Charles Mason and Jeremiah Dixon,

arrive in Philadelphia in November to begin establishing the borders of Pennsylvania. They start by fixing the latitude of the southern boundary of Philadelphia.

James Cook, working for the British Admiralty, commences the first exact survey of the coast of Newfoundland, a task that lasts until 1767.

1764

Early in the year, Harvard Hall is destroyed by fire, along with the collection of scientific and experimental equipment built up by Isaac Greenwood and John Winthrop, Jr. Winthrop appeals to the public for funds to replace the collection, and with the help of Franklin, then in England, he is able to build the largest and most up-to-date instrument collection of any colonial institution.

During the summer, Charles Mason and Jeremiah Dixon trace the north-south line dividing Pennsylvania from Delaware.

The College of Rhode Island, later Brown University, is founded.

1765

John Winthrop, Jr., is admitted as a fellow of the Royal Society on February 20 with the sponsorship of Benjamin Franklin.

In the spring, Mason and Dixon begin establishing the east-west Mason-Dixon Line between Maryland and Pennsylvania.

John Bartram is appointed king's botanist and explores the southeastern British colonies, including Florida, recently acquired from Spain.

Dr. John Morgan, armed with a medical degree from Edinburgh and a letter dated February 15 from the proprietor of Pennsylvania, Thomas Penn, begins agitating for the creation of an American medical school. A talk he gives is published as *Discourse upon the Institution of Medical Schools in America*. Morgan's program for medical education includes an emphasis on science. The medical school of the College of Philadelphia is founded under his leadership.

A state-run botanical garden is founded on the British-held island of St. Vincent.

1766

Several medical societies are formed. On February 14, the Philadelphia Medical Society is founded by a group of physicians led by John Morgan. In July, the Medical Society of New Jersey is formed; concerned primarily with regulating and improving medical practice, it also holds meetings at which scientific papers are read. Another medical society is formed in Litchfield County, Connecticut.

The Young Junto takes on more formal organization and a new name, the American Society for Promoting and Propagating Useful Knowledge.

Queen's College, later Rutgers University, is founded.

An anonymous pamphlet published in Boston, *Direc-tions for Making Calcined or Pearl-Ashes*, promotes the manufacture of pearlash, a refined form of potash.

1767

The American Philosophical Society is revived in Philadelphia.

The Society of the Hospital of the City of New York is founded to encourage the building of a hospital in the city.

On August 14, the medical school of King's College is founded by the action of the trustees.

On October 7, Mason and Dixon make their last measurement, at the mouth of Dunkard Creek.

Two treatises on potash production and American potash are published in London, Robert Dossie's *Observations on the Pot-Ash Brought from America* and W.M.B. Lewis's *Experiments and Observations on American Potashes*. Dossie is a leader in the Society of Arts.

The Charles Town physician Lionel Chalmers publishes *An Essay on Fevers*. It will attract European interest, being republished in London in 1768 and in German translation in 1773.

1768

On November 4, the Philadelphia Medical Society is dissolved as its members are admitted to the American Society for Promoting and Propagating Useful Knowledge. On December 20, the American Society and the American Philosophical Society merge to form the American Philosophical Society for Promoting Useful Knowledge, America's first enduring scientific society.

A chair of mathematics and natural philosophy is established at the College of New Jersey; however, this position will not be filled until William Charles Houston takes the chair in 1771.

A German scholar, Cornelius de Pauw, publishes in Berlin *Philosophical Researches on the Americans*. Following the French natural historian Buffon, de Pauw argues that American animals and peoples are naturally inferior to those of the Old World, particularly Europe. This sets off a controversy lasting several decades, involving Thomas Jefferson and Alexander von Humboldt, among others.

1769

On January 2, at the first meeting of the American Philosophical Society, Benjamin Franklin is elected president in absentia. In January, a member of the society, the military officer Lewis Nicola, publishes the first issue of *The American Magazine, and General Repository*. This periodical, which lasts for only nine months, includes much scientific material (mostly reprinted from European sources) and unofficial transactions of the American Philosophical Society.

The second transit of Venus on June 3 occasions more observations and widespread interest in the American colonies. A French expedition to Baja California led by the astronomer Jean-Baptiste Chappe d'Auteroche is nearly wiped out by an epidemic; the sole survivor brings the data back to Paris.

The Royal Society sends an expedition to Hudson Bay to observe the transit. For health reasons, John Winthrop, Jr., turns down an invitation from the Royal Society to observe the transit at Lake Superior. (The expedition is later abandoned due to a lack of funding.) He observes the transit from Harvard, communicating his results directly to *Philosophical Transactions*. The American Philosophical Society also sponsors and gathers over twenty observations.

On August 1, Benjamin Rush is appointed professor of chemistry at the College of Philadelphia.

Dartmouth College is founded in Hanover, New Hampshire.

1770

The physician Benjamin Gale is awarded a special gold medal by the London Society of Arts for an improved drill-plow for sowing grain. This accomplishment builds on the work of Thomas Clap and Gale's father-in-law Jared Eliot.

Benjamin Rush publishes the first American chemistry textbook, *A Syllabus of a Course of Lectures on Chemistry*.

1771

The first volume of the *Transactions of the American Philosophical Society* is published in February, including observations of the 1769 transit.

The Hudson's Bay Company sends the first of four large collections of natural history specimens to the Royal Society. (The others will be sent once a year for the next three years.)

The Society of Arts sends James Stewart to Maryland to encourage the potash industry.

New York Hospital is chartered.

David Rittenhouse completes work on the first orrery built in America. This mechanical representation of the motions of the planets and moons of the solar system provokes much interest and is eventually bought by Princeton University.

1772

The Virginia physician James McClurg publishes *Experiments upon the Human Bile*.

1773

William Bartram, son of botanist John Bartram, leaves on a series of expeditions through southeastern British America, which will last until 1776.

Benjamin Rush publishes *Experiments and Observations on the Mineral Waters of Philadelphia, Abingdon, and Bristol*.

The Virginian Society for the Promotion of Usefull Knowledge is founded, with John Clayton as its first president.

The first insane asylum in British America, at Williamsburg, Virginia, opens its doors.

1775

The fourth edition of Mitchell's map is published as *A Map of the British Colonies in North America with the Roads, Distances, Limits and Extent of the Settlements*.

The Dutch engineer and surveyor Bernard Romans publishes *Concise Natural History of East and West Florida* along with coastal charts for sailors.

Henry Monzon's *An Accurate Map of North and South Carolina with Their Indian Frontiers* is published.

A Yale student, David Bushnell, invents and builds a one-man submarine for use against the British.

1776

The American Revolution leads to the suspension of the meetings of the American Philosophical Society. These meetings will not resume until 1779.

The shortage of gunpowder for the American armies leads to increased interest in gunpowder manufacture, particularly the scarcest ingredient, potassium nitrate, known as saltpeter. Benjamin Rush publishes *Essays upon the Making of Salt-Petre and Gun Powder*.

Around this time, Jeremiah Wilkinson of Cumberland, Rhode Island, devises a technique for making nails out of cold iron rather than through heated forging.

Lionel Chalmers's *An Account of the Weather and Diseases of South-Carolina* is published. In it, he attempts to systematically correlate changes in the weather with epidemics.

1777

The Continental Congress commissions the Corps of Engineers. At first composed of four French officers, the corps will remain dominated by foreign engineers, such as Thaddeus Kosciuszko, throughout the war.

1778

The surveyor Thomas Hutchins publishes *Topographical Description of Virginia, Pennsylvania, Maryland and North Carolina*.

The first original American pharmacopoeia, *Pharmacopoeia simpliciorum et efficaciorum* by William Brown, is published.

1779

In an order dated March 10, Benjamin Franklin follows French example by directing captains of American ships not to molest the British scientific and geographical expedition of Captain Cook. Franklin lacks authority for this order, which also is too late. Cook has already been killed by native Hawaiians on February 4, after mapping much of the northwestern seacoast of North America.

1780

At the urging of John Adams and others, the Boston Academy of Arts and Sciences is founded with a charter from the Massachusetts General Court.

The American Philosophical Society is formally chartered by the Pennsylvania Assembly.

1781

The Massachusetts Medical Society is incorporated November 1. It combines the function of advancing medical science with the right to examine and license medical and surgical practitioners.

Thomas Clap's *Conjectures upon the Nature and Motion of Meteors*, in which he argues meteors are comets that orbit the earth, is published posthumously.

1782

The Harvard Medical School is founded in November. A library will be added the following year.

William E. Burns

Caribbean

Before 1492

Before Columbus's landing in 1492, three main groups inhabit the Caribbean islands. All are fairly recent migrants, most likely from South America. The Ciboney (Siboney), Arawak (or Lucayan), and Carib languages are interrelated, and the three are mutually intelligible. Most natives live on or near the coasts of the islands, since the sea provides them with a rich array of food and resources.

"Ciboney" refers to many small groups of people. They live in rock shelters and caves along the northwest coasts of Cuba and Hispaniola and have been in the Caribbean longer than the Arawaks and Caribs. They subsist by collecting fruit and shellfish and by hunting fish and turtles. Later archaeological sites reveal chipped and ground stone tools but no evidence of pottery or weaponry.

The Arawaks and Caribs are the second and third groups to settle the Caribbean. Both groups farm, hunt, fish, weave clothing, and build homes in similar ways, although they do not get along with each other. They practice *conuco* agriculture (a system of raising such root plants as yuca or manioc, by burning brush and piling topsoil into fertile mounds). Yuca is the main ingredient in the natives' traditional, flat, unleavened bread.

The Arawaks live on the Bahamas, the Greater Antilles (Cuba, Jamaica, Hispaniola, and Puerto Rico), and Trinidad. They produce pottery and baskets. Collecting gold from riverbeds, the Arawaks also produce gold nose rings and earrings, as well as necklaces and masks. And they participate in ball games, played in a rectangular court at the village center. Hispaniola is divided into five or six paramount chiefdoms.

The Caribs live mainly on the Virgin Islands and many of the Lesser Antilles (such as Anguilla, Barbuda, Antigua, Guadeloupe, and Martinique). Their government is more decentralized than that of their Arawak neighbors, and their gendered division of labor (men hunt, fish, and practice military skills, while women practice agriculture and maintain the home) is more strict than that of the Arawaks.

When the Spanish arrive, they classify the Caribs as vicious cannibals and the Arawaks as a peace-loving people. The accounts are exaggerated and colored by the fact that the Caribs more frequently resist the Spanish invaders with violence.

1492

Christopher Columbus, a Genoan sailor employed by King Ferdinand and Queen Isabella of Spain to reach the Indies, instead reaches San Salvador (Watling's Island) in the Bahamas. He mistakenly believes that he has achieved his goal and labels the people he meets on his voyage "Indians." (Until his death in 1506, Columbus will continue to claim that the islands he found are part of Asia.)

Later in 1492, Columbus reaches Cuba and Hispaniola, where he establishes the Spanish colony of Navidad. He returns to Spain with some pieces of gold and six Lucayo (Arawak) natives.

1493

A much larger expedition, made up of seventeen ships instead of three, sails from Spain under the direction of Columbus, who has been named an admiral. He tours most of the Lesser Antilles and Puerto Rico before arriving in Hispaniola in 1494.

On Hispaniola, Columbus disrupts native agricultural practices by forcing the Arawaks to find set amounts of gold. He also alienates the Spanish colonists (who probably resented serving a Genoan). Both Christopher and his brother Bartholomew mismanage the island.

1496

Columbus's brother Bartholomew moves the capital from Isabella to Santo Domingo. It will remain the administrative capital of the Spanish empire in the Americas for thirty years. San Domingo also will be the main port for Spanish shipping, until it is replaced by Havana in the 1560s.

1500

Francisco de Bobadilla, recently named royal governor of the Indies, arrives at Hispaniola in the midst of a civil war. He arrests both Columbus brothers and sends them back to Spain. Bobadilla increases gold production by licensing the mines and providing incentives.

1502

A hurricane destroys most of the gold Bobadilla has collected, along with his records, and he dies in the fierce summer storm.

Nicholas de Ovando arrives and establishes royal control over Hispaniola. He grants *encomiendas*, the rights to the labor of specific Native American communities, to Spaniards who are able to wield this power effectively. Ovando's administration, while severe, allows Hispaniola to flourish briefly. The population grows from 300 in 1502 to around 8,000 in 1509. The number of native people, however, who are forced to labor intensely and have no resistance to the epidemic diseases brought by the Europeans, drops catastrophically.

1508

Juan Ponce de León founds the colony of Puerto Rico, establishing towns near the richest gold deposits. Gold supplies are soon exhausted, and most of the settlers move to Hispaniola, Cuba, or Panama.

1509

Juan de Esquivel leads an expedition to Jamaica, where no gold is found. Within a few years, the island's natives are dead or serving Spanish masters in other parts of the New World. Most of the Spanish colonists leave.

1511

Cuba becomes the second most important Spanish possession (after Hispaniola). Pánfilo Narváez leads a wave of unprovoked massacres of Native Americans, and within a year, the entire island is under Spanish control. By 1519, gold supplies will be exhausted and most of the Arawaks will be dead or dispersed to labor in other parts of Spain's New World empire.

1513

The Spanish government begins to issue licenses to individuals to import slaves from Africa. This is an attempt to gain the advantage over Portuguese slave dealers, as well as an effort to prevent the extermination of the Arawaks, much lamented by church officials, by forcing black slaves to work in their stead.

1519–1521

The Spanish discovery of the Aztec empire and its subsequent conquest diminish the role that the Caribbean plays in the empire. The gold and silver carried out of Mexico and South America draw the attention of English, French, and Dutch pirates.

1542

The Spanish Crown outlaws Native American slavery. This decree has almost no effect in the Caribbean, where native populations have been virtually erased (save for a few villages) by a half-century of Spanish occupation. By this time, the Arawak population has dropped from approximately 225,000 to perhaps a few hundred.

1564

In response to pirate attacks, Spain requires that all treasure-bearing ships must sail in one fleet from Havana to Seville on their return voyages. This affords smaller, lighter ships (such as caravels) the protection of more heavily armed galleons and greatly reduces the number of ships lost to pirates. Spanish settlements in the New World still prove easy targets for raiding parties.

The new shipping rules require that the massive annual fleet gather at Havana, which helps the economy of that city. Through the second half of the sixteenth century, Cuba will become a center of tobacco and, to a lesser extent, sugar production.

1570s

The Spanish sugar industry, which enjoyed modest success in Santo Domingo, Puerto Rico, and Jamaica, collapses. The Spanish authorities focus more intently on removing precious metals and protecting their shipment across the Atlantic.

1580s

The Spanish own sugar-producing areas in Brazil from 1580 until the 1630s. Production in these areas undercuts the prices of Caribbean sugar, further weakening the Spanish Caribbean sugar industry.

1585

After astonishing success in taking Peruvian silver, the English sea captain Sir Francis Drake turns his attention to the Caribbean, sacking Santo Domingo and Cartagena. Although he does not carry off treasure, his actions spur more fortress construction on the part of the Spanish.

1595

Rather than issuing licenses to individual slave traders, the Spanish Crown sells monopolies to a series of Portuguese merchants. The monopoly, known as the *asiento*, limits the number of slaves, though this proved impossible to enforce.

1598

The Treaty of Vervins ends about 70 years of continuous strife between France and Spain. A secret addendum to the treaty excludes the Caribbean from the peace. "Beyond the lines"—that is, south of the tropic of Cancer and west of the Azores—ships are still fair game. Most European nations recognize that the customary rules of trade and diplomacy do not apply in the Caribbean.

1599–1609

Following the disappearance of the Puerto Rican sugar industry, only a few thousand inhabitants (many freed slaves and blacks) raise open-range cattle and farm for subsistence. Jamaica, still technically ruled by Columbus's heirs, falls under the misrule of a series of petty tyrants.

The Dutch, engaged in a long struggle against the Spanish in Europe, begin to flex their naval muscles in the Caribbean; they start to trade extensively in salt and tobacco, while at the same time raiding Spanish ships. By 1606, Spanish coastal shipping has stopped almost entirely as a result of Dutch depredations.

1621

The Dutch establish the Dutch West India Company in an effort to expand their role in the Caribbean and to weaken already deflated Spanish interest The company focuses intently on Brazil (taking it for a time in the 1630s and 1640s), while seeking to further damage Spanish shipping in the Caribbean.

1624

Sir Thomas Warner, with a force of less than twenty men, founds the first permanent British Caribbean colony at St. Kitts. After dispatching a group of hostile Caribs, Warner and his followers plant tobacco, which they later ship to London. As a reward, Warner is granted the position of governor of St. Kitts, Nevis, Barbados, and Montserrat.

1627

Permanent English settlement begins on Barbados. Within decades, Barbados's population will reach almost 69,000; 47,000 of these residents will be African slaves. In fact, Barbados will be more densely populated than most of England.

Barbados thrives as the result of the booming sugar industry. This allows for a strictly hierarchical society, with wealthy planters, those who own the most land and slaves, at the top. Barbadian planters employ a mix of indentured servants and African slaves in their sugar plantations and accompanying mills. By the 1660s, however, worsening conditions in Barbados, improving conditions in England, and increasing migration to North America will lead to the decline of indentured servitude on Barbados.

1628

Dutch ships under the command of Piet Heyn trap the entire Spanish fleet carrying Mexican treasure in Matanzas Bay, Cuba. The company's plunder is estimated at 11 million guilders.

1631

The Dutch occupy Sint Maarten and take advantage of its high-quality salt flats. The Spanish attack the small Dutch garrison in 1633 and occupy the island. After 1648, the island will come under joint Dutch and French control.

1634

The West India Company takes control of Curaçao, following this success by adding Bonaire and Aruba in 1636. Over the next 20 years, Curaçao proves to be a drain on company resources but an effective staging point for military adventures.

1635

The French undertake the colonization of the Lesser Antilles, when they settle colonies on Martinique and Guadeloupe. These colonies differ from the British and Dutch ventures in that they have been created by state guidance, not commercial interests. The French will experience conflicts among themselves and with the Carib peoples on the islands for decades.

1651

The English Commonwealth sends a fleet to Barbados, which has recognized the exiled Charles Stuart as king. When the fleet reaches Barbados, it is too weak to take the island, and the islanders agree to take on a new governor in exchange for the ability to trade with the Dutch and other concessions. The 1650s and 1660s mark the height of profitability for sugar production in Barbados. This period also sees a marked decline in white population and an increase in African slaves; poor and middle-class whites (and even some planters) flee the island as it becomes increasingly devoted to a harsh slave labor regime and sugar plantations.

1655

Britain conquers Jamaica. Though the plan (the Western Design) is to conquer all of Spain's colonies and remove that nation from the Caribbean entirely, the British are only able to hold on to Jamaica.

In January, the British try to take Santo Domingo by land and sea but fail twice to even reach the city (internal strife between the commanders plays a role).

In May, commanders of the British fleet (fearing a return to Cromwellian England with nothing to show for their trouble) turn their attention to Jamaica. The small Spanish garrison, allied with runaway slaves, loses its forts right away but manages to hold out in the mountains for two years. Eventually, the slaves join the British side. Cromwell rules Jamaica under martial law. After the Stuart restoration, King Charles II rules it as a Crown colony.

1660 and 1663

Two sets of Navigation Acts are enacted by England's restored monarchy under Charles II. These laws force the British possessions in the Caribbean to conduct trade only with Britain. Commodities such as sugar and tobacco must be carried in British ships to England or other British colonies.

1661–1664

Louis XIV assumes power as king of France. During his reign, independent proprietorships cease to exist, and the

French Caribbean increasingly comes under royal control. In 1664, the French West India Company is chartered, based on the Dutch West India Company; the company, an economic failure, will be liquidated in 1671.

1665

The French establish control over the western third of Hispaniola, which they call Saint-Domingue (today, the Republic of Haiti). Bertrand d'Ogéron is entrusted with the tasks of settling farmers on the western coast of Hispaniola and imposing order on Tortuga, a small island that has been functioning as a de facto pirate kingdom. Within a decade, d'Ogéron will accomplish both of these goals. Tobacco becomes the first successful cash crop of Saint-Domingue.

1665–1667

The Second Dutch War essentially removes the Spanish from the colonization of the Caribbean. Up to this point, Northern Europeans have usually worked together against Spanish interests. After 1665, the contest between France and England becomes more important and forces massive governmental expenditures in support of more than a century of warfare.

The war begins in Africa, where British forces capture Dutch strongholds on the slave coast. The Dutch respond by retaking the forts and proceeding to the Caribbean to wreak havoc on British shipping, destroying cargoes of sugar on the way to England.

The Jamaican government under Thomas Modyford convinces pirates operating out of Port Royal to attack Dutch interests. After early successes, however, the fleet chooses not to attack the more heavily armed island of Curaçao.

The French enter the war on the side of the Dutch and take St. Kitts while they raid the coast of Barbados. Both England and France dispatch warships to the region, and the British fleet defeats a combined Dutch-French fleet.

In 1667, the Treaty of Breda ends the war by returning almost all colonies to their previous owners.

1671

The Danish West India Company is chartered by King Christian V of Denmark and Norway. This company functions in much the same way as the Dutch West India Company, meaning that it seeks to monopolize the slave trade and shipping, but it never makes much of a profit. Denmark controls the small islands of St. Thomas, St. Croix, and St. John.

1672–1678

The Third Dutch War pits England and France (still enemies in the Caribbean) against the Dutch in an effort to diminish Dutch supremacy in commerce and shipping. Britain withdraws from the war in its opening stages, and the Caribbean on the whole plays a relatively minor role. Two French expeditions against Curaçao, in 1673 and 1678, fail terribly when the ships are repulsed by the Dutch and sink in a hurricane, respectively.

Though few colonies change hands, the war does bankrupt the Dutch West India Company. The French and British emerge as the major colonial powers in the region as a result of waning Dutch interest and because the Dutch are unable to protect their ships adequately from French and British pirates.

1689–1697

The Nine Years' War (also known as King William's War) pits England, Holland, and Spain against France. The English and French each wreak havoc on the other nation's Caribbean possessions.

In 1689, the French destroy Dutch settlements on Sint Eustasius and take the British part of St. Kitts. Under the leadership of Christopher Codrington, governor of the Leeward Islands, the English strike back, retaking St. Kitts and Anguilla in 1690. Codrington takes the additional precaution of sending the French settlers of St. Kitts to Saint-Domingue. He goes on to inflict serious damage on Guadeloupe but fails to retain possession of the island.

Disease decimates the crews of two joint Spanish-English vessels, preventing them from taking Saint-Domingue. As in the Second and Third Dutch Wars, the colonies taken are returned to their previous rulers after a peace treaty is signed.

1697

The French government begins to encourage the production of sugar on Saint-Domingue.

1702–1713

The War of the Spanish Succession, known in the Americas as Queen Anne's War, pits Austria, England, and the Netherlands against France and Spain in an effort to prevent the unification of the Spanish and French empires.

The war strengthens pirate control of the Bahamas, and French raiders continue to harass British interests. In one 1712 episode, the French carry off 1,200 slaves from British-held Montserrat.

1714

The Spanish retain Cuba, Puerto Rico, and the eastern portion of Hispaniola (Santo Domingo), although none of these colonies is particularly profitable.

A general cessation of hostilities in Europe, brought about by the signing of the Treaty of Utrecht in 1713, allows plantation agriculture in Jamaica to take off in an astonishing way. The number of white settlers shrinks, while the number of black slaves expands, and they outnumber whites by more than seven to one. The British also own Barbados, St. Kitts, Antigua, Montserrat, and Nevis.

The French maintain Martinique and Guadeloupe. In Saint-Domingue, the French sugar industry also grows by leaps and bounds, since the French now have access to slaves imported through Jamaica.

The British and French, seeking to profit from Europe's rapidly increasing demand for sugar, strive to produce as much sugar as they can in the Caribbean. Sugar plantations will grow larger and more efficient throughout the eighteenth century.

1730s

The colony of Saint-Domingue begins sugar production in earnest, using an elaborate irrigation system to bring increasing acreage under the plow. By 1740, Saint-Domingue is producing almost as much sugar as all of the British West Indies combined.

1733

Slaves on the island of St. John, a Danish possession, capture the island's only fort, burn many of its plantations, and kill most of the whites. They repel successive invasion attempts by British forces and control the island for six months, until an experienced French force of around 230 soldiers is able to subdue them.

1738–1739

Jamaica, which is heavily wooded and mountainous, proves to be an ideal location for the settlement of large Maroon communities. Jamaicans sign two treaties with the Maroons (long-term escaped slaves). The terms of this treaty guarantee the Maroons several homelands and complete autonomy. Interestingly, the Maroons also agree to return more recently escaped slaves from Jamaican plantations, a service for which they receive 2 pounds per slave.

1739–1748

The War of Jenkins' Ear (1739–1743) pits England against France and Spain. The British accuse the Spanish of piracy and intend to force British trade upon the Spanish, as well as to conquer the Spanish Caribbean. In 1741, the British seize Guantánamo Bay, Cuba, intending to march on Santiago; their mission fails when most of the soldiers die from disease.

Despite some minor successes by a British militia deployed from Anguilla, the Treaty of Aix-la-Chapelle in 1748 returns the colonial possessions to their former owners.

1740s

Up to this point, wars, raids by Maroons, low sugar prices, and a lack of available capital have held back Jamaica's full production potential. Following the signing of the treaties between the Jamaican planters and the Maroons, British traders bring in increasing numbers of African slaves. By 1758, 18,000 whites will rule over 180,000 slaves on the island's 455 sugar plantations.

1750

By 1750, the Leeward Islands (Nevis, St. Kitts, Montserrat, Anguilla, Antigua, and the Virgin Islands) are producing three times as much sugar as Barbados.

Substantial Maroon communities thrive in the mountainous region between French Saint-Domingue and Spanish Santo Domingo. In 1752, a charismatic Maroon leader named Mackandal unites the Maroons and creates a secret organization that includes both runaways and slaves on plantations.

1756

Britain and France are the main combatants in the Seven Years' War (called the French and Indian War in North America), a global contest for supremacy between the two emerging world powers. Both Britain and France covet each other's sugar colonies in the Caribbean; these colonies also are vulnerable to attack because of their tiny white minorities and large slave populations.

During the war, the British occupy Guadeloupe and Martinique. On Guadeloupe, the British, weakened again by illness, attack outlying plantations and settlements. They offer French deserters generous terms of surrender, allowing them to continue running the plantations as before, except for the fact that they will have access to British markets and cheaper British slaves. On both Guadeloupe and Martinique, the result of British conquest is to speed up sugar production.

1760

A huge slave rebellion breaks out on Easter Monday in Jamaica. Its leader, Tacky, is a Coromantee man from the Gold Coast. He leads an army of approximately 30,000 blacks, who intend to kill all the whites and rule Jamaica. Tacky's forces are finally defeated in the summer by a combined army of Maroons, the Jamaican militia, and the British army.

1762

The British take Havana. By the terms of the Treaty of Paris, the British return Havana to Spain in exchange for Florida. They also take Canada from the French and return the sugar-producing islands of Guadeloupe and Martinique.

1776–1783

As a result of the booming trade in sugar, St. Kitts has become the richest colony in the British Empire by 1776. The English colonies in the Caribbean are more closely tied to Great Britain than their North American counterparts; as a result, when the thirteen North American British colonies declare their independence in July, none of the British colonies in the Caribbean breaks away from England. Though West Indians continue to trade with American ships and support American independence, their connection to Great

Britain (and their reliance on British naval protection) makes independence impractical. Still, from 1776 to 1783, Britain and France challenge each other again on a global scale, and, this time, France wins.

After the siege of Yorktown, Virginia, in 1781, the French fleet under Admiral de Grasse does manage to take St. Kitts, Nevis, and Montserrat. In April 1782, however, the British fleet under Admiral Sir George Rodney pulls off a stunning victory and forces the French to surrender. In 1783, the Treaty of Paris once again returns most of the Caribbean colonies to their previous owners.

Matthew Jennings

Connecticut

1632

Edward Winslow and William Bradford try, unsuccessfully, to convince authorities in the Massachusetts Bay Colony to exploit trade opportunities with Native American communities in the Connecticut River Valley. John Oldham, an English trader from Watertown, travels in the area and brings back descriptions of large amounts of beaver, wild hemp, and graphite.

At approximately the same time, the Dutch build a small fort on the Hartford River in an effort to secure more trade with the region's Native American communities.

1633

The Plymouth Colony establishes a trading post on the west side of the Connecticut River, just south of the Farmington River.

1634

In the fall, John Oldham and a small group of followers begin to settle at Pyquag (present-day Wethersfield). The establishment of households indicates that English settlers are beginning to recognize the quality of the area's farmland.

In September, the Massachusetts General Court forbids the inhabitants of Newtown (present-day Cambridge), and their pastor—Thomas Hooker—from migrating to the Connecticut River country. The Newtown people feel pinched by strict Massachusetts land policies and hope that a move would give them more room. Governor John Winthrop denies their petition, believing that such a departure would deprive Massachusetts Bay not only of Hooker's followers, but also of prospective settlers from England.

1635

The Massachusetts Bay Colony begins to spin off the towns of Windsor and Hartford. A particularly harsh winter drives many of these initial English settlers back to the relative security of the colony, though most will return the following spring.

1636

John Winthrop, Jr., arrives from England as the representative of several important Puritan gentlemen and claims that the settlements on the Connecticut River are illegal. Massachusetts Bay Colony calls a commission to investigate the claims. New groups of English men and women move into the area. In May of 1636, Thomas Hooker sets out from Newtown to found the colony of Hartford. As earlier settlement efforts largely failed, this is generally considered the founding date of Connecticut.

Connecticut is founded as a Puritan colony. Though ministers do not usually hold actual political office, the Congregational Church remains powerful in local and colony-wide affairs. Puritanism is a community-based faith, and serves as a means of social control, as well as personal holiness. The Congregational Church, as the officially established church of Connecticut, will continue to receive governmental support from taxes for many years.

1637–1638

The Pequot War rips through southern New England. In the main action of the war, the English burn hundreds of Pequot noncombatants at a fort on the Mystic River. The war results in the near-total destruction of the Pequot and the opening of the fertile Connecticut River valley to new waves of English settlement. Surviving Pequots are sold into slavery in the West Indies, and it becomes illegal to identify oneself as Pequot.

1638

Reverend John Davenport and Theophilus Eaton, a merchant, found New Haven. An independent Puritan colony, New Haven never receives an official charter, and, as such, has little claim to the land it occupies. New Haven remains friendly with the colony of Connecticut for most of its short history.

1639

Connecticut Puritans draft and adopt the Fundamental Orders. The Orders state that a General Court consisting of a governor and six magistrates should meet twice yearly, and stand for election once a year at the spring meeting. Freemen can vote for all elected officials, but non-Puritan "admitted inhabitants" are forbidden from voting for the positions of governor and magistrate. The Fundamental Orders remain in force until 1662, when Connecticut obtains its royal charter.

1641

The General Court instates wage controls for seasonal labor. Skilled artisans—carpenters, coopers, and masons, for instance—can expect to receive 20 pence for an eleven-hour day in the summer and 18 pence for a nine-hour day in the winter. Less skilled workers receive 17 pence in the summer and 14 pence in the winter. Connecticut is not alone in this move; other Puritan colonies institute wage and price controls in order to maintain a tight grip on the economy.

1643

The United Colonies of New England—sometimes called the New England Confederation—band together during the English Civil War. Connecticut, New Haven, Massachusetts Bay, and Plymouth send commissioners to this federal body. Rhode Island is excluded because of its unorthodox status. The main goal of the United Colonies is to protect English interests against the Dutch, as the two empires hold overlapping claims in Connecticut and on Long Island.

1650

The United Colonies and the Dutch sign a treaty at Hartford. At this point, the English outnumber the Dutch by a significant margin. The treaty alleviates some tensions between the two groups, but problems remain. Although the document establishes boundaries, and both sides agree to return outlaws for prosecution, a Dutch settlement is allowed to remain in the Hartford area, and the United Colonies' commissioners live in constant suspicion of collusion between Dutch and Native American forces. When the Dutch and English go to war later in the decade, Connecticut seizes the trading post on the Connecticut River.

The Code of 1650, adopted by the General Assembly, provides legal guidelines for the treatment of servants and slaves. It provides harsh penalties for those who ignore their obligations, and stipulates that captured Native Americans can be shipped out of the colony and exchanged for black slaves.

1657

The popular John Winthrop, Jr. is elected governor. Interestingly, he is popular not only for his skills as a leader, but also as a medical practitioner. He is the first American colonist to be elected to the Royal Society. Like his father, a longtime leader of the Massachusetts Bay Colony, Winthrop serves almost continuously as governor until his death in 1676.

1662

Connecticut receives a royal charter from King Charles II. The effects on Connecticut's de facto self-governing status are relatively slight. The number of deputies serving each town is capped at two. The charter also replaces the General Court with a General Assembly, but the legislative body continues to perform most of the same functions as it had before the charter was granted. Most of the colony-wide political power remains in the hands of the legislature, while the governor and council act when the legislature is out of session.

Also in 1662, Massachusetts adopts the Half-way Covenant, which allows churchgoers who have not experienced conversion to baptize their children, thereby attaining a limited sort of church membership. Connecticut faces similar problems, namely fewer conversion experiences, and disputes break out within the colony's congregations. In 1669, the assembly allows various sects, whether they allow baptism of nonconverted people's children or not, to continue to worship, as long as they remain basically orthodox in the fundamentals of faith.

1665

At the urging of the United Colonies of New England, New Haven is absorbed into the larger Connecticut colony.

1675–1676

Metacom's (King Philip's) War consumes New England. Fighting breaks out between the Wampanoags, the Plymouth Colony, and the Massachusetts Bay Colony in response to increased dispossession and mission activity. Most of the actual fighting takes place outside of Connecticut's borders, but Connecticut commits a significant number of soldiers to the Puritans' war effort. Connecticut will aid western Massachusetts in a number of colonial wars throughout the eighteenth century as well. Interestingly, Edmund Andros, New York's governor, uses the chaos of King Philip's War to assert the Duke of York's claim to much of Connecticut, but after a brief, armed standoff, Andros backs down.

During the war, Connecticut's leaders quarrel with other Puritan military minds over how their troops might best be deployed. Connecticut's armies are employed first as guards for western Massachusetts towns, which displeases Connecticut's government. Additionally, Connecticut's official stance toward Native American communities along the Connecticut River is much less aggressive than that of the Massachusetts Bay Colony and Plymouth, whom Connecticut accuses of unnecessarily antagonizing Native Americans. In the Great Swamp Fight, the climactic battle of Metacom's War, Connecticut's forces suffer a higher casualty rate than those of the other Puritan colonies.

1685

England continues the long process of securing its empire and making it more profitable. Edward Randolph, at the request of the Lords of Trade, charges that Connecticut is in violation of the laws of England and seeks to revoke its charter. (Massachusetts Bay Colony's charter had been revoked in the previous year.) Connecticut's leadership is divided on how to proceed; some favor the acceptance of English rule, assuming they will have high positions no matter who actually rules the colony, while others urge delaying tactics, wavering between joining New York and Massachusetts Bay. In the fall of 1687, Edmund Andros takes control of Connecticut, bringing it into the political entity known as the Dominion of New England. Connecticut never technically surrenders its charter, and legend has it that it was hidden in the Charter Oak in Hartford.

On paper, the effects of the Dominion government on Connecticut appear devastating. The Congregational Church, the backbone of Connecticut society, would no longer receive support from taxes, and Anglicans and members of other denominations would attain legal equality. Militia members could no longer vote for their own leadership; instead, militia officers were to be appointed by Andros. In reality, life in Connecticut under the Dominion of New England changes relatively little.

1689

Following the Glorious Revolution in England, Massachusetts imprisons Governor Andros, thereby ending the Dominion of New England. Connecticut soon returns to business as usual, although some disputes do arise over whether the colony can hold new elections or must wait for a royal appointee to govern.

1690

The General Assembly decides that public grammar schools should be established in New Haven and Hartford. Educational institutions have been in existence since the colony's earliest years, but the new schoolmasters will be supported partly by the colony treasury and partly by the towns.

1693

Governor Benjamin Fletcher of New York, citing a royal commission, seeks to take control of Connecticut's militia. Connecticut lodges a symbolic protest by calling out drummers to play loudly while Fletcher reads his commission, and acts quickly to protect the colony's sovereignty on legal grounds. The Connecticut towns vote overwhelmingly to support an appeal to the king, and they appoint Fitz-John Winthrop (son of John Winthrop, Jr.) to travel to England and secure the colonial charter and the colony's right to control its own militia.

Winthrop, citing a distinction between the king's and Connecticut's militias, is able to forge a compromise. Connecticut will retain its charter and its liberties, and 120 Connecticut men will serve under New York's governor. Connecticut continues to rely on its charter until several decades after the War for Independence.

1701

The General Assembly establishes Connecticut's first institution of higher education in Killingworth (now Clinton), supplying it with ten ministers as trustees and providing 120 pounds a year to support it. The college trains ministers

in orthodox doctrine, but it also trains colonial leaders in classical university subjects, following the British model. In 1707, the college will move to Saybrook; in 1716, it will move to New Haven. In 1718, it will be renamed Yale College, following a large donation by Elihu Yale, a wealthy Englishman.

1708

In a Presbyterian reaction to the growing autonomy and diversity of Connecticut's Congregational churches, a group of ministers adopt the Saybrook Platform. This document is an attempt to enforce "ecclesiastical discipline," according to its authors. Pastors from the various churches are to meet together annually to resolve disputes. The platform gains the support of the General Assembly, and it becomes law. Individual congregations lose power, and churchgoers see their control over their specific congregations weakened as well.

1717

Captain John Munson of New Haven inaugurates wagon service between New Haven and Hartford. Munson transports both passengers and goods, and the monopoly granted him by the colonial legislature stipulates that he make at least one trip per month during the spring, summer, and fall.

1740

The Reverend George Whitefield travels through Connecticut, inaugurating a period of religious revival in the colony. There had been earlier revivalistic stirrings, such as in 1721 when the Windham congregation witnessed eighty conversions in six months, but Whitefield's presence ignites a much broader revival. Whitefield's skills as an orator are legendary, and his message leaves no gray area: men are utterly sinful and are totally dependent on God's grace for salvation. Though Connecticut's ministers at first welcome the spiritual fervor and mass conversions of the Great Awakening, they soon begin to mistrust the movement, which splits colonial society between Old Lights (those who question the sincerity of new converts and the effect that they might have on established congregations) and New Lights (those who follow the revivalist preachers).

1741

Jonathan Edwards, an itinerant preacher from Northampton, Massachusetts, delivers his most famous sermon at Enfield, Connecticut. Titled "Sinners in the Hands of an Angry God," this Great Awakening masterpiece makes people painfully aware of their wickedness and the fact that the only barrier separating them from eternal damnation is God's mercy. Edwards' language is as eloquent as his message is terrifying: "You hang by a slender thread . . . nothing to keep off the flames of wrath, nothing of your own, nothing that you have ever done, nothing that you can do, to induce God to spare you one moment."

1754–1763

Connecticut is an active participant in the major campaigns of the French and Indian War (the North American theater of the Seven Years' War). During the course of the conflict, Connecticut commits to raising 28,000 troops to support the British. The actual number of Connecticut soldiers in the field falls short of this ideal, but up to 25 percent of Connecticut's militia is on duty outside of the colony for much of the war. The war does not do too much damage to Connecticut's economy, since farmers and merchants are able to profit from supplying various armies.

1765

In response to George Grenville's proposal to place tax stamps on many colonial documents, newspapers, and other products, protests break out throughout Britain's mainland North American colonies. The Sons of Liberty and other activist groups demand the resignation of Jared Ingersoll, Connecticut's appointed stamp distributor. Interestingly, the storm of protest in Connecticut is mild compared to other hotbeds of anti-Stamp Act activity, most notably Boston.

1769

Connecticut merchants begin to support nonimportation of British goods, following the lead of merchants in Boston, New York, and Philadelphia. Nonimportation as a protest movement arises in reaction to the Townshend Duties, a series of taxes that many people in Connecticut see as burdensome and unfair.

1775

On an official level, Connecticut remains loyal to the king and parliament, but individual Connecticut towns express outrage over the treatment of Massachusetts by the British government. After the fighting at Lexington and Concord, Connecticut prepares for war, calling up one-fourth of its militia, and sending some of its soldiers to fight in Massachusetts and the Continental army.

1776

Connecticut, along with twelve other colonies, declares its independence from Great Britain. Estimates place the adult male population of loyalists, many of them Anglicans, at about 6 percent.

Connecticut fights in the War for Independence largely to maintain the rights guaranteed by its charter. As such, it sees no need to call a new state constitutional convention during or after the war.

Matthew Jennings

Delaware

Prior to the Arrival of Europeans

Most of the Native Americans living along the Delaware River consider themselves Lenni Lenapes, meaning the "original people." They speak a language belonging to the Algonquian family of languages, and they live in a loose confederation of autonomous villages, essentially wedged in between the Five Nations of the Iroquois and the Susquehannock, with whom they fight intermittently. Within villages, a relatively strict gender division is observed. Men hunt individually, while women farm in groups. The major exception to this rule is the fall deer kill, which involves whole communities.

1609

Henry Hudson, an Englishman commanding the Dutch ship *Half Moon*, becomes perhaps the first European to lay eyes on Delaware Bay. Hudson is searching in vain for the Northwest Passage, but accounts of his travels spark interest among the Dutch and the English, who will become the main European players in the Delaware River Valley.

1610

The English captain Samuel Argall, sailing in the employ of the Virginia Company, names Delaware Bay in honor of Thomas West, Baron De La Warr, the governor of the struggling Virginia colony. The name, originally applied to the bay, eventually refers to the river that feeds the bay, the Lenni Lenape living along the river, the lower three counties of Pennsylvania that make up the colony, and, finally, the state of Delaware.

1614

The Dutch name the entire mid-Atlantic region, basically extending from Jamestown to Quebec, New Netherland. They intend to extract beaver pelts and fish from the environs of Delaware Bay.

1621

The Dutch West India Company receives a monopoly from the States-General covering trade with the west coast of Africa and the Americas. This company is responsible for the earliest European settlements in the region, though none of these earliest colonies and trading posts is permanent. Dutch interest in the region remains high, or at least higher than English interest, but the Amsterdam government has other pressing concerns, such as the battle for independence from Spain, and concentrates on raiding wealthy Spanish colonies farther to the south.

1629

The charter of "Freedoms and Exemptions" is approved by the States-General. This statute provides that any independent settlers have a right to as much land as they can cultivate properly. It also stipulates that any stockholder in the West India Company who can settle fifty adults in New Netherland will become the patroon of a large swath of land, which can be passed along to the patroon's heirs. The original patroonships include 16 miles of riverfront property, and extend inland as far as is practical.

1631–1633

Samuel Godyn commissions a colonizing party of twenty-eight men to land on Delaware Bay, where they establish the first European settlement in what is now Delaware. The colony is called Swanendael, a reference to the number of swans in the area. Godyn intends that his settlers begin a profitable trade in whale oil, but they arrive too late in the season. The settlers who remain at Swanendael quarrel with local Native Americans and are all killed by the time reinforcements arrive.

1638

The first permanent European settlement in present-day Delaware occurs when a joint Dutch-Swedish trading corporation, the New Sweden Company, begins construction of Fort Christina (named for Sweden's young queen). The colony is funded by the Dutch—and run initially by Peter Minuit—but most of the colonists are Swedes. In 1641, Swedish investors buy out the last of the Dutch stockholders.

1643

Johan Printz becomes governor of New Sweden. He will govern for a decade and oversee the high point of the colony of New Sweden. By the end of his tenure in 1653, he has assured the survival of New Sweden and its cultural distinctiveness, even though it will eventually be surrounded and overtaken by other colonies.

1651

Peter Stuyvesant, seeking to divert fur trade from New Sweden, sails a fleet of eleven ships up and down the Delaware in a show of force. Though the population of New Sweden is greater than the resulting Dutch settlement, the Dutch presence continues to grow. The settlers build New Castle, which will eventually become Delaware's colonial capital.

1655

An ailing Peter Stuyvesant mounts an expedition against New Sweden. Few shots are actually fired, but the superior Dutch force succeeds in intimidating the Swedish garrison. The Dutch also persuade neighboring native tribes to raid Swedish farms. The governor of New Sweden leaves for Europe, as do some of the Swedish settlers, but many remain behind, free to practice their religion under the governance of the Dutch operating out of New Amsterdam. Under Dutch rule, the population of Delaware becomes more diverse, and it includes people from all over Western Europe, as well as African slaves.

1663

The main European settlement in Delaware, known as the City Colony—so named because it is not under the jurisdiction of the West India Company, is a diverse blend of Dutch, Swedish, and Finnish settlers. The settlers farm grain, brew beer to sell to the growing population of Maryland, raise large amounts of livestock, and engage in trade with local Native Americans for furs.

1664

King Charles II of England grants his brother, James, Duke of York, a huge chunk of the American coast, including the Dutch colony of New Netherland. New Netherland's government tries to prepare a defensive force, but the colony is caught by surprise when four ships and 450 soldiers appear at New Amsterdam. English rule over the former Dutch possessions turns out to be relatively mild. The main winners are London merchants, and the main losers are those operating out of Amsterdam.

1673

The Dutch again briefly regain control over the Delaware River Valley, but by the terms of a treaty signed at Westminster in 1674, they return the region to English control the next year. The new governor, Edmund Andros, insists on an Anglicization program for the Dutch, Swedes, and Finns. Still, much of the distinctive ethnic character of the region remains intact. One of the downsides of the rule of Andros and the Duke of York is the fact that they discourage representative government.

1682

William Penn, the proprietor of the Quaker colony of Pennsylvania, petitions the Duke of York for the pieces of New York on the west side of the Delaware River and is given a charter for them. Late in the year, representatives from Delaware vote to join Pennsylvania. William Penn and Lord Baltimore, the proprietor of Maryland, will clash intermittently over the boundaries of Pennsylvania, Maryland, and Delaware.

1688–1689

James II of England, the former Duke of York and William Penn's close friend, flees England. William of Orange, the stadholder of the Netherlands, and his wife Mary assume the throne of England. Many of the former king's friends, including Penn, end up in jail. Penn is eventually released, but during his absence, the colony of Delaware all but secedes from Pennsylvania for a period of three years. Penn attempts to calm the situation by appointing a separate governor for the Lower Counties. The Lower Counties have developed along slightly different lines than Pennsylvania and contain a much higher percentage of Anglicans than the more heavily Quaker north.

1691

In an effort to modernize the administration of the empire, the Lords of Trade propose that Penn's colony should be placed under royal control. Two years later, when Benjamin Fletcher, already governor of New York, takes power in Pennsylvania and Delaware, he satisfies Lower Counties colonists by appointing one of their own, William Markham, as lieutenant governor.

1694

William Penn's friends regain their influence over the English Crown, and Penn petitions for the return of his rights to govern—his ownership of the land was never really in doubt—which he receives in July. The English government forces Penn to accept all of the laws that have been enacted during Fletcher's administration. Penn also has to pledge loyalty to William and Mary and accept the fact that William Markham will continue to run Pennsylvania until Penn himself can take over the job.

1696

Feeling like little is being accomplished in the way of effective government, Markham dismisses the elected officials of Delaware and Pennsylvania and replaces them with appointees. He also holds legislative elections based on Fletcher's model, which gave New Castle County (Delaware) and Philadelphia County (Pennsylvania) equal representation. Later in the 1690s, Lower Counties delegates will refuse to attend legislative sessions; some counties, even in the face of fines, will refuse to hold elections, furthering the notion that the Lower Counties are independent of Pennsylvanian control.

1699

William Penn returns to America, and relations between Pennsylvania and the Lower Counties improve. Soon after, though, both provinces began to petition for a new charter. The Lower Counties fear that Pennsylvania, with its larger population, will begin to exert an inordinate amount of legislative power.

1700

Called by Penn to New Castle, a new colonial assembly meets and passes more than 100 laws, many of them codifying statutes that have been on the books for years. When the legislature adjourns, however, it still has not provided a new governmental structure for Pennsylvania and the Lower Counties.

1701

A special legislative assembly meets, ostensibly to deal with a royal command regarding the reinforcement of the New York frontier. The Delaware River delegates are frustrated by the decree, since they have no forts and do not want to be forced to finance forts in other colonies while their own shipping interests are in danger. They also object to pacifist Quaker policies that they feel keep them from providing adequate security.

Pennsylvania proper also has problems with the special legislative session, since some delegates question whether laws passed outside of Pennsylvania can be applied inside the colony. Lower Counties representatives counter that if laws passed at New Castle do not apply to Pennsylvania, then Pennsylvania's laws hold no sway over Delaware and promptly walk out of the session. Penn finally concedes that within three years, if either Pennsylvania or Delaware desire to leave the union, he will grant each a separate assembly. Complicated legislative wrangling will continue for the foreseeable future.

1704

In November, the first Delaware assembly meets at New Castle, with four representatives from each of the Lower Counties. The assembly confirms all the old joint assembly laws, and also increases each county's delegation to six. Trouble is brewing, however, between New Castle, the most profitable of Delaware's counties, and the other counties. New Castle seeks to establish itself as Delaware's commercial center, but those outside of New Castle, particularly merchants operating out of Philadelphia, prefer to retain some ties to Pennsylvania. Despite its political independence, Delaware is drawn increasingly into the commercial world of colonial Philadelphia.

1712

William Penn, who has fallen on financial hard times, makes an effort to sell his rights to govern Pennsylvania and Delaware to the British Crown. Penn eventually sells the rights for 12,000 pounds, though he retains title to the land. Before the transaction can be completed, Penn suffers a massive stroke. He never fully recovers and dies in 1718, leaving his wife Hannah to direct the colonies' affairs.

1717

After suffering through the government of Charles Gookin, Delaware receives a new governor, William Keith. His appointment is not without controversy, since the Earl of Sutherland has also applied for the job. When the Delaware assembly addresses Keith, in a somewhat surprising shift, they remind him of their loyalty to the Penn interests and their desire to remain connected to Pennsylvania.

1718

When William Penn dies, he leaves behind two proprietary colonies and considerable confusion. Hannah Penn is the sole executrix of William's will, and she has to deal with several problems: Penn's oldest son has been disinherited in favor of sons from his second marriage, there are different groups of trustees assigned to the American lands and their governments, and there are mortgagees who have kept Penn out of debtor's prison. Hannah is able to retain the Penn family's grip on Delaware for a few more years.

1720s

While the Penn estate is being sorted out in England, William Keith begins to act independently as a sort of royal governor for Delaware. Keith appoints new courts, institutes a new criminal code, and moves to New Castle County, purchasing an extensive tract he calls Keithsborough, and opening an iron works. He exceeds his authority in 1724, however, when he expands the boundaries of New Castle and gives it a new charter as a city. Keith has issued the charter in the name of the king, and it does not mention the Penns at all. The action gets Keith recalled, and in 1726, Major Patrick Gordon takes over as governor. Keith does not go quietly; he spends several years working behind the scenes and in the Pennsylvania assembly against Gordon's government.

1730s

The Lower Counties survive as a distinct political entity despite several claims, the most forceful of which are made by Charles Calvert, Fifth Lord Baltimore.

1739

The town of Wilmington, which has previously been a commercial settlement known as Willingtown, is chartered. The urban plan follows that of Philadelphia: a rectangle laid out on the banks of a river. In 1739 Wilmington's population is 600; by the outbreak of the War for Independence, it may be as high as 2,000.

Also in 1739, the Reverend George Whitefield arrives

in Delaware, preaching to large crowds and inspiring the sort of religious revivals that will eventually come to be called the Great Awakening. The response to Whitefield, however, is muted in Delaware because of the number of Anglicans in the population.

1754–1763

During the French and Indian War, Pennsylvania accuses Delaware of not aiding appropriately in matters of defense. The quarrels continue after the war is over.

Early 1760s

The Academy of Newark opens in New Castle County. The institution, similar in curriculum to other colonial colleges, will eventually become the University of Delaware.

1764

The boundaries of Delaware, most significantly the troublesome western boundary with Maryland, are surveyed and marked by none other than Charles Mason and Jeremiah Dixon. Just before the War for Independence breaks out, Delaware takes on its final shape.

1765

Delaware's reaction to the Stamp Act is much more muted than those of Philadelphia, Boston, and other colonial cities. The assembly cautiously insists on maintaining English rights and liberties, while remaining loyal to the king.

1767–1768

John Dickinson, who has lived in both Delaware and Pennsylvania, publishes the widely read *Letters from a Farmer in Pennsylvania to the Inhabitants of the British Colonies,* which criticizes imperial taxation.

1770

Tobacco, which has been an important factor in the settlement of Delaware, declines in importance, and, in fact, ceases to be cultivated in the colony. Correspondingly, slavery reaches its peak in the years before the American Revolution and will decline throughout the early national period.

1774–1775

The Lower Counties participate actively in the Continental Congresses, and their leadership includes such revolutionaries as Caesar Rodney. Still, there is a significant loyalist population in Delaware. The outbreak of hostilities moves most of Delaware's residents into the patriot camp.

1776

The Delaware assembly, meeting at New Castle under the guidance of Caesar Rodney, votes to sever all ties with the British Crown. Rodney also plays an instrumental role (though his famous horseback ride to rush to their side is probably fictional) in convincing the Delaware delegation to Philadelphia to vote for independence on July 2.

Matthew Jennings

French Colonies on Mainland North America

1491

Christopher Columbus, seeking patronage for Atlantic exploration, plans to join his brother Bartholomew at the French court of King Charles VIII if his final effort to win the support of Queen Isabella of Castile fails.

1492

Bartholomew Columbus is still seeking French financial backing when his brother gains the sponsorship of Castile and sails with three ships in August.

1493

In March, Christopher Columbus returns from his trans-Atlantic voyage, believing he has reached the Indies (having, in fact, been in the Caribbean). At Queen Isabella's request, Pope Alexander VI validates Castile's claims to new lands and demarcates the areas of exploration between Castile and Portugal to the exclusion of all other nations, including France.

1494–1495

King Charles VIII of France does not protest the papal decree since his interests center on the established trade routes of the Mediterranean. He leads an invasion of the Italian peninsula and sets the pattern for the next quarter century, whereby the French monarchy will become embroiled in a struggle to dominate Italy.

1497–1498

John Cabot, commissioned by King Henry VII of England, explores Newfoundland and its cod-rich waters, which will draw French fishermen, among others.

1506–1508

While King Louis XII of France continues to pursue French interests in Italy, individual Frenchmen become involved in Atlantic trade and exploration. In 1506, Jean Denys of Honfleur and, in 1508, Thomas Aubert of Dieppe, explore the coast of Newfoundland. Aubert returns to Rouen with seven Native Americans.

1523

Antonio Pigafetta, who has accompanied and chronicled the Magellan expedition's circumnavigation of the globe from 1519 to 1522, visits the court of King Francis I. The French king becomes interested in exploration and commissions the Florentine Giovanni da Verrazano to find a northwest passage to the Orient.

1524

In January, Verrazano sails in the royal vessel *La Dauphine* and makes landfall on the North American coast, which he explores from Florida to Cape Breton, Nova Scotia, including New York harbor. He names the lands Francesca in honor of his royal patron and returns to Dieppe in July. There is no papal support, however, for French claims to the discoveries, nor does Francis, involved in European warfare, sponsor Verrazano again.

1533

French officials persuade Pope Clement VII to revise the prior papal division of the world so that France can now claim any new lands it discovers.

1534

In March, King Francis I commissions Jacques Cartier, an experienced seaman, to explore beyond Newfoundland. In April, Cartier sails from his native Saint-Malo with two ships and, twenty days later, makes landfall. He explores the west coast of Newfoundland, Prince Edward Island, Chaleur Bay, and the Gaspé Peninsula, and claims these lands for France. He trades for furs with Native Americans and returns to Saint-Malo on September 5.

1535

King Francis sponsors a second voyage by Cartier, who sails with three ships in May. In September, the expedition sails up the St. Lawrence River to the native village of Stadacona, close to the future site of Quebec City. Cartier leads a party farther upriver to the native village of Hochelaga, near a mountain he names Mont Réal. At Sainte-Croix, their base camp near Stadacona, the French expedition endures a harsh winter before returning to France the following year.

1541

King Francis chooses Jean François de La Roque, Sieur de Roberval, to act as his lieutenant general in establishing a French colony in North America. Cartier is to serve under Roberval, but the two cross the Atlantic separately. Cartier, with five ships, sails on May 23. He goes beyond Sainte-Croix to found a new settlement, Charles-Bourg, but the settlers provoke hostilities with Native Americans.

1542

After a difficult winter, Cartier decides to return to France. Roberval, delayed in his preparations, finally sails from La Rochelle on April 16 with three ships and 200 men and women. On June 8, the two French parties cross paths off Newfoundland, but Cartier refuses to remain in North America. Roberval continues on to Charles-Bourg, where his settlers face a disease-ridden winter. After Cartier's return to France without any gold, Francis sends ships to bring back Roberval and his colonists the following year.

1547–1594

King Henry II, embroiled in ongoing European conflicts, does not sponsor colonization in North America, nor do his sons—Francis II, Charles IX, and Henry III. Instead, beginning in 1562, the French monarchy is weakened by a series of civil and religious wars in which French Calvinists, called Huguenots, fight for religious freedom. Upon the death of Henry III, the French throne passes to Henry of Bourbon, the leader of the Huguenots. When the Catholic majority does not readily accept a Protestant king, the pragmatic Henry IV converts to Catholicism in 1593 and triumphantly enters Paris in 1594.

1598

To end religious strife, King Henry grants the Huguenots religious toleration by the Edict of Nantes. He also revives the idea of a permanent French establishment in North America.

1599

Pierre de Chauvin, commissioned by Henry IV, makes two subsequent voyages of exploration, seeking suitable sites for settlement.

1603

In January, Henry convenes a commission at Rouen to discuss colonization, and, in November, he names Pierre de Gua, Sieur de Monts, who has sailed with Chauvin, to be his lieutenant general in "Acadia." Monts and his associates in the Company of New France are to found permanent settlements. In return, they are to enjoy a monopoly on the fur trade for ten years, although Henry, due to pressure from other merchants, will withdraw this privilege prior to its expiration.

1605

Samuel de Champlain, France's royal geographer, who has traveled through Spanish America and sailed the St. Lawrence with Chauvin, helps Monts establish a French colony at Port Royal (now Annapolis Royal, Nova Scotia).

1607

The first permanent English settlement in North America is made at Jamestown, Virginia.

1608

After exploring and mapping the region, Champlain lays the foundation for Quebec City on the St. Lawrence.

1609

Champlain establishes good relations with the Algonquin and Huron, and he joins them in their warfare against the Iroquois, who become enemies of the French. Champlain explores farther south, reaching the lake that today bears his name. The English navigator Henry Hudson, employed by the Dutch, sails up the river now named for him (first sighted by Verrazano in 1524). Dutch settlements on Manhattan Island and along the Hudson will constitute New Netherland.

1610

Champlain returns to France to gain additional support for Quebec, as he will continue to do for the next quarter century. The fur trade, however, is more lucrative for French merchants than permanent colonization, so the number of colonists will remain small. Missionaries, especially Jesuits, will play a major role in French colonial expansion as they work to convert Native Americans to Roman Catholicism. Henry Hudson, now employed by England, explores the straits and a large bay far to the northeast also named for him.

1615

Champlain, again joining the Huron against the Iroquois, journeys across Lake Ontario.

1620

English Puritans aboard the *Mayflower* land at Plymouth, Massachusetts, and establish the first colony in New England.

1621

King James I of England grants Nova Scotia to William Alexander. This puts the English in direct competition with the French, who claim this region as part of Acadia.

1627

Cardinal Richelieu, chief minister to King Louis XIII, interested in improving French commerce, authorizes a new

Company of New France, led by Isaac de Razilly, to help forward Champlain's plans for colonial expansion.

1629

Warfare between England and France in Europe spills over to North America when an English military expedition forces Champlain to surrender Quebec.

1632

Peace negotiations result in the return of Quebec to France. Champlain is accompanied back to Quebec by a French squadron commanded by Razilly.

1634

Champlain founds a trading post at Trois-Rivières.

1635

Samuel de Champlain, considered the father of New France, dies in Quebec. This same year, the Jesuits found a college there.

1642

Paul de Chomedy, Sieur de Maisonneuve, founds Ville-Marie, a permanent settlement at the confluence of the St. Lawrence and Ottawa Rivers, beneath Cartier's Mont Réal. The settlement, soon called Montreal, will become a center for the fur trade and a base for further exploration and missionary work.

1660

The first Catholic bishop appointed to Quebec, François Xavier de Laval-Montmorency, reports that there are twenty-six priests (mostly Jesuits), two orders of nuns, eleven churches, and a population of some 2,000 settlers in New France.

1663

Louis XIV makes New France a royal province. The first intendant, or royal administrator, at Quebec is Jean Talon. Under the direction of Louis's finance minister, Jean-Baptiste Colbert, Talon advances a program to encourage settlers to emigrate from France. The population will grow to about 7,000 in ten years, although the fur trade will remain the mainstay of the economy despite some diversification.

1664

The English fleet takes New Amsterdam. New Netherland will become New York.

1670

King Charles II of England grants the Hudson's Bay Company exclusive trading rights to the Hudson Bay territory, which threatens the French fur trade monopoly.

1672

Louis de Buade, Comte de Palluau et de Frontenac, begins a ten-year term as governor of New France, during which time

he will encourage further exploration and expansion westward, while keeping the Iroquois in check.

1673

Jacques Marquette, a French Jesuit missionary, and explorer Louis Jolliet journey to find the great river of which the native peoples speak. Beginning in Wisconsin, they explore the Mississippi River by canoe as far south as the confluence of the Arkansas, establishing that the Mississippi flows into the Gulf of Mexico.

1682

René-Robert Cavelier, Sieur de La Salle, explorer and frontier commander, follows the Mississippi to the Gulf of Mexico and claims the area for France, naming it Louisiana after King Louis XIV. The French claim to the continental heartland will bring them into conflict with the English colonists migrating westward from the Atlantic seaboard.

1684–1687

In 1684, La Salle sails from France to the Gulf of Mexico with 300 settlers to found a colony at the mouth of the Mississippi. In 1685, the ill-fated expedition lands 400 miles off-course at Matagorda Bay on the Texas coast. The settlers succumb to disease and hostile Native Americans, while La Salle fails to locate the Mississippi and is killed by his own men in 1687. The few survivors return to Montreal on foot.

1685

King Louis XIV revokes the Edict of Nantes. Some Huguenot émigrés settle in the English colonies in coastal towns from Boston to Charles Town.

1689

The Comte de Frontenac, returned as governor of New France, faces the hostilities of both the English and the Iroquois in King William's War, the colonial counterpart to the War of the League of Augsburg (1689–1697) being fought in Europe.

1690

In May, Sir William Phips of Massachusetts leads a successful attack on Port Royal, but his summer expedition against Quebec fails.

1698–1701

Pierre Le Moyne, Sieur D'Iberville, the victor in several naval actions against the English in Canada in the recent war, sails with an expedition from France in 1698. He establishes settlements at the mouth of the Mississippi River and builds forts at Biloxi and Mobile. D'Iberville is appointed governor of Louisiana.

1701

The Iroquois sign a peace treaty with the French. Antoine de la Mothe, Sieur de Cadillac, establishes Fort Pontchartrain du Detroit (present-day Detroit, Michigan) on Lake Claire with access to Lake Erie.

1702

The War of the Spanish Succession (1702–1713) begins in Europe. Known as Queen Anne's War in the colonies, it is fought between the French and British in Canada and New England.

1711

The planned British naval assault on Quebec fails when eleven ships are lost in the St. Lawrence River. This loss, in turn, halts the coordinated land expedition of New Englanders and Iroquois against Montreal.

1713

By the Treaty of Utrecht, the British receive Hudson Bay, Newfoundland, and Acadia (Nova Scotia) except for Cape Breton Island, where the French build the fortress of Louisbourg to guard the entrance to the St. Lawrence.

1717–1720

Philip II, Duke of Orléans, regent for King Louis XV, and facing huge debts left by Louis XIV's wars, follows the financial advice of Scottish financier John Law and establishes the Bank of France. Law creates the Company of the West, known as the Mississippi Company, to develop Louisiana. Given a monopoly on trade with Louisiana and eventually on all French foreign trade, the company experiences high demand for its stock and founds New Orleans in 1718. Wild speculation reaches its peak in 1720, when the bubble bursts and the stock declines precipitously, discrediting the company and all of Law's fiscal reforms for France.

1738

As fur traders move westward from the Great Lakes, the French build Fort Rouge (Winnipeg, Manitoba) on the Red River.

1745

King George's War (1744–1748), the North American portion of the larger War of the Austrian Succession (1740–1748). Governor William Shirley of Massachusetts orders William Pepperrell, a local merchant and official, to lead an expedition against Louisbourg on Cape Breton Island. With the assistance of the British navy, Pepperrell's colonial forces take the massive French fortress in June.

1748

By the Treaty of Aix-la-Chapelle, Great Britain returns Louisbourg to France.

1754

The French in North America, who number only some 75,000, are concerned about protecting their lands against expansion by the more populous (1.2 million) British colonists. To ensure a link between Canada and Louisiana, the French begin fortifying the Ohio Valley and build Fort Duquesne at a fork on the Ohio River. Virginians counter by building Fort Necessity, but a French attack in July forces the commandant, George Washington, to surrender his post.

1755

British General Edward Braddock, commanding British regulars and colonists, attempts to take Fort Duquesne in July. He is killed and his forces suffer high casualties when they are ambushed by the French and their Native American allies. The British, fearing an uprising among the French inhabitants of Nova Scotia, force the Acadians to relocate throughout the British colonies. Those who resettle in Louisiana later become known as Cajuns.

1756

The Seven Years' War (1756–1763) begins in Europe; the colonial counterpart is the French and Indian War, which, in fact, began in 1754. The French commander in New France is Louis Joseph, Marquis de Montcalm, who, taking the offensive, destroys the British fort and settlement at Oswego on Lake Ontario in New York.

1757

Montcalm, from his base at Fort Ticonderoga, captures Fort William Henry on Lake George, New York.

1758

The British Prime Minister, William Pitt (the Elder), is committed to defeating the French in North America. He relies on two talented officers, Jeffery Amherst and James Wolfe, who take Louisbourg in July, thus cutting Canada's main supply line with France. The French fortresses in the Ohio Valley and on the Great Lakes begin to fall to the British; these include Fort Duquesne, renamed Fort Pitt (present-day Pittsburgh, Pennsylvania). Montcalm falls back to the St. Lawrence.

1759

While Amherst takes Forts Ticonderoga and Crown Point in northern New York, Wolfe besieges Montcalm at Quebec. When the siege proves ineffective, the British climb an unguarded approach to Quebec, enabling them to surprise the French on the Plains of Abraham. On September 13, the British rout the French, but both Wolfe and Montcalm die in the action.

1760

On September 8, French Governor Pierre de Vaudreuil surrenders to Major General Amherst at Montreal.

1763

By the Treaty of Paris, Britain gains Canada and all lands east of the Mississippi River. The Louisiana territory to the west of the Mississippi passes to Spain. France no longer has colonies in North America.

1774

By the Quebec Act, the British government allows the French inhabitants of Canada to keep French civil law, their language, and their Catholic faith. The boundaries of Quebec are extended to include the Ohio Valley. The American colonists consider this act as part of the "Intolerable Acts" against their interests. The act, however, will help keep the French Canadians loyal to Britain during the American Revolution.

1778

The French government of King Louis XVI, seeing an opportunity to avenge the loss of its North American colonies and to weaken its traditional enemy Great Britain, signs a treaty supporting the United States in the American Revolution.

1783

French assistance has helped the United States gain independence from Great Britain. Independence is granted by the Treaty of Paris.

1800

Spain agrees to cede the Louisiana territory back to France by the secret Treaty of Ildefonso.

1803

Napoleon, First Consul of France, sells the Louisiana territory, including the port of New Orleans, to the U.S. government under President Thomas Jefferson for $15 million. The size of the United States is doubled, and France never again will be a colonial power in North America.

Florene S. Memegalos

Georgia

700s–1400s C.E.

The Mississippi culture of Native American mound builders thrives in the northern reaches of Georgia.

1400s–1600s

The Cherokee people push into the region from the north and east, forcing the Creek to move westward into what is now western Georgia and Alabama.

1566

Spanish missionaries moving north from Florida establish fortified outposts along the Atlantic coast, naming the region Guale. This expansion establishes Spain's lasting claim to the land in later years.

1686

Under pressure from the Native American allies of England and plagued by pirates, missionaries have long since begun pulling out of Guale, seeking the safety of other Spanish colonies. Military authorities consider Guale indefensible. By the end of this year, the Spanish withdrawal from the territory is complete.

1717

A Scottish baronet named Robert Montgomery proposes a new settlement below South Carolina in the area formerly known as Guale. Called Azilia, the project gets a favorable response from imperial sources but collapses due to money problems. Many of Montgomery's ideas—compact townships, citizen soldiers, silk production—are later used in the development of Georgia.

1732

King George II grants a twenty-one-year charter to the Trustees for Establishing the Colony of Georgia in America. Unable to raise sufficient funds to begin settlement, the trustees petition Parliament for a grant of 10,000 pounds. Over the next twenty years, the British government spends approximately 236,000 pounds on the colony's needs. Georgia thus becomes the first British colony funded from the beginning by public monies.

James Oglethorpe, one of the British trustees, leads the initial settlement effort on the journey across the Atlantic Ocean.

1733

James Oglethorpe, who is a philanthropist, publishes a pamphlet promoting Georgia as a place of exile and refuge for insolvent debtors and criminals to reform themselves through hard work. The first wave of settlers, including such debtors and criminals, establishes Savannah, which will become the province's leading port and political center. Though relations between the two settlements will soon sour, South Carolina initially supports its new neighbor by donating rice and cattle to help feed the newcomers.

1734

Tomo-chi-chi, chief of the Yamacraws, accompanies James Oglethorpe to England and meets with leading British officials.

A group of Protestant Salzburger exiles, under the leadership of Baron Philip Georg Friedrich von Reck and Johann Martin Bolzius, seeks refuge in Georgia. They establish the town of Ebenezer upriver from Savannah.

1735

The only three laws ever enacted under the Georgia trustees go into effect: One prohibits rum, another bans slaves, and a third regulates trade with Native Americans. South Carolina begins a lengthy and bitter protest over these policies, which the older colony sees as deliberately discriminating against Charles Town merchants.

The first organized pro-slavery letter, drawn up by a handful of settlers near Savannah, arrives in London.

The town of Augusta is established in the Georgia upcountry at the falls of the Savannah River. It quickly becomes the focal point for the colony's trade with Native Americans.

1736

On his second journey to Georgia, James Oglethorpe places the defensive settlement of Frederica on St. Simon's Island, at the southernmost portion of the colony.

Reverends John and Charles Wesley, who find fame in England as the founders of Methodism, arrive in Georgia as Christian missionaries. Frustrated by the religious apathy and constant bickering in Frederica, Charles Wesley returns to England in June, wanting nothing more to do with America.

1737

John Wesley, whose American religious mission ran afoul of political factionalism and a broken engagement scandal, also returns to England.

1738

A strongly worded petition, demanding a revision in land tenure rules and the legalization of slavery, is signed by 119 Georgia residents and delivered to London. The Georgia trustees dismiss the complaints of discontented colonists as coming from a handful of lazy and worthless "malcontents." The Germans at Ebenezer and Scottish Highlanders at Darien submit counterpetitions, supporting the slavery ban.

James Oglethorpe makes his third and final trip to Georgia, this time, as commander of the 42nd Regiment of Foot.

1740

After Spain and England declare war, Oglethorpe leads Georgia and South Carolina troops on an unsuccessful campaign against the Spanish fort at St. Augustine.

Following in the footsteps of the Wesleys before him, George Whitefield disembarks in Savannah and opens the Bethesda Orphanage for children. Whitefield then launches his famous tour of the American colonies, which helps fuel the eighteenth-century surge in religious sentiment known to future generations as the Great Awakening.

1741

Patrick Tailfer and several other pro-slavery malcontents publish *A True and Historical Narrative of the Colony of Georgia* in Charles Town and London. The pamphlet is a scathing indictment of trustee land and labor policies and portrays the colony's leaders as simultaneously malevolent and incompetent. This publication initiates a two-year print war between the malcontents and the Georgia trustees over who is to blame for the province's stagnant economy.

In order to govern the colony more effectively, the corporation splits Georgia into the districts of Savannah and Frederica.

1742

The Georgia malcontents in Savannah elect Thomas Stephens, son of the colony's secretary, to be their agent in London. The younger Stephens launches blistering criticisms of trustee policies in the press and in letters to British officials, and he successfully lobbies for a parliamentary investigation of Georgia's administration. Stephens's effectiveness as a representative ends in June when he is reprimanded and humbled on the floor of the House of Commons for impugning the reputations of the trustees.

In Georgia, the colony's future is threatened by a numerically superior Spanish invasion force that moves to capture Frederica as a prelude to marching on Savannah. Based on a combination of strong leadership, disinformation, and sheer luck, Oglethorpe convinces the Spanish commander that he must retreat to St. Augustine.

1743

After another failed attempt to capture St. Augustine, Oglethorpe returns to England to face an inquiry into his command decisions. He never again sets foot in America.

The trustees reorganize the colonial government by abolishing the district of Frederica and appointing their secretary, William Stephens (father of malcontent Thomas), to be the president of the entire province.

Savannah becomes the unquestioned capital of Georgia. Settlers petition the trustees for establishing the Colony of Georgia in America to permit slavery in the colony.

1749

Mary Musgrove Bosomworth, a Native American interpreter sometimes referred to as the "Queen of the Creeks," and her husband, Thomas, lay claim to several lush islands off the Georgia coast, based on their negotiations with local tribes. The dispute caused by the Bosomworth claims leads to deep divisions and factionalism in the province that linger for a decade before the issue is settled through compromise.

1750

Helpless to enforce a slavery prohibition in light of widespread colonial disregard of trustee policies, the Georgia Trust agrees to legalize the importation and ownership of African slaves. Georgia rapidly develops a plantation economy—growing rice, indigo, and long-staple cotton—modeled after that of South Carolina.

1751

Georgia's first elected assembly meets in Savannah. Charged by the trustees with providing information to England about the colony's needs, the assembly is authorized only to offer advice and make suggestions about what should be done. Frustrated by the Georgia board's monopolization of power in London, representatives ask for the power to make laws—a request firmly rejected by the trust.

1752

Unable to obtain further parliamentary funding and finding that most of their orders are ignored in Georgia, the trustees surrender their charter to the king a year before it is due to expire.

Puritans from Dorchester, South Carolina, emigrate en masse to the region surrounding the Midway River, adding large family groups and numerous slaves to Georgia's population.

1754

After a two-year interregnum, wherein holdover trustee officials govern by default, Governor John Reynolds arrives to implement royal control over the colony. The new royal council contains the leading incumbent government officials, giving the province a sense of continuity that some find refreshing and others find exasperating.

Italian silk workers establish silk production in Savannah. The project will prove economically unviable and will be abandoned in 1771.

1755

Georgia's first official legislative assembly convenes in January. Among other actions, it enacts the colony's first slave code, using South Carolina's as a model.

Unhappy with the outcome of the controversial and disputed lower house elections, candidate Edmund Gray and his followers leave Georgia proper and establish the town of New Hanover on contested land that the Spanish claim as part of Florida. The settlement creates diplomatic tension between the two nations for the next few years, as Spanish leaders in St. Augustine suspect that the settlement is a disguised act of British aggression.

1756

French-speaking Acadians expelled from Nova Scotia at the beginning of the French and Indian War arrive in Georgia. They are met with distrust and hostility.

1757

Governor Reynolds, a victim of his own political inexperience and excessive favoritism shown to his friend William Little, is recalled to England for examination by royal authorities. Lieutenant Governor Henry Ellis, a noted scientist and naturalist, assumes acting command of Georgia until he is officially elevated to the governorship the following year.

1758

After much debate and opposition, the Georgia Assembly establishes the Church of England as the official church in the province.

1760

Complaining that the hot Southern air has reduced his health, Henry Ellis leaves Georgia and soon obtains a posting as governor of Nova Scotia. Lieutenant Governor James Wright assumes command of the colony and is officially named to the governorship the following year. Wright will be the third and final governor of the Georgia colony.

1763

Savannah printer James Johnston launches the *Georgia Gazette*, the settlement's first regular newspaper.

The Creek people agree to cede approximately 2.4 million acres of land on the western and southern frontiers of the colony. Believing that the ceded Native American lands are part of Carolina's original charter, South Carolina governor Thomas Boone grants 90,000 acres of prime land to applicants from his province. Wright carries Georgia's protests against these claims to royal authorities in London, but the controversy remains unsettled through the Revolution and adds new fuel to the existing bitterness between the neighboring colonies.

1765

The Stamp Act passed by the English House of Commons evokes dire predictions from residents who believe that the burdensome tax will devastate Georgia's budding economy. The Liberty Boys hold their first meeting at McHenry's Tavern in Savannah to formulate opposition to the stamp measure. In November, crowds take to the streets of Savannah and other cities and towns to nonviolently yet vehemently protest the new tax.

1766

With the backing of his council and some local merchants, Lieutenant Governor Wright issues port clearances on stamped paper, making Georgia the only one of the colonies to enforce the stamp duty. After this symbolic gesture, Wright suspends further enforcement measures, pending Parliament's anticipated repeal of the measure.

When word arrives that Parliament has removed the Stamp Act, Reverend John J. Zubly preaches an influential sermon outlining the essential injustice of the tax and congratulating the mother country for seeing the justice of colonial arguments. Zubly's "The Stamp Act Repealed" is well received and is published in Savannah, Charles Town, and Philadelphia.

The Georgia lower house removes colonial agent William Knox from his position for writing a pamphlet endorsing Parliament's view of taxation.

1768

The *Georgia Gazette* reprints John Dickinson's *Letters from a Farmer in Pennsylvania*, a critique of imperial taxation written in light of the recently passed Townshend Acts. The year's assembly elections are marred by the threat of violence, as numerous voters carry weapons with them to the polls. Wright notes with regret that Dickinson's writings have "Plentifully Sown the Seeds of Faction & Sedition" in Georgia.

1769

A mass meeting in Savannah leads to the proposal of a nonimportation agreement with England in order to pressure the mother country into respecting colonial liberties.

1772

James Habersham, acting as governor while Wright is in England, dissolves the assembly in April 1772 because of the lower house's choice of Speaker. The third such legislative dissolution in thirteen months, this action is blamed on the Georgia assembly's perceived radicalism.

1773

Despite political unsettlement, Georgia's growth continues at a rapid rate. The Creek and Cherokee cede 2.1 million acres adjacent to the land handed over in the 1763 negotiations, giving the province enough land to sustain population expansion for the near future.

For the first time, recorded exports from Georgia exceed 100,000 pounds.

In a comprehensive survey of the colony, Wright finds that the number of inhabitants has grown to 18,000 whites and 13,000 slaves—nearly ten times the size of the population in 1754.

1774

Georgians react with mixed feelings to the passage by Parliament of the Intolerable Acts, which are designed to punish Massachusetts for the Boston Tea Party. Public meetings in July and August resist cooperation with other colonies; as a result, the Continental Congress convenes in Philadelphia minus any representatives from Georgia. Acting independently, St. John's Parish votes to send Dr. Lyman Hall to Philadelphia to monitor the proceedings, but Hall refuses to accept based on such uncertain authority.

1775

Georgia patriots finally organize themselves enough to summon a provincial congress in January. Over the course of the year, this body slowly usurps the powers exercised by Wright and the royal government.

When news of the battles of Lexington and Concord arrives on May 10, the people of Savannah are energized. The following night, Sons of Liberty break into the public magazine and strip it of most of its weapons and gunpowder.

Parochial committees in each parish replace the royal courts as the main judicial institutions in Georgia, and a newly created Council of Safety helps coordinate the activities of the various committees. At the Council of Safety's urging, militia units remove commanders loyal to Wright and the king and replace them with patriot officers.

1776

In January, British ships appear off the coast of Georgia. Fearing that Wright might conspire with naval officers, the Council of Safety orders him arrested and confined to Savannah.

In February, Wright slips away from his captors, fleeing to the protection of the British navy. His departure completes the transfer of power in Georgia from the British authorities to the colonists.

Andrew C. Lannen

Maryland

Prior to the Arrival of Europeans

The native population of the area that will become Maryland is hard to determine. Conservative estimates place the number at around 10,000. Most of the region's Native Americans speak languages related to Algonquian, but the Susquehanna speak a language similar to those of the Five Nations of the Iroquois. The Western Shore tribes include the Doeg, the Mattawoman, and the Patuxent. During the era of European colonization, most of these will fall under the jurisdiction of the Piscataway. The Eastern shore also is home to the sizable towns of the Nanticoke.

1629

George Calvert, Lord Baltimore, a Catholic nobleman, applies to King Charles I for a piece of Virginia on which to establish a colony. The king is lukewarm at first, but later agrees, over the objections of Virginians.

1632

Calvert dies, leaving his title and the work of establishing Maryland to his son Cecilius, who is still in his 20s. The charter of Maryland is not particularly clear concerning the boundaries of the colony; it will take a number of lawsuits to determine those boundaries in coming years. What is made clear, though, is the role that Lord Baltimore will play in the colony. In addition to millions of acres of land, Charles I gives him near-total authority over its settlement and government, naming Calvert as lord proprietor of Maryland.

1633–1634

The Calvert expedition prepares and leaves for Maryland. The first two ships carry about 130 people, including women, which early Virginia forays had not. Although Calvert does not make his intentions clear, he seems to conceive of Maryland as a haven for England's persecuted Catholics, as well as a means through which to increase his family's estate. Cecilius's younger brother Leonard becomes the first governor. On March 25, 1634, the party lands, erects a gigantic wooden cross, and celebrates Mass.

The early years of the Maryland colony differ from that of Virginia in several key aspects. There is not really a "starving time" in Maryland, as the settlers immediately plant enough corn for their own consumption with a small surplus. They also plant tobacco right away, securing the colony's financial future.

Lord Baltimore intends to set up a network of manors in Maryland. To this end, he drafts his "Conditions of Plantation," which states that anyone who can transport five laborers to Maryland will receive 2,000 acres of land. By the 1640s, only a handful of these large landholdings exist. Another, more popular option is the headright system, whereby individual planters receive land for settling servants and families in Maryland.

Finally, apart from sporadic violence, Maryland maintains peaceful relations with neighboring native tribes. Nevertheless, Maryland's Native American population will decline precipitously in the face of European disease, dispossession, and trade dependency. Fifty years after the English colony of Maryland is founded, few Native Americans will remain.

1635

Virginia and Maryland colonists clash in two minor naval battles, a result of the fact that Maryland was established in territory that had earlier been promised to Virginia. English authorities step in, and a tenuous peace ensues.

The provincial assembly meets for the first time on February 26 in St. Mary's City. The legislative body immediately sets about making laws, but Lord Baltimore conceives of its function differently. In his view, he will make the laws, and the Assembly can approve them or suggest changes.

1637

Tobacco becomes the de facto currency of Virginia. Demand for the crop is high, prices are high, and planters keep accounts, settle debts, and pay taxes with tobacco.

Also in 1637, Jesuits run afoul of Lord Baltimore when they begin to trade with Native Americans and negotiate land deals, a power expressly granted to the lord proprietor.

1638

Maryland's second assembly meets in January, and again runs into conflict with Lord Baltimore's desires for the colony. In theory, the assembly is a gathering of all free men in the colony, but many men depart the council after a day or two, in essence leaving behind a representative body. The assembly votes against Baltimore's veto of the earlier laws, and forwards its own statutes to him. The conflict is not as bitter as it may seem; the code of laws eventually includes measures proposed by Lord Baltimore.

1639

A more regular body of legislators meets at St. Mary's City; these men are chosen by constituents from their home areas. Governor Calvert also personally summons five men to sit as an advisory council, which would later become the Council of State.

1642

Records indicate that the first Africans are imported into St. Mary's City around this date. For fifty years, however, Maryland's planters rely mainly on European indentured servants.

1643

Governor Calvert commissions an abortive expedition against the Susquehannas; the two forces fight to a stalemate. The uneasy truce between Maryland and the Susquehannas survives Opechancanough's devastating 1644 attack on Virginia's English settlements.

1645

During the English Civil War, Richard Ingle, a supporter of Parliament, wrests control of Maryland's government from the Calverts. Governor Calvert regroups in Virginia and returns with a sizable army, only to find that Ingle himself has sailed back to England. Proprietary control is secure for the time being.

1648

Lord Baltimore appoints a Protestant, William Stone of Virginia, to the post of governor. One of Stone's first acts is to extend religious toleration to a group of Puritans, who have fled persecution at the hands of Virginia's Anglican governor, William Berkeley.

1649

Both William Stone and William Berkeley run afoul of Parliament when they declare Charles II the legal sovereign following the execution of Charles I.

The first "Act Concerning Religion" guarantees toleration to all sects of Christianity within the boundaries of Maryland.

1650

The Assembly divides into two distinct houses when the elected representatives get their own meeting chamber and speaker.

1654

A group of ten Puritan commissioners convenes at Patuxent and begins to govern Maryland as a Puritan commonwealth, outlawing Catholic religious practices, as well as drunkenness, swearing, and fornication. Interestingly, back in En-

gland, Cromwell sides with Lord Baltimore and reprimands the Puritan Commission.

1655

Governor Stone attempts to regain his position. When his forces engage those of the Puritans at the Battle of the Severn, the proprietary party is forced to retreat after losing almost fifty men. Stone and his council are held prisoner for more than a month. Troubles continue until 1657, when Lord Baltimore and Richard Bennett of the Puritans sign a treaty ensuring general amnesty and the return of the original "Act Concerning Religion."

1660

In an event known as Fendall's Rebellion, Governor Josias Fendall meets with both his council and the lower house of the Assembly as a single body, essentially handing over the government to the speaker of the Assembly. Lord Baltimore responds by appointing his younger brother Philip as governor of Maryland. Charles II's restoration also discourages those hoping to establish some sort of commonwealth in Maryland.

1661

After King Charles II is returned to the English throne, Cecilius Calvert's son and heir, Charles, becomes governor. He shares his father's authoritarian philosophy and will rule until 1684, when he returns permanently to England.

1666

George Alsop, a former indentured servant from Baltimore County, publishes *A Character of the Province of Maryland*. The pamphlet describes Maryland as a land of plenty, which in some cases is true, but overlooks the miserable lives of many of the colony's indentured servants.

Also in 1666, in the midst of a severe tobacco price crisis, Maryland and Virginia planters agree to cease planting tobacco for a full year, hoping that ridding the market of excess tobacco will raise prices to an acceptable level. Governor Calvert is behind the plan, but Lord Proprietor Calvert vetoes the agreement.

1672

George Fox, the founder of the Religious Society of Friends, oversees a number of Quaker meetings in Maryland. Eventually, Quakers, renowned for their sobriety and honest dealing, will make up an important component of the colony's merchant class.

1675

Cecilius Calvert dies in England, and Charles Calvert, the third Lord Baltimore, returns to England for two years, leaving his 9-year-old son Cecil—more accurately, the boy's regents—in charge of Maryland. Opponents of proprietary government seize the opportunity.

1676

A corollary to Bacon's Rebellion disturbs the peace in Maryland, when a group of Protestant planters, worried about Native American attacks, appear to threaten to overthrow the government because of a perceived failure on the government's part to protect planters from such attacks. In reality, native communities in Maryland are too weak and dependent to pose a significant threat.

1682

Charles Calvert meets with William Penn in an effort to solve a boundary dispute. Not only has the city of Philadelphia been laid out within the original limits of the Maryland proprietorship, but the Duke of York (later King James II) has granted Penn Delaware (or the Lower Counties) as well. The meeting does not accomplish anything, and in 1684 Calvert leaves for England to advance his claims.

1688

Lord Baltimore appoints William Joseph, a Catholic, as governor. Joseph addresses the Assembly, and the results are disastrous. He implores the legislators to take various oaths of allegiance and to set aside the prince's birthday as a holy day each year. He also accuses the representatives, and the residents of Maryland in general, of drunken and adulterous conduct.

1689

In the midst of the turmoil in Maryland's government, news arrives from England that James II has been replaced on the throne by William and Mary. In July, the Protestant Association, a hastily thrown together group that opposes the proprietary, essentially overturns Lord Baltimore's government without firing a shot. The Associators, as they are sometimes labeled, quickly pass a law forbidding any Catholics to occupy the colony's civil or military offices. Throughout the colony, new elections are held.

1690–1691

Maryland becomes a royal colony when Lionel Copley is appointed governor by William of Orange. The Associators, generally speaking, welcome Copley, a staunch Protestant.

1692

The first Assembly convenes under royal government, passing a large number of acts, many simply continuing earlier legislation. One major exception is an act that establishes the Church of England in the colony, but this does not actually go into effect for another ten years.

1693–1694

In 1693 Governor Copley dies and is replaced by Francis Nicholson, an experienced and skilled colonial administrator. In 1695 Nicholson is instrumental in designing the new capital, Annapolis.

1697

The African American population of Maryland stands at about 3,000, of a total population of about 30,000. In the decades that follow, Maryland planters will come to rely increasingly on slave labor, and ever-increasing numbers of Africans will be imported. By 1710, the slave population is nearly 8,000. This influx of labor helps to solidify the planter class in power, as well as to increase the average size of plantations.

1715

In the aftermath of the War of the Spanish Succession, royal government in Maryland comes to a sudden end. Queen Anne's death in 1714 paves the way for an obscure German prince to become King George I of England. Benedict Leonard, Charles Calvert's Protestant son, becomes Lord Baltimore and dies eight weeks later. His young son Charles, the new Lord Baltimore, is now heir to Maryland.

Maryland retains many of the characteristics that had marked the "royal period" of its history. The Assembly remains strong, and Marylanders are increasingly wary of factors that might infringe upon their rights.

1718

The last remnants of religious toleration vanish from Maryland as the Assembly disfranchises Catholics, requiring those who wish to vote to take an oath.

1722–1725

The Assembly begins to divide along lines that will become clearer as the eighteenth century progresses. Though political parties do not really exist, country and court interests collide. The country party claims to stand for the welfare of the entire colony, and it casts the court party as a tiny pocket of councilors and high officials surrounding the governor.

1726

William Parks arrives in Annapolis and opens a printing house. He quickly earns contracts for post office functions, printing the acts of the legislature. The next year, Parks begins printing the first newspaper in the Southern colonies, the *Maryland Gazette*.

1728

Daniel Dulany, the leader of the anti-proprietary party, publishes *The Right of the Inhabitants of Maryland to the Benefit of the English Laws*. The pamphlet is one of the earliest American documents to explore the theory of natural rights.

1732

Charles Calvert, Lord Baltimore, becomes the first proprietor to visit Maryland in almost fifty years. While Lord Baltimore and his lady energize an opulent social scene in Maryland, he also brings about a compromise with Daniel Dulany by granting Dulany several posts, including attorney general. The end result of Baltimore's visit is, as much as possible, a return to the absolute authority vested in earlier proprietors. The country party is weakened significantly.

1738

The election of 1738 brings about a shift in Maryland politics. Charles Carroll, a wealthy Protestant landowner, intellectual, merchant, and iron producer is one of several prominent new faces. The Assembly once again begins to grumble about the authoritarian leanings of the proprietorship. Governor Ogle dismisses the legislature, and Calvert eventually replaces him with Thomas Bladen.

1754

Fighting breaks out in the Ohio River Valley, and within a matter of years, England and France are waging war on a global scale. Maryland only barely joins with the other British colonies in what begins as an effort to defend the colonies against Native American and French aggression and turns into a battle for North America.

1756

The Assembly passes a piece of legislation known as the 40,000 Pound Act of 1756. The Act taxes all landholdings, including those of the proprietor, and taxes Catholic landholders at twice the usual rate. Representatives discover that the British Crown and the proprietor can be brought into conflict with one another, particularly during wartime. Painted into a corner, the proprietor allows the act to stand.

1765

Maryland's reaction to the Stamp Act lacks the fever pitch present in other colonies, most notably Pennsylvania and Massachusetts. But a small Sons of Liberty movement does appear, and Marylanders rejoice when the Act is repealed.

1770

About 220,000 people live in Maryland. The population has not only grown in terms of sheer numbers, but in diversity as well. English, Irish, Scots, and many recent German immigrants have swelled its ranks.

1776

Following the lead of Britain's other North American colonies, Maryland breaks away from the British Empire, and declares its independence. The Revolution in Maryland at first takes on a decidedly conservative tint, as the assembly institutes property requirements for both voting and office holding when it issues the Form of Government. The Assembly also passes a Declaration of Rights.

Matthew Jennings

Massachusetts

Prior to the Arrival of Europeans

In the areas that will become Plymouth and Massachusetts Bay Colony, the main native groups are the Wampanoag (including Pokanokets and Pocassets), the Narragansett, the Mohegan, the Nipmuc, the Massachusett, and the Nauset. As fur trading with Europeans increases, the Pequot and other tribes from closer to the Connecticut River Valley will move east to take part as well. Most of the native men and women who live in Massachusetts speak languages belonging to the Eastern Algonquian family.

Southern New England's native peoples live in villages led by sachems, mostly male but some female, though a sachem's control over his or her people is hardly ever absolute. (In the early seventeenth century, Massasoit will become grand sachem of all the Wampanoag villages.) Villages are semipermanent settlements situated along rivers and bays that allow for a varied diet of agricultural products, fish and shellfish, and wild game. Generally speaking, hunting, fishing, warfare, and politics are male activities, while agriculture and domestic work are performed by women.

Though beliefs vary widely from community to community, most native New Englanders have a concept akin to the Massachusetts's *Manitou*. Manitou refers to both spiritual beings and the spirit world in general. Religious practitioners (*pawauog*—"powwows" to the early English) seek manitou through fasting, dreams, and visions, and their access to spiritual power makes them valuable to their communities as healers, prophets, and advisors to sachems.

1497

John Cabot, under the flag of England, explores the northeast coast of North America in a futile attempt to find the Northwest Passage to the Indies. His voyage does not immediately bear fruit in terms of settlement or establishing trade, but it does form the legal basis for later English claims to North America.

1524

Giovanni da Verrazano, sailing for France, probes the American coast from the Carolinas to Maine.

1525

Esteban Gómez, a Portuguese captain commissioned by Spain, makes landfall near Massachusetts Bay. In the summer, he maps the bay as far as Cape Cod.

1602

Bartholomew Gosnold, an English sailor, lands and tries to establish a small colony on one of the Elizabeth Islands. He names Cape Cod for the vast amount of fish he sees in the bay. Running short on food, Gosnold and his settlers return to England with some cedar logs and sassafras.

Shortly after Gosnold's colony fails, Samuel de Champlain spends two years charting the New England coast in the hope of establishing a French colony. He gives up this effort and returns to France in 1607.

1606

Inspired by James Rosier's *True Relation of the Most Prosperous Voyage*—a rosy account of Captain George Weymouth's adventures in Maine—Sir Ferdinando Gorges, Sir John Popham, and Richard Hakluyt convince King James I to charter the Virginia Company, whose branches, the Plymouth Company and the London Company, will be responsible for establishing Massachusetts and Virginia respectively. The small colony in Maine fails when the English arrive too late in the season to plant.

1614

John Smith explores, and names, New England. He publishes his findings, and his influence leads to further English interest in the area.

1615–1620

The total native population of southern New England, which had been as high as 75,000, is cut in half by a series of epidemics. In some localities, the devastation is even greater—from 75 to 90 percent in the most extreme cases. This stunning decline dramatically alters native community life and paves the way for English colonization in the area.

1620

A group of 102 colonists, including many Separatists—known as the Pilgrims—completes a nine-week voyage when the *Mayflower* lands off Cape Cod. The Pilgrims, led by William Bradford, had intended to settle at the mouth of the Hudson River, which was within the territory claimed by the Virginia Company, but the trip around Cape Cod seems too risky, and they stop briefly at Provincetown before choosing Plymouth.

The remove to America is only the most recent for the Pilgrims. Facing persecution for their Separatist views, they had left Scrooby in Nottinghamshire for Amsterdam in the Netherlands, and then had moved from Amsterdam to Leyden. Though members of the group were prosperous and free from fines and prison in Leyden, some parents began to worry about their children growing up Dutch. They looked to American colonization as a better alternative.

1620s

Throughout the 1620s, Puritans become increasingly infatuated with the idea of establishing an American colony. They infuse more capital into the New England Company for a plantation in Massachusetts-Bay—the Massachusetts Bay Company—and assume leadership positions on its governing board. By 1629, the company has a royal charter allowing it to govern, a land grant, and a pool of disaffected English people ready to move to New England. The charter, for some unknown reason, does not require the company to hold meetings in London.

1630

Under the able leadership of John Winthrop, a mass migration of Puritans to Massachusetts Bay begins. The period between 1620 and 1640 sees approximately 60,000 English men and women leave England. Around 20,000 of these emigrants end up in the Massachusetts Bay area, earning the mass exodus the title of the "Great Migration."

By 1630, Puritans practicing their faith in certain parts of England have become targets for governmental persecution. In Suffolk, home of John Winthrop, harassment is only one of a number of problems. The area is also wracked by unemployment, high land prices, and general sinfulness, according to the Puritans.

On board the *Arabella,* Winthrop delivers his famous "Modell of Christian Charity" sermon. For Winthrop and like-minded Puritans, Massachusetts Bay is a chance to reform and purify church and society, both of which have been badly corrupted in England. Winthrop also speaks of two covenants. The first, between God and the Puritans, sets the Puritans apart as God's chosen people. The second covenant, among the Puritans themselves, is to set up a godly and orderly community. Once the godly community—Winthrop termed it a "city upon a hill"—is set up, it is to serve as a model for England.

1635

The General Court authorizes town government, and several of the Massachusetts towns, already holding scheduled town meetings, use this authorization to regularize their governments. Most towns are governed by a small group of selectmen chosen from a larger pool of freemen. Towns establish their own churches, hire and fire their own ministers, and deal with petty criminals. Most power in Massachusetts is held locally, though the General Court can step in to resolve disputes and handle colony-wide issues. Though Puritans are the dominant force in early Massachusetts, non-Puritans are involved from the start. Also, though Puritan laypeople dominate town meetings and the General Court, Puritan ministers are strictly forbidden from serving in the Court or holding high political office.

Thomas Hooker, pastor of the Cambridge church, leads his congregation to settle the town of Hartford. Puritans found other towns in Connecticut, New Haven (then a separate colony), Rhode Island, and New Hampshire.

The General Court establishes a fishing commission, and offers tax exemptions on boats and fishing equipment for seven years.

1636

Harvard College is founded. No other English colony possesses a comparable institution at such an early stage of its development. Though training for the ministry is the main reason for Harvard's existence, students receive a rigorous education in logic, language, and the other liberal arts.

Also in 1636, Thomas Pynchon founds the town of Agawam (present-day Springfield) on the Connecticut River. Pynchon dominates the early Massachusetts beaver pelt trade.

1637

Massachusetts Bay Colony and Connecticut declare war on the Pequot, who have moved into the Connecticut River Valley. In the main action of the war, Puritans under Captain John Underhill—along with their Narragansett allies—burn a palisaded village on the Mystic River, killing hundreds of Pequot noncombatants. Pequot warriors are dispersed to live among other tribes, killed, or sold into slavery in the West Indies, while the English try to erase any reminders of the Pequot from the landscape.

1640

The Bay Psalm Book is published for the first time. Religious music in America has lagged far behind that produced in Europe in terms of sophistication. Poor singing is a matter of some concern to colonial Massachusetts congregations. One town, Wilbraham, goes so far as to set up a committee to look into "the broken state of this town with regard to singing."

1641

Nathaniel Ward releases "The Body of Liberties," a bill of rights that evolves into the first legal code for English people in Massachusetts.

1643

Massachusetts bands together with Plymouth, Connecticut, and New Haven to form the United Colonies of New England. Heretical Rhode Island is not invited to join the union, which forms after the Pequot War for purposes of defense.

1646

John Eliot begins missionary activity among Massachusetts's native population. His "praying town," Natick, mirrors English towns, and brings native people together to work, study, and live. Eliot preaches in the Massachusett language, and also translates the Bible into a written form of Massachusett he develops. Thomas Mayhew and Richard Bourne work as missionaries on Martha's Vineyard and Cape Cod, respectively.

1647

The General Court passes a law requiring all towns of fifty or more households to provide a teacher to instruct children in reading and writing. The Puritans place great emphasis on education, and not for solely religious reasons. They view it as a means to improve society. Some students pay for their education, and others attend on public funds. Massachusetts boasts a 90 percent male (and 50 percent female) literacy rate. By 1700, Boston will be the second largest publishing center in the British Empire, behind only London.

1650

Anne Bradstreet's *The Tenth Muse Lately Sprung Up in America* is published in London. Using humor, warmth, and passion to great effect, Bradstreet's poetry, the first published work of an Englishwoman in America, shows an often overlooked side of Puritanism.

1660s

King Charles II, recently restored, attempts to regulate colonial trade with a series of Navigation Acts. Before goods can be shipped to the Americas, they have to pass through England and be taxed. Also, all goods moving around the empire have to be shipped by English or colonial vessels. Boston enforces these acts loosely; as a result, it becomes one of the most active port cities in the Americas.

1662

Some Massachusetts churches recognize a partial form of church membership in the Half-way Covenant. In the earliest years of the colony, a conversion experience was required to have one's children baptized. The Half-way Covenant allows persons who have not experienced conversion to have their children baptized, though they themselves are not allowed to take communion. Puritan leaders, and some later scholars, use the covenant to prove that Massachusetts Puritans are backsliding from their lofty goals. Solomon Stoddard, minister of Northampton and grandfather of Jonathan Edwards, allows "halfway" church members to take communion.

1675–1676

In June 1675, Wampanoags led by Metacom—known to the English colonists as King Philip—begin to harass settlements in western Massachusetts in response to colonial expansion and increased missionary activity. Large-scale warfare erupts between Plymouth and the Wampanoag, and soon people all over New England are forced to choose sides. Wampanoags, Narragansetts, and many Nipmucs fight the English, other Nipmucs, and a sizable contingent of Mohawks.

King Philip's War sees the destruction of some dozen English towns in New England. Other English settlements are partially burned or dispersed when their inhabitants flee toward the relative safety of Boston and other towns to the east. Mary Rowlandson, captured in the attack on Lancaster, leaves behind a lengthy account of her captivity; it will be published in 1682 as *The Soveraignty and Goodness of God* and will serve as the basis for future captivity narratives.

The effects of Metacom's War, as awful as they are for English people living in Massachusetts, are much worse for the region's native peoples. In the Great Swamp Fight, English soldiers kill hundreds of Narragansetts. Metacom's death in August 1676 weakens native resolve to keep up the fight. Native Americans will never really recover to the extent that they can challenge English authority in the area. Approximately 1,000 colonists perish in the fighting, and of a native population of around 20,000, three thousand lose their lives. Even Native Americans who fight alongside the English or remain neutral are subject to mistrust at best and outright violence at worst.

1683–1684

King Charles II begins the procedure to revoke the 1629 charter of Massachusetts Bay, citing numerous violations of English law. His death delays the process, but, by 1686, royal government is established in Massachusetts.

1686

The Dominion of New England takes shape. New Hampshire, Maine, Massachusetts Bay, and Plymouth become one administrative unit as part of an English effort to better control the empire. New York, East and West New Jersey, Connecticut, and Rhode Island become part of the Dominion shortly thereafter. Sir Edmund Andros, a professional soldier, is tapped by King James II to rule the Dominion. Andros, in conjunction with a royally appointed council, works diligently to bring New England under the rule of English law. Some provisions of this law would return land to the Crown and force religious toleration; both measures are unacceptable to Massachusetts Puritan leadership.

1689

Spurred on by resentment of the Andros government and news of England's Glorious Revolution that has placed William and Mary on the throne, rioters tear through Boston. Accompanied by armed militiamen, the rebels imprison many government officials, including Andros, who is shipped back to London but never prosecuted.

1690–1691

In spite of the fact that many Puritans prefer a return to the old charter government, King William III—and the Committee on Trade and Plantations—drafts a new charter that features a royal governor who can veto General Court decisions, sanctions religious toleration, and gives the governor broad powers when it came to matters of defense. The charter also gives Massachusetts jurisdiction over Maine and Plymouth, but not New Hampshire.

1691–1692

Massachusetts is engulfed by a series of witch hunts. The controversy originates in Salem village, where Reverend Samuel Parris's young daughter and niece blame their hysterical and strange behavior on a West Indian servant, Tituba. Soon afterward, more accusers—mainly young unmarried women—name more suspects, mostly older married women and widows. By the end of the controversy, scores of accused witches have been tried, and almost two dozen convicted and executed.

1702

Cotton Mather publishes *Magnalia Christi Americana*, a work that examines New England's history from a Puritan point of view. During his intellectual career, Mather publishes over 400 works on a variety of subjects, including religion, science, and politics.

1703

As part of the larger conflict known in the colonies as Queen Anne's War (the War of the Spanish Succession in Europe) French and Abenaki forces attack towns on the eastern frontier of Massachusetts, from Casco Bay to York.

1704

French and native forces fall on the town of Deerfield, killing or capturing half of its inhabitants. Most prominent among those captured is John Williams, the town's pastor. Upon Williams's release from Canada, he returns to Massachusetts and publishes *The Redeemed Captive Returning to Zion,* which, like other captivity narratives, tells the story of captivity at the same time as it reinforces the Puritan sense of mission. Much to Williams' chagrin, his daughter Eunice is never redeemed. She converts to Catholicism, marries Arosen, a Mohawk man, and lives with him in Kahnawake, an Iroquois mission community in southern Canada.

As Queen Anne's War wears on, settlements in western Massachusetts remain exposed to frequent attacks, and other colonies do little to alleviate the situation. Massachusetts soldiers participate in the capture of Port Royal, Acadia (Nova Scotia), in 1710. The Treaty of Utrecht, signed in 1713, brings the conflict to an end and secures Acadia as a British possession.

Publication of the *Boston News-Letter,* colonial America's first successful newspaper, begins. Other newspapers in colonial Boston will include the *Boston Gazette* and the *New England Courant.* Among Massachusetts towns, Salem, Newburyport, Worcester, and Cambridge all will have newspapers before the War for Independence begins.

1718

Around 1,000 Scots-Irish migrate from Northern Ireland to Boston. Some settle in Worcester, where locals burn their church to the ground. Most Scots-Irish settle outside of Boston, in Sutton, Rutland, Ware, Dracut, and Andover, or move northward into Maine, which is still part of Massachusetts.

1724–1725

Governor Dummer's War rages between Abenakis, allied with the French under the Marquis de Vaudreuil and the Jesuit Sebastien Râle, and Massachusetts forces. In 1725, following the death of Captain John Lovewell and many of his men at Pigwacket, hostilities cease.

1726

Nathaniel Ames, a medical practitioner and tavern owner, publishes an almanac that sells approximately 60,000 copies. Ames's almanac includes charts on astronomy and weather forecasts, as well as literary excerpts and witty sayings.

1732

Massachusetts Anglicans attempt to disestablish the Congregational (or Puritan) Church. Although the attempt fails, the fact that it is made at all indicates Puritanism's grip is weakening over colonial society in New England.

1733

Parliament passes the Molasses Act, which has little effect on Massachusetts's burgeoning merchant class. Designed to protect West Indian sugar planters and distillers from competition with non-English sources, the act places taxes on rum and molasses in an effort to enforce mercantilism. The act is enforced only on a limited basis, and foreign products continue to pass through Massachusetts ports. Massachusetts sea captains devise a number of ways to avoid paying customs duties on goods shipped around the Atlantic.

1734–1735

Jonathan Edwards, minister at Northampton, reports on religious revivals in the Connecticut River Valley. These are the first rumblings of what will become known as the Great Awakening—a series of spiritual renewals occurring throughout Great Britain's American colonies.

1740

The famed English preacher George Whitefield arrives in Massachusetts, and revivals increase in number and intensity. Whitefield preaches ten sermons in one week in Boston, and the meetings regularly draw several thousand people. His farewell speech reportedly draws 30,000 listeners. White-field emphasizes the senses over the mind in faith. The next year at Enfield, Connecticut, Edwards preaches his masterful "Sinners in the Hands of an Angry God" sermon. Edwards's imagery is terrifyingly realistic. At one point, he asks listeners to imagine that "after millions and millions of ages, your torment would be no nearer to an end, than ever it was; and that you never, never should be delivered!"

Edwards and other revivalists are not universally accepted, however. During the 1740s, Charles Chauncy of Boston's First Church and Edwards engage in a heated pamphlet battle. Chauncy argues against passionate faith, and in favor of reason. Conflicts emerge throughout the colony between New Lights (revivalists) and Old Lights (those skeptical about the revivals).

Samuel Waldo persuades forty German families to settle on his lands in Maine. They found the town of Waldoborough, which struggles to produce crops in a harsh climate. Reinforcements continue to arrive, however, and they help to rebuild the settlement after it is destroyed by natives in 1746.

1741

During the War of Jenkins' Ear—named in honor of an English sea captain's removed ear—Massachusetts, complying with an imperial quota, sends 500 soldiers to aid in the British attack on Cartagena in Colombia. The attack fails miserably, and only fifty of the Massachusetts men return alive.

1745

During King George's War, known in Europe as the War of the Austrian Succession, Massachusetts Governor William Shirley outfits an expedition to take the French fortress at Louisbourg, a massive outpost guarding the mouth of the St. Lawrence River. Led by William Pepperrell, a colonial, and Peter Warren, a British commodore, the attack forces a French surrender. The capture of Louisbourg is a matter of great pride for Pepperrell and all of colonial Massachusetts. When, in negotiations at Aix-la-Chapelle in 1748, British diplomats agree to return the fortress to the French, Massachusetts takes the action as a slap in the face.

1754

In a conference among colonial leaders regarding Iroquois relations, Benjamin Franklin proposes the Albany Plan of Union. Massachusetts has eagerly sent delegates to the conference, including Thomas Hutchinson, who iterates the need for some sort of union. The General Court votes down the Albany plan as a violation of the rights of individual colonies.

1756

The French and Indian War—the American theater of the global Seven Years' War—comes to Massachusetts as Gov-ernor Shirley orders 2,000 militiamen to root out French Acadian resistance in Nova Scotia. The Acadians are forced to disperse throughout British America.

Shirley also enlists 5,000 soldiers for attacks on Crown Point and Fort Niagara. After Braddock's death, William Shirley becomes commander of all the British forces in North America. Neither attack succeeds, in part, because of inclement weather. Shirley is replaced in his military duties by the Earl of Loudoun and in his civil duties by Thomas Pownall.

In 1758, as William Pitt, the Elder, guides a renewed war effort from London, nearly 10,000 Massachusetts troops are serving in British units and colonial militias. The colony earns special praise from the royal governor as the colonial leader in the fight against the French in Canada. During and immediately after the war, Anglo-Americans in Massachusetts experience a surge in both self-assurance and British patriotism.

1763

The British Empire confronts a number of pressing issues in the aftermath of the Seven Years' War. Pitt's wartime spending has put the empire in serious debt. Great Britain now faces the task of administering and defending all of its newly acquired territories and reorganizing the old ones. Finally, a serious postwar depression has hurt trade around the Atlantic world. In response to these problems, Great Britain, now under the leadership of Prime Minister George Grenville, begins to enforce the Navigation Acts more stringently and explore alternative methods for raising money.

Boston also suffers from a postwar depression. Almost a third of Boston's adult males hold no property, and unemployment is high. To make matters worse, Philadelphia and New York have grown continuously since the 1740s, weakening Boston's commercial position.

1764

Parliament passes the Sugar Act of 1764. Massachusetts merchants benefit from many of its clauses that reduce duties on trade goods, most notably molasses, but they sense that customs officials will be more diligent in the collection of the reduced duties and that Parliament intends to raise revenue from the process. Both of these suspicions draw their ire. Merchants are not the only ones protesting the acts, however. Political leaders and lawyers, such as Samuel Adams and James Otis, Jr., begin to criticize the Sugar Act for undermining the rights of the British Empire's American citizens. Otis pens *The Rights of the British Colonies Asserted and Proved* to convince Parliament to repeal the tax. Tellingly, he does so as a British citizen: "See here the grandeur of the British constitution! See here the wisdom of our ancestors."

William Billings, one of colonial America's few professional musicians, opens his music shop in Boston. In 1770, Billings publishes the *New England Psalm Singer*. His most famous composition is "Chester"—a song popular during the War for Independence.

1765

Parliament passes the Stamp Act, which places duties on such legal documents as wills and deeds. Newspapers, pamphlets, broadsides, and almanacs also require stamps indicating that the tax had been paid. While the Sugar Act has affected a relatively narrow segment of Massachusetts society, the echoes from the Stamp Act reverberate through a wide range of social classes, occupations, and regions. In response, the Massachusetts House of Representatives sends a circular letter to the other colonial legislatures, calling a Stamp Act Congress to convene in New York.

Before the Stamp Act Congress meets in New York, events on the streets of Boston and other colonial cities overshadow any unified legislative response. A group of shopkeepers and artisans, including one prominent newspaper printer, calling themselves the Loyal Nine, meet to prevent the Stamp Act from taking effect. Along with Ebenezer Mackintosh, a shoemaker and gang leader, the group sets its sights on Andrew Oliver, whom they assume will be the stamp collector. A mob hangs Oliver in effigy, destroys his alleged stamp office, and then attacks his house. The crowd also attacks Thomas Hutchinson's house and empties it of papers and valuables, an action that a town meeting the next day roundly condemns as excessive. At the same time, Boston's merchants agree not to import British goods until the Stamp Act is repealed.

1766

Upon news of the Stamp Act's repeal, enthusiastic celebrations break out in Boston. Lost in the celebration is the passage of the 1766 Declaratory Act, which simply declares that Parliament retains power to make binding decisions regarding the colonies.

The Quartering Act of 1765 also feeds into the growing controversy between Britain and its American colonies. Though most of the burden falls on New York, Boston is also required to shelter British troops. Samuel Adams, who opposes the specific act, still advocates the quartering of troops based on previous custom.

1767

Britain tries to enforce the Navigation Acts ever more strictly by creating a new vice-admiralty court at Halifax, Nova Scotia, to try American smugglers away from Boston. Parliament also creates an American Board of Customs Commissioners to oversee the Navigation Acts enforcement.

Also in 1767, under the leadership of Charles Townshend, Chancellor of the Exchequer, Parliament levies taxes known as the Townshend Duties on the importation of tea, glass, paper, and paint. The Massachusetts Circular Letter goes out to other colonies, which generally refuse to accept the new taxes. Boston merchants again agree to nonimportation of British goods, and a series of boycotts and nonconsumption agreements ensues.

1768

Customs officers seize John Hancock's sloop *Liberty* for suspected violations, but the price of their actions proves great when an angry crowd roughs up one of the collectors and burns a boat belonging to his father. Following the incident, most of the royal officials relocate to Castle William, in the harbor, under the protection of the warship *Romney*.

1770

The new prime minister, Lord North, repeals the Townshend Duties, except for the duty on tea, which remains as a symbol of Parliament's authority over the colonies.

In March, a group of British guards, provoked by a mob of Bostonians taunting them and throwing snow, ice, and clubs, opens fire on the crowd, killing five and wounding others. Paul Revere's imaginative recreation of the scene provokes widespread anger over the incident, which will become known as the Boston Massacre.

1772

In response to the increasing confrontation between British troops and the people of Massachusetts, Samuel Adams convenes a committee of correspondence to disseminate information, in this case Adams's "Boston Pamphlet," about the situation. Other similar committees meet throughout the colonies, and, on a grassroots level, opposition to British policies begins to take shape. In opposition to Adams, now-Governor Thomas Hutchinson essentially argues that either the colonies should accept Parliament's authority or become independent—Hutchinson, and many others, do not consider independence a real option, of course. Hutchinson's argument pushes many colonial moderates toward independence.

1773

In opposition to the tax on tea, a group of Boston patriots gathers to prevent the importation of a shipload of du010ed tea. At first, they petition Hutchinson to send the ship back to England, but he refuses. The group picks up support from the entire spectrum of colonial society, and, crudely disguised as Mohawks, they begin to empty the tea into Boston Harbor. The Boston Tea Party results in the destruction of English tea worth more than 10,000 pounds.

1774

Infuriated by the Boston Tea Party, King George III and Parliament pass a number of Coercive Acts, which the more rebellious among the colonists label the Intolerable Acts. Among these is the Boston Port Bill, which closes the port of Boston until such time as the Tea Party participants can be brought to justice, the East India Company repaid for its loss, and the Crown assured of the colony's obedience in the future. Other Massachusetts ports and American cities aid

Boston through the crisis, and Boston's plight becomes lightning rod for protests around the American colonies.

The Massachusetts House of Representatives meets secretly to call a Continental Congress. Shortly thereafter, Governor Gage—Hutchinson has moved to England—dissolves the body, further inflaming popular opinion against British rule. Gage also bans town meetings. The Continental Congress meets and adjourns, resolving to oppose British policies as a group of colonies.

Daniel Leonard, writing as "Massachusettensis," advocates a loyalist course of action, arguing that Parliament is the supreme authority in the British Empire. Interestingly, Leonard also prophesies that a future King George might rule his empire from a prosperous, secure British America. John Adams, responding as "Novanglus," advocates total independence from Great Britain. Most Massachusetts colonists are in between these two camps, though patriots outnumber loyalists.

1775

The Massachusetts Provincial Congress meets and places military preparedness at the top of its agenda. It proposes an all-volunteer army and later appoints officers.

In April, General Gage, on orders from Lord Dartmouth, sends a force out of Boston to capture patriot ammunition stores at Concord. A skirmish breaks out at Lexington, and by the time the British reach Concord, hundreds of militiamen oppose them, word having been sent by Paul Revere and others. As the British retreat to Boston, they fight a series of battles against the militia.

Fighting resumes in June at the Battle of Bunker Hill, which actually takes place on Breed's Hill. Massachusetts loses the battle but inflicts a large number of casualties.

1776–1783

Though Massachusetts is the leader of the continental movement toward independence, its own government continues to operate along the lines of the 1691 charter, although, obviously, it excludes the authority of the Crown and Parliament.

In 1778, the General Court offers a new constitution to the people, which many towns reject. A provisional government continues to administer the war effort and the state's finances. The Constitution of 1780 proves longer-lasting, and it is still in force today.

Matthew Jennings

New Hampshire

Prior to the Arrival of Europeans

Perhaps as many as 3,000 Algonquian-speaking native people live in what will become the English colony of New Hampshire. Several distinct native cultures exist in the region, the most widespread being that of the Pennacook.

Like other Algonquian-speaking peoples in New England, the Pennacook split their time between semipermanent agricultural settlements and smaller, more mobile, hunting and fishing camps. Women do all of the farming, while men are responsible for hunting, warfare, and other pursuits.

Before the arrival of the English, a series of catastrophes befalls the Pennacook. In the closing decades of the sixteenth century, some Mohawk communities relocate to the east, bringing them into competition and conflict with the Pennacook.

1603

A group of merchant adventurers from Bristol, England, explores the Piscataqua River area, hoping to pay for the voyage and perhaps turn a profit by collecting sassafras. The mission fails to find sufficient sassafras, though it does identify the Piscataqua inlet as a promising site for settlement.

1615–1620

An epidemic decimates the native peoples of New England, altering native life and paving the way for English colonization in the area.

In 1620, Sir Ferdinando Gorges is instrumental in creating the Council for New England, of which he becomes the first president. The Council for New England has the authority to grant land, control trade, and administer colonies north of Virginia. David Thomson, Gorges, and John Mason—all of whom would figure in New Hampshire's early history—will be issued patents by the council. Gorges's time will be occupied with fighting against Spain and France, but John Mason will continue to devote money and energy to exploring and settling New Hampshire.

1629

The Maine patent is split into two portions; the northern portion remains under the control of Gorges, while Mason comes into possession of the lower half, which he names New Hampshire, after the county in England that is home to his family's estate.

Also in 1629, Gorges and Mason receive a charter for the Laconia Company, which is intended to divert beaver pelts from the Dutch and French operating in the area. The company goes bankrupt in 1634.

1635

John Mason dies suddenly. English interest in New England focuses on Massachusetts Bay, and, following Mason's death, the colonization of New Hampshire abruptly halts. Only a handful of colonists are living in the Piscataqua watershed, and most of them move to Massachusetts Bay or Maine.

1637

For a short time, New Hampshire is led by Captain John Underhill, a powerful and unstable Puritan, who has run afoul of the Massachusetts Bay Colony leadership due to his support of Anne Hutchinson during the Antinomian Controversy. Underhill eventually returns to Massachusetts.

1638

Thomas Wheelwright, a Puritan minister and relative of Anne Hutchinson, sets up a dissenting community at Squamscott (now Exeter). Puritan officials disapprove of Wheelwright's settlement, but they encourage a group of Puritans to found a town at Winnacunnet (present-day Hampton).

1640

A sizeable English population lives between the northern border of the Bay Colony and Piscataqua. More than half of these recent immigrants have moved from Massachusetts Bay in search of increased economic opportunity and less Puritan social control. In fact, John Winthrop, governor of Massachusetts Bay, writes that Piscataqua is a hotbed of whoring, drunkenness, and conflict. Piscataqua settlers often quarrel with Massachusetts Bay over land claims, many of which overlap.

Most of the English settlement of New Hampshire occurs along the lines laid out by the Massachusetts towns farther to the south. That is to say, the town is the central unit of community organization, providing behavioral controls and protection against external enemies. The region quite naturally falls under the economic and political influence of the larger and more prosperous Massachusetts Bay Colony.

1641

The General Court of Massachusetts Bay accepts responsibility for the government of Hampton and the newly created Dover (combining two earlier settlements). The deal that brings Dover under Massachusetts' jurisdiction allows Anglicans to participate in town government. Soon after, Exeter became a Massachusetts town as well.

As for Thomas Wheelwright's community at Squamscott (Exeter), both he and his opponents apply to the Massachusetts General Court to become official towns. The Court rules in favor of Wheelwright's opposition, and he and his few remaining followers move farther north into present-day Maine.

1664

A royal commission lands in the Piscataqua region as part of an effort to determine whether the Massachusetts Bay Colony is governing territories beyond the purview of its charter. The commission breeds some dissension in the four towns of New Hampshire, where many of the residents have strong religious and economic ties to Massachusetts. The move to bring New Hampshire under royal control fails, largely because it is ignored by Parliament and the Crown.

1672

Upon hearing that Massachusetts Bay intends to purchase the titles to both Maine and New Hampshire, King Charles II sends another commission to New Hampshire after urging the owners of the various patents (still descendants of Gorges and Mason) not to sell the land. This action will eventually result in New Hampshire's permanent separation from Massachusetts and its establishment as a royal colony.

1677

An English court rules that since Captain John Mason has never received permission to govern New Hampshire, his grandson Joseph can make no such claim. The ruling prevents Mason from establishing a proprietary colony in the Piscataqua region, and it also determines that the ownership of New Hampshire must be debated before Massachusetts courts.

1679

Anthony Ashley Cooper, first Earl of Shaftesbury, and the Lords of Trade punish Massachusetts's charter violations by removing New Hampshire from Massachusetts's control and establishing it as a separate royal colony with its own government. The leaders of New Hampshire take advantage of a loophole to appoint many of the men who have ruled New Hampshire while it was under the influence of Massachusetts.

1680

The English population of New Hampshire stands at approximately 2,000. Most of these people are involved in agriculture and animal husbandry, both for use in New Hampshire and for export. New Hampshire, in particular, has become known for its forest products, and a lively trade has developed between Portsmouth and Dover and the West Indies.

1682

Edward Cranfield, the newly appointed royal governor of New Hampshire, arrives. Within a year and half of his appointment, he has removed every single official who has governed before his arrival. He replaces these former officials with men who try to weaken Puritan influence, gain acceptance for Quakers, and enforce the largely ignored Navigation Acts. As part of this process, Cranfield oversteps his authority to settle disputes over land. His far-reaching attempt to force New Hampshire to accept royal authority succeeds primarily in alienating most of the colony's residents.

1684

Edward Gove leads an abortive armed rebellion against Cranfield's royal government. Gove is convicted of treason and sentenced to die, but he eventually wins a pardon. Cranfield's hold on New Hampshire, always tenuous, has weakened to the point that he moves to Boston and seeks a different appointment. He becomes the customs official for Barbados.

1685

New Hampshire is subsumed into the Dominion of New England as King James II and his colonial officials seek to exert greater control over the colonies. Though the effects on everyday life in New Hampshire are slight—in fact, many unpopular holdovers from the Cranfield administration move to Boston—it is unclear whether New Hampshire is a distinct entity within the Dominion.

1689

In the wake of England's "Glorious Revolution," which removed James II from power and replaced him with King William III and Queen Mary II, Massachusetts deposes Edmund Andros, the Dominion governor. New Hampshire, which has town governments but no overarching political structure, is left in the lurch.

Pennacooks and Abenakis, the former having been recently dispossessed of their homeland, attack Dover. As France and England again go to war, native warriors in the region ally with the French against the English. The English settlers have their own native allies, the Iroquois. The two sides continue to fight sporadically for two decades. New Hampshire becomes a dangerous place to live for both native and non-native people as a series of retaliatory raids plague the region. Colonists refer to the conflicts as King William's (1689–1697) and Queen Anne's (1702–1713) Wars. The wars seriously slow New Hampshire's population growth and hurt the fishing industry, even as they prove a boon to the Piscataqua-area naval stores producers.

1690

Leading citizens of Portsmouth circulate a petition for reannexation by Massachusetts. The Massachusetts governor, council, and General Court accept the petition, and New Hampshire is once again part of Massachusetts.

1691–1692

Massachusetts battles Samuel Allen, an English merchant, in court for control of the four New Hampshire towns. Allen wins and becomes lieutenant governor in addition to proprietor, having purchased the post from Mason's heirs. Allen's tenure is plagued by political infighting. Massachusetts and New Hampshire share a governor at this point, though each maintains its own government at lower levels.

1693

Legislation is enacted that requires all New Hampshire towns to maintain grammar schools. Despite this legal requirement, many towns do not have schools, and teachers' salaries remain well below those of day laborers.

1724–1725

Dummer's War, named for the Massachusetts official who directs it, removes the Abenakis from the area along the eastern boundary of New Hampshire. White settlement increases in the area shortly thereafter. In fact, by the 1730s, very few native people remain in New Hampshire.

1730s

Portsmouth builds an Anglican church. Although Congregationalism remains the dominant faith in colonial New Hampshire, its influence weakens throughout the eighteenth century as increasing immigration sees the founding of Anglican, Presbyterian, and other churches.

1740

The Privy Council appoints a commission to establish New Hampshire's southern boundary. The commission accomplishes the task, and actually enlarges the colony by a few hundred square miles. The Privy Council also appoints Benning Wentworth independent governor of the newly expanded colony.

Also in 1740, George Whitefield visits New Hampshire. The well-known revivalist receives an ambivalent reception at first, but when he returns in 1744, he remarks upon the newly revitalized congregations. As in other colonies, the division between Old Light and New Light congregations and pastors causes some consternation. The New Light movement (pro-revivalist) eventually loses steam.

1741

Benning Wentworth becomes governor of New Hampshire. His successful tenure lasts until 1767, and he leads New Hampshire through a series of midcentury wars.

1745

New Hampshire contributes men and supplies to the English attack on the fort at Louisbourg, the most remarkable colonial success in what the colonists refer to as King George's War. The growing military might of the New England colonies troubles the French and their native allies.

1754–1763

New Hampshire provides hundreds of soldiers per year to the British war effort during the French and Indian War. Robert Rogers's famous "rangers" serve as scouts for the British and also disperse the Catholic Native American community at St. Francis, which had served as the jumping-off point for a number of invasions. The end of the war, with the collapse of French Canada and the signing of the Treaty of Paris in 1763, secures the northern part of New Hampshire as an area safe for English settlement.

1756

Daniel Fowle, a printer operating out of Boston, moves to Portsmouth and founds the *New Hampshire Gazette*. Prior to Fowle's paper, most New Hampshire news and advertisements ran in Massachusetts newspapers.

1765

In response to the Stamp Act handed down by Parliament, a local Sons of Liberty movement develops in Portsmouth. The governor, Benning Wentworth, refuses to enforce the act, but is accused by protestors of not acting passionately enough in defense of New Hampshire's rights.

1767

John Wentworth, the newly appointed governor of New Hampshire and nephew of the popular Benning, arrives. Wentworth immediately comes under fire when he decides not to oppose the Townshend Duties, a series of taxes meant to replace the Stamp Act. Throughout New Hampshire, merchants demonstrate their concerns by adopting nonimportation resolutions.

1768

Massachusetts circulates a letter asking that all of the British colonies stand together against the Townshend Act. Though most of the Assembly supports the cause, Wentworth and his associates prevent the measure from going forward, and the normally cordial political atmosphere grows more tense and rancorous.

1773

New Hampshirites join Massachusetts in protesting the Tea Act, not by dumping tea in the harbor, but by entering into nonconsumption pacts.

1774

Wentworth's authority continues to deteriorate. On December 14, a crowd of 400 men attacks Fort William and Mary, which they think will be reinforced by British troops. Wentworth calls out the militia, which does not respond.

1775

Reflecting dramatic population growth that occurred all along the eastern seaboard in the second half of the eighteenth century, particularly between 1765 and 1775, the population of New Hampshire stands at approximately 75,000.

In April, following the outbreak of hostilities at Lexington and Concord, hundreds of New Hampshire militiamen flood into Massachusetts to assist colonists there. Wentworth responds by delaying the sitting of the legislature, which infuriates the patriot movement even more.

The old Assembly begins to refer to itself as the "Provincial Congress," and in 1776 becomes the House of Representatives. Most of the power to govern in New Hampshire remains firmly entrenched at the town level.

1776

By July, when the Continental Congress meets at Philadelphia to declare independence, New Hampshire is already functioning as a self-governing, independent entity.

During the War for Independence, no fighting takes place within the borders of New Hampshire. The population of the state continues to grow rapidly, reaching 95,000 by the mid-1780s.

Matthew Jennings

New Jersey

Prior to the Arrival of Europeans

The most populous group of Native Americans in what will become New Jersey is the Lenni Lenape (Delaware). The Lenni Lenape, who speak variants of the Algonquian language, live in riverside villages in New Jersey, Delaware, Pennsylvania, and New York. Approximately 3,000 Lenni Lenapes live in New Jersey before the arrival of large numbers of Europeans.

The village is the basic unit of Lenni Lenape political life, and the people engage in a variety of subsistence activities, including fishing, hunting, and growing corn, beans, and squash. The Five Nations of the Iroquois, living north and west of the Lenni Lenape, are the dominant native power in the region and will continue in that capacity, expanding their role as colonization takes hold.

1497

John Cabot skirts the coast of New Jersey during his voyage of discovery. This voyage forms the shaky legal basis for later English claims to the region.

1609

During his futile search for a northwest passage, Henry Hudson, an English navigator working for the Dutch, sails up the river now bearing his name. Hudson's voyage prompts increased Dutch interest in the area.

1623

The States-General formally establishes the colony of New Netherland. It commissions small numbers of settlers to move into Fort Orange (Albany), Fort Nassau (near present-day Philadelphia), and the Fort of Good Hope (on the Connecticut River).

1626

Dutch colonization begins on the island of Manhattan. Most early Dutch ventures in the region are exclusively fur-trading outposts.

1629

Lessening its financial commitment to American colonization, the Dutch West India Company establishes a handful of patroonships in New York, New Jersey, and Delaware. The landowner, or patroon, holds feudal rights over a swath of land extending out indefinitely from a riverbank. Under the patroonship system, Michael Pauw becomes the first European to own land in New Jersey, calling his estate Pavonia.

1638

Willem Kieft becomes director-general of the colony of New Netherland. In an effort to revitalize the colony, he badly damages Native American–Dutch relations, first by threatening to tax Native Americans—payable in furs—and then by inciting a race war, which devastates both the Dutch and native populations. Kieft's War, which lasts from 1643 to 1645, eliminates nearly all Dutch settlements on the west side of the Hudson River.

1640

A small Swedish community is established on the New Jersey side of the Delaware River. By the 1650s, relatively few of the Swedes remain, though their relations with the Dutch are, for the most part, peaceful.

1655

A large Native American force attacks New Amsterdam. Though the assault is driven back, all Dutch settlement on the west side of the Hudson ceases. During the same year, Peter Stuyvesant forces the surrender of the colony of New Sweden.

1656

In a conciliatory move, Stuyvesant forces the purchase of Native American lands and commands that new immigrants to the region settle in villages, not on dispersed individual farms.

1660

Tielman Van Vleeck founds the town of Bergen, the first permanent European settlement in New Jersey. Bergen is laid out as a palisaded village, featuring two perpendicular main streets, with gardens and livestock pasture outside the palisade.

1664

A small English force—the exact number is not known, but far fewer than the 2,000 that Stuyvesant was convinced of—blockades the harbor at New Amsterdam. Stuyvesant surrenders without firing a shot.

Just before this "conquest," King Charles II of England grants his brother James, the Duke of York, all of the lands between the Connecticut and Delaware Rivers. The charter makes James the proprietor of the colony, with no provision for an elected assembly. James proceeds to grant two of his friends, Lord John Berkeley and Sir George Carteret, the proprietorship of New Jersey, which is named after the isle of Jersey, where Carteret had been born. Richard Nicolls, the governor, believes New Jersey to be the most valuable part of the proprietorship, and urges James not to give it up.

Nicolls grants an association of Baptists, Quakers, and disillusioned Puritans 400,000 acres. The grant results in the founding of Elizabethtown and Piscataway. The years that followed see Middletown, Woodbridge, Newark, and Shrewsbury established in much the same fashion.

1665

Nicolls issues the Duke's Laws. The Duke's Laws allow for town government and broad-based tolerance for all Protestant denominations.

The new proprietors, Carteret and Berkeley, draw up the Concessions and Agreements, guaranteeing a general assembly and freedom of trade and conscience—at least for Protestants. Meanwhile, the Dutch town of Bergen is allowed to keep all of its institutions and local officials, as long as they take an oath of allegiance to England.

1667–1670

A group of Barbadian planters purchases large tracts of land in Bergen County and brings in a substantial number of African slaves.

1673–1674

A Dutch fleet occupies New York and New Jersey, with relatively little impact on the lives of the New Jersey colonists. When residents of some of the towns petition for confirmation of their rights, they are told that they have the same rights as Dutch citizens, including liberty of conscience and the right to own their lands peacefully. A 1674 treaty restores New Jersey to the English.

Also in 1674, John Berkeley sells his proprietorship to two Quakers, Edward Byllynge (Billing) and John Fenwick.

1676

George Carteret agrees to partition the territory, creating the colonies of West Jersey (formerly Berkeley's grant) and East Jersey. His heir governs the East Jersey colony.

The East Jersey assembly enacts a code of criminal law, based on earlier laws and the Duke's Laws of 1665. The code is fairly strict, and is, in fact, based on New England law, though it provides for restitution, as well as corporal punishment and, therefore, is more lenient.

Also in 1676, Byllynge drafts the West Jersey Concessions, which become law in 1677. The Concessions, a fundamentally Quaker document, mark a watershed moment in colonial political development. Nearly all adult males will be able to vote, and the elected assembly will wield a comparatively large amount of power. William Penn encourages Quaker settlement in West Jersey, citing the proprietors' commitment to purchasing Native American lands, trial by jury, and other liberal aspects of the Concessions. Once Pennsylvania is founded, far greater numbers of Quakers migrate to that colony.

Late 1670s

Governor Carteret of East Jersey fights a series of legal battles with Sir Edmund Andros, the governor of New York, over customs collection on ships entering the Delaware River. At one point, Carteret is arrested, tried in New York and instructed not to assume the powers of government. Andros's takeover will end in 1680, and Governor Carteret will return to power until his death in 1682.

1682

Hoping the proprietorship's sale will increase the Carteret family's shrinking fortune, East Jersey goes up on the auction block. William Penn and a group of eleven associates purchase the colony, and, combined with the Lower Counties (Delaware), most of the land between Maryland and New York is administered by Quakers. Robert Barclay, a brilliant Scottish Quaker, becomes governor, but he never sets foot in East Jersey. His appointment leads to increased immigration, not only among Scottish Quakers, but the more numerous Presbyterians and Dissenters as well.

The early 1680s also witnesses dramatic change in the New Jersey proprietorships. William Penn's group, now expanded to twenty-four proprietors, controls East Jersey, while all of West Jersey comes under the control of Daniel Coxe, a Cambridge-trained royal physician, who has acquired more than 1 million acres of land in America.

1688

The Dominion of New England expands to encompass New York and the two Jerseys under the leadership of Sir Edmund Andros. The seeds are sown during this period for the establishment of East and West Jersey as royal colonies, but the Glorious Revolution and King William's War (or the War of the League of Augsburg) eventually delay proceedings and restore the status quo, albeit temporarily.

1690s

Both Jerseys experience unrest as colonists fight against the proprietors in a number of venues, including the assemblies and town governments. At the same time, the proprietors are fighting to uphold their monopoly on land sales in the region and establish Perth Amboy's port as a free port; ships are generally required to land at New York City first and pay customs duties. The Crown becomes increasingly interested in the right of government, a dispute that lingers from the colonies' earliest days.

1701

The proprietors propose the terms by which they would surrender East and West Jersey to the Crown. The most notable of these are that the proprietors will give up all rights of government; Perth Amboy, Burlington, and Cohansey will be free ports; and New Jersey will become a single colony with an elective assembly.

1703

Colonial politics begin to be dominated by the "Cornbury ring," named after the governor, Lord Cornbury. Cornbury spends most of his energy placing his friends in high offices and trying to control the legislature. Cornbury's party also tries to disfranchise the Quakers.

1707

John Lovelace, a colonel in the military, arrives to replace Cornbury as governor. Although he tries to reconcile the conflicts between the different levels of government, he dies the next year. Lovelace's lieutenant governor, Richard Ingoldsby, replaces him. Ingoldsby runs afoul of the legislature immediately, and the legislature repeatedly refuses to raise money for various projects, including Queen Anne's War.

1710

Robert Hunter takes office, and ushers in a new period of reconciliation and prosperity for New Jersey. Hunter is able to control the more reactionary elements of the council, and, at the same time, work with the assembly, until he runs into conflict with Daniel Coxe, the speaker of the assembly. One of the running themes of New Jersey's—and many of the colonies'—history during this time period is the increasing power and independence of colonial legislatures.

1720

William Burnet becomes governor. At first, Burnet's tenure is marred by conflicts with the assembly, but later he governs more tactfully.

1723

The Loan Office Act sets up a government-controlled bank that allows colonists to take out money, using their land as collateral.

1738

Lewis Morris is appointed governor of New Jersey. For the first time, New Jersey has its own governor, the post having been combined with that of New York in the past. Morris tries to impose his will on the assembly whenever possible, and often refers to his prerogative as governor and the power of the Crown's authority. The colonial assembly, not to be outdone, frequently withholds money—even during the War of Jenkins' Ear and King George's War—and distributes tax revenues as it sees fit.

1745–1746

The assemblies that meet during these years quarrel openly with Governor Morris, and Morris threatens to veto all legislation unless the assembly passes a support act and a militia act. The house finally does both, but when New England plans an attack on Louisbourg, the French fortress at the mouth of the St. Lawrence, New Jersey's legislature drags its feet, further infuriating the governor.

1747

Governor Jonathan Belcher arrives, promising an end to the conflicts that have racked New Jersey. As a result of land policy, he faces a new round of riots. Belcher works to gain Crown approval of measures that would provide amnesty for rioters. The house refuses to grant money to quell the disturbances.

1751

Governor Belcher dissolves the legislature when it refuses to pay his salary, and a slightly more conservative legislature takes its place. Finally, when New Jersey's debt is high and the treasury empty, the legislature begins to tax in earnest. The effect of Belcher's power is fading, the council is the main upholder of royal authority, and the lower house controls the power of the purse. A similar situation exists in other colonies.

1756–1763

The Seven Years' War, known in America as the French and Indian War, engulfs Great Britain and France in an all-out struggle for North America. Britain requires its colonies to provide men and money to support the war effort. New Jersey's legislature ties its support for the war to another Loan Office Act and generally supports the war in the most grudging manner. New Jersey is the only American colony that does not meet its wartime quotas, making it unpopular with the military and the Crown.

1763

In the aftermath of the war, William Franklin, Benjamin Franklin's son, becomes governor. His administration is particularly affected by the reining in of Britain's American colonies. New Jersey, which has issued more paper money than any other American colony, also finds that practice disallowed.

1765

Parliament passes the Stamp Act, which requires tax stamps to be affixed to legal documents and newspapers, igniting a firestorm of protest in several American colonies. New Jersey lawyers gather at Perth Amboy to propose a moderate course: not to buy the stamps, but to strongly oppose disorderly behavior. New Jersey participates in the Stamp Act Congress minimally and does not enter into any nonimportation agreements.

New Jersey is home to some Sons of Liberty activity, particularly in Woodbridge, Elizabethtown, Piscataway, and Freehold.

1767

The Townshend Acts—taxes on tea, glass, paper, and paint—cause more uproar in the colonies. Without the knowledge of Governor Franklin, New Jersey's assembly petitions the king directly to repeal the tax.

1775–1776

New Jersey's population stands at about 130,000, most of whom are involved in the production of cereal grains. African American slaves constitute less than 10 percent of the population, and Native Americans have all but disappeared from the area.

In New Jersey, Governor Franklin hopes fervently that reconciliation between the Crown and the colonies can be brought about. In New Jersey, as in the other colonies, committees of correspondence meet to voice their approval for a continental congress. Most New Jersey residents do not approve of independence.

Even after the hostilities at Lexington and Concord, New Jersey plots a cautious course. There are no newspapers and no organized resistance to imperial policies, partially because imperial policies rarely have relevance to the lives of New Jersey's largely rural population. Eventually, and reluctantly, New Jersey joins the cause of independence, but the colony also is home to fierce Tory resistance. As late as 1782, bands of patriots and Tories fight each other throughout the state.

New Jersey's 1776 Constitution is essentially a conservative document. It aims to correct royal and parliamentary abuses, not to institute a new state government and disrupt long-established patterns in the colony's society and economy.

Matthew Jennings

New York and New Netherland

Prior to the Arrival of Europeans

The Native Americans living in the region that will become New York are primarily members of either the Algonquian or Iroquoian linguistic groups. The Algonquin (consisting of tribes such as the Mahican and Delaware, among others) reside in the eastern regions of New York, while the western regions are occupied by Iroquois, who had migrated from farther west, beginning perhaps as early as 1300 C.E.

By the early sixteenth century, the Iroquoians living to the west have formed the League of Five Nations (or "League of Peace"), consisting of the Mohawk, Oneida, Onondaga, Cayuga, and Seneca tribes. The League not only maintains peace within the bounds of the confederacy, but it also reinforces its superiority over both the eastern Algonquin and other non-League Iroquois farther to the west and south (such as the Huron and Susquehanna peoples).

1579

Meeting in Utrecht, seven Low Countries provinces in the Netherlands form the United Provinces (and its governing body, the States-General), a mutual defense league against their common enemy Spain. With this more unified arrangement, the Dutch will increase their position relative to other European nation-states and become perhaps the preeminent commercial power in Western Europe, trading not only on their own continent, but with Africa, Asia, and eventually the Americas as well.

1602

The States-General incorporates the Dutch East India Company.

1609

Henry Hudson, an English captain in the employ of the Dutch East India Company, sails the *Half Moon* to the North American coastline, searching for the fabled Northwest Passage to Asia. On August 26, he enters Delaware Bay, and on September 12, Hudson arrives at Manhattan Island. This excursion becomes the basis for the eventual Dutch claim to the lands of the North American coastline stretching from Cape Cod to Delaware Bay.

1611

On a second voyage to North America, this time under the English flag, Hudson navigates the Canadian Shield, including the bay that bears his name. He and a few others are set adrift in Hudson Bay by his mutinous crew before the crew sails back to England; a search the following year will reveal no trace of the explorer.

1614

Three Dutch businessmen form the United New Netherland Company, which receives from the States-General a monopoly on trading privileges in the area called New Netherland, defined as stretching from Cape Cod to Delaware Bay. The company's intent is to begin trade in furs with the natives of the region; in its brief existence, the company will charter four voyages to America, none of which will further this goal. By 1617, the United New Netherland Company has failed and its monopoly privileges have been revoked.

1621

The truce that has existed between Spain and the Netherlands expires, prompting a renewed Dutch interest in gaining an even larger share of maritime and colonial trade at the expense of Spain. To this end, in June, the Dutch West India Company is incorporated; it will begin operations in 1623.

1624

In the spring, the Dutch West India Company settles some thirty Walloon (French-speaking refugees from the southern Low Countries) families at Fort Orange (present-day Albany) on the Hudson River. This is the first settlement of the New Netherland colony.

1626

Peter Minuit, the first director general of New Netherland, arrives at Manhattan Island in May. Minuit will "purchase" the island from its resident natives for goods worth some sixty Dutch florins. Each party seems to have interpreted the transaction differently, however, with the natives envisioning Minuit's bargain as one for the use—rather than the exclusive possession—of the land. Minuit, however, names the settlement New Amsterdam, and it becomes the colony's principal settlement. Reversing its initial policy of dispersing settlements, the company decrees that settlers will be concentrated here, while outposts like Fort Orange will be limited to a handful of licensed traders. By 1628, there will be approximately 270 European residents of Manhattan Island, while Fort Orange will be home to only fourteen traders.

1629

The directors of the West India Company authorize the *Vryheden* (or "Charter of Freedoms and Exemptions"), a document that creates the basis for the "patroon" system. Qualified shareholders could earn the title of patroon (patron) by transporting at least fifty settlers to New Netherland. Patroon status confers upon its holder an extensive grant of land (4 leagues—over 70 miles in length), as well as seigneurial privileges (judicial and administrative powers) within that grant and limited access to the fur trade. Several patroonships will be established during the 1630s, but the only one that will have any measure of sustained success will be Kiliaen Van Rensselaer's Rensselaerwyk.

1638

In March, the colony of New Sweden is established with Fort Christina at Cape Henlopen on the Delaware Bay. The expedition of Swedish and Dutch settlers is commanded by Peter Minuit, who had left the service of New Netherland in 1632 and is now employed by the Swedish and Dutch sponsors of the colonial venture.

In the next four years, subsequent expeditions sponsored by the Swedish Crown will add a small number of settlers to New Sweden, which will become a Swedish royal colony in 1642.

1642

Sir Edwin Plowden, an Englishman, attempts to create a settlement at Salem Creek, in the southern portion of the lands claimed by New Netherland. Dubbing his settlement "New Albion," Plowden has to reckon with a number of problems, including a mutinous crew that abandons him and competition from New Sweden. The venture will ultimately prove unsuccessful, and Plowden will be forced to return to England in 1648, where he will be imprisoned for debt.

1643–1645

A period of warfare between the colonists of New Netherland and surrounding native peoples, dubbed "Kieft's War" after the governor (Willem Kieft), whose policies sparked the conflict, nearly decimates New Netherland. At one point, the colonists are pushed back and confined to New Amsterdam by numerous and well-armed native warriors. Only by mobilizing the entire strength of the colony will the Dutch be able to force the natives into suing for peace.

1647

The Dutch West India Company's monopoly on trade with New Netherland ends. It will, however, retain its policy-making powers and recommend that the colony's chronic labor shortage be remedied through the increased use of African slaves. European laborers, the company reasons, cost too much to transport and are undependable workers.

In May, Peter Stuyvesant, a veteran colonial administrator, becomes Director-General of New Netherland.

1650

The Treaty of Hartford is concluded between the Dutch and English, defining the boundary between New Netherland and the New England colonies at 10 miles east of the Hudson River. The treaty represents a major concession to New England's claims.

1651

In September, Peter Stuyvesant leads an expedition into the area claimed by both New Netherland and New Sweden, erecting Fort Casimir 6 miles below the Swedish Fort Christina. Fort Casimir will be a lightly populated outpost, home to only fourteen Dutch families by the spring of 1653.

1652–1654

Increasing commercial restrictions and tensions spark war between the Netherlands and England, the first in what will become a series of Anglo-Dutch conflicts over the next two decades.

1654

In May, Johann Rising leads an expedition from New Sweden that takes Fort Casimir. Stuyvesant decides to respond with an overwhelming show of force and end what he sees as New Sweden's encroachment in New Netherland. On August 18, a fleet of seven Dutch ships, with 317 soldiers on board, retakes Fort Casimir, and forces the surrender of Fort Christina as well. This action effectively incorporates the colony of New Sweden into Dutch New Netherland.

1660

The end of the English Civil War and Oliver Cromwell's Interregnum sees the Restoration of the monarchy in the person of King Charles II. English interest in New Netherland intensifies with the Restoration, as the Dutch remain England's most significant commercial rival and the object of renewed focus on the part of the Crown.

1663

In July, the English ministry's Council for Foreign Plantations appoints a special committee to examine the feasibility of taking New Netherland by force.

1664

King Charles II confers a large grant of land—in particular the area between the Delaware and Connecticut Rivers—to his brother James, Duke of York. James has significant personal interest in any project affecting Dutch commercial interests. As the director of the Royal African Company, James has already become the principal rival to Dutch control of the transatlantic slave trade; as admiral of the Royal Navy, he is attracted to any project that would help establish dominance of the English in the Atlantic world at the expense of the Dutch.

In April, a parliamentary committee issues a report declaring that the Dutch are England's chief commercial enemies, providing the rationale for James's planned conquest of New Netherland.

On August 28, an English expedition commanded by Richard Nicolls, James's appointee as lieutenant governor, reaches the narrows of the Hudson River near New Amsterdam and demands a formal surrender of New Netherland. Prompted by his advisors to admit his position is an unfeasible one—the Dutch garrisons refuses to fight and English forces from Connecticut take Long Island by force—Stuyvesant will accede to Nicolls's demands and surrender New Amsterdam on August 29.

A formal treaty of surrender is signed on September 8, transforming the Dutch colony of New Netherland to the English proprietary colony of New York. The terms of surrender include continued recognition of Dutch property rights (i.e., homes and land), while all European inhabitants of the province are recognized as "free denizens," regardless of nationality.

On a practical level, there is significant continuity in terms of Dutch politics and culture in the early years of New York as an English proprietorship. James, as proprietor, makes enormous grants of land to his supporters, including all of the territory between the Hudson and Delaware Rivers (most of which eventually will become the colony of New Jersey).

1665

Acting Governor of New York Richard Nicolls promulgates the "Duke's Laws," the first codification of English law in New York. Reflecting the gradual nature of the Anglicization process, however, the laws at first cover only the towns of Long Island, the majority of which were English settlements even before 1664. Not until 1674 will Manhattan Island fall under the jurisdiction of the Duke's Laws, and these laws will not apply to the whole colony until 1676.

1667

In April, the Duke of York appoints Francis Lovelace to replace Nicolls as lieutenant (and therefore acting) governor. Lovelace will arrive in the colony eleven months later.

1672–1674

The third Anglo-Dutch War begins in the spring of 1672. During the conflict, the Dutch will reoccupy New York for over a year, beginning in July 1673. The October 1674 Treaty of Westminster ending the war returns the colony to England permanently.

1674

Edmund Andros becomes lieutenant governor of New York, beginning a period of more active oversight of the colony on the part of the English government. Andros concludes a firm alliance with the Iroquois Five Nations, and he will consolidate royal authority in New York. The latter becomes the most divisive aspect of the Andros regime, as his autocratic style and promotion of the economic interests of his friends make him many enemies. Adding to residents' dislike of Andros is his refusal to summon the colony's legislature; Andros will instead rule via courts of assize, whose members he alone appoints.

1677

New York City's cartmen go on strike and are prosecuted on contempt charges. Twelve are ultimately dismissed in what becomes the first instance of prosecuting striking workers in New York. In 1680, coopers in the city attempt to set collective prices for their labor; they are indicted and convicted on conspiracy charges—foreshadowing judicial tactics that will be used against organized labor in later eras.

1679

A smallpox epidemic sweeps through New York City, killing hundreds.

1681

The Duke of York recalls Edmund Andros to England, after receiving reports of civil unrest in the colony. Even after his recall, continued reports of strife and political breakdown force James to significantly reconsider how he governs his colony.

1683

Andros's replacement, Thomas Dongan, arrives in New York in August. He brings with him instructions from James, allowing for the creation of a colony-wide legislature, an attempt to alleviate political tensions within the colony.

The legislature will first meet at Fort James in October and issue the *Charter of Libertyes and Priviledges*. The document provides protections for individual liberties, as well as formalizing the prerogatives of the legislature. Dongan and his council approve it, as will James the next year. It will, however, never become the royally sanctioned law of the colony, as King Charles II will begin a reorganization of colonial administration in 1684 that will take a significantly different direction from that outlined by the *Charter*.

1684

The first intercolonial conference with Native Americans takes place in Albany, at Thomas Dongan's behest. Present are delegates from New York, Virginia, Maryland, and Massachusetts, as well as representatives from various Iroquois tribes.

1685

After the death of King Charles II in February, the Duke of York becomes King James II. Concurrently, the Lords of Trade meet and reconsider certain colonial charters, among them New York's. Acting on the recommendation of the board, as well as on his suspicion that the colony is moving too far out of the royal ambit, James II officially revokes New York's charter on March 3.

France's revocation of the Edict of Nantes sparks a surge of Huguenot immigration into New York. More French and Dutch will enter the colony than English during the 1680s and 1690s.

1686

In May, Governor Dongan receives instructions from the royal court detailing the revocation of New York's colonial charter. This revocation is part of James II's larger project, the creation of the Dominion of New England. The Dominion includes New York, New Jersey, and all of the New England colonies, and it will be administered by a royally appointed governor based in Boston. The consolidation of authority represented by the Dominion is highly unpopular in the colonies, especially since the colonial legislatures are dissolved.

New York's legislature is curtailed in 1686, and the colony will become completely absorbed into the Dominion by 1688. Adding to the controversy is the appointment by James II of the controversial Edmund Andros as governor of the Dominion; his administration is based in Boston.

1688

The centralization of authority undertaken by James II in the colonies is matched in England, according to his critics, who are also concerned about the king's Catholicism and stated desire to normalize relations with England's longtime enemy France. The opposition crests in June, when a self-designated "council" convenes in England, declares itself Parliament, and offers the throne to James II's daughter Mary and her husband William of Orange, currently ruler of the Netherlands. On November 5, William and a small army arrive in England to force James II from the throne.

1688–1689

In the "Glorious Revolution" in England, James II is overthrown. He and his followers will ultimately be vanquished at the Battle of the Boyne in 1690.

William and Mary are installed as joint monarchs, after giving their assent to the Parliament-crafted Declaration of Rights.

1689

When news of James II's overthrow reaches Boston in April, a crowd will chase and imprison Edmund Andros, forcing him to surrender the reins of government. In New York, Andros's deputy flees the province.

Into the power vacuum steps Jacob Leisler, a German immigrant and devout Calvinist. In June, Leisler issues a proclamation for the authority of William and Mary; in August, a meeting of nine towns will appoint Leisler commander-in-chief of the province. From this point on, Leisler will be the de facto ruler of New York. His seizure of power represents not only current instability, but also a reaction by Dutch elements to the consolidation of English authority and a general antipathy in New York to the Catholicism of King James and Governor Dongan.

King William's War, which will last until 1697, is the first in a series of Anglo-French wars that will stretch into the 1760s.

1690

Two hundred French and native attackers from Montreal sack Schenectady on February 9, killing sixty-two British and Dutch colonists and capturing twenty-seven. Albany, previously hesitant to recognize Leisler's authority, reconsiders its position after the attack on Schenectady and reverses its position in March. In April, Leisler convenes an intercolonial conference at Albany to discuss the French threat. The conference is attended by representatives from Plymouth, Massachusetts, and Connecticut, but it accomplishes nothing constructive.

Also in April, a revived colonial assembly convenes in response to writs issued by Leisler, calling for elections. Unbeknown to the colonists, though, King William has appointed Henry Sloughter as New York's governor in January, rendering these activities technically illegal.

1691

Governor Sloughter arrives at New York on April 19 and demands that Leisler surrender the fort at New York City. Leisler refuses three times before doing so, and Sloughter has him arrested and charged with treason. Leisler's trial takes place from March 31 to April 17; he is found guilty and is executed on May 16. Leisler's Rebellion, as this period becomes known, comes to an end.

In April, Governor Sloughter convenes a new legislature, which issues a declaration of "Rights and Priviledges" for New York. Because of its expansive interpretation of the legislature's powers, the document will be disallowed by the Lords of Trade in 1696.

Later in the summer, Sloughter dies. He is replaced the following year by Benjamin Fletcher, who also is an avid anti-Leislerian. His administration is a corrupt one, marked by bribery, embezzlement from customs revenue, and Fletcher's profiteering from trade with Native Americans.

1693

The Ministry Act provides for public support of the Anglican Church in four New York counties, an initiative that arouses the antipathy of the numerous members of the Dutch Reformed congregations.

1696

To stem Dutch discontent, Governor Fletcher issues a charter of incorporation to the Dutch Reformed ministers, which effectively places that denomination alongside the Anglicans as the colony's "established" church.

1698

Fletcher is replaced as governor by Richard Coote, Lord Bellomont, who inherits a colony in serious economic trouble. New York will be essentially insolvent by 1700.

1701

On the eve of war between England and France, New York concludes a treaty with the Iroquois Five Nations, establishing an uneasy armed neutrality between the two parties. (The Iroquois also reach similar accommodations with the French.)

The Assembly passes an act granting suffrage to freeholders whose property has a net value of forty pounds. This group makes up approximately half of the colony's adult white males.

1702

A yellow fever epidemic kills over 10 percent of New York City's population.

Lord Cornbury becomes the new governor of New York. Cornbury's tenure (to 1710) will be marked by controversy and scandal, as he attempts consolidation of both his own political power and the religious sway of the Anglican churches by methods of dubious legality. Adding to the disdain and skepticism held toward Cornbury is his notorious habit of publicly parading in the latest English women's fashions.

1702–1713

Queen Anne's War rages between the English and French. As during King William's War, New York is the most vulnerable of England's North American colonies, with its frontier abutting French possessions in the Great Lakes and St. Lawrence regions.

In 1703, the Assembly orders the construction of two roads—one to Connecticut through New York and Westchester Counties, the other across Long Island to East Hampton. Similar projects for the Hudson River Valley are envisioned for the future.

1709

For the first time, the Assembly orders the issuance of paper money to act as the colony's circulating medium of exchange.

1710

Lord Cornbury is replaced as governor by Robert Hunter, who will be replaced by William Burnet shortly thereafter.

1711

The City of New York's Common Council establishes the city's first slave market with its declaration that all slaves for hire should, for employers' convenience, congregate at the Wall Street Market. By the early eighteenth century, over 10 percent of the city's population will be enslaved, and the figure will reach 15 percent by the 1720s.

1712

Latent fears of slave revolt are realized on the night of April 6–7, as about twenty-five slaves rendezvous and arm themselves with a cache of weapons they had stored earlier. Lighting outhouses and a barn on fire, the group waits for white townsmen to respond to the alarm. When they do, the slaves attack, killing nine and wounding seven.

A manhunt ensues on April 7, and the slaves involved in the uprising are either captured or killed. A total of twenty-seven African Americans are tried for conspiracy; twenty-one are found guilty and executed.

1713

The Treaty of Utrecht ends Queen Anne's War. Significantly for New York, the French promise to leave the peoples of the Five Nations within the British sphere of influence alone, seemingly ending the threat of violence on New York's frontier.

1722

A conference takes place in September at Albany, attended by delegates from New York, Pennsylvania, and Virginia, who meet with members of the Five Nations. The agreement reached between the colonists and the Iroquois stipulates that the native peoples will have freedom of travel throughout the region and will refrain from attacking any of the tribes to the south, reflecting the colonists' goal of intertribal stability along their frontiers.

1727

The colony extends its frontier defenses with the construction of Fort Oswego, on the Niagara frontier at the site of a two-year-old trading post.

1728

Governor Burnet is transferred to Massachusetts. After a three-year interregnum, William Cosby will receive royal appointment as governor of New York (his only apparent qualification is his being a favorite of the Duke of Newcastle). Cosby's administration, as was the case with many of his predecessors, is marked by corruption and controversy.

1734–1735

John Peter Zenger, printer of the *New York Weekly Journal,* stands trial for libel when the paper (the organ of a faction opposed to Governor Cosby) publishes several editorials scathingly critical of the governor. Zenger's defense argues that such statements, if they can be proved truthful, do not constitute libel, and the defense seeks to therefore convince the jury of the essential truth of the criticisms leveled at Cosby. The jury agrees, and Zenger is acquitted.

The short-term result of the case is that political opposition to royal prerogative (in the person of the governor) is legitimized. The case's lasting significance is in the precedent it sets, which will ultimately become the basis for freedom of the press in the American republic.

James Alexander, a prominent member of the anti-Cosby faction, will write an account of the case (*Brief Narrative of the Case and Tryal of John Peter Zenger*), published by Zenger in 1736. The *Narrative* becomes one of the more significant expressions of the libertarian impulse within the colonies' developing political culture.

1737–1741

New York is governed by Lord De La Warr, who is an absentee governor for most of this period.

1739

The Assembly triumphs in its struggle with the governor over revenue, winning the right to make specific annual appropriations, rather than the vague long-term grants that had been the custom. This change effectively bestows the power of the purse on the Assembly, as these types of appropriations include the salary and miscellaneous funds for the governor. The Assembly is now able to also appropriate the salaries of other appointees, giving it significant leverage over the governor's power of appointment by the implication that an unpopular appointee's salary may simply be withheld by the Assembly. The Assembly's new power is symbolic of the process by which the assemblies (especially the lower, popularly-elected houses) throughout the colonies have been growing in sovereignty and significance in the eighteenth century.

From October 24 through November 19, English revivalist George Whitefield preaches to New York City crowds totaling in the thousands. Whitefield is the most prominent voice of the revivalist surge of evangelical Protestantism known as the Great Awakening, which has spread like wildfire through the colonies in the early decades of the eighteenth century. Originally strongest in the backcountry, the movement of "New Light" religion has permeated the older, more established communities of the Eastern seaboard by the 1730s, as evidenced by the massive attendance at Whitefield's sermons in New York.

1741

Striking bakers in New York City are put on trial in April, accused of forming an unlawful conspiracy in their refusal to bake bread for a week due to the high price of wheat. No convictions result from the trial, and the precedent is thus set for the utility of the strike, or "combination," as a tactic for New York laborers' future collective protests. This strike is only one of the several incidents that dramatically spike the levels of tension and fear in the city, the most dramatic result of which is the city's reaction to a rumored slave conspiracy.

On April 8, Fort George burns to the ground, and the next few weeks see a series of fires throughout the city that destroy both public and private buildings. Suspicions that the fires are arson combine with more general fears of African American unrest to produce a wave of anti-black hysteria among white residents. The city's population is almost 20 percent African American, and the specter of slave revolt has been present since the uprising of 1712.

Rumors about the fires being part of a larger conspiracy appear to be confirmed with the testimony of a 16-year-old indentured servant. Mary Burton takes advantage of the city leaders' promise of freedom and a hundred pounds in exchange for information by testifying she has heard the plans for a rebellion of workers and slaves being hatched in the tavern where she worked. The tavern's owner, his wife, two of their slaves, and a prostitute are all implicated, tried, and put to death. Burton's accusations continue, though, implicating more people—many of them black—as instigators of this conspiracy. The panic subsides only when Burton begins to accuse wealthy members of the city's white establishment of complicity as well; at this point, she is paid her one hundred pounds and dismissed.

A total of thirty-one blacks are executed (thirteen of them burned at the stake), and over seventy are deported from the colony, based upon evidence proffered by either Burton's accusations or coerced confessions and narratives of dubious legal validity. The conspiracy scare of 1741 is evidence of the power of racial fears and social unrest to spark outbreaks of public hysteria. Many historians remain skeptical whether such a conspiracy ever existed in the form imagined by New Yorkers.

1743

George Clinton becomes royal governor of the colony. He will serve until 1753, in what proves to be the longest tenure of any English-appointed governor.

1748

The Treaty of Aix-la-Chapelle ends King George's War between the English and the French. After the war, the French position in North America is a strong one, particularly in the upper Ohio Valley. The French in America embark upon an attempt to forge an alliance with the Iroquois, the only natives of the region who are still allied with the British colonists. Due to the aggressive expansion and cultivation of native alliances by the French in the Ohio/Great Lakes region following the treaty, New York becomes the most vulnerable of the British colonies.

1754

The French construct Fort Duquesne, at the point where the Allegheny and Monongahela Rivers join to form the Ohio River—a vital strategic location on the British colonial frontier. An expedition of Virginia militia, led by George Washington, surrenders to the French in early July after a failed attempt to oust them from Fort Duquesne.

To address the issues of western defense and the French and Native American threat, an intercolonial conference convenes at Albany in June and July. Twenty-three delegates from seven colonies agree on the need for mutual defense, but a formal plan of union (proposed by Pennsylvanian Benjamin Franklin) that would create an intercolonial agency to supervise frontier defenses is rejected by the individual colonies' legislatures, as well as by the British ministry.

1755

British general Edward Braddock devises a three-pronged strategy to seize the most important French forts in the Ohio Valley and Great Lakes region, including Niagara and Crown Point (near Lake George in the upper Hudson River Valley). The attacks are a failure; Braddock and his forces are massacred in July along the Monongahela River.

William Johnson's troops, however, are able to defeat a force of French and native warriors, who had ambushed them at Lake George, although they suffer heavy casualties in doing so.

1756

Britain and France officially declare war on one another, and the conflict, begun in America in 1754, becomes global. This latest war between the two colonial powers is called the Seven Years' War in Europe and the French and Indian War in the colonies.

William Johnson succeeds where the British had failed during King George's War, when he concludes an alliance with the Iroquois, now considered British subjects.

In August, the British and their colonists suffer one of their worst defeats, as the French capture Fort Oswego, forcing a general British retreat eastward to Albany.

The Assembly passes a Stamp Act to raise revenue for defense; similar measures are passed annually for the next three years.

1758

In July, the British attack on the French forces at Fort Ticonderoga fails spectacularly. The British fail to penetrate the French outer defenses and are slaughtered by French musket fire and artillery in the attempt. The British regulars suffer over 1600 casualties, while colonial militia units lose more than 330 men.

King's College, in New York City, graduates its first class. The new college is sponsored primarily by the Anglican elite (with some support from conservative Dutch Reformed families). Its establishment represents, in part, a reaction of the "Old Light" religious orthodox to what they see as the dangerous "New Light" groups of the Great Awakening.

1759

By this time, the tide of war is turning in favor of the British. Confirming this shift in momentum is the defeat of the French at Fort Niagara in July. This victory snaps the French link between Lakes Ontario and Erie. At the same time, Fort Ticonderoga falls to the British and colonists, and the French abandon Crown Point.

1760

With the surrender of the French at Montreal on September 8, the last step in the capitulation of all French Canada, the American phase of the Seven Years' War, known as the French and Indian War, comes to an end.

1763

The Treaty of Paris ends the Seven Years' War; under its terms, the French cede their colonial dominion in North America to the British. The British government issues the Proclamation of 1763, which forbids land surveying expeditions or colonial settlement west of the Appalachians. Influencing this policy is the outbreak of Pontiac's Rebellion, provoked by Native American fears regarding the increasing scope and speed of English expansion westward. It takes almost two years for British forces and colonial militia to restore calm on the frontier.

1764

In October, the New York assembly sends three petitions to England protesting the Sugar Act, the Currency Act, and the impending Stamp Act, characterizing these measures as arbitrary and objecting to their being passed without the colonists' consent.

1765

The "Stamp Act Congress" meets from October 7 to October 24 in New York City. Delegates from nine colonies pass resolutions that judge the Stamp Act to be against Britain's unwritten constitution, arguing "[t]hat the only representatives of the people of these colonies, are persons chosen therein by themselves, and that no taxes ever have been, or can be constitutionally imposed on them, but by their respective legislatures." A nonimportation agreement is also implemented in an attempt to exert economic pressure upon Parliament.

Crowd action against the royally appointed stamp agents is significant enough to prevent the law from being enforced in New York, when it is due to go into effect on November 1. In December, New York's lawyers concur in a resolution to continue doing business without the required revenue stamps.

Parliament also passes a Quartering Act, mandating that the colonies pay the costs of their defense by British soldiers. The New York assembly resists doing so, refusing to appropriate funds for this purpose.

1767

As a result of New York's defiance of the Quartering Act, Parliament passes the "Restraining Act" in December 1767, dissolving the Assembly until New York complies with the Quartering Act. The law never formally goes into effect, as word of its impending passage proves sufficient to force a reversal of the assembly's policy.

1768

In the fall, the largest colonial/Native American conference to date occurs at Fort Stanwix. The treaty that emerges from the proceedings represents a massive cession of American Indian lands; much of what will be modern-day central and southwestern New York comes under English control.

1771

The famous portrait artist John Singleton Copley takes up residence in New York City and enjoys a rush of clients. He will paint some of his best and most famous portraits of the revolutionary period.

1773–1774

Parliament passes the Tea Act in 1773, granting the East India Company and its licensed colonial brokers a monopoly on tea sales in the colonies. The law arouses a firestorm of protest, the most famous example of which is the Boston Tea Party of December 1773.

In New York, popular disapproval of the law is equally intense. The royal governor decides to send the East India tea back to England immediately after its landing in New York City. New York's Sons of Liberty have different plans, however. The first East India vessel arrives on April 19, 1774; three days later, a group of colonists, again disguised as Mohawk Indians, board the ship and dump its cargo over-

board as had patriots in Boston the year before. The remaining East India ships turn around and sail back to England.

Responding to Boston's Tea Party, Parliament passes the Coercive Acts, a series of measures dubbed the "Intolerable Acts" by the colonies. One law closes the port of Boston until the East India Company is compensated for its lost property. On July 4, 1774, a large public meeting in New York City issues a formal protest against the law and collects funds for the aid of Boston's townspeople.

New York elects eight delegates to represent the colony in the Continental Congress, which convenes September 5 in Philadelphia. Among the measures agreed upon by the Congress is the "Continental Association," an intercolonial nonimportation movement.

1775

In January, the colonial Assembly (dominated by conservative loyalists) adjourns for what proves to be the final time. It conducts no more business thereafter and is prorogued permanently by the governor by early 1776.

In April, the first in a series of "provincial congresses" is elected. These bodies represent the growing revolutionary sentiment in New York and quickly assume the function of the colony's de facto government.

1776

The members of the Second Continental Congress approve and sign the Declaration of Independence. On July 9, New York's provincial congress ratifies the document and then reconvenes itself as the Convention of Representatives of the State of New York.

Also that day, a large New York City crowd celebrates independence by pulling down a large statue of King George III mounted on a horse, which had been erected in 1770. The lead statue is subsequently melted down to make bullets for patriot muskets.

From August through November, British and American troops fight battles in and around New York City and northern New Jersey, culminating in George Washington's forces retreating from the city and southward to Valley Forge, Pennsylvania. From this point until the end of the Revolutionary War, New York City will be occupied by the British, including the commanders of the British forces in America, Lord Admiral John Howe and Sir Henry Clinton.

Kevin M. Gannon

North Carolina

Before 1500

North Carolina is home to several large Native American communities, including the Cherokee in the west and the Tuscarora in the east; these large tribes are linguistically related to the Iroquois. They subsist by maize agriculture and hunting. Numerous smaller tribes of Algonquian speakers inhabit resource-rich coastal areas. The Siouan-speaking ancestors of the Catawba live in the Piedmont region. Native North Carolina is strikingly diverse.

1524

Giovanni da Verrazano, a Florentine sailing under the auspices of King Francis I of France, sights land near Cape Fear (in modern-day North Carolina). He reports friendly natives, abundant wildlife, and stunning foliage, though he mistakenly believes, never seeing the mainland, that he has found the Pacific Ocean.

1526

Intrigued by Verrazano's voyage, Spanish official Lucas Vásquez de Ayllón lands 500 men and women from Hispaniola at the mouth of the Cape Fear River. Their provision ship sinks, they choose unhealthy swampland for their colony, and they begin to die of disease at an alarming rate. Less than a year later, 150 survivors return to the Caribbean.

1540

Hernando de Soto's *entrada*, or expedition, passes through the mountains of North Carolina on the way to Tennessee and parts west. The Cherokees entertain and provision the Spaniards with corn while they search fruitlessly for gold for about a month.

1584

A landing party financed by Sir Walter Raleigh, a staunch advocate of colonization with the ear of Queen Elizabeth, comes ashore on Roanoke Island in July. The party of explorers, including the artist John White, remains on or around Roanoke for the next six weeks. They collect samples of American flora and fauna and establish friendly trading relations with local Native Americans. Two Native Americans, Manteo and Wanchese, return to London with the party, where they become instant celebrities.

1585–1586

Another Raleigh-sponsored expedition, this one intended to establish a permanent English military presence, arrives at Roanoke in July. After barely surviving the first winter, the colonists return to England.

1587

Governor John White and 115 men, women, and children arrive at Roanoke in the summer. Virginia Dare is born—the first English child born in North America. John White returns to England for supplies. When he returns in 1590, the colony has disappeared. White discovers destroyed buildings, a ransacked fort, and the word "Croatoan" scratched into one of the stockade posts. Though search parties look for the colonists through the late sixteenth and early seventeenth centuries, they are never found. Their disappearance is shrouded in rumor and legend. They may have been assimilated into local tribes, killed by local tribes, or killed by Powhatan during his conquest of the area in the early 1600s.

1607–1620

Expeditions from Jamestown report fertile territory and friendly natives in North Carolina. English settlement begins slowly.

1650

Virginia officials begin to grant land in North Carolina to hunters, trappers, traders, farmers, and gentlemen. By 1663, more than 500 English people live on Albemarle Sound. By 1665, Albemarle County government is established, along Virginian lines, with a governor and legislative council. Planters begin to grow tobacco for profit, using indentured servants and African slaves, though Africans never constitute the same percentage of North Carolina's population as they do in South Carolina or Virginia.

1663

King Charles II rewards the political allies who helped him to the throne in 1660 by naming eight of them lords proprietors of the new province of Carolina. The charter granted by Charles II defines Carolina broadly as the territory stretching from the present Virginia–North Carolina border to below Spanish St. Augustine, and from the Atlantic to the Pacific. The lords proprietors are granted expansive powers to govern and design Carolina society.

1664–1665

A colony is established by John Vassall of Barbados on the Cape Fear River. Other Barbadians and New Englanders join him. The colony does not prosper and is abandoned by the summer of 1667.

1669

The lords proprietors draft the Fundamental Constitutions, trying to establish a hierarchical, orderly society in Carolina. For a time, the colonial legislature loses its power to initiate legislation. The Fundamental Constitutions undergo constant revision and are never fully enacted by the colonists.

1677

Culpeper's Rebellion strikes Albemarle County. Upset with misgovernment and a tax on tobacco, the area's most profitable export, a group of angry colonists jail and try the colony's governor, John Miller. Though Miller escapes and flees to England, Culpeper's Rebellion succeeds in reestablishing representative government. The proprietors respond first by appointing an incompetent and corrupt governor, and later by abandoning the Fundamental Constitutions altogether.

1701

The Church of England is established in North Carolina. A tax is approved to support ministers and build churches. Quakers oppose these measures, and Quaker and Anglican factions battle each other for control of the government for more than a decade. Colonial North Carolina is also home to Baptists, Presbyterians, and Moravians. The Church of England remains relatively weak here throughout the colonial period.

1706

The town of Bath, on the Pamlico River, is formally incorporated. By now, there are five English counties, though Bath County (like future settlements) receives fewer representatives in the colonial assembly than its older neighbors. Bath soon rivals Albemarle as the population center of North Carolina.

1709

Baron Christoph von Graffenried, a Swiss nobleman, secures permission to settle 650 Swiss and Germans on 17,500 acres of land on the Neuse River. He names his settlement Neuse-Bern, which the English hear as "New Bern." Though von Graffenried has paid colonial officials, John Lawson, the surveyor-general, and local Native Americans for the land, the Tuscarora are particularly upset by the new colony. The colony struggles to survive.

1711

The Tuscarora, together with other Native American allies, angered by sharp traders, English encroachment, and the continuing enslavement of native women and children, attack the settlement at New Bern. On September 22, 1711, a coordinated surprise attack devastates the Europeans along the Neuse, Pamlico, and Trent Rivers. The Tuscarora take twenty or thirty prisoners and kill between 130 and 140 Europeans. The survivors of the attack attempt to retaliate, but only end up suffering further loss of life. Bath County is all but abandoned during the Tuscarora War.

1712

South Carolina sends a force of 500 Native Americans, largely Yamasees, and thirty white men under Colonel John Barnwell to the aid of North Carolina. Barnwell and his men march through the North Carolina countryside, taking a Tuscarora fort, destroying more than 350 Tuscarora houses, and burning thousands of bushels of corn. The Yamasee also take native slaves at a rate that terrifies the Tuscarora.

In February, Barnwell's army lays siege to the Tuscarora stronghold of Hancock's Town. He is forced to withdraw as he is sick, many of his Native American allies have deserted, the Tuscarora hold several white hostages, and provisions are running low. Barnwell negotiates a treaty that he feels will end hostilities, although on the return march, he and his allies capture more slaves. The Tuscarora, enraged by this slave raid, resume their attacks in the fall.

1713

South Carolina forces, this time under Colonel James Moore, and numbering thirty-three whites and 1,000 Native Americans, including Cherokees, attack the Tuscarora at Fort Nohoroco on March 25. The result is a crushing defeat for the Tuscarora—some 950 men, women, and children are killed or captured. This effectively ends Tuscarora resistance to colonization, although a formal treaty is not drawn up until 1715. Many Tuscaroras decide to abandon North Carolina entirely and relocate to New York, where they join the Five Nations of the Iroquois in 1722.

1715

A law is passed allowing planters to continue the practice of manumitting their slaves, provided the freed slaves leave North Carolina within six months.

1718

Edward Teach, the pirate known as Blackbeard, sets up shop in Bath. From this base of operations, he terrorizes not only foreign vessels, but English and colonial ships as well. In November, Blackbeard is killed in combat off Okracoke Inlet. Also in November, Major Stede Bonnet, known as the "gentleman pirate," is captured. In December, he is hanged.

1729

The proprietors yield to Crown demands to sell their interests in Carolina. After years of mismanagement and crisis, North Carolina becomes a Crown colony and comes under the purview of an efficient, powerful, and rapidly expanding British colonial bureaucracy. The Crown concerns itself with matters of empire, and the colonial legislature focuses on local issues. These two bodies come into conflict a number of times before the War for Independence begins.

At this point, North Carolina contains a population of 30,000 white people and 6,000 enslaved Africans, most of them workers on tobacco plantations, although some also serve urban masters. North Carolina's population will increase nine times by 1776; it will eventually be the fourth most populous colony, behind Massachusetts, Virginia, and Pennsylvania.

North and South Carolina, which have been administered by separate colonial governments since 1691, begin negotiations to draw an official boundary line between the two colonies.

1730s

A massive movement of people from other North American colonies and Europe settles the Piedmont region of North Carolina. These immigrants are predominately Scots-Irish, but Germans (some of them the mislabeled Pennsylvania Dutch) form a sizable minority in the region. Most of the Scots-Irish and Germans come from Pennsylvania, while other groups arrive from New Jersey, Virginia, and Maryland. These colonies suffer from overcrowding, while North Carolina has a seemingly inexhaustible supply of land for settlement.

1731

A road connecting Cape Fear to Virginia is completed, using Native American guides and white laborers. This opens up Cape Fear to increased white settlement and facilitates trade between North Carolina and Virginia.

1732–1733

Highland Scots begin to receive grants up the Cape Fear River, in what would become Bladen County. A steady stream of immigration from Scotland continues throughout the colonial period. In the Highlands, the Scots had lived in exceedingly poor conditions. In North Carolina, the ready availability of timber allows the construction of substantial homes, and the newcomers are able to maintain strong community ties through the continued use of the Gaelic language and traditional Scottish clothing.

1739–1743

The War of Jenkins' Ear, a conflict between England and Spain erupts, and King George II calls upon all the American colonies to fight Spanish interests in the Americas. North Carolina responds by raising an army of 400 men to join forces with other colonies to attack Cartagena, on the mainland of South America in present-day Colombia. The attack is an unmitigated disaster, as the invaders face a skilled, entrenched opponent and a tropical disease-infested environment with which they are unfamiliar and ill prepared. Only twenty-five of the 400 men return. During the war, Spanish ships also wreak havoc on North Carolina shipping.

1744–1748

The War of Jenkins' Ear turns into King George's War, which pits England and Austria against France and Prussia. This begins a period of cooperation between colonies, particularly North Carolina, Virginia, and South Carolina, which would last through the remainder of the colonial period.

1753

A group of Moravians, under the leadership of Bishop August Gottlieb Spangenberg, settles in the Piedmont region, at a town they name Wachovia. The Moravians advocate communal ownership of property and cooperation among the various members of their society.

1758

During the French and Indian War, 300 North Carolinians, including some Native Americans, participate in the capture of Fort Duquesne.

1759

An attack by Cherokees allied with the French inflicts considerable damage on the North Carolina backcountry. Both Carolinas combine to send an expeditionary force into Cherokee territory, forcing their removal to remote mountain country.

1763

The French and Indian War concludes, and France relinquishes any claim it has to North America. The Proclamation Line of 1763, much maligned by colonists and land speculators in Virginia, has little effect on North Carolina, as there are hardly any white North Carolinians living in the mountains.

Governor Dobbs meets with other colonial governors and John Stuart, a British Indian agent at Augusta. They host a meeting of about 700 Native Americans from throughout the southeast. North Carolina pledges peace and perpetual alliance with the Cherokee, Chickasaw, Choctaw, Creek, and Catawba.

1765

North Carolina, like other American colonies, vehemently opposes the Stamp Act. At the grassroots level, the Sons of Liberty organize rural resistance. In Wilmington, at the end of October, they protest, shouting and drinking toasts to liberty.

1766

The legislature passes an act designating New Bern as the permanent capital of North Carolina. To this point, the assembly had met variously at New Bern, Wilmington, Bath, and Edenton.

1767

Governor William Tryon, with troops, Native American guides, and interpreters, undertakes an expedition to define the western boundary of North Carolina. The country proves too rugged, and Tryon's party turns back. In fact, the boundary line has little effect, as hunters, traders, and later farmers cross through Cherokee territory on the way to farmland in Tennessee and Kentucky.

1768

The Regulators, a group of disaffected settlers from the western counties of North Carolina who desire the right to regulate their own local government, formally organize. They believe that powerful interests along the coast are mismanaging the colony. The Regulators are not simply vigilantes; they are also a formidable political movement, whose efforts are interrupted by the onset of the War for Independence.

1770

In an effort to weaken the Townshend Act duties, Cape Fear merchants pledge their support of nonimportation.

1771

Queens College is chartered in Charlotte, Mecklenburg County. It is the first and only college to be founded in North Carolina by the colonial government, although it reverts to private ownership in 1772.

1774

At Edenton, fifty-one women led by Penelope Barker sign an agreement to do whatever they can to support the American cause. The Edenton Tea Party is an early example of female political activity in association with the resistance to the British.

The early 1770s also see the formation of a number of Committees of Safety, designed to keep up pressure on the British and enforce nonimportation among colonists.

1775

In response to the deteriorating situation in Boston, the Hillsborough Congress convenes. The Congress authorizes the use of 1,000 professional soldiers and 3,000 less skilled minutemen. Despite this, North Carolina is sharply divided and poorly prepared to fight a war.

1776

The Provincial Congress meets at Halifax. This body draws up a constitution that establishes the supremacy of the legislature. On April 12, the Congress votes to send a delegate to the Second Continental Congress, thereby declaring itself independent from Great Britain and tying its fate to the other rebellious colonies.

Matthew Jennings

Pennsylvania

Before 1600

Human occupation of the area today known as Pennsylvania began more than 16,000 years ago. The earliest evidence of these settlements is found in present-day Washington County.

When Europeans first arrive in this area, Pennsylvania is occupied by native peoples, including the Lenni Lenape (later called the Delaware), the Susquehannock, the Shawnee, and members of the Iroquois Confederacy, otherwise known as the Five Nations (later, the Six Nations when the Tuscarora joined). Other tribes (not yet identified with certainty) occupy western Pennsylvania.

1609

An expedition under Henry Hudson explores the Delaware River.

1638

Swedish settlers arrive in the Delaware Valley on the ships *Kalmar Nyckel* and *Fogel Grip* after sailing for four months from Gothenburg. They construct Fort Christina at present-day Wilmington, Delaware, and leave behind a garrison of twenty-four men, who begin trading with the Native Americans. The settlement, named New Sweden, will eventually include parts of present-day New Jersey, Delaware, and Pennsylvania.

1639

The *Fogel Grip* arrives at Fort Christina from St. Kitts with an Angolan slave, Anthony Swartz, the first slave in the Pennsylvania colony.

1640

The first families arrive in New Sweden on the return voyage of the *Kalmar Nyckel*.

1643

The ships *Fama* and *Swan* arrive from Sweden with fifty more settlers and the first colonial governor, Johan Printz. Printz constructs Fort New Gothenburg on Tinicum Island, southwest of the future site of Philadelphia.

1645

At Kingsessing, in what is now Philadelphia, the first gristmill is constructed on Cobbs Creek.

1655

Peter Stuyvesant and an armada of seven ships with 317 soldiers on board invade New Sweden. The colonists offer no opposition and surrender to the Dutch, to whom they pledge their loyalty.

1656

The ship *Mercutius* arrives at Tinicum Island with fourteen Swedish and ninety-two Finnish settlers. The Finns settle at what will become Marcus Hook, Pennsylvania.

1662

Governor Printz's daughter sells Tinicum Island to Joost de la Grange, a Dutchman.

1669

The French begin their exploration and survey of lands in western Pennsylvania.

1681

William Penn, a Quaker, receives Pennsylvania in the form of a land grant from King Charles II in payment for a royal debt owed to Penn's father. Penn sends William Markham, his cousin, to take control of the land grant and makes him governor.

1682–1683

In October, the ship *Welcome* brings Penn to an area near Chester, Pennsylvania. The First Frame of Government is written, and the first three counties are created: (1) Philadelphia County, whose name means "brotherly love." (2) Chester County, whose name is derived from Cheshire, England, home of many early settlers; it will become an inland county in 1789, when a part of it is taken to create Delaware County. (3) Bucks County, named for Buckinghamshire, England, where the Penns had resided for generations.

Penn summons the first General Assembly to Chester. The Assembly joins the Delaware counties with Pennsylvania and adopts a naturalization act.

A large wave of immigrants arrives from the British Isles and Germany.

The Great Law is adopted. It guarantees liberty of conscience and becomes the basis of Pennsylvania laws. The death penalty is applied only to acts of murder and treason.

From 1682 into 1683, the second Assembly, with

Penn's cooperation, creates the Second Frame of Government. Philadelphia, Bucks, and Chester County courts replace the Upland Court, which had been established by the Duke of York in the 1670s with jurisdiction over parts of New Jersey and Pennsylvania. The English, who have become the majority with the arrival of hundreds of Quaker settlers, require the Swedish settlers to naturalize as English subjects and employ them to negotiate treaties with the native peoples.

Also in 1683, German immigrants, arriving in Pennsylvania, form Germantown outside of Philadelphia.

1684

Penn sets aside land for future Swedish settlement in the present Upper Merion Township and Montgomery County area. Many Swedes and Finns sell their land and move out of Pennsylvania into West Jersey.

1688

The first official written protest against slavery in North America is signed by the Germantown Quakers.

1690

The first paper mill in North America is built near Germantown by William Bradford.

1693

The Wicaco and Crane Hook congregations write to King Charles XI of Sweden asking for Swedish Bibles, new ministers, and hymnals.

Whites in Philadelphia are permitted to imprison blacks found without passes.

1694

Members of German Pietist sects settle in Pennsylvania.

1698

The first public school is established in Philadelphia.

1701

Philadelphia officially becomes a city.

Andreas Rudman, pastor at Wicaco, successfully persuades Penn to put aside 10,000 more acres specifically for future Swedish immigrants. This land is located near Manatawny Creek alongside the Schuylkill River.

Penn grants the Charter of Privileges to his colony of Pennsylvania, establishing a unicameral legislature and a policy of religious freedom.

1703

Delaware separates from Pennsylvania, forming its own government.

1711

A new law is passed banning slavery in Pennsylvania, but it is overruled by Queen Anne and becomes ineffective.

1712

A law is passed outlawing the slave trade in Pennsylvania.

1714

Amish settlers begin to inhabit Berks County.

1716

Plays, music, and dancing are condemned by the Quakers in a public statement.

1721

Pennsylvania creates its first game law and officially declares its first deer season.

1723

The Pennsylvania Land Bank issues its first notes, which are secured by the property of the bank owners.

1726

The poor riot over food prices in Philadelphia.

1727

Horticulturalist John Bartram begins to explore the forests of western Pennsylvania.

The Junto antislavery group is organized by Benjamin Franklin.

1728

Benjamin Franklin starts his own printing shop in Philadelphia.

The first botanical garden in North America is opened in Philadelphia by John Bartram.

1729

Benjamin Franklin publishes *A Modest Enquiry into the Nature and Necessity of a Paper Currency*. He receives a contract to print the third issue of notes of the Pennsylvania Land Bank and becomes the publisher and proprietor of the *Pennsylvania Gazette*.

The first music is printed in Philadelphia.

1730

In spite of Quaker opposition to slavery, 4,000 slaves are brought to Pennsylvania.

1731

Benjamin Franklin establishes the first public library in the colonies in Philadelphia.

1732

Poor Richard's Almanack is published by Benjamin Franklin.

The "Colony of Schuylkill," the first known fishing club in the colonies, is created in Pennsylvania.

1733

English immigrant and entrepreneur John Harris receives the right to operate a ferry across the Susquehanna River in what later becomes Harrisburg.

1736

The Union Fire Company is established by Benjamin Franklin.

1737

Benjamin Franklin is appointed postmaster of Philadelphia.

Pennsylvania fraudulently acquires 1,200 square miles of land that belongs to the Lenni Lenape. The fraud is known as the Walking Purchase. Colonial officials show an old, unsigned draft of a deed to the native people, presenting it as a legal contract, and tell the Lenni Lenape negotiators that their tribal ancestors signed it. The supposed contract says that the Penns can have as much land as the Penns can cover in a day-and-a-half's walk. The Lenni Lenape agree to let the Penns do the walk. The Penns clear a straight path and hire the three fastest runners who run instead of walk. Even though the Lenni Lenape are unhappy with the way the runners "walk," they feel they have to respect the wishes of their ancestors and move westward.

1739

Johann Klemm of Philadelphia finishes the first pipe organ built entirely in the colonies.

Benjamin Franklin and others petition the Pennsylvania Assembly to remove tanneries from commercial districts and stop waste dumping, because both lower property values and compromise disease control and fire fighting. Even though the Assembly accepts the requests, the waste dumping continues.

1740

George Whitefield, a renowned traveling preacher, gives numerous public sermons in Philadelphia.

Members of the American Band establish the first association to support concerts in the colonies.

1741

The first magazine in the colonies, *The American Magazine,* is published by Andrew Bradford in Philadelphia.

1742

Gustavus Hesselius, an immigrant from Sweden, manufactures the first American spinets and virginals.

Many pastures and crops in Pennsylvania are destroyed by flocks of grasshoppers.

1743

The American Philosophical Society, the first association in America to be dedicated to the natural sciences, is formed.

Christopher Sower in Philadelphia publishes the first Bible printed in the colonies.

1745

Susanna Wright, a poet and frontierswoman, becomes the first female notary public of the colony. She serves as legal counselor to her neighbors, who are mostly illiterate, and also as an arbitrator in disputes involving property.

1748

The Ohio Company is created mainly to trade on a large scale with Native Americans and to influence settlement in southwestern Pennsylvania.

1749

Benjamin Franklin is named the first president of the Academy, a proposed school that later becomes the University of Pennsylvania.

The first acting company to present several plays in one theater within a season is created in Philadelphia.

Captain Pierre-Joseph Céleron de Blainville claims France's right to the Indian God Rock region, located south of Franklin.

1751

In honor of Penn's Charter of Privileges, the Liberty Bell is cast.

The Free Charity School opens in September, following the opening of the Academy, first proposed in 1749, in January.

Benjamin Franklin publishes *Experiments and Observations on Electricity* in London. Franklin and Dr. Thomas Bond establish Pennsylvania Hospital. On May 11, they are granted a charter by the legislature to establish a hospital that will provide care for the poor and mentally ill.

1752

Benjamin Franklin performs his famous electricity experiment with a kite.

1753

The French build forts in western Pennsylvania, claiming the region.

George Washington orders the French to move out of northwestern Pennsylvania.

1754

Washington loses a battle against the French at Fort Duquesne (present-day Pittsburgh).

Franklin's "Plan of the Union" is adopted by English colonies.

The Pennsylvania Gazette contains the first recorded American political cartoon. Created by Benjamin Franklin, the cartoon attacks the fragmentation of the colonists concerning frontier defense.

1755

The British, in cooperation with Virginia militiamen, try to take Fort Duquesne, but are massacred in an ambush.

Settlers in the Lehigh River Valley of northeastern Pennsylvania are attacked by Native Americans. As a result, they move to the more settled southeast for safety.

The College of Philadelphia, which later merges with the Philadelphia Academy to form the University of Pennsylvania, is founded.

1756

Declaring war on the Shawnee and Delaware, Pennsylvania begins to build forts along the frontier and fills them with men and supplies.

1757

Francis Hopkinson produces *Alfred*, a masque by Thomas Arne, at the College of Philadelphia.

John Palma directs the first public concert in Philadelphia. When the second concert is given, George Washington attends.

1758

Pennsylvania signs a peace treaty with the Shawnee and the Delaware.

The Society for the Propagation of the Gospel in Philadelphia, trains slaves in singing the Psalms.

The French retreat from Fort Duquesne. As they leave, they burn the fort down. Now under British control, a better fort is built in the same place, named Fort Pittsborough, or Fort Pitt, in an area today known as Pittsburgh. This region is of great importance, because whoever controls the fort also controls the trade that goes through it, which affects the northeastern parts of the Mississippi valley and surrounding areas.

British colonial commander George Washington surrenders to the French at Fort Necessity in southwestern Pennsylvania.

The British build Fort Bedford in south-central Pennsylvania.

The first school for black children is founded in Philadelphia.

1759

The French move out of western Pennsylvania.

Michael Hillegas, who will become the first treasurer of the United States, opens the first music store in the colonies in Philadelphia.

1760

An organ, which Francis Hopkinson will often play, is installed in Philadelphia College Hall.

1762

Pennsylvania makes plans to connect to the western territories via a canal.

William Allen, Chief Justice of Pennsylvania's Supreme Court and founder of Northamptontown, draws up plans for his rural village. It is later renamed Allentown since almost everyone refers to it as "Allen's Town."

In Philadelphia, Dr. William Shippen opens the first school of anatomy in North America.

1763

Native Americans start attacking settlers along the frontier. Fort Pitt is reinforced by more British troops. The Paxton Boys massacre the Conestoga Indians of Lancaster County in December.

1765

The first medical school in the colonies is established in Philadelphia.

Sons of Liberty groups are formed in Philadelphia and other colonial towns and cities.

1766

The Southwark Theatre, the first in the colonies to be known as an opera house, is established by the Old American Opera Company.

1767

Pennsylvania and Maryland are divided by the Mason-Dixon Line. This solves the boundary dispute that had existed between the Penns of Pennsylvania and the Calverts of Maryland.

Andrew Barton composes the first ballad opera by an American, titled *The Disappointment*. Due to its satirical plot, the show is cancelled.

1768

The settling of southwestern Pennsylvania causes problems with Native Americans, who claim the land as theirs. Initially, the Provincial Assembly reacts by threatening those who do not move out of native lands with the death penalty. When this action proves unsuccessful, the Proprietary Government of Pennsylvania is forced to purchase the land, extending westward to the Allegheny and Ohio Rivers, from the indigenous peoples.

John Dickinson publishes *Letters from a Farmer in Pennsylvania*.

1769

Offices are opened to sell the land purchased from the Native Americans; 3,200 applications are received during the first month.

Obadiah and Daniel Gore, two blacksmiths, manage to use anthracite coal successfully in their forge.

1773

A public road connecting Bedford County to Cumberland, Maryland, is opened.

1774

A committee selected by the residents of York County protests against British taxes and oppressive measures.

The Pennsylvania Assembly selects its representatives for the Continental Congress, which meets for the first time in Philadelphia on September 5.

The Continental Congress passes a Declaration and Resolves, which states that only colonial legislative bodies may enact legislation for the colonies and enacts a law creating the Continental Association in order to suspend commerce with Britain.

The Continental Congress asks colonists to forgo expensive activities like horse racing, cock fighting, and gambling, in order to concentrate on political protests against Britain.

1775

The colonies' first postal system is established, with Benjamin Franklin as its first postmaster.

Franklin is elected president of the Pennsylvania Society for the Abolition of Slavery, organized by the Quakers.

John Behrent builds the first American-made piano.

Imports from Pennsylvania are banned in Britain.

The Second Continental Congress meets in Philadelphia, starting on May 5. It declares a new name for the American colonies, "The United Colonies of America" and approves the creation of a Continental army of around 20,000 troops.

George Washington is appointed the Commander-in-Chief of the Continental army by the Continental Congress.

The Continental Congress approves the distribution of Colonel John Dickinson's *Declaration of the Causes and Necessity of Taking Up Arms*; the document attempts to justify the colonies' right to defend themselves. Thomas Jefferson originally had composed a similar document, but it was deemed far too militant.

The Continental Congress's Olive Branch Petition, a last attempt to offer a solution to the differences between the colonies and the Crown, is sent to the King, requesting that he end his military activities in the colonies.

The Continental Congress selects delegates to reach agreements with Native Americans.

The *Pennsylvania Gazette* publishes a story on how Parliament plans to try rebels in England for their offenses.

The Continental Congress establishes a secret committee to deal with spies and espionage in the impending war, passes a law creating the American Navy, and appoints a second secret committee to seek out foreign assistance in the struggle with Britain.

1776

The first official flag of the Continental navy is flown aboard the *USS Alfred* on the Delaware River.

Pennsylvania is the third largest English colony in North America, and Philadelphia is the second largest English-speaking city in the world after London.

Common Sense by Thomas Paine is published in Philadelphia by W&T Bradford. The pamphlet supports American independence, attacks the ideas of hereditary monarchies, and describes the future economic benefits of independence.

The Continental Congress allows for the enlistment of black soldiers, authorizes privateering against British ships, moves to suspend the slave trade, and opens all ports to any nation except for Britain.

Virginia delegate Richard Henry Lee proposes independence at a session of the Continental Congress, proclaiming that "these united colonies are, and of right ought to be, free and independent states."

Pennsylvania shifts control away from the Quakers and overthrows the Penn family's government. During this period, the state convention, which meets in Philadelphia, creates a Council of Safety that draws up the constitution and rules during the transitional period. The state constitution is adopted on September 28.

The Continental Congress appoints a committee to draft a declaration of independence, and selects Thomas Jefferson to compose the first draft.

The Continental Congress also adopts the first official United States flag, containing thirteen red and white stripes and thirteen stars on blue; begins to print paper money; and declares that loyalists are guilty of treason against the united American colonies.

The importation of slaves in the thirteen colonies is forbidden by the Continental Congress.

The Continental Congress passes a resolution calling for independence from Great Britain. John Hancock approves and signs the Declaration of Independence. The Congress declares independence on July 2, and it adopts the Declaration of Independence on July 4. The Declaration is read publicly for the first time on July 8 in Philadelphia.

The United Colonies are renamed the United States by the Continental Congress.

Pennsylvania approves its Declaration of Rights, which guarantees certain rights and freedoms to the state's citizens, and it ratifies its constitution.

The Continental Congress gives General George Washington dictatorial powers to be used for making urgent war decisions.

1777

The Declaration of Independence is reprinted, containing the signatures of all the signers, and Congress decides on the design of the new flag.

British and American forces battle at Brandywine Creek. Congress votes to buy blankets for soldiers in the Continental army.

Congress is forced to flee from Philadelphia as British troops advance to occupy the city. It meets in Lancaster, Pennsylvania, for three days and then moves to York, Pennsylvania, where it remains until June 27, 1778.

In the battle of Germantown, Washington tries to stop the British from occupying Philadelphia, but fails due to strong resistance by the British at Chew Mansion. The British manage to capture Philadelphia, and Washington and his army retreat to Valley Forge.

The British take over Fort Mercer and Fort Mifflin, guaranteeing access to the sea through the Delaware River and making it possible for them to resupply their troops and continue to occupy Philadelphia.

The Articles of Confederation, the United States' first plan of government, is agreed upon by the Continental Congress, but the plan is not completely ratified by the states until 1781.

1778

The British leave Philadelphia in the spring.

Fort Roberdeau is built during the spring and summer in present-day Tyrone Township to serve as a storage depot for ammunition and as a refuge for soldiers, miners, and settlers.

Congress ratifies an alliance with France and adopts the Articles of Confederation.

Pennsylvania takes over the College of Philadelphia and renames it the University of the State of Pennsylvania.

Congress authorizes a $100 bounty for enlistment into the Continental army.

1780

Robert Morris establishes the Pennsylvania Bank, the first public bank in the United States.

Pennsylvania passes the Emancipation Act, ending slavery throughout the state. It becomes the first state to abolish slavery.

1781

Congress legislates the establishment of the finance, war, and marine departments.

The American Revolution ends in October with the British surrender to the Americans at Yorktown.

John Hanson is elected to the presidency of the United States under the Articles of Confederation.

1782

Congress adopts the new country's official seal.

1783

Benjamin Franklin publishes *Remarks concerning the Savages of North America.*

Pennsylvania soldiers protest the state's failure to pay them by surrounding Independence Hall. Congress relocates to Princeton, New Jersey.

The Treaty of Paris is signed, officially ending the war and stipulating British recognition of American independence.

1785

The Adgate Free School, a singing school, which operates until 1793, is found by the Urania Society. Andrew Adgate publishes several music instruction lessons.

Dr. Benjamin Rush, Robert Morris, Richard Peters, and others found the Philadelphia Society for Promoting Agriculture. It promotes improved methods to preserve soil, prevent disease, and discover better types of seeds used in farming.

1786

John Fitch operates the first vessel ever moved by steam on the Delaware River.

1787

The U.S. Constitutional Convention meets in Philadelphia.

John Aitken and Thomas Dobson establish a music publishing shop, the first in the country to print sheet music.

Black churchmen Richard Allen and Absalom Jones found the Free African Society to fight for African American rights.

Delegates convene in Philadelphia on May 17 to discuss possible revisions of the Articles of Confederation.

George Washington is elected on May 25 to preside over the Constitutional Convention. Instead, the delegates decide to write an entirely new governing document for the country.

Edmund Randolph presents the "Virginia Plan" to what is now the Constitutional Convention, which calls for a bicameral legislature with representation in the lower house based upon population.

Congress, still constituted under the Articles of Confederation, passes the Northwest Ordinance, which proposes the eventual creation of three to five states in the Northwest Territory. Also, delegates agree that slavery is to be barred from the territory.

Elbridge Gerry and George Mason put forward a proposal on the topic of a "Bill of Rights."

Thirty-nine out of 42 delegates who attend the Constitutional Convention sign the Constitution of the United States, and it is sent to Congress for approval.

Congress reaches an agreement to send the Constitution to the states for ratification.

Pennsylvania ratifies the Constitution, becoming the second state to do so.

1789

Benjamin Franklin changes his will to appropriate funds to be used to build a pipeline that will bring fresh water to Philadelphia. Dirty water has caused disease in the area and the deaths of one-quarter of the city's population in just a few years.

The first Congress of the United States meets in Congress Hall in Philadelphia.

Arthur Holst

Rhode Island

Prior to the Arrival of Europeans

The original inhabitants of the Rhode Island area are the Wampanoag and Narragansett. Both speak variants of Algonquian. When Giovanni da Verrazano visits the region in the 1520s, both tribes will claim the island of Aquidneck (the site of Newport), although the Wampanoag temporarily have the upper hand. (Verrazano will rename the island Rhodes, because of its similarity to the famous Greek island of the same name.)

The Narragansett are probably the largest and most formidable tribe in southern New England, both before and after the arrival of the English. Ruled by two sachems, their territory is rich in natural resources. The Narragansett develop a semisedentary lifestyle based on hunting, fishing—particularly for shellfish—and corn agriculture. They also become the major wampum producers in the colonial era. A strict gender division orders village life: men are hunters, deep-sea fishers, diplomats, and warriors; women are farmers and producers of many goods used in Narragansett homes.

1524

Verrazano visits Narragansett Bay, and "discovers" dense populations of Wampanoags and Narragansetts. The explorer praises the harbor, but his French sponsors do not take an interest in the area. The Narragansett population is over 5,000, and its density is among the highest in North America—only in Mexico's central valley and the pueblos of the Southwest are these figures higher.

1614

Adriaen Block, a Dutch sea captain, visits the region. His voyage results in a reasonably accurate map and the naming of Block Island, but no significant Dutch colonizing activity follows.

1620

Religious refugees found the English colony of Plymouth on Wampanoag land made available as a result of a series of epidemics that ravage the area from 1616 to 1619. The militarily weak English ally themselves with the Wampanoag sachem, Massasoit (Ousamequin), but they are careful not to run afoul of the Narragansett.

1630

The Massachusetts Bay Company, led by John Winthrop, founds Massachusetts Bay Colony to the north of the Plymouth colony. The Great Migration begins, and native peoples throughout the region become alarmed at the sheer numbers of English people moving into New England. For the first few decades of English settlement, approximately 10,000 people per decade immigrate. By contrast, the Narragansett number around 5,000, and the Wampanoag fewer than 3,000. The Narragansett reach a tenuous agreement with the English, based largely upon the fact that both mistrust the intentions of the Pequot and Mohegan tribes farther to the west.

1635

Roger Williams, who had arrived in Massachusetts several years prior, battles Winthrop's General Court over theological and governmental matters. Williams, the pastor in Salem, asks his church to repudiate the other Puritans because they remain tied to the Church of England. He eventually accuses the General Court of trying to subvert the authority of individual congregations and is banished, supposedly to return to England. Instead, prompted by Winthrop—the two men respect each other, though they disagree—Williams moves into a Wampanoag village. When Plymouth governor Edward Winslow insists that Williams leave his jurisdiction, he moves west.

1636

Williams founds Providence on land granted to him by the Narragansett sachems Canonicus and Miantonomo. He has met both leaders on previous trading missions, and probably impressed them by learning their language.

Also in 1636, a new controversy, the Antinomian Controversy, rips Massachusetts Bay and spins off another community of dissenters, led by Anne Hutchinson. After a dramatic trial, Hutchinson and some of her followers are banished in 1637.

1637–1638

The Narragansett join the English and other native forces in destroying the Pequot during the Pequot War.

1638

Antinomian refugees obtain the island of Aquidneck (also known as Rhode Island) from local Narragansetts through a treaty and establish the town of Pocasset (Portsmouth). This settlement includes eighty families.

1639

After a dispute with the Antinomians, William Coddington, a wealthy Puritan, moves to the south end of Aquidneck and founds Newport. With a prime location on the bay, and a population more inclined to commerce, Newport eventually becomes one of the largest cities in colonial America.

Also in the late 1630s, Samuel Gorton, a Puritan mystic, moves around Narragansett Bay, eventually settling at Warwick. Gorton believes in the equality of the sexes and in direct communication with God. Eccentrics like Gorton, Williams, and Hutchinson arouse suspicion in the larger Massachusetts Bay Colony, where people jokingly call the new territories "Rogue's Island."

1643

Williams, in London to obtain official sanction for Rhode Island, publishes *A Key into the Language of America*, a book describing the Narragansett language and customs, as well as a tract outlining his principles regarding religious liberty.

Also in 1643, Plymouth, Connecticut, and Massachusetts Bay Colony form the United Colonies of New England and seek to divide heretical Rhode Island between them. The United Colonies periodically attack the Narragansett as well.

1644

A parliamentary patent obtained by Williams creates the colony of Rhode Island from the towns scattered around Narragansett Bay. Bringing the towns together proves more difficult, however. They meet for the first time in 1647, but the makeshift government falls apart in 1649. Threats from Plymouth and Massachusetts Bay force Rhode Islanders to band together. Still, the Rhode Island political situation is unstable and chaotic, and, at one point, several different men claim to govern the colony.

The patent itself allows the people of Rhode Island to select their own leaders and make their own laws, as long as they do not contravene English laws. Parliament reserves the right to govern at the highest level. The document lacks royal sanction, however, as King Charles I and Parliament are engaged in a bloody struggle for hegemony.

1658–1660

Williams unites the various factions within Rhode Island under a single government. This signals the end of a period of political chaos and factionalism.

In 1660, Quakers, heavily persecuted in both old and New England, begin to arrive on Aquidneck. In 1672, George Fox, the founder of the Religious Society of Friends,

will visit the island. Following his visit, the Aquidneck Friends will keep meticulous records and participate actively in the political and economic life of the colony.

1663

After much legal wrangling with Connecticut—led by John Winthrop, Jr.—in London, Rhode Island receives a royal charter from the new king, Charles II. A boundary dispute with Connecticut will continue for decades, but Rhode Island's right to exist is confirmed.

1664

According to the charter, Rhode Island's General Assembly meets at Newport, and determines a distribution of magistrates that prevents Newport from dominating the council, though it does retain the largest delegation. Much of the power still rests in the hands of individual towns.

1675–1676

Increasing Puritan missionary activity and land grabbing provokes Massasoit's son Metacom (King Philip) to attack Plymouth and Massachusetts Bay. The conflict soon widens to include most of southern New England, both native and non-native. The Narragansett try to stay out of the fight at first, but United Colonies aggression forces them to join the Wampanoag. Connecticut's militia, aided by the Mohegan, inflicts severe damage on Narragansett villages. Many of the captives are sold as slaves. From a native perspective, the end of King Philip's War is an unmitigated disaster. Both the Wampanoag and Narragansett are reduced to insignificance in regional politics; Rhode Island, which has done little to support the war, stands to gain immensely from their defeat.

1687

As part of King James II's plan to bring all of the New England colonies under royal control, Rhode Island's government is subsumed by the Dominion of New England, a massive administrative unit that includes Massachusetts, Plymouth, Connecticut, New York, and the two New Jerseys. Edmund Andros, a military man, is elevated to the position of governor.

1688–1689

In the wake of the Glorious Revolution, Dominion government collapses. Rhode Island towns refuse to pay taxes to support the Andros regime, and when Andros escapes a Boston jail for Newport, he is temporarily imprisoned there. In 1689 Rhode Island resumes government under the earlier model set up by royal charter, over the objections of some men whose fortunes have risen during the Dominion.

During King William's War, a French fleet attacks Block Island, but it is foiled in its attempt to take Newport.

1696

In response to the increasing number of towns and a growing population, Rhode Island's colonial assembly expands to two houses. More magistrates and justices also are elected and appointed during this period.

1698

The General Assembly chooses Samuel Cranston as governor.

Cranston will serve for almost twenty-nine years. His able administration brings Rhode Island into the empire economically, while at the same time maintaining the local political privileges outlined in the colony's charter. Commercial interests in the growing city of Newport come to the fore during Cranston's tenure.

1699

Richard Coote, the Earl of Bellomont, becomes governor of Massachusetts, a position that has recently been upgraded to include command of Rhode Island's militia, much to the chagrin of that colony's residents. Upon his arrival in Rhode Island in 1699, Bellomont writes a scathing report, accusing the government of aiding pirates, overstepping its chartered authority, and generally behaving poorly. Cranston, his back against the wall, is forced to accept many of Bellomont's critiques. Bellomont dies suddenly, and Rhode Island is able to maintain some measure of independence. The assembly votes wholeheartedly to support Queen Anne's War and to pay an agent in London to represent its interests.

The border dispute with Connecticut continues to simmer, and each colony continues arresting the other's local officials.

1702–1713

During Queen Anne's War, Rhode Island sends men to aid in the failed invasions of Canada. More successful are the privateering missions carried out by Newport's sea captains. The colony holds its own in some minor naval battles with the French.

1708

In a reply to a questionnaire sent by the Board of Trade, Cranston indicates the nature of Rhode Island's economy. Centered at Newport, a serious shipbuilding industry has begun to develop; between 1698 and 1708, 100 ships have been built. Most of these are smaller ships, but larger vessels are also being built. With other colonies from Massachusetts to the Caribbean, Newport is engaged in Atlantic trade and has recently begun a profitable trade in African slaves. Local distilleries provide Newport with one of its most profitable exports: rum.

1714–1715

The government of Rhode Island begins to issue paper money after a serious shake-up in the government costs many officials their jobs. The bills are based on land and fairly quickly fall below their face values. Rhode Island's repeated issuance of paper money in the first half of the eighteenth century brings the colony into conflict with the Board of Trade in London and merchants in the Massachusetts Bay Colony. Still, the abundance of currency helps to finance public works projects, including new facilities for Rhode Island's government and military.

1719

Rhode Island publishes a compilation of its laws, with an eye toward centralizing authority over land sales and bringing Rhode Island's laws into compliance with the charter and English law.

1739

The War of Jenkins' Ear breaks out between Spain and Great Britain. As in previous colonial wars, Newport's privateering and commercial enterprises benefit from the conflict and do especially brisk business with non-British ports in the Caribbean.

1756

The Seven Years' War, the contest between Britain and France for North America that is known as the French and Indian War in the colonies, begins in earnest. Rhode Island raises the appointed number of men, but they do not see much combat in the first phases of the conflict. They participate in a failed attack on Fort Ticonderoga and help protect New York's frontier; they also take part in the campaign that sees Cuba fall into British hands. After the Treaty of Paris in 1763, Rhode Island finds itself deeply in debt, racked with internal dissension, and facing a reduced role in the Atlantic world.

1758

Publication of the *Mercury,* a newspaper, begins in Newport. The pages contain news and advertisements, as well as social announcements, indicating the Newport gentry's growing prosperity and taste for refinement in the years before the War for Independence. Providence's newspaper opens for business in 1762.

1760s

Rhode Island is the site of a bitter internal conflict between Samuel Ward and Stephen Hopkins, each of whom serves as governor on and off through the late 1750s and 1760s. Each spearheads a political party; Hopkins's is most powerful in Providence and the northern towns, while Ward generally wins elections in the southern towns. The two square off on matters of taxation, currency, and patronage. Interestingly, both Ward and Hopkins journey to Philadelphia for the First Continental Congress.

1764–1765

Rhode Island protests the passage of the Sugar Act and the proposed Stamp Act. Governor Hopkins pens *The Rights of the Colonies Examined*, a treatise concerning the right of Parliament to represent and tax American colonies, many of which have their own legislatures. The publication touches off a pamphlet war between patriots and loyalists in the colony.

In 1765, Samuel Ward is elected governor, and faces the Stamp Act crisis. Some street violence occurs in association with the Stamp Act, but the distributor resigns, and the General Assembly declares the act void and sends delegates to the Stamp Act Congress. On the day the Stamp Act is to take effect, business in Rhode Island goes on as usual, although a mock funeral procession lays a casket marked "Liberty" to rest.

1772

John Brown of Providence organizes a party of men to attack the run-aground *Gaspee*, a royal ship stationed in the port. They seize the ship's cargo and burn the vessel to the water line. An investigation is launched, but half-hearted investigators declare punishing the culprits a lost cause.

1776

Rhode Island asserts its independence from Great Britain on May 4, almost two months before the Second Continental Congress does so. The General Assembly votes to repudiate allegiance to George III, and accuses the king of tyranny. During the war that follows, Newport is held alternately by British and American forces, and in the closing years, by a French force. Newport continues to decline in commercial importance, as Boston and New York dominate regional commerce ever more effectively.

Matthew Jennings

South Carolina

Prior to the Arrival of Europeans

A wide variety of Native American groups inhabit South Carolina. They range in size from single-village communities on the resource-rich Atlantic coast, to larger interior nations, such as the Cherokees and Creeks, to centralized Mississippian chiefdoms, such as that at Cofitachequi (near present-day Camden). They speak a wide range of mutually unintelligible languages from the Muskogean, Siouan, and Iroquoian language groups. South Carolina's native population is stunningly diverse.

The southeastern native peoples do share some common cultural traits, though. They tend toward decentralized, village-centered forms of government (except in the case of Mississippian chiefdoms). They also divide society strictly along gender lines: Agriculture and domestic tasks are primarily female roles, while warfare and hunting are almost exclusively male provinces.

The period before the arrival of Europeans is one of major cultural change for Native Americans. Smaller, multiethnic, and, in some cases, multilingual polities (the forerunners of colonial-period tribes) are replacing centralized societies like those created by the Mississippians. In many cases, the shift is already underway before Native Americans encounter Europeans. In the case of Cofitachequi, Spanish disease will accelerate the process.

1494

The Treaty of Tordesillas divides the New World between Spain and Portugal. South Carolina theoretically falls under the control of Spain.

1520–1521

Lucas Vásquez de Ayllón, an official from Hispaniola, sponsors a slaving voyage to the Carolina coast, which brings seventy native Carolinians to the Caribbean to replace Arawaks.

1524

Giovanni da Verrazano, a Florentine sailing for the king of France, explores the coast of South Carolina.

1526

Ayllón undertakes an even larger voyage and establishes a short-lived colony somewhere on the South Carolina or Georgia coast. Five hundred men and women leave Hispaniola, but only 150 return. His flagship, carrying most of the supplies, sinks. Ayllón himself perishes in the undertaking, and his native interpreters run off into the woods.

1540

Hernando de Soto's deadly *entrada*, or invasion, cuts its way through South Carolina. Bringing horses, pigs, and war dogs (mastiffs), de Soto and his army move through the entire Southeast (ten future states) from 1539–1543, searching for treasure. At Cofitachequi, de Soto meets the female chief, or "Lady of Cofitachequi." Although he finds the pearls collected by the Native Americans to be irregular and inferior, he orders his men to remove around 200 pounds of them from ceremonial burial complexes, some from the body cavities of deceased natives. De Soto's trip through South Carolina results in epidemics and bitterness among the region's native peoples.

1562

The French, under the command of Jean Ribaut, found Charlesfort on Port Royal Sound. The colony fails miserably when Ribaut returns to France for supplies. The settlers mutiny, construct a boat, and sail for France. They make it home, but to survive the journey have to resort to cannibalism en route.

1565–1570

Pedro Menéndez de Avilés founds Santa Elena as a joint missionary, military, and colonial outpost. It becomes the administrative capital of *la Florida,* the Spanish name for the southeastern part of North America. Attacks by Sir Francis Drake and others force Santa Elena to consolidate with St. Augustine, farther to the South.

1629

King Charles I of England grants Sir Robert Heath "Carolana," a territory stretching from Virginia to Florida and from the Atlantic to the Pacific. Heath finances several failed attempts at settlement by the English and a handful of French Huguenots.

1663

Shortly after his restoration to the throne, Charles II grants Carolina to a group of eight lords proprietors, led by Anthony Ashley Cooper, soon to become the first Earl of Shaftesbury. The king gives them broad powers to develop a society by distributing land and constructing a government.

1669

The lords proprietors draft the Fundamental Constitutions of Carolina, a document designed to govern settlement of the new colony. The Anglican Church will technically be "established," or supported by the state, but Carolinians will be free to worship however they see fit. The Constitutions also divide the territory into provinces and counties, and they provide for the establishment of a new class of nobleman, the landgrave, who wields an extraordinary amount of political power. Essentially visionary in character, the Constitutions exert a relatively small effect on the actual white settlement of the colony. The colonial legislature never approves the measures, even though the proprietors modify them several times between 1669 and 1705.

1670

Settlers land on the Ashley River and officially found the colony of Carolina. A group of planters, dissatisfied with life on Barbados, moves into the area and quickly draws the ire of the proprietors, especially Anthony Ashley Cooper, who avers that John Yeamans, the first governor, is more concerned with personal profit than creating a utopian society in Carolina. The "Goose Creek men," Barbadian Anglicans who lived along Goose Creek (a tributary of the Cooper River), dominate colonial politics for years, opposing the actions of the proprietors in nearly every regard. Meanwhile, African slavery begins to take hold in South Carolina, when Africans from the West Indies accompany their masters to the region. In fact, between 1670 and 1690, more than half of the colony's black population comes from the Caribbean.

1680–1683

The population center of the colony relocates to the carefully planned city of Charles Town (present-day Charleston), at the mouth of the Ashley and Cooper Rivers. The proprietors hope that colonists will settle in orderly towns like those of Puritan New England and avoid the dangers and irregularities of the sort that have befallen Virginia. Also in 1680, the proprietors begin a successful drive to recruit French Huguenots to settle in Carolina.

From 1680 to 1683, Carolinian colonists battle the Westo Indians, who had formerly been allied with the colony in a profitable Native American slave trade. The Westo are defeated and dispersed; most of the survivors trickle westward and are absorbed by the Creek nation.

1684

Lord Cardross and 150 Scots land at Charles Town in 1684, intending to settle between the Spanish and the English, at Stuart's Town on Port Royal. The Spanish destroy the settlement in 1686, and the twenty-five surviving Scots return home.

1691

South Carolina and North Carolina separate to a certain degree when a deputy governor of Carolina begins work in North Carolina. A separate colonial legislature convenes in North Carolina, and by 1712, the proprietors acknowledge the split and appoint separate governors for the two colonies.

1692

The Commons House of Assembly is established in South Carolina. There are two legislative bodies in the colony at this point: the elected commons house and the appointed council. This system is replaced by a unicameral parliamentary body. Although the exact date is unknown, rice has been introduced to South Carolina. Relying on the expertise of their slaves (preferring those with rice-growing experience in the Senegambia region of West Africa), white planters begin to produce the crop throughout the low country. Within decades, rice has become South Carolina's, and perhaps all of colonial North America's, most valuable export. The decade of the 1690s also sees a dramatic increase in the trade in deerskins with neighboring, and occasionally more distant, Native American communities.

1702

In an action related to the larger conflict of Queen Anne's War, Carolinians and Native American allies under James Moore capture and burn the Spanish city of St. Augustine, although they are unable to take the stone fortress of San Marcos.

1703–1706

Moore leads a new expedition to the panhandle of Florida, where a combined force of English and Native Americans destroy Spain's most populous and prosperous mission province, Apalachee. Moore's party succeeds in carrying off hundreds of slaves. The attacks impress Native Americans, who join the English in increasing numbers and shun the Spanish, who are not able to offer military protection or trade goods at the same level as the English.

In an era of increasing competition between Anglican and Dissenter factions in colonial government, in 1704, the Anglicans push through legislative acts (without Dissenter delegations present) that exclude Dissenters from serving in the Commons House of Assembly and establish the Church of England. The Dissenters send emissaries to London to plead their case with the proprietors. In 1706, both acts are repealed, and a new act for the establishment of the Anglican

Church is passed. The Church of England will remain the official religious organization of South Carolina from 1706 to 1778.

1708

South Carolina becomes the first, and only, mainland North American colony with a significant African majority. Throughout the colonial period, African-born and African American slaves outnumber their masters. The demographic situation, which more closely resembles that of the British West Indies, is not lost on white slave masters, who attempt to regulate the lives of their slaves in increasingly intrusive ways.

1711–1713

Angered by unscrupulous white trading practices and the rapid expansion of European settlement in the region, Tuscarora Indians attack North Carolina; South Carolina raises an army of Yamasees and other allied Native Americans to come to that colony's aid. John Barnwell leads the army to some early success, but fails to take the main Tuscarora stronghold, King Hancock's Fort. James Moore, Jr., leads another expedition, which finally succeeds in bringing the Tuscarora under control. The remaining Tuscaroras migrate north to New York, where they join the Five Nations of the Iroquois in 1722.

1715

The Yamasee, formerly allies of South Carolina, launch a surprise attack on the colony. All along the frontier, Yamasees, Creeks, and their allies kill traders living in their communities. By 1718, when an alliance of the Cherokees and the English defeats the combined forces of most of the region's Native Americans, South Carolina lies in ruins. One half of the colony's farmland is deserted, and 6 percent of the white population is killed. Losses among Native Americans who opposed the English are even more severe. The Yamasee leave for the protection of Spanish Florida, where they continue to suffer at the hands of English slaving expeditions; only a handful survive the colonial period.

1719

The Revolution of 1719 brings the beginning of the end of proprietary rule to South Carolina. This is a well-planned and well-executed bloodless coup. Dissenters and the Goose Creek men agree to cooperate for the purposes of ending the proprietorship. Although all of the individual proprietors will not be bought out until 1729, 1719 marks the end of their effective rule. In addition, the position of royal governor in South Carolina does not retain much power. Real authority rests instead in the Commons House of Assembly in Charles Town and the Board of Trade in London.

1724

Parliament drops the bounty, or subsidy, it had previously given to Carolina's producers of naval stores. A year earlier,

floods had destroyed a third of the rice crop. These factors, combined with inflation caused by an excess of paper money, produce a minor economic crisis in the colony.

1728

Yellow fever sweeps through Charles Town, adding an epidemiological crisis to an already tense economic and political situation.

1733

The founding of the colony of Georgia adds a layer of protection between South Carolina and the Spanish at St. Augustine. The skilled leadership of James Oglethorpe brings many Native American groups into alliance with the English in the 1730s.

1739

In what became known as the Stono Rebellion, a group of approximately twenty Angolan slaves under the leadership of Jemmy, attacked a store at Stono, about 15 miles outside of Charles Town. They seize powder and firearms and take off into the countryside, gathering followers along the way. By afternoon, the rebellious slaves number between sixty and 100. The revolt takes several days to quell entirely. By the time it is over, more than twenty whites, and an untold number of slaves are dead. The revolt, one of the largest in America, though relatively small by Caribbean standards, terrifies South Carolina's white population and spurs the development of a harsh new slave code in 1740.

The War of Jenkins' Ear, pitting the English against the Spanish, lasts from 1739 to 1743. Though trade is the main impetus behind the conflict, it provides a convenient excuse to attack St. Augustine. South Carolina participates in an expedition led by James Oglethorpe. A poorly timed naval and overland attack fails to take the fortress, and the English are forced to retreat.

1740

A massive fire sweeps through Charles Town, burning about one third of the city's buildings. Though no lives are lost, property damage is severe.

1750

Rice and, to a lesser extent, indigo have made the planter class of South Carolina the richest group of individuals in what would become the United States. Fully recovered from the effects of the Yamasee War, South Carolina also takes an increasing interest in the settlement of the midland and the Piedmont region of the colony.

1759–1761

Carolinians incite the largely pointless Cherokee War as their part of the larger French and Indian War (known as the Seven Years' War in Europe). Forces, under Governor William Henry Lyttelton and later under the British commander James Grant, succeed in routing the Cherokees and establishing a semipermanent border between South Carolina and the Cherokee towns. British and provincial troops quarrel continually, and on one occasion their officers duel.

1765

In the weeks leading up to the Stamp Act's enactment, Charles Town is the site of serious public disturbances, largely sparked by the Sons of Liberty. The protests are at once violent and creative. Some colonists, for example, parade a coffin labeled "American Liberty" through the streets and bury it in a solemn ceremony.

1766–1767

In successive years, crime waves sweep through the backcountry, now a fairly densely populated region. The leading men of the backcountry band together in what will become known as the Regulator movement. They seek law and order in the form of courts, jails, schools, and more proportionate representation in the Commons House, all four of which are lacking in the backcountry. In 1768, they pass the Plan of Regulation, which basically governs all of South Carolina outside of a 50-mile stretch along the coast. Eventually, after gaining some reforms, the group loses influence.

1776 and Beyond

The Revolutionary War is fought in South Carolina as a sort of civil war between those loyal to the king and those who support the American cause. When loyalists leave the state for Canada, the Caribbean, and elsewhere, they take about 5,000 slaves with them. An additional 25,000 slaves leave upon the departure of the British forces.

South Carolina also loses Britain as its primary trading partner as a result of the American victory in the War for Independence. After 1783 and the Treaty of Paris, however, South Carolina will remain a very profitable area devoted to plantation agriculture, African slavery, and the maintenance of an extraordinarily wealthy, and fractious, class of planters.

Matthew Jennings

Spanish Colonies on Mainland North America

Prior to the Arrival of Europeans

The areas eventually colonized by the Spanish include the western mountain and coastal portions of the North American continent, ranging from what is now the U.S. Pacific Northwest to Florida. The Native American population of these regions is extraordinarily diverse.

The Pacific Coast region is home to several major linguistic groups, including the Penutian, Athapascan, and Uto-Aztecan. These groups encompass hundreds of individual societies and tribes.

By 1000 C.E., sophisticated farming societies like the Anasazi, Hohokam, and Mogollon have developed in what is now Arizona and New Mexico, utilizing such methods as irrigation canals to practice intensive agricultural cultivation with maize (corn) as their primary crop. By the thirteenth century, however, these pueblo cultures have been affected by both climatological and social change. The environment has become more difficult for agriculture, and warfare between various groups contributes to the fragmented and smaller-scale cultures that will be encountered by the Spaniards in the sixteenth century.

In Florida, the Apalachee (the southernmost of the Eastern Woodlands peoples) are the largest native tribe, occupying what is now the Western Panhandle of Florida. For the most part, smaller, more dispersed, and nomadic groups such as the Caloosa and Timucua occupy the Florida peninsula.

1469

King Ferdinand and Queen Isabella are married, uniting the two largest Catholic kingdoms on the Iberian Peninsula, thus paving the way for the creation of the nation-state of Spain. The final stages of the *Reconquista*—the expulsion of the Moors (North African Muslims who had occupied Iberia since the eighth century)—commences with their marriage.

1481

Queen Isabella rejects a request from a Genoese sailor, Christopher Columbus, to sponsor his expedition aimed at reaching the East Indies. His plan is to sail westward across the Atlantic, instead of along the route currently being explored by the Portuguese, which goes eastward and southward around the Horn of Africa.

1483

With the Crown's explicit approval, the Inquisition begins operation in Spain. The primary targets of this strenuous (and often violent) enforcement of rigid Catholic orthodoxy are the *conversos*—Jews who have only recently converted to Catholicism and are therefore suspected of disloyal tendencies in the militaristic and xenophobic environment of the *Reconquista*.

1491

Christopher Columbus, unsuccessful in his bids to acquire sponsorship for his voyages from other European governments, once again applies to Isabella for funds. This time, with the *Reconquista* nearly complete and Spain positioned to enter into maritime competition with Portugal, the queen grants his request, providing three ships and royal sanction for his planned voyage.

1492

The *Reconquista* reaches its conclusion in January, when the last remaining Moorish enclave in Granada (on the southern coast of Spain) is defeated. Spain is completely reclaimed by Catholics.

A royal decree expels those of Jewish extraction from Spain. Many go underground, and some migrate to Spanish colonies in the Western Hemisphere.

In August, Christopher Columbus begins his voyage across the Atlantic. On October 12, he reaches land at what is now Watling's Island in the Bahamas. Columbus is convinced that he is near the Asian coast, as he has significantly underestimated the earth's circumference in his calculations. He names the island San Salvador and claims it in the name of God and the Spanish Crown. Kidnapping some of the Taino natives he encounters, as well as taking flora and fauna samples from his explorations in the immediate region around the Bahamas (including Hispaniola, meaning "Spanish Isle"), Columbus and his crew sail for Europe.

1493

Christopher Columbus arrives in Portugal in March. Ferdinand and Isabella reward Columbus by naming him Admiral of the Ocean Sea and governor of the islands he has "discovered." They grant him a share in all the wealth he might find in the region.

Columbus organizes a larger expedition to return to Hispaniola. He establishes a permanent Spanish colony there, although relations quickly deteriorate between the Spanish soldiers and the Taino natives. Columbus returns to Spain, leaving an interim governor in his place.

The problems between the Spanish and natives continue, but diseases introduced by the Spanish are already taking their toll on the native population. Where the population in early 1492 was estimated to have been over 5 million, by 1540, only a few thousand Taino will remain on Hispaniola. Adding to the natives' troubles will be the *encomienda,* a grant from the Crown of land and native labor that will first be made to Columbus in 1499. Over time, this practice will become prevalent in the Spanish colonial empire and will be the source of much misery and hardship for natives, who will become essentially enslaved by Spanish *encomenderos.*

Columbus will make two more voyages to the New World, still believing he is near Asia. Doubts will creep in, however, as he sails around the Caribbean and Gulf of Mexico without finding a break in what he thinks is a chain of barrier islands off the Asian coast. Columbus will die in 1506, embittered at having failed in his ultimate objective.

The pope grants Spain the right to conquer all non-Christian peoples and lands more than 100 leagues west of the Azores. This dispensation reinforces Spain's role as the leading Catholic nation in Europe, and it is also a large part of Spain's rationale for its overseas colonial conquests.

1494

To reconcile their separate papal dispensations, Spain and Portugal conclude the Treaty of Tordesillas. This moves the line of demarcation to 350 leagues west of the Azores and grants Portugal the right of conquest in all non-Christian lands east of that line.

1513

Don Juan Ponce de León leads a Spanish expedition to the east coast of "La Florida," seeking gold and slaves. He also searches for a mythical fountain of youth, whose existence has been hinted at in encounters with other native groups in the Caribbean region.

The expedition is met by the hostile Ais, who drive away the Spaniards. The ships sail around the Florida Keys and up Florida's west coast, where the Spaniards encounter the equally hostile Caloosa. Faced with the hostility of the native peoples, Ponce de León temporarily abandons his quest for wealth in Florida.

1519

Hernando Cortéz and approximately 1,000 Spanish soldiers land on the east coast of Mexico. They begin an expedition into the heart of the Aztec Empire, subduing the native societies they encounter along the way through either intimidation or force. Cortéz and his men reach the Aztec capital of Tenochtitlán within several months, where they are cautiously welcomed by the Aztec emperor Montezuma II. Cortéz's intent, however, is not diplomacy but conquest.

1521

In May, Cortéz completes the conquest of the Aztec Empire when the Spanish (along with native allies, who also desire an end to Aztec rule) defeat the Aztec in a climactic battle in Tenochtitlán. The Spanish conquistadores will become *encomenderos,* and the Aztec will suffer significant depopulation, not only from the violence of conquest, but also from the diseases brought by the Spanish. Mexico becomes the center of the viceroyalty of New Spain, which becomes the base for further Spanish expansion and colonization in the area that is today the United States.

Ponce de León returns to Florida with the intention of constructing a fort to serve as a base for expeditions into the Florida interior. Once again, the Caloosa attack the expedition, seriously wounding Ponce de León in the process; he dies a few days later in Cuba.

1527–1528

Panfilo Narváez, who earlier had conquered Cuba, receives royal permission to claim the lands previously explored by Ponce de León. He launches an expedition to West Florida, but four of its five ships are either destroyed by storm or are forced to turn back to Cuba. Undaunted, Narváez lands north of Caloosa territory, where he and his men encounter the Timucua. To avoid conflict with the encroaching Spanish, the Timucua direct Narváez and his men northward into Apalachee lands.

The Apalachee are a more populous and less dispersed and nomadic society than either the Caloosa or Timucua, and thus their hostile stance towards the Spanish proves far more deadly. The Apalachee destroy the expedition, and Narváez himself is killed along with some 300 of his men. Four Spaniards survive, including the expedition's treasurer, Cabeza de Vaca, and an African slave named Esteban.

For the next eight years, the four men will wander throughout the regions of the Gulf of Mexico's coast—through Louisiana, Texas, and finally into northern Mexico. Eventually, de Vaca and Esteban will become separated from the other two Spaniards. Cabeza de Vaca will publish a narrative of the journey, detailing his encounters with various tribes, from nomads to cannibals, and the roles, from slaves to holy men, that he and Esteban played in order to survive. Despite de Vaca's grim descriptions of the regions and peoples of the "borderlands," other conquistadores will continue to launch expeditions into these regions in subsequent decades.

1539

Hernando de Soto leads an expedition of approximately 600 Spanish soldiers to western Florida in search of land, slaves, and riches. For the next three years, de Soto will travel throughout what is now the southeastern United States. In the process, he will become the first European to reach the Mississippi River.

De Soto's expedition lays waste to the Native Americans of the region. Diseases brought by the Spaniards decimate the area's various populations, who tend to interact with one another commercially and politically and thus help to spread the deadly microbes at an accelerated rate. Additionally, de Soto, who has a significant capacity for violence, deals harshly with any natives who exhibit hostility or resistance towards the Spanish. Eventually, however, de Soto's forces are attacked and split in two.

Although he could meet a Spanish naval force on the Gulf coast, de Soto, still enthralled by visions of a fabled city of gold, instead turns northwards to continue his search. He will fall ill by early 1542 and die in May at the Mississippi River. The bedraggled remnants of his force will journey southward and reach the comparative safety of Spanish settlements approximately a year later.

1540–1542

Francisco Vázquez de Coronado commands an expedition journeying throughout what is now the southwestern United States (concurrently with de Soto's movements through the southeast). For approximately two years, Coronado and his men search for one of the fabled seven cities of gold. Journeying throughout the region—from the Grand Canyon and lower California in the west to Kansas and the Great Plains in the east—Coronado and his men generally enjoy good relations with the native peoples they encounter; some natives even accompany the Spanish as fellow warriors and guides.

This changes, however, when Coronado arrives at the Hawikuh pueblo, a group of villages north of the Zuni River. Seeking to feed his men, Coronado offers the Pueblo peoples the protection of the Spanish Crown in exchange for food. The natives respond by attacking Coronado; his force counterattacks. The Pueblo retreat to another, more fortified, village, but Coronado's force has essentially worn out its welcome in the area. Faced with hostile native populations and mutinous and hungry troops, Coronado resorts to attacking any natives who refuse to cooperate with the Spanish.

By the end of 1541, Coronado retreats southward to Mexico in April 1542, leaving in his wake many Native Americans killed by either violence or disease. There are other long-term effects of this European contact: Spanish horses, sheep, and cows will remain in Pueblo country and alter both the diets and wardrobes of the region's native peoples.

1565

An expedition of French Huguenots constructs Fort Caroline at the mouth of the St. John's River in Florida, a cause for serious concern among the Catholic Spanish authorities toward what they regard as a dangerous encroachment into their lands. In September, Pedro Menéndez de Avilés leads a force of some 500 Spanish soldiers to dislodge the French. The Spanish completely surprise the French community at Fort Caroline and kill most residents; most of those who surrender also are executed, as Menéndez deems this a justifiable punishment for Protestant "heretics" who refuse to convert to Catholicism.

Forty miles south of the Fort Caroline site, Menéndez constructs the fortress town of St. Augustine. It is the first permanent European colonial settlement in the area that will become the United States.

Menéndez will go on to construct a network of coastal fortifications along both the Gulf and Atlantic coasts to prevent both future French encroachment and European privateers' preying upon Spanish vessels. The principal settlement in this network is Saint Helena, on Port Royal Sound (in what is now South Carolina).

1570–1572

Pedro Menéndez de Avilés sends a Jesuit mission north to the Chesapeake Bay. The mission, however, becomes a tragic failure within a year. The Jesuits' guide is a native who had been captured by Spanish soldiers in 1561, taken to Spain, and baptized. Seemingly assimilated into European culture, the young man promises to help the Jesuits convert the peoples of his native region. Once in the Chesapeake, however, the guide deserts the Jesuits and exhorts the region's natives to resist the Spaniards.

In February 1571, a force of Native Americans surprises and massacres the Jesuits, leaving only one survivor—a child taken into captivity. Menéndez leads a retaliatory expedition to the Chesapeake in 1572; although he kills some thirty-five Native Americans, he cannot find the erstwhile guide who has undone the Jesuit mission. After this incursion, the Spanish will withdraw from the Chesapeake region.

1573

A new decree from the Spanish Crown, the Royal Orders for New Discoveries, mandates that future expeditions launched by conquistadores will be "pacifications" rather than "conquests" of the Native Americans. The Crown instructs conquistadores to proceed "peacefully and charitably" toward the native peoples. In their practical effect, the orders do not substantially alter the modus operandi of Spanish expeditions into North America.

1574

Menéndez dies in Florida. The erosion of Spanish settlement in the face of difficult conditions and hostile natives is strikingly evident at this point, with St. Augustine and Santa Elena the only remaining Spanish outposts in Florida.

1588

Decades of tension between England and Spain climax with an attempt by Spain's King Philip II to launch an invasion of England with a huge naval armada, consisting of 130 ships and over 22,000 soldiers and sailors. The confrontation between the Spanish Armada and the English navy begins on July 30; for two weeks, the opposing fleets engage one another, until the Spanish are forced to withdraw. As the Armada sails around Ireland and Scotland before heading back to Iberian waters, several storms decimate the fleet, and only a small crippled remnant makes it back to Spain.

The defeat and decimation of the Spanish Armada mark the beginning of a long, slow decline in Spain's imperial power vis-à-vis its principal European rivals, England and the Netherlands. From this point forward, Spain's dominance on the oceans and in the Americas will no longer stand uncontested. Other European nations will begin to create significant colonial dominions of their own alongside those of the Spanish in the Western Hemisphere.

1598–1607

Don Juan de Oñate is appointed by the viceroy of New Spain to lead a "pacification" expedition to the valley of the Rio Grande River and to found a Spanish colony (to be named New Mexico). The initial settlement in this venture, which includes some 130 Spanish troops and a handful of Franciscan friars, is founded in the midst of the Pueblo.

By 1599, Oñate and the Spanish manage to antagonize their Pueblo neighbors—mostly due to the Spanish soldiers' habit of taking whatever they need in the way of food or clothing by force from the Pueblo. When natives kill a few Spaniards engaged in this plundering in 1599, Oñate decides to make an example of them. Attacking one of the Pueblo villages, Oñate and the Spaniards kill several hundred Pueblo men, women, and children, and they enslave the survivors.

The Spaniards' ultimate goal—discovering rumored silver mines in the region—is never achieved, despite Oñate's willingness to launch more and more widespread expeditions into the North American interior (one even retraces the earlier route of Coronado). By 1602, many of the Spanish settlers, who had come with Oñate, are tired of arduous conditions without the promised returns, and they go back to Mexico. Faced with what is essentially a mutiny on the northern frontier, the viceroy recalls Oñate in 1607, strips him of his titles and honors, and orders him to keep away from New Mexico in the future.

1609

Under orders from the viceroy, Oñate's replacement as governor of "New Mexico," Don Pedro de Peralta, relocates the principal Spanish settlement in the region to the newly founded mission town of Santa Fe. The colony is to be rededicated to the ideal of pacification rather than conquest, with strict limits placed upon the conduct of the soldiers and civilian authorities; expanded powers are bestowed upon the Franciscans as well. The New Mexico colony, however, will never become more than an isolated backwater, far away from the main centers of Spanish colonization in the Americas—an enclave of a European minority in the midst of a large Pueblo majority.

1659

Approximately 10,000 of the native peoples housed in or near Spanish frontier missions die from a measles epidemic.

1680

A large, coordinated Pueblo revolt occurs in New Mexico. The uprising is a product of both short- and long-term causes, both revolving around decades of a Spanish presence. Diseases brought by the Spaniards have ravaged the Pueblo population, and harsh weather over the last several years has produced poor harvests and famine conditions throughout the region. These factors, combined with the aggressive methods with which the Spanish missionaries seek to acculturate the Pueblo, including beatings and executions of "heretic" Pueblo shamans, in an effort to enforce Christian practices, produce significant unrest. Some 17,000 to 18,000 Pueblos rise up in August in an attempt to force the Spanish out of New Mexico. They succeed in killing a number of the Spanish colonists and chasing the survivors as far as El Paso, farther eastward along the Rio Grande. The Pueblo insurgents take special pains to destroy any vestiges of Spanish culture, including churches, statues, and missions.

1687

Jesuit missionary Eusebio Francisco Kino establishes a mission in Baja California. From this base of operations, Kino extends missionary activity farther north, into what is now Arizona, as far as the Gila and Colorado rivers. Over the next twelve years, Kino will establish a significant Jesuit presence in the area.

1692

The remnant of Spain's New Mexico colonists, along with additional reinforcements from Spanish Mexico, reenter New Mexico in an attempt to reestablish Spanish hegemony in the region. The most significant fighting occurs at Santa Fe. Once the Pueblo are defeated there, Spanish control over the region is, for all intents and purposes, reestablished.

1696

Another revolt by the Pueblo of New Mexico against Spanish authority breaks out. Unlike the great rebellion of 1680, this insurgency is quickly suppressed by the governor, Diego de Vargas. But Vargas and the Spanish are unable to pacify the Hopi and Zuni peoples to the west, and these areas will become a refuge for Pueblo insurgents for the next several generations. This rebellion will prove to be the last organized uprising on the part of the Pueblo against Spanish authority.

1718

In the same year that the French establish New Orleans along the coast of the Gulf of Mexico, the Spanish move their range of northern settlements farther east to meet this perceived incursion. Indeed, the French have reached the Gulf of Mexico by cleaving the eastern half of Spanish settlement (Florida) from the western half (New Mexico and Texas). The settlement of San Antonio de Bexar and its mission, the Alamo, are founded in an attempt to redress what has been relative inattention to these northern regions. Additional Spanish expeditions range even farther northward, reaching present-day North Platte, Nebraska.

Although the French will not be dislodged from the North American interior until the 1760s, Spanish settlements in Texas reflect a gradual awareness on the part of the Spanish colonial bureaucracy that there is a French threat that needs to be met. For the next few decades, however, the northern regions of Spanish colonization remain distinctly secondary priorities to both the colonial authorities and the royal ministry back in Spain, and they are essentially regarded as lightly settled backwaters.

1763

The Spanish settlements in North America are reordered and expanded as a result of Spain's alliance with victorious Britain during the Seven Years' War (known in North America as the French and Indian War). The 1763 Treaty of Paris awards much of France's North American dominions to Spain, including the Mississippi River Valley, later known as the Louisiana Territory. The French division of Spain's northern settlements is therefore alleviated, as is the possibility of further encroachment by the French into lands nominally claimed by the Spanish. Spain, however, loses territory as well, with the cession of Florida to the British by the terms of the treaty.

1769

Jesuit missionary Junípero Serra leads an expedition into California, the last North American region to be settled by the Spanish. He establishes a mission and settlement at San Diego Bay. The year 1769 is regarded as the beginning of the "mission period" in California history, as from this point through the 1820s, a network of over twenty Spanish missions is created, stretching from San Diego to what is now northern California. Missions that will be founded in this period include San Francisco, Santa Barbara, and San José.

1783

The Treaty of Paris ends the Revolutionary War between Britain and its North American colonies. Spain had allied with France and the fledgling United States, and its reward for this support is winning back Florida from Great Britain as part of the settlement.

1810

While the Spanish monarchy undergoes internal conflict and eventual abdication as a result of the Napoleonic Wars in Europe, Spain's American colonies begin to take advantage of the power vacuum created by these dislocations in the homeland. The first of Spain's colonies to rebel against the authority of the mother country is Mexico. In September, an uprising breaks out in northern Mexico, led by the Creole priest Father Miguel Hidalgo. Hidalgo's insurgency has significant nationalist and peasant overtones, as it is led by the banner of the Virgin of Guadalupe, an indigenous and mestizo (people of mixed Spanish and native blood) symbol.

While Hidalgo's uprising will be quelled within two years, and Hidalgo himself will be captured and executed, the rebellion proves to be the beginning of over ten years of warfare. This violent period of revolution and upheaval will culminate in 1821 in the independent state of Mexico, which will include northern settlements in New Mexico, Texas, and California.

1819

In the Adams-Onís Treaty, Spain cedes Florida to the United States, in return for the U.S. government's assumption of 5 million dollars in American claims against the Spanish. The cession is perhaps the inevitable result of Spain's dramatically declining power in Florida, mirroring its loosening hold upon all its colonies during this era of Latin American revolutions.

The immediate occasion for the United States' interest in Florida emerges from General Andrew Jackson's incursion into Spanish territory early in the year. Jackson had been charged with pacifying the Seminole, who had been attacking American settlements in Georgia and Alabama. He interprets his orders broadly, choosing to strike at what he sees as the source of the Seminoles' strength—Spanish authorities in Pensacola. Entering Florida, Jackson forces the Spanish governor to lower the Spanish colors at Pensacola and executes two Britons he suspects of arming the Seminoles, thus causing an international incident. Despite Spain's protests against this violation of its sovereignty, U.S. Secretary of State John Quincy Adams realizes Jackson's expedition only underscores the weakness of Spanish authority in Florida, and he leverages this into what turns out to be a favorable treaty for the United States, which had desired the acquisition of Florida for years.

1821

Mexican forces defeat the last of Spain's Royal Army troops, completing the complex and violent process by which Mexico gains its independence from Spain. At first, Mexico is governed as an empire by the self-styled "emperor" Augustín de Iturbide. By 1824, however, Iturbide is deposed, and Mexico has become a constitutional republic.

The defined borders of Mexico include the regions of New Mexico, Arizona, Texas, and Alta California (the modern-day California in the United States)—the northern frontier of Spanish colonization in earlier years. These northern regions remain lightly settled by Mexicans and will become a target of U.S. expansionism by the 1830s.

Kevin M. Gannon

Virginia

Prior to the Arrival of Europeans

In the latter part of the sixteenth century, the chieftain Powhatan, who has inherited several villages between the James and Mattaponi Rivers through his mother's line, expands Tsenacommacah (which might have meant "densely inhabited land") through intimidation, diplomacy, and conquest to include most of the eastern half of what the English will later call Virginia.

Most of the tribes in this area share a language (of the eastern Algonquian type) and culture, but Powhatan's chiefdom is not a monolithic cultural entity. Each village maintains a *werowance*, a vassal chief, who rules with Powhatan's approval. In fact, Powhatan often appoints one of his numerous relations to the position.

There has been some disagreement by historians over the nature of Powhatan's authority. While he probably never held the same type or amount of power as paramount chiefs farther to the southeast, his chiefdom was more centralized than other eastern Algonquian polities. Powhatan ruled with the assistance of a wide-ranging network of chiefs and priests. Virginia is considered a Southern colony because of the sort of Anglo-American society that grew up there; however, in terms of Native American culture, it had more in common with that of New England.

The population of the eastern portion of Virginia around the turn of the seventeenth century possibly numbers around 20,000—perhaps over 100,000 for the entire future state, and Powhatan's authority extends over about thirty smaller chiefdoms. Each of these lesser chiefdoms consists of a network of villages. Life at the village level is divided along lines of gender. Men hunt, fish, and conduct war and diplomacy, while women farm, forage for food, and perform most of the domestic work.

1560–1570

The Spanish sail into Chesapeake Bay to explore, and Don Luis de Velasco, a young Powhatan chief, returns with them to Mexico. Don Luis lives in Mexico and Havana, and in between his journeys he studies at the court of King Philip II in Spain. The Spanish return in 1570 and establish a short-lived mission on Chesapeake Bay. Velasco, who has converted to Catholicism, draws the missionaries' ire by taking several wives and moving away from the mission. When the priests attempt to coax him back to the mission, he kills all but one of them, though he does give the victims Christian burials.

1572

A Spanish supply ship engages some Powhatan Indians and makes off with about thirty captives. The soldiers pick up the survivor of the mission but fail in their attempt to capture Velasco. Both Powhatan and Opechancanough, cousins and future paramount chiefs, are old enough to witness or participate in the killings. This has led some scholars to conclude that all three were related, and some to speculate that Velasco was either Powhatan or Opechancanough.

1584

An expedition funded by Walter Raleigh reaches the Outer Banks of present-day North Carolina. Walter Raleigh names the country Virginia in honor of Elizabeth I, the "Virgin Queen," and in return he is knighted.

1585

Raleigh sends another group of adventurers to Roanoke. The group returns home the following spring with Francis Drake, though the work of John White and Thomas Harriot will continue to increase English interest in the region.

1587

Raleigh sends out another larger group of adventurers, this time intending to stay, under the leadership of John White. White, however, returns with the ship. Hostilities with Spain (including the famous 1588 naval battle) prevent a supply ship from reaching the colony for four years. By the time White returns, the settlement has been abandoned, and the word "Croatoan" has been scratched into a stockade post. The fate of the colonists is unclear. They may have been killed by local natives or assimilated into a native community, only to be destroyed when Powhatan conquered the region in the first decade of the seventeenth century.

1606

Sir Ferdinando Gorges, Sir John Popham, and Richard Hakluyt, among others, convince King James I to charter the Virginia Company, whose branches, the Plymouth Company and the London Company, will be responsible for establishing colonies in Massachusetts and Virginia respectively. The

London Company is made up of merchants, lawyers, and other well-to-do men and is designed as a joint-stock company.

1607

Around 100 men and boys arrive in Virginia on the *Susan Constant* and establish Jamestown, named after the monarch. Company officials instruct the colonists not to let Native Americans see them die, thinking the natives perceive the English to be immortal.

Professional soldier John Smith, later appointed leader of the colony, is captured in December 1607. He is shown about Powhatan's territory and finally meets the paramount chief. Through a series of rituals, Powhatan accepts Smith's, and the English, presence in Tsenacommacah, perhaps sensing they will make allies in his effort to subdue the Monacan. In the last of these rituals, Smith is symbolically rescued from death by Pocahontas, Powhatan's young daughter.

From 1607 to 1622, the Virginia Company transports 10,000 people to Virginia, and only about 20 percent of these manage to stay alive. Of the first 100 colonists, fewer than 40 survive their first winter; in the winter of 1609–1610, 160 of the 220 colonists perish. The Jamestown colonists die (of malaria and other diseases, salt poisoning, and starvation) because of their colony's poor location on a stagnant swamp. One woman is killed by her starving husband and subsequently eaten. To compound all of these tragedies, many of the colonists refuse to plant crops or work, insisting on searching for gold instead. John Smith does eventually force the colonists to plant food, but he returns to England in 1609.

1610

Thomas West, Lord De La Warr, takes charge of the Jamestown colony and forces colonists to work, assigning each one a specific task with a work schedule.

1611

Sir Thomas Gates and Sir Thomas Dale are appointed to lead Jamestown, and Dale, drawing on both civil and military law, establishes a code of laws that will become the "Lawes Divine, Morall, and Martiall." Though Virginia colonists die at a slightly slower pace, the company continues to lose money.

1613

Tension between the Powhatan people and the English subsides after Samuel Argall takes Pocahontas hostage.

1614

John Rolfe produces four experimental barrels of tobacco for export to London. Fashionable English people have developed a taste for the plant, and Rolfe uses a West Indian variety, *Nicotiana tabacum*, in favor of the more bitter native plant. King James I denounces tobacco as unhealthy and disgusting, but his warnings have little effect. By 1617,

Virginia planters are shipping around 50,000 pounds of tobacco annually, and the tobacco explosion is just getting started. In 1624, Virginia exports 200,000 pounds, and by 1638, this figure is 3 million. Tobacco begins to operate as currency in colonial Virginia—it can purchase goods and services, pay debts, and provide salaries for colonial officials.

Pocahontas and John Rolfe wed, and tensions between the English and Powhatan peoples, who have been fighting almost continuously, ease yet further. Pocahontas returns to England with Rolfe. Taking the name Rebecca and accepting baptism, she becomes the talk of the town in London; she dies there in 1617.

1617

In an effort to attract more colonists, the Virginia Company institutes a "headright" system, which assures 50 acres of land to any man able to pay his own way to the colony, and 50 additional acres for each dependent he brings with him.

1618

The Virginia Company undertakes a large-scale recovery effort. The colony has yet to make its investors any money, and the company is near bankruptcy. Edwin Sandys becomes treasurer and promptly replaces the earlier military laws with ones more closely reflective of English common law. He also attracts new settlers, including more women, to Virginia.

Powhatan dies, and his chiefdom passes to his brother or cousin Opechancanough. The new chief is less willing to accommodate English expansion than his predecessor, especially since English settlements are expanding rapidly beyond the territory originally granted them by Powhatan.

1619

Governor Yeardley, a Sandys appointee, convenes an assembly at Jamestown. Yeardley meets with his six appointed councilors, and twenty elected representatives known as burgesses. The House of Burgesses, the first elected representative body in English America, will continue to meet until 1775.

A Dutch captain trading in Jamestown sells "twenty Negars" to Virginia planters. The legal status of the first Africans in Virginia is not precisely clear. In the first half of the seventeenth century, chattel slavery is not the only labor option. Some Africans work toward their freedom, and a few—most notably Anthony Johnson—even own their own tobacco plantations. This will become increasingly rare as slavery takes root during the second half of the seventeenth century and Virginia society begins to divide along strict racial lines.

Among the first acts of the General Assembly is a provision delineating the status of indentured servants. Not surprisingly, colonial laws perceive indentured servitude as a harsher form of apprenticeship and usually favor the master, although servants do have access to courts. Most indentures last from four to seven years, and indentured servants can be bought, sold, and willed like other forms of property.

1622

In what Anglo-Virginians will call the "Great Massacre," Opechancanough leads a furious assault on settlements that he feels have extended too far up the James River. To prove a point, some of the Powhatan use the farmers' own tools to kill them. Some scholars view this as an attempt to rid Virginia of the English altogether, but the intention was probably to keep English settlements within reasonable boundaries.

The attack has devastating consequences for the English colonists, 347 of whom—about one-third of the population—die in the attack. The colonists launch a series of counterattacks to open up new lands to English settlement, severely weakening their native neighbors, including groups who had nothing to do with the attack.

The Virginia Company leadership is devastated by news of the attack and never fully recovers from the shock. James I initiates *quo warranto* ("by what authority") proceedings, which will force the company to prove it should be allowed to continue operations. James I's untimely death in 1625 brings King Charles I to the throne; shortly thereafter, he declares Virginia to be a royal colony and removes the Virginia Company from control.

1634

Virginia organizes into counties, which become the main political units of the colony. County-level courts handle civil matters, and their decisions can be appealed to the General Assembly. Each county receives some appointed officials, including justices of the peace, sheriffs, clerks, and deputies.

1639

King Charles I secures the uncertain future of the Virginia general assembly when he authorizes it to continue. The assembly had been meeting regularly under his appointed governor, but with no official legal sanction since the Virginia Company's removal from power.

1644–1646

In another effort to punish English encroachment, Opechancanough, now around 100 years old, orders an attack on English settlements. The English respond quickly and capture the old warrior. To increase his own prestige, Governor William Berkeley intends to send Opechancanough to England, but is unable to do so, as one of the men guarding the prisoner shoots the chief in the back.

In 1646, treaty negotiations take place that give most of Tsenacommacah over to the English. The Powhatan people, now led by Necotowance, accept the sovereignty of the English king. They do not, however, give up their own sovereignty in the reservations that the treaty provides for them.

1651

England's civil war reaches Virginia when Governor Berkeley, a staunch supporter of the Stuarts, refuses to meet with a Puritan commission sent by the Commonwealth government. The commission threatens to attack the capital, and Berkeley backs down. Oliver Cromwell's Puritan regime has relatively little effect on the government and everyday life in Virginia.

1662

The General Assembly begins to define the legal status of Virginia's African slaves, who are steadily growing in number—though nothing like the population explosion of the eighteenth century.

1675–1676

Nathaniel Bacon leads a revolt against Berkeley's government. Bacon—incidentally, a second cousin of Berkeley—is an extraordinarily wealthy recent arrival in the Chesapeake. His plantations and those of his neighbors, near present-day Richmond, are the scene of hostilities between planters and a group of Doeg Indians, pressured by the expansion of English plantations. Bacon and his followers are upset by what they perceive to be Berkeley's lax Indian policies, which they believe favor his friends in the fur trade and do not provide enough money for defense.

Bacon and his followers retaliate against the Doeg— who are responding to a corrupt deal with a local planter— but they also kill fourteen Susquehannocks, a linguistically Iroquoian people who had been at peace with the Virginia colony for decades. The Susquehannock attack Virginia in the winter of 1675–1676, and kill thirty-six colonists. Western Virginians in turn attack some reservations of the Appomattox and Pamunkeys. Nathaniel Bacon rises to the fore of a movement that calls for the destruction of the region's native peoples. Berkeley refuses Bacon a commission for this purpose, but Bacon goes ahead anyway.

Following a series of attacks on Native Americans, Bacon turns his army toward Jamestown and captures the capital in September 1676, sending Berkeley to the Eastern shore, where he awaits the arrival of royal troops. Bacon dies of dysentery in October and his rebellion collapses shortly thereafter. The effects on Virginia society are much longer lasting. Virginia comes to be dominated by a class of great planters who are more responsive than their predecessors to those they govern. Racial solidarity becomes the order of the day, and the tributary Native Americans suffer a crushing defeat.

1677–1680s

The royal commission sent to smash Bacon's Rebellion runs into trouble with Berkeley and his cronies, who refuse to give up their government or pardon lesser rebels, as King Charles II has instructed. The new military commander, Sir Herbert Jeffreys, makes a mess of Virginia's government. His immediate successors—Culpeper and Lord Effingham, both of whom clash with the great planters—fare no better. All of these administrations are marred by legislative wrangling. By the close of the 1680s, Virginia's planter class grudgingly accepts its subservient position to England, whose hand has become increasingly strong in colonial affairs.

The issue of founding towns comes up repeatedly. The Crown prefers that Virginia settle at least one town on every river. Trade could then flow through these set points, thus making the Navigation Acts easier to enforce. Some Virginians advocate the founding of towns, since they believe the presence of towns will encourage manufacturing in the colony. In fact, the steady rise of a plantation society with its attendant risks and profits retards the development of any seriously concentrated settlements, in marked contrast to the Massachusetts Bay Colony farther to the north.

1690

Francis Nicholson serves as deputy governor from 1690 to 1692. He works closely with the leading men in Virginia and uses his military experience to reorganize the colony's defenses.

1691

The assembly, the first after the Glorious Revolution that put William and Mary on the throne, convenes and sends Reverend James Blair to England to secure a charter for a college. Blair spends more than a year in England garnering support and donations for the college. Funds are also raised in Virginia; in 1693, the College of William and Mary receives its royal charter. Construction begins on a building in 1695, and the search for a faculty starts in 1700.

1693

Edmund Andros, who had been imprisoned in Massachusetts at the end of the Dominion period, is transferred by King William III to govern Virginia. He eventually comes into conflict with James Blair and other council members and burgesses. He sends money to aid in the defense of New York and ends up dissolving the legislature on two separate occasions. Andros and Blair butt heads repeatedly, and Blair is removed from the council and reinstated intermittently.

1696

A new committee, the Lords Commissioners of Trade and Plantations, known as the Board of Trade, meets in London to oversee colonial affairs. Notable members include William Blathwayt and John Locke. The Board of Trade finds that Andros has badly mismanaged Virginia and abused his power. Francis Nicholson, a friend of James Blair, is tapped to replace Andros.

1697

The tobacco market, which has slowed during King William's War, strengthens during the period before Queen Anne's War. Three thousand African slaves come to Virginia during this five-year span, and more than a million acres of land are sold.

1698

The Crown cancels the monopoly the Royal African Company has held on the importation of slaves into British colonies. The Royal African Company focuses most of its efforts on transporting African slaves to the sugar-rich West Indies, but the decision officially opens up the Atlantic slave trade with Virginia to private enterprise. By the close of the seventeenth century, Africans comprise around 10,000 of Virginia's total population of roughly 75,000. Most of these slaves labor on tobacco plantations on the Northern Neck and the land between the James and York Rivers.

1699

Francis Nicholson adjourns the General Assembly to Middle Plantation, where construction has already begun on the College of William and Mary. Nicholson intends to design a new capital for Virginia, as he had previously in Annapolis during his stay in Maryland. Williamsburg is to be the beneficiary of the latest Enlightenment urban design, in which radial streets converge at the capitol, the church, and the college.

Nicholson is charged with implementing reforms demanded by the Board of Trade. Chief among these concerns are the increasing size of individual plantations in place of a farming middle class and the holding of multiple offices by individuals. Nicholson tries to end the headright bonanza for large slave owners but is thwarted by the council, and the Board of Trade eventually rescinds the order. Nicholson does succeed in increasing royal revenues from Virginia.

1702

Queen Anne's War—the War of the Spanish Succession in Europe—breaks out between ancient adversaries England and France, and Virginia is required to send 240 men and money to New York. The burgesses refuse to do so. Nicholson is gradually losing control over the planter class that has previously supported him.

1703

Six council members, including James Blair, petition Queen Anne to remove Nicholson. The ensuing conflict pits Nicholson, the burgesses, the clerical community, and some militia companies against Blair and the council. In 1705, Nicholson is transferred to Nova Scotia; he will also serve in South Carolina later in his career. The new governor—technically a lieutenant governor—is Edward Nott, who allows the council to run things and dies after just a year in office.

1705

Robert Beverley publishes *The History and Present State of Virginia, in Four Parts* (revised and republished in 1722). He criticizes Virginians for not establishing towns for industry and commerce, and relying on Great Britain for manufactured goods. He also describes the development of the institution of plantation slavery, which he compares favorably to the lives of white laborers in England and the colonies.

1710

Alexander Spotswood becomes lieutenant governor, and reinstates the House of Burgesses, although he is displeased with the low quality of men that Virginians elect.

1712

Responding to a Tuscarora attack on colonists in North Carolina, Spotswood begins to negotiate with friendly native groups with the intention of forming a buffer against attack. Money for a military expedition gets tied up in a battle between the burgesses and the council.

1716

Sixty-three horsemen known as the Knights of the Golden Horseshoe mount an expedition across the Blue Ridge. Accompanying the rangers are native scouts, servants, and historians. The adventure serves as a public relations coup, signaling that the western portion of Virginia is available for Anglo-American settlement.

1717

Governor Spotswood makes great strides toward ending piracy by sending Robert Maynard on an expedition against Edward Teach, or "Blackbeard," who is operating off the North Carolina coast. Maynard and his men kill Teach and execute thirteen of the crewmen they capture.

1718

Elections reflect the rising power of the lower house of the legislature. Men who openly oppose the policies of the governor are elected, and many of the burgesses favor petitioning the king against Spotswood. He in turn succeeds in having some of his fiercest opposition removed from the council. Spotswood, who to this point has acted very much like a royal appointee, also begins to speculate on western lands like his planter subordinates.

1720

Construction is finally completed on Governor Spotswood's palace, among the most sophisticated and elegant structures in British America. The great planters, not to be outdone by the governor's lavish residence, inaugurate a new golden age of great house construction along Virginia's rivers. Among these are William Byrd II's Westover, Robert Carter II's Nomini Hall, and Landon Carter's Sabine Hall.

From this time into the 1730s, Virginia planters begin to diversify their crops. Though tobacco will remain the most profitable export, more planters will turn to the production of cereal grains, which are not subject to the same violent price swings.

1721

Wary of upsetting the balance of power between native communities in and around Virginia, Governor Spotswood negotiates a treaty with the Iroquois. It stipulates that they will stay north of the Potomac and west of the Blue Ridge, provided that southern tribes honor the same line.

1730

Governor William Gooch proposes an act for the inspection of tobacco. The bill calls for the inspection of tobacco at public warehouses, the destruction of inferior tobacco, and generally standardizes the tobacco industry. After an intense struggle, the bill passes both houses of the legislature and receives royal support in 1731.

1732

Opponents of the Tobacco Act riot, destroying warehouses full of tobacco. The action moves many of the great planters, who detest such disorderly conduct, to support Gooch's plan. The Tobacco Act stands as an example of how a colony and the empire can both benefit from prudent economic policies. Things go smoothly as long as tobacco prices stay high, which they do from the 1730s to the 1750s.

The House of Burgesses invites William Parks to fulfill the newly created post of public printer. In 1736, Parks founds colonial Virginia's first newspaper, the *Virginia Gazette*.

1736

The town of Norfolk, home to many Scottish tobacco factors, is incorporated. Williamsburg and Jamestown are the only other incorporated towns in Virginia.

1740

About 400 Virginians, drawn from a wide range of colonial society, participate in the botched British attack on Cartagena during the War of the Austrian Succession. Governor Gooch is crippled for life by a cannonball, but many of his men are not so lucky. About half of the colonial force lose their lives to yellow fever and other diseases.

1747

The capitol building in Williamsburg burns. Some leading Virginians want to move the capital to more closely reflect the shifting population of Virginia, but the building is rebuilt, and Williamsburg remains the capital for several more decades.

1748–1749

The Virginia Assembly undertakes a large-scale restructuring of the colony's laws. Several of these laws are disallowed by the Board of Trade, but word of the disallowance takes years to reach Virginia. Great Britain is taking new interest in colonial administration, but the process is slow and inefficient.

1749

The Ohio Company's huge land grant in the Ohio River Valley is confirmed by the Privy Council. Thomas Lee, acting as governor, declares that the area will be a boon to settlement and a way to block French aspirations.

1751

Robert Dinwiddie becomes governor and institutes a quit-rent tax on the land claimed by speculators. Not surprisingly, his actions create an uproar in the House of Burgesses, which claims in 1754 that such a tax hinders settlement and violates the rights of landowners. The Privy Council in London determines that Dinwiddie has the right to impose a tax, but limits the effectiveness of the tax so as to render it negligible.

1754

The French and Indian War, the American theater of the worldwide Seven Years' War between France and Great Britain, begins in a dispute over the Ohio River Valley. Prominent members of the Ohio Company include Governor Dinwiddie, George Washington, Richard Henry Lee, and George Mason. The French move in the early 1750s to secure their claim to the region. Virginia responds by dispatching George Washington, who attacks a small group of French soldiers led by Joseph Coulon, Sieur de Jumonville, who dies in the attack. Washington proceeds to build Fort Necessity, which he later surrenders to a much larger French force.

1755

General Braddock lands at Alexandria with two regiments of British regulars. A combined force of British regulars and American militia, including George Washington, launches an ill-conceived attack on Fort Duquesne (near present-day Pittsburgh). The attack fails miserably, and with Braddock dead, Washington leads a quick retreat. In 1758, thanks largely to the leadership of Prime Minister William Pitt, the Elder, and Sir William Johnson's close ties to the Mohawk, the momentum shifts to the British.

1759

Parliament disallows two laws that permit Virginians to pay their clergymen in currency instead of tobacco. Parliament also issues a warning concerning the growing power of the General Assembly. This is a victory for the clergy, but a resulting court case, argued by Patrick Henry, awards dam-

ages of one penny. Henry uses the 1764 case against Reverend James Maury to argue against Parliament and the king as well as to advance his own political career.

1763

The Treaty of Paris ends the Seven Years' War, known as the French and Indian War in the colonies, which essentially removes France from North America. In the aftermath of the conflict, England faces a massive war debt, a postwar depression, and the challenge of defending and administering all of its new lands. One measure, the Proclamation of 1763, angers Virginia's elite, many of whom hold huge quantities of land over the mountains, in anticipation of a stream of white settlers.

1765

The British Parliament passes the Stamp Act, which requires a stamp—indicating that a tax has been paid—on legal documents, newspapers, pamphlets, and broadsides. The act ignites a firestorm of protest in the colonies. In Virginia, the reaction is somewhat more subdued. Petitions and letters are drafted by leading men and sent to British officials.

The mid-1760s are particularly lean years for Virginia's planter class, which finds itself in a downward spiral of debt and low tobacco prices. This probably contributes to that usually conservative group's adoption of radical, even revolutionary, ideas.

Led by Patrick Henry, among others, the assembly considers a series of Stamp Act resolves, which declare that the people of Virginia are not subject to taxes they do not approve in their colonial assembly, and that any person who upholds the authority of Parliament should be labeled an enemy of Virginia. The conservative leadership in the assembly does not support Henry's assertions, and Governor Fauquier dissolves the assembly. Local protests do emerge on the Northern Neck, with effigies of stamp distributors hanged and burned. The *Gazette* suspends operations rather than pay for stamps, and several courts open for business without the required stamps. The Stamp Act does go into effect in some parts of Virginia, but it will be repealed in 1766.

1766

British Parliament passes the Declaratory Act, a reminder to the colonies that it retains complete legislative authority over them.

Also, in a blow to the old-school politics of Virginia's elite, John Robinson, longtime Speaker of the House of Burgesses, dies. It is discovered that he had been using retired currency to loan to friends and political associates.

1767–1769

Charles Townshend, Chancellor of the Exchequer, proposes new duties to raise money. The Townshend Duties include taxes on paint, paper, and tea. Reaction to the duties in Virginia is more muted than during the Stamp Act crisis, but Virginia does sign on to the circular letter sent by Massachusetts. Virginia merchants agree not to import goods from Great Britain, and to favor goods produced in Virginia. There are relatively few British troops stationed in Virginia, and there are few aggressive British officials there, so the movement toward independence and revolution takes shape more slowly and along different lines than it does in Massachusetts, for instance.

1770

Under the leadership of Lord North, Parliament repeals all of the Townshend Duties, save for that on tea, which remains as a symbol of Parliament's right to tax the colonies in any manner it sees fit.

The inspector general for the American Board of Customs Commissioners arrives in Virginia and complains about the amount of tobacco exported illegally from the colony.

1771

The Earl of Dunmore, the new royal governor, arrives in Virginia, and immediately runs into trouble with the people of Virginia. His administration is further hampered by a deepening financial crisis, which causes some British merchants to attempt to collect on planter debt, which, in turn, pushes the planters toward a more revolutionary position.

1773

In the Tea Act, Parliament lowers the duty on tea, but colonists perceive this as another measure designed to interfere with their trade. Massachusetts is hardest hit by the Coercive Acts that follow, but Virginia and the other colonies pitch in to help Boston, which has its harbor shut down by the British.

1774

Meetings—sometimes referred to as committees of correspondence—occur throughout Virginia to determine an appropriate response to British actions in Boston. Several meetings decide they will shut down local courts to hurt the cases of British creditors. Many meetings also enter into more stringent nonimportation agreements. In the Continental Congress, Peyton Randolph and Richard Henry Lee argue for limiting the consumption of luxury goods, widespread nonimportation of British goods, and the formation of a Continental Association that would draw representatives from each of Britain's American colonies. Virginia's counties also begin to form independent militia companies.

1775

In a March convention, Patrick Henry, advocating the raising of regiments for Virginia, concludes a speech with the memorable phrase, "Give me liberty, or give me death!"

Lord Dunmore's proclamation offers freedom to any slaves who desert their masters and serve the British military. It is unclear how many slaves take advantage of this, but thousands of slaves will fight on each side during the War for Independence, despite the Continental army's often-ignored prohibition, and many will earn their freedom as a result.

Lord Dunmore also moves his government, along with some royal and loyalist forces, to Norfolk. As Virginia's governor, Patrick Henry stations his troops in Williamsburg. In December, the forces collide at Great Bridge, and the British are forced to withdraw to Norfolk's harbor. American forces ransack the loyalist town.

1776

Dunmore's forces evacuate Virginia for New York. On May 14, formal debate begins in Virginia regarding the colony's independence. The next day, a resolution passes that declares Virginia an independent state. Virginia, England's oldest colony, provides much of the leadership during and after the War for Independence. Richard Henry Lee, Peyton Randolph, George Washington, Thomas Jefferson, George Mason, and James Madison all contribute greatly to the American effort.

Matthew Jennings

General Index

F

G

K

Biographical Index

Geographical Index

Colonial America

AN ENCYCLOPEDIA OF SOCIAL, POLITICAL, CULTURAL, AND ECONOMIC HISTORY

Volume Five

EDITED BY JAMES CIMENT

WITH AN INTRODUCTION BY
MICHAEL ZUCKERMAN, UNIVERSITY OF PENNSYLVANIA

SHARPE REFERENCE
an imprint of M.E. Sharpe, Inc.

SHARPE REFERENCE

Sharpe Reference is an imprint of M.E. Sharpe, Inc.

M.E. Sharpe, Inc.
80 Business Park Drive
Armonk, NY 10504

© 2006 by M.E. Sharpe, Inc.

Cover Photo: Tontine Coffee House, c. 1797 (oil on linen), Francis Guy (1760–1820) / © New York Historical Society, New York, United States; www.bridgeman.co.uk.

Maps: Adapted by Carto-Graphics from the following sources:

Kwame Anthony Appiah and Henry Louis Gates, Jr., eds., *Africana: The Encyclopedia of the African and African American Experience* (New York: Basic Books, 1999). See map: Volume 3, page 788.

Geoffrey Barraclough, ed., *The Times Atlas of World History,* 6th edition (Maplewood, NJ: Hammond, 1982). See maps: Volume 1, pages xlii, xliii, 15, 214; Volume 2, pages xx, xxi; Volume 3, pages xx, xxi; Volume 4, pages xx, xxi, 850; Volume 5, pages xx, xxi.

James Ciment, ed. *Encyclopedia of American Immigration* (Armonk, NY: M.E. Sharpe, 2001). See map: Volume 1, page 55.

James Henretta, et al. *America's History.* 2nd edition (New York: Worth Publishers, 1993). See maps: Volume 1, pages xli, xlii, xliii, 59; Volume 2, pages xix, xx, xxi, 327, 362; Volume 3, pages xix, xx, xxi, 581, 738, 788; Volume 4, pages xix, xx, xxi; Volume 5, pages xix, xx, xxi.

Mary Beth Norton, et al. *A People and a Nation.* 6th edition (Boston: Houghton Mifflin, 2001). See maps: Volume 1, pages xliv, xlv; Volume 2, pages xxii, xxiii, 324; Volume 3, pages xxii, xxiii, 812; Volume 4, pages xxii, xxiii.

Library of Congress Cataloging-in-Publication Data

Colonial America: An encyclopedia of social, political, cultural, and economic history/James Ciment, editor.
    p. cm.
  Includes bibliographical references and index.
  ISBN 0-7656-8065-3 (Set: alk. paper)
  1. United States—Civilization—To 1783—Encyclopedias. I. Ciment, James.

E162.C68 2005
973.2′03—dc22
                                               2003023235

Printed and bound in the United States of America

Publisher: Myron E. Sharpe
Vice President and Editorial Director: Patricia Kolb
Vice President and Production Director: Carmen Chetti
Executive Editor and Manager of Reference: Todd Hallman
Senior Development Editor: Jeff Hacker
Project Editor: Laura Brengelman
Program Coordinator: Cathleen J. Prisco
Text Design: Carmen Chetti and Jesse Sanchez
Cover Design: Jesse Sanchez

Contents

iii

List of Maps

VOLUME 5

Topic Finder

Biographies

British Colonies

Religion

Maps

ARCTIC OCEAN

BERING SEA

ALEUT

INUIT

TLINGIT

HAIDA

TSIMSHIAN

DENE

DOGRIB

CHIPEWYAN

CREE

BLACKFOOT

SALISH

NOOTKA

KOOTENAI

CROW

NEZ PERCE

ASSINIBOINE

OJIBWA (CHIPPEWA)

DAKOTA (SIOUX)

CHEYENNE

PAWNEE

PAIUTE

SHOSHONE

IOWA

POMO

ARAPAHO

UTE

KIOWA

YOKUT

NAVAJO

PUEBLO

PAPAGO

HOPI PUEBLO

APACHE PUEBLO

COCHIMI

PIMA

COAHUILTEC

ZACATEC

Hudson Bay

INUIT

INUIT

NASKAPI

MONTAGNAIS

BEOTHUK

CREE

ALGONQUIN

MICMAC

ABENAKI

HURON

IROQUOIS

MOHAWK

ONONDAGA

CAYUGA

SENECA

ONEIDA

ERIE

SAUK

OTTAWA

POTAWATOMI

SUSQUEHANNOCK

LENNI LENAPE (DELAWARE)

NARRAGANSETT

PEQUOT

ATLANTIC OCEAN

PACIFIC OCEAN

ILLINOIS

SHAWNEE

POWHATAN

TUSCARORA

Roanoke (English, 1587)

CHEROKEE

CHICKASAW

NATCHEZ

YAMASEE

COMANCHE

CHOCTAW

CREEK

St. Augustine

CALUSA

LUCAYO

Rio Grande River

Gulf of Mexico

SEMINOLE

Havana

CIBONEY

SUB TAINO

ARAWAK

ARAWAK

TAINO

CARIB

Zacatecas

TOLTEC

Guadalajara

Tenocutitúan (Mexico City)

NAHUATL (AZTEC)

Acapulco

Vera Cruz

Mérida

MIXTEC

MAYA

Santo Domingo

CARIBBEAN SEA

ZAPOTEC

MISKITO

Guatemala

CUNA

Panama

GUAYMI

Spanish

0   500   1000 Miles

0   500   1000 Kilometers

North America, 1600. The above map shows the multiplicity of native peoples on the North American continent in 1600, as well as the extensive Spanish presence in Mexico, Central America, the Caribbean, and southwestern portions of what is now the United States. Note that the English colony of Roanoke mysteriously disappeared shortly after its establishment in 1587. *(Carto-Graphics)*

North America, 1700. The above map shows the presence of European colonial powers on the North American continent circa 1700. Note that the presence of Europeans varied: British holdings in the Hudson Bay region were little more than claims on maps, while settlements along the Atlantic seaboard of what is now the United States included tens of thousands of European settlers and African slaves, as well as the remaining native peoples. *(Carto-Graphics)*

North America, 1775. The above map shows the presence of European colonial powers on the North American continent on the eve of the American Revolution. Note that some regions—particularly in the heart of Mexico and along the Atlantic seaboard of what is now the United States—were more heavily populated by colonists than other areas. *(Carto-Graphics)*

European Settlement Areas, Eastern North America, 1650. The above map shows the thin line of European settlements along the Atlantic seaboard and the St. Lawrence River Valley. At the time, the total European and African populations in the British colonies stood at about 50,000, with a few thousand more in the Dutch, French, and Spanish colonies. *(Carto-Graphics)*

British Colonies, Mainland North America, 1765. By 1750, British settlements on mainland North America had pushed westward to the eastern edge of the Appalachian Mountains. The population of the thirteen colonies in 1750 was roughly 1.2 million, including about a quarter of a million slaves. *(Carto-Graphics)*

Colonial America

Volume Five

Documents

Columbus's Letter Announcing His Discoveries in the New World (1493)

Christopher Columbus transmitted his discoveries in the New World to Luis de Sant' Angel, the treasurer of Aragon. Sant' Angel was instrumental in securing the Spanish monarch's endorsement for Columbus's expedition, especially when it did not seem that support would be forthcoming. This letter was written aboard the *Niña* during Columbus's return trip to Spain. It is the first official account of the voyage and was almost certainly shared with King Ferdinand and Queen Isabella.

SIR:

As I know you will be rejoiced at the glorious success that our Lord has given me in my voyage, I write this to tell you how in thirty-three days I sailed to the Indies with the fleet that the illustrious King and Queen, our Sovereigns, gave me, where I discovered a great many islands, inhabited by numberless people; and of all I have taken possession for their Highnesses by proclamation and display of the Royal Standard without opposition. To the first island I discovered I gave the name of San Salvador, in commemoration of His Divine Majesty, who has wonderfully granted all this. The Indians call it Guanaham. The second I named the Island of Santa Maria de Concepcion; the third, Fernandina; the fourth, Isabella; the fifth, Juana; and thus to each one I gave a new name. When I came to Juana, I followed the coast of that isle toward the west, and found it so extensive that I thought it might be the mainland, the province of Cathay; and as I found no towns nor villages on the sea-coast, except a few small settlements, where it was impossible to speak to the people, because they fled at once, I continued the said route, thinking I could not fail to see some great cities or towns; and finding at the end of many leagues that nothing new appeared, and that the coast led northward, contrary to my wish, because the winter had already set in, I decided to make for the south, and as the wind also was against my proceeding, I determined not to wait there longer, and turned back to a certain harbor whence I sent two men to find out whether there was any king or large city. They explored for three days, and found countless small communities and people, without number, but with no kind of government, so they returned.

I heard from other Indians I had already taken that this land was an island, and thus followed the eastern coast for one hundred and seven leagues, until I came to the end of it. From that point I saw another isle to the eastward, at eighteen leagues' distance, to which I gave the name of Hispaniola. I went thither and followed its northern coast to the east, as I had done in Juana, one hundred and seventy-eight leagues eastward, as in Juana. This island, like all the others, is most extensive. It has many ports along the sea-coast excelling any in Christendom—and many fine, large, flowing rivers. The land there is elevated, with many mountains and peaks incomparably higher than in the centre isle. They are most beautiful, of a thousand varied forms, accessible, and full of trees of endless varieties, so high that they seem to touch the sky, and I have been told that they never lose their foliage. I saw them as green and lovely as trees are in Spain in the month of May. Some of them were covered with blossoms, some with fruit, and some in other conditions, according to their kind. The nightingale and other small birds of a thousand kinds were singing in the month of November when I was there. There were palm trees of six or eight varieties, the graceful peculiarities of each one of them being worthy of admiration as are the other trees, fruits and grasses. There are wonderful pine woods, and very extensive ranges of meadow land. There is honey, and there are many kinds of birds, and a great variety of fruits. Inland there are numerous mines of metals and innumerable people. Hispaniola is a marvel. Its hills and mountains, fine plains and open country, are rich and fertile for planting and for pasturage, and for building towns and villages. The seaports there are incredibly fine, as also the magnificent rivers, most of which bear gold. The trees, fruits and grasses differ widely from those in Juana. There are many spices and vast mines of gold and other metals in this island. They have no iron, nor steel, nor weapons, nor are they fit for them, because although they are well-made men of commanding stature, they appear extraordinarily timid. The only arms they have are sticks of cane, cut when in seed, with a sharpened stick at the end, and they are afraid to use these. Often I have sent two or three men ashore to some town to converse with them, and the natives came out in great numbers, and as soon as they saw our men arrive, fled without a moment's delay although I protected them from all injury.

At every point where I landed, and succeeded in talking to them, I gave them some of everything I had—cloth and many other things—without receiving anything in return, but they are a hopelessly timid people. It is true that since they have gained more confidence and are losing this fear, they are so unsuspicious and so generous with what they possess, that no one who had not seen it would believe it. They never refuse anything that is asked for. They even offer it themselves, and show so much love that they would give their very hearts. Whether it be anything of great or small value, with any trifle of whatever kind, they are satisfied. I forbade worthless things being given to them, such as bits of broken bowls, pieces of glass, and old straps, although they were as much pleased to get them as if they were the finest jewels in the world. One sailor was found to have got for a leathern strap, gold of the weight of two and a half castellanos, and others for even more worthless things much more; while for a new blancas they would give all they had, were it two or three castellanos of pure gold or an arroba or two of spun cotton. Even bits of the broken hoops of wine casks they accepted, and gave in return what they had, like fools, and it seemed wrong to me. I forbade it, and gave a thousand good and pretty things that I had to win their love, and to induce them to become Christians, and to love and serve their Highness and the whole Castilian nation, and help to got for us things they have in abundance, which are necessary to us. They have no religion, nor idolatry, except that they all believe power and goodness to be in heaven. They firmly believed that I, with my ships and men, came from heaven, and with this idea I have been received everywhere, since they lost fear of me. They are, however, far from being ignorant. They are most ingenious men, and navigate these seas in a wonderful way, and describe everything well, but they never before saw people wearing clothes, nor vessels like ours. Directly I reached the Indies in the first isle I discovered, I took by force some of the natives, that from them we might gain some information of what there was in these parts; and so it was that we immediately understood each other, either by words or signs. They are still with me and still believe that I come from heaven. They were the first to declare this wherever I went, and the others ran from house to house, and to the towns around, crying out, "Come! come! and see the men from heaven!" Then all, both men and women, as soon as they were reassured about us, came, both small and great, all bringing something to eat and to drink, which they presented with marvellous kindness. In these isles there are a great many canoes, something like rowing boats, of all sizes, and most of them are larger than an eighteen-oared galley. They are not so broad, as they are

made of a single plank, but a galley could not keep up with them in rowing, because they go with incredible speed, and with these they row about among all these islands, which are innumerable, and carry on their commerce. I have seen some of these canoes with seventy and eighty men in them, and each had an oar. In all the islands I observed little difference in the appearance of the people, or in their habits and language, except that they understand each other, which is remarkable. Therefore I hope that their Highnesses will decide upon the conversion of these people to our holy faith, to which they seem much inclined.

I have already stated how I sailed one hundred and seven leagues along the sea-coast of Juana, in a straight line from west to east. I can therefore assert that this island is larger than England and Scotland together, since beyond these one hundred and seven leagues there remained at the west point two provinces where I did not go, one of which they call Avan, the home of men with tails. These provinces are computed to be fifty or sixty leagues in length, as far as can be gathered from the Indians with me who are acquainted with all these islands. This there, Hispaniola, is larger in circumference than all Spain from Catalonia to Fuentarabia in Biscay, since upon one of its four sides I sailed one hundred and eighty-eight leagues from west to east. This is worth having, and must on no account be given up. I have taken possession of all these islands, for their Highnesses, and all may be more extensive than I know, or can say, and I hold them for their Highnesses, who can command them as absolutely as the kingdoms of Castile. In Hispaniola, in the most convenient place, most accessible for the gold mines and all commerce with the mainland on this side or with that of the great Khan, on the other, with which there would be great trade and profit, I have taken possession of a large town, which I have named the City of Navidad. I began fortifications there which should be completed by this time, and I have left in it men enough to hold it, with arms, artillery, and previsions for more than a year; and a boat with a master seaman skilled in the arts necessary to make others; I am so friendly with the king of that country that he was proud to call me his brother and hold me as such. Even should he change his mind and wish to quarrel with my men, neither he nor his subjects know what arms are, nor wear clothes, as I have said. They are the most timid people in the world, so that only the men remaining there could destroy the whole region, and run no risk if they know how to behave themselves properly. In all these islands the men seem to be satisfied with one wife, except they allow as many as twenty to their chief or king. The women appear to me to work harder than the men, and so far I can hear they have nothing of their own, for I think I perceived that what one had others shared, especially food. In the islands so far, I have found no monsters, as some expected, but, on the contrary, they are people of very handsome appearance. They are not black as in Guinea, though their hair is straight and coarse, as it does not grow where the sun's rays are too ardent. And in truth the sun has extreme power here, since it is within twenty-six degrees of the equinoctial line. In these islands there are mountains where the cold this winter was very severe, but the people endure it from habit, and with the aid of the meat they eat with very hot spices.

As for monsters, I have found no trace of them except at the point in the second isle as one enters the Indies, which is inhabited by a people considered in all the isles as most ferocious, who eat human flesh. They possess many canoes, with which they overrun all the isles of India, stealing and seizing all they can. They are not worse looking than the others, except that they wear their hair long like women, and use bows and arrows of the same cane, with sharp stick at the end for want of iron, of which they have none. They are ferocious compared to these other races, who are extremely cowardly; but I only hear this from the others. They are said to make treaties of marriage with the women in the first isle to be met with coming from Spain to the Indies, where there are no men. These women have no feminine occupation, but use bows and arrows of cane like those before mentioned, and cover and arm themselves with plates of copper, of which they have a great quantity. Another island, I am told, is larger than Hispaniola, where the natives have no hair, and where there is countless gold; and from them all I bring Indians to testify to this. To speak, in conclusion, only of what has been done during this hurried voyage, their Highnesses will see that I can give them as much gold as they desire, if they will give me a little assistance, spices, cotton, as much as their Highnesses may command to be shipped, and mastic as much as their Highnesses choose to send for, which until now has only been found in Greece, in the isle of Chios, and the Signoria can get its own price for it; as

much lign-aloe as they command to be shipped, and as many slaves as they choose to send for, all heathens. I think I have found rhubarb and cinnamon. Many other things of value will be discovered by the men I left behind me, as I stayed nowhere when the wind allowed me to pursue my voyage, except in the City of Navidad, which I left fortified and safe. Indeed, I might have accomplished much more, had the crews served me as they ought to have done. The eternal and almighty God, our Lord, it is Who gives to all who walk in His way, victory over things apparently impossible, and in this case signally so, because although these lands had been imagined and talked of before they were seen, most men listened incredulously to what was thought to be but an idle tale. But our Redeemer has given victory to our most illustrious King and Queen, and to their Kingdoms rendered famous by this glorious event, at which all Christendom should rejoice, celebrating it with great festivities and solemn Thanksgivings to the Holy Trinity, with fervent prayers for the high distinction that will accrue to them from turning so many peoples to our holy faith; and also from the temporal benefits that not only Spain but all Christian nations will obtain.

Thus I record. What has happened in a brief note written on board the Caravel, off the Canary Isles, on the 15th of February, 1493.

Yours to command,
THE ADMIRAL.

Source: Charles W. Eliot, ed., *American Historical Documents, 1000–1904. Harvard Classics,* Vol. 43 (New York: P. F. Collier & Son, 1910).

John Cabot's Discovery of North America (1497)

John Cabot (Giovanni Caboto) was a Venetian citizen who settled in England in the 1480s among merchants interested in the discovery of new lands. With their financial support and a patent granted by King Henry VII, Cabot set sail aboard the *Matthew,* discovering the mainland of North America. England based its claims to North America on Cabot's discoveries. Contemporary accounts of Cabot's discoveries are detailed in these dispatches.

Letter from Lorenzo Pasqualigo to His Brothers Alvise and Francesco.[1]

London, 23rd August, 1497

Our Venetian, who went with a small ship from Bristol to find new islands, has come back, and says he has discovered, 700 leagues off, the mainland of the country of the Gran Cam, and that he coasted along it for 300 leagues, and landed, but did not see any person. But he has brought here to the king certain snares spread to take game, and a needle for making nets, and he found some notched trees, from which he judged that there were inhabitants. Being in doubt, he came back to the ship. He has been away three months on the voyage, which is certain, and, in returning, he saw two islands to the right, but he did not wish to land, lest he should lose time for he was in want of provisions. This king has been much pleased. He says that the tides are slack, and do not make currents as they do here. The king has promised for another time, ten armed ships as he desires, and has given him all the prisoners, except such as are confined for high treason, to go with him, as he has requested; and has granted him money to amuse himself till then. Meanwhile, he is with his Venetian wife and his sons at Bristol. His name is Zuam Talbot,[2] and he is called the Great Admiral, great honour being paid to him, and he goes dressed in silk. The English are ready to go with him, and so are many of our rascals. The discoverer of these things has planted a large cross in the ground with a banner of England, and one of St. Mark, as he is a Venetian; so that our flag has been hoisted very far away.

First Despatch of Raimondo di Soncino to the Duke of Milan.[3] (Extract.)

24th August, 1497

Some month afterwards His Majesty sent a Venetian, who is a distinguished sailor, and who was much skilled in the discovery of new islands, and he has returned safe, and has discovered two very large and fertile islands, having, it would seem, discovered the seven cities 400 leagues from England to the westward. These successes led His Majesty at once to entertain the intention of sending him with fifteen or twenty vessels.

Second Despatch of Raimondo di Soncino to the Duke of Milan.[4]

London, 18th December, 1497

My most illustrious and most excellent Lord,

Perhaps amidst so many occupations of your Excellency it will not be unwelcome to learn how this Majesty has acquired a part of Asia without drawing his sword. In this kingdom there is a certain Venetian named Zoanne Caboto, of gentle disposition, very expert in navigation, who, seeing that the most serene Kings of Portugal and Spain had occupied unknown islands, meditated the achievement of a similar acquisition for the said Majesty. Having obtained royal privileges securing to himself the use of the dominions he might discover, the sovereignty being reserved to the Crown, he entrusted his fortune to a small vessel with a crew of 18 persons, and set out from Bristo, a port in the western part of this kingdom. Having passed Ibernia, which is still further to the west, and then shaped a northerly course, he began to

1. Calendar of State Papers (Venice), i. p. 262, No. 752.
2. A misprint: "T" for "C."
3. Calendar of State Papers (Venice), iii. p. 260, No. 750.
4. Annuario Scientifico, Milan, 1866, p. 700; Archiv d'Etat Milan,

reprinted by Harrisse in his John Cabot, p. 324, from the Intorno of Desimoni, and translated from his text for the Hakluyt Society, with his permission.

navigate to the eastern part, leaving (during several days) the North Star on the right hand; and having wandered thus for a long time, at length he hit upon land, where he hoisted the royal standard, and took possession for his Highness, and, having obtained various proofs of his discovery, he returned. The said Messer Zoanne, being a foreigner and poor, would not have been believed if the crew, who are nearly all English, and belonging to Bristo, had not testified that what he said was the truth. This Messer Zoanne has the description of the world on a chart, and also on a solid sphere which he has constructed, and on which he shows where he has been; and, proceeding towards the east, he has passed as far as the country of the Tanais. And they say that there the land is excellent and [the climate?] temperate, suggesting that brasil and silk grow there. They affirm that the sea is full of fish, which are not only taken with a net, but also with a basket, a stone being fastened to it in order to keep it in the water; and this I have heard stated by the said Messer Zoanne.

The said Englishmen, his companions, say that they took so many fish that this kingdom will no longer have need of Iceland, from which country there is an immense trade in the fish they call stock-fish. But Messer Zoanne has set his mind on higher things, for he thinks that, when that place has been occupied, he will keep on still further towards the east, where he will be opposite to an island called Cipango, situated in the equinoctial region, where he believes that all the spices of the world, as well as the jewels, are found. He further says that he was once at Mecca, whither the spices are brought by caravans from distant countries; and having inquired from whence they were brought and where they grow, they answered that they did not know, but that such merchandize was brought from distant countries by other caravans to their home; and they further say that they are also conveyed from other remote regions. And he adduced this argument, that if the eastern people tell those in the south that these things come from a far distance from them, presupposing the rotundity of the earth, it must be that the last turn would be by the north towards the west;

and it is said that in this way the route would not cost more than it costs now, and I also believe it. And what is more, this Majesty, who is wise and not prodigal, reposes such trust in him because of what he has already achieved, that he gives him a good maintenance, as Messer Zoanne has himself told me. And it is said that before long his Majesty will arm some ships for him, and will give him all the malefactors to go to that country and form a colony, so that they hope to establish a greater depot of spices in London than there is in Alexandria. The principal people in the enterprise belong to Bristo. They are great seamen, and, now that they know where to go, they say that the voyage thither will not occupy more than 15 days after leaving Ibernia. I have also spoken with a Burgundian, who was a companion of Messer Zoanne, who affirms all this, and who wishes to return because the Admiral (for so Messer Zoanne is entitled) has given him an island, and has given another to his barber of Castione,[5] who is a Genoese, and both look upon themselves as Counts; nor do they look upon my Lord the Admiral as less than a Prince. I also believe that some poor Italian friars are going on this voyage, who have all had bishopricks promised to them. And if I had made friends with the Admiral when he was about to sail, I should have got an archbishoprick at least; but I have thought that the benefits reserved for me by your Excellency will be more secure. I would venture to pray that, in the event of a vacancy taking place in my absence, I may be put in possession, and that I may not be superseded by those who, being present, can be more diligent than I, who am reduced in this country to eating at each meal ten or twelve kinds of victuals, and to being three hours at table every day, two for love of your Excellency, to whom I humbly recommend myself.

Your Excellency's most humble servant,
RAIMUNDUS.

Source: Charles W. Eliot, ed., *American Historical Documents 1000–1904. Harvard Classics,* Vol. 43 (New York: P. F. Collier & Son, 1910), 47–50.

---

5. Perhaps Catiglione, near Chiavari.

The Founding of St. Augustine (1565)

The only such account available in English, this document describes the 1565 Spanish expedition establishing St. Augustine, Florida, the first permanent European settlement and the oldest city in the United States. The ship's chaplain, Father Lopez de Mendoza Grajalas, relates how the French Huguenot colony in the area was routed in the name of King Philip II of Spain, ending French hegemony in Florida.

YOUR LORDSHIP will remember that, when the fleet was in preparation in Spain, I went to see the captain-general at the harbor of St. Mary, and, as I told you, he showed me a letter from his Royal Highness Philip II, signed with his name. In this letter his Majesty told him that on May 20 some ships had left France carrying seven hundred men and two hundred women. As I have stated, we learned at St. John's of Porto Rico that our despatch-boat had been captured. This fact, joined to the reflection that our fleet was much injured by the storm, and that of the ten vessels which left Cadiz only four remained, besides the one bought at the last port to transport the horses and troops—all this made it evident to our captain-general, a man of arms, that the French would likely be waiting for him near the harbors, a little farther on; that is, off Monte Christi, Havana, and the Cape of Las Canas, which lie on the same side, and precisely on our route to Florida. This was all the more to be expected since the French had come in possession of our plan to unite our forces at Havana. Not wishing, however, to encounter the French, having now lost our ships, and having but feeble means of defense, the general decided to take a northerly course, and pursue a new route, through the Bahama Channel, leaving the enemy to the windward. When I suggested this route to the admiral and the pilot, they said it was important and necessary to abandon the usual route, by way of Havana.

Following this dangerous navigation, the Lord permitted the admiral to arrive safely in port on Sunday, the 20th of August. We saw two islands, called the Bahama Islands. The shoals which lie between them are so extensive that the billows are felt far out at sea. The general gave orders to take soundings. The ship purchased at Porto Rico got aground that day in two and a half fathoms of water. At first, we feared she might stay there; but she soon got off and came to us. Our galley, one of the best ships afloat, found herself all day in the same position, when suddenly her keel struck three times violently against the bottom. The sailors gave

themselves up for lost, and the water commenced to pour into her hold. But, as we had a mission to fulfill for Jesus Christ and His blessed mother, two heavy waves, which struck her abaft, set her afloat again, and soon after we found her in deep water, and at midnight we entered the Bahama Channel.

ON Saturday, the 25th, the captain-general [Menendez] came to visit our vessel and get the ordnance for disembarkment at Florida. This ordnance consisted of two rampart pieces, of two sorts of culverins, of very small caliber, powder and balls; and he also took two soldiers to take care of the pieces. Having armed his vessel, he stopped and made us an address, in which he instructed us what we had to do on arrival at the place where the French were anchored. I will not dwell on this subject, on which there was a good deal said for and against, although the opinion of the general finally prevailed. There were two thousand (hundred) [sic] Frenchmen in the seaport into which we were to force an entrance. I made some opposition to the plans, and begged the general to consider that he had the care of a thousand souls, for which he must give a good account. . . .

On Tuesday, the 4th, the fleet left the place of which I have been speaking—and we took a northerly course, keeping all the time close to the coast. On Wednesday, the 5th, two hours before sunset, we saw four French ships at the mouth of a river. When we were two leagues from them, the first galley joined the rest of the fleet, which was composed of four other vessels. The general concerted a plan with the captains and pilots, and ordered the flagship, the San Pelayo, and a chaloupe to attack the French flagship, the Trinity, while the first galley and another chaloupe would attack the French galley, both of which vessels were very large and powerful. All the ships of our fleet put themselves in good position; the troops were in the best of spirits, and full of confidence in the great talents of the captain-general. They followed the galley; but, as our general is a very clever and artful officer, he did not fire, nor seek to make any attack on the enemy. He went straight to the French galley, and cast anchor about eight paces from her. The other vessels went to the windward, and very near the enemy. During the maneuvers, which lasted until about two hours after sunset, not a word was said on either side. Never in my life have I known such stillness. Our general inquired of the French galley, which was the vessel nearest his.

"Whence does this fleet come?"

They answered, "From France."

"What are you doing here?" said the Adelantado. "This is the territory of King Philip II. I order you to leave directly; for I neither know who you are nor what you want here."

The French commander then replied, "I am bringing soldiers and supplies to the fort of the King of France."

He then asked the name of the general of our fleet, and was told, "Pedro Menendez de Aviles, Captain-general of the King of Spain, who have come to hang all Lutherans I find here."

Our general then asked him the name of his commander, and he replied, "Lord Gasto."

While this parleying was going on, a long-boat was sent from the galley to the flagship. The person charged with this errand managed to do it so secretly that we could not hear what was said; but we understood the reply of the French to be, "I am the admiral," which made us think he wished to surrender, as they were in so small a force.

Scarcely had the French made this reply, when they slipped their cables, spread their sails, and passed through our midst. Our admiral, seeing this, followed the French commander, and called upon him to lower his sails, in the name of King Philip, to which he received an impertinent answer. Immediately our admiral gave an order to discharge a small culverin, the ball from which struck the vessel amidships, and I thought she was going to founder. We gave chase, and some time after he again called on them to lower their sails.

"I would sooner die first than surrender!" replied the French commander.

The order was given to fire a second shot, which carried off five or six men; but, as these miserable devils are very good sailors, they maneuvered so well that we could not take one of them; and, notwithstanding all the guns we fired at them, we did not sink one of their ships. We only got possession of one of their large boats, which was of great service to us afterwards. During the whole night our flagship [the San Pelayo] and the galley chased the French flagship [Trinity] and galley. . . .

The next morning, being fully persuaded that the storm had made a wreck of our galley, or that, at least, she had been driven a hundred leagues out to sea, we decided that so soon as daylight came we would weigh anchor, and withdraw in good order, to a river [Seloy] which was below the French colony, and there disembark, and construct a fort, which we would defend until assistance came to us. . . .

OUR fort is at a distance of about fifteen leagues from that of the enemy [Fort Caroline]. The energy and talents of those two brave captains, joined to the efforts of their brave soldiers, who had no tools with which to work the earth, accomplished the construction of this fortress of defense; and, when the general disembarked, he was quite surprised with what had been done.

On Saturday, the 8th, the general landed with many banners spread, to the sound of trumpets and salutes of artillery. As I had gone ashore the evening before, I took a cross and went to meet him, singing the hymn Te Deum laudamus. The general marched up to the cross, followed by all who accompanied him, and there they all kneeled and embraced the cross. A large number of Indians watched these proceedings and imitated all they saw done. The same day the general took formal possession of the country in the name of his Majesty, and all the captains took the oath of allegiance to him, as their general and governor of the country. . . .

Our general was very bold in all military matters, and a great enemy of the French. He immediately assembled his captains and planned an expedition to attack the French settlement and fort on the river with five hundred men; and, in spite of the opinion of a majority of them, and of my judgment and of another priest, he ordered his plan to be carried out. Accordingly, on Monday, September 17, he set out with five hundred men, well provided with fire-arms and pikes, each soldier carrying with him a sack of bread and supply of wine for the journey. They also took with them two Indian chiefs, who were the implacable enemies of the French, to serve as guides. . . .

They marched the whole distance until Tuesday evening, the 18th of September, 1565, when they arrived within a quarter of a league of the enemy's fort [Caroline], where they remained all night up to their waists in water. When daylight came, Captains Lopez, Patino, and Martin Ochoa had already been to examine the fort, but, when they went to attack the fort, a greater part of the soldiers were so confused they scarcely knew what they were about.

On Thursday morning our good captain-general, accompanied by his son-in-law, Don Pedro de Valdes and Captain Patino, went to inspect the fort. He showed so much vivacity that he did not seem to have suffered by any of the hardships to which he had been exposed, and, seeing him march off so brisk, the others took courage, and without exception followed his example. It appears the enemy did not perceive their approach until the very moment of the attack, as it was very early in the morning and had rained in torrents. The greater part of the soldiers of the fort were still in bed. Some arose in their shirts, and others, quite naked, begged for quarter; but, in spite of that, more than one hundred and forty were killed.

A great Lutheran cosmographer and magician was found among the dead. The rest, numbering about three hundred, scaled the walls, and either took refuge in the forest or on their ships floating in the river, laden with treasures, so that in an hour's time the fort was in our possession, without our having lost a single man, or even had one wounded.

The taking of this fort gained us many valuable objects, namely, two hundred pikes, a hundred and twenty helmets, a quantity of arquebuses and shields, a quantity of clothing, linen, fine cloths, two hundred tons of flour, a good many barrels of biscuit, two hundred bushels of wheat, three horses, four asses, and two she-asses, hogs, tallow, books, furnace, flour-mill, and many other things of little value. But the greatest advantage of this victory is certainly the triumph which our Lord has granted us, and which will be the means of the Holy Gospel being introduced into this country, a thing necessary to prevent the loss of many souls. . . .

When we had reached the sea, we went about three leagues along the coast in search of our comrades. It was about ten o'clock at night when we met them, and there was a mutual rejoicing at having found each other. Not far off we saw the camp fires of our enemies, and our general ordered two of our soldiers to go and reconnoiter them, concealing themselves in the bushes, and to observe well the ground where they were encamped, so as to know what could be done. About two o'clock the men returned, saying that the enemy was on the other side of the river, and that we could not get at them. Immediately the general ordered two soldiers and four sailors to return to where we had left the boats, and bring them down the river, so that we might pass over to where the enemy was. Then he marched his troops forward to the river and we saw a great many of the enemy go down to the river to get shell-fish for food.

Our general, who was observing all that, enlightened by the Holy Spirit, said to us,

"I intend to change these clothes for those of a sailor, and take a Frenchman with me (one of those whom we had brought with us from Spain), and we will go and talk with these Frenchmen. Perhaps they are without supplies, and would be glad to surrender without fighting."

He had scarcely finished speaking before he put his plan into execution. As soon as he had called to them, one of them swam towards and spoke to him; told him of their having been shipwrecked and the distress they were in; that they had not eaten bread for eight or ten days; and, what is more, stated that all, or at least the greater part of them. Immediately the general sent him back to his countrymen, to say they must surrender, and give up their arms, or he would put them all to death. A French gentleman, who was a sergeant, brought back the reply that they would surrender on condition their lives should be spared.

After having parleyed a long time, our brave captain-general answered "that he would make no promises, that they must surrender unconditionally, and lay down their arms, because, if he spared their lives, he wanted them to be grateful for it, and, if they were put to death, that there should be no cause for complaint." Seeing that there was nothing else left for them to do, the sergeant returned to the camp; and soon after he brought all their arms and flags, and gave them up to the general, and surrendered unconditionally. Finding they were all Lutherans, the captain-general ordered them all to be put to death; but, as I was a priest, and had bowels of mercy, I begged him to grant me the favor of sparing those whom we might find to be Christians. He granted it; and I made investigations, and found ten or twelve of the men Roman Catholics, whom we brought back. All the others were executed, because they were Lutherans and enemies of our Holy Catholic faith.

All this took place on Saturday (St. Michael's Day), September 29, 1565. . . .

Source: America, Great Crises in Our History Told by Its Makers, Vol. II, Colonization (Chicago: Veterans of Foreign Wars of the United States, 1925), 30–39.

The Constitution of the Iroquois Nations (c. 1570)

Roughly around 1570, the prophet Deganawidah and his disciple Hiawatha founded the confederacy of the Iroquois. This confederacy was created to end intermittent warfare among the five Native American nations who occupied what is now New York State and surrounding territory. Power was carefully shared among the five nations, and there were numerous checks and balances designed to prevent one nation from gaining hegemony over the others. Benjamin Franklin cited this document as an important source for the American Constitution.

The Great Binding Law, Gayanashagowa

1. I am Deganawidah and with the Five Nations' Confederate Lords I plant the Tree of Great Peace. I plant it in your territory, Adodarhoh, and the Onondaga Nation, in the territory of you who are Firekeepers.

I name the tree the Tree of the Great Long Leaves. Under the shade of this Tree of the Great Peace we spread the soft white feathery down of the globe thistle as seats for you, Adodarhoh, and your cousin Lords.

We place you upon those seats, spread soft with the feathery down of the globe thistle, there beneath the shade of the spreading branches of the Tree of Peace. There shall you sit and watch the Council Fire of the Confederacy of the Five Nations, and all the affairs of the Five Nations shall be transacted at this place before you, Adodarhoh, and your cousin Lords, by the Confederate Lords of the Five Nations.

2. Roots have spread out from the Tree of the Great Peace, one to the north, one to the east, one to the south and one to the west. The name of these roots is The Great White Roots and their nature is Peace and Strength.

If any man or any nation outside the Five Nations shall obey the laws of the Great Peace and make known their disposition to the Lords of the Confederacy, they may trace the Roots to the Tree and if their minds are clean and they are obedient and promise to obey the wishes of the Confederate Council, they shall be welcomed to take shelter beneath the Tree of the Long Leaves.

We place at the top of the Tree of the Long Leaves an Eagle who is able to see afar. If he sees in the distance any evil approaching or any danger threatening he will at once warn the people of the Confederacy.

3. To you Adodarhoh, the Onondaga cousin Lords, I and the other Confederate Lords have entrusted the caretaking and the watching of the Five Nations Council Fire.

When there is any business to be transacted and the Confederate Council is not in session, a messenger shall be dispatched either to Adodarhoh, Hononwirehtonh or Skanawatih, Fire Keepers, or to their War Chiefs with a full statement of the case desired to be considered. Then shall Adodarhoh call his cousin [associate] Lords together and consider whether or not the case is of sufficient importance to demand the attention of the Confederate Council. If so, Adodarhoh shall dispatch messengers to summon all the Confederate Lords to assemble beneath the Tree of the Long Leaves.

When the Lords are assembled the Council Fire shall be kindled, but not with chestnut wood, and Adodarhoh shall formally open the Council.

Then shall Adodarhoh and his cousin Lords, the Fire Keepers, announce the subject for discussion.

The Smoke of the Confederate Council Fire shall ever ascend and pierce the sky so that other nations who may be allies may see the Council Fire of the Great Peace.

Adodarhoh and his cousin Lords are entrusted with the Keeping of the Council Fire.

4. You, Adodarhoh, and your thirteen cousin Lords, shall faithfully keep the space about the Council Fire clean and you shall allow neither dust nor dirt to accumulate. I lay a Long Wing before you as a broom. As a weapon against a crawling creature I lay a staff with you so that you may thrust it away from the Council Fire. If you fail to cast it out then call the rest of the United Lords to your aid.

5. The Council of the Mohawk shall be divided into three parties as follows: Tekarihoken, Ayonhwhathah and Shadekariwade are the first party; Sharenhowaneh, Deyoenhegwenh and Oghrenghrehgowah are the second party, and Dehennakrineh, Aghstawenserenthah and Shoskoharowaneh are the third party. The third party is to listen only to the discussion of the first and second parties and if an error is made or the proceeding is irregular they are to call attention

to it, and when the case is right and properly decided by the two parties they shall confirm the decision of the two parties and refer the case to the Seneca Lords for their decision. When the Seneca Lords have decided in accord with the Mohawk Lords, the case or question shall be referred to the Cayuga and Oneida Lords on the opposite side of the house.

6. I, Deganawidah, appoint the Mohawk Lords the heads and the leaders of the Five Nations Confederacy. The Mohawk Lords are the foundation of the Great Peace and it shall, therefore, be against the Great Binding Law to pass measures in the Confederate Council after the Mohawk Lords have protested against them.

No council of the Confederate Lords shall be legal unless all the Mohawk Lords are present.

7. Whenever the Confederate Lords shall assemble for the purpose of holding a council, the Onondaga Lords shall open it by expressing their gratitude to their cousin Lords and greeting them, and they shall make an address and offer thanks to the earth where men dwell, to the streams of water, the pools, the springs and the lakes, to the maize and the fruits, to the medicinal herbs and trees, to the forest trees for their usefulness, to the animals that serve as food and give their pelts for clothing, to the great winds and the lesser winds, to the Thunderers, to the Sun, the mighty warrior, to the moon, to the messengers of the Creator who reveal his wishes and to the Great Creator who dwells in the heavens above, who gives all the things useful to men, and who is the source and the ruler of health and life.

Then shall the Onondaga Lords declare the council open.

The council shall not sit after darkness has set in.

8. The Firekeepers shall formally open and close all councils of the Confederate Lords, and they shall pass upon all matters deliberated upon by the two sides and render their decision.

Every Onondaga Lord (or his deputy) must be present at every Confederate Council and must agree with the majority without unwarrantable dissent, so that a unanimous decision may be rendered.

If Adodarhoh or any of his cousin Lords are absent from a Confederate Council, any other Firekeeper may open and close the Council, but the Firekeepers present may not give any decisions, unless the matter is of small importance.

9. All the business of the Five Nations Confederate Council shall be conducted by the two combined bodies of Confederate Lords. First the question shall be passed upon by the Mohawk and Seneca Lords, then it shall be discussed and passed by the Oneida and Cayuga Lords. Their decisions shall then be referred to the Onondaga Lords, (Fire Keepers) for final judgement.

The same process shall obtain when a question is brought before the council by an individual or a War Chief.

10. In all cases the procedure must be as follows: when the Mohawk and Seneca Lords have unanimously agreed upon a question, they shall report their decision to the Cayuga and Oneida Lords who shall deliberate upon the question and report a unanimous decision to the Mohawk Lords. The Mohawk Lords will then report the standing of the case to the Firekeepers, who shall render a decision as they see fit in case of a disagreement by the two bodies, or confirm the decisions of the two bodies if they are identical. The Fire Keepers shall then report their decision to the Mohawk Lords who shall announce it to the open council.

11. If through any misunderstanding or obstinacy on the part of the Fire Keepers, they render a decision at variance with that of the Two Sides, the Two Sides shall reconsider the matter and if their decisions are jointly the same as before they shall report to the Fire Keepers who are then compelled to confirm their joint decision.

12. When a case comes before the Onondaga Lords (Fire Keepers) for discussion and decision, Adodarho shall introduce the matter to his comrade Lords who shall then discuss it in their two bodies. Every Onondaga Lord except Hononwiretonh shall deliberate and he shall listen only. When a unanimous decision shall have been reached by the two bodies of Fire Keepers, Adodarho shall notify Hononwiretonh of the fact when he shall confirm it. He shall refuse to confirm a decision if it is not unanimously agreed upon by both sides of the Fire Keepers.

13. No Lord shall ask a question of the body of Confederate Lords when they are discussing a case, question or proposition. He may only deliberate in a low tone with the separate body of which he is a member.

14. When the Council of the Five Nation Lords shall convene they shall appoint a speaker for the day. He shall be a Lord of either the Mohawk, Onondaga or Seneca Nation.

The next day the Council shall appoint another speaker, but the first speaker may be reappointed if there is no objection, but a speaker's term shall not be regarded more than for the day.

15. No individual or foreign nation interested in a case, question or proposition shall have any voice in the Confederate Council except to answer a question put to him or them by the speaker for the Lords.

16. If the conditions which shall arise at any future time call for an addition to or change of this law, the case shall be carefully considered and if a new beam seems necessary or beneficial, the proposed change shall be voted upon and if adopted it shall be called, "Added to the Rafters."

Rights, Duties, and Qualifications of Lords

17. A bunch of a certain number of shell [wampum] strings each two spans in length shall be given to each of the female

families in which the Lordship titles are vested. The right of bestowing the title shall be hereditary in the family of the females legally possessing the bunch of shell strings and the strings shall be the token that the females of the family have the proprietary right to the Lordship title for all time to come, subject to certain restrictions hereinafter mentioned.

18. If any Confederate Lord neglects or refuses to attend the Confederate Council, the other Lords of the Nation of which he is a member shall require their War Chief to request the female sponsors of the Lord so guilty of defection to demand his attendance of the Council. If he refuses, the women holding the title shall immediately select another candidate for the title.

No Lord shall be asked more than once to attend the Confederate Council.

19. If at any time it shall be manifest that a Confederate Lord has not in mind the welfare of the people or disobeys the rules of this Great Law, the men or women of the Confederacy, or both jointly, shall come to the Council and upbraid the erring Lord through his War Chief. If the complaint of the people through the War Chief is not heeded the first time it shall be uttered again and then if no attention is given a third complaint and warning shall be given. If the Lord is contumacious the matter shall go to the council of War Chiefs. The War Chiefs shall then divest the erring Lord of his title by order of the women in whom the titleship is vested. When the Lord is deposed the women shall notify the Confederate Lords through their War Chief, and the Confederate Lords shall sanction the act. The women will then select another of their sons as a candidate and the Lords shall elect him. Then shall the chosen one be installed by the Installation Ceremony.

When a Lord is to be deposed, his War Chief shall address him as follows:

"So you, _____, disregard and set at naught the warnings of your women relatives. So you fling the warnings over your shoulder to cast them behind you.

"Behold the brightness of the Sun and in the brightness of the Sun's light I depose you of your title and remove the sacred emblem of your Lordship title. I remove from your brow the deer's antlers, which was the emblem of your position and token of your nobility. I now depose you and return the antlers to the women whose heritage they are."

The War Chief shall now address the women of the deposed Lord and say:

"Mothers, as I have now deposed your Lord, I now return to you the emblem and the title of Lordship, therefore repossess them."

Again addressing himself to the deposed Lord he shall say:

"As I have now deposed and discharged you so you are now no longer Lord. You shall now go your way alone, the rest of the people of the Confederacy will not go with you, for we know not the kind of mind that possesses you. As the Creator has nothing to do with wrong so he will not come to rescue you from the precipice of destruction in which you have cast yourself. You shall never be restored to the position which you once occupied."

Then shall the War Chief address himself to the Lords of the Nation to which the deposed Lord belongs and say:

"Know you, my Lords, that I have taken the deer's antlers from the brow of _____, the emblem of his position and token of his greatness."

The Lords of the Confederacy shall then have no other alternative than to sanction the discharge of the offending Lord.

20. If a Lord of the Confederacy of the Five Nations should commit murder the other Lords of the Nation shall assemble at the place where the corpse lies and prepare to depose the criminal Lord. If it is impossible to meet at the scene of the crime the Lords shall discuss the matter at the next Council of their Nation and request their War Chief to depose the Lord guilty of crime, to "bury" his women relatives and to transfer the Lordship title to a sister family.

The War Chief shall address the Lord guilty of murder and say:

"So you, _____ (giving his name) did kill _____ (naming the slain man), with your own hands! You have committed a grave sin in the eyes of the Creator. Behold the bright light of the Sun, and in the brightness of the Sun's light I depose you of your title and remove the horns, the sacred emblems of your Lordship title. I remove from your brow the deer's antlers, which was the emblem of your position and token of your nobility. I now depose you and expel you and you shall depart at once from the territory of the Five Nations Confederacy and nevermore return again. We, the Five Nations Confederacy, moreover, bury your women relatives because the ancient Lordship title was never intended to have any union with bloodshed. Henceforth it shall not be their heritage. By the evil deed that you have done they have forfeited it forever."

The War Chief shall then hand the title to a sister family and he shall address it and say:

"Our mothers, _____, listen attentively while I address you on a solemn and important subject. I hereby transfer to you an ancient Lordship title for a great calamity has befallen it in the hands of the family of a former Lord. We trust that you, our mothers, will always guard it, and that you will warn your Lord always to be dutiful and to advise his people to ever live in love, peace and harmony that a great calamity may never happen again."

21. Certain physical defects in a Confederate Lord make him ineligible to sit in the Confederate Council. Such defects are infancy, idiocy, blindness, deafness, dumbness and impotency. When a Confederate Lord is restricted by any of these conditions, a deputy shall be appointed by his sponsors to act for him, but in case of extreme necessity the restricted Lord may exercise his rights.

22. If a Confederate Lord desires to resign his title he shall notify the Lords of the Nation of which he is a member of his intention. If his coactive Lords refuse to accept his resignation he may not resign his title.

A Lord in proposing to resign may recommend any proper candidate, which recommendation shall be received by the Lords, but unless confirmed and nominated by the women who hold the title the candidate so named shall not be considered.

23. Any Lord of the Five Nations Confederacy may construct shell strings (or wampum belts) of any size or length as pledges or records of matters of national or international importance.

When it is necessary to dispatch a shell string by a War Chief or other messenger as the token of a summons, the messenger shall recite the contents of the string to the party to whom it is sent. That party shall repeat the message and return the shell string and if there has been a summons he shall make ready for the journey.

Any of the people of the Five Nations may use shells (or wampum) as the record of a pledge, contract or an agreement entered into and the same shall be binding as soon as shell strings shall have been exchanged by both parties.

24. The Lords of the Confederacy of the Five Nations shall be mentors of the people for all time. The thickness of their skin shall be seven spans—which is to say that they shall be proof against anger, offensive actions and criticism. Their hearts shall be full of peace and good will and their minds filled with a yearning for the welfare of the people of the Confederacy. With endless patience they shall carry out their duty and their firmness shall be tempered with a tenderness for their people. Neither anger nor fury shall find lodgement in their minds and all their words and actions shall be marked by calm deliberation.

25. If a Lord of the Confederacy should seek to establish any authority independent of the jurisdiction of the Confederacy of the Great Peace, which is the Five Nations, he shall be warned three times in open council, first by the women relatives, second by the men relatives and finally by the Lords of the Confederacy of the Nation to which he belongs. If the offending Lord is still obdurate he shall be dismissed by the War Chief of his nation for refusing to conform to the laws of the Great Peace. His nation shall then install the candidate nominated by the female name holders of his family.

26. It shall be the duty of all of the Five Nations Confederate Lords, from time to time as occasion demands, to act as mentors and spiritual guides of their people and remind them of their Creator's will and words. They shall say:

"Hearken, that peace may continue unto future days!
"Always listen to the words of the Great Creator, for he has spoken.

"United people, let not evil find lodging in your minds.
"For the Great Creator has spoken and the cause of Peace shall not become old.
"The cause of peace shall not die if you remember the Great Creator."

Every Confederate Lord shall speak words such as these to promote peace.

27. All Lords of the Five Nations Confederacy must be honest in all things. They must not idle or gossip, but be men possessing those honorable qualities that make true royaneh [nobility]. It shall be a serious wrong for anyone to lead a Lord into trivial affairs, for the people must ever hold their Lords high in estimation out of respect to their honorable positions.

28. When a candidate Lord is to be installed he shall furnish four strings of shells (or wampum) one span in length bound together at one end. Such will constitute the evidence of his pledge to the Confederate Lords that he will live according to the constitution of the Great Peace and exercise justice in all affairs.

When the pledge is furnished the Speaker of the Council must hold the shell strings in his hand and address the opposite side of the Council Fire and he shall commence his address saying: "Now behold him. He has now become a Confederate Lord. See how splendid he looks." An address may then follow. At the end of it he shall send the bunch of shell strings to the opposite side and they shall be received as evidence of the pledge. Then shall the opposite side say:

"We now do crown you with the sacred emblem of the deer's antlers, the emblem of your Lordship. You shall now become a mentor of the people of the Five Nations. The thickness of your skin shall be seven spans—which is to say that you shall be proof against anger, offensive actions and criticism. Your heart shall be filled with peace and good will and your mind filled with a yearning for the welfare of the people of the Confederacy. With endless patience you shall carry out your duty and your firmness shall be tempered with tenderness for your people. Neither anger nor fury shall find lodgement in your mind and all your words and actions shall be marked with calm deliberation. In all of your deliberations in the Confederate Council, in your efforts at law making, in all your official acts, self interest shall be cast into oblivion. Cast not over your shoulder behind you the warnings of the nephews and nieces should they chide you for any error or wrong you may do, but return to the way of the Great Law, which is just and right. Look and listen for the welfare of the whole people and have always in view not only the present but also the coming generations, even those whose faces are yet beneath the surface of the ground—the unborn of the future Nation."

29. When a Lordship title is to be conferred, the candidate Lord shall furnish the cooked venison, the corn bread and

the corn soup, together with other necessary things and the labor for the Conferring of Titles Festival.

30. The Lords of the Confederacy may confer the Lordship title upon a candidate whenever the Great Law is recited, if there be a candidate, for the Great Law speaks all the rules.

31. If a Lord of the Confederacy should become seriously ill and be thought near death, the women who are heirs of his title shall go to his house and lift his crown of deer antlers, the emblem of his Lordship, and place them at one side. If the Creator spares him and he rises from his bed of sickness he may rise with the antlers on his brow. The following words shall be used to temporarily remove the antlers:

"Now our comrade Lord (or our relative Lord) the time has come when we must approach you in your illness. We remove for a time the deer's antlers from your brow, we remove the emblem of your Lordship title. The Great Law has decreed that no Lord should end his life with the antlers on his brow. We therefore lay them aside in the room. If the Creator spares you and you recover from your illness you shall rise from your bed with the antlers on your brow as before and you shall resume your duties as Lord of the Confederacy and you may labor again for the Confederate people."

32. If a Lord of the Confederacy should die while the Council of the Five Nations is in session the Council shall adjourn for ten days. No Confederate Council shall sit within ten days of the death of a Lord of the Confederacy.

If the Three Brothers [the Mohawk, the Onondaga and the Seneca] should lose one of their Lords by death, the Younger Brothers [the Oneida and the Cayuga] shall come to the surviving Lords of the Three Brothers on the tenth day and console them. If the Younger Brothers lose one of their Lords then the Three Brothers shall come to them and console them. And the consolation shall be the reading of the contents of the thirteen shell [wampum] strings of Ayonhwhathah. At the termination of this rite a successor shall be appointed, to be appointed by the women heirs of the Lordship title. If the women are not yet ready to place their nominee before the Lords the Speaker shall say, "Come let us go out." All shall leave the Council or the place of gathering. The installation shall then wait until such a time as the women are ready. The Speaker shall lead the way from the house by saying, "Let us depart to the edge of the woods and lie in waiting on our bellies."

When the women title holders shall have chosen one of their sons the Confederate Lords will assemble in two places, the Younger Brothers in one place and the Three Older Brothers in another. The Lords who are to console the mourning Lords shall choose one of their number to sing the Pacification Hymn as they journey to the sorrowing Lords. The singer shall lead the way and the Lords and the people shall follow. When they reach the sorrowing Lords they shall hail the candidate Lord and perform the rite of Conferring the Lordship Title.

33. When a Confederate Lord dies, the surviving relatives shall immediately dispatch a messenger, a member of another clan, to the Lords in another locality. When the runner comes within hailing distance of the locality he shall utter a sad wail, thus: "Kwa-ah, Kwa-ah, Kwa-ah!" The sound shall be repeated three times and then again and again at intervals as many times as the distance may require. When the runner arrives at the settlement the people shall assemble and one must ask him the nature of his sad message. He shall then say, "Let us consider." Then he shall tell them of the death of the Lord. He shall deliver to them a string of shells (wampum) and say "Here is the testimony, you have heard the message." He may then return home.

It now becomes the duty of the Lords of the locality to send runners to other localities and each locality shall send other messengers until all Lords are notified. Runners shall travel day and night.

34. If a Lord dies and there is no candidate qualified for the office in the family of the women title holders, the Lords of the Nation shall give the title into the hands of a sister family in the clan until such a time as the original family produces a candidate, when the title shall be restored to the rightful owners.

No Lordship title may be carried into the grave. The Lords of the Confederacy may dispossess a dead Lord of his title even at the grave.

Election of Pine Tree Chiefs

35. Should any man of the Nation assist with special ability or show great interest in the affairs of the Nation, if he proves himself wise, honest and worthy of confidence, the Confederate Lords may elect him to a seat with them and he may sit in the Confederate Council. He shall be proclaimed a "Pine Tree sprung up for the Nation" and shall be installed as such at the next assembly for the installation of Lords. Should he ever do anything contrary to the rules of the Great Peace, he may not be deposed from office—no one shall cut him down—but thereafter everyone shall be deaf to his voice and his advice. Should he resign his seat and title no one shall prevent him. A Pine Tree chief has no authority to name a successor nor is his title hereditary.

Names, Duties and Rights of War Chiefs

36. The title names of the Chief Confederate Lords' War Chiefs shall be:

Ayonwaehs, War Chief under Lord Takarihoken (Mohawk)
Kahonwahdironh, War Chief under Lord Odatshedeh (Oneida)
Ayendes, War Chief under Lord Adodarhoh (Onondaga)

Wenenhs, War Chief under Lord Dekaenyonh (Cayuga)
Shoneradowaneh, War Chief under Lord Skanyadariyo (Seneca)

The women heirs of each head Lord's title shall be the heirs of the War Chief's title of their respective Lord.

The War Chiefs shall be selected from the eligible sons of the female families holding the head Lordship titles.

37. There shall be one War Chief for each Nation and their duties shall be to carry messages for their Lords and to take up the arms of war in case of emergency. They shall not participate in the proceedings of the Confederate Council but shall watch its progress and in case of an erroneous action by a Lord they shall receive the complaints of the people and convey the warnings of the women to him. The people who wish to convey messages to the Lords in the Confederate Council shall do so through the War Chief of their Nation. It shall ever be his duty to lay the cases, questions and propositions of the people before the Confederate Council.

38. When a War Chief dies another shall be installed by the same rite as that by which a Lord is installed.

39. If a War Chief acts contrary to instructions or against the provisions of the Laws of the Great Peace, doing so in the capacity of his office, he shall be deposed by his women relatives and by his men relatives. Either the women or the men alone or jointly may act in such a case. The women title holders shall then choose another candidate.

40. When the Lords of the Confederacy take occasion to dispatch a messenger in behalf of the Confederate Council, they shall wrap up any matter they may send and instruct the messenger to remember his errand, to turn not aside but to proceed faithfully to his destination and deliver his message according to every instruction.

41. If a message borne by a runner is the warning of an invasion he shall whoop, "Kwa-ah, Kwa-ah," twice and repeat at short intervals; then again at a longer interval.

If a human being is found dead, the finder shall not touch the body but return home immediately shouting at short intervals, "Koo-weh!"

Clans and Consanguinity

42. Among the Five Nations and their posterity there shall be the following original clans: Great Name Bearer, Ancient Name Bearer, Great Bear, Ancient Bear, Turtle, Painted Turtle, Standing Rock, Large Plover, Deer, Pigeon Hawk, Eel, Ball, Opposite-Side-of-the-Hand, and Wild Potatoes. These clans distributed through their respective Nations, shall be the sole owners and holders of the soil of the country and in them is it vested as a birthright.

43. People of the Five Nations members of a certain clan shall recognize every other member of that clan, irrespective of the Nation, as relatives. Men and women, therefore, members of the same clan are forbidden to marry.

44. The lineal descent of the people of the Five Nations shall run in the female line. Women shall be considered the progenitors of the Nation. They shall own the land and the soil. Men and women shall follow the status of the mother.

45. The women heirs of the Confederated Lordship titles shall be called Royaneh [Noble] for all time to come.

46. The women of the Forty Eight (now fifty) Royaneh families shall be the heirs of the Authorized Names for all time to come.

When an infant of the Five Nations is given an Authorized Name at the Midwinter Festival or at the Ripe Corn Festival, one in the cousinhood of which the infant is a member shall be appointed a speaker. He shall then announce to the opposite cousinhood the names of the father and the mother of the child together with the clan of the mother. Then the speaker shall announce the child's name twice. The uncle of the child shall then take the child in his arms and walking up and down the room shall sing: "My head is firm, I am of the Confederacy." As he sings the opposite cousinhood shall respond by chanting, "Hyenh, Hyenh, Hyenh, Hyenh," until the song is ended.

47. If the female heirs of a Confederate Lord's title become extinct, the title right shall be given by the Lords of the Confederacy to the sister family whom they shall elect and that family shall hold the name and transmit it to their (female) heirs, but they shall not appoint any of their sons as a candidate for a title until all the eligible men of the former family shall have died or otherwise have become ineligible.

48. If all the heirs of a Lordship title become extinct, and all the families in the clan, then the title shall be given by the Lords of the Confederacy to the family in a sister clan whom they shall elect.

49. If any of the Royaneh women, heirs of a titleship, shall willfully withhold a Lordship or other title and refuse to bestow it, or if such heirs abandon, forsake or despise their heritage, then shall such women be deemed buried and their family extinct. The titleship shall then revert to a sister family or clan upon application and complaint. The Lords of the Confederacy shall elect the family or clan which shall in future hold the title.

50. The Royaneh women of the Confederacy heirs of the Lordship titles shall elect two women of their family as cooks for the Lord when the people shall assemble at his house for business or other purposes.

It is not good nor honorable for a Confederate Lord to allow his people whom he has called to go hungry.

51. When a Lord holds a conference in his home, his wife, if she wishes, may prepare the food for the Union Lords who

assemble with him. This is an honorable right which she may exercise and an expression of her esteem.

52. The Royaneh women, heirs of the Lordship titles, shall, should it be necessary, correct and admonish the holders of their titles. Those only who attend the Council may do this and those who do not shall not object to what has been said nor strive to undo the action.

53. When the Royaneh women, holders of a Lordship title, select one of their sons as a candidate, they shall select one who is trustworthy, of good character, of honest disposition, one who manages his own affairs, supports his own family, if any, and who has proven a faithful man to his Nation.

54. When a Lordship title becomes vacant through death or other cause, the Royaneh women of the clan in which the title is hereditary shall hold a council and shall choose one from among their sons to fill the office made vacant. Such a candidate shall not be the father of any Confederate Lord. If the choice is unanimous the name is referred to the men relatives of the clan. If they should disapprove it shall be their duty to select a candidate from among their own number. If then the men and women are unable to decide which of the two candidates shall be named, then the matter shall be referred to the Confederate Lords in the Clan. They shall decide which candidate shall be named. If the men and the women agree to a candidate his name shall be referred to the sister clans for confirmation. If the sister clans confirm the choice, they shall refer their action to their Confederate Lords who shall ratify the choice and present it to their cousin Lords, and if the cousin Lords confirm the name then the candidate shall be installed by the proper ceremony for the conferring of Lordship titles.

Official Symbolism

55. A large bunch of shell strings, in the making of which the Five Nations Confederate Lords have equally contributed, shall symbolize the completeness of the union and certify the pledge of the nations represented by the Confederate Lords of the Mohawk, the Oneida, the Onondaga, the Cayuga and the Seneca, that all are united and formed into one body or union called the Union of the Great Law, which they have established.

A bunch of shell strings is to be the symbol of the council fire of the Five Nations Confederacy. And the Lord whom the council of Fire Keepers shall appoint to speak for them in opening the council shall hold the strands of shells in his hands when speaking. When he finishes speaking he shall deposit the strings on an elevated place (or pole) so that all the assembled Lords and the people may see it and know that the council is open and in progress.

When the council adjourns the Lord who has been appointed by his comrade Lords to close it shall take the strands of shells in his hands and address the assembled Lords. Thus will the council adjourn until such time and place as appointed by the council. Then shall the shell strings be placed in a place for safekeeping.

Every five years the Five Nations Confederate Lords and the people shall assemble together and shall ask one another if their minds are still in the same spirit of unity for the Great Binding Law and if any of the Five Nations shall not pledge continuance and steadfastness to the pledge of unity then the Great Binding Law shall dissolve.

56. Five strings of shell tied together as one shall represent the Five Nations. Each string shall represent one territory and the whole a completely united territory known as the Five Nations Confederate territory.

57. Five arrows shall be bound together very strong and each arrow shall represent one nation. As the five arrows are strongly bound this shall symbolize the complete union of the nations. Thus are the Five Nations united completely and enfolded together, united into one head, one body and one mind. Therefore they shall labor, legislate and council together for the interest of future generations.

The Lords of the Confederacy shall eat together from one bowl the feast of cooked beaver's tail. While they are eating they are to use no sharp utensils for if they should they might accidentally cut one another and bloodshed would follow. All measures must be taken to prevent the spilling of blood in any way.

58. There are now the Five Nations Confederate Lords standing with joined hands in a circle. This signifies and provides that should any one of the Confederate Lords leave the council and this Confederacy his crown of deer's horns, the emblem of his Lordship title, together with his birthright, shall lodge on the arms of the Union Lords whose hands are so joined. He forfeits his title and the crown falls from his brow but it shall remain in the Confederacy.

A further meaning of this is that if any time any one of the Confederate Lords choose to submit to the law of a foreign people he is no longer in but out of the Confederacy, and persons of this class shall be called "They have alienated themselves." Likewise such persons who submit to laws of foreign nations shall forfeit all birthrights and claims on the Five Nations Confederacy and territory.

You, the Five Nations Confederate Lords, be firm so that if a tree falls on your joined arms it shall not separate or weaken your hold. So shall the strength of the union be preserved.

59. A bunch of wampum shells on strings, three spans of the hand in length, the upper half of the bunch being white and the lower half black, and formed from equal contributions of the men of the Five Nations, shall be a token that the men have combined themselves into one head, one body and one thought, and it shall also symbolize their ratification of the peace pact of the Confederacy, whereby the Lords of the Five Nations have established the Great Peace.

The white portion of the shell strings represent the

women and the black portion the men. The black portion, furthermore, is a token of power and authority vested in the men of the Five Nations.

This string of wampum vests the people with the right to correct their erring Lords. In case a part or all the Lords pursue a course not vouched for by the people and heed not the third warning of their women relatives, then the matter shall be taken to the General Council of the women of the Five Nations. If the Lords notified and warned three times fail to heed, then the case falls into the hands of the men of the Five Nations. The War Chiefs shall then, by right of such power and authority, enter the open council to warn the Lord or Lords to return from the wrong course. If the Lords heed the warning they shall say, "we will reply tomorrow." If then an answer is returned in favor of justice and in accord with this Great Law, then the Lords shall individually pledge themselves again by again furnishing the necessary shells for the pledge. Then shall the War Chief or Chiefs exhort the Lords urging them to be just and true.

Should it happen that the Lords refuse to heed the third warning, then two courses are open: either the men may decide in their council to depose the Lord or Lords or to club them to death with war clubs. Should they in their council decide to take the first course the War Chief shall address the Lord or Lords, saying: "Since you the Lords of the Five Nations have refused to return to the procedure of the Constitution, we now declare your seats vacant, we take off your horns, the token of your Lordship, and others shall be chosen and installed in your seats, therefore vacate your seats."

Should the men in their council adopt the second course, the War Chief shall order his men to enter the council, to take positions beside the Lords, sitting between them wherever possible. When this is accomplished the War Chief holding in his outstretched hand a bunch of black wampum strings shall say to the erring Lords: "So now, Lords of the Five United Nations, harken to these last words from your men. You have not heeded the warnings of the women relatives, you have not heeded the warnings of the General Council of women and you have not heeded the warnings of the men of the nations, all urging you to return to the right course of action. Since you are determined to resist and to withhold justice from your people there is only one course for us to adopt." At this point the War Chief shall let drop the bunch of black wampum and the men shall spring to their feet and club the erring Lords to death. Any erring Lord may submit before the War Chief lets fall the black wampum. Then his execution is withheld.

The black wampum here used symbolizes that the power to execute is buried but that it may be raised up again by the men. It is buried but when occasion arises they may pull it up and derive their power and authority to act as here described.

60. A broad dark belt of wampum of thirty-eight rows, having a white heart in the center, on either side of which are two white squares all connected with the heart by white rows of beads shall be the emblem of the unity of the Five Nations.

The first of the squares on the left represents the Mohawk nation and its territory; the second square on the left and the one near the heart, represents the Oneida nation and its territory; the white heart in the middle represents the Onondaga nation and its territory, and it also means that the heart of the Five Nations is single in its loyalty to the Great Peace, that the Great Peace is lodged in the heart (meaning the Onondaga Lords), and that the Council Fire is to burn there for the Five Nations, and further, it means that the authority is given to advance the cause of peace whereby hostile nations out of the Confederacy shall cease warfare; the white square to the right of the heart represents the Cayuga nation and its territory and the fourth and last white square represents the Seneca nation and its territory.

White shall here symbolize that no evil or jealous thoughts shall creep into the minds of the Lords while in Council under the Great Peace. White, the emblem of peace, love, charity and equity surrounds and guards the Five Nations.

61. Should a great calamity threaten the generations rising and living of the Five United Nations, then he who is able to climb to the top of the Tree of the Great Long Leaves may do so. When, then, he reaches the top of the tree he shall look about in all directions, and, should he see that evil things indeed are approaching, then he shall call to the people of the Five United Nations assembled beneath the Tree of the Great Long Leaves and say: "A calamity threatens your happiness."

Then shall the Lords convene in council and discuss the impending evil.

When all the truths relating to the trouble shall be fully known and found to be truths, then shall the people seek out a Tree of Ka-hon-ka-ah-go-nah, [a great swamp Elm], and when they shall find it they shall assemble their heads together and lodge for a time between its roots. Then, their labors being finished, they may hope for happiness for many days after.

62. When the Confederate Council of the Five Nations declares for a reading of the belts of shell calling to mind these laws, they shall provide for the reader a specially made mat woven of the fibers of wild hemp. The mat shall not be used again, for such formality is called the honoring of the importance of the law.

63. Should two sons of opposite sides of the council fire agree in a desire to hear the reciting of the laws of the Great Peace and so refresh their memories in the way ordained by the founder of the Confederacy, they shall notify Adodarho. He then shall consult with five of his coactive Lords and they

in turn shall consult with their eight brethren. Then should they decide to accede to the request of the two sons from opposite sides of the Council Fire, Adodarho shall send messengers to notify the Chief Lords of each of the Five Nations. Then they shall despatch their War Chiefs to notify their brother and cousin Lords of the meeting and its time and place.

When all have come and have assembled, Adodarhoh, in conjunction with his cousin Lords, shall appoint one Lord who shall repeat the laws of the Great Peace. Then shall they announce who they have chosen to repeat the laws of the Great Peace to the two sons. Then shall the chosen one repeat the laws of the Great Peace.

64. At the ceremony of the installation of Lords if there is only one expert speaker and singer of the law and the Pacification Hymn to stand at the council fire, then when this speaker and singer has finished addressing one side of the fire he shall go to the opposite side and reply to his own speech and song. He shall thus act for both sides of the fire until the entire ceremony has been completed. Such a speaker and singer shall be termed the "Two Faced" because he speaks and sings for both sides of the fire.

65. I, Deganawidah, and the Union Lords, now uproot the tallest pine tree and into the cavity thereby made we cast all weapons of war. Into the depths of the earth, down into the deep under-earth currents of water flowing to unknown regions we cast all the weapons of strife. We bury them from sight and we plant again the tree. Thus shall the Great Peace be established and hostilities shall no longer be known between the Five Nations but peace to the United People.

Laws of Adoption

66. The father of a child of great comeliness, learning, ability or specially loved because of some circumstance may, at the will of the child's clan, select a name from his own (the father's) clan and bestow it by ceremony, such as is provided. This naming shall be only temporary and shall be called, "A name hung about the neck."

67. Should any person, a member of the Five Nations' Confederacy, specially esteem a man or woman of another clan or of a foreign nation, he may choose a name and bestow it upon that person so esteemed. The naming shall be in accord with the ceremony of bestowing names. Such a name is only a temporary one and shall be called "A name hung about the neck." A short string of shells shall be delivered with the name as a record and a pledge.

68. Should any member of the Five Nations, a family or person belonging to a foreign nation submit a proposal for adoption into a clan of one of the Five Nations, he or they shall furnish a string of shells, a span in length, as a pledge to the clan into which he or they wish to be adopted. The

Lords of the nation shall then consider the proposal and submit a decision.

69. Any member of the Five Nations who through esteem or other feeling wishes to adopt an individual, a family or number of families may offer adoption to him or them and if accepted the matter shall be brought to the attention of the Lords for confirmation and the Lords must confirm adoption.

70. When the adoption of anyone shall have been confirmed by the Lords of the Nation, the Lords shall address the people of their nation and say: "Now you of our nation, be informed that such a person, such a family or such families have ceased forever to bear their birth nation's name and have buried it in the depths of the earth. Henceforth let no one of our nation ever mention the original name or nation of their birth. To do so will be to hasten the end of our peace.

Laws of Emigration

71. When any person or family belonging to the Five Nations desires to abandon their birth nation and the territory of the Five Nations, they shall inform the Lords of their nation and the Confederate Council of the Five Nations shall take cognizance of it.

72. When any person or any of the people of the Five Nations emigrate and reside in a region distant from the territory of the Five Nations Confederacy, the Lords of the Five Nations at will may send a messenger carrying a broad belt of black shells and when the messenger arrives he shall call the people together or address them personally displaying the belt of shells and they shall know that this is an order for them to return to their original homes and to their council fires.

Rights of Foreign Nations

73. The soil of the earth from one end of the land to the other is the property of the people who inhabit it. By birthright the Ongwehonweh (Original beings) are the owners of the soil which they own and occupy and none other may hold it. The same law has been held from the oldest times.

The Great Creator has made us of the one blood and of the same soil he made us and as only different tongues constitute different nations he established different hunting grounds and territories and made boundary lines between them.

74. When any alien nation or individual is admitted into the Five Nations the admission shall be understood only to be a temporary one. Should the person or nation create loss, do wrong or cause suffering of any kind to endanger the peace of the Confederacy, the Confederate Lords shall order one of their war chiefs to reprimand him or them and if a similar offence is again committed the offending party or

parties shall be expelled from the territory of the Five United Nations.

75. When a member of an alien nation comes to the territory of the Five Nations and seeks refuge and permanent residence, the Lords of the Nation to which he comes shall extend hospitality and make him a member of the nation. Then shall he be accorded equal rights and privileges in all matters except as after mentioned.

76. No body of alien people who have been adopted temporarily shall have a vote in the council of the Lords of the Confederacy, for only they who have been invested with Lordship titles may vote in the Council. Aliens have nothing by blood to make claim to a vote and should they have it, not knowing all the traditions of the Confederacy, might go against its Great Peace. In this manner the Great Peace would be endangered and perhaps be destroyed.

77. When the Lords of the Confederacy decide to admit a foreign nation and an adoption is made, the Lords shall inform the adopted nation that its admission is only temporary. They shall also say to the nation that it must never try to control, to interfere with or to injure the Five Nations nor disregard the Great Peace or any of its rules or customs. That in no way should they cause disturbance or injury. Then should the adopted nation disregard these injunctions, their adoption shall be annulled and they shall be expelled.

The expulsion shall be in the following manner: The council shall appoint one of their War Chiefs to convey the message of annulment and he shall say, "You (naming the nation) listen to me while I speak. I am here to inform you again of the will of the Five Nations' Council. It was clearly made known to you at a former time. Now the Lords of the Five Nations have decided to expel you and cast you out. We disown you now and annul your adoption. Therefore you must look for a path in which to go and lead away all your people. It was you, not we, who committed wrong and caused this sentence of annulment. So then go your way and depart from the territory of the Five Nations and from the Confederacy."

78. Whenever a foreign nation enters the Confederacy or accepts the Great Peace, the Five Nations and the foreign nation shall enter into an agreement and compact by which the foreign nation shall endeavor to persuade other nations to accept the Great Peace.

Rights and Powers of War

79. Skanawatih shall be vested with a double office, duty and with double authority. One-half of his being shall hold the Lordship title and the other half shall hold the title of War Chief. In the event of war he shall notify the five War Chiefs of the Confederacy and command them to prepare for war and have their men ready at the appointed time and place for engagement with the enemy of the Great Peace.

80. When the Confederate Council of the Five Nations has for its object the establishment of the Great Peace among the people of an outside nation and that nation refuses to accept the Great Peace, then by such refusal they bring a declaration of war upon themselves from the Five Nations. Then shall the Five Nations seek to establish the Great Peace by a conquest of the rebellious nation.

81. When the men of the Five Nations, now called forth to become warriors, are ready for battle with an obstinate opposing nation that has refused to accept the Great Peace, then one of the five War Chiefs shall be chosen by the warriors of the Five Nations to lead the army into battle. It shall be the duty of the War Chief so chosen to come before his warriors and address them. His aim shall be to impress upon them the necessity of good behavior and strict obedience to all the commands of the War Chiefs. He shall deliver an oration exhorting them with great zeal to be brave and courageous and never to be guilty of cowardice. At the conclusion of his oration he shall march forward and commence the War Song and he shall sing:

> Now I am greatly surprised
> And, therefore I shall use it—
> The power of my War Song.
> I am of the Five Nations
> And I shall make supplication
> To the Almighty Creator.
> He has furnished this army.
> My warriors shall be mighty
> In the strength of the Creator.
> Between him and my song they are
> For it was he who gave the song
> This war song that I sing!

82. When the warriors of the Five Nations are on an expedition against an enemy, the War Chief shall sing the War Song as he approaches the country of the enemy and not cease until his scouts have reported that the army is near the enemies' lines when the War Chief shall approach with great caution and prepare for the attack.

83. When peace shall have been established by the termination of the war against a foreign nation, then the War Chief shall cause all the weapons of war to be taken from the nation. Then shall the Great Peace be established and that nation shall observe all the rules of the Great Peace for all time to come.

84. Whenever a foreign nation is conquered or has by their own will accepted the Great Peace their own system of internal government may continue, but they must cease all warfare against other nations.

85. Whenever a war against a foreign nation is pushed until that nation is about exterminated because of its refusal to accept the Great Peace and if that nation shall by its obstinacy

become exterminated, all their rights, property and territory shall become the property of the Five Nations.

86. Whenever a foreign nation is conquered and the survivors are brought into the territory of the Five Nations' Confederacy and placed under the Great Peace the two shall be known as the Conqueror and the Conquered. A symbolic relationship shall be devised and be placed in some symbolic position. The conquered nation shall have no voice in the councils of the Confederacy in the body of the Lords.

87. When the War of the Five Nations on a foreign rebellious nation is ended, peace shall be restored to that nation by a withdrawal of all their weapons of war by the War Chief of the Five Nations. When all the terms of peace shall have been agreed upon a state of friendship shall be established.

88. When the proposition to establish the Great Peace is made to a foreign nation it shall be done in mutual council. The foreign nation is to be persuaded by reason and urged to come into the Great Peace. If the Five Nations fail to obtain the consent of the nation at the first council a second council shall be held and upon a second failure a third council shall be held and this third council shall end the peaceful methods of persuasion. At the third council the War Chief of the Five Nations shall address the Chief of the foreign nation and request him three times to accept the Great Peace. If refusal steadfastly follows the War Chief shall let the bunch of white lake shells drop from his outstretched hand to the ground and shall bound quickly forward and club the offending chief to death. War shall thereby be declared and the War Chief shall have his warriors at his back to meet any emergency. War must continue until the contest is won by the Five Nations.

89. When the Lords of the Five Nations propose to meet in conference with a foreign nation with proposals for an acceptance of the Great Peace, a large band of warriors shall conceal themselves in a secure place safe from the espionage of the foreign nation but as near at hand as possible. Two warriors shall accompany the Union Lord who carries the proposals and these warriors shall be especially cunning. Should the Lord be attacked, these warriors shall hasten back to the army of warriors with the news of the calamity which fell through the treachery of the foreign nation.

90. When the Five Nations' Council declares war any Lord of the Confederacy may enlist with the warriors by temporarily renouncing his sacred Lordship title which he holds through the election of his women relatives. The title then reverts to them and they may bestow it upon another temporarily until the war is over when the Lord, if living, may resume his title and seat in the Council.

91. A certain wampum belt of black beads shall be the emblem of the authority of the Five War Chiefs to take up the weapons of war and with their men to resist invasion. This shall be called a war in defense of the territory.

Treason or Secession of a Nation

92. If a nation, part of a nation, or more than one nation within the Five Nations should in any way endeavor to destroy the Great Peace by neglect or violating its laws and resolve to dissolve the Confederacy, such a nation or such nations shall be deemed guilty of treason and called enemies of the Confederacy and the Great Peace.

It shall then be the duty of the Lords of the Confederacy who remain faithful to resolve to warn the offending people. They shall be warned once and if a second warning is necessary they shall be driven from the territory of the Confederacy by the War Chiefs and his men.

Rights of the People of the Five Nations

93. Whenever a specially important matter or a great emergency is presented before the Confederate Council and the nature of the matter affects the entire body of the Five Nations, threatening their utter ruin, then the Lords of the Confederacy must submit the matter to the decision of their people and the decision of the people shall affect the decision of the Confederate Council. This decision shall be a confirmation of the voice of the people.

94. The men of every clan of the Five Nations shall have a Council Fire ever burning in readiness for a council of the clan. When it seems necessary for a council to be held to discuss the welfare of the clans, then the men may gather about the fire. This council shall have the same rights as the council of the women.

95. The women of every clan of the Five Nations shall have a Council Fire ever burning in readiness for a council of the clan. When in their opinion it seems necessary for the interest of the people they shall hold a council and their decisions and recommendations shall be introduced before the Council of the Lords by the War Chief for its consideration.

96. All the Clan council fires of a nation or of the Five Nations may unite into one general council fire, or delegates from all the council fires may be appointed to unite in a general council for discussing the interests of the people. The people shall have the right to make appointments and to delegate their power to others of their number. When their council shall have come to a conclusion on any matter, their decision shall be reported to the Council of the Nation or to the Confederate Council (as the case may require) by the War Chief or the War Chiefs.

97. Before the real people united their nations, each nation had its council fires. Before the Great Peace their councils were held. The five Council Fires shall continue to burn as before and they are not quenched. The Lords of each nation in future shall settle their nation's affairs at this council fire governed always by the laws and rules of the council of the Confederacy and by the Great Peace.

98. If either a nephew or a niece see an irregularity in the performance of the functions of the Great Peace and its laws, in the Confederate Council or in the conferring of Lordship titles in an improper way, through their War Chief they may demand that such actions become subject to correction and that the matter conform to the ways prescribed by the laws of the Great Peace.

Religious Ceremonies Protected

99. The rites and festivals of each nation shall remain undisturbed and shall continue as before because they were given by the people of old times as useful and necessary for the good of men.

100. It shall be the duty of the Lords of each brotherhood to confer at the approach of the time of the Midwinter Thanksgiving and to notify their people of the approaching festival. They shall hold a council over the matter and arrange its details and begin the Thanksgiving five days after the moon of Dis-ko-nah is new. The people shall assemble at the appointed place and the nephews shall notify the people of the time and place. From the beginning to the end the Lords shall preside over the Thanksgiving and address the people from time to time.

101. It shall be the duty of the appointed managers of the Thanksgiving festivals to do all that is needed for carrying out the duties of the occasions.

   The recognized festivals of Thanksgiving shall be the Midwinter Thanksgiving, the Maple or Sugar-making Thanksgiving, the Raspberry Thanksgiving, the Strawberry Thanksgiving, the Cornplanting Thanksgiving, the Corn Hoeing Thanksgiving, the Little Festival of Green Corn, the Great Festival of Ripe Corn and the complete Thanksgiving for the Harvest.

   Each nation's festivals shall be held in their Long Houses.

102. When the Thanksgiving for the Green Corn comes the special managers, both the men and women, shall give it careful attention and do their duties properly.

103. When the Ripe Corn Thanksgiving is celebrated the Lords of the Nation must give it the same attention as they give to the Midwinter Thanksgiving.

104. Whenever any man proves himself by his good life and his knowledge of good things, naturally fitted as a teacher of good things, he shall be recognized by the Lords as a teacher of peace and religion and the people shall hear him.

The Installation Song

105. The song used in installing the new Lord of the Confederacy shall be sung by Adodarhoh and it shall be:

> "Haii, haii Agwah wi-yoh
> "   "   A-kon-he-watha
> "   "   Ska-we-ye-se-go-wah
> "   "   Yon-gwa-wih
> "   "   Ya-kon-he-wa-tha
>
> Haii, haii It is good indeed
> "   "   [That] a broom,—
> "   "   A great wing,
> "   "   It is given me
> "   "   For a sweeping instrument."

106. Whenever a person properly entitled desires to learn the Pacification Song he is privileged to do so but he must prepare a feast at which his teachers may sit with him and sing. The feast is provided that no misfortune may befall them for singing the song on an occasion when no chief is installed.

Protection of the House

107. A certain sign shall be known to all the people of the Five Nations which shall denote that the owner or occupant of a house is absent. A stick or pole in a slanting or leaning position shall indicate this and be the sign. Every person not entitled to enter the house by right of living within it upon seeing such a sign shall not approach the house either by day or by night but shall keep as far away as his business will permit.

Funeral Addresses

108. At the funeral of a Lord of the Confederacy, say: "Now we become reconciled as you start away. You were once a Lord of the Five Nations' Confederacy and the United People trusted you. Now we release you for it is true that it is no longer possible for us to walk about together on the earth. Now, therefore, we lay it [the body] here. Here we lay it away. Now then we say to you, 'Persevere onward to the place where the Creator dwells in peace. Let not the things of the earth hinder you. Let nothing that transpired while yet you lived hinder you. In hunting you once took delight; in the game of Lacrosse you once took delight and in the feasts and pleasant occasions your mind was amused, but now do not allow thoughts of these things to give you trouble. Let not your relatives hinder you and also let not your friends and associates trouble your mind. Regard none of these things.' "

   " 'Now then, in turn, you here present who were related to this man and you who were his friends and associates, behold the path that is yours also! Soon we ourselves will be left in that place. For this reason hold yourselves in restraint as you go from place to place. In your actions and in your conversation do no idle thing. Speak not idle talk neither gossip. Be careful of this and speak not and do not give way to evil behavior. One year is the time that you must abstain from unseemly levity but if you can not do this for ceremony, ten days is the time to regard these things for respect.' "

109. At the funeral of a War Chief, say:

"Now we become reconciled as you start away. You were once a War Chief of the Five Nations' Confederacy and the United People trusted you as their guard from the enemy." (The remainder is the same as the address at the funeral of a Lord.)

110. At the funeral of a Warrior, say:

"Now we become reconciled as you start away. Once you were a devoted provider and protector of your family and you were ever ready to take part in battles for the Five Nations' Confederacy. The United People trusted you." (The remainder is the same as the address at the funeral of a Lord.)

111. At the funeral of a young man, say:

"Now we become reconciled as you start away. In the beginning of your career you are taken away and the flower of your life is withered away." (The remainder is the same as the address at the funeral of a Lord.)

112. At the funeral of a chief woman, say:

"Now we become reconciled as you start away. You were once a chief woman in the Five Nations' Confederacy. You once were a mother of the nations. Now we release you for it is true that it is no longer possible for us to walk about together on the earth. Now, therefore, we lay it [the body] here. Here we lay it away. Now then we say to you, 'Persevere onward to the place where the Creator dwells in peace. Let not the things of the earth hinder you. Let nothing that transpired while you lived hinder you. Looking after your family was a sacred duty and you were faithful. You were one of the many joint heirs of the Lordship titles. Feastings were yours and you had pleasant occasions. . . . ' " (The remainder is the same as the address at the funeral of a Lord).

113. At the funeral of a woman of the people, say:

"Now we become reconciled as you start away. You were once a woman in the flower of life and the bloom is now withered away. You once held a sacred position as a mother of the nation . . . (etc.) Looking after your family was a sacred duty and you were faithful. Feastings . . . (etc.)" [The remainder is the same as the address at the funeral of a Lord.]

114. At the funeral of an infant or young woman, say:

"Now we become reconciled as you start away. You were a tender bud and gladdened our hearts for only a few days. Now the bloom has withered away . . . (etc.). Let none of the things that transpired on earth hinder you. Let nothing that happened while you lived hinder you." [The remainder is the same as the address at the funeral of a Lord.]

115. When an infant dies within three days, mourning shall continue only five days. Then shall you gather the little boys and girls at the house of mourning and at the funeral feast a speaker shall address the children and bid them be happy once more, though by a death, gloom has been cast over them. Then shall the black clouds roll away and the sky shall show blue once more. Then shall the children be again in sunshine.

116. When a dead person is brought to the burial place, the speaker on the opposite side of the Council Fire shall bid the bereaved family cheer their minds once again and rekindle their hearth fires in peace, to put their house in order and once again be in brightness for darkness has covered them. He shall say that the black clouds shall roll away and that the bright blue sky is visible once more. Therefore shall they be in peace in the sunshine again.

117. Three strings of shell one span in length shall be employed in addressing the assemblage at the burial of the dead. The speaker shall say:

"Hearken you who are here, this body is to be covered. Assemble in this place again ten days hence for it is the decree of the Creator that mourning shall cease when ten days have expired. Then shall a feast be made."

Then at the expiration of ten days the speaker shall say: "Continue to listen you who are here. The ten days of mourning have expired and your minds must now be freed of sorrow as before the loss of a relative. The relatives have decided to make a little compensation to those who have assisted at the funeral. It is a mere expression of thanks. This is to the one who did the cooking while the body was lying in the house. Let her come forward and receive this gift and be dismissed from the task." In substance this shall be repeated for every one who assisted in any way until all have been remembered.

Source: Constitution Society Web site, www.constitution.org/cons/iroquois.txt. Prepared by Gerald Murphy (The Cleveland Free-Net-AA300). Distributed by the Cybercasting Services Division of the National Public Telecomputing Network (NPTN). Reprinted with permission.

A Call for English Colonization of America (1584)

At the request of Sir Walter Raleigh, Richard Hakluyt presented a compelling case to Queen Elizabeth I, English merchants, and the gentry to invest in the colonization of America. The following are selections from the final chapter of Hakluyt's *Discourse Concerning Western Planting*.

1. The soil yieldth and may be made to yield all the several commodities of Europe, and of all kingdomes, dominions, and territories that England tradeth with that by trade of merchandise cometh into this realm.

2. The passage thither and home is neither to long nor to short but easy and to be made twice in the year. . . .

5. And where England now for certain hundreth years last passed, by the peculiar commodity of wools, and of later years by clothing of the same, hath raised itself from meaner state to greatr wealth and much highr honour, mighty and power than before, to the equaling of the princes of the same to the greatst potentates of this part of the world it cometh now so to passe, that by the great endeavour of the increase of the trade of wools in Spain and in the West Indies, now daily more and more multiplying that the wools of England, and the clothe made of the same, will become base, and every day more base then other; which, prudently weighed yet behoveth this realm if it mean not to return to former olde means and baseness but to stand in present and late former honour, glory, and force, and not negligently and sleepingly to slide into beggery, to foresee and to plant at Norumbega [New England] or some like place, were it not for any thing else but for the hope of the vent of our wool endraped, the principal and in effect the only enriching continuing natural commodity of this realm. And effectually pursuing that course, we shall not only find on that tract of land, and especially in that firm northward (to whom warm clothe shall be right welcome), an ample vent, but also shall, from the north side of that firm, find out known and unknown islands and dominions replenished with people that may fully vent the abundance of that our commodity, that else will in few years wax of none or of small value by foreign abundance &c.; so as by this enterprise we shall shun the imminent mischief hanging over our heads that else must needs fall upon the realm without breach of peace or sword drawn against this realm by any foreign state; and not offer our ancient riches to scornful neighbors at home, nor sell the same in effect for nothing, as we shall shortly, if presently it be not provided for. . . .

6. This enterprise may stay the Spanish King from flowing over all the face of that waste firm of America, if we seat and plant there in time, in time I say, and we by planting shall [prevent] him from making more short and more safe returns out of the noble ports of the purposed places of our planting, then by any possibility he can from the part of the firm that now his navys by ordinary courses come from, in this that there is no comparison between the ports of the coasts that the King of Spain doth now possess and use and the ports of the coasts that our nation is to possess by planting at Norumbega. . . . And England possessing the purposed place of planting, her Majesty may, by the benefit of the seat having won good and royall havens, have plenty of excellent trees for request masts of goodly timber to build ships and to make great navys, of pitch, tar, hemp, and all things incident for a navy royall, and that for no price, and without money for. How easy a matter may yet be to this realm, swarming at this day with valiant youths, rusting and hurtful by lack of employment, and having good makers of cable and of all sorts of cordage, and the best and most cunning shipwrights of the world, to be lords of all those seas, and to spoil Phillip's Indian navy, and to deprive him of yearly passage of his treasure into Europe, and consequently to abate the pride of Spain and of the suporter of the great Anti-Christ of Rome and to pull him down in equality to his neighbour princes, and consequently to cut of the common mischiefs that come to all Europe by the peculiar abundance of his Indian treasure, and this without difficulty.

7. . . . this realm shall have by that mean ships of great burden and of great strength for the defense of this realm, and for the defense of that new seat as need shall require, and with all great increase of perfect seamen, which great princes in time of wars want, and which kind of men are neither nourished in few days nor in few years. . . .

10. No foreign commodity that comes into England comes without payment of custom once, twice, or thrice, before it come into the realm, and so all foreign commodities become dearer to the subjects of this realm; and by this course to Norumbega foreign princes customs are avoided; and the foreign commodities cheaply purchased, they become cheap to the subjects of England, to the common benefit of the people, and to the saving of great treasure in the realm; whereas now the realm become the poor by the purchasing of foreign commodities in so great a mass at so excessive prices.

11. At the first traffic with the people of those parts, the subjects of this realm for many years shall change many cheap commodities of these parts for things of high valor there not esteemed; and this to the great enriching of the *realm*, if common use fail not.

12. By the great plenty of those regions the merchants and their factors shall lie there cheap, buy and repair their ships cheap, and shall return at pleasure without stay or restraint of foreign prince; whereas upon stays and restraints the merchant raiseth his charge in sale over of his ware; and, buying his wares cheap, he may maintain trade with small stock, and without taking up money upon interest; and so he shall be rich and not subject to many hazards, but shall be able to afford the commodities for cheap prices to all subjects of the realm.

13. By making of ships and by preparing of things for the same, by making of cables and cordage, by planting of vines and olive trees, and by making of wine and oil, by husbandry, and by thousands of things there to be done, infinite numbers of the English nation may be set on work, to the unburdening of the realm with many that now live chargeable to the state at home.

14. If the sea coast serve for making of salt, and the inland for wine, oils, oranges, lemons, figs, &c., and for making of iron, all which with much more is hoped, without sword drawn, we shall cut the comb of the French, of the Spanish, of the Portingal, and of enemies, and of doubtful friends, to the abating of their wealth and force, and to the great saving of the wealth of the realm. . . .

16. Wee shall by planting there enlarge the glory of the gospel, and from England plant sincere religion, and provide a safe and a sure place to receive people from all parts of the world that are forced to flee for the truth of God's word.

17. If frontier wars there chance to arise, and if thereupon we shall fortify, yet will occasion the training up of our youth in the discipline of war, and make a number fit for the service of the wars and for the defense of our people there and at home.

18. The Spaniards govern in the Indies with all pride and tyranny; and like as when people of contrary nature at the sea enter into gallies, where men are tied as slaves, all yell and cry with one voice, *Liberta, liberta,* as desirous of liberty and freedom, so no doubt whensoever the Queen of England, a prince of such clemency, shall seat upon that firm of America, and shall be reported throughout all that tract to use the natural people there with all humanity, curtesy, and freedom, they will yield themselves to her government, and revolt clean from the Spaniard, and specially when they shall understand that she hath a noble navy, and that she aboundeth with a people most valiant for their defense. And her Majesty having Sir Frances Drake and other subjects already in credit with the Symerons, a people or great multitude already revolted from the Spanish government, she may with them and a few hundreths of this nation, trained up in the late wars of France and Flanders, bring great things to pass, and that with great ease; and this brought so about, her Majesty and her subjects may both enjoy the treasure of the mines of gold and silver, and the whole trade and all the gain of the trade of merchandise, that now passeth thither by the Spaniards only hand, of all the commodities of Europe; which trade of merchandise only were of it self sufficient (without the benefit of the rich mine) to enrich the subjects, and by customs to fill her Majesty's coffers to the full. And if it be high policy to maintain the poor people of this realm in work, I dare affirm that if the poor people of England were five times so many as they be, yet all might be set on work in and by working linen, and such other things of merchandise as the trade into the Indies doth require.

19. The present short trades causeth the mariner to be cast of, and often to be idle, and so by poverty to fall to piracy. But this course to Norumbega being longer, and a continuance of the employment of the mariner, doth keep the mariner from idleness and from necessity; and so it cutteth of the principal actions of piracy, and the rather because no riche pray for them to take cometh directly in their course or any thing near their course.

20. Many men of excellent wits and of divers singular gifts, overthrown by . . . some folly of youth, that are not able to live in England, may there be raised again, and do their country good service; and many needful uses there may (to great purpose) require the saving of great numbers, that for trifles may otherwise be devoured by the gallows.

21. Many soldiers and servitors, in the end of the wars, that might be hurtful to this *realm*, may there be unladen, to the common profit and quiet of this *realm*, and to our foreign benefi[t] there, as they may be employed.

22. The frye [children] of the wandering beggars of England, that grow up idly, and hurtful and burdenous to this

realm, may there be unladen, better bred up, and may people waste countries to the home and foreign benefit, and to their own more happy state.

23. If England cry out and affirm, that there is so many in all trades that one cannot live for another, as in all places they doe, this Norumbega (if it be thought so good) offereth the remedy.

Source: Charles Deane, et al., eds., *Documentary History of the State of Maine*, Vol. 2 (Portland: Bailey and Noyes, 1869–1916), 152–61.

The Jamestown Settlement (1607–1609)

The Jamestown Company sent three ships to Virginia in 1607 to found the Jamestown Colony, the first permanent English settlement in America. This account, by Captain John Smith and others, records the difficult early years of the colony, describing the sickness and near starvation of the settlers, the squabbling among the leadership, and encounters with Native Americans. Only the arrival of new settlers and supplies in 1610 saved the colony from failing.

The occasion of sicknesse.

Being thus left to our fortunes, it fortuned that within ten dayes scarce ten amongst us could either goe, or well stand, such extreame weaknes and sicknes oppressed us. And thereat none need marvaile, if they consider the cause and reason, which was this; whilest the ships stayed, our allowance was somewhat bettered, by a daily proportion of Bisket, which the sailers would pilfer to sell, give, or exchange with us, for money, Saxefras, furres, or love. But when they departed, there remained neither taverne, beere house, nor place of reliefe, but the common Kettell. Had we beene as free from all sinnes as gluttony, and drunkennesse, we might have beene canonized for Saints; But our President would never have beene admitted, for ingrossing to his private, Oatmeale, Sacke, Oyle, Aquavitæ, Beefe, Egges, or what not, but the Kettell; that indeed he allowed equally to be distributed, and that was halfe a pint of wheat, and as much barley boyled with water for a man a day, and this having fryed some 26. weekes in the ships hold, contained as many wormes as graines; so that we might truely call it rather so much bran then corne, our drinke was water, our lodgings Castles in the ayre: with this lodging and dyet, our extreame toile in bearing and planting Pallisadoes, so strained and bruised us, and our continuall labour in the extremitie of the heat had so weakened us, as were cause sufficient to have made us as miserable in our native Countrey, or any other place in the world. From May, to September, those that escaped, lived upon Sturgeon, and Sea-crabs, fiftie in this time we buried, the rest seeing the Presidents projects to escape these miseries in our Pinnace by flight (who all this time had neither felt want nor sicknes) so moved our dead spirits, as we deposed him; and established Ratcliffe in his place, (Gosnoll being, dead) Kendall deposed, Smith newly recovered, Martin and Ratcliffe was by his care preserved and relieved, and the most of the souldiers recovered, with the skilfull diligence of Mr. Thomas Wotton our Chirurgian generall. But now was all our provision spent, the Sturgeon gone, all helps abandoned, each houre expecting the fury of the Salvages; when God the patron of all good indevours, in that desperate extremitie so changed the hearts of the Salvages, that they brought such plenty of their fruits, and provision, as no man wanted.

A bad President. Plentie unexpected.

And now where some affirmed it was ill done of the Councell to send forth men so badly provided, this incontradictable reason will shew them plainely they are too ill advised to nourish such ill conceits; first, the fault of our going was our owne, what could be thought fitting or necessary we had, but what we should find, or want, or where we should be, we were all ignorant, and supposing to make our passage in two moneths, with victuall to live, and the advantage of the spring to worke; we were at Sea five moneths, where we both spent our victuall and lost the opportunitie of the time, and season to plant, by the unskilfull presumption of our ignorant transporters, that understood not at all, what they undertooke.

Such actions have ever since the worlds beginning beene subject to such accidents, and every thing of worth is found full of difficulties, but nothing so difficult as to establish a Common wealth so farre remote from men and meanes, and where mens mindes are so untoward as neither doe well themselves, nor suffer others. But to proceed.

The building of James Towne.

The new President and Martin, being little beloved, of weake judgement in dangers, and lesse industrie in peace, committed the managing of all things abroad to Captaine Smith: who by his owne example, good words, and faire promises, set some to mow, others to binde thatch, some to build houses, others to thatch them, himselfe always bearing the greatest taske for his owne share, so that in short time, he provided most of them lodgings, neglecting any for himselfe. This done, seeing the Salvages superfluitie beginne to decrease (with some of his workemen) shipped himselfe in the

Shallop to search the Country for trade. The want of the language, knowledge to mannage his boat without sailes, the want of a sufficient power (knowing the multitude of the Salvages), apparell for his men, and other necessaries, were infinite impediments, yet no discouragement. Being but six or seaven in company he went downe the river to Kecoughtan, where at first they scorned him, as a famished man, and would in derision offer him a handfull of Corne, a peece of bread, for their swords and muskets, and such like proportions also for their apparell. But seeing by trade and courtesie there was nothing, to be had, he made bold to try such conclusions as necessitie inforced, though contrary to his Commission: Let fly his muskets, ran his boat on shore, whereat they all fled into the woods. So marching towards their houses, they might see great heapes of corne: much adoe he had to restraine his hungry souldiers from present taking of it, expecting as it hapned that the Salvages would assault them, as not long after they did with a most hydeous noyse. Sixtie or seaventie of them, some blacke, some red, some white, some party-coloured, came in a square order, singing and dauncing out of the woods, with their Okee (which was an Idoll made of skinnes, stuffed with mosse, all painted and hung with chaines and copper) borne before them: and in this manner being well armed, with Clubs, Targets, Bowes and Arrowes, they charged the English, that so kindly received them with their muskets loaden with Pistoll shot, that downe fell their God, and divers lay sprauling on the ground; the rest fled againe to the woods, and ere long sent one of their Quiyoughkasoucks to offer peace, and redeeme their Okee. Smith told them, if onely six of them would come unarmed and loade his boat, he would not onely be their friend, but restore them their Okee, and give them Beads, Copper, and Hatchets besides: which on both sides was to their contents performed: and then they brought him Venison, Turkies, wild foule, bread, and what they had, singing and dauncing in signe of friendship till they departed. In his returne he discovered the Towne and Country of Warraskoyack.

> Thus God unboundlesse by his power,
> Made them thus kind, would us devour.

Amoris, a Salvage his best friend slaine for loving us. The Discovery of Chickahamine.

Smith perceiving (notwithstanding their late miserie) not any regarded but from hand to mouth (the company being well recovered) caused the Pinnace to be provided with things fitting to get provision for the yeare following; but in the interim he made 3 or 4 journies and discovered the people of Chickahamania: yet what he carefully provided the rest carelessly spent. Wingfield and Kendall living in disgrace, seeing all things at randome in the absence of Smith, the companies dislike of their Presidents weaknes, and their small love to Martins never mending sicknes, strengthened themselves with the sailers, and other confederates to regaine

their former credit and authority, or at least such meanes abord the Pinnace.

Another project to abandon the country.

[The pinnace] being fitted to saile as Smith had appointed (for trade) to alter her course and to goe for England. Smith unexpectedly returning had the plot discovered to him, much trouble he had to prevent it, till with store of sakre and musket shot he forced them stay or sinke in the river, which action cost the life of captaine Kendall. These brawles are so disgustfull, as some will say they were better forgotten, yet all men of good judgement will conclude, at were better their basenes should be manifest to the world, then the busines beare the scorne and shame of their excused disorders. The President and captaine Archer not long after intended also to have abandoned the country, which project also was curbed, and suppressed by Smith. The Spaniard never more greedily desired gold then he victuall, nor his souldiers more to abandon the Country, then he to keepe it. But finding plentie of Corne in the river of Chickahamania where hundreds of Salvages in divers places stood with baskets expecting his comming. And now the winter approaching, the rivers became so covered with swans, geese, duckes, and cranes, that we daily feasted with good bread, Virginia pease, pumpions, and putchamins, fish, fowle, and diverse sorts of wild beasts as far as we could eate them: so that none of our Tuftaffaty humorists desired to goe for England. But our Comædies never endured long without a Tragedie; some idle exceptions being muttered against Captaine Smith, for not discovering the head of Chickahamania river, and taxed by the Councell, to be too slow in so worthy an attempt. The next voyage hee proceeded so farre that with much labour by cutting of trees in sunder he made his passage, but when his Barge could passe no farther, he left her in a broad bay out of danger of shot, commanding none should goe a shore till his returne: himselfe with two English and two Salvages went up higher in a Canowe, but hee was not long absent, but his men went a shore, whose want of government, gave both occasion and opportunity to the Salvages to surprise one George Cassen, whom they slew, and much failed not to have cut of the boat and all the rest. Smith little dreaming of that accident, being got to the marshes at the rivers head, twentie myles in the desert, had his two men slain (as is supposed) sleeping by the Canowe, whilst himselfe by fowling sought them victuall, who finding he was beset with 200 Salvages, two of them hee slew, still defending himselfe with the ayd of a Salvage his guid, whom he bound to his arme with his garters, and used him as a buckler, yet he was shot in his thigh a little, and had many arrowes that stucke in his cloathes but no great hurt, till at last they tooke him prisoner. When this newes came to James towne, much was their sorrow for his losse, fewe expecting what ensued. Six or seven weekes those Barbarians kept him prisoner, many strange triumphes and conjurations they made of him, yet hee so demeaned himselfe amongst them, as he not onely diverted them from surprising the Fort, but procured his owne libertie, and got himselfe and his company such estimation amongst them, that those Salvages admired him more then their owne Quiyouckosucks. The manner how they used and delivered him, is as followeth. . . .

Captaine Smith taken prisoner.

The Salvages having drawne from George Cassen whether Captaine Smith was gone, prosecuting that opportunity they followed him with 300. bowmen, conducted by the King of Pamaunkee, who in divisions searching the turnings of the river, found Robinson and Emry by the fire side, those they shot full of arrowes and slew. Then finding the Captaine, as is said, that used the Salvage that was his guide as his shield (three of them being slain and divers other so gauld [galled, or wounded]) all the rest would not come neere him. Thinking thus to have returned to his boat, regarding them, as he marched, more then his way, slipped up to the middle in an oasie creeke & his Salvage with him, yet durst they not come to him till being neere dead with cold, he threw away his armes. Then according to their composition they drew him forth and led him to the fire, where his men were slaine. Diligently they chafed his benummed limbs. He demanding for their Captaine, they shewed him Opechankanough, King of Pamaunkee, to whom he gave a round Ivory double compass Dyall. Much they marvailed at the playing of the Fly and Needle, which they could see so plainely, and yet not touch it, because of the glasse that covered them. But when he demonstrated by that Globe-like Jewell, the roundnesse of the earth, and skies, the sphaere of the Sunne, Moone, and Starres, and how the Sunne did chase the night round about the world continually; the greatnesse of the Land and Sea, the diversitie of Nations, varietie of complexions, and how we were to them Antipodes, and many other such like matters, they all stood as amazed with admiration. Notwithstanding, within an houre after they tyed him to a tree, and as many as could stand about him prepared to shoot him, but the King holding up the Compass in his hand, they all laid downe their Bowes and Arrowes, and in a triumphant manner led him to Orapaks, where he was after their manner kindly feasted, and well used.

The order they observed in their triumph.

Their order in conducting him was thus; Drawing themselves all in fyle, the King in the middest had all their Peeces and Swords borne before him. Captaine Smith was led after him by three great Salvages, holding him fast by each arme: and on each side six went in fyle with their Arrowes nocked. But arriving at the Towne (which was but onely thirtie or fortie hunting houses made of Mats, which they remove as they please, as we our tents) all the women and children staring to behold him, the souldiers first all in fyle performed the forme of a Bissom so well as could be, and on each flanke

officers as Serjeants to see them keepe their orders. A good time they continued this exercise, and then cast themselves in a ring, dauncing in such severall Postures, and singing and yelling out such hellish notes and screeches; being strangely painted, every one his quiver of Arrowes, and at his backe a club; on his arme a Fox or an Otters skinne, or some such matter for his vambrace; their heads and shoulders painted red, with Oyle and Pocones mingled together, which Scarlet-like colour made an exceeding handsome shew; his Bow in his hand, and the skinne of a Bird with her wings abroad dryed, tyed on his head, a peece of copper, a white shell, a long feather, with a small rattle growing at the tayles of their snaks tyed to it, or some such like toy. All this while Smith and the King stood in the middest guarded, as before is said, and after three dances they all departed. Smith they conducted to a long house, where thirtie or fortie tall fellowes did guard him, and ere long more bread and venison was brought him then would have served twentie men, I thinke his stomacke at that time was not very good; what he left they put in baskets and tyed over his head. About midnight they set the meate againe before him, all this time not one of them would eate a bit with him, till the next morning they brought him as much more, and then did they eate all the old, & reserved the new as they had done the other, which made him thinke they would fat him to eat him. Yet in this desperate estate to defend him from the cold, one Maocassater brought him his gowne, in requitall of some beads and toyes Smith had given him at his first arrivall in Virginia.

How he should have beene slaine at Orapacks.

Two dayes after a man would have slaine him (but that the guard prevented it) for the death of his sonne, to whom they conducted him to recover the poore man then breathing his last. Smith told them that at James towne he had a water would doe it, if they would let him fetch it, but they would not permit that; but made all the preparations they could to assault James towne, craving his advice, and for recompence he should have life, libertie, land, and women. In part of a Table booke he writ his minde to them at the Fort, what was intended, how they should follow that direction to affright the messengers, and without fayle send him such things as he writ for. And an Inventory with them. The difficultie and danger, he told the Salvages, of the Mines, great-gunnes, and other Engins exceedingly affrighted them, yet according to his request they went to James towne, in as bitter weather as could be of frost and snow, and within three dayes returned with an answer.

How he saved James towne from being surprised.

But when they came to James towne, seeing men sally out as he had told them they would, they fled; yet in the night they came againe to the same place where he had told them they should receive an answer, and such things as he had promised them, which they found accordingly, and with which they returned with no small expedition, to the wonder of them all that heard it, that he could either divine, or the paper could speake: then they led him to the Youthtanunds, the Mattapanients, the Payankatanks, the Nantaughtacunds, and Onawmanients upon the rivers of Raphanock, and Patawomek, over all those rivers, and backe againe by divers other severall Nations, to the Kings habitation at Pamaunkee, where they entertained him with most strange and fearefulle Conjurations; As if neare led to hell, Amongst the Devils to dwell.

How they did Conjure him at Pamaunkee.

Not long after, early in a morning a great fire was made in a long house, and a mat spread on the one side, as on the other; on the one they caused him to sit, and all the guard went out of the house, and presently came skipping in a great grim fellow, all painted over with coale, mingled with oyle; and many Snakes and Wesels skins stuffed with mosse, and all their tayles tyed together, so as they met on the crowne of his head in a tassell; and round about the tassell was as a Coronet of feathers, the skins hanging round about his head, backe, and shoulders, and in a manner covered his face; with a hellish voyce and a rattle in his hand. With most strange gestures and passions he began his invocation, and environed the fire with a circle of meale; which done, three more such like devils came rushing in with the like antique tricks, painted halfe blacke, halfe red: but all their eyes were painted white, and some red stroakes like Mutchato's, along their cheekes: round about him those fiends daunced a pretty while, and then came in three more as ugly as the rest; with red eyes, and white stroakes over their blacke faces, at last they all sat downe right against him; three of them on the one hand of the chiefe Priest, and three on the other. Then all with their rattles began a song, which ended, the chiefe Priest layd downe five wheat cornes: then strayning his armes and hands with such violence that he sweat, and his veynes swelled, he began a short Oration: at the conclusion they all gave a short groane; and then layd down three graines more. After that, began their song againe, and then another Oration, ever laying downe so many cornes as before, till they had twice incirculed the fire; that done, they tooke a bunch of little stickes prepared for that purpose, continuing still their devotion, and at the end of every song and Oration, they layd downe a sticke betwixt the divisions of Corne. Till night, neither he nor they did either eate or drinke, and then they feasted merrily, with the best provisions they could make. Three dayes they used this Ceremony; the meaning whereof they told him, was to know if he intended them well or no. The circle of meale signified their Country, the circles of corne the bounds of the Sea, and the stickes his Country. They imagined the world to be flat and round, like a trencher, and they in the middest. After this they brought him a bagge of gunpowder, which they carefully preserved

till the next spring, to plant as they did their corne; because they would be acquainted with the nature of that seede.

Opitchapam the Kings brother invited him to his house, where, with as many platters of bread, foule, and wild beasts, as did environ him, he bid him wellcome; but not any of them would eate a bit with him, but put up all the remainder in Baskets. At his returne to Opechancanoughs, all the Kings women, and their children, flocked about him for their parts, as a due by Custome, to be merry with such fragments.

> But his waking mind in hydeous dreames did oft
>   see wondrous shapes,
> Of bodies strange, and huge in growth, and of
>   stupendious makes.

How Powhatan entertained him.

At last they brought him to Meronocomo, where was Powhatan their Emperor. Here more then two hundred of those grim Courtiers stood wondering at him, as he had beene a monster; till Powhatan and his trayne had put themselves in their greatest braveries. Before a fire upon a seat like a bedsted, he sat covered with a great robe, made of Rarowcun skinnes, and all the tayles hanging by. On either hand did sit a young wench of 16 or 18 yeares, and along on each side the house, two rowes of men, and behind them as many women, with all their heads and shoulders painted red; many of their heads bedecked with the white downe of Birds; but every one with something: and a great chayne of white beads about their necks. At his entrance before the King, all the people gave a great shout. The Queene of Appamatuck was appointed to bring him water to wash his hands, and another brought him a bunch of feathers, in stead of a Towell to dry them: having feasted him after their best barbarous manner they could, a long consultation was held, but the conclusion was, two great stones were brought before Powhatan: then as many as could layd hands on him, dragged him to them, and thereon laid his head, and being ready with their clubs, to beate out his braines, Pocahontas the Kings dearest daughter, when no intreaty could prevaile, got his head in her armes, and laid her owne upon his to save him from death: whereat the Emperour was contented he should live to make him hatchets, and her bells, beads, and copper; for they thought him as well of all occupations as themselves. For the King himselfe will make his owne robes, shooes, bowes, arrowes, pots; plant, hunt, or doe any thing so well as the rest.

How Pocahontas saved his life.

> They say he bore a pleasant shew,
> But sure his heart was sad.
> For who can pleasant be, and rest,
> That lives in feare and dread:
> And having life suspected, doth
> It still suspected lead.

How Powhatan sent him to James Towne.

Two dayes after, Powhatan having disguised himselfe in the most fearefull manner he could, caused Capt. Smith to be brought forth to a great house in the woods, and there upon a mat by the fire to be left alone. Not long after from behinde a mat that divided the house, was made the most dolefullest noyse he ever heard; then Powhatan more like a devill then a man with some two hundred more as blacke as himselfe, came unto him and told him now they were friends, and presently he should goe to James towne, to send him two great gunnes, and a gryndstone, for which he would give him the Country of Capahowosick, and for ever esteeme him as his sonne Nantaquoud. So to James towne with 12 guides Powhatan sent him. That night they quarterd in the woods, he still expecting (as he had done all this long time of his imprisonment) every houre to be put to one death or other: for all their feasting. But almightie God (by his divine providence) had mollified the hearts of those sterne Barbarians with compassion. The next morning betimes they came to the Fort, where Smith having used the Salvages with what kindnesse he could, he shewed Rawhunt, Powhatans trusty servant two demi-Culverings & a millstone to carry Powhatan: they found them somewhat too heavie; but when they did see him discharge them, being loaded with stones, among the boughs of a great tree loaded with Isickles, the ice and branches came so tumbling downe, that the poore Salvages ran away halfe dead with feare. But at last we regained some conference with them, and gave them such toyes; and sent to Powhatan, his women, and children such presents, as gave them in generall full content. Now in James Towne they were all in combustion, the strongest preparing once more to run away with the Pinnace; which . . . with the hazzard of his life, with Sakre falcon and musket shot, Smith forced now the third time to stay or sinke. Some no better then they should be, had plotted with the President, the next day to have put him to death by the Leviticall law, for the lives of Robinson and Emry, pretending the fault was his that had led them to their ends: but he quickly tooke such order with such Lawyers, that he layd them by the heeles till he sent some of them prisoners for England. Now ever once in foure or five dayes, Pocahontas with her attendants, brought him so much provision, that saved many of their lives, that els for all this had starved with hunger.

> Thus from numbe death our good God sent reliefe,
> The sweete asswager of all other griefe.

A true proofe of Gods love to the action.

His relation of the plenty he had seene, especially at Werawocomoco, and of the state and bountie of Powhatan (which till that time was unknowne) so revived their dead spirits (especially the love of Pocahontas) as all mens feare was abandoned. Thus you may see what difficulties still crossed any good indevour: and the good success of the businesse being thus oft brought to the very period of destruction; yet you see by what strange means God hath still delivered it. As for the insufficiency of them admitted in Commission, that error could not be prevented by the Electors; there being no other choise, and all strangers to each others education, qualities, or disposition. And if any deeme it a shame to our Nation to have any mention made of those inormities, let them peruse the Histories of the Spanyards Discoveries and Plantations, where they may see how many mutinies, disorders, and dissentions have accompanied them, and crossed their attempts: which being knowne to be particular mens offences; doth take away the generall scorne and contempt, which malice, presumption, covetousnesse, or ignorance might produce; to the scandall and reproach of those, whose actions and valiant resolutions deserve a more worthy respect.

Of two evils the lesse was chosen.

Now whether it had beene better for Captaine Smith, to have concluded with any of those severall projects, to have abandoned the Countrey, with some ten or twelve of them, who were called the better sort, and have left Mr. Hunt our Preacher, Master Anthony Gosnoll, a most honest, worthy, and industrious Gentleman, Master Thomas Wotton, and some 27 others of his Countrymen to the fury of the Salvages, famine, and all manner of mischiefes, and inconveniences (for they were but fortie in all to keepe possession of this large Country); or starve himselfe with them for company, for want of lodging: or but adventuring abroad to make them provision, or by his opposition to preserve the action, and save all their lives; I leave to the censure of all honest men to consider.

> But We men imagine in our Jolitie,
> That 'tis all one, or good or bad to be.
> But then anone wee alter this againe,
> If happily wee feele the sence of paine;
> For then we're turn'd into a mourning vaine.

Written by Thomas Studley, the first Cape Merchant in Virginia, Robert Fenton, Edward Harrington, and J.S.

Source: John Smith, *The Generall Historie of Virginia, New England, and the Summer Isles* (1624; Glasgow: J. MacLehose, 1907; New York: Macmillan, 1907).

The Mayflower Compact (1620)

This agreement, drawn up and signed by male heads of household aboard the *Mayflower*, recognized that the new settlement would need rules by which it could be governed. As such, this civil covenant established the principle that all members of the community agreed to live in a society governed by laws established for the greater good of the majority.

IN THE NAME OF GOD, AMEN. We, whose names are underwritten, the Loyal Subjects of our dread Sovereign Lord King *James*, by the Grace of God, of *Great Britain*, *France*, and *Ireland*, King, *Defender of the Faith*, &c. Having undertaken for the Glory of God, and Advancement of the Christian Faith, and the Honour of our King and Country, a Voyage to plant the first Colony in the northern Parts of *Virginia*; Do by these Presents, solemnly and mutually, in the Presence of God and one another, covenant and combine ourselves together into a civil Body Politick, for our better Ordering and Preservation, and Furtherance of the Ends aforesaid: And by Virtue hereof do enact, constitute, and frame, such just and equal Laws, Ordinances, Acts, Constitutions, and Officers, from time to time, as shall be thought most meet and convenient for the general Good of the Colony; unto which we promise all due Submission and Obedience.

IN WITNESS whereof we have hereunto subscribed our names at *Cape-Cod* the eleventh of November, in the Reign of our Sovereign Lord King *James*, of *England*, *France*, and *Ireland*, the eighteenth, and of *Scotland* the fifty-fourth, *Anno Domini*; 1620.

Mr. John Carver,	Mr. Samuel Fuller,	Edward Tilly,
Mr. William Bradford,	Mr. Christopher Martin,	John Tilly,
Mr Edward Winslow,	Mr. William Mullins,	Francis Cooke,
Mr. William Brewster,	Mr. William White,	Thomas Rogers,
Isaac Allerton,	Mr. Richard Warren,	Thomas Tinker,
Myles Standish,	John Howland,	John Ridgdale,
John Alden,	Mr. Steven Hopkins,	Edward Fuller,
John Turner,	Digery Priest,	Richard Clark,
Francis Eaton,	Thomas Williams,	Richard Gardiner,
James Chilton,	Gilbert Winslow,	Mr. John Allerton,
John Craxton,	Edmund Margesson,	Thomas English,
John Billington,	Peter Brown,	Edward Doten,
Joses Fletcher,	Richard Britteridge,	Edward Liester.
John Goodman,	George Soule,	

Source: The Federal and State Constitutions, Colonial Charters, and Other Organic Laws of the States, Territories, and Colonies Now and Heretofore Forming the United States of America. Compiled and edited under the Act of Congress of June 30, 1906, by Francis Newton Thorpe (Washington, DC: Government Printing Office, 1909).

Rights and Privileges of Patroons (1629)

The Charter of Freedoms and Exemptions for New Netherland was granted by the Dutch West India Company on June 7, 1629. It provided for the perpetual proprietorship of vast estates, called patroonships, to those members of the company founding settlements of fifty or more persons on land purchased from the Indians. In return for a pledge of loyalty to the company, patroons were given complete jurisdiction over their territory. Under the terms of this charter, a handful of patroons quickly took control of most of the Hudson River Valley, the choicest portion of New Netherland.

Disputes within the company and difficulty with the native peoples doomed the system, however, so that by 1680 only two of the original grants remained in force. The colony itself had already fallen under British control in 1664.

All such shall be acknowledged patroons of New Netherland who shall, within the space of four years next after they have given notice to any of the chambers of the Company here, or to the commander or council there, undertake to plant a colony there of fifty souls, upward of fifteen years old; one-fourth within one year, and within three years after the sending of the first, making together four years, the remainder, to the full number of fifty persons, to be shipped from hence, on pain, in case of willful neglect, of being deprived of the privileges obtained; but it is to be observed that the Company reserve the island of the Manhattes [Manhattan] to themselves.

They shall, from the time they make known the situation of the places where they propose to settle colonies, have the preference to all others of the absolute property of such lands as they have there chosen, but, in case the situation should not afterward please them, or that they have been mistaken as to the quality of the land, they may, after remonstrating concerning the same to the commander and council there, be at liberty to choose another place.

The Patroons, by virtue of their power, shall and may be permitted, at such places as they shall settle their colonies, to extend their limits four miles along the shore, that is, on one side of a navigable river, or two miles on each side of a river, and so far into the country as the situation of the occupiers will permit; providing and conditioned that the Company keep to themselves the lands lying and remaining between the limits of colonies, to dispose thereof, when and at such time as they shall think proper, in such manner that no person shall be allowed to come within seven or eight miles of them without their consent, unless the situation of the land thereabout were such that the commander and council, for good reasons, should order otherwise; always

observing that the first occupiers are not to be prejudiced in the right they have obtained, other than, unless the service of the Company should require it, for the building of fortifications or something of that sort; remaining, moreover, the command of each bay, river, or island of the first-settled colony, under the supreme jurisdiction of their High Mightinesses the States General and the Company. But that, on the next colonies being settled on the same river or island, they may, in conjunction with the first, appoint one or more council in order to consider what may be necessary for the prosperity of the colonies on the said river and island.

They shall forever possess and enjoy all the lands lying within the aforesaid limits . . . and, in case any one should in time prosper so much as to found one or more cities, he shall have the power and authority to establish officers and magistrates there and to make use of the title of his colony, according to his pleasure and to the quality or the persons.

The patroons and colonists shall be privileged to send their people and effects thither in ships belonging to the Company, provided they take the oath and pay to the Company for bringing over the people.

Inasmuch as it is intended to people the island of the Manhattes first, all fruits and wares that are produced on the lands situate on the North River and lying thereabout shall, for the present, be brought there before they may be sent elsewhere; excepting such as are from their nature unnecessary there, or such as cannot, without great loss to the owner thereof be brought there; in which case the owners thereof shall be obliged to give timely notice in writing of the difficulty attending the same to the Company here, or the commander and council there, that the same may be remedied as the necessity thereof shall be found to require.

All the patroons of colonies in New Netherland and

of colonies on the island of Manhattes shall be at liberty to sail and traffic all along the coast from Florida to Terra Neuf, provided that they do again return with all such goods as they shall get in trade to the island of Manhattes and pay 5 percent for recognition to the Company, in order, if possible, that, after the necessary inventory of the goods shipped be taken, the same may be sent hither. . . .

In case the ships of the patroons, in going from Florida to Terra Neuf and no further without our grant, should overpower any of the prizes of the enemy, they shall be obliged to bring, or cause to be brought, such prize to the college of the place from whence they sailed out, in order to be rewarded by them; the Company shall keep the one-third part thereof, and the remaining two-thirds shall belong to them, in consideration of the cost and risk they have been at, all according to the orders of the Company.

It shall be also free for the aforesaid patroons to traffic and trade all along the coast of New Netherland and places circumjacent, with such goods as are consumed there, and receive in return for them all sorts of merchandise that may be had there, except beavers, otters, minks, and all sorts of peltry, which trade the Company reserve to themselves. . . .

The Company promises the colonists of the patroons that they shall be free from customs, taxes, excise, imposts, or any other contributions for the space of ten years; and, after the expiration of the said ten years at the highest, such customs as the goods are taxable with here for the present.

They will not take from the service of the patroons any of their colonists, either man or woman, son or daughter, manservant or maidservant; and, though any of them should desire the same, they will not receive them, much less permit them to leave their patroons and enter into the service of another, unless on consent obtained from their patroons in writing; and this for and during so many years as they are bound to their patroons; after the expiration whereof, it shall be in the power of the patroons to send hither all such colonists as will not continue in their service and until then shall not enjoy their liberty. And all such colonists as shall leave the service of his patroon and enter into the service of another or shall, contrary to his contract, leave his service, we promise to do everything in our power to apprehend and deliver the same into the hands of his patroon, or attorney, that he may be proceeded against. . . .

In regard to such private persons as on their own account, or others in the service of their masters here (not enjoying the same privileges of the patroons), shall be inclined to go thither and settle, they shall, with the approbation of the director and council there, be at liberty to take up as much land, and take possession thereof, as they shall be able properly to improve and shall enjoy the same in full property either for themselves or masters.

They shall have free liberty of hunting and fowling, as well by water as by land, generally, and in public and private woods and rivers, about their colonies, according to the orders of the director and council.

Whosoever, whether colonists of patroons for their patroons or free persons for themselves or other particulars for their masters, shall discover any shores, bays, or other fit places for erecting fisheries or the making of salt ponds, they may take possession thereof and begin to work on them in their own absolute property, to the exclusion of all others. . . .

In case any of the colonists should, by his industry and diligence, discover any minerals, precious stones, crystals, marbles, or suchlike or any pearl fishery, the same shall be and remain the property of the patroon or patroons of such colony, giving and ordering the discoverer such premium as the patroon shall beforehand have stipulated with such colonists by contract. And the patroons shall be exempt from all recognition to the Company for the term of eight years and pay only for freight to bring them over, 2 percent, and after the expiration of the aforesaid eight years, for recognition and freight, the one-eighth part of what the same may be worth.

The Company will take all the colonists, free as well as those that are in service, under their protection and the same, against all outlandish and inlandish wars and powers, with the forces they have there, as much as lies in their power, defend.

Whosoever shall settle any colony out of the limits of the Manhattes Island shall be obliged to satisfy the Indians for the land they shall settle upon, and they may extend or enlarge the limits of their colonies if they settle a proportionate number of colonists thereon.

The patroons and colonists shall in particular, and in the speediest manner, endeavor to find out ways and means whereby they may support a minister and schoolmaster, that thus the service of God and zeal for religion may not grow cool and be neglected among them; and that they do for the first, procure a comforter of the sick there.

The colonies that shall happen to lie on the respective rivers or islands (that is to say, each river or island for itself) shall be at liberty to appoint a deputy, who shall give information to the commander and council of that Western quarter, of all things related to his colony, and who are to further matters relating thereto, of which deputies there shall be one altered, or changed, in every two years; and all colonies shall be obliged, at least once every twelve months, to make exact report of their colony and lands thereabout to the commander and council there, in order to be transmitted hither.

The colonists shall not be permitted to make any woolen, linen, or cotton cloth, nor weave any other stuffs there on pain of being banished, and as perjurers to be arbitrarily punished.

The Company will use their endeavors to supply the colonists with as many blacks as they conveniently can, on the conditions hereafter to be made; in such manner, however, that they shall not be bound to do it for a longer time than they shall think proper.

Source: E. B. O'Callaghan, *History of New Netherland; or, New York Under the Dutch* (New York, 1846), 112–20.

A Modell of Christian Charity (1630)

Written by John Winthrop as he sailed to New England aboard the *Arabella*, this essay was a statement of the principles that would guide the Puritan Commonwealth. The new community offered the settlers a chance to practice their religion freely, and Winthrop saw the establishment of the colony as a divine mission. Theirs would be an inspired "city upon a hill," which would be an example to others in the creation of a more perfect society.

**Written on Board the Arabella,
on the Atlantic Ocean.**

By the Hon. John Winthrop Esqr. In his passage (with a great company of Religious people, of which Christian tribes he was the Brave Leader and famous Governor;) from the Island of Great Brittaine to New-England in the North America. Anno 1630.

**Christian Charitie.
*A Modell hereof.***

GOD ALMIGHTY in his most holy and wise providence, hath soe disposed of the condition of mankind, as in all times some must be rich, some poore, some high and eminent in power and dignitie; others mean and in submission.

The Reason hereof.

1 *Reas{on}.* First to hold conformity with the rest of his world, being delighted to show forth the glory of his wisdom in the variety and difference of the creatures, and the glory of his power in ordering all these differences for the preservation and good of the whole; and the glory of his greatness, that as it is the glory of princes to have many officers, soe this great king will have many stewards, Counting himself more honoured in dispensing his gifts to man by man, than if he did it by his owne immediate hands.

2 *Reas.* Secondly that he might have the more occasion to manifest the work of his Spirit: first upon the wicked in moderating and restraining them: soe that the riche and mighty should not eate upp the poore nor the poore and dispised rise upp against and shake off theire yoake.

2ly. In the regenerate, in exerciseing his graces in them, as in the grate ones, theire love, mercy, gentleness, temperance &c., in the poore and inferior sorte, theire faithe, patience, obedience &c.

3 *Reas.* Thirdly, that every man might have need of others, and from hence they might be all knitt more nearly together in the Bonds of brotherly affection. From hence it appears plainly that noe man is made more honourable than another or more wealthy &c., out of any particular and singular respect to himselfe, but for the glory of his creator and the common good of the creature, man. Therefore God still reserves the propperty of these gifts to himself as Ezek[ial]. 16. 17. he there calls wealthe, *his gold and his silver*, and Prov[erbs]. 3. 9. he claims theire service as his due, *honor the Lord with thy riches* &c.—All men being thus (by divine providence) ranked into two sorts, riche and poore; under the first are comprehended all such as are able to live comfortably by their owne meanes duely improved; and all others are poore according to the former distribution.

There are two rules whereby we are to walk one towards another: Justice and Mercy. These are always distinguished in their act and in their object, yet may they both concurre in the same subject in eache respect; as sometimes there may be an occasion of showing mercy to a rich man in some sudden danger or distresse, and alsoe doeing of meere justice to a poor man in regard of some perticular contract &c.

There is likewise a double Lawe by which wee are regulated in our conversation towardes another; in both the former respects, the lawe of nature and the lawe of grace, or the morrall lawe or the lawe of the gospell, to omitt the rule of justice as not propperly belonging to this purpose otherwise than it may fall into consideration in some perticular cases. By the first of these lawes man as he was enabled soe withall is commanded to love his neighbour as himself. Upon this ground stands all the precepts of the morrall lawe, which concernes our dealings with men. To apply this to the works of mercy; this lawe requires two things. First that every man afford his help to another in every want or distresse. Secondly, that hee performe this out of the same affection which makes him carefull of his owne goods, according to that of our Savior, *Whatsoever ye would that men should do to you* (Math.).

This was practised by Abraham and Lot in entertaining the angells and the old man of Gibea.

The lawe of Grace or of the Gospell hath some difference from the former; as in these respects, First the lawe of nature was given to man in the estate of innocency; this of the Gospell in the estate of regeneracy. 2ly, the former propounds one man to another, as the same flesh and image of God; this as a brother in Christ allsoe, and in the communion of the same Spirit, and soe teacheth to put a difference between christians and others. *Doe good to all, especially to the household of faith*; upon this ground the Israelites were to putt a difference betweene the brethren of such as were strangers though not of the Canaanites.

3ly. The Lawe of nature would give no rules for dealing with enemies, for all are to be considered as friends in the state of innocency, but the Gospell commands love to an enemy. Proofe. *If thine Enemy hunger, feed him; Love your Enemies, doe good to them that hate you.* Math[ew]. 5. 44.

This lawe of the Gospell propounds likewise a difference of seasons and occasions. There is a time when a christian must sell all and give to the poor, as they did in the Apostles times. There is a time allsoe when christians (though they give not all yet) must give beyond their abillity, as they of Macedonia, Cor[inthians]. 2, 6. Likewise community of perills calls for extraordinary liberality, and soe doth community in some speciall service for the churche. Lastly, when there is no other means whereby our christian brother may be relieved in his distress, we must help him beyond our ability rather than tempt God in putting him upon help by miraculous or extraordinary meanes.

This duty of mercy is exercised in the kinds, Giveing, lending and forgiving.—

Quest{ion}. What rule shall a man observe in giveing in respect of the measure?

Ans. If the time and occasion be ordinary he is to give out of his abundance. *Let him lay aside as God hath blessed him.* If the time and occasion be extraordinary, he must be ruled by them; taking this withall, that then a man cannot likely doe too much, especially if he may leave himselfe and his family under probable means of comfortable subsistence.

Object{ion}. A man must lay upp for posterity, the fathers lay upp for posterity and children, and *he is worse than an infidell that provideth not for his owne.*

Ans{wer}. For the first, it is plaine that it being spoken by way of comparison, it must be meant of the ordinary and usuall course of fathers, and cannot extend to times and occasions extraordinary. For the other place the Apostle speaks against such as walked inordinately, and it is without question, that he is worse than an infidell who through his owne sloathe and voluptuousness shall neglect to provide for his family.—

Object. The wise man's Eyes are in his head, saith Solomon, *and foreseeth the plague*; therefore he must forecast and lay upp against evill times when he or his may stand in need of all he can gather.

Ans. This very Argument Solomon useth to persuade to liberallity, Eccle[siastes].: *Cast thy bread upon the waters*, and *for thou knowest not what evill may come upon the land.* Luke 26. *Make you friends of the riches of iniquity*; you will ask how this shall be? Very well. For first he that gives to the poore, lends to the lord and he will repay him even in this life an hundredfold to him or his.—*The righteous is ever mercifull and lendeth and his seed enjoyeth the blessing*; and besides wee know what advantage it will be to us in the day of account when many such witnesses shall stand forth for us to witnesse the improvement of our tallent.

And I would know of those whoe pleade soe much for laying up for time to come, whether they holde that to be Gospell, Math[ew]. 16. 19. *Lay not upp for yourselves Treasures upon Earth &c.* If they acknowledge it, what extent will they allowe it? if only to those primitive times, let them consider the reason whereopon our Saviour groundes it. The first is that they are subject to the moathe, the rust, the theife. Secondly, They will steale away the hearte; *where the treasure is there will ye heart be allsoe.* The reasons are of like force at all times.

Therefore the exhortation must be generall and perpetuall, withallwayes in respect of the love and affection to riches and in regard of the things themselves when any speciall service for the churche or perticular Distresse of our brother doe call for the use of them; otherwise it is not only lawfull but necessary to lay upp as Joseph did to have ready uppon such occasions, as the Lord (whose stewards wee are of them) shall call for them from us; Christ gives us an Instance of the first, when hee sent his disciples for the Ass, and bids them answer the owner thus, the Lord hath need of him: soe when the Tabernacle was to be built, he sends to his people to call for their silver and gold, &c; and yeildes noe other reason but that it was for his worke. When Elisha comes to the widow of Sareptah and findes her preparing to make ready her pittance for herselfe and family, he bids her first provide for him, he challengeth first God's parte which she must first give before shee must serve her owne family.

All these teach us that the Lord lookes that when hee is pleased to call for his right in any thing wee have, our owne interest wee have, must stand aside till his turne be served. For the other, wee need looke noe further then to that of John 1. *He whoe hath this world's goodes and seeth his brother to neede and shutts upp his compassion from him, how dwelleth the love of God in him*, which comes punctually to this conclusion; if thy brother be in want and thou canst help him, thou needst not make doubt, what thou shouldst doe; if thou lovest God thou must help him.

Quest. What rule must wee observe in lending?

Ans. Thou must observe whether thy brother hath present or probable or possible means of repaying thee, if there be none of those, thou must give him according to his necessity, rather then lend him as he requires; if he hath present means of repaying thee, thou art to look at him not as an act of mercy, but by way of Commerce, wherein thou arte to walk by the rule of justice; but if his means of repaying thee be only probable or possible, then is hee an object of thy mercy, thou must lend him, though there be danger of losing it, Deut[eronomy]. 15. 7. *If any of thy brethren be poore &c., thou shalt lend him sufficient.* That men might not shift off this duty by the apparent hazzard, he tells them that though the yeare of Jubile were at hand (when he must remitt it, if hee were not able to repay it before) yet he must lend him and that chearefully. *It may not grieve thee to give him* (saith hee) and because some might object, why soe I should soone impoverishe myself and my family, he adds with all thy worke &c; for our Saviour, Math[ew]. 5. 42. *From him that would borrow of thee turne not away.*

Quest. What rule must we observe in forgiving?

Ans. Whether thou didst lend by way of commerce or in mercy, if he hath nothing to pay thee, must forgive, (except in cause where thou hast a surety or a lawfull pleadge) Deut[eronomy]. 15. 2. Every seaventh yeare the Creditor was to quitt that which he lent to his brother if he were poore as appears ver[se]. 8. *Save when there shall be no poore with thee.* In all these and like cases, Christ was a generall rule, Math[ew]. 7. 22. *Whatsoever ye would that men should doe to you, doe yee the same to them allsoe.*

Quest. What rule must wee observe and walke by in cause of community of perill?

Ans. The same as before, but with more enlargement towards others and lesse respect towards ourselves and our owne right. Hence it was that in the primitive Churche they sold all, had all things in common, neither did any man say that which he possessed was his owne. Likewise in theire returne out of the captivity, because the worke was greate for the restoring of the church and the danger of enemies was common to all, Nehemiah directs the Jews to liberallity and readiness in remitting theire debts to theire brethren, and disposing liberally to such as wanted, and stand not upon their owne dues which they might have demanded of them. Thus did some of our Forefathers in times of persecution in England, and soe did many of the faithful of other churches, whereof wee keepe an honorable remembrance of them; and it is to be observed that both in Scriptures and latter stories of the churches that such as have beene most bountifull to the poore saintes, especially in those extraordinary times and occasions, God hath left them highly commended to posterity, as Zacheus, Cornelius, Dorcas, Bishop Hooper, the Cuttler of Brussells and divers others. Observe againe that the

Scripture gives noe caussion to restraine any from being over liberall this way; but all men to the liberall and cherefull practise hereof by the sweeter promises; as to instance one for many, Isaiah 58. 6. *Is not this the fast I have chosen to loose the bonds of wickedness, to take off the heavy burdens, to lett the oppressed go free and to breake every yoake, to deale thy bread to the hungry and to bring the poore that wander into thy house, when thou seest the naked to cover them; and then shall thy light brake forth as the morning and thy healthe shall growe speedily, thy righteousness shall goe before God, and the glory of the Lord shalt embrace thee; then thou shall call and the Lord shall answer thee &c.,* Ch[ronicles]. 2. 10. *If thou power out thy soule to the hungry, then shall thy light spring out in darkness, and the Lord shall guide thee continually, and satisfie thy soule in draught, and make falt thy bones, thou shalt be like a watered garden, and they shalt be of thee that shall build the old wast places &c.*

On the contrary most heavy cursses are layed upon such as are straightened towards the Lord and his people, Judg[es]. 5. *Cursse the Meroshe because he came not to help the Lord. Hee whoe shutteth his eares from hearing the cry of the poore, he shall cry and shall not be heard;* Math[ew]. 25. *Goe ye cursed into everlasting fire &c. I was hungry and ye fedd mee not,* Cor[rinthians]. 2. 9. 16. He that soweth sparingly shall reape sparingly. Haveing already sett forth the practice of mercy according to the rule of God's lawe, it will be useful to lay open the groundes of it allsoe, being the other parte of the Commandment and that is the affection from which this exercise of mercy must arise, the Apostle tells us that this *love is the fullfilling of the lawe,* not that it is enough to love our brother and soe noe further; but in regard of the excellency of his partes gieveing any motion to the other as the soule to the body and the power it hath to sett all the faculties on worke in the outward exercise of this duty; as when wee bid one make the clocke strike, he doth not lay hand on the hammer, which is the immediate instrument of the sound, but setts on worke the first mover or maine wheele; knoweing that will certainely produce the sound which he intends. Soe the way to drawe men to the workes of mercy, is not by force of Argument from the goodness or necessity of the worke; for though this cause may enforce, a rationall minde to some present act of mercy, as is frequent in experience, yet it cannot worke such a habit in a soule, as shall make it prompt upon all occasions to produce the same effect, but by frameing these affections of love in the hearte which will as naturally bring forthe the other, as any cause doth produce the effect.

The deffinition which the Scripture gives us of love is this. *Love is the bond of perfection,* first it is a bond or ligament. 2ly, it makes the worke perfect. There is noe body but consists of partes and that which knitts these partes together, gives the body its perfection, because it makes eache parte soe contiguous to others as thereby they doe mutually participate with each other, both in strengthe and infirmity, in pleasure and paine. To instance in the most perfect of all bodies; Christ and his Church make one body; the severall partes of this body considered a parte before they were united, were as disproportionate and as much disordering as soe many contrary quallities or elements, but when Christ comes, and by his spirit and love knitts all these partes to himselfe and each to other, it is become the most perfect and best proportioned body in the world, Eph[esians]. 4. 16. *Christ, by whome all the body being knitt together by every joint for the furniture thereof, according to the effectuall power which is in the measure of every perfection of partes, a glorious body without spott or wrinkle;* the ligaments hereof being Christ, or his love, for Christ is love, 1 John 4. 8. Soe this definition is right. *Love is the bond of perfection.*

From hence we may frame these conclusions. 1. First of all, true Christians are of one body in Christ, 1 Cor[rinthians]. 12. 12. 13. 17. *Ye are the body of Christ and members of their parte.* All the partes of this body being thus [u]nited are made soe contiguous in a speciall relation as they must needes partake of each other's strength and infirmity; joy and sorrowe, weale and woe. 1 Cor[rinthians]. 12. 26. *If one member suffers, all suffer with it, if one be in honor, all rejoyce with it.* 2ly. The ligaments of this body which knitt together are love. 3ly. Noe body can be perfect which wants its proper ligament . . . 5ly. This sensibleness and sympathy of each other's conditions will necessarily infuse into each parte a native desire and endeavour, to strengthen, defend, preserve and comfort the other. To insist a little on this conclusion being the product of all the former, the truthe hereof will appeare both by precept and patterne. 1 John 3. 10. *Yee ought to lay downe your lives for the brethren.* Gal[atians]. 6. 2. *beare ye one another's burthen's and soe fulfill the lawe of Christ.* For patterns wee have that first of our Saviour whoe out of his good will in obedience to his father, becomeing a parte of this body and being knitt with it in the bond of love, found such a native sensibleness of our infirmities and sorrowes as he willingly yielded himselfe to deathe to ease the infirmities of the rest of his body, and soe healed theire sorrowes. From the like sympathy of partes did the Apostles and many thousands of the Saintes lay downe theire lives for Christ. Againe the like wee may see in the members of this body among themselves. 1 Rom[ans]. 9. Paule could have been contented to have been separated from Christ, that the Jewes might not be cutt off from the body. It is very observable what hee professeth of his affectionate partaking with every member; *whoe is weake* (saith hee) *and I am not weake? whoe is offended and I burne not;* and againe, 2 Cor[rinthians]. 7. 13. *therefore wee are comforted because yee were comforted.* Of Epaphroditus he speaketh, Phil[ippians]. 2. 30. *that he regarded not his owne life to do him service.* Soe Phebe and others are called *the servants of the churche.* Now it is apparent that they served not for wages, or by constrainte, but out of love. The like we shall finde in the histories of the churche, in all ages; the sweete sympathie of affections which was in the members of this body one towards another; theire chearfullness in serveing and suffering together; how liberall they were without repineing, harbourers without grudgeing, and helpfull without reproaching; and

all from hence, because they had fervent love amongst them; which onely makes the practise of mercy constant and easie.

The next consideration is how this love comes to be wrought. Adam in his first estate was a perfect modell of mankinde in all their generations, and in him this love was perfected in regard of the habit. But Adam, rent himselfe from his Creator, rent all his posterity allsoe one from another; whence it comes that every man is borne with this principle in him to love and seeke himselfe onely, and thus a man continueth till Christ comes and takes possession of the soule and infuseth another principle, love to God and our brother, and this latter haveing continuall supply from Christ, as the head and roote by which he is united, gets the predomining in the soule, soe by little and little expells the former. 1 John 4. 7. *love cometh of God and every one that loveth is borne of God,* soe that this love is the fruite of the new birthe, and none can have it but the new creature. Now when this quallity is thus formed in the soules of men, it workes like the Spirit upon the drie bones. Ezek[ekial]. 39. *bone came to bone.* It gathers together the scattered bones, or perfect old man Adam, and knitts them into one body againe in Christ, whereby a man is become againe a living soule.

The third consideration is concerning the exercise of this love, which is twofold, inward or outward. The outward hath beene handled in the former preface of this discourse. From unfolding the other wee must take in our way that maxime of philosophy. *Simile simili gaudet,* or like will to like; for as of things which are turned with disaffection to eache other, the ground of it is from a dissimilitude or ariseing from the contrary or different nature of the things themselves; for the ground of love is an apprehension of some resemblance in the things loved to that which affects it. This is the cause why the Lord loves the creature, soe farre as it hathe any of his Image in it; he loves his elect because they are like himselfe, he beholds them in his beloved sonne. So a mother loves her childe, because shee throughly conceives a resemblance of herselfe in it. Thus it is betweene the members of Christ; eache discernes, by the worke of the Spirit, his owne Image and resemblance in another, and therefore cannot but love him as he loves himself. Now when the soule, which is of a sociable nature, findes anything like to itselfe, it is like Adam when Eve was brought to him. She must be one with himselfe. *This is flesh of my flesh* (saith he) *and bone of my bone.*

Soe the soule conceives a greate delighte in it; therefore shee desires nearness and familiarity with it. Shee hath a greate propensity to doe it good and receives such content in it, as fearing the miscarriage of her beloved, shee bestowes it in the inmost closett of her heart. Shee will not endure that it shall want any good which shee can give it. If by occasion shee be withdrawne from the company of it, shee is still looking towardes the place where shee left her beloved. If shee heard it groane, shee is with it presently. If shee finde it sadd and disconsolate, shee sighes and moanes with it. Shee hath noe such joy as to see her beloved merry and thriving. If shee see it wronged, shee cannot hear it without passion. Shee setts noe boundes to her affections, nor hath any thought of reward. Shee findes recompense enough in the exercise of her love towardes it.

Wee may see this acted to life in Jonathan and David. Jonathan a valiant man endued [imbued] with the spirit of love, soe soone as he discovered the same spirit in David had presently his hearte knitt to him by this ligament of love; soe that it is said he loved him as his owne soule, he takes soe great pleasure in him, that hee stripps himselfe to adorne his beloved. His father's kingdome was not soe precious to him as his beloved David, David shall have it with all his hearte. Himself desires noe more but that hee may be neare to him to rejoyce in his good[ness]. Hee chooseth to converse with him in the wildernesse even to the hazzard of his owne life, rather than with the greate Courtiers in his father's Pallace. When hee sees danger towards him, hee spares neither rare paines nor perill to direct it. When injury was offered his beloved David, hee would not beare it, though from his owne father. And when they must parte for a season onely, they thought theire heartes would have broake for sorrowe, had not theire affections found vent by abundance of teares. Other instances might be brought to showe the nature of this affection; as of Ruthe and Naomi, and many others; but this truthe is cleared enough. If any shall object that it is not possible that love shall be bred or upheld without hope of requitall, it is graunted; but that is not our cause; for this love is allwayes under reward. It never gives, but it allwayes receives with advantage; First in regard that among the members of the same body, love and affection are reciprocall in a most equall and sweete kinde of commerce.

2nly. In regard of the pleasure and content that the exercise of love carries with it, as wee may see in the naturall body. The mouth is at all the paines to receive and mince the foode which serves for the nourishment of all the other partes of the body; yet it hath noe cause to complaine; for first the other partes send backe, by severall passages, a due proportion of the same nourishment, in a better forme for the strengthening and comforting the mouthe. 2ly, the laboure of the mouthe is accompanied with such pleasure and content as farre exceedes the paines it takes. Soe is it in all the labour of love among Christians. The partie loving, reapes love again, as was showed before, which the soule covetts more then all the wealthe in the world. 3ly. Nothing yieldes more pleasure and content to the soule then when it findes that which it may love fervently; for to love and live beloved is the soule's paradise both here and in heaven. In the State of wedlock there be many comforts to learne out of the troubles of that Condition; but let such as have tryed the most, say if there be any sweetness in that Condition comparable to the exercise of mutuall love.

From the former Considerations arise these Conclusions.—1. First, This love among Christians is a reall thing, not imaginarie. 2ly. This love is as absolutely necessary to the being of the body of Christ, as the sinews and other ligaments of a naturall body are to the being of that body.

3ly. This love is a divine, spirituall, nature; free, active, strong, couragious, permanent; undervaluing all things beneathe its propper object and of all the graces, this makes us nearer to resemble the virtues of our heavenly father. 4thly. It rests in the love and wellfare of its beloved. For the full certain knowledge of those truthes concerning the nature, use, and excellency of this grace, that which the holy ghost hath left recorded, 1 Cor[rinthians]. 13, may give full satisfaction, which is needful for every true member of this lovely body of the Lord Jesus, to worke upon theire heartes by prayer, meditation continuall exercise at least of the speciall [influence] of this grace, till Christ be formed in them and they in him, all in each other, knitt together by this bond of love.

It rests now to make some application of this discourse, by the present designe, which gave the occasion of writing of it. Herein are 4 things to be propounded; *first* the persons, 2ly the worke, 3ly the end, 4thly the meanes. 1. For *the persons.* Wee are a company professing ourselves fellow members of Christ, in which respect only though wee were absent from each other many miles, and had our imployments as farre distant, yet wee ought to account ourselves knitt together by this bond of love, and, live in the exercise of it, if wee would have comforte of our being in Christ. This was notorious in the practise of the Christians in former times; as is testified of the Waldenses, from the mouth of one of the adversaries *Aeneas Sylvius* "mutuo ament pere antequam norunt," they use to love any of theire owne religion even before they were acquainted with them. 2nly, for the *worke* wee have in hand. It is by a mutuall consent, through a speciall overvaluing providence and a more than an ordinary approbation of the Churches of Christ, to seeke out a place of cohabitation and Consorteshipp under a due forme of Government both civill and ecclesiasticall. In such cases as this, the care of the publique must oversway all private respects, by which, not only conscience, but meare civill pollicy, dothe binde us. For it is a true rule that particular Estates cannot subsist in the ruin of the publique. 3ly. The *end* is to improve our lives to doe more service to the Lord; the comforte and encrease of the body of Christe, whereof we are members; that ourselves and posterity may be the better preserved from the common corruptions of this evill world, to serve the Lord and worke out our Salvation under the power and purity of his holy ordinances. 4thly, for the *meanes* whereby this must be effected. They are twofold, a conformity with the worke and end wee aime at. These wee see are extraordinary, therefore wee must not content ourselves with usuall ordinary meanes. Whatsoever wee did, or ought to have, done, when wee lived in England, the same must wee doe, and more allsoe, where wee goe. That which the most in theire churches mainetaine as truthe in profession only, wee must bring into familiar and constant practise; as in this duty of love, wee must love brotherly without dissimulation, wee must love one another with a pure hearte fervently. Wee must beare one anothers burthens. We must not looke onely on our owne things, but allsoe on the things of our brethren. Neither must wee thinke that the Lord will beare with such faileings at our hands as he dothe from those among whome wee have lived; and that for these 3 Reasons; 1. In regard of the more neare bond of mariage between him and us, wherein hee hath taken us to be his, after a most strickt and peculiar manner, which will make them the more jealous of our love and obedience. Soe he tells the people of Israell, *you onely have I knowne of all the families of the Earthe, therefore will I punish you for your Transgressions.* 2ly, because *the Lord will be sanctified in them that come neare him.* We know that there were many that corrupted the service of the Lord; some setting upp altars before his owne; others offering both strange fire and strange sacrifices allsoe; yet there came noe fire from heaven, or other sudden judgement upon them, as did upon Nadab and Abihu, whoe yet wee may think did not sinne presumptuously. 3ly. When God gives a speciall commission he lookes to have it strictly observed in every article; When he gave Saule a commission to destroy Amaleck, Hee indented with him upon certain articles, and because hee failed in one of the least, and that upon a faire pretense, it lost him the kingdom, which should have beene his reward, if hee had observed his commission. Thus stands the cause betweene God and us. We are entered into Covenant with Him for this worke. Wee have taken out a commission. The Lord hath given us leave to drawe our owne articles. Wee have professed to enterprise these and those accounts, upon these and those ends. Wee have hereupon besought Him of favour and blessing. Now if the Lord shall please to heare us, and bring us in peace to the place we desire, then hath hee ratified this covenant and sealed our Commission, and will expect a strict performance of the articles contained in it; but if wee shall neglect the observation of these articles which are the ends wee have propounded, and, dissembling with our God, shall fall to embrace this present world and prosecute our carnall intentions, seeking great things for ourselves and our posterity, the Lord will surely breake out in wrathe against us; be revenged of such a [sinful] people and make us knowe the price of the breache of such a covenant.

Now the onely way to avoyde this shipwracke, and to provide for our posterity, is to followe the counsell of Micah, *to doe justly, to love mercy, to walk humbly with our God.* For this end, wee must be knitt together, in this worke, as one man. Wee must entertaine each other in brotherly affection. Wee must be willing to abridge ourselves of our superfluities, for the supply of other's necessities. Wee must uphold a familiar commerce together in all meekeness, gentlenes, patience and liberality. Wee must delight in each other; make other's conditions our owne; rejoice together, mourne together, labour and suffer together, allwayes haveing before our eyes our commission and community in the worke, as members of the same body. Soe shall wee *keepe the unitie of the spirit in the bond of peace.* The Lord will be our God, and delight to dwell among us, as his owne people, and will command a blessing upon us in all our wayes. Soe that wee shall see much more of his wisdome, power, goodness and truthe, than formerly wee have been acquainted with. Wee shall finde that the God of Israell is among us, when ten of us shall be able to resist a thousand of our enemies; when hee shall make us a prayse and glory that men shall say of succeeding plantations, "the Lord make it likely that of *New England.*" For wee must consider that wee shall be as a citty upon a hill. The eyes of all people are uppon us. Soe that if wee shall deale falsely with our God in this worke wee have undertaken, and soe cause him to withdrawe his present help from us, wee shall be made a story and a by-word through the world. Wee shall open the mouthes of enemies to speake evill of the wayes of God, and all professors for God's sake. Wee shall shame the faces of many of God's worthy servants, and cause theire prayers to be turned into curses upon us till wee be consumed out of the good land whither wee are a goeing.

I shall shutt upp this discourse with that exhortation of Moses, that faithfull servant of the Lord, in his last farewell to Israell, Deut[eronomy]. 30. *Beloved there is now sett before us life and good, Death and evill, in that wee are commanded this day to love the Lord our God, and to love one another, to walke in his wayes and to keepe his Commandements and his Ordinance and his lawes,* and the articles of our Covenant with him, that *wee may live and be multiplied, and that the Lord our God may blesse us in the land whither wee goe to possesse it. But if our heartes shall turne away, soe that wee will not obey, but shall be seduced, and worshipp and serve other Gods,* our pleasure and proffitts, *and serve them*; it is propounded unto us this day, *wee shall surely perishe out of the good land whither wee passe over this vast sea to possesse it;*

> Therefore lett us choose life
> that wee, and our seede
> may live, by obeyeing His
> voyce and cleaveing to Him,
> for Hee is our life and
> our prosperity.

Source: Collections of the Massachusetts Historical Society, 3rd ser. (Boston: Massachusetts Historical Society, 1838), 7:31–48.

The Trial of Anne Hutchinson (1637)

The educated daughter of a minister, Anne Hutchinson had an abiding interest in theology, which she did not hesitate to express. Her outspokenness on religious matters made the Puritan ministers of Massachusetts Bay uncomfortable. Not only did she hold informal group discussions of their weekly sermons in her home, she also professed antinomian beliefs, based on the feeling that one could achieve salvation through faith alone. As her views threatened the orthodoxy of the colony, she was brought to trial at the General Court at Newton on charges of heresy. She was condemned upon her stating that God had revealed himself to her directly. Banished from the colony, she relocated to Rhode Island, along with family members and supporters. What follows is an excerpt from the transcript of her trial.

Mr. {John} Winthrop, Governor: Mrs. Hutchinson, you are called here as one of those that have troubled the peace of the commonwealth and the churches here; you are known to be a woman that hath had a great share in the promoting and divulging of those opinions that are the cause of this trouble, and to be nearly joined not only in affinity and affection with some of those the court had taken notice of and passed censure upon, but you have spoken divers things, as we have been informed, very prejudicial to the honour of the churches and ministers thereof, and you have maintained a meeting and an assembly in your house that hath been condemned by the general assembly as a thing not tolerable nor comely in the sight of God nor fitting for your sex, and notwithstanding that was cried down you have continued the same. Therefore we have thought good to send for you to understand how things are, that if you be in an erroneous way we may reduce you that so you may become a profitable member here among us. Otherwise if you be obstinate in your course that then the court may take such course that you may trouble us no further. Therefore I would intreat you to express whether you do assent and hold in practice to those opinions and factions that have been handled in court already, that is to say, whether you do not justify Mr. Wheelwright's sermon and the petition.

Mrs. Hutchinson: I am called here to answer before you but I hear no things laid to my charge.

Gov.: I have told you some already and more I can tell you.

Mrs. H.: Name one, Sir.

Gov.: Have I not named some already?

Mrs. H.: What have I said or done?

Gov.: Why for your doings, this you did harbor and countenance those that are parties in this faction that you have heard of.

Mrs. H.: That's matter of conscience, Sir.

Gov.: Your conscience you must keep, or it must be kept for you.

Mrs. H.: Must not I then entertain the saints because I must keep my conscience.

Gov.: Say that one brother should commit felony or treason and come to his brother's house, if he knows him guilty and conceals him he is guilty of the same. It is his conscience to entertain him, but if his conscience comes into act in giving countenance and entertainment to him that hath broken the law he is guilty too. So if you do countenance those that are transgressors of the law you are in the same fact.

Mrs. H.: What law do they transgress?

Gov.: The law of God and of the state.

Mrs. H.: In what particular?

Gov.: Why in this among the rest, whereas the Lord doth say honour thy father and thy mother.

Mrs. H.: Ey Sir in the Lord.

Gov.: This honour you have broke in giving countenance to them.

Mrs. H.: In entertaining those did I entertain them against any act (for there is the thing) or what God has appointed?

Gov.: You knew that Mr. Wheelwright did preach this sermon and those that countenance him in this do break a law.

Mrs. H.: What law have I broken?

Gov.: Why the fifth commandment.

Mrs. H.: I deny that for he [Mr. Wheelwright] saith in the Lord.

Gov.: You have joined with them in the faction.

Mrs. H.: In what faction have I joined with them?

Gov.: In presenting the petition.

Mrs. H.: Suppose I had set my hand to the petition. What then?

Gov.: You saw that case tried before.

Mrs. H.: But I had not my hand to [not signed] the petition.

Gov.: You have councelled them.

Mrs. H.: Wherein?

Gov.: Why in entertaining them.

Mrs. H.: What breach of law is that, Sir?

Gov.: Why dishonouring the commonwealth.

Mrs. H.: But put the case, Sir, that I do fear the Lord and my parents. May not I entertain them that fear the Lord because my parents will not give me leave?

Gov.: If they be the fathers of the commonwealth, and they of another religion, if you entertain them then you dishonour your parents and are justly punishable.

Mrs. H.: If I entertain them, as they have dishonoured their parents I do.

Gov.: No but you by countenancing them above others put honor upon them.

Mrs. H.: I may put honor upon them as the children of God and as they do honor the Lord.

Gov.: We do not mean to discourse with those of your sex but only this: you so adhere unto them and do endeavor to set forward this faction and so you do dishonour us.

Mrs. H.: I do acknowledge no such thing. Neither do I think that I ever put any dishonour upon you.

Gov.: Why do you keep such a meeting at your house as you do every week upon a set day?

Mrs. H.: It is lawful for me to do so, as it is all your practices, and can you find a warrant for yourself and condemn me for the same thing? The ground of my taking it up was, when I first came to this land because I did not go to such meetings as those were, it was presently reported that I did not allow of such meetings but held them unlawful and therefore in that regard they said I was proud and did despise all ordinances. Upon that a friend came unto me and told me of it

and I to prevent such aspersions took it up, but it was in practice before I came. Therefore I was not the first.

Gov.: . . . By what warrant do you continue such a course?

Mrs. H.: I conceive there lies a clear rule in Titus that the elder women should instruct the younger and then I must have a time wherein I must do it.

Gov.: All this I grant you, I grant you a time for it, but what is this to the purpose that you Mrs. Hutchinson must call a company together from their callings to come to be taught of you? . . .

Mrs. H.: If you look upon the rule in Titus it is a rule to me. If you convince me that it is no rule I shall yield.

Gov.: You know that there is no rule that crosses another, but this rule crosses that in the Corinthians. But you must take it in this sense that elder women must instruct the younger about their business and to love their husbands and not to make them to clash. . . .

Mrs. H.: Will it please you to answer me this and to give me a rule for then I will willingly submit to any truth. If any come to my house to be instructed in the ways of God what rule have I to put them away? . . . . Do you think it not lawful for me to teach women and why do you call me to teach the court?

Gov.: We do not call you to teach the court but to lay open yourself. . . .

[They continue to argue over what rule she had broken.]

Gov.: Your course is not to be suffered for. Besides that we find such a course as this to be greatly prejudicial to the state. Besides the occasion that it is to seduce many honest persons that are called to those meetings and your opinions and your opinions being known to be different from the word of God may seduce many simple souls that resort unto you. Besides that the occasion which hath come of late hath come from none but such as have frequented your meetings, so that now they are flown off from magistrates and ministers and since they have come to you. And besides that it will not well stand with the commonwealth that families should be neglected for so many neighbors and dames and so much time spent. We see no rule of God for this. We see not that any should have authority to set up any other exercises besides what authority hath already set up and so what hurt comes of this you will be guilty of and we for suffering you.

Mrs. H.: Sir, I do not believe that to be so.

Gov.: Well, we see how it is. We must therefore put it away from you or restrain you from maintaining this course.

Mrs. H.: If you have a rule for it from God's word you may.

Gov.: We are your judges, and not you ours and we must compel you to it.

Mrs. H.: If it please you by authority to put it down I will freely let you for I am subject to your authority. . . .

Deputy Governor, Thomas Dudley: I would go a little higher with Mrs. Hutchinson. About three years ago we were all in peace. Mrs. Hutchinson, from that time she came hath made a disturbance, and some that came over with her in the ship did inform me what she was as soon as she was landed. I being then in place dealt with the pastor and teacher of Boston and desired them to enquire of her, and then I was satisfied that she held nothing different from us. But within half a year after, she had vented divers of her strange opinions and had made parties in the country, and at length it comes that Mr. Cotton and Mr. Vane were of her judgment, but Mr. Cotton had cleared himself that he was not of that mind. But now it appears by this woman's meeting that Mrs. Hutchinson hath so forestalled the minds of many by their resort to her meeting that now she hath a potent party in the country. Now if all these things have endangered us as from that foundation and if she in particular hath disparaged all our ministers in the land that they have preached a covenant of works, and only Mr. Cotton a covenant of grace, why this is not to be suffered, and therefore being driven to the foundation and it being found that Mrs. Hutchinson is she that hath depraved all the ministers and hath been the cause of what is fallen out, why we must take away the foundation and the building will fall.

Mrs. H.: I pray, Sir, prove it that I said they preached nothing but a covenant of works.

Dep. Gov.: Nothing but a covenant of works. Why a Jesuit may preach truth sometimes.

Mrs. H.: Did I ever say they preached a covenant of works then?

Dep. Gov.: If they do not preach a covenant of grace clearly, then they preach a covenant of works.

Mrs. H.: No, Sir. One may preach a covenant of grace more clearly than another, so I said. . . .

Dep. Gov.: When they do preach a covenant of works do they preach truth?

Mrs. H.: Yes, Sir. But when they preach a covenant of works for salvation, that is not truth.

Dep. Gov.: I do but ask you this: when the ministers do preach a covenant of works do they preach a way of salvation?

Mrs. H.: I did not come hither to answer questions of that sort.

Dep. Gov.: Because you will deny the thing.

Mrs. H.: Ey, but that is to be proved first.

Dep. Gov.: I will make it plain that you did say that the ministers did preach a covenant of works.

Mrs. H.: I deny that.

Dep. Gov.: And that you said they were not able ministers of the New Testament, but Mr. Cotton only.

Mrs. H.: If ever I spake that I proved it by God's word.

Court: Very well, very well.

Mrs. H.: If one shall come unto me in private, and desire me seriously to tell them what I thought of such an one, I must either speak false or true in my answer.

Dep. Gov.: Likewise I will prove this that you said the gospel in the letter and words holds forth nothing but a covenant of works and that all that do not hold as you do are in a covenant of works.

Mrs. H.: I deny this for if I should so say I should speak against my own judgment. . . .

Mr. Hugh Peters: That which concerns us to speak unto, as yet we are sparing in, unless the court command us to speak, then we shall answer to Mrs. Hutchinson notwithstanding our brethren are very unwilling to answer.

[The Governor says to do so. Six ministers then testify to the particular charges and that she was "not only difficult in her opinions, but also of an intemperate spirit"]

Mr. Peters: . . . . [I asked her] What difference do you conceive to be between your teacher and us? . . . Briefly, she told me there was a wide and broad difference. . . . He preaches the covenant of grace and you the covenant of works, and that you are not able ministers of the New Testament and know no more than the apostles did before the resurrection of Christ. I did then put it to her, What do you conceive of such a brother? She answered he had not the seal of the spirit.

Mrs. H.: If our pastor would shew his writings you should see what I said, and that many things are not so as is reported.

Mr. Wilson: . . . what is written [here now] I will avouch.

Mr. Weld: [Agrees that Peters related Hutchinson's words accurately.]

Mr. Phillips: [Agrees that Peters related Hutchinson's words accurately.] Then I asked her of myself (being she spake rashly of them all) because she never heard me at all. She likewise said that we were not able ministers of the New Testament and her reason was because we were not sealed.

Mr. Simmes: [Agrees that Peters related Hutchinson's words accurately.]

Mr. Shephard: [Also to Same.]

Mr. Eliot: [Agrees that Peters related Hutchinson's words accurately.]

Dep. Gov.: I called these witnesses and you deny them. You see they have proved this and you deny this, but it is clear.

You say they preached a covenant of works and that they were not able ministers of the New Testament; now there are two other things that you did affirm which were that the scriptures in the letter of them held forth nothing but a covenant of works and likewise that those that were under a covenant of works cannot be saved.

Mrs. H.: Prove that I said so.

Gov.: Did you say so?

Mrs. H.: No, Sir, it is your conclusion.

Dep. Gov.: What do I do charging of you if you deny what is so fully proved?

Gov.: Here are six undeniable ministers who say it is true and yet you deny that you did say that they preach a covenant of works and that they were not able ministers of the gospel, and it appears plainly that you have spoken it, and whereas you say that it was drawn from you in a way of friendship, you did profess then that it was out of conscience that you spake. . . .

Mrs. H.: . . . They thought that I did conceive there was a difference between them and Mr. Cotton. . . . I might say they might preach a covenant of works as did the apostles, but to preach a covenant of works and to be under a covenant of works is another business.

Dep. Gov.: There have been six witnesses to prove this and yet you deny it. [And then he mentions a seventh, Mr. Nathaniel Ward.]

Mrs. H.: I acknowledge using the words of the apostle to the Corinthians unto him, [Mr. Ward] that they that were ministers of the letter and not the spirit did preach a covenant of works.

Gov.: Mrs. Hutchinson, the court you see hath laboured to bring you to acknowledge the error of your way that so you might be reduced, the time grows late, we shall therefore give you a little more time to consider of it and therefore desire that you attend the court again in the morning . . .

[The next morning]

Gov.: We proceeded . . . as far as we could . . . There were divers things laid to her charge: her ordinary meetings about religious exercises, her speeches in derogation of the ministers among us, and the weakening of the hands and hearts of the people towards them. Here was sufficient proof made of that which she was accused of, in that point concerning the ministers and their ministry, as that they did preach a covenant of works when others did preach a covenant of grace, and that they were not able ministers of the New Testament, and that they had not the seal of the spirit, and this was spoken not as was pretended out of private conference, but out of conscience and warrant from scripture alleged the fear of man is a snare and seeing God had given her a

calling to it she would freely speak. Some other speeches she used, as that the letter of the scripture held forth a covenant of works, and this is offered to be proved by probable grounds. . . . Controversy—should the witnesses should be recalled and made swear an oath, as Mrs. Hutchinson desired. . . . I see no necessity of an oath in this thing seeing it is true and the substance of the matter confirmed by divers, yet that all may be satisfied, if the elders will take an oath they shall have it given them. . . .

Mrs. H.: After that they have taken an oath I will make good what I say.

Gov.: Let us state the case, and then we may know what to do. That which is laid to Mrs. Hutchinson charge is that, that she hath traduced the magistrates and ministers of this jurisdiction, that she hath said the ministers preached a covenant of works and Mr. Cotton a covenant of grace, and that they were not able ministers of the gospel, and she excuses it that she made it a private conference and with a promise of secrecy, &c. Now this is charged upon her, and they therefore sent for her seeing she made it her table talk, and then she said the fear of man was a snare and therefore she would not be affeared of them. . . .

Dep. Gov.: Let her witnesses be called.

Gov.: Who be they?

Mrs. H.: Mr. Leveret and our teacher and Mr. Coggeshall.

Gov.: Mr. Coggeshall was not present.

Mr. Coggeshall: Yes, but I was. Only I desired to be silent till I should be called.

Gov.: Will you, Mr. Coggeshall, say that she did not say so?

Mr. Coggeshall: Yes, I dare say that she did not say all that which they lay against her.

Mr. Peters: How dare you look into the court to say such a word?

Mr. Coggeshall: Mr. Peters takes upon him to forbid me. I shall be silent.

Mr. Stoughton {assistant of the Court}: Ey, but she intended this that they say.

Gov.: Well, Mr. Leveret, what were the words? I pray, speak.

Mr. Leveret: To my best remembrance when the elders did send for her, Mr. Peters did with much vehemency and intreaty urge her to tell what difference there was between Mr. Cotton and them, and upon his urging of her she said "The fear of man is a snare, but they that trust upon the Lord shall be safe." And being asked wherein the difference was, she answered that they did not preach a covenant of grace so clearly as Mr. Cotton did, and she gave this reason of it: because that as the apostles were for a time without the spirit so until they had received the witness of the spirit they could not preach a covenant of grace so clearly.

Gov.: Don't you remember that she said they were not able ministers of the New Testament?

Mrs. H.: Mr. Weld and I had an hour's discourse at the window and then I spake that, if I spake it. . . .

Gov.: Mr. Cotton, the court desires that you declare what you do remember of the conference which was at the time and is now in question.

Mr. Cotton: I did not think I should be called to bear witness in this cause and therefore did not labor to call to remembrance what was done; but the greatest passage that took impression upon me was to this purpose. The elders spake that they had heard that she had spoken some condemning words of their ministry, and among other things they did first pray her to answer wherein she thought their ministry did differ from mine. How the comparison sprang I am ignorant, but sorry I was that any comparison should be between me and my brethren and uncomfortable it was. She told them to this purpose that they did not hold forth a covenant of grace as I did. But wherein did we differ? Why she said that they did not hold forth the seal of the spirit as he doth. Where is the difference there? Say they, why saith she, speaking to one or other of them, I know not to whom. You preach of the seal of the spirit upon a work and he upon free grace without a work or without respect to a work; he preaches the seal of the spirit upon free grace and you upon a work. I told her I was very sorry that she put comparisons between my ministry and theirs, for she had said more than I could myself, and rather I had that she had put us in fellowship with them and not have made that discrepancy. She said, she found the difference. . . .

   This was the sum of the difference, nor did it seem to be so ill taken as it is and our brethren did say also that they would not so easily believe reports as they had done and withal mentioned that they would speak no more of it, some of them did; and afterwards some of them did say they were less satisfied than before. And I must say that I did not find her saying that they were under a covenant of works, nor that she said they did preach a covenant of works.

[More back and forth between Rev. John Cotton, trying to defend Mrs. Hutchinson, and Mr. Peters, about exactly what Mrs. Hutchinson said.]

Mrs. H.: If you please to give me leave I shall give you the ground of what I know to be true. Being much troubled to see the falseness of the constitution of the Church of England, I had like to have turned Separatist. Whereupon I kept a day of solemn humiliation and pondering of the thing; this scripture was brought unto me—he that denies Jesus Christ to be come in the flesh is antichrist. This I considered of and in considering found that the papists did not deny him to be come in the flesh, nor we did not deny him—who then

was antichrist? Was the Turk antichrist only? The Lord knows that I could not open scripture; he must by his prophetical office open it unto me. So after that being unsatisfied in the thing, the Lord was pleased to bring this scripture out of the Hebrews. he that denies the testament denies the testator, and in this did open unto me and give me to see that those which did not teach the new covenant had the spirit of antichrist, and upon this he did discover the ministry unto me; and ever since, I bless the Lord, he hath let me see which was the clear ministry and which the wrong. Since that time I confess I have been more choice and he hath left me to distinguish between the voice of my beloved and the voice of Moses, the voice of John the Baptist and the voice of antichrist, for all those voices are spoken of in scripture. Now if you do condemn me for speaking what in my conscience I know to be truth I must commit myself unto the Lord.

Mr. Nowel {assistant to the Court}: How do you know that was the spirit?

Mrs. H.: How did Abraham know that it was God that bid him offer his son, being a breach of the sixth commandment?

Dep. Gov.: By an immediate voice.

Mrs. H.: So to me by an immediate revelation.

Dep. Gov.: How! an immediate revelation.

Mrs. H.: By the voice of his own spirit to my soul. I will give you another scripture, Jer[emiah]. 46: 27–28—out of which the Lord showed me what he would do for me and the rest of his servants. But after he was pleased to reveal himself to me I did presently, like Abraham, run to Hagar. And after that he did let me see the atheism of my own heart, for which I begged of the Lord that it might not remain in my heart, and being thus, he did show me this (a twelvemonth after) which I told you of before. . . . Therefore, I desire you to look to it, for you see this scripture fulfilled this day and therefore I desire you as you tender the Lord and the church and commonwealth to consider and look what you do. You have power over my body but the Lord Jesus hath power over my body and soul; and assure yourselves thus much, you do as much as in you lies to put the Lord Jesus Christ from you, and if you go on in this course you begin, you will bring a curse upon you and your posterity, and the mouth of the Lord hath spoken it.

Dep. Gov.: What is the scripture she brings?

Mr. Stoughton {assistant to the Court}: Behold I turn away from you.

Mrs. H.: But now having seen him which is invisible I fear not what man can do unto me.

Gov.: Daniel was delivered by miracle; do you think to be deliver'd so too?

Mrs. H.: I do here speak it before the court. I look that the Lord should deliver me by his providence. . . . [Because God had said to her] though I should meet with affliction, yet I am the same God that delivered Daniel out of the lion's den, I will also deliver thee.

Mr. Harlakenden {assistant to the Court}: I may read scripture and the most glorious hypocrite may read them and yet go down to hell.

Mrs. H.: It may be so. . . .

Gov.: I am persuaded that the revelation she brings forth is delusion.

[The trial text here reads:] All the court but some two or three ministers cry out, we all believe it—we all believe it. [Mrs. Hutchinson was found guilty.]

Gov.: The court hath already declared themselves satisfied concerning the things you hear, and concerning the trouble-someness of her spirit and the danger of her course amongst us, which is not to be suffered. Therefore if it be the mind of the court that Mrs. Hutchinson for these things that appear before us is unfit for our society, and if it be the mind of the court that she shall be banished out of our liberties and imprisoned till she be sent away, let them hold up their hands.

[All but three did so.]

Gov.: Mrs. Hutchinson, the sentence of the court you hear is that you are banished from out of our jurisdiction as being a woman not fit for our society, and are to be imprisoned till the court shall send you away.

Mrs. H.: I desire to know wherefore I am banished?

Gov.: Say no more. The court knows wherefore and is satisfied.

Source: Charles F. Adams, *Antinomianism in the Colony of Massachusetts Bay* (Boston: Prince Society Publications, 1894).

Fundamental Orders of Connecticut (1639)

Often considered the first written constitution in America, the Fundamental Orders were adopted by freemen from the three Connecticut towns of Windsor, Hartford, and Wethersfield. This compact embodied democratic ideals that stressed the good of the community over individuals, and it provided guidelines under which all could live.

For as much as it hath pleased Almighty God by the wise disposition of his divine providence so to order and dispose of things that we the Inhabitants and Residents of Windsor, Hartford and Wethersfield are now cohabiting and dwelling in and upon the River of Connectecotte and the lands thereunto adjoining; and well knowing where a people are gathered together the word of God requires that to maintain the peace and union of such a people there should be an orderly and decent Government established according to God, to order and dispose of the affairs of the people at all seasons as occasion shall require; do therefore associate and conjoin ourselves to be as one Public State or Commonwealth; and do for ourselves and our successors and such as shall be adjoined to us at any time hereafter, enter into Combination and Confederation together, to maintain and preserve the liberty and purity of the Gospel of our Lord Jesus which we now profess, as also, the discipline of the Churches, which according to the truth of the said Gospel is now practiced amongst us; as also in our civil affairs to be guided and governed according to such Laws, Rules, Orders and Decrees as shall be made, ordered, and decreed as followeth:

1. It is Ordered, sentenced, and decreed, that there shall be yearly two General Assemblies or Courts, the one the second Thursday in April, the other the second Thursday in September following; the first shall be called the Court of Election, wherein shall be yearly chosen from time to time, so many Magistrates and other public Officers as shall be found requisite: Whereof one to be chosen Governor for the year ensuing and until another be chosen, and no other Magistrate to be chosen for more than one year: provided always there be six chosen besides the Governor, which being chosen and sworn according to an Oath recorded for that purpose, shall have the power to administer justice according to the Laws here established, and for want thereof, according to the Rule of the Word of God; which choice shall be made by all that are admitted freemen and have taken the Oath of Fidelity, and do cohabit within this Jurisdiction having been admitted Inhabitants by the major part of the Town wherein they live or the major part of such as shall be then present.

2. It is Ordered, sentenced, and decreed, that the election of the aforesaid Magistrates shall be in this manner: every person present and qualified for choice shall bring in (to the person deputed to receive them) one single paper with the name of him written in it whom he desires to have Governor, and that he that hath the greatest number of papers shall be Governor for that year. And the rest of the Magistrates or public officers to be chosen in this manner: the Secretary for the time being shall first read the names of all that are to be put to choice and then shall severally nominate them distinctly, and every one that would have the person nominated to be chosen shall bring in one single paper written upon, and he that would not have him chosen shall bring in a blank; and every one that hath more written papers than blanks shall be a Magistrate for that year; which papers shall be received and told by one or more that shall be then chosen by the court and sworn to be faithful therein; but in case there should not be six chosen as aforesaid, besides the Governor, out of those which are nominated, than he or they which have the most written papers shall be a Magistrate or Magistrates for the ensuing year, to make up the aforesaid number.

3. It is Ordered, sentenced, and decreed, that the Secretary shall not nominate any person, nor shall any person be chosen newly into the Magistracy which was not propounded in some General Court before, to be nominated the next election; and to that end it shall be lawful for each of the Towns aforesaid by their deputies to nominate any two whom they conceive fit to be put to election; and the Court may add so many more as they judge requisite.

4. It is Ordered, sentenced, and decreed, that no person be chosen Governor above once in two years, and that the Governor be always a member of some approved Congregation, and formerly of the Magistracy within this Jurisdiction; and that all the Magistrates, Freemen of this Commonwealth; and that no Magistrate or other public officer shall execute any part of his or their office before they are severally sworn, which shall be done in the face of the court if they be present, and in case of absence by some deputed for that purpose.

5. It is Ordered, sentenced, and decreed, that to the aforesaid Court of Election the several Towns shall send their deputies, and when the Elections are ended they may proceed in any public service as at other Courts. Also the other General Court in September shall be for making of laws, and any other public occasion, which concerns the good of the Commonwealth.

6. It is Ordered, sentenced, and decreed, that the Governor shall, either by himself or by the Secretary, send out summons to the Constables of every Town for the calling of these two standing Courts one month at least before their several times: And also if the Governor and the greatest part of the Magistrates see cause upon any special occasion to call a General Court, they may give order to the Secretary so to do within fourteen days' warning: And if urgent necessity so required, upon a shorter notice, giving sufficient grounds for it to the deputies when they meet, or else be questioned for the same; And if the Governor and major part of Magistrates shall either neglect or refuse to call the two General standing Courts or either of them, as also at other times when the occasions of the Commonwealth require, the Freemen thereof, or the major part of them, shall petition to them so to do; if then it be either denied or neglected, the said Freemen, or the major part of them, shall have the power to give order to the Constables of the several Towns to do the same, and so may meet together, and choose to themselves a Moderator, and may proceed to do any act of power which any other General Courts may.

7. It is Ordered, sentenced, and decreed, that after there are warrants given out for any of the said General Courts, the Constable or Constables of each Town, shall forthwith give notice distinctly to the inhabitants of the same, in some public assembly or by going or sending from house to house, that at a place and time by him or them limited and set, they meet and assemble themselves together to elect and choose certain deputies to be at the General Court then following to agitate the affairs of the Commonwealth; which said deputies shall be chosen by all that are admitted Inhabitants in the several Towns and have taken the oath of fidelity; provided that none be chosen a Deputy for any General Court which is not a Freeman of this Commonwealth. The aforesaid deputies shall be chosen in manner following: every person that is present and qualified as before expressed, shall bring the names of such, written in several papers, as they desire to have chosen for that employment, and these three or four, more or less, being the number agreed on to be chosen for that time, that have the greatest number of papers written for them shall be deputies for that Court; whose names shall be endorsed on the back side of the warrant and returned into the Court, with the Constable or Constables' hand unto the same.

8. It is Ordered, sentenced, and decreed, that Windsor, Hartford, and Wethersfield shall have power, each Town, to send four of their Freemen as their deputies to every General Court; and Whatsoever other Town shall be hereafter added to this Jurisdiction, they shall send so many deputies as the Court shall judge meet, a reasonable proportion to the number of Freemen that are in the said Towns being to be attended therein; which deputies shall have the power of the whole Town to give their votes and allowance to all such laws and orders as may be for the public good, and unto which the said Towns are to be bound.

9. It is Ordered, sentenced, and decreed, that the deputies thus chosen shall have power and liberty to appoint a time and a place of meeting together before any General Court, to advise and consult of all such things as may concern the good of the public, as also to examine their own Elections, whether according to the order, and if they or the greatest part of them find any election to be illegal they may seclude such for present from their meeting, and return the same and their reasons to the Court; and if it be proved true, the Court may fine the party or parties so intruding, and the Town, if they see cause, and give out a warrant to go to a new election in a legal way, either in part or in whole. Also the said deputies shall have power to fine any that shall be disorderly at their meetings, or for not coming in due time or place according to appointment; and they may return the said fines into the Court if it be refused to be paid, and the Treasurer to take notice of it, and to escheat or levy the same as he does other fines.

10. It is Ordered, sentenced, and decreed, that every General Court, except such as through neglect of the Governor and the greatest part of the Magistrates the Freemen themselves do call, shall consist of the Governor, or some one chosen to moderate the Court, and four other Magistrates at least, with the major part of the deputies of the several Towns legally chosen; and in case the Freemen, or major part of them, through neglect or refusal of the Governor and major part of the Magistrates, shall call a Court, it shall consist of the major part of Freemen

that are present or their deputies, with a Moderator chosen by them: In which said General Courts shall consist the supreme power of the Commonwealth, and they only shall have power to make laws or repeal them, to grant levies, to admit of Freemen, dispose of lands undisposed of, to several Towns or persons, and also shall have power to call either Court or Magistrate or any other person whatsoever into question for any misdemeanor, and may for just causes displace or deal otherwise according to the nature of the offense; and also may deal in any other matter that concerns the good of this Commonwealth, except election of Magistrates, which shall be done by the whole body of Freemen. In which Court the Governor or Moderator shall have power to order the Court, to give liberty of speech, and silence unseasonable and disorderly speakings, to put all things to vote, and in case the vote be equal to have the casting voice. But none of these Courts shall be adjourned or dissolved without the consent of the major part of the Court.

11. It is Ordered, sentenced, and decreed, that when any General Court upon the occasions of the Commonwealth have agreed upon any sum, or sums of money to be levied upon the several Towns within this Jurisdiction, that a committee be chosen to set out and appoint what shall be the proportion of every Town to pay of the said levy, provided the committee be made up of an equal number out of each Town.

14th January 1639 the 11 Orders above said are voted.

Source: The Federal and State Constitutions, Colonial Charters, and Other Organic Laws of the States, Territories, and Colonies Now or Heretofore Forming the United States of America, compiled and edited under the Act of Congress of June 30, 1906, by Francis Newton Thorpe (Washington, DC: Government Printing Office, 1909).

Psalm 23 from The Bay Psalm Book (1640)

❦ ～ ❦

The Bay Psalm Book, more correctly entitled *The Whole Book of Psalmes Faithfully Translated into English Metre,* was the first book printed and bound in the British colonies. This work replaced the earlier *Ainsworth Psalter,* which the Puritans brought to the colony from the Netherlands. *The Bay Psalm Book* is generally thought to have been written by Cotton Mather, with the help of other clergy of the Massachusetts Bay Colony, although some scholars believe it was written by Mather's grandfather John Cotton. One of the most widely known selections from *The Bay Psalm Book* is Psalm 23.

The Lord to me a shepherd is,
Want therefore I shall not,
He in the folds of tender grass
Doth make me down to lie

To waters calm he gently leads
Restore my soul doth he
He doth in paths of righteousness
For his names sake lead me.

Yea though in valley of death's shade
I walk none ill I'll fear,
Because thou art with me, thy rod,
and staff my comfort are.

For me a table thou hast spread
In presence of my foes;
Thou dost annoint my head with oil
My cup it over-flows.

Goodness and mercy surely shall
All my days follow me;
And in the Lord's house I shall dwell
So long as days shall be.

Source: The Whole Book of Psalmes Faithfully Translated into English Metre (Cambridge, MA: Imprinted by S. Daye, 1640).

Maryland Toleration Act (1649)

From the beginning, the colony of Maryland had always enjoyed religious tolerance. The following act guarded Lord Baltimore against charges that Maryland was a Catholic colony, and it officially spread the mantle of protection to Protestants as the Puritan party in Parliament increased. When the Puritans gained political control of Maryland in 1654, protection of Catholics was withdrawn, but it was restored when Lord Baltimore regained leadership.

An Act Concerning Religion

Forasmuch as in a well governed and Christian Commonwealth matters concerning Religion and the honor of God ought in the first place to be taken, into serious consideration and endeavoured to be settled, be it therefore ordered and enacted by the Right Honourable Cecilius Lord Baron of Baltemore absolute Lord and Proprietary of this Province with the advise and consent of this Generall Assembly:

That whatsoever person or persons within this Province and the Islands thereunto belonging shall from henceforth blaspheme God, that is Curse him, or deny our Saviour Jesus Christ to be the son of God, or shall deny the holy Trinity the father son and holy Ghost, or the Godhead of any of the said three persons of the Trinity or the Unity of the Godhead, or shall use or utter any reproachfull speeches, words or language concerning the said Holy Trinity, or any of the said three persons thereof, shall be punished with death and confiscation or forfeiture of all his or her lands and goods to the Lord Proprietary and his heires.

And be it also enacted by the authority and with the advise and assent aforesaid, that whatsoever person or persons shall from henceforth use or utter any reproachfull words or speeches concerning the blessed Virgin Mary the Mother of our Saviour or the holy apostles or evangelists or any of them shall in such case for the first offence forfeit to the said Lord Proprietary and his heirs Lords and proprietaries of this province the summe of five pound Sterling or the value thereof to be levyed on the goods and chattells of every such person soe offending, but in case such offender or offenders, shall not then have goods and chattells sufficient for the satisfyeing of such forfeiture, or that the same bee not otherwise speedily satisfyed that then such offender or offenders shalbe publically whipped and be imprisoned during the pleasure of the Lord Proprietary or the lieutenant or chief governor of this Province for the time being. And that every such offender or offenders for every second offence shall forfeit tenne pound sterling or the value thereof to bee levyed as aforesaid, or in case such offender or offenders shall not then have goods and chattells within this Province sufficient for that purpose then to be publically and severely whipped and imprisoned as before is expressed. And that every person or persons before mentioned offending herein the third time, shall for such third offence forfeit all his lands and goods and be for ever banished and expelled out of this Province.

And be it also further enacted by the same authority advise and assent that whatsoever person or persons shall from henceforth upon any occasion of offence or otherwise in a reproachful manner or Way declare call or denominate any person or persons whatsoever inhabiting, residing, traffiqueing, trading or comerceing within this Province or within any the ports, harbors, creeks or havens to the same belonging an heritick, scismatick, idolator, puritan, independant, Prespiterian popish prest, Jesuite, Jesuited papist, Lutheran, Calvenist, Anabaptist, Brownist, Antinomian, Barrowist, Roundhead, Separatist, or any other name or terme in a reproachfull manner relating to matter of religion shall for every such offence forfeit and loose the somme of tenne shillings sterling or the value thereof to bee levyed on the goods and chattells of every such offender and offenders, the one half thereof to be forfeited and paid unto the person and persons of whom such reproachfull words are or shalbe spoken or uttered, and the other half thereof to the Lord Proprietary and his heires Lords and Proprietaries of this Province. But if such person or persons who shall at any time utter or speake any such reproachfull words or language shall not have goods or chattells sufficient and overt within this Province to be taken to satisfie the penalty aforesaid or that the same bee not otherwise speedily satisfyed, that then the person or persons so offending shall be publically whipped, and shall suffer imprisonment without bail or maineprise [bail] untill he, she or they respectively shall satisfy the party so offended or greived by such reproachfull language by asking him or her respectively forgivenes publically for such his offence before the Magistrate of chief officer or officers of the town or place where such offence shal be given.

And be it further likewise enacted by the authority and consent aforesaid that every person and persons within this Province that shall at any time hereafter prophane the Sabbath or Lords day called Sunday by frequent swearing, drunkennes or by any uncivil or disorderly recreacion, or by working on that day when absolute necessity doth not require it shall for every such first offence forfeit 2s 6d sterling or the value thereof, and for the second offence 5s sterling or the value thereof, and for the third offence and so for every time he shall offend in like manner afterwards 10s sterling or the value thereof. And in case such offender and offenders shall not have sufficient goods or chattells within this Province to satisfy any of the said Penalties respectively hereby imposed for prophaning the Sabbath or Lords day called Sunday as aforesaid, That in Every such case the partie so offending shall for the first and second offence in that kind be imprisoned till he or she shall publickly in open Court before the chief Commander Judge or Magistrate, of that County Town or precinct where such offence shall be committed acknowledge the scandall and offence he hath in that respect given against God and the good and civil governement of this Province, And for the third offence and for every time after shall also bee publically whipped.

And whereas the enforcing of the conscience in matters of religion hath frequently fallen out to be of dangerous consequence in those commonwealthes where it hath been practised, and for the more quiet and peaceable governement of this Province, and the better to preserve mutual love and amity among the inhabitants thereof, be it therefore also by the Lord Proprietary with the advise and consent of this Assembly ordered and enacted (except as in this present Act is before declared and set forth) that no person or persons whatsoever within this Province, or the islands, ports, harbors, creekes, or havens thereunto belonging professing to beleive in Jesus Christ, shall from henceforth be any waies troubled, molested or discountenanced for or in respect of his or her religion nor in the free exercise thereof within this Province or the islands thereunto belonging nor any way compelled to the beleif or exercise of any other religion against his or her consent, so as they be not unfaithfull to the Lord Proprietary, or molest or conspire against the civil governement established or to be established in this Province under him or his heires. And that all and every person and persons that shall presume contrary to this Act and the true intent and meaning thereof directly or indirectly either in person or estate willfully to wrong disturbe trouble or molest any person whatsoever within this Province professing to beleive in Jesus Christ for or in respect of his or her religion or the free exercise thereof within this Province other than is provided for in this Act that such person or persons so offending, shall be compelled to pay treble damages to the party so wronged or molested, and for every such offence shall also forfeit 20s sterling in money or the value thereof, half thereof for the use of the Lord Proprietary, and his heires Lords and Proprietaries of this Province, and the other half for the use of the party so wronged or molested as aforesaid, or if the partie so offending as aforesaid shall refuse or be unable to recompense the party so wronged, or to satisfy such fine or forfeiture, then such offender shall be severely punished by public whipping and imprisonment during the pleasure of the Lord Proprietary, or his Lieutenant or chief Governor of this Province for the time being without baile or maineprise.

And be it further also enacted by the authority and consent aforesaid that the sheriff or other officer or officers from time to time to be appointed and authorized for that purpose, of the county towne or precinct where every particular offence in this present Act conteyned shall happen at any time to be committed and whereupon there is hereby a forfeiture fine or penalty imposed shall from time to time distraine and seise the goods and estate of every such person so offending as aforesaid against this present Act or any part thereof, and sell the same or any part thereof for the full satisfaccion of such forfeiture, fine, or penalty as aforesaid, Restoring unto the partie so offending the remainder or overplus of the said goods or estate after such satisfaccion so made as aforesaid.

The freemen have assented.

Source: W. H. Browne, et al., eds. *Archives of Maryland: Vol. I, Proceedings and Acts of the General Assembly of Maryland, January 1637/8–September 1664* (Baltimore: Maryland Historical Society, 1883), 244–47.

Connecticut Blue Laws (1650)

Blue laws originated in New Haven through social legislation. These laws covered all social concerns from arrests, capital offenses, children, and gaming, to regulations regarding marriage and schooling. The following are excerpts from the 1650 Code of the Connecticut General Court, which enacted laws to support and expand on the Fundamental Orders of 1639. Many other colonies established similar legislation to control their societies.

Forasmuch as the free fruition of such liberties, immunities, privileges as humanity, civility and Christianity call for, as due to every man in his place and proportion, without impeachment and infringement, has ever been and ever will be the tranquility and stability of churches and commonwealths; and the denial or deprival thereof, the disturbance, if not ruin of both: It is thereof ordered by this Court, and authority thereof, that no man's life shall be taken away; no man's honor or good name shall be stained; no man's person shall be arrested, restrained, banished, dismembered, nor any way punished; no man shall be deprived of his wife or children; no man's goods or estates shall be taken away from him nor anyways damaged, under color of law, or countenance of authority; unless it be by the virtue or equity of some express law of the country warranting the same, established by a General Court and sufficiently published, or in case of the defect of a law, in any particular case, by the Word of God.

Arrests

It is ordered and decreed by this Court, and authority thereof, that no person shall be arrested or imprisoned for any debt or fine if the law can find any competent means of satisfaction otherwise from his estate, and if not, his person may be arrested and imprisoned, where he shall be kept at his own charge, not the plaintiff's, till satisfaction be made, unless the court that had cognizance of the cause, or some superior court, shall otherwise determine; provided, nevertheless, that no man's person shall be kept in prison for debt, but when there appears some estate which he will not produce, to which end, any court or commissioners authorized by the General Court, may administer an oath to the party, or any others suspected to be privy in concealing his estate, he shall satisfy by service, if the creditor require it; but shall not be sold to any but of the English nation. . . .

Capital Laws

1. If any man after legal conviction shall have or worship any other God but the Lord God, he shall be put to death (Deut. 13: 6, 17: 2, Ex. 22: 20).

2. If any man or woman be a witch, that is, has or consults with a familiar spirit, they shall be put to death (Ex. 22: 18; Lev. 20: 27; Deut. 18: 10, 11).

3. If any person shall blasphemy the name of God the Father, Son or Holy Ghost with direct, express, presumptuous, or high-handed blasphemy, or shall curse in the like manner, he shall be put to death.

4. If any person shall commit any willful murder, which is manslaughter, committed upon malice, hatred, or cruelty, not in a man's necessary and just defense, nor by mere casualty against his will, he shall be put to death (Ex. 21: 12–14; Num. 35: 30, 31).

5. If any person shall slay another through guile, either by poisoning or other such devilish practice, he shall be put to death (Ex. 21: 14).

6. If any man or woman shall lie with any beast or brute creature, by carnal copulation, they shall surely be put to death, and the beast shall be slain and buried (Lev. 20: 15, 16).

7. If any man lies with mankind as he lies with woman, both of them have committed abomination, they both shall surely be put to death (Lev. 20: 10, 18: 20; Deut. 22: 23,24).

8. If any person commits adultery with a married or espoused wife, the adulterer and the adulteress shall surely be put to death (Lev. 20: 10, 18: 20; Deut. 22: 23, 24).

9. If any man shall forcibly, and without consent, ravish any maid or woman that is lawfully married or contracted, he shall be put to death (Deut. 22: 25).

10. If any man steals a man or mankind, he shall be put to death (Ex. 21: 16).

11. If any man rise up by false witness, wittingly and of purpose to take away any man's life, he shall be put to death (Deut. 19: 16, 18, 19).

12. If any man shall conspire or attempt any invasion, insurrection, or rebellion against the Commonwealth, he shall be put to death.

13. If any child or children above sixteen years old and of sufficient understanding shall curse or smite their natural father or mother, he or they shall be put to death; unless it can be sufficiently testified that the parents have been very unchristianly negligent in the education of such children, or so provoke them by extreme and cruel correction that they have been forced thereunto to preserve themselves from death, maiming (Ex. 21: 15, 17; Lev. 20).

14. If any man have a stubborn and rebellious son of sufficient years and understanding, viz., sixteen years of age, which will not obey the voice of his father or the voice of his mother, and that when they have chastened him will not hearken unto them, then may his father and mother, being his natural parents, lay hold on him and bring him to the magistrates assembled in Court, and testify unto them that their son is stubborn and rebellious and will not obey their voice, and chastisement, but lives in sundry notorious crimes, such a son shall be put to death (Deut. 21: 20, 21). . . .

Children

Forasmuch as the good education of children is of singular behoof and benefit to any commonwealth; and whereas many parents and masters are too indulgent and negligent of their duty in that kind: It is therefore ordered by this Court and authorized hereof that the selectmen of every town in the several precincts and quarters where they dwell shall have a vigilant eye over their bretheren and neighbors, to see, first, that none of them shall suffer so much barbarism in any of their families, as not to endeavor to teach by themselves or others their children and apprentices so much learning as may enable them perfectly to read the English tongue, and knowledge of the capital laws, upon penalty of 20 s[hillings] for such neglect therein. Also, that all masters of families do, once a week, at least, catecize their children and servants in the grounds and principles of religion, and if any be unable to do so much, that then, at the least, they procure such children or apprentices to learn some short orthodox catechism, without book, that they may be able to answer to the questions that shall be propounded to them out of such catechisms by their parents or masters, or any of the selectmen where they shall call them to a trial of what they have learned in this kind. And further, that all parents and masters do breed and bring up their children and apprentices in some honest, lawful calling, labor, or employment, either in husbandry or some other trade profitable for themselves and Commonwealth, if they will not nor cannot train them up in learning, to fit them for higher employments. And if any of the selectmen, after admonition by them given to such masters of families, shall find them still negligent of their duty in the particulars aforementioned, whereby children and servants become rude, stubborn, and unruly, the said selectmen, with the help of two magistrates, shall take such children or apprentices from them and place them with such masters for years, boys till they come to twenty-one, and girls, eighteen years of age complete, which will more strictly look unto and force them to submit unto government, according to the rules of this order, if by fair means and former instructions they will not be drawn unto it. . . .

Cruelty

It is ordered by this Court, and authority thereof, that no man shall exercise any tyranny or cruelty toward any brute creatures, which are usually kept for the use of man.

Damages Pretended

Forasmuch as the open contempt of God's Word, and messengers thereof, is the desolating sin of civil states and churches, and that the preaching of the Word by those whom God does send is that chief ordinary means ordained by God for the converting, edifying, and saving the souls of the elect, through the presence and power of the Holy Ghost thereunto promised; and that the ministry of the Word is set up by God in His churches for those holy ends; and accordingly to the respect or contempt of the same, and of those whom God has set apart for His own work and employment, the weal or woe of all Christian states, is much furthered and promoted; It is therefore ordered and decreed, that if any Christian, so called, within this jurisdiction, shall contemptuously bear himself toward the Word preached, or the messengers that are called to dispense the same in any congregation, when he does faithfully execute his service and office therein, according to the Will and Word of God, either by interrupting him in his preaching or by charging him falsely with an error, which he has not taught, in the open face of the church, or like a son of Korah, cast upon his true doctrine, or himself, any reproach to the dishonor of the Lord Jesus, who has sent him, and to the disparagement of that His Holy Ordinance, and making God's ways contemptible and ridiculous, that every such person or persons, whatsoever censure the church may pass, shall, for the first scandal, be convented and reproved openly by the magistrates, at some lecture, and bound to their good behavior. And if a second time they break forth into the like contemptuous carriages, they shall either pay 5 pounds to the public treasure, or stand two hours, openly, upon a block or stool four foot high, upon a lecture day, with a paper fixed on his breast written with capital letters AN OPEN AND OBSTINANTE CONTEMNER OF GOD'S HOLY ORDINANCES, that others may fear and be ashamed of breaking out into the like wickedness.

It is ordered and decreed by this Court, and authority thereof, that wheresoever the ministry of the Word is established, according to the order of the Gospel, throughout this jurisdiction, every person shall duly resort and attend thereunto respectively upon the Lord's Day, and upon such public fast days and days of thanksgiving as are to be generally kept by the appointment of authority. And if any person within this jurisdiction shall, without just and necessary cause, withdraw himself from hearing the public ministry of the Word, after due means of conviction used, he shall forfeit for his absence, from every such public meeting, 5 s[hillings]; all such offenses to be heard and determined by any one magistrate, or more, from time to time.

Forasmuch as the peace and prosperity of churches, and members thereof, as well as civil rights and liberties, are carefully to be maintained; it is ordered by this Court and decreed, that the civil authority here established has power and liberty to see the peace, ordinances, and rules of Christ be observed in every church, according to His Word; as also to deal with any church member in a way of civil justice, notwithstanding any church relation, office, or interest, so it be done in a civil and not in an ecclesiastical way; nor shall any church censure degrade or depose any man from any civil dignity, office, or authority he shall have in the Commonwealth. . . .

Gaming

Upon complaint of great disorder, by the use of the game called shuffleboard, in houses of common entertainment, whereby much precious time is spent unfruitfully, and much waste of wine and beer occasioned; It is therefore ordered and enacted by the authority of this Court, that no person shall henceforth use the said game of shuffleboard in any such house, nor in any other house used as common for such purpose, upon pain for every keeper of such house to forfeit for every such offence 20 s[hillings]; and for every person playing at the said game in any such house, to forfeit for every such offense 5 s[hillings].; the like penalty shall be for playing in any place at any unlawful game. . . .

Source: The Code of 1650, Being a Compilation of the Earliest Laws and Orders of the General Court of Connecticut (Hartford, 1822), 20–94.

Virginia Slave Laws (1660s)

While both African Americans and whites served as indentured servants in the colonies, by the mid-seventeenth century, laws began appearing in Virginia statutes distinguishing between white servants and African American slaves. The excerpts that follow reveal the bondage of African Americans and their treatment as property.

December 1662

Whereas some doubts have arisen whether children got by any Englishman upon a Negro woman should be slave or free, *be it therefore enacted and declared by this present Grand Assembly*, that all children born in this country shall be held bond or free only according to the condition of the mother; and that if any Christian shall commit fornication with a Negro man or woman, he or she so offending shall pay double the fines imposed by the former act.

September 1667

Whereas some doubts have risen whether children that are slaves by birth, and by the charity and piety of their owners made partakers of the blessed sacrament of baptism, should by virtue of their baptism be made free, *it is enacted and declared by this Grand Assembly, and the authority thereof*, that the conferring of baptism does not alter the condition of the person as to his bondage or freedom; that diverse masters, freed from this doubt may more carefully endeavor the propagation of Christianity by permitting children, though slaves, or chose of greater growth if capable, to be admitted to that sacrament.

September 1668

Whereas it has been questioned whether servants running away may be punished with corporal punishment by their master or magistrate, since the act already made gives the master satisfaction by prolonging their time by service, *it is declared and enacted by this Assembly* that moderate corporal punishment inflicted by master or magistrate upon a runaway servant shall not deprive the master of the satisfaction allowed by the law, the one being as necessary to reclaim them from persisting in that idle course as the other is just to repair the damages sustained by the master.

October 1669

Whereas the only law in force for the punishment of refractory servants resisting their master, mistress, or overseer cannot be inflicted upon Negroes, nor the obstinacy of many of them be suppressed by other than violent means, *be it enacted and declared by this Grand Assembly* if any slave resists his master (or other by his master's order correcting him) and by the extremity of the correction should chance to die, that his death shall not be accounted a felony, but the master (or that other person appointed by the master to punish him) be acquitted from molestation, since it cannot be presumed that premeditated malice (which alone makes murder a felony) should induce any man to destroy his own estate.

Source: William Waller Hening, *Statutes at Large; Being a Collection of All the Laws of Virginia,* Vol. 2 (New York : R. & W. & G. Bartow, 1819–1923).

Upon the Burning of Our House (1666)

America's first published American poet was Anne Bradstreet. She wrote about the common experiences—childbirth, death, and so on—of seventeenth-century residents of Massachusetts. This poem vividly recounts the ever-present danger of fire and the effect it had on families.

In silent night when rest I took,
For sorrow near I did not look,
I waken'd was with thund'ring noise
And piteous shrieks of dreadful voice.
That fearful sound of "fire" and "fire,"
Let no man know is my Desire.

I starting up, the light did spy,
And to my God my heart did cry
To straighten me in my Distress
And not to leave me succourless.
Then coming out, behold a space
The flame consume my dwelling place.

And when I could no longer look,
I blest his grace that gave and took,
That laid my goods now in the dust.
Yea, so it was, and so 'twas just.
It was his own; it was not mine.
Far be it that I should repine.

He might of all justly bereft
But yet sufficient for us left.
When by the Ruins oft I past
My sorrowing eyes aside did cast
And here and there the places spy
Where oft I sate and long did lie.

Here stood that Trunk, and there that chest,
There lay that store I counted best,
My pleasant things in ashes lie
And them behold no more shall I.

Under the roof no guest shall sit,
Nor at thy Table eat a bit.

No pleasant talk shall 'ere be told
Nor things recounted done of old.
No Candle 'ere shall shine in Thee,
Nor bridegroom's voice ere heard shall bee.
In silence ever shalt thou lie.
Adieu, Adieu, All's Vanity.

Then straight I 'gin my heart to chide:
And did thy wealth on earth abide,
Didst fix thy hope on mouldring dust,
The arm of flesh didst make thy trust?
Raise up thy thoughts above the sky
That dunghill mists away may fly.

Thou hast a house on high erect
Fram'd by that mighty Architect,
With glory richly furnished
Stands permanent, though this be fled.
It's purchased and paid for too
By him who hath enough to do.

A price so vast as is unknown,
Yet by his gift is made thine own.
There's wealth enough; I need no more.
Farewell, my pelf; farewell, my store.
The world no longer let me love;
My hope and Treasure lies above.

Source: John Harvard Ellis, ed., *The Works of Anne Bradstreet in Prose and Verse* (New York: Peter Smith, 1867; reprinted 1932).

John Eliot and His Work with Native Americans (1670)

In 1646, John Eliot began ministering to the native peoples of New England in their own language, becoming known as the "Apostle to the Indians." He subsequently translated the Bible into Algonquian (1661) and established Native American "praying towns," where he attempted to convert the natives to both Christianity and the ways of English civilization. The report that follows is Eliot's last narrative on the progress of his evangelization. His efforts were subsequently halted by King Philip's War (1675–1676).

To the Right Worshipful the Commissioners under his Majesties' Great-Seal, for Propagation of the Gospel amongst the poor blind Indians in New-England

Right Worshipful and Christian Gentlemen:

THAT brief Tract of the present state of the Indian-Work in my hand, which I did the last year on the sudden present you with when you call'd for such a thing; That falling short of its end, and you calling for a renewal thereof, with opportunity of more time, I shall begin with our last great motion in that Work done this Summer, because that will lead me to begin with the state of the Indians under the hands of my Brethren Mr. Mahew and Mr. Bourn.

Upon the 17th day of the 6th month, 1670, there was a Meeting at Maktapog near Sandwich in Plimouth-Pattent, to gather a Church among the Indians: There were present six of the Magistrates, and many Elders (all of them Messengers of the Churches within that Jurisdiction) in whose presence, in a day of Fasting and Prayer, they making confession of the Truth and Grace of Jesus Christ, did in that solemn Assembly enter into Covenant, to walk together in the Faith and Order of the Gospel; and were accepted and declared to be a Church of Jesus Christ. These Indians being of kin to our Massachuset-Indians who first prayed unto God, conversed with them, and received amongst them the light and love of the Truth; they desired me to write to Mr. Leveredge to teach them: He accepted the Motion: and performed the Work with good success; but afterwards he left that place, and went to Long-Island, and there a godly Brother, named Richard Bourne (who purposed to remove with Mr. Leveredge, but hindered by Divine Providence) undertook the teaching of those Indians, and hath continued in the work with good success to this day; him we ordained Pastor: and one of the Indians, named Jude, should have been ordained Ruling-Elder, but being sick at that time, advice was given that he should be ordained with the first opportunity, as also a Deacon to manage the present Sabbath-Day Collections, and other parts of that Office in their season. The same day also were they, and such of their Children as were present, baptized.

From them we passed over to the Vineyard, where many were added to the Church both men and women, and were baptized all of them, and their Children also with them; we had the Sacrament of the Lords Supper celebrated in the Indian-Church, and many of the English-Church gladly joyned with them; for which cause it was celebrated in both languages. On a day of Fasting and Prayer, Elders were ordained, two Teaching-Elders, the one to be a Preacher of the Gospel, to do the Office of a Pastor and Teacher; the other to be a Preacher of the Gospel, to do the Office of a Teacher and Pastor, as the Lord should given them ability and opportunity; Also two Ruling-Elders, with advice to ordain Deacons also, for the Service of Christ in the Church. Things were so ordered by the Lord's guidance, that a Foundation is laid for two Churches more; for first, these of the Vineyard dwelling at too great a distance to enjoy with comfort their Sabbath-communion in one place, Advice was given them, that after some experience of walking together in the Order and Ordinances of the Gospel, they should issue forth into another Church; and the Officers are so chosen, that when they shall do so, both Places are furnished with a Teaching and Ruling-Elder.

Also the Teacher of the Praying Indians of Nantuket, with a Brother of his were received here, who made good Confessions of Jesus Christ; and being asked, did make report unto us that there be about ninety Families who pray unto God in that Island, so effectual is the Light of the Gospel among them. Advice was given, that some of the chief Godly

People should joyn to this Church (for they frequently converse together, though the Islands be seven leagues asunder) and after some experience of walking in the Order of the Gospel, they should issue forth into Church-estate among themselves, and have Officers ordained amongst them.

The Church of the Vineyard were desirous to have chosen Mr. Mahew to be their Pastor: but he declined it, conceiving that in his present capacity he lieth under greater advantages to stand their Friend, and do them good, to save them from the hands of such as would bereave them of their Lands, &c., but they shall alwayes have his counsel, instruction and management in all their Church-affairs, as hitherto they have had; he will die in this service of Jesus Christ. The Praying-Indians of both these islands depend on him, as God's Instrument for their good. Advice also was given for the setling of Schools; every Child capable of learning, equally paying, whether he make use of it or no: Yet if any should sinfully neglect Schooling their Youth, it is a transgression liable to censure under both Orders, Civil and Ecclesiastical, the offence being against both. So we walk at Natick.

In as much as now we have ordained Indian Officers unto the Ministry of the Gospel, it is needed to add a word or two of Apology: I find it hopeless to expect English Officers in our Indian Churches; the work is full of hardship, hard labour, and chargeable also, and the Indians not yet capable to give considerable support and maintenance; and Men have bodies, and must live of the Gospel: And what comes from England is liable to hazard and uncertainties. On such grounds as these partly, but especially from the secret wise governance of Jesus Christ, the Lord of the Harvest, there is no appearance of hope for their souls feeding in that way: they must be trained up to be able to live of themselves in the ways of the Gospel of Christ; and through the riches of God's Grace and Love, sundry of themselves who are expert in the Scriptures, are able to teach each other: An English young man raw in that language, coming to teach among our Christian-Indians, would be much to their loss; there be of themselves such as be more able, especially being advantaged that he speaketh his own language, and knoweth their manners. Such English as shall hereafter teach them, must begin with a People that begin to pray unto God (and such opportunities we have many) and then as they grow in knowledge, he will grow (if he be diligent) in ability of speech to communicate the knowledge of Christ unto them. And seeing they must have Teachers amongst themselves, they must also be taught to be Teachers: for which cause I have begun to teach them the Art of Teaching, and I find some of them very capable. And while I live, my purpose is (by the grace of Christ assisting) to make it one of my chief cares and labours to teach them some of the Liberal Arts and Sciences, and the way how to analize, and lay out into particulars both the Works and Word of God; and how to communicate knowledge to others methodically and skilfully, and especially the method of Divinity. There be sundry Ministers who live in an opportunity of beginning with a

People, and for time to come I shall cease my importuning of others, and onely fall to perswade such unto this service of Jesus Christ, it being one part of our Ministerial Charge to preach to the World in the Name of Jesus, and from amongst them to gather Subjects to his holy Kingdom. The Bible, and the Catechism drawn out of the Bible, are general helps to all parts and places about us, and are the groundwork of Community amongst all our Indian-Churches and Christians.

I find a blessing, when our Church of Natick doth send forth fit Persons unto some remoter places, to teach them the fear of the Lord. But we want maintenance for that Service; it is chargeable matter to send a Man from his Family: The Labourer is worthy of his Hire: And when they go only to the High-wayes and Hedges, it is not to be expected that they should reward them: If they believe and obey their Message, it is enough. We are determined to send forth some (if the Lord will, and that we live) this Autumn, sundry ways. I see the best way is, up and be doing: In all labour there is profit; Seek and ye shall find. We have Christ's Example, his Promise, his Presence, his Spirit to assist; and I trust that the Lord will find a way for your encouragement.

Natick is our chief Town, where most and chief of our Rulers, and most of the Church dwells; here most of our chief Courts are kept; and the Sacraments in the Church are for the most part here administered: It is (by the Divine Providence) seated well near in the center of all our praying Indians, though Westward the Cords of Christ's Tents are more enlarged. Here we began Civil Government in the year 1650. And here usually are kept the General-Trainings, which seven years ago looked so big that we never had one since till this year, and it was at this time but a small appearance. Here we have two Teachers, John Speen and Anthony; we have betwixt forty and fifty Communicants at the Lord's Table, when they all appear, but now, some are dead, and some decriped with age; and one under Censure, yet making towards a recovery; one died here the last Winter of the Stone, a temperate, sober, godly man, the first Indian that ever was known to have that disease; but now another hath the same disease: Sundry more are proposed, and in way of preparation to joyn unto the Church.

Ponkipog, or Pakeunit, is our second Town, where the Sachems of the Bloud (as they term the Chief Royal-Line) had their Residence and Rights, which are mostly Alienated to the English Towns: The last Chief Man, off that Line, was last year slain by the Mauquzogs, against whom he rashly (without due Attendants and Assistance, and against Counsel) went; yet all, yea, his Enemies say, He died valiantly; they were more afraid to kill him, than we was to died; yet being deserted by all (some knowingly say through Treasoon) he stood long, and at last feel alone: Had he had but 10 Men, yea 5 in good order with him, he would have driven all his Enemies before him. His Brother was resident with us in this Town, but he is fallen into sin, and from praying to God. Our Chief Ruler is Ahauton, an old stedfast and trusty friend to the English, and loveth his Country. He is more loved than feared; the reins of his bridle are too long. Waken is sometimes necessarily called to keep Courts here, to add live and zeal in the punishment of Sinners. Their late Teacher, William, is deceased; He was a man of eminent parts, all the English acknowledge him, and he was known to many: He was of a ready wit, sound judgment, and affable; he is gone unto the Lord; And William, the Son of Ahauton, is called to be Teacher in his stead. He is a promising young-man, of a single and upright heart, a good judgment, he Prayeth and Preacheth well, he is studious and industrious, and well accounted of among the English.

Hassunnimesut is the next Town in order, dignity, and antiquity; sundry of our chief Friends in the great work of Praying to God, came from them, and there lived their Progenitors, and there lieth their Inheritance, and that is the place of their desires. It lieth upon Nichmuke River; the people were well known to the English so long as Connecticot Road lay that way, and their Religion was judged to be real by all that travelled that journey, and had occasion to lodge, especially to keep a Sabbath among them. The Ruler of the Town is Anuweekin, and his brother Tuppukkoowillin is Teacher, both sound and godly Men. This Ruler, last Winter, was overtaken with a Passion, which was so observable, that I had occasion to speak with him about it; he was very penitent; I hold him, That as to man, I, and all men were ready to forgive him. Ah! said he, I find it the greatest difficulty to forgive myself. For the encouragement of this place, and for the cherishing of a new Plantation of Praying Indians beyond them, they called Monatunkanet to be a Teacher also in that Town, and both of them to take care of the new Praying-Town beyond them. And for the like encouragement, Captain Gookins joyned Petahheg with Anuweekin. The aged Father of this Ruler and Teacher, was last year Baptized, who hath many Children that fear God. In this place we meditate ere long (if the Lord will, and that we live) to gather a Church, that so the Sabbath-Communion of our Christian Indians may be the more agreeable to the Divine Institution, which we make too bold with while we live at such distance.

Ogquonikongquamesut is the next Town; where, how we have been afflicted, I may not say. The English Town called Marlborough doth border upon them, as did the lines of the Tribes of Judah and Benjamin; the English Meeting-house standeth within the line of the Indian Town, although the contiguity and co-inhabitation is not barren in producing matters of interfering; yet our godly Indians do obtain a good report of the godly English, which is an argument that bringeth light and evidence to my heart, that our Indians are really godly. I was very lately among them; they desired me to settle a stated Lecture amongst them, as it is in sundry other Praying Towns, which I did with so much the more gladness and hope of blessing in it, because through Grace the Motion did first spring from themselves. Solomon is their Teacher, whom we judge to be a serious and sound Christian;

their Ruler is Owannamug, whose grave, faithful, and discreet Conversation hath procured him real respect from the English. One that was a Teacher in this place, is the man that is now under Censure in the Church; his sin was that adventitious sin which we have brought unto them, Drunkenness, which was never known to them before they knew us English. But I account it our duty, and it is much in my desire, as well to teach them Wisdom to Rule such heady Creatures, as skill to get them to be able to bridle their own appetites, when they have means and opportunity of high-spirited enticements. The Wisdom and Power of Grace is not so much seen in the beggarly want of these things, as in the bridling of our selves in the use of them. It is true Dominion, to be able to use them, and not to abuse ourselves by them.

Nashope is our next Praying Town, a place of much Affliction; it was the chief place of Residence, where Tahattawans lived, a Sachem of the Blood, a faithful and zealous Christian, a strict yet gentle Ruler; he was a Ruler of 50 in our Civil Order; and when God took him, a chief man in our Israel was taken away from us. His only Son was a while vain, but proved good, except in the Scripture, was Elected to rule in his Father's place, but soon died, insomuch that this place is now destitute of a Ruler. The Teacher of the place is John Thomas, a godly understanding Christian, well esteemed of by the English: his Father was killed by the Mauquaogs, shot to death as he was in the River doing his Eele-wyers. This place lying in the Road-way which the Mauquaogs haunted, was much molested by them, and was one year wholly deserted; but this year the People have taken courage and dwell upon it again.

In this place after the great Earthquake, there was some eruption out of the Earth, which left a great Hiatus or Cleft a great way together, and out of some Cavities under great Rocks, by a great Pond in that place, there was a great while after often heard an humming noise, as if there were frequent eruptions out of the Ground at that place: yet for Healthfulness thee place is much as other places be. For Religion, there be amongst them some Godly Christians, who are received into the Church, and baptized, and others looking that way.

Wamesut is our next Praying-Town; it lyeth at the bottom of the great Falls, on the great River Merymak, and at the falling-in of Concord River; the Sachem of this Place is named Nomphon, said to be a Prince of the Bloud, a Man of a real Noble Spirit: A Brother of his was slain by the Mauquaogs as he was upon a Rock fishing in the great River. In revenge whereof he went in the forementioned rash Expedition, but had such about him, and was so circumspect, that he came well off, though he lost one principal Man. This place is very much annoyed by the Mauquaogs, and have much ado to stand their ground.

In this Place Captain Gookins ordered a Garrison to be kept the last year, which Order while they attended they were safe; but when the Northern Sachems and Souldiers came, who stirred up ours to go with them on their unsuccessful Expedition, the Town was for the most part scatter'd and their Corn spoyled.

The Teacher of this Place is named George: they have not much esteem for Religion, but I am hopefully perswaded of sundry of them; I can go unto them but once in a year.

Panatuket is the upper part of Merimak-Falls; so called, because of the noise which the Waters make. Thither the Penagwog-Indians are come, and have built a great Fort; Their Sachems refused to pray to God, so signally and sinfully, that Captain Gookins and my self were very sensible of it, and were not without some expectation of some interposure of a Divine-Hand, which did eminently come to pass; for in the forenamed expedition they joyned with the Northern Sachems, and were all of them cut off; even all that had so signally refused to pray unto God were now as signally rejected by God, and cut off. I hear not that it was ever known, that so many Sachems and Men of Note were killed in one imprudent Expedition, and that by a few scattered people; for the Mauquaogs were not imbodied to received them, nor prepared, and few at home, which did much greaten the Overthrow of so many great Men, and shews a divine over-ruling hand of God. But now, since the Penaguag-Sachems are cut off, the People (sundry of them) dwelling at Panatuket-Fort do bow the ear to hear, and submit to pray unto God; to whom Jethro, after he had confest Christ and was baptized, was sent to preach Christ to them.

Magunkukquok is another of our Praying-Towns at the remotest Westerly borders of Natick; these are gathering together of some Nipmuk Indians who left their own places, and sit together in this place, and have given up themselves to pray unto God. They have called Pomham to be their Ruler, and Simon to be their Teacher. This latter is accounted a good and lively Christian; he is the second man among the Indians that doth experience that afflicting disease of the Stone. The Ruler hath made his Preparatory Confession of Christ, and is approved of, and at the next opportunity is to be received and baptized.

I obtained of the General-Court a Grant of a Tract of Land, for the settlement and encouragement of this People; which though as yet it be by some obstructed, yet I hope we shall find some way to accomplish the same.

Quanatusset is the last of our Praying-Towns, whose beginnings have received too much discouragement; but yet the Seed is alive: they are frequently with me; the work is at the birth, there doth only want strength to bring forth. The care of this People is committed joyntly to Monatunkanit, and Tuppunkkoowillin, the Teachers of Hassunemeesut, as is abovesaid; and I hope if the Lord continue my life, I shall have a good account to give of that People.

Thus I have briefly touched some of the chiefest of our present Affairs, and commit them to your Prudence, to do with them what you please; committing your Selves, and all your weighty Affairs unto the Guidance and Blessing of the Lord, I rest, Your Worships to serve you in the Service of our Lord Jesus.

JOHN ELLIOT [sic].
Roxbury, this 20th of the 7th month, 1670.

Source: John Eliot, *A Brief Narrative of the Progress of the Gospel Amongst the Indians in New England, in the Year 1670* (London: Printed for John Allen, 1671).

Probate Inventory of a Plymouth Colony Estate (1672)

This probate inventory of the estate of Ester Woodfeild, from Plymouth Colony, offers insights into the modest household of a woman who owned farm animals, linens, spinning wheels, and various other household implements. She was apparently literate, as evidenced by mention of not only a Bible but other books as well. It is likely that she died intestate, that is, without having left behind a will, since it was customary in such cases for the court to require an inventory and appraisal of the decedent's possessions.

A true Inventory of the estate of Ester Woodfeild of Scittuate lately deceased exhibited to the Court of his Matie holden att Plymouth in New England the fift of June 1672 on the oath of henery Ewell; taken and apprised by Rodulphus Elmes and Steven Vinall; as followeth

Item her purse and apparrell both woolen and linnine 36 [pounds] 00 [shillings] 00 [pence]

Item bookes viz: bibles and other bookes 00 12 00

Item bedds and beding both woolen and linnine 16 00 00

Item brasse pewter and Iron houshold stuffe 01 15 00

Item Cowes and Calfe mare and Colt and swine 20 00 00

Item three Chistes and Iron tooles 01 15 00

Item Corne meale seiues trenchers baggs and four Caske 01 00 00

Item spining wheeles Cards and Flax 00 18 00

Item bedsteeds Chernes tubb and other Lumber 02 10 00

Aprised by vs
Rodulphus Elmes
Steven Vinall

Source: *Plymouth Colony Wills*, Vol. III (Plymouth Colony Archive Project, University of Virginia Library), 38.

Marquette's Travels on the Mississippi (1673)

The French Jesuit priests Jacques Marquette and former seminary student Louis Jolliet traveled over 2,500 miles on the Mississippi, preaching to native settlements along the way. Jolliet made maps, and Marquette kept a detailed journal of their observations. On the return trip, Marquette lost his notes, and so wrote his account from memory.

Taken from his *Travels and Discoveries in North America,* Marquette's narrative comments on their diet along the way, animals and vegetation, rock drawings, iron mines, climate, and the hazards of the Mississippi and other waterways, which they monitored for depth using a sounding line. Their expedition ventured as far as the Arkansas and Louisiana border, where, realizing that the river flowed into the Gulf of Mexico and not California, they turned back to avoid capture by the Spanish.

I embarked with M. Joliet, who had been chosen to conduct this enterprise, on the 13th May, 1673, with five other Frenchmen, in two bark canoes. We laid in some Indian corn and smoked beef for our voyage. We first took care, however, to draw from the Indians all the information we could, concerning the countries through which we designed to travel, and drew up a map, on which we marked down the rivers, nations, and points of the compass to guide us in our journey. The first nation we came to was called the Folles-Avoines, or the nation of wild oats. I entered their river to visit them, as I had preached among them some years before. The wild oats, from which they derive their name, grow spontaneously in their country. . . .

I acquainted them with my design of discovering other nations, to preach to them the mysteries of our holy religion, at which they were much surprized, and said all they could to dissuade me from it. They told me I would meet Indians who spare no strangers, and whom they kill without any provocation or mercy; that the war they have one with the other would expose me to be taken by their warriors, as they are constantly on the look-out to surprize their enemies. That the Great River was exceedingly dangerous, and full of frightful monsters who devoured men and canoes together, and that the heat was so great that it would positively cause our death. I thanked them for their kind advice, but told them I would not follow it, as the salvation of a great many souls was concerned in our undertaking, for whom I should be glad to lose my life. I added that I defied their monsters, and their information would oblige us to keep more upon our guard to avoid a surprize. And having prayed with them, and given them some instructions, we set out for the Bay of Puan, where our missionaries had been successful in con-

verting them. . . . The next day, being the 10th of June, the two guides [Miamies] embarked with us in sight of all the village, who were astonished at our attempting so dangerous an expedition. We were informed that at three leagues from the Maskoutens, we should find a river which runs into the Mississippi, and that we were to go to the west-south-west to find it, but there were so many marshes and lakes, that if it had not been for our guides we could not have found it. . . .

Before embarking we all offered up prayers to the Holy Virgin, which we continued to do every morning, placing ourselves and the events of the journey under her protection, and after having encouraged each other, we got into our canoes. The river upon which we embarked is called Mesconsin [Wisconsin]; the river is very wide, but the sand bars make it very difficult to navigate, which is increased by numerous islands covered with grape-vines. The country through which it flows is beautiful; the groves are so dispersed in the prairies that it makes a noble prospect; and the fruit of the trees shows a fertile soil. These groves are full of walnut, oak, and other trees unknown to us in Europe. We saw neither game nor fish, but roebuck and buffaloes in great numbers. After having navigated thirty leagues we discovered some iron mines, and one of our company who had seen such mines before, said these were very rich in ore. They are covered with about three feet of soil, and situate near a chain of rocks, whose base is covered with fine timber. After having rowed ten leagues farther, making forty leagues from the place where we had embarked, we came into the Mississippi on the 17th of June [1673].

The mouth of the Mesconsin [Wisconsin] is in about 42½° N. lat. Behold us, then, upon this celebrated river, whose singularities I have attentively studied. The Mississippi takes its rise in several lakes in the North. Its channel is very narrow at the mouth of the Mesconsin, and runs south until it is affected by very high hills. Its current is slow, because of its depth. In sounding we found nineteen fathoms of water. A little further on it widens nearly three-quarters of a league, and the width continues to be more equal. We slowly followed its course to the south and southeast to the 42°, N. lat. Here we perceived the country change its appearance. There were scarcely any more woods or mountains. The islands are covered with fine trees, but we could not see any more roebucks, buffaloes, bustards, and swans. We met from time to time monstrous fish, which struck so violently against our canoes, that at first we took them to be large trees, which threatened to upset us. We saw also a hideous monster; his head was like that of a tiger, his nose was sharp, and somewhat resembled a wildcat; his beard was long; his ears stood upright; the color of his head was gray; and his neck black. He looked upon us for some time, but as we came near him our oars frightened him away. When we threw our nets into the water we caught an abundance of sturgeons, and another kind of fish like our trout, except that the eyes and nose are much smaller, and they have near the nose a bone like a woman's busk, three inches broad and a foot and a half long, the end of which is flat and broad, and when it leaps out of the water the weight of it throws it on its back.

Having descended the river as far as 41° 28' we found that turkeys took the place of game, and the Pisikious that of other animals. We called the Pisikious wild buffaloes, because they very much resemble our domestic oxen; they are not so long, but twice as large. We shot one of them, and it was as much as thirteen men could do to drag him from the place where he fell. . . .

We continued to descend the river, not knowing where we were going, and having made a hundred leagues without seeing anything but wild beasts and birds, and being on our guard we landed at night to make our fire and prepare our repast, and then left the shore to anchor in the river, while one of us watched by turns to prevent a surprize. We went south and southwest until we found ourselves in about the latitude of 40° and some minutes, having rowed more than sixty leagues since we entered the river.

We took leave of our guides about the end of June, and embarked in presence of all the village, who admired our birch canoes, as they had never before seen anything like them. We descended the river, looking for another called Pekitanoni [Missouri], which runs from the northwest into the Mississippi. . . .

As we were descending the river we saw high rocks with hideous monsters painted on them, and upon which the bravest Indians dare not look. They are as large as a calf, with head and horns like a goat; their eyes red; beard like a tiger's; and a face like a man's. Their tails are so long that they pass over their heads and between their fore legs, under their belly, and ending like a fish's tail. They are painted red, green, and black. They are so well drawn that I cannot believe they were drawn by the Indians. And for what purpose they were made seems to me a great mystery. As we fell down the river, and while we were discoursing upon these monsters, we heard a great rushing and bubbling of waters, and small islands of floating trees coming from the mouth of the Pekitanoni [Missouri], with such rapidity that we could not trust ourselves to go near it. The water of this river is so muddy that we could not drink it. It so discolors the Mississippi as to make the navigation of it dangerous. This river comes from the northwest, and empties into the Mississippi, and on its banks are situated a number of Indian villages. We judged by the compass, that the Mississippi discharged itself into the Gulf of Mexico. It would, however, have been more agreeable if it had discharged itself into the South Sea or Gulf of California. . . .

Having satisfied ourselves that the Gulf of Mexico was in latitude 31° 40', and that we could reach it in three or four days' journey from the Akansea [Arkansas River], and that the Mississippi discharged itself into it, and not to the eastward of the Cape of Florida, nor into the California Sea, we resolved to return home. We considered that the advantage of our travels would be altogether lost to our nation if we fell into the hands of the Spaniards, from whom we could expect no other treatment than death or slavery; besides, we saw that we were not prepared to resist the Indians, the allies of the Europeans, who continually infested the lower part of this river; we therefore came to the conclusion to return, and make a report to those who had sent us. So that having rested another day, we left the village of the Akansea, on the seventeenth of July, 1673, having followed the Mississippi from the latitude 42° to 34°, and preached the Gospel to the utmost of my power, to the nations we visited. We then ascended the Mississippi with great difficulty against the current, and left it in the latitude of 38° north, to enter another river [Illinois], which took us to the lake of the Illinois [Michigan], which is a much shorter way than through the River Mesconsin [Wisconsin], by which we entered the Mississippi. . . .

Source: America, Great Crises in Our History Told by its Makers, Vol. 2, Colonization (Chicago: Veterans of Foreign Wars of the United States, 1925), 198–204.

Governor William Berkeley on Bacon's Rebellion (1676)

≈≈ ~ ~ ≈≈

Bacon's Rebellion was the first popular revolt in the British colonies. Led by Nathaniel Bacon, the rebellion was fueled by a perception of disenfranchisement by landowners, heavy taxes, a low financial return on tobacco, and inadequate protection from native raids in Virginia. In this excerpt, Governor Berkeley, who was temporarily overthrown by Bacon, discusses how he resumed control and justifies his assessment of treason on the part of Bacon. The rebel leader died of dysentery in the midst of his campaign.

The declaration and Remonstrance of Sir William Berkeley his most sacred Majesties Governor and Captain Generall of Virginia

Sheweth That about the yeare 1660 Coll. Mathews the then Governor dyed and then in consideration of the service I had don the Country, in defending them from, and destroying great numbers of the Indians, without the loss of three men, in all the time that warr lasted, and in contemplation of the equall and uncorrupt Justice I had distributed to all men, Not onely the Assembly but the unanimous votes of all the Country, concurred to make me Governor in a time, when if the Rebells in England had prevailed, I had certainly dyed for accepting itt, 'twas Gentlemen an unfortunate Love, shewed to me, for to shew myselfe gratefull for this, I was willing to accept of this Governement againe, when by my gracious Kings favour I might have had other places much more proffitable, and lesse toylesome then this hath beene. Since that time that I returned into the Country, I call the great God Judge of all things in heaven and earth to wittness, that I doe not know of any thing relateive to this Country wherein I have acted unjustly, corruptly, or negligently in distributeing equall Justice to all men, and takeing all possible care to preserve their proprietys, and defend the from their barbarous enimies.

But for all this, perhapps I have erred in things I know not of, if I have I am soe conscious of humane frailty, and my owne defects, that I will not onely acknowledge them, but repent of, and amend them, and not like the Rebell Bacon persist in an error, onely because I have comitted itt, and tells me in diverse of his Letters that itt is not for his honnor to confess a fault, but I am of opinion that itt is onely for divells to be incorrigable, and men of principles like the worst of divells, and these he hath, if truth be reported to

me, of diverse of his ex pressions of Atheisme, tending to take away all Religion and Laws.

And now I will state the Question betwixt me as a Governor and Mr. Bacon, and say that if any enimies should invade England, any Councellor Justice of peace or other inferiour officer, might raise what forces they could to protect his Majesties subjects, But I say againe, if after the Kings knowledge of this invasion, any the greatest peere of England, should raise forces against the kings prohibition this would be now, and ever was in all ages and Nations accompted treason. Nay I will goe further, that though this peere was truly zealous for the preservation of his King, and subjects, and had better and greater abillitys then all the rest of his fellow subjects, doe his King and Country service, yett if the King (though by false information) should suspect the contrary, itt were treason in this Noble peere to proceed after the King's prohibition, and for the truth of this I appeale to all the laws of England, and the Laws and constitutions of all other Nations in the world, And yett further itt is declaired by this Parliament that the takeing up Armes for the King and Parliament is treason, for the event shewed that what ever the pretence was to seduce ignorant and well affected people, yett the end was ruinous both to King and people, as this will be if not prevented, I doe therefore againe declair that Bacon proceedeing against all Laws of all Nations modern and ancient, is Rebell to his sacred Majesty and this Country, nor will I insist upon the sweareing of men to live and dye togeather, which is treason by the very words of the Law.

Now my friends I have lived 34 yeares amongst you, as uncorrupt and dilligent as ever Governor was, Bacon is a man of two yeares amongst you, his person and qualities unknowne to most of you, and to all men else, by any vertuous action that ever I heard of, And that very action which he boasts of, was sickly and fooleishly, and as I am informed treacherously carried to the dishonnor of the English Nation, yett in itt, he lost more men then I did in three yeares Warr, and by the grace of God will putt myselfe to the same daingers and troubles againe when I have brought Bacon to acknowledge the Laws are above him, and I doubt not but by God's assistance to have better success then Bacon hath had, the reason of my hopes are, that I will take Councell of wiser men then my selfe, but Mr. Bacon hath none about him, but the lowest of the people.

Yett I must further enlarge, that I cannot without your helpe, doe any thinge in this but dye in defence of my King, his laws, and subjects, which I will cheerefully doe, though alone I doe itt, and considering my poore fortunes, I can not leave my poore Wife and friends a better legacy then by dyeing for my King and you: for his sacred Majesty will easeily distinguish betweene Mr. Bacons actions and myne, and Kinges have long Armes, either to reward or punish.

Now after all this, if Mr. Bacon can shew one precedens or example where such actings in any Nation what ever, was approved of, I will mediate with the King and you for a pardon, and excuce for him, but I can shew him an hundred examples where brave and great men have beene putt to death for gaineing Victorys against the Comand of their Superiors.

Lastly my most assured friends I would have preserved those Indians that I knew were howerly att our mercy, to have beene our spyes and intelligence, to finde out our bloody enimies, but as soone as I had the least intelligence that they alsoe were trecherous enimies, I gave out Commissions to distroy them all as the Commissions themselves will speake itt.

To conclude, I have don what was possible both to friend and enimy, have granted Mr. Bacon three pardons, which he hath scornefully rejected, suppoaseing himselfe stronger to subvert then I and you to maineteyne the Laws, by which onely and Gods assisting grace and mercy, all men m[igh]t hope for peace and safety. I will add noe more though much more is still remaineing to Justifie me and condemne Mr. Bacon, but to desier that this declaration may be read in every County Court in the Country, and that a Court be presently called to doe itt, before the Assembly meet, That your approbation or dissattisfaction of this declaration may be knowne to all the Country, and the Kings Councell to whose most revered Judgments itt is submitted.

Given the xxixth [29th] day of May, a happy day in the xxv'ith [25th] yeare of his most sacred Majesties Reigne, Charles the second, who God grant long and prosperously to Reigne, and lett all his good subjects say Amen.

Source: Massachusetts Historical Society Collections, 4th series, ix, 178–81.

Protest of German Quakers Against Slavery (1688)

More than any other group, Quakers consistently objected to the practice of slavery in America, even though some of their own members were slaveholders. This resolution from a group in Germantown, Pennsylvania, is the first known condemnation of slavery in the colonies. By 1777, the majority of Quakers were strongly advocating abolition.

These are the reasons why we are against the traffic of men-body, as followeth: Is there any that would be done or handled at this manner? viz., to be sold or made a slave for all the time of his life? How fearful and faint-hearted are many at sea, when they see a strange vessel, being afraid it should be a Turk, and they should be taken, and sold for slaves into Turkey. Now, what is this better done, than Turks do? Yea, rather it is worse for them, which say they are Christians; for we hear that the most part of such negers are brought hither against their will and consent, and that many of them are stolen. Now, though they are black, we cannot conceive there is more liberty to have them slaves, as it is to have other white ones. There is a saying, that we should do to all men like as we will be done ourselves; making no difference of what generation, descent, or colour they are. And those who steal or rob men, and those who buy or purchase them, are they not all alike? Here is liberty of conscience, which is right and reasonable; here ought to be likewise liberty of the body, except of evil-doers, which is another case. But to bring men hither, or to rob and sell them against their will, we stand against. In Europe there are many oppressed for conscience sake; and here there are those oppressed which are of a black colour. And we who know that men must not commit adultery some do commit adultery in others, separating wives from their husbands, and giving them to others: and some sell the children of these poor creatures to other men. Ah! do consider well this thing, you who do it, if you would be done at this manner and if it is done according to Christianity! You surpass Holland and Germany in this thing. This makes an ill report in all those countries of Europe, where they hear of [it], that the Quakers do here handel men as they handel there the cattle. And for that reason some have no mind or inclination to come hither. And who shall maintain this your cause, or plead for it? Truly, we cannot do so, except you shall inform us better hereof, viz.: that Christians have liberty to practice these things. Pray, what thing in the world can be done worse towards us, than if men should rob or steal us away, and sell us for slaves to strange countries; separating husbands from their wives and children. Being now this is not done in the manner we would be done at; therefore, we contradict, and are against this traffic of men-body. And we who profess that it is not lawful to steal, must, likewise, avoid to purchase such things as are stolen, but rather help to stop this robbing and stealing, if possible. And such men ought to be delivered out of the hands of the robbers, and set free as in Europe. Then is Pennsylvania to have a good report, instead, it hath now a bad one, for this sake, in other countries; Especially whereas the Europeans are desirous to know in what manner the Quakers do rule in their province; and most of them do look upon us with an envious eye. But if this is done well, what shall we say is done evil?

If once these slaves (which they say are so wicked and stubborn men,) should join themselves fight for their freedom, and handel their masters and mistresses, as they did handel them before; will these masters and mistresses take the sword at hand and war against these poor slaves, like, as we are able to believe, some will not refuse to do? Or, have these poor negers not as much right to fight for their freedom, as you have to keep them slaves?

Now consider well this thing, if it is good or bad. And in case you find it to be good to handel these blacks in that manner, we desire and require you hereby lovingly, that you may inform us herein, which at this time never was done, viz., that Christians have such a liberty to do so. To the end we shall be satisfied on this point, and satisfy likewise our good friends and acquaintances in our native country, to whom it is a terror, or fearful thing, that men should be handelled so in Pennsylvania.

This is from our meeting at Germantown, held ye 18th of the 2d month, 1688, to be delivered to the monthly meeting at Richard Worrell's.

Garret Henderich
Derick op de Graeff
Francis Daniel Pastorius
Abram op de Graeff.

Source: Pennsylvania Magazine of History and Biography, IV (1880), 28–30.

John Clayton's Report on Virginia (1688)

John Clayton's firsthand report to the Royal Society of London about Virginia was written some two years after Clayton returned to England. Having lost his books and scientific instruments at sea, Clayton draws upon memory and gives detailed observations on the hazardous journey over water, as well as the climate and vegetation of the area. He compares the weather of England and Virginia, being struck by the intense heat of the latter, comments on the effects of thunder and lightning, and describes medicinal cures used in Virginia.

A LETTER FROM Mr. JOHN CLAYTON Rector of Crofton at Wakefield in Yorkshire, TO THE ROYAL SOCIETY, May 12, 1688, giving an Account of several Observables in Virginia, and in his Voyage thither, more particularly concerning the Air.

Having oftentimes been urged to give an Account of Virginia, by several of the Worthy Members of the Royal Society, I cannot but, as far forth as I am able, obey Commands whereby I'm so much honour'd, and shew my Respect by my ready Compliance; tho' I am so sensible of my own Weakness and Incapacity to answer your Expectations, that before-hand I must Apologize for my self. And indeed by Sea I lost all my Books, Chymical Instruments, Glasses and Microscopes, which rendred me uncapable of making those Remarks and Observations I had designed, they were all cast away in Captain Win's Ship, as they were to follow me; and Virginia being a Country where one cannot furnish ones self again with such things, I was discourag'd from making so diligent a Scrutiny as otherwise I might have done, so that I took very few Minutes down in Writing; and therefore, since I have only my Memory to rely on, which too has the Disadvantage of it's own Weakness, and of the Distance of two Years since now I left the Country, if future Relations shall in some small Points, make out my Mistake, I thought this requisite to justify my Candor; for I ever judg'd it villanous to impose in matters of Fact; but Descriptions of things that depend on Memory may be liable to Mistakes; and yet the Sincerity of the Person that delivers them intire. But hereof I shall be as cautious as possible, and shall rather wave some things whereof I have some Doubts, and am uncapable now of satisfying my self, than in any sort presume too far. The Method I design is, first, to give an Account of the Air, and all such Observations as refer thereto; then of the Water, the Earth and Soil; the Birds, the Beasts, the Fishes, the Plants, the Insects; and lastly, the present State of the Inhabitants: But at present I shall neither trouble you nor my self with any more than an Account of what refers to the Air alone, being conscious the honourable Society may receive such a Glut with the Imperfection of this, as to excuse me from a farther Relation.

But before I begin, perhaps it may not be impertinent to acquaint you with some things that happen'd in our Voyage. We sail'd in the Ship Judith, Captain Trim Commander,'twas Flyboat built, about 200 or 250 Tuns; she sprung a considerable Leak. When the Captain had made long and diligent Search, had tried all Methods that Sea-men use upon such Occasions, or he could think of, all in vain, and that the Leak encreased, he came pensively to consult me. Discoursing with him about it, and understanding that the Ship was cieled within; so that though the Leak might possibly be in the Fore-part, it would fill the whole Cavity betwixt the Cieling and the Planks, and so run into the Hold at all the Crevices of the Cieling up and down: I thereupon conceived, that where it burst in betwixt the Cieling and the Planks, it must needs make some Noise. He told me, they had endeavoured to find it out that Way, and according to custom had clapt Cans to their Ears to hear with; but the working of the Ship, the Tackle and the Sea made such a Noise, that they could discover nothing thereby. I happily bethought my self of the Speaking Trumpet; and having one which I had contrived for some other Conveniences, of a differing Shape from the common Sorts, I bid him take it and apply the broad End to the Side of the Ship, the narrow End to his Ear, and it would encrease his Hearing as much as it augmented the Voice the other Way, and would ward the Ear the too from the Confusion of foreign Noise. Upon the first Application, accordingly they heard it, tho' it happened to be at a considerable Distance; and when they removed the Trumpet nigher, they heard it as if it had been the Current of a mighty River, even so distinctly, as to have Apprehensions of the bigness and figure of the Hole that the Water came in at; so that cutting there the Cieling of the Ship, they immediately stopt the Leak.

In the Sea I saw many little things which the Seamen

call Carvels; they are like a Jelly, or Starch that is made with a cast of Blue in it; they Swim like a small Sheeps Bladder above the Water, downwards there are long fibrous Strings, some whereof I have found near half a Yard long. This I take to be a Sort of Sea-Plant, and the Strings its Roots growing in the Sea, as Duck-weed does in Ponds. It may be reckon'd among the Potential Cauteries; for when we were one Day becalm'd, getting some to make Observations thereof, the sportful People rub'd it on one anothers Hands and Faces, and where it touch'd it would make it look very Red, and make it smart worse than a Nettle. In my Return for England we struck a Hauks-bill Turtle, in whose Guts I found many of these Carvels; so that it's manifest they feed thereon. 'Tis commonly asserted by the Seamen, that they can smell the Pines at Virginia several Leagues at Sea before they see Land, but I could receive no Satisfaction as to this Point; I could not discern any such thing when at a moderate Distance, I fear much of this may be attributed to Fancy; for one Day there came three or four full Scent to tell me they were certain they smelt the Pines; but it afterwards prov'd that we were at that Time two hundred Leagues from the Shoar, so that I was satisfied that was therefore meer Fancy. Indeed we thought, by the general Accounts of the Ship, that we had been just on the Coast, but all were deceived by a Current we me with, that at that Time set about South-East, or East South-East, which when once becalmed we tried thus: We hoised out a Boat, and took one of the Scuttles that covered one of the Hatches of the Ship, tying thereto a great Weight, and a strong long Rope, we let it sink a considerable Depth, and then fastning it to the Boat, it serv'd as an Anchor, that the Boat could not drive: then with the Glass and log Line we found the Current set, as I say, Eastward, at the rate of a Mile and a half an Hour. This Current is of mischievous Consequence, it does not always run one way, but as it sets sometimes as we proved Easterly, so does it as they say, set at other Times Westerly, whereby many Ships have been lost; for then the Ships being before their Accounts, they fall in with the Land before they are aware. Thus one Year many Ships were lost on Cape Hattarasse, and thereabouts.

Of the AIR.

THE Cape called Cape Henry, lies in 36 1/2 of the Northern Latitude. The Air and Temperature of the Seasons is much govern'd by Winds in Virginia, both as to heat and cold, driness and moisture, whose Variations being very notable, I the more lamented the Loss of my Barometers and Thermometers, for considerable Observations might be made thereby, there being often great and suddain Changes. The Nore and Nore-West are very nitrous and piercing, cold and clear, or else stormy. The South-East and South hazy and sultry hot: their Winter is a fine clear Air, and dry, which renders it very pleasant: Their Frosts are short, but sometimes very sharp, that it will freeze the Rivers over three Miles broad; nay, the Secretary of State assured me, it had frozen clever over Potomack River, over against his House, where

it is near nine Miles over: I have observed it freezes there the hardest, when from a moist South East, on a sudden the Wind passing by the Nore, a nitrous sharp Nore-West blows; not with high Gusts, but with a cutting brisk Air; and those Vales then that seem to be shelter'd from the Wind, and lie warm, where the Air is most stagnant and moist, are frozen the hardest, and seized the soonest; and there the Fruits are more subject to blast than where the Air has a free Motion. Snow falls sometimes in pretty Quantity, but rarely continues there above a Day or two: Their Spring is about a Month earlier than in England; in April they have frequent Rain, sometimes several short and suddain Gusts. May and June the Heat encreases, and it is much like our Summer, being mitigated with gentle Breezes that rise about nine of the Clock, and decrease and incline as the Sun rises and falls. July and August those Breezes cease, and the Air becomes stagnant that the Heat is violent and troublesome. In September the Weather usually breaks suddenly, and there falls generally very considerable Rains. When the Weather breaks many fall Sick, this being the Time of an endemical Sickness, for Seasonings, Cachexes, Fluxes, Scorbutical Dropsies, Gripes, or the like which I have attributed to this Reason. That by the extraordinary Heat, the Ferment of the Blood being raised too high, and the Tone of the Stomach relaxed, when the Weather breaks the Blood palls, and like overfermented Liquors is depauperated, or turns eager and sharp, and there's a crude Digestion, whence the named Distempers may be supposed to ensue. And for Confirmation, I have observed the carminative Seeds, such as warm, and whose Oil sheaths the acid humors that ever result from crude Digestions. But Decoctions that retain the Tone of the Stomach, as I suppose, by making the little Glands in the Tunicles of Stomach, squeeze out their Juice (for what is bitter may be as well offensive to the Stomach, as to the Palate) and then Chalibiates that raise the decayed Ferment, are no bad Practice; after which, I conceive, Armoniack Spirits might be very beneficial. But their Doctors are so learned, that I never met with any of them that understood what Armoniack Spirits were: Two or three of them one Time ran me clear down by Consent, that they were Vomitive, and that they never used any thing for that Purpose but Crocus Metallorum, which indeed every House keeps; and if their Finger, as the Saying is, ake but, they immediately give three or four Spoonfuls thereof; if this fail, they give him a second Dose, then perhaps Purge them with fifteen or twenty Grains of the Rosin of Jalap, afterwards Sweat them with Venice Treacle, Powder of Snake-root, or Gascoin's Powder; and when these fail conclamatum est. But to return. 'Tis wonderful what influence the Air has over Men's Bodies, whereof I had my self sad Assurances; for tho' I was in a very close warm Room, where was a Fire constantly kept, yet there was not the least Alteration or Change, whereof I was not sensible when I was sick of the Gripes, of which Distemper I may give a farther Account in it's proper Place. When a very ingenious Gentlewoman was visited with the same Distemper, I had the Opportunity of making very considerable

Observations. I stood at the Window, and could view the Clouds arise: for there small black fleeting Clouds will arise, and be swiftly carry'd cross the whole Element; and as these Clouds arose, and came nigher, her Torments were encreased, which were grievous as a labouring Womans; there was not the least Cloud but lamentably affected her, and that at a considerable Distance; but by her Shrieks it seemed more or less, according to the Bigness and nearness of the Clouds. The Thunder there is attended often with fatal Circumstances: I was with my Lord Howard of Effingham the Governor, when they brought Word that one Dr. A. was killed therewith after this Manner. He was Smoaking a Pipe of Tobacco, and looking out at his Window when he was struck dead, and immediately became so stiff, that he did not fall, but stood leaning in the Window, with the Pipe in his Mouth, in the same Posture he was in when struck: But this I only deliver as Report, tho' I heard the same Account from several, without any contradicting it. These things are remarkable, that it generally breaks in at the Gavel End of the Houses, and often kills Persons in, or near the Chimney's Range, darting most fiercely down the Funnel of the Chimney; more especially if there be a Fire (I speak here confusedly of Thunder and Lightning) for when they do any Mischief, the Crash and Lightning are at the same Instant, which must be from the nearness of the Cloud. One Time when the Thunder split the Mast of a Boat at James Town, I saw it break from the Cloud, which it divided in two, and seemed as if it had shot them immediately a Mile asunder, to the Eye: It is dangerous when it thunders standing in a narrow Passage, where there's a thorough Passage, or in a Room betwixt two Windows; tho' several have been kill'd in the open Fields. 'Tis incredible to tell how it will strike large Oaks, shatter and shiver them, sometimes twisting round a Tree, sometimes as if it struck the Tree backwards and forwards. I had noted a fine spreading Oak in James Town Island, in the Morning I saw it fair and flourishing, in the Evening I observed all the Bark of the Body of the Tree, as if it had been artificially peeled off, was orderly spread round the Tree, in a Ring, whose Semidiameter was four Yards, the Tree in the Center; all the Body of the Tree was shaken and split, but its Boughs had all their Bark on; few Leaves were fallen, and those on the Boughs as fresh as in the Morning, but gradually afterwards withered, as on a Tree that is fallen. I have seen several vast Oaks and other Timber Trees twisted, as if it had been a small Willow that a Man had twisted with his Hand, which I could suppose had been done by nothing but the Thunder. I have been told by very serious Planters, that thirty or forty Years since, when the Country was not so open, the Thunder was more fierce, and that sometimes after violent Thunder and Rain, the Roads would seem to have perfect casts of Brimstone; and 'tis frequent after much Thunder and Lightning for the Air to have a perfect sulphureous Smell. Durst I offer my weak Reasons when I write to so great Masters thereof, I should here consider the Nature of Thunder, and compare it with some sulphureous Spirits

which I have drawn from Coals, that I could no way condense, yet were inflamable; nay, would burn after they pass'd through Water, and that seemingly fiercer, if they were not over-power'd therewith. I have kept of this Spirit a considerable time in Bladders; and though it appeared as if they were only blown with Air, yet if I let it forth, and fired it with a Match or Candle, it would continue burning till all were spent. It might be worthy Consideration likewise, whether those frequent Thunders proceeded from the Air's being more stagnant, the Motion of the Winds being impeded by the Trees, or whether the Motion of the Winds being obstructed by them below, the Motion might not be more violent aloft; and how far that may promote Inflammability; for Stacks of Hay or Corn that ferment with Moisture, never burn, unless when brisk Winds blow, that agitate and fan the little fermenting Sparks, and often kindle them into an actual Fire. And Observance of the Meteors there might pehaps not be impertinent, as both what are more rare, and what are more frequent, as of Gosimore in great Abundance, and of those small Cobwebs in a Morning, which some have supposed to be Meteors: Ignes fatui, though there be many boggy Swamps and Marshes, are seldom, if any are seen there. There be frequent little sorts of Whirl-winds, whose Diameter may be sometimes not past two or three Yards, sometimes forty, which whisking round in a Circle, pass along the Earth, according to the Motion of the Cloud, from whence they issue; and as they pass along with their gyrous or circular Motion, they carry aloft the dry Leaves into the Air, which fall again often in places far remote. I have seen them descend in a calm Sun-shine Day, as if they had come from the Heavens in great Showers thereof, so that all the Elements seemed filled therewith. And I could perceive them to descend from on high as far as I could possibly discern a Leaf. I remember a roguish Expression of a Seaman, otherwise silly enough, who wondering thereat, cry'd out, Sure now 'tis manifest there is a World above! And now with them 'tis the Fall of the Leaf. But to proceed, I thought this made it manifest, whence many preternatural Showers have happen'd. I remember at Sir Richard Atherton's in Lancashire, some few Years ago, there fell a great Number of Seeds of Ivy-berries; at first we admir'd what they were, for they were cover'd with a thin Skin that was red, and resembled the Figure of a small Wheat Corn; but afterwards they fully manifested what they were; for many sprouted and took Root. I suppose they were carry'd aloft by some such Whirl-wind, and let fall there. I have purposely gone into the Place where I perceived this Gust, which is notorious enough by the Noise it makes, with ratling the Leaves as it carries them aloft, and have found a fine sharp Breeze of Wind.

Yours, &c.

Source: Tracts and Other Papers, Relating Principally to the Origin, Settlement, and Progress of the Colonies in North America, from the Discovery of the Country to the Year 1776, Vol. III, collected by Peter Force (New York: Peter Smith, 1947).

Commission of Sir Edmund Andros for the Dominion of New England (1688)

The Dominion of New England was a manifestation of the British Crown's tightening of control over the colonies. As governor-in-chief, Edmund Andros, along with his designees, had wide authority over lands stretching from Maryland to Maine. Additionally, the Dominion combined the New England, New York, and New Jersey colonies into one, abolishing their elected assemblies and charters. In 1689, Andros was deposed by Boston colonists.

James the Second by the Grace of God King of England, Scotland France and Ireland Defender of the Faith &c. To our trusty and welbeloved Sr Edmund Andros Knt Greeting: Whereas by our Commission under our Great Seal of England, bearing date the third day of June in the second year of our reign wee have constituted and appointed you to be our Captain Generall and Governor in Cheif in and over all that part of our territory and dominion of New England in America known by the names of our Colony of the Massachusetts Bay, our Colony of New Plymouth, our Provinces of New Hampshire and Main and the Narraganset Country or King's Province. And whereas since that time Wee have thought it necessary for our service and for the better protection and security of our subjects in those parts to join and annex to our said Government the neighboring Colonies of Road Island and Connecticutt, our Province of New York and East and West Jersey, with the territories . . . hereunto belonging, as wee do hereby join annex and unite the same to our said government and dominion of New England. Wee therefore reposing especiall trust and confidence in the prudence courage and loyalty of you the said Sir Edmund Andros, out of our especiall grace certain knowledge and meer motion, have thought fit to constitute and appoint as wee do by these presents constitute and appoint you the said Sr Edmund Andros to be our Captain Generall and Governor in Cheif in and over our Colonies of the Massachusetts Bay and New Plymouth, our Provinces of New Hampshire and Main, the Narraganset country or King's Province, our Colonys of Road Island and Connecticutt our Province of New York and East and West Jersey, and of all that tract of land circuit continent precincts and limits in America lying and being in breadth from forty degrees of Northern latitude from the Equinoctiall Line to the River of St. Croix Eastward, and from thence directly Northward to the river of Canada, and in length and longitude by all the breadth aforesaid and throughout the main land from the Atlantick or Western Sea or Ocean on the East part, to the South Sea on the West part, with all the Islands, Seas, Rivers, waters, rights, members, and appurtenances, thereunto belonging (our province of Pensilvania and country of Delaware only excepted), to be called and known as formerly by the name and title of our territory and dominion of New England in America.

And for your better guidance and direction Wee doe hereby require and command you to do & execute all things in due manner, that shall belong unto the said office and the trust wee have reposed in you, according to the severall powers instructions and authoritys mentioned in these presents, or such further- powers instructions and authoritys mentioned in these presents, as you shall herewith receive or which shall at any time hereafter be granted or appointed You under our signet and sign manual or by our order in our Privy Councill and according to such reasonable lawes and statutes as are now in force or such others as shall hereafter be made and established within our territory & dominion aforesaid.

And our will and pleasure is that You the said Sr Edmund Andros having, after publication of these our Letters Patents, first taken the Oath of duly executing the office of our Captain Generall and Governor in Cheif of our said territory and dominion, which our Councill there or any three of them are hereby required authorized and impowered to give and administer unto you, you shall administer unto each of the members of our Councill the Oath for the due execution of their places and trusts.

And Wee do hereby give and grant unto you full power and authority to suspend any member of our Councill from sitting voting and assisting therein, as you shall find just cause for so doing.

And if it shall hereafter at any time happen that by the death, departure out of our said territory, or suspension of any of our Counselors, or otherwise, there shall be a vacancy in our said Councill (any five whereof wee do hereby appoint to be a Quorum) Our will and pleasure is that you signify the same unto us by the first oppurtunity, that Wee may under our Signet and Sign Manuall constitute and appoint others in their room.

And Wee do hereby give and grant unto you full power and authority, by and with the advise and consent of our said Councill or the major part of them, to make constitute and ordain lawes statutes and ordinances for the public peace welfare and good governmt of our said territory & dominion and of the people and inhabitants thereof, and such others as shall resort thereto, and for the benefit of us, our heires and successors. Which said lawes statutes and ordinances, are to be, as near as conveniently may be, aggreeable to the lawes & statutes of this our kingdom of England: Provided that all such lawes statutes and ordinances of what nature or duration soever, be within three months, or sooner, after the making of the same, transmitted unto Us, under our Seal of New England, for our allowance or disapprobation of them, as also duplicates thereof by the next conveyance.

And Wee do by these presents give and grant unto you full power and authority by and with the advise and consent of our said Councill, or the major part of them, to impose assess and raise and levy rates and taxes as you shall find necessary for the support of the government within our territory and dominion of New England, to be collected and leveyed and to be imployed to the uses aforesaid in such manner as to you & our said Councill or the major part of them shall seem most equall and reasonable.

And for the better supporting the charge of the governmt of our said Territory and Dominion, our will and pleasure is and wee do by these presents authorize and impower you the sd Sr Edmund Andros and our Councill, to continue such taxes and impositions as are now laid and imposed upon the Inhabitants thereof; and to levy and distribute or cause the same to be levyed and distributed to those ends in the best and most equall manner, untill you shall by & with the advise and consent of our Councill agree on and settle such other taxes as shall be sufficient for the support of our government there, which are to be applied to that use and no other.

And our further will and pleasure is, that all publick money raised or to be raised or appointed for the support of the government within our said territory and dominion be issued out by warrant or order from you by & with the advise and consent of our Councill as aforesaid.

And our will and pleasure is that you shall and may keep and use our Seal appointed by Us for our said territory and dominion.

And Wee do by these presents ordain constitute and appoint you or the Commander in Cheif for the time being, and the Councill of our said territory & dominion for the time being, to be a constant and setled Court of Record for

ye administration of justice to all our subjects inhabiting within our said Territory and Dominion, in all causes as well civill as Criminall with full power and authority to hold pleas in all cases, from time to time, as well in Pleas of the Crown and in all matters relateing to the conservation of the peace and punishment of offenders, as in Civill causes and actions between party and party, or between us and any of our subjects there, whether the same do concerne the realty and relate to any right of freehold & inheritance or whether the same do concerne the personality and relate to matter of debt contract damage or other personall injury; and also in all mixt actions which may concern both realty and personalty; and therein after due and orderly proceeding and deliberate hearing of both sides, to give judgement and to award execution, as well in criminall as in Civill cases as aforesaid, so as always that the forms of proceedings in such cases and the judgment thereupon to be given, be as consonant and agreeable to the lawes and statutes of this our realm of England as the present state and condition of our subjects inhabiting within our said Territory and Dominion and the circumstances of the place will admit.

And Wee do further hereby give and grant unto you full power and authority with the advise and consent of our said Councill to erect constitute and establish such and so many Courts of Judicature and public Justice within our said Territory and Dominion as you and they shall think fit and necessary for the determining of all causes as well Criminall as Civill according to law and equity, and for awarding of execution thereupon, with all reasonable and necessary powers authorities fees and privileges belonging unto them.

And Wee do hereby give and grant unto you full power and authority to constitute and appoint Judges and in cases requisite Commissioners of Oyer and Terminer, Justices of the Peace, Sheriffs, & all other necessary Officers and Ministers within our said Territory for the better administration of Justice and putting the lawes in execution, & to administer such oath and oaths as are usually given for the due execution and performance of offices and places and for the cleering of truth in judiciall causes.

And our further will and pleasure is and Wee doe hereby declare that all actings and proceedings at law or equity heretofore had or don or now depending within any of the courts of our said Territory, and all executions thereupon, be hereby confirmed and continued so fare forth as not to be avoided for want of any legall power in the said Courts; but that all and every such judiciall actings, proceeding and execution shall be of the same force effect and virtue as if such Courts had acted by a just and legall authority.

And Wee do further by these presents will and require you to permit Appeals to be made in cases of Error from our Courts in our said Territory and Dominion of New England unto you, or the Commander in Cheif for the time being and the Council, in Civill causes: Provided the value appealed for do exceed the sum of one hundred pounds sterling, and that security be first duly given by the Appellant to answer such charges as shall be awarded in case the first sentence shall be affirmed.

And whereas Wee judge it necessary that all our subjects may have liberty to Appeal to our Royall Person in cases that may require the same: Our will and pleasure is that if either party shall not rest satisfied with the judgement or sentence of you (or the Commander in Cheif for the time being) and the Councill, they may Appeal unto Us in our Privy Councill: Provided the matter in difference exceed the value and summ of three hundred pounds stern and that such Appeal be made within one fortnight after sentence, and that security be likewise duly given by the Appellant to answer such charges as shall be awarded in case the sentence of you (or the Commander in Cheif for the time being) and the Councill be confirmed; and provided also that execution be not suspended by reason of any such appeal unto us.

And Wee do hereby give and graunt unto you full power where You shall see cause and shall judge any offender or offenders in capitall and criminall matters, or for any fines or forfeitures due unto us, fit objects of our mercy, to pardon such offenders and to remit such fines & forfeitures, treason and wilfull murder only excepted, in which case you shall likewise have power upon extraordinary occasions to grant reprieves to the offenders therein untill and to the intent our pleasure may be further known.

And Wee do hereby give and grant unto you the said Sr Edmd Andros by your self your Captains and Commanders, by you to be authorized, full power and authority to levy arme muster command or employ, all persons whatsoever residing within our said Territory and Dominion of New England, and, as occasion shall serve, them to transfers from one place to another for the resisting and withstanding all enemies pyrats and rebells, both at land and sea, and to transfers such forces to any of our Plantations in America or the Territories thereunto belonging, as occasion shall require for the defence of the same against the invasion or attempt of any of our enemies, and then, if occasion shall require to pursue and prosecute in or out of the limits of our said Territories and Plantations or any of them, And if it shall so please God, them to vanquish; and, being taken, according to the law of arms to put to death or keep and preserve alive, at your discretion. And also to execute martiall law in time of invasion insurrection or warr, and during the continuance of the same, and upon soldiers in pay, and to do and execute all and every other thing which to a Captain Generall doth or ought of right to belong, as fully and amply as any our Captain Generall doth or hath usually don.

And Wee do hereby give and grant unto you full power and authority to erect raise and build within our Territory and Dominion aforesaid, such and so many forts, platformes, Castles, cities, boroughs, towns, and fortifications as you shall judge necessary; and the same or any of them to fortify and furnish with ordnance ammunition and all sorts of armes, fit and necessary for the security & defence of our said territory; and the same again or any of them to demolish or dismantle as may be most convenient.

And Wee do hereby give and grant unto you the said Sr Edmund Andros full power and authority to erect one or more Court or Courts Admirall within our said Territory and Dominion, for the hearing and determining of all marine and other causes and matters proper therein to be heard & determined, with all reasonable and necessary powers, authorities fees and priviledges.

And you are to execute all powers belonging to the place and office of Vice Admirall of and in all the seas and coasts about your Government; according to such commission authority and instructions as you shall receive from ourself under the Seal of our Admiralty or from High Admirall of our Foreign Plantations for the time being.

And forasmuch as divers mutinies & disorders do happen by persons shipped and imployed at Sea, and to the end that such as shall be shipped or imployed at Sea may be better governed and ordered; Wee do hereby give and grant unto you the said Sr Edmund Andros our Captain Generall and Governor in Cheif, full power and authority to constitute and appoint Captains, Masters of Ships, and other Commanders, commissions to execute the law martial, and to use such proceedings authorities, punishment, correction and execution upon any offender or offenders who shall be mutinous seditious, disorderly or any way unruly either at sea or during the time of their abode or residence in any of the ports harbors or bays of our said Territory and Dominion, as the Cause shall be found to require, according to martial law. Provided that nothing herein conteined shall be construed to the enabling you or any by your authority to hold plea or have jurisdiction of any offence cause matter or thing committed or don upon the sea or within any of the havens, rivers, or creeks of our said Territory and Dominion under your government, by any Captain Commander Lieutenant Master or other officer seaman soldier or person whatsoever, who shall be in actuall service and pay in and on board any of our ships of War or other vessels acting by immediat commission or warrant from our self under the Seal of our Admiralty, or from our High Admirall of England for the time being; but that such Captain Commander Lieut Master officer seaman soldier and other person so offending shall be left to be proceeded against and tryed, as the merit of their offences shall require, either by Commission under our Great Seal of England as the statute of 28 Henry VIII directs, or by commission from our said High Admirall, according to the Act of Parliament passed in the 13th year of the reign of the late King our most dear and most intirely beloved brother of ever blessed memory (entituled An Act for the establishing articles and Orders for the regulating and better governmt of His Matys navys, shipps or warr, and Forces by sea) and not otherwise. Saving only, that it shall and may be lawfull for you, upon such Captains and Commanders refusing or neglecting to execute. Or upon his negligent or undue execution of any the written orders he shall receive from You for our service, & the service of our said Territory and Dominion. to suspend him the said Captain or Commander from the exercise of the said office of Commander and commit him safe custody, either on board his own ship or elsewhere, at the discretion of you, in order to his being brought to answer for the same by commission either under our Great Seal of England or from our said High Admirall as is before expressed. In which case our will and pleasure is that the Captain or Commander so by you suspended shall during his suspension and commitmt be succeeded in his said office, by such commission or Warrant Officer of our said ship appointed by our self or our High Admirall for the time being, as by the known practice and discipline of our Navy doth and ought next to succeed him, as is case of death sickness of other ordinary disability hapning to the Commander of any of our ships & not otherwise; you standing also accountable to us for the truth & importance of the crimes and misdemeanours for which you shall so proceed to the suspending of such our said Captain or Commander. Provided also that all disorders and misdemeanors committed on shore by any Captain Commander, Lieutent, Master, or other officer seaman soldier or person whatsoever belonging to any of our ships of warr or other vessel acting by immediate commission or warrt from our self under the Great Seal of our Admiralty or from our High Admll from England for the time being may be tryed & punished according to the lawes of the place where any such disorders off'ences and misdemeanors shall be so committed on shore, notwithstanding such offender be in our actuall service and borne in our pay on board any such out shipps of warr or other vessels acting by immediate Commission or warrant from ourself or our High Admirall as aforesaid; so as he shall not receive any protection (for the avoiding of justice for such offences committed on shore) from any presence of his being improved in our service at sea.

And Wee do likewise give and grant unto you full power and authority by and with the advice and consent of our said Councill to agree with the planters and inhabitants of our said Territory and Dominion concerning such lands, tenements & hereditaments as now are or hereafter shall be in our power to dispose of, and them to grant unto any person or persons for such terms and under such moderat Quit Rents, Services and acknowledgements to be thereupon reserved unto us as shall be appointed by us. Which said grants are to pass and be sealed by our Seal of New England and (being entred upon record by such officer or officers as you shall appoint thereunto, shall be good and effectual in law against us, our heires and successors.

And Wee do hereby give you full power and authority to appoint so many faires martes and markets as you with the advise of the said Councill shall think fitt.

As likewise to order and appoint within our said Territory such and so many ports harbors, bayes havens and other places for the convenience and security of shipping, and for the better loading and unloading of goods and merchandise as by you with the advice and consent of our Councill shall be thought flit and necessary; and in them or any of them to erect nominal and appoint Cuxtom houses ware houses and officers relating thereto; and them to alter change, place, or displace from time to time, as with the advice aforesaid shall be thought fitt.

And forasmuch as pursuant to the lawes & customes of our Colony of the Massachusetts Bay and of our other Colonies and Probes aforementioned, divers marriages have been made and performs by the Magstrats of our said territory; Our royall will and please is hereby to confirm all the said marriages and to direct that they be held good and valid in the same manner to all intents and purposes whatsoever as if they had been made and contracted according to the lawes established within our kingdom of England.

And Wee do hereby require and command all officers and ministers, civill and military and all other inhabitants of our said Territory and Dominion to be obedient aiding and assisting unto you the said Sr Edmd Andros in the execution of this our commission and of the powers and authorityes therein contained, and upon your death or absence out of our said Territory unto our Lieut. Governor, to whom wee do therefore by these presents give and grant all and singular the powers and authorityes aforesaid to be exercised and enjoyed by him in case of your death or absence during our pleasure, or untill your arrival within our said Territory and Dominion; as Wee do further hereby give and grant full power and authority to our Lieut. Governor to do and execute whatsoever he shall be by you authorized and appointed to do and execute, in pursuance of and according to the powers granted to you by this Commission.

And if in the case of your death or absence there be no person upon the place, appointed by us to be Commander in Cheif; our will and pleasure is, that the then' present Councill of our Territory aforesaid, do take upon them the administration of the Governmt and execute this commission and the severall powers and authorityys herein contained; and that the first Counselor who shall be at the time of yor death or absence residing within the same, do preside in our said Councill, with such powers and preheminencies as any former President hath used and enjoyed within our said territory, or any other our plantations in America, untill our pleasure be further known, or your arrivall as aforesaid.

And lastly, our will and pleasure is that you the said Sr Edmund Andros shall and may hold exercise and enjoy the office and place of Captain Generall and Governor in Cheif in and over our Territory and Dominion aforesaid, with all its rights members and appurtenances whatsoever, together with all and singular the powers and authorityes hereby granted unto you, for and during our will and pleasure.

In Witness whereof Wee have caused these our letters to be made Patents. Witness our self at Westminster the seventh day of Aprill in the fourth year of our reign.

By Writ of Privy Seal
Clerke

Source: The Federal and State Constitutions, Colonial Charters, and Other Organic Laws of the States, Territories, and Colonies Now or Heretofore Forming the United States of America, compiled and edited under the Act of Congress of June 30, 1906, by Francis Newton Thorpe (Washington, DC: Government Printing Office, 1909).

The Salem Witch Trial of Susanna Martin (1692)

The Salem witch trials were a low point in the life of the Puritan community of Plymouth. In a climate of hysteria, intolerance, and superstition, the judicial system convicted the innocent on specious evidence. In the end, some twenty individuals were found guilty of witchcraft and executed.

Following is the transcript of the trial of Susanna Martin. The fact that Cotton Mather termed her "one of the most Impudent, Scurrilous, wicked creatures" did not help her case. Convicted of the capital offense of witchcraft, she was hanged on July 19, 1692.

The Tryal of Susanna Martin, At the Court of Oyer and Terminer, Held by Adjournment at Salem, June 29, 1692.

I. Susanna Martin, pleading Not Guilty to the Indictment of Witchcraft brought in against her, there were produced the evidences of many persons very sensibly and grievously Bewitched; who all complaned of the prisoner at the Bar, as the person whom they Believed the cause of their Miseries. And now, as well as in the other Trials, there was an extraordinary endeavour by Witchcrafts, with Cruel and Frequent Fits, to hinder the poor sufferers from giving in their complaints; which the Court was forced with much patience to obtain, by much waiting and watching for it.

II. There was now also an Account given, of what passed at her first examination before the Magistrates. The cast of her eye then striking the Afflicted People to the ground, whether they saw that Cast or no; there were these among other passages between the Magistrates and the Examinate.

Magistrate: Pray, what ails these People?

{Susanna} Martin: I don't know.

Magistrate: But what do you think ails them?

Martin: I don't desire to spend my Judgment upon it.

Magistrate: Don't you think they are Bewitch'd?

Martin: No, I do not think they are.

Magistrate: Tell us your thoughts about them then.

Martin: No, my thoughts are my own when they are in, but when they are out, they are anothers. Their Master—

Magistrate: Their Master? who do you think is their Master?

Martin: If they be dealing in the Black Art, you may know as well as I.

Magistrate: Well, what have you done towards this?

Martin: Nothing at all.

Magistrate: Why, tis you or your Appearance.

Martin: I cannot help it.

Magistrate: Is it not Your Master? How comes your Appearance to hurt these?

Martin: How do I know? He that appeared in the shape of Samuel, a Glorify'd Saint, may Appear in any ones shape.

It was then also noted in her, as in others like her, that if the Afflicted went to approach her, they were flung down to the Ground. And, when she was asked the Reason of it, she said, "I cannot tell; it may be, the Devil bears me more Malice than another."

III. The Court accounted themselves Alarum'd by these things, to Enquire further into the Conversation of the Prisoner; and see what there might occur, to render these Accusations further credible. Whereupon, John Allen, of Salisbury, testify'd, That he refusing, because of the weakness of his Oxen, to Cart some Staves, at the request of this Martin, she was displeased at it; and said, "It had been as good that he had; for his Oxen should never do him much more Service." Whereupon this Deponent said, "Dost thou threaten me, thou old Witch? I'l throw thee into the Brook": Which to avoid, she flew over the Bridge, and escaped. But, as he was going home, one of his Oxen Tired, so that he was forced to Unyoke him, that he might get him home. He then put his Oxen, with many more, upon Salisbury Beach, where Cattle did use to get Flesh. In a few days, all the Oxen upon the Beach were found by their Tracks, to have run unto the mouth of Merrimack-River, and not returned; but the next day they were found come ashore upon Plum-Island. They that sought them used all imaginable gentleness, but they would still run away with a violence that seemed wholly Diabolical, till they came near the mouth of Merrimack-

River; when they ran right into the Sea, swimming as far as they could be seen. One of them then swam back again, with a swiftness amazing to the Beholders, who stood ready to receive him, and help up his Tired Carcass: But the Beast ran furiously up into the Island, and from thence, through the Marishes, up into Newbury Town, and so up into the Woods; and there after a while found near Amesbury. So that, of Fourteen good Oxen, there was only this saved: the rest were all cast up, some in one place, and some in another, Drowned.

IV. John Atkinson Testify'd, That he Exchanged a Cow with a Son of Susanna Martin, whereat she muttered, and was unwilling he should have it. Going to Receive this Cow, tho' he Hamstring'd her, and Halter'd her, she of a Tame Creature grew so mad, that they could scarce get her along. She broke all the Ropes that were fastned unto her, and though she were Ty'd fast unto a Tree, yet she made her Escape, and gave them such further Trouble, as they could ascribe to no cause but Witchcraft.

V. Bernard Peache testify'd, That being in Bed on a Lords-day Night, he heard a scrabbling at the Window, whereat he then saw Susanna Martin come in, and jump down upon the Floor. She took hold of this Deponents Feet, and drawing his Body up into an Heap, she lay upon him near Two Hours; in all which time he could neither speak nor stirr. At length, when he could begin to move, he laid hold on her Hand, and pulling it up to his mouth, he bit three of her Fingers, as he judged, unto the Bone. Whereupon she went from the Chamber, down the Stairs, out at the Door. This Deponent there-upon called unto the people of the House, to advise them of what passed; and he himself did follow her. The people saw her not; but there being a Bucket at the Left-hand of the Door, there was a drop of Blood found on it; and several more drops of Blood upon the Snow newly fallen abroad. There was likewise the print of her two Feet just without the Threshold; but no more sign of any Footing further off.

At another time this Deponent was desired by the Prisoner, to come unto an Husking of Corn, at her House; and she said, If he did not come, it were better that he did! He went not; but the Night following, Susanna Martin, as he judged, and another came towards him. One of them said, "Here he is!" but he having a Quarter-staff, made a Blow at them. The Roof of the Barn broke his Blow; but following them to the Window, he made another Blow at them, and struck them down; yet they got up, and got out, and he saw no more of them.

About this time, there was a Rumour about the Town, that Martin had a Broken Head; but the Deponent could say nothing to that.

The said Peache also testify'd the Bewitching of Cattle to Death, upon Martin's Discontents.

VI. Robert Downer testifyed, That this Prisoner being some years ago prosecuted at Court for a Witch, he then said unto her, He believed she was a Witch. Whereat she being dissatisfied, said, That some Shee-Devil would Shortly fetch him away! Which words were heard by others, as well as himself. The Night following, as he lay in his Bed, there came in at the Window the likeness of a Cat, which Flew upon him, took fast hold of his Throat, lay on him a considerable while, and almost killed him. At length he remembered what Susanna Martin had threatned the Day before; and with much striving he cryed out, "Avoid, thou Shee-Devil! In the Name of God the Father, the Son, and the Holy Ghost, Avoid!" Whereupon it left him, leap'd on the Floor, and Flew out at the Window.

And there also came in several Testimonies, that before ever Downer spoke a word of this Accident, Susanna Martin and her Family had related, How this Downer had been Handled!

VII. John Kembal testifyed, that Susanna Martin, upon a Causeless Disgust, had threatned him, about a certain Cow of his, That she should never do him any more Good: and it came to pass accordingly. For soon after the Cow was found stark Dead on the dry Ground, without any Distemper to be discerned upon her. Upon which he was followed with a strange Death upon more of his Cattle, whereof he lost in One Spring to the value of Thirty Pounds. But the said John Kembal had a further Testimony to give in against the Prisoner which was truly admirable.

Being desirous to furnish himself with a Dog, he applied himself to buy one of this Martin, who had a Bitch with Whelps in her House. But she not letting him have his Choice, he said, he would supply himself then at one Blezdels. Having mark'd a puppy which he lik'd at Blezdels, he met George Martin, the Husband of the prisoner, going by, who asked him, Whether he would not have one of his Wives Puppies? and he answered, No. The same Day, one Edmund Eliot, being at Martins House, heard George Martin relate, where this Kembal had been, and what he had said. Whereupon Susanna Martin replyed, "If I live, I'll give him Puppies enough!" Within a few Dayes after, this Kembal coming out of the Woods, there arose a little Black Cloud in the N.W. and Kembal immediately felt a Force upon him, which made him not able to avoid running upon the stumps of Trees, that were before him, albeit he had a broad, plain Cart way, before him; but tho' he had his Ax also on his Shoulder to endanger him in his Falls, he could not forbear going out of his way to tumble over them. When he came below the Meeting-House, there appeared unto him a little thing like a Puppy, of a Darkish Colour; and it shot backwards and forwards between his Legs. He had the Courage to use all possible Endeavours of Cutting it with his Ax; but he could not Hit it; the Puppy gave a jump from him, and went, as to him it seem'd, into the Ground. Going a little further, there appeared unto him a Black Puppy, somewhat bigger than the first, but as Black as a Cole. Its motions were quicker than those of his Ax; it Flew at his Belly, and away; then at his Throat; so, over his Shoulder one way, and then over his Shoulder another way. His heart now began to fail him, and he thought the Dog would have Tore his Throat out. But he recovered himself, and called upon God in his Distress; and Naming the Name of Jesus Christ, it Vanished away at once. The Deponent Spoke not one Word of these Accidents, for fear of affrighting his wife. But the next Morning, Edmond Eliot going into Martins House, this woman asked him where Kembal was? He Replyed, At home, a bed, for ought he knew. She returned, "They say, he was frighted last Night." Eliot asked, "With what?" She answered, "With Puppies." Eliot asked, Where she heard of it, for he had heard nothing of it? She rejoined, "About the Town." Altho' Kembal had mentioned the Matter to no Creature Living.

VIII. William Brown testify'd, that Heaven having blessed him with a most Pious and prudent wife, this wife of his one day mett with Susanna Martin; but when she approch'd just unto her, Martin vanished out of sight, and left her extremely affrighted. After which time, the said Martin often appear'd unto her, giving her no little trouble; and when she did come, she was visited with Birds that sorely peck't and Prick'd her; and sometimes a Bunch, like a pullets egg, would Rise in her throat, ready to Choak her, till she cry'd out, "Witch, you shan't choak me!" While this good Woman was in this Extremity, the Church appointed a Day of Prayer, on her behalf; whereupon her Trouble ceas'd; she saw not Martin as formerly; and the Church, instead of their Fast, gave Thanks for her Deliverance. But a considerable while after, she being Summoned to give in some Evidence at the Court, against this Martin, quickly thereupon this Martin came behind her, while she was milking her Cow, and said unto her, "For thy defaming me at Court, I'l make thee the miserablest Creature in the World." Soon after which, she fell into a strange kind of Distemper, and became horribly Frantick, and uncapable of any Reasonable Action; the Physicians declaring, that her Distemper was preternatural, and that some Devil had certainly Bewitched her; and in that Condition she now remained.

IX. Sarah Atkinson testify'd, That Susanna Martin came from Amesbury to their House at Newbury, in an extraordinary Season, when it was not fit for any one to Travel. She came (as she said unto Atkinson) all that long way on Foot. She brag'd and show'd how dry she was; nor could it be perceived that so much as the Soles of her Shoes were wet. Atkinson was amazed at it; and professed, that she should her self have been wet up to the knees, if she had then came so far; but Martin reply'd, She scorn'd to be Drabbled! It was noted, that this Testimony upon her Trial cast her in a very singular Confusion.

X. John Pressy testify'd, That being one Evening very unaccountably Bewildred, near a field of Martins, and several times, as one under an Enchantment, returning to the place he had left, at length he saw a marvellous Light, about the Bigness of an Half-Bushel, near two Rod out of the way. He went, and struck at it with a Stick, and laid it on with all his might. He gave it near forty blows; and felt it a palpable substance. But going from it, his Heels were struck up, and he was laid with his Back on the Ground, Sliding, as he thought, into a Pit; from whence he recover'd, by taking hold on the Bush; altho' afterwards he could find no such Pit in the place. Having, after his Recovery, gone five or six Rod, he saw Susanna Martin standing on his Left-hand, as the Light had done before; but they changed no words with one another. He could scarce find his House in his Return; but at length he got home, extreamly affrighted. The next day, it was upon Enquiry understood, that Martin was in a miserable condition by pains and hurts that were upon her.

It was further testify'd by this Deponent, That after he had given in some Evidence against Susanna Martin, many years ago, she gave him foul words about it; and said, He should never prosper more; particularly, That he should never have more than two Cows; that tho' he were never so likely to have more, yet he should never have them. And that from that very Day to this, namely for Twenty Years together, he could never exceed that Number; but some strange thing or other still prevented his having of any more.

XI. Jervis Ring testifyed, that about seven years ago, he was oftentimes and grievously Oppressed in the Night, but saw not who Troubled him, until at last he, Lying perfectly Awake, plainly saw Susanna Martin approach him. She came to him, and forceably Bit him by the Finger; so that the Print of the Bite is now so long after to be seen upon him.

XII. But besides all of these Evidences, there was a most wonderful Account of one Joseph Ring, produced on this Occasion.

This man has been strangely carried about by Dæmons, from one Witch-Meeting to another, for near two years together; and for one Quarter of this Time, they have made him and kept him Dumb, tho' he is now again able to speak. There was one T. H. who having, as tis judged, a Design of engaging this Joseph Ring in a Snare of Devillism, contrived a wile, to bring this Ring two Shillings in Debt unto him.

Afterwards, this poor man would be visited with unknown shapes, and this T. H. sometimes among them; which would force him away with them, unto unknown Places, where he saw meetings, Feastings, Dancings; and after his Return, wherein they hurried him along thro' the Air, he gave Demonstrations to the Neighbours, that he had indeed been so transported. When he was brought unto these Hellish meetings, one of the First things they still did unto him, was to give him a knock on the Back, whereupon he was ever as if Bound with Chains, uncapable of Stirring out of the place, till they should Release him. He related, that there often came to him a man, who presented him a Book, whereto he would have him set his Hand; promising to him, that he should then have even what he would; and presenting him with all the Delectable Things, persons, and places, that he could imagine. But he refusing to subscribe, the business would end with dreadful Shapes, Noises and Screeches, which almost scared him out of his witts. Once with the Book, there was a Pen offered him, and an Inkhorn with Liquor in it, that seemed like Blood: but he never toucht it.

This man did now affirm, that he saw the Prisoner at several of those Hellish Randezvouzes.

Note, This Woman was one of the most Impudent, Scurrilous, wicked creatures in the world; and she did now throughout her whole Trial discover herself to be such an one. Yet when she was asked, what she had to say for her self? her Cheef Plea was, That she had Led a most virtuous and Holy Life!

Source: George Lincoln Burr, *Narratives of the Witchcraft Cases, 1648–1706* (New York: Charles Scribner's Sons, 1914).

Thomas Brattle on the Salem Trials (1692)

The Boston gentleman and business leader Thomas Brattle offered his opinion of the Salem proceedings in the following letter to an unknown English minister. He questioned the contradictions in evidence and the scanty proofs used to uncharitably accuse hundreds of witchcraft. Many of those accused were imprisoned, and some twenty were condemned to death. In this missive, Brattle also wrote of the many pious men in the Boston area who questioned the "irregular and dangerous methods" used in the trials.

October 8, 1692.

Reverend Sir,

Your's I received the other day, and am very ready to serve you to my uttmost. I should be very loath to bring myself into any snare by my freedom with you, and therefore hope that you will put the best construction on what I write, and secure me from such as would interpret my lines otherwise than they are designed. Obedience to lawfull authority I evermore accounted a great duty; and willingly I would not practise any thing that might thwart and contradict such a principle. Too many are ready to despise dominions, and speak evil of Dignities; and I am sure the mischiefs, which arise from a factious and rebellious spirit, are very sad and notorious; insomuch that I would sooner bite my finger's ends than willingly cast dirt on authority, or any way offer reproach to it: Far, therefore, be it from me, to have any thing to do with those men your letter mentions, whom you acknowledge to be men of a factious spirit, and never more in their element than when they are declaiming against men in public place, and contriving methods that tend to the disturbance of the common peace. I never accounted it a credit to my cause, to have the good liking of such men. My son! (says Solomon) fear thou the Lord and the King, and meddle not with them that are given to change. Prov[verbs]. xxiv. 21. However, Sir, I never thought Judges infallible; but reckoned that they, as well as private men, might err; and that when they were guilty of erring, standers by, who possibly had not half their judgment, might, notwithstanding, be able to detect and behold their errors. And furthermore, when errors of that nature are thus detected and observed, I never thought it an interfering with dutifullness and subjection for one man to communicate his thoughts to another thereabout; and with modesty and due reverence to debate the premised failings; at least, when errours are fundamental, and palpably pervert the great end of authority

and government: for as to circumstantial errours, I must confesse my principle is, that it is the duty of a good subject to cover with his silence a multitude of them. But I shall no longer detain you with my preface, but passe to some things you look for, and whether you expect such freedome from me, yea or no, yet shall you find, that I am very open to communicate my thoughts unto you, and in plain terms to tell you what my opinion is of the Salem proceedings.

First, as to the method which the Salem Justices do take in their examinations, it is truly this: A warrant being issued out to apprehend the persons that are charged and complained of by the afflicted children, (as they are called); said persons are brought before the Justices, (the afflicted being present.) The Justices ask the apprehended why they afflict those poor children; to which the apprehended answer, they do not afflict them. The Justices order the apprehended to look upon the said children, which accordingly they do; and at the time of that look, (I dare not say by that look, as the Salem Gentlemen [S.G.] do) the afflicted are cast into a fitt. The apprehended are then blinded, and ordered to touch the afflicted; and at that touch, tho' not by the touch, (as above) the afflicted ordinarily do come out of their fitts. The afflicted persons then declare and affirm, that the apprehended have afflicted them; upon which the apprehended persons, tho' of never so good repute, are forthwith committed to prison, on suspicion for witchcraft. One of the Salem Justices was pleased to tell Mr. Alden, (when upon his examination) that truly he had been acquainted with him these many years; and had always accounted him a good man; but indeed now he should be obliged to change his opinion. This, there are more than one or two did hear, and are ready to swear to, if not in so many words, yet as to its natural and plain meaning. He saw reason to change his opinion of Mr. Alden, because that at the time he touched the poor child, the poor child came out of her fitt.

I suppose his Honour never made the experiment,

whether there was not as much virtue in his own hand, as there was in Mr. Alden's, to cure by a touch. I know a man that will venture two to one with any Salemite whatever, that let the matter be duly managed, and the afflicted person shall come out of her fitt upon the touch of the most religious hand in Salem. It is worthily noted by some, that at some times the afflicted will not presently come out of their fitts upon the touch of the suspected; and then, forsooth, they are ordered by the Justices to grasp hard, harder yet, etc. insomuch that at length the afflicted come out of their fitts; and the reason is very good, because that a touch of any hand, and process of time, will work the cure; infallibly they will do it, as experience teaches.

I cannot but condemn this method of the Justices, of making this touch of the hand a rule to discover witchcraft; because I am fully persuaded that it is sorcery, and a superstitious method, and that which we have no rule for, either from reason or religion. The Salem Justices, at least some of them, do assert, that the cure of the afflicted persons is a natural effect of this touch; and they are so well instructed in the Cartesian philosophy, and in the doctrine of effluvia, that they undertake to give a demonstration how this touch does cure the afflicted persons; and the account they give of it is this; that by this touch, the venemous and malignant particles, that were ejected from the eye, do, by this means, return to the body whence they came, and so leave the afflicted persons pure and whole. I must confesse to you, that I am no small admirer of the Cartesian philosophy; but yet I have not so learned it. Certainly this is a strain that it will by no means allow of.

I would fain know of these Salem Gentlemen, but as yet could never know, how it comes about, that if these apprehended persons are witches, and, by a look of the eye, do cast the afflicted into their fitts by poisoning them, how it comes about, I say, that, by a look of their eye, they do not cast others into fitts, and poison others by their looks; and in particular, tender, fearfull women, who often are beheld by them, and as likely as any in the whole world to receive an ill impression from them. This Salem philosophy, some men may call the new philosophy; but I think it rather deserves the name of Salem superstition and sorcery, and it is not fitt to be named in a land of such light as New-England is. I think the matter might be better solved another way; but I shall not make any attempt that way, further than to say, that these afflicted children, (as they are called,) do hold correspondence with the devill, even in the esteem and account of the S.G.; for when the black man, i.e. (say these gentlemen,) the Devill, does appear to them, they ask him many questions, and accordingly give information to the inquirer; and if this is not holding correspondence with the devill, and something worse, I know not what is.

But furthermore, I would fain know of these Salem Justices what need there is of further proof and evidence to convict and condemn these apprehended persons, than this look and touch, if so be they are so certain that this falling down and arising up, when there is a look and a touch, are natural effects of the said look and touch, and so a perfect demonstration and proof of witchcraft in those persons. What can the Jury or Judges desire more, to convict any man of witchcraft, than a plain demonstration, that the said man is a witch? Now if this look and touch, circumstanced as before, be a plain demonstration, (as their Philosophy teaches,) what need they seek for further evidences, when, after all, it can be but a demonstration?

But let this pass with the S.G. for never so plain and natural a demonstration; yet certain is it, that the reasonable part of the world, when acquainted herewith, will laugh at the demonstration, and conclude that the said S.G. are actually possessed, at least, with ignorance and folly.

I most admire that Mr. N. N. the Reverend Teacher at Salem, who was educated at the School of Knowledge, and is certainly a learned, a charitable, and a good man, though all the devils in Hell, and all the possessed girls in Salem, should say to the contrary; at him, (I say,) I do most admire; that he should cry up the above mentioned philosophy after the manner that he does. I can assure you, that I can bring you more than two, or twice two, (very credible persons) that will affirm, that they have heard him vindicate the above mentioned demonstration as very reasonable.

Secondly, with respect to the confessours, (as they are improperly called,) or such as confesse themselves to be witches, (the second thing you inquire into in your letter), there are now about fifty of them in Prison; many of which I have again and again seen and heard; and I cannot but tell you, that my faith is strong concerning them, that they are deluded, imposed upon, and under the influence of some evil spirit; and therefore unfitt to be evidences either against themselves, or any one else. I now speak of one sort of them, and of others afterward.

These confessours, (as they are called) do very often contradict themselves, as inconsistently as is usual for any crazed, distempered person to do. This the S.G. do see and take notice of; and even the Judges themselves have, at some times, taken these confessours in flat lyes, or contradictions, even in the Courts; By reason of which, one would have thought, that the Judges would have frowned upon the said confessours, discarded them, and not minded one tittle of any thing that they said; but instead thereof, (as sure as we are men,) the Judges vindicate these confessours, and salve their contradictions, by proclaiming, that the Devill takes away their memory, and imposes upon their brain. If this reflects any where, I am very sorry for it: I can but assure you, that, upon the word of an honest man, it is truth, and that I can bring you many credible persons to witnesse it, who have been eye and ear wittnesses to these things.

These confessours then, at least some of them, even in the Judges' own account, are under the influence of the Devill; and the brain of these Confessours is imposed upon by the Devill, even in the Judges' account. But now, if, in the Judges' account, these confessours are under the influence of the Devill, and their brains are affected and imposed upon by the Devill, so that they are not their own men, why then should these Judges, or any other men, make such account of, and set so much by, the words of these Confessours, as they do? In short, I argue thus:

If the Devill does actually take away the memory of them at some times, certainly the Devill, at other times, may very reasonably be thought to affect their fancyes, and to represent false ideas to their imagination. But now, if it be thus granted, that the Devill is able to represent false ideas (to speak vulgarly) to the imaginations of the confessours, what man of sense will regard the confessions, or any of the words, of these confessours?

The great cry of many of our neighbours now is, What, will you not believe the confessours? Will you not believe men and women who confesse that they have signed to the Devill's book? that they were baptized by the Devill; and that they were at the mock-sacrament once and again? What! will you not believe that this is witchcraft, and that such and such men are witches, altho' the confessours do own and assert it?

Thus, I say, many of our good neighbours do argue; but methinks they might soon be convinced that there is nothing at all in all these their arguings, if they would but duly consider of the premises.

In the mean time, I think we must rest satisfyed in it, and be thankfull to God for it, that all men are not thus bereft of their senses; but that we have here and there considerate and thinking men, who will not thus be imposed upon, and abused, by the subtle endeavours of the crafty one.

In the next place, I proceed to the form of their inditements, and the Trials thereupon.

The Inditement runs for sorcery and witchcraft, acted upon the body of such an one, (say M. Warren), at such a particular time, (say April 14, '92,) and at divers other times before and after, whereby the said M. W. is wasted and consumed, pined, etc.

Now for the proof of the said sorcery and witchcraft, the prisoner at the bar pleading not guilty.

1. The afflicted persons are brought into Court; and after much patience and pains taken with them, do take their oaths, that the prisoner at the bar did afflict them: And here I think it very observable, that often, when the afflicted do mean and intend only the appearance and shape of such an one, (say G. Proctour) yet they positively swear that G. Proctour did afflict them; and they have been allowed so to do; as tho' there was no real difference between G. Proctour and the shape of G. Proctour. This, methinks, may readily prove a stumbling block to the Jury, lead them into a very fundamental errour, and occasion innocent blood, yea the innocentest blood imaginable, to be in great danger. Whom it belongs unto, to be eyes unto the blind, and to remove such stumbling blocks, I know full well; and yet you and every one else, do know as well as I who do not.

2. The confessours do declare what they know of the said prisoner; and some of the confessours are allowed to give their oaths; a thing which I believe was never heard of in this world; that such as confesse themselves to be witches, to have renounced God and Christ, and all that is sacred, should yet be allowed and ordered to swear by the name of the great God! This indeed seemeth to me to be a grosse taking of God's name in vain. I know the S.G. do say, that there is hopes that the said Confessours have repented; I shall only say, that if they have repented, it is well for themselves; but if they have not, it is very ill for you know who. But then,

3. Whoever can be an evidence against the prisoner at the bar is ordered to come into Court; and here it scarce ever fails but that evidences, of one nature and another, are brought in, tho', I think, all of them altogether aliene to the matter of inditement; for they none of them do respect witchcraft upon the bodyes of the afflicted, which is the alone matter of charge in the inditement.

4. They are searched by a Jury; and as to some of them, the Jury brought in, that [on] such or such a place there was a preternatural excrescence. And I wonder what person there is, whether man or woman, of whom it cannot be said but that, in some part of their body or other, there is a preternatural excrescence. The term is a very general and inclusive term.

Some of the S.G. are very forward to censure and condemn the poor prisoner at the bar, because he sheds no tears: but such betray great ignorance in the nature of passion, and as great heedlessnesse as to common passages of a man's life. Some there are who never shed tears; others there are that ordinarily shed tears upon light occasions, and yet for their lives cannot shed a tear when the deepest sorrow is upon their hearts; and who is there that knows not these things? Who knows not that an ecstasye of Joy will sometimes fetch teares, when as the quite contrary passion will shutt them close up? Why then should any be so silly and foolish as to take an argument from this appearance? But this is by the by. In short, the prisoner at the bar is indited for sorcery and witchcraft acted upon the bodyes of the afflicted. Now, for the proof of this, I reckon that the only pertinent evidences brought in are the evidences of the said afflicted.

It is true, that over and above the evidences of the afflicted persons, there are many evidences brought in, against the prisoner at the bar; either that he was at a witch meeting, or that he performed things which could not be done by an ordinary natural power; or that she sold butter to a saylor, which proving bad at sea, and the seamen exclaiming against her, she appeared, and soon after there was a storm, or the like. But what if there were ten thousand evidences of this nature; how do they prove the matter of inditement! And if they do not reach the matter of inditement, then I think it is clear, that the prisoner at the bar is brought in guilty, and condemned, merely from the evidences of the afflicted persons.

The S.G. will by no means allow, that any are brought

in guilty, and condemned, by virtue of spectre Evidence, (as it is called,) i.e. the evidence of these afflicted persons, who are said to have spectral eyes; but whether it is not purely by virtue of these spectre evidences, that these persons are found guilty, (considering what before has been said,) I leave you, and any man of sense, to judge and determine. When any man is indited for murthering the person of A. B. and all the direct evidence be, that the said man pistolled the shadow of the said A. B. tho' there be never so many evidences that the said person murthered C. D., E. F. and ten more persons, yet all this will not amount to a legal proof, that he murthered A. B.; and upon that inditement, the person cannot be legally brought in guilty of the said inditement; it must be upon this supposition, that the evidence of a man's pistolling the shadow of A. B. is a legal evidence to prove that the said man did murther the person of A. B. Now no man will be so much out of his witts as to make this a legal evidence; and yet this seems to be our case; and how to apply it is very easy and obvious. As to the late executions, I shall only tell you, that in the opinion of many unprejudiced, considerate and considerable spectatours, some of the condemned went out of the world not only with as great protestations, but also with as good shews of innocency, as men could do.

They protested their innocency as in the presence of the great God, whom forthwith they were to appear before: they wished, and declared their wish, that their blood might be the last innocent blood shed upon that account. With great affection they intreated Mr. C. M. to pray with them: they prayed that God would discover what witchcrafts were among us; they forgave their accusers; they spake without reflection on Jury and Judges, for bringing them in guilty, and condemning them: they prayed earnestly for pardon for all other sins, and for an interest in the pretious blood of our dear Redeemer; and seemed to be very sincere, upright, and sensible of their circumstances on all accounts; especially Proctor and Willard, whose whole management of themselves, from the Goal to the Gallows, and whilst at the Gallows, was very affecting and melting to the hearts of some considerable Spectatours, whom I could mention to you:—but they are executed, and so I leave them.

Many things I cannot but admire and wonder at, an account of which I shall here send you.

And 1. I do admire that some particular persons, and particularly Mrs. Thatcher of Boston, should be much complained of by the afflicted persons, and yet that the Justices should never issue out their warrants to apprehend them, when as upon the same account they issue out their warrants for the apprehending and imprisoning many others.

This occasions much discourse and many hot words, and is a very great scandal and stumbling block to many good people; certainly distributive Justice should have its course, without respect to persons; and altho' the said Mrs. Thatcher be mother in law to Mr. Corwin, who is one of the Justices and Judges, yet if Justice and conscience do oblige them to apprehend others on the account of the afflicted their complaints, I cannot see how, without injustice and violence to conscience, Mrs. Thatcher can escape, when it is well known how much she is, and has been, complained of.

2. I cannot but admire that Mr. H. U. (whom we all think innocent,) should yet be apprehended on this account, and ordered to prison, by a mittimus under Mr. Lynd's his hand, and yet that he should be suffered, for above a fortnight, to be in a private house; and after that, to quitt the house, the town, and the Province, and yet that authority should not take effectual notice of it. Methinks that same Justice, that actually imprisoned others, and refused bail for them on any terms, should not be satisfyed without actually imprisoning Mr. U. and refusing bail for him, when his case is known to be the very same with the case of those others.

If he may be suffered to go away, why may not others? If others may not be suffered to go, how in Justice can he be allowed herein?

3. If our Justices do think that Mrs. C. Mr. E. and his wife, Mr. A. and others, were capital offenders, and justly imprisoned on a capital account, I do admire that the said Justices should hear of their escape from prison, and where they are gone and entertained, and yet not send forthwith to the said places, for the surrendering of them, that Justice might be done them. In other Capitalls this has been practised; why then is it not practised in this case, if really judged to be so heinous as is made for?

4. I cannot but admire, that any should go with their distempered friends and relations to the afflicted children, to know what their distempered friends ayl; whether they are not bewitched; who it is that afflicts them, and the like. It is true, I know no reason why these afflicted may not be consulted as well as any other, if so be that it was only their natural and ordinary knowledge that was had recourse to: but it is not on this notion that these afflicted children are sought unto; but as they have a supernatural knowledge; a knowledge which they obtain by their holding correspondence with spectres or evill spirits, as they themselves grant. This consulting of these afflicted children, as abovesaid, seems to me to be a very grosse evill, a real abomination, not fitt to be known in N.E. [New England] and yet is a thing practised, not only by Tom and John—I mean the ruder and more ignorant sort—but by many who professe high, and passe among us for some of the better sort. This is that which aggravates the evil, and makes it heinous and tremendous; and yet this is not the worst of it, for, as sure as I now write to you, even some of our civil leaders, and spiritual teachers, who, (I think,) should punish and preach down such sorcery and wickedness, do yet allow of, encourage, yea, and practise this very abomination.

I know there are several worthy Gentlemen in Salem, who account this practise as an abomination, have trembled to see the methods of this nature which others have used, and have declared themselves to think the practise to be very evill and corrupt; but all avails little with the abettours of the said practice.

A person from Boston, of no small note, carried up his child to Salem, (near 20 miles,) on purpose that he might consult the afflicted about his child; which accordingly he did; and the afflicted told him, that his child was afflicted by Mrs. Cary and Mrs. Obinson. The man returned to Boston, and went forthwith to the Justices for a warrant to seise the said Obinson, (the said Cary being out of the way); but the Boston Justices saw reason to deny a warrant. The Rev. Mr. I. M. of Boston, took occasion severely to reprove the said man; asking him whether there was not a God in Boston, that he should go to the Devill in Salem for advice; warning him very seriously against such naughty practices; which, I hope, proved to the conviction and good of the said person; if not, his blood will be upon his own head.

This consulting of these afflicted children, about their sick, was the unhappy begining of the unhappy troubles at poor Andover: Horse and man were sent up to Salem Village, from the said Andover, for some of the said afflicted; and more than one or two of them were carried down to see Ballard's wife, and to tell who it was that did afflict her. I understand that the said B. took advice before he took this method; but what pity was it, that he should meet with, and hearken to such bad Counsellours? Poor Andover does now rue the day that ever the said afflicted went among them; they lament their folly, and are an object of great pity and commiseration. Capt. B. and Mr. St. are complained of by the afflicted, have left the town, and do abscond. Deacon Fry's wife, Capt'n Osgood's wife, and some others, remarkably pious and good people in repute, are apprehended and imprisoned; and that that is more admirable, the forementioned women are become a kind of confessours, being first brought thereto by the urgings and arguings of their good husbands, who, having taken up that corrupt and highly pernicious opinion, that whoever were accused by the afflicted, were guilty, did break charity with their dear wives, upon their being accused, and urge them to confesse their guilt; which so far prevailed with them as to make them say, they were afraid of their being in the snare of the Devill; and which, through the rude and bar barous methods that were afterwards used at Salem, issued in somewhat plainer degrees of confession, and was attended with imprisonment. The good Deacon and Captain are now sensible of the errour they were in; do grieve and mourn bitterly, that they should break their charity with their wives, and urge them to confesse themselves witches. They now see and acknowledge their rashnesse and uncharitablenesse, and are very fitt objects for the pity and prayers of every good Christian. Now I am writing concerning Andover, I cannot omit the opportunity of sending you this information; that Whereas there is a report spread abroad the country, how that they were much addicted to Sorcery in the said town, and that there were fourty men in it that could raise the Devill as well as any astrologer, and the like; after the best search that I can make into it, it proves a mere slander, and a very unrighteous imputation.

The Rev'd Elders of the said place were much surprized upon their hearing of the said Report, and faithfully made inquiry about it; but the whole of naughtiness, that they could discover and find out, was only this, that two or three girls had foolishly made use of the sieve and scissors, as children have done in other towns. This method of the girls I do not Justifye in any measure; but yet I think it very hard and unreasonable, that a town should lye under the blemish and scandal of sorceryes and conjuration, merely for the inconsiderate practices of two or three girls in the said town.

5. I cannot but admire that the Justices, whom I think to be well-meaning men, should so far give ear to the Devill, as merely upon his authority to issue out their warrants, and apprehend people. Liberty was evermore accounted the great priviledge of an Englishman; but certainly, if the Devill will be heard against us, and his testimony taken, to the siezing and apprehending of us, our liberty vanishes, and we are fools if we boast of our liberty. Now, that the Justices have thus far given ear to the Devill, I think may be mathematically demonstrated to any man of common sense: And for the demonstration and proof hereof, I desire, only, that these two things may be duly considered, viz.

1. That several persons have been apprehended purely upon the complaints of these afflicted, to whom the afflicted were perfect strangers, and had not the least knowledge of imaginable, before they were apprehended.

2. That the afflicted do own and assert, and the Justices do grant, that the Devill does inform and tell the afflicted the names of those persons that are thus unknown unto them.

Now these two things being duly considered, I think it will appear evident to any one, that the Devill's information is the fundamental testimony that is gone upon in the apprehending of the aforesaid people.

If I believe such or such an assertion as comes immediately from the Minister of God in the pulpitt, because it is the word of the everliving God, I build my faith on God's testimony: and if I practise upon it, this my practice is properly built on the word of God: even so in the case before us.

If I believe the afflicted persons as informed by the Devill, and act thereupon, this my act may properly be said to be grounded upon the testimony or information of the Devill. And now, if things are thus, I think it ought to be for a lamentation to you and me, and all such as would be accounted good Christians.

If any should see the force of this argument, and upon it say, (as I heard a wise and good Judge once propose,) that they know not but that God almighty, or a good spirit, does give this information to these afflicted persons; I make answer thereto, and say, that it is most certain that it is neither almighty God, nor yet any good Spirit, that gives this information; and my Reason is good, because God is a God of truth; and the good Spirits will not lye; whereas these informations have several times proved false, when the accused were brought before the afflicted.

6. I cannot but admire that these afflicted persons should be so much countenanced and encouraged in their accusations as they are: I often think of the Groton woman, that was afflicted, an account of which we have in print, and is a most certain truth, not to be doubted of. I shall only say, that there was as much ground, in the hour of it, to countenance the said Groton woman, and to apprehend and imprison, on her accusations, as there is now to countenance these afflicted persons, and to apprehend and imprison on their accusations. But furthermore, it is worthy of our deepest consideration, that in the conclusion, (after multitudes have been imprisoned, and many have been put to death,) these afflicted persons should own that all was a mere fancy and delusion of the Devill's, as the Groton woman did own and acknowledge with respect to herself; if, I say, in after times, this be acknowledged by them, how can the Justices, Judges, or any else concerned in these matters, look back upon these things without the greatest of sorrow and grief imaginable? I confesse to you, it makes me tremble when I seriously consider of this thing. I have heard that the chief judge has expressed himself very hardly of the accused woman at Groton, as tho' he believed her to be a witch to this day; but by such as knew the said woman, this is judged a very uncharitable opinion of the said Judge, and I do not understand that any are proselyted thereto.

Rev'd Sir, these things I cannot but admire and wonder at. Now, if so be it is the effect of my dullness that I thus admire, I hope you will pity, not censure me: but if, on the contrary, these things are just matter of admiration, I know that you will join with me in expressing your admiration hereat.

The chief Judge is very zealous in these proceedings, and says, he is very clear as to all that hath as yet been acted by this Court, and, as far as ever I could perceive, is very impatient in hearing any thing that looks another way. I very highly honour and reverence the wisdome and integrity of the said Judge, and hope that this matter shall not diminish my veneration for his honour; however, I cannot but say, my great fear is, that wisdome and counsell are withheld from his honour as to this matter, which yet I look upon not so much as a Judgment to his honour as to this poor land.

But altho' the Chief Judge, and some of the other Judges, be very zealous in these proceedings, yet this you may take for a truth, that there are several about the Bay, men for understanding, Judgment, and Piety, inferiour to few, (if any,) in N.E. that do utterly condemn the said proceedings, and do freely deliver their Judgment in the case to be this, viz. that these methods will utterly ruine and undoe poor N.E. I shall nominate some of these to you, viz. The hon'ble Simon Bradstreet, Esq. (our late Governor); the hon'ble Thomas Danforth, Esq. (our late Deputy Governor); the Rev'd Mr. Increase Mather, and the Rev'd Mr. Samuel Willard. Major N. Saltonstall, Esq. who was one of the Judges, has left the Court, and is very much dissatisfyed with the proceedings of it. Excepting Mr. Hale, Mr. Noyes, and

Mr. Parris, the Rev'd Elders, almost throughout the whole Country, are very much dissatisfyed. Several of the late Justices, viz. Thomas Graves, Esq. N. Byfield, Esq. Francis Foxcroft, Esq. are much dissatisfyed; also several of the present Justices; and in particular, some of the Boston Justices, were resolved rather to throw up their commissions than be active in disturbing the liberty of their Majesties' subjects, merely on the accusations of these afflicted, possessed children.

Finally; the principal Gentlemen in Boston, and thereabout, are generally agreed that irregular and dangerous methods have been taken as to these matters.

Sir, I would not willingly lead you into any errour, and therefore would desire you to note,

1. That when I call these afflicted "the afflicted children," I would not be understood as though I meant, that all that are afflicted are children: there are several young men and women that are afflicted, as well as children: but this term has most prevailed among us, because of the younger sort that were first afflicted, and therefore I make use of it.

2. That when I speak of the Salem Gentlemen, I would not be understood as tho' I meant every Individual Gentleman in Salem; nor yet as tho' I meant, that there were no men but in Salem that run upon these notions: some term they must have, and this seems not improper, because in Salem this sort of Gentlemen does most abound.

3. That other Justices in the Country, besides the Salem Justices, have issued out their warrants, and imprisoned, on the accusations of the afflicted as aforesaid; and therefore, when I speak of the Salem Justices, I do not mean them exclusively.

4. That as to the above mentioned Judges, that are commissionated for this Court at Salem, five of them do belong to Suffolk county; four of which five do belong to Boston; and therefore I see no reason why Boston should talk of Salem, as tho' their own Judges had had no hand in these proceedings at Salem.

Nineteen persons have now been executed, and one pressed to death for a mute: seven more are condemned; two of which are reprieved, because they pretend their being with child; one, viz. Mrs. Bradbury of Salisbury, from the intercession of some friends; and two or three more, because they are confessours.

The Court is adjourned to the first Tuesday in November, then to be kept at Salem; between this and then will be [the] great assembly, and this matter will be a peculiar matter of their agitation. I think it is matter of earnest supplication and prayer to almighty God, that he would afford his gracious presence to the said assembly, and direct them aright in this weighty matter. Our hopes are here; and if, at this Juncture, God does not graciously appear for us, I think we may conclude that N.E. is undone and undone.

I am very sensible, that it is irksome and disagreeable to go back, when a man's doing so is an implication that he has been walking in a wrong path: however, nothing is more honourable than, upon due conviction, to retract and undo, (so far as may be,) what has been amiss and irregular.

I would hope that, in the conclusion, both the Judges and Justices will see and acknowledge that such were their best friends and advisers as disswaded from the methods which they have taken, tho' hitherto they have been angry with them, and apt to speak very hardly of them.

I cannot but highly applaud, and think it our duty to be very thankfull, for the endeavours of several Elders, whose lips, (I think,) should preserve knowledge, and whose counsell should, I think, have been more regarded, in a case of this nature, than as yet it has been: in particular, I cannot but think very honourably of the endeavours of a Rev'd person in Boston, whose good affection to his countrey in general, and spiritual relation to three of the Judges in particular, has made him very solicitous and industrious in this matter; and I am fully persuaded, that had his notions and proposals been hearkened to, and followed, when these troubles were in their birth, in an ordinary way, they would never have grown unto that heigth which now they have. He has as yet mett with little but unkindness, abuse, and reproach from many men; but I trust that, in after times, his wisdom and service will find a more universal acknowledgment; and if not, his reward is with the Lord.

Two or three things I should have hinted to you before, but they slipped my thoughts in their proper place.

Many of these afflicted persons, who have scores of strange fitts in a day, yet in the intervals of time are hale and hearty, robust and lusty, as tho' nothing had afflicted them. I Remember that when the chief Judge gave the first Jury their charge, he told them, that they were not to mind whether the bodies of the said afflicted were really pined and consumed, as was expressed in the inditement; but whether the said afflicted did not suffer from the accused such afflictions as naturally tended to their being pined and consumed, wasted, etc. This, (said he,) is a pining and consuming in the sense of the law. I add not.

Furthermore: These afflicted persons do say, and often have declared it, that they can see Spectres when their eyes are shutt, as well as when they are open. This one thing I evermore accounted as very observable, and that which might serve as a good key to unlock the nature of these mysterious troubles, if duly improved by us. Can they see Spectres when their eyes are shutt? I am sure they lye, at least speak falsely, if they say so; for the thing, in nature, is an utter impossibility. It is true, they may strongly fancye, or have things represented to their imagination, when their eyes are shutt; and I think this is all which ought to be allowed to these blind, nonsensical girls; and if our officers and Courts have apprehended, imprisoned, condemned, and executed our guiltlesse neighbours, certainly our errour is great, and we shall rue it in the conclusion. There are two or three other things that I have observed in and by these afflicted persons, which make me strongly suspect that the Devill imposes upon their

brains, and deludes their fancye and imagination; and that the Devill's book (which they say has been offered them) is a mere fancye of theirs, and no reality: That the witches' meeting, the Devill's Baptism, and mock sacraments, which they oft speak of, are nothing else but the effect of their fancye, depraved and deluded by the Devill, and not a Reality to be regarded or minded by any wise man. And whereas the Confessours have owned and asserted the said meetings, the said Baptism, and mock Sacrament, (which the S.G. and some others, make much account of) I am very apt to think, that, did you know the circumstances of the said Confessours, you would not be swayed thereby, any otherwise than to be confirmed, that all is perfect Devilism, and an Hellish design to ruine and destroy this poor land: For whereas there are of the said Confessours 55 in number, some of them are known to be distracted, crazed women, something of which you may see by a petition lately offered to the chief Judge, a copy whereof I may now send you; others of them denyed their guilt, and maintained their innocency for above eighteen hours, after most violent, distracting, and draggooning methods had been used with them, to make them confesse. Such methods they were, that more than one of the said confessours did since tell many, with teares in their eyes, that they thought their very lives would have gone out of their bodyes; and wished that they might have been cast into the lowest dungeon, rather than be tortured with such repeated buzzings and chuckings and unreasonable urgings as they were treated withal.

They soon recanted their confessions, acknowledging, with sorrow and grief, that it was an hour of great temptation with them; and I am very apt to think, that as for five or six of the said confessours, if they are not very good Christian women, it will be no easy matter to find so many good Christian women in N.E. But, finally, as to about thirty of these fiftyfive Confessours, they are possessed (I reckon) with the Devill, and afflicted as the children are, and therefore not fitt to be regarded as to any thing they say of themselves or others. And whereas the S.G. do say that these confessours made their Confessions before they were afflicted, it is absolutely contrary to universal experience, as far as ever I could understand. It is true, that some of these have made their confession before they had their falling, tumbling fitts, but yet not absolutely before they had any fitts and marks of possession, for (as the S.G. know full well) when these persons were about first confessing, their mouths would be stopped, and their throats affected, as tho' there was danger of strangling, and afterward (it is true) came their tumbling fitts. So that, I say, the confessions of these persons were in the beginning of their fitts, and not truly before their fitts, as the S.G. would make us believe.

Thus, (Sir,) I have given you as full a narrative of these matters as readily occurs to my mind, and I think every word of it is matter of fact; the several glosses and descants whereupon, by way of Reasoning, I refer to your Judgment, whether to approve or disapprove.

What will be the issue of these troubles, God only knows; I am afraid that ages will not wear off that reproach and those stains which these things will leave behind them upon our land. I pray God pity us, Humble us, Forgive us, and appear mercifully for us in this our mount of distress:

Herewith I conclude, and subscribe myself,
Reverend Sir, your real friend and humble servant,
T. B.

Source: George Lincoln Burr, *Narratives of the Witchcraft Cases, 1648–1706* (New York: Charles Scribner's Sons, 1914).

A Poem Recalling the Hanging of a Relative due to the Salem Witch Trials (in 1692; pub. 1857)

The Quaker poet John Greenleaf Whittier was known for his strong interest in the Puritan colonies of New England. His was more than a passing interest, however. He was related to Susanna Martin, who was condemned as a witch and hanged in 1692 as a result of the Salem witch trials.

The "Witch's Daughter" was originally published as a separate poem in 1857, but it was reissued in Whittier's expanded version of the poem as "Mabel Martin: A Harvest Idyl" (1875). This narrative poem captures the flavor of the period leading up to and following the trials and the effect such a judgment would have had on a child of a "witch." Note that it is a fictionalized account; Susanna Martin did not have a daughter named Mabel.

I call the old time back: I bring my lay
In tender memory of the summer day
When, where our native river lapsed away,

We dreamed it over, while the thrushes made
Songs of their own, and the great pine-trees laid
On warm noonlights the masses of their shade.

And she was with us, living o'er again
Her life in ours, despite of years and pain,
The Autumn's brightness after latter rain.

Beautiful in her holy peace as one
Who stands, at evening, when the work is done,
Glorified in the setting of the sun!

Her memory makes our common landscape seem
Fairer than any of which painters dream;
Lights the brown hills and sings in every stream;

For she whose speech was always truth's pure gold
Heard, not unpleased, its simple legends told,
And loved with us the beautiful and old.

I. THE RIVER VALLEY

. . . Here, in the dim colonial time
Of sterner lives and gloomier faith,
A woman lived, tradition saith,

Who wrought her neighbors foul annoy,
And witched and plagued the county side,
Till at the hangman's hand she died. . . .

III. THE WITCH'S DAUGHTER

But still the sweetest voice was mute
That river-valley ever heard
From lips of maid or throat of bird;

For Mabel Martin sat apart,
And let the hay-mow's shadow fall
Upon the loveliest face of all.

She sat apart, as one forbid,
Who knew that none would condescend
To own the Witch-wife's child a friend.

The seasons scarce had gone their round,
Since curious thousands thronged to see
Her mother at the gallows-tree;

And mocked the prison-palsied limbs
That faltered on the fatal stairs,
And wan lip trembling with its prayers!

Few questioned of the sorrowing child,
Or, when they saw the mother die,
Dreamed of the daughter's agony.

They went up to their homes that day,
As men and Christians justified:
God willed it, and the wretch had died!

Dear God and Father of us all,
Forgive our faith in cruel lies,
Forgive the blindness that denies!

Forgive thy creature when he takes,
For the all-perfect love Thou art,
Some grim creation of his heart.

Cast down our idols, overturn
Our bloody altars; let us see
Thyself in Thy humanity!

Young Mabel from her mother's grave
Crept to her desolate hearth-stone,
And wrestled with her fate alone;

With love, and anger, and despair,
The phantoms of disordered sense,
The awful doubts of Providence!

Oh, dreary broke the winter days,
And dreary fell the winter nights
When, one by one, the neighboring lights

Went out, and human sounds grew still,
And all the phantom-peopled dark
Closed round her hearth-fire's dying spark

And summer days were sad and long,
And sad the uncompanioned eves,
And sadder sunset-tinted leaves,

And Indian Summer's airs of balm;
She scarcely felt the soft caress,
The beauty died of loneliness!

The school-boys jeered her as they passed,
And, when she sought the house of prayer,
Her mother's curse pursued her there.

And still o'er many a neighboring door
She saw the horseshoe's curved charm,
To guard against her mother's harm:

That mother, poor and sick and lame,
Who daily, by the old arm-chair,
Folded her withered hands in prayer;

Who turned, in Salem's dreary jail,
Her worn old Bible o'er and o'er,
When her dim eyes could read no more!

Sore tried and pained, the poor girl kept
Her faith, and trusted that her way,
So dark, would somewhere meet the day.

And still her weary wheel went round
Day after day, with no relief:
Small leisure have the poor for grief.

IV. THE CHAMPION

So in the shadow Mabel sits;
Untouched by mirth she sees and hears,
Her smile is sadder than her tears.

But cruel eyes have found her out,
And cruel lips repeat her name,
And taunt her with her mother's shame.

She answered not with railing words,
But drew her apron o'er her face,
And, sobbing, glided from the place.

And only pausing at the door,
Her sad eyes met the troubled gaze
Of one who, in her better days,

Had been her warm and steady friend,
Ere yet her mother's doom had made
Even Esek Harden half afraid.

He felt that mute appeal of tears,
And, starting, with an angry frown,
Hushed all the wicked murmurs down.

"Good neighbors mine," he sternly said,
"This passes harmless mirth or jest;
I brook no insult to my guest.

"She is indeed her mother's child,
But God's sweet pity ministers
Unto no whiter soul than hers.

"Let Goody Martin rest in peace;
I never knew her harm a fly,
And witch or not, God knows—not I.

"I know who swore her life away;
And as God lives, I'd not condemn
An Indian dog on word of them."

The broadest lands in all the town,
The skill to guide, the power to awe,
Were Harden's; and his word was law.

None dared withstand him to his face,
But one sly maiden spake aside:
"The little witch is evil-eyed!

"Her mother only killed a cow,
Or witched a churn or dairy-pan;
But she, forsooth, must charm a man!"

V. IN THE SHADOW

Poor Mabel, homeward turning, passed
The nameless terrors of the wood
And saw, as if a ghost pursued,

Her shadow gliding in the moon;
The soft breath of the west-wind gave
A chill as from her mother's grave.

How dreary seemed the silent house!
Wide in the moonbeams' ghastly glare
Its windows had a dead man's stare!

And, like a gaunt and spectral hand,
The tremulous shadow of a birch
Reached out and touched the door's low porch,

As is to lift its latch; hard by,
A sudden warning call she heard,
The night-cry of a boding bird.

She leaned against the door; her face,
So fair, so young, so full of pain,
White in the moonlight's silver rain.

The river, on its pebbled rim,
Made music such as childhood knew;
The door-yard tree was whispered through

By voices such as childhood's ear
Had heard in moonlights long ago;
And through the willow-boughs below

. . . She strove to drown her sense of wrong,
And, in her old and simple way,
To teach her bitter heart to pray.

Poor child ! the prayer, begun in faith,
Grew to a low, despairing cry
Of utter misery: "Let me die!

"Oh! take me from the scornful eyes,
And hide me where the cruel speech
And mocking finger may not reach!

"I dare not breathe my mother's name:
A daughter's right I dare not crave
To weep above her unblest grave!

"Let me not live until my heart,
With few to pity, and with none
To love me, hardens into stone.

"O God ! have mercy on Thy child,
Whose faith in Thee grows weak and small,
And take me ere I lose it all!"

A shadow on the moonlight fell,
And murmuring wind and wave became
A voice whose burden was her name . . .

Source: The Complete Poetical Works of John Greenleaf Whittier
(Boston and New York: Houghton Mifflin, 1891).

Raising Colonial Children (1699)

In this essay, Cotton Mather gives moral guidance to his congregation, recognizing that parents need to exercise authority over their children to help maintain an orderly society. He urges parents to be examples to their children and to raise them in faith. Beyond their spiritual health, parents are exhorted to instruct children in civility and ensure that they can read and write. Widowed three times and the father of sixteen children, Mather well understood the responsibilities of parenthood.

The Duties of Parents to Their Children

I know him, That he will command his Children And his Household after him, And they shall keep the way of the Lord. (Gen{esis}. 18:19)

As the Great God, who at the Beginning said, Let Us make man after our Image, hath made man a Sociable creature, so it is evident, That Families are the Nurseries of all Societies; and the First combinations of mankind. Well-ordered Families naturally produce a Good Order in other Societies. When Families are under an ill Discipline, all other Societies being therefore ill Disciplined, will feel that Error in the First Concoction.

To Serve the Families of our Neighborhood, will be a Service to all our Interests. Every serious Christian is concerned, That he may be Serviceable in the World; And many a serious Christian is concerned, because he sees himself to be furnished with no more Opportunities to be Serviceable.

But art thou not a Member of some Family? If that Family may by thy means, O Christian, become a Well-regulated Family, in that point thou wilt become Serviceable; I had almost said, Incomprehensibly Serviceable.

They that have the Government of some Family, do make up no Little part of this Great Assembly. And, Sirs, are there any of you, that would forfeit that Honorable Title, of all the Faithful, The Children of Abraham? Give your Attention, ye Children of Abraham, while I set before you, the Example of your Father for your imitation.

Our Glorious Lord-Messiah, is here going to Communicate unto Abraham some of His Heavenly Counsels. And we have a Text before us, that assigns a Reason for that gracious Communication. The Reason is, the care which this Good man, would thereupon take to bring up his Family in the Fear of God.

In this Text there are some Remarkable Things; and things that some Wise men have often remarked. There was

an Excellent man, sometimes a Preacher of the Lord Jesus Christ, in this very place; whose custom it was, not only to Read a portion of the Scripture before his Prayers with his Family, but also to Infer and Apply brief Notes out of what he Read. He professed, That he found none of all his weary Studies in Divinity, so profitable to him, as this one Exercise, for the Rare and Rich Thoughts, which he therein found himself supplied withal, And he Declared, "that he looked on it as an accomplishment of this very word; Shall I hide from Abraham, the thing which I do? I know him, that he will command his Children, and his Household.

Moreover, You may here Observe a most comfortable Connection, between, He will, and They Shall. Say's the Lord, He will Command his Children, and They shall keep the way of the Lord. It seems, If every one that is Owner of a Family, would faithfully Command, and manage those that belong unto him, through the Blessing of God, they would generally Keep His Way, and His Law.

I find a famous Writer in the Church, therefore thus expressing himself; 'If Parents did their Duties as they ought, the Word Publically Preached would not be the ordinary means of Regeneration in the Church, but only without the Church, among Infidels:' God would so pour out His Grace upon the Children of His people, and Hear Prayers for them, and bless Endeavours for their Holy Education, that we should see the Promises made Good unto our Seed."

We will now Dismiss these Reflections; and Repair to that Grand Case, which hence offers itself unto us.

The Case

What May Be Done by Pious Parents, to Promote the Piety and Salvation of Their Children?

The Case Inquires, What may be done? You will take it for granted, that the Answer to it will tell you, What Should be done? For you will readily grant, that in such an Important Case as this, All that May be done, Should be done!

In the Case We Inquire after what is to be done, by Pious Parents. Other Parents will take no due Notice, of the Injunctions that God has Laid upon them concerning their Children.

Parents, If you don't first become yourselves Pious, you will do nothing to purpose to make your Children so.

Except you do yourselves walk in the Way of the Lord, you will be very careless about bringing your Children to such a Walk.

It is not a Cain, or a Cham, or any Enemy of God; that will do anything to make his Children become the Children of God. The Psalmist in Psal[ms]. 34:1, 4, 11, could first say I will bless the Lord and I sought the Lord, and then he says, Come ye Children, and I will teach you the Fear of the Lord.

O Parents, In the Name of God, Look after your own miserable Souls; How should those wretched people do anything for the Souls of their Children, that never did anything for their own?

In the Case, we Inquire, after what is to be done by Parents for their Children. But let it be Remembered, That our Servants [others in our home] are in some sort likewise our Children. Our whole Household, as well as the Children that are our Offspring, are to be taught the Way of the Lord. An Abraham will have his Trained Servants. We read concerning a certain Person of Quality, in 2 Ki[ngs]. 5:13. His servants came near and spake unto him, and said, My Father.

Let not those of my Hearers, that are without such Invaluable Blessings of God, as Children, count themselves unconcerned in our Discourse, if they have any Servants under them. A considerable part of what is to be done for our Children, I pray, Masters, think, as we go along; Think, without our particular inculcation, whether nothing. This may be done for your Servants: and, God make Eliezers of them for you!

Attend Now to the Counsils of God

I. Parents, Consider the Condition of your Children; and the loud cry of their Condition unto you, to Endeavour their Salvation! What an Army of powerful Thoughts, do at once now show themselves, to beseige your Hearts, and subdue them unto a just care for the Salvation of your Children!

Know you not, that your Children have precious and Immortal Souls within them? They are not all Flesh. You that are the Parents of their Flesh, must know, That your Children have Spirits also, whereof you are told, in Heb[rews]. 12:9. God is the Father of them; and in Eccles[iastes]. 12:7. God is the Giver of them.

The Souls of your Children, must survive their Bodies, and are transcendently Better and Higher & Nobler Things than their Bodies. Are you sollicitous that their Bodies may be Fed? You should be more sollicitous that their Souls may not be Starved, or go without the Bread of Life.

Are you sollicitous that their Bodies may be Cloath'd: you should be more sollicitous that their Souls may not be Naked, or go without the Garments of Righteousness.

Are you Loath to have their Bodies Labouring under Infimities, or Deformaties? You should be much more Loath to have their Souls pining away in their Iniquities.

Man, Are thy Children, but the Children of Swine? If thou art Regardless of their Souls, truly thou dost call them so!

One of the Ancients, namely Cyprian, has a pungent comparison for this matter; Pray, Consider; (said that Great man) He that minds his Childs Body more than his Soul, is like, one, that if his Child and his Dog were like to be drowned, should be sollicitous to save his Dog, but let the Child perish in the water.

How deaf art thou, that thou dost not hear a loud cry from the Souls of thy Children in thine Ears, Oh, my Father, my Mother, look after me!

But more than so; Don't you know, That your Children, are the Children of Death, and the Children of Hell, and the Children of Wrath, by Nature: And that from you, this Nature is derived and conveyed unto them!

You must know, Parents, that your Children are by your means Born under the dreadful Wrath of God: And if they are not New-Born before they die, it had been Good for them, that they never had been Born at all.

The law of equity was in Exodus 21:19 If one man wound another, he shalt cause him to be throughly healed. Your Children are born with deadly wounds of Sin upon their Souls; and they may Thank you for those wounds: Unjust men, will you now do nothing for their Healing?

Man, thy Children are dying of an horrid poison, in their Bowels; and it was thou that poison'd them. What! Wilt thou do nothing for the succour [help]! Thy Children are thrown into a Devouring Fire; and it is from thee that the Fiery Vengeance of God has taken Hold of them. What! Wilt thou do nothing to Help them out!

There is a Corrupt Nature in thy children, which is a Fountain of all Wickedness and Confusion. The very Pagans were not insensible of this Corrupt Nature; they styled it our Congenite [congenital] Sin, and our Domestick Evil, and cried out, with Tully, *"Simul ac Editi sumus in Lucem, ac suscepti, in omni continue pravitate versamur."*

The Jews have been yet more Sensible of this Corrupt Nature; they have Stil'd it, our Evil Frame and the poison of the old Serpent; and This they understand by The Enemy, so often mentioned in the Scripture; And, The Heart of Stone and, the Wicked that watches the Righteous.

Will not you that are Christians, then show your Christianity, by Sensibly doing what you can, that your Children may have a Better Nature infused into them?

What shall I Say? I may say, The Time would fail me to mention a thousanth part of what might be said. But, in short: Is it not a sad Thing to be the Father of a fool?

Alas, man, till thy Children become Regenerate, thou

art the Father of a Fool; Thy Children are but the Wild Asses Colt! I add; would it not Break thy Heart, if thy Children, were in Slavery to Turks, or Moors, or Indians?

Devils are worse than Indians, and Infidels: till thy Children are brought home to God, they are the slaves of Devils.

In a word; Can thy Heart Endure, that thy Children, should be Banished from the Lord Jesus Christ, and Languishing under the Torments of Sin among Devils, in outer Darkness throughout Eternal Ages?

Don't call thyself a Parent; Thou art an Ostrich [they care not for their offspring]. Call not these, the Children of thy Bowels; thou hast no Bowels! I will not say, that Zipporah call'd her Husband, A Bloody Husband. But all the Angels in Heaven call thee, A Bloody Father, and A Bloody Mother; and are astonished at the Adamantine Hardness of that Bloody Heart of thine; and those Heartstrings that are Sinewes of Iron!

II. Improve the Baptism of your children, as an obligation, and an encouragement unto you, parents, to endeavour the salvation of your Baptised little ones.

Of your children, you may say, with Jacob, in Gen[esis]. 33:5 These are the children that God hath graciously given to me. Now, will not you heartily give back those children to God again: their Baptism is to be the sign and seal of your doing so.

You generally bring your infant children unto the Baptism of the Lord: I suppose, it is because you are satisfied, that the children of believers were in the Covenant with God, in the days of the Old Testament; and, that the children of believers then had a right unto the initial seal of the Covenant, and, that in the days of the New Testament they have not lost this priviledge.

Well, but when you bring your children to the Sacred Baptism, what is it for? Oh, let it not be done, as an empty formality; as if the Baptism of your children were for nothing, but only a formal and a pompous putting of a name upon them.

No, but let the serious language of your souls, in this action, be that of Hannah, in I Sam[uel] 1:28: I have given this child unto the Lord, as long as he lives, he shall be given unto the Lord.

I find in the private writings of an holy man, who died in this place, not much above a year ago; That the day before one of his children was to be Baptised, he spent the time in giving up himself and his child unto the Lord, and in taking hold of the Covenant for both of them, and in praying that he might on the morrow, be able in much faith and love and Covenant obedience, to do it, at the Baptism of the Lord. Oh, which he writes it is not easy, though common, to offer a child unto God in Baptism.

Sirs, when you have done this for your Children, you have a singular advantage to plead for the fulfillment of that word upon them in Is[aiah]. 44:3 I will pour my Spirit upon thy Soul, and my blessing upon thy offspring. You may go before the Lord, and plead, Lord, Was not the Baptismal water poured by thy command upon my children! Oh, do thou now pour upon them the heavenly grace, which that Baptismal water signified.

And now, no sooner let those Children become able to understand it, than you shall make them understand what the design of their Baptism was. Parents, I am to tell you, that if you let your Children grow up, without ever telling them, that, and, why, they were Baptised into the Name of the Lord, you are fearfully guilty of taking the name of the Lord in vain.

It was the manner of an excellent minister, upon the Baptising of a child, solemnly to deliver the child into the hands of the Parents, with such words as those, here, take this child now, and bring it up for the Lord Jesus Christ, I charge you.

God from Heaven speaks the like words to you, O Parents, upon all your Baptised Children. And that you may bring up your Children for the Lord Jesus Christ, you must as soon as you can, let them know, that in Baptism, they were dedicated unto Him.

Show them that when they were Baptised, they were listed among the servants and soldiers of the Lord Jesus Christ, and that if they live in rebellion against Him, Woe unto them!

Show them, from Matthew 28:19, 20. That since they are Baptised into the Name of the Father, and the Son, and the Holy Spirit, they must observe all things, whatsoever the Lord Jesus Christ, has commanded them.

Show them from Romans 6:4, that since they are Baptised, they are Buried with Christ in baptism, and must live no longer in sin, but be Dead unto all the Vanities of the World.

Show them from Galatians 3:27, that since they are Baptised, they have put on Christ, and must follow His Example, and be as He was in the World.

Show them from I Peter 3:21, that being Baptised, they must now make the Answer of a good conscience, to all the proposals of the New-Covenant: and God propounding to them, shall my Christ be thine, and wilt thou be His? They must conscientiously answer, Lord, with all my heart!

Put this very solemnly unto your children; My child, shall God the Father, be thy Father? Shall God the Son, be thy Saviour! Shall God the Spirit, be thy Sanctifier; and are thou willing to be the servant of that one God, who is, Father, Son, and Spirit?

Leave them not, until their little hearts are conquered unto that for which they have been Baptised. It has been the judgment of some Judicious men; that If infant baptism were more improved, it would be less disputed. Oh, that it were thus Improved.

III. Instruct your children in the great matters of Salvation; Oh, Parents, do not let them die without instruction.

There is indeed, an Instruction in Civil Matters which we owe unto our Children. It is very pleasing to our Lord Jesus Christ, that our Children be well formed with, and well informed in the rules of Civility, and not be left a Clownish, and Sottish, and Ill Bred sort of Creatures. An Unmannerly Brood is a Dishonour to Religion.

And, there are many points of a Good Education that we should bestow upon our Children; they should Read, and Write, and Cyphar, and be put unto some Agreeable Callings; and not only our Sons, but our Daughters also should be taught such things, as will afterwards make them useful in their places. There is a little Foundation of Religion laid in such an Education. But besides, and beyond all this, there is an Instruction in Divine Matters, which our Children are to be made partakers of.

Parents, Instruct your Children, in the Articles of Religion; and acquaint them with God, and Christ, and the Mysteries of the Gospel, and the Doctrines and Methods of the Great Salvation.

It was Required, in Psalm 78:5 He commanded our Fathers, to make known to their Children, that the Generation to come might know, who should arise and declare them to their children, that they might set their Hope in God, and keep His commandments.

It was required in Eph[esians]. 6:4 Fathers, bring up your children in the Nurture and Admonitions of the Lord. Would you have your Children to be Wise and Good? I know not why you should expect it, unless you take abundance of pains, by your Instruction to make them so.

There was a Wise and Good son, who gave that account how he became what he was; in Prov[erbs] 4:3, 4. I was my Fathers son, and he taught me. O Begin betimes, to Tell your Children who is their Maker, and who is their Saviour, and what they are Themselves, and what is like to become of them; and by no means let them want that Advantage in 2 Tim[othy] 3:15 From a child thou hast known the Holy Scriptures, which are able to make thee wise unto Salvation.

Cause them to look often into their Bibles, and here and there Single out some special Sentences from those Oracles of Heaven for them to get into their Memories. And for the better management of their Instruction there are especially two Handles, to be laid hold upon; the one is, a Proper Catachism, the other is the Public Ministry.

Be sure that they learn their Catachism very perfectly; but then content not yourselves with hearing them say by Rote the Answers in their Catachism; Question them very distinctly over again about every clause in the Answer and bring all to it so plain before them, that by their saying only, Yes, or No, you may perceive that the sense of the Truth is entered into their souls.

And then, what they hear in the Evangelical Ministry, do you Apply it unto them after their coming Home; Confer with them familiarly about the Things that have been handled in the [proper and true] Ministry of the Word: go over one Thing after another, with them, till you see they have got clear Ideas of it; Then put it unto them, Are not you now to Avoid such a thing; or perform such a thing! And must not you now make such and such a prayer unto God? Bid them then, go do accordingly.

Hence also, 'twere very desireable, that you should watch all opportunities, to be instilling your Instructions into the souls of your little Folks. They are narrow-mouthed Vessles, and things must be drop after drop instilled into them. It was required in Deut[eronomy]. 6:6, 7 The words which I command thee, Thou shalt teach them Diligently unto thy Children, and shalt Talk of them, when thou sittest in thine House, and when thou walkest by the way, and when thou sittest down and when thou riseth up.

How often in a week, are we Diverting ourselves, with our Children in our Houses? There thy stand before us; There is nothing to hinder our saying some very profitable thing for them to think upon; well, can you let fall Nothing upon them, that it will be worth their while, for them to think upon?

What, Nothing of God, and Christ, and of another World, and of their own Souls, and of the Sins that may Endanger them, and of the Ways which they may take to be Happy? Doubtless, you may say something.

And who can tell? It may be after you are gone to behold the Face of the Lord Jesus Christ in Glory, these your Children will Remember Hundreds of profitable Instructions, that you have given them; and Live upon them when you that gave them, are Dead.

With Two Strokes I will clench this advice. The one is that in Proverbs 22:6 Train up a Child in the way he should go, and when he is old, he will not Depart from it. The other is that in Prov 17:25. A Foolish Son is a grief to his Father, and a bitterness to her that bare him.

IV. Parents, with a Sweet Authority over your Children, Rebuke them for, and Refrain them from, everything that may prove prejudicial unto their Salvation.

Sirs, You can do little for the Welfare of your Children, if once you have lost your Authority over them. Would you bring your Children to the Fear of God? Your character then must be that in 1 Tim[othy] 3:4 One that ruleth well his own House, having his Children in subjection, with all gravity.

Don't by your Lightness and Weakness and Folly, suffer them to Trample upon you; but keep up so much Authority, that your Word may be a Law unto them. Nevertheless,

Let not your Authority be strained with such Harshness and Fierceness, as may discourage your Children. To treat our Children like Slaves, and with such Rigour, that they shall always Tremble and Abhor to come into our presence, This will be very unlike to our Heavenly Father.

Our Authority should be so Tempered with Kindness, and Meekness, and Loving Tenderness, that our Children may Fear us with Delight, and see that we Love them, with as much Delight.

Now, Let our Authority, effectually keep in our Children, from all their unruly Exorbitancies and Extravagancies. If we let our Young Folks grow Head-Strong, and if we grow Afraid of compelling them to the Wholesome Orders of our Families, we have even given them up to Ruin. God brought that Son to an Untimely and a Terrible End, of whom its reported in I Kings 1:6 His Father had not Displeased him at any time, in saying, Why hast thou done so?

I beseech you, Parents, Interpose your Authority to stop and check the Carrier of your Children, when they will be running into the paths of the Destroyer.

Gratify them with Rewards of Well doing, when they Do well; but let them not be gratified with every Ungodly Vanity, that their Vain Minds may be set upon.

Wherefore keep a strict Inspection upon their Conversations; Examine, How they spend their Time; Examine, What Company they keep? Examine, Whether they take no Bad Courses.

Be not such Foolish Enemies to yourselves, and your Children as to count them your Enemies, that shall friendly advise you of their Miscarriages. That wretched Folly, is a very Frequent One!

When you Find out their Miscarriages, effectually Rebuke them, and Restrain them. Incurr not the Indignation of Heaven, once Incurred by a Fond Father, in 1 Sam[uel] 3: 13; I will Judge his House forever, for the Iniquity which he knoweth; because his Sons made themselves vile, and he Restrained them not.

Ah, Thou Indulgent Parent; if you canst not Cross thy Children, when they are disposed unto that which is for the Dishonour of God, God will make thy Children to become Crosses unto thee.

Sirs, When your Children do amiss, call them Aside; set before them the Precepts of God which they have broken, and the Threatenings of God, which they provoked. Demand of them, to profess their sorrow for their fault, and Resolve that they will be no more so Faulty.

Yes, there may be occasion for you, to consider that Word of God in Proverbs 13:24 He that spareth his Rod, hateth his son, but he that loveth him, chasteneth him betimes; and that Word in Proverbs 19:18 Chasten thy son while there is Hope, and let not thy soul spare for his Crying; and that word, in Proverbs 23:13, 14. Withold not Correction from the Child; for if thou beatest him with the Rod, he shall not Die; Thou shalt beat him with the Rod, and shalt deliver his Soul from Hell.

But if it must be so, Remember this Counsel; Never give a Blow in a passion. Stay till your passion is over; and let the Offenders plainly see, that you deal thus with them,

out of a pure Obedience unto God, and for their true Repentance.

One of the ancients, has this Ingenious gloss In the tabernacle, Aarons Rod, and the Pot of Manna, were together; so (says he) when the Rod is used, the sweetness and goodness of the Manna must accompany it: and Mercy be joined with Severity. Let me leave that premonition with you, in Proverbs 29:15 A child left unto himself, bringeth his Mother to shame.

V. Lay your Charges upon your Children; Parents, Charge them to Work about their own Salvation.

The Charges of Parents have a great Efficacy upon many Children; To Charge them vehemently, is to Charm them wonderfully.

Command your Children, and it may be they will Obey. Let Gods commands be your commands, and it may be your Children will obey them.

Lay upon your Children, the Charges of God, as David once upon his, in 1 Chron[icles] 28:9 My Son, know thou the God of thy Father, and serve Him with a perfect heart, and with a willing mind; if thou seek Him, He will be found of thee, but if thou forsake Him, He will cast thee off forever.

Now, Sirs, You will do well, to single out some singular Charges of God, and calling your Children one by one before you, Lay those Charges upon them, in the Name of the God that made them, and obtain from them, if you can, a promise that they will observe those Charges, with the Help of that God. I will set before you, three or four of those Charges.

Let one of your Charges upon your Children, be that in 1 John 3:23 This is His commandment, that we should believe on the Name of His Son Jesus Christ.

Charge them to carry their poor, guilty, ignorant and polluted and Enslaved souls unto the Lord Jesus Christ, that He may Save them from their Sins, and Save them from the Wrath to come.

Charge them, to mind how the Lord Jesus Christ Executes the Office of a Prophet, and a Priest, and a King, and Cry to Him, that He would Save them in the Execution of all those Blessed Offices.

Let another of your Charges be that in Hag[gai] 1:5, 7 Thus saith the Lord of Hosts, Consider Your Ways. Charge them to set apart a few minutes now and then, for Consideration; and in those minutes,

Charge them to Consider, what they have been doing, and what they should have been doing, ever since they came into the World, and if they should immediately go out of the World, what will become of them throughout Eternal Ages.

I have read of a Dying Parent, who laid this Charge upon his wild Son, That he would allow one quarter of an Hour every Day to Consider on something or other, any Thing, as his Fancy led him. The Young men having for some while done so, at last began to consider, why his Dying

Parent should lay such a Charge upon him. This brought on so many Devout Thoughts, that before long, in the Conversion of the Young man, the Desire of the Dying Parent was accomplished.

Oh! If you could Engage your Children to Think Upon Their Ways, there would be Hopes of their Turning to God.

But, Let a Third of your Charges, be that in Matthew 6:6 Enter into thy closet, and when thou hast shut thy door, pray to thy Father that sees in secret.

Charge them to retire for Secret Prayer, every Day that comes over their Heads, Talk with them, till you see, that they can tell, what they should Pray for: and then, often Charge them to Pray every day; yea, sometimes Ask them, Do you Remember the charge I Laid upon you?

Ah, Parent, thy children will do well, while it can be said, Behold, They Pray. And thy House filled with thy Childrens Prayers, would be better accommodated, than if it were filled, with all the Riches of the Indies.

Let a Fourth of your Charges be That, in Proverbs 9: 6, Forsake the Foolish and Live.

Charge them to avoid the snares of Evil Company; Terrify them with Warnings of those Deadly Snares.

Often Repeat this Charge unto them, That if there be any Vicious Company, they shun them, as they would the Plague or the Devil.

Often say, "My son, if Sinners entice thee, consent thou not."

Often say, "My child, walk with the Wise, and thou shalt be wise, but a Companion of Fools shall be destroyed."

Oh, Do Not let the Beasts of prey, carry away thy Children alive.

Shall I add; it is here intimated, That an Abraham, is to Command his Children, very particularly, about, The Way of the Lord. The Way of the Lord, is the Way of his Right, Pure, Instituted Worship. Well, then, Command your Children, that they do not Forsake the Holy Institutions of the Lord Jesus Christ, and Embrace a Vain Worship, consisting of things that He never Instituted.

There are some clauses in the Second Commandment, which intimate, That if Parents would see the Mercies of God upon their Children, they must Charge them, to Worship God, only in those Ways of Worship that God hath appointed.

Thus keep Charging of your Children, while you Live. And if you are capable so to Do, Do it once more with all possible Solemnity, when you come to Die. The words of a Dying Parent, will probably be Living Words, and Lively Ones.

When our Excellent Mitchel was a Dying, he let fall such a Speech as This, unto a Young Gentleman, that Lodged in his House, My Friend, as a Dying man, I now charge you, that you don't meet me out of Christ in the Day of Christ. This one Speech, brought into Christ, the soul of that Young Gentleman! Truly, if your Dying Lips, may utter such Dying

Words unto your Children, who can tell, but they may then be brought into Christ, if they were never so before!

But, lest you should have no opportunity to Speak in a Dying Hour, why should you not Write such things, as you would have them to Think upon, when you shall be Dead and Gone? An unknown deal of Good, may your Children reap, from the Admonitions, that a Dying Parent may Leave unto them.

VI. Parents, be Exemplary:

Your Example may do much towards the Salvation of your Children, your Works will more Work upon your Children, than your Words; your Patterns will do more than your Precepts; your Copies than your Counsels.

What was then said unto Pastors, may very fitly be said unto Parents, in Titus 2:2, In all Things show thyself a pattern of good works; and in Timothy 4:12 Be thou an Example in Word, in Conversation, in Charity, in Spirit, in Faith, in Purity.

It will be impossible for you to infuse any Good into your Children, if you appear void of that Good yourselves. If the Old Crab go backward, it is to no purpose, for the Young One to be directed to go forward: Sirs, Young Ones, will Crawl after the Old Ones.

Would you have your Children, well principled with the Fear and Faith of God? Mind that passage, in Acts 10:2, Cornelius was a devout man, and one that Feared God, with all his House.

Mind that passage in Acts 18:8 Crispus Believed on the Lord, with all his House. It seems, the whole House, is like to do, as the Parents do. It is as Austin {Augustine} expresses it, the ususal cry, Nolumus esse meliores quam patres, We will be no Better than our Parents, If the Parents will make their Cakes to the Queen of Heaven, the Children will kindle their Fires for them.

Justin Martyr somewhere Inquires why the Prophet Elisha imprecated the Revenges of Heaven upon the Children that mocked him, when they hardly understood what they did? and he answers, The Children Learned their wicked Language from their Parents, and now God punished both of them together.

Parents, let your Children see nothing by you, but what shall be commendable and imitable. Be able to say unto your Children, My child, follow me, as you have seen me follow Christ.

Let them from your Seriousness, and your Prayerfulness, and your Watchfulness, and your Sanctification of the Lord's Day, be taught, how they should walk and please God. You "Bid" them well; "Show" them How!

VII. Prayer, Prayer, must be the Crown of all:

Parents, is it your Hearts Desire? Let it be also your Prayer, for your Children, that they may be Saved.

Prayer for the Salvation of any Sinners, availith much.

How much may it avail for the Salvation of our Sinful Children? Much availed that Prayer of David in 1 Chron[icles]. 29:19, Lord, Give unto my Son a perfect Heart, to keep thy Commandments.

Parents, Make such a prayer for your Children, Lord, Give unto my Child, a New Heart, and a Clean Heart, and a Soft Heart; and an Heart after thy own Heart.

We have been told, that Children once were brought unto our Lord Jesus Christ, for Him to Put His hands upon them; and He Put His hands upon them, and blessed them. Oh! Thrice, and Four Times Blessed Children! Well, Parent, Bring your Children unto the Lord Jesus Christ; it may be, He will put His Blessing, and Healing, and Saving Hands upon them: Then, they are Blessed, and shall be Blessed for evermore! If Abraham cry to God, O that my son Ishmael may live in thy sight! God will say to Abraham, concerning Ishmael, I have heard thee!

Pray for the Salvation of thy Children, and carry the Names of every one of them, every day before the Lord, with Prayers, the Cries whereof shall pierce the very Heavens. Holy Job did so! Job 1:5 He offered according to the number of all his Children; Thus did Job continually.

Address Heaven with daily Prayers, That God would make thy Children the Temples of His Spirit, the Vessels of His Glory; and the Care of His Holy Angels.

Address the Lord Jesus Christ, with Prayers, like them of old, That all the Maladies upon the Souls of thy Children may be cured and that the Evil One may have no possession of them.

Yea, when thou do cast thine Eyes upon the Little Folks, often in a day dart up an Ejaculatory Prayer to Heaven for them; Lord, let this child be thy servant for ever.

If your Prayers are not presently answered, be not Disheartened: Remember the Word of the Lord, in Luke 18: 1, That men ought always to pray, and not to faint.

Redouble your Importunity, until thou speed for thy child, as the poor Woman of Canaan did.

Join Fasting to thy Prayer; it may be, the evil in the soul of your child, will not go out, without such a Remedy. David sets himself to Fasting, as well as Prayer, for the Life of his Child. Oh, Do as much for the Soul of thy Child!

Wrestle with the Lord. Receive no Denial. Earnestly protest, Lord, I will not let thee go, except thou Bless this poor Child of mine, and make it thy own! Do this, until, if it may be, thy Heart is Raised by a Touch of Heaven, to a particular Faith; that God has blessed this child, and it shall be Blessed and Saved Forever.

But is this all that is to be done? There is more. Parents, Pray with your Children, as well as for them.

Family prayer must be maintained by all those Parents, that would not have their Children miss of Salvation, and that would not have the Damnation of their Children horribly fall upon themselves. Man, thy Family is a Pagan Family, if it be a Prayerless Family: And the Children going down to the place of Dragons from this thy Family, will pour out their Execrations upon thee, in the Bottom of Hell, until the very Heavens be no more.

But, besides your Family Prayers, Oh, parents, why should you not now and then, take one capable Child after another, alone before the Lord? Carry the Child with you, into your Secret Chambers; make the Child kneel down by you, while you present it unto the Lord, and Implore His Blessing upon it.

Let the Child, hear the Groans, and See the Tears, and be a witness of the Agonies, wherewith you are Travailing for the Salvation of it. The Children will never Forget what you do; it will have a marvelous Force upon them.

Thus, Oh, Parents, You have been told, what you have to do, for the Salvation of your Children; and certainly, their Salvation is worth all of this!

Your Zeal about the Salvation of your Children, will be a symptom of your own Sincerity. A total want of Zeal, will be a Spot upon you, that is not a Spot of the Children of God.

God will Reward the Zeal. It is very probable, That the Children thus cared for, will be the Saved of the Lord. Your Glad Hearts will one day see it, if they are so: it will augment your Heaven, through all eternity, to have These in Heaven with you.

And let it be Remembered, That the Fathers, are not the only Parents obliged thus to pursue the Salvation of their Children: You that are Mothers, have not a little to do for the Souls of your Children, and you have Opportunity to do more than a Little.

Bathsheba the Mother of Solomon, and Eunice the Mother of Timothy, did greatly Contribute unto the Salvation of their famous and worthy Sons.

God has Commanded Children, Forsake not the Law of thy Mother. Then, a Mother must give the Law of God unto them.

It is said of the Virtuous Woman, She looks well to the ways of her Household; Then a Virtuous Mother looks well to the Ways of her Children.

Your Children may say, In sin did my Mother Conceive me. Oh, Then let Mothers do what they can, to Save their Children out of Sin!

And especially, Mothers, do you Travail for your Children over again, with your Earnest Prayers for their Salvation, until it may be said unto you, as it was unto Monica the Mother of Austin, concerning him: "Tis impossible, that thy Child should perish, after thou hast Employed so many Prayers and Tears for the Salvation of it."

Now God give a Good Success to these Poor Endeavours!

Source: Cotton Mather, *A family well-ordered, or, An essay to render parents and children happy in one another handling two very important cases: I. What are the duties to be done by pious parents, for the promoting of piety in their children, II. What are the duties that must be paid by children that they may obtain the blessings of the dutiful.* (Boston: Printed by B. Green & J. Allen, 1699).

Founding of New Sweden (1700s)

The eighteenth-century Swedish Lutheran minister Israel Acrelius gives an account of the earlier settlement of New Sweden, an area that today encompasses Delaware and parts of New Jersey and Pennsylvania.

In 1633, the King of Sweden granted a charter for the establishment of the New Sweden Company, which initially had Dutch and Swedish backing. Peter Minuit (also spelled Minuet), the former director of New Netherland, headed the Swedish settlement, but conflicts arose with neighboring Dutch settlements. In 1655, Peter Stuyvesant, who had replaced Minuit as director of New Netherland, claimed New Sweden. This diversion of resources, however, weakened New Netherland's defenses. In 1664, the British conquered New Netherland, which included lands extending to the Delaware River.

After that the magnanimous Genoese, Christopher Columbus, had, at the expense of Ferdinand, King of Spain, in the year 1492, discovered the western hemisphere, and the illustrious Florentine, Americus Vespucius, sent out by King Emanuel of Portugal, in the year 1502, to make a further exploration of its coasts, had had the good fortune to give the country his name, the European powers have, from time to time, sought to promote their several interests there. Our Swedes and Goths were the less backward in such expeditions, as they had always been the first therein. They had already, in the year 996 after the birth of Christ, visited America, had named it Vinland the Good, and also Skrællinga Land, and had called its inhabitants "the Skrællings of Vinland." It is therefore evident that the Northmen had visited some part of North America before the Spaniards and Portuguese went to South America. But the question is, What would have been thought about Vinland if no later discoveries had been made, and what they thought about it before the time of Columbus?

Every region in America was discovered in its own separate time. Virginia was discovered in the year 1497 by Sebastian Cabot, a Portuguese, who was then the captain of an English ship. Its coasts were afterwards visited by those brave knights, Sir Francis Drake and Sir Walter Raleigh, the latter of whom called the land VIRGINIA, after Queen Elizabeth of England, who lived unmarried. Under this name was included all the country stretching from Cape Florida to the St. Lawrence River, which was formerly called Florida, when separate names were not yet given to its coasts. That was done about the year 1584. Captain De la Ware, under the hand of the English Admiral James Chartiers, was the first who discovered the bay in which the Indian river Pou-

taxat debouched, and gave his name, Delaware, to both the river and the bay, in the year 1600. These countries were repeatedly visited by the English: first by those sent out by Sir Walter Raleigh from Bristol, in the year 1603, and afterwards by Sir G. Popham and Captain James Davis, but little more was accomplished than that they learned to know the people, erected me small places and forts, which, however, were soon destroyed by the savages. In the year 1606 body of emigrants was sent to the northern regions, by two companies, called the London and the Bristol Companies. The former settled southward on the Chesapeake Bay; the latter, on the Kennebeck, or Sagadahoc River. Each had its territorial rights secured by a patent. In the year 1620, a dispute arose between them about the fisheries at Cape Cod, when a new patent was given. The Bristol Company, which received an accession of some persons of rank and distinction, changed its name to that of the Plymouth Council, and obtained a right to all the lands lying above the 40th degree up to the 48th degree of north latitude, which was three degrees farther north than the former grant, and included the greater part of Acadia, or New Scotland, and also extended westward from the Atlantic to the Pacific Ocean: all this was included in New England. The rest remained under Virginia.

About the same time the Hollanders undertook to steal into these American harbors. They took a fancy to the shores of the bay called by the Indians Menahados, and the river Mohaan Henry Hudson, an Englishman in the service of the Holland East India Company, had first discovered those places, and called the bay after his own name, Hudson's Bay. 'P his East India Company, in the year 1608, sold its right to the country, which it based upon its priority of discovery, to some Hollanders. These obtained from the

States-General of Holland an exclusive privilege (*privilegium exclusivum*) to the country, and took the name of "The West India Company of Amsterdam." In the year 1610 they began to traffic with the Indians, and in the year 1613 built a trading post (*magazin*) at the plat now called Albany, and in the following year placed some cannon there. Samuel Argall, the Governor of Virginia, drove them out in 1618; but King James I. gave them permission to remain, that their ships might obtain water there in their voyages to Brazil. From that time until 1623, when the West India Company obtained its charter, their trade with the Indians was conducted almost entirely on shipboard, and they made no attempts to build any house or fortress until 1629. Now, whether that was done with or without the permission of England, the town of New Amsterdam was built and fortified, as also the place Aurania, Orange, now called Albany, having since had three general-governors, one after the other. But that was not yet enough. They wished to extend their power to the river Delaware also, and erected on its shores two or three small forts, which were, however, soon after destroyed by the natives of the country.

It now came in order for Sweden also to take part in this enterprise. William Usselinx, a Hollander, born at Antwerp in Brabant, presented himself to King Gustaf Adolph, and laid before him a proposition for a Trading Company, to be established in Sweden, and to extend its operations to Asia, Africa, and Magellan's Land (Terra Magellanica), with the assurance that this would be a great source of revenue to the kingdom. Full power was given him to carry out this important project; and thereupon a contract of trade was drawn up, to which the Company was to agree and subscribe it. Usselinx published explanations of this contract, wherein he also particularly directed attention to the country on the Delaware, its fertility, convenience, and all its imaginable resources. To strengthen the matter, a charter (octroy) was secured to the Company, and especially to Usselinx, who was to receive a royalty of one thousandth upon all articles bought or sold by the Company.

The powerful king, whose zeal for the honor of God was not less ardent than for the welfare of his subjects, availed himself of this opportunity to extend the doctrines of Christ among the heathen, as well as to establish his own power in other parts of the world. To this end, he sent forth Letters Patent, dated at Stockholm on the 2d of July, 1626, wherein all, both high and low, were invited to contribute something to the Company, according to their means. The work was completed in the Diet of the following year, 1627, when the estates of the realm gave their assent, and confirmed the measure. Those who took part in this Company were: His Majesty's mother, the Queen Dowager Christina, the Prince John Casimir, the Royal Council, the most distinguished of the nobility, the highest officers of the army, the bishops and other clergymen, together with the burgomasters and aldermen of the cities, as well as a large number of the people generally. The time fixed for paying in the subscriptions was the 1st of May of the following year (1628). For the management and working of the plan there were appointed an admiral, vice-admiral, chipman, under-chipman, assistants, and commissaries; also a body of soldiers duly officered.

But when these arrangements were now in full progress, and duly provided for, the German war and the king's death occurred, which caused this important work to he laid aside. The Trading Company was dissolved, its subscriptions nullified, and the whole project seemed about to die with the king. But, just as it appeared to be at its end, it received new life. Another Hollander, by the name of PETFR MENEWE, sometimes called MENUET made his appearance in Sweden. He had been in the service of Holland in America, where he became involved in difficulties with the officers of their Rest India Company, in consequence of which lie was recalled home and dismissed from their service. But he was not discouraged by this, and went over to Sweden, where he renewed the representations which Usselinx had formerly made in regard to the excellence of the country and the advantages that Sweden might derive from it.

Queen Christina, who succeeded her royal father in the government, was glad to have the project thus renewed. The royal chancellor, Count Axel Oxenstierna, understood well how to put it in operation. He took the West India Trading Company into his own hands, as its president, and encouraged other noblemen to take shares in it. King Charles I of England had already, in the year 1631, upon representations made to him by John Oxenstierna, at that time Swedish ambassador in London, renounced, in favor of the Swedes, all claims and pretensions of the English to that country, growing out of their rights as its first discoverers. Hence everything seemed to be settled upon a firm foundation, and all earnestness was employed in the prosecution of the plans for a colony.

As a good beginning, the first colony was sent off; and Peter Menewe was placed over it, as being best acquainted in those regions. They set sail from Götheborg, in a ship-of-war called the *Key of Colmar*, followed by a smaller vessel bearing the name of the *Bird Griffin*, both laden with people, provisions, ammunition, and merchandise, suitable for traffic and gifts to the Indians. The ships successfully reached their place of destination. The high expectations which our emigrants had of that new land were well met by the first views which they lead of it. They made their first landing on the bay or entrance to the river Poutaxat, which they called the river of New Sweden; and the place where they landed they called *Paradise Point*.

A purchase of land was immediately made from the Indians; and it was determined that all the land on the western side of the river, from the point called Cape Inlopen or Hinlopen, up to the fall called Santickan, and all the country inland, as much is was ceded, should belong to the Swedish crown forever. Posts were driven into the ground as landmarks, which were still seen in their places sixty years afterwards. A deed was driven up for the land thus purchased.

This was written in Dutch, because no Swede was yet able to interpret the language of the heathen. The Indians subscribed their hands and marks. The writing was sent home to Sweden to be preserved in the royal archives. Mans Kling was the surveyor. He laid out the land and made a map of the whole river, with its tributaries, islands, and points, which is still to be found in the royal archives in Sweden. Their clergyman was Reorus Torkillus of East Gothland.

The first abode of the newly arrived emigrants was at a place called by the Indians Hopokahacking. There, in the year 1638, Peter Menuet built a fortress which he named Fort Christina, after the reigning queen of Sweden. The place, situated upon the west side of the river, was probably chosen so as to be out of the way of the Hollanders, who claimed the eastern side, a measure of prudence, until the arrival of a greater force from Sweden. The fort was built upon an eligible site, not far from the mouth of the creek, so as to secure them in the navigable water of the Maniquas, which was afterwards called Christina Kihl, or creek.

The country was wild and uninhabited by the Hollanders. They had had two or three forts on the river—Fort Nassau, where Gloucester now stands, and another at Horekihl, down on the bay. But both of these were entirely destroyed by the Americans, and their occupants driven away. The following extract from the History of the New Netherlands, which Adrian van der Donck published in the year 1655, with the license and privilege as well of the States-General as of the Nest India Company, will serve as proof of what we have said.

"The place is called Hore-kihl, but why so called we know not. But this is certain: that some years back, before the English and the Swedes came hither, it was taken up and settled as a colony by Hollanders, the arms of the States being at the same time set up in brass. These arms having been pulled down by the villany of the Indians, the commissary there resident demanded that the head of the traitor should be delivered to him. The Indians, unable to escape in any other way, brought him the head, which was accepted as a sufficient atonement of their offence. But some time afterwards, when we were at work in the fields, and unsuspicious of danger, the Indians came as friends, surrounded the Hollanders with overwhelming numbers, fell upon them, and completely exterminated them. Thus was the colony destroyed, though sealed with blood, and dearly enough purchased."

Notwithstanding all this, the Hollanders believed that they had the best right to the Delaware River; yea, a better right than the Indians themselves. It was their object to secure at least all the land lying between said river and their city of New Amsterdam, where was their stronghold, and which country they once called "The New Netherlands." But, as their forces were still too weak, they always kept one or another of their people upon the east side of the river to watch those who might visit the country. As soon, therefore, as Menuet landed with his Swedish company, notice of the fact was given to the Director-General of the Hollanders in New Amsterdam. He waited for some time, until he could ascertain Menuet's purpose; but, when it appeared that he was erecting a fortress for the Swedes, he sent him the following protest:

Thursday, May 6, 1638.

"I, William Kieft, Director-General of the New Netherlands, residing upon the island of Manhattan, in the Fort Amsterdam, under the government belonging to the High and Mighty States-General of the United Netherlands, and the West India Company, chartered by the Council Chamber in Amsterdam, make known to you, Peter Menuet, who style yourself Commander in the service of Her Royal Majesty, the Queen of Sweden, that the whole South River of the New Netherlands, both above and below, hath already, for many years, been our property, occupied by our forts, and sealed with our blood, which was also done when you were in service in the New Netherlands, and you are, therefore, well aware of this. But whereas you have now come among our forts to build a fortress to our injury and damage, which we shall never permit; as we are also assured that Her Royal Majesty of Sweden has never given you authority to build forts upon our rivers and coasts, nor to settle people on the land, nor to traffic in peltries, or to undertake anything to our injury: We do, therefore, protest against all the disorder and injury, and all the evil consequences of bloodshed, uproar, and wrong which our Trading Company may thus suffer: And that we shall protect our rights in such manner as we may find most advisable." Then follows the usual conclusion.

In his History of the New Netherlands, already cited, Adrian van der Donck likewise relates how protest was made against the building of Fort Christina; but there, also, he gives evidence of the weakness of the Hollanders in the river, on the first arrival of the Swedes, and that their strength consisted almost entirely in great words.

"On the river," he says, "lies, first, Maniqua's Kihl, where the Swedes have built Fort Christina, where the largest ships can load and unload at the shore. There is another place on the river called Schulkihl, which is also navigable. That, also, was formerly under the control of the Hollanders, but is now mostly under the government of the Swedes. In that river (Delaware) there are various islands and other places, formerly belonging to the Hollanders, whose name they still bear, which sufficiently shows that the river belongs to the Hollanders, and not to the Swedes. Their very commencement will convict them. Before the year 1638, one Minnewits, who had formerly acted as director for the Trading Company at Manhatans, came into the river in the ship *Key of Colmar*, and the yacht called the *Bird Griffin*. He gave out to the Hollander, Mr. van der Nederhorst, the agent of the

West India Company in the South River, that he was on a voyage to the West India Islands, and that he was staying there to take in wood and water. Whereupon said Hollander allowed him to go free. But, some time after, some of our people going thither found him still there, and he had planted a garden, and the plants were growing in it. In astonishment eve asked the reasons for such procedure, and if he intended to stay there. To which he answered evasively, alleging various excuses for his conduct. The third time they found them settled and building a fort. Then we saw their purpose. As soon as he was informed of it, Director Kieft protested against it, but in vain."

Thus Peter Menuet made a good beginning for the settlement of the Swedish colony in America. He guarded his little fort for over three years, and the Hollanders neither attempted nor were able to overthrow it. After some years of faithful service he died at Christina. In his place followed Peter Hollendare, a native Swede, who did not remain at the mead of its affairs more than a year and a half. He returned home to Sweden, and was a major at Skepsholm, in Stockholm, in the year 1655.

The second emigration took place under Lieutenant Colonel JOHN PRINTZ, who went out with the appointment of Governor of New Sweden. He had a grant of four hundred six dollars for his travelling expenses, and one thousand two hundred dollars silver as his annual salary. The Company was invested with the exclusive privilege of importing tobacco into Sweden, although that article was even then regarded as unnecessary and injurious, although indispensable since the establishment of the bad habit of its use. Upon the same occasion was also sent out Magister John Campanius Holm, who was called by their excellencies the Royal Council and Admiral Claes Flemming, to become the government chaplain, and watch over the Swedish congregation.

The ship on which they sailed was called the "Fama." It went from Stockholm to Götheborg, and there took in its freight. Along with this went two other ships of the line, the *Swan* and the *Charitas*, laden with people, and other necessaries. Under Governor Printz, ships came to the colony in three distinct voyages. The first ship was the *Black Cat*, with ammunition, and merchandise for the Indians. Next, the ship *Swan*, on a second voyage, with emigrants, in the year 1647. Afterwards, two other ships, called the *Key* and *The Lamp*. During these times the clergymen, Mr. Lawrence Charles Lockenius and Mr. Israel Holgh, were sent out to the colony. The instructions for the governor were as follows:—

Instructions, according to which Her Royal Majesty, our Most Gracious Queen, will have the Lieutenant Colonel, now also the appointed governor over New Sweden, the noble and well-born JOHN PRINTZ, to regulate himself as well during his voyage as upon his arrival in that country. Given at Stockholm, the 15th of August, 1642.

. . . Inasmuch as some of the subjects of Her Royal Majesty and of the crown of Sweden have, for some time past, undertaken to sail to the coasts of the Rest Indies, and have already succeeded in conquering and purchasing a considerable tract of land, and in promoting commerce, with the especial object of extending the jurisdiction and greatness of Her Royal Majesty and of the Swedish crown, and have called the country NEW SWEDEN; wherefore and inasmuch as Her Royal Majesty approves and finds this their undertaking and voyaging not only laudable in itself, but reasonable, and likely, in the course of time, to benefit and strengthen Her Royal Majesty and the Swedish throne: so has Her Royal Majesty, for the promotion of that work and for the assistance of those who participate therein, furnished them for the making of that important voyage, and also for the confirming and strengthening of that important work thus begun in New Sweden, for said voyage, two ships, named the *Fama* and the *Swan*, as well as some other means necessary thereto, under a certain Governor, whom Her Majesty has provided with sufficient and necessary powers, having thereunto appointed and legitimated Lieutenant Colonel John Printz, whom she has, accordingly, seen good to instruct upon the points following.

2. The ships above named having proceeded to Götheborg, John Printz, the Governor of New Sweden, shall now, without any delay, take his departure to said place, so arranging his journey by land that he may reach there by the first opportunity. Going down to Götheborg, he shall assist in ordering and arranging everything in the best manner possible, and especially in accordance with the best regulations that the members of the company can have made; and as concerns his own person, and that of his attendants, he shall so arrange his affairs that he may immediately, in the month of September next following, set sail from this country and proceed to sea.

3. But either before, or at the time when the ships are about to set sail from Götheborg, the Governor shall consult with the skippers and officers of the ships, considering and deciding, according to the state of the wind and other circumstances, whether he shall direct his course to the north of Scotland, or through the channel between France and England.

4. Under Way, and on the journey, he must see to it that the officers and people of the ships perform their duties at sea truly and faithfully; and in all important and serious matters he can always avail himself of the aid and counsel of the persons aforesaid, who usually form the council of a ship; he shall also have every important occurrence carefully noted, causing a correct log or journal thereof to be kept, of which, also, he shall, by every opportunity, send hither a correct copy.

5. The Governor, God willing, having arrived in New Sweden, he must, for his better information, bear in mind that the boundaries of the country of which our subjects have taken possession extend, in virtue of the articles of the contract entered into with the wild inhabitants of the country, as its rightful lords, from the seacoast at Cape Hinlopen, upwards along the west side of Godin's Bay, and so up the Great South River, onwards to Minque's Pil, where Fort Christina is built, and thence still farther along the South River, and up to a place which the wild inhabitants call Sankikans, where the farthest boundaries of New Sweden are to be found. This tract or district of country extends in length about thirty (30) German miles; but in breadth, and into the interior, it is, in and by tile contract, conditioned that Her Royal Majesty's subjects, and the participants in this Company of navigators, may hereafter occupy as much land as they may desire.

6. Recently, and in the year last past—viz., 1641—several English families, probably amounting to sixty persons in all, settled, and begun to build and cultivate the land elsewhere, namely, upon the east side of the above-mentioned South River, on a little stream named Ferken's Kil; so have also the above-named subjects of Her Majesty, and participants in the Company, purchased for themselves of the wild inhabitants of the country the whole of this eastern side of the river, from the mouth of the aforesaid great river at Cape May up to a stream named Narraticen's Kil, which tract extends about twelve (12) German miles, including also the said Ferken's Kil, with the intention of thus drawing to themselves the English aforesaid. This purchase the Governor shall always, with all his power, keep intact, and thus bring these families under the jurisdiction and government of Her Royal Majesty and the Swedish crown; especially as we are informed that they themselves are not indisposed thereto; and should they be induced, as a free people, voluntarily to submit themselves to a government which can maintain and protect them, it is believed that they might shortly amount to some hundred strong. But, however that may be, the Governor is to seek to bring these English under the government of the Swedish crown, inasmuch as Her Royal Majesty finds it to be thus better for herself and the crown as partners in this undertaking; and they might also, with good reason, be driven out and away from said place; therefore Her most Royal Majesty aforesaid will most graciously leave it to the on of Governor Printz so to consider and act in the premises as can be done with propriety and success.

7. There is no doubt that the Holland West India Company will seek to appropriate to themselves the place aforesaid, and the large tract of land upon which the English have settled, and the whole of the above-named east side of the Great South River, and that so much the rather as their fort or fortification of Nassau, which they have manned with about twenty (20) men, is not very far therefrom, upon the same eastern side of the river; just as they also make pretensions to the whole western side of the aforesaid South River, and, consequently, to all that of which our subjects aforesaid have taken possession, which they have seized, relying upon their Fort Nassau, whereby they would take possession of the whole South River, and of the whole country situated upon both sides of the same river. It is for this that they have protested against the beginning which her before-mentioned Majesty's subjects have made in settling and building; and, so far as they could, have always opposed and sought to prevent our people from going up the South River and past their Fort Nassau. Therefore shall the Governor take measures for meeting the agents and participants of said Holland West India Company in a proper manner; and with mildness, but firmly, remonstrate, and make known to them the upright intentions of Her Royal Majesty and her subjects in the premises, that nothing has herein been sought, or is now sought, other than a free opening for commerce; that Her Royal Majesty's subjects have, in a just and regular manner, purchased of the proper owners and possessors of the country that district of which they have taken possession, and which they have begun to cultivate; and that they cannot, therefore, without injustice, oppose Her Royal Majesty or her subjects, or seek to disturb them in their possessions without doing them great injury. But should the same Holland Company, contrary to all better hopes, allow themselves to undertake any hostility, or make any attack, then, in such case, it will only be proper to be prepared with the best means that circumstances will allow, and so seek to repel force by force; therefore, as this, like everything else, is best judged of and decided on the ground, so also does Her Royal Majesty place it in the Governor's discretion to meet such vexations, in the first instance, with kind admonitions, but, if these are not effective, then with severity, according to the best of his understanding, so as to arrange everything to the best advantage and honor alike of Her Royal Majesty and the members of the Company. But if no such troubles arise, which it is hoped will be the case, and Her Royal Majesty and her subjects remain undisturbed in that which they have rightfully brought into their possession, then shall the Governor hold good friendship and neighborhood with the aforesaid Hollanders at Fort Nassau, and with those who dwell upon the North River at Mankatan's, or New Amsterdam, as also with the English who dwell in the country of Virginia, and make no inroads upon any of them, nor interfere with that of which they are in the actual possession. Especially, since the adjacent English in Virginia have already commenced to offer Her Royal

Majesty's subjects in New Sweden all kinds of useful assistance, and to let them procure, upon reasonable payment, such cattle and seed-corn as they may desire; therefore shall the Governor continually seek to give free and undisturbed course to the correspondence and commerce thus begun with the English, to the use and benefit of Her Royal Majesty's subjects aforesaid.

8. Those Hollanders who have emigrated to New Sweden, and settled there under the protection of Her Royal Majesty and the Swedish crown, over whom Jost von deco Boyandh has command, the Governor shall treat, according to the contents of the charter and privileges conferred by Her Royal Majesty, of the principles whereof the Governor has been advised; but in other respects he shall show them all good-will and kindness, yet so that he shall hold them also to the same, that they, also, upon their side, comply with the requisitions of their charter which they have received. And inasmuch as notice has already been given them that they have settled too near to Fort Christina, and as houses are said to be built at the distance of almost three miles from that place, they should therefore leave that place, and betake themselves to a somewhat greater distance from the said fort. So also does Her Royal Majesty leave it to the good pleasure and prudence of the Governor, when on the ground, duly to consider the deportment of said Hollanders and the situation of the place of which they have taken possession; and, according to his judgment, either let them remain there quietly or make such a disposition and settlement of the matter as lie shall find most suitable and advantageous to Her Royal Majesty and the participants in said Company of navigation.

9. The wild nations, bordering upon all other sides, the Governor shall understand how to treat with all humanity and respect, that no violence or wrong be done to them by Her Royal Majesty or her subjects aforesaid; but he shall rather, at every opportunity, exert himself that the same wild people may gradually be instructed in the truths and worship of the Christian religion and in other Ways brought to civilization and good government, and in this manner properly guided. Especially shall he seek to gain their confidence, and impress upon their minds that neither he, the Governor, nor his people and subordinates are come into those parts to do them any wrong or injury, but much more for the purpose of furnishing them with such things as they may need for the ordinary wants of life; and so, also, for such things as are found among them which they themselves cannot make for their own use, or buy, or exchange. Therefore shall the Governor also see thereto that the people of Her Royal Majesty, or of the Company who are engaged in trading in those parts, allow the wild people to obtain such things as they need, at a price somewhat more moderate than they are getting them of the Hollanders at Fort Nassau, or the adjacent English; so that said wild people may be withdrawn from them, and be so much the more won to our people.

10. In regard to the Governor's place of residence, Her Royal Majesty leaves it to him to provide and choose the same according as he finds the case to be in the place, or it can be continued where it now is, and the residence arranged and ordered in the most convenient manner possible; in like manner shall the Governor also provide a suitable place for a fortress, either at Cape Henlopen or the island called "James' Island," or wherever else a good site for the same may be found: wherein he has especially to keep in view these considerations above all others, namely, that by such a fortification it should be possible to close up the South River, having it commanded by the same fortress, and that there should also be found there, without great difficulty, a suitable harbor wherein the ships of Her Royal Majesty and her subjects could be in security, and, if need so were, continue to lie there over winter.

11. And if the Governor does not find it necessary at once and hastily to fortify another new place, but can for the present properly defend himself by Fort Christina, then shall he so much the more zealously at once arrange and urge forward agriculture and the improvement of the land, setting and urging the people thereto with zeal and energy, exerting him the ground that the people may derive from it their necessary food.

12. Next to this, he shall pay the necessary attention to the culture of tobacco, and appoint thereto a certain number of laborers, so arranging that the produce may be large, more and more being set out and cultivated from time to time, so that he can send over a good quantity of tobacco on all ships coming hither.

13. That better arrangements may be made for the production of cattle, both great and small, the Governor shall at once exert himself to obtain a good breed of cattle of all kinds, and especially of that which is sent out from this country, and also seek to obtain a supply from the neighboring English, dividing everything with those who will use and employ it in agriculture in exchange for seed, and with such prudence as he shall find most serviceable to the members of the Company.

14. Among and above other things, he shall direct his attention to sheep, to obtain them of good kinds, and, as soon as may be, seek to arrange as many sheep-folds as he conveniently can, so that presently a considerable supply of wool of good quality may be sent over to this country.

15. The peltry-trade with the natives he shall, also, so far as possible, seek to sustain in a good state, exercise a careful inspection of all engaged in it, prevent all frauds in

established commissions, and take care that Her Royal Majesty and her subjects, and the members of the Company, may have reason to expect good returns for their cargoes. In like manner, he shall provide that no other persons whatever be permitted to traffic with the natives in peltries; but this trade shall be carried on only by persons thereto appointed in the name of the whole Company, and in its ways.

16. Whatever else it may at present be necessary to do in that country will be best committed to the hands of the Governor in the country, according to the circumstances of the time and place; more especially as the same land of New Sweden is situated in the same climate with Portugal; so, apparently, it is to be expected that salt-works might be arranged on the sea coasts. But, if the salt could not be perfectly evaporated by the heat of the sun, yet, at the least, the salt water might be brought to such a grade that it might afterwards be perfectly condensed by means of fire, without great labor or expense which the Governor must consider, and make such experiment, and, if possible, put it into operation and make it effective.

17. And, as almost everywhere in the forests wild grapevines and grapes are found, and the climate seems to be favorable to the production of wine, so shall the Governor also direct his thoughts to the timely introduction of this culture, and what might herein be devised and effected.

18. He can also have careful search made everywhere as to whether any metals or minerals are to be found in the country, and, if any are discovered, send hither correct information, and then await further orders from this place.

19. Out of the abundant forests, the Governor shall examine and consider how and in what manner profit may be derived from the country; especially what kind of advantages may be expected from oak-trees and walnut-trees, and whether a good quality of them might be sent over here as ballast. So also it might be examined whether oil might not be advantageously pressed out of the walnuts.

20. The Governor shall likewise take into consideration and correctly inform himself how and where fisheries might be most profitably established; especially as it is said that at a certain season of the year the whale fishery can be advantageously prosecuted in the aforesaid Godin's Bay, and adjacently; lie shall therefore have an eye upon this and send over hither all needed information as to what can be done in this and other matters connected with the country, and what further hopes may be entertained in reference thereto.

21. The Governor shall also carefully inquire and inform himself in regard to the food and convenience for keeping great number of silkworms, wherewith a manufacture might be established; and, if he discovers that something useful might thus be accomplished, he shall take measures for the same.

22. Whatever else could be done in connection with the successful cultivation of the land, but cannot be introduced just for the present, this Her Royal Majesty will graciously have entrusted to the fidelity, foresight, and zeal of the Governor, with the earnest command and admonition that he seek in all matters to uphold the service and dignity of Her Royal Majesty and the crown of Sweden, as also to promote the advantage and interest of the members of the Company, in the conservation of the same land of New Sweden, its culture in every way possible, and the increase of its profitable commerce.

23. But, far above all this, as to what belongs to the political government and administration of justice, everything of this kind must be conducted under the name of Her Royal Majesty and the crown of Sweden, for no less reason than that the country enjoys the protection of Her Royal Majesty and of the crown, and that the interest of the crown is in the highest degree involved in the protection of that country, its cultivation, and active trade and commerce. To give the Governor specific information herein cannot so well and effectually be done at so great a distance; it must therefore be left to his own discretion and good sense that lie upon the ground provide, arrange, and execute whatever conduces to bring matters into good order and a proper constitution, according as he finds the necessities of the time and place to require. At first, and until matters can be brought into a better form, the Governor may use his own seal, but in a somewhat larger form, in briefs, contracts, correspondence, and other written documents of a public character.

24. He shall decide all matters of controversy which may arise, according to Swedish law and right, custom and usage; but in all other matters, also, so far as possible, he shall adopt and employ the laudable customs, habits, and usages of this most praiseworthy realm.

25. He shall also have power, through the necessary and proper means of compulsion, to bring to obedience and a quiet life the turbulent and disorderly, who will not live quietly and peacefully, and especially gross offenders, who may possibly be found; he may punish, not only with imprisonment and the like duly proportioned means of correction, but, also, according to their misdeeds or crimes, with the loss of life itself, yet not in any other than the usual manner, and after the proper hearing and consideration of the case, with the most

respectable people and the most prudent associate judges who can be found in the country as his counsellors.

26. Above all things, shall the Governor consider and see to it that a true and due worship, becoming honor, laud, and praise be paid to the Most High God in all things, and to that end all proper care shall be taken that divine service be zealously performed, according to the unaltered Augsburg Confession, the Council of Upsala, and the ceremonies of the Swedish Church; and all persons, but especially the young, shall be duly instructed in the articles of their Christian faith; and all good church discipline shall, in like manner, be duly exercised and received. But so far as relates to the Holland colonists that live and settle under the government of Her Royal Majesty and the Swedish crown, the Governor shall not disturb them in the indulgence granted them as to the exercise of the Reformed religion according to the aforesaid Royal Charter.

27. In all else which cannot here be set down in writing, the Governor shall conduct himself as is suitable and becoming to a faithful patriot, and take into due consideration whatever is correspondent to his office, according to the best of his understanding and with the greatest zeal and care, also regulating himself in accordance with that which may be here communicated to him by word of mouth; and there is herewith given him a special list of the people who accompany him, and of the means and equipment of his office.

28. Finally, Her Royal Majesty is also well satisfied that the said office of his government shall continue and exist for three years, after the lapse of which he, the said John Printz, shall be free to return hither again, after the necessary arrangements have been made in regard to his successor, or some substitute in the said service. Should he, the said John Printz, have a desire to continue longer in this charge, he shall have the preference over others therefor, provided that the advantage and service of Her Majesty and the crown, and of the Company, so demand. Given as above.

PAEHR BRAHE,
HERMAN WRANGEL,
CLAES FLEMMING,
AXEL OXENSTIERNA,
GABRIEL BENGTSSON OXENSTEIRNA
AND. GYLLENKLOU.

The voyage to New Sweden was at that time quite long. The watery way to the West was not yet well discovered, and, therefore, for fear of the sand-banks off Newfoundland, they kept their course to the east and south as far as to what were then called the Brazates. The ships which went under the command of Governor Printz sailed along the coast of Portugal, and down the coast of Africa, until they found the eastern passage, then directly over to America, leaving the Canaries high up to the north. They landed at Antigua, then continued their voyage northward, past Virginia and Maryland, to Cape Hinlopen. Yet, in view of the astonishingly long route which they took, the voyage was quick enough in . . . from Stockholm on August 16, 1642, to the new fort of Christina, in New Sweden, on February 15, 1643.

The Swedes who emigrated to America belonged partly to a trading company, provided with a charter, who, for their services, according to their condition or agreement, were to receive pay and monthly wages; a part of them also went at their own impulse to try their fortune. For these it was free to settle and live in the country as long as they pleased or to leave it, and they were therefore, by way of distinction from the others, called freemen. At first, also, malefactors and vicious people were sent over, who were used as slaves to labor upon the fortifications. They were kept in chains and not ale [allowed] intercourse With the other settlers; moreover, a separate place of abode was assigned to them. The neighboring people and country were dissatisfied that such wretches should come into the colony. It was also, in fact, very objectionable in regard to the heathen, who might be greatly offended by it. Whence it happened that, when such persons came over in Governor Printz's time, it was not permitted that one of them should set foot upon the shore, but they had all to be carried back again, whereupon a great part of them died during the voyage or perished in some other way. Afterwards it was forbidden at home in Sweden, under a penalty, to take for the American voyage any persons of bad fame; nor was there ever any lack of good people for the colony.

Governor Printz was now in a position to put the government upon a safe footing to maintain the rights of the Swedes, and to put down the attempts of the Hollanders. They had lately, before his arrival, pitched their little Fort Nassau. On this account he selected the island of Tenackong as his residence, which is sometimes also called Tutaeaenung and Tenicko, about three Swedish miles from Fort Christina. The convenient situation of the place suggested its selection, as also the location of Fort Nassau, which lay some miles over against it, to which he could thus command the passage by water. The new fort, which was erected and provided with considerable armament, was called New Götheborg. His place of residence, which he adorned with orchards, gardens, a pleasure-house, etc., he named Printz Hall. A handsome wooden church was also built at the same place, which Alagister Campanius consecrated, on the last great prayer-day which was celebrated in New Sweden, on the 4th of September, 1646. Upon that place also all the most prominent freemen had their residences and plantations.

Source: "The Founding of New Sweden," in *Old South Leaflets,* Vol. IV (Boston: Directors of the Old South Work, Old South Meeting House, 1898).

Pennsylvania Charter of Privileges (1701)

William Penn, proprietor of an extensive land grant called Pennsylvania, gave the colonists a new frame of government through the 1701 charter of privileges. This charter increased the powers of the general assembly, setting the stage for self-government. It secured the rights of the accused to representation and was the colony's equivalent of the Magna Carta, guaranteeing religious liberty in Pennsylvania. The charter remained in force until it was replaced by the state constitution in 1776. What we know as the Liberty Bell was cast to commemorate the fiftieth anniversary of this charter of privileges.

[28 October 1701]

William Penn Proprietary and Governour of the Province of Pennsilvania and Territories thereunto belonging To all to whom these presents shall come Sendeth Greeting.

WHEREAS King Charles the Second by his Letters Patents under the Great Seale of England beareing Date the fourth day of March in the Yeare one thousand, Six hundred and Eighty was Graciously pleased to Give and Grant unto me my heires and Assignes forever this Province of Pennsilvania with divers great powers and Jurisdictions for the well Governement thereof.

AND WHEREAS the King's dearest Brother James Duke of York and Albany &c by his Deeds of Feofment under his hand and Seale duely perfected beareing date the twenty fourth day of August one thousand Six hundred Eighty and two Did Grant unto me my heires and Assignes All that Tract of Land now called the Territories of Pennsilvania together with powers and Jurisdictions for the good Govern-ment thereof.

AND WHEREAS for the Encouragement of all the Freemen and Planters that might be concerned in the said Province and Territories and for the good Governement thereof I the said William Penn in the yeare one thousand Six hundred Eighty and three for me my heires and Assignes Did Grant and Confirme unto all the Freeman Planters and Adventurers therein Divers Liberties Franchises and properties as by the said Grant Entituled the Frame of the Government of the Province of Pensilvania and Territories thereunto belonging in America may Appeare which Charter or Frame being found in Some parts of it not soe Suitable to the present Circumstances of the Inhabitants was in the third Month in the yeare One thousand Seven hundred Delivered up to me by Six parts of Seaven of the Freemen of this Province and Territories in Generall Assembly mett provision being made in the said Charter for that End and purpose.

AND WHEREAS I was then pleased to promise that I would restore the said Charter to them againe with necessary Alterations or in liew thereof Give them another better adapted to Answer the present Circumstances and Conditions of the said Inhabitants which they have now by theire Representatives in a Generall Assembly mett at Philadelphia requested me to Grant.

KNOW YE THEREFORE that for the further well being and good Governement of the said Province and Territories and in pursuance of the Rights and Powers before mencioned I the said William Penn doe Declare Grant and Confirme unto all the Freemen Planters and Adventurers and other Inhabitants in this Province and Territories these following Liberties Franchises and Priviledges soe far as in me lyeth to [be] held Enjoyed and kept by the Freemen Planters and Adventurers and other Inhabitants of and in the said Province and Territories thereunto Annexed for ever.

FIRST Because noe people can be truly happy though under the Greatest Enjoyments of Civil Liberties if Abridged of the Freedom of theire Consciences as to theire Religious Profes-sion and Worship. And Almighty God being the only Lord of Conscience Father of Lights and Spirits and the Author as well as Object of all divine knowledge Faith and Worship who only [can] Enlighten the mind and perswade and Con-vince the understandings of people.

I doe hereby Grant and Declare that noe person or persons Inhabiting in this Province or Territories who shall Confesse and Acknowledge one Almighty God the Creator upholder and Ruler of the world and professe him or them-selves Obliged to live quietly under the Civill Governement shall be in any case molested or prejudiced in his or theire person or Estate because of his or theire Conscientious perswasion or practice nor be compelled to frequent or mentaine any Religious Worship place or Ministry contrary to his or theire mind or doe or Suffer any other act or thing contrary to theire Religious perswasion.

And that all persons who also professe to beleive in Jesus Christ the Saviour of the world shall be capable (notwithstanding theire other perswasions and practices in point of Conscience and Religion) to Serve this Governement in any capacity both Legislatively and Executively he or they Solemnly promiseing when lawfully required Allegiance to the King as Soveraigne and fidelity to the Proprietary and Governour.

And takeing the Attests as now Establisht by the law made at Newcastle in the yeare One thousand Seven hundred Intituled an Act directing the Attests of Severall Officers and Ministers as now amended and Confirmed this present Assembly.

SECONDLY For the well Governeing of this Province and Territories there shall be an Assembly yearly Chosen by the Freemen thereof to Consist of foure persons out of each County of most note for Virtue wisdome and Ability (Or of a greater number at any time as the Governour and Assembly shall agree) upon the first day of October forever And shall Sitt on the Fourteenth day of the said Month in Philadelphia unless the Governour and Councell for the time being shall See cause to appoint another place within the said Province or Territories. Which Assembly shall have power to choose a Speaker and other theire Officers and shall be judges of the Qualifications and Elections of theire owne Members Sitt upon theire owne Adjournments, Appoint Committees prepare Bills in or to pass into Laws Impeach Criminalls and Redress Greivances and shall have all other Powers and Priviledges of an Assembly according to the Rights of the Freeborne Subjects of England and as is usuall in any of the Kings Plantations in America.

And if any County or Counties shall refuse or neglect to choose theire respective Representatives as aforesaid or if chosen doe not meet to Serve in Assembly those who are soe chosen and mett shall have the full power of an Assembly in as ample manner as if all the representatives had beene chosen and mett Provided they are not less then two thirds of the whole number that ought to meet.

And that the Qualifications of Electors and Elected and all other matters and things Relateing to Elections of Representatives to Serve in Assemblies though not herein perticulerly Exprest shall be and remaine as by a Law of this Government made at Newcastle in the Yeare One thousand [Seven] hundred Intituled An act to ascertaine the number of members of assembly and to Regulate the elections.

THIRDLY That the Freemen [in Ea]ch Respective County at the time and place of meeting for Electing [th]eire Representatives to serve in Assembly may as often as there shall be Occasion choose a Double number of persons to present to the Governour for Sheriffes and Coroners to Serve for three Yeares if they Soe long behave themselves well out of which respective Elections and Presentments the Governour shall nominate and Commissionate one for each of the said Officers the third day after Such Presentment or else the first named in Such Presentment for each Office as aforesaid shall Stand and Serve in that Office for the time before respectively Limitted.

And in case of Death and Default Such Vacancies shall be Supplyed by the Governour to serve to the End of the said Terme Provided allwayes that if the said Freemen shall at any time neglect or decline to choose a person or persons for either or both the aforesaid Offices then and in Such case the persons that are or shall be in the respective Offices of Sheriffes or Coroner at the time of Election shall remaine therein untill they shall be removed by another Election as aforesaid.

And that the Justices of the respective Counties shall or may nominate and present to the Governour three persons to Serve for Clerke of the Peace for the said County when there is a vacancy, one of which the Governour shall Commissionate within Tenn dayes after Such Pressentment or else the first Nominated shall Serve in the said Office dureing good behaviour.

FOURTHLY That the Laws of this Government shall be in this Stile Vizt "By the Governour with the Consent and Approbation of the Freemen in Generall Assembly mett" And shall be after Confirmation by the Governour forthwith Recorded in the Rolls Office and kept at Philadelphia unless the Governour and Assembly shall Agree to appoint another place.

FIFTHLY that all Criminalls shall have the same Priviledges of Wittnesses and Councill as theire Prosecutors.

SIXTHLY That noe person or persons shall or may at any time hereafter be obliged to answer any Complaint matter or thing whatsoever relateing to Property before the Governour and Councill or in any other place but in the Ordinary courts of Justice unless Appeales thereunto shall be hereafter by law appointed.

SEVENTHLY That noe person within this Governement shall be Licensed by the Governour to keep Ordinary Taverne or house of publick entertainment but Such who are first recommended to him under the hands of the Justices of the respective Counties Signed in open Court which Justices are and shall be hereby Impowred to Suppress and forbid any person keeping Such publick house as aforesaid upon theire Misbehaviour on such penalties as the law doth or shall Direct and to recommend others from time to time as they shall see occasion.

EIGHTHLY If any person through Temptation or Melancholly shall Destroy himselfe his Estate Reall and personall shall notwithstanding Descend to his wife and Children or Relations as if he had dyed a Naturall Death. And if any person shall be Destroyed or kill'd by casualty or Accident there shall be noe forfeiture to the Governour by reason thereof And noe Act Law or Ordinance whatsoever shall at any time hereafter be made or done to Alter Change or Diminish the forme or Effect of this Charter or of any part or Clause therein Contrary to the True intent and meaning thereof without the Consent of the Governour for the [time being and] six parts of Seven of the Assembly [mett].

But because the happiness of Mankind Depends So much upon the Enjoying of Libertie of theire Consciences as aforesaid I Doe hereby Solemnly Declare Promise and Grant for me my heires and Assignes that the first Article of this Charter Relateing to Liberty of Conscience and every part and Clause therein according to the True Intent and meaneing thereof shall be kept and remaine without any Alteration Inviolably for ever.

AND LASTLY I the said William Penn Proprietary and Governour of the Province of Pensilvania and Territories thereunto, belonging for my Selfe my heires and Assignes Have Solemnly Declared Granted and Confirmed And doe hereby Solemnly Declare Grant and Confirme that neither I my heires or Assignes shall procure or doe any thing or things whereby the Liberties in this Charter contained and expressed nor any part thereof shall be Infringed or broken And if any thing shall be procured or done by any person or persons contrary to these presents it shall be held of noe force or Effect.

IN WITTNES WHEREOF I the said William Penn at Philadelphia in Pensilvania have unto this present Charter of Liberties Sett my hand and Broad Seale this twenty Eighth day of October in the Yeare of our Lord one thousand Seven hundred and one being the thirteenth yeare of the Reigne of King William the Third over England Scotland France and Ireland &c And in the Twenty first Yeare of my Government.

AND NOTWITHSTANDING the closure and Test of this present Charter as aforesaid I think fitt to add this following Provisoe thereunto as part of the same That is to say that notwithstanding any Clause or Clauses in the above mencioned Charter obligeing the Province and Territories to Joyne Together in Legislation I am Content and doe hereby Declare That if the representatives of the Province and Territories shall not hereafter Agree to Joyne togather in Legislation and that the same shall be Signifyed to me or my Deputy In open Assembly or otherwise from under the hands and Seales of the Representatives (for the time being) of the Province or Territories or the Major part of either of them any time within three yeares from the Date hereof That in Such case the Inhabitants of each o' the three Counties of this Province shall not have less then Eight persons to represent them in Assembly for the Province and the Inhabitants of the Towne of Philadelphia (when the said Towne is Incorporated). Two persons to represent them in Assembly and the Inhabitants of each County in the Territories shall have as many persons to represent them in a Distinct Assembly for the Territories as shall be requested by them as aforesaid. Notwithstanding which Seperation of the Province and Territories in Respect of Legislation I doe hereby promise Grant and Declare that the Inhabitants of both Province and Territories shall Seperately Injoy all other Liberties Priviledges and Benefitts granted Joyntly to them in this Charter Any law usage or Custome of this Governement heretofore made and Practised or any law made and Passed by this Generall Assembly to the Contrary hereof Notwithstanding.

Wm Penn

Edwd. Shippen
Phineas Pemberton
Sam. Carpenter Propry and
Griffith Owen Governours Council
Caleb Pusey Tho. Story

Endorsed: This Charter of priviledges being Distinctly read in Assembly & the whole & Every part thereof being Approved of and Agreed to by us. Wee do Thankfully receive the Same from our proprietary & Governour At Philadelphia this Twenty Eighth day of October 1701. Further endorsed: Signed on behalf and by order of the Assembly per Jos. Growdon Speaker.

Source: Recorded in the Rolls Office at Philadelphia in Patent Book A, Vol. 2, the 31st 8mo 1701. Miscellaneous Manuscript Collection, Quaker Information Center, Philadelphia, 125–29.

The Journal of Sarah Kemble Knight (1704)

Sarah Kemble Knight, a Boston widow, traveled on business to New York City in 1704. She kept a journal of her adventures over a five-month period, relating her use of guides, her dangerous travels over land and water, her accommodations, and her observations of various towns along the way. She comments, for example, on the rigidity of punishment exacted in the colony of Connecticut and makes comparisons in the Sabbath observances in Boston and New York.

MONDAY, Oct[o]b[e]r ye 2d, 1704.—About three o'clock afternoon, I begun my Journey from Boston to New-Haven; being about two Hundred Mile. My Kinsman, Capt. Robert Luist, waited on me as farr as Dedham, where I was to meet ye Western post.

I vissitted the Reverd. Mr. Belcher, ye Minister of ye town, and tarried there till evening, in hopes ye post would come along. But he not coming, I resolved to go to Billingses where he used to lodg, being 12 miles further. But being ignorant of the way, Madm Billings, seing no persuasions of her good spouses or hers could prevail with me to Lodg there that night, Very kindly went wyth me to ye Tavern, where I hoped to get my guide, And desired the Hostess to inquire of her guests whether any of them would go with mee. But they being tyed by the Lipps to a pewter engine, scarcely allowed themselves time to say what clownish. . . .

[Here half a page of the MS. is gone.]

. . . Peices of eight, I told her no, I would not be accessary to such extortion.

Then John shan't go, sais shee. No, indeed, shan't hee; And held forth at that rate a long time, that I began to fear I was got among the Quaking tribe, beleeving not a Limbertong'd sister among them could out do Madm. Hostes.

Upon this, to my no small surprise, son John arrose, and gravely demanded what I would give him to go with me? Give you, sais I, are you John? Yes, says he, for want of a Better; And behold! this John look't as old as my Host, and perhaps had bin a man in the last Century. Well, Mr. John, sais I, make your demands. Why, half a pss. of eight and a dram, sais John. I agreed, and gave him a Dram (now) in hand to bind the bargain.

My hostess catechis'd John for going so cheep, saying his poor wife would break her heart. . . .

[Here another half page of the MS. is gone.]

. . . His shade on his Hors resembled a Globe on a Gate post. His habitt, Hors and furniture, its looks and goings Incomparably answered the rest.

Thus jogging on with an easy pace, my Guide telling mee it was dangero's to Ride hard in the Night, (whch his horse had the sence to avoid,) Hee entertained me with the Adventurs he had passed by late Rideing, and eminent Dangers he had escaped, so that, Remembring the Hero's in Parismus and the Knight of the Oracle, I didn't know but I had mett wth a Prince disguis'd.

When we had Ridd about an how'r, wee come into a thick swamp, wch. by Reason of a great fogg, very much startled mee, it being now very Dark. But nothing dismay'd John: Hee had encountered a thousand and a thousand such Swamps, having a Universall Knowledge in the woods; and readily Answered all my inquiries wch. were not a few.

In about an how'r, or something more, after we left the Swamp, we come to Billinges, where I was to Lodg. My Guide dismounted and very Complasantly help't me down and shewd the door, signing to me Wth his hand to Go in; wch I Gladly did—But had not gone many steps into the Room, ere I was Interogated by a young Lady I understood afterwards was the Eldest daughter of the family, with these, or words to this purpose, (viz.) Law for mee—what in the world brings You here at this time a night?—I never see a woman on the Rode so Dreadfull late, in all the days of my versall life. Who are You? Where are You going? I'me star'd out of my witts—with much now of the same Kind. I stood aghast, Prepareing to reply, when in comes my Guide—to him Madam turn'd, Roreing out: Lawfull heart, John, is it You?—how de do! Where in the world are you going with this woman? Who is she? John made no Ansr. but sat down in the corner, fumblèd out his black Junk', and saluted that instead of Debb; she then turned agen to mee and fell anew into her silly questions, without asking me to sitt down.

I told her shee treated me very Rudely, and I did not think it my duty to answer her unmannerly Questions. But

1175

to get ridd of them, I told her I come there to have the post's company with me to-morrow on my Journey, & c. Miss star'd awhile, drew a chair, bid me sitt, And then run up stairs and putts on two or three Rings, (or else I had not seen them before,) and returning, sett herself just before me, showing the way to Reding, that I might see her Ornaments, perhaps to gain the more respect. But her Granam's new Rung s sow, had it appeared, would affected me as much. I paid honest John wth money and dram according to contract, and Dismist him, and pray'd Miss to shew me where I must Lodg. Shee conducted me to a parlour in a little back Lento, wch was almost fill'd wth the bedsted, wch was so high that I was forced to climb on a chair to gitt up to ye wretched b,.d that lay on it; on wch having Stretcht my tired Limbs, and lay'd my head on a Sad-coloured pillow, I began to think on the transactions of ye past day.

Tuesday, October ye 3d, about 8 in the morning, I with the Post proceeded forward without observing any thing remarkable; And about two, on, Arrived at the Post's second stage, where the western Post mett him and exchanged Letters. Here, having called for something to eat, ye woman bro't in a Twisted thing like a cable, but something whiter; and laying it on the bord, tugg'd for life to bring it into a capacity to spread; wch having wth great pains accomplished, shee serv'd in a dish of Pork and Cabage, I suppose the remains of Dinner. The sause was of a deep Purple, wch I tho't was boil'd in her dye Kettle; the bread was Indian, and every thing on the Table service Agreeable to these. I, being hungry, gott a little down; but my stomach was soon cloy'd, and what cabbage I swallowed serv'd me for a Cudd the whole day after.

Having here discharged the Ordnary for self and Guide; (as I understood was the custom,) About Three afternoon went on with my Third Guide, who Rode very hard; and having crossed Providence Ferry, we come to a River wch they Generally Ride thro'. But I dare not venture; so the Post got a Ladd and Cannoo to carry me to tother side, and hee rid thro' and Led my hors. The Cannoo was very small and shallow, so that when we were in she seem'd redy to take in water, which greatly terrified mee, and caused me to be very circumspect, sitting with my hands fast on each side, my eyes stedy, not daring so much as to lodg my tongue a hair's breadth more on one side of my mouth then tother, nor so much as think on Lott's wife, for a wry thought would have oversett our wherey: But was soon put out of this pain, by feeling the Cannoo on shore, wch I as soon almost saluted with my feet; and Rewarding my sculler, again mounted and made the best of our way forwards. The Rode here was very even and ye day pleasant, it being now near Sunsett. But the Post told mee we had neer [?] miles to Ride to the next Stage, (where we were to Lodg.) I askt him of the rest of the Rode, foreseeing wee must travail in the night. Hee told mee there was a bad River we were to Ride thro', was so very firce a hors could sometimes hardly stem it: But it was but narrow,

and wee should soon be over. I cannot express The concern of mind this relation sett me in: no thoughts but those of the dang'ros River could entertain my Imagination, and they were as formidable as varios, still Tormenting me with blackest Ideas of my Approaching fate—Sometimes seing my self drowning, otherwhiles drowned, and at the best like a holy Sister just come out of a Spiritual Bath in dripping Garments.

Now was the Glorious Luminary, wth his swift Coursers arrived at his Stage, leaving poor me wth the rest of this part of the lower world in darkness, with which wee were soon Surrounded. The only Glimering we now had was from the spangled Skies, Whose Imperfect Reflections rendered every Object formidable. Each lifeless Trunk, with its shatter'd Limbs, appear'd an Armed Enymie; and every little stump like a Ravenous devourer. Nor could I so much as discern my Guide, when at any distance, which added to the terror.

Thus, absolutely lost in Thought, and dying with the very thoughts of drowning, I come up wth the post, who I did not see till even with his Hors: he told mee he stopt for mee; and wee Rode on Very deliberatly a few paces, when we entred a Thickett of Trees and Shrubbs, and I perceived by the Hors's going, we were on the descent of a Hill, wch, as wee come neerer the bottom,'twas totaly dark wth the Trees that surrounded it. But I knew by the Going of the Hors wee had entred the water, wch my Guide told mee was the hazzardos River he had told me off; and bee, Riding up close to my Side, Bid me not fear we should be over Imediatly. I now ralyed all the Courage I Was mistriss of, Knowing that I must either Venture my fate of drowning, or be left like ye Children in the wood. So, as the Post bid me, I gave Reins to my Nagg; and sitting as Stedy as just before in the Cannoo, in a few minutes got safe to the other side, which bee told mee was the Narragansett country.

Here We found great difficulty in Travailing, the way being very narrow, and on each side the Trees and bushes gave us very unpleasant welcomes wth their Branches and bow's, wch wee could not avoid, it being so exceeding dark. My Guide, as before so now, putt on harder than I, wth my weary bones, could follow; so left mee and the way beehind him. Now Returned my distressed aprehensions of the place where I was: the dolesome woods, my Company next to none, Going I knew not whither, and encompased wth Terrifying darkness; The least of which was enough to startle a more Masculine courage. Added to which the Reflections, as in the afternoon of ye day that my Call was very Questionable, wch till then I had not so Prudently as I ought considered. Now, coming to ye foot of a hill, I found great difficulty in ascending; But being got to the Top, was there amply recompenced with the friendly Appearance of the Kind Conductress of the night, Just then Advancing above the Horisontall Line. The Raptures wch the Sight of that fair Planett produced in mee, caused mee, for the Moment, to forgett my present wearyness and past toils; and Inspir'd me for most of the remaining way with very divirting tho'ts, some of which, with the other Occurances of the day, I reserved to note down when I should come to my Stage. My tho'ts on the sight of the moon were to this purpose:

Fair Cynthia, all the Homage that I may
Unto a Creature, unto thee I pay;
In Lonesome woods to meet so kind a guide,
To Mee's more worth than all the world beside.
Some Joy I felt just now, when safe got or'e
Yon Surly River to this Rugged shore,
Deeming Rough welcomes from these clownish Trees,
Better than Lodgings wth Nereidees.
Yet swelling fears surprise; all dark appears—
Nothing but Light can disipate those fears.
My fainting vitals can't lend strength to say,
But softly whisper, O I wish 'twere day.
The murmer hardly warma the Ambient air,
E' re thy Bright Aspect rescues from dispair:
Makes the old Hagg her sable mantle loose,
And a Bright joy do's through my Soul diffuse.
The Boistero's Trees now Lend a Passage Free,
And pleasent prospects thou giv'st light to see.

From hence wee kept on, with more ease yn before: the way being smooth and even, the night warm and serene, and the Tall and thick Trees at a distance, especially wn the moon glar'd light through the branches, fill'd my Imagination wth the pleasent delusion of a Sumpteous citty, fill'd wth famous Buildings and churches, wth their spiring steeples, Balconies, Galleries and I know not what: Granduers woh I had heard of, and wch the stories of foreign countries had given me the Idea of.

Here stood a Lofty church—there is a steeple,
And there the Grand Parade—O see the people!
That Famous Castle there, were I but nigh,
To see the mote and Bridg and walls so high—
They'r very fine! sais my deluded eye.

Being thus agreably entertained without a thou't of any thing but thoughts themselves, I on a suden was Rous'd from these pleasing Imaginations, by the Post's sounding his horn, which assured mee hee was arrived at the Stage, where we were to Lodg: and that musick was then most musickall and agreeable to mee.

Being come to mr. Havens', I was very civilly Received, and courteously entertained, in a clean comfortable House; and the Good woman was very active in helping off my Riding clothes, and then ask't what I would eat. I told her I had some Chocolett, if shee would prepare it; which with the help of some Milk, and a little clean brass Kettle, she soon effected to my satisfaction. I then betook me to my Apartment, wch was a little Room parted from the Kitchen by a single bord partition; where, after I had noted the Occurrances of the past day, I went to bed, which, tho' pretty hard, Yet neet and handsome. But I could get no sleep,

because of the Clamor of some the of Town tope-ers in next Room, Who were entred into a strong debate concerning ya Signifycation of the name of their Country, (viz.) Narragan-set. One said it was named so by ya Indians, because there grew a Brier there, of a prodigious Highth and bigness, the like hardly ever known, called by the Indians Narragansett; And quotes an Indian of so Barberous a name for his Author, that I could not write it. His Antagonist Replyed no—It was from a Spring it had its name, wch hee well knew where it was, which was extreem cold in summer, and as Hott as could be imagined in the winter, which was much resorted too by the natives, and by them called Narragansett, (Hott and Cold,) and that was the originall of their places name—with a thousand Impertinances not worth notice, wch He utter'd with such a Roreing voice and Thundering blows with the fist of wickedness on the Table, that it peirced my very head. I heartily fretted, and wish't 'um tongue tyed; but wth as little succes as a freind of mine once, who was (as shee said) kept a whole night awake, on a Jorny, by a country Left.' and a Sergent, Insigne and a Deacon, contriving how to bring a triangle into a Square. They kept calling for tother Gill, wah while they were swallowing, was some Intermission; But presently, like Oyle to fire, encreased the flame. I set my Candle on a Chest by the bed side, and setting up, fell to my old way of composing my Resentments, in the following manner:

I ask thy Aid, O Potent Rum!
To Charm these wrangling Topers Dum.
Thou hast their Giddy Brains possest—
The man confounded wth the Beast—
And I, poor I, can get no rest.
Intoxicate them with thy fumes:
O still their Tongues till morning comes!

And I know not but my wishes took effect, for the dispute soon ended wth 'tother Dram; and so Good night!

Wednesday, Octob{e}r 4th. About four in the morning, we set out for Kingston (for so was the Town called) with a french Docter in our company.—lee and ye Post put on very furiously, so that I could not keep up with them, only as now and then they'd stop till they see mee. This Rode was poorly furnished wth accommodations for Travellers, so that we were forced to ride 22 miles by the post's account, but neerer thirty by mine, before wee could bait so much as our Horses, wch I exceedingly complained of. But the post encourag'd mee, by saying wee should be well accommodated anon at mr. Devil's, a few miles further. But I questioned whether we ought to go to the Devil to be helpt out of affliction. However, like the rest of Deluded souls that post to ye Infernal denn, Wee made all posible speed to this Devil's Habitation; where alliting, in full assurance of good accommodation, wee were going in. But meeting his two daughters, as I suposed twins, they so neerly resembled each other, both in features and habit, and look't as old as the

Divel himselfe, and quite as Ugly, We desired entertainm't, but could hardly get a word out of 'um, till with our Importunity, telling them our necesity, & c. they call'd the old Sophister, who was as sparing of his words as his daughters had bin, and no, or none, was the reply's bee made us to our demands. Hee differed only in this from the old fellow in to'ther Country: bee let us depart. However, I thought it proper to warn poor Travailers to endeavour to Avoid falling into circumstances like ours, wch at our next Stage I sat down and did as followeth:

May all that dread the cruel feind of night
Keep on, and not at this curs't Mansion light.
'Tis Hell; 'tis Hell! and Devills here do dwell:
Here dwells the Devill—surely this's Hell.
Nothing but Wants: a drop to cool yo'r
Tongue Cant be procur'd these cruel Feinds among.
Plenty of horrid Grins and looks sevear,
Hunger and thirst, But pitty's bannish'd here—
The Right hand keep, if Hell on Earth you fear!

Thus leaving this habitation of cruelty, we went forward; and arriving at an Ordinary about two mile further, found tollerable accommodation. But our Hostes, being a pretty full mouth'd old creature, entertain'd our fellow travailer, ye french Docter, wth Inumirable complaints of her bodily infirmities; and whispered to him so lou'd, that all ye House had as full a hearing as bee: which was very divirting to ye company, (of which there was a great many,) as one might see by their sneering. But poor weary I slipt out to enter my mind in my Jornal, and left my Great Landly with her Talkative Guests to themselves.

From hence we proceeded (about ten forenoon) through the Narragansett country, pretty Leisurely; and about one afternoon come to Paukataug River, wch was about two hundred paces over, and now very high, and no way over to to'ther side but this. I darid not venture to Ride thro, my courage at best in such cases but small, And now at the Lowest Ebb, by reason of my weary, very weary, hungry and uneasy Circumstances. So takeing leave of my company, tho' wth no little Reluctance, that I could not proceed wth them on my Jorny, Stop at a little cottage just by the River, to wait the Waters falling, web the old man that lived there said would be in a little time, and he would conduct me safe over. This little Hutt was one of the wretchedest I ever saw a habitation for human creatures. It was suported with shores enclosed with Clapbords, laid on Lengthways, and so much asunder, that the Light come throu' every where; the doore tyed on 'Nch a cord in ye place of hinges; The floor the bear earth; no windows but such as the thin covering afforded, nor any furniture but a Bedd wth a glass Bottle hanging at ye head on't; an earthan cupp, a small pewter Bas on, A Bord wth sticks to stand on, instead of a table, and a block or two in ye corner instead of chairs. The family were the old man, his wife and two Children; all and every part being the picture of poverty. Notwithstanding both the Hutt and its

Inhabitance were very clean and tydee: to the crossing the Old Proverb, that bare walls make giddy bows-wifes.

I Blest myselfe that I was not one of this misserable crew; and the Impressions their wretchedness formed in me caused mee on ye very Spott to say:

Tho' Ill at éase, A stranger and alone,
All my fatigues shall not extort a grone.
These Indigents have hunger wth their ease;
Their best is worn behalfe then my disease.
Their Misirable butt wch Heat and Cold
Alternately without Repulse do hold;
Their Lodgings thyn and hard, their Indian fare,
The mean Apparel which the wretches wear,
And their ten thousand ills wch can't be told,
Makes nature er'e 'tis midle age'd look old.
When I reflect, my late fatigues do seem
Only a notion or forgotten Dreem.

I had scarce done thinking, when an Indian-like Animal come to the door, on a creature very much like himselfe, in mien and feature, as well as Ragged cloathing; and having 'litt, makes an Awkerd Scratch wth his Indian shoo, and a Nodd, situ on Ye block, fumbles out his black Junk, dipps it in ye Ashes, and presents it piping hott to his muscheeto's, and fell to sucking like a calf, without speaking, for near a quarter of an bower. At length the old man said how do's Sarah do? who I understood was the wretches wife, and Daughter to yr old man: he Replyed—as well as can be expected, & c. So I remembred the old say, and suposed I knew Sarah's case. Butt bee being, as I understood, going over the River, as ugly as bee was, I was glad to ask him to show me ye way to Saxtons, at Stoningtown; wch he promising, I ventur'd over wth the old mans assistance; who having rewarded to content, with my Tatter tailed guide, I Ridd on very slowly thro' Stoningtown, where the Rode was very Stony and uneven. I asked the fellow, as we went, divers questions of the place and way, & c. I being arrived at my country Saxtons, at Stonington, was very well accommodated both as to victuals and Lodging, the only Good of both I had found since my setting out. Here I heard there was an old man and his Daughter to come that way, bound to N. London; and Ueing now destitute of a Guide, gladly waited for them, being in so good a harbour, and accordingly, *Thirsday, Octob{e}r ye 5th,* about 3 in the afternoon, I sat forward with neighbour Polly and Jemima, a Girl about 18 Years old, who hee said he had been to fetch out of the Narragansetts, and said they had Rode thirty miles that day, on a sory lean jade, wth only a Bagg under her for a pillion, which the poor Girl often complain'd was very uneasy.

Wee made Good speed along, wch made poor Jemima make many a sow'r face, the mare being a very hard trotter; and after many a hearty and bitter Oh, she at length Low'd out: Lawful Heart father! this bare mare hurts mee Dingeely, I'me direfull sore I vow; with many words to that purpose: poor Child sais Gaffer—she us't to serve your mother so. I don't care how mother us't to do, quoth Jemima, in a pasionate tone. At which the old man Laught, and kik't his jade o' the side, which made her jolt ten times harder.

About seven that Evening, we come to New London Ferry: here, by reason of a very high wind, we mett with great difficulty in getting over—the Boat tos't exceedingly, and our Horses capper'd at a very surprizing Rate, and set us all in a fright; especially poor Jemima, who desired her father to say so jack to the jade, to make her stand. But the careless parent, taking no notice of her repeated desires, She Rored out in a Passionate manner: Pray suth father, Are you deaf? Say so Jack to the jade, I tell you. The Dutiful Parent obey's; saying so Jack, so Jack, as gravely as if hee'd bin to saying Catechise after Young Miss, who with her fright look't of all coullers in ye Rain Bow.

Being safely arrived at the house of Mrs. Prentices in N. London, I treated neighbour Polly and daughter for their divirting company, and bid them farewell; and between nine and ten at night waited on the Revd Mr. Gurdon Saltonstall, minister of the town, who kindly Invited me to Stay that night at his house, where I was very handsomely and plentifully treated and Lodg'd; and made good the Great Character I had before heard concerning him: viz. that hee was the most affable, courteous, Genero's and best of men.

Friday, Octo{be}r 6th. I got up very early, in Order to hire somebody to go with mee to New Haven, being in Great parplexity at the thoughts of proceeding alone; which my most hospitable entertainer observing, himselfe went, and soon return'd wth a young Gentleman of the town, who he could confide in to Go with mee; and about eight this morning, Wth Mr. Joshua Wheeler my new Guide, takeing leave of this worthy Gentleman, Wee advanced on towards Seabrook. The Rodes all along this way are very bad, Incumbred wth Rocks and mountainos passages, wch were very disagreeable to my tired carcass; but we went on with a moderate pace wel' made ye Journy more pleasent. But after about eight miles Rideing, in going over a Bridge under wch the River Run very swift, my hors stumbled, and very narrowly 'scaped falling over into the water; wch extreemly frightened mee. But through God's Goodness I met with no harm, and mounting agen, in about half a miles Rideing, come to an ordinary, were well entertained by a woman of about seventy and vantage, but of as Sound Intellectuals as one of seventeen. Shee entertain'd Mr. Wheeler wth some passages of a Wedding awhile ago at a place hard by, the Brides-Groom being about her Age or something above, Saying his Children was dredfully against their fathers marrying, wch shee condemned them extreemly for.

From hence wee went pretty briskly forward, and arriv'd at Saybrook ferry about two of the Clock afternoon; and crossing it, wee call'd at an Inn to Bait, (foreseeing we should not have such another Opportunity till we come to Killingsworth.) Landlady come in, with her hair about her ears, and hands at full pay scratching. Shee told us shee had some mutton wch shee would broil, wch I was glad to hear; But I supose forgot to wash her scratchers; in a little time shee brot it in; but it being pickled, and my Guide said it smelt strong of head sause, we left it, and pd sixpence a piece for our Dinners, wch was only smell.

So wee putt forward with all speed, and about seven at night come to Killingsworth, and were tollerably well with Travillers fare, and Lodgd there that night.

Saturday, Oct{ober} 7th, we sett out early in the Morning, and being something unaquainted wth the way, having ask't it of some wee mett, they told us wee must Ride a mile or two and turne down a Lane on the Right hand; and by their Direction wee Rode on but not Yet comeing to ye turning, we mett a Young fellow and ask't him how farr it was to the Lane which turn'd down towards Guilford. Hee said wee must Ride a little further, and turn down by the Corner of uncle Sams Lott. My Guide vented his Spleen at the Lubber; and we soon after came into the Rhode, and keeping still on, without any thing further Remarkabell, about two a clock afternoon we arrived at New Haven, where I was received with all Possible Respects and civility. Here I discharged Mr. Wheeler with a reward to his satisfaction, and took some time to rest after so long and toilsome a journey; And Inform'd myselfe of the manners and customs of the place, and at the same time employed myselfe in the afair I went there upon.

They are Govern'd by the same Laws as wee in Boston, (or little differing,) thr'out this whole Colony of Connecticot, And much the same way of Church Government, and many of them good, Sociable people, and I hope Religious too: but a little too much Independant in their principalls, and, as I have been told, were formerly in their Zeal very Riggid in their Administrations towards such as their Lawes made Offenders, even to a harmless Kiss or Innocent merriment among Young people. Whipping being a frequent and counted an easy Punishment, about wch as other Crimes, the judges were absolute in their Sentantes. They told mee a pleasant story about a pair of justices in those parts, wch I may not omit the relation of.

A negro Slave belonging to a man in ye Town, stole a hogs head from his master, and gave or sold it to an Indian, native of the place. The Indian sold it in the neighbourhood, and so the theft was found out. Thereupon the Heathen was Seized, and carried to the justices House to be Examined. But his worship (it seems) was gone into the feild, with a Brother in office, to gather in his Pompions. Whither the malefactor is hurried, And Complaint made, and satisfaction in the name of justice demanded. Their Worships cann't proceed in form without a Bench: whereupon they Order one to be Imediately erected, which, for want of fitter materials, they made with pompions—which being finished, down sets their Worships, and the Malefactor call'd, and by the Senior Justice Interrogated after the following manner. You Indian why did You steal from this man? You sho'dn't do so—it's a Grandy wicked thing to steal. Hol't Hol't, cryes justice Junr. Brother, You speak negro to him. I'le ask him. You sirrah, why did You steal this man's Hoggshead? Hoggshead? (replys the Indian,) me no stomany. No? says his Worship; and pulling off his hatt, Patted his own head with his hand, sais, Tatapa-You, Tatapa-you; all one this. Hoggshead all one this. Hah! says Netop, now me stomany that. Whereupon the Company fell into a great fitt of Laughter, even to Roreing. Silence is comanded, but to no effect: for they continued perfectly Shouting. Nay, sais his worship, in an angry tone, if it be so, take mee off the Bench.

Their Diversions in this part of the Country are on Lecture days and Training days mostly: on the former there is Riding from town to town.

And on training dayes The Youth divert themselves by Shooting at the Target, as they call it, (but it very much resembles a pillory,) where hee that hitts neerest the white has some yards of Red Ribbin presented him, Wch being tied to his hattband, the two ends streeming down his back, he is Led away in Triumph, wth great applause, as the winners of the Olympiack Games. They generally marry very young: the males oftener as I am told under twentie than above; they generally make public wedings, and have a way something singular (as they say) in some of them, viz. Just before Joyning hands the Bridegroom quitts the place, who is soon followed by the Bridesmen, and as it were, dragg'd back to duty—being the reverse to ye former practice among us, to steal ma Pride.

There are great plenty of Oysters all along by the sea side, as farr as I Rode in the Collony, and those very good. And they Generally lived very well and comfortably in their famelies. But too Indulgent (especially ye farmers) to their slaves: sufering too great familiarity from them, permitting ym to sit at Table and eat with them, (as they say to save time,) and into the dish goes the black hoof as freely as the white hand. They told me that there was a farmer lived nere the Town where I lodgd who had some difference Wth his slave, concerning something the master had promised him and did not punctualy perform; wch caused some hard words between them; But at length they put the matter to Arbitration and Bound themselves to stand to the award of such as they named—wch done, the Arbitrators Having heard the Allegations of both parties, Order the master to pay 40' to black face, and acknowledge his fault. And so the matter ended: the poor master very honestly standing to the award.

There are every where in the Towns as I passed, a Number of Indians the Natives of the Country, and are the most salvage of all the salvages of that kind that I had ever Seen: little or no care taken (as I heard upon enquiry) to make them otherwise. They have in some places Landes of their owne, and Govern'd by Law's of their own making; they marry many wives and at pleasure put them away, and on the ye least dislike or fickle humour, on either side, saying stand away to one another is a sufficient Divorce. And indeed those uncomely Stand sways are too much in Vougue among the English in this (Indulgent Colony) as their Records plentifully prove, and that on very trivial matters, of which some have been told me, but are not proper to be Related by a Female pen, tho some of that foolish sex have had too large a share in the story.

If the natives committ any crime on their own precincts among themselves, ye English takes no Cognezens of. But if on the English ground, they are punishable by our Laws. They mourn for their Dead by blacking their faces, and cutting their hair, after an Awkerd and frightfull manner; But can't bear You should mention the names of their dead Relations to them: they trade most for Rum, for wch theyd hazzard their very lives; and the English fit them Generally as well by seasoning it plentifully with water.

They give the title of merchant to every trader; who Rate their Goods according to the time and spetia they pay in: viz. Pay, mony, Pay as mony, and trusting. Pay is Grain, Pork, Beef, & c. at the prices sett by the General Court that Year; mony is pieces of Eight, Ryalls, or Boston or Bay shillings (as they call them,) or Good hard money, as sometimes silver coin is termed by them; also Wampom, vizt. Indian beads wch serves for change. Pay as mony is provisions, as aforesd one Third cheaper then as the Assembly or Gene' Court sets it; and Trust as they and the mercht agree for time.

Now, when the buyer comes to ask for a comodity, sometimes before the merchant answers that he has it, he sais, is Your pay redy? Perhaps the Chap Reply's Yes: what do You pay in? say's the merchant. The buyer having answered, then the price is set; as suppose he wants a sixpenny knife, in pay it is 12d-in pay as money eight pence, and hard money its own price, viz. 6d. It seems a very Intricate way of trade and what Lex Mercatoria had not thought of.

Being at a merchants house, in comes a tall country fellow, wth his alfogeos full of Tobacco; for they seldom Loose their Cudd, but keep Chewing and Spitting as long as they'r eyes are open,—he advanc't to the midle of the Room, makes an Awkward Nodd, and spitting a Large deal of Aromatick Tincture, he gave a scrape with his shovel like shoo, leaving a small shovel full of dirt on the floor, made a full stop, Hugging his own pretty Body with his hands under his arms, Stood staring rown'd him, like a Catt let out of a Basket. At last, like the creature Balaam Rode on, he opened his mouth and said: have You any Ribinen for Hatbands to sell I pray? The Questions and Answers about the pay being past, the Ribin is bro't and opened. Bumpkin Simpers, cryes its confounded Gay I vow; and beckning to the door, in comes Jone Tawdry, dropping about 50 curtsees, and stands by him: hee shows her the Ribin. Law, You, sais shee, its right Gent, do You, take it, tis dreadfull pretty. Then she enquires, have You any hood silk I pray? wch being brought and bought, Have You any thred silk to sew it wth, says shee, wch being accomodated wth they Departed. They Generaly stand after they come in a great while speachless, and sometimes dont say a word till they are askt what they want, which I Impute to the Awe they stand in of the merchants, who they are constantly almost Indebted too; and must take what they bring without Liberty to choose for themselves; but they serve them as well, making the merchants stay long enough for their pay.

We may Observe here the great necessity and bennifitt both of Education and Conversation; for these people have as Large a portion of mother witt, and sometimes a Larger, than those who have bin brought up in Cities; But for want of emprovements, Render themselves almost Ridiculos, as above. I should be glad if they would leave such follies, and am sure all that Love Clean Houses (at least) would be glad on't too.

They are generaly very plain in their dress, throuout all ye Colony, as I saw, and follow one another in their modes; that You may know where they belong, especially the women, meet them where you will.

Their Cheif Red Letter day is St. Election, wch is annualy Observed according to Charter, to choose their Govenr: a blessing they can never be thankfull enough for, as they will find, if ever it be their hard fortune to loose it. The present Govenor in Conecticott is the Honlbe John Winthrop Esq. A Gentleman of an Ancient and Honourable Family, whose Father was Govenor here sometime before, and his Grand father had bin Gov, of the Massachusetts. This gentleman is a very curteous and afable person, much Given to Hospitality, and has by his Good services Gain'd the affections of the people as much as any who had bin before him in that post.

Dec{embe}r 6th. Being by this time well Recruited and rested after my Journy, my business lying unfinished by some concerns at New York depending thereupon, my Kinsman, Mr. Thomas Trowbridge of New Haven, must needs take a Journy there before it could be accomplished, I resolved to go there in company wth him, and a man of the town wch I engaged to wait on me there. Accordingly, Dec[ember] 6th we set out from New Haven, and about 1 t same morning came to Stratford ferry; wch crossing, about two miles on the other side Baited our horses and would have eat a morsell ourselves, But the Pumpkin and Indian mixt Bred had such an Aspect, and the Bare-legg'd Punch so awkerd or rather Awfull a sound, that we left both, and proceeded forward, and about seven at night come to Fairfield, where we met with good entertainment and Lodg'd; and early next morning set forward to Norowalk, from its halfe Indian name North-walk, when about 12 at noon we arrived, and Had a Dinner of Fryed Venison, very savoury. Landlady wanting some pepper in the seasoning, bid the Girl hand her the spice in the little Gay cupp on ye shelfe. From hence we Hasted towards Rye, walking and Leading our Horses neer a mile together, up a prodigios high Hill; and so Riding till about nine at night, and there arrived and took up our Lodgings at an ordinary, wch a French family kept. Here being very hungry, I desired a fricasee, wch the Frenchman undertake-

ing, mannaged so contrary to my notion of Cookery, that I hastned to Bed superless; And being shewd the way up a pair of stairs wch had such a narrow passage that I had almost stopt by the Bulk of my Body; But arriving at my apartment found it to be a little Lento Chamber furnisht amongst other Rubbish with a High Bedd and a Low one, a Long Table, a Bench and a Bottomless chair,—Little Miss went to scratch up my Kennell wch Russelled as if shee'd bin in the Barn amongst the Husks, and supose such was the contents of the tickin nevertheless being exceeding weary, down I laid my poor Carkes (never more tired) and found my Covering as scanty as my Bed was hard. Annon I heard another Russelling noise in Y, Room—called to know the matter—Little miss said shee was making a bed for the men; who, when they were in Bed, complained their leggs lay out of it by reason of its shortness—my poor bones complained bitterly not being used to such Lodgings, and so did the man who was with us; and poor I made but one Crone, which was from the time I went to bed to the time I Ris, which was about three in the morning, Setting up by the Fire till Light, and having discharged our ordinary wch was as dear as if we had had far Better fare—wee took our leave of Monsier and about seven in the morn come to New Rochell a french town, where we had a good Breakfast. And in the strength of that about an how'r before sunsett got to York. Here I applyd myself to Mr. Burroughs, a merchant to whom I was recommended by my Kinsman Capt. Prout, and received great Civilities from him and his spouse, who were now both Deaf but very agreeable in their Conversation, Diverting me with pleasant stories of their knowledge in Brittan from whence they both come, one of which was above the rest very pleasant to me viz. my Lord Darcy had a very extravagant Brother who had mortgaged what Estate bee could not sell, and in good time dyed leaving only one son. Him his Lordship (having none of his own) took and made him Heir of his whole Estate, which he was to receive at the death of his Aunt. He and his Aunt in her widowhood held a right understanding and lived as become such Relations, shee being a discreat Gentlewoman and he an Ingenios Young man. One day Hee fell into some Company though far his inferiors, very freely told him of the Ill circumstances his fathers Estate lay under, and the many Debts he left unpaid to the wrong of poor people with whom he had dealt. The Young gentleman was put out of countenance—no way bee could think of to Redress himself—his whole dependance being on the Lady his Aunt, and how to speak to her he knew not—Hee went home, sat down to dinner and as usual sometimes with her when the Chaplain was absent, she desired him to say Grace, wch he did after this manner:

> Pray God in Mercy take my Lady Darcy
> Unto his Heavenly Throne,
> That little John may live like a man,
> And pay every man his own.

The prudent Lady took no present notice, But finishd dinner, after wch having sat and talk't awhile (as Customary) He Riss, took his Hat, and Going out she desired him to give her leave to speak to him in her Clossett, Where being come she desired to know why hee prayed for her Death in the manner aforesaid, and what part of her deportment towards him merritted such desires. Hee Reply'd, none at all, But he was under such disadvantages that nothing but that could do him service, and told her how he had been affronted as above, and what Impressions it had made upon him. The Lady made him a gentle reprimand that he had not informed her after another manner, Bid him see what his father owed and he should have money to pay it to a penny, And always to lett her know his wants and he should have a redy supply. The Young Gentleman charm'd with his Aunts Discrete management, Beggd her pardon and accepted her kind offer and retrieved his fathers Estate, & c. and said Hee hoped his Aunt would never dye, for shee had done better by him than hee could have done for himself.—Mr. Burroughs went with me to Vendue where I bought about 100 Rheem of paper wch was retaken in a flyboat from Holland and sold very Reasonably here—some ten, some Eight shillings per Rheem by the Lott wch was ten Rheem in a Lott. And at the Vendue I made a great many acquaintants amongst the good women of the town, who curteosly invited me to their houses and generously entertained me.

The Cittie of New York is a pleasant, well compacted place, situated on a Commodius River wch is a fine harbour for shipping. The Buildings Brick Generaly, very stately and high, though not altogether like ours in Boston. The Bricks in some of the Houses are of divers Coullers and laid in Checkers, being glazed look very agreeable. The inside of them are neat to admiration, the wooden work, for only the walls are plasterd, and the Sumers and Gist are plained and kept very white scowr'd as so is all the partitions if made of Bords. The fire places have no Jambs (as ours have) But the Backs run flush with the walls, and the Hearth is of Tyles and is as farr out into the Room at the Ends as before the fire, wch is Generally Five foot in the Low'r rooms, and the peice over where the mantle tree should be is made as ours with Joyners work, and as I supose is fasten'd to iron rodds inside. The House where the Vendue was, had Chimney Corners like ours, and they and the hearths were laid wth the finest file that I ever see, and the stair cases laid all with white tile which is ever clean, and so are the walls of the Kitchen wch had a Brick floor. They were making Great preparations to Receive their Govenor, Lord Cornbury from the jerseys, and for that End raised the militia to Gard him on shore to the fort.

They are Generaly of the Church of England and have a New England Gentleman for their minister, and a very fine church set out with all Customary requsites. There are also a Dutch and Divers Conventicles as they call them, viz. Baptist, Quakers, & c. They are not strict in keeping the Sabbath as in Boston and other places where I had bin, But

seem to deal with great exactness as farr as I see or Deall with. They are sociable to one another and Curteos and Civill to strangers and fare well in their houses. The English go very fasheonable in their dress. Dut the Dutch, especially the middling sort, differ from our women, in their habitt go loose, were French muches wch are like a Capp and a head band in one, leaving their ears bare, which are sett out Wth Jewells of a large size and many in number. And their fingers hoop't with Rings, some with large stones in them of many Coullers as were their pendants in their ears, which You should see very old women wear as well as Young.

They have Vendues very frequently and make their Earnings very well by them, for they treat with good Liquor Liberally, and the Customers Drink as Liberally and Generally pay for't as well, by paying for that which they Bidd up Briskly for, after the sack has gone plentifully about, tho' sometimes good penny worthy are got there. Their Diversions in the Winter is Riding Sleys about three or four Miles out of Town, where they have Houses of entertainment at a place called the Bowery, and some go to friends Houses who handsomely treat them. Mr. Burroughs cary'd his spouse and Daughter and myself out to one Madame Dowes, a Gentlewoman that lived at a farm House, who gave us a handsome Entertainment of five or six Dishes and choice Beer and metheglin, Cyder, & c. all which she said was the produce of her farm. I believe we mett 50 or 60 slays that day—they fly with great swiftness and some are so furious that they'le turn out of the path for none except a Loaden Cart. Nor do they spare for any diversion the place affords, and sociable to a degree, they'r Tables being as free to their Naybours as to themselves.

Having here transacted the affair I went upon and some other that fell in the way, after about a fortnight's stay there I left New-York with no Little regrett, and *Thursday, Dec{ember} 21,* set out for New Haven wth my Kinsman Trowbridge, and the man that waited on me about one afternoon, and about three come to half-way house about ten miles out of town, where we Baited and went forward, and about 5 come to Spiting Devil, Else Kings bridge, where they pay three pence for passing over with a horse, which the man that keeps the Gate set up at the end of the Bridge receives.

We hoped to reach the french town and Lodg there that night, but unhapily lost our way about four miles short, and being overtaken by a great storm of wind and snow which set full in our faces about dark, we were very uneasy. But meeting one Gardner who lived in a Cottage thereabout, offered us his fire to set by, having but one poor Bedd, and his wife not well, & c. or he would go to a Housr with us, where he thought we might be better accommodated— thither we went, But a surly old shoe Creature, not worthy the name of woman, who would hardly let us go into her Door, though the weather was so stormy none but shee would have turnd out a Dogg. But her son whose name was gallop, who lived just by Invited us to his house and shewed me two pair of stairs, viz. one up the loft and tother up the Bedd, wh was as hard as it was high, and warmed it with a hott stone at the feet. I lay very uncomfortably, insomuch that I was so very cold and sick I was forced to call them up to give me something to warm me. They had nothing but milk in the house, wch they Boild, and to make it better sweetened wth molasses, which I not knowing or thinking oft till it was down and coming up agen woh it did in so plentifull a manner that my host was soon paid double for his portion, and that in specia. But I believe it did me service in Cleering my stomach.

So after this sick and weary night at East Chester, (a very miserable poor place,) the weather being now fair, *Friday the 22d Dec{ember}* we set out for New Rothell, where being come we had good Entertainment and Recruited ourselves very well. This is a very pretty place well compact, and good handsome houses, Clean, good and passable Rodes, and situated on a Navigable River, abundance of land well fined and Cleerd all along as wee passed, which caused in me a Love to the place, wch I could have been content to live in it. Here wee Ridd over a Bridge made of one entire stone of such a Breadth that a cart might pass with safety, and to spare—it lay over a passage cutt through a Rock to convey water to a mill not farr off. Here are three fine Taverns within call of each other, very good provision for Travailers.

Thence we travailed through Merrinak, a neet, though little place, wth a navigable River before it, one of the pleasantest I ever see—Here were good Buildings, Especialy one, a very fine seat, wch they told me was Col. Hethcoats, who I had heard was a very fine Gentleman.

From hence we come to Hors Neck, where wee Baited and they told me that one Church of England parson officiated in, all these three towns once every Sunday in turns throughout the Year; and that they all could but poorly maintaine him, which they grudg'd to do, being a poor and quarelsome crew as I understand by our Host; their Quarelling about their choice of Minister, they chose to have none—But caused the Government to send this Gentleman to them. Here wee took leave of York Government, and Descending the Mountainos passage that almost broke my heart in ascending before, we come to Stamford, a well compact Town, but miserable meeting house, wch we passed, and thro' many and great difficulties, as Bridges which were exceeding high and very tottering and of vast Length, steep and Rocky Hills and precipices, (Buggbears to a fearful female travailer.) About nine at night we come to Norrwalk, having crept over a timber of a Broken Bridge about thirty foot long, and perhaps fifty to ye water. I was exceeding tired and cold when we come to our Inn, and could get nothing there but poor entertainment, and the impertinant Bable of one of the worst of men, among many others of which our Host made one, who, had he bin one degree Impudenter, would have outdone his Grandfather. And this I think is the most perplexed night I have yet had.

From hence, *Saturday, Dec{ember} 23,* a very cold and windy day, after an Intolerable night's Lodging, wee hasted forward only observing in our way the Town to be situated on a Navigable river wth indiferent Buildings and people more refind than in some of the Country towns wee had passed, tho' vicious enough, the Church and Tavern being next neighbours. Having Ridd thro a difficult River wee come to Fairfield where wee Baited and were much refreshed as well with the Good things wch gratified our appetites as the time took to rest our wearied Limbs, woh Latter I employed in enquiring concerning the Town and manners of the people, & c. This is a considerable town, and filled as they say with wealthy people—have a spacious meeting house and good Buildings. But the Inhabitants are Litigious, nor do they well agree with their minister, who (they say) is a very worthy Gentleman.They have aboundance of sheep, whose very Dung brings them great gain, with part of which they pay their Parsons sallery, And they Grudg that, prefering their Dung before their minister. They Lett out their sheep at so much as they agree upon for a night; the highest Bidder always caries them, And they will sufficiently Dung a Large quantity of Land before morning. But were once Bitt by a sharper who had them a night and sheared them all before morning—From hence we went to Stamford, the next Town, in which I observed but few houses, and those not very good ones. But the people that I conversed with were civill and good natured. Here we staid till late at night, being to cross a Dangerous River ferry, the River at that time full of Ice; but after about four hours waiting with great difficulty wee got over. My fears and fatigues prevented my here taking any particular observation. Being got to Milford, it being late in the night, I could go no further; my fellow travailer going forward, I was invited to Lodg at Mrs.—, a very kind and civill Gentlewoman, by whom I was handsomely and kindly entertained till the next night. The people here go very plain in their apparel (more plain than I had observed in the towns I had passed) and seem to be very grave and serious. They told me there was a singing Quaker lived there, or at least had a strong inclination to be so, His Spouse not at all affected that way. Some of the singing Crew come there one day to visit him, who being then abroad, they sat down (to the woman's no small vexation) Humming and singing and groneing after their conjuring way—Says the woman are you singing quakers? Yea says They—Then take my squalling Brat of a child here and sing to it, says she, for I have almost split my throat wth singing to him and cant get the Rogue to sleep. They took this as a great Indignity, and mediately departed. Shaking the dust from their Heels left the good woman and her Child among the number of the wicked.

This is a Seaport place and accomodated with a Good Harbour, But I had not opportunity to make particular observations because it was Sabbath day—This Evening.

December 24. I set out with the Gentlewomans son who she very civilly offered to go with me when she see no parswasions would cause me to stay which she pressingly desired, and crossing a ferry having but nine miles to New Haven, in a short time arrived there and was Kindly received and well accommodated amongst my Friends and Relations.

The Government of Connecticut Collony begins westward towards York at Stanford (as I am told) and so runs Eastward towards Boston (I mean in my range, because I dont intend to extend my description beyond my own travails) and ends that way at Stonington—And has a great many Large towns lying more northerly. It is a plentiful Country for provisions of all sorts and its Generally Healthy. No one that can and will be dilligent in this place need fear poverty nor the want of food and Rayment.

January 6th. Being now well Recruited and fitt for business I discoursed the persons I was concerned with, that we might finnish in order to my return to Boston. They delays as they had hitherto done hoping to tire my Patience. But I was resolute to stay and see an End of the matter let it be never so much to my disadvantage.

So *January 9th* they come again and promise the Wednesday following to go through with the distribution of the Estate which they delayed till Thursday and then come with new amusements. But at length by the mediation of that holy good Gentleman, the Rev. Mr. James Pierpont, the minister of New Haven, and with the advice and assistance of other our Good friends we come to an accommodation and distribution, which having finished though not till February, the man that waited on me to York taking the charge of me I sit out for Boston. We went from New Haven upon the ice (the ferry being not passable thereby) and the Rev. Mr. Pierpont wch Madam Prout Cuzin Trowbridge and (livers others were taking leave wee went onward without any thing Remarkabl till wee come to New London and Lodged again at Mr. Saltonstalls—and here I dismist my Guide, and my Generos entertainer provided me Mr. Samuel Rogers of that place to go home with me—I stayed a day here Longer than I intended by the Commands of the Honh'e Govenor Winthrop to stay and take a supper with him whose wonderful civility I may not omitt. The next morning I Crossed ye Ferry to Groton, having had the Honor of the Company, of Madam Livingston (who is the Govenors Daughter) and Mary Christophers and divers others to the boat—And that night Losga at Stonington and had Rost Beef and pumpkin sause for supper. The next night at Haven's and had Rost fowle, and the next day wee come to a river which by Reason of Ye Freshetts coming down was swell'a so high wee feara it impassable and the rapid stream was very terryfying—However we must over and that in a small Cannoo. Mr. Rogers assuring me of his good Conduct, I after a stay of near an how'r on the shore for consultation went into the Cannoo, and Mr. Rogers paddled about 1oo yards up the Creek by the shore side, turned into the swift stream and dexterously steering her in a moment wee come to the other side as swiftly passing as an arrow shott out of the Bow by a strong arm. I staid on ye shore till Hee returned to fetch our horses, which he caused to swim over himself bringing the furniture in the Cannoo. But it is past my skill to express the Exceeding fright all their transactions formed in me.

Wee were now in the colony of the Massachusetts and taking Lodgings at the first Inn we come too had a pretty difficult passage the next day which was the *second of March* by reason of the sloughy ways then thawed by the Sunn. Here I mett Capt. John Richards of Boston who was going home, So being very glad of his Company we Rode something harder than hitherto, and missing my way in going up a very steep Hill, my horse dropt down under me as Dead; this new surprize no little hurt me meeting it just at the Entrance into Dedham from whence we intended to reach home that night. But was now obliged to gett another Hors there and leave my own, resolving for Boston that night if possible. But in going over the Causeway at Dedham the Bridge being overflowed by the high waters comming down I very narrowly escaped falling over into the river Hors and all wch twas almost a miracle I did not—now it grew late in the afternoon and the people having very much discouraged us about the sloughy way wch they said wee should find very difficult and hazardous it so wrought on mee being tired and dispirited and disapointed of my desires of going home that I agreed to Lodg there that night wch wee did at the house of one Draper, and the next day being *March 3d* wee got safe home to Boston, where I found my aged and tender mother and my Dear and only Child in good health with open arms redy to receive me, and my Kind relations and friends flocking in to welcome mee and hear the story of my transactions and travails I having this day bin five months from home and now I cannot fully express my joy and Satisfaction. But desire sincearly to adore my Great Benefactor for thus graciously carying forth and returning in safety his unworthy handmaid.

Source: Sarah Kemble Knight, "The Journal of Madam Knight," *The Puritans,* edited by Perry Miller and Thomas H. Johnson (New York: American Book Company, 1938).

The French and the Fur Trade (1724)

Cadwallader Colden, then the surveyor general in the province of New York, reports to Governor Burnet on what he sees as French encroachment on New York safety and its trade. He monitors the activities of the French both in the New York area and along the Mississippi, observing their forts, their priests' conversions of native peoples, and their use of inland travel routes used by the natives. Colden advocates extending the frontiers of the province to check the French presence and safeguard commerce with the natives.

A Memorial concerning the Fur Trade of the province of New-York. Presented to his Excellency William Burnet, Esq. Captain-General and Governor, &c. by Cadwallader Colden, Surveyor-General of the said province, the 10th of December, 1724.

It has of late been generally believed, that the inhabitants of the province of New-York are so advantageously situated, with respect to the Indian trade, and enjoy so many advantages as to trade in general, that it is in their power not only to rival the French of Canada, who have almost entirely engrossed the Fur Trade of America, but that it is impossible for the French to carry on that trade in competition with the people of this province. The inquiring into the truth of this proposition, may not only be of some consequence, as to the riches and honour of the British nation (for it is well known how valuable the fur trade of America is) but likewise as to the safety of all the British colonies in North America. New France, as the French now claim, extends from the mouth of the river Mississippi, to the mouth of the river St. Lawrence, by which the French plainly show their intention of enclosing the British settlements, and cutting us off from all commerce with the numerous nations of Indians, that are every where settled over the vast continent of North America. The English in America have too good reason to apprehend such a design, when they see the French king's geographer publish a map, by which he has set bounds to the British empire in America, and has taken in many of the English settlements both in South Carolina and New-York, within these boundaries of New France. And the good services they intend us with the Indians, but too plainly appears at this day, by the Indian war now carried on against New-England.

I have therefore for some time past, endeavoured to inform myself from the writings of the French, and from others who have travelled in Canada, or among the Indians, how far the people of this province may carry on the Indian trade with more advantage than the French can; or what

disadvantages they labour under more than the French do. As all endeavours for the good of one's country are excusable, I do not doubt but my intention in this will be acceptable to your excellency, though I be not capable of treating the subject as it deserves.

I shall begin with Canada, and consider what advantages they have either by their situation or otherwise. Canada is situated upon the river of St. Lawrence, by which the five great lakes (which may properly be called the five inland seas of North America) empty themselves into the ocean. The mouth of this great river is in the latitude of 50°, over against the body of Newfoundland. It rises from the Cataracui, now Lake Ontario, the easternmost of the five great lakes, about the latitude of 44°, and runs from thence about north-east to the ocean, and is about nine hundred miles in length, from that lake to the ocean. The five great lakes which communicate with each other, and with this river, extend about one thousand miles westward further into the continent. So far the French have already discovered, and their discoveries make it probable, that an inland passage may be found to the South Sea, by the rivers which run into these lakes, and rivers which run into the South Sea.

The method of carrying goods upon the rivers of North America, into all the small branches and over land, from the branches of one river to the branches of another, was learned from the Indians, and it is the only method practicable through such large forests and deserts as the traders pass through, in carrying from one nation to another—it is this; the Indians make a long narrow boat, made of the bark of the birch tree, the parts of which they join very neatly. One of these canoes that can carry a dozen men, can itself be easily carried on two men's shoulders; so that when they have gone as far by water as they can, which is further than is easily to be imagined, because their loaded canoes don't sink six inches into the water, they unload their canoes, and carry both goods and canoes upon their shoulders over land, into the nearest branch of the river they intend to follow. Thus the French have an easy communication with all the countries bordering upon the river of St. Lawrence, and its branches, with all the countries bordering upon these inland seas, and the rivers which empty themselves into these seas, and can thereby carry their burdens of merchandise through all these large countries, which could not by any other means than water-carriage be carried through so vast a tract of land.

This, however, but half finishes the view the French have as to their commerce in North America. Many of the branches of the river Mississippi come so near to the branches of several of the rivers which empty themselves into the great lakes, that in several places there is but a short land-carriage from the one to the other. As soon as they have got into the River Mississippi, they open to themselves as large a field for traffic in the southern parts of North America, as was before mentioned with respect to the northern parts. If one considers the length of this river and its numerous branches, he must say, that by means of this river and the lakes, there is opened to his view such a scene of inland navigation as cannot be paralleled in any other part of the world.

The French have, with much industry, settled small colonies, and built stockaded forts at all the considerable passes between the lakes, except between Cataracui Lake, called by the French Ontario, and Lake Erie, one of our Five Nations of Indians, whom we call Senecas, and the French Sonontouans, having hitherto refused them leave to erect any buildings there.

The French have been indefatigable in making discoveries, and carrying on their commerce with nations, of whom the English know nothing but what they see in the French maps and books. The barrenness of the soil, and the coldness of the climate of Canada, obliges the greatest number of the inhabitants to seek their living by travelling among the Indians, or by trading with those who do travel. The Governor, and other officers, have but a scanty allowance from the king, and could not subsist were it not by the perquisites they have from this trade; neither could their priests find any means to satisfy their ambition and luxury without it. So that all heads and hands are employed to advance it, and the men of best parts think it the surest way to advance themselves by travelling among the Indians, and learning their languages; even the bigotry and enthusiasm of some hot heads, has not been a little useful in advancing this commerce; for that government having prudently turned the edge of the zeal of such hot spirits upon converting the Indians, many of them have spent their lives under the greatest hardships, in endeavouring to gain the Indians to their religion, and to love the French nation, while, at the same time, they are no less industrious to represent the English as the enemies of mankind. So that the whole policy of that government, both civil and religious, is admirably turned to the general advancement of this trade. Indeed the art and industry of the French, especially that of their religious missions, has so far prevailed upon all the Indians in

North America, that they are every where directed by French councils. Even our own Five Nations, the Iroquois, who formerly were mortal enemies of the French, and have always lived in the strictest amity with the English, have of late, by the practices of the French priests, been so far gained, that several of the Mohawks who live nearest the English, have left their habitations, and are gone to settle near Montreal in Canada; and all the rest discover a dread of the French power. That much of this is truly owing to the priests, appears from many of the Sachems of the Iroquois wearing crucifixes when they come to Albany. And those Mohawk Indians that are gone to Canada, are now commonly known, both to the French and English, by the name of the Praying Indians, it being customary for them to go through the streets of Montreal with their beads, praying and begging alms.

But notwithstanding all these advantages, the French labour under difficulties that no art or industry can remove. The mouth of the river St. Lawrence, and more especially the bay of St. Lawrence, lies so far north, and is thereby so often subject to tempestuous weather and thick fogs, that the navigation there is very dangerous, and never attempted but during the summer months. The wideness of this bay, together with the many strong currents that run in it, the many shelves and sunken rocks that are every where spread over both the bay and river, and the want of places for anchoring in the bay, all increase the danger of this navigation; so that a voyage to Canada is justly esteemed much more dangerous than to any other part of America. The many shipwrecks that happen in this navigation, are but too evident proofs of the truth of this, particularly the miscarriage of the last expedition against Canada. The channel is so difficult, and the tides so strong, that after their shipping get into the river, they never attempt to sail in the night, though the wind be fair, and the weather good. These difficulties are so considerable, that the French never attempt above one voyage a year to Europe or the West Indies, though it be really nearer Europe than any of the English colonies, where the shipping that constantly use the trade, always make two voyages in the year.

The navigation between Quebec and Montreal is likewise very dangerous and difficult. The tide rises about eighteen or twenty feet at Quebec, which occasions so strong a stream, that a boat of six oars cannot make way against it; the river in many places very wide, and the channel at the same time narrow and crooked; there are many shelves and sunken rocks, so that the best pilots have been deceived; for which reasons vessels that carry goods to Montreal, are always obliged to anchor before night, though both wind and tide be fair. The flood goes no further than Trois Rivieres, half way to Montreal, and about ninety miles from Quebec.

After they pass this place they have a strong stream always against them, which requires a fair wind and a strong gale to carry the vessels against the stream. And they are obliged in this part of the river, as well as under the Trois Rivieres, to come to anchor at night though the wind be good. These difficulties make the common passages take up three or four weeks, and sometimes six weeks; though if they have the chance of a wind to continue so long, they may run it in five or six days. After they pass Montreal, they have a strong stream against them till they come near the Lakes; so that in all that, which is about one hundred and fifty miles in length, they force their canoes forward with setting poles, or drag them with ropes along shore; and at five or six different places in that way the river falls over rocks with such force, that they are obliged to unload their canoes, and carry them upon their shoulders. They never make this voyage from Montreal to Lake Ontario in less than twenty days, and frequently, twice that time is necessary.

Now we are come so far as the lake, my design leads me no further, for at this lake all the far Indians that go to Canada must pass by our traders. And from thence the road to the Indian countries is the same from Albany as it is from Montreal.

Besides these difficulties in the transportation, the French labour under greater in purchasing of the principal goods proper for the Indian market; for the most considerable and most valuable part of their cargo consists in strouds, duffils, blankets, and other woollens, which are bought at a much cheaper rate in England than in France. The strouds, which the Indians value more than any other clothing, are only made in England, and must be transported into France before they can be carried to Canada. Rum is another considerable branch of the Indian trade with the French have not, by reason they have no commodities in Canada fit for the West India market. This they supply with brandy, at a much dearer rate than rum can be purchased at New-York, though of no more value to with the Indians. Generally, all the goods used in the Indian trade, except gunpowder, and a few trinkets, are sold at Montreal for twice their value at Albany. To this likewise must be added, the necessity they are under of laying the whole charge of supporting their government on the Indian trade. I am not particularly informed of their duties or imposts, but I am well assured, that they commonly give six or seven hundred livres for a licence for one canoe, in proportion to her largeness, to go with her loading into the Indian country to trade.

I shall next consider the advantages the inhabitants of New-York have in carrying on this trade. In the first place, the ships that constantly use the trade to England, perform their voyage to and from London twice every year; and those that go to Bristol, the port from whence the greatest part of the goods for the Indian trade are exported, frequently return in four months. These goods are bought much cheaper in England than in France: they are transported in less time, with less charge, and much less risk, as appears by the premium for insurance between London and New-York, being only two per cent. Goods are easily carried from New-York to Albany up the Hudson River, the distance being only 140 miles, the river very straight all the way, and bold, and very free from sand banks, as well as rocks; so that

the vessels always sail as well by night as by day, and have the advantage of the tide upwards as well as downwards, the flood flowing above Albany. It may therefore be safely concluded, that all sorts of goods can be carried to Albany at a cheaper rate than they can to Quebec, which is also three times further from the Indian country than Albany is. To put the truth of this out of all dispute, I need only observe what is well known both at New-York and Albany, viz. That almost all the strouds carried by the French into the Indian countries, as well as large quantities of other goods, for the use of the French themselves, are carried from Albany to Montreal. There has been an account kept of nine hundred pieces of strouds transported thither in one year, besides other commodities of very considerable value. The distance between Albany and Montreal, is about two hundred miles, all by water, except twelve miles between Hudson River and Wood Creek, where they carry their bark canoes over land, and about sixteen miles between Chambly and La Prairie, over against Montreal. And though the passage be so short and easy, these goods are generally sold at double their value in Albany.

But as this path hath been thought extremely prejudicial to the interests of this colony, I shall leave it and go on to another that leads directly from Albany into the Cataracui or Ontario Lake, without going near any of the French settlements.

From Albany the Indian traders commonly carry their goods sixteen miles over land, to the Mohawk River at Schenectady, the charge of which carriage is nine shillings New-York money, or five shillings sterling each waggon-load. From Schenectady they carry them in canoes up the Mohawk River, to the carrying-place between the Mohawk River and the river which runs into the Oneida Lake; which carrying-place between is only three miles long, except in very dry weather, when they are obliged to carry them two miles further. From thence they go with the current down the Onondaga River to Lake Ontario. The distance between Albany and Lake Ontario this way, is nearly the same with that between Albany and Montreal; and likewise with that between Montreal and Lake Ontario, and the passage much easier than the last, because the stream of the Mohawk River is not near so strong as the river St. Lawrence between the Lake and Montreal, and there is no fall in the river save one short one; whereas there are, as I have said, at least five in the river St. Lawrence, where the canoes must be unloaded. Therefore it plainly follows, that the Indian goods may be carried at as cheap a rate from Albany to Lake Ontario, as from Albany to Montreal. So that the people of Albany plainly save all the charge of carrying goods two hundred miles from Montreal to that part of the Ontario Lake, which the French have to carry before they bring them to the same place from Montreal, besides the advantage which the English have in the price of their goods.

I have said, that when we are in Lake Ontario, we are upon the level with the French, because here we can meet with all the Indians that design to go to Montreal. But besides this passage by the lakes, there is a river which comes from the country of the Senecas, and falls into the Onondaga River, by which we have an easy carriage into that country, without going near Lake Ontario. The head of this river goes near to Lake Erie, and probably may give a very near passage into that Lake, much more advantageous than the way the French are obliged to take by the great fall of Niagara, because narrow rivers are much safer for canoes than lakes, where they are obliged to go ashore if there be any wind upon the water. But as this passage depends upon a further discovery, I shall say nothing more of it at this time.

Whoever then considers these advantages New-York has of Canada, in the first buying of their goods, and in the safe, speedy, and cheap transportation of them from Britain to the Lakes, free of all manner of duty or imposts, will readily agree with me, that the traders of New-York may sell their goods in the Indian countries at half the price the people of Canada can, and reap twice the profit they do. This will admit of no dispute with those that know that strouds, the staple Indian commodity, this year are sold for ten pounds a piece at Albany, and at Montreal for twenty-five pounds, notwithstanding the great quantity of strouds said to be brought directly into Quebec from France, and the great quantities that have been clandestinely carried from Albany. It cannot therefore be denied that it is only necessary for the traders of New-York to apply themselves heartily to this trade, in order to bring it wholly into their own hands; for in every thing besides diligence, industry, and enduring fatigues, the English have much the advantage of the French. And all the Indians will certainly buy, where they can at the cheapest rate.

It must naturally be objected, that if these things are true, how is it possible that the traders of New-York should neglect so considerable and beneficial trade for so long time?

In answering this objection, I shall show the difficulties New-York has laboured under, by giving a short history of the country, so far as it relates to this trade. Which method, I think, can be liable to the least objection, and put the whole in the truest light.

When this country (the province of New-York) came first under the crown of Great Britain, our Five Nations of Indians were mortal enemies of the French at Canada, and were in a continual war with them, and all the nations of Indians around the lakes; so that then it was not safe for the English to travel further than the countries of the Five Nations; nor would our Indians permit the far Indians, with whom they had constant war, to pass through their countries to Albany. Besides, the Five Nations of Indians were at that time so numerous, consisting of ten times the number of fighting men they now do, that the trade with them alone was very considerable for so young and small a colony. In the latter end of King Charles's reign, when the duke of York and popish councils prevailed, the Governor of New-York, who was likewise a papist, had orders to use all his endeavours

to make up a peace between our nations (the Iroquois) and the French; and that he should persuade the Five Nations to admit French priests among them, in order to civilize them. The consequence of which was, that the French thereby obtained a free commerce upon the lakes, and obtained leave to build Cataraqui Fort upon the north side of Lake Ontario, and have two vessels of force upon the same lake. From this time, during all king James's reign, the French, whenever they had any differences with our Five Nations, threatened that the English of New-York would join with them, and destroy the Five Nations; by which, and the practices of the French priests, our Five Nations became very much alienated in their affections from the English, and looked upon them as a people depending upon the French. The consequences of this appeared so dangerous to Colonel Dungan, the Governor of New-York, though, as I have said, a papist, that he again and again complained to his master of the ill offices the French priests did the English among our nations. When the English had thus procured a peace for the French, they thought they might justly reap some advantages from it; and it's hardly to be doubted but that they had promises of that kind. They were therefore encouraged to send forty men, with great quantities of goods, into the lakes, under the command of Major McGregory, to trade with the far nations. At this time, Mr. Denonville, Governor of Canada, was gathering together all the force of Canada, and of the Indians, enemies of the Five Nations, in order to surprise the Five Nations and destroy them, at the time they thought themselves secure by the peace so lately made. Major McGregory and his company, were met by a French officer on Lake Erie, coming with a great number of men to the general rendezvous of the French, and he, with all the English, were made prisoners. They were used with such severity as has never been practised between Christian nations in open war, though the two crowns at that time were not only at peace, but under the strictest ties of mutual friendship; for the French used these people as slaves in building Cataraqui fort, and a poor Frenchman that had conducted them, was publicly shot to death, as if he had brought an enemy into their country. Such were their apprehensions then of the English getting any footing among the Indians.

The French Governor surprised a village of the Five Nations, who, on the French faith, lived in great security but seven or eight leagues from the French fort, and sent these miserable people to the galleys in France. He afterwards fell upon the Senecas, and burnt their villages, but without any advantage to the French, they having lost more men than the Indians did. This renewed the war with greater fury than ever, between the French and our Indians. For some time afterwards our Indians, in a great body, fell upon the island of Montreal, while Mr. Denonville was in the town. They burnt and destroyed all the villages and houses around Montreal, and killed some hundreds of men, women, and children. Afterwards they came into the open fields before Montreal, and there defied the French Governor, who did not think it proper to fight them. And when they had done all the mischief they could, they retired without any loss.

About this time the revolution happened in Great Britain, which was succeeded by a war between Great Britain and France. In February 1689–90. A party of three hundred men, consisting of equal numbers of French and Indians, surprised Schenectady in the night-time, when the poor people were in their beds, in the greatest security, where they barbarously murdered sixty-three men, women, and children, in cold blood, laid the village in ashes, and then retired, without reaping any other advantage besides this cruel revenge on innocent people, for the mischief our Indians had done them. This raised a cruel war between the two colonies, in which there was much mischief done, and blood shed, without any advantage to either side.

In time of this war, the most Christian king's Governor of Canada was so much provoked, that he thought fit to follow the example of our barbarous Indians, and burn his Indian prisoners alive in the most cruel manner, in sight of all the inhabitants of Quebec, and to deliver up the English prisoners to the French Indians, who indeed had more mercy, for they killed none of them.

King William's peace put an end to this war; but the peace lasted so short a while, that the people of this province hardly had time to re-settle their farms on the frontiers, which they had deserted in the time of the war, much less to adventure trading in the Indian countries, so lately the scene of so much cruelty. But both colonies having now an abhorrence of the cruelties of the last war, agreed on a kind of neutrality for the Indians, during Queen Anne's war, in which time we lost much ground with our own Indians. For the French having learned, by dear experience, that it was not possible for them to conquer our Five Indian Nations, resolved to try all means to gain their affections, and in this art the French are always more successful than in that of war; and the English failing in two ill-concerted expeditions against Canada, the Indians lost much of the opinion they had of the English power and valour.

In time of this last war, the clandestine trade to Montreal began to be carried on by Indians from Albany to Montreal. This gave rise to the Kahnuaga, or Praying Indians, who are entirely made up of deserters from the Mohawks and river Indians, and were either enticed thither by the French priests, or by our merchants, in order to carry goods from Albany to Montreal, or run away for some mischief done here. These Indians now consist of about eighty fighting men, and live about four leagues above Montreal. They neither plant nor hunt, but depend chiefly upon this private trade for their subsistence. These Indians, in time of war, gave the French intelligence of all designs here against them. By them likewise the French engaged our Five Nations in a war with the Indians, friends of Virginia, and from them we might expect the greatest mischief in time of war, seeing every part of the province is as well known to them as to any of the inhabitants. But if this trade was entirely at an end,

we have reason to believe, that these Indians would return to their own tribes, for they then could not long subsist where they now are.

As soon as the peace was proclaimed, an open trade with Montreal was carried on with such earnestness, that Montreal was filled with Indian goods, and Albany exhausted; by which means Montreal became the principal, if not the only Indian market, and the Indians depended entirely on the French for what they wanted.

Our merchants were fond of the Canada trade, because they sold large quantities of goods without any trouble, the French taking them from their doors; whereas the trade with the Indians is carried on with a great deal of toil and fatigue; and as to the interest of the country, they either never thought any thing about it, or if they did, had no regard to it.

Now I have brought this account to the time your excellency arrived; what has happened since, your excellency knows better than I can by any means inform you. From the whole, it seems plain that any difficulties and disadvantages this province has been under, have only proceeded from the wars, which have continued since the first settling of the province, to the beginning of the last general peace. But now, that not only this province, but likewise our Six Nations of Indians are at peace, and in amity both with the French and all the Indian nations with whom we can have any commerce, these difficulties are all removed, and we now enjoy the most favourable time, that at any time can be hoped for, in order to extend the British commerce in North America, while the French not only labour under the difficulties which I have shown to be inseparable from the situation of their colony, but likewise under another disadvantage, not before taken notice of, by the fur trade of Canada being restrained to one Company. This company is obliged to pay heavy duties in France upon the importation of beaver or any other fur; for which reason they always fix a price upon beaver and their other furs in Canada; and the Indian traders of Canada being restrained from selling to any but the company's agents there, they cannot raise the price of Indian goods as the price of European rise, or as their profit on the goods they sell to the Indians is lessened.

The merchants of New-York allow our Indian traders double the price for beaver, that the French company allow their Indian traders, the price established by the company for beaver in Canada, being two livres, or eighteen pence sterling the pound weight; and the current price of beaver in New-York being five shillings New-York money, or three shillings sterling the pound weight. Therefore it plainly follows, that our Indian traders could undersell the French traders, though they were to give as great a price for European goods as the French do, and did transport them at as great charge, because of the double price they have for their furs in New-York.

But as our Indian traders not only have a double price for their Indian goods, but likewise buy the goods they sell to the Indians, at half the price the French Indian traders do, the French traders must be ruined by carrying on this trade, in competition with the English of New-York. And the French Indian traders had been ruined before now, if they had not found means to carry their beaver to Albany, where they got double the price they must have sold for in Canada.

It may be objected against this argument, that the Canada Company as soon as they find that the traders cannot sell at their established price, will allow a greater price. But if we consider the duties the French company is obliged to pay to the king, they cannot allow so great a price as the English can at New-York. And if it should be insisted, that the French company may obtain a remission of those, yet if the clandestine trade with Albany be entirely stopt, the French traders will be ruined before such remission can be obtained, and their trade will be at an end.

My inclination led me to show what advantages not only the Indian trade would reap by extending our frontiers as far as the lakes, but likewise the British trade in some other branches, which the parliament of Great Britain seem to have much at heart, viz. naval stores; for the soil on both sides of the Mohawk River being as rich as it is possible, I believe, for any land to be, will be found the most proper for raising of hemp of any part of America, and the whole country round it being full of the largest pines, the royal navy is as likely to be well provided with masts there, and at as cheap a rate as any where else. But I have already too far presumed on your excellency's patience.

CADWALLADER COLDEN

Source: David Hosack, *Memoir of De Witt Clinton: With an Appendix, Containing Numerous Documents, Illustrative of the Principal Events of his Life* (New York: Printed by J. Seymour, 1829), 232–45.

A Modest Enquiry into the Nature and Necessity of a Paper Currency (1729)

Since the supply of any official currency was limited in the colonies, a number of items served as money: wampum, furs, cash crops (tobacco, rice, indigo), and various foreign coinages. Some colonies issued their own paper money, but determining its value was problematic. To counteract depreciation in its value, Benjamin Franklin proposed that printed paper money be tied to land secured by mortgages. Franklin favored the circulation of money through public banks such as the Pennsylvania Land Bank, and he received a contract for the printing of the bank's third issue of notes in 1729.

THERE is no Science, the Study of which is more useful and commendable than the Knowledge of the true Interest of one's Country; and perhaps there is no Kind of Learning more abstruse and intricate, more difficult to acquire in any Degree of Perfection than This, and therefore none more generally neglected. Hence it is, that we every Day find Men in Conversation contending warmly on some Point in Politicks, which, altho' it may nearly concern them both, neither of them understand any more than they do each other.

Thus much by way of Apology for this present Enquiry into the Nature and Necessity of a Paper Currency. And if any Thing I shall say, may be a Means of fixing a Subject that is now the chief Concern of my Countrymen, in a clearer Light, I shall have the Satisfaction of thinking my Time and Pains well employed.

To proceed, then,

There is a certain proportionate Quantity of Money requisite to carry on the Trade of a Country freely and currently; More than which would be of no Advantage in Trade, and Less, if much less, exceedingly detrimental to it.

This leads us to the following general Considerations.

FIRST, A great Want of Money in any Trading Country, occasions Interest to be at a very high Rate. And here it may be observed, that it is impossible by any Laws to restrain Men from giving and receiving exhorbitant Interest, where Money is suitably scarce: For he that wants Money will find out Ways to give 10 per Cent. when he cannot have it for less, altho' the Law forbids to take more than 6 per Cent. Now the Interest of Money being high is prejudicial to a Country several Ways: It makes Land bear a low Price, because few Men will lay out their Money in Land, when they can make a much greater Profit by lending it out upon Interest: And much less will Men be inclined to venture their Money at Sea, when they can, without Risque or Hazard, have a great and certain Profit by keeping it at home; thus Trade is discouraged. And if in two Neighbouring Countries the Traders of one, by Reason of a greater Plenty of Money, can borrow it to trade with at a lower Rate than the Traders of the other, they will infallibly have the Advantage, and get the greatest Part of that Trade into their own Hands; For he that trades with Money he hath borrowed at 8 or 10 per Cent. cannot hold Market with him that borrows his Money at 6 or 4. On the contrary, A plentiful Currency will occasion Interest to be low: And this will be an Inducement to many to lay out their Money in Lands, rather than put it out to Use, by which means Land will begin to rise in Value and bear a better Price: And at the same Time it will tend to enliven Trade exceedingly, because People will find more Profit in employing their Money that Way than in Usury; and many that understand Business very well, but have not a Stock sufficient of their own, will be encouraged to borrow Money; to trade with, when they can have it at a moderate Interest.

SECONDLY, Want of Money in a Country reduces the Price of that Part of its Produce which is used in Trade: Because Trade being discouraged by it as above, there is a much less Demand for that Produce. And this is another Reason why Land in such a Case will be low, especially where the Staple Commodity of the Country is the immediate Produce of the Land, because that Produce being low, fewer People find an Advantage in Husbandry, or the Improvement of Land. On the contrary, A Plentiful Currency will occasion the Trading Produce to bear a good Price: Because Trade being encouraged and advanced by it, there will be a much greater Demand for that Produce; which will be a great Encouragement of Husbandry, who probably might otherwise have Sought some more profitable Employment.

As we have already experienced how much the Increase of our Currency by what Paper Money has been made, has encouraged our Trade; particularly to instance only in one Article, Ship-Building; it may not be amiss to observe under this Head, what a great Advantage it must be to us as a Trading Country, that has Workmen and all the Materials proper for that Business within itself, to have Ship-Building as much as possible advanced: For every Ship that is built here for the English Merchants, gains the Province her clear Value in Gold and Silver, which must otherwise have been sent Home for Returns in her Stead; and likewise, every Ship built in and belonging to the Province, not only saves the Province her first Cost, but all the Freight, Wages and Provisions she ever makes or requires as long as she lasts; provided Care is taken to make This her Pay Port, and that she always takes Provisions with her for the whole Voyage, which may easily be done. And how considerable an Article this is yearly in our Favour, every one, the least acquainted with mercantile Affairs, must needs be sensible; for if we could not Build our selves, we must either purchase so many Vessels as we want from other Countries, or else Hire them to carry our Produce to Market, which would be more expensive than Purchasing, and on may other Accounts exceedingly to our Loss. Now as Trade in general will decline where there is not a plentiful Currency, so Ship-Building must certainly of Consequence decline where Trade is declining.

THIRDLY, Want of Money in a Country discourages Labouring and Handicrafts Men (which are the chief Strength and Support of a People) from coming to settle in it, and induces many that were settled to leave the Country, and seek Entertainment and Employment in other Places, where they can be better paid. For what can be more disheartning to an industrious labouring Man, than this, that after he hath earned his Bread with the Sweat of his Brows, he must spend as much Time, and have near as much Fatigue in getting it, as he had to earn it. And nothing makes more bad Paymasters than a general Scarcity of Money. And here again is a Third Reason for Land's bearing a low Price in such a Country, because Land always increases in Value in Proportion with the Increase of the People settling on it, there being so many more Buyers; and its Value will infallibly be diminished, if the Number of its Inhabitants diminish. On the contrary, A Plentiful Currency will encourage great Numbers of Labouring and Handicrafts Men to come and Settle in the Country, by the same Reason that a Want of it will discourage and drive them out. Now the more Inhabitants, the greater Demand for Land (as is said above) upon which it must necessarily rise in Value, and bear a better Price. The same may be said of the Value of House-Rent, which will be advanced for the same Reasons; and by the Increase of Trade and Riches People will be enabled to pay greater Rents. Now

the Value of House-Rent rising, and Interest becoming low, many that in a Scarcity of Money practised Usury, will probably be more inclined to Building; which will likewise sensibly enliven Business in any Place; it being an Advantage not only to Brickmakers, Bricklayers, Masons, Carpenters, Joiners, Glaziers, and several other Trades immediately employed by Building, but likewise to Farmers, Brewers, Bakers, Taylors, Shoemakers, Shop-keepers, and in short to every one that they lay their Money out with.

FOURTHLY, Want of Money in such a Country as ours, occasions a greater Consumption of English and European Goods, in Proportion to the Number of the People, than there would otherwise be. Because Merchants and Traders by whom abundance of Artificers and labouring Men are employed, finding their other Affairs require what Money they can get into their hands, oblige those who work for them to take one half, or perhaps two thirds Goods in Pay. By this Means a greater Quantity of Goods are disposed of, and to a greater Value; because Working Men and their Families are thereby induced to be more profuse and extravagant in fine Apparel and the like, than they would if they were obliged to pay ready Money for such Things after they had earn'd and received it, or if such Goods were not imposed upon them, of which they can make no other Use: For such People cannot send the Goods they are paid with to a Foreign Market, without losing considerably by having them sold for less than they stand 'em in here; neither can they easily dispose of them at Home, because their Neighbours are generally supplied in the same Manner; But how unreasonable would it be, if some of those very Men who have been a Means of thus forcing People into unnecessary Expence, should be the first and most earnest in accusing them of Pride and Prodigalty. Now tho' this extraordinary Consumption of Foreign Commodities may be a Profit to particular Men, yet the Country in general grows poorer by it apace.— On the contrary, As A plentiful Currency will occasion a less Consumption of European Goods, in Proportion to the Number of the People, so it will be a means of making the Balance of our Trade more equal than it now is, if it does not give it in our Favour because our own Produce will be encouraged at the same Time. And it is to be observed, that tho' less Foreign Commodities are consumed in Proportion to the Number of People, yet this will be no Disadvantage to the Merchant, because the Number of People increasing, will occasion an increasing Demand of more Foreign Goods in the Whole.

Thus we have seen some of the many heavy Disadvantages a Country (especially such a Country as ours) must labour under, when it has not a sufficient Stock of running Cash to manage its Trade currently. And we have likewise seen some of the Advantages which accrue from having Money sufficient, or a Plentiful Currency.

The foregoing Paragraphs being well considered, we shall naturally be led to draw the following Conclusions with

Regard to what Persons will probably be for or against Emitting a large Additional Sum of Paper Bills in this Province.

1. Since Men will always be powerfully influenced in their Opinions and Actions by what appears to be their particular Interest: Therefore all those, who wanting Courage to venture in Trade, now practise Lending Money on Security for exhorbitant Interest, which in a Scarcity of Money will be done notwithstanding the Law, I say all such will probably be against a large Addition to our present Stock of Paper Money; because a plentiful Currency will lower Interest, and make it common to lend on less Security.

2. All those who are Possessors of large Sums of Money, and are disposed to purchase Land, which is attended with a great and sure Advantage in a growing Country as this is; I say, the Interest of all such Men will encline them to oppose a large Addition to our Money. Because their Wealth is now continually increasing by the large Interest they receive, which will enable them (if they can keep Land from rising) to purchase More some time hence than they can at present; and in the mean time all Trade being discouraged, not only those who borrow of them, but the Common People in general will be impoverished, and consequently obliged to sell More Land for less Money than they will do at present. And yet, after such Men are possessed of as much Land as they can purchase, it will then be their Interest to have Money made Plentiful, because that will immediately make Land rise in Value in their Hands. Now it ought not to be wondered at, if People from the Knowledge of a Man's Interest do sometimes make a true Guess at his Designs; for, Interest, they say, will not Lie.

3. Lawyers, and others concerned in Court Business, will probably many of them be against a plentiful Currency; because People in that Case will have less Occasion to run in Debt, and consequently less Occasion to go to Law and Sue one another for their Debts. Tho' I know some even among these Gentlemen, that regard the Publick Good before their own apparent private Interest.

4. All those who are any way Dependants on such Persons as are above mentioned, whether as holding Offices, as Tenants, or as Debtors, must at least appear to be against a large Addition; because if they do not, they must sensibly feel their present Interest hurt. And besides these, there are, doubtless, many well-meaning Gentlemen and Others, who, without any immediate private Interest of their own in View, are against making such an Addition, thro' an Opinion they may have of the Honesty and sound Judgment of some of their Friends that oppose it (perhaps for the Ends aforesaid), without having given it any thorough Consideration themselves. And thus it is no Wonder if there is a powerful Party on that Side. On the other Hand, Those who are Lovers of Trade, and delight to see Manufactures encouraged, will be for having a large Addition to our Currency: For they very well know, that People will have little Heart to advance Money in Trade, when what they can get is scarce sufficient to purchase Necessaries, and supply their Families with Provision. Much less will they lay it out in advancing new Manufactures; nor is it possible new Manufactures Should turn to any Account, where there is not Money to pay the Workmen, who are discouraged by being paid in Goods, because it is a great Disadvantage to them.

Again, Those who are truly for the Proprietor's Interest (and have no separate Views of their own that are predominant) will be heartily for a large Addition: Because, as I have shewn above, Plenty of Money will for several Reasons make Land rise in Value exceedingly: And I appeal to those immediately concerned for the Proprietor in the Sale of his Lands, whether Land has not risen very much since the first Emission of what Paper Currency we now have, and even by its Means. Now we all know the Proprietary has great Quantities to sell.

And since a Plentiful Currency will be so great a Cause of advancing this Province in Trade and Riches, and increasing the Number of its People; which, tho' it will not sensibly lessen the Inhabitants of Great Britain, will occasion a much greater Vent and Demand for their Commodities here; and allowing that the Crown is the more powerful for its Subjects increasing in Wealth and Number, I cannot think it the Interest of England to oppose us in making as great a Sum of Paper Money here, as we, who are the best Judges of our own Necessities, find convenient. And if I were not sensible that the Gentlemen of Trade in England, to whom we have already parted with our Silver and Gold, are misinformed of our Circumstances, and therefore endeavour to have our Currency stinted to what it now is, I should think the Government at Home had some Reasons for discouraging and impoverishing this Province, which we are not acquainted with.

It remains now that we enquire, Whether a large Addition to our Paper Currency will not make it sink in Value very much; And here it will be requisite that we first form just Notions of the Nature and Value of Money in general.

As Providence has so ordered it, that not only different Countries, but even different Parts of the same Country, have their peculiar most suitable Productions; and likewise that different Men have Genius's adapted to Variety of different Arts and Manufactures, Therefore Commerce, or the Exchange of one Commodity or Manufacture for another, is highly convenient and beneficial to Mankind. As for Instance A may be skilful in the Art of making Cloth, and B understand the raising of Corn; A wants Corn, and B Cloth; upon which they make an Exchange with each other for as much as each has Occasion, to the mutual Advantage and Satisfaction of both.

But as it would be very tedious, if there were no other Way of general Dealing, but by an immediate Exchange of Commodities; because a Man that had Corn to dispose of, and wanted Cloth for it, might perhaps in his Search for a Chapman to deal with, meet with twenty People that had

Cloth to dispose of, but wanted no Corn; and with twenty others that wanted his Corn, but had no Cloth to suit him with. To remedy such Inconveniences, and facilitate Exchange, men have invented MONEY, properly called a Medium of Exchange, because through or by its Means Labour is exchanged for Labour, or one Commodity for another. And whatever particular Thing Men have agreed to make this Medium of, whether Gold, Silver, Copper, or Tobacco; it is, to those who possess it (if they want any Thing) that very Thing which they want, because it will immediately procure it for them. It is Cloth to him that wants Cloth, and Corn to those that want Corn; and so of all other Necessaries, it is whatsoever it will procure. Thus he who had Corn to dispose of, and wanted to purchase Cloth with it, might sell his Corn for its Value in this general Medium, to one who wanted Corn but had no Cloth; and with this Medium he might purchase Cloth of him that wanted no Corn, but perhaps some other Thing, as Iron it may be, which this Medium will immediately procure, and so he may be said to have exchanged his Cloth for Iron; and thus the general Exchange is soon performed, to the Satisfaction of all Parties, with abundance of Facility.

For many Ages, those Parts of the World which are engaged in Commerce, have fixed upon Gold and Silver as the chief and most proper Materials for this Medium; they being in themselves valuable Metals for their Fineness, Beauty, and Scarcity. By these, particularly by Silver, it has been usual to value all Things else: But as Silver it self is no certain permanent Value, being worth more or less according to its Scarcity or Plenty, therefore it seems requisite to fix upon Something else, more proper to be made a Measure of Values, and this I take to be Labour.

By Labour may the Value of Silver be measured as well as other Things. As, Suppose one Man employed to raise Corn, while another is digging and refining Silver; at the Year's End, or any other Period of Time, the compleat Produce of Corn, and that of Silver, are the natural Price of each other; and if one be twenty Bushels, and the other twenty Ounces, then an Ounce of that Silver is worth the Labour of raising a Bushel of that Corn. Now if by the Discovery of some nearer, more easy or plentiful Mines, a Man may get Forty Ounces of Silver as easily as formerly he did Twenty, and the same Labour is still required to raise Twenty Bushels of Corn, then Two Ounces of Silver will be worth no more than the same Labour of raising One Bushel of Corn, and that Bushel of Corn will be as cheap at two Ounces, as it was before at one; ceteris paribus.

Thus the Riches of a Country are to be valued by the Quantity of Labour its Inhabitants are able to purchase, and not by the Quantity of Silver and Gold they possess; which will purchase more or less Labour, and therefore is more or less valuable, as is said before, according to its Scarcity or Plenty. As those Metals have grown much more plentiful in Europe since the Discovery of America, so they have sunk in Value exceedingly; for, to instance in England, formerly one

Penny of Silver was worth a Days Labour, but now it is hardly worth the sixth Part of a Days Labour; because not less than Six-pence will purchase the Labour of a Man for a Day in any Part of that Kingdom; which is wholly to be attributed to the much greater Plenty of Money now in England than formerly. And yet perhaps England is in Effect no richer now than at that Time; because as much Labour might be purchas'd or Work got done of almost any kind, for 100 then, as will now require or is now worth 600.

In the next Place let us consider the Nature of Banks emitting Bills of Credit, as they are at this Time used in Hamburgh, Amsterdam, London and Venice.

Those Places being Seats of vast Trade, and the Payment of great sums being for that Reason frequent, Bills of Credit are found very convenient in Business; because a great Sum is more easily counted in Them, lighter in Carriage, concealed in less Room, and therefore safer in Travelling or Laying up, and on many other Accounts they are very much valued. The Banks are the general Cashiers of all Gentlemen, Merchants, and great Traders in and about those Cities; there they deposit their Money, and may take out Bills to the Value, for which they can be certain to have Money again at the Bank at any Time: This gives the Bills a Credit; so that in England they are never less valuable than Money, and in Venice and Amsterdam they are generally worth more. And the Bankers always reserving Money in hand to answer more than the common Run of Demands (and some People constantly putting in while others are taking out) are able besides to lend large Sums, on good Security, to the Government or others, for a reasonable Interest, by which they are paid for their Care and Trouble; and the Money which otherwise would have lain dead in their Hands, is made to circulate again and thereby among the People: and thus the Running Cash of the Nation is as it were doubled; for all great Payments being made in Bills, Money in lower Trade becomes much more plentiful: And this is an exceeding great Advantage to a Trading Country, that is not over-stock'd with Gold and Silver.

As those who take Bills out of the Banks in Europe, put in Money for Security; so here, and in some of the neighbouring Provinces, we engage our Land. Which of these Methods will most effectually secure the Bills from actually sinking in Value, comes next to be considered.

Trade in general being nothing else but the Exchange of Labour for Labour, the Value of all Things is, as I have said before, most justly measured by Labour. Now suppose I put my Money into a Bank, and take out a Bill for the Value; if this Bill at the Time of my receiving it, would purchase me the Labour of one hundred Men for twenty Days; but some time after will only purchase the Labour of the same Number of Men for fifteen Days; it is plain the Bill has sunk in value one fourth Part. Now Silver and Gold being of no permanent Value; and as this Bill is founded on Money, and therefore to be esteemed as such, it may be that the Occasion of this Fall is the increasing Plenty of Gold and Silver, by which Money is one fourth Part less valuable than before, and therefore one fourth more is given of it for the same Quantity of Labour; and if Land is not become more plentiful by some proportionate Decrease of the People, one fourth Part more of Money is given for the same Quantity of Land, whereby it appears that it would have been more profitable to me to have laid that Money out in Land which I put into the Bank, than to place it there and take a Bill for it. And it is certain that the Value of Money has been continually sinking in England for several Ages past, because it has been continually increasing in Quantity. But if Bills could be taken out of a Bank in Europe on a Land Security, it is probable the Value of such Bills would be more certain and steady, because the Number of Inhabitants continue to be near the same in those Countries from Age to Age.

For as Bills issued upon Money Security are Money, so Bills issued upon Land, are in Effect Coined Land.

Therefore (to apply the Above to our own Circumstances) If Land in this Province was falling, or any way likely to fall, it would behove the Legislature most carefully to contrive how to prevent the Bills issued upon Land from falling with it. But as our People increase exceedingly, and will be further increased, as I have before shewn, by the Help of a large Addition to our Currency; and as Land in consequence is continually rising, So, in case no Bills are emitted but what are upon Land Security, the Money-Acts in every Part punctually enforced and executed, the Payments of Principal and Interest being duly and strictly required, and the Principal bona fide sunk according to Law, it is absolutely impossible such Bills should ever sink below their first Value, or below the Value of the Land on which they are founded. In short, there is so little Danger of their sinking that they would certainly rise as the Land rises, if they were not emitted in a proper Manner for preventing it; that is, by providing in the Act That Payment may be made, either in those Bills, or in any other Bills made current by any Act of the Legislature of this Province; and that the Interest, as it is received, may be again emitted in Discharge of Publick Debts; whereby circulating it returns again into the Hands of the Borrowers, and becomes Part of their future Payments; and thus as it is likely there will not be any Difficulty for want of Bills to pay the Office, they are hereby kept from rising above their first Value; For else, supposing there should be emitted upon mortgaged Land its full present Value in Bills; as in the Banks in Europe the full value of the Money deposited is given out in Bills; and supposing the Office would take nothing but the same Sum in those Bills in Discharge of the Land; as in the Banks aforesaid, the same Sum in their Bills must be brought in, in order to receive out the Money: In such Case the Bills would most surely rise in Value as the Land rises; as certain as the Bank Bills founded on Money would fall if that Money was falling. Thus if I were to mortgage to a Loan-Office, or Bank, a Parcel of Land now valued at 100 in Silver, and receive for it the like Sum in Bills, to be paid in again at the Expiration of a certain

Term of Years; before which, my Land rising in Value becomes worth 150 in Silver: 'Tis plain, that if I have not these Bills in Possession, and the Office will take nothing but these Bills, or else what it is now become worth in Silver, in Discharge of my Land; I say it appears plain, that those Bills will now be worth 150 in Silver to the Possessor; and if I can purchase them for less, in order to redeem my Land, I shall by so much be a Gainer.

I need not say any Thing to convince the Judicious that our Bills have not yet sunk, tho' there is and has been some Difference between them and Silver; because it is evident that that Difference is occasioned by the Scarcity of the latter, which is now become a Merchandize, rising and falling, like other Commodities, as there is a greater or less Demand for it, or as it is more or less Plenty.

Yet farther, in order to make a true Estimate of the Value of Money, we must distinguish between Money as it is Bullion, which is Merchandize, and as by being coin'd it is made a Currency: For its Value as a Merchandize, and its Value as a Currency, are two distinct Things; and each may possibly rise and fall in some Degree independent of the other. Thus if the Quantity of Bullion increases in a Country, it will proportionably decrease in Value; but if at the same Time the Quantity of current Coin should decrease (supposing Payments may not be made in Bullion) what Coin there is will rise in Value as a Currency, i.e. People will give more Labour in Manufactures for a certain Sum of ready Money.

In the same Manner must we consider a Paper Currency founded on Land; as it is Land, and as it is a Currency

Money as Bullion, or as Land, is valuable by so much Labour as it costs to procure that Bullion or Land.

Money, as a Currency, has an Additional Value by so much Time and Labour as it saves in the Exchange of Commodities.

If, as a Currency, it saves one Fourth Part of the Time and Labour of a Country; it has, on that Account, one Fourth added to its original Value.

When there is no Money in a Country, all Commerce must be by Exchange. Now if it takes one fourth Part of the Time and Labour of a Country, to exchange or get their Commodities exchanged; then, in computing their Value, that Labour of Exchanging must be added to the Labour of manufacturing those Commodities: But if that Time or Labour is saved by introducing Money sufficient, then the additional Value on Account of the Labour of Exchanging must be abated, and Things sold for only the Value of the Labour in making them; because the People may now in the same Time make one Fourth more in Quantity of Manufactures than they could before.

From these Considerations it may be gathered, that in all the Degrees between having no Money in a Country, and Money sufficient for the Trade, it will rise and fall in Value as a Currency, in Proportion to the Decrease or Increase of its Quantity: and if there may be at some Time more than enough, the Overplus will have no Effect towards making the Currency, as a Currency, of less value than when there was but enough; because such Overplus will not be used in Trade, but be some other way disposed of.

If we enquire, How much per Cent. Interest ought to be required upon the Loan of these Bills; we must consider what is the Natural Standard of Usury: And this appears to be, where the Security is undoubted, at least the Rent of so much Land as the Money lent will buy: For it cannot be expected that any Man will lend his Money for less than it would fetch him in as Rent if he laid it out in Land, which is the mose [most] secure Property in the World. But if the Security is casual, then a kind of Ensurance must be enterwoven with the simple natural Interest, which may advance the Usury very consciably to any height below the Principal it self. Now among us, if the Value of Land is twenty Years Purchase, Five per Cent. is the just Rate of Interest for Money lent on undoubted Security. Yet if Money grows scarce in a Country, it becomes more difficult for People to make punctual Payments of what they borrow, Money being hard to be raised; likewise Trade being discouraged, and Business impeded for want of a Currency, abundance of People must be in declining Circumstances, and by these Means Security is more precarious than where Money is plenty. On such Accounts it is no wonder if People ask a greater Interest for their Money than the natural Interest; and what is above is to be look'd upon as a kind of Premium for the Ensurance of those Uncertainties, as they are greater or less. Thus we always see, that where Money is scarce, Interest is high, and low where it is plenty. Now it is certainly the Advantage of a Country to make Interest as low as possible, as I have already shewn; and this can be done no other way than by making Money plentiful. And since, in Emitting Paper Money among us, the Office has the best of Security, the Titles to the Land being all skilfully and strictly examined and ascertained; and as it is only permitting the People by Law to coin their own Land, which costs the Government nothing, the Interest being more than enough to pay the charges of Printing, Officers Fees, &c. I cannot see any good Reason why Four per Cent. to the Loan-Office should not be thought fully sufficient. As a low Interest may incline more to take Money out, it will become more plentiful in Trade; and this may bring down the common Usury, in which Security is more dubious, to the Pitch it is determined at by Law.

If it should be objected, That the Emitting It at so low an Interest, and on such easy Terms, will occasion more to be taken out than the Trade of the Country really requires: It may be answered, That, as has already been shewn, there can never be so much of it emitted as to make it fall below the Land it is founded on; because no Man in his Senses will mortgage his Estate for what is of no more Value to him than That he has mortgaged, especially if the Possession of what he receives is more precarious than of what he mortgages, as that of Paper Money is when compared to Land: And if it should ever become so plenty by indiscreet Persons

continuing to take out a large Overplus, above what is necessary in Trade, so as to make People imagine it would become by that Means of less Value than their mortgaged Lands, they would immediately of Course begin to pay it in again to the Office to redeem their Land, and continue to do so till there was no more left in Trade than was absolutely necessary. And thus the Proportion would find it self, (tho' there were a Million too much in the Office to be let out) without giving any one the Trouble of Calculation.

It may perhaps be objected to what I have written concerning the Advantages of a large Addition to our Currency, That if the People of this Province increase, and Husbandry is more followed, we shall overstock the Markets with our Produce of Flower, &c. To this it may be answered, that we can never have too many People (nor too much Money) For when one Branch of Trade or Business is overstocked with Hands, there are the more to spare to be employed in another. So if raising Wheat proves dull, more may (if there is Money to support and carry on new Manufactures) proceed to the raising and manufacturing of Hemp, Silk, Iron and many other Things the Country is very capable of, for which we only want People to work, and Money to pay them with.

Upon the Whole it may be observed, That it is the highest Interest of a Trading Country in general to make Money plentiful; and that it can be a Disadvantage to none that have honest Designs. It cannot hurt even the Usurers, tho' it should sink what they receive as Interest; because they will be proportionably more secure in what they lend; or they will have an Opportunity of employing their Money to greater Advantage, to themselves as well as to the Country. Neither can it hurt those Merchants who have great Sums out-standing in Debts in the Country, and seem on that Account to have the most plausible Reason to fear it; to wit, because a large Addition being made to our Currency, will increase the Demand of our Exporting Produce, and by that Means raise the Price of it, so that they will not be able to purchase so much Bread and Flower with 100 when they shall receive it after such an Addition, as they now can, and may if there is no Addition: I say it cannot hurt even such, because they will get in their Debts just in exact Proportion so much the easier and sooner as the Money becomes plentier; and therefore, considering the Interest and Trouble saved, they will not be Losers; because it only sinks in Value as a Currency, proportionally as it becomes more plenty. It cannot hurt the Interest of Great Britain, as has been shewn; and it will greatly advance the Interest of the Proprietor. It will be an Advantage to every industrious Tradesman, &c. because his Business will be carried on more freely, and Trade be universally enlivened by it. And as more Business in all Manufactures will be done, by so much as the Labour and Time spent in Exchange is saved, the Country in general will grow so much the richer.

It is nothing to the Purpose to object the wretched Fall of the Bills in New-England and South-Carolina, unless it might be made evident that their Currency was emitted with the same Prudence, and on such good Security as ours is; and it certainly was not.

As this Essay is wrote and published in Haste, and the Subject in it self intricate, I hope I shall be censured with Candour, if, for want of Time carefully to revise what I have written, in some Places I should appear to have express'd my self too obscurely, and in others am liable to Objections I did not foresee. I sincerely desire to be acquainted with the Truth, and on that Account shall think my self obliged to any one, who will take the Pains to shew me, or the Publick, where I am mistaken in my Conclusions, And as we all know there are among us several Gentlemen of acute Parts and profound Learning, who are very much against any Addition to our Money, it were to be wished that they would favour the Country with their Sentiments on this Head in Print; which, supported with Truth and good Reasoning, may probably be very convincing. And this is to be desired the rather, because many People knowing the Abilities of those Gentle-men to manage a good Cause, are apt to construe their Silence in This, as an Argument of a bad One. Had any Thing of that Kind ever yet appeared, perhaps I should not have given the Publick this Trouble: But as those ingenious Gentlemen have not yet (and I doubt never will) think it worth their Concern to enlighten the Minds of their erring Countrymen in this Particular, I think it would be highly commendable in every one of us, more fully to bend our Minds to the Study of What is the true Interest of PENNSYLVANIA; whereby we may be enabled, not only to reason pertinently with one another; but, if Occasion requires, to transmit Home such clear Representations, as must inevitably convince our Superiors of the Reasonableness and Integrity of our Designs.

B. F.

Philadelphia, April 3, 1729.

Source: Andrew MacFarland Davis, *Colonial Currency Reprints, 1682–1751*, Vol. II (Boston: Prince Society, 1910–1911), 336–57.

Oglethorpe's Vision for the Founding of Georgia (1733)

As the last English colony established in America, Georgia was designed as a refuge where British debtors and criminals could have a new beginning and become self-sustaining. Hopes were high for the new colony, which was established with no slavery, and the mother country expected it to produce a steady stream of exports such as silk, oil, dyes, and medicines. The following, by James Oglethorpe, was published as a pamphlet in 1733 under the title "Some Account of the Designs of the Trustees for Establishing the Colony of Georgia in America."

In America there are fertile lands sufficient to subsist all the useless Poor in *England*, and distressed Protestants in Europe; yet Thousands starve for want of mere sustenance. The distance makes it difficult to get thither. The same want that renders men useless here, prevents their paying their passage; and if others pay it for 'em, they become servants, or rather slaves for years to those who have defrayed the expense. Therefore, money for passage is necessary, but is not the only want; for if people were set down in America, and the land before them, they must cut down trees, build houses, fortify towns, dig and sow the land before they can get in a harvest; and till then, they must be provided with food, and kept together, that they may be assistant to each other for their natural support and protection.

The Romans esteemed the sending forth of Colonies, among their noblest works; they observed that Rome, as she increased in power and empire, drew together such a conflux of people from all parts that she found herself over-burdened with their number, and the government brought under an incapacity to provide for them, or keep them in order. Necessity, the mother of invention, suggested to them an expedient, which at once gave ease to the capital, and increased the wealth and number of industrious citizens, by lessening the useless and unruly multitude; and by planting them in colonies on the frontiers of their empire, gave a new Strength to the whole; and *This* they looked upon to be so considerable a service to the commonwealth, that they created peculiar officers for the establishment of such colonies, and the expence was defrayed out of the public treasury.

FROM THE CHARTER.—His Majesty having taken into his consideration, the miserable circumstances of many of his own poor subjects, ready to perish for want: as likewise the distresses of many poor foreigners, who would take refuge here from persecution; and having a Princely regard to the great danger the southern frontiers of South Carolina are exposed to, by reason of the small number of white inhabitants there, hath, out of his Fatherly compassion towards his subjects, been graciously pleased to grant a charter for incorporating a number of gentlemen by the name of *The Trustees for establishing the Colony of Georgia in America.* They are impowered to collect benefactions; and lay them out in cloathing, arming, sending over, and supporting colonies of the poor, whether subjects or foreigners, in Georgia. And his Majesty farther grants all his lands between *Savannah and Alatamaha,* which he erects into a Province by the name of GEORGIA, unto the Trustees, in trust for the poor, and for the better support of the Colony. At the desire of the Gentlemen, there are clauses in the Charter, restraining them and their successors from receiving any salary, fee, perquisite, or profit, whatsoever, by or from this undertaking; and also from receiving any grant of lands within the said district, to themselves, or in trust for them. There are farther clauses granting to the Trustees proper powers for establishing and governing the Colony, and liberty of conscience to all who shall settle there.

The Trustees intend to relieve such unfortunate persons as cannot subsist here, and establish them in an orderly manner, so as to form a well regulated town. As far as their fund goes, they will defray the charge of their passage to Georgia; give them necessaries, cattle, land, and subsistence, till such time as they can build their houses and clear some of their land. They rely for success, first on the goodness of Providence, next on the compassionate disposition of the people of England; and, they doubt not, that much will be spared from luxury, and superfluous expenses, by generous tempers, when such an opportunity is offered them by the giving of £20 to provide for a man or woman, or £10 to a child for ever.

In order to prevent the benefaction given to this purpose, from ever being misapplied; and to keep up, as far as human Precaution can, a spirit of Disinterestedness, the Trustees have established the following method: That, each Benefactor may know what he has contributed is safely lodged, and justly accounted for, all money given will be deposited in the Bank of England; and entries made of every benefaction, in a book to be kept for that purpose by the Trustees; or, if concealed, the names of those, by whose hands they sent their money. There are to be annual accounts of all the money received, and how the same has been disposed of, laid before the Lord High Chancellor, the Lord Chief Justice of the King's Bench, the Master of the Rolls, the Lord Chief Justice of the Common Pleas, and the Lord Chief Baron of the Exchequer, or two of them, will be transmitted to every considerable Benefactor.

By such a Colony, many families, who would otherwise starve, will be provided for, and made masters of houses and lands; the people in Great Britain to whom these necessitous families were a burden, will be relieved; numbers of manufacturers will be here employed, forr supplying them with clothes, working tools, and other necessaries; and by giving refuge to the distressed Saltzburgers, and other persecuted Protestants, the power of Britain, as a reward for its hospitality, will be encreased by the addition of so many religious and industrious subjects.

The Colony of Georgia lying about the same latitude with part of China, Persia, Palestine, and the Madeiras, it is highly probable that when hereafter it shall be well-peopled and rightly cultivated, ENGLAND may be supplied from thence with raw Silk, Wine, Oil, Dyes, Drugs, and many other materials for manufactures, which she is obliged to purchase from Southern countries. As towns are established and grow populous along the rivers Savannah and Alatamaha, they will make such a barrier as will render the southern frontier of the British Colonies on the Continent of America, safe from Indian and other enemies.

All human affairs are so subject to chance, that there in no answering for events; yet from reason and the nature of things, it may be concluded, that the riches and also the number of the inhabitants in Great Britain will be increased, by importing at a cheap rate from this new Colony, the materials requisite for carrying on in Britain several manufactures. For our Manufacturers will be encouraged to marry and multiply, when they find themselves in circumstances to provide for their families, which must necessarily be the happy effect of the increase and cheapness of our materials of those Manufactures, which at present we purchase with our money from foreign countries, at dear rates; and also many people will find employment here, on account such farther demands by the people of this Colony, for those manufactures which are made for the produce of our own country; and, as has been justly observed, the people will always abound where there is full employment for them.

CHRISTIANITY will be extended by the execution of this design; since, the good discipline established by the Society, will reform the manners of those miserable objects, who shall be by them subsisted; and the example of a whole Colony, who shall behave in a just, moral, and religious manner, will contribute greatly towards the conversion of the Indians, and taking off the prejudices received from the profligate lives of such who have scarce any thing of Christianity but the name.

The Trustees in their general meetings, will consider of the most prudent methods for effectually establishing a regular Colony; and that it may be done, is demonstrable. Under what difficulties, was Virginia planted?—the coast and climate then unknown; the Indians numerous, and at enmity with the first Planters, who were forced to fetch all provisions from England; yet it is grown a mighty Province, and the Revenue receives £100,000 for duties upon the goods that they send yearly home. Within this 50 years, Pennsylvania was as much a forest as Georgia is now; and in these few years, by the wise economy of William Penn, and those who assisted him, it now gives food to 80,000 inhabitants, and can boast of as fine a City as most in Europe.

This new Colony is more likely to succeed than either of the former were, since Carolina abounds with provisions, the climate is known, and there are men to instruct in the seasons and nature of cultivating the soil. There are but few Indian families within 400 miles; and those, in perfect amity with the English:—*Port* Royal (the station of his Majesty's ships) is within 30, and *Charlestown* (a great mart) is within 120 miles. If the Colony is attacked, it may be relieved by sea, from Port Royal, or the Bahamas; and the Militia of South Carolina is ready to support it, by land.

For the continuing the relief which is now given, there will be lands reserved in the Colony; and the benefit arising from them is to go to the carrying on of the trust. So that, at the same time, the money by being laid out preserves the lives of the poor, and makes a comfortable provision for those whose expenses are by it defrayed; their labor in improving their own lands, will make the adjoining reserved lands valuable; and the rents of those reserved lands will be a perpetual fund for the relieving more poor people. So that instead of laying out the money upon lands, with the income thereof to support the poor, this is laying out money upon the poor; and by relieving those who are now unfortunate, raises a fund for the perpetual relief of those who shall be so hereafter.

There is an occasion now offered for every one, to help forward this design; the smallest benefaction will be received, and applied with the utmost care:—every little will do something; and a great number of small benefactions will amount to a sum capable of doing a great deal of good.

If any person, moved with the calamities of the unfortunate, shall be inclined to contribute towards their relief, they are desired to pay their benefactions into the Bank of England, on account of the Trustees for establishing the Colony of Georgia in America; or else, to any of the Trustees, who are, &c.

Source: Peter Force, *Tracts*, Vol. 1, no. 2 (Washington, DC, 1836), 4–7.

The Trial of Peter Zenger (1735)

Beginning in 1733, John Peter Zenger, the publisher of the *New York Weekly Journal*, printed critical articles in his newspaper about New York Governor William Cosby. Zenger was arrested for seditious libel and came before Chief Justice James Delancey, a judge handpicked by Cosby.

During the trial, Zenger was represented by the eloquent Philadelphia attorney Andrew Hamilton, who argued that Zenger had indeed printed the statements in question, however, they were not libelous but true. Ignoring Delancey's instructions, the jury found Zenger not guilty, and he was acquitted. This landmark case helped establish the democratic principle of freedom of the press in the colonies.

The Trial Begins—August 4, 1735

James Delancey, Chief Justice of the Province of New York
Frederick Philipse, Associate Justice
[Attorney, General Richard Bradley]

Mr. Attorney: . . . "The case before the Court is whether Mr. Zenger is guilty of libeling His Excellency the Governor of New York, and indeed the whole administration of the government. Mr. Hamilton has confessed the printing and publishing, and I think nothing is plainer than that the words in the information are 'scandalous, and tend to sedition, and to disquiet the minds of the people' of this Province. If such papers are not libels, I think it may be said that there can be no such thing as a libel."

Mr. Hamilton: "May it please Your Honor, I cannot agree with Mr. Attorney. For although I freely acknowledge that there are such things as libels, yet I must insist at the same time that what my client is charged with is not a libel. And I observed just now that Mr. Attorney, in defining a libel, made use of the words 'scandalous, seditious, and tend to disquiet the people.' But, whether with design or not I will not say, he omitted the word 'false.'"

Mr. Attorney: "I think that I did not omit the word 'false.' But it has been said already that it may be a libel notwithstanding that it may be true."

Mr. Hamilton: "In this I must still differ with Mr. Attorney. For I depend upon it that we are to be tried upon this information now before the Court and the jury, and to which we have pleaded 'Not guilty.' By it we are charged with printing and publishing 'a certain false, malicious, seditious, and scandalous libel.' This word 'false' must have some meaning, or else how came it there? I hope Mr. Attorney will not say he put it there by chance, and I am of the opinion that his information would not be good without it. But to show that it is the principal thing which, in my opinion, makes a libel, suppose that the information had been for printing and publishing a certain true libel, would that be the same thing? Or could Mr. Attorney support such an information by any precedent in the English law? No, the falsehood makes the scandal, and both make the libel. And to show the Court that I am in good earnest, and to save the Court's time and Mr. Attorney's trouble, I will agree that if he can prove the facts charged upon us to be false, I shall own them to be scandalous, seditious, and a libel. So the work seems now to be pretty much shortened, and Mr. Attorney has now only to prove the words false in order to make us guilty."

Mr. Attorney: "We have nothing to prove. You have confessed the printing and publishing. But if it were necessary, as I insist it is not, how can we prove a negative? I hope some regard will be had to the authorities that have been produced, and that supposing all the words to be true, yet that will not help them. Chief Justice Holt, in his charge to the jury in the case of Tutchin, made no distinction whether Tutchin's papers were true or false; and as Chief Justice Holt has made no distinction in that case, so none ought to be made here; nor can it be shown that, in all that case, there was any question made about their being false or true."

Mr. Hamilton: "I did expect to hear that a negative cannot be proved. But everybody knows there are many exceptions to that general rule. For if a man is charged with killing another, or stealing his neighbor's horse, if he is innocent in the one case he may prove the man said to be killed to be really alive, and the horse said to be stolen never to have been out of his master's stable, etc. And this, I think, is proving a negative.

"But we will save Mr. Attorney the trouble of proving

a negative, take the onus probandi [burden of proof] on ourselves, and prove those very papers that are called libels to be true."

Mr. Chief Justice: "You cannot be admitted, Mr. Hamilton, to give the truth of a libel in evidence. A libel is not to be justified; for it is nevertheless a libel that it is true."

Mr. Hamilton: "I am sorry the Court has so soon resolved upon that piece of law. I expected first to have been heard to that point. I have not, in all my reading, met with an authority that says we cannot be admitted to give the truth in evidence upon an information for libel."

Mr. Chief Justice: "The law is clear that you cannot justify a libel."

Mr. Hamilton: "I own that, may it please Your Honor, to be so. But, with submission, I understand the word 'justify' there to be a justification by plea, as it is in the case upon an indictment for murder or an assault and battery. There the prisoner cannot justify, but pleads 'Not guilty.' Yet it will not be denied but he may be, and always is, admitted to give the truth of the fact, or any other matter, in evidence, which goes to his acquittal. As in murder he may prove that it was in defense of his life, his house, etc.; and in assault and battery he may give in evidence that the other party struck first: and in both cases he will be acquitted. In this sense I understand the word 'justify' when applied to the case before the Court."

Mr. Chief Justice: "I pray, show that you can give the truth of a libel in evidence."

Mr. Hamilton: "How shall it be known whether the words are libelous, that is, true or false, but by admitting us to prove them true, since Mr. Attorney will not undertake to prove them false? Besides, is it not against common sense that a man should be punished in the same degree for a true libel, if any such thing could be, as for a false one? I know it is said that truth makes a libel the more provoking, and therefore the offense is greater, and consequently the judgment should be the heavier. Well, suppose it were so, and let us agree for once that truth is a greater sin than falsehood. Yet, as the offenses are not equal, and as the punishment is arbitrary, that is, according as the judges in their discretion shall direct to be inflicted, is it not absolutely necessary that they should know whether the libel is true or false, that they may by that means be able to proportion the punishment?

"For would it not be a sad case if the judges, for want of a due information, should chance to give as severe a judgment against a man for writing or publishing a lie, as for writing or publishing a truth? And yet this, with submission, as monstrous and ridiculous as it may seem to be, is the natural consequence of Mr. Attorney's doctrine that truth makes a worse libel than falsehood, and must follow from his not proving our papers to be false, or not suffering us to prove them to be true.

"In the case of Tutchin, which seems to be Mr. Attorney's chief authority, that case is against him; for Tutchin was, at his trial, put upon showing the truth of his papers; but he did not. At least the prisoner was asked by the king's counsel whether he would say that they were true. And as he never pretended that they were true, the Chief Justice was not to say so.

"But the point will be clearer on our side from Fuller's case.' Here you see is a scandalous and infamous charge against the late king; here is a charge no less than high treason, against the men in public trust, for receiving money of the French king, then in actual war with the crown of Great Britain; and yet the Court were far from bearing him down with that star chamber doctrine, to wit, that it was no matter whether what he said was true or false. No, on the contrary, Lord Chief Justice Holt asks Fuller, 'Can you make it appear that they are true? Have you any witnesses? You might have had subpoenas for your witnesses against this day. If you take it upon you to write such things as you are charged with, it lies upon you to prove them true, at your peril. If you have any witnesses, I will hear them. How came you to write those books which are not true? If you have any witnesses, produce them. If you can offer any matter to prove what you wrote, let us hear it.' Thus said, and thus did, that great man, Lord Chief Justice Holt, upon a trial of the like kind with ours; and the rule laid down by him in this case is that he who will take upon him to write things, it lies upon him to prove them, at his peril. Now, sir, we have acknowledged the printing and publishing of those papers set forth in the information and, with the leave of the Court, agreeable to the rule laid down by Chief Justice Holt, we are ready to prove them to be true, at our peril."

Mr. Chief Justice: "Let me see the book."

Mr. Chief Justice: "Mr. Attorney, you have heard what Mr. Hamilton has said, and the cases he has cited, for having his witnesses examined to prove the truth of the several facts contained in the papers set forth in the information. What do you say to it?"

Mr. Attorney: "The law, in my opinion, is very clear. They cannot be admitted to justify a libel, for by the authorities I have already read to the Court it is not the less a libel because it is true. I think I need not trouble the Court over again. The thing seems to be very plain, and I submit it to the Court."

Mr. Chief Justice: "Mr. Hamilton, the Court is of the opinion that you ought not to be permitted to prove the facts in the papers. these are the words of the book, 'It is far from being a justification of a libel that the contents thereof are true, or that the person upon whom it is made had a bad reputation, since the greater appearance there is of truth in any malicious invective, so much the more provoking it is.'"

Mr. Hamilton: "These are Star Chamber cases, and I was in hopes that practice had been dead with the court."

Mr. Chief Justice: "Mr. Hamilton, the Court have delivered their opinion, and we expect that you will use us with good manners. You are not to be permitted to argue against the opinion of the Court."

Mr. Hamilton: "With submission, I have seen the practice in very great courts, and never heard it deemed unmannerly to-"

Mr. Chief Justice: "After the Court have declared their opinion, it is not good manners to insist upon a point in which you are overruled."

Mr. Hamilton: "I will say no more at this time. The Court, I see, is against us in this point-and that I hope I may be allowed to say."

Mr. Chief Justice: "Use the Court with good manners and you shall be allowed all the liberty you can reasonably desire."

Mr. Hamilton: "I thank Your Honor. Then, Gentlemen of the Jury, it is to you that we must now appeal for witnesses to the truth of the facts we have offered, and are denied the liberty to prove. Let it not seem strange that I apply myself to you in this manner. I am warranted by both law and reason.

"The law supposes you to be summoned out of the neighborhood where the fact is alleged to be committed; and the reason of your being taken out of the neighborhood is because you are supposed to have the best knowledge of the fact that is to be tried. Were you to find a verdict against my client, you must take it upon you to say that the papers referred to in the information, and which we acknowledge we printed and published, are false, scandalous, and seditious.

"But of this I can have no apprehension. You are citizens of New York. You are really what the law supposes you to be, honest and lawful men; and according to my brief, the facts which we offer to prove were not committed in a corner. They are notoriously known to be true. Therefore in your justice lies our safety. And as we are denied the liberty of giving evidence to prove the truth of what we have published, I will beg leave to lay it down as a standing rule in such cases that the suppressing of evidence ought always to be taken for the strongest evidence; and I hope it will have that weight with you.

"But since we are not admitted to examine our witnesses, I will endeavor to shorten the dispute with Mr. Attorney, and to that end I desire he would favor us with some standard definition of a libel by which it may be certainly known whether a writing be a libel, yes or no."

Mr. Attorney: "The books, I think, have given a very full definition of libel."

Mr. Hamilton: "Ay, Mr. Attorney, but what standard rule have the books laid down by which we can certainly know whether the words or signs are malicious? Whether they are defamatory? Whether they tend to the breach of the peace, and are a sufficient ground to provoke a man, his family, or his friends to acts of revenge: especially the ironical sort of words? What rule have you to know when I write ironically? I think it would be hard when I say, 'Such a man is a very worthy honest gentleman, and of fine understanding,' that therefore I mean, 'He is a knave or a fool.'"

Mr. Attorney: "I think the books are very full. It is said in Hawkins, just now read, 'Such scandal as is expressed in a scoffing and ironical manner makes a writing as properly a libel as that which is expressed in direct terms.' I think nothing can be plainer or more full than these words."

Mr. Hamilton: "I agree the words are very plain, and I shall not scruple to allow (when we are agreed that the words are false and scandalous, and were spoken in an ironical and scoffing manner) that they are really libelous. But here still occurs the uncertainty which makes the difficulty to know what words are scandalous, and what are not. For you say that they may be scandalous, whether true or false.

"Besides, how shall we know whether the words were spoken in a scoffing and ironical manner, or seriously? Or how can you know whether the man did not think as he wrote? For by your rule, if he did, it is no irony, and consequently no libel.

"But under favor, Mr. Attorney, I think the same book, and under the same section, will show us the only rule by which all these things are to be known. The words are these, 'which kind of writing is as well understood to mean only to upbraid the parties with the want of these qualities as if they had directly and expressly done so.' Here it is plain that the words are scandalous, scoffing, and ironical only as they are understood. I know no rule laid down in the books but this, I mean, as the words are understood."

Mr. Chief Justice: "Mr. Hamilton, do you think it so hard to know when words are ironical or spoken in a scoffing manner?"

Mr. Hamilton: "I own it may be known. But I insist that the only rule by which to know is—as I do or can understand them. I have no other rule to go by but as I understand them."

Mr. Chief Justice: "That is certain. All words are libelous or not as they are understood. Those who are to judge of the words must judge whether they are scandalous, or ironical, or tend to the breach of the peace, or are seditious. There can be no doubt of it."

Mr. Hamilton: "I thank Your Honor. I am glad to find the Court of this opinion. Then it follows that these twelve men must understand the words in the information to be scandalous—that is to say, false. For I think it is not pretended they are of the ironical sort. And [only] when they understand the words to be so, they will say that we are guilty of publishing a false libel, and not otherwise."

Mr. Chief Justice: "No, Mr. Hamilton, the jury may find that Zenger printed and published those papers, and leave it to the Court to judge whether they are libelous. You know this is very common. It is in the nature of a special verdict, where the jury leave the matter of the law to the court."

Mr. Hamilton: "I know, may it please Your Honor, the jury may do so. But I do likewise know that they may do otherwise. I know that they have the right beyond all dispute to determine both the law and the fact; and where they do not doubt of the law, they ought to do so. Leaving it to judgment of the court whether the words are libelous or not in effect renders juries useless (to say no worse) in many cases. But this I shall have occasion to speak to by and by.

"Although I own it to be base and unworthy to scandalize any man, yet I think it is even more villainous to scandalize a person of public character. I will go so far into Mr. Attorney's doctrine as to agree that if the faults, mistakes, nay even the vices of such a person be private and personal, and do not affect the peace of the public, or the liberty or property of our neighbor, it is unmanly and unmannerly to expose them either by word or writing. But when a ruler of a people brings his personal failings, but much more his vices, into his administration, and the people find themselves affected by them either in their liberties or properties, that will alter the case mightily; and all the things that are said in favor of rulers and of dignitaries, and upon the side of power, will not be able to stop people's mouths when they feel themselves oppressed. I mean, in a free government."

Mr. Attorney: "Pray, Mr. Hamilton, have a care what you say, don't go too far. I don't like those liberties."

Mr. Hamilton: "Surely, Mr. Attorney, you won't make any applications. All men agree that we are governed by the best of kings, and I cannot see the meaning of Mr. Attorney's caution. My well-known principles, and the sense I have of the blessings we enjoy under His Majesty, make it impossible for me to err, and I hope even to be suspected, in that point of duty to my king."

Hamilton's Summation for Zenger

"May it please Your Honor, I was saying that notwithstanding all the duty and reverence claimed by Mr. Attorney to men in authority, they are not exempt from observing the rules of common justice either in their private or public capacities. The laws of our mother country know no exemptions. It is true that men in power are harder to be come at for wrongs they do either to a private person or to the public, especially a governor in The Plantations, where they insist upon an exemption from answering complaints of any kind in their own government. We are indeed told, and it is true, that they are obliged to answer a suit in the king's courts at Westminster for a wrong done to any person here. But do we not know how impracticable this is to most men among us, to leave their families, who depend upon their labor and care for their livelihood, and carry evidence to Britain, and at a great, nay, a far greater expense than almost any of us are able to bear, only to prosecute a governor for an injury done here?

"But when the oppression is general, there is no remedy even that way. No, our Constitution has—blessed be God—given us an opportunity, if not to have such wrongs redressed, yet by our prudence and resolution we may in a great measure prevent the committing of such wrongs by making a governor sensible that it is in his interest to be just to those under his care. For such is the sense that men in general—I mean free men—have of common justice, that when they come to know that a chief magistrate abuses the power with which he is trusted for the good of the people, and is attempting to turn that very power against the innocent, whether of high or low degree, I say that mankind in general seldom fail to interpose, and, as far as they can, prevent the destruction of their fellow subjects.

"And has it not often been seen—I hope it will always be seen that when the representatives of a free people are by just representations or remonstrances made sensible of the sufferings of their fellow subjects, by the abuse of power in the hands of a governor, that they have declared (and loudly too) that they were not obliged by any law to support a governor who goes about to destroy a Province or Colony, or their privileges, which by His Majesty he was appointed, and by the law he is bound, to protect and encourage? But I pray that it may be considered—of what use is this mighty privilege if every man that suffers is silent? And if a man must be taken up as a libeler for telling his sufferings to his neighbor?

"I know that it may be answered, 'Have you not a legislature? Have you not a House of Representatives to whom you may complain?' To this I answer, 'We have.' But what then? Is an Assembly to be troubled with every injury done by a governor? Or are they to hear of nothing but what those in the administration will please to tell them? And what sort of trial must a man have? How is he to be remedied, especially if the case were, as I have known to happen in America in my time, that a governor who has places—I will not say pensions, for I believe they seldom give that to another which they can take to themselves—to bestow can keep the same Assembly, after he has modeled them so as to get a majority of the House in his interest, for near twice seven years together? I pray, what redress is to be expected for an honest man who makes his complaint against a governor to an Assembly who may properly enough be said to be made by the same governor against whom the complaint is made? The thing answers itself.

"No, it is natural, it is a privilege, I will go farther, it is a right, which all free men claim, that they are entitled to complain when they are hurt. They have a right publicly to remonstrate against the abuses of power in the strongest terms, to put their neighbors upon their guard against the craft or open violence of men in authority, and to assert with courage the sense they have of the blessings of liberty, the value they put upon it, and their resolution at all hazards to preserve it as one of the greatest blessings heaven can bestow.

"When a House of Assembly composed of honest freemen sees the general bent of the people's inclination, that is it which must and will, I am sure it ought to, weigh with a legislature in spite of all the craft, caressing, and cajoling made use of by a governor to divert them from harkening to the voice of their country. As we all very well understand the true reason why gentlemen take so much pains and make such great interest to be appointed governors, so is the design of their appointment not less manifest. We know His Majesty's gracious intentions toward his subjects. He desires no more than that his people in The Plantations should be kept up to their duty and allegiance to the crown of Great Britain, that peace may be preserved among them, and justice impartially administered; so that we may be governed so as to render us useful to our mother country by encouraging us to make and raise such commodities as may be useful to Great Britain.

"But will anyone say that all or any of these good ends are to be effected by a governor s setting his people together by the ears, and by the assistance of one part of the people to plague and plunder the other? The commission that governors bear while they execute the powers given them according to the intent of the royal grantor requires and deserves very great reverence and submission. But when a governor departs from the duty enjoined on him by his sovereign, and acts as if he were less accountable than the royal hand that gave him all that power and honor that he is possessed of, this sets people upon examining and inquiring into the power, authority, and duty of such a magistrate, and to comparing those with his conduct. And just as far as they find he exceeds the bounds of his authority, or falls short in doing impartial justice to the people under his administration, so far they very often, in return, come short in their duty to such a governor.

"For power alone will not make a man beloved, and I have heard it observed that the man who was neither good nor wise before his being made a governor never mended upon his preferment, but has been generally observed to be worse. For men who are not imbued with wisdom and virtue can only be kept in bounds by the law; and by how much the further they think themselves out of the reach of the law, by so much the more wicked and cruel men are. I wish there were no instances of the kind at this day.

"Wherever this happens to be the case of a governor, unhappy are the people under his administration, and in the end he will find himself so too, for the people will neither love him nor support him.

"I make no doubt but there are those here who are zealously concerned for the success of this prosecution, and yet I hope they are not many; and even some of those, I am persuaded, when they consider to what lengths such prosecutions may be carried, and how deeply the liberties of the people may be affected by such means, will not all abide by their present sentiments. I say 'not all,' for the man who from an intimacy and acquaintance with a governor has conceived a personal regard for him, the man who has felt none of the strokes of his power, the man who believes that a governor has a regard for him and confides in him, it is natural for such men to wish well to the affairs of such a governor. And as they may be men of honor and generosity, may, and no doubt will, wish him success so far as the rights and privileges of their fellow citizens are not affected. But as men of honor I can apprehend nothing from them. They will never exceed that point.

"There are others that are under stronger obligations, and those are such as are in some sort engaged in support of the governor's cause by their own or their relations' dependence on his favor for some post or preferment. Such men have what is commonly called duty and gratitude to influence their inclinations and oblige them to go his lengths. I know men's interests are very near to them, and they will do much rather than forgo the favor of a governor and a livelihood at the same time. But I can with very just grounds hope, even from those men, whom I will suppose to be men of honor and conscience too, that when they see the liberty of their country in danger, either by their concurrence or even by their silence, they will like Englishmen, and like themselves, freely make a sacrifice of any preferment or favor rather than be accessory to destroying the liberties of their country and entailing slavery upon their posterity.

"There are indeed another set of men, of whom I have no hopes. I mean such who lay aside all other considerations and are ready to join with power in any shape, and with any man or sort of men by whose means or interest they may be assisted to gratify their malice and envy against those whom they have been pleased to hate; and that for no other reason than because they are men of ability and integrity, or at least are possessed of some valuable qualities far superior to their own. But as envy is the sin of the Devil, and therefore very hard, if at all, to be repented of, I will believe there are but few of this detestable and worthless sort of men, nor will their opinions or inclinations have any influence upon this trial.

"But to proceed. I beg leave to insist that the right of complaining or remonstrating is natural; that the restraint upon this natural right is the law only; and that those restraints can only extend to what is false. For as it is truth alone that can excuse or justify any man for complaining of a bad administration, I as frankly agree that nothing ought to excuse a man who raises a false charge or accusation even against a private person, and that no manner of allowance ought to be made to him who does so against a public magistrate.

"Truth ought to govern the whole affair of libels. And yet the party accused runs risk enough even then; for if he fails in proving every title of what he has written, and to the satisfaction of the court and jury too, he may find to his cost that when the prosecution is set on foot by men in power it seldom wants friends to favor it.

"From thence (it is said) has arisen the great diversity of opinions among judges about what words were or were not scandalous or libelous. I believe it will be granted that there is not greater uncertainty in any part of the law than about words of scandal. It would be misspending of the Court's time to mention the cases. They may be said to be numberless. Therefore the utmost care ought to be taken in following precedents; and the times when the judgments were given, which are quoted for authorities in the case of libels, are much to be regarded.

"I think it will be agreed that ever since the time of the Star Chamber, where the most arbitrary judgments and opinions were given that ever an Englishman heard of, at least in his own country; I say, prosecutions for libel since the time of that arbitrary Court, and until the Glorious Revolution, have generally been set on foot at the instance of the crown or its ministers. And it is no small reproach to the law that these prosecutions were too often and too much countenanced by the judges, who held their places 'at pleasure,' a disagreeable tenure to any officer, but a dangerous one in the case of a judge. Yet I cannot think it unwarrantable to show the unhappy influence that a sovereign has sometimes had, not only upon judges, but even upon parliaments themselves.

"It has already been shown how the judges differed in their opinions about the nature of a libel in the case of the Seven Bishops.

"There you see three judges of one opinion, that is, of a wrong opinion in the judgment of the best men in England, and one judge of a right opinion. How unhappy might it have been for all of us at this day if that jury had understood the words in that information as the Court did? Or if they had left it to the Court to judge whether the petition of the Bishops was or was not a libel? No, they took upon them[selves]—to their immortal honor—to determine both law and fact, and to understand the petition of the Bishops to be no libel, that is, to contain no falsehood or sedition; and therefore found them not guilty.

"If then upon the whole there is so great an uncertainty among judges—learned and great men—in matters of this kind, if power has had so great an influence on judges, how cautious ought we to be in determining by their judgments especially in The Plantations, and in the case of libels?

"There is heresy in law as well as in religion, and both have changed very much. We well know that it is not two centuries ago that a man would have been burned as a heretic for owning such opinions in matters of religion as are publicly written and printed at this day. They were fallible men, it seems, and we take the liberty not only to differ from them in religious opinions, but to condemn them and their opinions too. I must presume that in taking these freedoms in thinking and speaking about matters of faith or religion, we are in the right; for although it is said that there are very

great liberties of this kind taken in New York, yet I have heard of no information preferred by Mr. Attorney for any offenses of this sort. From which I think it is pretty clear that in New York a man may make very free with his God, but he must take a special care what he says of his governor.

"It is agreed upon by all men that this is a reign of liberty. While men keep within the bounds of truth I hope they may with safety both speak and write their sentiments of the conduct of men in power. I mean of that part of their conduct only which affects the liberty or property of the people under their administration. Were this to be denied, then the next step may make them slaves; for what notions can be entertained of slavery beyond that of suffering the greatest injuries and oppressions without the liberty of complaining, or if they do, to be destroyed, body and estate, for so doing?

"It is said and insisted on by Mr. Attorney that government is a sacred thing; that it is to be supported and reverenced; that it is government that protects our persons and estates, prevents treasons, murders, robberies, riots, and all the train of evils that overturns kingdoms and states and ruins particular persons. And if those in the administration, especially the supreme magistrate, must have all their conduct censured by private men, government cannot subsist. This is called a licentiousness not to be tolerated. It is said that it brings the rulers of the people into contempt, and their authority not to be regarded, and so in the end the laws cannot be put into execution.

"These, I say, and such as these, are the general topics insisted upon by men in power and their advocates. But I wish it might be considered at the same time how often it has happened that the abuse of power has been the primary cause of these evils, and that it was the injustice and oppression of these great men that has commonly brought them into contempt with the people. The craft and art of such men is great, and who that is the least acquainted with history or law can be ignorant of the specious pretenses that have often been made use of by men in power to introduce arbitrary rule, and to destroy the liberties of a free people?

"This is the second information for libeling of a governor that I have known in America. The first, although it may look like a romance, yet as it is true I will beg leave to mention it.

"Governor Nicholson, who happened to be offended with one of his clergy, met him one day upon the road; and as usual with him (under the protection of his commission) used the poor parson with the worst of language, and threatened to cut off his ears, slit his nose, and at last to shoot him through the head. The parson, being a reverend man, continued all this time uncovered in the heat of the sun, until he found an opportunity to fly for it. Coming to a neighbor's house, he felt himself very ill of a fever, and immediately writes for a doctor. And that his physician might the better judge of his distemper, he acquainted him with the usage he had received; concluding that the Governor was certainly mad, for that no man in his senses would have behaved in that manner.

"The doctor unhappily showed the parson's letter. The Governor came to hear of it. And so an information was preferred against the poor man for saying he believed the Governor was mad. It was laid down in the information to be false, scandalous, and wicked, and written with intent to move sedition among the people, and to bring His Excellency into contempt. But by an order from the late Queen Anne there was a stop put to that prosecution, with sundry others set on foot by the same Governor against gentlemen of the greatest worth and honor in that government.

"And may not I be allowed, after all this, to say that by a little countenance almost anything that a man writes may, with the help of that useful term of art called an innuendo, be construed to be a libel, according to Mr. Attorney's definition of it—to wit, that whether the words are spoken of a person of a public character or of a private man, whether dead or living, good or bad, true or false, all make a libel. For according to Mr. Attorney, after a man hears a writing read, or reads and repeats it, or laughs at it, they are all punishable. It is true that Mr. Attorney is so good as to allow it must be after the party knows it to be a libel, but he is not so kind as to take the man's word for it.

"If a libel is understood in the large and unlimited sense urged by Mr. Attorney, there is scarce a writing I know that may not be called a libel, or scarce a person safe from being called to an account as a libeler. For Moses, meek as he was, libeled Cain; and who is it that has not libeled the Devil?

"For according to Mr. Attorney it is no justification to say that one has a bad name. Echard has libeled our good King William; Burnet has libeled, among others, King Charles and King James; and Rapin has libeled them all. How must a man speak or write; or what must he hear, read, or sing; or when must he laugh so as to be secure from being taken up as a libeler?"

"I sincerely believe that were some persons to go through the streets of New York nowadays and read a part of the Bible, if it was not known to be such, Mr. Attorney, with the help of his innuendos, would easily turn it into a libel. As for instance Isaiah 9:16: 'The leaders of the people cause them to err; and they that are led by them are destroyed.' Should Mr. Attorney go about to make this a libel, he would read it thus: 'The leaders of the people (innuendo, the Governor and Council of New York) cause them (innuendo, the people of this Province) to err, and they (the people of this Province meaning) that are led by them (the Governor and Council meaning) arc destroyed (innuendo, are deceived into the loss of their liberty), which is the worst kind of destruction.'

"Or if some person should publicly repeat, in a manner not pleasing to his betters, the fourth and fifth verses of the 56th chapter of the same book, there Mr. Attorney would have a large field to display his skill in the artful application

of his innuendos. The words are: 'His watchmen are blind, they are all ignorant, . . . Yea, they are greedy dogs which can never have enough.' To make them a libel there is, according to Mr. Attorney's doctrine, no more wanting but the aid of his skill in the right adapting of his innuendos. As for instance: 'His watchmen (innuendo, the Governors Council and his Assembly) are blind, they are all ignorant (innuendo, will not see the dangerous designs of His Excellency). Yea, they (the Governor and Council meaning) are greedy dogs which can never have enough (innuendo, enough of riches and power).'

"Such an instance as this seems only fit to be laughed at; but I appeal to Mr. Attorney himself whether these are not at least equally proper to be applied to His Excellency and his ministers as some of the inferences and innuendos in his information against my client. Then if Mr. Attorney is at liberty to come into court and file an information in the king's name, without leave, who is secure whom he is pleased to prosecute as a libeler

"And give me leave to say that the mode of prosecuting by information, when a grand jury will not find a true bill, is a national grievance, and greatly inconsistent with that freedom that the subjects of England enjoy in most other cases. But if we are so unhappy as not to be able to ward off this stroke of power directly, yet let us take care not to be cheated out of our liberties by forms and appearances. Let us always be sure that the charge in the information is made out clearly even beyond a doubt; for although matters in the information may be called form [sic] upon trial, yet they may be, and often have been found to be, matters of substance upon giving judgment.

"Gentlemen: The danger is great in proportion to the mischief that may happen through our too great credulity. A proper confidence in a court is commendable, but as the verdict, whatever it is, will be yours, you ought to refer no part of your duty to the discretion of other persons. If you should be of the opinion that there is no falsehood in Mr. Zenger's papers, you will, nay pardon me for the expression, you ought, to say so—because you do not know whether others—I mean the Court—may be of that opinion. It is your right to do so, and there is much depending upon your resolution as well as upon your integrity.

"The loss of liberty, to a generous mind, is worse than death. And yet we know that there have been those in all ages who for the sake of preferment, or some imaginary honor, have freely lent a helping hand to oppress, nay to destroy, their country.

"This brings to my mind that saying of the immortal [Marcus] Brutus when he looked upon the creatures of Caesar, who were very great men but by no means good men. 'You Romans, said Brutus, 'if yet I may call you so, consider what you are doing. Remember that you are assisting Caesar to forge those very chains that one day he will make you yourselves wear.' This is what every man who values freedom ought to consider. He should act by judgment and not by affection or self-interest; for where those prevail, no ties of either country or kindred are regarded; as upon the other hand, the man who loves his country prefers its liberty to all other considerations, well knowing that without liberty life is a misery.

"A famous instance of this you will find in the history of another brave Roman of the same name, I mean Lucius Junius Brutus, whose story is well known, and therefore I shall mention no more of it than only to show the value he put upon the freedom of his country. After this great man, with his fellow citizens whom he had engaged in the cause, had banished Tarquin the Proud, the last king of Rome, from a throne that he ascended by inhuman murders and possessed by the most dreadful tyranny and proscriptions, and had by this means amassed incredible riches, even sufficient to bribe to his interest many of the young nobility of Rome to assist him in recovering the crown; the plot being discovered, the principal conspirators were apprehended, among whom were two of the sons of Junius Brutus. It was absolutely necessary that some should be made examples of, to deter others from attempting the restoration of Tarquin and destroying the liberty of Rome. To effect this it was that Lucius Junius Brutus, one of the consuls of Rome, in the presence of the Roman people, sat judge and condemned his own sons as traitors to their country. And to give the last proof of his exalted virtue and his love of liberty, he with a firmness of mind only becoming so great a man caused their heads to be struck off in his own presence. When he observed that his rigid virtue occasioned a sort of horror among the people, it is observed that he said only, 'My fellow citizens, do not think that this proceeds from any want of natural affection. No, the death of the sons of Brutus can affect Brutus only. But the loss of liberty will affect my country.'

"Thus highly was liberty esteemed in those days, that a father could sacrifice his sons to save his country. But why do I go to heathen Rome to bring instances of the love of liberty? The best blood in Britain has been shed in the cause of liberty; and the freedom we enjoy at this day may be said to be in a great measure owing to the glorious stand the famous Hampden, and others of our countrymen, made against the arbitrary demands and illegal impositions of the times in which they lived; who, rather than give up the rights of Englishmen and submit to pay an illegal tax of no more, I think, than three shillings, resolved to undergo, and for the liberty of their country did undergo, the greatest extremities in that arbitrary and terrible Court of the Star Chamber, to whose arbitrary proceedings—it being composed of the principal men of the realm, and calculated to support arbitrary government—no bounds or limits could be set, nor could any other hand remove the evil but Parliament.

"Power may justly be compared to a great river. While kept within its due bounds it is both beautiful and useful. But when it overflows its banks, it is then too impetuous to be stemmed; it bears down all before it, and brings destruc-tion and desolation wherever it comes. If, then, this is the nature of power, let us at least do our duty, and like wise men who value freedom use our utmost care to support liberty, the only bulwark against lawless power, which in all ages has sacrificed to its wild lust and boundless ambition the blood of the best men that ever lived.

"I hope to be pardoned, Sir, for my zeal upon this occasion. It is an old and wise caution that when our neighbor's house is on fire we ought to take care of our own. For though—blessed be God—I live in a government where liberty is well understood and freely enjoyed, yet experience has shown us all—I am sure it has to me—that a bad precedent in one government is soon set up for an authority in another. And therefore I cannot but think it my, and every honest man's, that while we pay all due obedience to men in authority we ought at the same time to be upon our guard against power wherever we apprehend that it may affect ourselves or our fellow subjects.

"I am truly very unequal to such an undertaking on many accounts. You see that I labor under the weight of many years, and am bowed down with great infirmities of body. Yet, old and weak as I am, I should think it my duty, if required, to go to the utmost part of the land where my services could be of any use in assisting to quench the flame of prosecutions upon informations, set on foot by the government to deprive a people of the right of remonstrating and complaining, too, of the arbitrary attempts of men in power."

"Men who injure and oppress the people under their administration provoke them to cry out and complain, and then make that very complaint the foundation for new oppressions and prosecutions. I wish I could say that there were no instances of this kind.

"But to conclude. The question before the Court and you, Gentlemen of the jury, is not of small or private concern. It is not the cause of one poor printer, nor of New York alone, which you are now trying. No! It may in its consequence affect every free man that lives under a British government on the main of America. It is the best cause. It is the cause of liberty. And I make no doubt but your upright conduct this day will not only entitle you to the love and esteem of your fellow citizens, but every man who prefers freedom to a life of slavery will bless and honor you as men who have baffled the attempt of tyranny, and by an impartial and uncorrupt verdict have laid a noble foundation for securing to ourselves, our posterity, and our neighbors, that to which nature and the laws of our country have given us a right to liberty of both exposing and opposing arbitrary power (in these parts of the world at least) by speaking and writing truth."

Court's Instruction to Jury

Mr. Chief Justice: "Gentlemen of the Jury: The great pains Mr. Hamilton has taken to show how little regard juries are to pay to the opinion of judges, and his insisting so much upon the conduct of some judges in trials of this kind, is done no doubt with a design that you should take but very little notice of what I might say upon this occasion. I shall therefore only observe to you that as the facts or words in the information are confessed, the only thing that can come in question before you is whether the words as set forth in the information make a libel. And that is a matter of law, no doubt, and which you may leave to the Court."

Mr. Hamilton: "I humbly beg Your Honor's pardon, I am very much misapprehended if you suppose that what I said was so designed.

"Sir, you know I made an apology for the freedom that I found myself under a necessity of using upon this occasion. I said there was nothing personal designed. It arose from the nature of our defense."

The Verdict

The jury withdrew to begin deliberations, but quickly returned with their verdict. Asked by the clerk whether whether John Peter Zenger was guilty of printing and publishing the libels in the information, Thomas Hunt, the jury foreman replied: "Not guilty."

Source: John Peter Zenger, *A Brief Narrative of the Case and Trial of John Peter Zenger* (New York: John Peter Zenger, 1736).

Maxims from Poor Richard's Almanack (1739)

One of the most popular and enduring works to emerge from the colonial era was Benjamin Franklin's *Poor Richard's Almanack*. Read by all classes in society, some 10,000 copies of the *Almanack* were published annually from 1732 to 1757. All enjoyed the *Almanack* for its wit and common sense. Many of its adages, such as those quoted here, are still familiar today.

When Death puts out our Flame, the Snuff will tell,
If we were Wax, or Tallow by the Smell.

At a great Pennyworth, pause a while.

As to his Wife, John minds St. Paul. He's one
That hath a Wife, and is as if he'd none.

Kings a be an Honour to them tho' they are dead.

If thou wouldst live long, live well; for Folly and Wickedness shorten Life.

Prythee isn't Miss Cloe's a comical Case?
She lends out her Tail, and she borrows her Face.

Trust thy self, and another shall not betray thee.

He that pays for Work before it's done, has but a pennyworth for twopence.

Historians relate, not so much what is done, as what they would have believed.

O Maltster! break that cheating Peck; 'tis plain,
When e'er you use it, you're a Knave in Grain . . .

Grace thou thy House, and let not that grace thee.

Thou canst not joke an Enemy into a Friend; but thou may'st a Friend into an Enemy.

Eyes & Priests
Bear no Jests.

He that falls in love with himself, will have no Rivals.

Let thy Child's first Lesson be Obedience, and the second may be what thou wilt.

Blessed is he that expects nothing, for he shall never be disappointed.

Rather go to bed supperless, than run in debt for a Breakfast.

Let thy Discontents be Secrets.

An infallible Remedy for the Tooth-ach, viz Wash the Root of an aching Tooth, in Elder Vinegar, and let it dry half an hour in the Sun; after which it will never ach more; Probatum est [it is proved].

A Man of Knowledge like a rich Soil, feeds
If not a world of Corn, a world of Weeds.

A modern Wit is one of David's Fools.

No Resolution of Repenting hereafter, can be sincere.

Pollio, who values nothing that's within,
Buys books as men hunt Beavers,—for their Skin.

Honour thy Father and Mother, i.e. Live so as to be an Honour to them tho' they are dead.

If thou injurest Conscience, it will have its Revenge on thee.

Hear no ill of a Friend, nor speak any of an Enemy.

Pay what you owe, and you'll know what's your own.

Be not niggardly of what costs thee nothing, as courtesy, counsel, & countenance.

Thirst after Desert, not Reward.

Beware of him that is slow to anger: He is angry for something, and will not be pleased for nothing.

No longer virtuous no longer free; is a Maxim as true with regard to a private Person as a Common-wealth.

When Man and Woman die, as Poets sung,
His Heart's the last part moves, her last, the tongue.

Proclaim not all thou knowest, all thou owest, all thou hast, nor all thou canst.

Let our Fathers and Grandfathers be valued for their Goodness, ourselves for our own.

Industry need not wish.

Sin is not hurtful because it is forbidden but it is forbidden because it's hurtful. Nor is a Duty beneficial because it is commanded, but it is commanded, because it's beneficial.

A——, they say, has Wit; for what?
For writing?—No; For writing not.

George came to the Crown without striking a Blow.
Ah! quoth the Pretender, would I could do so.

Love, and be lov'd.

O Lazy-Bones! Dost thou think God would have given thee Arms and Legs, if he had not design'd thou should'st use them.

A Cure for Poetry,
Seven wealthy Towns contend for Homer, dead,
Thro' which the living Homer beg'd his Bread.

Great Beauty, great strength, & great Riches, are really & truly of no great Use; a right Heart exceeds all.

Source: Poor Richard: An Almanack for the Year of Christ 1739 (Philadelphia: Benjamin Franklin, 1739).

The Demand for Slavery in Georgia (1743)

Slavery was originally outlawed in Georgia in 1735. Many of its settlers demanded in 1743 that it be allowed in order to stem "want and famine." Following is an excerpt from their petition.

The Trustees for Establishing the Colony of Georgia in America opposed the demand for slavery. By 1749, however, they relented and, out of what was considered economic necessity, rescinded the slavery ban in early 1750.

But as if the difficulties arising from indifferent lands, and discouraging tenures, were not sufficient to humble and prepare them for the other severities they have met with, they were totally prohibited the importation, use, or even sight of negroes. In spite of all endeavors to disguise this point, it is as clear as light itself, that negroes are essentially necessary to the cultivation of Georgia, as axes, hoes, or any other utensil of agriculture. So that if a colony was designed able to but to subsist itself, their prohibition was inconsistent; if a garrison only was intended, the very inhabitants were needless: but all circumstances considered, it looked as if the assistance of human creatures, who have been called slaves, as well as subject to the treatment of such, were incongruous with a system that proceeded to confer the thing, but to spare the odium of the appellation. Experience would too soon have taught them the parity of their conditions, in spite of a mere nominal difference. The only English clergymen, who were ever countenanced there, declared they never desired to see Georgia a rich, but a godly colony; and the blind subjection the poor Saltzburgers are under to the Rev. Mr. Boltzius, who has furnished such extraordinary extracts in some accounts of Georgia, published here, will be too evident from some of the annexed depositions to call for any descant.

The pretended content and satisfaction of the people of Ebenezer, without negroes, will plainly appear to be the dictates of spiritual tyranny, and only the wretched acquiescence of people, who were in truth unacquainted with the privilege of choosing for themselves.

It is acknowledged indeed that the present war, and late invasion, may furnish the enemies of the colony with the most plausible objections that could occur, against the allowance of black slaves; but these reasons have not always existed, nor have the trustees ever declared any resolution to admit them, at any other juncture. But if it plainly appears that Georgia, as a colony, cannot barely exist without them, surely an admission of them under limitations, suitable to the present situation of affairs, is absolutely necessary to its support; since want and famine must be more dreadful and insuperable invaders, than any living enemy: besides, the honorable trustees were informed by a letter from Mr. Stirling and others, of the falsehood, of the contended and comfortable situation of the people of Darien were affirmed to be in; and that they were brought with a number of cattle, and extensive promises of future rewards, when they signed their petition against negroes. . . .

Source: "A Brief Account of the Causes Have that Retarded the Progress of the Colony of Georgia in America, 1743." In *Collections of the Georgia Historical Society*, Vol. 2 (Savannah, 1842), 92–94.

Rules of Civility & Decent Behaviour in Company and Conversation (c. 1744)

As a schoolboy of 14, George Washington copied maxims on proper behavior from an early French text ("Bienseance de la conversation entre les Hommes," prepared in 1595), which had been adapted and translated into English. It is thought that this exercise was a formative influence on Washington, who was known in later life as a gentleman of impeccable manners and rectitude.

1st. Every Action done in Company, ought to be with Some Sign of Respect, to those that are Present.

2d. When in Company, put not your Hands to any Part of the Body, not usualy Discovered.

3d. Shew Nothing to your Freind that may affright him.

4[d]. In the Presence of Others Sing not to yourself with a humming Noise, nor Drum with your Fingers or Feet.

5th. If You Cough, Sneeze, Sigh, or Yawn, do it not Loud but Privately; and Speak not in your Yawning, but put Your handkercheif or Hand before your face and turn aside.

6th. Sleep not when others Speak, Sit not when others stand, Speak not when you Should hold your Peace, walk not on when others Stop.

7th. Put not off your Cloths in the presence of Others, nor go out your Chamber half Drest.

8th. At Play and at Fire its Good manners to Give Place to the last Commer, and affect not to Speak Louder than Ordinary.

9th. Spit not in the Fire, nor Stoop low before it neither Put your Hands into the Flames to warm them, nor Set your Feet upon the Fire especially if there be meat before it.

10th. When you Sit down, Keep your Feet firm and Even, without putting one on the other or Crossing them.

11th. Shift not yourself in the Sight of others nor Gnaw your nails.

12th. Shake not the head, Feet, or Legs rowl not the Eys lift not one eyebrow higher than the other wry not the mouth, and bedew no mans face with your Spittle, by appr[oaching too nea]r him [when] you Speak.

13th. Kill no Vermin as Fleas, lice ticks &c in the Sight of Others, if you See any filth or thick Spittle put your foot Dexteriously upon it, if it be upon the Cloths of your Companions, Put it off privately, and if it be upon your own Cloths return Thanks to him who puts it off.

14th. Turn not your Back to others especially in Speaking, Jog not the Table or Desk on which Another reads or writes, lean not upon any one.

15th. Keep your Nails clean and Short, also your Hands and Teeth Clean yet without Shewing any great Concern for them.

16th. Do not Puff up the Cheeks, Loll not out the tongue rub the Hands, or beard, thrust out the lips, or bite them or keep the Lips too open or too Close.

17th. Be no Flatterer, neither Play with any that delights not to be Play'd Withal.

18th. Read no Letters, Books, or Papers in Company but when there is a Necessity for the doing of it you must ask leave: come not near the Books or Writings of Another so as to read them unless desired or give your opinion of them unask'd, also look not nigh when another is writing a Letter.

19th. Let your Countenance be pleasant but in Serious Matters Somewhat grave.

20th. The Gestures of the Body must be Suited to the discourse you are upon.

21st. Reproach none for the Infirmaties of Nature, nor Delight to Put them that have in mind thereof.

22d. Shew not yourself glad at the Misfortune of another though he were your enemy.

23d. When you see a Crime punished, you may be inwardly Pleased; but always shew Pity to the Suffering Offender.

[24th. Do not laugh too loud or] too much at any Publick [Spectacle].

25th. Superfluous Complements and all Affectation of Ceremonie are to be avoided, yet where due they are not to be Neglected.

26th. In Pulling off your Hat to Persons of Distinction, as Noblemen, Justices, Churchmen &c make a Reverence, bowing more or less according to the Custom of the Better Bred, and Quality of the Person. Amongst your equals expect not always that they Should begin with you first, but to Pull off the Hat when there is no need is Affectation; in the Manner of Saluting and resaluting in words keep to the most usual Custom.

27th. Tis ill manners to bid one more eminent than yourself be covered as well as not to do it to whom it's due, Likewise he that makes too much haste to Put on his hat does not well, yet he ought to Put it on at the first, or at most the Second time of being ask'd; now what is herein Spoken, of Qualification in behaviour in Saluting, ought also to be observed in taking of Place, and Sitting down for ceremonies without Bounds is troublesome.

28th. If any one come to Speak to you while you are Sitting, Stand up tho he be your Inferiour, and when you Present Seats let it be to every one according to his Degree.

29th. When you meet with one of Greater Quality than yourself, Stop, and retire especially if it be at a Door or any Straight place to give way for him to Pass.

30th. In walking the highest Place in most Countrys Seems to be on the right hand therefore Place yourself on the left of him whom you desire to Honour: but if three walk together the mid[dest] Place is the most Honourable the wall is usually given to the most worthy if two walk together.

31st. If any one far Surpassess others, either in age, Estate, or Merit [yet] would give Place to a meaner than hims[elf in his own lodging or elsewhere] the one ought not to except it, S[o he on the other part should not use much earnestness nor offer] it above once or twice.

32d. To one that is your equal, or not much inferior you are to give the chief Place in your Lodging and he to who 'tis offered ought at the first to refuse it but at the Second to accept though not without acknowledging his own unworthiness.

33d. They that are in Dignity or in office have in all places Preceedency but whilst they are Young they ought to respect those that are their equals in Birth or other Qualitys, though they have no Publick charge.

34th. It is good Manners to prefer them to whom we Speak befo[re] ourselves especially if they be above us with whom in no Sort we ought to begin.

35th. Let your Discourse with Men of Business be Short and Comprehensive.

36th. Artificers & Persons of low Degree ought not to use many ceremonies to Lords, or Others of high Degree but Respect and high[ly] Honour them, and those of high Degree ought to treat them with affibility & Courtesie, without Arrogancy.

37th. In Speaking to men of Quality do not lean nor Look them full in the Face, nor approach too near them, at lest Keep a full Pace from them.

38th. In visiting the Sick, do not Presently play the Physicion if you be not Knowing therein.

39th. In writing or Speaking, give to every Person his due Title According to his Degree & the Custom of the Place.

40th. Strive not with your Superiers in argument, but always Submit your Judgment to others with Modesty.

41st. Undertake not to Teach your equal in the art himself Proffesses; it Savours of arrogancy.

[42d. Let thy ceremonies in] Courtesie be proper to the Dignity of his place [with whom thou conversest for it is absurd to ac]t the same with a Clown and a Prince.

43d. Do not express Joy before one sick or in pain for that contrary Passion will aggravate his Misery.

44th. When a man does all he can though it Succeeds not well, blame not him that did it.

45th. Being to advise or reprehend any one, consider whether it ought to be in publick or in Private; presently, or at Some other time in what terms to do it & in reproving Shew no Sign of Cholar but do it with all Sweetness and Mildness.

46th. Take all Admonitions thankfully in what Time or Place So ever given but afterwards not being culpable take a Time [&] Place convenient to let him know it that gave them.

[4]7th. Mock not nor Jest at any thing of Importance, break [n]o Jest that are Sharp Biting and if you Deliver any thing witty and Pleasent, abtain from Laughing thereat yourself.

48th. Wherein you reprove Another be unblameable yourself; for example is more prevalent than Precepts.

[4]9[th]. Use no Reproachfull Language against any one, neither Curse nor Revile.

[5]0th. Be not hasty to believe flying Reports to the Disparag[e]ment of any.

51st. Wear not your Cloths, foul, unript or Dusty but See they be Brush'd once every day at least and take heed tha[t] you approach not to any Uncleaness.

52d. In your Apparel be Modest and endeavour to accomodate Nature, rather than to procure Admiration keep to the Fashio[n] of your equals Such as are Civil and orderly with respect to Times and Places.

53d. Run not in the Streets, neither go t[oo s]lowly nor wit[h] Mouth open go not Shaking yr Arms [kick not the earth with yr feet, go] not upon the Toes, nor in a Dancing [fashion].

54th. Play not the Peacock, looking every where about you, to See if you be well Deck't, if your Shoes fit well if your Stokings sit neatly, and Cloths handsomely.

55th. Eat not in the Streets, nor in the House, out of Season.

56th. Associate yourself with Men of good Quality if you Esteem your own Reputation; for 'tis better to be alone than in bad Company.

57th. In walking up and Down in a House, only with One in Compan[y] if he be Greater than yourself, at the first give him the Right hand and Stop not till he does and be not the first that turns, and when you do turn let it be with your face towards him, if he be a Man of Great Quality, walk not with him Cheek by Joul but Somewhat behind him; but yet in Such a Manner that he may easily Speak to you.

58th. Let your Conversation be without Malice or Envy, for 'tis a Sig[n o]f a Tractable and Commendable Nature: And in all Causes of Passion [ad]mit Reason to Govern.

59th. Never express anything unbecoming, nor Act agst the Rules Mora[l] before your inferiours.

60th. Be not immodest in urging your Freinds to Discover a Secret.

61st. Utter not base and frivilous things amongst grave and Learn'd Men nor very Difficult Questians or Subjects, among the Ignorant or things hard to be believed, Stuff not your Discourse with Sentences amongst your Betters nor Equals.

62d. Speak not of doleful Things in a Time of Mirth or at the Table; Speak not of Melancholy Things as Death and Wounds, and if others Mention them Change if you can the Discourse tell not your Dreams, but to your intimate Friend.

63d. A Man o[ug]ht not to value himself of his Atchievements, or rare Qua[lities of wit; much less of his rich]es Virtue or Kindred.

64th. Break not a Jest where none take pleasure in mirth Laugh not aloud, nor at all without Occasion, deride no mans Misfortune, tho' there Seem to be Some cause.

65th. Speak not injurious Words neither in Jest nor Earnest Scoff at none although they give Occasion.

66th. Be not forward but friendly and Courteous; the first to Salute hear and answer & be not Pensive when it's a time to Converse.

67th. Detract not from others, neither be excessive in Commanding.

68th. Go not thither, where you know not, whether you Shall be Welcome or not. Give not Advice with[out] being Ask'd & when desired [d]o it briefly.

[6]9th. If two contend together take not the part of either unconstrain[ed]; and be not obstinate in your own Opinion, in Things indiferent be of the Major Side.

70th. Reprehend not the imperfections of others for that belong[s] to Parents Masters and Superiours.

71st. Gaze not on the marks or blemishes of Others and ask not how they came. What you may Speak in Secret to your Friend deliver not before others.

72d. Speak not in an unknown Tongue in Company but in your own Language and that as those of Quality do and not as the Vulgar; Sublime matters treat Seriously.

73d. Think before you Speak pronounce not imperfectly nor bring ou[t] your Words too hastily but orderly & distinctly.

74th. When Another Speaks be attentive your Self and disturb not the Audience if any hesitate in his Words help him not nor Prompt him without desired, Interrupt him not, nor Answer him till his Speec[h] be ended.

75th. In the midst of Discourse ask [not of what one treateth] but if you Perceive any Stop because of [your coming you may well intreat him gently] to Proceed: If a Person of Quality comes in while your Conversing it's handsome to Repeat what was said before.

76th. While you are talking, Point not with your Finger at him of Whom you Discourse nor Approach too near him to whom you talk especially to his face.

77th. Treat with men at fit Times about Business & Whisper not in the Company of Others.

78th. Make no Comparisons and if any of the Company be Commended for any brave act of Vertue, commend not another for the Same.

79th. Be not apt to relate News if you know not the truth thereof. In Discoursing of things you Have heard Name not your Author always A [Se]cret Discover not.

80th. Be not Tedious in Discourse or in reading unless you find the Company pleased therewith.

81st. Be not Curious to Know the Affairs of Others neither approach those that Speak in Private.

82d. Undertake not what you cannot Perform but be Carefull to keep your Promise.

83d. When you deliver a matter do it without Passion & with Discretion, howev[er] mean the Person be you do it to.

84th. When your Superiours talk to any Body hearken not neither Speak nor Laugh.

85th. In Company of these of Higher Quality than yourself Speak not ti[l] you are ask'd a Question, then Stand upright put of your Hat & Answer in few words.

86th. In Disputes, be not So Desireous to Overcome as not to give Liberty to each one to deliver his Opinion and Submit to the Judgment of the Major Part especially if they are Judges of the Dispute.

[87th. Let thy carriage be such] as becomes a Man Grave Settled and attentive [to that which is spoken. Contra]dict not at every turn what others Say.

88th. Be not tedious in Discourse, make not many Digressigns, nor rep[eat] often the Same manner of Discourse.

89th. Speak not Evil of the absent for it is unjust.

90th. Being Set at meat Scratch not neither Spit Cough or blow your Nose except there's a Necessity for it.

91st. Make no Shew of taking great Delight in your Victuals, Feed no[t] with Greediness; cut your Bread with a Knife, lean not on the Table, neither find fault with what you Eat.

92[d]. Take no Salt or cut Bread with your Knife Greasy.

93[d]. Entertaining any one at table it is decent to present him wt. meat, Undertake not to help others undesired by the Master.

[9]4th. If you Soak bread in the Sauce let it be no more than what you [pu]t in your Mouth at a time and blow not your broth at Table [bu]t Stay till Cools of it Self.

[95]th. Put not your meat to your Mouth with your Knife in your ha[nd ne]ither Spit forth the Stones of any fruit Pye upon a Dish nor Cas[t an]ything under the table.

[9]6th. It's unbecoming to Stoop much to ones Meat, Keep your Fingers clea[n &] when foul wipe them on a Corner of your Table Napkin.

[97]th. Put not another bit into your Mouth 'til the former be Swallowed [l]et not your Morsels be too big for the Gowls.

98th. Drink not nor talk with your mouth full, neither Gaze about you while you are a Drinking.

99th. Drink not too leisurely nor yet too hastily. Before and after Drinking wipe your Lips breath not then or Ever with too Great a Noise, for its uncivil.

100th. Cleanse not your teeth with the Table Cloth Napkin Fork or Knife but if Others do it let it be done wt. a Pick Tooth.

101st. Rince not your Mouth in the Presence of Others.

102d. It is out of use to call upon the Company often to Eat nor need you Drink to others every Time you Drink.

103d. In Company of your Betters be no[t longer in eating] than they are, lay not your Arm but o[nly your hand upon the table].

104th. It belongs to the Chiefest in Company to unfold his Napkin and fall to Meat first, But he ought then to Begin in time & to Dispatch [w]ith Dexterity that the Slowest may have time allowed him.

[1]05th. Be not Angry at Table whatever happens & if you have reason to be so, Shew it not but on a Chearfull Countenance especially if there be Strangers for Good Humour makes one Dish of Meat a Feas[t].

[1]06th. Set not yourself at the upper of the Table but if it Be your Due or that the Master of the house will have it So, Contend not, least you Should Trouble the Company.

107th. If others talk at Table be attentive but talk not with Meat in your Mouth.

108th. When you Speak of God or his Atributes, let it be Seriously & [wt.] Reverence. Honour & Obey your Natural Parents altho they be Poor.

109th. Let your Recreations be Manfull not Sinfull.

110th. Labour to keep alive in your Breast that Little Spark of Ce[les]tial fire Called Conscience.

Source: The Papers of George Washington Web site (Alderman Library, University of Virginia, 1996–2004), http://gwpapers. virginia.edu.

Advice to a Young Tradesman (1748)

In the following letter, Benjamin Franklin, a self-made man, known for his industry and common sense, gives sound advice to a young man beginning his career. No doubt, Franklin drew upon his own experiences of time and money management.

TO MY FRIEND, A. B.:

As you have desired of me, I write the following hints, which have been of service to me, and may, if observed, be so to you.

Remember that time is money. He that can earn ten shillings a day by his labour and goes abroad or sits idle one-half of that day, though he spends but sixpence during his diversion or idleness, ought not to reckon that the only expense; he has really spent, or rather thrown away, five shillings besides.

Remember that credit is money. If a man lets his money lie in my hands after it is due, he gives me the interest, or so much as I can make of it during that time. This amounts to a considerable sum where a man has good and large credit and makes good use of it.

Remember that money is of the prolific, generating nature. Money can beget money, and its offspring can beget more, and so on. Five shillings turned is six; turned again it is seven and threepence, and so on till it becomes a hundred pounds. The more there is of it the more it produces every turning, so that the profits rise quicker and quicker. He that kills a breeding sow destroys all her offspring to the thousandth generation. He that murders a crown destroys all that might have produced even scores of pounds.

Remember that six pounds a year is but a groat a day. For this little sum (which may be daily wasted either in time or expense unperceived) a man off credit may, on his own security, have the constant possession and use of a hundred pounds. So much in stock briskly turned by an industrious man produces great advantage.

Remember this saying, "The good paymaster is lord of another man's purse." He that is known to pay punctually and exactly to the time he promises may at any time and on any occasion raise all the money his friends can spare. This is sometimes of great use. After industry and frugality, nothing contributes more to the raising of a young man in the world than punctuality and justice in all his dealings; therefore never keep borrowed money an hour beyond the time you promised, lest a disappointment shut up your friend's purse for ever.

The most trifling actions that affect a man's credit are to be regarded. The sound of your hammer at five in the morning or nine at night heard by a creditor makes him easy six months longer, but if he sees you at a billard-table or hears your voice at a tavern, when you should be at work, he sends for his money the next day; demands it, before he can receive it, in a lump.

It shows, besides, that you are mindful of what you owe; it makes you appear a careful as well as an honest man, and that still increases your credit.

Beware of thinking all your own that you possess and of living accordingly. It is a mistake that many people who have credit fall into. To prevent this, keep an exact account for some time, both of your expenses and your income. If you take the pains at first to mention particulars, it will have this good effect: you will discover how wonderfully small, trifling expenses mount up to large sums, and will discern what might have been and may for the future be saved without occasioning any great inconvenience.

In short, the way to wealth, if you desire it, is as plain as the way to market. It depends chiefly on two words, industry and frugality; that is, waste neither time nor money, but make the best use of both. Without industry and frugality nothing will do, and with them everything. He that gets all he can honestly and saves all he gets (necessary expenses excepted), will certainly become rich, if that Being who governs the world, to whom all should look for a blessing on their honest endeavours, doth not, in his wise providence, otherwise determine.

AN OLD TRADESMAN.

Source: The Complete Works in Philosophy, Politics, and Morals of the Late Dr. Benjamin Franklin, Vol. 3 (London: J. Johnson, 1806), 463–66.

Gottlieb Mittelberger on Immigration to the Colonies (c. 1750)

In the mid-18th century, the German pastor Gottlieb Mittelberger investigated the immigration of his countrymen to Pennsylvania. His report gave a vivid account of the hardships of travel, the unsanitary conditions, and the large numbers of deaths. In addition, the burden of payment for the trip bound many into work indentures.

Upon his return to Germany, Mittelberger published his findings to dispel the illusions of many immigrants and to alert others as to what fate awaited them. Below is a selection from this publication.

Both in Rotterdam and in Amsterdam the people are packed densely, like herrings so to say, in the large sea-vessels. One person receives a place of scarcely 2 feet width and 6 feet length in the bedstead, while many a ship carries four to six hundred souls; not to mention the innumerable implements, tools, provisions, water-barrels and other things which likewise occupy much space.

On account of contrary winds it takes the ships sometimes 2, 3 and 4 weeks to make the trip from Holland to . . . England. But when the wind is good, they get there in 8 days or even sooner. Everything is examined there and the custom-duties paid, whence it comes that the ships ride there 8, 10 to 14 days and even longer at anchor, till they have taken in their full cargoes. During that time every one is compelled to spend his last remaining money and to consume his little stock of provisions which had been reserved for the sea; so that most passengers, finding themselves on the ocean where they would be in greater need of them, must greatly suffer from hunger and want. Many suffer want already on the water between Holland and Old England.

When the ships have for the last time weighed their anchors near the city of Kaupp [Cowes] in Old England, the real misery begins with the long voyage. For from there the ships, unless they have good wind, must often sail 8, 9, 10 to 12 weeks before they reach Philadelphia. But even with the best wind the voyage lasts 7 weeks.

But during the voyage there is on board these ships terrible misery, stench, fumes, horror, vomiting, many kinds of sea-sickness, fever, dysentery, headache, heat, constipation, boils, scurvy, cancer, mouth-rot, and the like, all of which come from old and sharply salted food and meat, also from very bad and foul water, so that many die miserably.

Add to this want of provisions, hunger, thirst, frost, heat, dampness, anxiety, want, afflictions and lamentations, together with other trouble, as . . . the lice abound so frightfully, especially on sick people, that they can be scraped off the body. The misery reaches the climax when a gale rages for 2 or 3 nights and days, so that every one believes that the ship will go to the bottom with all human beings on board. In such a visitation the people cry and pray most piteously.

When in such a gale the sea rages and surges, so that the waves rise often like high mountains one above the other, and often tumble over the ship, so that one fears to go down with the ship; when the ship is constantly tossed from side to side by the storm and waves, so that no one can either walk, or sit, or lie, and the closely packed people in the berths are thereby tumbled over each other, both the sick and the well—it will be readily understood that many of these people, none of whom had been prepared for hardships, suffer so terribly from them that they do not survive it.

I myself had to pass through a severe illness at sea, and I best know how I felt at the time. These poor people often long for consolation, and I often entertained and comforted them with singing, praying and exhorting; and whenever it was possible and the winds and waves permitted it, I kept daily prayer-meetings with them on deck. Besides, I baptized five children in distress, because we had no ordained minister on board. I also held divine service every Sunday by reading sermons to the people; and when the dead were sunk in the water, I commended them and our souls to the mercy of God.

Among the healthy, impatience sometimes grows so great and cruel that one curses the other, or himself and the day of his birth, and sometimes come near killing each other. Misery and malice join each other, so that they cheat and rob one another. One always reproaches the other with having persuaded him to undertake the journey. Frequently children cry out against their parents, husbands against their wives and wives against their husbands, brothers and sisters, friends and acquaintances against each other. But most against the soul-traffickers.

Many sigh and cry: "Oh, that I were at home again, and if I had to lie in my pig-sty!" Or they say: "O God, if I only had a piece of good bread, or a good fresh drop of water." Many people whimper, sigh and cry piteously for their homes; most of them get home-sick. Many hundred people necessarily die and perish in such misery, and must be cast into the sea, which drives their relatives, or those who persuaded them to undertake the journey, to such despair that it is almost impossible to pacify and console them.

No one can have an idea of the sufferings which women in confinement have to bear with their innocent children on board these ships. Few of this class escape with their lives; many a mother is cast into the water with her child as soon as she is dead. One day, just as we had a heavy gale, a woman in our ship, who was to give birth and could not give birth under the circumstances, was pushed through a loop-hole [port-hole] in the ship and dropped into the sea, because she was far in the rear of the ship and could not be brought forward.

Children from 1 to 7 years rarely survive the voyage. I witnessed misery in no less than 32 children in our ship, all of whom were thrown into the sea. The parents grieve all the more since their children find no resting-place in the earth, but are devoured by the monsters of the sea. . . .

That most of the people get sick is not surprising, because, in addition to all other trials and hardships, warm food is served only three times a week, the rations being very poor and very little. Such meals can hardly be eaten, on account of being so unclean. The water which is served out on the ships is often very black, thick and full of worms, so that one cannot drink it without loathing, even with the greatest thirst. Toward the end we were compelled to eat the ship's biscuit which had been spoiled long ago; though in a whole biscuit there was scarcely a, piece the size of a dollar that had not been full of red worms and spiders nests. . . .

At length, when, after a long and tedious voyage, the ships come in sight of land, so that the promontories can be seen, which the people were so eager and anxious to see, all creep from below on deck to see the land from afar, and they weep for joy, and pray and sing, thanking and praising God. The sight of the land makes the people on board the ship, especially the sick and the half dead, alive again, so that their hearts leap within them; they shout and rejoice, and are content to bear their misery in patience, in the hope that they may soon reach the land in safety. But alas!

When the ships have landed at Philadelphia after their long voyage, no one is permitted to leave them except those who pay for their passage or can give good security; the others, who cannot pay, must remain on board the ships till they are purchased, and are released from the ships by their purchasers. The sick always fare the worst, for the healthy are naturally preferred and purchased first; and so the sick and wretched must often remain on board in front of the city for 2 or 3 weeks, and frequently die, whereas many a one, if

he could pay his debt and were permitted to leave the ship immediately, might recover and remain alive. . . .

The sale of human beings in the market on board the ship is carried on thus: Every day Englishmen, Dutchmen and High-German people come from the city of Philadelphia and other places, in part from a great distance, say 20, 30, or 40 hours away, and go on board the newly arrived ship that has brought and offers for sale passengers from Europe, and select among the healthy persons such as they deem suitable for their business, and bargain with them how long they will serve for their passage money, which most of them are still in debt for. When they have come to an agreement, it happens that adult persons bind themselves in writing to serve 3, 4, 5 or 6 years for the amount due by them, according to their age and strength. But very young people, from 10 to 15 years, must serve till they are 21 years old.

Many parents must sell and trade away their children like so many head of cattle; for if their children take the debt upon themselves, the parents can leave the ship free and unrestrained; but as the parents often do not know where and to what people their children are going, it often happens that such parents and children, after leaving the ship, do not see each other again for many years, perhaps no more in all their lives. . . .

It often happens that whole families, husband, wife, and children, are separated by being sold to different purchasers, especially when they have not paid any part of their passage money.

When a husband or wife has died at sea, when the ship has made more than half of her trip, the survivor must pay or serve not only for himself or herself, but also for the deceased.

When both parents have died over half-way at sea, their children, especially when they are young and have nothing to pawn or to pay, must stand for their own and their parents' passage, and serve till they are 21 years old. When one has served his or her term, he or she is entitled to a new suit of clothes at parting; and if it has been so stipulated, a man gets in addition a horse, a woman, a cow.

When a serf has an opportunity to marry in this country, he or she must pay for each year which he or she would have yet to serve, 5 to 6 pounds. But many a one who has thus purchased and paid for his bride, has subsequently repented his bargain, so that he would gladly have returned his exorbitantly dear ware, and lost the money besides.

If some one in this country runs away from his master, who has treated him harshly, he cannot get far. Good provision has been made for such cases, so that a runaway is soon recovered. He who detains or returns a deserter receives a good reward.

If such a runaway has been away from his master one day, he must serve for it as a punishment a week, for a week a month, and for a month half a year. . . .

Source: Gottlieb Mittelberger, *Journey to Pennsylvania in the year 1750 and Return to Germany in the Year 1754*, translated by Carl Theo. Eben (Philadelphia: J. J. McVey, 1898), 16–29.

Captivity Narrative of Mary Jemison in the 1750s (pub. 1824)

During the French and Indian War, Mary Jemison was captured by Native Americans when she was some 15 years of age. Having lost her family and home during the raid, she feared for her life as she was taken to the Ohio frontier. It was customary for Seneca Indians who lost kin during battle to exact revenge by killing the enemy or to adopt a captive as a replacement for their lost family member. Mary Jemison, fortunately, was adopted by her captors.

Although she was illiterate, Jemison's story was captured in an interview by James Seaver in the 1820s and published in 1824. Her narrative describes the daily life of indigenous peoples, their family roles, and character.

Chapter 3.

The night was spent in gloomy forebodings. What the result of our captivity would be, it was out of our power to determine, or even imagine. At times, we could almost realize the approach of our masters to butcher and scalp us; again, we could nearly see the pile of wood kindled on which we were to be roasted; and then we would imagine ourselves at liberty, alone and defenseless in the forest, surrounded by wild beasts that were ready to devour us. The anxiety of our minds drove sleep from our eyelids; and it was with a dreadful hope and painful impatience that we waited for the morning to determine our fate.

The morning at length arrived, and our masters came early and let us out of the house, and gave the young man and boy to the French, who immediately took them away. Their fate I never learned, as I have not seen nor heard of them since.

I was now left alone in the fort, deprived of my former companions, and of every thing that was near or dear to me but life. But it was not long before I was in some measure relieved by the appearance of two pleasant looking squaws, of the Seneca tribe, who came and examined me attentively for a short time, and then went out. After a few minutes' absence, they returned in company with my former masters, who gave me to the squaws to dispose of as they pleased.

The Indians by whom I was taken were a party of Shawnees, if I remember right, that lived, when at home, a long distance down the Ohio.

My former Indian masters and the two squaws were soon ready to leave the fort, and accordingly embarked—the Indians in a large canoe, and the two squaws and myself in a small one—and went down the Ohio. When we set off, an Indian in the forward canoe took the scalps of my former friends, strung them on a pole that he placed upon his shoulder, and in that manner carried them, standing in the stern of the canoe directly before us, as we sailed down the river, to the town where the two squaws resided.

On the way we passed a Shawnee town, where I saw a number of heads, arms, legs, and other fragments of the bodies of some white people who had just been burned. The parts that remained were hanging on a pole, which was supported at each end by a crotch stuck in the ground, and were roasted or burnt black as a coal. The fire was yet burning; and the whole appearance afforded a spectacle so shocking that even to this day the blood almost curdles in my veins when I think of them.

At night we arrived at a small Seneca Indian town, at the mouth of a small river that was called by the Indians, in the Seneca language, She-nan-jee, about eighty miles by water from the fort, where the two squaws to whom I belonged resided. There we landed, and the Indians went on; which was the last I ever saw of them.

Having made fast to the shore, the squaws left me in the canoe while they went to their wigwam or house in the town, and returned with a suit of Indian clothing, all new, and very clean and nice. My clothes, though whole and good when I was taken, were now torn in pieces, so that I was almost naked. They first undressed me, and threw my rags into the river; then washed me clean and dressed me in the new suit they had just brought, in complete Indian style; and then led me home and seated me in the center of their wigwam.

I had been in that situation but a few minutes before all the squaws in the town came in to see me. I was soon surrounded by them, and they immediately set up a most dismal howling, crying bitterly, and wringing their hands in all the agonies of grief for a deceased relative.

Their tears flowed freely, and they exhibited all the signs of real mourning. At the commencement of this scene, one of their number began, in a voice somewhat between speaking and singing, to recite some words to the following purport, and continued the recitation till the ceremony was ended; the company at the same time varying the appearance of their countenances, gestures, and tone of voice, so as to correspond with the sentiments expressed by their leader.

"Oh, our brother! alas! he is dead—he has gone; he will never return! Friendless he died on the field of the slain, where his bones are yet lying unburied! Oh! who will not mourn his sad fate? No tears dropped around him: oh, no! No tears of his sisters were there! He fell in his prime, when his arm was most needed to keep us from danger! Alas! he has gone, and left us in sorrow, his loss to bewail! Oh, where is his spirit? His spirit went naked, and hungry it wanders, and thirsty and wounded, it groans to return! Oh, helpless and wretched, our brother has gone! No blanket nor food to nourish and warm him; nor candles to light him, nor weapons of war! Oh, none of those comforts had he! But well we remember his deeds! The deer he could take on the chase! The panther shrunk back at the sight of his strength! His enemies fell at his feet! He was brave and courageous in war! As the fawn, he was harmless; his friendship was ardent; his temper was gentle; his pity was great! Oh! our friend, our companion, is dead! Our brother, our brother! alas, he is gone! But why do we grieve for his loss? In the strength of a warrior, undaunted he left us, to fight by the side of the chiefs! His warwhoop was shrill! His rifle well aimed laid his enemies low: his tomahawk drank of their blood: and his knife flayed their scalps while yet covered with gore! And why do we mourn? Though he fell on the field of the slain, with glory he fell; and his spirit went up to the land of his fathers in war! They why do we mourn? With transports of joy, they received him, and fed him, and clothed him, and welcomed him there! Oh, friends, he is happy; then dry up your tears! His spirit has seen our distress, and sent us a helper whom with pleasure we greet. Dickewamis has come: then let us receive her with joy!—she is handsome and pleasant! Oh! she is our sister, and gladly we welcome her here. In the place of our brother she stands in our tribe. With care we will guard her from trouble; and may she be happy till her spirit shall leave us."

In the course of that ceremony, from mourning they became serene,—joy sparkled in their countenances, and they seemed to rejoice over me as over a long-lost child. I was made welcome among them as a sister to the two squaws before mentioned, and was called Dickewamis; which, being interpreted, signifies a pretty girl, a handsome girl, or a pleasant, good thing. That is the name by which I have ever since been called by the Indians.

I afterward learned that the ceremony I at that time passed through was that of adoption. The two squaws had lost a brother in Washington's war, sometime in the year before, and in consequence of his death went up to Fort Du Quesne on the day on which I arrived there, in order to receive a prisoner, or an enemy's scalp, to supply their loss. It is a custom of the Indians, when one of their number is slain or taken prisoner in battle, to give to the nearest relative of the dead or absent a prisoner, if they have chanced to take one; and if not, to give him the scalp of an enemy. On the return of the Indians from the conquest, which is always announced by peculiar shoutings, demonstrations of joy, and the exhibition of some trophy of victory, the mourners come forward and make their claims. If they receive a prisoner, it is at their option either to satiate their vengeance by taking his life in the most cruel manner they can conceive of, or to receive and adopt him into the family, in the place of him whom they have lost. All the prisoners that are taken in battle and carried to the encampment or town by the Indians are given to the bereaved families, till their number is good. And unless the mourners have but just received the news of their bereavement, and are under the operation of a paroxysm of grief, anger, or revenge; or, unless the prisoner is very old, sickly, or homely, they generally save them, and treat them kindly. But if their mental wound is fresh, their loss so great that they deem it irreparable, or if their prisoner or prisoners do not meet their approbation, no torture, let it be ever so cruel, seems sufficient to make them satisfaction. It is family and not national sacrifices among the Indians, that has given them an indelible stamp as barbarians, and identified their character with the idea which is generally formed of unfeeling ferocity and the most barbarous cruelty.

It was my happy lot to be accepted for adoption. At the time of the ceremony I was received by the two squaws to supply the place of their brother in the family; and I was ever considered and treated by them as a real sister, the same as though I had been born of their mother.

During the ceremony of my adoption, I sat motionless, nearly terrified to death at the appearance and actions of the company, expecting every moment to feel their vengeance, and suffer death on the spot. I was, however, happily disappointed; when at the close of the ceremony the company retired, and my sisters commenced employing every means for my consolation and comfort.

Being now settled and provided with a home, I was employed in nursing the children, and doing light work about the house. Occasionally, I was sent out with the Indian hunters, when they went but a short distance, to help them carry their game. My situation was easy; I had no particular hardships to endure. But still, the recollection of my parents, my brothers and sisters, my home, and my own captivity, destroyed my happiness, and made me constantly solitary, lonesome, and gloomy.

My sisters would not allow me to speak English in their hearing; but remembering the charge that my dear mother gave me at the time I left her, whenever I chanced to be alone I made a business of repeating my prayer, catechism, or something I had learned, in order that I might not forget my own language. By practicing in that way, I retained it till I came to Genesee flats, where I soon became acquainted with English people, with whom I have been almost daily in the habit of conversing.

My sisters were very diligent in teaching me their language; and to their great satisfaction, I soon learned so that I could understand it readily, and speak it fluently. I was very fortunate in falling into their hands; for they were kind, good-natured women; peaceable and mild in their dispositions; temperate and decent in their habits, and very tender and gentle toward me. I have great reason to respect them, though they have been dead a great number of years. . . .

Chapter 7.

After the conclusion of the French war, our tribe had nothing to do till the commencement of the American Revolution. For twelve or fifteen years, the use of the implements of war was not known, nor the warwhoop heard, save on days of festivity, when the achievements of former times were commemorated in a kind of mimic warfare, in which the chiefs, and warriors displayed their prowess, and illustrated their former adroitness, by laying the ambuscade, surprising their enemies, and performing many accurate maneuvers with the tomahawk and scalping knife; thereby preserving, and banding to their children, the theory of Indian warfare. During that period they also pertinaciously observed the religious rites of their progenitors, by attending with the most scrupulous exactness, and a great degree of enthusiasm, to the sacrifices, at particular times, to appease the anger of the Evil Deity; or to excite the commiseration of the Great Good Spirit, whom they adored with reverence, as the author, governor, supporter, and disposer of every good thing of which they participated.

They also practiced in various athletic games, such as running, wrestling, leaping, and playing ball, with a view that their bodies might be more supple—or, rather, that they might not become enervated, and that they might be enabled to make a proper selection of chiefs for the councils of the nation, and leaders for war.

While the Indians were thus engaged in their round of traditional performances, with the addition of hunting, their women attended to agriculture, their families, and a few domestic concerns of small consequence and attended with but little labor.

No people can live more happy than the Indians did in times of peace, before the introduction of spiritous liquors among them. Their lives were a continual round of pleasures. Their wants were few, and easily satisfied, and their cares were only for to-day—the bounds of their calculation for future comfort not extending to the incalculable uncertainties of to-morrow. If peace ever dwelt with men, it was in former times, in the recess from war, among what are now termed barbarians. The moral character of the Indians was (if I may be allowed the expression) uncontaminated. Their fidelity was perfect, and became proverbial. They were strictly honest; they despised deception and falsehood; and chastity was held in high veneration, and a violation of it was considered sacrilege. They were temperate in their desires, moderate in their passions, and candid and honorable in the expression of their sentiments, on every subject of importance.

Thus, at peace among themselves and with the neighboring whites—though there were none at that time very near—our Indians lived quietly and peaceably at home, till a little before the breaking out of the Revolutionary War. . . .

Chapter 9.

Soon after the close of the Revolutionary War, my Indian brother, Kau-jises-tau-ge-au, (which being interpreted signifies Black Coals) offered me my liberty, and told me that if it was my choice I might go to my friends.

My son Thomas was anxious that I should go; and offered to go with me, and assist me on the journey, by taking care of the younger children, and providing food as we traveled through the wilderness. But the chiefs of our tribe, suspecting, from his appearance, actions, and a few warlike exploits, that Thomas would be a great warrior, or a good counselor, refused to let him leave them on any account whatever.

To go myself, and leave him, was more than I felt able to do; for he had been kind to me, and was one on whom I placed great dependence. The chiefs refusing to let him go was one reason for my resolving to stay; but another, more powerful if possible, was, that I had got a large family of Indian children that I must take with me; and that, if I should be so fortunate as to find my relatives, they would despise them, if not myself, and treat us as enemies, or, at least, with a degree of cold indifference, which I thought I could not endure.

Accordingly, after I had duly considered the matter, I told my brother that it was my choice to stay and spend the remainder of my days with my Indian friends, and live with my family as I hitherto had done. He appeared well pleased with my resolution, and informed me that, as that was my choice, I should have a piece of land that I could call my own, where I could live unmolested, and have something at my decease to leave for the benefit of my children.

Source: James E. Seaver, *The Life of Mary Jemison: The White Woman of the Genesee* (Buffalo, NY: Matthews & Warren, 1877).

A Report on the Kite Experiment (1752)

Benjamin Franklin's letters to his English friend Peter Collinson concerning electricity were read to the Royal Society of London, and Collinson collected them for publication in 1751. The Royal Society recognized Franklin's work and, in 1753, awarded him their highest scientific honor, the Copley Medal. This singular honor helped secure Franklin's reputation as a scientist.

The following is from a letter describing the kite experiment. Written on October 19, 1752, from Franklin to Collinson, this letter was subsequently published in *The Pennsylvania Gazette*.

As frequent Mention is made in the News Papers from Europe, of the Success of the Philadelphia Experiment for drawing the Electric Fire from Clouds by Means of pointed Rods of Iron erected on high Buildings, &c. it may be agreeable to the Curious to be inform'd, that the same Experiment has succeeded in Philadelphia, tho' made in a different and more easy Manner, which any one may try, as follows.

Make a small Cross of two light Strips of Cedar, the Arms so long as to reach to the four Corners of a large thin Silk Handkerchief when extended; tie the Corners of the Handkerchief to the Extremities of the Cross, so you have the Body of a Kite; which being properly accommodated with a Tail, Loop and String, will rise in the Air, like those made of Paper; but this being of Silk is fitter to bear the Wet and Wind of a Thunder Gust without tearing. To the Top of the upright Stick of the Cross is to be fixed a very sharp pointed Wire, rising a Foot or more above the Wood. To the End of the Twine, next the Hand, is to be tied a silk Ribbon, and where the Twine and the silk join, a Key may be fastened. This Kite is to be raised when a Thunder Gust appears to be coming on, and the Person who holds the String must stand within a Door, or Window, or under some Cover, so that the Silk Ribbon may not be wet; and Care must be taken that the Twine does not touch the Frame of the Door or Window. As soon as any of the Thunder Clouds come over the Kite, the pointed Wire will draw the Electric Fire from them, and the Kite, with all the Twine, will be electrified, and the loose Filaments of the Twine will stand out every Way, and be attracted by an approaching Finger. And when the Rain has wet the Kite and Twine, so that it can conduct the Electric Fire freely, you will find it stream out plentifully from the Key on the Approach of your Knuckle. At this Key the Phial may be charg'd; and from Electric Fire thus obtain'd, Spirits may be kindled, and all the other Electric Experiments be perform'd, which are usually done by the Help of a rubbed Glass Globe or Tube; and thereby the Sameness of the Electric Matter with that of Lightning compleatly demonstrated.

Source: "Letter from B. Franklin to Peter Collinson, dated October 19, 1752," in *Benjamin Franklin Representative Selections, With Introduction, Bibliography, and Notes,* edited by Frank Luther Mott and Chester E. Jorgenson (New York: American Book, 1936).

Correspondence of Benjamin Franklin
(1752, 1753, 1769)

The Magical Circle

Benjamin Franklin corresponded with learned men of his day, and his letters reveal his wide-ranging interests. He communicated regarding experiments on electricity with the scientifically oriented London merchant Peter Collinson. Here, in a letter to Collinson, Franklin shares his mathematical "magical circle" algorithm.

1752?

SIR,

I am glad the perusal of the magical squares afforded you any amusement. I now send you the magical circle.

Its properties, besides those mentioned in my former, are these.

Half the number in any radial row, added with half the central number, make 180, equal to the number of degrees in a semi-circle.

Also half the numbers in any one of the concentric circles, taken either above or below the horizontal double line, with half the central number, make 180.

And if any four adjoining numbers, standing nearly in a square, be taken from any part, and added with half the central number, they make 180.

There are, moreover, included four other sets of circular spaces, excentric with respect to the first, each of these sets containing five spaces. The centers of the circles that bound them, are at A, B, C, and D. Each set, for the more easy distinguishing them from the first, are drawn with a different colour'd ink, red, blue, green, and yellow.

These sets of excentric circular spaces intersect those of the concentric, and each other; and yet the numbers contained in each of the twenty excentric spaces, taken all around, make, with the central number, the same sum as those in each of the 8 concentric, viz. 360. The halves, also of those drawn from the centers A and C, taken above or below the double horizontal line, and of those drawn from centers B and D, taken to the right or left of the vertical line, do, with half the central number, make just 180.

It may be observed, that there is not one of the numbers but what belongs at least to two of the different circular spaces; some to three, some to four, some to five; and yet they are all so placed as never to break the required number 360, in any of the 28 circular spaces within the primitive circle.

These interwoven circles make so perplexed an appearance, that it is not easy for the eye to trace every circle of numbers one would examine, through all the maze of circles intersected by it; but if you fix one foot of the compasses in either of the centers, and extend the other to any number in the circle you would examine belonging to that center, the moving foot will point the others out, by passing round over all the numbers of that circle successively.

I am, &c.

Electricity, the Transit of Mercury, and a Northwest Passage

This letter to Cadwallader Colden, then a Philadelphia scientist and physician, apparently relates to a scientific text being readied for publication by Franklin. In the letter, Franklin flatters Colden for his mathematical ability, downplaying his own aptitude for the subject. The letter also mentions Franklin's work on electricity, reveals his astronomical interest, and indicates his support of a ship ready to undertake a voyage to secure a Northwest Passage.

Philada[delphia] Feb[ruary] 28, 1753

Dear Sir

I return you herewith Professor Kanster's Remarks. As far as I am able to judge, the Translation is just, and your Answer a good one. I am pleas'd with the Omission of that part of a Paragraph relating to the German and Pensilvanian Electricians, and have corrected the Copy as you direct. I have but one other Alteration to propose, which is, to omit some Part of the last Paragraph, and read the rest thus;—"After all, Mr. Colden must think himself obliged to the Professor, for exposing the Difficulties his Treatise lies under in the Opinion of others, as thereby an Opportunity is given of explaining his Doctrine more fully to their Satisfaction." For it seems to me not so proper to make Acknowledgement for his Translating your Piece, as if it were a Favour, when he tells the World he did it by Command: And I apprehend it unnecessary, and that it may look like too great a Fondness for Complement, to draw one from him by Consequence; viz. That he did not think it a trifling Performance, or he would not have taken the Trouble, &c. since he himself freely says, that the many new, good and just Thoughts contain'd in it, made him willingly undertake the Task enjoin'd him. Besides that it is not clear he could have refus'd to obey the Command he received, whatever might have been his private Sentiments. The Ship I intended to forward these Papers by to Mr. Collinson, has stay'd much longer than I expected, and now I am told will not sail before the End of next Month, so that I may possibly receive your Directions concerning this propos'd Alteration before she sails.

I find I was not wrong in my Apprehensions that your Book would be incorrectly printed. I hope however, that the Errata will be in England time enough to be published with the Work; and I thank you for sending them to me. I have corrected the Book accordingly, and given it one Reading; but it is not a Piece to make sudden Remarks on, as one might of a Poem or other Performance on common Subjects.

I must read and consider it yet more attentively; at present I can only tell you, that some Things in it please me exceedingly; some I do not yet clearly understand; and one or two Positions I think wrong; of all which you shall hear more fully in my next. On the whole it gives me great Satisfaction, when I consider it as a Work that will not only improve Philosophy, but do Honour to America.

I am sorry I have not, as you expect, anything new to communicate to you on the Subject of Electricity. My Time and Thoughts have of late been much engag'd in other Matters: And ever since I heard of your being furnish'd with an Apparatus, I have hoped rather to receive Information of new Discoveries from you, than expected to send you any. If your other philosophical Pursuits do not prevent your Application to the Experiments you propos'd to make on various Salts, &c. I shall still hope it. Your Skill and Expertness in Mathematical Computations, will afford you an Advantage in these Disquisitions, that I lament the want of, who am like a Man searching for something in a dark Room, where I can only grope and guess; while you proceed with a Candle in your Hand.

We are preparing here to make accurate Observations on the approaching Transit of Mercury over the Sun. You will oblige us much by sending the Account you have received from Lord Macclesfield of his great mural Quadrant. I congratulate you on your Discovery of a new Motion in the Earth's Axis: You will, I see, render your Name immortal.

I believe I have not before told you, that I have procur'd a Subscription here of pounds 1500 to fit out a Vessel in Search of a NWest Passage: she sails in a few Days, and is called the Argo, commanded by Mr. Swaine, who was in the last Expedition in the California, Author of a Journal of that Voyage in two Volumes. We think the Attempt laudable, whatever may be the Success. . . . *Magnis tamen excidit ausis.* [A great venture even though unsuccessful.]

With great Esteem, I am, Dear Sir, Your most humble Servant

The King's Botanist

This letter to the Philadelphia naturalist John Bartram is the warmest of the three selections here. Franklin encourages his friend Bartram, the king's royal botanist in America, to record his observations for publication, indicating that there is interest in his work. Franklin also places an order for seed samples with Bartram, who supplied many scientists of the day with specimens, and offers to send some in return.

London July 9, 1769

Dear Friend,

It is with great Pleasure I understand by your Favour of April 10. that you continue to enjoy so good a Share of Health. I hope it will long continue. And altho' it may not now be suitable for you to make such wide Excursions as heretofore, you may yet be very useful to your Country and to Mankind, if you sit down quietly at home, digest the Knowledge you have acquired, compile and publish the many Observations you have made, and point out the Advantages that may be drawn from the whole, in publick Undertakings or particular private Practice. It is true many People are fond of Accounts of old Buildings, Monuments, &c. but there is a Number who would be much better pleas'd with such Accounts as you could afford them: And for one I confess that if I could find in any Italian Travels a Receipt for making Parmesan Cheese, it would give me more Satisfaction than a Transcript of any Inscription from any old Stone whatever.

I suppose Mr. Michael Collinson, or Dr. Fothergill have written to you what may be necessary for your Information relating to your Affairs here. I imagine there is no doubt but the King's Bounty to you will be continued; and that it will be proper for you to continue sending now and then a few such curious Seeds as you can procure to keep up your Claim. And now I mention Seeds, I wish you would send me a few of such as are least common, to the Value of a Guinea, which Mr. Foxcroft will pay you for me. They are for a particular Friend who is very curious. If in any thing I can serve you here, command freely,

Your affectionate Friend

P.S. Pray let me know whether you have had sent you any of the Seeds of the Rhubarb describ'd in the enclos'd Prints. It is said to be of the true kind. If you have it not, I can procure some Seeds for you.

Source: Benjamin Franklin, *The Writings of Benjamin Franklin,* edited by Albert Henry Smyth (New York: Macmillan Company, 1905–1907).

Founding Colleges in America (1754)

Colonial colleges usually were founded for religious purposes and most especially for the training of the ministry. The College of New Jersey (now Princeton University) came into existence in 1764, in part, due to the Great Awakening. Its charter prohibited the exclusion of any student on the basis of religion, a provision that was to prove advantageous in fund raising.

In 1752, the College of New Jersey described its origins and policies in a promotional brochure, which was reprinted in Britain in 1754. The following is text from that brochure.

NOTHING has a more direct tendency to advance the happiness and glory of a community than the founding of public schools and seminaries of learning for education of youth, and adorning their minds with useful knowledge and virtue. Hereby, the rude and ignorant are civilized and rendered human; persons who would otherwise be useless member[s] of society are qualified to sustain with honor the offices they may be invested with for the public service reverence of the Deity, filial piety, and obedience to the laws are inculcated and promoted. The sciences have nowhere flourished with more success than in our mother country. The universities and seminaries of Learning in England and Scotland a[re] annually sending abroad into the Kingdom proficients in all kinds of literature; men of refined sentiments, solid judgments, and noble principles, who spread (if the expression may be allowed) a kind of literary glory over the British nation.

America remained, during a long period, in the thickest darkness of ignorance and barbarism, till Christianity, at the introduction of the Europeans, enlightened her hemisphere with the salutary beams of life and immortality. Science, her constant attendant, soon raised her depressed head, and the arts began to flourish. New England first felt her nigh influences, whose sons she inspired with a generous emulation of erecting schools and colleges for the instruction of their youth, and instilling into the tender mind the principles of [pious] . . . learning. The southwestward colonies, except Virginia, continued a considerable number of years without any public institutions for the cultivation of the sciences. At length, several gentlemen residing in and near the province of New Jersey, who were well-wishers to the felicity of their count[ry] and real friends of [religious] . . . learning, having observed the vast increase of those colonies, with the denseness and ignorance of their inhabitants for want of the necessary means of improvement, first projected the scheme of a collegiate education in that province.

The immediate motives to this generous design were: the great number of Christian societies then lately formed in various parts of the country, where many thousands of the inhabitants, ardently desirous of the administration of religious ordinances, were entirely destitute of the necessary means of instruction and incapable of being relieved; the urgent applications that were annually made by those vacant congregations to the clergy in their collective bodies; complaining in the most moving manner of their unhappy circumstances in being deprived of the ordinary means of salvation and left to grope after happiness, almost in the obscurity of paganism, though the light of revelation shone on their surrounding neighbors; the great scarcity of candidates for the ministerial function to comply with these pious and Christian demands; the colleges of New England educating hardly a competent number for the service of its own churches—these considerations were the most urgent arguments for the immediate prosecution of the above mentioned scheme of education.

Accordingly, in the year 1747, a petition was presented to His Excellency Jonathan Belcher, Esq., governor of that province (a gentleman who has long signalized himself as a patron of religion and learning), praying His Majesty's grant of a charter for the establishment of a public seminary of literature in New Jersey. His Excellency, with the approbation of the council and attorney general of the said province, was pleased to comply with their request; and ordered a charter to pass the seals, incorporating sundry gentlemen, to the number of twenty-three, by the name of the Trustees of [th]e College of New Jersey [Princeton]; and appointing the governor of New Jersey, for the time being, who is His Majesty's representative, to act as their president when convened. This charter places the society upon the most catholic foundation—all Protestants of every denomination who are loyal subjects to Our Most Gracious Sovereign (the happy effects of whose mild and equal administration the remotest colonies of the British empire sensibly experience and gratefully acknowledge) are admitted to the enjoyment of all its privileges and allowed the unlimited exercise of their religion.

The trustees, thus authorized with ample powers for the execution of this laudable design, in conformity to the plan of their charter, applied themselves with the utmost deliberation to form and enact such rules and orders for the regulation of the methods of instruction and conduct of the students as might tend to prevent the entrance of vice into the society, and the introduction of idleness, vanity, and extravagant expenses among its members. It would be repugnant to the design of a general narrative, as well as impertinent to the reader, to enter into a minute detail of these several private regulations. It will suffice to say that the two principal objects the trustees had in view were science and religion. Their first concern was to cultivate the minds of the pupils in all those branches of erudition which are generally taught in the universities abroad; and, to perfect their design, their next care was to rectify the heart by inculcating the great precep[ts] of Christianity order to make them good. Upon the views this society was founded. Providence so far smiled upon the undertaking, in the first instance, as to point out a gentleman, possessed of every requisite endowment, to be placed at the head of such an academy. The Rev. Mr. Aaron Burr has been long known in these parts of America for his piety, affability, universal acquaintance with the arts and sciences, his easy, familiar methods of instruction. Under his immediate tuition and government, this society has flourished far beyond the most raised and sanguine expectations. The number of students has increased, in the short space of five years, from eight or ten, to about sixty; besides near forty in the grammar school. As no human institutions in a world of imperfection and error are so completely modeled to exclude the possibility of further emendation, it may be said, without any intention of disparagement to other learned seminaries, that the governors of this college have endeavored to improve upon the commonly conceived plans of education. They proceed not so much in the method of a dogmatic institution, by prolix discourses on the different branches of the sciences, by burdening the memory and imposing heavy and disagreeable tasks, as in the Socratic way of free dialogue between teacher and pupil, or between the students themselves under the inspection of their tutors. In this manner, the attention is engaged, the mind entertained, and the scholar animated in the pursuit of knowledge. In fine, the arts and sciences are conveyed into the minds of youth in a method, the most easy, natural, and familiar.

But as religion ought to be the end of all instruction and gives it the last degree of perfection; as one of the primary views of this foundation was to educate young gentlemen for the sacred office of the ministry and fit them for the discharge of so noble an employment; divinity, the mistress the sciences, engages the peculiar attention of the governors of this

society. Stated times are set apart for the study of the Holy Scriptures in the original languages, and stated hours daily consecrated to the service of religion. The utmost care is taken to discountenance vice and to encourage the practice of virtue and a manly, rational, and Christian behavior in the students. Enthusiasm, on the one hand, and profaneness, on the other, are equally guarded against and meet with the severest checks.

Under such management, this seminary, from the smallest beginnings, quickly drew the public attention, enlarged the number of her pupils, raised her reputation; and now . . . her ancient sisters upon the Continent. Daily observation evidences that in proportion as learning makes its progress in a country, it softens the natural roughness, eradicates the prejudices, and transforms the genius and disposition of its inhabitants. New Jersey and the adjacent provinces already feel the happy effects of this useful institution. A general desire of knowledge seems to be spreading among the people. Parents are inspired with emulation of cultivating the minds of their offspring; public stations are honorably filled by gentlemen who have received their education here; and, from hence, many Christian assemblies are furnished with men of distinguished talents for the discharge of the pastoral office. . . .

From the above representation of the ends for which this corporation was founded, the happy effects of its institution, and its present necessitous circumstances, it is hoped that the pious and benevolent in Great Britain, into who[se] hands these papers may fall, will extend their generous aids in the prosecution and completion of so excellent and useful a design. A Design! upon the success of which the happiness of multitudes in sundry colonies, and their numerous posterity, in the present and future ages far distant, in a great measure depends. A Design! which not only tends to promote the weal of the British inhabitants but also of the German emigrants; and to spread the gospel of salvation among the benighted Indian tribes and attach them to His Majesty's government. A Design! which is not calculated to promote the low purposes of a party, but in its views and consequences affects the Protestant interest in general, and Great Britain in particular, both in religious and civil respects; since, by this, the filial duty of her descendants will be inculcated, their manners reformed, and her trade increased; which is the basis of her empire, glory, and felicity.

The inhabitants of the infant colonies, dependent upon this seminary, unable to relieve themselves, are constrained to solicit and implore the assistance of others. And to whom shall they look but to their tender and powerful parent? To move her compassion, they plead their relation as children, as fellow subjects, as Christian and Protestant brethren with her sons that still enjoy the advantages of residing in their native country. They plead the deplorable circumstances of the church, and the exigencies of the state, for want of such an institution brought to maturity. And they beg leave modestly to intimate their importance to their mother country, as they enlarge the British dominions upon a vast continent, whither the industrious Poor may transplant themselves and find a comfortable subsistence, as they are a check upon the growth of the French power in America; engage the Indian natives to the British interest; furnish various assistances in time of war against the common enemy; and carry on sundry branches of trade advantageous to Great Britain, which will undoubtedly flourish more in proportion to their improvements in the liberal arts and sciences—for history and observation assure us that learning and trade mutually promote each other.

Source: A General Account of the Rise and State of the College, Lately Established in the Province of New-Jersey . . . [republished with some alterations and additions . . . by . . . Gilbert Tennent and Samuel Davies] (Edinburgh, 1754).

Colonial Recipe for Apple Tansey (1754)

After a meal, possibly of peanut soup and Carolina fish muddle, a favorite colonial dessert was a simple apple tansey, cooked like a custard in a pot or dish over a hearth.

Apple Tansey

To make an Apple Tansey,

Take three pippins, slice them round in thin slices, and fry them with butter.

Then beat four eggs, with six spoonfuls of cream, a little rosewater, nutmeg, and sugar

Stir them together, and pour it over the apples.

Let it fry a little, and turn it with a pye-plate.

Garnish with lemon and sugar strew'd over it.

Source: Eliza Smith, *The Compleat Housewife, or, Accomplished Gentlewoman's Companion* (London: Printed for J. Pemberton, 1727; 1754).

Evangeline, A Tale of Acadie (in 1755; pub. 1847)

➤ ～ ➤

Henry Wadsworth Longfellow's narrative poem "Evangeline" tells the sad story of the French Acadians, banished from their lush, forested homeland (in the area now known as Nova Scotia, New Brunswick, and eastern Maine) by the British in 1755. In this poem, Evangeline and her betrothed, Gabriel, are separated as their settlement is dispersed. Evangeline spends a lifetime searching for him, narrowly missing him several times. As a ministering Sister of Mercy, she finally finds him in a Philadelphia almshouse, just moments before his death.

THIS is the forest primeval. The murmuring pines and the
    hemlocks,
Bearded with moss, and in garments green, indistinct in
    the twilight,
Stand like Druids of eld, with voices sad and prophetic,
Stand like harpers hoar, with beards that rest on their
    bosoms.
Loud from its rocky caverns, the deep-voiced neighboring
    ocean
Speaks, and in accents disconsolate answers the wail of the
    forest.

This is the forest primeval; but where are the hearts that
    beneath it
Leaped like the roe, when he hears in the woodland the
    voice of the huntsman?
Where is the thatch-roofed village, the home of Acadian
    farmers,—
Men whose lives glided on like rivers that water the
    woodlands,
Darkened by shadows of earth, but reflecting an image of
    heaven?
Waste are those pleasant farms, and the farmers forever
    departed!
Scattered like dust and leaves, when the mighty blasts of
    October
Seize them, and whirl them aloft, and sprinkle them far
    o'er the ocean.
Naught but tradition remains of the beautiful village of
    Grand-Pré.

Ye who believe in affection that hopes, and endures, and is
    patient,
Ye who believe in the beauty and strength of woman's
    devotion,
List to the mournful tradition still sung by the pines of the
    forest;
List to a Tale of Love in Acadie, home of the happy.

PART THE FIRST.

. . . in silence the crowd awaited the will of the soldiers.
Then uprose their commander, and spake from the steps
    of the altar,
Holding aloft in his hands, with its seals, the royal
    commission.
"You are convened this day," he said, "by his Majesty's
    orders.
Clement and kind has he been; but how you have an-
    swered his kindness,
Let your own hearts reply! To my natural make and my
    temper
Painful the task is I do, which to you I know must be
    grievous.
Yet must I bow and obey, and deliver the will of our
    monarch;
Namely, that all your lands, and dwellings, and cattle of
    all kinds
Forfeited be to the crown; and that you yourselves from
    this province
Be transported to other lands. God grant you may dwell
    there
Ever as faithful subjects, a happy and peaceable people!
Prisoners now I declare you; for such is his Majesty's
    pleasure!" . . .

PART THE SECOND.

MANY a weary year had passed since the burning of
    Grand-Pré,
When on the falling tide the freighted vessels departed,
Bearing a nation, with all its household gods, into exile,
Exile without an end, and without an example in story.
Far asunder, on separate coasts, the Acadians landed;
Scattered were they, like flakes of snow, when the wind
    from the northeast

Strikes aslant through the fogs that darken the Banks of
Newfoundland.
Friendless, homeless, hopeless, they wandered from city to
city,
From the cold lakes of the North to sultry Southern sa-
vannas,—

. . . But Evangeline's heart was sustained by a vision, that
faintly
Floated before her eyes, and beckoned her on through the
moonlight.
It was the thought of her brain that assumed the shape of
a phantom.
Through those shadowy aisles had Gabriel wandered before her,
And every stroke of the oar now brought him nearer and
nearer . . .
. . . There from the troubled sea had Evangeline landed,
an exile,
Finding among the children of Penn a home and a
country. . . .

. . . Something at least there was in the friendly streets of
the city,
Something that spake to her heart, and made her no
longer a stranger;
And her ear was pleased with the Thee and Thou of the
Quakers,
For it recalled the past, the old Acadian country,
Where all men were equal, and all were brothers and
sisters.
So, when the fruitless search, the disappointed endeavor,
Ended, to recommence no more upon earth,
uncomplaining,
Thither, as leaves to the light, were turned her thoughts
and her footsteps. . . .

. . . Thus, on a Sabbath morn, through the streets, deserted and silent,
Wending her quiet way, she entered the door of the
almshouse.
Sweet on the summer air was the odor of flowers in the
garden;
And she paused on her way to gather the fairest among
them,
That the dying once more might rejoice in their fragrance
and beauty.
Then, as she mounted the stairs to the corridors, cooled by
the east wind,
Distant and soft on her ear fell the chimes from the belfry
of Christ Church,
While, intermingled with these, across the meadows were
wafted
Sounds of psalms, that were sung by the Swedes in their
church at Wicaco.

Soft as descending wings fell the calm of the hour on her
spirit;
Something within her said, "At length thy trials are
ended";
And, with light in her looks, she entered the chambers of
sickness.

Noiselessly moved about the assiduous, careful attendants,
Moistening the feverish lip, and the aching brow, and in
silence
Closing the sightless eyes of the dead, and concealing
their faces,
Where on their pallets they lay, like drifts of snow by the
roadside.
Many a languid head, upraised as Evangeline entered,
Turned on its pillow of pain to gaze while she passed, for
her presence
Fell on their hearts like a ray of the sun on the walls of a
prison.
And, as she looked around, she saw how Death, the
consoler,
Laying his hand upon many a heart, had healed it forever.
Many familiar forms had disappeared in the night-time;
Vacant their places were, or filled already by strangers.

Suddenly, as if arrested by fear or a feeling of wonder,
Still she stood, with her colorless lips apart, while a
shudder
Ran through her frame, and, forgotten, the flowerets
dropped from her fingers,
And from her eyes and cheeks the light and bloom of the
morning.
Then there escaped from her lips a cry of such terrible
anguish,
That the dying heard it, and started up from their
pillows.
On the pallet before her was stretched the form of an old
man.
Long, and thin, and gray were the locks that shaded his
temples;
But, as he lay in the morning light, his face for a moment
Seemed to assume once more the forms of its earlier man-
hood;
So are wont to be changed the faces of those who are
dying.
Hot and red on his lips still burned the flush of the fever,
As if life, like the Hebrew, with blood had besprinkled its
portals,
That the Angel of Death might see the sign, and pass
over.
Motionless, senseless, dying, he lay, and his spirit
exhausted
Seemed to be sinking down through infinite depths in the
darkness,
Darkness of slumber and death, forever sinking and
sinking.

Then through those realms of shade, in multiplied
    reverberations,
Heard he that cry of pain, and through the hush that
    succeeded
Whispered a gentle voice, in accents tender and saint-like,
"Gabriel! O my beloved!" and died away into silence.
Then he beheld, in a dream, once more the home of his
    childhood;
Green Acadian meadows, with sylvan rivers among them,
Village, and mountain, and woodlands; and, walking un-
    der their shadow,
As in the days of her youth, Evangeline rose in his vision.
Tears came into his eyes; and as slowly he lifted his
    eyelids,
Vanished the vision away, but Evangeline knelt by his
    bedside.
Vainly he strove to whisper her name, for the accents
    unuttered
Died on his lips, and their motion revealed what his
    tongue would have spoken.
Vainly he strove to rise; and Evangeline, kneeling beside
    him,
Kissed his dying lips, and laid his head on her bosom.
Sweet was the light of his eyes; but it suddenly sank into
    darkness,
As when a lamp is blown out by a gust of wind at a
    casement.

All was ended now, the hope, and the fear, and the sorrow,
All the aching of heart, the restless, unsatisfied longing,
All the dull, deep pain, and constant anguish of patience!
And, as she pressed once more the lifeless head to her
    bosom,
Meekly she bowed her own, and murmured, "Father, I
    thank thee!"

STILL stands the forest primeval; but far away from its
    shadow,
Side by side, in their nameless graves, the lovers are
    sleeping.
Under the humble walls of the little Catholic churchyard,
In the heart of the city, they lie, unknown and unnoticed.
Daily the tides of life go ebbing and flowing beside them,
Thousands of throbbing hearts, where theirs are at rest
    and forever,
Thousands of aching brains, where theirs no longer are
    busy,
Thousands of toiling hands, where theirs have ceased from
    their labors,
Thousands of weary feet, where theirs have completed
    their journey!
Still stands the forest primeval; but under the shade of its
    branches
Dwells another race, with other customs and language.
Only along the shore of the mournful and misty Atlantic
Linger a few Acadian peasants, whose fathers from exile
Wandered back to their native land to die in its bosom.
In the fisherman's cot the wheel and the loom are still
    busy;
Maidens still wear their Norman caps and their kirtles of
    homespun,
And by the evening fire repeat Evangeline's story.
While from its rocky caverns the deep-voiced, neighbor-
    ing ocean
Speaks, and in accents disconsolate answers the wail of the
    forest.

Source: Henry Wadsworth Longfellow, *Evangeline, A Tale of Acadie*
(New York: Van Cleve-Andrews, 1895).

Rights of the British Colonies Asserted and Proved (1764)

James Otis, a political leader from Boston, defends colonial rights, asserting that Parliament cannot levy direct taxes on the colonists. In this pamphlet, he maintains that the colonists can only be taxed by a legislature that represents them, and he bases this proposition on provincial charters, common law, and the British constitution itself. Otis also asserts that black men are entitled to the same natural rights as white men.

It is . . . true in fact and experience, as the great, the incomparable Harrington has most abundantly demonstrated in his Oceana and other divine writings, that empire follows the balance of property. 'Tis also certain that property in fact generally confers power, though the possessor of it may not have much more wit than a mole or a musquash: and this is too often the cause that riches are sought after without the least concern about the right application of them. But is the fault in the riches, or the general law of nature, or the unworthy possessor? It will never follow from all this that government is rightfully founded on property alone. What shall we say then? Is not government founded on grace? No. Nor on force? No. Nor on compact? Nor property? Not altogether on either. Has it any solid foundation, any chief cornerstone but what accident, chance, or confusion may lay one moment and destroy the next? I think it has an everlasting foundation in the unchangeable will of GOD, the author of nature, whose laws never vary. The same omniscient, omnipotent, infinitely good and gracious Creator of the universe who has been pleased to make it necessary that what we call matter should gravitate for the celestial bodies to roll round their axes, dance their orbits, and perform their various revolutions in that beautiful order and concern which we all admire has made it equally necessary that from Adam and Eve to these degenerate days the different sexes should sweetly attract each other, form societies of single families, of which larger bodies and communities are as naturally, mechanically, and necessarily combined as the dew of heaven and the soft distilling rain is collected by the all-enlivening heat of the sun. Government is therefore most evidently founded on the necessities of our nature. It is by no means an arbitrary thing depending merely on compact or human will for its existence. . . .

The end of government being the good of mankind points out its great duties: it is above all things to provide for the security, the quiet, and happy enjoyment of life, liberty, and property. There is no one act which a government can have a right to make that does not tend to the advancement of the security, tranquillity, and prosperity of the people. If life, liberty, and property could be enjoyned in as great perfection in solitude as in society there would be no need of government. But the experience of ages has proved that such is the nature of man, a weak, imperfect being, that the valuable ends of life cannot be obtained without the union and assistance of many. Hence 'tis clear that men cannot live apart or independent of each other. In solitude men would perish, and yet they cannot live together without contests. These contests require some arbitrator to determine them. The necessity of a common, indifferent, and impartial judge makes all men seek one, though few find him in the sovereign power of their respective states or anywhere else in subordinaton to it. . . .

I know of no human law founded on the law of nature to restrain him from separating himself from all the species if he can find it in his heart to leave them, unless it should be said it is against the great law of self-preservation: but of this every man will think himself his own judge.

The few hermits and misanthropes that have ever existed show that those states are unnatural. If we were to take out from them those who have made great worldly gain of their godly hermitage and those who have been under the madness of enthusiasm or disappointed hopes in their ambitious projects for the detriment of mankind, perhaps there might not be left ten from Adam to this day.

The form of government is by nature and by right so far left to the individuals of each society that they may alter it from a simple democracy or government of all over all to any other form they please. Such alteration may and ought to be made by express compact. But how seldom this right has been asserted, history will abundantly show. For once that it has been fairly settled by compact, fraud, force, or accident have determined it an hundred times. As the people have gained upon tyrants, these have been obliged to relax only till a fairer opportunity has put it in their power to encroach again.

But if every prince since Nimrod had been a tyrant, it would not prove a right to tyrannize. There can be no prescription old enough to supersede the law of nature and the grant of GOD Almighty, who has given to all men a natural right to be free, and they have it ordinarily in their power to make them-selves so if they please . . .

In order to form an idea of the natural rights of the colonists, I presume it will be granted that they are men, the common children of the same Creator with their brethren of Great Britain. Nature has placed all such in a state of equality and perfect freedom to act within the bounds of the laws of nature and reason without consulting the will or regarding the humor, the passions, or whims of any other man, unless they are formed into a society or body politic. . . .

The colonists are by the law of nature freeborn, as indeed all men are, white or black. No better reasons can be given for enslaving those of any color than such as Baron Montesquieu has humorously given as the foundation of that cruel slavery exercised over the poor Ethiopians, which threatens one day to reduce both Europe and America to the ignorance and barbarity of the darkest ages. Does it follow that tis right to enslave a man because he is black? Will short curled hair like wool instead of Christian hair, as tis called by those whose hearts are as hard as the nether millstone, help the argument? Can any logical inference in favor of slavery be drawn from a flat nose, a long or a short face? Nothing better can be said in favor of a trade that is the most shocking violation of the law of nature, has a direct tendency to diminish the idea of the inestimable value of liberty, and makes every dealer in it a tyrant, from the director of an African company to the petty chapman in needles and pins on the unhappy coast. It is a clear truth that those who every day barter away other men's liberty will soon care little for their own.

The colonists, being men, have a right to be considered as equally entitled to all the rights of nature with the Europeans, and they are not to be restrained in the exercise of any of these rights but for the evident good of the whole community.

By being or becoming members of society they have not renounced their natural liberty in any greater degree than other good citizens, and if 'tis taken from them without their consent they are so far enslaved.

I also lay it down as one of the first principles from whence I intend to deduce the civil rights of the British colonies, that all of them are subject to and dependent on Great Britain, and that therefore as over subordinate governments the Parliament of Great Britain has an undoubted power and lawful authority to make acts for the general good that, by naming them, shall and ought to be equally binding as upon the subjects of Great Britain within the realm. This principle, I presume, will be readily granted on the other side the Atlantic. It has been practised upon for twenty years to my knowledge, in the province of the Massachusetts Bay; and I have ever received it that it has been so from the beginning in this and the sister provinces through the continent. . . .

That the colonists, black and white, born here are freeborn British subjects, and entitled to all the essential civil rights of such is a truth not only manifest from the provincial charters, from the principles of the common law, and acts of Parliament, but from the British constitution, which was re-established at the Revolution with a professed design to secure the liberties of all the subjects to all generations. . . .

The liberties of the subject are spoken of as their best birthrights. No one ever dreamed, surely, that these liberties were confined to the realm. At that rate no British subjects in the dominions could, without a manifest contradiction, be declared entitled to all the privileges of subjects born with[in] the realm to all intents and purposes which are rightly given foreigners by Parliament after residing seven years. These expressions of Parliament as well as of the charters must be vain and empty sounds unless we are allowed the essential rights of our fellow subjects in Great Britain.

Now can there be any liberty where property is taken away without consent? Can it with any color of truth, justice, or equity be affirmed that the northern colonies are represented in Parliament? Has this whole continent of near three thousand miles in length, and in which and his other American dominions His Majesty has or very soon will have some millions of as good, loyal, and useful subjects, white and black, as any in the three kingdoms, the election of one member of the House of Commons?

Is there the least difference as to the consent of the colonists whether taxes and impositions are laid on their trade and other property by the crown alone or by the Parliament? As it is agreed on all hands the crown alone cannot impose them, we should be justifiable in refusing to pay them, but must and ought to yield obedience to an act of Parliament, though erroneous, till repealed. I can see no reason to doubt but the imposition of taxes, whether on trade, or on land, or houses, or ships, on real or personal, fixed or floating property, in the colonies is absolutely irreconcilable with the rights of the colonists as British subjects and as men. I say men, for in a state of nature no man can take my property from me without my consent: if he does, he deprives me of my liberty and makes me a slave. If such a proceeding is a breach of the law of nature, no law of society can make it just. The very act of taxing exercised over those who are not represented appears to me to be depriving them of one of their most essential rights as freemen, and if continued seems to be in effect an entire disfranchisement of every civil right. . . .

We all think ourselves happy under Great Britain. We

love, esteem, and reverence our mother country, and adore our King. And could the choice of independency be offered the colonies or subjection to Great Britain upon any terms above absolute slavery, I am convinced they would accept the latter. The ministry in all future generations may rely on it that British America will never prove undutiful till driven to it as the last fatal resort against ministerial oppression, which will make the wisest mad, and the weakest strong. . . .

The sum of my argument is: that civil government is of God that the administrators of it were originally the whole people; that they might have devolved it on whom they pleased; that this devolution is fiduciary, for the good of the whole; that by the British constitution this devolution is on the King, Lords and Commons, the supreme, sacred and uncontrollable legislative power not only in the realm but through the dominions; that by the abdication, the original compact was broken to pieces; that by the Revolution it was renewed and more firmly established, and the rights and liberties of the subject in all parts of the dominions more fully explained and confirmed; that in consequence of this establishment and the acts of succession and union, His Majesty GEORGE III is rightful King and sovereign, and, with his Parliament, the supreme legislative of Great Britain, France, and Ireland, and the dominions thereto belonging; that this constitution is the most free one and by far the best now existing on earth; that by this constitution every man in the dominions is a free man; that no parts of His Majesty's dominions can be taxed without their consent; that every part has a right to be represented in the supreme or some subordinate legislature; that the refusal of this would seem to be a contradiction in practice to the theory of the constitution; that the colonies are subordinate dominions and are now in such a state as to make it best for the good of the whole that they should not only be continued in the enjoyment of subordinate legislation but be also represented in some proportion to their number and estates in the grand legislature of the nation; that this would firmly unite all parts of the British empire in the greater peace and prosperity, and render it invulnerable and perpetual.

Source: James Otis, *Rights of the British Colonies, Asserted and Proved* (Boston: Edes and Gill, 1764).

Townshend Revenue Act (1767)

Through the Townshend Act, British Parliament placed duties on various imports to the American colonies. Paper in every imaginable form was notably targeted, but other items such as tea, earthenware, and fabrics also were included in the duties.

Replacing the Stamp Act, the Townshend Act was expected to yield some 40,000 pounds annually and defray the costs of paying the salaries of the colonial royal governors and judges who managed civil government and the administration of justice. The colonists strongly objected to the act, as evidenced by the subsequent Boston Tea Party and the Boston Massacre.

British Parliament
June 29, 1767

An act for granting certain duties in the British colonies and plantations in America; for allowing a drawback of the duties of customs upon the exportation, from this kingdom, of coffee and cocoa nuts of the produce of the said colonies or plantations; for discontinuing the drawbacks payable on china earthen ware exported to America; and for more effectually preventing the clandestine running of goods in the colonies and plantations.

WHEREAS it is expedient that a revenue should be raised in your Majesty's dominions in America, for making a more certain and adequate provision for defraying the charge of the administration of justice, and the support of civil government, in such provinces where it shall be found necessary; and towards further defraying the expenses of defending, protecting, and securing, the said dominions; we, your Majesty's most dutiful and loyal subjects, the commons of Great Britain, in parliament assembled, have therefore resolved to give and grant unto your Majesty the several rates and duties herein after mentioned; and do most humbly beseech your Majesty that it may be enacted, and be it enacted by the King's most excellent majesty, by and with the advice of the lords spiritual and temporal, and commons, in this present parliament assembled, and by the authority of the same, That from and after the twentieth day of November, one thousand seven hundred and sixty seven, there shall be raised, levied, collected, and paid, unto his Majesty, his heirs, and successors, for and upon the respective goods herein after mentioned, which shall be imported from Great Britain into any colony or plantation in America which now is, or hereafter may be, under the dominion of his Majesty, his heirs, or successors, the several rates and duties following; that is to say,

For every hundred weight avoirdupois [a system of weights based on a 16-ounce pound] of crown, plate, flint, and white glass, four shillings and eight pence.

For every hundred weight avoirdupois of green glass, one shilling and two pence.

For every hundred weight avoirdupois of red lead, two shillings.

For every hundred weight avoirdupois of white lead, two shillings.

For every hundred weight avoirdupois of painters colours, two shillings.

For every pound weight avoirdupois of tea, three pence.

For every ream of paper, usually called or known by the name of Atlas Fine, twelve shillings.

For every ream of paper called Atlas Ordinary, six shillings.

For every ream of paper called Bastard, or Double Copy, one shilling and six pence.

For every single ream of blue paper for sugar bakers, ten pence halfpenny.

For every ream of paper called Blue Royal, one shilling and six pence.

For every bundle of brown paper containing forty quires, not made in Great Britain, six pence.

For every ream of paper called Brown Cap, not made in Great Britain, nine pence.

For every ream of paper called Brown Large Cap, made in Great Britain, four pence halfpenny.

For every ream of paper called Small Ordinary Brown, made in Great Britain, three pence.

For every bundle, containing forty quires, of paper called Whited Brown, made in Great Britain, four pence halfpenny.

For every ream of cartridge paper, one shilling and one penny halfpenny.

For every ream of paper called Chancery Double, one shilling and six pence.

For every ream of paper called Genoa Crown Fine, one shilling and one penny halfpenny.

For every ream of paper called Genoa Crown Second, nine pence.

For every ream of paper called German Crown, nine pence.

For every ream of paper called Fine Printing Crown, nine pence.

For every ream of paper called Second Ordinary Printing Crown, six pence three farthings.

For every ream of paper called Crown Fine, made in Great Britain, nine pence.

For every ream of paper called Crown Second, made in Great Britain, six pence three farthings.

For every ream of paper called Demy Fine, not made in Great Britain, three shillings.

For every ream of paper called Demy Second, not made in Great Britain, one shilling and four pence halfpenny.

For every ream of paper called Demy Fine, made in Great Britain, one shilling and one penny halfpenny.

For every ream of paper called Demy Second, made in Great Britain, nine pence.

For every ream of paper called Demy Printing, one shilling and three pence.

For every ream of paper called Genoa Demy Fine, one shilling and six pence.

For every ream of paper called Genoa Demy Second, one shilling and one penny halfpenny.

For every ream of paper called German Demy, one shilling and one penny halfpenny.

For every ream of paper called Elephant Fine, six shillings.

For every ream of paper called Elephant Ordinary, two shillings and five pence farthing.

For every ream of paper called Genoa Fools Cap Fine, one shilling and one penny halfpenny.

For every ream of paper called Genoa Fools Cap Second, nine pence.

For every ream of paper called German Fools Cap, nine pence.

For every ream of paper called Fine Printing Fools Cap, nine pence.

For every ream of paper called Second Ordinary Printing Fools Cap, six pence three farthings.

For every ream of any other paper called Fools Cap Fine, not made in Great Britain, one shilling and ten pence halfpenny.

For every ream of any other paper called Fools Cap Fine Second, not made in Great Britain, one shilling and six pence.

For every ream of paper Fools Cap Fine, made in Great Britain, nine pence.

For every ream of paper called Fools Cap Second, made in Great Britain, six pence three farthings.

For every ream of paper called Imperial Fine, twelve shillings.

For every ream of paper called Second Writing Imperial, eight shillings and three pence.

For every ream of paper called German Lombard, nine pence.

For every ream of paper called Medium Fine, four shillings and six pence.

For every ream of paper called Genoa Medium, one shilling and ten pence halfpenny.

For every ream of paper called Second Writing Medium, three shillings.

For every ream of painted paper, not made in Great Britain, six shillings.

For every ream of paper called Fine Large Post, one shilling and ten pence halfpenny.

For every ream of paper called Small Post, one shilling and one penny halfpenny.

For every ream of paper called Fine Genoa Post, six pence three farthings.

For every ream of paper called Second Genoa Post, six pence three farthings.

For every ream of other paper called Superfine Post, not made in Great Britain, one shilling and six pence.

For every ream of other paper called Second Fine Post, not made in Great Britain, one shilling and one penny halfpenny.

For every ream of paper called Ordinary Post, not made in Great Britain, six pence three farthings.

For every ream of paper called Fine Post, made in Great Britain, nine pence.

For every ream of paper called Second Post, made in Great Britain, four pence halfpenny.

For every ream of paper called Super Royal Fine, nine shillings.

For every ream of paper called Royal Fine, six shillings.

For every ream of paper called Fine Holland Royal, two shillings and five pence farthing.

For every ream of paper called Fine Holland Second, one shilling and six pence.

For every ream of paper called Second Fine Holland Royal, one shilling and six pence.

For every ream of paper called Ordinary Royal, nine pence.

For every ream of paper called Genoa Royal, two shillings and five pence farthing.

For every ream of paper called Second Writing Royal, four shillings and one penny halfpenny.

For every ream of paper called Second Writing Super Royal, six shillings.

For every hundred weight avoirdupois of paste-boards, mill-boards, and scale-boards, not made in Great Britain, three shillings and nine pence.

For every hundred weight avoirdupois of paste-boards, mill-boards, and scale-boards, made in Great Britain, two shillings and three pence.

And for and upon all paper which shall be printed, painted, or stained, in Great Britain, to serve for hangings or other uses, three farthings for every yard square, over and above the duties payable for such paper by this act, if the same had not been printed, painted, or stained; and after those rates respectively for any greater or less quantity.

II. And it is hereby further enacted by the authority aforesaid, That all other paper (not being particularly rated and charged in this act) shall pay the several and respective duties that are charged by this act, upon such paper as is nearest above in size and goodness to such unrated paper.

III. And be it declared and enacted by the authority aforesaid, That a ream of paper, chargeable by this act, shall be understood to consist of twenty quires, and each quire of twenty-four sheets.

IV. And it is hereby further enacted by the authority aforesaid, That the said rates and duties, charged by this act upon goods imported into any British American colony or plantation, shall be deemed, and are hereby declared to be, sterling money of Great Britain; and shall be collected, recovered, and paid to the amount of the value which such nominal sums bear in Great Britain; and that such monies may be received and taken, according to the proportion and value of five shillings and six pence the ounce in silver; and shall be raised, levied, collected, paid, and recovered, in the same manner and form, and by such rules, ways, and means, and under such penalties and forfeitures, as any other duties, now payable to his Majesty upon goods imported into the said colonies or plantations, may be raised, levied, collected, paid, and recovered, by any act or acts of parliament now in force, as fully and effectually, to all intents and purposes, as if the several clauses, powers, directions, penalties, and forfeitures, relating thereto, were particularly repeated, and again enacted, in the body of this present act: and that all the monies that shall arise by the said duties (except the necessary charges of raising, collecting, levying, recovering, answering, paying, and accounting for the same) shall be applied, in the first place, in such manner as is herein after mentioned, in making a more certain and adequate provision for the charge of the administration of justice, and the support of civil government, in such of the said colonies and plantations where it shall be found necessary; and that the residue of such duties shall be paid into the receipt of his Majesty's exchequer, and shall be entered separate and apart from all other monies paid or payable to his Majesty, his heirs, or successors; and shall be there reserved, to be from time to time disposed of by parliament towards defraying the necessary expences of defending, protecting, and securing, the British colonies and plantations in America.

V. And be it further enacted by the authority aforesaid, That his Majesty and his successors shall be, and are hereby, impowered, from time to time, by any warrant or warrants under his or their royal sign manual or sign manuals, countersigned by the high treasurer, or any three or more of the commissioners of the treasury for the time being, to cause such monies to be applied, out of the produce of the duties granted by this act, as his Majesty, or his successors, shall think proper or necessary, for defraying the charges of the administration of justice, and the support of the civil government, within all or any of the said colonies or plantations.

VI. And whereas the allowing a drawback of all the duties of customs upon the exportation, from this kingdom, of coffee and cocoa nuts, the growth of the British dominions in America, may be a means of encouraging the growth of coffee and cocoa in the said dominions; be it therefore enacted by the authority aforesaid, That from and after the said twentieth day of November, one thousand seven hundred and sixty seven, upon the exportation of any coffee or cocoa nuts, of the growth or produce of any British colony or plantation in America, from this kingdom as merchandize, the whole duties of customs, payable upon the importation of such coffee or cocoa nuts, shall be drawn back and repaid; in such manner, and under such rules, regulations, penalties, and forfeitures, as any drawback or allowance, payable out of the duties of customs upon the exportation of such coffee or cocoa nuts, was, could, or might be paid, before the passing of this act; any law, custom, or usage, to the contrary notwithstanding.

VII. And it is hereby further enacted by the authority aforesaid, That no drawback shall be allowed for any china earthen ware sold, after the passing of this act, at the sale of the united company of merchants of England trading to the East Indies, which shall be entered for exportation from Great Britain to any part of America; any law, custom, or usage, to the contrary notwithstanding.

VIII. And it is hereby further enacted by the authority aforesaid, That if any china earthen ware sold, after the passing of this act, at the sale of the said united company, shall be entered for exportation to any part of America as china earthen ware that had been sold at the sale of the said company before that time; or, if any china earthen ware shall be entered for exportation to any parts beyond the seas, other than to some part of America, in order to obtain any drawback thereon, and the said china earthen ware shall nevertheless be carried to any part of America, and landed there contrary to the true intent and meaning of this act; that then, in each and every such case, the drawback shall be forfeited; and the merchant or other person making such entry, and the master or person taking the charge of the ship or vessel on board which the said goods shall be loaden for exportation, shall forfeit double the amount of the drawback paid, or to be paid, for the same, and also treble the value of the said goods;

one moiety to and for the use of his Majesty, his heirs, and successors; and the other moiety to such officer of the customs as shall sue for the same; to be prosecuted, sued for, and recovered, in such manner and form, and by the same rules and regulations, as other penalties inflicted for offences against any laws relating to the customs may be prosecuted, sued for, and recovered, by any act or acts of parliament now in force.

IX. And for the more effectual preventing the clandestine running of goods in the British dominions in America, be it further enacted by the authority aforesaid, That from and after the said twentieth day of November, one thousand seven hundred and sixty seven, the master or other person having or taking the charge or command of every ship or vessel arriving in any British colony or plantation in America shall, before he proceeds with his vessel to the place of unlading, come directly to the custom house for the port or district where he arrives, and make a just and true entry, upon oath, before the collector and comptroller, or other principal officer of the customs there, of the burthen, contents, and lading of such ship or vessel, with the particular marks, numbers, qualities, and contents, of every parcel of goods therein laden, to the best of his knowledge; also where and in what port she took in her lading; of what country built; how manned; who was master during the voyage, and who are owners thereof; and whether any, and what goods, during the course of such voyage, had or had not been discharged out of such ship or vessel, and where: and the master or other person having or taking the charge or command of every ship or vessel, going out from any British colony or plantation in America, before he shall take in, or suffer to be taken into or laden on board any such ship or vessel, any goods, wares, or merchandize, to be exported, shall, in like manner, enter and report outwards such ship or vessel, with her name and burthen, of what country built, and how manned, with the names of the master and owners thereof, and to what port or place he intends to pass or sail: and before he shall depart with such ship or vessel out of any such colony or plantation, he shall also bring and deliver unto the collector and comptroller, or other principal officer of the customs at the port or place where he shall lade, a content in writing, under his hand, of the name of every merchant, or other person who shall have laden, or put on board any such ship or vessel, any goods or merchandize, together with the marks and numbers of such goods or merchandize: and such master or person having or taking the charge or command of every such ship or vessel, either coming into, or going out of, any British colony or plantation as aforesaid, whether such ship or vessel shall be laden or in ballast, or otherwise, shall likewise publickly, in the open custom house, to the best of his knowledge, answer upon oath to such questions as shall be demanded of him by the collector and comptroller, or other principal officer of the customs for such port or place, concerning such ship or vessel, and the destination of her voyage,

or concerning any goods or merchandize that shall or may be laden on board her, upon forfeiture of one hundred pound sterling money of Great Britain, for each and every default or neglect; to be sued for, prosecuted, recovered, and divided, in the same manner and form, by the same rules and regulations in all respects, as other pecuniary penalties, for offences against the laws relating to the customs or trade of his Majesty's colonies in America, may, by any act or acts of parliament now in force, be prosecuted, sued for, recovered, and divided.

X. And whereas by an act of parliament made in the fourteenth year of the reign of King Charles the Second, intituled, An act for preventing frauds, and regulating abuses, in his Majesty's customs, and several other acts now in force, it is lawful for any officer of his Majesty's customs, authorized by writ of assistance under the seal of his majesty's court or exchequer, to take a constable, headborough, or other public officer inhabiting near unto the place, and in the day-time to enter and go into any house, shop, cellar, warehouse, or room or other place, and, in case of resistance, to break open doors, chests, trunks, and other package there, to seize, and from thence to bring, any kinds of goods or merchandize whatsoever prohibited or uncustomed, and to put and secure the same in his Majesty's store-house next to the place where such seizure shall be made: and whereas by an act made in the seventh and eighth years of the reign of King William the Third, intituled, An act for preventing frauds, and regulating abuses, in the plantation trade, it is, amongst other things, enacted, that the officers for collecting and managing his Majesty's revenue, and inspecting the plantation trade, in America, shall have the same powers and authorities to enter houses or warehouses, to search for and seize goods prohibited to be imported or exported into or out of any of the said plantations, or for which any duties are payable, or ought to have been paid; and that the like assistance shall be given to the said officers in the execution of their office, as, by the said recited act of the fourteenth year of King Charles the Second, is provided for the officers in England: but, no authority being expressly given by the said act, made in the seventh and eighth years of the reign of King William the Third, to any particular court to grant such writs of assistance for the officers of the customs in the said plantations, it is doubted whether such officers can legally enter houses and other places on land, to search for and seize goods, in the manner directed by the said recited acts: To obviate which doubts for the future, and in order to carry the intention of the said recited acts into effectual execution, be it enacted, and it is hereby enacted by the authority aforesaid, That from and after the said twentieth day of November, one thousand seven hundred and sixty seven, such writs of assistance, to authorize and impower the officer of his Majesty's customs to enter and go into any house, warehouse, shop, cellar, or other place, in the British colonies or plantations of America, to search for and seize prohibited or uncustomed goods, in the manner directed by the said recited acts, shall and may be granted by the said superior or supreme courts of justice having jurisdiction within such colony or plantation respectively.

XI. And be it further enacted by the authority aforesaid, That if any action or suit shall be commenced either in Great Britain or America, against any person or persons for any thing done in pursuance of this act, the defendant or defendants in such action or suit may plead the general issue, and give this act, and the special matter, in evidence at any trial to be had thereupon; and that the same was done in pursuance and by the authority of this act: and if it shall appear so to have been done, the jury shall find for the defendant or defendants: and if the plaintiff shall be nonsuited, or discontinue his action after the defendant or defendants shall have appeared, or if judgement shall be given upon any verdict or demurrer against the plaintiff; the defendant or defendants shall recover treble costs, and have the like remedy for the same as defendants have in other cases by law.

CAP. XLVII.

An act for discontinuing the duties on logwood exported; for taking off the duties on Succus Liquoritiae imported, and for granting other duties in lieu thereof; for explaining such parts of two acts made in the tenth and twelfth years of the reign of Queen Anne, as relate to certain duties on silks, printed, painted, or stained, in Great Britain; for granting a duty upon the exportation of such rice as shall have been imported duty-free, in pursuance of an act made in this session of parliament: and for more effectually preventing the wear of foreign lace and needle work which are prohibited to be imported into this kingdom,

WHEREAS the discontinuing the duty payable upon the exportation of logwood from this kingdom, may be a means of encouraging the importation thereof; May it please your Majesty that it may be enacted, and be it enacted by the King's most excellent majesty, by and with the advice and consent of the lords spiritual and temporal, and commons, in this present parliament assembled, and by the authority of the same, That from and after the twentieth day of July, one thousand seven and sixty seven, the duty now payable upon logwood, exported from this kingdom to any parts beyond the seas, shall cease, determine, and be no longer paid or payable; any law, custom or usage, to the contrary notwithstanding.

II. Provided always, and it is hereby further enacted by the authority aforesaid, That due entries shall be made at the custom-house of all such logwood, upon which the duty is taken off by this act; and such logwood shall be shipped outwards in the presence of the proper officers of the customs appointed for that purpose; and the exportation thereof shall be in British built ships or vessels, navigated according to law; and the said logwood shall be liable to the same duty as

if this act had never been made; any thing herein before contained to the contrary notwithstanding.

III. And whereas Succus Liquoritiae is rated in the book of rates made in the twelfth year of the reign of King Charles the Second, at one shilling per pound weight; according to which value, the duties now payable upon Succus Liquoritiae, imported into this kingdom, amount to seven pounds, two shillings, and six pence, for every hundred weight thereof: and whereas it has been found, by experience, that the said duties are too high; which has induced many persons to import clandestinely great quantities of such Succus Liquoritiae, to the prejudice of the revenue and the fair trader: For remedy whereof, be it enacted by the authority aforesaid, That from and after the twentieth day of July, one thousand seven hundred and sixty seven, the several duties payable upon the importation of Succus Liquoritiae shall cease, determine, and be no longer paid; and in lieu thereof, there shall be paid and payable to his Majesty, his heirs, and successors, for every hundred weight avoirdupois of Succus Liquoritiae, which from and after the said twentieth day of July, one thousand seven hundred and sixty seven, shall be imported into Great Britain, the sum of thirty shillings.

IV. And it is hereby further enacted by the authority aforesaid, That the said duty by this act granted shall be paid down in ready money, without any discount or allowance; and shall not be afterwards drawn back or repaid upon the exportation of the same goods; and shall be raised, levied, collected, and paid, in the same manner and form, and by such rules, ways, and means, and under such penalties and forfeitures, as the duties upon Succus Liquoritiae hereby determined, or any of them, might have been raised, levied, recovered, and paid, if the same, or any of them, had continued.

V. And it is hereby enacted by the authority aforesaid, That the duties to arise upon the importation of Succus Liquoritiae pursuant to this act (the necessary charges of management excepted) shall be appropriated and applied, as near as may be, to the same uses and purposes as the present duties upon drugs, rated by the book of rates made in the twelfth year of the reign of King Charles the Second, are applicable, or ought to be applied.

VI. And whereas by an act passed in the tenth year of the reign of her late majesty Queen Anne, intituled, An act for laying several duties upon all sope and paper made in Great Britain, or imported into the same; and upon chequered and striped linen imported; and upon certain silks, callicoes, linens, and stuffs, printed, painted, or stained; and upon several kinds of stampt vellum, parchment, and paper, and upon certain printed papers, pamphlets, and advertisements; for raising the sum of one million eight hundred thousand pounds, by way of a lottery, towards her Majesty's supply; and for licensing an additional number of hackney chairs; and for charging certain stocks of cards and dice; and for better securing her Majesty's duties to arise in the office of stamp duties by licences for marriages, and otherwise; and for relief of persons who have not claimed their lottery tickets in due time, or have lost exchequer bills or lottery tickets; and for borrowing money upon stock (part of the capital of the South Sea company) for the use of the public; it is, amongst other things, enacted, that there should be raised, levied, collected, and paid, to and for the use of her Majesty her heirs, and successors, for and upon all silks, calicoes, linens, and stuffs, of what kind soever, which, at any time or times, within or during the term of thirty two years, to be reckoned from the twentieth day of July, one thousand seven hundred and twelve, should be printed, stained, painted, or dyed, in Great Britain (such calicoes, linens, and fustians, as should be dyed throughout of one colour only; and stuffs made of woollen, or whereof the greatest part in value should be woollen; always excepted) the several and respective rates and duties herein after expressed (over and above the duties payable upon the importation of them, or any of them) that is to say,

For and upon all silks so printed, stained, or painted, in Great Britain (silk handkerchiefs excepted) the sum of six pence for every yard in length, reckoning half a yard for the breadth.

And for all silk handkerchiefs so printed, stained, or painted, in Great Britain, the sum of three pence for every yard square; and in those proportions for wider or narrower silks.

And whereas by an act passed in the third year of the reign of his late majesty King George the First, intituled, And act for redeeming the duties and revenues which were settled to pay off principal and interest on the orders made forth at four lottery acts passed in the ninth and tenth years of her late Majesty's reign; and for redeeming certain annuities payable on orders out of the hereditary excise, according to a former act in that behalf; and for establishing a general yearly fund, not only for the future payment of annuities at several rates, to be payable and transferrable at the bank of England, and redeemable by parliament, but also to raise monies for such proprietors of the said orders as shall choose to be paid their principal and arrears of interest in ready money; and for making good such other deficiencies and payments as in this act are mentioned; and for taking off the duties on linseed imported, and British linen exported; the said several rates and duties are made perpetual: And whereas by an act of parliament made in the twelfth year of the reign of her said late majesty Queen Anne, intituled, An act for laying additional duties on sope and paper; and upon certain linens, silks, callicoes, and stuffs; and upon starch, and exported coals; and upon stampt vellum, parchment, and paper, for raising one million four hundred thousand pounds, by way of a lottery, for her Majesty's supply; and for allowances on exporting made wares of leather, sheep skins, and lamb skins; and for distribution of four thousand pounds due to the officers and seamen for gun money; and to adjust the

property of tickets in former lotteries; and touching certain shares of stock in the capital of the South Sea company; and for appropriating the monies granted to her Majesty; it is, amongst other things, enacted, That there should be raised, levied, collected, and paid, to and for the use of her Majesty, her heirs, and successors, for and upon all silks, callicoes, linens, and stuffs, of what kind soever, which, at any time or times within or during the term of thirty two years, to be reckoned from the second day of August, one thousand seven hundred and fourteen, should be printed, stained, painted, or dyed, in Great Britain (such callicoes, linens, and fustians, as shall be dyed throughout of one colour only; and stuffs made of woollen, or whereof the greatest parts in value shall be woollen; always excepted) the several and respective rates and duties therein and herein after expressed (over and above all other duties payable for the same, or any of them) that is to say,

For and upon all silks so printed, stained, or painted, within or during the term aforesaid, in Great Britain (silk handkerchiefs excepted) the sum of six pence for every yard in length, reckoning half a yard for the breadth.

And for all silk handkerchiefs so printed, stained, or painted, within or during the term aforesaid, in Great Britain, the sum of one penny for every yard square; and in those proportions for wider or narrower silks.

And whereas by an act of parliament made in the sixth year of the reign of his said late majesty King George the First, intituled, An act for enabling the South Sea company to encrease their present capital and fund, by redeeming such publick debts and incumbrances as are therein mentioned; and for raising money, to be applied for lessening several of the publick debts and incumbrances; and for calling in the present exchequer bills remaining uncancelled; and for making forth new bills in lieu thereof, to be circulated and exchanged upon demand at or near the exchequer; the said several rates and duties last mentioned are made perpetual: And whereas some doubts have arisen, whether ribbands and silks so printed, stained, or painted, being less than half a yard in breadth, are within the meaning of the said recited acts, and liable to the said several rates and duties by the said acts imposed: Now, for obviating all such doubts, be it declared by the authority aforesaid, That all ribbands and silks printed, stained, or painted, in Great Britain, though less than half a yard in breadth, are, within the true intent and meaning of the said acts, liable to the several rates and duties by the said two first mentioned acts imposed, according to the proportions in which such ribbands or silks are or shall be made.

VII. And whereas by an act made in this present session of parliament, intituled, An act for allowing the free importation of rice, sago powder, and vermicelli, into this kingdom, from his Majesty's colonies in North America, for a limited time, it is, amongst other things, enacted, That it shall and may be lawful for any person or persons to import into Great

Britain, from any of his Majesty's colonies in North America, at any time or times before the first day of December, one thousand seven hundred and sixty seven, any rice, without the payment of any subsidy, custom, duty, or imposition whatsoever: Now, to the end the advantage intended to this kingdom, by the said recited act, may not be evaded by the exportation of such rice into foreign parts; we your Majesty's most dutiful and loyal subjects the commons of Great Britain, in parliament assembled, do give and grant unto your Majesty, and do humbly beseech your Majesty that it may be enacted; and be it enacted by the authority aforesaid, That for and upon all rice which hath been or shall be, imported into this kingdom duty-free, by virtue of the said recited act, and which shall be again exported thereout, there shall be paid and answered to his Majesty, his heirs, and successors, a subsidy of poundage of six pence in the pound, according to the value or rate set upon rice imported, in the book of rates referred to by the act of the twelfth year of King Charles the Second; which said subsidy of six pence in the pound upon such rice so exported, shall be raised, levied, collected, and recovered, by such ways and means, and under such rules, regulations, penalties, and forfeitures, as the subsidy or poundage for any goods or merchandizes exported from Great Britain may be raised, levied, collected, or recovered, by any act of parliament now in force, as fully and effectually, to all intents and purposes, as if the several clauses, powers, directions, penalties, and forfeitures, relating thereto, were particularly repeated and again enacted into the body of this present act.

VIII. And be it further enacted by the authority aforesaid, That the said duties granted by this act upon rice exported shall (the necessary charges of management excepted) be paid into the receipt of his Majesty's exchequer, and be there reserved for the disposition of parliament.

IX. And whereas the permitting foreign lace made of silk or thread and foreign needle-work, to be worn or used in Great Britain, after the same had been seized and condemned, gives the unfair dealer in those commodities, opportunity to secure from seizures great quantities thereof, which are clandestinely imported: Now to prevent a practice so very prejudicial to the publick revenue, and the manufacturers of such goods in this kingdom; be it therefore enacted by the authority aforesaid, That from and after the seventh day of July, one thousand seven hundred and sixty seven, no foreign lace made of silk or thread, or foreign needle-work, which shall have been, or shall be, seized and condemned in Great Britain, for any cause of forfeiture, shall be sold or delivered out of any custom-house warehouse wherein the same shall be secured, otherwise than on condition to be exported under the like securities, regulations, and restrictions, penalties, and forfeitures, as are prescribed by law, for the due exportation of East India goods prohibited to be worn or used in Great Britain; any law, custom, or usage to the contrary notwithstanding.

X. And be it further enacted by the authority aforesaid, That if any action or suit shall be commenced against any person or persons for any thing done in pursuance of this act, the defendant or defendants, in any such action or suit, may plead the general issue, and give this act, and the special matter, in evidence, at any trial to be had thereupon; and that the same was done in pursuance and by the authority of this act; and if it shall appear so to have been done, the jury shall find for the defendant or defendants; and if the plaintiff shall be nonsuited, or discontinue his action after the defendant or defendants shall have appeared; or if judgement shall be given upon any verdict or demurrer against the plaintiff; the defendant or defendants shall recover treble costs, and have the like remedy for the same, as any defendant or defendants hath or have in other cases by law.

Source: Henry Steel Commager, ed., *Documents of American History* (New York: F. S. Crofts & Company, 1934).

Newspaper Account of the Boston Massacre (1770)

Festering antagonisms between the Boston populace and British troops, sent to keep order and enforce the Townshend Acts, culminated in an incident in which five individuals were killed. A shocked citizenry objected to the peacetime presence of the troops and demanded their removal.

THE Town of Boston affords a recent and melancholy Demonstration of the destructive consequences of quartering troops among citizens in time of Peace, under a pretence of supporting the laws and aiding civil authority; every considerate and unprejudic'd Person among us was deeply imprest with the apprehension of these consequences when it was known that a number of regiments were ordered to this town under such a pretext, but in reality to inforce oppressive measures; to awe and controul the legislative as well as executive power of the province, and to quell a spirit of liberty, which however it may have been basely opposed and even ridicul'd by some, would do honour to any age or country. A few persons among us had determin'd to use all their influence to procure so destructive a measure, with a view to their securely enjoying the profits of an American revenue, and unhappily both for Britain and this country, they found means to effect it.

It is to Governor Bernard, the commissioners, their confidents and coadjutors, that we are indebted as the procuring cause of a military power in this capital.—The Boston Journal of Occurrences printed in Mr. Holt's York Journal, from time to time, afforded many striking instances of the distresses brought upon the inhabitants by this measure; and since those Journals have been discontinued, our troubles from that quarter have been growing upon us: We have known a party of soldiers in the face of day fire off a loaded musket upon the inhabitants, others have been prick'd with bayonets, and even our magistrate assaulted and put in danger of their lives, where offenders brought before them have been rescued and why those and other bold and base criminals have as yet escaped the punishment due to their crimes, may be soon matter of enquiry by the representative body of this people.—It is natural to suppose that when the inhabitants . . . saw those laws which had been enacted for their security, and which they were ambitious of holding up to the soldiery, eluded, they should most commonly resent for themselves—and accordingly if so has happened; many have been the squabbles between them and the soldiery; but it seems their being often worsted by our youth in those

encounters, has only serv'd to irritate the former.—What passed at Mr. Gray's rope walk, has already been given the public, and may be said to have led the way to the late catastrophe.—That the rope walk lads when attacked by superior numbers should defend themselves with so much spirit and success in the club-way, was too mortifying, and perhaps it may hereafter appear, that even some of their officers, were unhappily affected with this circumstance: Divers stories were propagated among the soldiery, that serv'd to agitate their spirits particularly on the Sabbath, that one Chambers, a serjeant, represented as a sober man, had been missing the preceding day, and must therefore have been murdered by the townsmen; an officer of distinction so far credited this report, that he enter'd Mr. Gray's rope-walk that Sabbath; and when enquired of by that gentleman as soon as he could meet him, the occasion of his so doing, the officer reply'd, that it was to look if the serjeant said to be murdered had not been hid there; this sober serjeant was found on the Monday unhurt in a house of pleasure.—The evidences already collected shew that many threatnings had been thrown out by the soldiery, but we do not pretend to say there was any preconcerted plan; when the evidences are published, the world will judge.—We may however venture to declare, that it appears too probable from their conduct, that some of the soldiery aimed to draw and provoke the townsmen into squabbles, and that they then intended to make use of other weapons than canes, clubs or bludgeons,

Our readers will doubtless expect a circumstantial account of the tragical affair on Monday night last; but we hope they will excuse our being so particular as we should have been, had we not seen that the town was intending an inquiry and full representation thereof.

On the evening of Monday, being the 5th current, several soldiers of the 29th regiment were seen parading the streets with their drawn cutlasses. . . . A few minutes after nine o'clock, four youths, named Edward Archbald, William Merchant, Francis Archbald, and John Leech, jun. came down Cornhill together, and separated at Doctor Loring's corner, the two former were passing the narrow alley leading to

Murray's barrack, in which was a soldier brandishing a broad sword of an uncommon size against the walls, but of which he struck fire plentifully. A person of mean countenance armed with a large cudgel bore him company. Edward Archbald admonished Mr. Merchant to take care of the sword, on which the soldier turned round and struck Archbald on the arm, then push'd at Merchant and pierced thro' his clothes inside the arm close to the arm pit and grazed the skin. Merchant then struck the soldier with a short stick he had; and the other person ran to the barrack and brought with him two soldiers, one armed with a pair of tongs, the other with a shovel. He with the tongs pursued Archbald back through the alley, collar'd and laid him over the head with the tongs. The noise brought people together, and John Hix a young lad, coming up, knock'd the soldier down, but let him get up again; and more lads gathering, drove them back to the barrack, where the boys stood some time as it were to keep them in. In less than a minute 10 or 12 of them came out with drawn cutlasses, clubs, and bayonets, and set upon the unarmed boys and young folks, who stood them a little while but, finding the inequality of their equipment, dispersed.—

On hearing the noise, one Samuel Atwood, came up to see what was the matter, and entering the alley from dock square, heard the latter part of the combat, and when the boys dispersed he met the 10 or 12 soldiers aforesaid rushing down the alley towards the square, and asked them if they intended to murder the people? They answered Yes, by G—d, root and branch! With that one of them struck Mr. Atwood with a club, which was repeated by another and being unarmed, he turned to go off, and received a wound on the left shoulder which reached the bone and gave him much pain. Retreating a few steps Mr. Atwood met two officers and said, Gentlemen what is the matter? They answered, you'll see by and by. Immediately after, those heroes appeared in the square, asking where were the boogers? where were the cowards? But notwithstanding their fierceness to naked men, one of them advanced towards a youth who had a split of a raw stave in his hand, and said damn them here is one of them. . . . But the young man seeing a person near him with a drawn sword and a good cane ready to support him, held up his stave in defiance, and they quietly passed by him, up the little alley by Mr. Silsby's to King Street, where they attacked single and unarmed persons till they raised much clamour, and then turned down Cornhill street insulting all they met in like manner, and pursuing some to their very doors.

Thirty or forty persons, mostly lads, being by this means gathered in Kingstreet, Capt. Preston with a party of men with charged bayonets, came from the main guard to the Commissioner's house the soldiers pushing their bayonets, crying, Make way! They took place by the custom-house, and continuing to push, to drive the people off, pricked some in several places; on which they were clamorous, and, it is said, threw snow balls. On this, the Captain

commanded them to fire, and more snow balls coming, he again said, Damn you, Fire, be the consequence what it will! One soldier then fired, and a townsman with a cudgel struck him over the hands with such force that he dropt his firelock; and rushing forward aimed a blow at the Captain's head, which graz'd? hat and fell pretty heavy upon his arm: However, the soldiers continued the fire, successively, till 7 or 8, or as some say, 11 guns were discharged.

By this fatal manoeuvre, three men were laid dead on the spot, and two more struggling for life; but what shewed a degree of cruelty unknown to British troops, at least since the house of Hanover has directed their operations, was an attempt to fire upon, or push with their bayonets the persons who undertook to remove the slain and wounded!

Mr. Benjamin Leigh, now undertaker in Delph Manufactory, came up, and after some conversation with Capt. Preston, relative to his conduct in this affair, advised him to draw off his men, with which he complied.

The dead are Mr. Samuel Gray, killed on the spot, the ball entering his head and beating off a large portion of his skull.

A mulatto man, named Crispus Attucks, who was born in Framingham, but lately belonged to New Providence and was here in order to go for North Carolina, also killed instantly; two balls entering his breast, one of them in special goring the right lobe of the lungs, and a great part of the liver most horribly.

Mr. James Caldwell, mate of Capt. Morton's vessel, in like manner killed by two balls entering his back.

Mr. Samuel Maverick, a promising youth of 17 years of age, son of the widow Maverick, and an apprentice of Mr. Greenwood, Ivory Turner, mortally wounded; a ball went through his belly, and was cut out at his back: He died the next morning.

A lad named Christopher Monk, about 17 years of age, an apprentice to Mr. Walker, Shipwright, wounded, a ball entered his back about 4 inches above his left kidney, near the spine, and was cut out of the breast on the same side. Apprehended he will die.

A lad named John Clark, about 17 years of age, whose parents live at Medford, and an apprentice to Capt. Samuel Howard of this town; wounded, a ball entered just above his groin and came out at his hip, on the opposite side. Apprehended he will die.

Mr. Edward Payne, of this town, merchant, standing at his entry door, received a ball in his arm, which shattered some of the bones.

Mr. John Green, Taylor, coming up Leverett's Lane, received a ball just under his hip, and lodged it in the under part of his thigh, which was extracted[.]

Mr. Robert Patterson, a seafaring man, who was the person that had his trowsers shot through in Richardson's affair, wounded; a ball went through his right arm, and he suffered great loss of blood.

Mr. Patrick Carr, about 30 years of age, who work'd

with Mr. Field, Leather-Breeches maker in Queen-street, wounded; a ball enter'd near his hip, and went out at his side.

A lad named David Parker, an apprentice to Mr. Eddy the Wheelwright, wounded; a ball enter'd in his thigh.

The people were immediately alarmed with the report of this horrid massacre, the bells were set a ringing, and great numbers soon assembled at the place where this tragical scene had been acted; their feelings may be better conceived than expressed; and while some were taking care of the dead and wounded, the rest were in consultation what to do in these dreadful circumstances.

But so little intimidated were they, notwithstanding their being within a few yards of the main-guard, and seeing the 29th regiment under arms, and drawn up in King-street; that they kept their station, and appear'd as an officer of rank express'd it, ready to run upon the very muzzles of their muskets.—The Lieut. Governor soon came into the Town House, and there met some of his Majesty's Council, and a number of civil Magistrates; a considerable body of people immediately enter'd the Council chamber and expressed themselves to his Honour with a freedom and warmth becoming the occasion. He used his utmost endeavoure to pacify them, requesting that they would let the matter subside for the night, and promised to do all in his power that justice should be done, and the law have its course; men of influence and weight with the people were not wanting on their part to procure their compliance with his Honour's request, by representing the horrible consequences of a promiscuous and rash engagement in the night, and assuring them that such measures should be entered upon in the morning, as would be agreeable to their dignity, and more likely way of obtaining the best satisfaction for the blood of their fellow-townsmen.—The inhabitants attended to these suggestions, and the regiment under arms being ordered to the barracks which was insisted upon by the people, they then separated and return'd to their dwellings, by one o'clock. At 3 o'clock Capt. Preston was committed, as were the soldiers who fir'd, a few hour after him.

Tuesday morning presented a most shocking scene, the blood of our fellow-citizens running like water thro' King-street, and the Merchant's Exchange, the principal spot of the military parade for about 18 months past. Our blood might also be track'd up to the head of Long-Lane, and thro' divers other streets and passages.

At eleven o'clock, the inhabitants met at Faneuil Hall, and after some animated speeches, becoming the occasion, they chose a Committee of 15 respectable Gentlemen, to wait upon the Lieut. Governor in Council, to request of him to issue his orders for the immediate removal of the troops. . . .

Source: The Boston Gazette and Country Journal, March 12, 1770.

On the Death of the Rev. Mr. George Whitefield (1770)

George Whitefield was a charismatic, evangelistic, English minister whose American tours stimulated the "Great Awakening" of religious revivals throughout the colonies. Phillis Wheatley, an educated black servant in a prominent Boston household, became widely known for her poem commemorating Whitefield. She is remembered as the first published African American writer in the colonies.

Hail, happy saint, on thine immortal throne,
Possest of glory, life, and bliss unknown;
We hear no more the music of thy tongue,
Thy wonted auditories cease to throng.
Thy sermons in unequall'd accents flow'd,
And ev'ry bosom with devotion glow'd;
Thou didst in strains of eloquence refin'd
Inflame the heart, and captivate the mind.
Unhappy we the setting sun deplore,
So glorious once, but ah! it shines no more.
Behold the prophet in his tow'ring flight!
He leaves the earth for heav'n's unmeasur'd height,
And worlds unknown receive him from our sight.
There *Whitefield* wings with rapid course his way,
And sails to *Zion* through vast seas of day.
Thy pray'rs, great saint, and thine incessant cries
Have pierc'd the bosom of thy native skies.
Thou moon hast seen, and all the stars of light,
How he has wrestled with his God by night.
He pray'd that grace in ev'ry heart might dwell,
He long'd to see America excel;
He charg'd its youth that ev'ry grace divine
Should with full lustre in their conduct shine;
That Saviour, which his soul did first receive,
The greatest gift that ev'n a God can give,
He freely offer'd to the num'rous throng,

That on his lips with list'ning pleasure hung.
"Take him, ye wretched, for your only good,
"Take him, ye starving sinners, for your food;
"Ye thirsty, come to this life-giving stream,
Ye preachers, take him for your joyful theme;
"Take him, my dear *Americans*," he said,
"Be your complaints on his kind bosom laid:
Take him, ye *Africans*, he longs for you,
"*Impartial Saviour* is his title due
"Was'd in the fountain of redeeming blood,
"You shall be son, and kings, and priests to God."
Great *Countess*, we *Americans* revere
Thy name, and mingle in thy grief sincere;
New England deeply feels, the *Orphans* mourn
Their more than father will no more return.
But, though arrested by the hand of death,
Whitefield no more exerts his lab'ring breath,
Yet let us view him in th' eternal skies,
Let ev'ry heart to this bright vision rise;
While the tomb safe retains its sacred trust,
Till life divine re-animates his dust.

Source: *Massachusetts Spy*, October 11, 1770. Later published as *An Elegiac Poem, on the Death of that Celebrated Divine, and Eminent Servant of Jesus Christ, the Reverend and Learned George Whitefield . . .* (Boston: printed and sold by Ezekiel Russell and John Boyles, 1770).

On Being Brought from Africa to America
(early 1770s)

Internationally recognized even in her own lifetime, the African-born poet Phillis Wheatley was the slave of Boston tailor John Wheatley until he freed her in 1773. That same year, her first book of poetry was published in London.

In the following poem, Wheatley says it was mercy that brought her from a pagan land—Africa—to one where she could learn of Christianity. Some scholars have argued that Wheatley, while seeming to endorse her forced transport to America, was, in fact, using irony to comment on a situation that brought her to slavery but also to her cherished Christian faith.

Twas mercy brought me from my *Pagan* land,
Taught my benighted soul to understand
That there's a God, that there's a *Saviour* too:
Once I redemption neither sought nor knew.
Some view our sable race with scornful eye,
"Their colour is a diabolic die."
Remember, *Christians, Negroes*, black as *Cain*,
May be refin'd, and join th' angelic train.

Source: Phillis Wheatley, *Poems on Various Subjects, Religious and Moral* (London: A. Bell, 1773).

A Tutor and his Pupils (1773–1774)

Philip Fitian was employed as a tutor in the home of Councillor Robert Carter in Westmoreland County, Virginia. Fitian had graduated from Princeton College in 1770 in the same class as Aaron Burr, intending to enter the ministry. When he took a temporary tutoring position with the Carter family, he was surprised at the elegant, cultured lifestyle he encountered. Fitian's journal gives an account of life in a gentleman's household, the education of his children, and the recreational activities of his family and neighbors.

Monday, November 1. We began school. The school consists of eight. Two of Mr. Carters sons, one nephew, and five daughters. The eldest son is reading Sallust; grammatical exercises, and Latin grammar. The second son is reading English grammar, and reading English writing, and ciphering in subtraction. The nephew is reading and writing as above; and ciphering in reduction. The eldest daughter is reading the Spectator, writing, and beginning to cipher. The second is reading now out of the spelling-book, and beginning to write. The next is reading in the spelling-book. The fourth is spelling in the beginning of the spelling-book. And the last is beginning her letters.

Thursday, November 25. Rode this morning to Richmond Courthouse, where two horses ran for a purse of 500 pounds: besides small bets almost innumerable. One of the horses belonged to Colonel John Tayloe, and is called Yorick; the other to Dr. Flood, and is called Gift. The Assembly was remarkably numerous; beyond my expectation and exceedingly polite in general. The horses started precisely at five minutes after three; the course was one mile in circumference, they performed the first round in two minutes, the third in two minutes and a half. Yorick came out the fifth time round about 40 rods ahead of Gift; both horses, when the riders dismounted proved very lame; they ran five miles, and carried 180 pounds . . .

Almost every lady wears a red cloak; and when they ride out they tie a red handkerchief over their head and face, so that when I first came into Virginia, I was distressed whenever I saw a lady, for I thought she had the toothache. The people are extremely hospitable, and very polite, both of which are most certainly universal characteristics of the gentlemen in Virginia. Some swear bitterly, but the practice seems to be generally disapproved. I have heard that this country is notorious for gaming; however that may be, I have not seen a pack of cards, nor a die, since I left home, nor gaming nor betting of any kind except at the Richmond-race. Almost every gentleman of condition, keeps a chariot and four; many drive with six horses. I observe that all the merchants and shopkeepers in the sphere of my acquaintance are young Scotchmen, several of whom I know . . . It has been the custom heretofore to have all their tutors, and schoolmasters from Scotland, tho' they begin to be willing to employ their own countrymen.

In the evening Ben Carter and myself had a long dispute on the practice of fighting. He thinks it best for two persons who have any dispute to go out in good-humour and fight manfully, and says that they will be sooner and longer friends than to brood and harbour malice. Mr. Carter is practicing this evening on the guitar. He has here at home a harpsichord, forte-piano, harmonica, guitar, violin, and German flutes, and at Williamsburg, he has a good pipe organ.

In the morning so soon as it is light a boy knocks at my door to make a fire; after the fire is kindled, I rise which now in the winter is commonly by seven, or a little after. By the time I am drest the children commonly enter the school-room, which is under the room I sleep in; I hear them round one lesson, when the bell rings for eight o-clock (for Mr. Carter has a large good bell which may be heard some miles, and this is always rung at meal times ;) the children then go out; and at half after eight the bell rings for breakfast, we then repair to the dining-room; after breakfast, which is generally about half after nine, we go into school, and sit till twelve, when the bell rings, and they go out for noon; the dinner-bell rings commonly about half after two, often at three, but never before two. After dinner is over, which in common, when we have no company, is about half after three we go into school, and sit til the bell rings at five, when they separate til the next morning. We go into supper commonly about half after eight or at nine and I usually go to bed between ten and eleven.

Saturday, December 18. After breakfast, we all retired into the dancing room, and after the scholars had their lesson singly round Mr. Christian, very politely, requested me to step a minuet; I excused myself, however, but signified my peculiar pleasure in the accuracy of their performance. There were several minuets danced with great ease and propriety; after which the whole company joined in country-dances, and it was indeed beautiful to admiration, to see such a number of young persons, set off by dress to the best advantage, moving easily, to the sound of well performed music, and with perfect regularity, tho' apparently in the utmost disorder. The dance continued till two, we dined at half after three. Soon after dinner we repaired to the dancing-room again; I observe in the course of the lessons, that Mr. Christian is punctual, and rigid in his discipline, so strict indeed that he struck two of the young Misses for a fault in the course of their performance, even in the presence of the mother of one of them! And he rebuked one of the young fellows so highly as to tell him he must alter his manner, which he had observed through the course of the dance, to be insolent, and wanton, or else absent himself from the school. I thought this a sharp reproof to a young gentleman of seventeen, before a large number of ladies! Nothing is now to be heard of in conversation, but the balls, the fox-hunts, the fine entertainments, and the good fellowship, which are to be exhibited at the approaching Christmas. Mr. Goodlet was barred out of his school last Monday by his scholars, for Christmas holidays, which are to continue till twelfth-day; but my scholars are of a more quiet nature, and have consented to have four or five days now, and to have their full holiday in May next, when I propose by the permission of Providence to go home, where I hope to see the good and benevolent Laura.

When the candles were lighted, we all repaired, for the last time, into the dancing-room; first each couple danced a minuet; then all joined as before in the country dances, these continued till half after seven when at the proposal of several, we played Button, to get pawns for redemption; here I could join with them, and indeed it was carried on with sprightliness, and decency; in the course of redeeming my pawns I had several kisses of the ladies!

Half after eight we were rung in to supper. The room looked luminous and splendid; four very large candles burning on the table where we supped; three others in different parts of the room; a gay, sociable assembly, and four well instructed waiters! So soon as we rose from supper, the company formed into a semicircle round the fire, and Mr. Lee, by the voice of the Company was chosen Pope and the rest of the company were appointed Friars, in the Play called "Break the Pope's Neck." Here we had great diversion in the respective judgments upon offenders, but we were all dismissed by ten, and retired to our several rooms.

Saturday, December 25. I was waked this morning by guns fired all round the house. The morning is stormy, the wind at south east and it rains hard. Nelson the boy who makes my fire, blacks my shoes, does errands, &c. was early in my room . . . He made me a vast fire, blacked my shoes, set my room in order, and wished me a joyful Christmas, for which I gave him half a bit. Soon after he left the room and before I was drest, the fellow who makes the fire in our school room, dressed very neatly in green, but almost drunk, entered my chamber with three or four profound bows, and made me the same salutation; I gave him a bit, and dismissed him as soon as possible. Soon after my clothes and linen were sent in with a message for a Christmas box, as they call it; I sent the poor slave a bit, and my thanks. I was obliged for want of small change, to put off for some days the barber who shaves and dresses me.

There were at table Mrs. Carter and her five daughters that are at school with me Miss Priscilla, Nancy, Fanny, Betsy, and Harriot, five as beautiful delicate, well-instructed children as I have ever known! Ben is abroad; Bob and Harry are out.

Ben, the eldest, is a youth of genius: of warm impetuous disposition; desirous of acquiring knowledge, docile, vastly inquisitive and curious in mercantile, and mechanical matters, very fond of horses and takes great pleasure in exercising them.

Bob, the other brother, is by no means destitute of capacity. He is extremely volatile and unsettled in his temper, which makes it almost wholly impossible to fix him for any time to the same thing, on which account he has made but very little advancement in any one branch of study, and this is attributed to barrenness of genius. He is slovenly, clumsy, very fond of shooting, of dogs, and of horses, but a very stiff rider, good natured, pleased with the society of persons much below his family, and estate and tho' quick and wrathful in his temper, yet he is soon moderated, and easily subdued.

Harry, the nephew, is rather sullen in his make. He is obstinate, tho' steady, and makes a slow uniform advance in his learning, he is vastly kind to me, but in particular to my horse.

Miss Priscilla, the eldest daughter, about 16 years old, is steady, studious, docile, quick of apprehension, and makes good progress in what she undertakes; she is small of her age, has a mild winning presence, a sweet obliging temper, never swears, which is here a distinguished virtue, dances finely, plays well on keyed instruments, and is on the whole in the first class of the female sex.

Nancy, the second, is not without some few of those qualities which are by some (I think with great ill-nature, and with little or no truth) said to belong intirely to the fair sex. I mean great curiosity, eagerness for superiority, and or in friendship, but bitterness and rage where there is enmity. She is not constant in her disposition, nor diligent nor attentive to her business. But she has her excellencies; she is cheerful, tender in her temper, easily managed by perswasion, and is never without what seems to have been a common gift of Heaven to the fair-sex, readiness of expression!

Fanny, the next, is in her person, according to my

judgment the flower of the family. She has a strong resemblance to her Mamma, who is an elegant, beautiful woman. Miss Fanny seems to have a remarkable sedateness, and simplicity in her countenance, which is always rather cheerful than melancholy; she has nothing with which we can find fault in her person, but has something in the features of her face which insensibly pleases us, and always when she is in sight draws our attention, and much the more because there seems to be for every agreeable feature a corresponding action which improves and adorns it.

Betsy, the next, is young, quiet, and obedient.

Harriet is bold, fearless, noisy and lawless; always merry, almost never displeased; she seems to have a heart easily moved by the force of music; she has learned many tunes and can strike any note, or succession of notes perfectly with the flute or harpsichord, and is never wearied with the sound of music either vocal or instrumental.

These are the persons who are at present under my direction, and whose general character I have very imperfectly attempted to describe.

Source: Albert Bushnell Hart with Blanche E. Hazard, *Colonial Children* (New York: Macmillan, 1902).

The Boston Port Act (1774)

The Boston Port Act was the first of five so-called Intolerable Acts passed by British Parliament to punish Boston for its famous Tea Party. Through this act, the port of Boston was closed to all commerce, except for food and fuel. Reopening the port was predicated on payment of damages sustained by the East India Company and all other losses resulting from the riots of 1773 and 1774.

[March 31, 1774]

WHEREAS dangerous commotions and insurrections have been fomented and raised in the town of Boston, in the province of Massachuset's Bay, in New England, by divers ill-affected persons, to the subversion of his Majesty's government, and to the utter destruction of the publick peace, and good order of the said town; in which commotions and insurrections certain valuable cargoes of teas, being the property of the East India Company, and on board certain vessels lying within the bay or harbour of Boston, were seized and destroyed: And whereas, in the present condition of the said town and harbour, the commerce of his Majesty's subjects cannot be safely carried on there, nor the customs payable to his Majesty duly collected; and it is therefore expedient that the officers of his Majesty's customs should be forthwith removed from the said town: May it please your Majesty that it may be enacted; and be it enacted by the King's most excellent majesty, by and with the advice and consent of the lords spiritual and temporal, and commons, in this present parliament assembled, and by the authority of the same, That from and after the first day of June, one thousand seven hundred and seventy-four, it shall not be lawful for any person or persons whatsoever to lade put, or cause or procure to be laden or put, off or from any quay, wharf, or other place, within the said town of Boston, or in or upon any part of the shore of the bay, commonly called The Harbour of Boston, between a certain headland or point called Nahant Point, on the eastern side of the entrance into the said bay, and a certain other headland or point called Alderton Point, on the western side of the entrance into the said bay, or in or upon any island, creek, landing place, bank, or other place, within the said bay or headlands, into any ship, vessel, lighter, boat, or bottom, any goods, wares, or merchandise whatsoever, to be transported or carried into any other country, province or place whatsoever, or into any other part of the said province of the Massachuset's Bay, in New England; or to take up, discharge, or lay on land, or cause or procure to be taken up, discharged, or laid on land, within the said town, or in or upon any of the places aforesaid, out of any boat, lighter, ship, vessel, or bottom, any goods, wares, or merchandise whatsoever, to be brought from any other country, province, or place, or any other part of the said province of the Massachuset's Bay in New England, upon pain of the forfeiture of the said goods, wares, and merchandise, and of the said boat, lighter, ship, or vessel or other bottom into which the same shall be taken, and of the guns, ammunition, tackle, furniture, and stores, in or belonging to the same: And if any such goods, wares, or merchandise, shall, within the said town, or in any the places aforesaid, be laden or taken in from the shore into any barge, hoy, lighter, wherry, or boat, to be carried on board any ship or vessel coming in and arriving from any other country or province, or other part of the said province of the Massachuset's Bay in New England, such barge, hoy, lighter, wherry, or boat, shall be forfeited and lost.

II. And be it further enacted by the authority aforesaid, That if any warfinger, or keeper of any wharf, crane, or quay, of their servants, or any of them, shall take up or land, or knowingly suffer to be taken up or landed, or shall ship off, or suffer to be waterborne, at or from any of their said wharfs, cranes, or quays, any such goods, wares, or merchandise; in every such case, all and every such wharfinger, and keeper of such wharf, crane, or quay, and every person whatever who shall be assisting, or otherwise concerned in the shipping or in the loading or putting on board any boat, or other vessel for that purpose, or in the unshipping such goods, wares, and merchandise, or to whose hands the same shall knowingly come after the loading, shipping, or unshipping thereof, shall forfeit and lose treble the value thereof, to be computed at the highest price which such sort of goods, wares, and merchandise, shall bear at the place where such offence shall be committed, together with the vessels and boats, and all the horses, cattle, and carriages, whatsoever made use of in the shipping, unshipping, landing, removing, carriage, or conveyance of any of the aforesaid goods, wares, and merchandise.

III. And be it further enacted by the authority aforesaid, That if any ship or vessel shall be moored or lie at anchor, or be seen hovering within the said bay, described and bounded as aforesaid, or within one league from the said bay so described, or the said headlands, or any of the islands lying between or within the same, it shall and may be lawful for any admiral, chief commander, or commissioned officer, of his Majesty's fleet or ships of war, or for any officer of his Majesty's customs, to compel such ship or vessel to depart to some other port or harbour, or to such station as the said officer shall appoint, and to use such force for that purpose as shall be found necessary: And if such ship or vessel shall not depart accordingly, within six hours after notice for that purpose given by such person as aforesaid, such ship or vessel, together with all the goods laden on board thereon, and all the guns, ammunition, tackle, and furniture, shall be forfeited and lost, whether bulk shall have been broken or not.

IV. Provided always, That nothing in this act contained shall extend, or be construed to extend, to any military or other stores for his Majesty's use, or to the ships or vessels whereon the same shall be laden, which shall be commissioned by, and in the immediate pay of, his Majesty, his heirs or successors; nor to any fuel or victual brought coastwise from any part of the continent of America, for the necessary use and sustenance of the inhabitants of the said town of Boston, provided the vessels wherein the same are to be carried shall be duly furnished with a cocket and let-pass, after having been duly searched by the proper officers of his Majesty's customs at Marblehead, in the port of Salem, in the said province of Massachuset's Bay; and that some officer of his Majesty's customs be also there put on board the said vessel, who is hereby authorized to go on board, and proceed with the said vessel, together with a sufficient number of persons, properly armed, for his defence, to the said town or harbour of Boston; nor to any ships or vessels which may happen to be within the said harbour of Boston on or before the first day of June, one thousand seven hundred and seventy four, and may have either laden or taken on board, or be there with intent to load or take on board, or to land or discharge any goods, wares, and merchandise, provided the said ships and vessels do depart the said harbour within fourteen days after the said first day of June, one thousand seven hundred and seventy-four.

V. And be it further enacted by the authority aforesaid, That all seizures, penalties, and forfeitures, inflicted by this act, shall be made and prosecuted by any admiral, chief commander, or commissioned officer, of his Majesty's fleet, or ships of war, or by the officers of his Majesty's customs, or some of them, or by some other person deputed or authorised, by warrant from the lord high treasurer, or the commissioners of his Majesty's treasury for the time being, and by no other person whatsoever: And if any such officer, or other person authorised as aforesaid, shall, directly or indirectly, take or receive any bribe or reward, to connive at such lading or unlading, or shall make or commence any collusive seizure, information, or agreement for that purpose, or shall do any other act whatsoever, whereby the goods, wares, or merchandise, prohibited as aforesaid, shall be suffered to pass, either inwards or outwards, or whereby the forfeitures and penalties inflicted by this act may be evaded, every such offender shall forfeit the sum of five hundred pounds for every such offence, and shall become incapable of any office or employment, civil or military; and every person who shall give, offer, or promise, any such bribe or reward, or shall contract, agree, or treat with any person, so authorised as aforesaid, to commit any such offence, shall forfeit the sum of fifty pounds.

VI. And be it further enacted by the authority aforesaid, That the forfeitures and penalties inflicted by this act shall and may be prosecuted, sued for, and recovered, and be divided, paid, and applied, in like manner as other penalties and forfeitures inflicted by any act or acts of parliament, relating to the trade or revenues of the British colonies or plantations in America, are directed to be prosecuted, sued for, or recovered, divided, paid, and applied, by two several acts of parliament, the one passed in the fourth year of his present Majesty (intituled, An act for granting certain duties in the British colonies and plantations in America; for continuing, amending, and making perpetual, an act passed in the sixth year of the reign of his late majesty King George the Second, intituled, An act for the better securing and encouraging the trade of his Majesty's sugar colonies in America: for applying the produce of such duties, and of the duties to arise by virtue of the said act, towards defraying the expences of defending, protecting, and securing, the said colonies and plantations; for explaining an act made in the twenty-fifth year of the reign of King Charles the Second, intituled, An act for the encouragement of the Greenland and Eastland trades, and for the better securing the plantation trade; and for altering and disallowing several drawbacks on exports from this kingdom, and more effectually preventing the clandestine conveyance of goods to and from the said colonies and plantations, and improving and securing the trade between the same and Great Britain;) the other passed in the eighth year of his present Majesty's reign (intituled, An act for the more easy and effectual recovery of the penalties and forfeitures inflicted by the acts of parliament relating to the trade or revenues of the British colonies and plantations in America.)

VII. And be it further enacted by the authority aforesaid, That every charter party bill of loading, and other contract for consigning shipping, or carrying any goods, wares, and merchandize whatsoever, to or from the said town of Boston, or any part of the bay or harbour thereof, described as aforesaid, which have been made or entered into, or which shall be made or entered into, so long as this act shall remain in full force, relating to any ship which shall arrive at the said town or harbour, after the first day of June, one thousand seven hundred and seventy-four, shall be, and the same are hereby declared to be utterly void, to all intents and purposes whatsoever.

VIII. And be it further enacted by the authority aforesaid, That whenever it shall be made to appear to his Majesty, in his privy council, that peace and obedience to the laws shall be so far restored in the said town of Boston, that the trade of Great Britain may safely be carried on there, and his Majesty's customs duly collected, and his Majesty, in his privy council, shall adjudge the same to be true, it shall and may be lawful for his Majesty, by proclamation, or order of council, to assign and appoint the extent, bounds, and limits, of the port or harbour of Boston, and of every creek or haven within the same, or in the islands within the precincts thereof; and also to assign and appoint such and so many open places, quays, and wharfs, within the said harbour, creeks, havens, and islands, for the landing, discharging, lading, and shipping of goods, as his Majesty, his heirs or successors, shall judge necessary and expedient; and also to appoint such and so many officers of the customs therein as his Majesty shall think fit, after which it shall be lawful for any person or persons to lade or put off from, or to discharge and land upon, such wharfs, quays, and places, so appointed within the said harbour, and none other, any goods, wares, and merchandise whatever.

IX. Provided always, That if any goods, wares, or merchandize, shall be laden or put off from, or discharged or landed upon, any other place than the quays, wharfs, or places, so to be appointed, the same, together with the ships, boats, and other vessels employed therein, and the horses, or other cattle and carriages used to convey the same, and the person or persons concerned or assisting therein, or to whose hands the same shall knowingly come, shall suffer all the forfeitures and penalties imposed by this or any other act on the illegal shipping or landing of goods.

X. Provided also, and it is hereby declared and enacted, That nothing herein contained shall extend, or be construed, to enable his Majesty to appoint such port, harbour, creeks, quays, wharfs, places, or officers in the said town of Boston, or in the said bay or islands, until it shall sufficiently appear to his Majesty that full satisfaction hath been made by or on behalf of the inhabitants of the said town of Boston to the united company of merchants of England trading to the East Indies, for the damage sustained by the said company by the destruction of their goods sent to the said town of Boston, on board certain ships or vessels as aforesaid; and until it shall be certified to his Majesty, in council, by the governor, or lieutenant governor, of the said province, that reasonable satisfaction hath been made to the officers of his Majesty's revenue, and others, who suffered by the riots and insurrections above mentioned, in the months of November and December, in the year one thousand seven hundred and seventy-three, and in the month of January, in the year one thousand seven hundred and seventy-four.

XI. And be it further enacted by the authority aforesaid, That if any action or suit shall be commenced, either in Great Britain or America, against any person or persons, for any thing done in pursuance of this act of parliament, the defendant or defendants, in such action or suit, may plead the general issue, and give the said act, and the special matter, in evidence, at any trial to be had thereupon, and that the same was done in pursuance and by the authority of this act: and if it shall appear so to have been done, the jury shall find for the defendant or defendants; and if the plaintiff shall be nonsuited, or discontinue his action, after the defendant or defendants shall have appeared: or if judgment shall be given upon any verdict or demurrer, against the plaintiff, the defendant or defendants shall recover treble costs, and have the like remedy for the same, as defendants have in other cases by law.

Source: Danby Pickering, *Statutes at Large . . . {from 1225 to 1867}* (Cambridge, UK: Printed by Benthem, for C. Bathhurst, 1762–1869).

Slave Petition to the Governor, Council, and House of Representatives of the Province of Massachusetts (1774)

Influenced by the rhetoric and actions of American patriots beginning their struggle for freedom from the British Crown, a number of slaves—particularly those in the urban areas of the North—began to petition for their freedom. This 1774 petition, submitted by Massachusetts slaves to officials of the colony, reflects some of the language and sentiments of other patriots at the time.

25 May 1774

The Petition of a Grate Number of Blackes of this Province who by divine permission are held in a state of Slavery within the bowels of a free and christian Country

Humbly Shewing. . . . That your Petitioners apprehind we have in common with all other men a naturel right to our freedoms without Being depriv'd of them by our fellow men as we are a freeborn Pepel and have never forfeited this Blessing by aney compact or agreement whatever. But we were unjustly dragged by the cruel hand of power from our dearest frinds and sum of us stolen from the bosoms of our tender Parents and from a Populous Pleasant and plentiful country and Brought hither to be made slaves for Life in a Christian land. Thus are we deprived of every thing that hath a tendency to make life even tolerable, the endearing ties of husband and wife we are strangers to for we are no longer man and wife then our masters or mestreses thinkes proper marred or onmarred. Our children are also taken from us by force and sent maney miles from us wear we seldom or ever see them again there to be made slaves of for Life which sumtimes is vere short by Reson of Being dragged from their mothers Breest Thus our Lives are imbittered to us on these accounts By our deplorable situation we are rendered incapable of shewing our obedience to Almighty God how can a slave perform the duties of a husband to a wife or parent to his child How can a husband leave master and work and cleave to his wife How can the wife submit themselves to there husbands in all things. How can the child obey thear parents in all things. There is a grat number of us sencear . . . members of the Church of Christ how can the master and the slave be said to fulfil that command Live in love let Brotherly Love contuner and abound Beare yea onenothers Bordenes How can the master be said to Beare my Borden when he Beares me down whith the Have chanes of slavery and operson against my will and how can we fulfill our parte of duty to him whilst in this condition and as we cannot searve our God as we ought whilst in this situation Nither can we reap an equal benefet from the laws of the Land which doth not justifi but condemns Slavery or if there had bin aney Law to hold us in Bondege we are Humbely of the Opinon ther never was aney to inslave our children for life when Born in a free Countrey. We therefor Bage your Excellency and Honours will give this its deu weight and consideration and that you will accordingly cause an act of the legislative to be pessed that we may obtain our Natural right our freedoms and our children be set at lebety at the yeare of Twenty one for whoues sekes more petequeley your Petitioners is in Duty ever to Pray.

Source: Massachusetts Historical Society Collections, 5th ser., 3:432–33.

A Case for Non-Interference by Parliament (1775)

John Adams wrote a series of letters for the Boston *Gazette*, under the pseudonym Novanglus, in which he demonstrated a penetrating understanding of the nature of government. Adams argued that New England derived its rights from the charters granted by the British Crown and that Parliament did not have authority to control America. He equated Britain and America as separate states, maintaining that, even though both shared allegiance to the Crown and America had given its assent to Parliament in matters of foreign trade, it was local government that had authority in the colonies.

February 6, 1775

I agree, that "two supreme and independent authorities cannot exist in the same state," any more than two supreme beings in one universe; And, therefore, I contend, that our provincial legislatures are the only supreme authorities in our colonies. Parliament, notwithstanding this, may be allowed an authority supreme and sovereign over the ocean, which may be limited by the banks of the ocean, or the bounds of our charters; our charters give us no authority over the high seas. Parliament has our consent to assume a jurisdiction over them. And here is a line fairly drawn between the rights of Britain and the rights of the colonies, namely, the banks of the ocean, or low-water mark; the line of division between common law, and civil or maritime law. . . .

"If then, we are a part of the British empire, we must be subject to the supreme power of the state, which is vested in the estates in parliament."

Here, again, we are to be conjured out of our senses by the magic in the words "British empire," and "supreme power of the state." But, however it may sound, I say we are not a part of the British empire; because the British government is not an empire. The governments of France, Spain, &c. are not empires, but monarchies, supposed to be governed by fixed fundamental laws, though not really. The British government is still less entitled to the style of an empire. It is a limited monarchy. If Aristotle, Livy, and Harrington knew what a republic was, the British constitution is much more like a republic than an empire. They define a republic to be a government of laws, and not of men. If this definition is just, the British constitution is nothing more nor less than a republic, in which the king is first magistrate. This office being hereditary, and being possessed of such ample and splendid prerogatives, is no objection to the government's being a republic, as long as it is bound by fixed laws, which the people have a voice in making, and a right to defend. An empire is a despotism, and an emperor a despot, bound by no law or limitation but his own will; it is a stretch of tyranny beyond absolute monarchy. For, although the will of an absolute monarch is law, yet his edicts must be registered by parliaments. Even this formality is not necessary in an empire

"If the colonies are not subject to the authority of parliament, Great Britain and the colonies must be distinct states, as completely so as England and Scotland were before the union, or as Great Britain and Hanover are now." There is no need of being startled at this consequence. It is very harmless. There is no absurdity at all in it. Distinct states may be united under one king. And those states may be further cemented and united together by a treaty of commerce. This is the case. We have, by our own express consent, contracted to observe the Navigation Act, and by our implied consent, by long usage and uninterrupted acquiescence, have submitted to the other acts of trade, however grievous some of them may be. This may be compared to a treaty of commerce, by which those distinct states are cemented together, in perpetual league and amity. . . .

The only proposition in all this writer's long string of pretended absurdities, which he says follows from the position that we are distinct states, is this: That, "as the king must govern each state by its parliament, those several parliaments would pursue the particular interest of its own state; and however well disposed the king might be to pursue a line of interest that was common to all, the checks and control that he would meet with would render it impossible." Every argument ought to be allowed its full weight; and therefore candor obliges me to acknowledge, that here lies all the difficulty that there is in this whole controversy. There has been, from first to last, on both sides of the Atlantic, an idea, an apprehension that it was necessary there should be some superintending power, to draw together all the wills, and unite all the strength of the subjects in all the dominions, in case of war, and in the case of trade. The necessity of this, in case of trade, has been so apparent, that, as has often been said, we have consented that parliament should exercise such a power. In case of war, it has by some been thought necessary. But, in fact and experience, it has not been found so. . . . The inconveniences of this were small, in comparison of the absolute ruin to the liberties of all which must follow the submission to parliament, in all cases, which would be giving up all the popular limitations upon the government.

But, admitting the proposition in its full force, that it is absolutely necessary there should be a supreme power, coextensive with all the dominions, will it follow that parliament, as now constituted, has a right to assume this supreme jurisdiction? By no means.

A union of the colonies might be projected, and an American legislature; for, if America has 3,000,000 people, and the whole dominions 12,000,000, she ought to send a quarter part of all the members to the house of commons; and instead of holding parliaments always at Westminister, the haughty members for Great Britain must humble themselves, one session in four, to cross the Atlantic, and hold the parliament in America.

There is no avoiding all inconveniences in human affairs. The greatest possible, or conceivable, would arise from ceding to parliament power over us without a representation in it. . . . The least of all would arise from going on as we began, and fared well for 150 years, by letting parliament regulate trade, and our own assemblies all other matters.

But perhaps it will be said, that we are to enjoy the British constitution in our supreme legislature, the parliament, not in our provincial legislatures. To this I answer, if parliament is to be our supreme legislature, we shall be under a complete oligarchy or aristocracy, not the British constitution, which this writer himself defines a mixture of monarchy, aristocracy, and democracy. For king, lords, and commons, will constitute one great oligarchy, as they will stand related to America, as much as the deceivers did in Rome; with this difference for the worse, that our rulers are to be three thousand miles off. . . . If our provincial constitutions are in any respect imperfect, and want alteration, they have capacity enough to discern it, and power enough to effect it, without interposition of parliament. . . . America will never allow that parliament has any authority to alter their constitution at all. She is wholly penetrated with a sense of the necessity of resisting it at all hazards. . . . The question we insist on most is, not whether the alteration is for the better or not, but whether parliament has any right to make any alteration at all. And it is the universal sense of America, that it has none.

That a representation in parliament is impracticable, we all agree; but the consequence is, that we must have a representation in our supreme legislatures here. This was the consequence that was drawn by kings, ministers, our ancestors, and the whole nation, more than a century ago, when the colonies were first settled, and continued to be the general sense until the last peace; and it must be the general sense again soon, or Great Britain will lose her colonies.

"It is our highest interest to continue a part of the British empire; and equally our duty to remain subject to the authority of parliament," says Massachusettensis.

We are a part of the British dominions, that is, of the King of Great Britain, and it is our interest and duty to continue so. It is equally our interest and duty to continue subject to the authority of parliament, in the regulation of our trade, as long as she shall leave us to govern our internal policy, and to give and grant our own money, and no longer.

Novanglus

Source: Boston Gazette, February 6, 1775.

Petition of London Merchants for Reconciliation with the Colonies (1775)

Amid a devastating decline in trade with the colonies, London merchants pleaded with Parliament for a tempering of the onerous commercial policies that resulted in an American embargo of British goods. While numerous such petitions were delivered to Parliament, this one is a particularly detailed account of the materials traded, and it gives a clear picture of the pressing need to restore standard trading practices.

Mr. Alderman Hayley said he had a petition from the merchants of the city of London concerned in the commerce to North America, to that honourable House, and desired leave to present the same, which being given, it was brought up and read, setting forth:

That the petitioners are all essentially interested in the trade to North America, either as exporters and importers, or as venders of British and foreign goods for exportation to that country; and that the petitioners have exported, or sold for exportation, to the British colonies in North America, very large quantities of the manufacture of Great Britain and Ireland, and in particular the staple articles of woollen, iron, and linen, also those of cotton, silk, leather, pewter, tin, copper, and brass, with almost every British manufacture; also large quantities of foreign linens and other articles imported into these kingdoms, from Flanders, Holland, Germany, the East Countries, Portugal, Spain, and Italy, which are generally received from those countries in return for British manufactures; and that the petitioners have likewise exported, or sold for exportation, great quantities of the various species of goods imported into this kingdom from the East-Indies, part of which receive additional manufacture in Great Britain; and that the petitioners receive returns from North America to this kingdom directly, viz. pig and bar iron, timber, staves, naval stores, tobacco, rice, indigo, deer, and other skins, beaver and furs, train oil, whalebone, bees wax, pot and pearl ashes, drugs and dying woods, with some bullion, and also wheat flour, Indian corn and salted provisions, when, on account of scarcity in Great Britain, those articles are permitted to be imported; and that the petitioners receive returns circuitously from Ireland (for flax seed, &c. exported from North America) by bills of exchange on the merchants of this city trading to Ireland, for the proceeds of linens, &c. imported into these kingdoms from the West Indies; in return for provisions, lumber and cattle, exported from North America, for the use and support of the West India islands, by bills of exchange on the West India merchants, for the proceeds of sugar, molasses, rum, cotton, coffee, or other produce, imported from those islands into these kingdoms; from Italy, Spain, Portugal, France, Flanders, Germany, Holland, and the East Countries, by bills of exchange or bullion in return for wheat flour, rice, Indian corn, fish, and lumber, exported from the British colonies in North America, for the use of those countries; and that the petitioners have great reason to believe, from the best informations they can obtain, that on the balance of this extensive commerce, there is now due from the colonies in North America, to the said city only, 02,000,000 sterling, and upwards; and that, by the direct commerce with the colonies, and the circuitous trade thereon depending, some thousands of ships and vessels are employed, and many thousands of seamen are bred and maintained, thereby increasing the naval strength and power of Great Britain; and that, in the year 1765, there was a great stagnation of the commerce between Great Britain and her colonies, in consequence of an Act for granting and applying certain stamp duties, and other duties, in the British colonies and plantations in America, by which the merchants trading to North America, and the artificers employed in the various manufactures consumed in those countries, were subjected to many hardships; and that, in the following year, the said Act was repealed, under an express declaration of the legislature, that the continuance of the said Act would be attended with many inconveniences, and might be productive of consequences greatly detrimental to the commercial interests of these kingdoms; upon which repeal, the trade to the British colonies immediately resumed its former flourishing state; and that in the year 1767 an Act passed for granting certain duties in the British colonies and plantations in America, which imposed certain duties, to be paid in America, on tea, glass, red and white lead, painters' colours, paper, paste-board, mill-board, and scale-board, when the commerce with the colonies was again interrupted; and that in the year 1770, such parts of the said Act as imposed duties on glass, red and white lead, painters' colours, paper, paste-board, mill-board, and scale-board, were repealed, when the trade to America soon revived, except in the article of tea, on which a duty was continued, to be demanded on its importation into America, whereby that branch of our commerce was nearly lost; and that, in the year 1773, an Act passed, to allow a drawback of the duties of customs on the exportation of tea to his Majesty's colonies or plantations in America, and to empower the commissioners of the Treasury to grant licenses to the East India Company, to export tea, duty free; and by the operation of those and other laws, the minds of his Majesty's subjects in the British colonies have been greatly disquieted, a total stop is now put to the export trade with the greatest and most important part of North America, the public revenue is threatened with a large and fatal diminution, the petitioners with grievous distress, and thousands of industrious artificers and manufacturers with utter ruin; under these alarming circumstances, the petitioners receive no small comfort, from a persuasion that the representatives of the people, newly delegated to the most important of all trusts, will take the whole of these weighty matters into their most serious consideration; and therefore praying the House, that they will enter into a full and immediate examination of that system of commercial policy, which was formerly adopted, and uniformly maintained, to the happiness and advantage of both countries, and will apply such healing remedies as can alone restore and establish the commerce between Great Britain and her colonies on a permanent foundation; and that the petitioners may be heard by themselves, or agents, in support of the said petition.

Source: T. C. Hansard, *The Parliamentary History of England, Vol. XVIII, 1774–1777* (London: R. Bagshaw, 1812–1820), 168–71.

Tobacco Growing (1775)

This early account details the cultivation of tobacco in the colonies. Though grown in all of the colonies, tobacco was primarily a cash crop exported from Maryland, Virginia, and North Carolina.

This plant [tobacco] is cultivated in all parts of North America, from Quebec to Carolina, and even the West Indies; but, except in Maryland, Virginia, and North Carolina, they plant no more than for private use, making it an object of exportation only in these provinces, where it is of such immense consequence. . . .

One of the greatest advantages attending the culture of tobacco, is the quick, easy, and certain method of sale. This was effected by the inspection law, which took place in Virginia in the year 1730, but not in Maryland till 1748. The planter, by virtue of this, may go to any place and sell his tobacco, without carrying a sample of it along with him, and the merchant may buy it, though lying a hundred miles, or at any distance from his store, and yet be morally sure both with respect to quantity and quality. For this purpose, upon all the rivers and bays of both provinces, at a distance of about twelve or fourteen miles from each other, are erected warehouses, to which all the tobacco in the country must be brought, and there lodged, before the planters can offer it for sale; and inspectors are appointed to examine all the tobacco brought in, receive such as is good and merchantable, condemn and burn what appears damnified or insufficient. The greatest part of the tobacco is prized, or put up into hogsheads by the planters themselves, before it is carried to the warehouses. Each hogshead, by an act of assembly, must be 950 lb. neat, or upwards; some of them weigh 14 cwt. and even 18 cwt. and the heavier they are the merchants like them the better; because four hogsheads, whatsoever their weight be, are esteemed a tun, and pay the same freight. The inspectors give notes of receipt for the tobacco, and the merchants take them in payment for their goods, passing current indeed over the whole colonies; a most admirable invention, which operates so greatly, that in Virginia they have no paper currency.

The merchants generally purchase the tobacco in the country, by sending persons to open stores for them; that is, warehouses in which they lay in a great assortment of British commodities and manufactures, to these, as to shops, the planters resort, and supply themselves with what they want,

paying, in inspection receipts, or taking on credit according to what will be given them; and as they are in general a very luxurious set of people, they buy too much upon credit; the consequence of which is, their getting in debt to the London merchants, who take mortgages on their plantations, ruinous enough, with the usury of eight per cent. But this is apparently the effect of their imprudence in living upon trust. . . .

There is no plant in the world that requires richer land, or more manure than tobacco; it will grow on poorer soils, but not to yield crops that are sufficiently profitable to pay the expences of negroes, &c. The land they found to answer-best is fresh woodlands, where many ages have formed a stratum of rich black mould. Such land will, after clearing, bear tobacco many years, without any change, prove more profitable to the planter than the power of dung can do on worse lands: this makes the tobacco planters more solicitous for new land than any other people in America, they wanting it much more. Many of them have very handsome houses, gardens, and improvements about them, which fixes them to one spot; but others, when they have exhausted their grounds, will sell them to new settlers for corn-fields, and move backwards with their negroes, cattle, and tools, to take up fresh land for tobacco; this is common, and will continue so as long as good land is to be had upon navigable rivers: this is the system of business which made some, so long ago as 1750, move over the Allegany mountains, and settle not far from the Ohio, where their tobacco was to be carried by land some distance, which is a heavy burthen on so bulky a commodity, but answered by the superior crops they gained: the French encroachments drove these people all back again; but upon the peace, many more went, and the number increasing, became the occasion of the new colony which has been settled in that country.

Source: American Husbandry I (London, 1775), 222. Reprinted in *Selections from the Economic History of the United States, 1765–1860,* edited by Guy Steven Callender (Boston: Ginn and Company, 1909), 22–25.

Common Sense (1776)

Thomas Paine's pamphlet *Common Sense*, dated January 10, 1776, made a compelling case that the problems with England went well beyond taxation. Paine's inspiring essay rallied American resolve to fight for independence from the mother country. Over 100,000 copies of this seminal work were sold within three months of its printing.

Volumes have been written on the subject of the struggle between England and America. Men of all ranks have embarked in the controversy, from different motives, and with various designs: but all have been ineffectual. . . .

I have heard it asserted by some, that as America hath flourished under her former connection with Great Britain, the same connection is necessary towards her future happiness, and will always have the same effect. Nothing can be more fallacious than this kind of argument. We may as well assert that because a child has thriven upon milk, that it is never to have meat, or that the first twenty years of our lives is to become a precedent for the next twenty. But even this is admitting more than is true; for I answer roundly, that America would have flourished as much, and probably much more, had no European power taken any notice of her. The commerce by which she hath enriched herself are the necessaries of life, and will always have a market while eating is the custom of Europe.

But she has protected us, say some. That she hath engrossed us is true, and defended the continent at our expense as well as her own is admitted; and she would have defended Turkey from the same motive . . . for the sake of trade and dominion.

Alas! we have long been led away by ancient prejudices, and made large sacrifices to superstition. We have boasted the protection of Great Britain without considering that her motive was interest, not attachment; and that she did not protect us from our enemies on our account, but from her enemies on her own account, from those who had no quarrel with us on any other account, but who will always be our enemies on the same account. Let Britain waive her pretensions to the continent, or the continent throw off her dependence, and we should be at peace with France and Spain were they at war with Britain. . . .

But Britain is the parent country, say some. Then the more shame upon her conduct. Even brutes do not devour their young, nor savages make war upon their families; wherefore, the assertion, if true, turns to her reproach; but it happens not to be true, or only partly so, and the phrase parent or mother country hath been jesuitically adopted by the king and his parasites, with a low, papistical design of gaining an unfair bias on the credulous weakness of our minds. Europe, not England, is the parent country of America. This new world hath been the asylum for the persecuted lovers of civil and religious liberty from every part of Europe. Hither have they fled, not from the tender embraces of a mother, but from the cruelty of a monster; and it is so far true of England, that the same tyranny which drove the first emigrants from home, pursues their descendants still. . . .

I challenge the warmest advocate for reconciliation to show a single advantage that this continent can reap, by being connected to Great Britain. . . . Our corn will fetch its price in any market in Europe, and our imported goods must be paid for, buy them where we will.

But the injuries and disadvantages we sustain by that connection are without number; and our duty to mankind at large, as well as to ourselves, instructs us to renounce the alliance: because any submission to, or dependence on, Great Britain tends directly to involve this continent in European wars and quarrels, and sets us at variance with nations who would otherwise seek our friendship, and against whom we have neither anger nor complaint. As Europe is our market for trade, we ought to form no partial connection with any part of it. 'Tis the true interest of America to steer clear of European contentions, which she never can do while by her dependence on Britain she is made the makeweight in the scale of British politics.

Europe is too thickly planted with kingdoms to be long at peace, and whenever a war breaks out between England and a foreign power, the trade of America goes to ruin, because of her connection with Britain. The next war may not turn out like the last, and should it not, the advocates for reconciliation now will be wishing for separation then, because neutrality in that case would be a safer convoy than a man of war. Everything that is right or natural pleads for separation. The blood of the slain, the weeping voice of nature cries, "TIS TIME TO PART." Even the distance at which the Almighty hath placed England and America is a strong and natural proof that the authority of one over the other was never the design of heaven. . . .

It is the good fortune of many to live distant from the scene of present sorrows; the evil is not sufficiently brought to their doors to make them feel the precariousness with which all American property is possessed. But let our imaginations transport us for a few moments to Boston; that seat of wretchedness will teach us wisdom, and instruct us to forever renounce a power in whom we can have no trust. The inhabitants of that unfortunate city, who but a few months ago were in ease and affluence, have now no other alternative than to stay and starve, or turn out to beg. Endangered by the fire of their friends if they continue within the city, and plundered by the soldiery if they leave it, in their present situation they are prisoners without the hope of redemption. . . .

But if you say, you can still pass the violations over, then I ask, Hath your house been burnt? Hath your property been destroyed before your face? Are your wife and children destitute of a bed to lie on, or bread to live on? Hath you lost a parent or child by their hands, and yourself the ruined and wretched survivor? If you have not, then you are not a judge of those who have. But if you have, and can still shake hands with the murderers, then you are unworthy of the name of husband, father, friend, or lover; and whatever might be your rank or title in life, you have the heart of a coward, and the spirit of a sycophant. . . .

Every quiet method for peace hath been ineffectual. Our prayers have been rejected with disdain; and have tended to convince us that nothing flatters vanity or confirms obstinacy in kings more than repeated petitioning—and nothing hath contributed more than that very measure to make the kings of Europe absolute. . . . Wherefore, since nothing but blows will do, for God's sake let us come to a final separation, and not leave the next generation to be cutting throats under the violated unmeaning names of parent and child. . . .

As to government matters, it is not in the power of Britain to do this continent justice . . . for if they cannot conquer us, they cannot govern us. To be always running three or four thousand miles with a tale or petition, waiting four or five months for an answer, which, when obtained, requires five or six more to explain it in, will in a few years be looked upon as folly and childishness. There was a time when it was proper, and there is a proper time for it to cease.

Small islands not capable of protecting themselves are the proper objects for kingdoms to take under their care; but there is something very absurd in supposing a continent to be perpetually governed by an island. In no instance hath nature made the satellite larger than its primary planet; and as England and America, with respect to each other, reverse the common order of nature, it is evident that they belong to different systems. England to Europe—America to itself. . . .

[The king] hath shown himself such an inveterate enemy to liberty, and discovered such a thirst for arbitrary power, is he, or is he not, a proper person to say to these colonies, "You shall make no laws but what I please!" And is there any inhabitant in America so ignorant as not to know, that according to what is called the present constitution, this continent can make no laws but what the King gives leave to; and is there any man so unwise as not to see, that (considering what has happened) he will suffer no law to be made but such as suits his purpose? . . . [C]an there be any doubt but the whole power of the Crown will be exerted to keep this continent as low and as humble as possible? Instead of going forward we will go backward. . . . We are already greater than the King wishes us to be, and will he not hereafter endeavor to make us less? To bring the matter to one point, is the power jealous of our prosperity, a proper power to govern us? Whosoever says No to this question is an independent, for independency means no more than this, whether we shall make our own laws, or whether the king, the greatest enemy which this continent hath, or can have, shall tell us, "There shall be no laws but such as I like. . . ."

But where, say some, is the king of America? I'll tell you, friend, he reigns above, and doth not make havoc of mankind like the Royal Brute of Great Britain. . . . [L]et it be brought forth placed on the divine law, the Word of God; let a crown be placed thereon, by which the world may know, that so far as we approve of monarchy, that in America THE LAW IS KING. For in absolute governments the king is law, so in free countries the law ought to BE king, and there ought to be no other. But lest any ill use should afterwards arise, let the crown at the conclusion of the ceremony be demolished. . . .

A government of our own is our natural right; and when a man seriously reflects on the precariousness of human affairs, he will become convinced, that it is infinitely wiser and safer to form a constitution of our own in a cool deliberate manner, while we have it in our power, than to trust such an interesting event to time and chance. . . .

Ye that tell us of harmony and reconciliation, can ye restore to us the time that is passed? Can ye give to prostitution its former innocence? Neither can ye reconcile Britain and America. The last cord is now broken. . . . There are injuries which nature cannot forgive; she would cease to be nature if she did. As well can the lover forgive the ravisher of his mistress, as the continent forgive the murders of Britain. The Almighty hath implanted in us these inextinguishable feelings for good and wide purposes. They are the guardians of his image in our hearts. They distinguish us from the herd of common animals. The social compact would dissolve, and justice be extirpated from the earth, or have only a casual existence, were we callous to the touches of affection. The robber and the murderer would often escape unpunished, did not the injuries which our tempers sustain, provoke us into justice.

O ye that love mankind! Ye that dare oppose not only the tyranny but the tyrant, stand forth! Every spot of the old world is overrun with oppression. Freedom hath been hunted round the globe. Asia and Africa have long expelled her. Europe regards her like a stranger, and England hath given her warning to depart. O receive the fugitive, and prepare in time an asylum for all mankind. . . .

Source: Thomas Paine, *Common Sense: addressed to the inhabitants of America* . . . (Philadelphia: Printed and sold by W. and T. Bradford, 1791).

Letters between Abigail Adams and John Adams (1776)

Abigail and John Adams corresponded regularly when he was away on official duties. She discussed the politics of the time, and he valued her insights.

While independence was being debated in the Continental Congress, Abigail Adams questioned her husband on the colonies' readiness for defense. In her letter of March 31, she also pointed out that women might rebel if they were not accorded representation.

In his April 14 response to his wife, John Adams detailed what he saw as the defense strengths, especially of Virginia and North Carolina, and he spoke of the aristocratic tendencies of a number of the representatives. Adams was obviously amused by his wife's "saucy" request that he "remember the ladies," and his teasing reply suggests that men "are the subjects" and "have only the Name of Masters."

Abigail Adams to John Adams

March, 31, 1776

I wish you would ever write me a Letter half as long as I write you; and tell me if you may where your Fleet are gone? What sort of Defence Virginia can make against our common Enemy? Whether it is so situated as to make an able Defence? Are not the Gentery Lords and the common people vassals, are they not like the uncivilized Natives Brittain represents us to be? I hope their Riffel Men who have shewen themselves very savage and even Blood thirsty; are not a specimen of the Generality of the people.

I am willing to allow the Colony great merrit for having produced a Washington but they have been shamefully duped by a Dunmore.

I have sometimes been ready to think that the passion for Liberty cannot be Eaequelly Strong in the Breasts of those who have been accustomed to deprive their fellow Creatures of theirs. Of this I am certain that it is not founded upon that generous and christian principal of doing to others as we would that others should do unto us. . . .

I long to hear that you have declared an independancy—and by the way in the new Code of Laws which I suppose it will be necessary for you to make I desire you would Remember the Ladies, and be more generous and favourable to them than your ancestors. Do not put such unlimited power into the hands of the Husbands. Remember all Men would be tyrants if they could. If perticuliar care and attention is not paid to the Laidies we are determined to foment a Rebelion, and will not hold ourselves bound by any Laws in which we have no voice, or Representation.

That your Sex are Naturally Tyrannical is a Truth so thoroughly established as to admit of no dispute, but such of you as wish to be happy willingly give up the harsh title of Master for the more tender and endearing one of Friend. Why then, not put it out of the power of the vicious and the Lawless to use us with cruelty and indignity with impunity. Men of Sense in all Ages abhor those customs which treat us only as the vassals of your Sex. Regard us then as Beings placed by providence under your protection and in immitation of the Supreem Being make use of that power only for our happiness.

Source: Abigail Smith Adams, *The Book of Abigail and John: Selected Letters of the Adams Family, 1762–1784,* edited by L. H. Butterfield, et al. (Cambridge, MA: Harvard University Press, 1975).

John Adams to Abigail Adams

April 14, 1776

You justly complain of my short Letters, but the critical State of Things and the Multiplicity of Avocations must plead my Excuse. You ask where the Fleet is. The inclosed Papers will inform you. You ask what Sort of Defence Virginia can make. I believe they will make an able Defence. Their Militia and minute Men have been some time employed in training them selves, and they have Nine Battallions of regulars as they call them, maintained among them, under good Officers, at the Continental Expence. They have set up a Number of Manufactories of Fire Arms, which are busily employed. They are tolerably supplied with Powder, and are successfull and assiduous, in making Salt Petre. Their neighbouring Sister or rather Daughter Colony of North Carolina, which is a warlike Colony, and has several Battallions at the Continental Expence, as well as a pretty good Militia, are ready to assist them, and they are in very good Spirits, and seem determined to make a brave Resistance.—The Gentry are very rich, and the common People very poor. This Inequality of Property, gives an Aristocratical Turn to all their Proceedings, and occasions a strong Aversion in their Patricians, to Common Sense. But the Spirit of these Barons, is coming down, and it must submit.

It is very true, as you observe they have been duped by Dunmore. But this is a Common Case. All the Colonies are duped, more or less, at one Time and another. A more egregious Bubble was never blown up, than the Story of Commissioners coming to treat with the Congress. Yet it has gained Credit like a Charm, not only without but against the clearest Evidence. I never shall forget the Delusion, which seized our best and most sagacious Friends the dear Inhabitants of Boston, the Winter before last. Credulity and the Want of Foresight, are Imperfections in the human Character, that no Politician can sufficiently guard against.

You have given me some Pleasure, by your Account of a certain House in Queen Street. I had burned it, long ago, in Imagination. It rises now to my View like a Phoenix.— What shall I say of the Solicitor General? I pity his pretty Children, I pity his Father, and his sisters. I wish I could be clear that it is no moral Evil to pity him and his Lady. Upon Repentance they will certainly have a large Share in the Compassions of many. But [illegible] let Us take Warning and give it to our Children. Whenever Vanity, and Gaiety, a Love of Pomp and Dress, Furniture, Equipage, Buildings, great Company, expensive Diversions, and elegant Entertainments get the better of the Principles and Judgments of Men or Women there is no knowing where they will stop, nor into what Evils, natural, moral, or political, they will lead us.

Your Description of your own Gaiety de Coeur, charms me. Thanks be to God you have just Cause to rejoice—and may the bright Prospect be obscured by no Cloud.

As to Declarations of Independency, be patient. Read our Privateering Laws, and our Commercial Laws. What signifies a Word.

As to your extraordinary Code of Laws, I cannot but laugh. We have been told that our Struggle has loosened the bands of Government every where. That Children and Apprentices were disobedient—that schools and Colledges were grown turbulent—that Indians slighted their Guardians and Negroes grew insolent to their Masters.

But your Letter was the first Intimation that another Tribe more numerous and powerfull than all the rest were grown discontented.—This is rather too coarse a Compliment but you are so saucy, I wont blot it out.

Depend upon it, We know better than to repeal our Masculine systems. Altho they are in full Force, you know they are little more than Theory. We dare not exert our Power in its full Latitude. We are obliged to go fair, and softly, and in Practice you know We are the subjects. We have only the Name of Masters, and rather than give up this, which would compleatly subject Us to the Despotism of the Peticoat, I hope General Washington, and all our brave Heroes would fight. I am sure every good Politician would plot, as long as he would against Despotism, Empire, Monarchy, Aristocracy, Oligarchy, or Ochlocracy.—A fine Story indeed. I begin to think the Ministry as deep as they are wicked. After stirring up Tories, Landjobbers, Trimmers, Bigots, Canadians, Indians, Negroes, Hanoverians, Hessians, Russians, Irish Roman Catholicks, Scotch Renegadoes, at last they have stimulated the to demand new Priviledges and threaten to rebell.

Source: L.H. Butterfield, ed. *Adams Family Correspondence,* Vol. 1 (Cambridge, MA: Harvard University Press, 1963).

The Declaration of Independence (1776)

This document called for the independence of the thirteen American colonies from Britain. Unanimously adopted in Philadelphia by the Second Continental Congress on July 4, 1776, the text was written primarily by Thomas Jefferson, who drew, in part, from John Locke's theories of natural rights and government deriving its power from the governed.

Originally signed only by John Hancock, the presiding officer of the Continental Congress at the time of its passage, the Declaration of Independence was copied and sent to the colonial legislatures on January 18, 1777. Meanwhile, the other members of the Congress signed this document on August 2, 1776.

Action of Second Continental Congress, July 4, 1776
The unanimous Declaration of the thirteen United States of America

WHEN in the Course of human Events, it becomes necessary for one People to dissolve the Political Bands which have connected them with another, and to assume among the Powers of the Earth, the separate and equal Station to which the Laws of Nature and of Nature's God entitle them, a decent Respect to the Opinions of Mankind requires that they should declare the causes which impel them to the Separation.

WE hold these Truths to be self-evident, that all Men are created equal, that they are endowed by their Creator with certain unalienable Rights, that among these are Life, Liberty and the Pursuit of Happiness—That to secure these Rights, Governments are instituted among Men, deriving their just Powers from the Consent of the Governed, that whenever any Form of Government becomes destructive of these Ends, it is the Right of the People to alter or to abolish it, and to institute new Government, laying its Foundation on such Principles, and organizing its Powers in such Form, as to them shall seem most likely to effect their Safety and Happiness. Prudence, indeed, will dictate that Governments long established should not be changed for light and transient Causes; and accordingly all Experience hath shewn, that Mankind are more disposed to suffer, while Evils are sufferable, than to right themselves by abolishing the Forms to which they are accustomed. But when a long Train of Abuses and Usurpations, pursuing invariably the same Object, evinces a Design to reduce them under absolute Despotism, it is their Right, it is their Duty, to throw off such Government, and to provide new Guards for their future Security. Such has been the patient Sufferance of these Colonies; and

such is now the Necessity which constrains them to alter their former Systems of Government. The History of the present King of Great-Britain is a History of repeated Injuries and Usurpations, all having in direct Object the Establishment of an absolute Tyranny over these States. To prove this, let Facts be submitted to a candid World.

HE has refused his Assent to Laws, the most wholesome and necessary for the public Good.

HE has forbidden his Governors to pass Laws of immediate and pressing Importance, unless suspended in their Operation till his Assent should be obtained; and when so suspended, he has utterly neglected to attend to them.

HE has refused to pass other Laws for the Accommodation of large Districts of People, unless those People would relinquish the Right of Representation in the Legislature, a Right inestimable to them, and formidable to Tyrants only.

HE has called together Legislative Bodies at Places unusual, uncomfortable, and distant from the Depository of their public Records, for the sole Purpose of fatiguing them into Compliance with his Measures.

HE has dissolved Representative Houses repeatedly, for opposing with manly Firmness his Invasions on the Rights of the People.

HE has refused for a long Time, after such Dissolutions, to cause others to be elected; whereby the Legislative Powers, incapable of the Annihilation, have returned to the People at large for their exercise; the State remaining in the mean time exposed to all the Dangers of Invasion from without, and the Convulsions within.

HE has endeavoured to prevent the Population of these States; for that Purpose obstructing the Laws for Naturalization of Foreigners; refusing to pass others to encourage their Migrations hither, and raising the Conditions of new Appropriations of Lands.

HE has obstructed the Administration of Justice, by refusing his Assent to Laws for establishing Judiciary Powers.

HE has made Judges dependent on his Will alone, for the Tenure of their Offices, and the Amount and Payment of their Salaries.

HE has erected a Multitude of new Offices, and sent hither Swarms of Officers to harrass our People, and eat out their Substance.

HE has kept among us, in Times of Peace, Standing Armies, without the consent of our Legislatures.

HE has affected to render the Military independent of and superior to the Civil Power.

HE has combined with others to subject us to a Jurisdiction foreign to our Constitution, and unacknowledged by our Laws; giving his Assent to their Acts of pretended Legislation:

FOR quartering large Bodies of Armed Troops among us;

FOR protecting them, by a mock Trial, from Punishment for any Murders which they should commit on the Inhabitants of these States:

FOR cutting off our Trade with all Parts of the World:

FOR imposing Taxes on us without our Consent:

FOR depriving us, in many Cases, of the Benefits of Trial by Jury:

FOR transporting us beyond Seas to be tried for pretended Offences:

FOR abolishing the free System of English Laws in a neighbouring Province, establishing therein an arbitrary Government, and enlarging its Boundaries, so as to render it at once an Example and fit Instrument for introducing the same absolute Rules into these Colonies:

FOR taking away our Charters, abolishing our most valuable Laws, and altering fundamentally the Forms of our Governments:

FOR suspending our own Legislatures, and declaring themselves invested with Power to legislate for us in all Cases whatsoever.

HE has abdicated Government here, by declaring us out of his Protection and waging War against us.

HE has plundered our Seas, ravaged our Coasts, burnt our Towns, and destroyed the Lives of our People.

HE is, at this Time, transporting large Armies of foreign Mercenaries to compleat the Works of Death, Desolation, and Tyranny, already begun with circumstances of Cruelty and Perfidy, scarcely paralleled in the most barbarous Ages, and totally unworthy the Head of a civilized Nation.

HE has constrained our fellow Citizens taken Captive on the high Seas to bear Arms against their Country, to become the Executioners of their Friends and Brethren, or to fall themselves by their Hands.

HE has excited domestic Insurrections amongst us, and has endeavoured to bring on the Inhabitants of our Frontiers, the merciless Indian Savages, whose known Rule of Warfare, is an undistinguished Destruction, of all Ages, Sexes and Conditions.

IN every stage of these Oppressions we have Petitioned for Redress in the most humble Terms: Our repeated Petitions have been answered only by repeated Injury. A Prince, whose Character is thus marked by every act which may define a Tyrant, is unfit to be the Ruler of a free People.

NOR have we been wanting in Attentions to our British Brethren. We have warned them from Time to Time of Attempts by their Legislature to extend an unwarrantable Jurisdiction over us. We have reminded them of the Circumstances of our Emigration and Settlement here. We have appealed to their native Justice and Magnanimity, and we have conjured them by the Ties of our common Kindred to disavow these Usurpations, which, would inevitably interrupt our Connections and Correspondence. They too have been deaf to the Voice of Justice and of Consanguinity. We must, therefore, acquiesce in the Necessity, which denounces our Separation, and hold them, as we hold the rest of Mankind, Enemies in War, in Peace, Friends.

WE, therefore, the Representatives of the UNITED STATES OF AMERICA, in GENERAL CONGRESS, Assembled, appealing to the Supreme Judge of the World for the Rectitude of our Intentions, do, in the Name, and by Authority of the good People of these Colonies, solemnly Publish and Declare, That these United Colonies are, and of Right ought to be, FREE AND INDEPENDENT STATES; that they are absolved from all Allegiance to the British Crown, and that all political Connection between them and the State of Great-Britain, is and ought to be totally dissolved; and that as FREE AND INDEPENDENT STATES, they have full Power to levy War, conclude Peace, contract Alliances, establish Commerce, and to do all other Acts and Things which INDEPENDENT STATES may of right do. And for the support of this Declaration, with a firm Reliance on the Protection of divine Providence, we mutually pledge to each other our Lives, our Fortunes, and our sacred Honor.

John Hancock.

GEORGIA, *Button Gwinnett, Lyman Hall, Geo. Walton.*

NORTH-CAROLINA, *Wm. Hooper, Joseph Hewes, John Penn.*

SOUTH-CAROLINA, *Edward Rutledge, Thos Heyward, junr., Thomas Lynch, junr., Arthur Middleton.*

MARYLAND, *Samuel Chase, Wm. Paca, Thos. Stone, Charles Carroll, of Carrollton.*

VIRGINIA, *George Wythe, Richard Henry Lee, Ths. Jefferson, Benja. Harrison, Thos. Nelson, jr., Francis Lightfoot Lee, Carter Braxton.*

PENNSYLVANIA, *Robt. Morris, Benjamin Rush, Benja. Franklin, John Morton, Geo. Clymer, Jas. Smith, Geo. Taylor, James Wilson, Geo. Ross.*

DELAWARE, *Caesar Rodney, Geo. Read.*

NEW-YORK, *Wm. Floyd, Phil. Livingston, Frank Lewis, Lewis Morris.*

NEW-JERSEY, *Richd. Stockton, Jno. Witherspoon, Fras. Hopkinson, John Hart, Abra. Clark.*

NEW-HAMPSHIRE, *Josiah Bartlett, Wm. Whipple, Matthew Thornton.*

MASSACHUSETTS-BAY, *Saml. Adams, John Adams, Robt. Treat Paine, Elbridge Gerry.*

RHODE-ISLAND AND PROVIDENCE, *C. Step. Hopkins, William Ellery.*

CONNECTICUT, *Roger Sherman, Saml. Huntington, Wm. Williams, Oliver Wolcott.*

IN CONGRESS, JANUARY 18, 1777.

Source: Journals of the American Congress: from 1774 to 1788, Vol. 1, Thursday, July 4, 1776 (Washington, DC: 1823).

Glossary

A

Abatis. A defensive obstacle made by laying felled trees on top of one another with the branches, sometimes sharpened, facing the enemy.

Absentee landlord. A proprietor who lives in a country or district other than that where his estate or business is located. Also called an absentee.

Ad valorem. A term that describes a tax or duty on goods that is set at a percentage of the value of the goods.

Adelantado. The Spanish term for the governor of a province or colony.

Adjutant. *See* Aide-de-camp.

Aide-de-camp. Usually a military officer, but occasionally a civilian, acting as secretary and confidential assistant to a superior officer of general or flag rank. Also may be called an adjutant.

Albany Congress of 1754. Often mistakenly referred to as the Albany Convention, the 1754 Albany Congress was a conclave of colonial representatives who met to work out collective relations with Native Americans and to push for a collective colonial government.

Albany Convention. 1) An independent ruling body formed in Albany, New York, in 1689, which was opposed to rebel leader Jacob Leisler's control of the colony of New York, because it feared that his policies would alienate the colony's Iroquois allies. Following a combined French and Native American raid on Schenectady in 1690, the convention relinquished its opposition in favor of mutual defense. 2) This also is an alternate name for the Albany Congress of 1754.

Almshouse. A home for the poor that is maintained by private charity.

Alum. A white crystalline double sulfate of aluminum. It may be used medically as an astringent or styptic, as well as to set dyes in fibers or fabrics.

Amaranth. 1) Any of several annuals of the genus *Amaranthus* with dense clusters of tiny green, purplish, or crimson flowers. 2) The seed of amaranth plants used as a native cereal in Central and South America.

American Academy of Arts and Sciences. A society dedicated to scientific and philosophical studies. Founded in Boston in 1780, it is still in existence.

Amish. A major Anabaptist sect that took its name from Jacob Amman, a Swiss Mennonite leader, who came into conflict with other Mennonites over a practice known as "banning and shunning." Amman believed in the maintenance of this strict system of punishment for followers who broke the rules, as well as complete repudiation of all forms of "worldliness."

Animistic. Relating to animism, the belief in the existence of spirits that inhabit natural objects and phenomena, or of spirits separate from bodies.

Antinomian. One who follows the belief of antinomianism, a theological doctrine that originated in Germany around 1535, with John Agricola. Antinomianism maintains that through faith and the Gospel, man is saved and freed from the need to follow either Mosaic law—that is, the laws of the Old Testament—or the laws of man.

Apothecary. One who prepares and sells drugs and various compounds for medicinal purposes.

Apprentice. A trainee to a master craftsman in a given craft or trade in the guild system. (*See also* Guild system.)

Apprenticeship. *See* Guild system.

Arminians. Followers of Protestant religious leader Jacob Arminius. The sect rejected the Calvinist doctrines of predestination and election and believed that human free will is compatible with God's sovereignty. Also called Remonstrants or Remonstrators.

Assiento. A contract between Spain and other nations to provide African slaves to the Spanish colonies in the Americas, especially the contract made with Great Britain in 1713.

Azimuth. The horizontal angle of the observer's bearing in surveying, measured clockwise from a referent direction, as from the north.

B

Backcountry. Any sparsely inhabited or remote, rural region. In colonial America, the term was used to refer especially to the western reaches of the colonies.

Baronet. A British hereditary title of honor reserved for commoners, ranking immediately below the barons and above all orders of knighthood, except the order of the Garter.

Basque. An ethnic group of unknown origin, inhabiting the western Pyrenees and the Bay of Biscay in France and Spain.

Bastion. 1) A projecting part of a rampart or other fortification. 2) A fortified stronghold.

Bawdy house. A brothel.

Bayonet. A dagger-like blade adapted to fit on the muzzle of a rifle or musket for use in close combat.

Belles-lettres. Literature created as an end in itself, rather than for didactic purposes or informative content, such as most fiction, poetry, and drama.

Belletristic. Of, or pertaining to, belles-lettres, i.e., light, entertaining, and more sophisticated literature.

Benefit of clergy. The exemption of a clergyman from trial in a civil court.

Bermuda Company. A land company chartered by King James I in 1615 to govern Bermuda. The charter was rescinded in1684, and Bermuda became a British Crown colony.

Bicameral legislature. A system of government where the legislature is composed of two legislative chambers or branches. Examples of bicameral legislatures include the British government's House of Commons and House of Lords, and the United States Congress, composed of the Senate and the House of Representatives.

Bill of exchange. A document binding the signer or signers to pay a certain sum to the bearer either on a specific date or on demand, with or without interest, as specified in the document.

Bison. Popularly known as buffaloes, a wild bovine with a shaggy mane. Once roamed in the millions from the Appalachians to the Rockies, serving as many native peoples' main source of meat and hides.

Blockade. 1) The act of isolating a nation, city, or harbor by using enemy ships to prevent the entrance and exit of traffic and supplies. 2) The ships enforcing such isolation.

Bog iron. A variety of brown iron ore, or limonite, found in boggy or swampy land.

Borough. In England, an incorporated town with certain political and legal rights, such as self-government and the right to send a representative to Parliament.

Boston Latin School. A boys' school founded in Boston in 1635 and the first public school in North America.

Boycott. To refuse to use or buy certain goods and/or to deal with certain persons or companies as an expression of protest or disfavor.

Broadsheet. *See* Broadside.

Broadside. 1) In military terms, a broadside may refer to all the guns along one side of a ship, or to the firing of all the guns on one side of a ship simultaneously. 2) In printing, a broadside may be either a large sheet of paper, usually printed on one side, or a published piece, such as an advertisement or public notice, that is printed on a broadside. Such a publication also may be called a broadsheet.

C

Cacique. 1) Spanish adaptation of the Taino word for "chief." 2) An Indian chief, especially in the Spanish West Indies and other parts of Latin America during colonial and postcolonial times.

Cajun. A corruption of Acadian, used to describe the descendants of the Acadians, who migrated to Louisiana after their expulsion from what would become the Maritime Provinces of Canada.

Calabash. A variety of gourd that can be dried and used to make containers or utensils.

Camp meeting. A religious gathering, usually held outdoors or in a tent and lasting for several days, during which attendees may lodge in tents or temporary houses. Also called a revival or revival meeting.

Carrying trade. The business of transporting goods from one place to another, usually carried out by someone other than the producer of the goods.

Casa de Contratación. In English, the "House of Trade." Founded in 1503 in Seville, the *Casa* was established by the Spanish monarchy to regulate trade in the Americas, which the Spanish considered private property. The *Casa* was also the agency that maintained the Spanish maps of the New World.

Cassava. The tuberous root of a tropical American shrub, also known as manioc. The sweet variety may be eaten as a vegetable. The bitter variety, which must be processed to remove its poisonous sap, yields a nutritious starch, the source of tapioca.

Catalan. The people of, and the language spoken in, Catalonia, a region of northeast Spain bordering on France and the Mediterranean Sea.

Catechism. A form of instruction, especially religious, by means of questions and answers. A set series of questions are asked, and the student must be able to answer them correctly.

Causeway. A roadway raised above ground level, usually across water or marshlands.

Cavaliers. The nickname for the Royalist supporters in the English Civil War.

Chancellor of the Exchequer. The member of the British cabinet in charge of the government income and expenditure.

Charter. A document issued by a sovereign or legislature that creates and defines the privileges and purposes of a public or private corporation, such as a colony, city, college, or bank.

Chattel. 1) A piece of movable property, such as coinage, furniture, or domestic animals. 2) Slaves were considered to be chattel.

Cholera. An acute infectious intestinal disease, caused by ingestion of contaminated water or food. Symptoms include profuse watery diarrhea, vomiting, muscle cramps, severe dehydration, depletion of electrolytes. If untreated, this disease causes death in many cases.

Circumferentor. A surveying instrument used for taking horizontal angles and bearings, also known as a surveyor's compass. It consists of a compass marked in degrees and a horizontal brass bar with uprights with narrow slits for sighting at each end. The whole instrument is usually supported on a tripod by a ball-and-socket joint.

Civet. A collective name for several catlike mammals. The North American species is a member of the skunk family, and it also releases a foul-smelling musk when in danger. It also is known as a civet cat, ringtail cat, or miner's cat (because it was used by miners to catch rodents).

Clapboard. 1) A long plank with one edge thicker than the other, used as siding for buildings by overlapping one board over the board below it. 2) The act of siding a building using clapboards.

Coin clipping. A crime involving slicing off slivers of silver or gold from the edges of coins and then melting those slivers down into bullion. Since the value of the coin was equal to the value of the metal, a clipped coin would be of lesser value than an unclipped coin. If the clipping was done discreetly, however, the debased coin could be spent as a whole coin, while the criminal could profit by selling the metal shaving.

Coldstream Guards. An elite regiment of the British Army.

Column. In military terms, a body of troops formed in even ranks, one behind the other.

Commonplace book. A personal journal in which quotable passages, literary excerpts, comments, and ideas or events one wishes to remember are recorded.

Commons. 1) A building or hall for dining at a university or college. 2) Land set aside for common use by members of the community.

Compagnie de la Nouvelle-France. See *Compagnie des Cent Associes.*

Compagnie des Cent Associes. One of the companies chartered by the King of France for the exploration and development of New France. Created in 1627 by Cardinal de Richelieu, it brought together approximately 100 associates who promised to populate New France by sending 4,000 Catholic settlers to North America over a fifteen-year period. The company failed in this promise and was dissolved in 1663. Also called the *Compagnie de la Nouvelle-France.*

Company of One Hundred Associates. *See Compagnie des Cent Associes.*

Company of Royal Adventurers to Africa. A trading company that was granted a monopoly over the African slave trade by Charles II of England in 1660. The company collapsed in 1667, to be succeeded by the Royal African Company in 1672.

Congregationalism. 1) In general, a type of church government in which each local congregation is self-governing. 2) The system of government and religious beliefs of the Congregationalists, a Protestant denomination.

Continental army. Formed in Massachusetts after the first battle of the Revolution at Lexington and Concord in April 1775, this became the regular army of patriots who fought for colonial independence. After the Second Continental Congress in July 1776, it was led by George Washington.

Consistory. In the Anglican Church, a diocesan court presided over by a bishop's chancellor or commissary.

Cooper. An artisan who builds and repairs wooden barrels, casks, and tubs.

Cooperage. A cooper's place of business.

Cordage. 1) Rope or cord. 2) Anything made of rope or cord, especially the ropes in a ship's rigging.

Coulter. A vertical blade or wheel mounted on a plow that cuts the ground ahead of the plowshare.

Council for New England. Founded in 1621, the Council for New England was granted a royal charter for the lands between Philadelphia and the south coast of Newfoundland. The governor and head of this council, Frederic Gorges, was responsible only to the Crown and had the right to grant land charters. The council was dissolved in 1639.

Counting house. A building or office used by the accounting and bookkeeping part of a business.

Coureurs des bois. 1) Literally, "woods runners." 2) A woodsman or guide employed by a fur company to transport goods and supplies between remote stations in Canada. Also called *voyageurs.*

Covenant Chain. A military and trade alliance between the Iroquois Confederation and non-Iroquois tribes of New York, Pennsylvania, and the Ohio River Valley. The non-Iroquois tribes had no vote or direct representation in the ruling Iroquoian Council. The terms of the arrangement made the Iroquois the only group permitted to negotiate trade and alliances with the Europeans. In return, the Iroquois agreed to protect those in the alliance from intertribal warfare.

Covenanter. A Scottish Presbyterian who supported either the National Covenant of 1638 or the Solemn League and Covenant of 1643, both documents that defended Presbyterianism.

Coverture. 1) Literally, concealment, shelter, or protection. 2) Legally, the state of a woman during marriage, because she is considered under the power and protection of her husband.

Creole. 1) In linguistics, a language or dialect that arises from contact between two other languages and has features of both. Also called a pidgin. 2) In terms of ethnicity, a person from one of the following groups: descendants of the original French settlers of the southern United States (especially Louisiana), those of European descent born in South America or the West Indies, descendants of the Spanish or Portuguese settlers of the Gulf States, or those of mixed African and European ancestry who speak a creolized language, especially one based on French or Spanish.

Criollo. Spanish for creole.

Crop rotation. A system of planting the same land with

different crops over successive seasons or years, in order to replenish the nutrients in the soil.

Crown colony. An overseas territory of Britain that was governed directly by officials appointed by the British government (as opposed to a colony founded by a land investment company, which was governed by systems established by the company and the colonists). Also called a royal colony.

Curtesy. In English common law, the right of a man to use, but not sell, his wife's property after her death.

Customs house. A building where customs and duties on imported and exported goods are collected, and where ships are cleared for entering or leaving the country.

Cyclometer. An instrument that records the revolutions of a wheel to indicate distance traveled.

D

Deacon. A layman elected by the congregation of a church to assist the minister in worship, in pastoral care, and on administrative committees.

Dead reckoning. A method of estimating the position of a ship without using celestial observations. Taking the last known position of the ship, one uses the compass heading and distance traveled since that position to determine the current position.

Dengue. An acute, infectious, tropical viral disease transmitted by mosquitoes and characterized by high fever, rash, headache, and severe muscle and joint pain. If untreated, it can be fatal.

Diggers. A radical political group in England during the Interregnum, the period from 1649–1660 between the reign of King Charles I and Charles II. Diggers were mainly peasants, who advocated a form of primitive communism. They argued that all land belonged equally to the whole of the English people, a position in direct opposition to the English social structure, which was based on a landed gentry and tenant farmers.

Diphtheria. A very dangerous, contagious disease, in which the air passages, especially the throat, become coated with a false membrane, causing difficulty in breathing, high fever, and weakness. The disease may cause permanent damage to the heart and central nervous system, and, possibly, death.

Disorderly house. A legal term for a house in which the residents' conduct is likely to become a public nuisance or a house where persons congregate in a way that is likely to cause a disturbance of the peace or other crime. This would include brothels, gaming and betting houses, and other disorderly places of entertainment.

Dockyard. An area with facilities for building and repairing ships. Also called a shipyard.

Doctrina. A Spanish mission compound, including the church complex and surrounding Native American villages, which provided crops and labor to support the community.

Doublet. A close-fitting garment for men, covering the body from the neck to the waist or just below, either with or without sleeves. It was worn by European men from the fifteenth through the seventeenth century.

Dower. The right of a widow to use, but not sell, the property of her late husband.

Dowry. 1) Most commonly, money or property brought by a bride to her husband when they marry. 2) Dowry may also be equated with the bride price (a sum paid to the bride's father by the groom for permission to wed), or a gift of money or lands from the groom to the bride on marriage.

Dropsy. A swelling from excessive accumulation of watery fluid in tissue. In modern medical terminology, edema.

Dysentery. An inflammatory intestinal disease, usually caused by a bacterial, parasitic, or protozoan infection. Characterized by pain, fever, and severe diarrhea, often accompanied by the passage of blood and mucus, it was often fatal in colonial times.

E

Ecumenism. A movement promoting unity among Christian churches or denominations through greater cooperation and improved understanding.

Enclosure. In Great Britain, chiefly in the seventeenth through nineteenth centuries, the landed gentry were permitted under a series of acts of Parliament to claim lands that had previously been public or common property and literally enclose them using walls, hedges, or fences. The loss of the use of these lands forced many farmers and villagers into poverty, as they no longer had access to land where they could grow food or graze livestock.

Encomienda. 1) A system formulated by the Spanish in the New World by which native lands and people were "commended" to Spanish landlords, or *encomenderos*. The indigenous people were obligated to render goods and services as tribute to their *encomenderos*, who, in return, protected them and indoctrinated them to be Christians. While the Native Americans could not be sold, the system was often tantamount to slavery, due to abusive *encomenderos*. 2) The estate granted to the Spanish landlord under the *encomienda* system.

Engraving. 1) A print or illustration made from a block of wood or metal plate that has the design carved into it in reverse. The block or plate is inked to transfer the design to the paper. 2) The process of making such a block or plate.

Entailment. To limit the inheritance of property to a designated succession of heirs.

Entrada. 1) Spanish term literally meaning "entrance." 2) A term used to describe an expedition into unexplored territory for purposes of exploration or conquest. Especially used to mean Spanish expeditions in America during the colonial period.

Entrepôt. A center of trade, marketing, or commercial shipping.

Escheat. 1) A legal term describing the reversion of property of a deceased person to the state due to a lack of legal heirs or claimants. 2) The forfeiture of property to the state as a consequence of a crime committed, usually against the state. 3) The property in question.

Ethnography. The branch of anthropology that studies and describes human cultures.

Evangelicalism. A Christian doctrine that stresses the ultimate authority of the Bible and the importance of personal conversion and faith as the means of salvation.

Exogamy. A system requiring, by either law or custom, that members of a clan, tribe, or class marry someone from outside the group.

F

Fall line. 1) The geological feature that forms a boundary between an upland region and a coastal plain, across which rivers from the upland region drop to the plain as falls or rapids. 2) The low, east-facing cliff that parallels the Atlantic coastline from New Jersey to the Carolinas.

Fealty. 1) In the feudal system, the obligation of the tenant or vassal to be faithful to his lord. 2) The special oath by which this obligation was assumed.

Femme covert. 1) In Latin, "hidden women." 2) Signifies a woman's loss of legal rights and property once she became married and her legal identity was folded into that of her husband's.

Femme sole. Legal term for a single woman. (*See also Femme Covert.*)

Feudal system. The political and economic system of Europe in the medieval period (about the ninth century to the fifteenth century), in which the holding of land depended on the obligation of vassals to provide service to their feudal superior or the king, either in labor at the peasant level or in military service at the level of landholders.

Five Nations. Another name for the Iroquois Confederation before the inclusion of the sixth nation, the Tuscarora, in 1722. Refers to the original nations of the Iroquois Confederation: the Mohawk, Seneca, Cayuga, Oneida, and Onondaga.

Flax. 1) A plant that yields a textile fiber,which is woven to produce linen fabric. 2) The textile fiber itself.

Fleming. A native or inhabitant of the region of Flanders.

Flintlock. 1) A type of firearm, named for the method of firing. When a flintlock is fired, a hammer bearing a small piece of flint strikes the steel lid to a pan containing the primer (a small amount of gunpowder), which ignites and, in turn, ignites the main charge of powder in the barrel of the weapon, propelling a lead ball out of the barrel and toward its target. 2) The lock mechanism itself. Beginning in the seventeenth century, muskets, rifles, and pistols were manufactured with flintlock mechanisms.

Flying column. A force of troops equipped and organized to move swiftly and independently of the principal unit to which it is attached.

Freedman. A person who has been freed from slavery.

Freedom dues. A sum of money paid to an indentured servant at the end of his indenture. This payment also could be made in tools, seed, or, sometimes, property.

Freeholder. A person who holds land in fee simple, that is, outright, without limitation to any class of heirs or restrictions on transfer of ownership.

Froe. A cleaving tool with a sharp blade perpendicular to the handle, usually used to create wood shavings and shingles.

Fulling. A method of cleaning and increasing the weight and bulk of cloth by moistening, heating, and pressing.

Fulling mill. 1) A machine for fulling cloth. 2) The building that holds such a machine.

Fusilier. A soldier armed with a fusil, which is a light flintlock musket.

G

Garrison. 1) A fortified military post. 2) The troops at such a post. 3) When used as a verb, the act of supplying or assigning troops to a military post or the creation of a military post to defend an area.

Gauntlet. A form of torture used by some Native American tribes, in which two lines of men armed with clubs or other weapons were formed, facing each other. The individual to be tortured was then forced to run between the lines while being struck from either side.

Geechee. *See* Gullah.

General Council of the Massachusetts Bay Colony. *See* Massachusetts General Court.

General Court of the Massachusetts Bay Colony. *See* Massachusetts General Court.

Gimlet. A small hand tool for boring holes. It has a screw tip and a spiral grooved shank, with a handle perpendicular to the shank.

Grammar school. In British usage, a secondary school, teaching Greek and Latin, as well as other subjects, that prepares students for attending a university.

Gray's Inn. *See* Inns of Court.

Great and General Court of the Massachusetts Bay Colony. *See* Massachusetts General Court.

Great League of Peace and Power. Another name for the Iroquois Confederation.

Great Migration. A large-scale immigration between 1630 and 1640, when roughly 10,000 Puritans settled in the Massachusetts Bay Colony.

Great Negro Plot of 1741. A supposed conspiracy among slaves and poor laborers in New York City, both black and white, to burn down the city. The trials following the alleged conspiracy resulted in the death by burning or hanging of several slaves and laborers. Ultimately, almost a hundred slaves were tortured, hung, burned, or resold into slavery in the West Indies. Also called the

New York Conspiracy, Great New York Conspiracy, or New York Slave Revolt of 1741.

Great New York Conspiracy. *See* Great Negro Plot of 1741.

Great Seal. *See* Privy Seal.

Great Wagon Road. A wagon trail used by colonial settlers to move from Pennsylvania southward through the Shenandoah Valley along the flank of the Blue Ridge Mountains through Virginia and the Carolinas to Georgia. The road followed a Native American trail known as the Warrior's Path.

Great War for Empire. Another name for the Seven Years' War, known in the colonies as the French and Indian War.

Grenadier. 1) Originally, a soldier armed with grenades. 2) A member of the British Grenadier Guards (the first regiment of the royal household infantry) or a member of a special corps or regiment.

Gristmill. A mill for grinding grain.

Guild system. A system whereby craftsmen and those who wished to train in a given craft belonged to a guild. This association of persons in the same trade was formed to protect mutual interests, maintain standards, regulate the wages paid to workers, and the prices charged for goods. A guild member began as an apprentice to a master craftsman, who trained him in the craft and often supplied him with room and board in lieu of wages. Apprentices were usually contracted to a master for a set period of time. As his training proceeded and his skills increased, the apprentice could be promoted to journeyman and be considered a skilled craftsman, but he could not afford to open his own business and thus continued to work for a master for a wage. A master craftsman usually owned his own business, and he employed and trained journeymen and apprentices.

Gullah. 1) A people of African ancestry inhabiting the Sea Islands and coastal areas of South Carolina, Georgia, and northern Florida. 2) The creolized Gullah language (also called Geechee), which is spoken in isolated communities from eastern South Carolina to northern Florida. It is based on English but includes vocabulary elements and grammatical features from several African languages.

H

Habeas corpus. A legal writ to bring a person before a court or judge, especially to inquire into the cause of a person's imprisonment or detention, in order to protect his or her right to personal liberty.

Haberdasher. A dealer in small items commonly included in clothing and sewing, such as needles, pins, buttons, and trims. Also, a dealer in men's furnishings, such as shirts, ties, hats, gloves, and other items.

Haberdashery. The goods sold by a haberdasher, or a haberdasher's shop.

Habitant. 1) A vassal of a seigneur under the feudal system. Used in both France and French colonial Canada. 2) A settler of French descent in either Canada or Louisiana.

Half-way Covenant. An attempt by the Puritans to resolve a crisis of faith and increase church membership. Originally, in Puritan communities in America, only church members had the right to vote in church matters and take communion. Membership was attained by testifying before the congregation to a conversion experience or moment of revelation. As time passed, fewer children of members were testifying, and thus they were denied church membership. In 1662, a Massachusetts synod agreed that adults who had been baptized would be allotted a "half-way" membership. They could have their children baptized in the church, but neither they nor their children could vote or take communion until they had experienced conversion.

Handbill. A printed sheet or pamphlet, usually containing an advertisement or other announcement, intended for wide distribution.

Handfasting. A Scottish tradition of trial marriage. In handfasting, a couple agreed, before at least two witnesses, to live together for a year and a day. At the end of that period, if both were content with the marriage, or if the woman became pregnant, they would marry in the church or in a civil ceremony. Otherwise, they were free to separate.

Harrow. 1) In agriculture, a farm tool consisting of a heavy frame with sharp teeth or upright disks, used to break up and even off plowed ground. 2) The act of using this tool.

Headright. A grant of land for immigration. The Virginia Company granted fifty acres of land per person, or head, transported to the Virginia colony. The land was granted to the person who had paid the passage, rather than to the person transported. In Maryland, one hundred acres was granted to a settler, with an additional hundred acres for his wife, fifty acres for each of his children, and additional acreage for servants. Headright was intended to encourage settlers to bring their families and servants to increase the viability of the colony. It also encouraged wealthy people to pay for the transport of numerous indentured servants in order to gain title to lands, without necessarily immigrating themselves.

Hellfire Club. An exclusive English club that met irregularly from 1746 to around 1763, run by Sir Francis Dashwood. The club is rumored to have held sexual rites and satanic meetings at Medmenham Abbey beside the Thames. Also called the Medmenham Monks.

Hemp. 1) The fiber of the skin or rind of the cannabis plant, used to make rope, cordage, and coarse cloth. 2) Various fibers resembling true hemp.

Highwayman. One who stops and robs travelers on public roads or "highways."

Hogshead. 1) A unit of liquid measure that varied from 63 to 140 gallons. 2) A large barrel or cask with the capacity to hold this liquid measure; these containers were also used to store and transport dry goods, such as tobacco.

Hortatory. Marked by strong urging or encouragement, as in a speech or sermon.

Hosier. A tradesman who deals in hosiery and other knit goods.

House of Commons. The lower house of the British Parliament, composed of elected members from various towns, counties, and boroughs.

House of correction. An institution for the confinement of persons convicted of minor criminal offenses, such as vagrancy or disorderly behavior.

House of Lords. The upper house of the British Parliament, composed of members of the hereditary nobility and the clergy.

Howitzer. A short-barreled, muzzle-loading cannon that fires shells with high trajectories for a relatively short range (similar to a mortar).

Hudson's Bay Company. A trading company created by a royal charter from Charles II of England in 1670. The charter granted the company a monopoly over all trade with the Native Americans, especially the fur trade, in the region watered by the rivers and streams flowing into Hudson Bay in northern Canada.

Humanism. A Renaissance philosophy emphasizing secular concerns. Humanism advocated a belief in human dignity and man's capacity for fulfillment through reason and scientific method, and it often rejected religion. This intellectual and cultural movement was triggered by the rediscovery and study of the literature, art, and civilization of ancient Greece and Rome.

Humanist. One who supports the beliefs of humanism.

Humors. The four fluids of the body—blood, phlegm, choler (or yellow bile), and black bile—the proportions of which were thought to determine a person's disposition and general health.

Hutterites. Members of a major Anabaptist sect, named after Jacob Hutter, whom they chose as their leader in 1533. Hutter was burned at the stake in 1536 for refusing to renounce his faith.

I

Impress. To compel a person to serve in a military force. The British Navy sometimes impressed sailors by picking up drunks at dockside bars, or by forcibly removing sailors from colonial ships to serve on its naval vessels.

Infrastructure. Underlying base of an organization or system, especially the basic facilities and services necessary to the functioning of a community. These include communication, transportation, water supplies, sanitation, and public institutions such as schools, postal services, and prisons.

Inner Temple. *See* Inns of Court.

Inns of Court. The collective name of the four legal societies in London—Lincoln's Inn, Gray's Inn, the Inner Temple, and the Middle Temple—that have the exclusive right of admission to the British bar. Established sometime before the fourteenth century, each society takes its name from one of the buildings where schools of law were originally held.

Intendant. 1) The chief administrative official of a French province or colony, usually appointed by the monarch. 2) A royal governor.

Internecine. 1) Relating to struggle within a nation or organization. 2) A struggle that is ruinous or fatal to both sides.

Interregnum. 1) The period between the end of a ruler's reign and the beginning of his/her successor's reign. 2) In English history, this term is commonly used to refer to the period of Puritan rule after the English Civil War from 1649, when Charles I was executed, to 1660, when Charles II ascended to the throne.

Iroquois League. Another name for the Iroquois Confederation.

J

Jacobite. A supporter of James II (the last Stuart monarch), after his deposition in favor of William of Orange and James II's daughter Mary in 1688. Most Jacobites were Highland Scots or Irish, along with some groups from northern England. The name Jacobite comes from the Latin for James, which is Jacobus.

Jacobite Rising of 1745. The last major rebellion of the Jacobite sympathizers against the British Crown. The '45, as it became known, came to an inglorious end for the Jacobites with the defeat and near destruction of the Highland clans at the Battle of Culloden.

Janissary. A loyal soldier or official.

Jansenist. A follower of Cornelius Jansen, a seventeenth-century Roman Catholic bishop of Ypres, in Flanders, who espoused a doctrine that emphasized predestination, denied free will, and maintained that humans, by their very nature, are incapable of good. Jansen and his doctrines were condemned as heretical by the Roman Catholic Church.

Jargon. 1) In linguistics, a hybrid language or dialect. 2) Terms applicable to a specific subject.

Jeremiad. 1) A literary work or speech telling a tale of sorrow or disappointment, expressing a bitter complaint, or making a prophecy of doom. 2) A lamentation.

Joiner. A skilled woodworker who joins pieces of wood to make furniture and cabinetry.

Jurist. 1) A public official authorized to decide questions brought before a court of justice. 2) A legal scholar.

Justice of the peace. A judicial officer or subordinate magistrate appointed for the conservation of the peace in a specified district, with the authority to act upon minor offenses, commit cases to a higher court for trial, perform marriages, and administer oaths.

K

King William's War. The first of four wars between the French and the British in America over control of North America, which lasted from 1689 to 1697. The associated conflict in Europe was known as the War of the League of Augsburg.

King's Bench. The highest court of common law in England, which tries both civil and criminal cases. When the sovereign is a woman, it is called the Queen's Bench.

Kiva. An underground or partly underground chamber in a Pueblo village, used by the men for ceremonies or councils.

L

Land Bank. A 1740 institution in Massachusetts, which issued paper money to borrowers, whose loans were secured by real estate. The bank was dissolved by Parliament in 1741, on the grounds that it violated the Bubble Act of 1720. The dissolution of the bank left the subscribers and partners in economic turmoil.

Latitudinarians. A group of Anglicans active from the seventeenth through the nineteenth century, who were opposed to dogmatic positions of the Church of England and believed in allowing reason to inform theological interpretation and judgment.

Letters of marque. A license granted by a government to a private person to equip and arm a privateer in order to attack and seize the ships and merchandise of an enemy nation.

Levellers. Members of an English radical political movement that evolved in the parliamentarian forces during the English Civil War. The Levellers advocated the dissolution of Parliament as a corrupt body, universal male suffrage, equality before the law, parliamentary democracy, and religious tolerance.

Liberty Boys. Another name for the Sons of Liberty.

Liberty pole. *See* Liberty tree.

Liberty tree. A flagstaff or tree flying a flag that indicated support for the Revolutionary cause. Also called a Liberty pole.

Lime. Oxide of calcium, a caustic substance obtained by heating limestone or shells to a high temperature. Lime may be used to treat hides to remove the hair, to eliminate smells in privies, or to treat sails to whiten them.

Limner. An archaic term for a portrait painter.

Lincoln's Inn. *See* Inns of Court.

Lingua franca. A common language used by speakers of different languages, often for commercial purposes. It may be a hybrid language or creole.

Linsey-woolsey. A type of rough woven cloth made from a mixture of linen and wool. The mixture may occur in the spinning of the thread used to weave the cloth, or in the weaving itself, using linen for the warp (lengthwise) threads and wool for the woof (crosswise) threads.

Littoral. 1) A coastal region. 2) The shore between the water and the high water mark.

Liturgy. 1) A prescribed formula for public worship. 2) A book or collection of documents containing such a formula.

Lockjaw. *See* Tetanus.

London Society of Arts. *See* Society for the Encouragement of Arts, Manufactures and Commerce.

Long hunters. Professional trappers and hunters, who took hunting trips lasting for months at a time into the unexplored lands of what is now Kentucky and Tennessee, as well as into the Ohio River Valley. In the course of these extended hunts, they gained extensive knowledge of the native peoples, terrain, plants, and animals of these territories, knowledge that was passed along to other hunters and potential settlers.

Longhouse. A long communal dwelling, typical of the Iroquois tribes and built of poles and bark with a central corridor bordered by family compartments on either side.

Lord Privy Seal. The person who has custody of the Privy Seal. The office of Lord Privy Seal is a traditional sinecure office in the British cabinet, whose holder has no defined function within the government.

Low country. A low-lying area of land, especially the coastal plains of the Carolinas and Georgia. Sometimes used as one word: lowcountry.

Loyal Land Company. A land speculation company founded in 1749 by several prominent Virginia citizens, which received a patent for 800,000 acres located along the southern border of Virginia (now southeastern Kentucky), with the provision that the land be settled within four years. The Loyal Company obtained two renewals of the grant. In 1763, however, the Crown rejected further extension of the grant as part of the ban on western settlements that accompanied the Proclamation of 1763. The company's land claims were later upheld, and legal activities involving the company continued until 1842.

Lygonia. A semi-independent province created in 1643, granted to George Cleeves, between Cape Porpoise and the Kennebec River in what is now Maine. The province was annexed by the Massachusetts Bay Colony in 1658.

M

Magistrate. A civil officer, such as a judge or a justice of the peace, with the power to administer and enforce laws.

Malt house. A house in which malt is made from grain. This product is used in making alcoholic beverages, such as beer, ale, porter, and whiskey.

Manioc. *See* Cassava.

Manumission. The formal act of freeing a person from slavery. A manumitted slave usually had to carry legal documentation to prove that he or she was a free person.

Marian martyrs. Protestants executed for their beliefs during the reign of Mary I of England during the mid-sixteenth century.

Maritime. 1) Of, relating to, or bordering on the sea. 2) Relating to navigation or commerce on the sea.

Maroon. 1) A fugitive black slave, often living in communities in remote or wilderness areas. 2) To abandon with little or no hope of rescue.

Maroon Wars. A series of unsuccessful slave uprisings in Jamaica in 1725–1739 and 1795–1797.

Marrano. A Spanish or Portuguese Jew, who converted outwardly to Christianity in order to avoid persecution or expulsion. These forced converts often continued to practice Judaism in secret.

Marron. A variant spelling of maroon.

Marronage. Flight from slavery. Petit marronage was a temporary flight, to escape punishment, to visit communities of escaped slaves, or sometimes to negotiate for better treatment. Grand marronage was a flight with no intent to return.

Massachusetts General Court. The governing body of the colony of Massachusetts, formed in 1691. After the Revolutionary War, the legislature of the state of Massachusetts retained the name. Also referred to as the Great and General Court of the Massachusetts Bay Colony, and occasionally as the General Council of the Massachusetts Bay Colony.

Massachusetts Provincial Congress. A body formed after the Massachusetts Government Act of 1774 revoked the Massachusetts colonial charter. This congress operated as the government of Massachusetts outside British-controlled Boston. Its functions included promoting communications between towns, making decisions regarding the colony's future, and raising recruits and supplies for the Continental army.

Matrilineal. Tracing descent, and usually inheritance, through the maternal line.

Matrilocal. Centered around the residence of the wife's family. In a matrilocal society, a husband moves in with his wife's family after marriage.

Mennonites. A major Anabaptist sect, which traced its spiritual beliefs to the teachings of Menno Simons, a Dutch Catholic priest who renounced Catholicism in 1536.

Mestizo. A person born in Mexico, or in former Mexican territory in the United States, of an indigenous and a European parent.

Metacom's War. Another name for King Philip's War.

Métis. A child of mixed French-Canadian and Native American ancestry.

Mezzotint. 1) A type of engraving on copper, steel, or other metal, made by drawing upon a roughened surface, and removing the roughness in places by scraping in order to create shading. 2) An engraving produced by the mezzotint process.

Middle Passage. 1) The area of the Atlantic Ocean between the west coast of Africa and the West Indies. 2) The voyage through these waters by African slaves captured in Africa.

Middle Temple. *See* Inns of Court.

Militia. A force of civilians trained as soldiers but not part of the regular army.

Millennialism. A belief in some Christian denominations, literature, and folk religion that, at some point in the future, there will be a golden age of peace and prosperity, when Christ will reign. This is believed by some to be the final age before the end of the world.

Millwright. A craftsman who designs, builds, repairs, or maintains mills or mill machinery.

Miniature. A small painting, often a portrait, executed with great detail, usually on parchment or ivory.

Minor orders. In the Catholic Church, those of a lower rank than deacon in the church hierarchy, such as an acolyte, reader, or doorkeeper.

Moiety. One of two subdivisions of a tribe or clan, based on kinship traced through one parent.

Moravian. A member of a Protestant denomination founded in Saxony in 1722 by Hussite emigrants from Moravia, in central Czechoslovakia. There were colonial Moravian settlements in Pennsylvania and North Carolina.

Mortar. In military terms, a portable muzzle-loading cannon, used to fire shells at low velocities, short ranges, and high trajectories (similar to a howitzer).

Mourning war. A custom of the Iroquois and other native peoples, in which raids were conducted on outside groups to obtain captives, as part of the mourning process for a deceased family member. Sometimes the captives were killed to allow the bereaved to vent their grief; other times, the captives were adopted into the bereaved family as a replacement for the deceased member.

M. P. An abbreviation for Member of Parliament.

Mulatto. A person of mixed white and African ancestry.

Muscovado. Unrefined or raw sugar.

Musket. A long-barreled, smoothbore, muzzle-loading shoulder gun.

N

Nahuatl. The language of the Aztecs.

Narváez Expedition. A disastrous expedition commanded by Pánfilo de Narváez in 1527, under charter from the Spanish government, to establish a colony on the north rim of the Gulf of Mexico. Narváez took a party of 300 men to explore the Florida coast on foot. The party was stranded after becoming lost and separated from their ships. Only four men survived the expedition.

Negro Act. *See* Stono Rebellion.

New England Confederation. In 1643, representatives of the colonies of Massachusetts Bay, Plymouth, Connecticut, and New Haven met in Boston and adopted a written constitution to create a league for "mutual safety and welfare." The primary purpose of the league was the coordination of defense and the settlement of boundary disputes. Each colony was to manage its own internal affairs. Also called the United Colonies of New England.

New Learning. The fundamental precepts of deism, based on the writings of Francis Bacon, John Locke, and Isaac Newton.

New Sweden Company. A company established in 1637,

under the aegis of King Gustavus Adolphus of Sweden, for the purpose of trading furs and tobacco in North America. The company established a colony of Swedish, Dutch, and German merchants and traders called Fort Christina (named for the Swedish queen) on the site of what is now Wilmington, Delaware.

New York Conspiracy. *See* Great Negro Plot of 1741.

New York Slave Revolt of 1741. *See* Great Negro Plot of 1741.

O

Ohio Company. A land company formed in 1748 by investors from Virginia to sell Ohio Country land to settlers. The stockholders were granted 200,000 acres in the Ohio Country by the British Crown, on the understanding that they would sell it to colonists and build a fort to ensure the colonists' safety.

Oligarchy. 1) A form of government where the power is resident in a small group of people, who are often related to one another by blood and/or marriage, or are members of the same political faction. 2) The group itself.

Olive Branch Petition of 1775. A petition sent directly to King George III of England, bypassing Parliament, from the Second Continental Congress in a final attempt to avoid a war for independence. The petition asked for a moderation of taxation and other harsh measures imposed on the colonies by the British government, and it assured the king of the colonists' desire to remain loyal. George III chose to deny the petition.

Ordinary. 1) A weekly community gathering in New England towns, where the citizens prayed, ate, drank, and gossiped. 2) The bill of fare at a tavern. 3) An establishment at which food and drink is served.

Ordination. Consecration to the ministry, usually through a formal religious ceremony.

Orrery. A mechanical model of the solar system, which illustrates the relative positions and motions of bodies in the solar system by rotation and revolution of balls moved by an arrangement of gears and wheels.

P

Palatinate. A territory in what is now southwestern Germany, ruled by the counts palatine. Geographically, the Palatinate consisted of two areas: the Lower or Rhenish Palatinate (Niederpfalz or Rheinpfalz in German) in southwest Germany between Luxembourg and the Rhine River; the Upper Palatinate (Oberpfalz in German) in northern Bavaria, on both sides of the Naab River as it flows south toward the Danube, and eastward to the Bohemian Forest.

Palatine Germans. People from the area of southern Germany known as the Palatinate.

Paleo-Indians. A term used to refer to prehistoric Native Americans from the time they arrived in the Americas until around 5000 B.C.E.

Pandemic. 1) General, widespread. 2) In medical terms, an epidemic disease that spreads over a wide area and affects the majority of the population.

Pandering. Procuring customers for prostitutes; pimping.

Papacy. The system of church government headed by the pope.

Papal bull. An official edict or letter issued by the pope, often stating the Church's official position on a controversial issue or sanctioning or forbidding a given activity.

Papist. 1) A derogatory term for a Roman Catholic. 2) Used as an adjective to describe practices in a Protestant church that have Roman Catholic overtones.

Parson's Cause. A legal dispute involving the Anglican clergy in Virginia. The General Assembly passed a law commuting the salaries of the clergy from tobacco to currency, setting the rate of two pence per pound of tobacco for salaries, when tobacco was selling for six pence per pound. When the King vetoed the act in 1759, several clergymen sued for back salary. The most famous suit was by Reverend James Maury against a Hanover County parish in 1763. Patrick Henry defended the parish, decrying the interference of the king in repealing a law ratified by the colonial government. This case established Henry's reputation.

Pastel. 1) A drawing medium of dried paste formed into crayons. The paste is made of ground pigments and a water-based binder. 2) A drawing made with such pastel crayons.

Patronage. The power to make appointments to governmental or political positions, especially for political advantage.

Pays d'en haut. The French name for the Upper Ohio River Valley.

Pearlash. A crystalline substance produced from potash (made from wood ash) used in making soap, glass, enamels, and dyes.

Philomath. 1) Literally, a lover of learning. 2) A scholar.

Physiognomy. 1) The supposed science of discovering the predominant nature, characteristics, and qualities of the mind of a person, or a race of people, by examining the outward appearance, especially the features of the face. 2) The facial features, or general appearance, of a person or race.

Pidgin. *See* Creole.

Pillory. A wooden framework on a post, with holes for the head and hands, in which offenders were locked to be exposed to public scorn as punishment for relatively minor crimes.

Pinnace. A light boat propelled by sails or oars, which was used as a ship's boat for merchant and war vessels.

Pitch. A thick, dark, sticky substance, obtained from the distilled residue of coal tar, wood tar, or petroleum, that is used for waterproofing, roofing, caulking, and paving.

Plebeian. 1) Of or pertaining to the common people, or large groups of people. 2) Also may be used to mean vulgar.

Plowshare. The part of the plow that cuts the slice of earth or sod at the bottom of the furrow (trench made by the plow).

Polemic. An argument or debate, usually refuting or attacking a specific opinion or doctrine.

Polity. 1) An organized society with a specific form of government. 2) The manner of government and underlying principles of a society or organization.

Polymath. A person who is knowledgeable in many fields.

Porphyria. A genetic abnormality of the metabolism, which causes abdominal pains, sensitivity to light, and mental confusion.

Portage. 1) To carry boats and supplies overland between two waterways or around an obstacle to navigation. 2) The road or track used for the activity.

Potash. Crude potassium carbonate, a caustic substance derived from leaching, or soaking, wood ash. In a liquid solution, it is also called lye; evaporation of the liquid produces pearlash, a crystalline substance. Potash is used in making soap, glass, dyes, and enamels.

Predestination. A religious doctrine that teaches that God has chosen a selected group of people, known only to God, who will receive forgiveness of their sins and enter heaven upon death.

Presbytery. In the Presbyterian Church, an assembly or court consisting of all the ministers within a district and one ruling elder from each parish or church. This select group has general jurisdiction over the churches in the district, and it is next below the provincial synod in authority.

Presidio. A military outpost in the Spanish colonies of North and Central America, intended to control the Native American population in the area.

Privateer. 1) A privately owned and manned armed ship, which is commissioned by a government to fight or harass enemy ships. 2) The person who owns or captains such a ship.

Privy Council. A body of officials chosen by the British monarch as an advisory council to the Crown.

Privy Seal. The seal that the British sovereign uses in proof of assent to a document. In matters of minor importance, it is only necessary for a document to pass the Privy Seal; those of greater significance must also have the Great Seal.

Probate. The process of legally establishing the validity of a will before a judicial authority. A will must go through this process, which may be done in a special court, before the provisions of the will can be carried out.

Profiteering. To make excessive profits on goods in short supply, often through unfair practices, such as price fixing or gouging.

Proprietor. 1) A person, or group of persons, granted the ownership of a colony, with the right to establish a colonial government and distribute land. 2) The owner or anyone with controlling rights to a business, plantation, or other endeavor or property.

Prothonotary. The chief clerk in certain courts of law.

Publican. 1) Keeper of a public house (inn or hostelry). 2) Tavern keeper.

Pueblo Revolt of 1680. After years of religious persecution, forced conversion, and exploitation of their labor, the majority of the Pueblo tribes united to drive the Spanish out of New Mexico. They were so successful that it was twelve years before the Spanish returned.

Q

Quadrivium. In medieval education, the higher division of the seven liberal arts, consisting of geometry, astronomy, arithmetic, and music. (*See also* Trivium.)

Quartermaster. 1) In military usage, an officer responsible for the purchase and distribution of supplies for an army, especially food, clothing, and equipment. 2) In naval usage, the quartermaster is responsible for navigation, steering, communications, and bridge watch, and he supervises lookout.

Queen Anne's War. Another name for the War of the Spanish Succession.

Queen's Bench. *See* King's Bench.

Quinine. A bitter, colorless alkaloid powder or crystalline substance extracted from the bark of a chinchona tree. Used as a drug to treat malaria, other illnesses involving fever, and some forms of heart disease.

Quinoa. 1) A plant native to the Andes cultivated for its edible seeds. 2) The dried seeds of this plant, used as a high protein food staple and also ground into flour.

Quitrent. Dating from the Middle Ages, a fee paid in money by a freeman in lieu of services to a landlord.

Quivira. A legendary Native American city of immense wealth sought by Francisco Vázquez de Coronado, thought to be located in what is now central Kansas. It is generally accepted that the story of the city was a hoax engineered by the Pueblos to remove Coronado and his army from their lands.

R

Rack-renting. A practice of auctioning newly expired land leases to the highest bidder that usually resulted in exorbitant rents, called rack-rents, which the existing tenants could not pay. This, in turn, resulted in tenants being evicted from the lands their families had occupied, sometimes for generations.

Recollects. A French branch of the Franciscan order, established at Nevers in 1592.

Reconquista. 1) The Spanish word for "reconquest." 2) The centuries-long struggle between Christians and Muslims for the control of the Iberian Peninsula. The *Reconquista* ended in 1492 with the defeat of Granada, the last Muslim kingdom in Spain, by the combined forces of Aragon and Castile.

Redemptioner. An emigrant from Europe to America who paid for the voyage upon arrival by serving for a specified period as a bondservant. While indentured servants obtained written contracts to pay for their entire passage before they left Europe, a redemptioner usually paid part of his own passage in advance and promised to establish a contract to pay the remainder once he arrived in America. If a redemptioner did not establish a contract within a given period of time after arrival, his or her services were auctioned off to the highest bidder.

Redoubt. A small fort, usually intended to be temporary and often without flanking defenses, used especially to fortify the top of a hill, or for defense in hostile territory.

Reformed Protestantism. Another name for Calvinism.

Regenerate. Spiritually or morally reformed.

Regicide. 1) The act of killing a king. 2) The person who commits such acts. Specifically, in English history, one of the judges who condemned Charles I to death.

Regular. In military terms, a soldier who is part of a permanent standing army, as opposed to a militiaman.

Remonstrants or Remonstrators. *See* Arminians.

Repartimiento. 1) Spanish for a partition or distribution of property, especially of slaves. 2) An assessment of taxes.

Restoration. The return of the British monarchy under Charles II in 1660, after the Commonwealth era under Oliver Cromwell.

Revival. *See* Camp meeting.

Revival meeting. *See* Camp meeting.

Rigging. The lines and chains used aboard a ship for working sail and supporting masts and spars.

Rigging house. A building or business where rigging for a ship is prepared.

Ring shout. A traditional African American form of music, which combines a counterclockwise dance-like movement, call-and-response singing, and the percussion of hand clapping and a stick beating a rhythm on wood. The ring shout influenced later musical forms such as spiritual, jubilee, gospel, and jazz music.

Ropewalk. A long narrow pathway or building where strands of fiber, such as hemp, are twisted to manufacture rope.

Rosin. A translucent resin, yellowish to dark brown in color, derived from the sap of various pine trees, which is used to increase sliding friction, as on the bows of certain stringed instruments. It may be used to manufacture a wide variety of products, including varnish, ink, paper, and adhesive.

Roundheads. The nickname for the parliamentary forces in the English Civil War.

Royal Academy of Arts. The national academy of art for Great Britain, founded by George III in 1768. It is governed by the Academicians, selected from the most skilled British artists in all areas of the fine arts.

Royal Academy of Sciences. *See* Royal Society of London.

Royal colony. *See* Crown colony.

Royal Society of London. A society of leading scientists and scholars founded in London in 1660 to promote scientific discussion, particularly in the physical sciences.

It is considered the national academy of science for the United Kingdom.

S

Sachem. The chief of a Native American tribe, especially the chief of a confederation of the Algonquin tribes of the North Atlantic coast.

Sail loft. A loft or room where sails for ships are cut out and made.

Salting. A method of curing or preserving foodstuffs, especially fish and meat, using salt and/or a brine solution.

Saltpeter. Potassium nitrate or niter, one of the chief ingredients in gunpowder. It also may be used as an antiseptic agent in curing meat, as well as medicinally as a diuretic, an asthma medication, and an agent to induce perspiration and reduce fevers.

Sassafras. 1) A North American tree with brittle wood and aromatic leaves and bark. 2) The dried root bark of the sassafras tree, which may be used as a flavoring and is the source of sassafras oil. The oil may be used as a disinfectant; the bark has been used as a fever medicine and diuretic, as well as to treat kidney stones. The dried leaves produce the Southern seasoning and thickener called filé.

Sawmill. A mill for cutting raw lumber into boards.

Scabies. A contagious skin disease caused by a parasitic mite, characterized by intense itching and skin irritation.

Scarlet fever. An acute contagious disease, occurring predominantly among children, causing a scarlet rash, high fever, and, sometimes, death.

Schwenkfelder. A member of a religious sect founded by Kaspar von Schwenkfeld, a reformer who disagreed with Luther, especially on the deification of the body of Christ.

Scrapple. A mush of ground meat and meal, usually pork combined with cornmeal or flour, which is set in a mold and then sliced and fried.

Scurvy. A disease caused by a deficiency of vitamin C, characterized by spongy and bleeding gums, bleeding under the skin, and extreme weakness. Sometimes fatal, it was common among soldiers and sailors, as well as among laborers and prisoners without access to sufficient fresh fruit and vegetables.

Seigneur. A vassal of the French king under the feudal system. Used in both France and French colonial Canada.

Selectman. One of a board of officials chosen annually in New England towns to serve as the administrative authority of the town. Selectmen were empowered to make appointments and judicial decisions, as well as to see to the daily administration of town business.

Sephardic Jews. Jews descended from Jewish families driven from Spain by the Inquisition in 1492. Also called the Sephardim, or Spanish or Portuguese Jews.

Seven Years' War. A war over territorial control that began in 1756 and extended through Europe, North America, and India. Known as the French and Indian War in America, it was ended with the Treaty of Paris in 1763.

Sextant. A navigational instrument for measuring angular distances between objects, in order to ascertain latitude and longitude.

Shallop. A small open boat, fitted with oars and/or sails, used mainly in shallow waters.

Shaman. 1) A Native American spiritual leader and healer. 2) One who acts as a medium between the visible world and the invisible spirit world, and who practices magic or sorcery for purposes of healing, divination, and control over natural events.

Shilling. A silver coin of Great Britain, equal to twelve pence or one twentieth of a pound (before the British changed to a decimal currency in the 1970s).

Ship money. A tax levied on English maritime towns and shires to provide ships for war. Charles I's attempt to reinstate this tax was one of the factors that led to his deposition and execution.

Shipwright. A craftsman who builds and repairs wooden ships.

Shipyard. *See* Dockyard.

Shire. 1) A portion of Great Britain that was under the supervision of an earl. A shire was usually roughly equivalent to a county, but was sometimes a smaller area. 2) The division of land into shires.

Six Nations. Another name for the Iroquois Confederation after the accession of the Tuscarora in 1722. Along with the Tuscarora, the Six Nations included the Mohawk, Seneca, Cayuga, Oneida, and Onondaga.

Smallpox. An acute, highly infectious disease common during colonial times. Caused by the variola virus, symptoms include high fever and the eruption of blisters, and, untreated, it often leads to death. It was particularly virulent among Native Americans, who had little or no natural immunity to the disease.

Snuff. 1) A finely pulverized tobacco that can be drawn up into the nostrils by inhaling. 2) To take snuff.

Society for Promoting Christian Knowledge. A society founded by the Anglican Church in 1698 to distribute Anglican literature abroad.

Society for the Encouragement of Arts, Manufactures and Commerce. A society founded in London in 1754 by William Shipley to encourage the development of the arts, creativity, and commerce. Although the Society sponsored the first public art exhibition in 1760, its primary focus became industrial design and technology rather than fine art.

Society for the Propagation of the Gospel in Foreign Parts. A missionary body founded by the Anglican Church in 1701 to spread their beliefs and win converts abroad, including the American colonies.

Society of Arts. *See* Society for the Encouragement of Arts, Manufactures and Commerce.

Society of Friends. The formal name of the Protestant denomination commonly known as the Quakers.

South Sea Bubble. *See* South Sea Company.

South Sea Company. A British trading company founded in 1711 by Robert Harley, which was given a monopoly on trade in Spanish South America in return for assuming part of the government's debt. A frenzy of speculation in the company's stock ensued over the period from 1711–1720, but the company's profits from its trading ventures did not meet the claims it had made to investors. The South Sea Company collapsed in September 1720, after the level of trade in its stock led to a drastic drop in stock prices. The buildup and subsequent crash of stock prices is known as the South Sea Bubble, which had a disastrous effect on the British economy.

Speaking in tongues. To believers, the phenomenon of speaking a language unknown to the speaker during an episode of religious ecstasy, which to nonbelievers sounds like babbling.

Specie. Hard money, coin.

Spermaceti. A white, waxy substance obtained from the head of the sperm whale, used for making candles, ointments, cosmetics, and other products.

Stadholder. The governor of a province in the Netherlands. Also spelled *stadtholder*.

Stamp distributor. A British government official responsible for the sale of the stamps, required on newspapers, pamphlets, legal documents, commercial bills, advertisements, and other papers issued in the colonies, under the Stamp Act of 1765.

Star Chamber. 1) A fifteenth-century to seventeenth-century English court consisting of judges appointed by the Crown, which conducted its business in closed sessions on cases involving state security. Their judgments were often overly severe and arbitrary. 2) Any court or group that engages in secret, harsh, or arbitrary procedures.

States-General. The legislative body of the Netherlands.

Stays. A women's undergarment stiffened by metal or whalebone (or baleen). The stays were fitted to the upper part of the body and laced; various styles, shapes, and lengths were in vogue during different periods.

Stockade. 1) A defensive barrier made of timbers driven into the ground in an upright position, with each timber in contact with the next to form a wall or fence. 2) The area protected by such a barrier.

Stocks. A timber frame with holes in which the ankles and wrists of criminals were confined by way of punishment for relatively minor crimes. The stocks were usually located in a public area of a town, such as a marketplace, in order to shame the offender into better behavior.

Stono Rebellion. A slave rebellion that took place on September 9, 1739, near the Stono River in South Carolina. Approximately 20 slaves attacked a general store, killing the proprietors and stealing weapons, including firearms. They marched south, recruiting slaves at the homes and businesses they passed, and ultimately killing about 20 white people. The rebellion was quickly suppressed, and it resulted in the passage of the Negro Act in 1740, which forbade slaves to grow their own food, assemble in groups, earn their own money, or learn to read.

Subcutaneous. Beneath the skin. Usually used in reference to inoculations and other medical procedures.

Subscription library. A library, usually owned by a society or company, which extended borrowing privileges only to members. Each member paid a fee, or subscription, which supported the purchase of books, the housing of the collection, and the salaries of the staff.

Sumptuary laws. Laws intended to govern what different classes of citizens were allowed to spend on clothing, furniture, and so on, and to forbid or restrict the use of certain items, such as food, drink, or fabrics. The main purpose of such laws was to mark class distinctions and to prevent anyone from assuming the appearance of a superior class.

Swamp fever. Another name for malaria.

Syncretism. Reconciliation or fusion of differing systems of belief, as in philosophy or religion.

Synod. 1) Usually, an ecclesiastical council, or an assembly of church officials or churches. 2) A secular council.

T

Tacky's Revolt. An unsuccessful slave rebellion in Jamaica in 1760.

Tallow. The suet or fat of animals, such as cattle, sheep, or horses, which was used in foodstuffs and to make candles, leather dressing, soap, and lubricants.

Tan. To convert skins or hides into leather, often by treating with tannin (a vegetable-based astringent).

Tanner. An artisan who tans hides.

Tannery. A place of business where hides are tanned.

Tariff. A duty, or fee, imposed by a government on imported or exported goods.

Tetanus. An acute infection of the central nervous system caused by bacterial infection of open wounds. An early symptom of tetanus is spasms of the jaw and laryngeal muscles; this causes the jaw to lock and inspired the colloquial name "lockjaw" for the disease.

Thatch. 1) Plant stalks or foliage, such as reeds or straw, used as a roofing material. 2) To cover a building with such materials.

Theocracy. A government ruled by religious authority.

Theodolite. An instrument consisting of a small telescope, mounted so that it can be rotated both horizontally and vertically. It is used to measure angles in surveying, meteorology, and navigation.

Thresh. In agriculture, to beat the stems and husks of grain or cereal plants with a flail to separate the grains or seeds from the straw and chaff.

Tithe. A tenth part of one's annual income, either contributed voluntarily or due as a tax, often for the support of the clergy or church.

Tonsure. 1) The act of shaving all or part of the head, especially in preparation for becoming a priest or joining a monastic order. 2) The part of a monk's or priest's head that has been shaved.

Tory. 1) A British political party, now known as the Conservative Party. 2) During the Revolutionary War, Americans loyal to the British Crown were called Tories, or Loyalists.

Town meeting. A legislative gathering of the voters of a town for the transaction of public business, such as electing officials, passing laws, levying taxes, and settling disputes. Usually held annually.

Township. A subdivision of a county, having the status of a unit of local government with varying governmental powers.

Tract. A leaflet or pamphlet containing a brief treatise on a given subject, usually of a religious, philosophical, or political nature.

Transportation. In the penal system, the deportation of a convicted offender to a penal colony in lieu of other sentencing. The convict could be transported for life, or for a set period of time. In either case, he served his sentence as a laborer in the colony.

Transylvania Company. A land company formed in 1775 by Richard Henderson of North Carolina to exploit and colonize the area now comprising much of Kentucky and Tennessee. Henderson purchased approximately 20 million acres from the Cherokee Indians, in hopes of creating a fourteenth colony. The company was denounced by both North Carolina and Virginia, since the land in question lay within their charters. Neither the British Crown nor the Continental Congress recognized the colony. Although it failed as a company and a colony, the Transylvania Company succeeded in furthering the settlement of Tennessee and Kentucky.

Treenails. Wooden pegs used to hold structures together in lieu of more expensive metal nails.

Trivium. In medieval education, the lower division of the seven liberal arts, consisting of grammar, logic, and rhetoric. (*See also* Quadrivium.)

Turner. A skilled woodworker who carves or uses a lathe to form turned wooden pieces for furniture or architectural details.

Typhoid fever. A communicable disease marked by fever, diarrhea, prostration, headache, intestinal inflammation, and, sometimes, death. It is caused by a bacterium (*Salmonella typhi*) usually ingested with food or water.

Typhus. Any of several infectious diseases caused by the rickettsia bacterium, usually transmitted by fleas, lice, or mites. Symptoms of typhus include severe headache, sustained high fever, depression, delirium, and the eruption of red rashes on the skin. Sometimes fatal, it also is called prison fever, ship fever, and jail fever.

U

Unchurched. Not belonging to or participating in a church.

Unfree labor. Workers who were unable to leave their place of employment at will. Unfree labor included both slaves and indentured servants.

Unicameral legislature. A system of government where the legislature is a single legislative chamber.

Unitarianism. A Christian doctrine derived in part from the precepts of deism. Unitarianism denies the doctrine of the Trinity, believing that God exists only in one person. Unitarianism also puts great importance on rationalism and ethical living, with reason and conscience considered the only guides to religious truth. The tenets of complete religious toleration, innate human goodness, and universal salvation are central.

United Colonies of New England. *See* New England Confederation.

Universalism. A Christian doctrine, derived in part from the precepts of deism. The central tenet is the belief in universal salvation. Universalism places great importance on reason as the route to spiritual truth.

Ursulines. An order of nuns of the Roman Catholic Church, founded in the early sixteenth century and devoted to the education of girls.

V

Variolation. Inoculation against smallpox by deliberately infecting a healthy person through an incision in the skin. (*See also* Subcutaneous.)

Vestry. A committee of members elected to administer the temporal affairs of a parish.

Vestryman. A man who is a member of a vestry.

Vicinal. Belonging to or restricted to a limited area or neighborhood.

Visitas. Spanish missionary stations without resident priests, which were periodically visited by priests from an established mission.

Viticulture. The cultivation of grapes, usually for wine making.

Voyageurs. *See* Coureurs des bois.

W

Walloon. A French-speaking people of Celtic descent inhabiting southern and southeast Belgium and adjacent regions of France.

Wampum. A seventeenth-century currency made from drilled shell beads strung together in various lengths, which also had spiritual significance for some Native Americans.

War of the Austrian Succession. The name for the larger European conflict, the colonial portion of which is known as King George's War (1744–1748).

War of the League of Augsburg. *See* King William's War.

War of the Spanish Succession. The name for the European portion of the war from 1702 to 1713, known in the United States as Queen Anne's War.

Warrior's Path. The Native American trail that ran north and south through the Shenandoah Valley, extending from New York to the Carolinas. A major artery for hunting, trade, and warfare, it also had a branch that ran westward from what is now east Tennessee through the Cumberland Gap into what is now Kentucky.

Wattle and daub. A building method that uses interwoven rods and laths or twigs (wattle) plastered with mud or clay (daub) to form walls of simple dwellings or to fill in spaces in timber framed walls.

Werowance. A Native American chief who owed allegiance and tribute to the head chief of the Powhatan tribe.

Wheel. In addition to the common uses, a wheel could also be used as an instrument for torture or the punishment of heinous crimes, to which the offender was bound spread-eagled. His limbs were broken by striking them with an iron bar or other heavy tool, whereupon he was left to die. An executioner might also administer several blows to the chest to kill the offender. Thus, offenders were literally "broken upon the wheel."

Wheelwright. An artisan who builds and repairs wheels for vehicles.

Whig. 1) An eighteenth- and nineteenth-century British political party that was opposed to the Tories. 2) A supporter of the war against England during the American Revolution. 3) A nineteenth-century American political party formed to oppose the Democratic Party.

Whooping cough. A highly contagious respiratory disease, usually affecting children, characterized in its advanced stage by spasms of coughing interspersed with deep, noisy inhalations, sometimes resulting in death.

Wigwam. A Native American dwelling, usually having an oval or circular framework covered by bark, hides, or mats.

Wilderness Road. The road cleared through the Cumberland Gap by Daniel Boone and his companions, in order to allow settlers to travel to Kentucky more easily. The Wilderness Road followed a portion of the western branch of the Warrior's Path. Also known as the Wilderness Trail.

Windward Passage. The channel connecting the Atlantic Ocean with the Caribbean Sea (between Cuba and Haiti).

Winnow. 1) To separate the chaff, or husks of grain, from the grain itself by means of a current of air, after threshing. 2) A tool to perform this separation process.

Workhouse. A poorhouse where the town poor were maintained at public expense. Its residents were provided with labor, which was usually compulsory for the able-bodied.

Writs of assistance. Unlimited search warrants issued to customs officials under the Townshend Acts, which allowed them to search any vessel for smuggled goods at will. These warrants were seen by American colonists as an invasion of privacy, and contrary to common law.

Y

Yellow fever. An infectious disease common in tropical regions, which is caused by a virus transmitted by mosquito bites. During epidemics, the death rate could go as high as 85 percent. The name "yellow" fever arose from the jaundice of the skin that is a prominent symptom.

Primary Sources

Published Sources

"Acts, Orders and Resolutions of the General Assembly of Virginia, July 1, 1644," *Virginia Magazine of History and Biography*, 23 (July 1915).

Alvord, Clarence W., and Clarence E. Carter, eds. *Collections of the Illinois State Historical Library*. 40 vols. Chicago: R. R. Donnelley and Sons, 1915.

American Historical Documents, 1000–1904: With introductions, notes, and illustrations. The Harvard Classics. New York: P. F. Collier & Sons, 1909–1914.

Anderson, Robert Charles, George F. Sanborn, Jr., and Melinde Lutz Sanborn, eds. *The Great Migration: Immigrants to New England, 1634–1635*. 3 vols. Boston: New England Historical and Genealogical Society, 1999.

Andrews, Charles McLean. *Guide to the Manuscript Materials for the History of the United States to 1782*. Washington, DC: Carnegie Institution of Washington, 1908.

———. *Guide to the Materials for American History, to 1783, in the Public Record Office of Great Britain*. Washington, DC: Carnegie Institution of Washington, 1912–1914. New York: Kraus Reprint Corporation, 1965.

———. *Narratives of the Insurrections, 1675–1690*. New York: Charles Scribner's Sons, 1915.

Andrews, William L., ed. *Journeys in New Worlds: Early American Women's Narratives*. Wisconsin Studies in American Autobiography. Madison: University of Wisconsin Press, 1990.

Arber, Edward, ed. *The True Story of the Pilgrim Fathers, 1606–1623, A.D.; As Told by Themselves, Their Friends, and Their Enemies*. London: 1897.

Armstrong, Virginia Irving, ed. *I Have Spoken American History Through the Voices of the Indians*. Chicago: Sage, 1971.

Axtell, James, ed. *The Indian Peoples of Eastern America: A Documentary History of the Sexes*. New York: Oxford University Press, 1981.

Bain, James, ed. *Alexander Henry Travels and Adventures in Canada and the Indian Territories Between the Years 1760 and 1776*. New York: Burt Franklin Press, 1969.

Bakeless, John. *America as Seen by Its First Explorers, the Eyes of Discovery*. New York: Dover Publications, 1961.

Barbot, John. "A Description of the Coasts of North and South Guinea." In *Collection of Voyages and Travels*. Edited by Thomas Astley and John Churchill. London: 1732.

Barclay, Donald A., et al., eds. *Into the Wilderness Dream: Exploration Narratives of the American West, 1500–1805*. Reprint, Salt Lake City: University of Utah Press, 1994.

Barlett, John R., ed. *Records of the Colony of Rhode Island and Providence Plantation in New England*. 10 vols. Providence, RI: Printed by A. C. Greene by order of the State Legislature, 1856–1865.

Barreiro, Jose, ed. *Indian Roots of American Democracy*. Ithaca, NY: Cornell University Press, 1992.

Bartram, William. *Travels of William Bartram*. Edited by Mark Van Doren. New York: Dover Publications, 1955.

Baumgarten, Linda. *Eighteenth-Century Clothing at Williamsburg*. Williamsburg, VA: Colonial Williamsburg Foundation, 1989.

Beckerdite, Luke. "Architect-Designed Furniture in Eighteenth-Century Virginia: The Work of William Buckland and William Bernard Sears." In *American Furniture*. Milwaukee, WI: Chipstone Foundation, 1994.

———. "William Buckland and William Bernard Sears: The Designer and the Carver." *Journal of Early Southern Decorative Arts* 8 (November 1982): 7–40.

Bell, Whitfield J., Jr., ed. *A Journey from Pennsylvania to Onondaga in 1743 by John Bartram, Lewis Evans, Conrad Weiser*. Barre, MA: Imprint Society, 1973.

Benton, Helen H., ed. *The Annals of America*. 18 vols. Chicago: Encyclopedia Britannica, 1968.

Berkin, Carol. "Bibliographical Essay." In *First Generations: Women in Colonial America*. New York: Hill and Wang, 1996.

Berkin, Carol, and Leslie Horowitz, eds. *Women's Voices, Women's Lives: Documents in Early American History*. Boston: Northeastern University Press, 1998.

Betanzos, Juan de. *Narrative of the Incas*. Reprint, Austin: University of Texas Press, 1996.

Beverley, Robert. *The History and Present State of Virginia*. Edited by Louis Wright. Reprint of the 1705 edition, Chapel Hill: University of North Carolina Press, 1947.

Biedma, Luys Hernandez de. *Narratives of the Career of Hernando de Soto in the Conquest of Florida*. Edited by Edward G. Bourne; translated by Buckingham Smith. 2 vols. New York: Allerton Book Company, 1922.

Billings, Warren M., ed. *The Old Dominion in the Seventeenth Century: A Documentary History of Virginia, 1606–1689*. Chapel Hill: University of North Carolina Press, 1973.

Bluett, Thomas. *Some Memoirs of the Life of Job, the Son of Solomon the high priest of Boonda in Africa; who was a slave about two years in Maryland* . . . London: Printed for R. Ford, 1734.

Bond, Henry, ed. *Genealogies of the Families and Descendants of the Early Settlers of Watertown, Massachusetts, and Watertown Records.* Boston: New England Historical and Genealogical Society, 2002.

Book of the General Lawes and Libertyes Concerning the Inhabitants of the Massachusetts. 1648. Facsimile edition reprint, Cambridge, MA: Harvard University Press, 1929.

Bougainville, Comte Louis-Antoine de. *Adventure in the Wilderness: The American Journals of Louis-Antoine de Bougainville, 1756–1760.* Translated by Edward P. Hamilton. American Exploration and Travel Series, vol. 42. Norman: University of Oklahoma Press, 1990.

Bouton, Nathaniel, et al., eds. *New Hampshire State Papers.* 40 vols. Manchester, NH: 1867–1941.

Boyer, Paul, and Stephen Nissenbaum, eds. *The Salem Witchcraft Papers: Verbatim Transcripts of the Legal Documents of the Salem Witchcraft Outbreak of 1692.* 3 vols. New York: DaCapo, 1977.

Bradford, William. *History of Plimoth Plantation.* Boston: Wright & Potter, 1899.

———. *Of Plymouth Plantation, 1620–1647.* c. 1650. Edited by Samuel Eliot Morison. New York: Alfred A. Knopf, 1962.

Bray, Warwick, ed. *The Meeting of Two Worlds: Europe and the Americas, 1492–1650.* Oxford. UK: Oxford University Press, 1993.

Bridenbaugh, Carl, ed. *Gentleman's Progress: The Itinerarium of Dr. Alexander Hamilton, 1744.* Chapel Hill: University of North Carolina Press, 1948.

Brown, Alexander. *The Genesis of the United States: A narrative of the movement in England, 1605–1616, which resulted in the plantation of North America by Englishmen, disclosing the contest between England and Spain for the possession of the soil now occupied by the United States of America, set forth through a series of historical manuscripts now first printed together with a reissue of rare contemporaneous tracts, accompanied by bibliographical memoranda, notes, and brief biographies.* 2 vols. Boston: Houghton, Mifflin, 1890.

Brown, Rodney Hilton. *American Polearms, 1526–1865.* New Milford, CT: N. Fleyderman, 1967.

Bruce, Philip A. *Economic History of Virginia in the Seventeenth Century: An Inquiry into the Material Condition of the People, Based on Original and Contemporaneous Records.* New York: Macmillan, 1896.

Bucher, Bernadette. *Icon and Conquest: A Structural Analysis of the Illustrations of de Bry's Great Voyages.* Translated by Basia Miller Galati. Chicago: University of Chicago Press, 1981.

Buck, Solon Justus, ed. *Illinois Historical Collections.* 10 vols. Springfield: Illinois State Historical Library, 1914.

Burton, Clarence M., ed. *Journal of Pontiac's Conspiracy 1763.* Detroit, MI: Speaker-Hines Printing, 1910.

Byrd, William. *William Byrd's Histories of the Dividing Line Betwixt Virginia and North Carolina.* 1728. New York: Dover Publications, 1967; 1987.

Calder, Isabel M. *Colonial Captivities, Marches, and Journeys.* Edited under the auspices of the National Society of the Colonial Dames of America. Port Washington, NY: Kennikat Press, 1967.

Calloway, Colin G., ed. *Dawnland Encounters: Indians and Europeans in Northern New England.* Hanover, NH: University Press of New England, 1991.

———. *The World Turned Upside Down: Indian Voices from Early America.* Boston: St. Martin's, 1994.

The Cambridge History of English and American Literature in 18 Volumes. New York: G. P. Putnam's Sons; Cambridge, UK: University Press, 1907–21.

Campbell, Richard L. *Historical Sketches of Colonial Florida.* 1829. Facsimile Series, Gainesville: University of Florida Press, 1975.

Carey, Arthur Merwyn. *American Firearm Makers: When, Where, and What They Made From the Colonial Period to the End of the Nineteenth Century.* New York: Thomas Y. Crowell, 1953.

———. *English, Irish, and Scottish Firearms Makers: When, Where, and What They Made, From the Middle of the Sixteenth Century to the End of the Nineteenth Century.* New York: Thomas Y. Crowell, 1954.

Cariana, Adrian B. *Grasshoppers and Butterflies: The Light 3 Pounders of Pattison and Townshend.* Bloomfield, Ontario, Canada: Museum Restoration Service, 1979.

Carver, Jonathan. *Jonathan Carver's Travels through America, 1766–1768: An Eighteenth-Century Explorer's Account of Uncharted America.* Edited by Norman Gelb. New York: Wiley, 1993.

———. *Travels Through the Interior Parts of North America in the Years 1766, 1767, 1768.* 1778. Reprint, Minneapolis, MN: Ross and Maines, 1956.

Casas, Bartolome de las. *The Devastation of the Indies: A Brief Account.* 1552. Reprint, Baltimore: Johns Hopkins University Press, 1992.

Castillo, Edward D., ed. *Native American Perspectives on the Hispanic Colonization of Alta California.* New York: Garland Publishers, 1991.

Champagne, Duane. *The Native American Almanac.* Detroit, MI: Gale Press, 1994.

Chapa, Juan Bautista. *Texas and Northeastern Mexico, 1630–1690.* Edited by William C. Foster. Translated by Ned F. Brierley. Reprint, Austin: University of Texas Press, 1997.

Clinton, Catherine, and Michele Gillespie, eds. *The Devil's Lane: Sex and Race in the Early South.* New York: Oxford University Press, 1997.

Coe, Michael, Dean Snow, and Elizabeth Benson, eds. *Atlas of Ancient America.* New York: Facts on File, 1986.

Colket, Meredith B., Jr. *Founders of Early American Families.* 2nd ed. Cleveland: The Ohio Society for the General Court of the Order of the Founders and Patriots of America, 2002.

Colón, Fernando. *The Life of the Admiral Christopher Columbus, by his son Ferdinand.* Translated by Benjamin Keen. New Brunswick, NJ: Rutgers University Press, 1992.

Columbus, Christopher. *The Diary of Christopher Columbus's First Voyage to America, 1492–1493.* The American Exploration and Travel Series. Norman: University of Oklahoma Press, 1988.

———. *The Four Voyages of Columbus: A Documentary History.* Edited by Cecil Jane. New York: Dover Publications, 1988.

———. *The Log of Christopher Columbus.* Translated by Robert H. Fuson. Camden, ME: International Marine, 1987.

Commager, Henry Steele, ed. *Documents of American History.* 7th ed. New York: Appleton-Century-Crofts, 1934.

Condie, Carol J., and Don D. Fowler, eds. *Anthropology of the Desert West.* Salt Lake City: University of Utah Press, 1986.

Connecticut Particular Court. *Records of the Particular Court of Connecticut, 1639–1663.* Hartford: Connecticut Historical Society, 1928.

Connecticut Superior Court. *The Superior Court Diary of William Samuel Johnson, 1772–1773.* Washington, DC: American Historical Association, 1942.

Cooke, Jacob Earnest, et al., eds. *Encyclopedia of the North American Colonies.* 3 vols. New York: Charles Scribner's Sons, 1993.

Cooper, James F., Jr., and Kenneth P. Minkema, eds. *The Sermon Notebook of Samuel Parris 1689–1694.* Boston: Colonial Society of Massachusetts, 1993.

Copeland, David A. *Debating the Issues in Colonial Newspapers: Primary Documents on Events of the Period.* Westport, CT: Greenwood Press, 2000.

Cortés, Hernán. *Letters from Mexico.* Edited and translated by Anthony Pagden. New Haven, CT: Yale University Press, 1986.

Cortés y de Olarte, José Maria. *Views from the Apache Frontier: Report on the Northern Provinces of New Spain.* Edited by A. H. Elizabeth; translated by John Wheat. Norman: University of Oklahoma Press, 1989.

Costello, Julia G., ed. *Documentary Evidence for the Spanish Missions of Alta California.* New York: Garland Publishers, 1991.

Coto, Rupert, and Jeannette Henry Costo, eds. *The Missions of California: A Legacy of Genocide.* San Francisco: Indian Historian Press, 1987.

Coues, Elliot, ed. *The Manuscript Journals of Alexander Henry and of David Thompson.* 3 vols. New York: Francis P. Harper, 1897. Minneapolis, MN: Ross & Haines, 1965.

Coxe, Daniel. *A Description of the English Province of Carolina, by the Spaniards call'd Florida, and by the French La Louisiane.* 1722. Facsimile Series, Gainesville: University of Florida Press, 1976.

Crawford, Michael H. *The Origins of Native Americans: Evidence from Anthropological Genetics.* Cambridge, UK; New York: Cambridge University Press, 1998.

Daniel, Elizabeth, and Jeanne E. Sawtelle, eds. *Thomas Rogers,*

Pilgrim, and Some of His Descendants. Baltimore: Gateway Press, 1980.

Davis, David Brian. *Foundation of America Series.* Williamsburg, VA: Colonial Williamsburg Foundation, 1986.

Davis, David Brian, and Steven Mintz. *The Boisterous Sea of Liberty: A Documentary History of America from Discovery through the Civil War.* New York: Oxford University Press, 1998.

De Fuentes, Patricia, ed. *The Conquistadors: First Person Accounts of the Conquest of Mexico.* Norman: University of Oklahoma Press, 1993.

De Vorsey, Louis, Jr. *Keys to the Encounter: A Library of Congress Resource Guide for the Age of Discovery.* Washington, DC: Library of Congress, 1992.

Delaware. County Court, Kent County. *Court Records of Kent County, Delaware.* (Counties of New Castle, Kent, and Sussex upon Delaware.) Washington, DC: American Historical Association, 1959.

Delaware. New Castle Court. *Records of the Court of New Castle on Delaware.* 2 vols. Lancaster: Colonial Society of Pennsylvania, 1904–1935.

Deloria, Vine, comp. *Of Utmost Good Faith.* San Francisco: Straight Arrow, 1971.

Denevan, W. M., ed. *The Native Population of the Americas in 1492.* 2nd ed. Madison: University of Wisconsin Press, 1992.

Derounian-Stodola, Kathryn Zabelle, ed. *Women's Indian Captivity Narratives.* New York: Penguin Press, 1998.

Dibble, Ernest W., and Earle W. Newton, eds. *In Search of Gulf Coast Colonial History.* Pensacola, FL: Historic Preservation Board, 1970.

Dobyns, Henry F., and Robert C. Euler. *Indians of the Southwest: A Critical Bibliography.* Bloomington: Indiana University Press, 1980.

Drimmer, Frederick, ed. *Captured by the Indians: 15 Firsthand Accounts, 1750–1870.* New York: Dover Publications, 1961; 1985.

Drinker, Elizabeth. *The Diary of Elizabeth Drinker.* Edited by Elaine Forman Crane. 3 vols. Boston: Northeastern University Press, 1991.

Ebersole, Gary L. *Captured by Texts: Puritan to Postmodern Images of Indian Captivity.* Charlottesville: University Press of Virginia, 1995.

Ellot, C. W., ed. *Voyages and Travels: Ancient and Modern, with Introductions, Notes and Illustrations.* The Harvard Classics, vol. 33. New York: P. F. Collier and Son, c. 1910.

Emerson, Everett, ed. *Letters from New England: The Massachusetts Bay Colony, 1629–1638.* Commonwealth Series. Amherst: University of Massachusetts Press, 1976.

Equiano, Olaudah. *The Interesting Narrative of the Life of Olaudah Equiano or Gustavus Vassa the African.* 1789. New York: W. Durell, 1791.

Farish, Hunter Dickinson, ed. *Journal and Letters of Philip Vickers Fithian, 1773–1774: A Plantation Tutor of the Old Dominion.* Charlottesville: The University Press of Virginia, 1957.

Farkas, Alexander Boloni. *Journey in North America.* Edited and translated by Theodore Schoenman and Helen Benedek Schoenman. Philadelphia: American Philosophical Society, 1977.

Farmer, Silas, ed. *A History of Detroit and Michigan.* 4 vols. Detroit, MI: Silas Farmer, 1884.

Flick, Alexander C., ed. *History of the State of New York.* 10 vols. Port Washington, NY: Ira J. Friedman, 1962.

Forbes, Harriette Merrifield. *New England Diaries, 1602–1800, a Descriptive Catalog of Diaries, Orderly Books, and Sea Journals.* Topsfield, MA: Privately Printed, 1923.

Forbes, James Grant. *Sketches, Historical and Topographical of the Floridas: More Particularly of East Florida.* 1821. Facsimile reproduction with an introduction by James W. Covington. Gainesville: University of Florida Press, 1964.

Force, Peter. *Tracts and other papers relating principally to the Origin, Settlement, and Progress of the Colonies in North America, from the Discovery of the Country to the Year 1776.* 4 vols. New York: P. Smith, 1947. Reprinted in 3 vols. Gloucester, MA: Peter Smith, 1963.

Ford, Worthington C., ed. *The Writings of George Washington.* 14 vols. New York: G. P. Putnam's Sons, 1889.

Franklin, Benjamin. *An Autobiographical Portrait.* Edited by Alfred H. Tamarin. New York: Macmillan, 1969.

———. *Autobiography and Other Writings.* Edited by Kenneth Silverman. New York: Penguin, 1986.

———. *The Autobiography and Selections from His Other Writings.* Indianapolis, IN: Bobbs-Merrill, 1952.

———. *The Autobiography of Benjamin Franklin.* Edited by Louis P. Masur. Boston: Bedford/St. Martin's, 1993.

———. *The Autobiography of Benjamin Franklin, Poor Richard's Almanack, and Other Papers.* Reading, PA: Spencer Press, 1936.

———. *Benjamin Franklin: His Life as He Wrote It.* Edited by Esmond Wright. Cambridge, MA: Harvard University Press, 1990.

———. *Writings.* Edited by J. A. Leo Lemay. New York: Literary Classics of the United States, 1987.

Franklin, Jameson J. *Original Narratives of Early American History.* Reproduced under the auspices of the American Historical Association. 19 vols. New York: Charles Scribner's Sons, 1906–1917.

Frohnen, Bruce, ed. *The American Republic: Primary Sources.* Indianapolis, IN: Liberty Fund, 2002.

Glasrud, Bruce A., and Alan M. Smith, eds. *Race Relations in British North America, 1660–1783.* Chicago: Nelson-Hall Press, 1982.

Gluckman, Arcadi. *United States Muskets, Rifles and Carbines.* Harrisburg, PA: Stackpole, 1959.

Goddard, Ives, and Kathleen J. Bragdon. *Native Writings in Massachusetts.* Philadelphia: American Philosophical Society, 1988.

Goetzmann, William H., ed. *The Colonial Horizon: America in the Sixteenth and Seventeenth Centuries: interpretive articles and documentary sources.* Reading, MA: Addison Wesley, 1969.

Goldstein, Robert A. *French-Iroquois Diplomatic and Military Relations, 1609–1701.* The Hague: Mouton Press, 1969.

Goodborne, John. "A Virginian Minister's Library, 1635." Edited by R. G. Marsden. *American Historical Review* 11 (January 1906): 328–32.

Greene, Jack P., ed. *Great Britain and the American Colonies, 1606–1763.* Columbia: University of South Carolina Press, 1970.

Grimshaw, Polly. *Images of the Other: A Guide to Microfilm Manuscripts on Indian-White Relations.* Urbana: University of Illinois, 1991.

Gunn, Giles, ed. *Early American Writing.* New York: Penguin, 1994.

Hall, David D., ed. *Witch-Hunting in Seventeenth-Century New England: A Documentary History, 1638–1692.* Boston: Northeastern University Press, 1991. 2nd ed., Boston: Northeastern University Press, 1999.

Hamilton, Edward P. "Colonial and Revolutionary Artillery." *Bulletin of the Fort Ticonderoga Museum* 12 (December 1969): 313–27.

Hamilton, Milton W., ed. *The Papers of Sir William Johnson.* 14 vols. Albany: University of the State of New York Press, 1921–1965.

Harvey, David, and Gregory Brown, eds. *Common People and Their Material World: Free Men and Women in the Chesapeake, 1700–1830.* Williamsburg, VA: The Colonial Williamsburg Foundation, 1995.

Hauptman, Lawrence M., and Jack Campisi, eds. *Neighbors and Intruders: An Ethnohistorical Exploration of the Indians of Hudson's River.* Ottawa: National Museum of Canada, 1978.

Hawke, David Freeman, ed. *Captain John Smith's History of Virginia.* Indianapolis, IN: Bobbs-Merrill, 1970.

Hazard, Samuel, ed. *Pennsylvania Colonial Records.* 16 vols. Philadelphia: Jo. Swerns, 1852.

Heimert, Alan, ed. *The Puritans in America, A Narrative Anthology.* Cambridge, MA: Harvard University Press, 1985.

Heizer, Robert F, ed. *Indians of California: A Critical Bibliography.* Bloomington: Indiana University Press, 1976.

Hening, William Waller, ed. *The Statutes at Large; Being a Collection of All the Laws of Virginia, from the First Session of the Legislature in the Year 1619.* Vol. 1. New York: Printed for the editor, 1819–1823.

Hill, Edward E. *Guide to the Records in the National Archives of the United States Relating to American Indians.* Washington, DC: National Archives, 1981.

Hirschfelder, Arlene, ed. *Native Heritage: Personal Accounts by American Indians, 1790 to the Present.* New York: Macmillan, 1995.

Hotten, John Camden. *The Original Lists of Persons of Quality, Emigrants, Religious Exiles, Political Rebels, Serving Men Sold for a Term of Years, Apprentices, Children Stolen, Maidens*

Pressed, and Others Who Went from Great Britain to the American Plantations, 1600–1700. Baltimore: Genealogical Publishing, 1962.

Hough, Franklin B., ed. *Diary of the Siege of Detroit in the War with Pontiac.* Albany, NY: J. Munsell, 1860.

Hutchins, Thomas. *An Historical Narrative and the Graphical Description of Louisiana, and West Florida.* 1784. Facsimile series, Gainesville: University of Florida Press, 1968.

Jacobs, Wilbur R. *The Letters of Francis Parkman.* 2 vols. Norman: University of Oklahoma Press, 1960.

James, James A., ed. *Illinois Historical Collections.* 10 vols. Springfield: Illinois Historical Library, 1912.

Jensen, Merrill. *American Colonial Documents to 1776.* New York: Oxford University Press, 1955.

———, ed. *English Historical Documents: American Colonial Documents to 1776.* Vol. 9. New York: Oxford University Press.

Jodziewicz, Thomas W. *Birth of America: The Year in Review, 1763–1783; A Chronological Guide and Index to the Contemporary Colonial Press.* Glen Rock, NJ: Microfilming Corporation of America, 1976. (Also available in microform.)

Johnson, Emery R. "Geographic Influences Affecting the Early Development of American Commerce." *Bulletin of the American Geographical Society* 40 (1908): 129–43.

Johnson, Steven L. *Guide to American Indian Documents in the Congressional Serial Set.* New York: Clearwater Press, 1977.

Josephy, Alvin, Jr., and Frederick E. Hoxie, eds. *America in 1492.* New York: Alfred A. Knopf, 1992.

Joutel, Henri. *A Journal of LaSalle's Last Voyage.* New York: Corinth, 1962.

Joyner, Georgina Louise. *William Buckland in England and America: His Apprenticeship, English Early Georgian Influences on his Style and New Evidence at Gunston Hall.* Master's thesis, University of Notre Dame, 1985.

Katz, Jane B., ed. *I Am the Fire of Time: The Voices of Native American Women.* New York: Dutton, 1977.

Kennedy, Melissa S., ed. *Thomas Hariot's A Briefe and True Report of the New Found Land of Virginia.* University of Virginia Archive Edition.

Kimber, Edward. *A Relation, or Journal, of a Late Expedition to the Gates of Saint Augustine, on Florida.* 1744. Facsimile Series, Gainesville: University of Florida Press, 1976.

Knox, John. *Campaigns in North America 1757–1760.* Edited by Arthur G. Doughty. 3 vols. Toronto: Champlain Society, 1914. Freeport, NY: Books for Libraries, 1970.

Konig, David Thomas, ed. *Plymouth Court Records 1686–1859.* Boston: NEHGS/Pilgrim Society, 2002.

Kupperman, Karen Ordahl. *Major Problems in American Colonial History: Documents and Essays.* Lexington, MA: D. C. Heath, 1993.

Larsen, Clark Spencer, ed. *Native American Demography in the Spanish Borderlands.* New York: Garland, 1991.

Leon-Portilla, Miguel, ed. *The Broken Spears: The Aztec Account of the Conquest of Mexico.* Boston: Beacon Press, 1992.

Lestringant, Frank. *Mapping the Renaissance World: The Geographical Imagination in the Age of Discovery.* Translated by David Fausett. Los Angles: University of California Press, 1997.

Lockhart, James, ed. and trans. *We People Here: Nahauatl Accounts of the Conquest of Mexico.* Berkeley: University of California Press, 1993.

López de Gómara, Francisco. *Cortéz: The Life of the Conqueror by His Secretary.* Edited and translated by Leslie Byrd Simpson. Berkeley: University of California Press, 1964.

Lunenfeld, Marvin, ed. *1492—Discovery, Invasion, Encounter: Sources and Interpretation.* Sources in Modern History Series. Lexington, MA: D. C. Heath, 1991.

Mancall, Peter C., ed. *Envisioning America: English Plans for the Colonization of North America, 1580–1640.* Boston: Bedford/St. Martin's, 1995.

Manuel, Espinosa, J., ed. *The Pueblo Indian Revolt of 1696 and the Franciscan Missions in New Mexico: Letters of the Missionaries and Related Documents.* Norman: University of Oklahoma Press, 1988.

Manwaring, Charles William. *A Digest of the Early Connecticut Probate Records.* 3 vols. Baltimore: Genealogical Publishing, 1995.

Martin, Wendy, ed. *Colonial American Travel Narratives: A True History of the Captivity and Restoration of Mrs. Mary Rowlandson, The Journal of Madam Knight, The Secret History of the Line by William Byrd II, and The Itinararium of Dr. Alexander Hamilton.* New York: Penguin, 1994.

Maryland. *Proceedings of the Provincial Court of Maryland, 1663–1666.* Archives of Maryland, 49. Baltimore: 1932.

Massachusetts (Colony). County Court, Essex County. *Records and Files of the Quarterly Courts of Essex County, Massachusetts.* Vols. 1–8. Salem, MA: Essex Institute, 1911–1921.

Matter, Robert Allen. *Pre-Seminole Florida: Spanish Soldiers, Friars, and Indian Missions, 1513–1763.* New York: Garland Press, 1991.

McNickle, D'Arcy. *Center for American History Annual Bibliography of Recent Books and Articles in American Indian History.* Chicago: The Center, 1992.

Meynen, Emil, ed. *Bibliography on the Colonial Germans of North America; Especially the Pennsylvania Germans and Their Descendants.* Baltimore: Genealogical Publishing, 1982.

Michigan Historical Commission. *Michigan Pioneer and Historical Collections.* 40 vols. Lansing, MI: Robert Smith and Company, State Printers, 1894.

Milanich, Jerald T., ed. *Earliest Hispanic/Native America Interactions in the American Southeast.* New York: Garland Press, 1991.

Miller, John Chester, ed. *The Colonial Image: Origins of American Culture.* New York: G. Braziller, 1962.

Millner, Clyde A., ed. *Major Problems in American Colonial History: Documents and Essays.* Major Problems in American History Series. Lexington, MA: D. C. Heath, 1993.

Mintz, Steven, ed. *Native American Voices: A History and Anthology.* New York: Brandywine Press, 1995.

Moquin, Wayne, comp. *Great Documents in American Indian History*. New York: Da Capo, 1995.

Mowat, Charles Loch. *East Florida as a British Province, 1763–1784*. Facsimile Series, Gainesville: University of Florida Press, 1964.

Murray, David. *Forked Tongues: Speech, Writing, and Representation in North American Indian Texts*. Bloomington: Indiana University Press, 1991.

Mylne, William. *Travels in the Colonies in 1773–1775: Described in the Letters of William Mylne*. Edited by Ted Ruddock. Athens: University of Georgia Press. 1993.

Nabokov, Peter. *Native American Testimony: A Chronicle of Indian-White Relations from Prophecy to the Present*. New York: Viking Press, 1991.

Nade, Mason, ed. *The Journals of Francis Parkman*. 2 vols. New York: Harper and Brothers, 1947.

Namias, June. *White Captives: Gender and Ethnicity on the American Frontier*. Chapel Hill: University of North Carolina Press, 1993.

New York. *Papers: Admiralty Court and Other Records of the Administration of New York Governor Thomas Dongan, 1683–1688*. 2 vols. Syracuse, NY: Syracuse University Press, 1993–1995.

Nickerson, Warren Sears. *Early Encounters—Native Americans and Europeans in New England*. Edited by Delores Bird Carpenter. East Lansing: Michigan State University Press, 1994.

Nordquist, Joan. *Native American: Social, Economic, and Political Aspects, A Bibliography*. Santa Cruz, CA: Research and Reference Service, 1998.

Notson, Adelia White, ed. *Stepping Stones: The Pilgrims' Own Story*. Portland, OR: Binford & Mort, 1987.

Nuñez Cabeza de Vaca, Alvar. *The Account: Alvar Nuñez Cabeza de Vaca's Relacion*. Translated and annotated by Martin A. Favata and José A. Fernandez. Houston, TX: Arte Publico Press, 1993.

O'Callaghan, Edmund B., ed. *Calendar of N.Y. Colonial Manuscripts, Indorsed Land Papers: In the Office of the Secretary of State of New York, 1643–1803*. Harrison, NY: Harbor Hill, 1987.

Pagden, Anthony. *European Encounters With the New World from Renaissance to Romanticism*. New Haven, CT: Yale University Press, 1993.

Pargellis, Stanley McCrory, ed. *Military Affairs in North America, 1748–1765; Selected Documents from the Cumberland Papers in Windsor Castle*. New York: D. Appleton-Century, 1936.

Parkman, Francis. *The Conspiracy of Pontiac and the Indian War After the Conquest of Canada*. 10th ed. 2 vols. Reprint Series, Lincoln: University of Nebraska Press, 1851.

Peckham, Howard Henry. *Historical Americana: Books from which Our Early History Is Written*. Ann Arbor: University of Michigan Press, 1980.

———, ed. *Narratives of Colonial America, 1704–1765*. Chicago: R. R. Donnelley and Sons, 1971.

Peterson, Harold L. *Arms and Armor in Colonial America 1526–1783*. Harrisburg, PA: Stackpole, 1956.

———. "The Military Equipment of the Plymouth and Bay Colonies: 1620–1690." *New England Quarterly* 20 (July 1947): 197–208.

Peyer, Bernd. *The Elders Wrote: An Anthology of Early Prose by North American Indians, 1768–1931*. Berlin: Reimer, 1982.

Pittman, Phillip. *The Present State of the European Settlements on the Mississippi*. 1770. Reprint, Gainesville: University of Florida Press, 1973.

Polishook, Irwin H. *Roger Williams, John Cotton and Religious Freedom: A Controversy in New and Old England*. American Historical Sources Series: Research and Interpretation. Englewood Cliffs, NJ: Prentice-Hall, 1967.

Prucha, Francis Paul. *Atlas of American Indian Affairs*. Lincoln: University of Nebraska Press, 1990.

———. *A Bibliographical Guide to the History of Indian-White Relations in the United States*. Chicago: University of Chicago Press, 1977.

———. *Indian-White Relations: A Bibliography of Works Published 1975–1980*. Lincoln: University of Nebraska Press, 1982.

Quaife, Milo M., ed. *Alexander Henry's Travels and Adventures in the Years 1760–1776*. Chicago: R. R. Donnelley and Sons, 1921.

———. *The Conquest of the Illinois by George Rogers Clark*. Chicago: R. R. Donnelley and Sons, 1928.

———. *The Siege of Detroit in 1763: The Journal of Pontiac's Conspiracy and John Rutherford's Narrative of a Captivity*. Chicago: R. R. Donnelley and Sons, 1958.

Quimby, George Irving. *Indian Culture and European Trade Goods: The Archaeology of the Historic Period in the Western Great Lakes Region*. Madison: University of Wisconsin Press, 1966.

Richter, Daniel K. *Facing East from Indian Country: A Native History of Early America*. Cambridge, MA: Harvard University Press, 2001.

Riley, Edward Miles, ed. *The Journal of John Harrower: An Indentured Servant in the Colony of Virginia, 1773–1776*. Williamsburg, VA: Colonial Williamsburg Foundation, 1963.

Riley, Patricia, ed. *Growing Up Native American*. New York: Morrow, 1993.

Rolle, Denys. *To the Right Honorable the Lords of His Majesty's Most Honourable Privy Council. The Humble Petition of Denys Rolle, Esq; Setting Forth the Hardships, Inconveniencies, and Grievances, which have Attended Him in East Florida, Humbly Praying such Relief, as their Lordships Wisdom Shall Seem Meet*. 1765. Facsimile Series, Gainesville: University of Florida Press, 1977.

Ronda, James P., and James Axtell. *Indian Missions: A Critical Bibliography*. Bloomington: Indiana University Press, 1978.

Rosengarten, J. G. *French Colonists and Exiles in the United*

States. Philadelphia: J. B. Lippincott, 1907. Reprint, 1989.

Ross, Thomas E., and Tyrel G. Moore, eds. A *Cultural Geography of North American Indians.* Boulder, CO: West-view Press, 1987.

Rumsey, Jean. *First Congregational Church of Westbrook, Connecticut, 1725–1899.* Dixon, IL: Print Shop, 1979.

Rutherford, John. "A Journal of an Indian Captivity During Pontiac's Rebellion in the Year 1763." Edited by Milo M. Quaife. *American Heritage* 10:3 (April 1958): 65–81.

Rutherford, William Kenneth, and Anna Clay (Zimmerman) Rutherford, comp. *Genealogical History of Our Ancestors.* Lexington, MO: Privately printed, 1970.

St. John de Crèvecoeur, J. Hector. *Letters from an American Farmer.* Gloucester, MA: P. Smith, 1968.

Salls, Timothy, ed. *Guide to the Manuscript Collections of the New England Historic Genealogical Society.* Boston: New England Historic and Genealogical Society, 2002.

Sandoz, Ellis, ed. *Political Sermons of the American Founding Era, 1730–1805.* Indianapolis, IN: Liberty Press, 1991.

Saucer, Carl Ortwin. *Sixteenth Century North America: The Land and the People as Seen by Europeans.* Berkeley: University of California Press, 1971.

Schechter, Stephen. *Roots of the Republic: American Founding Documents Interpreted.* Madison, WI: Madison House, 1990.

Shirley, William. *Correspondence of William Shirley, Governor of Massachusetts and Military Commander in America, 1731–1760.* Edited by Charles Henry Lincoln, under the auspices of the National Society of the Colonial Dames of America. 2 vols. New York: Macmillan Press, 1912.

Simmons, William C., ed. *Handbook of North American Indians.* Washington, DC: Smithsonian Institution, 1978.

Smith, Billy G., and Richard Wojtowic. *Blacks Who Stole Themselves: Advertisements for Runaways in the Pennsylvania Gazette, 1728–1790.* Philadelphia: University of Pennsylvania Press, c. 1989.

Smith, John. *Captain John Smith: A Select Edition of His Writings.* Edited by Karen Ordahl Kupperman. Chapel Hill: University of North Carolina Press, 1991.

Smith, Joseph H, ed., *Colonial Justice in Western Massachusetts (1639–1702): The Pynchon Court Record, An Original Judges' Diary of the Administration of Justice in the Springfield Courts in the Massachusetts Bay Colony.* Cambridge, MA: Harvard University Press, 1961.

Smith, Venture. *A Narrative of the Life and Adventures of Venture, A Native of Africa, but Resident above Sixty Years in the United States of America.* New London, CT: 1798. Middletown, CT: J. S. Stewart, 1897.

Snow, Dean R. *The Archaeology of New England.* New York: Academic Press, 1980.

Soderland, Jean R., ed. *William Penn and the Founding of Pennsylvania: A Documentary History.* Philadelphia: University of Pennsylvania Press, 1983.

Stevens, Sylvester K., and Donald H. Kent, eds. *The Papers of Col. Henry Bouqet.* 17 vols. Harrisburg: Pennsylvania Historical Commission, 1940.

———. *Wilderness Chronicles of Northwestern Pennsylvania.* Harrisburg: Pennsylvania Historical Commission, 1941.

Stewart, Omer C. *Indians of the Great Basin: A Critical Bibliography.* Bloomington: Indiana University Press, 1982.

Stiles, T. J., comp. *In Their Own Words: The Colonizers: Early European Settlers and the Shaping of North America.* New York: Berkley Publishing Group, 1998.

Stockley, Andrew. *Britain and France at the Birth of America: The European Powers and the Peace Negotiations of 1782–1783.* Exeter, UK: University of Exeter Press, 2001.

Stone, William L., ed. *The Historical Writings of the Late Orsamus H. Marshall Relating to the Early History of the West.* Albany, NY: Joel Munsell's Sons, 1887.

Stott, Clifford, ed. *Vital Records of Springfield, Massachusetts to 1850.* Boston: NEHGS, 2002.

Strong, Pauline Turner. *Captive Selves, Captivating Others: The Politics and Poetics of Colonial American Captivity Narratives.* Boulder, CO: Westview Press, 1999.

Stryker-Rodda, Harriet. *Understanding Colonial Handwriting.* Baltimore: Genealogical Publishing Company, 1986.

Swem, Earl G., and John M. Jennings. *A Selected Bibliography of Virginia, 1607–1699.* Williamsburg: Virginia 350th Anniversary Celebration Corporation, 1957.

Tanner, Helen Hornbeck, et al., eds. *Atlas of Great Lakes Indian History.* Norman: University of Oklahoma Press, 1987.

Taxay, Don. *Money of the American Indians and Other Primitive Currencies of the Americas.* New York: Nummus Press, 1970.

Thatcher, Oliver J., ed. *The Library of Original Sources.* 9th to 16th Centuries, vol. 5. Milwaukee, WI: University Research Extension, 1907.

Thorpe, Francis Newton, ed. *The Federal and State Constitutions Colonial Charters, and Other Organic Laws of the States, Territories, and Colonies Now or Heretofore Forming the United States of America.* Compiled and edited under the Act of Congress of June 30, 1906. Washington, DC: Government Printing Office, 1909.

Thwaites, Reuben Gold, ed. *Early Western Travels.* 32 vols. Cleveland, OH: Burrows Brothers, 1849.

———. *France in America 1497–1763.* New York: Harper and Brothers, 1905.

———. *The Jesuit Relations and Allied Documents.* 73 vols. Cleveland, OH: Burrows Brothers, 1849.

Tillson, Albert. "The Southern Backcountry: A Survey of Current Research." *Virginia Magazine of History and Biography* 98 (1990): 387–422.

Trask, Richard B., comp. *Salem Village and the Witch Hysteria.* New York: Grossman Publishers, 1975.

Treckel, Paul A. "Bibliographical Essay." In *To Comfort the Heart: Women in Seventeenth-Century America.* New York: Twayne Press, 1996.

Trent, William. "Journal at Fort Pitt, 1763." Edited by A. T. Volwiler. *Mississippi Valley Historical Review* 11 (1924): 400–410.

Unser, Daniel H., Jr., ed. *Indians, Settlers, and Slaves in a Frontier Exchange Economy: The Lower Mississippi Valley Before 1783.* Chapel Hill: University of North Carolina, 1992.

Vanderwerth, W. C., comp. *Indian Oratory.* Norman: University of Oklahoma Press, 1971.

Vargas, Diego de. *Letters from the New World: Selected Correspondence of Don Diego de Vargas to His Family, 1615–1706.* Edited by John L. Kessell, Rich Hendricks, and Meredith Dodge. Albuquerque: University of New Mexico Press, 1992.

Vega, Garcilaso de la. *The Florida of the Inca: A History of Adelantado, Hernando de Soto, Governor and Captain General of the Kingdom of Florida, and Other Heroic Spanish and Indian Cavaliers.* Edited and translated by Jeanette Johnson Varner. Austin: University of Texas Press, 1980.

Vespucci, Amerigo. *Letters from a New World: Amerigo Vespucci's Discovery of America.* New York: Marsilio, 1992.

Vogel, Virgil J. *This Country Was Ours: A Documentary History of the American Indians.* New York: Harper & Row, 1972.

Vorsey, Louis De, Jr. *The Atlantic Pilot.* Facsimile series, Gainesville: University of Florida Press, 1772.

Waldman, Carl. *Atlas of the North American Indian.* New York: Facts on File Press, 1985.

Walsh, Lorena S. *From Calabar to Carter's Grove: The History of a Virginia Slave.* Charlottesville: University of Virginia Press, 1997.

Warhus, Mark. *Another America: Native American Maps and the History of Our Land.* New York: St. Martin's, 1997.

Washington, George. *The Diaries of George Washington.* Edited by Donald Jackson. Charlottesville: University Press of Virginia, 1976–1979.

———. *George Washington: A Collection.* Edited and compiled by W. B. Allen. Indianapolis, IN: Liberty Classics, 1988.

Weddle, Robert S., ed. *La Salle, the Mississippi, and the Gulf: Three Primary Documents.* College Station: Texas A & M University Press, 1987.

Weeks, Lyman Horace, and Edwin M. Bacon, eds. *An Historical Digest of the Provincial Press; Being a Collation of All Items of Personal and Historic Reference Relating to American Affairs Printed in the Newspapers of the Provincial Period Beginning with the Appearance of the Present State of New York/Massachusetts.* Boston: Society for Americana, 1911.

White, Phillip M. *American Indian Studies: A Bibliographic Guide.* Englewood, NJ: Libraries Unlimited, 1995.

Wigglesworth, Michael. *The Diary of Michael Wigglesworth, 1653–1657: The Conscience of a Puritan.* Edited by Edmund S. Morgan. Gloucester, MA: Peter Smith, 1970.

Willard, Samuel. "A briefe account of a strange & unusuall Providence of God befallen to Elizabeth Knap of Groton." Edited by Samuel A. Green. In *Groton In The Witchcraft Times.* Groton, MA: 1883.

Williams, Daniel E., comp. *Pillars of Salt: An Anthology of Early American Criminal Narratives.* Reprinted from 1699–1796 edition, Madison, WI: Madison House, 1993.

Winship, George Parker, ed. and trans. *The Journey of Coronado 1540–1542 from the City of Mexico to the Grand Canon of the Colorado and the Buffalo Plains of Texas, Kansas and Nebraska as Told by Himself and his Followers.* New York: Greenwood Press, 1969. Reprint, Golden, CO: Fulcrum Publishing, 1990.

Winthrop, John. *A Modell of Christian Charity (1630).* Collections of the Massachusetts Historical Society, 3rd series, 7:31–48. Boston: 1838.

Wish, Harvey, ed. *William Bradford of Plymouth Plantation, The Pilgrims in America.* New York: Capricorn, 1962.

Witt, Shirley H., and Stan Steiner, eds. *The Way.* New York: Vintage Books, 1972.

Woolsey, Anne I., and John C. Ravesloot, eds. *Culture and Contact: Charles C. Di Peso's Gran Chichimeca.* Albuquerque: University of New Mexico Press, 1993.

Wrone, David R., and Russell S. Nelson, Jr., eds. *Who's the Savage?* Greenwich, CT: Fawcett Publications, 1973.

Zuckerman, Michael. "Tocqueville, Turner, and Turds: Four Stories of Manners in Early America." *Journal of American History* 85 (1998): 13–42.

Internet Sources

Amdocs Documents for the Study of American History. Website includes documents from the 1650s to the present with access by time period and subject. Created by Lynn Nelson, University of Kansas. http://history.cc.ukans.edu/carrie/docs/amdocs_index.html.

American and British Full-text Documents by Period. This is a useful site for identifying historical document collections. http://www.libraries.rutgers.edu/rul/rr_gateway/research_guides/history/by_period.shtml.

American Women's History: A Research Guide: Colonial America. Provides sources and links regarding women in the colonial era. Created by Ken Middleton, Middle Tennessee State University Library. http://www.mtsu.edu/~kmiddlet/history/women/wh-colonial.html.

Archiving Early America: Historical Documents from 18th Century America. Provides maps, newspapers and other primary source material in the original format. http://www.earlyamerica.com.

The Avalon Project. Yale Law School. Covers diplomatic and legal documents from all historical periods. http://www.yale.edu/lawweb/avalon/avalon.htm.

Documenting the American South. Contains primary source material on Southern history, literature, and culture from colonial times through the early twentieth century. Provided by the University of North Carolina at Chapel Hill. http://docsouth.unc.edu.

Doing History: Document Archives. The Lawrence University

History Department site provides a list of websites where primary documents are available online. http://www.lawrence.edu/dept/history/HistoryDocuments.htm.

Gilder Lehrman Institute of American History. Contains materials from all historical periods. http://www.gliah.uh.edu/index.cfm.

Graphic Works for Historians. This list of websites contains art, images, and material artifacts of interest to historians. http://www.lawrence.edu/dept/history/HistoryGraphics.htm.

Humbul Humanities Web. A service of the United Kingdom Resource Discovery Network that provides annotated information for many primary sources. http://www.humbul.ac.uk/output/subout.php?subj=history.

The Internet History Sourcebooks Project. Edited by Paul Halsall of Fordham University, this website provides collections of historical texts for educational use. http://www.fordham.edu/halsall.

Library of Congress. This site includes exhibits, the Library Catalog, and digitalized historical collections such as American Memory. http://www.loc.gov.

The National Archives and Records Administration. Provides online guides to federal archives and a virtual library. (The National Archives has regional branches throughout the United States.) http://www.archives.gov.

The National Union Catalog of Manuscript Collections. Provides information about archives and manuscript repositories and Library of Congress resources. http://lcweb.loc.gov/coll/nucmc.

Online Archive of California. A database of "finding aids" of primary manuscripts, photographs, and artwork found in California institutions. http://www.oac.cdlib.org.

The Plymouth Colony Archive Project at the University of Virginia. Includes court records, legal documents, and building structures of the Colony 1620–1691. http://etext.virginia.edu/users/deetz.

Repositories of Primary Sources. List of websites describing manuscripts, archives, rare books, and other primary sources. http://www.uidaho.edu/special-collections/Other.Repositories.

UNESCO Archives Portal. An international gateway to archives and primary sources. http://www.unesco.org/webworld/portal_archives/pages/index.shtml.

Virtual Jamestown. Site of the Virginia Center for Digital History in Charlottesville, Virginia. http://www.virtualjamestown.org.

Microfilm Sources

Note: All sources are found on microfilm, unless otherwise noted.

Adams, John, Benjamin Franklin, George Washington, Thomas Jefferson, and Thomas Paine. 4 reels.

Adams, Samuel. Middlebury College and Yale University Library. *The Samuel Adams Papers, 1635–1826.* These two collections include microfilm of official documents and correspondence. 5 reels each.

Adams Family. Massachusetts Historical Society. *Microfilms of the Adams Papers Microform, Owned by the Adams Manuscript Trust and Deposited in the Massachusetts Historical Society.* Includes materials for John Adams, John Quincy Adams, Abigail Adams, and other members of the family. Accompanied by index. 608 reels.

Andrews, Charles McLean. *Guide to the Manuscript Materials for the History of the United States to 1783, in the British Museum, in Minor London Archives, and in the Libraries of Oxford and Cambridge.*

Carter Family Papers, 1659–1797, in the Sabine Hall Collection, University of Virginia. Includes land documents, correspondence, and diaries. 4 reels.

Folliott, George. *Diary of George Folliott, New York Merchant, 1765–1766.*

Franklin, Benjamin. *Benjamin Franklin's Account Books (1743–1768).* Accompanied by guide. 3 reels.

Hazard, Ebenezer. *Historical Collections: Consisting of State Papers, and Other Authentic Documents; Intended as Materials for an History of the United States of America.* Philadelphia: Printed by T. Dobson, for the author, 1792–1794. Microform.

Hobhouse, Isaac, and Company. *The Hobhouse Letters, 1722–1755: Letters and Other Papers of Isaac Hobhouse and Company.* Bristol Merchants. Microform.

Jefferson, Thomas. University of Virginia Library. *Guide to the Microfilm Edition of the Jefferson Papers of the University of Virginia, 1732–1788.*

Knox, Henry. *Papers, 1719–1825.* Army officer and Secretary of War; includes correspondence with Nathaniel Greene and George Washington. 55 reels.

Laurens, Henry. *The Papers of Henry Laurens in the South Carolina Historical Society.* Includes letters, documents, and miscellaneous papers, 1747–1792. 19 reels.

Lee Family Papers, 1742–1795. Microform. 8 reels.

Penn, Thomas. *Guide to the Microfilm Edition of the Thomas Penn Papers.*

Penn, William. *Guide to the Microfilm of the Papers of William Penn.*

———. *The Papers of William Penn.* Vols. 1–5.

Peters, Samuel. *The Papers of Loyalist Samuel Peters: A Survey of the Contents of His Notebooks-Correspondence during His Flight to England, Exile, and the Last Years of His Life.*

Royal Society of Arts. *American Correspondence of the Royal Society of Arts, London, 1755–1840: Guard Books (1755–1770) and Loose Archives (1755–1840).* Microform.

Sabin, Joseph. *Selected Americana from Sabin's Dictionary of Books Relating to America, from Its Discovery to the Present Time.* Based on Joseph Sabin's *Bibliotheca Americana. A Dictionary of Books Relating to America, from Its Discovery to the Present Time.* Microfiche.

Shirley, William. *Correspondence of William Shirley, Governor of Massachusetts and Military Commander in America.*

Travels in the Old South, I, II, and III. Based on Thomas Dionysius Clark, *Travels in the Old South, a Bibliography.* Microfilm and microfiche.

U.S. Bureau of the Census. *Historical Statistics of the United States on CD-ROM: Colonial Times to 1970.* New York: Cambridge University Press, 1997.

Vargas, Diego de. *By Force of Arms: The Journals of Don Diego de Vargas, New Mexico, 1691–1693.*

———. *Letters from the New World: Selected Correspondence of Don Diego de Vargas to His Family, 1675–1706.*

———. *Remote Beyond Compare: Letters of Don Diego de Vargas to His Family from New Spain and New Mexico, 1675–1706.*

———. *To the Royal Crown Restored: The Journals of Don Diego de Vargas, New Mexico, 1692–1694.*

Washington, George. *The Diaries of George Washington, 1748–1799.* Vols. 1–4.

———. *Papers (1697–1799).* 124 reels.

———. *The Papers of George Washington.* 29 vols. in 4 series.

Williams, Roger. *Complete Writings.* Vols. 1–7.

———. *The Correspondence of Roger Williams.* Vols. 1–2.

Colonial Records and Laws on Microfilm

Connecticut. *The Civil and Executive Officers' Assistant: Containing the Forms of Bonds, Bills, Deeds, Letters of Attorney, Policies of Insurance; Releases, Wills, Writs, Pleas, Officers Returns and Justices Records of Court.* Early American Imprints. First Series. No. 25556.

Connecticut. *The Code of 1650, Being a Compilation of the Earliest Laws and Orders of the General Court of Connecticut.*

Connecticut. *The First Laws of the State of Connecticut.*

Connecticut. *The Public Records of the Colony of Connecticut, 1636–1776.* 15 vols.

Connecticut. Swift, Zephaniah. *A System of the Laws of the State of Connecticut.* Early American Imprints, First Series.

Continental Congress. *Papers of the Continental Congress, 1774–1789.*

Delaware. *The First Laws of the State of Delaware.*

England and Wales, Sovereign. *British Royal Proclamations Relating to America, 1603–1783.*

Florida. *Archivo General de Indias. Further English Voyages to Spanish America, 1583–1594: Documents from the Archives of the Indies at Seville Illustrating English Voyages to the Caribbean, the Spanish Main, Florida, and Virginia.*

Georgia. *The Colonial Records of the State of Georgia.*

Georgia. *The First Laws of the State of Georgia.*

Maine. *The Probate Records of Lincoln County, Maine: 1760–1800.* Edited by William Davis Patterson.

Maine. *Province and Court Records of Maine.*

Maryland. *The First Laws of the State of Maryland.*

Maryland, County Court, Prince Georges County. *Court Records of Prince Georges County.*

Massachusetts. *A Bibliography of the Laws and Resolves of the Massachusetts Bay, 1642–1780.*

Massachusetts. *The First Laws of the Commonwealth of Massachusetts.*

Massachusetts. Middlesex County Registry of Deeds. *Records of the South Registry of Deeds, Middlesex County (Record Books) 1st Series, 1639–1799.* Excerpts. 1 reel.

Massachusetts. *The Colonial Laws of Massachusetts, 1672–1686.*

Massachusetts. *Plymouth Court Records, 1686–1859.* 5 reels.

Massachusetts. Court of Assistants. *Records of the Court of Assistants of the Colony of the Massachusetts Bay, 1630–1692.*

Massachusetts. Courts, Hampshire County. *Colonial Justice in Western Massachusetts, 1639–1702: The Pynchon Court Records, an Original Judges' Diary of the Administration of Justice in the Springfield Courts in the Massachusetts Bay Colony.*

Massachusetts. General Court. House of Representatives. *Journal, 1715–1779.*

Massachusetts. Superior Court of Judicature. *Reports of Cases Argued and Adjudged in the Superior Court of Judicature of the Province of Massachusetts Bay, between 1761 and 1772.*

Mississippi. Department of Archives and History. *Mississippi Provincial Archives: French Dominion.*

Native Americans. *Early American Indian Documents: Treaties and Laws, 1607–1789.* Includes treaties, conference reports, council minutes, commissioners' reports, scouts' and interpreters' records, and deeds of land sales. 20 volumes, 10 of which have been produced thus far.

New Hampshire. *The First Laws of the State of New Hampshire.*

New Jersey. *The First Laws of the State of New Jersey.*

New Mexico. *The Spanish Archives of New Mexico.* Translated by Ralph Emerson Twitchell.

New Mexico. *Spanish Archives of New Mexico, 1621–1821.* 22 reels.

New Netherland. Council. *Council Minutes, 1655–1656.*

New Netherland. Inferior Court of Justice, Beverwyck, New York. *Fort Orange Court Minutes, 1652–1660.*

New Netherland. West-Indische Compagnie (Netherlands). *Documents Relating to New Netherland, 1624–1626.*

New York. *An Account of Her Majesty's Revenue in the Province of New York, 1701–09: The Customs Records of Early Colonial New York.*

New York. *The First Laws of the State of New York.*

New York Council. *Journal of the Legislative Council of the Colony of New York.*

New York. Mayors Court. *Select Cases of the Mayor's Court of New York City, 1674–1784.*

North Carolina. *The First Laws of the State of North Carolina.*

Pennsylvania. *Colonial Records of Pennsylvania.* Vols. 1–16.

Pennsylvania. *The First Laws of the Commonwealth of Pennsylvania.*

Pennsylvania. *Journals and Minutes of the Pennsylvania Assembly, 1776–1790.* 3 reels.

Pennsylvania. *Records of the Provincial Council, 1682–1776.*

Documents the executive government of Pennsylvania, from the establishment of the provincial council under William Penn until the overthrow of the proprietary government in 1776. 26 reels.

Pennsylvania. Court of Quarter Sessions of the Peace, Bucks County. *Records of the Courts of Quarter Sessions and Common Pleas of Bucks County, Pennsylvania, 1684–1700.*

Pennsylvania. Historical Society of Pennsylvania Library. *The Charlemagne Tower Collection of American Colonial Laws.*

Rhode Island. *The First Laws of the State of Rhode Island.*

Rhode Island. *Records of the Colony of Rhode Island and Providence Plantation in New England, 1636–1677.* Compiled by John Russell Bartlett.

Rhode Island. Court of Vice-Admiralty. *Records of the Vice-Admiralty of Rhode Island, 1716–1752.*

South Carolina. *Biographical Directory of the South Carolina House of Representatives.* Includes the colonial era.

South Carolina. *The First Laws of the State of Carolina.*

South Carolina. Court of Chancery. *Records of the Court of Chancery of South Carolina, 1671–1779.*

Virginia. *Archivo General de Indias. Further English Voyages to Spanish America, 1583–1594: Documents from the Archives of the Indies at Seville Illustrating English Voyages to the Caribbean, the Spanish Main, Florida, and Virginia.*

Virginia. *Criminal Proceedings in Colonial Virginia. (Records of) Fines, Examination of Criminals, Trials of Slaves, etc. from March 1710 (1711) to (1754).*

Virginia. Daily records of the proceedings of Virginia's elected lower house-reports, petitions, orders, declarations, and other papers covering subjects such as defense, agriculture, the slave trade, and education, 1619–1776. 13 vols.

Virginia. *The First Laws of the State of Virginia.*

Virginia. Council. *Legislative Journals of the Council of Colonial Virginia.*

Virginia. Council. *Minutes of the Council and General Court of Colonial Virginia, 1622–1632, 1670–1676, with Notes and Excerpts from Original Council and General Court Records, into 1683, Now Lost.*

Virginia. General Assembly. House of Burgesses. *The Journals of the House of Burgesses of Virginia. The Journals of the House of Burgesses of Virginia, 1619–1776.* 4 reels.

Virginia. County Court, Northampton County. *County Court Records of Accomack-Northampton, Virginia.* Two sets: 1632–1640 and 1640–1645.

Secondary Sources

Thematic

Arts and Culture

Agnew, Jean-Christophe. *Worlds Apart: The Market and the Theater in Anglo-American Thought, 1550–1750.* Cambridge, UK: Cambridge University Press, 1986.

Aldridge, A. Owen. *Early American Literature: A Comparatist Approach.* Princeton, NJ: Princeton University Press, 1982.

Axtell, James. *The School upon a Hill: Education and Society in Colonial New England.* New Haven, CT: Yale University Press, 1974.

Belknap, Waldron P. *American Colonial Painting: Materials for a History.* Cambridge, MA: Harvard University Press, 1959.

Bertelson, David. *The Lazy South.* New York: Oxford University Press, 1967.

Breen, T. H. *Tobacco Culture: The Mentality of the Great Tidewater Planters on the Eve of Revolution.* Princeton, NJ: Princeton University Press, 1985.

Bridenbaugh, Carl. *The Colonial Craftsman.* Chicago: University of Chicago Press, 1961.

Brown, Richard D. *Knowledge Is Power: The Diffusion of Information in Early America, 1700–1865.* New York: Oxford University Press, 1991.

Bushman, Richard. *The Refinement of America: Persons, Houses, Cities.* New York: Alfred A. Knopf, 1992.

Caldwell, Patricia. *The Puritan Conversion Narrative: The Beginnings of American Expression.* Cambridge, UK: Cambridge University Press, 1983.

Canup, John. *Out of the Wilderness: The Emergence of an American Identity in Colonial New England.* Middletown, CT: Wesleyan University Press, 1990.

Carroll, Peter N. *Puritanism and the Wilderness: The Intellectual Significance of the New England Frontier, 1629–1700.* New York: Columbia University Press, 1969.

Carson, Cary, Ronald Hoffman, and Peter J. Albert, eds. *Of Consuming Interests: The Style of Life in the Eighteenth Century.* Charlottesville: University Press of Virginia, 1994.

Clark, Charles E. *The Public Prints: The Newspaper in Anglo-American Culture, 1665–1740.* New York: Oxford University Press, 1994.

Cohen, Patricia C. *A Calculating People: The Spread of Numeracy in Early America.* Chicago: University of Chicago Press, 1983.

Craven, Wayne. *Colonial American Portraiture: The Economic, Religious, Social, Cultural, Philosophical, Scientific, and Aesthetic Foundations.* New York: Cambridge University Press, 1986.

Cremin, Lawrence A. *American Education: The Colonial Experience, 1607–1783.* New York: Harper and Row, 1970.

Davidson, Cathy N. *Revolution and the Word: The Rise of the Novel in America.* New York: Oxford University Press, 1986.

Davis, Richard B. *A Colonial Southern Bookshelf: Reading in the Eighteenth Century.* Athens: University of Georgia Press, 1979.

———. *Intellectual Life in the Colonial South, 1585–1763.* 3 vols. Knoxville: University of Tennessee, 1978.

Deetz, James. *In Small Things Forgotten: The Archaeology of Early American Life.* Garden City, NY: Doubleday, 1977.

Elliott, Emory. *Revolutionary Writers: Literature and Authority in the New Republic, 1725–1810.* New York: Oxford University Press, 1982.

Emerson, Everett, ed. *Major Writers of Early American Literature.* Madison: University of Wisconsin Press, 1972.

Fischer, David H. *Albion's Seed: Four British Folkways in America.* New York: Oxford University Press, 1991.

Fliegelman, Jay. *Prodigals and Pilgrims: The American Revolution Against Patriarchal Authority, 1750–1800.* Cambridge, UK: Cambridge University Press, 1982.

Forman, Henry C. *The Architecture of the Old South: The Medieval Style, 1585–1850.* New York: Russell & Russell, 1967.

Foster, Stephen. *Their Solitary Way: The Puritan Social Ethic in the First Century of Settlement in New England.* New Haven, CT: Yale University Press, 1971.

Franklin, Wayne. *Discoverers, Explorers, Settlers: The Diligent Writers of Early America.* Chicago: University of Chicago Press, 1979.

Fries, Sylvia D. *The Urban Idea in Colonial America.* Philadelphia: Temple University Press, 1977.

Gay, Peter. *A Loss of Mastery: Puritan Historians in Colonial America.* Berkeley: University of California Press, 1966.

Gilje, Paul A. *The Road to Mobocracy: Popular Disorder in New York City, 1763–1834.* Chapel Hill: University of North Carolina Press, 1987.

Grafton, Anthony. *New Worlds, Ancient Texts: The Power of Tradition and the Shock of Discovery*. Cambridge, MA: Harvard University Press, 1992.

Granger, Bruce. *American Essay Serials from Franklin to Irving*. Knoxville: University of Tennessee Press, 1978.

Greenblatt, Stephen. *Marvelous Possessions: The Wonder of the New World*. Chicago: University of Chicago Press, 1992.

Greene, Jack P. *Imperatives, Behaviors, and Identities: Essays in Early American Cultural History*. Charlottesville: University Press of Virginia, 1992.

Gummere, Richard M. *The American Colonial Mind and the Classic Tradition: Essays in Comparative Culture*. Cambridge, MA: Harvard University Press, 1963.

Habermas, Jurgen. *The Structural Transformation of the Public Sphere*. Cambridge, MA: Harvard University Press, 1989.

Hawke, David F. *Every Day Life in Early America*. New York: HarperCollins, 1989.

Hench, John B., ed. *The Press and the American Revolution*. Boston: Northeastern University Press, 1997.

Hoffman, Ronald, and Peter J. Albert, eds. *Of Consuming Interests: The Style of Life in the Eighteenth Century*. Charlottesville: University Press of Virginia, 1994.

Hollifield, E. Brooks. *Era of Persuasion: American Thought and Culture, 1521–1680*. Boston: Twayne, 1989.

Jones, Howard M. *O Strange New World: American Culture, the Formative Years*. Westport, CT: Greenwood, 1982.

Jordan, Terry G., and Matti Kaups. *The American Backwoods Frontier: An Ethnic and Ecological Interpretation*. Baltimore: Johns Hopkins University Press, 1989.

Joyce, William L. et al, eds. *Printing and Society in Early America*. Worcester, MA: American Antiquarian Society, 1983.

Ketcham, Ralph. *From Colony to Country: The Revolution in American Thought, 1750–1820*. New York: Macmillan, 1975.

Kimball, Fiske. *Domestic Architecture of the American Colonies and of the Early Republic*. New York: Scribner's, 1922.

Kirk, John T. *American Furniture and the British Tradition to 1830*. New York: Alfred A. Knopf, 1982.

Koch, Arienne. *Power, Morals, and the Founding Fathers: Essays in the Interpretation of the American Enlightenment*. Ithaca, NY: Cornell University Press, 1961.

Kupperman, Karen O., ed. *America in European Consciousness, 1493–1750*. Chapel Hill: University of North Carolina Press, 1995.

Labaree, Leonard W. *Conservatism in Early American History*. Ithaca, NY: Cornell University Press, 1965.

Landsman, Ned C. *From Colonials to Provincials: American Thought and Culture, 1680–1760*. Ithaca, NY: Cornell University Press, 2000.

Laugher, Charles T. *Thomas Bray's Grand Design: Libraries of the Church of England in America, 1695–1785*. Chicago: American Library Association, 1973.

Leighton, Ann. *American Gardens in the Eighteenth Century: "For use of delight."* Amherst: University of Massachusetts Press, 1986.

———. *Early American Gardens: "For meate or medicine."* Amherst: University of Massachusetts Press, 1986.

Levernez, David. *The Language of Puritan Feeling: An Exploration in Literature, Psychology, and Social History*. New Brunswick, NJ: Rutgers University Press, 1980.

Levine, Lawrence W. *Highbrow, Lowbrow: Emergence of Cultural Hierarchy in America*. Cambridge, MA: Harvard University Press, 1988.

Lockridge, Kenneth A. *Literacy in Colonial New England: An Enquiry into the Social Context of Literacy in the Early Modern West*. New York: W. W. Norton, 1974.

Lowens, Irving. *Music and Musicians in Early America*. New York: W. W. Norton, 1964.

Ludwig, Allan I. *Graven Images: New England Stonecarving and Its Symbols, 1650–1815*. Middletown, CT: Wesleyan University Press, 1966.

Maccubin, Robert P., and Peter Martin, eds. *British and American Gardens in the Eighteenth Century: Eighteen Illustrated Essays on Garden History*. Williamsburg, VA: Colonial Williamsburg Foundation, 1984.

Mates, Julian. *The American Musical Stage before 1800*. New Brunswick, NJ: Rutgers University Press, 1962.

May, Henry F. *The Enlightenment in America*. New York: Oxford University Press, 1976.

McNamara, Brooks. *The American Playhouse in the Eighteenth Century*. Cambridge, MA: Harvard University Press, 1969.

Meserve, Walter J. *An Emerging Entertainment: The Drama of the American People to 1828*. Bloomington: Indiana University Press, 1977.

Middlekauf, Robert. *Ancients and Axioms: Secondary Education in Eighteenth-Century New England*. New Haven, CT: Yale University Press, 1963.

Morison, Samuel E. *The Intellectual Life of Colonial New England*. New York: New York University Press, 1970.

Morrison, Hugh. *Early American Architecture: From the First Colonial Settlements to the National Period*. New York: Dover Publications, 1987.

O'Connor, Hyla. *The Early American Cookbook*. Englewood Cliffs, NJ: Prentice-Hall, 1974.

Poesch, Jessie J. *The Art of the Old South: Painting, Sculpture, Architecture, and the Products of Craftsmen, 1560–1860*. New York: Harrison House, 1989.

Quimby, Ian M., ed. *American Painting to 1776: A Reappraisal*. Charlottesville: University Press of Virginia, 1971.

———. *Arts of the Anglo-American Community in the Seventeenth Century*. Charlottesville: University Press of Virginia, 1975.

Rankin, Hugh F. *The Theatre in Colonial America*. Chapel Hill: University of North Carolina Press, 1965.

Rice, Kym S. *Early American Taverns: For the Entertainment of Friends and Strangers*. Chicago: Regnery Gateway, 1983.

Richardson, E. P. *Painting in America, from 1502 to the Present.* New York: Crowell, 1965.

Robson, David W. *Educating Republicans: The College in the Era of the American Revolution, 1750–1800.* Westport, CT: Greenwood, 1985.

Saunders, Richard H., and Ellen G. Miles. *American Colonial Portraits, 1700–1776.* Washington, DC: Smithsonian Institution Press, 1987.

Savelle, Max. *Seeds of Liberty: The Genesis of the American Mind.* Seattle: University of Washington Press, 1965.

Shalhope, Robert E. *The Roots of Democracy: American Thought and Culture, 1760–1800.* Boston: Twayne, 1990.

Shields, David S. *Civil Tongues and Polite Letters in British America.* Chapel Hill: University of North Carolina Press, 1997.

———. *Oracles of Empire: Poetry, Politics, and Commerce in British America, 1690–1750.* Chicago: University of Chicago Press, 1990.

Silverman, Kenneth, ed. *Colonial American Poetry.* New York: Hafner, 1968.

Slotkin, Richard. *Regeneration through Violence: The Mythology of the American Frontier, 1600–1860.* Middletown, CT: Wesleyan University Press, 1973.

Smith, Jeffrey A. *Printers and Press Freedom: The Ideology of Early American Journalism.* New York: Oxford University Press, 1988.

Sonneck, O. G. *Early Concert-Life in America (1731–1800).* New York: Musurgia, 1949.

St. George, Robert B. *Conversing by Signs: The Poetics of Implication in Colonial New England Culture.* Chapel Hill: University of North Carolina Press, 1998.

———. *Material Life in America, 1600–1860.* Boston: Northeastern University Press, 1988.

Stowell, Marion B. *Early American Almanacs: The Colonial Weekday Bible.* New York: Burt Franklin, 1977.

Thompson, Peter. *Rum Punch & Revolution: Taverngoing & Public Life in Eighteenth Century Philadelphia.* Philadelphia: University of Pennsylvania Press, 1998.

Tichi, Cecelia. *New World, New Earth: Environmental Reform in American Literature from the Puritans through Whitman.* New Haven, CT: Yale University Press, 1970.

Warner, Michael. *The Letters of the Republic: Publication and the Public Sphere in Eighteenth-Century America.* Cambridge, MA: Harvard University Press, 1990.

Waterman, Thomas T. *The Dwellings of Colonial America.* Chapel Hill: University of North Carolina Press, 1950.

Whitehill, Walter M. *The Arts in Early American History: An Essay by Walter Muir Whitehill.* Chapel Hill: University of North Carolina Press, 1965.

Wright, Louis B. *The Cultural Life of the American Colonies, 1607–1763.* New York: Harper, 1957; 1962.

———. *The Dream of Prosperity in Colonial America.* New York: New York University Press, 1965.

Wright, Louis B., et al. *The Arts in America: The Colonial Period.* New York: Scribner's, 1966.

Wroth, Lawrence C. *The Colonial Printer.* Charlottesville, VA: Dominion, 1964.

Ziff, Larzer. *Puritanism in America: New Culture in a New World.* New York: Viking, 1973.

Economy, Labor, and Business

Anderson, Terry L. *The Economic Growth of Seventeenth-Century New England: A Measurement of Regional Income.* New York: Arno, 1975.

Anderson, Virginia D. "King Philip's Herds: Indians, Colonists, and the Problem of Livestock in Early New England." *William and Mary Quarterly*, 3rd ser., 51 (October 1994): 601–24.

Anderson, William G. *The Price of Liberty: The Public Debt of the American Revolution.* Charlottesville: University Press of Virginia, 1983.

Andrews, Kenneth R. *Trade, Plunder, and Settlement: Maritime Enterprise and the Genesis of the British Empire, 1480–1630.* New York: Cambridge University Press, 1984.

Appleby, Joyce O. *Economic Thought and Ideology in Seventeenth-Century England.* Princeton, NJ: Princeton University Press, 1978.

Bailyn, Bernard. *The New England Merchants in the Seventeenth Century.* Cambridge, MA: Harvard University Press, 1955.

Barrow, Thomas C. *Trade and Empire: The British Customs Service in Colonial America, 1660–1775.* Cambridge, MA: Harvard University Press, 1967.

Berlin, Ira. *Many Thousands Gone: The First Two Centuries of Slavery in North America.* Cambridge, MA: Harvard University Press, 1998.

Berlin, Ira, and Philip D. Morgan, eds. *Cultivation and Culture: Labor and the Shaping of Slave Life in the Americas.* Charlottesville: University Press of Virginia, 1993.

Blackburn, Robin. *The Making of New World Slavery: From the Baroque to the Modern, 1492–1800.* New York: Verso, 1997.

Boxer, C. R. *The Dutch Seaborne Empire, 1600–1800.* New York: Penguin, 1989.

Braund, Kathryn E. *Deerskins and Duffels: The Creek Indian Trade with Anglo-America, 1685–1815.* Lincoln: University of Nebraska Press, 1993.

Breen, T. H. " 'Baubles of Britain': The American and Consumer Revolutions of the Eighteenth Century." *Past and Present* 119 (May 1988): 73–104.

Brock, Leslie V. *The Currency of the American Colonies, 1700–1764: A Study in Colonial Finance and Imperial Relations.* New York: Arno, 1975.

Brown, Jennifer S. *Strangers in Blood: Fur Trade Company Families in Indian Country.* Vancouver: University of British Columbia Press, 1980.

Bruchey, Stuart. *The Roots of American Economic Growth, 1607–1861: An Essay in Social Causation.* New York: Harper and Row, 1965.

Bushman, Richard L. "Markets and Composite Farms in Early America." *William and Mary Quarterly*, 3rd ser., 55 (1998): 351–74.

Canny, Nicholas, and Alaine Low, eds. *The Origins of Empire: British Overseas Enterprise to the Close of the Seventeenth Century*. New York: Oxford University Press, 1998.

Carroll, Charles F. *The Timber Economy of Puritan New England*. Providence, RI: Brown University Press, 1973.

Chaplin, Joyce E. *An Anxious Pursuit: Agricultural Innovation and Modernity in the Lower South, 1730–1815*. Chapel Hill: University of North Carolina Press, 1993.

Curtin, Philip D. *The Atlantic Slave Trade: A Census*. Madison: University of Wisconsin Press, 1969.

———. *The Rise and Fall of the Plantation Complex: Essays in Atlantic History*. New York: Cambridge University Press, 1998.

Davis, David B. *The Problem of Slavery in Western Culture*. New York: Oxford University Press, 1966.

Davis, Ralph. *The Rise of the Atlantic Economies*. Ithaca, NY: Cornell University Press, 1973.

Devine, T. M. *The Tobacco Lords: A Study of the Tobacco Merchants of Glasgow and Their Trading Activities, c. 1740–90*. Edinburgh, UK: John Donald, 1975.

Ernst, Joseph A. *Money and Politics in America, 1755–1775: A Study in the Currency Act of 1764 and the Political Economy of Revolution*. Chapel Hill: University of North Carolina Press, 1973.

Fabel, Robin F. *The Economy of British West Florida, 1763–1783*. Tuscaloosa: University of Alabama Press, 1987.

Ferguson, E. James. *The Power of the Purse: A History of American Public Finance, 1776–1790*. Chapel Hill: University of North Carolina Press, 1961.

Fisher, David H. *The Great Wave: Price Revolutions and the Rhythm of History*. New York: Oxford University Press, 1996.

Foner, Philip S. *Labor and the American Revolution*. Westport, CT: Greenwood, 1977.

Francis, Daniel, and Toby Morantz. *Partners in Furs: A History of the Fur Trade in Eastern James Bay, 1600–1870*. Kingston, Ontario, Canada: McGill-Queen's University Press, 1983.

Galenson, David. *Traders, Planters, and Slaves: Market Behavior in Early English America*. Cambridge, UK: Cambridge University Press, 1986.

———. *White Servitude in Colonial America: An Economic Analysis*. New York: Cambridge University Press, 1984.

Gemery, Henry A., and Jan S. Hogendorn, eds. *The Uncommon Market: Essays in the Economic History of the Atlantic Slave Trade*. New York: Academic Press, 1979.

Hancock, David. *Citizens of the World: London Merchants and the Integration of the British Atlantic Community, 1735–1785*. Cambridge, UK: Cambridge University Press, 1997.

Hartley, E. N. *Ironworks on the Saugus*. Norman: University of Oklahoma Press, 1957.

Henretta, James A. *The Origins of American Capitalism: Collected Essays*. Boston: Northeastern University Press, 1991.

Hughes, J. R. *Social Control in the Colonial Economy*. Charlottesville: University Press of Virginia, 1976.

Innes, Stephen. *Creating the Commonwealth: The Economic Culture of Puritan New England*. New York: W. W. Norton, 1995.

———, ed. *Work and Labor in Early America*. Chapel Hill: University of North Carolina Press, 1988.

Jernegan, Marcus W. *Laboring and Dependent Classes in Colonial America, 1607–1783*. Chicago: University of Chicago Press, 1931.

Jones, Alice H. *Wealth of a Nation to Be: The American Colonies on the Eve of the Revolution*. New York: Columbia University Press, 1980.

Klein, Herbert. *The Atlantic Slave Trade*. New York: Cambridge University Press, 1999.

———. *Slavery in the Americas: A Comparative Study of Virginia and Cuba*. Chicago: University of Chicago Press, 1967.

Kolchin, Peter. *American Slavery, 1619–1877*. New York: Hill & Wang, 1993.

Kulikoff, Allan. *The Agrarian Origins of American Capitalism*. Charlottesville: University Press of Virginia, 1992.

Kussmaul, Ann. *Servants in Husbandry in Early Modern England*. New York: Cambridge University Press, 1981.

Lang, James. *Conquest and Commerce: Spain and England in the Americas*. New York: Academic Press, 1975.

Lewis, Ronald L. *Coal, Iron, and Slaves: Individual Slavery in Maryland and Virginia, 1715–1865*. Westport, CT: Greenwood, 1979.

Liss, Peggy K. *Atlantic Empires: The Network of Trade and Revolution, 1713–1826*. Baltimore: Johns Hopkins University Press, 1983.

Malone, Joseph J. *Pine Trees and Politics: The Naval Stores and Forest Policy in Colonial New England, 1691–1775*. New York: Arno, 1979.

Mannix, Daniel P. *Black Cargoes: A History of the Atlantic Slave Trade, 1518–1865*. New York: Viking, 1962.

Martin, John Frederick. *Profits in the Wilderness: Entrepreneurship and the Founding of New England Towns in the Seventeenth Century*. Chapel Hill: University of North Carolina Press, 1991.

McCusker, John J. *Money and Exchange in Europe and America, 1600–1775*. Chapel Hill: University of North Carolina Press, 1978.

McCusker, John J., and Russell R. Menard. *The Economy of British America, 1607–1789*. Chapel Hill: University of North Carolina Press, 1985.

McKendrick, Neil, John Brewer, and J. H. Plumb. *The Birth of a Consumer Society: The Commercialization of Eighteenth-Century England*. Bloomington: Indiana University Press, 1982.

McManus, Edgar J. *Black Bondage in the North*. Syracuse, NY: Syracuse University Press, 1973.

Menard, Russell. "Financing the Low Country Export Boom: Capital and Growth in Early Carolina." *William and Mary Quarterly*, 3rd ser., 51 (1994): 659–76.

Middleton, Arthur P. *Tobacco Coast: A Maritime History of Chesapeake Bay in the Colonial Era*. Newport News, VA: Mariners' Museum, 1953.

Morgan, Kenneth. "The Organization of the Colonial American Rice Trade." *William and Mary Quarterly*, 3rd ser., 53 (1995): 433–52.

Mullin, Michael. *Africa in America: Slave Acculturation and Resistance in the American South and the British Caribbean, 1736–1831*. Urbana: University of Illinois Press, 1992.

Nettels, Curtis P. *The Money Supply of the American Colonies before 1720*. Madison: University of Wisconsin Press, 1934.

Newell, Margaret E. *From Dependency to Independence: Economic Revolution in Colonial New England*. Ithaca, NY: Cornell University Press, 1998.

Pares, Richard. *Yankees and Creoles: The Trade between North America and the West Indies before the American Revolution*. Cambridge, MA: Harvard University Press, 1956.

Parry, J. H. *Trade and Dominion: The European Overseas Empire in the Eighteenth Century*. London: Weidenfeld and Nicolson, 1971.

Perkins, Edwin J. *The Economy of Colonial America*. New York: Columbia University Press, 1980.

Pope-Hennessy, James. *Sins of the Fathers: A Study of the Atlantic Slave Traders, 1441–1807*. New York: Alfred A. Knopf, 1968.

Price, Jacob M. *Capital and Credit in British Overseas Trade: The View from the Chesapeake, 1700–1776*. Cambridge, MA: Harvard University Press, 1980.

Rabb, Theodore K. *Enterprise and Empire: Merchant and Gentry Investment in the Expansion of England, 1575–1630*. Cambridge, MA: Harvard University Press, 1967.

Rawley, James A. *The Transatlantic Slave Trade: A History*. New York: W. W. Norton, 1981.

Ray, Arthur J. *Indians in the Fur Trade: Their Role as Trappers, Hunters, and Middlemen in the Lands Southwest of Hudson Bay, 1660–1870*. Toronto: University of Toronto Press, 1974.

Rediker, Marcus. *Between the Devil and the Deep Blue Sea: Merchant Seamen, Pirates, and the Anglo-American Maritime World, 1700–1750*. Cambridge, UK: Cambridge University Press, 1987.

Rorabaugh, W. J. *The Craft Apprentice: From Franklin to the Machine Age in America*. New York: Oxford University Press, 1986.

Russell, Howard S. *A Long, Deep Furrow: Three Centuries of Farming in New England*. Hanover, NH: University Press of New England, 1976.

Schlesinger, Arthur M. *The Colonial Merchants and the American Revolution, 1763–1776*. New York: Columbia University Press, 1918.

Schumacher, Max G. *The Northern Farmer and His Markets during the Late Colonial Period*. New York: Arno, 1975.

Shammas, Carole. *The Pre-Industrial Consumer in England and America*. New York: Oxford University Press, 1990.

Shepherd, James F., and Gary M. Walton. *Shipping, Maritime Trade and the Economic Development of Colonial North America*. Cambridge, UK: Cambridge University Press, 1972.

Smith, Abbot E. *Colonists in Bondage: White Servitude and Convict Labor in America, 1607–1776*. Chapel Hill: University of North Carolina Press, 1947.

Steinberg, Robert J. *The Invention of Free Labor: The Employment Relation in English and American Law and Culture, 1350–1850*. Chapel Hill: University of North Carolina Press, 1991.

Tolles, Frederick B. *Meeting House and Counting House*. Chapel Hill: University of North Carolina Press, 1948.

Truxes, Thomas M. *Irish-American Trade, 1660–1783*. Cambridge, UK: Cambridge University Press, 1988.

Walton, Gary M., and James F. Shepherd. *The Economic Rise of Early America*. Cambridge, UK: Cambridge University Press, 1979.

Walvin, James. *Black Ivory: A History of British Slavery*. London: Fontana, 1992.

Family, Community, and Society

Altman, Ida, and James Horn, eds. *"To Make America": European Emigration in the Early Modern Period*. Berkeley: University of California Press, 1991.

Anderson, Virginia D. *New England's Generation: The Great Migration and the Formation of Society and Culture in the Seventeenth Century*. New York: Cambridge University Press, 1991.

Bailyn, Bernard. *The Peopling of British North America: An Introduction*. New York: Vintage Books, 1988.

———. *Voyagers to the West: A Passage in the Peopling of America on the Eve of the Revolution*. New York: Alfred A. Knopf, 1986.

Bailyn, Bernard, and Philip D. Morgan, eds. *Strangers Within the Realm: Cultural Margins of the First British Empire*. Chapel Hill: University of North Carolina Press, 1991.

Balmer, Randall H. *A Perfect Babel of Confusion: Dutch Religion and English Culture in the Middle Colonies*. New York: Oxford University Press, 1989.

Bender, Thomas. *Community and Social Change in America*. New Brunswick, NJ: Rutgers University Press, 1978.

Berlin, Ira. "Time, Space, and the Evolution of Afro-American Society on British Mainland North America." *American Historical Review* 85 (January 1980): 44–78.

Bitterli, Urs. *Cultures in Conflict: Encounters between European and Non-European Cultures, 1492–1800*. Stanford, CA: Stanford University Press, 1989.

Breen, T. H. *Tobacco Culture: The Mentality of the Great Tidewater Planters on the Eve of Revolution*. Princeton, NJ: Princeton University Press, 1985.

Bridenbaugh, Carl. *Cities in Revolt: Urban Life in America, 1742–1776*. New York: Oxford University Press, 1985.

———. *Cities in the Wilderness: The First Century of Urban Life in America, 1625–1742*. New York: Oxford University Press, 1971.

Brown, Richard D. *Modernization: The Transformation of American Life, 1600–1865*. New York: Farrar, Straus and Giroux, 1976.

Bumsted, J. M. *Land, Settlement, and Politics on Eighteenth-Century Prince Edward Island*. Kingston, Ontario, Canada: McGill-Queen's University Press, 1987.

———. *The People's Clearance: Highland Emigration to British North America, 1770–1815*. Edinburgh, UK: Edinburgh University Press, 1982.

Butler, Jon. *The Huguenots in America: A Refugee People in a New World Society*. Cambridge, MA: Harvard University Press, 1983.

Canny, Nicholas, ed. *Europeans on the Move: Studies in European Migration, 1500–1800*. New York: Oxford University Press, 1994.

Carroll, Peter N. *Puritanism and the Wilderness: The Intellectual Significance of the New England Frontier, 1629–1700*. New York: Columbia University Press, 1969.

Cayton, Andrew R., and Fredrika J. Teute, eds. *Contact Points: American Frontiers from the Mohawk Valley to the Mississippi, 1750–1830*. Chapel Hill: University of North Carolina Press, 1998.

Cell, Gillian T. *English Enterprise in Newfoundland, 1577–1660*. Toronto: University of Toronto Press, 1969.

Clark, Charles E. *The Eastern Frontier: The Settlement of Northern New England, 1610–1763*. New York: Alfred A. Knopf, 1970.

Colley, Linda. *Britons: Forging the Nation, 1707–1837*. New Haven, CT: Yale University Press, 1992.

Cook, Edward M. *The Fathers of the Town: Leadership and Community Structure in Eighteenth-Century New England*. Baltimore: Johns Hopkins University Press, 1976.

Crane, Verner W. *The Southern Frontier, 1670–1732*. New York: W. W. Norton, 1981.

Cremin, Lawrence A. *American Education: The Colonial Experience*. New York: HarperCollins, 1972.

Cressy, David. *Coming Over: Migration and Communication Between England and New England in the Seventeenth Century*. New York: Cambridge University Press, 1987.

Demos, John. *The Unredeemed Captive: A Family Story from Early America*. New York: Vintage Books, 1995.

Dickson, R. J. *Ulster Emigration to Colonial America, 1718–1775*. London: Routledge and Kegan Paul, 1966.

Ditz, Toby L. *Property and Kinship: Inheritance in Early Connecticut, 1750–1820*. Princeton, NJ: Princeton University Press, 1986.

Dobson, David. *Scottish Emigration to Colonial America, 1607–1785*. Athens: University of Georgia Press, 1994.

Dunn, Richard S. *Puritans and Yankees: The Winthrop Dynasty of New England, 1630–1717*. Princeton, NJ: Princeton University Press, 1962.

Ekirch, A. Roger. *Bound for America: The Transportation of British Convicts to the Colonies, 1718–1775*. Oxford, UK: Clarendon Press, 1987.

Fabend, Firth H. *A Dutch Family in the Middle Colonies, 1660–1800*. New Brunswick, NJ: Rutgers University Press, 1991.

Fischer, David H. *Growing Old in America*. New York: Oxford University Press, 1978.

Flaherty, David H. *Privacy in Colonial New England*. Charlottesville: University Press of Virginia, 1972.

Fliegelman, Jay. *Prodigals and Pilgrims: The American Revolution Against Patriarchal Authority, 1750–1800*. Cambridge, UK: Cambridge University Press, 1982.

Frost, J. William. *The Quaker Family in Colonial America: A Portrait of the Society of Friends*. New York: St. Martin's, 1973.

Graham, Ian. C. *Colonists from Scotland: Emigration to North America, 1707–1783*. Ithaca, NY: Cornell University Press, 1956.

Gray, Edward G. *New World Babel: Languages and Nations in Early America*. Princeton, NJ: Princeton University Press, 1999.

Greene, Jack P. *Pursuits of Happiness: The Social Development of Early Modern British Colonies and the Formation of American Culture*. Chapel Hill: University of North Carolina Press, 1988.

Grumet, Robert S. *Historic Contact: Indian Peoples and Colonists in Today's Northeastern United States in the Sixteenth and Seventeenth Centuries*. Norman: University of Oklahoma Press, 1996.

Haffenden, Philip S. *New England in the English Nation, 1689–1713*. New York: Oxford University Press, 1974.

Hann, John H. *Apalachee: The Land Between the Rivers*. Gainesville: University of Florida Press, 1988.

Henretta, James A., Michael G. Kammen, and Stanley N. Katz, eds. *The Transformation of Early American History: Society, Authority, and Ideology*. New York: Alfred A. Knopf, 1991.

Henretta, James A., and Gregory H. Nobles. *Evolution and Revolution: American Society, 1600–1820*. Lexington, MA: Heath, 1987.

Hoffer, Peter C. *Law and People in Colonial America*. Baltimore: Johns Hopkins University Press, 1992.

Hofstadter, Richard. *America at 1750: A Social Portrait*. New York: Alfred A. Knopf, 1971.

Jimenez, Mary Ann. *Changing Faces of Madness: Early American Attitudes and Treatment of the Insane*. Hanover, NH: Brandeis University Press, 1987.

Johnson, Richard R. *Adjustment to Empire: The New England Colonies, 1675–1715*. New Brunswick, NJ: Rutgers University Press, 1981.

Kammen, Michael. *People of Paradox: An Inquiry Concerning*

the Origins of American Civilization. Ithaca, NY: Cornell University Press, 1990.

Kulikoff, Allan. *Tobacco and Slaves: The Development of Southern Culture in the Chesapeake, 1680–1800*. Chapel Hill: University of North Carolina Press, 1986.

Leach, Douglas E. *The Northern Colonial Frontier, 1607–1763*. New York: Holt, Rinehart and Winston, 1966.

Lockhart, Audrey. *Some Aspects of Emigration from Ireland to the North American Colonies between 1660 and 1775*. New York: Arno, 1976.

Main, Jackson T. *The Social Structure of Revolutionary America*. Princeton, NJ: Princeton University Press, 1965.

Mancall, Peter C. *Deadly Medicine: Indians and Alcohol in Early America*. Ithaca, NY: Cornell University Press, 1995.

McConnell, Michael N. *A Country Between: The Upper Ohio Valley and Its Peoples, 1724–1774*. Lincoln: University of Nebraska Press, 1992.

Miller, Christopher L., and George R. Hamell. "A New Perspective on Indian-White Contact: Cultural Symbols and Colonial Trade." *Journal of American History* 73 (1986): 311–28.

Morgan, Edmund S. *The Puritan Family: Religion and Domestic Relations in Seventeenth-Century New England*. Westport, CT: Greenwood, 1980.

Murrin, John. "Beneficiaries of Catastrophe: The English Colonies in America." In *The New American History*, edited by Eric Foner. Philadelphia: Temple University Press, 1997.

Nash, Gary B. *The Urban Crucible: Social Change, Political Consciousness, and the Origins of the American Revolution*. Cambridge, MA: Harvard University Press, 1979.

Nobles, Gregory H. "Breaking Into the Backcountry: New Approaches to the Early American Frontier." *William and Mary Quarterly*, 3rd ser., 46 (1989): 641–70.

Powell, Sumner C. *Puritan Village: The Formation of a New England Town*. Middletown, CT: Wesleyan University Press, 1963.

Reps, John W. *Town Planning in Frontier America*. Columbia: University of South Carolina Press, 1980.

Rorabaugh, W. J. *The Alcoholic Republic: An American Tradition*. New York: Oxford University Press, 1981.

Rutman, Darrett B., and Anita H. Rutman. *Small Worlds, Large Questions: Explorations in Early American Social History, 1600–1850*. Charlottesville: University Press of Virginia, 1994.

Scholten, Catherine M. *Childbearing in American Society: 1650–1850*. New York: New York University Press, 1985.

Slater, Peter G. *Children in the New England Mind: In Death and Life*. Hamden, CT: Archon, 1977.

Smith, Daniel B. *Inside the Great House: Planter Family Life in Eighteenth-Century Chesapeake Society*. Ithaca, NY: Cornell University Press, 1980.

Sobel, Mechal. *The World They Made Together: Black and White*

Values in Eighteenth-Century Virginia. Princeton, NJ: Princeton University Press, 1987.

Spielmann, Katherine A., ed. *Farmers, Hunters, and Colonists: Interaction Between the Southwest and the Southern Plains*. Tucson: University of Arizona Press, 1991.

Steele, Ian K. *The English Atlantic, 1675–1740: An Exploration of Communication and Community*. New York: Oxford University Press, 1986.

Tate, Thad W., and David L. Ammerman, eds. *The Chesapeake in the Seventeenth Century: Essays on Anglo-American Society*. Chapel Hill: University of North Carolina Press, 1979.

Trigger, Bruce G. "Early Native American Responses to European Contact: Romantic versus Rationalistic Interpretations." *Journal of American History* 77:4 (March 1991): 1195–215.

Usner, Daniel H. *Indians, Settlers, and Slaves in a Frontier Exchange Economy: The Lower Mississippi Valley Before 1783*. Chapel Hill: University of North Carolina Press, 1992.

Wall, Helena M. *Fierce Communion: Family and Community in Early America*. Cambridge, MA: Harvard University Press, 1990.

Wells, Robert V. *The Population of the British Colonies in America Before 1776*. Princeton, NJ: Princeton University Press, 1975.

White, Richard. *"It's Your Misfortune and None of My Own": A New History of the American West*. Norman: University of Oklahoma Press, 1991.

Yazawa, Melvin. *From Colonies to Commonwealth: Familial Ideology and the Beginnings of the American Republic*. Baltimore: Johns Hopkins University Press, 1985.

Zuckerman, Michael. *Peaceable Kingdoms: New England Towns in the Eighteenth Century*. Westport, CT: Greenwood, 1983.

Gender Issues

Beard, Mary. *Women as a Force in History: A Study in Traditions and Realities*. New York: Macmillan, 1946.

Benson, Mary S. *Women in Eighteenth-Century America: A Study of Opinion and Social Usage*. New York: Columbia University Press, 1935.

Berkin, Carol. *First Generations: Women in Colonial America*. New York: Hill & Wang, 1997.

Brown, Kathleen M. *Good Wives, Nasty Wenches, and Anxious Patriarchs: Gender, Race, and Power in Colonial Virginia*. Chapel Hill: University of North Carolina Press, 1996.

Buel, Joy D., and Richard Buel. *The Way of Duty: A Woman and Her Family in Revolutionary America*. New York: W. W. Norton, 1984.

Clepp, Susan E. "Revolutionary Bodies: Women and the Fertility Transition in the Mid-Atlantic Region, 1760–1820." *Journal of American History* 85 (1998): 910–45.

Cott, Nancy F. *The Bonds of Womanhood: "Women's Sphere" in New England, 1780–1835*. New Haven, CT: Yale University Press, 1977.

Dayton, Cornelia H. *Women Before the Bar: Gender, Law, and*

Society in Connecticut, 1639–1789. Chapel Hill: University of North Carolina Press, 1995.

Donegan, Jane B. *Women and Men Midwives: Medicine, Morality, and Misogyny in Early America.* Westport, CT: Greenwood, 1978.

Hoffer, Peter C., and N. E. Hull. *Murdering Mothers: Infanticide in England and New England, 1558–1803.* New York: New York University Press, 1981.

Hoffman, Ronald, and Peter J. Albert, eds. *Women in the Age of the American Revolution.* Charlottesville: University Press of Virginia, 1989.

James, Janet W. *Changing Ideas about Women in the United States, 1776–1825.* New York: Garland, 1981.

Jensen, Joan M. *Loosening the Bonds: Mid-Atlantic Farm Women, 1750–1850.* New Haven, CT: Yale University Press, 1986.

Jester, Susan. *Disorderly Women: Sexual Politics & Evangelicalism in Revolutionary New England.* Ithaca, NY: Cornell University Press, 1994.

Kerber, Linda. *Women of the Republic: Intellect and Ideology in Early America.* Chapel Hill: University of North Carolina Press, 1980.

Koehler, Lyle. *A Search for Power: The "Weaker Sex" in Seventeenth-Century New England.* Urbana: University of Illinois Press, 1980.

Norton, Mary Beth. *Founding Mothers and Fathers: Gendered Power and the Forming of American Society.* New York: Alfred A. Knopf, 1996.

———. *Liberty's Daughters: The Revolutionary Experience of American Women, 1750–1800.* Ithaca, NY: Cornell University Press, 1996.

Price, Mary, ed. *Women in English Society, 1500–1800.* New York: Methuen, 1985.

Reis, Elizabeth. *Damned Women: Sinners and Witches in Puritan New England.* Ithaca, NY: Cornell University Press, 1999.

Salmon, Marylynn. *Women and the Law of Property in Early America.* Chapel Hill: University of North Carolina Press, 1986.

Spruill, Julia C. *Women's Life and Work in the Southern Colonies.* Chapel Hill: University of North Carolina Press, 1938.

Thompson, Roger. *Women in Stuart England and America: A Comparative Study.* Boston: Routledge & Kegan Paul, 1974.

Ulrich, Laurel T. *Good Wives: Image and Reality in the Lives of Women in Northern New England, 1650–1750.* New York: Alfred A. Knopf, 1982.

Van Kirk, Sylvia. *Many Tender Ties: Women in Fur-Trade Society, 1670–1870.* Norman: University of Oklahoma Press, 1980.

Military and Diplomatic

Alden, John R. *John Stuart and the Southern Colonial Frontier.* New York: Gordian Press, 1966.

Anderson, Fred. *Crucible of War: The Seven Years' War and the Fate of Empire in British North America, 1754–1766.* New York: Alfred A. Knopf, 2000.

Aquila, Richard. *The Iroquois Restoration: Iroquois Diplomacy on the Colonial Frontier, 1701–1754.* Detroit, MI: Wayne State University Press, 1983.

Bellesiles, Michael. *Revolutionary Outlaws: Ethan Allen and the Struggle for Independence on the Early American Frontier.* Charlottesville: University Press of Virginia, 1993.

Black, Jeremy. *Britain as a Military Power, 1688–1715.* London: University College London Press, 1999.

Black, Jeremy, and Philip Woodfine, eds. *The British Navy and the Use of Naval Power in the Eighteenth Century.* Leicester, UK: Leicester University Press, 1988.

Bowler, R. Arthur. *Logistics and the Failure of the British Army in America, 1775–1783.* Princeton, NJ: Princeton University Press, 1975.

Carp, E. Wayne. *To Starve the Army at Pleasure: Continental Army Administration and American Political Culture, 1775–1783.* Chapel Hill: University of North Carolina Press, 1984.

Cave, Alfred A. *The Pequot War.* Amherst: University of Massachusetts Press, 1996.

Christie, Ian R. *Wars and Revolutions: Britain, 1760–1815.* Cambridge, MA: Harvard University Press, 1982.

Cress, Lawrence D. *Citizens in Arms: The Army and the Militia in American Society to the War of 1812.* Chapel Hill: University of North Carolina Press, 1982.

Draper, Theodore. *A Struggle for Power: The American Revolution.* New York: Random House, 1996.

Dull, Jonathan R. *The French Navy and American Independence: A Study of Arms and Diplomacy, 1774–1787.* Princeton, NJ: Princeton University Press, 1975.

Ferling, John E. *A Wilderness of Miseries: War and Warriors in Early America.* Westport, CT: Greenwood, 1980.

Fischer, David H. *Paul Revere's Ride.* New York: Oxford University Press, 1995.

Fowler, William M. *Rebels under Sail: The American Navy during the Revolution.* New York: Scribner's, 1976.

Frey, Sylvia R. *The British Soldier in America: A Social History of Military Life in the Colonial Period.* Austin: University of Texas Press, 1981.

Gipson, Lawrence H. "The American Revolution as an Aftermath of the Great War for Empire, 1754–1763." *Political Science Quarterly* 65 (1950): 86–104.

Gross, Robert. *The Minutemen and Their World.* New York: Hill & Wang, 1976.

Gruber, Ira D. *The Howe Brothers and the American Revolution.* New York: Atheneum, 1972.

Haynes, Robert V. *The Natchez District and the American Revolution.* Jackson: University Press of Mississippi, 1976.

Higginbotham, Don, ed. *The War of American Independence: Military Attitudes, Policies, and Practice, 1763–1789.* New York: Macmillan, 1971.

Hoffman, Ronald, and Peter J. Albert, eds. *Arms and Inde-*

pendence: The Military Character of the American Revolution. Charlottesville: University Press of Virginia, 1984.

———. Diplomacy and Revolution: The Franco-American Alliance of 1778. Charlottesville: University Press of Virginia, 1981.

———. Peace and the Peacemakers: The Treaty of 1783. Charlottesville: University Press of Virginia, 1986.

Hutson, James H. John Adams and the Diplomacy of the American Revolution. Lexington: University Press of Kentucky, 1980.

Jacobs, W. R. Diplomacy and Indian Gifts: Anglo-French Rivalry along the Ohio and Northwest Frontier, 1748–1763. Stanford, CA: Stanford University Press, 1950.

Jones, Dorothy V. License for Empire: Colonialism by Treaty in Early America. Chicago: University of Chicago Press, 1982.

Kaplan, Lawrence S. Colonies Into Nation: American Diplomacy, 1763–1801. New York: Macmillan, 1972.

Karr, Ronald D. " 'Why Should You Be So Furious?': The Violence of the Pequot War." Journal of American History 85 (December 1998): 876–909.

Keegan, John. Fields of Battle: The Wars for North America. New York: Vintage Books, 1997.

Leach, Douglas E. Arms for Empire: A Military History of the British Colonies in North America, 1607–1763. New York: Macmillan, 1973.

———. Roots of Conflict: British Armed Forces and Colonial Americans, 1677–1763. Chapel Hill: University of North Carolina Press, 1986.

Lepore, Jill. The Name of War: King Philip's War and the Origins of American Identity. New York: Alfred A. Knopf, 1998.

Mackesy, Piers. The War for America, 1775–1783. Cambridge, MA: Harvard University Press, 1964.

Malone, Patrick D. The Skulking Way of War: Technology and Tactics Among the New England Indians. Lanham, MD: Madison, 1991.

Marcus, G. J. The Conquest of North America. New York: Oxford University Press, 1981.

Marshall, P. J., ed. The Oxford History of the British Empire. Vol. 2. The Eighteenth Century. New York: Oxford University Press, 1998.

Martin, James K., and Mark E. Lender. A Respectable Army: The Military Origins of the Republic, 1763–1789. Arlington Heights, IL: Harlan Davidson, 1982.

Morrison, Kenneth M. The Embattled Northeast: The Elusive Ideal of Alliance in Abenake-Euroamerican Relations. Berkeley: University of California Press, 1984.

Peckham, Howard M. The Colonial Wars, 1689–1762. Chicago: University of Chicago Press, 1965.

———, ed. The Toll of Independence: Engagements and Battle Casualties of the American Revolution. Chicago: University of Chicago Press, 1974.

Ritchie, Robert C. Captain Kidd and the War Against the Pirates. Cambridge, MA: Harvard University Press, 1989.

Rogers, Alan. Empire and Liberty: American Resistance to British

Authority, 1755–1763. Berkeley: University of California Press, 1974.

Royster, Charles. A Revolutionary People at War: The Continental Army and American Character, 1775–1783. Chapel Hill: University of North Carolina Press, 1979.

Savelle, Max. The Origins of American Diplomacy: The International History of Anglo-America, 1492–1763. New York: Macmillan, 1967.

Searcy, Martha C. The Georgia-Florida Contest in the American Revolution, 1776–1778. Tuscaloosa: University of Alabama Press, 1985.

Shy, John. A People Numerous and Armed: Reflections on the Military Struggle for American Independence. Ann Arbor: University of Michigan Press, 1990.

———. Toward Lexington: The Role of the British Army in the Coming of the American Revolution. Princeton, NJ: Princeton University Press, 1965.

Steele, Ian K. Betrayals: Fort William Henry and the Massacre. New York: Oxford University Press, 1990.

———. Warpaths: Invasions of North America. New York: Oxford University Press, 1994.

Stinchcombe, William C. The American Revolution and French Alliance. Syracuse, NY: Syracuse University Press, 1969.

Stone, Lawrence, ed. An Imperial State at War: Britain from 1689 to 1815. New York: Routledge, 1994.

Stourzh, Gerald. Benjamin Franklin and American Foreign Policy. Chicago: University of Chicago Press, 1954.

Swanson, Carl E. Predators and Prizes: American Privateering and Imperial Warfare, 1739–1748. Columbia: University of South Carolina Press, 1991.

Varg, Paul A. Foreign Policies of the Founding Fathers. East Lansing: Michigan State University Press, 1964.

Wallace, Willard M. Appeal to Arms: A Military History of the American Revolution. New York: Harper, 1951.

Zobel, Hiller. The Boston Massacre. New York: W. W. Norton, 1996.

Politics and Government

Adams, Willi P. The First American Constitutions: Republican Ideology and the Making of the State Constitutions in the Revolutionary Era. Translated by Rita Kimber and Robert Kimber. Chapel Hill: University of North Carolina Press, 1980.

Ammerman, David L. In the Common Cause: American Response to the Coercive Acts of 1774. Charlottesville: University Press of Virginia, 1974.

Andrews, Charles. The Colonial Period of American History. 4 vols. New Haven, CT: Yale University Press, 1934–1938.

Arieli, Yehoshua. Individualism and Nationalism in American Ideology. Baltimore: Penguin, 1966.

Bailyn, Bernard. The Ideological Origins of the American Revolution. Cambridge, MA: Harvard University Press, 1967.

———. The Origins of American Politics. New York: Random House, 1970.

Barrow, Thomas C. *Trade and Empire: The British Customs Service in Colonial America, 1660–1775.* Cambridge, MA: Harvard University Press, 1967.

Becker, Carl. *The Declaration of Independence: A Study in the History of Political Ideas.* New York: Alfred A. Knopf, 1942.

Becker, Robert A. *Revolution, Reform, and the Politics of American Taxation, 1763–1783.* Baton Rouge: Louisiana State University Press, 1980.

Beeman, Richard, Stephen Botein, and Edward C. Carter, eds. *Beyond Confederation: Origins of the Constitution and American National Identity.* Chapel Hill: University of North Carolina Press, 1987.

Bliss, Robert M. *Revolution and Empire: English Politics and the American Colonies in the Seventeenth Century.* Manchester, UK: Manchester University Press, 1990.

Bonomi, Patricia. *The Lord Cornbury Scandal: The Politics of Reputation in British America.* Chapel Hill: University of North Carolina Press, 1998.

Botein, Stephen. *Early American Law and Society.* New York: Alfred A. Knopf, 1983.

Breen, T. H. *The Character of the Good Ruler: A Study of Puritan Political Ideas in New England, 1630–1730.* New Haven, CT: Yale University Press, 1970.

Bremer, Francis J. *Puritan Crisis: New England and the English Civil Wars, 1630–1670.* New York: Garland, 1989.

Brewer, John. *Party Ideology and Popular Politics at the Accession of George III.* Cambridge, UK; New York: Cambridge University Press, 1976.

Bullion, John L. *A Great and Necessary Measure: George Grenville and the Genesis of the Stamp Act, 1763–1765.* Columbia: University of Missouri Press, 1982.

Canny, Nicholas P. "The Ideology of English Colonization: From Ireland to America." *William and Mary Quarterly,* 3rd ser., 30 (1973): 575–98.

Christie, Ian K., and Benjamin W. Labaree. *Empire or Independence: A British-American Dialogue on the Coming of the American Revolution.* New York: W. W. Norton, 1976.

Colbourn, H. Trevor. *The Lamp of Experience: Whig History and the Intellectual Origins of the American Revolution.* Chapel Hill: University of North Carolina Press, 1965.

Craven, Wesley F. *The Colonies in Transition, 1660–1713.* New York: Harper & Row, 1968.

Daniels, Bruce C., ed. *Power and Status: Officeholding in Colonial America.* Middletown, CT: Wesleyan University Press, 1986.

———. *Town and Country: Essays on the Structure of Local Government in the American Colonies.* Middletown, CT: Wesleyan University Press, 1978.

Dargo, George. *Roots of the Republic: A New Perspective on Early American Constitutionalism.* New York: Praeger, 1974.

Dinkin, Robert J. *Voting in Provincial America: A Study of Elections in the Thirteen Colonies, 1680–1776.* Westport, CT: Greenwood, 1977.

Donoughue, Bernard. *British Politics and the American Revolution: The Path to War, 1773–75.* New York: St. Martin's, 1964.

Douglass, Elisha P. *Rebels and Democrats: The Struggle for Equal Political Rights and Majority Rule during the American Revolution.* Chapel Hill: University of North Carolina Press, 1955.

Egnal, Marc. *A Mighty Empire: The Origins of the American Revolution.* Ithaca, NY: Cornell University Press, 1988.

Elliot, J. H. *Imperial Spain, 1469–1716.* New York: Penguin, 1990.

Flaherty, David H., ed. *Essays in the History of Early American Law.* Chapel Hill: University of North Carolina Press, 1969.

Forster, Cornelius. *The Uncontrolled Chancellor: Charles Townshend and His American Policy.* Providence: Rhode Island Bicentennial Foundation, 1978.

Gipson, Lawrence H. *The Coming of the Revolution, 1763–1775.* New York: HarperCollins, 1954.

Greene, Jack P. *The Intellectual Construction of America: Exceptionalism and Identity from 1492–1800.* Chapel Hill: University of North Carolina Press, 1997.

———. *Negotiated Authorities: Essays in Colonial Political and Constitutional History.* Charlottesville: University Press of Virginia, 1994.

———. *Peripheries and Center: Constitutional Development in the Extended Polities of the British Empire and the United States, 1607–1788.* Athens: University of Georgia Press, 1986.

———. *The Quest for Power: The Lower Houses of Assembly in the Southern Royal Colonies, 1689–1776.* Chapel Hill: University of North Carolina Press, 1963.

Guttridge, George H. *English Whiggism and the American Revolution.* Berkeley: University of California Press, 1963.

Haffenden, Philip S. *New England in the English Nation, 1689–1713.* Oxford, UK: Clarendon, 1974.

Henderson, H. James. *Party Politics in the Continental Congress.* New York: McGraw-Hill, 1974.

Henretta, James. *"Salutary Neglect": Colonial Administration Under the Duke of Newcastle.* Princeton, NJ: Princeton University Press, 1972.

Hinderaker, Eric. *Elusive Empires: Constructing Colonialism in the Ohio Valley, 1673–1800.* New York: Cambridge University Press, 1997.

Hoffer, Peter C., and N. E. Hull. *Impeachment in America, 1635–1805.* New Haven, CT: Yale University Press, 1984.

Hofstadter, Richard. *The Idea of a Party System: The Rise of Legitimate Opposition in the United States, 1740–1840.* Berkeley: University of California Press, 1969.

Horwitz, Morton J. *The Transformation of American Law, 1780–1860.* Cambridge, MA: Harvard University Press, 1977.

Johnson, Richard R. *Adjustment to Empire: The New England Colonies, 1675–1715.* New Brunswick, NJ: Rutgers University Press, 1981.

Kammen, Michael. *Empire and Interest: The American Colonies and the Politics of Mercantilism.* Philadelphia: University of Pennsylvania Press, 1970.

———. *A Rope of Sand: The Colonial Agents, British Politics, and the American Revolution.* Ithaca, NY: Cornell University Press, 1968.

Katz, Stanley N., John M. Murrin, and Douglas Greenberg, eds. *Colonial America: Essays in Politics and Social Development.* New York: McGraw-Hill, 1993.

Ketcham, Ralph L. *From Colony to Country: The Revolution in American Thought, 1750–1820.* New York: Macmillan, 1975.

Kettner, James H. *The Development of American Citizenship, 1608–1870.* Chapel Hill: University of North Carolina Press, 1978.

Labaree, Leonard W. *Royal Government in America: A Study of the British Colonial System Before 1783.* New Haven, CT: Yale University Press, 1930.

Landsman, Ned C. "Nation, Migration, and the Province in the First British Empire: Scotland and the Americas, 1600–1800." *American Historical Review* 105 (April 1999): 463–75.

Leder, Lawrence H. *Liberty and Authority: Early American Political Ideology, 1689–1763.* Chicago: Quadrangle, 1968.

Levy, Leonard W. *The Emergence of a Free Press.* New York: Oxford University Press, 1985.

Lockridge, Kenneth A. *Settlement and Unsettlement in Early America: The Crisis of Political Legitimacy before the Revolution.* Cambridge, UK: Cambridge University Press, 1981.

Lonn, Ella. *The Colonial Agents of the Southern Colonies.* Gloucester, MA: Smith, 1965.

Lovejoy, David S. *The Glorious Revolution in America.* New York: Harper & Row, 1972.

Maier, Pauline. *American Scripture: Making the Declaration of Independence.* New York: Vintage Books, 1998.

———. *From Resistance to Revolution: Colonial Radicals and the Development of American Opposition to Britain, 1775–1776.* New York: W. W. Norton, 1992.

Main, Jackson T. *Political Parties before the Constitution.* Chapel Hill: University of North Carolina Press, 1973.

———. *The Upper House in Revolutionary America, 1763–1788.* Madison: University of Wisconsin Press, 1967.

Marston, Jerrilyn G. *King and Congress: The Transfer of Political Legitimacy, 1774–1776.* Princeton, NJ: Princeton University Press, 1987.

Martin, James K. *Men in Rebellion: Higher Government Leaders and the Coming of the American Revolution.* New Brunswick, NJ: Rutgers University Press, 1973.

Matthews, Richard K. *Virtue, Corruption, and Self-Interest: Political Values in the Eighteenth Century.* Bethlehem, PA: Lehigh University Press, 1994.

Middlekauf, Robert. *The Glorious Cause: The American Revolution, 1763–1789.* New York: Oxford University Press, 1982.

Middleton, Richard. *The Bells of Victory: The Pitt-Newcastle Ministry and the Conduct of the Seven Years' War, 1757–1762.* Cambridge, UK: Cambridge University Press, 1985.

Morgan, Edmund S. *The Birth of the Republic, 1763–1789.* Chicago: University of Chicago Press, 1956.

———. *Inventing the People: The Rise of Popular Sovereignty in England and America.* New York: W. W. Norton, 1988.

Morgan, Edmund S., and Helen Morgan. *The Stamp Act Crisis: Prologue to Revolution.* Chapel Hill: University of North Carolina Press, 1995.

Namier, Lewis. *England in the Age of the American Revolution.* 2nd ed. New York: St. Martin's, 1961.

Olson, Alison G. *Anglo-American Politics, 1660–1775: The Relationship Between Parties in England and Colonial America.* New York: Oxford University Press, 1973.

———. *Making the Empire Work: London and American Interest Groups, 1690–1790.* Cambridge, MA: Harvard University Press, 1997.

Osgood, Herbert L. *The American Colonies in the Eighteenth-Century.* 4 vols. Gloucester, MA: Smith, 1957.

Pagden, Anthony. *Lords of All the World: Ideologies of Empire in Spain, Britain, and France, c. 1500–c. 1800.* New Haven, CT: Yale University Press, 1995.

Pahl, Jon. *Paradox Lost: Free Will and Political Liberty in American Culture, 1630–1760.* Baltimore: Johns Hopkins University Press, 1992.

Palmer, Robert R. *The Age of the Democratic Revolution: A Political History of Europe and America, 1760–1800.* 2 vols. Princeton, NJ: Princeton University Press, 1959–1964.

Pole, J. R. *The Gift of Government: Political Responsibility from the English Restoration to American Independence.* Athens: University of Georgia Press, 1983.

———. *Political Representation in England and the Origins of the American Republic.* New York: St. Martin's, 1966.

Potter, Janice. *The Liberty We Seek: Loyalist Ideology in Colonial New York and Massachusetts.* Cambridge, MA: Harvard University Press, 1983.

Rakove, Jack. *The Beginnings of National Politics: An Interpretive History of the Continental Congress.* Baltimore: Johns Hopkins University Press, 1979.

Reid, John P. *In a Rebellious Spirit: The Argument of Facts, the Liberty Riot, and the Coming of the American Revolution.* University Park: Pennsylvania State University Press, 1979.

———. *In Defiance of the Law: The Standing-Army Controversy, the Two Constitutions, and the Coming of the American Revolution.* Chapel Hill: University of North Carolina Press, 1981.

Ritcheson, Charles R. *British Politics and the American Revolution.* Norman: University of Oklahoma Press, 1954.

Robinson, Donald L. *Slavery in the Structure of American Politics, 1765–1820.* New York: Harcourt Brace Jovanovich, 1971.

Rossiter, Clinton L. *Seedtime of the Republic: The Origin of the*

American Tradition of Political Liberty. New York: Harcourt, Brace, 1953.

Sosin, Jack M. *English America and Imperial Inconstancy, The Rise of Provincial Autonomy, 1696–1715*. Lincoln: University of Nebraska Press, 1985.

———. *English America and the Revolution of 1688*. Lincoln: University of Nebraska Press, 1991.

Thomas, P. D. *British Politics and the Stamp Act Crisis: The First Phase of the American Revolution, 1763–1767*. New York: Oxford University Press, 1975.

Tucker, Robert W., and David C. Hendrickson. *The Fall of the First British Empire: Origins of the War for American Independence*. Baltimore: Johns Hopkins University Press, 1982.

Tully, Alan. *Forming American Politics: Ideals, Interests, and Institutions in Colonial New York and Pennsylvania*. Baltimore: Johns Hopkins University Press, 1994.

Voorhees, David W. "The 'Fervent Zeale' of Jacob Leisler." *William and Mary Quarterly,* 3rd ser., 51 (July 1994): 447–72.

Webb, Stephen S. *1676: The End of American Independence*. New York: Alfred A. Knopf, 1984.

———. *Lord Churchill's Coup: The Anglo-American Empire and the Glorious Revolution Reconsidered*. Syracuse, NY: Syracuse University Press, 1998.

Wickwire, Franklin B. *British Subministers and Colonial America, 1763–1783*. Princeton, NJ: Princeton University Press, 1966.

Wiecek, William M. *The Sources of Antislavery Constitutionalism in America, 1760–1848*. Ithaca, NY: Cornell University Press, 1977.

Wood, Gordon S. *The Creation of the American Republic, 1776–1787*. Chapel Hill: University of North Carolina Press, 1969.

———. *The Radicalism of the American Revolution*. Cambridge, MA: Harvard University Press, 1979.

Race and Ethnicity

Axtell, James. *After Columbus: Essays in the Ethnohistory of Colonial North America*. New York: Oxford University Press, 1988.

———. *Beyond 1492: Encounters in Colonial North America*. New York: Cambridge University Press, 1992.

———. *The European and the Indian: Essays in the Ethnohistory of Colonial North America*. New York: Oxford University Press, 1981.

———. *The Indians' New South: Cultural Change in the Colonial Southeast*. Baton Rouge: Louisiana State University Press, 1997.

———. *The Invasion Within: The Contest of Cultures in Colonial North America*. New York: Oxford University Press, 1985.

Boucher, Philip P. *Cannibal Encounters: Europeans and Island Caribs, 1492–1763*. Baltimore: Johns Hopkins University Press, 1992.

Bourne, Russell. *The Red King's Rebellion: Racial Politics in New England, 1675–1678*. New York: Oxford University Press, 1991.

Bragdon, Kathleen J. *Native People of Southern New England, 1500–1650*. Norman: University of Oklahoma Press, 1996.

Breen, T. H. "Creative Adaptations: Peoples and Cultures." In *Colonial British America: Essays in the New History of the Early Modern Era*, edited by Jack P. Green and J. R. Pole. Baltimore: Johns Hopkins University Press, 1984.

Brock, William R. *Scotus Americanus: A Survey of the Sources for Links Between Scotland and America in the Eighteenth Century*. Edinburgh, UK: Edinburgh University Press, 1982.

Butler, Jon. *The Huguenots in America: A Refugee People in New World Society*. Cambridge, MA: Harvard University Press, 1983.

Calloway, Colin G., ed. *After King Philip's War: Presence and Persistence in Indian New England*. Hanover, NH: University Press of New England, 1997.

———. *New Worlds for All: Indians, Europeans, and the Remaking of Early America*. Baltimore: Johns Hopkins University Press, 1997.

Canny, Nicholas, and Anthony Pagden, eds. *Colonial Identity in the Atlantic World, 1500–1800*. Princeton, NJ: Princeton University Press, 1987.

Corkran, David H. *The Carolina Indian Frontier*. Columbia: University of South Carolina Press, 1970.

———. *The Cherokee Frontier: Conflict and Survival, 1740–1762*. Norman: University of Oklahoma Press, 1962.

———. *The Creek Frontier, 1540–1783*. Norman: University of Oklahoma Press, 1967.

Daniels, John D. "The Indian Population of North America in 1492." *William and Mary Quarterly,* 3rd ser., 49 (April 1992): 298–320.

Dennis, Matthew. *Cultivating a Landscape of Peace: Iroquois-European Encounters in Seventeenth-Century America*. Ithaca, NY: Cornell University Press, 1993.

Dickason, Olive P. *Canada's First Nations: A History of Founding Peoples from Earliest Times*. Norman: University of Oklahoma Press, 1992.

Dickson, R. J. *Ulster Emigration to Colonial America, 1718–1775*. London: Routledge, 1966.

Fitzhugh, William W., ed. *Cultures in Contact: The Impact of European Contacts on Native American Cultural Institutions, A.D. 100–1800*. Washington, DC: Smithsonian Institution Press, 1985.

Fogelman, Aaron S. *Hopeful Journeys: German Immigration, Settlement, and Political Culture in Colonial America, 1717–1775*. Philadelphia: University of Pennsylvania Press, 1996.

Forbes, Jack D. *Africans and Native Americans: The Language of Race and the Evolution of Red-Black Peoples*. Urbana: University of Illinois Press, 1993.

Frazier, Patrick. *The Mohicans of Stockbridge*. Lincoln: University of Nebraska Press, 1992.

Frey, Sylvia. *Water from the Rock: Black Resistance in a Revolutionary Age*. Princeton, NJ: Princeton University Press, 1991.

Galloway, Patricia K. *Choctaw Genesis, 1500–1700*. Lincoln: University of Nebraska Press, 1995.

Gibson, Arrell M. *The Chickasaw*. Norman: University of Oklahoma Press, 1971.

Gomez, Michael A. *Exchanging Our Country Marks: The Transformation of African Identities in the Colonial and Antebellum South*. Chapel Hill: University of North Carolina Press, 1998.

Graham, Ian C. *Colonists from Scotland: Emigration to North America, 1707–1783*. Ithaca, NY: Cornell University Press, 1956.

Greene, Lorenzo J. *The Negro in Colonial New England, 1620–1776*. New York: Columbia University Press, 1942.

Hall, Gwendolyn M. *Africans in Colonial Louisiana: The Development of Afro-Creole Culture in the Eighteenth Century*. Baton Rouge: Louisiana State University Press, 1995.

Hauptman, Laurence M., and James D. Wherry, eds. *The Pequots in Southern New England: The Fall and Rise of an American Indian Nation*. Norman: University of Oklahoma Press, 1990.

Higginbotham, A. Leon. *In the Matter of Color: Race and the American Legal Process, the Colonial Period*. New York: Oxford University Press, 1978.

Hoffman, Ronald, Mechal Sobol, and Fredrika J. Teute, eds. *Through A Glass Darkly: Reflections on Personal Identity in Early America*. Chapel Hill: University of North Carolina Press, 1997.

Hudson, Charles, and Carmen T. Tesser, eds. *The Forgotten Centuries: Indians and Europeans in the American South, 1521–1704*. Athens: University of Georgia Press, 1994.

Jennings, Francis. *The Ambiguous Iroquois Empire*. New York: W. W. Norton, 1984.

———. *The Invasion of America: Indians, Colonialism, and the Cant of Conquest*. Chapel Hill: University of North Carolina Press, 1975.

Johnson, Amandus. *The Swedish Settlements on the Delaware: Their History and Relation to the Indians, Dutch, and English, 1638–1664, With an Account of the South, the New Sweden, and the American Companies, and the Efforts of Sweden to Regain the Colony*. 2 vols. New York: Franklin, 1970.

Jordan, Winthrop D. *White Over Black: American Attitudes Toward the Negro, 1550–1812*. New York: W. W. Norton, 1977.

Jordan, Winthrop D., and Sheila L. Skemp, eds. *Race and Family in the Colonial South: Essays*. Jackson: University Press of Mississippi, 1987.

Karras, Alan L. *Sojourners in the Sun: Scottish Migrants to Jamaica and the Chesapeake, 1740–1800*. Ithaca, NY: Cornell University Press, 1992.

Kolchin, Peter. *American Slavery, 1619–1877*. New York: Hill & Wang, 1994.

Leyburn, James G. *The Scotch-Irish: A Social History*. Chapel Hill: University of North Carolina Press, 1962.

MacLeod, Duncan J. *Slavery, Race, and the American Revolution*. Cambridge, UK: Cambridge University Press, 1974.

Mandell, Daniel. " 'To Live More Like My Christian English Neighbors': Natick Indians in the Eighteenth Century." *William and Mary Quarterly,* 3rd ser., 48 (October 1991): 552–79.

Merrell, James. *The Indians' New World: Catawbas and Their Neighbors from European Contact Through the Era of Removal*. Chapel Hill: University of North Carolina Press, 1989.

Mintz, Sidney W., and Richard Price. *The Birth of African-American Culture: An Anthropological Perspective*. Boston: Beacon, 1992.

Moffitt, John F., and Santiago Sebastián. *O Brave New People: The European Invention of the American Indian*. Albuquerque: University of New Mexico Press, 1996.

Morgan, Philip D. *Slave Counterpoint: Black Culture in the Eighteenth Century Chesapeake and Lowcountry*. Chapel Hill: University of North Carolina Press, 1998.

Mullin, Michael. *Africa in America: Slave Acculturation and Resistance in the American South and British Caribbean, 1736–1831*. Urbana: University of Illinois, 1995.

Nash, Gary B. *Red, White, and Black: The Peoples of Early America*. Englewood Cliffs, NJ: Prentice-Hall, 1982.

———. "Social Development." In *Colonial British America: Essays in the New History of the Early Modern Era*, edited by Jack P. Green and J. R. Pole. Baltimore: Johns Hopkins University Press, 1984.

Perdue, Theda. *Slavery and the Evolution of Cherokee Society, 1540–1866*. Knoxville: University of Tennessee Press, 1979.

Piersen, William D. *Black Yankees: The Development of an Afro-American Subculture in Eighteenth-Century New England*. Amherst: University of Massachusetts Press, 1988.

Richter, Daniel K. *The Ordeal of the Longhouse: The Peoples of the Iroquois League in the Era of European Colonization*. Chapel Hill: University of North Carolina Press, 1992.

Richter, Daniel K., and James H. Merrell, eds. *Beyond the Covenant Chain: The Iroquois and Their Neighbors in Indian North America, 1600–1800*. Syracuse, NY: Syracuse University Press, 1987.

Roeber, A. G. *Palatines, Liberty, and Property: German Lutherans in Colonial British America*. Baltimore: Johns Hopkins University Press, 1993.

Rountree, Helen C. *The Powhatan Indians of Virginia: Their Traditional Culture*. Norman: University of Oklahoma Press, 1989.

Rouse, Irving. *The Taínos: The Rise and Decline of the People Who Created Columbus*. New Haven, CT: Yale University Press, 1992.

Russell, Howard S. *Indian New England before the Mayflower*. Hanover, NH: University Press of New England, 1980.

Salisbury, Neal. "The Indians' Old World: Native Americans and the Coming of Europeans." *William and Mary Quarterly*, 3rd ser., 53 (July 1996): 435–58.

Sauer, Carl O. *Sixteenth-Century North America: The Land and the People as Seen by the Europeans*. Berkeley: University of California Press, 1971.

Simmons, William S. *Spirit of the New England Tribes: Indian History and Folklore, 1620–1984*. Hanover, NH: University Press of New England, 1986.

Snow, Dean R. *The Iroquois*. Cambridge, MA: Blackwell, 1994.

Thornton, John. *Africa and Africans in the Making of the Atlantic World, 1400–1680*. New York: Cambridge University Press, 1992.

Vaughan, Alden T. *New England Frontier: Puritans and Indians*. Norman: University of Oklahoma Press, 1995.

———. *Roots of American Racism: Essays on the Colonial Experience*. New York: Oxford University Press, 1995.

Wahlgren, Erik. *The Vikings and America*. New York: Thames and Hudson, 1986.

Wallace, Anthony F. C. *The Death and Rebirth of the Seneca*. New York: Alfred A. Knopf, 1969.

Weslager, C. A. *The Delaware Indians: A History*. New Brunswick, NJ: Rutgers University Press, 1972.

White, Richard. *The Middle Ground: Indians, Empires, and Republics in the Great Lakes Region, 1650–1815*. New York: Cambridge University Press, 1991.

———. *The Roots of Dependency: Subsistence, Environment, and Social Change among the Choctaws, Pawnees, and Navajos*. Lincoln: University of Nebraska Press, 1983.

———. "The Winning of the West: The Expansion of the Western Sioux in the Eighteenth and Nineteenth Centuries." *Journal of American History* 65 (September 1978): 319–43.

Wood, Peter H., Gregory A. Waselkov, and M. Thomas Hatley, eds. *Powhatan's Mantle: Indians in the Colonial Southeast*. Lincoln: University of Nebraska Press, 1989.

Wright, J. Leitch. *The Only Land They Knew: The Tragic Story of the American Indians in the Old South*. New York: Free Press, 1981.

Religion

Anderson, Virginia D. "Migrants and Motives: Religion and the Settlement of New England." *New England Quarterly* 58 (1985): 339–83.

Baker, Frank. *From Wesley to Asbury: Studies in Early American Methodism*. Durham, NC: Duke University Press, 1976.

Balmer, Randall. *A Perfect Babel of Confusion: Dutch Religion and English Culture in the Middle Colonies*. New York: Oxford University Press, 1989.

Berens, John F. *Providence and Patriotism in Early America, 1640–1815*. Charlottesville: University Press of Virginia, 1978.

Bloch, Ruth H. *Visionary Republic: Millennial Themes in American Thought, 1756–1800*. Cambridge, UK: Cambridge University Press, 1985.

Bolton, Charles S. *Southern Anglicanism: The Church of England in Colonial South Carolina*. Westport, CT: Greenwood, 1982.

Bonomi, Patricia U. *Under the Cope of Heaven: Religion, Society, and Politics in Colonial America*. New York: Oxford University Press, 1986.

Boyer, Paul, and Stephen Nissenbaum. *Salem Possessed: The Social Origins of Witchcraft*. Cambridge, MA: Harvard University Press, 1974.

Bozeman, Theodore D. *To Live Ancient Lives: The Primitivist Dimension in Puritanism*. Chapel Hill: University of North Carolina Press, 1988.

Brekus, Catherine A. *Strangers and Pilgrims: Female Preaching in America, 1740–1845*. Chapel Hill: University of North Carolina Press, 1998.

Bremer, Francis J. *The Puritan Experiment: New England Society from Bradford to Edwards*. New York: St. Martin's, 1976.

Bumsted, J. M., and E. Van de Wetering. *What Must I Do to Be Saved? The Great Awakening in Colonial America*. Hinsdale, IL: International Thomson Publishing, 1976.

Bushman, Richard L., ed. *The Great Awakening: Documents on the Revival of Religion, 1740–1745*. Chapel Hill: University of North Carolina Press, 1970.

Butler, Jon. *Awash in a Sea of Faith: Christianizing the American People*. Cambridge, MA: Harvard University Press, 1990.

———. "Enthusiasm Described and Decried: The Great Awakening as Interpretive Fiction." *Journal of American History* 69 (1982): 302–25.

Crawford, Michael J. *Seasons of Grace: Colonial New England's Revival Tradition in Its British Context*. New York: Oxford University Press, 1991.

Cohen, Charles L. *God's Caress: The Psychology of Puritan Religious Experience*. New York: Oxford University Press, 1986.

Davidson, James W. *The Logic of Millennial Thought: Eighteenth-Century New England*. New Haven, CT: Yale University Press, 1977.

Demos, John P. *Entertaining Satan: Witchcraft and the Culture of Early New England*. New York: Oxford University Press, 1982.

Ellis, John T. *Catholics in Colonial America*. Baltimore: Helicon, 1965.

Endy, Melvin B. *William Penn and Early Quakerism*. Princeton, NJ: Princeton University Press, 1973.

Ferguson, Roberta A. *The American Enlightenment, 1750–1820*. Cambridge, MA: Harvard University Press, 1997.

Foster, Stephen. *The Long Argument: English Puritanism and the Shaping of New England Culture, 1570–1700*. Chapel Hill: University of North Carolina Press, 1991.

Garrett, Clarke. *Spirit Possession and Popular Religion: From the Camisards to the Shakers*. Baltimore: Johns Hopkins University Press, 1987.

Gaustad, Edwin S. *The Great Awakening in New England.* Chicago: Quadrangle, 1968.

———. *Historical Atlas of Religion in America.* New York: Harper & Row, 1962.

Gewehr, Wesley M. *The Great Awakening in Virginia, 1740–1790.* Durham, NC: Duke University Press, 1930.

Godbeer, Richard. *The Devil's Dominion: Magic and Religion in Early New England.* New York: Cambridge University Press, 1982.

Goen, C. C. *Revivalism and Separatism in New England, 1740–1800: Strict Congregationalists and Separate Baptists in the Great Awakening.* Middletown, CT: Wesleyan University Press, 1987.

Greven, Philip. *The Protestant Temperament: Patterns of Child Rearing, Religious Experience, and the Self in America.* New York: Random House, 1978.

Gura, Philip L. *A Glimpse of Sion's Glory: Puritan Radicalism in New England, 1620–1660.* Middletown, CT: Wesleyan University Press, 1986.

Hall, David D., ed. *Lived Religion in America: Toward a History of Practice.* Princeton, NJ: Princeton University Press, 1997.

———. *Worlds of Wonder, Days of Judgment: Popular Religious Belief in Early New England.* New York: Alfred A. Knopf, 1989.

Hall, Timothy. *Contested Boundaries: Itinerancy and the Reshaping of the Colonial American Religious World.* Durham, NC: Duke University Press, 1994.

Hambrick-Stowe, Charles E. *The Practice of Piety: Puritan Devotional Disciplines in Seventeenth-Century New England.* Chapel Hill: University of North Carolina Press, 1982.

Hansen, Chadwick. *Witchcraft in Salem.* New York: New American Library, 1970.

Heimert, Alan. *Religion and the American Mind: From the Great Awakening to the Revolution.* Cambridge, MA: Harvard University Press, 1968.

Heyrman, Christine L. *Southern Cross: The Beginnings of the Bible Belt.* New York: Alfred A. Knopf, 1997.

Holifield, E. Brooks. *The Covenant Sealed: The Development of Puritan Sacramental Theology in Old and New England, 1570–1720.* New Haven, CT: Yale University Press, 1974.

Holstun, James. *A Rational Millennium: Puritan Utopias of Seventeenth-Century England and America.* New York: Oxford University Press, 1987.

Hunt, William. *The Puritan Movement: The Coming of Revolution in an English County.* Cambridge, MA: Harvard University Press, 1983.

James, Sydney W. *A People among Peoples: Quaker Benevolence in Eighteenth-Century America.* Cambridge, MA: Harvard University Press, 1963.

Jones, James W. *The Shattered Synthesis: New England Puritanism before the Great Awakening.* New Haven, CT: Yale University Press, 1973.

Karlsen, Carol F. *The Devil in the Shape of a Woman: Witchcraft in Colonial New England.* New York: W. W. Norton, 1987.

Lambert, Frank. *Inventing the "Great Awakening."* Princeton, NJ: Princeton University Press, 1999.

———. *"Pedlar in Divinity": George Whitefield and the Transatlantic Revivals, 1737–1770.* Princeton, NJ: Princeton University Press, 1994.

Larson, Rebecca. *Daughters of Light: Quaker Women Preaching and Prophesying in the Colonies and Abroad, 1700–1775.* New York: Alfred A. Knopf, 1999.

Lovejoy, David S. *Religious Enthusiasm in the New World: Heresy to Revolution.* Cambridge, MA: Harvard University Press, 1985.

Marcus, Jacob R. *The Colonial American Jew, 1492–1776.* 3 vols. Detroit, MI: Wayne State University Press, 1970.

Marietta, Jack D. *The Reformation of American Quakerism, 1748–1783.* Philadelphia: University of Pennsylvania Press, 1984.

Mathews, Donald G. *Religion in the Old South.* Chicago: University of Chicago Press, 1977.

May, Henry F. *The Enlightenment in America.* New York: Oxford University Press, 1976.

McEwan, Bonnie G., ed. *The Spanish Missions of La Florida.* Gainesville: University of Florida Press, 1993.

McLoughlin, William G. *New England Dissent, 1630–1833: The Baptists and the Separation of Church and State.* 2 vols. Cambridge, MA: Harvard University Press, 1971.

———. *Revivals, Awakenings, and Reform: An Essay on Religion and Social Change in America, 1607–1977.* Chicago: University of Chicago Press, 1978.

Mead, Sydney E. *The Lively Experiment: The Shaping of Christianity in America.* New York: Harper and Row, 1963.

Miller, Perry. *The New England Mind: The Seventeenth Century.* New York: Belknap Press, 1983.

Morais, Herbert M. *Deism in Eighteenth-Century America.* New York: Russell & Russell, 1966.

Morgan, Edmund S. *The Puritan Dilemma: The Story of John Winthrop.* Boston: Little, Brown, 1958.

Morrison, Dane. *A Praying People: Massachusetts Acculturation and the Failure of the Puritan Mission, 1600–1690.* New York: Peter Lang, 1995.

Newlin, Claude M. *Philosophy and Religion in Colonial America.* New York: Greenwood, 1968.

Noll, Mark A. *A History of Christianity in the United States and Canada.* Grand Rapids, MI: Eerdmans, 1992.

———, ed. *Religion and American Politics: From the Colonial Period to the 1980s.* New York: Oxford University Press, 1990.

Noll, Mark A., David W. Bebbington, and George A. Rawlyk, eds. *Evangelicalism: Comparative Studies of Popular Protestantism in North America, the British Isles, and Beyond, 1700–1990.* New York: Oxford University Press, 1994.

Peterson, Mark A. *The Spiritual Economy of Puritan New England.* Palo Alto, CA: Stanford University Press, 1997.

Pope, Robert G. *The Half-Way Covenant: Church Membership*

in Puritan New England. Princeton, NJ: Princeton University Press, 1969.

Roeber, A. G. *Palatines, Liberty, and Property: German Lutherans in Colonial British America*. Baltimore: Johns Hopkins University Press, 1998.

Salisbury, Neal. *Manitou and Providence: Indians, Europeans, and the Making of New England, 1500–1643*. New York: Oxford University Press, 1982.

Scherer, Lester B. *Slavery and the Churches in Early America, 1619–1819*. Grand Rapids, MI: Eerdmans, 1975.

Scott, Donald M. *From Office to Profession: The New England Ministry, 1750–1850*. Philadelphia: University of Pennsylvania Press, 1978.

Simmons, Marc. *Witchcraft in the Southwest: Spanish and Indian Supernaturalism on the Rio Grande*. Lincoln: University of Nebraska Press, 1974.

Simmons, William S. "Red Yankees: Narragansett Conversion in the Great Awakening." *American Ethnologist* 10 (May 1983): 253–71.

Stoeffler, F. Ernest, ed. *Continental Pietism and Early American Christianity*. Grand Rapids, MI: Eerdmans, 1976.

Stoever, William K. *"A Faire and Easie Way to Heaven": Covenant Theology and Antinomianism in Early Massachusetts*. Middletown, CT: Wesleyan University Press, 1978.

Stout, Harry S. *"The Divine Dramatist": George Whitefield and the Rise of Modern Evangelicalism*. Grand Rapids, MI: Eerdmans, 1991.

———. *The New England Soul: Preaching and Religious Culture in Colonial New England*. New York: Oxford University Press, 1986.

Stout, Harry S., and D. G. Hart, eds. *New Directions in American Religious History*. New York: Oxford University Press, 1997.

Tanis, James. *Dutch Calvinistic Pietism in the Middle Colonies: A Study in the Life and Theology of Theodorus Jacobus Frelinghuysen*. The Hague: Martinus Nijhoff, 1967.

Tracy, Patricia J. *Jonathan Edwards, Pastor: Religion and Society in Eighteenth-Century Northampton*. New York: Hill & Wang, 1979.

Trinterud, Leonard J. *The Forming of an American Tradition: A Re-examination of Colonial Presbyterianism*. Philadelphia: Westminster, 1949.

Versluis, Arthur. *Sacred Earth: The Spiritual Landscape of Native America*. Rochester, VT: Inner Traditions International, 1992.

Westerkamp, Marilyn J. *Triumph of the Laity: Scots-Irish Piety and the Great Awakening, 1624–1760*. New York: Oxford University Press, 1988.

———. *Women and Religion in Early America, 1600–1850: The Puritan and Evangelical Traditions*. New York: Routledge, 1999.

Winship, Michael. *Seers of God: Puritan Providentialism in the Restoration and Early Enlightenment*. Baltimore: Johns Hopkins University Press, 1996.

Winslow, Ola E. *Meetinghouse Hill: 1630–1783*. New York: W. W. Norton, 1972.

Wood, Betty, and Sylvia R. Frey. *Come Shouting to Zion: African American Protestantism in the American South and British Caribbean to 1830*. Chapel Hill: University of North Carolina Press, 1998.

Woolverton, John F. *Colonial Anglicanism in North America*. Detroit, MI: Wayne State University Press, 1984.

Worrall, Arthur J. *Quakers in the Colonial Northeast*. Hanover, NH: University Press of New England, 1980.

Wright, Conrad. *The Beginning of Unitarianism in America*. Boston: Beacon, 1955.

Science, Technology, and the Environment

Anderson, M. Kat, and Thomas C. Blackburn, eds. *Before the Wilderness: Environmental Management by Native Californians*. Menlo Park, CA: Ballena Press, 1992.

Bedini, Silvio A. *Thinkers and Tinkers: Early American Men of Science*. New York: Scribner's, 1975.

Bell, Whitfield J. *The Colonial Physician and Other Essays*. New York: Science History, 1975.

———. *Early American Science*. Chapel Hill: University of North Carolina Press, 1955.

Boorstin, Daniel. *The Discoverers: A History of Man's Search to Know His World and Himself*. New York: Random House, 1985.

Cassedy, James H. *Demography in Early America: Beginnings of the Statistical Mind, 1600–1800*. Cambridge, MA: Harvard University Press, 1969.

Childs, St. Julien R. *Malaria and Colonization in the Carolina Low Country, 1526–1696*. Baltimore: Johns Hopkins University Press, 1940.

Cochran, Thomas C. *Frontiers of Change: Early Industrialism in America*. New York: Oxford University Press, 1981.

Cook, Noble D., and George W. Lovell, eds. *"Secret Judgments of God": Old World Disease in Colonial Spanish America*. Norman: University of Oklahoma Press, 1991.

Cronon, William. *Changes in the Land: Indians, Colonists, and the Ecology of New England*. New York: Hill & Wang, 1983.

Crosby, Alfred W. *The Columbian Exchange: Biological and Cultural Consequences of 1492*. Westport, CT: Greenwood, 1972.

———. *Ecological Imperialism: The Biological Expansion of Europe, 900–1900*. New York: Cambridge University Press, 1986.

Diamond, Jared. *Guns, Germs, and Steel: The Fates of Human Societies*. New York: W. W. Norton, 1998.

Duffy, John. *Epidemics in Colonial America*. Baton Rouge: Louisiana State University Press, 1971.

Estes, J. Worth. *Hall Jackson and the Purple Foxglove: Medical Practice and Research in Revolutionary America, 1760–1820*. Hanover, NH: University Press of New England, 1979.

Goldenberg, Joseph A. *Shipbuilding in Colonial America*. Charlottesville: University Press of Virginia, 1976.

Hindle, Brooke. *The Pursuit of Science in Revolutionary America, 1735–1789*. Chapel Hill: University of North Carolina Press, 1956.

———. *Technology in Early America: Needs and Opportunities for Study, with a Directory of Artifact Collections by Lucius F. Ellsworth*. Chapel Hill: University of North Carolina Press, 1966.

Kipple, Kenneth F. *The Caribbean Slave: A Biological History*. New York: Cambridge University Press, 1984.

Kipple, Kenneth F., and Stephen V. Beck, eds. *Biological Consequences of the European Expansion, 1450–1800*. Brookfield, VT: Ashgate, 1997.

Krech, Shepard. *The Ecological Indian: Myth and History*. New York: W. W. Norton, 1999.

———, ed. *Indians, Animals, and the Fur Trade: A Critique of Keepers of the Game*. Athens: University of Georgia Press, 1981.

Leventhal, Herbert. *In the Shadow of the Enlightenment: Occultism and Renaissance Science in Eighteenth-Century America*. New York: New York University Press, 1976.

Ludlum, David M. *Early American Hurricanes, 1492–1870*. Boston: American Meteorological Society, 1963.

Martin, Calvin. *The Keepers of the Game: Indian-Animal Relationships and the Fur Trade*. Berkeley: University of California Press, 1985.

McManis, Douglas R. *Colonial New England: A Historical Geography*. New York: Oxford University Press, 1975.

Melville, G. K. *A Plague of Sheep: Environmental Consequences of the Conquest of Mexico*. New York: Cambridge University Press, 1994.

Merchant, Carolyn. *Ecological Revolutions: Nature, Gender, and Science in New England*. Chapel Hill: University of North Carolina Press, 1989.

Mokyr, Joel. *The Lever of Riches: Technological Creativity and Economic Progress*. New York: Oxford University Press, 1990.

Mulholland, James A. *A History of Metals in Colonial America*. Tuscaloosa: University of Alabama Press, 1981.

Nash, Roderick. *Wilderness and the American Mind*. New Haven, CT: Yale University Press, 1967.

Numbers, Ronald, ed. *Medicine in the New World: New Spain, New France, and New England*. Knoxville: University of Tennessee Press, 1987.

Nussbaum, Frederick L. *The Triumph of Science and Reason, 1660–1685*. New York: HarperCollins, 1953.

Oleson, Alexandra, and Sanborn C. Brown, eds. *The Pursuit of Knowledge in the Early American Republic: American Scientific and Learned Societies from Colonial Times to the Civil War*. Baltimore: Johns Hopkins University Press, 1976.

Perlin, Jonathan. *A Forest Journey*. Cambridge, MA: Harvard University Press, 1989.

Porter, Roy. *The Greatest Benefit to Mankind: A Medical History of Humanity*. New York: W. W. Norton, 1998.

Shyrock, Richard H. *Medicine and Society in America, 1660–1860*. New York: New York University Press, 1960.

Silver, Timothy. *A New Face on the Countryside: Indians, Colonists, and Slaves in South Atlantic Forests, 1500–1800*. New York: Cambridge University Press, 1990.

Stearns, Raymond P. *Science in the British Colonies of America*. Urbana: University of Illinois Press, 1970.

Stilgoe, John R. *Common Landscape of America, 1580 to 1845*. New Haven, CT: Yale University Press, 1982.

York, Neil L. *Mechanical Metamorphosis: Technological Change in Revolutionary America*. Westport, CT: Greenwood, 1985.

Regional

Caribbean

Beckles, Hilary M. *Black Rebellion in Barbados: The Struggle Against Slavery, 1627–1838*. Barbados: Antilles Publications, 1984.

———. *Natural Rebels: A Social History of Enslaved Black Women in Barbados*. New Brunswick, NJ: Rutgers University Press, 1989.

———. "A 'Riotous and Unruly Lot': Irish Indentured Servants and Freemen in the English West Indies, 1644–1713." *William and Mary Quarterly,* 3rd ser., 48 (October 1990): 503–22.

———. *White Servitude and Black Slavery in Barbados, 1627–1715*. Knoxville: University of Tennessee Press, 1989.

Bennett, J. Harry. *Bondsmen and Bishops: Slavery and Apprenticeship on the Codrington Plantations of Barbados, 1710–1838*. Berkeley: University of California Press, 1958.

Brathwaite, Edward. *The Development of Creole Society in Jamaica, 1770–1820*. New York: Oxford University Press, 1971.

Bridenbaugh, Carl, and Roberta Bridenbaugh. *No Peace Beyond the Line: The English in the Caribbean, 1624–1690*. New York: Oxford University Press, 1972.

Bush, Barbara. *Slave Women in Caribbean Society, 1650–1838*. Bloomington: Indiana University Press, 1990.

Cox, Edward L. *Free Coloreds in the Slave Societies of St. Kitts and Grenada, 1763–1833*. Knoxville: University of Tennessee Press, 1984.

Craton, Michael. *A History of the Bahamas*. London: Collins, 1968.

———. *Testing the Chains: Resistance to Slavery in the British West Indies*. Ithaca, NY: Cornell University Press, 1982.

Craton, Michael, and James Walvin. *A Jamaican Plantation: The History of Worthy Park, 1670–1970*. New York: W. H. Allen, 1970.

Dunn, Richard S. *Sugar and Slaves: The Rise of the Planter Class in the English West Indies, 1624–1713*. Chapel Hill: University of North Carolina Press, 1972.

Exquemelin, A. O. *The Buccaneers of America*. Baltimore: Penguin, 1969.

Fortune, Stephen A. *Merchants and Jews: The Struggle for British West Indian Commerce, 1650–1750*. Gainesville: University Presses of Florida, 1984.

Gaspar, David B. *Bondmen and Rebels: A Study of Master-Slave Relations in Antigua, with Implications for Colonial British America*. Baltimore: Johns Hopkins University Press, 1985.

Geggus, David P. *Slavery, War, and Revolution: The British Occupation of Saint Dominique, 1793–1798*. New York: Oxford University Press, 1982.

Goveia, Elsa V. *Slave Society in the British Leeward Islands at the End of the Eighteenth Century*. New Haven, CT: Yale University Press, 1965.

Handler, Jerome S., and Frederick W. Lange. *Plantation Slavery in Barbados: An Archaeological and Historical Investigation*. Cambridge, MA: Harvard University Press, 1978.

Haring, Clarence H. *The Buccaneers in the West Indies in the Seventeenth Century*. New York: E. P. Dutton, 1910.

Harlow, Vincent T., ed. *Colonising Expeditions to the West Indies and Guiana, 1623–1667*. London: Bedford, 1925.

———. *A History of Barbados, 1625–1685*. New York: Oxford University Press, 1926.

Higham, C. S. *The Development of the Leeward Islands under the Restoration, 1660–1688: A Study of the Foundations of the Old Colonial System*. Cambridge, UK: Cambridge University Press, 1921.

Hoffman, Paul E. *The Spanish Crown and the Defense of the Caribbean, 1535–1585: Precedent, Patrimonialism, and Royal Parsimony*. Baton Rouge: Louisiana State University Press, 1980.

Kipple, Kenneth E. *The Caribbean Slave: A Biological History*. Cambridge, UK: Cambridge University Press, 1984.

Kopytoff, Barbara K. "The Early Political Development of Jamaican Maroon Societies." *William and Mary Quarterly*, 3rd ser., 35 (April 1978): 287–307.

Metcalf, George. *Royal Government and Political Conflict in Jamaica, 1729–1783*. London: Longmans, 1965.

Newton, Arthur P. *The European Nations in the West Indies, 1493–1688*. London: A. and C. Black, 1933.

Pares, Richard. *War and Trade in the West Indies, 1739–1763*. London: Frank Cass, 1963.

Puckrein, Gary. *Little England: Plantation Society and Anglo-Barbadian Politics, 1627–1700*. New York: New York University Press, 1984.

Sheridan, Richard. *Sugar and Slavery: An Economic History of the British West Indies, 1623–1775*. Baltimore: Johns Hopkins University Press, 1973.

Spurdle, F. G. *Early West Indian Government: Showing the Progress of Government in Barbados, Jamaica, and the Leeward Islands, 1660–1783*. Palmerston North, New Zealand: Spurdle, 1963.

Watson, Karl. *The Civilized Island, Barbados: A Social History, 1750–1816*. Barbados: K. Watson, 1979.

Watts, David. *The West Indies: Patterns of Development, Culture, and Environmental Change since 1492*. Cambridge, UK: Cambridge University Press, 1987.

Weddle, Robert S. *The Adventurers of Bermuda: A History of the Island from Its Discovery until . . . 1694*. New York: Oxford University Press, 1933.

———. *The French Thorn: Rival Explorers in the Spanish Sea, 1682–1762*. College Station: Texas A & M University Press, 1991.

Wilkinson, Henry. *Bermuda in the Old Empire: A History of the Island . . . 1684–1784*. New York: Oxford University Press, 1950.

Williams, Eric. *From Columbus to Castro: The History of the Caribbean*. New York: Vintage Books, 1984.

Connecticut

Buel, Richard, Jr. *Dear Liberty: Connecticut's Mobilization for the Revolutionary War*. Middletown, CT: Wesleyan University Press, 1980.

Bushman, Richard L. *From Puritan to Yankee: Character and the Social Order in Connecticut, 1690–1765*. Cambridge, MA: Harvard University Press, 1970.

Daniels, Bruce C. *The Connecticut Town: Growth and Development, 1635–1790*. Middletown, CT: Wesleyan University Press, 1979.

Ditz, Toby L. *Property and Kinship: Inheritance in Early Connecticut, 1750–1820*. Princeton, NJ: Princeton University Press, 1986.

Garvan, Anthony. *Architecture and Town Planning in Colonial Connecticut*. New Haven, CT: Yale University Press, 1951.

Grant, Charles S. *Democracy in the Connecticut Frontier Town of Kent*. New York: Columbia University Press, 1961.

Hosley, William N. *Great River: Art and Society of the Connecticut Valley, 1635–1820*. Hartford, CT: Wadsworth Atheneum, 1985.

Jones, Mary J. *Congregational Commonwealth: Connecticut, 1636–1662*. Middletown, CT: Wesleyan University Press, 1968.

Lacey, Barbara F. "Gender, Piety, and Secularization in Connecticut Religion, 1720–1775." *Journal of Social History* 24 (Summer 1991): 799–821.

Lucas, Paul R. *Valley of Discord: Church and Society along the Connecticut River, 1636–1725*. Hanover, NH: University Press of New England, 1976.

Main, Jackson T. *Society and Economy in Colonial Connecticut*. Princeton, NJ: Princeton University Press, 1985.

Mann, Bruce H. *Neighbors and Strangers: Law and Community in Early Connecticut*. Chapel Hill: University of North Carolina Press, 1987.

Selesky, Harold E. *War and Society in Colonial Connecticut*. New Haven, CT: Yale University Press, 1990.

Taylor, Robert J. *Colonial Connecticut: A History*. Millwood, NY: KTO, 1979.

Weaver, Glenn. *Jonathan Trumbull, Connecticut's Merchant*

Magistrate, 1710–1785. Hartford: Connecticut Historical Society, 1956.

Delaware

Herman, Bernard L. *Architecture and Rural Life in Central Delaware, 1700–1900.* Knoxville: University of Tennessee Press, 1987.

Levy, Barry. *Quakers and the American Family: Settlement in the Delaware Valley.* New York: Oxford University Press, 1988.

Munroe, John A. *Colonial Delaware: A History.* Millwood, NY: KTO, 1978.

———. *Federalist Delaware, 1775–1815.* New Brunswick, NJ: Rutgers University Press, 1954.

Weslager, C. A. *Dutch Explorers, Traders, and Settlers in the Delaware Valley, 1609–1644.* Philadelphia: University of Pennsylvania Press, 1961.

French Colonies in Mainland North America

Brandao, José A. *"Your Fyre Shall Burn No More": Iroquois Policy Toward New France and Its Native Allies to 1701.* Lincoln: University of Nebraska Press, 1997.

Brasseaux, Carl A. *The Founding of New Acadia: The Beginnings of Acadian Life in Louisiana, 1765–1803.* Baton Rouge: Louisiana State University Press, 1987.

Briggs, Winstantley. "Le Pays des Illinois." *William and Mary Quarterly,* 3rd ser., 47 (January 1990): 30–56.

Bumstead, J. M., ed. *Interpreting Canada's Past.* Vol. 1. Toronto: Oxford University Press, 1993.

Desbarats, Catherine M. "The Cost of Early Canada's Native Alliances: Reality and Scarcity's Rhetoric." *William and Mary Quarterly,* 3rd ser., 52 (October 1995): 609–30.

Dickason, Olive P. *Canada's First Nations: A History of Founding Peoples from Earliest Times.* Norman: University of Oklahoma Press, 1992.

Eccles, W. J. *The Canadian Frontier, 1534–1760.* Albuquerque: University of New Mexico Press, 1983.

———. *Essays on New France.* Toronto: Oxford University Press, 1987.

———. *France in America.* East Lansing: Michigan State University Press, 1990.

Edmunds, R. David, and Joseph L. Peyser, eds. *The Fox Wars: The Mesquakie Challenge to New France.* Norman: University of Oklahoma Press, 1993.

Frégault, Guy. *Canada: The War of the Conquest.* Translated by Margaret M. Cameron. New York: Oxford University Press, 1969.

Galloway, Patricia K., ed. *La Salle and His Legacy: Frenchmen and Indians in the Lower Mississippi Valley.* Jackson: University Press of Mississippi, 1982.

Giraud, Marcel. *The Métis in the Canadian West.* Translated by George Wookcock. 2 vols. Lincoln: University of Nebraska Press, 1986.

Greer, Allan. *Peasant, Lord, and Merchant: Rural Society in Three Quebec Parishes, 1740–1840.* Toronto: University of Toronto Press, 1985.

———. *The People of New France.* Toronto: University of Toronto, 1997.

Harris, Richard C. *The Seigneurial System in Early Canada: A Geographical Study.* Madison: University of Wisconsin Press, 1966.

Jaenen, Cornelius J. *Friend and Foe: Aspects of French-Amerindian Cultural Contact in the Sixteenth and Seventeenth Centuries.* Toronto: University of Toronto Press, 1976.

———. *The Role of the Church in New France.* Toronto: McGraw-Hill Ryerson, 1976.

Johnston, A. J. *Religion in Life at Louisbourg, 1713–1758.* Kingston, Ontario, Canada: McGill-Queen's University Press, 1984.

Miquelon, Dale. *New France, 1701 to 1744: A Supplement to Europe.* Toronto: McClelland and Stewart, 1987.

Moogk, Peter N. "Reluctant Exiles: Emigrants from France in Canada before 1760." *William and Mary Quarterly,* 3rd ser., 46 (1989): 463–505.

Noel, Jan. *Women in New France.* Ottawa: Canadian Historical Association, 1998.

O'Neill, Charles E. *Church and State in French Colonial Louisiana: Policy and Politics to 1732.* New Haven, CT: Yale University Press, 1966.

Ouellet, Fernand. *Economic and Social History of Quebec, 1760–1850.* Translated under the auspices of the Institute of Canadian Studies. Toronto: Macmillan, 1980.

Sayre, Gordon M. *Les Sauvages Américains: Representations of Native Americans in French and English Colonial Literature.* Chapel Hill: University of North Carolina Press, 1997.

Smith, G. Hubert, and Raymond W. Wood, eds. *The Explorations of the La Vérendryes in the Northern Plains, 1738–1743.* Lincoln: University of Nebraska Press, 1980.

Stanley, George F. *New France: The Last Phase, 1744–1760.* Toronto: McClelland and Stewart, 1968.

Trigger, Bruce G. *Natives and Newcomers: Canada's "Heroic Age" Reconsidered.* Kingston, Ontario: McGill-Queen's University Press, 1985.

Trudel, Marcel. *The Beginnings of New France, 1524–1663.* Translated by Patricia Claxton. Toronto: McClelland and Stewart, 1973.

———. *Introduction to New France.* Toronto: Holt, Rinehart and Winston, 1968.

Turgeon, Laurier. "French Fishers, Fur Traders, and Amerindians during the Sixteenth Century: History and Archeology." *William and Mary Quarterly,* 3rd ser., 50 (1998): 585–610.

Wood, Peter H. "La Salle: Discovery of a Lost Explorer." *American Historical Review* 89 (April 1984): 294–323.

Wood, W. Raymond, and Thiessen Thomas, eds. *Early Fur Trade on the Northern Plains: Canadian Traders Among the Mandan and Hidatsa Indians, 1738–1818.* Norman: University of Oklahoma Press, 1985.

Woods, Patricia D. *French-Indian Relations on the Southern Frontier, 1699–1762*. Ann Arbor, MI: UMI Research Press, 1980.

Georgia

Abbot, W. W. *The Royal Governors of Georgia, 1754–1775*. Chapel Hill: University of North Carolina Press, 1959.

Coleman, Kenneth. *Colonial Georgia: A History*. New York: Kraus, 1976.

Davis, Harold E. *The Fledgling Province: Social and Cultural Life in Colonial Georgia, 1733–1776*. Chapel Hill: University of North Carolina Press, 1976.

Gallay, Alan. "Jonathan Bryan's Plantation Empire: Land Politics and the Formation of a Ruling Class in Colonial Georgia." *William and Mary Quarterly,* 3rd ser., 45 (1988): 253–79.

Jackson, Harvey H., and Phinzy Spalding, eds. *Forty Years of Diversity: Essays on Colonial Georgia*. Athens: University of Georgia Press, 1984.

———. *Oglethorpe in Perspective: Georgia's Founder After Two Hundred Years*. Tuscaloosa: University of Alabama Press, 1999.

Lanning, John T. *The Diplomatic History of Georgia: A Study of the Epoch of Jenkins' Ear*. Chapel Hill: University of North Carolina Press, 1936.

Reese, Trevor R. *Colonial Georgia: A Study in British Imperial Policy in the Eighteenth Century*. Athens: University of Georgia Press, 1963.

Taylor, Paul S. *Georgia Plan: 1732–1752*. Berkeley: University of California Press, 1972.

Wood, Betty. *Slavery in Colonial Georgia, 1730–1775*. Athens: University of Georgia Press, 1984.

Maryland

Barker, Charles A. *The Background of the Revolution in Maryland*. New Haven, CT: Yale University Press, 1940.

Carr, Lois G., and David W. Jordan. *Maryland's Revolution of Government, 1682–1692*. Ithaca, NY: Cornell University Press, 1974.

Carr, Lois G., and Lorena A. Walsh. "The Planter's Wife: The Experience of Women in Seventeenth-Century Maryland." *William and Mary Quarterly*, 3rd ser., 34 (1977): 542–65.

Carr, Lois G., Lorena S. Walsh, and Russell R. Menard. *Robert Cole's World: Agriculture and Society in Early Maryland*. Chapel Hill: University of North Carolina Press, 1991.

Clemens, Paul G. *The Atlantic Economy and Colonial Maryland's Eastern Shore: From Tobacco to Grain*. Ithaca, NY: Cornell University Press, 1980.

Crowl, Philip A. *Maryland During and After the Revolution: A Political and Economic Study*. Baltimore: Johns Hopkins University Press, 1943.

Day, Alan F. *A Social Study of Lawyers in Maryland, 1660–1775*. New York: Garland, 1989.

Earle, Carville V. *The Evolution of a Tidewater Settlement System: All Hallow's Parish, Maryland, 1650–1783*. Chicago: University of Chicago Press, 1975.

Hoffman, Ronald. *A Spirit of Dissension: Economics, Politics, and the Revolution in Maryland*. Baltimore: Johns Hopkins University Press, 1973.

Jordan, David W. *Foundations of Representative Government in Maryland, 1632–1715*. Cambridge, UK: Cambridge University Press, 1987.

Land, Aubrey C. *Colonial Maryland: A History*. Millwood, NY: KTO, 1981.

Land, Aubrey C., Lois G. Carr, and Edward C. Papenfuse, eds. *Law, Society, and Politics in Early Maryland, 1650–1720*. Baltimore: Johns Hopkins University Press, 1977.

Lemay, J. A. *Men of Letters in Colonial Maryland*. Knoxville: University of Tennessee Press, 1972.

Main, Gloria L. *Tobacco Colony: Life in Early Maryland, 1650–1720*. Princeton, NJ: Princeton University Press, 1982.

Murdock, Kenneth B. *Literature and Theology in Colonial New England*. Cambridge, MA: Harvard University Press, 1949.

Owings, Donnell M. *His Lordship's Patronage: Offices of Profit in Colonial Maryland*. Baltimore: Maryland Historical Society, 1953.

Petter, Henri. *The Early American Novel*. Columbus: Ohio State University Press, 1971.

Quinn, David B., ed. *Early Maryland in a Wider World*. Detroit, MI: Wayne State University Press, 1982.

Rozbicki, Michal J. *Transformation of the English Cultural Ethos in Colonial America: Maryland, 1634–1720*. Lanham, MD: University Press of America, 1998.

Russo, Jean B. *Free Workers in a Plantation Economy: Talbot County, Maryland, 1650–1759*. New York: Garland, 1989.

Steffen, Charles G. *From Gentlemen to Townsmen: The Gentry of Baltimore County, 1660–1776*. Lexington: University Press of Kentucky, 1993.

———. *The Mechanics of Baltimore, Maryland: Workers and Politics in the Age of Revolution, 1763–1812*. Urbana: University of Illinois Press, 1984.

Stiverson, Gregory. *Poverty in a Land of Plenty: Tenancy in Eighteenth-Century Maryland*. Baltimore: Johns Hopkins University Press, 1977.

Massachusetts

Allen, David G. *In English Ways: The Movement of Societies and the Transferal of English Local Law and Custom to Massachusetts Bay in the Seventeenth Century*. Chapel Hill: University of North Carolina Press, 1981.

Anderson, Fred. *A People's Army: Massachusetts Soldiers and Society in the Seven Years' War*. Chapel Hill: University of North Carolina Press, 1984.

Baxter, William T. *The House of Hancock: Business in Boston, 1724–1775*. Cambridge, MA: Harvard University Press, 1945.

Boyer, Paul, and Stephen Nissenbaum. *Salem Possessed: The Social Origins of Witchcraft*. Cambridge, MA: Harvard University Press, 1976.

Breslaw, Elaine. *Tituba, Reluctant Witch of Salem*. New York: New York University Press, 1996.

Brooke, John L. *The Heart of the Commonwealth: Society and Political Culture in Worcester County, Massachusetts, 1713–1861*. Cambridge, UK: Cambridge University Press, 1989.

Brown, Richard D. *Revolutionary Politics in Massachusetts: The Boston Committee of Correspondence and the Towns, 1772–1774*. Cambridge, MA: Harvard University Press, 1970.

Brown, Robert E. *Middle-Class Democracy and the Revolution in Massachusetts, 1691–1780*. New York: Harper & Row, 1969.

Bushman, Richard L. *King and People in Provincial Massachusetts*. Chapel Hill: University of North Carolina Press, 1985.

Byers, Edward. *The Nation of Nantucket: Society and Politics in an Early American Commercial Center, 1660–1820*. Boston: Northeastern University Press, 1986.

Chu, Jonathan. *Neighbors, Friends, or Madmen: The Puritan Adjustment to Quakerism in Seventeenth-Century Massachusetts Bay*. Westport, CT: Greenwood, 1985.

Conroy, David W. *In Public Houses: Drink and the Revolution of Authority in Colonial Massachusetts*. Chapel Hill: University of North Carolina Press, 1995.

Demos, John. *A Little Commonwealth: Family Life in Plymouth Colony*. New York: Oxford University Press, 1970.

Faler, Paul G. *Mechanics and Manufacturers in the Early Industrial Revolution: Lynn, Massachusetts, 1780–1860*. Albany: State University of New York Press, 1981.

Gawalt, Gerald W. *The Promise of Power: The Emergence of the Legal Profession in Massachusetts, 1760–1840*. Westport, CT: Greenwood, 1979.

Gildrie, Richard P. *Salem, Massachusetts, 1626–1683: A Covenant Community*. Charlottesville: University Press of Virginia, 1975.

Gragg, Larry. *The Salem Witchcraft Crisis*. New York: Praeger, 1992.

Greven, Philip. *Four Generations: Population, Land, and Family in Colonial Andover, Massachusetts*. Ithaca, NY: Cornell University Press, 1970.

Haskins, George L. *Law and Authority in Early Massachusetts: A Study in Tradition and Design*. Hamden, CT: Archon, 1968.

Heyrman, Christine L. *Commerce and Culture: The Maritime Communities of Colonial Massachusetts, 1690–1750*. New York: W. W. Norton, 1984.

Hoerder, Dirk. *Crowd Action in Revolutionary Massachusetts, 1765–1780*. New York: Academic Press, 1977.

Hoffer, Peter C. *The Devil's Disciples: Makers of the Salem Witchcraft Trials*. Baltimore: Johns Hopkins University Press, 1996.

———. *The Salem Witchcraft Trials: A Legal History*. Lawrence: University Press of Kansas, 1998.

Holmes, Richard. *Communities in Transition: Bedford and Lincoln, Massachusetts, 1729–1850*. Ann Arbor, MI: UMI Research Press, 1980.

Hull, N. E. *Female Felons: Women and Serious Crime in Colonial Massachusetts*. Urbana: University of Illinois Press, 1987.

Innes, Stephen. *Labor in a New Land: Economy and Society in Seventeenth-Century Springfield*. Princeton, NJ: Princeton University Press, 1983.

Jones, Douglas L. *Village and Seaport: Migration and Society in Eighteenth-Century Massachusetts*. Hanover, NH: University Press of New England for Tufts University Press, 1981.

Kawashima, Yasuhide. *Puritan Justice and the Indian: White Man's Law in Massachusetts, 1630–1763*. Middletown, CT: Wesleyan University Press, 1986.

Knight, Janice. *Orthodoxies in Massachusetts: Rereading American Puritanism*. Cambridge, MA: Harvard University Press, 1997.

Konig, David Thomas. *Law and Society in Puritan Massachusetts: Essex County, 1629–1692*. Chapel Hill: University of North Carolina Press, 1979.

Labaree, Benjamin W. *Colonial Massachusetts: A History*. Millwood, NY: KTO, 1979.

Langdon, George D., Jr. *Pilgrim Colony; A History of New Plymouth, 1620–1691*. New Haven, CT: Yale University Press, 1966.

Lockhart, Audrey. *Some Aspects of Emigration from Ireland to the North American Colonies between 1660 and 1775*. New York: Arno, 1976.

Lockridge, Kenneth A. *A New England Town: The First Hundred Years, Dedham, Massachusetts, 1636–1736*. New York: W. W. Norton, 1985.

Melvoin, Richard I. *New England Outposts: War and Society in Colonial Deerfield*. New York: W. W. Norton, 1989.

Miller, Perry. *Orthodoxy in Massachusetts, 1630–1650: A Genetic Study*. Cambridge, MA: Harvard University Press, 1933.

Nelson, William E. *Americanization of the Common Law: The Impact of Legal Change on Massachusetts Society, 1760–1830*. Cambridge, MA: Harvard University Press, 1975.

———. *Dispute and Conflict Resolution in Plymouth County, Massachusetts, 1725–1825*. Chapel Hill: University of North Carolina Press, 1981.

Nobles, Gregory H. *Divisions Throughout the Whole: Politics and Society in Hampshire County, Massachusetts, 1740–1775*. Cambridge, UK: Cambridge University Press, 1983,

O'Brien, Jean M. *Dispossession by Degrees: Indian Land and Identity in Natick, Massachusetts, 1650–1790*. New York: Cambridge University Press, 1997.

Patterson, Stephen E. *Political Parties in Revolutionary Massachusetts*. Madison: University of Wisconsin Press, 1973.

Pencak, William. *War, Politics, and Revolution in Provincial Massachusetts.* Boston: Northeastern University Press, 1981.

Puglisi, Michael J. *Puritans Besieged: The Legacies of King Philip's War in the Massachusetts Bay Colony.* Lanham, MD: University Press of America, 1991.

Rosenthal, Bernard. *Salem Story: Reading the Witch Trials of 1692.* Cambridge, UK: Cambridge University Press, 1993.

Rothenberg, Winifred B. *From Market Places to a Market Economy: The Transformation of Rural Massachusetts, 1750–1850.* Chicago: University of Chicago Press, 1992.

Rutman, Darrett B. *Husbandmen of Plymouth: Farms and Villages in the Old Colony, 1620–1692.* Boston: Beacon for Plimoth Plantation, 1967.

———. *Winthrop's Boston: Portrait of a Puritan Town, 1630–1649.* Chapel Hill: University of North Carolina Press, 1965.

Salisbury, Neal. "Red Puritans: The 'Praying Indians" of Massachusetts Bay and John Eliot." *William and Mary Quarterly*, 3rd ser., 31 (January 1974): 27–54.

Schutz, John A. *William Shirley: King's Governor of Massachusetts.* Chapel Hill: University of North Carolina Press, 1961.

Simmons, Richard C. *Studies in the Massachusetts Franchise, 1631–1691.* New York: Garland, 1989.

Taylor, Alan. *Liberty Men and Great Proprietors: The Revolutionary Settlement on the Maine Frontier, 1760–1820.* Chapel Hill: University of North Carolina Press, 1990.

Taylor, Robert J. *Western Massachusetts in the Revolution.* Providence, RI: Brown University Press, 1954.

Thompson, Roger. *Sex in Middlesex: Popular Mores in a Massachusetts County, 1649–1699.* Amherst: University of Massachusetts Press, 1986.

Tyler, John W. *Smugglers and Patriots: Boston Merchants and the Advent of the American Revolution.* Boston: Northeastern University Press, 1986.

Vickers, Daniel. *Farmers and Fisherman: Two Centuries of Work in Essex County, Massachusetts, 1630–1850.* Chapel Hill: University of North Carolina Press, 1994.

Wall, Robert E. *Massachusetts Bay: The Crucial Decade, 1640–1650.* New Haven, CT: Yale University Press, 1972.

Warden, G. B. *Boston, 1689–1776.* Boston: Little, Brown, 1970.

Waters, John J. *The Otis Family in Provincial and Revolutionary Massachusetts.* Chapel Hill: University of North Carolina Press, 1968.

Whitehill, Walter M. *Boston: A Topographical History.* Cambridge, MA: Belknap Press, 1968.

Young, Christine A. *From "Good Order" to Glorious Revolution: Salem, Massachusetts, 1628–1689.* Ann Arbor, MI: UMI Research Press, 1980.

Zakai, Avihu. *Theocracy in Massachusetts: Reformation and Separation in Early Puritan New England.* San Francisco: Mellen Research University Press, 1993.

New Hampshire

Clark, Charles E. *The Eastern Frontier: The Settlement of Northern New England, 1610–1763.* New York: Alfred A. Knopf, 1970.

Daniel, Jere R. *Colonial New Hampshire: A History.* Millwood, NY: KTO, 1981.

Turner, Lynn W. *The Ninth State: New Hampshire's Formative Years.* Chapel Hill: University of North Carolina Press, 1983.

Van Deventer, David. *The Emergence of Provincial New Hampshire, 1623–1741.* Baltimore: Johns Hopkins University Press, 1976.

New Jersey

Batinksi, Michael C. *The New Jersey Assembly, 1738–1775: The Making of a Legislative Community.* Lanham, MD: University Press of America, 1987.

Cohen, David S. *The Folklore and Folklife of New Jersey.* New Brunswick, NJ: Rutgers University Press, 1983.

Craven, Wesley F. *New Jersey and the English Colonization of North America.* Princeton, NJ: Van Nostrand, 1964.

Gerlach, Larry R. *Prologue to Independence: New Jersey in the Coming of the American Revolution.* New Brunswick, NJ: Rutgers University Press, 1975.

Landsman, Ned C. *Scotland and Its First American Colony, 1683–1765.* Princeton, NJ: Princeton University Press, 1985.

Leiby, Adrian C. *The Early Dutch and Swedish Settlers of New Jersey.* Princeton, NJ: Van Nostrand, 1964.

Levitt, James H. *For Want of Trade: Shipping and the New Jersey Ports, 1680–1783.* Newark: New Jersey Historical Society, 1981.

Pomfret, John E. *Colonial New Jersey: A History.* New York: Charles Scribner's Sons, 1973.

———. *The Province of East Jersey, 1609–1702: The Rebellious Proprietary.* Princeton, NJ: Princeton University Press, 1962.

———. *The Province of West New Jersey, 1609–1702.* Princeton, NJ: Princeton University Press, 1956.

Purvis, Thomas L. *Proprietors, Patronage, and Paper Money: Legislative Politics in New Jersey, 1703–1776.* New Brunswick, NJ: Rutgers University Press, 1986.

Ryan, Dennis P. "Landholding, Opportunity, and Mobility in Revolutionary New Jersey." *William and Mary Quarterly*, 3rd ser., 36 (October 1979): 571–92.

Wacker, Peter O., and Paul G. Clemens. *Land Use in Early New Jersey: A Historical Geography.* New Brunswick, NJ: Rutgers University Press, 1995.

New York and New Netherland

Archdeacon, Thomas. *New York City, 1664–1710: Conquest and Change.* Ithaca, NY: Cornell University Press, 1976.

Bachman, Van Cleaf. *Peltries or Plantations: The Economic*

Policies of the Dutch West India Company in New Netherland, 1623–1639. Baltimore: Johns Hopkins University Press, 1970.

Becker, Carl L. *The History of Political Parties in the Province of New York, 1760–1776*. Madison: University of Wisconsin Press, 1909.

Biemer, Linda. *Women and Property in Colonial New York: The Transition from Dutch to English Law, 1643–1727*. Ann Arbor: University of Michigan Press, 1983.

Bonomi, Patricia U. *A Factious People: Politics and Society in Colonial New York*. New York: Columbia University Press, 1971.

Bonomi, Patricia U., and Eric Nooter, eds. *Colonial Dutch Studies: An Interdisciplinary Approach*. New York: New York University Press, 1988.

Burke, Thomas E. *Mohawk Frontier: The Dutch Community of Schenectady, New York, 1661–1710*. Ithaca, NY: Cornell University Press, 1991.

Cohen, David. "How Dutch Were the Dutch of New Netherland." *New York History* 62 (1981): 51.

Condon, Thomas J. *New York Beginnings: The Commercial Origins of New Netherland*. New York: New York University Press, 1968.

Countryman, Edward. *A People in Revolution: The American Revolution and Political Society in New York, 1760–1790*. Baltimore: Johns Hopkins University Press, 1981.

Cray, Robert E. *Paupers and Poor Relief in New York City and Its Rural Environs, 1700–1830*. Philadelphia: Temple University Press, 1988.

Davis, Thomas J. *A Rumor of Revolt: The "Great Negro Plot" in Colonial New York*. New York: Free Press, 1985.

Goebel, Julius, Jr., and T. Raymond Naughton. *Law Enforcement in Colonial New York: A Study in Criminal Procedure*. New York: The Commonwealth Fund, 1944.

Goodfriend, Joyce D. *Before the Melting Pot: Society and Culture in Colonial New York City, 1664–1730*. Princeton, NJ: Princeton University Press, 1992.

Greenberg, Douglas. *Crime and Law Enforcement in the Colony of New York, 1691–1776*. Ithaca, NY: Cornell University Press, 1974.

Hartog, Hendrik. *Public Property and Private Power: The Corporation of the City of New York in American Law, 1730–1870*. Chapel Hill: University of North Carolina Press, 1983.

Higgins, Ruth L. *Expansion in New York, with Especial Reference to the Eighteenth Century*. Philadelphia: Porcupine, 1976.

Hodges, Graham R. *New York City Cartmen, 1667–1850*. New York: New York University Press, 1986.

Hummel, Charles F. *With Hammer in Hand: The Dominy Craftsmen of East Hampton, New York*. Charlottesville: University Press of Virginia, 1980.

Israel, Jonathan I. *The Dutch Republic: Its Rise, Greatness, and Fall, 1477–1806*. New York: Oxford University Press, 1998.

Johnson, Herbert A. *Essays on New York Colonial Legal History*. Westport, CT: Greenwood, 1981.

Kaestle, Carl F. *The Evolution of an Urban School System: New York City, 1750–1850*. Cambridge, MA: Harvard University Press, 1973.

Kammen, Michael. *Colonial New York: A History*. New York: Oxford University Press, 1975.

Katz, Stanley N. *Newcastle's New York: Anglo-American Politics, 1732–1753*. Cambridge, MA: Harvard University Press, 1968.

Kim, Sung B. *Landlord and Tenant in Colonial New York: Manorial Society, 1664–1775*. Chapel Hill: University of North Carolina Press, 1978.

Klein, Milton M. *Politics of Diversity: Essays in the History of Colonial New York*. Port Washington, NY: Kennikat, 1974.

Kross, Jessica. *The Evolution of an American Town: Newtown, New York, 1642–1775*. Philadelphia: Temple University Press, 1983.

Leder, Lawrence H. *Robert Livingston, 1654–1728, and the Politics of Colonial New York*. Chapel Hill: University of North Carolina Press, 1961.

Lustig, Mary L. *Robert Hunter, 1666–1734: New York's Augustan Statesman*. Syracuse, NY: Syracuse University Press, 1983.

Matson, Cathy. "'Damned Scoundrels' and 'Libertisme of Trade': Freedom and Regulation in Colonial New York's Fur and Grain Trades." *William and Mary Quarterly*, 3rd ser., 51 (1994): 389–418.

Merwick, Donna. *Possessing Albany, 1630–1710: The Dutch and English Experiences*. New York: Cambridge University Press, 1990.

Middlekauf, Robert. *Ancients and Axioms: Secondary Education in Eighteenth-Century New England*. New Haven, CT: Yale University Press, 1963.

Miller, Howard. *The Revolutionary College: American Presbyterian Higher Education, 1707–1837*. New York: New York University Press, 1976.

Narrett, David E. *Inheritance and Family Life in Colonial New York City*. Ithaca, NY: Cornell University Press, 1992.

Norton, Thomas E. *The Fur Trade in Colonial New York, 1686–1776*. Madison: University of Wisconsin Press, 1974.

Pencak, William, and Conrad E. Wright, eds. *Authority and Resistance in Early New York*. New York: New York Historical Society, 1988.

Price, J. L. *The Dutch Republic in the Seventeenth Century*. New York: St. Martin's, 1998.

Rink, Oliver A. *Holland on the Hudson: An Economic and Social History of Dutch New York*. Ithaca, NY: Cornell University Press, 1986.

Ritchie, Robert C. *The Duke's Province: A Study of New York Politics and Society, 1664–1691*. Chapel Hill: University of North Carolina Press, 1977.

Schwartz, Philip J. *The Jarring Interests: New York's Boundary*

Makers, 1664–1776. Albany: State University of New York Press, 1979.

Smith, George L. *Religion and Trade in New Netherland: Dutch Origins and American Development*. Ithaca, NY: Cornell University Press, 1973.

Trelease, Allen W. *Indian Affairs in Colonial New York: The Seventeenth Century*. Ithaca, NY: Cornell University Press, 1960.

White, Philip L. *The Beekmans of New York in Politics and Commerce, 1647–1877*. New York: New York Historical Society, 1956.

———. *Beekmantown, New York: Forest Frontier to Farm Community*. Austin: University of Texas Press, 1979.

Young, Alfred E. *The Democratic Republicans of New York: The Origins, 1763–1797*. Chapel Hill: University of North Carolina Press, 1967.

North Carolina

Clarke, Desmond. *Arthur Dobbs, Esquire, 1689–1765: Surveyor-General of Ireland, Prospector and Governor of North Carolina*. Chapel Hill: University of North Carolina Press, 1957.

Ekirch, A. Roger. *"Poor Carolina": Politics and Society in Colonial North Carolina, 1729–1762*. Chapel Hill: University of North Carolina Press, 1981.

Ganyard, Robert L. *The Emergence of North Carolina's Revolutionary State Government*. Raleigh: North Carolina Department of Cultural Resources, 1978.

Kars, Marjoleine. *"Breaking Loose Together": How North Carolina Farmers Came to Fight the War of the Regulation*. Chapel Hill: University of North Carolina Press, 2001.

Lee, Lawrence. *The Lower Cape Fear in Colonial Days*. Chapel Hill: University of North Carolina Press, 1965.

Lefler, Hugh T., and William S. Powell. *Colonial North Carolina: A History*. New York: Scribner's 1973.

Merrens, Harry R. *Colonial North Carolina in the Eighteenth Century: A Study in Historical Geography*. Chapel Hill: University of North Carolina Press, 1964.

Meyer, Duane. *The Highland Scots of North Carolina, 1732–1776*. Chapel Hill: University of North Carolina Press, 1953.

Powell, William S. *Colonial North Carolina: A History*. Chapel Hill: University of North Carolina Press, 1988.

Ramsey, Robert W. *Carolina Cradle: Settlement of the Northwest Carolina Frontier, 1747–1762*. Chapel Hill: University of North Carolina Press, 1964.

Rankin, Hugh F. *The North Carolina Continentals*. Chapel Hill: University of North Carolina Press, 1971.

Sensbach, Jon A. *A Separate Canaan: The Making of an Afro-Moravian World in North Carolina, 1763–1840*. Chapel Hill: University of North Carolina Press, 1998.

Spindell, Donna. *Crime and Society in North Carolina, 1673–1776*. Baton Rouge: Louisiana State University Press, 1989.

Thorp, Daniel B. "Assimilation in North Carolina's Moravian Community." *Journal of Southern History* 52 (February 1986): 19–42.

———. *The Moravian Community in Colonial North Carolina: Pluralism on the Southern Frontier*. Knoxville: University of Tennessee Press, 1989.

Ver Steeg, Clarence L. *Origins of a Southern Mosaic: Studies of Early Carolina and Georgia*. Athens: University of Georgia Press, 1975.

Pennsylvania

Alexander, John K. *Render Them Submissive: Responses to Poverty in Philadelphia, 1760–1800*. Amherst: University of Massachusetts Press, 1980.

Bridenbaugh, Carl, and Jessica Bridenbaugh. *Rebels and Gentlemen: Philadelphia in the Age of Franklin*. Westport, CT: Greenwood, 1970.

Bronner, Edwin B. *William Penn's "Holy Experiment": The Founding of Pennsylvania, 1681–1701*. New York: Temple University Publications, 1962.

Doerflinger, Thomas M. *A Vigorous Spirit of Enterprise: Merchants and Economic Development in Revolutionary Philadelphia*. Chapel Hill: University of North Carolina Press, 1986.

Dunn, Mary M. *William Penn, Politics and Conscience*. Princeton, NJ: Princeton University Press, 1967.

Dunn, Richard S., and Mary M. Dunn, eds. *The World of William Penn*. Philadelphia: University of Pennsylvania Press, 1986.

Fletcher, Stevenson W. *Pennsylvania Agriculture and Country Life, 1640–1840*. Harrisburg: Pennsylvania Historical and Museum Commission, 1950.

Frantz, George W. *Paxton: A Study of Community Structure in the Colonial Pennsylvania Backcountry*. New York: Garland, 1989.

Hanna, William S. *Benjamin Franklin and Pennsylvania Politics*. Stanford, CA: Stanford University Press, 1964.

Hutson, James H. *Pennsylvania Politics, 1747–1770: The Movement for Royal Government and Its Consequences*. Princeton, NJ: Princeton University Press, 1972.

Illick, Joseph. *Colonial Pennsylvania: A History*. New York: Charles Scribner's Sons, 1976.

Jensen, Arthur L. *The Maritime Commerce of Colonial Philadelphia*. Madison: State Historical Society of Wisconsin, 1966.

Klein, Randolph S. *Portrait of an Early American Family: The Shippens of Pennsylvania across Five Generations*. Philadelphia: University of Pennsylvania Press, 1975.

Klepp, Susan E. *Philadelphia in Transition: A Demographic History of the City and Its Occupation Groups, 1720–1830*. New York: Garland, 1989.

Lemon, James T. *The Best Poor Man's Country: A Geographical Study of Early Southeastern Pennsylvania*. Baltimore: Johns Hopkins University Press, 1972.

Levy, Barry. *Quakers and the American Family: British Settlement in the Delaware Valley.* New York: Oxford University Press, 1988.

Nash, Gary B. *Forging Freedom: The Formation of Philadelphia's Black Community, 1720–1840.* Cambridge, MA: Harvard University Press, 1991.

———. *Quakers and Politics: Pennsylvania, 1681–1726.* Boston: Northeastern University Press, 1993.

Offutt, William M. *Of Good Laws and Good Men: Law and Society in the Delaware Valley, 1680–1710.* Urbana: University of Illinois Press, 1995.

Ousterhout, Anne M. *A State Divided: Opposition in Pennsylvania to the American Revolution.* Westport, CT: Greenwood, 1987.

Paskoff, Paul F. *Industrial Evolution: Organization, Structure, and Growth of the Pennsylvania Iron Industry, 1750–1860.* Baltimore: Johns Hopkins University Press, 1983.

Rosswurm, Steven. *Arms, Country, and Class: The Philadelphia Militia and the "Lower Sort" during the American Revolution.* New Brunswick, NJ: Rutgers University Press, 1987.

Rothermund, Dietmar. *The Layman's Progress: Religious and Political Experience in Colonial Pennsylvania, 1740–1770.* Philadelphia: University of Pennsylvania Press, 1962.

Salinger, Sharon V. *"To Serve Well and Faithfully": Labor and Indentured Servitude in Pennsylvania, 1682–1800.* New York: Heritage, 2000.

Schwartz, Sally. *"A Mixed Multitude": The Struggle for Toleration in Colonial Pennsylvania.* New York: New York University Press, 1988.

Schweitzer, Mary M. *Custom and Contract: Household, Government, and the Economy in Colonial Pennsylvania.* New York: Columbia University Press, 1987.

Smaby, Beverly P. *The Transformation of Moravian Bethlehem: From Communal Mission to Family Economy.* Philadelphia: University of Pennsylvania Press, 1988.

Smith, Billy G. *The "Lower Sort": Philadelphia's Laboring People, 1750–1800.* Ithaca, NY: Cornell University Press, 1990.

———. "The Material Lives of Laboring Philadelphians, 1750 to 1800." *William and Mary Quarterly,* 3rd ser., 38 (April 1981): 163–202.

Thayer, Theodore. *Pennsylvania Politics and the Growth of Democracy, 1740–1776.* Harrisburg: Pennsylvania Historical and Museum Commission, 1953.

Tolles, Frederick B. *Meeting House and Counting House: The Quaker Merchants of Colonial Philadelphia, 1682–1763.* Chapel Hill: University of North Carolina Press, 1948.

Tully, Alan. *William Penn's Legacy: Politics and Social Structure in Provincial Pennsylvania, 1726–1755.* Baltimore: Johns Hopkins University Press, 1977.

Wolf, Stephanie G. *Urban Village: Population, Community, and Family Structure in Germantown, Pennsylvania, 1683–1800.* Princeton, NJ: Princeton University Press, 1976.

Wood, Jerome H. *Conestoga Crossroads: Lancaster, Pennsylvania, 1730–1790.* Harrisburg: Pennsylvania Historical and Museum Commission, 1979.

Yogg, Michael R. *"The Best Place for Health and Wealth": A Demographical and Economic Analysis of the Quakers of Bucks County, Pennsylvania.* New York: Garland, 1988.

Rhode Island

Bridenbaugh, Carl. *Fat Mutton and Liberty of Conscience: Society in Rhode Island, 1636–1690.* Providence, RI: Brown University Press, 1974.

Cheyt, Stanley F. *Lopez of Newport: Colonial American Merchant Prince.* Detroit, MI: Wayne State University Press, 1970.

Coughtry, Jay. *The Notorious Triangle: Rhode Island and the American Slave Trade, 1700–1807.* Philadelphia: Temple University Press, 1981.

Crane, Elaine F. *A Dependent People: Newport, Rhode Island, in the Revolutionary Era.* New York: Fordham University Press, 1985.

Daniels, Bruce C. *Dissent and Conformity on Narragansett Bay: The Colonial Rhode Island Town.* Middletown, CT: Wesleyan University Press, 1983.

Hedges, James B. *The Browns of Providence Plantations.* 2 vols. Providence, RI: Brown University Press, 1952–1968.

James, Sydney V. *Colonial Rhode Island: A History.* New York: Charles Scribner's Sons, 1975.

Lovejoy, David S. *Rhode Island Politics and the American Revolution, 1760–1776.* Providence, RI: Brown University Press, 1958.

McLoughlin, William G. *Rhode Island: A Bicentennial History.* New York: W. W. Norton, 1978.

Withey, Lynne. *Urban Growth in Colonial Rhode Island: Newport and Providence in the Eighteenth Century.* Albany: State University of New York Press, 1984.

South Carolina

Brown, Richard M. *The South Carolina Regulators.* Cambridge, MA: Harvard University Press, 1963.

Canady, Hoyt P. *Gentlemen of the Bar: Lawyers in Colonial South Carolina.* New York: Garland, 1987.

Clowse, Converse D. *Economic Beginnings in Colonial South Carolina.* Columbia: University of South Carolina Press, 1971.

Coclanis, Peter A. *The Shadow of a Dream: Economic Life and Death in the South Carolina Low Country, 1670–1920.* New York: Oxford University Press, 1989.

Frakes, George E. *Laboratory for Liberty: The South Carolina Legislative Committee System 1719–1776.* Lexington: University Press of Kentucky, 1970.

Greene, Jack P. "Colonial South Carolina and the Caribbean Connection." *South Carolina Historical Magazine* 88 (1987): 192–210.

Hatley, M. Thomas. *The Dividing Paths: Cherokees and South*

Carolinians through the Era of Revolution. New York: Oxford University Press, 1993.

Littlefield, Daniel C. *Rice and Slaves: Ethnicity and the Slave Trade in Colonial South Carolina.* Baton Rouge: Louisiana State University Press, 1981.

Meriwether, Robert L. *The Expansion of South Carolina, 1729–1765.* Kingsport, TN: Southern Publishers, 1940.

Nadelhaft, Jerome J. *The Disorders of War: The Revolution in South Carolina.* Orono: University of Maine at Orono Press, 1981.

Olwell, Robert. *Masters, Slaves, and Subjects: The Culture of Power in the South Carolina Low Country, 1740–1790.* Ithaca, NY: Cornell University Press, 1998.

Rogers, George C. *Charleston in the Age of the Pinckneys.* Norman: University of Oklahoma Press, 1969.

Sherman, Richard P. *Robert Johnson: Proprietary and Royal Governor of South Carolina.* Columbia: University of South Carolina Press, 1966.

Sirmans, M. Eugene. *Colonial South Carolina: A Political History, 1663–1763.* Chapel Hill: University of North Carolina Press, 1966.

Smith, Warren B. *White Servitude in Colonial South Carolina.* Columbia: University of South Carolina Press, 1961.

Walsh, Richard. *Charleston's Sons of Liberty: A Study of the Artisans, 1763–1789.* Columbia: University of South Carolina Press, 1959.

Waterhouse, Richard. *A New World Gentry: The Making of a Merchant and Planter Class in South Carolina, 1670–1770.* New York: Garland, 1989.

Weir, Robert M. *Colonial South Carolina: A History.* Millwood, NY: KTO, 1983.

Wood, Peter H. *Black Majority: Negroes in Colonial South Carolina from 1670 Through the Stono Rebellion.* New York: Alfred A. Knopf, 1974.

Spanish Colonies in Mainland North America

Bannon, John F. *The Spanish Borderlands Frontier, 1513–1821.* New York: Holt, Rinehart and Winston, 1970.

Bethell, Leslie, ed. *Colonial Spanish America.* New York: Cambridge University Press, 1987.

Bushnell, Amy. *The King's Coffer: Proprietors of the Spanish Florida Treasury, 1565–1702.* Gainesville: University of Florida Press, 1981.

Chipman, Donald E. *Spanish Texas, 1519–1821.* Austin: University of Texas Press, 1992.

Clendinnen, Inga. *Aztecs: An Interpretation.* New York: Cambridge University Press, 1991.

Cook, Warren L. *Flood Tide of Empire: Spain and the Pacific Northwest, 1543–1819.* New Haven, CT: Yale University Press, 1973.

Cruz, Gilbert R. *Let There Be Towns: Spanish Municipal Origins in the American Southwest, 1610–1810.* College Station: Texas A & M University Press, 1988.

Elliott, J. H. *Imperial Spain, 1469–1716.* London: Edward Arnold, 1963.

Fireman, Janet R. *The Spanish Royal Corps of Engineers in the Western Borderlands: Instrument of Bourbon Reform, 1764 to 1815.* Glendale, CA: Clark, 1977.

Forbes, Jack D. *Apache, Navaho, and Spaniard.* Norman: University of Oklahoma Press, 1994.

Gibson, Charles. *Spain in America.* New York: Harper & Row, 1966.

Gold, Robert L. *Borderland Empires in Transition: The Triple Nation Transfer of Florida.* Carbondale: Southern Illinois University Press, 1969.

Gutiérrez, Ramon A. *When Jesus Came, the Corn Mothers Went Away: Marriage, Sexuality, and Power in New Mexico, 1500–1846.* Stanford, CA: Stanford University Press, 1991.

Gutiérrez, Ramon A., and Richard J. Orsi, eds. *Contested Eden: California Before the Gold Rush.* Berkeley: University of California Press, 1998.

Hall, Thomas D. *Social Change in the Southwest, 1350–1880.* Lawrence: University Press of Kansas, 1989.

Hanke, Lewis. *The Spanish Struggle for Justice in the Conquest of America.* Dallas, TX: Southern Methodist University Press, 2002.

Hann, John H. *Apalachee: The Land Between the Rivers.* Gainesville: University Presses of Florida, 1988.

Hoffman, Paul E. *A New Andalucia and a Way to the Orient: The American Southeast during the Sixteenth Century.* Baton Rouge: Louisiana State University Press, 1990.

Howard, David A. *Conquistador in Chains: Cabeza de Vaca and the Indians of the Americas.* Tuscaloosa: University of Alabama Press, 1997.

Jackson, Jack. *Los Mesteños: Spanish Ranching in Texas, 1721–1821.* College Station: Texas A & M University Press, 1986.

Jackson, John B. *A Sense of Place, A Sense of Time.* New Haven, CT: Yale University Press, 1994.

John, Elizabeth A. H. *Storms Brewed in Other Men's Worlds: The Confrontation of Indians, Spanish, and French in the Southwest, 1540–1795.* Norman: University of Oklahoma Press, 1996.

Jones, Oakah L. *Los Paisanos: Spanish Settlers on the Northern Frontier of New Spain.* Norman: University of Oklahoma Press, 1979.

———. *Pueblo Warriors and Spanish Conquest.* Norman: University of Oklahoma Press, 1966.

Kessell, John L. *Friars, Soldiers, and Reformers: Hispanic Arizona and the Sonora Mission Frontier, 1767–1856.* Tucson: University of Arizona Press, 1976.

Knaut, Andrew L. *The Pueblo Revolt of 1680: Conquest and Resistance in Seventeenth-Century New Mexico.* Norman: University of Oklahoma Press, 1997.

Landers, Jane. "Garcia Real de Santa Teresa de Mose: A Free Black Town in Spanish Colonial Florida." *American Historical Review* 95 (1990): 9–30.

Lockhart, James, and Stuart B. Schwartz. *Early Latin America:*

A History of Colonial Spanish America and Brazil. New York: Cambridge University Press, 1983.

Lowery, Woodbury. *The Spanish Settlements within the Present Limits of the United States, 1513–1561.* New York: Russell and Russell, 1959.

Lyon, Eugene. *The Enterprise of Florida: Pedro Menéndez de Avilés and the Spanish Conquest of 1565–1568.* Gainesville: University of Florida Press, 1976.

McAlister, Lyle N. *Spain and Portugal in the New World, 1492–1700.* Minneapolis: University of Minnesota Press, 1984.

Moore, John P. *Revolt in Louisiana: The Spanish Occupation, 1766–1770.* Baton Rouge: Louisiana State University Press, 1976.

Moorhead, Max L. *The Apache Frontier: Jacobo Ugarte and Spanish Indian Relations in Northern New Spain, 1769–1791.* Norman: University of Oklahoma Press, 1968.

———. *The Presidio: Bastion of the Spanish Borderlands.* Norman: University of Oklahoma Press, 1991.

Nasatir, Abraham P. *Borderland in Retreat: From Spanish Louisiana to the Far Southwest.* Albuquerque: University of New Mexico Press, 1976.

Sauer, Carl O. *The Early Spanish Main.* Berkeley: University of California Press, 1966.

Sluiter, Engel. *The Florida Situado: Quantifying the First Eighty Years, 1571–1651.* Gainesville: University of Florida Libraries, 1985.

Spicer, Edward H. *Cycles of Conquest: The Impact of Spain, Mexico, and the United States on the Indians of the Southwest, 1533–1960.* Tucson: University of Arizona Press, 1962.

Te Paske, John J. *The Governorship of Spanish Florida, 1700–1763.* Durham, NC: Duke University Press, 1964.

Thomas, David H., ed. *Columbian Consequences,* vol. 2, *Archaeological and Historical Perspectives on the Spanish Borderlands East.* Washington, DC: Smithsonian Institution Press, 1990.

Vigil, Ralph H., Francis W. Kaye, and John R. Wunder, eds. *Spain and the Plains: Myths and Realities of Spanish Exploration and Settlement on the Great Plains.* Niwot: University Press of Colorado, 1994.

Wagner, Henry R. *The Spanish Southwest, 1542–1794: An Annotated Bibliography.* New York: Arno, 1968.

Weber, David J., ed. *New Spain's Far Northern Frontier: Essays on Spain in the American West.* Albuquerque: University of New Mexico Press, 1979.

———. *The Spanish Frontier in North America.* New Haven, CT: Yale University Press, 1992.

Weddle, Robert S. *Spanish Sea: The Gulf of Mexico in North American Discovery, 1500–1685.* College Station: Texas A & M University Press, 1985.

Wright, J. Leitch. *Anglo-Spanish Rivalry in North America.* Athens: University of Georgia Press, 1971.

Virginia

Abernethy, Thomas P. *Three Virginia Frontiers.* Baton Rouge: Louisiana State University Press, 1940.

Bailey, Kenneth P. *The Ohio Company of Virginia and the Westward Movement, 1748–1792: A Chapter in the History of the Colonial Frontier.* Glendale, CA: Clark, 1939.

Bailey, Raymond C. *Popular Influence Upon Public Policy: Petitioning in Eighteenth-Century Virginia.* Westport, CT: Greenwood, 1979.

Beeman, Richard R. *The Evolution of the Southern Backcountry: A Case Study of Lunenburg County, Virginia, 1746–1832.* Philadelphia: University of Pennsylvania Press, 1989.

Billings, Warren M. *Virginia's Viceroy: Their Majesties' Governor General Francis Howard, Baron Howard of Effingham.* Fairfax, VA: George Mason University Press, 1991.

Billings, Warren M., John E. Selby, and Thad W. Tate. *Colonial Virginia: A History.* White Plains, NY: KTO, 1986.

Breen, T. H., and Stephen Innes. *"Myne Owne Ground": Race and Freedom on Virginia's Eastern Shore, 1640–1676.* New York: Oxford University Press, 1982.

Brown, Robert E., and Katherine B. Brown. *Virginia, 1705–1786: Democracy or Aristocracy?* East Lansing: Michigan State University Press, 1964.

Buckley, Thomas E. *Church and State in Revolutionary Virginia, 1776–1787.* Charlottesville: University Press of Virginia, 1977.

Carr, Lois G., Philip D. Morgan, and Jean B. Russo, eds. *Colonial Chesapeake Society.* Chapel Hill: University of North Carolina Press, 1988.

Craven, Wesley, F. *The Southern Colonies in the Seventeenth Century, 1607–1689.* Baton Rouge: Louisiana State University Press, 1970.

———. *White, Red, and Black: The Seventeenth-Century Virginian.* Charlottesville: University Press of Virginia, 1971.

Davis, Richard B. *Literature and Society in Early Virginia, 1608–1840.* Baton Rouge: Louisiana State University Press, 1973.

Gleach, Frederic. *Powhatan's World and Colonial Virginia: A Conflict of Cultures.* Lincoln: University of Nebraska Press, 1997.

Greene, Jack P. *Political Life in Eighteenth-Century Virginia.* Williamsburg, VA: Colonial Williamsburg Foundation, 1986.

Griffith, Lucille. *The Virginia House of Burgesses, 1750–1774.* Tuscaloosa: University of Alabama Press, 1970.

Hemphill, John M. *Virginia and the English Commercial System, 1689–1733: A Study in the Development and Fluctuations of a Colonial Economy Under Imperial Control.* New York: Garland, 1985.

Hofstra, Warren R. " 'The Extention of His Majesties Dominions': The Virginia Backcountry and the Reconfiguration of Imperial Frontiers." *Journal of American History* 84 (March 1998): 1281–312.

Horn, James. *Adapting to a New World: English Society in the Seventeenth-Century Chesapeake.* Chapel Hill: University of North Carolina Press, 1994.

Hughes, Sarah S. *Surveyors and Statesmen: Land Measuring in Colonial Virginia.* Richmond: Virginia Surveyors Foundation and Virginia Association of Surveyors, 1979.

Hume, Ivor N. *The Virginia Adventure, Roanoke to Jamestown: An Archaeological and Historical Odyssey.* Charlottesville, VA: University Press of Virginia, 1997.

Isaac, Rhys. *The Transformation of Virginia, 1740–1790.* Chapel Hill: University of North Carolina Press, 1982.

Johnston, James H. *Race Relations in Virginia and Miscegenation in the South, 1776–1860.* Amherst: University of Massachusetts Press, 1970.

Kolp, John Gilman. *Gentlemen and Freeholders: Electoral Politics in Colonial Virginia.* Baltimore: Johns Hopkins University Press, 1998.

Kukla, Jon. *Political Institutions in Virginia, 1619–1660.* New York: Garland, 1989.

Kupperman, Karen O. *Roanoke: The Abandoned Colony.* Totowa, NJ: Rowman & Allanheld, 1984.

Morgan, Edmund. *American Slavery, American Freedom: The Ordeal of Colonial Virginia.* New York: W. W. Norton, 1975.

Morgan, Gwenda. *The Hegemony of the Law: Richmond County, Virginia, 1692–1776.* New York: Garland, 1989.

Morton, Louis. *Robert Carter of Nomini Hall: A Virginia Tobacco Planter of the Eighteenth Century.* Charlottesville, VA: Dominion, 1964.

Mullin, Gerald W. *Flight and Rebellion: Slave Resistance in Eighteenth-Century Virginia.* New York: Oxford University Press, 1972.

O'Mara, James. *An Historical Geography of Urban System Development: Tidewater Virginia in the Eighteenth Century.* Downsview, UK: York University, 1983.

Perry, James R. *The Formation of a Society on Virginia's Eastern Shore, 1615–1655.* Chapel Hill: University of North Carolina Press, 1990.

Quinn, David B. *Set Fair for Roanoke: Voyages and Colonies, 1584–1606.* Chapel Hill: University of North Carolina Press, 1985.

Quitt, Martin H. "Trade and Acculturation at Jamestown, 1607–1609: The Limits of Understanding." *William and Mary Quarterly*, 3rd ser., 52 (1995): 227–58.

———. *Virginia House of Burgesses, 1660–1706: The Social,*

Educational and Economic Bonds of Political Power. New York: Garland, 1989.

Rainbolt, John C. *From Prescription to Persuasion: Manipulation of Eighteenth Century Virginia Economy.* Port Washington, NY: Kennikat, 1974.

Reps, John W. *Tidewater Towns: City Planning in Colonial Virginia and Maryland.* Williamsburg, VA: Colonial Williamsburg Foundation, 1972.

Roeber, A. G. *Faithful Magistrates and Republican Lawyers: Creators of Virginia Legal Culture, 1680–1810.* Chapel Hill: University of North Carolina Press, 1981.

Roundtree, Helen C. *Pocahontas's People: The Powhatan Indians of Virginia Through Four Centuries.* Norman: University of Oklahoma Press, 1990.

———. *The Powhatan Indians of Virginia: Their Traditional Culture.* Norman: University of Oklahoma Press, 1989.

Rutman, Darrett B., and Anita H. Rutman. *A Place in Time: Middlesex County, Virginia, 1650–1750.* New York: W. W. Norton, 1984.

Schwarz, Philip J. *Twice Condemned: Slaves and the Criminal Laws of Virginia, 1705–1865.* Baton Rouge: Louisiana State University Press, 1988.

Selby, John E. *The Revolution in Virginia, 1775–1783.* Williamsburg: University Press of Virginia, 1988.

Shea, William L. *The Virginia Militia in the Seventeenth Century.* Baton Rouge: Louisiana State University Press, 1983.

Sluiter, Engel. "New Light on the '20 and Odd Negroes' Arriving in Virginia, August, 1619." *William and Mary Quarterly,* 3rd ser., 54 (1997): 396–98.

Soltow, James H. *The Economic Role of Williamsburg.* Williamsburg, VA: Colonial Williamsburg, 1965.

Sydnor, Charles S. *Gentlemen Freeholders: Political Practices in Washington's Virginia.* Westport, CT: Greenwood, 1984.

Thornton, John. "The African Experience of the '20 and Odd Negroes' Arriving in Virginia in 1619." *William and Mary Quarterly* 54 (1997): 421–34.

Tillson, Albert H. *Gentry and Common Folk: Political Culture on a Virginia Frontier, 1740–1789.* Lexington: University Press of Kentucky, 1991.

Titus, James. *The Old Dominion at War: Society, Politics, and Warfare in Late Colonial Virginia.* Columbia: University of South Carolina Press, 1991.

Vaughan, Alden T. *American Genesis: Captain John Smith and the Founding of Virginia.* Boston: Little, Brown, 1975.

Washburn, Wilcomb E. *The Governor and the Rebel: A History of Bacon's Rebellion in Virginia.* New York: W. W. Norton, 1972.

General Index

Biographical Index

Geographical Index